International Dictionary of Theatre-3
ACTORS, DIRECTORS
and
DESIGNERS

International Dictionary of Theatre-3

Volume 1
PLAYS

Volume 2
PLAYWRIGHTS

Volume 3
ACTORS, DIRECTORS AND DESIGNERS

International Dictionary of Theatre-3
ACTORS, DIRECTORS
and
DESIGNERS

EDITOR
DAVID PICKERING

PICTURE EDITOR
JUDITH M. KASS

ST. JAMES PRESS
An ITP Information/Reference Group Company

I(T)P

Changing the Way the World Learns

NEW YORK • LONDON • BONN • BOSTON • DETROIT • MADRID
MELBOURNE • MEXICO CITY • PARIS • SINGAPORE • TOKYO
TORONTO • WASHINGTON • ALBANY NY • BELMONT CA • CINCINNATI OH

While every effort has been made to ensure the reliability of the information presented in this publication, St. James Press does not guarantee the accuracy of the data contained herein. St. James accepts no payment for listing; and inclusion of any organization, agency, institution, publication, service, or individual does not imply endorsement of the editors or publisher.

Errors brought to the attention of the publisher and verified to the satisfaction of the publisher will be corrected in future editions.

∞™ This book is printed on acid-free paper that meets the minimum requirements of American National Standard for Information Sciences—Permanence Paper for Printed Library Materials, ANSI Z39.48-1984.

A CIP record is available from the British Library

Printed in the United States of America

I(T)P™ Gale Research Inc., an International Thomson Publishing Company.
ITP logo is a trademark under license.

10 9 8 7 6 5 4 3 2 1

CONTENTS

EDITOR'S NOTE

The *International Dictionary of Theatre* is in three volumes: *Plays* (Volume 1), *Playwrights* (Volume 2), and *Actors, Directors and Designers* (Volume 3).

The selection of people and plays appearing in the *Dictionary* is based on the recommendations of the advisers listed in the separate volumes. The book's focus, as the titles of the individual volumes suggest, is primarily on the various genres of drama (both as literature and performance) as distinct from the other performing arts such as opera, dance, mime, the musical, performance art, and folk, ritual, and community theatre.

The scope of the *Dictionary* is historical (ranging from the theatre of Ancient Greece to that of the present day) and international, covering plays of some 20 languages and playwrights, actors, directors, and designers of many nationalities. Many entries are illustrated with photographs of productions, designs, portraits or, engravings.

VOLUME 3: Actors, Directors and Designers

Volume 3 contains entries on 300 actors, directors, and designers for the stage. Most are widely recognised as major figures in both their own countries and beyond, and many of them have had a significant and lasting effect upon the development of world drama. Some are familiar names, still studied today, while others are less well known, but of considerable historical importance, or are still active and yet to complete their work. Many more figures arguably deserve a place in this volume, but have reluctantly had to be sacrificed in the interests both of space and of establishing a reasonable spread over periods and nationalities.

A NOTE ON THE ENTRIES

Each entry contains: a summary of the subject's life and career; a list of relevant productions and roles, including film, television, and radio credits; a list of publications by the subject; a list of publications about the entrant; a signed critical overview of the entrant's work for the stage by one of the *Dictionary*'s contributors.

*

Each entry starts with a **Biographical Summary** of its subject. The summary begins with details (where known) of birth, education and training, and marriage(s), before giving a chronological resumé of the subject's life. Awards, honours, and honorary degrees are listed at the end.

The biographical summary is followed by a listing of the entrant's **Productions** or **Roles** (comprehensive where this has been possible, otherwise incorporating the most significant only). Where known, dates, names of parts played, the authors of the plays, and the venues are included in this list, though these are sometimes conjectural, particularly in the case of historical figures, and should be accepted as certain only with caution. When a role was repeated by a performer many times the details of the first assumption of the part are generally given, sometimes with notes of important revivals. If only a few details are known about an entrant's repertoire, roles or productions are listed alphabetically. In most instances, the titles of plays are given in the language in which they were performed, with English translations following.

Significant achievements in areas related to the theatre are listed under **Films**, **Television**, and **Radio** and any publications by the entrant, from autobiographies to plays, and works on the practice and theory of drama, are listed under **Publications**. Periodical publications and individual essays and contributions to joint publications are not included.

*

The various categories of an entrant's works are then followed, where relevant, by two categories of **Bibliography** dealing with the subject. Important biographical commentaries and critical studies in book form are listed with details of author(s), place of publication, and dates. These are generally confined to works published in English, or in French, German, Italian, Spanish, and Portuguese, with a particular emphasis upon books published in recent decades. Books in the less familiar East- and Central-

European languages and in languages using non-Roman alphabets are excluded, as are those dealing not specifically with the person in question but with a dramatic period/movement/genre in a more general way. Where there are no substantial books available, relevant articles (usually in English) in various theatrical periodicals may also be detailed.

*

Each entry concludes with the **Critical Overview** of the subject by one of the *Dictionary*'s contributors.

ACKNOWLEDGEMENTS

I should like to thank the following for their help on this volume: all the contributors (including those whose contributions had to be omitted for reasons of space); Mark Hawkins-Dady, who oversaw the early stages of the project and obliged with invaluable assistance throughout; the staff of the Bodleian Library, Oxford, and of various other institutions consulted; Zoe Chung, for help with entries on the Far East; Lesley Ripley Greenfield; Philippe Barbour; Kate Berney; Laura Standley Berger; and, lastly, Jan, Edward, and Charles Pickering for their crucial supporting roles.

ADVISERS

Arnold Aronson
Martin Banham
Eugene Benson
Michael Billington
David Bradby
James Brandon
Jarka M. Burian
Marvin Carlson
John Russell Brown
Ruby Cohn
Tish Dace
Daniel Gerould
Vera Gottlieb
Peter Holland
William D. Howarth

Christopher Innes
Bruce King
Felicia Hardison Londré
Frederick J. Marker
Walter J. Meserve
Michael Patterson
Kenneth Richards
Laurence Senelick
Peter Thomson
Stanley Wells
George E. Wellwarth
Margaret Williams
George Woodyard
Katharine Worth

CONTRIBUTORS

Asbjørn Aarseth
David Allen
Stanley Allen
Arnold Aronson
Chris Banfield
Susan Bassnett
Mark Batty
Christopher Baugh
Richard C. Beacham
Jean Benedetti
Joss Bennathan
Günther Berghaus
Michael Billington
David Bradby
George Brandt
Kazimierz Braun
Kirsten Broch
William Brooks
John Russell Brown
Jarka M. Burian
Charles Calder
Roger N. Casey
Janet Clarke
Nancy Copeland
David Cottis
Peter A. Davis
Jim Davis
Terence Dawson
Sarah-Jane Dickenson
Suzanne Burgoyne Dieckman
William Dolby
Margaret Eddershaw
Robert Findlay
Helena Forsås-Scott
Richard Foulkes
Daniel Gerould

Melissa Gibson
S. E. Gontarski
Robert Gordon
Kiki Gounaridou
Marjorie L. Hoover
William D. Howarth
Martin Hunter
Raymond Ingram
R. D. S. Jack
David Jeffery
Samantha Johnson
Dennis Kennedy
Laurence Kitchin
Margaret M. Knapp
Robert Knopf
Michal Kobialka
Edward A. Langhans
Andrew Lavender
Robert Leach
Jill Line
Felicia Hardison Londré
Colin MacKerras
Michelle F. Mazza
Howard McNaughton
Anthony Meech
Pieter van der Merwe
George C. Mielke
Margery Morgan
J. R. Mulryne
Ronald Naversen
Alison J. L. Oddey
Tom J. A. Olsen
John Osborne
David Payne-Carter
Andy Piasecki
David Pickering

Ron Popenhagen
Colin Radford
Lesley Rathkamp
Michael Read
Leslie du S. Read
Joseph Reed
Kenneth Richards
Francesca Richards
Kenneth Richards
Hugh Rorrison
Margaret Rose
John Rothenberg
Donald Roy
Claude Schumacher
Virginia Scott
Laurence Senelick
Robert Shaughnessy

Christopher Smith
Christopher Sutcliffe
George Taylor
Val Taylor
Philip Thody
Richard Trousdell
Delbert Unruh
Carla Waal
Daniel J. Watermeier
Carl Weber
Rudolf Weiss
David Whitton
Jytte Wiingaard
David Williams
Simon Williams
Leigh Woods
Nick Worrall
Kathryn Wylie-Marques

International Dictionary of Theatre-3
ACTORS, DIRECTORS
and
DESIGNERS

A-Z LIST OF ACTORS, DIRECTORS AND DESIGNERS

Konrad Ackermann
André Acquart
Maude Adams
Nikolai Akimov
Ira Aldridge
George Alexander
Edward Alleyn
Andreini family
Margaret Anglin
André Antoine
Adolphe Appia
Robert Armin
Boris Aronson
Antonin Artaud
Peggy Ashcroft

Squire and Marie Bancroft
Eugenio Barba
Jean-Louis Barrault
Lawrence Barrett
Spranger Barry
Elizabeth Barry
John Barrymore
Ethel Barrymore
André Barsacq
John Barton
Gaston Baty
Norman Bel Geddes
David Belasco
George Anne Bellamy
Luigi Bellotti-Bon
Frank Benson
Ingmar Bergman
Sarah Bernhardt
Benno Besson
Thomas Betterton
Biancolelli family
Bibiena family
Bjørn Bjørnson
Roger Blin
William Edward Bloch
Claire Bloom
Augusto Boal
Michael Bogdanov
Junius Brutus Booth
Edwin Booth
Anne Bracegirdle
Anton Giulio Bragaglia
Otto Brahm
Lee Breuer
Peter Brook
Johannes Finne Brun
Richard Burbage
Emil František Burian
John Bury

Zoë Caldwell

Mrs Patrick Campbell
William Capon
Morris Carnovsky
Maria Casarès
Lewis Casson
Michael Chekhov
Cheng Changgeng
Pierre-Luc-Charles Ciceri
Mlle Clairon
Alec Clunes
Harold Clurman
Fay Compton
George Frederick Cooke
Jacques Copeau
Constant-Benoît Coquelin
Katharine Cornell
Gordon Craig
Hume Cronyn
Charlotte Cushman

Jean Dasté
Edward Loomis Davenport
Jean-Baptiste Gaspard Deburau
Judi Dench
George Devine
Emil Devrient
Ludwig Devrient
Colleen Dewhurst
John Dexter
Pauline-Virginie Déjazet
Marie Dorval
John Drew
Mrs John Drew
Gerald du Maurier
William Dudley
Charles Dullin
Eleonora Duse
Johanne Dybwad

Oleg Efreimov
Anatoly Efros
Bengt Ekerot
Konrad Ekhof
Mariya Ermolova
Edith Evans
Maurice Evans
Nikolai Evreinov
Richard Eyre

Helen Faucit
Glikeriya Fedotova
Albert Finney
Tiberio Fiorilli
Minnie Maddern Fiske
Floridor
Johnston Forbes-Robertson
Edwin Forrest

David Garrick
Jean Gascon
Bill Gaskill
John Gielgud
William Gillette
Mordecai Gorelik
Terence Gray
Ben Greet
Grieve family
Joseph Grimaldi
Jerzy Grotowski
Gustaf Gründgens
Alec Guinness
John Forsyth Gunter
Tyrone Guthrie

Peter Reginald Frederick Hall
Terry Hands
Charles Hawtrey
Helen Hayes
Jocelyn Herbert
Wendy Hiller
John Hirsch
John Houseman
Alan Howard
August Wilhelm Iffland
Henry Irving

Barry Jackson
Glenda Jackson
Derek Jacobi
Joseph Jefferson III
Jodelet
Robert Edmond Jones
Inigo Jones
Margo Jones
Louis Jouvet

Vasili Kachalov
Josef Kainz
Tadeusz Kantor
Elia Kazan
Edmund Kean
Charles Kean
Fanny Kemble
Charles Kemble
John Philip Kemble
Will Kemp
Ralph Koltai
Vera Kommisarjevskaya
Theodore Kommisarjevsky

Heinrich Laube
Charles Laughton
Eva Le Gallienne
Adrienne Lecouvreur
Ming Cho Lee
Eugene Lee
Henri-Louis Lekain
Frédérick Lemaître
Per Lindberg

John Liston
Joan Littlewood
Philip James de Loutherbourgh
Aurélien Lugné-Poë
Alfred Lunt and Lynn Fontanne
Yuri Lyubimov

Charles Macklin
William Charles Macready
Laurent Mahelot
Richard Mansfield
Julia Marlowe
Charles Marowitz
Mlle Mars
Raymond Massey
Charles James Mathews
Guthrie McClintic
Ian McKellen
Gregan McMahon
Mei Lanfang
Anne Merry
Oliver Messel
Vsevolod Meyerhold
Jo Mielziner
Jonathan Miller
Ariane Mnouchkine
Pavel Mochalov
Gustavo Modena
Helena Modjeska
Tanya Moiseiwitsch
Alexander Moissi
Olof Molander
Montdory

John Napier
Vladimir Nemirovich-Danchenko
Friederike Caroline Neuber
John Neville
Hans Jacob Nilsen
Adrian Keith Noble
Trevor Robert Nunn

Nikolai Okhlopkov
Anne Oldfield
Laurence Olivier
Teo Otto

Geraldine Page
Peter Palitzsch
Ben Iden Payne
Claus Peymann
Samuel Phelps
Gérard Philipe
Erwin Piscator
Georges Pitoëff
Roger Planchon
Joan Plowright
William Poel
Lyubov Popova
Hannah Pritchard
Philip Prowse

Anthony Quayle
James Quin
José Quintero

Élisa Rachel
Sergei Radlov
Vanessa Redgrave
Michael Scudamore Redgrave
Ada Rehan
Kate Reid
Max Reinhardt
Gabrielle-Charlotte Réjane
Riccoboni family
John Rich
Ralph Richardson
Adelaide Ristori
Jason Robards
Paul Robeson
Flora Robson
Luca Ronconi
Jean Rosenthal
Ernesto Rossi
Ruggero Ruggeri

Michel Saint-Denis
Tommaso Salvini
Leon Schiller
Friedrich Ludwig Schröder
Paul Scofield
George C. Scott
Peter Sellars
Ekaterina Semionova
Andrei Serban
Sebastiano Serlio
Giovanni Servandoni
Karl Seydelmann
Mikhail Shchepkin
Sarah Siddons
Lee Simonson
Alf Sjöberg
Otis Skinner
Maggie Smith

E.H. Sothern
Luigi Squarzina
Konstantin Stanislavsky
Maureen Stapleton
Peter Stein
Josef Anton Stranitzky
Lee Strasberg
Giorgio Strehler
Janet Suzman
Josef Svoboda
Jósef Szajna

Alexander Tairov
François-Joseph Talma
Jessica Tandy
Laurette Taylor
Ellen Terry
Sybil Thorndike
J.L. Toole
Giacomo Torelli
Georgyi Tovstonogov
Herbert Beerbohm Tree

Evgeny Vakhtangov
"Madame" Lucia Elizabeth Vestris
Jean Vilar
Luchino Visconti
Antoine Vitez

Helene Weigel
Manfred Wekwerth
Orson Welles
Nicol Williamson
Robert M. Wilson
Peg Woffington
Donald Wolfit
Irene Worth

Ermete Zacconi
Yuri Zavadsky
Franco Zeffirelli

A

ACKERMANN, Konrad (Ernst). German actor-manager. Born in Schwerin, Germany, 1 February 1712. Trained as a surgeon. Served with Russian army in Turkish wars. Married actress Sophie Charlotte Schröder in 1749, two daughters. Stage debut, with company of Johann Friedrich Schönemann, Lüneburg, 1740; actor, Sophie Shröder's troupe, from 1742; toured widely in northern Germany, central and eastern Europe, and Russia with his future wife, returning to Germany, 1751; established his own company, 1753; toured Poland and Russia; opened theatre built at his own expense in Königsberg, 1755; abandoned Königsberg on approach of Russian soldiers in the Seven Years' War, 1756; toured Switzerland and Alsace, 1757–61; settled in Hamburg and recruited actor Konrad Ekhof, 1764; toured Bremen, 1764; first performance in Schauspielhaus am Ğnsemarkt, Hamburg, 1765; lost control of company, which became the Hamburg National Theatre, 1767; regained control and returned to touring, 1769; director (with part of his company) at Hanover and Brunswick, 1769; final appearance, September 1771. Died in Hamburg, 13 November 1771.

Principal productions

As actor-manager:
1754   Harpagon in *Der Geizige* (Molière), first performed, Glogau.

Mithridates in *Mithridates* (Racine), first performed, Glogau.

Orosman in *Zaire* (Voltaire), first performed, Glogau.

Rodrigo in *Le Cid* (Corneille), first performed, Glogau.

Ulfo in *Canut* (Schlegel), first performed, Frankfurt an der Oder.

1755   Mellefont in *Miss Sara Sampson* (Lessing), first performed, Frankfurt an der Oder.

1767   Werner in *Minna von Barnhelm* (Lessing), first performed, National Theater, Hamburg.

Other productions included: *Alzire* (Voltaire), 1754; *Der Spieler* (Moore), 1754; *Der Kranke in der Einbildung* (Molière), 1754; *Oedip* (Voltaire), 1754; *Das errettete Venedig* (Otway), 1754; *Demetrius* (Metastasio), 1754; *Der dumme Herr und der kluge Knecht* (Molière), 1754; *Cato* (Gottsched), 1754; *Der verschwenderische Sohn* (Voltaire), 1754; *Der kluge Arzt* (Molière), 1754; *Iphigenia* (Racine), 1754; *Polyeuctes* (Corneille), 1754; *Democrit* (Regnard), 1754; *Der Hausknecht* (Leeuw), 1754; *Die ungleiche Liebe* (Gottsched), 1755; *Die stumme Schönheit* (Schlegel), 1755;

Der Ehrsüchtige (Destouches), 1755; *Sylvia* (Gellert), 1755; *Die Raserei des Orestes* (Schlegel), 1755; *Das Orakel* (St Foix), 1755; *Der faule Bauer* (Uhlich), 1755; *Jean de France* (Holberg), 1755; *Le Medicin malgré lui* (Molière), 1755; *Der Graf von Essex* (Corneille), 1755; *Der Franzos in London* (Boissy), 1755; *Der Tod des Cäsar* (Voltaire), 1755; *Oratin und Mascarilla* (Molière), 1755; *Cinna* (Corneille), 1755; *Der Kaufmann von London* (Lillo), 1755; *Atalanta* (Gottsched), 1755; *Phädra* (Racine), 1755; *Die erzwungene Heirat* (Molière), 1755; *Tartuffe* (Molière), 1755; *Die Kandidaten* (Krüger), 1757; *Herzog Michel* (Krüger), 1757; *Die Schule der Frauen* (Molière), 1757; *Der Freigeist* (Lessing), 1757; *Merope* (Voltaire), 1757; *Johanna Gray* (Wieland), 1758; *Der sterbende Cato* (Gottsched), 1758; *Pamela* (Goldoni), 1758; *Der natürliche Sohn* (Diderot), 1759; *Orest und Pylades* (Schlegel), 1759; *Vertumnus* (Vorspiel), 1759; *Eduard und Eleonore* (Thompson), 1759; *Codrus* (Cronegk), 1760; *Die Weiberschule* (Molière), 1760; *Der Sonderling* (Destouches), 1760; *Timoleon* (Behrmann), 1760; *Das Kaffeehaus* (Voltaire), 1761; *Die Mütterschule* (Marivaux), 1762; *Bramarbas* (Holberg), 1763; *Die gelehrten Frauen* (Molière), 1764; *Richard III* (Weisse), 1764; *Jean de France* (Holberg), 1764; *Brutus* (Voltaire), 1764; *Die Huernte*, 1764; *Der Poet vom Lande* (Destouches), 1764; *Der verliebte Verdruss* (Molière), 1764; *Das falsche Kammermädchen* (Marivaux), 1765; *Das Herrenrecht* (Voltaire), 1765; *Die stumme Schönheit* (Schlegel), 1765; *Die Komödie im Tempel der Tugend* (Löwen), 1765; *Der Advokat Patelin* (Bruyes), 1765; *Die schlaue Witwe* (Goldoni), 1765; *Der verstellte Sterndeuter* (Corneille), 1765; *Der Mann nach der Welt* (Boissy), 1765; *Die kluge Ehefrau* (Goldoni), 1765; *Der blinde Ehemann* (Krüger), 1765; *Der erzürnte Ehemann* (Vanbrugh), 1766; *Der Bauer mit der Erbschaft* (Marivaux), 1766; *Der Triumph der guten Frauen* (Schlegel), 1766; *Der Diener zweier Herren* (Goldoni), 1766; *Die Belagerung von Calais* (Belloy), 1766; *Der Talismann* (De la Motte), 1766; *Das Testament* (Gottsched), 1766; *Amphytrion* (Molière), 1766; *Der Geheimnisville* (Schlegel), 1766; *Die Kornente*, 1766; *Rodogune* (Corneille), 1766; *La serva padrona* (Pergolesi), 1766; *Die Trojanerinnen* (Schlegel), 1766; *Don Juan* (Molière), 1766; *Amalia* (Weisse), 1766; *Tancred* (Voltaire), 1766; *Philosophie marié* (Destouches), 1767; *Rosemunde* (Weisse), 1767; *Zelmire* (Belloy), 1767; *Das Blendwerk* (Corneille), 1767; *Der Hausvater* (Diderot), 1769; *Romeo und Julia* (Weisse), 1769; *Eugenie* (Beaumarchais), 1769; *Der Vorschlag* (Calderón), 1770; *Der Arzt wider Willen* (Molière), 1770; *Der Lügner* (Goldoni), 1770; *Verwirrung über Verwirrung* (Calderón), 1770; *Der Sizilianer* (Molière), 1770; *Der adlige Bürger* (Molière), 1770; *Der Arglistige*

(Congreve), 1771; *Die Juden* (Lessing), 1771; *Die Guebern* (Voltaire), 1771.

*

Bibliography

Books:

W. H. Bruford, *Theatre, Drama and Audience in Goethe's Germany*, London, 1950.

Herbert Eichhorn, *Konrad Ernst Ackermann*, Emsdetten, Westfalia, 1965.

Paul Möhring, *Von Ackermann bis Ziegel-Theater in Hamburg*, Hamburg, 1970.

Articles:

Heinz Kindermann, "Ackermann's Wegbereitung", *Theatergeschichte der Goethezeit*, 1948.

Max Fehr, "Die wandernden Theatertruppen in der Schweiz", *Jahrbuch der Schweizerischen Gesellschaft für Theatergeschichte*, 18, 1948.

Herbert Eichhorn, "Konrad Ernst Ackermann: Ein deutscher Theaterprinzipal", *Die Schaubühne*, 64, 1965.

* * *

Few actors of the 18th century have aroused such admiration, both for their acting and for the excellence of their character, as Konrad Ackermann. "He was a proper man," wrote Eduard Devrient, "of sterling German worth, of healthy bluntness and simplicity. His performances, models of colourful freshness and natural proportion, had no precedent, but came unconstrainedly from his upright nature". While Devrient's judgement was undoubtedly influenced by his unswerving determination to prove a respectable bourgeois genesis for the fledgling German theatre during the middle decades of the 18th century, even in his lifetime, during his long career as an actor and manager, Ackermann earned the extraordinary respect of his contemporaries.

When Ackermann began his career in 1740, in the newly-formed Schönemann troupe that was in effect a reconstituted version of the troupe once led by Caroline Neuber, the German theatre was still undeveloped. There were no standing theatres with German companies as permanent occupants; court theatres were still occupied exclusively by French players and Italian singers. Consequently, Ackermann was forced to make a living by travelling in Northern Germany, the Baltic states, and Russia, first in a troupe led by Schönemann, then in one led by Sophie Schröder, whom he married. After becoming manager of his own troupe in 1753, he attempted to establish a permanent home, building at his own expense a theatre in Königsberg. Had he been able to remain here, he would have enjoyed the distinction of being the first German actor-manager to found an independent standing theatre. However, he and his family took flight as Russian troops advanced on Königsberg in the course of the Seven Years' War and even after peace was restored he was never able to return to Königsberg to reclaim his property. He avoided hostilities by touring in Switzerland, which rendered a service to that country as, until that time, theatre in Switzerland was virtually non-existent. Later, in the 1760's, he centred his activities on Hamburg, where again he attempted to establish a permanent theatre. He lacked, however, any

sense for business and because of his improvidential ways was eventually forced to sell his interest in the Schauspielhaus am Gänsemarkt, which then for two years became the famous Hamburg National Theatre. After the collapse of this institution, Ackermann regained the leadership of his troupe but was forced to take to the road again. It would be left to his stepson, Friedrich Ludwig Schröder, to complete the search for a permanent home for the company.

In its heyday, during the 1750's and early 1760's, Ackermann's company was known for the excellence of its ensemble, the quality of its individual players, for its attention to the details of physical production, and for the development of a natural style of acting that challenged the stiff, rhetorical manner based on French acting, in which the majority of German actors performed. At various times, most of the leading actors of the period played in Ackermann's troupe. These included Konrad Ekhof, Heinrich Koch, David Borchers, and Marie Hensel, not to mention the extraordinarily talented family of Ackermann himself, his wife Sophie, his stepson Friedrich Schröder, and his daughters Dorothea and Charlotte.

As an actor, Ackermann was imposing. He had a powerful and genial personality and it would seem that he relied upon this, not upon any rhetorical skills or mimetic techniques, to impress his audience. Despite some corpulence, several years' practice as a fencer, dancer and skier meant that Ackermann was physically agile. This, combined with his notably well-developed vocal powers, ensured that he had little difficulty in adapting himself to whatever role came his way. At a time when casting in German theatre troupes was strictly by systemized typecasting, Ackermann's versatility made audiences and actors alike aware of how flexible an individual actor might be. He had considerable success at playing the heroes of neoclassical tragedies by both French and native German writers, particularly because the naturalness of his speech and gesture struck audiences as pleasantly novel. In contrast to other actors, Ackermann made the heroes of Corneille and Racine strikingly human — but he was most successful and probably most at home in comedy. No other German actor of his generation could bring Molière's figures so close to the audiences' experience and at the same time realise their full complexity. Harpagon was the most celebrated of all his roles. But versatility was the principal mark of Ackermann's acting. His stepson Schröder, who had no cause to love him due to their passionate and often jealous rivalry, claimed that there was no role he could not undertake and that he never exaggerated on stage.

Perhaps Ackermann's chief legacy as an actor and manager was to acclimatize the bourgeois tragedy to the German stage. Although the Ackermann company was responsible for few German premieres, it gave important works such as Lillo's *The London Merchant*, Moore's *The Gambler*, and Lessing's *Miss Sara Sampson*, *Minna von Barnhelm*, and *Emilia Galotti* in performances that were close to exemplary and hence helped establish a drama that would both give the German theatre an identity of its own and encourage actors to adopt a manner of acting that was natural rather than overtly rhetorical. Ackermann's historical importance has perhaps been clouded by the ill-fortune that he died just at the onset of a period in which the German theatre underwent remarkable growth and attained a cohesion that has marked it to this day. Although

Ackermann did not live to see this, he did much to prepare it.

—Simon Williams

————

ACQUART, André. French designer. Born in Vincennes, Paris, 12 November 1922. Educated at the École Nationale des Beaux Arts, Algiers, 1937–40. Married Barbara Richlowska, one son. Debut as set designer, Algeria, 1950; moved to Paris, 1951; acclaimed for designs for productions by Roger Blin, Jean Vilar, and other leading French directors, especially for the plays of Jean Genet in the early 1960's; has also worked in Germany.

Selected productions

1950   *Le Bal des voleurs* (Anouilh), Centre Culturel, Algiers.

1951   *Le Sicilien* (Molière), L'Équipe Théâtrale, Paris.
       Monsieur de Pourceaugnac (Molière), Centre Culturel, Algiers.
       Le Bourgois gentilhomme (Molière), Centre Culturel, Algiers.

1952   *Léocadia* (Anouilh), Centre Culturel, Algiers.
       Les Mariés de la tour Eiffel (Cocteau), Centre Culturel, Algiers.

1953   *Pasiphae* (Montherlant), Centre Culturel, Algiers.
       Don Perlimplin (Garcia Lorca), L'Équipe Théâtrale, Paris.
       Le Tambourin (anon.), L'Équipe Théâtrale, Paris.
       Au Grand large (Vane), Les Comédiens d'Algier.

1954   *La Supplément au voyage de Cook* (Giraudoux), Centre Culturel, Algiers.
       Le Pauvre Jean (Giraudoux), L'Équipe Théâtrale, Paris.
       Le Jeune homme pressé (Labiche), L'Équipe Théâtrale, Paris.
       Le Commencement des tatous (Kipling), L'Équipe Théâtrale, Paris.
       L'Enfant d'éléphant (Kipling), L'Équipe Théâtrale, Paris.
       On ne saurait penser à tout (Musset), L'Équipe Théâtrale, Paris.
       La Cruche cassée (Kleist), Stage National d'Art Dramatique, Bordeaux.
       La Première famille (Supervielle), Stage National d'Art Dramatique, Bordeaux.

1955   *Un Inspector vous demande* (Priestley), L'Équipe Théâtrale, Algiers.
       La Tempête (Shakespeare), L'Équipe Théâtrale, Algiers.
       Mercator (Plautus), Théâtre de la Gaîté-Montparnasse, Paris.

1956   *Saint Elie de Gueuce* and *Catherine d'Aulnac* (Tour du Pin), Théâtre de Poche, Paris.

1957   *Les Coréens* (Vinaver), Théâtre de l'Alliance, Paris.

         Les Bâtisseurs d'Empire (Vian), Théâtre National Populaire-Récamier, Paris.

1959   *Les Nègres* (Genet), Théâtre de Lutèce, Paris.

1960   *Le Barrage contre le Pacifique* (Duras and Serreau), Studio des Champs-Élysées, Paris.
       Monsieur Biedermann and the Firebugs (Frisch), Théâtre de Lutèce, Paris.
       La Résistible ascension d'Arturo Ui (Brecht), Théâtre National Populaire, Paris.
       La Bonne âme de Se-Tchouan (Brecht), Théâtre National Populaire-Récamier, Paris.
       Altanima (Audiberti), Théâtre de la Cité Universitaire, Paris.
       La Logeuse (Audiberti), Théâtre des Nations, Paris.
       Le Lion (Kenan), Théâtre de Lutèce, Paris.
       Spectacle de Tennessee Williams, Studio des Champs-Élysées, Paris.

1961   *Apprendre à marcher* (Ionesco), Théâtre de l'Étoile, Paris.
       L'Histoire de Tobie et de Sarah (Claudel), Kirche Maria Himmelfahrt, Cologne.
       Roses rouges pour moi (O'Casey), Théâtre National Populaire, Paris.
       Pantomimes d'un sou (Ségal), Odéon-Théâtre de France, Paris.
       Les Nuits blanches (Dostoevsky, adapted by Adamov), Théâtre de Lutèce, Paris.

1962   *Un Certain Monsieur Blot* (Rocca), Théâtre Gramont, Paris.
       Carmen (Bizet), Opernhaus, Cologne.
       Les Témoins (Soria), Théâtre du Vieux-Colombier, Paris.
       On ne sait comment (Pirandello, adapted by Artaud), Théâtre du Vieux-Colombier, Paris.
       Tartuffe (Molière), Coimbra.
       Antigone (Sophocles), Festival de Nantes.
       Don Juan (Ghelderode), Festival d'Arras.
       La Vie est un songe (Calderón), Festival de la Rochelle.
       La Bête dans la jungle (Lord and Duras), Théâtre de l'Athénée, Paris.
       La Brigitta (Audiberti), Théâtre de l'Athénée, Paris.
       Lulu (Wedekind), Théâtre de l'Athénée, Paris.
       Les Parapluies (Ségal), Théâtre de l'Odéon, Paris.
       Antigone (Brecht), Comédie de Provence and Théâtre National Algérien.

1963   *Les Officiers* (Lenz, adapted by Leroi and Moatti), Théâtre Récamier, Paris.
       Tchin-Tchin (Billetdoux), Fontainebleau.
       Les Troyennes (Euripides), Théâtre Récamier, Paris.
       O'Man Chicago (Planchon), Théâtre de la Cité, Villeurbanne.
       Horace (Corneille), Comédie de l'Est, Strasburg, and Baalbeck Festival.
       Divines parôles (Valle-Inclan), Théâtre de l'Odéon, Paris.
       Charles XII (Strindberg), Festival d'Aubervilliers.
       Les Passions contraires (Soria), Théâtre de la Bruyère, Paris.

Monsieur Pourceaugnac (Molière), Comédie de Saint-Etienne.

Roses rouges pour moi (O'Casey), Théâtre National Algérien.

1964   *Troilus and Cressida* (Shakespeare), Théâtre de la Cité, Villeurbanne, and Odéon-Théâtre de France, Paris.

Un Banquier sans visage (Weideli), Grand Théâtre, Geneva.

Coriolan (Shakespeare), Festival d'Aubervilliers.

Le Dossier Oppenheimer (Vilar and Kipphardt), Théâtre de l'Athénée, Paris.

1965   *Macbeth* (Shakespeare), Théâtre de l'Est Parisien, Paris.

L'Elu (Mann), Éducation National.

La Mort d'un commis voyageur (Miller), Théâtre de la Commune, Aubervilliers.

Les Séquestrés d'Altona (Sartre), Théâtre de l'Athénée, Paris.

Les Chiens (Brulé), Théâtre de l'Athénée, Paris.

Turcaret (Lesage), Théâtre de l'Est Parisien, Paris.

Les Paravents (Genet), Odéon-Théâtre de France, Paris.

Mesure pour mesure (Shakespeare), Théâtre de l'Est Parisien, Paris.

Les Hasards du coin du feu (Vilar), Théâtre de l'Est Parisien, Paris.

Other productions have included: *Les Libertins* (Planchon), Théâtre de la Cité, Villeurbanne, 1967; *Minamata and Co.* (Takahashi), Théâtre de la Commune d'Aubervilliers, 1978; *Triptyque* (Frisch), Théâtre de l'Odéon, Paris, 1983; *Faut pas tuer Maman* (Keatley), Gaité-Montparnasse, Paris, 1989.

* * *

André Acquart has been an active scene designer in France for some 45 years. His work in the 1950's and 1960's was associated with the New Theatre movement, and he has always remained close to contemporary trends that are on the cutting edge. While only marginally known outside Europe, Acquart has, nonetheless, been a collaborator on several productions of great historical significance. His designs for the French metteur en scène Roger Blin are among his most stunning achievements. Perhaps Acquart's most remarkable quality as a designer is his capacity to develop and build upon a director's visual concept; he is far more concerned about creating a sense of unity in a production, than in making a bold individual statement. His sensitivity to actors and metteurs en scène has been the key to his imaginative, yet subtle, constructions.

Acquart approaches stage space with the eye of an architect. It was this spatial aspect of his work that drew the attention of Roger Blin. Blin was interested in minimalist staging that was functional without sacrificing a certain "magic". He wanted a designer who was interested in serving the text in the same manner that he, as director, wished to serve it. Acquart agreed with Blin's approach and also shared his adventurous quest to stage the work of new playwrights. The complicity between Acquart and Blin found its proper outlet in the plays of Jean Genet. Acquart

did the design for the 1959 production of *Les Nègres* (*The Blacks*). This outlandish presentation rocked the foundations of the Paris theatre. Acquart's skeletal series of platforms was constructed from pipes textured with a white plaster-like material. The texturing eliminated the cold stark lines of the piping, while maintaining the abstract quality through the form. Blin desired a setting that the actors could touch and play with, not one that was simply a background for the performers. Acquart, too, believed in the concept of scenery in action: the setting as another element of play.

Since Acquart had lived a long time in Algeria, Blin especially wanted to work with him on the Genet plays. His awareness of space, colour, and light in Africa was utilized in the designs of both *Les Nègres* and *Les Paravents*. With the assistance of his wife, Acquart also designed outrageous costumes and masks for the Genet productions. Form was again the main concern. Exaggerated profiles, distinctively shaped costumes, and strong horizontal and vertical lines defined the stage space. In *Les Nègres* levels were arranged in the manner of scaffolding. In *Les Paravents* the moveable screens in white were vast easels for the bold and striking images drawn by the actors. Both sets were simple, dynamic solutions to the complex needs of the text. Acquart worked as an inventive problem-solver. His costumes for *Les Paravents* also exhibited his playfulness and sense of humour. The pyramidal forms of Warda (performed by Madeleine Renaud) and La Mère (performed by Maria Casarès) topped with colourful — almost oriental — make-up and gargantuan wigs are images that have marked the annals of modern French theatre.

Acquart also designed for Blin's mise en scène of *Divines parôles* by Valle-Inclan, *Minimata and Co.* by Takahashi, and Max Frisch's *Triptyque*. The two later productions were characterized by stark open spaces with an oriental simplicity in the use of objects. Both made very little use of colour, relying primarily upon contrast achieved from the use of variations on black and white. *Triptyque*, Blin's last mise en scène before his death in 1984, was a large-scale production at the Odéon that utilized five turntables in the stage floor. Acquart was able to create intimate spaces within a broad expanse by isolating areas with light and incorporating minimal furniture pieces. A dreamlike quality and stunning silences were created by moving the actors in the world of the dead, and in reality, through the use of the turntables.

For Blin's mise en scène of *Divines parôles*, Acquart, together with his wife and Blin himself, travelled to Spain to obtain a sense of the space recreated in Valle-Inclan's text. All were greatly moved by the landscape's intense beauty. On their return to Paris, Acquart utilized newspaper and plastic to attain the special colour, light, and space that they had experienced in Spain. Acquart treated the granite rocks of the region in an abstract manner, but, unfortunately, the result was not one of abstraction, but one of extreme realism. Both Acquart and Blin were stimulated and amused by this paradoxical realisation.

Acquart makes considerable use of basic, quotidien materials like plastic and fabric. There is an element of "objets trouvés" in his stage designs. This may be the result of working in less than ideal circumstances in the 1950's, making the most of small playing spaces and even smaller budgets. As a scenographer in the 1980's and 1990's, designing for operas directed by Claude Confortès and

Jean-Claude Fall, Acquart continued to use similar materials and minimal colour. At his best, the designs propose a visual poetry that is highly engaging.

Acquart has worked with many of the innovative metteurs en scène in France, including Jean Vilar, Jean-Marie Serreau, and Roger Planchon. Recently he has returned to work with moveable panels, as in *Les Paravents* and in Planchon's *Troilus and Cressida*, for a production of Charlotte Keatley's *Faut pas tuer Maman* (*My Mother Said I Never Should*). In a very restricted performing space, Acquart provided director Michel Fagadeau with a "fluid" setting that projected the actor into a close physical contact with the spectators. Through the use of transparent materials, he created silhouettes that aptly illustrated the drama's passages from generation to generation.

—Ron Popenhagen

ADAMS, Maude. US actress. Born Maude Adams Kiskadden in Salt Lake City, Utah, 11 November 1872. Educated at schools in San Francisco and subsequently at the Collegiate Institute, Salt Lake City, 1882–83. Stage debut at nine months with her parents' Salt Lake City theatre company; first major success, aged five, in *Fritz, Our German Cousin*, 1878; New York debut, Star Theatre, 1888; played regularly opposite John Drew under the management of Charles Frohman, 1890–1915; emerged as a star in plays by J. M. Barrie, from 1897; left professional stage, 1918; lighting consultant, General Electric, 1920's; returned to stage, 1931; final retirement, 1937. Professor of Dramatic Arts, Stephens College, Columbia, Missouri, 1937–50. LL.D: University of Wisconsin, 1927. Died in Tannersville, New York, 17 July 1953.

Roles

1875   Little Schneider in *Fritz, Our German Cousin* (Emmett), California Theatre, San Francisco.
1878   Alice Redding in *Kit, The Arkansas Traveller* (De Walden and Spencer), California Theatre, San Francisco.
        Pussy in *Saratoga* (Howard and Marshall), Virginia City, Nevada.
        Little Eva in *Uncle Tom's Cabin* (adapted from H. B. Stowe), Bush Theatre, San Francisco.
1879   Adrienne in *A Celebrated Case* (D'Ennery and Cormon), Bush Theatre, San Francisco.
1881   Alfred in *Queen's Evidence* (Conquest and Pettitt), Bush Theatre, San Francisco.
1887   Mary Stuart in *Caught in a Corner* (W. J. Shaw), Alcazar Theatre, New York.
1888   Moyna Sullivan in *The Paymaster* (Harrison), Star Theatre, New York.
1889   Louisa in *The Highest Bidder* (Belasco), Grand Opera House, New York.
        Jessie Deane in *Lord Chumley* (Belasco), Grand Opera House, New York.
        Dot Bradbury in *A Midnight Bell* (Hoyt), Bijou Theatre, New York.

1890   Evangeline Bender in *All the Comforts of Home* (Gillette), Proctor's 23rd Street Theatre, New York.
        Dora in *Men and Women* (De Mille and Belasco), Proctor's 23rd Street Theatre, New York.
1891   Nell in *The Lost Paradise* (De Mille), Proctor's 23rd Street Theatre, New York.
1892   Suzanne Blondet in *The Masked Ball* (Bisson and Carre), Palmer's Theatre, New York.
1894   Miriam in *The Butterflies* (Carleton), Palmer's Theatre, New York.
1895   Jessie Keber in *The Bauble Shop* (Carton), Empire Theatre, New York.
        Marion in *That Imprudent Young Couple* (Carleton), Empire Theatre, New York.
        Dora in *Christopher, Jr* (Ryley), Empire Theatre, New York.
1896   Adele in *The Squire of Dames* (Carton), Palmer's Theatre, New York.
        Dorothy Cruikshanks in *Rosemary* (Parker and Carson), Empire Theatre, New York.
1897   Lady Babbie in *The Little Minister* (Barrie), Empire Theatre, New York.
        Mrs Hilary in *Mrs Hilary Regrets* (Smith), Knickerbocker Theatre, New York.
1899   Juliet in *Romeo and Juliet* (Shakespeare), Empire Theatre, New York.
1900   Duke of Reichstadt in *L'Aiglon* (Rostand), Knickerbocker Theatre, New York.
1901   Phoebe Throssell in *Quality Street* (Barrie), Knickerbocker Theatre, New York.
1903   Pepita in *The Pretty Sister of José* (Burnett), Empire Theatre, New York.
1905   Amanda Affleck in *'Op o' me Thumb* (Fenn and Pryce), Empire Theatre, New York.
1905–07 Peter Pan in *Peter Pan* (Barrie), Empire Theatre, New York.
1908   Maggie Wylie in *What Every Woman Knows* (Barrie), Atlantic City and Empire Theatre, New York.
        Rene in *The Jesters* (Zamacoïs), Empire Theatre, New York.
        Viola in *Twelfth Night* (Shakespeare), Sanders Theatre, Harvard University.
1909   St Joan in *Joan of Arc* (adapted from Schiller), Stadium, Harvard University.
1910   Rosalind in *As You Like It* (Shakespeare), Greek Theatre, Berkeley, California.
1911   Chantecler in *Chantecler* (Rostand, adapted by Parker), Knickerbocker Theatre and US tour.
1914   Rosalind in *Rosalind* (Barrie), Rochester, New York.
        Leonora in *The Legend of Leonora* (Barrie), Empire Theatre, New York.
1916   Miss Thing in *A Kiss for Cinderella* (Barrie), Empire Theatre, New York.
1931   Portia in *The Merchant of Venice* (Shakespeare), US tour.
1934   Maria in *Twelfth Night* (Shakespeare), Ogunquit, Maine.

Other roles (mostly as a child) included: Chrystal in *Chums* (Belasco); Flower Girl in *Michael Strogoff* (Byron); Little

Adele in *Jane Eyre* (Wills); Little Marie in *The Sea of Ice* (Robertson); Newsboy in *The Streets of New York* (Boucicault); Paul in *The Octoroon* (Boucicault); and roles in *Across the Continent* (McCloskey), *Barney's Courtship* (anon.), *La Belle Russe* (Belasco), *Diplomacy* (Scott and Stephenson), *Harbour Lights* (Sims and Pettitt), *Jack Shepard* (Boucicault), *Monte Cristo* (Dumas *père*), *My Geraldine* (Campbell), *Ninon* (Wills), *Oliver Twist* (Dickens), *The Planter's Wife* (Tillotson), *The Stepmother* (Howard), *Too Happy by Half* (Field), *The Wages of Sin* (Harvey), *The Wandering Boys* (Pixérécourt), *A Woman of the People* (Webster).

*

Bibliography

Books:
Acton Davies, *Maude Adams*, New York, 1901.
A. Patterson, *Maude Adams: A Biography*, New York, 1907.
Phyllis Robbins, *Maude Adams: An Intimate Portrait*, New York, 1956.

* * *

One of the most popular actresses of her age, Maude Adams was among the first US performers to emphasize personal charm and virtue over classical acting skills. While never attaining the critical stature of Charlotte Cushman, Mary Anderson, Fanny Janauschek, or Helena Modjeska, Adams was the top box-office draw in the country, largely due to her performances in the plays of J. M. Barrie.

Adams was the daughter of James Kiskadden, a Salt Lake City businessman, and Ansenath Ann (née Adams) Kiskadden, an actress in a local Mormon stock company. Adams, who eventually took her mother's maiden name, made her theatrical debut at the age of nine months, carried on stage by her mother in a production of *The Lost Child*. In 1875, the family moved to San Francisco, where Adams began a career as a child star, performing her first professional role as Little Schneider in *Fritz, Our German Cousin*. She returned to Salt Lake City in 1882 to attend the Collegiate Institute, having outgrown her child characters, but within a year her schooling was cut short when her father died and she joined her mother on the theatrical circuit. In 1888, Maude Adams made her adult debut at the Star Theatre in New York City, where she was discovered by E. H. Sothern and cast as Jessie Deane in *Lord Chumley*. The next year she was working for Charles Hoyt and in 1890 she signed with Charles Frohman, in whose company she became a leading star. Her early parts included the leading role of Dora in *Men and Women*, which was written especially for her by David Belasco and H. C. De Mille at Frohman's insistence.

It was not surprising, therefore, when Adams was paired with the great romantic comedian John Drew in H. C. De Mille's *The Lost Paradise*. From 1892 to 1896 she was the female lead in Drew's company, establishing a loyal following and creating the image of wholesome innocence and sprightly whimsy that became her hallmark. It was her performance in 1896 of the title character in *Rosemary* that first attracted the attention of J. M. Barrie. Upon Frohman's urging, Barrie adapted his novel *The Little Minister* for the stage, casting Adams in the starring role of Lady Babbie. The 1897 premiere at the Empire Theatre was both a critical and financial success and lasting starring status was assured. Over the next 20 years, Adams continued to win leading roles in Barrie's plays, performing in the US premieres of *Quality Street*, *What Every Woman Knows*, *The Legend of Leonora*, and *A Kiss for Cinderella*. But it was her performance of the title role in *Peter Pan*, a part written specifically for her, for which she is now best remembered.

Peter Pan was the perfect vehicle for Adams's stage persona. While not a striking beauty, according to the prevailing standards, she had a boyish countenance and elfin-like presence that suited the role exactly. Her portrayal of the boy who refused to grow up highlighted her innate performance qualities, while she in turn defined the role in perpetuity. The role also established her fondness for androgenous characters, reflected in her subsequent performances of Viola in *Twelfth Night*, Joan of Arc, Rosalind in *As You Like It*, and the title roles in *L'Aiglon* and *Chantecler*. While less successful in Shakespeare, she was praised for her interpretations of Rostand's works, in which her melodic voice and youthful energy combined to great effect.

Her early retirement from the stage in 1918 at the height of her career is attributed to both ill-health and a growing dissatisfaction with Frohman's firm after his death on the *Lusitania* in 1915. For the next 14 years she lived a fiercely private and reclusive life, devoting her energies to her alternate passions in theatrical lighting and technical theatre. In the early 1920's, in association with General Electric, she developed a prototype of the kleig light, a standard instrument in modern cinematic photography. Despite numerous offers, she remained in retirement until 1931, when Otis Skinner persuaded her to play Portia to his Shylock in a national tour of *The Merchant of Venice*. She last performed on stage in a 1934 summer stock production of *Twelfth Night*, playing Maria. She then turned her attentions to education and for 10 years she taught acting and directed plays as a founding faculty member of the theatre department at Stephens College in Columbia, Missouri.

Although Adams never married, she projected a public image of her private life that was beyond reproach. Her popularity rested largely on her perceived innocence and purity. Her skill as a performer was her instinctive ability to capitalize on her public image. While her performances lacked the passion required for romantic leads, her talent for emotional sincerity, playfulness, and youthful sentiment captured the US audience as no other performer had.

—Peter A. Davis

———

AKIMOV, Nikolai (Pavlovitch). Soviet designer, director, graphic artist, portraitist, and teacher. Born in Kharkov, Russia (now Kharkov, Ukraine), 3 April 1901. Trained in the studios of artists Dobouzhinsky, Yakovlev, and Shukhaev, 1915–19. Began career in design at Kharkov Children's Theatre, 1922; worked in Moscow and Leningrad from 1923; debut as director, 1929; artistic director of Leningrad Theatre of Comedy, 1939–49 and 1955–68; artistic director of Lensoviet Theatre, Leningrad, 1951–55; also acclaimed for paintings, playbills, and book illustrations. People's Artist of the USSR, 1960. Died in Moscow, 6 September 1968.

Productions

As designer:

1926   *Konets Krivorylska* [The End of Krivorylsk] (Romashov), Pushkin Theatre, Leningrad.

1927   *Bronepoezd 14—69* [Armoured Train 14—69] (Ivanov), Pushkin Theatre, Leningrad.

1928   *Chelovek s portfelem* [The Man with a Briefcase] (Faiko), Theatre of the Revolution, Moscow.

       Razlom [The Breakthrough] (Lavrenev), Vahktangov Theatre, Moscow.

1929   *Tartuffe* (Molière), Pushkin Theatre, Leningrad; also directed.

       Zagovor chustv [A Conspiracy of Feelings] (Olesha), Pushkin Theatre, Leningrad.

1930   *Kabale und Liebe* [Love and Intrigue] (Schiller), Vakhtangov Theatre, Moscow.

       Iarost' [Jealousy] (Ianovsky), Pushkin Theatre, Leningrad.

1931   *Strakh* [Fear] (Afinogenov), Pushkin Theatre, Leningrad.

1932   *Hamlet* (Shakespeare), Vakhtangov Theatre, Moscow.

1934   *Pravda* [Truth] (Korneichuk), Theatre of the Revolution, Moscow.

1935   *Gibel' eskadry* [The Destruction of the Squadron] (Korneichuk), Pushkin Theatre, Leningrad.

1936   *Liubov Iarovaia* [Schoolmistress Liubov Iarovaia] (Trenev), Art Theatre, Moscow.

       El perro del hortelano (Vega Carpio), Theatre of Comedy, Leningrad; also directed.

1938   *Twelfth Night* (Shakespeare), Theatre of Comedy, Leningrad; revived there, 1964; also directed.

1939   *The Widow of Valencia* (Vega Carpio), Theatre of Comedy, Leningrad; also directed.

1940   *The School for Scandal* (Sheridan), Art Theatre, Moscow.

       Ten' [The Shadow] (Shvarts), Theatre of Comedy, Leningrad; revived there, 1960; also directed.

1944   *Drakon* [The Dragon] (Shvarts), Theatre of Comedy, Leningrad; revived there, 1962; also directed.

1945   *The Naval Officer* (Kron), Art Theatre, Moscow.

1953   *Teni* [Shadows] (Saltykov-Shchedrin), Lensoviet Theatre, Leningrad; also directed.

1955   *Delo* [The Deal] (Sukhovo-Kobylin), Lensoviet Theatre, Leningrad; revived there, 1964; also directed.

1956   *Obyknovennoe chudoe* [An Ordinary Miracle] (Shvarts), Theatre of Comedy, Leningrad; also directed.

1960   *Pëstrye rasskazy* [Motley Stories] (Chekhov), Theatre of Comedy, Leningrad.

1963   *Don Juan* (Byron), Theatre of Comedy, Leningrad; also directed.

1966   *Svadba Krechinskogo* [Krechinsky's Wedding] (Sukhovo-Kobylin), Theatre of Comedy, Leningrad.

Other productions included: *Avan gard* [Avant garde] (Kataev); *Vragi* [The Enemy] (Gorky); *Zena* [The Wife] (Trenev).

Films

Cinderella.

Publications

O teatre [About Theatre], 1962; *Ne tol'ko o teatre* [Not Only About Theatre], 1966; *Teatral'noe nasledie* [Theatre Legacy], 1978.

*

Bibliography

Books:
Nikolai A. Gorchakov, *The Theater in Soviet Russia*, translated by Edgar Lehrman, New York, 1957.
Mordecai Gorelik, *New Theaters for Old*, New York, 1962.

* * *

Nikolai Akimov was among the most innovative and controversial stage designers of his generation and it was largely through his efforts that the Leningrad Theatre of Comedy became established as one of the most exciting Soviet ensembles. Starting out as a designer only, he soon attracted attention with his radical designs for such plays as Afinogenov's *Fear*, on which he collaborated with the Meyerhold-influenced director Nikolai Petrov. Branded "giantist" and "expressionist", his design was intended to emphasise the theme of a people driven by fear and comprised a huge raked stage with a hole of darkness in the background. The characters themselves were reduced to pygmies, as one critic observed, running frantically about the stage.

Akimov combined design and direction for the first time in 1929 and went on to treat established Russian and European classics as well as new plays by contemporary Soviet writers in a similar vein of unilinear extremism in order to point out a Communist moral. The theatre historian Gorchakov remarked that "The national record for revising Shakespeare was set by Akimov's production of *Hamlet* in 1932 at the Vakhtangov Theatre" and this certainly proved one of the most contentious of all his works. He abridged the great soliloquy "To be or not to be", which he felt would be boring or foreign to a Soviet audience, and had a single-mindedly ambitious Hamlet speak it with a crown in his hand to underline his determination to regain his purloined throne. The ghost, meanwhile, was depicted as a figment of his imagination and Ophelia came on not mad but drunk.

Another classic production followed in 1930 with Friedrich Schiller's *Love and Intrigue*, the success of which owed more to Akimov's designs than to the work of the directors. A tragedy about a son's resistance to his politician-father's plans to marry him off for the sake of political advancement (rather than to a poor musician's daughter), the production opened with a celebrated stage picture, in which the poor musician was seen conducting an invisible orchestra "in the middle of a huge circle, which sparkled with silver and sloped sharply toward the footlight" (as described by Gorchakov). Another striking visual image was created by Akimov for the end of the play, the two lovers' bodies lying in the same shining circle while the poor musician, now mad with grief, stood threatening some power in the sky as his unseen orchestra played a sequence of final mourning chords.

Akimov is sometimes ignored as one of the foremost designers of the 20th century, but his mastery of both design and direction, with his use of colour, motion, and fantasy, was unique. Akimov himself claimed "I am an incorrigible realist" and his designs were remarkable for their simplicity (an approach he adopted while designing for children, who require a simplified version of reality). His famous portraits of his friends (and of himself) were simplified almost to the point of caricature, though critics found in this simplification a tendency to neglect other salient traits. His stage designs were clean and effective (in contrast to the cluttered designs associated with the Moscow Art Theatre) and well-suited to conveying the Communist ideology then required of the Soviet theatre. Akimov was among the first wave of Communist directors and designers and proved one of the most adept. His design for *Armoured Train 14—69*, only the second for which he was solely responsible, was a particularly successfully evocation of revolutionary ideals, depicting as it did the heroism and tragedy of the crew of an armoured train in the civil war that split Russia after the 1917 Revolution. Highlights of the production included the 'vertical' stage picture that was used to support the illusion of overhead attacks on the train and the so-called 'clean changes' that allowed one scene to fade seamlessly into another (a technique intended to bring the instant scene changes of the cinema to the live stage).

Akimov's use of a raked stage was another characteristic of his work, forcing performers downstage and assisting in the illusion of vast panoramas. Other special effects employed in his productions included the use of a turntable (though this was prone to technical failure and did not work on the opening night of Chekhov's *Man with a Briefcase*).

Political criticism remained central to Akimov's productions throughout his career, though it became less open as the years went by. Notable expressions of his antipathy towards bureaucratic corruption included his productions of plays by Schiller and of the political fairytales of Evgeny Shvarts, which implied daring criticisms of both Hitler and Stalin. Some of these plays have dated badly, but Akimov himself is remembered for his colourful designs and melodramatically exaggerated movement and blocking.

—Marjorie L. Hoover

ALDRIDGE, Ira (Frederick). US actor. Born in New York (some sources, Baltimore or even Senegal) c.24 July 1807 (some sources, as early as 1804), son of a strawvendor. Educated at the African Free School, New York, 1820–24; possibly also at Glasgow University, 1825. Married 1) Margaret Gill in 1825 (died 1864); 2) Amanda Pauline von Brandt in 1865, two daughters and one son; one son by unidentified woman. Stage debut, African Theatre, New York, c.1822; travelled to England, as servant to the actor Edmund Kean, 1824; British debut, playing Othello, Royal Coburg Theatre, London, 1825; acclaimed as 'The African Roscius' on tour throughout Britain over next 25 years; succeeded Edmund Kean in *Othello*, Covent Garden, 1833; returned to provinces; toured successfully in Europe, particularly in Germany and Russia, from 1852; finally won acceptance as a black actor on London stage, 1858; took British nationality, 1863; embarked on last European tour, 1865. Hon. Captain, Republican Army of Haiti, 1827. Member: Imperial and Archducal Institution of Our Lady of the Manger (Austria), 1856; Royal Saxon Ernestinischen House Order (Saxe-Meiningen), 1858; Royal Bohemian Conservatoire of Prague, 1858; National Dramatic Conservatoire of Hungary, 1858; Russian Hofversamlung of Riga, 1859; Imperial Academy of Beaux Arts, St Petersburg, 1858. Recipient: Gold Medal, Prussian Academy of Arts and Sciences, 1853; White Cross of Switzerland, 1854; Grand Cross, Order of Leopold (Austria), 1854. Died in Lødz, Poland, 10 August 1867.

Principal roles

c.1822–23	Rolla in *Pizarro* (Kotzebue), African Theatre, New York.
	Romeo in *Romeo and Juliet* (Shakespeare), African Theatre, New York.
1825	Oroonoko in *The Revolt of Surinam; or, A Slave's Revenge* (adapted from Southerne), Royal Coburg Theatre, London.
	Gambia in *The Slave* (Morton), Royal Coburg Theatre, London.
	Christophe in *The Death of Christophe, King of Hayti* (Amherst), Royal Coburg Theatre, London.
	Othello in *Othello* (Shakespeare), Royal Coburg Theatre, London.
1827	Lear in *King Lear* (Shakespeare), British provinces.
	Zanga in *The Revenge* (Young), British provinces.
	Mungo in *The Padlock* (Bickerstaff), British provinces.
	Hassan in *The Castle Spectre* (Lewis), British provinces.
	Ginger Blue in *The Virginian Mummy* (Rice), British provinces.
1829	Kalkanco in *The Savage of the Desert* (Roberds), British provinces.
	Aboan in *The Revolt of Surinam; or, A Slave's Revenge* (adapted from Southerne), British provinces.
	Alhambra in *Paul and Virginia* (Cobb), British provinces.
1830	Captain Dick Hatteraick in *Guy Mannering* (Scott and Terry), Kendal.
	Jack in *Obi; or, Three-Fingered Jack* (Fawcett, adapted by Murray), Theatre Royal, Bristol.
1831	Macbeth in *Macbeth* (Shakespeare), Hull.

Ira Aldridge

Shylock in *The Merchant of Venice* (Shakespeare), Adelphi Theatre, Hull.

Bertram in *Bertram; or, The Castle of St Aldobrand* (Maturin), Theatre Royal, Derby.

Alessandro in *The Brigand; or, Alessandro Massaroni* (Planché), Adelphi Theatre, Hull.

Rob Roy in *Rob Roy* (Sloane, adapted from Scott), Adelphi Theatre, Hull.

1832   Sambo in *Laugh While You Can* (Reynolds), Hull.

Richard III in *Richard III* (Shakespeare), Hull.

Muley Hassan in *Fiesco; or, The Conspiracy of Genoa* (Schiller), Theatre Royal, Dublin.

1837   Tomba in *Captain Ross; or, The Hero of the Arctic Regions* (anon.), Hull.

c.1847 Fabian in *The Black Doctor* (adapted from Anicet-Bourgeois and Dumanoir), Bath and Dublin.

c.1849 Aaron in *Titus Andronicus* (Shakespeare, adapted by Aldridge and Somerset), British provinces.

1860   Man Friday in *Robinson Crusoe; or, The Bold Buccaneer* (Pocock), Glasgow.

Also acted roles in: *The Afghanistan War* (anon.); *The African's Vengeance* (anon.); *Banks of the Hudson; or, The Congress Trooper* (anon.); *Bond of Blood* (anon.); *The Cannibal King* (anon.); *The Coronation Day of William IV* (anon.); *Father and Son; or, The Rock of La Carbonniere* (Fitzball); *Frankenstein; or, The Man and Monster* (Milner); *The French Pirate* (anon.); *The Negro's Curse; or, The Foulah Son* (Milner); *The Siberian Exile* (Reynolds); *Valentine and Orson* (T. Dibdin); *William Tell* (Knowles).

*

Bibliography

Books:
Herbert Marshall and Mildred Stock, *Ira Aldridge – The Negro Tragedian*, London, 1958.
Mary Malone, *Actor in Exile: The Life of Ira Aldridge*, New York, 1969.
Herbert Marshall, *Further Research on Ira Aldridge, the Negro Tragedian*, Carbondale, Illinois, 1973.

Articles:
Anon., "Mr Ira Aldridge", *Tallis's Dramatic Magazine*, June 1851.
Fountain Peyton, "A Glance at the Life of Ira Frederick Aldridge" (pamphlet), Washington, 1917.

* * *

Considered by most historians to be the USA's first great African-American actor, Ira Frederick Aldridge is credited with anticipating the psychological school of realistic acting decades before its widespread popularization. He was the first US-born actor to achieve critical and popular acclaim on the European stage.

Little is known about Aldridge's early life. His place of birth is variously listed as Maryland, New York, and even Senegal, where he was reported to be descended from the royal family of the Fulah tribe. The year of his birth is similarly vague, estimates ranging from 1804 to as late as 1820 (a mere five years before his London debut). His father, Daniel Aldridge, who may have served as a lay minister in the community, saw to it that his son got a respectable education and before he left school the young man had already begun his theatrical career with the shortlived African Theatre under the guidance of the company's leading actor, James Hewlett. By most accounts Aldridge made his debut as Rolla in Kotzebue's *Pizarro* and may have performed the male lead in *Romeo and Juliet* as well. In June 1823, amid growing hostility against the company from Whites, the African Theatre was closed by the authorities shortly after the opening of *The Drama of King Shotaway*, in which Hewlett portrayed the leader of a Black insurrection on a Caribbean island. Within a year Aldridge had left the USA for England and was launched on one of the most illustrious careers of the 19th-century stage.

Speculation that Aldridge briefly attended the University of Glasgow is supported by his delayed arrival on the London stage, for it was not until October 1825, apparently at the age of 18, that he made his English theatrical debut. The mixed notices he received in the press were as much a reflection of his youthful inexperience as they were of the inherent bigotry of English critics. Despite his sudden popularity among audiences, Aldridge was forced to spend much of the next 25 years touring the provinces, where he developed an enormous following and an outstanding critical reputation, perfecting such roles as Othello, Macbeth, Zanga from Edward Young's *The Revenge*, and Mungo in Bickerstaff's *The Padlock*. In 1833, Aldridge made his only appearance at Covent Garden when he took over as Othello for two performances upon the death of Edmund Kean. As expected, the critical response was mixed; the enlightened press acknowledged his brilliance and insight while the rest echoed the racial slurs and blatant bigotry of his earlier London debut. Nevertheless, for the first time a US actor (and more significantly one of African descent) had performed one of the greatest tragic roles on one of the greatest stages in the English-speaking world.

In the wake of his Covent Garden performance, Aldridge returned to his usual pattern of provincial tours through England, Ireland, and Scotland with occasional stints at London's lesser houses, including the Surrey, the City, and the Britannia theatres. The provincial audiences were far more accommodating and appreciative of his genius. Hence he was able, as well as encouraged, to expand his repertoire to include most of Shakespeare's leading roles — Lear, Titus Andronicus, Shylock, Richard III, and perhaps Hamlet — opportunities unavailable to him in the West End.

Yet despite his growing reputation and repertoire, Aldridge was ignored by the major London theatres and in the summer of 1852, hoping to find more appreciative audiences elsewhere, he left England on his first Continental tour. The repertory included his best known works, *Othello*, *Titus Andronicus*, *The Padlock*, and *Macbeth*, in which he appeared in the major cities of northern Europe. He was particularly popular in the German states, where he became a favourite of royalty and the recipient of numerous honours. It appears from surviving records that he continued to perform in his native English, while the supporting cast spoke in German or other European languages, and for some roles — notably Lear — he even donned white facial make-up (though his hands were left dark).

Upon his return to England in 1855, Aldridge sought unsuccessfully to break into the West End once more but was forced to resort again to touring the provinces and playing the minor London houses. His reputation on the Continent, however, continued to grow and by 1858, after another brief tour through northern Europe, Aldridge returned to London and an offer to perform Othello at the Lyceum in the West End. Despite the well-deserved but long-delayed acclaim of the West End audiences that ensued, Aldridge continued to find greater satisfaction on the Continent. In 1865 he left England for the last time, dying while performing at Lødz in Poland. Aldridge never returned to the USA. He made England his adopted home and became a British subject in 1863. Later in his career he was favourably compared to Macready and praised for his dignified, restrained, and intelligent interpretations. He played a wide range of classical and contemporary characters and was equally adept at tragedy and comedy.

—Peter A. Davies

ALEXANDER, (Sir) George. British actor-manager. Born George Alexander Gibb Samson in Reading, 19 June 1858. Educated at Dr Benham's, Clifton; Relton's, Ealing; High School, Stirling; apprenticed to London draper's firm; entered business, 1875. Married Florence Jane Théleur in 1882. Began acting as amateur; professional debut, Theatre Royal, Nottingham, 1879; London debut, Standard Theatre, Bishopsgate, 1881; actor, Henry Irving's company at the Lyceum Theatre, 1881–89; also acted alongside W. H. Kendal and John Hare with the St James's Theatre company and elsewhere; accompanied Irving on US tours, 1884–85 and 1887–88; entered management, Avenue Theatre, London, 1890; lessee and manager, St James's Theatre, 1891–1918; championed presentation of plays by British authors, including works by Bennett, Hardy, Galsworthy, Wilde, and Pinero; Royal Command performances, 1895 and 1908; briefly manager of the Royalty Theatre, 1896; last appearance, St James's Theatre, 1917. Member: Royal General Theatrical Fund (president); Actors' Benevolent Fund (vice-president); Actors' Association; Theatres Mutual Insurance Company (chairman); London County Council (representing South St Pancras), 1907–13. LL.D, University of Bristol, 1912. Liveryman, Turner's Company; Justice of the Peace. Knighted, 1911. Died in Chorley Wood, Hertfordshire, 16 March 1918.

Roles

1879	Charles in *His Last Legs* (Bernard), Theatre Royal, Nottingham, England.
	Harry Prendergast in *Snowball* (Grundy), Theatre Royal, Nottingham, England.
1879–80	Hawtree and George D'Alroy in *Caste* (Robertson), British tour.
	Angus in *Ours* (Robertson), British tour.
	Lord Beaufoy in *School* (Robertson), British tour.
	Colonel White in *Home* (Robertson), British tour.
	Sydney Daryl in *Society* (Robertson), British tour.
	Chudleigh Dunscombe in *M.P.* (Robertson), British tour.
1881	Freddy Butterscotch in *The Guv'nor* (Reece), Standard Theatre, Bishopsgate, London, and British tour.
	Caleb Deecie in *The Two Roses* (Albery), Lyceum Theatre, London.
1882	Paris in *Romeo and Juliet* (Shakespeare), Lyceum Theatre, London.
	Claude Gwynne in *The Parvenu* (Godfrey), Court Theatre, London.
	Orlando in *As You Like It* (Shakespeare), British tour.
	Romeo in *Romeo and Juliet* (Shakespeare), British tour.
	Benedick in *Much Ado About Nothing* (Shakespeare), British tour.
	Posthumus Leonatus in *Cymbeline* (Shakespeare), British tour.
1883	Cecil Cassilis in *Ranks and Riches* (Collins), Adelphi Theatre, London.
1884	D'Aulnay in *Comedy and Tragedy* (Gilbert), Lyceum Theatre, London.
	Octave in *The Iron-Master* (Pinero), St James's Theatre, London.
	De Mauprat in *Richelieu* (Bulwer-Lytton), Lyceum Theatre, London.

1884–85   Orsino in *Twelfth Night* (Shakespeare), US tour.

Bassanio in *The Merchant of Venice* (Shakespeare), US tour.

Don Pedro in *Much Ado About Nothing* (Shakespeare), US tour.

Lord Moray in *Charles I* (Wills), US tour.

Nemours in *Louis XI* (Boucicault), US tour.

Christian in *The Bells* (Lewis), US tour.

Laertes in *Hamlet* (Shakespeare), US tour.

Courriol in *The Lyons Mail* (Reade), US tour.

1885–86   Valentine and Faust in *Faust* (Wills), Lyceum Theatre, London.

1886–89   Ulric in *Werner* (Lord Byron), Lyceum Theatre, London.

Claudio in *Much Ado About Nothing* (Shakespeare), Lyceum Theatre, London.

Squire Thornhill in *Olivia* (Wills), Lyceum Theatre, London.

Silvio in *The Amber Heart* (Calmour), Lyceum Theatre, London.

Macduff in *Macbeth* (Shakespeare), Lyceum Theatre, London.

1889   Frank Granville in *London Day by Day* (Sims and Pettitt), Adelphi Theatre, London.

1890   Dr. William Brown in *Dr Bill* (Aidé), Avenue Theatre, London.

François Legoez in *The Grandsire* (Woodhouse), Avenue Theatre, London.

Paul Astier in *The Struggle for Life* (Buchanan and Horner), Avenue Theatre, London.

George Addis in *Sunlight and Shadow* (Carton), Avenue Theatre, London; St James's Theatre, London, 1891.

1891   Sir Harry Lovel in *The Gay Lothario* (Calmour), St James's Theatre, London.

Mark Cross in *The Idler* (Chambers), St James's Theatre, London.

Rupert Lee in *Lord Annerley* (Quinton and Hamilton), St James's Theatre, London.

Mr. Hamilton in *Forgiveness* (Carr), St James's Theatre, London.

1892   Lord Windermere in *Lady Windermere's Fan* (Wilde), St James's Theatre, London.

Mister Owen in *Liberty Hall* (Carton), St James's Theatre, London; Balmoral, Scotland, 1895.

1893   Aubrey Tanqueray in *The Second Mrs. Tanqueray* (Pinero), St James's Theatre, London; revived there, 1913.

1894   David Remon in *The Masqueraders* (Jones), St James's Theatre, London.

1895   Jack Worthing in *The Importance of Being Earnest* (Wilde), St James's Theatre, London.

Guy Domville in *Guy Domville* (James), St James's Theatre, London.

Sir Valentine Fellowes in *The Triumph of the Philistines* (Jones), St James's Theatre, London.

Mr. Corquordale in *The Misogynist* (Godfrey), St James's Theatre, London.

Gaunt Humeden in *The Divided Way* (Esmond), St James's Theatre, London.

George Alexander

1896   Rudolf Rassendyll, Prince Rudolf, and Rudolf V in *The Prisoner of Zenda* (Hope), St James's Theatre, London.

Orlando in *As You Like It* (Shakespeare), St James's Theatre, London.

1897   Sir George Lamorant in *The Princess and the Butterfly* (Pinero), St James's Theatre, London.

Nigel Stanton in *The Tree of Knowledge* (Carton), St James's Theatre, London.

1898   Benedick in *Much Ado About Nothing* (Shakespeare), St James's Theatre, London.

Lord St Orbyn in *The Ambassador* (Hobbes), St James's Theatre, London.

Eric von Rodeck in *The Conquerors* (Potter), St James's Theatre, London.

1899   The Friar in *A Repentance* (Hobbes), St James's Theatre, London.

Armyn Beddart in *In Days of Old* (Rose), St James's Theatre, London.

1900   Rudolf V and Rudolf Rassendyl in *Rupert of Hentzau* (Hope), St James's Theatre, London.

George Carlyon in *A Debt of Honour* (Grundy), St James's Theatre, London.

Duke of St Asaph in *The Wisdom of the Wise* (Hobbes), St James's Theatre, London.

Lee Fanshawe in *The Man of Forty* (Frith), St James's Theatre, London.

1901   James St John Trower in *The Awakening* (Chambers), St James's Theatre, London.

1902   Sir Harry Milanor in *The Wilderness* (Esmond), St James's Theatre, London.

Giovanni Malatesta in *Paolo and Francesca* (Phillips), St James's Theatre, London.

François Villon in *If I Were King* (M'Carthy), St James's Theatre, London.

1903   Prince Karl Heinrich in *Old Heidelberg* (Meyer-Forster and Bleichmann), St James's Theatre, London.

1904   Hans Rudorff in *Love's Carnival* (Hartleben and Bleichmann), St James's Theatre, London.

Denis Mallory in *The Garden of Lies* (Forman and Grundy), St James's Theatre, London.

Lord Culvert in *Saturday to Monday* (Fenn and Pryce), St James's Theatre, London.

1905   Oscar Stephenson in *The Prodigal Son* (Caine), Theatre Royal, Drury Lane, London.

John Loder and John Chilcote in *John Chilcote, M.P.* (E. T. and K. C. Thurston), St James's Theatre, London.

Maurice Darlay in *The Man of the Moment* (Melville, Capus, and Arène), St James's Theatre, London.

1906   Hilary Jesson in *His House in Order* (Pinero), St James's Theatre, London; revived there, 1914.

1907   John Glayde in *John Glayde's Honour* (Sutro), St James's Theatre, London.

Richard Chelford in *The Thief* (Bernstein and Gordon-Lennox), St James's Theatre, London.

1908   Thaddeus Mortimore in *The Thunderbolt* (Pinero), St James's Theatre, London.

Edward Thursfield in *The Builder of Bridges* (Sutro), St James's Theatre, London, and Sandringham, Norfolk, England.

1909   Colonel Smith in *Colonel Smith* (Mason), St James's Theatre, London.

Lorrimer Sabiston in *Lorrimer Sabiston, Dramatist* (Carton), St James's Theatre, London.

1910   Hon. John D'Arcy in *D'Arcy of the Guards* (Shipman), St James's Theatre, London.

Earl of Comberdene in *Eccentric Lord Comberdene* (Carton), St James's Theatre, London.

1911   Henry Thresk in *The Witness for the Defence* (Mason), St James's Theatre, London.

Alfred Evelyn in *Money* (Bulwer-Lytton), Theatre Royal, Drury Lane, London.

Dr. Isaacson in *Bella Donna* (Fagan), St James's Theatre, London.

Nicholas Fawsitt in *The Ogre* (Jones), St James's Theatre, London.

1912   Lieutenant-Colonel Felt in *The Turning Point* (Kistemaeckers and Le Marchant), St James's Theatre, London.

1913   John Herrick in *Open Windows* (Mason), St James's Theatre, London.

Tommy Dixon in *A Social Success* (Beerbohm), Palace Theatre, London.

1914   Alexandre Mérital in *The Attack* (Bernstein and Egerton), St James's Theatre, London.

Jeffery Panton in *The Two Virtues* (Sutro), St James's Theatre, London.

Viscount Goring in *An Ideal Husband* (Wilde), St James's Theatre, London.

Michael Trent in *Those Who Sit in Judgment* (Orme), St James's Theatre, London.

1915   Frederick IV in *Kings and Queens* (Besier), St James's Theatre, London.

Sir Richard Gauntlett in *The Panorama of Youth* (Manners), St James's Theatre, London.

Other roles included: *Mammon* (Grundy), Theatre Royal, Nottingham, England, 1879; *A Lesson in Love* (Cheltnam), Theatre Royal, Nottingham, England, 1879; *Living at Ease* (Sketchley), Theatre Royal, Nottingham, England, 1879; *Impulse* (Stephenson), St James's Theatre, London, 1883; *Young Folks' Ways* (Burnett and Gilette), St James's Theatre, London, 1883; *The Aristocrat* (Parker), St James's Theatre, London, 1917.

Publications

Parts I Have Played, 1909.

*

Bibliography

Books:
A. E. W. Mason, *Sir George Alexander and the St James's Theatre*, London, 1935.

* * *

Sir George Alexander's individuality as an actor largely corresponded to the nature of his own personality: he was a perfect gentleman on and off the stage, the matinée idol of the fashionable St James's audience. Elegance, refinement, restraint, and charm were the qualities most admired in his acting. However, true emotion and genuine passion were also within his range of expression. A good voice, while not free of mannerisms, effective modulation, and excellent timing counted among his strengths, though he seems to have lacked humour and spontaneity. It bespeaks his stature as an actor that a number of insignificant plays are only remembered for Alexander's performances in them, even if he occasionally resorted to "a finished impersonation of Mr. George Alexander", as Shaw remarked caustically, in order to "fill his empty parts". Nevertheless, boundless praise was lavished on him by the dramatists whose characters he had brought to life on the stage, A. W. Pinero, H. A. Jones, and Stephen Phillips being the most important of them. Only Oscar Wilde was a striking exception.

Usually associated with immaculately dressed protagonists in drawing-room dramas and heroes in plays of a romantic mould, Alexander's versatility in the choice and interpretation of his numerous roles was remarkable all the same. Such diverse parts as the dual role of Rassendyll and the King in *The Prisoner of Zenda*, the boyish German Prince Karl Heinrich in *Old Heidelberg* (at the age of 45), Dr. Isaccson in *Bella Donna*, John Worthing in *The Importance of Being Earnest*, Aubrey Tanqueray in *The Second Mrs. Tanqueray*, and, most notably, the raisonneur Hilary Jesson in *His House in Order* were among his triumphs. Without excelling as a Shakespearean actor, he gave competent performances of Orlando and Benedick. His impersonation of the demanding title role in Henry James's *Guy Domville* won him much respect. Furthermore, his compelling portrayal of Giovanni Malesta in *Paolo and Francesca*, the fierce, tormented warrior-husband not being his line at all, greatly added to his reputation as an actor. Outside his own St James's Theatre, Alexander distinguished himself in the difficult part of Alfred Evelyn in Bulwer-Lytton's *Money* at a gala performance at Drury Lane in 1911 among an all-star cast including Hare, Tree, and Wyndham.

Alexander's significance as a leading actor of his time is surpassed by his acheivement as a theatrical manager. Various factors contributed to the commercial and artistic success of his 27 years' management at the St James's Theatre, in particular conscientious pre-rehearsal preparations, whenever possible together with the dramatist, carefully paced and perfectly timed rehearsals with an emphasis on punctuality, discipline, and efficiency, and well-balanced, unselfish casting — not a common virtue in actor-managers. Although not necessarily the star on the stage, Alexander was the soul of every production, at least behind the scenes. His tact, politeness, and poise were conducive to a pleasant yet productive working climate. He also afforded a number of young actors and actresses the opportunity to make their names. Countless anecdotes cluster around Alexander's martyrdom at the hands of the most famous of them, the temperamental and capricious Mrs Patrick Campbell, whose Paula Tanqueray took the town by storm in 1893. The house style of Alexander's St James's Theatre may be seen as a continuation and adaptation of the attempts at stage realism by the Bancrofts and Robertson, with a view to attracting a socially superior segment of the theatre-going public.

By and large Alexander's repertoire was also attuned to the taste of his audience. Henry Arthur Jones's compliment, "Alec was the best judge of a play of any man in London", required the modification "with regard to its suitability for his own theatre". Although Alexander deserves credit for his preference for and encouragement of British dramatists, he generally spared his clientele every confrontation with the unconventional, let alone the experimental, in drama. The majority of the authors of costume dramas, romances, comedies, and society plays in the wake of Jones and Pinero seen at the theatre were at best solid craftsmen.

However, Alexander was also associated with a few authors of greater literary merit. The production of Henry James's *Guy Domville* won some praise from the critics, though it failed with the St James audience. The verse tragedy *Paolo and Francesca*, which Alexander commissioned from Stephen Phillips, was received much more favourably. With the exception of *The Masqueraders*, Henry Arthur Jones's works for Alexander's theatre (*The Triumph of the Philistines* and *The Ogre*) never became popular. It was chiefly Alexander's co-operation with Oscar Wilde and Arthur Wing Pinero that secured him a prominent position in the history of English drama. Both *Lady Windermere's Fan*, which came to incorporate some textual improvements suggested by the actor-manager, and *The Importance of Being Earnest*, one of his major successes (though only in a later revival), were first produced by Alexander. His collaboration with Pinero, not without

friction in later years — mostly due to the dramatist's autocratic attitude — was a fruitful one. Of the seven plays altogether performed, *The Second Mrs. Tanqueray* was the most important, whereas *His House in Order* provided Alexander with an ideal part and earned him the longest run of his management. *The Thunderbolt* and *Mid-Channel* turned out to be much less attractive; in the former, the provincial setting, the theme, and Alexander's role were not to the audience's taste. In the latter case, Alexander's absence from the cast, notwithstanding a central part for the raisonneur, guaranteed its failure.

Harley Granville-Barker, an exponent of the alternative theatre and a champion against censorship, had considerable respect for Alexander, the manager of a commercial theatre and defender of censorship. In a letter to John Gielgud, Barker remembers and comments on Alexander's unpretentious assessment of his own services to the theatre: "I've not done much for the drama (though in a carefully limited fashion he had) but I've paid salaries every Friday night without fail, and *that's* to my credit." And it was.

—Rudolf Weiss

ALLEYN, Edward. English actor-manager. Born in Bishopsgate, London, 1 September 1566. Married 1) Joan Woodward, stepdaughter of theatre manager Phillip Henslowe, in 1592 (died 1623); 2) Constance Donne, daughter of poet John Donne, in 1623. Acting professionally with Worcester's Men by 1583; actor, Admiral's Men, by 1589; actor, combined Lord Admiral's company and Lord Strange's Men, Rose Theatre, Southwark, 1592–94; following marriage to Joan Woodward, partnered Henslowe in his entrepreneurial activities, eventually controlling Rose and Fortune theatres, the Paris Garden, and the Bear Garden among other venues for entertainment; toured provinces during outbreak of plague, 1593; created roles in plays by Marlowe, among other writers; left stage in 1597, returned in 1599; built Fortune Theatre, Cripplegate, in partnership with Henslowe, 1600, and appeared regularly there with the Admiral's Men, 1599–c.1604; retired from the stage, c.1604; made congratulatory speech, welcoming James I to the City of London, and took part in coronation procession, 1604; received joint patent with Henslowe as "Master of the Royal Game of Bears, Bulls, and Mastiff Dogs", 1604; bought Dulwich Manor, 1605; became churchwarden, 1610; inherited share in Hope Theatre, 1616; opened The College and Hospital of God's Gift (Dulwich College), 1619; became patron of Dekker and other writers; unsuccessfully attempted to acquire a knighthood, 1624. Died in Dulwich, 25 November 1626.

Documented roles

c.1587–88   Tamburlaine in *Tamburlaine the Great* (Marlowe), Rose Theatre, London.
c.1588   Faustus in *Doctor Faustus* (Marlowe), Bel Savage or Rose Theatre, London.
c.1589   Muly Mahomet in *The Battle of Alcazar* (Peele), Rose Theatre, London.
   Barabas in *The Jew of Malta* (Marlowe), several London theatres.

c.1591   Orlando in *Orlando Furioso* (Greene), venue
        unknown.
c.1592   Hieronimo in *The Spanish Tragedy* (Kyd),
        venue unknown.
c.1596   Tamar Cam in *Tamar Cam, part 1* (anon.,
        possibly by Alleyn), Rose Theatre, London.

Conjectured roles

The Beggar in *The Blind Beggar of Alexandria* (Chapman);
Cutlack in *Cutlack* (anon.); Sebastian in *Frederick and
Basilea* (anon.); role in *Friar Bacon and Friar Bungay*
(Greene); King Edgar in *A Knack to Know a Knave*
(anon.); role in *A Knack to Know an Honest Man* (anon.);
role in *The Wise Man of West Chester* (anon.).

*

Bibliography

Books:
J. P. Collier, *Memoir of Edward Alleyn*, London, 1841.
J. P. Collier, *Alleyn Papers*, London, 1843.
G. L. Hosking, *Life and Times of Edward Alleyn*, London,
1952.
A. D. Wraight, *Christopher Marlowe and Edward Alleyn*,
Chichester, 1993.

* * *

Without doubt, Edward Alleyn and Richard Burbage
were the two greatest actors of the Elizabethan era. In
attempting to understand their particular achievements,
Burbage's acting is often characterised as an advance on
and a development of Alleyn's more rhetorical style. Such a
clear-cut sequential view is misleading as their careers, in
the main, ran side by side. Alleyn was, at the most, no more
than two or three years older than his rival (Burbage's exact
date of birth is unknown) and was acting professionally by
1583 (whereas, according to his brother Cuthbert, Burbage's histrionic career began in 1584). However, fame
came early for Alleyn, probably initiated by the phenomenal success of *Tamburlaine* in 1587–88 and certainly
consolidated by his remarkable season at the Rose Playhouse in the winter and spring of 1591–92. "Famous Ned
Allen" is eulogized by Nashe in *Pierce Penilesse* (1592), and
in *Strange News* (1592) his contemporary eminence is
suggested when Nashe writes of Edmund Spenser that "his
very name (as that of Ned Allen on the common stage) was
able to make an ill matter good".

From 1594 onwards, it is clear that Burbage, as founder-
member of the Lord Chamberlain's Men and leading
interpreter of Shakespeare's growing repertoire, began to
challenge Alleyn's pre-eminence. Both actors played major
roles during the important and financially successful years
leading up to the dark days surrounding the Privy Council
Order of 1597, when the future of the public playhouses
seemed about to be curtailed. It was at this moment that
Alleyn chose to retire from the stage. Why he did so must
remain conjecture, but it surely relates to future prospects
and his own situation rather than to his acting being
outmoded. The view that his style was by then old-fashioned is untenable for, when he returned to acting in 1600
at the request of the Queen and after the fortune of the

playhouses had revived, he gave some five years of
"unimitable" performances before deciding to leave playing for good and to devote his money and time to the
foundation and management of the College of God's Gift at
Dulwich. At the coronation procession of James I, he
appeared as the Genius of the City "with excellent action
and a well-tun'de, audible voyce". He outlived Burbage by
seven years, maintaining an interest in the theatre and
becoming a patron of his former profession. It was this
longevity and his years off the stage that seems to have
kindled this sense of his being out of fashion, though
Thomas Heywood was among those who clearly cherished
the memory: "Among so many dead let me not forget one
yet alive, in his time the most worthy, famous Maister
Edward Allen."

The misleading stress on Alleyn's "earlier" and "less
sophisticated" style of acting springs from comparison
between Marlowe and Shakespeare and identification of
their leading interpreters with the literary differences that
are so apparent. Marlowe died in 1593, while Alleyn
survived another 20 or so years, stranded perhaps by
changes in the repertoire rather than by some evolution
within acting. What can be gleaned from Henslowe's
accounts of the 1594–97 seasons allows us to assume that
Alleyn was as outstanding in comedy as he was in tragedy.
That this was true of his earlier career is suggested by the
revival of such plays as Greene's *Friar Bacon and Friar
Bungay* in the repertoire of the Fortune Theatre alongside
Kyd's *The Spanish Tragedy* and Peele's *The Battle of
Alcazar* and by the quite exceptional ascription to *A Knack
to Know a Knave*: "as it hath sundrye tymes been plaid by
Ned. Allen and his Companie". The remarkable perfor-
mance records of *A Knack to Know an Honest Man*, *The
Wise Man of West Chester*, and Chapman's *The Blind
Beggar of Alexandria* must have owed much to Alleyn.
Chapman's play (*the* success of the 1596 season at the
Rose) was revived, along with *The Jew of Malta*, for
Alleyn's return to the stage in 1600 and the role of the
Beggar, like that of Barabas, must have been chosen to
confirm his rank as a "Proteus for shapes", as Heywood
described him. The principal character is a blind soothsay-
er who affects a dazzling variety of disguises, just as
Marlowe's Jew astounds by his duplicity. In different ways,
both are vehicles for considerable comic skill.

Humour and bathos are evident in the alterations made
to the role of Orlando, in Greene's *Orlando Furioso*, which
survives in Alleyn's handwriting among his papers in
Dulwich. In the mad scene, changes include a descent from
grave latin to the more colloquial "a peny for a pott of beer
and six pence for a peec of beife wounds!" together with
judiciously farcical stage directions. Abrupt changes of
mood and an exhilarating rapidity in self-alteration seem to
have been as much a feature of Alleyn's style as oratory and
pathos. Undoubtedly his rhetorical skills were well-suited
to the role of Tamburlaine, as they were to that of
Hieronimo, but his range was wide, wider even that the
seven roles of which we have direct evidence. In the parts
of Barabas and Faustus something of the nature of this
range can be discerned. They were among his most
successful "personations" and held the stage for a decade.
Faustus, to take but one of these, demands eloquence and
pathos but also a robust sense of satire and farce. It was a
range that made Alleyn a master on the stage of his era, in
the words of Thomas Heywood: "a man whom we may

rank with (doing no one wrong) Proteus for shapes, and Roscius for a tongue, so he could speak, so vary."

—Leslie du S. Read

ANDREINI family. Italian actor-managers, comprising Francesco Andreini, his wife Isabella Andreini, their eldest son Giovan Battista Andreini, and other family members. Francesco Andreini was an actor-manager and playwright, born Francesco Cerrachi in Pistoia, c.1548. Isabella Andreini was an actress, playwright, and poet, born Isabella Canali in Padua, 1562. Both made stage debuts with Flamineo Scala's commedia dell'arte company before co-founding the Gelosi acting company, c.1588; Francesco taken prisoner by Turks for eight years, returning to Italy and to the Gelosi, 1578; Isabella celebrated in role of the Innamorata, becoming the most famed member of the family; Francesco popular as the Sicilian doctor and the young lover, but later excelled as the braggart soldier Capitano Spavento da Vall'Inferno; Gelosi acclaimed on tour to Paris, 1603–04; company dissolved on Isabella's death during childbirth in Lyons, 10 June 1604. Francesco Andreini died in Mantua, 20 August 1624. Giovan Battista Andreini was an actor, playwright, and poet, born in Florence, 9 February 1576 or 1579. Educated at the University of Bologna. Married 1) actress Virginia Ramponi (died 1630); 2) actress Virginia Rotari in 1634. Stage debut with the Gelosi; played role of the Innamorato under the stagename Lelio; left the Gelosi and co-founded the Fedeli company with Tristano Martinelli; toured Italy with the Fedeli, 1613–14; acclaimed in France, becoming favourite of Louis XIII; continued acting until the age of 73. Died in Reggio Emilia, Italy, 7 or 8 June c.1654.

Publications

Francesco Andreini:
Il felicissimo arrivo del Serenissimo Don Vittorio Principe di Savoia insieme al Serenissimo Don Filiberto suo fratello nella famosa citta di Torino, 1605; *Le bravure del Capitan Spavento*, 1607; *L'ingannata Proserpina*, 1611; *L'Alterezza di Narciso*, 1611; *I Ragionamenti fantastici posti in forma di dialoghi rappresentativi*, 1612.

Isabella Andreini:
La Mirtilla (pastoral play), 1588; *Rime* (verse), 1601; *Lettere*, 1607; *Fragmenti di alcune scritture*, 1620.

Giovan Battista Andreini:
La Saggia egiziana, 1604; *La Divina visione* (verse), 1604; *Il Pianto di Apollo* (verse), 1606; *Florinda* (play, produced 1608); *La Turca* (play), 1608; *La Maddalena* (verse), 1610; *Lo Schiavetto* (play), 1612; *L'Adamo* (play), 1613; *La Maddalena* (play), 1617; *La Veneziana* (play), 1619; *Lelio bandito* (play), 1620; *Mincio ubbidiente* (play), 1620; *La Sultana* (play), 1622; *La Ferinda* (play), 1622; *L'amor nello specchio* (play), 1622; *Li due Lelii simili* (play), 1622; *La Centaura* (play), 1622; *Le due comedie in comedia* (play), 1623; *La Tecla vergine e martire* (verse), 1623; *Lo Specchio della commedia*, 1625; *La Ferza contro le accuse date alla commedia e a' professori di lei*, 1625; *Il teatro celeste*, 1625; *La Rosella* (play), 1632; *I Due baci* (play), 1634; *La Rosa* (play), 1638; *L'Olivastro overo il poeta sfortunato* (verse), 1642; *Il Cristo sofferente* (verse), 1651; *La Maddalena lasciva e penitente* (play), 1652.

*

Bibliography

Books:
Rosamond Gilder, *Enter The Actress: The First Women in the Theatre*, New York, 1931.
K. M. Lea, *Italian Popular Comedy: A Study in the Commedia dell'Arte 1560–1630 with Special Reference to the English Stage*, Oxford, 1934.
Allardyce Nicoll, *The World of Harlequin: A Critical Study of the Commedia dell'Arte*, Cambridge, England, 1963.
Roberto Tessari, *La Commedia dell'Arte nel Seicento "Industria" e "Arte giocosa" della civiltà barocca*, Florence, 1981.
Ferdinando Taviani and Mirella Schino, *Il Segreto della Commedia dell'Arte, La Memoria delle compagnie italiane del XVI, XVII e XVIII secolo*, Florence, 1982.
Christopher Cairns (ed.), *The Commedia dell' Arte from the Renaissance to Dario Fo*, Lewiston, Queenston, and Lampeter, 1988.

* * *

When Rosamond Gilder included a chapter on Isabella Andreini in her book on early actresses, *Enter the Actress*, she was making a deliberate attempt to correct a misconception still widespread in theatre history — the mistaken idea that there were no women players until the late 17th century. This misconception has arisen because of the absence of women from the Elizabethan and Jacobean stages in England, but elsewhere in Europe the actress was by no means unfamiliar, as the accounts of the skills of such women as Isabella Andreini or Vicenza Armani show.

Isabella seems to have been exceptionally talented, or at least we may infer this from the extent of her following and from the public response to her state funeral in Lyons. She has been compared by Italian critics to Eleonora Duse in that she endeavoured to create a new image of women in the theatre and she became established as a stock type in commedia performances in her own right. *La Pazzia di Isabella* (The Madness of Isabella), performed in Florence in 1589 for the wedding of the Grand Duke Ferdinand was just one of many celebrated triumphs in which she appeared, contemporary accounts praising her for her "marvellous eloquence". There is a well-known story of an evening at the home of Cardinal Aldobrandini, when Isabella came close to winning a competition to determine the best poet, being beaten into second place by Torquato Tasso, and Tasso himself wrote a sonnet in praise of her.

From what we know about Isabella, we can conclude that she was unusually well-educated (she knew several languages) and had an exceptional talent for poetry. As a performer, she was beautiful and is said to have had a wonderful voice, but obviously her ability to improvise in excellent verse was a talent ideally suited for a commedia player. Ferdinando Taviani has suggested that the women players were especially skilled in improvisation techniques, a point that is worth further examination, especially since the traditional view of the female player in commedia was to suggest that a woman simply "played herself", being decorative rather than a virtuoso actor. Commedia players worked in two ways, either performing plays or performing in stock roles, using these as the basis for improvisation in the construction of a stylized performance. Isabella's fluency with poetic language would have given her a great advantage over many other players.

Recent work on commedia has also revealed a great deal of information on the period of transition in the 16th century, when the companies became established on a commercial basis rather than operating under the older system of patronage. Earlier in the century, companies were hired to perform on special occasions such as weddings, civic holidays, religious festivals, etc. but once the companies began to work on a professional basis, the entire concept of theatre changed. Playing spaces acquired a new significance, the idea of a theatre season came into being, and actors now had to earn their living in the open marketplace as it were. What appears very apparent from the career of Isabella Andreini, for example, is that she worked at establishing an image and a reputation for herself as a star performer. When she died, Francesco Andreini, himself a popular performer, abandoned his own acting career and dissolved the company, and although the traditional view was to attribute this to grief, it is more likely that he realized the impossibility of maintaining the company without its star attraction. Giovan Battista had already set up his own company shortly before his mother's death and established his own style of work.

Besides spanning the moment of transition to professional theatre, the career of the Andreini family also developed during the period of the Counter-Reformation. Great emphasis was placed on Isabella's chastity and devout behaviour by contemporaries and, indeed, four of her daughters all entered the convent. Giovan Battista's work is even more markedly religious and his "sacre rappresentazioni", or religious plays, reflect this tendency. He also wrote an impassioned defence of the theatre, arguing for the importance of technical skills in the performers as a prime component of good theatre.

The tradition of the "famiglia d'arte", the company composed of members of the same family, had begun long before the 16th century and was to continue in one way or another into the 20th century. The Andreini family, however, have become legendary as the first of the great family companies and the fact that they toured abroad and became as well-known in France as in Italy has further increased their reputation. We know very little about how they worked — there are contemporary accounts, some drawings of performers, some scenarii, and later there are the actors' handbooks, which contain some clues about what they did on stage, but we do know that they enjoyed great success in an age of tough competition from many talented companies endeavouring to attract the same audiences.

Isabella Andreini, who died so tragically in childbirth at the age of 42, was a legend in her own lifetime and was obviously one of the great performers of her era. As more work is done on the theatre of this period, we may yet discover details of the Andreini family's technique. It would also be helpful to learn more about the way in which the history of female performers in the European theatre has come to be so poorly documented that the atypical model of the mysogynist English theatre of Shakespeare and his contemporaries is taken to be the norm, while the work of great actresses in Italy, France, and Spain has been ignored.

—Susan Bassnett

ANGLIN, Margaret (Mary). Canadian actress and director. Born in Ottawa, Ontario, Canada, 3 April 1876, daughter of T. W. Anglin, Speaker of Canadian House of Commons. Educated at Loretto Abbey, Toronto, and the Convent of the Sacred Heart, Montreal; studied briefly for the stage under Charles Frohman at the Empire Dramatic School, New York, 1893–94. Married actor Howard Hull in 1911. Stage debut, Academy of Music, New York, 1894; played a season with James O'Neill's touring company, 1896–97; actress, E. H. Sothern's touring company, 1897–98, and Richard Mansfield's touring company, 1898–99; toured Canada with her own company, 1898; leading lady in Charles Frohman's company, Empire Theatre, New York, 1899–1903; toured with Henry Miller's company, 1903; began producing the plays she appeared in, from 1904; Australian tour, 1908; pursued career primarily on the New York stage, but also acclaimed for her appearances in Greek tragedies in Berkeley, California, from 1910; also made numerous radio broadcasts; retired from the stage, 1943. Died in Toronto, 7 January 1958.

Roles

1894	Madeline West in *Shenandoah* (Howard), Academy of Music, New York.
1896–97	Jeannette in *The Courier of Lyons* (Reade), US tour.
	Mercedes in *Monte Cristo* (Dumas *fils*), US tour.
	Ophelia in *Hamlet* (Shakespeare), US tour.
	Virginia in *Virginius* (Knowles), US tour.
	Julie de Mortemar in *Richelieu* (Bulwer-Lytton), US tour.
1898	Meg in *Lord Chumley* (Sothern), US tour.
	Rosalind in *As You Like It* (Shakespeare), Canadian tour.
	Roxanne in *Cyrano de Bergerac* (Rostand), Garden Theatre, New York.
1899	Constance in *The Musketeers* (Grundy), Broadway Theatre, New York.
	Heloise Tyson in *Citizen Pierre* (Coghlan), Miner's Theatre, New York.
	Mimi in *The Only Way* (Wills), Herald Square Theatre, New York.
1899–1900	Baroness Royden in *Brother Officers* (Trevor), Empire Theatre, New York.
	Millicent Denbigh in *The Bugle Call* (Parker and Bright), Empire Theatre, New York.
1900	Mrs Dane in *Mrs Dane's Defence* (Jones), Empire Theatre, New York.
1900–03	Dora in *Diplomacy* (Scott and Stephenson), Empire Theatre, New York.
	Lady Ursula in *Lady Ursula* (Hope), Empire Theatre, New York.

Mabel Vaughan in *The Wilderness* (Esmond), Empire Theatre, New York.

Guiditta in *The Twin Sister* (Fuldo, translated by Parker), Empire Theatre, New York.

Gwendolen in *The Importance of Being Earnest* (Wilde), Empire Theatre, New York.

Margaret Fielding in *The Unforseen* (Marshall), Empire Theatre, New York.

1903   Camille in *Camille* (Wills), US tour.

1905   Zira in *Zira* (adapted from Wilkie Collins's *The New Magdalen*), Princess Theatre, New York.

Hester Trent in *Zira* (adapted from Collins's *The New Magdalen*), Princess Theatre, New York.

1906   Carey Fernald in *Young Fernald*, Boston, Massachusetts.

Lady Eastney/Mrs Dane in *Mrs Dane's Defence* (Jones), Lyric Theatre, New York.

1906–07   Ruth Jordan in *The Great Divide* (Moody), Princess Theatre, New York.

1908   Helen Ritchie in *The Awakening of Helen Ritchie*, Savoy Theatre, New York.

Katherine in *The Taming of the Shrew* (Shakespeare), Australian tour.

Viola in *Twelfth Night* (Shakespeare), Australian tour.

1910   Antigone in *Antigone* (Sophocles, adapted by Plumtree), Greek Theatre, Berkeley, California; also directed.

1911   Celia Faraday in *Green Stockings* (Mason), New Britain, US tour, and 39th Street Theatre, New York.

Barbara Milne in *The Rival*, Detroit and US tour.

1912   Lydia Gilmore in *Lydia Gilmore* (H. A. Jones), Lyceum Theatre, New York.

Egypt Komello in *Egypt*, Albany Theatre, New York.

1913   Electra in *Electra* (Euripides), Greek Theatre, Berkeley, California; also directed.

1913–14   Viola in *Twelfth Night* (Shakespeare), US tour and Hudson Theatre; also directed.

Rosalind in *As You Like It* (Shakespeare), US tour and Hudson Theatre, New York; also directed.

Katherine in *The Taming of the Shrew* (Shakespeare), US tour and Hudson Theatre, New York; also directed.

Cleopatra in *Antony and Cleopatra* (Shakespeare), US tour; also directed.

1914   Mrs Erlynne in *Lady Windermere's Fan* (Wilde), Hudson Theatre, New York.

1915   Beverley Dinwiddie in *Beverley's Balance*, Lyceum Theatre, New York.

Maria of Magdala in *The Divine Friend*, Columbia Theatre, San Francisco.

Iphigenia in *Iphigenia in Tauris* (Euripides), Greek Theatre, Berkeley, California; also directed.

Medea in *Medea* (Euripides), Greek Theatre, Berkeley, California; also directed.

1916   Ida Compton in *The Voice of Gold*, Alvin Theatre, Pittsburgh, Pennsylvania.

Mrs Arbuthnot in *A Woman of No Importance* (Wilde), Fulton Theatre, New York.

Caroline Ashley in *Caroline* (Maugham), Empire Theatre, New York.

1917   Betty Tarradine in *Billeted* (Jesse and Harwood), Playhouse Theatre, New York.

1920   Mrs Vivian Hunt in *The Woman of Bronze*, Powers Theatre, Chicago and Frazee Theatre, New York.

Joan in *The Trial of Joan of Arc*, Columbia Theatre, San Francisco and Century Theatre.

1921   Clytemnestra in *Iphigenia in Aulis* (Euripides), Manhattan Opera House, New York; also directed.

1923   Phaedra in *Hippolytus* (Euripides), Greek Theatre, Berkeley, California; also directed.

1923–24   Lady Dedlock/Hortense in *The Great Lady Dedlock* (adapted from Dickens), US tour.

1924   Iris Bellamy in *Iris* (Pinero), Rutland, Vermont.

Stéphanie de Mohrivart in *Foot-loose* (Merivale and Grove), US tour.

1926–27   Peg Woffington in *Peg the Actress*, San Francisco and Los Angeles.

Candida in *Candida* (G. B. Shaw), San Francisco and Los Angeles.

Role in *Gypsy* (Anderson), US tour.

1927   *Erlanger*, Gallo Theatre, New York.

1928   Lady Henry Fairfax in *Diplomacy* (Scott and Stephenson), Gallo Theatre, New York.

1929   Jane Mapleson in *Security* (Pieterson), Maxine Elliott Theatre, New York.

Lady Dedlock/Hortense in *The Great Lady Dedlock* (adapted from Dickens), US tour; also directed.

1934   Lady Mary Crabbe in *Fresh Fields* (Novello), Blackstone Theatre, Chicago.

1936   Mrs Malaprop in *The Rivals* (Sheridan), Empire Theatre, New York.

1937   Empress Theresa in *Marriage Royal*, Dennis, Massachusetts.

Flora Lowell in *Retreat from Folly* (Gould and Russell), Blackstone Theatre, Chicago; also directed.

1943   Sara Müller in *Watch on the Rhine* (Hellman), US tour.

Also acted roles in: *Christopher Jr* (Ryley), Canadian tour, 1898; *The Mysterious Mr Bugle* (Ryley), Canadian tour, 1898; *The Liars* (H. A. Jones), Empire Theatre, New York, 1900–03; *Lord and Lady Algy* (Carton), Empire Theatre, New York, 1900–03; *The Devil's Disciple* (G. B. Shaw), US tour, 1903; *The Aftermath* (Vynne), US tour, 1903; *The Taming of Helen* (Davis), US tour, 1903; *Cynthia* (Davies), US tour, 1903; *The Eternal Feminine*, New Haven, Connecticut, 1904; *A Wife's Strategy*, Albany Theatre, New York, 1905; *The Marriage of Kitty* (Gordon-Lennox), San Francisco, 1905; *The Lady Paramount*, San Francisco, 1905; *Frou-Frou* (Meilhac and Halévy), San Francisco, 1905; *Mariana* (Graham), San Francisco, 1905; *The Second Mrs Tanqueray* (Pinero), San Francisco, 1905; *The Correct Thing* (Sutro), Broadway Theatre, New York, 1906; *The Sabine Woman* (Moody, adapted from *The Great Divide*), Chicago, Illinois, 1906; *Shifting Sands*, Seattle, Washington, 1910; *The Wager*, US tour, 1917; *The Open Fire*, US tour, 1921; *The Sea Woman* (Robertson), US tour, 1923; *Nature versus Art*, Palace Theatre, New York, 1926; *Smarty's Party* (Kelly), New York, 1928; *Macbeth* (Shakespeare), New York, 1928.

*

Bibliography

Books:
John LeVay, *Margaret Anglin: A Stage Life*, 1988.

Articles:
Matthew White, "Margaret Anglin", *Munsey's*, 35, July 1906.

* * *

Although born in Canada, Margaret Anglin spent most of her professional life in the USA and was almost universally regarded as a US actress. Her extensive early training in elocution gave her the melodious and flexible speaking voice and perfect diction that would be praised by critics throughout her career, while her private school education provided her with an aura of stateliness and gentility that would serve her well in many of her roles, particularly in her revivals of plays by Oscar Wilde. Entering the professional theatre at the end of the 19th century, Anglin quickly proved herself adept at the 'emotional' style then popular among actresses, using her energy and passion to ignite the scenes of suffering and recrimination so frequent in the plays of the period. But she was soon able to move beyond this to develop subtle, complex, and sustained characterizations, most notably her performance as the repressed New Englander Ruth Jordan in William Vaughn Moody's *The Great Divide*.

When she was 28, Anglin began to produce the plays in which she appeared, and for the greater part of her career she oversaw every aspect of her productions. Quite frequently, she was forced to tour with an inferior play in order to raise enough money to pay for the plays she really wanted to do. Although she had some success with Shakespeare and Wilde, her reputation as both actress and manager rests mainly on a series of Greek tragedies that she produced at the outdoor Greek Theatre on the campus of the University of California at Berkeley: *Antigone, Electra, Iphigenia in Aulis, Medea*, and *Hippolytus*.With simple yet evocative settings designed by Livingston Platt (a disciple of the 'new stagecraft' of Edward Gordon Craig), the Berkeley performances were the first large-scale, professional productions of Greek tragedy that attempted to give US audiences an experience approximating to that in an ancient Greek theatre.

Critics praised Anglin as both producer and actress, finding her performances of Electra and Medea particularly stirring. The actress's Medea was generally recognized as her finest achievement, and indeed the 'grand manner' that critics ascribed to her, combined with the prodigious energy she was able to bring to emotional scenes and the variety and clarity of her declamation, made the barbarian princess an ideal role for her. Critics were particularly struck by Anglin's complete transformation in each of the tragic roles she played, her voice, movements, and gestures changing completely as she moved in a single season from the pathetic Iphigenia to the turbulent Medea to the vengeful Electra.

The success of her Berkeley productions encouraged Anglin to revive them at different times for special performances at New York's Carnegie Hall and Manhattan Opera House (these performances were often rehearsed when Anglin was also appearing in one of her less distinguished plays at a Broadway theatre). On these occasions the New York reviewers echoed the praises that had been heaped on her by the San Francisco critics.

The acclaim she received for her productions of Greek tragedy can obscure the fact that Anglin was one of the most versatile actresses of her day. She was praised by critics for her lighthearted and vivacious portrayals of Shakespeare's comic heroines and at different stages of her career she garnered laudatory reviews for her performances as Camille, Candida, Joan of Arc, and Mrs Malaprop. In the 1930's, Anglin's stage performances were less frequent as she became a sought-after radio personality, both as a reader of poetry and as a performer in condensed dramatizations of her great stage successes.

Margaret Anglin was in some respects a transitional figure in the history of US acting. Schooled in the florid, 'emotional' acting of the late 19th century, she carried with her throughout her career the vestiges of the 'grand manner'. Her emotionalism and intensity, as well as her vocal flexibility, served her well in Greek tragedy and in a number of contemporary melodramas that called for larger-than-life displays of passion. Anglin's success kept the older style of acting alive, even as some of her contemporaries (notably Minnie Maddern Fiske) were developing more 'modern' methods.

Perhaps sensing that audiences were gradually losing interest in bravura performances of heart-wrenching dramas, Anglin moved more and more into comedy, impressing critics with both her boisterous performance in *The Taming of the Shrew* and her deft handling of drawing-room witticisms in *Lady Windermere's Fan*. As late as the 1940's critics were hailing her understated interpretation of Mrs Malaprop in the Theatre Guild's revival of Sheridan's *The Rivals*, as well as the light comedy touch she brought to her role when she replaced another actress in Lillian Hellman's drama *Watch on the Rhine*. But despite her many fine comic portrayals, Margaret Anglin is best remembered for first interesting US theatre audiences in Greek tragedy through her series of remarkable performances in Berkeley. No other major actress before or since has undertaken as many roles in Greek tragedy, or with as much critical and popular success.

—Margaret M. Knapp

ANTOINE, André. French actor-manager, director, and critic. Born in Limoges, 31 January 1858. Educated at schools in Limoges and Paris, until 1871. National service with French army, 1879–83. First married in 1881 (separated 1883); married Pauline Verdovaine c.1900 (died 1913); two sons. Worked as a clerk in the Paris Gas Company until 1887; founded Théâtre Libre in Paris, 1887; staged many new plays by French and European authors, 1887–94; Théâtre Libre moved to the Théâtre Montparnasse, 1887, and then to the Salle des Menus-

Plaisirs, 1888; made many innovations in design and acting; following decline of the Théâtre Libre, worked mainly as an actor, 1895–97, and briefly managed the Théâtre de l'Odéon, Paris, 1896; directed at the Théâtre des Menus-Plaisirs, Paris, renaming it the Théâtre-Antoine, 1897–1906; director, Théâtre de l'Odéon, 1906–14; after World War I, worked in films as screenwriter, adapter, and director and became a theatre and film critic. Officer, Légion d'Honneur, 1900. Died in Paris, October 1943.

Productions

As director:
1887   *Mademoiselle Pomme* (Duranty and Alexis), Passage de l'Élysées des Beaux Arts, Paris.

Un Préfet (Byl), Passage de l'Élysées des Beaux Arts, Paris.

Jacques d'Amour (Hennique, adapted from Zola), Passage de l'Élysées des Beaux Arts, Paris.

La Cocarde (Vidal), Passage de l'Élysées des Beaux Arts, Paris.

La Nuit Bergamesque (Bergerat), Passage de l'Élysées des Beaux Arts, Paris.

En Famille (Métènier), Passage de l'Élysées des Beaux Arts, Paris.

Soeur Philomène (Byl and Vidal), Passage de l'Élysées des Beaux Arts, Paris.

L'Évasion (L'Isle-Adam), Passage de l'Élysées des Beaux Arts, Paris.

Belle-Petite (Corneau), Théâtre Montparnasse, Paris.

La Femme de Tabarin (Mendès), Théâtre Montparnasse, Paris.

Esther Brandès (Hennique), Théâtre Montparnasse, Paris.

La Sérénade (Jullien), Théâtre Montparnasse, Paris.

1888   *Le Baiser* (Banville), Théâtre Montparnasse, Paris.

Tout pour l'honneur (Céard, adapted from Zola's *Captaine Burle*), Théâtre Montparnasse, Paris.

La Puissance des ténèbres (Tolstoy), Théâtre Montparnasse, Paris.

La Pelote (Bonnetain and Descaves), Théâtre Montparnasse, Paris.

Pierrot assassin de sa femme (Margueritte), Théâtre Montparnasse, Paris.

Les Quarts d'heure (Guiches and Lavedan), Théâtre Montparnasse, Paris.

Le Pain du Péché (Arène), Théâtre Montparnasse, Paris.

Matapan (Moreau), Théâtre Montparnasse, Paris.

La Prose (Salandri), Théâtre Montparnasse, Paris.

Monsieur Lamblin (Ancey), Théâtre Montparnasse, Paris.

La Fin de Lucie Pellegrin (Alexis), Théâtre Montparnasse, Paris.

Les Bouchers (Icres), Théâtre des Menus-Plaisirs, Paris.

Chevalerie rustique (Verga), Théâtre des Menus-Plaisirs, Paris.

L'Amante du Christ (Darzens), Théâtre des Menus-Plaisirs, Paris.

Rolande (Gramont), Théâtre des Menus-Plaisirs, Paris.

La Chance de Françoise (Porto-Riche), Théâtre des Menus-Plaisirs, Paris.

La Mort du duc d'Enghien (Hennique), Théâtre des Menus-Plaisirs, Paris.

Le Cor fleuri (Mikhaël), Théâtre des Menus-Plaisirs, Paris.

1889   *La Reine Fiammette* (Mendès), Théâtre des Menus-Plaisirs, Paris.

Les Résignés (Céard), Théâtre des Menus-Plaisirs, Paris.

L'Echéance (Jullien), Théâtre des Menus-Plaisirs, Paris.

La Patrie en Danger (Goncourt), Théâtre des Menus-Plaisirs, Paris.

L'Ancien (Cladel), Théâtre des Menus-Plaisirs, Paris.

Madeleine (Zola), Théâtre des Menus-Plaisirs, Paris.

Les Inséparables (Alcey), Théâtre des Menus-Plaisirs, Paris.

Le Comte Witold (Rzewuski), Théâtre des Menus-Plaisirs, Paris.

Le Coeur révélateur (Laumann, adapted from Poe), Théâtre des Menus-Plaisirs, Paris.

La Casserole (Méténier), Théâtre des Menus-Plaisirs, Paris.

Dans le Guignol (Aicard), Théâtre des Menus-Plaisirs, Paris.

Le Père Lebonnard (Aicard), Théâtre des Menus-Plaisirs, Paris.

Au temps de la ballade (Bois), Théâtre des Menus-Plaisirs, Paris.

L'Éole des veufs (Ancey), Théâtre des Menus-Plaisirs, Paris.

1890   *Le Pain d'autrui* (Turgenev), Théâtre des Menus-Plaisirs, Paris.

En Détresse (Févre), Théâtre des Menus-Plaisirs, Paris.

Les Frères Zemganno (Alexis and Méténier, adapted from Goncourt), Théâtre des Menus-Plaisirs, Paris.

Deux tourtereaux (Ginisty and Guérin), Théâtre des Menus-Plaisirs, Paris.

Ménages d'artistes (Brieux), Théâtre des Menus-Plaisirs, Paris.

Le Maître (Jullien), Théâtre des Menus-Plaisirs, Paris.

Jacques Bouchard (Wolff), Théâtre des Menus-Plaisirs, Paris.

Une Nouvelle École (Mullem), Théâtre des Menus-Plaisirs, Paris.

La Tante Léontine (Boniface and Bodin), Théâtre des Menus-Plaisirs, Paris.

Les Revenants (Ibsen), Théâtre des Menus-Plaisirs, Paris.

La Pêche (Céard), Théâtre des Menus-Plaisirs, Paris.

André Antoine

Myrane (Bergerat), Théâtre des Menus-Plaisirs, Paris.

Les Chapons (Descaves and Darien), Théâtre des Menus-Plaisirs, Paris.

L'Honneur (Fèvre), Théâtre des Menus-Plaisirs, Paris.

Monsieur Bute (Biollay), Théâtre des Menus-Plaisirs, Paris.

L'Amant de sa femme (Scholl), Théâtre des Menus-Plaisirs, Paris.

La Belle Opération (Sermet), Théâtre des Menus-Plaisirs, Paris.

La Fille Élisa (Ajalbert, adapted from Goncourt), Théâtre des Menus-Plaisirs, Paris.

Conte de Noël (Linert), Théâtre des Menus-Plaisirs, Paris.

1891   *La Meule* (Lecomte), Théâtre des Menus-Plaisirs, Paris.

Jeune premier (Ginisty), Théâtre des Menus-Plaisirs, Paris.

Le Canard sauvage (Ibsen, translated by Ephraïm and Lindenlaub), Théâtre des Menus-Plaisirs, Paris.

Nell Horn (Rosny), Théâtre des Menus-Plaisirs, Paris.

Leurs filles (Wolff), Théâtre des Menus-Plaisirs, Paris.

Les Fourches caudines (Corbellier), Théâtre des Menus-Plaisirs, Paris.

Lidoire (Courteline), Théâtre des Menus-Plaisirs, Paris.

Coeurs simples (Sutter-Laumann), Théâtre des Menus-Plaisirs, Paris.

Le Pendu (Bourgeois), Théâtre des Menus-Plaisirs, Paris.

Dans le rêve (Mullem), Théâtre des Menus-Plaisirs, Paris.

Le Père Goriot (Tarabant, adapted from Balzac), Théâtre des Menus-Plaisirs, Paris.

La Rançon (Salandri), Théâtre des Menus-Plaisirs, Paris.

L'Abbé Pierre (Prévost), Théâtre des Menus-Plaisirs, Paris.

Un beau soir (Vaucaire), Théâtre des Menus-Plaisirs, Paris.

La Dupe (Ancey), Théâtre des Menus-Plaisirs, Paris.

Son petit coeur (Marsolleau), Théâtre des Menus-Plaisirs, Paris.

1892   *L'Envers d'une sainte* (Curel), Théâtre des Menus-Plaisirs, Paris.

Seul (Guinon), Théâtre des Menus-Plaisirs, Paris.

Simone (Gramont), Théâtre des Menus-Plaisirs, Paris.

Les Maris de leurs filles (Wolff), Théâtre des Menus-Plaisirs, Paris.

La Fin du vieux temps (Anthelme), Théâtre des Menus-Plaisirs, Paris.

Pêche d'amour (Carré *fils* and Loiseau), Théâtre des Menus-Plaisirs, Paris.

Les Fenêtres (Perrin and Couturier), Théâtre des Menus-Plaisirs, Paris.

Mélie (Docquois, adapted from Reibrach), Théâtre des Menus-Plaisirs, Paris.

Le Grappin (Salandri), Théâtre des Menus-Plaisirs, Paris.

L'Affranchie (Biollay), Théâtre des Menus-Plaisirs, Paris.

Les Fossiles (Curel), Théâtre des Menus-Plaisirs, Paris.

1893   *Le Ménage Brésile* (Coolus), Théâtre des Menus-Plaisirs, Paris.

Mademoiselle Julie (Strindberg), Théâtre des Menus-Plaisirs, Paris.

A bas le progrès (Goncourt), Théâtre des Menus-Plaisirs, Paris.

Le Devoir (Bruyerre), Théâtre des Menus-Plaisirs, Paris.

Mirages (Lecomte), Théâtre des Menus-Plaisirs, Paris.

Valet de coeur (Vaucaire), Théâtre des Menus-Plaisirs, Paris.

Boubouroche (Courteline), Théâtre des Menus-Plaisirs, Paris.

Les Tisserands (Hauptmann), Théâtre des Menus-Plaisirs, Paris.

Ahasvère (Heijermans), Théâtre des Menus-Plaisirs, Paris.

Blanchette (Brieux), Italian tour.

Mariage d'argent (Bourgeois), Théâtre des Menus-Plaisirs, Paris.

La Belle au bois rêvant (Mazade), Théâtre des Menus-Plaisirs, Paris.

Une Faillite (Björnson), Théâtre des Menus-Plaisirs, Paris.

Le Poète et le financier (Vaucaire), Théâtre des Menus-Plaisirs, Paris.

L'Inquietude (Perrin and Couturier), Théâtre des Menus-Plaisirs, Paris.

Amants éternels (Corneau and Gerbault), Théâtre des Menus-Plaisirs, Paris.

1894   *L'Assomption de Hannele Mattern* (Hauptmann), Théâtre des Menus-Plaisirs, Paris.

En l'attendant (Roux), Théâtre des Menus-Plaisirs, Paris.

Une Journée parlementaire (Barrès), Théâtre des Menus-Plaisirs, Paris.

Le Missionaire (Luguet), Théâtre des Menus-Plaisirs, Paris.

1895   *Elën* (Isle-Adam), Théâtre Libre, Paris.

L'Argent (Fabre), Théâtre Libre, Paris.

Grand-papa (Berton), Théâtre Libre, Paris.

Si c'était . . . (Lheureux), Théâtre Libre, Paris.

La Lumée puis la flamme (Caraguel), Théâtre Libre, Paris.

Le Cuivre (Adam and Picard), Théâtre Libre, Paris.

1896   *L'Ame invisible* (Berton), Théâtre Libre, Paris.

Mademoiselle Fifi (Méténier), Théâtre Libre, Paris.

Inceste d'âmes (Laurenty and Hauser), Théâtre Libre, Paris.

Soldat et mineur (Malafayde), Théâtre Libre, Paris.

La Fille d'Artaban (Mortier), Théâtre Libre, Paris.

La Nébuleuse (Dumur), Théâtre Libre, Paris.

Dialogue inconnu (Vigny), Théâtre Libre, Paris.

Britannicus (Racine), Théâtre de l'Odéon, Paris.

Le Médécin malgré lui (Molière), Théâtre de l'Odéon, Paris.

La Capitaine Fracasse (Bergerat), Théâtre de l'Odéon, Paris.

Don Carlos (Schiller), Théâtre de l'Odéon, Paris.

Tartuffe (Molière), Théâtre de l'Odéon, Paris.

1897–98   *Le Repas du Lion* (Curel), Théâtre Antoine, Paris.

La Parisienne (Becque), Théâtre Antoine, Paris.

Le Bien d'autrui (Fabré), Théâtre Antoine, Paris.

Dix ans après (Veber), Théâtre Antoine, Paris.

Les Amis (Dreyfus), Théâtre Antoine, Paris.

L'Infidèle (Porte-Riche), Théâtre Antoine, Paris.

La Brebis (Sée), Théâtre Antoine, Paris.

Herakléa (Villeroy), Théâtre Antoine, Paris.

Joseph d'Arimathée (Travieux), Théâtre Antoine, Paris.

Hors des lois (Marsolleau and Byl), Théâtre Antoine, Paris.

Le Petit Lord (Lemaire and Bournet), Théâtre Antoine, Paris.

Le Fardeau de la liberté (Bernard), Théâtre Antoine, Paris.

L'Epidémie (Mirbeau), Théâtre Antoine, Paris.

Son petit coeur (Marsolleau), Théâtre Antoine, Paris.

Le Retour de l'aigle (Labruyere), Théâtre Antoine, Paris.

Le Départ (Becque), Théâtre Antoine, Paris.

1898–99   *La Nouvelle Idole* (Curel), Théâtre Antoine, Paris.

L'Avenir (Ancey), Théâtre Antoine, Paris.

L'Empreinte (Hermant), Théâtre Antoine, Paris.

Les Gaietés de l'Escadron (Courteline), Théâtre Antoine, Paris.

Judith Renaudin (Loti), Théâtre Antoine, Paris.

Le Gendarme est sans pitié (Courteline), Théâtre Antoine, Paris.

Le Doute (Jullien), Théâtre Antoine, Paris.

La Farce du Polichinelle (Kahn and Tailhade), Théâtre Antoine, Paris.

Coeur blette (Coolus), Théâtre Antoine, Paris.

Les Girouettes (Vaucaire), Théâtre Antoine, Paris.

Vallabra (Alexis), Théâtre Antoine, Paris.

Résultat des courses (Brieux), Théâtre Antoine, Paris.

Une pièce nouvelle (Donnay and Descaves), Théâtre Antoine, Paris.

La Mort d'Hypathie (Trarieux), Théâtre Antoine, Paris.

Père naturel (Depré and Charton), Théâtre Antoine, Paris.

En Paix (Bruyère), Théâtre Antoine, Paris.

1899–1900   *La Clairière* (Donnay and Descaves), Théâtre Antoine, Paris.

Poil de Carotte (Renard), Théâtre Antoine, Paris.

La Gitane (Richepin), Théâtre Antoine, Paris.

Le Marché (Bernstein), Théâtre Antoine, Paris.

1900–01   *Les Remplaçantes* (Brieux), Théâtre Antoine, Paris.

Les Avariés (Brieux), Théâtre Antoine, Paris.

L'Article 330 (Courteline), Théâtre Antoine, Paris.

Sur la foi des étoiles (Travieux), Théâtre Antoine, Paris.

La Petite Paroisse (adapted from Daudet), Théâtre Antoine, Paris.

1901–02   *La Fille Sauvage* (Curel), Théâtre Antoine, Paris.

L'Honneur (Sudermann), Théâtre Antoine, Paris.

Les Balances (Courteline), Théâtre Antoine, Paris.

La Terre (Hugot and St-Arroman), Théâtre Antoine, Paris.

La Compagne (Schnitzler), Théâtre Antoine, Paris.

Boule de Suif (Méténier), Théâtre Antoine, Paris.

1902–03   *La Bonne Espérance* (Heijermans), Théâtre Antoine, Paris.

L'Indiscret (Sée), Théâtre Antoine, Paris.

M Vernet (Renard), Théâtre Antoine, Paris.

1903–04   *Maternité* (Brieux), Théâtre Antoine, Paris.

Oiseaux de Passage (Donnay and Descaves), Théâtre Antoine, Paris.

La Paix chez soi (Courteline), Théâtre Antoine, Paris.

La Guerre au village (Trarieux), Théâtre Antoine, Paris.

1904–05   *Le Meilleur Parte* (Maindron), Théâtre Antoine, Paris.

1905–06   *Le Coup d'Aile* (Curel), Théâtre Antoine, Paris.

Vers l'amour (Gandillot), Théâtre Antoine, Paris.

La Pitié (Leblanc), Théâtre Antoine, Paris.

1906   *Vieil Heidelberg* (Meyer-Förster), Théâtre de l'Odéon, Paris.

Le Vray Mistère de la Passion (Gréban), Théâtre de l'Odéon, Paris.

La Préférée (Descaves), Théâtre de l'Odéon, Paris.

La Recommandation (Maurey), Théâtre de l'Odéon, Paris.

Les Honnêtes femmes (Becque), Théâtre de l'Odéon, Paris.

Discipline (Conring), Théâtre de l'Odéon, Paris.

La Race (Thorel), Théâtre de l'Odéon, Paris.

Les Experts (Bénière), Théâtre de l'Odéon, Paris.

Un Client sérieux (Courteline), Théâtre de l'Odéon, Paris.

Le Florentin (La Fontaine), Théâtre de l'Odéon, Paris.

Polyeucte (Corneille), Théâtre de l'Odéon, Paris.

L'Honneur (Sudermann), Théâtre de l'Odéon, Paris.

Les Précieuses ridicules (Molière), Théâtre de l'Odéon, Paris.

Andromaque (Racine), Théâtre de l'Odéon, Paris.

Jules César (Shakespeare), Théâtre de l'Odéon, Paris.

Don Juan (Molière), Théâtre de l'Odéon, Paris.

Britannicus (Racine), Théâtre de l'Odéon, Paris.

Les Plaideurs (Racine), Théâtre de l'Odéon, Paris.

Le Philosophie sans le savoir (Sedaine), Théâtre de l'Odéon, Paris.

1907   *Le Jeu de l'amour et du hasard* (Marivaux), Théâtre de l'Odéon, Paris.

Le Barbier de Séville (Beaumarchais), Théâtre de l'Odéon, Paris.

Le Maison des Juges (Leroux), Théâtre de l'Odéon, Paris.

Depuis six mois (Maurey), Théâtre de l'Odéon, Paris.

Chatterton (Vigny), Théâtre de l'Odéon, Paris.

La Grand'mère (Hugo), Théâtre de l'Odéon, Paris.

La Faute de l'Abbé Mouret (Bruneau), Théâtre de l'Odéon, Paris.

Florise (Banville), Théâtre de l'Odéon, Paris.

Joseph d'Arimathée (Trarieux), Théâtre de l'Odéon, Paris.

L'Arlesienne (Daudet), Théâtre de l'Odéon, Paris.

Le Chandelier (Musset), Théâtre de l'Odéon, Paris.

La Française (Brieux), Théâtre de l'Odéon, Paris.

Les Goujons (Bénière), Théâtre de l'Odéon, Paris.

L'Otage (Trarieux), Théâtre de l'Odéon, Paris.

Monsieur de Prévan (Gumpel and Delaquys), Théâtre de l'Odéon, Paris.

Le Maître á aimer (Veber and Delorme), Théâtre de l'Odéon, Paris.

Les Plumes du Paon (Bisson and Turique), Théâtre de l'Odéon, Paris.

L'Alouette (Wildenruch, translated by Lutz), Théâtre de l'Odéon, Paris.

Tartuffe (Molière), Théâtre de l'Odéon, Paris.

Son Père (Guinon and Bouchinet), Théâtre de l'Odéon, Paris.

Le Voyage au Caire (Fauré), Théâtre de l'Odéon, Paris.

La Jeunesse du Cid (Castro, translated by Dieulafoy), Théâtre de l'Odéon, Paris.

Le Trésor (Coppée), Théâtre de l'Odéon, Paris.

Le Cid (Corneille), Théâtre de l'Odéon, Paris.

L'Avare (Molière), Théâtre de l'Odéon, Paris.

Phèdre (Racine), Théâtre de l'Odéon, Paris.

La Farce de la marmite (Plautus, translated by Tailhade), Théâtre de l'Odéon, Paris.

1908   *L'Apprentie* (Geffroy), Théâtre de l'Odéon, Paris.

Le Chevalier avare (Pushkin, adapted by Bienstock), Théâtre de l'Odéon, Paris.

L'Impromptu de Versailles (Molière), Théâtre de l'Odéon, Paris.

L'Avare chinois (Julien), Théâtre de l'Odéon, Paris.

Électre (Euripides, adapted by Hérold), Théâtre de l'Odéon, Paris.

Iphigénie en Taurid (Goethe, translated by Dwelhauvers), Théâtre de l'Odéon, Paris.

Ramuntcho (Loti), Théâtre de l'Odéon, Paris.

Les Euménides (Aeschylus, adapted by Lisle), Théâtre de l'Odéon, Paris.

Petite Holland (Guitry), Théâtre de l'Odéon, Paris.

La Comédie des familles (Géraldy), Théâtre de l'Odéon, Paris.

Le Chauffeur (Maurey), Théâtre de l'Odéon, Paris.

Alibi (Trarieux), Théâtre de l'Odéon, Paris.

Une Vieille contait (Gumpel and Delaquys), Théâtre de l'Odéon, Paris.

Le Nirvana (Vérola), Théâtre de l'Odéon, Paris.

La Voix frêle (Thierry and Bertaux), Théâtre de l'Odéon, Paris.

Velléda (Magre), Théâtre de l'Odéon, Paris.

L'Autre (André Dumas), Théâtre de l'Odéon, Paris.

Les Corbeaux (Becque), Théâtre de l'Odéon, Paris.

Le Domino á quatre (Becque), Théâtre de l'Odéon, Paris.

Á Pierre Corneille (compilation), Théâtre de l'Odéon, Paris.

Stances á la marquise (Corneille), Théâtre de l'Odéon, Paris.

Le Coeur et la Dot (Mallefille), Théâtre de l'Odéon, Paris.

Parmi les Pierres (Sudermann, translated by Rémon and Valentin), Théâtre de l'Odéon, Paris.

Karita (Sonniès), Théâtre de l'Odéon, Paris.

L'Éole des femmes (Molière), Théâtre de l'Odéon, Paris.

La Critique de l'Éole des femmes (Molière), Théâtre de l'Odéon, Paris.

La Dévotion á la croix (Calderón), Théâtre de l'Odéon, Paris.

Don Pietro Caruso (Bracco, translated by Sansot-Orland), Théâtre de l'Odéon, Paris.

Les Fausses confidences (Marivaux), Théâtre de l'Odéon, Paris.

Le Poussin (Guiraud), Théâtre de l'Odéon, Paris.

Pylade (Legendre), Théâtre de l'Odéon, Paris.

Bienheureuse (Bouchor), Théâtre de l'Odéon, Paris.

Les Fourberies de Scapin (Molière), Théâtre de l'Odéon, Paris.

Saint Genest (Rotrou), Théâtre de l'Odéon, Paris.

1909   *La Tragédie Royale* (Bouhélier), Théâtre de l'Odéon, Paris.

La Mort de Pan (Arnoux), Théâtre de l'Odéon, Paris.

Laurent (Céard and Croze), Théâtre de l'Odéon, Paris.

Molière et sa femme (Pottecher), Théâtre de l'Odéon, Paris.

Les Grands (Veber and Basset), Théâtre de l'Odéon, Paris.

Cinna (Corneille), Théâtre de l'Odéon, Paris.

Andromaque (Euripides, adapted by Hérold), Théâtre de l'Odéon, Paris.

Beethoven (Fauchois), Théâtre de l'Odéon, Paris.

Le Mariage de Figaro (Beaumarchais), Théâtre de l'Odéon, Paris.

Poil de carotte (Renard), Théâtre de l'Odéon, Paris.

Les Danicheff (Newsky), Théâtre de l'Odéon, Paris.

Les Deux génies (Bénédict), Théâtre de l'Odéon, Paris.

George Dandin (Molière), Théâtre de l'Odéon, Paris.

Cavalleria rusticana (Verga, translated by Solanges and Darsenne), Théâtre de l'Odéon, Paris.

Les Emigrants (Hirsch), Théâtre de l'Odéon, Paris.

La Bigote (Renard), Théâtre de l'Odéon, Paris.

La Moralité nouvelle d'un empereur (Rial-Faber, adapted from Janet and Fournier), Théâtre de l'Odéon, Paris.

La Farce du chauldronnier (Rial-Faber), Théâtre de l'Odéon, Paris.

L'Aveugle et le Boiteux (Vigne), Théâtre de l'Odéon, Paris.

Le Cry (Gringoire), Théâtre de l'Odéon, Paris.

Male fin, ou le repas trop copieux (Chesnaye), Théâtre de l'Odéon, Paris.

Jarnac (Hennique and Gravier), Théâtre de l'Odéon, Paris.

Les Sept contre Thèbes (Aeschylus, adapted by Hérold), Théâtre de l'Odéon, Paris.

Comme les feuilles (Giacosa, translated by Darsenne), Théâtre de l'Odéon, Paris.

Les Femmes savantes (Molière), Théâtre de l'Odéon, Paris.

Sur la lisière d'un bois (Hugo), Théâtre de l'Odéon, Paris.

Horace (Corneille), Théâtre de l'Odéon, Paris.

Charles VII chez ses grands vassaux (Dumas père), Théâtre de l'Odéon, Paris.

1910   *Turcaret* (Lesage), Théâtre de l'Odéon, Paris.

La Maison (Arnoux), Théâtre de l'Odéon, Paris.

Petite femme (Reynold), Théâtre de l'Odéon, Paris.

Phèdre et Hippolyte (Pradon), Théâtre de l'Odéon, Paris.

Antar (Chekri-Ganem), Théâtre de l'Odéon, Paris.

Lazare le pâtre (Bouchardy), Théâtre de l'Odéon, Paris.

Le Légataire universel (Regnard), Théâtre de l'Odéon, Paris.

L'Éole des Ménages (Balzac), Théâtre de l'Odéon, Paris.

Manette Salomon (Goncourt), Théâtre de l'Odéon, Paris.

Le Malade Imaginaire (Molière), Théâtre de l'Odéon, Paris.

Coriolan (Shakespeare, translated by Sonniès), Théâtre de l'Odéon, Paris.

Le Candidat (Flaubert), Théâtre de l'Odéon, Paris.

Mademoiselle Molière (Leloir and Nigond), Théâtre de l'Odéon, Paris.

Thérèse Raquin (Zola), Théâtre de l'Odéon, Paris.

Athalie (Racine), Théâtre de l'Odéon, Paris.

Monsieur de Pourceaugnac (Molière), Théâtre de l'Odéon, Paris.

Les Plus beaux jours (Traversi, adapted by Darsenne), Théâtre de l'Odéon, Paris.

Un Soir (Trarieux), Théâtre de l'Odéon, Paris.

Iphigénie en Aulide (Racine), Théâtre de l'Odéon, Paris.

Le Menteur (Corneille), Théâtre de l'Odéon, Paris.

Zaïre (Voltaire), Théâtre de l'Odéon, Paris.

Les Trois Sultanes (Favart), Théâtre de l'Odéon, Paris.

Les Affranchis (Lenéru), Théâtre de l'Odéon, Paris.

Roméo et Juliet (Shakespeare, translated by Gramont), Théâtre de l'Odéon, Paris.

Le Médecin malgré lui (Molière), Théâtre de l'Odéon, Paris.

1911 *Rodogune* (Corneille), Théâtre de l'Odéon, Paris.

L'Inquiète (Richard), Théâtre de l'Odéon, Paris.

L'Épreuve (Marivaux), Théâtre de l'Odéon, Paris.

La Femme d'intrigues (Dancourt), Théâtre de l'Odéon, Paris.

La Boulangère (Marlet), Théâtre de l'Odéon, Paris.

Le Pacha (Benjamin), Théâtre de l'Odéon, Paris.

Le Misanthrope (Molière), Théâtre de l'Odéon, Paris.

Mère (Dick-May), Théâtre de l'Odéon, Paris.

Maud (Nouy), Théâtre de l'Odéon, Paris.

La Cour d'amour de Romanin (Puyfontaine), Théâtre de l'Odéon, Paris.

L'Armée dans la ville (Romains), Théâtre de l'Odéon, Paris.

Rivoli (Fauchois), Théâtre de l'Odéon, Paris.

La Revanche de Boileau (Galzy), Théâtre de l'Odéon, Paris.

Chapelain décoiffé (Boileau), Théâtre de l'Odéon, Paris.

Les Héros de roman (Boileau), Théâtre de l'Odéon, Paris.

La Lumière (Duhamel), Théâtre de l'Odéon, Paris.

Vers l'amour (Gandillot), Théâtre de l'Odéon, Paris.

Coeur maternel (Franck), Théâtre de l'Odéon, Paris.

L'Apôtre (Loyson), Théâtre de l'Odéon, Paris.

Le Jouer (Regnard), Théâtre de l'Odéon, Paris.

Les Mages sans étoiles (Schneider), Théâtre de l'Odéon, Paris.

L'Assomption de Verlaine (Raynaud), Théâtre de l'Odéon, Paris.

Les Uns et les Autres (Verlaine), Théâtre de l'Odéon, Paris.

Diane de Poitiers (Faramond), Théâtre de l'Odéon, Paris.

Le Bourgois Gentilhomme (Molière), Théâtre de l'Odéon, Paris.

Musotte (Maupassant and Normand), Théâtre de l'Odéon, Paris.

La Mort de Sénèque (Tristan L'Hermite), Théâtre de l'Odéon, Paris.

Le Tribut (Karcher and Jeanne), Théâtre de l'Odéon, Paris.

David Copperfield (Maurey, adapted from Dickens), Théâtre de l'Odéon, Paris.

Aux jardins de Murcie (Feliu y Codina), Théâtre de l'Odéon, Paris.

Les Frères Lambertier (Hell and Villeroy), Théâtre de l'Odéon, Paris.

Madame Dandin (Croze), Théâtre de l'Odéon, Paris.

Bajazet (Racine), Théâtre de l'Odéon, Paris.

1912 *Le Pédant joué* (Bergerac), Théâtre de l'Odéon, Paris.

Le Redoutable (Lenéru), Théâtre de l'Odéon, Paris.

L'Âne de Buridan (Lafenestre), Théâtre de l'Odéon, Paris.

La Coupe enchantée (La Fontaine), Théâtre de l'Odéon, Paris.

Esther, princesse d'Israël (André Dumas and Leconte), Théâtre de l'Odéon, Paris.

Près de lui (Amiel), Théâtre de l'Odéon, Paris.

La Sentence (Barot-Forlière), Théâtre de l'Odéon, Paris.

L'Épée (Passillé), Théâtre de l'Odéon, Paris.

Troïlus et Cressida (Shakespeare, translated by Vedel), Théâtre de l'Odéon, Paris.

La Reine Margot (Dumas *père* and Maquet), Théâtre de l'Odéon, Paris.

L'Étoile de Séville (Vega), Théâtre de l'Odéon, Paris.

L'Honneur japonais (Anthelme), Théâtre de l'Odéon, Paris.

Amphitryon (Molière), Théâtre de l'Odéon, Paris.

La Foi (Brieux), Théâtre de l'Odéon, Paris.

Le Soulier de Corneille (Gautier), Théâtre de l'Odéon, Paris.

Les Perses (Aeschylus, adapted by Hérold), Théâtre de l'Odéon, Paris.

Dans l'ombre des statues (Duhamel), Théâtre de l'Odéon, Paris.

Le Dépit amoureux (Molière), Théâtre de l'Odéon, Paris.

Madame de Châtillon (Vérola), Théâtre de l'Odéon, Paris.

La Locandiera (Goldoni, adapted by Darsenne), Théâtre de l'Odéon, Paris.

Le Double Madrigal (Auzanet), Théâtre de l'Odéon, Paris.

L'Heure des tziganes (Larguier), Théâtre de l'Odéon, Paris.

Faust (Goethe, translated by Vedel), Théâtre de l'Odéon, Paris.

1913 *Sylla* (Mortier), Théâtre de l'Odéon, Paris.

Héraclius (Corneille), Théâtre de l'Odéon, Paris.

La Maison divisée (Fernet), Théâtre de l'Odéon, Paris.

La Nuit florentine (Bergerat, adapted from Machiavelli), Théâtre de l'Odéon, Paris.

La Rue du Sentier (Decourcelle and Maurel), Théâtre de l'Odéon, Paris.

L'Éole de la médisance (Sheridan, translated by Oudine and Bazile), Théâtre de l'Odéon, Paris.

Esther (Racine), Théâtre de l'Odéon, Paris.

La Grand-rue (Mortier), Théâtre de l'Odéon, Paris.

Réussir (Zahori), Théâtre de l'Odéon, Paris.

Dannémorah (Puyfontaine), Théâtre de l'Odéon, Paris.

Le Galant précepteur (Hollande), Théâtre de l'Odéon, Paris.

Moïse (Chateaubriand), Théâtre de l'Odéon, Paris.

Est-il bon? Est-il méchant? (Diderot), Théâtre de l'Odéon, Paris.

Le Mariage forcé (Molière), Théâtre de l'Odéon, Paris.

La Poudre aux yeux (Labiche and Martin), Théâtre de l'Odéon, Paris.

L'Homme n'est pas parfait (Thiboust and Barrière), Théâtre de l'Odéon, Paris.

Histoire de Manon Lescaut (Gold), Théâtre de l'Odéon, Paris.

L'Étourdi (Molière), Théâtre de l'Odéon, Paris.

Le Diplomate (Scribe and Delavigne), Théâtre de l'Odéon, Paris.

La Demoiselle à marier (Scribe and Mélesville), Théâtre de l'Odéon, Paris.

Rachel (Grillet), Théâtre de l'Odéon, Paris.

Le Voyage à Dieppe (Vafflard and Fulgence), Théâtre de l'Odéon, Paris.

Indiana et Charlemagne (Bayard and Dumanoir), Théâtre de l'Odéon, Paris.

Oscar ou le mari qui trompe sa femme (Scribe and Duveyrier), Théâtre de l'Odéon, Paris.

Les Vieux péchés (Mélesville and Dumanoir), Théâtre de l'Odéon, Paris.

1914 *Guillaume Tell* (Schiller, translated by Vedel), Théâtre de l'Odéon, Paris.

Geneviève ou la jalousie paternelle (Scribe), Théâtre de l'Odéon, Paris.

Michel Perrin (Mélesville and Duveyrier), Théâtre de l'Odéon, Paris.

Il ne faut jurer de rien (Musset), Théâtre de l'Odéon, Paris.

Le Bourgeois aux Champs (Brieux), Théâtre de l'Odéon, Paris.

Le Seul rêve (Grawitz), Théâtre de l'Odéon, Paris.

Bruno le fileur (Cogniard brothers), Théâtre de l'Odéon, Paris.

Faut s'entendre (Duveyrier), Théâtre de l'Odéon, Paris.

Don Juan (Molière), Théâtre de l'Odéon, Paris.

Le Jeune mari (Mazères), Théâtre de l'Odéon, Paris.

Le Feu au convent (Barrière), Théâtre de l'Odéon, Paris.

La Petite ville (Picard), Théâtre de l'Odéon, Paris.

Le Gamin de Paris (Bayard and Vanderburch), Théâtre de l'Odéon, Paris.

Le Dîner de Madelon (Désaugiers), Théâtre de l'Odéon, Paris.

Psyché (Molière), Théâtre de l'Odéon, Paris.

Films

Les Frères corses, 1916; *Le Coupable*, 1917; *Les Travailleurs de la mer*, 1917; *Israël*, 1918; *La Terre*, 1921; *Madame de Seiglière*, 1921; *L'Arlésienne*, 1922; *L'Hirondelle et le mésange*, 1922.

Publications

Le Théâtre Libre, 1890; *Mes souvenirs sur le Théâtre Libre*, 1921 (translated as *Memories of the Théâtre Libre*, 1964); *Mes Souvenirs sur le Théâtre Libre et sur l'Odéon*, 1928; *Le Théâtre de 1870 à nos jours*, 1932; *Lettres à Pauline*, edited by Pruner, 1962.

*

Bibliography

Books:
Adolphe Thalasso, *Le Théâtre Libre*, Paris, 1909.
Samuel Waxman, *Antoine and the Théâtre Libre*, Harvard, 1926.
F. Prince, *André Antoine et le renouveau du théâtre hollandais*, 1880–1900, Amsterdam, 1941.
M. Rousseau, *André Antoine*, Paris, 1954.
Francis Pruner, *Le Théâtre Libre d'Antoine*, Paris, 1958.
André Antoine, *Antoine — Père et fils*, Paris, 1962.
Francis Pruner, *Les Luttes d'Antoine*, Paris, 1964.
James Sanders, *André Antoine, directeur á l'Odéon*, Paris, 1978.
James Sanders (ed.), *La Correspendence d'André Antoine*, Quebec, 1987.
Jean Chothia, *André Antoine*, Cambridge, 1991.

* * *

André Antoine, the founder of the Théâtre Libre, is often referred to as "the father of modern *mise en scène*"; he was also a fine actor in his own right, a film director, and, later in life, an influential theatre and film critic. Yet, his first direct contact with the official world of theatre was a disappointment: in 1878 he failed to get a place at the Conservatoire, the drama school of the Comédie-Française. The following year he joined the army and was in national service until 1883. On his return to civilian life he became a very active member of an amateur theatre group, the Cercle Gaulois, where he gained his first experience as a director. It was from within the Cercle Gaulois that he was to found his own Théâtre Libre, which gave its first performance on 29 March 1887. The programme consisted of four plays, including an adaptation by Léon Hennique of Zola's short story, *Jacques d'Amour*. Between 1887 and 1894, the golden years of the Théâtre Libre, Antoine directed 124 plays by 114 different authors, 64 of whom, including Brieux, Porto-Riche, Icres, Courteline, and Renard, thus made their debut as playwrights. As well as works by French writers, Antoine introduced the best European playwrights to the French stage (among them, Hauptmann, Ibsen, Strindberg, and Tolstoy). He championed new writing throughout his career and was instrumental in fostering a new interest in Shakespeare. So devoted was he to new drama that, after the failure of Curel's *Les Fossiles*, he said that he was prouder of having discovered this play than vexed at having played it badly, the essential thing being to assure young writers that their plays would be read and performed.

An artistic success that was to inspire theatre people for generations, the Théâtre Libre was a financial disaster. After its demise, Antoine was briefly co-director of the Théâtre de l'Odéon (France's second "national theatre") before taking over a commercial house, the Théâtre des

Menus-Plaisirs, renaming it the Théâtre Antoine. In 1906 he was appointed sole director of the Odéon, where he tried to introduce some of the excitement of the Théâtre Libre by pursuing once again a policy of encouraging new writing. His stated aim was to run "a model theatre which lives by and for French literature" and he exhausted himself by putting on a new play every week: during the seven years of his directorship the Odéon presented no less than 364 plays! But, once again, Antoine's business acumen did not match his artistic flair and mounting debts forced him to give up the theatre's direction in 1914.

That same year, Antoine turned his attention to the cinema and during the following 10 years he adapted for the screen a number of works by his favourite authors, including Zola and Hugo. As a film director, Antoine warned that there should be no confusion between the aesthetics of the stage and the specific requirements of the screen. Whereas the theatre is an "art of imitation", he affirmed that the cinema must be "living creation". He forced the studio-bound cinema of his day into outside locations, liberated the static camera, and insisted on the importance of a multiple point of view. He encouraged actors to ignore the camera, just as he had asked the stage actors to perform as if they were inside the "fourth wall". As he went on directing films, Antoine became increasingly innovative and created an elliptic, symbolic, and at times expressionistic style that anticipated some of the best post-World War II cinema.

Nonetheless, Antoine's name is forever linked primarily with Zola and the cause of naturalism in the theatre. The actor and theatre director found his inspiration in the novelist's critical work and owed a great deal to the ideas expressed in *Le Naturalisme au théâtre*. To reform the theatre of the 1880s, Zola prayed for the coming of "a powerful personality who would revolutionize the tired conventions". No doubt he would have liked to cast himself in that role. Instead of a playwright, however, the personality he sought emerged in a director, or rather *the* director, the modern *metteur en scène*. In his productions, and in his rare theoretical writings, Antoine insisted on the importance of the set and of the creation of an all-encompassing environment. An original set, says Antoine, should be properly researched and based on exact observation and the fourth-wall convention should be strictly adhered to by designers and actors alike. But it would be a mistake to restrict Antoine's influence to the introduction of naturalistic devices, like building the set for *Ghosts* in its minutest details with wood specially imported from Norway or displaying sides of mutton in *Les Bouchers*. Ironically, critics at the time and historians ever since are guilty of misrepresentation: Fernand Incres's romantic verse drama, a tragic love story set in a butcher's shop, was directed by Antoine in an expressionistic style — mutton offals were strewn all over the stage to create a morbid atmosphere, not to imitate the neat appearance of a French "boucherie". Antoine always refused to be straitjacketed into any given school of thought and always tried to be receptive to new ideas.

His influence was felt in Berlin (Freie Bühne), Moscow (Arts Theatre), and London (Independent Theatre Society). His example is still inspiring the best of today's theatre people: he introduced seriousness, commitment, and intellectual honesty into a profession that was too often frivolous. He insisted on directing only quality texts and in practical terms instilled into the profession the need for long, painstaking, and questioning preparation, followed by intensive rehearsals. In his company he abolished the star system and emphasized the importance of the ensemble. By getting rid of footlights, by lowering the lights in the auditorium, and by using new lighting technology creatively he radically transformed the theatrical experience. The highest tribute paid to his revolutionary innovations is that today they are taken for granted. Yet Antoine's lifework will still be inspirational in the 21st century.

—Claude Schumacher

———

APPIA, Adolphe. Swiss theorist and designer. Born in Geneva, Switzerland, 1862. Educated at the Collège de Vevey, 1873–79; studied music in Geneva, 1880–81, and at the Leipzig Conservatory of Music, 1882. Apprentice, Dresden Hoftheater, 1889; worked backstage at the Vienna Burgtheater and the Hofoper, 1890; moved to Bière, Switzerland, and began work on ideas for staging Wagnerian opera, 1891; numerous innovations in lighting and staging technique; launched collaboration with the creator of eurhythmics, Emile Jaques-Dalcroze, 1906; contributed to the designs and plans for an institute of eurhythmics to be built in Hellerau, 1910, and to the two Hellerau Festivals, 1912 and 1913; exhibited designs in Zürich, 1914, and in London and Amsterdam, 1922; ended collaboration with Dalcroze after resigning from the Dalcroze Institute in Geneva, 1923; designs exhibited in Magdeburg, 1927. Died near Geneva, 29 February 1928.

Productions

1903	Act Two of *Carmen* with a scene from *Manfred* (Lord Byron, adapted by Schumann), Comtesse de Béarn's private theatre, Paris.
1912	*Descent into Hades* from *Orfeo et Euridice* (Gluck), Festival of the Hellerau Institute, Germany.
	Echo and Narcissus (mime), Festival of the Hellerau Institute, Germany.
1913	*Orfeo et Euridice* (Gluck), Festival of the Hellerau Institute, Germany.
	Tidings Brought to Mary (Claudel), Festival of the Hellerau Institute, Germany.
1914	*Fête de Juin* (pageant), Geneva.
1919	*Echo and Narcissus* (reworking), Dalcroze Institute, Geneva.
1923	*Tristan und Isolde* (Wagner), Teatro La Scala, Milan.
1924	*Das Reingold* (Wagner), Basle Theatre, Basle.
1925	*Die Walküre* (Wagner), Basle Theatre, Basle.
	Prometheus Bound (Aeschylus), Basle Theatre, Basle.

Unstaged designs included: *Parsifal* (Wagner), 1896 and 1922; *Les Jumeaux de Bergame* (Dalcroze), 1907; *A Midsummer Night's Dream* (Shakespeare), 1922; *Hamlet* (Shakespeare), 1922; *Die Meistersinger* (Wagner), 1922; *Siegfried* (Wagner), 1923; *Götterdämmerung* (Wagner), 1923; *Orfeo ed Euridice* (Gluck), 1926; *King Lear* (Shakespeare), 1926; *Macbeth* (Shakespeare), 1926; *Lohengrin* (Wagner), 1926; *Iphigénie en Tauride* (Gluck), 1926; *Iphigénie en Aulide* (Gluck), 1926; *Faust* (Goethe), 1927.

Publications

La Mise-en-scène du drame Wagnérien, 1895; *Die Musik und die Inscenierung*, 1899; *L'Oeuvre d'art vivant*, 1921.

*

Bibliography

Books:
Henry C. Bonifas, *Adolphe Appia*, Zurich, 1929.
W. Volbach, *Adolphe Appia, Prophet of the Modern Theatre*, Middletown, Connecticut, 1968.
Ferruccio Marotti, *Adolphe Appia: Attore, Musica e Scena*, Milan, 1981.
Richard C. Beacham, *Adolphe Appia — Theatre Artist*, Cambridge, 1987.
Richard C. Beacham (ed.), *Adolphe Appia, Essays, Scenarios and Designs*, UMI, 1989.

Articles:
Jacques Copeau, "L'Art et l'oeuvre d'Adolphe Appia", *Comoedia*, 1928.
Edmond Stadler, "Adolphe Appia and Oskar Wälterlin", *Neue Zürcher Zeitung*, 1963.
Richard C. Beacham, "Adolphe Appia and Eurhythmics", *Maske und Kothern*, vol. 29, 1983.
Richard C. Beacham, "Adolphe Appia and the Staging of Wagnerian Opera", *Opera Quaterly*, 1983.
Richard C. Beacham, "Adolphe Appia, Emile Jaques-Dalcroze, and Hellerau", two parts, *New Theatre Quaterly*, 1985.

* * *

In the last decade of the 19th century, Adolphe Appia, working virtually in isolation, laid out both the theoretical and practical foundations for a fundamental and permanent change in theatrical art. Through his extensive commentary, detailed scenarios, and unprecedented designs — all inspired by his analysis of Wagnerian opera — Appia first provided a complete and devastating critique of the disastrous state of theatre practice, and then, with quite astonishing foresight, suggested the solutions which, in time and frequently at the hands of others, would re-establish it upon an entirely different basis.

In his revolutionary work, *Die Musik und die Inscenierung* (*Music and the Art of the Theatre*), Appia suggested that essentially music was the measure of all things. The score itself should dictate not only the duration of the performance, but also all movement and gestures of the actors, and by extension, the physical area itself, the scenic space in which the performance took place. Appia built upon this radical concept what became known as the "New Art" of the theatre. He called for three-dimensional scenery, for the use of creative form-revealing light (developing the concept of the "lighting plot"), and for settings, the overall conception of which would be expressive of the inner reality *as art* of works of musical drama. Through music all the arts of the theatre could be integrated into an hierarchically ordered, balanced, conceptually coherent, and uniquely expressive new form of art.

Appia demanded that the actor be set free from the mockery of flat painted settings, in order to practice a purified craft within a supportive and responsive setting. Light, symbolic colouring, and a dynamic sculptured space would be used to evoke for the first time atmosphere and psychological nuance, with all these expressive elements harmoniously correlated by the new theatrical artist, whom Appia termed the 'designer-director', whose work of art would be the production itself. The audience, benefiting in turn from such reforms, should no longer be thought of as mere passive spectators, for Appia believed that experiments along the lines he suggested could more fully involve them in the theatrical act in order to both experience and determine it more directly.

The second phase of Appia's creative career arose from his involvement with the system of eurhythmics devised by his fellow-countryman Emile Jaques-Dalcroze. This was designed to enhance performers' perception of musical nuance and sensitivity to musical rhythm and tempo through the responsive movement of their own bodies in space. In 1906 Appia encountered it for the first time and perceived at once that it provided the key to realising his earlier theoretical principle that the actor must be motivated by music and through his movement determine the nature of the scenic environment. He began to prepare for Dalcroze's use a series of designs, termed "rhythmic spaces", which were destined to revolutionise future scenic practice still further. These were essentially abstract arrangements of solid stairs, platforms, podia, and the like, whose rigidity, sharp lines and angles, and immobility, when confronted by the softness, subtlety, and movement of the body, would by opposition, take on a kind of borrowed life. Settings were no longer to be thought of as illustrations of fictive environments, but as particular spaces for a performance to take place, simultaneously themselves evoking the inner meaning of the drama.

Together with Dalcroze, Appia helped to plan and present a series of extraordinary demonstrations highlighting the potential of eurhythmics both for performance and design, at Dalcroze's institute in Hellerau, near Dresden in Germany. The proscenium arch was abolished and the lighting, operated from a central "organ", was carefully co-ordinated with the music and movement as well as the emotional flow of the performance. Attended by the leading theatrical artists of the day, the festivals at Hellerau in 1912 and 1913 caused astonishment and admiration and exercised a profound influence upon later scenic practice, as well as directly and indirectly upon the development of modern dance.

In the last decade of his life, Appia added to his earlier work even more radical ideas for the future evolution of what he now termed "living art". He realised that what he had begun as an analysis and critique of the state of the theatre must end in a fundamental attack on contemporary culture itself and, crucially, on the role which art was forced to play within it. People observed art passively and if it moved them at all it did so *artificially*, having lost its power to activate emotionally and spiritually an audience that could now only contemplate but no longer enter into it. It was necessary to return to the well-spring of all art, the living experience of the human body, and from there to express and share both the reality of oneself and simultaneously, one's communal relationship with the rest of society, from which one would no longer be isolated, but reintegrated into living contact. The theatre of the future would no longer confine itself to enacting stories, but would instead use in their purest form the primary expressive elements that Appia had identified earlier — light, movement, music, and space, all in the service of the human body — to create less "literary" and representational forms of art, analagous to abstract painting, sculpture, and indeed, music.

In his book *L'Oeuvre d'art vivant* (*The Work of Living Art*), a collection of essays, Appia detailed the social implications of this new collaborative art. These speculative treatments tend inevitably to be less concrete than his earlier writings but provide a programme and descriptions of many of the developments and expressions that have characterized theatrical art in the latter part of the 20th century.

Appia himself was a shy and reclusive person, who despite the eminently practical basis of most of his ideas, found collaborative work extremely difficult and frustrating (early in his life he twice attempted suicide, in 1888 and 1890). His realised productions were very few as his radical ideas brought him into conflict with traditionalists and his contribution has been inadequately recognised. Appia was a pioneering genius who, arguably more than any other individual, may justly be termed not just the "prophet" but the "father" of the modern theatre.

—Richard C. Beacham

ARMIN, Robert. English actor and playwright. Born probably in King's Lynn, Norfolk, c.1568. Education included study of Latin and Italian. Records of the burial of one daughter, 1600, and a son, 1606, and of the birth of a daughter, 1603. Apprentice, London Company of Goldsmiths, 1581–92; established reputation as writer of ballads and anecdotes; joined service of Lord Chandos as actor, touring 1595–97; enjoyed outstanding success in clown parts after studying the acting of Richard Tarlton; acting at the Globe Theatre by 1600, and with Lord Chamberlain's Men (later renamed King's Men) inheriting clown roles of Will Kemp, c.1598–1610. Died in London, November 1615.

Roles (venues uncertain)

1599	Touchstone in *As You Like It* (Shakespeare).
	Carlo Buffone in *Every Man Out of His Humour* (Jonson).
c.1600	Feste in *Twelfth Night* (Shakespeare).
c.1602	Lavache in *All's Well that Ends Well* (Shakespeare).
	Thersites in *Troilus and Cressida* (Shakespeare).
1604	Passarello in *The Malcontent* (Marston).
1605	Fool in *King Lear* (Shakespeare).
	Frog in *The Fair Maid of Bristow* (anon.).
	The Porter in *Macbeth* (Shakespeare).
	A Gravedigger in *Hamlet* (Shakespeare).
1606	The Fool in *The Miseries of Enforced Marriage* (Wilkins).
	The Clown in *Othello* (Shakespeare).
	The Clown in *Antony and Cleopatra* (Shakespeare).
c.1609	Dogberry in *Much Ado About Nothing* (Shakespeare).

Other conjectured roles included: Abel Drugger in *The Alchemist* (Jonson); Apemantis in *Timon of Athens* (Shakespeare); Autolycus in *The Winter's Tale* (Shakespeare); Caliban in *The Tempest* (Shakespeare); Casca in *Julius Caesar* (Shakespeare); Civet in *The London Prodigal* (anon.); Cloten in *Cymbeline* (Shakespeare); Menenius in *Coriolanus* (Shakespeare); Nano, the Dwarf in *Volpone* (Jonson); Nym in *Henry V* (Shakespeare); Pandarus in *Troilus and Cressida* (Shakespeare); Robin in *Doctor Faustus* (adapted from Marlowe).

Publications

Quips upon Questions, 1600 (as Clonnico de Curtanio Snuffe); *Foole upon Foole; or, Six Sorts of Sottes* (comic tales), 1600 (as Clonnico de Curtanio Snuffe); *A Nest of Ninnies* (enlarged version of *Foole upon Foole*), 1609; *The Italian Taylor and His Boy* (ballads, adapted from Straparda), 1609; *The History of the Two Maids of Moreclacke* (play), 1609.

*

Bibliography

Books:
J. P. Collier, *Memoirs of the Principal Actors in the Plays of Shakespeare*, London, 1846.
Charles S. Felver, *Robert Armin, Shakespeare's Fool*, Kent State University, Ohio, 1961.
David Wiles, *Shakespeare's Clown: Actor and Text in the Elizabethan Playhouse*, Cambridge, 1987.

Articles:
Austin K. Gray, "Robert Armine, The Foole", *PMLA*, 42, 1927.
Charles S. Felver, "Robert Armin, Shakespeare's Source for Touchstone", *Shakespeare Quarterly*, 7, 1956.
John Feather, "A Check-list of the Works of Robert Armin", *The Library*, 26, 1971.
John Feather, "Robert Armin and the Chamberlain's Men", *Notes and Queries*, 217, 1972.
Raymong Gardette, "La vie, le péché et la mort dans une version élisabéthaine de la nef des fous: le Suite des fous de Robert Armin", *Caliban*, 10, 1973.
H. F. Lippincott, "*King Lear* and the Fools of Robert Armin", *Shakespeare Quarterly*, 26, 1975.
Jane Belfield, "Robert Armin, Citizen and Goldsmith of London", *Notes and Queries*, 225, 1980.
Guy Butler, "Shakespeare and the Two Jesters", *Hebrew University Studies in Literature and the Arts*, 11, 1983.

* * *

According to an anecdote in *Tarlton's Jests*, printed in London in 1611, the young Robert Armin so impressed

Richard Tarlton, the most famous clown of the Elizabethan age, by a piece of extemporised rhyming on the fate of a debtor that Tarlton prophesied:

> As I am,
> So in time thou'lt be the same,
> My adopted sonne therefore be,
> To enjoy my clownes sute after me.

Whatever the truth of the anecdote (and it may indeed be true), Armin was clearly well versed in the Tarltonian tradition of clowning, a tradition he was to expand as a solo performer before becoming the leading comic player with the Lord Chamberlain's Men, the position to which he largely owed his fame.

Even if he had not achieved his later eminence with "Shakespeare's company", Armin's contribution to our understanding of the comic performances of his time would have been considerable. Of his early career as a player with the Lord Chandos's Men in Gloucestershire little can be said with any degree of certainty. However, he also spent some time as a peripatetic solo clown, with mixed financial success according to his own comment that he sometimes slept "in the fields, wanting a house o'er my head". His solo repertoire provided him with some of the material for two of his printed works: *Quips upon Questions* and *Foole upon Foole*, both 1600, by which time he had become established as a London player and thus no longer needed it. Even though much of the material, especially in *Quips*, is self-consciously literary, even pietistic, when read as performance texts these two reworkings provide glimpses of Armin as a remarkably skilled and sophisticated performer.

Quips records his answers in verse to questions thrown at him by an audience. Tarlton was reputedly a master of extemporisation, though the few examples of his wit that have survived are frankly unimpressive. Armin expanded the tradition by creating duologues between himself and his "marotte" (Sir Timothie Truncheon, to whom the work is dedicated). At their best they show lively, comic crosstalk between the lofty but stupid, animate clown and the worldly-wise, earthy, inanimate "marotte". There is little that is bawdy. On occasions clown and "marotte" combine to mock a member of the audience or an imagined third party. In one piece clown and "marotte" agree to go off and have a drink. These performance pieces combine verbal wit with visual interest and vocal dexterity, creating a surreal world of human and object, confusion and illusion. The audience, by being interrogators, became participants rather than spectators, absorbed into an absurd world where normal concepts and behaviours were suspended. The same surreal world can be seen in *Foole*, a collection of stories about six Elizabethan household fools. At times the material, dressed up as "reportage", shows Armin as a highly sophisticated monipolyloguist. Armin, through his gallery of fools, creates anarchy in the orderly world of the great halls of England. His fools fight, trundle burning wheelbarrows, eat hawks, steal quince pies, and walk on ice. In addition to the fools, Armin played such other characters as the dramas required, whilst also acting as narrator, in which role he reassured his audience of their collective wisdom. Armin's fools are "naturals" or imbeciles; their behaviour irrational, their emotions stunted. They are figures to be held up for inspection and ridicule: it is a cruel humour. It is also highly theatrical — a bravura

solo presentation by one who described himself as "this poore Petite of transformation" of kings, knights, gentlemen, minstrels, cobblers, messengers, and selected members of the great genus fool. Further evidence of Armin's interest in and presentation of folly occurs in his one extant play, *The History of the Two Maids of More-clacke*. In this sprawling, convoluted Jacobean expansion of an Elizabethan original, Armin provided himself with a starring vehicle in which he played not just Blue John, a "natural" who also appears in *Foole*, but also Tutch, an artificial fool. Tutch is a very different clown from the illiterate rustics of Tarlton and Kemp; he is a street-wise Londoner, wearing livery, quoting Latin, using language with skill, victimising others — an Elizabethan English Scapino. At the very end of the play Armin appears as Tutch disguised as John, a symbiosis of old and new fool. The character of the witty fool may be said to have arrived.

One further element of Armin's repertoire as a solo clown should be noted: his mocking personal attacks on others. In *The Two Maids* he attacks John Stone, an old-fashioned tavern fool, while elsewhere he directs his venom against Ben Jonson among others.

Armin can thus be seen as a performer in the Tarltonian tradition, performing anywhere, creating a world of anarchy, delivering personal attacks, extemporising, and — like Carlo Buffone — talking "crackers and fireworks". Both could claim, like Autolycus, that "We may do anything extempore". Armin expanded the tradition, bringing to it his skill as multi-vocal performer and his control of dramatic structure. It is therefore something of a surprise that this is precisely what he did not do after he had become the leading comic player with the Lord Chamberlain's Men.

The date of Armin's first association with the Lord Chamberlain's Men is debatable. It may be that he joined as early as 1598, being employed initially as a singer to play Balthasar in *Much Ado* and then Amiens in *As You Like It*, a role easily doubled with Touchstone, so-named to celebrate the new player's first major part. Singing was clearly an important strength in his repertoire, as it was of Tarlton's (Armin himself suggests that he was a countertenor).

Following the departure of the erratic Kemp, Armin provided Shakespeare with the skills demanded by the roles of the witty fools, written to appeal to a more select and educated audience as part of the company's attempt to move upmarket. He appears to have abandoned improvisation and direct address, following Hamlet's advice "Let not your Clowne speak more than is set down". Arminian roles are always part of the stage picture, integrated into the play, yet standing to one side, commenting on the action.

The reason for this lay not just in the writing of the roles. David Wiles concludes "For Armin's contemporaries, the clown's deformity was too obvious to require direct comment". Armin was a deformed, possibly grotesque, dwarf. Whereas Kemp whirled and leapt in the jig, Armin stood aside, pointing out the folly of the dance.

It is not possible to assess the influence that Armin may have had on Shakespeare. What can be said is that Shakespeare made full use of the talents of this remarkable player, who insisted that just because he played the fool did not mean that he was one. Without Armin the roles, and thus the plays, would not be as they are. Shakespeare was indeed fortunate to have such a man to create both with and for.

—Christopher Sutcliffe

———

ARONSON, Boris. US designer, painter, and sculptor. Born in Kiev, Russia, 15 October 1900 (some sources, 1898). Educated at the State Art School, Kiev, graduated 1916; trained as set designer under Aleksandra Ekster at the School of Theatre, Kiev, under Ilya Mashkov at the School of Modern Painting, Moscow, and under Herman Struch in Berlin, 1922. Married Lisa Jalowetz in 1945, one son. Co-founder, Museum of Modern Art, Kiev, 1917; designed posters and decorations for state-sponsored street theatre, 1918–22; left Kiev for Berlin, 1922; settled in New York, 1923; debut as stage designer, Unser Theatre, New York, 1924; worked with the Unser Theatre, the Yiddish Art Theatre, and, in the 1930's, on Broadway and with the Group Theatre, New York; acclaimed for musicals in collaboration with Harold Prince in the 1960's; innovations included use of projections. Member: United Scenic Artists. Recipient: Guggenheim Fellowship, 1950; Tony Award for Stage Designs, 1950–51, 1966, 1968, 1970, 1971, 1976; Ford Foundation Grant, 1962; New York Drama Critics Award, 1964; Maharam Award for Set Design, 1965, 1967, 1970, 1971, 1976; Creative Arts Award, Brandeis University, 1969. Died in Hyack, New York, 16 November 1980.

Productions

As set designer:

1919   *Romeo and Juliet* (Shakespeare), Kamerny Theatre, Moscow; also designed costumes.

1924   *Day and Night* (Ansky), Unser Theatre, New York; also designed costumes.

1925   *The Final Balance* (Pinski), Unser Theatre, New York; also designed costumes.

The Bronx Express (Dymov), Schildkraut Theatre, New York; also designed costumes.

String of Pearls (Asch), Yiddish Art Theatre, New York; also designed costumes.

1926   *The Tenth Commandment* (Goldfaden), Yiddish Art Theatre, New York; also designed costumes.

1927   *Yoshe Musikant* [Singer of his Own Sadness] (Dymov), Yiddish Art Theatre, New York.

Menschen Stoib (Dymov), Yiddish Art Theatre, New York; also designed costumes.

Red, Yellow and Black (Wolfe), Civic Repertory Theatre, New York; also designed costumes.

2×2=5 (Wied), Civic Repertory Theatre, New York; also designed costumes.

The Tragedy of Nothing (Nadir), Irving Place Theatre, New York; also directed and designed costumes.

1929   *Jew Süss* (Feuchtwanger), Yiddish Art Theatre, New York.

Stempenyu, The Fiddler (Aleichem), Yiddish Art Theatre, New York; also designed costumes.

Angels on Earth (Gottesfeld), Yiddish Art Theatre, New York; also designed costumes.

1930   *Roaming Stars* (Schwartz), Yiddish Art Theatre, New York.

Jim Cooperkop (Godiner), Princess Theatre, New York.

1932   *Walk a Little Faster* (Perelman), St James's Theatre, New York.

1934   *Small Miracle* (Krasna), John Golden Theatre, New York.

Ladies' Money (Abbott), Ethel Barrymore Theatre, New York.

1935   *Battleship Gertie* (Brennan), Lyceum Theatre, New York.

Awake and Sing (Odets), Belasco Theatre, New York.

The Body Beautiful (Rossen), Plymouth Theatre, New York.

Weep for the Virgins (Child), 46th Street Theatre, New York.

Paradise Lost (Odets), Longacre Theatre, New York.

Three Men on a Horse (Holm and Abbott), The Playhouse, New York; also designed costumes.

1937   *Western Waters* (Carlson), Hudson Theatre, New York; also designed costumes.

1938   *The Merchant of Yonkers* (Wilder), Guild Theatre, New York.

1939   *The Time of Your Life* (Saroyan), Shubert Theatre, New York; also designed costumes.

The Gentle People (I. Shaw), Belasco Theatre, New York; also designed costumes.

Ladies and Gentlemen (Hecht and MacArthur), Martin Beck Theatre, New York; also designed costumes.

1940   *The Unconquered* (Rand), Biltmore Theatre, New York.

The Great American Goof (ballet by Loring, Brant, and Saroyan), Centre Theatre, New York; also designed costumes.

Heavenly Express (Bein), National Theatre, New York; also designed costumes.

Cabin in the Sky (Root), Martin Beck Theatre, New York; also designed costumes.

1941   *The Night Before Christmas* (L. and S. J. Perelman), Morosco Theatre, New York.

Clash by Night (Odets), Belasco Theatre, New York.

1942   *Café Crown* (Kraft), Cort Theatre, New York.

R.U.R. (Čapek), Ethel Barrymore Theatre, New York.

The Russian People (Simonov), Guild Theatre, New York.

The Snow Maiden (ballet by Nijinska, Glazunov, and Denham), Metropolitan Opera House, New York; also designed costumes.

1943   *The Family* (Wolfson), Windsor Theatre, New York.

What's Up (Lerner and Pierson), National Theatre, New York.

Boris Aronson

South Pacific (Rigsby and Heyward), Cort Theatre, New York.

The Red Poppy (Schwezoff and Glière), Music Hall Theatre, Cleveland; also designed costumes.

1944 *Sadie Thompson* (Dietz and Mamoulian), Alvin Theatre, New York.

Pictures at an Exhibition (ballet by Nijinska and Moussorgsky), Metropolitan Opera House, New York; also designed costumes.

1945 *The Desert Song* (Harbach, Hammerstein, and Mandel), Philharmonic Auditorium, Los Angeles.

The Assassin (Shaw), National Theatre, New York.

The Stranger (Reade), The Playhouse, New York; also designed lighting.

1946 *Truckline Café* (Anderson), Belasco Theatre, New York.

The Fortune Teller (Smith and Herbert), Philharmonic Auditorium, Los Angeles.

Sweet Bye and Bye (Perelman, Hirschfeld, Duke, and Nash), Shubert Theatre, New York.

1947 *The Big People* (Young), Lyric Theatre, Bridgeport, Connecticut.

1948 *Skipper Next to God* (Hartog), Maxine Elliott's Theatre, New York.

Love Life (Lerner and Weill), 46th Street Theatre, New York.

The Survivors (Viertel and Shaw), The Playhouse, New York; also designed lighting.

1949 *Detective Story* (Kingsley), Hudson Theatre, New York.

1950 *The Bird Cage* (Laurents), Coronet Theatre, New York; also designed lighting.

Season in the Sun (Gibbs), Cort Theatre, New York; also designed lighting.

The Country Girl (Odets), Lyceum Theatre, New York; also designed lighting.

1951 *The Rose Tattoo* (T. Williams), Martin Beck Theatre, New York.

I Am a Camera (van Druten), Empire Theatre, New York.

Barefoot in Athens (Anderson), Martin Beck Theatre, New York; also designed lighting.

1952 *I've Got Sixpence* (van Druten), Ethel Barrymore Theatre, New York.

Ballade (ballet by Robbins and Debussy), New York City Centre, New York; also designed costumes.

1953 *The Crucible* (Miller), Martin Beck Theatre, New York.

My Three Angels (S. and B. Spewack), Morosco Theatre, New York.

The Frogs of Spring (Benchley), Broadhurst Theatre, New York; also designed lighting.

1954 *Mademoiselle Colombe* (Anouilh), Longacre Theatre, New York.

1955 *The Master Builder* (Ibsen), Phoenix Theatre, New York.

Bus Stop (Inge), Music Box Theatre, New York.

Once Upon a Tailor (Lumet), Cort Theatre, New York.

A View from the Bridge and *A Memory of Two Mondays* (Miller), Coronet Theatre, New York.

The Diary of Anne Frank (Goodrich and Hackett), Cort Theatre, New York.

Dancing in the Chequered Shade (van Druten), McCarter Theatre, Princeton, New Jersey.

1956 *Girls of Summer* (Nash), Longacre Theatre, New York.

1957 *Small War on Murray Hill* (Sherwood), Ethel Barrymore Theatre, New York.

A Hole in the Head (Schulman), Plymouth Theatre, New York.

Orpheus Descending (T. Williams), Martin Beck Theatre, New York.

The Rope Dancers (Wishengrad), Cort Theatre, New York.

1958 *This Is Goggle* (Plagemann), McCarter Theatre, Princeton, New Jersey.

The Firstborn (Fry), Coronet Theatre, New York.

The Cold Wind and the Warm (Behrman), Morosco Theatre, New York.

J. B. (MacLeish), ANTA Theatre, New York.

1959 *Coriolanus* (Shakespeare), Shakespeare Memorial Theatre, Stratford-upon-Avon.

Flowering Cherry (Bolt), Lyceum Theatre, New York.

A Loss of Roses (Inge), Eugene O'Neill Theatre, New York.

1960   *Semi-Detached* (Joudry), Martin Beck Theatre, New York.

Do Re Mi (Kanin, Styne, Comden, and Green), St James's Theatre, New York.

1961   *The Garden of Sweets* (Hansen), ANTA Theatre, New York.

1962   *A Gift of Time* (Kanin), Ethel Barrymore Theatre, New York.

Judith (Giraudoux), Her Majesty's Theatre, London.

1963   *Andorra* (Frisch), Biltmore Theatre, New York.

1964   *Fiddler on the Roof* (Stein, Bock, and Harnick), Imperial Theatre, New York.

Incident at Vichy (Miller), ANTA Washington Square Theatre, New York.

1965   *L'Histoire du Soldat* (Stravinsky, Ramuz, and Sokolow), Grand Ballroom, Waldorf-Astoria Hotel, New York.

1966   *Cabaret* (Masteroff, Kander, and Ebb), Broadhurst Theatre, New York.

1967   *Mourning Becomes Electra* (opera by Lavy and Butler), Metropolitan Opera House, New York; also designed costumes.

1968   *Zorba* (Stein, Kander, and Ebb), Imperial Theatre, New York.

The Price (Miller), Morosco Theatre, New York; also designed costumes.

1970   *Company* (Furth and Sondheim), Alvin Theatre, New York.

Fidelio (opera by Beethoven and Sonnleithner), Metropolitan Opera House, New York; also designed costumes.

1971   *Follies* (Goldman and Sondheim), Winter Garden Theatre, New York.

1972   *The Creation of the World and Other Business* (Miller), Shubert Theatre, New York.

The Great God Brown (O'Neill), Lyceum Theatre, New York.

1973   *A Little Night Music* (Wheeler and Sondheim), Shubert Theatre, New York.

1974   *The Tzaddick* (ballet by Feld and Copland), Newman Theatre, New York; also designed costumes.

1975   *Dreyfus in Rehearsal* (Grumberg), Ethel Barrymore Theatre, New York.

1976   *Pacific Overtures* (Weidman and Sondheim), Winter Garden Theatre, New York.

The Nutcracker (ballet by Tchaikovsky and Baryshnikov), Kennedy Centre, Washington, D.C.

Films

The Diary of Anne Frank (as consultant), 1957.

Television

The Nutcracker, 1977.

Publications

Marc Chagall, 1923; *Contemporary Jewish Graphic Art*, 1924.

*

Bibliography

Books:
Waldemar George, *Boris Aronson et L'art du théâtre*, Paris, 1928.
Thor E. Wood, Harold Clurman, Garson Kanin, and Harold Prince, *Boris Aronson: From His Theatre Work*, New York, 1981.
Frank Rich and Lisa Aronson, *Boris Aronson's Theatre Art*, New York, 1987.

Articles:
C. Glassold, "Art in the Theatre: Boris Aronson", *Arts*, January 1928.
Anon., "Aronson of Russia", *Art Digest*, 15 January 1931.

* * *

The designer Donald Oenslager claimed that Boris Aronson "designs as a painter in the theatre", while critic Frank Rich began his biography of Aronson with the words: "This is a book about an artist." When Aronson himself began working with projected scenery, notably in *The Great American Goof* in 1940, he called it "painting with light", a phrase subsequently appropriated by the Museum of Modern Art in New York as the title for an exhibition of the designs from the show in 1947. While Aronson was certainly not the first person to come to theatre design through painting, virtually no other US designer was so thoroughly informed by the aesthetics of painting and sculpture. Aronson came of age in Russia around the time of the Revolution, when the theatre and art communities there were in the forefront of the avant-garde, and he became immersed in this world of radical innovation and artistic exploration. He was introduced early on to the paintings of Matisse and Picasso, he was a friend of the artist Marc Chagall and published a book on him in 1923, and he studied with Alexandra Ekster, a Russian painter and the primary designer for Alexander Tairov at the Kamerny Theatre in Moscow. Thus, at a time when US designers were still experimenting with realism, Aronson in Moscow and then Berlin was soaking up Cubism, Constructivism, Expressionism, and a range of anti-realist developments. He admired the work of Russian director Vsevelod Meyerhold, who practiced a style of theatre best described as 'theatricalism'. He worked directly with Tairov as Ekster's assistant on a 1919 production of *Romeo and Juliet* — an angular, abstract production that included the use of mirrors. The influence of Tairov and Meyerhold, especially the rejection of naturalism in favour of a poetic, metaphoric theatricality, would remain with him throughout his career.

Aronson brought this background with him to the USA, unaware that most of these ideas were still unknown or unwelcome. Frank Rich makes a keen insight when he notes that the architecture, technology, and energy of the New York City in which Aronson settled contained the avant-garde spirit of the European art world he left behind, but the New York theatre, ironically, was still mired in the 19th century. Part of the difficulty that Aronson faced in gaining acceptance was a matter of being 30 or 40 years ahead of his time.

Aronson's early work in the USA was with the Yiddish theatres and his Constructivist background showed in these productions. Some aspects of his design for *The Tenth Commandment*, for instance, seems to anticipate the Living Theatre's scenography for their production of *Frankenstein* some 40 years later. His contributions at these theatres were so unlike anything seen on Broadway at the time that they attracted notice and led to more mainstream work. Through the 1930's he designed for productions ranging from the Radio City Music Hall extravaganzas to Max Reinhardt's intimate production of *The Merchant of Yonkers*. Other notable productions included *Walk a Little Faster* and *Three Men on a Horse*. He developed a close relationship with Group Theatre director Harold Clurman and designed several productions for the Group. Despite this, and despite the admiration he received from his colleagues, however, Aronson was not achieving the success and popularity of some of his contemporaries.

Aronson's 1939 design for William Saroyan's *The Gentle People* seemed to anticipate the style of poetic realism soon to be popularized by Jo Mielziner. The Coney Island pier was created not in a detailed realistic manner but more in the style of a Japanese woodcut. Unlike such designers as Bel Geddes, Mielziner, and Howard Bay, who were willing to create hyper-realistic sets on occasion, Aronson constantly listened to his inner voice and the lessons learned from Tairov and Ekster that rejected naturalistic decor. Furthermore, he felt that each scene should contain the mood of the whole production. This latter idea, however, did not necessitate a stylistic consistency from one scene to the next, at least in the way that is usually understood. Designer John Lee Beatty once observed of Aronson's work that his "theatricality and inconsistency [made] for a certain rhythm in his work. His design for *Cabaret*, for instance, had very realistic scenery in one scene and painted effects in the next; it kept things alive." Aronson insisted on consistency, but this could apply to a mood or feeling within a design. Just as Tairov believed that naturalism had to give way to theatrical truth, Aronson noted that "for each play you first and foremost must create a space which, inherent in its design, already holds the mystique of the entire event."

During the 1950's Aronson was associated with some of the best serious drama on Broadway, but he did not gain widespread fame and acceptance until the mid-1960's, when he began his collaboration with director/producer Harold Prince on a series of musicals, including *Fiddler on the Roof, Cabaret, Company,* and *Follies*. It is arguable that Prince's success is attributable in part to Aronson. Musicals, because of their inherent theatricality and poeticism, allowed Aronson to blossom. Moreover, the musicals of the 1960's and 1970's moved into a realm of complexity and social consciousness that meshed with Aronson's sensibilities. The Chagall-inspired settings of *Fiddler on the Roof,* the sliding plexiglas panels with painted birch trees of *A Little Night Music,* the audience-reflecting mirror of *Cabaret,* the Constructivist-inspired vision of New York apartment life in *Company,* and the metaphorical empty stage of *Follies* brought all of Aronson's artistry to bear and produced some of the most memorable designs of the 20th-century US theatre.

—Arnold Aronson

ARTAUD, Antonin. French poet, theorist, director, actor, designer, and playwright. Born Antoine-Marie-Joseph Artaud in Marseilles, 4 September 1896. Military service in French army 1914–15; medical discharge. Stage debut, as an actor, Paris, 1921; actor and designer with Paris companies of Lugné-Poë, Charles Dullin, and George Pitöeff, 1921–24; aligned with the Surrealists; made many film appearances, 1923–35; director, Bureau of Surrealist Research, 1925; co-founded, with Roger Vitrac and Robert Aron, Théâtre Alfred-Jarry, Paris, 1926; lectured on theatre at the Sorbonne, Paris, 1928, 1931, and 1933; developed concept of theatre of cruelty, 1933; founder, shortlived Théâtre de Cruauté at the Folies-Wagram, 1935; visited Mexico and Ireland, 1936; inmate in various psychiatric hospitals, notably Rodez, 1937–46. Recipient: Prix Sainte-Beuve, 1948. Died in Ivry-sur-Seine, 4 March 1948.

Productions

As actor:

1921–23   Carlo in *Huon de Bordeaux* (Arnoux), Théâtre de l'Atelier, Paris.
The King in *La Vita est un songe* (Calderón), Théâtre de l'Atelier, Paris.

Other roles included: *Piacere dell'onesta* (Pirandello) and *Monsieur Pygmalion* (Giau), both Théâtre de l'Atelier, Paris.

As director:

1927   *Les Mystères de l'amour* (Vitrac), Théâtre Alfred-Jarry, Paris.
Le Ventre brûlé; ou, La Mère folle (Jacob), Théâtre Alfred-Jarry, Paris.

1928   *Le Partage de midi* (Claudel), Théâtre Alfred-Jarry, Paris.
Pièce des rêves (Strindberg), Théâtre Alfred-Jarry, Paris; also acted the Theologian.
Victor; ou, Les Enfants au Pouvoir (Vitrac), Théâtre Alfred-Jarry, Paris.

1935   *Les Cenci* (Artaud, adapted from Shelley), Folies Wagram, Paris.

Films

As actor:

Fait divers, 1923; *Mathusalem*, 1924; *Surcouf*, 1925; *Graziella*, 1925; *Le Juif errant*, 1926; *Napoléon*, 1926; *La Coquille et le Clergyman*, 1927; *Verdun, visions d'histoire*, 1928; *La Passion de Jeanne d'Arc*, 1928; *L'Argent*, 1929; *Tarakanova*, 1929; *La Femme d'une nuit*, 1930; *Faubourg Montmartre*, 1931; *L'Opéra de quat'sous*, 1931; *Coups de feu á l'aube*, 1932; *L'Enfant de ma soeur*, 1932; *Les Croix de Bois*, 1932; *Mater dolorosa*, 1933; *Sidonie Panache*, 1934; *Liliom*, 1934; *Koenigsmark*, 1935; *Lucrèce Borgia*, 1936.

Antonin Artaud (1928).

As screenwriter:
La Coquille et le clergyman, 1927.

Publications

Tric-trac du ciel (verse), 1923; *Jet de Sang* (play), 1925; *Le Pese-nerfs*, 1925; *L'Ombilic des limbes*, 1927; *Correspondance*, 1927; *L'Art et la mort*, 1929; *Le Théâtre Alfred Jarry et l'hostilité public* (with Vitrac), 1930; *Le Théâtre de la cruauté*, 1933; *Héliogabale; ou, L'Anarchiste couronné*, 1934; *Le Théâtre de Séraphin*, 1936; *Les Nouvelles Révélations de l'être*, 1937; *Le Théâtre et son double*, 1938 (*The Theatre and Its Double*, 1958); *D'Un Voyage au pays de Tarahumaras* (essays and letters), 1945; *Lettres de Rodez*, 1946; *Van Gogh, Le suicidé de la société*, 1947; *Artaud le Mômo* (verse), 1947; *Ci-gîtt, précedé de la culture indienne* (verse), 1947; *Pour en finir avec le jugement de Dieu*, 1948; *Supplément aux Lettres de Rodez suivi de Coleridge le traître*, 1949; *Lettres contre la Cabbale*, 1949; *Lettres á Jean-Louis Barrault*, 1952; *La Vie et mort de Satan le feu*, 1953 (*The Death of Satan and Other Mystical Writings*, 1974); *Les Tarahumaras* (letters and essays), 1955 (*The Peyote Dance*, 1976); *Galapagos, Les Îles du bout du monde* (travel), 1955; *Oeuvres complètes*, 1956–81; *Autre chose que l'enfant beau*, 1957; *Voici un endroit*, 1958; *Mexico*, 1962; *Lettres à Anaïs Nin*, 1965; *Artaud Anthology* (edited by Jack Hirschman), 1965; *Poète noir et autres textes* (edited by Paul Zweig), 1966; *Collected Works*, 1968–75; *Lettres á Génica Atha-*nasiou, 1969; *Les Cenci* (play, produced 1935), 1970; *Selected Writings* (edited by Susan Sontag), 1976; *Nouvelles écrits de Rodez*, 1977; *Lettres à Anie Besnard*, 1978.

*

Bibliography

Books:
O. Hahn, *Portrait d'Antonin Artaud*, Paris, 1968.
Eric Sellin, *The Dramatic Concepts of Artaud*, Chicago, Illinois, 1968.
Naomi Greene, *Artaud: Poet Without Words*, New York, 1970.
Alan Virmaux, *Artaud et le théâtre*, Paris, 1970.
Jean-Louis Brau, *Antonin Artaud*, Paris, 1970.
Bettina Knapp, *Artaud: Man of Vision*, New York, 1971.
Martin Essler, *Artaud*, London, 1976.
Ronald Hayman, *Artaud and After*, Oxford, 1977.
Elena Kapralik, *Antonin Artaud, 1896–1948*, Munich, 1977.
Julia F. Costich, *Artaud*, Boston, Massachusetts, 1978.
Thomas Maeder, *Antonin Artaud*, Paris, 1978.
Alan and Odette Virmaux, *Artaud: un bilan critique*, Paris, 1979.
Alan Virmaux, *Artaud vivant*, Paris, 1980.
Cécile Schrammer, *Souvenirs familiers sur Antonin Artaud*, Gouy, 1980.
Françoise Bonardel, *Antonin Artaud: ou la fidelité à l'infini*, Paris, 1987.
Stephen Barber, *Antonin Artaud: Blows and Bombs*, London, 1993.

* * *

Antonin Artaud was above all a poet, a writer, a seer. In the theatre he was actor, designer, playwright, director, and theorist. He acted in films and wrote a number of scenarios. His theatrical career began in the early 1920s and was over by 1935. It got off to a promising start: Artaud had the good luck to work with the most creative French directors of the time, from the veteran Lugné-Poë to the young and avant-garde Dullin and Pitoëff. Unfortunately, from a professional point of view, Artaud was unable to follow the strict discipline of rehearsals and he soon fell out with the directors who had given him the opportunity to gain valuable experience. Very soon the young man grew very impatient with, to his mind, the unimaginative and tame theatre of his day, and he performed for the last time in a play not directed by himself in 1924.

That same year Artaud joined the Surrealist movement and in 1925 he became director of the Surrealist "think-tank" known as "la Centrale Surréaliste". Although his collaboration with the surrealist poets was equally short-lived, it put him in touch with kindred minds, confirmed him in his revolutionary ideas, and brought about his encounter with Roger Vitrac. In 1926 Artaud, with Vitrac and Robert Aron, founded the Théâtre Alfred-Jarry, which gave eight performances between June 1927 and January 1929. The aim of the Jarry Theatre, expressed in a number of manifestos, was not to present plays in the conventional way but "to uncover the mind's obscure, hidden, unrevealed aspects" by assaulting the spectator's whole being: "Audiences coming to our theatre know they are present at a real operation involving not only the mind but all their senses and their flesh ... we can make them scream". The Jarry Theatre's most notable production was Vitrac's *Victor, ou les enfants au pouvoir* (*Victor, or Power to the Children*), a satire of the bourgeoisie and its most cherished values (marriage, family, respectability, hypocrisy), but not even its success could insure the theatre's survival. This early failure only strengthened Artaud's desire to impose his vision of theatre, since for him theatre was never an end in itself but a means to an end; and that end is nothing less than to change life itself.

Versed in oriental mysticism, in esoteric doctrines, and haunted by the manifestations of the irrational, Artaud had "true theatre" revealed to him with the visit of a Balinese dance company to the Paris Colonial Exhibition of 1931. Galvanised by the experience, he gave a series of lectures and wrote numerous articles, later to be published under the title *Le Théâtre et son double* (*The Theatre and Its Double*). Artaud summarily dismisses all forms of Western theatre, sick with psychologism and divorced from authentic reality, and pronounces that mankind, in order to survive, must return to the very roots of life itself. And in the search theatre must play the crucial role: "The aim of the theatre is not to solve social or psychological conflicts, nor to provide a battleground for moral conflicts, but to express the truth objectively". Theatrically speaking, this means that the true language of the stage is not speech, but mise en scène — the actor must not be the mere mouthpiece of the playwright, lamely relaying his words and his thoughts, but a medium in whom metaphysical truths are made flesh. Theatre is "a crucible of fire" where mankind can renew itself and where life is, *literally*, shown in the making, "where the mythical act of creating a body is shown physically and plainly". In his famous manifesto, *The Theatre of Cruelty*, he writes: "Theatre will never be itself again unless it provides the audience with truthful distillations of dreams in which its taste for crime, its erotic obsessions, its savageness, its fantasies, are satisfied". Artaud never realised his dream. The only play produced by his Théâtre de la Cruauté, *The Cenci*, was a melodramatic parody: Artaud's wordy script and the haphazard quality of the production obscured rather than illuminated Artaud's revolutionary vision.

The theatre of cruelty (Artaud's central concept) is founded on the idea of abolishing the distance between life and art, of communion between spectator and actor. Theatre must regain its ritualistic and sacred dimension and rely on a gestural, physical, emotional language, operating a kind of "therapeutic of the soul".

Artaud's influence is widespread and reaches playwrights (Adamov, who knew the poet personally, Genet, and particularly Arrabal, but also Ionesco and Beckett), actors (Alain Cuny, Maria Casarès), and directors (Jean-Louis Barrault and Roger Blin, who both worked with Artaud, Roger Planchon, Patrice Chéreau, Charles Marowitz, and Peter Brook). The work of such important and revolutionary companies as Jerzy Grotowski's Wrocław Theatre Laboratory, Judith Malina and Julian Beck's Living Theatre, or Ariane Mnouchkine's Théâtre du Soleil have in their different ways put into practice Artaud's ideas so that his word, long after his death, has indeed become flesh.

—Claude Schumacher

ASHCROFT, (Dame) Peggy. British actress. Born Edith Margaret Emily Ashcroft in Croydon, Surrey, England, 22 December 1907. Educated at Woodford School, Croydon; studied for the stage at the Central School of Dramatic Art, London. Married 1) Rupert Charles Hart-Davies in 1929 (divorced 1932); 2) director Theodore Komisarjevsky in 1934 (divorced 1936); 3) Jeremy Nicholas Hutchinson in 1940 (divorced 1966); one son, one daughter. Stage debut, Birmingham Repertory Theatre, 1926; first London appearance, 1927; film debut, 1933; first New York appearance, 1937; television debut, 1959; joined newly-formed Royal Shakespeare Company, 1960; opening of Ashcroft Theatre, Croydon, named in her honour, 1962; director, from 1968, then associate artist, Royal Shakespeare Company. Member: Council of the English Stage Company, from 1957; Arts Council, 1962–65; Shakespeare Memorial Theatre Council, 1962–65; Apollo Society, from 1964 (founder and president); Council of Equity. Recipient: Ellen Terry Award, 1947; Sketch Award for outstanding achievement in the theatre, 1949; King's Gold Award Medal, 1955 (Norway); Evening Standard Drama Award, 1956, 1964, 1976; Plays and Players Award, 1956, 1969, 1971; Paris Theatre Festival Award for Best Actress, 1962; Variety Club of Great Britain Award for Best Actress, 1964; Society of West End Theatre Award, 1976; British Academy of Film and Television Arts Award, 1980, 1984, 1985, 1990 (special); Festival International de Télévision de Monte Carlo Award, 1981; British Press Guild Award, 1981; British Theatre Association Award, 1983; Royal Television Society Award, 1984; Broadcasting Press Guild Television Award, 1984; Golden Globe Award, National Board of Review Award, New York Film Critics' Best Actress Award, 1984; Oscar for Best Supporting Actress, 1984; Los Angeles Film Critics' Award, 1984; Hollywood South Award, 1985; International TV Movies Festival USA Award, 1985; Venice Film Festival Award, 1989. D.Litt: University of Oxford, 1961, University of Leicester, 1964, University of London, 1965, University of Cambridge, 1972, University of Warwick, 1974, Open University, 1986, and University of Bristol, 1986; fellowship, St Hugh's College, University of Oxford. CBE (Commander of the British Empire), 1951; DBE (Dame of the British Empire), 1956; Commander, Order of St Olav, 1976. Died in London, 14 June 1991.

Roles

1926   Margaret in *Dear Brutus* (Barrie), Repertory Theatre, Birmingham.
1927   Bessie Carvil in *One Day More* (Conrad), Playroom Six, London.
          Mary Dunn in *The Return* (Bennett), Everyman Theatre, London.
          Eve in *When Adam Delved* (Paston), Q Theatre, London.
          Joan Greenleaf in *Bird in Hand* (Drinkwater), Repertory Theatre, Birmingham.
          Betty in *The Way of the World* (Congreve), Wyndham's Theatre, London.
1928   Anastasia Vullimay in *The Fascinating Foundling* (Shaw), Arts Theatre, London.
          Mary Bruin in *The Land of Heart's Desire* (Yeats), Arts Theatre, London.

Hester in *The Silver Cord* (Howard), British tour.

Edith Strange in *Earthbound* (Goddard and Weir), Q Theatre, London.

Kristina in *Easter* (Strindberg), Arts Theatre, London.

Eulalia in *A Hundred Years Old* (Quinteros), Lyric Theatre, Hammersmith, London.

1929   Lucy Deren in *Requital* (Kerr), Everyman Theatre, London.

Sally Humphries in *Bees and Honey* (Maltby), Strand Theatre, London.

Constance Neville in *She Stoops to Conquer* (Goldsmith), British tour.

Naemi in *Jew Süss* (Feuchtwanger, adapted by Dukes), Duke of York's Theatre, London.

1930   Desdemona in *Othello* (Shakespeare), Savoy Theatre, London.

Judy Battle in *The Breadwinner* (Maugham), Vaudeville Theatre, London.

1931   Pervaneh in *Hassan* (Flecker), New Theatre, Oxford.

Angela in *Charles the Third* (Götz, adapted by Wallace), Wyndham's Theatre, London.

Anne in *A Knight Passed By* (Fabricus, adapted by Darlington), Ambassador's Theatre, London.

Fanny in *Sea Fever* (Pagnol, adapted by Lee and van Druten), New Theatre, London.

Marcela in *Take Two from One* (Sierras, adapted by Granville-Barker), Haymarket Theatre, London.

1932   Juliet in *Romeo and Juliet* (Shakespeare), New Theatre, Oxford; New Theatre, London, 1936.

Stella in *The Magnificent Cuckold* (Crommelynck), Globe Theatre, London.

Salome Westaway in *The Secret Woman* (Phillpots), Duchess Theatre, London.

Cleopatra in *Caesar and Cleopatra* (Shaw), Old Vic Theatre, London.

Imogen in *Cymbeline* (Shakespeare), Old Vic Theatre, London.

Rosalind in *As You Like It* (Shakespeare), Old Vic Theatre, London.

Portia in *The Merchant of Venice* (Shakespeare), Old Vic Theatre, London; Queen's Theatre, London, 1938; Shakespeare Memorial Theatre, Stratford-upon-Avon, England, 1953.

Elsa in *Fräulein Elsa* (Schnitzler), Kingsway Theatre, London.

1933   Perdita in *The Winter's Tale* (Shakespeare), Old Vic Theatre, London.

Kate Hardcastle in *She Stoops to Conquer* (Goldsmith), Old Vic Theatre, London.

Mary Stuart in *Mary Stuart* (Drinkwater), Old Vic Theatre, London.

Lady Teazle in *The School for Scandal* (Sheridan), Old Vic Theatre, London; Queen's Theatre, London, 1937.

Miranda in *The Tempest* (Shakespeare), Old Vic Theatre, London.

Peggy Ashcroft

Inken Peters in *Before Sunset* (Hauptmann), Shaftesbury Theatre, London.

1934   Vasantesena in *The Golden Toy* (Zuckmayer), Coliseum, London.

Lucia Maubel in *The Life that I Gave Him* (Pirandello), Little Theatre, London.

1935   Thérèse Paradis in *Mesmer* (Nichols), British tour.

1936   Nina in *The Seagull* (Chekhov), New Theatre, London.

1937   Lise in *High Tor* (Anderson), Martin Beck Theatre, New York.

The Queen in *Richard II* (Shakespeare), Queen's Theatre, London.

1938   Irina in *Three Sisters* (Chekhov), Queen's Theatre, London.

Yeliena Talberg in *The White Guard* (Bulgakov, adapted by Ackland), Phoenix Theatre, London.

Viola in *Twelfth Night* (Shakespeare), Phoenix Theatre, London; Old Vic Theatre, London, 1950.

1939   Isolde in *Weep for the Spring* (Haggard), British tour.

Cecily Cardew in *The Importance of Being Earnest* (Wilde), Globe Theatre, London.

1940   Dinah Sylvester in *Cousin Muriel* (Dane), Globe Theatre, London.

Miranda in *The Tempest* (Shakespeare), Old Vic Theatre, London.

1941   Mrs de Winter in *Rebecca* (D. du Maurier), British tour.

1942   Cecily Cardew in *The Importance of Being Earnest* (Wilde), Phoenix Theatre, London.

1943   Catherine Lisle in *The Dark River* (Ackland), Whitehall Theatre, London.

1944   Ophelia in *Hamlet* (Shakespeare), Haymarket Theatre, London, and British tour.

1945   Titania in *A Midsummer Night's Dream* (Shakespeare), Haymarket Theatre, London.
        The Duchess in *The Duchess of Malfi* (Webster), Haymarket Theatre, London; Aldwych Theatre, London, 1960.

1947   Evelyn Holt in *Edward, My Son* (Morley and Langley), His Majesty's Theatre, London; Martin Beck Theatre, New York, 1948.

1949   Catherine Sloper in *The Heiress* (R. and A. Goetz), Haymarket Theatre, London.

1950   Beatrice in *Much Ado About Nothing* (Shakespeare), Shakespeare Memorial Theatre, Stratford-upon-Avon, England; Palace Theatre, London, and European tour, 1955.
        Cordelia in *King Lear* (Shakespeare), Shakespeare Memorial Theatre, Stratford-upon-Avon, England; European tour and Palace Theatre, London, 1955.

1951   Electra in *Electra* (Sophocles), Old Vic Theatre, London.
        Mistress Page in *The Merry Wives of Windsor* (Shakespeare), Old Vic Theatre, London.

1952   Hester Collyer in *The Deep Blue Sea* (Rattigan), Duchess Theatre, London.

1953   Cleopatra in *Antony and Cleopatra* (Shakespeare), Shakespeare Memorial Theatre, Stratford-upon-Avon, England, Prince's Theatre, London, and European tour.

1954   Hedda in *Hedda Gabler* (Ibsen), Lyric Theatre, Hammersmith, London, Westminster Theatre, London, and European tour.

1956   Miss Madrigal in *The Chalk Garden* (Bagnold), Haymarket Theatre, London.
        Shen Te/Shui Ta in *The Good Woman of Setzuan* (Brecht), Royal Court Theatre, London.

1957   Rosalind in *As You Like It* (Shakespeare), Shakespeare Memorial Theatre, Stratford-upon-Avon, England.
        Imogen in *Cymbeline* (Shakespeare), Shakespeare Memorial Theatre, Stratford-upon-Avon, England.

1958   *Portraits of Women* (solo recital devised by Ashcroft and O. Ellis), Edinburgh Festival, Scotland.
        Julia Rajk in *Shadow of Heroes* (Ardrey), Piccadilly Theatre, London.

1959   Eve Delaware in *The Coast of Coromandel* (Sadler), British tour.
        Rebecca West in *Rosmersholm* (Ibsen), Royal Court Theatre, London, and Comedy Theatre, London.

1960   Katharina in *The Taming of the Shrew* (Shakespeare), Shakespeare Memorial Theatre, Stratford-upon-Avon, England.

Paulina in *The Winter's Tale* (Shakespeare), Shakespeare Memorial Theatre, Stratford-upon-Avon, England.

1961   Several roles in *The Hollow Crown* (Barton), Aldwych Theatre, London; European tour, 1962; Ottawa, Canada, 1974; Swan Theatre, Stratford-upon-Avon, England, 1986.
        All roles in *Some Words on Women and Some Women's Words* (Ashcroft), Senate House, University of London.
        Emilia in *Othello* (Shakespeare), Royal Shakespeare Theatre, Stratford-upon-Avon, England.
        Madame Ranevsky in *The Cherry Orchard* (Chekhov), Royal Shakespeare Theatre, Stratford-upon-Avon, England, and Aldwych Theatre, London.

1962   Several roles in the anthology *The Vagaries of Love* (Barton), Belgrade Theatre, Coventry, England.

1963   Margaret in *The Wars of the Roses* (Shakespeare, adapted by Barton), Royal Shakespeare Theatre, Stratford-upon-Avon, England; Aldwych Theatre, London, 1964.

1964   Madame Arkadina in *The Seagull* (Chekhov), Queen's Theatre, London.

1966   Mother in *Days in the Trees* (Duras), Aldwych Theatre, London.

1967   Mrs Alving in *Ghosts* (Ibsen), Aldwych Theatre, London.

1969   Agnes in *A Delicate Balance* (Albee), Aldwych Theatre, London.
        Beth in *Landscape* (Pinter), Aldwych Theatre, London; revived there and for European tour, 1973.
        Queen Katharine in *Henry VIII* (Shakespeare), Royal Shakespeare Theatre, Stratford-upon-Avon, England; Aldwych Theatre, London, 1970.

1970   Volumnia in *The Plebians Rehearse the Uprising* (Grass), Aldwych Theatre, London.

1971   Claire Lannes in *The Lovers of Viorne* (Duras), Royal Court Theatre, London.

1972   The Wife in *All Over* (Albee), Aldwych Theatre, London.
        Lady Boothroyd in *Lloyd George Knew My Father* (Douglas-Home), Savoy Theatre, London.

1973   Flora in *A Slight Ache* (Pinter), European tour and Aldwych Theatre, London.

1974   Lilian Baylis in *Tribute to the Lady* (May), Aldwych Theatre, London; Old Vic Theatre, London, 1976.

1975   Ella Rentheim in *John Gabriel Borkman* (Ibsen), Old Vic Theatre, London.
        Winnie in *Happy Days* (Beckett), Old Vic Theatre, London; Citadel, Edmonton, Canada, 1977; National Theatre, London, 1980.
        Mrs Patrick Campbell in *Dear Liar* (Kilty, adapted from the letters of G. B. Shaw), Citadel, Edmonton, Canada.

1976   Lidya Vasilyevna in *Old World* (Arbuzov), Aldwych Theatre, London, and Royal Shakespeare Theatre, Stratford-upon-Avon, England.

1980   Fanny Farelly in *Watch on the Rhine* (Hellman), National Theatre, London.

1981   Voice 2 in *Family Voices* (Pinter), National Theatre, London.

Countess of Rousillon in *All's Well That Ends Well* (Shakespeare), Royal Shakespeare Theatre, Stratford-upon-Avon, England, and Barbican Theatre, London.

1986   Lilian Baylis in *Save the Wells* (May), Royal Opera House, London.

Films

Olalla Qintana in *The Wandering Jew*, 1933; Margaret Crofter in *The Thirty-Nine Steps*, 1935; Anna Carpenter in *Rhodes of Africa*, 1936; The Woman in *Channel Incident*, 1940; Fleur Lisle in *Quiet Wedding*, 1941; ATS Girl in *New Lot*, 1942; Mother Matilde in *The Nun's Story*, 1958; Aunt Hanna in *Secret Ceremony*, 1968; Belle in *Three into Two Won't Go*, 1969; Mrs Greville in *Sunday, Bloody Sunday*, 1971; Lady Gray in *Der Fussgänger*, 1975; Lady Tattle in *Joseph Andrews*, 1977; Lady Gee in *Hullabaloo over George and Bonnie's Pictures*, 1978; Mrs Moore in *A Passage to India*, 1984; Hilda (voice) in *When the Wind Blows*, 1987; Lady Emily in *Madame Sousatzka*, 1988.

Television

The Tempest, 1939; *Twelfth Night*, 1939; *Shadow of Heroes*, 1959; *The Class*, 1961; *The Cherry Orchard*, 1962; *The Wars of the Roses*, 1964; *Rosmersholm*, 1965; *Days in the Trees*, 1966; *Dear Liar*, 1966; *From Chekhov with Love*, 1968; *The Last Journey*, 1971; *Edward and Mrs Simpson*, 1978; *Caught on a Train*, 1980; *Cream in My Coffee*, 1980; *Little Eyolf*, 1982; *The Jewel in the Crown*, 1984; *Six Centuries of Verse*, 1984; *Murder by the Book*, 1986; *A Perfect Spy*, 1987; *Two Loves*, 1987; *Heat of the Day*, 1988; *Coming Home*, 1988; *She's Been Away*, 1989.

Radio

Danger, 1930; *Hamlet*, 1931; *Othello*, 1932; *A Hundred Years Old*, 1932; *Twelfth Night*, 1933; *Measure for Measure*, 1934; *Cymbeline*, 1934; *Berkeley Square*, 1935; *The Lover*, 1935; *The Breadwinner*, 1935; *Cyrano de Bergerac*, 1939; *Arms and the Man*, 1939; *I Was Hitler's Prisoner*, 1940; *This is Illyria, Lady*, 1940; *The Barretts of Wimpole Street*, 1940; *The Importance of Being Earnest*, 1940; *A Month in the Country*, 1941; *Alexander Nevsky*, 1941; *Mary Rose*, 1941; *Distant Point*, 1942; *Quality Street*, 1942; *The Rape of the Lock*, 1942; *Twelfth Night*, 1942; *Alexander Nevsky*, 1942; *Homage to a King*, 1942; *Dnieper Dam*, 1942; *The Seagull*, 1942; *The Spirit of France*, 1943; *The Battle of the Marne*, 1943; *Butterfly on the Wheel*, 1943; *Epithalamium*, 1943; *Distant Point*, 1944; *The Hostage*, 1944; *The Blessed Damosel*, 1944; *A Midsummer Night's Dream*, 1945; *The Barretts of Wim-*

pole Street, 1946; *Comus*, 1946; *Island Anthology*, 1946; *She Married Again*, 1946; *Twelfth Night*, 1947; *Romeo and Juliet*, 1947; *The Bronze Horse*, 1948; *The Rape of Lucrece*, 1948; *Romeo and Juliet*, 1953; *The Merchant of Venice*, 1953; *Antony and Cleopatra*, 1953; *By Heart*, 1954; *The Duchess of Malfi*, 1954; *A Lover's Complaint*, 1954; *The Good Woman of Setzuan*, 1957; *Hedda Gabler*, 1957; *Cymbeline*, 1957; *As You Like It*, 1957; *The Ring and the Book Part V*, 1958; *The Hollow Crown*, 1961; *Macbeth*, 1966; *Madam Liberality*, 1967; *Side*, 1968; *Landscape*, 1968; *The Lady of Shallott*, 1970; *The Father*, 1971; *Hay Fever*, 1971; *Emperor of the Sea*, 1972; *Days in the Trees*, 1972; *Lady Caroline Lamb*, 1974; *Tribute to the Lady*, 1976; *The Waves*, 1976; *Vivat Rex*, 1977; *A Bit of Singing and Dancing*, 1978; *Moments of Being*, 1978; *The Girl Who Came to Supper*, 1979; *Dearest Hope*, 1979; *In the Unlikely Event of an Emergency*, 1979; *The Day War Broke Out*, 1979; *Ouida*, 1980; *A Generation of Giants*, 1980; *Family Voices*, 1981; *Chances*, 1981; *Yesterday's News*, 1981; *A Lady's Life in the Rockie Mountains*, 1981; *You Can't Shut Out the Human Voice*, 1984; *Sense and Nonsense*, 1985; *Days in the Trees*, 1985; *The Blue Jug*, 1986.

*

Bibliography

Books:
Eric Keown, *Peggy Ashcroft*, London, 1955.
Robert Tanitch, *Ashcroft*, London, Melbourne, Auckland, Johannesburg, 1987.
Michael Billington, *Peggy Ashcroft*, London, 1988.

* * *

Peggy Ashcroft was not just a great actress. She also had a major influence on modern British theatre. The whole story of her career is of a quest for permanence and continuity: for the satisfaction of working in a company rather than achieving the egotistical thrill of star billing. She unhesitatingly lent her support to John Gielgud in his attempt to set up classical companies in the West End in the 1930's and 1940's. She was the first major performer — before Olivier in *The Entertainer* — to appear with the English Stage Company at the Royal Court. She instantly agreed to sign a two-year contract to appear with Peter Hall's newly-founded Royal Shakespeare Company in 1960 and was for many years a member of the Advisory Directorate (along with John Barton, Peter Brook, and Trevor Nunn). And, typically, she was the first artist to appear on the stage of the new National Theatre in 1976 in a performance of Beckett's *Happy Days*. Her career was, in a nutshell, exemplary.

Ashcroft's life as an actress was shaped by many things, most crucially by reading Stanislavsky's *My Life in Art* in 1924 when she was a student at the Central School. The book became her bible: her sustaining dream was of working for an English equivalent of the Moscow Art Theatre. But that was a long time coming. She first made her mark, at the age of 22, playing Desdemona to Robeson's Othello in the West End — a performance full of innocence, gaiety, and heartfelt adoration. This was quickly followed by a race through the major classical roles in the 1932–33 Old Vic season: 10 parts in eight months with scant time for rehearsal. It was only when she worked with

Gielgud at the New Theatre in 1935–36, playing Juliet and Nina in *The Seagull*, that she began to get a glimmer of what could be achieved through settled, dedicated teamwork.

She nursed the vision of a company, something only fully realised when Peter Hall took over the reins at Stratford in 1960. But, while cherishing her idealistic dream, she gave many fine performances characterised by vocal clarity, an extraordinary emotional directness, and a quality of all-out attack. As Gielgud once noted: "She takes a part by the throat, as Olivier does, and she absolutely puts it over the way she wants to."

Numerous examples come to mind. In 1954 she was a legendary Hedda Gabler, all frozen fire and flinty malice. Three years later at Stratford, when nudging 50, she was the perfect Imogen in *Cymbeline*, lending the character an impulsiveness, emotional passion, and sexual ecstacy that made nonsense of her years. And, in 1963, again at Stratford, she gave arguably her greatest-ever performance as Margaret of Anjou in the three parts of the Peter Hall and John Barton's *The Wars of the Rose*s. In the course of the three plays she moved from a light, lisping, girlish bride to a troop-rallying termagant and finally a wrinkled, cursing crone. What was so astonishing was the demonism and ferocity with which she invested the character: imaginative qualities that had rarely been tapped before. But her own personal clue to the character lay in getting the sound exactly right — against Peter Hall's wishes, she insisted on giving Margaret a distinctive French 'r' sound to establish her permanent sense of alienation and foreignness.

The RSC was Ashcroft's natural home, the kind of institution she had always dreamed of. But it also gave her the freedom to explore the most challenging living dramatists and give the lie to the notion, fostered by Tynan in the 1950's, that her forté was Kensingtonian graciousness. She played a gross, vulgar, chain-jangling parvenu in Marguerite Duras's *Days in the Trees*. She was an elegant, New England mixture of serenity and steel in Edward Albee's *A Delicate Balance*. And as Beth in Pinter's *Landscape* she combined the quality of remembered ecstacy with current isolation and solitude. Peggy Ashcroft had long been a great classical actress: she now brought to the best modern writers her supreme gifts of energy, directness, and emotional attack. Like many of her contemporaries (Gielgud and Richardson specifically), Peggy Ashcroft resisted an autumnal twilight by responding boldly to contemporary dramatists and the modern media. In the 1980's she won a vast new audience of admirers through her work in television and the cinema. She bullied her way across Europe as an upper-middle-class Viennese in Stephen Poliakoff's marvellous television film *Caught on a Train*, while her Barbie Batchelor in *The Jewel in the Crown* embodied the waddling eccentricity and touching ordinariness of Paul Scott's missionary misfit. And as Mrs Moore in David Lean's film of *A Passage to India* (for which she won a Hollywood Oscar) she imbued a rather shadowy character with a kindly good sense and radiant spirituality.

But the heart of Peggy Ashcroft's achievement lay in the theatre. She tackled most of the great classic roles (though, oddly enough, neither Lady Macbeth nor Saint Joan) and proved herself equal to the challenge of Beckett or Pinter. But transcending individual achievement was the power of her example and her passionate commitment to the idea that you cannot have truly great theatre without permanent, properly-subsidised companies.

—Michael Billington

B

BANCROFT, (Sir) Squire and (Lady) Marie. British actor-managers. Squire Bancroft born Squire Butterfield in Rotherhithe, London, 14 May 1841. Educated at private schools in England and France. Marie Bancroft born Marie Effie Wilton in Doncaster, 12 January 1839. No formal education. Bancroft and Wilton married in 1867; one son (playwright and novelist George Pleydell Bancroft). Marie Wilton, daughter of a provincial actor, made her stage debut as a child in Norwich, 1845; appeared with William Charles Macready among others, notably in burlesque; earned nickname "The Queen of Burlesque"; made London debut, Lyceum Theatre, 1856; entered management with H. J. Byron, Prince of Wales's Theatre, London, 1865. Squire Bancroft made stage debut, Theatre Royal, Birmingham, 1861; actor, provincial stock companies in Cork, Dublin, Devonport, Liverpool, and elsewhere, reputedly playing 346 roles, 1861–65. Wilton and Bancroft first acted together, Liverpool, 1865; jointly managed the Prince of Wales's Theatre, also playing many leading roles there, 1867–78; established vogue for drawing-room comedies and dramas and made numerous reforms in staging technique; jointly took over the Haymarket Theatre, London, and, following rebuilding, reopened it, 1880; jointly managed and acted at the Haymarket, 1880–85; retired from the stage together, 1885. Squire Bancroft returned to play three roles at the Lyceum Theatre, with Henry Irving, 1889, and at the Garrick Theatre, 1893; also gave public readings of Dickens's *A Christmas Carol* to raise money for hospitals in the UK and Canada, 1893–1913. Marie Bancroft appeared at the Garrick Theatre, 1893, and at the Haymarket Theatre, 1895, and also wrote a novel and three plays. Squire Bancroft: president of the Royal Academy of Dramatic Art; member, advisory board to the Lord Chamberlain for the licensing of plays; president, Green Room theatrical club. LL.D: St. Andrew's University, 1922. Knighted, 1897. Marie Bancroft died in Folkestone, Kent, 22 May 1921. Squire Bancroft died in London, 19 April 1926.

Roles

Squire Bancroft:
1861 Lieutenant Manley in *St Mary's Eve* (Bernard), Theatre Royal, Birmingham.
1861–65 Marcellus, Rosencrantz, Laertes, Second Player, and Osric in *Hamlet* (Shakespeare), Cork, Ireland.
Captain Murphy Maguire in *The Serious Family* (Barnett), Devonport.

Captain Hawkesley in *Still Waters Run Deep* (Taylor), Devonport.
Lord Dundreary in *Our American Cousin* (Taylor), Devonport.
Malcolm in *Macbeth* (Shakespeare), Theatre Royal, Dublin.
King John in *King John* (Shakespeare), Theatre Royal, Dublin.
Captain Thornton in *Rob Roy* (Scott), Theatre Royal, Dublin.
Counsel for the Defence in *The Trial of Effie Deans* (Boucicault), Theatre Royal, Birmingham.
John Mildmay in *Still Waters Run Deep* (Taylor), Theatre Royal, Dublin.
Fernando Villabella in *The Maid and the Magpie* (H. J. Byron), Theatre Royal, Dublin.
Beppo in *Fra Diavolo* (H. J. Byron), Theatre Royal, Dublin.
Lord Dundreary in *Sam's Arrival* (Oxenford), Theatre Royal, Dublin.
Captain Howard in *Peep o'Day* (Falconer), Theatre Royal, Dublin.
Oscar de Beaupré in *Retribution* (Bennett), Theatre Royal, Dublin.
Bob Brierley in *The Ticket-of-Leave Man* (Taylor), Theatre Royal, Dublin.
Dick Dowlas in *The Heir at Law* (Colman the Younger), Theatre Royal, Dublin.
Paul in *Paul's Return* (Phillips), Liverpool.
Antipholus of Syracuse in *The Comedy of Errors* (Shakespeare), Liverpool.
Courriol in *The Courier of Lyons* (Reade), Liverpool.
Ironbrace in *Used Up* (Boucicault), Liverpool.
Duke of Albemarle in *Court Favour* (Planché), Liverpool.
Captain Dudley Smooth in *Money* (Bulwer-Lytton), Liverpool.
1865 Jack Crawley in *A Winning Hazard* (Wooler), Prince of Wales's Theatre, London.
Sidney Daryl in *Society* (Robertson), Prince of Wales's Theatre, London.
Captain Thistleton in *War to the Knife* (H. J. Byron), Prince of Wales's Theatre, London.
Don Giovanni in *Don Giovanni* (H. J. Byron), Prince of Wales's Theatre, London.
1866 Angus Macalister in *Ours* (Robertson), Prince of Wales's Theatre, London.

General Gerald Goodwin in *A Hundred Thousand Pounds* (H. J. Byron), Prince of Wales's Theatre, London.

1867   Captain Hawtree in *Caste* (Robertson), Prince of Wales's Theatre, London.

Beecher Sprawley in *How She Loves Him* (Boucicault), Prince of Wales's Theatre, London.

1868   Chevalier Brown in *Play* (Robertson), Prince of Wales's Theatre, London.

1869   Jack Poyntz in *School* (Robertson), Prince of Wales's Theatre, London.

1870   Talbot Piers in *M.P.* (Robertson), Prince of Wales's Theatre, London.

Hugh Chalcot in *Ours* (Robertson), Prince of Wales's Theatre, London.

Sir Benjamin Backbite in *The School for Scandal* (Sheridan), Theatre Royal, Drury Lane, London.

Dazzle in *London Assurance* (Boucicault), Prince of Wales's Theatre, London.

1872   Sir Frederick Blount in *Money* (Bulwer-Lytton), Prince of Wales's Theatre, London; Haymarket Theatre, London, 1880–85.

1873   Speedwell in *Man and Wife* (Collins), Prince of Wales's Theatre, London.

1874   Joseph Surface in *The School for Scandal* (Sheridan), Prince of Wales's Theatre, London.

1875   The Prince of Morocco in *The Merchant of Venice* (Shakespeare), Prince of Wales's Theatre, London.

Triplet in *Masks and Faces* (Reade and Taylor), Prince of Wales's Theatre, London; Her Majesty's Theatre, London, 1918.

Mr Honeyton in *A Happy Pair* (Smith), Prince of Wales's Theatre, London.

1876   Sir George Ormond in *Peril* (Scott and Stephenson), Prince of Wales's Theatre, London.

Bob Blewitt in *Wrinkles* (H. J. Byron), Prince of Wales's Theatre, London.

1877   Blenkinsop in *The Unequal Match* (Taylor), Prince of Wales's Theatre, London.

1878   Count Orloff in *Diplomacy* (adapted from Sardou), Prince of Wales's Theatre, London; Garrick Theatre, London, and Balmoral Castle, 1891.

1882   Lord Henry Trevene in *Odette* (Sardou, adapted by Scott and Stephenson), Haymarket Theatre, London.

Fouché in *Plot and Passion* (Taylor and Lang), Haymarket Theatre, London.

Tom Dexter in *The Overland Route* (Taylor), Haymarket Theatre, London.

1883   Jean de Siriex and Loris Ipanoff in *Fédora* (Sardou, adapted by Merivale), Haymarket Theatre, London.

Tom Jervoise in *Lords and Commons* (Pinero), Haymarket Theatre, London.

Dr Thornton in *Peril* (Scott and Stephenson), Haymarket Theatre, London.

1884   Faulkland in *The Rivals* (Sheridan), Haymarket Theatre, London.

Henry Beauclerc in *Diplomacy* (adapted from Sardou), Haymarket Theatre, London.

1889   Abbé Latour in *The Dead Heart* (Pollock), Lyceum Theatre, London.

Other roles included: *The Bottle* (Taylor), Theatre Royal, Birmingham, 1861–65; *The Lonely Man of the Ocean* (Blake), Theatre Royal, Birmingham, 1861–65; *Susan Hopley* (Pitt), Theatre Royal, Birmingham, 1861–65; *The Green Bushes* (Buckstone), Theatre Royal, Birmingham, 1861–65; *The Flowers of the Forest* (Buckstone), Theatre Royal, Birmingham, 1861–65; *The Brigands of the Abruzzi*, Cork, Ireland, 1861–65; *Sweeney Todd* (Pitt), Theatre Royal, Birmingham, 1861–65; *Thirty Years of a Gambler's Life* (Milner), Theatre Royal, Birmingham, 1861–65; *Much Ado About Nothing* (Shakespeare), Theatre Royal, Dublin, 1861–65; *A Cure for the Heartache* (Morton), Theatre Royal, Dublin, 1861–65; *To Parents and Guardians* (Taylor), Theatre Royal, Dublin, 1861–65; *My Own Victim* (Morton), Liverpool, 1861–65; *A Fair Pretender* (Simpson), Prince of Wales's Theatre, London, 1865; *A Lover by Proxy* (Boucicault), Prince of Wales's Theatre, London, 1865; *Allow Me to Explain* (Gilbert), Prince of Wales's Theatre, London.

Marie Wilton:

1845–56   Emperor of Lilliput in *Gulliver's Travels* (adapted from Swift), Theatre Royal, Manchester.

Fleance in *Macbeth* (Shakespeare), Theatre Royal, Manchester.

Jo in *Bleak House* (adapted from Dickens), Theatre Royal, Manchester.

Arthur in *King John* (Shakespeare), Theatre Royal, Manchester.

1856   Henri in *Belphegor* (Webb), Lyceum Theatre, London.

Perdita in *Perdita* (Brough, adapted from Shakespeare's *The Winter's Tale*), Lyceum Theatre, London.

Serena in *Conrad and Medora* (Brough), Lyceum Theatre, London.

Pippo in *The Maid and the Magpie* (Byron), Strand Theatre, London.

Sir Walter Raleigh in *Kenilworth* (Scott), Strand Theatre, London.

Albert in *William Tell* (Knowles), Strand Theatre, London.

Karl in *The Miller and His Men* (Talfourd and H. J. Byron), Strand Theatre, London.

Aladdin in *Aladdin; or, The Wonderful Scamp* (H. J. Byron), Strand Theatre, London.

Pierre Gringoire in *Esmeralda*, Strand Theatre, London.

Lucy Morton in *Court Favour* (Planché), Strand Theatre, London.

Myles-na-Coppaleen in *The Colleen Bawn* (H. J. Byron), Strand Theatre, London.

Orpheus in *Orpheus and Eurydice* (H. J. Byron), Strand Theatre, London.

1857   Cupid in *Atalanta* (Talfourd), Haymarket Theatre, London.

Cupid in *Cupid and Psyche* (Burnand), Adelphi Theatre, London.

1864	Juliet in extract from *Romeo and Juliet* (Shakespeare), Strand Theatre, London.
1865	Alessio in *La !Somnambula!* (H. J. Byron), Prince of Wales's Theatre, London.
	Maud Hetherington in *Society* (Robertson), Prince of Wales's Theatre, London.
	Mrs Delacour in *War to the Knife* (H. J. Byron), Prince of Wales's Theatre, London.
1866	Alice Barlow in *A Hundred Thousand Pounds* (H. J. Byron), Prince of Wales's Theatre, London.
	Mary Netley in *Ours* (Robertson), Prince of Wales's Theatre, London.
1867	Polly Eccles in *Caste* (Robertson), Prince of Wales's Theatre, London.
	Miss Atalanta Cruiser in *How She Loves Him* (Gilbert), Prince of Wales's Theatre, London.
1868	Rosie Fanquehere in *Play* (Robertson), Prince of Wales's Theatre, London.
1869	Naomi Tighe in *School* (Robertson), Prince of Wales's Theatre, London.
1870	Cecilia Dunscombe in *M.P.* (Robertson), Prince of Wales's Theatre, London.
	Lady Gay Spanker in *London Assurance* (Boucicault), Princess's Theatre, London.
1872	Georgina Vesey in *Money* (Bulwer-Lytton), Prince of Wales's Theatre, London.
1873	Blanche Lundie in *Man and Wife* (Collins), Prince of Wales's Theatre, London.
1874	Jenny Northcott in *Sweethearts* (Gilbert), Prince of Wales's Theatre, London.
	Lady Teazle in *The School for Scandal* (Sheridan), Prince of Wales's Theatre, London.
1875	Lady Franklin in *Money* (Bulwer-Lytton), Prince of Wales's Theatre, London; Garrick Theatre, London, 1894.
	Peg Woffington in *Masks and Faces* (Reade and Taylor), Prince of Wales's Theatre, London.
1876	Winifred Piper in *Wrinkles* (H. J. Byron), Prince of Wales's Theatre, London.
1877	Mrs Haygarth in *The Vicarage* (Scott), Prince of Wales's Theatre, London.
	Pert in *London Assurance* (Boucicault), Prince of Wales's Theatre, London.
	Hester Grazebrook in *An Unequal Match* (Taylor), Prince of Wales's Theatre, London.
1878	Countess Zicka in *Diplomacy* (adapted from Sardou), Prince of Wales's Theatre, London.
	Nan in *Good for Nothing* (Buckstone), Prince of Wales's Theatre, London.
1881	Kate Reeve in *A Lesson* (Burnand), Haymarket Theatre, London.
1882	Lady Walker in *Odette* (Scott and Stephenson, adapted from Boucicault), Haymarket Theatre, London.
	Mrs Sebright in *The Overland Route* (Taylor), Haymarket Theatre, London.
1883	Countess Olga Soukareff in *Fédora* (Sardou, adapted by Merivale), Haymarket Theatre, London; revived there, 1895.
	Miss Maplebeck in *Lords and Commons* (Pinero), Haymarket Theatre, London.
1884	Lady Henry Fairfax in *Diplomacy* (adapted from Sardou), Haymarket Theatre, London; Garrick Theatre, London, 1893.

Other roles included: *Heart of Midlothian* (Scott), St James's Theatre, London, 1856; *The Little Treasure* (Harris), Adelphi Theatre, London, 1856; *Unlimited Confidence* (Troughton), Strand Theatre, London, 1856; *Mazourka* (H. J. Byron), Strand Theatre, London, 1856; *A Fair Pretender* (Simpson), Prince of Wales's Theatre, London, 1865.

Publications

Mr. and Mrs. Bancroft On and Off the Stage: Written by Themselves (autobiography), 1886 (revised and expanded in 1909 as *The Bancrofts: Recollections of Sixty Years*); *The Shadow of Neeme* (novel by Marie Wilton), 1912; *Empty Chairs* (autobiographical essays by Squire Bancroft), 1925.

*

Bibliography

Books:
George Pleydell Bancroft, *Stage and Bar*, London, 1939.
Robert C. Buzecky, *The Bancrofts at the Prince of Wales's and Haymarket Theatres, 1865–1885*, Madison, Wisconsin, 1970.

* * *

Marie Wilton must have received the most thorough training available to a woman in the Victorian theatre, for, from her earliest youth until she was 25, she specialized in playing boys, from the noble Prince Arthur in *King John* and the pathetic Henri in Charles Dillon's *Belphegor* to her more usual "urlesque boys" like Pippo in H. J. Byron's *The Maid and the Magpie*, which so astonished Charles Dickens: "it is perfectly free from offence ... the manner, the appearance, the levity, impulse, and spirits of it are exactly like a boy, that you cannot think of anything like her sex in association with it". From 1856 she was the star of H. J. Byron's burlesques at the Strand Theatre, where the range of styles she had to perform, albeit in parody, was listed by Tom Robertson in his *Theatrical Types: the Burlesque Actress*: "She can waltz, polk, dance a *pas seul* or a sailor's hornpipe, La Sylphide, or Genu-wine Transatlantic Cape Cod Skedaddle, with equal grace and spirit; and as for acting, she can declaim á la Phelps or Fechter; is serious, droll; and must play farce, tragedy, opera, comedy, melodrama, pantomime, ballet, change her costume, fight a combat, make love, poison herself, die, and take one encore for a song and another for a dance, in the short space of ten minutes".

However, Wilton also wished to play in more legitimate comedy and this led her into independent management in 1865, when she acquired a small and dilapidated theatre off Tottenham Court Road, which she refurbished as the Prince of Wales's. Although she continued to play some burlesques — H. J. Byron was in the partnership — her aim was to attract a more discriminating and fashionable audience. For Tom Robertson's comedy *Society* she hired two actors she had met on tour in Liverpool, Squire

Bancroft and John Hare, neither of whom had been brought up to the profession as she had. Although Hare was a clever mimic, specialising in eccentric old men, Bancroft's attraction was his air of social ease. Although he had experienced four years of provincial stock theatre, at the age of 24 he seemed the epitome of the "gentleman amateurs" who, during the 1860's and 1870's, were to transform the "disreputable" profession. Many, such as Alfred Wigan, William Kendal, Charles Calvert, and Herman Vezin, married actresses more professionally experienced than themselves and Bancroft and Wilton were similarly married in 1867. Bancroft, of course, took over responsibility for his wife's financial commitments as manager of the Prince of Wales's, but she remained the star attraction of the partnership.

Nonetheless, the house-style of the Prince of Wales's Theatre was not one of star attractions but of a carefully balanced ensemble. Following the success of *Society* and, more significantly, the intimate comedy *Caste*, Tom Robertson's "naturalistic" drama became their speciality. Although many of his plays for the Bancrofts remained essentially melodramatic in plot and sentiment, their meticulous settings and carefully balanced playing were acclaimed by Clement Scott of the *Daily Telegraph* as "The Dawn of the Renaissance" and by the French critic Augustin Filon as "a new era for English comedy - the era of Robertson". Nevertheless, despite the 'cup-and-saucer' detail of the Bancrofts' production methods, Robertson continued to provide opportunities for Marie Bancroft to display her purely theatrical talents in vivacious comedy roles, in which the characters contrived to sing and dance as well as indulge in extravagant comic business. William Archer wrote that these "practical-humorous heroines — Mary Netley, Polly Eccles, Naomi Tighe — always fell to the lot of Mrs Bancroft, whose alert and expressive face, humid-sparkling eyes, and small compact figure seemed to have been expressly designed for these characters. She possessed, too, the faculty of approaching the borderline of vulgarity without overstepping it — an essential gift for the actress who has to deal with Robertsonian pertness." In fact, Robertson's comedies were not particularly naturalistic as scripts, but, because they expected them to run for several months in their small theatre, the Bancrofts could provide solidly built and well-dressed sets, maintain a relatively small company of actors, specifically cast to strength, and, above all, rehearse the company so as to achieve the integration of an ensemble. These rehearsals were led by Robertson, who, according to John Hare, "had a gift peculiar to himself ... of conveying by some rapid almost electric suggestion to the actor an insight into the character assigned to him". W. S. Gilbert, whose comedy *Sweethearts* was directed for the Bancrofts by Robertson in 1879, "learnt a great deal from his method of stage management, which in those days was quite a novelty ... I look upon stage management as now understood, as having been invented by him." This directorial control by the author was to be emulated and extended by Gilbert himself, H. A. Jones, Pinero, and George Bernard Shaw.

The new style was also highly profitable. During their management of the Prince of Wales's, by increasing prices — with orchestra stalls carpeted, upholstered, and antimacassared — and by restricting the evening's entertainment to a single play, which might run for hundreds of performances, the Bancrofts were able to increase their actors' salaries and by 1880 had made enough to take over the large and prestigious Haymarket Theatre, refurbishing it throughout along the same fashionable and comfortable lines. Henry James wrote of the new Haymarket: "Brilliant, luxuriant, softly cushioned and perfectly aired, it is almost entertainment enough to sit there and admire the excellent device by which the old-fashioned and awkward proscenium has been suppressed and the stage set all around in an immense gilded frame, like that of some magnificent picture". In this way the theatre's architecture reinforced the naturalistic convention of the invisible "fourth wall", emphasizing the contained comedy style of the Bancrofts, so different from the drollery of the earlier Victorian comedians, who had played out over the footlights to more volatile audiences than the middle-class patrons that the Bancrofts had cultivated. The financial success of their policy was such that they retired from management in their mid-forties, although they continued to act. Squire Bancroft, though never very versatile, increased his range with such roles as Triplet in Charles Reade's *Masks and Faces* and the Abbé Latour in *The Dead Heart* with Irving at the Lyceum in 1889. In 1897, after the couple finally retired from the stage, he was awarded a knighthood — becoming only the second actor (the first was Irving) to be thus honoured.

—George Taylor

———

BARBA, Eugenio. Italian director and theorist. Born in Brindisi, Italy, 29 October 1936. Educated at schools in Gallipoli, Italy, and at the Naples Military College, 1951–54; University of Oslo, 1954–65. Married Judy Jones. Migrated to Norway, 1954; worked as welder and sailor, 1954–56; subsequently studied direction under Jerzy Grotowski at the Polish Laboratory Theatre, Opole, Poland, 1961–64; studied theatre forms in India, 1963; founded the Odin Teatret in Oslo, 1964, with which he has since been associated; Odin Teatret relocated in Holstebrö, Denmark, financially supported by the Danish Ministry of Culture, 1966, as part of the larger Nordiskteaterlaboratorium umbrella organisation; has since toured with the Odin Teatret throughout the world; founded International School of Theatre Anthropology (ISTA) to study intercultural performance and acting techniques, 1979.

Productions

1965   *Ornitofilene* [The Bird Lovers] (Bjørneboe), Odin Teatret, Oslo, and tour.
1967   *Kaspariana* (Sarvig), Odin Teatret, Hostelbrö.
1969   *Ferai* (Seeberg), Odin Teatret, Hostelbrö, Théâtre des Nations Festival, Paris, and European tour.
1972   *Min Fars Hus* [My Father's House] (Barba and company, adapted from Dostoevsky), Odin Teatret, Hostelbrö, and European tour.
1974   *Johan Sebastian Bach* (Barba and company), Odin Teatret, Carpignano, Italy; revived, 1979.

Dansenes Bog [The Book of Dances] (Barba and company), Odin Teatret, Carpignano, Italy, and tour.

1976 *Come! And the Day Will Be Ours* (Barba and company), Caracas, Venezuela, and tour.

1977 *Anabasis* (Barba and company), Odin Teatret, Hostelbrö; revived, 1982–84.

1979 *Millionen — Første Rejse* [The Million] (Barba and company), Odin Teatret, Hostelbrö; revived, 1982–84.

1982 *Brechts Aske 2* [Brecht's Ashes 2] (Barba and company), Odin Teatret, Hostelbrö.

1984 *El Romancero de Edipo*, Basho company, Nordiskteaterlaboratorium, Holstebrö.

Bryllup Med Gud [Marriage with God], Farfa company, Nordiskteaterlaboratorium, Holstebrö.

1985 *Såret af vinden* [Wait for the Dawn] (Fowler), Canada Project, Nordisk Teaterlaboratorium, Canadian tour.

Oxyrhyncus Evangeliet [The Gospel According to Oxyrhyncus] (Barba), Odin Teatret, Hostelbrö, and tour.

1988 *Talabot* (Barba and company), Odin Teatret, Hostelbrö.

1993 *Kaosmos: The Ritual of the Door* (Barba and company), Odin Teatret, Temuco, Chile, and tour.

Publications

Alla Ricerca del Teatro Perduto, 1965 (translated as *In Search of the Lost Theatre*, 1965); *The Kathakali Theatre*, 1967; *Towards a Poor Theatre* (as editor and contributor), 1967; *The Floating Islands*, 1979 (revised as *Beyond the Floating Islands*, 1986); *Modsaetningernes spil*, 1980; *Il Brecht dell'Odin*, 1981; *Theatre Anthropology: First Hypothesis*, 1981; *Teaterkultur*, 1982; *Theatre Anthropology*, 1982; *The Way of Opposites*, 1982; *The Dilated Body*, 1985; *The Nature of Dramaturgy*, 1985; *Odin Teatret, dets historie*, 1985; *Det forgår i Helvede*, 1985; *Anatomie de l'acteur*, with Nicola Savarese, 1986; *The Way of Refusal*, 1986; *The Actor's Energy: Male-Female versus Animus-Anima*, 1987; *The Etymological Intellectual*, 1987; *Eurasian Theatre*, 1988; *Eugenio Barba to Phillip Zarrilli*, 1988; *Anthropological Theatre*, 1988; *The Dictionary of Theatre Anthropology*, with Nicola Savarese, 1991; *The Secret Art of the Performer*, with Nicola Savarese, 1991; *La Canoa di Carta*, 1993.

*

Bibliography

Books:

Tony D'Urso and Ferdinando Taviani, *L'Étragner qui danse — Album de l'Odin Teatret 1972–77*, Rennes, 1977.

Frank Coppieters, *Eugenio Barba et son École Internationale d'Anthropologie Théâtrale*, Brussels, 1981.

Richard Fowler, *Denmark: Grotowski and Barba, a Canadian Perspective*, Toronto, 1981.

Piergiorgio Giacche, *ISTA che scuola*, Milan, 1981.

Piergiorgio Giacche, *La scuola si Barba e il teatro di gruppo*, Milan, 1981.

Richard Schechner, *Third Theater: An Interview with Jerzy Grotowski About Eugenio Barba*, New York, 1984.

Monique Bori, *Eugenio Barba et son école*, Paris, 1986.

Nicola Savarese, *ISTA-Salento, Dialoghi Teatrali*, Lecce, 1987.

Magaly Muguercia, *Barba: trascender la literalidad*, Havana, 1988.

Hector Noguera, *Castro y Barba: Teatro en la diversidad cultural*, Santiago, 1988.

Ian Watson, *Towards a Third Theatre: Eugenio Barba and the Odin Teatret*, London, 1993.

* * *

Born in Italy, based in Scandinavia and truly a citizen of world theatre through his frequent touring, Eugenio Barba claims that: "My body is my country. The only place where I always *am*". This internationalism has been evident from the very start of his career, when he emerged from his studies with Grotowski and a revelatory introduction to Indian ritual theatre with the express ambition of promoting Western performance standards through the influence of Oriental modes of expression. In 1964 he wrote a much-translated essay upon the Indian art of Kathakali, thus generating new interest in a whole new genre of theatre. As creator of the Odin Teatret in Oslo, and from 1966 in Hostelbrö, he dedicated himself to the task of defining a theatre language that benefited from a new emphasis upon body movement and gesture, characteristic of many forms of Eastern theatre.

The Odin Teatret began inauspiciously enough, with Barba bringing together a small group of inexperienced performers who had failed to gain entrance to conventional theatre schools. Teaching themselves the essence of their craft, they developed a programme of intensive rehearsal in which finished productions grew through improvisation, initially based loosely on a written text but later as a product of the group's own contributions, always closely monitored by Barba himself (who insists upon a high level of discipline in his troupe). The performance of *Ferai* at the Théâtre des Nations in Paris in 1969 announced the arrival of a theatre enterprise of major importance, and Barba has since established himself as a leading theorist, disseminating his ideas not only through his productions but through his many writings and through seminars and other gatherings organised under the aegis of the Nordiskteaterlaboratorium, which he founded in 1966, and of the International School of Theatre Anthropology, which he founded in 1979.

At the heart of Barba's extensive research into the theatre is the need to understand better the nature of "acting". Studies of Oriental theatre revealed to him unrealised possibilities in the incorporation of the tiniest movements during a performance and much of his rehearsal technique is based on the process of deconstructing an actor's stance and gestures so as to bring them under control. Identifying "tensions" and "oppositions" in modes of movement, speech and gesture is, according to Barba, "at the root of various performing techniques", and an actor must be made aware of these before going on to think of broader characterisation and meaning. In fact, he maintains that use of such movements is of equal importance to understanding the social or political milieu of a play.

Barba has summarised his thoughts on the sociology of the theatre in terms of a "third theatre", a form of community-based theatre that has evolved over recent years alongside the more immediately recognisable institutionalised theatre and the intellectually self-absorbed avant-garde. This "third theatre" surfaces, according to Barba, most often in the countries of the Third World, where the other two forms have a weaker hold, and is characterised by the presence of dedicated "theatre workers" whose activities lie on the fringe of accepted culture and who are concentrating on cultivating a new language of performance, free of political interests and dependent on the interplay of group dynamics. In pursuit of developing awareness of this third theatre, Barba has staged a variety of street entertainments in several continents and has worked to establish links between his own company and many other like-minded organisations around the globe. A specific example of this approach in practice was the "barter" system he promoted in the 1970's — his own group performed for the local population, who then completed the exchange by offering their own efforts. The process goes on in Barba's company to the present day, with visitors to their base being encouraged to share their own perceptions of the theatre for the mutual benefit of all.

As a theorist, Barba denies the validity of frontiers and boundaries between one theatre genre and another, and his company (and ISTA), boasting performers from a wide range of cultural backgrounds, works as a meeting-place for all manner of theatrical traditions. Critics have sometimes taken issue with his directorial style, accusing him of lacking a clear political standpoint and of obscurity — but Barba himself protests that political drama all too often reduces itself to polemics not theatre and further that in suggesting a host of conclusions from a single piece he is presenting a much richer work; thus, it is not what a production has to say that interests him most, but how it goes about saying it. To Barba, theatre is a form of social action: "What is theatre? If I try to reduce this word to something tangible, what I discover are men and women, human beings who have joined together. Theatre is a particular relationship in an elected context. First between people who gather together in order to create something, and then, later, between the creation made by this group and this public".

Most recently, he has done further work to integrate his theatre with the local community through the inauguration of what he calls "festuges", informal festivals of music and drama that are deliberately aimed to involve the inhabitants of Hostelbrö, always with the emphasis on breaking down intercultural barriers and promoting, through performance, contact between various groups and organisations.

—David Pickering

BARRAULT, Jean-Louis. French actor, director, and manager. Born in Le Vésinet, Seine-et-Oise, Paris, 8 September 1910. Educated at private school from 1916 and at the Collège Chaptal, Paris; studied painting at the École du Louvre, Paris; studied mime under Étienne Decroux at Charles Dullin's theatre school at the Théâtre de l'Atelier, Paris, 1931–35. Married actress Madeleine Renaud in 1940. Acting debut, in Jonson's *Volpone*, Théâtre de l'Atelier, Paris, 1932; debut as director, Théâtre de l'Atelier, 1935; formed Le Grenier des Augustins theatre company, 1936; film debut, 1936; took over Théâtre de l'Atelier, 1938; acted and directed with the Comédie Française, 1940–46; with his wife, formed the Compagnie Madeleine Renaud — Jean-Louis Barrault, based at the Théâtre Marigny, Paris, 1946; first of many tours, to Belgium, Holland, and Switzerland, 1946; toured worldwide with the company during the 1950's, including appearances at the Edinburgh Festival, 1948; London, 1951; Montreal and New York, 1952; London, 1956; New York, 1957; Edinburgh Festival, 1957; London, 1958; opened Le Petit Marigny studio theatre, Paris, 1954; company left the Théâtre Marigny, moving for two seasons to the Théâtre Sarah Bernhardt; following offer from André Malraux, Minister of State: the company inaugurated a national theatre, the Théâtre de France de l'Odéon in Paris, where Barrault was made director, 1959; toured the USSR, 1962; acted, with his company, in New York and Venice, 1964, and at the second World Theatre Season in London, 1965; director, Théâtre des Nations, 1965–67, 1972–74; managed, acted, and directed at l'Odéon until dismissed from post following his toleration of an occupation by students during the student riots in Paris, 1968; resumed touring after 1968; co-founder, with Peter Brook, International Centre for Theatre Research, Paris, 1970; converted the Orsay station in Paris into a performance area, 1972; director, Théâtre d'Orsay, 1974–81; moved to the Théâtre du Rond Pont, Paris, 1981. Officier, Légion d'Honneur; Commander, Ordre des Arts et des Lettres. Died in Paris, 22 January 1994.

Productions

As actor/director:

1935   *Autour d'une Mère* (Barrault, adapted from Faulkner), Théâtre de l'Atelier, Paris.
        Numancia (Cervantes), Théâtre Antoine, Paris.
1938   *La Terre est Ronde* (Salacrou), Théâtre de l'Atelier, Paris; acted Silvio.
        Hamlet ou Les Suites de la piété filiale (Laforgue), Théâtre de l'Atelier, Paris.
1939   *La Faim* (Barrault, adapted from Hamsun), Théâtre de l'Atelier, Paris; acted Tangen.
1942   *Phèdre* (Racine), Comédie Française, Paris.
        The Suppliant Women (Barrault, adapted from Aeschylus), Coubertin Stadium, Paris.
        Huit cents Mètres (Obey), Coubertin Stadium, Paris.
1943   *Le Soulier de satin* (Claudel), Comédie Française, Paris.
1945   *Antony and Cleopatra* (Shakespeare), Comédie Française, Paris.
1946   *La Princesse d'Elide* (Molière), Comédie Française, Paris; acted Moron.
        Hamlet (Shakespeare, translated by Gide), Théâtre de Marigny, Paris; later on tour; acted Hamlet.
        Les Fausses Confidences (Marivaux), Théâtre de Marigny, Paris.

Baptiste (mime by Prévert), Théâtre de Marigny, Paris.

Les Nuits de la Colère (Salacrou), Théâtre de Marigny, Paris.

1947   *Le Procès* (adapted by Barrault and Gide from Kafka), Théâtre de Marigny, Paris.

Le Pays des Cerisiers (Dhotel), Théâtre de Marigny, Paris.

L'Ours (Chekhov), Théâtre de Marigny, Paris.

Amphitryon (Molière), Théâtre de Marigny, Paris; acted Mercurio.

La Fontaine de Jouvence (Kochno), Théâtre de Marigny, Paris.

1948   *Occupe-toi d'Amélie* (Feydeau), Théâtre de Marigny, Paris.

L'État de Siège (Camus), Théâtre de Marigny, Paris.

Partage de Midi (Claudel), Théâtre de Marigny, Paris.

1949   *Les Fourberies de Scapin* (Molière), Théâtre de Marigny, Paris.

La Seconde Surprise de l'Amour (Marivaux), Théâtre de Marigny, Paris.

Elizabeth d'Angleterre (Bruckner, translated by Cave), Théâtre de Marigny, Paris.

Le Bossu (Féval and Bourgeois), Théâtre de Marigny, Paris.

1950   *On purge bébé* (Feydeau), Théâtre de Marigny, Paris.

Marlborough s'en va-t-en guerre (Achard), Théâtre de Marigny, Paris.

Les Mains sales and *Crime passionel* (Sartre), Théâtre de Marigny, Paris.

L'Impromptu (Molière), Théâtre de Marigny, Paris.

La Répétition ou l'Amour puni (Anouilh), Théâtre de Marigny, Paris.

Malatesta (Montherlant), Théâtre de Marigny, Paris.

1951   *Oedipe* (Gide), Théâtre de Marigny, Paris.

Maguelone (Clavel), Théâtre de Marigny, Paris.

L'Épreuve (Marivaux), Théâtre de Marigny, Paris.

Lazare (Obey), Théâtre de Marigny, Paris.

On ne badine pas avec l'Amour (Musset), Théâtre de Marigny, Paris.

L'Échange (Claudel), Théâtre de Marigny, Paris.

Bacchus (Cocteau), Théâtre de Marigny, Paris.

1952   *Connaissance de Paul Claudel* (Barrault), Théâtre de Marigny, Paris.

1953   *Christophe Colomb* (Claudel), Théâtre de Marigny, Paris.

Pour Lucrèce (Giraudoux), Théâtre de Marigny, Paris.

1954   *Renard* (mime by Stravinsky and Ramuz), Théâtre de Marigny, Paris.

La Soirée des Proverbs (Schehadé), Théâtre de Marigny, Paris.

Le Misanthrope (Molière), Théâtre de Marigny, Paris.

Le Cocu magnifique (Crommelynck), Théâtre de Marigny, Paris.

Jean-Louis Barrault

La Cerisaie (Chekhov, translated by Neveux), Théâtre de Marigny, Paris.

Il faut qu'une porte soit ouverte ou fermée (Musset), Théâtre de Marigny, Paris.

Irène Innocente (Betti), Théâtre de Marigny, Paris.

1955   *Bérénice* (Racine), Théâtre de Marigny, Paris.

Le Songe des Prisonniers (Fry, translated by Morvan-Lebesque), Théâtre de Marigny, Paris.

Volpone (Jonson, adapted by Romains and Zweig), Théâtre de Marigny, Paris.

Intermezzo (Giraudoux), Théâtre de Marigny, Paris.

L'Orestiea (Aeschylus, adapted by Obey), Théâtre de Marigny, Paris.

Le Chien du Jardinier (Vega, adapted by Neveux), Théâtre de Marigny, Paris.

Les Suites d'une Course (mime by Supervielle and Sauguet), Théâtre de Marigny, Paris.

1956   *Le Personnage combattant* (Vauthier), Théâtre de Marigny, Paris.

Histoire de Vasco (Schehadé), Schauspielhaus, Zürich; acted Cesar.

1957   *Le Château de Kafka* (Quentin), Théâtre de Marigny, Paris; acted Joseph K.

Madame sans Gêne (Sardou and Moreau), Théâtre de Marigny, Paris.

1958   *La Vie Parisienne* (Meilhac, Halévy, and Offenbach), Palais-Royal, Paris; acted Brazilian.

Le Soulier de Satin (Claudel), Théâtre de Marigny, Paris.

1959   *Le Tie Clara* (Roncoroni), Théâtre de Marigny, Paris.

Tête d'Or (Claudel), Théâtre de l'Odéon, Paris.

1960   *Rhinocéros* (Ionesco), Théâtre de l'Odéon, Paris; acted Berenger.

1963   *Divine Paroles* (Vallé-Inclan), Théâtre de l'Odéon, Paris; acted Lucero.

1964   *Le Mariage de Figaro* (Beaumarchais), City Centre, New York; acted Count Almaviva.

Andromaque (Racine) City Centre, New York; acted Orestes.

Le Piéton de l'Air (Ionesco), City Centre, New York; acted Monsieur Bérenger.

Salut à Molière, City Centre, New York; acted Narrator, Arnolphe, and Alceste.

1965   *Ne se Promène Donc Pas Toute Nue*, Aldwych Theatre, London.

1968   *Rabelais* (Barrault), Elysée-Montmartre, Paris.

1985   *Le Cid* (Corneille), Théâtre du Rond Pont, Paris.

Other productions included: *Jarry sur la butte*, 1970; *Harold et Maude*, 1973; *Zarathustra*, 1974. Other roles included: Servant in *Volpone* (Jonson), Théâtre de l'Atelier, Paris, 1932; Third Clerk in *The Pleasure of Honesty* (Pirandello), Théâtre de l'Atelier, Paris, 1935; Rodrigue in *Le Cid* (Corneille), Comédie Française, Paris, 1940; Willie in *Oh, les Beaux jours!* (Beckett), Venice Festival, 1964; and roles in: *Georges Dandin* (Molière); *Un Homme comme les autres* (Passeur), *Richard III* (Shakespeare); *Numance*; *The Rape of Lucrece*; *Tandis que j'agonise*.

Films

Les Beaux Jours, 1935; *Sous les yeux d'Occident*, 1936; *A nous deux*, 1936; *Madame la Vie*, 1936; *Un grand amour de Beethoven*, 1936; *Hélène*, 1936; *Jenny*, 1936; *Mademoiselle Docteur*, 1937; *Police mondaine*, 1937; *Le Puritan*, 1937; *Les Perles de la Couronne*, 1937; *Mirages*, 1937; *Drôle de drame*, 1937; *Altitude 3200*, 1937; *Nous les Jeunes*, 1938; *Orage*, 1938; *Le Piste du Sud*, 1938; *Farinet oder das falsche Geld*, 1939; *Parade en Sept Nuits*, 1941; *Le Destin fabuleux de Desirée Clary*, 1941; *Montmartre-sur-Seine*, 1941; *La Symphonie fantastique*, 1942; *Lumière d'été*, 1943; *L'Ange de la Nuit*, 1943; *Les Enfants du Paradis*, 1945; *La Part de l'Ombre*, 1945; *Le Cocu magnifique*, 1946; *D'Hommes à hommes*, 1948; *La Ronde*, 1950; *Si Versailles m'était conté*, 1953; *Le Dialogue des Carmélites*, 1960; *Le Miracle des Loups*, 1961; *Le Testament du Docteur Cordelier*, 1961; *The Longest Day*, 1962; *Répétition chez Jean-Louis Barrault*, 1964; *Le Grande frousse*, 1964; *Chappaqua*, 1966; *La Nuit de Varennes*, 1981.

Publications

Réflexions sur le Théâtre, 1949; *Nouvelles Réflexions sur le Théâtre*, 1959; *Journal de Bord*, 1961; *Souvenirs pour Demain*, 1972; *Comme je le Pense*, 1975; *Paris Notre Siècle* (with Madeleine Renaud), 1983; *Saisir le Présent*, 1984.

*

Bibliography

Books:
Léon Chancerel, *Jean-Louis Barrault*, Paris, 1953.
André Frank, *Jean-Louis Barrault*, Paris, 1971.

Articles:
Roger Wallis, "Jean-Louis Barrault's *Rabelais*", *Theatre Quarterly*, I, 3, 1971.

* * *

Jean-Louis Barrault embodied developments of both modernism and post-modernism in the theatre through his perfection of the binary rays of Actor as Creator and of Director as textual Interpreter and Image-maker. Throughout his six decades of theatrical invention, Barrault pushed the limits of stifling convention with the goal of aerating and refreshing the spectator's dialogue with the moving body in space. Barrault injected the actor with a new technique of dramatic action through refinements in the quality of movement and through the incorporation of breath into the delivery of words and gesture. Barrault taught through his own example as an actor and through his visceral contact with other actors when working as a director. He was, at once, the intellectual and the naïf, the prophet and the child, the histrionic aristocrat and the Bohemian artist, the diplomat and the anarchist.

From the outset of his career in the 1930's, Barrault perceived the theatrical space as a centre impatient for ritualized presentations of the passions. The actor — as speaker and mime — was, metaphorically, a rooted tree on the "boards" that transformed ordinary space, lifting it into the higher realm of poetic space. Naturalism (and, perhaps, even realism) was beneath Barrault's vibrating atmosphere of "total theatre", negating, as is so often the case, the mystical and unpredictable elements of the dream. Linear time and spatial fixity were never assured in the theatre of Jean-Louis Barrault. His search was always for the non-quotidian and the extraordinary.

Barrault carried the torch of Copeau's stripped-down theatre, Dullin's festive theatre, and Artaud's alchemic, cruel theatre from the era of the German Occupation of Paris into the era of absurdity and fragmentation. As a partner in Étienne Decroux's research on mime techniques, Barrault discovered a language of gesture that he brilliantly applied to Faulkner's novel *As I Lay Dying* and to Hamsun's *Hunger*. These virtuoso mime creations (performed with friends from the Dullin school) sounded a break between Barrault and Decroux by their appeal to the pleasure of the spectator over the choice of appeal to the purist aesthete. Barrault's mime legacy is still visible in the performances of Marcel Marceau and in certain aspects of the pedagogy of Jacques Lecoq. His collaboration with Decroux was renewed, temporarily, during the shooting of *Les Enfants du Paradis*, in which Barrault played Debureau and Decroux and Marceau played supporting roles.

In the 1940's, with his feet firmly planted in gestural techniques, Barrault's building of the actor-self leaped to a confrontation with the classics of dramatic literature. He moved quickly from silence to rhythmic dialogue and musical renditions of the monologue and soliloquy. Barrault's renewed work with texts coincided with his new friendship with the great actress Madeleine Renaud. His union with Renaud was as stunning a theatrical marriage as that of his first metteur-en-scène/teacher, Georges Pitoëff, with his wife, the actress Ludmilla Pitoëff. Soon, within the illustrious throng of the Comédie-Française, Barrault began the expansion of his gestural performance into a dynamized torso of the tragic, romantic hero. Here Barrault built upon his extended apprenticeship with Charles Dullin at the Atelier, which served as the foundation for all his work in the theatre. Dwarfed by the vocal bravura of his colleagues, Barrault encountered the limitations of his own vocal technique, and the need to put his theory of the voice/word as a "gesture of the body" into a more developed and exemplary posture.

In Paul Claudel, Barrault found a spiritual father whose theories and texts allowed the young actor/director to engage the total body in a dance of word and gesture. Claudel had refused production of some of his plays for over 40 years until Barrault convinced him to permit his mise-en-scène. *Le Soulier de satin* and *Partage de midi* were the greatest successes that ensued. In these productions Barrault trained himself to be a master of direction and vocal projection, completing his construction of the hero body from the feet to the head. He transformed himself from the rough material of a provincial dilettante to a fine-tuned, three-dimensional actor. Barrault's influence from the Surrealist writers and painters, the Japanese Noh theatre, and the masks of Asia and the Americas combined with his enthusiasm for the words of Cervantes, Corneille, Molière, Racine, and Shakespeare to create one complete whole 'Renaissance' person.

Initially, the partnership of Jean-Louis Barrault and Madeleine Renaud focused upon impassioned interpretations of the standard French repertoire and new French-language playwrights like Anouilh, Camus, Montherlant, Obey, and translations/adaptations by André Gide. Soon, however, the internationalism that was one of the most notable aspects of their collaboration established itself in earnest. The Claudel productions, for example, were taken on world tours. Barrault had always been a friend of expatriate artists in Paris, and an avid reader of literature from all cultures. In the 1950's Barrault welcomed and encouraged the exponents of the 'New Theatre', including Beckett, Ionesco, and France's own outcast Jean Genet. Jean-Louis Barrault acted with Renaud in several of Roger Blin's mises-en-scène of Beckett plays, and he was instrumental in finally arranging for Blin to direct *The Screens* at the Théâtre de France in 1966 (with Renaud playing a major role). Also at this time, Barrault proposed a multicultural and multi-lingual production of *The Tempest* to be directed by Peter Brook in Paris.

The political events of May 1968 separated Barrault from the national theatres because of his sympathies with, and assistance to, the protesters. He soon triumphed, however, with *Rabelais*, in a former boxing arena, and with an invited performance by Bunraku puppeteers. Laurence Olivier followed with an invitation to produce a season in London. In another twist of fate, Barrault's US tour of *Rabelais* arrived at the University of California at Berkeley during the Kent State riot of 1969, resulting in another theatre/street event — a communal moment — that inspired Barrault's investigation of actor/spectator rapport. The immediate result of this experience was a European tour in a circus tent with a mise-en-scène of yet another Claudel text.

Barrault's career was never at a standstill. He recognized the ephemeral qualities of the theatre and the theatre's constant need to be reborn through inspirations from its past history, and from the contributions of new writers like Marguerite Duras. The theatre, for Barrault, was an act of perpetual rebirth, a flirtation with eternal youth. He revelled in its silences and its immobilities, waiting for the next gesture to prompt another rupture of its conventions.

—Ron Popenhagen

BARRETT, Lawrence (Patrick). US actor-manager. Born in Paterson, New Jersey, 4 April 1838. No formal education. Married Mary F. Mayer in 1859, three daughters. Worked as call boy and apprentice at Metropolitan Theatre, Detroit, from 1852; stage debut, Detroit, 1853; actor, Grand Opera House, Pittsburgh, 1854–56; New York debut, Chamber's Street Theatre, 1857; actor, Metropolitan Theatre, Boston's Museum, and Howard Athenaeum companies, 1858–61; served as captain in 28th Massachusetts Volunteer Regiment, 1861–62; appeared in Philadelphia and Washington, DC, 1861–62; acclaimed in classical roles on both sides of Atlantic, often appearing alongside Edwin Booth at the Winter Garden Theatre and Booth's Theatre, New York, and on tour, from 1862; co-manager, with John McCullough, California Theatre, San Francisco, 1869–70, Variety Theatre, New Orleans, 1871–73, and Lyceum Theatre, London, 1884–85; toured with Booth, 1886–91; last appearance, in *Richelieu*, 18 March 1891. Died in New York, 20 March 1891.

Roles

1853	Murad in *The French Spy* (Haines), Metropolitan Theatre, Detroit.
1857	Sir Thomas Clifford in *The Hunchback* (Knowles), Chamber's Street Theatre, New York.
	Fazio in *Fazio* (Milman), Chamber's Street Theatre, New York.
	Armand in *Camille* (Wills), Chamber's Street Theatre, New York.
	Lord Townley in *The Provoked Husband* (Cibber and Vanbrugh), Chamber's Street Theatre, New York.
	The Stranger in *The Stranger* (Kotzebue), Chamber's Street Theatre, New York.
	Ingomar in *Ingomar* (Lovell), Chamber's Street Theatre, New York.
	Claude Melnotte in *The Lady of Lyons* (Bulwer-Lytton), Chamber's Street Theatre, New York.
	Matthew Bates in *Time Tries All* (Jerrold), Metropolitan Theatre, New York.
1858	Frederick Bramble in *The Poor Gentleman* (Colman the Younger), Boston Museum.
1862–63	Richard in *Richard III* (Shakespeare), Winter Garden Theatre, New York.

	Hamlet in *Hamlet* (Shakespeare), Winter Garden Theatre, New York.
1871	Adrian de Mauprat in *Richelieu* (Bulwer-Lytton), Booth's Theatre, New York.
	Othello in *Othello* (Shakespeare), Booth's Theatre, New York.
	Iago in *Othello* (Shakespeare), Booth's Theatre, New York.
	James Harebell in *Harebell; or, The Man O'Airlie* (Wills), Booth's Theatre, New York.
	Leontes in *The Winter's Tale* (Shakespeare), Booth's Theatre, New York.
1875	Cassius in *Julius Caesar* (Shakespeare), Booth's Theatre, New York.
1877–78	Bartlett in *A Counterfeit Presentment* (Howell), US tour.
	Yorick in *Yorick's Love* (Howells, adapted from Tamayo y Baus), US tour.
	Macduff in *Macbeth* (Shakespeare), US tour.
	Garrick in *David Garrick* (Robertson), US tour.
	Edgar in *King Lear* (Shakespeare), US tour.
	Laertes in *Hamlet* (Shakespeare), US tour.
1888	The Ghost in *Hamlet* (Shakespeare), Metropolitan Opera House, New York.
1889	Ganelon in *Ganelon* (Young), US tour.

Other roles included: King Arthur in *Pendragon* (Young); Benedick in *Much Ado About Nothing*; Elliot Grey in *Rosedale*; Gringoire in *The King's Pleasure* (Thompson); Lear in *King Lear* (Shakespeare); Lanciotto in *Francesca da Rimini* (Boker); Richelieu in *Richelieu* (Bulwer-Lytton); Raphael in *The Marble Heart* (Selby); Rienzi in *Rienzi* (Mitford); Romeo in *Romeo and Juliet* (Shakespeare); Shylock in *The Merchant of Venice* (Shakespeare); and roles in *A Blot in the 'Scutcheon* (Browning), *Dan'l Druce* (Gilbert), *Don Cesar de Bazan* (Boucicault), *The Fool's Revenge* (Taylor), *Guido Ferranti* (Wilde, US title of *The Duchess of Padua*), *Hernani* (adapted from Hugo), and *Katherine and Petruchio* (Garrick).

Publications

Edwin Forrest, 1881; *Edwin Booth and His Contemporaries*, 1886.

*

Bibliography

Books:
Elwyn Alfred Barron, *Lawrence Barrett: A Professional Sketch*, Chicago, 1889.
Charles H. Shattuck, *Shakespeare on the American Stage: From Booth and Barrett to Sothern and Marlowe*, Washington, 1987.

Articles:
Edith Barrett, "The Real Lawrence Barrett", *Theatre*, March 1905.
Melvin R. White, "Lawrence Barrett and the Role of Cassius", *Quarterly Jounal of Speech*, 50, October 1964.

* * *

Below average height, with limited vocal capabilities, Lawrence Barrett succeeded through diligence, intellectual application, and passionate, intense energy. Undoubtedly his best features were his broad forehead — "noble" it was often called — and his deep-set eyes. His close friend, the drama critic William Winter, described the latter as "dark ... deeply sunken and glowing with intense light" and Clara Morris called them "hungry eyes", while Otis Skinner preferred the adjective "burning". But apart from the eyes, his face was not particularly expressive, nor easily disguised. As Shattuck writes, Barrett looked the same whether the role was Richard III, Romeo, Richelieu or James Harebell. Regular elocutionary exercises developed his vocal range and strength and many admired his delivery, but others criticized his peculiar vocal mannerisms and artificiality. One contemporary spectator remembered that Barrett used his vocal range far more than the part or the particular emotion demanded: "Inordinately fond of the linguals, for example, he would cover more than an octave in pitch before releasing the vowel." He was at his best, according to Winter, at moments when "after long repression, the torrent of passion broke loose in a tumult of frenzy and a wild strain of eloquent words". Examples included Cassius's "terrible exultation ... after the fall of Caesar" or "the ecstacy of Lanciotto when he first believes himself to be loved by Francesca". Skinner also recollected the "tempestuous, torrential character" to Barrett's acting in many parts which "swept his audiences into enthusiasm".

These passionate outbursts, resonating the earlier Romantic style of Edwin Forrest, Charlotte Cushman, and G. V. Brooke, were widely admired, even if some complained that they seemed more calculated amd planned than spontaneous. Indeed, critics often noted his "consistency" in performance. In this respect, Barrett stood in distinct contrast to Booth's intuitive, subtler, more natural, but occasionally emotionally lacklustre style. As Winter wrote, "his deep and burning desire to be understood, his anxiety lest his acting should not be appreciated, his inveterate purpose of conquest — the overwhelming solicitude of ambition — often led him to insist upon points, to over-elaborate and enforce them, and in that way his art to some extent defeated itself by the excess of his eager zeal." Unlike Booth, Barrett also failed to convey personal warmth or charms. He was admired for his technique, but he never achieved Booth's popularity.

He was most effective in portraying characters that were close to his own intellectually austere, ambitious, moody, sometimes impetuous personality. Certainly Cassius fitted Barrett's temperament, appearance, and technique like a glove and his reading of the part was widely regarded as the definitive interpretation of his era. Winter called it "an achievement of genius" and lauded Barrett's "variety of expression and fire of eloquence". He especially praised his demeanour in the Senate scene — "at first watchful calm, the silence of concentrated purpose, then the awful energy of the dagger thrust; then the wild, half-joyous, frenzied outburst of triumph". For Winter he "made and sustained a complete illusion". Shattuck has written, however, that when Booth and Barrett were touring *Julius Caesar* in 1887–88, Barrett "learned to bank his fires and relate his Cassius closer to Booth's more naturalistic Brutus". Toning down his energetic displays of passion, Barrett's Cassius became more controlled and dignified. A San Francisco critic observed that Booth and Barrett were not like the earlier actors who represented Brutus and Cassius as "big lunged fellows who orated instead of talked", but rather they seemed "Roman gentlemen quietly considering the best means to remove a danger that menaced their country".

Barrett's Hamlet, Shylock, and Lear also impressed audiences and critics. Lawrence Hutton, for example, thought that next to Cassius, Barrett's Hamlet was "the best thing he does ... vigorous, consistent and unfailingly tender", but it was a performance inspired and overshadowed by Booth's interpretation. Winter, while admitting that Barrett's Shylock, following the interpretations of Edmund Kean and the elder Booth, was not an original treatment, praised him for his "exactness and beauty of execution". Similarly he was often lauded for his touching and eloquent portrayal of Lear, though as Winter observed it was a performance that "might fitfully be typified by a broken medallion rather than by a fallen statue". While he played most of the principal Shakespearean roles, on balance he remained (with the exception of Cassius) second to Booth in this arena.

Unlike Booth, however, Barrett achieved considerable popular and critical success in a wide range of non-Shakespearean roles, usually in historical romantic verse melodramas. Winter called his Lanciotto a "torrent of light — luminous throughout its whole extent with his electric spirit". Skinner lauded Harebell as Barrett's "one true masterpiece" in which his "usual mannerisms" and "artificial elocution" were "thrown completely overboard".

Barrett was particularly interested in developing a body of US dramatic literature. He commissioned new plays, adaptations, and translations from many native US authors. He also revived both US and European romantic dramas, presented the US premiere of Oscar Wilde's *The Duchess of Padua*, and encouraged Minnie Maddern Fiske to produce Ibsen's *A Doll's House*. Other contributions included essays on the US theatre, including grateful biographical sketches of Edwin Forrest and Charlotte Cushman.

Barrett was, furthermore, an outstanding theatrical producer and manager. He significantly raised the performance and production standards during his managements of both the California and New Orleans Variety Theatres. When he toured at the head of his own company in the 1880s, his productions were noted for the quality of the supporting casts, carefully rehearsed ensemble effects, and handsome, historically accurate scenery and costumes. His highly successful management of Booth's five national tours, in three of which he also starred, was his crowning achievement as a producer.

A few days after Barrett's death, Booth, his professional associate and long time friend, retired. With their passing, an epoch ended in the annals of the US stage. Winter hoped that their example would have an "abiding influence", but for the most part their influence was short-lived as the fin-de-siècle American theatre abandoned the outmoded high Victorian style and haltingly embraced modernism.

—Daniel J. Watermeier

BARRY, Elizabeth. English actress. Born c.1658, daughter of a barrister. Educated privately under guardianship of playwright William Davenant; trained as an actress under Davenant and under John Wilmot, Earl of Rochester. Never married but is thought to have borne a daughter each to playwright Sir George Etherege and to Wilmot. Stage debut, Dorset Garden Theatre, c.1673; leading actress, often opposite Thomas Betterton, with Duke's Company, by 1680; co-manager, with Betterton, of United company, Theatre Royal, Drury Lane, from late 1680's; formed own company with Betterton and Anne Bracegirdle, Lincoln's Inn Fields Theatre, 1694; temporary retirement from stage, 1708; last stage appearance, 1710. Died in Acton, London (allegedly after being bitten by her infected lapdog), 7 November 1713.

Principal roles

c.1673   Isabella in *Mustapha* (Orrery), Dorset Garden Theatre, London.

1675   Draxilla in *Alcibiades* (Otway), Dorset Garden Theatre, London.

1676   Leonora in *Abdelazer* (Behn), Dorset Garden Theatre, London.

Elvira in *The Wrangling Lovers* (Ravenscroft), Dorset Garden Theatre, London.

Theodoria in *Tom Essence* (Rawlins), Dorset Garden Theatre, London.

Constantia in *Madam Fickle* (D'Urfey), Dorset Garden Theatre, London.

Phaenice in *Titus and Berenice* (Otway), Dorset Garden Theatre, London.

Lucia in *The Cheats of Scapin* (Otway), Dorset Garden Theatre, London.

1677   Helena in *The Rover* (Behn), Dorset Garden Theatre, London.

Emilla in *The Fond Husband* (D'Urfey), Dorset Garden Theatre, London.

Clarina in *The French Conjuror* (Porter), Dorset Garden Theatre, London.

Philisides in *The Constant Nymph* (anon.), Dorset Garden Theatre, London.

1678   Mrs Goodville in *Friendship in Fashion* (Otway), Dorset Garden Theatre, London.

Clara in *The Counterfeits* (Leanerd), Dorset Garden Theatre, London.

Sophia in *Squire Oldsapp* (D'Urfey), Dorset Garden Theatre, London.

Polyxena in *The Destruction of Troy* (Banks), Dorset Garden Theatre, London.

1679   Cornelia in *The Feigned Courtesans* (Behn), Dorset Garden Theatre, London.

Lavinia in *Caius Marius* (Otway), Dorset Garden Theatre, London.

1679–80   Mrs Gripe in *The Woman-Captain* (Shadwell), Dorset Garden Theatre, London.

Olivia in *The Virtuous Wife* (D'Urfey), Dorset Garden Theatre, London.

1680   Camilla in *The Loving Enemies* (Maidwell), Dorset Garden Theatre, London.

Lady Dunce in *The Soldier's Fortune* (Otway), Dorset Garden Theatre, London.

Corina in *The Revenge* (Behn), Dorset Garden Theatre, London.

Monimia in *The Orphan* (Otway), Dorset Garden Theatre, London.

Athenais in *Theodosius* (Lee), Dorset Garden Theatre, London.

1680–81 Princess of Cleve in *The Princess of Cleve* (Lee), Dorset Garden Theatre, London.

Leonora in *The Spanish Friar* (Dryden), Dorset Garden Theatre, London.

Cordelia in *King Lear* (Shakespeare, adapted by Tate), Dorset Garden Theatre, London.

1682 Belvidera in *Venice Preserved* (Otway), Dorset Garden Theatre, London.

1683 Porcia in *The Atheist* (Otway), Dorset Garden Theatre, London.

1682–95 Olivia in *The Plain Dealer* (Wycherley), Theatre Royal, Drury Lane, London.

Lucina in *Valentinian* (Rochester), Theatre Royal, Drury Lane, London.

Queen of England in *Richard III* (Shakespeare), Theatre Royal, Drury Lane, London.

Mrs Loveit in *Man of Mode* (Etherege), Theatre Royal, Drury Lane, London.

Laetitia in *The Old Bachelor* (Congreve), Theatre Royal, Drury Lane, London.

Lady Touchwood in *The Double Dealer* (Congreve), Theatre Royal, Drury Lane, London.

1688 Borzana in *Darius* (Crowne), Theatre Royal, Drury Lane, London.

1690 Roxana in *The Rival Queens* (Lee), Theatre Royal, Drury Lane, London.

1692 Cassandra in *Cleomenes, The Spartan Hero* (Dryden and Southerne), Theatre Royal, Drury Lane, London.

1694 Isabella in *The Fatal Marriage* (Southerne), Theatre Royal, Drury Lane, London.

1695 Mrs Frail in *Love for Love* (Congreve), Lincoln's Inn Fields Theatre, London; Theatre Royal, Drury Lane, London, 1709.

1696 Lady Grumble in *The City Lady* (Dilke), Lincoln's Inn Fields Theatre, London.

1697 Lady Brute in *The Provoked Wife* (Vanbrugh), Lincoln's Inn Fields Theatre, London.

Boadicea in *Boadicea* (Hopkins), Lincoln's Inn Fields Theatre, London.

Zara in *The Mourning Bride* (Congreve), Lincoln's Inn Fields Theatre, London.

1698 Armida in *Rinaldo and Armida* (Dennis), Lincoln's Inn Fields Theatre, London.

1699 The Queen in *Iphigenia* (Dennis), Lincoln's Inn Fields Theatre, London.

1700 Mrs Marwood in *The Way of the World* (Congreve), Lincoln's Inn Fields Theatre, London.

1703 Calista in *The Fair Penitent* (Rowe), Lincoln's Inn Fields Theatre, London.

Lady Easy in *The Careless Husband* (Cibber), Lincoln's Inn Fields Theatre, London; Queen's Theatre, London, 1709 and 1710, her last appearance.

Calpurnia in *Julius Caesar* (Shakespeare), Lincoln's Inn Fields Theatre, London.

Elizabeth Barry

1704 Mrs Ford in *The Merry Wives of Windsor* (Shakespeare), Lincoln's Inn Fields Theatre, London.

1704–07 Evadne in *The Maid's Tragedy* (Beaumont and Fletcher), Lincoln's Inn Fields Theatre, London; Queen's Theatre, London, 1710.

Queen Katherine in *Henry VIII* (Shakespeare), Lincoln's Inn Fields Theatre, London.

1707 Lady Macbeth in *Macbeth* (Shakespeare), Haymarket Theatre, London; Queen's Theatre, London, 1709–10.

1708 Sophonisba in *Sophonisba* (Lee), Haymarket Theatre, London.

1709–10 Queen Elizabeth in *The Earl of Essex; or, The Unhappy Favourite* (Banks), Queen's Theatre, London.

The Queen in *The Spanish Friar* (Dryden), Queen's Theatre, London.

Angelica in *The Rover* (Behn), Queen's Theatre, London.

Margaretta in *Rule a Wife and Have a Wife* (Fletcher), Queen's Theatre, London.

Alcmena in *Amphitryon* (Dryden), Queen's Theatre, London.

Lady Cockwood in *She Would if She Could* (Etherege), Queen's Theatre, London.

Almeria in *The Indian Emperor* (Dryden), Queen's Theatre, London.

The Queen in *Edward III* (Bancroft and Mountfort), Queen's Theatre, London.

Other roles included: *Liberty Asserted* (Dennis), Lincoln's Inn Fields Theatre, London, 1704.

*

Bibliography

Colley Cibber, *An Apology for the Life of Mr Colley Cibber, Comedian*, London, 1740.

* * *

Although Elizabeth Barry may have begun her career on the stage at the age of 17 and, within a year was unusually busy for a newcomer at the Dorset Garden Theatre in the 1676–77 season, her great talent was not fully recognized until late February 1680. Her original Monimia in *The Orphan* by Thomas Otway was the first of three outstanding roles that John Downes in his *Roscius Anglicanus* (1708) records as having "gain'd her the Name of Famous Mrs Barry, both at Court and City". Something of her experience as a child under the protection of nobility, as the mistress of the Earl of Rochester and the mother of their illegitimate daughter Betty, must have been transmuted in her rendering of this part, which in the words of Colley Cibber "forc'd Tears from the Eyes of her Auditory, especially those who have any Sense of Pity for the Distres't". Pathos was, throughout her career, one of her best effects, as Cibber observed: "When Distress or Tenderness possess'd her, she subsided into the most affecting Melody and Softness. In the Art of exciting Pity she had a Power beyond all the Actresses I have yet seen, or what your Imagination can conceive."

This power established her as the leading lady in the Duke's Company, playing opposite Betterton, and it was for this combination that Otway (who was reputedly obsessed by Barry) wrote *Venice Preserved*. Belvidera was the second of her great roles where "the softer passions" moved her audience to tears, and Isabella in *The Fatal Marriage* was the third.

Pathos, however, was not the sum and substance of her skill. Control, charm, and variety feature in accounts of her performances, which ranged from heroic tragedy to comedy. She was the original Lady Touchwood in *The Double Dealer*, Lady Brute in *The Provoked Wife*, and Mrs Marwood in *The Way of the World*. Anthony Aston records that in comedy her gestures were full of variety and that she was alert, easy, and genteel. No doubt she made use in her more mature comic roles of what Edmund Curll described as that "peculiar Smile which made her look the most genteely malicious Person that can be imagined". But it was in serious drama, in Dryden, Lee, and Otway, that she excelled. "In Scenes of Anger, Defiance, or Resentment, while she was impetuous and terrible, she pour'd out the Sentiment with an enchanting Harmony", as Cibber enthused. When jealous, as Roxana in Lee's *The Rival Queens*, she "seemed to feel a Fever within, which by Debate and Reason she would quench. This was not done in a ranting Air, but as if she were struggling with her Passions, and trying to get the Mastery of them". The emotional intensity of her acting was disturbing, but Barry always kept control and shaped her characterizations so that they remained believable.

Contrast appears to have been an important part of this shaping, as John Dennis highlighted when praising her performance in his heroic drama *Liberty Asserted*, set among Canadian Indians: "That incomparable Actress changing like Nature which she represents, from Passion to Passion, from Extream to Extream, with piercing Force, and with easie Grace, changes the Hearts of all who see her with irresistible Pleasure". The ease and penetration were presumably due to a careful balance between artistry and spontaneity. Barry herself is said to have given the advice that in acting one must thoroughly enter into the part, acquainting oneself with the person one is to represent, but then one must "leave the Figure and Action to Nature". Notions of "nature" and "naturalness" in accounts of acting are notoriously slippery, bound up as they are in social constructs of the time, but it is clear that there was something in her manner of personation that sprang from an open but *total* absorption in the time and place of each performance. As Gildon quotes Betterton as saying: "I have frequently observed her change her countenance several times as the discourse of others on the stage have affected her in the part she acted. This is being thoroughly concern'd, this is to know her part, this is to express the passions in the countenance and gesture." It is a quality that distinguishes the "Grace", "Harmony", and "elevated Dignity" ascribed to her style from the formality and vocal affectation that was such a feature on the stage during the first half of the 18th century. It was a quality that, in her time, transformed her appearance, for offstage she was "indifferent plump" and "not handsome" (a fact that many a satire or discourse capitalized on, one concluding that she was "the finest woman in the world upon the stage, and the ugliest woman off on't"). Above all, it is the quality that made her the first great English actress.

—Leslie du S. Read

———

BARRY, Spranger. Irish actor-manager. Born in Dublin, c.20 November 1719. Trained as apprentice silversmith in father's business, until his bankruptcy. Married 1) Anne (died c.1750), two sons; 2) Ann Dancer in 1768. Stage debut, Smock Alley Theatre, Dublin, 1744; first appearance at Theatre Royal, Drury Lane, London, 1746; acted with Charles Macklin, David Garrick, and Peg Woffington, particularly acclaimed in the role of lover; engaged at Covent Garden, in direct rivalry with Garrick, 1750–58; actor, Smock Alley Theatre, 1754–55; ruined financially by costs of building and managing Crow Street Theatre, Dublin, 1755–58; returned to London, acting at the King's Theatre, the Haymarket, and at Drury Lane, 1766; appearances restricted by ill health from 1770; engaged at Covent Garden, from 1774; last appearance, 1776. Died in London, 10 January 1777.

Principal roles

1744   Othello in *Othello* (Shakespeare), Smock Alley Theatre, Dublin, and Aungier Street Theatre, Dublin; Theatre Royal, Drury Lane, London, 1746; King's Theatre, London, 1766; Theatre Royal, Drury Lane, London, 1767.

Pierre (and later Jaffeir) in *Venice Preserved* (Otway), Smock Alley Theatre, Dublin; revived there, 1745–46; Theatre Royal, Drury Lane, London, 1747; Covent Garden, London, 1751 and 1752.

Varennes in *Theodosius* (Lee), Smock Alley Theatre, Dublin; revived there, 1745–46; Theatre Royal, Drury Lane, London, 1746.

1745–46   Bajazet in *Tamerlane* (Rowe), Smock Alley Theatre, Dublin; Theatre Royal, Drury Lane, London, 1747–48.

Castalio in *The Orphan* (Otway), Smock Alley Theatre, Dublin; Theatre Royal, Drury Lane, London, 1746 and 1747.

Antony in *All for Love* (Dryden), Smock Alley Theatre, Dublin; Theatre Royal, Drury Lane, London, 1747.

Torrismond in *The Spanish Friar* (Dryden), Smock Alley Theatre, Dublin.

Edgar in *King Lear* (Shakespeare), Smock Alley Theatre, Dublin.

Orestes in *The Distresst Mother* (Racine), Smock Alley Theatre, Dublin; Theatre Royal, Drury Lane, London, 1747–48.

Altamont in *The Fair Penitent* (Rowe), Smock Alley Theatre, Dublin.

Hotspur in *Henry IV, part 1* (Shakespeare), Smock Alley Theatre, Dublin; Theatre Royal, Drury Lane, London, 1747.

Oroonoko in *Oroonoko* (Southerne), Smock Alley Theatre, Dublin; Covent Garden, London, 1751.

1746   Macbeth in *Macbeth* (Shakespeare), Theatre Royal, Drury Lane, London; revived there, 1747.

1747   Lord Townly in *The Provoked Husband* (Cibber and Vanbrugh), Theatre Royal, Drury Lane, London.

Henry in *Henry V* (Shakespeare), Theatre Royal, Drury Lane, London; Covent Garden, London, c.1750–54.

Bevil Junior in *The Conscious Lovers* (Steele), Theatre Royal, Drury Lane, London.

Hamlet in *Hamlet* (Shakespeare), Theatre Royal, Drury Lane, London; Crow Street Theatre, Dublin, 1758.

Julius Caesar in *Julius Caesar* (Shakespeare), Theatre Royal, Drury Lane, London.

Hastings and Dumont in *Jane Shore* (Rowe), Theatre Royal, Drury Lane, London; Covent Garden, London, 1752.

Lothario and Horatio in *The Fair Penitent* (Rowe), Theatre Royal, Drury Lane, London; Covent Garden, London, 1751; Theatre Royal, Drury Lane, London, 1771.

1748   Sir Charles Raymond in *The Foundling* (Moore), Theatre Royal, Drury Lane, London.

Romeo in *Romeo and Juliet* (Shakespeare), Theatre Royal, Drury Lane, London; Covent Garden, London, 1750.

1749   Mahomet in *Mahomet and Irene* (Johnson), Theatre Royal, Drury Lane, London.

1751   Phocyas in *The Siege of Damascus* (Hughes), Covent Garden, London; Theatre Royal, Drury Lane, London, 1770.

Philip the Bastard in *King John* (Shakespeare), Covent Garden, London.

1752   Osmyn in *Zara* (Voltaire, adapted by Hill), Covent Garden, London.

1753   Essex in *The Earl of Essex* (Jones), Covent Garden, London.

1756   Alexander in *The Rival Queens* (Cibber), Covent Garden, London.

Lear in *King Lear* (Shakespeare), Covent Garden, London; Haymarket Theatre, London, 1766–67; Theatre Royal, Drury Lane, London, 1769.

Busiris in *Busiris, King of Egypt* (Young), Covent Garden, London.

Osmyn in *The Mourning Bride* (Congreve), Covent Garden, London.

1757   Douglas in *Douglas* (Home), Covent Garden, London.

1766–67   Macheath in *The Beggar's Opera* (Gay), Haymarket Theatre, London.

1768   Rhadamistus in *Zenobia* (Murphy), Theatre Royal, Drury Lane, London.

1771   Timon in *Timon of Athens* (Shakespeare, adapted by Cumberland), Theatre Royal, Drury Lane, London.

1772   Evander in *The Grecian Daughter* (Murphy), Theatre Royal, Drury Lane, London; Edinburgh and Covent Garden, London (his last appearance), 1776.

1774   Lusignan in *Zara* (Garrick, adapted from Hill), Covent Garden, London.

Jaques in *As You Like It* (Shakespeare), Covent Garden, London.

1775   Sciolto in *The Fair Penitent* (Rowe), Covent Garden, London.

Selim in *Edward and Eleonora* (Thomson), Covent Garden, London.

1776   Old Norval in *Douglas* (Home), Covent Garden, London.

Orellan in *The Fatal Discovery* (Home), Covent Garden, London.

*

Bibliography

Books:
I. Wenman, *Mr Barry in the Character of Othello*, London, 1777.
Nancy E. Copeland, *Spranger Barry, Garrick's "Great Rival"* (thesis), University of Toronto, 1985.

* * *

In theatrical histories the third quarter of the 18th century is known, inevitably, as The Age of Garrick — a deserved tribute to a great actor and innovator. But in his own day Garrick was rivalled in the Shakespearean repertoire at least by his slightly younger contemporary Spranger Barry. Like that other brilliant Irishman Charles Macklin, Barry was a gifted exponent of the major tragic roles. He did not have the range of Garrick, who excelled in comedy as in tragedy, but as Romeo, Antony, Othello, and Lear, Barry was in his natural element and as leading actor at Covent Garden in the 1750's he supplied strong opposition to Garrick at Drury Lane.

Observers agree in identifying Barry's virtues: noble bearing, richness of voice, and expressiveness of feature. Those characteristics suited him admirably when he came to play Othello or Lear, though the truculence, energy, and jocularity of Philip the Bastard in *King John* were not within his grasp. Harold Child states flatly that as Philip "Barry failed . . . he showed no ease, humour, gaiety, or gallantry". Much more suited to him was the grandeur of Henry V, one of many parts he played at both Drury Lane and Covent Garden.

It was in tragedy that Barry came into his own. Here it is evident that he was a competitor of Garrick but also a beneficiary who had gained from his example. Garrick had been primarily responsible for supplanting the declamatory manner and studied recitative practised by actors of the old school represented by James Quin. Barry had a debt of a more particular kind, for as a member of the Drury Lane company in the 1740s he had learned a good deal from playing opposite Garrick. C. B. Young notes that as Romeo he "owed his finest strokes to his previous pupillage in tragic parts under Garrick". Garrick, indeed, had allowed Barry to play the role at Drury Lane in 1748 to Mrs Cibber's Juliet — a valuable rehearsal for Barry's Covent Garden appearances, when he and Garrick starred simultaneously in rival productions of the play at the two theatres. The competition between the two actors attracted much attention at the time. Cecil Price records that: "Barry was said to excel in the first three acts, and Garrick in the last two. Mrs Pritchard declared that Garrick's passion was so fiery that she expected to see him climbing up to the balcony, but Barry's voice was so winning that she knew she would have gone down to greet him".

Barry and Mrs Cibber must indeed have been an "incomparable pair of lovers". If Garrick possessed the vivacity and fire, Barry had the keen diction, vocal finesse, and handsome presence. In 1766 he returned to the Garrick fold, playing his last Romeo two years later at the age of 49 (Garrick had given up the part in 1761). It was a long inhabiting of a role for which his gifts were completely suited.

Barry was a celebrated Othello, being well equipped to convey the nobility, grandeur, and anguish of the Moor. Contemporary descriptions indicate the power and musical expressivity of his voice and his capacity to rise to the great moments. John Hill, in *The Actor* (1755), recorded his delivery of the ferocious vow in the fifth act: "When Othello says 'Had all his hairs been lives my great revenge had stomach for them all' we see Mr Barry redden thro' the very black of his face; his whole visage becomes inflamed; his eyes sparkle with successful vengeance, and he seems to raise himself above the ground while he pronounces it." This was undoubtedly an occasion on which Barry surpassed the great Garrick. His Lear, however, received rather faint praise from Thomas Davies in his *Life of Garrick* (1781), in which he compared Barry's "very respectable" account with Garrick's "perfect exhibition". Barry was at any rate content to understudy Garrick's Lear after returning to the Lane. He also played Timon, but this was in Richard Cumberland's adaptation, in which Timon's affairs are subordinated to the love-interests involv-

ing his daughter Evanthe. Outside Shakespeare, Barry was a noted Lord Townly in *The Provoked Husband*.

Tate Wilkinson wrote an amusing account of the contrasts between old and new style playing while describing a 1747 Covent Garden production of *The Orphan*, which assembled from the older generation Quin and Ryan and from the younger Barry and Mrs Cibber. In the midst of the resulting absurdities and incongruities that Wilkinson depicts, he gives a pleasing glimpse of the 28-year-old Barry: "Old Ryan was the strong and lusty Polydore, with a red face, and voice truly horrible . . . not near so well dressed as Quin's Chamont, though in much the same extraordinary manner; and by them stood Mr Barry in Castalio, in a neat bag wig . . . in his bloom and prime of life".

There are certain performers who leave behind an impress of personality, a suggestion of grace and amiability. Such a performer was Spranger Barry — "one of the handsomest men ever seen on or off the stage".

—Charles Calder

BARRYMORE, Ethel. US actress and manager. Born Edith Blythe Barrymore in Philadelphia, Pennsylvania, 15 August 1879; sister of Lionel and John Barrymore. Married Russell Griswold Colt (divorced), two sons and one daughter. Stage debut, Empire Theatre, New York, 1894; subsequently trained under her grandmother Mrs John Drew and her uncle John Drew and also under Sir Henry Irving in England, 1897–98; admired opposite Irving in *The Bells*, 1897; won immediate acclaim on appearing in her first leading role on Broadway, 1901; film debut, 1914; Ethel Barrymore Theatre, New York, opened 1928; concentrated on film career from 1944; also performed on radio and television. Recipient: Oscar, 1944. Died in Hollywood, California, 18 June 1959.

Roles

1894	Julia in *The Rivals* (Sheridan), Empire Theatre, New York.
	Kate Fennell in *The Bauble Shop* (Jones), Empire Theatre, New York.
1895	Katherine in *That Imprudent Young Couple*, Empire Theatre, New York.
1896	Zoë in *The Squire of Dames* (Carton), Palmer's Theatre, New York.
	Priscilla in *Rosemary* (Parker and Carson), Empire Theatre, New York.
1897	Miss Kittridge in *Secret Service* (Gillette), Adelphi Theatre, London.
	Annette in *The Bells* (Lewis), English tour.
1898	Euphrosine in *Peter the Great* (L. Irving), Lyceum Theatre, London.
	Madeleine in *Catherine*, Garrick Theatre, London.
1900	Stella de Gex in *His Excellency the Governor* (Marshall), Garrick Theatre, New York.
1901	Madame Trentoni in *Captain Jinks of the Horse Marines* (Fitch), Garrick Theatre, New York; revived, 1906.

1901–03   Carrots in *Carrots* (Sutro), New York.
           Angela Muir in *A Country Mouse* (Law), New York.
1903   Kate Curtis in *Cousin Kate* (Davies), New York.
           Sunday in *Sunday* (Raceward), New York.
           Gwendolyn Cobb in *The Painful Predicament of Sherlock Holmes*.
           Nora Helmer in *A Doll's House* (Ibsen), New York.
           Mrs Grey in *Alice-Sit-by-the-Fire* (Barrie), New York; tour, 1905–06.
1904   Cynthia in *Cynthia* (Davies), Wyndham's Theatre, London.
1907   Mrs Jones in *The Silver Box* (Galsworthy), Empire Theatre, New York.
1908   Lady Frederick in *Lady Frederick* (Maugham), Hudson Theatre, New York.
1910   Zoë Blundell in *Mid-Channel* (Pinero), Empire Theatre, New York, and tour.
1911   Rose Trelawney in *Trelawney of the Wells* (Pinero), Empire Theatre, New York.
           Kate in *The Twelve Pound Look* (Barrie), Empire Theatre, New York.
           Stella Ballantyne in *The Witness for the Defence* (Mason), Trenton, New Jersey, and Empire Theatre, New York.
1912   Kate Spencer in *Cousin Kate* (Davies), Empire Theatre, New York.
1913   Madame Okraska in *Tante*, Empire Theatre, New York.
1914   Suzanne de Ruseville in *A Scrap of Paper* (Simpson), New York.
1915   Berthe Tregnier in *The Shadow*, Empire Theatre, New York.
           Emma McChesney in *Our Mrs McChesney*, Lyceum Theatre, New York; tour, 1916–17.
1917   Marguerite Gautier in *The Lady of the Camelias* (Dumas), Empire Theatre, New York.
1918   Lady Cardonnell in *The Off-Chance*, New York.
           Belinda Barrington in *Belinda* (Milne), New York.
1919   Lady Helen Haden in *Déclassé*, New York; tour, 1920–21.
1921   The Queen in *Clair de Lune*, Empire Theatre, New York.
1922   Rose Bernd in *Rose Bernd* (Hauptmann), Longacre Theatre, New York.
           Juliet in *Romeo and Juliet* (Shakespeare), New York.
1923   Lady Marjorie Colladine in *The Laughing Lady* (Sutro), New York.
           Lady Teazle in *The School for Scandal* (Sheridan), Lyceum Theatre, New York.
           Princess Amelia in *A Royal Fandango*, Plymouth Theatre, New York.
1924   Paula in *The Second Mrs Tanqueray* (Pinero), Cort Theatre, New York.
1925   Ophelia in *Hamlet* (Shakespeare), Hampden's Theatre, New York.
           Portia in *The Merchant of Venice* (Shakespeare), Hampden's Theatre, New York.

Ethel Barrymore (1952).

1926   Constance Middleton in *The Constant Wife* (Maugham), Maxine Elliott Theatre, New York, and tour.
1928   Sister Gracia in *The Kingdom of God* (Sierra), Ethel Barrymore Theatre, New York.
1929   She in *The Love Duel*, New York.
1930   Sister Mary in *Scarlet Sister Mary*, New York.
1938   Gran in *Whiteoaks* (De la Roche), New York.
1940   Miss Moffat in *The Corn is Green* (Williams), New York.

Other roles included: *Miss Civilization*, New York, 1903, and Palace Theatre, New York, 1913; *Her Sister* (Fitch and Gordon-Lennox), tour and Hudson Theatre, New York, 1907; *A Slice of Life* (Barrie), Empire Theatre, New York, 1912; *Drifting Apart* (Herne), tour, 1914.

Films

The Nightingale, 1914; *The Final Judgement*, 1915; *The Awakening of Helen Ritchie*, 1916; *Kiss of Hate*, 1916; *The White Raven*, 1917; *The Lifted Veil*, 1917; *The Eternal Mother*, 1917; *The American Widow*, 1917; *Life's Whirlpool*, 1917; *The Call of Her People*, 1917; *Our Miss Chesney*, 1918; *The Divorcee*, 1919; *Rasputin and the Empress*, 1932; *None but the Lonely Heart*, 1944; *The Spiral Staircase*, 1946; *The Farmer's Daughter*, 1947; *Moss Rose*, 1947; *The Paradine Case*, 1948; *Night Song*, 1948; *Moonrise*, 1949; *Portrait of Jennie*, 1949; *The Great*

Sinner, 1949; *That Midnight Kiss*, 1949; *Pinky*, 1949; *The Red Danube*, 1949; *The Secret of Convict Lake*, 1951; *Kind Lady*, 1951; *It's a Big Country*, 1952; *Deadline*, 1952; *Just for You*, 1952; *The Story of Three Loves*, 1953; *Main Street to Broadway*, 1953; *Young at Heart*, 1954; *Johnny Trouble*, 1957.

Publications

Memories, 1956.

*

Bibliography

Books:
Lionel Barrymore, *We Barrymores*, New York, 1951.
Hollis Alpert, *The Barrymores*, New York, 1964.
James Kotsilibas-Davis, *The Barrymores: The Royal Family in Hollywood*, New York, 1981.

* * *

It is hard to perceive from the surviving evidence of Ethel Barrymore's screen appearances the full strength of her talents as a stage actress. In contrast to her brother John, who concentrated much more upon his film career, Ethel Barrymore abandoned the cinema altogether after making a number of silent films of generally only passing interest, and made only one screen appearance — alongside her brothers in *Rasputin* (the only time all three acted together in front of the cameras) — between 1919 and 1944. Relatively late in life she returned to the cinema and became a Hollywood favourite, specialising in cantakerous but warmhearted old ladies and picking up an Oscar for her performance in *None but the Lonely Heart* — but history suggests that she was past her prime by this late stage in her career.

As an actress on Broadway, however, Ethel Barrymore was one of the legends of her generation. Her physical beauty in her youth (preserved in still photographs from her early roles) and her regal bearing did much to promote the image of the Barrymores as the "royal family" of the US stage and screen, and she was the quintessence of "glamour" to audiences and social commentators on both sides of the Atlantic in the first decade of the century. The term "glamour girl" was invented specifically in reference to her. Aspiring young men in the highest circles competed for her favours and the young Winston Churchill was one of the suitors whose proposal of marriage was politely declined.

In fact, before achieving such heady success she had served several years as a performer in supporting roles under the tutelage of her grandmother, Mrs John Drew, and her uncle, John Drew, and also had some education as an actress under Henry Irving, before she was finally entrusted with leading roles. English audiences applauded her to the echo for her performances opposite Irving in *The Bells* in 1897, but it was her performance in Fitch's *Captain Jinks of the Horse Marines* (1901) that established her as a major star on Broadway, before either of her brothers had made their mark. Subsequently she employed her beauty and intelligence to maximum effect in a wide range of plays, from Ibsen and Shakespeare to Pinero and Dumas

fils. Under the experienced guidance of manager Charles Frohman, many roles she played were tailor-made for her and were in reality little more than star vehicles, examples including the title role in *Cousin Kate* and parts in such forgotten successes as *Alice-Sit-By-the-Fire* and *Lady Frederick*. That Barrymore was more than just a pretty face was, though, proved beyond doubt by her repeated triumphs in such challenging roles as Portia and Juliet, and she was also much admired in classic comedy parts like Lady Teazle. Critics were almost unanimous in their praise of her characterisations, voicing the public's adulation and highlighting by turn her beauty, her intelligent reading of her roles and her fluid, graceful movement on stage.

The opening of the Ethel Barrymore Theatre in 1928 provided a permanent monument to her status in the American theatre and the inaugural production appropriately showcased the star herself in Martinez Sierra's *The Kingdom of God*, in which she portrayed three ages of woman. By now firmly established as the "First Lady of the American Theatre", she gradually switched to more mature roles by the 1930's and began, perhaps wisely as her looks faded to a more homely elegance, to concentrate on the roles of truculent but appealing dowagers and mothers. Perhaps her last significant stage role was that of Miss Moffat in Emlyn Williams's *The Corn is Green* (1940), and she continued to play variations of this character in various guises throughout her Indian summer as a Hollywood character actress.

The film legacy Ethel Barrymore left behind may not be adequate as a memento of her stage achievements, but as the actress herself observed: "We who play, who entertain for a few years, what can we leave that will last?" Her reputation, however, has long outlived her, while the image of her youth remains the epitome of the star fin-de-siècle actress.

—David Pickering

———

BARRYMORE, John (Sydney Blythe). US actor. Born in Philadelphia, 15 February 1882, into the theatrical Drew-Barrymore family; brother of Ethel Barrymore (q.v.). Educated at the Georgetown Academy, Philadelphia; Seton Hall Academy, East Orange, New Jersey, until 1897; King's College, Wimbledon, London, 1897–98; Slade School of Art, London, 1898. Married 1) Katherine Corri Harris in 1910 (divorced 1917); 2) poet "Michael Strange" (Blanche Thomas; née Oelrichs) in 1920 (divorced 1928), one daughter; 3) actress Dolores Costello in 1928 (divorced 1935), one son; 4) Elaine Barry Jacobs in 1936 (divorced 1941). Stage debut, Cleveland's Theatre, Chicago, October 1903; New York debut at the Savoy Theatre, December 1903; first London appearance, Comedy Theatre, 1905; film debut, 1912; acclaimed as stage Hamlet, 1922; left the stage for Hollywood, 1925; concentrated on film career, 1926–38, before returning to stage in 1939; formed radio comedy partnership with Rudy Vallee, 1937; health in decline, as a result of alcoholism, from the early 1930's. Died in Los Angeles, California, 29 May 1942.

Roles

1903   Max in *Magda* (Parker), Cleveland's Theatre, Chicago, and US tour.
Corley in *Glad of It* (Fitch), Savoy Theatre, New York.

1904   Polk in *Glad of It* (Fitch), Savoy Theatre, New York.
Charley Hine in *The Dictator* (Davis), Criterion Theatre, New York.
Signor Valreali in *Yvette*, Knickerbocker Theatre, New York; tour of Australia and England, 1905.

1905   Jackey in *Sunday* (Raceward), US tour.
Clown in *Pantaloon* (Barrie), Criterion Theatre, New York.
Stephen Rollo in *Alice Sit by-the-Fire* (Barrie), Criterion Theatre, New York.

1906   Brick Meakin in *Miss Civilisation* (Davis), Broadway Theatre, New York.

1907   Tony Allen in *The Boys of Company B* (Young), Lyceum Theatre, New York, and US tour.

1908   Lord Meadows in *Toddles* (Fitch), Savoy Theatre, New York.
Mac in *A Stubborn Cinderella*, Chicago; Broadway Theatre, New York, 1909.

1909   Jack Sweet in *The Candy Shop*, Knickerbocker Theatre, New York.
Nathaniel Duncan in *The Fortune Hunter* (Gilbert), Gaiety Theatre, New York; US tour, 1910–11.

1911   Robert Hudson in *Uncle Sam* (Shipman and Hoffman), Reading, Pennsylvania, and Liberty Theatre, New York.
Pete in *Princess Zim-Zim*, US tour.

1912   Mr. Hyphen-Brown in *A Slice of Life* (Barrie), Empire Theatre, New York.
Anatol in *The Affairs of Anatol* (Schnitzler), Little Theatre, New York.

1913   Robert E. W. Pitt in *A Thief for a Night* (Stapleton and Wodehouse), McVicker's Theatre, Chicago.
George MacFarland in *Believe Me Xantippe* (Ballard), 39th Street Theatre, New York, and US tour.

1914   Julian Rolfe in *The Yellow Ticket* (Morton), Eltinge Theatre, New York, and US tour.
Chick Hewes in *Kick In* (Mack), Longacre Theatre, New York.

1916   William Falder in *Justice* (Galsworthy), Candler Theatre, New York.

1917   Peter Ibbetson in *Peter Ibbetson* (G. Du Maurier), Republic Theatre, New York, and US tour.

1918   Fedor Vasilyevich Protosov in *Redemption* (Tolstoy), Plymouth Theatre, New York.

1919   Gianette Malespini in *The Jest* (Carson and Parker), Plymouth Theatre, New York.

1920   Richard in *Richard III* (Shakespeare), Plymouth Theatre, New York.

1921   Gwymplane in *Clair de Lune* (Strange), Empire Theatre, New York.

1922   Hamlet in *Hamlet* (Shakespeare), Sam H. Harris Theatre, New York; US tour, 1923–24; Haymarket Theatre, London, 1925.

1939   Allan Manville in *My Dear Children*, McCarter Theatre, Princeton, New Jersey, and US tour; Belasco Theatre, New York, 1940.

Other roles included: *The Dictator* (Davis), Australian tour, 1906; *Half a Husband*, Shubert Theatre, Rochester, New York, and US tour, 1912.

Films

The Dictator, 1912; *An American Citizen*, 1914; *The Man from Music*, 1914; *Are You a Mason?*, 1915; *The Director*, 1915; *The Incorrigible Dukane*, 1915; *Nearly a King*, 1916; *The Lost Bridegroom*, 1916; *The Man from Mexico*, 1916; *The Red Widow*, 1916; *Raffles, the Amateur Cracksman*, 1917; *On the Quiet*, 1918; *Here Comes the Bride*, 1919; *The Test of Honor*, 1919; *Dr Jekyll and Mr Hyde*, 1920; *The Lotus Eater*, 1921; *Sherlock Holmes*, 1922; *Beau Brummell*, 1924; *The Sea Beast*, 1926; *Don Juan*, 1926; *When a Man Loves (His Lady)*, 1927; *The Beloved Rogue*, 1927; *Twenty Minutes at Warner Brothers Studios*, 1927; *Tempest*, 1928; *Eternal Love*, 1929; *Song of Songs*, 1929; *The Show of Shows*, 1930; *General Crack*, 1930; *The Man from Blankley's*, 1930; *Moby Dick*, 1930; *Svengali*, 1931; *The Mad Genius*, 1931; *Arsène Lupin*, 1932; *Grand Hotel*, 1932; *State's Attorney (Cardigan's Last Case)*, 1932; *A Bill of Divorcement*, 1932; *Rasputin and the Empress (Rasputin the Mad Monk)*, 1932; *Topaze*, 1933; *Reunion in Vienna*, 1933; *Dinner at Eight*, 1933; *Night Flight*, 1933; *Counsellor-at-Law*, 1934; *Long Lost Father*, 1934; *Twentieth Century*, 1934; *Romeo and Juliet*, 1936; *Maytime*, 1937; *Bulldog Drummond Comes Back*, 1937; *Night Club Scandal*, 1937; *Bulldog Drummond's Revenge*, 1937; *True Confession*, 1937; *Romance in the Dark*, 1938; *Bulldog Drummond's Peril*, 1938; *Marie Antoinette*, 1938; *Spawn of the North*, 1938; *Hold that Co-ed (Hold that Gal)*, 1938; *The Great Man Votes*, 1939; *Midnight*, 1939; *The Great Profile*, 1941; *The Invisible Woman*, 1941; *World Premiere*, 1941; *Playmates*, 1941; *Screen Snapshots No. 107*, 1942.

Publications

Confessions of an Actor, 1926; *We Three: Ethel — Lionel — John*, 1935.

*

Bibliography

Books:
Alma Power-Waters, *John Barrymore, The Legend and the Man*, New York, 1941.
Gene Fowler, *Good Night, Sweet Prince: The Life and Times of John Barrymore*, New York, 1944.
Lionel Barrymore, *We Barrymores*, New York, 1951.
Ethel Barrymore, *Memories*, New York, 1956.
James Card, *The Films of John Barrymore*, Rochester, New York, 1969.

John Barrymore

Spencer M. Berger, *Tribute to John Barrymore*, Rochester, New York, 1969.

Hollis Alpert, *The Barrymores*, New York, 1969.

John Koblen, *Damned in Paradise: The Life of John Barrymore*, New York, 1977.

James Kotsilibas-Davis, *The Barrymores: The Royal Family in Hollywood*, New York, 1981.

* * *

John Barrymore first established a reputation as an actor in light comedy. His striking looks made him the matinée idol of the day (he was dubbed "The Great Profile"). At this stage, Garson Kanin recalls, he worked superficially, "using no more than the tip of his talent ... But despite his lack of drive, he was soon building a reputation as a charming, expert, sure-fire *farceur*, who connected magically with audiences from the moment of every entrance".

It was the playwright Edward Sheldon who urged Barrymore to test his ability beyond comedy roles. "In fact", Barrymore admitted, "I'm not sure that he didn't make me a serious actor". His appearance as the tragic clerk in John Galsworthy's *Justice* was a revelation. *The New York Times* wrote: "For Barrymore the first night of *Justice* was a milestone. By his simple, eloquent, deeply touching performance as young Falder, he arrested the attention of the city and gained overnight a prestige ... which all his work in trivial entertainment would not give him. This comes now to a player whose years in the theatre have been lackadaisical".

It was Sheldon, again, who encouraged Barrymore to take on classical roles. On a visit to the Bronx zoo, they stopped to observe a red tarantula with a grey bald spot on its back. "It was peculiarly sinister and evil looking", Barrymore recalled, "the personification of a crawling power. I said to Sheldon: 'It looks just like Richard III'. 'Why don't you play it?' was his only comment".

Barrymore's voice at this time was slightly nasal; it lacked range and his diction was slipshod. To prepare for Richard, Barrymore trained with Margaret Carrington, a retired opera singer. They worked incessantly for six weeks, not only on voice and breath control, but also on text. The final transformation of Barrymore, from matinée idol to the USA's leading classical actor, was to a considerable extent due to Carrington's training.

As Richard, Barrymore was "unforgettable", as the director Arthur Hopkins later testified. "He had fire, humour, beauty, cajolery, chilling cruelty. Shakespeare tragedy, for the first time in that period, became thrillingly alive". Barrymore himself felt this was "the first genuine acting I ever managed to achieve, and perhaps my own best. It was the first time I ever actually got inside the character I was playing".

The performance revealed Barrymore's delight in transforming himself physically. He "glided across the stage like some unearthly spider" Gene Fowler observed. Asked how he achieved this effect, he replied: "I merely turned my right foot inward, pointing it towards the instep of my left foot. I let it stay in that position and then forgot all about it. I did not try to walk badly, I walked as *well* as I could".

At the same time as he was playing Richard, Barrymore was filming *Dr Jekyll and Mr Hyde*. As Hyde, he "managed the most striking malformation of his body and face, often without the benefit of make-up", Hollis Alpert notes. "It was as though he did the utmost to distort his handsome features into the most fearsome ugliness". Barrymore himself observed: "The only time I'm at ease is when I can bury this damned profile beneath false whiskers, putty noses, and pasteboard foreheads. I need a barrier — something to hide behind".

Barrymore's performance as Hamlet caused a sensation. "Careless and indeed ignorant of tradition", wrote Robert Speaight, "Barrymore acted the part as if he had never even read the play before". This was not the conventional "sweet prince". Reviewing the London revival, *The Times* wrote: "the aim of all actors we have ever seen in *Hamlet* has been to slur over the mysterious parts and to smooth down the strangeness; their tendency has been to put before us not so much the queer Hamlet as a plausible Hamlet. The distinction of the new American Hamlet is, that he makes the queerness plausible".

The performance was a mixture of naturalism and bravura. It was "tremendously athletic" — "See him gyrate like a top in the play scene! See him take a running jump at the King at the end!" The closet scene with Gertrude was played as if it was a love scene — a reading that was both novel and daring for the time. Some critics, however, felt that Barrymore's prince lacked warmth. George Jean Nathan said it was "glittering, vari-coloured, brilliant — but cold, intensely cold. We get from it the reflected rays of intelligence, but never — or at best rarely — the rays of heat".

After the London production in 1925, Barrymore quit the stage. He was drawn by the greater financial rewards of

Hollywood — but was also, perhaps, exhausted by the demands he made of himself as a performer. Constance Collier (who played the Queen in London) observed: "He gave so much of himself to every performance that each one seemed a chip off his life. He was really obsessed when on stage".

Barrymore's personality in some ways overshadowed his acting. He was notorious for his behaviour offstage, and sometimes on. He hated coughing in the audience and would reprimand offenders. Once, during a performance of *Peter Ibbetson*, a spotlight was misdirected onto Barrymore's feet instead of his face; he left the stage, knocked the hapless lighting operator to the ground, and returned in time to pick up his next cue and continue the scene.

Many years of heavy drinking finally began to take their toll. His unreliability caused a rapid decline in his film career. He began to forget his lines; for one scene in *Counsellor-at-Law* in 1933 he needed over 56 takes. He hoped to film *Hamlet*, but the tests were a disaster. "The trouble with Jack", Charlie Chaplin concluded, "was that he had a naive, romantic, conception of himself as a genius doomed to self-destruction, which he eventually achieved in a vulgar, boisterous way by drinking himself to death".

When he finally returned to the stage in *My Dear Children* in 1939 he was like a caricature of his former self. Audiences went to see him make a fool of himself, and he obliged — peppering the script with his ad-libs, belching, staggering as if drunk. Some of this at least was deliberate (the audience, he said, "have a right to their innocent amusement"). Observing Barrymore's decline, Ashton Stevens commented: "No one can run downhill as fast as a thoroughbred". His health destroyed, he ended his career playing stooge to Rudy Vallee in a popular radio show. On 19 May 1942, while attending a rehearsal for the programme, he collapsed in the dressing-room. He did not recover and died on 29 May.

—David Allen

BARSACQ, André. French designer and director. Born Anatole Sophocle Barsacq in Theodosia, the Crimea, Russia, 24 January 1909. Educated in Paris at the Lycée Henri IV, 1920–25; studied architecture at l'École des Arts Décoratifs, Paris, 1925–26. Military service, 1931. Married Mila Kliatchko in 1929, two sons, two daughters. Emigrated to France with mother, 1919; began collaboration with Charles Dullin at the Théâtre de l'Atelier, Paris, 1927; first stage design, *Volpone* by Ben Jonson, at the Théâtre de l'Atelier, 1928; left Théâtre de l'Atelier to collaborate with Michel Saint-Denis and the Compagnie des Quinze, 1930; first collaboration with Jacques Copeau, 1933; co-founder of the Théâtre des Quatre Saisons, 1936; designed the Théâtre Volant and the Théâtre de Verdure for the l'Exposition Internationale de Paris, 1937; worked with the Compagnie des Quatre Saisons at the French Theatre of New York, 1937–40; toured USA and Brazil, 1938; succeeded Dullin as director of the Théâtre de l'Atelier, 1940; made regular tours of European countries from end of World War II; founded Syndicat National des Metteurs en Scène, 1948, and the Nouveau Cartel with, among others, Jean-Louis Barrault, 1958; co-founder of the "Théâtres Associés", 1962; toured USSR, 1965 and 1971; toured

Egypt, 1966; founder and president of "Théâtre de l'Enfance et la Jeunesse de Paris", 1970; president of the Centre français du Théâtre, 1971. Recipient: Prix Dominique, 1955. Chevalier de la Légion d'Honneur, 1950; Chevalier de l'Ordre des Arts et Lettres, 1959. Died in Paris, 3 February 1973.

Productions

As designer:
1928   *Volpone* (Jonson, adapted by Zweig and Romains), Théâtre de l'Atelier, Paris; designed set and costumes.
1930   *Le Stratagème des Roués* (Constantin-Weyer, adapted from Farquhar), Théâtre de l'Atelier, Paris; designed set and costumes.
         Le Fils de Don Quichotte (Frondaie), Théâtre de l'Atelier, Paris; designed set and costumes.
         Musse ou l'École de l'hypocrisie (Romains), Théâtre de l'Atelier, Paris; designed set and costumes.
         Le Bourgeois de Falaise (Thiriet), Théâtre de l'Opéra-Comique, Paris; designed set.
1931   *Noé* (Obey), Théâtre du Vieux-Colombier, Paris; designed set.
         Le Viol de Lucrèce (Obey), Théâtre du Vieux-Colombier, Paris; designed set and costumes.
         La Bataille de la Marne (Obey), Théâtre du Vieux-Colombier, Paris; designed set.
1933   *Violante* (Ghéon, adapted from Tirso de Molina), Théâtre du Vieux-Colombier, Paris; designed set and costumes.
         Mystère de Santa Uliva (anon.), Santa Croce, Florence; designed set.
1934   *Perséphone* (Gide and Stravinsky), Opéra de Paris; designed set and costumes.
         Sémiramis (Valéry and Honegger), Ballets d'Ida Rubinstein, Opéra de Paris; designed costumes.
1935   *Médecin de son honneur* (Arnoux, adapted from Calderón), Théâtre de l'Atelier, Paris; designed set and costumes.
         Savanarole (Alessi), Piazza Signoria, Florence; designed set.
1936   *Beaucoup de bruit pour rien* (Shakespeare, adapted by Sarment), Théâtre de la Madeleine, Paris; designed set and costumes.
         Napoléon unique (Raynal), Théâtre de la Porte Saint-Martin, Paris; designed set and costumes.
1937   *Un Caprice* (Musset), French Theatre, New York; designed set.
1939   *Les Précieuses ridicules* (Molière), French Theatre of New York; designed set and costumes.
1940   *Lèocadia* (Anouilh), Théâtre de la Michodière, Paris; designed set.

As director:
1937   *Roi Cerf* (Gozzi), Comédie des Champs-Elysées, Paris; also designed set.
         Le Voyage de Monsieur Perrichon (Labiche), French Theatre, New York; also designed set and costumes.

Les 37 sous de Monsieur de Montaudoin (Labiche), French Theatre, New York; also designed set and costumes.

Knock (Romains), French Theatre, New York; also designed set and costumes.

Jean de la lune (Achard), French Theatre, New York; also designed set and costumes.

Nationale 6 (Bernard), French Theatre, New York; also designed set and costumes.

Y'avait un prisonnier (Anouilh), French Theatre, New York; also designed set and costumes.

La Farce des bossus, French Theatre, New York; also designed set and costumes.

Fantasio (Musset), French Theatre of New York.

1938   *Le Bal des voleurs* (Anouilh), Théâtre des Arts, Paris; also designed set and costumes.

Maïe (Purnel), Théâtre des Arts, Paris.

Chacun sa vérité (Pirandello, adapted by Crémieux), French Theatre, New York; also designed set.

1939   *Les Fourberies de Scapin* (Molière), French Theatre, New York; also designed set and costumes.

Siegfried (Giraudoux), French Theatre, New York; also designed set and costumes.

L'Enterrement (Monnier), French Theatre, New York; also designed set and costumes.

1940   *Marie-Jeanne*, (Dennery and Mallian, adapted by Anouilh), Théâtre des Arts, Paris; also designed set.

1941   *Rendez-vous de Senlis* (Anouilh), Théâtre de l'Atelier, Paris; also designed set.

Vêtir ceux qui sont nus (Pirandello), Théâtre de l'Atelier, Paris; also designed set.

Eurydice (Anouilh), Théâtre de l'Atelier, Paris; also designed set.

1942   *Sylvie et le fantôme* (Adam and Beydts), Théâtre de l'Atelier, Paris; also designed set.

1943   *L'Honorable Monsieur Pepys* (Couturier), Théâtre de l'Atelier, Paris; also designed set.

1944   *Antigone* (Anouilh), Théâtre de l'Atelier, Paris; also designed set.

A quoi rêvent les jeunes filles (Musset), Théâtre de l'Atelier, Paris; also designed set.

1945   *Agrippa ou La Folle journée* (Barsacq), Théâtre de l'Atelier, Paris; also designed set.

Frères Karamazov (Dostoevsky, adapted by Copeau and Croué), Théâtre de l'Atelier, Paris; also designed set.

1946   *Roméo et Jeanette* (Anouilh), Théâtre de l'Atelier, Paris; also designed set.

1947   *L'invitation au château* (Anouilh), Théâtre de l'Atelier, Paris; also designed set.

1948   *Revizor* (Gogol, adapted by Barsacq), Théâtre de l'Atelier, Paris.

1949   *Pain dur* (Claudel), Théâtre de l'Atelier, Paris; also designed set.

La Nuit des hommes (Bernard-Luc), Théâtre de l'Atelier, Paris; also designed set.

1950   *Voyageur sans bagage* (Anouilh), Théâtre Montparnasse, Paris; also designed set.

Henry IV (Pirandello), Théâtre de l'Atelier, Paris.

1951   *Colombe* (Anouilh), Théâtre de l'Atelier, Paris; also designed set.

Chéri (Colette and Marchand), Teatro Eliseo, Rome.

1952   *La Tête des autres* (Aymée), Théâtre de l'Atelier, Paris.

1953   *Medea* (Cherubini), Teatro Communale, Florence.

Frères Karamazov (adapted from Dostoevsky), Teatro Eliseo, Rome.

1954   *Quatre vérités* (Aymée), Théâtre de l'Atelier, Paris.

1955   *La Mouette* (Chekhov, adapted by Pitoëff), Théâtre de l'Atelier, Paris.

Oiseaux de lune (Aymée), Théâtre de l'Atelier, Paris.

1956   *L'Oeuf* (Marceau), Théâtre de l'Atelier; Habimah Theatre, Tel Aviv, 1958.

1957   *Les Acteurs de bonne foi* (Marivaux), Théâtre de l'Atelier, Paris.

Le Légataire universel (Regnard), Théâtre de l'Atelier, Paris.

1958   *L'Épouvantail* (Rolin), Théâtre de l'Oeuvre, Paris.

Turcaret (Lesage), Théâtre de l'Atelier, Paris.

La Bonne soupe (Marceau), Théâtre du Gymnase, Paris.

1959   *La Punaise* (Mayakovsky, adapted by Barsacq), Théâtre de l'Atelier, Paris.

Un Beau dimanche de septembre (Betti), Théâtre de l'Atelier, Paris.

Bérénice (Racine), Théâtre du Gymnase, Paris.

Un Demande en mariage (Chekhov), Théâtre de l'Atelier, Paris.

1960   *Château en Suède* (Sagan), Théâtre de l'Atelier, Paris.

La Tosca (Puccini), Opéra de Paris.

L'Étouffe-chrétien (Marceau), Théâtre de la Renaissance, Paris.

1961   *Les Ambassades* (Antoine and Dorian), Théâtre des Bouffes-Parisiens, Paris.

Le Barbier de Séville (Beaumarchais), Théâtre de l'Atelier, Paris.

Les Maxibules (Aymée), Théâtre des Bouffes-Parisiens, Paris.

1962   *L'Avare* (Molière), Théâtre de l'Atelier, Paris.

Les Cailloux (Marceau), Théâtre de l'Atelier, Paris.

La Fourmi dans le corps (Audiberti), Comédie-Française, Paris.

L'Oeuf (Marceau), Flemish Theatre of Brussels.

Frank V (Dürrenmatt), Théâtre de l'Atelier, Paris.

1963   *La Bonne soupe* (Marceau), Théâtre du Parc, Brussels.

Satyre de la Villette (Obaldia), Théâtre de l'Atelier, Paris.

Un Mois à la campagne (Turgenev, adapted by Barsacq), Théâtre de l'Atelier, Paris.

1964   *Les Maxibules* (Aymée), Théâtre du Parc, Brussels.

Monstre Turquin (Gozzi, adapted by Arnaud and Barsacq), Théâtre de l'Atelier, Paris.

1965   *Le tour d'écrou* (Britten), Opéra de Marseille.
Ce Soir on improvise (Pirandello, adapted by Arnaud), Théâtre de l'Atelier, Paris.
Sud (Coe), Opéra de Marseille.
La Provinciale (Turgenev, adapted by Barsacq), Odéon-Théâtre de France, Paris.

1966   *L'Idiot* (Dostoevsky, adapted by Barsacq), Théâtre de l'Atelier, Paris; in Amsterdam, 1967.
Trois Soeurs (Chekhov), Théâtre Hébertot, Paris.

1967   *Un Jour j'ai rencontré la vérité* (Marceau), Comédie des Champs-Elysées, Paris.
Duel (Chekhov, adapted by Barsacq and Couturier), Théâtre de l'Atelier, Paris.
Opéra pour un tyran (Rey), Théâtre de l'Atelier, Paris.
La Giaconda (Ponchielli), Opéra de Marseille.

1968   *Les Chemins de fer* (Labiche), Théâtre de l'Atelier, Paris.
L'Aide-mémoire (Carrière), Théâtre de l'Atelier, Paris.
Siegfried (Giraudoux), Théâtre des Celestins, Lyons.

1969   *Mon destin moqueur* (Chekhov, adapted by Maliouguine and Soria), Théâtre de l'Atelier, Paris.
Le Babour (Marceau), Théâtre de l'Atelier, Paris.

1970   *La Forêt* (Ostrovsky), Théâtre de l'Atelier, Paris.
Madame de . . . (Damase and Anouilh), Opéra de Monte-Carlo.
Un Piano dans l'herbe (Sagan), Théâtre de l'Atelier, Paris.

1971   *Au Bal des chiens* (Foriani), Théâtre de l'Atelier, Paris.
Haggerty, où es-tu? (Mercer, adapted by Dubillard), Théâtre de l'Atelier, Paris.
Doux Oiseau de la jeunesse (T. Williams), Théâtre de l'Atelier, Paris.

1972   *David la nuit tombe* (Kops, adapted by Zerline), Théâtre de l'Atelier, Paris.
Crime et châtiment (Dostoevsky, adapted by Barsacq), Théâtre de l'Atelier, Paris; Kameri Theatre, Tel Aviv.

Other productions included: (as director and designer) *Zamore* (Neveux), 1953; *Jouer* (Betti, adapted by Clavel), 1953; *Caterina* (Marceau), 1954; *Les Fourberies de Scapin* (Molière), 1956.

Films

As designer:
Maldone, 1927; *L'Argent*, 1928; *Gardiens de phare*, 1929; *Le Martyre de l'obèse*, 1932; *Courrier Sud*, 1935; *Yoshiwara*, 1937; *La Comédie du bonheur*, 1939; *L'Honorable Catherine*, 1942; *Lumière d'été*, 1942.

As director:
La Dolorosa (as assistant to Gremillon), 1934; *Le Rideau rouge*, 1952.

Television

As director:
Château en Suède, 1964; *Un Mois à la campagne*, 1965; *Le Roi cerf*, 1966; *L'Idiot*, 1967; *Revizor*, 1969; *Madame de . . .* , 1971; *David la nuit tombe*, 1972; *Les Vilains*, 1972; *Le Babour*, 1972; *Les Oiseaux de lune*, 1972.

Publications

Adaptations:
Le Revizor (adaptation from Gogol), 1949; *La Mouette*, 1955; *Un Mois á la campagne* (adaptation from Turgenev), 1964; *L'Idiot* (adaptation from Dostoevsky), 1966; *La Forêt* (adaptation from Ostrovsky), 1970.

Other:
L'Agrippa (play), 1947; *Le Voyage de Monsieur Perrichon*, 1954.

*

Bibliography

Books:
Marie Françoise Christout, *André Barsacq: Cinquante Ans de Théâtre*, Paris, 1978.

* * *

André Barsacq inherited and developed the tradition of Charles Dullin, an early member of Copeau's company who soon left to set up his own theatre. He had a serious view of the director's art, but felt it should always be put at the service of a text. Dullin called his theatre L'Atelier, because he saw it as an experimental workshop. In 1940 he handed it over to Barsacq, who continued the policy of experimentation, as well as putting on revivals of the classics and his own adaptations of the Russian repertoire.

Barsacq was no doctrinaire theorist. He wrote little about his work and was typically modest in his definition of the director's function, "which simply consists in organising and balancing all the elements of the dramatic work". An instinctive practical man of the theatre, he said that he "always avoided a dangerous excess of abstract researches, preferring to work through human contact".

He began his career as a designer, working with Dullin, Copeau, Michel Saint-Denis, and major film directors of the 1930's such as Max Ophüls. His use of costume and décor continued to be an important element in his success and he designed nearly all his productions into the late 1950's. Later, he collaborated with leading French designers such as Bakst, Allio, and Jacques Noël, while keeping control of the basic stage layout. His simple, elegant designs for Dullin's production of Jonson's *Volpone* in 1929 helped make this into the Atelier's first big box-office success. The Act 1 set had dark red walls criss-crossed with a bold diamond pattern in white with gold arched doors and windows. The simple strong colours are typical of his designs. By way of contrast, for his own production of Labiche's *Le voyage de Monsieur Perrichon*, he used backdrops and flats painted in the style of line drawings to underscore the theatricality of the farce.

Barsacq's first company, the Théâtre des Quatre Saisons, co-founded with Jean Dasté in 1936, was a theatre co-operative aiming to find new audiences in the provinces and to collaborate directly with new young authors. Jean Anouilh saw their first major production, the comedy *Le Roi cerf* by Carlo Gozzi, which charmed and impressed him: the most important partnership in Barsacq's career was set to begin. It was really an equal partnership, especially in the early years. Barsacq tells how Anouilh and himself spent the next summer working on *Le Bal des voleurs*: while he designed the sets and sketched out a productions the author was revising his text. They discussed each other's ideas, surprising people on the beach when they performed a wild dance they had just devised for the comic thieves around whom the play revolves. Anouilh, in his own writings, claimed that they effectively taught each other the art of the theatre. They also rehearsed the company together, agreeing so closely that actors nicknamed them "the twins".

Because Barsacq came to rehearsal with such a detailed vision of the play, and after extensive preparation, he tended to be demanding with actors. Jean Vilar once wrote to him asking to be given more time to find his own interpretation and not to be pushed so hard. Actors did, however, appreciate his enthusiasm and his quiet authority and the list of those who worked with him includes nearly all the great performers of the period, from Pierre Arditi and Jean-Paul Belmondo to Jeanne Moreau, Delphine Seyrig, and Simone Valère. Lacking formal training as an actor himself, he was coached by his co-director Dasté in 1937 and subsequently sometimes took small parts in his own productions.

Barsacq made brilliant use of music in his work. Leading composers collaborated with him on some plays, Poulenc requesting very exact information about timing for *L'Invitation au château*, for instance, in which music was played continually from Act 2 to the final curtain. Similar use was made of a detailed musical score in *Le Bal des voleurs*, on which Milhaud collaborated, with comic characters making entrances and exits to given musical themes.

Although Barsacq was drawn to comedy — it is noticeable that all his revivals of the classics were comedies — his best-known creation is Anouilh's *Antigone* in 1944, which ran for 645 performances. A neutral décor with a semi-circular tier of steps backstage and simple openings for the two doorways gave the play a classical feel, while the use of black and white for both costumes and set echoed the theme of pure idealism against reasonable compromise. Barsacq's decision to put all the characters in evening dress created a somber dignified mood, while placing the action firmly in the present. The guards, in glistening black oilskins over dinner-jackets epitomized for many of the audience the brutal menace of the Nazis and Monelle Valentin's thin tormented features were ideal to set against the solid certainty of Jean Davy as the tyrant Créon.

After the war, Anouilh began to intervene more and more in the production of his work and Barsacq felt his skills were not being used in the partnership. He went on to discover other new playwrights and to "help them to enter the magic world of the theatre". He said this when discussing the first play of Jean-Claude Carrière, *L'Aide-mémoire*, just one writer whose career was effectively launched through involvement with L'Atelier in the 1960's. Other postwar discoveries included Félicien Marceau, whose *L'Oeuf* and *La Bonne Soupe* had long runs, and Françoise Sagan, who acknowledged the director's help in creating her first play, *Château en Suède*, in 1960. It was this readiness to work creatively with dramatists, together with a willingness to take risks, financial and artistic, that were probably the most important elements in Barsacq's contribution to the French theatre.

—John Rothenberg

BARTON, John (Bernard Adie). British director. Born in London, 26 November 1928. Educated at Eton College; King's College, Cambridge, until 1951. Married Anne Righter in 1969. Early theatrical experience with the Marlowe Society and the Amateur Dramatic Club at Cambridge University; first London production, Westminster Theatre, 1953; lecturer in drama, University of California at Berkeley, 1953–54; Fellow of King's College, Cambridge, 1954–59; subsequent theatrical career almost wholly with the Royal Shakespeare Company, as assistant director, from 1960, associate director, 1964–91, company director at Stratford-upon-Avon, 1968–74, and advisory director, from 1991; has also worked as fight director on numerous RSC productions. CBE (Commander of the British Empire), 1981.

Productions

As director:

1952 *Romeo and Juliet* (Shakespeare), Cambridge and Phoenix Theatre, London.

1953 *Henry V* (Shakespeare), Westminster Theatre, London.

1954–59 *Henry IV, parts 1 and 2* (Shakespeare), Cambridge.

    Julius Caesar (Shakespeare), Cambridge.

1960 *The Taming of the Shrew* (Shakespeare), Shakespeare Memorial Theatre, Stratford-upon-Avon.

    Troilus and Cressida (Shakespeare), Shakespeare Memorial Theatre, Stratford-upon-Avon.

1961 *Carmen* (Bizet), Sadler's Wells Theatre, London.

    The Hollow Crown (Shakespeare anthology devised by Barton), Aldwych Theatre, London; also acted; Henry Miller Theatre, New York, 1962.

1962 *The Art of Seduction* (adapted by Barton from *Les Liaisons Dangereuses* by De Laclos), Aldwych Theatre, London; also narrated.

    The Vagaries of Love (devised by Barton), Belgrade Theatre, Coventry; also acted.

1963   *The Wars of the Roses* (adapted and co-directed by Barton from Shakespeare's *Henry VI, parts 1–3* and *Richard III*), Royal Shakespeare Theatre, Stratford-upon-Avon; Aldwych Theatre, London, 1964.

Beatrice et Benedict (Berlioz), Festival Hall, London; also acted.

1964   *Richard II* (Shakespeare; as co-director), Royal Shakespeare Theatre, Stratford-upon-Avon.

Henry IV, parts 1 and 2 (Shakespeare; as co-director), Royal Shakespeare Theatre, Stratford-upon-Avon; revived, 1966.

Henry V (Shakespeare; as co-director), Royal Shakespeare Theatre, Stratford-upon-Avon; Aldwych Theatre, London, 1965; Royal Shakespeare Theatre, Stratford-upon-Avon, 1966.

1965   *Love's Labour's Lost* (Shakespeare), Royal Shakespeare Theatre, Stratford-upon-Avon.

1967   *All's Well that Ends Well* (Shakespeare), Royal Shakespeare Theatre, Stratford-upon-Avon; Aldwych Theatre, London, 1968.

Coriolanus (Shakespeare), Royal Shakespeare Theatre, Stratford-upon-Avon; Aldwych Theatre, London, 1968.

1968   *Julius Caesar* (Shakespeare), Royal Shakespeare Theatre, Stratford-upon-Avon; Aldwych Theatre, London, 1968.

Troilus and Cressida (Shakespeare), Royal Shakespeare Theatre, Stratford-upon-Avon; Aldwych Theatre, London, 1969.

1969   *Twelfth Night* (Shakespeare), Royal Shakespeare Theatre, Stratford-upon-Avon; Aldwych Theatre, London, 1970; Royal Shakespeare Theatre, Stratford-upon-Avon, 1971.

1970   *When Thou Art King* (adapted by Barton from *Henry IV, parts 1 and 2* and *Henry V*), Royal Shakespeare Company Theatregoround, The Roundhouse, London; Aldwych Theatre, London, 1970.

Measure for Measure (Shakespeare), Royal Shakespeare Theatre, Stratford-upon-Avon.

The Tempest (Shakespeare), Royal Shakespeare Theatre, Stratford-upon-Avon; revived, 1971.

1971   *Richard II* (Shakespeare), Royal Shakespeare Company Theatregoround, British tour.

Henry V (Shakespeare), Royal Shakespeare Company Theatregoround, British tour.

Othello (Shakespeare), Royal Shakespeare Theatre, Stratford-upon-Avon; Aldwych Theatre, London, 1972.

Titus Andronicus (Shakespeare; as co-director), Royal Shakespeare Theatre, Stratford-upon-Avon.

1973   *Richard II* (Shakespeare), Royal Shakespeare Theatre, Stratford-upon-Avon; Aldwych Theatre, London, 1974.

1974   *Doctor Faustus* (Marlowe, adapted by Barton), Aldwych Theatre, London.

King John (Shakespeare, adapted and co-directed by Barton), Royal Shakespeare Theatre, Stratford-upon-Avon; Aldwych Theatre, London.

Cymbeline (Shakespeare; as co-director), Royal Shakespeare Theatre, Stratford-upon-Avon; Aldwych Theatre, London.

1975   *Perkin Warbeck* (Ford; as co-director), Other Place, Stratford-upon-Avon.

1976   *Much Ado about Nothing* (Shakespeare), Royal Shakespeare Theatre, Stratford-upon-Avon; Aldwych Theatre, London, 1977.

The Winter's Tale (Shakespeare; as co-director), Royal Shakespeare Theatre, Stratford-upon-Avon.

Troilus and Cressida (Shakespeare; as co-director), Royal Shakespeare Theatre, Stratford-upon-Avon.

King Lear (Shakespeare; as co-director), Royal Shakespeare Theatre, Stratford-upon-Avon.

1977   *A Midsummer Night's Dream* (Shakespeare), Aldwych Theatre, London.

Pillars of the Community (Ibsen), Aldwych Theatre, London.

1978   *The Way of the World* (Congreve), Aldwych Theatre, London.

The Merchant of Venice (Shakespeare), Other Place, Stratford-upon-Avon; Warehouse Theatre, London, 1979.

Love's Labour's Lost (Shakespeare), Royal Shakespeare Theatre, Stratford-upon-Avon; Aldwych Theatre, London, 1979.

1980   *Hamlet* (Shakespeare), Royal Shakespeare Theatre, Stratford-upon-Avon; Aldwych Theatre, London, 1981.

The Greeks (devised by Barton), Aldwych Theatre, London.

1981   *The Merchant of Venice* (Shakespeare), Royal Shakespeare Theatre, Stratford-upon-Avon and Aldwych Theatre, London.

Titus Andronicus (Shakespeare), Royal Shakespeare Theatre, Stratford-upon-Avon.

Two Gentlemen of Verona (Shakespeare), Royal Shakespeare Theatre, Stratford-upon-Avon.

1982   *La Ronde* (Schnitzler), Aldwych Theatre, London.

1983   *The School for Scandal* (Sheridan), Haymarket Theatre, London, and Duke of York's Theatre, London.

Life's a Dream (Calderón), Other Place, Stratford-upon-Avon.

The Vikings at Helgeland (Ibsen, adapted by Barton), Nationale Scene, Bergen, Norway.

1984   *The Devils* (Whiting), The Pit, London.

Waste (Granville-Barker), The Pit, London, and Lyric Theatre, London.

1985   *Dream Play* (Strindberg), The Pit, London.

1986   *The Rover* (Behn, adapted by Barton), Swan Theatre, Stratford-upon-Avon; Mermaid Theatre, London, 1987.

1988   *The Three Sisters* (Chekhov), Barbican Theatre, London.

1989   *Coriolanus* (Shakespeare), Royal Shakespeare Theatre, Stratford-upon-Avon.

1990   *Peer Gynt* (Ibsen), Oslo.
1991   *Measure for Measure* (Shakespeare), Oslo.
         As You Like It (Shakespeare), Oslo.
1994   *Peer Gynt* (Ibsen, adapted by Fry), Swan Theatre, Stratford-upon-Avon.

As adapter only:
1965   *The Peloponnesian War* (from the dialogues of Thucydides and Socrates), Aldwych Theatre, London.
1966   *The Revenger's Tragedy* (Tourneur), Royal Shakespeare Theatre, Stratford-upon-Avon.
         The Shepherd's Play (anon.), Royal Shakespeare Company Theatregoround, British tour.

Television

Hamlet (Shakespeare; as adapter), 1970; *Playing Shakespeare* (series; as writer and director), 1982; *Mallory's Morte d'Arthur* (as writer and narrator), 1983; *The War That Never Ends* (as writer), 1990.

Radio

The Rape of Lucrece (Shakespeare; as adapter and actor), 1964.

Publications

The Hollow Crown, 1962; *The Vagaries of Love*, 1962; *The Wars of the Roses* (with Peter Hall), 1963; *The Revenger's Tragedy*, 1966; *King John*, 1974; *Doctor Faustus*, 1974; *The Greeks*, 1981; *Playing Shakespeare*, 1984.

*

Bibliography

Books:
Michael L. Greenwald, *Directions by Indirections: John Barton of the Royal Shakespeare Company*, Newark, Delaware, and London, New Jersey, 1985.

* * *

John Barton has been and remains one of the most notable and controversial directors of the post-war British theatre. As an undergraduate at Cambridge he came under the influence of the Cambridge English school, with its emphasis on the close reading of literary texts, but was less sympathetic to the critical methods of F. R. Leavis than his Cambridge near-contemporaries Peter Hall and Trevor Nunn. Barton directed widely at Cambridge, especially for the ADC and the Marlowe Society, where among other productions he co-directed *Romeo and Juliet* (1952) with the renowned Cambridge don and theatre scholar George Rylands. Among other notable Cambridge productions directed by Barton were *Henry IV, parts 1 and 2*, with Clive Swift as Falstaff, Ian McKellen as Justice Shallow, and Derek Jacobi as Hal, and a *Julius Caesar* that made use of 16th-century settings and language practices. Though his directing career has been largely occupied with the work of

Shakespeare and his contemporaries, Barton by his own statement remains a passionate Chekhovian, and commonly includes Chekhovian elements in his productions, an inclination that may be traced back to the influence of the Moscow Arts *Three Sisters*, seen in London in the 1950's.

In 1960, Barton was invited to join Peter Hall at Stratford, where he concentrated on verse-speaking, and where he was deeply involved in studio work with the company, in association with such figures as Michel Saint-Denis, Peggy Ashcroft, Donald Sinden, Litz Pisk and Cicely Berry. His 1960 production of *The Taming of the Shrew*, incorporating material from the anonymous *A Shrew*, drew both approval and ridicule from the critics, and his rehearsal methods met with some opposition from members of the company. In 1963, he co-directed with Peter Hall a trilogy of history plays known as *The Wars of the Roses*, incorporating the three *Henry VI* plays and *Richard III*, and including much newly-written material offering explanatory historical infilling, cross-references and a narrative focus that construed the plays as the political legacy of Henry V. Despite academic and other hostility, the trilogy was well received at the box office and remains a testament to what Hall describes as Barton's formidable literary technique. With set designer John Bury's "cruel, harsh world of decorated steel, cold and dangerous" (as Hall described it), the production portrayed a vicious world of "real politik". The second tetralogy of history plays followed in the next season, with Barton again preparing the texts, but this time avoiding serious interference with Shakespeare's mature writing. The sequence showed England's historical decline, from the white and gold finery of *Richard II* to the black leather and harsh materialism of *Richard III*, and included such controversial features as the deglamourising of Hotspur, including a graphically sexual leave-taking from his wife. In 1965, Barton, Clifford Williams and Trevor Nunn restaged the plays, with significant cast changes.

Barton has shown a particular directorial interest in *Troilus and Cressida*, finding in the play what he calls "a deliberate and organic orchestration of dissonances" and seeing it as a piece that is "unique and brilliant and resists labelling". His 1960 production with Peter Hall, with its prominent use of a sandpit as a stage setting, gave a grim view of the play that was nevertheless popularly well-received. The 1968 Stratford production, transferring to the Aldwych in 1969, despite some critics and audiences finding it offensive, was acclaimed as "one of the peak achievements of contemporary British theatre" (*The Daily Telegraph*). Centring on Thersites and his distorted vision of wars and lechery, and with Alan Howard as a bisexual Achilles symbolising Greek decadence, the production showed "the real savagery of erotic art", according to Irving Wardle. The 1976 *Troilus*, directed with Barry Kyle, was generally thought a weaker version of these earlier interpretations.

Barton's work with Shakespearean comedy has generally emphasised the darker tones of the plays. His versions of *Love's Labour's Lost* in 1965 and 1978 both saw the fragility of the play's artifice, the latter in particular giving a sense of the complexity of emotion in the piece, including a wonderfully poignant final scene. The 1969 *Twelfth Night*, which Barton regarded as "very much an actor's play" in which he "wanted to sound all the notes that are there" was kept in the repertory until 1972, with Judi

Dench playing Viola in a production very much aware of the play's melancholy elements. The production eventually ran for 200 performances in Stratford, London, Australia and Japan. A 1978 *Merchant of Venice* at The Other Place in Stratford was set in Edwardian England, with some Chekhovian overtones, and with Patrick Stewart playing Shylock so as to emphasise his human rather than his racial characteristics. A revival in the Stratford main house in 1981, with David Suchet (himself a Jew) as Shylock, was a pungent reinterpretation, but generally less well-received. Another comedy presented in a non-Elizabethan setting was the Indian Raj *Much Ado* (1976), with Judi Dench and Donald Sinden as Beatrice and Benedick, and with John Woodvine playing Dogberry as a Sikh constable not fully in control of his English. Questions were raised about racial stereotyping, but the production was generally praised for its interpretation of social and sexual rituals through the Victorian setting. A 1977 *Midsummer Night's Dream* evoked the delicacy and the darkness of 16th-century woodland spirits, with Patrick Stewart playing Oberon as a wood-god reminiscent of Nijinsky in *L'Après-midi d'un faune*, and with memorable effect as "a thin silvery woodland chord" was sounded at the death of Pyramus.

The problem comedies and the late comedies have also drawn Barton's attention as a director. *All's Well* in 1967 proved much more stageworthy than this difficult play was until then thought to be, with Ian Richardson playing Bertram rather more lightly than expected, Estelle Kohler giving an innocent rather than a calculating Helena and the production drawing out the melancholy of a society with an emotional and social gap between the generations. *Measure for Measure* in 1970 was another production that explored the ambiguities of the text, in its final scene preserving rather than resolving questions and contradictions: at the end Isabella did not join the Duke but remained staring out over the audience, lost in thought. For *The Tempest* (1970), a nearly nude Ariel (Ben Kingsley) was joined by a gross Caliban (Barry Stanton) and a somewhat melancholy Prospero (Ian Richardson). *Cymbeline* (1974) was cut by 820 lines, and staged after the manner of Jacobean masques. *The Winter's Tale* (1976) drew on Nordic mythology and fused the role of the Bear with John Nettles' Time Chorus.

Among the histories, Barton returned to *Richard II* and *King John* in the 1970's. *Richard II* was notable for the device of swapping Richard Pasco and Ian Richardson in the roles of Richard and Bolingbroke to reflect the symmetry Barton detected in the text. *King John* provided Barton with another opportunity to reorder the Shakespeare text, incorporating material from the anonymous *The Troublesome Reign of King John* and from John Bale's *King Johan*. Once more controversial, the production reflected "our world of outward order and inner instability, of shifting ideologies and self-destructive pragmatism".

Othello (1971) was set in the Victorian period and put the emphasis on social and military rank and on sexual motivation. *Hamlet* (1980), by way of contrast, was interpreted in the light of Anne Barton's view of the play as "unique in the density and pervasiveness of its theatrical self-reference", with a setting resembling a back-stage space, with wicker basket, property throne and props table all on view.

Notable non-Shakespearean productions have included Marlowe's *Dr Faustus*, in which most of the comic scenes were excised and the action was confined to Faustus's study; Sheridan's *The School for Scandal*, which discovered a Chekhovian melancholy in the script; and works by Congreve, Schnitzler and Ibsen. Most important of all was *The Greeks* (1980), which combined the work of Euripides, Aeschylus, Sophocles and Barton himself, drawing on Homer.

Barton brings to his work a scholar's knowledge of the texts, a keen sense for the details of human interaction, a creative writer's fascination with and skill in language, and a sense for the importance of sensitive and flexible verse-speaking. His influence on the Royal Shakespeare Company and therefore on theatre performance in Britain and internationally has been profound.

—J. R. Mulryne

BATY, (Jean-Baptiste-Marie-) Gaston. French director, manager, theorist, designer, and playwright. Born in Pélussin, Loire, 26 May 1885. Educated at the Dominican Collège d'Oullins, Rhône; studied law in Lyon, 1903–06, and German literature at the University of Monte Carlo, 1906–08. Assistant to Firmin Gémier, Cirque d'Hiver, Paris, 1919–20; directed and designed at various Parisian theatres through the 1920's; founder and manager, Théâtre Montparnasse-Gaston Baty, Paris, 1930–47, where he was acclaimed for expressionist productions of classical and modern plays; worked with the Comédie-Française, 1936–48; also presented marionette plays. Died in Paris, 13 October 1952.

Productions

As director:
1920   *La Grande Pastorale* (Hellem and Estoc), Cirque d'Hiver, Paris.
    Les Esclaves (Bouhélier), Théâtre des Arts, Paris; also designed set and costumes.
    (With Gémier) *Oedipe, roi de Thèbes* (Bouhélier), Cirque d'Hiver, Paris.
    Le Simoun (Lenormand), Comédie Montaigne-Gémier, Paris; Théâtre Pigalle, Paris, 1930; Comédie-Française, Paris, 1936; also designed set and costumes.
1921   *L'Avare* (Molière), Comédie Montaigne-Gémier, Paris.
    29 Vingt-neuf degrés à l'Ombre (Labiche), Comédie Montaigne-Gémier, Paris; Studio des Champs-Élysées, Paris, 1925; also designed set.
    Les Amants puérils (Crommelynck), Comédie Montaigne-Gémier, Paris; also designed set and costumes.
    Le Héros et le soldat (G. B. Shaw), Comédie Montaigne-Gémier, Paris; Théâtre de l'Odéon, Paris, 1924; also designed set and costumes.
    L'Annonce faite à Marie (Claudel), Comédie Montaigne-Gémier, Paris.
1922   *Haya* (Grégoire), Comédie des Champs-Élysées, Paris.

La Belle de Haguenau (Variot), Comédie des Champs-Élysées, Paris.

Césaire (Schlumberger), Comédie des Champs-Élysées, Paris.

La Farce de Popa Ghéorghé (Orna), Comédie des Champs-Élysées, Paris.

Martine (Bernard), Théâtre des Mathurins, Paris; Studio des Champs-Élysées, Paris, 1925.

Intimité (Pellerin), Théâtre des Mathurins, Paris; Studio des Champs-Élysées, Paris, 1925; also designed set.

La Revue de la Cigale (Vautel and Eddy), Batignolles-Cigale-Odéon, Paris.

1923   *Le Voyageur* (Amiel), Baraque de la Chimère, Paris; Studio des Champs-Élysées, Paris, 1925; also designed set.

Je veux revoir ma Normandie (Besnard), Baraque de la Chimère, Paris.

Cyclone (Gantillon), Baraque de la Chimère, Paris; Théâtre de l'Odéon, Paris, 1924; Théâtre Montparnasse, Paris, 1934; also designed set.

L'Aube et le Soir de Sainte Geneviève (Diémer), Baraque de la Chimère, Paris; also designed set.

Le Fardeau de la Liberté (Bernard), Théâtre de l'Odéon, Paris.

Empereur Jones (O'Neill), Théâtre de l'Odéon, Paris; also designed set.

La Souriante Madame Beudet (Amiel and Obey), Théâtre de l'Odéon, Paris; also designed set.

Le Voile du souvenir (Turpin and Fournier), Théâtre de l'Odéon, Paris; also designed set.

1924   *L'Invitation au Voyage* (Bernard), Théâtre de l'Odéon, Paris, and Studio des Champs-Élysées, Paris; also designed set.

Alphonsine (Haurigot), Théâtre du Vaudeville, Paris; also designed set.

Suite de Parades (Guellette, adapted by Crémieux), Studio des Champs-Élysées, Paris; also designed set.

Maya (Gantillon), Studio des Champs-Élysées, Paris; revived there, 1927; Théâtre de l'Avenue, Paris, 1928; Théâtre Montparnasse, Paris, 1931, 1939, and 1948; also designed set and costumes.

À l'ombre du Mal (Lenormand), Studio des Champs-Élysées, Paris; Théâtre Montparnasse, Paris, 1932; also designed set.

1925   *Mademoiselle Julie* (Strindberg), Studio des Champs-Élysées, Paris; also designed set.

Déjeuner d'Artistes (Gaument and Cé), Studio des Champs-Élysées, Paris; also designed set.

L'Étrange Épouse du Professeur Stierbecke (Albert-Jean), Studio des Champs-Élysées, Paris.

La Cavalière Elsa (Demasy), Studio des Champs-Élysées, Paris; Théâtre Montparnasse, Paris, 1930; also designed set.

La Chapelle Ardente (Marcel), Théâtre du Vieux-Colombier, Paris; also designed set.

1925–26 *Les Chevaux du Char* (Zogheb), Théâtre Antoine, Paris.

Le Dompteur ou l'Anglais tel qu'on le mange (Savoir), Théâtre Michel, Paris; also designed set.

L'Homme du Destin (G. B. Shaw), Studio des Champs-Élysées, Paris; also designed set.

Fantasie amoureuse (Lang), Studio des Champs-Élysées, Paris; also designed costumes.

Le Couvre-Feu (Saint-Marc), Studio des Champs-Élysées, Paris; also designed costumes.

1926   *Le Bourgeois romanesque* (Blanchon), Studio des Champs-Élysées, Paris; Théâtre Montparnasse, Paris, 1940; also designed set.

Têtes de Rechange (Pellerin), Studio des Champs-Élysées, Paris; Théâtre Montparnasse, Paris, 1932; also designed set.

Une Visite (Valray), Studio des Champs-Élysées, Paris; also designed set.

L'Amour magicien (Lenormand), Studio des Champs-Élysées, Paris; also designed set.

1927   *Les Précieuses ridicules* (Molière), Dutch tour.

La Machine à calculer (Rice), Studio des Champs-Élysées, Paris.

Amilcar (Fauré-Frémiet), Studio des Champs-Élysées, Paris; also designed set.

1928   *Le Dibbouk* (An-Ski), Studio des Champs-Élysées, Paris; Théâtre de l'Avenue, Paris, 1929; Théâtre Montparnasse, Paris, 1931; also designed set.

Cris des Coeurs (Pellerin), Théâtre de l'Avenue, Paris; Théâtre Montparnasse, Paris, 1935 and 1937; also designed set.

Le premier Hamlet (Lascaris, adapted from Shakespeare), Théâtre de l'Avenue, Paris; also designed set.

La Farce du Pâté et de la Tarte (Brulies), Dutch tour.

Terminus (Soumagne), Théâtre de l'Avenue, Paris.

Départs (Gantillon), Théâtre de l'Avenue, Paris.

1929   *Le Malade imaginaire* (Molière), Théâtre de l'Avenue, Paris; Théâtre Montparnasse, 1931; also designed set.

Karl et Anna (Frank), Théâtre de l'Avenue, Paris; also designed set.

La Voix de sa Maîtresse (Oulmont and Masson), Théâtre de l'Avenue, Paris; also designed set.

Prise (Pascal and Albert-Jean), Théâtre de l'Avenue, Paris.

1930   *Feu du Ciel* (Dominique), Théâtre Pigalle, Paris.

L'Opéra de Quat' sous (Gay and Brecht), Théâtre Montparnasse-Gaston Baty, Paris; also designed set and costumes.

Le Médecin malgré lui (Molière), Théâtre Montparnasse-Gaston Baty, Paris; also designed set and costumes.

1931   *Terrain Vague* (Pellerin), Théâtre Montparnasse-Gaston Baty, Paris.

Le Sourd ou l'Auberge pleine (Choudard-Des-forges), Théâtre Montparnasse-Gaston Baty, Paris; also designed set and costumes.

Beau Danube rouge (Zimmer), Théâtre Montparnasse-Gaston Baty, Paris.

1932   *Bifur* (Gantillon), Théâtre Montparnasse-Gaston Baty, Paris; also designed set and costumes.

Le Déménagement (adapted from Guignol Lyonnais), Théâtre Montparnasse, Paris.

Chambre d'Hôtel (Rocher), Théâtre Montparnasse, Paris.

Café-Tabac (Amiel), Théâtre Montparnasse-Gaston Baty, Paris.

Comme tu me veux (Pirandello), Théâtre Montparnasse-Gaston Baty, Paris.

1933   *Crime et Châtiment* (Baty, adapted from Dostoevsky), Théâtre Montparnasse-Gaston Baty, Paris; revived there, 1933–34; also designed set.

1934   *Voyage circulaire* (Chabannes), Théâtre Montparnasse-Gaston Baty, Paris.

Prosper (Favre, adapted by Baty), Théâtre Montparnasse-Gaston Baty, Paris; Théâtre de la Renaissance, Paris, 1948; also designed set.

1935   *Hôtel des Masques* (Albert-Jean), Théâtre Montparnasse-Gaston Baty, Paris.

Les Caprices de Marianne (Musset), Théâtre Montparnasse-Gaston Baty, Paris; Théâtre Montparnasse, Paris, 1937 and 1940.

1936   *Madame Bovary* (Flaubert, adapted by Baty), Théâtre Montparnasse-Gaston Baty, Paris; revived there, 1941; also designed set and costumes.

Le Chandelier (Musset), Comédie-Française, Paris.

1937   *Les Ratés* (Lenormand), Théâtre Montparnasse-Gaston Baty, Paris.

Faust (Goethe, adapted by Fleg), Théâtre Montparnasse-Gaston Baty, Paris.

Madame Capet (Maurette), Théâtre Montparnasse, Paris.

1938   *Un Chapeau de paille d'Italie* (Labiche), Comédie-Française, Paris.

Arden de Feversham (Lenormand), Théâtre Montparnasse, Paris.

Dulcinée (Baty), Théâtre Montparnasse, Paris; also designed set.

1939   *Manon Lescaut* (Maurette), Théâtre Montparnasse, Paris.

1939–40   *Phèdre* (Racine), Théâtre Montparnasse, Paris.

1940–41   *Un Garçon de chez Véry* (Labiche), Théâtre Montparnasse, Paris.

1941   *La Mégère apprivoisée* (Fouchardière, adapted from Shakespeare), Théâtre Montparnasse, Paris; revived there, 1942 and 1946.

1941–42   *Marie Stuart* (Maurette), Théâtre Montparnasse, Paris; also designed set.

1942–43   *Macbeth* (Shakespeare), Théâtre Montparnasse, Paris; also designed set.

1943–44   *Le Grand Poucet* (Puget), Théâtre Montparnasse, Paris; also designed set.

La Queue de la Poële (Baty), Pavillon de Marsan, Paris; also designed set.

1944–45   *Emily Brontë* (Simone), Théâtre Montparnasse, Paris; also designed set.

1945–46   *Lorenzaccio* (Musset), Théâtre Montparnasse, Paris; also designed set.

1946–47   *Bérénice* (Racine), Comédie-Française, Paris.

Arlequin poli par l'amour (Baty and Charon), Comédie-Française, Paris.

L'Amour des Trois Oranges (Arnoux), Théâtre Montparnasse, Paris.

1947–48   *Sapho* (Daudet and Belot), Comédie-Française, Paris.

La Langue des Femmes (Baty), Marionnettes á la Française, Paris.

La Marjolaine (Baty), Marionnettes á la Française, Paris.

Au Temps où Berthe filait (Fabry), Marionnettes á la Française, Paris.

1948–49   *L'Inconnu d'Arras* (Salacrou), Comédie-Française, Paris; also designed set and costumes.

Publications

La Passion (play), 1905; *Blancheneige* (play), 1911; *Le Masque et l'encensoir*, 1926; *Masques*, 1926–42; *Théâtre nouveau*, 1927; *Visage de Shakespeare*, 1928; *Théâtre classique de Guignol*, 1932; *Vie de l'art théâtral des origines á nos jours*, 1932; *Crime et châtiment*, 1933; *Guignol*, 1934; *Madame Bovary* (adaptation from Flaubert), 1936; *Le Théâtre Joly*, 1937; *Dulcinée* (adaptation from Martínez), 1938; *Conférence de M Gaston Baty (á) l'ouverture du Théâtre des Célestins*, 1941; *trois p'tits tours et puis s'en vont ... Les théâtres forains de marionettes á fils et leur répertoire*, 1942; *Rideau baissé*, 1949; *Les Caprices de Marianne*, 1952; *Lettre á une jeune comédienne*, 1953; *Histoire des Marionettes* (with René Chanvance), 1959.

*

Bibliography

Books:
Paul Blanchart, *Gaston Baty*, Paris, 1939.
Raymond Cogniat, *Gaston Baty*, Paris, 1953.
Arthur Simon, *Gaston Baty, théoricien du théâtre*, Paris, 1972.
Gisela Meiler, *Kunst und Kult im Werk von Gaston Baty*, Munich, 1984.

* * *

Theorist, scholar, art historian, and director, Gaston Baty was the most theatricalist of the four-man Cartel that dominated the French stage between the wars. Alone among the four, he was not an actor and the only member of the Cartel to challenge the assumption that the director's role is to serve the playwright. Regarding theatre as a microcosmic universe, he was less interested in communicating a text than in creating a form of total theatre with the text as its nucleus. Working at a time when the prestige of the playwright was at its height in French theatre and respect for the text held sway as the directorial orthodoxy, he acquired an exaggerated reputation as a "dictatorial" director because of the importance he attached to non-verbal means of expression. In fact, this worried the critics more than the playwrights. Whilst a vociferous group of critics branded him the enemy of the text, writers with whom he worked, such as Lenormand and Bernard, all declared themselves fully satisfied with his productions. To the public he became known as "the magician of mise en scène", thanks to his unrivalled mastery of subtle pictorial techniques.

Baty was a disciple of Max Reinhardt, from whom he derived his idea of a dramaturgy created by a "regisseur" orchestrating voice, movement, music, and setting. He was also influenced by Firmin Gémier, a director noted for his masterly large-scale productions and one of the pioneers of the People's Theatre movement in France. But the ultimate source of Baty's theatrical programme lay in his vision of man's place in the universe and his views on the origins and purpose of drama. He believed that the humanistic Renaissance had produced a narrow egoistical accent on man isolated from the mysteries of creation, and had turned theatre into a thinking, not feeling, art. Inspired by the Thomist doctrine of his Dominican upbringing, he sought to replace verbal theatre with a holistic drama that would integrate man into the rest of creation.

His object, then, was to use the text as a springboard to the world that lay beyond the play. He came to believe that beyond or above the play itself there was another drama that had been revealed to the author but of which the text was an incomplete shadow. At this point the director must take over from the playwright, deploying the non-verbal language of the stage to communicate all that words are incapable of expressing.

These ideas made Baty the natural director of the "school of silence", also known as the "theatre of the unexpressed", of which Jean-Jacques Bernard and Jean-Victor Pellerin were the principal exponents. Together with Henri-René Lenormand and Simon Gantillon with their plays of the subconscious, these writers provided the showcases for Baty's expressionist techniques in the 1920's.

As a producer of the classics, to which he turned in the 1930's, Baty was viewed with suspicion by traditionalists, partly because of his unorthodox interpretations and partly because his views on the limitations of the spoken word were felt to be incompatible with the respect due to Shakespeare, Molière, Racine, and Marivaux. In retrospect, his experiments with the classics, although they were not well received at the time, might be said to have been vindicated by later developments. By deliberately challenging the critics' hide-bound and proprietorial attitude to the classics he helped to open the way for more adventurous interpretations.

His finest productions, the culmination of his search for total theatre, were his own adaptations of novels such as *Crime and Punishment*, *Madame Bovary*, and *Manon Lescaut*. Here he was able to mould scripts to his vision of man, society and nature, while tailoring them perfectly to his own staging methods. His adaptations, which he spent many years finishing, translated the narrative flow of the novels into a succession of unforgettable pictorial tableaux. The productions were miracles of staging. *Crime and Punishment* was presented in some 60 scenes involving 13 different settings. To achieve the necessary continuity he divided the stage into compartments, illuminating the different scenes in turn. For *Madame Bovary* entire settings were constructed on mobile platforms so that as one set was trucked off to the wings, another took its place. Literary critics may have objected to his interpretation of the stories, but theatrically these were unblemished productions executed with unrivalled pictorial and technical skill.

In his last years, Baty became pessimistic about the state of the theatre. He recognised that the ultimate problem, which theatre had failed to resolve, was that of creating a new public other than elitist middle-class audiences. His life's mission was based on a conviction that theatrical renewal depended on restoring the stage to its central place in the collective life and beliefs of the community. But this depended on a complete cultural transformation, a re-emergence of the overall order that had welded audiences together in earlier ages, and no amount of scenic reform could accomplish that. By the end of the war even the relatively restricted but cultivated audiences that had gathered around the Cartel were dispersed and the unified public remained as much an elusive and nostalgic ideal as ever. After his last production at the Comédie-Française in 1948, Baty worked mainly with puppets. Although he supported the development of a decentralized theatre, he had little confidence in the possibility of a new public re-grouping around a more politically-motivated theatre — in which direction, as it happened, the best hopes for a popular theatre now lay.

—David Whitton

BELASCO, David. US actor-manager and playwright. Born David Valasco in San Francisco, 25 July 1853. Educated at Lincoln College, California, and at local schools in San Francisco, until 1871. Married Cecilia Loverich in 1873, two daughters. Worked as call-boy and first undertook duties of director, Metropolitan Theatre, San Francisco, 1873; stage manager, Baldwin Theatre, 1876, Grand Opera House, and Metropolitan Theatre, all in San Francisco; stage manager, Madison Square Theatre, New York, 1882–84; joined Daniel Frohman at the Lyceum Theatre, New York, 1886; debut as producer, 1890; subsequently directed or produced over 300 Broadway plays and also worked in London; acquired Republic Theatre, New York, and renamed it the Belasco Theatre, 1902; built and opened Stuyvesant Theatre, New York, also later renamed the Belasco Theatre, 1910; wrote numerous novels, plays, and adaptations for the stage. Chevalier, Légion d'Honneur. Died in New York, 14 May 1931.

Productions

As director:
1873   *A Morning Call* (Dance), Metropolitan Theatre, San Francisco.

            The Colleen Bawn (Boucicault), Metropolitan Theatre, San Francisco.

            Darling; or, Woman and Her Master (De Walden), Metropolitan Theatre, San Francisco.

            Little Don Giovanni (H. J. Byron), Metropolitan Theatre, San Francisco.

The Gold Demon, Metropolitan Theatre, San Francisco.

Checkmate (Halliday), Metropolitan Theatre, San Francisco.

Schermerhorn's Boy, Metropolitan Theatre, San Francisco.

The Wonderful Scamp; or, Aladdin Number Two, Metropolitan Theatre, San Francisco.

The Statue Lover (Jerrold), Metropolitan Theatre, San Francisco.

Pluto, Metropolitan Theatre, San Francisco.

Cinderella, Metropolitan Theatre, San Francisco.

The New Magdalen (Belasco and Le Roy, adapted from Collins), Shiel's Opera House, San Francisco.

Maum Cre, Shiel's Opera House, San Francisco.

Help (Maeder), Shiel's Opera House, San Francisco.

Ireland and America, Shiel's Opera House, San Francisco.

The Rising Moon, Shiel's Opera House, San Francisco.

Out at Sea (Newton), Shiel's Opera House, San Francisco.

Uncle Tom's Cabin (Rowe), Shiel's Opera House, San Francisco.

Twice Saved; or, Bertha the Midget, Shiel's Opera House, San Francisco.

The Woman in Red (Coyne), Shiel's Opera House, San Francisco.

Dark Deeds, Shiel's Opera House, San Francisco.

More Blunders Than One (Rodwell), Shiel's Opera House, San Francisco.

Little Katy; or, The Hot Corn Girl, Shiel's Opera House, San Francisco.

The Stage Struck Chambermaid, Shiel's Opera House, San Francisco.

Man and Wife (Collins), Shiel's Opera House, San Francisco.

The Mexican Tigress, Shiel's Opera House, San Francisco.

Evenings at Home, Shiel's Opera House, San Francisco.

1873–74   *Our American Cousin* (Taylor), Piper's Opera House, Virginia City, Nevada.

Donna Diana; or, Love's Masque (Marston, adapted from Moreto), Piper's Opera House, Virginia City, Nevada.

Lucretia Borgia (adapted from Donizetti), Piper's Opera House, Virginia City, Nevada.

The Jealous Wife (Colman), Piper's Opera House, Virginia City, Nevada.

East Lynne (Kempe, adapted from Wood), Piper's Opera House, Virginia City, Nevada.

Mary Stuart (Wills), Piper's Opera House, Virginia City, Nevada.

Pygmalion and Galatea (Gilbert), Piper's Opera House, Virginia City, Nevada.

1874–80   *Marie Antoinette* (Simpson), Piper's Opera House, Virginia City, Nevada.

The School for Scandal (Sheridan), Piper's Opera House, Virginia City, Nevada.

Bianca Visconti (Willis), Piper's Opera House, Virginia City, Nevada.

Love (Knowles), Piper's Opera House, Virginia City, Nevada.

Much Ado About Nothing (Shakespeare), Piper's Opera House, Virginia City, Nevada.

Lady Audley's Secret (Roberts), Piper's Opera House, Virginia City, Nevada.

1874   *Charity* (Gilbert), Maguire's New Theatre, San Francisco.

Alixe (Daly, adapted from Prevois and Barriére's *La Comtesse de Somerive*), Maguire's New Theatre, San Francisco.

War to the Knife (Gilbert), Maguire's New Theatre, San Francisco.

Mr. and Mrs. White, Maguire's New Theatre, San Francisco.

The French Spy (Haines), Maguire's New Theatre, San Francisco.

The Pretty Housebreaker (Halliday and Brough), Maguire's New Theatre, San Francisco.

Nita; or, Woman's Constancy, Maguire's New Theatre, San Francisco.

Mazeppa (Milner, adapted from Lord Byron), Maguire's New Theatre, San Francisco.

The Wept of the Wish-Ton-Wish (adapted from Fenimore Cooper), Maguire's New Theatre, San Francisco.

Rip Van Winkle (Herne), Maguire's New Theatre, San Francisco.

Parepa Rosa (burlesque), Maguire's New Theatre, San Francisco.

Blind Beggars (Farnie), Maguire's New Theatre, San Francisco.

The People's Lawyer (J. S. Jones), Maguire's New Theatre, San Francisco.

Alphonse (Daly, adapted from Dumas *fils*), Maguire's New Theatre, San Francisco.

Lady Madge (Le Roy), Maguire's New Theatre, San Francisco.

Charles O'Malley (Herne, adapted from Lever), Maguire's New Theatre, San Francisco.

The Sphinx (adapted from Ohnet), Maguire's New Theatre, San Francisco.

Oliver Twist (Herne, adapted from Dickens), Maguire's New Theatre, San Francisco.

Carlotta! Queen of the Arena, Maguire's New Theatre, San Francisco.

Terrible Hymen, Maguire's New Theatre, San Francisco.

Jenny Lind, Maguire's New Theatre, San Francisco.

The Enchantress (Bunn), Maguire's New Theatre, San Francisco.

1874–75   *East Lynne* (adapted from Wood), US tour.

Camille (Lander), US tour.

Frou-Frou (Daly, adapted from Meilhac and Halévy), US tour.

A Conjugal Lesson (Danvers), US tour.

A Happy Pair (Smith), US tour.

The Antics of a Clown (Belasco), US tour.

Black Ey'd Susan (Jerrold), California Theatre.

The Bohemian (Ceprico, adapted from Dumas's *Edmund Kean*), US tour.

1875–76 *Gaspardo; or, The Three Banished Men of Milan*, Thorne's Palace Theatre, San Francisco.

The Miser's Daughter, Thorne's Palace Theatre, San Francisco.

The Dawn of Freedom (Leffingwell), Thorne's Palace Theatre, San Francisco.

The Fool's Revenge (Taylor), Thorne's Palace Theatre, San Francisco.

The Forty Thieves (Reece and Lutz), Thorne's Palace Theatre, San Francisco.

Who Killed Cock Robin (C. Mathews), Thorne's Palace Theatre, San Francisco.

Faustus, a Romantic Spectacle, Thorne's Palace Theatre, San Francisco.

The Black Hand; or, The Lost Will (Hurst), Thorne's Palace Theatre, San Francisco.

1876 *Richard II* (Shakespeare, adapted by Cibber), Baldwin's Theatre, San Francisco.

The Wonder (Centlivre), Baldwin's Theatre, San Francisco.

Hamlet (Shakespeare), Baldwin's Theatre, San Francisco.

Macbeth (Shakespeare), Baldwin's Theatre, San Francisco.

The Gamester (Moore), Baldwin's Theatre, San Francisco.

King Lear (Shakespeare), Baldwin's Theatre, San Francisco.

Othello (Shakespeare), Baldwin's Theatre, San Francisco.

The Merchant of Venice (Shakespeare), Baldwin's Theatre, San Francisco.

A Match for a King (C. Mathews, adapted from Dumanois and D'Ennery's *Don César de Bazan*), Baldwin's Theatre, San Francisco.

A New Way to Pay Old Debts (Massinger), Baldwin's Theatre, San Francisco.

The Wife (Knowles), Baldwin's Theatre, San Francisco.

1876–77 *The Creole* (Brooks), US tour.

The Willing Hand, US tour.

Uncle Tom's Cabin (Belasco), US tour.

The Octoroon (Boucicault), US tour.

The Stranger (Thompson, adapted from Kotzebue), US tour.

The Love Chase (Knowles), US tour.

Henry IV, part 1 (Shakespeare), US tour.

The Pearl of Savoy, US tour.

The Ticket-of-Leave Man (Taylor), US tour.

Lost in London (Phillips), US tour.

The Bonnie Fish Wife (Selby), US tour.

Meg's Diversion (Craven), US tour.

Meg Merrilies (adapted from Scott's *Guy Mannering*), US tour.

1877 *The Haunted House* (Belasco), Egyptian Hall, San Francisco.

Faust (Belasco), Egyptian Hall, San Francisco.

The Mysterious Inn (Belasco), Egyptian Hall, San Francisco.

A Storm of Thoughts (Belasco), Egyptian Hall, San Francisco.

The Persecuted Traveller (Belasco), Egyptian Hall, San Francisco.

Our Mysterious Boarding House (Belasco), Egyptian Hall, San Francisco.

The Prodigal's Return (Belasco), Egyptian Hall, San Francisco.

Wine, Women, and Cards (Belasco), Egyptian Hall, San Francisco.

Christmas Night; or, The Convict's Return (Belasco), Egyptian Hall, San Francisco.

The Lady of Lyons (Bulwer-Lytton), Petaluma, California.

The Young Widow (Rodwell), Petaluma, California.

The Hidden Hand (Taylor), Petaluma, California.

Robert Macaire (Selby), Petaluma, California.

The Wife (Knowles), Petaluma, California.

My Turn Next (T. J. Williams), Petaluma, California.

The Streets of New York (Boucicault), Petaluma, California.

The Rough Diamond (Buckstone), Petaluma, California.

Deborah (Daly, adapted from Mosenthal), Petaluma, California.

Solon Shingle, Petaluma, California.

The Ticket-of-Leave Man (Taylor) US tour.

1877–78 *Agnes* (adapted from Sardou's *Andrea*), US tour.

One Hundred Years Old (Jackson, adapted from D'Ennery and Plouvier's *Le Centenaire*), US tour.

Saratoga (Howard), US tour.

A Celebrated Case (D'Ennery and Cormon), US tour.

The Danites (Miller), US tour.

1878–79 *The Octoroon* (Boucicault, adapted by Belasco), Baldwin's Theatre, San Francisco.

Olivia (Belasco, adapted from *The Vicar of Wakefield*), Baldwin's Theatre, San Francisco.

A Woman of the People (Wills, adapted by Belasco), Baldwin's Theatre, San Francisco.

Struck Oil (Greene and Thompson), Baldwin's Theatre, San Francisco.

The Chinese Question (Greene), Baldwin's Theatre, San Francisco.

The Unequal Match (Taylor), Baldwin's Theatre, San Francisco.

The Loan of a Lover (Planché), Baldwin's Theatre, San Francisco.

Honi Soit Qui Mal Y Pens (Godor), Baldwin's Theatre, San Francisco.

Conscience (Lancaster), Baldwin's Theatre, San Francisco.

Article 47 (Daly), Baldwin's Theatre, San Francisco.

Macbeth (Shakespeare), Baldwin's Theatre, San Francisco.

Not Guilty (Phillips, adapted by Belasco), Baldwin's Theatre, San Francisco.

Loyal Till Death, Baldwin's Theatre, San Francisco.

Ours (Robertson), Baldwin's Theatre, San Francisco.

He Would and He Would Not, Baldwin's Theatre, San Francisco.

The Governess (adapted from Brontë's *Jane Eyre*), Baldwin's Theatre, San Francisco.

Within an Inch of His Life (Belasco, adapted from Gaboriau), Baldwin's Theatre, San Francisco.

The Passion Play (Morse), Baldwin's Theatre, San Francisco.

A Fast Family (Belasco, adapted from Sardou's *La Famille Benoiton*), Baldwin's Theatre, San Francisco.

The Millionaire's Daughter (Belasco), Baldwin's Theatre, San Francisco.

The Fool of the Family (H. J. Byron), Baldwin's Theatre, San Francisco.

Camille (Landor, adapted from Dumas *fils*), Baldwin's Theatre, San Francisco.

London Assurance (Boucicault and Brougham), Baldwin's Theatre, San Francisco.

Marriage by Moonlight (Belasco and Herne), Baldwin's Theatre, San Francisco.

L'Assommoir (Belasco, adapted from Zola), Baldwin's Theatre, San Francisco.

Cupid's Lawsuit, Baldwin's Theatre, San Francisco.

Chums (Belasco and Herne), Baldwin's Theatre, San Francisco.

Hearts of Oak (Belasco and Herne), Hamlin's Theatre, Chicago; Fifth Avenue Theatre, New York, 1880.

Romeo and Juliet (Shakespeare), Baldwin's Theatre, San Francisco.

As You Like It (Shakespeare), Baldwin's Theatre, San Francisco.

The Hunchback (Knowles), Baldwin's Theatre, San Francisco.

Amy Robsart (Halliday, adapted from Scott's *Kenilworth*), Baldwin's Theatre, San Francisco.

The School for Scandal (Sheridan), Baldwin's Theatre, San Francisco.

The Lady of Lyons (Bulwer-Lytton), Baldwin's Theatre, San Francisco.

1879–80   *Paul Arniff; or, The Love of a Serf* (Belasco), Baldwin's Theatre, San Francisco.

Deception (Piercy), Baldwin's Theatre, San Francisco.

An Orphan of the State, Baldwin's Theatre, San Francisco.

Richelieu (Bulwer-Lytton), Baldwin's Theatre, San Francisco.

True to the Core (Cooke, adapted by Belasco), Baldwin's Theatre, San Francisco.

Ninon (W. G. Wills), Baldwin's Theatre, San Francisco.

Forget Me Not (Merivale and Grove), Baldwin's Theatre, San Francisco.

The Galley Slave (Campbell), Baldwin's Theatre, San Francisco.

Fairfax (Campbell), Baldwin's Theatre, San Francisco.

Golden Game (Campbell), Baldwin's Theatre, San Francisco.

Louis XI (Reade), Baldwin's Theatre, San Francisco.

Wild Oats (O'Keeffe), Baldwin's Theatre, San Francisco.

The Lady of Lyons (Bulwer-Lytton), Baldwin's Theatre, San Francisco.

The Merchant of Venice (Shakespeare), Baldwin's Theatre, San Francisco.

A New Way to Pay Old Debts (Massinger), Baldwin's Theatre, San Francisco.

Othello (Shakespeare), Baldwin's Theatre, San Francisco.

The Lyons Mail (Reade), Baldwin's Theatre, San Francisco.

1880–82   *The World* (Merritt, Pettitt, and Harris), Baldwin's Theatre, San Francisco.

La Belle Russe (Belasco), Baldwin's Theatre, San Francisco.

The Stranglers of Paris (Belasco, adapted from Belot), Baldwin's Theatre, San Francisco.

The Eviction (Belasco), Baldwin's Theatre, San Francisco.

Wedded by Fate (Field and McDowell), Baldwin's Theatre, San Francisco.

Back from the Grave (Darrell), Baldwin's Theatre, San Francisco.

Four Fates, Baldwin's Theatre, San Francisco.

Transported for Life, Baldwin's Theatre, San Francisco.

The Curse of Cain (Belasco), Baldwin's Theatre, San Francisco.

The Great Divorce Case (Scott and Matthison), Baldwin's Theatre, San Francisco.

Caryswold, Baldwin's Theatre, San Francisco.

American Born (Belasco, adapted from Merritt and Pettitt's *British Born*), Baldwin's Theatre, San Francisco.

Mary Warner (Taylor), US tour.

Our Boys (H. J. Byron), US tour.

The Woman in Red (Coyne), US tour.

1882   *La Belle Russe* (Belasco), Wallack's Theatre, New York.

Young Mrs Winthrop (Howard), Madison Square Theatre, New York.

1883   *A Russian Honeymoon* (Harrison), Madison Square Theatre, New York.

The Rajah; or, Wyncot's Ward (Young, adapted by Belasco), Madison Square Theatre, New York.

The Stranglers of Paris (Belasco), New Park Theatre, New York.

Delmar's Daughter; or, Duty (De Mille), Madison Square Theatre, New York.

1884   *Alpine Roses* (Boyesen), Madison Square Theatre, New York.

May Blossom (Belasco), Madison Square Theatre, New York.

Called Back (Conway, adapted by Belasco), Fifth Avenue Theatre, New York.

1886   *Valerie* (Belasco, adapted from Sardou's *Fernande*), Wallack's Theatre, New York, and Baldwin Theatre, San Francisco.

The Marble Heart (Selby), Baldwin Theatre, San Francisco.

Anselma (adapted from Sardou's *Andrea*), Baldwin Theatre, San Francisco.

The Lady of Lyons (Bulwer-Lytton), Baldwin Theatre, San Francisco.

Alone in London (Buchanan and Jay), Baldwin Theatre, San Francisco.

The Main Line; or, Rawson's Y (De Mille and Barnard), Lyceum Theatre, New York.

A Wall Street Bandit (Gunter, adapted by Belasco), Standard Theatre, New York.

Faust (Gilbert), Lyceum Theatre, New York.

Frou-Frou (Daly), Lyceum Theatre, New York.

King René's Daughter (Martin, adapted from Herz), Lyceum Theatre, New York.

Sweethearts (Gilbert), Lyceum Theatre, New York.

1887   *Les Précieuses Ridicules* (Molière), Lyceum Theatre, New York.

The Highest Bidder (Belasco, adapted from Morton and Reece's *Trade*), Lyceum Theatre, New York.

Pawn Ticket 210 (Belasco and Greene), McVicker's Theatre, Chicago.

Editha's Burglar (Thomas and Smith), Lyceum Theatre, New York.

The Wife (Belasco and De Mille) Lyceum Theatre, New York.

She (Gillette), Niblo's Garden, New York.

1888   *Lord Chumley* (Belasco and De Mille), Lyceum Theatre, New York.

The Kaffir Diamond (Schwartz, adapted by Belasco), Broadway Theatre, New York.

1889   *Electra* (Sophocles), Lyceum Theatre, New York.

The Marquise (Belasco, adapted from Sardou's *Ferréol*), Lyceum Theatre, New York.

Robert Elsmere (Gillette, adapted from Ward), Union Square Theatre, New York.

Featherbrain (Alberry), Madison Square Theatre, New York.

The Charity Ball (Belasco and De Mille), Lyceum Theatre, New York.

1890   *The Prince and the Pauper* (Richardson), Broadway Theatre, New York.

Men and Women (De Mille and Belasco), Proctor's 23rd Street Theatre, New York.

The Ugly Duckling (Potter), Broadway Theatre, New York.

1891   *Miss Helyett* (Belasco, adapted from Boucheron), Star Theatre, New York.

1893   *The Younger Son* (Belasco, adapted from Vischer's *Schlimme Saat*), Empire Theatre, New York.

1895   *The Heart of Maryland* (Belasco), Herald Square Theatre, New York.

1897   *The First Born* (Powers), Manhattan Theatre, New York.

1899   *Zaza* (Belasco, adapted from Berton and Simon), Garrick Theatre, New York; Criterion Theatre, New York, 1900; Belasco Theatre, New York, 1903 and 1905.

1900   *Naughty Anthony* (Belasco), Herald Square Theatre, New York.

Madame Butterfly (Belasco, adapted from Long), Herald Square Theatre, New York.

1901   *Under Two Flags* (Potter), Garden Theatre, New York.

The Auctioneer (Arthur and Klein), Bijou Theatre, New York; Victoria Theatre, New York, 1903; Belasco Theatre, New York, 1913; Manhattan Opera House, New York, 1918.

Du Barry (Belasco), Criterion Theatre, New York; Belasco Theatre, New York, 1902, 1903, and 1905.

1902   *The Darling of the Gods* (Long and Belasco), Belasco Theatre, New York.

1903   *Sweet Kitty Bellairs* (Belasco, adapted from the Castles' *The Bath Comedy*), Belasco Theatre, New York; revived there, 1904.

1904   *The Music Master* (Klein), Belasco Theatre, New York; Bijou Theatre, New York, 1905 and 1906; Knickerbocker Theatre, New York, 1916.

1905   *Adrea* (Long and Belasco), Belasco Theatre, New York.

The Girl of the Golden West (Belasco), Belasco Theatre, New York; Academy of Music, New York, 1908.

1906   *The Rose of the Rancho* (Tully and Belasco), Belasco Theatre, New York.

1907   *A Grand Army Man* (Phelps, Short, and Belasco), Stuyvesant Theatre, New York, and Belasco Theatre, New York.

The Warrens of Virginia (De Mille), Belasco Theatre, New York.

1908   *The Fighting Hope* (Hurlbut), Stuyvesant Theatre, New York; Belasco Theatre, New York, 1909.

1909   *The Easiest Way* (Walter), Stuyvesant Theatre, New York; Lyceum Theatre, New York, 1921.

Is Matrimony a Failure? (Ditrichstein, adapted from Blumenthal and Kadelberg), Belasco Theatre, New York.

The Lily (Belasco, adapted from Wolff and Leroux), Stuyvesant Theatre, New York.

1910   *Just a Wife* (Walter), Belasco Theatre, New York.

The Concert (Ditrichstein, adapted from Bahr), Belasco Theatre, New York.

Nobody's Widow (Hopwood), Hudson Theatre, New York.

1911   *The Woman* (De Mille), Republic Theatre, New York.

The Return of Peter Grimm (Belasco), Belasco Theatre, New York; Belasco Theatre, New York, 1921.

1912   *The Governor's Lady* (Bradley), Republic Theatre, New York.

The Case of Becky (Locke), Belasco Theatre, New York.

David Belasco

Tainted Philanthropy (Goldknopf), Belasco Theatre, New York.

Years of Discretion (Hatton), Belasco Theatre, New York.

1913   *A Good Little Devil* (Strong, adapted from Gerard and Rostand), Republic Theatre, New York.

The Temperamental Journey (Ditrichstein, adapted from Rivoire and Mirandeis's *Pour Vivre Heureux*), Belasco Theatre, New York.

The Man Inside (Molineux), Criterion Theatre, New York.

The Secret (Bernstein), Belasco Theatre, New York.

1914   *The Phantom Rival* (Molnar), Belasco Theatre, New York.

1915   *Marie-Odile* (Knoblock), Belasco Theatre, New York.

The Boomerang (Smith and Mapes), Belasco Theatre, New York.

1916   *The Heart of Wetona* (Scarborough), Lyceum Theatre, New York.

Seven Chances (Megrue), Cohan Theatre, New York.

Little Lady in Blue (Hodges and Percyval), Belasco Theatre, New York.

1917   *The Very Minute* (Meehan), Belasco Theatre, New York.

Polly with a Past (Middleton and Bolton), Belasco Theatre, New York.

Tiger Rose (Mack), Lyceum Theatre, New York.

1918   *Daddies* (Hobble), Belasco Theatre, New York.

Tiger! Tiger! (Knoblock), Belasco Theatre, New York.

1919   *Dark Rosaleen* (Hepenstall and Kane), Belasco Theatre, New York.

The Gold Diggers (Hopwood), Lyceum Theatre, New York.

The Son-Daughter (Scarborough and Belasco), Belasco Theatre, New York.

1920   *Call the Doctor* (Archibald), Empire Theatre, New York.

One (Knoblock), Belasco Theatre, New York.

Deburau (Granville-Barker, adapted from Guitry), Belasco Theatre, New York.

1921   *The Grand Duke* (Abdullah, adapted from Guitry), Lyceum Theatre, New York.

Kiki (Belasco, adapted from Picard), Belasco Theatre, New York.

1922   *Shore Leave* (Osborne), Lyceum Theatre, New York.

The Merchant of Venice (Shakespeare), Lyceum Theatre, New York.

1923   *The Comedian* (Belasco, adapted from Guitry), Lyceum Theatre, New York.

Mary, Mary, Quite Contrary (Ervine), Belasco Theatre, New York.

Laugh, Clown, Laugh! (Cushing and Belasco, adapted from Martini), Belasco Theatre, New York.

The Other Rose (Middleton, adapted from Bourdet), Morosco Theatre, New York.

1924   *Tiger Cats* (Bramson, adapted from Orme), Belasco Theatre, New York.

The Harem (Hopwood, adapted from Vajda), Belasco Theatre, New York.

Ladies of the Evening (Gropper), Lyceum Theatre, New York.

1925   *The Dove* (Mack), Empire Theatre, New York.

Canary Dutch (Mack), Lyceum Theatre, New York.

1926   *Lulu Belle* (Sheldon and MacArthur), Belasco Theatre, New York.

Fanny (Mack and Belasco), Lyceum Theatre, New York.

Lily Sue (Mack), Lyceum Theatre, New York.

1928   *The Bachelor Father* (Carpenter), Belasco Theatre, New York.

Mima (Belasco, adapted from Molnar's *The Red Mill*), Belasco Theatre, New York.

1929   *It's a Wise Child* (Johnson), Belasco Theatre, New York.

1930   *Dancing Partner* (Engel and Grunwald, adapted by Hatton), Belasco Theatre, New York.

Tonight or Never (Hatton, adapted from Hatvany), Belasco Theatre, New York.

Other productions included: *The Ballad Monger* (Pollock and Besant); *The Beauty and the Brigands* (H. J. Byron); *Box and Cox* (Morton); *A Bull in a China Shop* (C. Mathews); *The Child of the Regiment* (Blaney); *The Corsican Brothers* (Boucicault); *Damon and Pythias* (Danim); *The Dead Heart* (Phillips); *Enoch Arden* (Matthison); *Fritz in a Madhouse*; *Green Bushes* (Buckstone); *A Hard Struggle* (Marston); *The Haunted Man*; *Ingomar* (Lovell); *The Jibbenainosay*; *Julius Caesar* (Shakespeare); *Katharine and Petruchio* (Garrick); *Katy*; *The Lancashire Lass* (H. J. Byron); *The Light-House Cliff*; *The Lone Pine* (Belasco); *The Long Strike* (Boucicault); *A Life's Revenge* (Suter); *Lost in London* (Phillips); *Medea* (Euripides); *Mimi* (Boucicault); *Money* (Bulwer-Lytton); *Nobody's Child* (Phillips); *Pizarro* (Sheridan); *The Red Pocketbook* (adapted from the French); *Rory O'Moore* (Lever); *She Stoops to Conquer* (Goldsmith); *The Spectre Bridegroom* (Rowe); *The Toodles* (Burton); *The Two Orphans* (Oxenford); *A Yankee in Cuba*.

Publications

Plays and adaptations included:
Hearts of Oak (produced 1880); *La Belle Russe* (adaptation of Merivale and Groves's *Forget-Me-Not* and Collins's *The New Magdalen*, produced 1882); *The Stranglers of Paris* (adaptation of Belot's *Les Etrangleurs de Paris*, produced 1883); *May Blossom* (produced 1884); *Valerie* (adaptation of Sardou's *Fernande*, produced 1886); *The Highest Bidder* (adaptation of Morton and Reece's *Trade*, produced 1887); *Baron Rudolph* (with Howard, produced 1887); *The Wife* (with De Mille, produced 1887); *Lord Chumley* (with De Mille, produced 1888); *The Charity Ball* (with De Mille, produced 1889); *Men and Women* (with De Mille, produced 1890); *Miss Helyett* (adaptation from Boucheron, produced 1891); *The Senator's Wife* (produced 1892); *The Girl I Left Behind Me* (with Fyles, produced 1893); *The Younger Son* (adaptation of Vischer's *Schlimme Saat*, produced 1893); *The Heart of Maryland* (produced 1895); *Zaza* (adaptation from Berton and Simon, produced 1899); *Naughty Anthony* (produced 1900); *Madame Butterfly* (adaptation from Long, produced 1900); *Du Barry* (produced 1901); *The Darling of the Gods* (with Long, produced 1902); *Sweet Kitty Bellairs* (adaptation of the Castles' *The Bath Comedy*, produced 1903); *The Music Master* (with Klein, produced 1904); *Adrea* (with Long, produced 1905); *The Girl of the Golden West* (produced 1905); *The Rose of the Rancho* (with Tully, produced 1906); *A Grand Army Man* (with Phelps and Short, produced 1907); *The Lily* (adaptation of Wolff and Leroux's *Le Lys*, produced 1909); *The Return of Peter Grimm* (produced 1911); *The Governor's Lady* (with Bradley, produced 1912); *The Secret* (adaptation from Bernstein, produced 1913); *Van Der Decken* (produced 1915); *The Son-Daughter* (with Scarborough, produced 1919); *Kiki* (adaptation from Picard, produced 1921); *Timothy* (with Hurlbut, produced 1921); *The Comedian* (adaptation from Guitry, produced 1923); *Laugh, Clown, Laugh!* (adaptation with Cushing of Martini's *Ridi Pagliaccio*, produced 1923); *Fanny* (with Mack, produced 1926); *Mima* (adaptation of Molnár's *The Red Mill*).

Other:
The Theatre Through Its Stage Door, edited by L. V. Devoe, 1919.

*

Bibliography

Books:
William Winter, *The Life of David Belasco*, 2 vols., New York, 1918.
Craig Timberlake, *The Bishop of Broadway: The Life and Work of David Belasco*, New York, 1954.
Lise-Lone Marker, *David Belasco: Naturalism in the American Theatre*, Princeton, New Jersey, 1975.
Samuel L. Leiter, *From Belasco to Brook: Representative Directors of the English-Speaking Stage*, New York, 1991.

* * *

One of the most compelling figures of the turn-of-the-century US stage, David Belasco understood the power of the image and the appeal of sentiment, not to mention emotional display, all of which he exploited to enhance his own mystique as well as to win success with the plays he wrote, directed, and produced. He was also the creator of star performers, owner of two theatres, and a prolific author of journal articles on theatrical practice and artistic philosophy. A self-styled autocrat of the theatre, he habitually wore a clerical collar (hence the epithet "bishop of Broadway") and maintained a legendary studio office crammed with books, memorabilia, curios, technical devices, and works in progress. One of his ploys for making an impression in rehearsal or business dealings was to fly into such a rage that he stamped on and smashed his pocketwatch; little did the cowed observer suspect that Belasco kept a supply of cheap watches for just such occasions. Thus, David Belasco himself was one of the greatest creations of this son of Portuguese Hebrew immigrants originally named Valasco.

Belasco began acting as a child in Victoria, British Columbia. In San Francisco in the 1860's and 1870's, he gave recitations, did imitations of famous actors, and played small roles at various venues. The generous encouragement of tragedian John McCullough was to motivate Belasco in later years to accommodate the flocks of would-be actors who wanted to recite for him. His experience of performing in California mining camps gave him an understanding of the appeals of sensation melodrama. While playing minor roles at Maguire's Theatre in San Francisco, he also worked as an assistant stage manager, prompter, secretary, and play adapter. He learned much during brief associations with Dion Boucicault and James A. Herne. As Herne's co-author and director of *Hearts of Oak* in 1880, Belasco made his first visit to New York, where he settled in 1882, writing plays and directing first at Mallory's Madison Square Theatre, later at the Lyceum, and eventually in his own two theatres, to which he gave his own name.

Belasco's skill as a director accounted for the success of his hackneyed melodramas. A fruitful collaboration with Henry C. De Mille included *The Wife* (1887), *The Charity Ball* (1889), and *Men and Women* (1890). With Franklin Fyles, he wrote *The Girl I Left Behind Me* (1893). His outstanding plays as sole author were *The Heart of Maryland* (1895), *Madame Butterfly* (1900), *Du Barry* (1901), *Sweet Kitty Bellairs* (1903), *The Girl of the Golden West* (1905), *The Rose of the Rancho* (1906), and *The Return of Peter Grimm* (1911). He also did adaptations from the French, including *Zaza* (1899) and *Kiki* (1921). He may have written or adapted as many as 200 plays in his lifetime, of which 34 were produced in New York.

It was said that Belasco practiced the most up-to-date stagecraft on the most out-of-date plays. His plays were "out-of-date" in their reliance upon melodramatic plot devices and their failure to grapple with social issues. Nor did he direct the classics, exceptions being an ambitious amateur production of Sophocles's *Electra* in 1888 and a visually opulent *Merchant of Venice*, starring David Warfield as Shylock, in 1922. Critics often took Belasco to task for the lack of substance in the plays he produced, noting his proclivity for what George Jean Nathan called "the sentimental vapourings of third- and fourth-rate writers". They acknowledged, however, that he "brought to that theatre a standard of tidiness in production" (as Nathan conceded), and "brought to it mood and atmosphere and sensuous beauty" born of "detailed discipline" (according to Walter Prichard Eaton). In other words, Belasco is most remembered for pushing stage realism to the level of naturalism in visual terms (despite hokey, overwrought plots and performances) and using the most advanced technical resources of the theatre to achieve stunning pictorial effects.

Numerous examples illustrate Belasco's genius for creating the illusion of reality on the stage. For Eugene Walter's *The Easiest Way* he bought authentic boarding-house wallpaper and furnishings, which critic Alan Dale called "indescribably real" and "absolutely perfect" in "the detail, the touches, the atmosphere". For the final scene of Alice Bradley's *The Governor's Lady* he replicated a Child's Restaurant, complete with coffee and cooking aromas. He imported antique French furniture for *Du Barry* and Japanese artefacts for *The Darling of the Gods*. In his memoir, *The Theatre Through Its Stage Door*, he mentioned engaging, when possible, actors of the same nationality as the characters they were to play.

Above all, Belasco was interested in the play of light and colour, and conducted numerous, endless experiments (often while actors waited, dropping with fatigue) to achieve a precise effect. The Belasco Theatre was touted as "the only playhouse in New York that has a machine-shop operated by power" and there, in the second sub-cellar, Belasco's lighting apparatus was manufactured. "Lights are to drama what music is to the lyrics of a song", he wrote. He boasted of having spent $5000 "in an effort to imitate certain delicate colourings of a sunset, and ... ended by throwing aside the scene altogether". For *The Girl of the Golden West* and *The Rose of the Rancho*, he persevered until he achieved a particular atmospheric quality of California light. He used lighting for striking ghostly effects in *The Darling of the Gods* and *The Return of Peter Grimm*. These efforts were supplemented by careful attention to sound effects and a melodious interplay of vocal qualities among the actors he cast.

As a "star-maker", Belasco had several important successes, beginning with Mrs Leslie Carter, a socialite whose scandalous divorce brought notoriety. However, instead of putting her on stage immediately while she was still in the news, Belasco spent over a year putting her through a rigorous training programme. It paid off with her stunning emotional performance in *The Heart of Maryland*. Other

stars made (and controlled) by Belasco were Blanche Bates, Frances Starr, David Warfield, and Lenore Ulric.

—Felicia Hardison Londré

BEL GEDDES, Norman. US designer and director. Born Norman Melancton Geddes in Adrian, Michigan, 27 April 1893. Educated at public schools in Michigan, Ohio, Pennsylvania, Illinois, and Indiana; Cleveland School of Art; Chicago Art Institute. Married 1) Helen Sneider in 1916 (died), two daughters; 2) Frances Waite in 1933 (died); 3) Anne Howe in 1944. First exhibition of designs, Saginaw, 1913; anticipated development of theatre-in-the-round with stage lacking proscenium arch, 1915; staged first of some 200 plays, introduced first focus spot lamps, and developed first lenses for stage lights, Los Angeles, 1916; stage designer, Little Theatre, Los Angeles, 1916; first New York production, 1918; designed first combined focus and flood lamp unit, 1919; designer of illumination and consultant, Architectural Commission of the Chicago World's Fair, 1929; experimented with composite settings in the 1930's; also designed numerous theatres and stage spaces; outside the theatre, he won acclaim for his many industrial designs, including cars, cameras, refrigerators, prefabricated housing, ships, furniture, and board games. Member: Art Committee of New York, from 1935; USA Inventors' Council; Authors League of America; National Academy of Science; National Research Council. Recipient: Prize for Design, Ukrainian State Theatre, Kharkov, 1930. Died in New York, 8 May 1958.

Selected productions

As set designer:
1916   *Nju* (Perelman), Little Theatre, Los Angeles.
        Papa (Akins), Little Theatre, Los Angeles.
1923   *The Miracle* (Volmöller), Century Theatre, New York.
1924   *Poor Richard* (Kerr), Hayes Theatre, New York.
        Lady Be Good (Bolton, Thompson, and Gershwin), Liberty Theatre, New York.
1925   *Follies* (Ziegfeld), New Amsterdam Theatre, New York.
1926   *The Devil in the Cheese* (Cushing), Hopkins Theatre, New York.
1927   *Damn the Tears* (Gaston), Garrick Theatre, New York.
        Spread Eagle (Brooks and Lister), Martin Beck Theatre, New York.
        Creoles (Shipman and Perkins), Klaw Theatre, New York.
        John (Barry), Klaw Theatre, New York.
1929   *Fifty Million Frenchmen* (Porter and Fields), Lyric Theatre, New York.
1936   *Dead End* (Kingsley), Belasco Theatre, New York.
        Iron Men (Gallagher), Longacre Theatre, New York.
1937   *Siege* (I. Shaw), Longacre Theatre, New York.

The Eternal Road (Werfel, adapted by Lewisohn and Drake), Manhattan Opera House,
New York.

1943   Sons and Soldiers (I. Shaw), Morosco Theatre,
New York.

Other productions included: Shanewis, 1918; Erminie
(Bellamy and Paulton), 1920; The Truth about Blayds
(Milne), 1922; The Comic Supplement (Conrad), 1924;
Quarantine, 1924; Arabesque, 1925; Julius Caesar (Shake-
speare), 1927; The Five o'Clock Girl (Bolton, Thompson,
Kalmar, and Ruby), 1927; The Patriot, 1928; Lysistrata
(Aristophanes), 1930; Hamlet (Shakespeare), 1931; Flying
Colors (Courville and Pink), 1932; It Happens on Ice, 1940;
Seven Lively Arts (Porter), 1944.

Films

As designer:
Lief the Lucky, 1919; Feet of Clay, 1924; The Sorrows of
Satan, 1925; The Pit and the Pendulum, 1925; Bermuda,
1933.

As director:
Nathan Hale, 1917; Helen of Troy, 1926; Amphibia, 1927;
Reptilia, 1927; Insects, 1927; Battle of Tushima, 1928;
Tuxedo, 1928; Juxtaposition, 1928; Atlantic Crossing,
1930, Hokus Pocus, 1930; Bicycle Boys of Barbizon, 1930;
Hamlet in Production, 1931; Mayan Architecture, 1936;
Bull Fight, 1936; Mexico Goes to Market, 1936; City of
Tomorrow, 1937.

As writer:
Nathan Hale, 1917; New York, 1925; The Pit and the
Pendulum, 1925.

Publications

A Project for a Theatrical Presentation of the Divine
Comedy of Dante Alighieri, 1923; Horizons, 1934; Magic
Motorways, 1940; Miracle in the Evening (autobiogra-
phy), edited by W. Kelley, 1960.

*

Bibliography

Articles:
Bruce Bliven, "Norman Bel Geddes: His Art and Ideas",
Theatre Arts Magazine, 3, July 1919.
Arthur Strawn, "Norman Bel Geddes", The Outlook, 12
February 1930.
"Bel Geddes", Fortune, 11, July 1930.
Hiram Motherwell, "Geddes: An Engineer in the Theatre",
Theatre Guild Magazine, November 1931.
"Geddes — The Great", The Scratch Pad, 3, July 1934.
Lucius Beebe, "From Hamlet to the World's Fair", New
York Herald-Tribune, 28 May 1939.
M. Sanchez Cobos, "Norman Bel Geddes, the Man That
Revolutionized Theatre Architecture", El Diario, 23
October 1956.
Fredrick Hunter, "Norman Bel Geddes", Texas Quarterly,
5, 1962.
Fredrick Hunter, "Norman Bel Geddes: Renaissance Man
of the Theatre", Innovations in Stage and Theatre Design,
New York, 1972.

* * *

Norman Bel Geddes was one of the most visionary and
wide-ranging of 20th-century US designers, his work spanning theatre design, stage technology, architecture, film,
and industrial design. Sometimes referred to as the "father
of streamlining", he had a profound influence upon the
development of functional and futuristic industrial design.
Many of his ideas were published in his book Horizons and
this led, among other things, to the development of the
Chrysler Airflow car. Other non-theatre projects included
an ocean liner interior, gas stoves, refrigerators, and the
Futurama exhibit at the 1939 New York World's Fair.
European influences, notably Constructivism and the work
of Le Corbusier, were evident in his architectural work and
these, together with his melding of style and function in the
objects he designed, were applied in various ways to his
theatre work. In Horizons he states: "Drama goes hand in
hand with the progress and achievements of humanity. The
theatre today needs the same aggressive spirit of experimentation that characterized progressive industry. The
quality of our drama would be enhanced if the theatre were
industrialized, which implies a modern and economical
organization, financial structure, and stabilization."

Bel Geddes rejected the ornate, Rococo-style proscenium
theatres of the day in favour of highly-mechanized and
functionally designed theatres in which the auditorium and
stage were a unified architectural entity. He began drawing
plans for several such theatres in the early 1920's, contributed plans for further theatre projects for the 1933 Century
of Progress Exposition in Chicago, and designed still more
in relation to specific productions, but none were ever
constructed. By eliminating balconies and boxes in his
proposed theatres Bel Geddes echoed Richard Wagner's
"democratic" seating and the sense of communion within
the audience. The unified stage and auditorium seemed to
echo Adolphe Appia, while the open stage plan and
mechanization allowed for continuity and fluidity in production and paralleled some of the work of the German
director Max Reinhardt.

Bel Geddes's architectural proposals focused not only on
the theatre interior, but also on its relationship to its
external environment. Presaging recent practices, his proposals included office towers and automobile ramps that
brought people right into the buildings. Most of these plans
were published in theatre and architecture journals and
monographs and thus exerted great influence on the
development of theatre architecture in the USA. The post-
World War II trend towards thrust and flexible stages owes
much to Bel Geddes's visions. At the same time he was
making technological improvements to lighting systems
and by 1919 he had developed a method that eliminated
the footlights and illuminated the stage with lights from the
bridge and balcony rail in eight Broadway theatres.

Bel Geddes's approach to scenic design was based
primarily on actor movement rather than pictorial considerations or metaphor. He was also a successful director and
saw design and direction as aspects of the same discipline.
His early stage designs included grandiose but unrealized
projects that combined the influence of Appia and Edward

Gordon Craig with multilevel sculptural and architectural stages. The most colossal of these was the project for staging Dante's *The Divine Comedy*, for which he also designed a special theatre. A model was constructed and it was finally scheduled for production at the 1933 Chicago World's Fair, but it was never done. The design envisaged a two-hour performance incorporating *Inferno*, *Purgatory*, and *Paradise*. The dominant image for the massive set was a "gyre". As described by Bel Geddes in *Miracle in the Evening*, the stage, 135 feet wide by 165 feet deep, "would be modelled on the form of the funnel". The rear wall of the funnel, made of steps and levels, was to rise some five stories above stage level, with four towers rising even higher toward the domed roof of the theatre some 120 feet above the centre of the pit.

Bel Geddes achieved theatrical fame in 1924 with the transformation of the Century Theatre into a Gothic cathedral for Max Reinhardt's New York production of *The Miracle*. It was, at the time, the largest theatrical spectacle ever mounted in New York, including not just a set but a complete environment that camouflaged the auditorium and created the awe-inspiring atmosphere of a cathedral throughout. The reviews were as laudatory of his contribution as they were of Reinhardt's. Bel Geddes performed a similar transformation once more, though on a smaller scale, in 1936 when he tore out the proscenium of the Manhattan Opera House for the production of Franz Werfel's *The Eternal Road*, for which the set rose out of the orchestra pit and soared up to 50 feet above the rear of the stage.

Ironically, his best-known Broadway production after *The Miracle* was a hyper-realistic setting of an apartment building overlooking the East River in New York, complete with water tank in the orchestra pit, for Sidney Kingsley's *Dead End*. Although Bel Geddes was virtually the only US designer or director with the vision and sense of Craig, Reinhardt, or Appia, Broadway economics and tastes limited and circumscribed his work. His creativity had to find other outlets that the commercial theatre was unable to provide.

—Arnold Aronson

BELLAMY, George Anne. Irish actress. Born in Fingal, Ireland, c.1727 (23 April 1733, or 1731, according to Bellamy), illegitimate daughter of Lord Tyrawley (misnamed George Anne possibly in error for Georgiana). Educated in a convent in Boulogne between the ages of five and 11. Bigamously married actor West Digges; eloped with George Montgomery Metham in 1749, one son; lovers included politician John Calcraft, by whom she had one son and one daughter. Stage debut, 1741; first appearance at Covent Garden, London, under Christopher Rich, 1741; appeared with David Garrick for the first time, 1743; actress, Smock Alley Theatre and Aungier Street Theatre, both in Dublin, under Thomas Sheridan, 1745–46; returned to Covent Garden, 1748–50; joined Garrick at the Theatre Royal, Drury Lane, 1750–53; hugely acclaimed in chiefly tragic roles; engaged at Covent Garden, opposite Spranger Barry, 1753–59, Smock Alley Theatre, 1760–61, Covent Garden, 1761–62; acted in Edinburgh, 1764, then returned to Covent Garden, 1764–70; suffered ill health

from 1757; retired, 1770; last appearance, 1780. Died in London, 16 February 1788.

Roles

1741   Columbine's Servant in *Harlequin Barber* (anon.), Covent Garden, London.
1742   Miss Prue in *Love for Love* (Congreve), Covent Garden, London.
1743   Andromache in *The Distresst Mother* (Racine, adapted by Philips), private performance, Kington.
1744   Monimia in *The Orphan* (Otway), Covent Garden, London.
        Aspasia in *The Maid's Tragedy* (Beaumont and Fletcher), Covent Garden, London.
1745   Celia in *Volpone* (Jonson), Covent Garden, London.
        Arsinoe in *Mariamne* (Fenton), Covent Garden, London.
        Mrs Bullen in *Henry VIII* (Shakespeare), Covent Garden, London.
        Desdemona in *Othello* (Shakespeare), Smock Alley Theatre, Dublin.
        Cleopatra in *All for Love* (Dryden), Smock Alley Theatre, Dublin.
        Queen in *The Spanish Friar* (Dryden), Smock Alley Theatre, Dublin.
        Queen in *Richard III* (Shakespeare), Smock Alley Theatre, Dublin.
        Cherry in *The Beaux' Stratagem* (Farquhar), Smock Alley Theatre, Dublin.
1746   Calista in *The Fair Penitent* (Rowe), Smock Alley Theatre, Dublin.
        Cordelia in *King Lear* (Shakespeare), Smock Alley Theatre, Dublin.
        Andromache in *Orestes* (Theobald), Smock Alley Theatre, Dublin.
        Athenias in *Theodosius* (Lee), Smock Alley Theatre, Dublin.
        Imoinda in *Oroonoko* (Southerne), Smock Alley Theatre, Dublin.
        Almeyda in *Don Sebastian, King of Portugal* (Dryden), Smock Alley Theatre, Dublin.
        Jane Shore in *Jane Shore* (Rowe), Smock Alley Theatre, Dublin.
        Marcia in *Cato* (Addison), Smock Alley Theatre, Dublin.
        Leonora in *The Revenge* (Behn), Smock Alley Theatre, Dublin.
        Arpasia in *Tamerlane* (Rowe), Smock Alley Theatre, Dublin.
        Indiana in *The Conscious Lovers* (Steele), Smock Alley Theatre, Dublin.
        Portia in *The Merchant of Venice* (Shakespeare), Smock Alley Theatre, Dublin.
1747   Doris in *Aesop* (Vanbrugh), Smock Alley Theatre, Dublin.
        Lady Townly in *The Provoked Husband* (Cibber and Vanbrugh), Smock Alley Theatre, Dublin.
        Sigismunda in *Tancred and Sigismunda* (Thomson), Smock Alley Theatre, Dublin.

George Anne Bellamy as the Comic Muse.

Mrs Biddy in *Miss in Her Teens* (Garrick), Smock Alley Theatre, Dublin.

Belvidera in *Venice Preserved* (Otway), Smock Alley Theatre.

Clarinda in *The Suspicious Husband* (Hoadly), Smock Alley Theatre, Dublin.

Lady Macbeth in *Macbeth* (Shakespeare), Smock Alley Theatre, Dublin.

Amanda in *Love's Last Shift* (Cibber), Smock Alley Theatre, Dublin.

Flippanta in *The Confederacy* (Vanbrugh), Smock Alley Theatre, Dublin.

Mrs Sullen in *The Beaux' Stratagem* (Farquhar), Smock Alley Theatre, Dublin.

1748   Lady Sadlife in *The Double Gallant* (Cibber), Smock Alley Theatre, Dublin.

Lady Betty Modish in *The Careless Husband* (Cibber), Smock Alley Theatre, Dublin.

Alinda in *The Loyal Subject* (Fletcher), Smock Alley Theatre, Dublin.

Constance in *King John* (Shakespeare), Smock Alley Theatre, Dublin.

Almeria in *The Mourning Bride* (Congreve), Smock Alley Theatre, Dublin.

Laetitia in *The Old Bachelor* (Congreve), Smock Alley Theatre, Dublin.

Lady Froth in *The Double-Dealer* (Congreve), Smock Alley Theatre, Dublin.

Millamant in *The Way of the World* (Congreve), Smock Alley Theatre, Dublin.

1748–49   Elcria in *The Emperor of the Moon* (Behn), Covent Garden, London.

Volumnia in *Coriolanus* (Shakespeare), Covent Garden, London.

Eudocia in *The Siege of Damascus* (Hughes), Covent Garden, London.

Statira in *The Rival Queens* (Cibber), Covent Garden, London.

Harriet in *The Man of Mode* (Etherege), Covent Garden, London.

Lady Percy in *Henry IV* (Shakespeare), Covent Garden, London.

1750   Juliet in *Romeo and Juliet* (Shakespeare), Covent Garden, London, and Theatre Royal, Drury Lane, London.

Octavia in *All for Love* (Dryden), Covent Garden, London.

Eltruda in *Alfred* (Kotzebue), Theatre Royal, Drury Lane, London.

1751   Ismena in *Phaedra and Hippolytus* (Smith), Theatre Royal, Drury Lane, London.

1752   Countess of Rutland in *The Earl of Essex* (Jones), Theatre Royal, Drury Lane, London.

Lady Jane Gray in *Lady Jane Gray* (Rowe), Theatre Royal, Drury Lane, London.

Eugenia in *Eugenia* (Francis), Theatre Royal, Drury Lane, London.

1754   Empress Fulvia in *Constantine* (Francis), Covent Garden, London.

1755   Eurydice in *Oedipus* (Dryden and Lee), Covent Garden, London.

Zara in *Zara* (Garrick, adapted from Hill), Covent Garden, London.

1757   Lady Randolph in *Douglas* (Home), Covent Garden, London.

Alzira in *Alzira* (Voltaire), Covent Garden, London.

1758   Cleone in *Cleone* (Dodsley), Covent Garden, London.

1762   Estifania in *Rule a Wife and Have a Wife* (Fletcher), Edinburgh.

Veturia in *Coriolanus* (Thomson), Covent Garden, London.

Lady Fanciful in *The Provoked Wife* (Vanbrugh), Covent Garden, London.

1769–70   Alicia in *Jane Shore* (Rowe), Covent Garden, London; revived there, 1780 (her last appearance).

Berinthia in *The Relapse* (Vanbrugh), Covent Garden, London.

Roxana in *The Rival Queens* (Cibber), Covent Garden, London.

Isabella in *Isabella* (Southerne), Covent Garden, London.

Other roles included: *The Provoked Wife* (Vanbrugh), Covent Garden, London, 1748–49.

Publications

An Apology for the Life of George Anne Bellamy (autobiography, with Alexander Bicknell), 6 vols., 1785.

*

Bibliography

Books:
"Gentleman of Covent Garden Theatre", *Memoirs of George Anne Bellamy*, London, 1785.
Cyril H. Hartmann, *Enchanting Bellamy*, London, 1956.

* * *

George Anne Bellamy was strictly speaking among the second rank of actresses, but during her prime she challenged the best of her contemporaries in pathetic tragedy and outstripped even Susanna Cibber's fame by virtue of her scandalous private life. Her greatest performances were as characters of suffering innocence, such as Juliet and Desdemona, Monimia in Otway's *The Orphan*, and Belvidera in his *Venice Preserved*. More violent roles, like Lady Macbeth, were thought to be "out of character" for her. She also played leading roles in comedies of manners and in sentimental comedies, including Lady Townly in Cibber's *The Provoked Husband* and Indiana in Steele's *The Conscious Lovers*, but she remained primarily known as a tragic actress.

Bellamy's success in tragedy owed much to her considerable beauty and her "softness", which together made an embodiment of the feminine ideal for many of her contemporaries. A poem addressed to her near the beginning of her career praised her in these terms:

> The Grace-adorning Smile! the feign'd Despair!
> The soft'ning Sigh! the Soul-dissolving Tear!
> Each magic Charm, lamented Oldfield knew,
> Inchanting Bellamy! revives in you.

When she participated in the 1750 *Romeo and Juliet* contest between Drury Lane and Covent Garden, as Garrick's Juliet, she successfully rivalled Mrs Cibber, not because she was a more skilful actress but because of her greater youth and beauty. The author of a comparison between the two actresses found that he "shed more tears on seeing Mrs Cibber", but was "more delighted in seeing Mrs Bellamy" and Francis Gentleman noted that "Mrs Bellamy was an object of love, Mrs Cibber of admiration". Similarly, as Monimia, Bellamy "looked and spoke all the passages of amorous feeling, much better" than Mrs Cibber.

An essential component of her success was her ability to display tenderness with the apparent sincerity that was highly valued in contemporary acting. The author of the *Theatrical Review for 1757* wrote admiringly that her performances demonstrated that "habit has not yet steeled her heart, nor dried her eyes of the precious fluid ... real, undissembled tears speak her feeling". In his treatise on acting, John Hill commended her Juliet and her Cordelia in his chapter on the benefits of "an amorous disposition", attributing her success in these characters to "an heart ... more susceptible of tenderness than any other passion".

Hill's comment also suggests the contribution that her notorious love-life made to her reputation as an actress.

Bellamy's credibility in the expression of pathetic tenderness was achieved despite monotonous delivery and stilted deportment. She had a "strong taint of the old fashioned titumiti utterance" and her "motions ... savoured too much of the looking-glass", according to Gentleman. In her *Apology*, however, she claims to have pioneered a "simple" performance style when she originated the virtuous and victimized heroine of Dodsley's tragedy *Cleone*. "The language was simple, and I determined that my performance of it should be the same," she reports. "The unaffected naiveté, which I intended to adopt in the representation, was accompanied by the same simplicity in my dress": that is, she wore no hoop. Her representation of Cleone's madness was so different from the "noise and violence" with which "*mad* stage ladies" were usually performed that the author feared for the success of the attempt, but, according to Bellamy, "I succeeded ... beyond my most sanguine hopes". Although the *Apology* is chronically inaccurate and self-serving, she was so well-received that she was credited with the play's success.

Bellamy's career was, however, ultimately tied to her appearance. Her beauty played an important part in her original, precocious success and as it declined with age (from about 1760) her status dwindled. Nevertheless, she played Juliet, among other leading roles, into her last season.

The *Apology*, which may or may not have been actually written by her, is a sensational and romanticized version of her life that emphasizes the love affairs that, to a great degree, shaped her career and reputation. It is an entertaining, if unreliable, attempt at legend-making and a classic example of actress (auto)biography.

—Nancy Copeland

BELLOTTI-BON, Luigi. Italian actor-manager and playwright. Born Luigi Bellotti in Udine, 17 April 1820. Trained under his adoptive father F. A. Bon. Stage debut as a child in Bon's company; acted as a young man with the company of Gustavo Modena, 1845, among others, at Verona, Milan, Padua and elsewhere; appeared alongside Adelaide Ristori and Cesare Rossi as a member of the Reale Sarda, from 1854; director of the Reale Sarda, from 1855; toured Europe, 1856–58; founded his own company, 1859; promoted the work of young playwrights; expanded company into three troupes, 1873, but got into severe and lasting financial difficulties. Died (suicide) in Milan, 31 January 1883.

Principal productions

1845   *Il Bicchier d'acqua* (Scribe), Verona; acted Lord Bolingbroke.
            Camaraderie (Scribe), Verona; acted Bernadet.
1850   *Notte di S. Silvestro* (Castellvecchio).
1854   *Niente di male* (Bellotti-Bon), Compagnia Reale Sarda.
            Spensieratizza e buon cuore (Bellotti-Bon), Compagnia Reale Sarda.

1863   *Il Vero blasone* (Testa), Compagnia Bellotti-
        Bon.
1867   *I Mariti* (Torelli), Florence.

Publications

Van Dyck á Londres (translated from Carré and Narrey),
1875; *Condizioni dell'arte drammatica in Italia*, 1875.
Plays included: *Lo Studente di Salamanca*; *Spensieratez-
za e buon cuore*; *L'Arte di far fortuna*; *I Lancieri*; *Un
Cappello che vola*; *Alice e storione*.

*

Bibliography

Books:
Enrico Montasio, *Luigi Bellotti-Bon, cenni biografici*, Flor-
    ence, 1865.
Guiseppe De Abate, *Bellotti-Bon e la Reale Sarda*, Rome,
    1903.

* * *

The Italian theatre of the 19th century was dominated by
the great international touring stars and the lavish and
passionate operas of Giuseppe Verdi. Extravagance and
flair characterize our impression of the Italian performers
of the era, in which distinct, personal interpretations of the
classical repertoire prevailed in both the dramatic and the
operatic theatre. Shakespeare was in the ascendancy and
the darling of the virtuoso performers.

Against this backdrop of colour and flamboyance stands
the steady figure of Luigi Bellotti-Bon, the antithesis of the
eccentric or savage and sublime actor-celebrity. Bellotti-
Bon, in the centuries-old tradition, had learned his craft
from his family from an early age, being particularly
influenced by his adoptive father, the actor-manager and
dramatist Francesco Augusta Bon. By the age of 17 he was
already playing "young lover" roles in productions presented by Bon and Tassani. Over the next 15 years he appeared
with numerous Italian companies, playing a great variety of
roles and establishing himself as a formidable comic actor.
Most notable was his work with the company led by
Gustavo Modena. Modena, a heralded actor-manager and
teacher, had travelled extensively throughout Europe and
had spent a period of time in London during the political
unrest of the 1830's. Perhaps Modena had seen the theatre
of William Charles Macready and was aware of Macready's
progressive approach to management, rehearsal techniques,
and unity in productions. Modena transferred an interest
in Shakespeare to his students and promoted a dramatic
repertoire that included works by new French writers.
Bellotti-Bon's employment with the company began in
1845 alongside another budding Italian actor, Tommaso
Salvini, and it is apparent that his acting in dramatic and
tragic roles under the tutorship of Modena was significant
in his evolution as a theatre artist.

Bellotti-Bon's performance style had little in common
with the powerful animal-like force that Salvini later
displayed. On the contrary, Bellotti-Bon's stage aura was
one of dignity, reserve, and self-confidence. While both
Salvini and Bellotti-Bon were famous for their portrayals of
the Ludro character in F. A. Bon's plays, their interpreta-

tions were very different. Bellotti-Bon emphasized ease and
natural spontaneity rather than brilliant premeditated
effects. He was instinctive — eager, open, and jovial —
with a stability and diplomacy that endowed him with
outstanding leadership qualities. His acting was not characterized by the sudden burst of fury or orchestrated losses of
control that made Salvini such a stunning performer.

Bellotti-Bon had performance experience with all three of
the great Italian touring performers: Adelaide Ristori,
Cesare Rossi, and Tommaso Salvini. In the mid-1850's,
when he was 35 years old, he had established himself as the
equal of Rossi and Salvini (who were slightly younger than
he was) and as a member of the Reale Sarda company often
shared with Rossi the honour of playing leading man to
Ristori, in which role he was seen on tour in France,
Germany, Britain, and the Low Countries. These international tours gave Bellotti-Bon a chance to observe a variety
of theatre and acting styles and it is possible that he saw
Rachel perform in Paris, or Emil Devrient and Bogumil
Dawison on the German stage.

Bellotti-Bon's career did not develop, however, in parallel
with his fellow-stars. While most successful Italian actors
were enthusiastic in pursuing their profession outside Italy,
Bellotti-Bon chose to remain and to concentrate on influencing the profession at home. This was a challenging task,
given the political uncertainties surrounding Italian unification and the lack of support for the dramatic theatre.
While Ristori had brought Italy to the attention of international theatre audiences, theatre in Italy was still seen as a
minor art when compared to the theatre in Paris or London
and especially when viewed alongside Italian opera. Bellotti-Bon had the determination and personality to make a
difference in this perception.

Having formed his own company in Italy in 1859,
inspired in part by the ensemble work of the Meynadier
Company in France, Bellotti-Bon devoted himself to high-
quality drama that encouraged the ensemble rather than
the individual and aimed for unity in productions as a
whole. Reminiscent of Macready in England and foresha-
dowing the Duke of Saxe-Meiningen in Germany, he
became an actor-manager whose role was close to the
modern concept of the stage director.

No one did more to establish a new Italian dramatic
tradition than Bellotti-Bon. He encouraged the production
of contemporary drama dealing with social issues, promoting the plays of Paolo Ferrari and then Achille Torelli
before later switching to historical dramas and romantic
comedies by such authors as Pietro Cossa and Giuseppe
Giacosa. He was the driving force behind the development
of at least a dozen new Italian playwrights and also
presented many notable French plays by the likes of Augier,
Dumas *fils*, and Sardou, effectively paving the way in Italy
for the dramas of Henrik Ibsen.

The success of Bellotti-Bon's company inspired him to
expand by dividing his troupe into three distinct companies but this proved a serious miscalculation as financial
troubles disrupted further progress and led to a deteriora-
tion in quality. From 1875, two years after the expansion,
the problems steadily worsened. Tragically, in 1883, the
firm, admirable, and vivacious Bellotti-Bon could no
longer endure the difficulties and committed suicide. His
sacrifice sent shock waves through the theatre community
and brought to the forefront the massive obstacles —
funding, an indigenous literature, and a universally accept-

ed dialect — that blocked the way to the establishment of an exemplary prose theatre in Italy.

—Ron Popenhagen

BENSON, (Sir) Frank. British actor-manager. Born Francis Robert Benson in Alresford, Hampshire, England, 4 November 1858. Educated at Winchester College, 1871–78; New College, Oxford University, 1878–81, no degree. Married actress Gertrude Constance Featherstonhaugh Samwell in 1886, one son and one daughter. Early theatrical experience as a founder of what became the Oxford University Dramatic Society; professional debut, under Henry Irving, Lyceum Theatre, London, 1882; acquired control of touring company, 1883; conducted numerous provincial tours over succeeding years, winning particular acclaim for his Shakespeare productions, frequently seen at Stratford-upon-Avon; first London season, Globe Theatre, 1889–90; acted alongside Ellen Terry, 1902; tour of USA and Canada, 1913–14; served as Red Cross ambulance driver in France during World War I, 1916–18; staged theatrical comeback, 1920; tour of South Africa, 1921–22; last appearance as a director at Stratford-upon-Avon festival (his 26th), 1919; last London appearance, 1933; granted civil list pension, 1933. Governor of Shakespeare Memorial Theatre; trustee of Shakespeare Birthplace. LL.D, University of Montreal, 1913–14. Freedom of the borough of Stratford-upon-Avon, 1910; Freedom of Cork. Croix de Guerre (France), 1918. Knighted in theatre at close of performance of *Julius Caesar*, 1916. Died in London, 31 December 1939.

Roles

1882   Paris in *Romeo and Juliet* (Shakespeare), Imperial Theatre, London, and British tour; US and Canadian tour, 1913–14.
Fabian in *The Corsican Brothers* (Boucicault), British tour.
Hamlet in *Hamlet* (Shakespeare), British tour; Lyceum Theatre, London, 1900; US and Canadian tour, 1913–14; St Martin's Theatre, London, 1920; South African tour, 1921–22; British tour, 1925–26.
Claude Melnotte in *The Lady of Lyons* (Bulwer-Lytton), British tour.
Shylock in *The Merchant of Venice* (Shakespeare), British tour; British tour, 1890; US and Canadian tour, 1913–14; Kensington Theatre, London, 1920; South African tour, 1921–22; British tour, 1926 and 1932.
Sir Frederick Blount in *Money* (Bulwer-Lytton), Lyceum Theatre, London.
1883   Sir Anthony Absolute in *The Rivals* (Sheridan), British tour.
Doricourt in *The Belle's Stratagem* (Daly), British tour.
Evelyn in *Money* (Bulwer-Lytton), British tour.
Glavis in *The Lady of Lyons* (Bulwer-Lytton), British tour.

Rosencrantz in *Hamlet* (Shakespeare), British tour.
1884   Othello in *Othello* (Shakespeare), British tour.
1885   Macbeth in *Macbeth* (Shakespeare), British tour; British tour, 1903.
Charles Surface in *The School for Scandal* (Sheridan), British tour.
1886   Richard in *Richard III* (Shakespeare), Shakespeare Memorial Theatre, Stratford-upon-Avon; South African tour, 1921–22.
Caius in *The Merry Wives of Windsor* (Shakespeare); US and Canadian tour, 1913–14; South African tour, 1921–22; Winter Garden Theatre, London, 1932.
1887   Young Marlow in *She Stoops to Conquer* (Goldsmith), British tour.
Randinelli in *Priest or Painter* (Poel), Shakespeare Memorial Theatre, Stratford-upon-Avon.
1888   Quince in *A Midsummer Night's Dream* (Shakespeare), Shakespeare Memorial Theatre, Stratford-upon-Avon.
1889   Lysander in *A Midsummer Night's Dream* (Shakespeare), Globe Theatre, London; Lyceum Theatre, London, 1900.
1890   Caesar in *Julius Caesar* (Shakespeare), British tour; Theatre Royal, Drury Lane, London, 1916.
1891   Rosmer in *Rosmersholm* (Ibsen), British tour.
1891–99 Caliban in *The Tempest* (Shakespeare), British tour; Lyceum Theatre, London, 1900.
Timon in *Timon of Athens* (Shakespeare), British tour.
Coriolanus in *Coriolanus* (Shakespeare), British tour.
Henry in *Henry IV, part 2* (Shakespeare), British tour.
Richard in *Richard II* (Shakespeare), British tour; Lyceum Theatre, London, 1900; US and Canadian tour, 1913–14; British tour, 1925–26.
1892   Orlando in *As You Like It* (Shakespeare), British tour.
1899   Beaufort in *Henry VI, part 2* (Shakespeare), Shakespeare Memorial Theatre, Stratford-upon-Avon.
Dick the butcher in *Henry VI, part 2* (Shakespeare), Shakespeare Memorial Theatre, Stratford-upon-Avon.
Richelieu in *Richelieu* (Bulwer-Lytton), Shakespeare Memorial Theatre, Stratford-upon-Avon.
1900   Henry in *Henry V* (Shakespeare), Lyceum Theatre, London; Shaftesbury Theatre, London, 1914.
Captain Absolute in *The Rivals* (Sheridan), Lyceum Theatre, London; British tour, 1927–29.
Malvolio in *Twelfth Night* (Shakespeare), Lyceum Theatre, London; US and Canadian tour, 1913–14; South African tour, 1921–22; Worthing, 1932.
Mark Antony in *Antony and Cleopatra* (Shakespeare), Lyceum Theatre, London.

1900–01	Diarmuid in *Diarmuid and Grania* (Yeats and Moore), British tour.
1901	Bottom in *A Midsummer Night's Dream* (Shakespeare), Birmingham.
	Second Executioner in *King John* (Shakespeare), Shakespeare Memorial Theatre, Stratford-upon-Avon.
	Cardinal Wolsey in *Henry VIII* (Shakespeare), British tour.
1902	Lear in *King Lear* (Shakespeare), British tour.
1903	Aylmer in *Aylmer's Secret* (Phillips), Strand Theatre, London.
	Bobadil in *Every Man In His Humour* (Jonson), Shakespeare Memorial Theatre, Stratford-upon-Avon.
	Giovanni in *Paolo and Francesca* (Walcott), Shakespeare Memorial Thearte, Stratford-upon-Avon.
	Leontes in *The Winter's Tale* (Shakespeare), Shakespeare Memorial Theatre, Stratford-upon-Avon.
1904	Edward in *Edward II* (Marlowe), Shakespeare Memorial Theatre, Stratford-upon-Avon.
	Antipholus in *The Comedy of Errors* (Shakespeare), Shakespeare Memorial Theatre, Stratford-upon-Avon.
	Orestes in *Orestes* (Morshead and Warre), Shakespeare Memorial Thearte, Stratford-upon-Avon.
1906	Talbot in *Henry VI, part 1* (Shakespeare), Shakespeare Memorial Theatre, Stratford-upon-Avon.
1907	Belville in *The Country Girl* (Daly), Shakespeare Memorial Theatre, Stratford-upon-Avon.
	Berowne in *Love's Labour's Lost* (Shakespeare), Shakespeare Memorial Theatre, Stratford-upon-Avon.
	Don Quixote in *Don Quixote* (Morrison and Stewart, adapted from Cervantes), Shakespeare Memorial Theatre, Stratford-upon-Avon.
1908	John in *King John* (Shakespeare), British tour.
1909	Crabtree in *The School for Scandal* (Sheridan), British tour.
	Posthumus Leonatus in *Cymbeline* (Shakespeare), Shakespeare Memorial Theatre, Stratford-upon-Avon.
1910	The Piper in *The Piper* (Peabody), St James's Theatre, London.
	First Outlaw in *The Two Gentlemen of Verona* (Shakespeare), Shakespeare Memorial Theatre, Stratford-upon-Avon.
1911	Puff in *The Critic* (Sheridan), Shakespeare Memorial Theatre, Stratford-upon-Avon.
1912	Villon in *If I Were King* (M'Carthy), Shakespeare Memorial Theatre, Stratford-upon-Avon.
	Cnaeius Pompeius Magnus in *Pompey the Great* (Masefield), British tour; St Martin's Theatre, London, 1920.
1913–14	Benedick in *Much Ado About Nothing* (Shakespeare), His Majesty's Theatre, Montreal.
	Petruchio in *The Taming of the Shrew* (Shakespeare), US and Canadian tour; South African tour, 1921–22.
	Jaques in *As You Like It* (Shakespeare), US and Candian tour.
1914	Friar Laurence in *Romeo and Juliet* (Shakespeare), British tour.
1915	Theseus in *A Midsummer Night's Dream* (Shakespeare), Court Theatre, London.
1916	Parolles in *All's Well That Ends Well* (Shakespeare), Shakespeare Memorial Theatre, Stratford-upon-Avon.
1921–22	Matthias in *The Wandering Jew* (Whiting), South African tour.
	Mark Antony in *Julius Caesar* (Shakespeare), South African tour.
1923	Sir Peter Teazle in *The School for Scandal* (Sheridan), British tour.
1925	Edgar in *King Lear* (Shakespeare), British tour.
	First Witch in *Macbeth* (Shakespeare), British tour.
1926	First Witch in *Faust* (Wills), British tour.
1927	Beau Nash in *Monsieur Beaucaire* (Tarkington), British tour.
	Hardcastle in *She Stoops to Conquer* (Goldsmith), British tour.

Other roles included: The Ghost in *Hamlet* (Shakespeare); Mercutio in *Romeo and Juliet* (Shakespeare); and role in *Elizabethan Triumph* (pageant), Earl's Court, London, 1912.

Films

Richard III, 1910; *Julius Caesar*, 1910; *Macbeth*, 1910; *The Taming of the Shrew*, 1910; *Becket*, 1923.

Publications

My Memoirs, 1930; *I Want to Go on the Stage*, 1931.

*

Bibliography

Books:
Constance Benson, *Bensonian Memories*, London, 1926.
J. C. Trewin, *Benson and the Bensonians*, London, 1960.

* * *

The son of a well-to-do lawyer, Frank Benson entered the theatre via the Oxford University Dramatic Society, where he attracted the attention of Henry Irving and Ellen Terry with his performance as Clytemnestra in Aeschylus's *Agamemnon*. Irving was sufficiently impressed to say that should Benson decide upon a stage career "I shall be only too glad to give you any help I can".

Always an athlete, Benson possessed a striking "Roman" appearance, with a mop of ill-kempt hair. Prior to making his professional debut with Irving at the Lyceum in September 1882, he sought the tutelage of various masters of elocution, all of them by then distinctly venerable:

Walter Lacy, William Creswick, and Hermann Vezin. Vocally, therefore, Benson was moulded in the traditions of the mid-19th century stage. At this point in his career he was criticised for his awkward, angular movements, unnatural, sing-song delivery, and ungraceful and ill-timed gestures. Through his long acting career (he played Hamlet when he was 73) Benson never completely eradicated these mannerisms; indeed, they became entrenched. There was always something of the amateur about Benson's acting, the true consistency of the professional eluding him. As his biographer J. C. Trewin wrote: "he had to be met upon his night; his quality could rise and fall like a fever chart". In comedy he tended toward broad effects. His Petruchio in *The Taming of the Shrew* was boorish, becoming farcically knock-about and brutal in his treatment of Katherine. His Malvolio was judged to be over-acted, lacking in those touches of pathos (tragedy even) which other subtler actors brought out.

Benson was forthrightly heroic as Henry V, but he received his greatest acclaim (from C. E. Montague) as Richard II. Montague found in Benson's performance the complete artist-king: "the exercise of exquisite responsiveness to the appeal made to his artistic sensibility by whatever life throws for the moment in his way". Thus he revelled in the 'idea' of a king's fall, his separation from his wife, and even his death. Perhaps this concept of the unhappy monarch owed more to the critic than the actor; nevertheless, the part remained one of Benson's most celebrated creations.

However, it was as a manager that Benson sustained his career. Although he played a London season at the Lyceum Theatre during 1890, the response to it did not encourage any metropolitan aspirations. Instead he devoted his life to touring the English provinces, with the annual Stratford-upon-Avon Festivals being a regular engagement in the period 1886–1919. In his heyday, Benson had four companies touring concurrently; he also visited Canada and the USA (1913–14) and South Africa (1921). Despite all this managerial activity, Benson was no businessman and in February 1911 he ceded control to F. R. Benson and Company Limited ("The Syndicate"), which paid him a salary of £20 a week.

Benson was an idealist. Sidney Lee listed the five points of Benson's creed: that the full range of Shakespeare's plays should be performed; the programme should be changed regularly, giving no play a disproportionate run; all actors should be trained in speaking blank verse; plays should not be adapted for the sake of one part; and, finally, the scenery should be simple and subordinate to dramatic interest. Whatever Benson's own shortcomings as an actor may have been, his company became a recognised training ground for the profession. Benson's wife Constance took a leading role in this training function, despite the fact that her own acting was the subject of a dispute between Benson and the governors of the Stratford Memorial Theatre, who in May 1911 intimated that they did not regard her as a suitable leading lady.

Team spirit was the essence of Benson's regime. Max Beerbohm couched his review of Henry V in the language of the cricket field: "As a branch of university cricket, the whole performance was indeed beyond praise. But as a form of acting, it was not impressive". Sport played an important part in the life of Benson's companies — indeed Oscar Ashe reckoned that his engagement owed more to his prowess as a wicket-keeper than to his acting talent. Sporting fixtures were part of the touring lifestyle and Benson was still playing football at the age of 56; he was even reputed to punt along the Avon during Leontes' lengthy absence from the stage in *The Winter's Tale*.

Absurd as much of this sounds in retrospect, Benson made a serious and sustained contribution to the English theatre over half a century. He brought Shakespeare to mass audiences, earnestly liaising with schools for special matinée performances. The productions and much of the acting may have bordered on the makeshift, but there was enthusiasm and dedication in abundance. Robert Morley leaves a vivid picture of Benson in later life: making do with stock scenery (Morley was positioned to obscure a deckchair painted on the backcloth pressed into service for the sea-coast of Illyria in *Twelfth Night*) and forgetful of his lines, even of which part he was playing, but going everywhere at a jog-trot and delivering himself of an immensely effective speech to the audience at the fall of the curtain.

Benson's was a peculiarly English form of theatre through which he secured a special place in the affections of audiences across the land. In 1910 he became the second actor (Garrick was the first) to receive the Freedom of the Borough of Stratford-upon-Avon; he was knighted by George V in the royal box during the Shakespeare Tercentenary performance at Drury Lane in May 1916. On each occasion his fellow professionals enthusiastically endorsed the public recognition conferred on him.

Appropriately, Benson's achievements have a lasting memorial in the Benson Memorial window in the Picture Gallery at the (now) Royal Shakespeare Theatre, Stratford-upon-Avon.

—Richard Foulkes

BERGMAN, (Ernst) Ingmar. Swedish director. Born in Uppsala, Sweden, 14 July 1918. Educated at the University of Stockholm. Married Ingrid Karleboven Rosen in 1971; eight children by previous marriages. Led amateur theatre group at university; artistic director, City Theatre, Hälsingborg, 1944–46; debut as film director, 1946; director, City Theatre, Gothenburg, 1946–49; directed at the Intima Teatern, Stockholm, 1950; first of many productions at the Dramaten [Royal Dramatic Theatre], Stockholm, 1951; artistic director, City Theatre, Malmö, 1952–58, and at the Dramaten, Stockholm, 1963–66; first production outside Sweden, 1967; lived in Munich for nine years after argument with Swedish tax authorities, 1976; retired from films, 1982; returned to the Dramaten, 1985; director, Madame de Sade Theatre, 1989. Member: European Cinema Society (chairman, from 1989); Swedish Academy of Letters. Recipient: Cannes Film Festival Special Prize, 1956; Oscar, 1959, 1961; Erasmus Prize, 1965; National Society of Film Critics Award, 1970; Order of the Yugoslav Flag, 1971; Luigi Pirandello International Theatre Prize, 1971; Goethe Prize, 1976; Gold Medal, Swedish Academy, 1977; European Film Award, 1988; Le Prix Sonning, 1989; Praemium Imperiale Prize (Japan), 1991. Honorary doctorate: University of Rome, 1988. Commander, Légion d'honneur, 1985.

Ingmar Bergman

Productions

1944   *Ascheberskan på Widtskövle* (von Horn and Collin), City Theatre, Hälsingborg.
Hvem er Jeg? [Who Am I?] (Soya), City Theatre, Hälsingborg.
Macbeth (Shakespeare), City Theatre, Hälsingborg.

1945   *Kriss-Krass-filibom* (revue), City Theatre, Hälsingborg.
Sagan [The Legend] (H. Bergman), City Theatre, Hälsingborg.
Reducera moralen [Morality Reduced] (Bergström), City Theatre, Hälsingborg.
Jacobowsky and the Colonel (Werfel), City Theatre, Hälsingborg.
Rabies (Hedberg), City Theatre, Hälsingborg.
Pelikanen [The Pelican] (Strindberg), Intimate Stage, City Theatre, Malmö.

1946   *Rekviem* (Höijer), City Theatre, Hälsingborg.
Rakel och biografvakmästaren [Rachel and the Cinema Doorman] (I. Bergman), Intimate Stage, City Theatre, Malmö.
Caligula (Camus), City Theatre, Gothenburg.

1947   *Magic* (Chesterton), City Theatre, Gothenburg.
Dagen slutar tidigt [Early Ends the Day] (I. Bergman), City Theatre, Gothenburg.
Mig till skräck [To My Terror] (I. Bergman), City Theatre, Gothenburg.

1948   *Dans på bryggan* [Dance on the Wharf] (Höijer), City Theatre, Gothenburg.
Macbeth (Shakespeare), City Theatre, Gothenburg.
Thieves' Carnival (Anouilh), City Theatre, Gothenburg.

1949   *La Sauvage* (Anouilh), City Theatre, Gothenburg.
A Streetcar Named Desire (T. Williams), City Theatre, Gothenburg.

1950   *Divine Words* (Valle-Inclán), City Theatre, Gothenburg.
The Threepenny Opera (Brecht), Intima Teatern, Stockholm.
En skugga [A Shadow] (H. Bergman), Intima Teatern, Stockholm.
Medea (Anouilh), Intima Teatern, Stockholm.

1951   *Det lyser i kåken* [Light in the Hovel] (Höijer), Dramaten, Stockholm.
The Rose Tattoo (T. Williams), Municipal Theatre, Norrköping.

1952   *Mordet i Barjärna* [The Murder at Barjärna] (I. Bergman), City Theatre, Malmö.
Kronbruden [The Crown-Bride] (Strindberg), City Theatre, Malmö.

1953   *Six Characters in Search of an Author* (Pirandello), City Theatre, Malmö.
The Castle (Brod, adapted from Kafka), City Theatre, Malmö.

1954   *Spöksonaten* [The Ghost Sonata] (Strindberg), City Theatre, Malmö.
The Merry Widow (Lehár), City Theatre, Malmö.

1955   *Dom Juan* (Molière), City Theatre, Malmö.
Teahouse of the August Moon (Patrick), City Theatre, Malmö.
Trämålning [Painting on Wood] (I. Bergman), City Theatre, Malmö.
Lea och Rakel [Leah and Rachel] (Moberg), City Theatre, Malmö.

1956   *The Poor Bride* (Ostrovsky), City Theatre, Malmö.
Cat on a Hot Tin Roof (T. Williams), City Theatre, Malmö.
Erik XIV (Strindberg), City Theatre, Malmö.

1957   *Peer Gynt* (Ibsen), City Theatre, Malmö.
Le Misanthrope (Molière), City Theatre, Malmö.

1958   *Sagan* [The Legend] (H. Bergman), City Theatre, Malmö; revived there and at the Théâtre Sarah Bernhardt, Paris, 1959.
Ur-Faust (Goethe), City Theatre, Malmö; London, 1959.
Värmlänningarna [The People of Värmland] (Dahlgren), City Theatre, Malmö.

1961   *The Seagull* (Chekhov), Dramaten, Stockholm.
The Rake's Progress (Stravinsky and Auden), Royal Opera, Stockholm.

1963   *Who's Afraid of Virginia Woolf?* (Albee), Dramaten, Stockholm.
Sagan [The Legend] (H. Bergman), Dramaten, Stockholm.

1964   *Tre knivar från Wei* [Three Knives from Wei] (Martinson), Dramaten, Stockholm.

Hedda Gabler (Ibsen), Dramaten, Stockholm; revived at Helsingfors and at the Dramaten, Stockholm, and in Berlin, 1967; Aldwych Theatre, London, 1968.

1965   *Dom Juan* (Molière), Dramaten, Stockholm.
Tiny Alice (Albee), Dramaten, Stockholm.

1966   *The Investigation* (Weiss), Dramaten, Stockholm.
The School for Wives (Molière), Dramaten, Stockholm.

1967   *Six Characters in Search of an Author* (Pirandello), Nationaltheatret, Oslo.

1969   *Woyzeck* (Büchner), Dramaten, Stockholm.

1970   *Ett dröspel* [A Dream Play] (Strindberg), Dramaten, Stockholm; Aldwych Theatre, London, 1971.
Hedda Gabler (Ibsen), Cambridge Theatre, London.

1971   *Show* (Forssell), Dramaten, Stockholm.

1972   *Vildanden* [The Wild Duck] (Ibsen), Dramaten, Stockholm; Aldwych Theatre, London, 1973.

1973   *Spöksonaten* [The Ghost Sonata] (Strindberg), Dramaten, Stockholm.
Le Misanthrope (Molière), Danish Royal Theatre, Copenhagen; Dramaten, Stockholm, 1974.

1974   *Till Damaskus* [To Damascus] (Strindberg), Dramaten, Stockholm.

1975   *Twelfth Night* (Shakespeare), Dramaten, Stockholm.

1977   *Ett dröspel* [A Dream Play] (Strindberg), Residenztheater, Munich.

1978   *The Three Sisters* (Chekhov), Residenztheater, Munich, and German tour.

1979   *Tartuffe* (Molière), Residenztheater, Munich.
Hedda Gabler (Ibsen), Residenztheater, Munich.
Twelfth Night (Shakespeare), Dramaten, Stockholm; Paris, 1980.

1980   *Yvonne, Princess of Burgundy* (Gombrowicz), Residenztheater, Munich.

1981   *Nora and Julie* (Ibsen's *A Doll's House* and Strindberg's *Miss Julie*), Residenztheater, Munich.
Scener ur ett äktenskap [Scenes from a Marriage] (I. Bergman), Theater im Marstall, Munich.
Fröken Julie [Miss Julie] (Strindberg), Dramaten, Stockholm.

1983   *Dom Juan* (Molière), Salzburg.

1984   *King Lear* (Shakespeare), Dramaten, Stockholm.

1985   *Fröken Julie* [Miss Julie] (Strindberg), Dramaten, Stockholm.
Ett dröspel [A Dream Play] (Strindberg), Dramaten, Stockholm.
John Gabriel Borkman (Ibsen), Munich.

1986   *Hamlet* (Shakespeare), Dramaten, Stockholm.
Ett dröspel [A Dream Play] (Strindberg), Dramaten, Stockholm.

Films

As screenwriter:
Hets [Frenzy], 1944; *Kvinna utan ansikte* [Woman Without a Face], 1947; *Eva*, 1948; *Medan staden sover* [While the City Sleeps], 1950; *Frånskild* [Divorced], 1951; *Sista paret ut* [Last Couple Out], 1956; *Lustgården* [The Pleasure Garden], 1961; *Good Intentions*, 1989.

As director:
Kris [Crisis], 1946; *Det regnar på vår kärlek* [It Rains on Our Love], 1946; *Musik i mörker* [Music in the Dark], 1947; *Skepp till Indialand* [A Ship Bound for India], 1947; *Hamnstad* [Port of Call], 1948; *Fängelse* [Prison/The Devil's Wanton], 1949; *Törst* [Three Strange Loves/Thirst], 1949; *Till glädje* [To Joy], 1950; *Sånt händer inte här* [This Can't Happen Here], 1950; *Sommarlek* [Summer Interlude/Illicit Interlude], 1951; *Kvinnors väntan* [Waiting Women], 1952; *Sommaren med Monika* [Summer with Monika], 1952; *Gycklornas Afton* [The Naked Night/Sawdust and Tinsel], 1953; *En lektion i kärlek* [A Lesson in Love], 1954; *Det sjunde inseglet* [The Seventh Seal], 1955; *Kvinnodröm* [Dreams/Journey into Autumn], 1955; *Sommarnattens leende* [Smiles of a Summer Night], 1955; *Nära livet* [So Close to Life], 1957; *Smultronstället* [Wild Strawberries], 1957; *Ansiktet* [The Face/The Magician], 1958; *Jungfrukällen* [The Virgin Spring], 1959; *Djävulens öga* [The Devil's Eye], 1959; *Såsom i en spegel* [Through a Glass Darkly], 1961; *Nattvardsgästerna* [Winter Light], 1962; *Tystnaden* [The Silence], 1962; *För att inte tala om alla dessa kvinnor* [Now About These Women], 1964; *Persona*, 1966; *Vargtimmen* [The Hour of the Wolf], 1968; *Skammen* [The Shame], 1968; *En passion* [Passion], 1969; *The Touch*, 1971; *Viskningar och rop* [Cries and Whispers], 1973; *Das Schlangenei*, 1977; *Herbstsonate* [Autumn Sonata], 1978; *Aus dem Leben der Marionetten*, 1980; *Fårö-dokument 1979* [Fårö Document 1979], 1980; *Fanny och Alexander* [Fanny and Alexander], 1982; *After the Rehearsal*, 1984.

As actor:
Kallelsen [The Vocation], 1974; *Paradistorg* [Summer Paradise], 1976; *A Look at Liv*, 1977.

Television

As director:
Herr Sleeman kommer [Mr Sleeman is Coming], 1957; *The Venetian*, 1958; *Rabies*, 1958; *Oväder* [Storm Weather], 1960; *Första varningen* [First Warning], 1960; *Leka med elden* [Playing with Fire], 1961; *Ett dröspel* [A Dream Play], 1963; *Don Juan*, 1965; *Riten* [The Rite], 1969; *Reservatet* [Sanctuary], 1970; *Scener ur ett äktenskap* [Scenes from a Marriage] (series), 1973; *The Misanthrope*, 1974; *Trollflöjten* [The Magic Flute], 1975; *Ansikte mot ansikte* [Face to Face], 1975.

Radio

Leka med elden [Playing with Fire], 1947; *The Dutchman*, 1947; *Mother Love*, 1948; *Staden* [The City], 1951; *Brott och brott* [Crimes and Crimes], 1952; *Easter*, 1952;

Blodsbröllop [Blood Wedding], 1952; *The Dutchman*, 1953.

Publications

Jack hos skådespelerna, 1946; *Moraliteter*, 1948; *Trämålning: En moralitat*, 1956; *Four Screenplays*, 1960; *The Virgin Spring*, 1960; *Three Films by Ingmar Bergman*, 1967; *Persona and Shame*, 1972; *Filmberättelser*, 3 vols., 1973; *Bergman on Bergman*, 1973; *Scenes from a Marriage*, 1974; *Face to Face*, 1976; *Four Stories*, 1977; *The Serpent's Egg*, 1978; *Autumn Sonata*, 1979; *From the Life of the Marionettes*, 1980; *The Magic Lantern* (autobiography), 1988; *Fanny and Alexander*, 1989; *My Life in Films*, 1993; *Sunday's Child*, 1994.

*

Bibliography

Books:
Peter Cowie, *Ingmar Bergman*, London, 1962.
Birgitta Steene, *Ingmar Bergman*, Boston, 1968.
Arthur Gibson, *The Silence of God*, New York, 1969.
Robin Wood, *Ingmar Bergman*, New York, 1969.
Vernon Young, *Cinema Borealis: Ingmar Bergman and the Swedish Ethos*, New York, 1972.
Jörn Donner, *The Films of Ingmar Bergman*, New York, 1972.
John Simon, *Ingmar Bergman Directs*, New York, 1972.
Stuart M. Kaminsky (ed.), *Ingmar Bergman: Essays in Criticism*, Oxford, 1975.
Maria Bergom-Larsson, *Ingmar Bergman and Society*, London and South Brunswick, New Jersey, 1978.
Vilgot Sjöman, *L 136: Diary with Ingmar Bergman*, Ann Arbor, Michigan, 1978.
Lise-Lone Marker and Frederick J. Marker, *Ingmar Bergman, A Life in the Theatre*, Cambridge, 1992.

* * *

Incessantly innovative and indeed revolutionary in his approaches, Ingmar Bergman has become one of the most influential directors in European theatre since World War II. In declaring his love of the theatre, he has characteristically foregrounded the actors: "to work with them ... learning to listen to the playwright's words and to his heart together with the actors ... that is a way of living; that is the best of all". The refined simplicity that has become a hallmark of many of Bergman's productions stems from a growing reliance on the suggestive powers of the actors on the stage.

A self-taught theatre director, Bergman has acknowledged the role of Swedish predecessors such as Olof Molander and Alf Sjöberg; and the influence of Torsten Hammerén, under whom he worked at the Gothenburg City Theatre, became seminal. Prominent among Bergman's more than 80 major productions are works by 20th-century European, US, and Swedish playwrights, including Pirandello and Anouilh, O'Neill and Albee, Hjalmar Bergman and Per Olov Enquist; his relatively few productions of Shakespeare include *Twelfth Night* (1975) and notoriously bleak versions of *King Lear* (1984) and *Hamlet* (1986). However,

Bergman has become best known for his productions of Molière and, especially, Strindberg.

Bergman has testified to the impact of his encounter with Molière at the Comédie Française in 1949; and his productions, which have included *Dom Juan* (1955, 1965, 1983), *Le Misanthrope* (1957, 1973), and *Tartuffe* (1979), have brought to the fore a theatricality that can be seen to be fundamental to Bergman's work in the theatre. It is, he has said, "tremendously important ... that you take the pretence utterly seriously and that you remain aware all the time that it is pretence and never imagine anything else". His 1955 and 1956 productions of *Dom Juan* made use of a stage within the stage, in line with Bergman's conviction that each stage has a focal point, an optimum of communication between actors and audience around which the production should be constructed. His 1957 *Le Misanthrope*, pivotal to the interpretation of Molière in Sweden, placed actors and spectators in a shared space by extending the acting area into the auditorium, the meticulously choreographed movements of the characters on the chequer-board of the stage highlighting the significance of erotic tension in the play.

The radical simplification of Bergman's productions of Ibsen has focused the inner, psychological drama. While his *Peer Gynt* in 1957 initially found himself among realistic props, these gradually gave way to projections and then to an increasingly bare stage as the spiritual journey of the central character was illuminated. In an epoch-making production of *Hedda Gabler* in 1964, the foregrounding of Hedda's inner room, with her piano and her father's pistols, focused her sense of entrapment, the phases of her personal plight relentlessly exposed to the audience. Bergman's *Et Dukkehjem* [A Doll's House], retitled *Nora* and performed together with Strindberg's *Miss Julie* in Munich in 1981, developed the theme of entrapment in the context of masquerade and role-playing, perceived by Bergman as the play's central metaphor. In his much-acclaimed version of *Vildanden* [The Wild Duck] in 1972, Bergman focused the role of illusion and escapism by locating the attic in the space between the stage and the audience and making it wholly dependent on the suggestive powers of the actors; and his production of *John Gabriel Borkman* in Munich in 1985 assumed the proportions of a reckoning with artistic obsession and ruthlessness.

Bergman has produced more works by Strindberg than by any other playwright, Strindberg having been his "companion and teacher" since he was 10. These have included *Pelikanen* [The Pelican], *Kronbruden* [The Crown-Bride], and *Erik XIV*; but the breakthrough came with *Ett drömspel* [A Dream Play] in 1970. Bergman's version marginalised the Eastern mysticism and gave the Poet a crucial role: his desk, centre stage, became the focal point of the action, with the other characters emerging as projections of his imagination. Bergman's 1986 *Drömspel*, again in Stockholm, strengthened many of these features but also drew on a kaleidoscope of back projections to reinforce the pictorial fluidity of a dream. His *Till Damaskus* [To Damascus] in 1974 was a daring synthesis of the first two parts of the work, relying on swift transformations to give a dreamlike quality to the movement inwards and down into the mind of The Unknown.

Strindberg's *Spöksonaten* [The Ghost Sonata] has been hailed by Bergman as "the most remarkable play ever to be written in Swedish", and his three productions (1941,

1954, 1973) testify to an affinity that has generated a growing boldness. While his 1954 production, as Bergman pointed out in his programme note, took its starting-point in the tradition established by Molander and simultaneously freed itself from this model, the 1973 production amounted to a radical innovation in that it presented the entire drama as a dream. By suggesting that the dreamer was sinking ever deeper into a dream that was becoming increasingly grotesque, Bergman was able to integrate the notoriously difficult final act, his Student embarking on a verbal unmasking of the Lady that emerged as a parallel of the Mummy's unmasking of Hummel in the previous act. In a starkly simple setting, the mercilessness of the plight of humankind was underlined by the suggestion of a cyclical pattern, the Student and the Lady eventually on their way to becoming another Hummel and another Mummy.

A theatre performance, Bergman has stressed, is first and foremost an emotional experience, similar to the experience of a piece of music or a film, with any intellectual consequences necessarily being secondary. It is a conviction that illuminates his seemingly paradoxical claim that his intention "is not to be an innovator": "I want only to present the play and make it live in the hearts of an audience".

—Helen Forsås-Scott

BERNHARDT, Sarah. French actress and playwright. Born Sarah Henriette Rosine Bernard in Paris, France, 22 October 1844. Educated at schools in Paris; studied acting at the Paris Conservatoire, from 1860. Married Jacques Damala in 1882 (separated 1883); one son by previous partner. Stage debut, Théâtre de la Tour d'Auvergne, 1861; actress, Comédie-Française, 1862; first appearance at Gymnase, 1863; debut at Théâtre de l'Odéon, 1866; organized hospital for wounded at the Odéon during siege of Paris, 1870; rejoined Comédie-Française, 1872; made sociétaire of the Comédie-Française, 1875; London debut, 1879; controversial departure from Comédie-Française, 1880; entered management with own company, 1880; first tour of many US tours, 1881; co-manager (with son Maurice), Théâtre Ambigu, 1881; manager, Théâtre du Porte Saint-Martin, 1883–86; declared bankrupt, 1883; world tour, 1891–93; manager, Théâtre de la Renaissance, 1893–99; manager, Théâtre des Nations, renamed Théâtre Sarah Bernhardt, 1899–1923; raised funds for the wounded in World War I; right leg amputated, 1915; farewell tour of USA, 1916–18; last London season, 1921. Légion d'Honneur, 1913. Died in Paris, 26 March 1923.

Roles

1861	Edouard V in *Les Enfants d'Edouard* (Delavigne), Théâtre de la Tour d'Auvergne, Paris; London, 1880.
	Richelieu in *Les premières armes de Richelieu* (Bayard and Dumanoir), Théâtre de la Tour d'Auvergne, Paris.
1862	Iphigénie in *Iphigénie* (Racine), Comédie-Française, Paris.

	Valérie in *Valérie* (Scribe), Comédie-Française, Paris; tour, 1883.
	Henriette in *Les Femmes Savantes* (Molière), Comédie-Française, Paris.
	Hippolyte in *L'Étourdi* (Molière), Comédie-Française, Paris.
1863	Madame de Rives in *La Maison sans Enfants* (Dumanoir), Gymnase, Paris.
	Anita in *Le Père de la Débutante* (Théaulon and Bayars), Gymnase, Paris.
	Amélie de Villefontaine in *Le Démon du Jeu* (Barrière), Gymnase, Paris.
	Jeannette in *Un Soufflet n'est Jamais Perdu* (Bayard), Gymnase, Paris.
	Anita in *L'Étourneau* (Bayard and Laya), Gymnase, Paris.
	Clémence in *Le Premier Pas* (Labiche and Delacour), Gymnase, Paris.
1864	Duchinka in *Un Mari Qui Lance sa Femme* (Deslandes), Gymnase, Paris.
1865	Princess Désirée in *La Biche Aux Bois* (Coignard), Gymnase, Paris.
1866	Silvia in *Le Jeu de L'Amour et du Hasard* (Marivaux), Théâtre de L'Odéon, Paris.
	Aricie in *Phèdre* (Racine), Théâtre de l'Odéon, Paris; revived, 1873.
1867	Armande in *Les Femmes Savantes* (Molière), Théâtre de L'Odéon, Paris.
	Amélie in *Aux Arrêts* (De Boissières), Théâtre de L'Odéon, Paris.
	Albine then Junie in *Britannicus* (Racine), Théâtre de l'Odéon, Paris; Comédie-Françoise, Paris, 1872 (as Junie).
	Angélique in *Le Malade Imaginaire* (Molière), Théâtre de L'Odéon, Paris.
	Hortense in *Le Legs* (Marivaux), Théâtre de L'Odéon, Paris.
	Zacharie in *Athalie* (Racine), Théâtre de L'Odéon, Paris.
	Baronne d'Arglade in *Le Marquis de Villemer* (Sand), Théâtre de L'Odéon, Paris.
	Mariette in *François le Champi* (Sand), Théâtre de L'Odéon, Paris.
1868	Hortense in *Le Testament de César Girodot* (Belot and Villetard), Théâtre de L'Odéon, Paris.
	Anna Damby in *Kean* (Dumas *père*), Théâtre de L'Odéon, Paris.
	Cordelia in *Le Roi Lear* (Shakespeare), Théâtre de L'Odéon, Paris.
	Laure Dufour in *La Loterie du mariage* (Barbier), Théâtre de L'Odéon, Paris.
	Julia Vidal in *Le Drame de la Rue de la Paix* (Belot), Théâtre de L'Odéon, Paris.
1869	Zanetto in *Le Passant* (Coppée), Théâtre de L'Odéon, Paris.
	Jeanne in *Le Bâtard* (Touroude), Théâtre de L'Odéon, Paris.
1870	Bérénice in *L'Affranchi* (de Saint Ybars), Théâtre de L'Odéon, Paris.
	Hélène de Mérangis in *L'Autre* (Sand), Théâtre de L'Odéon, Paris.

1871   Thérèse in *Jean-Marie* (Theuriet), Théâtre de l'Odéon, Paris, and London; Théâtre de la Renaissance, Paris, 1895; Théâtre Sarah Bernhardt, Paris, 1902.

Marthe in *Fais ce que dois* (Coppée), Théâtre de L'Odéon, Paris.

Geneviève in *La Baronne* (Foussier), Théâtre de L'Odéon, Paris.

1872   Mlle Aïssé in *Mlle Aïssé* (Bouilhet), Théâtre de L'Odéon, Paris.

Doña Maria de Neubourg in *Ruy Blas* (Hugo), Odéon; Comédie-Française, Paris, and London, 1879.

Gabrielle in *Mlle de Belle-Isle* (Dumas *père*), Comédie-Française, Paris.

1873   Chérubin in *Le Mariage de Figaro* (Beaumarchais), Comédie-Française, Paris.

Hélène in *Mademoiselle de la Seiglière* (Sandeau), Comédie-Française, Paris.

Léonora Falconieri in *Dalila* (Feuillet), Comédie-Française, Paris; Théâtre Sarah Bernhardt, Paris, 1899.

Mistress Douglas in *L'Absent* (Manuel), Comédie-Française, Paris.

Marthe in *Chez l'Avocat* (Ferrier), Comédie-Française, Paris.

Andromaque in *Andromaque* (Racine), Comédie-Française, Paris; London and Théâtre Sarah Bernhardt, Paris, 1912.

1874   Caroline de la Roseraie in *Le Péril dans la demeure* (Feuillet), Comédie-Française, Paris.

Berthe de Savigny in *Le Sphinx* (Feuillet), Comédie-Française, Paris.

Henri de Ligniville in *La Belle Paule* (Decayrouse), Comédie-Française, Paris.

Zaïre in *Zaïre* (Voltaire), Comédie-Française, Paris.

Phèdre in *Phèdre* (Racine), Comédie-Française, Paris; Théâtre de la Renaissance, Paris, 1893; Théâtre Sarah Bernhardt, Paris, 1899, 1902, 1909, 1911, and 1914.

1875   Berthe in *La Fille de Roland* (de Bournier), Comédie-Française, Paris.

Gabrielle in *Gabrielle* (Augier), Comédie-Française, Paris.

1876   Mistress Clarkson in *L'Étrangère* (Dumas *fils*), Comédie-Française, Paris; London, 1877.

La Muse in *La Nuit de mai* (Musset), Comédie-Française, Paris; Théâtre Sarah Bernhardt, Paris, 1900.

Posthumia in *Rome vaincue* (Parodi), Comédie-Française, Paris, and London.

1877   Doña Sol in *Hernani* (Hugo), Comédie-Française, Paris; London, 1879.

1878   Desdemona in *Othello* (Shakespeare), Comédie-Française, Paris.

Alcmène in *Amphitryon* (Molière), Comédie-Française, Paris; Théâtre de la Renaissance, Paris, 1895.

1879   Monime in *Mithridate* (Racine), Comédie-Française, Paris.

1880   Doña Clorinde in *L'Aventurière* (Augier), Comédie-Française, Paris.

Adrienne Lecouvreur in *Adrienne Lecouvreur* (Scribe), London; revived in London, 1905, and at the Théâtre Sarah Bernhardt, Paris, 1907.

Gilberte in *Froufrou* (Meilhac and Halévy), London; Théâtre du Porte Saint-Martin, 1883.

Marguerite Gautier in *La Dame aux Camélias* (Dumas *fils*), Booth Theatre, New York; London, 1881; Théâtre de la Gaîté, Paris, 1882; Théâtre du Porte Saint-Martin, 1883; Théâtre des Variétés, Paris, 1889; Théâtre de la Renaissance, Paris, 1893 and 1896, and at the Théâtre Sarah Bernhardt, Paris, 1899, 1905, 1908, 1909, 1912, and 1914.

1881   Blanche de Chelles in *Le Sphinx* (Feuillet), London.

The Princess in *La Princesse Georges* (Dumas *fils*), Boston.

1882   Esther in *Les Faux Ménages* (Pailleron), Lyon and London.

Fédora in *Fédora* (Sardou), Vaudeville, Paris; London, 1883; Théâtre du Porte Saint-Martin, Paris, 1886; Théâtre de la Renaissance, Paris, 1893; Théâtre Sarah Bernhardt, Paris, 1902 and 1909.

1883   Djemma in *Nana Sahib* (Richepin), Théâtre du Porte Saint-Martin, Paris.

1884   Macbeth in *Macbeth* (Shakespeare), Théâtre du Porte Saint-Martin, Paris, and London.

Théodora in *Théodora* (Sardou), Théâtre du Porte Saint-Martin, Paris; Théâtre Sarah Bernhardt, Paris, 1902.

1885   Marion Delorme in *Marion Delorme* (Hugo), Théâtre du Porte Saint-Martin, Paris.

1886   Ophelia in *Hamlet* (Shakespeare), Théâtre du Porte Saint-Martin, Paris.

Claire de Beaulieu in *Le Maître de Forges* (Ohnet), Buenos Aires.

1887   Tosca in *La Tosca* (Sardou), US tour; Lyceum Theatre, London, 1888; Théâtre de la Renaissance, Paris, 1894 and 1897; Théâtre Sarah Bernhardt, Paris, 1899 and 1909.

1888   Francine de Riverolles in *Françillon* (Dumas *fils*), Lyceum Theatre, London.

Comtesse Marthe de Rocca in *L'Aveu* (Bernhardt), US tour.

Thérèse in *Thérèse Raquin* (Zola), US tour.

1889   Léna Despard in *Léna* (Berton), Théâtres des Variétés, Paris, and London.

1890   Jeanne d'Arc in *Jeanne d'Arc* (Barbier), Théâtre du Porte Saint-Martin, Paris, and London.

Cléopâtre in *Cléopâtre* (Sardou and Moreau), Théâtre du Porte Saint-Martin, Paris; London, 1892.

1891   Pauline in *Pauline Blanchard* (Darmont and Humblot), London and Australian tour.

1892   Léah in *Léah* (Darmont), Boston and London.

Camille in *On ne badine pas avec l'amour* (Musset), New York.

1893   Princesse Wilhelmine in *Les Rois* (Lemaître), Théâtre de la Renaissance, Paris; London, 1894.

Sarah Bernhardt

1894 Césarine in *La Femme de Claude* (Dumas *fils*), Théâtre de la Renaissance, Paris, and London; Théâtre Sarah Bernhardt, Paris, 1902 and 1904.

Gismonda in *Gismonda* (Sardou), Théâtre de la Renaissance, Paris.

1895 Magda in *Magda* (Sudermann), Théâtre de la Renaissance, Paris, and London; Théâtre Sarah Bernhardt, Paris, 1902 and 1904.

Mélissinde in *La Princesse Lointaine* (Rostand), Théâtre de la Renaissance, Paris, and London.

1896 Lorenzo in *Lorenzaccio* (Musset, adapted by D'Artois), Théâtre de la Renaissance, Paris; London, 1897; Théâtre Sarah Bernhardt, Paris, 1912.

1897 Simone d'Aubenas in *Spiritisme* (Sardou), Théâtre de la Renaissance, Paris, and London.

La Samaritaine in *La Samaritaine* (Rostand), Théâtre de la Renaissance, Paris; Théâtre Sarah Bernhardt, Paris, 1899, 1902, 1904, 1909 and 1912; Coliseum Theatre, London, 1913.

Madeleine in *Les Mauvais Bergers* (Mirbeau), Théâtre de la Renaissance, Paris.

1898 Anne in *La Ville Morte* (D'Annunzio), Théâtre de la Renaissance, Paris.

1899 Hamlet in *Hamlet* (Shakespeare, adapted by Marcel Schwob), Théâtre Sarah Bernhardt, Paris; and Adelphi Theatre, London.

1900 The King of Rome in *L'Aiglon* (Rostand), Théâtre Sarah Bernhardt, Paris; Théâtre Sarah Bernhardt, Paris, and London, 1901; Théâtre Sarah Bernhardt, Paris, 1903, 1905, 1909, 1912, 1914, 1918, and 1922.

Léonie de Rénat in *L'Etincelle* (Pailleron), Théâtre Sarah Bernhardt, Paris.

Roxane in *Cyrano de Bergerac* (Rostand), New York.

1902 Francesca in *Francesca da Rimini* (Crawford), Théâtre Sarah Bernhardt, Paris, and London.

1903 Hermione in *Andromaque* (Racine), Théâtre Sarah Bernhardt, Paris, and London.

Circé in *Circé* (Richet), Monte-Carlo.

Fanny Legrand in *Sapho* (Daudet), His Majesty's Theatre, London.

Joséphine de Beauharnais in *Plus que reine* (Bergerat), London.

Cabestaing in *La Légende du Coeur* (Aicard), Théâtre antique d'Orange.

Jane in *Jane Wedeking* (Philippe), Théâtre Sarah Bernhardt, Paris.

Zoraya in *La Sorcière* (Sardou), Théâtre Sarah Bernhardt, Paris; London, 1904 and 1907.

1904 Madame de Maujordain in *Le Festin de la Mort* (De Castellanne), Théâtre Sarah Bernhardt, Paris.

Marie-Antoinette in *Varennes* (Lenôtre and Lavedan), Théâtre Sarah Bernhardt, Paris.

Pelléas in *Pelléas et Mélisande* (Maeterlinck), London, 1905.

1905 La Tisbé in *Angelo, Tyran de Padoue* (Hugo), Théâtre Sarah Bernhardt, Paris, and London.

Assuérus in *Esther* (Racine), Théâtre Sarah Bernhardt, Paris.

1906 Soeur Thérèse in *La Vierge D'Avila* (Mendès), Théâtre Sarah Bernhardt, Paris.

1907 Jacasse in *Les Bouffons* (Zamaçois), Théâtre Sarah Bernhardt, Paris; revived, 1910.

Queen Margaret in *Le Vert galant* (Moreau), Théâtre Sarah Bernhardt, Paris.

Thérèze de Mégée in *Le Réveil* (Hervieu), Théâtre-Français, London.

Landry in *La Belle au Bois Dormant* (Richepin and Cain), Théâtre Sarah Bernhardt, Paris.

1908 Cléonice in *La Courtisane de Corinthe* (Carré and Bilhaud), Théâtre Sarah Bernhardt, Paris.

Dominique Brienne in *Le Passé* (Portoriche), Théâtre Sarah Bernhardt, Paris.

1909 Joan in *Le Procès de Jeanne d'Arc* (Moreau), Théâtre Sarah Bernhardt, Paris; Coliseum Theatre, London, 1911.

1910 Gianetto Malespine in *La Beffa* (Benelli and Richepin), Théâtre Sarah Bernhardt, Paris.

Jacqueline Fleuriot in *La Femme X ...* (Bisson), Théâtre Sarah Bernhardt, Paris.

1911 Béatrice in *Soeur Béatrice* (Maeterlinck), Chicago.

Lucrèce in *Lucrèce Borgia* (Hugo), Théâtre Sarah Bernhardt, Paris; Coliseum Theatre, London, 1912.

Dorine in *Tartuffe* (Molière), Théâtre Sarah Bernhardt, Paris.

1912 Élisabeth in *La Reine Élisabeth* (Moreau), Théâtre Sarah Bernhardt, Paris; Coliseum Theatre, London.

Marion in *Une Nuit de Noël sous La Terreur* (Maurice Bernhardt and Cain), Coliseum Theatre, London.

Sarah Bernhardt Jubilee, Théâtre Sarah Bernhardt, Paris.

1913 Jeanne in *Jeanne Doré* (Tristan Bernhardt), Théâtre Sarah Bernhardt, Paris.

1914 Cléopâtre in *La Mort de Cléopâtre* (Maurice Bernhardt and Cain), Théâtre Sarah Bernhardt, Paris; Coliseum Theatre, London.

Marquise de Chalonne in *Tout á Coup* (De Cassagnac), Théâtre Sarah Bernhardt, Paris.

1920 Athalie in *Athalie* (Racine), Théâtre Sarah Bernhardt, Paris.

Other roles included: *La Gloire de Molière* (de Banville), Théâtre de L'Odéon, Paris, 1869; *Pierrot assassin* (Richepin), Trocadéro, Paris, 1883; *La Passion* (Haraucourt), Cirque d'Hiver, Paris, 1890; *La Dame de Chalant* (Giacosa), Cincinnati, 1891; *Izéyl* (Silvestre and Morand), Théâtre de la Renaissance, Paris, and London, 1894; *Lysiane* (Coolus), Théâtre de la Renaissance, Paris, 1894; *Médée* (Mendès), Théâtre de la Renaissance, Paris, 1894; *Les Précieuses ridicules* (Molière), Théâtre Sarah Bernhardt, Paris, 1901; *Théroigne de Méricourt* (Hervieu), Théâtre Sarah Bernhardt, Paris, 1902; *Werther* (Decourcelle), Théâtre Sarah Bernhardt, Paris, 1903; *Bohèmos* (Zamaçois), Monte-Carlo and London, 1903; *La Fille de Rabenstein* (Remon); Théâtre Sarah Bernhardt, Paris, 1909; *Judas* (De Kay), Globe Theatre, New York, 1910;

Les Cathédrales (Morand), Théâtre Sarah Bernhardt, Paris, 1915; *Du Théâtre au Champ d'Honnête*, Coliseum Theatre, London, 1915–20; *Daniel* (Verneuil), Théâtre Sarah Bernhardt, Paris, 1920; *La Gloire* (Rostand), Paris, 1921; *La Mort de Molière* (Rostand), Théâtre Sarah Bernhardt, Paris, 1922; *Régine Armand* (Verneuil), Théâtre Sarah Bernhardt, Paris, 1922.

Films

Hamlet's Duel, 1900; *Tosca*, 1908; *La Dame aux Camélias*, 1911; *Queen Elizabeth*, 1912; *Adrienne Lecouvreur*, 1913; *Jeanne Doré*, 1914; *Mères Françaises*, 1917; *La Voyante*, 1923.

Publications

L'Aveu (one act play), Paris, 1888; "A Christmas Story", *The Strand Magazine*, December 1893; "Men's Roles as Played by Women", *Harper's Bazaar*, December 1900; *Ma Double vie: mémoires de Sarah Bernhardt*, 1907 and 1923 (*The Memoirs of Sarah Bernhardt*, 1907 and 1924); *Adrienne Lecouvreur* (play), 1908; *Un coeur d'homme* (play), 1911; *La Petite idole* (novel), 1920 (*The Idol of Paris*, 1921); *Jolie Sosie* (novel), 1922; *L'Art du théâtre*, 1923 (*The Art of the Theatre*, 1924); *The Memoirs of Sarah Bernhardt*, edited by Sandy Lesberg, 1977.

*

Bibliography

Books:
Marie Colombier, *Les Mémoires de Sarah Bernhardt*, Paris and London, 1884.
A. L. Renner, *Sarah Bernhardt: Artist and Woman*, New York, 1896.
Jules Huret, *Sarah Bernhardt: acteurs et actrices d'aujourd'hui*, Paris, 1899.
Thérèse Berton, *Sarah Bernhardt as I Knew Her; Memoirs of Mme Pierre Berton as told to Basil Woon*, London, 1923.
Reynaldo Hahn, *La Grande Sarah*, Paris, 1929.
G.-J. Geller, *Sarah Bernhardt*, Paris, 1931.
Maurice Baring, *Sarah Bernhardt*, London, 1938.
Louis Verneuil, *The Fabulous Life of Sarah Bernhardt*, New York and London, 1942.
Lysiane Bernhardt, *Sarah Bernhardt: ma grand' mère*, Paris, 1945.
May Agate, *Madame Sarah*, London, 1945.
Maurice Rostand, *Sarah Bernhardt*, Paris, 1950.
Suze Rueff, *I Knew Sarah Bernhardt*, London, 1951.
Arthur William Row, *Sarah the Divine*, New York, 1957.
Joanna Richardson, *Sarah Bernhardt*, London, 1959.
André Castelot, *Sarah Bernhardt*, Paris, 1961.
Gerda Taranov, *Sarah Bernhardt – The Art within the Legend*, Princeton, 1972.
William Emboden, *Sarah Bernhardt*, London, 1974.
Joanna Richardson, *Sarah Bernhardt and Her World*, London, 1977.
Eric Salmon (ed.), *Bernhardt and the Theatre of Her Time*, Westport, Connecticut, and London, 1984.
John Stokes, Michael R. Booth, and Susan Bassnett, *Bernhardt Terry Duse: The Actress in Her Time*, Cambridge, 1988.
Elaine Aston, *Sarah Bernhardt: A French Actress on the English Stage*, Oxford, 1989.

* * *

Sarah Bernhardt was the most famous actress who ever lived — and one of the most enduring. Although there is no truth in the legend that she played the role of Hamlet with a wooden leg — she performed the part in 1899, 16 years before having her right leg amputated — she allowed neither age nor sex to discourage her from playing leading roles in such plays as Rostand's *La Gloire* and Racine's *Athalie* right up to the end of her life. One of her most famous parts was in *L'Aiglon*, Rostand's play about the only son of Napoleon, who died at the age of 21 — a role Bernhardt essayed when she was 56. Even in her last years, though, Bernhardt's voice retained the pure, silver quality, like a golden bell in living water, that inspired the young Marcel Proust to give her immortality in the pages of *A la recherche du temps perdu* (*Remembrance of Things Past*) as the great tragic actress La Berma after he saw her as Racine's *Phèdre*.

Bernhardt left the Comédie-Française relatively early in her career, when she was only 35, impatient at the constraints of the traditional style of acting that it imposed upon its members and anxious to play the full range of modern as well as classical roles. In this first incarnation as a star of the Comédie-Française she had notched up many notable triumphs, among them her performances as Cordelia in *King Lear* and the Queen in *Ruy Blas*, the play in which, in her own words, she "introduced the whole rainbow of different feelings" in a role that had hitherto been overshadowed by the other characters in the drama. Others included her central role in *Athalie*, in which she quite renewed the interpretation of the character, playing her not as a violent, tempestuous, externally aggressive tyrant, but employing instead a cooing sweetness that allowed Racinian poison to seep through every word.

Bernhardt worked in a theatrical tradition in which audiences went to see the actress rather than the play, and it was her fame as one of the great "monstres sacrés" that enabled her to play Racine, an author with whom English 19th-century audiences had little sympathy, with such success in London. In 1880, she scored one of her greatest successes in both London and New York in the role of the 18th-century French actress Adrienne Lecouvreur, in the play of the same name by Scribe. The fact that the original Adrienne had been refused burial in consecrated ground provided the opportunity for emphasizing both her sufferings and the changed status of the actress in contemporary society, of which Sarah Bernhardt herself was the living embodiment. The French romantic repertoire gave her a multitude of parts and she was at her best in the role of the unhappy courtesan in Alexandre Dumas *fils's* adaptation of his novel *La Dame aux Camélias* in 1884. When she performed the role in Vienna, in 1889, her deathbed scene was so overwhelming that several of the ladies in the Court fainted clean away. In Paris, where theatre performances traditionally ended with the singing of the *Marseillaise*, she could electrify audiences with the power of her voice, coming back to lead the singing for a third or fourth time, everyone standing with tears streaming down their faces.

Recordings of her voice were made too early for its quality to be heard above the crackling and the film extract of *Hamlet*, which she played when she was in her mid fifties, give little indication of how good she was. In fact, she revolutionized the interpretation of the play for English as well as for French audiences, reciting "To be or not to be" in a meditative but always half-audible whisper, instead of declaiming it in the rhetorical style made fashionable by the great English tragic actors of the early 19th century, and suddenly appearing behind the King at the climax of the play-within-a-play *The Murder of Gonzago* to scare him out of his wits by drawing his attention to the parallel with his own crime. In this respect, her acting looked forward to the innovations of the 20th century and Maurice Baring considered that it was only with her interpretation, in a prose translation written especially for her, that the French public began to understand what kind of playwright Shakespeare really was. She was, in the tradition of the 19th century, no respecter of texts, and there were occasions when this worked splendidly. Her triumph as Hamlet in 1899 was preceded by what the French critics thought of as her greatest role, that of Lorenzo in Musset's *Lorenzaccio*. Wisely, in view of Musset's rather self-indulgent if modernistic stage craft, she cut the play down to actable length and the resulting version remained unequalled until the play's revival by Gérard Philipe in the 1950's.

In her physical prime, Bernhardt was tall, slender, with dark eyes, a totally commanding presence on stage and a woman of considerable culture and independence of mind. She was an accomplished painter and sculptress and the author of a number of the plays in which she appeared. She gave her name to the Théâtre Sarah Bernhardt, Paris and is now widely remembered as the dominant actress on the French stage over a period of some 50 years.

—Philip Thody

BESSON, Benno. Swiss director and actor. Born in Switzerland, 1922. Educated at the University of Zurich. Stage debut, under Jean-Marie Serreau, Lyon, 1942; director and actor, Zurich, 1943–47; first meeting with Bertolt Brecht, Paris, 1947; toured French occupation zone in Germany as actor and director with Serreau's company, 1947–49; invited to join Brecht in East Berlin, 1949: collaborated with him on numerous adaptations for the stage as actor and director with the Berliner Ensemble, 1949–58; director, Deutsches Theater, 1962–69, and at the Volksbühne, Berlin, 1969–77; artistic director, Théâtre de la Comédie, Geneva, 1982–89; also made regular appearances at the Avignon Festival. Member: German Academy of Art; Council of the Theatre Union. Recipient: Nationalpreis der DDR (East Germany), 1974; Reinhart-Ring Award (Switzerland), 1985.

Productions

As director:
1945   *Die drei Soldaten* (Brecht), Yverdon.

1952   *Don Juan* (Brecht, adapted from Molière), Volkstheater, Rostock; Theater am Schiffbauerdamm, Berlin, 1954; Teatro Bellini, Palermo, 1964; Deutsches Theater, 1968; Burgtheater, Vienna, 1986; Comédie de Genève, Geneva, 1987.

1953   *Der Prozess der Jeanne d'Arc zu Rouen 1431* (Brecht), Deutsches Theater, Berlin.
          Volpone oder Der Fuchs (Jonson, adapted by Brecht, Besson, and Hauptmann), Neues Theater, Vienna.

1955   *Pauken und Trompeten* (Farquhar, adapted by Brecht, Besson, and Hauptmann), Theater am Schiffbauerdamm, Berlin.

1956   *Die Tage der Commune* (Brecht), Städttheater, Karl-Marx-Stadt, East Germany.
          Die gute Mensch von Setzuan (Brecht), Volkstheater, Rostock; Theater am Schiffbauerdamm, Berlin, 1957; Volksbühne, Berlin, 1970, 1971; Teatro Stabile, Rome, 1973.

1958   *Mann ist Mann* (Brecht), Volkstheater, Rostock (two separate productions); Comédie de Genève, Geneva, Centre Théâtral de Namur, Maison des Arts de Créteil, and Schauspielhaus, Zurich, 1988.

1959   *Die Dreigroschenoper* (Brecht and Weill), Volkstheater, Rostock.
          Die zwei edlen Herren aus Verona (Shakespeare), Städtische Bühnen, Frankfurt am Main; Deutsches Theater, Berlin, 1963.

1960   *Die Holländerbraut* (Strittmatter), Deutsches Theater, Berlin, and Theater am Schiffbauerdamm, Berlin.

1961   *Die heilige Johanna der Schlachthöfe* (Brecht), Württemberische Staatstheater, Stuttgart; Volkstheater, Rostock, 1961; Théâtre Municipal, Lausanne, 1962; Kammerspiele, Munich, 1973; Kungliga Dramatiska Teatern, Stockholm, 1981.

1962   *Der Frieden* (Aristophanes, adapted by Hacks), Deutsches Theatre, Berlin.

1963   *Der Tartüff* (Molière), Deutsches Theater, Berlin.

1964   *Die schöne Helena* (Hacks), Deutsches Theater, Berlin; Volksbühne, Berlin, 1971.

1965   *Der Drache* (Schwarz), Deutsches Theater, Berlin; Comédie de Genève, Geneva, 1985; Théâtre de la Ville, Paris, 1986.
          Moritz Tassow (Hacks), Volksbühne, Berlin.

1967   *Ödipus Tyrann* (Sophocles, adapted by Hölderlin and Müller), Deutsches Theater, Berlin; Associazione Teatri Emilia Romagna, Correggio, 1980.
          Ein Lorbass (Salomon), Deutsches Theater, Berlin.

1969   *Turandot oder Der Kongress der Weisswäscher* (Brecht), Schauspielhaus, Zurich.
          Horizonte (Winterlich), Volksbühne, Berlin.

1970   *Der Arzt wider Willen* (Molière), Volksbühne, Berlin.

1971   *König Hirsch* (Gozzi), Volksbühne, Berlin.

1973   *Das letzte Paradies* (Müller), Volksbühne, Berlin.
          Margarete in Aix (Hacks), Volksbühne, Berlin.

1975   *Was ihr wollt* (Shakespeare), Volksbühne, Berlin, and Dramatic Theatre, Sofia; Avignon and Théâtre de l'Est Parisien, 1976.
        Die Schlacht (Müller), Volksbühne, Berlin.

1977   *Hamlet* (Shakespeare), Volksbühne, Berlin, Théâtre de l'Est Parisien, l'Atelier théâtral de Louvain-la-Neuve, and Avignon; Comédie de Genève, Geneva, and Schauspielhaus, Zurich, 1983; Lilla Teatern, Helsinki, 1985; Comédie de Genève, Geneva, 1986.

1978   *Le Cercle de craie caucasien* (Brecht), l'Atelier théâtral de Louvain-la-Neuve, Théâtre National de Chaillot, and Avignon.

1982   *Der neue Menoza* (Lenz), Burgtheater, Vienna.
        L'Oiseau vert (Besson, adapted from Gozzi), Comédie de Genève, Geneva.

1984   *Le Sexe Faible* (Flaubert), Comédie de Genève, Geneva.
        Moi! (Labiche and Martin), Comédie de Genève, Geneva.
        Le Dîner de Mademoiselle Justine (Ségur), Comédie de Genève, Geneva.

1985   *Le Médecin malgré lui* (Molière), Comédie de Genève, Geneva.

1986   *Lapin Lapin* (Bourquin), Comédie de Genève, Geneva; Théâtre de la Ville, Paris, 1987.

1987   *La Flûte enchantée* (Mozart), Grand Théâtre de Genève, Geneva.

1988   *Le Théâtre de verdure* (Bourquin), Comédie de Genève, Geneva.

1989   *Jonas und sein Veteran — Ein Palaver* (Frisch), Schauspielhaus, Zurich, and Théâtre Vidy-Lausanne.

1990   *Mille Francs de Récompense* (Hugo), Théâtre Vidy-Lausanne.

Publications

Jahre mit Brecht, with Christa Neubert-Herwig and Ulrike Janslin-Simon, Willisau, 1990.

*

Bibliography

Books:
André Müller, *Der Regisseur Benno Besson*, Berlin, 1967.

* * *

Benno Besson holds a unique position in the contemporary European theatre. As a native of Switzerland, where he worked for many years as artistic director of the Comédie de Genève, Besson has had the opportunity to blend characteristic styles of the French and German theatres. His voluptuous mises en scène are simultaneously disturbing, entertaining, and intellectually challenging. Besson's productions are sterling examples of theatre where the word and the image work together; his interpretations and adaptations of modern and classical drama are theatrical, thought-provoking, and dynamic.

Besson performed under the direction of Jean-Marie Serreau in Lyon and Paris in the 1940's and with Jean Marie and Geneviève Serreau was responsible for the first productions of Brecht's plays in the French capital. While these early productions were not particularly successful, they did prepare the way for more noteworthy interpretations by Jean Vilar and the true successes of Jean Dasté in Brechtian works. Besson met Brecht on several occasions in Switzerland after Brecht's return to Europe from exile in the USA. He also toured in 1947–49 in Serrau's production of Brecht's *L'Exception et la Règle* in the French-occupied zone in Germany. His attraction to the theatre of Brecht was immediate and intense. Ultimately, he was invited by Brecht to work as an actor and assistant for mise en scène for the Berliner Ensemble in East Berlin. This provided Besson with the opportunity to combine his initial theatre experiences based upon a French tradition (Serreau had been a student of Charles Dullin) with the ideas of Brecht, the most influential figure in the theatre of the time. Previously, only Gaston Baty, who had studied at the Reinhardt Seminar, had utilized his experiences in the German theatre to influence 20th century mise en scène in France (the process continues today through such individuals as the Swiss director Luc Bondy).

During Besson's nine years with the Berliner Ensemble, he imposed a vibrant, visual style of performance that attempted to establish a solid rapport between the actor and the audience. He produced theatre that was "vivant", in sharp contrast to the grey image Westerners then had of Germany and its drama. His productions of Molière's *Don Juan* and Farquhar's *Drums and Trumpets* were playful and colourful, stylistically influenced by the French tradition. As principal metteur en scène with the Berliner Ensemble, he had particular success with Brecht's *The Good Woman of Setzuan* and the première of *Days in the Commune*. Besson stresses that he never took a theoretical approach in his work with the company and that during the period he worked so intimately with Brecht he never heard the latter so much as mention the term "Verfremdungsaffekt" to describe the distancing he desired in performance. Social comment and Marxist philosophy were important, but remained within the context of artistic freedom.

Besson continued to work in Berlin after Brecht's death. He was director of the Deutsches Theater from 1960 to 1969 and subsequently served as director of the Volksbühne. As well as Brecht, he also developed significant ties with playwrights Peter Hacks and Heiner Müller during his 25 years in the East German theatre. His masked and gestural production of Aristophanes' *Peace* (as *Der Frieden*), in an adaptation by Peter Hacks, caused a sensation in the West. His mises en scène for Hacks' *Der Drache* and *Die Schöne Helena* also scored great critical and popular successes. His choice of repertoire contrasted Molière and Shakespeare with Brecht and new treatments of old texts, like Heiner Müller's *Oedipus*.

By the mid-1970's, Besson was growing weary of working exclusively in the German language. Critics claimed that his productions were "losing their bite". In response, Besson returned to the French theatre through three successive mises en scène at the Festival d'Avignon. His versions of *As You Like It*, *Hamlet*, and *The Caucasian Chalk Circle* established his reputation in France, bringing invitations from theatres throughout Europe. He was also noted for his translations and adaptations of drama in French, German, English, and Italian.

Benno Besson's love for theatricality found a perfect marriage in maskmaker Werner Strub. In the mises en scène for Brecht, Shakespeare, Molière, and Gozzi, Strub has provided fantastic, powerful, and grotesque forms for Besson's actors. In Besson's *L'Oiseau vert*, for example, commedia dell'arte masks were mixed with elaborate animal masks and fantastic costumes to produce a memorable feast of visual surprises. This use of masks, together with a muscular physicality, has characterized much of Besson's later work, particularly that with the Comédie de Genève, which remains unique in contemporary European theatre.

—Ron Popenhagen

———————

BETTERTON, Thomas. English actor-manager and playwright. Born in Westminster, London, c.12 August 1635. Educated at local schools in London. Married actress Mary Saunderson c.1662. Son of under-cook to Charles I; apprenticed to bookseller, 1650's; stage debut under Sir William Davenant, Opera House, Charter House Yard, London, c.1656; appeared with company of John Rhodes at the Cockpit, Drury Lane, London, 1659–60; actor, and later shareholder in, Davenant's Duke's Company, Lincoln's Inn Fields Theatre, London, from 1661; studied scene designs on the Paris stage, 1661; actor, Duke's Company, Dorset Garden Theatre, from 1671, and with the United Company, from 1682; lost fortune in speculation in the East Indies, 1692; quarrelled with management of Christopher Rich and formed own company at Lincoln's Inn Fields, 1695; retired from management, 1704; appearances restricted by gout from 1705; last appearance, benefit performance, 25 April 1710. Died in London, 28 April 1710.

Roles

1659–60	Archas in *The Loyal Subject* (Fletcher), Cockpit, Drury Lane, London.
	Pericles in *Pericles* (Shakespeare), Cockpit, Drury Lane, London.
1660	Deflores in *The Changeling* (Middleton and Rowley), Cockpit, Drury Lane, London.
	Memnon in *The Mad Lover* (Fletcher), Cockpit, Drury Lane, London.
1661	Solyman in *The Siege of Rhodes* (Davenant), Lincoln's Inn Fields Theatre, London.
	Elder Palatine in *The Wits* (Davenant), Lincoln's Inn Fields Theatre, London.
	Hamlet in *Hamlet* (Shakespeare), Lincoln's Inn Fields Theatre, London.
	Sir Toby Belch in *Twelfth Night* (Shakespeare), Lincoln's Inn Fields Theatre, London.
	Prince Alvaro in *Love and Honour* (Davenant), Lincoln's Inn Fields Theatre, London.
	Colonel Jolly in *Cutter of Coleman Street* (Cowley), Lincoln's Inn Fields Theatre, London.
1662	Mercutio in *Romeo and Juliet* (Shakespeare), Lincoln's Inn Fields Theatre, London.
	Bosola in *The Duchess of Malfi* (Webster), Lincoln's Inn Fields Theatre, London.

	Monsieur Brisac in *The Villain* (Porter), Lincoln's Inn Fields Theatre, London.
1662–63	Faustus in *Doctor Faustus* (Marlowe), Lincoln's Inn Fields Theatre, London.
1663	Don Henrique in *The Adventures of Five Hours* (Tuke), Lincoln's Inn Fields Theatre, London.
	Iberio in *The Slighted Maid* (Stapylton), Lincoln's Inn Fields Theatre, London.
	Filamor in *The Step-Mother* (Stapylton), Lincoln's Inn Fields Theatre, London.
	Henry in *Henry VIII* (Shakespeare), Lincoln's Inn Fields Theatre, London.
1664	Lord Beaufort in *The Comical Revenge* (Etherege), Lincoln's Inn Fields Theatre, London.
	Owen Tudor in *Henry V* (Orrery), Lincoln's Inn Fields Theatre, London.
	Philander in *The Rivals* (Davenant), Lincoln's Inn Fields Theatre, London.
	Macbeth in *Macbeth* (Shakespeare, adapted by Davenant), Lincoln's Inn Fields Theatre, London.
1665	Solyman in *Mustapha* (Orrery), Lincoln's Inn Fields Theatre, London.
1667	Richard III in *The English Princess* (Caryll), Lincoln's Inn Fields Theatre, London.
1668–69	Lovemore in *The Amorous Widow* (Betterton), Lincoln's Inn Fields Theatre, London.
1669	Virginius in *The Roman Virgin* (Betterton), Lincoln's Inn Fields Theatre, London.
	Mr Art in *Mr Anthony* (Orrery), Lincoln's Inn Fields Theatre, London.
1670	Sir Salomon in *Sir Salomon* (Caryll), Lincoln's Inn Fields Theatre, London.
	Alcippus in *The Forced Marriage* (Behn), Lincoln's Inn Fields Theatre, London.
1671	Cambyses in *Cambyses* (Settle), Dorset Garden Theatre, London.
	Ladislaus in *Juliana* (Crowne), Dorset Garden Theatre, London.
	Charles in *Charles VIII* (Crowne), Dorset Garden Theatre, London.
1672	Townlove in *The Morning Ramble* (Payne), Dorset Garden Theatre, London.
	Bevil in *Epsom Wells* (Shadwell), Dorset Garden Theatre, London.
1673	Grimalhaz in *The Empress of Morocco* (Settle), Dorset Garden Theatre, London.
1675	Don Juan in *The Libertine* (Shadwell), Dorset Garden Theatre, London.
	Alcibiades in *Alcibiades* (Otway), Dorset Garden Theatre, London.
1676	Ramble in *The Country Wit* (Crowne), Dorset Garden Theatre, London.
	Solyman in *Ibrahim* (Settle), Dorset Garden Theatre, London.
	Dorimant in *The Man of Mode* (Etherege), Dorset Garden Theatre, London.
	Longvil in *The Virtuoso* (Shadwell), Dorset Garden Theatre, London.
	Philip II in *Don Carlos* (Otway), Dorset Garden Theatre, London.
	Abdelazer in *Abdelazer* (Behn), Dorset Garden Theatre, London.

Lord Bellamore in *Madam Fickle* (D'Urfey), Dorset Garden Theatre, London.

Titus Vespasian in *Titus and Berenice* (Otway), Dorset Garden Theatre, London.

Sylvano in *Pastor Fido* (Settle), Dorset Garden Theatre, London.

1677   Antony in *Antony and Cleopatra* (Sedley), Dorset Garden Theatre, London.

Belvile in *The Rover* (Behn), Dorset Garden Theatre, London.

Orestes in *Circe* (Davenant), Dorset Garden Theatre, London.

Orontes in *The Siege of Babylon* (Pordage), Dorset Garden Theatre, London.

1678   Timon in *Timon of Athens* (Shakespeare, adapted by Shadwell), Dorset Garden Theatre, London.

Wittmore in *Sir Patient Fancy* (Behn), Dorset Garden Theatre, London.

Goodvile in *Friendship in Fashion* (Otway), Dorset Garden Theatre, London.

Vitelli in *The Counterfeits* (Leanerd), Dorset Garden Theatre, London.

Welford in *Squire Oldsapp* (D'Urfey), Dorset Garden Theatre, London.

Oedipus in *Oedipus* (Dryden and Lee), Dorset Garden Theatre, London.

Achilles in *The Destruction of Troy* (Banks), Dorset Garden Theatre, London.

1679   Galliard in *The Feigned Courtesans* (Behn), Dorset Garden Theatre, London.

Troilus in *Troilus and Cressida* (Shakespeare, adapted by Dryden), Dorset Garden Theatre, London.

Caesar in *Caesar Borgia* (Lee), Dorset Garden Theatre, London.

Caius in *Caius Marius* (Otway), Dorset Garden Theatre, London.

Earl of Warwick in *The Misery of Civil War* (Crowne), Dorset Garden Theatre, London.

Theocrin in *The Loyal General* (Tate), Dorset Garden Theatre, London.

1680   Lorenzo in *The Loving Enemies* (Maidwell), Dorset Garden Theatre, London.

Castalio in *The Orphan* (Otway), Dorset Garden Theatre, London.

Beaugard in *The Soldier's Fortune* (Otway), Dorset Garden Theatre, London.

Varanes in *Theodosius* (Lee), Dorset Garden Theatre, London.

Torrismond in *The Spanish Friar* (Otway), Dorset Garden Theatre, London.

Lucius Junius Brutus in *Lucius Junius Brutus* (Lee), Dorset Garden Theatre, London.

1680–81   Lear in *King Lear* (Shakespeare, adapted by Tate), Dorset Garden Theatre, London.

1681   Gloucester in *Henry VI, part 1* (Shakespeare, adapted by Crowne), Dorset Garden Theatre, London.

1682   Jaffeir in *Venice Preserv'd* (Otway), Dorset Garden Theatre, London.

Piercy in *Virtue Betrayed* (Banks), Dorset Garden Theatre, London.

Thomas Betterton

Tom Wilding in *The City Heiress* (Behn), Dorset Garden Theatre, London.

Michael Perez in *Rule a Wife and Have a Wife* (Fletcher), Dorset Garden Theatre, London.

The Duke of Guise in *The Duke of Guise* (Lee and Dryden), Theatre Royal, Drury Lane, London.

Duke Nemours in *The Princess of Cleve* (Lee), Theatre Royal, Drury Lane/Dorset Garden Theatre, London.

1682–83   Arbaces in *A King and No King* (Beaumont and Fletcher), Theatre Royal, Drury Lane/Dorset Garden Theatre, London.

1683   Beaugard in *The Atheist* (Otway), Dorset Garden Theatre, London.

Crispus in *Constantine* (Lee), Theatre Royal, Drury Lane/Dorset Garden Theatre, London.

1683–84   Brutus in *Julius Caesar* (Shakespeare), Theatre Royal, Drury Lane, London.

Manly in *The Plain Dealer* (Wycherley), Theatre Royal, Drury Lane/Dorset Garden Theatre, London.

1684   Aecius in *Valentinian* (Fletcher, adapted by Rochester), Theatre Royal, Drury Lane, London.

Alphonso in *The Disappointment* (Southerne), Theatre Royal, Drury Lane/Dorset Garden Theatre, London.

1686   Gayman in *The Lucky Chance* (Behn), Theatre Royal, Drury Lane/Dorset Garden Theatre, London.

1688   Rheusanes in *The Injured Lovers* (Mountfort), Theatre Royal, Drury Lane, London.

1689   Lord Bellamy in *Bury Fair* (Shadwell), Theatre Royal, Drury Lane/Dorset Garden Theatre, London.
Admiral of France in *The Massacre of Paris* (Lee), Theatre Royal, Drury Lane/Dorset Garden Theatre, London.
Dorax in *Don Sebastian* (Dryden), Theatre Royal, Drury Lane/Dorset Garden Theatre, London.

1689–90   Othello in *Othello* (Shakespeare), Theatre Royal, Drury Lane, London.

1690   Jupiter in *Amphitryon* (Dryden), Theatre Royal, Drury Lane, London.

1690–91   Sir Ralph Jerningham in *The Merry Devil of Edmonton* (anon.), Theatre Royal, Drury Lane, London.

1691   Arthur in *King Arthur* (Dryden), Theatre Royal, Drury Lane, London.
Lovemore in *The Wives' Excuse* (Southerne), Theatre Royal, Drury Lane, London.

1691–92   Edward IV in *Richard III* (Shakespeare), Theatre Royal, Drury Lane, London.

1692   Gunderic in *The Rape* (Brady), Theatre Royal, Drury Lane, London.
Cleomenes in *Cleomenes, The Spartan Hero* (Dryden and Southerne), Theatre Royal, Drury Lane, London.
Regulus in *Regulus* (Crowne), Theatre Royal, Drury Lane, London.
Henry in *Henry II* (Bancroft), Theatre Royal, Drury Lane, London.

1693   Heartwell in *The Old Bachelor* (Congreve), Theatre Royal, Drury Lane, London.
Maskwell in *The Double Dealer* (Congreve), Theatre Royal, Drury Lane, London.

1693–94   Alexander in *The Rival Queens* (Lee), Theatre Royal, Drury Lane, London.

1694   Alphonso in *Love Triumphant* (Dryden), Theatre Royal, Drury Lane, London.
Villeroy in *The Fatal Marriage* (Southerne), Theatre Royal, Drury Lane, London.
Polidor in *The Married Beau* (Crowne), Theatre Royal, Drury Lane, London.

1695   Valentine in *Love for Love* (Congreve), Lincoln's Inn Fields Theatre, London.
Bellair in *The Lover's Luck* (Dilke), Lincoln's Inn Fields Theatre, London.
Cyrus in *Cyrus the Great* (Banks), Lincoln's Inn Fields Theatre, London.
Bellamour in *The She-Gallants* (Granville), Lincoln's Inn Fields Theatre, London.

1696   Woodvill in *The Country Wake* (Doggett), Lincoln's Inn Fields Theatre, London.
Osman in *The Royal Mischief* (Manley), Lincoln's Inn Fields Theatre, London.
Railmore in *Love's a Jest* (Motteux), Lincoln's Inn Fields Theatre, London.

1697   Sir John Brute in *The Provoked Wife* (Vanbrugh), Lincoln's Inn Fields Theatre, London.
Duke de Sanserre in *The Intrigues at Versailles* (D'Urfey), Lincoln's Inn Fields Theatre, London.
Grammont in *The Unfortunate Couple* (Motteux, adapted from Filmer's *The Unnatural Brother* as part of *The Novelty*), Lincoln's Inn Fields Theatre, London.
Sir Charles Beauclair in *The Innocent Mistress* (Pix), Lincoln's Inn Fields Theatre, London.
Cassibelan in *Boadicea* (Hopkins), Lincoln's Inn Fields Theatre, London.
Melitu Bondi in *The Deceiver Deceived* (Pix), Lincoln's Inn Fields Theatre, London.

1698   Agamemnon in *Heroic Love* (Lansdowne), Lincoln's Inn Fields Theatre, London.
Gramont in *Fatal Friendship* (Trotter), Lincoln's Inn Fields Theatre, London.
Don Vincentio in *Beauty in Distress* (Motteux), Lincoln's Inn Fields Theatre, London.
Owen Tudor in *Queen Catharine* (Pix), Lincoln's Inn Fields Theatre, London.
Melantius in *The Maid's Tragedy* (Beaumont and Fletcher), Lincoln's Inn Fields Theatre, London.
Rinaldo in *Rinaldo and Armida* (Dennis), Lincoln's Inn Fields Theatre, London.

1699   Attabanus in *Xerxes* (Cibber), Lincoln's Inn Fields Theatre, London.
Doria in *The Princess of Parma* (Smith), Lincoln's Inn Fields Theatre, London.
Zoilus in *Friendship Improved* (Hopkins), Lincoln's Inn Fields Theatre, London.
Orestes in *Iphigenia* (Dennis), Lincoln's Inn Fields Theatre, London.

1700   Falstaff in *Henry IV* (Shakespeare, adapted by Betterton), Lincoln's Inn Fields Theatre, London.
Angelo in *Measure for Measure* (Shakespeare, adapted by Gildon), Lincoln's Inn Fields Theatre, London.
Fainall in *The Way of the World* (Congreve), Lincoln's Inn Fields Theatre, London.
Virginius in *The Fate of Capua* (Southerne), Lincoln's Inn Fields Theatre, London.
Memnon in *The Ambitious Stepmother* (Rowe), Lincoln's Inn Fields Theatre, London.

1701   Courtine in *The Ladies Visiting Day* (Burnaby), Lincoln's Inn Fields Theatre, London.
Rhesus, King of Wales in *Love's Victim* (Gildon), Lincoln's Inn Fields Theatre, London.
Bassanio in *The Jew of Venice* (Lansdowne, adapted from Shakespeare's *The Merchant of Venice*), Lincoln's Inn Fields Theatre, London.
Clorimon in *Altemira* (Orrery, adapted by Boyle), Lincoln's Inn Fields Theatre, London.
Tamerlane in *Tamerlane* (Rowe), Lincoln's Inn Fields Theatre, London.

1703   Iopano in *The Governor of Cyprus* (Oldmixon), Lincoln's Inn Fields Theatre, London.

Bevil in *As You Find It* (Boyle), Lincoln's Inn Fields Theatre, London.

Horatio in *The Fair Penitent* (Rowe), Lincoln's Inn Fields Theatre, London.

1704   Mahomet IV in *Abra Mule* (Trapp), Lincoln's Inn Fields Theatre, London.

Marc Antony in *All for Love* (Dryden), Lincoln's Inn Fields Theatre, London.

Miramont in *Liberty Asserted* (Dennis), Lincoln's Inn Fields Theatre, London.

Lovewell in *Squire Trelooby* (Congreve, Vanbrugh, and Walsh), Lincoln's Inn Fields Theatre, London.

Falstaff in *The Merry Wives of Windsor* (Shakespeare), Lincoln's Inn Fields Theatre, London.

Sir Timothy Tallapoy in *The Biter* (Rowe), Lincoln's Inn Fields Theatre, London.

1705   Lovewell in *The Gamester* (Centlivre), Lincoln's Inn Fields Theatre, London.

Ulysses in *Ulysses* (Rowe), Haymarket Theatre, London.

Don Alvarez in *The Mistake* (Vanbrugh), Haymarket Theatre, London.

1706   Marus in *The Faithful General* (anon.), Haymarket Theatre, London.

Count Arwide in *The Revolution of Sweden* (Trotter), Haymarket Theatre, London.

Caelius in *The British Enchanters* (Lansdowne), Haymarket Theatre, London.

Sir Thomas Beamont in *The Platonic Lady* (Centlivre), Haymarket Theatre, London.

Caliph Almanzor in *Almyna* (Manley), Haymarket Theatre, London.

1707   Morose in *The Silent Woman* (Jonson), Haymarket Theatre, London.

Montezuma in *The Indian Emperor* (Dryden), Haymarket Theatre, London.

Don Antonio in *The Adventures of Five Hours* (Tuke), Haymarket Theatre, London.

Marius senior in *Caius Marius* (Otway), Haymarket Theatre, London.

Dominic in *The Spanish Friar* (Dryden), Haymarket Theatre, London.

Theseus in *Phaedra and Hippolitus* (Smith), Haymarket Theatre, London.

1708   Old Emperor in *Aureng-Zebe* (Dryden), Haymarket Theatre, London.

Mithridates in *Mithridates* (Lee), Haymarket Theatre, London.

1709   Virginius in *Appius and Virginia* (Dennis), Haymarket Theatre, London.

Leontius in *The Humorous Lieutenant* (Fletcher), Haymarket Theatre, London.

Thersites in *Troilus and Cressida* (Shakespeare, adapted by Dryden), Haymarket Theatre, London.

Other roles included: *The Unfortunate Lovers* (Davenant), Cockpit, Drury Lane, London, 1659–60; *Rule a Wife and Have a Wife* (Fletcher), Cockpit, Drury Lane, London, 1659–60; *A Wife for a Month* (Fletcher), Cockpit, Drury Lane, London, 1659–60; *A Wild Goose Chase* (Fletcher), Cockpit, Drury Lane, London, 1659–60; *The Woman's Prize* (Fletcher), Cockpit, Drury Lane, London, 1659–60; *The Spanish Curate* (Fletcher and Massinger), Cockpit, Drury Lane, London, 1659–60; *The Maid in the Mill* (Fletcher and Rowley), Cockpit, Drury Lane, London, 1659–60; *Aglaura* (Suckling), Cockpit, Drury Lane, London, 1659–60; *The Bondman* (Massinger), Cockpit, Drury Lane, London, 1660; *The Grateful Servant* (Shirley), Lincoln's Inn Fields Theatre, London, 1661; *The Valiant Cid* (Rutter, adapted from Corneille's *Le Cid*), Lincoln's Inn Fields Theatre, London, 1662; *A Woman is a Weathercock* (Field), Lincoln's Inn Fields Theatre, London, 1666–67; *The Witty Fair One* (Shirley), Lincoln's Inn Fields Theatre, London, 1666–67; *Love Tricks* (Shirley), Lincoln's Inn Fields Theatre, London, 1667; *The Woman Made a Justice* (Betterton), Lincoln's Inn Fields Theatre, London, 1669–70; *An Evening's Love* (Dryden), Theatre Royal, Drury Lane/Dorset Garden Theatre, London; 1685–86; *The Prophetess* (Fletcher and Massinger, adapted by Betterton), Theatre Royal, Drury Lane/Dorset Garden Theatre, London, 1689–90.

Publications

The Amorous Widow; or, The Wanton Wife (adaptation of Corneille's *Le Baron d'Albikrac* and Molière's *George Dandin*), 1668–69; *The Roman Virgin; or, The Unjust Judge* (adaptation of Webster's *Appius and Virginia*), 1669; *The Woman Made a Justice* (adaptation from Montfleury), 1670; *The Prophetess; or, The History of Dioclesian* (adaptation from Fletcher and Massinger), 1690; *King Henry IV, with the Humours of Sir John Falstaff* (adaptation of Shakespeare's *Henry IV, part 1*), 1700; *The Miller's Tale*, "Chaucer's Characters, or the Introduction to the Canterbury Tales", *Miscellaneous Poems and Translations by Several Hands* (verse), 1712; *A History of the English Stage*, 1741 (probably the work of William Oldys and Edmund Curll).

*

Bibliography

Books:

Charles Gildon, *The Life of Mr Thomas Betterton*, London, 1710.

Anon., *An Account of the Life of That Celebrated Tragedian Mr. Thomas Betterton*, London, 1749.

Anon., *The Life and Times of that Excellent and Renowned Actor Thomas Betterton*, London, 1888.

Robert W. Lowe, *Thomas Betterton*, London, 1891.

G. C. D. Odell, *Shakespeare from Betterton to Irving*, London, 1921.

Frederick F. Seely, *Thomas Betterton, Dramatist*, Iowa City, 1942.

Thomas W. Schmunk, *The Acting Style of Thomas Betterton*, Medford, 1964.

Bruce D. Podewell, *The Acting of Thomas Betterton*, New York, 1975.

Cornelia R. Rathke, *The Career of Thomas Betterton*, New Orleans, 1976.

Judith Milhous, *Thomas Betterton and the Management of Lincoln's Inn Fields 1695–1708*, Carbondale, Illinois, 1979.
Joseph Roach, *The Player's Passion*, London, 1985.

* * *

Though Thomas Betterton's acting style would be considered "stagy" today, he was in his time (like his contemporary Molière) admired for becoming the character he portrayed, for tightly controlling his voice and body, and for conserving his artistic and physical energy. The playwright George Farquhar in his *Discourse* in 1702 praised Betterton's ability to *be* Alexander in *The Rival Queens*, and "Yet the whole audience at the same time knows that this is Mr Betterton who is strutting upon the stage and tearing his lungs for a livelihood". The performer Tony Aston in his *Brief Supplement* (1747) to Colley Cibber's *Apology* noted Betterton's passion for remaining in character: he kept his costume on to the end of a performance, even if he was not in the final scene.

Cibber, like Betterton an actor-playwright-manager, left a vivid description of Betterton's first encounter with the Ghost in *Hamlet* ("the Passion never rises beyond an almost breathless Astonishment, or an Impatience, limited by filial Reverence"), while *The Laureate* in 1740 discussed his second meeting with the Ghost in detail: "his Countenance (which was naturally ruddy and sanguin) in this Scene ... thro' the violent and sudden Emotions of Amazement and Horror, turned instantly on the Sight of his Father's Spirit, as pale as his Neckcloth, when every Article of his Body seem'd to be affected with a Tremor inexpressible". To an astounding control over his voice and body Betterton, according to the prompter W. R. Chetwood in his *General History* (1949), added harbouring of his energy: in the two Ghost scenes, for instance, he acted with restraint in the first so as to top it with the second.

A study of the Hamlet text used by Betterton shows that he (or his mentor and theatre manager during his formative years, Sir William Davenant) cut the script to keep it fast-moving and melodramatic. The cuts probably helped make up for what we would find fairly static staging, which depended largely upon carefully selected movements and gestures and posing in striking stances ('points') throughout the play. The result was a highly theatrical yet believable performance that commanded attention in auditoria that could not be fully darkened and where spectators were very aware of themselves and of theatregoing as a social and not just a theatrical event.

The diarist Samuel Pepys, who saw Betterton in his prime in the 1660s, confided again and again to his diary how dazzled he was by Betterton, especially in tragedy and most particularly as Macbeth and Hamlet. Many of the actor's tragic characters are rarely played today but were standard vehicles for stars of the Restoration and the 18th century, Jaffier in Otway's *Venice Preserved* and Alexander in Lee's *The Rival Queens* being just two examples. But Betterton tested himself, and won critical approval, in the great Shakespearean roles (albeit usually in adaptations of the originals, which were too rough-hewn for neoclassical tastes). In addition to Hamlet and Macbeth, he was praised for his Brutus, Othello, and Hotspur. A survey of the roles Betterton played, over 180 of them in more than 50 years on the stage (and the records for his period are not

complete), shows that he was equally at home in comedy and tragedy and presumably brought to the former all the passion for detail and control that he gave to the latter.

Yet Betterton must have been nature's least likely candidate for a stage career. Aston described him as "clumsily made, having a great Head, a short thick Neck, stoop'd Shoulders, and ... fat short Arms, which he rarely lifted higher than his Stomach". But, as fellow-actor Barton Booth said, "divinity hung round that man!" Betterton evidently had, in common with most fine performers, that indescribable quality known as stage presence and even his painted image in the Kneller masterpiece at the National Portrait Gallery in London bears witness to his striking, commanding eyes.

Betterton had other theatrical skills besides. He was a playwright of sorts (a successful play doctor and adapter would perhaps be more accurate) and served as an acting coach and manager. As manager he mounted several spectacular shows — *The Prophetess*, *King Arthur*, and *The Fairy Queen*, all with music by Henry Purcell, were among the most notable — that gained him a considerable reputation as what later became identified as a director. His managerial expertise, however, attracted criticism. *The Lunatick* in 1705, for example, accused Betterton and his fellow-managers Elizabeth Barry and Anne Bracegirdle of tinkering with the company accounts and the attack probably had a basis in truth.

Thomas Betterton's first appearance on stage is cloaked in obscurity, but his last is documented — Melantius in Beaumont and Fletcher's *The Maid's Tragedy* on 13 April 1710 at the close of a run of his most popular roles, some of which he had acted for years (he was still playing Hamlet at 74!). He died two weeks later and befitting his status was buried in the East Cloister of Westminster Abbey on 2 May 1710. Steele in the *Tatler* that day said he went to the funeral to "see the last office done to a man whom I had always very much admired, and from whose action I had received more strong impressions of what is great and noble in human nature, than from the arguments of the most solid philosophers, or the descriptions of the most charming poets I have read".

Lacking information about Shakespeare's chief player, Richard Burbage, we cannot judge whether Betterton was the first or the second great English actor. He was clearly the most important before the arrival of David Garrick in the middle of the 18th century and the tightly-controlled, majestic, highly theatrical style of Betterton remained the model for English performers for years.

—Edward A. Langhans

———

BIANCOLELLI family. French-Italian actors, comprising Francesco Biancolelli, his son Giuseppe Domenico Biancolelli, his grandson Pietro Francesco Biancolelli, and other family members. Francesco Biancolelli was born in Bologna, Italy, c.1600; married actress Isabella Franchini; acted in France and Italy (roles unknown); died c.1640. Isabella Franchini was the daughter of Pantalone actor Francesco Franchini; celebrated in the role of Columbina; took Francesco Biancolelli as her third husband; appeared with the Duke of Modena's company in Bologna, Milan, and Verona, 1651; on Francesco Biancolelli's death, married Carlo Cantù, popular in zanni role of Buffeto; died c.1651. Their son Giuseppe Domenico Biancolelli was born in Italy, c.1636; married actress Orsola Cortesi in 1663; eleven children; made stage debut, trained by Cantù, as a child under the name Menghino; appeared in Parma, Paris, 1645–46, at the Farnese court in Rome, and with Tabarin in Vienna in his youth; won acclaim throughout Europe as the definitive commedia dell'arte character Arlequin, using stagename Dominique; actor, with company of Domenico Locatelli in Paris, from 1661; won permission from Louis XIV to perform in French rather than Italian; actor, Comédie-Italienne, Hôtel de Bourgogne, from 1680; died in Paris (of pneumonia after an exhausting performance), 2 August 1688. Orsola Cortesi was born in Bologna, c.1632, daughter of Antonio Cortesi and actress Barbara Minuti (Florinda); married Giuseppe Biancolelli in 1663; acted under the name Eularia; appeared with the company of Giovan Battista Andreini and also with her own company in Italy in the 1650's; acclaimed in the role of the Innamorata with Locatelli's Paris company, 1660; left the stage, 1691, and retired to a convent, 1704; died in Paris, 11 June 1718. Their daughter Françoise Maria Apolline Biancolelli was born in Paris, 1664; married Charles-Constantin de Turgis in 1691 (annulled 1695); acted under the name Isabella; acclaimed alongside her sister in Fatouville's *Arlequin Prothée*, Comédie-Italienne, 1683; excelled in the role of the Innamorata; left the stage, 1697; retired to a convent, 1713; died in Paris, 3 September 1747.

Catherine Biancolelli was born in Paris, 1665; married actor Fontainebleau Pierre Lenoir de La Thorillière in 1685; acted under the name Isabella, as Columbine, and in various male roles, such as Arlequin in *Retour de la foire de Bezons*, 1695; left the stage, 1697; died in Paris, 22 February 1716. Pierre François Biancollelli was born in Paris, 20 September 1680; educated by the Jesuits in Paris; married 1) Jeanne Jaquette Tortoriti in 1703, 2) Marie-Thérèse de Lalande in 1729; acted in Toulouse and elsewhere in the French provinces with Giuseppe Tortoriti's company and won acclaim as Arlequin in Grenoble, Venice, Milan, Pavia, Mantua, and Genoa, using stagename Dominique *fils*; returned to France, 1710; also popular as Pierrot in Fréret's *Force du naturel*, 1717, and in straight plays with Luigi Riccoboni's company, from 1717; manager, Opéra-Comique, Paris, and, with Riccoboni, Comédie-Italienne, from 1716; also wrote numerous scenarios as a basis for improvisation; died 18 April 1734. Jeanne Jaquette Tortoriti was born in Orange in 1683; daughter of actor-manager Giuseppe Tortoriti; acted opposite her husband in the role of Columbine; died in Paris, 12 October 1725. Pierre's daughter Marie Thérèse de Lalande was born in Paris in 1723; acted under the name Madamoiselle Biancolelli; popular in Boissy's *Surprise de la haine*, 1738, and in the role of the Innamorata; left the stage, 1762; died in Paris, 16 December 1788.

*

Bibliography

Books:

Charles-Simon Favart, *Baiocco et Serpille: parodie du Joueur*, Paris, 1771.

* * *

The most celebrated of the Biancolellis was Domenico, who was brought up in the traditions of the commedia dell'arte. Both his parents were popular performers and his stepfather, Carlo Cantù, who was himself famous in the role of the First Zanni, Buffeto, undertook the boy's training as the Second Zanni, Arlecchino. Called to Paris to substitute for the seriously ill Domenico Locatelli, Biancolelli — known in France as Dominique — stayed on until his death in 1688. Although we do not know when, or even if, he became the official "capocomico" of the Comédie-Italienne, he was certainly its "orateur", the actor who welcomed the audience with graceful compliments and whetted appetites for the day's activities. With Tiberio Fiorilli, Scaramouche, he was one of the company's two great stars. Although famous as an acrobat, he was the first of the Italian actors to play in French, specializing in "harangues", or set speeches, added to the improvised plays in Italian.

A small man who became rather too stout for the ideal Arlequin, Dominique developed a character that both reflected the Italian tradition of the Second Zanni and appealed to the French taste for parody and satire. Like his Italian precursors, Dominique's Arlequin was gluttonous, occasionally lecherous, and none too bright, unable to reason from cause to effect or predict the consequences of his actions. He was the "patsy" to the First Zanni's bully, the target of everyone's blows and beatings. After the introduction of a new repertory in 1668, Arlequin began to specialize in travesties, or disguises. Once merely a means to carry out the schemes of the First Zanni or the "amoureux", disguise became an end in itself, an unexpected and much appreciated element of Dominique's play. In some entertainments he donned as many as eight disguises, from the parodistic — an absurd "petit marquis" — to the fantastic — an orange tree or an English bulldog.

Dominique's play is known to us from a "zibaldone", or actor's aide-memoire, which he apparently kept to remind himself of his ever-increasing repertory. Although the entries give only his scenes, the document is one of the most valuable for the recreation of the comic elements of the commedia dell'arte. A typical entry begins with Scaramouche as First Zanni scolding Arlequin: "He says that I will never be anything but a simpleton and a fool. He says that I must get into the streetlight in front of the Docteur's door. He lowers the lamp and puts me in ... The Docteur enters and stands under the lamp, I light some scraps of paper that I throw on his head; he looks around, I hide in the lamp. I light more papers, he sees them and exits in a rage. Cinthio enters and draws his pistol to shoot out the light, I shout at him, don't shoot, it's me, Arlequin. He exits, but the Docteur enters with two pistols and fires at the lamp; I shout 'ohimé', lower the lamp. The police enter and want to know what the matter is, I answer that we have a wounded streetlight here ... "

Dominique was a noted dancer who performed in court ballets. He was less celebrated as a musician and, indeed, performed his role with a squawking or parrot voice. A number of anecdotes suggest that he was well-read, even intellectual, in spite of having had little formal education. He was a devoted husband and father, the head of a family noted for its regularity of manners, and a favourite of King Louis XIV.

His wife, Orsola Cortesi, was born like him into a commedia dell'arte family. Already well-known in Italy before she came to France, she played with the troupe of Giovan Battista Andreini in the early 1650's and led her own troupe under the protection of the Duke of Mantua later in the decade. She was "tall, well made, and very attractive without being beautiful". Like many other actresses who followed in the footsteps of the great Isabella Andreini, she published a play translated from the Spanish to establish her literary credentials. Her roles were for the most part conventional, although she did play an occasional love scene with Arlequin, usually in disguise as his master or another gentleman, probably because the audience enjoyed seeing the husband and wife together on stage. Orsola Cortesi was the only member of the troupe who played for the full 35 years it was established in Paris, although she rarely appeared in the French repertory that was introduced after 1680.

The Biancolelli couple were the parents of 11 children, eight of whom survived to adulthood. Three had careers in the theatre. They were Françoise, Catherine, and Pierre-François. The daughters joined the Comédie-Italienne in April 1683 and had huge success in their respective roles of the Innamorata and Columbine. Donneau de Visé wrote in the *Mercure galant* that "never has been seen such intelligence for theatre combined with such great youth. There is no point of character into which they do not enter, and they acquit themselves with such good grace that whenever they appear in whatever scene, they seem uniquely born for the characters that they play."

Françoise and Catherine appeared primarily in the French repertory; since they had been born and raised in France they were native speakers of the language. Although they were able to act improvisationally, most of the time they played French texts written by French playwrights. As a result, their characters are less consistent than the fixed characters developed by earlier actors, more dependent on the intentions of the writers. However, they did perform in a sequence of plays featuring young women who were independent, even emancipated, who lived by their wits, and who led the action. Catherine was especially popular with audiences, the first female star of the Comédie-Italienne.

Their brother Pierre-Françoise Biancolelli was only 17 when the Comédie-Italienne was dismissed by Louis XIV and had not made his debut. He joined a company organised by one of the Italian actors to play in the provinces and returned to Paris in 1710 to play Arlequin at the fairs. In 1717 he was admitted to the new Comédie-Italienne, formed the previous year by the regent, the duc d'Orléans. His role was Trivelin, but he played a variety of characters and wrote, alone and in collaboration, a great number of comedies and parodies for his troupe.

The third generation of Biancolellis in France included Marie-Thérèse Biancolelli, the daughter of Pierre-François, who played young lovers at the Comédie-Italienne with great success from 1738 to 1762. She and a cousin, the son of Catherine Biancolelli and the French actor Lenoir de la

Thorillière, who entered the Comédie-Française in cape and sword roles, were the last of the family to appear on the Paris stage.

—Virginia Scott

BIBIENA family. Italian designers, comprising Ferdinando Bibiena, his brother Francesco Bibiena, Ferdinando's sons Alessandro Bibiena, Giuseppe Bibiena, Antonio Bibiena and Giovanni Maria Bibiena, and his grandson Carlo Bibiena. Ferdinando Bibiena was born in Bologna, Italy, 18 August 1657. Studied painting under Cignani and G. Trogli and architecture under M. Aldovrandini and G. A. Mannini. Collaborated on design of Teatro Farnese, Bologna; contributed stage settings for the theatres in Parma, 1688–92, Bologna, 1697, Venice, Turin, Rome, Naples, 1699, Milan, 1700, Florence and elsewhere in Italy; designed decorations for marriage of Charles III of Spain, Barcelona, 1708, and appointed court painter, Vienna, 1711; noted also for the development of perspective sets in Vienna, 1712–17, alongside his brother and sons; designer, Teatro della Fortuna, Fano, 1718–19; gave up imperial post in Vienna to Giuseppe, 1726; worked in Bologna as teacher, painter and architect, 1726–43; built Teatro del Castello, Mantua, 1732. Died in Bologna, 1743. Francesco Bibiena was born in Bologna, Italy, 12 December 1659. Studied painting under Pasinelli and Cignani. Executed first wall decorations, Bologna, 1679; subsequently spent three years as set designer in Rome and also designed settings for the theatres in Bologna, 1697 and 1703, Genoa and Naples, 1702; built opera houses in Vienna, 1704, and Nancy, 1707–09; contributed opera sets for the theatres in Vienna, 1710–12, and Venice, 1712; built Teatro Filarmonico, Verona, and Teatro Aliberti (or Delle Dame), Rome, both 1720; designed further settings in Bologna, 1717, 1727, 1730, 1731 and 1737. Died in Bologna, 20 January 1739. Alessandro Bibiena was born in Parma, Italy, 1687. Designed catafalque for Joseph I of Austria, 1711; worked with his father Ferdinando in Vienna, 1712; built Jesuit church and college in Mannheim, 1733–56; also designed opera house there, 1737–42; architectural adviser, Stuttgart, 1746–47. Died in Mannheim, 1748. Giuseppe Bibiena was born in Parma, Italy, 5 January 1696. Studied under his father in Barcelona, 1708, and elsewhere. Designed over 30 catafalques in Vienna, 1715–45; worked in theatre sacra in Vienna as early as 1717; also executed opera sets for the Viennese stage; designed opera sets for the wedding of Augustus III of Saxony, Munich, 1722, and for theatres in Prague, 1723–29; invented transparent settings for *L'Asile d'Amore*, Linz, 1732; also designed settings for theatres in Vienna and Graz, 1732–41, for the Teatro Sant Giovanni Chrisostomo, Venice, 1742, and Dresden, 1747–48; designed Bayreuth Opera House, 1744–48; redecorated old opera house in Dresden, 1749–51; further opera sets in Berlin and Dresden, 1751–56. Died in Berlin, 1757. Antonio Bibiena was born in Parma, Italy, 1700. Studied under his father, Giuseppe del Sole, Felice Torelli and M. A. Franceschini. Worked with his father on stage sets for the Teatro della Fortuna, Fano, 1718–19; subsequently collaborated with Francesco in Rome and with his father at the Teatro Malvezzi, Bologna, 1720–21; designed sets for theatres in Austria,

Hungary and Germany, from 1721, and also in Milan; rebuilt Teatro dei Rinnuovati, Sienna, 1751–53; built theatre in Colle and decorated Teatro della Pergola, Florence; altered Teatro Manzoni, Pistoia, 1755; designed Teatro Comunale, Bologna, 1756, and Teatro Rossini, Lugo, 1758–61; designed opera sets in Parma, 1761, 1763 and 1765; worked as set designer in Reggio nell'Emilia; began remodelling of the theatre of the Academia dei Timidi, Mantua, 1767, but relinquished project, 1769; built Teatro de' Quattro Cavalieri, Pavia, 1773. Died in Milan, 1774. Giovanni Maria Bibiena was born in 1700. Worked as painter and architect in Prague, c.1739–69; may have remodelled Teatro San Carlo, Naples, 1762. Died 1774. Carlo Bibiena was born in Vienna, 1728 (some sources, 1725). Designed opera sets and wedding decorations and collaborated with his father on decoration of Opera House, Bayreuth, 1746–53; executed opera sets in Munich, Bayreuth and Brunswick, 1753; spent a year in Rome and then worked in Bologna before returning to Bayreuth and Brunswick, 1758; worked in France and the Netherlands, 1759–60; further opera sets in Bayreuth and Brunswick, 1760; Worked in London, until 1763; set designer in Berlin, 1765–66; designed opera sets for baptism of daughter of Ferdinand IV, King of the Two Sicilies, Naples, 1772; may have built theatre in Pavia, 1773; designed opera sets for wedding of Duke of Södermanland, Stockholm, 1774; subsequently worked in St Petersburg until 1778. Died in Florence, 1787.

Productions

Ferdinando Bibiena:
1687   *Didio Giulano* (Lotti), Piacenza.
1690   *Il Favore degli dei* (Benedetti), Teatro Farnese, Parma.
         L'Età dell'oro (Tosi), Teatrino di corte, Parma.
         Teodora clemente (anon.), Teatro Ducale, Piacenza.
1692   *Endimione* (Magni and Griffini), Lodi.
1694   *Demetrio tiranno* (Sabadini), Teatro Nuovo, Piacenza.
1696   *La Finta pazzia di Ulisse* (Ziani), Teatro di San Salvador, Venice.
1697   *Ajace* (Magni and others), Teatro Capranica, Rome.
1700   *Eraclea* (Scarlatti), Naples.
1707   *Svanvita* (Fioré), Milan.
1709   *L'Inimico generoso* (Caldara), Teatro Malvezzi, Bologna.
1714   *Alba Cornelia* (Conti), Teatro di corte, Vienna.
         I Satiri in Arcadia (Conti), Teatro di corte, Vienna.
         Scaramucci et Arlecchini (ballet), Teatro di corte, Vienna.
         Zingani e zingane (ballet), Teatro di corte, Vienna.
         Mascherate (ballet), Teatro di corte, Vienna.

Francesco Bibiena:
1690   *L'Età dell'oro* (Tosi), Teatrino di corte, Parma.
1693   *Seleuco* (anon.), Teatro Tordinona, Rome.
1695   *Giustino* (Legrenzi), Teatro Tordinona, Rome.
         Penelope casta (Perti), Teatro Tordinona, Rome.
         Muzio Scevola (anon.), Teatro Tordinona, Rome.
1698   *Ulisse sconosciuto in Itaca* (Pollorolo), Teatro Comunale, Reggio Emilia.
         Apollo generoso (Perti), Teatro Formagliari, Bologna.
1699   *Ariovisto* (Perti, Magni and Ballarotti), Milan.
1702   *Tiberio imperatore di Oriente* (Gasparini), Teatro San Bartolomeo, Naples.
1710   *I Rivali generosi* (Monari), Teatro Comunale, Reggio Emilia.
         Cajo Gracco e Tirgane (Bononcini), Teatro di corte, Vienna.
1711   *La Vittoria dell'amicizia e dell'amore* (Conti), Teatro di corte, Vienna.
1715   *Il Tartaro nella Cina* (Gasparini), Teatro Comunale, Reggio Emilia.
1716   *L'Enigma disciolto* (Pollarolo), Teatro Molza, Modena.
         Ciro (Gasparini), Teatro Comunale, Reggio Emilia, and Teatro Capranica, Rome.
1717   *La Conquista del vello d'oro* (Bononcini), Teatro Comunale, Reggio Comunale.
         Merope (Orlandini), Teatro Formagliari, Bologna.
1719   *Lucio Vero*, Teatro Alibert, Rome.
         Astianatte (Gasparini), Teatro Alibert, Rome.
1720   *Amore e Maestà*, Teatro Alibert, Rome.
         Faramondo, Teatro Alibert, Rome.
1721   *Griselda* (Scarlatti), Teatro Capranica, Rome.
1726   *La Fedeltà coronata* (Orlandini), Teatro Malvezzi, Bologna.
1730   *La Finda Ninfa* (Vivaldi), Teatro Nuovo dell'Academie, Verona.

Giuseppe Bibiena:
1717   *La Verità nell'inganno* (Caldara), Gardens of the Imperial Favorita, Vienna.
1718   *Ifigenia in Aulide* (Caldara), Gardens of the Imperial Favorita, Vienna.
         Paraninfi (ballet), Gardens of the Imperial Favorita, Vienna.
1719   *Don Chisciotte in Sierra Morena* (Conti), Gardens of the Imperial Favorita, Vienna.
1721   *Ascanio* (Lotti), Hoftheater, Vienna.
         Orsmida (Caldara), Hoftheater, Vienna.
1722   *Scipione nell Spagne* (Caldara), Hoftheater, Vienna.
1723   *Costanza e fortezza* (Fu), Prague.
1724   *Gianguir* (Caldara), Hoftheater, Vienna.
1726   *Il Due dittatori* (Caldara), Hoftheater, Vienna.
         Spartaco (Porsile), Hoftheater, Vienna.
1727   *Don Chisciotte* (Caldara), Hoftheater, Vienna.
1728   *La Forza dell'amicizia* (Caldara), Hoftheater, Vienna.
1729   *I Disinganni* (Caldara), Hoftheater, Vienna.
1732   *Asilo d'amore* (Caldara), Linz.
1733   *Sancio Panza Governatore dell'Isola di Barattaria* (Caldara), Hoftheater, Vienna.
1740   *Zenobia* (Predieri), Hoftheater, Vienna.
1742   *Baiazet* (Bernasconi), Teatro di Sant Giovanni Crisostomo, Venice.

Publications

Ferdinando Bibiena:
L'Architettura civile, 1711; *Direzioni ai giovani*, 1731; *Direzioni della prospettiva teorica*, 1731.

Francesco Bibiena:
L'Architettura Maestra dell'Arti che la compongono (never printed).

Giuseppe Bibiena:
Architetture e Prospettive, 1740.

*

Bibliography

Books:
Corrado Ricci, *I Bibiena — Architetti teatrali 1625–1780*, Milan, 1915.
Alpheus Hyatt Mayor, *The Bibiena Family*, New York, 1945.
Franz Hadamowsky, *Die Familie Galli-Bibiena in Wien*, Vienna, 1962.
Diane Kelder, *Drawings by the Bibiena Family*, Philadelphis, 1968.

Articles:
Kalman A. Burnim, "La Scena per Angelo — Magic by the Bibienas", *Theatre Survey 2*, 1961.
Kalman A. Burnim, "The Theatrical Career of Giuseppe Galli-Bibiena", *Theatre Survey 6*, 1965.

* * *

The Bibiena family of scene designers and architects is by far the best known of the 18th century. They covered a span of some 100 years, from about 1680, and they worked throughout Europe: Italy, Austria, Germany, Sweden, England, France, Russian, Spain and the Netherlands. Yet, considering their output, importance, widespread influence in Europe and the numerous examples of their work, including existing scenery and buildings, no full-dress theatrical study of the Bibienas has been attempted and perhaps never can be. We have collections of the work of some members of the group (variously listed under their family name, Galli, or their town name, Bibiena or Bibbiena), but many illustrations can only be labelled "by a member of the Bibiena family", making evaluation of the work of individual Bibienas extremely difficult.

Generally then, the Bibiena use of chiaroscuro is striking, giving a sense of great three dimensionality; their intricate use of angular perspective ("scena per angolo"), which Ferdinando mastered and popularized if he did not actually invent, is dazzling, coaxing the eye into the deeper reaches of the often maze-like designs; their use of the traditionally soft colours is boldly handsome in the few examples we have; and their monumentality is often overwhelming. Indeed, as a group, their chief fault is that they appeal to the eye so much that one would have difficulty focusing attention on performers working in front of the scenery. But frequently the Bibienas use a common Baroque practice to counter that: keeping the background lighter and less distinct, to help bring the eye back to the foreground, but the scale is often so grand and the diminishing architectural details so intriguing, that only the strongest performers could hold their own against such stage decorations. The fascinating Vienna collection of Bibiena sketches, gathered by Hadamowsky, reveal many typical features: regular use of "scena per angolo", so popular in the 18th century, so dazzlingly used by the Bibienas, and so much more interesting visually than the single-point perspectives of the previous century; a generally more organized, less carefree approach than similar sketches by another important 18th-century designer, Filippo Juvarra; frequent use of arches, often repeated, adding curves to otherwise blocky architectural features, but without Juvarra's exciting but sometimes distracting swirls; and, almost always, an awesome sense of space.

Those designs that can be attributed to particular members of the family allow at least some description of the individual styles of the major members. Ferdinando, the earliest and perhaps the most influential because of his writings, designed with great exactness and a sense of organisation; Francesco used rich and fanciful ornamentations; Giuseppe, the best known, especially because his fabulous interior design of the Markgräflisches Operhaus in Bayreuth (1744–48) can still be seen, was the most inventive; Antonio was especially careful and correct and the only Bibiena really skilled at figure drawing; and Carlo, who at first used his father Giuseppe's rich, decorative quality but moved toward the realism that by the end of the 18th century was appearing more frequently in European scene designs.

What audiences were dazzled by were not only the Bibiena settings, but the magical changes of them and the fantastic flying and sea machinery. Lady Mary Wortley Montague in September 1716 described in a letter to Alexander Pope a celebratory production created by Ferdinando and Giuseppe Bibiena in Vienna, and it is worth noting what she did and did not pay attention to: "Nothing of the kind was ever more magnificent; and I can easily believe, what I am told, that the decorations and habits cost the Emperor thirty thousand pounds sterling. The stage was built over a very large canal, and at the beginning of the second act, divided into two parts, discovering the water, on which there immediately came, from different parts, two fleets of little gilded vessels, that gave the representation of a naval fight ... The story of the opera is the enchantment of Alcina, which gives opportunities for a great variety of machines, and changes of the scenes, which are performed with a surprising swiftness. The theatre is so large, that 'tis hard to carry the eye to the end of it, and the habits in the utmost magnificence to the number of one hundred and eight".

The costumes were probably not by the Bibienas, who avoided that field, but the machines would have been theirs. The composer, librettist, and performers received short shrift from Lady Mary: it was a designer's show.

We should imagine when studying a Bibiena design a stage setting painted on flats standing at various positions on the stage (wherever needed, but probably all or most units set parallel to the front of the stage). The scenery would have been dimly lit, with the chandeliers above the performing area providing the most light along the centre line. Spectators were fully or partly illuminated and very aware of themselves, their elegant architectural surroundings and the social event they were attending. The Bibiena penchant for monumentality was right for the kind of production they were commissioned — usually by princes — to design.

What makes the Bibienas so distinct from other designers of the 18th century? They did not usually have the élan, the brio one finds in Juvarra. What the Bibienas had was a power, a sureness that one does not find so often in their contemporaries. Their designs do not just attract your attention, they command it. That monumentality provides a kind of security, a no-nonsense, businesslike quality that is overwhelming yet comforting. To use a musical comparison, the Bibienas are like Bach, Juvarra more like Tellemann, and it is quite possible to like them both.

—Edward A. Langhans

BJØRNSON, Bjørn. Norwegian director, actor and playwright. Born in Christiania (renamed Kristiania, 1877–24, and Oslo, 1925), 15 November 1859; son of writer Bjørnstjerne Bjørnson. Educated in Vienna. Married 1) Jenny Sandberg in 1886 (d. 1914); 2) Ingeborg Aas in 1893; 3) Eileen Bendix in 1909. Stage debut, as actor with the Saxe-Meiningen company, 1880–82; worked in St Gallen, Paris, 1882–83, and Hamburg, 1883–84; actor and director, Kristiania Theatre, 1884–93; director, Dagmar Teater, Copenhagen, 1894–96; co-founder and first director, Nationalteatret, Kristiania, 1899; resigned from Nationalteatret due to ill-health, 1907; subsequently lived in Germany and Italy; returned to Nationalteatret, 1923–27. Died in Oslo, 14 April 1942.

Principal productions

As actor:
1880   Spiegelberg in *Die Raüber* (Schiller), Saxe-Meiningen.
        Casca in *Julius Caesar* (Shakespeare), Saxe-Meiningen.
1883   Riis in *En Hanske* [A Gauntlet] (Bjørnstjerne Bjørnson), Kristiania Theatre, Kristiania.
1884   Richard in *Richard III* (Shakespeare), Kristiania Theatre, Kristiania.
1884–92 Darnley and Rizzio in *Maria Stuart i Skotland* [Mary Stuart in Scotland] (Bjørnstjerne Bjørnson), Kristiania Theatre, Kristiania.
1889   Professor Tygesen in *Geografi og Kjaerlighed* [Geography and Love] (Bjernstjerne Bjørnson), Kristiania Theatre, Kristiania.
1892   Peer Gynt in *Peer Gynt* (Ibsen), Kristiania Theatre, Kristiania.
1898   Paul Lange in *Paul Lange og Tora Parsberg* [Paul Lange and Tora Parsberg] (Bjørnstjerne Bjørnson), Dagmar Teater, Copenhagen.

Other roles included: Petruchio in *Trold kan taemmes* [The Taming of the Shrew] (Shakespeare); Sigurd Slembe in *Sigurd Slembe* [Sigurd the Bad] (Bjørnstjerne Bjørnson).

As director:
1883   *En Hanske* [A Gauntlet] (Bjørnstjerne Bjørnson), Kristiania Theatre, Kristiania.
1884   *Richard III* (Shakespeare), Kristiania Theatre, Kristiania.
1884–92 *Maria Stuart i Skotland* [Mary Stuart in Scotland] (Bjørnstjerne Bjørnson), Kristiania Theatre, Kristiania.
        Vildanden [The Wild Duck] (Ibsen), Kristiania Theatre, Kristiania.
1892   *Peer Gynt* (Ibsen), Kristiania Theatre, Kristiania.
1898   *Paul Lange og Tora Parsberg* [Paul Lange and Tora Parsberg] (Bjørnstjerne Bjørnson), Dagmar Teater, Copenhagen.
1902   *Kongen* [The King] (Bjørnstjerne Bjørnson), Nationalteatret, Kristiania.

Other productions included: *Brand* (Ibsen); *Gengangere* [Ghosts] (Ibsen); *Kejser og Galilaeer* [The Emperor and the Galilean] (Ibsen); *Over Aevne* [Beyond Our Power] (Bjørnstjerne Bjørnson); *Stjaalen Lykke* [Falling Leaves] (Giacosa), all at the Nationalteatret, Kristiania.

Publications

Johanne (play), 1898; *Solen skinner jo* [The Sun Shines] (play), 1913; *Vom deutschen Wesen*, 1917; *En tørstig kamel* [The Thirsty Camel] (play), 1919; *Far barndommen dage* (memoir), 1922; *Mit livs historier* [Story of My Life], 1922; *Bjørnstierne Bjørnson, Hiemmet og vennene. Aulestadsminner*, 1932; *Bare ungdom* (memoir), 1934; *Det gamle teater, Kunster og menneskene*, 1937.

* * *

The national theatre movement in Norway in the second half of the 19th century produced a number of distinguished actors and actresses, but the art of directing had not been given much attention prior to the arrival of the young Bjørn Bjørnson. he saw the need of modernizing acting and directing in the Norwegian theatre. It was clear that a proper education for an ambitious young man of the theatre in the 1870's could only be had abroad. Bjørnson's influential father, the well-known poet and playwright Bjørnsterne Bjørnson, introduced him to two of the most prominent theatre managers and directors in Vienna, Heinrich Laube at the Stadttheater and Franz von Dingelstadt at the Burgtheater.

The purpose of any stage production was for these directors to create dramatic illusion. Laube was an innovator in the direction of actors, working particularly on their language. He kept his eye on the performance of each actor in relation to the effect of the whole, and would take great care in developing a genuine tone of conversation. In Dingelstadt's view the way to achieve this was through the total stage effect, not so much by means of verbal language as by means of the visual aspects and the atmosphere of the performance. While Laube stressed clarity of diction and intellectual understanding, Dingelstadt aimed more at the emotional receptivity of the audience.

During his stay in Vienna, Bjørnson was a keen observer of the two directors and their specialities. Since both of them had one common aim, the effect of dramatic illusion, it was possible to learn from both, in spite of their differences. The new ideas concerning the art of theatre direction developed in Vienna in the 1860's and 1870's were given favourable conditions at the theatre of Georg II, Duke of Meiningen, who pursued his interests in directing along similar lines, convinced that the true task of theatrical art is to picture a piece of real life on stage, as accurately as possible. The work of the Duke was particularly successful in the staging of history plays, where he insisted that every historical detail was to be truthfully reproduced.

In spite of his handicap as a non-native speaker of German, Bjørnson became a member of the company of the Duke of Meiningen in 1880. He was given several important parts, such as Spiegelberg in Schiller's *The Robbers* and Casca in *Julius Caesar*. When he returned to Norway to work both as an actor and as a director, he brought with him strong impressions of the directing style in the contemporary German theatre, and it was his ambition to realise a similar programme for the Norwegian theatre of the 1880's and 1890's.

Together with his natural disposition for display of energy and will-power, Bjørnson's determination to introduce modern acting and principles of direction on the Norwegian stage impressed his contemporaries. One of the critics who had a good chance of observing the young man on stage at this time, Hjalmar Christensen, writes about a certain air of sovereignity and of being a born ruler, which often manifested itself in the characters Bjørnson portrayed. Occasionally this reportedly led to a certain exaggeration in his acting. At other times the same quality was fitting for the part he played. One of the greatest triumphs he enjoyed both as an actor and as a director was the production of *Richard III* at the Kristiania Theatre in 1884, where he played Richard. This was his first appearance on the Norwegian stage since his return, and the expectations were unusually high. The ruthlessness and energy with which he personified the king made a great impact on the audience.

In spite of this appearance of primitive force in his expression as an actor, Bjørnson was on the whole self-conscious and calculating in relation to the parts he played. According to Christensen, he seemed to maintain a distance between the characters he presented and himself, as if he was observing his own embodiment of the character in question. Bjørnson had a great talent for direct imitation of people he knew. Playing the leading part of Professor Tygesen in his father's comedy *Geography and Love* (1889), he wore the characteristic mask of Bjørnson senior. Imitations of this kind were not at all unusual among Norwegian actors at the time, and were generally appreciated by the audience.

A certain unscrupulousness combined with mental and physical strength also made itself felt when he worked as a director, which he did with great power and enthusiasm. This might in some cases have an intimidating effect on young actors. The critic Christenson adds that Bjørnson in his mature years had learned to modify his powerful appearance both in acting and in directing.

As a director, Bjørnson would carefully select scenographical and musical expressions to achieve the appropriate atmosphere on the stage. When history plays such as *Richard III* and Bjørnson senior's *Mary Stuart in Scotland* were presented at the old Kristiania Theatre, the critics immediately perceived a historical change in the principle of arrangement; the traditional style of symmetry had to yield before the modern principle of picturesque arrangement, with the use of a large number of well-rehearsed walkers-on as well as carefully calculated effects of sound, light, shadow and movement.

The ancient declamatory style was to a great extent replaced by a quickened pace that was felt to be more lifelike, particularly in the modern prose plays. In Ibsen's *Wild Duck*, one of Bjørnson's greatest artistic successes, the photographer's studio was not merely a background for the dialogue, it clearly fulfilled a dramatic function. When a short version of *Peer Gynt* (the first three acts) was performed in 1892, with Bjørnson playing the central character, the judgement of the critics varied as to the actor, but the director was unanimously praised. The production was very expensive, and the effect seems to have met the popular taste of the age.

When Bjørn Bjørnson became manager of the new Nationalteatret in Copenhagen in 1899, he had less opportunity to develop his art as actor and director further. His innovatory contribution to theatre art in Norway belongs mainly to the 19th century.

—Asbjørn Aarseth

BLIN, Roger (Paul Jules). French actor-manager, director, and designer. Born in Neuilly-sur-Seine, 22 March 1907. Educated at Sainte-Croix Collège, Neuilly; University of the Sorbonne, Paris, 1925–26; studied art at the Grande Chaumière, Paris, 1927–29. Began career working as a film extra, studying mime, and writing film criticism; joined October Group and made stage debut, 1935; actor in films and plays with Antonin Artaud, Charles Dullin, and Jean-Louis Barrault, 1936–39; actor in mime and teacher, Jean-Marie Conty's Education by Theatre project during World War II; manager, Théâtre Gaîté-Montparnasse company, 1948–50; acclaimed as director of Theatre of the Absurd in the 1950's, directing avant-garde plays by Arthur Adamov, Samuel Beckett, and Jean Genet among others; staged world premiere of *Waiting for Godot*, 1953; banned from government-supported media after signing Manifesto des 121 supporting right to insubordination in Algeria, 1955; continued to act in and direct new plays in the theatre and make numerous film and television appearances until 1984; open-heart surgery, 1971; Compagnie Roger Blin founded in his honour, 1976. Recipient: Grand Prix National des Arts et Lettres, 1976. Died in Paris, 20 January 1984.

Productions

As actor:
1935   Mute assassin in *Les Cenci* (adapted from Shelley), Folies Wagram, Paris.
1937   First Free Man in *Ubu enchaîné* (Jarry), Comédie des Champs-Élysées, Paris.
        Tahitian leper in *Pacifique* (Lenormand), Théâtre aux Ambassadeurs, Paris.
        Peasant in *La Cruche cassée* (Kleist), Théâtre des Ambassadeurs, Paris.
        Several roles in *Numance* (Cervantes), Théâtre Antoine, Paris.
1939   Laforgue in *Hamlet ou Les Suites de la piété filiale* (Laforgue, adapted from Shakespeare), Théâtre de l'Atelier, Paris.
1940   Buckingham in *Richard III* (Shakespeare), Théâtre de l'Atelier, Paris.
1947   The Devil in *Les Épiphanies* (Pichette), Théâtres des Noctambules, Paris.
1950   The Mutilated One in *La Grande et la Petite Manoeuvre* (Adamov), Théâtre des Noctambules, Paris.
1959   Bishop Tickone in *Les Possédés* (Dostoevsky, adapted by Camus), Théâtre Antoine, Paris.
1960   Davies in *Le Gardien* (Pinter), Théâtre de Lutèce, Paris.
        The Envoy in *Le Balcon* (Genet), Théâtre du Gymnase, Paris.
1964   Cardinal Cibo in *Lorenzaccio* (Musset), Théâtre Sarah Bernhardt, Paris.
1967   Rapaccini in *Rapaccini's Daughter* (Paz, adapted from Hawthorne), French tour.
        The Watchman in *Le Jardin aux betteraves* (Dubillard), Théâtre de Lutèce, Paris.
1974   The Solitary One in *Le Cochon noir* (Planchon), Théâtre National Populaire, Villeurbanne.

Other roles included: *La Faim* (Hamson, adapted by Barrault), Théâtre de l'Atelier, Paris, 1939; *Le Bal des voleurs* (Anouilh), Théâtre de l'Atelier, Paris, 1939; *Le Cocu magnifique* (Crommelynck), tour, 1939; *Marie-Jeanne* (Dennery and Mallian, adapted by Anouilh), Théâtre des Arts, Paris, 1939; *L'Ombre de la ravine* (Synge), Fondation Lyjo and Théâtre Monceau, 1941; *Le Baladin du monde occidental* (Synge), Fondation Lyjo and Théâtre Monceau, Paris, 1943; *La Tragédie de l'amour* (Heiberg), Théâtre du Vieux-Colombier, Paris, 1943; *Le Véritable Blanco Posnet* (Shaw), Théâtre du Vieux Colombier, Paris, 1947; *La Route au tabac* (Caldwell), Swiss tour, 1955.

As director:
1949   *La Lune dans la fleuve Jaune* (Johnston), Théâtre Gaîté-Montparnasse, Paris.
        La Sonate des spectres (Strindberg), Théâtre Gaîté-Montparnasse, Paris; acted The Student.
1950   *Le Bourrea s'impatiente* (Silvant), Théâtre Gaîté-Montparnasse, Paris.
1952   *La Parodie* (Adamov), Théâtre Lancry, Paris.
1953   *En Attendant Godot* (Beckett), Théâtre de Babylone, Paris, and Arnheim, the Netherlands; Schauspielhaus, Zurich, 1954; Théâtre Hébértot, Paris, 1956; Grenier de Toulouse, 1966; Théâtre Récamier, Paris, 1970; Comédie-Française, Paris, 1978; Théâtre de l'Odéon, Paris, 1979; acted Pozzo.
1956   *Marée basse* (Duvignaud), Théâtre des Noctambules, Paris.
1957   *Endgame* (Beckett), Royal Court Theatre, London, and Studio des Champs-Élysées, Paris; Fleismarket Theatre, Vienna, 1958; Théâtre Alpha 347, Paris; acted Hamm.
1958   *L'Ombre de la ravine* (Synge), Théâtre du Faubourg St-Jacques, Paris.
1959   *Les Nègres* (Genet), Théâtre de Lutèce, Paris; Théâtre de la Renaissance, Paris, 1960; Royal Court, London, 1961; Odéon-Théâtre de France, Paris, 1962.
1960   *La Dernière bande* (Beckett), Théâtre Récamier, Paris.
        Le Lion (Kenan), Théâtre de Lutèce, Paris.
1963   *Divines paroles* (Valle-Inclán), Théâtre de l'Odéon, Paris; Ljubljana, Yugoslavia, 1972; acted Pedro Gailo.
        Oh, les beaux jours (Beckett), Venice Drama Festival and l'Odéon-Théâtre de France, Paris; Teatro Stabile, Turin, 1965.
1964   *Le Tragédie du roi Christophe* (Césaire), Festival of Experimental Art, Knokke-le-Zoute, and Théâtre de Lutèce, Paris.
1965   *Hommes et pierres* (Faye), l'Odéon-Théâtre de France, Paris.
1966   *Les Paravents* (Genet), Odéon-Théâtre de France, Paris, and Nieuw Rotterdams Toneel; Buhnen der Stadt, Essen, 1967.
1967   *Le Balcon* (Genet), Rotterdam.
1968   *Les Charognards* (Weingarten), Théâtre de Carouge, Grand Théâtre de Lausanne, and Comédie de Genève, Geneva.

1969   *Les Nonnes* (Manet), Théâtre de Poche-Mont-
        parnasse, Paris.
1971   *La Nuit des assassins* (Triana), Théâtre
        Récamier, Paris.
1972   *Macbeth* (Shakespeare), Théâtre de Strasbourg.
        Où boivent les vaches (Dubillard), Théâtre
        Récamier, Paris.
1974   *Les Émigrés* (Mrozek), Petit-Orsay, Paris.
1975   *Songe* (Strindberg), Schauspielhaus, Zurich.
1976   *Boesman et Léna* (Fugard), Théâtre de la Cité
        internationale, Paris; Théâtre National de
        Chaillot, Paris, 1979.
1977   *Lady Strass* (Manet), Théâtre de Poche-Mont-
        parnasse, Paris.
1978   *Minamata and Co.* (Takahashi), Théâtre de la
        Commune d'Aubervilliers.
1979   *M'Appelle Isabelle Langrenier* (Bauer), Petit-
        T.E.P, Paris.
1979–83 *Ai-je dit que je suis bossu?* (Billetdoux), Théâtre
        Petit-Montparnasse, Paris.
        Le Président (Bernhart), Théâtre de la Micho-
        dière, Paris.
        Le Bleu de l'eau de vie (Maura), Petit-Odéon,
        Paris.
1983   *Triptych* (Frisch), Théâtre de l'Odéon, Paris.
        Rue Noire (Diguet), l'Épée de Bois, Cartoucher-
        ie de Vincennes.

Films

As actor:
Zouzou, 1934; *Les Mutinés de l'Elseneur*, 1936; *Sous les
yeux d'Occident*, 1936; *Un grand amour de Beethoven*,
1936; *Jenny*, 1936; *La vie est à nous*, 1936; *Le Temps des
cerises*, 1937; *La Citadelle du silence*, 1937; *L'Alibi*, 1937;
L'Affaire Lafarge, 1937; *La Dame de pique*, 1937; *Rendez-vous Champs-Élysées*, 1937; *La Tragédie impériale*,
1937; *Adrienne Lecouvreur*, 1938; *Entrée des artistes*,
1938; *Louise*, 1939; *Battement de couer*, 1939; *L'Esclave
blanche*, 1939; *Le monde tremblera*, 1939; *Premier refuge*,
1939; *Volpone*, 1940; *L'Age d'or*, 1941; *Le Capitaine
Fracasse*, 1942; *Dernier atout*, 1942; *La Vie de bohème*,
1942; *Les Visiteurs du soir*, 1942; *Adieu Léonard*, 1943;
Le Colonel Chabert, 1943; *Le Corbeau*, 1943; *Raspoutine*,
1943; *Douce*, 1943; *Premier de cordée*, 1943; *Le Couple
idéal*, 1945; *Le Jugement dernier*, 1945; *Pour une nuit
d'amour*, 1946; *Hans le marin*, 1948; *Histoires extraordi-
naires*, 1949; *Orphée*, 1949; *Le Bagnard*, 1950; *La
Taverne de La Nouvelle-Orléans*, 1951; *Pied d'Alu fait
des miracles*, 1952; *Torticola contre Frank Sberg*, 1952;
Le Chevalier de la nuit, 1954; *Á toi de jouer, Callaghan*,
1955; *Notre-Dame de Paris*, 1956; *Les Étoiles de midi*,
1958; *Tripes au soleil*, 1959; *Paris-Blues*, 1961; *Marie-
Soleil*, 1964; *La Loi du survivant*, 1966; *Le Désordre à
vingt ans*, 1967; *Le Traité du rossignol*, 1971; *La Ligne
d'ombre*, 1973; *Dada au coeur*, 1973; *Lili, aime-moi*,
1974; *Aloïse*, 1974; *Dragées au poivre*, 1974; *Jamais plus
toujours*, 1975; *Il faut vivre dangereusement*, 1977;
L'Adolescente, 1978.

As actor and director/screenwriter:
The Nameless Street (with Pierre Chenal), 1933.

As director:
Oh, les beaux jours, 1971.

Television

1960–80:   *Que voyez-vous, miss Ellis?*; *Mesure pour me-
            sure*; *La Croisée*; *Le Petit Clos et le Grand
            Clos*; *Oil*; *En route pour Cardiff*; *La Mortelle*;
            Quatre petits soirs; *La Neige et la cendre*;
            L'Hôpital de Leningrad; *Vendredi ou La Vie
            sauvage*; *Bouclage*; *L'Ordre*; *Les Trois Soeurs*;
            Alexandra; *La Père Gobert*; *L'Illusion co-
            mique*; and others.

Publications

Roger Blin: Souvenirs et Propos, edited by Lynda Peskine,
1986.

*

Bibliography

Books:
Jean Genet, *Lettres à Roger Blin*, Paris, 1968.
Andree Waintrop, *Les Mises en scène de Beckett par Roger
    Blin*, Paris, 1969.
Odette Aslan (translated by Ruby Cohn), *Roger Blin and
    Twentieth-Century Playwrights*, Cambridge, 1988.

Articles:
Anonymous, "Roger Blin aux prises avec Les Nègres",
    Lettres nouvelles, 1959.
John Fletcher, "Roger Blin at Work", *Modern Drama*,
    1966.
Brigitte Salino, "Roger Blin, fin de partie", *L'Avant-scène
    théâtre*, 1984.
Anonymous, "Adieu Roger Blin", *Acteurs*, 1984.

* * *

Roger Blin made no contributions to the theory of the
stage; he distrusted theory. He never headed a major state-
subsidized theatre. He did not create a distinctive form of
"scenic writing", seeking instead an "invisible" mise en
scène. But if for no other reason, he has earned his niche in
theatre history as the preferred director of Samuel Beckett
and Jean Genet.

Following in the footsteps of Copean and the Cartel, Blin
viewed the author as the primary creator of the theatrical
experience. His interest lay not in the French classics,
however, but in new playwrights; the majority of the plays
he directed were premieres. Legend has it that Beckett
submitted *Waiting for Godot* to Blin after seeing the young
director's production of Strindberg's *The Ghost Sonata*
because of Blin's fidelity to the text — and because the
theatre was empty.

With his instinct for recognizing a major talent, Blin set
out to produce *Godot*; three years and several cast changes
later, *Godot* opened at the Théâtre de Babylone on 4
January 1953, with a reluctant Blin (who had seen himself
in a dream playing Lucky) in the role of Pozzo. By all
accounts, the collaboration between Blin and Beckett was a

close one, Blin suggesting cuts and changes in the text and Beckett vetoing ideas that he considered too obvious, such as Blin's initial concept of staging the play as a circus performance.

Blin, who had studied mime and dance, took a physical approach to the mise en scène of *Godot*. He approached each part through the character's primary ailment (Estragon's sore feet, Vladimir's prostate problem), working with the actors to find a movement pattern based on the ailment that also expressed the character's inner being (Estragon's lethargy, Vladimir's restlessness). Circular blocking emphasized the circular structure of the text.

Following the success of *Godot*, Beckett dedicated *Endgame* to Blin, who later viewed his creation of Hamm as his best performance. The Blin/Beckett collaboration continued with Blin directing the premieres of *Endgame*, *Krapp's Last Tape*, and *Happy Days*, as well as revivals and foreign productions of *Godot*.

Scholars have persisted in labelling Blin a disciple of Artaud, a classification that Blin just as persistently denied. Although a loyal friend of the demented poet, Blin found Artaud's theoretical work too stylized and his directorial approach dictatorial. The label "Artaudian" may seem most appropriate for Blin's mises en scène of Genet, to whose texts the label is also — debatably — applied.

For *The Blacks*, Blin reluctantly renounced his ideal of the "invisible" mise en scène because he believed the metatheatrical structure of the text required directorial intervention to break the illusion and remind the audience they were witnessing a theatrical performance. Blin, a visual artist since his youth, did the preliminary scenic designs himself. André Acquart's multi-levelled scaffolding of metal tubing wound in asbestos cloth provided an image of multiple audiences: Blacks and Whites performing for each other as well as for the theatre public. The grotesque half-masks of the Whites, the ceremonial quality of the performance, the striking contrasts of rhythm ranging from slow-motion to frenzy, evoked an Artaudian image while faithfully translating Genet's own brand of cruelty. Most critics consider *The Blacks* Blin's best production and Genet himself called the mise en scène "perfection".

The Genet/Blin collaboration on *The Screens*, produced at Barrault's invitation at the Odéon-Théâtre de France in 1966, has been documented in Genet's published rehearsal notes, *Lettres à Roger Blin*. As in the Beckett/Blin ventures, author input was extensive and Blin often found himself in the role of mediator between the actors and their demanding playwright. Artaudian elements in the mise en scène included ceremonial costumes, a formulaic performance style drawing on Oriental traditions, and symbolic make-up designed by Blin himself, who had an ongoing interest in the art of make-up.

Although the production of *The Screens* aroused a furore of right-wing protest in the wake of the Algerian rebellion, Blin was never an overtly political director. A self-proclaimed atheist with leftist leanings, Blin was attracted to plays that offered anti-Establishment provocation, but never wandered down the Brechtian path. Aside from *The Screens*, Blin's most politically hard-hitting production was *Mishima and Co.*, an environmentalist play in which he used marionettes to represent pollution victims. The suffering puppets, joined in the last scene by actors moving like marionettes, presented an image of the malignant power exercised by corporations upon the human body.

While Blin sought a mise en scène that rendered the author's vision so faithfully as to remain unnoticeable, his work nonetheless demonstrated stylistic characteristics related to his early involvement with the Surrealists. He described his ideal setting as being animate, subjective, "a street as it appears when you're drunk". His mise en scène was rigorously choreographed, physically and vocally rhythmic. When appropriate, he designed movement to create a dreamlike atmosphere, as in his use of turntables rotating at various speeds in opposite directions for Max Frisch's *Triptych* to create a land of the dead in which characters moved through a field of hypnotic forces. Blin preferred scenic transformations in view of the audience to give an impression of fluidity and ambiguity, as in his mise en scène of *Divine Words*, *The Screens*, and *Macbeth*. Other directorial "tricks" of which he was fond included use of a "double" for a character, which allowed the audience simultaneous views of the character, and scenes in which actors spoke to a fixed point in the house instead of to each other. Blin was noted for strong casting choices and an attraction to the strange and striking; his three witches in *Macbeth* were portrayed by a man, a short actress, and a dwarf — all enveloped in a single costume.

Another hallmark of Blin's directorial work was his flexibility. Not having a theatre of his own, rarely having a subsidy, he adapted to theatrical spaces — and budgets — large and small. In rehearsal, observers commented on his unobtrusive style. Sometimes sitting through an entire rehearsal without speaking, he did not theorize about the play but directed by indirection, so that by the end of rehearsal, the actors had absorbed his concept by osmosis. His directions tended to take the form of demonstration more than verbal comment, but he remained open to input from actors as well as authors.

A man who became an actor because of his stutter (he never stuttered in performance), Blin was a director who thrived on challenges. His determination and insight brought Samuel Beckett, among others, to the attention of the modern theatre.

—Suzanne Burgoyne Dieckman

BLOCH, William Edward. Danish director and playwright. Born in Copenhagen, 30 March 1845. Educated at the Borgerdyd School, Copenhagen; graduated in law, 1871. Married actress Anna Kristine Lindemann in 1887. Worked initially in an insurance office but established reputation as playwright; director, Kongelige Teater, Copenhagen, 1881; particularly admired for his productions of Henrik Ibsen and introduced naturalistic staging there; resigned from the Kongelige Teater, 1893; returned, 1899–1909; also acclaimed for his productions of Ludvig Holberg. Died in Copenhagen, 1 November 1926.

Productions

1881   *Umyndige i Kærlighed* [Minors in Love] (Topsøe), Kongelige Teater, Copenhagen; revived there, 1892.

1882   *Et Eventyr i Rosenborg Have* [An Adventure in Rosenborg Gardens] (Heiberg), Kongelige Teater, Copenhagen.

Den forvandlede Brudgom [The Transformed Bridegroom] (Holberg), Kongelige Teater, Copenhagen.

1883   *En Folkefjende* [An Enemy of the People] (Ibsen), Kongelige Teater, Copenhagen.

1884   *Tartuffe* (Moliére), Kongelige Teater, Copenhagen; revived there, 1899.

En Skandale [A Scandal] (Benzon), Kongelige Teater, Copenhagen.

1885   *Vildanden* [The Wild Duck] (Ibsen), Kongelige Teater, Copenhagen.

Geografi of Kærlighed [Geography and Love] (Bjørnson), Kongelige Teater, Copenhagen.

1886   *Tilfældigheder* [Coincidences] (Benzon), Kongelige Teater, Copenhagen.

Karens Garde [Karen's Guards] (Hostrup), Kongelige Teater, Copenhagen.

1887   *Der var engang* [Once Upon a Time] (Drachmann), Kongelige Teater, Copenhagen.

Frøken Nelly [Miss Nelly] (Bloch), Kongelige Teater, Copenhagen.

Fruentimmerskolen [The School for Wives] (Molière), Kongelige Teater, Copenhagen.

Pernilles korte Frøkenstand [Pernille's Brief Ladyship] (Holberg), Kongelige Teater, Copenhagen.

1888   *Ninon* (Hertz), Kongelige Teater, Copenhagen.

Under Snefog [During the Snowstorm] (Hostrup), Kongelige Teater, Copenhagen.

Aprilsnarrene [The April Fools] (Heiberg), Kongelige Teater, Copenhagen.

1889   *Fruen fra Havet* [The Lady from the Sea] (Ibsen), Kongelige Teater, Copenhagen.

De Danske i Paris [Danes in Paris] (Heiberg), Kongelige Teater, Copenhagen.

Amors Genistreger [Love's Blunders] (Hertz), Kongelige Teater, Copenhagen.

Pottemager Walter [Walter the Potter] (Heiberg), Kongelige Teater, Copenhagen.

Generationer [Generations] (Christiansen), Kongelige Teater, Copenhagen.

Et Rejse-Eventyr [A Marvellous Journey] (Arnesen), Kongelige Teater, Copenhagen.

1890   *Kong Midas* [King Midas] (Heiberg), Kongelige Teater, Copenhagen.

De Forelskede [The Lovers] (Goldoni), Kongelige Teater, Copenhagen.

Mange Aar efter [Many Years Later] (Steenbuch), Kongelige Teater, Copenhagen.

Det nye System [The New System] (Bjørnson), Kongelige Teater, Copenhagen.

Hr Poirier og hans Svigersøn [Mr Poirier and His Son-in-Law] (Augier and Sandeau), Kongelige Teater, Copenhagen.

Tilfældet har Ret [The Justice of Chance] (Goldoni), Kongelige Teater, Copenhagen; revived there, 1903.

I Provinsen [In the Provinces] (Esmann), Kongelige Teater, Copenhagen.

De Fattiges Dyrehave [The Zoo of the Poor] (Hertz), Kongelige Teater, Copenhagen.

En Advarsel [A Warning] (Gad), Kongelige Teater, Copenhagen.

Aladdin (Oehlenschlager), Kongelige Teater, Copenhagen.

1891   *Gregers* (Holm), Kongelige Teater, Copenhagen.

Hedda Gabler (Ibsen), Kongelige Teater, Copenhagen; revived there, 1902.

En Historietime [A History Lesson] (Heckscher), Kongelige Teater, Copenhagen.

En Skavank [A Flaw] (Goldschmidt), Kongelige Teater, Copenhagen.

I Ravnekrogen [In the Hole] (Høyer), Kongelige Teater, Copenhagen.

Et Kompagniskab [A Partnership] (Picard), Kongelige Teater, Copenhagen.

Grænsen [The Boundary] (Steenbuch), Kongelige Teater, Copenhagen.

Marianna (Musset), Kongelige Teater, Copenhagen.

Gulddaasen [The Golden Box] (Olufsen), Kongelige Teater, Copenhagen.

1892   *En Gøgeunge* [A Cuckoo in the Nest] (Hansen), Kongelige Teater, Copenhagen.

Hagbarth og Signe [Hagbarth and Signe] (Oehlenschlager), Kongelige Teater, Copenhagen.

Hjertets Ret [Justice of the Heart] (Nordau), Kongelige Teater, Copenhagen.

Den kære Familie [The Beloved Family] (Esmann), Kongelige Teater, Copenhagen.

Erik og Abel [Erik and Abel] (Oehlenschlager), Kongelige Teater, Copenhagen.

En lykkelig Aften [A Pleasant Evening] (Hansen), Kongelige Teater, Copenhagen.

Unge Folk [Young People] (Nielsen), Kongelige Teater, Copenhagen.

Helligtrekongers [Twelfth Night] (Shakespeare), Kongelige Teater, Copenhagen.

1893   *Et Samfundsoffer* [A Victim of Society] (Hansen), Kongelige Teater, Copenhagen.

Bygmester Solness [The Master Builder] (Ibsen), Kongelige Teater, Copenhagen.

Den Stundesløse [The Fussy Man] (Holberg), Kongelige Teater, Copenhagen.

1899   *Den Vægelsindede* [The Weathercock] (Holberg), Kongelige Teater, Copenhagen.

Middelalderlig [Middle-Aged] (Drachmann), Kongelige Teater, Copenhagen.

Det gamle Hjem [The Old Home] (Esmann), Kongelige Teater, Copenhagen.

Doktoren imod sin Vilje [The Doctor in Spite of Himself] (Molière), Kongelige Teater, Copenhagen.

1900   *Moderate Løjer* [Reasonable Pranks] (Benzon), Kongelige Teater, Copenhagen.

Mester Gert Westphaler [Master Gert Westphaler] (Holberg), Kongelige Teater, Copenhagen.

Mørkets [The Power of Darkness] (Tolstoy), Kongelige Teater, Copenhagen.

Erasmus Montanus (Holberg), Kongelige Teater, Copenhagen.

En Sillingsmand [A Person of Status] (Hansen), Kongelige Teater, Copenhagen.

1901   *Ulysses von Ithacia* (Holberg), Kongelige Teater, Copenhagen.
   Skærmydsler [Quarrels] (Wied), Kongelige Teater, Copenhagen.
   Den ellevte Juni [The 11th of June] (Holberg), Kongelige Teater, Copenhagen.

1902   *Da vi var en og tyve* [When We Were One-and-Twenty] (Esmond), Kongelige Teater, Copenhagen.
   Det gamle Færgested [The Old Ferry Dock] (Nielsen), Kongelige Teater, Copenhagen.
   Den gamle Pavillon [The Old Pavilion] (Wied), Kongelige Teater, Copenhagen.
   Paa Storhove [At Storhove] (Bjørnson), Kongelige Teater, Copenhagen.

1903   *Jeppe paa Bjerget* [Jeppe on the Hill] (Holberg), Kongelige Teater, Copenhagen.
   Figurantinden [The Mannequin] (Curel), Kongelige Teater, Copenhagen.

1904   *Forretning er Forretning* [Business Is Business] (Mirbeau), Kongelige Teater, Copenhagen.
   Et Opgør [A Reckoning] (Wied), Kongelige Teater, Copenhagen.
   Den gamle Præst [The Old Minister] (Knudsen and Lange), Kongelige Teater, Copenhagen.
   Barselstuen [The Lying-In Room] (Holberg), Kongelige Teater, Copenhagen.

1905   *Landlov* [Shore Leave] (Nielsen), Kongelige Teater, Copenhagen.
   Fader og Søn [Father and Son] (Esmann), Kongelige Teater, Copenhagen.
   Hekseri eller blind Alarm [Sorcery or False Alarm] (Holberg), Kongelige Teater, Copenhagen.
   Kærlighed og Købmandsskab [Love and Commerce] (Knudsen), Kongelige Teater, Copenhagen.

1906   *Taget med Storm* [Taken by Storm] (Donnay), Kongelige Teater, Copenhagen.
   Mellem Læger [Between Doctors] (Kistemaecker), Kongelige Teater, Copenhagen.

1907   *Den gode Borger* [The Good Citizen] (Nathansen), Kongelige Teater, Copenhagen.
   Den politiske Kandestøber [The Political Tinker] (Holberg), Kongelige Teater, Copenhagen.
   Kvinder [Women] (Larsen), Kongelige Teater, Copenhagen.

1908   *Forældre* [Parents] (Benzon), Kongelige Teater, Copenhagen.

1909   *Daniel Hertz* (Nathansen), Kongelige Teater, Copenhagen.

Publications

En Fix Idé [A Fixed Idea] (play, with Nicolai Bøgh); *Kanarienfuglen* [The Canary] (play, with Nicolai Bøgh); *De hvide Rose* [The White Roses] (play, with Nicolai Bøgh, produced Kongelige Teater, 1872); *Lygtemaend* [Will-o-the-Wisps] (play, with Nicolai Bøgh, produced Kongelige Teater, 1875); *Naar möbler flyttes* [When the Furniture is Moved] (play, produced Kongelige Teater, 1879), 1879; *Konsekvenzer* [Consequences] (play, with

Richard Kaufmann, produced Kongelige Teater, 1881), 1881; *Frøken Nelly* [Miss Nelly] (play, produced Kongelige Teater, 1886), 1887; *Paa rejse med H. C. Andersen, dagsbogoptegnelser af William Bloch*, 1942.

*

Bibliography

Books:
Marker and Marker, *The Scandinavian Theatre: A Short History*, Oxford, 1975.

Articles:
Carla Waal, "William Bloch's *The Wild Duck*", Educational Theatre Journal, 30, 1978.

* * *

William Bloch made his first impression as a playwright, his first comedies being produced by the Folk Theatre while he was still a student. Though the Kongelige Teater produced his comedy *The White Roses* in 1872, he (and co-author Nikolai Bøgh) won more attention with *Will-o-the-Wisps*, which provoked serious rioting at the theatre due to its attack on young social reformers of the period. Subsequent works included *Miss Nelly*, his most personal play, which was written expressly for his future wife.

As a playwright, Bloch was much influenced by French literature (he also translated several plays from French) but the detailed stage directions in his scripts regarding movement, scenery, and the characters' psychological reactions were early evidence of a talent for modern naturalistic directing. This latent potential was one reason why the artistic director Edvard Fallesen proposed hiring him in July 1881 as director at the Kongelige Teater, where he was to have his first big breakthrough with Ibsen's *An Enemy of the People*.

In his naturalist style of directing William Bloch concentrated on both the tangible and the intangible. The tangible — external realism — was a milieu with authentic details, scenery based on nature, and an acting style resembling realistic behaviour. The intangible — inner realism — consisted of the atmosphere and mood of the performance as well as a psychological approach to the dialogue. Naturalism for Bloch, therefore, was twofold, because the external realism represented an inner world. He did not try to create a mirror image of reality, but to present a reflection of "the hidden life of the soul", which would affect the spectator through sensory impressions.

To carry out his naturalistic programme, Bloch drew extensively on technical resources. Electric lighting, which was installed gradually toward the end of the 19th century, made it possible to have even illumination over the whole stage, so that the action could take place everywhere. Twilight, daylight, moonlight, and sunlight effects gave the stage just the atmosphere and mood suitable for Danish naturalism. By combining the walls, furniture, and backdrops from different productions, Bloch was able without much expense to create the milieu he wanted. Pietro Kohn, who was engaged at the theatre in 1880, added to the Bloch style authentic dress, thereby laying the foundation for a modern approach to costuming.

Beyond the theatre's technical capabilities, Ibsen's drama also contributed to the introduction of naturalism. Bloch directed several of Ibsen's plays, learning in the process how to create a modern technique of vocal delivery with pauses and silences appropriate to a psychological style of acting.

The fact that Bloch was especially interested in contemporary drama gradually led to his being criticized, especially by the actors at the Kongelige Teater itself. The actors considered him an outsider and dilettante because he had not been trained as a performer. People also thought that he was too modern in his directing methods, had too many rehearsals (about 20 per production), and did not allow the actors to develop their own interpretations. The criticism he received led to Bloch leaving the theatre in 1893.

When Einar Christiansen was invited to become the head of the Kongelige Teater in 1899 he agreed only on condition that Bloch would return. This engagement lasted until 1909, and with younger actors, trained in naturalism at the new theatre school, Bloch was better able to carry out his ideas. In his last period as a director, Bloch continued to stage a number of contemporary plays, but his greatest contribution was a new approach to the comedies of Ludvig Holberg. The first Holberg play he directed after returning to the theatre was *Master Gert Westphaler* in 1900. Thorolf Pederson designed a new set, a pleasant little provincial marketplace, which framed the action, and Anna Bloch's Leonora was also new. Her naturalistic acting style, with significant pauses and subtle nuances of line delivery, supported her husband's direction.

The theatre had maintained a Holberg tradition, because the comedies were presented continuously. Bloch took what he could use from that tradition and adjusted its form to his own times, so that the comedies had an immediacy and appeal that stimulated the audience's imagination. Holberg's plays in Bloch's direction became almost as logical as Henrik Ibsen's, because the scene changes were logical and the characters' actions had a psychological basis.

Bloch's naturalism therefore brought new life to Holberg's old comedies, but around 1900 a problem arose regarding his interpretation of new plays. The author Herman Bang, who considered Bloch an excellent director, perceived Bloch's lack of passion to be a serious weakness. "William Bloch has taught his actors a great deal," he wrote. "But he has forgotten to teach them one thing — occasionally to forget themselves."

Another problem for Bloch was his lack of ability to interpret the symbolism that was present in naturalistic plays. As time went on, symbols, for example in Ibsen, became more prominent, and Bloch's last Ibsen productions were therefore only partially realised. The theatre did not discover until much later that Ibsen in his plays made concrete what Sigmund Freud in his book *The Interpretation of Dreams* tried to establish scientifically.

Every style has its limitations, and this was true of Bloch's somewhat pale and colourless naturalism. It was best suited for psychological drama and entertaining comedies. But even if the style seems dated today, Bloch established Danish theatrical naturalism and his principles of directing are still used.

—Jytte Wiingaard

Claire Bloom

BLOOM, Claire. British actress. Born Patricia Claire Bloom in Finchley, London, 15 February 1931. Educated at Badminton School, Bristol; Fern Hill Manor, New Milton; New York City public schools, 1940–43; scholarship in acting under Eileen Thorndike at the Guildhall School of Music and Drama, London, 1944–46; Central School of Speech and Drama, London, 1947–48. Married 1) actor Rod Steiger in 1959 (divorced 1969), one daughter; 2) director Hillard Elkins in 1969 (divorced 1972); 3) novelist Philip Roth in 1990. Stage debut, Oxford Repertory Theatre, 1946; London debut, Duchess Theatre, 1947; film debut, 1948; actress, Old Vic company, 1952–54; Broadway debut, Winter Garden Theatre, 1956; won acclaim as Juliet and in other Shakespearean roles; Canadian and US tour with Old Vic company, 1956–57; acted at the Spoleto Festival of Two Worlds, 1963; British and US tour, 1982–83. Member: Guildhall School of Music (Fellow). Distinguished Visiting Professor, Hunter College, New York, 1989. Recipient: British Film Award, 1952; *Elle* Award, 1952; Drama Desk Award, 1971; Outer Circle Award, 1971; *London Evening Standard* Award, 1974; *Plays and Players* Award, 1974; British Academy of Film and Television Arts Award, 1985.

Roles

1946   Private Jessie Killigrew in *It Depends What You Mean* (Bridie), Oxford Repertory Theatre.

Helen in *An Italian Straw Hat* (Labiche), Oxford Repertory Theatre.

Jessie in *Pink String and Sealing Wax* (Pertwee), Oxford Repertory Theatre.

1947   Lady-in-waiting in *The White Devil* (Webster), Duchess Theatre, London.

Circus performers in *He Who Gets Slapped* (Andreyev), Duchess Theatre, London.

Erinna in *The Wanderer* (Kotzebue), His Majesty's Theatre, London.

1948   Blanch in *King John* (Shakespeare), Shakespeare Memorial Theatre, Stratford-upon-Avon.

Ophelia in *Hamlet* (Shakespeare), Shakespeare Memorial Theatre, Stratford-upon-Avon; Edinburgh Festival, 1953; Old Vic Theatre, London, 1953–54.

Perdita in *The Winter's Tale* (Shakespeare), Shakespeare Memorial Theatre, Stratford-upon-Avon.

1949   Daphne Randall in *The Damask Cheek* (Van Druten), Lyric Theatre, Hammersmith, London.

Alizon Eliot in *The Lady's Not For Burning* (Fry), Globe Theatre, London.

1950   Isabelle in *Ring Round the Moon* (Anouilh, translated by Fry), Globe Theatre, London.

1952–53   Juliet in *Romeo and Juliet* (Shakespeare), Old Vic Theatre, London; revived there and on US and Canadian tour, 1956–57.

Jessica in *The Merchant of Venice* (Shakespeare), Old Vic Theatre, London.

1953–54   Helena in *All's Well That Ends Well* (Shakespeare), Old Vic Theatre, London.

Viola in *Twelfth Night* (Shakespeare), Old Vic Theatre, London.

Virgilia in *Coriolanus* (Shakespeare), Old Vic Theatre, London.

Miranda in *The Tempest* (Shakespeare), Old Vic Theatre, London; Palace Theatre, London, 1955.

1955   Cordelia in *King Lear* (Shakespeare), Palace Theatre, London.

1956–57   The Queen in *Richard II* (Shakespeare), US and Canadian tour.

1958   Lucile in *Duel of Angels* (Giraudoux, translated by Fry), Apollo Theatre, London.

1959   The Wife in *Rashomon* (F. and M. Kanin), Music Box Theatre, New York.

1961   Johanna in *Altona* (Sartre), Royal Court Theatre, London, and Saville Theatre, London.

1963   Andromache in *The Trojan Women* (Euripides), Spoleto Festival of Two Worlds, Italy.

1965   Sasha in *Ivanov* (Chekhov), Phoenix Theatre, London.

1971   Nora in *A Doll's House* (Ibsen), Playhouse Theatre, New York and Eisenhower Theatre, Kennedy Centre, Washington; Criterion Theatre, London, 1973.

Hedda in *Hedda Gabler* (Ibsen), Playhouse Theatre, New York.

1972   Mary Queen of Scots in *Vivat! Vivat Regina!* (Bolt), Broadhurst Theatre, New York.

1974   Blanche du Bois in *A Streetcar Named Desire* (Williams), Piccadilly Theatre, London.

1976   Miss Giddens in *The Innocents* (Archibald), Morosco Theatre, New York.

1977   Rebecca West in *Rosmersholm* (Ibsen), Haymarket Theatre, London.

1981   Madame Ranevskaya in *The Cherry Orchard* (Chekhov), Chichester Festival.

1982–83   All roles in *These Are Women, a Portrait of Shakespeare's Heroines* (Shakespeare compilation), British and US tour.

1990   Irene in *When We Dead Waken* (Ibsen), Almeida Theatre, London.

Films

The Blind Goddess, 1948; *Limelight*, 1952; *Innocents in Paris*, 1953; *The Man Between*, 1953; *Richard III*, 1956; *Alexander the Great*, 1956; *The Brothers Karamazov*, 1958; *The Buccaneer*, 1958; *Look Back in Anger*, 1959; *Schnachnovelle*, 1960; *Three Steps to Freedom*, 1960; *Royal Game*, 1960; *Brainwashed*, 1961; *The Wonderful World of the Brothers Grimm*, 1962; *The Chapman Report*, 1962; *The Haunting*, 1963; *80,000 Suspects*, 1963; *Alta Infedelità*, 1963; *Il Maestro de Vigevano*, 1963; *The Outrage*, 1964; *The Spy Who Came in from the Cold*, 1966; *Charly*, 1968; *Three into Two Won't Go*, 1969; *The Illustrated Man*, 1969; *Red Sky at Morning*, 1970; *A Severed Head*, 1971; *A Doll's House*, 1973; *The Going Up of David Lev*, 1973; *Islands in the Stream*, 1977; *Clash of the Titans*, 1981; *Shadowlands*, 1985; *Déjà*, 1985; *Sammy and Rosie Get Laid*, 1987; *Crimes and Misdemeanors*, 1989.

Television

Cyrano de Bergerac, 1956; *Caesar and Cleopatra*, 1956; *Romeo and Juliet*, 1957; *Misalliance*, 1959; *Shirley Temple's Storybook*, 1959; *Anna Karenina*, 1961; *Wuthering Heights*, 1962; "Claire Bloom Reads Poetry", *Camera Three*, 1964; *A Time to Love*, 1967; *Soldier in Love*, 1967; *Ivanov*, 1967; *A Legacy*, 1975; *In Praise of Love*, 1975; *The Oresteia*, 1978; *Henry VIII*, 1979; *Brideshead Revisited*, 1979; *Backstairs at the White House*, 1979; *Hamlet*, 1980; *Cymbeline*, 1982; *Separate Tables*, 1982; *The Ghost Writer*, 1982; *King John*, 1983; *Time and the Conways*, 1984; *Ellis Island*, 1984; *Florence Nightingale*, 1984; *Oedipus the King*, 1985; *Lightning Always Strikes Twice*, 1985; *Promises to Keep*, 1985; *Liberty*, 1986; *Anastasia: the Mystery of Anna*, 1986; *The Belle of Amherst*, 1986; *Consenting Adults*, 1987; *Intimate Contact*, 1987; *Queenie*, 1987; *Hold the Dream*, 1987; *A Shadow on the Sun*, 1988; *The Lady and the Highwayman*, 1989; *The Camomile Lawn*, 1992.

Publications

Limelight and After: The Education of an Actress (autobiography), 1982.

* * *

Claire Bloom is an actress of rather remote, poetic beauty who moves with the grace of a dancer. She was, indeed, trained in dance as well as in acting and came to the attention of audiences worldwide when Charlie Chaplin selected her to play the young dancer in his last major film, *Limelight*. Since then, she has worked equally in films and on the stage. She had already played her first Shakespearean roles at Stratford and continued, in the next few years, to move through the range of Shakespeare's enchanting girls — Perdita, Helena, Viola, Miranda, and Juliet — along with the gently suffering Ophelia and Cordelia and Virgilia, Coriolanus's "gracious silence". This youthful acting experience confirmed the quality of the dream-girl, of a flower-like innocence at its brief point of perfection, as the dominant aspect of her stage personality. It also brought her the benefit of playing opposite some of the finest actors of the period, including Laurence Olivier.

In diverging for a while from Shakespeare in the early 1950's to appear in modern plays, Bloom found herself matched with the young Richard Burton (with whom she was later re-united in the film *The Spy Who Came in from the Cold*) in John Gielgud's production of Christopher Fry's *The Lady's Not for Burning* and also acted opposite Paul Scofield, who played the twin brothers, in Anouilh's *Ring Round the Moon* (adapted by Fry). The absence of realism from the lyric charm of Fry's work led to its rejection by the new movement associated with the Royal Court Theatre in the second half of the decade and it might be supposed that the actress's career was similarly at risk. The fact that she was soon to be seen as Helena in the highly successful film of *Look Back in Anger*, the flagship of the new realism, and appeared with Kenneth Haigh (the original Jimmy Porter) in Sartre's *Altona* at the Royal Court in 1961, testifies both to the intelligence and adaptability of the actress as well as to the persistent attraction of the feminine image she projected.

Comparison with Vanessa Redgrave, the outstanding impersonator of the young Shakespearean heroines of her generation, helps define the careful limitations of so much of Claire Bloom's acting. The robustness, humour, and generous warmth in Vanessa Redgrave's performances show up in contrast the limited animation, controlled vitality, and absence of humour that preserve the ideal quality Bloom most frequently communicates, the inner stillness conveyed with grave, large-eyed facial immobility and setting off a masculine dynamism in the actors she partners. Some critics have expressed their reservations about her work in such terms as "austere" and even "frosty", while recognising that her dignity is not simply that of the lady, the manner of a social class, but nearer to a quality of spirit, fitting her to play Andromache in *The Trojan Women* and the heroines of Ibsen's plays in pursuit of some absolute beyond life. Though so much of her subsequent career has been dominated by typecasting, some of her most considerable triumphs have involved a breaking of the mould.

Limelight and success as Juliet in the USA opened the way for Bloom to spend as much of her acting life in the USA and Canada as in England. Her first husband was the US actor Rod Steiger, after Marlon Brando the best known of the "Method" actors who emerged from the Actors' Studio where Lee Strasberg and Elia Kazan practised their experimental adaptation of Stanislavsky's ideas on the training of actors. In her autobiography, which says little about the marriage, Claire Bloom puts the "Method" in its place as an alternative to classical disciplines, which opened the theatre to actors of working-class origins. Yet the emphasis laid by the Actors' Studio on internal activity, on intensely *being* in character, in preference to more overt rhetorical techniques of acting, was congenial to her own approach and encouraged her to try a more emotion-centred naturalism (this was a period when the whole acting profession was busy debating the ideas of the Actors' Studio and everyone who had the opportunity paid a visit to see Strasberg at work).

Turning to Ibsen, playing Nora in *A Doll's House* and Hedda Gabler, was perhaps predictable in a leading serious actress in her maturity: this was classical repertoire still and Ibsen offered a gallery of major roles for actresses. At the same time, his roots in the thought and feeling of 19th-century romanticism nourish the social and psychological naturalism of his prose plays with a quality appropriate to this particular actress: above all else, Nora waits for the wonderful revelation of the truth she believes marriage must hold, while Hedda's longings are for a nobility and beauty she cannot find in everyday life. Yet it was one of the plays most closely associated with the Actors' Studio, Tennessee Williams's *A Streetcar Named Desire*, which provided her with what became her favourite role. Through Blanche du Bois she was able to explore and express the experience of the break-up of the image (a man-determined ideal in her feminist interpretation) under the assaults of time, a bullying society hungry for victims, and the impulses of the woman's vitality, discovering the rich variety of the part from haunting terror through dignity to a self-mocking humour. This was preparation for taking on the heroines of Ibsen's late plays, Rebecca West in *Rosmersholm* and Irene in *When We Dead Awaken*. Rebecca, looking back on a passionate and wilful life from the vantage-point of a wisdom without hope in this world, then steadfastly moving towards transcendance, dominated the performance rather to the exclusion of the intensely ambitious, political creature who is still fighting and contriving her way through the first two acts of the play. In Irene, in Ibsen's rarely performed final work, she took on perhaps the most difficult part of her career and largely mastered it with acting intelligence of a high order. Irene is both a symbol and a character, human and inhuman, the soul or ghost of a woman, the muse of an ageing artist. Turning to avenging fury, she walks the dizzying edge between sanity and madness. As she had done with Blanche, so here again Bloom held the coherence of the character while shifting easily from facet to facet.

Television producers have continued to typecast her, whether as the tragic heroine of *Anna Karenina* or the femme fatale, half-aristocratic socialite, half-nun, in *Brideshead Revisited*. Although she has had her share of appearances in films unworthy of her, the cinema has also rewarded her with greater variety of material, ranging from the *Brothers Karamazov*, in which her performance was singled out for critical praise, through *A Severed Head* to *The Chapman Report* (directed by George Cukor) and *Three into Two Won't Go* (with Rod Steiger, directed by Peter Hall).

—Margery Morgan

BOAL, Augusto. Brazilian theoretician, director and playwright. Born in Brazil, 1931. Educated at Columbia University, USA. Married actress Cecilia Boal. Artistic director, Arena Theatre, San Paulo, 1953–68, collaborating with Gianfrancesco Guarnieri on various classical plays; lost post in revolution of 1968; imprisoned and tortured for radical political views, 1971; subsequently exiled to Argentina, 1971–76, and also worked in Peru; developed impromptu documentary drama technique based on contemporary issues, often performed unannounced in public places; directed in Europe, 1976–86; founded Centre du Théâtre de l'Opprimé, Paris, 1979; returned to Brazil, 1986, and founded Theatre of the Oppressed centre in Rio de Janeiro. Recipient: Unesco Pablo Picasso Medal, 1994.

Principal productions

As director:
1953–68   *Mandragola* (Machiavelli), Arena Theatre, San Paulo.
        El mejor alcalde, el rey (Vega), Arena Theatre, San Paulo.
        Tartuffe (Molière), Arena Theatre, San Paulo.
1957   *Mulher magra, marido chato* (Boal), Arena Theatre, San Paulo.
1961   *Revolução na América do Sul* (Boal), Arena Theatre, San Paulo.
1962   *José, do parto a sepultura* (Boal), Teatro Oficina.
1965   *Arena conte Zumbi* (Boal and Guarnieri), Arena Theatre, San Paulo.
        Arena conte Tirandentes (Boal and Guarnieri), Arena Theatre, San Paulo.
        Arena conte Bolívar (Boal and Guarnieri), Arena Theatre, San Paulo.
1973–78   *El público* (Garcia Lorca), Schauspielhaus, Wuppertal.
        Strike the Point of a Knife (Boal), Austria.

Other productions have included: *O Corsario do rei* (Boal), 1985; *We Are Thirty One Million People, Now What?* (Boal).

Publications

Mulher magra, marido chato (play), 1957; *Revoluçãna América do Sul* (play), 1961; *José, do parto a sepultura* (play), 1962; *Arena conta* series (with Gianfrancesco Guarnieri), from 1965; *Teatro latinoamericano de agitacíon*, 1972; *Teatro do Oprimido* (translated as *Theatre of the Oppressed*, 1979), 1973; *A tempestade; As mulheras de atenas*, 1977; *Técnicas latinamericanas de teatro popular*, 1979; *Miragle no Brasil* (novel), 1979; *O Corsario do rei*, 1985; *Teatro de Augusto Boal*, 1986; *The Rainbow of Desire*, 1990; *Jeux pour acteurs et non-acteurs*, 1992.

*

Bibliography

Books:
Mady Schutzman, *Playing Boal: Theatre, Therapy, Activism*, London, 1994.

* * *

Augusto Boal had no special training as a director, writer or teacher. He studied Chemical Engineering at university in the USA but was particularly interested in theatre as a student. As artistic director of the Arena Theatre, San Paulo, for 15 years, he spent the first decade directing a wide range of plays, including the works of 12 new Brazilian playwrights alongside plays by Machiavelli, Lope de Vega, and Molière. A second coup d'état and military dictatorship in 1968 forced him to seek alternative means of providing theatre and political awareness in Brazil. He developed the "Newspaper Theatre", which transformed and demystified the latest news into theatrical events using 11 or 12 simple techniques, such as some of the company singing a politician's speech on censorship as Gregorian chant in an attempt perhaps to emphasize the medieval aspects of the words. In January 1971, he was imprisoned and tortured, an experience that provided material for his first novel, *The Miracle in Brazil*.

Inspired by Brazilian carnival, circus, and music, Boal claims to have been influenced by "all intelligent and creative people". His list includes Cervantes, Brecht, Shakespeare, and all those who have studied with him. In 1973, he wrote *The Theatre of the Oppressed*, which has been published worldwide in 25 languages. The first part is a series of scholarly essays written between 1962 and 1973, in which he examines the European tradition of dramatic theory from Aristotle to Brecht. His line of argument in these essays is pursued through practice in the second part of the book with descriptions of his work in both Brazil and Peru. He offers a "poetics of the oppressed", which gives theatre back to the people and no longer accepts the spectator in the passive role. Theatre becomes a rehearsal for social change, dealing with the concerns of its audience and the process of change in reality. Perhaps the latter section is less developed and articulate than the theory of the earlier essays. However, a better balance is struck in his latest theoretical book, *The Rainbow of Desire*, published some 17 years later in France. Here he establishes the hypothesis that theatre is the first invention of mankind developing the concepts of the "spect-actor" and the "aesthetic space". He analyses the three characteristics of this space as being dichotomic, telemicroscopic, and plastic. The second part of the book is practical and describes the newer "Cop in the Head" techniques, which are supported by examples from his own work, including the experiences of working with psychotic children. The reader is given an explanation of how the techniques work and the emotional involvement provoked by their use.

In Argentina, Boal directed plays under a different dictatorship, which resulted in the creation and practice of "Invisible Theatre" in order to avoid detection by the police. Invisible Theatre is a meeting of fiction and reality, play and living. Clandestine plays were structured, rehearsed and then presented in public places, for example, markets, restaurants or trains, to people unaware that they were an audience. The company prepared the work in detail for every possible intervention, reaction, and response from those witnessing the performance. Such hidden theatrical events allowed Boal to popularize old Argentinian laws, questioning the differences between reality and fiction in these presentations. In Peru under the centre-left government of General Velasco Alvarado, Boal developed the technique of "Simultaneous Playwriting", which invited spectators to suggest endings for the play that the actors could then improvise according to the choices of the audience. This was the start of the spectator penetrating the fiction created from that community's oppression.

The 1970's saw Boal directing a range of plays across Europe, among them the first production of *The Public* by Lorca at the Schauspielhaus, Wuppertal, in Germany and his own play *Strike the Point of a Knife* in Austria. From 1978 to 1986, he wrote and directed many "Forum Theatre" productions with his Paris-based company. These were written or improvised performances in which the audience was asked to look at the protagonist's problem and work with the actors in order to learn a possible solution together. Forum Theatre as a method requires actors to devise a play in response to a particular group's oppression. Having watched the play, the group concerned is then encouraged to "stop" the action when it sees a better direction for a character to follow. The spectator then replaces the protagonist and acts out his or her chosen alternative action. This process is facilitated by the "Joker" who functions as go-between audience and performers. In Boal's form of pedagogical theatre, he offers the "spect-actor" a theatrical language to use to look at the possibilities of a situation, enabling him or her to make a choice and potentially to change the real life situation.

From the Theatre of the Oppressed, Boal has developed the work educationally, politically, and therapeutically. The range of exercises, games, and techniques is described in his book *Games for Actors and Non-Actors* and illustrates the breadth of material available for this participatory form of theatre. The therapeutic side naturally came about from his work in Paris and other cities of Europe during the early 1980's. The "Cop in the Head" techniques attempt to visualise the oppressors internalized in an individual's head and try to show the relation between those cops and the headquarters outside the person. They try to clarify what is obscure and is often concealed in the pre-conscious. Boal endeavours to help the individual "track down" his or her oppressions, which are obvious to others. These can then be "pluralized" and form the basis of the collective experience of Forum Theatre.

Currently, Boal uses workshops to experiment and invent new techniques as applied to different countries, cultures, and situations all over the world. He describes himself as having many aspects to his career, which include directing, writing both theory and fiction, teaching, and political work. He divides his time between Brazil, Europe, and the USA. His most recent productions in Brazil range from the spectacular large-scale musical *The King's Corsaire* to his own play *We Are Thirty One Million People, Now What?*, which resulted from his collaboration with the trade unions after they lost an election and was played in the form of Forum Theatre in order to ascertain how the workers saw their future.

—Alison J. L. Oddey

BOGDANOV, Michael. British director and playwright. Born in London, 15 December 1938. Educated at Lower School of John Lyon, Harrow; Trinity College, University of Dublin, MA; University of Munich; University of the Sorbonne, Paris. Married Patricia Ann Warwick in 1966; two sons, one daughter. Producer and director, Telefis Eireann, 1966–68; stage debut, Oxford Playhouse, 1968; London debut, 1969; assistant director, Royal Shakespeare Company, 1970–71; associate to Jean-Louis Barrault, Rabelais Theatre, 1971; associate director, Tyneside Theatre Company, 1971–73; associate director, Leicester Theatre Trust, 1973–77; director, Phoenix Theatre, Leicester, 1974–77; director, Young Vic Theatre, 1978–80; associate director, National Theatre, 1980–88; co-founder and joint artistic director, English Shakespeare Company, 1986; artistic director and executive producer, Deutsche Schauspielhaus, Hamburg, 1988–92; also guest director at theatres in Dublin, London, Stratford, Ontario, and Tokyo. Has also written revues, plays, adaptations, and children's theatre pieces. Hon. Professor, University of Wales; Senior Fellow, De Montfort University, Leicester. Recipient: Society of West End Theatre Award for Director of the Year, 1979 and 1989.

Productions

1968	*The Bootleg Gentleman* (adapted by Bogdanov from Molière's *Le Bourgeois Gentilhomme*), Playhouse, Oxford.
1969	*A Comedy of the Changing Years* (Cregan), Theatre Upstairs, Royal Court Theatre, London.
1970	*A Midsummer Night's Dream* (Shakespeare; associate director under Peter Brook), Royal Shakespeare Theatre, Stratford-upon-Avon; New York, 1971; world tour, 1972.
1971	Two Gentlemen of Verona (Shakespeare), São Paulo, Brazil.
1976	*He That Plays the King* (compilation of Shakespeare's *Richard III*, *Hamlet*, and *The Tempest*), Phoenix Theatre, Leicester.
	The Recruiting Officer (Farquhar), Haymarket Theatre, Leicester.
1977	*Sir Gawain and the Green Knight* (adapted by Bogdanov), National Theatre, London.
	The Hunchback of Notre Dame (Hill), National Theatre, London.
1978	*The Taming of the Shrew* (Shakespeare), Royal Shakespeare Theatre, Stratford-upon-Avon; London, 1979.
	Bartholomew Fair (Jonson), Young Vic Theatre, London.
	The Canterbury Tales (adapted from Chaucer), Young Vic Theatre, London.
1978–79	*Richard III* (Shakespeare), Young Vic Theatre, London.
	Hamlet (Shakespeare), Young Vic Theatre, London.
	The Tempest (Shakespeare), Young Vic Theatre, London.
1979	*Faust!*, Young Vic Theatre, London.
1980	*Shadow of a Gunman* (O'Casey), Royal Shakespeare Company.

The Seagull (Chekhov), Toho Theatre, Tokyo.

The Romans in Britain (Brenton), National Theatre, London.

Hiawatha (Bogdanov), National Theatre, London.

1981   *The Knight of the Burning Pestle* (Beaumont), Royal Shakespeare Company.

One Woman Plays (Rame), National Theatre, London.

The Mayor of Zalamea (Calderón), National Theatre, London; Washington D.C., 1984.

The Hypochondriac (Molière, adapted by Drury), National Theatre, London.

1982   *Uncle Vanya* (Chekhov), National Theatre, London.

The Spanish Tragedy (Kyd), National Theatre, London.

1983   *Romeo and Juliet* (Shakespeare), Imperial Theatre, Tokyo.

Lorenzaccio (Musset), National Theatre, London.

You Can't Take It With You (Kaufman), National Theatre, London.

Hamlet (Shakespeare), Abbey Theatre, Dublin.

1984   *Strider* (Chekhov), National Theatre, London.

1985   *Measure for Measure* (Shakespeare), Festival Theatre, Stratford, Ontario.

Mutiny! (Crane), Piccadilly Theatre, London.

Donnerstag aus Licht (Stockhausen), Royal Opera House, Covent Garden, London.

1986   *Julius Caesar* (Shakespeare), Deutsche Schauspielhaus, Hamburg.

Romeo and Juliet (Shakespeare), Barbican Theatre, London.

1986–87   *Henry IV, parts 1 and 2* (Shakespeare), British and European tour, Old Vic Theatre, London, and Canada.

Henry V (Shakespeare), British and European tour, Old Vic Theatre, London, and Canada.

1987   *Reineke Fuchs*, Schauspielhaus, Hamburg.

The Canterbury Tales (adapted from Chaucer), Prince of Wales Theatre.

1987–89   *The Wars of the Roses* (compilation of seven Shakespeare history plays), British, European, and world tour.

1988   *Montag* (Stockhausen), La Scala, Milan.

1989   *Hamlet* (Shakespeare), Schauspielhaus, Hamburg.

1990–91   *Coriolanus* (Shakespeare), Aldwych Theatre, London, and world tour.

The Winter's Tale (Shakespeare), British and world tour.

Reynard the Fox (Bogdanov, adapted from Goethe), London.

1992   *Macbeth* (Shakespeare), Royalty Theatre, London, and British tour.

The Tempest (Shakespeare), Royalty Theatre, London, 1992.

1993   *The Venetian Twins* (Goldoni), Swan Theatre, Stratford-upon-Avon.

Romeo and Juliet (Shakespeare), Lyric Theatre, Hammersmith, London.

Hair (MacDermot, Ragni, and Rado), Old Vic Theatre, London.

Television

Broad and Narrow (series, as co-author with Terence Brady), 1965; *Shakespeare Lives* (as deviser and presenter), 1983; *Julius Caesar*, 1986.

Publications

Hiawatha; *The Rime of the Ancient Mariner*; *The English Shakespeare Company* (with Michael Pennington), 1990.

*

Bibliography

Books:
M. J. Ballard, *In Search of Michael Bogdanov. A Director of the 1980's* (thesis), Leicester Polytechnic, 1982–83.

Articles:
Andrew Rissik, "The Henry Trilogy", *Plays and Players*, 1987.
Liz Gibney, "Michael Bogdanov", *Plays International*, June 1990.

* * *

Like most contemporary stage directors, Michael Bogdanov's territory ranges over a wide range of plays, including Shakespeare, continental classics, opera, musicals, and dramatic adaptations. While his approach to staging has sometimes been fairly conservative — as, for example, in his productions of *The Spanish Tragedy*, *Lorenzaccio*, and *The Mayor of Zalamea* — he is best known for his inventive, provocative approach to Shakespeare. Although his distinctive style with Shakespeare was discernable as early as his 1978 productions of *Richard III*, *Hamlet*, and *The Tempest* for the Young Vic company, it has reached a peak of refinement and control in his more recent stagings of *Measure for Measure*, *Romeo and Juliet*, and especially *The Wars of the Roses*.

In staging these plays, Bogdanov tried to find associations in the plots, language, and characters that would resonate in our own time and that are reflected in our popular media, in contemporary incidents and events, and in prevailing societal attitudes, values, and tensions. The historical world of the play, its character relationships, and thematic concerns are then juxtaposed with our own time in large part by contemporizing the mise-en-scène.

Bogdanov has said, for example, that it was a goal of his English Shakespeare Company in particular to take Shakespeare to audiences that had either never seen a play by Shakespeare of "not gone to Shakespeare for a long time." Furthermore, he wanted a style that would appeal especially to young people. In part, he attempted to reach this audience "by using contemporary references, contemporary props, contemporary costumes … " Modern dress is used not merely as a "style", however, but also to suggest a trait of personality in a character or to associate character with contemporary social groups or character-types in an emblematic fashion. He has said that he discovered that by using modern dress he removed an artificial barrier between his audiences and Shakespeare's language.

In Bogdanov's productions of *Romeo and Juliet* and *Measure for Measure*, for instance, all the characters wore various modes of contemporary dress. The dominant male authority figures — Capulet, Montague, Vincentio — in their carefully tailored business suits suggested powerful industrial tycoons, Mafia dons, or politicians. The Ladies Capulet and Montague, Mariana, and the Nurse also wore elegant contemporary cocktail dresses or stylish suits and blouses. Isabel wore simple black outfits, Tybalt wore modish black leather jacket, pants, and boots, while Mercutio, either nursing a hangover or tipsy with drink, was a brash, derisive post-adolescent in a bold plaid shirt, black jeans, and crumpled panama hat. Friar Lawrence was a harried, cigarette-smoking parish priest in black slacks and cassock. Romeo (in a casual cotton sportsuit) and Juliet (in simple, summery skirts and blouses) were blond, attractive, slightly unkempt, unaffected, but dangerously naive, idealistic "yuppie-puppies". Lucio, a "fantastic", wore baggy, pleated trousers, white shoes, a thigh-length sports jacket, a long white scarf, and a white fedora. Pompey was a dark, small-boned, oily Levantine pimp in a seedy, electric blue suit and a slimy black shirt with a garish gold neck chain. Overall, the "look" of both productions — reliant mainly on the costumes — reflected an affluent, but shallow, spiritually debased society of our own time, the same sort of society, as several reviewers observed, reflected in the movies of Fellini and Antonioni, and to a lesser extent in US soap operas or in the pages of *Oggi* or *Vogue*.

Bogdanov tends to prefer a certain Spartan economy of style in his use of scenery. Typical was his use in *Measure for Measure* of the unaltered essentially bare Festival Theatre stage. The set for *The Wars of the Roses* consisted mainly of two pairs of rolling iron pipe construction scaffolds. Following the tendencies of the Brechtian epic theatre, moreover, lighting instruments, microphones, amplifiers, and speakers are usually fully exposed to the view of the audience. But within these "empty spaces" Bogdanov is at his most inventive, creating by fairly economic means striking pieces of business and visual images — "speaking pictures" — of an explicit social world.

Often he will set the locale and tone with some elaborate, mainly visual "pre-show" activity. In *Measure for Measure* a pre-show entertainment established an atmosphere of a sensually depraved and decadent Vienna. The stage was set with black cocktail tables and café chairs. A rock band played moody heavy metal music and the air was heavy with incense as transvestites in leather skirts and blouses invited spectators (actually members of the ensemble) to dance with them onstage. A Master of Ceremonies, resplendent in black leather pants, a hot pink shirt open to the navel, and lion's mane of blond and brunette hair, breathily addressed the audience through a hand-held microphone: "Welcome. We are here for your pleasure". *Romeo and Juliet* opened with a display of bustling urban activity around a town square or mall complete with bicycles, motor scooters, and a child on roller skates. Teenaged Capulets and Montagues in designer sportswear and dark glasses rowdily swaggered about. New wave rock music throbbed from a rock band at stage right. The opening fight was an exciting, realistic gang "rumble", à la *West Side Story*, with flick knives and chains.

Generally the atmosphere and period established by such pre-show activities are consistently maintained throughout the production. The Capulet banquet in *Romeo and Juliet*, for example, became a boisterous teenage bash with party-crashing Montagues, rock and roll music, and dancing, with several drunken guests plunging fully-clothed into a swimming pool located downstage. In the morning-after scene Benvolio and Mercutio shared an Alka-Seltzer in the piazza. The brawl and resulting deaths of Mercutio and Tybalt in the third act were brutally violent. In the last act, when Romeo received the news of Juliet's death, he rushed into the street to find the Apothecary and found himself in the middle of a Mantuan carnival complete with giant puppet caricatures of Margaret Thatcher, Ronald Reagan, and Mikhail Gorbachev. The Apothecary, meanwhile, was portrayed as a drug-dealer rather than a druggist and later Romeo injected the poison, as a deliberate overdose. The finale was perhaps the most striking and original scene in the production, the Prince standing between two golden statues of Romeo and Juliet and delivering his eulogy in a perfunctory, rushed style from his notecards to a television crew. At the end of his remarks, reporters attempted to interview him and Friar Lawrence, but they rushed off without comment. The Capulets and Montagues were photographed shaking hands in front of the statues in a half-hearted public display of reunion, the grief-stricken Benvolio standing to one side, isolated from the hypocrisy of the families and the hollow, cynical "memorial service". This staging reinforced the social tragedy in the play and made it an indictment of a materialistic, hedonistic, ethically confused society that individually and collectively victimizes its youth.

Many of the scenes in the 25 hours of *The Wars of the Roses* were similarly inventively but simply staged. The first scene of *Henry IV, part 1*, for example, was presented as a political press conference, King Henry, Westmoreland, and Lancaster broadcasting their speeches before individual microphones in front of two enormous floor to ceiling banners — the flags of England and France — on an otherwise bare stage. At the end of the scene Mozart's Coronation Mass "Gloria" provided an ironic musical comment. At the close of *Richard III*, following the defeat of Richard in a traditional sword fight, the action switched to a television studio and Richmond's final soliloquy was transmitted to the populace. Highlights of *Henry IV, part 2* included the military embarkation for France, Nell Quickly recounting the death of Falstaff as a "soldier" played an ironic solo guitar rendition of Frank Sinatra's "My Way" and the shadows of departing soldiers were cast onto a screen in the background; the eulogy over, the bridge and scaffold towers were peopled with rowdy young men in football scarves waving Union flags and singing "'Ere we go, 'ere we go, 'ere we go" as they unfurled banners reading "Fuck the Frogs", thus putting Harry's military adventure in the context of British soccer fans on the rampage and incidentally evoking the jingoistic farewells attending the departure of troops for the Falklands War. Some scenes deliberately sounded echoes of other moments in the cycle of plays, the staging of scenes in the Boar's Head Tavern paralleling the coronation scene at the end of *Henry IV, part 2*, which in turn paralleled the embarkation scene in *Henry V* and certain of the Jack Cade scenes, while Harry's exhortation on top of a tank at Harfleur echoed Hotspur's speech from on top of a baggage cart and in turn Falstaff's parody of King Henry in *Henry IV, part 1*.

Bogdanov's distinctive directorial style draws on several different tendencies in the modern theatre, including the work of Brecht, Brook, and perhaps that of Giorgio Strehler and Peter Stein as well. But without question there is a daringly imaginative, iconoclastic spirit to Bogdanov's approach, an effort — as he has put it himself — to "cut through the fustian of history and classical tradition".

—Daniel J. Watermeier

BOOTH, Edwin (Thomas). US actor and manager. Born in Belair, Maryland, 13 November 1833, son of actor Junius Brutus Booth (*q.v.*). Educated at local schools of Miss Susan Hyde, Mr Louis Dugas, and Mr Kearney. Married 1) actress Mary Devlin in 1860 (died 1863); one daughter; 2) actress Mary McVicker in 1869 (died 1881). Stage debut, Holliday Street Theatre, Baltimore, 1847; New York debut, 1850; accompanied father to California, 1852; played San Francisco, Sacramento, and mining camp towns; Australian tour with Laura Keene, 1854–55; returned to New York stage, 1857; British tour, 1861–62; managed several theatres, including the Walnut Street Theatre in Philadelphia, 1863–70, the Winter Garden Theatre in New York, 1864–67; and his own Booth's Theatre, New York, 1869–74; went into temporary retirement on assassination of President Lincoln by his brother, John Wilkes Booth, 1865; declared bankrupt, 1873; toured USA, 1874–82, and England and Germany, 1882; alternated roles of Othello and Iago with Henry Irving at the Lyceum Theatre, London, 1881–82; toured with Lawrence Barrett, 1887–91; founded Players' theatrical club, 1888; last performance, as Hamlet, Brooklyn Academy of Music, 1891. Recipient: Hamlet Medal, 1867. Died in New York, 7 June 1893.

Roles

1847	Walk-on role in *The Spectre Bridegroom* (Moncrieff), Holliday Street Theatre, Baltimore.
1849	Tressel in *Richard III* (Shakespeare, adapted by Cibber), Boston Museum.
	Cassio in *Othello* (Shakespeare), Providence, Rhode Island.
1849–51	Titus in *Brutus; or, The Fall of Tarquin* (Payne), Boston Museum.
	Wilford in *The Iron Chest* (Colman the Younger), Arch Street Theatre, Philadelphia.
	Gratiano in *The Merchant of Venice* (Shakespeare), US tour.
	Laertes in *Hamlet* (Shakespeare), US tour.
	Macduff in *Macbeth* (Shakespeare), US tour.
	Edgar in *King Lear* (Shakespeare), US tour.
1851	Richard in *Richard III* (Shakespeare), National Theatre, New York.
1852	Jaffier in *Venice Preserved* (Otway), Sacramento, California.
1852–54	Iago in *Othello* (Shakespeare), US tour.
	Sir Giles Overreach in *A New Way To Pay Old Debts* (Massinger), Jenny Lind Theatre, San Francisco; Boston, 1857; revived notably, Haymarket Theatre, London, 1861.

Hamlet in *Hamlet* (Shakespeare), Jenny Lind Theatre, San Francisco; Winter Garden Theatre, New York, 1864–65; Booth's Theatre, New York, 1870.

Macbeth in *Macbeth* (Shakespeare), Jenny Lind Theatre, San Francisco; revived notably, Booth's Theatre, New York, 1869–74.

Petruchio in *The Taming of the Shrew* (Shakespeare), Jenny Lind Theatre, San Francisco.

1854	Shylock in *The Merchant of Venice* (Shakespeare), Sydney, Australia; Haymarket Theatre, London, 1861; revived notably, Winter Garden Theatre, New York, 1867.
1855	Benedick in *Much Ado About Nothing* (Shakespeare), Metropolitan Theatre, San Francisco; revived notably, Booth's Theatre, New York, 1871.
	Raphael in *The Marble Heart* (Selby), Sacramento Theatre, Sacramento, California.
	Claude Melnotte in *The Lady of Lyons* (Bulwer-Lytton), Honolulu; Metropolitan Theatre, New York, 1857.
1856	Sir Edward Mortimer in *The Iron Chest* (Colman the Younger), Forrest Theatre, Sacramento, California.
	Lear in *King Lear* (Shakespeare, adapted by Tate), Sacramento Theatre, Sacramento, California; revived notably, London, 1880.
	Cardinal Richelieu in *Richelieu* (Bulwer-Lytton), Sacramento, California; revived notably, Haymarket Theatre, London, 1861; Winter Garden Theatre, New York, 1866; Booth's Theatre, New York, 1871.
	Romeo in *Romeo and Juliet* (Shakespeare), Richmond, Virginia; revived notably, Booth's Theatre, New York, 1869–74.
1856–57	The Stranger in *The Stranger* (Kotzebue), Metropolitan Theatre, New York.
	Pescara in *The Apostate* (Sheil), Metropolitan Theatre, New York.
1861	Othello in *Othello* (Shakespeare), Manchester; revived notably, Booth's Theatre, New York, 1869–74; Lyceum Theatre, London, 1881–82.
1863	Ruy Blas in *Ruy Blas* (Hugo), Winter Garden Theatre, New York.
1864	Brutus in *Julius Caesar* (Shakespeare), Winter Garden Theatre, New York; revived notably, Booth's Theatre, New York, 1871–72.
	Bertuccio in *The Fools' Revenge* (Taylor, adapted from Hugo's *Le Roi s'amuse*), Winter Garden Theatre, New York; revived notably, Booth's Theatre, New York, 1871.
	Mark Antony in *Antony and Cleopatra* (Shakespeare), Booth's Theatre, New York.
	Cassius in *Julius Caesar* (Shakespeare), Booth's Theatre, New York.
1875	Richard in *Richard II* (Shakespeare), US tour; Lyceum Theatre, New York, 1876.

Edwin Booth

Publications

The Break Between Player and Poet: Letters from Edwin Booth to Richard Henry Stoddard, New York, 1903.
Between Actor and Critic: Selected Letters of Edwin Booth and William Winter, edited by Daniel J. Watermeier, 1971.

*

Bibliography

Books:
William Winter, *Edwin Booth in Twelve Dramatic Characters*, Boston, 1872.
Asia Booth, *The Elder and the Younger Booth*, Boston, 1882.
William Winter, *The Edwin Booth Prompt Books*, 6 vols., New York, 1890.
Laurence Hutton, *Edwin Booth*, New York, 1893.
William Winter, *The Life and Art of Edwin Booth*, London, 1894.
Edwina Booth Grossman, *Edwin Booth: Recollections by His Daughter and Letters to Her and to His Friends*, New York, 1894.
Charles Townsend Copeland, *Edwin Booth*, Boston, 1901.
Katherine Goodale, *Behind the Scenes with Edwin Booth*, Boston and New York, 1931.
Richard Lockridge, *Darling of Misfortune: Edwin Booth, 1833–1893*, London and New York, 1932.

Stanley Kimmel, *The Mad Booths of Maryland*, New York, 1940.
Edwin Milton Royle, *Edwin Booth As I Knew Him*, New York, 1933.
Otis Skinner, *The Last Tragedian: Booth Tells His Own Story*, New York, 1939.
Eleanor Ruggles, *Prince of Players: Edwin Booth*, New York, 1953.
Alma Power-Waters, *The Story of Young Edwin Booth*, New York, 1955.
Charles H. Shattuck, *The Hamlet of Edwin Booth*, Urbana, Illinois, and London, 1969.
Mary Isabella Stone, *Edwin Booth's Performances: The Mary Isabella Stone Commentaries*, Ann Arbor, Michigan, and London, 1990.

Articles:
O. B. Frothingham, "The Acting of Mr. Edwin Booth", *Nation*, 2, 1866.
Edmund Clarence Stedman, "Edwin Booth", *Atlantic*, 16, 1866.
Lucia Gilbert Calhoun, "Edwin Booth", *Galaxy*, 7, 1869.
William Winter, "Edwin Booth", *Harper's*, 63, 1881.
Henry Austin Clapp, "Edwin Booth", *Atlantic*, 72, 1893.
Laurence Hutton, "Edwin Booth", *Harper's Weekly*, 37, 1893.
J. R. Lows, "Edwin Booth", *Nation*, 56, 1893.
Laurence Hutton, "Edwin Booth, Man and Actor", *Living Age*, 216, 1898.
Walter Prichard Eaton, "Edwin Booth", *Theatre Arts*, 16, 1932.
Arthur E. Waterman, "The Acting of Edwin Booth", *Journal of Popular Culture*, 3, 1969.

* * *

Edwin Booth was the finest US tragedian of his time and the first to gain an international reputation. Darkly handsome and gifted with a slender, graceful, figure ("lithe as an Indian" as his friend the critic William Winter once called it), a clear, musical, voice, and luminous, expressive eyes, Booth was a versatile actor. He was undoubtedly at his best in the portrayal of brooding, melancholy characters like Hamlet — his greatest creation — or Brutus or in capturing darkly sinister characters like Iago or Bertuccio. He was also successful, however, in such playfully comic roles as Benedick and Petruchio and especially as the wily, histrionic Cardinal Richelieu.

One of the hallmarks of Booth's acting style was his vocal, physical, and emotional restraint or "quietude." It was the chief quality that distinguished his acting from the often violent excesses of the earlier Romantic school to which his father, Junius Brutus Booth, belonged. Booth himself, in response to Otis Skinner's question as to how his father's acting compared to his own, reportedly said: "I think I must be somewhat quieter". Mollie Devlin, Booth's first wife, called his style, the "conversational, colloquial school".

Booth spoke Shakespeare's verse or the lesser stuff of Bulwer-Lytton or Payne as if it were "natural conversation". He did this in part with pauses and stresses that sometimes broke up the regular, formal metre, but which also created a new rhythm emphasizing meaning. Booth, in his notes to H. H. Furness's *Variorum Othello*, advises readings like the following: "Hesitatingly — break up the line with well-timed pauses, not to mar the metre." At another time he indicates an emphasis that "violates the metre". Booth admitted that he had "never practised with any elocutionist or teacher" and reportedly his voice was not particularly powerful, but it was flexible and clear and distinctively musical.

An amateur Booth-watcher, Mary Isabella Stone, called Booth's voice "naturally penetrating". She observed that without "apparent force" Booth could "carry on a conversation with another actor on the stage in the low tones natural to the occasion or their proximity or even whisper, etc. and yet make every word audible to the spectators". She thought, however, that the "great charm" of Booth's voice was "its marvellous modulations so perfectly adapted to the thought or emotion expressed". In note after note on his Hamlet and Iago, she celebrates not only the "naturalness" of his speaking, but his complex, richly suggestive, tonalities of "exquisite sarcasm" or of "sincere friendly interest and sympathy" or of "mingled grief, astonishment and anger". Booth in his notes to the *Variorum* editions of *Othello* and *The Merchant of Venice*, describes readings in terms of "a reflective tone", "subdued tones", or a voice with "a tinge of anxiety". And always, as both his *Variorum* notes and his observers reveal, there was an effort to restrain, to suppress, or to play down. "Not too loud" was Booth's constant watchword even in highly impassioned moments.

Booth did frequently gesture, vary his facial expressions, and change his stance and position — occasionally perhaps too much so — but generally his physical actions were regarded as "natural" and appropriate. A close examination of Booth's *Variorum* notes, his promptbooks, and the contemporary performance annotations reveals a language of motivated, carefully orchestrated, but uncomplicated and economical physical actions, arising "naturally" out of the interplay between dialogue, character, and scene. He did not exaggerate or strain after effect. Rather, he took great pains, as he once wrote for the *Variorum Othello*, to make sure that "every movement, gesture, look, and tone should be in harmony".

Moreover, although Booth's physical actions were carefully planned, they appeared spontaneous and dynamic, as "if for the first time". For Booth, the foundation for physical actions was sincerely-felt emotion. He cautions a would-be Iago, for instance, to "be sincere" or to "feel the curiousness". At one point he advises Cassio: "Don't preach; be not violent, avoid rant, yet be impassioned — *feel* thoroughly disgusted with yourself and you'll be natural".

Perhaps because of his concentration on feeling, Booth seems to have lost his own personality in a role, creating vivid, completely different, utterly believable, characters. He also unfolded these characters gradually and incrementally with a remarkable degree of sustained strength and cumulative completeness and consistency. Stone observed, for example, that one admired Booth's character development even more in "backward reflection" than at any particular moment. She continued: "Though Booth greatly alters his tones and manner in different scenes to suit varying moods ... throughout any one play, he is always the same person. But when he comes to act in another drama, or to assume a different character, the alteration is very different; it is immense and fundamental, radical: he

seems as if actually another individual, more so than would seem possible ... never does he remind you during a play of one of his other characters".

Although Booth was attentive to the details of costuming and make-up, the distinctiveness of his wide-ranging characterizations depended, as Stone suggests, on much more fundamental factors. No matter whether the character was Hamlet, Lear, Petruchio, Bertuccio, or Richelieu, Booth's acting "naturalized" these extraordinary individuals and made them seem recognizably human — that is, he represented *real* human natures. Yet, although Booth's representation was natural, it was not "naturalistic". Following Hamlet's advice to the players, he did not "O'erstep the modesty of nature". Rather, he aimed — as G. H. Lewes wrote in *On Natural Acting* — to select, heighten, sublimate nature: "to represent ideal character with such truthfulness that it shall affect us as real, not to drag down ideal character to the vulgar level". That is to say, the outward details of his acting seemed natural and his expression of feeling real, but the general effect produced by each separate detail and expression impressed his viewers, in their words, as "poetic", "philosophical", "intellectual", or even "spiritual" — that is, ideal. Thus Booth's portrayals were simultaneously intimate — human and natural — and distant — poetic and ideal. In this respect, Booth's acting style echoed the prevailing aesthetic values and tastes of his era, a dialectical interplay between reality and ideality.

Booth's Theatre, which opened on 3 February 1869, was the most innovative theatre to be built in the USA up to that time. Among its several technical innovations were a hydraulic system for changing scenery and a forced air heating and cooling system. Booth's management of this theatre was distinguished by his carefully mounted, visually spectacular productions of *Romeo and Juliet*, *Hamlet*, *Julius Caesar*, *The Merchant of Venice*, *Othello*, and *Richelieu*. Had Booth not lost his theatre, the result of poor financial management and the Panic of 1873, he might have built a reputation as a "regisseur" equal to his position as the USA's foremost actor.

—Daniel J. Watermeier

BOOTH, Junius Brutus. US actor-manager. Born in London, 1 May 1796. Married 1) Adelaide Delannoy in 1815 (divorced 1851), one son; 2) Mary Ann Holmes in 1851, ten children (including actors Junius Brutus Booth, Edwin Thomas Booth (*q.v.*), and John Wilkes Booth). Stage debut, Deptford, London, 1813; continental tour, 1814–15; acted alongside Edmund Kean in Brighton and Worthing, 1816; actor, Covent Garden, London, 1817; bested by Kean when both actors appeared in open rivalry at the Theatre Royal, Drury Lane, London, 1818, and returned to Covent Garden; deserted wife and son and emigrated to USA, 1821; toured widely as leading romantic actor on the US stage, 1821–52, with a repertoire of less than a dozen roles; returned to England, 1825–26 and 1836–37; suffered from drunkenness, melancholia, and madness in last years; last stage appearance, New Orleans, 1852. Died on a Missipi River steamboat near Louisville, Ohio, 30 November 1852.

Principal roles

1813   Campillo in *The Honeymoon* (Tobin), Deptford, London.
1817   Richard in *Richard III* (Shakespeare, adapted by Cibber), Covent Garden, London; revived there, 1818; Richmond, Virginia, and US tour, 1821 (and subsequently).
1818   Iago in *Othello* (Shakespeare), Theatre Royal, Drury Lane, London.
1820   Shylock in *The Merchant of Venice* (Shakespeare), Covent Garden, London.
1821–52   Cassio in *Venice Preserved* (Otway), US tour.
       Sir Edward Mortimer in *The Iron Chest* (Colman the Younger), US tour.
       Sir Giles Overreach in *A New Way to Pay Old Debts* (Massinger), US tour.
       Hamlet in *Hamlet* (Shakespeare), US tour.
       Jerry Sneak in *The Mayor of Garratt* (Foote), US tour.
       Lear in *King Lear* (Shakespeare, adapted by Tate), US tour.
       Oreste in *Andromaque* (Racine), US tour.
       Othello in *Othello* (Shakespeare), US tour.
       Pescara in *The Apostate* (Shiel), US tour.
       Second Gravedigger in *Hamlet* (Shakespeare), US tour; Baltimore, 1831.

Publications

Memoirs of Junius Brutus Booth, from His Birth to the Present Time, 1817.

*

Bibliography

Books:
Anon., *Memoirs of the Life of Mr Booth*, London, 1817.
Anon., *The Actor; or, A Peep Behind the Curtain. Being Passages in the Lives of Booth and Some of His Contemporaries*, New York, 1846.
Thomas Ridgeway Gould, *The Tragedian; An Essay on the Histrionic Genius of Junius Brutus Booth*, New York, 1868.
Asia Booth Clarke, *Booth Memorials: Passages, Incidents, and Anecdotes in the Life of Junius Brutus Booth*, New York, 1886.
Stanley Kimmel, *The Mad Booths of Maryland*, New York, 1940.
Stephen Archer, *Junius Brutus Booth: Theatrical Prometheus*, 1992.

*   *   *

In his 1885 essay "The Old Bowery" Walt Whitman perhaps let memory and affection distort his judgement too much when he described Junius Brutus Booth as "the grandest histrion of modern times", yet there is much in his appreciation of an actor whose place is assured in the annals of the US stage that is accurate and discerning. On the one hand Whitman cannot ignore the fact that well before the end of the 19th century Booth's inflated and stagey style of performing Shakespeare had become quite unfashionable, but on the other he pays tribute to Booth's "own electric personal idiosyncrasy". It vitalised his playing, not only making him the "royal heir and legitimate representative of the Garrick-Kemble-Siddons dramatic tradition", but also enabling him to add to it the tempestuous energy and mercurial moodiness that the Romantic movement expected to be displayed on stage, especially in the interpretation of Shakespearean heroes. The unfortunate circumstances of possessing a notoriously unstable temperament, though adding to the strains of working, undoubtedly attracted the attention of a public that particularly at that time liked to draw parallels between what was revealed on stage and an actor's private life.

To what extent Booth consciously modelled his style on Edmund Kean's is a moot point. In the absence of positive evidence that the younger man had opportunities of observing the methods of an established star who was some nine years his senior, it seems probably, on balance, that personal temperament and the temper of the times ought to be allowed as much weight as direct imitation, and in any case both actors can be seen as heirs of the so-called realistic school of performance associated with George Frederick Cooke. However that may be, it was not long after Booth's debut in London that Kean became aware of a potential rival with a manner and physique distinctly similar to his own. The outcome was a famous theatrical showdown, with Kean inviting the younger man over from Covent Garden to Drury Lane on 20 February 1818 to play Iago to his Othello and providing the London public with compelling proof of his superiority. After this, it was in the USA that Booth had to make his career. This he did with considerable success, travelling far and wide to present to the most varied audiences plays by Shakespeare (including *Richard III* in Colley Cibber's version and *King Lear* in Nahum Tate's) and Massinger (in whose *A New Way to Pay Old Debts* he played Sir Giles Overreach with great success), 18th-century classics, and quite a lot of modern drama (for instance, Shiel's *The Apostate*) that was important in its own day, even if it has by now been largely dropped from the repertory. For the most part he chose to play the roles of villains and other problematic characters, which gave the opportunity of depicting such strong emotions as fear, hatred, and jealousy. He had, however, the versatility to shine in the role of Jerry Sneak in Samuel Foote's farce *The Mayor of Garratt*, and he was not above taking the part of Second Grave Digger when he gave Charles Kean the opportunity of playing Hamlet in Baltimore in 1831. Even if Booth had not played all these roles and managed a number of theatres over the years, he would still merit a place in the history of US theatre as the father of the fine actor Edwin Booth.

Junius Brutus Booth was, to quote Walt Whitman again, "a moderate sized man, almost small", shorter than Kean, who was himself of no more than average height. Perhaps his modest stature bred a need for assertion; at all events, it was never suggested that Booth did not have a commanding stage presence. He had a muscular, but spare frame and a powerful neck and chest. His thick hair was dark, and until 1838 when he attacked his manager, Thomas Flynn, and came out of the encounter with a broken nose, he had a handsome profile. His mobile face was pale, which was thought to reflect the force of the passions that coursed through his veins, and he knew how to use his blue eyes most expressively to convey emotion. Though his legs were decidedly bandy, Booth was renowned for the way he bestrode the stage, moving across it repeatedly to convey a great reserve of nervous energy. Above all, Booth's voice was famous not just for its strength, though that was an essential pre-requisite in the tumultuous theatres of his day, but also for its flexible melodiousness.

Booth had, in particular, the inner concentration to be outstandingly effective as a soliloquist, and, perhaps profiting from earlier indiscretions when he had exhausted his voice and nerves, and possibly his audiences too, by screwing emotions too high from the very outset, he developed the art of starting quite calmly so that he could rise the more readily to an overwhelming climax.

A man of education and, by all accounts, a fine linguist, Booth is said to have played Shylock in Hebrew. He also delighted a francophone public in New Orleans with his interpretation of Oreste in Racine's *Andromaque*. Though the tragedy is, of course, in the classical mould, the role of Oreste gave Booth every opportunity to reveal his powers as a Romantic actor as he showed how the character was first a bundle of barely contained contradictions and then descended into trammels of furious madness in the concluding scenes of the fifth act. Members of the audience showed their appreciation by crying out "Talma! Talma!". To Booth, who had not proved equal to comparison with Kean, the greatest of the English Romantic actors, it must have been particularly gratifying to hear himself hailed as the peer of the finest of their French counterparts.

—Christopher Smith

BRACEGIRDLE, Anne. English actress. Born in Northamptonshire, England, c.13 November 1671 (some sources, as early as 1663). Supposed mistress, possibly wife, of playwright William Congreve. Stage debut reputedly at the Dorset Garden Theatre, London, as a child, under her guardians Thomas and Mary Betterton, 1680; subsequently appeared at the Theatre Royal, Drury Lane, 1688, winning acclaim in both comic and tragic roles, especially in breeches parts; acted with United Company until 1695; joined Betterton's new company at the Lincoln's Inn Fields Theatre as co-manager, 1695; created major roles in several of William Congreve's plays; reputedly first female to play Shakespeare's Portia; retired, 1707, but made final appearance at benefit for Betterton, 1709. Died in London, 12 September 1748.

Roles

1680   (Possibly) Cordelio in *The Orphan* (Otway), Dorset Garden Theatre, London.
1685   (Possibly) Clita in *A Commonwealth of Women* (D'Urfey), Theatre Royal, Drury Lane, London.
1688   Atelina in *The Injured Lovers* (Mountfort), Theatre Royal, Drury Lane, London.
         Lucia in *The Squire of Alsatia* (Shadwell), Theatre Royal, Drury Lane, London.
1689   Semernia in *The Widow Ranter* (Behn), Theatre Royal, Drury Lane, London.

1690   Biancha in *The Successful Strangers* (Mountfort), Theatre Royal, Drury Lane, London.
         Marcelia in *The Treacherous Brothers* (Powell), Theatre Royal, Drury Lane, London.
         Statira in *The Rival Queens* (Lee), Theatre Royal, Drury Lane, London.
         Julia in *The English Friar* (Crowne), Theatre Royal, Drury Lane, London.
         Rosania in *The Amorous Bigot* (Shadwell), Theatre Royal, Drury Lane, London.
         Cleomira in *Distressed Innocence* (Settle), Theatre Royal, Drury Lane, London.
         Charlott in *Sir Anthony Love* (Southerne), Theatre Royal, Drury Lane, London.
         Maria in *Edward III* (Bancroft and Mountfort), Theatre Royal, Drury Lane, London.
         Urania in *Alphonso King of Naples* (Powell), Theatre Royal, Drury Lane, London.
         Clara in *The Scowrers* (Shadwell), Theatre Royal, Drury Lane, London.
         Miranda in *The Mistakes* (Harris), Theatre Royal, Drury Lane, London.
c.1690–91 Dorinda in *Win Her and Take Her* (Smyth and Underhill), Theatre Royal, Drury Lane, London.
         Millicent in *The Merry Devil of Edmonton* (anon.), Theatre Royal, Drury Lane, London.
1691   Mirtilla in *Love for Money* (D'Urfey), Theatre Royal, Drury Lane, London.
         Tamira in *Bussy d'Ambois* (Chapman, adapted by D'Urfey), Theatre Royal, Drury Lane, London.
         Emmeline in *King Arthur* (Dryden), Theatre Royal, Drury Lane, London.
         Mrs Sightly in *The Wives' Excuse* (Southerne), Theatre Royal, Drury Lane, London.
c.1691–92 Lady Anne in *Richard III* (Shakespeare), Theatre Royal, Drury Lane, London.
         Desdemona in *Othello* (Shakespeare), Theatre Royal, Drury Lane, London.
1692   Phaebe in *The Marriage-Hater Matched* (D'Urfey), Theatre Royal, Drury Lane, London.
         Eurione in *The Rape* (Brady), Theatre Royal, Drury Lane, London.
         Amidea in *The Traitor* (Rivers), Theatre Royal, Drury Lane, London.
         Cleora in *Cleomenes* (Dryden), Theatre Royal, Drury Lane, London.
         Elisa in *Regulus* (Crowne), Theatre Royal, Drury Lane, London.
         Rosamond in *Henry II* (Bancroft), Theatre Royal, Drury Lane, London.
         Clara in *The Volunteers* (Shadwell), Theatre Royal, Drury Lane, London.
         Countess of Essex in *The Unhappy Favourite* (Banks), Theatre Royal, Drury Lane, London.
1693   Lady Trickett in *The Maid's Last Prayer* (Southerne), Theatre Royal, Drury Lane, London.
         Araminta in *The Old Bachelor* (Congreve), Theatre Royal, Drury Lane, London.
         Fulvia in *The Richmond Heiress* (D'Urfey), Theatre Royal, Drury Lane, London.

Anne Bracegirdle as Semernia in *The Widow Ranter.*

Mariana in *The Female Virtuosos* (Wright), Theatre Royal, Drury Lane, London.

Cynthia in *The Double Dealer* (Congreve), Theatre Royal, Drury Lane, London.

1693–94 Europa in *The Rape of Europa* (anon.), Theatre Royal, Drury Lane, London.

1694 Celidea in *Love Triumphant* (Dryden), Theatre Royal, Drury Lane, London.

Victoria in *The Fatal Marriage* (Southerne), Theatre Royal, Drury Lane, London.

Clarismunda in *The Ambitious Slave* (Settle), Theatre Royal, Drury Lane, London.

Camilla in *The Married Beau* (Crowne), Theatre Royal, Drury Lane, London.

Marcella in *Don Quixote, part 1* (D'Urfey), Theatre Royal, Drury Lane, London.

Marcella in *Don Quixote, part 2* (D'Urfey), Theatre Royal, Drury Lane, London.

1695 Angelica in *Love for Love* (Congreve), Lincoln's Inn Fields Theatre, London; revived for final appearance at Betterton benefit, 1709.

Charlot in *She Ventures and He Wins* (anon.), Lincoln's Inn Fields Theatre, London.

Mrs Purflew in *The Lover's Luck* (Dilke), Lincoln's Inn Fields Theatre, London.

Lausaria in *Cyrus the Great* (Banks), Lincoln's Inn Fields Theatre, London.

Angelica in *The She-Gallants* (Lansdowne), Lincoln's Inn Fields Theatre, London.

1696 Bassima in *The Royal Mischief* (Manley), Lincoln's Inn Fields Theatre, London.

Flora in *The Country Wake* (Doggett), Lincoln's Inn Fields Theatre, London.

Christina in *Love's a Jest* (Motteux), Lincoln's Inn Fields Theatre, London.

Venus in *The Loves of Mars and Venus* (Motteux), Lincoln's Inn Fields Theatre, London.

1697 Almeria in *The Mourning Bride* (Congreve), Lincoln's Inn Fields Theatre, London.

Bellinda in *The Provoked Wife* (Vanbrugh), Lincoln's Inn Fields Theatre, London.

Countess de Sanserre in *The Intrigues at Versailles* (D'Urfey), Lincoln's Inn Fields Theatre, London.

Mrs Beauclair in *The Innocent Mistress* (Pix), Lincoln's Inn Fields Theatre, London.

Camilla in *Boadicea Queen of Britain* (Hopkins), Lincoln's Inn Fields Theatre, London.

Ariana in *The Deceiver Deceived* (Pix), Lincoln's Inn Fields Theatre, London.

1698 Briseis in *Heroic Love* (Lansdowne), Lincoln's Inn Fields Theatre, London.

Felicia in *Fatal Friendship* (Trotter), Lincoln's Inn Fields Theatre, London.

Placentia in *Beauty in Distress* (Motteux), Lincoln's Inn Fields Theatre, London.

Isabella in *Queen Catharine* (Pix), Lincoln's Inn Fields Theatre, London.

1699 Almira in *The Princess of Parma* (Smith), Lincoln's Inn Fields Theatre, London.

Lovisa in *The False Friend* (Pix), Lincoln's Inn Fields Theatre, London.

Locris in *Friendship Improved* (Hopkins), Lincoln's Inn Fields Theatre, London.

Iphigenia in *Iphigenia* (Dennis), Lincoln's Inn Fields Theatre, London.

Mrs Brittle in *The Amorous Widow* (Betterton, adapted from Corneille's *Le Baron d'Albikrac* and Molière's *Georges Dandin*), Lincoln's Inn Fields Theatre, London.

1700 Isabella in *Measure for Measure* (Shakespeare, adapted by Gildon), Lincoln's Inn Fields Theatre, London.

Millamant in *The Way of the World* (Congreve), Lincoln's Inn Fields Theatre, London.

Lady Landsworth in *The Beau Defeated* (Pix), Lincoln's Inn Fields Theatre, London.

Marcella in *The Comical History of Don Quixote* (D'Urfey, combined version of *Don Quixote, parts 1 and 2*), Lincoln's Inn Fields Theatre, London.

Amestris in *The Ambitious Stepmother* (Rowe), Lincoln's Inn Fields Theatre, London.

1701 Fulvia in *The Ladies Visiting Day* (Burnaby), Lincoln's Inn Fields Theatre, London.

Portia in *The Jew of Venice* (Lansdowne, adapted from Shakespeare's *The Merchant of Venice*), Lincoln's Inn Fields Theatre, London.

Cytheria in *The Double Distress* (Pix), Lincoln's Inn Fields Theatre, London.

Venus in *The Judgment of Paris* (Congreve), Lincoln's Inn Fields Theatre, London.

Guinoenda in *Love's Victim* (Gildon), Lincoln's Inn Fields Theatre, London.

Victoria in *The Fatal Marriage* (Southerne), Lincoln's Inn Fields Theatre, London.

Cordelia in *King Lear* (Shakespeare, adapted by Tate), Lincoln's Inn Fields Theatre, London.

Selima in *Tamerlane* (Rowe), Lincoln's Inn Fields Theatre, London.

1702   Evandra in *Timon of Athens* (Shakespeare, adapted by Shadwell), Lincoln's Inn Fields Theatre, London.

1703   Caesaria in *Love Betrayed* (Burnaby), Lincoln's Inn Fields Theatre, London.

Amintas in *The Fickle Shepherdess* (anon.), Lincoln's Inn Fields Theatre, London.

Orinda in *As You Find It* (Boyle), Lincoln's Inn Fields Theatre, London.

Lavinia in *The Fair Penitent* (Rowe), Lincoln's Inn Fields Theatre, London.

1704   Abra Mule in *Abra Mule* (Trapp), Lincoln's Inn Fields Theatre, London.

Octavia in *All for Love* (Dryden), Lincoln's Inn Fields Theatre, London.

Irene in *Liberty Asserted* (Dennis), Lincoln's Inn Fields Theatre, London.

Julia in *Sir Salomon Single* (Caryll), Lincoln's Inn Fields Theatre, London.

Julia in *Squire Trelooby* (Congreve, Vanbrugh, and Walsh), Lincoln's Inn Fields Theatre, London.

Mrs Ford in *The Merry Wives of Windsor* (Shakespeare), Lincoln's Inn Fields Theatre, London.

Antimora in *Zelmane* (anon.), Lincoln's Inn Fields Theatre, London.

Mariana in *The Biter* (Rowe), Lincoln's Inn Fields Theatre, London.

1705   Angelica in *The Gamester* (Centlivre), Haymarket Theatre, London.

Flippanta in *The Confederacy* (Vanbrugh), Haymarket Theatre, London.

Semanthe in *Ulysses* (Rowe), Haymarket Theatre, London.

1706   Oriana in *The British Enchanters* (Lansdowne), Haymarket Theatre, London.

Phillis in *The Temple of Love* (Motteux), Haymarket Theatre, London.

Laura in *Adventures in Madrid* (Pix), Haymarket Theatre, London.

Aspasia in *The Maid's Tragedy* (Beaumont and Fletcher), Haymarket Theatre, London.

Harriet in *The Man of Mode* (Etherege), Haymarket Theatre, London.

Estifania in *Rule a Wife and Have a Wife* (Fletcher), Haymarket Theatre, London.

Lucinda in *The Platonic Lady* (Centlivre), Haymarket Theatre, London.

Countess of Rutland in *The Unhappy Favourite* (Banks), Haymarket Theatre, London.

Arbella in *The Committee* (Howard), Haymarket Theatre, London.

Gatty in *She Would If She Could* (Etherege), Haymarket Theatre, London.

Ophelia in *Hamlet* (Shakespeare), Haymarket Theatre, London.

Zoradia in *Almyna* (Manley), Haymarket Theatre, London.

1706–07   Lady Laycock in *The Amorous Widow* (Betterton), Haymarket Theatre, London.

1707   Portia in *Julius Caesar* (Shakespeare), Haymarket Theatre, London.

Helena in *The Rover* (Behn), Haymarket Theatre, London.

Melantha in *Marriage á la Mode* (Dryden, adapted by Cibber), Haymarket Theatre, London.

Lavinia in *Caius Marius* (Otway, adapted from Shakespeare's *Romeo and Juliet*), Haymarket Theatre, London.

Other roles included: *Justice Busy* (Crowne), Lincoln's Inn Fields Theatre, London, 1698–99.

*

Bibliography

Books:
Lucyle Hook, *Mrs Elizabeth Barry and Mrs Anne Bracegirdle, Actresses*, New York, 1945.
Joanna Lafler, *The Celebrated Mrs Oldfield*, Carbondale, Illinois, 1989.

Articles:
Lucyle Hook, "Anne Bracegirdle's First Appearance", *Theatre Notebook*, 1959.
Lucyle Hook, "Portraits of Elizabeth Barry and Anne Bracegirdle", *Theatre Notebook*, 1961.
Stoddard Lincoln, "Eccles and Congreve: Music and Drama on the Restoration Stage", *Theatre Notebook*, 1963.
Jean Haynes, "Anne Bracegirdle", *Times Literary Supplement*, 2 May 1986.

* * *

Anne Bracegirdle was the English theatre's first great comedienne. Bright, pretty, witty, and so far as we can now determine, chaste, she evidently drove men in Restoration London to distraction. "The Celebrated Virgin" she was called in *A Comparison between the Two Stages* in 1702, and rightly or wrongly she fostered that reputation, which made her ideal for the kind of heroines William Congreve created for her in his plays. Her most perfect role, perhaps, was Millamant in *The Way of the World* — as devastating a beauty and wit as one can find in English comedy: it is said that Bracegirdle herself, with all her virtues, was both the model Congreve used for the character and the perfect interpreter of the part. "Here she comes, i'faith", says Mirabell at Millamant's first entrance, "full sail, with her fan spread and her streamers out, and a shoal of fools for tenders". It might well have been a description of the actress rather than the character she played. Of Bracegirdle's physical beauty evidence remains in Kneller's large equestrian portrait of William III, preserved at Hampton Court, in which she is depicted kneeling in homage with her fellow-actress Elizabeth Barry.

Tony Aston, actor and author of the frank *Brief Supplement* (1747) to Colley Cibber's *Apology*, was unusually complimentary when it came to Bracegirdle. She was, he says, "of a lovely Height, with dark-brown Hair and Eyebrows, black sparkling Eyes, and a fresh blushy Complexion; and, whenever she exerted herself, had an involuntary Flushing in her Breast, Neck and Face, having continually a chearful Aspect, and a fine Set of even white Teeth." Cibber said that no other woman "was in such general Favour of her Spectators, which, to the last Scene of her Dramatick Life, she maintain'd by not being unguarded in her private Character. This Discretion contributed not a little to make her the *Cara*, the Darling of the Theatre ... " Congreve pined: "Wou'd she cou'd make of me a Saint, or I of her a Sinner!"

Bracegirdle was good in "breeches" parts (roles requiring women to don men's clothes), for, said Aston, she was "finely shap'd, and had very handsome Legs and Feet; and her Gait, or Walk, was free, manlike, and modest, when in Breeches". She seems to have been so physically attractive that few of her contemporaries thought of recording her vocal attributes. Colley Cibber said "her Voice and Action gave a Pleasure which good Sense, in those Days, was not asham'd to give Praise to" — but that devious statement does not tell us much, and one wonders whether her line readings were perhaps flawed in some way. But she could sing. The poet-playwright John Dryden was enthusiastic about her in this regard, writing to his friend Walsh in May 1693 of her "wonderfully good" singing in *The Richmond Heiress*. Indeed, Bracegirdle was the English-speaking theatre's first really accomplished actress-singer, taught by the composer John Eccles.

Though her forté was comedy, Mrs Bracegirdle (as she was regularly called after she reached maturity, though she never actually married) was admired for her tender quality in tragedy. A review of her roles shows some memorable parts: Lady Anne in *Richard III*, Desdemona in *Othello*, Ophelia in *Hamlet*, Cordelia in *King Lear*, Lavinia in Otway's *Caius Marius* (altered from *Romeo and Juliet*), and Lavinia in Rowe's *The Fair Penitent* — all very much in the pathetic cast. In a period when theatrical records are far from complete, Anne is known to have acted 115 roles, most of them major or leading parts, in a stage career of about 20 years. In the early 18th century she also shared with Elizabeth Barry and Thomas Betterton the management (or mismanagement, according to the satirists) of the Lincoln's Inn Fields Theatre.

Anne Bracegirdle's popularity was the more remarkable in the context of the formidable competition she faced in her day. Perhaps her nearest equal in her own company was Mrs Barry, who specialized in the more powerful tragic characters, like Lady Macbeth and Calista in *The Fair Penitent*. She and Anne appear to have been friendly rivals and complimented each other's playing. A more serious threat, however, emerged in 1700, when the young Anne Oldfield emerged to challenge Bracegirdle in comedy. The story (first related in Oldfield's sometimes unreliable *Authentick Memoirs* in 1730) goes that there was a competition between the two Annes in 1706-07, the actresses playing the leading role in *The Amorous Widow* on alternate nights: Oldfield won. The Memoirs say that Mrs Oldfield's grace and beauty, "the harmony of her Voice and softness of her Delivery" and her inimitable action "charm'd the whole Audience to that Degree, they almost forgot they had ever seen Mrs Bracegirdle ... " Anne left the stage, either in a fit of pique or else simply recognizing

that her unchallenged reign was over, before the end of that season, her last appearance being as the Countess of Rutland in *The Unhappy Favourite* at the Queen's Theatre on 19 February 1707. Recently uncovered baptismal evidence suggests that she retired at 36, when she was still very much in her prime.

—Edward A. Langhans

———

BRAGAGLIA, Anton Giulio. Italian director, designer, theatre historian, theorist, and critic. Born in Rome, 11 February 1890. Educated at schools in Rome. Editor, *Cronache d'attualita* journal, 1916–22; founder, Casa d'Arte Bragaglia arts centre, Rome, 1918; founder and director, avant-garde Teatro degli Indipendenti company, Rome, 1922–31; introduced numerous radical staging reforms and argued for spectacular futurist theatre, presenting influential range of modern and classic plays; toured South America, 1937 and 1939; director, Teatro delle Arti, Rome, 1937–43; wrote extensively on the theatre and also worked intermittently in the cinema. Died in Rome, 1960.

Productions

As director:

1923   *L'Uomo dal fiore in bocca* (Pirandello), Teatro degli Indipendente, Rome.
Siepe a Nord-Ovest (Bontempelli), Teatro degli Indipendente, Rome.
Bianco e rosso (Marinetti), Teatro degli Indipendente, Rome.
Sansone (Spaini), Teatro degli Indipendente, Rome.
Giramondo (Spaini), Teatro degli Indipendente, Rome.
Un Vigliacco (Vergani), Teatro degli Indipendente, Rome.
Il Paese e la Città (Alvaro), Teatro degli Indipendente, Rome.
Serata in famiglia (Soffici), Teatro degli Indipendente, Rome.
Il Carosello (Patti), Teatro degli Indipendente, Rome.
Ecce Homo (Moscardelli), Teatro degli Indipendente, Rome.
All'uscita (Pirandello), Teatro degli Indipendente, Rome.
La Morte e il diavolo (Wedekind), Teatro degli Indipendente, Rome.
1925   *Dramma di sogni* (Bonelli), Teatro degli Indipendenti, Rome.
Fantocci elettrici (Marinetti), Teatro degli Indipendenti, Rome.
La Felicità (Moscardelli), Teatro degli Indipendente, Rome.
Il Fiore necessario (San Secondo), Teatro degli Indipendente, Rome.
La Notte di un nevrastenico (Bacchelli), Teatro degli Indipendente, Rome.

Storienko (Bonelli), Teatro degli Indipendente, Rome.

Dramma di sogni (Bonelli), Teatro degli Indipendente, Rome.

La Casa del passeggero (Savarese), Teatro degli Indipendente, Rome.

Ciaccona (Giovannetti), Teatro degli Indipendente, Rome.

Un Commiato (Stefani), Teatro degli Indipendente, Rome.

La Metempsicosi di Yo-Ceu (adapted from Yupetuen), Teatro degli Indipendente, Rome.

Centocinquanta la gallina canta (Camanile), Teatro degli Indipendente, Rome.

Il Ciambellone (Campanile), Teatro degli Indipendente, Rome.

L'Inventore del cavallo (Campanile), Teatro degli Indipendente, Rome.

Quitte pour la peur (Maeterlinck), Teatro degli Indipendente, Rome.

Amore africano (Mérimée), Teatro degli Indipendente, Rome.

La Danza degli spettri (Strindberg), Teatro degli Indipendente, Rome.

Il Giudizio (Strindberg), Teatro degli Indipendente, Rome.

Pierrot fumiste (Laforgue), Teatro degli Indipendente, Rome.

Il Castello di Wetterstein (Wedekind), Teatro degli Indipendente, Rome.

Fedra (Unamuno), Teatro degli Indipendente, Rome.

1926   *Don Chisciotte* (Bragaglia), Teatro degli Indipendenti, Rome.

Il Medico e la signora malata (Bonelli), Teatro degli Indipendente, Rome.

Il Topo (Bonelli), Teatro degli Indipendente, Rome.

Il Principo pauroso (Savarese), Teatro degli Indipendente, Rome.

Salomè (Stefani), Teatro degli Indipendente, Rome.

Snob (Sternheim), Teatro degli Indipendente, Rome.

La Femmina del toro (Aniante), Teatro degli Indipendente, Rome.

Bob Taft (Aniante), Teatro degli Indipendente, Rome.

Corpus Domini (Lanza), Teatro degli Indipendente, Rome.

L'Affare Makropulos (Čapek), Teatro degli Indipendente, Rome.

Il Messia col clakson (Gallian), Teatro degli Indipendente, Rome.

Gelsomino d'Arabia (Aniante), Teatro degli Indipendente, Rome.

Eco e Narciso (Pavolini), Teatro degli Indipendente, Rome.

Dimmidolce (Solari), Teatro degli Indipendente, Rome.

La Smorfia (Bacchelli), Teatro degli Indipendente, Rome.

Socrate immaginario (Galiani), Teatro degli Indipendente, Rome; Naples, 1949.

Tintagile (Maeterlinck), Teatro degli Indipendente, Rome.

La Provinciale (Turgenev), Teatro degli Indipendente, Rome.

Girotondo (Schintzler), Teatro degli Indipendente, Rome.

Re Ubu (Jarry), Teatro degli Indipendente, Rome.

1927   *Voulez-vous jouer avec moi?* (Achard), Teatro degli Indipendenti, Rome.

L'Imperatore (Bonelli), Teatro degli Indipendente, Rome.

Le Mammelle di Tiresia (Apollinaire), Teatro degli Indipendente, Rome.

1928   *Lo Scimmione peloso* (O'Neill), Teatro degli Indipendente, Rome.

Il Fecondatore di Siviglia (Solari and Aniante), Teatro degli Indipendente, Rome.

Scalari e vettori (Barbaro), Teatro degli Indipendente, Rome.

L'Avventuriero davanti alla porta (Begovic), Teatro degli Indipendente, Rome.

La Morte del dottor Faust (Ghelderode), Teatro degli Indipendente, Rome.

1929   *La Casa di Lazzaro* (Gallian), Teatro degli Indipendenti, Rome.

Il Grande Dio Brown (O'Neill), Teatro degli Indipendente, Rome.

Ancorato al cuore di Maria (Barbaro), Teatro degli Indipendente, Rome.

Il Venditore di fumo (Napolitano), Teatro degli Indipendente, Rome.

1930   *La Veglia dei lestofanti* (Brecht), tour; Naples, 1951.

Il Suggeritore nudo (Marinetti), Teatro degli Indipendente, Rome.

Ultimi avvenimenti (Gallian), Teatro degli Indipendente, Rome.

Carmen darling (Aniante), Teatro degli Indipendente, Rome.

1930–31   *Frangiallo* (Libero), Teatro degli Indipendente, Rome.

Carmen 1930 (Aniante), Teatro degli Indipendente, Rome.

Le Corna di del sor Friolera (Inclán), Teatro degli Indipendente, Rome.

1932   *La Costa azzurra* (Birabeau and Dolley), Teatro Valle, Rome.

La Ronda di notte (Viola), Teatro Argentina, Rome.

1937   *Il Signor Bruschino* (Rossini), Maggio Museum, Florence.

La Finestrina (Alfieri), Teatro delle Arti, Rome.

1938   *La Foresta pietrificata* (Sherwood), Teatro delle Arti, Rome.

La Niña boba (Vega), Teatro delle Arti, Rome.

Partita a carte (Pesce), Teatro delle Arti, Rome.

La Dirindina (Gigli), Teatro delle Arti, Rome.

1939   *Nozze di sangue* (Lorca), Teatro delle Arti, Rome.

Delitto e castigo (Dostoevsky, adapted by Baty), Teatro delle Arti, Rome.
Icaro (Landi), Teatro delle Arti, Rome.
La Cortigiana (Aretino), Teatro delle Arti, Rome.
Oltre l'orizzonte (O'Neill), Teatro delle Arti, Rome.
Anna Christie (O'Neill), Teatro delle Arti, Rome.

1940   *La Sconosciuta di Arras* (Salacrou), Teatro delle Arti, Rome.
Winterset (Anderson), Teatro delle Arti, Rome.
O Giovanni o la morte (Murolo), Teatro delle Arti, Rome.
La Nuova colonia (Pirandello), Teatro delle Arti, Rome.
I Fratelli Karamazoff (Dostoevsky, adapted by Alvaro), Teatro delle Arti, Rome.

1941   *Rosso e nero* (Stendhal, adapted by Marcellini), Teatro delle Arti, Rome.
Catene (Martin), Teatro delle Arti, Rome.
Il Fornaretto di Venezia (Ongaro), Teatro delle Arti, Rome.
Lo Spirito della morte (San Secondo), Teatro delle Arti, Rome.
Le Piccole volpi (Hellman), Teatro delle Arti, Rome.
Cavalleria rusticana (Verga), Teatro delle Arti, Rome.
La Lupa (Verga), Teatro delle Arti, Rome.
Pioggia (Maugham and Colton), Teatro delle Arti, Rome.
Luciella Catena (Russo), Teatro delle Arti, Rome.
Occhi consacrati (Bracco), Teatro delle Arti, Rome.

1942   *La Via fiorita* (Kataev), Teatro delle Arti, Rome.
Caterina Ivonovna (Andreev), Teatro delle Arti, Rome.
Desiderio sotto gli olmi (O'Neill), Teatro delle Arti, Rome.
La Voce nella tempesta (Brontë, adapted by Moltedo), Teatro delle Arti, Rome.
La Gibigianna (Bertolazzi), Teatro delle Arti, Rome.

1943   *Oro* (O'Neill), Teatro delle Arti, Rome.
Per sempre (O'Neill), Teatro delle Arti, Rome.
Anfissa (Andreev), Teatro delle Arti, Rome.
Don Giovanni involontario (Brancati), Teatro delle Arti, Rome.

1948   *Peccato che fosse una sgualdrina* (Ford), Teatro del Ridotto, Venice.
Ragazzo d'oro (Odets), Teatro del Ridotto, Venice.
Delitto senze passione (Hecht), Teatro del Ridotto, Venice.
Yerma (Lorca), Palermo.

1952   *La Vedova* (Simoni), Venice Festival.

As designer:
1934   *Cefalo e Procri* (Křenek), Venice International Festival.
1939   *Piccola città* (Wilder), Teatro delle Arti, Rome.

1941   *Il Lutto si addice ad Elettra* (O'Neill), Teatro delle Arti, Rome.

Films

Perfido incanto, 1916; *Thais*, 1916; *Vele ammainate*, 1931.

Publications

Fotodinamismo, 1911; *Nuovo archeologia romana*, 1915; *I Tedeschi e le canzoni di guerra*, 1916; *Territori tedeschi di Roma*, 1917; *Spionaggio miliatre, civile e commerciale*, 1917; *La Maschera mobile*, 1926; *La Bella danzante*, 1926; *Del Teatro teatrale, ossia del teatro*, 1927; *Scultura vivente*, 1927; *Il Film sonoro. Nuovi orizzonti della cinematografia*, 1929; *Il Teatro della rivoluzione*, 1929; *Evoluzione del mimo*, 1930; *El Nuevo teatro Argentino*, 1930; *Jazz band*, 1930; *Scenografie del '900*, 1932; *Il Segreto di Tabarrino*, 1932; *Il maestro fiorentino del teatro italiano*, 1933; *Scenografia moderna*, 1933; *Il Teatro di massa*, 1934; *Sacre rappresentazioni di Bolsena*, 1934; *Giacomo Torelli de Fano*, 1935; *Nicola Sabbatini*, 1935; *Sottopalco, saggi sul teatro*, 1937; *Commedia dell'arte*, 1943; *Le Maschere romane*, 1947; *Danze popolari italiane*, 1952; *Pulcinella*, 1953; *Dell'arte rapprasentativa* (editor), 1960.

*

Bibliography

Books:
Mario Verdone, *Anton Giulio Bragaglia*, Rome, 1965.
Antonella Vigliani Bragaglia and W. Zettl, *Anton Giulio Bragaglia*, 1966.
Alberto Cesare Alberti, *Il Teatro nel fascismo, Pirandello e Bragaglia. Documenti inediti negli archivi italiani*, Rome, 1974.
Alberto Cesare Alberti, *Poetica teatrale e bibliografia di Anton Giulio Bragaglia*, Rome, 1978.

* * *

The novelty and importance of Anton Giulio Bragaglia's work lay essentially in the facts that first, he helped to establish the role of the director in the Italian theatre, and second, he was a prime mover in developing in Italy in the 1920's the concept of a specialist and serious art theatre. Involved from early in his career in the iconoclastic Futurist movement, Bragaglia was to remain at the forefront of the Italian avant-garde for some 30 years. Fired by the example of European-wide avant-garde movements, he championed a number of artistic activities, including particularly the theatre, seeking a thorough renovation of the moribund Italian stage by the development of an independent "little" theatre movement comparable to that which had helped to effect significant change in the English, French, and German theatres through the activities of groups like Grein's Independent Theatre, Antoine's Théâtre Libre, and Otto Brahm's Free Theatre.

In 1922 he founded his own Teatro degli Indipendenti in Rome (modelled, as its name suggests, on Grein's London-based Independent Theatre) and sought to re-establish the idea of a theatrical theatre. But the implications of his theory he never fully carried through. While his experimental theatre was certainly not one wholly dominated by literary texts, nonetheless the notion of a theatrical theatre was distinctly qualified in practice, and although he mounted there a number of pantomimes and dance dramas as well as plays proper, his artistic policy was ultimately orientated to play texts, notably perhaps those of the European intellectual stage, including works by Strindberg, Jarry, Apollinaire, and Maeterlinck as well as Italian dramas by such playwrights as Bacchelli and Bontempelli. This certainly provided a refined artistic repertoire, but it was not perhaps one rooted in any clear idea of the possible social functions of theatre.

In these early years Bragaglia was involved too with the cinema, and again in an innovative and experimental capacity, although his engagement was only intermittent. One of the most important of his ventures was the first, and perhaps the only, Futurist film, *Perfido incanto* (1916). Of the same year was another experimental piece, *Thais*. But Bragaglia was more committed to the theatre, and he made nothing more in the cinema until *Vele ammainate* in 1931. He did, however, take a number of ideas from the cinema into his theatre productions and importantly he recognised the need for theatre to be distinct from the cinema, an art form in its own right — an idea much argued for by Edward Gordon Craig, then a resident in Italy.

In 1937 Bragaglia became director of the Teatro dell Arti in Rome, which he ran until 1943, mounting an ambitious programme of modern and classic plays of international range. He took on the important responsibility of exploring the classic national repertory and as a consequence helped to obtain modern stagings for many old plays, like those by Ruzante, which had not been performed since their own day. There was perhaps a touch of aestheticism in his approach. Again, while the staging was interesting and ambitious, he remained quite strongly wedded to the literary text, recognizing the dangers of vapidity implicit in too unrestrained a commitment to theatrical theatre. Only rarely after the war did he undertake directorial work, concentrating instead on his writing and editing.

In fact, right from the beginning many of Bragaglia's more ambitious staging ideas found expression in occasional writings and his first book, *Del Teatro teatrale, ossia del teatro*, made a strong impression on those in Italy concerned in revitalising theatre. There was an element of the antiquarian in Bragaglia's practical work, which often saw him exploring the ancient repertory and recovering neglected masterpieces; it was to be complemented later by his energetic forays into historical writing, twin interests and activities shared by so many of the new wave of directors in the early 20th century — among them Poel, Craig, and Copeau. But he also produced much contemporary Italian and foreign work.

Bragaglia was a skilfully capable and eclectic director rather than a distinctively original one. By the same token his writings on contemporary theatre illuminatingly chronicle the more interesting work of the age, but are not themselves writings of any great theoretical significance. In this regard, Bragaglia may be said to have been an Italian equivalent of J. T. Grein rather than Stanislavski or Meyerhold.

Bragaglia was keenly interested in all aspects of the theatrical past, but more particularly in popular theatre

forms and the theatre of the commedia dell'arte, and while his writings are not always academically reliable on points of detail, his wide knowledge, enthusiasm, and instinctive understanding have helped to make some of them standard accounts. Thus his *Pulcinella* (1960) is a brilliantly suggestive and richly documented and illustrated account of this traditional Neapolitan mask, while his edition of Andrea Perrucci's *Dell'arte rapprasentativa* (1960) is a most important modern version of a 1699 text discussing aspects of the performance of amateur improvisational theatre that is difficult to obtain in the original.

—Francesca Richards

BRAHM, Otto. German director and critic. Born Otto Abrahamsohn in Hamburg, 5 February 1856. Studied in Berlin under Wilhelm Scherer, Heidelberg, with Erich Schmidt, and in Jena with Eduard Sievers; Doctor of Philosophy, 1879. Began as drama critic for the *Vossichte Zeitung* and *Die Nation* newspapers in Berlin, 1881–85; founded the Freie Bühne theatre club, Berlin, to present contemporary naturalistic drama, 1889; particularly acclaimed for his productions of the plays of Henrik Ibsen and Gerhart Hauptmann; director, Deutsches Theater, Berlin, 1894–1904, and Lessing-Theater, Berlin, from 1904. Died in Berlin, 28 November 1912.

Principal productions

1889   *Spettri* (Ibsen), Lessing-Theater, Berlin.
          Vor Sonnenaufgang (Hauptmann), Lessing-Theater, Berlin.
1890   *Das Friedenfest* and *Einsame Menschen* (Hauptmann), Ostendtheater, Berlin.
1891   *Einsame Menschen* (Hauptmann), Residenztheater, Berlin.
1894   *Esther* (Grillparzer), Deutsches Theater, Berlin.
          Der Talisman (Fulda), Deutsches Theater, Berlin.
          Das vierte Gebot e Der Doppelselbstmord (Anzengruber), Deutsches Theater, Berlin.
          Die Weber (Hauptmann), Deutsches Theater, Berlin.
          Der Kaufmann von Venedig (Shakespeare), Deutsches Theater, Berlin.
          Hamlet (Shakespeare), Deutsches Theater, Berlin.
          Die Katakomben (Davis), Deutsches Theater, Berlin.
          Kabale und Liebe (Schiller), Deutsches Theater, Berlin.
1895   *Weh dem der lügt!* (Grillparzer), Deutsches Theater, Berlin.
          Der Mann im Schatten (Reuling), Deutsches Theater, Berlin.
          Der G'wissenswurm (Anzengruber), Deutsches Theater, Berlin.
          Das Lumpengesindel (Wolzogen), Deutsches Theater, Berlin.
          Don Carlos (Schiller), Deutsches Theater, Berlin.

Prinz Friedrich von Homburg (Kleist), Deutsches Theater, Berlin.

Der Widerspenstigen Zähmung (Shakespeare), Deutsches Theater, Berlin.

Romeo und Julia (Shakespeare), Deutsches Theater, Berlin.

Der Meister von Palmyra (Wilbrandt), Deutsches Theater, Berlin.

Robinsons Eiland (Fulda), Deutsches Theater, Berlin.

Der Talisman (Fulda), Deutsches Theater, Berlin.

Lille Eyolf (Ibsen), Deutsches Theater, Berlin.

1896 *Florian Geyer* (Hauptmann), Deutsches Theater, Berlin.

Romeo und Julia (Shakespeare), Deutsches Theater, Berlin.

Der zerbrochne Krug (Kleist), Deutsches Theater, Berlin.

König Heinrich IV (Shakespeare), Deutsches Theater, Berlin.

König Richard III (Shakespeare), Deutsches Theater, Berlin.

Zu Hause (Hirschfeld), Deutsches Theater, Berlin.

Lumpazivagabundus (Nestroy), Deutsches Theater, Berlin.

Die Stützen des Gesellschaft (Ibsen), Deutsches Theater, Berlin.

Der Meister von Palmyra (Wilbrandt), Deutsches Theater, Berlin.

Jugend (Halbe), Deutsches Theater, Berlin.

Julius Cäsar (Shakespeare), Deutsches Theater, Berlin.

Morituri (Sudermann), Deutsches Theater, Berlin.

Freiwild (Schnitzler), Deutsches Theater, Berlin.

Die versunkene Glocke (Hauptmann), Deutsches Theater, Berlin.

1897 *Die Wildente* (Ibsen), Deutsches Theater, Berlin.

John Gabriel Borkmann (Ibsen), Deutsches Theater, Berlin.

Romeo und Julia (Shakespeare), Deutsches Theater, Berlin.

Der Sohn des Kalifen (Fulda), Deutsches Theater, Berlin.

Die Jüdin von Toledo (Grillparzer), Deutsches Theater, Berlin.

Einsame Menschen (Hauptmann), Deutsches Theater, Berlin.

Das Ewig-Männliche (Braun and Suppé), Deutsches Theater, Berlin.

Die Räuber (Schiller), Deutsches Theater, Berlin.

Faust (Goethe), Deutsches Theater, Berlin.

Mutter Erde (Halbe), Deutsches Theater, Berlin.

Agnes Jordan (Hirschfeld), Deutsches Theater, Berlin.

Das Käthchen von Heilbronn (Kleist), Deutsches Theater, Berlin.

1898 *Johannes* (Sudermann), Deutsches Theater, Berlin.

Der Biberpelz (Hauptmann), Deutsches Theater, Berlin.

Nathan der Weise (Lessing), Deutsches Theater, Berlin.

Cyrano de Bergerac (Rostand), Deutsches Theater, Berlin.

Das Vermächtnis (Schnitzler), Deutsches Theater, Berlin.

Fuhrmann Henschel (Hauptmann), Deutsches Theater, Berlin.

Weh dem, der lügt! (Grillparzer), Deutsches Theater, Berlin.

1899 *Die drei Reiherfedern* (Sudermann), Deutsches Theater, Berlin.

Pauline (Hirschfeld), Deutsches Theater, Berlin.

Die Hochzeit der Sobeide (Hofmannsthal), Deutsches Theater, Berlin.

Mutterherz (Bacano), Deutsches Theater, Berlin.

Der grüne Kakadu (Schnitzler), Deutsches Theater, Berlin.

Der Talisman (Fulda), Deutsches Theater, Berlin.

Einsame Menschen (Hauptmann), Deutsches Theater, Berlin.

Prinz Friedrich von Homburg (Kleist), Deutsches Theater, Berlin.

Die Räuber (Schiller), Deutsches Theater, Berlin.

Kollege Crampton (Hauptmann), Deutsches Theater, Berlin.

Rosmersholm (Ibsen), Deutsches Theater, Berlin.

Das Friedensfest (Hauptmann), Deutsches Theater, Berlin.

Der Meister von Palmyra (Wilbrandt), Deutsches Theater, Berlin.

Ein Gastspiel (Wolzogen and Olden), Deutsches Theater, Berlin.

Der Probekandidat (Dreyer), Deutsches Theater, Berlin.

Der Vielgeprüfte (Meyer-Förster), Deutsches Theater, Berlin.

1900 *Schluck und Jau* (Hauptmann), Deutsches Theater, Berlin.

Das tausendjährige Reich (Halbe), Deutsches Theater, Berlin.

Der grüne Kakadu (Schnitzler), Deutsches Theater, Berlin.

Gespenster (Ibsen), Deutsches Theater, Berlin.

Faust (Goethe), Deutsches Theater, Berlin.

Rosenmontag (Hartleben), Deutsches Theater, Berlin.

Die Macht der Finsternis (Tolstoy), Deutsches Theater, Berlin.

Michael Kramer (Hauptmann), Deutsches Theater, Berlin.

1901 *Der Tag* (Bacano), Deutsches Theater, Berlin.

Der junge Goldner (Hirschfeld), Deutsches Theater, Berlin.

Wiederfinden (Rittner), Deutsches Theater, Berlin.

Das Lumpengesindel (Wolzogen), Deutsches Theater, Berlin.

Fuhrmann Henschel (Hauptmann), Deutsches Theater, Berlin.

Jugend (Halbe), Deutsches Theater, Berlin.

Die versunkene Glocke (Hauptmann), Deutsches Theater, Berlin.

Der Probekandidat (Dreyer), Deutsches Theater, Berlin.

Gespenster (Ibsen), Deutsches Theater, Berlin.

Der Biberpelz (Hauptmann), Deutsches Theater, Berlin.

Ein Volksfeind (Ibsen), Deutsches Theater, Berlin.

Die Macht der Finsternis (Tolstoy), Deutsches Theater, Berlin.

Michael Kramer (Hauptmann), Deutsches Theater, Berlin.

Johannes (Sudermann), Deutsches Theater, Berlin.

Nora (Ibsen), Deutsches Theater, Berlin.

Die Hoffnung (Heijermans), Deutsches Theater, Berlin.

Die Wildente (Ibsen), Deutsches Theater, Berlin.

Der rote Hahn (Hauptmann), Deutsches Theater, Berlin.

1902   *Lebendige Stunden* (Schnitzler), Deutsches Theater, Berlin.

Es lebe das Leben (Sudermann), Deutsches Theater, Berlin.

Ecclesia triumphans (Dreyer), Deutsches Theater, Berlin.

Der Weg zum Licht (Hirschfeld), Deutsches Theater, Berlin.

Der grüne Kakadu (Schnitzler), Deutsches Theater, Berlin.

Liebelei (Schnitzler), Deutsches Theater, Berlin.

Die Hoffnung (Heijermans), Deutsches Theater, Berlin.

Jugend (Halbe), Deutsches Theater, Berlin.

Die Wildente (Ibsen), Deutsches Theater, Berlin.

Fuhrmann Henschel (Hauptmann), Deutsches Theater, Berlin.

Der Probekandidat (Dreyer), Deutsches Theater, Berlin.

Monna Vanna (Maeterlinck), Deutsches Theater, Berlin.

D'Mali (Bernstein), Deutsches Theater, Berlin.

Der arme Heinrich (Hauptmann), Deutsches Theater, Berlin.

1903   *Rose Bernd* (Hauptmann), Deutsches Theater, Berlin.

Der Puppenspieler (Schnitzler), Deutsches Theater, Berlin.

1904   *Der einsame Weg* (Schnitzler), Deutsches Theater, Berlin.

1905   *Elga* (Hauptmann), Lessing-Theater, Berlin.

Stein unter Steinen (Sudermann), Lessing-Theater, Berlin.

1906   *Und Pippa tanzt!* (Hauptmann), Lessing-Theater, Berlin.

Der Ruf des Lebens (Schnitzler), Lessing-Theater, Berlin.

Das Blumenboot (Sudermann), Lessing-Theater, Berlin.

1907   *Die Jungfrau vom Bischofsberg* (Hauptmann), Lessing-Theater, Berlin.

1908   *Kaiser Karls Geisel* (Hauptmann), Lessing-Theater, Berlin.

1909   *Griselda* (Hauptmann), Lessing-Theater, Berlin.

1911   *Die Ratten* (Hauptmann), Lessing-Theater, Berlin.

Das weite Land (Schnitzler), Lessing-Theater, Berlin.

Other productions included: *Von Gottes Gnaden* (Fitger), *Die Familie Selicke* (Holz and Schlaf), *Angele* (Hartleben), *Ohne Liebe* (Ebner-Eschenbach), *Henriette Maréchal* (Goncourt), *Les Corbeaux* (Becque), *Padre* (Strindberg), *La Portenza delle tenebre* (Tolstoy), *Thérèse Raquin* (Zola), *La Signorina Giulia* (Strindberg), *Dämmerung* (Rosmer), all 1890–94.

Publications

Das deutsche Ritterdrama im 18. Jahrhundert, 1880; *Goethe und Berlin*, 1880; *Heinrich von Kleist*, 1884; *Henrik Ibsen*, 1887; *Schiller*, 1888–92; *Karl Stauffer-Bern, Sein Leben, Seine Briefe, Seine Gedichte*, 1892; *Kainz, Gesehenes und Gelebtes*, 1910; *Das Leben Heinrich von Kleists*, 1911; *Kritische Schriften aus dem Nachlass*, 1913; *Kritische Schriften über Drama und Theater*, 1913-15; *Theater — Dramatiker — Schauspieler*, 1961; *Kritiken und Essays*, 1964.

*

Bibliography

Books:
Willi Simon (ed.), *Otto Brahm — Kundgebungen su seinem Gedenken*, Berlin, 1913.
Georg Hirschfeld, *Otto Brahm. Briefe und Erinnerungen*, Berlin, 1925.
Herbert Henze, *Otto Brahm und das Deutsche Theater in Berlin*, Berlin, 1930.
Oskar Koplowitz (Oskar Seidlin), *Otto Brahm als Theaterkritiker*, Zurich and Leipzig, 1936.
Maxim Newmark, *Otto Brahm — The Man and the Critic*, New York, London, Paris, Leipzig, 1938.
Max Osborn, *Freie Bühne: Otto Brahm*, 1945.
Oskar Seidlein (ed.), *Der Briefwechsel Arthur Schnitzler — Otto Brahm*, Berlin, 1953.
Gernot Schley, *Die Freie Bühne in Berlin*, Berlin, 1967.
Horst Claus, *The Theatre Director Otto Brahm*, Ann Arbor, Michigan, 1981.

* * *

The leading theatre director of the German naturalist movement, Otto Brahm provides a link between the illusionist theatre of the late 19th century, as exemplified in the productions of the Meiningen theatre, which the young Brahm reviewed, and modern directors' theatre, as exemplified by Max Reinhardt, who spent his early career as an actor in Brahm's company at the Deutsches Theater in Berlin.

Like his lifelong friend Paul Schlenther (director of the Burgtheater in Vienna, 1898–1910), Brahm began his career as a scholar and critic. The positivist methodology he acquired from his teacher, Wilhelm Scherer, and which he applied in his early critical studies of the dramatists Kleist and Schiller, made him particularly receptive to the determinist element in naturalist doctrine. At the same time his grounding in literary history gave him a sureness of judgement possessed by few of his contemporaries. When, in the 1880's, he began to develop a more active interest in contemporary literature he immediately recognised the stature of Ibsen and played a major role in the reception of the work of the Norwegian dramatist in the German theatre. Together with the older Theodor Fontane he shared in the discovery of Gerhart Hauptmann and from 1896 onwards he added the dramas of Schnitzler to his repertoire.

The earlier part of Brahm's career can be seen as preparatory to his 18-year period as director, first at the Deutsches Theater then, from 1904, at the Lessing-Theater in Berlin. His early theatre criticism shows an awareness of the potential of stage direction, but this is qualified by a distrust of superficial theatricality, spectacular visual effects, and excessively declamatory acting styles, together with the suspicion that mise-en-scène could sometimes be just a way of compensating for poor acting.

His entry into the practical theatre came in 1889 with the founding of the Freie Bühne (Free Theatre), a private theatre society based on the example of the Antoine's Parisian Théâtre Libre. Brahm, a man of great administrative skill and a somewhat authoritarian temperament, was the initiator of this venture, which brought the leadership of the naturalist movement back to Berlin and established the drama as the central genre. The programme, which opened with Ibsen's *Ghosts*, at that time still banned from public performance in Germany, included Hauptmann's first three plays and clearly shows Brahm's influence. Once Hauptmann's plays began to be accepted for performance by the commercial theatres the work of the Freie Bühne was complete and Brahm successfully bid for the lease of the Deutsches Theater from Adolf L'Arronge.

Brahm's greatest achievements date from this period, although he began with a failure that determined his policy for the rest of his directing career. In 1894 he opened with a production of Schiller's *Kabale und Liebe*, making a conscious attempt at a modern realistic production of this canonical social drama with a strongly romantic and rhetorical element. The casting of Rudolf Rittner, a restrained naturalistic actor, in the heroic role of Ferdinand, while Josef Kainz, the most celebrated and passionate Ferdinand of the day, took the part of the villain, Wurm, was more than critics and public could yet accept. Brahm henceforth gave up the attempt at a synthesis of the new production style and the mainstream repertoire, leaving the classics to his assistant, Emil Lessing. As a result he soon lost the services of his two most celebrated actors, Kainz and Agnes Sorma, but he succeeded in building a powerful ensemble that excelled in the modern repertoire: Rittner, Emanuel Reicher, Oscar Sauer, Else Lehmann, Rose Ber-

tens, and Albert Bassermann. Even Brahm's modern repertoire, however, was fairly exclusive; when experiments in poetic and early expressionist drama were becoming increasingly prominent in the theatres, he remained largely true to the realism of Ibsen and Hauptmann. During his years at the Deutsches Theater he produced no works by Strindberg, Wedekind, or Wilde, and Maeterlinck's *Monna Vanna* appeared only in the 1902–03 season. After the turn of the century younger members of his company began to feel restricted by the sobriety of the Brahm style and, under Reinhardt's leadership, set themselves up in the Kleines Theater, eventually taking over the Deutsches Theater in 1905. Brahm continued with notable productions of Ibsen and Hauptmann in the Lessing-Theater until his death in 1912. His last great series of productions was an Ibsen cycle from *The League of Youth* to *When We Dead Awaken*.

Brahm differed from the other great naturalist directors, the actors Antoine and Stanislavsky, in that he came to the theatre late and with an academic and journalistic background. It was not his name that appeared on the playbills as director, but that of his senior assistant, Emil Lessing, who carried out for him the role of intermediary, much as Ludwig Chronegk had done for Duke Georg of Meiningen. The latter, for whose work Brahm, like Antoine and Stanislavsky, expressed distinct, but qualified admiration, provided Brahm with certain of his principles: the importance of dramaturgical analysis of the text, careful casting, precise observation of environmental details, the importance of ensemble; his achievement, again like Antoine and Stanislavsky, was to apply these principles to the work of the major contemporary dramatists, developing a style of theatre appropriate to their specific kind of modernity.

—John Osborne

BREUER, Lee. US director, playwright, and actor. Born in Philadelphia, 6 February 1937. Educated at University of California, Los Angeles, BA 1958; San Francisco State University. Married actress and director Ruth Maleczech in 1978, two children. Director, San Francisco Actors' Workshop, 1963–65; studied with Berliner Ensemble and Polish Theatre Laboratory, 1965–70; founder, 1969, and artistic director, 1969–76, Mabou Mines avant-garde theatre company, New York; choreographed and directed at American Dance Festival, 1976; subsequently explored Asian and African drama; teacher and lecturer, New York University, Yale Drama School, 1978–80, Harvard Extension, 1981–82, New York University, 1981–82, University of California, and elsewhere; artistic director, Re.Cher.Chez. Studio for the experimental performing arts. Member: panel for National Endowment for the Arts; board of directors, Theatre Communications Group, 1979–81; Inter-Art. Recipient: Obie Award, 1978, 1980 (twice); Creative Arts Public Service Programme Fellowship, 1980; Guggenheim Foundation Fellowship, 1980; National Endowment for the Arts Fellowship, 1980, 1982; Rockefeller Foundation Fellowship, 1981.

Productions

As director:

1963   *The House of Bernarda Alba* (Lorca), San Francisco Actors' Workshop, San Francisco.

1967   *Mother Courage* (Brecht), Paris, France.

1968   *The Messingkauf Dialogues* (Brecht), Edinburgh Festival, Edinburgh.

1969   *Play* (Beckett), Paris; New York, 1970.

1970   *The Red Horse Animation* (Breuer), Guggenheim Museum, New York; La Mama Experimental Theatre Club, New York, 1972.

1974   *The B. Beaver Animation* (Breuer), Whitney Museum of American Art, New York; Public Theatre, New York, 1977.

1975   *Mabou Mines Performs Samuel Beckett* (Beckett compilation), Mabou Mines, New York.

1976   *The Saint and the Football Players* (Breuer), American Dance Festival; also choreographed.

1978   *The Shaggy Dog Animation* (Breuer), Public Theatre, New York.

A Prelude to Death in Venice (Breuer), Public Theatre, New York.

1980   *Sister Suzie Cinema* (Breuer), Public Theatre, New York.

The Screens (Genet), New York Shakespeare Festival, New York.

Lulu (adapted from Wedekind), American Repertory Theatre, Cambridge, Massachusetts.

1981   *The Tempest* (Shakespeare), New York Shakespeare Festival, Delacorte Theatre, New York.

1982   *Hajj* (Breuer, Maleczech, Jones, and Archer), Public Theatre, New York.

1983   *The Gospel at Colonus* (adapted by Breuer), Brooklyn Academy of Music, New York, and Grand Opera House, Houston, Texas; Arena Stage, Washington, DC, 1984; Lunt-Fontanne Theatre, New York, 1988.

1984   *It's a Man's World* (Breuer), Mabou Mines, New York.

Other productions included: *King Lear* (Shakespeare).

Publications

The Best Ones (produced Theatre for the New City, New York, 1976, and Mark Taper Forum, Los Angeles, 1979); *Red Horse Animation* (produced Mabou Mines, 1970); *B. Beaver Animation* (produced Mabou Mines, 1974); *Shaggy Dog Animation* (produced Mabou Mines, 1978); *A Prelude to Death in Venice* (produced Mabou Mines, 1980), 1982; *Sister Suzie Cinema* (produced Mabou Mines, 1980); *Hajj* (produced Mabou Mines, 1982), 1983; *The Gospel at Colonus*, 1983; *Animations* (trilogy of plays, produced 1971–77), 1979.

* * *

Lee Breuer is one of the seminal figures of the US avant-garde of the 1970's and 1980's, yet one of the more difficult to define. Unlike his most prominent contemporaries, Richard Foreman and Robert Wilson, his work does not emanate from a clearly articulated or readily apparent theoretical basis, nor is there a distinct visual or directorial style. Breuer's limited theoretical and explicatory writings are often purposely vague, pretentious, or obscure. Some of these writings are intentional parodies, some are indicative of the associative and bricollage-like thought processes out of which his work is created over a long gestation period. Much of his work possesses the formalist, minimalist, and structuralist qualities of the most significant work of the period, yet there is also a strong sense of the individual personality of both the creator and performers, and intense emotion and manipulation more typical of the ensemble works of groups like the Open Theatre. Like Foreman and virtually all the performance artists of the time, Breuer utilizes the self as subject, notably in his "animations", yet the self is not quite as distilled, distanced, or objectified. There is almost a sense of personal catharsis in some of these works reminiscent of a playwright like Eugene O'Neill. And Breuer has hardly limited himself to purely original creations: his productions include adaptations of Samuel Beckett novels and explorations of classical scripts including *Oedipus at Colonus*, which became *The Gospel at Colonus*, and *King Lear*. The roots of his work lie in his love of theatre and in his fascination by its origins, impact, possibilities, and, significantly, its relation to contemporary culture and society. He refuses to be pinned down or locked into a particular style or method.

Many of the leading avant-garde theatre practitioners of the post-1960 generation came out of the art world or some other non-theatre aesthetic, but Breuer trained in the ensemble, neo-Expressionist tradition of the 1960's. Influences included his work with the San Francisco Actors' Workshop, the Berliner Ensemble, and with Jerzy Grotowski as well as the ideology of Bertolt Brecht and Antonin Artaud. Yet Mabou Mines, the group of which he is a founding director, is unlike almost any other ensemble of the period; it does not bear the stamp of a single dominant director or aesthetic. Rather, it is a true collective of individuals who draw inspiration and support from each other but who each pursue distinct interests and sensibilities. Both Ruth Maleczech and JoAnne Akalaitis, for instance, have enjoyed equal acclaim as directors and performers with the group.

The Beckett adaptations Breuer created with Mabou Mines in the 1970's were evocative, emotionally-charged mood pieces that found visual and performative metaphors for the author's narrative. His production of *The Lost Ones*, for example, with actor David Warrilow, involved the manipulation of a small army of figurines placed within a miniaturized landscape. The lighting for all the Beckett productions was generally dim, creating a sense of entering into a dreamlike world. The "animations", on the other hand — *Red Horse*, *B. Beaver*, and *Shaggy Dog* — were a form of monodrama in which Breuer explored his spiritual self through performance pieces that he described as combinations of animated cartoons and Kafka fables. Each contains a central "character" who in some metaphoric way stands for the playwright, yet these are not narratives. The ideas are brought to life, or animated, through parallel texts presented simultaneously, voice-overs, choral sections, physical action, visual images, and music. There is no dialogue as such but the language used here and in other Breuer works is rich with puns, word games, and jazz-like riffs. They are ambiguous, associative, provocative, even mythological works dealing with the transformation of the spirit, vulnerability, sexual and artistic impotence, and triumph. But unlike the formalists, whose work the animations resemble, the Breuer pieces *do* have direct social and political overtones. They may not have the form of traditional theatre, but they can be analyzed, at least to some extent, in traditional terms.

The animations are rich in references to popular culture and mythology and by the late 1970's Breuer took these themes and turned from the inner-directed explorations of these works to creating mythologizing theatre that would reflect the time and society. Central to all Breuer creations is music. The early pieces often had music by Philip Glass, the post-animation work generally involved collaboration with composer Bob Telson. *Sister Suzie Cinema*, a "doo-wop opera" based on a poem Breuer wrote, was the first of the post-animation works. It was, said Breuer, the "synthesis of my lyric and ironic modes". The poem and the opera are a collage of rhythm and blues, movie imagery, and US pop landscape. *The Gospel at Colonus*, on the other hand, was an attempt to fuse gospel music and Black church services with the oral tradition of Greek theatre. The result was a moral lesson related by a gospel preacher and suffused with gospel music. The play was thus removed from standard Western traditions and re-presented in a distinctly US milieu. Interestingly, the presence of well-known gospel singers attracted an audience that generally did not go to the theatre and their response, especially to the music, was much more spontaneous and demonstrative than that usually seen in the theatre. The result was a rarely achieved excitement.

With *King Lear*, Breuer placed himself firmly in the post-modern tradition. The production switched the gender of all the characters and located the play in the southern USA in the 1950's. By so doing, Breuer felt that he could make the acknowledged themes of ageing, power, and love resonate in the USA of the 1990's. The production simultaneously challenged views of violence, aggression, and power as male traits and possessions, and the privileging of men in the theatre itself. As in his other productions, *Lear* constantly quotes images of popular culture so the play seems to shift wildly from comedy, to pathos, to travesty, and ultimately to tragedy. Some critics and audiences found that as a result of domesticizing the situation and transferring the locale to one so uncomfortably near and familiar the play was diminished and trivialised. But as with all Breuer works, no one left bored, uninterested, or unopinionated. By and large, Breuer's theatre is not contemplative or distanced — it assaults the viewer emotionally, intellectually, and psychologically. He searches for a theatre that will be relevant both theatrically and politically. Breuer and Mabou Mines had an avid following through the 1970's and were constantly listed among the four or five leading exponents of avant-garde theatre, yet they never achieved quite the same acclaim as Foreman or Wilson. Now, however, as the culture and history-cannibalizing, eclectic, and ironic aesthetics of post-modernism emerge as the dominant form in new theatre, Breuer seems to have been a prescient leader.

—Arnold Aronson

BROOK, Peter (Stephen Paul). British director. Born in London, 21 March 1925. Educated at Westminster School; Gresham's School; Magdalen College, Oxford University, 1942–44. Married actress Natasha Parry in 1951, one daughter and one son. Debut as director, Torch Theatre, London, 1942; ballet critic briefly for *The Observer* in the 1940's; co-director, Royal Shakespeare Company, 1962–70; founder, International Centre for Theatre Research, Paris, 1970; worked in Africa and the USA, 1971–73; moved to permanent base at Théâtre des Bouffes du Nord, Paris, 1974. Fellow, Magdalen College, University of Oxford, 1991. Recipient: New York Drama Critics Award for Best Director, 1965–66; Freiherr von Stein Foundation Shakespeare Award, 1973; Grand Prix Dominique, 1975; Brigadier Prize, 1975; Emmy Award, 1983; Society of West End Theatre Award, 1983; Prix Italia, 1984; European Community Theatre Prize, 1989; International Emmy Award, 1990. D.Litt, University of Birmingham, University of Strathclyde, 1990. Officier, Légion d'Honneur, 1987. CBE (Commander of the British Empire), 1965.

Productions

1942	*Doctor Faustus* (Marlowe), Torch Theatre, London.
1945	*The Infernal Machine* (Cocteau), Chanticleer Theatre Club, London.
	The Barretts of Wimpole Street (Besier), Q Theatre, London.
	Pygmalion (G. B. Shaw), ENSA tour of UK and Germany.
	Man and Superman (G. B. Shaw), Birmingham Repertory Theatre.
	King John (Shakespeare), Birmingham Repertory Theatre.
	The Lady from the Sea (Ibsen), Birmingham Repertory Theatre.
1946	*Love's Labour's Lost* (Shakespeare), Shakespeare Memorial Theatre, Stratford-upon-Avon.
	The Brothers Karamazov (Dostoevsky, adapted by Guinness), Lyric Theatre, Hammersmith, London.
	Vicious Circle (Sartre), Arts Theatre, London.
1947	*Romeo and Juliet* (Shakespeare), Shakespeare Memorial Theatre, Stratford-upon-Avon.
	Men without Shadows and *The Respectable Prostitute* (Sartre), Lyric Theatre, Hammersmith, London.
1948	*Boris Godunov* (Mussorgsky), Royal Opera House, Covent Garden, London.
	La Bohème (Puccini), Royal Opera House, Covent Garden, London.
1949	*Dark of the Moon* (Richardson and Berney), Lyric Theatre, Hammersmith, London.
	The Marriage of Figaro (Mozart), Royal Opera House, Covent Garden, London.
	The Olympians (Bliss), Royal Opera House, Covent Garden, London.
	Salome (Strauss), Royal Opera House, Covent Garden, London.

1950   *Ring Round the Moon* (Anouilh, adapted by Fry), Globe Theatre, London.

Measure for Measure (Shakespeare), Shakespeare Memorial Theatre, Stratford-upon-Avon.

The Little Hut (Roussin, adapted by Mitford), Lyric Theatre, Hammersmith, London.

1951   *La Mort d'un Commis Voyageur* (Miller), Belgian National Theatre, Brussels.

A Penny for a Song (Whiting), Haymarket Theatre, London.

The Winter's Tale (Shakespeare), Phoenix Theatre, London.

Colombe (Anouilh, adapted by Cannan), New Theatre, London.

1953   *Venice Preserved* (Otway), Lyric Theatre, Hammersmith, London.

The Little Hut (Roussin), Coronet Theatre, New York.

Faust (Gounod), Metropolitan Opera, New York.

1954   *The Dark Is Light Enough* (Fry), Aldwych Theatre, London.

Both Ends Meet (Macrae), Apollo Theatre, London.

House of Flowers (Capote), Alvin Theatre, New York.

1955   *The Lark* (Anouilh, translated by Fry), Lyric Theatre, Hammersmith, London.

Titus Andronicus (Shakespeare), Shakespeare Memorial Theatre, Stratford-upon-Avon.

Hamlet (Shakespeare), Phoenix Theatre, London.

1956   *The Power and the Glory* (Cannan and Bost, adapted from the novel by Greene), Phoenix Theatre, London.

The Family Reunion (Eliot), Phoenix Theatre, London.

A View from the Bridge (Miller), Comedy Theatre, London.

La Chatte sur un Toit Brûlant (T. Williams, translated by Obey), Théâtre Antoine, Paris.

1957   *The Tempest* (Shakespeare), Shakespeare Memorial Theatre, Stratford-upon-Avon, and Theatre Royal, Drury Lane, London.

Eugene Onegin (Tchaikovsky), Metropolitan Opera, New York.

1958   *Vue du pont* (Miller, translated by Aymé), Théâtre Antoine, Paris.

The Visit (Dürrenmatt, adapted by Valency), Lynn Fontane Theatre, New York.

Irma la Douce (Breffort), Lyric Theatre, Hammersmith, London.

1959   *The Fighting Cock* (Hill, translated from Anouilh's *L'Hurluberlu*), ANTA Theatre, New York.

1960   *Le Balcon* (Genet), Théâtre de Gymnase, Paris.

1962   *King Lear* (Shakespeare), Royal Shakespeare Theatre, Stratford-upon-Avon.

1963   *The Physicists* (Dürrenmatt, translated by Kirkup), Aldwych Theatre, London.

The Tempest (Shakespeare), Royal Shakespeare Theatre, Stratford-upon-Avon.

Peter Brook

The Perils of Scobie Prilt (More and Norman), New Theatre, Oxford.

La Danse de Sergent Musgrave (Arden), Théâtre de l'Athénée, Paris.

Le Vicaire (Hochhuth), Théâtre de l'Athénée, Paris.

1964   *Theatre of Cruelty Season*, LAMDA Theatre, London.

The Screens (Genet), Donmar Rehearsal Rooms, Covent Garden, London.

Marat/Sade (Weiss), Aldwych Theatre, London.

1965   *The Investigation* (Weiss), Aldwych Theatre, London.

1966   *US* (Cannan, Mitchell, and others), Aldwych Theatre, London.

1968   *Oedipus* (Seneca, adapted by Hughes), Old Vic Theatre, London.

The Tempest (Shakespeare), Round House, London.

1970   *A Midsummer Night's Dream* (Shakespeare), Royal Shakespeare Theatre, Stratford-upon-Avon.

1971   *Orghast*, Shiraz International Festival of Arts, Persepolis, Iran.

1972   *Kaspar* (Handke), Théâtre Récamier, Paris.

1974   *Timon d'Athènes* (Shakespeare, translated and adapted by Carrière), Théâtre des Bouffes du Nord, Paris.

1975   *Les Iks*, Théâtre des Bouffes du Nord, Paris.

1977   *Ubu aux Bouffes* (adapted from Jarry), Théâtre des Bouffes du Nord, Paris.

1978   *Antony and Cleopatra* (Shakespeare), Royal Shakespeare Theatre, Stratford-upon-Avon.

Mesure pour Mesure (Shakespeare, translated and adapted by Carrière), Théâtre des Bouffes du Nord, Paris.

1979   *La Conférence des Oiseaux* ('Attar, adapted by Carrière), Théâtre des Bouffes du Nord, Paris.

L'Os (adapted from Diop), Théâtre des Bouffes du Nord, Paris.

1981   *La Cerisale* (Chekhov), Théâtre des Bouffes du Nord, Paris.

La Tragédie de Carmen (Constant and Carrière, adapted from Bizet, Merimée, Meilhac, and Halévy), Théâtre des Bouffes du Nord, Paris; Glasgow, 1989.

1983   *Tchin-Tchin*, Théâtre Montparnasse, Paris.

1985   *Le Mahabharatu* (adapted by Carrière from the Sanskrit), Festival d'Avignon and Théâtre des Bouffes du Nord, Paris.

1988   *The Cherry Orchard* (Chekhov), Majestic Theatre, New York.

1989   *Woza Albert!* (Ngema, Mtewa, and Simon, adapted by Carrière), Théâtre des Bouffes du Nord, Paris.

1990   *La Tempête* (Shakespeare, adapted and translated by Carrière), Théâtre des Bouffes du Nord, Paris.

1992   *Impressions de Pelléas*, Paris.

1993   *L'Homme Qui*, Paris.

Films

A Sentimental Journey, 1944; *The Beggar's Opera*, 1952; *Moderato Cantabile*, 1960; *Lord of the Flies*, 1963; *Marat/Sade*, 1967; *Tell Me Lies*, 1968; *King Lear*, 1971; *Meetings with Remarkable Men*, 1979; *La Tragédie de Carmen*, 1983; *Swann in Love*, 1984; *The Mahabharata*, 1989.

Television

Box for One, 1953; *King Lear*, 1953; *The Birthday Present*, 1955; *Report from Moscow*, 1955; *Heaven and Earth*, 1955.

Publications

The Empty Space, 1968; *The Shifting Point* (autobiography), 1987; *The Mahabharata*, 1988; *Le Diable c'est l'ennui*, 1991.

*

Bibliography

Books:
J. C. Trewin, *Peter Brook: A Biography*, London, 1971.
A. C. H. Smith, *Orghast at Persepolis*, London, 1972.
John Heilpern, *Conference of the Birds: The Story of Peter Brook in Africa*, Harmondsworth, England, 1979.
Margaret Croyden, *The Centre: A Narrative*, Paris, 1980.
David Selbourne, *The Making of A Midsummer Night's Dream*, London, 1982.
Georges Banu (ed.), *Les Voies de la Création Théâtrale, 13: Peter Brook*, Paris, 1985.
Edward Trostle Jones, *Following Directions: A Study of Peter Brook*, New York, 1985.
Olivier Ortolani, *Peter Brook: Regie im Theater*, Frankfurt, 1988.
David Williams (ed.), *Peter Brook: A Theatrical Casebook*, London, 1988.
Garry O'Connor, *The Mahabharata: Peter Brook's Epic in the Making*, London, 1989.
David Williams (ed.), *"The Great Poem of the World": Critical Perspectives on Peter Brook's Mahabharata*, London, 1991.

* * *

Peter Brook is unquestionably one of this century's most innovative and productive directors. In an immensely industrious career spanning more than 40 years, he has approached every kind of text, performance, and creative medium. Although perhaps recognised in Britain primarily for his productions of Shakespeare, Brook has directed a number of major operas (he was a precocious Covent Garden director at the age of 22), including, at the age of 24, a sinisterly erotic and capricious reworking of Strauss's *Salome* with designs and special effects by Salvador Dali. During the formative years of his professional life, he managed to juggle productions of major European voices (Cocteau, Sartre, Anouilh, Genet, Dürrenmatt) with works by seminal modernists (Eliot, Fry, Miller, and others). He also involved himself in overtly commercial forms: "boulevard" and musical comedy, television drama, even a string of quirkily original television advertisements. He collaborated with many of the greatest performers of his generation, including Alec Guinness, Orson Welles, Laurence Olivier, John Gielgud, and Paul Scofield. The only constant appeared to be wilfully abrupt changes of gear between forms, styles, themes, and working conditions and processes. Later, Brook himself described this hyperactive period in terms of a conscious determination to immerse himself in as many different forms as possible: "I have really spent all of my working life in looking for opposites. This is a dialectical principle of finding a reality through opposites".

Although necessarily reductive, it is possible to divide Brook's career into three periods, the first of which he has referred to as "a theatre of images". An escapist aesthetic informed his elegant treatment of *Love's Labour's Lost*, for example — a bitter-sweet "fête champêtre" indebted visually to Watteau and atmospherically to Molière and Marivaux. All was wistful luminosity and movement, lyricism and imagination, blazing colour and silken conceits, for this was a constructed world deliberately separated from the everyday gloom and dowdiness of postwar Britain.

Titus Andronicus in the mid-1950's marked the end of romantic fantasy, decoration, and escape for Brook. He salvaged this "lost" play once and for all from the scorn of academics, successfully transforming a grotesque neo-Senecan melodrama of primitive bloodlust into a rite of authentic passions and suffering. Brook was now edging towards a theatre of darkness and austerity, a forum for confronting modern sensibilities: a theatre of direct event in which what occurred on stage could no longer be a separate reality.

With hindsight, this production signalled the genesis of fresh concerns and a new aesthetic, explored exhaustively throughout the 1960's — Brook's second period. His aim became a theatre of provocation and "disturbance", focused on disinterring the specificity of a contemporary theatre idiom: the study of the actor as primary creative and expressive source in an unadorned empty space and of rehearsal as 'process' in search of means and meaning; the investigation and generation of ensemble creation; the prioritisation of scenographic starkness, clarity, and visibility, in an uneasy fusion of Artaud, Beckett, and Brecht — the ideal remaining a discontinuous and prismatic density of form, to reflect the intellectual and sensory contradictions underpinning the "zeitgeist". Productions included a Kott-inspired absurdist *Lear*, the paroxystic madness and theatricality of the *Marat/Sade*, a collage "group-happening-collaborative-spectacle" in response to the Vietnam War (*US*), and a ritualistic *Oedipus*, in which Ted Hughes's text served as a jagged musical score. The decade ended with Brook's swansong with the Royal Shakespeare Company: his airborne *A Midsummer Night's Dream*, with its roots in Chinese circus, was a celebration of theatricality and showmanship, an ode to the actor and the liberating joy of "play". Emphasizing the physical, presentational, and frankly dangerous, Brook's startling re-reading of the text chipped away cultural accretions in order to concretize a contemporary experience of "magic".

The third period began in 1970 with Brook's departure from England to establish an "international centre for theatre research" in Paris. Since that time, cushioned by government subsidy from the crippling demands and impositions of commercial theatre, he has collaborated with a multi-cultural group in a radically utopian search for an intercultural theatre language. Initial research was structured around a series of questions: can certain elements communicate directly without passing through the channels of a single culture's shared linguistic signs? Is there an "objective" tonal consciousness common to all? Are there archetypal "deep structures" of a vocal or gestural kind? Is the human need for make-believe an organic necessity or an obsolete anachronism?

Since his company's move to a permanent performing base in the distressed shell of an abandoned 19th-century "théâtre à l'italienne", Les Bouffes du Nord, Brook's pursuit of a 'necessary' theatre has come to focus increasingly on myth and storytelling, culminating in his nine-hour adaptation of the sprawling Sanskrit epic, *The Mahabharata*. Like Ottomar Krejca, Brook insists that theatre can only embrace the modern world by retreating from it, re-enacting past narratives as a means of spiritual and political self-reappropriation. The material he selects proposes a critique of liberalist-humanist ethics, suggesting that mankind's greatest threat remains the ignorance and misanthropy of our fellow human beings, the results of the desolation of rampant materialism. Nevertheless, these fables are ultimately restorative, outlining an itinerary in which fragmentation necessarily precedes reintegration and healing. Certain commentators have read this material as

evidence of a political myopia, thematically reflecting an amoral and factitious pessimism. And yet the work is consistently confrontational, for it rejects mystical or quietist retreats from social engagement and repeatedly offers a compelling provocation to personal action.

Like all popular theatre forms, Brook's actor-based scenography is founded broadly on ellipsis, suggestion, and refusal of closure at every level: his model remains the fluidity of Elizabethan staging, with its representational, temporal, and geographical mobility. Using metonym and synecdoche, it is an idiom that invites active participation in the audience's imagination, for the spectator is accredited as co-creator here. At the same time, the Centre's theatre practice has remained rigorously syncretic, rather than synthetic. Cultural difference has been consistently cherished as a source of creative friction, never erased in a quest for some imaginary theatrical "esperanto" — indeed, the company's structure itself implicitly offers a paradigm in microcosm of social and cultural coexistence. And the performative ideal remains a non-homogeneous multi-textuality, within which style and form evolve to meet the demands of the moment. For Brook, the pragmatic showman ever sceptical of all dogma, the ultimate theatrical sanction is that whatever is direct and effective in a particular context "works", and a play must always be "play".

—David Williams

―――――――

BRUN, Johannes Finne. Norwegian actor and director. Born in Vaerdal, Norway, 10 March 1832. Married actress Louise B. Gulbrandsen in 1851 (died 1866). Leading actor, Norske Teater, Bergen, 1850–57; study tour to Copenhagen, with Henrik Ibsen, 1852; actor, Christiania Theatre (Kristiania Theatre from 1877), 1857–84; played nearly 400 roles and created many parts in Ibsen's plays, also appearing in Stockholm and Copenhagen; debut as director, 1879. Died in Kristiania (Oslo), 7 March 1890.

Principal productions

As actor:
1850   Henrik in *Den Vaegelsindede* [The Waverer] (Holberg), Norske Teater, Bergen.
1853   Julian Poulsen in *Sankthansnatten* [St John's Night] (Ibsen), Norske Teater, Bergen.
1855   Olaf Skaktavl in *Fru Inger til Østråt* [Lady Inger of Østraat] (Ibsen), Norske Teater, Bergen.
1856   Bengt Gauteson in *Gildet pa Solhaug* [The Feast at Solhaug] (Ibsen), Norske Teater, Bergen.
1857   Arne of Guldvik in *Olaf Liljekrans* (Ibsen), Norske Teater, Bergen.
1869   Daniel Hejre in *De unges forbund* [The League of Youth] (Ibsen), Christiania Theatre, Christiania.
1873   Straamand in *Kjaerlighedens komedie* [Love's Comedy] (Ibsen), Christiania Theatre, Christiania.

1875	Jacobsen in *En Fallit* [A Bankrupt] (Bjørnson), Nya Teatern, Stockholm.
1876	The Dovre King in *Peer Gynt* (Ibsen), Christiania Theatre, Christiania.
1877	Aune in *Samfundets støtter* [The Pillars of Society] (Ibsen), Möllergaten Theatre, Kristiania.
1885	Old Ekdal in *Vildanden* [The Wild Duck] (Ibsen), Norske Teater, Bergen.
	Professor Turman in *Geografi og kjaerlighed* [Love and Geography] (Bjørnson), Kristiania Theatre, Kristiania.

Other roles included: Falstaff in *Henry IV* (Shakespeare); Jacob in *Jacob von Tyboe* (Holberg); Jeppe in *Jeppe på Bierget* [Jeppe of the Hill] (Holberg); Old Kampe in *Det ny System* [The New System] (Bjørnson); Karker in *Earl Hakon* (Oehlenschläger); Deacon Per in *Erasmus Montanus* (Holberg); Sganarelle in *Don Juan* (Molière); Vielgeschrey in *Den Stundesløse* [Scatterbrains] (Holberg).

As director:

1879	*Samfundets støtter* [The Pillars of Society] (Ibsen), Kristiania Theatre, Kristiania.
1880	*Et dukkehjem* [A Doll's House] (Ibsen), Kristiania Theatre, Kristiania.
1883	*En folkefiende* [An Enemy of the People] (Ibsen), Kristiania Theatre, Kristiania.

Publications

Johannes Brun: Et Mindeblad, 1890.

* * *

Johannes Finne Brun was Norway's first professional native actor. His acting career started with the opening performance of Ole Bull's Norwegian Theatre in Bergen on 2 January 1850, where he played Henrik in Ludvig Holberg's comedy *The Waverer*, with immediate success. His final appearance on the stage was on 9 December 1889, as old Ekdal in Ibsen's *The Wild Duck* at the Kristiania Theatre. The 40 years between these two dates witnessed the foundation and growth of an independent Norwegian dramatic art. With his versatile acting talent and his infectious delight in performing, he immediately became a favourite of audiences both in Bergen and Christiania, and his influence on Norwegian acting in the age of Ibsen and Bjørnson was considerable.

The stage language in Norway around the middle of the 19th century was mainly Danish, due to the many Danish actors in Christiania and elsewhere. When the transition from Danish to Norwegian took place in the second half of the century, the dominant norm was based on a cultivated version of the Bergen dialect. This was the contribution of a number of actors, who had received their training in Bergen, with Johannes Brun and his wife Louise as the pioneers.

Brun's acting ability was primarily in comedy. He wanted to move rather than to shake his audience. His formative years had been in the happy age of vaudeville comedy and this seems to have influenced his art in other kinds of plays as well. Sometimes his critics found that he had made his character *too* good-natured and sympathetic. An example was his representation of Daniel Hejre in Ibsen's comedy *The League of Youth*, whom other actors would make more sarcastic and biting. When the production of another Ibsen play, *Love's Comedy*, was discussed in 1872, the playwright — who knew Brun as an actor both from his years in Bergen and in Christiania — wrote to the manager of the Christiania Theatre suggesting that Brun would not be suitable for the part of Guldstad, the grocer to whom Svanhild finally gives herself: "I doubt that he will be able to give the part the right tone. If he plays it in his comic manner, then Svanhild's decision — that most dangerous point in the play — might easily come to stand out too crudely. If he plays it with dignity, without comedy, then he is in unfamiliar territory". In the event, Brun played Pastor Straamand instead and was very well received.

During his years at the Christiania Theatre, Brun made numerous appearances in French and German farces as well as in the national repertory. His most famous Holberg characters included Jeppe in *Jeppe of the Hill*, Deacon Per in *Erasmus Montanus*, the title role in *Jacob von Tyboe*, and Vielgeschrey in *The Restless One*. With his somewhat stout figure he was also a very successful Falstaff.

Brun's special inclination for comedy made him less fit for Romantic history plays, although he played a number of parts in the genre as well, among others Karker in Oehlenschläger's *Earl Hakon* and Olaf Skaktavl in Ibsen's *Lady Inger of Østraat*. When the other early plays by Ibsen were staged at the Bergen theatre in the 1850's, Brun played characters like the student Julian Poulsen in *St John's Night*, Bengt Gauteson in *The Feast at Solhaug*, and Arne of Guldvik in *Olaf Liljekrans*. In the first performance of *Peer Gynt* he created the Dovre-Master and contributed greatly to the production's outstanding success.

During his 33 years at the Christiania Theatre, Brun played altogether around 400 different roles. Of particular importance to the art of the theatre in Norway was his involvement in the performance of contemporary Norwegian drama, both as an actor and as a stage manager. He staged several major Ibsen works and also played many of the most important characters in new plays by both Ibsen and Bjørnson. His popularity as an actor was unsurpassed in his time in Norway and he also made a number of acclaimed appearances as a guest on the stages of Stockholm and Copenhagen.

—Asbjørn Aarseth

———

BURBAGE, Richard. English actor. Born probably in Shoreditch, London, c.1567. Married Winifred c.1601; six daughters and two sons. Early career obscure; stage debut, the Theatre, Shoreditch, c.1584; actor with the Earl of Leicester's Men (renamed the Earl of Derby's company), the Lord Chamberlain's Men, and the King's Men, from c.1588; actor with the Admiral's Men at the Theatre, c.1590; actor with Strange's Men, until 1594; first performed before Elizabeth I, with Will Kemp and Shakespeare, 1594; joint-payee, Lord Chamberlain's Men, by 1595; with his brother Cuthbert and sister Alice inherited Blackfriars Theatre from his father, 1597; demolished the Theatre and rebuilt it as the Globe in Southwark, 1599; listed as patentee of King's Men, 1603; narrowly survived

Globe's destruction by fire, 1613; appeared in Royal pageant, 1613; Globe rebuilt, 1614. Died in Shoreditch, London, 13 March 1619.

Documented roles (venues uncertain)

Berowne in *Love's Labour's Lost* (Shakespeare); Ferdinand in *The Duchess of Malfi* (Webster), c.1616; Gorboduc and Tereus in *The Seven Deadly Sins* (Tarlton), c.1590; Hamlet in *Hamlet* (Shakespeare); Hieronimo in *The Spanish Tragedy* (Kyd), c.1588; Lear in *King Lear* (Shakespeare); Malevole in *The Malcontent* (Marston); Othello in *Othello* (Shakespeare); Richard III in *Richard III* (Shakespeare); and roles in *The Alchemist* (Jonson), 1610; *Catiline His Conspiracy* (Jonson), 1611; *Every Man in his Humour* (Jonson), 1598; *Every Man out of his Humour* (Jonson), 1599; *Sejanus His Fall* (Jonson), 1603; *Volpone* (Jonson), 1605.

Conjectured roles

Aecius in *Valentinian* (Fletcher), c.1611–14; Amintor in *The Maid's Tragedy* (Beaumont and Fletcher); Angelo in *Measure for Measure* (Shakespeare); Antonio in *Antonio and Mellida* (Marston); Antony in *Antony and Cleopatra* (Shakespeare); Arbaces in *A King and No King* (Beaumont and Fletcher); Archas in *The Loyal Subject* (Fletcher), 1618; Arcite in *The Two Noble Kinsmen* (Fletcher and Shakespeare); Bassanio in *The Merchant of Venice* (Shakespeare); Bertram in *All's Well That Ends Well* (Shakespeare); Brachiano in *The White Devil* (Webster); Brutus in *Julius Caesar* (Shakespeare); Caratach in *Bonduca* (Beaumont and Fletcher), c.1613–14; Claudio in *Much Ado About Nothing/Measure for Measure* (Shakespeare); Coriolanus in *Coriolanus* (Shakespeare); Demetrius in *A Midsummer Night's Dream* (Shakespeare); Don John in *The Chances* (Beaumont and Fletcher); Edward in *Edward III/Edward II* (Marlowe); Ford in *The Merry Wives of Windsor* (Shakespeare); Frankford in *A Woman Killed with Kindness* (Heywood); Henry V in *Henry V* (Shakespeare); John in *King John* (Shakespeare); Leontes in *The Winter's Tale* (Shakespeare); Lucentio in *Measure for Measure* (Shakespeare); Lucius in *Titus Andronicus* (Shakespeare); Macbeth in *Macbeth* (Shakespeare); Memnon in *The Mad Lover* (Fletcher); Orlando in *As You Like It* (Shakespeare); Orsino in *Twelfth Night* (Shakespeare); Pericles in *Pericles* (Shakespeare); Philaster in *Philaster; or, Love Lies A-Bleeding* (Beaumont and Fletcher); Posthumus in *Cymbeline* (Shakespeare); Prince Henry in *Henry IV, part 1* (Shakespeare); Prospero in *The Tempest* (Shakespeare); Proteus in *The Two Gentlemen of Verona* (Shakespeare); Richard II in *Richard II* (Shakespeare); Richard Plantaganet in *Henry VI, parts 2 and 3* (Shakespeare); role in *The Captain* (Beaumont and Fletcher), c.1612; role in *The Dead Man's Fortune* (anon.), c.1590; role in *The Knight of Malta* (Fletcher and Massinger), c.1618; role in *The Queen of Corinth* (Fletcher and Massinger), c.1617; Romeo in *Romeo and Juliet* (Shakespeare); Talbot in *Henry VI, part 1* (Shakespeare); Theoderet in *Thierry, King of France, and His Brother, Theoderet* (Beaumont, Fletcher, and Massinger); Timon in *Timon of Athens* (Shakespeare); Vendice in *The Revenger's Tragedy* (Tourneur); Wolsey in *Henry VIII* (Shakespeare).

*

Bibliography

Books:
J. P. Collier, *Lives of the Actors in Shakespeare's Plays*, London, 1846.
C. C. Stopes, *Burbage and Shakespeare's Stage*, London, 1913.
Martin Holmes, *Shakespeare and Burbage*, Chichester, 1978.

* * *

From the last years of the 16th century until his death in 1619, Richard Burbage was both an actor of considerable merit who was entrusted with the first performances of many very important roles and also a major figure in the management and financing of the theatre in London. Without him, Shakespeare would most likely have had less opportunity to develop his talents, and it is at least arguable that creating parts to suit Burbage's particular characteristics and temperament inspired him to explore more complex dramatic characters than might otherwise have been the case.

As the son of James Burbage, who owned the first playhouse in London, The Theatre in Shoreditch, Richard Burbage no doubt made his stage debut as a child in walk-on parts before going on to play female roles as a boy-actor, which he would have played into his teens, using a light head-voice after puberty. After that he became one of the leading adult actors of his time. A cynic might suggest that since he was the son of a theatre proprietor when he started out on his career and a major shareholder in a theatre-owning enterprise in his maturity he had every chance to make the most of his potential. The fact remains, however, that he did not neglect the opportunities open to him as an actor — in contrast to his brother Cuthbert, whose interests in theatres were largely financial and who did not, for some reason, seek a reputation on the stage itself.

In his *Short Discourse of the English Stage* in 1664, Richard Flecknoe recorded that Burbage had "all the parts of an excellent orator". Such a statement had a precise meaning at the time. Oratory was considered as having six parts. Three of them concerned the composition of speeches (and so would be the province of the playwright), but the remainder had to do with their delivery. The first of these was memory, and though prompters and prompt-books were indispensable in the theatres of the day, there can be little doubt that Burbage had a remarkable capacity for memorising his lines, for he played the substantial leading roles in a considerable number of plays every year and his audiences would have been unforgiving if he had stumbled over his words. The ability to present a speech with apt gestures, which were often stylised to quite a high degree, was recognised as the second skill of a good orator. The third was the ability to pronounce the text clearly and with the right emotion. Though Burbage did not possess the stentorian tones of Edward Alleyn, his great London rival, and seems to have excelled in smaller-scale productions before private audiences, he must nonetheless have been able to project his voice in open-air theatres before

Richard Burbage

inward-looking personalities in a more profound fashion. The contrast between the presentation of Tamburlaine and that of Richard III is some indication of the difference in Alleyn and Burbage as actors, the latter making such an impression in his role that "My kingdom for a horse" seems to have become (and remains) a catchphrase. Burbage went on to score further triumphs as Hamlet, Lear, and Othello, helping move tragedy away from blustering rhetoric and on to a form of drama that presented multi-faceted characterisation with more insight and sympathy. To a modern audience Burbage's acting would no doubt seem very stagey, with a good deal of studied expansive posturing, but his contemporaries seem to have been impressed by what was felt to be an unusually high degree of realism in his interpretations. Shakespeare, who was never backward in criticising over-acting, appears to have found Burbage very satisfactory in his greatest roles.

Ben Jonson, like Marston, was also pleased to have Burbage play the lead in his plays. It is some measure of John Webster's regard for the actor — who towards the end of a long career played Ferdinand in *The Duchess of Malfi* — that he included in the sixth (posthumous) edition of Sir Thomas Overbury's *Characters* a flattering portrait of an anonymous actor who has been persuasively identified as Burbage. The most telling comment in his warm appreciation is a remark that is a condemnation of many of the other actors of Burbage's time: he did not, writes Webster, "strive to make nature monstrous".

—Christopher Smith

audiences that were not by any means always ready to listen in solemn silence.

Flecknoe goes on to pay tribute to Burbage's gift for "animating his words with speaking, and speech with action". He adds too that he was an actor who knew the important art of keeping up dramatic tension when he was not himself speaking by responding and reacting with body language and facial expression to everything said by his interlocutor. Furthermore, unlike the actors at the universities, he did not, it seems, pause and stand still to deliver his speech, but rather moved about as he spoke. He was a versatile actor, playing in comedy as well as in tragedy, and he certainly possessed a number of ancillary skills, as a singer (at least in his early days) and a dancer, and, in *Hamlet*, for instance, enough ability as a swordsman to carry off the last act fencing bout with the confidence and style needed to satisfy an audience that was both knowledgeable and demanding. To a somewhat conventional remark about the way Burbage always carried conviction as a character, Flecknoe adds the unusual and therefore probably reliable detail that from the moment he donned his costume to the end of the play he kept up the role he had assumed, not only on stage but even in the "tiring house".

Though tending to stoutness, Burbage was not as tall a man as Edward Alleyn or the possessor of so commanding a stage presence. It appears that Shakespeare either felt obliged to tailor roles to suit Burbage's particular capacities or else, far more likely, perceived that his gifts and style offered the possibility of exploring more rounded, more

BURIAN, Emil František. Czech director, actor, composer and playwright. Born in Plzeň, Czechoslovakia, 11 June 1904. Studied at the Prague Conservatoire, until 1927. Stage debut, as composer, musician, and subsequently actor, with various avant-garde companies in Prague, 1928–29; developed Voice Band concept, combining music and recitation, and led Voice Band music group on tour, 1927–39; also participated in the Festival of Modern Music at Siena, 1928; worked at the Modern Studio, Prague, 1929–30; director, Národní Divadlo [National Theatre], Brno, 1930–31 and 1932–33, and Communal Theatre, Olomouc, 1931–32; founded D34 theatre collective in Prague, 1933 (the number changing with each season); imprisoned in Nazi concentration camp, 1941–45; founded *Kulturní Politika* [Political Culture] weekly magazine, 1946; elected to Czech Parliament, 1948; D51 company renamed the Armádní Umělecké Divadlo [Theatre of the Czech Army], 1951; also composed six operas, 300 songs and film soundtracks as well as writing poetry and a novel. Czech National Artist, 1954. Died in Prague, 9 August 1959.

Productions

1934   *Život za našich dnu* [The Life of Our Days] (Kästner and Nick), D34, Prague.

Pljas manekenov [The Dance of the Dummies] (Jasenskij), D34, Prague.

Činžak Evropa (Melíšek), D34, Prague.

Kavárna na hlavní třídě [The Café on the Main Road] (Včelička), D34, Prague.

Lakomec [The Miser] (Burian, adapted from Molière's *L'Avare*), D34, Prague.

Chceme žit [Desire Lives] (Nový), D34, Prague.

1935   *Máj* [May] (Mácha), D35, Prague.

Dobrý voják Švejk [The Brave Soldier Shwejk] (Hašek), D35, Prague.

Cantico dei Cantici [Song of Songs], D35, Prague.

Vojna [War] (Burian, adapted from Erben), D35, Prague.

Dreigroschenoper [The Threepenny Opera] (Brecht), D35, Prague.

Mládí ve hře [Youth at Play] (Hoffmeister), D35, Prague.

Kupec benátský (Burian, adapted from Shakespeare's *The Merchant of Venice*), D35, Prague.

1936   *Aristocratici* [Aristocrats] (Pogodin), D36, Prague.

Milenci z kiosku [Lovers of the Kiosk] (Nezval), D36, Prague.

Frühlings erwachen (Wedekind), D36, Prague.

1937   *Le Barbier de Séville* (Beaumarchais), D37, Prague.

Evgenij Onegin [Eugene Onegin] (Puskhin), D37, Prague.

Hamlet III [Hamlet III] (Burian, adapted from Shakespeare's *Hamlet*), D37, Prague.

1938   *Die Leiden des jungen Werthers* (Goethe), D38, Prague.

Pařiž hraje prim [Paris Comes First] (Villon compilation), D38, Prague.

První lidová suita [First Popular Suite], D38, Prague.

1939   *Věra Lukášová* (Benešová), D39, Prague.

Druhá lidová suita [Second Popular Suite], D39, Prague.

1940   *Manon Lescaut* (Sternheim), D40, Prague.

The Village of Stepanchikovo (Dostoevsky), D40, Prague.

Krysař [The Rat Charmer] (Dyk), D40, Prague.

1941   *Pohádka o tanci* [Story of the Dance] (Přecechtěl), Prague.

1946   *White Nights* (Dostoevsky), D46, Prague.

Žalář nejtemnější [The Gloomier Prison] (Olbracht), D46, Prague.

Esther (Höchwalder), D46, Prague.

Sen Jednoho vězně [Dream of a Prisoner] (Burian, adapted from Shakespeare's *Romeo and Juliet*), D46, Prague.

1947   *Výlet pana Broučka do XV století* [Brouček's Excursions in the Fifteenth Century] (Čech), D47, Prague.

Láska, Vzdor a smrt [Love, Spite and Death] (Halas and Holan), D47, Prague.

Vánoční hry českého lidu [Native Comedy of the Czech People] (trad.), D47, Prague.

Hráze mezi námi [The Dykes Between Us] (Burian), D47, Prague.

1948   *The Emperor's New Clothes* (Andersen), D48, Prague.

Láska ze všech nejkrásnější [Love Most Beautiful] (Burian), D48, Prague.

Neni pozdě na štěstí [Never Too Late for the Truth] (Burian), D48, Prague.

Krčma na Břehu [The Pub on the Shore] (Burian), D48, Prague.

1949   *Parta brusiče Karhana* (Káňa), D49, Prague.

1952   *Winterschlact* (Becher), Armádní Umělecké Divadlo, Prague.

1953   *Pan Kobkán vdává dceru* [Mister Kobkán Finds a Husband for His Daughter] (Hašek), Armádní Umělecké Divadlo, Prague.

Psohlavci [The Book of the Dog] (adapted from Jirásek), Armádní Umělecké Divadlo, Prague.

Čelovek s ružěm [The Man with a Gun] (Pogodin), Armádní Umělecké Divadlo, Prague.

1954   *Švejk* (adapted from Hašek), Armádní Umělecké Divadlo, Prague.

Publications

O Moderní ruské hudbé [Of Modern Russian Music], 1926; *Polydynamika*, 1926; *Jazz*, 1928; *Černošske tance* [Negro Dance], 1929; *Památník bratří Burianu* [Album of Comrade Burian], 1929; *Zamette jeviště* [Sweeping the Stage], 1936; *Pražská dramaturgie* [Prague Dramaturgy], 1937; *Dejte nám divadlo*, 1939; *O nové divadlo* [Towards a New Theatre], 1946; *Viděno slzami* [Seen Through Tears] (verse), 1947; *Osm odtemtud* [Eight from There] (short stories), 1954; *Vítězové* [The Winner] (novel), 1955.

* * *

Emil František Burian's small studio theatre D34 in Prague became an internationally known avant-garde showcase in the 1930's. Burian himself exemplifies the stresses inevitably found in a highly gifted, individualistic artist who has committed himself to a political ideology that demands subordination of individuality for a presumably greater good. In Burian's case, it was Marxist-Leninist Communism that at first inspired him to some of his most significant work, but which also came to frustrate him and eventually to contribute to a falling off of his creativity.

A conservatory-educated composer, he first began to work in the theatre as a composer, musician and later actor in the mid-1920's, primarily in avant-garde groups, most notably with the Osvobozene Divadlo [The Liberated Theatre]. He soon developed a small ensemble of his own, known as Voice Band, which presented highly individual, syncopated music-poems for which the human voice created musical, rhythmic effects in addition to the works of various poetic texts (for instance, Wolker's *Ballads*). This emphasis on choral expression and the musicality of stage speech carried over to many of his more conventional stage productions in later years.

After acquiring experience in directing in the state theatre in Brno, he returned to Prague to launch his own theatre and ensemble in 1933, naming it D34, the D representing the Czech word for theatre and the numerals the forthcoming year. The repertoire consisted of works that alternated between rather overtly anti-capitalist propaganda and works that expressed more subjective, poetic, lyrical material, most of which at least implied criticism of the socio-economic system. Of special interest to Burian were folk materials, the life of village and country people and their legends and ceremonies (*Vojna*, 1935) as if such material was inherently not only more colourful but also somehow more authentic than urban life in depicting human experience.

Several key characteristics marked virtually all of the productions. First, Burian hardly ever worked with a finished playscript, and even when he did, he felt free to edit or rewrite it thoroughly. He preferred to adapt material from other forms — fiction, documentary information, poetry — or to create his own scenarios, sometimes with collaborators. In this, as in other ways, he echoed the practice of his model, if not idol, the great Soviet director Vsevolod Meyerhold. Burian became the creator of the total production, in which the text was simply one element. As the creator, Burian always exercised nearly total control of the shaping of what eventually became the production text. Given the great significance of music in his productions, perhaps libretto would be a better term than text.

The staging of the works embodied Burian's musical orientation in several ways. Not only were music, song and dance important components in most productions, but the very shaping and structuring of the stage action also reflected Burian's musical sense of form and rhythm, in which all elements, visual as well as auditory, were orchestrated by Burian's creative sensibility. His mises-en-scène achieved fullest expressiveness in those works that employed what Burian came to call the 'theatregraph' technique, which supplemented conventional staging practice with a system that combined sophisticated lighting with static slide and cinematic projections. Such projections, unlike those of his notable predecessor Erwin Piscator, were not primarily documentary, but poetically evocative and symbolic, and they virtually enveloped the stage action in that Burian used not only opaque projection screens behind the curtain line but scrims that filled the proscenium opening of the stage; he thus allowed frontal projections onto the scrim along with other projections behind the scrim, as well as sharply delineated illumination of the actors' live action within this total projection space. For this form of staging, Burian blended literary text, lighting, sound and projection cues, and stage directions for the actors into a master scenario. His adaptations of Wedekind's *Spring's Awakening* (1936), Pushkin's *Eugene Onegin* (1937) and Goethe's *Sorrows of Young Werther* (1938) were outstanding examples, all the more remarkable for their being produced within the extremely limited facilities of his theatre, which was converted from a small chamber recital hall. Eventually, in 1940, he was able to move his operations to a larger building in the heart of Prague.

Burian's Marxist tendentiousness and lyrical expressiveness operated compatibly for several years, but in 1936 and 1937 his creative spirit began to resent the official socialist realism doctrine of the Communist Party, which dogmatically rejected individualistic creativity in favour of readily understandable works with a strong Marxist message. Burian's distress, which was heightened by his awareness of the muzzling of Meyerhold in the Soviet Union, culminated in his production of *Hamlet III* (1937), in which he combined elements of Shakespeare's drama and Jules Laforgue's novel of the same name, accentuating the plight of the unjustly inhibited free critical spirit.

The overwhelming fascist threat of the late 1930's brought Burian back to the fold. He and his theatre were allowed to operate even after the occupation of Czechoslovakia by Germany in 1939, no doubt because of the Communist-Nazi pact of 1939. Although his free days were numbered, Burian continued to stage provocative although politically muted works until the closing of his theatre and his own arrest, in 1941.

Burian returned to his own theatre from concentration camp internment after the war, but his productions never matched the artistic impact of the work of the 1930's, not even after Czechoslovakia became a Communist satellite in 1948. Burian seemed disoriented in the new socio-cultural milieu. Although ostensibly proud of his theatre being officially renamed the Theatre of the Czech Army, and of the uniform he rather ostentatiously wore, Burian seemed unable to rediscover the creative secret of his earlier years. He tried one experiment after another, from socialist realism to Shakespeare and neo-Voice Band, but died before finding the right formula that would integrate his talents with Czechoslovakia's postwar culture.

—Jarka M. Burian

BURY, John. British designer. Born in Aberystwyth, Wales, 27 January 1925. Educated at Hereford Cathedral School, 1935–40; University College, London, 1941–42. Served as Observer with the Fleet Air Arm of the Royal Navy, 1942–46. Married 1) Margaret Greenwood in 1947 (divorced 1962), one son; 2) Elizabeth Duffield in 1966, two sons and one daughter. Actor and designer with Joan Littlewood and the Theatre Workshop, Theatre Royal, Stratford East, London, 1946–63; associate designer, 1963–73, and head of design, 1965–68, Royal Shakespeare Company; associate director and head of design, National Theatre, London, 1973–85; has also designed for plays and operas in New York and Tokyo. Member: Arts Council Drama Panel, 1960–68 and 1975–77; Arts Council Designers' Working Group, 1962–78 (chairman); Society of British Theatre Designers, 1975–85 (chairman); Scenographic Commission, Organisation Internationale des Scenographs, Techniciens et Architectes du Théâtre, from 1990. Recipient: Tony Awards for Best Set Design and Best Lighting, both 1981; Gold Medal for Scene Design, Prague Quadrienale, 1976 and 1979. Fellow, Royal Society of Arts, 1970. OBE (Order of the British Empire), 1979.

Productions

1954   *An Enemy of the People* (Ibsen), Theatre Royal, Stratford East, London; also acted Captain Horster.
            The Cruel Daughters (adapted by Littlewood), Theatre Royal, Stratford East, London.
            The Chimes (adapted by Littlewood), Theatre Royal, Stratford East, London.
            Jupiter's Night Out, Theatre Royal, Stratford East, London.

The Good Soldier Schweik (McColl, adapted from Hasek), Theatre Royal, Stratford East, London, and Comedy Theatre, London.

1955   *Richard II* (Shakespeare), Theatre Royal, Stratford East, London.

Volpone (Jonson), Theatre Royal, Stratford East, London.

Mother Courage and Her Children (Brecht), Devon Festival, Barnstaple.

1956   *Edward II* (Marlowe), Theatre Royal, Stratford East, London.

Captain Brassbound's Conversion (G. B. Shaw), Theatre Royal, Stratford East, London.

The Quare Fellow (Behan), Theatre Royal, Stratford East, London, and Comedy Theatre, London.

1957   *Macbeth* (Shakespeare), Theatre Royal, Stratford East, London.

You Won't Always Be on Top (Chapman), Theatre Royal, Stratford East, London.

And the Wind Blew, Theatre Royal, Stratford East, London.

1958   *Celestina* (Casona), Theatre Royal, Stratford East, London.

Love and Lectures, Theatre Royal, Stratford East, London.

The Man of Destiny (G. B. Shaw), Theatre Royal, Stratford East, London.

The Glass Menagerie (T. Williams), Theatre Royal, Stratford East, London.

Unto Such Glory (Green), Theatre Royal, Stratford East, London.

The Respectful Prostitute (Sartre), Theatre Royal, Stratford East, London.

A Taste of Honey (Delaney), Theatre Royal, Stratford East, London, and Wyndham's Theatre, London.

A Christmas Carol (Dickens, adapted by Littlewood), Theatre Royal, Stratford East, London.

1959   *The Dutch Courtesan* (Marston), Theatre Royal, Stratford East, London.

Fings Ain't Wot They Used T'Be (Norman and Bart), Theatre Royal, Stratford East, London.

1960   *Sam, the Highest Jumper of Them All*, Theatre Royal, Stratford East, London.

Ned Kelly, Theatre Royal, Stratford East, London.

Every Man in his Humour (Jonson), Theatre Royal, Stratford East, London.

Sparrers Can't Sing (Lewis), Theatre Royal, Stratford East, London.

Progress to the Park, Theatre Royal, Stratford East, London.

Henry V (Shakespeare), Old Vic Theatre, London.

1962   *Measure for Measure* (Shakespeare), Royal Shakespeare Theatre, Stratford-upon-Avon.

Macbeth (Shakespeare), Royal Shakespeare Theatre, Stratford-upon-Avon.

The Collection (Pinter), Aldwych Theatre, London.

Playing with Fire (Strindberg), Aldwych Theatre, London.

Afore Night Come (Rudkin), Arts Theatre, London; Aldwych Theatre, London, 1964.

1963   *Mystery Cycle* (adapted from medieval plays), York.

Oh! What a Lovely War (Theatre Workshop), Theatre Royal, Stratford East, London, and Wyndham's Theatre, London; Broadhurst Theatre, New York, 1964.

Julius Caesar (Shakespeare), Royal Shakespeare Theatre, Stratford-upon-Avon.

The Wars of the Roses (Shakespeare compilation), Royal Shakespeare Theatre, Stratford-upon-Avon, and Aldwych Theatre, London.

The Physicists (Dürrenmatt), Aldwych Theatre, London; New York, 1964.

1964   *The History Cycle* (Shakespeare compilation), Royal Shakespeare Theatre, Stratford-upon-Avon, and Aldwych Theatre, London.

Eh? (Livings), Aldwych Theatre, London.

Andorra (Frisch), Old Vic Theatre.

The Blood Knot (Fugard), Arts Theatre, London.

1965   *Hamlet* (Shakespeare), Royal Shakespeare Theatre, Stratford-upon-Avon, and Aldwych Theatre, London.

The Homecoming (Pinter), Aldwych Theatre, London.

Moses and Aaron (Schoenberg opera), Royal Opera House, Covent Garden, London.

1966   *The Meteor* (Dürrenmatt), Aldwych Theatre, London.

The Government Inspector (Gogol), Aldwych Theatre, London.

The Magic Flute (Mozart opera), Royal Opera House, Covent Garden, London.

1967   *Coriolanus* (Shakespeare), Royal Shakespeare Theatre, Stratford-upon-Avon.

Macbeth (Shakespeare), Royal Shakespeare Theatre, Stratford-upon-Avon, and Aldwych Theatre, London.

The Criminals (Triana), Aldwych Theatre, London.

1968   *Indians* (Kopit), Aldwych Theatre, London.

1969   *Henry VIII* (Shakespeare), Royal Shakespeare Theatre, Stratford-upon-Avon.

A Delicate Balance (Albee), Aldwych Theatre, London.

Dutch Uncle (Gray), Aldwych Theatre, London.

Landscape and *Silence* (Pinter), Aldwych Theatre, London.

The Silver Tassie (O'Casey), Aldwych Theatre, London.

Hamlet (Shakespeare), Shiki Theatre, Tokyo.

Honour and Offer (Livings), Fortune Theatre, London.

The Lionel Touch, Strand Theatre, London.

1970   *Calisto* (Cavalli opera), Glyndebourne.

The Battle of Shrivings (P. Shaffer), Apollo Theatre, London.

When Thou Art King, British tour.

The Knot Garden (Tippett opera), Royal Opera House, Covent Garden, London.

The Rothschilds, Lynne Fontaine Theatre, New York.

1971	*Old Times* (Pinter), Aldwych Theatre, London.
	Tristan and Isolde (Wagner opera), Royal Opera House, Covent Garden, London.
	A Doll's House (Ibsen), 48th Street Theatre, New York; Criterion Theatre, London, 1973.
	Hedda Gabler (Ibsen), 48th Street Theatre, New York.
1972	*All Over* (Albee), Aldwych Theatre, London.
	The Return of Ulysses to His Homeland (opera), Glyndebourne.
	Via Galactica, Uris Theatre, New York.
1973	*Landscape* and *A Slight Ache* (Pinter), Aldwych Theatre, London, and British tour.
	Sleuth (A. Shaffer), Shiki Theatre, Tokyo.
	Phaedra (Racine), Shiki Theatre, Tokyo.
	The Marriage of Figaro (Mozart opera), Glyndebourne.
1974	*The Freeway* (Nichols), Old Vic Theatre, London.
	Grand Manoeuvres (Ellis), Old Vic Theatre, London.
	The Tempest (Shakespeare), Old Vic Theatre, London.
	Happy Days (Beckett), Old Vic Theatre, London, and National Theatre, London.
1975	*Hamlet* (Shakespeare), Old Vic Theatre, London, and National Theatre, London.
	No Man's Land (Pinter), Old Vic Theatre, London, and National Theatre, London.
1976	*Tamburlaine* (Marlowe), National Theatre, London.
	Counting the Ways (Albee), National Theatre, London.
1977	*Julius Caesar* (Shakespeare), National Theatre, London.
	Volpone (Jonson), National Theatre, London.
	Judgement (Collins), National Theatre, London.
	The Country Wife (Wycherley), National Theatre, London.
	Don Giovanni (Mozart opera), Glyndebourne.
1978	*Cosi fan Tutti* (Mozart opera), Glyndebourne.
	The Cherry Orchard (Chekhov), National Theatre, London.
	Macbeth (Shakespeare), National Theatre, London.
	Betrayal (Pinter), National Theatre, London; New York, 1979.
	Strife (Galsworthy), National Theatre, London.
1979	*The Fruits of Enlightenment* (Frayn), National Theatre, London.
	Amadeus (P. Shaffer), National Theatre, London; Broadhurst Theatre, New York, 1980.
1980	*Boris Godunov* (Mussorgsky opera), Australian Opera.
	Othello (Shakespeare), National Theatre, London.
1981	*A Midsummer Night's Dream* (Britten opera), Glyndebourne.
1982	*Macbeth* (Verdi opera), Metropolitan Opera, New York.
	Other Places (Pinter), National Theatre, London.

1984	*Coriolanus* (Shakespeare), National Theatre, London.
1985	*The Bartered Bride* (Smetana opera), Coliseum Theatre, London.
1986	*Yonadab* (P. Shaffer), National Theatre, London, and New York.
1987	*Romeo and Juliet* (Shakespeare), Shiki Theatre, Tokyo.
	Salome (Strauss opera), Los Angeles Opera; Royal Opera House, Covent Garden, London, 1988.
1988	*Cosi fan Tutti* (Mozart opera), Los Angeles Opera.
1991	*The Homecoming* (Pinter), Comedy Theatre, London.

*

Bibliography

Books:

David Addenbrooke, *The Royal Shakespeare Company*, London, 1974.

John Goodwin (ed.), *British Theatre Design — the Modern Age*, London, 1989.

* * *

Design, for John Bury, is essentially creating tangible, tactile environments that define the spaces performers must inhabit and communicate what he has called his and the director's "image" of a play or opera. Fundamental to his schemes are the establishment of a work's atmosphere and momentum, and its performers' physicality: their dynamic actuality, solidity, and size within their world. The 'image' must include what Bury has called "the volume side of things": the acting area's shape, the spatial relationships it compels and its association with the auditorium. Only when the "image" is defined does Bury ask "How can I get it on stage?" In answer to this he has, over some 40 years, introduced new materials and methods into the theatre. His style is distinctive, not for consistency of techniques but of approach. It has been called "selective realism" and has complemented that of the two directors of companies for whom much of his work has been undertaken — Joan Littlewood and Peter Hall. Both, in their distinct ways, have stressed the integrity of theatre, its provision of experiences that are real. "Real" is no synonym of "natural"; Littlewood, Hall, and Bury do not seek to persuade audiences that what is witnessed could happen elsewhere, but to affirm the actuality of performance. Their concern is with the selectivity and shaping that define art while emphasising its application to life. For this reason Bury's designs frequently employ life-related shapes and textures, but in ways that direct natural associations towards emotive and intellectual implications.

Bury's pragmatic approach may derive from his pre-theatre experience: studying chemistry and serving in the Fleet Air Arm. Experimental method, teamwork, and practical efficiency replaced for him the designer's usual art school training. After demobilisation he became assistant electrician with Littlewood's touring Theatre Workshop; there he learned the evocative but inexpensive potential of lighting used creatively. In 1954 the Theatre Workshop became resident at the Theatre Royal, East London, with

Bury as resident designer. Because productions were minimal budget, single-play runs, he literally built sets from "knocked-down houses and bits of ships ... we never simulated anything; it was all totally real". In 1960 he designed the scenery for the Old Vic company's *Henry V* and in 1962 began his long association with the Royal Shakespeare Company. As these were both repertoire organisations, whose sets were changed daily, Bury had to answer an additional question concerning play "images": "how can the stage staff handle the components?" Thus began his exploration for techniques that simulated, practically, the shapes and textures of reality.

Early set designs for the RSC concentrated attention on the stage floor, that reality with which actors must make contact. Both *Measure for Measure* and *Macbeth* (1962) featured tongues of pale planking thrusting towards the audience over dark stone. One architectural feature — an irregular stone wall for the former play and a granite arch for the latter — gave elevation; angled light on the textured floor and structure indicated each play's various locations. For *The Wars of the Roses* Bury created an influential, highly dramatic scheme from the imagery of medieval weaponry. Everything was metallic — burnished or rusting. Civil war's barbarism became actual when actors struck sparks from the steel floor or crashed against the pivoted metal walls, which could confine or expand the acting area. Lighting picked from the predominant darkness the vibrance of spilt blood and the resonance of judiciously selected, recurrent, properties: a metal council table, huge swords, and a throne whose elegant perpendicular lines contrasted with its gleaming steel construction. For most of the previous productions Bury had designed only the sets; for *The Wars of the Roses* he also oversaw the costumes. With Anne Curtis, thereafter a frequent collaborator, he determined to "take the fancy dress out of costumes" and contrived garments in which functional evocation superseded period detail. Clothes were treated with latex, grit, and metal dust to achieve craggy shapes and unyielding textures. Against these the untreated coarse woollen robe of gentle King Henry marked him as a stranger within his own kingdom. When, in 1964, the RSC added Shakespeare's other history plays to chart the cycle of events from Richard II to Richard III, Bury expanded his scheme to show England's metamorphosis from "a tarnished jewel" to a dark "bunker". The design and the production by Hall, John Barton, and Clifford Williams, organically embodied an historical process.

With Hall as director, Bury has designed the premieres of many Pinter plays. These economical, enigmatically menacing works are confined within rooms. To each room Bury's versatile selective realism has imparted its peculiar status and atmosphere. Angularity and bleak space characterised the shabby living-room of *The Homecoming*; a riven set — part country-house kitchen, part reflective limbo — matched environment to ill-matched couple in *Landscape*; the comfortable Hampstead lounge for *No Man's Land* was an ovoid within darkness, its curves symbolic of the characters' uncertain relationships. *Betrayal* required several rooms: Hall's *Diaries* record Bury's struggle to achieve the image that author and director both pronounced "a triumph" — a triangular ceiling below which the corners of different rooms revolved into place, without walls and ceiling quite meeting. The gap emblematised the time-jumps and faulty relationships in a menage à trois. These rooms, like those designed for plays by Albee, Dürrenmatt, and Ibsen, combined surface with subtextual reality.

By contrast, Bury has rejoiced in stage mechanics for works of overt theatricality. *The Magic Flute* and Verdi's *Macbeth* had painted flats and backdrops; the masque-like *Return of Ulysses* and *The Tempest* had sliding panels and flying devices for the immortals. In Britten's *A Midsummer Night's Dream* "tree-actors" within a mirrored box constantly rearranged the forest in response to the shifting musical images, while in Strauss's *Salome* reflective surfaces, painted gauzes, projections, and a floating moon created "a seamless sequence of visual transformations". Over the years Bury's palette has strengthened, but always within a confined colour range for individual works; sharply defining lighting has remained a consistent characteristic.

Concern for the apt image has made Bury a fervently collaborative designer, refining ideas in response to colleagues' reactions; it has also influenced his contributions to the planning of the Barbican and Olivier theatres. For these he sought spaces that did not impose one particular design approach; however, both do demand the strongly sculptural textural style that is Bury's.

—Raymond Ingram

C

CALDWELL, Zoë. Australian actress and director. Born Ada Caldwell in Hawthorn, Victoria, Australia, 14 September 1933. Educated at the Methodist Ladies College, Melbourne. Married producer Robert Whitehead; two sons. Actress, Union Theatre Repertory Company, Melbourne, from 1953; first appeared at the Shakespeare Memorial Theatre, Stratford-upon-Avon, 1958; London debut, 1960; New York debut, 1965; taught Shakespearean drama at the Neighborhood Playhouse, New York, 1970; has also made a number of television appearances. Recipient: New York Drama Critics' Award, 1965–66; Tony Award, 1966, 1968, 1982. OBE (Order of the British Empire), 1970.

Productions

As actress:
1954–57	Bubba in *The Summer of the Seventeenth Doll* (Lawler), Elizabethan Theatre Trust, Sydney.
	Ophelia in *Hamlet* (Shakespeare), Elizabethan Theatre Trust, Sydney.
1958–59	Daughter of Antiochus in *Pericles* (Shakespeare), Shakespeare Memorial Theatre, Stratford-upon-Avon.
	Margaret in *Much Ado About Nothing* (Shakespeare), Shakespeare Memorial Theatre, Stratford-upon-Avon.
1959	Bianca in *Othello* (Shakespeare), Shakespeare Memorial Theatre, Stratford-upon-Avon.
	Helena in *All's Well That Ends Well* (Shakespeare), Shakespeare Memorial Theatre, Stratford-upon-Avon.
	A Fairy in *A Midsummer Night's Dream* (Shakespeare), Shakespeare Memorial Theatre, Stratford-upon-Avon.
	Cordelia in *King Lear* (Shakespeare), Shakespeare Memorial Theatre, Stratford-upon-Avon.
1960	Ismène in *Antigone* (Anouilh), Royal Court Theatre, London.
	The Whore in *Cob and Leach*, part of *Trials by Logue* (Logue), Royal Court Theatre, London.
1961	Isabella in *The Changeling* (Middleton), Royal Court Theatre, London.
	Jacqueline in *Jacques* (Ionesco), Royal Court Theatre, London.

Rosaline in *Love's Labour's Lost* (Shakespeare), Stratford Shakespearean Festival, Stratford, Ontario.

Sonja Downfahl in *The Canvas Barricade*, Stratford Shakespearean Festival, Stratford, Ontario.

Pegeen Mike in *The Playboy of the Western World* (Synge), Manitoba Theatre Centre, Winnipeg, Manitoba.

1962	Joan in *Saint Joan* (Shaw), Adelaide Festival of the Arts and tour.
	Role in *The Ham Funeral* (White), Elizabethan Theatre Trust, Sydney.
	Nola Boyle in *The Season at Sarsaparilla* (White), Union Theatre, Melbourne.
1963	Frosine in *The Miser* (Molière), Tyrone Guthrie Theatre, Minneapolis; Tyrone Guthrie Theatre, Minneapolis, 1965.
	Natasha in *The Three Sisters* (Chekhov), Tyrone Guthrie Theatre, Minneapolis.
1964	Mother Courage in *Mother Courage* (Brecht), Manitoba Theatre Centre, Winnipeg, Manitoba.
	Countess Aurelia in *The Mad Woman of Chaillot* (Giraudoux), Goodman Theatre, Chicago.
1965	Millamant in *The Way of the World* (Congreve), Tyrone Guthrie Theatre, Minneapolis.
	Grusha in *The Caucasian Chalk Circle* (Brecht), Tyrone Guthrie Theatre, Minneapolis.
	The Prioress in *The Devils* (Whiting), New York.
1966	Polly in *Gnädiges Fraulein*, part of *Slapstick Tragedy* (Williams), Longacre Theatre, New York.
	Orinthia in *The Apple Cart* (Shaw), Shaw Festival, Niagara-on-the-Lake.
	Lena Szezepanowska in *Misalliance* (Shaw), Shaw Festival, Niagara-on-the-Lake.
1967	Cleopatra in *Antony and Cleopatra* (Shakespeare), Stratford Shakespearean Festival, Stratford, Ontario.
	Lady Anne in *Richard III* (Shakespeare), Stratford Shakespearean Festival, Stratford, Ontario.
	Mrs Page in *The Merry Wives of Windsor* (Shakespeare), Shakespearean Festival, Stratford, Ontario.

1968	Jean Brodie in *The Prime of Miss Jean Brodie* (Spark), Helen Hayes Theatre, New York.
1970	Colette in *Colette*, Ellen Stewart Theatre, New York.
	Emma Hamilton in *A Bequest to the Nation* (Rattigan), Haymarket Theatre, London.
1972	Eve in *The Creation of the World and Other Business* (Miller), Shubert Theatre, New York.
1974	Alice in *The Dance of Death* (Strindberg), Vivian Beaumont Theatre, Lincoln Centre, New York.
1975	Mary Tyrone in *Long Day's Journey into Night* (O'Neill), Eisenhower Theatre, Washington, D.C.
1982	Medea in *Medea* (adapted by Jeffers), Court Theatre, New York.

Has also acted roles in: *Hamlet* (Shakespeare), tour of Soviet Union, 1958–59; *Twelfth Night* (Shakespeare), tour of Soviet Union, 1958–59; *Romeo and Juliet* (Shakespeare), tour of Soviet Union, 1958–59; *Love and Master Will*, Kennedy Centre, Washington, D.C., 1973, and Brooklyn Academy, New York, 1976.

As director:

1977	*An Almost Perfect Person*, Belasco Theatre, New York.
1979	*Richard II* (Shakespeare), Stratford Shakespearean Festival, Stratford, Ontario.
1980	*These Men*, New York.
1981	*Othello* (Shakespeare; as co-director), Winter Garden Theatre, New York.
	Macbeth, New York.

Television

Roles in:

Witness to Yesterday, 1974; *The Seagull*; *Sarah*; *The Apple Cart*; *Macbeth*; *The Lady's Not for Burning*.

* * *

Zoe Caldwell began her professional theatre career at the age of nine in her native Melbourne. The daughter of a dancer, she studied tap and ballet but her powerful voice, likened by one London critic to "a wolf baying at the moon" and her ability to express strong emotions led her into a career in the theatre rather than in dance. She gained extensive radio experience and was a founding member of the Union Theatre Repertory Company in Melbourne, where her roles ranged from Ophelia to Bubba in *The Summer of the Seventeenth Doll*. She turned down the chance to go to London with this play but by 1960 was appearing with the Royal Shakespeare Company in the UK and on tour in Russia in a variety of small parts. She soon attracted the attention of Tyrone Guthrie, for whom she went on to play Helena in *All's Well That Ends Well* and Rosaline in *Love's Labour's Lost*, as well as playing Cordelia in Charles Laughton's *King Lear*.

Caldwell rapidly established herself as an actress of vibrant theatricality. She believes it is important for a performer to maintain absolute control over the audience through the use of both technique and a strong personal magnetism. She speaks with admiration of Sarah Bernhardt and Mrs Patrick Campbell and sees herself as working in the tradition of these great 'divas', whom she refers to as "theatrical ancestors". Success in London was followed by similar acclaim in the USA, where she made an indelible mark as Cleopatra to Christopher Plummer's Antony at Stratford, Ontario, in a portrayal that was characterised as "sexy, foul-mouthed and funny". She returned to Australia to play Saint Joan and went on to demonstrate her versatility in a range of theatre, from Chekhov's *The Three Sisters* and Congreve's *The Way of the World* to Brecht's *Mother Courage*, O'Neill's *Long Day's Journey into Night*, and Rattigan's *Bequest to the Nation*.

Among her more notable contributions to radio drama have been her portrayals of Arkadina in *The Seagull* for the BBC and Sarah Bernhardt in *Sarah* for CBC, a role that she initially resisted: "I told John Hirsch it was a mistake to hire one rococco actress to play another rococco actress, but in fact I enjoyed it thoroughly." In time, she essayed almost all the big bravura roles in the classical and modern canon, in her own words "hanging them like scalps from my belt" and refusing to be daunted by any theatrical challenge, her imagination being especially fuelled by roles requiring extravagance and eccentricity. Typical performances combine a proletarian vigour with aristocratic hauteur and an irrepressible sense of humour evidenced by her crooked smile, described as "the grin of a gleeful witch".

Based in New York since her marriage, Caldwell has scored notable triumphs on Broadway in such roles as Polly in *Gnädiges Fraulein*, Muriel Spark's Jean Brodie, and as Medea (succeeding to the part after Judith Anderson elected to play the Nurse); all three performances were rewarded with Tony Awards, establishing Caldwell as one of the most versatile and potent actresses working on the US stage.

Since the 1960's Caldwell has worked sporadically but effectively as a director, her projects including *Richard II* at Stratford, Ontario, *An Almost Perfect Person*, which featured Colleen Dewhurst, and *Macbeth*, starring Christopher Plummer. Opinionated, outspoken, practical, yet audacious, her vibrant personality and utter candour appeal to actors but sometimes frighten managers. She remains unconcerned by this; having played virtually all the major roles in the repertoire, she professes to be undismayed at the prospect of lengthy periods away from the stage.

Caldwell tours occasionally with her own one-woman show, which comprises a collage of favourite roles together with pieces by her own hand and reflections upon her experiences both on and off the stage. Other highlights include renditions of such songs as the unofficial Australian national anthem 'Waltzing Matilda'.

—Martin Hunter

———

CAMPBELL, (Mrs) Patrick. British actress. Born Beatrice Rose Stella Tanner in Kensington, London, 9 February 1865. Educated, from 1875, at schools in Brighton and London, and under private tuition in Paris, until 1880; scholar, Guildhall School of Music, London,

1881–82. Married 1) Patrick Campbell in 1884 (died 1900), one son and one daughter; 2) George Cornwallis-West in 1914. Amateur actress, Anomalies Dramatic Club, 1886; professional debut, Alexandra Theatre, Liverpool, 1888; joined Ben Greet's touring company, 1889; London debut, Adelphi Theatre, 1890; established reputation under George Alexander in *The Second Mrs Tanqueray*, 1893; acclaimed in leading Shakespearean roles opposite Johnston Forbes-Robertson, 1896–99; first of several co-managements, Prince of Wales's Theatre, London, 1898–99; New York debut, 1902; acted with Sarah Bernhardt, 1904; created Bernard Shaw's Eliza Doolittle, 1914; film debut, 1930. Died in Pau, France, 9 April 1940.

Roles

1888	Sophia Moody in *Bachelors* (Buchanan), Alexandra Theatre, Liverpool.
	Rachel Denison in *Tares* (Beringer), British tour.
1889	Rosalind in *As You Like It* (Shakespeare), British tour; Shaftesbury Theatre, London, 1891.
	Viola in *Twelfth Night* (Shakespeare), British tour.
	Helena in *A Midsummer Night's Dream* (Shakespeare), British tour.
	Princess of France in *Love's Labour's Lost* (Shakespeare), British tour.
	Queen Eglamour in *Love in a Mist* (Cook), British tour.
1890	Helen in *The Hunchback* (Knowles), Adelphi Theatre, London.
	Stella Maris in *A Buried Talent* (Parker), Vaudeville Theatre, London.
1891	Lady Teazle in *The School for Scandal* (Sheridan), Adelphi Theatre, London; Lyceum Theatre, London, 1896.
	Astrea in *The Trumpet Call* (Sims and Buchanan), Adelphi Theatre, London.
1892	Elizabeth Cromwell in *The White Rose* (Sims and Buchanan), Adelphi Theatre, London.
	Tress Purvis in *The Lights of Home* (Sims and Buchanan), Adelphi Theatre, London.
1893	Belle Hamilton in *The Black Domino* (Sims and Buchanan), Adelphi Theatre, London.
	Paula in *The Second Mrs Tanqueray* (Pinero), St James's Theatre, London; Berlin, 1898; St James's Theatre, London, 1913; San Francisco, 1915; British tour, 1923–24.
1894	Dulcie Larondie in *The Masqueraders* (Jones), St James's Theatre, London.
	Kate Cloud in *John-a-Dreams* (Chambers), Haymarket Theatre, London.
1895	Agnes Ebbsmith in *The Notorious Mrs Ebbsmith* (Pinero), Garrick Theatre, London.
	Fédora in *Fédora* (Merivale), Haymarket Theatre, London.
	Juliet in *Romeo and Juliet* (Shakespeare), Lyceum Theatre, London.
1896	Militza in *For the Crown* (Davidson), Lyceum Theatre, London.

Magda in *Magda* (Sudermann, adapted by Parker), Lyceum Theatre, London; Republic Theatre, New York, 1902; British tour, 1923–24.

The Rat Wife and Rita in *Little Eyolf* (Ibsen), Avenue Theatre, London.

1897	Lady Hamilton in *Nelson's Enchantress* (Horne), Avenue Theatre, London.
	Ophelia in *Hamlet* (Shakespeare), Lyceum Theatre, London; Berlin, 1898.
1898	Lady Macbeth in *Macbeth* (Shakespeare), Berlin and Lyceum Theatre, London; Aldwych Theatre, London, 1920.
	Mélisande in *Pelléas et Mélisande* (Maeterlinck), Prince of Wales's Theatre, London; Vaudeville Theatre, London, 1904; Coronet Theatre, London, 1905; Lyceum Theatre, London, 1911.
1899	Vera in *Carlyon Sahib* (Murray), Prince of Wales's Theatre, London.
	Inamura Nanoya in *The Moonlight Blossom* (Fernald), Prince of Wales's Theatre, London.
	Jeffik Guillou in *The Sacrament of Judas* (Parker), Prince of Wales's Theatre, London.
	Mrs Martin Temple in *The Canary* (Fleming), Prince of Wales's Theatre, London.
1900	Dora Jordan in *Mrs Jordan* (Smedley), Royalty Theatre, London.
	Percinet in *The Fantasticks* (Fleming), Royalty Theatre, London.
	Hilda Daventry in *Mr and Mrs Daventry* (Harris), Royalty Theatre, London.
1901	Mariana in *Mariana* (Echegaray), Royalty Theatre, London.
	Mrs Clara Sang in *Beyond Human Power* (Bjornson), Royalty Theatre, London.
1902	Beata in *The Joy of Living* (Sudermann, translated by Wharton), Garden Theatre, New York; New Theatre, London, 1903.
	Aunt Jeannie in *Aunt Jeannie* (Benson), Garden Theatre, New York.
1904	Donia Maria de Neuborg in *A Queen's Romance* (Davidson, adapted from Hugo's *Ruy Blas*), Imperial Theatre, London.
	Theodosia Hemming in *Warp and Woof* (Lyttelton), Camden Theatre, London.
	Zoraya in *La Sorcière* (Sardou, translated by Parker), US tour.
1906	Countess of Ellingham in *The Whirlwind* (Melvill), Criterion Theatre, London.
	Undine in *Undine* (Courtney), Criterion Theatre, London.
	Margaretta Sinclair in *The Macleans of Bairness* (Lyttelton), Criterion Theatre, London.
	Greeba in *The Bondman* (Caine), Theatre Royal, Drury Lane, London.
1907	Hedda Tesman in *Hedda Gabler* (Ibsen), Court Theatre, London; Everyman Theatre, London, 1922.
1908	Electra in *Electra* (Sophocles), Garden Theatre, New York, and New Theatre, London.

Phyllis Mortimore in *The Thunderbolt* (Pinero), British tour.

Deirdre in *Deirdre* (Yeats), New Theatre, London.

1909   Olive in *Olive Latimer's Husband* (Besier), Vaudeville Theatre, London.

1909   Fabia in *His Borrowed Plumes* (Cornwallis-West), Hicks Theatre, London.

Mièris in *False Gods* (Fagan), His Majesty's Theatre, London.

Sonja in *A Russian Tragedy*, His Majesty's Theatre, London; US tour, 1910.

The Wife in *The Ambassador's Wife* (A. Campbell), Chicago.

Fanny Armawry in *The Foolish Virgin* (Bataille, translated by Besier), Knickerbocker Theatre, New York.

1911   Lady Patricia Cosway in *Lady Patricia* (Besier), Haymarket Theatre, London.

Olga Weather in *The Bridge*, Hippodrome, Brighton.

Mrs Chepstow in *Bella Donna* (Fagan), St James's Theatre, London; St James's Theatre, London, 1916.

1913   Leonora in *The Adored One* (Barrie), Duke of York's Theatre, London.

1914   Eliza Doolittle in *Pygmalion* (G. B. Shaw), His Majesty's Theatre, London, and Park Theatre, New York; US tour, 1914–15; Aldwych Theatre, London, and German tour, 1920.

1915   Mrs Blaine in *Searchlights* (Vachell), San Francisco.

1916   Enid Vane in *The Law of the Sands* (Hichens), London Opera House.

1917   Thérèse Bonnet in *Pro Patria* (Cornwallis-West), Coliseum Theatre, London.

Simaetha in *Simaetha* (Courtney), Coliseum Theatre, London.

Madame Rosalie la Grange in *The Thirteenth Chair* (Veiller), Duke of York's Theatre, London; British tour, 1923–24 and 1933.

1920   George Sand in *Madame Sand* (Bjornson), Duke of York's Theatre, London.

1922   Grandmother in *Voodoo* (Wiborg), Blackpool.

1925   Adela Rivers in *The Adventurous Age* (Witney), British tour and Grand Theatre, Fulham, London; Mansfield Theatre, New York, 1927.

1926   Countess Strong-i-th'-Arm in *What Might Happen* (Maltby), Savoy Theatre, London.

1927   Madame Kuranda in *Madame Kuranda*, British tour.

1928   Mrs Alving in *Ghosts* (Ibsen), Wyndham's Theatre, London; British tour, 1930.

Ella Rentheim in *John Gabriel Borkman* (Ibsen), Q Theatre, London.

1929   Anastasia in *The Matriarch* (Stern), Royalty Theatre, London.

1931   Countess Polaki in *The Sex Fable* (translated from the French), Henry Miller Theatre, New York.

1932   Clytemnestra in *Electra* (Sophocles), Selwyn Theatre, New York.

1933   Mrs MacDonald in *A Party* (Novello), Playhouse, New York.

Films

The Dancers, 1930; *Riptide*, 1934; *One More River*, 1934; *Outcast Lady*, 1934; *Crime and Punishment*, 1935.

Publications

My Life and Some Letters, 1922.

*

Bibliography

Books:
Alan Dent (ed.), *Bernard Shaw and Mrs Patrick Campbell: Their Correspondence*, London, 1952.
Alan Dent, *Mrs Patrick Campbell*, London, 1961.
Helen Spinola, *Nothing But the Truth: The Reminiscences*, London, 1961.
Margot Peters, *Mrs Pat: The Life of Mrs Patrick Campbell*, London, 1984.

* * *

During a long and tempestuous career, Mrs Patrick Campbell experienced, and adapted to, momentous transitions in the theatrical world as it evolved from the conservative 1880's to the new demands of a cinema-conscious public in the 1930's. Working with many of the famous actor-managers of the period, 'Mrs Pat' was renowned for her impetuous nature and also for her refusal to accept a subordinate role in terms of either acting or production within the theatre. Her suggestive beauty and excellent manipulation of publicity vehicles such as photography and the press made her a great favourite with audiences on both sides of the Atlantic. Admirably independent and self-supporting, she was nonetheless hounded by the debts that were accumulated through her generosity and extravagant lifestyle. Recollections of Mrs Pat veer from the absolutes of adoration to loathing, many contemporary performers resenting her egotism and temperamentalism upon the stage and accusing her of unprofessionalism. However, her instinctive talent and her personal charm, combined with an alluring sexuality and nervous intensity, won over countless fans and her most fervent admirers included the likes of J. M. Barrie, Sarah Bernhardt, A. W. Pinero, and, of course, George Bernard Shaw.

In her autobiography, Mrs Campbell offers the reader a carefully censored version of her private and public experiences. She uses memorabilia, letters, and reminiscences to corroborate the public image that she sought to establish throughout her stage career. Highlighting her Italian antecedents and her Romantic female relatives, she enshrouds herself with traditions of mystique and sensuality. Indeed, much of the autobiography does not concentrate on her theatrical achievements and professional associates, but rather upon her acquaintance with literary and social characters of the day. This conveys accurately her acceptance into extra-theatrical circles and avoids the self-congratulatory extremes of comparative memoirs, such as those of Lillie Langtry and Vesta Tilley. Mrs Campbell sought to retain her middle-class status, in spite of the onus against her profession, by maintaining a 'superior' lifestyle and attitude. It is important to note that in creating and developing these aspects of her public persona, she antagonised her acting and managerial colleagues. Using her beauty and popularity to ensure leading roles, she maintained a condescending manner towards dramatists and playwrights alike: many people, for instance, were shocked at her scornful dismissal of the then courted H. A. Jones and his play *Michael and His Lost Angel* in 1896. Her complicated private life likewise caused raised eyebrows among the most conservative members of the theatrical community.

Passing through a series of engagements with leading managers (the Gattis at the Adelphi, George Alexander at the St James's, Tree at the Haymarket, John Hare at the Garrick, and a longer period with Forbes-Robertson at the Lyceum), Mrs Campbell realised that only through leasing a theatre herself could she escape the routine of poor quality plays and clichéd roles. She therefore toured in the provinces in 1898 in an effort to attract financial backers and then took her own theatre, the Prince of Wales's in Kensington, in joint-management with Forbes-Robertson. Predictably, the pair clashed over dramatic tastes as Mrs Campbell demonstrated her interest in more unconventional plays and the partnership collapsed under the financial pressures of costly failures like the oriental *Moonlight Blossom*. Mrs Campbell was obliged to transfer to the smaller Royalty Theatre and to embark on a tour of the US to recoup her losses. Henceforth her career continued to follow this pattern: any new or innovative ventures into management, which included an attempt to establish a pseudo-repertory company, resulted invariably in financial losses that were only made good through provincial and overseas tours in popular plays. Particularly dangerous enterprises included her regular productions of important modern European drama, including translations of Bjornson, Sudermann, and Maeterlinck, which were all performed in front of minority audiences and brought in barely enough money to cover the costs. Dogged by ill health and increased reluctance on the part of managers to engage a notoriously difficult actress, Mrs Campbell was increasingly forced to rely upon borrowed funds. Even the months of affluence such as those following the production and US tour of *Pygmalion* in 1914 provided only temporary relief. Nonetheless, Mrs Campbell's enthusiasm for modern theatre, evidenced by her productions of Ibsen, Granville Barker, Barrie, and Shaw, remained undimmed, though her plans were often thwarted by the financial risks involved.

Mrs Campbell's acting talent remains a bone of contention even among modern critics. Whilst many choose to emphasize only her 'vampish' reputation, pointing out that she exploited her sexuality through the 'fallen woman' roles in which she made her mark, it can also be argued that a more sympathetic interpretation should be offered. Having begun her career on the London stage in Adelphi melodramas, it is certainly true that she established herself in the part of the archetypal 'fallen woman', creating a sensation as Paula Tanquerary in *The Second Mrs Tanqueray* and consolidating her fame in similar roles specially written for her by the likes of Pinero, Haddon Chambers, and Jones. When free to choose her own parts under her own

Mrs Patrick Campbell (credit: Hal Linden, London).

management, however, she proved capable of a much wider range. Her productions of *Pelléas and Mélisande*, *Madame Sand*, and *The Matriarch*, for instance, all offered her opportunities to develop powerful and original female characters. Although financially unsuccessful, these productions gained Mrs Campbell artistic acclaim both as an actress and as a director. Her collaboration in the creation of Eliza Doolittle proved a high point in her career, displaying both her skill as an actress and her intelligence as an interpreter as well as her ability to work with such martinets as Shaw. Although she called herself 'amateurish', it is clear that Mrs Campbell conscientiously sought to learn her art and to be accepted as a serious actress. Repeatedly forced back into revivals of popular roles, she was torn between financial necessity and an artistic integrity that rebelled against the stereotyping influences that affected her career from the outset.

When actually on the stage, much of Mrs Campbell's appeal rested in her appearance. As a young woman, she was described as willowy and fragile-looking, her height accentuated by an almost gaunt demeanour that reflected the anxieties of overwork and lack of funds. This contributed to the aura of nervous intensity and emotional spontaneity that made her portrayals of female suffering so remarkable. She was also admired for her fluidity of movement and gesture, although she did not always maintain a continuous balance of tension throughout a play. Indeed, it was suggested that once she lost interest in a part she assumed a mechanical deliverance of lines without any attempt to disguise her boredom. Her almost black eyes, which she highlighted by using kohl and considerable quantities of white chalk body make-up, and abundant dark hair contributed to her sensual Italianate image. Her choice of wardrobe tended towards the classical drapery and exotic designs of the fin de siècle, but as photographs show the extremely low-cut ornate modern dresses that she chose for her most famous roles maximised the effects of her well-proportioned figure. Her voice was characterised by a rich silkiness and excellent elocution, which long outlived her other physical attributes, enabling her to work in radio and to lecture on the theatre later in her career. In middle age, her changed physical appearance made her unsuited to the roles of her youth and her increased weight countered the advantages of her height. She felt restricted on a small stage as she believed that only a large auditorium corresponded to her size and vocal powers. In her later years, she resisted being typecast in 'matronly' roles, despite Shaw's encouragement that she should progress to more mature character types, as she refused to forfeit the psychological and financial bonuses of star status. Her attempts to adapt to the thriving film businesss in the 1930's, as co-star to Peter Lorre and Norma Shearer among others, display not only her indefatigable spirit but also the inability of the theatre to accommodate an original, determined, idiosyncratic, and wilful actress of Mrs Campbell's stature.

—Samantha Johnson

CAPON, William. British set designer, artist, and architect. Born in Norwich, 6 October 1757. Began as portraitist but then studied architecture, assisting in design of Italian Opera House and Ranelagh Gardens. Worked on refurbishment of Haymarket Theatre, London, 1791 and built theatre at Belan House, Kildare, 1794; appointed scenic director, Theatre Royal, Drury Lane, under J. P. Kemble, 1794; drawings of interiors of Drury Lane and Covent Garden exhibited, 1800 and 1802; appointed architectural draughtsman to Duke of York, 1804; assisted in design of Royal Circus and Theatre Royal, Bath, 1805; set designer, Covent Garden, also under Kemble, from 1802; celebrated for historically authentic theatrical settings; also designed churches and researched plans of old palace of Westminster. Died in London, 26 September 1827.

Productions

1794   Oratorio (Handel), Theatre Royal, Drury Lane, London.
        Macbeth (Shakespeare), Theatre Royal, Drury Lane, London.
        The Cherokee (Storace), Theatre Royal, Drury Lane, London.
1795   *Jack of Newbury* (anon.), Theatre Royal, Drury Lane, London.
1796   The Iron Chest (Colman the Younger), Theatre Royal, Drury Lane, London.
        Richard III (Shakespeare), Theatre Royal, Drury Lane, London.
        Vortigern (Ireland), Theatre Royal, Drury Lane, London.

1800   De Montfort (Baillie), Theatre Royal, Drury Lane, London.
1801   Adelmorn, the Outlaw (Lewis), Theatre Royal, Drury Lane, London.
1805   Jane Shore (Rowe), Covent Garden, London.
1811   *Richard III* (Shakespeare), Covent Garden, London.
1812   *Hamlet* (Shakespeare), Covent Garden, London.

*

Bibliography

Books:
James Boaden, *Memoirs of the Life of John Philip Kemble*, London, 1825.

* * *

The considerable enlargement of both the patent theatres, Drury Lane and Covent Garden, during their rebuilding of the 1790's is usually accounted for by the rapid growth in the size of London's population and therefore the potential audience. This, of course, was an important factor, but central too was the fact that theatre was increasingly being considered a spectacle and required an appropriate scale and stage technology. The stage of the 18th century was one of rhetoric with an actively engaged *listening* audience that was rapidly disappearing to be replaced by the vast, more anonymous, *observing* spectator. Garrick and Loutherbourgh had, during their short partnership of the 1770's, created entertainments that offered picturesque and sublime scenes along with settings of such topographical accuracy that the idea of the theatre experience as one which could transport its audience — mistaking art for reality — became current and rapidly developed towards the close of the century.

The stage work of William Capon offered another crucial ingredient to this theatre experience, which not only expanded upon the work of Loutherbourgh, Richards, and Rooker, but laid the foundation stone on which the great 19th-century managers (Macready, Kean, and Irving) were to build their image of a carefully studied, educational, and above all, respectable theatre. Whilst Loutherbourgh offered mountain scenes, waterfalls, and crumbling rocks, Capon contributed to the romantic stage meticulously detailed and researched architectural scenes that he undertook for his principal patron, John Kemble, at Drury Lane and later at Covent Garden.

Capon's work corresponds closely to that of the fashionable antiquarian painters, the novels of Sir Walter Scott, and the general romantic enthusiasm for England's medieval and Tudor past. It is equally significant that the period of Capon's work also coincided with the beginnings of modern antiquarian scholarship — especially the studies of Edmond Malone, to whom Kemble dedicated his early pamphlet, *Macbeth Reconsidered* — into the nature and historicity of Shakespeare's plays. The designer's attitude and contribution paralleled this growing desire to conceive of Shakespeare's and his contemporaries' plays as being firmly bound within a period context with their own significant and important visual and architectural styles.

It is clear, from the very first responses of the audiences, that the fine Gothic detail, authoritative historicism and advertised accuracy of Capon's paintings, were timely, important, and well-received innovations although, as was still customary, he worked alongside other painters who chose to design individual scenes in plays according to their speciality. He worked primarily with such painters as Marinari and Greenwood on scenes for *Jack of Newbury*, *Richard III*, and William Ireland's forged Shakespearean fantasy, *Vortigern*. He also produced, in the best 18th-century tradition, stock 'generic' scenes for use in any and every one of the increasingly popular 'old English plays' in the repertoire.

The rebuilding of the patent houses in the 1790's, and again when the Covent Garden and Drury Lane theatres were destroyed by fire in 1808 and 1809, necessitated the urgent restocking of their scenic stores and Capon provided scenes of Gothic streets, chambers, and Tudor halls, which in the case of Covent Garden were still regularly in use in 1828. But these huge new stages also required and encouraged a new stagecraft, which suggests that Capon's innovations have an important scenographic and technical element as well as the purely aesthetic response to audience taste. The size, variety, and the sheer quantity of scenery becomes important to remark upon as does the fact that Capon was beginning to break away from the regularity of the purely two-dimensional painted wing shutters and back-scenes and to introduce significant quantities of large three-dimensional constructed scenic pieces. Indeed, Capon's first commission for Kemble in March 1794 was to convert the Drury Lane stage into the interior of a Gothic cathedral for its inaugural concert of music by Handel, and Kemble's biographer, James Boaden, excitedly described this as "an actual building of a gothic chapel".

There were, however, some serious drawbacks to this aspect of Capon's work, which have lived with the theatre and its designers ever since. For example, the 15 new scenes prepared for Kemble's *Macbeth* required the services of a scene-drop, to hide the lengthy scene-changes, which a testy critic referred to as the "perpetual curtain". George Colman complained of Capon's contribution in the published text of his play *The Iron Chest*: "My consent was, abruptly, requested to a transposition of two of the most material scenes in the second act: and the reason given for this curious proposal, that the present stage of Drury ... was so bunglingly constructed, that there was not time for the carpenters to place the lumbering framework on which an abbey was painted, behind the representations of a Library, without a chasm of ten minutes in the action of the Play; and that in the middle of an act ... " But this play, along with M. G. Lewis's *Adelmorn, the Outlaw* and Joanna Baillie's *De Montfort*, all with Capon's scenes, might also be termed 'modern' in the sense that they are all really rather trivial works, made stageworthy only on account of the opportunities that they offered for spectacle and scenic effect. The *European Magazine* in May 1801 reported on Baillie's play that: "The audience, however, though they rapturously applauded the Composer and the Scene Painter, hissed the dialogue almost from beginning to end", while the *Gentleman's Magazine* at the same time said: "The Artist, at great pains and labour, followed the style of building of the 15th century ... whereby, the spectator, for a short space, might indulge his imagination to believe he was in some religious pile".

The surviving designs and sketchbooks show intricately drawn 'caprices' of Tudor chambers and street scenes and

it is important to note that in spite of his vast knowledge of antiquarian architecture, Capon's visual image of the past was frequently as 'constructed' as that portrayed in Scott's novels. Looking at the designs and reading of Capon's intentions, it is hard not to agree smilingly with the Drury Lane manager, Sheridan, who called the designer 'Pompous Billy'. However, it should also be borne in mind that his place within the development of the scenic language of theatre and within this history Capon gave the energy of authority and research to the role of the designer. His influence in this respect upon such later artists as Stanfield, the Grieves, Lloyds, and Telbin was enormous. More controversially, perhaps, his work also confirms scenery's ever-present potential for becoming the leading performer in the theatre, which indeed it was to become in the sensation melodrama of the late 19th century and in the musical spectacular of modern times.

—Christopher Baugh

CARNOVSKY, Morris. US actor, director and teacher. Born in St Louis, Missouri, 5 September 1897. Educated at Teatman High School, St Louis, Missouri; University of Washington, 1920; trained for the stage under Emanuel Reacher, 1922. Married 1) Florence Lasersohn in 1922 (divorced 1933); 2) actress Phoebe Brand in 1941; one son. Stage debut, Boston, Massachussetts, 1919; acted with the Henry Jewitt Players and E. E. Clive's company, 1919–22; New York debut, Provincetown Playhouse, 1922; actor, Theatre Guild, New York, 1923–30; Group Theatre, New York, 1931–41; film debut, 1937; London debut, 1938; acted and directed with the Actors Laboratory Theatre, Hollywood, California, 1940–50; also made regular appearances at the American Shakespeare Festival in Stratford, Connecticut, from 1956. Died 1 September 1992.

Productions

As actor:

1922	Reb Aaron in *The God of Vengeance* (Asch), Provincetown Playhouse, New York.
1923	Commissioner of Police and the Magistrate in *The Failures*, Garrick Theatre, New York.
	La Hire and Brother Martin in *Saint Joan* (Lenihan), Garrick Theatre, New York.
1926	Philip Speed in *The Creaking Chair* (Wilkes), Lyceum Theatre, New York.
	General and Priest in *Juarez and Maximilian* (Werfel), Guild Theatre, New York.
	Second Federal Man in *Ned McCobb's Daughter* (Howard), John Golden Theatre, New York.
1927	Alypsha in *The Brothers Karamazov* (adapted from Dostoevsky), Guild Theatre, New York.
	Centuri and Aggazi in *Right You Are (If You Think You Are)* (Pirandello), Guild Theatre, New York.
	Dr Schutzmacher in *The Doctor's Dilemma* (G. B. Shaw), Guild Theatre, New York.
1928	Kublai the Great Kaan in *Marco Millions* (O'Neill), Guild Theatre, New York.

The Judge in *Volpone* (Jonson), Guild Theatre, New York.

1929   Bezchyba in *Camel Through the Needle's Eye* (Langer), Martin Beck Theatre, New York.

Uncle Vanya in *Uncle Vanya* (Chekhov), Morosco Theatre, New York.

1930   Nicobar in *The Apple Cart* (G. B. Shaw), Martin Beck Theatre, New York.

Stephen Field in *Hotel Universe* (Barry), Martin Beck Theatre, New York.

Francis Bacon in *Elizabeth the Queen* (M. Anderson), Guild Theatre, New York.

1931   Uncle Bob in *The House of Connelly* (Green), Martin Beck Theatre, New York.

Several roles in *1931* (revue), Mansfield Theatre, New York.

1932   Father Martinez in *Night over Taos* (M. Anderson), 48th Street Theatre, New York.

Rufus Sonnenberg in *Success Story* (Lawson), Maxine Elliott Theatre, New York.

1933   Levering in *Both Your Houses* (M. Anderson), Royale Theatre, New York.

Dr Levine in *Men in White* (Kingsley), Broadhurst Theatre, New York.

1934   Dr Lewis Golden in *Gentlewoman* (Lawson), Cort Theatre, New York.

Will Parrot in *Gold Eagle Guy* (Levy), Morosco Theatre, New York.

1935   Fayette in *Waiting for Lefty* (Odets), Longacre Theatre, New York.

Jacob in *Awake and Sing!* (Odets), Belasco Theatre, New York.

Leo Gordon in *Paradise Lost* (Odets), Longacre Theatre, New York.

1936   The Speaker in *The Case of Clyde Griffiths* (adapted from Dreiser's *An American Tragedy*), Ethel Barrymore Theatre, New York.

Dr Mahodan in *Johnny Johnson* (Green), 44th Street Theatre, New York.

1937   Mr Bonaparte in *Golden Boy* (Odets), Belasco Theatre, New York; St James's Theatre, London, 1938.

1938   Ben Stark in *Rocket to the Moon* (Odets), Belasco Theatre, New York.

1939   Captain Joshua in *Thunder Rock* (Ardrey), Mansfield Theatre, New York.

1940   Rosenberger in *Night Music* (Odets), Broadhurst Theatre, New York.

John Adams Kent in *Susannah and the Elders* (Bridie), Morosco Theatre, New York.

Mr Appopolous in *My Sister Eileen* (Fields and Chodorov), Biltmore Theatre, New York.

1942   David Cole in *Café Crown*, Cort Theatre, New York.

1943   Kulkov in *Counterattack*, Windsor Theatre, New York.

1948   Sam Blumenfield in *Joy to the World*, Plymouth Theatre, New York.

1950   Peter Stockmann in *An Enemy of the People* (Ibsen), Broadhurst Theatre, New York.

1951   Ratchett in *Let Me Hear the Melody*, Playhouse, Wilmington, Delaware.

1953   Aaron Katz and the Presiding Angel in *The World of Sholom Aleichem* (Samuel), Barbizon-Plaza, New York.

1954   Tzaddik in *The Dybbuk* (Ansky), Fourth Street Theatre, New York.

1955   Andrei in *The Three Sisters* (Chekhov), Fourth Street Theatre, New York; Stratford, Connecticut, 1969.

Priam in *Tiger at the Gates* (Fry), Plymouth Theatre, New York.

1956   Probus in *The Lovers*, Martin Beck Theatre, New York.

Earl of Salisbury in *King John* (Shakespeare), American Shakespeare Festival, Stratford, Connecticut.

Provost in *Measure for Measure* (Shakespeare), American Shakespeare Festival, Stratford, Connecticut; Phoenix Theatre, New York, 1957.

Gremio in *The Taming of the Shrew* (Shakespeare), American Shakespeare Festival, Stratford, Connecticut; Phoenix Theatre, New York, 1957.

1957   Shylock in *The Merchant of Venice* (Shakespeare), American Shakespeare Festival, Stratford, Connecticut; Goodman Memorial Theatre, Chicago, 1959; Globe Theatre, San Diego, California, 1961; Stratford, Connecticut, 1967.

Antonio in *Much Ado About Nothing* (Shakespeare), American Shakespeare Festival, Stratford, Connecticut.

Jacob Friedland in *Nude with Violin* (Coward), Belasco Theatre, New York.

1958   Claudius in *Hamlet* (Shakespeare), American Shakespeare Festival, Stratford, Connecticut.

Quince in *A Midsummer Night's Dream* (Shakespeare), American Shakespeare Festival, Stratford, Connecticut.

Mr Sacher in *The Cold Wind and the Warm* (Behrman), Morosco Theatre, New York.

1959   Capulet in *Romeo and Juliet* (Shakespeare), American Shakespeare Festival, Stratford, Connecticut.

Dr Caius in *The Merry Wives of Windsor* (Shakespeare), American Shakespeare Festival, Stratford, Connecticut.

1960   Feste in *Twelfth Night* (Shakespeare), American Shakespeare Festival, Stratford, Connecticut.

Prospero in *The Tempest* (Shakespeare), American Shakespeare Festival, Stratford, Connecticut; revived there, 1971.

Lepidus in *Antony and Cleopatra* (Shakespeare), American Shakespeare Festival, Stratford, Connecticut.

1961   The Logician in *Rhinoceros* (Ionesco), Longacre Theatre, New York.

Mr Baker in *Come Blow Your Horn* (Simon), Brooks Atkinson Theatre, New York.

Malvolio in *Twelfth Night* (Shakespeare), Globe Theatre, San Diego, California.

Edward IV in *Richard III* (Shakespeare), Globe Theatre, San Diego, California.

1962   Morris Siegal in *A Family Affair* (Ostrovsky), Billy Rose Theatre, New York.
        Azdak in *The Caucasian Chalk Circle* (Brecht), Goodman Memorial Theatre, Chicago.
1963   Lear in *King Lear* (Shakespeare), American Shakespeare Festival, Stratford, Connecticut; Schoenberg Hall, University of California, Los Angeles, and Pilgrimage Theatre, Hollywood, California, 1964; Stratford, Connecticut, 1975.
1965   Dr Max Faessler in *The Man with the Perfect Wife*, Coconut Grove Playhouse, Miami.
1967   Creon in *Antigone* (Anouilh), Stratford, Connecticut.
1969   Polonius in *Hamlet* (Shakespeare), Stratford, Connecticut.
        Galileo Galilei in *Lamp at Midnight*, tour.
1971–72 Role in *Swan Song* (Chekhov), Long Wharf Theatre, New Haven, Connecticut.
1976   Role in *Awake and Sing* (Odets), McCarter Theatre, Princeton.
1983   Firs in *The Cherry Orchard* (Chekhov), Long Wharf Theatre, New Haven, Connecticut.

As director:
1940–50 *Volpone* (Jonson), Actors Laboratory Theatre, Hollywood, California.
        The Dragon (Shvarts), Actors Laboratory Theatre, Hollywood, California.
        Monday's Heroes, Actors Laboratory Theatre, Hollywood, California.
        Distant Isles, Actors Laboratory Theatre, Hollywood, California.
1975   *Volpone* (Jonson), Laboratory Theatre, New York.

Films

As actor:
The Life of Emile Zola, 1937; *Tovarich*, 1937; *Edge of Darkness*, 1943; *Address Unknown*, 1944; *The Master Race*, 1944; *Our Vines Have Tender Grapes*, 1945; *Rhapsody in Blue*, 1945; *Cornered*, 1945; *Miss Susie Slagle's*, 1945; *Dead Reckoning*, 1947; *Dishonoured Lady*, 1947; *The Knockout*, 1947; *Saigon*, 1948; *Maneater of Kumaon*, 1948; *Siren of Atlantis*, 1948; *Gun Crazy*, 1949; *Thieves' Highway*, 1949; *Western Pacific Agent*, 1950; *Cyrano de Bergerac*, 1950; *The Second Woman*, 1951; *A View from the Bridge*, 1962; *The Gambler*, 1974.

Television

As actor:
Medea, 1961; *The World of Sholom Aleichem*, 1961; *Chicago Eight Conspiracy Trial*.

Publications

Group Theatre Sketches, 1935; *The Actor's Eye*, 1984.

*

Bibliography

Books:
Harold Clurman, *The Fervent Years: The Group Theatre and the Thirties*, New York, 1945.

* * *

In 1942, after the break-up of the Group Theatre, Morris Carnovsky was featured on Broadway in the popular comedy *My Sister Eileen*. When he was asked how his recent success made him feel, Carnovsky answered: "I have been in a success for ten years". By this he was referring to his membership of the Group Theatre since its inception in 1931. The beginnings of his career as an actor were in the 1920's, when he joined the Theatre Guild; among the plays in which he appeared with Lynn Fontanne and Alfred Lunt were *Saint Joan* and *Elizabeth the Queen*. When Harold Clurman, Cheryl Crawford and Lee Strasberg founded the Group Theatre in New York, Morris Carnovsky was one of the first actors to be recruited as a member of the company. The Group Theatre reacted against the externalized acting style that was prevalent in the commercial theatre of the time, and they adopted Strasberg's version of Stanislavsky's system for the training of actors and the interpretation of roles. Strasberg's Method was introspective and emphasized the importance of the "sense of truth" for the actor; the source of this truth should be the actor's own self, his or her personal intellectual and emotional experience.

Carnovsky embraced the Method with enthusiasm and claimed that, before joining the Group Theatre, he had "good instincts", but that he "was capable of acting truthfully up to a certain point". During his years with the Group Theatre he gained critical acclaim for his acting in such productions as *Night Over Taos*, *Waiting for Lefty*, *Awake and Sing!*, *Paradise Lost*, *Golden Boy*, *Rocket to the Moon* and *Johnny Johnson*. His interpretation of Jacob in *Awake and Sing!* was a popular success: "It is almost an impertinence to praise such a performance, so complete, so perfectly judged and balanced, so authentic in every detail of character, feeling, and action" one reviewer wrote. In *Paradise Lost*, he portrayed Leo Gordon, a challenging character who develops from a naive dreamer into a serious philosopher. In *Johnny Johnson*, he played a psychiatrist who is crazier than his patients, and in *Rocket to the Moon*, he interpreted the character of Ben as a boyish man who yearns for life but has a hard time connecting to it.

Carnovsky was also famous for his gibberish improvisations. These improvisations were among the exercises that the Group members included in their training in order to explore the expression of emotion independent from language. Carnovsky, together with Joe Bromberg, created some of the most comic improvisations in gibberish; Carnovsky usually played the part of the optimist who tried to convince the pessimist Bromberg to feel better about the state of the world.

The other actors of the Group called Carnovsky "the Dean" because, although only 34, he was one of the oldest members; besides, he liked to act as protector and advocate for the younger members of the Group. Nevertheless, in spite of his generally good relations with most of the Group members, a serious conflict broke out between Carnovsky and Stella Adler, another member of the Group, during the rehearsals for Harold Clurman's production of *The Three*

Sisters in 1939. Adler did not accept Carnovsky's criticism that she was not "a truthful actress" and Clurman was unable to control the friction between the two actors. Adler resigned and so did Clurman. Soon the project was abandoned. In many ways, this marked the beginning of the end for the Group Theatre, which was to be disbanded in 1941.

Carnovsky also worked in Hollywood. One of his most acclaimed film roles was that of Anatole France in *The Life of Emile Zola* in 1937. During the 1940's, he taught and directed plays at the Actors' Laboratory in Hollywood and acted in Broadway hits. Morris Carnovsky, together with other members of the Group Theatre in the 1930's, had been politically committed to the left. He believed that the only hope for justice in the US system and for resistance against fascism was to be found in the ideology of the American left. And like so many other artists and intellectuals, he was called to testify before the House Committee on Un-American Activities in 1951. Carnovsky refused to submit to the pressures of the Committee and chose to take the Fifth Amendment. As a result, he and his wife Phoebe Brand, a former member of the Group Theatre as well, faced many financial difficulties, as they were unable to get jobs in either film or theatre for a long time thereafter.

In the 1960's, Carnovsky associated himself with the American Shakespeare Festival at Stratford, Connecticut, and later on with the New York Shakespeare Festival. He appeared in several plays, including *King John* and *The Taming of the Shrew*, but his most famous interpretation was that of King Lear. Since his early years with the Group Theatre, he had been interested in the exploration of speech in poetic drama, and especially in Shakespeare. Carnovsky put less emphasis than Strasberg did on the actor's personal emotions and thus attempted to unite the psychological realism of the Method with the stylistic elements of poetic drama. In his 1984 book *The Actor's Eye*, a transcript of a series of acting workshops that he conducted at the Theatre Department of Brandeis, Carnovsky summarized what he thought were the main components of Stanislavsky's system in order for the students to use them toward the performance of Shakespearean roles. These components were Self, Action and Object. The actor's Self must be 'free', 'self-contained', 'receptive' and 'loving'. This Self has to establish on stage a 'vital connection with an Object'. Action then is what happens between Self and Object. In Carnovsky's words, "it is in the repercussion from Self to Object that the excitement of the moment is generated".

Carnovsky had a long and successful career as an actor and teacher of acting. Yet he always considered the years with the Group Theatre as the most important in his life. In the final paragraph of *The Actor's Eye* he refers to his and his colleagues' work in the Group Theatre as "an act of love". And he concludes: "That's how I still think about everything that an actor does with all his truth and depth. An act of love".

—Kiki Gounaridou

CASARÈS, Maria. French actress. Born Maria Casarès Quiroga in La Coruña, Spain, 21 November 1922. Studied at the Paris Conservatoire, 1930's. Settled in Paris during the Spanish Civil War; stage debut, in Paris, 1942; film debut, 1945; first appearance at the Comédie-Française, 1952–53; actress, Théâtre National Populaire, 1955–59; member of the company of the Comédie-Française from 1960.

Principal roles

1942	Role in *Deidre of the Sorrows* (Synge), Théâtre des Mathurins, Paris.
1943	Martha in *Le Malentendu* (Camus), Théâtre des Mathurins, Paris.
1945	Grusenka in *Les Frères Karamazov* (Copeau and Croué), Théâtre de l'Atelier, Paris.
1946	Jeanette in *Roméo et Jeanette* (Anouilh), Théâtre de l'Atelier, Paris.
1947	Role in *Les Épiphanies* (Pichette), Théâtre des Noctambules, Paris.
1948	Victoria in *L'État de siège* (Camus), Théâtre Marigny, Paris.
1949	Dora in *Les Justes* (Camus), Théâtre Hébertot, Paris.
1951	Hilda in *Le Diable et le bon Dieu* (Sartre), Théâtre Antoine, Paris.
	Role in *La Seconde* (Colette and Marchand), Théâtre de la Madeleine, Paris.
1952	Role in *Don Juan* (Molière), Comédie-Française, Paris.
	Role in *Carosse du Saint Sacrement*, Comédie-Française, Paris.
	Constance in *King John* (Shakespeare), Festival d'Angiers.
1953	Role in *La Dévotion à la Croix* (Camus, adapted from Calderón), Festival d'Angiers.
	Jeanne in *Jeanne d'Arc* (Péguy), Festival de Lyons.
	Phèdre in *Phèdre* (Racine), Comédie-Française, Paris.
1954	Role in *L'Ennemi* (Green), Théâtres des Bouffes du Nord, Paris.
	Lady Macbeth in *Macbeth* (Shakespeare), Avignon Festival.
	Doña Sol in *Ruy Blas* (Hugo), Théâtre National Populaire, Paris.
1955	Marie Tudor in *Marie Tudor* (Hugo), Théâtre National Populaire.
	La Princesse in *Le Triomphe de l'Amour* (Marivaux), Théâtre National Populaire.
1966	La Mère in *Les Paravents* (Genet), Odéon-Théâtre de France, Paris; Nanterre, 1983.

Other roles include: Medée in *Medée*, 1967; Mère Courage in *Mère Courage* (Brecht), 1968; Queen Victoria in *Early Morning* (Bond), 1970; Cleopatra in *Antony et Cléopatre* (Shakespeare), 1975.

Films

Les Enfants du Paradis, 1945; *Les Dames du Bois de Boulogne*, 1945; *Roger-la-Honte*, 1946; *La Revanche de Roger-le-Honte*, 1946; *L'Amour autour de la maison*, 1947; *La Chartreuse de Parme*, 1948; *Bagarres*, 1948; *La*

Maria Casarès (1949).

Septième porte, 1948; *L'Homme qui revient de loin*, 1950; *Orphée*, 1950; *Ombre et lumière*, 1951; *Le Testament d'Orphée*, 1959; *The Rebel Nun*, 1974; *Flavia*, 1976.

Publications

Résidente privilégiée, 1980.

* * *

Maria Casarès brought Castilian intensity to the French stage, becoming one of its great tragic actresses. Her most famous literary associations are with two very different writers, Albert Camus and Jean Genet. The fact that she came to France as a political refugee when Franco overthrew the Spanish republic in the Civil War of 1936–39 created an immediate affinity with Camus, a writer intensely hostile to fascism, who was later to resign from UNESCO in 1952 in protest against the admission of Franco's Spain. She performed two of Camus's favourite roles, Martha in *Le Malentendu* (*Cross Purposes*) and Dora in *Les Justes*. Casarès's performance in the role of Martha saved a bad play from total disaster and her highly successful performance as Death in Jean Cocteau's film *Orphée* made her one of the leading figures in the French cinema. She had dark eyes, jet-black hair combed back with the straightest of white partings in the middle, and played the part of Dora in Camus's play about the Russian revolutions of 1905 with such commitment that even the most conservative members of the audience felt that there might be something to be said for terrorism after all.

Camus's death in 1960 came a year after her five-year membership of the Théâtre National Populaire had come to an end and she had moved to the longer-established Comédie-Française. He would certainly not have approved of her accepting the part of the Mother in Jean Genet's play *Les Paravents* (*The Screens*), a vast and rather rambling account of the defeat of the French by the Algerian Front de Libération Nationale in the 1954–60 war. The role nevertheless confirmed her status as a Grand Guignol character actress and showed that she could from time to time move out of the great tragic roles to which her physique and style naturally destined her.

While at the TNP, she had played a terrifying Lady Macbeth and in 1975 she consolidated her standing in Shakespeare by becoming perhaps the finest French actress to portray his Cleopatra. Her Phèdre in 1958 had been controversial, however, bringing against her the charge of over-acting. The incestuous passion that Thesée's wife feels for her stepson Hippolyte was more marked than the feelings of guilt that Racine's last pagan heroine feels for her crime and the view of the more hostile French critics tended to be that the role needed more intellectual awareness and less Castilian passion. Others saw it as one of the great performances of the role. Casarès, they maintained, was reacting against a tradition that had grown up whereby actresses played Phèdre as a woman sorry for herself — though this was not the way the actress herself saw the part, envisaging instead a woman who was consumed by passion and with burning self-hatred. When she seized Hippolyte's sword, it was not as a phallic object with which to pleasure herself but as the means whereby she might genuinely die by the hand of the man she most loved. Highlights of her career since then have ranged from the decrepit central role in Brecht's *Mother Courage* to a very interesting and dignified Queen Victoria in Bond's *Early Morning*.

Together with Gérard Philipe, Casarès was the great revelation of the Théâtre National Populaire, brilliant as the princess in disguise in the 1955 production of Marivaux's *Le Triomphe de l'Amour* and a superb Doña Sol in harmony with Philipe's Ruy Blas. Most of all, she remains an example of the catholicity of French theatrical culture and especially its ability to absorb talent from the Iberian peninsula, familiar as the source of inspiration for plays by Corneille and Molière and a setting for Beaumarchais.

—Philip Thody

CASSON, (Sir) Lewis (Thomas). British actor and director. Born in Birkenhead, 26 October 1875. Educated at Ruthin Grammar School. Married actress Sybil Thorndike (*q.v.*) in 1908, two sons and two daughters. Amateur debut, 1900; first professional appearance, Royalty Theatre, London, 1903; subsequently acted under the Barker-Vedrenne management at the Court Theatre, London, 1904–07, and with Annie Horniman's company at the Gaiety Theatre, Manchester, 1908–09; New York debut, 1910; director, Gaiety Theatre, Manchester, 1911–13; director, Royalty Theatre, Glasgow, 1914; served in Royal Engineers, 1915–18; director, Little Theatre, London, from 1920; manager, with Thorndike, of the New Theatre, London, from 1922; film debut, 1933; television debut, 1946; often appeared with and directed Thorndike both in London and on frequent British and overseas tours. Member: Council for the Encouragement of Music and the Arts (hon. drama adviser), 1940; Actors' Equity (president, 1940–45); Arts Council (drama director, 1942–45). Fellow, Imperial College of Science and Technology, 1959. LL.D: University of Glasgow, 1954, University of Wales, 1959; D.Litt: University of Oxford, 1966. MC (Military Cross), 1917. Knighted, 1945. Died in London, 16 May 1969.

Roles

As actor:

1903   Polixenes in *The Winter's Tale* (Shakespeare), Royalty Theatre, London.

        Cassius in *Julius Caesar* (Shakespeare), Royalty Theatre, London.

1904   First Outlaw and Eglamour in *The Two Gentlemen of Verona* (Shakespeare), Court Theatre, London.

        Servilius in *Timon of Athens* (Shakespeare), Court Theatre, London.

        Don Pedro in *Much Ado About Nothing* (Shakespeare), Court Theatre, London.

        Pico del Amare in *The Prayer of the Sword* (Fagan), Adelphi Theatre, London.

1904–07 Statue of Love in *Prunella* (Housman and Granville-Barker), Court Theatre, London; Duke of York's Theatre, London, 1910; Gaiety Theatre, Manchester, 1911.

        Octavius Robinson in *Man and Superman* (G. B. Shaw), Court Theatre, London.

        Castor in *Electra* (Euripides), Court Theatre, London.

        Sidi el Assif in *Captain Brassbound's Conversion* (G. B. Shaw), Court Theatre, London; Middle East and Australian tour, 1932.

        Mr Danby in *The Doctor's Dilemma* (G. B. Shaw), Court Theatre, London.

        The Magistrate's Clerk in *The Silver Box* (Galsworthy), Court Theatre, London.

        Allen Trent in *Votes for Women* (Robins), Court Theatre, London.

1905   Rosencrantz and Laertes in *Hamlet* (Shakespeare), Adelphi Theatre, London.

        Dante in *Beatrice*, Court Theatre, London.

1907   Troilus in *Troilus and Cressida* (Shakespeare), Great Queen Street Theatre, London.

        Chaplain Brudenell in *The Devil's Disciple* (G. B. Shaw), Savoy Theatre, London.

        Messenger in *Medea* (Euripides), Savoy Theatre, London; Holborn Empire, London, 1920; Prince's Theatre, London, 1927; South African tour, 1928; New Theatre, London, 1941.

1909   James Roden in *The Fires of Fate* (Conan Doyle), Haymarket Theatre, London.

1910   The Doctor in *Justice* (Galsworthy), Duke of York's Theatre, London.

        Mr Brigstock in *The Madras House* (Granville-Barker), Duke of York's Theatre, London.

        Osier in *The Sentimentalists* (Meredith), Duke of York's Theatre, London.

        Fenwick in *Chains* (Baker), Duke of York's Theatre, London.

        Fletcher in *Smith* (Maugham), Empire Theatre, New York.

1911   John Curtis in *Elaine* (Chapin), Gaiety Theatre, Manchester; Court Theatre, London, 1913.

1913   Brutus in *Julius Caesar* (Shakespeare), Gaiety Theatre, Manchester.

1914   John Tanner in *Man and Superman* (G. B. Shaw), Royalty Theatre, Glasgow.

1919   Constant in *The Provoked Wife* (Vanbrugh), King's Hall, Covent Garden, London.

        Le Bret in *Cyrano de Bergerac* (Rostand, adapted by Thomas and Guillemand), Garrick Theatre, London.

1920   Paul Marketel in *A Chinese Puzzle* (Bower and Lion), Grand Theatre, Croydon, London.

        Poseidon and Talthybius in *The Trojan Women* (Euripides), Holborn Empire, London.

        Reverend James Morrell in *Candida* (G. B. Shaw), Holborn Empire, London.

        Robert Darzac in *The Mystery of the Yellow Room* (Leroux, adapted by Bennett), St James's Theatre, London.

1922   Admiral Gravières and the Préfet in *The Scandal* (Hamilton), New Theatre, London.

        The Judge in *The Cenci* (Shelley), New Theatre, London; Empire Theatre, London, 1926.

1925   De Stogumber in *Saint Joan* (G. B. Shaw), Regent Theatre, London, 1925; Lyceum Theatre, London, 1926; Théâtre des Champs-Elysées, Paris, 1927; South African tour, 1928; His Majesty's Theatre, London, 1931; Middle East and Australian tour, 1932.

        Tom Edgeworthy in *The Verge* (Glaspell), Regent Theatre, London.

        The Passenger in *The Round Table* (Robinson), Wyndham's Theatre, London.

        Griffith in *Henry VIII* (Shakespeare), Empire Theatre, London.

1926   Father Silvain in *Israel* (Bernstein, adapted by Isaacs), Strand Theatre, London.

        The Nameless Man in *Granite* (Dane), Ambassadors' Theatre, London; British tour, 1930; Middle East and Australian tour, 1932.

        Buckingham and Griffith in *Henry VIII* (Shakespeare), British tour.

1927   Polusky and Colonel Schultz in *The Greater Love* (Fagan), Prince's Theatre, London.

        Valentine in *Angela* (Bell), Prince's Theatre, London.

        Petruchio in *The Taming of the Shrew* (Shakespeare), Lyric Theatre, Hammersmith, London.

        Shylock in *The Merchant of Venice* (Shakespeare), Lyric Theatre, Hammersmith, London.

        Benedick in *Much Ado About Nothing* (Shakespeare), Lyric Theatre, Hammersmith, London.

Lewis Casson

	Henry in *Henry V* (Shakespeare), Lyric Theatre, Hammersmith, London.
1928	Arrophernes in *Judith of Israel* (Baruch), Strand Theatre, London.
	Henry Clegg in *Jane Clegg* (Ervine), South African tour; Wyndham's Theatre, London, 1929.
1929	Professor Adolphus Cusins in *Major Barbara* (G. B. Shaw), Wyndham's Theatre, London.
	Reverend Benjamin Cobb in *Mariners* (Dane), Wyndham's Theatre, London.
	Jason in *Medea* (Euripides), Wyndham's Theatre, London.
	Sir Charles Denbury in *Exiled* (Galsworthy), Wyndham's Theatre, London.
	Napoleon Bonaparte in *Madame Plays Nap* (Girvin and Cozens), New Theatre, London; Middle East and Australian tour, 1932.
1930	Reverend Herbert Messiter in *The Devil* (Hamilton), Arts Theatre, London.
	Socrates in *Socrates*, Prince of Wales's Theatre, London.
	Professor Zeigher in *Moloch* (Carter), Strand Theatre, London.
1931	Armand Fontaine in *Marriage by Instalments* (Passeur, adapted by Clive), Embassy Theatre, London.
	Michael Townsend in *Late Night Final* (Weitzenkorn), Phoenix Theatre, London.

	Walter Fane in *The Painted Veil* (Maugham), Playhouse, London; Middle East and Australian tour, 1932.
	Lennox in *Bluestone Quarry*, Duchess Theatre, London.
1932	Macbeth in *Macbeth* (Shakespeare), Middle East and Australian tour.
1933	Baron Stein in *Diplomacy* (Stephenson and Scott), Prince's Theatre, London.
	Stanislas Rosing in *Ballerina* (Ackland), Gaiety Theatre, London.
	Sir Jafna Pandranath in *On the Rocks* (G. B. Shaw), Winter Garden Theatre, London.
1934	The English Chaplain in *Nurse Cavell* (Roberts and Forester), Q Theatre, London, and Vaudeville Theatre, London.
	Dr Braddock in *Men in White* (Kingsley), Lyric Theatre, London.
	The Mayor in *Overture 1920*, Phoenix Theatre, London.
	Supt. Harrison in *Line Engaged* (Leon and Celestin), Duke of York's Theatre, London.
	Reverend Percy Huntbach in *Flowers of the Forest* (Buckstone), Whitehall Theatre, London.
1935	Owen Glendower in *Henry IV, part 1* (Shakespeare), His Majesty's Theatre, London; King's Theatre, Hammersmith, London, 1953.
	Quince in *A Midsummer Night's Dream* (Shakespeare), Open Air Theatre, London.
	Lord Palmerston in *Victoria Regina* (Housman), Broadhurst Theatre, New York.
1937	George Loveless in *Six Men of Dorset* (Malleson), British tour.
	Judge Vlora in *Judgment Day* (Rice), Phoenix Theatre, London.
1938	Baron Krug in *Power and Glory* (Cannan and Bost, adapted from Greene), Savoy Theatre, London.
	Sir Anthony Absolute in *The Rivals* (Sheridan), Old Vic Theatre, London; Mediterranean tour, 1939.
1939	Polonius in *Hamlet* (Shakespeare), Mediterranean tour.
	Sir William Gower in *Trelawny of the Wells* (Pinero), Mediterranean tour.
	Judge Tuttington in *Libel* (Dorane), Mediterranean tour.
	Dr Gortler in *I Have Been Here Before* (Priestley), Mediterranean tour.
	Colonel Pickering in *Pygmalion* (G. B. Shaw), Haymarket Theatre, London.
1940	Gonzalo in *The Tempest* (Shakespeare), Old Vic Theatre, London.
1941	Pandulph in *King John* (Shakespeare), British tour and New Theatre, London.
	Philip, the Bastard, in *King John* (Shakespeare), British tour.
1941–42	Morell in *Candida* (G. B. Shaw), British tour.
	Prologue and First Chorus in *Jacob's Ladder* (Housman), British tour.
1943	Mayor Orden in *The Moon is Down* (Steinbeck), Whitehall Theatre, London.

1945	Warwick in *Saint Joan* (G. B. Shaw), British and European tour; King's Theatre, Hammersmith, London, 1946.
1946	President Woodrow Wilson in *In Time to Come* (Knoch and Huston), King's Theatre, Hammersmith, London.
1947	Dr Marshall in *A Sleeping Clergyman* (Bridie), Citizens' Theatre, Glasgow.
	The Priest in *The Righteous Are Bold*, Citizens' Theatre, Glasgow.
	Edmund, Duke of York, in *Richard II* (Shakespeare), New Theatre, London.
	Professor Robert Linden in *The Linden Tree* (Priestley), Duchess Theatre, London.
1949	Simon Bracken in *The Foolish Gentlewoman* (Sharp), Duchess Theatre, London.
	Eustace Mills in *Treasure Hunt* (Farrell and Perry), Apollo Theatre, London; British tour, 1950.
1950	Lord Randolph in *Douglas* (Home), Edinburgh Festival.
1951	Antigonus in *The Winter's Tale* (Shakespeare), Phoenix Theatre, London.
1952	Leonato in *Much Ado About Nothing* (Shakespeare), Phoenix Theatre, London.
	Friar Lawrence in *Romeo and Juliet* (Shakespeare), Old Vic Theatre, London.
1953	Tiresias in *Oedipus* (Sophocles), King's Theatre, Hammersmith, London.
	Earl of Gloucester in *King Lear* (Shakespeare), King's Theatre, Hammersmith, London.
	David Anson in *A Day by the Sea* (Hunter), Haymarket Theatre, London.
1955	Northbrook in *The Sleeping Prince* (Rattigan), tour of Australia and New Zealand.
	Mr Fowler in *Separate Tables* (Rattigan), tour of Australia and New Zealand.
1956	Dr Warburton in *The Family Reunion* (Eliot), Phoenix Theatre, London.
	Sir Patrick Cullen in *The Doctor's Dilemma* (G. B. Shaw), Saville Theatre, London.
1957	Dr Frederick Baston in *The Potting Shed* (Greene), Bijou Theatre, London.
	The Judge in *The Chalk Garden* (Bagnold), tour of Australia and New Zealand.
1959	Sir Horace Darke in *Eighty in the Shade* (Dane), Globe Theatre, London.
1960	Osgood Meeker in *Waiting in the Wings* (Coward), Duke of York's Theatre, London, and British tour.
1961	Father-General in *Teresa of Avila* (Williamson), Olympia Theatre, Dublin, and Vaudeville Theatre, London.
1962	Telyegin in *Uncle Vanya* (Chekhov), Festival Theatre, Chichester.
1963	Harding in *Queen B* (Guthrie), Theatre Royal, Windsor, and British tour.

Also acted roles in: *The Duke of Killicrankie* (Marshall), British tour, 1903; *Trelawny of the Wells* (Pinero), Duke of York's Theatre, London, 1910; *The Lie* (H. A. Jones), South African tour, 1928; *The Silver Cord* (Howard), South African tour, 1928; *The Squall* (Bart), British tour, 1930; *Ghosts* (Ibsen), British tour, 1930; *The Matchmaker's Arms*

(Dukes), British tour, 1930; *Milestones* (Bennett and Knoblock), Middle East and Australian tour, 1932; *Advertising April* (Farjeon and Horsnell), Middle East and Australian tour, 1932; *To-Night at 8.30* (Coward), British tour, 1936; *Village Wooing* (G. B. Shaw), British tour, 1936; *Hippolytus* (Euripides), British tour, 1936; *Romeo and Juliet* (Shakespeare), King's Theatre, Hammersmith, London, 1946; *The Wise Have Not Spoken* (Carroll), King's Theatre, Hammersmith, London, 1946; *Man and Superman* (G. B. Shaw), King's Theatre, Hammersmith, London, 1946; *Electra* (Euripides), King's Theatre, Hammersmith, London, 1946.

As director:

1908	*Hippolytus* (Euripides, translated by Murray), Gaiety Theatre, Manchester.
1911	The Marriage of Columbine (Chapin), Gaiety Theatre, Manchester.
1912	*Hindle Wakes* (Houghton), Gaiety Theatre, Manchester.
1912–13	*Jane Clegg* (Ervine), Gaiety Theatre, Manchester.
	Revolt (Calderón), Gaiety Theatre, Manchester; acted Vernon Hodder.
	The Whispering Well (Rose), Gaiety Theatre, Manchester.
1913	*The Shadow* (Phillpotts), Gaiety Theatre, Manchester.
	The Threshold, Gaiety Theatre, Manchester.
1914	*Marigold* (Harker and Pryor), Royalty Theatre, Glasgow.
	The Golden Fleece, Haymarket Theatre, London.
	A Woman Alone (Clifford), Little Theatre, London.
1920	*Jane Clegg* (Ervine), New Theatre, London; acted Mr Morrison.
1923	*Advertising April* (Farjeon and Horsnell), Criterion Theatre, London.
	Cymbeline (Shakespeare), New Theatre, London; acted Arviragus and Philario.
	The Lie (H. A. Jones), New Theatre, London.
1924	*Saint Joan* (G. B. Shaw), New Theatre, London; acted de Stogumber.
	Masses and Man (Toller), New Theatre, London; acted the Guide.
1926	*Macbeth* (Shakespeare), Prince's Theatre, London; acted Banquo.
1927	*Medea* (Euripides), Théâtre des Champs-Elysées, Paris; acted Jason.
1935	*Days Without End* (O'Neill), Grafton Theatre, London; British tour, 1945.
1936	*My Son, My Son* (Lawrence and Greenwood), British tour.
1937	*I Have Been Here Before* (Priestley), Royalty Theatre, London; acted Dr Gortler.
	The Trojan Women (Euripides), Adelphi Theatre, London; acted Talthybius and Poseidon.
1938	*Coriolanus* (Shakespeare), Old Vic Theatre, London.
	Henry V (Shakespeare), Theatre Royal, Drury Lane, London.
	Man and Superman (G. B. Shaw), Old Vic Theatre, London.

1940   *King Lear* (Shakespeare), Old Vic Theatre, London; acted Kent.
        Macbeth (Shakespeare), Welsh tour; acted Macbeth.
1945   *Sheppey* (Maugham), British tour.

*

Bibliography

Books:
John Casson, *Lewis and Sybil*, London, 1972.

* * *

Lewis Casson was a leader of his profession. A man of religious temperament and a stalwart socialist who believed in the deeply civilising power of theatre, he was one of the founders of the Arts Council (formerly the Council for the Encouragement of Music and the Arts) as the key organisation in state funding of the arts in Britain — and its first Drama Director. His devotion and organisational skills were also called on for a period of service as President of Equity, the actors' trade union. He had entered the profession relatively late, having decided that he had no vocation for the priesthood, and with experience of teaching as well as assisting his father in the building of organs. The route he took was through amateur performances of Shakespeare, under producers who had a strong and particular interest in vocal delivery: first a professor of elocution, Charles Fry, then the champion of Elizabethan staging, William Poel. Other Shakespeareans with whom he toured briefly in his early days were Ben Greet and Harcourt Williams.

Casson became an authority on Poel's methods of teaching and directing actors and was himself outstandingly successful in mastering the 'tunes', the intonational patterns and management of stresses to ensure maximum audibility and intelligibility in combination with brisk, speeded-up delivery. The doyenne of voice teachers and therapists in the first half of the 20th century, Elsie Fogerty, who had also acted for Poel, declared of Casson: "It's the best voice on the stage — the purest production"; and Sybil Thorndike, who became Mrs Casson in 1908, recalled the first time she observed him in rehearsal: "he spoke so fast that it woke you up and made you puzzle a bit". In old age she said: "Lewis used to have more notes in his voice than anyone I've ever known — three octaves — and a wonderful ear".

The formulation of Casson's vision of what the theatre might be was completed through his work with another of Poel's disciples, Harley Granville-Barker. When Casson was engaged to play in Barker's production of *The Two Gentlemen of Verona* in 1904 the latter was already responsible, with William Archer, for a 'Scheme and Estimates for a National Theatre' and was about to demonstrate at the Court Theatre over a three-year period the quality of work that such a theatre could give. Casson participated in those seasons, filling minor roles but thrilling audiences when, as the Statue of Love in *Prunella*, he revealed the full glory of his voice. He later recalled Barker's custom at that time of gathering his actors round a table to begin their mutual exploration of the play and even discouraging private study in the interests of a complete ensemble effect. Shortly afterwards, when Barker had no

company or theatre, Casson went to the Gaiety Theatre, Manchester, where Miss Annie Horniman's new company was to pursue similar aims to the historic Court Theatre enterprise and, indeed, to revive some of the plays first performed there. Sybil Thorndike also joined the Gaiety company and wrote at the time: "Casson's acting interests me — you're frightfully conscious of a brain, not so much that he's *become* the person but as if he was making *you* see the person and he was giving you suggestions ... and his speed is most exhilarating". This sounds rather like a Brechtian actor before his time.

However, Casson must have become aware quite soon that he lacked qualities that might transform him into more than a moderate, reliable performer. Even William Poel, when he went to Manchester to produce *Measure for Measure*, reluctantly demoted Casson to the role of Provost instead of allowing him to play the Duke as originally intended, finding him not sprightly enough. Not until he was over 70 did he achieve unqualified success in a leading role, in J. B. Priestley's *The Linden Tree*, though his playing of the Chaplain, de Stogumber, in the British première of *Saint Joan* was warmly received at an earlier date. Of the latter, his son, John Casson, recalled that he performed "with a realism, a humour, and a passion that I had never seen in his acting before". His name appeared on the programme as producer of the play; in fact, he assisted Bernard Shaw rather as Barker had assisted with most of the Shaw plays first produced at the Court Theatre. Though he quite often played the male leads in his own productions on tour, all his efforts were supportive of the true acting genius in the family: his wife.

Periods as director of the Manchester Gaiety company and of the Glasgow Repertory company followed on from occasional productions for experimental groups such as the Literary Theatre Society and gave way, in turn, to spells in management — with Bruce Winston, then with the backing of Lady Wyndham (handing on to her son Bronson Albery), or with his wife. His range as a director matched hers as an actress, embracing contemporary Grand Guignol as well as Greek tragedy, Shakespeare, modern naturalistic plays and Toller's expressionist *Masses and Man* for the Stage Society in 1924. Casson's idea of naturalism differed from that of most young actors after World War II. He used to say that the naturalness that won critics' praise at the Court Theatre in the early years of the century was the result of elaborately calculated artistry. He insisted that all acting is artifice and all stage speech a form of rhetoric, though the scale of a performance should always correspond to the size of the building in which it is given. In an article for the Citizens' Theatre Society's magazine, he called for the individual actor to assert himself and not be swamped by the co-operative art involving all the others who contribute to a production. In practice, he was a severe, meticulous, insistent director, who could drive actors half-mad until they had mastered the effects he sought. As an old man he admitted to having always paid most attention to vocal acting, and that not all actors responded well to practising exercises around a table, though he claimed to having tried to build their good ideas into his productions.

Casson never ceased to regret Granville-Barker's withdrawal from the theatre and succeeded in bringing him back to take three weeks' rehearsals for *King Lear* (with John Gielgud) at the Old Vic in 1940. His hope remained that Barker would return to head the National Theatre, when at last it was established. The role of disciple, not messiah, was always Lewis Casson's choice.

—Margery Morgan

CHEKHOV, Michael. Russian actor, director and theorist. Born Mikhail Aleksandrovich Chekhov in St Petersburg, 16 August 1891; nephew of playwright Anton Chekhov. Trained for the stage at A. S. Suvorin's theatre school in St Petersburg, 1908–11. Married 1) his cousin actress Olga Chekhov in 1914 (divorced 1918), one daughter; 2) Xenia Siller. Stage debut as actor with the Literary-Artistic Society, St Petersburg, 1911; actor, First Studio, Moscow Art Theatre, from 1913; film debut, 1913; director, Chekhov Studio, 1919–22; artistic director, Second Moscow Art Academic Theatre, 1924–28; emigrated, 1928; acted with Max Reinhardt's company in Berlin, 1928–30; subsequently worked in Vienna and Paris; actor, Latvian State Theatre, Riga, 1932–33; also worked as director in Kaunas, Lithuania, before travelling to New York with an emigré company, the Moscow Art Players, 1935; founder, Chekhov Theatre Studio, based at Dartington Hall, Devonshire, and (from 1939) at Ridgefield, Connecticut, 1936–42; subsequently concentrated on career as teacher and as an actor in Hollywood movies. Honoured Artist of the Republic, 1924. Died in Beverly Hills, California, 30 September 1955.

Roles

1911	Tsar Fyodor in *Tsar Fyodor Ivanovich* (A. Tolstoy), Suvorin Theatre, St Petersburg.
1913	Kobus in *Op Hoop van Zegen* [The Wreck of 'The Hope'] (Heijermans), First Studio, Art Theatre, Moscow.
1914	Caleb Plummer in *Svercok na peci* [The Cricket on the Hearth] (Suskevic and Uralsky, adapted from Dickens), First Studio, Art Theatre, Moscow.
1915	Frazer in *The Deluge* (Berger), First Studio, Art Theatre, Moscow.
1917	Malvolio in *Twelfth Night* (Shakespeare), First Studio, Art Theatre, Moscow.
1921	Erik in *Erik XIV* (Strindberg), First Studio, Art Theatre, Moscow.
	Khlestakov in *Revizor* [The Government Inspector] (Gogol), Art Theatre, Moscow; New York, 1935.
1924	Hamlet in *Hamlet* (Shakespeare), Art Theatre, Moscow; Paris, 1931–32.
1925	Senator Ableukhov in *The Death of a Senator* (adapted from Bely's *Petersburg*), Art Theatre, Moscow.
1927	Muromsky in *Delo* [The Case] (Sukhovo-Kobylin), Art Theatre, Moscow.
1928	Skid in *Artisten* (Watter and Hopkins), Deutsches Theater, Berlin.
1932–33	Ivan the Terrible in *Smert Ioanna grotznogo* [The Death of Ivan the Terrible] (A. Tolstoy), Latvian State Theatre, Riga.

	Foma Opiskin in *Foma* (adapted from Dostoevsky's *The Village of Stepanchikovo*), Latvian State Theatre, Riga.
1935	Ivan Alexandrovich in *Revizor* [The Government Inspector] (Gogol), Majestic Theatre, New York.
	Lyubim Tortsov in *Bednost ne porok* [Poverty is No Crime] (Ostrovsky), New York.

Productions as director included: *The Possessed* (Dostoevsky); *Twelfth Night* (Shakespeare); *The Cricket on the Hearth* (Dickens); *King Lear* (Shakespeare); all with the Chekhov Theatre Studio, from 1936.

Films

As actor:

Trechsotletie carstvovaniya Doma Romanovich, 1913; *Chirurgiya, 1913; Kogda zcucat struny serdca*, 1914; *Svercok na peci* [The Cricket on the Hearth], 1915; *Skaf s sjurprizom*, 1915; *Lyubvi sjurprizy tscetnye*, 1916; *Celovek iz retorana* [The Waiter], 1927; *Phantome des Glucks*, 1929; *Troika*, 1930; *In Our Time*, 1944; *Song of Russia*, 1944; *Spellbound*, 1945; *Spectre of the Rose*, 1945; *Cross My Heart*, 1945; *Abie's Irish Rose*, 1946; *Arch of Triumph*, 1947; *Texas, Brooklyn and Heaven*, 1948; *Invitation*, 1952; *Holiday for Sinners*, 1952; *Rhapsody*, 1954.

Publications

Put aktoryora [The Path of an Actor] (autobiography), 1928; *Chekhov Theatre Studio — Dartington Hall*, 1936; *Chekhov Theatre Studio*, 1939; *O tekhnike aktyora* [On the Actor's Technique], 1946; *To the Actor, on the Technique of Acting*, 1953; *To the Director and Playwright*, edited by Charles Leonard, 1963; *Lessons for the Professional Actor*, edited by Deirdre Hurst du Prey, 1985.

*

Bibliography

Books:
Lendley C. Black, *Mikhail Chekhov as Actor, Director and Teacher*, Ann Arbor, Michigan, 1987.

Articles:
Margarita Woloschin, "Michael Chekhov: The Actor as Conscious Artist", *Journal for Anthroposophy*, 27, 1978.
Michael Chekhov issue, *The Drama Review*, 27, 1983.
N. A. Krimova, "Mikhail Tchékov et Stanislavski", *Bouffonneries*, 20/21, 1989.
Deirdre Hurt du Prey, "Mikhail Tchékov: Le théâtre de l'avenir", *Bouffoneries*, 20/21, 1989.

* * *

Michael Chekhov was the son of a talented but alcoholic journalist and was a nephew of the writer Anton Chekhov. He first attracted attention as an actor when he played Tolstoy's Tsar Fyodor and subsequently entered the Moscow Art Theatre, where his creative personality continued to develop under the influence of Stanislavsky, Vakhtangov and Sulerzhitsky. Here he became acquainted with the yogic principle of 'prana', which helped the actor transfer his 'radiance' to the spectator. Acting for both the First Studio and the Moscow Art Theatre proper, he distinguished himself in such parts as the harried businessman Frazer in Berger's *The Deluge*, an untraditionally lecherous Malvolio in *Twelfth Night* and as the psychotic king in Strindberg's *Eric XIV*.

Chekhov walked a complicated path from abstract homilies of virtue, beauty and moral perfection to the incarnation of the tragedy of a person caught between two worlds. On the stage of the Moscow Art Theatre in 1924, he created a mythomaniacal Khlestakov in Gogol's *The Government Inspector*, a stunning performance that confirmed him as one of the most brilliant actors in the Soviet theatre.

As head of the Chekhov Studio (1919–22), he based his work on Stanislavsky's System, experimenting in perfecting the actor's technique; but he found the concept of 'emotional memory' less valuable than that of imagination. Many of his students, particularly Maria Knebel, were later to preserve and disseminate his ideas, long after Stanislavsky had become canonized at all Stalinist drama schools. After Vakhtangov died in 1922, Chekhov was named director of the First Studio, which was subsequently renamed the Moscow Art Theatre II.

The Revolution had bred acute depression in Chekhov, and he sought consolation in the mystical theories of the philosopher V. Solovyov, and particularly the anthroposophy of Rudolph Steiner and its theory of movement, eurhythmy. The notion of a spiritual world accessible to everyone's latent awareness led Chekhov to work towards an 'enhanced consciousness' to crystallize the perception of this transcendental sphere. Conventional critics read these motifs in his directing and acting as insistence on ruin and decay. His performances took on a tenebrous colouration, which accentuated the notes of suffering and unease. In *Hamlet* (1924), he underlined the theme of tragic desperation, interpreting the hero on a mystical plane bordering on true madness. This decadent philosophy took him beyond Stanislavsky to the latter's discomfort, and his considerable talent did wonders with such roles as Senator Ableukhov in Andrei Bely's *Petersburg* (1925) and Muromsky in Sukhovo-Kobylin's *The Case* (1927), both feeble old men caught in a web of intrigue. These interpretations were distinguished by novelty, audacity of concept and virtuosic transformations. The sharp outlines of the characters' outward appearance and a profound lyricism embodied in the subtle intonations of his melodic voice, brilliant improvisations and complete control of his physicality made his performances emotionally striking. But he insisted on his own distance from his creations, claiming that he imitated an image without introducing features of his own personality.

Chekhov began his film career in 1913 and made his best silent appearances in the 1915 version of *The Cricket on the Hearth* and in *The Waiter* (1927), a bitterly satirical work directed by Protazanov. Conflicts between his artistic vision and the demands of a Soviet bureaucracy that denounced his idealism, however, led him to leave the USSR in 1928 and to continue his career on stage and screen first in Europe and finally in the US. Notable were his creations of two new roles, Tolstoy's Ivan the Terrible

and Dostoevsky's hypocrite Foma Opiskin while at the Latvian State Theatre in Riga (1932–33).

Chekhov arrived in New York in 1935 with a troupe of emigré actors, and, though he won only modest praise as Khlestakov and Lyubim Tortsov, was subsequently invited by the wealthy young actress Beatrice Straight to found a school. The Chekhov Theatre Studio was based initially at Dartington Hall but, with the coming of war in 1939, was transferred to Ridgefield, Connecticut. Productions staged there between 1939 and 1942 were greeted by the critics with respectful disappointment. Despite his great charisma, Chekhov's pedagogic activities lacked an organic relation to the US theatre, particularly during wartime, and he moved to Hollywood, where he supported himself by acting in movies. He was usually cast as cute codgers, at his best as the crotchety psychiatrist in Hitchcock's *Spellbound* and as the campy impresario in Ben Hecht's *Spectre of the Rose*. As a teacher, his pupils there included Gregory Peck, Yul Brynner, Jack Palance and Marilyn Monroe.

During his American period, Chekhov published further theoretical writings. Although Stanislavsky had been disturbed by what he saw as Chekhov's mystical and stylistic excesses (after his Hamlet, he advised him not to play tragedy), Chekhov still sought to assimilate Stanislavsky's ideas into his own original researches. A leading tenet was the 'psychological gesture', which was to encapsulate a character and permeate the actor's psychology in early stages of rehearsal. As a teacher, he invested great importance in the cultivation of the body and the voice, concentration, imagination and the conjuring of atmosphere in the creation of highly imaginative characters. A number of his disciples carried on his work in the Michael Chekhov Studio in New York and in private acting classes, although schisms and variations gradually crept into their approaches. Over the last decade, there had been a revival of interest in his teaching methods.

—Laurence Senelick

CHENG CHANGGENG. Chinese actor. Born in Qianshan, Anhui, 1811 (personal names Chun and Wenhan; courtesy name, Yushan; nickname Jiaotion; often billed as Sizhentang). Educated at Anhui Regional Drama Training School; trained as actor under uncle in Beijing. May have run business selling musical instruments in Beijing before taking up the theatre; leader, celebrated Three Celebrations Troupe (Sanqingtuan), Beijing, 1845–61; guild head, Jongzhong Temple, Beijing, 1851–80; appeared in several imperial command performances from 1860; acclaimed playing in 'laosheng' roles, especially great warriors and rulers. Died in Beijing, 1880.

Principal roles

Guan Yu in *Hua-rong dao* [Huarong Road]; Guan Yu in *Zhan Chang-sha* [Fighting at Long Sands]; Liu Zhang in *Qu Cheng-du* [Taking Chengdu]; Lu Su in *Qu Nan-jun* [Taking Nanjun]; Lu Su in *Qun-ying hui* [Meeting of all the Heroes]; Wu Yuan in *Yu-chang jian* [Fish-maw Sword]; Wu Yuan in *Zhan Fan-cheng* [Fighting at Fan City]; Wu Yuan in *Zhao-guan* [Resplendent Pass]; Yuchi

Baolin in *Bai-liang Pass* [Bailiang Pass]; Yue Fei in *Zheng Tan-zhou* [Holding Tanzhou].

*

Bibliography

Books:
Colin Mackerras, *The Rise of the Peking Opera*, 1972.
W. Dolby, *A History of Chinese Drama*, 1976.

* * *

Cheng Changgeng is often, and with much justification, regarded as the father of Beijing Opera. Undoubtedly he was the most famous Beijing Opera actor of the 19th century and was revered almost as a god of the theatre by many performers of the early 20th century. His first public appearances were, however, inauspicious, the audience mocking him and he retired from the stage for three years to study under the celebrated 'laosheng' (old men) actor Mi Xizi, who died in 1832. He re-emerged at a feast given by imperial princes in the role of the ancient statesman and general Wu Yuan and was so imposing in the part that there was an uproar of applause, the audience even then regarding him in awe as godlike. His star reputation throughout Beijing and at the highest social levels was assured.

Cheng Changgeng shone mainly in the roles of powerful, dignified, faithful, and conscientious statesmen, notably as Wu Yuan, the mighty warrior and later Chinese god of war Guan Yu, the influential chief minister Lu Su, the governor Liu Zhang, and the much-adulated patriot general Yue Fei. These were all 'laosheng' roles, the 'laosheng' being thus established as the most popular characters of the period. Cheng was particularly admired for his punctilious enunciation of the lyrics and his resonant, clear-toned voice. A poem of 1853 ran:

> The Titan of Luantan, hand it to Changgeng,
> And flawless in Kunqu, perfect every word,
> So captivating the young peacock players,
> That they all revere him as teacher and as lord.

Kunqu ('Mount Kun melodies'), sometimes termed Junju ('Mount Kun drama'), is, incidentally, the supreme traditional intellectual Chinese theatre. Luantan ('disorderly strumming') describes other kinds of drama.

Cheng, Yu Sansheng (1802–66), and Zhang Erkui (1814–64) were known as The Three Laosheng Masters and also as The Three Top Graduates, the latter by analogy with their imperial examinations, but when Emperor Xuanxong summoned all three to perform in the palace with their respective troupes, it was Changgeng who was put in overall charge. Known respectively as 'Big Boss', he prospered through his kindness, conscientiousness, and orderly firmness and gathered together an outstanding company of players. They included Xu Xiaoxiang (1832–c.1902), He Guishan (dates unknown), and the actor-playwright Lu Shengkui (1822–90). When the troupe fell on hard times, Changgeng emerged from comfortable semi-retirement to assist it financially by the loan of his talents and fame. When invited to sing at private banquets, he would insist on the whole company being employed as well. Nor did he disdain to take supporting roles when so

asked, as he did in *Bai-liang Pass*. He was proud of his often maligned profession and in order to maintain the dignity of actors he strongly advocated the abolition of the somewhat debasing custom called 'Standing On the Stage' (zhantai), whereby female-role performers were required to entertain or titillate an audience before the play began.

A stickler for discipline in his company, Cheng was a courageous man, able to stand up against emperor, imperial clansmen, and mob-crowds alike. Altruistic, intensely patriotic, highly moral, and notably modest — vigorously according theatrical art precedence over his personal celebrity — he was a very Confucian gentleman of an actor.

It was Cheng Ghanggeng more than any other who ushered in the golden age of the Beijing Opera and Pihuang music in the last three decades of the 19th century and who nurtured the key actors for it. Tan Xinpei (1847–1917), Sun Juxian (1841–1931), and Wang Guifen (1860–1906), acclaimed as The Three New Laosheng Masters and The Three New Top Graduates, all received instruction from him. He also founded the Four Exhortations Drama Training School, which reared the renowned actors Chen Delin (1862–1930), Qian Jinfu (1862–1937), Zhang Qilin, and others. His adopted son, Cheng Zhangpu, was skilled at the clapper-drum ('bangu') and was at one time head of this school, later known as The Heaven-tree Longevity Hall Drama Training School. Zhangpu's son, Cheng Jixian (1875–1944) was a famous Beijing Opera actor of 'xiaosheng' (young men) roles.

Cheng Changgeng established a style of Beijing Opera performance known as 'the Chang school' or 'the Anhui school'. Beijing Opera is an eclectic genre and his skills also embraced Kunqu and Qinqiang ('Shaanxi music') and other styles of drama performance. Nor was he limited to 'laosheng' roles, but likewise excelled in the falsetto-voice 'dan' (young females) and 'xiaosheng' acting.

—William Dolby

———

CICERI, Pierre-Luc-Charles. French designer and artist. Born in Saint-Cloud, Paris, 17 or 18 August 1782. Trained as a singer then as an artist under F. J. Belanger, from 1802. Assistant, Séraphin's Chinese shadow theatre, from 1796; staff painter, Paris Opéra, from 1806; also worked in Germany; chief painter, Paris Opéra, 1818; established own studio, 1822; scenic director, Paris Opéra, 1822–47; acclaimed for landscapes and views of ruins; oversaw coronation of Charles X, 1825; also designed for the Comédie-Française, from 1826, and at other Parisian theatres. Died in Saint-Cléron, 22 August 1862.

Productions

1813	*Paul et Virginie* (Lesueur), Saint-Cloud Opéra, Paris.
1815	*Flore et Zéphire* (Didelot), Paris Opéra, Paris.
1818	*Zirphile et Fleur de myrte* (Catel), Paris Opéra, Paris.
	Proserpine (Schneitzhoeffer), Paris Opéra, Paris.
1819	Les Petites Danaïdes (Désaugiers and Gentil), Théâtre de la Porte-Saint-Martin, Paris.

1822   *Bertram ou Le Pirate* (Taylor), Panorama-Dramatique, Paris.
        Aladin ou La Lampe merveilleuse (Isouard), Paris Opéra, Paris.
        Florestan (Garcia), Paris Opéra, Paris.
        Alfred le grand (Aumer), Paris Opéra, Paris.
1823   *Cendrillon* (Albert), Paris Opéra, Paris.
        Lasthénie (Hérold), Paris Opéra, Paris.
        Vendôme en Espagne (Auber, Boïeldieu, and Hérold), Paris Opéra, Paris.
1824   *Ipsiboé* (Kreutzer), Paris Opéra, Paris.
        Zémire et Azor (Schneitzhoeffer), Paris Opéra, Paris.
1825   *La Belle au bois dormant* (Carafa), Paris Opéra, Paris.
        Pharamond (Boïeldieu, Berton, and Kreutzer), Paris Opéra, Paris.
        Don Sanche (Liszt), Paris Opéra, Paris.
        Mars et Vénus (Blache père), Paris Opéra, Paris.
        Léonidas (Pichat), Comédie-Française, Paris.
1826   *L'Assedio di Corinto* (Rossini), Paris Opéra, Paris.
1827   *Astolphe et Joconde* (Aumer), Paris Opéra, Paris.
        Le Somnambule (Aumer), Paris Opéra, Paris.
        Louis XI à Péronne (Mély-Janin), Comédie-Française, Paris.
1828   *La Muette de Portici* (Auber), Paris Opéra, Paris.
        Il Conte Ory (Rossini), Paris Opéra, Paris.
1829   *Guillaume Tell* (Rossini), Paris Opéra, Paris.
        Henry III et sa coeur (Dumas père), Comédie-Française, Paris.
        Le More de Venise (Vigny, adapted from Shakespeare), Comédie-Française, Paris.
1830   *Le Dieu et la Bayadère* (Auber), Paris Opéra, Paris.
        François I à Chambord (Gineste), Paris Opéra, Paris.
        Manon Lescaut (Aumer), Paris Opéra, Paris.
        Hernani (Hugo), Comédie-Française, Paris.
1831   *Robert le Diable* (Meyerbeer), Paris Opéra, Paris.
1832   *La Sylphide* (Taglioni), Paris Opéra, Paris.
        Le Roi s'amuse (Hugo), Comédie-Française, Paris.
1833   *Nathalie* (Taglioni), Paris Opéra, Paris.
        Gustave III (Auber), Paris Opéra, Paris.
        Ali Baba (Cherubini), Paris Opéra, Paris.
        La Revolte au sérail (Taglioni), Paris Opéra, Paris.
1834   *Don Giovanni* (Mozart), Paris Opéra, Paris.
        La Tempête (Coralli), Paris Opéra, Paris.
1836   *La Fille du Danube* (Taglioni), Paris Opéra, Paris.
        Dom Juan de Maraña (Dumas père), Théâtre de la Porte-Saint-Martin, Paris.
1841   *Le Comte de Carmagnola* (Thomas), Paris Opéra, Paris.
        Gisèle ou Les Willis (Coralli), Paris Opéra, Paris.
1842   *Le Jolie fille de Gand* (Albert), Paris Opéra, Paris.

1844   *Lady Henriette* (Mazilier), Paris Opéra, Paris.
1845   *Eucharis* (Coralli), Paris Opéra, Paris.
        Richard en Palestine (Adam), Paris Opéra, Paris.
        Le Diable à quatre (Adam), Paris Opéra, Paris.
1846   *David* (Mermet), Paris Opéra, Paris.
        Batty (Mazilier), Paris Opéra, Paris.
1847   *Ozaï* (Coralli), Paris Opéra, Paris.

*

Bibliography

Books:
M. A. Allévy, *La Mise en scène en France dans la première moitié du dix-neuvième siècle*, Paris, 1938.

* * *

In French theatre Romanticism did not only mean fundamental changes in philosophical outlook and in the concept of the hero; it also involved major developments in the styles and techniques of dramatic representation. The shift in emphasis away from the ideal and on to the characteristic, with the concomitant tendency to present together both the sublime and the grotesque, was naturally linked with a fresh interest in what is conveniently summed up in the catchphrases 'local colour' and 'historical colour'. For at that time the conviction was abroad that true art was to be found not only in those eternal, universal values cherished by Classicism, but also in the aspects of life that might be seen as fundamentally shaped by the circumstance of time and place.

When it is moreover recalled that the French Romantic dramatists, like their predecessors in the melodrama theatres of the Parisian boulevards, also cavilled at what they regarded as the irksome constraints of the Aristotelian unities because they sought to emulate the freer flow and wider scope of Shakespearean dramaturgy, it becomes clear why hidebound traditions of staging and costuming had to be abandoned. A single set with architectural features vaguely suggestive of Antiquity that had been used for dozens of Classical tragedies could no longer be regarded as adequate. Spectacle was restored to a high place in the hierarchy of theatrical values and the effects can be noted from the very start of the 19th century, though, of course, they had their impact at the ultra-conservative Comédie-Française only late in the 1820's when Alexandre Dumas père's *Henri III* and Victor Hugo's *Hernani* were presented there. The trend was strongly marked throughout the period on the operatic stage too.

Many of the artists of the age collaborated with dramatists, theatre managers, and actors (most notably François-Joseph Talma) in these developments. Among them none was more productive or more influential than Pierre-Luc-Charles Ciceri, 'the father of modern stage design' in the admiring words of Alexandre Dumas père. The fact that Ciceri was employed by theatres of all categories for shows of every variety, from the grandest to the far less prepossessing, is, moreover, evidence of the amount of contact and interaction between the different classes of theatre in the French capital.

Ciceri's obvious talent had won for him an early appointment as a painter of landscapes at the prestigious Opéra in the latter part of the Napoleonic era. His pre-eminence in his art was soon recognized, both at home and abroad, and he appears to have had no difficulty in retaining his post at the Opéra under the Restoration. He was also called up to work at the two 'official' theatres, the Comédie-Française and the rather more adventurous Odéon of the Left Bank. It was a mark of the regard in which he was held that he was also charged with such duties as the design of the costumes and the arrangement of the picturesque aspects of the coronation of Charles X in Rheims Cathedral. Such success did not, however, mean that Ciceri disdained opportunities to work for the less prestigious theatres. At the Panorama-Dramatique he collaborated with Daguerre, which must have contributed to his interest in stage lighting, and at such houses as the Porte-Saint-Martin, which specialised in historical drama, the Nouveautés, the Palais-Royal, and even the Cirque Olympique. He was no less ready to contribute elaborate and fanciful settings for productions of the 'grandes féeries' beloved of Parisian audiences than to design what at the time were widely, if mistakenly, admired as historically accurate sets for period drama and grand opera.

With real skill in exploiting perspective effects Ciceri excelled in the creation of medieval settings as, for instance, those he designed for Meyerbeer's opera *Robert le Diable* in 1832. There appears to be an immense amount of space for soloists and chorus under the arched colonnades, and light and darkness are mingled to create the air of mystery appropriate to the libretto. No less impressive are Ciceri's open-air scenes. Forest glades seem to stretch out endlessly, rocks jut upwards, and beetling crags stand out against skies that often seem to threaten storms. In the distance, a ruined castle is glimpsed in the mist. Unprecedented large sums of money were required for settings such as these, but theatre managers, knowing that there was a strong public demand for this sort of thing, were prepared to risk the financial commitment, and usually it paid off.

Dramatists and operatic composers were encouraged to make ever increasing demands and Ciceri again and again showed himself equal to the challenge. Among his most striking successes was the spectacle of Vesuvius in eruption at the climax of Auber's *La Muette de Portici* in 1828. For *La Belle au bois dormant*, which was described as a 'ballet-pantomime', Ciceri experimented with a moving panorama, using a pair of cylinders turned by means of handles to unwind a backcloth to create the impression of a landscape seen from a boat.

Even in Ciceri's own day there were critics who raised their voices against the ever-increasing elaboration of scenic effects, which was felt to be inimical to French traditions of psychological analysis through language. There can, however, be no doubt that Ciceri expressed the taste of the times, interpreting the wishes of dramatists and opera composers faithfully, to the utter delight of their public. He played a considerable part in enhancing the status of stage design and though a later generation might deplore his excesses, it is clear that Realism, when it came, would owe much to the Romantic developments in staging of which Ciceri was the notable French exponent. It is not fanciful to see his influence even in the historical epics of the early cinema.

—Christopher Smith

CLAIRON, Mlle. French actress. Born Claire-Josèphe-Hippolyte Léris de la Tude at Condé-sur-Escaut, France, 25 January 1723. No formal education. Stage debut, Comédie-Italienne, Paris, 1736; subsequently gained experience in Rouen and elsewhere in the French provinces before joining the Comédie-Française in Paris as an understudy and making her first appearance there to immediate acclaim, 1743; admired by David Garrick and hailed as the finest tragedienne of her age, especially in plays by Pierre Corneille, Racine, and Voltaire; promoted use of historically authentic costumes at the Comédie-Française; imprisoned over dispute with another performer, 1765; retired from the stage, 1765, and opened acting school; thenceforth confined herself to private theatricals; reduced to poverty by the Revolution, 1789. Died in Paris, 29 January 1803.

Principal roles

1736	Cléanthis in *L'Ile des esclaves* (Marivaux), Comédie-Italienne, Paris.
1743	Venere in *Hésione* (Danchet), Opéra, Paris.
	Phèdre in *Phèdre* (Racine), Comédie-Française, Paris.
	Dorine in *Tartuffe* (Molière), Comédie-Française, Paris.
1748	Arétie in *Denys le Tyran* (Marmontel), Comédie-Française, Paris.
1749	Léonide in *Aristomène* (Marmontel), Comédie-Française, Paris.
1755	Idamé in *L'Orphelin de Chine* (Voltaire), Comédie-Française, Paris.
1760	Aménaïde in *Tancrède* (Voltaire), Comédie-Française, Paris.
1761	Electre in *Oreste* (Voltaire), Comédie-Française, Paris.
1764	Olympie in *Olympie* (Voltaire), Comédie-Française, Paris.
1765	Abénor in *Siège de Calais* (Du Belloy), Comédie-Française, Paris.

Other roles included: Agrippine in *Britannicus* (Racine); Aricie in *Phèdre* (Racine); Camille in *Horace* (P. Corneille); Cléopatre in *Cléopatre* (Marmontel); Électre in *Électre* (Crébillon); Emilie in *Cinna* (P. Corneille); Éroxine in *Timoléon* (La Harpe); Hermione in *Andromaque* (Racine); Pauline in *Polyeucte* (P. Corneille); Pénélope in *Pénélope* (Genest); Roxane in *Bajazet* (Racine); Zénobie in *Rhadamiste et Zénobie* (Crébillon).

Publications

Mémoires d'Hippolyte Clairon et réflexions sure l'art dramatique, 1779.

*

Bibliography

Books:
Edmond de Goncourt, *Mademoiselle Clairon*, Paris, 1889.

*   *   *

Like Adrienne Lecouvreur a generation earlier, Mlle Clairon is memorable for having attempted to break the mould of received performance values. She was an actress of great single-mindedness, studied artistry, and, to judge by the memoirs that she published a few years before her death, no mean intelligence, despite her total lack of formal education. An illegitimate child, living in squalid and impoverished circumstances, she turned early to the stage as the protégée of an actor in the Comédie-Italienne, where she made her debut at the age of 13 as the remonstrative maidservant in *L'Ile des esclaves*. There followed a number of engagements with companies in the northern provinces before she returned to Paris early in 1743 to perform (once) at the Opéra and to seek a place at the Comédie-Française. This was soon achieved, for she made her first appearance there in September of that year as a very youthful but rapturously applauded Phèdre in Racine's tragedy, followed a few days later by the role of the down-to-earth Dorine in Molière's *Tartuffe*.

Over the next two decades Clairon's position in the company became a dominant one, particularly in tragedy. Within the traditional repertoire she was especially acclaimed as Camille in Corneille's *Horace* and as Roxane in Racine's *Bajazet*, but she was no less successful in the creation of tragic roles in the work of contemporary dramatists like Crébillon, Marmontel, La Harpe, and Du Belloy. Above all, she won the admiration of Voltaire, who dubbed her the "divine Melpomene" and fashioned several of his female protagonists with her in mind, notably the character of Aménaïde in *Tancrède*. In these parts she frequently appeared — to mutual advantage — alongside leading players with whom professional relations were decidedly strained, as with her most distinguished male counterpart, Lekain, and Mlle Dumesnil, an intuitive performer and her most contentious rival.

Of particular interest in this connection is the fact that her conception of tragic acting underwent a radical transformation in the second half of her career. At the outset her style had been indistinguishable from that of most legitimate actors of her day, one in which the musical properties of alexandrine verse were given full value and the use of voice and physical gesture was intended to underscore the formal rhetorical devices in the text. In her case, given the lengthy study she brought to the preparation of all her roles, the effect was often of calculation and, however impressive, of over-contrivance: as Baron Grimm said of her playing, "I perceive always the art and never the nature". Later, under the influence of Marmontel, who was for a time one of her many lovers, she experimented with a simpler, more straightforward form of diction which allowed for greater nuance, spontaneity, and even some naturalness of expression, a process that reached complete fruition in her performance as Idamé in Voltaire's *L'Orphelin de la Chine* in 1755 and again as Electre in the revival of his *Oreste* in 1761. Critics saw the change as little short of revolutionary and it must have enabled her to capitalize still further on what had always been her principal strengths as an actress, emotional subtlety and a capacity for tendernesss and vulnerability. In Corneille's *Polyeucte*, for instance, she is reported as having conveyed a sensitive differentiation between the love Pauline feels for Sévère and that she owes to her martyr-husband; as Hermione in Racine's *Andromaque* she kept the two aspects of the character, proud princess and woman in love, carefully in balance, and was

much appreciated in the same author's *Britannicus* for playing Agrippine without any of the fiery, impassioned stridency often associated with the role. Similarly she contrived to introduce variety and refinement into roles that are prone to emotional monotony, such as Electre or Emilie in Corneille's *Cinna*.

To greater delicacy of characterization she also added some sense of appropriateness and consistency in dress. At a time when stage costume was largely a pretext for the display of current fashion, supplemented by a few conventional accoutrements, and star quality could be judged in terms of elegance of attire, Mlle Clairon would often abandon its most extravagant features, such as paniers, frilled cuffs, and towering wigs, for plays set in mythological times or exotic locations. Thus, for Electre she adopted an unadorned garment with deep folds, a train, and a collar of black velvet that followed the general line, if not the detail, of classical Greek dress, while for Voltaire's mandariness she wore a costume embroidered with dragons and decorated with furs, with an aigrette on her head.

Both this and the change in her style of acting suggest that she had begun to develop a tentative concern for realism, or at least consistency, in stage performance. The same preoccupation is evident in her memoirs, which contain some interesting analyses of the tragic roles she had played and emphasize the importance of a good, all-round culture for the actor, a knowledge of mythology, history, and geography, as well as literature, which will afford him an insight into "the times, places, and characters" of a given play and thereby enable him to cultivate his "art". Her reference to the "reality without art" of Mlle Dumesnil's performances so incensed her old adversary that the latter published her own memoirs in the following year, presenting the ability to act as a gift of nature superior to any art, insisting on the universality of the tragic impulse and criticizing Mlle Clairon "for being all art ... for always allowing the great actress to show through in your so *finished* style of acting".

By this time the erstwhile star had been living in retirement for more than 30 years. She resigned from the Comédie in 1765 in circumstances that have never been satisfactorily explained but to which ill health and friction within the company may have contributed. Thereafter she never acted publicly again and only rarely in private performances or at court. Instead, she opened a school for young actors for a time and, from 1772, spent 17 years in Ansbach as the permanent house-guest of an adoring margrave. She returned to France on the eve of the Revolution and lived her last years in abject poverty, only slightly relieved by a modest state pension, and almost total obscurity.

—Donald Roy

CLUNES, Alec. British actor-manager and director. Born Alexander Sheriff de Moro Clunes in Brixton, London, 17 May 1912. Educated at Cliftonville, Margate. Married 1) Stella Richman in 1949 (divorced 1954); 2) Daphne Acott in 1956, one son and one daughter. Debut as amateur actor while working in advertising and journalism; actor, Ben Greet's touring company, 1934; joined Old Vic company, London, 1934; first of many appearances at Players'

Theatre Club, Covent Garden, London, 1938; first acted at Stratford-upon-Avon, 1939; founded Arts Theatre Group of Actors, Arts Theatre Club, London, 1942; presented over 100 plays at the Arts Theatre, 1942–53; also made many television and film appearances. Died in London, 13 March 1970.

Productions

As actor:

1934   Orlando in *As You Like It* (Shakespeare), Croydon Repertory Theatre, London.

Christopher Venables in *The Distaff Side* (Van Druten), Theatre Royal, Brighton.

Longaville in *Love's Labour's Lost* (Shakespeare), British tour.

Antonio in *Twelfth Night* (Shakespeare), British tour.

Lysander in *A Midsummer Night's Dream* (Shakespeare), British tour.

Proculeius and Octavius Caesar in *Antony and Cleopatra* (Shakespeare), Old Vic Theatre, London.

Bagot in *Richard II* (Shakespeare), Old Vic Theatre, London.

A Messenger and Friar Francis in *Much Ado About Nothing* (Shakespeare), Old Vic Theatre, London.

Gilles de Rais and A Soldier in *Saint Joan* (G. B. Shaw), Sadler's Wells Theatre, London.

1935   A Lord and Curtis in *The Taming of the Shrew* (Shakespeare), Sadler's Wells Theatre, London.

A Messenger and Lodovico in *Othello* (Shakespeare), Old Vic Theatre, London.

Leader of the Chorus of Huntsmen in *Hippolytus* (Euripides, adapted by Murray), Old Vic Theatre, London.

Charles Lomax in *Major Barbara* (G. B. Shaw), Old Vic Theatre, London.

Morton, Pistol, and the Earl of Westmoreland in *Henry IV, part 2* (Shakespeare), Old Vic Theatre, London.

Thomas Mowbray, Duke of Norfolk, Sir Stephen Scroop, and Sir Pierce of Exton in *Richard II* (Shakespeare), Old Vic Theatre, London.

Laertes in *Hamlet* (Shakespeare), Old Vic Theatre, London.

Tony Oldham in *Grief Goes Over* (Hodge), Opera House, Manchester.

Aslak the Smith in *Peer Gynt* (Ibsen), Old Vic Theatre, London.

A Cobbler, Artemidorus of Cnidos, and Octavius Caesar in *Julius Caesar* (Shakespeare), Old Vic Theatre, London.

Ferapont in *The Three Sisters* (Chekhov), Old Vic Theatre, London.

Third Witch and A Doctor in *Macbeth* (Shakespeare), Old Vic Theatre, London.

Trip in *The School for Scandal* (Sheridan), Old Vic Theatre, London.

1936   George, Duke of Clarence in *Richard III* (Shakespeare), Old Vic Theatre, London.

A Ship's Carpenter and Dr Antommarchi in *St Helena* (Sherriff and Casalis), Old Vic Theatre, London.

Autolycus in *The Winter's Tale* (Shakespeare), Old Vic Theatre, London.

Edmund in *King Lear* (Shakespeare), Sadler's Wells Theatre, London.

Flute in extract from *A Midsummer Night's Dream* (Shakespeare), Old Vic Theatre, London.

Aslak the Smith, A Strange Passenger, and A Lean Person in *Peer Gynt* (Ibsen), Sadler's Wells Theatre, London.

Pra in *The Simpleton of the Unexpected Isles* (G. B. Shaw), Theatre Royal, Brighton.

General Baron Gourgaud in *St Helena* (Sherriff and Casalis), Theatre Royal, Brighton.

Gilbert Kent in *Dusty Ermine* (Grant), Theatre Royal, Brighton.

Clive Monkhams in *After October* (Ackland), Theatre Royal, Brighton.

The Salesman in *Ah! Wilderness* (O'Neill), Theatre Royal, Brighton.

Sam Gridley in *Bees on the Boatdeck* (Priestley), Theatre Royal, Brighton.

Dunois in *Saint Joan* (G. B. Shaw), Theatre Royal, Brighton; Malvern Festival, 1938.

Berowne in *Love's Labour's Lost* (Shakespeare), Old Vic Theatre, London.

Mr Harcourt in *The Country Wife* (Wycherley), Old Vic Theatre, London.

Jim Lee in *Hell-for-Leather!* (Lyndon), Phoenix Theatre, London.

1937   Roger Garth-Bander in *George and Margaret* (Savory), Strand Theatre, London.

Harry Dornton in *The Road to Ruin* (Holcroft), Ambassadors' Theatre, London.

Lucentio in *The Taming of the Shrew* (Shakespeare), New Theatre, London.

Douglas Hall in *Yes, My Darling Daughter* (Reed, adapted by Ackland), St James's Theatre, London.

The Hon. Basil Trent in *Punch and Judy* (V. Gielgud), Vaudeville Theatre, London.

George, Duke of Clarence, and Sir James Tyrrel in *Richard III* (Shakespeare), Old Vic Theatre, London.

Klaus Tott in *Queen Christina* (Strindberg), Westminster Theatre, London.

Detective Raines in *I Killed the Count* (Coppel), Whitehall Theatre, London.

1938   Mr Bassett Laneworthy-Figg in *Late Joys* (revue), Players' Theatre, Covent Garden, London.

Peter Horlett in *Music at Night* (Priestley), Malvern Festival.

Tom Buchlyvie in *The Last Trump* (Bridie), Malvern Festival.

1939   Petruchio in *The Taming of the Shrew* (Shakespeare), Shakespeare Memorial Theatre, Stratford-upon-Avon.

Richmond in *Richard III* (Shakespeare), Shakespeare Memorial Theatre, Stratford-upon-Avon.

Iago in *Othello* (Shakespeare), Shakespeare Memorial Theatre, Stratford-upon-Avon; European tour, 1947.

Sir Andrew Aguecheek in *Twelfth Night* (Shakespeare), Shakespeare Memorial Theatre, Stratford-upon-Avon.

Benedick in *Much Ado About Nothing* (Shakespeare), Shakespeare Memorial Theatre, Stratford-upon-Avon.

Caius Marcius Coriolanus in *Coriolanus* (Shakespeare), Shakespeare Memorial Theatre, Stratford-upon-Avon.

Vivaldi in *The King of Nowhere* (Bridie), Playhouse, Oxford.

Sir William Gower in *Trelawny of the Wells* (Pinero), Playhouse, Oxford.

Jupiter and Amphitryon in *Amphitryon 38* (Giraudoux), Playhouse, Oxford.

Roland Spencer in *String Quartet* (Savory), Playhouse, Oxford.

Alastair Fitzfassenden in *The Millionairess* (G. B. Shaw), Playhouse, Oxford.

Robert Browning in *The Barretts of Wimpole Street* (Besier), Playhouse, Oxford; Garrick Theatre, London, 1948.

1940   Mr Horner in *The Country Wife* (Wycherley), Little Theatre, London.

Godfrey Kneller in *In Good King Charles's Golden Days* (G. B. Shaw), New Theatre, London.

1941   Young Marlow in *She Stoops to Conquer* (Goldsmith), British tour.

Taffy in *Trilby* (Potter, adapted from Du Maurier), British tour.

Malvolio in *Twelfth Night* (Shakespeare), British tour.

Enrique in *The World is Mine* (Granville-Barker, adapted from Sierra's *The Kingdom of God*), British tour.

1943   Mr Rencelaw in *The Drunkard* (Smith), Arts Theatre, London.

1945   Sir Fretful Plagiary and the Governor of Tilbury Fort in *The Critic* (Sheridan), Arts Theatre, London.

Hamlet in *Hamlet* (Shakespeare), Arts Theatre, Cambridge, and Arts Theatre, London; European tour, 1947.

Charles Surface in *The School for Scandal* (Sheridan), Arts Theatre, London.

1946   Mr Rafflin in *1066 and All That* (all-star matinée), Palace Theatre, London.

The Voice of Robert Singleton in *The Dove and the Carpenter* (L. E. Jones), Arts Theatre, London.

Don Juan in *Don Juan in Hell* (G. B. Shaw), Arts Theatre, London; European tour, 1947.

Higgins in *Pygmalion* (G. B. Shaw), Lyric Theatre, Hammersmith, London.

1948   Thomas Mendip in *The Lady's Not For Burning* (Fry), Arts Theatre, London.

Marry MacGog in *Gog and MacGog* (Bridie), Arts Theatre, London.

1949   Yegor Dimitrich Gloumov in *The Diary of a Scoundrel* (Ostrovsky, adapted by Ackland), Arts Theatre, London.

1950   Humphrey Waspe in *Bartholomew Fair* (Jonson), Assembly Hall, Edinburgh, and Old Vic Theatre, London.

Orsino in *Twelfth Night* (Shakespeare), Old Vic Theatre, London.

1951   Henry V in *Henry V* (Shakespeare), Old Vic Theatre, London.

Ford in *The Merry Wives of Windsor* (Shakespeare), Old Vic Theatre, London.

1952   Moses in *The Firstborn* (Fry), Winter Garden Theatre, London.

Major C. O. P. Carrington in *Carrington, V.C.* (Christie), Westminster Theatre, London.

Bassett Laneworthy-Figg in *The Burglar, the Child, and the Doll's House* (Anstey), Theatre Royal, Drury Lane, London.

1954   Allan Peters in *The Facts of Life* (MacDougall), Duke of York's Theatre, London, and Cambridge Theatre, London.

1955   Claudius in *Hamlet* (Shakespeare), Art Theatre, Moscow, and Phoenix Theatre, London.

1956   Professor Harry Peterson in *Who Cares?* (Lehman), Fortune Theatre, London.

1957   Philip the Bastard in *King John* (Shakespeare), Shakespeare Memorial Theatre, Stratford-upon-Avon.

Marcus Brutus in *Julius Caesar* (Shakespeare), Shakespeare Memorial Theatre, Stratford-upon-Avon.

Caliban in *The Tempest* (Shakespeare), Shakespeare Memorial Theatre, Stratford-upon-Avon, and Theatre Royal, Drury Lane, London.

1959   Higgins in *My Fair Lady* (Loewe and Lerner, adapted from Shaw's *Pygmalion*), Theatre Royal, Drury Lane, London.

1962   Sir Lewis Eliot in *The Affair* (Snow), Strand Theatre, London.

1967   Soames in *Getting Married* (G. B. Shaw), Strand Theatre, London.

1968   Bishop Bell in *Soldiers* (Hochhuth), New Theatre, London.

Also acted roles in: *Dangerous Corner* (Priestley), Seaford Repertory Theatre, 1934; *Rookery Nook* (Travers), Seaford Repertory Theatre, 1934; *Almost a Honeymoon* (Ellis), Seaford Repertory Theatre, 1934; *Peg o' My Heart* (Manners), Seaford Repertory Theatre, 1934; *The Importance of Being Earnest* (Wilde), Seaford Repertory Theatre, 1934.

As director:
1937   *Distant Fields* (Lauren), Players' Theatre, Covent Garden, London.

Tomorrow at Midnight (Wilder), Players' Theatre, Covent Garden, London.

1942   *Awake and Sing!* (Odets), Arts Theatre, London, and Cambridge Theatre, London.

Twelfth Night (Shakespeare), Arts Theatre, London; acted Feste.

The Swan Song (Chekhov, adapted by Garnett), Arts Theatre, London; acted Vassily Vassilyitch Svetlovidov.

The Proposal (Chekhov), Arts Theatre, London.

Magic (Chesterton), Arts Theatre, London; acted The Stranger.

House of Regrets (Ustinov), Arts Theatre, London.

1943   *Androcles and the Lion* (G. B. Shaw), Arts Theatre, London; acted Ferrovius.

The Well of the Saints (Synge), Arts Theatre, London.

Beyond (Ustinov), Arts Theatre, London.

Don Juan in Hell (G. B. Shaw), Arts Theatre, London; Winter Garden Theatre, London, 1952; acted Don Juan.

The Constant Couple (Farquhar), Arts Theatre, London; Arts Theatre, London, 1945; Winter Garden Theatre, London, 1952; acted Sir Harry Wildair.

The Magistrate (Pinero), Arts Theatre, London.

Misalliance (G. B. Shaw), Arts Theatre, London.

The Watched Pot (Munro and Maude), Arts Theatre, London.

The Recruiting Officer (Farquhar), Arts Theatre, London.

1944   *The Two Children* (Powell), Arts Theatre, London.

Bird in Hand (Drinkwater), Arts Theatre, London.

Mine Hostess (Goldoni), Arts Theatre, London; acted the Knight of Ripafratta.

1949   *A Pair of Spectacles* (Grundy), Arts Theatre, London.

Hindle Wakes (Houghton), Arts Theatre, London.

1950   *Macbeth* (Shakespeare), Arts Theatre, London; acted Macbeth.

Queen Elizabeth (Williamson), Arts Theatre, London.

Maria Marten (adapted by Clunes), Arts Theatre, London.

1953   *Arms and the Man* (G. B. Shaw), Arts Theatre, London; acted Bluntschli.

The Bespoke Overcoat (Mankowitz), Arts Theatre, London.

Films

Convoy, 1940; *Saloon Bar*, 1940; *Sailors Three*, 1941; *One of Our Aircraft is Missing*, 1942; *Now Barabbas Was a Robber*, 1949; *Melba*, 1953; *The Knights of the Round Table*, 1954; *The Brighton Story*, 1955; *The Adventures of Quentin Durward*, 1956; *Richard III*, 1956; *Tiger in the Smoke*, 1956; *Tomorrow at Ten*, 1962.

Television

The Lady's Not for Burning, 1950; *The Buccaneers*, 1956; *Amphitryon 38*, 1958; *The Great Adventure*, 1958; *The Heiress*, 1958; *The Franchise Affair*, 1958; *Hamlet*, 1964.

Radio

Island of Sheep, 1954.

Publications

The British Theatre, 1964.

*

Bibliography

Books:
J. C. Trewin, *Alec Clunes*, London, 1958.

* * *

As an actor of the first rank, Alec Clunes's record of performances was irregular and disappointingly limited. This was a necessary condition of a wider contribution to the theatre, bridging World War II and the period of the setting up of the Arts Council preparatory to the theatrical renaissance of the later 1950's and 1960's. Clunes took over the Arts Theatre Club near Leicester Square, within West End theatreland, in 1942 and for the next 10 years maintained a programme of short runs (usually up to three or four weeks) of a high quality international repertoire performed to an exacting standard of excellence. Within a year Clunes brought membership figures at the Arts from 200 to ten thousand as it became clear that he intended to provide for the wartime hunger for first-rate theatre rather than following the Stage Society in mounting one or two performances of each play for a specialist audience. Theatre membership reached thirty thousand in 1947. The Arts had a financial stability denied to other idealistic club theatres of the time; its small stage was well-equipped and its auditorium, with a small balcony, was intimate without being cramped and had good sightlines and acoustics. The club facilities, which Clunes cherished, made it a hospitable place for meeting and discussion with the civilised atmosphere at which later arts centres were to aim. Although the stage was end-on to the auditorium, the spatial relationships provided a model for later studio theatres, which profit from closeness between actors and audience in ways major London theatres could never discover.

The Arts had a separate Board of Management, but Clunes selected all the plays, directed many of them himself, and played roles that particularly attracted him. The other directors he brought in had talent and sometimes considerable experience (among them Lewis Casson). John Fernald's series of Chekhov productions exemplified the happy matching of directors to playwrights. Women were also quite prominent: Judith Furse was a regular director and several actresses, including Dorothy Green, Beatrix Lehmann, Catherine Lacey, Vivienne Bennett, and Lucy Mannheim, produced single plays. Clunes's perfectionism ensured that design was not overlooked and Maise Meiklejohn in particular became expert in devising practicable and effective sets for the small Arts Theatre stage.

Clunes as a director was demanding and even dictatorial. He worked on plays he loved and was totally clear about what he wanted. He aimed to share his own enjoyment and understanding with the audience and his productions were noted for their swift pace, liveliness, and often high spirits. His taste was wide-ranging and cultivated, generally intellectual, and he assumed a conventionally well-educated audience. Such terms as 'classical' and even 'literary' were not reproaches in his theatre. From the first he included Shakespeare and Restoration comedy alongside the modern masters, Ibsen, Chekhov, O'Neill, and Strindberg. Bernard Shaw was a particular favourite, but Clunes also presented plays by contemporary French dramatists, rediscovered Pinero's farces, and resurrected the Victorian melodrama for fun. Efforts were made to encourage emerging playwrights and the Arts gave a start to Peter Ustinov and Christopher Fry, though it was John Whiting who came to be regarded as the theatre's new playwright par excellence, defiantly backed by the management and leading actors in the face of uncertain audiences and mixed reviews. It was a logical development that Clunes's successor, Peter Hall, should use the Arts as a base for the further liberation of English theatre by bringing audiences to the work of Beckett and Pinter.

After touring with the Ben Greet players in 1934, Clunes had joined the Old Vic, where he applied himself incessantly to the study of technique, until there was not a more accomplished actor in the English theatre. As one critic observed: "He speaks elegantly and without affectation, his movements are at once graceful and spontaneous". His glorious tones were frequently admired, as was his ability to charm. He was also praised for his ease and naturalness and only rarely was 'too studied' the verdict. Not surprisingly, he excelled in comedy and among his best roles were Horner in *The Country Wife* and Don Juan. Humanity, as well as intelligence, imbued the comic mechanism of Clunes's Bluntschli and his Higgins. His version of this last role was to be seen and heard at Drury Lane, when he took over the lead in *My Fair Lady* from Rex Harrison.

Certain aspects of tragedy were outside Clunes's range. Lacking the necessary savagery, he failed as Macbeth, though his Iago, balanced in powerful irony against Jack Hawkins's Othello, made a deep impression. His Hamlet divided critical opinion: he interpreted the Prince as "too civilised for his environment" but this interpretation was considered narrow by those who judged the sweetness of the character over-emphasized. This performance, his fantastic witty Orsino, and even his Henry V shared qualities he had shown as Berowne in Guthrie's production of *Love's Labour's Lost*. Shakespeare at the Arts (and on overseas tours) proved in time Clunes's bridge back to full-time acting at the Old Vic, where his Henry V won high praise for its "compelling reality", a "combination of inflexibility and compassion", authority, and "winning humanity". His interpretation and his much-analysed rendering of the speech before Agincourt undoubtedly contributed to Olivier's more famous version. The imaginative freshness Clunes brought to his reading of the plays was never more evident than in the production of *Hamlet*, which was dominated by his depiction of Claudius "as a man who committed a crime passionel after an internal battle which has left scars on his conscience", in Kenneth

Tynan's words, so revealing the play by "miracles of reclamation" as a near-Sophoclean family tragedy.

—Margery Morgan

CLURMAN, Harold (Edgar). US director, manager, actor, author, and critic. Born in New York, 18 September 1901. Educated at University of Columbia, New York, 1919–21; University of the Sorbonne, Paris, diploma 1923; trained for the theatre under Jacques Copeau at the Théâtre du Vieux-Colombier, Paris, 1923–24, and under Richard Boleslavsky at the American Laboratory Theatre, New York, 1927. Married 1) actress Stella Adler in 1943 (divorced 1960); 2) actress Juleen Compton in 1960 (divorced 1962). Acting debut, in minor roles, Greenwich Village Playhouse, New York, 1924; assistant stage manager, Theatre Guild, New York, 1925; stage manager, Garrick Gaieties, 1926; playreader, Theatre Guild, 1929–31; co-founder and director, with Lee Strasberg and Cheryl Crawford, Group Theatre, New York, 1931–41; producer and director, 20th Century Fox, Paramount, and RKO Studios, Hollywood, 1941–45; independent producer and stage director, 1946–69; theatre critic, *Tomorrow Magazine*, 1946–52, *The New Republic*, 1949–52, *The Nation*, 1953–80, *London Observer*, 1959–63; Andrew Mellon lecturer on theatre, Carnegie-Mellon University, Pittsburgh, 1962–63; Executive Consultant, Repertory Theatre, Lincoln Centre for the Performing Arts, New York, 1963; Visiting Professor in the Theatre, Hunter College, New York, 1964–80. Member: Theatre Development Fund of New York City; Society of Stage Directors and Choreographers. Recipient: Donaldson Award for direction, 1950; George Jean Nathan Award, 1959; Medal of Achievement, Brandeis University, 1976. D.Litt: Bard College, Annandale-on-Hudson, New York, 1959; DFA: Carnegie-Mellon University, Pittsburgh, Ripon College, Wisconsin, and Boston University, all 1963. Chévalier, Légion d'Honneur, 1959. Died in New York, 9 September 1980.

Productions

As director:
1935   *Awake and Sing!* (Odets) Belasco Theatre, New York; revived, 1938.
        Paradise Lost (Odets), Longacre Theatre, New York.
1937   *Golden Boy* (Odets), Belasco Theatre, New York; London, 1938.
1938   *Rocket to the Moon* (Odets), Belasco Theatre, New York.
1939   *The Gentle People* (I. Shaw), Belasco Theatre, New York.
1940   *Night Music* (Odets), Broadhurst Theatre, New York.
        Retreat to Pleasure (I. Shaw), Belasco Theatre, New York.
1942   *The Russian People* (Simonov, adapted by Odets), Guild Theatre, New York.
1945   *Beggars Are Coming to Town* (Reeves), Coronet Theatre, New York.

1946   *Truckline Café* (Anderson), Belasco Theatre, New York.

1947   *The Whole World Over* (Simonov, adapted by Schnee), Biltmore Theatre, New York.

1948   *The Young and Fair* (Nash), Fulton Theatre, New York.

1949   *Montserrat* (Roblès), Tel Aviv, Israel.

1950   *The Member of the Wedding* (McCullers), Empire Theatre, New York.

        The Bird Cage (Laurents), Coronet Theatre, New York.

1951   *The Autumn Garden* (Hellman), Coronet Theatre, New York.

1952   *Desire Under the Elms* (O'Neill), Anta Theatre, New York.

        The Time of the Cuckoo (Laurents), Empire Theatre, New York.

1953   *The Emperor's Clothes* (Tabori), Ethel Barrymore Theatre, New York.

        The Ladies of the Corridor (Parker and d'Usseau), Longacre Theatre, New York.

1954   *Mademoiselle Colombe* (Anouilh), Longacre Theatre, New York.

1955   *Bus Stop* (Inge), Music Box Theatre, New York.

        Tiger at the Gates (Giraudoux, translated by Fry), Apollo Theatre, London and New York.

        Pipe Dream (Rodgers and Hammerstein), Shubert Theatre, New York.

1956   *The Waltz of the Toreadors* (Anouilh), Coronet Theatre, New York; US tour, 1957, 1958.

1957   *Orpheus Descending* (T. Williams), Martin Beck Theatre, New York.

1958   *The Day the Money Stopped* (Anderson and Gill), Belasco Theatre, New York.

        A Touch of the Poet (O'Neill), Helen Hayes Theatre, New York.

        The Cold Wind and the Warm (Behrman), Morosco Theatre, New York; revived, 1959.

1959   *Heartbreak House* (G. B. Shaw), Billy Rose Theatre, New York.

        Caesar and Cleopatra (G. B. Shaw), Tel Aviv, Israel.

1960   *Jeannette* (Anouilh), Maidman Theatre, New York.

1961   A Shot in the Dark (Kurnitz and Achard), Booth Theatre, New York.

1962   *Judith* (Giraudoux, translated by Fry), Her Majesty's Theatre, London.

1964   *Incident at Vichy* (Miller), Washington Square Theatre, New York.

1965   *Long Day's Journey into Night* (O'Neill), Tokyo.

1966   *Where's Daddy?* (Inge), Billy Rose Theatre, New York.

1968   *The Iceman Cometh* (O'Neill), Tokyo.

1969   *Uncle Vanya* (Chekhov), Mark Taper Forum, Los Angeles.

Films

Deadline at Dawn, 1946.

Publications

The Fervent Years: The Story of the Group Theatre and the Thirties, New York, 1945; *Lies Like Truths: Theatre Reviews and Essays*, 1958; *Famous Plays of the 1930's*, 1959; *The Naked Image: Observations on Modern Theatre*, 1966; *On Directing*, 1972; *The Divine Pastime: Theatre Essays*, 1974; *All People Are Famous: Instead of an Autobiography*, 1974; *Ibsen*, 1978.

* * *

Discussing Harold Clurman inevitably entails discussing the Group Theatre, even though the Group occupied only a decade of his more than 50-year theatrical career, a career in which he matured from a role as a minor actor and playreader to that of an esteemed director and valued critic. Today, his presence lingers on the US stage, most salient in the prominence of the 'Method' and in the voices of playwrights championed through his direction or critical support.

In his youth, Clurman attended New York's Yiddish theatre, for immigrants — as he later wrote — a "centre of social discourse. Here the problems of their life, past and present, could be given a voice". In the 1920's, he became an admirer of the Theatre Guild, whose daring works frequently captivated the New York drama scene. This vision of theatre as a "centre of social discourse" with daring allure was to form the quintessence of Clurman's aspirations for the US stage.

Clurman believed that Broadway attenuated or abandoned altogether meaningful issues and human concerns and that profit, not artistic development, was the ultimate preoccupation of contemporary producers. To counter this tendency, in 1930 he collaborated with Lee Strasberg and Cheryl Crawford and a group of other New York theatre artists on a seven-month series of Friday gatherings at which, shaman-like, he mystically intoned his passion for theatrical rebirth. Eventually these talks spawned the Group Theatre as an offshoot of the Theatre Guild.

Clurman's primary goal for the Group was to move from a "theatre of words", which venerated the dramatic text, toward a theatre reflecting the 'Zeitgeist' and producing plays more coherently staged, full of vibrant, believable acting. In *The Divine Pastime* he wrote: "The Group Theatre (1931–41) was the first ... conscious effort in America to create a theatre exemplifying both an aesthetic and a 'philosophic' attitude. Its first emphasis was on a unity of technique — particularly in regard to acting; its second was the enunciation of what it held to be the temper of American life of the time".

Clurman's artistic model was Stanislavsky and the Moscow Art Theatre. The Group adopted (and adapted) Stanislavsky's Method, which Clurman called "the grammar of acting", as the set approach for its work. In fact, the Group's most lasting influence on US theatre was this promulgation of the Method, which was further promoted through the various acting schools that were later started by Group members, some of which still exist — including one led by Clurman's first wife, Stella Adler. Adler met with Stanislavsky in 1934 and subsequently relayed from him correctives to the Method as practiced by the Group, primarily through Strasberg's direction. Strasberg's objec-

Harold Clurman (left) and Clifford Odets (c. 1945).

tions to her suggestions eventually led to a rift in US approaches to Stanislavsky that continues to this day.

In *On Directing* Clurman addressed the Group's use of Stanislavsky and the prominence of the Method in the USA: "I myself am convinced that the Stanislavsky system . . . has never really been practiced in the United States. It is understood by some, it is taught by many, but it has never been completely employed". Though many decry the Method's excesses, Clurman remained convinced "its general effect has been far more beneficial than harmful". Nevertheless, he realized the Method has often been misapplied: "the stress on emotional memory was embraced as a saving grace, as a universal answer. It became a fetish . . . the Method for many American actors is no longer a technique but a therapy".

Though often artistically successful, Clurman never could create a self-sustaining organization with resources enough to focus all its attention on artistic development. Instead, like every other Broadway producer, he found himself raising funds for each show. As for artistic direction, though not overtly political, the Group was socially conscious. As Clurman said: "a play didn't have to deal with obvious social themes in order to have social significance". The Group, as it proposed to do, reflected the social spirit of the age. Its collective nature paved the way for the shortlived Federal Theatre, part of Roosevelt's New Deal. Indeed, roots of the off-Broadway and experimental theatres of the 1960's and 1970's extend back to the Group.

Perhaps Clurman best summarized the organization's importance when he said: "The Group was stronger as a symbol and as an influence than it was as a theatre".

Following the Group's demise, Clurman was sought after as a respected director and critic and he directly and indirectly promoted the works of many of his contemporaries. His association with emerging playwrights began in the 1930's when he produced and directed Clifford Odets's *Awake and Sing!*, the first of six Odets plays that he directed in all. Clurman also promoted the career of other writers, including William Inge, Carson McCullers, and Arthur Miller, whose second play, *All My Sons*, he produced. He also directed works by US writers Lillian Hellman, Eugene O'Neill, and Tennessee Williams and brought to the English-speaking stage several modern French playwrights, directing plays by Anouilh in New York and by Giraudoux in London.

Clurman approached his criticism with equal zeal, arguing against the influence of the overnight review, which reigns over New York theatre. He thought a critic should be "concerned with causes, with the composition of human, social, formal substances which have produced the effect", not with hasty judgements.

Through the Group, Clurman demonstrated that the artistic development of actors could coincide with the technical development of a production. He espoused the virtues of a permanent acting company and its potential effect on generating new plays by new playwrights, a philosophy embraced by many US regional theatres today. Above all, he believed in a theatre of full experience; as he concluded in his "instead of an autobiography": "I believe life terrible and glorious". For Harold Clurman, the juxtaposition of extremes makes theatre vital and such theatre is essential in a vital society.

—Roger N. Casey

———

COMPTON, Fay. British actress. Born Virginia Lilian Emmiline Compton in West Kensington, London, 18 September 1894; daughter of actor Edward Compton (Mackenzie) and actress Virginia Bateman. Educated at Leatherhead Court School, Surrey, and in Paris. Married 1) Harry Gabriel Pélissier in 1911 (died 1913), one son; 2) actor Lauri de Frece (died 1921); 3) actor Leon Quartermaine in 1922 (divorced 1942); 4) actor Ralph Shotter in 1942 (divorced 1946). Professional stage debut with Follies revue troupe, Apollo Theatre, London, 1911; New York debut, 1914; established reputation in plays of J. M. Barrie and Somerset Maugham in early 1920's; acclaimed as Ophelia opposite John Barrymore, 1925, and subsequently opposite John Gielgud, 1939; also popular in pantomime and music hall. CBE (Commander of the British Empire), 1975. Died in Hove, Sussex, 12 December 1978.

Roles

1913	Denise in *Who's the Lady?* (Levy), Garrick Theatre, London.
1914	Miranda Peploe in *The Pearl Girl* (Hood, Felix, and Talbot), Shaftesbury Theatre, London.
	Cissie in *The Cinema Star* (Hulbert), Shaftesbury Theatre, London.
	Victoria in *To-Night's the Night* (Thompson), Shubert Theatre, New York.
1915	Ruth Wilson in *The Only Girl* (Blossom), Apollo Theatre, London.
1916	Lady Di in *Follow the Crowd* (Wimperis, Carrick, and Berlin), Empire Theatre, London.
	Virginia Xelva in *The Boomerang* (Smith and Mapes), Queen's Theatre, London.
	Annabel in *Innocent and Annabel* (Chapin), Coliseum Theatre, London.
	Lucy White in *The Professor's Love Story* (Barrie), Savoy Theatre, London.
1917	Annette in *The Bells* (Lewis), Savoy Theatre, London.
	Sheila West in *Sheila* (Sowerby), St James's Theatre, London.
	Helen Bransby in *The Invisible Foe* (Hackett), Savoy Theatre, London.
	Peter in *Peter Pan* (Barrie), New Theatre, London.
1918	Blanche Wheeler in *Fair and Warmer* (Hopwood), Prince of Wales's Theatre, London.
	Sylvia in *The Harbury Pearls*, Victoria Palace Theatre, London.
1919	Violet Little in *Caesar's Wife* (Maugham), Royalty Theatre, London.

	Silvia in *Summertime* (Betti), Royalty Theatre, London.
1920	The Wife in *Tea for Three* (Cooper-Megrue), Haymarket Theatre, London.
	Mary Rose in *Mary Rose* (Barrie), Haymarket Theatre, London; revived there, 1926.
	Juliet in extract from *Romeo and Juliet* (Shakespeare), His Majesty's Theatre, London.
1921	Elizabeth in *The Circle* (Maugham), Haymarket Theatre, London.
	Phoebe Throssel in *Quality Street* (Barrie), Haymarket Theatre, London.
1922	Mary and Lady Carlton in *Secrets* (Besier and Edginton), Comedy Theatre, London; revived there, 1929.
1923	Loyse in *The Ballad Monger* (Besant and Pollock), His Majesty's Theatre, London.
	Princess Flavia in *The Prisoner of Zenda* (Rose, adapted from Hope), Haymarket Theatre, London.
	Lady Babbie in *The Little Minister* (Barrie), Queen's Theatre, London.
1924	Diana Tunstall in *The Claimant* (Watts), Queen's Theatre, London.
	Madeleine in *Orange Blossom* (Birabeau and Dolley, adapted by Graham), Queen's Theatre, London.
	Yasmin in *Hassan* (Flecker), His Majesty's Theatre, London.
1925	Ophelia in *Hamlet* (Shakespeare), Haymarket Theatre, London; revived there, 1931; Lyceum Theatre, London, and Elsinore, Denmark, 1939.
	Ariadne Winter in *Ariadne; or, Business First* (Milne), Haymarket Theatre, London.
	The Lady in *The Man With a Load of Mischief* (Dukes), Haymarket Theatre, London.
1926	Crawford in *This Woman Business* (Levy), Haymarket Theatre, London.
	Jenny Bell in *The White Witch* (Herbert), Haymarket Theatre, London.
	Julie in *Liliom* (Molnar), Duke of York's Theatre, London.
1927	Constance Middleton in *The Constant Wife* (Maugham), Strand Theatre, London.
	Lisa Mordaunt in *The Bridge*, Arts Theatre, London.
	Gianella in *The Wandering Jew* (Thurston), Theatre Royal, Drury Lane, London.
1928	Femme de Chambre in *Other Men's Wives* (Hackett), St Martin's Theatre, London.
	Suzanne de Tournai in *The Scarlet Pimpernel* (Orczy and Barstow), Palace Theatre, London.
	Olympia, Princess Orsolini in *Olympia* (Molnar), Empire Theatre, New York.
1930	Julia March in *Virtue for Sale*, British tour.
	Madeleine Cary in *Dishonoured Lady* (Barnes and Sheldon), Playhouse, London.
	Dick in *Dick Whittington* (pantomime), Palace Theatre, Manchester.
1931	Fanny Grey in *Autumn Crocus* (Anthony), Lyric Theatre, London, and British tour.

Fay Compton

Dick in *Dick Whittington* (pantomime), Theatre Royal, Glasgow.

1932   Camilla Graham in *Once a Husband* (Neville and Hay), Haymarket Theatre, London.

Dick in *Dick Whittington* (Wylie and Leno), Hippodrome, London.

1933   Several roles in *This, That, and The Other* (variety show), British tour.

Norma Matthews in *Proscenium* (Novello), Globe Theatre, London.

1934   Christina in *Indoor Fireworks* (Macrae), Aldwych Theatre, London.

Mary Ventyre in *Murder in Mayfair* (Novello), Globe Theatre, London.

1935   Duchess of Shires in *Hervey House*, His Majesty's Theatre, London.

Titania in *A Midsummer Night's Dream* (Shakespeare), Open Air Theatre, London; revived there, 1937.

Rosaline in *Love's Labour's Lost* (Shakespeare), Open Air Theatre, London.

Dorothy Hilton in *Call it a Day* (Anthony), Globe Theatre, London; British tour, 1937.

1937   Calpurnia in *Julius Caesar* (Shakespeare), Open Air Theatre, London.

The Lady in *Comus* (Milton), Open Air Theatre, London.

Paulina in *The Winter's Tale* (Shakespeare), Open Air Theatre, London.

1938   Robin Hood in *Babes in the Wood* (pantomime), Theatre Royal, Drury Lane, London.

1939   Mrs Philips in *Drawing Room*, British tour.

Sanchia Carson in *Robert's Wife* (Ervine), British tour.

1940   Regan in *King Lear* (Shakespeare), Old Vic Theatre, London.

Virgin Mary in *Family Portrait* (Coffee and Cowen), British tour; Strand Theatre, London, 1948.

Doris Gow in *Fumed Oak* (Coward), British tour.

The Prince in *Cinderella* (pantomime), Palace Theatre, Manchester.

1941   Ruth in *Blithe Spirit* (Coward), Piccadilly Theatre, London.

1942   Regina Giddens in *The Little Foxes* (Hellman), Piccadilly Theatre, London.

The Prince in *Cinderella* (pantomime), Stoll Theatre, London.

1943   Madame Sans-Gêne in *The Duchess of Dantzig* (Caryll), British tour.

1944   Hannah Kernahan in *The Last of Summer* (O'Brien and Perry), Phoenix Theatre, London.

Martha Dacre in *No Medals* (McCracken), Vaudeville Theatre, London.

1946   Emilia in *Othello* (Shakespeare), European tour; Piccadilly Theatre, London, 1947.

Candida in *Candida* (G. B. Shaw), European tour; Piccadilly Theatre, London, 1947.

1948   Gina Ekdal in *The Wild Duck* (Ibsen), St Martin's Theatre, London.

1949   Sister Mary Bonaventure in *Bonaventure* (Hastings), Vaudeville Theatre, London.

1951   Yvonne in *Intimate Relations* (Cocteau, translated by Frank), Arts Theatre, London, and Strand Theatre, London.

1952   Lora Sutherland in *Red Letter Day* (Rosenthal), Garrick Theatre, London.

Esther Ledoux in *The Holy Terrors* (Cocteau), Arts Theatre, London.

1953   Martha in *Out of the Whirlwind*, Westminster Abbey, London.

Gertrude in *Hamlet* (Shakespeare), Edinburgh Festival and Old Vic Theatre, London.

Countess of Rossillion in *All's Well That Ends Well* (Shakespeare), Old Vic Theatre, London.

Constance of Bretagne in *King John* (Shakespeare), Old Vic Theatre, London.

Volumnia in *Coriolanus* (Shakespeare), Old Vic Theatre, London.

Juno in *The Tempest* (Shakespeare), Old Vic Theatre, London.

1954   Gertrude Blunt in *Witch Errant*, Q Theatre, London.

1955   Ruth Prendergast in *Tabitha* (Ridley and Borer), British tour.

1956   Lydia Sheridan in *Starlight*, British tour.

1957   Queen Margaret in *Richard III* (Shakespeare), Old Vic Theatre, London.

1958   Mrs St Maugham in *The Chalk Garden* (Bagnold), British tour.

1959   Kate Murphy in *God and Kate Murphy* (Tunney and Synge), 54th Street Theatre, New York.

Lady Bracknell in *The Importance of Being Earnest* (Wilde), Old Vic Theatre, London.

1960   Contesse de la Brière in *What Every Woman Knows* (Barrie), Old Vic Theatre, London.

1961   Mrs Malaprop in *The Rivals* (Sheridan), Pembroke Theatre, Croydon, London; Lyric Theatre, Hammersmith, London, 1963.

1962   Grausis in *The Broken Heart* (Ford), Chichester Festival Theatre.

Marya in *Uncle Vanya* (Chekhov), Chichester Festival Theatre; revived there, 1963.

1963   Mrs B in *The Workhouse Donkey* (Arden), Chichester Festival Theatre.

Mrs Caution in *The Gentleman Dancing Master* (Wycherley), British tour.

1965   Anna in *A Month in the Country* (Turgenev), Yvonne Arnaud Theatre, Guildford, and Cambridge Theatre, London.

Chorus in *Samson Agonistes* (Milton), Yvonne Arnaud Theatre, Guildford.

Also acted roles in: *Victoria Regina* (Housman), *To-Night at 8.30* (Coward), and *George and Margaret* (Savory), tour of Australia and New Zealand, 1937–38; *Hamlet* (Shakespeare), European tour, 1946.

Films

She Stoops to Conquer, 1914; *One Summer's Day*, 1917; *The Labour Leader*, 1917; *A Woman of No Importance*, 1921; *The Old Wives' Tale*, 1921; *Mary Queen of Scots*, 1922; *This Freedom*, 1923; *Robinson Crusoe*, 1927; *Fashions in Love*, 1929; *Tell England*, 1931; *Autumn Crocus*, 1934; *The Mill on the Floss*, 1935; *The Prime Minister*, 1941; *Odd Man Out*, 1946; *London Belongs to Me*, 1948; *Laughter in Paradise*, 1950; *Othello*, 1952; *Aunt Clara*, 1954; *The Story of Esther Costello*, 1957; *The Haunting*, 1963; *The Virgin and the Gypsy*, 1970.

Television

The Forsyte Saga, 1967.

Publications

Rosemary: Some Remembrances, 1926.

* * *

The key to Fay Compton's nature lies in the word 'trouper' employed eulogistically. As one of a family involved in drama and literature, she was introduced to the stage at an early age and gained her training in a company more closely associated with revue than classical theatre. The autobiography of her elder brother, writer Compton Mackenzie, stressed Fay's altruism and modesty in the face of her growing reputation. Nonetheless, he also recorded that Henry Irving, seeing the whole family, pointed dramat-

ically to Fay (then four) and prophesied: "That's the one who will make a success".

These attitudes are reflected in the extraordinary range of parts that Fay Compton played. The same actress who was hailed by James Agate for "the beauty and pathos of her Ophelia" also delighted audiences in Glasgow, Manchester, and London in the pantomime role of Dick Whittington. In the latter role, a reviewer in *The Times* noted the disappearance of all ethereal qualities — those natural skills that had made her the first and finest Mary Rose: instead there was "vivacity without archness, dash without affected swagger; she can sing with an exuberant lightness that can charm the house and she can dance in front of the Tiller girls". The range of her talents was further complemented by thoughtful interpretion, even in this light dramatic mode.

Compton's refusal to overact or to draw attention away from her fellow performers was consistently admired. Critics who had witnessed Ellaline Terriss's self-indulgent portrayal of Phoebe in *Quality Street*, for instance, were unaware that this young attractive heroine was meant to be plain and verging on middle age, and it was only when Compton came to play the character in the 1921 revival that her gentle underplaying revealed Barrie's true purpose to astonished critics for the first time.

This subtlety makes the actress's choice of favourite role less surprising than on the surface it might appear. She opted not for Ophelia nor for Mary Rose but for Paulina in *The Winter's Tale*, a relatively minor part that she played at the Open Air Theatre in 1937. Reviewers noted the skill with which her voice and her intelligent re-interpretation made her stand out from the rest of the cast while still subsuming her performance within the overall effect. Again it was the reviewer from *The Times* who summed up her achievement most effectively, in a series of negatives: "never flat, never dull, never pompous nor facetious, never 'just herself'". Her control of Shakespearean language also impressed those who saw her and ensured that her Paulina never lapsed into homily but compelled the audience to 'hear anew'.

These strengths may also (ironically) account for the fact that Compton's greatest plaudits came in the relatively early stages of her career, when she had two other notable advantages. The first of these was her association with J. M. Barrie, whose plays provided the material on which she matured from juvenile to star. Believing his work was more complex than audiences assumed, the Scottish playwright welcomed Compton's serious approach and receptive mind. She, in her turn, appreciated the accolade of being offered Peter Pan, having been promised — as she recalled in her autobiography — the chance to play the part by the author much earlier. She fell completely under Barrie's spell, just as Gladys Cooper and many others would. Not that her insights into his work were always sympathetic. Her assessment that Lucy White in *The Professor's Love Story* was one of her most difficult parts reflects as much on the dramatist's failure to integrate the heroine's role into the plot as on any imagined limitation on Compton's acting.

The other advantage Compton enjoyed at the start of her career was the greater range of parts open to her. She was not limited then to characters of her own age and was, indeed, drawn to the challenge of conveying the aging process. Thus, one of her greatest successes came with the dual role of Mary and Lady Carlton in *Secrets*. Nor did her outstanding redhaired beauty prove any more of an obstacle than her naturally sympathetic personality when faced with the test of presenting evil. John Gielgud was deeply impressed by her Regan, for instance. She played her, he recorded, as "a kind of cold pussy cat". The director, Granville Barker, was not slow to take advantage and added a piece of business where she made up her face, looking in a mirror, undisturbed by news of her widowhood. Equally, the failure of *The Little Foxes* in 1942 was carefully separated from her achievement as Regina Giddens. A. E. Wilson commented on the intensity with which she conveyed "that flint-hearted creature who, unmoved, watched her dying husband and refused to help him".

In the period after 1950, Compton did not lose in popularity but never enjoyed the same degree of acclaim. *Plays and Players 1953–68* mentions her only once and that is to record her Lady Bracknell as one of the two major disappointments of 1959. The root of her problem may well have been the series of such 'grande dame' parts that are usually expected of aging female stars. Most adapt well to these, but Compton's unselfish interest in overall effect and tendency to underplay were, arguably, not well served by cameo roles where self-indulgence and melodrama became virtues. Her brother's memory of her helping to shift cases on arrival in a new town catches the spirit of this inspired trouper more fittingly than her name in lights.

—R. D. S. Jack

COOKE, George Frederick. British actor. Born in Westminster, London (possibly in Dublin), 17 April 1756. Educated at schools in Berwick. Married 1) actress Alicia Daniels in 1796 (annulled in 1801); 2) a Miss Lamb in 1808; 3) a Mrs Behn in 1811. Apprenticed to printer while still at school; began in amateur theatre; professional stage debut, King's Lynn, 1774; strolling player with various provincial companies, 1774–82; possibly appeared at Haymarket Theatre, London, 1778; leading actor, Nottingham-Derby company, 1781–82; acclaimed as 'Manchester Roscius', Manchester, 1784; two visits to Dublin, one resulting in forcible but shortlived enlistment in army, 1796; engaged at Covent Garden, London, 1800–10; career much disrupted by alcoholism and debt; US debut, Park Theatre, New York, 1810; subsequently appeared in Philadelphia, Boston, and Baltimore; last appearance, as Sir Giles Overreach, Providence, July 1811. Died in New York, 26 September 1811.

Roles

1774   Lord Aimworth in *The Maid of the Mill* (Bickerstaff); last acted, 1792.
Alexander in *The Rival Queens* (Lee); last acted, 1797.
Beau Mizen in *The Fair Quaker of Deal* (Shadwell); last acted, 1775.
Belville in *The School for Wives* (Kelly); last acted, 1775.
Damaetas in *Midas* (O'Hara).

Lord Duke in *High Life Below Stairs* (Townley and Garrick).
Epicene in *The Macaroni* (Hitchcock).
Don Felix in *The Wonder* (Centlivre); last acted, 1808.
Ferdinand in *The Tempest* (Shakespeare); last acted, 1775.
Filch in *The Beggar's Opera* (Gay).
Fuzee in *The Modish Wife* (Gentleman); last acted, 1775.
Granville in *Clementina* (Kelly).
Hamlet in *Hamlet* (Shakespeare); last acted, 1802.
Lord Hardy in *The Funeral* (Steele).
Lord Hastings in *Jane Shore* (Rowe); last acted, 1805.
Sir George Hastings in *A Word to the Wise* (Kelly).
Henry in *The Deserter* (C. Dibdin); last acted, 1775.
Henry in *Henry II* (Hull); last acted, 1775.
Jaffier in *Venice Preserved* (Otway); last acted, 1793.
Lear in *King Lear* (Shakespeare); last acted, 1811.
Lionel in *Lionel and Clarissa* (Bickerstaff); last acted, 1775.
Mr Lovemore in *The Way to Keep Him* (Murphy); last acted, 1789.
Macbeth in *Macbeth* (Shakespeare); last acted, 1811.
Young Marlow in *She Stoops to Conquer* (Goldsmith); last acted, 1794.
Young Meadows in *Love in a Village* (Bickerstaff); last acted, 1775.
Jack Meggot in *The Suspicious Husband* (Hoadley).
Paris in *The Judgement of Paris* (Langford).
Posthumous in *Cymbeline* (Shakespeare); last acted, 1791.
Ramilie in *The Miser* (Fielding).
Revell in *The Note of Hand* (Cumberland); last acted, 1775.
Richard in *Richard III* (Shakespeare); last acted, 1811.
Riches in *Harlequin Fortunatus* (Woodward); last acted, 1775.
Spatter in *The English Merchant* (Colman the Elder); last acted, 1784.
Lord Trinket in *The Jealous Wife* (Colman the Elder).
Wilding in *The Gamesters* (Garrick).
Zanga in *The Revenge* (Young); last acted, 1811.

1775   Apollo in *Midas* (O'Hara).
King Arthur in *King Arthur* (Dryden).
Beverley in *All In The Wrong* (Murphy).
Beverley in *The Man of Business* (Colman the Elder).
Mr Dupely in *The Maid of the Oaks* (Burgoyne); last acted, 1791.
Hotspur in *Henry IV* (Shakespeare); last acted, 1794.

George Frederick Cooke (engraving by Rogers).

Charles Marlowe in *The Choleric Man* (Cumberland).

Marplot in *The Busybody* (Centlivre).

Morcar in *Matilda* (Francklin).

Lord Ogleby in *The Clandestine Marriage* (Colman the Elder and Garrick).

Oroonoko in *Oroonoko* (Southern); last acted, 1792.

Paris in *The Golden Pippin* (O'Hara).

Prattle in *The Deuce Is in Him* (Colman the Elder).

Romeo in *Romeo and Juliet* (Shakespeare); last acted, 1791.

Stockwell in *The West Indian* (Cumberland); last acted, 1800.

Tamerlane in *Tamerlane the Great* (Rowe); last acted, 1782.

Tom in *The Conscious Lovers* (Steele).

1776   Dumont in *Jane Shore* (Rowe); last acted, 1806.

Young Dudley in *The West Indian* (Cumberland); last acted, 1788.

1778   Lord Abbeville in *The Fashionable Lover* (Cumberland).

Bedamar in *Venice Preserved* (Otway).

George Bevil in *Cross Purposes* (O'Brien).

Castalio in *The Orphan* (Otway).

Charles in *The Busybody* (Centlivre).

Conjurer in *The Devil to Pay* (Coffey and Mottley).

Captain Constant in *The Ghost* (anon.).

Edgar in *King Lear* (Shakespeare); last acted, 1789.

Frederick in *The Miser* (Fielding); last acted, 1782.

Frederick in *The Wonder* (Centlivre).

Freeman in *A Bold Stroke for a Wife* (Centlivre).

Gayless in *The Lying Valet* (Garrick).

Glenalvon in *Douglas* (Home); last acted, 1811.

Mr Harlow in *The Old Maid* (Murphy).

Harry in *The Mock Doctor* (Fielding).

Hortensio in *Catherine and Petruchio* (Garrick).

Lovewell in *The Clandestine Marriage* (Colman the Elder and Garrick); last acted, 1791.

Modely in *The Country Lasses* (Johnson); last acted, 1790.

Sir Harry's Servant in *High Life Below Stairs* (Townley and Garrick).

Southampton in *The Earl of Essex* (James); last acted, 1792.

Tressel in *Richard III* (Shakespeare).

Trueman in *The London Merchant* (Lillo).

Tybalt in *Romeo and Juliet* (Shakespeare).

Young Wilding in *The Citizen* (Murphy); last acted, 1794.

1779   Young Belmont in *The Foundling* (Moore); last acted, 1787.

1781   Sir George Airy in *The Busybody* (Centlivre); last acted, 1797.

Eastern Magician in *Harlequin Sorcerer* (anon.); last acted, 1782.

Evander in *The Grecian Daughter* (Murphy); last acted, 1799.

Pierre in *Venice Preserved* (Otway); last acted, 1811.

Saville in *The Belle's Stratagem* (Cowley); last acted, 1785.

1782   Young Cape in *The Author* (Foote).

Clytus in *The Rival Queens* (Lee); last acted, 1811.

Frankly in *The Suspicious Husband* (Hoadley); last acted, 1794.

Earl of Pembroke in *Lady Jane Grey* (Rowe).

Salmandore in *The Rape of Proserpine* (Theobald).

Joseph Surface in *The School for Scandal* (Sheridan); last acted, 1810.

Lord Townly in *The Provoked Husband* (Vanbrugh and Cibber); last acted, 1808.

1784   Abbot in *Henry II* (Hull).

Aimwell in *The Beaux' Stratagem* (Farquhar); last acted, 1791.

Alonzo in *The Revenge* (Young); last acted, 1785.

Alwin in *The Countess of Salisbury* (Hartson); last acted, 1791.

Antonio in *The Merchant of Venice* (Shakespeare); last acted, 1790.

Barbarossa in *Barbarossa* (Brown).

Belair in *More Ways than One* (Cowley).

Benedick in *Much Ado About Nothing* (Shakespeare); last acted, 1799.

Lord Burleigh in *The Unhappy Favourite* (Banks).

Don Carlos in *Love Makes a Man* (Cibber); last acted, 1792.

Claudio in *Much Ado About Nothing* (Shakespeare); last acted, 1791.

Claudius in *Hamlet* (Shakespeare); last acted, 1785.

Douglas in *Douglas* (Home).

Fairfax in *King Charles I* (Havard).

Mr Fitzherbert in *Which is The Man?* (Cowley); last acted, 1791.

Gambler in *The Indian Chief* (Williams).

Glanville in *Cleone* (Dodsley).

King Henry in *Richard III* (Shakespeare); last acted, 1800.

Don Juan in *The Castle of Andalusia* (O'Keeffe).

Don Julio in *A Bold Stroke for a Husband* (Cowley); last acted, 1785.

Sir John Lambert in *The Hypocrite* (Bickerstaff).

Ensign Maclaymore in *The Reprisal* (Smollett); last acted, 1793.

Malville in *Know your own Mind* (Murphy); last acted, 1789.

Moneses in *Tamerlane* (Rowe); last acted, 1787.

Orestes in *The Distressed Mother* (Phillips).

Philotas in *The Grecian Daughter* (Murphy); last acted, 1787.

Sir Charles Pleasant in *The Fair Quaker* (Thompson).

Earl Raby in *Percy* (More); last acted, 1786.

Ranger in *The Suspicious Husband* (Hoadly); last acted, 1792.

Raymond in *The Countess of Salisbury* (Hartson); last acted, 1785.

Sciolto in *The Fair Penitent* (Rowe); last acted, 1805.

Siffridi in *Tancred and Sigismunda* (Thomson).

Sir Peter Teazle in *The School for Scandal* (Sheridan); last acted, 1788.

Friar Tuck/Baron Fitzherbert in *Robin Hood* (anon.); last acted, 1785.

Valerius in *The Roman Father* (Whitehead).

Villeroy in *Isabella* (Southern); last acted, 1786.

Wolsey in *Henry VII* (Shakespeare); last acted, 1793.

1785 Captain Absolute in *The Rivals* (Sheridan); last acted, 1796.

Adam in *As You Like It* (Shakespeare); last acted, 1792.

Aubrey in *The Fashionable Lover* (Cumberland); last acted, 1790.

Mr Beauchamp in *Which is the Man?* (Cowley).

Bertoldo in *The Maid of Honour* (Massinger, adapted by J. P. Kemble).

Count Baldwin in *Isabella* (Garrick, adapted from Southern's *The Fatal Marriage*).

Belville in *Which is the Man?* (Cowley); last acted, 1789.

Don Carlos in *A Bold Stroke for a Husband* (Cowley); last acted, 1804.

Carlton in *More Ways Than One* (Cowley).

Sir John Melville in *The Clandestine Marriage* (Coman the Elder and Garrick); last acted, 1792.

Spatterdash in *The Young Quaker* (O'Keeffe).

Stukeley in *The Gamester* (Moore); last acted, 1811.

1786 Comus in *Comus* (Milton, adapted by Colman the Elder); last acted, 1803.

Dashwood in *Know your own Mind* (Murphy).

Doricourt in *The Belle's Stratagem* (Cowley).

Durand in *Venice Preserved* (Otway).

King Edward in *The Earl of Warwick* (Francklin).

Gloster in *Jane Shore* (Rowe); last acted, 1807.

King in *The Mourning Bride* (Congreve).

Loveless in *A Trip to Scarborough* (Sheridan); last acted, 1800.

Othello in *Othello* (Shakespeare); last acted, 1801.

Petruchio in *Catherine and Petruchio* (Garrick); last acted, 1807.

Raymond in *The Count of Narbonne* (Jephson); last acted, 1787.

Sir John Restless in *All in the Wrong* (Murphy); last acted, 1788.

Rosse in *Macbeth* (Shakespeare).

Shylock in *The Merchant of Venice* (Shakespeare); last acted, 1811.

1787 John Cockle in *The King and the Miller of Mansfield* (Dodsley); last acted, 1809.

Earl Douglas in *Percy* (More); last acted, 1798.

Colonel Downright in *I'll Tell You What* (Inchbald).

Sir Clement Flint in *The Heiress* (Burgoyne); last acted, 1793.

Colonel Holberg in *The Disbanded Officer* (Johnstone).

The Natural Son in *The Natural Son* (Cumberland).

Mr Oakley in *The Jealous Wife* (Colman the Elder); last acted, 1808.

Mr Ordeal in *Fashionable Levities* (Macnally); last acted, 1788.

Sultan in *Such Things Are* (Inchbald).

Colonel Talbot in *He wou'd be a Soldier* (Pilon); last acted, 1798.

Sir George Touchwood in *The Belle's Stratagem* (Cowley); last acted, 1798.

Mr Vandercrab in *New Peerage* (Lee).

1788 Aboan in *Oroonoko* (Southern).

Archer in *The Beaux' Stratagem* (Farquhar).

Falstaff in *Henry IV, part 1* (Shakespeare); last acted, 1811.

Freeport in *The English Merchant* (Colman the Elder); last acted, 1794.

Grey in *The Chapter of Accidents* (Lee); last acted, 1800.

Haswell in *Such Things Are* (Inchbald); last acted, 1806.

Inkle in *Inkle and Yarico* (Colman the Younger); last acted, 1792.

Leonidas in *The Fate of Sparta* (Cowley); last acted, 1790.

Don Manuel in *The Regent* (Greathead); last acted, 1792.

Mentevole in *Julia* (Jephson).

Myrtle in *The Conscious Lovers* (Steele).

Varanes in *Theodosius* (Lee).

1789   Young Bevil in *The Conscious Lovers* (Steele); last acted, 1790.

Cato in *Cato* (Addison); last acted, 1810.

Chamont in *The Orphan* (Otway).

Clerimont in *The Old Maid* (Murphy); last acted, 1791.

The Duke in *Measure for Measure* (Shakespeare).

Colonel Feignwell in *A Bold Stroke for a Wife* (Centlivre).

Farmer Freehold in *The Farmhouse* (J. P. Kemble).

Iachimo in *Cymbeline* (Shakespeare); last acted, 1807.

Jaques in *As You Like It* (Shakespeare); last acted, 1808.

Leontes in *The Winter's Tale* (Shakespeare).

Loveless in *Reparation* (Andrews).

Moody in *The Country Girl* (Garrick); last acted, 1800.

Major Oakley in *The Jealous Wife* (Colman the Elder); last acted, 1810.

Captain Plume in *The Recruiting Officer* (Farquhar); last acted, 1792.

Prospero in *The Tempest* (Shakespeare); last acted, 1807.

Colonel Standard in *The Constant Couple* (Farquhar); last acted, 1790.

1790   Sir Christopher Curry in *Inkle and Yarico* (Colman the Younger); last acted, 1808.

Lord Davenant in *The Mysterious Husband* (Cumberland); last acted, 1806.

Dick in *The Confederacy* (Vanbrugh).

Sir John Dormer in *A Word to the Wise* (Kelly).

Sir William Douglas in *The English Merchant* (Colman the Elder); last acted, 1791.

Lord Guilford Dudley in *Lady Jane Grey* (Rowe).

Essex in *The Earl of Essex* (Jones).

Earl of Exeter in *Henry V* (Shakespeare).

Falstaff in *The Merry Wives of Windsor* (Shakespeare); last acted, 1811.

Gondibert in *The Battle of Hexham* (Colman the Younger).

The Guardian in *The Guardian* (Garrick); last acted, 1800.

Heartwell in *The Guardian* (Garrick).

Henry in *Henry V* (Shakespeare); last acted, 1805.

Lord Hildebrand in *The Carmelite* (Cumberland).

Robin Hood in *Robin Hood and Little John* (anon.).

Lusignan in *Zara* (Hill).

Mahomet in *Mahomet* (Miller).

Neville in *The Dramatist* (Reynolds); last acted, 1791.

Mr Strictland in *The Suspicious Husband* (Hoadly); last acted, 1807.

Valentine in *Love for Love* (Congreve).

Earl of Warwick in *The Earl of Warwick* (Francklin); last acted, 1791.

Zamor in *Alzira* (Hill); last acted, 1791.

1791   Dick Buskin in *Wild Oats* (O'Keeffe); last acted, 1793.

Cromwell in *King Charles I* (Havard); last acted, 1792.

Falconbridge in *King John* (Shakespeare).

Mr Hammond in *Modern Breakfast* (Siddons).

Mr Heartly in *The Guardian* (Garrick); last acted, 1803.

Macduff in *Macbeth* (Shakespeare); last acted, 1804.

Major O'Flaherty in *The West Indian* (Cumberland).

Rover in *Wild Oats* (O'Keeffe); last acted, 1794.

Sir George Splenderville in *Next Door Neighbours* (Inchbald); last acted, 1792.

Colonel Tamper in *The Deuce is in him* (Colman the Elder).

Tancred in *Tancred and Sigismunda* (Thomson).

1792   Count Almaviva in *The Follies of a Day* (Holcroft).

Banquo in *Macbeth* (Shakespeare).

George Barnwell in *The London Merchant* (Lillo); last acted, 1793.

Beverley in *The Gamester* (Moore).

Dr Cantwell in *The Hypocrite* (Bickerstaff).

Don Carlos in *Lovers' Quarrels* (King).

Clairville in *Notoriety* (Reynolds).

Sir John Classick in *The Married Man* (Inchbald).

Dionysius in *The Grecian Daughter* (Murphy).

Harry Dornton in *The Road to Ruin* (Holcroft); last acted, 1794.

Floriville in *The Dramatist* (Reynolds).

The Ghost in *Hamlet* (Shakespeare); last acted, 1804.

Horatius in *The Roman Father* (Whitehead); last acted, 1810.

Iago in *Othello* (Shakespeare); last acted, 1811.

Sir Pertinax MacSycophant in *The Man of the World* (Macklin); last acted, 1811.

Young Manley in *The Fugitive* (Richardson); last acted, 1793.

Orloff in *A Day in Turkey* (Cowley); last acted, 1793.

Count Ribemont in *The Surrender of Calais* (Colman the Younger); last acted, 1793.

Count Ribemont in *The Black Prince* (Boyle).

Richard in *Richard Coeur de Lion* (Burgoyne).

Count Connoly Villars in *The School for Arrogance* (Holcroft).

Warford in *How to Grow Rich* (Reynolds).

Mr Wingrove in *The Fugitive* (O'Keeffe).

1793   Alonzo in *Columbus* (Morton).

Biron in *Isabella* (Southern); last acted, 1799.

Edward in *Edward the Black Prince* (Shirley).

Harmony in *Everyone Has His Fault* (Inchbald); last acted, 1801.

King in *The King and the Miller of Mansfield* (Dodsley); last acted, 1809.

King in *The King in the Country* (Waldron).

Kiteley in *Every Man in his Humour* (Jonson); last acted, 1811.

Mark Antony in *Julius Caesar* (Shakespeare); last acted, 1796.

Old Norval in *Douglas* (Home); last acted, 1799.

Sealand in *The Conscious Lovers* (Steele).

1794 Sir Callaghan O'Brallaghan in *Love á la Mode* (Macklin).

Columbus in *Columbus* (Morton).

Eustace de St Pierre in *The Surrender of Calais* (Colman the Younger).

Faulkland in *The Rivals* (Sheridan).

Don Juan in *The Duke of Braganza* (Jephson).

Friar Lawrence in *Romeo and Juliet* (Shakespeare); last acted, 1799.

Octavian in *The Mountaineers* (Colman the Younger); last acted, 1802.

Sir Robert Ramble in *Everyone has his Fault* (Inchbald).

Tobine in *The Suicide* (Colman the Elder).

1795 Sir Anthony Absolute in *The Rivals* (Sheridan).

Sir George in *The Rage* (Reynolds).

Horatio in *The Fair Penitent* (Rowe); last acted, 1811.

Sir Oliver Surface in *The School for Scandal* (Sheridan).

1796 Dorington in *The Man of Ten Thousand* (Holcroft).

Iago in *Othello* (Shakespeare).

Marquis Almanza in *The Child of Nature* (Minchbald); last acted, 1798.

Captain Faulkner in *How to Get Married* (anon.); last acted, 1802.

John in *King John* (Shakespeare); last acted, 1811.

Sir Archy MacSarcasm in *Love á la Mode* (Macklin); last acted, 1811.

Sir Edward Mortimer in *The Iron Chest* (Colman the Younger); last acted, 1802.

Sir Giles Overreach in *A New Way to Pay Old Debts* (Massinger); last acted, 1811.

1797 Sir William Dorrillon in *Wives as They Were, and Maids as They Are* (Iinchbald); last acted, 1800.

Master of the Shop in *The Toyshop* (Dodsley).

McLaughlan in *Bantry Bay* (Reynolds).

Osmyn in *The Mourning Bride* (Congreve).

Penruddock in *The Wheel of Fortune* (Cumberland); last acted, 1811.

Sir Hubert Stanley in *A Cure for the Heartache* (Morton).

Sir Thomas Wildmay in *The Outcasts* (Cherry).

1798 Delaval in *He's Much to Blame* (Holcroft).

Sir John Flowerdale in *Lionel and Clarissa* (Bickerstaff).

Midas in *Midas* (O'Hara).

Stedfast in *The Heir-at-Law* (Colman the Younger); last acted, 1799.

1799 Austin in *The Count of Narbonne* (Jephson); last acted, 1800.

Captain Bertram in *The Birthday* (T. Dibdin); last acted, 1802.

Fairfield in *The Maid of the Mill* (Bickerstaff).

Captain Ironsides in *The Brothers* (Cumberland); last acted, 1807.

Earl Osmond in *The Castle Spectre* (Lewis); last acted, 1804.

Reginald in *The Castle Spectre* (Lewis).

Earl of Salisbury in *The Countess of Salisbury* (Hartson).

Dr Specific in *The Jew and the Doctor* (T. Dibdin).

The Stranger in *The Stranger* (Thomson); last acted, 1808.

Baron Wildenheim in *Lover's Vows* (Inchbald); last acted, 1809.

1800 Bastard in *King Lear* (Shakespeare).

Sir Stephen Bertram in *The Jew* (Cumberland).

Sir Phillip Blandford in *Speed the Plough* (Morton); last acted, 1803.

Las Casas in *Pizarro* (Sheridan).

Pizarro in *Pizarro* (Sheridan); last acted, 1806.

1801 Alberto in *The Child of Nature* (Inchbald).

Leon in *Rule a Wife and Have a Wife* (Beaumont and Fletcher).

Mercutio in *Romeo and Juliet* (Shakespeare).

1802 Bajazet in *Tamerlane the Great* (Rowe); last acted, 1805.

Orsino in *Alfonso, King of Castile* (Lewis); last acted, 1805.

1803 Angelo in *Measure for Measure* (Shakespeare).

John in *King John* (Shakespeare).

Macduff in *Macbeth* (Shakespeare).

1804 Cohenburg in *The Siege of Belgrade* (Cobb); last acted, 1805.

Hubert in *King John* (Shakespeare).

Peregrine in *John Bull* (Colman the Younger); last acted, 1809.

Rolla in *Rolla* (Lewis); last acted, 1805.

1805 Lord Avondale in *The School of Reform* (Morton); last acted, 1806.

Lavensforth in *To Marry or Not to Marry* (Inchbald).

Lennox in *Sprigs of Laurel* (O'Keeffe).

Donald MacIntosh in *The Register Office* (Reed).

Mortimer in *Laugh when you Can* (Reynolds).

1806 Prince of Altenburg in *Adrian and Orrila* (Dimond); last acted, 1808.

Ventidius in *All for Love* (Dryden).

1808 Catarach in *Bonduca* (Beaumont and Fletcher, adapted by Colman the Elder).

Kent in *King Lear* (Shakespeare).

Colonel Vortex in *Match Making* (Mrs C. Kemble).

1809 Gibby in *The Wonder* (Centlivre).

Colin Macleod in *The Fashionable Lover* (Cumberland); last acted, 1810.

1810 Henry in *Henry VIII* (Shakespeare); last acted, 1811.

Luke Traffic in *Riches* (Burges).

Also acted role in: *The Irish Widow* (Garrick), 1774.

*

Bibliography

Books:
William Dunlap, *Memoirs of George Frederick Cooke*, New York, 1813.
Arnold Hare, *George Frederick Cooke: The Actor and the Man*, London, 1980.
Dan B. Wilmeth, *George Frederick Cooke — Machiavel of the Stage*, Westport, Connecticut, 1984.

* * *

According to John Genest, George Frederick Cooke "did not play many parts well, but ... he played those which he did play well better than anybody else." The 'Old Playgoer', William Robson, conceded that Cooke was equal with John Philip Kemble in all characters "whose villainy was meant to create disgust", but that he was less effective as soon as charm, loftiness, elegance, or nobility were required. Cooke was certainly the great Richard III of his generation and in parts such as this many thought he actually usurped the primacy of Kemble. His features and his voice assisted him in such roles, as Leigh Hunt attests: "Cooke, a square-faced, hook-nosed, wide-mouthed, malignantly smiling man, was intelligent and peremptory, and a hard hitter; he seized and strongly held your attention; but he was never pleasant. He was too entirely the satirist, the hypocrite, and the villain. He loved too fully his own caustic and rascally words; so that his voice, which was otherwise harsh, was in the *habit* of melting and dying away inwardly in the secret satisfaction of its smiling malignity."

The originality of Cooke's performance as Richard was particularly notable: "He sometimes passes over what have been usually conceived to be *great points* in the character; and he exults other passages into importance which former Richards have not thought significant enough for particular notice." As Richard he put strong emphasis on the character's deformity, even regarding it as a justification for his behaviour, and on his satisfaction in doing evil. He made the character utterly "detestable" and his soliloquies seemed to reveal the "secret deliberations of the soul", rather than take the form of a direct address to this audience. Even though Charles Lamb was to criticise Cooke's Richard on the grounds that his dissimulation was too glaring, his jocularity too like the coarse humour of a low-minded assassin, and his reference to his deformity too full of distaste, most critics praised his discrimination and careful study of the role.

Inevitably, Cooke was also highly praised in roles such as Iago and Shylock. His Iago, like his Richard, avoided the temptation to make the audience party to his machinations; he focussed on Iago's personal malignity, but was praised for assuming a different disposition with each of the characters he deceived. As Shylock he particularly revealed the cunning, the servile, and the malign aspects of the role, but was less effective in demonstrating its quieter emotions. Nevertheless, he was generally considered the best Shylock since Charles Macklin.

Cooke proved himself to be, unlike Kemble, equally adept in comic roles. He was an effective Falstaff, rescuing this character from the vulgar buffooneries of the low comedian. In roles like Sir Pertinax MacSycophant he was particularly praised; Leigh Hunt regarded this as his most finished performance. Robson felt that Cooke's Scotsmen were his masterpieces, writing in praise of his Sir Archy MacSarcasm: "The dry sarcastic mirth, the perfect concentration of self-good opinion, the inward triumphant chuckle, and sneering *Scotch* laugh of Cooke were beyond belief fine!". A Scottish reviewer claimed that Cooke's Sir Archy was "in dialect and in manner the most forcible and characteristic representation of Macklin's baronet" he had ever seen or conceived. As with Shylock, Cooke inevitably drew comparisons, largely favourable, with Macklin's performance of the role.

Cooke's voice was considered by some to be a problem. Dunlap, for instance, recalling the opening night at the Park Theatre, felt that "the high key in which he pitched his voice, and its sharp and rather grating tones, caused a sensation of disappointment in some, and fear in others that such tones could not be modulated to the various cadences of nature, or such a voice have compass for the various expression of harmonious diction and distracting passion, which the characters of Shakespeare require." James E. Murdoch, however, whilst finding it rather hard and sharp, considered that it was remarkable in compass. Macready reckoned that Cooke's "varieties of tone seemed limited to a loud harsh croak descending to the lowest audible murmur; but there was such a significance in each inflection, look and gesture, and such impressive earnestness in his whole bearing, that he compelled your attention and interest."

Some considered Cooke, on account of his originality and individualism, one of the first romantic actors. Dunlap praised him for "seizing the perfect image of the person he would represent, and identifying it with his own feelings, so as to express every emotion designed by the author, as if that emotion were his own." This quality was probably enhanced by the fact that all Cooke's characters seemed to speak as if their words were totally unpremeditated. Leigh Hunt was dubious about Cooke's talents, partly on account of this characteristic, especially as far as Shakespearean roles were concerned: "As to his vaunted tragedy, it was a mere reduction of Shakespeare's poetry into indignant prose. He limited every character to its worst qualities, and had no idealism, no affections, no verse." Hazlitt, however, felt that Cooke discovered the "great actor" in his death scenes in *Macbeth* and *Richard III*. According to him: "He fell like the ruin of a state, like a King with his regalia about him."

Cooke certainly provoked varying critical responses, earning from Leigh Hunt the ambiguous epithet of "the Machiavel of the Modern Stage". Among his achievements were, in the words of Charles Lamb, the "infusion of some warm blood into the frozen declamatory style" towards which the theatre had degenerated in the early years of the 19th century. His visit to the USA was the first by a major British actor, thus setting a precedent for future visiting stars. His death in 1811 also left a gap in a particular line of roles that, three years later, Edmund Kean was to fill with such success. In many ways it was Cooke, more than any other actor of his time, who made possible the transition from the age of Kemble to the age of Kean.

—Jim Davis

———

COPEAU, Jacques. French actor-manager, director, playwright, essayist, and critic. Born in Paris, 1879. Educated at schools in Paris. Co-founder, *Nouvelle Revue Française*, 1909; debut as director, 1911; founded influential theatre company at the Théâtre du Vieux-Colombier, Paris, 1913; at the close of World War I, reformed company at the Garrick Theatre, New York, 1917–19; returned to Paris, 1920; withdrew to Pernand-Vergelesses, Burgundy, 1924, and founded "Les Copiaus" theatre group; subsequently directed sporadically, at the Comédie-Française, Paris, from 1936, and elsewhere; director, Comédie-Française, 1940–41. Died in Beaune, France, 20 October 1949.

Productions

1911   *Les Frères Karamazov* (Copeau, adapted from Dostoevsky), Théâtre des Arts, Paris.
1913   *Une Femme tuée par le douceur* (Heywood, adapted by Copeau and Croué), Théâtre du Vieux-Colombier, Paris.
        L'Amour médecin (Molière), Théâtre du Vieux-Colombier, Paris.
        Les Fils Louverné (Schlumberger), Théâtre du Vieux-Colombier, Paris.
        Barberine (Musset), Théâtre du Vieux-Colombier, Paris.
        L'Avare (Molière), Théâtre du Vieux-Colombier, Paris.
        Le Pain de ménage (Renard), Théâtre du Vieux-Colombier, Paris.
        La Peur des coups (Courteline), Théâtre du Vieux-Colombier, Paris.
        Le Jeu de Robin et Marion (Ruteboeuf), Théâtre du Vieux-Colombier, Paris.
        La Farce du savetier enragé (anon., adapted by Arnoux), Théâtre du Vieux-Colombier, Paris.
1914   *La Jalousie du Barbouillé* (Molière), Théâtre du Vieux-Colombier, Paris.
        L'Échange (Claudel), Théâtre du Vieux-Colombier, Paris.
        Le Testament du Père Leleu (Du Gard), Théâtre du Vieux-Colombier, Paris.
        La Navette (Becque), Théâtre du Vieux-Colombier, Paris.
        Les Frères Karamazov (Copeau and Croué, adapted from Dostoevsky), Théâtre du Vieux-Colombier, Paris.
        L'Eau de vie (Ghéon), Théâtre du Vieux-Colombier, Paris.
        La Nuit des rois (Shakespeare), Théâtre du Vieux-Colombier, Paris.
1917   *L'Impromptu du Vieux-Colombier* (Copeau), Garrick Theatre, New York.
        Les Fourberies de Scapin (Molière), Garrick Theatre, New York.

La Navette (Becque), Garrick Theatre, New York.
La Jalousie du Barbouillé (Molière), Garrick Theatre, New York.
Le Carosse du Saint-Sacrement (Mérimée), Garrick Theatre, New York.
Barberine (Musset), Garrick Theatre, New York.
Le Pain de ménage (Renard), Garrick Theatre, New York.
La Nuit des rois (Shakespeare), Garrick Theatre, New York.
1918   *La Nouvelle Idole* (Curel), Garrick Theatre, New York.
        Les Frères Karamazov (Copeau and Croué, adapted from Dostoevsky), Garrick Theatre, New York.
        La Surprise de l'amour (Marivaux), Garrick Theatre, New York.
        La Traverse (Villeroy), Garrick Theatre, New York.
        Poil de carotte (Renard), Garrick Theatre, New York.
        Les Mauvais Bergers (Mirbeau), Garrick Theatre, New York.
        La Petite Marquise (Meilhac and Halévy), Garrick Theatre, New York.
        L'Amour médecin (Molière), Garrick Theatre, New York.
        L'Avare (Molière), Garrick Theatre, New York.
        Le Carosse du Saint-Sacrement (Mérime), Garrick Theatre, New York.
        La Paix chez soi (Courteline), Garrick Theatre, New York.
        Le Testament du Père Leleu (Du Gard), Garrick Theatre, New York.
        La Chance de Françoise (Porto-Riche), Garrick Theatre, New York.
        Le Secret (Bernstein), Garrick Theatre, New York.
        Le Mariage de Figaro (Beaumarchais), Garrick Theatre, New York.
        Blanchette (Brieux), Garrick Theatre, New York.
        Georgette Lemeunier (Donnay), Garrick Theatre, New York.
        Crainquebille (France), Garrick Theatre, New York.
        Le Voile du bonheur (Clemenceau), Garrick Theatre, New York.
        La Femme du Claude (Dumas *fils*), Garrick Theatre, New York.
        Le Médecin malgré lui (Molière), Garrick Theatre, New York.
        Gringoire (Bonneville), Garrick Theatre, New York.
        Rosmersholm (Ibsen), Garrick Theatre, New York.
        Le Gendre de M. Poirier (Augier), Garrick Theatre, New York.
        Les Caprices de Marianne (Musset), Garrick Theatre, New York.
        Le Fardeau de la liberté (Bernard), Garrick Theatre, New York.

Les Romanesques (Rostand), Garrick Theatre, New York.

Boubouroche (Courteline), Garrick Theatre, New York.

L'Enigme (Hervieu), Garrick Theatre, New York.

1919   *L'Avare* (Molière), Garrick Theatre, New York.

Chatterton (Vigny), Garrick Theatre, New York.

Les Frères Karamazov (Copeau and Croué, adapted from Dostoevsky), Garrick Theatre, New York.

Le Menteur (Corneille), Garrick Theatre, New York.

L'Ami Fritz (Erckmann-Chatrian), Garrick Theatre, New York.

Pelléas et Mélisande (Maeterlinck), Garrick Theatre, New York.

Washington (Mackaye), Garrick Theatre, New York.

La Coupe enchantée (La Fontaine and Champmeslé), Garrick Theatre, New York.

La Veine (Capus), Garrick Theatre, New York.

Le Misanthrope (Molière), Garrick Theatre, New York.

1920   *Le Conte d'hiver* (Copeau and Bing), Théâtre du Vieux-Colombier, Paris.

Le Pacquebot Tenacity (Vildrac), Théâtre du Vieux-Colombier, Paris.

Le Carosse du Saint Sacrement (Mérimée), Théâtre du Vieux-Colombier, Paris.

L'Oeuvre des athlètes (Duhamel), Théâtre du Vieux-Colombier, Paris.

Les Fourberies de Scapin (Molière), Théâtre du Vieux-Colombier, Paris.

Cromedeyre-le-Vieil (Romains), Théâtre du Vieux-Colombier, Paris.

Phocas le jardinier (Vielé-Griffin), Théâtre du Vieux-Colombier, Paris.

La Folle journée (Mazaud), Théâtre du Vieux-Colombier, Paris.

La Coupe enchantée (La Fontaine and Champmeslé), Théâtre du Vieux-Colombier, Paris.

Le Médecin malgré lui (Molière), Théâtre du Vieux-Colombier, Paris.

La Folle journée (Mazaud), Théâtre du Vieux-Colombier, Paris.

La Coupe enchantée (La Fontaine and Champmeslé), Théâtre du Vieux-Colombier, Paris.

La Surprise de l'amour (Marivaux), Théâtre du Vieux-Colombier, Paris.

La Jalousie de Barbouillé (Molière), Théâtre du Vieux-Colombier, Paris.

Phocas le jardinier (Vielé-Griffin), Théâtre du Vieux-Colombier, Paris.

Le Pacquebot Tenacity (Vildrac), Théâtre du Vieux-Colombier, Paris.

Le Carosse du Saint-Sacrement (Mérimée), Théâtre du Vieux-Colombier, Paris.

La Nuit des rois (Shakespeare), Théâtre du Vieux-Colombier, Paris.

Les Fourberies de Scapin (Molière), Théâtre du Vieux-Colombier, Paris.

1921   *Le Pauvre sous l'escalier* (Ghéon), Théâtre du Vieux-Colombier, Paris.

La Mort de Sparte (Schlumberger), Théâtre du Vieux-Colombier, Paris.

Oncle Vania (Chekhov), Théâtre du Vieux-Colombier, Paris.

La Dauphine (Porche), Théâtre du Vieux-Colombier, Paris.

L'Amour médecin (Molière), Théâtre du Vieux-Colombier, Paris.

Un Caprice (Musset), Théâtre du Vieux-Colombier, Paris.

Le Testament du Père Leleu (Du Gard), Théâtre du Vieux-Colombier, Paris.

Au Petit Bonheur (France), Théâtre du Vieux-Colombier, Paris.

La Fraude (Fallens), Théâtre du Vieux-Colombier, Paris.

Le Mariage de Figaro (Beaumarchais), Théâtre du Vieux-Colombier, Paris.

Le Testament du Père Leleu (Du Gard), Théâtre du Vieux-Colombier, Paris.

La Navette (Becque), Théâtre du Vieux-Colombier, Paris.

Un Caprice (Musset), Théâtre du Vieux-Colombier, Paris.

Les Frères Karamazov (Copeau and Croué, adapted from Dostoevsky), Théâtre du Vieux-Colombier, Paris.

La Nuit des rois (Shakespeare), Théâtre du Vieux-Colombier, Paris.

Cromedeyre-le-Vieil (Romains), Théâtre du Vieux-Colombier, Paris.

1922   *Le Médecin malgré lui* (Molière), Théâtre du Vieux-Colombier, Paris.

Le Pain de ménage (Renard), Théâtre du Vieux-Colombier, Paris.

Le Misanthrope (Molière), Théâtre du Vieux-Colombier, Paris.

La Jalousie du Barbouillé (Molière), Théâtre du Vieux-Colombier, Paris.

L'Amour, livre d'or (Tolstoy, adapted by De Gramont), Théâtre du Vieux-Colombier, Paris.

La Mort joyeuse (Evreinov, adapted by Roche), Théâtre du Vieux-Colombier, Paris.

L'Avare (Molière), Théâtre du Vieux-Colombier, Paris.

La Coup enchantée (La Fontaine and Champmeslé), Théâtre du Vieux-Colombier, Paris.

Le Pacquebot Tenacity (Vildrac), Théâtre du Vieux-Colombier, Paris.

Les Plaisirs du hazard (Benjamin), Théâtre du Vieux-Colombier, Paris.

Saul (Gide), Théâtre du Vieux-Colombier, Paris.

Le Mariage de Figaro (Beaumarchais), Théâtre du Vieux-Colombier, Paris.

Le Carosse du Saint-Sacrement (Mérimée), Théâtre du Vieux-Colombier, Paris.

Un Caprice (Musset), Théâtre du Vieux-Colombier, Paris.

Le Pacquebot Tenacity (Vildrac), Théâtre du Vieux-Colombier, Paris.

Le Testament du Père Leleu (Du Gard), Théâtre du Vieux-Colombier, Paris.

Le Pain de ménage (Renard), Théâtre du Vieux-Colombier, Paris.

Sophie Arnould (Nigond), Théâtre du Vieux-Colombier, Paris.

La Pie borgne (Benjamin), Théâtre du Vieux-Colombier, Paris.

La Belle de Hagueneau (Variot), Théâtre du Vieux-Colombier, Paris.

Le Menteur (Corneille), Théâtre du Vieux-Colombier, Paris.

Maître Pierre Pathelin (Allard), Théâtre du Vieux-Colombier, Paris.

Les Plaisirs du hazard (Benjamin), Théâtre du Vieux-Colombier, Paris.

Le Misanthrope (Molière), Théâtre du Vieux-Colombier, Paris.

La Nuit des rois (Shakespeare), Théâtre du Vieux-Colombier, Paris.

Michel Auclair (Vildrac), Théâtre du Vieux-Colombier, Paris.

1923   *La Princesse Turandot* (Gozzi, adapted by Olivier), Théâtre du Vieux-Colombier, Paris.

Prologue improvisé (Copeau), Théâtre du Vieux-Colombier, Paris.

Le Médecin malgré lui (Molière), Théâtre du Vieux-Colombier, Paris.

Un Caprice (Musset), Théâtre du Vieux-Colombier, Paris.

Le Misanthrope (Molière), Théâtre du Vieux-Colombier, Paris.

La Coupe enchantée (La Fontaine and Champmeslé), Théâtre du Vieux-Colombier, Paris.

Dardamelle (Mazaud), Théâtre du Vieux-Colombier, Paris.

La Folle journée (Mazaud), Théâtre du Vieux-Colombier, Paris.

Bastos le hardi (Regis and De Veynes), Théâtre du Vieux-Colombier, Paris.

L'Imbécile (Bost), Théâtre du Vieux-Colombier, Paris.

La Locandiera (Goldoni, adapted by Darsenne), Théâtre du Vieux-Colombier, Paris.

Bastos le hardi (Regis and De Veynes), Théâtre du Vieux-Colombier, Paris.

Le Testament du Père Leleu (Du Gard), Théâtre du Vieux-Colombier, Paris.

La Pie borgne (Benjamin), Théâtre du Vieux-Colombier, Paris.

La Folle journée (Mazaud), Théâtre du Vieux-Colombier, Paris.

La Maison natale (Copeau), Théâtre du Vieux-Colombier, Paris.

1924   *Le Misanthrope* (Molière), Théâtre du Vieux-Colombier, Paris.

Il Faut que chacun soit à sa place (Benjamin), Théâtre du Vieux-Colombier, Paris.

Le Pacquebot Tenacity (Vildrac), Théâtre du Vieux-Colombier, Paris.

1925   *L'Impôt* (Copeau), Les Copiaus, Burgundy.

L'Objet (Copeau), Les Copiaus, Burgundy.

Le Veuf (Copeau), Les Copiaus, Burgundy.

Les Sottises de Gilles (Guelette), Les Copiaus, Burgundy.

Les Jeunes Filles à marier (Chancerel), Les Copiaus, Burgundy.

Mirandoline (Copeau, adapted from Goldoni's *La Locandiera*), Les Copiaus, Burgundy.

Le Médecin malgré lui (Molière), Les Copiaus, Burgundy.

Arlequin magicien (Copeau), Les Copiaus, Burgundy.

Les Vacances (Saint-Denis), Les Copiaus, Burgundy.

Les Cassis (Copeau, adapted from De Rueda), Les Copiaus, Burgundy.

L'Ecole des maris (Molière), Les Copiaus, Burgundy.

Fête de la vigne et des vignerons (Saint-Denis, Copeau, and others), Les Copiaus, Burgundy.

La Coupe enchantée (La Fontaine and Champmeslé), Les Copiaus, Burgundy.

1926   *La Pie borgne* (Benjamin), Les Copiaus, Burgundy.

L'Illusion (Copeau, adapted from De Rojas and P. Corneille), Les Copiaus, Burgundy.

1927   *L'Anconitaine* (Copeau, adapted from Ruzzante), Les Copiaus, Burgundy.

1928   *La Danse de la ville et des champs* (Villard and Saint-Denis), Les Copiaus, Burgundy.

1929   *Les Jeunes Gens et L'Araignée* (Villard and Saint-Denis), Les Copiaus, Burgundy.

1932   *Jeanne* (Duvernois), Théâtre des Nouveautés, Paris.

1933   *Il Miracolo di Sant'Uliva* (anon.) Santa Croce, Florence.

1934   *Persephone* (Gide), Opéra, Paris.

Rosalinde (adapted from Shakespeare's *As You Like It*), Théâtre de l'Atelier, Paris.

1935   *Savonarola* (Alessi), Piazza della Signoria, Florence.

1936   *Beaucoup de bruit pour rien* (Shakespeare), Théâtre de la Madeleine, Paris.

Napoléon unique (Raynal), Théâtre du Porte-Saint-Martin, Paris.

Le Misanthrope (Molière), Comédie-Française, Paris.

1938   *Come vi piace* (Shakespeare), Boboli Gardens, Florence.

Le Testament du Père Leleu (Du Gard), Comédie-Française, Paris.

1940   *Le Misanthrope* (Molière), Comédie-Française, Paris.

Un Caprice (Musset), Comédie-Française, Paris.

Le Pacquebot Tenacity (Vildrac), Comédie-Française, Paris.

Le Carosse du Saint-Sacrement (Mérimée), Comédie-Française, Paris.

Le Cid (Corneille), Comédie-Française, Paris.

La Nuit des rois (Shakespeare), Comédie-Française, Paris.

1943   Le Miracle du pain doré (adapted by Copeau), Hospices de Beaune, Burgundy.

Publications

Impromptu du Vieux Colombier, 1917; Souvenirs du Vieux-Colombier, 1931; Le Théâtre populaire, 1941; Le Petit Pauvre, 1946; Notes sur le métier de comédien, 1955; Correspondence Copeau-Martin Du Gard, 2 vols., 1972; Appels, 1974; Molière, 1976; Les Registres du Vieux-Colomber I, 1979; Les Registres du Vieux-Colombier II, 1984.

*

Bibliography

Books:

Maurice Kurtz, Jacques Copeau, Biographie d'un Théâtre, Paris, 1950.

Marcel Doisy, Jacques Copeau, ou l'Absolu dans l'Art, Paris, 1954.

France Anders, Jacques Copeau et le Cartel des Quatre, Paris, 1959.

Clément Borgal, Jacques Copeau, Paris, 1960.

Franco Cologni, Jacques Copeau — Il Vieux Colombier, Bologna, 1962.

Fabrizio Cruciani, Jacques Copeau, Rome, 1971.

Denis Gontard, Le Journal de Bord des Copiaus, Paris, 1974.

Hubert Gignoux, Histoire d'une Famille Théâtrale, Lausanne, 1984.

John Rudlin, Jacques Copeau, Cambridge, 1986.

David Whitton, Stage Directors in Modern France, Manchester, 1987.

John Rudlin and Norman H. Paul, Copeau: Texts on Theatre, London, 1990.

Paul-Louis Mignon, Jacques Copeau, Paris, 1993.

* * *

Known as the father of modern French theatre, Jacques Copeau influenced a whole generation of writers, actors, and directors. He is remembered for his success in reforming the French stage, both aesthetically and spiritually, through the founding of the Vieux-Colombier Theatre in 1913. Perhaps most important of all was his establishment, alongside this theatre, of a school, many of whose students left Paris to follow him when he closed down the theatre in 1924. His claim to fame rests as much on his education of others in the arts of theatre, as on his own achievements as a director.

Copeau grew up in the Faubourg Saint-Denis in Paris, where his father ran a business selling buckles and hooks-and-eyes. At 22, on the death of his father, he inherited the business, which provided him with some financial security while he developed a career as writer and critic. He contributed dramatic and art criticism to various journals and planned a novel. In 1902 he met André Gide, who was to become a life-long friend and mentor. In 1909, in collaboration with Gide and Schlumberger, he founded the Nouvelle Revue Française, still one of the most influential literary journals in France today. He was also appointed drama critic of the Grande Revue. Using these channels, he conducted a campaign against the frivolity and commercialism of the Paris theatre establishment of the banquet years. In 1911 he made his first practical attempt at offering an alternative, when he directed his own adaptation of The Brothers Karamazov at the Théâtre des Arts. In 1913 he set up his theatre company in the Théâtre du Vieux-Colombier on the then unfashionable Paris left bank. It was launched with the help of a poster campaign headed "Appel à la jeunesse" ("Call to youth") and a long article in the Nouvelle Revue Française entitled "Un essai de rénovation dramatique" ("An attempt at dramatic renewal"), in which he set out his beliefs regarding the causes of the decadence of French theatre, and his proposed solutions.

He was most insistent that the only way forward was to rediscover the values, moral as well as aesthetic, that had underpinned the great theatres of earlier times, notably the ancient Greeks, the commedia dell'arte, Shakespeare and his contemporaries in Elizabethan England, and Molière in seventeenth-century France. But he also believed in the need to cultivate a contemporary repertoire and to open the theatre to new writers. His first season at the Vieux-Colombier showed how he meant to continue: it included three plays by Molière (L'Avare, L'Amour médecin, La Jalousie du Barbouillé), one each by Shakespeare and Thomas Heywood (Twelfth Night, A Woman Killed with Kindness), his adaptation of The Brothers Karamazov, and several plays by new writers, including L'Échange by Paul Claudel, at a time when only one of Claudel's plays had been given a professional performance. The outbreak of war interrupted his plans, but he took the opportunity to travel and to learn from other theatre people: Edward Gordon Craig, Emile Jacques-Dalcroze, and Adolphe Appia.

As part of the campaign to persuade the Americans to enter the war, Copeau was allowed to reconvene his company and sent to play two seasons in New York (1917–19). They returned to the Vieux-Colombier in 1920 and performed on a stage remodelled by Louis Jouvet to achieve something close to an Elizabethan playing space. This was when Copeau set up his theatre school. After only four seasons, however, he decided that he could never realise his ambitions in Paris. He was convinced that only a long-term educative effort could bring about the theatre culture he desired, and he was also in the grips of a religious crisis. His most important collaborators, Charles Dullin and Louis Jouvet, had already left to set up their own theatres; Copeau invited some of the young company members and students from the school to follow him into a retreat in the Burgundy countryside. From 1925 to 1929, he encouraged them to develop an extreme suppleness of body and mind, performing in the open air on a bare stage devoid of modern technical effects, and drawing inspiration both from the peasant communities in which they lived and from popular theatre forms such as the medieval French farces and the commedia dell'arte.

When he once again withdrew from active involvement, some of his disciples formed the Compagnie des Quinze. Copeau himself never again found an established role in the French theatre, although he was widely respected and regarded as mentor to the generation who came to the theatre in the 1930's: Michel Saint-Denis, Jean Dasté,

Hubert Gignoux, André Barsacq, and others. He did occasional guest productions at the Comédie-Française, and was briefly its administrator (1940–41). He wrote plays of his own, translated much of Shakespeare in collaboration with Suzanne Bing, and published an influential essay, *Le Théâtre populaire*, in which he articulated the theoretical foundation for what was to become the post-war decentralization movement. But theatre historians agree that his most important work of this period was invested in the three large-scale open-air productions he undertook: *Il Miracolo di Sant'Uliva* and *Savonarola*, both in Florence, and *Le Miracle de pain doré*, in Beaune. In these, he felt he achieved the synthesis of a theatre drawing on popular traditions, inventive but simple performance styles, and grounded in a shared religious belief. His life-long search for a performance style capable of combining truthfulness with a strongly inventive, popular vein is still acknowledged as a source of inspiration by contemporary practitioners such as Ariane Mnouchkine, director of the Théâtre du Soleil.

—David Bradby

COQUELIN, Constant-Benoît. French actor. Born in Boulogne-sur-Mer, France, 23 January 1841. Trained as an actor at the Paris Conservatoire, from 1859. Stage debut, Comédie-Française, Paris, 1860; immediately acclaimed in comic roles in both classical and contemporary plays; first appearances in Britain, 1880; toured Europe and USA, 1886–89; returned briefly to Comédie-Française, 1890–92; appeared with Sarah Bernhardt at the Théâtre de la Renaissance, Paris, 1892; created Rostand's Cyrano, 1897, and subsequently played the part over 400 times at the Théâtre de la Porte-Saint-Martin, of which he became director that same year; founded Pont-aux-Dames retirement home for old actors; died while studying for the part of Rostand's Chantecler. Sociétaire, Comédie-Française, 1864. Died in Couilly-St-Germain, Seine-et-Marne, 27 January 1909.

Roles

1860	Gros-René in *Dépit amoureux* (Molière), Comédie-Française, Paris.
1861	Figaro in *Le Mariage de Figaro* (Beaumarchais), Comédie-Française, Paris.
1860–79	Petit-Jean in *Plaideurs* (Racine), Comédie-Française, Paris.
	Mascarille in *Dépit amoureux* (Molière), Comédie-Française, Paris.
	Purgon in *Le Malade imaginaire* (Molière), Comédie-Française, Paris.
	Figaro in *Barbier de Séville* (Beaumarchais), Comédie-Française, Paris.
	Cliton in *Menteur* (Corneille), Comédie-Française, Paris.
1866	Gringoire in *Gringoire* (de Banville), Comédie-Française, Paris.
1869	Georges in *Faux ménages* (Pailleron), Comédie-Française, Paris.

1876	Roblet in *Jean de Thommeray* (Augier), Comédie-Française, Paris.
	Filippo in *Luthier de Crémone* (Coppée), Comédie-Française, Paris.
1879	Don César de Bazan in *Ruy Blas* (Hugo), Comédie-Française, Paris.
1881	Paul Raymond in *Monde où l'on s'ennuie* (Pailleron), Comédie-Française, Paris.
1885	Thouvenin in *Denise* (Dumas *fils*), Comédie-Française, Paris.
1891	Labussière in *Thermidor* (Sardou), Comédie-Française, Paris.
1892	Role in *Gismonda* (Sardou) Théâtre de la Renaissance, Paris.
1895	Guesclin in *Monsieur de Guesclin* (Déroulède), Théâtre de la Porte-Saint-Martin, Paris.
1896	Valentin Salviat in *Bienfaiteurs* (Brieux), Théâtre de la Porte-Saint-Martin, Paris.
	Roquebrune in *Colonel Roquebrune* (Ohnet), Théâtre de la Porte-Saint-Martin, Paris.
1897	Cyrano in *Cyrano de Bergerac* (Rostand), Théâtre de la Porte-Saint-Martin, Paris.
1907	Abbé Griffard in *Affaire des poisons* (Sardou), Théâtre de la Porte-Saint-Martin, Paris.

Other roles included: Tartuffe in *Tartuffe* (Molière).

Publications

L'Art et le Comédien, 1880; *Molière et le Misanthrope*, 1881; *Un Poète du foyer: Eugène Manuel*, 1881; *Un Poète philosophe: Sully Prudhomme*, 1882; *L'Arnolphe de Molière*, 1882; *Les Comédiens par un Comédien*, 1883; *Tartuffe* (essay), 1884; *L'Art de Dire le Monologue*, 1884; *Scène tirée de "Démocrite" de Regnard*, 1887.

* * *

Constant-Benoît Coquelin rated amongst the most significant and most popular actors of the late 19th-century French stage. The elder of two sons of a baker from Bologne, he was popularly known as Coquelin aîné (the elder) to distinguish him from the other acting members of his family — his brother, Ernest Alexandre (known as Coquelin cadet - the younger) and his son, Jean Coquelin. To his peers and close colleagues he was known simply as 'Coq', an appropriate abbreviation which served to sum up the confident, charismatic and masculine qualities of his performance and the imposing way in which he would strut across the boards of the stage commanding both attention and admiration.

He left home for Paris in 1859 and entered directly into the Conservatoire to study under the master comedian Régnier. Here he quickly demonstrated a natural talent for comic acting, winning the first prize for comedy, and debuted the following year at the Comédie Française in the role of Gros-René in Molière's *Le Dépit amoureux*, initiating his life-long affection for and mastery of France's greatest comic writer. It was his overwhelming success in the role of Figaro in 1861 that assured his popular appeal and undoubtedly led to his being nominated a sociétaire of the Comédie-Française in 1864, a considerable accomplishment for an actor of 23 years of age. His reinterpretation of the Beaumarchais character, casting off the traditional gestures, stance and intonation expected of an actor in the part, and thereby lending the role greater realism, earned him a certain amount of early notoriety. Within the Comédie-Française he quickly became a member of the reading committee and by the age of 30 was a member of the highly influential administrative committee, replacing his master Régnier in 1871. In his first decade at the House of Molière he was accelerated to star status as the company's premiere comique or jeune premiere and played in every classic French comedy in the troupe's repertoire. By the late 1870's he had become so indispensable to the group that the management denied him the right to tour the Americas with Sarah Bernhardt in 1880 for fear that the company's identity would be too harshly damaged by his absence. By 1886 he had played in over 160 roles at the Comédie-Française and had created a number of original roles, most notably in *L'Étrangère* by Dumas fils, *Paul Forestier* by Augier and *Le Monde où l'on s'ennuie* by Pailleron. He nevertheless grew tired of the youthful and servant roles for which he had demonstrated such a flair and upon which he had constructed a healthy reputation and yearned instead to take on the great leading roles including the whole series of Molière's monomaniacs. This restlessness, coupled with further disagreements over plans to tour Europe and the States, led to his resignation from the Comédie-Française in 1886. He was to return in 1890 only to break permanently with the company another two years later.

As an independent artist at the Porte-Saint-Martin he continued to play Molière and also successfully took on a number of more serious roles in contemporary plays and, on his first tour, parts in light farces deemed unworthy of him by his former colleagues. Though he never played any serious roles from the canon of classical tragedy his stocky build and military bearing made him an appropriate actor to take on the swashbuckling roles of the romantic drama. Reputedly capable of stirring tears with his vocal inflection, he was also highly gifted at portraying affection and this, alongside his dignified gait and confident body language made him wholly suitable for the role of Cyrano de Bergerac, which Rostand wrote with his stage persona in mind and which he performed hundreds of times between its conception in 1897 and his death, of a heart attack during a rehearsal of Rostand's *Le Chantecler* in 1909. His name became synonymous with the role, as it had been with Figaro (to Parisians of the end of the nineteenth century he was 'le grand Figaro'), with Tartuffe and with Gringoire (from the 1866 play of the same name by Théodore de Banville), which he adopted as his favourite role in the years after his departure from the Comédie-Française.

As an actor, Coquelin's main instruments were his voice and expressive face. He believed in good clear diction and adopted a more realistic prose delivery than was the contemporary practice. This he blended with a musical lilt to make a listenable and comprehensible style, which equalled that employed by his close friend Sarah Bernhardt. His voice was deep and assertive with a distinctive nasal quality and he used it with great force, punctuating his delivery with bursts of emphasis on key words. As a young actor he spoke rapidly, matching his youthful vigour and spontaneity in performance, but in later years he had developed a more relaxed delivery to a considered and

Constant-Benoît Coquelin

pensive performance. His expressive face and subtle eye movements won him the admiration of the critics, who, at the turn of the century, advised the audience to bring opera-glasses with them to the performance the better to make out his facial control.

Constant Coquelin also provided an intelligent appraisal of the art of acting, published in two volumes; *L'Art et le Comédien* (1880) and *Les Comédiens par un Comédien* (1882). He advocated a considered and intellectual approach to performance and, speaking of the dual personality of the actor, believed in the emotional detachment of an actor from his role. He stated that the soul of the actor should concern itself with understanding a given character and should conceive it as fully as possible as created by its author. It should then be up to the other self, the actor's physical being (which is, he would have it, to the soul as an instrument is to a musician) to imitate this intellectually constructed vision — all the while the part of the actor that executes should be overseen and controlled by the part that sees and understands. Coquelin believed that this understanding of character was the starting point to all aspects of the interpretation of a role and he disapproved of flamboyant gestures and attractive poses as merely vacant posturing that did nothing to embellish a role. Though he despised the vulgarity of Naturalism, his pursuit of greater realism in the portrayal of a character later in his career took him to extreme conclusions, causing scandal in 1900 in New York when he appeared on stage as Scarpia without make-up, and in 1903 performing Molière in the court of Kaiser Wilhelm with only a table and two chairs.

Coquelin's studied method of interpretation and his modernising approach to classical and romantic drama served to pave the way for the developing interest in actor training at the turn of the century and for the growing public acceptance of the new experimental writers that followed Ibsen's lead in creating greater realism on the stage.

—Mark Batty

————

CORNELL, Katharine. US actress and manager. Born in Berlin, Germany, 16 February 1898. Educated at private school in Buffalo, New York; Oaksmere School, Mamaroneck, New York, until 1913. Married director Guthrie McClintic (*q.v.*) in 1921 (died 1961). New York debut, Washington Square Players, Comedy Theatre, 1916; actress, Jessie Bonstelle stock company, Buffalo and Detroit, 1918; London debut, 1919; acclaimed leading US actress of her generation, often directed by her husband from 1925; entered management, 1931; retired on her husband's death, 1961. Recipient: Chancellor's Medal, University of Buffalo, 1935; New York Drama League Award, 1935; Gold Medal, National Acheivement Award, 1937; Freedom Medal, 1945; Jane Addams Medal Award, Rockford College, 1950; Woman of the Year Award, American Friend of the Hebrew University, 1959; Medal for Good Speech on the Stage, American Academy of Arts and Letters, 1959. D.Litt: University of Wisconsin, 1936, Cornell University, Ithaca, New York, Elmira College, New York, Hobart College, Geneva, New York, University of Pennsylvania, all 1937–38, Kenyon College, Gambier, Ohio, 1956; LHD: Smith College, Northampton, Massachusetts, 1937; Middlebury College, Vermont, 1955; DFA: Clark University, 1941, Ithaca College, 1947, and Princeton University, 1948. Died in New York, 9 June 1974.

Roles

1916   Samuri Mother in *Bushido* (Idzumo), Comedy Theatre, New York.
1917   Offstage role in *The Life of Man* (Andreyev), Comedy Theatre, New York.
        One of the Three Fates in *The Death of Tintagiles* (Maeterlinck), Comedy Theatre, New York.
1919   Jo in *Little Women* (Alcott), New Theatre, London.
        Diane in *Seventh Heaven* (Strong), Detroit, Michigan.
1921   Eileen Baxter-Jones in *Nice People* (Crothers), Klaw Theatre, New York.
        Sydney Fairfield in *A Bill of Divorcement* (Dane), George M. Cohan Theatre, New York.
1923   Mary Fitton in *Will Shakespeare* (Dane), National Theatre, New York.
        Laura Pennington in *The Enchanted Cottage* (Pinero), Ritz Theatre, New York.
        Henriette in *Casanova* (Azertis), Empire Theatre, New York.

1924   Shirley Pride in *The Way Things Happen* (Dane), Lyceum Theatre, New York.
        Lalage Sturdee in *The Outsider* (Brandon), 49th Street Theatre, New York.
        Suzanne Chaumont in *Tiger Cats* (Orme), Belasco Theatre, New York.
        Candida in *Candida* (Shaw), 48th Street Theatre, New York; US tour, 1933–34; Empire Theatre, New York, 1937; Shubert Theatre, New York, 1942.
1925   Iris Fenwick in *The Green Hat* (Arlen), Chicago, Broadhurst Theatre, New York, and US tour.
1927   Leslie Crosbie in *The Letter* (Maugham), Morosco Theatre, New York.
1928   Ellen Olenska in *The Age of Innocence*, Empire Theatre, New York, and US tour.
1930   Madeleine Cary in *Dishonoured Lady* (Barnes and Sheldon), Empire Theatre, New York, and US tour.
1931   Elizabeth Barrett in *The Barretts of Wimpole Street* (Besier), Empire Theatre, New York; US tour, 1932, 1933–34; Martin Beck Theatre, New York, 1934; US Army tour, 1944–45; Ethel Barrymore Theatre, New York, 1945.
1932   Lucrece in *Lucrece* (Obey), Belasco Theatre, New York.
1933   Elsa Brandt in *Alien Corn* (Howard), Belasco Theatre, New York.
1934   Juliet in *Romeo and Juliet* (Shakespeare), US tour and Martin Beck Theatre, New York; revived there, 1935.
1935   Naomi Jacklin in *Flowers of the Forest* (Buckstone), Martin Beck Theatre, New York.
1936   Joan in *St Joan* (G. B. Shaw), Martin Beck Theatre, New York.
        Oparre in *The Wingless Victory* (Anderson), Empire Theatre, New York.
1938   Mariamne in *Herod and Mariamne* (Hebbel), US tour.
1939   Linda Easterbrook in *No Time for Comedy* (Behrman), Ethel Barrymore Theatre, New York; US tour, 1940.
1941   Jennifer Dubedat in *The Doctor's Dilemma* (G. B. Shaw), Shubert Theatre, New York, and US tour.
1942   Rose Burke in *Rose Burke*, Curran Theatre, San Francisco, California.
        Masha in *The Three Sisters* (Chekhov), Ethel Barrymore Theatre, New York, and US tour.
1943   Stella Boswell in *Lovers and Friends*, Plymouth Theatre, New York.
1946   Antigone in *Antigone* (Anouilh), Cort Theatre, New York.
1947   Cleopatra in *Antony and Cleopatra* (Shakespeare), Martin Beck Theatre, New York, and US tour.
1949   Ana de Mendoza in *That Lady* (O'Brien), Martin Beck Theatre, New York.
1950   Smilja Darde in *Captain Carvallo* (Cannan), US tour.

Katharine Cornell (1943).

1951	Constance Middleton in *The Constant Wife* (Maugham), National Theatre, New York, and US tour.
1953	Mary Prescott in *The Prescott Proposals* (Lindsay and Crouse), Broadhurst Theatre, New York.
1955	Countess Rosmarin Ostenburg in *The Dark is Light Enough* (Fry), ANTA Theatre, New York.
1958	Anath Bitniah in *The Firstborn* (Fry), Coronet Theatre, New York, and Habimah Theatre, Tel Aviv, Israel.
1959	Mrs Patrick Campbell in *Dear Liar* (Kilty), US tour; Billy Rose Theatre, New York, 1960.

Also acted roles in: *Plots and Playwrights* (Massey), Comedy Theatre, New York, 1917; *The Gypsy Trial*, Buffalo, New York, and Detroit, Michigan, 1918; *Daybreak*, Buffalo, New York, and Detroit, Michigan, 1918; *Broken Threads*, Buffalo, New York, and Detroit, Michigan, 1918; *Fanny's First Play* (G. B. Shaw), Buffalo, New York, and Detroit, Michigan, 1918; *Captain Kidd, Jr.* (Young), Buffalo, New York, and Detroit, Michigan, 1918; *Lilac Time* (adapted from Schubert), Buffalo, New York, and Detroit, Michigan, 1918; *Cheating Cheaters*, Buffalo, New York, and Detroit, Michigan, 1918; *The Man Who Came Back* (Goodman), US tour, 1918; *The Man Outside*, US tour, 1920.

Films

Stage Door Canteen, 1943; *Helen Keller in her Story*, 1954.

Television

The Barretts of Wimpole Street, 1956; *There Shall Be No Night*, 1957.

Publications

I Wanted to Be an Actress (autobiography), 1939.

*

Bibliography

Books:
Gladys Malvern (ed.), *Curtain Going Up! The Story of Katharine Cornell*, New York, 1943.
Guthrie McClintic, *Me and Kit*, Boston and Toronto, 1955.
Tad Mosel and Gertrude Macy, *Leading Lady: The World and Theatre of Katharine Cornell*, Boston and Toronto, 1978.

Articles:
Clara Beranger, "Katharine Cornell", *Woman's Home Companion*, 63, 1936.
Eric Johns, "Actress by Design", *Theatre World*, 34, 1941.
Ward Morehouse, "Katharine Cornell", *Hearst's*, 118, 1945.
Ward Morehouse, "Queen Katharine", *Theatre Arts*, 42, 1958.

* * *

Katharine Cornell shared the title of 'First Lady' of her generation of US actresses with Helen Hayes. She embodied the popular ideal of the 'leading lady' during her tenure on the stage and tended to the art of the theatre as a Vestal Virgin would have the flame of the hearth. Cornell forged a career in the theatre for herself despite almost overwhelming odds. Although she claimed to have been born in Buffalo, New York, in 1898, she was actually born in Berlin, the daughter of a physician turned theatre manager and a mother who had no interest in the theatre. As a young woman, Cornell was tall and gawky, unable to secure parts with which to build a technique. A robust, almost muscular person, her striking looks included large dark eyes set so far apart as to seem on the side of her head and brown hair that prematurely greyed.

Her career began to flourish, however, once she met Guthrie McClintic, a stage manager with the Jessie Bonstelle Stock Company, with whom Cornell was playing maids and scrub ladies, hoping to develop her talent. McClintic saw her potential, developed it, and directed her in most of her successes. They were also — and many claim only secondarily — husband and wife. Together they made popular Broadway successes of properties ranging from scorching melodramas like *The Green Hat* and *A Lady Dishonoured* to Shakespearean classics like *Romeo and Juliet* and *Antony and Cleopatra*.

Cornell consolidated her experience playing in shocking melodramas and rueful romances. In hindsight, her admirers thought she had squandered her talent for a decade. To the more astute, she was simply learning and perfecting her craft. She was also amassing enough capital to form her own production company (she or McClintic produced most of her later artistic and popular successes).

To define Cornell's style of acting is difficult, for it was based on an elemental communicative force rather than on external, describable elements. Her fans and critics alike never failed to be struck by the sheer power and incandescence of her desire to act. Perhaps the essence of her art lay in the relationship between this overwhelming personal charisma coupled with her determination to make the audience believe in the character in the play rather than to be noticed as a skilled actress. She above all eschewed inspiration and sought to build a solid technique. Whatever her intentions, she attained star status and used her reputation to take theatrical chances. She was, however, interested purely in the theatre: time and again she refused to make motion pictures, even as a record of her art for posterity.

Katharine Cornell's initial instinct, in her words, was to "make the audience believe in the character". This, under the tutelage of McClintic, she did by transforming her own rather potent personal aura, rather than disguising it. Each character she played was distinct, but also distinctly Cornell. She had a voice of considerable range, which at turns seemed shrill, liquid, or gutsy. Unlike her contemporaries, as a young actress she was unafraid to use chest tones in her portrayals of murderesses or adulteresses, roles she seemed to prefer. At the same time, she could be lyrical and romantic, exuding an evergreen youth. She used these two seemingly contradictory qualities in various measures for her later characterizations. Her two most successful portrayals were Elizabeth Barrett in *The Barretts of Wimpole Street* and Shakespeare's Juliet — both directed by McClintic. Her Elizabeth Barrett, the first role with which she gained widespread respect as an actress, was a combination of tenderness and dignity coupled with an ardour for Browning (played by Brian Aherne) that gave plausibility to the suggestions of incest with her father. Her Juliet was acclaimed as the finest of its time. Cornell was able to portray Juliet's youth and impetuosity and at the same time give a convincing account of the maturity of her emotions. Her achievement was the pinnacle of her collaboration with McClintic. Never again would the public so take to their special brand of theatre, well cast and colourful, direct yet full of hidden meanings and allusions.

As her art matured, Cornell was able to walk the fine line between committed actress and over-used, indulgent star. She seemed to do this by continually refining her technique, searching for the essentials of character and characterization rather than embroidering the obvious. Her absolute dedication to the art of the theatre made her truly a servant to the play and her ensemble skills became only sharper as she played a succession of difficult roles. She had a sure instinct for the significant, both in acting and in the theatrical marketplace.

Later in her career, Cornell attempted more maturely decadent roles and did not succeed. Her Cleopatra was amorous, but she could not successfully portray the character's abandon. Her Constance Middleton in Maugham's *The Constant Wife*, who leaves husband for lover, was unconvincing for she could not shake a certain respectability for which she always yearned both for herself and for her art.

Katharine Cornell will be remembered for the joy and intensity of her acting as well as for her dedication to the art of the theatre. In an era of light comedy and sensational escapism, she and McClintic raised the standards of US acting and made the Broadway stage a focus of culture as well as entertainment.

—David Payne-Carter

CRAIG, (Edward Henry) Gordon. British director, designer, actor-manager, and writer on stage theory. Born Edward Godwin in Harpenden, England, 16 January 1872. Educated at Tunbridge Wells, 1883–86, Bradfield College, 1886–88, and Heidelberg, Germany, 1888. Married May Gibson in 1893 (divorced c.1905), three sons and one daughter; several other children by various lovers, including a daughter by Isadora Duncan. Son of actress Ellen Terry; stage debut as a child, Court Theatre, London, 1878; trained as actor under Henry Irving at the Lyceum Theatre, London, 1889–97; concentrated on direction and design from 1897 and on design and theory from 1903; wrote and published first issues of *The Page*, 1898; designed in Germany under Otto Brahm and Eleonora Duse, from 1904; first collaboration with Isadora Duncan, 1905, and with Constantin Stanislavsky, 1908; lived in Florence, 1907–14; launched influential journal *The Mask*, 1908; designed screens for Abbey Theatre, Dublin, 1909; founded School for the Art of the Theatre, Florence, 1913 (closed in 1915); lived in Rome and Rapallo during war years; inaugurated first International Exhibition of Theatrical Art, Amsterdam, 1922; exhibited at Deutsche Theater-Austellung, Magdeburg, 1927; attended Convegno Volta, Rome, 1934; visited Moscow, 1935; interned in Paris during World War II; elected president of Mermaid Theatre, London, 1964. Member: Royal Society of Arts, 1938 (Royal Designer for Industry); French Syndicat des Metteurs en Scène, 1946; United Scenic Artists, 1961. Order of the Knights of Dannebrog, 1930; CH (Companion of Honour), 1956. Died in Vence, France, 29 July 1966.

Productions

As actor:
1878   Walk-on role in *Olivia* (Wills), Court Theatre, London.
1881   Walk-on role in *Charles I* (Wills), Alexandra Theatre, Liverpool.
1884   Walk-on role in *Hamlet* (Shakespeare), US tour.
            Walk-on role in *Much Ado About Nothing* (Shakespeare), US tour.
            Walk-on role in *Twelfth Night* (Shakespeare), US tour.
1885   Gardener's boy in *Eugene Aram* (Wills), Chicago.
1889   Arthur de St Valéry in *The Dead Heart* (Phillips), Lyceum Theatre, London.
1889–97   Cassio in *Othello* (Shakespeare), British tour.

Mercutio in *Romeo and Juliet* (Shakespeare), British tour.

1890   Moses in *Olivia* (Wills), Lyceum Theatre, London.

Caleb Deecie in *Two Roses* (Albery), Lyceum Theatre, London.

Henry Ashton in *Ravenswood* (Merivale), Lyceum Theatre, London.

Biondello in *The Taming of the Shrew* (Shakespeare), British tour.

1891   Messenger and one of the Watch in *Much Ado About Nothing* (Shakespeare), Lyceum Theatre, London.

Alexander Oldworthy in *Nance Oldfield* (Reade), Lyceum Theatre, London.

Abel Quick in *A Regular Fix* (Morton), Lyceum Theatre, London.

Charles Surface in *The School for Scandal* (Sheridan), British tour.

Malcolm in *Macbeth* (Shakespeare), British tour.

Lorenzo in *The Merchant of Venice* (Shakespeare), British tour.

1892   Cromwell in *Henry VIII* (Shakespeare), Lyceum Theatre, London.

Oswald in *King Lear* (Shakespeare), Lyceum Theatre, London.

Ford in *The Merry Wives of Windsor* (Shakespeare), Margate Theatre, Margate.

Petruchio in *The Taming of the Shrew* (Shakespeare), Margate Theatre, Margate.

1893   Youngest Knight Templar in *Becket* (Tennyson), Lyceum Theatre, London.

1894   Romeo in *Romeo and Juliet* (Shakespeare), British tour.

Gratiano in *The Merchant of Venice* (Shakespeare), British tour.

Richmond in *Richard III* (Shakespeare), British tour.

1895   Cavaradossi in *La Tosca* (Sardou), British tour.

1896   The brothers in *The Corsican Brothers* (Boucicault), British tour.

Arviragus in *Cymbeline* (Shakespeare), Lyceum Theatre, London.

Edward IV in *Richard III* (Shakespeare), Lyceum Theatre, London.

1897   Hamlet in *Hamlet* (Shakespeare), Olympic Theatre, London.

Young Marlow in *She Stoops to Conquer* (Goldsmith), Kingston-on-Thames Theatre.

Also acted roles in: *The Lyons Mail* (Reade), Lyceum Theatre, London, 1889–97; *The Day After the Wedding* (M. Kemble), British tour, 1890; *The Lady of Lyons* (Bulwer-Lytton), British tour, 1890; *The New Magdalen* (Collins), Paisley, 1895; *The Streets of London* (Boucicault), Paisley, 1895; *La Dame aux Camélias* (Dumas *fils*), Paisley, 1895; *François Villon* (Courte), Aberdeen and Dundee, 1985.

As designer:
1893   *No Trifling with Love* (De Musset), Town Hall, Uxbridge; also acted leading role and directed.

1896   *Romeo and Juliet* (Shakespeare), Parkhurst Theatre, London; also acted Romeo and directed.

Hamlet (Shakespeare), Parkhurst Theatre, London; also acted Hamlet and directed.

1897   *François Villon* (Courte), Theatre Royal, Croydon; also acted leading role and directed.

The New Magdalen (Collins), Theatre Royal, Croydon; also acted leading role and directed.

1900   *Dido and Aeneas* (Purcell), Hampstead Conservatoire of Music, London; also directed.

1901   *The Masque of Love* (Purcell), Coronet Theatre, London; also directed.

1902   *Acis and Galatea* (Handel and Gay), Great Queen Street Theatre, London; also directed.

Bethlehem (Housman), Imperial Institute, London; also directed.

1903   *For Sword or Song* (Legge), Shaftesbury Theatre, London; also directed.

The Vikings at Helgeland (Ibsen), Imperial Theatre, London; also directed.

Much Ado About Nothing (Shakespeare), Imperial Theatre, London; also directed.

1905   *Das Gerettete Vendig* (Otway), Lessing Theatre, Berlin; also directed.

1906   *Rosmersholm* (Ibsen), Pergola Theatre, Florence.

1912   *Hamlet* (Shakespeare), Moscow Art Theatre, Moscow; also directed.

1926   *The Pretenders* (Ibsen), Royal Theatre, Copenhagen; also directed.

1928   *Macbeth* (Shakespeare), Knickerbocker Theatre, New York.

Publications

What the Moon Saw (Pierrot show, produced, 1898); *The Gordon Craig Book of Penny Toys*, 1899; *Woodcuts and Some Words*, 1899 and 1924; *Bookplates*, 1900; *The Art of the Theatre*, 1905 (revised as *On the Art of the Theatre*, 1911); *Isadora Duncan: Six Movement Designs*, 1906; *Portfolio of Etchings*, 1908 and 1910; *The Mask* (quarterly journal), 1908–29; *Towards a New Theatre*, 1913; *The Marionette* (monthly journal), 1918–19; *The Theatre Advancing*, 1921; *Puppets and Poets*, 1921; *Scene* (marionette play), 1923; *Nothing*, 1925; *Books and Theatres*, 1925; *A Production, 1926*, 1926; *Hamlet*, 1929; *Henry Irving*, 1930; *Ellen Terry and her Secret Self*, 1931; *Fourteen Notes*, 1931; *Index to the Story of my Days, 1872–1907*, 1957.

*

Bibliography

Books:
Enid Rose, *Gordon Craig and the Theatre*, London, 1931.
Laurence Housman, *The Unexpected Ideas*, London, 1937.
Janet Leeper, *Edward Gordon Craig: Designs for the Theatre*, Harmondsworth, England, 1948.
Ferrucio Marotti, *Edward Gordon Craig*, Bologna, 1961.
Denis Bablet, *Edward Gordon Craig*, Paris, 1962.

Gordon Craig

Arnold Rood and Donald Oenslager, *Edward Gordon Craig: Artist of the Theater*, New York, 1967.

Edward A. Craig, *Gordon Craig: The Story of His Life*, New York, 1968.

Brian Arnott, *Edward Gordon Craig and Hamlet*, Ottawa, 1975.

Arnold Rood, *Gordon Craig on Movement and Dance*, New York, 1977.

Frederick Marker and Lisa Lone, *Edward Gordon Craig and The Pretenders*, Carbondale, Illinois, 1982.

Christopher Innes, *Edward Gordon Craig*, Cambridge, England, 1983.

Articles:
Haldane Macfall, "Some Thoughts on the Art of Gordon Craig", *The Studio*, vol. 22, 2, 1901.

Lee Simonson, "The Case of Gordon Craig", *Theatre Guild Magazine*, February, 1931.

Barnard Hewitt, "Gordon Craig and Post Impressionism", *Quarterly Journal of Speech*, vol. 30, 1, 1944.

Bernard Barshay, "Gordon Craig's Theories of Acting", *Theatre Annual*, 1947.

Eugene Ilyin, "How Stanislavski and Gordon Craig Produced *Hamlet*", *Plays and Players*, March 1957.

Morgens Hyllestod, "The Pretenders: Copenhagen 1926", *Theatre Research*, vol. 7, 3, 1966.

Edward Craig, "Gordon Craig and Hubert von Herkomer", *Theatre Research*, vol. 10, 1, 1969.

Edward Craig, "Gordon Craig and Bach's St Matthew Passion", *Theatre Notebook*, vol. 26, 4, 1972.

Laurence Senelick, "The Craig-Stanislavsky *Hamlet* at the Moscow Art Theatre", *Theatre Quarterly*, vol. 6, 22, 1976.

* * *

Edward Gordon Craig's parentage provides an important key to understanding this complex, irritating, and elusive theatre artist. His father, William Godwin, was a member of the Art and Craft movement whose revolt against the factory-produced products demanded by the material capitalism of the century essentially sought to expose and break down the hierarchical relationship between the artist (designing at the drawing board) and the craftsman (creating in the workshop). Through his mother, Ellen Terry, Craig found himself being brought up within the very traditional theatre structure of the late 19th century, exemplified by the romantic pictorialism of Henry Irving, to whom Craig was apprenticed as an actor.

As a craftsman, Craig believed that theatre had its own principles, laws, aesthetic codes, and 'tools of the trade' and that if theatre workers could be trained thoroughly in their crafts, then the theatre could create its own product — just as a skilled, sensitive wood-worker might create his own furniture. Theatre should not exist, Craig suggests, to service the playwright or simply to produce three-dimensional literature.

Irving's theatre tried to *realise* (and escape from) the world by picturing it and offering a vision into another more ordered and finished world. Completed images of characters within their environment, appropriately clothed, furnished, and 'propertied', expressed the reality of people through the physical materials of their existence. The darkening of the auditorium, practised late in the century, increasingly brightened the stage box and gave the impression that the spectator was eavesdropping on life — albeit a life that was heightened and emotionally picturesque.

Two strands of theatrical perception, therefore, run through Craig's life and work. There is a lifelong dedication to the values and ideals of craft: the meticulous wood-cut illustrations of theatre, the study of craft as the basis for creation, and the relishing of theatre as though it was a well-used box-wood craft tool. But there is also the romance and intangibility of 'the moment of pure theatre': the moment when paper snow swirled, canvas wind rasped on lath wood, limelight shone, violins were 'agitated', and Irving stood at the door of the Inn as Mathias in *The Bells* and the audience was transfixed. Craig found a unity within this. The combination of craft elements in the hands of Craig's theatre artist *might* serve to create an effect much greater than the sum of individual parts — to lead to the emotional mystery of which he felt the theatre was capable.

Craig's 'tools of the trade' were light, space, movement, and sound (just as a musician has time, pitch, tone, and silence or an architect has space, mass, volume, light, etc.). Theatre workers of the future, Craig says, will become skilled and adept users of, and ultimately creators with, their own tools rather than employing them solely at the service of the interpretation of dramatic literature. It is significant to note that in the same period, the painter Kandinsky was stating that in his future perception of art, the subject matter of the painting would be the aesthetic qualities of paint and painting rather than representations of nature. Craig's shortlived and typically impractical theatre school established in 1913 in the Arena Goldoni in Florence was a testament to this thinking and, of course, its training philosophy pre-dates Paul Klee's Bauhaus concepts of art training by several years.

Largely through the patronage of his mother, Craig was able to experiment with some of his visions of a 'total theatre' in Purcell's *Dido and Aeneas*, Handel's *Acis and Galatea*, and Ibsen's *The Vikings at Helgeland*. His ideas intrigued many, including Yeats, for whom he worked at the Abbey Theatre. Stanislavsky invited Craig to the Moscow Art Theatre to stage *Hamlet*, where he was intrigued by the possibilities of Craig's fluid scenography, which might more readily reflect and envelop the emotional momentum and movement of a play — a visual sub-text perhaps. To this end he designed and experimented with tall hinged flats (screens) that might be moved and re-arranged during the stage action to create different stage volumes and lighting surfaces. But their full potential was ultimately flawed by Craig's temperament, surprisingly limited grasp of stage technology, and artistic dissatisfaction.

At the close of his Moscow *Hamlet* experience in 1912, Craig recorded that henceforth his aim would be to "study the theatre. I do not want to waste time producing plays ... I want to leave behind me the seeds of the art — for it does not yet exist, and such seeds are not to be discovered in a moment." Craig encapsulated his ideas in his central theoretical texts, *The Art of the Theatre* and *On the Art of the Theatre*. In these he reiterates the central idea that "Today the theatre interprets, tomorrow it will create." His statement remains as provocative and stimulating as when first written and has served as a theoretical energy running through the century and finding significant forms of expression in Martha Graham's work, Peter Brook's research, and Grotowski's laboratory.

Craig's concept of the actor as Über-Marionette provoked the accusation that he wanted to reduce the art of the actor to that of a mere 'super-puppet' in the hands of a director. It is a point of debate, but Craig's defenders suggest that philosophically, Craig is simply saying that the theatre has no centre. It is wrong to say that actor, play, director, or whatever is most important: *all* are subservient to the art of the theatre.

Craig's drawings and wood-cuts should be seen as attempts to communicate something of the totality of theatre. The images of *Hamlet* and *Macbeth* are graphic metaphors for theatre, not 'designs' for realization. Trying to scale them up into practical existence in a theatre, reading them as workable propositions, as many critics frequently do, reveals only their sheer impracticality.

Craig is frequently 'paired' with Adolphe Appia and indeed 20th-century scenographic theory rests firmly upon a base of their works. Appia had a vision of a theatre-making process, but it was one which was ultimately circumscribed by the perception of theatre as interpretation. It was the music drama, as evolved by Wagner, which served as his vision of the theatre of the future. Craig's vision was equally one of process, but one which is limitless and ill-defined in its final form. Procrastination, absurd technical requirements, and eccentricity mark Craig's early withdrawal from the working theatre but he leaves behind a body of theoretical concepts as challenging and radical today as when they were written.

—Christopher Baugh

CRONYN, Hume. Canadian actor, director, and producer. Born in London, Ontario, 18 July 1911. Educated at Ridley College, St Catherine's, Ontario, until 1930; McGill University, Montreal, 1930–31; studied acting at the American Academy of Dramatic Art, 1933–34, the Mozarteum, Salzburg, Austria, 1932–33, and the New York School of the Theatre. Married actress Jessica Tandy (*q.v.*) in 1942, one son and one daughter. Stage debut, National Theatre stock company, 1931; production director, Barter Theatre Company, Abingdon, Virginia, 1934; Broadway debut, 1934; film debut, 1938; teacher, American Academy of Dramatic Art, 1938–39, and Actors' Laboratory, Los Angeles, 1945–46; London debut, 1962. Member: Board of Governors, Stratford (Ontario) Shakespearean Festival, 1978; Board of Governors, Tyrone Guthrie Theatre, Minneapolis. Recipient: Comedia Matinee Club Award, 1952; Tony Award, 1952, 1964, 1979; Barter Theatre Award, 1961; New York Drama League Delia Austria Medal, 1961; Variety New York Drama Critics' Award, 1964; American Academy of Dramatic Arts Award, 1964; Herald Theatre Award, 1967; Los Angeles Critics Circle Award, 1972, 1979; Straw Hat Award, 1972; Obie Award, 1973; Brandeis University Creative Arts Award, 1978; National Press Club Award, 1979; Commonwealth Award, 1983; Humanitas Award, 1985; Emmy Award, 1985; Best Television Script Award, 1985; Christopher Award, 1985, Writers Guild Award, 1985; Kennedy Centre Honours, 1986; Lifetime Achievement Award, 1986; Alley Theatre Award, 1987; National Medal Arts, 1990. LL.D: University of Western Ontario, London, Ontario, 1974; LHD: Fordham University, Bronx, New York, 1985.

Roles

As actor:
1931	Paper Boy in *Up Pops the Devil* (Hackett and Goodrich), National Theatre, Washington D.C.
1931–34	Austin Lowe in *The Second Man* (Behrman), Barter Theatre, Abingdon, Virginia.
	Dr Haggett in *The Late Christopher Bean* (E. Williams), Barter Theatre, Abingdon, Virginia.
	Jim Hipper in *He Knew Dillinger*, Barter Theatre, Abingdon, Virginia.
	Doke Odum in *Mountain Ivy*, Barter Theatre, Abingdon, Virginia..
1934	Janitor in *Hipper's Holiday*, Maxine Elliot's Theatre, New York.
1935	Stingo and Sir Charles Marlowe in *She Stoops to Conquer* (Goldsmith), US tour.
	Gideon Bloodgood in *The Streets of New York*, US tour.
1936	Erwin Trowbridge in *Three Men on a Horse* (Holm and Abbott), Cort Theatre, New York, and US tour.

Green in *Boy Meets Girl* (Spewack), Cort Theatre, New York, and US tour.

1937   Elkus in *High Tor* (Anderson), Martin Beck Theatre, New York.

Leo Davis in *Room Service* (Murray and Boretz), Cort Theatre, New York, and US tour.

1938   Abe Sherman in *There's Always a Breeze*, Windsor Theatre, New York.

Steve in *Escape This Night*, 44th Street Theatre, New York.

1939   Harry Quill in *Off to Buffalo*, Ethel Barrymore Theatre, New York.

Hutchens Stubbs in *Susan and God* (Crothers), Lakewood Theatre, Skowhegan, Maine.

Toby Cartwright in *Ways and Means* (Colman the Younger), Lakewood Theatre, Skowhegan, Maine.

George Davies in *Tonight at 8.30* (Coward), Lakewood Theatre, Skowhegan, Maine.

Francis O'Connor in *Shadow and Substance* (Carroll), Lakewood Theatre, Skowhegan, Maine.

Christy Dudgeon in *The Devil's Disciple* (G. B. Shaw), Lakewood Theatre, Skowhegan, Maine.

Lloyd Lloyd in *Kiss the Boys Goodbye* (Luce), Lakewood Theatre, Skowhegan, Maine.

Judas in *A Family Portrait* (Coffee and Cowen), Lakewood Theatre, Skowhegan, Maine.

Stage Manager in *Our Town* (Wilder), Lakewood Theatre, Skowhegan, Maine.

Denis Dillon in *The White Steed* (Carroll), Lakewood Theatre, Skowhegan, Maine.

Karl Baumer in *Margin for Error* (Boothe), Lakewood Theatre, Skowhegan, Maine.

Joe Bonaparte in *Golden Boy* (Odets), Lakewood Theatre, Skowhegan, Maine; Bucks County Playhouse, New Hope, Pennsylvania, 1941.

Andrei Prozoroff in *The Three Sisters* (Chekhov), Longacre Theatre, New York.

1940   Peter Mason in *The Weak Link*, John Golden Theatre, New York.

Lee Tatnall in *Retreat to Pleasure*, Belasco Theatre, New York.

1941   Harley L. Miller in *Mr Big*, Lyceum Theatre, New York.

1942   Several roles in *It's All Yours* (USO revue), US tour.

1944   Tommy Turner in *The Male Animal* (Thurber and Nugent), US tour.

1948   Jodine Decker in *The Survivors*, Playhouse Theatre, New York.

1949   Hamlet in *Hamlet* (Shakespeare), US tour.

1950   Gandersheim in *The Little Blue Light* (Wilson), Brattle Theatre, Cambridge, Massachusetts.

1951   Michael in *The Fourposter* (Hartog), Ethel Barrymore Theatre, New York; City Centre Theatre, New York, 1955.

1954   Several roles in *Face to Face* (concert readings), US tour.

1955   Curtis and Bennett Honey in *The Honeys*, Longacre Theatre, New York.

Hume Cronyn

Julian Anson in *A Day by the Sea* (Hunter), ANTA Theatre, New York.

1957   Oliver Walling in *The Man in the Dog Suit* (Beich and Wright), US tour; Coronet Theatre, New York, 1958.

1961   Jimmy Luton in *Big Fish, Little Fish* (Wheeler), ANTA Theatre, New York; Duke of York's Theatre, London, 1962.

1963   Harpagon in *The Miser* (Molière), Tyrone Guthrie Theatre, Minneapolis, Minnesota; revived there, 1965; Mark Taper Forum, Los Angeles, 1968.

Tchebutkin in *The Three Sisters* (Chekhov), Tyrone Guthrie Theatre, Minneapolis, Minnesota.

Willie Loman in *Death of a Salesman* (Miller), Tyrone Guthrie Theatre, Minneapolis, Minnesota.

1964   Polonius in *Hamlet* (Shakespeare), Lunt-Fontanne Theatre, New York.

Newton in *The Physicists* (Dürrenmatt), Martin Beck Theatre, New York.

1965   Richard in *Richard III* (Shakespeare), Tyrone Guthrie Theatre, New York.

Yephikodov in *The Cherry Orchard* (Chekhov), Tyrone Guthrie Theatre, New York.

Tobias in *A Delicate Balance* (Albee), Martin Beck Theatre, New York, and US tour.

1969	Frederick William Rolfe in *Hadrian VII* (Luke), Stratford (Ontario) Festival Theatre; US tour, 1970.
1971	Captain Queeg in *The Caine Mutiny Court Martial* (Wauk), Ahmanson Theatre, Los Angeles.
1972	Grandfather and Willie in *Promenade, All!* (Robison), Alvin Theatre, New York, and US tour; US tour, 1973.
	Krapp in *Krapp's Last Tape* (Beckett), Forum Theatre, New York, and US and Canadian tour.
	Willie in *Happy Days* (Beckett), Forum Theatre, New York.
	Player in *Act without Words 1* (Beckett), Forum Theatre, New York.
1973	Verner Conklin and Sir Hugo Latymer in *Suite in Three Keys* (Coward), Ethel Barrymore Theatre, New York, and US tour.
1976	Shylock in *The Merchant of Venice* (Shakespeare), Stratford (Ontario) Festival Theatre.
	Bottom in *A Midsummer Night's Dream* (Shakespeare), Stratford (Ontario) Festival Theatre.
1977	Weller Martin in *The Gin Game* (Coburn), Long Wharf Theatre, New Haven, Connecticut, John Golden Theatre, New York, and US tour.
1980	Hector Nations in *Foxfire* (Cronyn and Cooper), Stratford (Ontario) Festival Theatre; Tyrone Guthrie Theatre, Minneapolis, Minnesota, 1981; Ethel Barrymore Theatre, New York, 1982; Ahmanson Theatre, New York, 1986.
1986	Sir Edmund Milne in *The Petition* (Clark), John Golden Theatre, New York.

As director:

1946	*Portrait of a Madonna* (T. Williams), Las Palmas Theatre, Los Angeles; US tour, 1958; Playhouse Theatre, New York, 1959; acted the Doctor.
1949	*Now I Lay Me Down to Sleep* (Ryan), Stanford University, Stanford, California; Broadhurst Theatre, New York, 1950.
1950	*Hilda Crane* (Raphaelson), Coronet Theatre, New York.
1953	*Madam, Will You Walk?* (Howard), Phoenix Theatre, New York; acted Dr Brightlee.
1957	*The Egghead*, Ethel Barrymore Theatre, New York.
1958	*A Pound on Demand* (O'Casey), US tour; Playhouse Theatre, New York, 1959; acted Jerry.
	Bedtime Story (O'Casey), US tour; Playhouse Theatre, New York, 1959; acted John Jo Mulligan.
	Some Comments on the Harmful Effects of Tobacco (Chekhov monologue), US tour; Playhouse Theatre, New York, 1959; acted Ivan Ivanovitch Nyukhin.
1964	*Slow Dance on the Killing Ground* (Hanley), Plymouth Theatre, New York.

Films

Shadow of a Doubt, 1943; *The Cross of Lorraine*, 1943; *The Phantom of the Opera*, 1943; *Lifeboat*, 1944; *Main Street After Dark*, 1944; *The Seventh Cross*, 1944; *A Letter for Evie*, 1945; *The Sailor Takes a Wife*, 1945; *The Postman Always Rings Twice*, 1946; *The Green Years*, 1946; *The Ziegfeld Follies*, 1946; *The Secret Heart*, 1946; *Beginning or the End*, 1947; *Brute Force*, 1947; *The Bride Goes Wild*, 1948; *Top o' the Morning*, 1949; *People Will Talk*, 1951; *Crowded Paradise*, 1956; *Sunrise at Campobello*, 1960; *Cleopatra*, 1963; *Hamlet*, 1964; *The Arrangement*, 1969; *Gaily, Gaily*, 1969; *There Was a Crooked Man*, 1970; *Conrack*, 1974; *The Parallax View*, 1974; *Honky Tonk Freeway*, 1981; *Rollover*, 1981; *The World According to Garp*, 1982; *Impulse*, 1984; *Brewster's Millions*, 1985; *Cocoon*, 1985; **batteries not included*, 1987; *Cocoon: The Return*, 1988; *A Month of Sundays*, 1990.

Television

As actor:

Her Master's Voice, 1939; *The Marriage* (series), 1953–54; *Ben Hecht's Tales of the City*, 1953; *The Motorola Television Hour*, 1954; *The Fourposter*, 1955; *The Great Adventure*, 1956; *The Confidence Man*, 1956; *The Big Wave*, 1956; *The Five Dollar Bill*, 1957; *Member of the Family*, 1957; *The Bridge of San Luis Rey*, 1958; *The Moon and Sixpence*, 1959; *A Doll's House*, 1959; *Juno and the Paycock*, 1960; *John F. Kennedy Memorial Broadcast*, 1963; *Hamlet*, 1964; *The Oath: 33 Hours in the Life of God*, 1976; *The Many Faces of Love*, 1977; *The Gin Game*, 1984; *Hitchcock, Il brivido del genio*, 1985; *Foxfire*, 1987; *Everybody's Doing It*, 1988; *Onstage: 25 Years at the Guthrie*, 1988; *Day One*, 1989.

As director:

Portrait of a Madonna, 1948; *Actors' Studio*, 1948–50.

Radio

The Marriage, 1953.

Publications

Rope (screenplay), 1948; *Under Capricorn* (screenplay), with J. Bridie, 1949; *Foxfire* (play), with S. Cooper, 1980; *The Dollmaker* (television screenplay), with S. Cooper, 1985; *A Terrible Liar* (autobiography), 1991.

* * *

Hume Cronyn grew up in the small provincial city of London, Ontario, where his forbears included a member of parliament, a bishop, and a successful brewer. School and university prepared him to take his place in one of the professions (the church, law, politics) that were recognised as suitable for members of the Canadian upper middle class. Although he ran away from all this to become an actor in New York, he retained many of the managerial skills he must have absorbed as a boy. The enterprise, tenacity, and insistence on quality that he shares with his cousin producer Robert Whitehead has served him well (though it has sometimes led to acrimony, notably in his involvement as a board member of the Stratford Festival). Certainly it has been invaluable in the structuring of his own career and that of his wife, Jessica Tandy.

Elia Kazan has described how Cronyn, an early promoter of Tennessee Williams, showcased Tandy in Williams's one-act *Portrait of a Madonna*; this led to her being cast as Blanche in *A Streetcar Named Desire*, the role that established her as a star of the US stage. Tandy and Cronyn have maintained a cunning equilibrium in their theatrical careers; unlike such husband-and-wife teams as the Lunts, they have continued to appear in separate vehicles as well as working together, he playing a salty Polonius in John Gielgud's production of *Hamlet* starring Richard Burton while she displayed her capacity for subtle ensemble playing in *Five Finger Exercise*, he touring as the neo-Machiavellian homosexual pope Hadrian VII while she played the doomed courtesan Marguerite Gautier in *Camino Real* at the Lincoln Centre. They have contrived for over 40 years to juggle careers on both stage and screen. Cronyn's film debut was in Alfred Hitchcock's *Shadow of a Doubt* in 1943 and a year later he and Tandy appeared together in *The Seventh Cross*, for which Cronyn received an Academy Award nomination. Four decades later their sympathetic screen partnership was still evident in the two *Cocoon* films.

Unquestionably it is their work together that has consolidated the couple's commanding position in US theatre, culminating in a Lifetime Achievement Award in 1986. Like the Lunts, this ensemble of two depends on a special rapport, a keen sense of timing and a shared sensitivity to hidden motives and meanings. Yet Tandy and Cronyn employ radically differing techniques rooted in complementary but quite dissimilar personalities. Tandy is a fluid, intuitive actress whose performance changes from night to night whereas Cronyn plans his effects carefully and executes them with dependable precision, lays down, as it were, a steady groundbase over which Tandy can weave spontaneous improvisations, providing the element of surprise and a certain tension that gives their joint work vitality and freshness.

Over the years Cronyn has sought scripts that provide opportunities for them both to exploit their affinities and differences. Jan de Hartog's *The Fourposter* in 1951 allowed them to play out the vicissitudes of a marriage beginning with the hopes and confusions of the wedding night and extending over 40 years to the nostalgia and decay of old age. Edward Albee constructed for them a rueful, haunting, comedy, whose title — *A Delicate Balance* — might almost be a description of their art. They modulated two one-act plays from *Suite in Three Keys*, which Noël Coward had written to show off his own versatility, to suit their own rather different style. They chose two Beckett plays, *Krapp's Last Tape* and *Happy Days* to showcase their strengths as solo performers at the Lincoln Centre in 1972. With the help of Mike Nichols as director they developed a promising but only partially realised script by D. L. Coburn into the deftly constructed Broadway hit *The Gin Game*. They capitalised on the disparities of their relationship as Bottom and Titania in Robin Phillips' production of *A Midsummer Night's Dream* at Stratford in 1976. Finally, Cronyn collaborated with Susan Cooper on the writing of the play *Foxfire*, which won a Pulitzer Prize and was successfully adapted for television.

Though his development as a performer has been shaped by teamwork, Cronyn remains a highly distinctive actor. He evinced a flair for comedy from his very first Broadway appearance in George Abbott's *Three Men on a Horse* and he has honed his talent for acerbic delivery over the years. Cronyn's creations come across as dry, sly, sharp, scratchy, self-serving, and at the same time self-mocking. They suggest a dirt farmer who has come up in the world; above the flinty bedrock of early experience there is an overlay of acquired manners, a hard won appreciation of territorial boundaries and carefully weighed distinctions.

Cronyn's characters display a limited range of feeling but a palette of emotions only too familiar to a modern audience: ambition, self-doubt, rage, frustration, suppressed fears, affection soured but somehow surviving. His creatures scheme and strive, retract into their shells, then suddenly strike out. And usually at some point there is a penetrating moment of self-recognition when each character sees himself for what he is. Cronyn has perfected a complex but contained expression of a certain kind of Protestant bourgeois sensibility: cautious, sceptical, but persevering, motivated by an irrepressible compulsion to root out the truth.

—Martin Hunter

CUSHMAN, Charlotte (Saunders). US actress. Born in Boston, 23 July 1816. Educated at public schools in Boston until 1829. Professional debut in opera, as Countess Almaviva in *The Marriage of Figaro*, at the Tremont Theatre, Boston, 1835; debut as an actress, playing Lady Macbeth, St Charles Theatre, New Orleans, 1836; played minor roles at the Park Theatre, New York, 1837–40; stage manager, Walnut Street Theatre, Philadelphia, 1842–44; supported William Charles Macready on his US tours, 1843–44; London debut, alongside Edwin Forrest, Princess's Theatre, 1845; reunited with Macready at the Princess's Theatre, London, 1847; acclaimed on both sides of the Atlantic in a range of Shakespearean and other roles; toured USA, 1849–52; appeared infrequently after 1852; retired to England, 1852–57, and then to Rome, 1858–60; returned to the US stage despite cancer, 1869; last New York appearance, as Lady Macbeth, 1874. Died in Boston, 17 February 1876.

Roles

1836	Lady Macbeth in *Macbeth* (Shakespeare), St Charles Theatre, New Orleans, and Bowery Theatre, New York.
	Lucretia Borgia in *Lucretia Borgia* (Hugo), St Charles Theatre, New Orleans.
	Fatima in *Bluebeard* (Planché), St Charles Theatre, New Orleans.
	Mrs Haller in *The Stranger* (Kotzebue), Bowery Theatre, New York.
	Helen MacGregor in *Rob Roy* (Scott), Bowery Theatre, New York.
	Patrick in *The Poor Soldier* (O'Keeffe), Bowery Theatre, New York, and Franklin Theatre, New York.

Charlotte Cushman

Alicia in *Jane Shore* (Rowe), Bowery Theatre, New York.

Aladdin in *Aladdin of the Wonderful Lamp* (O'Keeffe), Franklin Theatre, New York.

Count Belino in *The Devil's Bridge* (Arnold), Pearl Street Theatre, Albany, New York.

Henry in *Speed the Plough* (Morton), Pearl Street Theatre, Albany, New York.

Floranthe in *The Mountaineers* (Colman the Younger), Pearl Street Theatre, Albany, New York.

Mrs Lionel Lynx in *Married Life* (Buckstone), Pearl Street Theatre, Albany, New York.

Joan in *Joan of Arc* (Serle), Pearl Street Theatre, Albany, New York.

Margaret in *Margaret of Burgundy* (anon.), Pearl Street Theatre, Albany, New York.

Jack Horner in *Greville Cross; or, The Druid's Stone* (anon.), Pearl Street Theatre, Albany, New York.

Louise in *Norman Leslie* (anon.), Pearl Street Theatre, Albany, New York.

Emilia in *Othello* (Shakespeare), Pearl Street Theatre, Albany, New York.

Alvedson in *The Two Galley Slaves* (Payne), Pearl Street Theatre, Albany, New York.

Lucy in *The Fiend of Eddystone* (anon.), Pearl Street Theatre, Albany, New York.

Henry Germain in *The Hut of the Red Mountain* (Milner), Pearl Street Theatre, Albany, New York.

Portia in *The Merchant of Venice* (Shakespeare), Pearl Street Theatre, Albany, New York.

Julia in *The Hunchback* (Knowles), Pearl Street Theatre, Albany, New York.

Tullia in *Brutus* (Payne), Pearl Street Theatre, Albany, New York.

Zorilda in *Timour the Tartar* (Oxenford), Pearl Street Theatre, Albany, New York.

Belvidera in *Venice Preserved* (Otway), Pearl Street Theatre, Albany, New York.

Roxana in *Alexander the Great* (Lee), Pearl Street Theatre, Albany, New York.

1837 George Fairman in *The Liberty Tree; or, Boston Bridge in 1773* (anon.), Pearl Street Theatre, Albany, New York.

Romeo in *Romeo and Juliet* (Shakespeare), Pearl Street Theatre, Albany, New York.

Meg Merrilies in *Guy Mannering* (Scott), National Theatre, Albany, New York.

Elvira in *Pizarro* (Kotzebue), National Theatre, New York.

Gertrude in *Hamlet* (Shakespeare), National Theatre, New York.

Madge Wildfire in *Heart of Midlothian* (Scott), Tremont Theatre, Boston.

Cordelia in *King Lear* (Shakespeare), Park Theatre, New York.

Nahmeokee in *Metamora* (Stone), Park Theatre, New York.

Goneril in *King Lear* (Shakespeare), Park Theatre, New York.

Laura in *The Genoese* (Sargent), Park Theatre, New York.

Volumnia in *Coriolanus* (Shakespeare), Park Theatre, New York.

1838 Madame Melnotte and Claude Melnotte in *The Lady of Lyons* (Bulwer-Lytton), Park Theatre, New York.

Hero in *Woman's Wit* (Knowles), Park Theatre, New York.

Evadne in *The Bridal* (Knowles), Park Theatre, New York.

Nancy Sykes in *Oliver Twist* (Simpson and Price, adapted from Dickens), Park Theatre, New York.

1839 Queen Katharine in *Henry VIII* (Shakespeare), Park Theatre, New York.

Lady Teazle in *The School for Scandal* (Sheridan), Park Theatre, New York.

1840 Mary Stuart in *Mary Stuart* (Schiller), Park Theatre, New York.

Mrs Page in *The Merry Wives of Windsor* (Shakespeare), Park Theatre, New York.

Lydia Languish in *The Rivals* (Sheridan), National Theatre, Philadelphia.

Ellen Rivers in *The Patriarch and the Parvenu* (anon.), National Theatre, Philadelphia.

Gabrielle in *Tom Noddy's Secret* (Bayly), National Theatre, Philadelphia.

Beatrice in *Much Ado About Nothing* (Shakespeare), National Theatre, Philadelphia.

Smike in *Nicholas Nickleby* (Dickens), National Theatre, Philadelphia.

Naiad Queen in *The Naiad Queen* (Dalrymple), National Theatre, Philadelphia.

1841   Oberon in *A Midsummer Night's Dream* (Shakespeare), Park Theatre, New York.

Lady Gay Spanker in *London Assurance* (Boucicault), Park Theatre, New York.

Lady Blanche in *Old Maids* (Knowles), Park Theatre, New York.

1842   Mrs Racket in *The Belle's Stratagem* (Cowley), Walnut Street Theatre, Philadelphia.

1844   Aldabella in *Fazio* (Milman), Walnut Street Theatre, Philadelphia.

Julie de Mortemar in *Richelieu* (Bulwer-Lytton), Melodeon Theatre, Boston.

Mrs Oakley in *The Jealous Wife* (Colman the Elder), Melodeon Theatre, Boston.

1845   Bianca in *Fazio* (Milman), Princess's Theatre, London.

Rosalind in *As You Like It* (Shakespeare), Princess's Theatre, London.

1846   Viola in *Twelfth Night* (Shakespeare), Haymarket Theatre, London.

1849   Juliana in *The Honeymoon* (Tobin), Broadway Theatre, New York.

Mariana in *Measure for Measure* (Shakespeare), Broadway Theatre, New York.

Cardinal Wolsey in *Henry VIII* (Shakespeare), US tour.

Hamlet in *Hamlet* (Shakespeare), US tour.

1850   La Tisbe in *The Actress of Padua* (Smith), Lyceum Theatre, New York.

1852   Eleanor in *Duchess Eleanor* (Chorley), Haymarket Theatre, London.

Also acted roles in: *The Tempest* (Shakespeare), St Charles Theatre, New Orleans, 1836; *Knight of the Golden Fleece* (anon.), Park Theatre, New York, 1837; *Infatuation* (Kenney), Princess's Theatre, London, 1845.

*

Bibliography

Books:

Emma Stebbins, *Charlotte Cushman: Her Letters and Memories of Her Life*, Boston, 1878.
Clara Clement Waters, *Charlotte Cushman*, Boston, 1882.
W. T. Price, *A Life of Charlotte Cushman*, New York, 1894.
Joseph Leach, *Bright, Particular Star: The Life and Time of Charlotte Cushman*, New Haven and London, 1970.

Articles:

George T. Ferris, "Charlotte Cushman", *Appleton's Journal*, 11, 1874.
R. G. White, "Charlotte Cushman", *Nation*, 19, 1874.
John D. Stockton, "Charlotte Cushman", *Scribner's*, 12, 1876.
Elizabeth M. Puknet, "Romeo Was a Lady, Charlotte Cushman's London Triumph", *Theatre Annual*, 1951.

* * *

Charlotte Cushman was the finest US actress of her time and the first to gain recognition abroad. She began her career as an opera singer, but her first professional engagement in New Orleans was a fiasco. On the advice of James Caldwell, manager of the St Charles Theatre there, she decided on a career as an actress rather than as a singer. Her engagement in London in 1845–46 established her international reputation and she remained a leading transatlantic star for almost 30 years.

Although Thomas Sully's flattering 1843 portrait captured a certain prettiness, Cushman was not considered physically attractive. With a strong jaw line and chin, her features were most often described as "mannish", an idea reinforced by her tall, big-boned figure, and forceful, husky voice. She discovered early in her career, however, that she could put these assets to good advantage playing wilful, domineering women and sometimes even men.

Among her masterpieces was the gypsy witch Meg Merrilies. The Boston critic Henry Austin Clapp remembered her performance as an absolutely convincing fusion of the natural and supernatural at once, being both "poignantly pathetic" and "a weird presence dominating the dark woods and the cavernous hills, an inspired Prophetess and an avenging Fury." Similarly her Nancy Sykes was widely regarded as a chillingly realistic portrait of "feminine sensibility blotted and trampled by human cruelty, slowly discovering a sense of honour and decency." Few Macbeths, including those of Edwin Booth and William Charles Macready, could match her powerful Lady Macbeth, costumed entirely in black — "a pantheress let loose" according to one critic — and her devastating emotional intensity. Towards the end of her career, her Queen Katharine likewise impressed many critics with its "unstudied eloquence" and tragic grandeur.

In an effort to expand her repertoire, though "prevented by nature from the whole range of delicate and physically beautiful woman characters", Cushman boldly broke across the sex barrier to play male roles. Early in her career, for example, she assumed the part of Oberon and at various times she also attempted, not always successfully, Hamlet, Cardinal Wolsey, and Claude Melnotte (in Bulwer-Lytton's *The Lady of Lyons*). As early as 1837, however, she had succeeded as a creditable Romeo and thereafter the role became part of her standard repertoire. During her first London engagement, she restored much of the original text omitted or otherwise 'improved' in David Garrick's stage version. It was a significant contribution "to the cause of textual integrity in the staging of Shakespeare", according to the critic Charles H. Shattuck. Her Romeo was, indeed, declared by one London critic as "the best ... that has appeared on the stage in 30 years." It was certainly true that throughout the length of her career Cushman never had any serious competition in the role.

The hallmarks of Cushman's style were undoubtedly emotional directness and energy. She intuitively grasped, as the actor James Murdock once observed, the "facts of a character" and her understanding was "keen and penetrating". But her characterizations lacked subtlety and imagination and even her admirers had to agree that the "conceits" of character "were beyond her reach".

—Daniel J. Watermeier

DASTÉ, Jean. French actor and director. Born in Paris, 18 September 1904. Trained for the stage at the École du Vieux-Colombier, Paris, under Jacques Copeau, 1922–24. Married actress Marie-Hélène Copeau. Stage debut, in minor roles, Théâtre du Châtelet, 1919; actor, Copeau's Copiaux de Bourgogne company, 1924–29; actor, Théâtre de l'Avenue, Paris, 1930–31; co-founder and actor, Compagnie des Quinze, from 1931; numerous appearances in the films of Jean Vigo and Jean Renoir, from 1933; co-founder, with André Barsacq and Maurice Jacquemont, Compagnie des Quatre-Saisons, 1937–39; US tour, 1937–39; actor, Théâtre de l'Atelier, Paris, 1940–44; led summer touring company during World War II; founder, first decentralised theatre company, the Comédiens de Grenoble, 1945; founded celebrated Comédie de St Étienne, 1947; acclaimed for productions of classics and contemporary plays; resigned as head at St Étienne, 1970.

Productions

As director:
1945–46   *Sept Couleurs* (adapted by Variot), Comédie de Grenoble.
    Le Retable des merveilles (Cervantes, adapted by Belon); 1947–48, Comédie de Grenoble.
    L'Exode (mime), Comédie de Grenoble.
    Chansons (Lafforgue), Comédie de Grenoble.
    Les Étoiles (Duvaleix), Comédie de Grenoble.
    La Fille folle (Cariffa), Comédie de Grenoble.
1946–47   *L'Etourdi* (Molière), Comédie de Grenoble.
    Ce que murmure la Sumida (adapted by Bing), Comédie de Grenoble.
    Tirant d'eau (Boutefeu), Comédie de Grenoble.
    La Chasse aux météores (Duvaleix), Comédie de Grenoble.
1947–48   *Le Médecin malgré lui* (Molière), Comédie de St Etiénne.
    Les Trente-Sept Sous de M. Montaudouin (Labiche), Comédie de St Etiénne.
    Le Voyage de M. Perrichon (Labiche), Comédie de St Etiénne.
    Les Fourberies de Scapin (Molière), Comédie de St Etiénne.
    Y'avait un prisonnier (Anouilh), Comédie de St Etiénne.
    L'Ecole des femmes (Molière), Comédie de St Etiénne.
1948   *Les Noces noires* (Lescure), Comédie de St Étienne.

1948–49   *Les Caprices de Marianne* (Musset), Comédie de St Etienne.
    Une Noce (Chekhov), Comédie de St Etienne.
    George Dandin (Molière), Comédie de St Etienne.
    Le Baladin du monde occidental (Synge), Comédie de St Etienne.
    La Sumida (Motokiyo, adapted by Bing), Comédie de St Etienne.
    L'Ecole des maris (Molière), Comédie de St Etienne.
    L'Epreuve (Marivaux), Comédie de St Etienne.
1949–50   *La Cagnotte* (Labiche), Comédie de St Etienne.
    Le Jeu de l'amour et du hasard (Marivaux), Comédie de St Etienne.
    La Nuit (Lescure), Comédie de St Etienne.
    Mesure pour mesure (Shakespeare), Comédie de St Etienne.
    Tartuffe (Molière), Comédie de St Etienne.
1950–51   *L'Illusion* (Copeau), Comédie de St Etienne.
    Polyeucte (Corneille), Comédie de St Etienne.
    Kagékyo (adapted by Bing), Comédie de St Etienne.
    La Savetière prodigieuse (Lorca), Comédie de St Etienne.
    Le Bourgeois gentilhomme (Molière), Comédie de St Etienne.
1951–52   *Les Fausses Confidences* (Marivaux), Comédie de St Etienne.
    A cheval vers la mer (Synge), Comédie de St Etienne.
    Amal ou la Lettre du roi (Tagore, adapted by Gide), Comédie de St Etienne.
    Les Précieuses ridicules (Molière), Comédie de St Etienne.
    Macbeth (Shakespeare), Comédie de St Etienne.
1952–53   *Le Mariage de Figaro* (Beaumarchais), Comédie de St Etienne.
    Montserrat (Roblès), Comédie de St Etienne.
    Hyménée (Gogol), Comédie de St Etienne.
    Le Mariage forcé (Molière), Comédie de St Etienne.
1953–54   *Chacun sa Vérité* (Pirandello), Comédie de St Etienne.
    Les Femmes savantes (Molière), Comédie de St Etienne.
    Irène innocente (Betti, adapted by Clavel), Comédie de St Etienne.

Jean Dasté (credit: Talbot, New York City).

Antigone (Sophocles, adapted by Florennes), Comédie de St Etienne.
L'Ile des esclaves (Marivaux), Comédie de St Etienne.

1954–55   *On ne badine pas avec l'amour* (Musset), Comédie de St Etienne.
L'Ours (Chekhov), Comédie de St Etienne.
L'Annonce faite à Marie (Claudel), Comédie de St Etienne.
L'Avare (Molière), Comédie de St Etienne.
La Tempête (Shakespeare), Comédie de St Etienne.

1955–56   *Le Malade imaginaire* (Molière), Comédie de St Etienne.
La Putain respectueuse (Sartre), Comédie de St Etienne.
Les Frères Karamazov (Dostoevsky, adapted by Copeau), Comédie de St Etienne.
Un Miracle de Notre-Dame (anon.), Comédie de St Etienne.

1956   *Le Cercle de craie caucasien* (Brecht), French tour; Théâtre de l'Odéon, Paris, 1960; acted Azdak.

1956–57   *Hérops et le soldat* (G. B. Shaw), Comédie de St Etienne.
La Cantatrice chauve (Ionesco), Comédie de St Etienne.
Les Méfaits du tabac (Chekhov), Comédie de St Etienne.

Le Misanthrope et l'Auvergnat (Labiche), Comédie de St Etienne.

1957–58   *Amphitryon* (Molière), Comédie de St Etienne.
Le Maquignon de Brandebourg (Le Porrier), Comédie de St Etienne.
Le Songe d'une nuit d'été (Shakespeare), Comédie de St Etienne.

1958–59   *Mais ne te promène donc pas toute nue* (Feydeau), Comédie de St Etienne.
Les Amants comiques (adapted from Shakespeare), Comédie de St Etienne.
La Queue du diable (Jamaique), Comédie de St Etienne.
La vie est un songe (Calderón), Comédie de St Etienne.

1959–60   *L'Exception et la règle* (Brecht), Comédie de St Etienne.
Les Coréens (Vinaver), Comédie de St Etienne.

1960–61   *M. Bonhomme et les incendiaires* (Max), Comédie de St Etienne.
La Lune se lève (Gregory), Comédie de St Etienne.
Oncle Vanya (Chekhov), Comédie de St Etienne.
Les Musiques magiques (children's play), Comédie de St Etienne.
Homme pour homme (Brecht), Comédie de St Etienne.

1961–62   *Un Chapeau de paille d'Italie* (Labiche), Comédie de St Etienne.
La Charrue et les étoiles (O'Casey), Comédie de St Etienne.
Don Juan (Molière), Comédie de St Etienne.

1962–63   *Cycloème le triste* (Salaman), Comédie de St Etienne.
Les Joueurs (Gogol), Comédie de St Etienne.
La Cruche cassée (Kleist), Comédie de St Etienne.
Le Zouave d'Eupatoria (Soula), Comédie de St Etienne.
Le Drame du Fukuriu Maru (Cousin); 1963–64.

1963–64   *Monsieur de Pourceaugnac* (Molière), Comédie de St Etienne.

1964–65   *L'Avare* (Molière), Comédie de St Etienne.
L'Officier recruteur (Webster), Comédie de St Etienne.
Andorra (Frisch), Comédie de St Etienne.
Lettres de Stalingrad (Salaman), Comédie de St Etienne.

1965–66   *Un Homme seul* (Gatti), Comédie de St Etienne.
Maître Puntila et son valet Matti (Brecht), Comédie de St Etienne.
Arlequin, valet de deux maîtres (Goldoni), Comédie de St Etienne.

1966–67   *La Double Inconstance* (Marivaux), Comédie de St Etienne.
Les Derniers (Gorky), Comédie de St Etienne.
Monsieur Fugue (Atlan), Comédie de St Etienne.

1967–68   *Le Revizor* (Gogol), Comédie de St Etienne.
Le Dragon (Shwartz), Comédie de St Etienne.

Le mal court (Audiberti), Comédie de St Etienne.

1968–69   *L'Opéra des gueux* (Gay), Comédie de St Etienne.

Avoir (Hay), Comédie de St Etienne.

1969–70   *La Famille de l'antiquaire* (Goldoni), Comédie de St Etienne.

L'Architecte et l'empereur d'Assyrie (Arrabal), Comédie de St Etienne.

Les Débuts de l'époque indienne (Haiks), Comédie de St Etienne.

Le Général inconnu (Obaldia), Comédie de St Etienne.

1970–71   *L'Illusion comique* (Corneille), Comédie de St Etienne.

Les Frelons (Aristophanes), Comédie de St Etienne.

La Chemise (Olmo), Comédie de St Etienne.

Les Bonnes (Genet), Comédie de St Etienne.

Also acted roles in: *Tour du monde en 80 jours* (Dennery and Verne), Théâtre du Châtelet, Paris, 1919; *Nuit des rois* (Shakespeare), Théâtre du Vieux-Colombier, Paris, 1922; 1924–29: *Arlequin poli par l'amour, Les Fâcheux*, Burgundy, *L'Illusion* (Copeau); *Noé* (Obey), French tour, Paris, and London, 1931; *Le Viol de Lucrèce* (Obey), Paris and London, 1932; *Autour d'une mère*, 1935; *Bataille de la Marne* (Obey), French tour, 1935; *Beaucoup de bruit pour rien* (Shakespeare), Théâtre de la Madeleine, Paris, 1936; Brighella in *Roi-Cerf* (Gozzi), Théâtre des Quatre Saisons, Paris, 1937; 1937–39: Perrichon in *Le Voyage de M. Perrichon* (Labiche), French Theatre, New York; Dr. Parpalaid and the Woman in Black in *Knock* (Romains), French Theatre, New York; *Le Bal des voleurs* (Anouilh), Théâtre de l'Atelier, Paris, 1939; *Le Rendez-vous de Senlis* (Anouilh), Théâtre de l'Atelier, Paris, 1941; *Eurydice* (Anouilh), Théâtre de l'Atelier, Paris, 1942; *Miracle du pain doré* (adapted by Copeau), Hospice de Beaune, 1943.

Films

As actor:

Boudu sauvé des eaux, 1932; *Zéro de conduite*, 1933; *L'Atalante*, 1934; *Le Crime de Monsieur Lange*, 1936; *La Grande Illusion*, 1937; *Remorques*, 1939; *Croisières sidérales*, 1942; *L'Enfant Sauvage*, 1970.

Publications

Qui êtes-vous?, 1987.

*

Bibliography

Books:

Phillip Aykroyd, *The Dramatic Art of La Compagnie des Quinze*, London, 1935.

P. L. Mignan, *Jean Dasté*, Paris, 1951.

* * *

Jean Dasté, director and actor, was a major force in the expansion of the French theatre in the post-war era. Following the enormous influence of the Cartel des Quatre during the inter-war years, a new generation of directors was needed to fill the gap left by Louis Jouvet, Georges Pitoëff, Gaston Baty, and Charles Dullin. Jean Dasté became one of the most important figures in French theatre during the 1950's, just prior to and during the emerging of the New Theatre in Paris. While most of the new directors appearing on the scene — like Jean Vilar, Roger Blin, and Jean-Marie Serreau — were trained at Dullin's Atelier, Jean Dasté was a student of "le patron" himself, Jacques Copeau. Dasté is responsible for continuing Copeau's dream of developing the theatre outside Paris, a dream also shared by Dullin and initially undertaken by Firmin Gémier in the early part of the century.

Building upon his experience with the Copiaus de Bourgogne and with the Compagnie des Quinze, Dasté returned to the French provinces with the intent of taking theatre to "the people", rather than of performing for a social elite. Dasté had the personality and the tenacity to make this happen. The research and training with popular theatre forms at the École du Vieux-Colombier and the touring with André Obey's *Noé, Le Viol de Lucrèce*, and *La Bataille de la Marne* to village squares with the 'Quinze' prepared Dasté for the task of accelerating the decentralisation of the French theatre and, as protegé (and son-in-law) of Jacques Copeau, he carried the spirit of Copeau's work into the second half of the century.

Dasté did not remain stationary or nostalgic, however. He moved the French theatre forward by recognizing the importance of Bertolt Brecht, whom he considered the most gifted 'popular' poet of the era and his 1956 production of *The Caucasian Chalk Circle* was the first critically successful Brecht play staged in France, reaching Paris after a lengthy provincial tour in 1958. The Berliner Ensemble first performed in Paris in 1954 and returned in 1960 during a revival of Dasté's production at the Odéon. Dasté embellished the visual aspects of the play by expanding the use of masks and by drawing on his knowledge of the Japanese Noh play tradition. He also elaborated upon the folk elements of the play, rendering it even more accessible to a popular audience. Stylistically, Dasté blended the Copeau tradition with the German tradition of the grotesque, accentuating the comic elements of the text.

Dasté's interest in masks, extending back to improvisations with Michel St-Denis, and his fascination with the commedia dell'arte were complemented by his work with Jean-Louis Barrault in the 1930's. He performed in Barrault's *Autour d'une mère* in 1935 and also helped organize the artistic gatherings at the Grenier des Augustins. These discussions and performances that took place in Barrault's apartment helped formulate the individual directions of writers like Antonin Artaud and the Surrealists. Barrault's mime work, evolved from Étienne Decroux, added another dimension to Dasté's physical performance style.

Like most of the great French directors, Jean Dasté continued to work as an actor throughout his career. He made his debut at the age of 15 and appeared regularly in the films of Jean Vigo and Jean Renoir in the 1930's. Subsequently he performed in many of his own productions, most notably as Azdak in *The Caucasian Chalk Circle*. He also collaborated with his wife, who acted, designed costumes, and also created mises en scène. Their versatility was a great asset to their work. Dasté's ability to combine silent acting skills with the interpretation of dramatic texts made it possible for him to present theatre ranging from silent choral mime pieces to Shakespeare, Calderón, Corneille, and Japanese Noh plays.

With André Barsacq and Maurice Jacquemont, Dasté created the Compagnie des Quatre-Saisons in Paris in 1937. This company produced a series of Molière and Marivaux plays that were well received at the Atelier and also in the course of two seasons in New York. With these texts and with a collection of improvisations, Dasté then took this company into the French provinces during the German occupation in the early 1940's. The success of this venture and the notoriety gained from the premieres of new plays by Jean Anouilh ultimately earned Dasté an invitation to establish a new company in Grenoble. When it became clear that this engagement was only temporary, Dasté accepted an invitation to establish a permanent regional company in the mining community of St Étienne, which was recognised as an official 'Centre Dramatique' by Jeanne Lauront in 1947.

The theatre of Jean Dasté was not limited to formal indoor spaces. He utilized unconventional performance sites near the homes of the non-theatre-going public and made an evening at the theatre an exciting event. Performances took place on outdoor platform stages, in boxing arenas, and in circus tents. Like Jean Vilar, Dasté attempted to attract a popular audience to his productions. Considering his successes in French villages and at St Étienne, his contact with people outside the artistic and intellectual circles was greater than that of Vilar's presentations in Paris and Avignon.

For Jean Dasté, the theatre was a festive event for all elements of the community. He was a director of actors; his companies established a simple and vital rapport with their spectators. In contrast to many contemporary directors, stage pictures did not diminish or dominate the role of the actor in his theatre; all spectacle was simple and discreet. The influence of his direction upon Jacques Lecoq — and subsequently upon Ariane Mnouchkine — confirms his importance and demonstrates his impact upon the contemporary French theatre.

—Ron Popenhagen

DAVENPORT, Edward Loomis. US actor-manager. Born in Boston, 15 November 1815. Educated at schools in New Haven, Connecticut, and at Mayhew School, Boston, until 1829. Married actress Fanny Vining in 1849; nine children (including actress Fanny Davenport). Professional stage debut, Lion Theatre or Brick Circus, Providence, Rhode Island, 1836; subsequently acted at the Tremont Theatre, Boston, and at the Walnut Street Theatre, Philadelphia; New York debut, 1843; actor, Mrs John Drew's company, from 1843; played regularly opposite Anna Cora Mowatt, from 1846; London debut, with Mowatt, 1847; remained in the UK for seven years, appearing often with William Charles Macready, 1847–54; returned to USA to lead his own company; acted regularly at the American Theatre, New York, Howard Athenaeum, Boston, Old Washington Theatre, and Chestnut Street Theatre, Philadelphia; manager, Howard Athenaeum, 1859–61; actor, Augustin Daly's

Fifth Avenue Theatre company, New York, 1869–70; manager, Chestnut Street Theatre, Philadelphia, 1870–74; last appearance, Howard Athenaeum, 1877. Died in Canton, Pennsylvania, 1 September 1877.

Roles

1836	Parson Willdo in *A New Way to Pay Old Debts* (Massinger), Lion Theatre or Brick Circus, Providence, Rhode Island.
	Young Norval in *Douglas* (Home), New Bedford, Massachusetts.
1841	Captain Crosstree in *Black-Eyed Susan* (Jerrold), Arch Street Theatre, Philadelphia.
1843	Frederick Fitzallen in *He's Not Amiss* (Dance), Niblo's Garden, New York.
	Baudon in *Military Manoeuvres* (anon.), Niblo's Garden, New York.
	Archard in *Mlle D'Angerville* (anon.), Niblo's Garden, New York.
	Farmer in *The Golden Farmer* (Webster), Niblo's Garden, New York.
	Titus in *Brutus* (Payne), Bowery Theatre, New York.
1844	Major Sapling in *Putnam; or, The Iron Son of '76* (Bannister), Bowery Theatre, New York.
1845	Littleton Coke in *Old Heads and Young Hearts* (Boucicault), Bowery Theatre, New York.
	Marchmont in *Robin Hood* (anon.), Bowery Theatre, New York.
	Hezekiah Pokeabout in *Everybody's Mess* (anon.), Bowery Theatre, New York.
	Ben in *Ben the Boatswain* (Wilks), Bowery Theatre, New York.
	Beauseant in *The Lady of Lyons* (Bulwer-Lytton), Niblo's Garden, New York.
	Sir Adelbert in *The Sleeping Beauty* (anon.), Bowery Theatre, New York.
	Charles in *Charles II* (Payne), Bowery Theatre, New York.
	Tom Truck in *The Wizard of the Wave* (anon.), Bowery Theatre, New York.
	Ivanhoe in *Ivanhoe* (Scott), Bowery Theatre, New York.
	Sultan Schariah in *The Last of the Thousand and One Nights* (Pittman), Bowery Theatre, New York.
	Wildrake in *The Love Chase* (Knowles), Bowery Theatre, New York.
1846	Claude Melnotte in *The Lady of Lyons* (Bulwer-Lytton), Albany, New York.
	Romeo in *Romeo and Juliet* (Shakespeare), Park Theatre, New York.
	Fazio in *Fazio* (Milman), Park Theatre, New York.
	Benedick in *Much Ado About Nothing* (Shakespeare), Park Theatre, New York.
	Armand in *Armand* (Mowatt), Park Theatre, New York.
1847	Sir Thomas Clifford in *The Hunchback* (Knowles), Princess's Theatre, London.
	Dudley Latymer in *The Lords of Ellingham* (Spicer), Olympic Theatre, London.

Iago in *Othello* (Shakespeare), Olympic Theatre, London.

Othello in *Othello* (Shakespeare), Olympic Theatre, London.

1848   Orlando in *As You Like It* (Shakespeare), Theatre Royal, Marylebone, London.

Luke in *The Shadow on the Wall* (Serle), Theatre Royal, Marylebone, London.

1849   Velasco in *Velasco* (Sargent), Theatre Royal, Marylebone, London.

Virginius in *Virginius* (St Ybar, translated by Oxenford), Theatre Royal, Marylebone, London.

Mercutio in *Romeo and Juliet* (Shakespeare), Theatre Royal, Marylebone, London.

Valentine in *The Two Gentlemen of Verona* (Shakespeare), Olympic Theatre, London.

Leon in *The Noble Heart* (Lewes), Olympic Theatre, London.

Brutus in *Brutus* (Payne), Olympic Theatre, London.

Laertes in *Hamlet* (Shakespeare), Olympic Theatre, London.

Adam Trueman in *Fashions* (Mowatt), Olympic Theatre, London.

William in *Black-Eyed Susan* (Jerrold), Haymarket Theatre, London.

1850   Macduff in *Macbeth* (Shakespeare), Haymarket Theatre, London.

1852   The Brothers in *The Corsican Brothers* (Boucicault), British tour.

Macbeth in *Macbeth* (Shakespeare), British tour.

Shylock in *The Merchant of Venice* (Shakespeare), British tour.

Richelieu in *Richelieu* (Bulwer-Lytton), British tour.

Ingomar in *Ingomar* (Lovell), British tour.

1853   George Sanford in *Gold* (Reade), Theatre Royal, Drury Lane, London.

1854   St Marc in *St Marc; or, A Husband's Sacrifice* (Wilkins), Broadway Theatre, New York.

Hamlet in *Hamlet* (Shakespeare), Broadway Theatre, New York.

Richard in *Richard III* (Shakespeare), Broadway Theatre, New York.

The Stranger in *The Stranger* (Kotzebue), Broadway Theatre, New York.

1855   William Tell in *William Tell* (Knowles), Boston Museum.

Duke of Aranza in *The Honeymoon* (Tobin), Boston Museum.

Abdas in *The Egyptian* (Wilkins), Broadway Theatre, New York.

Matthew Elmore in *Love's Sacrifice* (Lovell), Broadway Theatre, New York.

Jaques in *As You Like It* (Shakespeare), Walnut Street Theatre, Philadelphia.

Calaynos in *Calaynos* (Boker), Walnut Street Theatre, Philadelphia.

Sir Giles Overreach in *A New Way to Pay Old Debts* (Massinger), Broadway Theatre, New York.

Edward Loomis Davenport

Pythias in *Damon and Pythias* (Banim), Broadway Theatre, New York.

Lanciotto in *Francesca da Rimini* (Boker), Bowery Theatre, New York.

Prospero in *The Tempest* (Shakespeare), US tour.

1856   Matthew Hopkins in *The Witch Wife* (Spicer), Burton's Theatre, New York.

Walter in *The Poor Scholar* (anon.), Burton's Theatre, New York.

Charles Surface in *The School for Scandal* (Sheridan), Burton's Theatre, New York.

Maurice Landry in *Genevieve; or, The Reign of Terror* (Boucicault), Burton's Theatre, New York.

1857   King John in *King John* (Shakespeare), Bowery Theatre, New York.

De Soto in *De Soto; or, The Hero of the Mississippi* (Miles), Broadway Theatre, New York.

Brutus in *Julius Caesar* (Shakespeare), London; revived notably, Booth's Theatre, 1875.

1858   Richard Wilder in *A Struggle for Gold* (Patton), Burton's Theatre, New York.

Markham in *The Mormons* (anon.), Burton's Theatre, New York.

Cardinal Wolsey in *Henry VIII* (Shakespeare), Boston Theatre.

1859   Asa Trenchard in *Our American Cousin* (Taylor), Howard Athenaeum, Boston.

Mokorah in *The Cataract of the Ganges* (Moncrieff), Boston Theatre.

Captain John Smith in *Pocohontas* (anon.), Howard Athenaeum, Boston.

The Ghost in *Hamlet* (Shakespeare), Howard Athenaeum, Boston.

1862   Sir Benjamin Backbite in *The School for Scandal* (Sheridan), Winter Garden Theatre, New York.

1864   Philip Ray in *Enoch Arden* (Matthison, adapted from Tennyson), Boston Theatre.

Bill Sykes and Fagin in *Oliver Twist* (adapted from Dickens), Boston Theatre.

1865   Sir Francis Levison in *East Lynne* (Wood, adapted by Oxenford), Boston Theatre.

Rover in *Wild Oats* (O'Keeffe), Broadway Theatre, New York.

1866   Duke Tyrell, Felix Reybauld, Montani, and Hector de Riviers in *F; or, Branded* (anon.), Walnut Street Theatre, Philadelphia.

Long Tom Coffin in *The Pilot* (Cooper), Walnut Street Theatre, Philadelphia.

Rob Roy in *Rob Roy* (Scott), Walnut Street Theatre, Philadelphia.

1869   Dazzle in *London Assurance* (Boucicault), Walnut Street Theatre, Philadelphia.

Bruce Fanquehere in *Play* (Robertson), Fifth Avenue Theatre, New York.

Von Harfthal in *Dreams* (Robertson), Fifth Avenue Theatre, New York.

Sir Harcourt Courtly in *London Assurance* (Boucicault), Fifth Avenue Theatre, New York.

Don Cesar de Bazan in *Don Cesar de Bazan* (Webster and Boucicault), Fifth Avenue Theatre, New York.

Sir William Dorillon in *Wives as They Were and Maids as They Are* (Inchbald), Fifth Avenue Theatre, New York.

Gray in *Daddy Gray* (Halliday), Fifth Avenue Theatre, New York.

Master Walter in *The Hunchback* (Knowles), Fifth Avenue Theatre, New York.

Enoch Arden in *Enoch Arden* (anon.), Selwyn's Theatre, Boston.

1874   Jack Cade in *Jack Cade* (anon.), Howard Athenaeum, Boston.

1876   Edgar in *King Lear* (Shakespeare), Booth's Theatre, New York.

1877   Dan'l Druce in *Dan'l Druce* (Gilbert), Walnut Street Theatre, Philadelphia.

Also acted roles in: *Love* (Knowles), Park Theatre, New York, 1846; *The Bride of Lammermoor* (Scott), Boston Museum, 1855; *Love and Loyalty* (Robson), Broadway Theatre, New York, 1855; *A Morning Call* (Dance), Broadway Theatre, New York, 1855; *The Scalp Hunters* (anon.), US tour, 1855; *Charity's Love* (anon.), Bowery Theatre, New York, 1857; *Guy Mannering* (Scott), Boston Theatre, 1858; *The Actress of Padua* (Á Beckett), Boston Theatre, 1858; *She Stoops to Conquer* (Goldsmith), Boston Theatre, 1858; *Faint Heart Ne'er Won Fair Lady* (Planché), Selwyn's Theatre, Boston, 1869.

*

Bibliography

Books:

Edwin Francis Edgett, *Edward Loomis Davenport: A Biography*, New York, 1901; reprinted, New York, 1970.

Articles:

Bernard Bayle, "Mr Davenport", *Tallis's Dramatic Magazine*, 8, June 1851.

Henry P. Goddard, "Recollections of E. L. Davenport", *Lippincott's Magazine*, 21, April 1878.

Johnson Briscoe, "The Daring Davenports", *Green Book Magazine*, 9, March 1913.

* * *

Edward Loomis Davenport was among the more versatile actors of his era, equally adept at playing such broad farcical characters as Jerrold's William the Sailor or tragic heroes like Hamlet and Brutus. Until eclipsed by Edwin Booth, Davenport's Hamlet was considered by many critics the finest of its day. Similarly, his Brutus was highly regarded. Indeed, towards the end of his career when Davenport was invited to play Brutus in a sumptuous production staged by Henry Jarrett and Henry Palmer at Booth's Theatre in New York in 1875, the production ran for 103 performances, setting a record for the run of any Shakespeare play. It subsequently toured other Eastern cities for another 100 performances. Davenport's Sir Giles Overreach was also a forceful interpretation, equal to if not surpassing the performances of Edmund Kean and Junius Brutus Booth. Davenport himself counted Sir Giles among his favourite parts because of its "tremendous power and passion".

Although capable of projecting emotional energy and intensity and possessing an impressive physique and strong, melodious, voice, Davenport had a reputation as "a master of histrionic technique and a precisionist rather than an overwhelmer in performance." Except for his portrayal of Sir Giles, which over the years Davenport played him, became increasingly naturalistic and emotionally powerful, Davenport aimed for emotional restraint. The wisdom of such an approach was underlined by the declining popularity of his Overreach: the more vicious, vigorous, and horribly brilliant Davenport made him the more audiences avoided it. A contemporary, Henry Dickinson Stone, observed that in most of Davenport's other impersonations "calm judgement controls his impulses". Some critics, however, found he went too far in this opposite direction, judging him cold or overtly intellectual in some parts. William Winter, for example, complained that Davenport was "deficient in soul". This deficiency for Winter at least made even "his otherwise excellent Hamlet ... as metallic as the rapier he carried."

Ultimately, Davenport's very versatility may have worked to his disadvantage. As Henry P. Goddard noted, his "versatility led people to doubt his greatness in the highest walks of tragedy to which most actors confine themselves." Unwilling or unable to specialize but playing both great tragic heroes and vapid clowns, he "never won the popular recognition or the great pecuniary rewards that fell to ... men of less genius."

—Daniel J. Watermeier

DEBURAU, Jean-Baptiste Gaspard. French actor. Born Jan Kašpar Dvořák in Kolín, Bohemia, 31 July 1796, into a family of circus performers. Married for the first time in 1819 (his wife died a few months later); 2) Marie Trioullier in 1835; four sons (including actor Jean-Charles Deburau). Arrived in France, with his family, 1811; first appeared at the Théâtre des Funambules, Paris, 1816; excelled in mime under the stagename Baptiste, notably in the role of Pierrot, which he refashioned, from around 1820; retained popularity despite trial on a charge of killing a young man who insulted his wife, 1836. Died in Paris, 17 June 1846.

Roles

1827   Pierrot in *Harlequin Docteur*, Théâtre des Funambules, Paris.
      Pierrot in *Le Boeuf enragé*, Théâtre des Funambules, Paris.
      Pierrot in *Les Vingt-six infortunes de Pierrot*, Théâtre des Funambules, Paris.
      Pierrot in *La Génie du pauvre*, Théâtre des Funambules, Paris.
      Pierrot in *Pierrot nourrice*, Théâtre des Funambules, Paris.
      Pierrot in *Les Deux braconniers*, Théâtre des Funambules, Paris.
      Pierrot in *Le Poulailler ou Prenez garde à vous*, Théâtre des Funambules, Paris.

1828   Pierrot in *L'Homme-légume*, Théâtre des Funambules, Paris.
      Pierrot in *Kaleb*, Théâtre des Funambules, Paris.
      Pierrot in *Le Songe d'or ou L'Arlequin et l'avare*, Théâtre des Funambules, Paris.

1829   Pierrot in *Marchand de salade*, Théâtre des Funambules, Paris.
      Pierrot in *Ma mère l'oie ou Arlequin et l'oeuf d'or*, Théâtre des Funambules, Paris.

1832   Pierrot in *Le Lutin femelle*, Théâtre des Funambules, Paris.
      Pierrot in *Les Épreuves*, Théâtre des Funambules, Paris.
      Pierrot in *La Baleine*, Théâtre des Funambules, Paris.

1836   Pierrot in *Les Dupes ou Les Deux Georgettes*, Théâtre des Funambules, Paris.

1837   Pierrot in *Jack l'Orang-Outang*, Théâtre des Funambules, Paris.
      Pierrot in *Pierrot et ses créanciers*, Théâtre des Funambules, Paris.
      Pierrot in *Le Diable boiteux*, Théâtre des Funambules, Paris.
      Pierrot in *La Guerre des Cuisiniers*, Théâtre des Funambules, Paris.

1838   Pierrot in *Le Rempailleur de chaises*, Théâtre des Funambules, Paris.

      Pierrot in *Roberta chef de brigands*, Théâtre des Funambules, Paris.
      Pierrot in *Le Voile rouge*, Théâtre des Funambules, Paris.
      Pierrot in *En v'là des bamboches*, Théâtre des Funambules, Paris.

1840   Pierrot in *La Sorcière ou Le Démon protecteur*, Théâtre des Funambules, Paris.
      Pierrot in *Pierrot errant*, Théâtre des Funambules, Paris.
      Pierrot in *Le Tonnelier et le somnambule*, Théâtre des Funambules, Paris.
      Pierrot in *Le Rêve d'un conscrit*, Théâtre des Funambules, Paris.
      Pierrot in *Pierrot partout*, Théâtre des Funambules, Paris.
      Pierrot in *L'Amour et la folie ou Le Grelot mystificateur*, Théâtre des Funambules, Paris.

1841   Pierrot in *Les Cosaques ou La Ferme indendiée*, Théâtre des Funambules, Paris.
      Pierrot in *Pierrot Croquemitaine*, Théâtre des Funambules, Paris.
      Pierrot in *Biribi*, Théâtre des Funambules, Paris.

1842   Pierrot in *Satan ermite*, Théâtre des Funambules, Paris.
      Pierrot in *Pierrot en Afrique*, Théâtre des Funambules, Paris.
      Pierrot in *Les Trois godiches*, Théâtre des Funambules, Paris.

*

Bibliography

Books:
Jules Janin, *Deburau — Histoire du Théâtre a Quatre Sous*, Paris, 1881.
T. Rémy, *Jean-Gaspard Deburau*, Paris, 1954.

* * *

Jean-Baptiste Gaspard Deburau revitalized and revolutionized popular French theatre in the first half of the nineteenth century. The populace and the poets of that era hailed Deburau as their hero on the Paris stage and his name became synonymous with the character he performed — Pierrot, or Gilles, distinguishable by his white face, dead-pan expression, flowing white blouse, and wide trousers.

Before the appearance of Deburau's Pierrot, the character of Pierrot, or Pedrolino as he had been known in Italian, was below Harlequin in the hierarchical structure of the commedia dell'arte. Pierrot was Harlequin's servant, sometimes a friend or a cousin, usually embodying laziness, sexlessness, and gluttony. By the time Deburau appeared on the stage, his immediate predecessors had allowed Pierrot to degenerate into a lifeless stereotype, executing Harlequin's commands and passively gazing at Colombine. Deburau resuscitated the character of Pierrot and brought him into his true glory.

The exact dates of Pierrot's evolution are unclear. It probably began in the late 1810's or the early 1820's. Initially, Deburau's Pierrot played a small part alongside

Harlequin at the Théâtre des Funambules. However, very gradually and consistently, Deburau evolved as an actor and created the character that emerged as a leading box-office attraction for over 20 years. In his hands, Pierrot came to surpass Harlequin in importance, and his name similarly replaced Harlequin's in the titles of many plays and pantomimes. First and foremost, audiences came to see Pierrot.

Performing five times a day and nine times on Sundays, Deburau attracted packed houses at the Théâtre des Funambules. His audience was a mélange of the proletariat, artists, and socialites seeking the fashionable theatrical event. In Sacha Guitry's play *Deburau*, Guitry indicates that the stage was small and lit with candles, and that the auditorium was cramped. Perfumes of the world in the boxes mixed with the thick smells of garlic and orange peelings in the pit and galleries. Guitry's play, however, exaggerates the relationship between the principal characters, especially between Deburau and Marie Duplessis. Marcel Carné's film *Les Enfants du Paradis*, written by Jacques Prévert and with Jean-Louis Barrault playing the central role, marvellously reconstitutes the life of Deburau and accurately depicts the physical conditions of the Théâtre des Funambules, as well as immortalizing the physical actions of the Pierrot that Deburau invented and perfected.

Deburau changed the appearance of Pierrot as he had been presented by his predecessors. Deburau was tall and thin, and he had a long narrow face. He introduced changes in the costume that served to emphasize his comic lankiness and his subtle facial expressions. He replaced the tight-fitting jacket with a large cotton blouse and loose-fitting trousers, and entirely removed the frilled collarette. This new costume amplified the lines of his lyrical movements. He discarded the large white hat and used a black velvet skullcap to draw even more attention to his whitened face, creating a striking profile. Having said that, he assumed different costumes depending upon Pierrot's professions in the given play — for example, a soldier, a merchant, or an ecclesiastic. He even went as far as donning a wig or a moustache, but always retained the white face.

Deburau's Pierrot found himself in a variety of situations — reluctantly enlisted in the army, defending an unjustly persecuted brother, or in amorous pursuit of a girlfriend who had an unsympathetic father. Sometimes he was the protagonist, at other times he was the victim. Comic opportunities abounded in these pantomimes, which ranged from melodrama to everyday situations and encounters with fairies. Pierrot's character was complex and versatile; he was capable of love, revenge, compassion, and murder. At different times he was naive, mischievous, unscrupulous, diabolical, and libidinous. His female companion changed with each play, but she was always from the same social class.

Deburau was not a soloist on stage, being always in the company of other actors, but he remained mute while all of the others spoke dialogue. Some scholars argue that he performed in total silence, never uttering a word, using accessories that made no sound, and stepping lightly and noiselessly. Others maintain that he emitted sighs and made gutteral sounds but never pronounced actual words. Nevertheless, it is universally agreed that Deburau was a skilful and gifted pantomime. In silence, he created a

language of gesture, using his hands to convey his thoughts or intentions. He accompanied these movements with body postures — physical attitudes — and simultaneously used facial expressions. The audience was able to understand his dialogue and emotional state immediately. What appeared as effortless spontaneity was actually achieved through meticulous and constant rehearsal.

Pierrot's silence in itself was evocative of the repression and silent suffering of the proletariat and was in part the reason behind his appeal to "the people". The character was no longer a slave or a servant watching and assisting the follies of his master. He shunned submission, and looked his adversaries directly in the eye. Pierrot was not instigating a revolution; he was merely dealing with life as an individual worthy of respect, acting with rightful dignity. His white face functioned like a mask, betraying no emotion, no gaiety, no weakness, and no strength — only a stoic calm. His silence invited speculation and conjecture.

Deburau succeeded in elevating the character of Pierrot to a poetic level that intrigued and inspired his audience and subsequent generations of actors and directors. His audience remained in awe of him, and his admirers considered him a magician. Critics claimed he was almost faceless, mysteriously moving through space and reducing each gesture to its purest form. Deburau's influence is visible in the actor training and performance of Jacques Copeau, Étienne Decroux, Jean-Louis Barrault, and Jacques Lecoq. The tradition of the whitened face and the intricate posturing is continued by Marcel Marceau. The primary difference between Deburau and Marceau is that Deburau was a pantomime in silent dialogue with other characters and a real set, while Marceau is a mime creating the illusion of a place and other characters on a bare stage. Deburau's Pierrot was clearly the predecessor of Buster Keaton's and Charlie Chaplin's characters — pale-faced underdogs, survivors, charming and sympathetic, penniless and priceless.

—Ludvika Popenhagen

DÉJAZET, Pauline-Virginie. French actress and manager. Born in Paris, 30 August 1798. Virtually no formal education; trained for the stage as a child under her sister, actress Thérèse Déjazet. Unmarried; one son and one daughter. Stage debut, Théâtre des Jeunes Artistes, Paris, 1806; joined Thâtre du Vaudeville, Paris, 1807; first appearance at the Théâtre des Variétés, Paris, 1817; subsequently acted in Lyon and Bordeaux; joined Théâtre du Gymnase company, Paris, 1821 and established reputation in male roles; joined the Théâtre des Nouveautés, Paris, 1828; actress, Théâtre du Palais-Royal, Paris, 1831–44; returned to the Variétés, 1845; subsequently acted at the Vaudeville and elsewhere and took over the Folies-Nouvelles, renamed the Théâtre Déjazet, 1859; retired as manager, 1866, and resumed touring throughout Europe, to universal acclaim, continuing to play young men into her seventies in order to stave off poverty. Died in Paris, 1 December 1875.

Roles

1806   Fanchon in *Fanchon toute seule* (Ponet), Théâtre des Jeunes Artistes, Paris.

Hortense in *La Laitière* (Henrion), Théâtre des Jeunes Artistes, Paris.

Constance in *L'Amant Instituteur* (Redon and Defrénoy), Théâtre des Jeunes Artistes, Paris.

Rosine in *Avis aux pères, ou La Fille corrigée* (Redon and Defrénoy), Théâtre des Jeunes Artistes, Paris.

Virginie in *Se Fâchera-t-il? ou le Pari imprudent* (Ponet), Théâtre des Jeunes Artistes, Paris.

Colombine in *Une Espièglerie d'Arlequin, ou l'Enlèvement nocturne* (Redon and Defrénoy), Théâtre des Jeunes Artistes, Paris.

Pauline in *Pongo* (anon.), Théâtre des Jeunes Artistes, Paris.

1807   L'Amour in *Les Sirènes, ou les Sauvages de la montagne d'or* (Hapdé), Théâtre des Jeunes Artistes, Paris.

Young boy in *Le Fond du sac, ou la Préface de Lina* (Dieulafoi and Gersin), Théâtre du Vaudeville, Paris.

1808   Virginie in *L'Etourderie, ou Comment sortira-t-il de là?* (Radet), Théâtre du Vaudeville, Paris.

Young girl in *Bayard au Pont-Neuf, ou le Picotin d'avoine* (Dieulafoi and Gersin), Théâtre du Vaudeville, Paris.

1809   Virginie in *Adam-Montauciel, ou À qui la Gloire?* (Gersin, De Rougement, and Désaugiers), Théâtre du Vaudeville, Paris.

Petit Pichard in *Benoît, ou le Pauvre de Notre-Dame* (Pain and Dumersan), Théâtre du Vaudeville, Paris.

1810   Bernatt in *Les Sabotiers Béarnais, ou la Faute d'orthographe* (Moreau and Gentil), Théâtre du Vaudeville, Paris.

One of the family in *L'Auberge dans les nues, ou le Chemin de la gloire*, Théâtre du Vaudeville, Paris.

Jacquot in *Les Deux Lions* (Barré and Picard), Théâtre du Vaudeville, Paris.

Eugénie in *La Cendrillon des écoles, ou le Tarif des prix* (Saint-Rémy), Théâtre du Vaudeville, Paris.

1811   Fairy Nabotte in *La Belle au bois dormant* (Bouilly and Dumersan), Théâtre du Vaudeville, Paris.

1812   Nini Gobetout in *Paris volant, ou la Fabrique d'ailes* (Moreau, Ourry, and Théaulon), Théâtre du Vaudeville, Paris.

Flora in *Les Rendez-vous de minuit* (Dupin and Dartois), Théâtre du Vaudeville, Paris.

Page in *Bayard page, ou Vaillance et Beauté* (Théaulon and Dartois), Théâtre du Vaudeville, Paris.

Page in *Robert le Diable* (Bouilly and Dumersan), Théâtre du Vaudeville, Paris.

1813   Tippo's child in *Le Cimetière de Parnasse, ou Tippo malade* (Théoulon and Dartois), Théâtre du Vaudeville, Paris.

Adolphe in *Les Deux Ermites, ou la Confidence* (Delestre-Poirson and Ménissier), Théâtre du Vaudeville, Paris.

Louisette in *Greuze, ou l'Accordée de village* (Beaunoir and Valory), Théâtre du Vaudeville, Paris.

Jacquot in *Les Bêtes savantes* (Dumersan, Théaulon, and Dartois), Théâtre du Vaudeville, Paris.

Mlle Crépon in *Les Characeds en action, ou la Soirée bourgeoise* (Dumersan and Sewrin), Théâtre du Vaudeville, Paris.

1814   Jacques in *La Route de Paris, ou les Allants et les Venants* (Théaulon and Dartois), Théâtre du Vaudeville, Paris.

Jules in *Les Visites, ou les Compliments du jour de l'an* (Théaulon and Dartois), Théâtre du Vaudeville, Paris.

1815   Page in *Les Trois Saphos Lyonnaises, ou Une cour d'amour* (Barré, Radet, and Desfontaines), Théâtre du Vaudeville, Paris.

Juliette in *Nous aussi, nous l'aimons! ou la Fête du faubourg Saint-Antoine* (Maréchalle), Théâtre du Vaudeville, Paris.

Pierrot in *Le Vaudeville en vendanges* (Désaugiers, Moreau, and Gentil), Théâtre du Vaudeville, Paris.

Gouspignac in *La Pompe funèbre* (Dupin and Scribe), Théâtre du Vaudeville, Paris.

1816   Thérèse in *Les Visites bourgeoises, ou le Dehors et le Dedans* (Désaugiers, Moreau, and Gentil), Théâtre du Vaudeville, Paris.

Villager in *Le Revenant, ou l'Héritage* (Pain and Dupin), Théâtre du Vaudeville, Paris.

First dancer in *Flore et Zéphire* (Scribe and Delestre-Poirson), Théâtre du Vaudeville, Paris.

Virginie in *Les Garde-Marine, ou l'Amour et la Faim* (Dieulafoi and Gersin), Théâtre du Vaudeville, Paris.

Miss Scott in *La Rosière de Hartwell* (Dartois and Letournel), Théâtre du Vaudeville, Paris.

Mlle Sure in *Les Montagnes russes, ou le Temple de la mode* (Scribe, Delestre-Poirson, and Dupin), Théâtre du Vaudeville, Paris.

1817   Suzette in *Quinze ans d'absence* (Merle and Brazier), Théâtre des Variétés, Paris.

Félix in *Les Petits Braconniers, ou les Ecoliers en vacances* (Merle and Brazier), Théâtre des Variétés, Paris.

1820   Elise in *Le Cirque Bojolay, ou Pleuvra-t-il, ne pleuvra-t-il pas?* (Belfort, Lepeintre, and Leon), Théâtre-Français de Bordeaux, Bordeaux.

Rosine in *Honneur et Fatuité, ou le Prix des braves* (Belfort and Rodolphe), Théâtre-Français de Bordeaux, Bordeaux.

1821   Marianne in *Caroline* (Scribe and Ménissier), Théâtre du Gymnase, Paris.

Adeline de Préval in *La Meunière* (Scribe and Mélesville), Théâtre du Gymnase, Paris.

Léon in *La Petite Soeur* (Scribe and Mélesville), Théâtre du Gymnase, Paris.

Madeleine in *Le Comédien d'Etampes* (Moreau and Sewrin), Théâtre du Gymnase, Paris.

Octave de Ballainville in *Le Mariage enfantin* (Scribe and Delavigne), Théâtre du Gymnase, Paris.

Nanette in *Monsieur Courtois, ou la Saint-Louis* (Dupin), Théâtre du Gymnase, Paris.

Julienne in *L'Amant bossu* (Scribe, Mélesville, and Vandière), Théâtre du Gymnase, Paris.

Frosine in *Frosine, ou la Dernière venue* (Radet), Théâtre du Gymnase, Paris.

Victor in *Philibert marié* (Moreau and Scribe), Théâtre du Gymnase, Paris.

1822   Marinette in *Le Dépit amoureux* (Milière), Théâtre du Gymnase, Paris.

Suzanne in *Le Garde-moulin* (Moreau and Sewrin), Théâtre du Gymnase, Paris.

Félix in *Le Plaisant de société* (Scribe and Mélesvilles), Théâtre du Gymnase, Paris.

Clopin in *La Famille normande, ou le Cousin Marcel* (Mélesville and Brazier), Théâtre du Gymnase, Paris.

Claire in *Le Notaire* (Mazères, De Lurieu, and Vandière), Théâtre du Gymnase, Paris.

Tiennette in *Le Nouveau Pourceaugnac* (Scribe and Delestre-Poirson), Théâtre du Gymnase, Paris.

Mathilde in *Le Vieux Garçon et la Petite fille* (Scribe and Delavigne), Théâtre du Gymnase, Paris.

Petit Jacques in *La Nouvelle Clary*, Théâtre du Gymnase, Paris.

Fortuné in *L'Ecarté, ou Un coin de salon* (Scribe, Mélesville, and Saint-Georges), Théâtre du Gymnase, Paris.

Adolphe in *Le Bon Papa, ou la Proposition de marriage* (Scribe and Mélesville), Théâtre du Gymnase, Paris.

1823   Aladin in *La Petite Lampe merveilleuse* (Scribe and Mélesville), Théâtre du Gymnase, Paris.

Petit Jacob in *La Loge du portier* (Scribe and Mazères), Théâtre du Gymnase, Paris.

Marie-Jeanne in *L'Actrice* (Dupeuty and Villeneuve), Théâtre du Gymnase, Paris.

Toinette in *La Maison en loterie* (Picard and Radet), Théâtre du Gymnase, Paris.

Rose in *Le Menteur véridique* (Scribe and Mélesville), Théâtre du Gymnase, Paris.

Annette in *La Diligence versée* (Langlé, Rousseau, and Courcy), Théâtre du Gymnase, Paris.

Marie in *Le Pension bourgeoise* (Scribe, Dupin, and Dumersan), Théâtre du Gymnase, Paris.

Madeleine in *Partie et Revanche* (Scribe, Francis, and Brazier), Théâtre du Gymnase, Paris.

Jules in *Mon Ami Christophe* (Dupeuty, Villeneuve, and Lafontaine), Théâtre du Gymnase, Paris.

Mimi in *Les Grisettes* (Scribe and Dupin), Théâtre du Gymnase, Paris.

Inès in *La Fête Française* (Delestre and Poirson), Théâtre du Gymnase, Paris.

Pauline-Virginie Déjazet

Piedlevé in *L'Apthéose de Polichinelle* (Rochefort, Dupin, and Langlé), Théâtre du Gymnase, Paris.

Joséphine in *Le Bureau de loterie* (Mazères and Romieu), Théâtre du Gymnase, Paris.

Victor in *L'Atelier de peinture* (Sewrin and Tousez), Théâtre du Gymnase, Paris.

Louise in *Rodolphe, ou Frère et soeur* (Scribe and Mélesville), Théâtre du Gymnase, Paris.

Madeleine in *Rossini à Paris, ou le Grand dîner* (Scribe and Mazères), Théâtre du Gymnase, Paris.

Léveillé in *La Fête de la Victoire, ou le Rendez-vous militaire* (Villeneuve and Dupeuty), Théâtre du Gymnase, Paris.

Justin in *La Morale en action, ou les Promesses du jour de l'an* (Jaime, Rolland, and Villeneuve), Théâtre du Gymnase, Paris.

1824   Justine in *Le Coiffeur et le Perruquier* (Scribe, Mazères, and Saint-Laurent), Théâtre du Gymnase, Paris.

Jacqueline in *Les Petites Saturnales* (Brazier, Carmouche, and Mazères), Théâtre du Gymnase, Paris.

Denise in *Le Oui des jeunes filles* (Dupeuty, Villeneuve, and Lassalle), Théâtre du Gymnase, Paris.

Madelon in *Les Femmes romantiques, ou Lord X . . .* (Théaulon, Ramond, and Capelle), Théâtre du Gymnase, Paris.

Jeannette in *Le Leycester du faubourg* (Scribe, Saintine, and Carmouche), Théâtre du Gymnase, Paris.

Joséphine in *Le Bal champêtre, ou les Grisettes à la campagne* (Scribe and Dupin), Théâtre du Gymnase, Paris.

Madeline in *M. Tardif* (Scribe and Mélesville), Théâtre du Gymnase, Paris.

Juliette in *La Haine d'une femme, ou le Jeune homme à marier* (Scribe), Théâtre du Gymnase, Paris.

1825   Antonine in *Le Plus Beau Jour de la vie* (Scribe and Varner), Théâtre du Gymnase, Paris.

Nicole in *Le Jeune Werther* (Désaugiers and Gentil), Théâtre du Gymnase, Paris.

Auguste in *La Charge à payer, ou la Mère intrigante* (Scribe and Varner), Théâtre du Gymnase, Paris.

Modeste in *Les Eosières de Paris* (Brazier, Simonnin, and Carmouche), Théâtre du Gymnase, Paris.

Victoire in *Fenêtres à louer* (Désaugiers and Gentil), Théâtre du Gymnase, Paris.

Marie in *Les Ricochets* (Picard), Théâtre du Gymnase, Paris.

Louise in *Les Enfants du colon* (Duport, Saintine, and Duvert), Théâtre du Gymnase, Paris.

Henri in *L'An 1835, ou la Saint-Charles au village* (Désaugiers), Théâtre du Gymnase, Paris.

Alain in *La Chercheuse d'esprit* (Favart, Dumersan, Lafontaine, and Brazier), Théâtre du Gymnase, Paris.

1826   Catherine in *Le Confident* (Scribe and Mélesville), Théâtre du Gymnase, Paris.

Brigitte in *Les Manteaux* (Scribe, Varner, and Dupin), Théâtre du Gymnase, Paris.

Jules in *La Belle-Mère* (Scribe and Bayard), Théâtre du Gymnase, Paris.

Louise in *L'Oncle d'Amérique* (Scribe and Mazères), Théâtre du Gymnase, Paris.

Baronne de Wladimir in *La Lune de miel* (Scribe, Mélesville, and Carmouche), Théâtre du Gymnase, Paris.

Nicolle in *Clara Wendel* (Brazier and Dumersan), Théâtre du Gymnase, Paris.

Zanetta in *L'Ambassadeur* (Scribe and Mélesville), Théâtre du Gymnase, Paris.

Virginie in *Le Misanthrope de la rue de Clichy* (Dartoism, Francis, and Alhoy), Théâtre du Gymnase, Paris.

Adolphe in *La Coutume allemande, ou les Vacances* (Mazères and Rougemont), Théâtre du Gymnase, Paris.

Jeanneton in *La Fée du voisinage, ou la Saint-Charles au village* (Théaulon, Courcy, and Rousseau), Théâtre du Gymnase, Paris.

1827   Elisa in *Les Deux Elèves, ou l'Education particulière* (Rochefort, Langlé, Dittmer, Cavé, and Brunet), Théâtre du Gymnase, Paris.

Guillaume in *La Famille du faubourg* (Scribe and Varner), Théâtre du Gymnase, Paris.

René in *Le Myope* (Dupeuty, Saintine, and Laloue), Théâtre du Gymnase, Paris.

Georges in *Les Mémoires d'une Anglaise* (Rochefort and Duport), Théâtre du Gymnase, Paris.

Guilleri in *Les Elèves du Conservatoire* (Scribe and Saintine), Théâtre du Gymnase, Paris.

Adrien in *L'Arbitre, ou les Séductions* (Théaulon and Duport), Théâtre du Gymnase, Paris.

Rose in *Le Jeune Maire* (Dupeuty, Duvert, and Saintine), Théâtre du Gymnase, Paris.

Cécilia in *L'Ecrivain public* (Théaulon, Simonnin, and Courcy), Théâtre du Gymnase, Paris.

Gritly in *Le Mal du pays, ou la Batelière de Brienz* (Scribe and Méesville), Théâtre du Gymnase, Paris.

Ramplan in *Une Heure à Porte-Sainte-Marie* (Scribe), Théâtre des Tuileries, Paris.

Marie in *L'Intendant et le Garde-chasse* (Désaugiers and Anne), Théâtre des Tuileries, Paris.

1828   Catherine in *Le Mariage impossible* (Mélesville and Carmouche), Théâtre du Gymnase, Paris.

Jeannette in *Le Garçon de caisse, ou Comme on monte et comme on descend* (Gabriel and Ymbert), Théâtre des Nouveautés, Paris.

Dauphin in *Henri IV en famille* (Villeneuve, Vanderburch, and Desforges), Théâtre des Nouveautés, Paris.

Françoise in *Le Bourgeois de Paris, ou la Partie de plaisir* (Dartois, Varner, and Dupin), Théâtre des Nouveautés, Paris.

Georgette in *Valentine, ou la Chute des feuilles* (Saint-Hilaire and Villeneuve), Théâtre des Nouveautés, Paris.

Adélaïde Chopin in *Jean* (Théaulon and Signol), Théâtre des Nouveautés, Paris.

Didier in *La Maison du rempart* (Mélesville, Boirie, and Merle), Théâtre des Nouveautés, Paris.

Jaqueline in *Le Défunt et l'Héritier* (Mélesville and Dumersan), Théâtre des Nouveautés, Paris.

1829   Grandmother in *Aventures et Voyages du petit Jonas* (Scribe and Dupin), Théâtre des Nouveautés, Paris.

Léon and Jules in *Antoine, ou les Trois générations* (Mélesville and Brazier), Théâtre des Nouveautés, Paris.

Madame Pinchon in *Les Suites d'un mariage de raison* (Dartois, Brunswick, and Lhérie), Théâtre des Nouveautés, Paris.

Clair-de-lune in *Le Doge et le Dernier jour d'un condamné, ou le Canon d'alarme* (Simonnin, Vanderburch, and Brazier), Théâtre des Nouveautés, Paris.

Parchemin in *Jovial en prison* (Théaulon, Gabriel, and Anne), Théâtre des Nouveautés, Paris.

Babet in *Babet, ou la Petite bonne* (Desnoyer and Fontan), Théâtre des Nouveautés, Paris.

Firmin in *Le Bandit* (Théaulon, Saint-Laurent, and Anne), Théâtre des Nouveautés, Paris.

Blanchette in *Isaure* (Nézel, Antier, Cornu, and Payn), Théâtre des Nouveautés, Paris.

Sophie in *La Couturière* (Duvert, Desvergers, and Varin), Théâtre des Nouveautés, Paris.

Zisky in *La Paysanne de Livonie* (Saintine, Villeneuve, and Vanderburch), Théâtre des Nouveautés, Paris.

Ninie in *La Femme, le Mari et l'Amant* (Kock and Dupeuty), Théâtre des Nouveautés, Paris.

1830   Henriette in *Monsieur Sans-Gêne* (Désaugiers and Gentil), Théâtre des Nouveautés, Paris.

The Duchess in *La Femme innocente, malheureuse et persécutée* (Rougemont), Théâtre des Nouveautés, Paris.

Adélaïde Chopin in *Le Bal champêtre* (Théaulon and Grégoire), Théâtre des Nouveautés, Paris.

Seyton in *Henri V et ses compagnons* (Romieu and Royer), Théâtre des Nouveautés, Paris.

Mila in *Le Mari aux neuf femmes* (Théaulon), Théâtre des Nouveautés, Paris.

Zéphirine in *Le Bénéficiare* (Théaulon and Etienne), Théâtre des Nouveautés, Paris.

Léonora in *Rafaël* (Théaulon), Théâtre des Nouveautés, Paris.

Blanche in *Une Nuit du duc de Montfort* (Soulié and Arnould), Théâtre des Nouveautés, Paris.

Auguste in *A-propos patriotique* (Villeneuve and Masson), Théâtre des Nouveautés, Paris.

Louise in *André le chansonnier* (Fontan and Desnoyer), Théâtre des Nouveautés, Paris.

Séraphine in *Le Marchand de la rue Saint-Denis, ou le Magasin, la Mairie et la Cour d'assises* (Brazier, Villeneuve, and Vanderburch), Théâtre des Nouveautés, Paris.

Sister Sainte-Claire in *Les Dragons et les Religeuses* (Pigault-Lebrun), Théâtre des Nouveautés, Paris.

Bonaparte in *Bonaparte à l'Ecole de Brienne, ou le Petit Caporal* (Gabriel, Villeneuve, and Masson), Théâtre des Nouveautés, Paris.

Colombine in *La Chatte blanche* (pantomime), Théâtre des Nouveautés, Paris.

Candide in *Manette, ou le Danger d'être jolie fille* (Rougemont), Théâtre des Nouveautés, Paris.

Catherine Howard in *Les Trois Catherine* (Duport and Monnais), Théâtre des Nouveautés, Paris.

Betty in *Le Collier de perles* (Duvert and Duport), Théâtre des Nouveautés, Paris.

Duc de Reichstadt in *Le Fils de l'homme* (Lussan), Théâtre des Nouveautés, Paris.

1831   Juliette in *Juliette* (Morel), Théâtre des Nouveautés, Paris.

L'Illusion and Le Comète in *Les Pilules dramatiques, ou le Choléra-Morbus* (Rochefort, Villeneuve, Masson, and Leuven), Théâtre des Nouveautés, Paris.

Madeleine Jarry in *Les Jumeaux de la Réole, ou les Frères Faucher* (Rougemont and Decomberousse), Théâtre des Nouveautés, Paris.

Herminie in *Ils n'Ouvriront pas!* (Mélesville, Brazier, and Bayard), Théâtre du Palais-Royal, Paris.

Frédéric in *L'Audience du Prince* (Villeneuve, Anicet-Bourgeois, and Livry), Théâtre du Palais-Royal, Paris.

Catherine in *Le Philtre champenois* (Mélesville and Brazier), Théâtre du Palais-Royal, Paris.

The Fairy and The Dancer in *Le Tailleur et la Fée, ou les Chansons de Béranger* (Vanderburch, Langlé, and De Forges), Théâtre du Palais-Royal, Paris.

Catherine in *Catherine II, ou Un Caprice impérial* (Desvergers and Varin), Théâtre du Palais-Royal, Paris.

Ursule in *Les Jeunes bonnes et les vieux garçons* (Desvergers and Varin), Théâtre du Palais-Royal, Paris.

Anna Boleno, La Politique, and La Gaudriole in *Les Bouillons à domicile* (Gabriel, Villeneueve, and Livry), Théâtre du Palais-Royal, Paris.

Mariette in *Les Deux Novices* (Varner and Bayard), Théâtre du Palais-Royal, Paris.

Duc d'Orléans in *L'Enfance de Louis XII, ou la Correction de nos pères* (Mélesville, Simonnin, and Nézel), Théâtre du Palais-Royal, Paris.

1832   Manette in *La Chanteuse et l'Ouvrière* (Saintine and Villeneuve), Théâtre du Palais-Royal, Paris.

Vert-Vert in *Vert-Vert* (Leuven and De Forges), Théâtre du Palais-Royal, Paris.

Charlotte in *La Ferme de Bondy, ou les Deux réfractaires* (Gabriel, Villeneuve, and Masson), Théâtre du Palais-Royal, Paris.

Follet in *Follet, ou le Sylphe* (Rochefort, Varin, and Desvergers), Théâtre du Palais-Royal, Paris.

Joséphine in *Le Dernier Chapitre* (Mélesville, Dumanoir, and Mallian), Théâtre du Palais-Royal, Paris.

Coq-à-l'âne, Jocrisse, une Vivandière, and Le Plaisir in *Paris malade* (Bayard and Varner), Théâtre du Palais-Royal, Paris.

1833   Madeleine in *Les Trois Assiettes* (Masson, Saintine, and Villeneuve), Théâtre du Palais-Royal, Paris.

Célestin in *Le Cadet de famille* (Vanderburch, Brunswick, and D'Avrecourt), Théâtre du Palais-Royal, Paris.

Sophie Arnould in *Sophie Arnould* (Leuven, De Forges, and Dumanoir), Théâtre du Palais-Royal, Paris.

Atala in *Sous clef* (Leuven, De Forges, and Dumanoir), Théâtre du Palais-Royal, Paris.

Catherine Biancolelli in *La Fille de Dominique* (Villeneuve and Livry), Théâtre du Palais-Royal, Paris.

Zerbi in *La Danseuse de Venise* (Théaulon and De Forges), Théâtre du Palais-Royal, Paris.

1834   Madame Fromageot in *Un Scandale* (Duvert and Lauzanne), Théâtre du Palais-Royal, Paris.

J. J. Rousseau in *Les Charmettes, ou Une page des confessions* (Bayard, De Forges, and Vanderburch), Théâtre du Palais-Royal, Paris.

Charles Welstein in *Le Triolet bleu* (Gabriel, Villeneuve, and Masson), Théâtre du Palais-Royal, Paris.

Fifine in *Le Commis et la Grisette* (Kock, Labie, and Monier), Théâtre du Palais-Royal, Paris.

Thérésina in *Judith and Holopherne* (Théaulon, Nézel, and Overnay), Théâtre du Palais-Royal, Paris.

The Idiot in *L'Idiote* (Théaulon and Nézel), Théâtre du Palais-Royal, Paris.

Camille, or Frétillon, in *Frétillon, ou la Bonne fille* (Bayard and Decomberousse), Théâtre du Palais-Royal, Paris.

1835   Louis XV in *Les Beignets à la cour* (Antier), Théâtre du Palais-Royal, Paris.

Ascagne in *Un Raout chex M. Lupot, rue Greneta, 378* (Kock), Théâtre du Palais-Royal, Paris.

Christine in *La Croix d'or* (Rougemont and Dupeuty), Théâtre du Palais-Royal, Paris.

La Périchole in *La Périchole* (Théaulon and De Forges), Théâtre du Palais-Royal, Paris.

Baronne de Merville and Suzanne in *La Fiole de Cagliostro* (Anicent-Bourgeois, Dumanoir, and Brisebarre), Théâtre du Palais-Royal, Paris.

1836   Cadet-Buteux, Madame Denis, Rosine, Margot, La Duchesse, Le Franc-vaurien, and La Gaudriole in *Les Chansons de Désugiers* (Théaulon, Chazet, and Courcy), Théâtre du Palais-Royal, Paris.

La Marquise in *La Marquise de Prétintaille* (Bayard and Dumanoir), Théâtre du Palais-Royal, Paris.

Arthur de Wolferag in *L'Oiseau bleu* (Bayard and Varner), Théâtre du Palais-Royal, Paris.

Arouet in *Voltaire en vacances* (Villeneuve and Livry), Théâtre du Palais-Royal, Paris.

Marion Delorme in *Marion Carmélite* (Bayard and Dumanoir), Théâtre du Palais-Royal, Paris.

Marie Duronceray in *Madame Favart* (Saintine and Masson), Théâtre du Palais-Royal, Paris.

1837   Postillon de Lonjumeau in *L'Année sur la sellette* (Bayard, Théaulon, and Courcy), Théâtre du Palais-Royal, Paris.

Agathe de Servières in *L'Outrage* (Scribe and Dupin), Théâtre du Palais-Royal, Paris.

Jeanneton in *La Comtesse du Tonneau, ou les Deux Cousines* (Théaulon and Chazet), Théâtre du Palais-Royal, Paris.

Mimie in *Le Café des comédiens* (Cogniard), Théâtre du Palais-Royal, Paris.

Suzanne in *Suzanne* (Mélesville and Guinot), Théâtre du Palais-Royal, Paris.

1838   Circus rider and announcer in *L'Ile de la folie* (Cogniard), Théâtre du Palais-Royal, Paris.

Léonide in *La Maîtresse de langues* (Saint-Georges, Leuven, and Dumanoir), Théâtre du Palais-Royal, Paris.

Mlle Dangeville, Jacquot, Marquise de Nesle, and Tching-Ka in *Mademoiselle Dangeville* (Villeneuve and Livry), Théâtre du Palais-Royal, Paris.

Emmanuel in *Les Deux Pigeons* (Saintine and Masson), Théâtre du Palais-Royal, Paris.

Françoise and Francesca in *Françoise et Francesca* (Varner), Théâtre du Palais-Royal, Paris.

1839   Gîtana in *Rothomago* (Cogniard), Théâtre du Palais-Royal, Paris.

Nanon in *Nanon, Ninon and Maintrenon, ou les Trois boudoirs* (Théaulon, Dartois, and Lesguillon), Théâtre du Palais-Royal, Paris.

Flora in *Argentine* (Gabriel, Dupeuty, and Delaporte), Théâtre du Palais-Royal, Paris.

Richelieu in *Les Premières Armes de Richelieu* (Bayard and Dumanoir), Théâtre du Palais-Royal, Paris.

1840   Indiana in *Indiana et Charlemagne* (Bayard and Dumanoir), Théâtre du Palais-Royal, Paris.

1841   Mlle Sallé in *Mademoiselle Sallé* (Saintine, Bayard, and Dumanoir), Théâtre du Palais-Royal, Paris.

Létorières in *Le Vicomte de Létorières* (Bayard and Dumanoir), Théâtre du Palais-Royal, Paris.

1842   Coraline in *Une Femme sous les scellés* (Bayard and Saintine), Théâtre du Palais-Royal, Paris.

Charlotte Clapier in *Le Capitaine Charlotte* (Bayard and Dumanoir), Théâtre du Palais-Royal, Paris.

1843   Lisette in *La Lisette de Béranger* (Bérat), Théâtre du Palais-Royal, Paris.

Raphaël Potichon in *Les Deux Anes* (Mélesville and Carmouche), Théâtre du Palais-Royal, Paris.

Mlle Déjazet in *Mademoiselle Déjazet au sérail, ou le Palais-Royal en 1872* (Bayard and Lurieu), Théâtre du Palais-Royal, Paris.

Suzon in *La Marquise de Carabas* (Bayard and Dumanoir), Théâtre du Palais-Royal, Paris.

Génie of the Future in *La Cour de Gérolstein* (Bayard, Mélesville, and Dumanoir), Théâtre du Palais-Royal, Paris.

1844   Carlo Bertinazzi in *Carlo et Carlin* (Mélesville and Dumanoir), Théâtre du Palais-Royal, Paris.

1845   Marquise de Villani in *Un Conte de fées* (Leuven, Brunswick, and Dumas), Théâtre des Variétés, Paris.

Gothe in *Le Gardeuse de dindons* (Théaulon, Dartois, and Biéville), Théâtre des Variétés, Paris.

Gentil-Bernard in *Gentil-Bernard, ou l'Art d'aimer* (Dumanoir and Clairville), Théâtre des Variétés, Paris.

Jacques in *L'Enfant de l'amour, ou les Deux Marquis de Saint-Jacques* (Bayard and Guinot), Théâtre des Variétés, Paris.

Madame Caillette in *Le Moulin à paroles* (Gabriel and Dupeuty), Théâtre des Variétés, Paris.

1848   Lauzun in *Le Marquis de Lauzun* (Carmouche and Guinot), Théâtre des Variétés, Paris.

Mlle de Choisy in *Mademoiselle de Choisy* (Saint-Georges and Lopez), Théâtre des Variétés, Paris.

1850   Lully in *Lully, ou les Petits violons de Mademoiselle* (Dumanoir and Clairville), Théâtre des Variétés, Paris.

Thérésa Baletti in *Colombine, ou les Sept péchés capitaux* (Carmouche and Guinot), Théâtre des Variétés, Paris.

Douairière and Sébastien in *La Douairière de Brionne* (Bayard and Dumanoir), Théâtre du Vaudeville, Paris.

Jean in *Jean le postillon* (Carmouche and Guinot), Théâtre du Vaudeville, Paris.

1851   Hector de Blécourt in *Ouistiti* (Leuven and Lhérie), Théâtre du Vaudeville, Paris.

Cloud in *Quand on va cueillir la noisette* (Kock and Jallais), Théâtre du Vaudeville, Paris.

1852   Mathéus in *Les Rêves de Mathéus* (Mélesville and Carmouche), Théâtre du Vaudeville, Paris.

Scapin in *Scapin* (Carmouche and Guinot), Théâtre du Vaudeville, Paris.

Comtesse de Mailly in *Les Paniers de la comtesse* (Gozlan), Théâtre du Vaudeville, Paris.

1853   Fanfan in *Les Trois Gamins* (Venderburch and Clairville), Théâtres des Variétés, Paris.

1855   Frédéric in *Le Sergent Frédéric* (Vanderburch and Dumanoir), Théâtre de la Gaîté, Paris.

1857   Roger-Bontemps and Mère Toby in *Les Chants de Béranger* (Clairville and Lamber-Thiboust), Théâtre des Variétés, Paris.

1859   Chérubin in *Chérubin* (Dumanoir and Lambert-Thiboust), Théâtre des Variétés, Paris.

Figaro in *Les Premières Armes de Figaro* (Vanderburch and Sardou), Théâtre Déjazet, Paris.

1860   Françoise Giraudeau and Désiré in *P'tit-fils, p'tit mignon* (Gabriel and Dupeuty), Théâtre Déjazet, Paris.

Garat in *Monsieur Garat* (Sardou), Théâtre Déjazet, Paris.

1862   Prince de Conti in *Les Prés Saint-Gervais* (Sardou), Théâtre Déjazet, Paris.

1863   Mercure, Mlle de Scudéry, and Maclou in *L'Argent et l'Amour* (Jaime *fils*, Colin, and Polo), Théâtre Déjazet, Paris.

Hector de Bassompierre in *Le Dégel* (Sardou), Théâtre Déjazet, Paris.

1865   Lantara in *Lantara* (Montépin and Dornay), Théâtre Déjazet, Paris.

Chevalier de Belle-Isle in *Monsieur de Belle-Isle* (Jaime *fils*), Théâtre Déjazet, Paris.

1870   Chevalier de Gersac, Rosine Depuis, and Olympe in *Les Pistolets de mon père* (O'Squarr), Théâtre Déjazet, Paris.

*

Bibliography

Books:
Eugène Pierron, *Virginie Déjazet*, Paris, 1856.
Georges Duval, *Virginie Déjazet, 1797–1875*, Paris, 1876.
L. Henry Lecomte, *Virginie Déjazet*, Paris, 1892.
L. Henry Lecomte, *Un Amour de Déjazet, Histoire et Correspondence inédités, 1834–44*, Paris, 1907.
Léon Deutsch, *Déjazet*, Paris, 1928.

* * *

When Virginie Déjazet died in her late seventies in 1875 many of those who had seen her performing on the Paris stage grieved at the passing of a great actress, whose style was, they felt, eminently French in character, and commentators somewhat too readily drew attention to what they saw as a contrast between her public triumphs and the sorrows and poverty of her life, both at its start and at its end. Nowadays, with the benefit of hindsight, it is easier, while still sympathizing with her many personal misfortunes and the indomitable spirit with which she responded to them, to see in her career reflections of the unsatisfactory state of French drama in the first three-quarters of the 19th century.

The eleventh and youngest child of a poor Parisian tailor, Virginie Déjazet received enough training from her sister Thérèse, herself already a member of the corps de ballet at the Opéra, to be able to appear on stage for the first time at the age of five. After that she had a number of minor roles in the children's troupes pretending to provide practical training for youngsters that were a feature of theatre life in Paris at the time. Much has naturally been made of the value of the experience she gained in this way. It must, however, also be noted that Virginie Déjazet's general education was woefully neglected, and, in a period when whatever reform was made in French drama was spearheaded by literary men who had to fight hard against the complacency of actors and managers content with uninspiring, humdrum entertainments, she had little choice but to side, probably unconsciously to a large degree, with the forces of an intellectually unprepossessing popular theatrical conservatism.

Virginie Déjazet found a suitable outlet for her looks, her acting and dancing skills, and her singing voice in the countless "vaudevilles" that flourished both in the capital and in the provinces, where she toured whenever work was short in Paris, during the Restoration and the July Monarchy. For these shows any little incident could serve as the basis for a plot; originality was not really expected, though some neatness in treatment would generally come in for praise. A spice of topicality was always welcome, and this generally came across in the songs ("couplets"), which were commonly sung to the popular tunes of the day. Virginie Déjazet naturally took the role of the "soubrette", the pretty, often pert young thing. She also made a name for herself in "breeches roles", in which she specialized until the very end of her career. Her most notable part in this style was that of the callow young Duke in *Les Premières*

Armes de Richelieu of 1839, by Bayard and Dumanoir. The play, with what now seems its rather insipid amorous intrigue, is set in 1721 and allowed Déjazet the opportunity of wearing knee-breeches and embroidered half-length coat, which showed her figure to good advantage. The costume was completed with a tight-curled, powdered wig.

There can be no doubt that Virginie Déjazet gave much pleasure in these roles. She was small in stature, standing only a couple of inches above five feet tall. At a time when many actresses were built on regal proportions and affected a statuesque manner, she remained both slim and lively right into old age, and though she might herself comment pointedly on the absurdity of her playing in her seventies the role of sexually inexperienced noblemen in their teens, her public did not complain. Not even her most ardent admirers claimed that she was a "beauty" according to the somewhat limiting canons of mid-19th century taste, but she had charm and vigour to go with dark chestnut hair (though it could not always be seen) and an aquiline nose. Her singing voice is described as "extremely sweet", though it must have had the power to carry in theatres that were not always hushed, and her speaking voice, with a slightly nasal quality, was especially suited to cheeky repartee.

An exceptionally long career, a certain reputation for wit, even if some of her sallies may be apocryphal, and fortitude in the face of misfortune all helped endear Virginie Déjazet to a loyal public, and perhaps when her praises are sung there may be just a note of protest about progressive tendencies in the theatre, which did not appeal to everybody at the time. Even in the eulogies, however, it is notable that many saw in her the last representative of a tradition that was passing. Victorien Sardou, at the start of his career, could think of no better vehicle for her than the obviously backward-looking *Premières Armes de Figaro*, and the failure of the Théâtre Déjazet (formerly the Folie-Dramatiques) was not solely due to the fecklessness and financial incompetence of her son Eugène; times were changing, and Virginie Déjazet's style, like her repertory, was becoming outdated.

Early in the 1850's, Alexandre Dumas *fils* asked Déjazet for her opinion about *La Dame aux Camélias*. She had the insight to recognise the play's potential; she also had the self-knowledge to admit that the leading role would demand something more than she could give to it. Her range was, in fact, limited to something not far off a handful of theatrical stereotypes, and, though it is true that she created a huge number of roles over the years, it was, for the most part, a matter of variations on a theme. In the 19th century Talma was closely associated with many of the most exciting theatrical developments of his time, and Frédéric Lemaître brought unheard-of strength to boulevard melo-drama; Marie Dorval came across to reinvigorate the Comédie-Française, and Sarah Bernhardt, whose Hamlet doubtless owed something to Richelieu, had new fire to go with fresh aspirations. Virginie Déjazet's professional tragedy was that she accepted all too readily the unambitious and limiting theatricality to which she was introduced so young and served so gracefully all life long.

—Christopher Smith

DENCH, (Dame) Judi. British actress and director. Born Judith Olivia Dench in York, 9 December 1934. Educated at the Mount School, York; trained for the stage at the Central School of Speech Training and Dramatic Art, London. Married actor Michael Williams in 1971, one daughter. Stage debut, Old Vic Theatre, London, 1957; Broadway debut, 1958; actress, Old Vic Company, 1957–60; joined Royal Shakespeare Company, 1961; musical debut, in *Cabaret*, 1968; made record 100 appearances as Cleopatra with National Theatre, 1987; debut as director, Renaissance Theatre Company, 1988. Member: Royal Shakespeare Company (associate), from 1969; board of the Royal National Theatre, 1988–91. Recipient: Paladino d'Argentino Award, Venice Festival, 1961; British Academy of Film and Television Arts Award for Most Promising Newcomer, 1965; *Variety* London Critics Award, 1967; Guild of Directors Award, 1967; *Plays and Players* Award, 1980; Society of West End Theatre Award, 1980, 1983, 1987; *Evening Standard* Drama Award, 1980, 1983, 1987; British Academy of Film and Television Arts Award, 1981, 1985, 1987, 1988; American Cable Award, 1988. D.Litt: University of Warwick, Coventry, 1978, University of York, 1983, University of Birmingham, 1989, University of Loughborough, 1991, Open University, Milton Keynes, 1992. OBE (Order of the British Empire), 1970; DBE (Dame Commander of the British Empire), 1988.

Productions

As actress:
1957   Ophelia in *Hamlet* (Shakespeare), Old Vic Theatre, London.
       Juliet in *Measure for Measure* (Shakespeare), Old Vic Theatre, London.
       First Fairy in *A Midsummer Night's Dream* (Shakespeare), Old Vic Theatre, London.
1958   Maria in *Twelfth Night* (Shakespeare), Old Vic Theatre, London.
       Katherine in *Henry V* (Shakespeare), Old Vic Theatre, London, and New York; revived, 1960.
1959   Cynthia in *The Double-Dealer* (Congreve), Old Vic Theatre, London.
       Anne Page in *The Merry Wives of Windsor* (Shakespeare), Old Vic Theatre, London.
       Phebe in *As You Like It* (Shakespeare), Old Vic Theatre, London.
       Cecily Cardew in *The Importance of Being Earnest* (Wilde), Old Vic Theatre, London.
1960   The Queen in *Richard II* (Shakespeare), Old Vic Theatre, London.
       Juliet in *Romeo and Juliet* (Shakespeare), Old Vic Theatre, London.
       Kate Hardcastle in *She Stoops to Conquer* (Goldsmith), Old Vic Theatre, London.
       Hermia in *A Midsummer Night's Dream* (Shakespeare), Old Vic Theatre, London.
1961   Anya in *The Cherry Orchard* (Chekhov), Aldwych Theatre, London.
1962   Isabella in *Measure for Measure* (Shakespeare), Royal Shakespeare Theatre, Stratford-upon-Avon; Playhouse, Nottingham, 1965.

Judi Dench and Ian Holm (1985).

Titania in *A Midsummer Night's Dream* (Shakespeare), Royal Shakespeare Theatre, Stratford-upon-Avon.

Dorcas Bellboys in *A Penny for a Song* (Whiting), Aldwych Theatre, London.

1963 Lady Macbeth in *Macbeth* (Shakespeare), Playhouse, Nottingham, and West African tour; Royal Shakespeare Theatre, Stratford-upon-Avon, 1976; Aldwych Theatre, London, 1977–78.

Viola in *Twelfth Night* (Shakespeare), Playhouse, Nottingham, and West African tour; Royal Shakespeare Theatre, Stratford-upon-Avon, 1969; Aldwych Theatre, London, and Australian tour, 1970–71; Japanese tour, 1972.

Josefa Lautenay in *A Shot in the Dark* (Kurnitz), Lyric Theatre, London.

1964 Irina in *The Three Sisters* (Chekhov), Playhouse, Oxford.

Anna in *The Twelfth Hour* (Arbuzov), Playhouse, Oxford.

1965 Dol Common in *The Alchemist* (Jonson), Playhouse, Oxford.

Jeannette in *Romeo and Jeannette* (Anouilh), Playhouse, Oxford.

Jacqueline in *The Firescreen*, Playhouse, Oxford.

Amanda in *Private Lives* (Coward), Playhouse, Nottingham.

1966 Margery Pinchwife in *The Country Wife* (Wycherley), Playhouse, Oxford.

Barbara in *The Astrakhan Coat* (Macaulay), Playhouse, Nottingham.

Joan in *St Joan* (G. B. Shaw), Playhouse, Nottingham.

Lika in *The Promise* (Arbuzov), Playhouse, Oxford; Fortune Theatre, London, 1967.

Sila in *The Rules of the Game* (Pirandello), Playhouse, Oxford.

1968 Sally Bowles in *Cabaret* (Kander, Ebb, and Masteroff), Palace Theatre, London.

1969 Hermione and Perdita in *The Winter's Tale* (Shakespeare), Royal Shakespeare Theatre, Stratford-upon-Avon; Aldwych Theatre, London, 1970–71.

Bianca in *Women Beware Women* (Middleton), Royal Shakespeare Theatre, Stratford-upon-Avon.

1970 Grace Harkaway in *London Assurance* (Boucicault), Aldwych Theatre, London; New Theatre, London, 1972.

Barbara Undershaft in *Major Barbara* (G. B. Shaw), Aldwych Theatre, London.

1971 Portia in *The Merchant of Venice* (Shakespeare), Royal Shakespeare Theatre, Stratford-upon-Avon.

The Duchess in *The Duchess of Malfi* (Webster), Royal Shakespeare Theatre, Stratford-upon-Avon.

First Fieldmouse, a Brave Stoat, and Mother Rabbit in *Toad of Toad Hall* (Milne), Royal Shakespeare Theatre, Stratford-upon-Avon.

1973   Aurelia in *Content to Whisper*, Theatre Royal, York.

Vilma in *The Wolf* (Molnár), Playhouse, Oxford.

1974   Miss Trant in *The Good Companions* (Priestley), Her Majesty's Theatre, London.

1975   Sophie Fullgarney in *The Gay Lord Quex* (Pinero), Albery Theatre, London.

Sweetie Simpkins in *Too True to Be Good* (G. B. Shaw), Aldwych Theatre, London, and Globe Theatre, London.

1976   Beatrice in *Much Ado About Nothing* (Shakespeare), Royal Shakespeare Theatre, Stratford-upon-Avon; Aldwych Theatre, London, 1977–78.

Adriana in *The Comedy of Errors* (Shakespeare), Royal Shakespeare Theatre, Stratford-upon-Avon; Aldwych Theatre, London, 1977–78.

Regan in *King Lear* (Shakespeare), Royal Shakespeare Theatre, Stratford-upon-Avon.

1977   Lona Hessell in *Pillars of the Community* (Ibsen), Aldwych Theatre, London.

1978   Millamant in *The Way of the World* (Congreve), Aldwych Theatre, London.

1979   Imogen in *Cymbeline* (Shakespeare), Royal Shakespeare Theatre, Stratford-upon-Avon.

1980   Juno Boyle in *Juno and the Paycock* (O'Casey), Aldwych Theatre, London.

1981   Young Woman in *Village Wooing* (G. B. Shaw), New End Theatre, Hampstead, London.

1982   Deborah in *A Kind of Alaska* (Pinter), National Theatre, London.

Lady Bracknell in *The Importance of Being Earnest* (Wilde), National Theatre, London.

1983   Barbara Jackson in *Pack of Lies* (Whitemore), Lyric Theatre, London.

1984   Mother Courage in *Mother Courage* (Brecht), Barbican Theatre, London.

1985   Amy O'Connell in *Waste* (Granville-Barker), Barbican Theatre, London, and Lyric Theatre, London.

1987   Mrs Pooter in *Mr and Mrs Nobody* (Waterhouse), Garrick Theatre, London.

Cleopatra in *Antony and Cleopatra* (Shakespeare), National Theatre, London.

Sarah Eldridge in *Entertaining Strangers* (Edgar), National Theatre, London.

1989   Gertrude in *Hamlet* (Shakespeare), Royal National Theatre, London, and Dubrovnik Theatre Festival.

Madame Ranevskaya in *The Cherry Orchard* (Chekhov), Aldwych Theatre, London.

1991   Louise Rafi in *The Sea* (Bond), National Theatre, London.

Bessie Burgess in *The Plough and the Stars* (O'Casey), Young Vic Theatre, London.

1992   Volumnia in *Coriolanus* (Shakespeare), Chichester Festival Theatre.

Stepmother in *The Gift of the Gorgon* (P. Shaffer), Barbican Pit, London; Wyndham's Theatre, London, 1993.

1994   Arkadina in *The Seagull* (Chekhov), Royal National Theatre, London, 1994.

As director:
1988   Much Ado About Nothing (Shakespeare), Repertory Theatre, Birmingham.

1989   *Look Back in Anger* (Osborne), Belfast and London.

1991   *The Boys from Syracuse* (Rodgers and Hart), Open Air Theatre, London.

1993   *Romeo and Juliet* (Shakespeare), Open Air Theatre, London.

Films

The Third Secret, 1964; *A Study in Terror*, 1966; *He Who Rides a Tiger*, 1966; *Four in the Morning*, 1966; *A Midsummer Night's Dream*, 1968; *The Third Secret*, 1978; *Dead Cert*, 1985; *Wetherby*, 1985; *84 Charing Cross Road*, 1987; *A Handful of Dust*, 1987; *Henry V*, 1990.

Television

An Age of Kings, 1960; *Talking to a Stranger*, 1966; *Love in a Cold Climate*, 1980; *A Fine Romance*, 1981–84; *Going Gently*, 1981; *Saigon — Year of the Cat*, 1983; *The Browning Version*, 1985; *Behaving Badly*, 1989. Other productions include: *Hilda Lessways*; *Village Wooing*; *Major Barbara*; *Pink String and Sealing Wax*; *The Funambulists*; *Jackanory*; *Luther*; *Neighbours*; *Parade's End*; *Marching Song*; *On Approval*; *Days to Come*; *Emilie*; *The Comedy of Errors*; *Macbeth*; *Langrishe Go Down*; *On Giants Shoulders*; *The Cherry Orchard*; *Mr and Mrs Edgehill*; *Make or Break*; *Ghosts*; *Absolute Hell*; *Can You Hear Me Thinking?*; *As Time Goes By*.

*

Bibliography

Books:
Gerald Jacobs, *Judi Dench: A Great Deal of Laughter*, London, 1985.

* * *

While her acting may not exhibit the virtuoso technical skills of Dame Maggie Smith, Judi Dench remains unparalleled for the utter naturalness and unguarded humanity of her characterisations. She and Maggie Smith are the only actresses to emerge since the war who have unquestionably attained the stature of Peggy Ashcroft or Edith Evans. In the 1950's and 1960's Dench's work for the Old Vic and the Royal Shakespeare Company earned her respect and admiration from critics and colleagues but she was not widely known outside the theatrical profession, being somewhat overshadowed by Vanessa Redgrave, Dorothy Tutin, and

Maggie Smith until her acclaimed appearance on television in John Hopkins's powerful tetralogy *Talking to a Stranger* (1966) and her great critical success as Sally Bowles in the West End production of the musical *Cabaret* (1968). Although her appearance opposite her husband, Michael Williams, in the television situation comedy *A Fine Romance* brought her a huge popular following in the late 1970's, she has never really left the subsidised theatre in which she was nurtured as an actress, preferring to combine appearances in plays with the Royal Shakespeare Company and the National Theatre with occasional performances in television plays or series.

Dench's distinctive contribution to British theatre resides in the fact that she has for over 40 years dedicated her remarkable acting talent and her star status to realising the ideal of ensemble performance in productions at the major subsidised companies. Following in the footsteps of Dame Peggy Ashcroft at the RSC, she is among those who made the company the chief glory of the British theatre from the mid-1960's to the early 1980's, enhancing the prestige of subsidised theatre in order to guarantee its funding by a monetarist and philistine government.

As a performer, she has the gift of making ordinariness interesting by radiating the kind of charm that signifies suburban English niceness at its best. Her own unselfishness as an actress expresses itself in the warmth and generosity of her portrayals of decent characters and in the gleeful vitality of her characterisations of malevolence or egotism. No other actor of her generation is able to appear so spontaneous on stage: it is the untheatrical directness and intensity of her playing that sets her apart from almost all her contemporaries.

Dench's bubbly sincerity and unsparing truth of feeling distinguished her moving and unaffected performances for the Old Vic in the 1950's and for the RSC as Anya in *The Cherry Orchard*, Isabella in *Measure for Measure*, and Titania in *A Midsummer Night's Dream*. First recognition of the true depth of her talent took the form of a BAFTA Best Television Actress Award for her searing portrait of Teresa, the grown-up daughter of *Talking to a Stranger*. Here the slightly square set of her features with eyes that can blaze with startling aggression or melt with aching sadness was powerfully employed to evoke the neurotic self-destructiveness of a middle-class malcontent.

In *Cabaret* she gradually transformed Sally Bowles's initially fun-loving gurgle into the grim determination of the seedy survivor who rasped out Kander and Ebb's ironic anthem to the hedonism of show business, "Life is a cabaret, old chum, so come to the cabaret". Her Sally was no promising singing star: Dench portrayed her with a Brechtian complexity as childish, lonely, and corrupt. In both these performances, Dench's rather un-English volatility as an actress was apparent. Within seconds she could turn a mood of sunny delight into one of cold gloom, the twinkling eyes and creamy voice giving way to a stony stare and a cracked growl.

From this point onwards Dench has hardly put a foot wrong; indeed, her professional career has appeared to alternate between success and triumph. With Trevor Nunn as artistic director from 1968, Judi Dench, together with Janet Suzman, Alan Howard, and Ian McKellen, led the RSC to its position as "the greatest theatre company in the world". Her versatility was dazzling, her personality apparently placing no restrictions on the type of role she could

play. She gave memorable performances as an intelligent Viola in *Twelfth Night*, a poignant double of Hermione with her daughter, Perdita, in *The Winter's Tale*, the blue-stocking heroine of Boucicault's *London Assurance*, a passionate Barbara in *Major Barbara*, a middle-aged and rather earnest Beatrice that perfectly complemented Donald Sinden's hilarious confirmed-bachelor Benedick in *Much Ado About Nothing*. She was never inappropriately showy, maintaining her part in the ensemble with subtlety and wit.

Genius was apparent in Dench's portrayal of Lady Macbeth in Trevor Nunn's third attempt at *Macbeth* (1976). In an intimate production of the play that was performed in small theatres in the round, Ian McKellen as Macbeth created with Dench and the company an atmosphere of hushed concentration that allowed the audience's imagination to respond to the play with a fullness and intensity that made the production legendary. Her Lady Macbeth was a revelation, suggesting many more facets of the role than any English actress this century: she was sexual, affectionate, frustrated, cunning, resourceful, loyal to her husband, and ruthless by turns. There was a raw despair in her sleep-walking scene that made the observer instantly sympathetic, her natural empathy with an audience humanising the character without excusing her evil.

Dench's amazing versatility was displayed when in the same season she played a witty and glamorous Adriana, the seemingly neglected wife, in Trevor Nunn's razzle-dazzle musical version of *The Comedy of Errors*: Dench's many-faceted talent seemed to exemplify the company ethos. Since then she has continued to extend her range. Her tragic Juno in O'Casey's *Juno and the Paycock* was chiefly remarkable for her complete yet unobtrusive assumption of the persona of a working-class Dublin woman, her face and body coarsened by harsh experience, her spirit overflowing with generosity and love of life.

Dench won all the major British acting awards for her down-to-earth portrait of Lady Bracknell in *The Importance of Being Earnest* as a petit-bourgeois hausfrau, for her depiction of the childlike desolation of Deborah, a middle-aged woman who awakes after years of suffering from encephalitis lethargica in Pinter's *A Kind of Alaska*, and for her brilliant interpretation at the age of 52 of Shakespeare's Cleopatra as an unparalleled role-player, which gave definitive proof that "Age cannot wither her, nor custom stale her infinite variety".

—Robert Gordon

———

DEVINE, George (Alexander Cassady). British actor and director. Born in Hendon, London, 20 November 1910. Educated at Clayesmore public school, Hampshire; Wadham College, Oxford University, 1929–32, no degree. Married Sophia Harris in 1939 (died 1966), one daughter. President, Oxford University Dramatic Society, 1932; secretary, Motley stage designers, 1932–35; actor, Old Vic company, London, 1932–34; joined John Gielgud at the New Theatre, London, 1934–38; co-founded and taught at Michel Saint-Denis's London Theatre Studio, 1936–39; after war service with Royal Regiment of Artillery, 1940–46, co-founded Old Vic Theatre Centre, 1946; director, Young Vic touring company, 1946–51; directed at

Sadler's Wells Theatre, London, and at the Shakespeare Memorial Theatre, Stratford-upon-Avon, 1951–54; artistic director, English Stage Company, Royal Court Theatre, London, 1954–65. CBE (Commander of the British Empire), 1957. Died in London, 20 January 1966.

Productions

As actor:

1932   Salanio in *The Merchant of Venice* (Shakespeare), St James's Theatre, London.

The Herdsman in *Le Cocu Magnifique* (Crommelynck), Globe Theatre, London.

Luis Moreno in *Evensong* (Knoblock and Nichols), Queen's Theatre, London.

Lucius Septimus in *Caesar and Cleopatra* (G. B. Shaw), Old Vic Theatre, London.

Lord Worthington in *The Admirable Bashville* (G. B. Shaw), Old Vic Theatre, London.

Posthumus Leonatus in *Cymbeline* (Shakespeare), Old Vic Theatre, London.

1933   Tubal in *The Merchant of Venice* (Shakespeare), Old Vic Theatre, London.

1934   Moses in *The School for Scandal* (Sheridan), Old Vic Theatre, London; Queen's Theatre, London, 1937.

Mr Poyser in *Magnolia Street* (Golding and Rawlinson), Adelphi Theatre, London.

Bernardo and Player King in *Hamlet* (Shakespeare), New Theatre, London.

Reverend Colpus in *The Voysey Inheritance* (Granville-Barker), Sadler's Wells Theatre, London, and Shaftesbury Theatre, London.

The Bear and The Man in *Noah* (Wilmurt), New Theatre, London.

1935   Peter in *Romeo and Juliet* (Shakespeare), New Theatre, London.

1936   Shamraef in *The Seagull* (Chekhov), New Theatre, London.

1937   Gardener in *Richard II* (Shakespeare), Queen's Theatre, London.

1938   Vershinin in *Three Sisters* (Chekhov), Queen's Theatre, London.

Launcelot Gobbo in *The Merchant of Venice* (Shakespeare), Queen's Theatre, London.

Viktor Myschlajevsky in *The White Guard* (Bulgakov, adapted by Ackland), Phoenix Theatre, London.

Sir Toby Belch in *Twelfth Night* (Shakespeare), Phoenix Theatre, London.

1939   Dai Hippo in *Rhondda Roundabout* (J. Jones), Globe Theatre, London.

1945   Mr Antrobus in *The Skin of our Teeth* (Wilder), Piccadilly Theatre, London.

1952   Uncle Louis in *The Happy Time* (Taylor), St James's Theatre, London.

1954   George Tesman in *Hedda Gabler* (Ibsen), Lyric Theatre, Hammersmith, London.

1955   Dogberry in *Much Ado About Nothing* (Shakespeare), Palace Theatre, London.

Gloucester in *King Lear* (Shakespeare), Palace Theatre, London.

1956   Danforth in *The Crucible* (Miller), Royal Court Theatre, London.

Father Golden Orfe in *Cards of Identity* (Dennis), Royal Court Theatre, London.

Pinchwife in *The Country Wife* (Wycherley), Royal Court Theatre, London.

Mr Shu Fu in *The Good Woman of Setzuan* (Brecht), Royal Court Theatre, London.

1957   Old Man in *The Chairs* (Ionesco), Royal Court Theatre, London.

Frederick Compton in *The Making of Moo* (Dennis), Royal Court Theatre, London.

1958   Hamm in *Endgame* (Beckett), Royal Court Theatre, London.

1959   Herr von Putzeboum in *Look After Lulu* (Coward), Royal Court Theatre, London.

1961   Vicar General Staupitz in *Luther* (Osborne), Royal Court Theatre, London.

1962   Brecht in *Brecht on Brecht* (Tabori), Royal Court Theatre, London.

1964   Dorn in *The Seagull* (Chekhov), Queen's Theatre, London.

1965   David Cornwallis in *Miniatures* (Cregan), Royal Court Theatre, London.

Baron von Epp in *A Patriot for Me* (Osborne), Royal Court Theatre, London.

As director:

1936   *The Witch of Edmonton* (Dekker), Old Vic Theatre, London.

1937   *Macbeth* (Shakespeare), Old Vic Theatre, London.

1939   *Great Expectations* (Dickens, adapted by Guiness), Rudolf Steiner Hall, London.

1940   *Rebecca* (D. du Maurier), Queen's Theatre, London.

The Tempest (Shakespeare), Old Vic Theatre, London.

The Millionairess (G. B. Shaw), British tour.

1946   *The King Stag* (Gozzi), Lyric Theatre, Hammersmith, London.

1947   *The Shoemaker's Holiday* (Dekker), Young Vic tour.

1949   *A Midsummer Night's Dream* (Shakespeare), Young Vic tour.

The Servant of Two Masters (Goldoni), Young Vic tour.

The Knight of the Burning Pestle (Beaumont and Fletcher), Young Vic tour.

1950   *Bartholomew Fair* (Jonson), Old Vic Theatre, London.

The Provoked Wife (Vanbrugh), Arts Theatre, London.

1951   *Don Carlos* (Verdi opera), Sadler's Wells Theatre, London.

The Wedding (Chekhov), Old Vic Theatre, London.

1952   *The Mortimer Touch*, Shakespeare Memorial Theatre, Stratford-upon-Avon.

The Happy Time (Taylor), Shakespeare Memorial Theatre, Stratford-upon-Avon.

1953   *Romeo and Juliet* (Sutermeister opera), Sadler's Wells Theatre, London.

Volpone (Jonson), Shakespeare Memorial Theatre, Stratford-upon-Avon.

The Taming of the Shrew (Shakespeare), Shakespeare Memorial Theatre, Stratford-upon-Avon.

King John (Shakespeare), Old Vic Theatre, London.

King Lear (Shakespeare), Shakespeare Memorial Theatre, Stratford-upon-Avon.

1954   *A Midsummer Night's Dream* (Shakespeare), Shakespeare Memorial Theatre, Stratford-upon-Avon.

Nelson (Berkeley opera), Sadler's Wells Theatre, London.

Troilus and Cressida (Walton opera), Royal Opera House, Covent Garden, London.

1955   *The Magic Flute* (Mozart opera), Sadler's Wells Theatre, London.

King Lear (Shakespeare), Palace Theatre, London, and European tour.

1956   *The Mulberry Bush* (Wilson), Royal Court Theatre, London.

The Crucible (Miller), Royal Court Theatre, London.

Don Juan (Duncan), Royal Court Theatre, London.

The Death of Satan (Duncan), Royal Court Theatre, London.

The Good Woman of Setzuan (Brecht), Royal Court Theatre, London.

The Country Wife (Wycherley), Royal Court Theatre, London.

1957   *Nekrassov* (Sartre), Royal Court Theatre, London.

1958   *The Sport of My Mad Mother* (Jellicoe), Royal Court Theatre, London.

Major Barbara (G. B. Shaw), Royal Court Theatre, London.

Live Like Pigs (Arden), Royal Court Theatre, London.

Endgame (Beckett), Royal Court Theatre, London.

1959   *Cock-a-Doodle Dandy* (O'Casey), Royal Court Theatre, London.

Rosmersholm (Ibsen), Royal Court Theatre, London.

1960   *A Taste of Honey* (Delaney), Royal Court Theatre, New York.

Platonov (Chekhov), Royal Court Theatre, London.

1961   *August for the People* (Dennis), Royal Court Theatre, London, and Edinburgh Festival.

1962   *Twelfth Night* (Shakespeare), Royal Court Theatre, London.

Happy Days (Beckett), Royal Court Theatre, London.

1963   *Exit the King* (Ionesco), Royal Court Theatre, London, and Edinburgh Festival.

1964   *Play* (Beckett), Old Vic Theatre, London.

Television

Mr Justice Erskine in *A Subject of Scandal and Concern,* 1960.

*

Bibliography

Books:
Irving Wardle, *The Theatres of George Devine*, London, 1978.
Richard Findlater, *At the Royal Court: 25 Years of the English Stage Company*, London, 1981.

* * *

George Devine has been widely seen as one of the key figures in the development of postwar British drama. After an uneven early career as an actor, he moved into teaching and directing. Working at the London Theatre Studio in the prewar period, he was strongly influenced by Michel Saint-Denis and by Theodore Komisarjevsky, and his subsequent work reflected his attempts to introduce both the ideas and techniques of the contemporary European avant-garde and the traditions of the mask and the commedia dell'arte to the English theatre. In its commitment to the systematic training of the actor and exploration of theatrecraft — in particular the arts of comic improvisation — the Theatre Studio was unique in the prewar British theatre. Devine's central convictions as a director and producer were in the development of ensemble work in permanent acting companies and in loyalty to the text and the author. These were enshrined in his consistent advocacy of experiment and innovation in playwriting and the need to take risks independent of commercial considerations. His policy as director of the English Stage Company at the Royal Court was to support the author's 'right to fail'; from the outset the theatre was designated as a 'writer's theatre'. By offering a space for the performance of new drama that would have been ignored by the commercial theatre, the Royal Court fostered the early writing careers of, amongst others, John Osborne, John Arden, and N. F. Simpson; it also produced British premieres of work by Beckett, Ionesco, and Brecht.

In addition, Devine's theatrical philosophy favoured methods of production, direction, and design that placed the text, rather than the director's interpretation of it, to the forefront. In his 1955 production of *King Lear* at Stratford-upon-Avon this took the form of what Devine defined as 'essentialism': where the abstract quality of the scenery and the costumes reflected an attempt to eschew specific social and historical associations in order to project the timeless and universal 'essence' of the play. The experiment was widely regarded as unsuccessful; but as a reaction against traditional pictorial realism in Shakespearean production, it influenced later directors — in particular Peter Brook in his 1963 production of the play. This approach to the text, however, assumed a more practicable form in the style pioneered by Devine at the Royal Court: partly reflecting the influence of Brecht, it was on scenic economy and minimalism. The task of the director in the writer's theatre was not to impose his or her own vision upon the play but to reproduce faithfully the intentions of the author. In this sense, Devine's loyalty to the unadorned text made him the ideal director for the work of Beckett, and he was indeed given control over all English productions by the author. This close association between an author and a director was another of the important features of the Royal Court work instituted by Devine.

Alongside a belief that the theatre should support new writing, Devine wished to extend the cultural base of the English theatre, to engage the drama with the social, political, and intellectual life of its society. One aspect of this was cultural: Devine wanted the Royal Court to test new and experimental work beyond the confines of minority audiences. In the event this meant attracting a new audience in the 1950's and 1960's of educated, possibly disaffected, middle-class youth. But this also had a political aspect: although Devine did not identify himself or the English Stage Company with a specifically socialist position, there was a period during the 1950's when the identity of the theatre was aligned with a politics of liberal protest — in particular with the Campaign for Nuclear Disarmament. The commitment of the Royal Court, nonetheless, reflected Devine's idealist and humanist conception of theatre, being aesthetic rather than overtly political, and expressed through its struggles with the Lord Chamberlain's office over the censorship of plays — Devine himself was involved in a protracted battle over a line in Beckett's *Endgame* in 1958.

Apart from his achievements as an actor and a director, however, Devine's enduring legacy to the Royal Court and to the theatre as a whole lay in his skills as a negotiator, facilitator, and organiser; he saw theatre as a collective endeavour and was most successful as a teacher. Devine's significance has most often been valued in terms of his support of, and influence upon, other directors, actors, and writers. Towards the end of his life, however, Devine became increasingly disillusioned about the extent of his own achievement, in that while he had set out to change the role of theatre in society he felt that he had at best been only partly successful in realising this aim. But in his promotion of the ensemble idea and in providing a platform for a growing school of experimental and socially-committed playwriting, Devine played a formative role in the development of postwar English drama.

—Robert Shaughnessy

DEVRIENT, Emil. German actor. Born in Berlin, 3 September 1803; youngest brother of actors Carl and Eduard Devrient and nephew of actor Ludwig Devrient (*q.v.*). Married actress Dorothea Böhler in 1825. Stage debut with August Klingemann in Brunswick; subsequently acted in Bremen, Leipzig, Magdeburg and Hamburg, 1822–31; hired by August von Lüttichau to act at the Court Theatre, Dresden, 1831; subsequently acclaimed throughout Germany on series of guest tours in dramas by Goethe, Schiller, Shakespeare and others; led first company of German actors to play in England, appearing at St James's Theatre, 1852; played second London season, 1853; retired from stage after 37 years with the Dresden company, 1868. Died in Dresden, 7 August 1872.

Roles

1837–38   Hamlet in *Hamlet* (Shakespeare), Hamburg.
Guido in *Corona von Saluzzo*, Hamburg.
Rudolph in *Der Landwirth*, Hamburg.
Robert in *Die Leibrente*, Hamburg.
Fröhlich in *Die Leibrente*, Hamburg.
Baron Ringelstern in *Bürgerlich und Romantisch* (Bauernfeld), Hamburg.
Marquis Posa in *Don Carlos* (Schiller), Hamburg.
Harleigh in *Sie ist wahnsinnig*, Hamburg.
Heinrich in *Vetter Heinrich*, Hamburg.
Moritz in *Die Schwestern*, Hamburg.
Tasso in *Torquato Tasso* (Goethe), Leipzig.
Gaston in *Eiserne Maske*, Leipzig.
Don Ramiro in *Schule des Lebens*, Leipzig.
Ferdinand in *Kabale und Liebe* (Schiller), Leipzig.
Hans Sachs in *Hans Sachs* (Lortzing), Leipzig.
Hans in *Vorsatz*, Schwerin.
Rubens in *Rubens in Madrid*, Leipzig.

1838–39   Paul von Scharfeneck in *Der Majoratserbe*, Berlin.
Wehringer in *Braut aus der Residenz*, Berlin.
Richard Wanderer in *Richards Wanderleben*, Berlin.
Tasso in *Tasso's Tod*, Frankfurt-am-Maim.
Heinrich in *Lorbeerbaum und Bettelstab* (Holtei), Frankfurt-am-Maim.
Philipp Brook in *Die Mündel* (Iffland), Frankfurt-am-Maim.
Richard Savage in *Richard Savage* (Labat and Desnoyer), Frankfurt-am-Maim.
Wallenfeld in *Der Spieler* (Iffland), Frankfurt-am-Maim.
Philipp Rüstig in *Hundertjähriger Greis*, Frankfurt-am-Maim.
Romeo in *Romeo und Juliet* (Shakespeare), Frankfurt-am-Maim.
Antonio in *Correggio* (Oehlenschläger), Schwerin.
Clermont in *Der Maler* (Babo), Schwerin.
Jaromir in *Jaromir*, Schwerin.
Kean in *Kean* (Dumas père), Schwerin.

1839–40   Graf von Strahl in *Noch ist es Zeit*, Breslau.
Baron Wiburg in *Stille Wasser sind tief* (Schrödet), Breslau.
Jakob in *Verräter* (Berwald), Breslau.
Fiesko in *Fiesko* (Schiller), Breslau.
Spinarosa in *Spinarosa*, Frankfurt-am-Maim.
Baron Rosenthal in *Die Entführung* (Lenz), Munich.
Baron von Abendstern in *Nach Sonnenuntergang*, Munich.
Tempelherr in *Nathan* (Schiller), Munich.

1840–41   Havelin in *Der Fabrikant*, Chemnitz.
Chevalier St Georges in *Der Mulatte* (Andersen), Leipzig.
Bolingbroke in *Marquise von Villette* (Birch-Pfeiffer), Leipzig.
Heinrich von Jordan in *Werner* (Gutzkow), Munich.
Sancho Perez in *Schole des Lebens*, Pesth.

Wildenberg in *Die Geschwister* (Goethe), Pesth.

Don Cesar in *Donna Diana*, Pesth.

Baron von Nordeck in *Die seltsame wette*, Pesth.

William in *Der Heirathsantrag auf Helgoland*, Pesth.

Arthur Normann in *Der Sehn der Wellend*, Pesth.

1841–42 König Enzio in *König Enzio* (Raupach), St Petersburg.

Gustav in *Der beste Arzt*, St Petersburg.

Don Cesar in *Die Braut von Messina* (Schiller), Riga.

Ferdinand in *Drillinge* (Bonin), Riga.

Perin in *Donna Diana*, Riga.

1842–43 Robert in *Memoiren des Teufels* (Arago and Vermond), Pesth.

Gustav Holm in *Ein weisses Blatt* (Gutzkow), Pesth.

Zolky in *Der alte Student* (Maltitz), Pesth.

Herfort in *Warum*, Pesth.

Friedrich Günther in *Der Siegelring*, Pesth.

Graf von Nordheim in *Der beste Arzt*, Pesth.

Monaldeschi in *Monaldeschi* (Laube), Pesth.

Hauptmann von Linden in *Die Quälgeister* (Beck), Pesth.

1844–45 Molière in *Urbild des Tartüffe* (Gutzkow), Braunschweig.

Bruno in *Mutter und Sohn*, Breslau.

Wilhelm in *Der verwunschene Prinz* (Bäuerle), Breslau.

1845–46 Bolingbroke in *Glas Wasser* (Scribe), Braunschweig.

Don Cesar in *Der Graf von Irun*, Thaliatheater, Hamburg.

Garrick in *Doktor Robin*, Thaliatheater, Hamburg.

Graf Waltron in *Graf von Waltron* (Möller), Pesth.

1846–47 Richard in *Richard Wanderleben*, Braunschweig.

Schiller in *Die Karlsschüler* (Laube), Braunschweig.

Uriel Acosta in *Uriel Acosta* (Gutzkow), Bremen.

Egmont in *Egmont* (Goethe), Bremen.

Richard II in *Richard II* (Shakespeare), Breslau.

Baron Jakob in *Ball zu Ellerbrunn*, Breslau.

Von Brunnstädt in *Eine Familie*, Breslau.

1847–48 Reinhard in *Dorf und Stadt* (Birch-Pfeiffer), Bremen.

Mertens in *Der Pfarrherr*, Bremen.

Stolpe in *Breite Strasse und schamle Gasse*, Vienna.

Arthur Derwood in *Ein Arzt*, Vienna.

1848–49 Ulrich von Hutten in *Eins deutsches Herz*, Danzig.

1849–50 Tasso in *Tasso Traumbild*, Hamburg.

Unbekannter in *Menschenhass und Reue* (Kotzebue), Hamburg.

Petrucchio in *Bezähmte Widerspenstige*, Hamburg.

Theodor in *Sohn und Enkel*, Hamburg.

Emil Devrient

Gustav Bremont in *Besser früher wie später*, Hamburg.

Baron von Wallenfeld in *Revenge Prag*, Hamburg.

Graf Waldemar in *Graf Waldemar* (Freytag), Leipzig.

1850–51 Wilhelm Zorn in *Einer muss heiraten*, Frankfurt-am-Maim.

Belphegor in *Bajazzo und sie Familie*, Frankfurt-am-Maim.

Carl Moor in *Die Räuber* (Schiller), Weimar.

1851–52 Antipholus in *Komöde der Irrungen* (Shakespeare), Breslau.

1852–53 Tamburini in *Ein alter Musikant*, Koburg-Gotha.

Edward Gibbon in *Englisch*, Koburg-Gotha.

1853–54 Jules Franz in *Am Klavier*, Breslau.

Bolz in *Journalisten* (Freytag), Breslau.

Lear in *König Lear* (Shakespeare), Breslau.

Wilhelm Tell in *Wilhelm Tell* (Schiller), Darmstadt.

Bergheim in *Ein Lustspiel* (Kotzebue), Frankfurt-am-Maim.

1854–55 Sigismund in *Lenz und Söhne* (Gutzkow), Königsberg.

Waller in *Der letzte Trumpf*, Stettin.

1855–56 Narziss in *Narziss* (Brachvogel), Breslau.

Eduard in *Mit den Wölfen muss man heulen*, Breslau.

1856–57 Graf Essex in *Graf Essex* (Laube), Schwerin.

1858–59   Cato von Eisen in *Cato von Eisen* (Laube), Thaliatheater, Hamburg.
1859–60   Gluthen in *Das letzte Mittel*, Koburg-Gotha.
1861–62   Dr Löwe in *Oheim* (Iffland), Königsberg.

*

Bibliography

Books:
Emil Kneschke, *Emil Devrient*, Dresden, 1868.
Heinrich Hubert Houben, *Emil Devrient: sein Leben, sein Wirken, sein Nachlass*, Frankfurt, 1903.
Julius Bab, *Die Devrients: Geschichte einer deutschen Theaterfamilie*, Berlin, 1932.
Simon Williams, *German Actors of the 18th and 19th Centuries: Idealism, Romanticism and Realism*, Westport, Connecticut, 1985.

Articles:
Rudolf Gottschall, "Emil Devrient", *Literarische. Charakterköpfe, Porträts und Silhouetten*, vol. 6, Leipzig, 1876.
Paul Legband, "Emil Devrient", *Bühne und Welt*, 6, 1, 1903.

* * *

During his lifetime Emil Devrient was the most celebrated actor of his generation, but after his death his reputation suffered an eclipse. This was primarily because towards the end of the century, the Weimar style of acting, of which Emil Devrient was the master, went out of fashion due to the rise of naturalism. Towards the end of his career, therefore, Devrient was the last, and possibly the most splendid survivor of what might justly be called the classical tradition of German acting. In every regard his acting was the antithesis to that of his famous uncle, Ludwig Devrient.

Emil Devrient was ideally suited to practice the Weimar style of acting. His slender frame had a particularly noble bearing, while his sonorous voice was ideal for suggesting calmness and mastery, both over himself and those around him. Even in later years, he lost none of his physical and vocal graces and he never seemed to age. Initially he sang in opera as well as acted in spoken drama, a not unusual combination in those days, but as during the 1820's and 1830's greater specialisation developed in the acting profession, he turned to the spoken drama alone, his talents being most fit for it.

The beauty of Devrient's physical appearance and voice meant that he was ill-suited to represent characters who were rent by split and contradictory emotions. Instead he best played idealistic characters like the Marquis Posa in Schiller's *Don Carlos*, a role in which he made no effort to discover the ironies that have interested later actors. Perhaps his most celebrated role was Hamlet, surprisingly so, as in the 19th century as in the 20th, German actors were drawn to the part because of the savage contradictions that rend the character. Devrient would have none of this. Rather the sole unifying point of his interpretation was Hamlet's grief at the perfidy of his mother. As the disappointed son, Devrient invited the audience's pity; he became "the weak, affectionate son of his mother, the sweet beautiful speaker, the elegaic youth of moonlight", and pathos dominated his interpretation. As it was difficult

to encompass all aspects of the role within such an approach, Devrient was often forced to resort to manneristic devices that had little to do with the construction of a consistent or complete character. Nevertheless, when he played the role in London in 1852, as a member of the first company of German actors to visit England, he was a critical success and some of his more enthusiastic German partisans claimed to have heard members of the audience compare him favourably to such notables as John Philip Kemble and Edmund Kean.

Emil Devrient's good looks and flawless technique guaranteed him a widespread popular following in Germany; in essence he was what later generations would call a 'matinee idol'. However, the very talents that assured his success also led cognoscenti of the theatre to question his seriousness as an actor. His brother Eduard Devrient, author of the great *Geschichte der deutschen Schauspielkunst* and intendant of the Karlsruhe Court theatre, was consistently distressed by Emil's vanity and increasingly resisted cooperating with him in any theatrical venture. During the 1850's, the Polish actor Bohumil Dawison, whose acting foreshadowed naturalism, was engaged by the Dresden company. Emil Devrient considered his presence to be a slight on his own pre-eminence in the company and several performances in which both actors played were marked and, in most cases, marred by the intense rivalry between the two. Unfortunately, the theatrical excitement that could have been aroused by this conflict between acting styles that were perceived to be representative of different generations was spoiled by the personal antipathies that motivated the two actors.

Emil Devrient was remarkable as the last and possibly the most accomplished of German actors, who considered acting to be concerned less with the representation of character, more with the display of physical and vocal accomplishments. He was the supreme virtuoso, an artist whose work was best described by Gustav Freytag as: "a fixed tempo in speech and acting, gradual and established transitions from one mood to another, an aversion to all violence and subtle affectation, a striving always to be as gracious in bearing, gesture and speech, performing as beautifully and as nobly as the role possibly allows, developing most carefully the voice and powers of mimetic expression.

—Simon Williams

DEVRIENT, Ludwig. German actor-manager. Born in Berlin, 15 December 1784; senior member of celebrated acting family. Educated at local commercial school in Berlin. Married an actress by the name of Neefe in 1807, one daughter. Stage debut, under name of Ludwig Hertzberg, J. W. Lange's travelling company, Naumberg, Thuringia, 1804; actor, Hoftheater, Dessau, 1805; also appeared in Leipzig; actor, City Theatre, Breslau, 1809; recruited by August Wilhelm Iffland to act at the Königliches Schauspielhaus, Berlin, 1814; appointed stage manager (for comedy only), 1816; acclaimed in Romantic tragedy, but increasingly restricted against his wishes to comedy roles from 1816; toured regularly and was hugely acclaimed in Vienna, 1828; career ended by alcoholism. Died in Berlin, 30 December 1832.

Principal roles

1804	Messenger in *Die Braut von Messina* (Schiller), Naumberg, Thuringia.
1805	Count Schmetterling in *Die Jagd* (Weisse), tour.
	Rudenz in *Wilhelm Tell* (Schiller), tour.
	Franz Moor in *Die Räuber* (Schiller), Hoftheater, Dessau; City Theatre, Breslau; Königliches Schauspielhaus, Berlin, 1814.
1809–14	Lear in *King Lear* (Shakespeare), City Theatre, Breslau.
1815	Shylock in *Der Kaufman von Venedig* (Shakespeare), Königliches Schauspielhaus, Berlin.
1817	Falstaff in *Henry IV* (Shakespeare), Königliches Schauspielhaus, Berlin.
1828	Richard in *Richard III* (Shakespeare), Königliches Schauspielhaus, Berlin.
1831	Buttler in *Piccolomini* (Schiller), Königliches Schauspielhaus, Berlin.
1832	Chancellor Flessel in *Die Mündel* (Iffland), Königliches Schauspielhaus, Berlin.
	Schewa in *Der Jude* (Cumberland), Königliches Schauspielhaus, Berlin.

Other roles included: the three brothers in *Die Drillinge* (Bonin).

*

Bibliography

Books:
Franz Ermin, *Devrient in Wien*, Vienna, 1829.
Heinrich Smidt, *Ludwig Devrient*, Berlin, 1833.
Carl Gerold, *Ludwig Devrient*, Berlin, 1869.
Georg Altman, *Ludwig Devrient: Leben und Werke eines Schauspielers*, Berlin, 1926.
Julius Bab, *Die Devrients: Geschichte einer deutschen Theaterfamilie*, Berlin, 1932.
Eduard Devrient, *Geschichte der deutschen Schauspielkunst*, edited by Rolf Kabel and Christoph Trilse, Munich, 1967.
Simon Williams, *German Actors of the 18th and 19th Centuries: Idealism, Romanticism and Realism*, Westport, Connecticut, 1985.

Articles:
Ludwig Rellstab, "Ludwig Devrient", *Gesammelte Schriften*, 9, Leipzig, 1860.
Hermann Ulrici, "Ludwig Devrient als König Lear", *Jahrbuch der deutschen Shakespeare-Gesellschaft*, 2, 1867.
E. T. A. Hoffmann, "Seltsame Leiden eines Theaterdirektors", *Gesammelte Schriften*, 3, 1977.

* * *

Both in performance and as a public persona, this most legendary of German actors embodied several features popularly associated with the Romantic culture of his country. As an actor, Ludwig Devrient represented the antithesis of the Weimar school that encouraged the performer to project an impression of poise and control and to personify nobility in the character presented on the stage. Devrient was entirely unsuited to such a deliberate manner of acting. He was a master at transforming himself into characters utterly different to himself. Among his most popular plays were several in which he was required to appear in various disguises or else to act as a number of contrasting characters. The versatility with which he could accomplish this was a constant source of delight to his audiences. But he was never content to represent mediocre characters taken from everyday life: instead, in the words of his nephew Eduard Devrient: "with a sort of demonic air, his spirit hunted to the borders of humanity after its extreme manifestations ... the extraordinary, the terrible, the horrid, the bizarre, and the laughable". In the representation of the grotesque extremes of human experience he had no equal. But he was not a strident or noisy actor. Contemporary accounts suggest that his voice was at times so quiet that it was difficult to hear him, while his movement and gestures could be so subtle that unless one was fairly close to the stage the impact of his performance was lost. Those who were moved by his presence on stage found that he had a strangely visceral effect on them, which earned for him the soubriquet of a 'Nervenschauspieler', an actor who disrupts the nervous energies of the audience.

Perhaps the most distinctive mark of his acting was the manner in which he brought the unconscious mind of the characters he played to the fore. Devrient's great tragic roles were relatively few: he was famous for only three tragic parts in Shakespeare (Lear, Richard III, and Shylock) and one in Schiller (Franz Moor). Nevertheless, the originality of his interpretation of these characters, whose actions he represented as being determined by unconscious forces they could do nothing to control, had such an impact upon audiences and colleagues alike that a whole generation of later actors tried to recapture the unique quality and power of Devrient's performance. This was not necessarily to the theatre's advantage. The essence of Devrient's acting was its apparent spontaneity — he created, it appeared, solely from his own 'genius' and with none of the premeditation that was so obvious in the Weimar actor. However, while the Weimar style was useful precisely because it was accessible to the untrained actors of the German theatre of the time, most lacked Devrient's creative imagination. Hence, for a good generation after his death, Germany abounded with actors whose work was essentially a meagre imitation of Devrient's, in which shrillness substituted for passion and rant for powerful utterance.

As a personality, Devrient exemplified the popular idea of the Romantic artist, tormented by an imagination that seemed to drive him to extremes of self-indulgence. In fact, Devrient suffered from chronic alcoholism. Although this did not seem to impair his performance — indeed drink may even have ensured him access to powers of expression that seemed unique to him — it eroded his stamina. Karl von Holtei recalled seeing him play Lear in Breslau, when he fainted in the middle of the performance, having to be carried out "like a dead man from battle". He was often unable to complete this role in particular due to the demand it made upon his deficient energies. However, Devrient's imbibing added greatly to his mystique and public appeal. Especially celebrated were the great bouts of drinking he engaged in with the poet and writer E. T. A. Hoffmann, from soon after his arrival in Berlin to the latter's death in 1822. The two men served as mutual stimuli, as they frequently indulged in fantastic reveries by

Ludwig Devrient (portrait by Christoph Wohlin).

which they provided each other with material for their work in their respective creative spheres. Hoffmann, in his essay "Seltsame Leiden eines Theaterdirektors", wrote the most penetrating of all contemporary descriptions of Devrient's acting, explaining the process by which he created each performance as a form of self-induced mesmerism.

While Devrient acquired a formidable reputation and enthusiastic following during his lifetime, his career was not entirely a success. This was due only partially to his alcoholism. As a tragic actor, his style was not to the taste of Count von Brühl, who was intendant at the Berlin National Theatre for most of Devrient's tenure there and who preferred the Weimar style. In 1816, Brühl acquired Pius Alexander Wolff, Goethe's leading tragic actor, as a principal in the Berlin company. Wolff was given all the leading tragic roles, while Devrient had to stick to comedy, at which he was notably versatile. Only on tour could he perform tragic roles with any regularity, but touring did not provide him with the opportunity to expand his repertoire, which remained unusually narrow for an actor of his reputation. Only after Wolff's death in 1828 was Devrient once again given access to tragic roles on the Berlin stage. He celebrated the occasion by performing Richard III, but his energies had been so sapped by this time that audiences sensed the interpretation to be only a shadow of what it might once have been. Nevertheless, in this same year, he visited Vienna, where in a remarkable series of performances, he recreated all his major roles with great energy and in the process earned the adulation of his audiences.

Ludwig Devrient died, it is said, while listening to his wife play *Don Giovanni* on the piano, expiring at the point where the statue drags Giovanni down to hell. The story is no doubt apocryphal, but it captures well the demonic aura that surrounded the man and contributed to the extraordinary magic that must have emanated from his presence on the stage.

—Simon Williams

DEWHURST, Colleen. Canadian actress. Born in Montreal, Quebec, Canada, 3 June 1926. Educated at the Downer College for Young Ladies, Milwaukee, Wisconsin; trained for the stage at the American Academy of Dramatic Arts and with Harold Clurman and Joseph Anthony. Married 1) James Vickery; 2) actor George C. Scott (*q.v.*) in 1960 (divorced 1965); remarried George C. Scott in 1967 (divorced 1972), two sons. Stage debut, Carnegie Lyceum Theatre, Pittsburgh, Pennsylvania, 1946; first appearance in New York, ANTA Theatre, 1952; actress, New York Shakespeare Festival, 1956–59; film debut, 1959. Member: Actors' Equity (twice President); Save the Theatres (Vice-President); American Council for the Arts; TD Fund. Recipient: Obie Award, 1958, 1963; *Theatre World* Award, 1958; Sylvania Award, 1960; Lola D'Annunzion Award, 1961; Tony Award, 1962, 1974; Sarah Siddons Award, 1974; Gemini Award, 1986. Died in South Salem, New York, 22 August 1991.

Productions

As actress:
1946   Julia Cavendish in *The Royal Family* (Marshall), Carnegie Lyceum Theatre, Pittsburgh, Pennsylvania.
1952   Neighbour in *Desire Under the Elms* (O'Neill), ANTA Theatre, New York.
1956   Memphis Virgin and Turkish Concubine in *Tamburlaine the Great* (Marlowe), Winter Garden Theatre, New York.
        Tamora in *Titus Andronicus* (Shakespeare), Shakespeare Festival, New York.
        Camille in *Camille* (Dumas fils), Cherry Lane Theatre, New York.
        Kate in *The Taming of the Shrew* (Shakespeare), Emanuel Presbyterian Church, New York.
        Queen in *The Eagle Has Two Heads* (Rostand), Actors' Playhouse, New York.
1957   Penelope in *Maiden Voyage* (Osborn), Forrest Theatre, Philadelphia, Pennsylvania.
        Lady Macbeth in *Macbeth* (Shakespeare), Shakespeare Festival, New York.
        Mrs Squeamish in *The Country Wife* (Wycherley), Adelphi Theatre, New York.
1958   Laetitia in *Children of Darkness* (Mayer), Circle in the Square Theatre, New York.

Josie Hogan in *A Moon for the Misbegotten* (O'Neill), Festival of Two Worlds, Spoleto, Italy; Studio Arena Theatre, Buffalo, New York, 1965; Morosco Theatre, New York, 1973; Ahmanson Theatre, Los Angeles, California, 1974.

1959   Cleopatra in *Antony and Cleopatra* (Shakespeare), Heckscher Theatre, New York; Shakespeare Festival, Delacorte Theatre, New York, 1963.

1960   Caesonia in *Caligula* (Camus), 54th Street Theatre, New York.

1960–61 Mary Follet in *All the Way Home* (Mosel, adapted from Agee), Belasco Theatre, New York.

1962   Phoebe Flaherty in *Great Day in the Morning* (Norman and Wilson), Henry Miller Theatre, New York.

1963   Abbie Putnam in *Desire Under the Elms* (O'Neill), Circle in the Square Theatre, New York.
         Amelia Evans in *The Ballad of the Sad Café* (Albee), Martin Beck Theatre, New York.

1967   Sara in *More Stately Mansions* (O'Neill), Broadhurst Theatre, New York.

1969   Hester in *Hello and Goodbye*, Sheridan Square Playhouse, New York.

1970   Shen Teh in *The Good Woman of Setzuan* (Brecht), Vivian Beaumont Theatre, New York.

1971   The Mistress in *All Over* (Albee), Martin Beck Theatre, New York.
         Nel Denton in *The Big Coca-Cola Swamp in the Sky*, Westport Country Playhouse, Connecticut.

1972   Gertrude in *Hamlet* (Shakespeare), Shakespeare Festival, Delacorte Theatre, New York.
         Christie Mannon in *Mourning Becomes Electra* (O'Neill), Circle in the Square Theatre, New York.

1975   Margaret in *Artichoke*, Long Wharf Theatre, New Haven, Connecticut.

1976   Martha in *Who's Afraid of Virginia Woolf?* (Albee), Music Box Theatre, New York.

1977   Irene Porter in *An Almost Perfect Person*, Belasco Theatre, New York.

1978   Lillian Hellman in *Are You Now or Have You Ever Been ... ?*, Promenade Theatre, New York.

1979   Ruth Chandler in *Taken in Marriage*, Shakespeare Festival, Public Theatre, new York.

1982   Argia in *The Queen and the Rebels*, Plymouth Theatre, New York.

1983   Olga in *You Can't Take It with You* (Kaufman), Paper Mill Playhouse, Milburn, New Jersey, and Plymouth Theatre, New York.

1987   Carlotta O'Neill in *My Gene*, Shakespeare Festival, Public Theatre, New York.

Has also played roles in: *O'Neill and Carlotta*, Shakespeare Festival, Public Theatre, New York, 1979; *Night of 100 Stars*, Radio City Music Hall, New York, 1982; *The Only Woman General*, American Place Theatre, New York,

Colleen Dewhurst (1979).

1984; *Rainsnakes*, Long Wharf Theatre, New Haven, Connecticut, 1984; *Night of 100 Stars 2*, Radio City Music Hall, New York, 1985.

As director:
1981   *Ned and Jack*, Hudson Guild Theatre, New York, and Little Theatre, New York.

Films

The Nun's Story, 1959; *Man on a String*, 1960; *A Fine Madness*, 1966; *The Last Run*, 1971; *The Cowboys*, 1971; *McQ*, 1974; *Annie Hall*, 1977; *When a Stranger Calls*, 1979; *Ice Castles*, 1979; *Final Assignment*, 1980; *Tribute*, 1980; *The Dead Zone*, 1983; *The Boy Who Could Fly*, 1986.

Television

No Exit; *Antony and Cleopatra*; *Medea*; *Focus*; *The Price*; *The Crucible*; *The Hands of Cormac Joyce*; *Jacob and Joseph*, 1974; *Studs Lonigan*, 1979; *The Kitty O'Neal Story*; *Silent Victory*, 1979; *And Baby Makes Six*, 1979; *The Glitter Dome*, 1984; *The Blue and the Gray*, 1984; *A.D.*, 1985; *Anne of Green Gables*, 1985.

*   *   *

'Earth mother' has been a term frequently used in describing Colleen Dewhurst. A titan of a woman, powerful, sensual, down to earth, she is at once the embodiment of mother, sister and lover. Early in her career her five feet eight inches stature and enormous physical energy marked her out as ideally suited to play classical heroines on stage. A founding member of the New York Shakespeare Workshop, she played a succession of strong women in Joseph Papp's productions: Tamora in *Titus Andronicus*, Titania in *A Midsummer Night's Dream*, Kate in *The Taming of the Shrew*, Lady Macbeth in *Macbeth*, Cleopatra in *Antony and Cleopatra* and Gertrude in *Hamlet*. Dewhurst was the first actress in memory to make Gertrude a power instead of a victim. When Claudius warned the queen not to drink the poisoned wine, Dewhurst's Gertrude defiantly lifted the glass and said "I *will* my Lord" — knowingly committing suicide. Like Zoe Caldwell, with whom she has worked on several occasions, Dewhurst takes risks and is not afraid to make outrageous choices or to buck trends. When she played the traditionally weak and neurasthenic Mary Tyrone in *Long Day's Journey into Night*, she startled many critics by transforming her into a forceful character.

At the start of her career, Dewhurst's size limited the material she could play and made it difficult for her to find leading men that she did not totally overpower. She was not small enough for ingenues, nor was she mature enough for character parts in contemporary drama. Sometimes referred to as the Anna Magnani of Off-Broadway and combining sensuality, earthiness and size she was, however, uniquely qualified for the women of Albee and O'Neill. She earned Tony nominations for her performances in three Albee plays: the strapping Miss Amelia Evans in love with a dwarf in *The Ballad of the Sad Café* (1963), the Mistress in *All Over* (1971) directed by John Gielgud, and Martha in *Who's Afraid of Virginia Woolf?* opposite Ben Gazzara. As she grew older, she obtained the maturity and depth that resulted in her being labelled the foremost interpreter of O'Neill's heroines. Dewhurst had a preference for O'Neill women, because, as she stated in an interview with Rex Reed, "they move from the groin rather than the brain. To play O'Neill you have to be big. You can't sit around and play little moments of sadness and sweetness. You cannot phoney up O'Neill".

While she had notable successes as Christine in *Mourning Becomes Electra*, Abbie Putnam in *Desire Under the Elms*, Sara Melody in *More Stately Mansions*, Essie Miller in *Ah, Wilderness!* and Mary Tyrone in *Long Day's Journey into Night*, it was as Josie Hogan in *A Moon for the Misbegotten* opposite Jason Robards as Jamie Tyrone that she enjoyed her greatest Broadway acclaim and forged a permanent link between her own name and that of O'Neill. In 1974, at the age of 50, recently divorced from George Scott and living in a large farm house in upstate New York, she was ripe for a reprise of Josie, a role she had long familiarity with from two previous productions also directed by Jose Quintero. When Dewhurst appeared in *Moon* she presented a striking figure for audiences used to glamorous leading ladies. Barefoot, without make-up, sweating as she scrubbed the floor in a loose-fitting old cotton work dress, she embodied the plain large-boned farmer's daughter who could do the work of two men indicated in O'Neill's stage directions. The critic T. E. Kalem wrote that no actress had been big enough for the role before, "not physically but in that

generosity of heart, mind and spirit which Josie must convey".

Although Dewhurst began her stage career by studying with Harold Clurman and might have been termed a naturalistic actor, she did not indulge in the small details or business characteristic of many Method actors. She held the stage through a kind of rooted presence born of a strong inner power and keen ability to listen to her fellow actor. Vulnerability is a word that characterized her gifts as an actress. It is a word she frequently used, along with "survivor" and "ability to give" when she talked about why she likes O'Neill's women. She viewed O'Neill's dramaturgy as a slow peeling process in which characters let down their masks little by little and ultimately achieve redemption by baring their souls. She related that she found the key to Josie — triggering both her vulnerability and instinct to fight back — when her father enters the opening scene where she is scrubbing the floor and calls her an "overgrown cow". As the play progressed Dewhurst found that O'Neill keeps draining Josie so that by the final scene she is totally emotionally stripped and honest. It was this slow unveiling — typical of O'Neill's dramaturgy — that Dewhurst underwent on stage in a way that few actresses have before or since.

Dewhurst's voice and face are the raw conduits of the inner workings of the character. Her greatest physical attribute was a low, raspy voice that always touched the raw edge of deep feeling so that it quavers and breaks — conveying pain, vulnerability and suffering. Her titan structure was softened by the earthy sensuality of a high cheekboned face, generous mouth and crinkly eyes, which were able to model the play of the character's emotion to the last row in the house. It was a face that recalls the twin masks of tragedy and comedy. When in deep pain, the corners of the mouth turned down and one was in the presence of suffering, but in a second she could flash a smile and belt out a laugh that would light up the whole stage. Since she had been most often associated with the works of O'Neill, Albee and Shakespeare, it is not as apparent that Dewhurst also exceled in comic roles, exemplified by cameo appearances as the Grand Duchess Olga in the 1983 revival of *You Can't Take It with You* and as the mother in the television sitcom *Murphy Brown*. She had tremendous humour on stage and an irrepressible roar of a laugh, which spilled over even when doing tragic roles. She played Essie Miller, as a lovable dizzy 'mom' and, as Martha in *Who's Afraid of Virginia Woolf?*, combined tremendous humour with great depth.

—Kathryn Wylie-Marques

DEXTER, John. British director and actor. Born in Derby, 2 August 1925. Educated at schools in Derby until 1939. Began career as actor at the Derby Playhouse and on television and radio after army service; associate director, English Stage Company, Royal Court Theatre, London, 1957–63; associate director, National Theatre, London, 1963–66, 1971–75; director of production, Metropolitan Opera House, New York, 1974–81; production adviser, Metropolitan Opera House, New York, 1981–84; career hampered by ill-health from 1980. Recipient: Best Director of Drama Award, 1975; Shakespeare Prize, 1978. Died in London, 23 March 1990.

Productions

As director:

1957   Purgatory (Yeats), Devon Festival.
        Yes — and After (Hastings), Royal Court Theatre, London.

1958   Each in His Own Wilderness (Lessing), Royal Court Theatre, London.
        Chicken Soup With Barley (Wesker), Belgrade Theatre, Coventry; Royal Court Theatre, London, 1960.

1959   *Roots* (Wesker), Belgrade Theatre, Coventry, Duke of York's Theatre, London, and Royal Court Theatre, London.
        The Kitchen (Wesker), Royal Court Theatre, London.

1960   *I'm Talking About Jerusalem* (Wesker), Royal Court Theatre, London.
        Toys in the Attic (Hellman), Piccadilly Theatre, London.

1961   *The Keep* (Thomas), Royal Court Theatre, London.

1962   *England, Our England* (Hall and Waterhouse), London.
        Chips with Everything (Wesker), Royal Court Theatre, London, and Vaudeville Theatre, London; New York, 1963.
        The Blood of the Bambergs (Osborne), Royal Court Theatre, London.
        The Sponge Room (Waterhouse and Hall), Royal Court Theatre, London.
        Squat Betty (Waterhouse and Hall), Royal Court Theatre, London.

1963   *Jackie the Jumper* (Thomas), Royal Court Theatre, London.
        Half-a-Sixpence (Cross and Heneker), Cambridge Theatre, London.
        Saint Joan (Shaw), Chichester and Edinburgh Festivals and Old Vic Theatre, London.

1964   *Hobson's Choice* (Brighouse), Old Vic Theatre, London.
        Othello (Shakespeare), Old Vic Theatre, London.
        The Royal Hunt of the Sun (Shaffer), Old Vic Theatre, London, and Chichester Festival; New York, 1965.

1965   *Armstrong's Last Goodnight* (Arden), Old Vic Theatre, London, and Chichester Festival.
        Black Comedy and *White Lies* (Shaffer), Chichester Festival; Old Vic Theatre, London, 1966; New York, 1967.
        Do I Hear a Waltz? (Rodgers and Sondheim), New York.

1966   *A Bond Honoured* (Osborne, adapted from Vega), Old Vic Theatre, London.
        The Storm (Ostrovsky), Old Vic Theatre, London.

1967   *The Unknown Soldier and His Wife* (Ustinov), New York.

Wise Child (Gray), Wyndham's Theatre, London.

1968   *Benevenuto Cellini* (opera by Berlioz), Royal Opera House, Covent Garden, London; La Scala, Milan.

1969   *I Vespri siciliani* (opera by Verdi), Hamburg State Opera, Hamburg; Metropolitan Opera House, New York, and Paris Opéra, Paris, 1974; Coliseum Theatre, London, 1984.

1971   *A Woman Killed with Kindness* (Heywood), Old Vic Theatre, London.
        Tyger (Mitchell), New Theatre, London.
        The Good-Natured Man (Goldsmith), Old Vic Theatre, London.

1972   *The Old Ones* (Wesker), Royal Court Theatre, London.
        From the House of the Dead (opera by Janáček), Hamburg State Opera, Hamburg.
        Boris Godunov (opera by Mussorgsky), Hamburg State Opera, Hamburg.
        Billy Budd (opera by Britten), Hamburg State Opera, Hamburg.
        Un ballo in maschera (opera by Verdi), Hamburg State Opera, Hamburg.

1973   *The Devils of Loudun* (opera by Penderecki), Coliseum Theatre, London, and Sadler's Wells Theatre, London.
        The Misanthrope (Molière, adapted by Harrison), Old Vic Theatre, London; New York, 1975.
        Equus (Shaffer), Old Vic Theatre, London; New York, 1974.
        The Party (Griffiths), Old Vic Theatre, London.
        In Praise of Love (Rattigan), Duchess Theatre, London.

1974   *Pygmalion* (G. B. Shaw), Albery Theatre, London.

1975   *Phaedra Britannica* (Harrison, adapted from Racine's *Phèdre*), National Theatre, London.
        La Forza del Destino (opera by Verdi), Paris.

1976   *Aida* (opera by Verdi), Metropolitan Opera House, New York.

1977   *Le Prophète* (opera by Meyerbeer), Metropolitan Opera House, New York.
        Les Dialogues des Carmelites (opera by Poulenc), Metropolitan Opera House, New York, San Franscisco, and Salle Favart, Paris.
        Lulu (opera by Berg), Metropolitan Opera House, New York; revived there in revised version, 1980.
        Rigoletto (opera by Verdi), Metropolitan Opera House, New York.

1978   *Don Pasquale* (opera by Donzetti), Metropolitan Opera House, New York.
        The Bartered Bride (opera by Smetana), Metropolitan Opera House, New York.

1979   *Don Carlos* (opera by Verdi), Metropolitan Opera House, New York.
        Rise and Fall of the City of Mahagonny (opera by Brecht and Weill), Metropolitan Opera House, New York.
        Pygmalion (G. B. Shaw), Ahmanson Theatre, Los Angeles.

As You Like It (Shakespeare), National Theatre, London.

1980   *Life of Galileo* (Brecht), National Theatre, London.

1981   *Parade* (operatic compilation comprising Satie's *Parade*, Poulenc's *Les Mamelles de Tirésias*, and Ravel's *L'Enfant et les sortileges*), Metropolitan Opera House, New York; (in part) Royal Opera House, Covent Garden, London, 1982.

        The Shoemaker's Holiday (Dekker), National Theatre, London.

1982   Stravinsky tribute (operatic compilation comprising Stravinsky's *The Rite of Spring*, *The Nightingale*, and *Oedipus Rex*), Metropolitan Opera House, New York.

1980's   *Heartbreak House* (G. B. Shaw), Haymarket Theatre, London.

1982   *The Portage to San Christobal of A. H.* (Hampton), Mermaid Theatre, London.

        Valmouth (Wilson), Chichester Festival.

1984   *The Devil and the Good Lord* (Sartre), Lyric Theatre, Hammersmith, London.

        Das Entführung aus dem Serail (opera by Mozart), Chicago and Metropolitan Opera House, New York.

        The Glass Menagerie (T. Williams), New York.

1985   *La Buona figliuola* (opera by Piccinni), Buxton Festival, Buxton.

        Gigi (Lerner and Loewe), Lyric Theatre, London.

1986   *The Cocktail Party* (Eliot), Phoenix Theatre, London.

        Nabucco (opera by Verdi), Zurich.

1987   *Portraits* (Home), Malvern Festival, Malvern.

1988   *Madam Butterfly* (Hwang), New York; Shaftesbury Theatre, London, 1989.

1989   *The Threepenny Opera* (Brecht and Weill), New York.

        Julius Caesar (Shakespeare), Haymarket Theatre, Leicester.

        Creon (Sophocles), Haymarket Theatre, Leicester.

Films

As director:
The Virgin Soldiers, 1968; *Sidelong Glances of a Pigeon Kicker*, 1970; *I Want What I Want*, 1971.

*

Bibliography

Books:
John Elsom and Nicholas Tomalin, *The History of the National Theatre*, London, 1978.

* * *

Bill Gaskill once described the productions of Olivier's National Theatre as falling into two categories: 'green-brown' (dark, sparse, and realistic, like Gaskill's own *Mother Courage*) and 'red-gold' (bright, flashy, and theatrical, like *The Royal Hunt of the Sun*). It is a division that applies well to the work of Gaskill's National Theatre and Royal Court colleague John Dexter, with the two styles corresponding to the two main strands in his work and the two playwrights with whom he was most associated, Arnold Wesker and Peter Shaffer.

It was George Devine's policy at the Court to pair writers and directors (as, for instance, Lindsay Anderson with David Storey or Bill Gaskill with N. F. Simpson and, later, Edward Bond) and Dexter was linked with the Welsh playwright Gwyn Thomas and with Arnold Wesker. It was an inspired pairing, since Wesker's early plays were largely concerned with patterns of social class and the rhythms of everyday work, themes close to the heart of Dexter, the only non-university director at the Court. He soon became known for skilful choreography of large groups (especially in *The Kitchen*, with its almost ritualistic depiction of a working day) and with the realistic portrayal of working-class life. He also, with designer Jocelyn Herbert and lighting designer Andy Phillips, developed an austere, Brechtian aesthetic that was to become the dominant style of British theatre until the 1970's. Jim Hiley, in *Theatre at Work — The story of the National Theatre's production of Brecht's Galileo* in 1981, observed that Dexter "pioneered ideas that have since become commonplace, leaving visible the real, bare walls of the stage, for example, and using metals and polystyrene rather than the prettier materials popular at the time".

It was also at the Court that he developed his ability to draw towering performances from his leads, most obviously Joan Plowright as Beatie Bryant in *Roots*. At the National Theatre, which he joined in 1963, he continued this tradition with Laurence Olivier's swansong performances in *Othello* and *The Party*. His National Theatre work was characterised by a clarity, precision, and an awareness of the needs of each individual play, as in his workmanlike productions of *Hobson's Choice* and *A Woman Killed with Kindness*, and by a bold theatricality well suited to both the dazzling verbal pyrotechnics of Tony Harrison and the technically superb, if intellectually shallow, plays of Peter Shaffer. He also, less creditably, became known for his occasional poor judgement of scripts (most notably *Tyger* and *A Bond Honoured*) and as a directorial tyrant. Derek Jacobi, generally a very mild-mannered man, described him as one who "worked through terrorism".

Simon Callow, who appeared in *As You Like It* and *The Life of Galileo*, the productions with which Dexter returned to the National after seven years at New York's Metropolitan Opera House, has left one of the best accounts of Dexter at work, an account that focuses largely on his difficult manner and his limitations as a director of actors: "For rehearsals, he generally wears a tracksuit and plimsolls, circling the acting area, shouting out comments, criticisms or advice. His conception of acting is at heart athletic; it's a skill, requiring physical address and mental stamina. The intuitive aspect of the art is something you do at home ... He's not interested in the process, only the results". Despite his discomfort in it, Callow described *The Life of Galileo* as "the best the directocratic system can offer; a highly polished, crystal clear, gleaming great machine of a production". It also included another stunning central performance, this time from Michael Gambon. These two shows, and *The Shoemaker's Holiday*, are important historically as the first National Theatre productions to make full, effective use of the Olivier Theatre. Previously thought of as oversize and unwieldy, it was shown by Dexter (reunited with Herbert and Phillips) to be a dramatically effective space.

A lot of the work of Dexter's last decade was marred by a perverse choice of plays, apparently selected more for theatrical moments than any degree of substance. *The Devil and the Good Lord* and *The Portage to San Christobal of A. H.* were both little more than showcases for their central performers, respectively Gerard Murphy and Alec McCowen (who, as Hitler, gave a 25-minute speech justifying the Holocaust). McCowen also took the lead role in *The Cocktail Party*, a revival of Eliot's play intended to inaugurate a new West End company, a venture abandoned after the failure of its first production, which emerged as more a museum piece than a theatrical classic. Dexter's final British productions showed a return to form with both aspects of his work; *Julius Caesar* and *Creon* with their young, mostly little-known casts and almost bare stage seemed to signal a recreation of the powerful 'green-brown' austerity of his Royal Court days, while *Madam Butterfly*, a Shafferish play of ideas, was treated in a suitably 'red-gold' style that drew on Asian theatrical techniques.

—David Cottis

DORVAL, Marie. French actress. Born Marie-Thomase-Amélie Delaunay in Lorient, 7 January 1798. No formal education. Married 1) actor-manager Louis-Étienne Allan, known as Dorval, in 1813 (died 1819), two sons; 2) manager and playwright Jean Toussaint Merle in 1829; one daughter by lover Alessandro Piccinni. Stage debut, as a child in melodrama, 1806; spotted by the actor Potier while appearing in Strasbourg and finally made her Paris debut at the Théâtre de la Porte-Saint-Martin, 1818; acted to acclaim opposite Frédérick Lemaître, 1827; established as the most popular actress on the Boulevard du Temple by 1829; appeared in plays written for her by her lover, 1833–35, Alfred de Vigny; joined Comédie-Française, 1834, but left the company the following year due in part to the hostility of Mlle Mars; acted at the Théâtre de l'Odéon and the Gymnase before reappearing at the Comédie-Française in the 1840's at the request of George Sand; then went to the Odéon and subsequently back to the Boulevard theatres, 1845; spent her final years in poverty after the taste for Romantic drama faded. Died in Paris, 20 May 1849.

Principal roles

1827   Amélie in *Trente ans ou la Vie d'un jouer* (Ducange), Théâtre de la Porte-Saint-Martin, Paris.
1831   Adèle d'Hervey in *Antony* (Dumas *père*), Théâtre de la Porte-Saint-Martin, Paris.
       Marion in *Marion de Lorme* (Hugo), Théâtre de la Porte-Saint-Martin, Paris.
1835   Kitty Bell in *Chatterton* (Vigny), Comédie-Française, Paris.
       Catarina in *Angelo* (Hugo), Comédie-Française, Paris.

1840   Cosima in *Cosima* (Sand), Comédie-Française, Paris.
1842   Phèdre in *Phèdre* (Racine), Théâtre de l'Opéra, Paris.
1843   Lucrèce in *Lucrèce* (Ponsard), Théâtre de l'Odéon, Paris.
1845   Marie-Jeanne in *Marie-Jeanne* (Dennery), Théâtre de la Porte-Saint-Martin, Paris.
1846   Agnès in *Agnès de Méranie* (Ponsard), Théâre d'Italien, Paris.

Also acted roles in: *The Bride of Lammermoor* (adapted from Scott), Théâtre de la Porte-Saint-Martin, Paris, 1827; *Marino Faliero* (Delavigne), Théâtre de la Porte-Saint-Martin, Paris, 1829; *Quitte pour la peur* (Vigny), Théâtre de l'Opéra, Paris, 1833; *Le Proscrit* (Soulié), Théâtre de la Renaissance, Paris, 1839; *La Maréchal d'Ancre* (Vigny), Comédie-Française, Paris, 1840.

Publications

Lettres à A. de Vigny, edited by C. Gautier, Paris, 1942.

*

Bibliography

Books:
É. Coupy, *Marie Dorval*, Paris, 1868.
Nozière, *Madame Dorval*, Paris, 1930.
F. Moser, *Marie Dorval*, Paris, 1947.
Paul Hagenhauer, *La Vie douloureuse de Marie Dorval*, Paris, 1972.

* * *

The illegitimate daughter of two actors, Marie Dorval went on stage as a child and experienced the hard life of impoverished itinerant players; "Instead of being rocked in a cradle," she wrote, "I was jolted about in Ragotin's cart, and I never knew childish play or childish pleasures". Orphaned at 15, she was soon married to an equally impecunious man of the theatre called Dorval and then had to fend for herself once more when he died in 1819, leaving her with two small children. However, in the 1820's she began to make a name for herself in the popular boulevard theatres of Paris, being engaged at the Porte-Saint-Martin, where her career really took off as partner to Frédérick Lemaître in *Trente ans ou la Vie d'un joueur* and in such early Romantic works as *The Bride of Lammermoor* and *Marino Faliero*. Finally, she took the leading role of Adèle d'Hervey opposite Bocage in Alexandre Dumas's *Antony*, one of the first triumphs of the Romantic movement in the theatre. After another successful pairing with Bocage in Victor Hugo's *Marion de Lorme*, Dorval was being hailed as "the leading actress of the boulevard".

Dorval had none of the usual prejudice against the Romantic idiom — the revitalised alexandrine, the provocatively colourful vocabulary, the audacious mixture of styles — that was shown by traditionalists at the Comédie-Française. She brought to such roles as Marion the right sort of flexibility and was by now sufficiently well-established to be able to impose her terms on a playwright like Hugo, who was still aspiring towards complete success. The

Marie Dorval

name of Hugo's play was changed (from *A Duel under Richelieu*) to give due prominence to her role and the ending was adapted, Marion now being pardoned by her lover as he goes to his death, thus allowing for the expression of mutual love and forgiveness that makes the definitive ending so moving. With *Antony* there had been no problem of adaptation, for Dumas's style was much nearer that of the boulevard melodramas, and all accounts agree on the contribution made by Dorval to the play's outstanding success. To quote Gautier's narrative of the first night: "The house was in complete delirium: spectators were clapping, sobbing, weeping, shouting ... the notion of Romantic passion was admirably represented by Bocage and Dorval, who gave an extraordinary intensity to the couple of Antony and Adèle: Bocage the "homme fatal", Dorval the quintessence of feminine weakness".

The other great Romantic success with which Dorval was to be identified was Vigny's *Chatterton*. Vigny had been her lover since 1833, and the play was written with Dorval in mind for the role of Kitty Bell, the demure Quakeress who conceals her love for the young genius. "An almost silent role, expressing itself in a single cry at the end — but what a cry!" wrote Gautier, referring to the discovery of Chatterton's death. In Dorval's hands, Kitty's agonised cry was a cue for her famous "dégringolade", her collapse at the top of a specially constructed flight of stairs, followed by the sliding of her senseless body down the entire length of the bannister rail, coming to rest at the bottom. This "jeu de scène", invented by Dorval herself, was an obvious concession to popular taste; but more generally, the sentimental

tableau of Kitty and her two children, and the innocent purity of her love for the poet, leading to a sudden outburst of feeling in the last act, gave excellent scope to an actress who so well embodied the boulevard manner.

The production of *Chatterton* at the Comédie-Française had been delayed by hostility on the part of senior members of the company there — especially Mlle Mars — to the new Romantic drama and its exponents; and in spite of its success, Vigny's play was withdrawn while still playing to good houses so as to make way for a classical revival. In 1836 the two rivals clashed in Hugo's prose play *Angelo*, Mlle Mars using her prerogative to obtain the role of Tisbe, which seemed to call for "le style Dorval". To quote Madame Hugo: "The chaste, decent Catarina was ideal for the talents of Mlle Mars; Tisbe, uncontrolled, impulsive, a child of the streets, seemed to suit the free, bohemian manner of Mme Dorval. Mlle Mars therefore chose Tisbe ... ".

The late 1830's marked the peak of Marie Dorval's career. Disillusioned by her experience at the Comédie-Française, she returned to popular drama in boulevard theatres such as the Gymnase and the Renaissance before reappearing as Lucrèce in Ponsard's play of that name at the Odéon in 1843, a date that is conventionally accepted as signalling the end of the Romantic movement in the theatre. From this point onwards, Dorval fell remarkably quickly from the heights of success into solitude, poverty — with the increasing burden of a paralysed second husband to support — and premature old age, hastened by the death in 1848 of an adored grandson. On her death in 1849, all her possessions had to be sold to satisfy her creditors, and a special performance was held at the Comédie-Française in order to raise money for a suitable tombstone.

—William D. Howarth

DREW, John. US actor. Born in Philadelphia, 13 November 1853; son of actor John Drew and actress Louisa Lane (Mrs John Drew). Educated at boarding school in Andalusia, Pennsylvania; the Episcopal Academy, Philadelphia; also under private tutors. Married actress Josephine Baker in 1880 (died 1918), one daughter. Stage debut, under management of his mother, Arch Street Theatre, Philadelphia, 1873; New York debut, under management of Augustin Daly, 1875; hugely popular in comic roles, often opposite Ada Rehan, and dubbed 'the first gentleman of the stage'; London debut, 1884; further acclaimed under the management of Charles Frohman, from 1892. Member: Players' Club, New York (president). Died in Vancouver, Canada, 9 July 1927.

Roles

1873   Plumper in *Cool as a Cucumber* (C. Mathews), Arch Street Theatre, Philadelphia.
1873–75   Hornblower in *The Laughing Hyena* (Webster), Arch Street Theatre, Philadelphia.
          Lord Fitzfoley in *The Arkansas Traveller* (De Walden and Spencer), Arch Street Theatre, Philadelphia.

1875–77   Major Alfred Steele in *Women of the Day* (Morton), Arch Street Theatre, Philadelphia.

Bob Ruggles in *The Big Bonanza* (Moser, adapted by Daly), Fifth Avenue Theatre, New York, and US tour.

Thorsby Gyll in *Pique* (Daly), Fifth Avenue Theatre, New York.

Rosencrantz in *Hamlet* (Shakespeare), Fifth Avenue Theatre, New York.

Sir Pierce of Exton and Lord Willoughby in *Richard II* (Shakespeare), Fifth Avenue Theatre, New York.

Clavis in *The Lady of Lyons* (Bulwer-Lytton), Fifth Avenue Theatre, New York.

Lodovico in *Othello* (Shakespeare), Fifth Avenue Theatre, New York.

François in *Richelieu* (Bulwer-Lytton), Fifth Avenue Theatre, New York.

Francis in *The Stranger* (Kotzebue), Fifth Avenue Theatre, New York.

Hortensio in *The Taming of the Shrew* (Shakespeare), Fifth Avenue Theatre, New York.

Cloten in *Cymbeline* (Shakespeare), Fifth Avenue Theatre, New York.

Seth and Henrick Vedder in *Rip Van Winkle* (Boucicault), Booth's Theatre, New York.

Charles Surface in *The School for Scandal* (Sheridan, adapted by Daly), Arch Street Theatre, Philadelphia.

Mr Bronzley in *Wives as They Were and Maids as They Are* (Inchbald), Arch Street Theatre, Philadelphia.

1878–79   Algie Fairfax and Henry Beauclerc in *Diplomacy* (Scott and Stephenson), US tour.

1879   Tom Sanderson in *Newport* (Logan), Daly's Theatre, New York.

Chrisalde in *Wives* (Howard, adapted from Molière), Daly's Theatre, New York.

Reverend Harry Duncan in *Divorce* (Daly, adapted from Trollope), Daly's Theatre, New York.

Alexander Sprinkle in *An Arabian Night* (Moser, adapted by Daly), Daly's Theatre, New York.

1880   Geoffrey Knickerbocker in *Our First Families* (Fawcett), Daly's Theatre, New York.

Clyde Monograne in *The Way We Live* (L'Arronge, adapted by Daly), Daly's Theatre, New York.

Sir Jasper in *Rosemary* (Parker and Carson), Daly's Theatre, New York.

Tom Versus in *Needles and Pins* (Rosen, adapted by Daly), Daly's Theatre, New York.

The Adjutant in *The Passing Regiment* (Moser and Schönthan, adapted by Daly), Daly's Theatre, New York.

1882   Don Phillip in *She Would and She Would Not* (Cibber), Toole's Theatre, London.

Lieutenant Erick Thorndyke in *The Squire* (Pinero), Daly's Theatre, New York.

1883   Prince Serge Panine in *Serge Panine* (Ohnet, adapted by Daly), Daly's Theatre, New York.

John Drew

Courtney Corliss in *Seven Twenty-Eight; or, Casting the Boomerang* (Schönthan, adapted by Daly), Daly's Theatre, New York.

Harry Latimer in *Dollars and Sense* (L'Arronge, adapted by Daly), Daly's Theatre, New York.

1884   Belleville in *The Country Girl* (Wycherley and Garrick, adapted by Daly), Daly's Theatre, New York.

Tom Jervoice in *Lords and Commons* (Pinero), Daly's Theatre, New York.

Sidney Austin in *Love on Crutches* (Stobitzer, adapted by Daly), Daly's Theatre, New York.

1885   Captain Plume in *The Recruiting Officer* (Farquhar, adapted by Daly), Daly's Theatre, New York.

Colonel Lukyn in *The Magistrate* (Pinero), Daly's Theatre, New York.

Jack Mulberry in *A Night Off* (Schönthan, adapted by Daly), Daly's Theatre, New York.

1886   Francis Ford in *The Merry Wives of Windsor* (Shakespeare, adapted by Daly), Daly's Theatre, New York.

Kiefe O'Kiefe in *Nancy and Company* (Rosen, adapted by Daly), Daly's Theatre, New York.

Richard Brandagee in *After Business Hours* (Blumenthal, adapted by Daly), Daly's Theatre, New York.

Frederick in *Love in Harness* (Valabrègue, adapted by Daly), Daly's Theatre, New York.

Major Tarvor in *Dandy Dick* (Pinero), Daly's Theatre, New York.

1887   Petruchio in *The Taming of the Shrew* (Shakespeare, adapted by Daly), Fifth Avenue Theatre, New York.

Lieutenant Howell Everett in *The Railroad of Love* (Rosen, adapted by Daly), Daly's Theatre, New York.

1888   Demetrius in *A Midsummer Night's Dream* (Shakespeare, adapted by Daly), Daly's Theatre, New York.

Adolphus Doubledot in *The Lottery of Love* (Bisson and Mars, adapted by Daly), Daly's Theatre, New York.

1889   Young Mirabel in *The Inconstant* (Farquhar, adapted by Daly), Daly's Theatre, New York.

Lord Ravenstoke in *An International Match* (Schöthan, adapted by Daly), Daly's Theatre, New York.

Counsel in *Samson and Delilah* (Bisson and Moineaux, adapted by Daly), Daly's Theatre, New York.

Tom De Camp in *The Golden Widow* (Sardou, adapted by Daly), Daly's Theatre, New York.

Ned Dreemer in *The Great Unknown* (Schönthan, adapted by Daly), Daly's Theatre, New York.

Orlando in *As You Like It* (Shakespeare, adapted by Daly), Daly's Theatre, New York, and Chicago.

1891   The King of Navarre in *Love's Labour's Lost* (Shakespeare, adapted by Daly), Daly's Theatre, New York.

1892   Robin Hood in *The Foresters* (Tennyson, adapted by Daly), Daly's Theatre, New York.

Paul Blondet in *The Masked Ball* (Bisson, adapted by Fitch), Palmer's Theatre, New York.

1894   Frederick Ossian in *The Butterflies* (Carleton), Palmer's Theatre, New York.

1895   Viscount Clivebrook in *The Bauble Shop* (H. A. Jones), Empire Theatre, New York.

John Annesley in *That Imprudent Young Couple* (Carleton), Empire Theatre, New York.

Christopher Colt Jr in *Christopher Jr* (Ryley), Empire Theatre, New York.

Mr Kilroy in *The Squire of Dames* (Carton, adapted from Dumas fils's *L'Ami des Femmes*), Palmer's Theatre, New York.

1897   Comte de Condale in *A Marriage of Convenience* (Grundy), Empire Theatre, New York.

1898   Dick Rudyard in *One Summer's Day* (Esmond), Wallack's Theatre, New York.

Sir Christopher Deering in *The Liars* (H. A. Jones), Empire Theatre, New York.

1899   Mr Parbury in *The Tyranny of Tears* (Chambers), Empire Theatre, New York.

1900   Richard Carvel in *Richard Carvel* (Rose, adapted from Churchill), Empire Theatre, New York.

1901   Christopher Bingham in *The Second in Command* (Marshall), Empire Theatre, New York.

1902   Lord Lumley in *The Mummy and the Humming Bird* (Henderson), Empire Theatre, New York.

1903   Captain Dieppe in *Captain Dieppe* (Hope and Rhodes), Herald Square Theatre, New York.

1904   Duke of Killicrankie in *The Duke of Killicrankie* (Marshall), Empire Theatre, New York.

1905   James De Lancey in *De Lancey* (Thomas), Empire Theatre, New York.

1906   Hilary Jesson in *His House in Order* (Pinero), Empire Theatre, New York.

1907   Gerald Eversleigh in *My Wife* (Morton), Empire Theatre, New York.

1908   Jack in *Jack Straw* (Maugham), Empire Theatre, New York.

1909   George Ballin in *Inconstant George* (Unger), Empire Theatre, New York.

1910   Thomas Freeman in *Smith* (Maugham), Empire Theatre, New York.

1911   Robin Worthington in *A Single Man* (Davies), Empire Theatre, New York.

1912   Thomas Pelling in *The Perplexed Husband* (Sutro), Empire Theatre, New York.

1913   Benedick in *Much Ado About Nothing* (Shakespeare), Empire Theatre, New York.

Philip Ross in *The Will* (Barrie), Empire Theatre, New York.

1914   Prosper Couramont in *A Scrap of Paper* (Simpson), Empire Theatre, New York.

Michel Giroux in *The Prodigal Husband* (Wood), Empire Theatre, New York.

1915   Earl of Yester in *The Chief*, Empire Theatre, New York.

1916   Shakespeare in *Caliban by the Yellow Sands* (MacKaye), Stadium, New York College.

Major Arthur Pendennis in *Major Pendennis* (adapted from Thackeray), Criterion Theatre, New York.

1917   Marquis of Quex in *The Gay Lord Quex* (Pinero), 48th Street Theatre, New York.

1920   Martin Gloade in *The Cat-Bird* (Hughes), Maxine Elliott's Theatre, New York.

1921   Lord Porteous in *The Circle* (Maugham), Playhouse Theatre, New York.

1923   Sir Peter Teazle in *The School for Scandal* (Sheridan), Lyceum Theatre, New York.

1926   Sir William in *Trelawny of the Wells* (Pinero), US tour.

Also acted roles in: *London Assurance* (Boucicault), US tour, 1875–77; *Weak Women* (H. J. Byron), US tour, 1875–77; *The Rough Diamond* (Buckstone), US tour, 1875–77; *Charity* (Gilbert), US tour, 1875–77; *Oliver Twist* (adapted from Dickens), US tour, 1875–77; *Saratoga* (Howard), Fifth Avenue Theatre, New York, 1875–77; *The Apostate* (Shiel), Fifth Avenue Theatre, New York, 1875–77; *The Merchant of Venice* (Shakespeare), Fifth Avenue Theatre, New York, 1875–77; *King Lear* (Shakespeare), Fifth Avenue Theatre, New York, 1875–77; *The New Leah* (Daly), Fifth Avenue Theatre, New York, 1875–77; *Twelfth Night* (Shakespeare), Fifth Avenue Theatre, New York, 1875–77; *Money* (Bulwer-Lytton), Fifth Avenue Theatre, New York; *The Princess Royal* (Daly, adapted from Adenis and Rostaing's *L'Officier de fortune*),

Fifth Avenue Theatre, New York, 1877; *The Dark City and its Bright Side* (Daly, adapted from Cogniard and Nicolaïe's *Les Compagnons de la truelle*), Fifth Avenue Theatre, New York, 1877; *Tiote* (Drach, adapted by Daly), Daly's Theatre, New York, 1880; *Odette* (Sardou, adapted by Daly), Daly's Theatre, New York, 1882; *A Woman's Won't* (Röttinger, adapted by Daly), Daly's Theatre, New York, 1884; *A Tragedy Rehearsed* (Sheridan), Daly's Theatre, New York, 1888; *A Priceless Paragon* (adapted from Sardou's *Belle-Maman*), Daly's Theatre, New York, 1889; *Haroun Alraschid and His Mother-in-Law* (Grundy), Daly's Theatre, New York, 1889; *New Lamps for Old* (Jerome), Daly's Theatre, New York, 1889; *The Last Word* (Schönthan, adapted by Daly), Daly's Theatre, New York, 1890; *The Cabinet Minister* (Pinero), Daly's Theatre, New York, 1891; *Love in Tandem* (Bocage and Courcy, adapted by Daly), Daly's Theatre, New York, 1892.

Publications

My Years on the Stage (autobiography), 1922.

*

Bibliography

Books:
Edward A. Dithmar, *John Drew*, New York, 1900.
Peggy Wood, *A Splendid Gypsy: John Drew*, New York, 1927.

Articles:
Acton Davies, "John Drew", *Munsey's*, 34, February 1906.
Lawrence F. Abbott, "John Drew and His Art", *Outlook*, 145, 30 March 1927.

* * *

John Drew was the 'Dean' of his generation of US actors. Coming from a long line of theatrical performers, he continued a tradition of English and Irish acting families in the USA. This mantle he passed on, most notably to his niece Ethel Barrymore. So established was the Drew tradition in the minds of the popular audience that despite her being the child of Drew's sister Georgia, herself an accomplished comedienne, and Maurice Barrymore, a comparably prominent actor, at her debut a member of the audience is said to have called: "Speak up, Ethel, don't be afraid. The Drews is all good actors".

In addition to the familial tradition of performing, John Drew was the second in a line, after Edwin Booth, of prominent US actors who strove to establish the respectability of the acting profession in polite society. He was president of the Players' Club, a private men's club in New York that was founded by Booth to facilitate social intercourse between members of the theatrical profession and other, more socially acceptable professions. In this capacity Drew was tireless in giving example as the perfect actor-gentleman.

Drew was a quiet, polite man who was affectionately known in the profession as 'Uncle John', an appellation bestowed by Lionel Barrymore, his nephew. His generation of actors considered him the glass of fashion and the model of form. He was perceived by the public as the 'arbiter

dictum' of style, grace, and good manners and, as such, succeeded in establishing the actor as a positive (rather than merely fashionable) role model. Indeed, his personal aura began to overshadow his abilities as a classical actor and roles of dashing, polite, fair young men became known as 'John Drew parts'.

Drew's career falls roughly into two main periods. The first part was spent as a member of Augustin Daly's repertory company from 1875, just two years after his stage debut. Drew's potential was quickly recognised and Daly made him into the star of his company along with Ada Rehan, who was thought at the time to be the finest US actress. Their most famous pairing was as Katerina and Petruchio in Shakespeare's *The Taming of the Shrew* and Drew often claimed Petruchio as his favourite part. It is notable that Drew and Rehan played Shakespeare's text — more or less intact — rather than the simplified and at the time vastly more popular version, called *Katherine and Petruchio*, in which Edwin Booth had acted.

Drew's contribution to the development of the US theatre at this point in his career lay primarily in his recruitment of the public's attention and affection, to the degree that he was able to make the transition from hero of the provincial repertory system to leading figure in a lucrative star system of national scope. In this regard he was a worthy successor to Booth, perhaps the most famous US actor to date. His participation in, and success at, the standard repertoire in a classically-orientated 19th-century repertory company gave him the theatrical and dramatic weight to negotiate the more economically-based early 20th-century theatre with aplomb and dignity. His craft was a major stone in the foundation upon which the star system in the USA was based and his respectability was the basis upon which it claimed validity in the press as well as the mind of its audience.

The second part of Drew's career, 1892–1915, saw him as a star, a lode in the constellation of Charles Frohman, then the most successful producer of popular theatre in the USA. His extraordinary range, developed in repertory, was ignored and he became the epitome of the polite, dashing hero, whose insistence on fair play provided him with a niche not only in the audience's mind, but in their hearts as well. The ubiquitousness of this kind of part in early 20th-century light comedy owes its volume largely to John Drew. Each year when the Empire Theatre in New York opened its doors after a summer hiatus, offering Drew in another polished comedy, the theatrical — as well as the social — season was officially considered under way. The audience's identification of this kind of role with the actor became so thorough that they could not imagine him playing a range of characters. Audiences were shocked, for instance, when during a production of *The Chief* a child climbed up on his knee and mussed his hair. So perfect was his image as a person that his public could not accept that he could be subject to any sartorial imperfection.

While Drew's very chivalry made his career in the public eye, it served at the same time to limit him artistically. Although he had gained prominence as one of the USA's foremost interpreters of Shakespeare, his fame rests on his ability as a light comedian. This evidences one of the main shortcomings in the star system as it developed in the USA. Like Joseph Jefferson before him, Drew became identified with one kind of role and his development as an artist for all intents and purposes came to an abrupt halt. Too much of a gentleman to make what he considered unwarranted requests of his agents and producers, he continued to play the gentleman on stage and to stagnate as an artist. He was often criticised for merely 'playing himself' — a self that was like enough to the real person, but had been considerably simplified and heightened by Daly and Frohman. Drew had become not so much an actor as a commodity. Had Drew broken out of the mould that he had created (and that had been created for him) his reputation might be considerably different — that of an actor of range rather than merely a period personality.

Drew's enduring importance will continue to be that of a genuinely honourable actor whose immense talent allowed him to fill a number of roles at the same time. He was one of the finest products of the US stock company tradition and among the first superstars of the modern era.

—David Payne-Carter

DREW, (Mrs) John. US actress and manager. Born Louisa Lane in London, 10 January 1820. Educated at local schools in London and Baltimore. Married 1) singer Henry Blaine Hunt in 1836 (divorced 1847); 2) George Mossop in 1848 (died 1849); 3) actor John Drew in 1850 (died 1862), one son (actor John Drew, *q.v.*) and two daughters (one actress Georgiana Drew); also one illegitimate son (actor Sidney Drew), probably by actor Robert Craig. Made stage debut as an infant and appeared regularly in melodrama at the age of five; emigrated to USA as a child with her widowed mother, 1827; US stage debut, with Junius Brutus Booth, Walnut Street Theatre, Philadelphia, 1827; subsequently toured as a child star, acting with Edwin Booth, Joseph Jefferson, Edwin Forrest, and William Charles Macready; as an adult, particularly acclaimed for appearances with her husband John Drew in the 1850's; succeeded John Drew as manager of the Arch Street Theatre, Philadelphia, 1861–92; last appearance, Montauk Theatre, Brooklyn, 13 May 1897. Died in New York, 31 August 1897.

Roles

1825   Child in *Meg Murnock; or, The Hag of the Glen* (Barrymore), British provinces.
1826   Child in *Frankenstein* (adapted from Shelley), Liverpool.
1827   Child in *Damon and Pythias* (Banim), British provinces.
        Prince Agib in *Timour the Tartar* (Lewis), Cooke's Amphitheatre, Liverpool.
        Duke of York in *Richard III* (Shakespeare), Walnut Street Theatre, Philadelphia.
        Albert in *William Tell* (Knowles), Joe Cowell's Theatre, Baltimore.
        Therese in *Thérèse; or, The Orphan of Geneva* (Payne), Park Theatre, New York.
1828   Little Pickle in *The Spoiled Child* (anon.), Bowery Theatre, New York.
        Five roles in *Twelve Precisely* (Milner), Bowery Theatre, New York.

1828–30 Dr Pangloss in *The Heir-at-Law* (Colman the Younger), Bowery Theatre, New York.
        Goldfinch in *The Road to Ruin* (Holcroft), Bowery Theatre, New York.
        Seven roles in *Winning a Husband* (Macfarren), Bowery Theatre, New York.
        Five roles in *72 Piccadilly*, Bowery Theatre, New York.
        Six roles in *Actress of All Work* (Oxberry), Bowery Theatre, New York.
        Thaner in *The Secret*, Bowery Theatre, New York.
        Gregory in *Turn Out* (Kenney), Bowery Theatre, New York.
1833   Florabel in *The Wife* (Knowles), Bowery Theatre, New York.
1835   Julia in *Julia*, Portland, Maine.
        Maria in *The School for Scandal* (Sheridan), New Orleans.
1836–37 Second Bayadère in *Le Bayadère* (Horncastle), New Orleans.
1837–38 Pauline in *The Lady of Lyons* (Bulwer-Lytton), Natchez, Mississippi.
        Lady Macbeth in *Macbeth* (Shakespeare), Natchez, Mississippi.
        Cinderella in *Cinderella*, Natchez, Mississippi.
        Rosina in *Rosina* (Brooke), Natchez, Mississippi.
1840–42 Lady Gay Spanker in *London Assurance* (Boucicault), Pittsburgh, Pennsylvania.
        Richard III in *Richard III* (Shakespeare), Louisville, Kentucky.
        Beauty in *Beauty and the Beast*, Bowery Theatre, New York.
1847   Romeo in *Romeo and Juliet* (Shakespeare), Park Theatre, New York.
        Mark Antony in *Antony and Cleopatra* (Shakespeare), Park Theatre, New York.
1850   Hypolita in *She Would and She Would Not* (Cibber), Chestnut Street Theatre, Philadelphia.
1880   Mrs Malaprop in *The Rivals* (Sheridan), US tour.
1890   Lady Teazle in *The School for Scandal* (Sheridan), Arch Street Theatre, Philadelphia.
1893   Mother-in-Law in *An Arabian Night*, Standard Theatre, New York.

Other roles included: Desdemona in *Othello* (Shakespeare); Dot in *The Cricket on the Hearth* (Dickens); Juliet in *Romeo and Juliet* (Shakespeare); Queen Katharine in *Henry VIII* (Shakespeare); Lydia Languish in *The Rivals* (Sheridan); Mrs Oakley in *The Jealous Wife* (Colman the Elder); Ophelia in *Hamlet* (Shakespeare); Mistress Quickly in *The Merry Wives of Windsor* (Shakespeare); Rosalind in *As You Like It* (Shakespeare); Peg Woffington in *Peg Woffington* (Boucicault); and roles in *Fortunio, The Four Mowbrays, The Lecture Room, The Miseries of Human Life, The Octoroon* (Boucicault), *Our American Cousin* (Taylor); *Pauvrette* (Boucicault), *The Sea of Ice, The Sporting Duchess, The Swiss Cottage*.

Publications

Autobiographical Sketch of Mrs John Drew, 1900.

*

Bibliography

Books:
Montrose Moses, *Famous Actor-Families in America*, New York, 1906.
William C. Young, *Famous Actors and Actresses of the American Stage*, vol. 1, New York and London, 1975.
James Kotsilibas-Davis, *Great Times, Good Times: The Odyssey of Maurice Barrymore*, New York, 1977.
Donald Mullin, *Victorian Actors and Actresses in Review*, Westport, Connecticut, and London, 1983.
Mary M. Turner, *Forgotten Leading Ladies of the American Theatre*, Jefferson, North Carolina, and London, 1990.

* * *

Both as a widely acclaimed actress and the first woman in the USA to become a successful long-term manager Mrs John Drew was a leading figure in the development of the US theatre in the last half of the 19th century. Under five feet tall, with small, thrusting features, Mrs Drew was not particularly beautiful, but her pale blue eyes — "thrusting" according to Kotsilibas-Davis — were expressive, while her voice was clear and musical and her enunciation unusually distinct. Her contemporary T. Allston Brown wrote that her reading was "faultless; her voice clear, of great compass, and musical in tone; her enunciation so clear and distinct that you lose no word or syllable of the text in her most impassioned utterance." Her voice commanded attention both on and off stage, compensating for her diminutive stature. One reviewer, for example, thought that her Queen Katharine "suffered nothing by comparison" when she played in support of a statuesque Charlotte Cushman's formidable and celebrated Cardinal Wolsey: "The exquisitely queenly bearing, commingled with the scarcely concealed mental suffering of the trial scene, reached its climax in the stately exit from the courtroom when the crier whispers 'Madame, you are called back', and the Queen's pent-up indignation found vent in an angry smiting of the cushion borne before her, as, with thrilling tones, she replied: 'What need you note it ... when you are called, return'". The energy, vocal dynamics, and small but forceful and natural gestures were hallmarks of her style. Indeed, she was often praised for the energetic but contained 'naturalness' of her performances.

During a long career, she played hundreds of roles, including such standards as Lady Macbeth, Desdemona, Ophelia, and Juliet, as well as such novelties as Romeo, Dr Pangloss in *The Heir-at-Law*, and on one occasion Marc Antony. In her first three seasons at the Arch Street Theatre, for example, she played over 90 different parts. Undoubtedly she was at her best, however, playing characters in what were then called "the rare old English comedies". Brown, for instance, extolled her Hypolita as "fresh, natural, sparkling, and altogether charming", while the actress Clara Morris praised her "dashing" Lady Gay Spanker in *London Assurance*. As Lady Teazle and Mrs Malaprop in particular she was, as Montrose Moses writes, "the quintessence of comedy". Brown thought she played

Mrs Malaprop "gloriously, making her ludicrous verbal blunders with the most sublime unconsciousness, and embodying the part as she alone can do it."

Although justly acclaimed as a versatile, gifted performer, Mrs Drew's achievements in theatrical management are perhaps even more important in the annals of the US stage. In the course of her 30 year management, she built the Arch Street Theatre stock company into one of the finest of the time. She was an exacting manager and director and she maintained high standards in rehearsal, production, and performance. She refurbished the Arch Street Theatre, brought order and discipline to heretofore generally slipshod rehearsal procedures, and closely supervised settings, lights, and all of the backstage personnel. Her theatre and stock company was soon regarded as one of the best in the country and a training ground for some of the finest acting talent of the period. By changing the bill frequently and booking such stars as Edwin Booth, Charlotte Cushman, and Fanny Davenport — who were eager to play at Arch Street — she kept the theatre on a sound, even profitable financial footing. Among the actors who began their careers at the theatre were Ada Rehan, Clara Morris, Fanny Davenport, Louis James, Frank Murdoch, and of course her own children and grandchildren.

When Mrs Drew retired she had succeeded in raising not only the status of women managers, but of her entire profession and her methods provided a model for a later generation of women managers, most notably Eva Le Gallienne, Nina Vance, and Margo Jones.

—Daniel J. Watermeier

DUDLEY, William (Stuart). British designer. Born in London, 4 March 1947. Educated at Highbury School, London; studied art at St Martin's School of Art, London, and Slade School of Art, London, DipAd, BA in Fine Art; University College of London, postgraduate Diploma in Fine Art. Began career in London amateur fringe theatre; debut as professional designer, Nottingham Playhouse, 1970; designer, from 1974, and associate designer, from 1981, with the National Theatre, London; has also worked in New York, Berlin, Bayreuth, and Salzburg. Member: Society of British Theatre Designers. Recipient: Society of West End Theatre Designer of the Year Award, 1980; Laurence Olivier Designer of the Year Award, 1985, 1986.

Productions

As set designer:
1970   *Hamlet* (Shakespeare), Nottingham Playhouse, Nottingham.
1971   *The Duchess of Malfi* (Webster), Royal Court Theatre, London.
          Man is Man (Brecht), Royal Court Theatre, London.
1972   *Live Like Pigs* (Arden), Royal Court Theatre, London.
          I, Claudius (Mortimer, adapted from Graves), Newcastle.
          The Baker, the Baker's Wife and the Baker's Boy, Newcastle.

1973   *Rooted* (Buzo), Royal Court Theatre, London.
Magnificence (Brenton), Royal Court Theatre, London.
Sweet Talk (Abbensetts), Royal Court Theatre, London.
The Merry-Go-Round (Lawrence), Royal Court Theatre, London.

1974   *Tyger* (Mitchell), Old Vic Theatre, London.
The Duchess of Malfi (Webster), Old Vic Theatre, London.
Man is Man (Brecht), Old Vic Theatre, London.
Cato Street, Old Vic Theatre, London.
The Good-Natured Man (Goldsmith), Old Vic Theatre, London.
Ashes (Rudkin), Watford.
The Corn is Green (E. Williams), Watford.
Twelfth Night (Shakespeare), Royal Shakespeare Theatre, Stratford-upon-Avon.
Harding's Luck (Nichols), Greenwich Theatre, London.

1975   *Fish in the Sea* (McGrath), Royal Court Theatre, London.
The Fool (Bond), Royal Court Theatre, London.
As You Like It (Shakespeare), Nottingham Playhouse, Nottingham; Riverside Studios, London, 1976.

1976   *Small Change* (Gill), Royal Court Theatre, London.
Ivanov (Chekhov), Aldwych Theatre, London.
The Norman Conquests (Ayckbourn), Berlin.
Il barbiere di Siviglia (Rossini), Welsh National Opera, Cardiff.

1977   *The Cherry Orchard* (Chekhov), Riverside Studios, London.
That Good Between Us (Barker), Warehouse Theatre, London.
Lavender Blue (McKendrick), Old Vic Theatre, London.
Touched (Lowe), Old Vic Theatre, London.
The Passion (Dudley and Bryden), Old Vic Theatre, London.

1978   *The World Turned Upside Down*, Old Vic Theatre, London.
Has "Washington" Legs? (Wood), Old Vic Theatre, London.
Billy Budd (Britten), Metropolitan Opera House, New York.
Lark Rise (Thompson, adapted by Dewhurst), National Theatre, London; also designed lighting.
Lost Worlds, National Theatre, London; also designed lighting.

1979   *Dispatches* (Herr, adapted by Bryden), National Theatre, London.
Candleford (Thompson, adapted by Dewhurst), National Theatre, London.
Undiscovered Country (Schnitzler), National Theatre, London.

1980   *Tales of Hoffman* (Offenbach), Royal Opera House, Covent Garden, London.
Hamlet (Shakespeare), Royal Court Theatre, London.

1981   *Il barbiere di Siviglia* (Rossini), Opera House, Glyndebourne.
Don Giovanni (Mozart), Royal Opera House, Covent Garden, London.

1982   *The Good Soldier Shweyk* (adapted from Hasek), National Theatre, London.

1983   *The Ring* (Wagner), Bayreuth.
Cinderella, National Theatre, London.

1984   *Der Rosenkavalier* (Strauss), Bayreuth.
Richard III (Shakespeare), Royal Shakespeare Theatre, Stratford-upon-Avon.
The Party (Griffiths), Barbican Pit, London.
Today (Holman), Royal Shakespeare Theatre, Stratford-upon-Avon.

1985   *The Mysteries* (Harrison), Lyceum Theatre, London.
The Real Inspector Hound (Stoppard), National Theatre, London.
The Critic (Sheridan), National Theatre, London.
The Merry Wives of Windsor (Shakespeare), Royal Shakespeare Theatre, Stratford-upon-Avon; revived, 1992.
Mutiny! (Crane), Piccadilly Theatre, London.

1986   A Midsummer Night's Dream (Shakespeare), Royal Shakespeare Theatre, Stratford-upon-Avon.
Futurists (Hughes), National Theatre, London.
Kafka's Dick (Bennett), Royal Court Theatre, London.
Richard II (Shakespeare), Barbican Theatre, London.

1987   *Waiting for Godot* (Beckett), National Theatre, London.
Kiss Me Kate (adapted from Shakespeare), British tour.

1988   *The Shaughran* (Boucicault), National Theatre, London.
Cat on a Hot Tin Roof (T. Williams), National Theatre, London.
The Changeling (Middleton), National Theatre, London.
Bartholomew Fair (Jonson), National Theatre, London.

1989   *Un ballo in maschera* (Verdi), Salzburg Festival.

1990   *The Crucible* (Miller), National Theatre, London.
Etta Jenks (Meyer), Royal Court Theatre, London.
The Cunning Little Vixen (Janáček), Royal Opera House, Covent Garden, London.
The Ship (Bryden), Clydeside, Glasgow.

1991   *The Coup* (Matura), National Theatre, London.
Idomeneo (Mozart), Welsh National Opera, Cardiff.

1992   *Pygmalion* (Shaw), National Theatre, London.
Heartbreak House (Shaw), Haymarket Theatre, London.

1993   *On the Ledge* (Bleasdale), National Theatre, London.
The Deep Blue Sea (Rattigan), Almeida Theatre, London.

* * *

William Dudley's initial contributions as a designer tended toward a spare, undecorative, Brechtian style but his creative instincts subsequently revealed a hunger for a richer, neo-Romantic expressiveness. Now in his third decade as a major British designer with international credits, he still creates on a spectrum that ranges from work with minimal means in unconventional theatre spaces for a popular audience to elaborate spectacles in opera houses and other traditional venues for more sophisticated audiences.

While completing studies in landscape painting and, later, stage design at art school in the late 1960's, Dudley gained his first practical experience with amateur fringe theatre in the London area. His first extended association as a professional stage designer was in the first half of the 1970's with London's Royal Court Theatre, which specialized in new English plays (including works by Osborne, Wesker, and Gill) in unadorned realistic productions that represented, according to Dudley, "an English attitude toward a Brecht attitude". Jocelyn Herbert, the Royal Court's chief designer, exemplified this manner, and Dudley inevitably came under its influence as, earlier, he had admired work in a similar vein by the US painter Edward Hopper. In Dudley's stage designs these influences took the form of work that was stripped down and bare, "but what remained was to have strong echoes, be romantic, very humane, not harsh." Eventually Dudley came to feel restricted by the Royal Court approach and sought outlets for fuller expression on a grander scale, which he found primarily in opera. For *Billy Budd* at the Met in the late 1970's, he created the effect of a floating wooden city by constructing the frontal cross section of a sailing ship, which revealed its multiple decks as it rose or sank on hydraulic lifts. In the early 1980's, his *Tales of Hoffman* at Covent Garden displayed him at his most romantic: he saw the work not as a lightweight amusement but as full of mystery and strangeness, a blend of Victor Hugo grandness and Edgar Allan Poe fantasy, or as if Fellini were to film Dickens. It was the complete opposite of Royal Court spareness.

Dudley speaks of his basic approach to stage designing as being that of a landscape painter, by which he means that he is primarily concerned with establishing the proper 'landscape' or stage world inhabited by the characters. Usually this depends on the author's text, but sometimes the landscape may be determined by a production concept or by the special characteristics of a specific production space. Dudley's interest in popular entertainment, for example, includes street theatre, a form that he has employed in several productions both indoors and outdoors. With director Bill Bryden, he developed in the late 1970's a series of three plays, *The Passion* (based on the York medieval cycle plays), that traced the biblical story of humanity from the creation to doomsday as if it were being performed by the artisans and merchants of today rather than of the middle ages. Usual theatrical scenery was abolished and the performances took place as if on a street, in a space shared by the spectators, a form of staging often called 'promenade performance'. The properties and costumes used reflected the contemporary world; Noah and his wife were lifted in a mechanical scoop, mobile warehouse storage stacking equipment shunted objects around

or elevated the Christ figure toward heaven, and characters wore hardhats with functional flashlights attached. A variation of this approach was explored in *Lark Rise*, which traced one day's life in rural England, the movement of the sun being suggested by the light shifting from one spotlight to another hung above a gauze ceiling suspended over the long axis of the playing space shared by the audience. For Dudley, these production spaces were but other landscapes.

Street or promenade theatre has formed one of the two main streams of Dudley's work from the late 1970's to the present. The other has been his work on the grand scale, culminating in his 1983 production of Wagner's *Ring* at Bayreuth. In this he employed kinetic staging in the form of a 50 by 30 feet rectangular platform with a convex and concave surface. The platform could be tumbled, rotated, and lifted to a height of 30 feet. Essentially, Dudley wanted to suggest the idea of mountains not in the form of pointed peaks but "high, godlike plateaus". The platform also served other functions, such as that of a ceiling or gently sloping forest terrain, depending on the treatment of its surface and the presence of other scenic elements such as tress. The overall intent, developed in conjunction with director Peter Hall, was the creation of "a lyrical landscape, an exploration of nature, not painted but very physical, three dimensional: a pre-Raphaelite, romantic voyage of expression."

Dudley's interest in larger scale, more technical work increased in the late 1980's, along with his interest in forms of popular theatre, which he associates with more overt spectacle in staging. Several recent productions have embodied this special fascination with "visual language", as he puts it. For *A Midsummer Night's Dream* for the RSC, he created a storybook, magical, larger than life forest dominated by a huge cobweb of stainless steel cable on which actors, especially Puck, could scamper.

The Shaughran, a 19th-century romantic melodrama by Dion Boucicault, required a great many scenic locations, a challenge Dudley met by employing a previously unused high-tech turntable in the National Theatre. Half of the huge cylinder that formed the turntable could descend and ascend while turning, thus not only shifting locales by rotating the turntable but also enabling changes of scenery below the stage while another scene was playing at stage level.

Dudley's attraction to popular entertainment found natural resonance in a version of Jonson's *Bartholomew Fair*, updated to the turn of the century Victorian funfairs with their highly decorated, colourful, ingeniously mechanical carousels. The main attraction of the set were three turntable units plus a moveable funfair steam organ. All these pieces could also move together on the underlying turntable that supported them.

Despite his recent involvement with more elaborate productions, Dudley wishes to avoid pigeonholes, to do the widest range of things. He sees in street theatre "a thinking man's popular theatre, and a marvellous antidote to grand opera", but he is also disturbed by any critic's dismissal of more richly expressive scenography as mere spectacle, "as though Turner or Rembrandt were mere spectacle".

—Jarka M. Burian

DULLIN, Charles. French actor and director. Born in Yenne, Savoy, 12 May 1885. Educated at the Seminary de Pont-de-Beauvoisin, 1895–98; trained as an actor at the Lyon Conservatoire. Married actress Marcelle Jeanniot (known as Francine Mars) in 1919. Early stage experience as an amateur in Paris; professional stage debut, Paris, 1906; subsequently acted under Jacques Copeau at the Théâtre du Vieux-Colombier, Paris, from 1913; accompanied Copeau to the USA, 1917–19; returned to Paris and joined Firmin Gémier's company, 1919; founder and director, Théâtre de l'Atelier, Paris, 1921; pupils at his Atelier theatre school included Jean-Louis Barrault and Roger Blin; founder-member of the Cartel des Quatre, 1927; director, Comédie-Française, Paris, 1937–39; compiled report anticipating the development of the decentralisation movement, 1938; director, Théâtre Sarah Bernhardt, renamed the Théâtre de la Cité under the German Occupation, 1940–47. Died in Paris, 11 December 1949.

Productions

As actor:

1906   Vieux Rao in *Les Aventures du capitaine Corcoran*, Belville, Paris.
        Javert in *Les Misérables* (Hugo), Paris.

1910   Masurel in *Le Carnaval des enfants* (Bouhélier), Théâtre des Arts, Paris.
        Smerdiakov in *Les Frères Karamazov* (Copeau and Croué), Théâtre des Arts, Paris.

1911   Finet in *Le Pain* (Ghéon), Théâtre des Arts, Paris.

1913   Des Fonandrès in *L'Amour médecin* (Molière), Théâtre du Vieux-Colombier, Paris.
        Nicolas in *Une Femme tuée par le douceur* (Heywood, adapted by Copeau and Croué), Théâtre du Vieux-Colombier, Paris.
        Polacco in *Barberine* (Musset), Théâtre du Vieux-Colombier, Paris.
        Harpagon in *L'Avare* (Molière), Théâtre du Vieux-Colombier, Paris.

1914   Fossard in *L'Eau de vie* (Ghéon), Théâtre du Vieux-Colombier, Paris.
        Louis Laine in *L'Échange* (Claudel), Théâtre du Vieux-Colombier, Paris.

1918   Role in *Rosmersholm* (Ibsen), Garrick Theatre, New York.

1919   Marchand d'ombres in *Le Grande Pastorale* (Hellem and D'Estoc), Cirque d'Hiver, Paris.

1920   Soldier in *Les Esclaves* (Bouhélier), Théâtre des Arts, Paris.

1920–21 Harpagon in *L'Avare* (Molière), Comédie des Champs-Élysées, Paris.
        Profeta in *Simoun* (Lenormand), Comédie des Champs-Élysées, Paris.
        The Baron in *Les Amants puérils* (Crommelynck), Comédie des Champs-Élysées, Paris.
        J. Hury in *L'Annonce faite à Marie* (Claudel), Comédie des Champs-Élysées, Paris.

Also acted roles in: *Don César de Bazan* (Dumanoir and d'Ennery), Paris, 1906; *Le Courier de Lyon* (Moreau, Siraudin, and Delacour), Paris, 1906; *La Porteuse de pain*, Paris, 1906; *L'Éventail de Lady Windermere* (Wilde),

Théâtre des Arts, Paris, 1909; *Oeuvre posthume* (Mortier), Théâtre des Arts, Paris, 1909; *L'Esprit soutterain* (Lenormand), Grand Guignol, Paris, 1912; *Gringoire* (Bonneville), Garrick Theatre, New York, 1918.

As director:

1912   *Marie-Madeleine* (Hebbel), Théâtre des Arts, Paris.

1921–22 *Une Parade de Gueulette*, Château Landon, Paris, and Salle Pasdeloup, Paris.
        Le Divorce (Regnard), Château Landon, Paris, and Salle Pasdeloup, Paris.
        Les Boulingrins (Courteline), Château Landon, Paris, and Salle Pasdeloup, Paris.
        La Vie est un songe (Calderón), Salle Pasdeloup, Paris.
        L'Hotellerie (Cervantes), Salle Pasdeloup, Paris.
        Visites de condoléances (Calderón), Salle Pasdeloup, Paris.
        Les Olives (Lope de Rueda), Salle Pasdeloup, Paris.
        L'Occasion (Mérimée), Salle Pasdeloup, Paris.
        L'Avare (Molière), Salle Pasdeloup, Paris.
        Monsieur Sardony (Berubet), Salle de la Rue des Ursulines, Paris.
        Chantage (Jacob), Salle de la Rue des Ursulines, Paris.
        Moriana et Galvan (Arnoux), Salle de la Rue des Ursulines, Paris.
        La Vie est un songe (Calderón), Théâtre du Vieux-Colombier, Paris.
        L'Avare (Molière), Théâtre du Vieux-Colombier, Paris.
        Le Testament du père Leleu (Du Gard), Château Landon.
        Arlequin poli par l'amour (Marivaux), Château Landon.

1922   *La Vie est un songe* (Candlerón), Théâtre Montmartre, Paris.
        Carmosine (Musset), Théâtre Montmartre, Paris.
        La Mort de Souper (Chesnaye), Théâtre Montmartre, Paris.
        La Volupté de l'honneur (Pirandello), Théâtre Montmartre, Paris.
        Antigone (Sophocles), Théâtre Montmartre, Paris.

1923   *Monsieur de Pygmalion* (Gran), Théâtre Montmartre, Paris.
        Huon de Bordeaux (Arnoux), Théâtre Montmartre, Paris.
        La Promenade du prisonnier (Blanchon), Théâtre Montmartre, Paris.
        Celui qui vivait sa mort (Achard), Théâtre Montmartre, Paris.
        Cyprien ou l'amour à 18 ans (Pillement), Théâtre de l'Atelier, Paris.
        Mais un ange intervint (Dell), Théâtre de l'Atelier, Paris.
        Parade (Achard), Théâtre de l'Atelier, Paris.
        Les Risques de la vertu (Priel), Théâtre de l'Atelier, Paris.

Le Chevalier sans nom (Variot), Théâtre de l'Atelier, Paris.

Voulez-vous jouer avec moâ? (Achard), Théâtre de l'Atelier, Paris.

L'Homme rouge (Carriere), Théâtre de l'Atelier, Paris.

Pour vous dire je vous aime (Achard), Théâtre de l'Atelier, Paris.

Mentons bleus (Courteline and Bonaud), Théâtre de l'Atelier, Paris.

1924   *L'Eventail* (Goldoni), Théâtre de l'Atelier, Paris.

Le Veau gras (Zimmer), Théâtre de l'Atelier, Paris.

Petite Lumière et l'Ourse (Arnoux), Théâtre de l'Atelier, Paris.

Chacun sa vérité (Pirandello), Théâtre de l'Atelier, Paris.

Un imbécile (Pirandello), Théâtre de l'Atelier, Paris.

1925   *Les Zouaves* (Zimmer), Théâtre de l'Atelier, Paris.

Corilla (Nerval), Théâtre de l'Atelier, Paris.

La Révolte (Villiers de L'Isle Adam), Théâtre de l'Atelier, Paris.

George Dandin ou le mari confondu (Molière), Théâtre de l'Atelier, Paris.

Le Dieu de vengeance (Asch), Théâtre de l'Atelier, Paris.

La Lame sourde (Neis), Théâtre de l'Atelier, Paris.

Les Serments d'usage (Jonson), Théâtre de l'Atelier, Paris.

1926   *Irma* (Ferdinand), Théâtre de l'Atelier, Paris.

Je ne vous aime pas (Achard), Théâtre de l'Atelier, Paris.

Il faut qu'une porte soit ouverte ou fermée (Musset), Théâtre de l'Atelier, Paris.

Tout pour le mieux (Pirandello), Théâtre de l'Atelier, Paris.

La Grande Pénitence (Regis and Veynes), Théâtre de l'Atelier, Paris.

Chagrins d'amour (Regis and Veynes), Théâtre de l'Atelier, Paris.

La Comédie du bonheur (Evreinov), Théâtre de l'Atelier, Paris.

1927   *Hara-Kiri* (Blanchon), Théâtre de l'Atelier, Paris.

Pas encore (Passeur), Théâtre de l'Atelier, Paris.

Le Joueur d'échecs (Achard), Théâtre de l'Atelier, Paris.

La Vie est un songe (Calderón), Théâtre de l'Atelier, Paris.

La Volupté de l'honneur (Pirandello), Théâtre de l'Atelier, Paris.

Chacun sa vérité (Pirandello), Théâtre de l'Atelier, Paris.

Le Veau gras (Zimmer), Théâtre de l'Atelier, Paris.

La Danse de vie (Ould), Théâtre de l'Atelier, Paris.

1928   *Les Oiseaux* (Aristophanes), Théâtre de l'Atelier, Paris.

A quoi penses-tu? (Passeur), Théâtre de l'Atelier, Paris.

Volpone (Jonson, adapted by Romains), Théâtre de l'Atelier, Paris; acted Volpone.

1929   *L'Admirable visite* (Rouleau), Théâtre de l'Atelier, Paris.

Bilora (Ruzzante), Théâtre de l'Atelier, Paris.

1930   *Patchouli ou Les désordres de l'amour* (Salacrou), Théâtre de l'Atelier, Paris.

Le Stratagème des roués (Farquhar), Théâtre de l'Atelier, Paris.

Volpone (Jonson), Théâtre de l'Atelier, Paris.

Le Fils de Don Quichotte (Frondaie), Théâtre de l'Atelier, Paris.

Musse ou l'école de l'hypocrisie (Romains), Théâtre de l'Atelier, Paris.

1931   *La Quadrature du cercle* (Kataev), Théâtre de l'Atelier, Paris.

Fraternité (Fleuret and Girard), Théâtre de l'Atelier, Paris.

Atlas-Hôtel (Salacrou), Théâtre de l'Atelier, Paris.

Tzar Lénine (Porche), Théâtre de l'Atelier, Paris.

Village (Richaud), Théâtre de l'Atelier, Paris.

Musse ou l'école de l'hypocrisie (Romains), Théâtre de l'Atelier, Paris.

1932   *L'Ombre* (Sans), Théâtre de l'Atelier, Paris.

Les Tricheures (Passeur), Théâtre de l'Atelier, Paris.

La Comédie du bonheur (Evreinov), Théâtre de l'Atelier, Paris.

La Volupté de l'honneur (Pirandello), Théâtre de l'Atelier, Paris.

Le Château des Papes (Richaud), Théâtre de l'Atelier, Paris.

Cyprien ou l'amour à 18 ans (Pillement), Théâtre de l'Atelier, Paris.

La Paix (Aristophanes), Théâtre de l'Atelier, Paris.

Volpone (Jonson), Théâtre de l'Atelier, Paris.

1933   *Richard III* (Shakespeare, adapted by Obey), Théâtre de l'Atelier, Paris; acted Richard.

1934   *Les Coqs* (Klein), Théâtre de l'Atelier, Paris.

Dommage qu'elle soit une prostituée (Ford), Théâtre de l'Atelier, Paris.

1935   *Le Médecin de son honneur* (Calderón), Théâtre de l'Atelier, Paris.

Le Misanthrope et l'Auvergnat (Labiche), Théâtre de l'Atelier, Paris.

Le Méchant (Grasset), Théâtre de l'Atelier, Paris.

Mercadet ou Le Faiseur (Balzac), Théâtre de l'Atelier, Paris.

1936   *Le Camelot* (Vitrac), Théâtre de l'Atelier, Paris.

1937   *Jules César* (Shakespeare), Théâtre de l'Atelier, Paris.

Plutus (Aristophanes), Théâtre de l'Atelier, Paris.

1938   *La Terre est ronde* (Salacrou), Théâtre de l'Atelier, Paris.

Le Mariage de Figaro (Beaumarchais), Comédie-Française, Paris.

1939	*Richard III* (Shakespeare), Comédie-Française, Paris.
	Médée (Milhaud), Théâtre de l'Opéra, Paris.
1940	*Plutus* (Aristophanes), Théâtre de Paris.
	Le Ciel et l'Enfer (Mérimée), Théâtre de Paris.
	L'Avare (Molière), Théâtre de Paris.
1941	*Mamouret* (Sarment), Théâtre de Paris.
1942	*La Princesse des Ursins* (Jollivet), Théâtre de la Cité, Paris.
	La Volupté de l'honneur (Pirandello), Théâtre de la Cité, Paris.
	Le Misanthrope et l'Auvergnat (Labiche), Théâtre de la Cité, Paris.
	Les Amants de Galice (Lope de Vega), Théâtre de la Cité, Paris.
	Crainquebille (France), Théâtre de la Cité, Paris.
	La Matrone d'Ephèse (Morand), Théâtre de la Cité, Paris.
	Richard III (Shakespeare), Théâtre de la Cité, Paris.
	Mamouret (Sarment), Théâtre de la Cité, Paris.
1943	*Les Mouches* (Sartre), Théâtre de la Cité, Paris.
	Monsieur de Pourceaugnac (Molière), Théâtre de la Cité, Paris.
	Le Gendarme est sans pitié (Courteline), Théâtre de la Cité, Paris.
	La Vie est un songe (Calderón), Théâtre de la Cité, Paris.
1944	*Maurin des Maures* (Dumas), Théâtre de la Cité, Paris.
	Volpone (Jonson), Théâtre de la Cité, Paris.
1945	*Le Roi Lear* (Shakespeare), Théâtre de la Cité, Paris.
	Mercadet ou Le Faiseur (Balzac), Théâtre de la Cité, Paris.
1946	*Le Soldat et la sorcière* (Salacrou), Théâtre de la Cité, Paris.
	La Vie est un songe (Calderón), Théâtre de la Cité, Paris.
	La Terre est ronde (Salacrou), Théâtre de la Cité, Paris.
1947	*L'An mil* (Romains), Théâtre de la Cité, Paris.
	Cinna (Corneille), Théâtre de la Cité, Paris.
1948–49	*L'Archipel Lenoir* (Salacrou), Théâtre Montparnasse, Paris, tour, and Théâtre de Paris.
1949–50	*La Marâtre* (Balzac), Théâtre des Célestins, Lyon.
	L'Avare (Molière), French tour.

Films

Le Secret de Rosette Lambert, 1920; *L'Homme qui vendit son âme au diable*, 1921; *Les Trois Mousquetaires*, 1921; *Le Miracle des loups*, 1924; *Le Joueur d'échecs*, 1927; *Maldone*, 1927; *Cagliostro*, 1929; *Les Misérables*, 1933; *Mademoiselle Docteur*, 1937; *Volpone*, 1939; *Le Brieur de chaînes*, 1942; *Quai des Orfèvres*, 1947; *Les Jeux sont faits*, 1947.

Publications

Souvenirs et notes de travail d'un acteur, 1946; *L'Avare*, 1946; *Cinna*, 1948; *Ce sont les Dieux qu'il nous faut*, 1969.

*

Bibliography

Books:
Jean Sarment, *Charles Dullin*, Paris, 1950.
Alexandre Arnoux, *Charles Dullin — portrait brisé*, Paris, 1951.
Lucien Arnaud, *Charles Dullin*, Paris, 1952.
Pauline Teillon-Dullin and Charles Charras, *Charles Dullin ou les ensorcelés du Châtelard*, Paris, 1955.
Monique Surel-Tupin, *Charles Dullin*, Louvain, 1985.

* * *

Like his master, Jacques Copeau, and his colleagues of the Cartel des Quatre, Charles Dullin was a highly idiosyncratic actor and director. Like them, he used to declare that he was nothing but a modest interpreter of the author's voice. More than any of his contemporaries he reintroduced the idea of play and playfulness into the theatre. He espoused Evreinov's notion of "retheatricalizing the theatre" and he opened the French stage to foreign influences, mainly to the commedia dell'arte and, long before it became fashionable, to Far Eastern traditions like Noh and Kabuki.

Dullin's activities as director and teacher are intimately linked. It was not enough for him to create his own theatre; he was resolved to reform the art of the actor and, to that end, he needed to mould the future members of his company. In a manifesto (August 1921) he declared that "the Atelier is not a theatrical enterprise, but a laboratory of dramatic experimentation". The true art of the theatre, he added, shuns the amateur, the dilettante as well as the ham actor. He hoped for a "spiritual direction" in the theatre, away from all financial considerations, and for total commitment on the part of his students and actors. He identified the Conservatoire, the illustrious school of the Comédie-Française, as the source of all evils: there teachers produced (inadequate) clones of themselves and fostered a star mentality. The Atelier, in contrast, encouraged the student to find his own way and, always, to strive for total sincerity. In his teaching Dullin referred frequently to the soul and the inner life (of characters and interpreters). "Instead of working on the text, we work on the feelings", he used to say. If he suspected that an actor was faking an emotion, he would interrupt with a reproachful "You're cheating, love". Although he insisted that actors should be well-educated and informed, he stressed the prime importance of physical action, since the greatest theatrical masterpieces are not "literary" works, but "poetry in action".

For Dullin, improvisation was the best method to shape the student's personality as it forced him to find his inspiration and his means of expression in himself. Collective improvisation, based on everyday situations or events suggested by dramatic texts, led towards fluid exchanges between actors and the creation of an ensemble (as Antoine had called for in the 1880's and Brecht was to create at the

Berliner Ensemble in the 1940's). Exercises with full or half masks, derived from commedia and Japanese traditions, helped students towards a certain depersonalization, greater objectivity, and an extension of their powers of imagination.

Throughout his career, Dullin promoted new writing, since "the strength of western theatre is its dramatic literature". Yet he joined the chorus of modern directors in lamenting the absence of new playwrights. He took great risks in staging the first plays of young playwrights, the most memorable being Sartre's *Les Mouches* (*The Flies*) in 1943, during the German Occupation of Paris. He had a few successes with contemporary authors (Achard's *Voulez-vous jouer avec moá?*, Passeur's *Les Tricheurs*, Salacrou's *Patchouli* and *L'Archipel Lenoir*), but most have sunk without trace. Like Jouvet, he scored his greatest triumphs with classics: Shakespeare's *Richard III*, Molière's *L'Avare* (*The Miser*), and, above all, Jonson's *Volpone*, a money-spinner that he revived every time his hand-to-mouth existence became truly unbearable. Dullin is also remembered for introducing to the French stage Calderón (*Le Médecin de son honneur*), Evreinov (*La Comédie du bonheur*), and Pirandello (*La Volupté de l'honneur* and *Chacun sa vérité*). He acted in a handful of films only, which is a great pity as he was a very powerful and inspirational performer. In 1929 he turned down Fritz Lang's offer of five million francs to go to Hollywood, as acting could never be for him a mere business.

Music and lights played a central role in all Dullin's productions. For a truly satisfying experience in the theatre all senses must be stimulated, he said. He associated composers and musicians with his work on new plays from the very beginning to ensure that music would be perfectly integrated, not merely a pleasant background or a distraction during scene changes. Music had to create powerful atmospheres, participate to highly charged or intimate moments, and increase the impact of silence. Dullin experimented with recordings and special effects to expand the expressive range of sound and music. He designed lighting plots like a composer writes a musical score and was closer in his aesthetic conceptions to Robert Wilson than to his contemporaries.

Dullin believed passionately in the educational virtue of theatre. In 1938 the French government entrusted him with the task of conducting a feasibility study on the question of "decentralization": how could theatre be promoted in the provinces? Dullin's response was prophetic. He suggested dividing France into zones, and each zone (or region) would get its theatre, company, director, designer, and so on, and, naturally, an adequate state subsidy. If nothing came of the plan before the war, the post-war government, under the impulse of Jeanne Laurent, responsible for theatres in the Ministry of Culture, started to implement it with the creation of "centres dramatique" across France. After the war, Dullin, Jean-Louis Barrault, and Pierre Dux (director of the Comédie-Française, 1970–79) founded the CID (Culture par l'Initiation Dramatique), a short-lived association whose aim was to attract a new public to the theatre in order to educate it. Finally, in 1947, Dullin was appointed to two commissions: one to distribute subventions to Parisian theatres, the other to help the most promising young playwrights.

Dullin's pupils and younger collaborators took charge and shaped the immediate post-war theatre in France, and

their influence is felt to this day. They were Antonin Artaud, Jean-Louis Barrault, Alain Cuny, Madeleine Renaud, Michel Saint-Denis, and Jean Vilar. The Théâtre du Soleil and the many experimental companies working at the Cartoucherie de Vincennes, on the outskirts of Paris, share the ethic and aesthetic values of Dullin and continue his work.

—Claude Schumacher

---

du MAURIER, (Sir) Gerald (Hubert Edward). British actor-manager. Born in Hampstead, London, 26 March 1873; son of writer and artist George du Maurier. Educated at Harrow public school, Berkshire. Married Muriel Beaumont in 1903; three daughters (including novelist Daphne du Maurier). Stage debut, Garrick Theatre, London, 1894; toured with Johnson Forbes-Robertson, 1895; actor, Beerbohm Tree's company, from 1895; toured USA, 1896; acclaimed in plays by J. M. Barrie and, from 1902, in the role of Raffles; co-manager, with Frank Curzon, Wyndham's Theatre, London, 1910–25; served as Cadet in the Irish Guards, 1918; co-manager, with Gilbert Miller, St James's Theatre, London, 1925–29. Member: Actors' Orphanage Fund, 1914 (president); Denville Hall for aged actors and actresses, 1928 (president); Actors' Benevolent Fund, 1931 (president). Knighted, 1922. Died in London, 11 April 1934.

Roles

1894   Fritz in *An Old Jew* (Grundy), Garrick Theatre, London.
1895   Dodor in *Trilby* (George du Maurier), Haymarket Theatre, London; US tour, 1896.
1896   Gadshill in *Henry IV, part 1* (Shakespeare), Haymarket Theatre, London; US tour, 1896.
1897   Lieutenant Ferney in *The Seats of the Mighty* (Parker), Her Majesty's Theatre, London.
            Chamillac in *The Silver Key* (Grundy), Her Majesty's Theatre, London.
            Count Bohrenheim in *The Red Lamp* (Tristram), Her Majesty's Theatre, London.
            Ricordot in *A Man's Shadow* (Buchanan), Her Majesty's Theatre, London.
1900–01   Percy Burlingham in *The Canary* (Fleming), Royalty Theatre, London.
            Strephonal in *The Fantasticks* (Fleming), Royalty Theatre, London.
            Ashurst in *Mr and Mrs Daventry* (Harris), Royalty Theatre, London.
            Sir Sandford Cleeve in *The Notorious Mrs Ebbsmith* (Pinero), Royalty Theatre, London.
            Captain Hugh Ardale in *The Second Mrs Tanquerary* (Pinero), Royalty Theatre, London.
1902   Hon. Archibald Vyse in *A Country Mouse* (Law), Prince of Wales's Theatre, London.

Hon. Ernest Woolley in *The Admirable Crichton* (Barrie), Duke of York's Theatre, London; Duke of York's Theatre, London, 1908; Coliseum Theatre, London, and London Opera House, 1916.

1903   Lord Rolfe in *Little Mary* (Barrie), Wyndham's Theatre, London.

1904   Albert Jerrold in *Cynthia* (Newmarch), Wyndham's Theatre, London.

Peter in *Merely Mary Ann* (Zangwill), Duke of York's Theatre, London.

Captain Hook and Mr Darling in *Peter Pan* (Barrie), Duke of York's Theatre, London; revived there, 1905 and 1906; St James's Theatre, London, 1929.

1905   Pantaloon in *Pantaloon* (Barrie), Duke of York's Theatre, London.

Arthur Frederick Adolphus Taunton in *On the Love Path* (McLellan), Haymarket Theatre, London.

1906   Hon. Jimmy Keppel in *All-of-a-Sudden Peggy* (Denny), Duke of York's Theatre, London.

A. J. Raffles in *Raffles* (Presberg and Hornung), Comedy Theatre, London; Wyndham's Theatre, London, 1914.

1907   Montgommery Brewster in *Brewster's Millions* (McCuthcheon, Smith, and Ongley), Hicks Theatre, London.

1908   John Shand in *What Every Woman Knows* (Barrie), Duke of York's Theatre, London.

1909   Duc de Charmerace in *Arsène Lupin* (adapted from the French), Duke of York's Theatre, London.

1910   Lee Randall in *Alias Jimmy Valentine* (Armstrong), Comedy Theatre, London.

Mr Hyphen-Brown in *A Slice of Life* (Barrie), Duke of York's Theatre, London.

John Frampton in *Nobody's Daughter* (Paston), Wyndham's Theatre, London.

1911   Charles Lebrun in *Mrs Jarvis*, Wyndham's Theatre, London.

Peter Waverton in *Passers-By* (Chambers), Wyndham's Theatre, London.

The Governor of Tilbury Fort in *The Critic* (Sheridan), His Majesty's Theatre, London.

Thomas Pelling in *The Perplexed Husband* (Sutro), Wyndham's Theatre, London.

1912   Sam Weller in *Bardell v. Pickwick* (Hollingshead), Coliseum Theatre, London.

Geoffrey Lascelles in *The Dust of Egypt*, Wyndham's Theatre, London.

Richard Jelf in *Jelf's* (Vachell), Wyndham's Theatre, London.

Noel in *Doormats* (Davies), Wyndham's Theatre, London.

1913   Henry Beauclerc in *Diplomacy* (Stephenson and Scott), Wyndham's Theatre, London; Widsor Castle, 1914.

1914   Wilfred Callender in *The Clever Ones* (Sutro), Wyndham's Theatre, London.

Henry Corkett in *The Silver King* (H. A. Jones and H. Herman), His Majesty's Theatre, London.

Geoffrey in *Outcast* (Davies), Wyndham's Theatre, London.

Charles Sullivan in *A Quiet Rubber* (Coghlan), Theatre Royal, Drury Lane, London.

1915   Harold Tempest in *Gamblers All* (Martindale), Wyndham's Theatre, London.

Lord Sands in *Henry VIII* (Shakespeare), His Majesty's Theatre, London.

Sir Hubert Ware in *The Ware Case* (Pleydell), Wyndham's Theatre, London; Adelphi Theatre, London, and Wyndham's Theatre, London, 1924; British tour, 1931.

1916   Our Policeman and A Prince in *A Kiss for Cinderella* (Barrie), Wyndham's Theatre, London.

Mr Bantry in *Shakespeare's Legacy* (Barrie), Theatre Royal, Drury Lane, London.

James Lane Fountain in *The Old Country* (Calthrop), Wyndham's Theatre, London.

1917   Cuthbert Tunks in *London Pride* (Unger and Lyons), Wyndham's Theatre, London.

Harry Larcomb in *The Passing of the Third-Floor-Back* (Jerome), Coliseum Theatre, London.

Dick in *A Pair of Spectacles* (Grundy), Haymarket Theatre, London, and Wyndham's Theatre, London.

Ferdinand Gadd in *Trelawney of the Wells* (Pinero), New Theatre, London.

Mr Dearth in *Dear Brutus* (Barrie), Wyndham's Theatre, London; Wyndham's Theatre, London, 1922; Playhouse Theatre, London, 1929.

1918   Another in *A Well-Remembered Voice* (Barrie), Wyndham's Theatre, London.

1919   John Ingleby Cordways in *The Choice* (Sutro), Wyndham's Theatre, London.

1920   Captain André Le Briquet in *The Prude's Fall* (Besier and Edginton), Wyndham's Theatre, London.

1921   Captain Hugh Drummond in *Dull-Dog Drummond* (Gerald du Maurier and 'Sapper'), Wyndham's Theatre, London; revived there, 1922; Adelphi Theatre, London, 1932.

1923   Tony and the Earl of Chievely in *The Dancers* (Gerald du Maurier and V. Tree), Wyndham's Theatre, London.

1924   Felix Menzies in *Not in Our Stars* (Massingham, adapted from Maurice), Wyndham's Theatre, London.

Prince Michael in *To Have the Honour* (Milne), Wyndham's Theatre, London.

1925   Wilberforce East in *A Man With a Heart* (Sutro), Wyndham's Theatre, London.

Lord Arthur Dilling in *The Last of Mrs Cheyney* (Lonsdale), St James's Theatre, London.

1927   Sir John Marley in *Interference* (Pertwee and Dearden), St James's Theatre, London.

1928   Owen Heriot in *S.O.S.* (Ellis), St James's Theatre, London.

Dr Henry Fausting in *The Return Journey* (Bennett), St James's Theatre, London.

Sandor Turai in *The Play's the Thing* (Molnár), St James's Theatre, London.

1929   Paolo Gheradi in *Fame* (Carten), St James's Theatre, London.
1930   Jim Warlock in *Cynara* (Harwood and Browne), Playhouse Theatre, London.
1931   Paul Lauzun in *The Pelican* (Tennyson and Harwood), Playhouse Theatre, London.
   Baron Thomas Ullrich in *The Church Mouse* (Levy), Playhouse Theatre, London.
1932   Larry Deans in *The Green Pack* (Wallace), Wyndham's Theatre, London.
   Gordon Evers in *Behold, We Live* (Van Druten), St James's Theatre, London.

Also acted roles in: *Mrs Lessingham* (Fleming), Garrick Theatre, London, 1894; *Money* (Bulwer-Lytton), Garrick Theatre, London, 1894; *Slaves of the Ring* (Garrick), Garrick Theatre, London, 1894; *The Notorious Mrs Ebbsmith* (Pinero), Garrick Theatre, London, 1895; *A Pair of Spectacles* (Grundy), Garrick Theatre, London, 1895; *The Profligate* (Pinero), British tour, 1895; *Diplomacy* (Stephenson and Scott), British tour, 1895; *The Dancing Girl* (H. A. Jones), US tour, 1896; *Hamlet* (Shakespeare), US tour, 1896; *The Seats of the Mighty* (Parker), US tour, 1896; *The Red Lamp* (Tristram), US tour, 1896; *Ragged Robin* (Parker), Her Majesty's Theatre, London, 1897; *Carnac Sahib* (H. A. Jones), Her Majesty's Theatre, London, 1897; *An Interrupted Honeymoon* (Peile), Avenue Theatre, London, 1898–99; *The Fatal Typist* (Barrie), His Majesty's Theatre, London, 1915; *The Popular Novelist*, Palace Theatre, London, 1916.

Films

Escape, 1931; *Lord Camber's Ladies*, 1932.

Publications

A Royal Rival (play, adapted from *Don César de Bazan*), 1901; *An Englishman's Home*, with Guy du Maurier and J. M. Barrie, 1909; *The Dancers: The Beginning and the End of the Story in the Play*, with Viola Tree, 1923; *Bull-Dog Drummond* (play), with 'Sapper', 1925.

*

Bibliography

Books:
Daphne du Maurier, *Gerald: A Portrait*, London, 1934.
C. C. Hoyer Millar, *George du Maurier and Others*, London, 1937.
James Harding, *Gerald du Maurier*, London, 1989.

* * *

In *Gerald*, her affectionate biography of her father Gerald du Maurier, Daphne du Maurier recalls what a deep impression he made as Captain Hook in the premiere of J. M. Barrie's *Peter Pan* in 1904. "When Hook first paced his quarter-deck ... children were carried screaming from the stalls ... How he was hated, with his flourish, his poses, his dreaded diabolical smile! That ashen face, those blood-red lips, the long, dank, greasy curls; the sardonic laugh, the maniacal scream, the appalling courtesy of his gestures; and that above all most terrible of moments when he descended the stairs and with slow, most merciless cunning poured the poison into Peter's glass". Barrie had reason to be grateful to Gerald du Maurier for all he did to launch what has become a classic children's drama, and the youngsters themselves plainly had a great thrill. Their parents, however, especially if they were regular London theatregoers, would have enjoyed the performance all the more because they could appreciate that the role had been cast against type. Gerald du Maurier could plaster his face with make-up, put on a wig, and dress up in a period pirate costume; he could rant and rave, sawing the air with grand gestures, striding about with an air of authority and making the audience's flesh creep as he embarked on his next devilish deed. But that was not his usual style. Mr Darling, which he also played at the premiere of *Peter Pan*, was much more in his line.

As was officially acknowledged by his knighthood in 1895, Henry Irving was the leader of the acting profession at the time when the young du Maurier entered it after leaving Harrow. From a background more cultured and better off than many and with a better education than most actors, du Maurier did not choose to compete with the titans of the Victorian stage. Indeed, his Hook can be seen as an ironic comment on their style, for du Maurier appears to have been suggesting that the impersonation of larger than life-size extraordinary characters with every device of theatrical illusion and rhetorical extravagance was really old-fashioned fustian that may still work with children but by then, in the Edwardian period, needed to be replaced by something far less stagey if it was to appeal to an intelligent public. His attitude is summed up in a comment, recorded by Raymond Massey in *A Hundred Different Lives*, that sets up an even longer historical perspective: "I couldn't do some of the plays — realistic plays like *Alias Jimmy Valentine*, *Raffles* ... — in that declamatory style which everybody had been using since David Garrick. I had to find another way".

Du Maurier did not smother his features with thick make-up as if to hide himself in impenetrable disguise, but preferred to allow audiences to perceive his own personality within the roles he played. Costume drama, the great stand-by of the previous generation, had little appeal to an actor who found success in plays set in his own time and felt no obligation to scale the heights of Shakespeare. Another quotation from Daphne du Maurier is very revealing about the naturalness he aimed at, the understatement and the abhorrence of gross histrionic effects. He considered extravagant displays of affection on stage 'very bad theatre'. "Must you kiss her as though you were having steak and onions for lunch?" he would say. "It may be what you feel, but it's damned unattractive from the front row of the stalls. Can't you just say 'I love you', and yawn, and light a cigarette, and walk away?"

Du Maurier did not bestride the stage like a conqueror, but sauntered around it looking the image of the Hampstead gentleman that he liked to be in real life. His cigarette was an emblem of his relaxation and informality. Typically enough, however, when a brand of cigarettes named after him was launched in 1903, they were noted for the mildness of the tobacco. So great was du Maurier's skill in conveying an air of naturalness that audiences and critics alike were sometimes tempted to imagine that he was not really acting at all but merely walking through his part, throwing away his lines. Such views were mistaken and there is abundant evidence that he went to immense pains to perfect his style. Unlike the Victorians he reacted against, he sought to conceal his artistry, but it was no less real, no less hardly won for that. In particular he possessed a remarkable vocal technique, for he was able to project a speech (without electronic amplification, of course) while seeming just to be speaking naturally.

More serious criticisms are that his naturalness of manner tended to limit the scope of drama to a single type and that even within the confines of a naturalistic manner he preferred to entertain fashionable, complacent audiences with plays that were undemanding, both intellectually and theatrically. In *An Actor and His Times*, Sir John Gielgud pays tribute to du Maurier's qualities, only to conclude: "If only he had brought such skill and expertise to Ibsen and Chekhov! But he had little appreciation of great plays".

Within his limits, however, du Maurier certainly gave a great deal of pleasure, particularly in works by J. M. Barrie. An important figure in the raising of the status of the acting profession, he also made a crucial contribution to the emergence of the less stagey acting style. That was something that would be increasingly needed in the cinema, in which he took a considerable interest both as a performer and as a director of Associated Talking Pictures at Ealing, and, a generation later, in the even more intimate medium of television.

—Christopher Smith

DUSE, Eleonora. Italian actress and manager. Born in Vigevano, Italy, 3 October 1859; into family of strolling players. Little formal education. Married Tebaldo Cecchi; one daughter; lovers included actor Flavio Andò, composer and librettist Arrigo Boito, and poet and playwright Gabriele D'Annunzio. Stage debut, at the age of four with her parents' company, 1863; debut as Shakespeare's Juliet at the age of 14, Verona, 1873; joined Giocinta Pezzana's company in Naples and subsequently Turin, 1879; became leading lady with the company, 1881; first appearance in Rome, 1883; first overseas tour, to South America, 1886; co-founded Compagnia Città di Roma, 1887; acclaimed on tour to Russia, 1891; first London appearance, 1893; first US tour, 1893; acted in London in rivalry with Sarah Bernhardt, 1895; continued to tour extensively in the great tragic roles until retirement in 1909; came out of retirement due to financial problems, 1921, and was touring the USA at the time of her death. Died in Pittsburgh, USA, 21 April 1924.

Roles

1863   Cosetta in *Les Misérables* (Hugo), tour.
1873   Giulietta in *Romeo e Giulietta* (Shakespeare), Verona, Italy.
1878–80 Adele in *Marcellina* (Marenco), Naples, Italy.
        Matilde in *L'onore della Famiglia* (Battu), Naples, Italy.
        Lia in *Kean* (Dumas *père*), Naples, Italy.

Angela in *Domino rosso* (Delacour and Hennequin), Naples, Italy.
Jvon in *Serafina la devota* (Sardou), Naples, Italy.
Maja in *Les Fourchambault* (Augier), Naples, Italy.
Giovanna in *La Duchessa di Bracciano* (Agnillo), Naples, Italy.
Contessa Costanza in *Dope tre anni* (Corbo), Naples, Italy.
Debora in *Milton* (Gattinelli), Naples, Italy.
Cecilia in *La Calunnia* (Scribe), Naples, Italy.
Maria in *Una Cristiana* (Marenco), Naples, Italy.
Delia in *Sullivan* (Melville), Naples, Italy.
Amalia in *I Masnadieri* (Schiller), Naples, Italy.
Jolanda in *Rambaldo* (traditional), Naples, Italy.
Amanda in *Fernanda* (Sardou), Naples, Italy.
Ofelia in *Amleto* (Shakespeare), Naples, Italy.
Alina in *Babbo cattivo* (Piccioli), Naples, Italy.
Marcella in *Borghesi di Pontarcy* (Sardou), Naples, Italy.
Marcella in *Demi-monde* (Dumas *fils*), Naples, Italy.
Nanà in *Nanà* (Barbieri), Naples, Italy.
Susanna in *Il Matrimonio di Figaro* (Beaumarchais), Naples, Italy.
Elettra in *Oreste* (Alfieri), Naples, Italy.
Teresa in *Teresa Raquin* (Zola), Naples, Italy, 1879.
1880–84 La Princesse in *La Princesse de Baghdad* (Dumas *fils*), Turin, Italy.
Cypriana in *Facciamo divorzio* (Sardou), Venice, Italy, 1881; European tour, 1891; New York, 1893.
Giorgina in *Fernanda* (Sardou), Turin, Italy.
Mirandolina in *La Locandiera* (Goldoni), Turin, Italy; European tour, 1891; New York, 1893; Windsor Castle, England, 1894.
Pamela in *Pamela nubile* (Goldoni), Turin, Italy.
Livia in *Amore senza stima* (Ferrari), Turin, Italy.
Eugenia in *L'Innamorata* (Praga), Turin, Italy.
Giulia in *La Moglie ideale* (Praga), Turin, Italy.
Bianca in *La Porte chiusa* (Praga), Turin, Italy.
Santuzza in *Cavalleria Rusticana* (Verga), Turin, Italy, 1884.
Contessa Teresa in *Scrollina* (Torelli).
Emma in *Tristi amori* (Giacosa).
Bianca Maria in *La Signora de Challant* (Giacosa).
Costanza Giulia di Saint Florent in *La Badessa di Jouarre* (Renan).
Desdemona in *Otello* (Shakespeare), Milan, Italy, 1887.
Cleopatra in *Antonio e Cleopatra* (Shakespeare, translated by Boito); Teatro Manzoni, Milan, Italy, 1888; London, 1893.
Marguerite Gautier in *La Signora dalle Camelie* (Dumas *fils*), Florence, Italy; Rome, 1883; St Petersburg, Russia, 1891; Lyric Theatre, London, 1893.

Lidia in *Una Visita di Nozze* (Dumas *fils*).

Severina in *La Principessa Giorgio* (Dumas *fils*).

Cesarina in *La Moglie di Claudio* (Dumas *fils*), European tour, 1891; New York, 1893.

Dionisia in *Dionisia* (Dumas *fils*).

Francine in *Francillon* (Dumas *fils*), European tour, 1891; New York, 1893.

Teodora in *Teodora* (Sardou).

Odette in *Odette* (Sardou).

Clothilde in *Fernanda* (Sardou).

Adriana Lecouvreur in *Adriana Lecouvreur* (Scribe and Legouvé).

Fernanda in *Fernanda* (Sardou).

Gilberta in *Frou-Frou* (Meilhac and Halévy), Florence, Italy, 1882.

Clara in *L'altro pericolo* (Donnay).

Paula in *La Seconda Moglie* (Pinero).

Nora in *La Casa di Bambola* (Ibsen), European tour, 1891.

Tosca in *La Tosca* (Sardou), Berlin, 1892.

Fédora in *Fédora* (Sardou), European tour, 1891; New York, 1893.

Hedda in *Hedda Gabler* (Ibsen), 1898; Adelphi Theatre, London, 1903.

Rebecca West in *Rosmersholm* (Ibsen), 1907.

Ellida Wangel in *The Lady from the Sea* (Ibsen), 1909; Teatro Balbo, Turin, 1921.

Magda in *Casa Paterna* (Sudermann), London, 1895.

Anna in *La Città Morta* (D'Annunzio), 1898.

Silvia Settala in *La Gioconda* (D'Annunzio), 1898; Adelphi Theatre, London, 1903.

Elena Komnena in *La Gloria* (D'Annunzio), 1899.

Francesca in *Francesca da Rimini* (D'Annunzio), 1901; Adelphi Theatre, London, 1903.

La Demente in *Il Sogno di un Mattino di Primavera* (D'Annunzio), 1898.

Role in *Sogno di un Tramonto d'Autunno* (D'Annunzio), 1898.

Vassilissa in *I Bassifondi* (Gorky).

Klärchen in *Egmont* (Goethe).

Monna Vanna in *Monna Vanna* (Maeterlinck).

Le madre in *Così sia* (Gallarati Scotti), 1921.

Ella in *John Gabriel Borkman* (Ibsen), 1921.

Signora Alving in *Spettri* (Ibsen), 1923.

Films

Cenere, 1916.

*

Bibliography

Books:

Alfred Fried, *Führer durch das Gastpiel der Eleonora Duse*, Berlin and Leipzig, 1892.

C. Bullo, *Eleonora Duse e suo Nonno*, Venice, 1897.

Victor Mapes, *Duse and the French*, New York, 1898.

Luigi Rasi, *La Duse*, Florence, 1901.

Gemma Ferruggia, *La Nostra Vera Duse*, Milan, 1924.

Jeanne Bordeaux, *Eleonora Duse: The Story of Her Life*, New York, 1925.

Camillo Antona Traversi, *Eleonora Duse, sua Vita, sua Gloria, suo Martirio*, Pisa, 1926.

Ofelia Mazzoni, *Con la Duse*, Milan, 1927.

Arthur Symons, *Eleonora Duse*, New York and London, 1927.

Edouard Schneider, *Eleonora Duse*, Paris, 1927.

E. A. Reinhardt, *The Life of Eleonora Duse*, London, 1930.

Oreste Cimoroni, *Eleonora Duse*, Milan, 1940.

Luciano Nicastro, *Confessioni di Eleonora Duse*, Milan, 1945.

Bertitia Harding, *Age Cannot Wither: The Story of Duse and D'Annunzio*, London, 1949.

Olga Signorelli, *Eleonora Duse*, Rome, 1955.

Frances Winwar, *Wingless Victory*, New York, 1956.

Leonardo Vergani, *Eleonora Duse*, Milan, 1958.

Nino Bolla, *Eleonora Duse nell'amore e nell'arte*, Rome, 1960.

Olga Signorelli, *Vita di Eleonora Duse*, Bologna, 1962.

Eva Le Gallienne, *The Mystic in the Theatre: Eleonara Duse*, London, 1965.

Lucio Ridenti, *La Duse minore*, Rome, 1966.

Memo Benassi, *L'Ultima Viaggio di Eleonora*, Vicenza, 1967.

Jean Stubbs, *Eleonora Duse*, New York, 1970.

Clemente Fusero, *Eleonora Duse*, Milan, 1971.

Giovanni Pontiero, *Duse on Tour: Guido Noccioli's Diaries 1906–07*, Manchester, 1982.

William Weaver, *Duse: A Biography*, London, 1984.

Giovanni Pontiero, *Eleonora Duse in Life and Art*, Frankfurt, Bern, and New York, 1986.

John Stokes, Michael Booth, and Susan Bassnett, *Bernhardt, Terry, Duse: The Actresses in Her Time*, Cambridge, 1988.

* * *

There is a huge body of writing about Eleonora Duse, a lot of it highly speculative or sensationalist, which is perhaps to be expected in view of the almost mythical reputation that Duse established during her own lifetime. Her theatrical career lasted over 60 years, during which time she travelled continuously and became as well known in theatres in North and South America as in theatres in Europe.

Silvio d'Amico has argued that Duse's career falls into three phases: a first stage, when she was principally playing realist roles, a second stage that coincided with her relationship with D'Annunzio, when she entered what he calls her "aestheticist" phase, and a final stage that he terms her "religious period". This assessment of Duse's career has coloured the views of a large number of biographers and theatre historians, and accounts of Duse's "mysticism" are manifold.

In the 1980's, which heralded a period of reassessment of Duse, this traditional view has come to be seen as misguided at best, as downright wrong at worst. Certainly, Duse had many of her early successes playing realist roles — the Lady of the Camelias, Santuzza in *Cavalleria Rusticana*, Sudermann's Magda, and many others, but it is far too simplistic to divide her career into clearly separate phases. Once she had established a reputation for herself as an actress, Duse's great concern was to enlarge her reper-

Eleonora Duse

toire, and the drive to find new roles is a key factor in her life and art. She believed, with many of her contemporaries, that the Italian theatre was in a state of decadence and needed revitalization. She was irritated by the predominance of the French drama, and in a letter of 1882 she complained that in one season she had played "seven Odettes, four Frou-Frous, two Lady of the Camelias, two Fernandes, three Scrollinas and six Femmes de Claude". Once she set up her own company in 1887, the drive for new material was allowed free rein. Her relationship with the writer Arrigo Boito, which lasted from 1887 to 1897, when she fell in love with D'Annunzio, resulted in an unsatisfactory experiment to create a new Italian Shakespeare. Boito's version of *Antony and Cleopatra*, although relatively successful on overseas tours, was not well received in Italy, and with the role of Cleopatra Duse encountered the limits of her own carefully crafted acting style. Her greatest strength was always with characters who had a strong inner life, often combining that with a contradictory outer life. The role of Cleaopatra made different demands, and Duse was accused by a number of Italian critics of not having a feeling for tragedy.

The relationship with D'Annunzio, which has fascinated so many biographers, was a fraught one, and Duse lent her talent and her money to promoting D'Annunzio as a playwright. He wrote several works for her, but ironically his first successful play was performed with another actress in the lead, and although Duse insisted on touring such works as *Il Sogno d'un Mattino di Primavera* and *La Figlia di Iorio*, she never had much success in these parts. What the seven year relationship with D'Annunzio did for her, apart from the pain and public humiliation that she suffered, was to show her where her greatest strengths as an actress lay. Far from entering into a "religious" or "mystical" phase, as some have termed it, Duse's work became more powerful after 1904.

Duse first played Ibsen in 1891, when she performed the role of Nora in *A Doll's House*, the first Ibsen production in Italy. Boito had attempted to dissuade her from Ibsen, but Duse's interest in the parts offered by the Norwegian writer bordered on obsession. She added *Hedda Gabler* to her repertoire in 1898, then *Rosmersholm* in 1907, *The Lady from the Sea* in 1909, *John Gabriel Borkman* in 1921, and *Ghosts* in 1923. Her farewell to the theatre in 1909 was in *The Lady from the Sea*, and when she returned to the stage in 1921 it was in the same role of Ellida Wangel. In Ibsen, Duse finally found the writer whose roles gave her the possibility of both expanding her repertoire and extending the range of her own acting style. She insisted on adding Ibsen to her repertoire despite the contrary arguments of both Boito and D'Annunzio, a point that mitigates against the traditional view of Duse as a helpless little woman dominated by stronger men. After 1907, her choice of roles and her work for other actresses shows a very definite sense of purpose and considerable strength of mind.

Duse's earliest roles portray women trapped by social constraints that force them into positions of unhappiness and loss. The plays written for her by D'Annunuzio demonstrate his misogyny and fear of women, and those roles show women mutilated, abused, murdered. But the roles that Duse began to take for herself, particularly the roles created by Ibsen, portray women who impose their will on the world around them. They may suffer, but they survive and are a source of life.

Contemporary reviewers describe Duse in almost metaphysical terms — she is "luminous", she wears no make-up, she does not act, she simply is. Fellow performers provide a different view — Noccioli recounts the skill with which Duse positioned herself on stage for maximum effect, the care she took with her make-up and costumes, while Adelaide Ristori, the grand old lady of the Italian theatre, analyzed the careful way in which Duse created her own gestural and vocal styles. Far from being an actress who worked from the soul, Duse seems to have been a master craftswoman, a technician of great skill who knew exactly how to work her audience. It is ironic that she should be remembered so often not for her theatrical skills, but for her personal life and for the image that critics and audiences imposed upon her.

The new work that has begun to appear on Duse's acting moves away from theories of mystical inspiration and concentrates instead on the realities of performance. It is suggested, for example, that one of the reasons for the failure of D'Annunzio's plays (apart from their melodramatic, hyperbolic qualities) lay in Duse's difficulty with the acting style demanded by his roles. She had established a reputation for herself as Italy's foremost actress, and had worked long and hard on her technique, so that by the time she met D'Annunzio she already knew how she wanted to work. By forcing herself to play roles that did not fit her style of work, and submitting to D'Annunzio's amateur directing, Duse did herself a disservice. Why she did this is significant; until the break-up with D'Annunzio Duse seems to have seen herself as an instrument rather than as an initiator. She wanted to create great Art and she wanted to raise the standards of Italian theatre, but she doubted her own ability to do this unaided. She needed D'Annunzio, just as she needed Boito, and it was not until she could overcome that need both on the personal and professional plane, that she was finally able to work for herself and become a genuinely innovative performer.

—Susan Bassnett

DYBWAD, Johanne (Juell). Norwegian actress and director. Born in Christiania (renamed Kristiania, 1877–24 and Oslo, 1925), Norway, 2 August 1867. Educated at schools in Bergen, Norway. Stage debut, National Scene, Bergen, 1887; actress, Kristiania Theatre, Kristiania, 1888–99; leading actress, Nationalteatret, Kristiania, from 1899; appeared regularly under her own direction, from 1906; toured extensively, including visits to Germany, 1907, Helsinki and Copenhagen, 1908–09, and Paris, 1937; last appearance at the Nationalteatret, 1947. Died 1950.

Productions

As actress:
1887   Gertrude Howard in *Gertrude* (Harris), National Scene, Bergen.
1887–88   Nora in *Et Dukkehjem* [A Doll's House] (Ibsen), National Scene, Bergen; Christiania Theatre, Oslo, 1890; Nationalteatret, Oslo, 1906.

Sophie in *Syv Militaire Piger*, National Scene, Bergen.

Claire Macassar in *Landsted til Salg*, National Scene, Bergen.

Nora Holm in *Det ny System* [The New System] (Bjørnson), National Scene, Bergen.

Else Top in *Løitnant Tobiesen*, National Scene, Bergen.

Ingeborg in *Søstrene paa Kinnekullen*, National Scene, Bergen.

Salle Pomuchelskopp in *Landmandsliv* [A Farmer's Life] (Fristrup, adapted from Reuter), National Scene, Bergen; Kristiania Theatre, Kristiania, 1889.

En Butikkjomfru in *Ultimo* (Moser), National Scene, Bergen.

Fanchon Vivieux in *En liden Hex* (Birch-Pfeiffer, adapted from Sand), National Scene, Bergen; Christiania Theatre, Oslo, 1888.

En gammel Dame in *Nordlandstrompeten*, National Scene, Bergen.

Cupid in *Orfeus i Underverdenen* [Orpheus in the Underworld], National Scene, Bergen.

En Opvarterske in *Han gaar paa Komers*, National Scene, Bergen.

William Taylor in *Maria Stuart i Skotland* [Mary Stuart of Scotland] (Bjørnson), National Scene, Bergen.

En spansk Foendrik in *Alt for Foedrelandet*, National Scene, Bergen.

Axel Sparre in *Tordenskjold*, National Scene, Bergen.

Baronesse de Préfont in *Fabrikanten*, National Scene, Bergen.

Ida in *I telefonen* [On the Telephone] (Ahlgren), National Scene, Bergen.

1888   Amanda in *Fernande* (Sardou), Kristiania Theatre, Kristiania.

Bertha in *Rejsen til Kina* [The Journey to China] (Recke, adapted from Labiche and Delacour), Kristiania Theatre, Kristiania.

Germaine in *Germaine* (Legouvé), Kristiania Theatre, Kristiania.

One of the girls in *I telefonen* [On the Telephone] (Ahlgren), Kristiania Theatre, Kristiania.

Ingeborg Blytaekkers in *Barselstuen* [The Lying-in Room] (Holberg), Kristiania Theatre, Kristiania.

La Miotte in *Lille-mor* [Little-Mother] (Meilhac and Halévy), Kristiania Theatre, Kristiania.

1889   Herma in *Den berømte kone* [The Renowned Wife] (Schönthan and Kadelburg), Kristiania Theatre, Kristiania.

Hilde Wangel in *Fruen fra havet* [The Lady from the Sea] (Ibsen), Kristiania Theatre, Kristiania.

Astrid in *På tremandshand* [A Triangular Secret] (Lange), Kristiania Theatre, Kristiania.

Ida in *Professoren* [The Professor] (Kielland), Kristiania Theatre, Kristiania.

Gertrude in *Cornevilles klokker* [The Bells of Corneville] (Clairville and Gabet), Kristiania Theatre, Kristiania.

Helene Liebenau in *Den vilde jakt* [The Wild Hunt] (Fulda), Kristiania Theatre, Kristiania.

Edith Marsland in *Bibliotekaren* [The Librarian] (Moser), Kristiania Theatre, Kristiania.

Helga in *Geografi of kjaerlighed* [Geography and Love] (Bjørnson), Kristiania Theatre, Kristiania.

Sylvine in *Andrea* (Sardou), Kristiania Theatre, Kristiania.

Emilie Willmer in *Ultimo* (Moser), Kristiania Theatre, Kristiania.

Leonora in *Den stundesløse* [The Fidgety Man] (Holberg), Kristiania Theatre, Kristiania.

Hedvig in *Vildanden* [The Wild Duck] (Ibsen), Kristiania Theatre, Kristiania; Nationalteatret, Kristiania, 1904.

Paula von Pernwald in *Cornelius Voss* (Schönthan), Kristiania Theatre, Kristiania.

1890   The Princess in *Svein Uraed* [Svein the Fearless] (Rolfsen), Kristiania Theatre, Kristiania.

Vera Alexandrovna in *Natalia* (Turgenev), Kristiania Theatre, Kristiania.

Grethe Dorn in *Våre koner* [Our Wives] (Moser and Schönthan), Kristiania Theatre, Kristiania.

Hanna in *Uden ansvar* [Without Responsibility] (Bull), Kristiania Theatre, Kristiania.

1891   Lydie in *Kampen for tilvaerelsen* [The Struggle for Existence] (Daudet), Kristiania Theatre, Kristiania.

Richard, Duke of York, in *Richard III* (Shakespeare), Kristiania Theatre, Kristiania.

Thea Elvsted in *Hedda Gabler* (Ibsen), Kristiania Theatre, Kristiania.

Clotilde de Rieux in *Krokodilletårer* [Crocodile Tears] (Siraudeu and Thiboust), Kristiania Theatre, Kristiania.

1892   Solveig in *Peer Gynt* (Ibsen), Kristiania Theatre, Kristiania.

Alvilde Lehmann in *Alvorsmaend* [Earnest Men] (Bull), Kristiania Theatre, Kristiania.

Emily Friis in *Den kjaere familie* [The Dear Family] (Esmann), Kristiania Theatre, Kristiania.

Kamma in *En Hanske* [A Gauntlet] (Bjørnson), Kristiania Theatre, Kristiania.

Emma Scarli in *Sorgfuld elskov* [Sorrowful Love] (Giacosa), Kristiania Theatre, Kristiania.

1893   Emilie Netland in *Viljer* [Wills] (Valset), Kristiania Theatre, Kristiania.

Hilde Wangel in *Bygmester Solness* (Ibsen), Kristiania Theatre, Kristiania; Nationalteatret, Oslo, 1910, also directed.

Else Werner in *Den kloge Else* [Wise Else], Kristiania Theatre, Kristiania.

Adele Dyring in *Ein seierherre* [A Victor] (Christensen), Kristiania Theatre, Kristiania.

1894   Kathrine, Duchess of Septmonts, in *Den frem-mede* [L'Étrangère] (Dumas fils), Kristiania Theatre, Kristiania.

Dunja in *Vanitas* (Krag), Kristiania Theatre, Kristiania.

Valeria Messalina in *Arria og Messalina* (Wilbrandt), Kristiania Theatre, Kristiania.

Franziska Spangenbach in *Vaeggepryd* [Wallflower] (Blumenthal and Kadelburg), Kristiania Theatre, Kristiania.

Paula in *Hr Tanquerays anden hustru* [The Second Mrs Tanqueray] (Pinero), Kristiania Theatre, Kristiania.

1895   Selma Bratsberg in *De unges forbund* [The League of Youth] (Ibsen), Kristiania Theatre, Kristiania.

Asta Allmers in *Lille Eyolf* [Little Eyolf] (Ibsen), Kristiania Theatre, Kristiania.

Sara Hegge in *Lystige koner* [Merry Wives] (Lie), Kristiania Theatre, Kristiania.

Margrethe Tondorf in *Henning Tondorf* (Rosenberg), Kristiania Theatre, Kristiania.

Regisse in *Svend Dyrings hus* [Svend Dyring's House] (Hertz), Kristiania Theatre, Kristiania.

Mandanika in *Vansantasena* (Sudraha), Kristiania Theatre, Kristiania.

Pierrot Junior in *L'Enfant prodigue* (Carré), Kristiania Theatre, Kristiania; also directed.

Else Høyer in *Folkets tjener* [The People's Servant] (Christensen), Kristiania Theatre, Kristiania.

Lina Kaarmo in *Mødre* [Mothers] (Garborg), Kristiania Theatre, Kristiania.

Gundel in *Han kommer* [He Is Coming] (Prydz), Kristiania Theatre, Kristiania.

Pernille in *Julestuen* [The Christmas Party] (Holberg), Kristiania Theatre, Kristiania.

1896   Susanne de Villiers in *Den kjedelige verden* [The Tiresome World] (Pailleron), Kristiania Theatre, Kristiania.

Ingeborg in *Daggry* [Dawn] (Rolfsen), Kristiania Theatre, Kristiania.

Thamar in *Iraka* (Sinding), Kristiania Theatre, Kristiania.

Teresita in *Livets spil* [The Game of Life] (Hamsun), Kristiania Theatre, Kristiania.

1897   Frida Foldal in *John Gabriel Borkman* (Ibsen), Kristiania Theatre, Kristiania.

Abigael in *Ambrosius* (Molbech), Kristiania Theatre, Kristiania.

Johanne Siems in *Ungdomsleg* [The Game of Youth], Kristiania Theatre, Kristiania.

Kirstine Rosenkrans in *Dansen på Koldinghus* [The Dance at Koldinghus] (Drachmann), Kristiania Theatre, Kristiania.

Ella in *Folkerådet* [The National Council] (Heiberg), Kristiania Theatre, Kristiania.

Alison Broch in *En og tre* [One and Three] (anon.), Kristiania Theatre, Kristiania.

Lalla Lisgaard in *Kundskabens trae* [The Tree of Knowledge] (Maurer), Kristiania Theatre, Kristiania.

Signe in *Gildet på Solhaug* [The Feast at Solhaug] (Ibsen), Kristiania Theatre, Kristiania.

1898   Anette St Clair in *Theatret* [The Theatre] (Esmann), Kristiania Theatre, Kristiania.

Johanne Sylow in *Johanne* (Bjørnson), Kristiania Theatre, Kristiania.

Lucie in *Under ballet* [Wonder Ballet] (Pailleron), Kristiania Theatre, Kristiania; also directed.

Clara Spohr in *Evig Kjaerlighed* [Eternal Love] (Faber), Kristiania Theatre, Kristiania.

Jonna Malling in *Aabent visir* [Open Visor] (Gad), Kristiania Theatre, Kristiania.

Birgitte in *Lille-mor* [Meilhac and Halévy], Kristiania Theatre, Kristiania.

1899   Helga Høeg in *De to magter* [The Two Powers] (Christensen), Kristiania Theatre, Kristiania.

Julie in *Romeo og Julie* [Romeo and Juliet] (Shakespeare), Kristiania Theatre, Kristiania.

Marguerite Gautier in *Kameliadamen* [La Dame aux camélias] (Dumas fils), Kristiania Theatre, Kristiania.

Engelche Hattemagers in *Barselstuen* (Holberg), Nationalteatret, Oslo.

Borghild av Dal in *Sigurd Jorsalfar* (Bjørnson), Nationalteatret, Oslo.

Fru Svan in *Harald Svans mor* [Harald Svan's Mother] (Heiberg), Nationalteatret, Oslo.

Klara Sang in *Over aevne I* [Beyond Our Power I] (Bjørnson), Nationalteatret, Oslo; directed in Stockholm, 1901, and Oslo, 1931.

1900   Karen Ejlersdatter in *Varulven* [The Werewolf] (Woldemar), Nationalteatret, Oslo.

Helga in *Geografi og kjaerlighed* (Bjørnson), Nationalteatret, Oslo.

Maja Rubek in *Når vi døde vågner* [When We Dead Awaken] (Ibsen), Nationalteatret, Oslo.

Tove in *Gurre* (Drachmann), Nationalteatret, Oslo.

Anna in *Ungdom* [Youth] (Halbe), Nationalteatret, Oslo.

1901   Tante Ulrikke in *Tante Ulrikke* [Aunt Ulrikke] (Heiberg), Nationalteatret, Oslo.

Aino in *Aino* (Prydz), Nationalteatret, Oslo.

Tora Parsberg in *Paul Lange og Tora Parsberg* (Bjørnson), Nationalteatret, Oslo.

Thea Elvsted in *Hedda Gabler* (Ibsen), Nationalteatret, Oslo.

Anna Møller in *Første fiolin* [First Violin] (Pettersen and Wied), Nationalteatret, Oslo.

1902   Eline Gyldenløve in *Fru Inger til Østråt* [Lady Inger of Østrat] (Ibsen), Nationalteatret, Oslo.

Helene Bording in *Under loven* [Under the Law] (Brandes), Nationalteatret, Oslo.

Widow Ring in *Om våren* [In the Spring] (Obstfelder), Nationalteatret, Oslo.

Clara Ernst in *Kongen* [The King] (Bjørnson), Nationalteatret, Oslo.

Jo in *Håpet* [Hope] (Heijermans), Nationalteatret, Oslo.

Maria Ura in *På Storhove* [At Storhove] (Bjørnson), Nationalteatret, Oslo.

Mathilde Krabbe in *Korsvei* [Crossroad] (Dickmar), Nationalteatret, Oslo.

1903   Puk in *En sommernattsdrøm* [A Midsummer Night's Dream] (Shakespeare), Nationalteatret, Oslo.

Cornelia in *Kjaerlighet til naesten* [Love Thy Neighbour] (Heiberg), Nationalteatret, Oslo.

Ilka in *Det store lod* [The Big Lottery] (Heiberg), Nationalteatret, Oslo.

1904   Tamara in *Dronning Tamara* [Queen Tamara] (Hamsun), Nationalteatret, Oslo.

Cathérine in *Madame Sans-Gêne* (Sardou and Moreau), Nationalteatret, Oslo.

Gerd in *Brand* (Ibsen), Nationalteatret, Oslo.

Maria Stuart in *Maria Stuart i Skotland* [Mary Stuart of Scotland] (Bjørnson), Nationalteatret, Oslo.

1905   Karen in *Kjaerlighetens tragedie* [Love's Tragedy] (Heiberg), Nationalteatret, Oslo.

Katarina Maslova in *Oppstandelse* [Resurrection] (L. Tolstoy), Nationalteatret, Oslo.

Kirstine Rosenkrans in *Dansen på Koldinghus* (Drachmann), Nationalteatret, Oslo.

Ragna in *Daglannet* (Bjørnson), Nationalteatret, Oslo.

Rebekka West in *Rosmersholm* (Ibsen), Nationalteatret, Oslo; also directed, 1922.

1906   Mélisande in *Pelléas og Mélisande* (Maeterlinck), Nationalteatret, Oslo; also directed.

Portia in *Kjøpmannen i Venedig* [The Merchant of Venice] (Shakespeare), Nationalteatret, Oslo.

Lady Chiltern in *Den ideale ektemann* [An Ideal Husband] (Wilde), Nationalteatret, Oslo.

1907   Veronica in *Sangen om Florens* [The Song of Florence] (Krag), Nationalteatret, Oslo.

1908   Anne Pedersdotter in *Anne Pedersdotter* (Wiers-Jenssen), Nationalteatret, Oslo; also directed, 1924.

Marie Louise Voysin in *Tyven* [The Thief], Nationalteatret, Oslo.

1909   Griselda in *Griselda* (Hauptmann), Nationalteatret, Oslo.

Mrs Worthley in *Mrs Dot* (Maugham), Nationalteatret, Oslo; also directed.

1910   Margaret Wolfe in *Den sterkeste makt* [The Woman in the Case] (Fitch), Nationalteatret, Oslo.

1911   Anna Karénin in *Anna Karénin* (Tolstoy, adapted by Guirand), Nationalteatret, Oslo.

Hélène Laroche in *Taifun* (Lengyel), Nationalteatret, Oslo.

A Lapp girl in *Sigurd Slembe* (Bjørnson), Nationalteatret, Oslo.

Marie de Lanjallay in *Marie Victoire* (Guiraud), Nationalteatret, Oslo; also directed.

1912   Inga Gar in *Idyllen* [The Idyll] (Egge), Nationalteatret, Oslo.

Maria in *Flekken som renser* [Mancha que limpa] (Echegary), Nationalteatret, Oslo; also directed.

Rosalinde in *Livet i skoven* [As You Like It] (Shakespeare), Nationalteatret, Oslo; also directed.

1913   Halla in *Bjerg-Eivind og hans hustru* [Bjerg-Eivind and His Wife] (Sigurjónsson), Nationalteatret, Oslo; also directed.

Toinette in *Den innbilt syke* [Le Malade Imaginaire] (Molière), Nationalteatret, Oslo.

Helene Bern in *Det store fund* [The Great Find] (Aadahl), Nationalteatret, Oslo; also directed.

1914   Lavinia Celius in *Det lykkelige valg* [The Happy Election] (Kjaer), Nationalteatret, Oslo.

Peggy Admeston in *Sommerfuglen i nettet* [The Butterfly in the Net] (Hemmerde and Neilson), Nationalteatret, Oslo; also directed.

Julia Cameron in *Robert Frank* (S. Ibsen), Nationalteatret, Oslo.

1915   Therese Hvass in *Therese* (Vogt), Nationalteatret, Oslo.

Beatrice in *Star ståhei for ingenting* [Much Ado About Nothing] (Shakespeare), Nationalteatret, Oslo; also directed.

Frida Breim in *Brist* [Flaws] (Egge), Nationalteatret, Oslo; also directed.

1916   Henriette in *Syndens sold* [There Are Crimes and Crimes] (Strindberg), Nationalteatret, Oslo.

Itine Kos in *Over vannene* [Over the Waters] (Engel), Nationalteatret, Oslo; also directed.

1917   The woman in *Fata morgana* (Vajda), Nationalteatret, Oslo.

1918   Margherita Cavallini in *Romantikk* [Romance] (Sheldon), Nationalteatret, Oslo.

Medea in *Medea* (Euripides), Nationalteatret, Oslo; also directed.

1919   Jennifer Dubedat in *Doktorens dilemma* [The Doctor's Dilemma] (G. B. Shaw), Nationalteatret, Oslo.

1920   Maria of Neuburg in *Ruy Blas* (Hugo), Nationalteatret, Oslo; also directed.

Norma McIntyre in *Vi mordere* [We Murderers] (Kamban), Nationalteatret, Oslo; also directed.

1921   Cornelia in *Kirken* [The Church] (Anker), Nationalteatret, Oslo.

Nini Aarvik in *Syndefald* [The Fall] (Fangen), Nationalteatret, Oslo; also directed.

1922   Hulda in *Halte Hulda* [Lame Hulda] (Bjørnson), Nationalteatret, Oslo; also directed.

1923   Madame Legros in *Madame Legros* (Mann), Nationalteatret, Oslo.

1924   Victoria in *Brennende jord* [Terre Inhumaine] (Curel), Nationalteatret, Oslo.

1925   Therese Borch in *Ansiktet på ruten* [The Face on the Window] (Christensen), Nationalteatret, Oslo.

Helena Alving in *Gengangere* [Ghosts] (Ibsen), Nationalteatret, Oslo; also directed.

1926   The Manager in *Seks personer søker en forfatter* [Six Characters in Search of an Author] (Pirandello), Nationalteatret, Oslo; also directed.

1927	Hjørdis in *Haermaendene på Helgeland* [The Vikings at Helgeland] (Ibsen), Nationalteatret, Oslo; also directed.
1928	Colette Bolbec in *Advokat Bolbec og hennes mann* [Attorney Bolbec and Her Husband] (Berr and Verneuil), Nationalteatret, Oslo; also directed.
	Ariel in *Stormen* [The Tempest] (Shakespeare), Nationalteatret, Oslo; also directed.
	Ceres in *Stormen* [The Tempest] (Shakespeare), Nationalteatret, Oslo.
1929	Elisabeth, Queen of England, in *Maria Stuart* (Schiller), Nationalteatret, Oslo; also directed.
1930	Janet Fraser in *Den først Mrs Fraser* [The First Mrs Fraser] (Ervine), Nationalteatret, Oslo; also directed.
	Celia Bottle in *Fru Bottle og kunsten* [Art and Mrs Bottle] (Levy), Nationalteatret, Oslo; also directed.
1931	Fru Inger Ottisdatter Rømer in *Fru Inger til Østråt* (Ibsen), Nationalteatret, Oslo.
1932	Elisabeth in *Elisabeth av England* [Elizabeth of England] (Bruckner), Nationalteatret, Oslo.
1933	Christine Mannon in *Sorgen klaer Elektra* [Mourning Becomes Electra] (O'Neill), Nationalteatret, Oslo; also directed.
1934	Paulina in *Et vintereventyr* [The Winter's Tale] (Shakespeare), Nationalteatret, Oslo, also directed.
	Mrs Phelps in *Det sterke bånd* [The Silver Cord] (Howard), Nationalteatret, Oslo.
1936	Volumnia in *Coriolan* [Coriolanus] (Shakespeare), Nationalteatret, Oslo; also directed.
	Aase in *Peer Gynt* (Ibsen), Nationalteatret, Oslo.
	Majorinnen in *Gösta Berlings saga* (Lagerlöf), Nationalteatret, Oslo.
1938	Elisabeth in *Elisabeth, kvinnen uten mann* [Elizabeth, the Woman Without a Man] (Josset), Nationalteatret, Oslo.
1940	The mother in *Møren* [The Mother] (Čapek), Nationalteatret, Oslo.
	Kaisa in *Ferjestedet* [The Ferry Landing] (Elvestad and Christensen), Nationalteatret, Oslo.
1942	The mother in *Brand* (Ibsen), Nationalteatret, Oslo.

Other roles included: Catharina in *Troll kan temmes* [The Taming of the Shrew] (Shakespeare); Grethe in *Kjaerligheten og døden* [Love and Death] (Lange); Jacqueline in *Hvem er hun* [Who Is She] (Bisson); Julie in *Balkonen* [The Balcony] (Genet); Karen in *Karen Bornemann* (Bergstrøm); regine in *Gengangere* [Ghosts] (Ibsen); the woman in *Femme X*; the woman in *Hundjaevelen* [Der Weibsteufel] (Schönherr).

As director only:

Barrabas (Grieg), 1927; *Hoppla, vi lever!* [Hoppla, wir leben!] (Toller), 1928; *Frøken* [The Spinster] (Deval), 1932; *Kvinnenes oprør* [Lysistrata] (Aristophanes), 1933; *Vår aere vår makt* [Our Power and Our Glory] (Grieg), 1935; *King Lear* (Shakespeare), 1937; *Mrs Dot* (Maugham), 1939.

*

Bibliography

Books:
Carla Waal, *Johanne Dybwad — Norwegian Actress*, Oslo, London and Boston, 1967.

* * *

Johanne Dybwad's achievements as actress and director earned the admirations of audiences during her lifetime and a position of stature in the annals of Norwegian theatre history. Intensely hard-working and serious in purpose, she maintained high artistic standards and exercised an influence upon authors, actors and the public. Through her uninhibited expressions of passion and of liberated views, she clarified the attitudes of modern women and encouraged others to act with tolerance and courage.

The quantity and variety of roles played by Dybwad are impressive. While engaged at the Kristiania Theatre she played 76 roles, and at the Nationalteatret, 96. Her individuality and intelligence were evident whether she appeared as an ingenue, a romantic heroine, a figure of fantasy, an eccentric character or a tragic heroine. With her understanding of human nature and a flair for theatricality, Dybwad brought to life the works of both Norwegian and foreign playwrights. Above all, she achieved memorable interpretations of the plays of Henrik Ibsen.

Having inherited acting talent from her parents, Johanne Juell Dybwad felt confident from the start of her career that she could rely on her own taste and instincts. The director Bjørn Bjørnson influenced her in the early years, but otherwise Dybwad learned from observing actors in Norway and abroad. She admired Sarah Bernhardt, to whom she was compared in talent and significance. Not everyone admired Johanne Dybwad without reservation, but always in her strongest performances there was discipline, emotional power and clarity.

In the first few decades of her career, Dybwad was praised for the gracefulness with which she moved; this was true of her agile and boisterous performance of Puck in *A Midsummer Night's Dream* and her tortured dance in Holger Drachmann's *The Dance at Koldinghus*. When her petite body grew matronly, she created physical images through control of gestures and poses. With its high forehead, penetrating eyes and expressive mouth, Dybwad's face had radiance and a classical simplicity. Having been raised in Bergen, she always retained the characteristic sounds of the local accent, but combined them with elements of the Oslo dialect to achieve a unique pronunciation. Her voice had a rare and somewhat harsh quality but also a wide range of pitch and musical inflections. Nowhere was this clearer than when she blended her voice as Aase with Grieg's music for the death scene in *Peer Gynt*.

Dybwad's brilliant mind and forceful personality were responsible for both triumphs and failures. Sometimes a performance was distorted because of her unique and powerful interpretation of a leading role, or because she functioned as both star and director and therefore could not observe the production with detachment. As the years went by, a younger generation of theatre-goers did not appreciate the larger-than-life dimensions of her playing or her continuing to take youthful roles. Admirers accepted the essence and imagination of her performances, and her efforts to break free of traditional realism.

Analysing the style of Johanne Dybwad's playing requires dividing her career into two major periods. In the early decades she did beautiful work with precise details in realistic dramas. Some of the outstanding roles in this genre were Hedvig in *The Wild Duck* and Klara Sang in Bjørnstjerne Bjørnson's *Beyond Human Power*. Later she developed a monumental, impressionistic style that was broad and elevated. The change is attributed in part to her frequent co-star, August Oddvar, who tended toward a broad, tense and declamatory manner of delivery. Exemplifying the power and brilliance of the later phase of Dybwad's career were such roles as Medea, Queen Elizabeth and Christine Mannon in *Mourning Becomes Electra*.

Although her work as a director was not universally praised, Dybwad contributed some distinctive and controlled productions to the history of Norwegian theatre. Of the seven productions she directed without appearing in the cast, two of the most significant were of plays by Nordahl Grieg, *Barrabas* and *Our Power and Our Glory*, with which she showed her affinity for expressionism and the newest Continental approaches to staging. Among the many productions for which she was both leading actress and director, two of the most successful were Ibsen's *Rosmersholm* and *Ghosts*. When she directed, Dybwad looked for a key to the essence of the play. Sometimes she would cut a script and rearrange scenes to make the action concentrated and fast-moving. In general there was the same trend from realism to monumentality in her directing that there was in her acting, but she always sought to establish the appropriate style for each play, ranging from the traditional and subdued to the bold and innovative.

Rather than analysing her technique, witnesses of Johanne Dybwad's great performances remembered the electrifying effect of her presence, which kept audiences spellbound. Critics wrote of her Puck as 'myth' rather than art, of Gerd in *Brand* as mystical and dazzling, of Hilde Wangel in *The Master Builder* as a fascinating Mona Lisa or a beautiful bird of prey. Although removed from the charisma of her stage presence, we can appreciate the tributes to the beauty, originality and depth of her interpretations.

—Carla Waal

EFREIMOV, Oleg (Nikolaievich). Russian director and actor. Born 1927. Trained at Moscow Art Theatre Studio School, until 1949. Actor, Central Children's Theatre, Moscow, from 1949; joined Communist Party, 1953; debut as director, 1955; founder and director, Studio of Young Actors, Moscow, 1957; installed company at Sovremennik Theatre, Moscow, 1958; acclaimed for productions of contemporary Russian and European dramas; director, Moscow Art Theatre, from 1971; elected to Parliament as a People's Deputy, 1989; has also appeared in films. Recipient: USSR State Prize, 1969. People's Artist of the USSR, 1976.

Productions

As director:
1957   *In Search of Joy* (Rozov), Young Actors' Studio, Moscow; also acted Fyodor.
1958   *Alive Forever* (Rozov), Moscow Hotel, Moscow; also acted Boris.
1959   *Two Flowers* (Volodin), Sovremennik Theatre, Moscow; also acted Boris.
1962   *Moya starshaya sestra* [My Older Sister] (Volodin), Sovremennik Theatre, Moscow.
       Goly Korol [The Naked King] (Shvarts), Sovremennik Theatre, Moscow.
1963   *The Appointment* (Volodin), Sovremeinik Theatre, Moscow.
       Two for the Seesaw (Gibson), Sovremennik Theatre, Moscow.
1964   *On the Wedding Day* (Rozov), Sovremennik Theatre, Moscow.
       Cyrano de Bergerac (Rostand), Sovremennik Theatre, Moscow.
1965   *Always on Sale* (Aksyonov), Sovremennik Theatre, Moscow.
1966   *Look Back in Anger* (Osborne), Sovremennik Theatre, Moscow.
1967   *The Reunion* (Rozov), Sovremennik Theatre, Moscow.
       Ballad of the Sad Café (Albee), Sovremennik Theatre, Moscow.
       An Ordinary Story (adapted from Goncharov), Sovremennik Theatre, Moscow.
       The Decembrists (Zorin), Sovremennik Theatre, Moscow; acted Nicholas I.
       The Populists (Svobodin), Sovremennik Theatre, Moscow; acted Zhelyabov.

       The Bolsheviks (Shatrov), Sovremennik Theatre, Moscow.
1969   *From Night to Noon* (Rozov), Sovremennik Theatre, Moscow.
       Na dne [The Lower Depths] (Gorky), Sovremennik Theatre, Moscow.
1970   *Chayka* [The Seagull] (Chekhov), Sovremennik Theatre, Moscow.
1972   *Dulcinea of El Toboso* (Volodin), Moscow Art Theatre, Moscow.
       Valentin and Valentina (Roshchin), Moscow Art Theatre, Moscow.
1973   *The Old New Year* (Roshchin), Moscow Art Theatre, Moscow.
       El sueno de razón (Buero Vallejo), Moscow Art Theatre, Moscow.
1974   *Steel-Workers* (Bokrev), Moscow Art Theatre, Moscow.
1975   *Echelon* (Roshchin), Moscow Art Theatre, Moscow.
       Sweet Bird of Youth (T. Williams), Moscow Art Theatre, Moscow.
1976   *Ivanov* (Chekhov), Moscow Art Theatre, Moscow.
1980   *Chayka* [The Seagull] (Chekhov), Moscow Art Theatre, Moscow.
1981   *Thus We Conquer* (Shatrov), Moscow Art Theatre, Moscow.
1985   *Dyadya Vanya* [Uncle Vanya] (Chekhov), Moscow Art Theatre, Moscow; London, 1989; acted Astrov.
1988   *Molière* (Bulgakov), Moscow Art Theatre, Moscow; acted Molière.
1989   *Vishnevy sad* [The Cherry Orchard] (Chekhov), Moscow Art Theatre, Moscow.

* * *

Oleg Efreimov is one of the most significant figures in the history of post-war Soviet theatre. His main achievement has been to advance production methods during the "period of stagnation" and to revitalise a moribund Moscow Art Theatre.

On graduation from the Moscow Art Theatre Studio School, he joined the Moscow Central Children's Theatre where he played a record 22 different roles. His work was distinguished by his ability to find the unusual, the special quality contained within a character. He observed the specific behaviour of his Soviet contemporaries and absorbed them into himself. His primary concern, in accordance with the Stanislavsky system was to create the inner psychological life of the character but his use of the system was more than the academic formality it had become for many of his colleagues. He rethought the fundamentals of the system, notably the search for genuine psychological truth. He was also able to provide a broader perspective to a role, putting the question: what is the character's aim in life, what does he want to achieve? Marya Knebbel, Stanislavsky's former colleague and an outstanding teacher at GITIS (State Institute for Theatre Arts) regarded him as a potential Michael Chekhov but he did not go on to create a career as a star actor. He played no major classical or Chekhovian roles. His true gifts lay elsewhere. Interviewed by Anatoly Smeliansky he stated: "Really I'm not a director in the full sense of the word ... I'm probably not an actor. My life has not been planned so that I went from one role to another. I've never been desperate to act or direct ... You know, there is something called 'a man of the theatre'. That's probably what I am."

Efreimov's self-assessment seems accurate. His work has consisted in the creation or revitalization of theatre companies. In 1957 he founded the Young Actors' Studio, which was composed not only of seasoned professionals but also outstanding graduates from the Moscow Art Theatre Studio School. Among them was Oleg Tabakov. The members of the new Studio rehearsed and performed where they could, while fulfilling their normal commitments. Among their first productions was *In Search of Joy* by Vasily Rozov, who was to become closely associated with the group. Official recognition came in 1958, when the Studio was transformed into the Sovremennik (Contemporary) Theatre. The name not only expressed the company's desire to perform new, more experimental plays, it evoked the memory of the most progressive literary magazine of the 19th century.

At the Sovremennik, with a company that was soon hailed as probably the best in Russia, Efreimov, benefiting from the 'thaw' following the 20th Party Congress, staged a series of new plays, extending the confines of the repertoire as far as it was possible to go in the prevailing political climate. The opening production was Rozov's wartime drama *Alive Forever*; among the works that followed were several plays by Volodin who became with Rozov one of the theatre's two most favoured dramatists. Plays by Shvarts brought them into conflict with the authorities in the early 1960's, but the programme also came to include items from the classical repertoire, beginning with Rostand's *Cyrano de Bergerac* in 1964, and several other foreign plays by the likes of William Gibson, John Osborne, and Edward Albee.

To celebrate the 50th anniversary of the Revolution, Efreimov staged a trilogy of plays based on that era before finally tackling Gorky's *The Lower Depths* and Chekhov's *The Seagull* almost as if in preparation for his eventual move to the Art Theatre, the established shrine of such Russian classics. The Art Theatre was badly in need of a shake-up when Efreimov was appointed. He had already demonstrated his ability to cover a wide repertoire of plays without causing repeated offence in officialdom and was deemed the natural choice as the Art Theatre's new head and thus the senior figure in the Russian theatrical hierarchy (Stalin had previously made the Art Theatre the model for all Russian theatres and had lavished considerable resources upon it). The Art Theatre had, however,

ossified since the Stalin era and change would be difficult to effect. It was understandable that Efreimov should have hesitated when he already had such a good company around him but he eventually accepted the post, reportedly under pressure, and took as many of his existing company as were willing to go with him. Some, like Tabakov, elected to stay at the Sovremennik.

On his arrival at the Moscow Art Theatre, Efreimov attempted to make the company aware of new writers and new methods. He gave a series of over 20 play readings and set up a number of short courses for young directors. In planning the repertoire he continued his policy of presenting modern drama and opened his regime with a production of Volodin's *Dulcinea of El Tobosco*, followed by plays by Roshchin, Buero Vallejo, and Tennessee Williams among others. At the same time he ensured that there were new productions of classic plays, including works by Gorky, Ostrovsky, and Pogodin. He also invited leading directors, such as Anatoly Efros, to direct guest productions.

In 1973 the Moscow Art Theatre company moved into a lavish new theatre on the Tverskoi Boulevard, which proved a mixed blessing. Few people, actors or audience, liked it. The vast stage swallowed up intimate plays and made actor-audience contact difficult if not impossible. For a time performances continued to be given in the original Art Theatre in Art Theatre Lane, but this was eventually closed for renovation.

In 1976 Efreimov began a cycle of productions of Chekhov, starting with *Ivanov*, with Smoktunovsky in the lead role; other major productions included Shatrov's *Thus We Conquer*, a play with Lenin as its central character, and Bulgakov's *Molière*, which had been removed from the Art Theatre's repertoire during the Stalinist period and was now one of the first new productions to be presented at the newly refurbished original Art Theatre.

Although the company's return to its proper home should have been a happy period for Efreimov, it was, in fact, fraught with difficulty. The Art Theatre was split into two, one group remaining at the modern building on Tverskoi Boulevard, the other moving back with Efreimov to Art Theatre Lane. After a short period both groups were in trouble. A number of actors, including Borisov, who like Smoktunovsky had joined the Art Theatre after working in Leningrad with Tovstonogov, left the company. One result was to restore Efreimov to the stage as an actor, his appearances included Borisov's role as Astrov in *Uncle Vanya* and the title part in *Molière*. To his work as actor and director he then added his responsibilities as a People's Deputy in the Soviet Parliament.

Efreimov's great gift as a director is his ability to elicit performances from actors. He brings to rehearsal his own intimate and sympathetic understanding of actors' problems. He does not swamp the cast with director's effects and is sensitive to the period and circumstances in which the play was written. Thus, in working on the sets for *Uncle Vanya*, he was inspired by the work of Chekhov's friend, the painter Levitan. This approach in current conditions tends to give him a conservative air. In the post-perestroika period, when all restrictions have been lifted and censorship has been abolished there has been a rush (not always discriminating) for the new and his genuine achievements have tended to be underestimated, not least his capacity to effect change in difficult political conditions and to control the destiny of the Art Theatre under four Presidents.

—Jean Benedetti

EFROS, Anatoly (Vasilievich). Soviet director and actor. Born 1925. Trained under N. V. Petrov and M. O. Knebel at the Moscow State Institute of Theatrical Art, until 1951. Debut as director, Ryazan; artistic director, Central Children's Theatre, Moscow, 1954–63, and Lenin Komsomol Theatre, Moscow, 1963–67; staff director, Malaya Bronaya Theatre, Moscow, 1967–85; artistic director, Taganka Theatre, Moscow, from 1985. Died 1986.

Principal productions

1959	*Die Gesichte der Simone Machard* (Brecht and Feuchtwanger), Sovremennik Theatre, Moscow.
1964	*Wedding Day* (Rozov), Lenin Komsomol Theatre, Moscow.
1965	*104 Pages about Love* (Radzinsky), Lenin Komsomol Theatre, Moscow.
	Making a Movie (Radzinsky), Lenin Komsomol Theatre, Moscow.
	My Poor Marat (Arbuzov), Lenin Komsomol Theatre, Moscow.
1967	*Molière* (adapted from Bulgakov's *A Cabal of Hypocrites*), Lenin Komsomol Theatre, Moscow; revived notably, Guthrie Theatre, Minneapolis, 1979.
	Tri sestri [The Three Sisters] (Chekhov), Malaya Bronaya Theatre, Moscow.
1970	*Romeo and Juliet* (Shakespeare), Malaya Bronaya Theatre, Moscow.
1971	*The Outsider* (Dvoretsky), Malaya Bronaya Theatre, Moscow.
1972	*Brother Alyosha* (Rozov, adapted from Dostoevsky's *The Brothers Karamazov*), Malaya Bronaya Theatre, Moscow.
	The Surgeon (Korneichuk), Malaya Bronaya Theatre, Moscow.
1973	*Don Juan* (Molière), Malaya Bronaya Theatre, Moscow.
1974	*Zhenitba* [Marriage] (Gogol), Malaya Bronaya Theatre, Moscow; revived notably, Guthrie Theatre, Minneapolis.
1975	*Echelon* (Roshchin), Moscow Art Theatre, Moscow.
	Vishnevy sad [The Cherry Orchard] (Chekhov), Taganka Theatre, Moscow.
1981	*Tartuffe* (Molière), Moscow Art Theatre, Moscow.
1985	*Na dne* [The Lower Depths] (Gorky), Taganka Theatre, Moscow.

Television

Molière.

Publications

Rehearsals are My Passion, 1975; *Profession: Director*, 1979; *Prodolzhenie Teatral'nogo Rasskaza*, 1985.

* * *

The death of Anatoly Efros at the comparatively early age of 61 in 1986 deprived the Soviet theatre of one of its most respected, talented, and at times controversial directors. He took over the direction of the Central Children's Theatre in 1954, when Oleg Efreimov was a member of the company, and was appointed to the Lenin Komsomol Theatre in 1963, where he spent four important years before being sacked for what were described as "ideological inadequacies".

During his time at the Lenin Komsomol Theatre he directed a number of contemporary plays that dealt openly, perhaps too openly, with the psychological and spiritual problems of Soviet life: Rozov's *Wedding Day*, Radzinsky's *104 Pages on Love*, and Arbuzov's *My Poor Marat*. Moreover, he did not endear himself to the authorities by his decision in 1967, long before the rehabilitation of Bulgakov, to stage his *Molière; or, The Cabal of Hypocrites*, with Lyubimov in the title role. Bulgakov's bitter protest against censorship and ideological sterility, written at the beginning of the Stalinist period, had even more force in 1967 than originally and soon Efros found himself removed from the Komsomol Theatre and transplanted in the ambiguous position of staff director at the Malaya Bronaya Theatre, which left him on the fringes of the Soviet theatrical establishment. It was, however, at the Malaya Bronaya that he did much of his best work, gathering around him a group of gifted and dedicated actors.

Efros's work was based on exploration of human individuality, of personality in all its diversity and contradictions. He was intensely aware of the powerful, often irrational forces driving human behaviour. Such an approach was far removed from the official view of the mind as a social product and the emphasis on producing the new Soviet man through conditioning. Efros insisted on dealing with items that were not on the agenda. His productions were distinguished not merely by their psychological truth and insight but by the often violent physical action through which feelings and states of being were expressed. It was Efros's contention that it should be possible to block off the proscenium arch with a perspex screen and for the audience still to read the action and feelings of the characters through the actors' physical behaviour. In that he was working in the tradition of Vakhtangov and the still disgraced Meyerhold.

His radical reinterpretations of classic plays staged during the 1970's made few concessions to the official line and provoked strong criticism. Where Tovstonogov had reinterpreted *The Three Sisters* as a study in individual selfishness, In Efros's version the characters' energy had been sapped through sexual repression. Their lack of inner energy was expressed in mechanical outer movements. Their dreams of the future became absurd. The problem of positive human values was explored in his two subsequent productions: in *Romeo and Juliet* he set the passion and vitality of the two young lovers against the corrupt, debilitated world of their parents, while in *Don Juan* the central character was portrayed as a man near the end,

A scene from *The Seagull,* directed by **Anatoly Efros** (1966).

physically faltering, going through the motions of seduction mechanically, out of lifelong habit. In Gogol's *Marriage* he expressed the negative emotions of the play — fear, jealousy, revenge, spite — in a nightmare world, in which the endlessly moving and revolving set was part of the nightmare.

Occasionally, Efros was rescued from the semi-ghetto of the Malaya Bronaya by friends and colleagues. In 1975 Efreimov invited him to direct the wartime drama *Echelon* for the Moscow Art Theatre and that same year Lyubimov arranged for him to direct *The Cherry Orchard* at the Taganka — another study of a dead and sterile world. In 1981 he directed Molière's *Tartuffe* at the Art Theatre's second house; the mad household he depicted has been likened to Marx Brothers films.

When, in 1985, Efros was named as Lyubimov's successor at the Taganka Theatre, many observers felt that Efros had little to gain from such a move. Anyone attempting to take Lyubimov's place was bound to provoke hostility: Lyubimov had become, rightly or wrongly, a symbol of resistance against the dead hand of state policy. Efros's approach, for all its physicality, was more intensely psychological than Lyubimov's. On moving to the Taganka, Efros lost the group of actors who knew him and understood his methods. He was faced with a ready-made company that by and large resented him, as they would have resented any outsider. The general opinion was that his work suffered. His production of *The Lower Depths* seemed lost in the wide expanse of the Taganka stage, conveying little of the claustrophobic atmosphere of the play. Rumours that Lyubimov, whose shadow hung over the theatre, might return, perhaps permanently, did little to consolidate his position. He died suddenly in 1986, having received no official honours and too soon to benefit from the artistic freedom that came with perestroika.

—Jean Benedetti

———————

EKEROT, Bengt. Swedish director and actor. Born in Stockholm, 8 February 1920. Trained at the Dramaten Drama School, Stockholm, 1938–41. Stage debut, as an actor, Dramaten, Stockholm, 1939; debut as director, New Theatre, Stockholm, 1946; worked at the Stadsteater, Malmö, 1947–50, and at the Stadsteater, Gothenburg, 1950–53; acclaimed for productions of plays by Garcia Lorca and Bertolt Brecht; joined the Dramaten, Stockholm, 1953; directed both classical and contemporary plays there and at the Stockholm Stadsteater until his death; also appeared in several films under director Ingmar Bergman; career hampered by ill-health from 1965. Died 1971.

Productions

As director:

1946   *Le Bal des voleurs* (Anouilh), Stadsteater, Mal-
        mö.

1949   *The Giaconda Smile* (Huxley), Stadsteater,
        Malmö.
        Yerma (Lorca), Stadsteater, Malmö.
        Les Mains sales (Sartre), Stadsteater, Malmö.
        Marius (Pagnol), Stadsteater, Malmö.
        The Three Sisters (Chekhov), Stadsteater, Mal-
        mö.
        Death of a Salesman (Miller), Stadsteater,
        Malmö.

1950   *Upptäcktsresanden* [The Explorer] (Dagerman),
        Stadsteater, Malmö.

1950–53 *Dona Rosita* (Lorca), Stadsteater, Gothenburg.
        Don't Go Away Mad (Saroyan), Stadsteater,
        Gothenburg.

1951   *Den kaukasiska kritcirkeln* [The Caucasian
        Chalk Circle] (Brecht), Stadsteater, Gothen-
        burg.
        Den döda drottningen [The Dead Queen]
        (Montherlant), Stadsteater, Gothenburg.

1952   *Den yttersta dagen* [The Day of Judgement]
        (Dagerman), Stadsteater, Gothenburg.
        Le Diable et le bon Dieu (Sartre), Stadsteater,
        Gothenburg.
        Blodsbröllop [Blood Wedding] (Lorca), Stads-
        teater, Gothenburg.
        Hamlet (Shakespeare), Stadsteater, Gothen-
        burg; acted Hamlet.

1956   *Lång dags färd mot natt* [Long Day's Journey
        Into Night] (O'Neill), Dramaten, Stockholm;
        US tour, 1962.

Other productions included: *Det lyser i kåken* [The Light in
the Hut] (Höijer), 1951; *The Coronation* (Forssell), 1956;
Hughie (O'Neill), 1958; *The Emperor Jones* (O'Neill),
1958; *Fadren* [The Father] (Strindberg), 1958; *Sunday
Promenade* (Forssell), 1963; *Madcap* (Forssell), 1964; *Mi-
santropen* [The Misanthrope] (Molière).

As actor:

1939   Reginald in *Gustav Vasa* (Strindberg), Drama-
        ten, Stockholm.

1940   Curley in *Of Mice and Men* (Steinbeck), Dra-
        maten, Stockholm.

1950–53 Baise Couture in *Asmodée* (Mauriac), Stads-
        teater, Gothenburg.
        Colby Simkins in *Privatsekreteraren* [The Con-
        fidential Clerk] (Eliot), Stadsteater, Gothen-
        burg.
        Pathelin in *Farsen om Mäster Pierre Pathelin*
        [Master Pathelin's Farce], Stadsteater, Goth-
        enburg.
        The Man in *Babels torn* [The Tower of Babel]
        (Helgesson), Stadsteater, Gothenburg.
        Hamlet in *Hamlet* (Shakespeare), Stadsteater,
        Gothenburg.

1957   Jimmy Porter in *Look Back in Anger* (Os-
        borne), Dramaten, Stockholm.

1958   Mesa in *Partage de Midi* (Claudel), Dramaten,
        Stockholm.

1965   Jean Paul Marat in *Marat-Sade* (Weiss), Dra-
        maten, Stockholm.

Films

As actor:
Med livet som insats [Life in Reverse], 1938; *Hanna i
societén* [Hanna in Society], 1940; *Snapphanar*, 1942;
Natt i hamn [The Gate of the Night], 1943; *Sonja*, 1943;
Kungliga Patrasket [Royal Rabble], 1945; *Rosen på
Tistelön* [The Rose of Tistelon], 1945; *Brott och straff*
[Crime and Punishment], 1945; *Brita i grosshandlarhuset*
[Brita of the Big Warehouse], 1946; *I dödens väntrum*
[Death's Waiting-room], 1946; *Dynamit* [Dynamite],
1947; *Det Sjunde inseglet* [The Seventh Seal], 1957.

As director:
Sceningång, 1956.

Television

As actor:
Hamlet, 1955.

* * *

Bengt Ekerot belonged to the Swedish generation to
whom Constantin Stanislavsky was of the greatest importance. Ekerot made his debut as an actor while still a
student in the Drama School of the Royal Dramatic
Theatre (Dramaten) in Stockholm in Strindberg's *Gustav
Vasa* and many of the critics who saw him recognised at
once a performer of great potential. Before he left Stockholm he had been seen in a large number of sensational
roles.

Ekerot's debut as a director came at a private theatre in
Stockholm with a comedy of minor importance. It was at
the Municipal Theatre in Malmö, though, that he first
appeared to advantage as one of the outstanding directors
in the Sweden of his day. His mastery of stage lighting
combined with his influence over his actors in a varied
series of productions notable for their smooth but realistic
tone. Works directed by Ekerot during his three years at
Malmö included plays by dramatists as varying as the
Swedes Hjalmar Bergman and Stig Dagerman, Jean Anouilh, Garcia Lorca, and Arthur Miller.

After Malmö Ekerot worked at the Gothenburg Municipal Theatre and proceeded steadily from one stage of
enlightenment to another, mostly as a director of plays by
Lorca and, for the first time in his career, Bertolt Brecht in
a fruitful combination of the theories of Brecht and
Stanislavsky. He crowned his work in Gothenburg with
Shakespeare's *Hamlet* in a young, aggressive, production
full of living tradition and new vitality.

Back in his father's house in Stockholm, Ekerot now
created the masterpiece of his whole career, directing the
world premiere of Eugene O'Neill's chef-d'oeuvre, *Long
Day's Journey Into Night* in 1956. In a subsequent interview, after the production had been hailed by critics from
all over the world, Ekerot said modestly that he had only
been sitting in the theatre during the rehearsals watching
the outstanding actors come together to build the Tyrone
family. But, as always, much of the success of the produc-

tion could be credited to the director's contribution, not least in his eye for realistic detail and his mastery of gradation in language, which he perfected in this very personal play, at once both richly symbolic and realistic. The play, together with Strindberg's *The Father*, also brilliantly directed by Ekerot, and *Miss Julie*, directed by another outstanding Swedish director, Alf Sjöberg, was to form the basis of the Dramaten's very first guest appearance on tour in the USA.

Ekerot never forgot that he was also an actor. Among his most admired roles was Jimmy Porter in John Osborne's *Look Back in Anger*, which consolidated his reputation as one of the leading actors in Sweden. In particular he was praised for his dovetailing of youthful fury with the smoothest sensitivity. In the cinema he included Death in Ingmar Bergman's *The Seventh Seal* among his most famous roles.

The dedication Ekerot gave the theatre eventually exhausted him and his death, at the premature age of 51, was a major loss. But he will always remain as an outstanding artist in Swedish theatre history, both as a director and as an actor.

—Tom J. A. Olsen

EKHOF, (Hans) Konrad (Dietrich). German actor, director, and playwright. Born in Hamburg, 12 August 1720. Educated at schools in Schwerin. Married actress Georgine Sophie Caroline Auguste Spiegelberg. Worked in clerical posts from 1734 before entering theatre; stage debut, Lüneberg, 1740; actor, touring company of Johann Schönemann, 1740–64; founder, Academy of Acting, Schwerin, 1753; inherited leadership of Schönemann company, 1757; amalgamated his company with that of Gottfried Koch, 1758; actor, company of Konrad Ackermann, 1764–71; leading actor, National Theatre, Hamburg, 1767; actor, Abel Seyler's touring company, 1769–74; settled in Weimar with Seyler's troupe at invitation of Anna-Amalia of Sachsen-Weimar, 1771; theatre in Weimar Castle destroyed by fire, 1774; artistic director, Gotha Court Theatre, 1774–78; acclaimed for promoting naturalistic acting style. Died in Gotha, Saxe-Gotha, 16 June 1778.

Principal roles

1740	Xipharès in *Mithridate* (Racine), Lüneberg.
1751–56	Mellefont in *Miss Sara Sampson* (Lessing), Schwerin.
	Barnwell in *Der Kaufmann von London, Georg Barnwell* (Lillo), Schwerin.
	Beverly in *The Gamester* (Moore), Schwerin.
1764–67	Canute in *Canut* (Schlegel), Ackermann company.
	Orbesson in *Père de famille* (Diderot), Ackermann company.
1767	Tellheim in *Minna von Barnhelm* (Lessing), Ackermann company.
1767–74	Odoardo in *Emilia Galotti* (Lessing), Seyler company.
	Capellet in *Romeo und Julie* (Weisse, adapted from Shakespeare), Seyler company.

1778	The Father in *The West-Indian* (Cumberland), Court Theatre, Botha.
	The Ghost in *Hamlet* (Shakespeare), Court Theatre, Gotha.

Other roles included: Bauer in *Der Bauer mit der Erbschaft* (Krüger and Marivaux); Harpagon in *The Miser* (Molière); Lusignan and Orosmane in *Zaïre* (Voltaire); Lord Oglesby in *The Clandestine Marriage* (Garrick and Colman).

Publications

Plays:
Die Mütterschule, adaptation from La Chaussée and Marivaux, 1753; *Das Blindekuhlspiel*, 1760; *Wucherer ein Edelmann, Die wüste Insel*, adaptation from Collet, 1762.

Other:
Denkmal wahrer Grösse, 1752; *Chronologie des deutschen Theatres*, 1775; *Geschichte des deutschen Theaters*, 1766; *Progrès des Allemands dans les sciences*, 1780.

*

Bibliography

Books:
Joseph Kurschner, *Conrad Ekhofs Leben und Wirken*, Vienna, 1872.
Hugo Fetting, *Conrad Ekhof: Ein Schauspieler des achtzehnten Jahrhunderts*, Berlin, 1954.
Heinz Kindermann, *Conrad Ekhofs Schauspielerakademie*, Vienna, 1956.
Gerhard Piens, *Conrad Ekhof und die erste deutsche Schauspielerakademie*, Berlin, 1956.
Heinz Kindermann, *Theatergeschichte Europas*, vol. 4, Salzburg, 1961.
Simon Williams, *German Actors of the Eighteenth and Nineteenth Centuries: Idealism, Romanticism and Realism*, Westport, Connecticut, 1985.

Articles:
A. W. Iffland, "Über Ekhof", *Almanach für Theater und Theaterfreunde auf das Jahr 1807*, 1807.
Hermann Uhde, "Konrad Ekhof", *Der neue Plutarch*, vol. 4, 1876.
John Terfloth, "The Pre-Meiningen Rise of the Director", *Theatre Quarterly*, 6, 21, 1976.

* * *

Regarded by most historians as 'the father of German acting', Konrad Ekhof was the first actor in the German theatre who attempted to define an aesthetic of acting and to determine principles by which actors could be trained. Such an endeavour was due partially to Ekhof making a virtue from necessity. His relatively undistinguished appearance and quiet, though rich, vocal powers meant that he was singularly unsuited to perform leading roles in the inflated neoclassical tragedies that were so prominent in the repertoire during his early years in the profession. Such roles were customarily taken by actors with imposing physique and loud, sonorous, voices. Nevertheless, despite the unsuitability of the dramatic material and the frequent-

Konrad Ekhof (engraving by F. Miller, from a portrait by A. Graff).

ly primitive environment in which the Schönemann company had to perform, Ekhof developed a style of acting that was quieter, simpler, less overtly artificial, and more suited to realistic characterization than the acting practised by his colleagues. As audiences warmed to his strikingly human representations, other members of the company began to imitate him.

Ekhof was aware of the dangers of pure imitation and in 1753 he founded an 'Academy' composed of members of the Schönemann company, the prime intention of which was to discover a 'grammar' of acting that would allow performers "to see to the root cause of everything" and would provide them with a methodology that would earn for them "the name of a free artist". The Academy was also intended to define standards for the acting profession. Due to the indifference and laziness of several of its participants, regular meetings were abandoned after 13 months and the important questions raised by Ekhof would not be systematically addressed in the German theatre for the next 150 years.

The high point in Ekhof's career as an actor occurred while he was the leading actor in the shortlived Hamburg National Theatre project between 1767 and 1769. Here he had the opportunity to work with Lessing, who was dramaturg for the theatre. Ekhof's acting, which encouraged audiences both to admire and sympathize with the characters he represented, served perfectly the function of theatre as envisioned by Lessing and expounded in the *Hamburg Dramaturgy*, namely that theatre should extend audiences' sympathies and understanding to those who, for social, national, religious, or racial reasons, are different from themselves. Whatever character he played, Ekhof was capable of revealing all its facets; being master of "all the sounds and tones of passion", he was able to disclose "all aspects and folds of the heart". By arousing in audiences a sense of commonality in the human race, Ekhof was supremely an actor of the Enlightenment. Furthermore, his capacity to mingle "composure and a certain coldness" with "fire and a certain enthusiasm" provided Lessing with a living example of the art of acting as one that "stands midway between the plastic arts and poetry".

Although in his final years Ekhof lost few of his powers as an actor, he turned his attention more to professional matters. As director of the Gotha Court Theatre, he had the distinction of forming the first company of German actors that was supported solely by a subvention from a royal patron, in this case the Duke of Gotha. He took the opportunity to make a number of important innovations. While neither he nor his actors received large salaries, they were paid regularly. In addition, Ekhof initiated a pension plan for actors, though he died before this came to fruition. In this final period of his life, perhaps the most important contribution to the theatre was the training of three young actors, Heinrich Beck, Johann Beil, and August Iffland, who, when the Gotha company broke up after Ekhof's death, went on to form the nucleus of the famous Mannheim National Theatre, which would put into practice several matters relating to theatrical organization and stage representation that Ekhof could only conceive of in principle, not realise in actuality.

Ekhof's lasting contribution to the history of the theatre may well lie in his recognition of the primacy of the actor in the performance event. No doubt, this was mainly the reason why he did not welcome the plays of Shakespeare that were beginning to appear on German stages in the years immediately before his death. Shakespeare's plays, he wrote: "will utterly spoil our actors. Everyone who speaks his splendidly powerful language has nothing else to do except say it. The rapture Shakespeare excites makes everything easy for the actor". Despite this, Ekhof may well have recognised Shakespeare's theatrical power and the final role he played was the Ghost in *Hamlet*.

—Simon Williams

ERMOLOVA, Mariya (Nikolaevna). Russian actress. Born in Moscow, 3 July 1853; daughter of the prompter at the Maly Theatre, Moscow. Trained for the stage at the Moscow Theatre School, until 1870. Stage debut, while still at acting school, 1866; appeared in first major role at the Maly Theatre, 1870; joined Maly Theatre company, 1871; subsequently highly acclaimed there in the great tragic roles, playing some 300 parts in all; career revived after 1917 Revolution; retired from the stage, 1921; studio at the Maly Theatre named after her, 1930. People's Artist of the Soviet Republics, 1920; Hero of Labour, 1924. Died in Moscow, 12 March 1928.

Principal roles

1866   Fansetta in *Zenich na raschvat* (Lensky), Moscow.

1870   Emilia Galotti in *Emila Galotti* (Lessing), Maly Theatre, Moscow.

1873   Katerina in *Groza* [The Storm] (Ostrovsky), Maly Theatre, Moscow.

1874   Sofia in *Gore ot Uma* [Woe from Wit] (Griboyedov), Maly Theatre, Moscow.

1876   Elvire in *Don Juan* (Molière), Maly Theatre, Moscow.

Laurencia in *Fuente Ovejuna* (Lope de Vega), Maly Theatre, Moscow.

Hero in *Much Ado About Nothing* (Shakespeare), Maly Theatre, Moscow.

1877   Margarite in *Faust* (Goethe), Maly Theatre, Moscow.

Elvira in *El Mejor alcalde el rey* (Lope de Vega), Maly Theatre, Moscow.

Julia Tugina in *Poslednyaya zhertva* [The Last Victim] (Ostrovsky), Maly Theatre, Moscow.

1878   Ophelia in *Hamlet* (Shakespeare); revived notably, 1891.

Lady Anne in *Richard III* (Shakespeare), Maly Theatre, Moscow.

1879   Judith in *Uriel Acosta* (Gutzkow), Maly Theatre, Moscow.

Marie Tudor in *Marie Tudor* (Hugo), Maly Theatre, Moscow.

1880   Evlalia in *Nevolnitsy* [Slaves] (Ostrovsky), Maly Theatre, Moscow.

1881   Negina in *Talanty i poklonniki* [Talents and Suitors] (Ostrovsky), Maly Theatre, Moscow.

Juliet in *Romeo and Juliet* (Shakespeare), Maly Theatre, Moscow.

Gulnara in *Korsikanka* [Gulnara la Còsa] (Gualtieri), Maly Theatre, Moscow.

1884   Joan of Arc in *Die Jungfrau von Orléans* (Schiller), Maly Theatre, Moscow.

Kruchinina in *Bezvinny vinovatye* [More Sinned Against Than Sinning] (Ostrovsky), Maly Theatre, Moscow.

1886   Maria Stuart in *Maria Stuart* (Schiller), Maly Theatre, Moscow.

1887   Hermione in *The Winter's Tale* (Shakespeare), Maly Theatre, Moscow.

1888   Clärchen in *Egmont* (Goethe), Maly Theatre, Moscow.

1889   Dona Sol in *Hernani* (Hugo), Maly Theatre, Moscow.

1890   Phèdre in *Phèdre* (Racine), Maly Theatre, Moscow.

1892   Sappho in *Sappho* (Grillparzer), Maly Theatre, Moscow.

1894   Tusnelda in *Der Fechter von Ravenna* (Halm), Maly Theatre, Moscow.

Elisabeth de Valois in *Don Carlos* (Schiller), Maly Theatre, Moscow.

1896   Lady Macbeth in *Macbeth* (Shakespeare), Maly Theatre, Moscow.

1900   Natalya Petrovna in *Mesyats v derevne* [A Month in the Country] (Turgenev), Maly Theatre, Moscow.

1902   Volumnia in *Coriolanus* (Shakespeare), Maly Theatre, Moscow.

1904   Ella Rentheim in *John Gabriel Borkman* (Ibsen), Maly Theatre, Moscow.

1909   Mrs Alving in *Gengangere* [Ghosts] (Ibsen), Maly Theatre, Moscow.

1921   Mamelfa Dmitrievna in *Viceroy* (A. K. Tolstoy), Maly Theatre, Moscow.

Princess Plavutina-Plavunca in *Cholopy* (Gnedich), Maly Theatre, Moscow.

Other roles included: Queen Anne in *Le Verre d'Eau* (Scribe); Lonina in *On the Threshold of the Business* (Soloyev).

* * *

Mariya Ermolova came from a theatrical family. Her paternal grandfather was Master of the Wardrobe at the Maly, her uncle, Aleksandr, was a dramatic actor and a friend and drinking companion of Mochalov, her father was the theatre's prompter. Her other relatives were either actors, dancers or technicians. It was, therefore, natural for her to follow in their footsteps. She received her theatrical training at ballet school, where it was the custom for pupils to be allowed to play children's roles in straight plays. She acquired her clarity of diction from a French teacher of speech, Saint-Amand, who noted her dramatic potential. As far as her notions of acting were concerned these she derived from Shchepkin.

Ermolova made her stage debut in 1866 and in January 1870 played the title role in Lessing's *Emilia Galotti*. She then joined the Maly company for the 1870–71 season and remained active on the Moscow stage until 1922.

During her career, in accordance with the practice of the time, Ermolova sometimes played as many as 10 or 12 roles in a season. Her range was wide and in her early years she encompassed not only contemporary plays but major classic roles, both Russian and foreign: Sofia in *Woe from Wit*, Elvire in Molière's *Don Juan*, Laurencia in Lope de Vega's *Fuente Ovejuna*, in which she made a great impression, Margarite in Goethe's *Faust* and Marie Tudor in Victor Hugo's play of the same name. Particular success came with the tragedies of Schiller, which appealed to Russian audiences in the last quarter of the century: Mary in *Maria Stuart*, Elisabeth de Valois in *Don Carlos* and Joan in *Der Jungfrau von Orléns*, a role she repeated many times. She also played Dona Sol in Victor Hugo's *Ernani* and the title role in Racine's *Phèdre*. Of her Shakespearean roles the most admired included Volumnia in *Coriolanus*.

She was famous for her interpretation of Ostrovsky's plays and gave a notable performance as Natalya Petrovna in Turgenev's *A Month in Country*. She was among the first to perform the plays of Ibsen and also had a gift for light comedy, which she displayed as Queen Anne in Scribe's *Le Verre d'Eau*. She was always a draw for audiences, but such plays as *Maria Stuart* and *The Winter's Tale*, in which she appeared with the other great actress of the company, Fedotova, were a sell-out.

Ermolova was Stanislavsky's favourite actress in his early days and he devoted a long passage to a description of her work in *My Life in Art* (Russian edition). He defined her as essentially a personality rather than a character actress, that is to say she worked entirely off her own emotional and psychological resources. She did not, however, play the same personality all the time: her characters all differed from each other, combining different aspects of herself. This was apparently achieved without recourse to external aid or stimulus. Off-stage, she was extremely modest and reserved, mistrustful of her own reputation. Stanislavsky's analysis is confirmed by other commentators. Her working method remained a mystery even to her closest collaborators. In the initial stages of rehearsal she gave free rein to her instincts and feelings, responding spontaneously to the material. She then shaped her performance carefully and conscientiously to make it theatrically viable. After her death it was said that she combined the best qualities of Russia's two most famous actors, Mochalov and Shchepkin: she had Mochalov's passion and emotional power and Shchepkin's sense of theatrical truth and discipline. She was careful to cultivate her mind, reading widely, visiting art galleries and museums, carrying reproductions of her favourite artists — Raphael, Titian, Michelangelo — around with her. In her apartment she had a copy of the Venus de Milo. She never consciously copied these forms in her performances, but interiorized them so that they emerged spontaneously.

It was, however, Ermolova's personality that appealed to audiences. Stanislavski said of her that with her beauty and depth of emotion she expressed 'der ewig Weibliche'. In 1900 the author Yuzhin (Sumbatov) defined her personality as being essentially Russian and was convinced that it was this Russianness that made her so attractive to the public.

In the early years of the century, she began to give a series of readings and recitals. This did not endear her to the authorities and unsuccessful attempts were made to remove her from the Maly. At one time she toyed with the idea of joining the Art Theatre, which she admired, but her home was the Maly, critical though she was of its production standards after seeing the Moscow Art Theatre's *Tsar Fiodor Ioannovich*.

After the Revoltion, Ermolova was honoured first by being named one of the first of the People's Artists and then as Hero of Labour. After Meyerhold's disgrace, his theatre on Gorky Street was renamed after her.

—Jean Benedetti

EVANS, (Dame) Edith (Mary). British actress. Born in London, 8 February 1888. Educated at St Michael's School, Chester Square, London, until 1913. Married George Booth in 1925 (died 1934). Professional stage debut, under William Poel, Shakespeare Memorial Theatre, Stratford-upon-Avon, Warwickshire, 1913; toured variety theatres in Shakespearean scenes with Ellen Terry, 1918; acted at numerous London theatres and for troops overseas during both world wars; actress, Old Vic company, 1925–26, 1936; co-manager, Wyndham's Theatre, London, 1927, and Prince of Wales's Theatre, London, 1930; New York debut, 1931; actress, Royal Shakespeare Company, 1959; especially admired on both sides of the Atlantic in comedy roles and in Elizabethan and Jacobean plays as well as in Shaw, Chekhov, Wilde and plays by contemporary playwrights; also made several film appearances; virtually retired from stage on medical advice, 1971. Recipient: British Film

Academy Award, 1967; New York Critics Award for Best Actress, 1967; Berlin Film Festival Award for Best Actress, 1967. D.Litt: University of London, 1950, University of Oxford, 1954; Litt.D.: University of Cambridge, 1951. DBE (Dame of the British Empire), 1946. Died in Kent, 14 October 1976.

Roles

1913	Cressida in *Troilus and Cressida* (Shakespeare), Shakespeare Memorial Theatre, Stratford-upon-Avon, England.
	Maid in *Elizabeth Cooper* (Moore), Haymarket Theatre, London.
1914	Queen Gertrude in *Hamlet* (Shakespeare), Little Theatre, London.
	Knowledge in *Everyman* (anon.), Crosby Hall, Chelsea, London.
	Isota in *The Ladies' Company* (Hewlett), Little Theatre, London.
	Mrs Taylor in *Acid Drops* (Jennings), Royalty Theatre, London.
	Moeder Kaatje and Miss Sylvia in *My Lady's Dress* (Knoblock), Royalty Theatre, London.
	Mrs Rhead in *Milestones* (Bennett and Knoblock), Royalty Theatre, London.
1916	Lady Frances Ponsonby in *The Conference* (Gray), Royal Court Theatre, London.
	Miss Myrtle in *The Man Who Stayed At Home* (Worrall and Terry), Royalty Theatre, London.
1917	Mistress Ford in *The Merry Wives of Windsor* (Shakespeare), London Coliseum, London; British tour, 1918.
1918	Nerissa in *The Merchant of Venice* (Shakespeare), London Coliseum, London; British tour, 1918; Royal Court Theatre, London, 1919.
	The Nurse in *The Dead City* (D'Annunzio), Royal Court Theatre, London.
	The Witch of the Alps and Destiny in *Manfred* (Lord Byron), Theatre Royal, Drury Lane, London.
1919	Nona in *The Player King* (Yeats), King's Hall, Covent Garden, London.
1920	The Wife and Salvation Officer in *From Morn to Midnight* (Kaiser, translated by Dukes), Lyric Theatre, Hammersmith, London.
	Moeder Kaatje and Lady Appleby in *My Lady's Dress* (Knoblock), Royalty Theatre, London.
	Mrs Hunter in *Wedding Bells* (Field), Playhouse, London.
	Aquilina in *Venice Preserved* (Otway), Lyric Theatre, Hammersmith, London.
1921	Madame Girard in *Daniel* (Verneuil, adapted by Harris), St James's Theatre, London.
	Mrs Van Zile in *Polly With a Past* (Middleton and Bolton), St James's Theatre, London.
	Ann Ratcliffe in *The Witch of Edmonton* (Dekker, Ford, and Rowley), Lyric Theatre, Hammersmith, London.

Mrs Chester in *Mother Eve* (Montagu), Ambassadors Theatre, London.

Mrs Barraclough in *Out to Win* (Pertwee and Calthrop), Shaftesbury Theatre, London.

Lady Utterword in *Heartbreak House* (Shaw), Royal Court Theatre, London; Malvern Festival, Malvern, 1929; Queen's Theatre, London, 1932.

1922   Mrs Faraker in *The Wheel* (Fagan), Apollo Theatre, London.

Cleopatra in *All for Love* (Dryden), Shaftesbury Theatre, London.

Kate Harding in *I Serve* (Pertwee), Kingsway Theatre, London.

Cynthia Dell in *The Laughing Lady* (Sutro), Globe Theatre, London.

Ruby in *The Rumour* (Munro), Globe Theatre, London.

1923   Marged in *Taffy* (Evans), Prince of Wales's Theatre, London.

The Serpent, The Oracle, She-Ancient, and Ghost of the Serpent in *Back to Methuselah* (Shaw), Birmingham Repertory Theatre, Birmingham; Royal Court Theatre, London, 1924 and 1928.

Mistress Page in *The Merry Wives of Windsor* (Shakespeare), Lyric Theatre, Hammersmith, London; Old Vic Theatre, London, 1925–26.

1924   Millamant in *The Way of the World* (Congreve), Lyric Theatre, Hammersmith, London; Wyndham's Theatre, London, 1927.

Daisy in *The Adding Machine* (Rice), Strand Theatre, London.

Suzanne in *Tiger Cats* (adapted from *Les Félines* by Karen Bramson), Savoy Theatre, London; Royalty Theatre, London, 1931.

Mrs George Collins in *Getting Married* (Shaw), Everyman Theatre, Hampstead, London.

Helena in *A Midsummer Night's Dream* (Shakespeare), Theatre Royal, Drury Lane, London.

1925   Ann in *The Painted Swan* (Bibesco), Everyman Theatre, Hampstead, London.

Evadne in *The Maid's Tragedy* (Beaumont and Fletcher), Scala Theatre, London.

1925–26   Portia in *The Merchant of Venice* (Shakespeare), Old Vic Theatre, London.

Queen Margaret in *Richard III* (Shakespeare), Old Vic Theatre, London; Shakespeare Memorial Theatre, Stratford-upon-Avon, England, 1961.

Katharina in *The Taming of the Shrew* (Shakespeare), Old Vic Theatre, London; Theatre Royal, Drury Lane, London, 1926; New Theatre, London, 1937.

Mariana in *Measure for Measure* (Shakespeare), Old Vic Theatre, London.

Cleopatra in *Antony and Cleopatra* (Shakespeare), Old Vic Theatre, London; Piccadilly Theatre, London, 1946.

The Angel in *The Child in Flanders* (Hamilton), Old Vic Theatre, London.

Kate Hardcastle in *She Stoops to Conquer* (Goldsmith), Old Vic Theatre, London.

Edith Evans (1963).

Portia in *Julius Caesar* (Shakespeare), Old Vic Theatre, London.

Rosalind in *As You Like It* (Shakespeare), Old Vic Theatre, London; Old Vic Theatre, 1936; New Theatre, 1937.

Dame Margery Eyre in *The Shoemaker's Holiday* (Dekker), Old Vic Theatre, London.

The Nurse in *Romeo and Juliet* (Shakespeare), Old Vic Theatre, London; New Theatre, London, 1935; New Theatre, Oxford, 1932; Martin Beck Theatre, New York, 1934; New Theatre, London, 1935; Shakespeare Memorial Theatre, Stratford-upon-Avon, England, 1961.

Beatrice in *Much Ado About Nothing* (Shakespeare), Old Vic Theatre, London.

1926   Maude Fulton in *Caroline* (Maugham), Playhouse, London.

Rebecca West in *Rosmersholm* (Ibsen), Kingsway Theatre, London.

1927   Mrs Sullen in *The Beaux' Stratagem* (Farquhar), Lyric Theatre, Hammersmith, London; Royalty Theatre, London, 1930.

Maître Bolbec in *The Lady in Law* (Berr and Verneuil, translated by Murrey), Wyndham's Theatre, London.

1928   Miriam Rooth in *The Tragic Muse* (James, adapted by Griffith), Arts Theatre, London.

Josephine in *Napoleon's Josephine* (O'Riordan), Fortune Theatre, London.

1929   Florence Nightingale in *The Lady with a Lamp* (Berkeley), Arts Theatre and Garrick Theatre, London; Maxine Elliott Theatre, New York, 1931.

Orinthia in *The Apple Cart* (Shaw), Malvern Festival, Malvern, and Queen's Theatre, London.

Constance Harker in *Wills and Ways* (Glover), Arts Theatre, London.

1930   Diana in *The Humours of the Court* (Bridges), Arts Theatre, London.

Delilah in *Delilah* (Barbor), Prince of Wales's Theatre, London.

1931   Mrs Carruthers in *O.H.M.S.* (Berkeley), Arts Theatre, London, and New Theatre, London.

Laetitia in *The Old Bachelor* (Congreve), Lyric Theatre, Hammersmith, London.

1932   Emilia in *Othello* (Shakespeare), Old Vic Theatre, London.

Viola in *Twelfth Night* (Shakespeare), Old Vic Theatre, London.

Irela in *Evensong* (Knoblock and Nichols), Queen's Theatre, London; Selwyn Theatre, New York, 1933.

Irma Petersen in *Bull-dog Drummond* (Munro), Adelphi Theatre, London.

1933   May Daniels in *Once in a Lifetime* (Hart and Kaufman), Queen's Theatre, London.

Gwenny in *The Late Christopher Bean* (Fauchois, adapted by E. Williams), St James's Theatre, London; Indian tour, 1945.

1934   The Duchess of Marlborough in *Viceroy Sarah* (Ginsbury), Arts Theatre, London.

1935   Agatha Payne in *The Old Ladies* (Ackland, adapted from Walpole), New Theatre, London.

1936   Irina Arcadina in *The Seagull* (Chekhov), New Theatre, London.

Lady Fidget in *The Country Wife* (Wycherley), Old Vic Theatre, London.

Mother Sawyer in *The Witch of Edmonton* (Dekker, Ford, and Rowley), Old Vic Theatre, London.

1937   Sanchia Carson in *Robert's Wife* (Ervine), Globe Theatre, London.

1939   Lady Bracknell in *The Importance of Being Earnest* (Wilde), Globe Theatre, London; Phoenix Theatre, London, 1942.

1940   Muriel Meilhac in *Cousin Muriel* (Dane), Globe Theatre, London.

Lady Epifania Fitzfassenden in *The Millionairess* (Shaw), British tour.

Several roles in *Diversion* (revue by Farjeon), Wyndham's Theatre, London.

1941   Several roles in *Diversion Number Two* (revue by Farjeon), Wyndham's Theatre, London.

Katherine Markham in *Old Acquaintance* (van Druten), Apollo Theatre, London.

1943   Hesione Hushabye in *Heartbreak House* (Shaw), Cambridge Theatre, London and overseas tour.

1945   Mrs Malaprop in *The Rivals* (Sheridan), Criterion Theatre, London.

1946   Katerina Ivanovna in *Crime and Punishment* (Dostoevsky, adapted by Ackland), New Theatre, London.

1948   Lady Wishfort in *The Way of the World* (Congreve), New Theatre, London.

Madame Ranevsky in *The Cherry Orchard* (Chekhov), New Theatre, London.

1949   Lady Pitts in *Daphne Laureola* (Bridie), Wyndham's Theatre, London; Music Box Theatre, New York, 1950.

1951   Helen Lancaster in *Waters of the Moon* (Hunter), Haymarket Theatre, London.

1954   Countess Rosmarin Ostenburg in *The Dark Is Light Enough* (Fry), Aldwych Theatre, London.

1956   Mrs St Maugham in *The Chalk Garden* (Bagnold), Alexandra Theatre, Birmingham, and Haymarket Theatre, London.

1958   Queen Katharine in *Henry VIII* (Shakespeare), Old Vic Theatre, London, and European tour.

1959   Countess of Roussillon in *All's Well That Ends Well* (Shakespeare), Shakespeare Memorial Theatre, Stratford-upon-Avon, England.

Volumnia in *Coriolanus* (Shakespeare), Shakespeare Memorial Theatre, Stratford-upon-Avon, England.

1963   Violet in *Gentle Jack* (Bolt), Queen's Theatre, London.

1964   Judith Bliss in *Hay Fever* (Coward), National Theatre, London.

1965   Mrs Forest in *The Chinese Prime Minister* (Bagnold), National Theatre, London.

1973–74   Herself in *Edith Evans ... and Friends* (Clifford), tour.

Films

A Welsh Singer, 1915; *East is East*, 1915; *The Queen of Spades*, 1948; *The Last Days of Dolwyn*, 1948; *The Importance of Being Earnest*, 1951; *Look Back in Anger*, 1959; *The Nun's Story*, 1959; *Tom Jones*, 1963; *The Chalk Garden*, 1964; *Young Cassidy*, 1965; *The Whisperers*, 1967; *Fitzwilly*, 1968; *Prudence and the Pill*, 1968; *Crooks and Coronets*, 1969; *The Madwoman of Chaillot*, 1969; *David Copperfield*, 1969; *Scrooge*, 1970; *A Doll's House*, 1973; *Craze*, 1973; *The Slipper and the Rose*, 1976; *Nasty Habits*, 1976.

Television

The Importance of Being Earnest, 1954; *A Question of Fact*, 1954; *The Old Ladies*, 1955; *Waters of the Moon*, 1959; *The Importance of Being Earnest*, 1959; *Hay Fever*, 1960; *Upon This Rock*, 1973; *QB VII*, 1974.

*

Bibliography

Books:
J. C. Trewin, *Edith Evans*, London, 1954.

Bryan Forbes, *Edith Evans. A Personal Memoir*, London, 1977.

Bryan Forbes, *Ned's Girl. The Authorised Biography of Dame Edith Evans*, London, 1977.

* * *

Sybil Thorndike, the only contemporary who might have disputed the title with her, called Edith Evans simply "our greatest actress". Evans first took the stage while working as a milliner, appearing with an amateur company in South London under a remarkable teacher, Miss E. C. Massey, for whom she played such leading Shakespearean roles as Viola in *Twelfth Night*, Beatrice in *Much Ado About Nothing*, and the Duchess of York in *Richard II*. The story has often been told of how William Poel saw her and chose her to play Cressida in the rarely seen *Troilus and Cressida* in four performances, experimentally conceived and addressed to an audience of keen and learned Shakespeareans. Her success in creating so fresh and original a portrait of a 'real' woman (in Elizabethan dress) determined her to turn professional. There can be no doubt that Poel's notorious and eccentric approach to vocal delivery helped in the creation of her remarkable stage voice, with its great range and flexibility, encompassing subtlety of tone but also extravagances of manner, perfectly controlled swoops, flounces, curlicues, and festoons of sound. She herself spoke on occasion of the lovely sense of words streaming from her like water from a fountain.

There are two contradictory versions of how her career went during the first decade: that she had a difficult struggle for recognition and alternatively that her route to fame was easy, with luck as well as talent on her side. The two views are reconcilable in that the work kept coming to her and awareness of an actress out of the ordinary spread among the profession and discerning critics, yet she remained unknown to the public at large, with little sign of progressing out of small parts in the commercial theatre. Her features were heavy, disqualifying her for conventional 'jeune première' roles and she found herself frequently having to assume age to play more or less elderly matrons. On the other hand, a genuinely elderly but most famous actress, Ellen Terry, sought her out to play Mistress Ford to her Mistress Page and Nerissa in scenes from *The Merry Wives of Windsor* and *The Merchant of Venice* performed in variety theatres — and she also gained experience in rarely seen drama of distinction through working with the Stage Society and the Phoenix Society, giving a triumphant foretaste of her most famous performances when she played Cleopatra in Dryden's *All for Love*. Then George Bernard Shaw, an appreciative follower of Poel's work and a keen talent spotter, lifted her out of the rut with some unusual and difficult roles: the Serpent in the Garden of Eden and a She-Ancient in *Back to Methuselah*, which she played with the Birmingham Repertory company. For the Serpent she invented strange body movements as well as a sinuous seductive voice punctuated with a faint hiss; as the She-Ancient of a far-distant future she was remote, gentle, seeming infinitely wise. There followed Millamant in *The Way of the World* for Nigel Playfair at the Lyric Theatre, Hammersmith, which represented one of the two great peaks of her acting career — the other being Lady Bracknell in John Gielgud's production of *The Importance of Being Earnest* in 1939. Her second Rosalind, at the Old

Vic, might be added, thanks to the special magic evoked by the private emotional relationship between her and her Orlando, Michael Redgrave, but there have been other captivating Rosalinds in this century. The minor role of the Nurse in *Romeo and Juliet* was virtually appropriated by her for her generation.

Evans's brilliance in Restoration comedy helped to re-establish it in the repertoire. Her style combined a perfection of period artifice with freshness and humanity; she wooed and won her audiences. The performances were the result of meticulous preparation, the actress working over single phrases and gestures until they seemed just right, then putting everything together with an effect of complete ease and spontaneity. Recognising a superb comedienne, the influential critic James Agate warned her against playing tragedy. Certainly, when she came to play Shakespeare's Cleopatra, she succeeded with the witty extravagant queen, but missed the transcendence of the last act. Mixed accounts of her Rebecca in Ibsen's *Rosmersholm* suggest an inadequate, perhaps otherwise undercast production, in which she struggled to bring her fellow players up to the same plane as her own performance. Her Arcadina in *The Seagull* was admired but found a little cold, which might be a legitimate reading of the part of a successful, self-regarding actress. As Ranevskaya in *The Cherry Orchard*, she established her command of tragi-comic pathos. Her film performances as the aged Countess in *The Queen of Spades* and a solitary down-at-heel pensioner in *The Whisperers* are enough in themselves to prompt a wish that she had been positively encouraged and guided into further exploration of the tragic repertoire. As early as 1933, she had shown in *The Late Christopher Bean* that she could play a simple Welsh maidservant as well as she could a mannered sophisticate.

Evans revealed her way of working, explaining that she approached each part without preconceptions, digging into the script and imagining a being with whom she could identify and who could exist truthfully within the author's lines. She was uninterested in theory: looking into Stanislavsky's writings, she could not be bothered to go on reading. The identification with her roles seemed total, the effect of complete concentration. Having thought her way into a character, she was prolific in ideas for original touches and risk-taking strokes and she had the disciplined technique to carry them through. Despite the surviving record on film and disc, legend has wrenched her Lady Bracknell out of context, even isolating a single phrase and rendering it grotesque in frequent imitation. In fact, Gielgud's production was beautifully balanced, united in a precision of style far removed from burlesque. Edith Evans knew the (now-vanished) social type she based the character upon and spoke of domineering women who rang a bell to fetch a maid to put a lump of coal on the fire; she knew their inhibited stiffness, their snobbery, and the tones and accents with which they spoke. That truth was raised to the edge of fantasy and its own kind of grace.

Edith Evans got herself into the Old Vic company against resistance from Lilian Baylis and she was there for a short period only, though she played many roles. Katharine of Aragon in Henry VIII, with Gielgud as Wolsey, lay ahead, as did the Countess of Roussillon under Tyrone Guthrie's direction and Volumnia under Peter Hall. Yet the conclusion is hard to resist that the theatre wasted her talents on a lot of indifferent material over the years and her two brief failed attempts in management for herself, like her reluctance to take as many Shaw roles as the playwright offered, may indicate faults of judgement on her own part.

—Margery Morgan

EVANS, Maurice (Hubert). British-born US actor and producer. Born in Dorchester, Dorset, England, 3 June 1901. Educated at the Grocers' Company School, London. Stage debut, Festival Theatre, Cambridge, 1926; first London appearance, Wyndham's Theatre, 1927; actor, Old Vic company, Sadler's Wells Theatre, London, 1934–35; New York debut, Martin Beck Theatre, 1935; acclaimed in Shakespearean roles, notably with Old Vic company and under Margaret Webster, 1930's; took US citizenship, 1941; served in US army, 1942–45; in charge of Army Entertainment Section, Central Pacific Area, 1942–45; honorary artistic supervisor, City Centre Theatre Company, New York, 1949–51; performed few roles after 1965. Member: Board of Trustees, American Shakespeare Festival, Stratford, Connecticut. Recipient: Pulitzer Critics' Prize, 1953; Emmy Award, 1961. LL.D: University of Hawaii; Lafayette College, Easton, Pennsylvania; Brandeis University, Waltham, Massachusetts. Legion of Merit, 1945. Died in Rottingdean, England, 12 March 1989.

Roles

1926   Orestes in *The Oresteia* (Aeschylus), Festival Theatre, Cambridge.
1927   P.C. Andrews in *The One-Eyed Herring* (Young), Wyndham's Theatre, London.
1928   Stephani in *Listeners* (Berkeley), Wyndham's Theatre, London.
        Sir Blayden Coote in *The Stranger in the House* (Morton and Traill), Wyndham's Theatre, London.
        Hector Frome and Edward Clements in *Justice* (Galsworthy), Wyndham's Theatre, London.
        Borring and Graviter in *Loyalties* (Galsworthy), Wyndham's Theatre, London.
        Jean in *The Man They Buried* (Bramson, translated by Murrey), Ambassadors' Theatre, London.
        Wyn Hayward in *Diversion* (van Druten), Little Theatre, London.
        Second Lieutenant Raleigh in *Journey's End* (Sherriff), Apollo Theatre, London; Savoy Theatre, London, 1929.
1930   Young Frenchman in *The Man I Killed* (Rostand), Savoy Theatre, London.
        The Sailor in *The Queen Bee* (Connell and Hawthorne), Savoy Theatre, London.
        Professor Agi in *The Swan* (Molnar), St James's Theatre, London.
        Owen Llewellyn in *To See Ourselves* (Delafield), Ambassadors' Theatre, London.
1931   Marius in *Sea Fever* (Lee and van Druten), New Theatre, London.

Eric Masters in *Those Naughty Nineties* (Graham and Simpson), Criterion Theatre, London.
        Ralph in *After All* (van Druten), British tour.
1932   Nigel Chelmsford in *Avalanche* (Nichols), Arts Theatre, London.
        Jean Jacques in *The Heart Line* (Puget), Lyric Theatre, London.
        Peter in *Will You Love Me Always?* (Halasz, translated by Aylmer), Globe Theatre, London.
        Reverend Peter Penlee in *Playground* (Scott), Royalty Theatre, London.
1933   Guy Daunt in *Cecilia* (Monkhouse), Arts Theatre, London.
        Dick in *The Soldier and the Gentlewoman* (adapted from the novel by Massingham and Lister), Vaudeville Theatre, London.
        Arnold Waite in *Other People's Lives* (Milne), Wyndham's Theatre, London.
        Aristide in *Ball at the Savoy* (Hammerstein), Theatre Royal, Drury Lane, London.
1934   Edward Voysey in *The Voysey Inheritance* (Granville-Barker), Sadler's Wells Theatre, London, and Shaftesbury Theatre, London.
        Octavius Caesar in *Antony and Cleopatra* (Shakespeare), Sadler's Wells Theatre, London.
        Richard in *Richard II* (Shakespeare), Sadler's Wells Theatre, London; US tour, 1937; St James Theatre, New York, 1937 and 1940; City Centre Theatre, New York, 1951.
        Benedick in *Much Ado About Nothing* (Shakespeare), Sadler's Wells Theatre, London.
        The Dauphin in *Saint Joan* (G. B. Shaw), Sadler's Wells Theatre, London; Martin Beck Theatre, New York, 1936.
1935   Petruchio in *The Taming of the Shrew* (Shakespeare), Sadler's Wells Theatre, London.
        Iago in *Othello* (Shakespeare), Sadler's Wells Theatre, London.
        Hippolytus in *Hippolytus* (Euripides), Sadler's Wells Theatre, London.
        Adolphus Cusins in *Major Barbara* (G. B. Shaw), Sadler's Wells Theatre, London.
        Silence in *Henry IV, part 2* (Shakespeare), Sadler's Wells Theatre, London.
        Hamlet in *Hamlet* (Shakespeare), Sadler's Wells Theatre, London; St James Theatre, New York, 1938; 44th Street Theatre, New York, 1939; (as *GI Hamlet*) Columbus Circle Theatre, New York, 1945; US tour, 1945–47; City Centre Theatre, New York, 1946.
1936   Napoleon in *St Helena* (Sherriff and Casilis), Lyceum Theatre, New York.
1935   Romeo in *Romeo and Juliet* (Shakespeare), Martin Beck Theatre, New York, and British tour.
1937   Falstaff in *Henry IV, part 1* (Shakespeare), Forrest Theatre, Philadelphia; St James Theatre, New York, 1939.
1940   Malvolio in *Twelfth Night* (Shakespeare), St James Theatre, New York, and US tour.

Maurice Evans (1968).

1941	Macbeth in *Macbeth* (Shakespeare), National Theatre, New York; US tour, 1942.
1947	John Tanner in *Man and Superman* (G. B. Shaw), Alvin Theatre, New York; US tour, 1948–49; City Centre Theatre, New York, 1949.
1949	Andrew Crocker-Harris in *The Browning Version* (Rattigan), Coronet Theatre, New York.
	Arthur Gosport in *Harlequinade* (Rattigan), Coronet Theatre, New York.
1950	Dick Dudgeon in *The Devil's Disciple* (G. B. Shaw), City Centre Theatre, New York, Royale Theatre, New York, and US tour.
1951	Hjalman Ekdal in *The Wild Duck* (Ibsen), City Centre Theatre, New York.
1952	Tony Wendice in *Dial M for Murder* (Knott), Plymouth Theatre, New York.
1956	King Magnus in *The Apple Cart* (Shaw), Plymouth Theatre, New York; US tour, 1957.
1959	Captain Shotover in *Heartbreak House* (G. B. Shaw), Billy Rose Theatre, New York.
1960	Reverend Brock in *Tenderloin* (Bock and Harnick), Shubert Theatre, New Haven, Connecticut, and 46th Street Theatre, New York.
1962	H. J. in *The Aspern Papers* (Redgrave, adapted from James), Playhouse Theatre, New York.
	Several roles in *Shakespeare Revisited: A Program for Two Players* (Shakespeare compilation), American Shakespeare Festival, Stratford, Connecticut; US tour, 1962–63.
1973	The Narrator in *The Plague*, National Symphony Orchestra, Washington, D.C.
	Oberon and other roles in *Shakespeare and the Performing Arts* (Shakespeare compilation), Festival of Shakespeare Dance and Drama, Kennedy Centre for the Performing Arts, Washington, D.C.
1981	Norman in *On Golden Pond* (Thompson), Florida.

Also acted roles in: *The Grass Is Greener* (H. and M. Williams), US tour, 1965; *Holiday* (Barry), Los Angeles, 1980.

Films

White Cargo, 1930; *Raise the Roof*, 1930; *Should a Doctor Tell?*, 1931; *Cupboard Love*, 1932; *Marry Me*, 1932; *Wedding Rehearsal*, 1932; *The Empress and I*, 1933; *The Only Girl*, 1934; *Bypass to Happiness*, 1934; *The Path of Glory*, 1934; *Checkmate*, 1935; *Scrooge*, 1935; *Kind Lady*, 1951; *Androcles and the Lion*, 1952; *The Great Gilbert and Sullivan*, 1953; *Macbeth*, 1963; *The War Lord*, 1965; *One of Our Spies Is Missing*, 1966; *Jack of Diamonds*, 1967; *Planet of the Apes*, 1968; *Rosemary's Baby*, 1968; *The Body Stealers*, 1969; *Beneath the Planet of the Apes*, 1970; *Terror in the Wax Museum*, 1973; *The Jerk*, 1979; *Sam Hughes' War*, 1984.

Television

As actor:
"Hamlet", *Hallmark Hall of Fame*, 1953; "Richard II", *Hallmark Hall of Fame*, 1954; "Macbeth", *Hallmark Hall of Fame*, 1954; "The Devil's Disciple", *Hallmark Hall of Fame*, 1955; "The Taming of the Shrew", *Hallmark Hall of Fame*, 1956; "Man and Superman", *Hallmark Hall of Fame*, 1956; "Twelfth Night", *Hallmark Hall of Fame*, 1957; "Dial M for Murder", *Hallmark Hall of Fame*, 1958; "The Tempest", *Hallmark Hall of Fame*, 1960; *Bewitched* (series), 1964–72; "Saint Joan", *Hallmark Hall of Fame*, 1967; *Batman*, 1967; *U.M.C.*, 1969; *Brotherhood of the Bell*, 1970; *The Girl, the Gold Watch, and Everything*, 1980; *Agatha Christie's "A Caribbean Mystery"*, 1983. Other appearances included roles in "Caesar and Cleopatra", *General Electric Theatre*; *Tarzan*; *The Six Million Dollar Man*.

As producer:
"The Devil's Disciple", *Hallmark Hall of Fame*, 1955; "Dream Girl", *Hallmark Hall of Fame*, 1955; "Alice in Wonderland", *Hallmark Hall of Fame*, 1955; "The Corn is Green", *Hallmark Hall of Fame*, 1956; "The Good Fairy", *Hallmark Hall of Fame*, 1956; "The Taming of the Shrew", *Hallmark Hall of Fame*, 1956; "The Cradle Song", *Hallmark Hall of Fame*, 1956.

Publications

Hamlet (adapted from Shakespeare), 1945; *All This ... And Evans Too* (autobiography), 1987.

* * *

Maurice Evans was 36 when he achieved fame with his New York Richard II in 1937; but the long period of preparation stood him in good stead. Before joining the Old Vic company in September 1934, Evans had gained a good deal of experience in modern plays. He had scored an early success as Second Lieutenant Raleigh in *Journey's End* in 1928, remaining in the cast when the play re-opened at the Savoy Theatre in January 1929, but it was not until the Old Vic season of 1934–35 that Evans had the opportunity of showing his abilities in the Shakespearean repertoire, his roles including Richard II, Hamlet, Iago, Octavius Caesar, Benedick, and Petruchio — a demanding series of parts that would hardly be expected of today's actors. It was apparent that a classical actor of stature had come onto the scene.

It was Evans's Richard that made, perhaps, the most striking impression; certainly it was this role that established him on the New York stage (the production also marked the Broadway debut of Margaret Webster as director and launched a fruitful Webster-Evans partnership). Here was sustained lyricism, mastery of Shakespearean idiom, and control of those luxuriant Ricardian verse-paragraphs. Robert Speaight noted the recording of Evans's Richard "reminded some listeners of Alexander Moissi; the work, it seemed, of a cantor rather an actor; and Richard, the most lyrical of Shakespeare's tragic protagonists, was particularly suited to his style." The comparison with Moissi is interesting, Moissi having been renowned for his vocal richness and musicality. Clearly *Richard* was the occasion for a splendid matching of a role's demands with the qualities of an actor; one thinks of Gielgud's triumph in the same play. Evans's delivery of "We are amazed ... " suggested to J. C. Trewin "the last flare before the sun of the Plantagenets fell beneath the horizon". Trewin also remembered the eloquence of the King's farewell to his Queen in the last act and the "long, flashing upward gesture" that accompanied his prophecy to Northumberland:

> Northumberland, thou ladder wherewithal
> The mounting Bolingbroke ascends my throne.

This Richard was well able to sustain comparison with Gielgud's.

As a Shakespearean actor Evans showed considerable versatility. He gave his US audiences not only Hamlet, Romeo, and Macbeth, but also the Falstaff of *Henry IV, part 1*, Silence, and Malvolio. He frequently re-worked and re-explored roles, in particular those of Hamlet and Richard II. He played Macbeth in 1941, returning to it in 1960, when he made a film version, again playing opposite Judith Anderson. This was a low-budget enterprise designed to attract television sales; one can only regret that Olivier's projected film had to be abandoned. Evans was also active as an exponent of Shaw: among other parts, he played John Tanner in his own production of *Man and Superman*, King Magnus, and Captain Shotover. Most of these productions

were taken on tour; Evans did much sterling work in bringing classical theatre to various US towns and cities. In the same spirit he presented (and later published) an abridged *Hamlet* for the forces (the "GI Hamlet"). A later venture (with Helen Hayes) was the recital *Shakespeare Revisited; A Program for Two Players*, which was toured throughout the USA in 1962–63. In addition he put on television versions of both Shakespeare and Shaw, confirming his reputation as an enthusiastic advocate of the best in English drama.

Observers are agreed on the virtues of Evans's style: thoughtful, disciplined playing, vocal command, and careful preparation. He brought to his work exactly the qualities required by Margaret Webster and the Theatre Guild. In comedy he was capable of creating odd and appealing effects. In the Theatre Guild *Twelfth Night*, for instance, he wore "a black bow tie, and wide, winged, upstanding ... collar. His genteel cockney accent brought the part closer to Pinero or Wilde than to Olivia's household." Critics have since seen in this performance a precursor of Olivier's celebrated Malvolio at Stratford in 1955. In tragedy he won praise for his positive virtues, but some critics felt there was a lack of dynamism. There was no doubting the princely credentials of his Hamlet; the scholar and student were well presented, although strenuousness and inner debate were less in evidence. As Macbeth, he used his intelligence and vocal resource to good purpose; he did not produce the large effects and volcanic power summoned up by certain of his contemporaries on the English stage. But that is only to say that Evans knew his strengths and played to them. He did not possess the iron quality and ruggedness of Wolfit or — in an earlier generation — Randle Ayrton and Baliol Holloway. He did not communicate the physicality and sense of danger associated with Olivier. But his *bravura* was of a different kind; perhaps Gielgud provides a more apt comparison. One recalls in fairness that when Evans was astonishing New York audiences with the virtuosity of his Richard II, Olivier (six years his junior) was in the midst of his early striving with the demands of Shakespearean blank verse.

—Charles Calder

———

EVREINOV, Nikolai (Nikolaivich). Russian director, playwright and theorist. Born in Moscow, 26 February 1879. Educated at the Conservatoire, St Petersburg. Co-founder, with Baron Nikolai Drizen, of the Ancient Theatre, St Petersburg, 1907–08 and 1911–12; co-director, Vera Kommisarjevskaya's Theatre, St Petersburg, 1908–09; co-founder, with Theodore Kommisarjevsky, Merry Theatre for Grown-up Children, St Petersburg, 1909; artistic director, Krivoye Zerkalo (Crooked Mirror) Theatre, Moscow, 1910–17; with the Revolution, largely withdrew from the theatre to concentrate on theoretical writings, 1917; emigrated to Paris, 1925. Died in Paris, 7 September 1953.

Productions

1907–08   *The Three Magi* (trad.), Ancient Theatre, St Petersburg.

The Miracle of Theophilus (Rutebeuf), Ancient Theatre, St Petersburg.

Play of Robin and Marion (De La Halle), Ancient Theatre, St Petersburg.

1910–17   *V kulisax dusi* [In the Stage-Wings of the Soul] (Evreinov), Krivoye Zerkalo Theatre, Moscow.

Revizor [The Government Inspector] (Gogol, adapted by Evreinov), Krivoye Zerkalo Theatre, Moscow.

Skola etualej [The School of the Stars] (Evreinov), Krivoye Zerkalo Theatre, Moscow.

Kuxnja smexna. Mirovoj konkurs ostroumija [A Feast of Laughter. The World Contest of Wit] (Evreinov), Krivoye Zerkalo Theatre, Moscow.

Kolombina segodnja [A Columbine of Today] (Evreinov), Krivoye Zerkalo Theatre, Moscow.

Vecnaja tancovscica [The Eternal Dancer] (Evreinov), Krivoye Zerkalo Theatre, Moscow.

Cetvertaja stena [The Fourth Wall] (Evreinov), Krivoye Zerkalo Theatre, Moscow.

O sesti krasavicax ne poxozix drug na druga [About Six Beautiful Women who Don't Resemble One Another] (El-Bassri, adapted by Evreinov), Krivoye Zerkalo, Theatre, Moscow.

Pod vlast'ju Pana [Under the Power of Pan] (Vengerova and Evreinov), Krivoye Zerkalo Theatre, Moscow.

Pesni Bilitis [Songs of Bilitis] (Evreinov), Krivoye Zerkalo Theatre, Moscow.

Veer [The Fan] (Evreinov), Krivoye Zerkalo Theatre, Moscow.

Karagez (Evreinov), Krivoye Zerkalo Theatre, Moscow.

The Doctor's Dilemma (G. B. Shaw, adapted by Evreinov), Krivoye Zerkalo Theatre, Moscow.

Eolovye arfy [Aeolian Harps] (Evreinov and Gejer), Krivoye Zerkalo Theatre, Moscow.

Sladkij pirog [A Sweet Pastry] (Evreinov and Urvancev), Krivoye Zerkalo Theatre, Moscow.

Ljubov k bliznemu [Love for One's Neighbour] (Andreyev), Krivoye Zerkalo Theatre, Moscow.

Prekrasnye sabinjanki [The Sabine Women] (Andreyev), Krivoye Zerkalo Theatre, Moscow.

Monument [Monument] (Andreyev), Krivoye Zerkalo Theatre, Moscow.

Voda zizni [Aqua Vitae] (Gejer), Krivoye Zerkalo Theatre, Moscow.

Son [Dream] (Gejer), Krivoye Zerkalo Theatre, Moscow.

Vospominanija [Reminiscences] (Gejer), Krivoye Zerkalo Theatre, Moscow.

Legenda o svj ascennom cernom lebede [The Legend of the Holy Black Swan] (Gejer), Krivoye Zerkalo Theatre, Moscow.

Solnecnye zajciki [Reflections of Sunrays] (Gejer), Krivoye Zerkalo Theatre, Moscow.

Nosovoj platok baronessy [The Handkerchief of the Baroness] (Gejer), Krivoye Zerkalo Theatre, Moscow.

Oprometcivyj turk [The Hasty Turk] (Prutkov), Krivoye Zerkalo Theatre, Moscow.

Torzestvennoe publicnoe zasedanie pamjati Kozmy Prutkova po slucaju pjatiletija ego konciny [A Solemn Public Conference Commemorating Kozma Prutkov on the Fifth Anniversary of His Death] (Smirnov and Scerbakov), Krivoye Zerkalo Theatre, Moscow.

The 29th of Martober (Vyskov), Krivoye Zerkalo Theatre, Moscow.

Vsegdasnie sasni [Everyday Affairs] (Sologub), Krivoye Zerkalo Theatre, Moscow.

Evoljucija djavola [The Evolution of the Devil] (Teffi), Krivoye Zerkalo Theatre, Moscow.

Cetvero [The Four] (Avercenko), Krivoye Zerkalo Theatre, Moscow.

Zamecatelnoe predstavlenie [A Wonderful Presentation] (Avercenko), Krivoye Zerkalo Theatre, Moscow.

Gastrol Rycalova [Rycalov's Tour] (Avercenko), Krivoye Zerkalo Theatre, Moscow.

Nravstennye osnovy celoveka [The Moral Bases of Man] (Smirnov and Scerbakov), Krivoye Zerkalo Theatre, Moscow.

Kolbasa iz babocek [Sausage from Butterflies] (Smirnov and Scerbakov), Krivoye Zerkalo Theatre, Moscow.

Bjuro poxoronnyx processij [The Bureau of the Funeral Services] (Smirnov and Scerbakov), Krivoye Zerkalo Theatre, Moscow.

Vasil Vasilic pomirilsja [Vasil Vasilic Reconciled] (Urvancev), Krivoye Zerkalo Theatre, Moscow.

Ne xvalis iduci na rat [Don't Shoot Your Mouth off Before Going into Battle] (Sac), Krivoye Zerkalo Theatre, Moscow.

Vostocnye sladosti [Eastern Delights] or *Bitva russkix s kabardincami* [The Russians' Battle with the Kabardinians] (Sac and Podgornyj), Krivoye Zerkalo Theatre, Moscow.

Rycarskaja ballada [A Chivalrous Ballad] (Erenberg), Krivoye Zerkalo Theatre, Moscow.

V Versale [In Versailles] (Erenberg), Krivoye Zerkalo Theatre, Moscow.

Sumurun (Erenberg), Krivoye Zerkalo Theatre, Moscow.

Torzestvennaja kantata [A Festive Cantata] (Erenberg), Krivoye Zerkalo Theatre, Moscow.

Zeltaja kofta [Yellow Jacket] (Erenberg), Krivoye Zerkalo Theatre, Moscow.

Vostorgi ljubvi [Love's Delights] (Erenberg), Krivoye Zerkalo Theatre, Moscow.

Mudrec Catamutra [The Sage of Catamutra] (Erenberg), Krivoye Zerkalo Theatre, Moscow.

Zenscina i smert [Woman and Death] (Antimonov), Krivoye Zerkalo Theatre, Moscow.

Cuzaja zena i muz pod krovatju [Someone Else's Wife and Husband under the Bed] (Antimonov, adapted from Dostoevsky), Krivoye Zerkalo Theatre, Moscow.

Muzja i zeny [Husbands and Wives] (Antimonov), Krivoye Zerkalo Theatre, Moscow.

A ne opustit li nam zanavesku? [Shouldn't We Lower the Curtain?] (Potemkin), Krivoye Zerkalo Theatre, Moscow.

Barometr [Barometer] (Potemkin), Krivoye Zerkalo Theatre, Moscow.

Starozily 1812–1912 [Old Timers 1812–1912] (Potemkin), Krivoye Zerkalo Theatre, Moscow.

Pod zvuki trombona [To the Accompaniment of a Trombone] (Saxarov), Krivoye Zerkalo Theatre, Moscow.

Nemaja zena [A Mute Wife] (France), Krivoye Zerkalo Theatre, Moscow.

Objavljaetsja pereryv [An Intermission is Announced] (Jonson), Krivoye Zerkalo Theatre, Moscow.

Primernye suprugi [Model Spouses], Krivoye Zerkalo Theatre, Moscow.

Stranicka romana [A Page from a Novel] (Esterejx), Krivoye Zerkalo Theatre, Moscow.

Vodevil 1812 goda [Vaudeville of 1812], Krivoye Zerkalo Theatre, Moscow.

Xorovod [La Ronde] (Schnitzler), Krivoye Zerkalo Theatre, Moscow.

Dekamerona cas [Decameron Hour] (Ljubosic-Ljubovnaja), Krivoye Zerkalo Theatre, Moscow.

1920   *Vzjatie Zimnego Dvorca* [The Storming of the Winter Palace] (pageant), Uritsky Square, Petrograd.

Films

Fécondité, 1929.

Publications

Stepik and Maniurochka (play), 1905; *The Beautiful Despot* (play), 1906; *A Merry Death* (play), 1908; *An Introduction to Monodrama*, 1909; *The Presentation of Love* (monodrama), 1910; *V kulisax dusi* [In the Stage-Wings of the Soul] (monodrama), 1911; *The Theatre as Such*, 1912; *The Theatre for Oneself*, 3 vols., 1915–17; *Pro Scena Sua*, 1915; *Cetvertajastena* [The Fourth Wall] (play), 1915; *The Chief Thing* (play), 1921; *The Theatre in Life*, translated and edited by A. I. Nazaroff, 1927; *The Ship of the Righteous* (play); *Le Théâtre en Russe Sovietique*, 1946; *Life as Theatre: Five Modern Plays*, translated and edited by C. Collins, 1973.

*

Bibliography

Books:
E. A. Znosko-Borovsky, *Evreinoff*, Paris, 1924.
Genia Cannac, *Nicolas Evreinoff en France*, Paris, 1978.
Ellendea Proffer, *Evreinov: A Pictorial Biography*, Ann Arbor, Michigan, 1981.
Spencer Golub, *Evreinov: The Theatre of Paradox and Transformation*.

* * *

Nikolai Evreinov was one of those geniuses so talented in so many fields that he never fully realised his potential in any of them. Born in 1879, by the age of 40 he was recognised as a major theatre director, a playwright and a theatrical historian and theoretician of the first rank; a philosopher, a social historian, a juggler and circus performer, and a prolific composer who had studied with Rimsky-Korsakov and was able to play many musical instruments, from the piano to the spoons.

As a playwright, his work was performed in all the major theatres of Russia. Some of his early plays, notably *Stepik and Maniurochka*, *The Beautiful Despot* and *A Merry Death*, retain a genuine freshness and theatricality. But by 1910 he was developing his theory of monodrama, in which the whole action of the play would be perceived and presented from the point of view of the protagonist. *In the Stage-Wings of the Soul* is probably the most successful of this type, though it has certain burlesque qualities that link it equally to Evreinov's plays for the Crooked Mirror Theatre-cum-cabaret, of which he was artistic director. These included his *The Government Inspector*, which presented the same scenes in different styles; and *The Fourth Wall*, a hilarious satire on naturalistic theatre that ends with the 'fourth wall' being built up to increase the 'truth' of the performance: the fact that the audience can no longer see is irrelevant!

The Chief Thing, in which actors are enlisted to help the inadequate characters face their major problems, and *The Ship of the Righteous*, which traces the attempt of a group of idealists to find — or found — a new utopia, are generally regarded as Evreinov's major plays. Certainly, they tackle complex issues in a thoroughly theatrical, even Pirandellian, manner — yet somehow today they seem rather self-conscious and dated.

Evreinov's directing work was probably more significant that his writing. He began by creating the 'Ancient Theatre', a venture that attempted to reconstruct the best work from earlier, more theatrical periods of dramatic history. Believing that naturalism had stifled the true strengths of the theatre, Evreinov presented a season of mainly medieval plays, which included the 11th-century liturgical drama *The Three Magi*, for which Evreinov wrote an important prologue, the 13th-century trouvere play *The Miracle of Theophilus*, and the pastoral *Play of Robin and Marion*, generally acknowledged to be the most interesting and successful of the group.

Robin and Marion was set in a knight's castle and the audience were assumed to be the knight's guests. The play was announced by a master of ceremonies and the simple, stylized set was erected before the spectators' eyes. *The Three Magi* began with a crowd asleep on stage as the audience entered; gradually they awoke and discussed the expected drama as well as the Black Death, their salvation and the like. During the play, this stage crowd interjected comments to which the actors responded. In both shows, real life and stage life were deliberately merged.

The success of this venture (which was repeated with a season of Spanish drama of the 'golden age' in 1911–12) was enough to spur Vera Kommisarjevskaya into inviting Evreinov to become joint director of her theatre along with her young brother, Theodore, and in 1909, when Kommisarjevskaya's theatre collapsed, bankrupt, these two initiated the Merry Theatre for Grown-up Children in the building for a season. This work was in turn probably largely responsible for Evreinov being selected by A. R. Kugel to be the artistic director of the Crooked Mirror theatre-cabaret. Here he developed a style for the typical Crooked Mirror 'miniatures', which drew on the ancient tradition he had already explored but in an original and highly contemporary way, suffused with paradox, irony and parody. His best work developed from ritual or mime and often included masks; he favoured such theatrical devices as the play-within-the-play and direct address to the audience; and he argued strongly that the director should be regarded as the 'author' of the theatrical work, as the writer was the author of the dramatic work.

When the Revolution came in 1917, the Crooked Mirror closed and Evreinov, a thoroughly non-political person, withdrew to continue his researches for a series of books. Nevertheless, he emerged to direct one more show, undoubtedly the most extraordinary, in which he finally almost achieved the blurring of the boundaries between art and life. The drama was *The Storming of the Winter Palace*, the biggest and most fabulous of all the 'mass spectacles' mounted in Russia in the immediate post-revolutionary period.

The work was a reconstruction (in the manner of the Ancient Theatre), three years to the day, of the moment of the revolution's victory. It employed approximately ten thousand performers, including actors, dancers, circus performers, students, soldiers and sailors as well as ordinary workers. Evreinov actively sought out people who had been present at the time, and asked them to play themselves. Over a hundred thousand spectators packed the huge square before the Winter Palace in spite of rain and snow, and were rewarded with an extraordinarily vivid spectacle, much of which has survived on old silent film, made during the dress rehearsal. The acting styles and the spatial configurations are alike fascinating, and on the night the finale of fireworks and red stars lighting the captured Palace created unprecedented fervour in the spectators.

But the spartan demands of the new Communist regime in Russia did not suit Evreinov's temperament, and in 1925 he left the country, not necessarily intending to emigrate. But he never returned. He mounted half a dozen or more productions in western Europe, wrote more plays and books, but never again achieved much of note in nearly 30 years of exile.

—Robert Leach

EYRE, Richard (Charles Hastings).   British director. Born in Barnstaple, Devon, 28 March 1943. Educated at Sher-
borne public school and Peterhouse, Cambridge. Married Sue Birtwistle in 1973, one daughter. Debut as director, Phoenix Theatre, Leicester, 1965; assistant director, Phoenix Theatre, 1966; associate director, 1967–72, and director of productions, 1970–72, Royal Lyceum Theatre, Edinburgh; directed British Council tour to West Africa, 1971, and south-east Asia, 1972; artistic director, Nottingham Playhouse, 1973–78; producer, BBC *Play for Today*, 1978–80; associate director, National Theatre, London, 1981–88; succeeded Sir Peter Hall as artistic director, Royal National Theatre, from 1988. Recipient: STV Award for Best Production in Scotland, 1969, 1970, 1971; Society of West End Theatre Director of the Year Award, 1982; *London Standard* Best Director Award, 1982; *Evening Standard* Best Film Award, 1983; Television Prize, Venice Film Festival, 1985; *Time Out* Best Production Award, 1986; Special Prize, Tokyo Television Festival, 1986; British Academy of Film and Television Arts Award, 1988; Italia RAI Prize, 1988; two Royal Television Society awards, 1988; Press Guild Award, 1988; Tokyo Prize, 1988; De Sica Award, Sorrento Film Festival, 1986. CBE (Commander of the British Empire), 1992.

Productions

1965	*The Knack* (Jellicoe), Phoenix Theatre, Leicester.
1967–72	*The Three Sisters* (Chekhov), Royal Lyceum Theatre, Edinburgh.
	The Cherry Orchard (Chekhov), Royal Lyceum Theatre, Edinburgh.
	Trumpets and Drums (Brecht, adapted from Farquhar's *The Recruiting Officer*), Royal Lyceum Theatre, Edinburgh.
	Schweyk in the Second World War (Brecht), Royal Lyceum Theatre, Edinburgh.
	The White Devil (Webster), Royal Lyceum Theatre, Edinburgh.
	The Changeling (Middleton and Rowley), Edinburgh Festival, Edinburgh.
	Random Happenings in the Hebrides (McGrath), Edinburgh Festival, Edinburgh.
	Confessions of a Justified Sinner, Edinburgh Festival, Edinburgh.
1968	*The Ha-Ha* (adapted by Eyre), London.
1970	*The Giveaway* (Jellicoe), London.
1972	*The Great Exhibition* (Hare), Hampstead Theatre, London.
1973–78	*Brassneck* (Brenton and Hare), Playhouse, Nottingham.
	The Government Inspector (Gogol), Playhouse, Nottingham.
	The Churchill Play (Brenton), Playhouse, Nottingham.
	Bendigo (Campbell, Hill, and Andrews), Playhouse, Nottingham.
	Comedians (Griffiths), Playhouse, Nottingham.
	Walking Like Geoffrey (Campbell, Hill, and Andrews), Playhouse, Nottingham.
	Jug! (Livings, adapted from Kleist's *De zerbrochene Krug*), Playhouse, Nottingham.
	The Plough and the Stars (O'Casey), Playhouse, Nottingham.

Bartholomew Fair (Jonson), Playhouse, Nottingham.

Othello (Shakespeare), Playhouse, Nottingham.

The Cherry Orchard (Chekhov), Playhouse, Nottingham.

The Alchemist (Jonson), Playhouse, Nottingham.

Deeds (Brenton, Campbell, Griffiths, and Hare), Playhouse, Nottingham.

1975   *Jingo* (Wood), Aldwych Theatre, London.

Comedians (Griffiths), Old Vic Theatre, London, and Wyndham's Theatre, London.

1977   *White Suit Blues*, Old Vic Theatre, London.

Touched (Lowe), Playhouse, Nottingham, and Old Vic Theatre, London.

1979   *Hamlet* (Shakespeare), Royal Court Theatre, London.

1982   *Guys 'n' Dolls* (Loesser), National Theatre, London.

The Beggar's Opera (Gay), National Theatre, London.

Schewyk in the Second World War (Brecht), National Theatre, London.

1985   *Edmond* (Mamet), Royal Court Theatre, London.

The Government Inspector (Gogol), National Theatre, London.

1986   *Kafka's Dick* (Bennett), Royal Court Theatre, London.

Futurists (Hughes), National Theatre, London.

1987   *High Society* (Porter), Victoria Palace Theatre, London.

1988   *The Changeling* (Middleton and Rowley), National Theatre, London.

Bartholomew Fair (Jonson), National Theatre, London.

1989   *Hamlet* (Shakespeare), Royal National Theatre, London.

The Voysey Inheritance (Granville-Barker), Royal National Theatre, London.

1990   *Racing Demon* (Hare), Royal National Theatre, London; revived there, 1993.

Richard III (Shakespeare), Royal National Theatre, London.

1991   *White Chameleon* (Hampton), Royal National Theatre, London.

Napoli Milionaria (De Filippo), Royal National Theatre, London.

Murmuring Judges (Hare), Royal National Theatre, London; revived there, 1993.

1992   *The Night of the Iguana* (T. Williams), Royal National Theatre, London.

1993   Macbeth (Shakespeare), Royal National Theatre, London.

1993   *The Absence of War* (Hare), Royal National Theatre, London.

Johnny on a Spot (McArthur), Royal National Theatre, London.

1994   *Sweet Bird of Youth* (T. Williams), Royal National Theatre, London.

Films

The Ploughman's Lunch, 1983; *Loose Connections*, 1983; *Laughterhouse*, 1984.

Television

The Imitation Game, 1980; *Pasmore*, 1980; *Country*, 1981; *The Insurance Man*, 1986; *Past Caring*, 1986; *v.*, 1988; *Tumbledown*, 1988; *Suddenly Last Summer*, 1993. Other productions include: *Waterloo Sunset*; *Comedians*.

Publications

Utopia and Other Places, 1993.

*

Bibliography

Articles:
Mark Hawkins-Dady, "Gogol's *The Government Inspector* at the National Theatre", *New Theatre Quarterly*, vol. 3, no. 12, 1987.

* * *

When Richard Eyre became Director of the National Theatre in 1988 he published a loose statement of intent in *The Independent*. Describing himself as a 'populist', he qualified the term as follows: "I mean that art can and should be popular and accessible even if its content is complex and disturbing". It is a characteristic assertion, decisive yet qualified. Eyre's work has usually displayed a fine understanding of contradictions: it certainly refuses straightforward categorisation.

Eyre had held executive posts (producer of BBC's *Play for Today*, Artistic Director of the Nottingham Playhouse) before he landed the top job in British subsidised theatre, but he cannot easily be conscripted to that nebulous collective, the Establishment. He has spoken up for the arts in an embattled era — although in this he is only doing his job. His reputation as an independent spirit had been confirmed, however, with his production of *Tumbledown* for BBC television in 1988. Charles Wood's television play dramatised the real story of Robert Lawrence, a Lieutenant in the Scots Guards who was wounded in action during the Falklands War, and claimed that the military establishment subsequently treated him shabbily. Amid the ensuing controversy it was less generally recognized that Eyre, as so often before and since, had caught the nuances of establishment England most tellingly. We are inescapably defined by our society, his productions proclaim.

Father figures loom large in Eyre's work, although not always in the most obvious ways. In his 1979 production of *Hamlet* at the Royal Court, with Jonathan Pryce in the title role, the Ghost was played by Pryce himself, tortuously uttering the lines as if his own father was erupting from within him. When Eyre directed the play again at the National Theatre the designer, John Gunter, provided a huge statue of Hamlet the elder in full military array, a permanent presence upstage. The shadow of the father towered over Hamlet throughout. For his own part, in his book *Utopia and Other Places*, Eyre refers to Harley

Granville-Barker as "something of a father figure for me", an altogether more benevolent shadow. The actor-playwright himself wrote about the theatre: not as a codifier but as an entertainer, committed to drama as subtle as it was strong-boned.

Eyre's productions — similarly layered — are grounded in social detail. His celebrated production of *Richard III* in 1990, for instance, was set in the Edwardian era and charted Richard's rise from post-World War I army officer to fascist dictator along the lines of Hitler and Mussolini. If this seems a version of early 20th-century European history, note that various mannerisms, costumes, and iconography — including the cross of St George — were decidedly English. One of the strengths of Eyre's work is that it sets up a series of contemporary cultural resonances; in this instance depicting a strong leader relying on an increasingly demagogic populism.

If Eyre can be called a 'state of the nation' director, however, the tag is most obviously deserved through his direction of the David Hare trilogy, three plays centring respectively on the Church of England, the penal and judicial system, and the Labour Party. They are to some extent contemporary epics. The first, *Racing Demon*, was presented in the National's smallest theatre, the Cottesloe, but proved successful enough to transfer to the Olivier Theatre, where the two subsequent plays were staged. The Olivier is a notoriously difficult space to handle, a cavernous semi-Epidorus. Eyre and his designer Bob Crowley relied on swiftly interchanging projected backdrops and items of set quickly flown or trucked in. The plays were thus given great pace and fluidity, while the production style threw emphasis on the dialogue and on the actors' performances.

As the Director of the National Theatre, Eyre will be assessed in part as a curator of the nation's drama. He has welcomed a wider range of theatre practices than did either of his predecessors, Laurence Olivier or Peter Hall. New plays by the likes of Caryl Churchill, Tony Harrison, and Tom Stoppard demonstrate his fidelity to an old guard of contemporary playwrights. He has shrewdly championed particular directors. Stephen Daldry provided the National with a production of J. B. Priestley's *An Inspector Calls* in 1992 that defined a deconstructive, concept-led approach to established texts. Declan Donnellan and Nick Ormerod, the director and designer of the impressive touring company, Cheek By Jowl, delivered a more robust, ensemble-based style of theatre. By inviting the British company Theatre de Complicite and the French-Canadian director Robert Lepage to present their own productions and to develop shows at the National in a more conventional in-house manner, Eyre proved himself open to newer forms of physical and visual theatre. Indeed, through the company he keeps he has to some extent blurred the distinctions between 'mainstream', 'fringe', and 'alternative' theatre.

Eyre has also turned to the USA for drama on the grand scale. New plays at the National have included Tony Kushner's epic fantasia *Angels in America*. A deal with the producer Cameron Mackintosh enabled the theatre to stage new productions of existing US musicals: Sondheim's *Sunday in the Park with George* and *Sweeney Todd* and Rodgers and Hammerstein's *Carousel*. Eyre himself directed Tennessee Williams' *The Night of the Iguana* and *Sweet Bird of Youth*, a commitment to the playwright's work that was sealed with his 1993 BBC production of *Suddenly Last Summer*.

It is not difficult to see why transatlantic drama excites Eyre. These are shows with robust narratives and strong characters, filled with social metaphor and extravagant passions. Eyre once expressed his admiration for "a kind of theatre that exploits the unique properties of the medium — its use of space, of light, of movement, of speech: its *theatreness*". This is a point about form; but there is also a theatricality of the emotions in his work. This is not to say that his productions ham it up for the gallery. They have great clarity, but they are also detailed and complicated. Eyre is a muscular liberal: a director of many shades and sensitivities, and a manager who asserts an inclusive artistic doctrine. In both respects he strikes a discord with the tenor of his age. "I recoil still from appeals to 'country' and 'national culture', and in this I reveal my Englishness", he has said: an appropriately sceptical attitude, surely, for a national theatre artist.

—Andrew Lavender

FAUCIT, Helen (Saville). British actress. Born in London, 1817; daughter of theatrical parents. Educated at boarding school in Greenwich, London. Married Theodore Martin in 1851. Stage debut, Covent Garden, London, 1836; particularly acclaimed in plays by Bulwer-Lytton and Shakespeare, often appearing as William Charles Macready's leading lady, Covent Garden, 1837–39; joined Macready at the Haymarket Theatre, London, 1839, and then at the Theatre Royal, Drury Lane, 1842; subsequently toured widely, sometimes with Macready, until her marriage, after which she made fewer appearances; became Lady Martin on her husband's knighthood, 1880. Died in Bryntysilio, Wales, 31 October 1898.

Roles

1836   Julia in *The Hunchback* (Knowles), Covent Garden, London.
Belvidera in *Venice Preserved* (Otway), Covent Garden, London.
Mrs Haller in *The Stranger* (Thompson), Covent Garden, London.
Lady Margaret in *Separation* (Baillie), Covent Garden, London.
Juliet in *Romeo and Juliet* (Shakespeare), Covent Garden, London.
Lady Townley in *The Provoked Husband* (Vanbrugh and Cibber), Covent Garden, London.
Florinda in *Don Juan of Austria* (translated from the French), Covent Garden, London.
Mariana in *The Wife* (Knowles), Covent Garden, London.
Clemanthe in *Ion* (Talfourd), Covent Garden, London.
Mrs Beverley in *The Gamester* (Moore), Covent Garden, London.
Katherine in *The Taming of the Shrew* (Shakespeare), Covent Garden, London.
Portia in *The Merchant of Venice* (Shakespeare), Covent Garden, London.
Desdemona in *Othello* (Shakespeare), Covent Garden, London.
Constance in *King John* (Shakespeare), Covent Garden, London.
Lady Teazle in *The School for Scandal* (Sheridan), Covent Garden, London.

1837   The Duchess in *The Duchess de la Vallière* (Bulwer-Lytton), Covent Garden, London.

Queen Catherine in *Henry VIII* (Shakespeare), Covent Garden, London.
Lucy, Countess of Carlisle in *Strafford* (Browning), Covent Garden, London.
Erina in *Brian Boroihme* (Knowles), Covent Garden, London.
Imogen in *Cymbeline* (Shakespeare), Covent Garden, London.
Hermione in *The Winter's Tale* (Shakespeare), Covent Garden, London.
Marion in *The Wrecker's Daughter* (Knowles), Covent Garden, London.
Clotilda Lilienstein in *The Novice*, Covent Garden, London.
Jane Carlton in *The Parole of Honour* (Serle), Covent Garden, London.
Cordelia in *King Lear* (Shakespeare), Covent Garden, London.

1838   Pauline Deschappelles in *The Lady of Lyons* (Bulwer-Lytton), Covent Garden, London.
Marina in *The Two Foscari* (Lord Byron), Covent Garden, London.
Creusa in *The Athenian Captive* (Talfourd), Covent Garden, London.
Hero in *Woman's Wit; or, Love's Disguises* (Knowles), Covent Garden, London.
Miranda in *The Tempest* (Shakespeare), Covent Garden, London.
Violante in *The Wonder* (Centlivre), Covent Garden, London.

1839   Julie de Mortemar in *Richelieu* (Bulwer-Lytton), Covent Garden, London.
Rosalind in *As You Like It* (Shakespeare), Covent Garden, London.
Violet in *The Sea Captain* (Bulwer-Lytton), Haymarket Theatre, London.

1840   Helen Campbell in *The Tragedy of Glencoe; or, The Fate of the MacDonalds* (Talfourd), Haymarket Theatre, London.
Lady Dorothy Cromwell in *Master Clarke* (Serle), Haymarket Theatre, London.

1840   Clara Douglas in *Money* (Bulwer-Lytton), Haymarket Theatre, London.

1841   Julia in *The Rivals* (Sheridan), Haymarket Theatre, London.
Nina in *Nina Zforza* (Troughton), Haymarket Theatre, London.
Beatrice in *Much Ado About Nothing* (Shakespeare), Haymarket Theatre, London.

1842   Sophronia in *Gisippus* (Griffin), Theatre Royal, Drury Lane, London.

Maddalene in *Plighted Troth* (Darley), Theatre Royal, Drury Lane, London.

Lady Macbeth in *Macbeth* (Shakespeare), Theatre Royal, Dublin.

Angelica in *Love for Love* (Congreve), Theatre Royal, Drury Lane, London.

1842   Angiolina in *Marino Falieri* (Lord Byron), Theatre Royal, Drury Lane, London.

Lady Mabel in *The Patrician's Daughter* (Marston), Theatre Royal, Drury Lane, London.

1843   Mildred Tresham in *A Blot in the 'Scutcheon* (Browning), Theatre Royal, Drury Lane, London.

The Lady in *Comus* (Milton), Theatre Royal, Drury Lane, London.

Virginia in *Virginius* (Knowles), Theatre Royal, Drury Lane, London.

Lady Laura Gaveston in *The Secretary* (Knowles), Theatre Royal, Drury Lane, London.

Portia in *Julius Caesar* (Shakespeare), Theatre Royal, Drury Lane, London.

Elfrida in *Athelwold* (W. Smith), Theatre Royal, Drury Lane, London.

1845   Ophelia in *Hamlet* (Shakespeare), Tuileries, Paris.

1846   Antigone in *Antigone* (Sophocles), Theatre Royal, Dublin.

Jane Shore in *Jane Shore* (Rowe), Theatre Royal, Dublin.

Isabella in *The Fatal Marriage* (Southerne), Theatre Royal, Dublin.

Iphigenia in *Iphigenia in Aulis* (Euripides), Theatre Royal, Dublin.

1847   Florence Delmar in *The Heart and the World* (Marston), Haymarket Theatre, London.

1848   Anne Bracegirdle in *The Tragedy Queen* (Fournier, adapted by Oxenford), Edinburgh.

Evadne in *Evadne; or, The Statue* (Sheil), Theatre Royal, Dublin.

1850   Iolanthe in *King René's Daughter* (Herz, adapted by Martin), Glasgow.

Marie in *Philip of France and Marie de Meranie* (Marston), Olympic Theatre, London.

1852   Adrienne Lecouvreur in *Adrienne Lecouvreur* (Scribe, adapted by Martin), Manchester.

1853   Colombe in *Colombe's Birthday* (Browning), Haymarket Theatre, London.

1855   Margaret in *Love's Martyrdom* (Saunders), Haymarket Theatre, London.

Publications

On Some of Shakespeare's Female Characters, 1892.

*

Bibliography

Books:
Theodore Martin, *Helen Faucit*, Edinburgh, 1900.

Ifor Edwards, *Lady Helena Faucit Martin (1817–98): Shakespearean Actress*, Wrexham, 1985.

* * *

Despite her mother's discouragement, Helen Faucit, like four of her five siblings, upheld the family tradition of a career on the stage. Her debut at Richmond, Surrey in 1833 arose by chance — the manager (Willis Jones), having overheard her playing Juliet to the Romeo of her elder sister Harriet, prevailed upon Helen to perform the role publicly, which she did with great success. Nearly three years elapsed, however, before she made her professional debut at Covent Garden. The play was Sheridan Knowles's *The Hunchback*, substituted for *Romeo and Juliet* due to the lack of a suitable Romeo. Of her Julia *The Morning Chronicle* wrote: "We have never witnessed a better first performance".

Helen Faucit was endowed with many natural qualities: a tall graceful figure, reminiscent of the idealised forms of classical Greek sculpture, and a face that in profile displayed perfect proportions of physiognomy upon "a pillar-like neck". Her voice was clear, full and mellow, easily suited to the expression of tender emotion, tending towards petulance in moments of violent passion. Prior to her appearance at Covent Garden Helen Faucit was instructed in the 'business' of her characters by Percy Farren (brother of William Farren the elder). At Covent Garden she was inevitable influenced by the style of the leading actor Charles Kemble (by then so deaf that he could not hear the prompter) from whom she learnt the practice of realising each line not only by vocal delivery but also with accompanying gesture. Accomplished though she became in perfecting this art, she did not have (and probably saw no need for) the art to conceal her art. Since during the remainder of her career Helen Faucit did not respond to the trend towards more natural acting, she ultimately became something of an acting anachronism.

In July 1837 Faucit commenced her celebrated professional partnership with William Charles Macready. As part of his campaign to reform the stage, Macready encouraged established authors to write plays and it was Faucit who created the female leads in many of these dramas, among them Bulwer-Lytton's *The Duchess de la Vallière*, *The Lady of Lyons*, *Richelieu*, and *Money*, Browning's *Strafford* and *A Blot on the 'Scutcheon*, and plays by T. N. Talfourd, Sheridan Knowles, and Westland Marston.

Forceful though he was, Macready found that in Helen Faucit he had a leading lady of independent mind. As Pauline Deschappelles she developed her own interpretation, making the character increasingly sympathetic. Thus, according to the *Athenaeum*, her pride (in rejecting her husband Claude Melnotte on discovering that he is a gardener's son and not the aristocrat she thought him to be) "is soon forgiven, and for the rest, she is the sufferer, not the inflicter of wrong, and therefore the natural object of pity". This tendency to seek (or in their absence introduce) sympathetic traits in characters was a recurrent feature of Helen Faucit's acting, displaying not only her own humanity, but her desire to appeal to her audiences' better nature.

Faucit accompanied Macready to Paris in 1845, where she was warmly received. Her acting commended itself to the French and her reception reinforced her rather artificial, self-consciously graceful style. Increasingly she pursued her career independently from Macready, whose retirement from the stage coincided with her marriage to Theodore Martin in 1851. Her marriage to Martin, a man of letters prominent in public life, further encouraged her ladylike ways both onstage and off. The couple lived in Onslow Square, neighbours of Thackeray and friends of Charles Kingsley, Matthew Arnold, Dean Stanley, and Nathaniel Hawthorne. They bought a country house in North Wales and as Martin progressed with his authorised biography of the late Prince Consort (for which he was knighted in 1880) their entrée into court circles was facilitated.

Although by 1885, when *Some of Shakespeare's Female Characters* ("Respectfully Dedicated by Permission to Her Most Gracious Majesty The Queen by Her Majesty's Grateful and Devoted Subject and Servant, Helena Faucit Martin") appeared, Helen Faucit had long since abandoned the stage, the chapters contained therein inevitably reflected her earlier performances. Her selection of Shakespearean heroines is indicative of her own predelictions, which themselves reflected public taste. Thus, although she had performed Lady Macbeth, Katherine, and Constance, these more equivocal characters found no place in her book, in which she discoursed on Ophelia, Portia, Desdemona, Juliet, Imogen, Rosalind, and Beatrice.

The essay on Portia had previously appeared in 1880 and was almost certainly conceived partly as a riposte to the Portia of a very different type of actress, Ellen Terry, who was then enjoying a huge popular success in *The Merchant of Venice* with Irving at the Lyceum. Faucit's intellectual and idealised approach to the character is apparent throughout her interpretation. On stage she had not been at her best in the opening banter with Nerissa at the expense of her suitors, but in Bassanio's 'casket-scene' her silent byplay had affected all. Despite the intensity of Portia's feelings for Bassanio Faucit remained resolute (on stage and page) that no hint should be given to direct Bassanio to the right casket. She conceived Portia as a "long-standing pupil of Bellario" and therefore believed that the loophole in the wording of the bond was apparent to her before she left Belmont (though she is not apprised on stage of its full content). Her Portia thus arrived at the trial confident of her ability to save Antonio and her appeals to Shylock for mercy were directed towards his salvation rather than his intended victim's. In the face of Shylock's obduracy, her Portia's desire to find extenuation for him vanished, though Faucit postulated an after-life for the characters in which Portia visited Shylock with gifts of wine and oil and her former antagonist found comfort in her likeness to Leah.

In later life, Helen Faucit used her social position to advance the cause of the theatre. In 1879 she emerged from retirement twice to support worthy causes. In April she played Shakespeare's Beatrice opposite Barry Sullivan's Benedict in the opening production at the Shakespeare Memorial Theatre, Stratford-upon-Avon and later wrote of her delight "of my last essay to present a living portraiture of the Lady Beatrice" — though one critic considered that "A more artificial and conscious Beatrice would be difficult to find". In October she appeared as Rosalind in Manchester to raise money for the widow and family of the actor-manager Charles Calvert. Although the actors (many of them amateurs) and audiences were deferential to this 'grande dame' of the theatre, they must have realised the redundancy of her style. But a great actress's ability to transcend changes in fashion is apparent from Herman Merivale's description recalled by Violet Vanbrugh: "the first sight of this Rosalind, in clothes of another tradition, speaking the lines after a half-forgotten convention, gradually merged into wonder and finally into intense admiration".

—Richard Foulkes

FEDOTOVA, Glikeriya (Nikolaevna). Russian actress. Born Glikeriya Nikolaevna Pozdnyakova in Orel, Russia, 10 October 1846. Trained at the Moscow Theatrical School under I. V. Samarin, 1856–63. Married actor-director Aleksandr Filipovich Fedotov (divorced 1871), one son. Stage debut, Maly Theatre, Moscow, 1858; joined Maly Theatre company, 1863; subsequently hailed as leading Russian actress of her generation, playing both comic and tragic roles; especially acclaimed for performances in plays by Ostrovsky and Shakespeare; promoted Stanislavsky and the Moscow Art Theatre; toured extensively; retired from stage and worked as teacher, 1905; made final stage appearance in 50th anniversary celebration of her debut, 1912. Chairman, Moscow Society of Art and Literature, from 1892. People's Artist of the Republic, 1924; Hero of Labour, 1924. Died in Moscow, 27 February 1925.

Principal roles

1862	Verochka in *Rebënok* [The Infant] (Boborykin), Maly Theatre, Moscow, 1863.
	Nina in *Maskarad* [Masquerade] (Lermontov), Maly Theatre, Moscow.
1863	Katerina in *Groza* [The Storm] (Ostrovsky), Maly Theatre, Moscow.
1865	Beatrice in *Much Ado About Nothing* (Shakespeare), Maly Theatre, Moscow.
1868	Isabella in *Measure for Measure* (Shakespeare), Maly Theatre, Moscow.
	Vasilisa in *Vasilisa Melentyeva* (Ostrovsky), Maly Theatre, Moscow.
1869	Parasha in *Gorjačee serce* [The Ardent Heart] (Ostrovsky), Maly Theatre, Moscow.
1870	Lidiia in *Besheny dengi* [Easy Money] (Ostrovsky), Maly Theatre, Moscow.
1871	Katherina in *The Taming of the Shrew* (Shakespeare), Maly Theatre, Moscow.
1872	Natalya Petrovna in *Mesyats v derevne* [A Month in the Country] (Turgenev), Maly Theatre, Moscow.
1875	Murzaveckaja in *Volki i ovsty* [Wolves and Sheep] (Ostrovsky), Alexandrinsky Theatre, Moscow.
1877	Portia in *The Merchant of Venice* (Shakespeare), Maly Theatre, Moscow.
1878	Larisa in *Bespridannitsa* [The Girl Without a Dowry] (Ostrovsky), Maly Theatre, Moscow.
1884	Kruchinina in *Bezvinny vinovatye* [More Sinned Against Than Sinning] (Ostrovsky), Maly Theatre, Moscow.

1890   Lady Macbeth in *Macbeth* (Shakespeare), Maly
        Theatre, Moscow.
        Mistress Page in *The Merry Wives of Windsor*
        (Shakespeare), Maly Theatre, Moscow.
1893   Cheboksarova in *Besheny dengi* [Easy Money]
        (Ostrovsky), Maly Theatre, Moscow.
1902   Volumnia in *Coriolanus* (Shakespeare), Maly
        Theatre, Moscow.
1912   Tsaritsa Marfa in *Dmitry Samozvanets i Vasily
        Shuysky* [The False Dmitrii and Vasilii Shuis-
        kii] (Ostrovsky), Maly Theatre, Moscow.

Other roles included: Atueva and Lidočka in *Svadba
Krečinskogo* [Krechinsky's Wedding] (Sukhovo-Kobylin),
Maly Theatre, Moscow; Cleopatra in *Antony and Cleopatra*
(Shakespeare), Maly Theatre, Moscow; Queen Elizabeth in
Maria Stuart (Schiller), Maly Theatre, Moscow; Paulina in
The Winter's Tale (Shakespeare), Maly Theatre, Moscow;
and roles in *Alcade de Zalamea* (Vega Carpio), Maly
Theatre, Moscow; *La Dame aux Camèlias* (Dumas), Maly
Theatre, Moscow; *Kabale und Liebe* (Schiller), Maly The-
atre, Moscow; *Les* [The Forest] (Ostrovsky), Alexandrinsky
Theatre, Moscow; *Snegurochka* [The Snow Maiden] (Os-
trovsky), Bolshoi Theatre, Moscow.

* * *

With Ermolova, Glikeriya Fedotova was one of the great
attractions of the Maly Theatre. During her adolescence
she was a pupil of Mikhail Shchepkin, with whom she
studied during the summer break from school. The account
she gave Stanislavsky of her lessons, which he reproduces
in *My Life in Art*, gives little detail of Shchepkin's methods,
except to indicate how rigorous he was in his demands. She
made her professional debut in Boborykin's *The Infant* in
1861 and was immediately received with enthusiasm.
While allowing her to enjoy her evening of success,
Shchepkin later provided her with a detailed analysis of her
performance. A proper mistrust of popular acclaim was one
of the lessons she later passed on to Stanislavsky. The
following year she joined the company of the Maly Theatre,
repeating her performance in *The Infant*. The general
opinion was that she had introduced a new tendency into
acting with her depth of dramatic insight and simplicity of
expression. She had considerable emotional power, which
she demonstrated in her performances in Lope de Vega's
Alcade de Zalamea and Schiller's *Kabale und Liebe*. She
also had a gift for comedy, to which she gave edge and bite.
As Beatrice in *Much Abo About Nothing* she delivered the
barbs of wit with relish and accomplishment. As Kate in
The Taming of the Shrew she successfully charted the
psychological progression of the character from wilfulness
and violence to love and submission.

After the mid-1870's the critics noted a greater simplicity
in her playing. This was particularly true of her performance as Marguerite Gautier in Dumas's *La Dame aux
Camèlias*, where the realism of her acting made audiences
forget they were in the theatre. She was at her best playing
strong-minded characters. Most notable was her Queen
Elizabeth in Schiller's *Maria Stuart*, in which she played
opposite Ermolova's Mary. The following year she again
played opposite Ermolova as Paulina to the latter's Hermione in *The Winter's Tale* and that season also appeared
in the part of Shakespeare's Cleopatra.

Fedotova and Ermolova were the perfect foils for one
another. Their personalities complemented each other:
both had great emotional power and technical control but
both in life and on stage Fedotova was the more assertive.
Ermolova, with her extreme reserve, contented herself with
working on her own role. Fedotova had an eye to everything concerning the production — costumes, props, and
staging to make sure all was in harmony with the text. The
management was not a little intimidated by her, but it must
be said that at a time of lax production methods her
interventions were usually justified.

There was, however, a negative side to Fedotova's acting
that perceptive critics had noted early in her career and
which she was not always able to rectify: the temptation of
being melodramatic and mannered. This was particularly
true of her Lady Macbeth in 1890. While in the early scenes
she showed great psychological understanding, in the
sleepwalking scene she became declamatory and artificial.

Apart from her own achievements as a star of the Maly,
Fedotova is important as a major influence on Stanislavsky's development as an actor. It was perhaps the unre-
solved contradiction in her own playing that enabled her to
understand Stanislavsky's early difficulties and his struggle
to achieve truth of character and avoid posturing. Stanislavsky was largely self-taught and apart from what he would
learn through observation and imitation, he received direct
training at the hands of Fedotova and her estranged
husband Aleksandr.

Stanislavsky's encounters with Fedotova were neither
planned nor regular. When he enrolled at a drama school in
1885 it was only to find that Fedotova, who had been
teaching there, had resigned. He was, however, a school-
fellow of her son, Aleksandr. Chance brought them together
in December 1889 when he was unexpectedly asked to fill
in for a sick actor in a performance of Nemirovich-
Danchenko's *The Lucky Man*. The cast included Ermolova
and Fedotova; Fedotova recognised his talent but also
pointed out his lack of technique. She told him firmly but
kindly that he was a "talented mess". As far as she could,
she passed on to him the lessons she herself had learned
from Shchepkin, thus forging the link between Stanislavsky
and the early tradition of Russian realism. It was from
Fedotova that Stanislavsky learned to address his partner
directly, to make eye contact, and play off others' reactions.
According to his notebooks, it was the memory of Fedotova's reworking of his interpretation of Imshin in Ostrovsky's *A Law Unto Themselves* in 1889 that led him to
formulate the principle of opposites in a role: look for the
good in an evil man and the evil in a good man. In 1892
Fedotova became chairman of the board of Stanislavsky's
Society of Art and Literature and characteristically introduced much greater professional discipline in rehearsals
and backstage generally. Although forced to retire for
reasons of ill-health in 1905, she followed the fortunes of
the Art Theatre with passionate interest.

—Jean Benedetti

FINNEY, Albert. British actor and director. Born in
Salford, Lancashire, 9 May 1936. Educated at Salford
Grammar School; trained for the stage at the Royal
Academy of Dramatic Art, London. Married 1) actress

Jane Wenham in 1957 (divorced 1961), one son; 2) actress Anouk Aimée in 1970 (divorced 1975). Stage debut, Birmingham Repertory Theatre, 1956; London debut, Old Vic Theatre, 1956; first film appearance, 1959; joined Shakespeare Memorial Theatre Company, 1959; Broadway debut, 1963; joined National Theatre company, 1965; founder, Memorial Enterprises film production company, 1965; associate artistic director, Royal Court Theatre, 1972–75; co-founder, United British Artists, 1983. Recipient: British Academy Award, 1960; Venice Festival Award, 1963; New York Film Critics' Award, 1963; Oscar, 1974; *London Standard* Award, 1986; Laurence Olivier Award, 1986. Litt.D: University of Sussex, 1965; University of Salford, 1979.

Productions

As actor:

1956–58	Decius Brutus in *Julius Caesar* (Shakespeare), Repertory Theatre, Birmingham.
	Belzanor in *Caesar and Cleopatra* (Shakespeare), Old Vic Theatre, London.
	Francis Archer in *The Beaux' Stratagem* (Farquhar), Repertory Theatre, Birmingham.
	Face in *The Alchemist* (Jonson), Repertory Theatre, Birmingham.
	Malcolm in *The Lizard on the Rock*, Repertory Theatre, Birmingham.
	Henry V in *Henry V* (Shakespeare), Repertory Theatre, Birmingham.
1958	Macbeth in *Macbeth* (Shakespeare), Repertory Theatre, Birmingham; National Theatre, London, 1978.
	Soya Marshall in *The Party* (Arden), New Theatre, London.
1959	Edgar in *King Lear* (Shakespeare), Shakespeare Memorial Theatre, Stratford-upon-Avon.
	Cassio in *Othello* (Shakespeare), Shakespeare Memorial Theatre, Stratford-upon-Avon.
	Lysander in *A Midsummer Night's Dream* (Shakespeare), Shakespeare Memorial Theatre, Stratford-upon-Avon.
	Coriolanus in *Coriolanus* (Shakespeare), Shakespeare Memorial Theatre, Stratford-upon-Avon.
1960	Ted in *The Lily-White Boys* (Cookson), Royal Court Theatre, London.
	Billy Fisher in *Billy Liar* (Hall and Waterhouse), Cambridge Theatre, London.
1961	Luther in *Luther* (Osborne), Paris International Festival, Théâtre des Nations, Paris, Holland Festival, and Royal Court Theatre, London; St James Theatre, New York, 1963.
1962	Feste in *Twelfth Night* (Shakespeare), Royal Court Theatre, London.
1963	Henry IV in *Henry IV* (Pirandello), Glasgow Citizens' Theatre, Glasgow.
1965	Don Pedro in *Much Ado About Nothing* (Shakespeare), Old Vic Theatre, London.
1966	Poche in *A Flea in Her Ear* (Feydeau, adapted by Mortimer), Old Vic Theatre, London.
	John Armstrong in *Armstrong's Last Goodnight* (Arden), Chichester Festival Theatre; Old Vic Theatre, London, 1983.
	Jean in *Miss Julie* (Strindberg), Chichester Festival Theatre.
	Harold Gorringe in *Black Comedy* (P. Shaffer), Chichester Festival Theatre.
1968	Bri in *A Day in the Death of Joe Egg* (Nichols), London and Brooks Atkinson Theatre, New York.
1972	Mr Elliot in *Alpha Beta* (Barker), Royal Court Theatre, London, and Apollo Theatre, London.
1973	Krapp in *Krapp's Last Tape* (Beckett), Royal Court Theatre, London.
	O'Hallaran in *Cromwell* (Storey), Royal Court Theatre, London.
1974	Phil in *Chez Nous* (Nichols), Globe Theatre, London.
1975	Hamlet in *Hamlet* (Shakespeare), Old Vic Theatre, London; National Theatre, London, 1976.
1976	Tamburlaine in *Tamburlaine the Great* (Marlowe), National Theatre, London.
	Narrator in *Tribute to a Lady* (May), Old Vic Theatre, London.
1977	Mr Horner in *The Country Wife* (Wycherley), National Theatre, London.
1978	Lopakhin in *The Cherry Orchard* (Chekhov), National Theatre, London.
	Vanya in *Uncle Vanya* (Chekhov), Royal Exchange Theatre, Manchester.
	Gary Essendine in *Present Laughter* (Coward), Royal Exchange Theatre, Manchester.
	John Bean in *Has "Washington" Legs?* (Wood), National Theatre, London.
1984	Musgrave in *Sergeant Musgrave's Dance* (Arden), Old Vic Theatre, London.
	The Lawyer in *The Biko Inquest* (Blair and Fenton), Riverside Studios, Hammersmith, London.
1986	Harold in *Orphans* (Kessler), Hampstead Theatre, London, and Apollo Theatre, London.

Has also acted roles in: *J. J. Farr*, Phoenix Theatre, London, 1987; *Another Time*, Wyndham's Theatre, London, 1989, and Chicago, 1991; *Reflected Glory*, Vaudeville Theatre, London, 1992, all by R. Harwood.

As director:

1963	*The Birthday Party* (Pinter), Glasgow Citizens' Theatre, Glasgow.
	The School for Scandal (Sheridan), Glasgow Citizens' Theatre, Glasgow.
1965	*Armstrong's Last Goodnight* (Arden), Old Vic Theatre, London.
1973	*The Freedom of the City* (Friel), Royal Court Theatre, London.
1975	*Loot* (Orton), Royal Court Theatre, London.
1983	*Armstrong's Last Goodnight* (Arden), Old Vic Theatre, London.
1984	*The Biko Inquest* (Blair and Fenton), Riverside Studios, Hammersmith, London.

Albert Finney

Sergeant Musgrave's Dance (Arden), Old Vic Theatre, London.

Films

As actor:
The Entertainer, 1959; *Saturday Night and Sunday Morning*, 1960; *The Victors*, 1963; *Tom Jones*, 1963; *Night Must Fall*, 1964; *Two for the Road*, 1967; *Charlie Bubbles*, 1968; *The Picasso Summer*, 1969; *Scrooge*, 1970; *Bleak Moment*, 1972; *Gumshoe*, 1972; *Alpha Beta*, 1973; *Murder on the Orient Express*, 1974; *The Adventures of Sherlock Holmes' Smarter Brother*, 1975; *The Duellists*, 1978; *Loophole*, 1980; *Looker*, 1981; *Wolfen*, 1981; *Shoot the Moon*, 1982; *Annie*, 1982; *The Dresser*, 1983; *Under the Volcano*, 1984; *Orphans*, 1987; *Miller's Crossing*, 1990; *The Playboys*, 1992; *Rich in Love*, 1992.

As director:
Charlie Bubbles, 1968.

Television

Pope John Paul II, 1984; *The Biko Inquest*, 1984; *The Endless Game*, 1989; *The Image*, 1989; *The Green Man*, 1990; *Grushko*, 1994. Other productions include: *Forget-*

Me-Not Lane; *View Friendship and Marriage*; *The Claverdon Road Job*; *The Miser.*

*

Bibliography

Books:
Quentin Falk, *Albert Finney in Character: A Biography*, London, 1992.

* * *

Albert Finney first attracted attention as an actor at the Birmingham Repertory Theatre, where he went after RADA training in the later 1950's. His stocky, youthful, Henry V, directed by Douglas Seale, demonstrated considerable stature and emotional maturity; "sturdy rather than royal, in the Burton tradition rather than the Olivier", according to *The Times*. A West End move became inevitable after Charles Laughton visited Birmingham to see Finney playing the leading role in *Macbeth* the following year.

Like contemporaries Tom Courtenay and Alan Bates, Albert Finney's solid northern roots proved advantageous during an era when a fashionable deluge of plays brought working-class characters into predominantly middle-class theatres, among them the eponymous hero of Willis Hall and Keith Waterhouse's *Billy Liar* at the Cambridge in 1960. Finney's ability to sustain the intrigues of the would-be scriptwriter's web of fantastic inventions showed that he was capable of playing modern comedy as well as majestic Shakespearean roles. His later appearance at the Old Vic, doubling as the suspected husband and the hotel porter in John Mortimer's adaptation of the Feydeau farce *A Flea in Her Ear*, confirmed the breadth of his stylistic range.

Interspersed with several highly successful film appearances, Finney made a significant contribution to the development of work at both the Royal Court Theatre and the National Theatre during the 1960's and 1970's. At the Royal Court — which had first staged his gritty, stubborn performance of John Osborne's *Luther* — he was appointed associate director in 1972, and the following year earned acclaim for his virtuoso characterisation of the deteriorating figure sifting through the spools in Beckett's *Krapp's Last Tape*. For the celebrated opening of the new, partially completed National Theatre on the South Bank, Peter Hall's production of *Hamlet* in 1976 transferred from the Old Vic to the Lyttleton's proscenium stage with Finney in the title role. Critical reaction to the sparse setting of the play was mixed, although the large white circle painted on the stage floor provided ample opportunity for the actor to prowl with threatening, yet equivocating menace at its edge until the violent denouement. Benedict Nightingale writing in the *Sunday New York Times* described Finney's performance as "full of scalding humour" and Peter Hall's diary record noted that this was "a powerful, passionate, sexy Hamlet, glowering with resentment".

Raw sexual energy came to the fore again in another Hall production, *Macbeth*, also at the National in 1978. Now 20 years closer to the part he had played in Birmingham as a 21-year-old, Finney was partnered by Dorothy Tutin as Lady Macbeth, making the infamous husband and wife team, as Bernard Levin put it, "the most erotic ever". Finney's dangerous volatility, the extent of his emotional range, and the ability to electrify and enthrall his audiences with almost unbearable tension had been hallmarks of his performance style at least since playing the title role in Pirandello's *Henry IV* at the Glasgow Citizens' in 1963.

Yet Finney's stage career has been interrupted by long absences, a factor which has contributed to the feeling that in spite of a sporadic series of major opportunities he has, thus far, failed to fulfil his early potential as a classical actor of consistent quality to rival the truly great performances of Laurence Olivier and Paul Scofield. Though Olivier, whose Coriolanus he understudied at Stratford in 1959, certainly regarded him as being the best of a generation of actors, to some extent one has to acknowledge that Finney's film work has inevitably been at the expense of his stage career. Perhaps ironically, it was Olivier who offered him his cinematic debut with a small part in *The Entertainer*. However, without his portrayal of the rumbustious hero in *Tom Jones* in 1963 Finney's international reputation is unlikely to have developed so swiftly. He has declared a desire one day to play Lear and Iago, but has consistently accepted stage work only if it generates his unbridled enthusiasm.

This selectivity, together with a propensity for extended breaks from directing or performance to pursue his equine interests (his father was a Salford bookmaker and horse-racing seems to run in the family) has meant that Finney was only seen in five productions on an English stage in the period 1970-90. He will be best remembered during this time for the part of Harold in Lyle Kessler's *Orphans*, originally produced by Chicago's Steppenwolf Theatre Company. The play, a psychological three-hander, transferred from the Hampstead Theatre to the West End after arousing much interest. For his role as the Chicago conman-turned-kidnap-victim who becomes the paternalistic redeemer in the emotionally battered lives of his two orphaned young captors, Finney won the London Standard Drama Award for Best Actor and a Laurence Olivier Award.

Often preferring film assignments, Finney has worked behind and in front of the camera for Memorial Enterprises, an independent production company he founded in the mid-1960's. The list of his directing credits for the stage suggests a political consciousness has informed the choice of such plays as Brian Friel's *The Freedom of the City*, set in Londonderry, *The Biko Inquest*, about the death in police custody of Black South African Steve Biko, and a revival at the Old Vic of John Arden's anti-war play *Sergeant Musgrave's Dance*, in which Finney played Musgrave.

Albert Finney's contribution to postwar theatre has been considerable, and the range of his work as performer and director belies the traditional reputation of his youth as a tough, earthy, northern character actor. Though more active on screen than stage over the years than some of his contemporaries, he has proved to be extraordinarily versatile in his stage career. From Restoration comedy to Chekhovian tragicomedy, French farce to the heroic epic of Marlowe's *Tamburlaine*, Finney's physical stature, rich tones, and ability to exude stage presence have all contributed to the high regard in which he is still held.

—Chris Banfield

FIORILLI, Tiberio. Italian actor. Born in Naples, Italy, 9 November 1608 (other sources, as early as 1604); probably son of actor Silvio Fiorillo. Married 1) actress Lorenza Elisabetta (or Isabella) Del Campo, known as Marinetta (separated 1664), three sons; 2) Marie-Robert Duval in 1688, one daughter; also one son by lover Anna Doffan. Began career in Italy around 1625, appearing in Mantua, Florence, Naples, Palermo, Rome and Milan; actor, with the Comédie-Italienne commedia dell'arte company in Paris, from 1644; appeared at the Théâtre du Petit-Bourbon, Paris, 1655-59, in alternation with Molière's company; highly acclaimed as Scaramouche, playing without the customary mask; made several extended return visits to Italy and also appeared at the Palais-Royal, Paris, from 1661; settled permanently in Paris, 1670; also acted in London, 1673 and 1675; made final appearance on the stage, 1690; retired officially at the end of the 1693-94 season. Died in Paris, 7 December 1694.

Roles

Scaramouche in: *La Rosaura imperatrice di Constantinopoli*, Comédie-Italienne, Paris, 1658; *Il Convitato di pietra*, Comédie-Italienne, Paris, 1658; *Colombine avocat pour et contre* (Fatouville), Paris, 1685; *Arlequin et Scaramouche juifs errans de Babilone*; *La Cruauté du docteur*; *Le Gelosie di Scaramuccia*; *Les Jugements du Duc d'Ossone*; *Lèhypocrite*; *Le Mari*; *Table de Scaramouche*; *Le Triomphe de la médecine*; many more.

*

Bibliography

Books:
Angelo Costantini, *La Vie de Scaramouche*, 1695 (translated by Cyril W. Beaumont), London, 1924.

* * *

Tiberio Fiorilli was one of the most famous improvisatory actors of all time and a star of the Comédie-Italienne, the Italian commedia dell'arte troupe that played in Paris in the 17th century. Fiorillo was with the company when it made its debut on 13 June 1644. He entered de facto retirement, according to his own claim, in 1690, and officially retired at the end of the 1693-94 season. He was probably 86 at the time of his death, which means he played until he was 81 or 82. Most of his professional life was spent in France. No records survive of his work in Italy before 1644, although he was certainly active, probably from 1625 or so. In later years he travelled back and forth on a number of occasions, sometimes performing in Italy, sometimes merely visiting his home outside Florence. After 1670 he remained in Paris.

Fiorilli's role was Scaramouche, a character first played in 1614 by Giovan Battista Fiorillo, very probably Tiberio Fiorilli's brother. His probable father, Silvio Fiorillo, played the Capitano, a precursor of Scaramouche. Although some scholars have denied that Fiorilli was a member of the famous Fiorillo family, the weight of evidence suggests that he was. His special skills as a mime and a musician required development over a long period of time, and it is hard to imagine him sprung, ready formed, from some nontheatrical lineage.

Fiorilli was a tall man whose Scaramouche was costumed in antique Spanish style with the black breeches, doublet and short cape of the early 17th century. On his head was a large black beret. He wore no mask but was 'enfarinée', in white face, with a curving handlebar moustache and a 'mouche', or tiny chin whisker. In portraits he usually carries a guitar. If we are to believe Callot's image of Scaramuccia in *I Balli de Sfessania* (1622), the character began as a conventional Capitano figure, but Fiorilli's version was essentially a zanni (one of the comic servant characters).

The first role we can be certain Fiorilli played was the servant of Count Partinopolis in *La Rosaura imperatrice di Constantinopoli*, performed by the Comédie-Italienne for a carnival in 1658. The gazetteer Loret reported that "among a hundred exquisite things which cause us happy surprise, among a quantity of happenings, what makes us laugh until our teeth ache, what would give delight to a stump, is the table of Scaramouche". This is a famous extended 'lazzi', or comic turn, in which a starving zanni, in this case Scaramouche, is prevented by all sorts of tricks and accidents from helping himself at a table magically provided with food. Gluttony was one of Scaramouche's most prominent characteristics, along with cowardice. *La Rasaura* provided the actor with two opportunities to perform the famous lazzi of fright, one during a thunderstorm, one when he was expected to fly to Paris on a dragon. It is probable that Fiorilli also played Don Juan's servant when *Il Convitato di pietra* was first performed, also in 1658. Fiorilli's first biographer, Angelo Costantini, wrote that this was the actor's favourite role because of the eating that was in it.

Unlike his colleague and co-star Domenico Biancolelli, who played Arlequin, Fiorilli left no personal record of his play. We find traces of it, however, in Biancolelli's 'zibaldone', or actor's aide-memoire, and in Evaristo Gherardi's *Le Théâtre Italien*. Very little is available from the traditional repertory played before 1670; in one piece entitled *La Cruauté du docteur*, Scaramouche fulfils a traditional Capitano function of rival suitor. In general, however, we can infer from material after 1670 that Scaramouche is usually a zanni. He can be either the 'fourbe intrigante', the clever rascal, or the 'fourbe balourde', the simpleton. He also appears from time to time, especially in later years, as a substitute 'vieillard', or old man.

The tall, stout Fiorilli performed many comic routines with Biancolelli, who was small and also rather stout. The difference in size is often played up, as in *Arlequin et Scaramouche juifs errans de Babilone*, when the two change clothes and Arlequin puts both of his legs into one leg of Scaramouche's breeches. Sometimes the two collaborate, as in *Le Mari*, when Arlequin notices that the Docteur's shoes need cleaning, and they each pick up one of his feet. Sometimes they are adversaries, as in *Lèhypocrite*, when Arlequin takes a bat made of cardboard from the back of his belt and beats his fellow zanni with it. Scaramouche falls and claims to be dead, but the Docteur — seeing the cardboard bat — announces that he is merely scared to death.

Fiorilli was known in his day as "the master of Molière". Molière's troupe shared theatres with the Comédie-Italianne, and the great French actor-playwright was apparent-ly much influenced by the acting style of the commedia dell'arte. The Italian actors improvised their plays, constructing them without the aid of a playwright. Improvisation led the Italians to develop what Sandro DèAmico calls "the novelty of perfectly executed action and the total identification of the actor with his character". The classical French actor used a formal declamatory style with very little physical action; the Italians introduced the French to acting that was lively, natural and focused, in the modern sense, on playing the moment.

Exactly what Molière owed to his Italian mentor as an actor cannot be recovered, but the two certainly shared comic business. We can often only speculate about which actor originated a piece of business and which actor borrowed it. In *Les Jugements du Duc d'Ossone*, Scaramouche performs the 'lazzi of the patrol', in which he speaks in different tones and different languages, as Molière does in *Les Fourberies de Scapin*, while in *Le Triomphe de la médecine*, Scaramouche plays a hypochondriac in the style of *Le Malade imaginaire*.

A star of the first established popular theatre in Europe, Tiberio Fiorilli's celebrity was based both on his own skills and on the relationship that develops through long experience between a stable audience and an actor playing a fixed character. Regardless of the specifics of plot and action, the character remains predictable, allowing the audience to think ahead and indulge in anticipatory enjoyment. Like Charlie Chaplin or Jack Benny in the 20th century, Tiberio Fiorilli played a form rather than a character in the conventional sense. His career of close on 50 years testifies to his success.

—Virginia Scott

FISKE, Minnie Maddern. US actress. Born Marie Augusta Davey in New Orleans, 19 December 1865; daughter of a theatrical manager. Educated in convents in Cincinnati, New Orleans, Montreal, and St Louis. Married playwright Harrison Grey Fiske in 1890. Stage debut, at the age of two, with Maddern family travelling company, 1868; New York debut, 1870; achieved fame by the age of 15; retired on marriage, 1890, but returned to stage, 1894; co-manager, with her husband, Manhattan Theatre, New York, 1901–07. LL.D: University of Wisconsin, 1927. Died in Hollis, New York, 15 February 1932.

Roles

1868	Duke of York in *Richard III* (Shakespeare), Little Rock, Arkansas; Niblo's Garden, New York, 1871.
1870	Little Fritz in *Fritz, Our German Cousin* (Gayler), Wallack's Theatre, New York.
1871	Willie Leigh in *Hunted Down* (Boucicault), Lina Edwin's Theatre, New York.
1872	Dollie in *Chicago Before the Fire*, Theatre Comique, New York.
1874	Prince Arthur in *King John* (Shakespeare), Booth's Theatre, New York.
1874–82	Damon's Son in *Damon and Pythias* (Banim), Philadelphia.

Paul in *The Octoroon* (Boucicault), Philadelphia.

Little Mary Morgan in *Ten Nights in a Barroom*, Boston.

The Boy in *Bosom Friends* (adapted from Sardou's *Nos Intimes*), Booth's Theatre, New York.

Lucy Fairweather in *The Streets of New York* (Boucicault), Olympic Theatre, New York.

The Sun God in *The Ice Witch*, New Orleans.

Ralph Rackstraw in *H.M.S. Pinafore* (Gilbert and Sullivan), Park Theatre, New York.

1882   Chip in *Fogg's Ferry* (Callahan), Park Theatre, New York.

1883   Juanita in *Juanita* (Callahan), Academy of Music, Chicago.

1884   Mercy Baxter in *Caprice* (Taylor), New Park Theatre, New York; US tour, 1885.

1885   Alice Clendenning in *In Spite of All* (MacKaye, adapted from Sardou's *Andrea*), Lyceum Theatre, New York, and US tour.

1889   Mrs Coney in *Featherbrain* (adapted from MacKaye's *Tête de Linotte*), Madison Square Theatre, New York.

1893   Hester Crewe in *Hester Crewe* (H. G. Fiske), Tremont Theatre, Boston.

Nora in *A Doll's House* (Ibsen), Empire Theatre, New York; Manhattan Theatre, New York, 1903.

Magda Gilberte in *Frou-Frou* (Meilhac and Halevy, adapted by Daly), Garden Theatre, New York.

1895   Marie Deloche in *Marie Deloche — The Queen of Liars* (Daudet and Hennique, adapted by H. G. Fiske), US tour and Garden Theatre, New York.

1896   Césarine in *Césarine* (Dumas *fils*), Garden Theatre, New York; Manhattan Theatre, New York, 1903.

The Marquis in *The White Pink* (Daudet, adapted by H. G. Fiske), Grand Opera House, San Antonio, Texas.

'Toinette in *A Light from St Agnes* (M. M. Fiske), Garden Theatre, New York.

Adelaide in *Not Guilty* (M. M. Fiske), Duquesne Theatre, Pittsburgh.

Madeline in *The Right to Happiness* (Merington), Grand Opera House, New Orleans.

1897   Tess in *Tess of the D'Urbervilles* (Stoddard, adapted from Hardy), Fifth Avenue Theatre, New York.

Cyprienne in *Divorçons* (Sardou), Fifth Avenue Theatre, New York; Manhattan Theatre, New York, 1903.

1898   Alexandra Victoria Belchamber in *A Bit of Old Chelsea* (Beringer), Fifth Avenue Theatre, New York; Manhattan Theatre, New York, 1903.

Madeline in *Love Finds the Way* (Merington), Fifth Avenue Theatre, New York.

1899   Magda Giulia in *Little Italy* (Fry), Fifth Avenue Theatre, New York.

Magda in *Magda* (Sudermann), Fifth Avenue Theatre, New York.

Minnie Maddern Fiske

Becky Sharp in *Becky Sharp* (Mitchell, adapted from Thackeray), Fifth Avenue Theatre, New York; Lyceum Theatre, New York, 1911.

1901   Miranda Warriner in *Miranda of the Balcony* (Flexner), Manhattan Theatre, New York.

Marian Lorimer in *The Unwelcome Mrs Hatch* (Harrison), Manhattan Theatre, New York.

1902   Mary in *Mary of Magdala* (Winter, adapted from Heyse), Manhattan Theatre, New York.

1903   Hedda in *Hedda Gabler* (Ibsen), Manhattan Theatre, New York.

1904   Leah in *Leah Kleschna* (McLellan), Manhattan Theatre, New York.

1906   Dolce, Contessa di Cassali in *Dolce* (Long), Manhattan Theatre, New York.

Cynthia Karslake in *The New York Idea* (Mitchell), Milwaukee and Lyric Theatre, New York.

1907   Rebecca West in *Rosmersholm* (Ibsen), Lyric Theatre, New York.

1908   Nell Sanders in *Salvation Nell* (Sheldon), Hackett's Theatre, New York.

1910   Lona Hessel in *The Pillars of Society* (Ibsen), Lyceum Theatre, New York.

Hannele in *Hannele* (Hauptmann), Lyceum Theatre, New York.

Mrs Bumpstead-Leigh in *Mrs Bumpstead-Leigh* (H. J. Smith), Chicago; Lyceum Theatre, New York, 1911; Klaw Theatre, New York, 1929.

1911   Agnes Bromley in *The New Marriage* (Mitchell), Syracuse, New York.
1912   Julia France in *Julia France* (Atherton), Princess Theatre, Toronto.
        Lady Patricia Cosway in *Lady Patricia* (Besier), Empire Theatre, New York.
        Mary Page in *The High Road* (Sheldon), Hudson Theatre, New York; US tour, 1913.
1914   Lady Betty Martingale in *Lady Betty Martingale* (Long and Stayton), US tour.
1916   Juliet Miller in *Erstwhile Susan* (Forest), Gaiety Theatre, New York.
1917   George Sand in *Madame Sand* (Moeller), Criterion Theatre, New York.
1918   Madame Eulin in *Service* (Lavedan, adapted by Taylor), Cohan Theatre, New York.
1919   Nellie Daventry in *Mis' Nelly o' New Orleans* (Eyre), Henry Miller's Theatre, New York.
1921   Marion Blake in *Wake Up, Jonathan* (Hughes and Rice), Henry Miller's Theatre, New York.
1923   Patricia Baird in *The Dice of the Gods* (Barrett), National Theatre, New York.
        Mary Westlake in *Mary, Mary, Quite Contrary* (Ervine), Belasco Theatre, New York.
1924   Helen Tilden in *Helena's Boys* (Erlich), Henry Miller's Theatre, New York.
1925   Mrs Malaprop in *The Rivals* (Sheridan), Hollis Street Theatre, Boston.
1927   Mrs Alving in *Ghosts* (Ibsen), Mansfield Theatre, New York.
1928   Mistress Page in *The Merry Wives of Windsor* (Shakespeare), Knickerbocker Theatre, New York.
        Beatrice in *Much Ado About Nothing* (Shakespeare), US tour.
1929   Mrs Livingston Baldwin Crane in *Ladies of the Jury* (Ballard), Erlanger's Theatre, New York.
1930   Helen Tyler in *It's a Grand Life* (Hughes and Williams), Cort Theatre, New York.
1931   Kate Gordon in *Against the Wind* (Drake), Blackstone Theatre, Chicago.

Other roles included: Alfred in *Divorce* (Daly); The Crowned Child in *Macbeth* (Shakespeare); Franko in *Guy Mannering* (Scott); The Child in *Across the Continent* (McCloskey); The Gamin and Peachblossom in *Under the Gaslight* (Daly); Marjorie in *The Rough Diamond* (Buckstone); The Girl in *The Little Rebel* (Coyne); Adrienne in *Monsieur Alphonse* (Dumas *fils*); Georgie in *Frou-Frou* (Meilhac and Halevy); Hendrick and Meenie in *Rip Van Winkle* (Boucicault); Clip in *A Messenger from Jarvis Section* (Locke); François in *Richelieu* (Bulwer-Lytton); Louise in *The Two Orphans* (Oxenford); Widow Melnotte in *The Lady of Lyons* (Bulwer-Lytton); Eva in *Uncle Tom's Cabin* (Stowe); and roles in *The Puritan Maid* (Ver Planck and Devereux) and *The Professional Beauty* (Ver Planck and Devereux).

Films

Tess of the D'Urbervilles, 1913; *Vanity Fair*, 1915.

Publications

The Countess Roudine (with Paul Kester), play (performed 1892); *A Light from St Agnes*, play (performed 1896); *Not Guilty*, play (performed 1896); *The Rose*, play (performed 1905); *The Eyes of the Heart*, play (performed 1905); *Fontenelle* (with H. G. Fiske), play; *Moses*, play; *John Doe*, play; *Selma*, play (unperformed); *Florian*, play (unperformed); *Verrick*, play (unperformed); *The Girls of Cloverton*, play (unperformed); *Common Clay*, scenario (unperformed); *Kathryn*, scenario (unperformed); *Mrs Fiske: Her Views on Actors, Acting, and the Problems of Production*, edited by Alexander Woolcott, 1917.

*

Bibliography

Books:
Frank Carlos Griffith, *Mrs Fiske*, New York, 1912.
Archie Binns and Olive Kooken, *Mrs Fiske and the American Theatre*, New York, 1955.

* * *

Sometimes referred to as the first 'modern' US actress, Minnie Maddern Fiske began her lifetime in the theatre when, as a child billed as "Little Minnie Maddern", she acted in support of some of the greatest 19th-century US actors, including John McCullough and Lawrence Barrett. In adolescence and early adulthood she toured across the country in melodramas and farces and had begun to develop a following when she retired from the professional stage in 1890 upon her marriage to Harrison Grey Fiske, editor of the influential *New York Dramatic Mirror*. Four years later, after receiving critical acclaim for her performance as Nora in a charity production of *A Doll's House*, she returned to the stage as "Mrs Fiske", and remained active in the theatre until a few months before her death in 1932.

Unlike most of her contemporaries, who appeared in revivals of the classics or in the heavily emotional costume melodramas of the period, Mrs Fiske preferred the new European drama of Ibsen and his followers as well as new plays by US playwrights. In doing this she was making a virtue of necessity, since she had little interest in Shakespeare and since she and her husband, as the only 'independent' managers to hold out completely against the monopolistic Theatrical Syndicate in the early years of the century, were unable to obtain the rights to the plays of hundreds of established writers who were represented by Syndicate-controlled literary agents.

Two of Mrs Fiske's earliest successes upon her return to the stage were adaptations of 19th-century novels: *Tess of the D'Urbervilles* and *Vanity Fair* (the latter dramatized as *Becky Sharp*). While *Tess* gave her an opportunity to demonstrate her capabilities as an emotional actress in the 19th-century style, the role of Becky Sharp more closely fitted Mrs Fiske's unique talents and marked a turning-point in her career. Thereafter she was known for her nervous, cerebral style, her tendency to speak lines quickly, as if conversing rather than declaiming, and her insistence on a 'naturalness' of acting that included turning her back to the audience when the action demanded it (something that would never have been tolerated in the 19th-century

US theatre). Her reputation as a 'modern' actress resulted from this brittle, almost neurotic, performance style as well as from her choice of plays and supervision of productions.

When Mrs Fiske returned to the New York stage in 1894, she brought with her an idealistic view of theatre that was at odds with the commercial practices of the day: she announced that she would perform only the best drama in carefully mounted productions with first-rate casts. At first she had to compromise these ideals in order to keep her name and her work before the public, but once she and her husband became independent producers and managers of their own New York playhouse, they made certain that every element in their productions met their high standards. Mrs Fiske quickly abandoned the tradition of the 'star' actress appearing with an inferior supporting company in favour of a carefully-selected ensemble in which all of the performers were appropriately cast and carefully rehearsed. Again and again, reviewers praised the ensemble effects that Mrs Fiske was able to achieve and marvelled at her generosity in sharing the stage with the rest of the cast at a time when most stars remained at the figurative and literal centre of their productions.

Although she was not the first actress to produce Ibsen's plays in the USA, Mrs Fiske was the first to achieve widespread success with them. Before appearing as Nora Helmer or Hedda Gabler or Rebecca West, she spent several years reading and studying each role, until she was intimately acquainted with every thought, every movement of the character. Meanwhile, she toured in whatever plays were available to her. When she felt that she was ready to perform an Ibsen play in public, she spent several months in consultation with her husband on every facet of the production, and then rehearsed it intensively with the best cast she could assemble. The results astounded the critics and her Ibsen tours proved highly profitable, despite predictions that Ibsen's plays would never be popular with audiences outside a few large cities.

In addition to her landmark productions of Ibsen, Mrs Fiske was noted for her support of young playwrights. Two of her biggest hits were by writers whom she had discovered and nurtured — The New York Idea by Langdon Mitchell (who had also created her adaptation of Vanity Fair) and Salvation Nell by Edward Sheldon. She also produced plays by several of the women playwrights who contributed to the New York stage in large numbers during the first decades of this century, including Anna Crawford Flexner, Gertrude Atherton, and Marian de Forest. Because she was herself a playwright, the author of a number of one-act plays that she or others produced professionally, Mrs Fiske was particularly adept at recognizing theatrical potential in the work of inexperienced playwrights and she spent a great deal of time restructuring and rewriting the plays she chose to produce.

During the years when she appeared under her own management Mrs Fiske directed her plays, and, in conjunction with her husband, supervised the design of sets, lighting, and costumes, and the choice of musical accompaniment. Critics heaped superlatives on the grimy realism of the slum setting for Salvation Nell and praised Mrs Fiske for choosing lighter, more cheerful scenery than had previously been used in an Ibsen production for The Pillars of Society. Several newspaper accounts of her working methods suggest that Mrs Fiske was a sensitive but demanding director who was able to bring out first-rate performances in her actors through a combination of individual attention and infinite patience.

After financial reversals forced Harrison Grey Fiske to declare bankruptcy in 1914, Mrs Fiske appeared under other managements. She added more comedy to her repertoire, touring successfully with modern plays such as Mrs Bumpstead-Leigh and, late in her career, with the classics she had earlier eschewed, giving memorable performances in The Merry Wives of Windsor and The Rivals.

Mrs Fiske toured indefatigably with her plays, taking them to parts of the USA and Canada that were rarely if ever visited by live theatrical productions. Her insistence on unity of mood and ensemble acting, combined with her innovative acting style and penchant for the 'new' realistic drama, gave US theatregoers higher standards, and helped to pave the way for the revolution in US theatre that took place in the period around World War I.

—Margaret M. Knapp

———————

FLORIDOR.   French actor-manager. Born Josias de Soulas, Sieur de Primefosse, in the Brie district of France, 1608. Educated in Paris. Served in French army. Married Marguerite Beloré in 1638, seven sons. Stage debut, as a strolling player in the French provinces, c. 1630; led touring company to London, appearing at the English Court and at the Phoenix and Cockpit theatres, Drury Lane, 1635; debut at the Théâtre du Marais, Paris, 1640; director, Théâtre du Marais, from 1642; acclaimed in plays by Corneille and Racine; led company at the Hôtel de Bourgogne, from 1647. Died August 1671.

Roles

1642–43	Sévère in *Polyeucte* (P. Corneille), Théâtre du Marais, Paris.
1643–44	Ptolémée in *La Mort de Pompée* (P. Corneille), Théâtre du Marais, Paris.
1642–47	Horace in *Horace* (P. Corneille), Théâtre du Marais, Paris; Hôtel de Bourgogne, Paris, 1657.
	Cinna in *Cinna* (P. Corneille), Théâtre du Marais, Paris; Hôtel de Bourgogne, Paris, 1657.
1659	*Oedipe* (P. Corneille), Théâtre de l'Hôtel de Bourgogne, Paris.
1660	*Stilicon* (T. Corneille), Théâtre de l'Hôtel de Bourgogne, Paris.
1663	Massinissa in *Sophonisbe* (P. Corneille), Théâtre de l'Hôtel de Bourgogne, Paris.
1664	Othon in *Othon* (P. Corneille), Fontainebleu.
1665	Alexandre in *Alexandre* (Racine), Théâtre du Palais-Royale, Paris.
1667	Pyrrhus in *Andromaque* (Racine), Théâtre de l'Hôtel de Bourgogne, Paris.
1669	Néron in *Britannicus* (Racine), Théâtre de l'Hôtel de Bourgogne, Paris.
1670	Titus in *Bérénice* (Racine), Théâtre de l'Hôtel de Bourgogne, Paris.

* * *

When Josias de Soulas, the son of a minor aristocrat, left the army, he gained early theatrical experience in London, where he acted in plays by Corneille and Scudéry at the Cockpit and other theatres, before joining a company touring the French provinces. On his return to Paris, by now known as Floridor, he established such a strong reputation at the Théâtre du Marais that he was transferred, reputedly by royal command, to the more prestigious Hôtel de Bourgogne, where he became the effective leader of the troupe with which his name was virtually synonymous for a quarter of a century.

The chronicler Tallemant des Réaux, who wrote bitterly and negatively about so many people, called him a mediocre actor, but other contemporaries praised his natural air, his lack of self-consciousness, his strength of voice and the clarity of his diction, and the impressive demeanour that made him a joy to watch as well as to hear. Perhaps because his talents were regarded as obvious (he was often described simply as the greatest actor of his age), praise of Floridor often consisted of enthusiastic but unspecific assertions of his excellence and his entitlement to the various honours and eulogies heaped upon him. Whenever he was compared with other actors, he was always accounted superior. He was tall and well-built, a well-educated, intelligent, cultured man, and a good friend, much loved not only as an actor but also as an individual.

An acting innovation with which Floridor is sometimes credited is that of speaking his roles instead of chanting them reverentially, thus allowing himself greater flexibility to develop character and to portray a full range of emotions. Indeed, his influence on the style of those actors who were later to form the Comédie-Française equalled that of Molière. When the latter in his *Impromptu de Versailles* cruelly mimicked the unsubtle over-emphatic acting, the striking of poses, and the bombastic mode of speech of some members of the Hôtel de Bourgogne company, and implied that they did not differentiate between roles and had no sense of characterization or life, he significantly avoided criticizing Floridor, in whom he must have recognised real talent.

Floridor played both heroes and villains, young and old (but mostly young). Whilst still at the Théâtre du Marais, he probably created the eponymous heroes Horace and Cinna in Pierre Corneille's plays as well as Sévère in *Polyeucte* and Ptolémée in *La Mort de Pompée*. Afterwards, he acted these same parts in revivals by the rival company. It was, of course, the Hôtel de Bourgogne that was reputed to be the most accomplished in the performance of tragedy and tragic playwrights increasingly preferred to have their works given there. It was there that Floridor acted major roles in several of Corneille's later plays and in works by such important secondary dramatists as Thomas Corneille and Quinault. He was Alexandre in Racine's play of that name and he created Pyrrhus in *Andromaque*, Néron in *Britannicus*, and Titus in *Bérénice*. He appeared with some of the greatest actresses of the century, including Mademoiselle Des Oeillets and Mademoiselle Duparc and, in *Bérénice*, Mademoiselle Champmeslé.

An associated talent for which he was renowned was that of stepping forward and delivering the 'annonces' or 'compliments' with which performances usually closed. These consisted of partly extemporized comments on the play just performed and on its reception by the audience and an exhortation to attend the next. A ready wit and the

Floridor

ability to engage in repartee would have been essential qualities. Sometimes, his 'annonces' received greater applause than the play that had preceded them. Floridor also enjoyed considerable success in addressing both prepared and extemporized 'harangues' (laudatory speeches) to members of the royal family and nobles who visited the theatre or in whose homes and palaces the company performed. Louis XIV and his brother (Monsieur) were among the most frequent recipients of these 'harangues'. In return, Floridor was showered with gifts and privileges. Partly, no doubt, because of his favoured position, he also became a successful businessman.

Exceptionally, for a leading actor in the period of Molière, Floridor seems not to have tried his hand at writing. He was a skilful administrator and he held his company together in the face of determined rivalry by the Marais troupe and later by Molière. Eighteen months after his death, the Hôtel de Bourgogne, under his protégé and successor Hauteroche, was able to withstand and even to profit from the disarray in the Paris theatre world following the death of Molière and, more important, to do so during the key early months of the inexorable rise to fortune of that impresario of quite a different stamp, Jean-Baptiste Lully.

—William Brooks

FORBES-ROBERTSON, (Sir) Johnston. British actor-manager. Born in London, 16 January 1853. Educated at Charterhouse public school and in France and Germany; student, Royal Academy School of Art, London, 1870. Married Gertrude Elliott (May Gertrude Dermot) in 1900, four daughters (including actress Jean Forbes-Robertson). Stage debut, Princess's Theatre, London, 1874; studied elocution under Samuel Phelps as actor with Charles Calvert's company, Prince's Theatre, Manchester, and elsewhere, 1874–78; toured with Ellen Terry, 1874; actor, various London theatres, 1875–83; joined the Bancrofts at the Prince of Wales's Theatre, London, 1878, and subsequently at the Haymarket Theatre, London, 1880 and 1883–85; first of several US tours, 1885; appeared regularly with Henry Irving's company at the Lyceum Theatre, London, 1882–95, and with John Hare's company at the Garrick Theatre, London, 1889–91; particularly acclaimed as Romeo, 1895, and as Hamlet, 1897; manager, Lyceum Theatre, 1896–1902, Comedy Theatre, London, 1901, Lyric Theatre, London, 1902, and Scala Theatre, London, 1905; provincial farewell tour, 1912; farewell season, Theatre Royal, Drury Lane, 1913; toured USA in most famous roles, 1913–16. MA: University of Columbia, New York, 1915. Knighted, 1913. Died at St Margaret's Bay, near Dover, 6 November 1937.

Productions

As actor:

1874   Chastelard in *Mary Queen of Scots* (Wills), Princess's Theatre, London.

James Annesley in *The Wandering Heir* (Reade), Astley's Theatre, London.

Prince Hal in *Henry IV, part 2* (Shakespeare), Prince's Theatre, Manchester.

Fenton in *The Merry Wives of Windsor* (Shakespeare), Gaiety Theatre, London.

1875   Lord Glossmore in *Money* (Bulwer-Lytton), Gaiety Theatre, London.

Beauseant in *The Lady of Lyons* (Bulwer-Lytton), Gaiety Theatre, London.

Hastings in *She Stoops to Conquer* (Goldsmith), Gaiety Theatre, London.

Lysander in *A Midsummer Night's Dream* (Shakespeare), Gaiety Theatre, London.

Chevalier de Vaudray in *The Two Orphans* (Oxenford), Olympic Theatre, London.

Borders in *The Spendthrift* (Jerrold), Olympic Theatre, London.

1876   Mark Smeaton in *Anne Boleyn* (Taylor), Haymarket Theatre, London.

Orsino in *Twelfth Night* (Shakespeare), Gaiety Theatre, London.

Baron Steinfort in *The Stranger* (Kotzebue), Gaiety Theatre, London.

Abbé de Larose in *Corinne* (Buchanan), Lyceum Theatre, London.

Geoffrey Wynyard in *Dan'l Druce, Blacksmith* (Gilbert), Haymarket Theatre, London.

1877   Jeremy Diddler in *Raising the Wind* (Kenney), Olympic Theatre, London.

Arthur Wardlaw in *The Scuttled Ship* (Boucicault and Reade), Olympic Theatre, London.

George Talboys in *Lady Audley's Secret* (Hazlewood), Olympic Theatre, London.

Sandro in *The Violin Maker of Cremona* (Neville), Olympic Theatre, London.

Clement Austin in *Henry Dunbar* (Taylor), Olympic Theatre, London.

Edgar Greville in *The Turn of the Tide* (Burnand), Olympic Theatre, London.

Gerard Seton in *The Ne'er-Do-Weel* (Gilbert), Olympic Theatre, London.

Richard Goodwin in *The Miser's Treasure*, Olympic Theatre, London.

Hercule in *Belphegor* (Boucicault), Olympic Theatre, London.

Squire Lockwood in *Love or Life* (Taylor and Meritt), Olympic Theatre, London.

1878   Count Orloff in *Diplomacy* (Stephenson and Scott), Prince of Wales's Theatre, London.

1879   Julian Beauclerc in *Diplomacy* (Stephenson and Scott), Prince of Wales's Theatre, London; Haymarket Theatre, London, 1884; Garrick Theatre, London, 1893.

Pierre Latouche in *Zillah* (Simpson and Templar), Lyceum Theatre, London.

Orsini in *Lucrezia Borgia* (H. J. Byron), Lyceum Theatre, London.

Sir Horace Welby in *Forget-Me-Not* (Merivale and Grove), Lyceum Theatre, London.

Dick Fanshawe in *Duty* (Albery), Prince of Wales's Theatre, London.

Sergeant Jones in *Ours* (Robertson), Prince of Wales's Theatre, London.

1880   Krux in *School* (Robertson), Haymarket Theatre, London.

Koenraad Deel in *Anne-Mie* (Scott), Prince of Wales's Theatre, London.

Maurice de Saxe in *Adrienne Lecouvreur* (Scribe), Court Theatre, London.

Armand Duval in *Heartsease* (Mortimer), Court Theatre, London.

Romeo in *Romeo and Juliet* (Shakespeare), Court Theatre, London; revived notably, Lyceum Theatre, London, 1895.

Don Carlos in *Juana* (Wills), Court Theatre, London.

Comte de Valreas in *Frou-Frou* (Daly), Princess's Theatre, London.

1882   Claude Glynne in *The Parvenu* (Godfrey), Court Theatre, London.

Claudio in *Much Ado About Nothing* (Shakespeare), Lyceum Theatre, London.

1883   Earl of Caryll in *Lords and Commons* (Pinero), Haymarket Theatre, London.

1884   Sir George Ormond in *Peril* (Stephenson and Scott), Haymarket Theatre, London.

Captain Absolute in *The Rivals* (Sheridan), Haymarket Theatre, London.

1885   Sir Charles Pomander in *Masks and Faces* (Reade and Taylor), Haymarket Theatre, London.

Petruchio in *Katherine and Petruchio* (Garrick), Haymarket Theatre, London.

Pygmalion in *Pygmalion and Galatea* (Gilbert), British and US tour.

Ingomar in *Ingomar* (Lovell), British and US tour.

Orlando in *As You Like It* (Shakespeare), British and US tour.

D'Aulnay in *Comedy and Tragedy* (Gilbert), British and US tour.

Sir Thomas Clifford in *The Hunchback* (Knowles), British and US tour.

Claude Melnotte in *The Lady of Lyons* (Bulwer-Lytton), British and US tour.

1887   Leontes in *The Winter's Tale* (Shakespeare), Lyceum Theatre, London.

1888   Nigel Chester in *Tares* (Beringer), Prince of Wales's Theatre, London.

Arthur Dimmesdale in *The Scarlet Letter* (Forbes and Coleridge), Royalty Theatre, London.

1889   Dunstan Renshaw in *The Profligate* (Pinero), Garrick Theatre, London.

Baron Scarpia in *La Tosca* (Grove and Hamilton), Garrick Theatre, London.

1890   Robert in *Dream Faces* (Miller), Garrick Theatre, London.

1891   Dennis Heron in *Lady Bountiful* (Pinero), Garrick Theatre, London.

Hugon in *Thermidor* (Sardou), Proctor's Theatre, New York.

1892   Buckingham in *Henry VIII* (Shakespeare), Lyceum Theatre, London.

1893   Hugh Rokeby in *Robin Goodfellow* (Carton), Garrick Theatre, London.

1894   George D'Alroy in *Caste* (Robertson), Garrick Theatre, London.

Walter Forbes in *Mrs Lessingham* (Fleming), Garrick Theatre, London.

Alfred Evelyn in *Money* (Bulwer-Lytton), Garrick Theatre, London.

Dr Alec Neill in *Dr and Mrs Neill*, British tour.

1895   Lancelot in *King Arthur* (Comyns Carr), Lyceum Theatre, London.

Lucas Cleeve in *The Notorious Mrs Ebbsmith* (Pinero), Garrick Theatre, London.

1897   Othello in *Othello* (Shakespeare), British tour.

1898   Golaud in *Pelleas and Mélisande* (Maeterlinck, translated by Mackail), Lyceum Theatre, London.

1899   Ito Arumo in *The Moonlight Blossom* (Fernald), Prince of Wales's Theatre, London.

Jacques Bernez in *The Sacrament of Judas* (Parker), Prince of Wales's Theatre, London.

1900   Mr Lepic in *Carrots* (Sutro), British tour.

Dick Dudgeon in *The Devil's Disciple* (G. B. Shaw), British tour.

1904   Jim Poulett in *The Edge of the Storm*, Duke of York's Theatre, London.

1906   Shylock in *The Merchant of Venice* (Shakespeare), Manchester.

1908   Captain Yule in *The High Bid* (James), Lyceum Theatre, Edinburgh.

The Stranger in *The Passing of the Third Floor Back* (Jerome), St James's Theatre, London, and Terry's Theatre, London.

1918   Mr Don in *A Well-Remembered Voice* (Barrie), Wyndham's Theatre, London.

Johnston Forbes-Robertson

1924   Hon Sir Richard Petworth in *The Ware Case* (Pleydell), Adelphi Theatre, London.

1927   The Priest in *Twelfth Night* (Shakespeare), St James's Theatre, London.

As actor-manager:

1895   *Romeo and Juliet* (Shakespeare), Lyceum Theatre, London; acted Romeo.

1896   *Michael and His Lost Angel* (Jones), Lyceum Theatre, London; acted the Priest.

1896   *For the Crown* (Davidson), Lyceum Theatre, London; acted Constantine.

Magda (Sudermann, adapted by Parker), Lyceum Theatre, London; acted Pastor Heffterdinck.

The School for Scandal (Sheridan), Lyceum Theatre, London; acted Joseph Surface.

1897   *Nelson's Enchantress* (Horne), Avenue Theatre, London; acted Lord Nelson.

Hamlet (Shakespeare), Lyceum Theatre, London; acted Hamlet.

1898   *The Second Mrs Tanqueray* (Pinero), German tour; acted Aubrey.

Macbeth (Shakespeare), German tour and Lyceum Theatre, London; acted Macbeth.

1901   *Count Tezma*, Comedy Theatre, London; acted Count David Tezma.

1902   *Mice and Men* (Ryley), Lyric Theatre, London; acted Mark Embury.

1903	*The Light That Failed* (Fleming), Lyric Theatre, London; acted Dick Heldar.
1903–04	*Love and the Man*, US tour.
1905	*The Conqueror* (Duchess of Sutherland), Scala Theatre, London; acted Morven Lord of Abivard.
	Mrs Grundy (Ryley), Scala Theatre, London; acted Edward Sotheby.
1906	*Caesar and Cleopatra* (Shaw), US tour; acted Caesar.

Films

Hamlet, 1912; *Masks and Faces*, 1916; *The Passing of the Third Floor Back*, 1917.

Publications

A Player Under Three Reigns (autobiography), 1925.

* * *

Shaw described Johnston Forbes-Robertson as "essentially a classical actor", by which he meant that "he can present a dramatic hero as a man whose passions are those which have produced the philosophy, the poetry, the art, and the state-craft of the world." Forbes-Robertson himself consciously saw his role as upholding the great tradition of English acting.

Forbes-Robertson joined Charles Calvert's company at the Prince's Theatre, Manchester, in 1874 and there came under the influence of the veteran Samuel Phelps. He wrote of this: "To be taken up so early in my career by one of the best of the old school was my supreme good fortune" and he traced his "histrionic pedigree" back through Phelps to Macready, Mrs Siddons, and Garrick. For *Henry IV, part 2*, Phelps, who was doubling Henry IV and Justice Shallow, took Forbes-Robertson through his part of Prince Hal, revealing how little the apprentice actor understood. Despite Phelps's tutelage Forbes-Robertson's Hal was found to be disappointing — he was refined, gentle, and melancholy, but he lacked the necessary fire and impetuous wilfulness of the character and emerged as a rather lackadaisical Prince.

Until his death in 1878, Phelps remained Forbes-Robertson's mentor (the young actor was a talented artist and painted a portrait of Phelps as Cardinal Wolsey; he was also co-author of his biography). When Forbes-Robertson joined Irving's Lyceum company in 1882 to play Claudio in *Much Ado About Nothing*, Ellen Terry's advice was that he should stick to painting — he did in fact produce a fine canvas of the church scene in Irving's production. Forbes-Robertson persevered, however, with his acting career, playing increasingly important roles for Irving — Buckingham in *Henry VIII* and Lancelot in *King Arthur* — and in 1895 took over the Lyceum during Irving's absence on tour for a production of *Romeo and Juliet* under his own management.

His Juliet, Mrs Patrick Campbell, admitted that the "Phelps School" meant nothing to her, but she was aware that Forbes-Robertson's work was built upon it. Shaw found clear evidence of Forbes-Robertson's artist's eye in his *Romeo and Juliet* but considered the effect to be essentially English. Forbes-Robertson's own performance as Romeo similarly lacked the fire and heat of Italy. According to one review, his duel with Tybalt was decorous and "a gentleman to the last he laid out Paris after killing him as carefully as if he were folding up his best suit of clothes."

The want of force and energy that detracted from his Hal and Romeo was less of an impediment to Hamlet, in which role he was received with a consensus of praise. Although he was by then middle-aged (44 in 1897), Forbes-Robertson's natural talents were well suited to the melancholy Dane. He seized upon every opportunity for philosophical discussion, be it with Ophelia, the players, the gravediggers, Horatio, or Rosencrantz and Guildenstern. Instead of being obtrusive, his own personality served the part admirably — in marked contrast to Irving's. Hamlet's grace, distinction, affability, melancholy, and intellectual discursiveness were harmonised to embody the many-faceted Prince. Forbes-Robertson's fine voice, moreover, came into its own in his resonant and sensitive delivery of the soliloquies, particularly "Oh, what a rogue and peasant slave am I."

Shaw's admiration of Forbes-Robertson resulted in the creation of the role of Julius Caesar in *Caesar and Cleopatra*, to which the actor's qualities were ideally suited: the Roman physique, the dignity, and above all the magnificent voice and elocution; though on the negative side he missed the humour and fun as a result of which Shaw's Caesar was in danger of becoming something of a bore.

Forbes-Robertson's achievements in contemporary drama were patchy. Courageously he played the guilt-torn cleric in H. A. Jones's *Michael and His Lost Angel*, but did nothing to mitigate the unpalatableness of the character by making him excessively solemn, joyless, and preachy. His involvement in *The High Bid* did something to redeem Henry James's reputation as a dramatist, but Forbes-Robertson's greatest success came from the lesser pen of Jerome K. Jerome. *The Passing of the Third Floor Back* took the old formula of a mysterious 'Passer-by' intervening in the lives of the residents of a shabby boarding-house with beneficent results. Forbes-Robertson's classic countenance (assisted by some judicial limelight) and saintly repose elevated Jerome's drama, but it remained in Max Beerbohm's view irretrievably tenth-rate and he was not alone in criticising Forbes-Robertson for prostituting his talents.

Unlike some of his contemporaries, Forbes-Robertson did not prolong his career into extreme old age. He took a characteristically graceful retirement in 1913 and received his knighthood during his farewell at Drury Lane. In the same year he committed his legendary Hamlet to film. At a cost of £10,000, Forbes-Robertson's *Hamlet* used elaborate sets and locations and ran (on six reels) for one hour and 40 minutes. By then Forbes-Robertson's age did "o'erstep the bounds of plausibility" for Hamlet, but his innate dignity, restraint, beautiful movement and gesture are nevertheless apparent, as is a surprising adeptness in using the new medium.

—Richard Foulkes

FORREST, Edwin. US actor. Born in Philadelphia, 9 March 1806. Educated at local schools in Philadelphia, until 1819. Married Catherine Norton Sinclair in 1837 (divorced 1852). Stage debut, as amateur, 1816; professional debut, Walnut Street Theatre, Philadelphia, 1820; strolling player, Pittsburgh, Lexington, Cincinnati, Louisville, and New Orleans, 1820–25; briefly entered management, Prune Street Theatre, Philadelphia, 1821; acted under Edmund Kean, Albany, New York, 1825; organized annual playwriting competitions to encourage US writers, 1829–35; alternated Iago and Othello with Junius Brutus Booth; European tour, 1834–36; London debut, Theatre Royal, Drury Lane, 1836; second British tour, 1845–46; rivalry with William Charles Macready culminated in tragic Astor Place Opera House riot, 1848; numerous US tours, 1850–72; opened Edwin Forrest Home for old actors, Philadelphia; last appearance, as Richelieu, 1872; presented Shakespeare readings after retirement as actor. Died in Philadelphia, 12 December 1872.

Principal roles

1820	Young Norval in *Douglas* (Home), Walnut Street Theatre, Philadelphia.
	Frederick in *Lovers' Vows* (Kotzebue), Walnut Street Theatre, Philadelphia.
	Octavian in *The Mountaineers* (Colman the Younger), Walnut Street Theatre, Phildelphia.
1821	Richard III in *Richard III* (Shakespeare), Prune Street Theatre, Philadelphia.
1823	Young Malfort in *The Soldier's Daughter* (Cherry), Columbia Street Theatre, Cincinatti.
	Blackface role in *The Tailor in Distress* (Smith), Columbia Street Theatre, Cincinnati.
	Tom Tipple in *Dandyism; or, Modern Fashions*, Columbia Street Theatre, Cincinatti.
	Sancho Panza in *Don Quixote*, Columbia Street Theatre, Cincinatti.
	Jaffier in *Venice Preserved* (Otway), Columbia Street Theatre, Cincinatti.
	George Barnwell in *George Barnwell* (Lillo), Columbia Street Theatre, Cincinatti.
1825	Iago in *Othello* (Shakespeare), New Orleans.
	Brutus in *Brutus* (Payne), New Orleans.
	Indian Chief in *She Would be a Soldier* (Noah), Albany Theatre, New York.
	Titus in *Brutus* (Payne), Park Theatre, New York.
	Richmond in *Richard III* (Shakespeare), Park Theatre, New York.
1826	Othello in *Othello* (Shakespeare), Park Theatre, New York, and Bowery Theatre, New York.
1827	Damon in *Damon and Pythias* (Banim), Bowery Theatre, New York.
	Mark Antony in *Antony and Cleopatra* (Shakespeare), Bowery Theatre, New York.
1828	William Tell in *William Tell* (Knowles), Bowery Theatre, New York.
1829	Metamora in *Metamora* (Stone), Park Theatre, New York.
1831	Spartacus in *The Gladiator* (Bird), Park Theatre, New York; revived notably, Theatre Royal, Drury Lane, London, 1836.
1836	Lear in *King Lear* (Shakespeare), Park Theatre, New York.
	Hamlet in *Hamlet* (Shakespeare), Park Theatre, New York.
	Macbeth in *Macbeth* (Shakespeare), Park Theatre, New York.

Other roles included: The Broker in *The Broker of Bogota* (Bird); Claude Melnotte in *The Lady of Lyons* (Bulwer-Lytton); Coriolanus in *Coriolanus* (Shakespeare); Jack Cade in *Jack Cade* (Conrad); Richelieu in *Richelieu* (Bulwer-Lytton); Shylock in *The Merchant of Venice* (Shakespeare); and roles in *Caius Marcus* (Smith), *Oralloosa* (Bird), *Rolla* (Kotzebue), and *Virginius* (Knowles).

*

Bibliography

Books:
James Rees (Colley Cibber), *The Life of Edwin Forrest with Reminiscences and Personal Recollections*, Philadelphia, 1874.
William Rounseville Alger, *Life of Edwin Forrest, The American Tragedian*, 2 vols., Philadelphia, 1877.
Lawrence Barrett, *Edwin Forrest*, Boston, 1881.
Gabriel Harrison, *Edwin Forrest: The Actor and the Man*, Brooklyn, 1889.
E. Robins, *Twelve Great Actors*, New York and London, 1900.
A. E. Newton, *Edwin Forrest and His Noble Creation*, Philadelphia, 1928.
Montrose Moses, *The Fabulous Forrest: The Record of an American Actor*, Boston, 1929.
Richard Moody, *Astor Place Riot*, Bloomington, Indiana, 1958.
Richard Moody, *Edwin Forrest: First Star of the American Stage*, New York, 1960.
Garff Wilson, *A History of American Acting*, Bloomington, Indiana, and London, 1966.
Charles H. Shattuck, *Shakespeare on the American Stage: From the Hallams to Edwin Booth*, Folger Shakespeare Library, Washington, D.C., 1976.

Articles:
Arthur Fleming, "Behind the Scenes", *Harpers'*, 34, December 1866.
Rufus Rockwell Wilson, "The Centenary of Edwin Forrest", *Theatre*, 6, March 1906.
Walter Prichard Eaton, "Edwin Forrest", *Atlantic*, 162, August 1938.
Iline Fife, "Edwin Forrest: The Actor in Relation to His Times", *Southern Speech Journal*, 9, March 1944.
Garff B. Wilson, "The Acting of Edwin Forrest", *Quarterly Journal of Speech*, 36, 1950.
Barbara Alden, "Edwin Forrest's Othello", *Theatre Annual*, 14, 1956.
Marvin Rosenberg, "Othello to the Life", *Theatre Arts*, 42, June 1958.

Edwin Forrest

Richard E. Mennen, "Edwin Forrest's 'Improved' King Lear", *Theatre Southwest*, 7, April 1981.

* * *

Edwin Forrest was the first native-born US actor to achieve 'star' status in his own country and recognition abroad in England. For over 40 years, until eclipsed by Edwin Booth, his forceful portraits of Shakespeare's tragic heroes and of such romantic rebels as Jack Cade, Metamora, and Spartacus, dominated the US stage.

A hallmark of Forrest's mature acting style was his powerful phsyicality. Although frail as a boy, through a regimen of strenuous daily exercise, he developed an unusually muscular body. When actress Fanny Kemble saw him for the first time, she reportedly exclaimed: "What a mountain of a man!". In several of his favourite roles he appeared in costumes that exposed his bulging biceps, calves, and shoulders. His voice, moreover, was as powerful as his physique. At full power, in moments of rage, for example, Forrest could make the theatre walls tremble. He was not just a roarer and ranter, however. He could "roar like a hurricane" but also "sigh like a zephyr" or speak in tones of "quiet loving tenderness". Indeed, his elocution was considered by some contemporaries to be impressive though sometimes also over-elaborate and artificial. Undoubtedly his physical and vocal power shaped his acting style and his interpretation of the characters he played. Strength was the predominant characteristic of his acting and he was best at expressing strong, violent states such as revenge, scorn, hatred, rage, and indignation rather than subtler passions.

A modern critic has characterized Forrest's style as "strenuous realism". Certainly he aimed for detailed, realistic, character portrayals and complemented his physical assets with diligent attention to the text and to the real life situations of characters. For his portrayal of Lear, for example, he visited asylums and homes for the ageing, carefully noting the physical manifestations of mental illness and senility. Once, as a young man, he had befriended an American Indian chief and had lived with his tribe for several weeks observing and adopting their lifestyle. When he created the role of Metamora, he drew extensively on this experience.

There were undoubtedly many who were moved by the realism of his characterizations, but some critics and commentators thought that he so exaggerated or "muscularized" effects that he sometimes strained the limits of credibility. Despite his textual and life study, Forrest painted characters with a bold stroke. He was most effective playing Metamora, Spartacus, or William Tell, roles which allowed a display of passionate energy — democratic heroes pitted against arrogant, aristocratic, tyrants. Such characters, and Forrest's interpretation of them, struck a common chord with US audiences of the time, particularly that portion of the audience drawn from the working class, the masses. As one of his contemporaries, the actor-manager Noah Ludlow opined, Forrest "both physically and in his artistic execution" was a "complete living illustration" of "the *masses* of American character". Hence, his enormous popularity.

Forrest played Shakespeare's leading characters because he was expected to, but he was "temperamentally out of tune" with them, as Shattuck notes: "Shakespeare gave him no democrats to work with". He could be effective with Othello and Lear "because he could construe them as noble and innocent men, much put-upon heroes who go down fighting". He played Hamlet, Macbeth, Richard III, and Shylock, but generally the complexities and ambiguities of these characters were beyond his grasp. As Ludlow observed, in Forrest's hands Lear and Hamlet were "frequently like enraged Titans" while Macbeth was "a ferocious chief of a barbarous tribe" and Othello "truly the ferocious and bloody Moor".

Despite his shortcomings, as his biographer Richard Moody writes: "In the middle 50 years of the past century no native-born, native trained actor climbed so high, summoned American writers to the drama with such fervour, spread the enduring glories of the mighty Shakespeare so widely, and carried the raging democratic fever to the stage with such fierce passion. And no actor compelled so many Americans to pay so much for a tempestuous evening in the theatre".

—Daniel J. Watermeier

G

GARRICK, David. British actor-manager and playwright. Born at the Angel Inn, Hereford, England, 19 February 1717. Educated at Ediall Hall School, Lichfield, under Samuel Johnson, 1735–37. Married ballerina Eva Maria Violette in 1749. Came to London with Johnson, 1737; read for the Bar and opened wine business with his brother; took up amateur theatricals; first play staged at Theatre Royal, Drury Lane, 1740; appeared under the name Lyddal, owing to family's disapproval, at Ipswich, 1741; debut as actor on London stage, Goodman's Fields Theatre, 1741; immediate success in role of Shakespeare's Richard III; joined company at Theatre Royal, Drury Lane, 1742; appeared at Smock Alley Theatre, Dublin, where he began affair with actress Peg Woffington, 1742; set up house with Charles Macklin and Peg Woffington in London, 1742; public quarrel with Macklin, 1743; estrangement from Woffington, 1745; co-manager of Smock Alley Theatre, 1745–46; actor, Covent Garden, 1746–47; joint-patentee, Drury Lane, from 1747; staged first spectacular Drury Lane pantomime, 1750; visited Paris, 1752; riots over Garrick's employment of French dancers at Drury Lane on the verge of war with France, 1755, and again over his abolition of half-price admission during the third–act intermission, 1762; in wake of furore embarked on European tour, 1763–65; presented Shakespeare Jubilee at Stratford-upon-Avon, 1769, hampered by heavy rain; engaged designer de Loutherbourgh at Drury Lane, 1773; suffered increasingly from gout and migraine; final appearance, 1776. Member: Theatrical Fund for Decayed Actors (first president). Died in London, 20 January 1779.

Roles

1741   Aboan in *Oroonoko* (Southerne), Ipswich, England.

Chamont in *The Orphan* (Otway), Ipswich, England; last acted, 1759–60.

Sir Harry Wildair in *The Constant Couple* (Farquhar), Ipswich, England.

Captain Brazen in *The Recruiting Officer* (Farquhar), Ipswich, England.

Richard III in *Richard III* (Shakespeare), Goodman's Fields Theatre, London; last acted, 1775–76.

Jack Smatter in *Pamela* (Dance), Goodman's Fields Theatre, London.

Sharp in *The Lying Valet* (Garrick, adapted from Motteux's *Novelty*), Goodman's Fields Theatre, London; last acted, 1742–43.

The Ghost in *Hamlet* (Shakespeare), Goodman's Fields Theatre, London; last acted, 1762–63.

Harlequin Student in *Harlequin Student* (anon.), Goodman's Fields Theatre, London.

1741–42   Lothario in *The Fair Penitent* (Rowe), Goodman's Fields Theatre, London; last acted, 1766–67.

Fondlewife in *The Old Bachelor* (Congreve), Goodman's Fields Theatre, London; last acted, 1743–44.

Clodio in *Love Makes a Man* (Cibber), Goodman's Fields Theatre, London; last acted, 1742–43.

Pierre in *Venice Preserved* (Otway), Goodman's Fields Theatre, London; last acted, 1759–60.

Duretete in *The Inconstant* (Farquhar), Goodman's Fields Theatre, London; 1760–61.

Witwou'd in *The Way of the World* (Congreve), Goodman's Fields Theatre, London.

Coster Pearmain in *The Recruiting Officer* (Farquhar), Goodman's Fields Theatre, London.

1742   Bayes in *The Rehearsal* (Villiers), Goodman's Fields Theatre, London; last acted, 1772–73.

Master Johnny in *The School Boy* (Cibber), Goodman's Fields Theatre, London; last acted, 1742–43.

Lear in *King Lear* (Shakespeare), Goodman's Fields Theatre, London; last acted, 1775–76.

Lord Foppington in *The Careless Husband* (Cibber), Goodman's Fields Theatre, London; last acted, 1775–76.

Hamlet in *Hamlet* (Shakespeare), Smock Alley Theatre, Dublin, and Theatre Royal, Drury Lane, London; last acted, 1775–76.

Captain Plume in *The Recruiting Officer* (Farquhar), Smock Alley Theatre, Dublin, and Theatre Royal, Drury Lane, London; last acted, 1748–49.

1742–43   Archer in *The Beaux' Stratagem* (Farquhar), Theatre Royal, Drury Lane, London; last acted, 1775–76.

Hastings in *Jane Shore* (Rowe), Theatre Royal, Drury Lane, London; last acted, 1775–76.

Abel Drugger in *The Alchemist* (Jonson), Theatre Royal, Drury Lane, London; last acted, 1775–76.

David Garrick

1743   Millamour in *The Wedding Day* (Fielding),
            Theatre Royal, Drury Lane, London.
1743–44   Biron in *The Fatal Marriage* (Southerne, adapt-
            ed by Garrick), Theatre Royal, Drury Lane,
            London; last acted, 1757.
            Townly in *The Provok'd Husband* (Cibber),
            Theatre Royal, Drury Lane, London; last
            acted, 1758–59.
            Regulus in *Regulus* (Havard), Theatre Royal,
            Drury Lane, London.
            Zaphna in *Mahomet the Imposter* (Miller),
            Theatre Royal, Drury Lane, London; last
            acted, 1744–45.
1744   Macbeth in *Macbeth* (Shakespeare), Theatre
            Royal, Drury Lane, London; last acted,
            1769–70.
1744–45   Sir John Brute in *The Provok'd Wife* (Van-
            brugh), Theatre Royal, Drury Lane, London;
            last acted, 1775–76.
            Scrub in *The Beaux' Stratagem* (Farquhar),
            Theatre Royal, Drury Lane, London; last
            acted, 1762–63.
            King John in *King John* (Shakespeare), Theatre
            Royal, Drury Lane, London.
            Othello in *Othello* (Shakespeare), Theatre Roy-
            al, Drury Lane, London; last acted, 1745–76.
            Tancred in *Tancred and Sigismunda* (Thom-
            son), Theatre Royal, Drury Lane, London;
            last acted, 1761–62.

1745–46   Orestes in *Orestes* (Theobald), Smock Alley
            Theatre, Dublin.
            Faulconbridge in *King John* (Shakespeare),
            Smock Alley Theatre, Dublin; last acted,
            1760–61.
            Iago in *Othello* (Shakespeare), Smock Alley
            Theatre, Dublin; last acted, 1752–53.
1746–47   Hotspur in *King Henry IV, Part One* (Shake-
            speare), Covent Garden, London.
1747   Fribble in *Miss in Her Teens* (Garrick), Covent
            Garden, London; last acted, 1761–62.
            Ranger in *The Suspicious Husband* (Hoadly),
            Covent Garden, London; last acted, 1775–76.
1747–48   Chorus in *King Henry V* (Shakespeare), Theatre
            Royal, Drury Lane, London; last acted,
            1748–49.
            Jaffier in *Venice Preserved* (Otway), Theatre
            Royal, Drury Lane, London; last acted,
            1762–63.
            Young Belmont in *The Foundling* (Moore),
            Theatre Royal, Drury Lane, London; last
            acted, 1749–50.
1748–49   Benedick in *Much Ado About Nothing* (Shake-
            speare, adapted by Garrick), Theatre Royal,
            Drury Lane, London; last acted, 1775–76.
            Dorilas-Eumenes in *Merope* (Hill), Theatre
            Royal, Drury Lane, London; last acted,
            1753–54.
            Frenchman, Drunken Man, Fine Gentleman,
            and Poet in *Lethe* (Garrick), Theatre Royal,
            Drury Lane, London; last acted, 1751–52.
1749   Demetrius in *Mahomet and Irene* (Johnson),
            Theatre Royal, Drury Lane, London.
            Comus in *Comus* (Milton), Theatre Royal,
            Drury Lane, London.
1749–50   Horatius in *The Roman Father* (Whitehead),
            Theatre Royal, Drury Lane, London; last
            acted, 1757–58.
            Edward in *Edward the Black Prince* (Shirley),
            Theatre Royal, Drury Lane, London.
1750   Romeo in *Romeo and Juliet* (Shakespeare),
            Theatre Royal, Drury Lane, London; last
            acted, 1761–62.
1750–51   Osmyn in *The Mourning Bride* (Congreve),
            Theatre Royal, Drury Lane, London; last
            acted, 1755–56.
1751   Alfred in *Alfred, a Masque* (Mallet), Theatre
            Royal, Drury Lane, London.
            Kitely in *Every Man in His Humour* (Jonson,
            adapted by Garrick), Theatre Royal, Drury
            Lane, London; last acted, 1775–76.
            Gil Blas in *Gil Blas* (Moore), Theatre Royal,
            Drury Lane, London.
1752   Mercour in *Eugenia* (Francis), Theatre Royal,
            Drury Lane, London.
1752–53   Demetrius in *The Brothers* (Young), Theatre
            Royal, Drury Lane, London.
            Loveless in *Love's Last Shift* (Cibber), Theatre
            Royal, Drury Lane, London; last acted,
            1753–54.
1753   Beverly in *The Gamester* (Moore), Theatre
            Royal, Drury Lane, London.
1753–54   Dumnorix in *Boadicea* (Glover), Theatre Roy-
            al, Drury Lane, London.

Virginius in *Virginia* (Crisp), Theatre Royal, Drury Lane, London.

Aletes in *Creusa* (Whitehead), Theatre Royal, Drury Lane, London; last acted, 1754–55.

Lusignan in *Zara* (Hill), Theatre Royal, Drury Lane, London; last acted, 1775–76.

Don Carlos in *The Mistake* (Vanbrugh), Theatre Royal, Drury Lane, London; last acted, 1762–63.

1754   Don John in *The Chances* (Villiers, adapted by Garrick), Theatre Royal, Drury Lane, London; last acted, 1774–75.

Achmet in *Barbarossa* (Brown), Theatre Royal, Drury Lane, London; last acted, 1775–76.

1755–56   Lord Chalkstone in *Lethe* (Garrick), Theatre Royal, Drury Lane, London; last acted, 1771–72.

Leon in *Rule a Wife and Have a Wife* (Fletcher), Theatre Royal, Drury Lane, London; last acted, 1775–76.

1756   Leontes in *Florizel and Perdita* (Garrick, adapted from Shakespeare's *The Winter's Tale*), Theatre Royal, Drury Lane, London; last acted, 1761–62.

Athelstan in *Athelstan* (Brown), Theatre Royal, Drury Lane, London.

Don Felix in *The Wonder* (Centlivre), Theatre Royal, Drury Lane, London; last acted, 1775–76.

1757   Wilding in *The Gamesters* (Garrick, adapted from Shirley's *The Gamester*), Theatre Royal, Drury Lane, London.

1757–58   Henry IV in *King Henry IV, Part Two* (Shakespeare), Theatre Royal, Drury Lane, London; last acted, 1769–70.

Lysander in *Agis* (Home), Theatre Royal, Drury Lane, London; last acted, 1760–61.

Pamphlet in *The Upholsterer* (Murphy), Theatre Royal, Drury Lane, London.

1758–59   Marplot in *The Busy Body* (Centlivre), Theatre Royal, Drury Lane, London.

Antony in *Antony and Cleopatra* (Shakespeare, adapted by Capel), Theatre Royal, Drury Lane, London.

Zamti in *The Orphan of China* (Murphy), Theatre Royal, Drury Lane, London; last acted, 1759–60.

Periander in *Eurydice* (Mallet), Theatre Royal, Drury Lane, London.

1759   Heartly in *The Guardian* (Garrick), Theatre Royal, Drury Lane, London; last acted, 1761–62.

1759–60   Lovemore in *The Way to Keep Him* (Murphy), Theatre Royal, Drury Lane, London; last acted, 1762–63.

Aemilius in *The Siege of Aquileia* (Home), Theatre Royal, Drury Lane, London.

Oroonoko in *Oroonoko* (Southerne), Theatre Royal, Drury Lane, London.

Sir Harry Gubbins in *The Tender Husband* (Steele), Theatre Royal, Drury Lane, London.

1760–61   Oakly in *The Jealous Wife* (Colman), Theatre Royal, Drury Lane, London; last acted, 1766–67.

Mercutio in *Romeo and Juliet* (Shakespeare), Theatre Royal, Drury Lane, London.

1761–62   Posthumus in *Cymbeline* (Shakespeare), Theatre Royal, Drury Lane, London; last acted, 1762–63.

1762   Dorilant in *The School for Lovers* (Whitehead), Theatre Royal, Drury Lane, London; last acted, 1762–63.

The Farmer in *The Farmer's Return from London* (Garrick), Theatre Royal, Drury Lane, London; last acted, 1762–63.

1763   Don Alonzo in *Elvira* (Mallet), Theatre Royal, Drury Lane, London.

Sir Anthony Branville in *The Discovery* (Mrs Sheridan), Theatre Royal, Drury Lane, London; last acted, 1775–76.

Sciolto in *The Fair Penitent* (Rowe), Theatre Royal, Drury Lane, London.

Publications

Plays:

Lethe; or, Esop in the Shades, 1741; *The Lying Valet*, from the play by Motteux, 1741; *Miss in Her Teens*, 1747; *Every Man in His Humour*, from the play by Jonson, 1751; *The Chances*, from the play by George Villiers, 1754; *Zara*, from the play by Hill, 1754; *Lilliput*, 1756; *The Male Coquette*, 1757; *The Fatal Marriage*, from the play by Southerne, 1757; *The Gamesters*, from Shirley's *The Gamester*, 1757; *The Guardian*, 1759; *Harlequin's Invasion; or, A Christmas Gambol*, pantomime with Colman the Elder, 1759; *The Farmer's Return*, 1762; *The Clandestine Marriage*, with Colman the Elder, 1766; *The Country Girl*, from Wycherley's *The Country Wife*, 1766; *Neck or Nothing*, from a play by Lesarge, 1766; *Cymon*, from Dryden's *Cymon and Iphigenia*, 1767; *Linco's Travels*, 1767; *A Peep Behind the Curtain; or, The New Rehearsal*, 1767; *The Jubilee*, Shakespeare pageant, 1769; *King Arthur*, from the play by Dryden, 1770; *The Institution of the Garter*, from the dramatic poem by Gilbert West, 1771; *The Irish Widow*, from Molière's *Le Mariage Forcé*, 1772; *A Christmas Tale*, 1773; *The Meeting of the Company*, 1774; *Bon Ton; or, High Life Above Stairs*, 1775; *The Theatrical Candidates*, 1775; *May Day; or, The Little Gypsy*, 1775.

Adaptations of Shakespeare:
King Lear, 1742; *Hamlet*, 1742; *Macbeth*, 1744; *Much Ado About Nothing*, 1748; *Romeo and Juliet*, 1750; *Katharine and Petruchio*, from *The Taming of the Shrew*, 1754; *Florizel and Perdita*, from *The Winter's Tale*, 1756; *Antony and Cleopatra*, 1758; *Cymbeline*, 1761; *Hamlet*, 1772.

Other:
An Essay on Acting: In Which Will Be Considered the Mimical Behaviour of a Certain Fashionable Faulty Actor . . . to Which Will be Added, A Short Criticism on His Acting Macbeth, 1744; *Poetical Works*, 2 vols., 1785; *The Private Correspondence of David Garrick with the Most Celebrated Persons of His Time*, 2 vols., 1832; *Some Unpublished Correspondence of David Garrick*, 1907; *The Diary of David Garrick: Being A Record of his Memorable*

Trip to Paris in 1751, 1928; *The Journal of David Garrick, Describing his Visit to France and Italy in 1763*, 1939; and numerous prologues, pamphlets, and poems.

*

Bibliography

Books:

Joseph Pittard, *Observations on Mr. Garrick's Acting*, London, 1758.

Thomas Davies, *Memoirs of the Life of David Garrick*, 2 vols., London, 1780.

Arthur Murphy, *The Life of David Garrick, Esq.*, 2 vols., London, 1801.

Percy H. Fitzgerald, *The Life of David Garrick: From Original Family Papers*, 2 vols., London, 1868.

Joseph Knight, *David Garrick*, London, 1894.

C. Gaehde, *David Garrick als Shakespeare Darsteller*, Berlin, 1904.

Mrs Clement Parsons, *Garrick and His Circle*, London, 1906.

Frank A. Hedgcock, *A Cosmopolitan Actor; David Garrick and His French Friends*, London, 1911.

E. P. Stein, *David Garrick Dramatist*, New York, 1941.

Margaret Barton, *Garrick*, New York, 1949.

A. B. Stewart, *Enter David Garrick*, Philadelphia and London, 1951.

R. G. Noyes, *The Thespian Mirror*, Providence, 1953.

M. E. Knapp, *Checklist of Verses by David Garrick*, Charlottesville, Virginia, 1955.

George Winchester Stone, Jr. and George M. Kahrl, *David Garrick — A Critical Biography*, Illinois, 1956.

Carola Oman, *David Garrick*, London, 1958.

Kalman A. Burnheim, *David Garrick: Director*, Pittsburgh, 1961.

David M. Little and George M. Kahrl, *The Letters of David Garrick*, 1963.

Leigh Woods, *Garrick Claims the Stage*, London, 1984.

Christopher Baugh, *Garrick and Loutherbourg*, Cambridge, 1990.

Articles:

Walter Herries Pollock, "Garrick's Acting as Seen in his Own Time", *Longman's Magazine*, VII, 1885.

Charles Riddell Williams, "David Garrick, Actor-Manager: Two Unpublished Letters", *Cornhill Magazine*, 1929.

William Angus, "An Appraisal of David Garrick: Based Mainly upon Contemporary Sources", *The Quarterly Journal of Speech*, 25, 1939.

G. W. Stone, "Shakespeare's Tempest at Drury Lane During Garrick's Management", *Shakespeare Quarterly*, 1956.

* * *

Of the list of actors inhabiting the Shakespearean tradition, David Garrick may have possessed the greatest range of all. In this connection, he seems to have resuscitated the qualities of Shakespeare's first Hamlet and contemporary, Richard Burbage, and to have foreshadowed the easy access between tragedy and comedy achieved by the 20th century's leading Shakespearean, Laurence Olivier.

Garrick acted from 1741, when he debuted in London as Richard III, until the spring of 1776, when he played,

together with contemporary roles, Hamlet, Lear, and Benedick. Garrick was pre-eminent in Shakespeare's plays at a time when the Bard was coming to the prominence in English repertories that he has held ever since. Indeed, Garrick's acting, directing, and adapting helped to elevate Shakespeare to the sort of idolatry and centrality we have since come to take for granted.

During his first run as Lear, when he was only 25, Garrick highlighted his versatility with an appearance in an afterpiece as an adolescent cut-up in Colley Cibber's *The School Boy*. Such tours de force typified his acting from the time of his debut, when he struck audiences with his departures from the conventional style of the familiar declamatory tradition. The actor James Quin was among those to recognise the fundamental change his acting represented, remarking in wonder "If the young fellow is right, I and the rest of the players have been all wrong". To the accepted practice of playing tragedy in heavy measure and with static dignity, Garrick added a seasoning of conversational speaking, rapid pantomimic movements, and lightened — to some, even trivialised — moments. Clearly, these qualities might serve him even better in comic characters, and such was the judgement of some of his most acute contemporary critics.

Small of stature and light of voice, Garrick was compelled toward a novel style by his divergence from the stockiness and rotundity that had been the model for actors in serious roles since the Restoration. Garrick reduced the scale of his tragic heroes by, for instance, stealing on tiptoes into Juliet's garden as Romeo "like a thief in the night" as one observer put it, and by whispering his way in manifest terror through Macbeth's scene with his wife immediately following the slaughter of Duncan. Although greeted by some as signs of degeneration in popular taste, Garrick's anti-heroic touches offered testimony among his apologists to a more refined and "feeling" theatre by the mid-point of his career. His acting also anticipated the sort of psychological detail associated with the advent of cinematic realism some 150 years after his death.

Garrick's style was legitimized in his own time through his diligent cultivation of the highest levels of European society. A tireless correspondent, Garrick wrote thousands of letters that have survived (as well as thousands of others, apparently, that did not), attended soirées among the elite of London's artistic, political, and intellectual communities, and twice extended his renown in tours of the Continent. In Paris during the early 1760's, he entertained exclusive gatherings with salon performances, largely in pantomime, from his great Shakespearean characterizations. In so doing he effectively stamped his vivacious and ingratiating style on a generation of French actors and audiences. Thus, descended from a line of French Huguenots who escaped their homeland under oppression in the 1680's, Garrick succeeded partly in reversing the long pattern of cultural hegemony that French letters and arts had enjoyed over their English counterparts. He was also known and imitated in Germany, where he travelled only briefly but where his acting was reported in great detail by a series of German tourists and journalists who had seen him in London.

As adapter of Shakespeare's plays for the contemporary stage, Garrick did much to consolidate the Bard's status as the greatest English playwright. His adaptations were sometimes eccentric — Ophelia's madness and the gravediggers scene were cut from *Hamlet*, while Romeo and Juliet were reunited in the tomb — but did much to restore public interest in the originals, some of which had not been staged since the Restoration. Together with these adaptations, Garrick also wrote a number of notable original comedies, usually short pieces including good roles for himself. For nearly 30 years he managed the Theatre Royal, Drury Lane with a mixed programme based on such plays and turned it into one of the most artistically rigorous and well-attended theatres in Europe. Under his regime it also became the most lucrative. On Garrick's retirement his share of the enterprise was bought by the playwright Richard Brinsley Sheridan who, for all his brilliance, only succeeded in undoing much of Garrick's good work and running the theatre into the ground. Garrick would have deplored Sheridan's improvidence, so different to his own canny commercialism, and in fact came out of retirement in 1777 to help with the mounting of Sheridan's first production of *The School for Scandal*.

Garrick's skill as an actor seems to have owed much to his broader acuity as a man of the stage able to write sharp and pointed dialogue in the contemporary vein, to reclaim lively dramatic action from antique plays, to shape and tailor the performances of other company members to his own taste, and to maintain a consistently high level both of activity and of quality as he did so. Garrick's managerial talent extended itself into more thorough rehearsal practices and more lavish and well-integrated uses of painted scenery and lighting equipment than had prevailed before him. His hiring of the Alsatian painter Phillipe De Loutherbourgh as resident set designer at Drury Lane in the 1770s marked a sea-change in the expense and care afforded to scenic elements on English stages and as such had a lasting influence on the national theatre. Other innovations included banning wealthy patrons from occupying their accustomed seats actually on the stage itself, where they might parade themselves before the audience almost alongside the performers.

Garrick's failures in great roles can be numbered on the fingers of one hand — Antony in *Antony and Cleopatra* and Othello among them — and his failures as a producer were almost as rare. More significantly, though, David Garrick brought to the art of acting an animation that was novel in its own time and which, taken in the larger context, typified the optimism and buoyancy of the English Enlightenment. His achievement was readily acknowledged in his own lifetime and on his death he was accorded the ultimate honour of a lavish public funeral and interrment in Poets' Corner in Westminster Abbey.

—Leigh Woods

GASCON, Jean. Canadian director and actor. Born in Montreal, Canada, 21 December 1921. Educated at the College Sainte Marie, Montreal, and studied medicine at L'Université de Montreal, 1940–45; trained as an actor at the Vieux-Colombier, Paris, 1946–49. Married 1) Marie Lalonde, one son, three daughters; 2) actress Marilyn Gardner. Stage debut, as an amateur, with the Compagnons de Saint-Laurent, Montreal, in the 1940's; studied theatre and worked as actor and director with the Centre Dramatique de l'Ouest, France, 1948–51; New York debut, 1951;

founded Le Théâtre du Nouveau Monde, Montreal, 1951; artistic director, Théâtre du Nouveau Monde, 1951–66; television debut, 1953; founder and director, National Theatre School of Canada, 1960–63; artistic director, Stratford (Ontario) Shakespeare Festival, 1967–74; artistic director, National Arts Centre, Ottawa, Canada, 1977–84. Recipient (selected): Prix du Québec for Theatre, 1985. Officer of the Order of Canada. Died in Stratford, Ontario, 20 April 1988.

Productions

As director:
1950   *L'Avare* (Molière), Centre Dramatique de l'Ouest, France; also acted Harpagon.
1951   An Evening of Farces (Molière), Phoenix Theatre, New York; Théâtre Sarah Bernhardt, Paris, 1955.
         The Imaginary Invalid (Molière), Phoenix Theatre, New York.
1956   *Nemo* (Rivemale), Gesu Theatre, Montreal; also acted Nemo.
1958   *An Evening of French Farces* (Molière), US, Canadian, and European tours; also acted Pancrace and Béralde.
1959   *Othello* (Shakespeare), Stratford Shakespeare Festival, Ontario.
         Cosi fan tutte (Mozart), Stratford Shakespeare Festival, Ontario.
         Lysistrata (Aristophanes), Phoenix Theatre, New York.
1963   *The Comedy of Errors* (Shakespeare), Stratford Shakespeare Festival, Ontario.
1964   *Le Bourgeois Gentilhomme* (Molière), Chichester Festival, England, and Stratford Shakespeare Festival, Ontario.
1965   *Mahagonny* (Weill), Stratford Shakespeare Festival, Ontario.
         The Marriage of Figaro (Mozart), Stratford Shakespeare Festival, Ontario.
         Klondyke, Old Vic Theatre, London.
         L'École des femmes (Molière), Old Vic Theatre, London; also acted Arnolphe.
1966   *Henry V* (Shakespeare), Stratford Shakespeare Festival, Ontario.
         The Dance of Death (Strindberg), Royal Shakespeare Theatre, Stratford-upon-Avon, England; also acted Edgar.
1968   *Tartuffe* (Molière), Stratford Shakespeare Festival, Ontario; revived there, 1970.
         The Seagull (Chekhov), Stratford Shakespeare Festival, Ontario.
1969   *Hadrian VII* (Luke), Stratford Shakespeare Festival, Ontario.
1970   *The Merchant of Venice* (Shakespeare), Stratford Shakespeare Festival, Ontario.
         Cymbeline (Shakespeare), Stratford Shakespeare Festival, Ontario.
1971   *The Duchess of Malfi* (Webster), Stratford Shakespeare Festival, Ontario.
         There's One in Every Marriage (Feydeau), Stratford Shakespeare Festival, Ontario.

1972   *Lorenzaccio* (Musset), Stratford Shakespeare Festival, Ontario.

The Threepenny Opera (Brecht), Stratford Shakespeare Festival, Ontario.

1973   *The Taming of the Shrew* (Shakespeare), Stratford Shakespeare Festival, Ontario, and European tour.

Pericles (Shakespeare), Stratford Shakespeare Festival, Ontario; revived there, 1974.

1974   *The Imaginary Invalid* (Molière), Stratford Shakespeare Festival, Ontario, and Australian tour.

La Vie Parisienne (Burnand), Stratford Shakespeare Festival, Ontario.

1975   *The Miser* (Molière), Lakewood, Ohio.

Cyrano de Bergerac (Rostand), Winnipeg.

1976   *Anatol* (Schnitzler), Montreal.

1977   *Le Médécin volant* and *Le Médécin malgré lui* (Molière), National Arts Centre, Ottawa.

1977–84 *Riel* (Coulter), National Arts Centre, Ottawa.

L'Annonce fait à Marie (Claudel), National Arts Centre, Ottawa.

1978   *The Father* (Strindberg), National Arts Centre, Ottawa; also acted The Captain.

1988   *My Fair Lady* (Loewe, Lerner, and Hart), Stratford Shakespeare Festival, Ontario.

As actor only:

1952   Don Juan in *Don Juan* (Molière), Théâtre du Nouveau Monde, Montreal.

1956   The Constable of France in *Henry V* (Shakespeare), Stratford Shakespeare Festival, Stratford, Ontario.

1967   Dr Caius in *The Merry Wives of Windsor* (Shakespeare), Stratford Shakespeare Festival, Ontario.

Other productions included: *Long Day's Journey into Night* (O'Neill); *The Alchemist* (Jonson); *La Ronde* (Schnitzler); *The Cherry Orchard* (Chekhov).

Films

As actor:
A Man Called Horse, 1970.

Television

Oedipus Rex; *L'Annonce faite à Marie*; many others.

* * *

When Jean Gascon was a student at the College de Sainte Marie, his days were devoted to meeting the rigorous demands of his Jesuit instructors but his evenings were spent rehearsing plays. He and fellow students Jean-Louis Roux, Jean Coutu, and Georges Groulx became members of an amateur company, Les Compagnons de Saint-Laurent, supervised by Père Emile Legault, a stage-struck cleric whose technical knowledge of theatre was limited but who proved to be an inspired animateur.

As soon as the European war ended Gascon extended his experience in Paris, where he was powerfully influenced by

the work of Le Cartel — Charles Dullin, Louis Jouvet, Georges Pitoeff, and Gaston Baty — as well as by the younger directors Jean-Louis Barrault and Jean Vilar. Gascon had already attracted the attention of Ludmilla Pitoeff when he played Hippolytus to her Phaedra in Montreal during the war years. In France he joined her company, overlaying the indoctrination in classical literature he had received from the Jesuits with a thorough grounding in acting technique.

When Gascon returned to Montreal in 1951 the theatre he helped to create reflected his Parisian models: vigorous, inventive, but firmly rooted in the traditions of classical French theatre. Le Théâtre du Nouveau Monde was conceived as an ensemble of equals. Many of the players had been in France with Gascon: Georges Groulx, Guy Hoffman, Denise Pelletier, Jean-Louis Roux. It had somewhat the ambience of a large French-Canadian family: high-spirited, quarrelsome, affectionate. Jean Gascon emerged as the father-figure, his irrepressible enthusiasm driving the company forward. His vision of theatre was summed up in his pungent motto: "Le théâtre, c'est comme la merde: ca se sent."

Gascon had already staged *L'Avare* at the Centre Dramatique de l'Ouest and once home in Canada he continued to produce Molière. His performances of Molière's Pancrace, Arnolphe, and especially Don Juan benefited greatly from his personal magnetism. His temperament was especially suited to comedy, blending intelligence, charm, and irreverent wit. He married the precision and theatricality of Jouvet and Barrault to the ribald energy of French Quebec. The work of the TNM was finely detailed but possessed an air of spontaneous invention that delighted audiences not only in Montreal but also in Europe and the USA when the company toured in the mid-1950's.

Gascon led his troupe of actors to Stratford (Ontario) in 1956, where they played the French court in Michael Langham's production of *Henry V*, starring Christopher Plummer, who hailed from the English community of Quebec. The production hit a political nerve. It also brought a fresh breath of theatrical invention and emotional liberation to the Stratford company. In return the French actors conceded that they learned something about organization and textual analysis. The success of this production led to invitations for Gascon to direct at the Stratford, a partnership that inspired his commedia dell'arte-inspired version of *The Comedy of Errors* and an extravagant staging of *Le Bourgeois Gentilhomme* among other productions.

Gascon gave up the leadership of the TNM after his first heart attack in 1963. After his initial exposure to Stratford he was no longer satisfied to work only in French. He embraced the idea that an original Canadian style could be developed that would blend the vivacity of French performers with the more cerebral control of English actors. Counselled by Michel St Denis, Gascon established the National Theatre School in Montreal in 1960, where he encouraged actors from both English and French backgrounds to work in harness together.

It proved to be a bit like yoking Clydesdales with carriage horses and it soon became apparent that even if the students were prepared to co-operate the teachers were not. The Quiet Revolution in Quebec was already underway and many leading theatre artists were avid separatists. In 1987, shortly before he died, Gascon confessed: "I see now we were deluded, but in the early 1960's we had this vision of a transcendant style that inspired us and led us on, until in the end nationalism destroyed us all." Whatever Gascon's delusions, the National Theatre School remains today the foremost Canadian training ground for actors working in either French of English.

Gason's early association with Stratford focussed on musical productions, notably Weill's *Mahagonny* and Mozart's *Cosi fan tutte*, but Gascon continued to act both large and small roles himself, as he had done with the TNM. Memorable were his cameo of Dr Caius in *The Merry Wives of Windsor* and his intensely tortured portrayal of Edgar in Strindberg's *The Dance of Death*, opposite Denise Pelletier. When finally he was offered the opportunity to become the first Canadian artistic director of the Stratford Festival he accepted the challenge with a zest and good humour that encouraged the company to break new ground.

As well as Shakespeare, Gascon staged Mozart, Weill, Offenbach, and Verdi. He introduced the company to the French repertoire, productions including Musset's *Lorenzaccio* and Feydeau's *There's One in Every Marriage*, but his most memorable productions were Molière's *Tartuffe* and *Le Malade imaginaire*, in which he inspired William Hutt to give two of the finest comic performances of his career. Gascon's admiration of Shakespeare was enormous: he had his greatest success with the late romances, *Cymbeline* and *Pericles*. He also had a feel for the dark convolutions of Jacobean drama and directed memorable productions of *The Alchemist* and *The Duchess of Malfi*.

Under Gascon's leadership, Stratford expanded its scope and toured successfully in Europe, Russia, the USA, and Australia. On these tours Gascon personally led his family of actors, but his health began to fail, his heart condition exacerbated by indulgence in alcohol. Never much interested in administration, he allowed his technical staff a free hand, which led to internal rivalry. There was also the strain of working constantly in a language that was not his mother tongue.

At the end of his eight years at the helm of Stratford Gascon was hailed as a major theatre artist but he had burned his bridges in Quebec and times had changed. Montreal theatre was dominated by playwrights writing in 'joual', the language of the streets. Gascon scolded his daughters for not speaking their own language properly on stage. He soon found he was considered 'vieux jeux' and 'vendu aux anglais'. He fretted and chafed but refused to retire into the shadows. In 1977 he was appointed Director-General of the National Arts Centre in Ottawa, where his most notable achievements included productions of John Coulter's Canadian epic *Riel* and Molière's *Le Médécin malgré lui*. He also gave passionate performances in Strindberg's *The Father* and in O'Neill's *Long Day's Journey into Night*. He left the NAC after another heart attack in 1983 but continued to work sporadically in the theatre until his death while preparing a production of *My Fair Lady* at Stratford.

—Martin Hunter

GASKILL, Bill. British director. Born William Gaskill in Shipley, Yorkshire, 24 June 1930. Educated at Salt High School, Shipley; Hertford College, Oxford University. Debut as director, Redcar Theatre, Redcar, Yorkshire, 1954; resident director, Granada Television, 1956–57; assistant artistic director, under George Devine, Royal Court Theatre, London, 1957–59; freelance director for the Royal Shakespeare Company and others, 1960–63; associate director to Laurence Olivier's National Theatre, 1963–65 and 1979; artistic director, English Stage Company, Royal Court Theatre, 1965–72; freelance director, from 1972; co-founder, Joint Stock touring company, 1974–83. Member: Council of the English Stage Company, 1978–87.

Productions

1954	*The First Mrs Fraser* (Ervine), Redcar Theatre, Redcar, Yorkshire.
1955	*The Country Wife* (Wycherley), Theatre Royal, Stratford, London; also acted Quack.
	The Hawthorn Tree, Q Theatre, London.
1957	*A Resounding Tinkle* (Simpson), Royal Court Theatre, London.
1958	*Epitaph for George Dillon* (Osborne and Creighton), Royal Court Theatre, London.
	A Resounding Tinkle and *The Hole* (Simpson), Royal Court Theatre, London.
	Brixham Regatta, London.
	The Deadly Game (Dürrenmatt), New York.
	One Way Pendulum (Simpson), Royal Court Theatre, London.
1960	*The Happy Haven* (Arden), Royal Court Theatre, London.
	Sugar in the Morning (Howard), Royal Court Theatre, London.
1961	*Richard III* (Shakespeare), Royal Shakespeare Theatre, Stratford-upon-Avon.
	Cymbeline (Shakespeare), Royal Shakespeare Theatre, Stratford-upon-Avon.
1962	*The Caucasian Chalk Circle* (Brecht), Aldwych Theatre, London.
	Infanticide in the House of Fred Ginger (Watson), Aldwych Theatre, London.
1963	*Baal* (Brecht), Phoenix Theatre, London.
	The Recruiting Officer (Farquhar), Old Vic Theatre, London.
1964	*Philoctetes* (Sophocles), Old Vic Theatre, London, and Chichester Festival Theatre, Chichester.
	The Dutch Courtesan (Marston), Old Vic Theatre, London, and Chichester Festival Theatre, Chichester.
1965	*Mother Courage* (Brecht), Old Vic Theatre, London.
	Armstrong's Last Good Night (Arden), Old Vic Theatre, London, and Chichester Festival Theatre, Chichester.
	Saved (Bond), Royal Court Theatre, London.
1966	*A Chaste Maid in Cheapside* (Middleton), Royal Court Theatre, London.
	The Performing Giant (Johnstone), Royal Court Theatre, London.
	Their Very Own and Golden City (Wesker), Royal Court Theatre, London.

Macbeth (Shakespeare), Royal Court Theatre, London.

1967 *The Three Sisters* (Chekhov), Royal Court Theatre, London.

Fill the Stage with Happy Hours (Wood), Vaudeville Theatre, London.

1968 *Early Morning* (Bond), Royal Court Theatre, London.

1969 *Saved* (Bond), Royal Court Theatre, London.

Early Morning (Bond), Royal Court Theatre, London.

The Double-Dealer (Congreve), Royal Court Theatre, London.

Hadrian VII (Luke), Thalia Theatre, Hamburg.

1970 *Beckett 3* (Beckett), Theatre Upstairs, London.

Cheek (Barker), Royal Court Theatre, London.

The Beaux' Stratagem (Farquhar), Old Vic Theatre, London, and US tour.

1971 *Man Is Man* (Brecht), Royal Court Theatre, London.

Lear (Bond), Royal Court Theatre, London.

1972 *Big Wolf* (Muellar, translated by Gooch), Royal Court Theatre, London.

Measure for Measure (Shakespeare), Exeter.

1973 *The Sea* (Bond), Royal Court Theatre, London.

Lear (Bond), Residentztheater, Munich.

Galileo (Brecht), Thalia Theatre, Hamburg.

1974 *The Speakers* (H. Williams), Joint Stock Theatre Group.

Snap, National Theatre of Belgium, Brussels.

The Kitchen (Wesker), National Theatre of Belgium, Brussels.

Love's Labour's Lost (Shakespeare), Sydney, Australia.

1975 *Fanshen* (Hare), Joint Stock Theatre Group.

The Government Inspector (Gogol), Edinburgh Festival.

1976 *Yesterday's News*, Joint Stock Theatre Group.

King Oedipus (Sophocles), Dubrovnik, Yugoslavia.

Oedipus at Colonus (Sophocles), Dubrovnik, Yugoslavia.

1977 *A Mad World, My Masters* (Keefe), Joint Stock Theatre Group.

The Madras House (Granville-Barker), National Theatre, London.

The Barber of Seville (Rossini), Welsh National Opera, Wales.

La Boheme (Puccini), Welsh National Opera, Wales.

1978 *The Ragged Trousered Philanthropists* (Lowe), Joint Stock Theatre Group.

1979 *A Fair Quarrel* (Middleton and Rowley), National Theatre, London.

The Gorky Brigade (Wright), Royal Court Theatre, London.

1980 *An Optimistic Thrust*, Joint Stock Theatre Group.

1981 *Touched* (Lowe), Royal Court Theatre, London.

Tibetan Inroads (Lowe), Royal Court Theatre, London.

Hamlet (Shakespeare), Sydney, Australia.

Bill Gaskill (credit: Hans Wild, London).

1982 *Pericles* (Shakespeare), Teatro Stabile, Genoa, Italy.

She Stoops to Conquer (Goldsmith), Lyric Theatre, Hammersmith, London.

1983 *The Crimes of Vautrin* (Wright), Joint Stock Theatre Group.

The Entertainer (Osborne), New York.

The Relapse (Vanbrugh), Lyric Theatre, Hammersmith, London.

1984 *Rents* (Wilcox), Lyric Theatre, Hammersmith, London.

The Way of the World (Congreve), Chichester Festival Theatre and London.

1985 *Infidelities* (Marivaux), Tyrone Guthrie Theatre, Minneapolis, and Lyric Theatre, Hammersmith, London.

Candida (G. B. Shaw), Tyrone Guthrie Theatre, Minneapolis.

1986 *Women Beware Women* (Middleton, adapted by Barker), Royal Court Theatre, London.

1990 *Man, Beast and Virtue* (Pirandello), Royal National Theatre, London.

1993 *The Mountain Giants* (Pirandello, adapted by Wood), Royal National Theatre, London.

Other productions include: *Jeppe of the Hill* (Holberg); *The Marriage of Figaro* (Beaumarchais); *Lucia Di Lammermoor* (Donizetti).

Television

Zoo Time, 1956.

Publications

A Sense of Direction, 1988.

* * *

Since his first productions for the English Stage Company at the Royal Court in the late 1950's, William Gaskill has become one of the most important and influential directors in the postwar British theatre, producing a distinctive body of work both in the area of new plays and in revivals of the classics. Gaskill has at various times directed productions for most of the major subsidised companies, although he has worked freelance in Britain and abroad since 1972. In his early productions at the Royal Court, he not only implemented the policies of fidelity to the text and author and clarity and precision of staging instituted by the theatre's first artistic director, George Devine, but also did much to define and develop an austere and direct style that became characteristic of Royal Court work as much as his own.

Seeing the director's function as first and foremost to discover and communicate the intentions of the author to the actors and thence to the audience, Gaskill has most often worked in a milieu of minimal, poetic, realism, which he has coupled with a scrupulous regard for dramatic speech; his maxim, taken from Samuel Beckett, being that "a theatre stage should have the maximum of verbal presence and the maximum of corporal presence". After successes in the 1950's with productions of verbal experimenters such as N. F. Simpson, Gaskill embraced work more directly concerned with social and political reality. He was strongly influenced by the work of the Berliner Ensemble, which visited Britain in the mid-1950's, and one of his most important contributions to the British theatre in the 1960's was as a director of Brecht and of the Epic drama that followed him: in particular, Edward Bond. Gaskill's *The Caucasian Chalk Circle* for the Royal Shakespeare Company in 1962 was an early attempt to introduce Brechtian theatrical methods — and, to an extent, politics — to the British theatre. More successful were Gaskill's productions of the work of Bond. Beginning with *Saved* in 1965, he directed all of Bond's work at the Royal Court up to *The Sea* in 1973. Between them, the writer and director evolved a political aesthetic that represented a significant development of Epic Theatre in Britain.

Gaskill also brought his initial experience in the direction of contemporary drama to bear on his productions of classic theatre, in particular that of the 17th and 18th centuries, applying the same criteria of social realism and theatrical clarity. The production of Farquhar's *The Recruiting Officer* that he directed at the National Theatre in 1963 was exemplary: strongly influenced by Brecht's *Trumpets and Drums*, it displayed an unprecedented grasp of the social and political content of the play. Gaskill also directed an uncompromisingly non-illusionistic *Macbeth* at the Royal Court in 1966, which, attempting to dispel conventional obfuscatory connotations of mysterious evil, presented the action under relentless white light in a bare, permanent, set; this also consciously displayed the influ-

ence of Brecht and Bond. More recently, Gaskill has directed work by Thomas Middleton, including Howard Barker's adaptation of *Women Beware Women* at the Royal Court in 1986. Lindsay Anderson said of Gaskill that he "directed classics like new plays and new plays like classics".

As artistic director of the English Stage Company, Gaskill helped move the Royal Court away from the 'angry young men' identity it had acquired in the 1950's and moved it towards more radically committed socialist drama and the experimental avant-garde. While continuing the commitment to 'writers' theatre', championing Bond in particular, Gaskill also reached out to the theatrical fringe and to the 1960's counter-culture — a move that culminated in the opening of the Royal Court's studio space, the Theatre Upstairs, which represented an extension of the theatre's commitment to new and experimental writing. During this period Gaskill was no stranger to controversy: he was frequently accused of modishness and artistic irresponsibility — as with the 1966 *Macbeth*, where the merits of the production were forgotten amid the controversy over the casting of Simone Signoret as Lady Macbeth. Similarly, there was heated debate over the casting of pop personality Marianne Faithfull in *The Three Sisters* in 1967. Gaskill responded to the adverse criticism of the former production by threatening to withdraw invitations to the British press to future Court productions. Many reviewers saw this as an arrogant stance, but the point about the superficial and uninformed quality of British theatrical reviewing was (and still is) a valid and significant one. More importantly, Gaskill was involved in legal and political controversy over Bond's *Saved* and *Early Morning*, productions that were instrumental in bringing about the abolition of the censorship powers of the Lord Chamberlain's office in 1968. Gaskill himself was arrested and prosecuted for his part in the production of *Saved*.

In 1974 Gaskill joined forces with Max Stafford-Clark to set up Joint Stock, a touring theatre company that did much to put into practice his long-held commitment to ensemble methods. The working practices, structure, and organisation of the group meant that it was able to sustain a rare quality of collective and collaborative achievement: the shared political perspective that developed through the rehearsal and performance process underpinned and enhanced the theatrical and political impact of the work produced by the company. The plays themselves were shared political statements by writer, director, and actors. In that the bulk of Gaskill's work had been, and continues to be, geared towards the productions of already-existing texts, working towards the production of a text from the basis of improvisation and research by the company as a whole represented something of a departure. But he nonetheless felt that the company "achieved the dream of the committed ensemble" and the work produced under the company's auspices includes some of the strongest Epic political drama produced in Britain in the 1970's — in particular, *Fanshen*, written by David Hare and directed by Gaskill in 1975.

Gaskill's work as a director has been distinctive, but he has repeatedly disavowed the idea that the director has an independent creative role or identity. The director in his view is initially and essentially responsive to the imagination of the writer. This perhaps reflects in part an attachment to the values of ensemble and collective work, as well as placing a central emphasis upon the quality of dramatic writing; but it also represents Gaskill's opposition to 'director's theatre'. In a way Gaskill's initial involvement with contemporary writing, and consequently his working relationship with contemporary writers before moving to the classics might explain this emphasis. Throughout his career, Gaskill's work has reflected a commitment to writers, to the actor, and to the responsibility of the theatre to engage with the life of its society; the quality of that work has stemmed from the degree of success with which he has achieved a balance between them.

—Robert Shaughnessy

GIELGUD, (Sir Arthur) John. British actor and director. Born in London, 14 April 1904; great-nephew of Ellen Terry. Trained for the stage at Lady Benson's School, 1921; Royal Academy of Dramatic Art, London, 1922. Stage debut, Old Vic Theatre, London, 1921; actor, Oxford Repertory Company, 1924–25; first film appearance, 1924; Broadway debut, 1928; joined Old Vic company, 1929; presented own season at the Queen's Theatre, London, 1937–38; first appearance at Stratford-upon-Avon, 1950; toured widely with Shakespearean recitals and in a range of classical and modern parts; London's Globe Theatre renamed the Gielgud Theatre in Gielgud's honour, 1994. Member: Actors' Benevolent Fund (President, from 1942); Shakespearean Reading Society (President, from 1958); American Academy of Arts and Sciences, 1961; Royal Academy of Dramatic Arts (President, from 1977). Recipient: New York Stage Award, 1936; British Film Academy Award for Best British Actor, 1955; Antoinette Perry (Tony) Award, 1959, 1961; Variety Club of Great Britain Award, 1968; Evening Standard Drama Award, 1970; Society of Film and Television Arts Award, 1974; Plays and Players Award, 1975; National Academy of Recording Arts and Sciences (Grammy) Award, 1979, 1983, 1986; Academy Award, 1982; Golden Globe Award, 1982; New York Film Critics Circle Award, 1982; Los Angeles Film Critics Award, 1982, 1986; Standard Award, 1983; Laurence Olivier Award, 1985. LL.D: St Andrew's University, Glasgow, 1950; Brandeis University, 1965; D.Litt: University of Oxford, 1955; University of London, 1977; D.Univ, Open University, Milton Keynes, 1980. Chevalier, Légion d'Honneur (France), 1957. Knighted, 1953; Companion of Honour, 1977.

Roles

1921   Soldier and English Herald in *Henry V* (Shakespeare), Old Vic Theatre, London.
1922   Walk-on role in *Peer Gynt* (Ibsen), Old Vic Theatre, London.
        Walk-on role in *King Lear* (Shakespeare), Old Vic Theatre, London.
        Walk-on role in *Wat Tyler* (Glover), Old Vic Theatre, London.
        Walk-on role in *Love is the Best Doctor* (Molière), Old Vic Theatre, London.
        Walk-on role in *The Comedy of Errors* (Shakespeare), Old Vic Theatre, London.

Walk-on role in *As You Like It* (Shakespeare), Old Vic Theatre, London.
Lieutenant Manners in *The Wheel* (Fagan), New Oxford Theatre, London.
1923   Younger Brother in *The Masque of Comus* (Milton), Middle Temple, London.
Felix in *The Insect Play* (Čapek, adapted by Playfair and Bax), Regent Theatre, London.
Aide to General Lee in *Robert E. Lee* (Drinkwater), Regent Theatre, London.
Charles Wykeham in *Charley's Aunt* (Thomas), Comedy Theatre, London.
1924   Johnson in *Captain Brassbound's Conversion* (G. B. Shaw), Playhouse, Oxford.
Valentine in *Love for Love* (Congreve), Playhouse, Oxford; Phoenix Theatre, London, 1943 (also directed); Haymarket Theatre, London, 1944 (also directed); National Theatre, Washington, and Boston, 1947 (also directed).
Brian Strange in *Mr Pym Passes By* (Milne), Playhouse, Oxford.
Young Marlow in *She Stoops to Conquer* (Goldsmith), Playhouse, Oxford.
Prinzivalle in *Monna Vanna* (Maeterlinck, translated by Sutro), Playhouse, Oxford.
Paris in *Romeo and Juliet* (Shakespeare), Royal Academy of Dramatic Art, London.
Romeo in *Romeo and Juliet* (Shakespeare), Regent Theatre, London; (extract) Coliseum Theatre, London, 1926; Old Vic Theatre, London, 1929; New Theatre, London, 1935 (also directed).
John Sherry in *The Return Half* (Van Druten), Royal Academy of Dramatic Art, London.
Eugene Marchbanks in *Candida* (G. B. Shaw), Playhouse, Oxford.
Naisi in *Deirde of the Sorrows* (Synge), Playhouse, Oxford.
Paul Roget in *A Collection Will Be Made* (Eckersley), Playhouse, Oxford; revived there, 1925.
A Domino in *Everybody's Husband* (Cannan), Playhouse, Oxford.
Antonio in *The Cradle Song* (Sierra, translated by Underhill), Playhouse, Oxford.
Erhart Borkman in *John Gabriel Borkman* (Ibsen, translated by Archer), Playhouse, Oxford.
Zurita in *His Widow's Husband* (Benavente, translated by Underhill), Playhouse, Oxford.
Augusto in *Madame Pepita* (Sierra, translated by Underhill), Playhouse, Oxford.
Lieutenant George Graham in *French Leave* (Berkeley), Charterhouse.
1925   Algernon Peppercorn in *Smith* (Maugham), Playhouse, Oxford.
Trofimov in *The Cherry Orchard* (Chekhov, translated by Calderon), Playhouse, Oxford; Lyric Theatre, Hammersmith, London, 1925.
Castalio in *The Orphan* (Otway), Aldwych Theatre, London.

John Gielgud (1979).

Ted Hewitt in *The Nature of the Evidence* (Peacey), Royal Academy of Dramatic Art, London.

Nicky Lancaster in *The Vortex* (Coward), Little Theatre, London.

Julien de Boys-Bourredon in *The High Constable's Wife* (Lewis, adapted from Balzac), Garden Theatre, London.

A Stranger in *The Lady from the Sea* (Ibsen, translated by Archer), Playhouse, Oxford.

The Man in *The Man with a Flower in his Mouth* (Pirandello, translated by Livingston), Playhouse, Oxford; Old Vic Theatre, London, 1930.

Valentine in *The Two Gentlemen of Verona* (Shakespeare), Apollo Theatre, London.

Konstantin in *The Seagull* (Chekhov, translated by Garnett), Little Theatre, London; Arts Theatre, London, 1929.

Good Angel in *Dr Faustus* (Marlowe), New Theatre, Oxford.

Robert in *L'École des Cocottes* (Armont and Gerbidon, adapted by Harwood), Prince's Theatre, London.

Second Shepherd in *Old English Nativity Play* (anon.), Daly's Theatre, London.

1926   Ferdinand in *The Tempest* (Shakespeare), Savoy Theatre, London.

Richard Southern in *Sons and Fathers* (Monkhouse), Royal Academy of Dramatic Art, London.

Baron Nickolay Tusenbach in *The Three Sisters* (Chekhov, translated by Garnett), Barnes Theatre, London.

Georg Stibelev in *Katerina* (Andreyev, adapted by Bernstein), Barnes Theatre, London.

Rosencrantz in *Hamlet* (Shakespeare), Royal Court Theatre, London.

Armand Duval in *The Lady of the Camellias* (Dumas *fils*, adapted by Orme), Garrick Theatre, London.

Wilfred Marlay in *Confession* (Casey), Royal Court Theatre, London.

Lewis Dodd in *The Constant Nymph* (Kennedy and Dean), New Theatre, London.

Sir John Harrington in *Gloriana* (John), Little Theatre, London.

1927   Cassio in *Othello* (Shakespeare), Apollo Theatre, London.

Dion Anthony in *The Great God Brown* (O'Neill), Strand Theatre, London.

1928   Grand Duke Alexander in *The Patriot* (Neumann, adapted by Dukes), Majestic Theatre, New York.

Oswald Alving in *Ghosts* (Ibsen, translated by Grein), Wyndham's Theatre, London; Arts Theatre, London.

Dr Gerald Marloe in *Holding Out The Apple* (Wynne-Bower), Globe Theatre, London.

Jacob Slovak in *Prejudice* (Acosta), Arts Theatre, London.

Captain Vernon Allenby in *The Skull* (McOwen and Humphrey), Shaftesbury Theatre, London.

Alberto in *Fortunato* (Quintero, translated by Granville-Barker), Royal Court Theatre, London.

Felipe Rivas in *The Lady from Alfâqueque* (Quintero, translated by Granville-Barker), Royal Court Theatre, London.

John Marstin in *Out of the Sea* (Marquis), Strand Theatre, London.

1929   Fédor in *Red Rust* (Kirchon and Ouspensky, adapted by Vernon), Little Theatre, London.

Paul de Tressailles in *Hunter's Moon* (Michaelis, adapted by Graham), Prince of Wales's Theatre, London.

Henry Tremayne in *The Lady with the Lamp* (Berkeley), Garrick Theatre, London.

Captain Jennings in *Shall We Join the Ladies?* (Barrie), Palace Theatre, London.

Bronstein (Trotsky) in *Red Sunday* (Griffith), Arts Theatre, London.

Antonio in *The Merchant of Venice* (Shakespeare), Old Vic Theatre, London.

Cléante in *The Imaginary Invalid* (Molière, adapted by Anstey), Old Vic Theatre, London.

Richard in *Richard II* (Shakespeare), Old Vic Theatre, London; Queen's Theatre, London, 1937 (also directed); Bulawayo, Rhodesia, 1953 (also directed).

Prologue in *Douaumont* (Moeller, adapted by Rawson), Prince of Wales's Theatre, London.

Oberon in *A Midsummer Night's Dream* (Shakespeare), Old Vic Theatre, London; Haymarket Theatre, London, 1945.

1930   Marcus Antonius in *Julius Caesar* (Shakespeare), Old Vic Theatre, London.

Ferdinand in *As You Like It* (Shakespeare), Old Vic Theatre, London.

The Emperor in *Androcles and the Lion* (G. B. Shaw), Old Vic Theatre, London.

Macbeth in *Macbeth* (Shakespeare), Old Vic Theatre, London; tour and Piccadilly Theatre, London, 1942 (also directed).

Mr Hughes in *The Rehearsal* (Baring), Old Vic Theatre, London.

Hamlet in *Hamlet* (Shakespeare), Old Vic Theatre, London; Queen's Theatre, London; New Theatre, London, 1934 (also directed); Royal Alexandra Theatre, Toronto, and Empire Theatre, New York, 1936; St James's Theatre, New York, and Shubert Theatre, Boston, 1937; Lyceum Theatre, London, and Kronborg Castle, Elsinore, Denmark, 1939 (also directed); Haymarket Theatre, London, 1944; Far East tour, 1945–46 (also directed).

John Worthing in *The Importance of Being Earnest* (Wilde), Lyric Theatre, Hammersmith, London; Globe Theatre, London, 1939 and 1942 (also directed); US and Canadian tour, 1947 (also directed).

Hotspur in *Henry IV, part 1* (Shakespeare), Old Vic Theatre, London.

Prospero in *The Tempest* (Shakespeare), Old Vic Theatre, London; revived there, 1940; Shakespeare Memorial Theatre, Stratford-upon-Avon, and Theatre Royal, Drury Lane, London, 1957; Old Vic Theatre, London, 1974.

Lord Trinket in *The Jealous Wife* (Colman), Old Vic Theatre, London.

Antony in *Antony and Cleopatra* (Shakespeare), Old Vic Theatre, London.

1931   Malvolio in *Twelfth Night* (Shakespeare), Old Vic Theatre and Sadler's Wells Theatre, London.

Major Segius Seranoff in *Arms and the Man* (G. B. Shaw), Old Vic Theatre and Sadler's Wells Theatre, London.

Benedict in *Much Ado About Nothing* (Shakespeare), Old Vic Theatre and Sadler's Wells Theatre, London; Shakespeare Memorial Theatre, Stratford-upon-Avon, 1950 (also directed); Phoenix Theatre, London, 1952 (also directed); Palace Theatre, London, 1955 (also directed); Cambridge Drama Festival, Boston, and Lunt-Fontanne Theatre, New York, 1959 (also directed).

Lear in *King Lear* (Shakespeare), Old Vic Theatre and Sadler's Wells Theatre, London; Old Vic Theatre, London, 1940; Shakespeare Memorial Theatre, Stratford-upon-Avon, 1950 (also directed, with Anthony Quayle); European tour and Palace Theatre, London, 1955 (also directed, with George Devine).

Inigo Jollifant in *The Good Companions* (Priestley), His Majesty's Theatre, London.

Joseph Schindler in *Musical Chairs* (Mackenzie), Arts Theatre, London; Criterion Theatre, London, 1932.

1932   Richard in *Richard of Bordeaux* (Daviot), Arts Theatre, London (also directed, with Harcourt Williams); New Theatre, London, 1933 (also directed).

1934   Roger Maitland in *The Maitlands* (Mackenzie), Wyndham's Theatre, London.

1935   Noah in *Noah* (Obey, translated by Wilmurt), New Theatre, London.

Mercutio in *Romeo and Juliet* (Shakespeare), New Theatre, London; also directed.

1936   Boris Trigorin in *The Seagull* (Chekhov, translated by Komisarjevsky), New Theatre, London.

1937   Mason in *He Was Born Gay* (E. Williams), Queen's Theatre, London; also directed.

Joseph Surface in *The School for Scandal* (Sheridan), Queen's Theatre, London; Haymarket Theatre, London, and Majestic Theatre, New York, 1962 (also directed).

1938   Vershinin in *The Three Sisters* (Chekhov), Queen's Theatre, London.

Shylock in *The Merchant of Venice* (Shakespeare), Queen's Theatre, London; also directed (with Glen Byam-Shaw).

Nicholas in *Dear Octopus* (Smith), Queen's Theatre, London.

1940   Macheath in *The Beggar's Opera* (Gay), Haymarket Theatre, London; also directed.

Henry Crow in *Fumed Oak* (Coward), Globe Theatre, London, and tour; also directed.

Peter Gilpin in *Hands Across the Sea* (Coward), Globe Theatre, London, and tour; also directed.

An Old Actor in *Hard Luck Story* (Chekhov, adapted by Gielgud), Globe Theatre, London, and tour; also directed.

William Shakespeare in *The Dark Lady of the Sonnets* (G. B. Shaw), Edinburgh; also directed.

1941   William Dearth in *Dear Brutus* (Barrie), Globe Theatre, London; also directed.

1943   Louis Dubedat in *The Doctor's Dilemma* (G. B. Shaw), Haymarket Theatre, London.

1944   Arnold Champion-Chesney in *The Circle* (Maugham), Haymarket Theatre, London.

1945   Ferdinand in *The Duchess of Malfi* (Webster), Haymarket Theatre, London.

1945–46   Charles Condomine in *Blithe Spirit* (Coward), Far East tour; also directed.

1946   Raskolnikoff in *Crime and Punishment* (Dostoevsky), New Theatre, London, and Globe Theatre, London; National Theatre, New York, 1947.

1947   Jason in *Medea* (Euripides, adapted by Jeffers), National Theatre, New York; also directed.

1948   Eustace Jackson in *The Return of the Prodigal* (Hankin), Globe Theatre, London.

1949   Thomas Mendip in *The Lady's Not For Burning* (Fry), Globe Theatre, London; Royale Theatre, New York, 1950; also directed, with Esme Percy.

1950   Angelo in *Measure for Measure* (Shakespeare), Shakespeare Memorial Theatre, Stratford-upon-Avon.
        Cassius in *Julius Caesar* (Shakespeare), Shakespeare Memorial Theatre, Stratford-upon-Avon.

1951   Leontes in *The Winter's Tale* (Shakespeare), Phoenix Theatre, London.

1953   Mirabell in *The Way of the World* (Congreve), Lyric Theatre, Hammersmith, London; also directed.
        Jaffeir in *Venice Preserved* (Otway), Lyric Theatre, Hammersmith, London.
        Julian Anson in *A Day by the Sea* (Hunter), Haymarket Theatre, London; also directed.

1956   Sebastien in *Nude with Violin* (Coward), Globe Theatre, London; also directed, with Coward.

1957   All roles in *The Ages of Man* (Rylands, adapted from Shakespeare), Edinburgh; tour, 1958; Queen's Theatre, London, 1959; Haymarket Theatre, London, 1960; Royal Shakespeare Theatre, Stratford-upon-Avon, 1961; British and European tour, 1962; Majestic Theatre, New York, and Lyceum Theatre, New York, and Australian tour, 1963; Playhouse, Nottingham, and tour, 1964; The Whitehouse, Washington, 1965; Norwegian tour, 1966; Los Angeles and Ankara, Turkey, 1967.

1958   James Callifer in *The Potting Shed* (Greene), Globe Theatre, London.
        Cardinal Wolsey in *Henry VIII* (Shakespeare), Old Vic Theatre, London, and European tour.

1960   Prince Ferdinand Cavanati in *The Last Joke* (Bagnold), Phoenix Theatre, London.

1961   Othello in *Othello* (Shakespeare), Royal Shakespeare Theatre, Stratford-upon-Avon.
        Gaev in *The Cherry Orchard* (Chekhov, adapted by Gielgud), Aldwych Theatre, London.

1963   Julius Caesar in *The Ides of March* (Wilder, adapted by Kilty), Haymarket Theatre, London.

1964   All roles in *Homage to Shakespeare* (Shakespeare compilation), Lincoln Centre, New York, McCarter Theatre, Princeton University, and Philharmonic Hall, New York.
        Julian in *Tiny Alice* (Albee), Billy Rose Theatre, New York.

1965   Ivanov in *Ivanov* (Chekhov, adapted by Gielgud), Phoenix Theatre, London; Shubert Theatre, New York, 1966; also directed.

1966   Roles in *Men, Women and Shakespeare* (Shakespeare compilation), tour of North and South America.

1967   Narrator in *Oedipus Rex* (Stravinsky), Festival Hall, London.
        Orgon in *Tartuffe* (Molière, translated by Wilbur), Old Vic Theatre, London.

1968   Oedipus in *Oedipus* (Seneca, adapted by Hughes), Old Vic Theatre, London.
        Headmaster in *Forty Years On* (Bennett), Apollo Theatre, London.

1970   Sir Gideon Petrie in *The Battle of Shrivings* (Shaffer), Lyric Theatre, London.
        Harry in *Home* (Storey), Royal Court Theatre, London, Apollo Theatre, London, and Morosco Theatre, New York.

1971   Caesar in *Caesar and Cleopatra* (G. B. Shaw), Festival Theatre, Chichester.

1972   Sir Geoffrey Kendle in *Veterans* (Wood), Royal Court Theatre, London.

1974   William Shakespeare in *Bingo* (Bond), Royal Court Theatre, London.

1975   Spooner in *No Man's Land* (Pinter), Old Vic Theatre, London, and Wyndham's Theatre, London; National Theatre, London, and Longacre Theatre, New York, 1976; National Theatre, London, 1977.

1977   Caesar in *Julius Caesar* (Shakespeare), National Theatre, London.
        Sir Politic Wouldbe in *Volpone* (Jonson), National Theatre, London.
        Sir Noel Cunliffe in *Half-Life* (Mitchell), National Theatre, London; Duke of York's Theatre, London, 1978.

1988   Sir Sydney Cockerell in *The Best of Friends* (Whitemore), Apollo Theatre, London.

As director only:

1932   *Romeo and Juliet* (Shakespeare), New Theatre, Oxford.
        Strange Orchestra (Daviot), Arts Theatre, London.
        The Merchant of Venice (Shakespeare), St Martin's Theatre, London.

1933   *Sheppey* (Maugham), Wyndham's Theatre, London.

1934   *Spring 1600* (E. Williams), Shaftesbury Theatre, London.
        Queen of Scots (Daviot), New Theatre, London.

1935   *The Old Ladies* (Ackland, adapted from Walpole), New Theatre, London.
        Punch Cartoons (Du Maurier), His Majesty's Theatre, London.

1936   *Richard II* (Shakespeare), New Theatre, Oxford.

1938   *Spring Meeting* (Farrell and Perry), Ambassadors Theatre, London.

1939   *Scandal in Assyria* (Kjellstrom, adapted by Bullett), Globe Theatre, London.
        Rhondda Roundabout (Jones), Globe Theatre, London.

1941   *Ducks and Drakes* (Farrell), Apollo Theatre, London.

1943   *Landslide* (Albertyn and Peel), Westminster Theatre, London.

1944   *The Cradle Song* (Sierra, translated by Granville-Barker), Apollo Theatre, London.

Crisis in Heaven (Linklater), Lyric Theatre, London.

The Last of Summer (O'Brien and Perry, adapted from O'Brien), Phoenix Theatre, London.

1945   *Lady Windermere's Fan* (Wilde), Haymarket Theatre, London.

1948   *The Glass Menagerie* (T. Williams), Haymarket Theatre, London.

Medea (Euripides, adapted by Jeffers), Royal Lyceum Theatre, Edinburgh, and Globe Theatre, London.

1949   *The Heiress* (Goetz, adapted from James), Haymarket Theatre, London.

Much Ado About Nothing (Shakespeare), Shakespeare Memorial Theatre, Stratford-upon-Avon.

Treasure Hunt (Farrell and Perry), Apollo Theatre, London.

1950   *Shall We Join the Ladies?* (Barrie), Lyric Theatre, Hammersmith, London.

The Boy with a Cart (Fry), Lyric Theatre, Hammersmith, London.

1951   *Indian Summer* (Watling), Criterion Theatre, London.

1952   *Macbeth* (Shakespeare), Shakespeare Memorial Theatre, Stratford-upon-Avon.

Richard II (Shakespeare), Lyric Theatre, Hammersmith, London.

1954   *Charley's Aunt* (Thomas), New Theatre, London.

The Cherry Orchard (Chekhov, adapted by Gielgud), Lyric Theatre, Hammersmith, London.

1955   *Twelfth Night* (Shakespeare), Shakespeare Memorial Theatre, Stratford-upon-Avon.

1956   *The Chalk Garden* (Bagnold), Haymarket Theatre, London.

1957   *The Trojans* (Berlioz), Royal Opera House, Covent Garden, London.

1958   *Variation on a Theme* (Rattigan), Globe Theatre, London.

Five Finger Exercise (Shaffer), Comedy Theatre, London; Music Box Theatre, New York, 1959.

1959   *The Complaisant Lover* (Greene), Globe Theatre, London.

1961   *A Midsummer Night's Dream* (Tippett), Royal Opera House, Covent Garden, London.

Big Fish, Little Fish (Wheeler), ANTA Theatre, New York.

Dazzling Prospect (Farrell and Perry), Globe Theatre, London.

1962   *The School for Scandal* (Sheridan), Haymarket Theatre, London.

1967   *Half Way up the Tree* (Ustinov), Queen's Theatre, London.

1968   *Don Giovanni* (Mozart), Coliseum Theatre, London.

1971   *All Over* (Albee), Martin Beck Theatre, New York.

1972   *Private Lives* (Coward), Queen's Theatre, London.

Irene (Wheeler, Stein, Tierney, and McCarthy), US tour.

1973   *The Constant Wife* (Maugham), Albery Theatre, London; US tour, 1974.

1974   *Private Lives* (Coward), US tour.

1975   *The Gay Lord Quex* (Pinero), Albery Theatre, London.

Films

Who is the Man?, 1924; *Michael Strogoff*, 1926; *The Clue of the New Pin*, 1929; *Insult*, 1933; *The Good Companions*, 1933; *Full Fathom Five*, 1934; *The Secret Agent*, 1936; *The Prime Minister*, 1941; *An Airman's Letter to his Mother*, 1941; *Unfinished Journey*, 1943; *Shakespeare's Country*, 1944; *A Diary for Timothy*, 1945; *Julius Caesar*, 1953; *Romeo and Juliet*, 1954; *Richard III*, 1955; *The Barretts of Wimpole Street*, 1957; *Saint Joan*, 1957; *Around the World in Eighty Days*, 1957; *The Immortal Land*, 1958; *Becket*, 1964; *The Loved One*, 1965; *Chimes at Midnight*, 1966; *Assignment to Kill*, 1967; *To Die in Madrid*, 1967; *October Revolution*, 1967; *Sebastian*, 1968; *The Charge of the Light Brigade*, 1968; *The Shoes of the Fisherman*, 1968; *Oh! What a Lovely War*, 1969; *Julius Caesar*, 1970; *Eagle in a Cage*, 1970; *The Lost Horizon*, 1973; *11 Harrowhouse*, 1974; *Gold*, 1974; *Frankenstein: The True Story*, 1974; *Murder on the Orient Express*, 1974; *Galileo*, 1974; *Aces High*, 1976; *Providence*, 1977; *Joseph Andrews*, 1977; *Caligula*, 1979; *Portrait of the Artist as a Young Man*, 1979; *Murder by Decree*, 1979; *The Human Factor*, 1980; *The Elephant Man*, 1980; *The Conductor*, 1981; *Omar Mukhtar — Lion of the Desert*, 1981; *Sphinx*, 1981; *Chariots of Fire*, 1981; *The Formula*, 1981; *Arthur*, 1981; *Priest of Love*, 1981; *Buddenbrooks*, 1982; *Gandhi*, 1982; *Invitation to the Wedding*, 1982; *The Wicked Lady*, 1982; *Scandalous*, 1982; *The Shooting Party*, 1985; *Wagner*, 1985; *Plenty*, 1985; *Leave All Fair*, 1986; *The Whistle Blower*, 1987; *Bluebeard, Bluebeard*, 1988; *Appointment with Death*, 1988; *Arthur on the Rocks*, 1988; *Prospero's Books*, 1991.

Television

The Browning Version, 1959; *A Day by the Sea*, 1959; *The Cherry Orchard*, 1962; *The Rehearsal*, 1963; *Hamlet*, 1964; *Ivanov*, 1966; *Conflict*, 1966; *The Love Song of Barney Kempinski*, 1966; *The Ages of Man*, 1966; *The Mayfly and the Frog*, 1966; *Alice in Wonderland*, 1966; *Romeo and Juliet*, 1967; *From Chekhov with Love*, 1968; *Saint Joan*, 1968; *Conversation at Night*, 1969; *In Good King Charles's Golden Days*, 1970; *Hassan*, 1971; *Hamlet*, 1971; *Streeter*, 1972; *Home*, 1972; *Deliver Us From Evil*, 1973; *QB VII* (1973); *Special Duties*, 1975; *Edward VII*, 1975; *The Picture of Dorian Gray*, 1976; *The Grand Inquisitor*, 1977; *Heartbreak House*, 1977; *Neck*, 1978; *No Man's Land*, 1978; *Richard II*, 1978; *Romeo and Juliet*, 1978; *Why Didn't They Ask Evans?*, 1980; *Les Misérables*, 1980; *Parson's Pleasure*, 1980; *The Seven*

Dials Mystery, 1981; *Brideshead Revisited*, 1981; *The Hunchback of Notre Dame*, 1982; *The Critic*, 1982; *The Scarlet and the Black*, 1983; *Inside the Third Reich*, 1983; *The Far Pavilions*, 1984; *The Master of Ballantrae*, 1984; *Frankenstein*, 1984; *Camille*, 1984; *Romance on the Orient Express*, 1985; *Time After Time*, 1986; *Marco Polo*, 1986; *Oedipus the King*, 1986; *Antigone*, 1986; *Quartermaine's Terms*, 1987; *The Canterville Ghost*, 1987; *War and Remembrance*, 1988; *A Summer's Lease*, 1989.

Radio

The Man with a Flower in his Mouth, 1929; *The Tempest*, 1931; *Will Shakespeare*, 1931; *Othello*, 1932; *Hamlet*, 1932; *The Tempest*, 1933; *He Was Born Gay*, 1937; *The School for Scandal*, 1937; *The Importance of Being Earnest*, 1939; *Hamlet*, 1939 and 1940; *The Laughing Woman*, 1940; *The Importance of Being Earnest*, 1940; *Prince of Behemia*, 1941; *King Lear*, 1941; *The Return of Mr Oakroyd*, 1941; *The Great Ship*, 1943; *Pilgrim's Progress*, 1943; *The Family Reunion*, 1948; *Hamlet*, 1948; *The Tempest*, 1948; *The Wreck of the Deutschland*, 1949; *Hero and Leander Parts I and II*, 1949; *The Importance of Being Earnest*, 1951; *The Cross and the Arrow*, 1951; *King Lear*, 1951; *Helena*, 1951; *Richard of Bordeaux*, 1952; *The Tempest*, 1953; *Ivanov*, 1954; *The Adventures of Sherlock Holmes*, 1954; *Scheherezade*, 1955; *Present Laughter*, 1956; *The Rime of the Ancient Mariner*, 1956; *The Browning Version*, 1957; *Lycidas*, 1958; *Oedipus at Colonus*, 1959; *The Way of the World*, 1960; *Richard II*, 1960; *Arms and the Man*, 1961; *The Butterfly that Stamped*, 1962; *In Memoriam*, 1966; *King Lear*, 1967; *Five Children With It*, 1967; *Leon Quartermain*, 1967; *I Don't Mind What They Do As Long As They Don't Do It In The Streets and Frighten The Horses*, 1970; *Two Knights Not a Round Table*, 1971; *Forty Years On*, 1973; *O Wild West Eind*, 1975; *Pilgrim's Progress*, 1975; *Mr Luby's Fear of Heaven*, 1975; *The Grand Inquisitor*, 1975; *Henry V*, 1976; *Disraeli's Reminiscences*, 1976; *Vivat Rex*, 1977; *Themes from Childhood*, 1978; *The Monogamist*, 1978; *Ode to the West Wind*, 1978; *Glory*, 1981; *Leave it to Psmith*, 1981; *The Winter's Tale*, 1981; *Passing Time*, 1983.

Publications

Early Stages, 1939; *Stage Directions*, 1963; *Distinguished Company*, 1972; *An Actor and His Time*, 1979.

*

Bibliography

Books:
Rosamund Gilder, *John Gielgud's Hamlet*, London, 1937.
Hallam Fordham, *John Gielgud — An Actor's Biography in Pictures*, London, 1952.
Ronald Hayman, *John Gielgud*, London, 1971.
Ronald Harwood (ed.), *The Ages of Gielgud: An Actor at Eighty*, London, 1984.
Robert Tanitch, *Gielgud*, London, 1988.

* * *

The criterion for evaluating actors in the English language is their record in accepted classics: tragedy or comedy. In them the performer and great literature are partners in the theatre, an influence both on scholarship and on the general public. Gielgud in the 20th century has had rivals in tragedy, but none at the highest level in comedy. Uniquely, he has been a master of both.

In the absence of all but the briefest evidence on film, we are left with the testimony of written criticism charting Gielgud's stage career, and James Agate, with space not available to critics in later years, pointed out the precise moment in which Gielgud first displayed the authority fitting an actor destined to be great. This was in *Richard of Bordeaux* by Gordon Daviot, when he made an entrance on a stage filled with actors collectively decades ahead of him in experience. Among them, it happened, was Donald Wolfit; but it was Gielgud who dominated the scene, even before he spoke.

Gielgud's vocal delivery is the highlight of his talent. His performances in the early 1930's rescued the heroic roles from bad habits dating from the Edwardian era, when tragedians were squeezing the life out of verse drop by drop in a parsonical drone. Gielgud arrived at a balance between Shakespeare's flowing poetry and a fluent, almost conversational delivery, acceptable to audiences able to listen. Conditions in the great Granville-Barker climate, emphasizing simple settings, rapid diction, and faithfulness to the text, were in his favour. High-tech visual elaboration was yet to come, and in 1934 Gielgud achieved what had been thought impossible in the commercial theatre: a 155-performance West End run as Hamlet.

Gielgud's Hamlet, considered the definitive interpretation of his time, had several characteristics. Foremost of these was his speaking of Shakespeare's verse, though he was equally convincing in the prose passages. Then there was the sense of an incurable inward melancholy, offset when called for by flashes of cynical humour. A brooding stage presence and gestures natural to a Tudor aristocrat bred on Castiglione's *Courtier* controlled the surface, so that a less than graceful walk and now and then too much lingering on open vowels was scarcely noticed.

Such qualities were deployed equally well in the sombre lyricism of Richard II, this time Shakespeare's. A sterner test was Lear, which he rehearsed under Granville-Barker himself. Although Wolfit's devastating power in that role could not be expected from Gielgud, he learned to catch what he had missed as Hamlet — a unique affinity with late Shakespeare's luminous resignation (a quality also evident in his Prospero). To convey what, for want of a better term, may be called tragic pathos was beyond the scope of any of Gielgud's contemporaries.

Still to come were his Angelo and Leontes, which were essays in brooding psychology. But in comedies of manners, ranging from Congreve to Wilde, he displayed total mastery, his tone subtly adapted to the demands of often finely wrought dialogue. One of the later triumphs was his Joseph Surface, seated in profile to the audience like some modern company director — icily manipulative behind his desk. By way of contrast, in romantic comedy he was sunnily expansive as Benedick. One episode in particular, in which Benedick is the victim of a practical joke, gave rise to as extraordinary a display of comic acting as one is ever likely to witness. Gielgud came across both as the deceived Benedick and, simultaneously, as actor in league with the audience enjoying the joke.

In the 1960's estimates of Gielgud were vitiated by changes in theatrical fashion in favour of shock tactics and a drift into the three-minute attention span induced by television. Socially, an anti-aristocratic prejudice reduced heroic acting to competition with high-tech visual effects by actors used to naturalistic dialogue rather than verse. Under the influence of impressionalistic journalism in drastically limited space, the musical element in Shakespeare's poetry was neglected and Gielgud, the unsurpassed speaker of the Shakespearean line, was somewhat overshadowed by the adulation afforded such equally great contemporaries as Olivier. Olivier and Gielgud's achievements were quite distinct, however, Olivier unrivalled as Macbeth, but Gielgud unmatched as Hamlet and in the comedy of manners. The most futile cliché was that Gielgud, the finest interpreter of Hamlet and Prospero, lacked "stomach" — whatever that may mean.

Gielgud's decision to refuse an offer to film his Hamlet may prove disastrous to his long-term reputation. Fortunately, however, his recordings of Hamlet and Richard II survive and are conclusive proof of his skill. So are his performances on screen of Cassius and, in *Richard III*, Clarence. For the towering remainder, posterity must rely on writers who saw and heard him in his prime.

—Laurence Kitchin

GILLETTE, William (Hooker). US actor and playwright. Born in Hartford, Connecticut, 24 July 1853. Educated at Hartford High School; Yale University, New Haven, Massachusetts; Harvard University, Cambridge, Connecticut; Massachusetts Institute of Fine Arts, BA. Married Helen Nickles in 1882 (died 1888). Stage debut, New Orleans, 1875; subsequently acted at the Globe Theatre, Boston, 1875, and in Cincinnatti and Louisville, Kentucky, 1875–87; wrote first play, 1881; retired temporarily from stage after serious illness, 1891; London debut, Adelphi Theatre, 1897; first of 1300 appearances as Sherlock Holmes, his greatest role, 1899; absent from stage, 1921–29; last stage appearance, Hartford, Connecticut, 1936. Member: American Academy of Arts and Letters, 1913. Honorary degrees: Yale University; University of Columbia, New York; Trinity College, Hartford; all 1930. Died in Hartford, 29 April 1937.

Roles

1875	Walk-on role in *Across the Continent* (McCloskey), New Orleans.
	Duff in *Colonel Sellers/The Gilded Age* (Raymond, adapted from Twain and Warner), Union Square Theatre, New York.
	Bailiff in *For Love or Money* (Halliday), Globe Theatre, Boston.

Guzman in *Faint Heart Ne'er Won Fair Lady* (Planché), Globe Theatre, Boston.

Malcolm in *Macbeth* (Shakespeare), Boston Museum.

Montano in *Othello* (Shakespeare), Boston Museum.

Benvolio in *Romeo and Juliet* (Shakespeare), Boston Museum.

Rosencrantz in *Hamlet* (Shakespeare), Boston Museum.

Master Wilford in *The Hunchback* (Knowles), Boston Museum.

Prince Florian in *Broken Hearts* (Gilbert), Boston Museum.

1877	Foreman of the Jury in *Colonel Sellers/The Gilded Age* (Raymond, adapted from Twain and Warner), New Park Theatre, New York.
1878	Marquis de Presles in *The Two Orphans* (Corman and d'Ennery), Brooklyn Academy of Music.
1881	Professor Hopkins in *The Professor* (Gillette), Madison Square Theatre, New York.
1883–84	Douglas Winthrop in *Young Mrs Winthrop* (Howard), US tour.
1884	Reverend Job McCosh in *Digby's Secretary* (Gillette, adapted from Moser's *Der Bibliothekar*, later retitled *The Private Secretary*), Comedy Theatre, New York; Empire Theatre, New York, 1910.
1886	Thomas Henry Bean in *Held by the Enemy* (Gillette), Criterion Theatre, Brooklyn, and Madison Square Theatre, New York.
1894	Augustus Billings in *Too Much Johnson* (Gillette), Standard Theatre, New York; Garrick Theatre, London, 1898; Empire Theatre, New York, 1910.
1895	Lewis Dumont in *Secret Service* (Gillette), Broad Street Theatre, Philadelphia; Garrick Theatre, New York, 1896; Adelphi Theatre, London, 1897; Empire Theatre, New York, 1910 and 1915.
1899	Sherlock Holmes in *Sherlock Holmes* (Gillette), Garrick Theatre, New York; Lyceum Theatre, London, 1901; Duke of York's Theatre, London, 1905; Boston and Empire Theatre, New York, 1910; Empire Theatre, New York, 1915; New Amsterdam Theatre, New York, 1929; US tour, 1931–32.
1903	Mr Crichton in *The Admirable Crichton* (Barrie), Lyceum Theatre, New York.
1905	Sherlock Holmes in *The Painful Predicament of Sherlock Homes* (Gillette), Metropolitan Opera House, New York, and Duke of York's Theatre, London.
	Doctor Carrington in *Clarice* (Gillette), Duke of York's Theatre, London, and US tour; Garrick Theatre, New York, 1906.
1908	Maurice Brachard in *Samson* (Gillette), Criterion Theatre, New York.
1914	Henry Beauclerc in *Diplomacy* (Scott and Stephenson), Empire Theatre, New York.
1917	Henry Wilton in *A Successful Calamity* (Kummer), Booth Theatre, New York.

William Gillette

1918	Mr Dearth in *Dear Brutus* (Barrie), Empire Theatre, New York.
1921	Dr Paul Clement in *The Dream Maker* (Gillette), Empire Theatre, New York.
1935	Role in *Three Wise Fools* (Strong), US tour.

Films

Sherlock Holmes, 1916.

Radio

Sherlock Holmes, 1935.

Publications

The Professor (play), 1881; *Esmeralda* (play, with Burnett), 1881; *Digby's Secretary* (play), 1884; *Held by the Enemy* (play), 1886; *She* (play, adapted from Rider Haggard), 1887; *A Legal Wreck* (play), 1888; *All the Comforts of Home* (play), 1890; *Mr Wilkinson's Widows*, 1891; *Settled Out of Court* (play), 1892; *Ninety Days* (play), 1893; *Too Much Johnson* (play), 1894; *Secret Service* (play), 1896; *Because She Loved Him So* (play), 1899; *Sherlock Holmes* (play, adapted from Conan Doyle), 1899; *The Painful Predicament of Sherlock Holmes* (play, adapted from Conan Doyle), 1905; *Clarice* (play), 1905; *The Red Owl* (vaudeville sketch), 1907; *That Little Affair at Boyd's*

(play), 1908; *Samson* (play), 1908; *The Robber* (play), 1909; *Among Thieves* (play), 1909; *Electricity* (play), 1910; *The Illusion of the First Time in Acting* (essay), 1915; *The Dream Maker* (play), 1921; *Winnie and the Wolves* (play), 1923.

*

Bibliography

Books:
Doris E. Cook, *Sherlock Holmes and Much More; or, Some of the Facts about William Gillette*, Hartford, Connecticut, 1970.

Articles:
Richard Burton, "William Gillette", *Book Buyer*, 16, February 1898.
Gertrude Lynch, "The Real William Gillette", *Theatre*, 13, April 1901.
W. P. Dodge, "William Gillette", *Strand*, 42, October 1911.
Peter Clark Macfarlane, "The Magic of William Gillette", *Everybody's Magazine*, 32, February 1915.
Clayton Hamilton, "William Gillette: Theatrical Craftsman", *Collier's*, 56, December 1915.
Harold J. Nichols, "William Gillette — Innovator in Melodrama", *Theatre Annual*, 31, 1975.

* * *

William Gillette's own judgement upon himself was: "I'm a pretty fair stage carpenter, and not altogether bad as an actor, after I have written myself a good part that suits me". The interdependence of Gillette's acting career and playwriting was such that the best indicators of his performance style are probably embedded in his own stage directions, rather than in his celebrated lecture published as *The Illusion of the First Time in Acting*. However, his quotation also reflects an aspect of his personality that seems to have been prominent in shaping his acting: an extreme unpretentiousness, which sometimes presented itself as self-disparagement.

Perhaps because of this trait, it has become usual to regard Gillette as an accomplished technician and scriptwriter rather than as any kind of innovator. William Archer wrote that *Secret Service* was "simply the best thing of its kind, the best drama of adventure and situation, written within my recollection in the English language", while Allardyce Nicoll demonstrated that *Sherlock Holmes* represented "the foundation for the whole of the popular school of drama to which are variously attached the terms 'crook', 'crime', 'detective', 'mystery', and 'thriller'". However, the most radical of Gillette's achievements was arguably not in his scripts but in the kind of performance on which *Sherlock Holmes* pivoted — a reflective, introverted characterisation in which a single utterance could convey volumes of significance. Thus, his method of underplaying parts offered an extreme contrast to the passionate, declamatory style of actors like James O'Neill, which epitomised late 19th-century drama.

Along with David Belasco, Gillette has always been associated with the pioneer realists of the US theatre. This association is substantiated not only by the anecdotes of his going to extraordinary lengths over trivial details to achieve an ambiance of authenticity, but also by his expansive stage directions, which were similar to those that T. W. Robertson was writing in England at much the same time. The essential difference between the two is that whereas Robertson understood and explored the effects of silent action, Gillette was concerned to represent all dimensions of behaviour, often not to advance the action significantly but to indulge character in itself within actions that are formulaic. He took issue with the historian A. H. Quinn's "evident opinion that the words constitute the play" and went on to assert that "I would much prefer that people read what my characters *do* — how they *behave* — and what is in their minds — than to merely get the words they utter". Archer, who found his acting "quietly original and impressive", commented on *Secret Service* as a whole that the "heroism is quiet and gentlemanlike, not rampant and robustious" — a remarkable feat at the Adelphi, which then seated 1500. The emphasis on non-verbal behaviour largely accounted for the play's striking success on television in the 1980's and for the acclaimed stage revivals of both *Secret Service* and *Sherlock Holmes* in the 1970's.

Gillette did only four, secondary Shakespeare roles, all of them in his student period before his New York debut. Apart from his own scripts, the most famous roles of his maturity were the lead parts in Barrie's *The Admirable Crichton* and *Dear Brutus*, where his subdued gentlemanly stage persona made him an obvious choice. He rejected notions that versatility goes with great acting, pointing out that when great actors "undertook parts ... unsuited to their personalities, they were great no longer and frequently quite the reverse". This attitude has sometimes been dismissed as 'typecasting', but for Gillette it was a matter of the actors' "successful use of their own strong and compelling personalities". Though his acting career did not allow opportunity for sustained study, he attended a number of universities for particular courses and constantly emphasized the intellectual preparation for acting. Quinn saw the central purpose of this preparation as discovering "the mental and emotional position" of a character, to be able to "simulate that gradual or sudden birth of motor impulses whose handling or mishandling draws the line between success and failure".

Although he was involved in the scripting of about 25 plays, less than half of these were fully original — a substantial writing output nevertheless for an actor who did as many as 1300 performances of a single role. His plays were by no means all written for his own performance and within conventional structures they cover a range of genres. *Esmeralda* is a pioneering comedy drama that was frequently revived and was even done in London by the Kendals. *The Professor*, *The Private Secretary* (originally titled *Digby's Secretary*), and *Too Much Johnson* are farcical comedies, all of which were stage successes, but it was through his Civil War melodramas *Held by the Enemy* and *Secret Service* that Gillette became a celebrity as a playwright. The cohesion of both plays in story terms comes from the deployment of a spy in a pivotal role; in both function and character type, the spy clearly anticipates the detective in the Conan Doyle adaptations.

Gillette was becoming very wealthy by the turn of the century, but he continued to develop his writing with the topical satire *Electricity* and with *Clarice*, a subtle domestic play that ends in comedy. Perhaps he is best remembered, affectionately, for mannerisms like the episode in *Clarice*,

where a stage direction of 111 words establishes the behavioural context for the line "Come, Clancy", after which the stage directions continue.

—Howard McNaughton

GORELIK, Mordecai. US designer and director. Born in Shchedrin (now Minsk), Russia, 25 August 1899. Educated at the Boys High School, Brooklyn, New York; Pratt Institute School of Fine Arts, New York, graduated 1920; studied design under Robert Edmond Jones, Norman Bel Geddes, and Serge Soudeikine. Married 1) Frances Strauss (died); 2) Loraine Kabler; two children. Instructor-designer, School of the Theatre, New York, 1921–22; scene-painter, Provincetown Playhouse, New York, 1921; teacher, Cornish School, Seattle, 1925, and American Academy of the Dramatic Arts, 1926–32; leading designer, Group Theatre, New York, 1930's; London debut, 1938; taught at the Drama Workshop of the New School of Social Research, 1940–41, the American University, Biarritz, France, 1945–46, and subsequently at the universities of Toledo, Ohio, Hawaii, New York, Bard College, San José, and Brigham Young University, Provo, Utah; consultant in theatre, US Military Government in Germany, 1949; designed for the Comédie-Française and the Old Vic Company on US visits, 1955; research professor, Southern Illinois University, Carbondale, 1960–72. Member: American Educational Theatre Association; Speech Communication Association; American Theatre Research Association. Recipient: Guggenheim Fellowship, 1936–37; Rockefeller Foundation Grant, 1949–51; Fulbright Scholarship, 1967; US Institute of Theatre Technology Award, 1981. Died in Sarasota, Florida, 7 March 1990.

Productions

1925   *King Hunger* (Andreyev), Hedgerow Theatre, Philadelphia.
        Processional (Lawson), Theatre Guild, New York.
1926   *Nirvana* (Lawson), Greenwich Village Theatre, New York.
        The Moon is a Gong (Dos Passos), Cherry Lane Theatre, New York.
1927   *Loud Speaker* (Lawson), 52nd Street Theatre, New York.
1928   *The Final Balance* (Pinsky), Provincetown Playhouse Theatre, New York.
        God, Man, and the Devil (Gordin), Yiddish Art Theatre, New York.
1931   *Uncle Moses* (Ash), Yiddish Art Theatre, New York.
        1931 (Cifton), Group Theatre, New York.
1932   *Success Story* (Lawson), Group Theatre, New York.
1933   *Men in White* (Kingsley), Group Theatre, New York.
        Gentlewoman (Lawson), Group Theatre, New York.
        Big Night (Powell), Group Theatre, New York.

Little Ol' Boy (Bein), Playhouse Theatre, New York.

All Good Americans (Perelman), Henry Miller Theatre, New York.

1934   *Sailors of Cattaro* (Wolf), Civic Repertory Theatre, New York.

1935   *Mother* (adapted from Brecht's *Mother Courage*), Civic Repertory Theatre, New York.

Let Freedom Ring (Bein), Broadhurst Theatre, New York.

The Young Go First (Martin, Scudder, and Friedman), Park Theatre, New York.

1937   Golden Boy (Odets), Group Theatre, New York.

1938   *Tortilla Flat* (Kirkland, adapted from Steinbeck), Henry Miller Theatre, New York.

Rocket to the Moon (Odets), Group Theatre, New York.

Casey Jones (Ardrey), Group Theatre, New York.

1939   *Thunder Rock* (Ardrey), Group Theatre, New York.

The Quiet City (I. Shaw), Group Theatre, New York.

1940   *Night Music* (Odets), Group Theatre, New York.

1944   *Volpone* (Jonson), Actors' Laboratory Theatre, Los Angeles.

1945   *Doctor Knock* (Romains), American University, Biarritz, France; also directed.

The Front Page (Hecht and MacArthur), American University, Biarritz, France; also directed.

Volpone (Jonson), American University, Biarritz, France.

The Time of Your Life (Saroyan), American University, Biarritz, France.

Winterset (Anderson), American University, Biarritz, France.

Paul Thompson Forever (Gorelik), Los Angeles; also directed.

1947   *All My Sons* (Miller), Coronet Theatre, New York.

1952   *Desire Under the Elms* (O'Neill), American National Theatre, New York.

Danger, Men Working (Steward), Circle Workshop, Los Angeles; also directed.

1954   *The Flowering Peach* (Odets), Belasco Theatre, New York.

St Joan (G. B. Shaw), Washington National Theatre, New York.

1955   *A Hatful of Rain* (Gazzo), Lyceum Theatre, New York.

1956   *Born Yesterday* (Kanin), Toledo, Ohio.

The Plough and the Stars (O'Casey), Barbizon Plaza Theatre, New York.

1957   *The Sin of Pat Muldoon* (McLiam), New Haven Theatre, New York.

1958   *Guests of the Nation*, New York.

1960   *A Distant Bell* (Morrill), New York.

1961   *The Dybbuk* (Ansky), Brigham Young University, Provo, Utah; also directed.

The Annotated Hamlet (adapted from Shakespeare), Southern Illinois University; also directed.

1962   *The House of Bernarda Alba* (Lorca), Southern Illinois University; also directed.

Marseilles (Howard), Southern Illinois University; also directed.

1964   *The Good Woman of Setzuan* (Brecht), Southern Illinois University; also directed.

1963   *The Firebugs* (Frisch, adapted by Gorelik); also co-directed.

1975   *The Firebugs* (Frisch, translated by Gorelik), Bouwerie Lane Theatre, New York.

Films

As designer:

Days of Glory, 1944; *None But the Lonely Heart*, 1944; *Give Us This Day*, 1949; *Salt to the Devil*, 1954; *Our Street*, 1954; *L'Ennemi publique No 1*, 1954.

Publications

New Theatres for Old, 1940; *Paul Thompson Forever* (play), 1945; *The Firebugs* (play, adapted from Frisch), 1963; *Toward a Larger Theatre*, 1988.

*

Bibliography

Articles:
D. Barnes, "Mordecai Gorelik", *Theatre Guild Magazine*, February 1931.
"Mordecai Gorelik", *Le Spectateur*, October 1945.

* * *

Mordecai Gorelik was not only a designer but a passionate theoretician and advocate for new ideas in the theatre. His book, *New Theatres for Old*, still in print, remains one of the best explications of the new theatre movements of Europe from the 1880's onward and was a major factor in the introduction of Brecht and Epic Theatre to the USA. Gorelik was also a playwright and the US translator of Max Frisch's *Biedermann und die Brandstifter* (as *The Firebugs*). The combination of his stage designing and writing — he continued to publish articles into the 1980's — made him a unique influence on US design.

Gorelik took a singular view of design, that it should make a statement in the service of the play. He was virtually the only designer to state that his first consideration was the audience: "Who are they; what is their purpose in coming to the theatre?". The next consideration was the social meaning of the play. On the one hand, this social commitment limited the number and types of plays that he would do, yet, at least theoretically, it altered the focus of stage design. No other designer, at least in the USA, ever suggested that scenography could be a force for social change. Some of this undoubtedly came from his training and influences. While studying art at the Pratt Institute, he became interested in theatre. He studied with the Russian emigré painter and designer Serge Soudeikine and took a few design classes with Norman Bel Geddes. Robert Edmond Jones, who was to become a lifelong friend, took an interest in his work, though their styles were very different. By and large, Gorelik did not follow the general tendencies of US design at the time; he avoided the symbolism and abstraction of many of his contemporaries as well as the later poetic realism of designers such as Mielziner. Perhaps through Soudeikine, the strongest influence seemed to be Constructivism. "A production," he once stated, "is, in a sense, a machine for the theatre. Scenery is the chassis and the actors are the engine". By Constructivism Gorelik meant "a form that proposes to fill the whole space of the stage". From his earliest productions, such as *King Hunger*, he used industrial materials as well.

Lest any of this suggest a dull didacticism, it should be noted that his designs could be stunning. One of the earliest was for John Howard Lawson's *Processional*. The collage-like setting representing a cross between a West Virginia coal town and a vaudeville stage was a visual expression of the popular culture embodied in the play, which was subtitled "A Jazz Symphony of American Life". Significantly, Gorelik's credits included designs for Minsky's burlesque. His fame, however, came with a series of productions for the socially committed Group Theatre in the 1930's. For the groundbreaking production of Sidney Kingsley's *Men in White*, Gorelik designed a simple surround of sliding panels and a wagon stage that allowed the smooth and rapid shifting of scenes among the various rooms of a hospital. For Clifford Odets's *Golden Boy* he designed a set in the style of suggestive realism, yet the groundplan was more like a boxing ring in which the antagonists stepped to the centre from corners of the stage with bright light shining down on them. The posts at the corners of the ring became decorative pillars in Gorelik's set. *Golden Boy* was an excellent example of Gorelik's idea of design as metaphor. He felt that finding the appropriate metaphor or metaphors would serve as inspiration for the designer and have an emotional effect upon the audience, although he cautioned that it should be "*felt, not seen*".

Gorelik's ideals were best summed up in his own words for a 1936 profile by Norris Houghton in *Theatre Arts Monthly*: "I still believe that the purpose of worthwhile theatre is to clarify life; that stage production must exist for the welfare of its audiences, not merely to show how well someone can write, act, direct or design. Therefore the designer must know what the play will mean to its public, and how he can contribute to that meaning. I define the setting as a documentation of environment ... and as a machine-for-theatre".

—Arnold Aronson

GRAY, Terence. British director, designer, and playwright. Born in Felixstowe, Suffolk, 14 September 1895. Educated at Eton public school; Magdalene College, Cambridge University. Co-founder, Festival Theatre, Cambridge, 1926; introduced numerous staging innovations as director and designer there, 1926–29 and 1930–33; retired from the theatre, 1933.

Productions

1926   *Oresteia* (Aeschylus), Festival Theatre, Cambridge.

1927   *Miss Julie* (Strindberg), Festival Theatre, Cambridge.
        Oedipus Tyrannus (Sophocles), Festival Theatre, Cambridge.
        A Florentine Irony, Festival Theatre, Cambridge.

1928   *The Carthaginian* (Taylor), Festival Theatre, Cambridge.
        Richard III (Shakespeare), Festival Theatre, Cambridge.
        The Pretenders (Ibsen), Festival Theatre, Cambridge.
        The Riding to Lithend (Bottomley), Festival Theatre, Cambridge.
        A Royal Audience (T. Gray), Festival Theatre, Cambridge.
        The Birds (Aristophanes), Festival Theatre, Cambridge.
        The Man Who Ate the Popomack (Turner), Festival Theatre, Cambridge.
        As You Like It (Shakespeare), Festival Theatre, Cambridge.
        From Morn to Midnight (Kaiser), Festival Theatre, Cambridge.
        The Hairy Ape (O'Neill), Festival Theatre, Cambridge.

1929   *Romeo and Juliet* (Shakespeare), Festival Theatre, Cambridge.
        Twelve Thousand (Frank), Festival Theatre, Cambridge.
        Salome (Wilde), Festival Theatre, Cambridge.

1931   *Henry VIII* (Shakespeare), Festival Theatre, Cambridge.
        The Insect Play (Čapek), Festival Theatre, Cambridge.
        The Wild Duck (Ibsen), Festival Theatre, Cambridge.
        Lysistrata (Aristophanes), Festival Theatre, Cambridge.
        Antigone (Sophocles), Festival Theatre, Cambridge.
        Hassan (Flecker), Festival Theatre, Cambridge.
        Gustav Vasa (Strindberg), Festival Theatre, Cambridge.
        The Eunuch (Terence), Festival Theatre, Cambridge.
        The Alcestis (Euripides), Festival Theatre, Cambridge.

1932   *The Makropoulos Secret* (Čapek), Festival Theatre, Cambridge.
        One More River (Cross), Festival Theatre, Cambridge.
        Caesar and Cleopatra (G. B. Shaw), Festival Theatre, Cambridge.
        The Merchant of Venice (Shakespeare), Festival Theatre, Cambridge.

1933   *The Suppliants* (Aeschylus), Festival Theatre, Cambridge.

Other productions included: *The Adding Machine* (Rice); *Twelfth Night* (Shakespeare).

* * *

Terence Gray is a unique instance of someone with almost no practical experience in the theatre, whose background was that of an enthusiastic, wealthy, and indulgent amateur, who nonetheless managed in his brief stage career to have a substantial impact upon the contemporary theatre. In 1926, together with the lighting designer Harold Ridge, he founded the Cambridge Festival Theatre and, although shortlived (it closed in 1939), the project had an influence and an importance that, had its achievement been more sustained and consistent, might have revolutionised the English theatre of the time. Innovative and iconoclastic in both its theatrical methods and its repertoire, the Festival Theatre under Gray's direction introduced European and US Expressionist drama into the English theatre as well as mounting a number of idiosyncratic, highly original, and controversial productions of the classics, particularly of Shakespeare.

Initially, Gray's work conspicuously demonstrated the influence of the ideas of Adolphe Appia and Edward Gordon Craig. He wrote several mime plays where the action consisted largely of movement and lighting, and designed for them abstract settings of geometrical shapes, screens, and columns, similar to the staging of Yeats's plays at the Abbey Theatre in Dublin in the previous decade. He was also a keen proponent of the use of split levels on the the stage. Gray, however, went further in his repudiation of naturalism and the picture-frame stage. In terms that are reminiscent of Piscator, Meyerhold, and Brecht, he rejected "the old game of illusion and glamour and all the rest of the 19th-century hocus pocus and bamboozle", and redesigned the Georgian Barnwell theatre in Cambridge so that illusionistic representation became impossible. The side walls of the proscenium arch and the footlights were removed and a forestage connected with the auditorium by a staircase, so that there was no definite boundary between audience and performers. On this open stage the mechanisms of the theatre were clearly exposed: actors, stagehands, prompter, props; while actors moved freely offstage into the auditorium, addressing themselves directly to the audience. The aim was to ensure that the audience did not surrender to the illusion of 'spying on reality'.

The repertory of the Cambridge Festival Theatre was wide-ranging and eclectic, its rapid turnover of plays determined more by the mode of production than by the drama itself. Expressionist and Symbolist drama were strongly represented, productions including Georg Kaiser's *From Morn to Midnight* and Eugene O'Neill's *The Hairy Ape*. Gray had a cheerful disrespect for the traditional authority of the playwright, seeing the role of the director not as the loyal interpreter of the author's intentions but as the creator of an 'independent work of theatre art'. Again, this recalled Meyerhold as well as Craig: the text was simply one element in the total theatre event. This approach was controversial — the trend towards 'directors' theatre', although well established in Europe, had not yet taken hold in Britain. When Gray came to apply this method to the classics, it was bound to unsettle traditional sensibilities: on the non-illusionist stage of the Festival Theatre imagination and outrageous invention were al-

lowed their full scope. There was a substantial number of productions of the Greek drama, from the opening *Oresteia* of Aeschylus in 1926 to Gray's final production, *The Suppliants*, in 1933: here at least the revolt against illusion could be tolerated. His productions of Shakespeare, however, were notorious. In *The Merchant of Venice* Gray overtly expressed his own boredom with the play and had Portia delivering the "quality of mercy" speech from a trapeze while the Duke played a yo-yo. *Twelfth Night* had characters on roller-skates and *Romeo and Juliet* had a flamenco treatment. His staging of the rarely-produced *Henry VIII* as a 'masque in the modern manner with the text attributed to Shakespeare and others' was the most radical departure from conventional methods. Heavily stylised throughout, the costuming and make-up made the court appear like playing cards, while smaller parts were indicated by cardboard cut-outs. Cardinal Wolsey appeared on stilts, which diminished together with his fortunes in the course of the play. The tempo alternated between slow and frenzied and much of the action was conducted through dance and mime. The play was staged on a metal ramp, which revolved madly in the final scene, which was played as grotesque slapstick, culminating in a ludicrous property baby representing the infant Queen Elizabeth being tossed into the audience. As an example of an independent work of theatre art, the production — like many of Gray's — infuriated Shakespearean loyalists as much as it delighted its admirers.

The work at the Cambridge Festival Theatre, daringly experimental and avant-garde as it was, was significantly at odds with the British theatre of the time. While Gray's own productions have been criticised as erratic, eccentric, and self-indulgent, they nonetheless presented a salutary challenge to the staid and conventional realism of the contemporary theatre. Certainly with regard to the Festival stage itself, the Cambridge Festival Theatre experiment was an important forerunner of subsequent theatre practice: in particular, the work of Tyrone Guthrie, who ran the theatre from 1929 to 1930. After an unsuccessful attempt to repeat the Cambridge experiment in London's Covent Garden, which was thwarted by the insistence of the local authority that the theatre building should have a fire curtain, Gray finally abandoned the theatre in 1933 to become a winegrower and breeder of racehorses.

—Robert Shaughnessy

GREET, (Sir) Ben. British actor-manager. Born Philip Barling Greet in London, 24 September 1857. Educated at Royal Naval School, New Cross. Began career as a school teacher in Worthing before making stage debut with J. W. Gordon's company in Southampton, 1879; acted with Sarah Thorne's company in Margate, 1880–83; London debut, Gaiety Theatre, 1883; joined Minnie Palmer's company, 1883; acted at the Lyceum Theatre, London, alongside Lawrence Barrett, 1884; first entered into management with his own touring company, 1886; staged series of plays at the Shakespeare Festival, Stratford-upon-Avon, 1894–95; toured widely with his own companies, 1890–1902; founder, Ben Greet Academy of Acting, 1896; acted chiefly in the USA, 1902–14; presented 24 Shakespearean plays as director of the Old Vic Theatre, London,

1914–18; led Shakespearean touring company from 1918; presented English plays in Paris, 1924–26; toured USA, 1929–32; reopened Oxford Repertory Company, 1930; co-founder, Open Air Theatre, Regent's Park, London, 1933; last appearance, as Shylock in *The Merchant of Venice*, 1936. Knighted, 1929. Died in London, 17 May 1936.

Productions

As actor only:

1883   Caius Lucius in *Cymbeline* (Shakespeare), Gaiety Theatre, London.
        Dudley Harcourt in *My Sweetheart* (Maeder and Gill), Grand Theatre, Islington, London, and Strand Theatre, London.

1884   Master Woodford in *Yorick's Love* (Howells, adapted from Tamayo y Baus), Lyceum Theatre, London.
        De Beringhen in *Richelieu* (Bulwer-Lytton), Lyceum Theatre, London.
        The Apothecary in *Romeo and Juliet* (Shakespeare), Lyceum Theatre, London.

1886   Dr Pettywise in *Jim the Penman* (Young), Haymarket Theatre, London.

1887   Joe Jeffcoat in *Hard Hit* (H. A. Jones), Haymarket Theatre, London.
        Mr May in *Man and Wife* (Collins), Haymarket Theatre, London.

1890   Maris in *A Buried Talent* (Parker), Vaudeville Theatre, London.

1897   George Romney in *Nelson's Enchantress* (Horne), Avenue Theatre, London.

As actor-manager:

1894   *Diplomacy* (Sardou), Shakespeare Festival, Stratford-upon-Avon.
        Masks and Faces (Reade and Taylor), Shakespeare Festival, Stratford-upon-Avon.
        Sowing the Wind (Grundy), Shakespeare Festival, Stratford-upon-Avon.

1895   *The Winter's Tale* (Shakespeare), Shakespeare Festival, Stratford-upon-Avon; acted Autolycus.
        Much Ado about Nothing (Shakespeare), Shakespeare Festival, Stratford-upon-Avon.
        As You Like It (Shakespeare), Shakespeare Festival, Stratford-upon-Avon.

1896–1902 *The Sign of the Cross* (Barrett), tour.
        The Little Minister (Barrie), tour.
        The Second in Command (Marshall), tour.
        The Belle of New York (Morton), tour.

1897   *Hamlet* (Shakespeare), Olympic Theatre, London.
        Antony and Cleopatra (Shakespeare), Olympic Theatre, London.
        The Merchant of Venice (Shakespeare), Olympic Theatre, London; acted Shylock.
        Macbeth (Shakespeare), Olympic Theatre, London.

1901   *Hamlet* (Shakespeare), tour; acted Hamlet.

1902   *Everyman* (anon.), British and US tour.

1910   *The Little Town of Bethlehem*, Garden Theatre, New York.

The Palace of Truth (Gilbert), Garden Theatre, New York.
The Tempest (Shakespeare), Garden Theatre, New York; acted Prospero.
A Midsummer Night's Dream (Shakespeare), Garden Theatre, New York; acted Bottom.

1911   *The Whirlwind* (Melvill), Daly's Theatre, New York; acted General the Duke de Brial.

1914–18 *King René's Daughter* (Martin), Old Vic Theatre, London.
        The Star of Bethlehem (Martens), Old Vic Theatre, London.
        Comedy and Tragedy (Gilbert), Theatre Royal, Worcester; acted role.
        Pygmalion and Galatea (Gilbert), His Majesty's Theatre, London; acted Chrysos.
        The Rivals (Sheridan), Stratford-upon-Avon.
        She Stoops to Conquer (Goldsmith), Stratford-upon-Avon.
        The School for Scandal (Sheridan), Stratford-upon-Avon.
        The Comedy of Errors (Shakespeare), Stratford-upon-Avon.
        Othello (Shakespeare), Stratford-upon-Avon.
        Much Ado About Nothing (Shakespeare), Stratford-upon-Avon.
        The Tempest (Shakespeare), Stratford-upon-Avon.
        The Winter's Tale (Shakespeare), Stratford-upon-Avon.
        The Two Gentlemen of Verona (Shakespeare), Stratford-upon-Avon.
        Hamlet (Shakespeare), Stratford-upon-Avon.
        Henry VIII (Shakespeare), Stratford-upon-Avon.
        Macbeth (Shakespeare), Stratford-upon-Avon.
        A Christmas Carol (adapted from Dickens), Old Vic Theatre, London.
        St Patrick's Day (Sheridan), Old Vic Theatre, London.
        The Critic (Sheridan), Old Vic Theatre, London.
        The Lady of Lyons (Bulwer-Lytton), Old Vic Theatre, London.
        Masks and Faces (Reade and Taylor), Old Vic Theatre, London.

1924   *The Chastening* (Kennedy), Mary Ward Settlement.
        The Admiral (Kennedy), Mary Ward Settlement.

1926   *Hamlet* (Shakespeare), Lyceum Theatre, London; acted First Gravedigger.

1927   *A Midsummer Night's Dream* (Shakespeare), Adelphi Theatre, London; acted Aegeus.

1933   *Hamlet* (Shakespeare, first quarto), Arts Theatre Club, London; acted Corambis/Polonius.

1935   *The Rivals* (Sheridan), Theatre Royal, Bournemouth; acted Sir Anthony Absolute.
        The School for Scandal (Sheridan), Theatre Royal, Bournemouth; acted Sir Peter Teazle.
        Everyman (anon.), Ambassadors' Theatre, London; acted The Messenger.
        The Miracle Man (Hicks), Victoria Palace Theatre, London; acted The Patriarch.

1934   *The Comedy of Errors* (Shakespeare), Open Air Theatre, London; acted Aegeon.

As You Like It (Shakespeare), Open Air Theatre, London; acted Touchstone.

Romeo and Juliet (Shakespeare), Open Air Theatre, London; acted Friar Lawrence.

* * *

If Ben Greet had remained solely an actor, he might not have achieved his later recognition. His first role in a major London production was gained through the superstitious beliefs of Mary Anderson, who was producing *Romeo and Juliet* at the Lyceum in 1884. While auditioning young actors for the Apothecary she realised that Greet was the twelfth she had seen so, not daring to risk a thirteenth, she offered him the part. Although in later years he was to play Prospero, Shylock, and other leading roles, Greet preferred supporting characters, such as Bottom, Friar Lawrence, and the First Gravedigger. As a man who inspired respect, his acting was rarely criticised, although G. B. Shaw dared to write of his "exasperatingly placid Polonius" and said that he was "as bad a Touchstone as a critic could desire to see". Whilst comparatively undistinguished as an actor, however, his real talent came to the fore when, at the early age of 25, he went into management.

The overwhelming passion of Greet's life was Shakespeare, who, according to Sybil Thorndyke, was "the nearest approach to Almighty God that B. G. knew". A devoted Anglican, pillar of the Actors' Church Union and the Church and Stage Guild, Greet had a confident belief that the words of Shakespeare, with their innate morality, could bring 'serenity of mind' to all who heard them. He aimed to bring Shakespeare to as wide an audience as possible and to this end toured companies throughout Britain and the USA for over 50 years. His energy, resourcefulness, and capacity to inspire devotion gained him early respect and later renown.

In 1896 he founded the Ben Greet Academy of Acting and this became a source of young actors for his companies, eager for experience and unafraid of low salaries and an exhausting regime of one-night stands in draughty church halls. The many famous names who trained under Greet's guidance included Sybil and Russell Thorndyke, Mrs Patrick Campbell, and the young Edward Gordon Craig, who played Hamlet at the Olympic Theatre in one of Greet's early companies.

Believing that one of the best ways of seeing Shakespeare was in the open air, Greet sent out many 'pastoral' tours. The necessary voice projection required for playing in public and private gardens, even football fields, provided invaluable training for his young companies. The outdoor productions continued for many years, including tours of the USA and finally came to fruition when, with Robert Atkins in 1933, he established the Open Air Theatre in Regent's Park, London.

Although some of his early theatre productions were lavishly staged, Greet became influenced by William Poel's belief that Shakespeare's plays should be performed, with no scenery and in Elizabethan costume, on the kind of stage for which they were written. The plays themselves should be uncut, there should be no break between scenes, and the verse should be spoken flowingly and at speed. He made a point of presenting *Hamlet* 'in its entirety' and also directed the First Quarto version of the play, believing it to be Shakespeare's early draft. With Poel he revived the medieval morality play *Everyman*, touring it extensively throughout Britain and the USA with outstanding success. Performed in a church setting, it was received enthusiastically by the clergy as a moral lesson and audiences seemed to find it an uplifting and moving experience.

Greet's simple, no-nonsense, policy and earnest style of direction, as well as his high moral beliefs, appealed to the equally crusading spirit of Lilian Baylis and, for the duration of World War I, he joined the Old Vic as her director. Against all the difficulties of the war years, they established a large popular following for Shakespeare at the Old Vic. With a new play each week and an annual Celebrity Matinée on Shakespeare's birthday, Greet was so successful that, in 1916, he was invited to take the company to Stratford for the Tercentenary season.

Before he went to the Old Vic, Greet had begun giving performances to evening school students and schoolchildren under the sponsorship of the Church and Stage Guild. By 1914 he was giving special matinées for schools at the Old Vic under the auspices of the London County Council. These proved enormously successful and also provided much-needed funds for the theatre. Long after he left the Old Vic, Greet continued to play schools' matinées in London theatres and took his touring companies into schools all over the country. It was to Ben Greet that many thousands of schoolchildren owed their first introduction to Shakespeare.

Largely forgotten by today's audiences, Greet is remembered with affection by the theatrical profession through the many stories still told of his exploits. Knighted in 1929 for his services to drama and education, it can truly be said that he achieved his goal of popularizing Shakespeare among diverse audiences on both sides of the Atlantic.

—Jill Line

GRIEVE family. British set designers and artists, comprising John Henderson Grieve, his sons Thomas Grieve and William Grieve, and his grandson by Thomas, Thomas Walford Grieve. John Henderson Grieve was born in Perth, 1770; first worked at the Theatre Royal, Drury Lane, London, c.1794; subsequently contributed designs to the Sadler's Wells Theatre, London, and the Theatre Royal, Bath, and became resident designer at Astley's Royal Amphitheatre, London, 1799–1807; produced first designs for Covent Garden, London, 1806, and subsequently painted scenery for the Shakespearean productions of J. P. Kemble there in the 1820's; with his sons continued to produce designs for Drury Lane and other leading London venues until his death; died 16 April 1845. Thomas Grieve was born in Lambeth, London, 11 June 1799; trained as a scene-painter at Covent Garden and worked alongside his father from 1817; was resident designer at Covent Garden for many years and also worked at the Theatre Royal, Drury Lane, 1835–39 and 1843–48, at the Royal Italian Opera House, at Her Majesty's Theatre, at the Princess's Theatre under Charles Kean, 1850–60, at the Lyceum Theatre, 1865–67, and at the Gaiety Theatre, from 1868; died in Lambeth, London, 16 April 1882. William Grieve was born in Lambeth, London, 1800; trained under his father at Covent Garden and joined him as an assistant there in 1818; resident designer, King's Theatre (later Her Majesty's), London, 1829–44; became first artist to be called before audience to take applause, 1832; also worked with his father and brother at the Theatre Royal, Drury Lane, 1835–39, and other London venues; died 12 November 1844. Thomas Walford Grieve was born 15 October 1841; joined the family business, 1862; supplied designs for Covent Garden, Drury Lane, the Lyceum, and other London theatres; retired early due to declining health; 1887; died 1899. Over 700 designs by the Grieve family survive, few attributable to individual members of the family.

Selected productions

1796	*The Magician of the Rocks*, Sadler's Wells Theatre, London.
1805	*Richard III* (Shakespeare), Theatre Royal, Bath.
	The Poor Soldier, Theatre Royal, Bath.
1806	*The Three Sisters and the Golden Bull*, Astley's Amphitheatre, London.
	The Tempest (Shakespeare), Covent Garden, London.
	Harlequin and Mother Goose (T. Dibdin), Covent Garden, London.
1819	*Marriage of Figaro* (Mozart), Covent Garden, London.
1820	*Harlequin and Friar Bacon* (pantomime), Covent Garden, London.
1821	*Undine*, Covent Garden, London.
	Kenilworth, (Scott), Theatre Royal, Bath.
1823	*The Vision of the Sun*, Covent Garden, London.
	Harlequin and Cock Robin (pantomime), Covent Garden, London.
1824	*The Spirits of the Moon*, Covent Garden, London.
	Der Freischutz (Weber), Covent Garden, London.
1824	*Oberon* (Weber), Covent Garden, London.
1825	*Harlequin and the Magic Rose*, Covent Garden, London.
1826	*Oberon* (Weber), Covent Garden, London.
1829	*The Devil's Elixir*, Covent Garden, London.
1830	*Harlequin Pat*, Covent Garden, London.
1831	*Kenilworth* (Deshayes), King's Theatre, London.
1832	*La Sylphide* (Nourrit and Schneitzhoeffer), Covent Garden, London.
	Puss in Boots (Farley), Covent Garden, London.
	Robert le Diable (Meyerbeer), King's Theatre, London.
1833	*Harlequin and Old Gammer Gurton*, Covent Garden, London.
1839	*Love's Labour's Lost* (Shakespeare), Covent Garden, London.
1840	*A Midsummer Night's Dream* (Shakespeare), Covent Garden, London.
1842	*Alma; ou, La Fille de feu* (Perrot and Cerrito), Covent Garden, London.
1843	*Zélia* (Perrot), Covent Garden, London.
	The Bohemian Girl (Balfe), Theatre Royal, Drury Lane, London.
	Ondine; ou, La Naïade (Perrot and Cerrito), Her Majesty's Theatre, London.
1845	*Maritana* (Wallace), Theatre Royal, Drury Lane, London.
1846	*The Maid of Artois* (Balfe), Theatre Royal, Drury Lane, London.
1847	*Semiramide* (Rossini), Covent Garden, London.
1850	*The Overland Route to India* (panorama), Gallery of Illustration, London.
1851	*Fidelio* (Beethoven), Her Majesty's Theatre, London.
	Il Flauto magico (Mozart), Covent Garden, London.
1851	*Favorita* (Donizetti), Covent Garden, London.
1852	*Pietro il Grande* (Jullien), Covent Garden, London.
1853	*Macbeth* (Shakespeare), Princess's Theatre, London.
	Sardanapalus (Lord Byron), Princess's Theatre, London.
1855	*Henry VIII* (Shakespeare), Princess's Theatre, London.
1856	*A Winter's Tale* (Shakespeare), Princess's Theatre, London.
1857	*Richard II* (Shakespeare), Princess's Theatre, London.
	The Tempest (Shakespeare), Princess's Theatre, London.
1858	*The Merchant of Venice* (Shakespeare), Princess's Theatre, London.
	King Lear (Shakespeare), Princess's Theatre, London.
1859	*Henry V* (Shakespeare), Princess's Theatre, London.
1862	*Goody Two Shoes* (Blanchard), Theatre Royal, Drury Lane, London.
1864	*St George and the Dragon* (H. J. Byron), Covent Garden, London.
	Cinderella (pantomime), Lyceum Theatre, London.
	Little Red Riding Hood (Buckingham), Lyceum Theatre, London.
1865	*Aladdin and the Wonderful Lamp* (Blanchard), Covent Garden, London.
	The Master of Ravenswood (Simpson), Lyceum Theatre, London.
1866	*The Corsican Brothers* (Boucicault), Lyceum Theatre, London.
	Rouge et Noir (Leslis), Lyceum Theatre, London.
1867	*The Lady of Lyons* (Bulwer-Lytton), Lyceum Theatre, London.
1868	*Robert the Devil* (Gilbert), Gaiety Theatre, London.
1869	*Dreams* (Robertson), Gaiety Theatre, London.
1874	*The Merry Wives of Windsor* (Shakespeare), Gaiety Theatre, London.
1879	*Gulliver* (H. J. Byron), Gaiety Theatre, London.

* * *

The Grieve family of scene-painters, who worked principally in London, were among the most famous and enduring of all nineteenth-century theatrical dynasties. John Henderson Grieve, a Scot from Perth, worked at various venues and by October 1805, when he collaborated on scenery for *Richard III* and *The Poor Soldier* at the Theatre Royal, Bath, he was being described as one of the "celebrated masters of the art" of theatrical design. He was the resident scene-painter at Astley's from 1799 to 1807 and, according to fellow-artist David Roberts, it was while so engaged that he was sent to assist Covent Garden in getting up a spectacle by which "the managers then found out that a scene might be painted in a day equally effective with those that had taken a month or perhaps more — and that a spectacle might be produced in a couple of weeks, at a fourth of the expense and equally effective with what used to occupy the greater part of the season". Roberts identifies the production as *Timour the Tartar*, but it was probably either *The Tempest* or the Christmas pantomime *Harlequin and Mother Goose*. By the season 1807–08 he was being paid five guineas a week, second only to the architectural specialist Phillips at six guineas, with whose highly-finished style, characteristic of eighteenth-century painters, the actor Joseph Cowell favourably compared Grieve's approach: "every day *splashing* into existence a cottage or a cavern with a pound brush in each hand".

It would appear from such comments that Grieve pioneered a broad, romantic handling of paint suited to a fast turnover of spectacular novelty, and likely to react well under gas light, which was first used on stage at Covent Garden and Drury Lane in 1817. His other innovation was to devise a form of scenic glaze, as in watercolour painting, to supplement previous sole use of solid distemper colours. Rivals called it "Scotch wash" in contempt, but Grieve lived to see it generally adopted, again presumably because of its effects under the strong illumination of gas. At a time when most scenery was painted in theatre scene-rooms, Grieve is the first artist we know of to have had an independent studio, near where he lived in Lambeth, and from which scenes were sent out to theatres by wagon. In this way, from 1815 to 1818, he augmented the in-house design of Robert Andrews (another fast worker) at Sadlers' Wells, on a piecework basis, as well as being engaged at Covent Garden: this practice continued and became common in the second half of the century. It was at Covent Garden, however, that by 1820 Grieve established his dominance of the scene-room, supported by his two sons. Together they raised the theatre to a scenic eminence that was only challenged after Drury Lane acquired Clarkson Stanfield and David Roberts in early 1823 and which the Grieves sustained into the 1840's, well beyond these rivals' retirements from the stage.

The Grieves' output ranged from romantic and exotic landscapes, real and imagined, to fantasy and historic architecture. From 1827 to 1833 they had the young A. W. N. Pugin as an assistant, and his influence as a source of gothic authenticity is particularly detectable in the spectacular ballet *Kenilworth*, painted for the King's Theatre in 1831. They otherwise provided scenery for everything from opera to pantomime. A particularly notable example of their pantomime scenery was that for *Harlequin and Friar Bacon* in 1820, for which they produced the first fully successful theatrical moving panorama, of a steam packet voyage from Holyhead to Dublin. This was a form they continued with great success, including at least one, a Rhine panorama as seen from a balloon, which moved vertically rather than across the stage, in *Harlequin and Old Gammer Gurton*.

Many of the 700 surviving Grieve designs are unidentified and apart from John Henderson's tendency to work in monochrome sketches, it is often difficult to separate which of them did what on style alone, or by relying on the playbill attributions of particular scenes. William excelled in moonlight scenes and is said to have been the first artist to be called before the curtain to receive the audience's appreciation of his work, on *Robert le Diable* in 1832. Thomas, meanwhile, had a particular success with the exhibition hall panorama of *The Overland Route to India* in 1850, the first of several such projects in which he became involved. He also won acclaim as a member of the team of artists employed by Charles Kean in "archaeologically authentic" revivals of Shakespeare and other historical plays at the Princess's Theatre in the 1850's.

Taken together, however, their bold and atmospheric handling, and the practical ingenuity of their settings, vindicate the melodramatist Edward Fitzball's perceptive comment that the Grieves were "the most perfect scene painters in the world as a combination", as well as being a close-knit family. His view of their generosity to other artists strongly contrasts with that of David Roberts, who worked beside them at Covent Garden in the 1820's and, albeit a biased rival, found them to be ruthless in suppressing any work they saw as a threat to their supremacy. Thomas Walford Grieve entered the family concern in 1862, and thereafter "the announcement that the scenery for any piece was by Grieve and son was a sufficient guarantee of the excellence of the work", the mainstay of which continued to be spectacular pieces for Covent Garden and Drury Lane, though they also supplied Charles Fechter's management at the Lyceum and other theatres. Thomas Walford finally sold his interest in the Grieve workshop in Macklin Street in 1887, but the building remains in similar use to this day, though altered internally.

—Pieter van der Merwe

GRIMALDI, Joseph. British actor. Born in Clare Market, London, 18 December 1778; grandson of Italian dancer John Baptist 'Iron Legs' Grimaldi, and illegitimate son of dancer and Pantaloon actor Giuseppe Grimaldi. Educated at Mr Ford's Boarding School, Putney. Married 1) Maria Hughes in 1798 (died 1800); 2) actress Mary Bristow in 1802 (died 1835), one son. Stage debut at the age of two, Sadler's Wells Theatre, London, 1781; became popular child performer with his father, at both Sadler's Wells and the Theatre Royal, Drury Lane, where he first appeared in 1782; established unsurpassed reputation as transformed pantomime clown from 1800; actor, Covent Garden, 1806–23; also made numerous provincial tours and visited Dublin; left Sadler's Wells, 1816, but returned on acquiring share in the theatre, 1818; crippled by injuries received during career, by 1823; appointed assistant manager, Sadler's Wells Theatre, 1825; farewell appearances, Covent Garden and Drury Lane, 1828. Died in London, 31 May 1837.

Roles

1794   Dwarf in *Valentine and Orson* (T. Dibdin), Sadler's Wells Theatre, London.

Morad in *The Talisman of Orosmanes; or, Harlequin Made Happy* (anon.), Sadler's Wells Theatre, London.

1796   Pero in *Robinson Crusoe* (Sheridan), Theatre Royal, Drury Lane, London.

1799   Countryman in *A Trip to Scarborough* (Sheridan), Theatre Royal, Drury Lane, London.

Maid in *Rule a Wife and Have a Wife* (Beaumont and Fletcher), Theatre Royal, Drury Lane, London.

Camazin in *Lodoiska* (J. P. Kemble), Theatre Royal, Drury Lane, London.

1800   Guzzle, The Drinking Clown in *Peter Wilkins; or, Harlequin in the Flying World* (C. Dibdin), Sadler's Wells Theatre, London.

Officer in *The Wheel of Fortune* (Cumberland), Theatre Royal, Drury Lane, London.

Jew Pedlar in *The Indian* (anon.), Theatre Royal, Drury Lane, London.

Second Gravedigger in *Hamlet* (Shakespeare), Theatre Royal, Drury Lane, London.

1801   Punch and Clown in *Harlequin Amulet; or, The Magick of Mona* (Powell), Theatre Royal, Drury Lane, London.

Clown in *Harlequin Benedick; or, The Ghost of Mother Shipton* (anon.), Sadler's Wells Theatre, London.

Deperado in *The Great Devil* (C. Dibdin), Sadler's Wells Theatre, London.

1803   Rufo the Robber in *Red Riding Hood* (C. Dibdin), Sadler's Wells Theatre, London.

Pedro in *Cinderella; or, The Little Glass Slipper* (anon.), Theatre Royal, Drury Lane, London.

Sir John Bull in *New Brooms* (C. Dibdin), Sadler's Wells Theatre, London.

1804   Punch in *Old Harlequin's Fireside* (anon.), Theatre Royal, Drury Lane, London.

1805   Pan in *Terpsichore's Return* (D'Egville), Theatre Royal, Drury Lane, London.

1806   Orson in *Valentine and Orson* (T. Dibdin), Covent Garden, London.

Squire Bugle and Clown in *Harlequin Mother Goose; or, The Golden Egg* (T. Dibdin), Covent Garden, London.

1807   Clown in *Harlequin and the Water Kelp* (anon.), Sadler's Wells Theatre, London.

1808   Second Champion in *Bonifacio and Bridgetina* (T. Dibdin), Covent Garden, London.

Clown in *Harlequin in his Element; or, Fire, Water, Earth, and Air* (T. Dibdin), Covent Garden, London.

Baptist in *Raymond and Agnes; or, The Bleeding Nun* (Grosette), Covent Garden, London.

Skirmish in *The Deserter of Naples* (C. Dibdin), Covent Garden, London.

1809   Scaramouch in *Don Juan* (anon.), Covent Garden, London.

The Wild Man in *The Wild Man* (C. Dibdin), Sadler's Wells Theatre, London.

Clown in *Fashion's Fools* (C. Dibdin), Covent Garden, London.

1810   Clown in *Harlequin in Asmodeus; or, Cupid on Crutches* (Farley), Covent Garden, London.

Clown in *The Astrologer; or, Harlequin and Moore's Almanack* (C. Dibdin), Sadler's Wells Theatre, London.

1811   Cayfacattadhri and Clown in *Harlequin and Padmanaba; or, The Golden Fish* (anon.), Covent Garden, London.

Clown in *Bang Up; or, Harlequin Prime* (C. Dibdin), Sadler's Wells Theatre, London.

Bob Acres in *The Rivals* (Sheridan), Covent Garden, London.

Napoleon in *Dulce Domum; or, England the Land of Freedom!* (anon.), Sadler's Wells Theatre, London.

1812   Clown in *Harlequin and the Red Dwarf* (anon.), Covent Garden, London.

Clown in *Fairlop Fair; or, The Genie of the Oak* (anon.), Sadler's Wells Theatre, London.

1813   Kasrac in *Aladdin* (Farley), Covent Garden, London.

1814   Clown in *The Rival Genii; or, Harlequin Wild Man* (anon.), Sadler's Wells Theatre, London.

Dame Cicely Suett in *Harlequin Whittington, Lord Mayor of London* (Farley), Covent Garden, London.

1815   Munchikoff and Clown in *Harlequin and Fortunio* (Farley), Covent Garden, London.

1816   Clown in *Harlequin and the Sylph of the Oak; or, The Blind Beggar of Bethnal Green* (anon.), Covent Garden, London.

1817   Clown in *Harlequin Gulliver; or, The Flying Island* (anon.), Covent Garden, London.

1818   Clown in *The Elements; or, Where is Harlequin?* (anon.), Sadler's Wells Theatre, London.

Fairy Grimalkin in *The Marquis de Carabas; or, Puss in Boots* (anon.), Covent Garden, London.

My Lord Humpy Dandy in *Harlequin Munchausen; or, The Fountains of Love* (Farley), Covent Garden, London.

Sancho Panza in *Harlequin and Don Quixote; or Sancho Panza in his Glory* (Farley), Covent Garden, London.

1819   Clown in *The Talking Bird; or, Perizade Columbine* (compilation), Covent Garden, London.

1820   Clown in *Harlequin and Cinderella* (anon.), Covent Garden, London.

Clown in *Scraps; or, Fun for the Gallery!* (compilation), Covent Garden, London.

Miles and Clown in *Harlequin and Friar Bacon; or, The Brazen Head* (Farley), Covent Garden, London.

1821   Clown in *Harlequin and Mother Bunch; or, The Yellow Dwarf* (anon.), Covent Garden, London.

1822   Clown in *Harlequin and the Ogress; or, The Sleeping Beauty of the Wood* (Farley), Covent Garden, London.

Joseph Grimaldi in *The Red Dwarf* (c. 1811).

Tycobrec in *The Vision of the Sun; or, The Orphan of Peru* (Farley), Covent Garden, London.

Other roles included: Friday in *Robinson Crusoe* (Sheridan); Kanko in *La Pérouse* (Fawcett); Ravin in *Ko and Zoa* (C. Dibdin); and roles in *The Ogre and Little Thumb; or, The Seven League Boots* (anon.), Covent Garden, London, 1807; *Sadak and Kalasrade* (Farley), Sadler's Wells Theatre, London, 1814; *Undine; or, The Spirit of the Waters* (Soane), Covent Garden, London, 1821.

*

Bibliography

Books:
Charles Dickens, *The Memoirs of Joseph Grimaldi*, 2 vols., London, 1838; edited by Richard Findlater, 1968.
Henry Downes Miles, *A Life of Grimaldi*, London, 1838.
Richard Findlater, *Grimaldi: King of Clowns*, London, 1955; revised edtion, Cambridge, 1978.
David Mayer, *Harlequin in his Element*, Cambridge, Massachusetts, 1969.
Giles Neville, *Incidents in the Life of Joseph Grimaldi*, London, 1980.

Articles:
A. Cervellati, "Il clown, maschera moderna. Vita di Joe Grimaldi", *Progresso d'Italia*, 1949.

* * *

In Shakespearean usage a 'Clown' was a rustic made comic by his uncouth and oafish ways. The current image of the clown as a mischievous, energetic red-and-white coloured creature, saucy and outrageous, was first promulgated by Joseph Grimaldi and circus folks have called a clown a 'Joey' in his honour ever since. Grimaldi was the latest in a dynasty of popular entertainers: his grandfather John Baptist 'Iron Legs' Grimaldi (otherwise known as Nicolini) and his father Giuseppe Grimaldi, who was noted for his agility and manners, performed in the relatively novel genre of pantomime, in which Joseph Grimaldi would become famous. The English pantomime evolved in the early 18th century and was bipartite in structure, the first part telling a story based on classical mythology or a fairy tale, which climaxed in the transformation of the characters into English versions of commedia dell'arte figures, notably Harlequin, Columbine, Pantaloon, and Clown, who then engaged in a mute, balletic, knockabout 'harlequinade'.

Young Joe underwent the customary initiation as a theatrical child, playing sprites and fairies. He made his debut at Sadler's Wells and Drury Lane at the age of four under the less than kindly eye of his father, who much mistreated him. Once, when impersonating a monkey to his father's Clown, the chain on which he was being swung broke and he was tossed into the audience, fortunately without mishap. For years he played villains and comics without much distinction, though he was praised by the press for his acrobatic fights and stunts. His first real acclaim came with the role of Clown in *Peter Wilkins; or, Harlequin in the Flying World* in 1800, in which he wore a costume more extravagant and motley than was usual and, instead of the usual ruddy complexion, a white face with two red half-moons on the cheek.

Grimaldi's great opportunity came in 1805 in the Covent Garden pantomime *Harlequin and Mother Goose; or, The Golden Egg*. The production was shabby judged by the spectacular standards of the time, with no impressive scenery or costumes and scant rehearsal time. Yet it proved to be such a hit that it made £20,000 for the theatre. Much of this success was due to Grimaldi, whose comic genius shone all the more brightly without the distraction of elaborate sets and effects. In the first part he played Squire Bugle, a bullying farmer who wooed Mother Goose's daughter; then, in the second part, he was transformed into Clown and dominated the stage with his extravagant lunacy. His white-floured face with enormous red mouth and red patches on the cheeks left the impression of an urchin who had been messing about in a jam jar and strange blue tufts erupted disconcertingly from his otherwise bald head. His countenance was in constant motion — the huge round eyes goggling and ogling, the turned-up nose pointed in all directions, the mouth stretching from ear to ear in sheer greed or dropping to his chest in fright. The costume with its buttons and frills, its baggy breeches with deep pockets capable of hiding everything from strings of sausages to live geese, suggested both the truant schoolboy and the braggart captain of Italian comedy.

Avid and amoral, out to glut his appetites, Grimaldi's Clown had the exuberant optimism of the born survivor and much of the fun derived from his overthrow of everyday inhibitions. His opening cry of 'Here we are again' was the signal for a succession of outrageous surprises and in time became the traditional greeting of clowns everywhere. Grimaldi perfected a vast range of tricks and antics: he sat down to a meal only to find the chairs soaring into the air; he cut open a pie and a duck walked out; he played a tune on a tin fish-kettle with a ladle and a whisk. Not least of the attractions were the verbal puns: he stole some letters, read "Sir, I'll trouble you with a line", and pulled out a tiny hangman's noose. Sometimes the puns were visual, employing the skill of the theatre's machinists: one example was the transformation scene in which a touch of Harlequin's bat turned a red-coated soldier (popularly nicknamed a 'lobster') into an actual lobster and back again.

Grimaldi's finest transformations were not magical but 'tricks of construction'. Clown would put together some odd combination of inanimate objects, Harlequin would bring it to life, and it would turn on the dismayed but ludicrous Frankenstein-Grimaldi. If Clown built a boxer out of cabbages and root vegetables, it would fight him off the stage. From a clothes hamper, two broomsticks, a rolling pin, and an umbrella — all stolen — he concocted a coach drawn by two dogs. His hussar's uniform was made up of two coal scuttles for boots, brass plates for spurs, a muff for a shako, and a black tippet for a beard. The army was a frequent butt of his ridicule and Clown would drill his squadron of pots and ale kegs, assembled to look like soldiers on parade. So keen was his satire that the Horse guards demanded a cessation of this exercise.

Much of Grimaldi's skill lay in his relaxed stage personality. Between the strenuous leaping about and popping in and out of trapdoors, he would banter with the audience in the most familiar terms and coax them into joining in the choruses of his celebrated songs 'Hot Codlins' and 'Tippiti-witchet'. Like a baby, Clown wanted whatever he saw and snatched whatever was in reach; when thwarted, he would hit a policeman or knock someone into a horsepond and then blame it on an innocent bystander. Clown's appetites were open and gross and his frank delinquency contagious, but his misdeeds were readily excused by his zest and good nature. The audience became an accomplice. "If he took physic," wrote *The Times*, "the moment he poured it out, we were sure it was salts — if he took a red-hot poker to anybody, we never could interfere, though it had been to save our father — and when he stole apples, we really doubted whether common honesty was not a kind of prejudice." Lord High Chancellor Eldon himself exclaimed: "Never, never did I see a leg of mutton stolen with such superhumanly sublime impudence as by that man".

Despite his popularity and the great influence of his incarnation of Clown, Grimaldi knew little happiness in his personal life. He groomed his only son Joseph (1802–32) to portray Clown in his footsteps, but the boy was irresponsible and died young of alcoholism. Grimaldi's limbs, once tireless and powerful, suffered from cramps and rheumatism brought on from years spent in draughty theatres, exacerbated by the many injuries he suffered. In his later years, stagehands waited in the wings to massage his legs when he made his exit, but by 1823 he was virtually crippled. Eventually, in 1828, when he gave two farewell performances at Sadler's Wells and Drury Lane, he had to play seated in a chair and conceded to his still-adoring public: "I am worse on my feet that I used to be on my head. It is four years since I jumped my last jump — filched my last oyster — boiled by last sausage — and set in for retirement". His last days were, as he is purported to have said, "grim-all-day". His memoirs, the manuscript of which is presently in a private collection, were edited by Charles Dickens in 1838. His grave in Pentonville is honoured annually by a conventicle of clowns.

—Laurence Senelick

GROTOWSKI, Jerzy. Polish director. Born in Rzezów, Poland, 11 August 1933. Trained for the stage at the National Advanced School of Theatre, Cracow, and in Moscow, 1951–55. Directed at the Teatr Stary, Cracow, 1957–59; lecturer, National Theatrical Academy, Cracow, 1959; founder, 1959, with critic Ludwik Flaszen, and director, 1959–64, of the Theatre of 13 Rows, Opole; renamed the company the Teatr Laboratorium [Laboratory Theatre] on its transfer to Wrocław, 1965; worked with the Royal Shakespeare Company in London, 1966, and at New York University; also ran courses for actors at the Odin Teatret, Hostebro, Denmark, 1966–69, and at Stockholm, from 1966; director, Ecole Supérieure d'Art Dramatique,

Aix-en-Provence, 1968–70; continued to lead the Laboratory Theatre until its disbanding in 1976; has since worked privately, usually without audiences; director, University of Explorations of Theatre of the Nations, Wrocław, from 1975; left Poland during the period of martial law, 1981–82, and settled in the USA; subsequently associated with the University of California (Irvine), 1983–86; director, Centro di Lavoro di Jerzy Grotowski in Pontedera, Italy, since 1986. Honorary Foreign Member, American Academy of Arts and Sciences, 1987. Recipient: Golden Prize, International Festival of Theatres, Belgrade, 1967; Ministry of Culture of Poland Award for Research into Pedagogics, 1967; Drama Desk Award, New York, 1969–70; Award of Polish Ministry of Foreign Affairs, 1970; State Prize, 1972; Smithsonian Institute Diploma, 1973; Honorary Citizen, Pontedera, 1986; McArthur Fellowship, 1991. Honorary doctorate: Wrocław, 1991. Knight's Cross, Order Polonia Restituta, 1974; Officer's Cross, Order Polonia Restituta, 1979; Commander, Ordre des Arts et Lettres (France), 1989.

Principal productions

Stage productions:
1960   *Cain* (Lord Byron), Theatre of 13 Rows, Opole.
Faust (Goethe), Theatre of 13 Rows, Opole.
Mystery-Bouffe (Mayakovsky), Theatre of 13 Rows, Opole.
Shakuntala (Kalidasa), Theatre of 13 Rows, Opole.
1961   *Dziady* [Forefathers' Eve] (Mickiewicz), Theatre of 13 Rows, Opole.
1962   *Kordian* (Słowacki), Theatre of 13 Rows, Opole.
1962–69 *Akropolis* (Wyspiański), Theatre of 13 Rows, Opole.
1963–64 *Tragical History of Doctor Faustus* (adapted from Marlowe), Theatre of 13 Rows, Opole.
1964   *Hamlet* (Shakespeare), Theatre of 13 Rows, Opole.
1965–70 *El Principe Constante* (adapted from Słwacki and Calderón), Teatr Laboratorium, Wrocław.
1968–81 *Apocalypsis cum figuris* (adapted from the Bible, Eliot, Dostoevsky and Weil), Teatr Laboratorium, Wrocław.

Research projects:
Holiday (Grotowski), 1971–74; *The Research University*, 1975; *The Mountain Project*, 1976–77; *Theatre of Sources*, 1977–82; *Objective Drama*, University of California, Irvine, 1983–86; *Workcentre Grotowski (Ritual Arts)*, since 1985.

Publications

Towards a Poor Theatre, 1968; *Le Jour Saint et les autres textes*, 1974; *Tecniche Originaire dell'Attore*, 1983; *Teksty z lat* [Text and Performer], 1990.

*

Bibliography

Books:
Raymonde Temkine, translated by Alex Szogyi, *Grotowski*, 1968.
Tadeusz Burzynski and Zbigniew Osiński, *Grotowski's Laboratory*, Warsaw, 1979.
Jennifer Kumiega, *The Theatre of Grotowski*, London, 1985.
Barbara Schwerin von Krosigh, *Der nackte Schauspieler: Die Entwicklung der Theatertheorie Jerzy Grotowski*, 1986.

* * *

Jerzy Grotowski has been acclaimed by many as the most significant theatrical innovator of the last half of the 20th century. His work is thus often compared with that of Stanislavsky, Copeau, Artaud and Brecht. Grotowski from the late 1950's into the 1990's has ranged in his explorations from theatre to paratheatre to active culture, source theatre and objective drama. In 1980, the critic August Grodzicki estimated that the worldwide bilbiography on Grotowski and the Polish Laboratory Theatre included more than 10,000 items.

Through the book *Towards a Poor Theatre*, edited by Eugenio Barba, and its subsequent publication in many languages, Grotowski's innovative ideas on actor training, use of actor/audience space and treatment of text became widely disseminated. Grotowski turned away from some of these methods in later years, as he proceeded into 'paratheatrical experiences' and 'active culture'. Nonetheless, the fundamentals of these techniques continue to be taught in most up-to-date actor-training programmes throughout the world.

In *Towards a Poor Theatre*, Grotowski spoke of a minimalist theatre that is the antithesis of the traditional 'rich' theatre. The 'rich' theatre is dependent upon spectacle and technology, seeking to approximate what might better be accomplished by film and television. Grotowski's poor theatre, on the other hand, sought through only basic essentials — the actor, the audience and a minimum of scenic elements and properties — to confront the spectator with archetypal images and myths in a contemporary context. While the poor theatre is akin to ceremony and ritual, it accomplishes efficacy without the traditional religious underpinnings. Though images from traditional religion may appear obliquely — the sufferings of Christ, the Second Coming, Lazarus rising from the dead, etc. — such images in Grotowski's productions often reflected as well the archetypes of 20th-century culture: the psychiatric ward (Słowacki's *Kordian*), the concentration camp (Wyspiański's *Akropolis*), a way station or gaol cell for drunks sobering up (*Apocalypsis cum figuris*).

To accomplish this confrontation for the audience member or 'witness', Grotowski spoke of the necessity of the 'holy actor': "I speak about 'holiness' as an unbeliever. I mean a secular 'holiness'". In performance, if one is such an actor, said Grotowski, "one must give oneself totally, in one's deepest intimacy, with confidence, as when one gives oneself in love". Such an actor performs a process of 'self donation' before the audience, working through the principle of 'via negativa', in other words, through the elimination of blocks to the creative employment of body, voice and mind.

To achieve such ends, Grotowski developed many rigorous physical, vocal and psychological exercises for the actor. But always the improvisational base stood as a principle of creative exploration. At first, few performers other than those of Grotowski's company were able to achieve such discipline. As a result, many actors from all over the world flocked to the Laboratory Theatre to study Grotowski's methods directly.

Ryszard Cieślak was Grotowski's prime example of the 'holy actor'. In such productions as *The Constant Prince*, in which Cieślak performed the role of Don Fernando, and *Apocalypsis cum figuris*, where he played the village idiot/returned saviour, Cieślak's 'total act' of vulnerability and giving as a performer achieved Grotowski's goal of 'self donation'. And in *Apocalypsis cum figuris* particularly, other members of the company — Antoni Jahołkowski, Elizabeth Cynkutis, Rena Mirecka, Elizabeth Albahaca, Zygmunt Molik and Stanisław Ścierski — also acheived this ideal. Consequently, *Apocalypsis* was lauded by critics internationally as Grotowski's theatrical masterpiece.

Despite Grotowski's mounting world acclaim as a theatrical director, in the early 1970's he 'excited' the theatre per se to pursue other closely related projects in 'paratheatrical experiences' and 'active culture'. Such activities eliminated the traditional separations between performers and spectators and were based on improvisational artistic interactions among groups of outsiders and company members for varying lengths of time up to several weeks.

Early in his work, Grotowski had been struck by the model of the Bohr Institute for physicists in Copenhagen, where advanced researchers came together to pool their knowledge. This is what he also sought to do in his subsequent projects from the mid-1970's into the 1990's. At the *Research University* in summer 1975, numerous improvisational 'ule' or 'beehives' were conducted by members of the Laboratory Theatre with large groups of theatrical workers, artists, social scientists, journalists, and so on from many parts of the world. *The Mountain Project* and *Tree of People* brought together outsiders and company members for more extended periods of exploration. In *Objective Drama*, which Grotowski conducted for several years in the mid-1980's at the University of California, Irvine, groups of outsiders were invited to work improvisationally with a team of 'technical specialists' (highly qualified performing artists from the Far East and South America) and university students. Each outsider was individually trained in the afternoon in 'The Motions', a complicated series of physically difficult ritualistic body positions and movements oriented on the position of the sun. At sunset, the total group of about 40 participants moved out onto a vast, hilly prairie and performed 'The Motions'. Throughout the night and eventually early morning, a series of improvisational activities occurred, culminating in the entire group once again at sunrise performing 'The Motions' on the topmost hill.

By 1990, Grotowski's work was focused both in California and at the Centre di Lavoro de Jerzy Grotowski in Pontedera, Italy.

—Robert Findlay

GRÜNDGENS, Gustaf. German actor and director. Born in Düsseldorf, 22 December 1899. Educated at Catholic boarding school from 1913; trained for the theatre at the Luise Dumont-Gustav Lindemann drama school, Düsseldorf. Married 1) Erika Mann in 1926 (divorced 1929); 2) actress Marianne Hoppe in 1934 (divorced 1945). Stage debut, after army service, at Saarbrücken, 1918; subsequently acted in a variety of minor parts throughout the German provinces, appearing in Halberstadt, Kiel, and at the Kammerspiele, Hamburg, until he was invited to Berlin by Max Reinhardt; worked as a director under Reinhardt at the Deutsches Theater until 1932, also winning acclaim in leading romantic roles and in Shaw and Shakespeare; appointed Intendant of the Prussian theatres by Hermann Göring, 1932, and promoted to Generalintendant, 1937; director, Staatstheater, Berlin, 1934–44, Deutsches Theater, Berlin, 1946–47, Städtische Bühnen, Düsseldorf, 1947–51, and Deutsches Schauspielhaus, Hamburg, 1955–62, also worked in films. Died in Manila (overdose of sleeping pills), 7 October 1963.

Productions

As actor:

1918   Philipp in *Jugendfreunde* (Fulda), Fronttheater, Saarbrücken.

Schüler in *Faust I* (Goethe), Fronttheater, Saarbrücken.

1919   Mephisto in *Faust I* (Goethe), Fronttheater, Saarbrücken; Vereinigte Städtische Theater, Kiel, 1922; Schauspielhaus am Gendarmenmarkt, Berlin, 1932 and 1941; Edinburgh Festival, 1948; Städtische Bühnen, Düsseldorf, 1949 and 1952; Deutsches Schauspielhaus, Hamburg, 1957; Städtische Bühnen, Düsseldorf, 1958.

1920   Paoulet in *Maria Stuart* (Schiller), Städttische Bühnen, Halberstadt.

Schäfer in *Wintermärchen* (Shakespeare), Städttische Bühnen, Halberstadt.

Max in *Anatol* (Schnitzler), Städttische Bühnen, Halberstadt.

Pastor Manders in *Gespenster* (Ibsen), Städttische Bühnen, Halberstadt.

Macchiavell in *Egmont* (Goethe), Städttische Bühnen, Halberstadt.

1921   Amynth in *Die Hochzeit der Schäferin* (Lahusen), Städttische Bühnen, Halberstadt.

Alexander Mill in *Candida* (G. B. Shaw), Städttische Bühnen, Halberstadt.

Waldschrat in *Die versunkene Glocke* (Hauptmann), Vereinigte Städtische Theater, Kiel.

Oberhofzeremonienmeister in *Der König* (Johst), Vereinigte Städtische Theater, Kiel.

Fürst von Klausthal-Agordo in *Die fünf Frankfurter* (Rössler), Vereinigte Städtische Theater, Kiel.

1922   Weislingen in *Götz von Berlichingen* (Goethe), Vereinigte Städtische Theater, Kiel.

Atalus in *Weh dem, der lügt* (Grillparzer), Vereinigte Städtische Theater, Kiel.

Graf Mancini in *Der, der di Maulschellen kriegt* (Andreyev), Vereinigte Städtische Theater, Kiel.

Der Chevalier in *Der verwandelte Komödiant* (Zweig), Vereinigte Städtische Theater, Kiel.

Fred O'Brixor in *Varieté* (Mann), Vereinigte Städtische Theater, Kiel.

Schlenker in *Schlemihl* (Zinn), Vereinigte Städtische Theater, Kiel.

Sascha in *Schrei aus der Strasse* (Laucker), Theater in der Kommandantenstrasse, Berlin.

1923   Maler in *Der Clown Gottes* (Philipp), Kammerspiele, Hamburg.

Priest in *Und das Licht scheinet in der Finsternis* (Tolstoy), Kammerspiele, Hamburg.

Geisterbeschwörer in *Die Komödie der Irrungen* (Shakespeare), Kammerspiele, Hamburg.

Ago von Bohna in *Das Fossil* (Sternheim), Kammerspiele, Hamburg.

Narrator in *Von Geistern und Gespenstern*, Kammerspiele, Hamburg.

First Man in *Nebendeinander* (Kaiser), Kammerspiele, Hamburg.

Mastyx in *Der ewige Traum* (Kornfeld), Kammerspiele, Hamburg.

1924   Guldenzier in *Blindermanns Weltlauf* (Walter), Kammerspiele, Hamburg.

Grimaldi in *Die Zwillinge* (Klinger), Kammerspiele, Hamburg.

Ssawelow in *Der Gedanke* (Andreyev), Kammerspiele, Hamburg.

Matrose in *Die Fahrt nach Orplid* (Schmidtbonn), Kammerspiele, Hamburg.

Palme in *Palme oder Der Gekränkte* (Kornfeld), Kammerspiele, Hamburg.

Bogoboj in *Bocksgesang* (Werfel), Kammerspiele, Hamburg.

Narrator in *Erotiker*, Kammerspiele, Hamburg.

Albert Becher in *Hans Sonnenstössers Höllenfahrt* (Apel), Kammerspiele, Hamburg.

Hyazinth in *Belinde* (Eulenberg), Kammerspiele, Hamburg.

Lord Stonbury in *Der Faun* (Knoblauch), Kammerspiele, Hamburg.

Baron Gard in *Prozess Bunterbart* (Brod), Kammerspiele, Hamburg.

Herzog in *Franziska* (Wedekind), Kammerspiele, Hamburg.

Xavier in *Geschäft ist Geschäft* (Mirbeau), Kammerspiele, Hamburg.

Andreas von Bleichenwang in *Was ihr Wollt* (Shakespeare), Kammerspiele, Hamburg.

Joseph in *Herodes und Mariamne* (Hebbel), Kammerspiele, Hamburg.

Acke in *Kolportage* (Kaiser), Kammerspiele, Hamburg.

Gley in *Komödie der Worte* (Schnitzler), Kammerspiele, Hamburg.

Der Versucher in *Nach Damaskus* (Strindberg), Kammerspiele, Hamburg.

Thamal in *Spiegelmensch* (Werfel), Kammerspiele, Hamburg.

1925   Pao in *Kreidekreis* (Klabund), Kammerspiele, Hamburg.

Günther in *Hassberg oder: Die neuen Karamasoffs* (Sakheim), Kammerspiele, Hamburg.

Bluntschli in *Helden* (G. B. Shaw), Kammerspiele, Hamburg.

Hettore Gonzaga in *Emilia Galotti* (Lessing), Kammerspiele, Hamburg; Schauspielhaus am Gendarmenmarkt, Berlin, 1937.

Wilde in *Oscar Wilde* (Sternheim), Kammerspiele, Hamburg.

Dr Jura in *Das Konzert* (Bahr), Kammerspiele, Hamburg; Schauspielhaus am Gendarmenmarkt, Berlin, 1933 and 1942.

Christian Maske in *Der Snob* (Sternheim), Kammerspiele, Hamburg; revived there, 1928; Deutsches Theater, Berlin, 1946; Städtische Bühnen, Düsseldorf, 1948.

Prinz Leonce in *Leonce und Lena* (Büchner), Kammerspiele, Hamburg.

Angelo in *Mass für Mass* (Shakespeare), Kammerspiele, Hamburg.

Der Tod in *Der Teufelspakt* (Klabund), Kammerspiele, Hamburg.

John Tanner in *Mensch und Übermensch* (G. B. Shaw), Kammerspiele, Hamburg.

1926   Zeckerdie in *Regina im Glas* (Palitzsch), Kammerspiele, Hamburg.

Jaques in *Wie es euch gefällt* (Shakespeare), Kammerspiele, Hamburg.

Sawin in *Sturmflut* (Paquet), Kammerspiele, Hamburg.

Algernon in *Bunbury* (Wilde), Kammerspiele, Hamburg.

Cederström in *Duell am Lido* (Rehfisch), Kammerspiele, Hamburg.

Kalaf, Prinz von Astrachan in *Turandot* (Gozzi and Schiller), Kammerspiele, Hamburg.

Aristeus and Pluto in *Orpheus in der Unterwelt* (Grimieux), Kammerspiele, Hamburg.

Florindo in *Cristinas Heimreise* (Hofmannsthal), Theater in der Josefstadt, Vienna.

1927   Aimwell in *Die zwei Abenteurer* (Farquhar, adapted by Zoff), Kammerspiele, Hamburg.

Kaspar Hauser in *Kaspar Hauser* (Ebermeyer), Kammerspiele, Hamburg.

Advokat in *Traumspiel* (Strindberg), Kammerspiele, Hamburg.

Bertram in *Robert und Bertram oder Die lustigen Vagabunden* (Räder), Kammerspiele, Hamburg.

Allan in *Revue zu Vieren* (Mann), Kammerspiele, Hamburg.

Ernest Ollier in *Papiermühle* (Kaiser), Kammerspiele, Hamburg.

Cäsar in *Cäsar und Cleopatra* (G. B. Shaw), Kammerspiele, Hamburg; Städtische Bühnen, Düsseldorf, 1959.

Hamlet in *Hamlet* (Shakespeare), Kammerspiele, Hamburg; Schauspielhaus am Gendarmenmarkt, Berlin, 1935; Kronborg Castle, Denmark, 1938; Städtische Bühnen, Düsseldorf, 1949.

Alonzo in *Blauer Dunst* (Paul), Kammerspiele, Hamburg.

Eugen Marchbanks in *Candida* (G. B. Shaw), Kammerspiele, Hamburg.

1928 Danton in *Dantons Tod* (Büchner), Kammerspiele, Hamburg.

Jean-Marc-Marrien in *Oktobertag* (Kaiser), Kammerspiele, Hamburg.

Narrator in *Die schöne Magelone* (Tieck), Kammerspiele, Hamburg.

Fernand Jolivet in *Der Unwiderstehliche* (Geraldy and Spitzer), Deutsches Theater, Berlin.

Ottfried in *Die Verbrecher* (Bruckner), Deutsches Theater, Berlin, and Theater in der Josefstadt, Vienna.

Alfremow in *Der lebende Leichnam* (Tolstoy), Berliner Theater, Berlin.

1929 Role in *Die oberen Zehntausend* (Maugham and Pogson), Theater in der Josefstadt, Vienna.

Pistol in *Die lustigen Weiber von Windsor* (Shakespeare), Deutsches Theater, Berlin.

Herzog von Bristol in *Zur gefl Ansicht* (Lonsdale and Berstl), Kammerspiele, Berlin.

1930 Frederick in *Victoria* (Maugham), Komödie, Berlin.

Grossherzog in *Haus Danieli* (Neumann), Lessing-Theater, Berlin.

Orest in *Iphigenie auf Tauris* (Goethe), Deutsches Theater, Berlin; Schauspielhaus am Gendarmenmarkt, Berlin, 1943.

Role in *Elga* (Hauptmann), Deutsches Theater, Berlin.

1931 Role in *Alles Schwindel* (Schiffer), Theater am Kurfürstendamm, Berlin.

Bacon in *Elisabeth von England* (Bruckner), Deutsches Theater, Berlin.

Lord John Lonsdale in *Der Domptoir* (Savoir), Theater am Schiffbauerdamm, Berlin.

Hofmarschall von Kalb in *Kabale und Liebe* (Schiller), Deutsches Theater, Berlin.

1933 Mephisto, Geiz and Phorkyas in *Faust II* (Goethe), Schauspielhaus am Gendarmenmarkt, Berlin; revived there, 1942.

Bolingbroke in *Das Glas Wasser* (Scribe), Schauspielhaus am Gendarmenmarkt, Berlin.

1934 Der König in *Friedrich der Grosse* (Boetticher), Schauspielhaus am Gendarmenmarkt, Berlin.

Fouché in *Hundert Tage* (Mussolini and Forzano), Schauspielhaus am Gendarmenmarkt, Berlin.

Riccaut de la Marlinière in *Minna von Barnhelm* (Lessing), Schauspielhaus am Gendarmenmarkt, Berlin.

1935 Jack Warren in *Himmel auf Erden* (Huth), Schauspielhaus am Gendarmenmarkt, Berlin.

Ludwig Capet in *Thomas Paine* (Johst), Schauspielhaus am Gendarmenmarkt, Berlin.

Hans Sonnenstosser in *Hans Sonnenstossers Höllenfahrt* (Apel), Schauspielhaus am Gendarmenmarkt, Berlin.

Don Juan in *Don Juan und Faust* (Grabbe), Schauspielhaus am Gendarmenmarkt, Berlin.

1937 Louis Dubedat in *Der Arzt am Scheideweg* (G. B. Shaw), Schauspielhaus am Gendarmenmarkt, Berlin.

1938 Friedrich der Grosse in *Der Siebenjährige Kriege* (Rehberg), Schauspielhaus am Gendarmenmarkt, Berlin.

1939 Richard II in *Richard II* (Shakespeare), Schauspielhaus am Gendarmenmarkt, Berlin.

St Just in *Dantons Tod* (Büchner), Schauspielhaus am Gendarmenmarkt, Berlin.

1940 Fiesco in *Die Verschwörung des Fiesco zu Genua* (Schiller), Schauspielhaus am Gendarmenmarkt, Berlin.

Lukull in *Kirschen für Rom* (Hömberg), Schauspielhaus am Gendarmenmarkt, Berlin; Städtische Bühnen, Düsseldorf, 1954.

1941 Julius Caesar in *Julius Caesar* (Shakespeare), Schauspielhaus am Gendarmenmarkt, Berlin.

Alexander in *Alexander* (Baumann), Schauspielhaus am Gendarmenmarkt, Berlin.

1943 Franz Moor in *Die Räuber* (Schiller), Schauspielhaus am Gendarmenmarkt, Berlin; Städtische Bühnen, Düsseldorf, 1951.

1946 Vassili Michailowitsch Worobjow in *Stürmischer Lebensabend* (Rachmaninov), Deutsches Theater, Berlin.

Oedipus in *König Oedipus* (Sophocles and Weinstock), Deutsches Theater, Berlin, and Städtische Bühnen, Düsseldorf.

1947 Marquis von Keith in *Der Marquis von Keith* (Wedekind), Deutsches Theater, Berlin.

Orest in *Die Fliegen* (Sartre), Städtische Bühnen, Düsseldorf.

1948 Trigórin in *Die Möwe* (Chekhov), Städtische Bühnen, Düsseldorf.

1949 Tasso in *Torquato Tasso* (Goethe), Städtische Bühnen, Düsseldorf.

Sir Robert Morton in *Der Fall Winslow* (Rattigan), Städtische Bühnen, Düsseldorf.

1950 Josef K in *Der Prozess* (Kafka, adapted by Gide and Barrault), Städtische Bühnen, Düsseldorf.

Sir Henry Harcourt-Reilly in *Die Cocktail Party* (Eliot), Städtische Bühnen, Düsseldorf.

1952 Heinrich IV in *Heinrich IV* (Pirandello), Städtische Bühnen, Düsseldorf.

Kardinal Zampi in *Bacchus* (Cocteau), Städtische Bühnen, Düsseldorf.

1953 Wallenstein in *Wallensteins Tod* (Schiller), Städtische Bühnen, Düsseldorf; Deutsches Schauspielhaus, Hamburg, 1955.

General Ramsay in *Herrenhaus* (Wolfe), Städtische Bühnen, Düsseldorf; Deutsches Schauspielhaus, Hamburg, 1956.

1955 Ruppert Forster in *Marschlied* (Whiting), Städtische Bühnen, Düsseldorf.

1956 Cliff Clifford in *Nichts Neues aus Hollywood* (Goetz), Städtische Bühnen, Düsseldorf.

1957 Archie Rice in *Der Entertainer* (Osborne), Städtische Bühnen, Düsseldorf.

1960 Kandaules in *Gyges und sein Ring* (Hebbel), Städtische Bühnen, Düsseldorf.

Prospero in *Der Sturm* (Shakespeare), Städtische Bühnen, Düsseldorf.

1962   Albert Heink in *Das Konzert* (Bahr), Städtische Bühnen, Düsseldorf.

Philipp II in *Don Carlos* (Schiller), Städtische Bühnen, Düsseldorf.

As director:

1921   *Die Hochzeit der Schäferin* (Lahusen), Städttische Bühnen, Halberstadt.

1924   *Geschäft ist Geschäft* (Mirbeau), Kammerspiele, Hamburg.

Kolportage (Kaiser), Kammerspiele, Hamburg.

Komödie um Rosa (Angermayer), Kammerspiele, Hamburg.

1925   *Helden* (G. B. Shaw), Kammerspiele, Hamburg.

Das Konzert (Bahr), Kammerspiele, Hamburg.

Leonce und Lena (Büchner), Kammerspiele, Hamburg.

1926   *Regina im Glas* (Palitzsch), Kammerspiele, Hamburg.

Die zärtlichen Verwandten (Benedix), Kammerspiele, Hamburg.

Frühlingserwachen (Wedekind), Kammerspiele, Hamburg.

Bunbury (Wilde), Kammerspiele, Hamburg.

Androklus und der Löwe (G. B. Shaw), Kammerspiele, Hamburg.

Orpheus in der Unterwelt (Grimieux), Kammerspiele, Hamburg.

1927   *Traumspiel* (Strindberg), Kammerspiele, Hamburg.

Robert und Bertram oder Die lustigen Vagabunden (Räder), Kammerspiele, Hamburg.

Revue zu Vieren (Mann), Kammerspiele, Hamburg.

Papiermühle (Kaiser), Kammerspiele, Hamburg.

Cäsar und Cleopatra (G. B. Shaw), Kammerspiele, Hamburg.

Blauer Dunst (Paul), Kammerspiele, Hamburg.

1928   *Dantons Tod* (Büchner), Kammerspiele, Hamburg.

Oktobertag (Kaiser), Kammerspiele, Hamburg.

Pension Schöller (Laufs), Kammerspiele, Hamburg.

Der Snob (Sternheim), Kammerspiele, Hamburg.

Der Unwiderstehliche (Geraldy and Spitzer), Deutsches Theater, Berlin.

1929   *Wann kommst Du wider?* (Maugham and Pogson), Theater in der Josefstadt, Vienna.

Zur gefl Ansicht (Lonsdale and Berstl), Kammerspiele, Berlin.

1930   *Die liebe Feindin* (Antoine and Zuckerkandl), Komödie, Berlin.

Menschen im Hotel (Baum), Theater am Nollendorfplatz, Berlin.

1914 (Müller), Deutsches Theater, Berlin.

Die zärtlichen Verwandten (Benedix), Deutsches Theater, Berlin.

1931   *Pariser Platz 13* (Baum), Deutsches Theater, Berlin.

Alles Schwindel (Schiffer), Theater am Kurfürstendamm, Berlin.

1934   *Rebell in England* (Schwarz), Schauspielhaus am Gendarmenmarkt, Berlin.

Minna von Barnhelm (Lessing), Schauspielhaus am Gendarmenmarkt, Berlin.

König Lear (Shakespeare, adapted by Tieck), Schauspielhaus am Gendarmenmarkt, Berlin.

1935   *Himmel auf Erden* (Huth), Schauspielhaus am Gendarmenmarkt, Berlin.

Egmont (Goethe), Schauspielhaus am Gendarmenmarkt, Berlin.

Gyges und sein Ring (Hebbel), Schauspielhaus am Gendarmenmarkt, Berlin.

1936   *Der Tolle Tag* (Beaumarchais), Schauspielhaus am Gendarmenmarkt, Berlin.

1937   *Was ihr wollt* (Shakespeare), Schauspielhaus am Gendarmenmarkt, Berlin.

Emilia Galotti (Lessing), Schauspielhaus am Gendarmenmarkt, Berlin.

Die Kameliendame (Dumas fils), Schauspielhaus am Gendarmenmarkt, Berlin.

1938   *Der Siebenjährige Kriege* (Rehberg), Schauspielhaus am Gendarmenmarkt, Berlin.

Südfrüchte (Pagnol and Teichs), Schauspielhaus am Gendarmenmarkt, Berlin.

1939   *Die Königin Isabella* (Rehberg), Schauspielhaus am Gendarmenmarkt, Berlin.

Dantons Tod (Büchner), Schauspielhaus am Gendarmenmarkt, Berlin.

1940   *Cavour* (Mussolini and Forzano), Schauspielhaus am Gendarmenmarkt, Berlin.

Wie es euch gefällt (Shakespeare and Schlegel), Schauspielhaus am Gendarmenmarkt, Berlin.

1941   *Alexander* (Baumann), Schauspielhaus am Gendarmenmarkt, Berlin.

Faust I (Goethe), Schauspielhaus am Gendarmenmarkt, Berlin.

Die lustigen Weiber von Windsor (Shakespeare and Schlegel), Schauspielhaus am Gendarmenmarkt, Berlin.

1942   *Faust II* (Goethe), Schauspielhaus am Gendarmenmarkt, Berlin.

1943   *Die Räuber* (Schiller), Schauspielhaus am Gendarmenmarkt, Berlin.

1946   *Kapitän Brassbounds Bekehrung* (G. B. Shaw), Deutsches Theater, Berlin.

1947   *Der Marquis von Keith* (Wedekind), Deutsches Theater, Berlin.

Der Schatten (Schwarz), Deutsches Theater, Berlin.

Die Fliegen (Sartre), Städtische Bühnen, Düsseldorf.

1948   *Die Möwe* (Chekhov), Städtische Bühnen, Düsseldorf.

Zwei Herren aus Verona (Shakespeare), Städtische Bühnen, Düsseldorf.

Frühlingserwachen (Wedekind), Städtische Bühnen, Düsseldorf.

Der Snob (Sternheim), Städtische Bühnen, Düsseldorf.

1949   *Torquato Tasso* (Goethe), Städtische Bühnen, Düsseldorf.

Faust I (Goethe), Städtische Bühnen, Düsseldorf.

1950   *Der Familientag* (Eliot), Städtische Bühnen, Düsseldorf.

Der Prozess (Kafka, adapted by Gide and Barrault), Städtische Bühnen, Düsseldorf.

Die Cocktail Party (Eliot), Städtische Bühnen, Düsseldorf.

1951   *Die Frau des Bäckers* (Pagnol), Städtische Bühnen, Düsseldorf.

Die Räuber (Schiller), Städtische Bühnen, Düsseldorf.

Wie es euch gefällt (Shakespeare and Schlegel), Städtische Bühnen, Düsseldorf.

Venus im Licht (Fry), Städtische Bühnen, Düsseldorf.

1952   *Der Alpenkönig und der Menschenfeind* (Raimund), Städtische Bühnen, Düsseldorf.

Faust I (Goethe), Städtische Bühnen, Düsseldorf.

Heinrich IV (Pirandello), Städtische Bühnen, Düsseldorf.

Bacchus (Cocteau), Städtische Bühnen, Düsseldorf.

Undine (Giraudoux), Städtische Bühnen, Düsseldorf.

1953   *Der Gasttenmord* (Rehberg), Städtische Bühnen, Düsseldorf.

Herrenhaus (Wolfe), Städtische Bühnen, Düsseldorf.

1954   *Ende gut, alles gut* (Shakespeare), Städtische Bühnen, Düsseldorf.

Der Privatsekretär (Eliot), Städtische Bühnen, Düsseldorf.

Um Lucretia (Giraudoux), Städtische Bühnen, Düsseldorf.

1955   *Marschlied* (Whiting), Städtische Bühnen, Düsseldorf.

Der Drachenthron (Hildesheimer), Städtische Bühnen, Düsseldorf.

Das kalte Licht (Zuckmayer), Städtische Bühnen, Düsseldorf.

Der Privatsekretär (Eliot), Städtische Bühnen, Düsseldorf.

1956   *Herrenhaus* (Wolfe), Städtische Bühnen, Düsseldorf.

Thomas Chatterton (Jahnn), Städtische Bühnen, Düsseldorf.

Nicht Neues aus Hollywood (Goetz), Städtische Bühnen, Düsseldorf.

1957   *Faust I* (Goethe), Städtische Bühnen, Düsseldorf.

Der Entertainer (Osborne), Städtische Bühnen, Düsseldorf.

1958   *Dantons Tod* (Büchner), Städtische Bühnen, Düsseldorf.

Faust II (Goethe), Städtische Bühnen, Düsseldorf.

1959   *Don Juan und Faust* (Goethe), Städtische Bühnen, Düsseldorf.

Die heilige Johanna der Schlachthöfe (Brecht), Städtische Bühnen, Düsseldorf.

Maria Stuart (Schiller), Städtische Bühnen, Düsseldorf.

Cäsar und Cleopatra (G. B. Shaw), Städtische Bühnen, Düsseldorf.

Wallensteins Tod (Schiller), Städtische Bühnen, Düsseldorf.

Sappho (Durrell), Städtische Bühnen, Düsseldorf.

Faust I (Goethe), Leningrad and Moscow.

1960   *Gyges und sein Ring* (Hebbel), Städtische Bühnen, Düsseldorf.

Fräulein Julie (Strindberg), Städtische Bühnen, Düsseldorf.

Von Bergamo bis morgen früh (Waldmann), Städtische Bühnen, Düsseldorf.

1961   *Actis* (Durrell), Städtische Bühnen, Düsseldorf.

Don Gil von den grünen Hosen (Tirso de Molina), Städtische Bühnen, Düsseldorf.

1962   *Das Konzert* (Bahr), Städtische Bühnen, Düsseldorf.

Don Carlos (Schiller), Städtische Bühnen, Düsseldorf.

1963   *Totentanz* (Strindberg), Städtische Bühnen, Düsseldorf.

Hamlet (Shakespeare), Städtische Bühnen, Düsseldorf.

Films

As actor:

Ich Glaub' nie Mehr an eine Frau, 1930; *Der Brand in der Oper*, 1930; *Hokuspokus*, 1930; *Va Banque*, 1930; *M*, 1931; *Der Raub der Mona Lisa*, 1931; *Luise, Königein von Preussen*, 1931; *Die Gräfin von Monte Christo*, 1931; *Yorck*, 1931; *Danton*, 1931; *Teilnehmer antwortet nicht*, 1932; *Eine Stadt steht Kopf*, 1932; *Liebelei*, 1933; *Die Schönen Tage von Aranjuez*, 1933; *Der Tunnel*, 1933; *So Endete eine Liebe*, 1934; *Das Mädchen Johanna*, 1934; *Schwarzer Jäger Johanna*, 1934; *Das Erbe in Pretoria*, 1934; *Hundert Tage*, 1935; *Das Mädchen Johanna*, 1935; *Pygmalion*, 1935; *Eine Frau ohne Bedeutung*, 1936; *Capriolen*, 1937; *Tanz auf dem Vulkan*, 1938; *Der Schritt vom Wege*, 1939; *Ohm Krüger*, 1941; *Friedemann Bach*, 1941; *Das Glas Wasser*, 1960; *Faust I*, 1961.

As director:

Die Finanzen des Grossherzogs, 1934; *Zwei Welten*, 1936; *Capriolan*, 1937.

Publications

Wirklichkeit des Theaters, 1953; *Briefe, Reden, Aufsätze*, 1967.

*

Bibliography

Books:

Alfred Mühr, *Gustaf Gründgens — Aus dem Tagewerk des Schauspielers*, Hamburg, 1943.

Alfred Mühr, *Grosses Theater — Begegnungen mit Gustaf Gründgens*, Berlin, 1950.

Friedrich Luft, *Gustaf Gründgens*, Berlin, 1958.

Rosemarie Clausen, *Theater — Gustaf Grüngens inszeniert*, Hamburg, 1960.

Henning Rischbieter, *Gustaf Gründgens — Schauspieler, Regisseur, Theaterleiter*, Hanover, 1963.

Curt Riess, *Gustaf Gründgens, eine Biographie*, Hamburg, 1965.

Edda Kuehlken, *Die Klassiker-Inszenierungen von Gustaf Gründgens*, Meisenheim, 1972.

Herbert Holba, Günther Knorr, and Peter Spiegel, *Gustaf Gründgens — Filme*, Vienna, 1978.

*   *   *

Gustaf Gründgens first stood on the stage as an amateur with fellow soldiers after he was drafted into the German army at the age of 17. He was an unexceptional student at Luise Dumont's drama school attached to the Düsseldorf Schauspielhaus but drew attention when given leads at the Kammerspiele, Hamburg, among them Marchbanks in Shaw's *Candida*, the title role in Schnitzler's *Anatol* and *Hamlet*. Invited to Berlin by Max Reinhardt, Gründgens played a variety of parts at Reinhardt's Deutsches Theater. He was also called upon to direct opera at the two State operas, the Unter den Linden and the small Kroll Oper, as well as at the Staatsoper. Reinhardt, however, was disappointed with Gründgens as a director and the two parted company in 1932.

Compared with his gradual growth as an actor, Gründgens's skill as director matured quickly. As administrator too he worked at a high level and was exacting in detail, while still focussing on the whole. In 1934 he was appointed by Göring Intendant (and in 1937 Generalintendant) of the Prussian theatres. As an actor he enjoyed success in such pieces as *Minna von Barnhelm*, though he also appeared in many supporting roles. As a director he headed the Staatstheater in Berlin, remodelling it to benefit from greater stage depth and updated technology; thus it was that under his direction the hero of Goethe's *Egmont* could ride on horseback a full 60 metres out of the darkness towards the audience and into bright light. In his third duty as administrator, Gründgens kept on the roster actors and directors who were considered politically questionable because married to Jewish spouses, and he even invited them to bring their wives or husbands with them to the safety of the theatre, especially at night when increasingly arrests and pogroms occurred. Many of his contemporaries have said that his very collaboration with the Nazis saved numerous theatre people from the camps. Above all, Gründgens helped a better German theatre to survive the Nazis and the years of World War II.

Klaus Mann, whose sister Erika was married to and subsequently divorced from Gründgens, presented a less favourable view of Gründgens when he used him as the model for the traitorous Henrik Höfgen in the novel *Mephisto*, though he softened this portrait in the second edition and in time came to deny that he had used the theatre director as his prototype. The book itself was made the subject of an injunction at the suit of Gründgens's adopted son Peter Gorski, and was unavailable in Germany until 1980.

At the end of the war Gründgens came closer to hell in reality than he ever did on stage as Mephisto when he was captured unrecognized by the Soviets and herded from one Russian prison camp to another for nine months, suffering the privations of cold and hunger. He was only traced and released after strenuous efforts by his second wife, actress Marianne Hoppe. He made his comeback with such productions as *Oedipus* and the hitherto forbidden *Drakon*, but did not feel free of surveillance in Berlin and so, in September 1947, unhesitatingly accepted an offer to head the Schauspielhaus in Düsseldorf.

In the red-velvet and gold 19th century interior of the Düsseldorf house, with its antiquated technology, Gründgens again staged a range of classic and contemporary drama. Among his most notable productions were Goethe's *Torquato Tasso*, in which he played Tasso, Schiller's *Wallensteins Tod*, in which he played Wallenstein on the play's 200th anniversary, Sartre's *Die Fliegen*, in which he was partnered by his former wife Marianne Hoppe, and opera. Less successful was John Osborne's *Der Entertainer*, which failed either because he was ill-suited to play the expansive Archie Rice or because the character was simply too British to identify with German audiences.

In 1955 he moved to Hamburg, with its rebuilt and re-equipped theatre, and there found it possible to stage both parts of Goethe's *Faust*, directing as well as playing Mephisto. He now chose to take older roles, among them Shakespeare's Prospero and Schiller's King Philip in *Don Carlos*. His Hamburg *Faust*, meanwhile, was filmed and he was on a world tour of Part I of the triumphant stage production when he died.

No theoretician, Gründgens espoused in his collected essays the belief that the actor and director should, without preconception, go as deep as possible to find the "key idea" of the part or the production within the play itself. No theory, not Stanislavskian empathy nor biomechanical techniques, for instance, dictated such effects as Gründgens's delivery of Mephisophelean monologues from a swing (though skill as a gymnast was employed). Rather his director's invention suggested the device as an inspired means of projecting the character's malicious delight in ensnaring a soul — "I feel like the cat with a mouse" — as he attuned the motion of the swing to the mood of each speech. To complete the effect he favoured a striking appearance, wearing Harlequin tights with a black skull cap and clown's whiteface (in contrast to the red of melodramatic folk drama).

Gründgens was always flexible in his attempts to find expressions for an author's meaning. He showed the same flexibility in the other aspects of his theatrical existence — on the one hand protecting Ernst Busch and other performers from the Nazis and on the other testifying on behalf of Emmy Göring at her trial for participation in Nazi crimes. The one straight course he followed without deviation was his pursuit of great theatre. His sensitivity to language and literature determined his choice of repertory, new and old, native and foreign, and he always resisted propaganda material. He was somewhat limited as an actor, perhaps, being at his best when projecting the ironic intellectual, but as a director his skills were almost boundless, and he succeeding in presenting ever interesting, fine theatre art to German audiences in the most difficult of circumstances.

—Marjorie L. Hoover

GUINNESS, (Sir) Alec. British actor. Born in London, 2 April 1914. Educated at Pembroke Lodge, Southbourne; Roborough, Eastbourne; trained for the stage at the Fay

Compton Studio of Dramatic Art. Married Merula Salaman in 1938, one son. Stage debut, Playhouse, London, 1934; recruited by John Gielgud as actor at the New Theatre, London, 1935; also appeared with the Old Vic company, playing Hamlet for the first time, 1938; served in Royal Navy during World War II, 1941–45; rejoined Old Vic company at New Theatre, London, 1946–48; first speaking role in films, 1946; debut as director, 1948. Fellow, British Academy of Film and Television Arts, 1989. Recipient: Best Actor Award, National Board of Review, 1950, 1957; *Picturegoer* Gold Medal for Most Popular Actor, 1950; Office Catholique Internationale du Cinema Award, 1956; Oscar for Best Actor, 1957; New York Film Critics' Circle Award, 1957; British Film Academy Award, 1957; Golden Globe Award, 1957; Oscar for Best Screenplay, 1958; *Evening Standard* Award, 1960; David O. Selznick Gold Laurel Award, Berlin Film Festival, 1962; *Plays and Players* Award, 1963; Tony Award, 1964; Variety Club Award, 1977; Special Academy Award, 1979; British Academy of Film and Television Arts Award, 1980, 1982; Shakespeare Prize, 1985; Golden Bear Award, Berlin Film Festival, 1988; Society of West End Theatre Special Award, 1989. DFA: Boston College, 1962; D.Litt: University of Oxford, 1977; Litt.D: University of Cambridge, 1991. CBE (Commander of the British Empire), 1955. Knighted, 1959.

Productions

As actor:

1934   Junior Counsel in *Libel!* (Wooll), Playhouse, London.

Chinese Coolie/French Pirate/English Sailor in *Queer Cargo* (Langley), Piccadilly Theatre, London.

Osric/Third Player in *Hamlet* (Shakespeare), New Theatre, London.

1935   The Wolf in *Noah* (Obey, translated by Wilmurt), New Theatre, London.

Sampson/Apothecary in *Romeo and Juliet* (Shakespeare), New Theatre, London.

1936   Workman/Yakov in *The Seagull* (Chekhov, translated by T. Komisarjevsky), New Theatre, London.

1936   Boyet in *Love's Labour's Lost* (Shakespeare), Old Vic Theatre, London.

Le Beau/William in *As You Like It* (Shakespeare), Old Vic Theatre, London.

Old Thorney in *The Witch of Edmonton* (Dekker, Rowley, and Ford), Old Vic Theatre, London.

1937   Reynaldo/Osric in *Hamlet* (Shakespeare), Old Vic Theatre, London.

Sir Andrew Aguecheek in *Twelfth Night* (Shakespeare), Old Vic Theatre, London.

Exeter in *Henry V* (Shakespeare), Old Vic Theatre, London.

Osric/Reynaldo/Player Queen in *Hamlet* (Shakespeare), Kronborg Castle, Elsinore, Denmark.

Aumerle/Groom in *Richard II* (Shakespeare), Queen's Theatre, London.

Snake in *The School for Scandal* (Sheridan), Queen's Theatre, London.

1938   Feodotik in *The Three Sisters* (Chekhov), Queen's Theatre, London.

Lorenzo in *The Merchant of Venice* (Shakespeare), Queen's Theatre, London.

Louis Dubedat in *The Doctor's Dilemma* (G. B. Shaw), Richmond Theatre, Surrey.

Arthur Gower in *Trelawny of the 'Wells'* (Pinero), Old Vic Theatre, London.

Hamlet in *Hamlet* (Shakespeare), Old Vic Theatre, London; Egyptian and European tour, 1939; New Theatre, London, 1951; also directed.

Bob Acres in *The Rivals* (Sheridan), Old Vic Theatre, London; Egyptian and European tour, 1939.

1939   Chorus in *Henry V* (Shakespeare), Egyptian and European tour.

Emile Flordon in *Libel!* (Wooll), Egyptian and European tour.

Michael Ransom in *The Ascent of F6* (Auden and Isherwood), Old Vic Theatre, London.

Romeo in *Romeo and Juliet* (Shakespeare), Perth, Scotland.

Herbert Pocket in *Great Expectations* (Dickens, adapted by Guinness), Rudolf Steiner Hall, London.

1940   Richard Meilhac in *Cousin Muriel* (Dane), Globe Theatre, London.

Ferdinand in *The Tempest* (Shakespeare), Old Vic Theatre, London.

Charleston in *Thunder Rock* (Ardrey), British tour.

1942   Flight-Lieutenant Graham in *Flare Path* (Rattigan), Henry Miller Theatre, New York.

1945   Nelson in *Hearts of Oak* (pageant), Albert Hall, London.

1946   Mitya Karamazov in *The Brothers Karamazov* (Dostoevsky, adapted by Guinness), Lyric Theatre, Hammersmith, London.

Garcin in *Vicious Circle* (Sartre, translated by Gabain and Swinstead), Arts Theatre, London.

1946   Fool in *King Lear* (Shakespeare), New Theatre, London.

Eric Birling in *An Inspector Calls* (Priestley), New Theatre, London.

Comte de Guiche in *Cyrano de Bergerac* (Rostand, translated by Hooker), New Theatre, London.

1947   Abel Drugger in *The Alchemist* (Jonson), New Theatre, London.

Richard II in *Richard II* (Shakespeare), New Theatre, London.

The Dauphin in *St Joan* (G. B. Shaw), New Theatre, London.

1948   Klestakov in *The Government Inspector* (Gogol, translated and adapted by Campbell), New Theatre, London.

Menenius Agrippa in *Coriolanus* (Shakespeare), New Theatre, London.

Alec Guinness

1949   Dr James Y. Simpson in *The Human Touch* (Thompson and Leslie), Savoy Theatre, London.

Sir Henry Harcourt-Reilly in *The Cocktail Party* (Eliot), Lyceum Theatre, Edinburgh; Henry Miller Theatre, New York, 1950; Chichester Festival Theatre and Wyndham's Theatre, London, 1968; Haymarket Theatre, London, 1969.

1952   The Ant Scientist in *Under the Sycamore Tree* (Spewack), Aldwych Theatre, London.

1953   Richard III in *Richard III* (Shakespeare), Shakespeare Festival, Stratford, Ontario.

King of France in *All's Well That Ends Well* (Shakespeare), Shakespeare Festival, Stratford, Ontario.

1954   The Cardinal in *The Prisoner* (Boland), Globe Theatre, London.

1956   Boniface in *Hotel Paradiso* (Feydeau and Desvallières, translated by Glenville), Winter Garden Theatre, London.

1960   Ross in *Ross* (Rattigan), Haymarket Theatre, London.

1963   Beringer in *Exit the King* (Ionesco, translated by Watson), Edinburgh Festival and Royal Court Theatre, London.

1964   Dylan Thomas in *Dylan* (Michaels), Plymouth Theatre, New York.

1966   Von Berg in *Incident at Vichy* (Miller), Phoenix Theatre, London.

Macbeth in *Macbeth* (Shakespeare), Royal Court Theatre, London.

1967   Mrs Artminster in *Wise Child* (Gray), Wyndham's Theatre, London.

1970   John in *Time Out of Mind* (Boland), Yvonne Arnaud Theatre, Guildford.

1971   Father in *A Voyage Round My Father* (Mortimer), Haymarket Theatre, London.

1973   Dr Arthur Wicksteed in *Habeas Corpus* (Bennett), Lyric Theatre, London.

1975   Dudley Gaveston in *A Family and a Fortune* (Mitchell, adapted from Compton-Burnett), Apollo Theatre, London.

1976   Jonathan Swift in *Yahoo* (Swift, adapted by Guinness and Strachan), Queen's Theatre, London.

1977   Hilary in *The Old Country* (Bennett), Queen's Theatre, London.

1984   Shylock in *The Merchant of Venice* (Shakespeare), Chichester Festival Theatre.

1988   Andrey Lvovich Botvinnik in *A Walk in the Woods* (Blessing), Comedy Theatre, London.

As director:
1949   *Twelfth Night* (Shakespeare), New Theatre, London.

Films

Evensong, 1934; *Great Expectations*, 1946; *Oliver Twist*, 1948; *King Hearts and Coronets*, 1949; *A Run for your Money*, 1949; *The Last Holiday*, 1950; *The Mudlark*, 1950; *The Lavender Hill Mob*, 1951; *The Man in the White Suit*, 1951; *The Card*, 1952; *Malta Story*, 1953; *The Square Mile*, 1953; *The Captain's Paradise*, 1953; *Father Brown*, 1954; *Stratford Adventure*, 1954; *To Paris With Love*, 1955; *The Prisoner*, 1955; *The Ladykillers*, 1955; *Richardson's England*, 1956; *The Swan*, 1956; *The Bridge on the River Kwai*, 1957; *Barnacle Bill*, 1957; *The Horse's Mouth*, 1958; *The Scapegoat*, 1958; *Our Man in Havana*, 1959; *Tunes of Glory*, 1960; *A Majority of One*, 1961; *H.M.S. Defiant*, 1962; *Lawrence of Arabia*, 1962; *The Fall of the Roman Empire*, 1964; *Situation Hopeless — But Not Serious*, 1965; *Dr Zhivago*, 1965; *Hotel Paradiso*, 1966; *The Quiller Memorandum*, 1966; *The Comedians*, 1968; *Cromwell*, 1970; *Scrooge*, 1970; *Fratello Sole, Sorella Luna*, 1972; *Hitler — The Last Ten Days*, 1973; *Murder by Death*, 1973; *Star Wars*, 1977; *The Empire Strikes Back*, 1980; *Raise the Titanic*, 1980; *Little Lord Fauntleroy*, 1980; *Lovesick*, 1983; *Return of the Jedi*, 1983; *A Passage to India*, 1984; *Little Dorrit*, 1987; *A Handful of Dust*, 1988.

Television

Baker's Dozen, 1955; *The Wicked Scheme of Jebal Deeks*, 1959; *Conversation at Night*, 1969; *Twelfth Night*, 1970; *Solo*, 1972; *The Gift of Friendship*, 1974; *Caesar and Cleopatra*, 1977; *Tinker, Tailor, Soldier, Spy*, 1979; *Smiley's People*, 1982; *Edwin*, 1984; *Monsignor Quixote*, 1985; *Tales from Hollywood*, 1991; *A Foreign Field*, 1993.

Radio

Doctor Faustus, 1938; *The Snowman*, 1938; *The Seagull*, 1939; extracts from *Romeo and Juliet*, 1939; *The Tempest*, 1940; *This is Illyria, Lady*, 1940; *A Month in the Country*, 1941; *Distant Point*, 1942; *The Rape of the Lock*, 1942; *Twelfth Night*, 1942; *The Fort*, 1942; *He Was Born Gay*, 1946; *A Time for Verse*, 1946; *Fourth Form Feature*, 1946; *Doctor Faustus*, 1946; *Vicious Circle*, 1946; *Theatre Programme Number Two*, 1946; *The Story of the Nativity*, 1946; *A Time for Verse*, 1947; *Richard II*, 1947; *Britain's Pleasure Parade*, 1947; *Antigone*, 1949; *A Christmas Carol*, 1950; *The Hunting of the Snark*, 1963; extract from *A Voyage Round My Father*, 1971; *My Own Right Hand Shall Do It*, 1974; *King Lear*, 1974; extract from *A Family and a Fortune*, 1975; *The Waste Land*, 1975; *Journey of the Magi*, 1975; *Confessions of a Primary Terrestrial Mental*, 1979; *Receiver and Communicator*, 1979; extract from *The Merchant of Venice*, 1984.

Publications

Blessings in Disguise (autobiography), 1985.

*

Bibliography

Books:
Kenneth Tynan, *Alec Guinness*, London, 1953.
John Russell Taylor, *Alec Guinness: A Celebration*, London, 1984.
Kenneth Von Gunden, *Alec Guinness: The Films*, Jefferson, North Carolina, 1987.
Robert Tanitch, *Guinness*, London, 1989.
Ronald Harwood (ed.), *Dear Alec — Guinness at Seventy-Five*, London, 1989.

* * *

Alec Guinness has never been the conventional idea of a great stage actor and he has readily admitted that he could never emulate the emotional pyrotechnics of Olivier or the classic formality of Gielgud with whom, alongside Ralph Richardson, he now ranks as one of the four most enduring English actors of the 20th century. Guinness's career has encompassed both stage and screen and has seen him take the roles of not only actor but director and scriptwriter as well. His first significant break came when Gielgud signed him for his New Theatre company. Working with Gielgud was to be a double-edged experience for Guinness. Whilst obviously learning from the already established Gielgud, he was hampered in his own acting development by attempts to imitate the other's style. However, by attending lessons with Michel Saint-Denis, Guinness began to discover and explore his ability to focus on detail, which, combined with his acute intelligence, provided the foundation for his skilful manipulation of the quality of essential ordinariness. Coupled with this, Guinness was brilliant at mime and had, as Michael Redgrave observed, the valuable natural asset for comedy, "the appearance of possessing an impenetrable secret". Even at this early stage his ability to make an audience feel as if they were eavesdroppers on a private gathering was evident, but the strength to carry a play was as yet unrealised. Proof of this came when he attempted Hamlet in 1938. The critics recognised the quality of the atmosphere of the play and Guinness's sensitive portrayal of a young intellectual, but they also agreed that in the final analysis the production failed to ignite. The director, Tyrone Guthrie, admitted that Guinness "had not yet quite the authority to support, as Hamlet must, a whole evening, or give the tragedy its full stature".

Guinness was called up to join the Navy in 1940 and was promoted to officer class for the last half of the conflict. He told the writer John Mortimer "the most difficult part I ever had to play was to be an officer and a gentleman for three years in the navy". It was the experience of serving in the forces during the war that enabled Guinness to gain the maturity and resourcefulness that would enhance his ability to carry a play.

After the war, Guinness was chosen as a leading actor for the Old Vic company, but it was in the playing of a supporting role, the Fool to Olivier's Lear, that his initial success came. He played the role in a clown's white face "wry, quiet, true, with a dog's devotion" and stole the show.

Although his successes on stage established him as a recognised actor, it was his work in the Ealing comedies that cemented his reputation as a performer with flexibility, range, and depth — and earned him the tag "the man of a thousand faces". It is arguable that his minimalistic style of acting lent itself to the medium of film and his versatility enabled him to become known as the actor who could disguise himself as often and as disparately as demanded. An early example of this was his multi-roled performance in the film *Kind Hearts and Coronets*, in which he played the whole of the Ascoyne-D'Ascoyne family.

Guinness was meticulous in his preparation and this was aided by his excellent memory, though his insistence on total control of the parts he played sometimes put him at odds with directors. During the filming of *The Lavender Hill Mob* he refused to have any pre-ordained moves set down for himself or to allow stand-ins to do distance shots for him.

While working on *The Ladykillers*, the director, Mackendrick, observed the way Guinness created his character, Marcus, by working from the outside in, initially relying on gimmicks and funny voices, "but then he gets down and discards the unessentials and finds the core of the character". This resulted in an empathetic, ironic, and multi-layered portrait displaying intellectual scrupulousness as well as terrifyingly large teeth.

Although the parts Guinness played in the Ealing comedies varied, he became synonymous with the quiet but rebellious 'little man', a character that was appropriate in its reflection of the moral ambivalence of English society in the confused postwar period.

It was in the role of Nicholson in *The Bridge on the River Kwai* that Guinness achieved international stardom as well as an Oscar, playing a 'little man' who has a limitless inner strength reinforced by a large dose of obstinacy. His ability to show with the smallest amount of movement the greatest amount of emotion was employed to great effect, although during the making of the film the director David Lean felt he was underplaying the character, an undeserved criticism that was to be levelled at Guinness again in later working associations. With the status of a great actor and now a knighthood, Guinness found himself in constant demand and during the next decade he undertook a veritable glut of work that was uneven in quality, yet he continued to work on and pare down his performance style. This fine tuning of an already eminent craft culminated in the polished and impressively structured performances of *Star Wars* and *Tinker, Tailor, Soldier, Spy*. The delicate shading concentrated within the characters implied a depth and range beyond the prescribed words and actions.

Guinness's skill as an actor is in his sense of balance. "A human personality is many sided and you have to be sufficiently balanced to know which side to bring out in a given situation". He achieves this by refusing to put on a performance of his private personality, leaving little for the public to dissect outside of his acting. It is this impersonality that is at the core of his creative process and that allows him to be a concentrated communicator of qualitative intimacy.

—Sarah-Jane Dickenson

GUNTER, John Forsyth. British designer. Born in Billericay, Essex, 31 October 1938. Educated at Bryanston public school, 1956; trained for the stage at the Central School of Art and Design, London, 1958–61. Married Micheline McKnight in 1969; two daughters. Resident designer, English Stage Society, Royal Court Theatre, London, 1965–66; first designed for Royal Shakespeare Company, 1968; resident designer, Zurich Schauspielhaus, Switzerland, 1970–73; head of theatre department, Central School of Art and Design, London, 1974–82; first designed for National Theatre, London, 1979; head of design, National Theatre, London, 1988–90; theatre design consultant and associate, Royal National Theatre, London, since 1990; has also designed in Germany, Austria, Australia, Argentina, the USA, Hong Kong, and Russia. Member: Arts Council Training Committee; Royal Society of Arts (Fellow), 1982. Recipient: Society of West End Theatre Award, 1982, 1984; *Drama Magazine* Best Design Award, 1982; *Plays and Players* Award, 1983, 1984; Olivier Award, 1984.

Productions

1965   *The D. H. Lawrence Trilogy* (Lawrence), Royal Court Theatre, London.
        Saved (Bond), Royal Court Theatre, London.
1966   *The Knack* (Jellicoe), Royal Court Theatre, London.
1967   *The Soldier's Fortune* (Otway), Royal Court Theatre, London.
        Marya (Hampton), Royal Court Theatre, London.
1968   *God Bless* (Feiffer), Aldwych Theatre, London.
        Julius Caesar (Shakespeare), Aldwych Theatre, London.
1969   *The Double-Dealer* (Congreve), Royal Court Theatre, London.
        The Contractor (Storey), Royal Court Theatre, London.

Insideout (Norman), Royal Court Theatre, London.
1968–70   *Landscape* and *Silence* (Pinter), Vivian Beaumont Theatre, New York.
        The Death and Resurrection of Mr. Roche (Kilroy), Lyceum Theatre, Edinburgh, and Hampstead Theatre Club, London.
1970   *AC/DC* (H. Williams), Royal Court Theatre, London.
        The Philanthropist (Hampton), Royal Court Theatre, London, and New York.
1971   *West of Suez* (Osborne), Royal Court Theatre, London, and Cambridge Theatre, London.
1973–76   *Falstaff* (Verdi), Opernhaus, Cologne, and Stadt Oper, Hamburg.
1975   *Entertaining Mr Sloane* (Orton), Royal Court Theatre, London.
        Comedians (Griffiths), Playhouse, Nottingham, Old Vic Theatre, London, and Wyndham's Theatre, London; Music Box Theatre, New York, 1977.
        Jingo (Wood), Aldwych Theatre, London.
1976   *The White Devil* (Webster), Old Vic Theatre, London.
1977   *Stevie* (Whitemore), Vaudeville Theatre, London.
        The Old Country (Bennett), Comedy Theatre, London.
        We Come to the River (Henze), Opernhaus, Cologne.
1978   *Deeds* (Brenton, Campbell, Griffiths, and Hare), Playhouse, Nottingham.
        Flying Blind (Morrison), Royal Court Theatre, London.
        Inadmissible Evidence (Osborne), Royal Court Theatre, London.
        The Cherry Orchard (Chekhov), Playhouse, Nottingham.
        Peter Grimes (Britten), Colon Teater, Buenos Aires, Argentina.
1979   *Tishoo* (Thompson), Wyndham's Theatre, London.
        Death of a Salesman (Miller), National Theatre, London; Thalia, Hamburg, 1980.
        Born in the Gardens (Nichols), Globe Theatre, London.
        Commedia (opera), Stadt Oper, Kassel, Germany.
        Die Meistersinger (Wagner), Cologne Oper, Cologne.
1980   *Rose* (Davies), Duke of York's Theatre, London; Cort Theatre, New York, 1981.
        Lord Arthur Savile's Crime (Cox), Malvern Festival and British tour.
        Heartbreak House (G. B. Shaw), Malvern Festival and British tour.
        Juno and the Paycock (O'Casey), Aldwych Theatre, London.
        We Come to the River (Henze), State Opera House, Nuremburg.
        Hamlet (opera), State Opera House, Nuremburg.
        Beatrice and Benedict (Berlioz), Buxton Festival.

1981   *The Cherry Orchard* (Chekhov), British tour.

All's Well That Ends Well (Shakespeare), Royal Shakespeare Theatre, Stratford-upon-Avon; Barbican Theatre, London, 1982; Martin Beck Theatre, New York, 1983.

We Come to the River (Henze), State Opera House, Nuremburg.

The Greek Passion (opera), Welsh National Opera, Wales.

Macbeth (Verdi), Grand Theatre, Leeds.

1982   *Andrea Chenier* (Giordano), Welsh National Opera, Wales.

King Lear (Berlioz), State Opera House, Nuremburg.

Guys and Dolls (Loesser), National Theatre, London.

The Beggar's Opera (Gay), National Theatre, London.

Plenty (Hare), Public Theatre, New York; Plymouth Theatre, New York, 1983.

1983   *The Rivals* (Sheridan), National Theatre, London.

Lorenzaccio (Musset), National Theatre, London.

Maydays (Edgar), Barbican Theatre, London.

Die Fledermaus (Strauss), Grand Theatre, Leeds.

The Turn of the Screw (Britten), Munich.

1984   *Wild Honey* (Frayn, adapted from Chekhov's *Platonov*), National Theatre, London; Ahmanson Theatre, Los Angeles, 1985.

St Joan (G. B. Shaw), National Theatre, London.

1985   *The Government Inspector* (Gogol), National Theatre, London.

Albert Herring (Britten), Glyndebourne Opera House; Royal Opera House, Covent Garden, 1989; Glyndebourne, 1990.

Faust (Gounod), Coliseum Theatre, London; revived there, 1986; English National Opera, London, 1990; Lyric Opera, Australia, 1991.

The Masked Ball (Verdi), Sydney Opera House, Sydney, Australia.

1986   *Guys and Dolls* (Loesser), Australian tour.

Méphisto (Mnouchkine), Barbican Theatre, London.

Made in Bangkok (Minghella), Aldwych Theatre, London.

Bay at Nice and *Wrecked Eggs* (Hare), National Theatre, London.

High Society (Barry and Porter), Haymarket Theatre, Leicester; Victoria Palace Theatre, London, 1987.

Simon Boccanegra (Verdi), Glyndebourne Opera House.

Porgy and Bess (Gershwin and Heyward), Glyndebourne Opera House.

Die Meistersinger (Wagner), Maggio Musicale, Florence; Australian Opera, Sydney, 1988.

1987   *La Traviata* (Verdi), Glyndebourne Opera House.

Fidelio (Beethoven), San Francisco Opera; Washington, DC, 1988; Sydney Opera House, Sydney, 1992.

Macbeth (Verdi), Grand Theatre, Leeds.

1988   *The Flying Dutchman* (Wagner), La Scala, Milan.

Falstaff (Verdi), Glyndebourne Opera House; revived there, 1990.

Mrs Klein (Wright), Royal National Theatre, London, and Apollo Theatre, London.

Secret Rapture (Hare), Royal National Theatre, London.

1989   *Hamlet* (Shakespeare), Royal National Theatre, London.

Jeffrey Bernard is Unwell (Waterhouse), Theatre Royal, Brighton, Theatre Royal, Bath, and Apollo Theatre, London.

The Marriage of Figaro (Mozart), Glyndebourne Opera House.

Tosca (Puccini), Los Angeles.

1990   *The School for Scandal* (Sheridan), Royal National Theatre, London.

Bookends (Waterhouse), Apollo Theatre, London.

1991   *The Marriage of Figaro* (Mozart), Salzburg, Austria.

Don Giovanni (Mozart), Cologne Opernhaus, Cologne.

1992   *All's Well That Ends Well* (Shakespeare), Swan Theatre, Stratford-upon-Avon.

* * *

John Gunter's English training and early practice was supplemented in the early 1970's by extensive stage design work on the Continent, where he had gone as an English designer for the new wave of English plays of social realism that had attracted interest there. From his English and Continental experiences he envisioned an ideal form of stage design that would blend the best of both worlds: the English respect for the text and careful selectivity in staging with the Continent's greater receptivity to heightened artistic expression. "The Continent is very heavy on ART, while in England we have been much more austere. The latter involves a very honest approach to plays, in which the writer is dominant. But I also like to see spectacle".

Prior to his engagements on the Continent, Gunter's most sustained work had been with the English Stage Society at London's Royal Court Theatre in the late 1960's. It was there, largely under the influence of the designer Jocelyn Herbert, that Gunter came to appreciate the attention to acutely observed realistic detail and special lighting that eliminated emotive coloration in favour or a near-Brechtian white light (Gunter's eye for significant detail and spatial proportion remains evident in the precise, small-scale models with which he prefers to work). The Royal Court specialized in new English drama and Gunter had the opportunity to work on new plays by Edward Bond, David Storey, and Christopher Hampton, as well as on a highly successful revival of D. H. Lawrence's trilogy of coalmining plays under Peter Gill's direction. The blend of selective naturalism with Brechtian theatricality (stage lighting instruments as well as the rear wall of the theatre were frankly exposed) not only defined the Royal Court style of those years but also remained characteristic of much of Gunter's subsequent work, even when he became more interested in greater spectacle, as did English theatre in general in the 1980's.

Two productions in the early 1980's were landmarks for Gunter. In *All's Well That Ends Well* for the RSC, the time frame became the Edwardian era. Gunter designed a set that combined his eye for essentials with the creation of an exciting environment for actors to work in and audiences to respond to. The basic scenic unit was a large, skeletal structure that with changing lighting and screens took on the appearance of a railroad station, a hotel lobby, a ballroom, a conservatory sitting-room, and other locations. Its transformable, elegant, but spare form gave the audience a chance to use its own fantasy to fill in the picture. Using an analogy to the way radio drama stimulates the imagination, Gunter admitted that it is "wonderful to go all the way with a stage setting, but that's not what I think a stage designer should do. A stage setting should be evocative, suggestive of ambience, lead the audience into it, but then the audience should carry on the fantasy with the actors".

The National Theatre's revival of *Guys and Dolls* in 1982 was an even greater breakthrough to lavish yet disciplined theatricality. The basic spatial configuration of the NT's Olivier stage with its enormous diagonals prompted Gunter to create a design that had the form of "a monumental film set" dominated by flamboyant Times Square neon advertising billboards, with complex scene changes involving sliding platforms and probably more flown scenery than had ever been seen before in the Olivier theatre. Yet the same principle of prompting the audience's imagination was again central: "If you can select the correct object you can excite an audience and set them off on a visual journey that they can almost complete for you". Collaborating with director Richard Eyre, who had recently been working in TV and films, Gunter evolved readily changeable theatrical equivalents to many film techniques, thus creating theatricality without lumbering stage machinery.

Two productions from the later 1980's ranging from selective realism to bold theatricality are further indication of Gunter's creative spectrum. Gogol's *The Government Inspector* was by Gunter's own admission "overdesigned". To represent a crushing bureaucratic system, he created a landscape of official papers cascading all over the stage and piled up in huge packages of legal documents at either side of the stage. An enormous cloth sheet covered everything like a spider web but could be lifted up in various positions by a series of lines attached to various parts of the sheet. An animated film of Czar Nicholas I belching was projected onto the cloth at the beginning of the production, cueing in the lifting of the sheet to reveal the chaos of papers. Much more discreet and understated was Gunter's scenography for *Secret Rapture*, a contemporary social realistic play by David Hare. Gunter strove to accentuate the play's basic distress at a society being destroyed by heedless economic programmes. Symbolizing the positive values of older times, a huge tree was deliberately framed as a permanent background to the many interior scenes of the play, which were designed to be enclosed by flexible walls that could move into different configurations, always encroaching on space. Other notable productions of more recent years have included *Fidelio* and *The Flying Dutchman*.

Gunter's contribution to English stage design has included a significant tenure of teaching and administration of theatrical design at London's Central School, as well as his work as head of design at the National Theatre since 1988.

—Jarka M. Burian

———

GUTHRIE, (Sir William) Tyrone. British director and playwright. Born in Tunbridge Wells, England, 2 July 1900. Educated at Wellington College; St John's College, Oxford, BA, 1923, MA, 1931. Married Judith Bretherton in 1931. Great-grandson of Irish actor Tyrone Power; began career as an amateur actor with the Oxford University Dramatic Society; made professional stage debut under J. B. Fagan at the Oxford Playhouse, 1924; worked for the BBC in Belfast and as director, 1926–28, of the Scottish National Players, Glasgow, before appointment as director, 1929–30, of the Festival Theatre, Cambridge; London debut, Westminster Theatre, 1931; director, Old Vic Theatre, London, 1933–36; succeeded Lilian Baylis as administrator of the Old Vic and Sadler's Wells theatres, 1937–45; director, Lyric, Hammersmith, London, from 1945; co-founder, Stratford (Ontario) Shakespeare Festival, 1953; also worked in New York, Australia, Finland, Poland, and Israel; founder and director, Tyrone Guthrie Theatre, Minneapolis, 1971. Recipient: Tony Award, 1955; Distinguished Service Award, Minneapolis Chamber of Commerce, 1964; Citation of the American Educational Theatre Association for Distinguished Service to the Theatre, 1967. Chancellor, Queen's University, Belfast, 1963–70. LL.D: St Andrew's University, Scotland, 1950, Queen's University, Belfast, 1964, Queen's University, Kingston, Ontario, 1964, University of Aberdeen, 1965; D.Litt, University of Western Ontario, 1954, The Citadel, Military College of South Carolina, 1964, Trinity College, Dublin, 1964, Franklyn and Marshall University, Pennsylvania, 1964, Wartburg College, Connecticut, 1965; fellowship, St John's College, University of Oxford, 1964; DFA, Ripon College, Wisconsin, 1964. Fellow, Royal Society of Arts, 1948. Knighted, 1961. Died in County Monaghan, Northern Ireland, 15 May 1971.

Productions

1924	*The Triumph of Death* (Scaife), Barn Theatre, Oxted, England.
1926–28	*The Glen is Mine* (Brandane), Scottish National Players, Scotland.
	C'est la Guerre (Graham), Scottish National Players, Scotland.
	Britain's Daughter (Bottomley), Scottish National Players, Scotland.
1929–30	*Six Characters in Search of an Author* (Pirandello), Festival Theatre, Cambridge.
	Iphigenia in Tauris (Euripides, adapted by Murray), Festival Theatre, Cambridge.
	The Rivals (Sheridan), Festival Theatre, Cambridge.
	The Machine Wreckers (Toller), Festival Theatre, Cambridge.
	Rosmersholm (Ibsen), Festival Theatre, Cambridge.

The Merry Wives of Windsor (Shakespeare), Festival Theatre, Cambridge.

Dandy Dick (Pinero), Festival Theatre, Cambridge.

Le Malade Imaginaire (Molière), Festival Theatre, Cambridge.

The Cherry Orchard (Chekhov), Festival Theatre, Cambridge.

Warren Hastings (Feuchtwanger), Festival Theatre, Cambridge.

1931   *The Anatomist* (Bridie), Westminster Theatre, London.

The Unquiet Spirit, Westminster Theatre, London.

A Pair of Spectacles (Grundy), Westminster Theatre, London.

Six Characters in Search of an Author (Pirandello), Westminster Theatre, London.

1932   *Love's Labour's Lost* (Shakespeare), Westminster Theatre, London.

Follow Me (Guthrie), Westminster Theatre, London.

Dangerous Corner (Priestley), Lyric Theatre, London.

1933   *Lady Audley's Secret* (Hazlewood), Arts Theatre, London.

Count Albany (Carswell), Arts Theatre, London.

The Lake (Massingham), Arts Theatre, London, and Westminster Theatre, London.

Richard II (Shakespeare), Shakespeare Memorial Theatre, Stratford-upon-Avon, England.

Twelfth Night (Shakespeare), Old Vic Theatre, London.

Henry VIII (Shakespeare), Old Vic Theatre, London.

Measure for Measure (Shakespeare), Old Vic Theatre, London.

Macbeth (Shakespeare), Old Vic Theatre, London.

The Cherry Orchard (Chekhov), Old Vic Theatre, London.

1934   *The Importance of Being Earnest* (Wilde), Old Vic Theatre, London.

Love for Love (Congreve), Old Vic Theatre, London.

Sweet Aloes (Carey), Wyndham's Theatre, London; National Theatre, Washington, and New York, 1936.

Mary Read (Bridie), His Majesty's Theatre, London.

Viceroy Sarah (Ginsbury), Arts Theatre, London; Whitehall Theatre, London, 1935.

Hervey House (Cowle, Avery, and Lawrence), His Majesty's Theatre, London.

Mrs Nobby Clarke (MacDonald), Comedy Theatre, London.

1936   *Call it a Day* (Smith), Morosco Theatre, New York.

Dance of Death (Auden), Westminster Theatre, London.

Love's Labour's Lost (Shakespeare), Old Vic Theatre, London.

Tyrone Guthrie

The Country Wife (Wycherley), Old Vic Theatre, London.

1937   *Hamlet* (Shakespeare), Old Vic Theatre, London.

Twelfth Night (Shakespeare), Old Vic Theatre, London.

Henry V (Shakespeare), Old Vic Theatre, London.

Love and How to Cure it (Wilder), Globe Theatre, London.

Paganini (Knepler and Jenbach, adapted by Herbert), Lyceum Theatre, London.

The School for Scandal (Sheridan), Queen's Theatre, London.

Pygmalion (G. B. Shaw), Old Vic Theatre, London.

Measure for Measure (Shakespeare), Old Vic Theatre, London.

Richard III (Shakespeare), Old Vic Theatre, London.

A Midsummer Night's Dream (Shakespeare), Old Vic Theatre, London.

1938   *Othello* (Shakespeare), Old Vic Theatre, London.

Goodness, How Sad! (Morley), Vaudeville Theatre, London.

Trelawny of the Wells, Old Vic Theatre, London.

Hamlet (Shakespeare), Old Vic Theatre, London.

A Midsummer Night's Dream (Shakespeare), Old Vic Theatre, London.

She Stoops to Conquer (Goldsmith), Old Vic Theatre, London.

An Enemy of the People (Ibsen), Old Vic Theatre, London.

The Taming of the Shrew (Shakespeare), Old Vic Theatre, London.

The Good Natured Man (Goldsmith), Opera House, Buxton, and Streatham Hill Theatre, London.

1941   *King John* (Shakespeare), Old Vic Theatre, London.

The Cherry Orchard (Chekhov), New Theatre, London.

1943   *La Traviata* (Verdi), British tour.

Abraham Lincoln (Drinkwater), Playhouse, London.

The Russians (Simonov), Playhouse, London.

1944   *The Last of Mrs Cheyney* (Lonsdale), Savoy Theatre, London.

Guilty (Boutall, adapted from Zola's *Thérèse Raquin), Lyric* Theatre, Hammersmith, London.

Hamlet (Shakespeare), New Theatre, London.

1944   *Uneasy Laughter (He Who Gets Slapped)* (Andreyev, adapted by Judith Guthrie), Playhouse, Liverpool; Booth Theatre, New York, 1946; Duchess Theatre, London, 1947.

Peer Gynt (Ibsen), New Theatre, London.

1945   *The Alchemist* (Jonson), Playhouse, Liverpool.

Cyrano de Bergerac (Rostand), New Theatre, London.

1947   *Oedipus Rex* (Sophocles), Habimah Theatre, Tel Aviv; Broadway Theatre, New York, and Svenska Theatre, Helsinki, 1948.

Peter Grimes (Britten), Royal Opera House, Covent Garden, London.

La Traviata (Verdi), Royal Opera House, Covent Garden, London.

1948   *The Three Estates* (Lyndsay), Assembly Hall, Edinburgh; revived there, 1949.

The Beggar's Opera (Gay, adapted by Britten), Dutch tour and Sadler's Wells Theatre, London.

1949   *Henry VIII* (Shakespeare), Shakespeare Memorial Theatre, Stratford-upon-Avon, England.

The Gentle Shepherd (Ramsay), Royal High School, Edinburgh.

The Taming of the Shrew (Shakespeare), Svenska Theatre, Helsinki.

Carmen (Bizet), Sadler's Wells Theatre, London; Metropolitan Opera House, New York, 1951–52.

1950   *The Miser* (Molière), New Theatre, London.

Hamlet (Shakespeare), Gate Theatre, Dublin.

The Barber of Seville (Rossini), Sadler's Wells Theatre, London.

Falstaff (Verdi), Sadler's Wells Theatre, London.

The Queen's Comedy (Bridie), Assembly Hall, Edinburgh.

The Atom Doctor (Linklater), Assembly Hall, Edinburgh.

Top of the Ladder (Guthrie), St James's Theatre, London.

1951   *The Passing Day* (Shiels), Lyric Theatre, Hammersmith, London.

The Sham Prince (Shadwell and Loudan), Lyric Theatre, Hammersmith, London.

Danger Men at Work (Stewart), Lyric Theatre, Hammersmith, London.

1951   *Tamburlaine the Great* (Marlowe), Old Vic Theatre, London.

1951–52   *A Midsummer Night's Dream* (Shakespeare), Old Vic Theatre, London.

Timon of Athens (Shakespeare), Old Vic Theatre, London.

1952   *The Highland Fair*, Assembly Hall, Edinburgh; revived there, 1953.

1953   *Henry VIII* (Shakespeare), Old Vic Theatre, London.

Richard III (Shakespeare), Shakespeare Festival Theatre, Stratford, Ontario.

All's Well That Ends Well (Shakespeare), Shakespeare Festival Theatre, Stratford, Ontario.

1954   *Pen Don* (Williams), Natural History Museum, Swansea, Wales.

The Taming of the Shrew (Shakespeare), Shakespeare Festival Theatre, Stratford, Ontario.

Oedipus Rex (Sophocles, adapted by Yeats), Shakespeare Festival Theatre, Stratford, Ontario; revived there, 1955; Assembly Hall, Edinbugh, 1956.

The Matchmaker (Wilder), Edinburgh Festival, Edinburgh, and Haymarket Theatre, London; Royale Theatre, New York, 1955.

1955   *The Bishop's Bonfire* (O'Casey), Gaiety Theatre, Dublin.

The Merchant of Venice (Shakespeare), Shakespeare Festival Theatre, Stratford, Ontario.

A Life in the Sun (Wilder), Assembly Hall, Edinburgh.

Six Characters in Search of an Author (Pirandello), Phoenix Theatre, New York.

1956   *Troilus and Cressida* (Shakespeare), Old Vic Theatre, London, and New York.

Tamburlaine the Great (Marlowe), Toronto and Winter Garden Theatre, New York.

Candide (Hellman and Bernstein), Martin Beck Theatre, New York.

1957   *La Traviata* (Verdi), Metropolitan Opera House, New York.

The First Gentleman (Ginsbury), Belasco Theatre, New York.

Twelfth Night (Shakespeare), Shakespeare Festival Theatre, Stratford, Ontario.

Mary Stuart (Schiller), Phoenix Theatre, New York.

The Makropoulos Secret (Capek), Phoenix Theatre, New York.

1958   *The Bonefire* (MacLarnon), Opera House, Belfast, and Lyric Theatre, Edinburgh.

1959   *The Merchant of Venice* (Shakespeare), Habimah Theatre, Tel-Aviv.

All's Well That Ends Well (Shakespeare), Shakespeare Memorial Theatre, Stratford-upon-Avon, England.

The Three Estates (Lyndsay), Assembly Hall, Edinburgh.

The Tenth Man (Chayefsky), Booth Theatre, New York.

1960   *H.M.S. Pinafore* (Gilbert and Sullivan), Avon Theatre, Stratford, Ontario, and Phoenix Theatre, New York; Her Majesty's Theatre, London, 1962.

Love and Libel (Davies), Martin Beck Theatre, New York.

The Pirates of Penzance (Gilbert and Sullivan), Avon Theatre, Stratford, Ontario, and Phoenix Theatre, New York; Her Majesty's Theatre, London, 1962.

Gideon (Chayefsky), Plymouth Theatre, New York.

1962   *A Time to Laugh* (Crean), Theatre Royal, Brighton.

The Alchemist (Jonson), Old Vic Theatre, London.

1963   *Hamlet* (Shakespeare), Tyrone Guthrie Theatre, Minneapolis.

The Three Sisters (Chekhov, co-adapted by Guthrie), Tyrone Guthrie Theatre, Minneapolis.

1964   *Henry V* (Shakespeare), Tyrone Guthrie Theatre, Minneapolis.

Volpone (Jonson), Tyrone Guthrie Theatre, Minneapolis.

Six Characters in Search of an Author (Pirandello), Scott Hall, University of Minnesota, Minneapolis.

1965   *Richard III* (Shakespeare), Tyrone Guthrie Theatre, Minneapolis.

The Cherry Orchard (Chekhov, co-adapted by Guthrie), Tyrone Guthrie Theatre, Minneapolis.

1966   *Measure for Measure* (Shakespeare), Theatre Royal, Bristol; US tour, 1967.

Dinner at Eight (Kaufman and Ferber), Alvin Theatre, New York.

1967   *Carmen* (Bizet), Metropolitan Opera House, New York; Opera House, Dusseldorf, 1968.

Harper's Ferry (Stavis), Tyrone Guthrie Theatre, Minneapolis.

The House of Atreus (Aeschylus, adapted by Lewin), Tyrone Guthrie Theatre, Minneapolis; Billy Rose Theatre, New York, and Mark Taper Forum, Los Angeles, 1968.

Tartuffe (Molière), Old Vic Theatre, London.

Peter Grimes (Britten), Metropolitan Opera House, New York; revived there, 1969.

1968   *Volpone* (Jonson), New Theatre, London.

The Anatomist (Bridie), Citizens' Theatre, Glasgow.

1969   *Lamp at Midnight* (Stavis), Mershon Auditorium, Columbus, Ohio, and US tour.

McCook's Corner, Opera House, Belfast, and Abbey Theatre, Dublin.

Swift (McCabe), Abbey Theatre, Dublin.

Uncle Vanya (Chekhov), Tyrone Guthrie Theatre, Minneapolis.

1970   *Oedipus the King* (Sophocles, adapted by Lewin), Clancy Auditorium, Sydney, Australia.

All's Well That Ends Well (Shakespeare), Princess Theatre, Melbourne, Australia.

1971   *The Barber of Seville* (Rossini), Theatre Royal, Brighton.

Films

As actor:
Vessel of Wrath, 1938; *St Martin's Lane*, 1938.

Radio

As director:
Iphigenia in Tauris, 1925; *The Land of Heart's Desire*, 1925; *Good Friday*, 1925; *A Night in a Victorian Drawing Room*, 1925; *The Romance of Canada*, 1930.

Publications

Squirrel's Cage (radio play), 1931; *The Flowers are not for you to Pick* (radio play), 1931; *Matrimonial News* (radio play), 1931; *Theatre Prospect*, 1932; *Top of the Ladder* (play), 1950; *Renown at Stratford*, 1953; *Twice have the Trumpets Sounded*, 1954; *Haste to the Wedding* (play), 1954; *Thrice the Brinded Cat hath Mew'd*, 1955; *A Life in the Theatre* (autobiography), 1959; *A New Theatre*, 1964; *In Various Directions*, 1966; *Tyrone Guthrie on Acting*, 1971.

*

Bibliography

Books:
James Forsyth, *Tyrone Guthrie*, London, 1976.

* * *

Tyrone (Tony) Guthrie exerted an immense influence upon the shape and development of 20th-century theatre. His reputation was established, nationally and internationally, by his work as producer and director, principally of Shakespeare and a wide range of classical plays but also of modern drama, opera, and comic opera. Whereas the work of most directors is related to individual productions and therefore ephemeral, Guthrie's influence has persisted through the important acting talents he helped to nurture; through his new, often daringly original approaches to theatrical production; and more concretely through his innovative contribution to modern theatrical architecture and stage design.

One feature of Guthrie's success was an unerring eye for talent, which enabled him to attract to his productions the very best actors and collaborators. Thus, at the height of his successful career, he worked with a host of actors and actresses who themselves had international reputations, among them Laurence Olivier, Ralph Richardson, Edith Evans, Irene Worth, Anthony Quayle, Donald Wolfit, Gladys Cooper, and even the elderly Marie Tempest, to name but a few. More significant, in a way, was his immense skill, even at an early stage in his career and before his reputation was established, in drawing together beginners and stars and moulding them into a team. Many famous performers, such as Flora Robson, Alec Guinness, James Mason, Robert Morley, and Michael Redgrave benefited from his inspiration; many owe their start in the acting profession or their first opportunity in a West End production to Guthrie's judgement. In his very earliest days at the Old Vic, his casts included Charles Laughton, Leon Quartermaine, Roger Livesey, and Laurence Olivier.

Another of Guthrie's numerous talents was his originality. He is remembered by English audiences for some of his reinterpretations of Shakespeare in modern dress at the Old Vic, notably *Hamlet*, with Alec Guinness in the title role in 1938, and *Troilus and Cressida* in 1956. This delight in novelty was apparent at the very outset of his lengthy career. It was typical of the man that he should have been attracted to the potential of radio when the BBC was in its infancy; as well as producing plays during his time with the BBC in Belfast he also adapted or wrote drama, while his production of *The Romance of Canada* for the Canadian National Radio was probably the first radio drama serial ever broadcast.

Without neglecting the minutest detail of his actors' performance, Guthrie was particularly happy with bold, sweeping, often majestic effects and pageantry, which were most fully realised in memorable large-scale productions of plays and operas both at home and abroad. These included *Carmen* at the Metropolitan Opera House in New York, *Peter Grimes* at Covent Garden, and *Oedipus Rex* in Tel-Aviv, and, in addition to plays by Shakespeare, ambitious productions of other European classics, such as *Tartuffe*, *The Miser*, and *Cyrano de Bergerac* as well as dramas by such modern figures as Ibsen, Pirandello, and Chekhov.

Guthrie's strong reaction against realism and naturalism in the theatre and years of experimentation with decor and stage design dating back to his earliest years at the Old Vic culminated in his production for the second Edinburgh Festival in 1948 of *Ane Satire of the Thrie Estaites*. The conversion of the huge Gothic Assembly Hall into an open Elizabethan stage for the hugely successful performances of the 16th-century allegory by Sir David Lyndsay can be seen as a landmark in 20th-century theatrical production. It was a vindication of Guthrie's belief that much theatre, including above all Shakespeare, suffers from the divisive conditions imposed upon actors and audience by the conventional proscenium arch. This conviction and Guthrie's powerful demonstrations of the arena or open stage were to influence the design of many modern theatres at home and abroad, including those at Chichester and Sheffield, numerous studio theatres in the UK and at US universities, the Shakespeare Festival at Stratford, Ontario, for which Guthrie staged *Richard III* in an enormous tent in 1953, and the Guthrie Theatre in Minneapolis.

As a practitioner rather than a theoretician, Guthrie wrote mainly for, rather than about, the theatre (for example, his play *Top of the Ladder*). For those unable to deduce his views from his theatrical productions, many important ideas and attitudes are expressed elegantly and forcefully in his autobiography, *A Life in the Theatre*, which gives a delightfully anecdotal account of his career, interspersed with chapters on the history of the Old Vic, the roles of the director and actor, and the shortcomings of the traditional "picture frame" design of the theatre.

Tyrone Guthrie was a big man in every sense. His height (six feet, five inches) may have been obstacle to an acting career, but as a director gave him a commanding presence, which, coupled with his natural authority and exceptional managerial skills, enabled him to put a decisive and truly personal stamp on all his work. His lightness of touch, charm, and considerable wit encouraged the best from those with whom he worked energetically and successfully over the course of his most influential career.

—Colin Radford

H

HALL, (Sir) Peter Reginald Frederick. British director and manager. Born in Bury St Edmunds, Suffolk, 22 November 1930. Educated at Perse School, Cambridge; St Catherine's College, Cambridge University. Married 1) actress Leslie Caron in 1956 (divorced 1965), one son and one daughter; 2) Jacqueline Taylor in 1965 (divorced 1981), one son and one daughter; 3) Maria Ewing in 1982 (divorced 1990), one daughter; 4) Nicola Frei in 1990, one daughter. Began career directing the Cambridge Amateur Dramatic Club and the Marlowe Society, Cambridge; London debut, Theatre Royal, Windsor, 1953; director, Oxford Playhouse, 1954–55; director, Arts Theatre, London, 1955–57; debut as director at Stratford-upon-Avon, 1956; New York debut, Cort Theatre, 1957; opera debut, 1957; founder, International Playwrights' Theatre production company, 1957; director, Royal Shakespeare Theatre, 1960; founder and managing director, Royal Shakespeare Company, 1961–68; film debut, 1966; associate professor of drama, University of Warwick, Coventry, from 1966; co-director, Royal Shakespeare Company, 1968–73; director of productions, Royal Opera House, Covent Garden, London, 1970–71; director, National Theatre, 1973–88; oversaw transfer of National Theatre from Old Vic Theatre, 1976; artistic director, Glyndebourne Festival Opera, 1984–90; founded the Peter Hall transatlantic production company, 1988. Fellow, St Catherine's College, University of Cambridge, 1964. Member: Arts Council of Great Britain, 1969–73; founder-member, Theatre Directors' Guild of Great Britain, 1983. Recipient: Shakespeare Prize (Germany), 1967; Tony Award, 1967, 1981; *Standard* Special Award, 1979; *Standard* Award for Best Director, 1981, 1987; *Standard* Opera Award, 1981. MA, Cambridge University, 1964; D.Litt: University of Reading, 1973; Litt.D: University of Liverpool, 1974; University of Leicester, 1977. Chevalier de l'Ordre des Arts et des Lettres (France), 1965; CBE (Commander of the British Empire), 1963. Knighted, 1977.

Productions

1954   *Blood Wedding* (Lorca), Arts Theatre, London.
The Immoralist (Goetz and Goetz), Arts Theatre, London.
The Lesson (Ionesco), Arts Theatre, London.
South (Green), Arts Theatre, London.

1955   *Mourning Becomes Electra* (O'Neill), Arts Theatre, London.
Waiting for Godot (Beckett), Arts Theatre, London.

Burnt Flower-Bed (Betti), Arts Theatre, London.
Listen to the Wind (Reaney), Arts Theatre, London.

1956   *The Waltz of the Toreadors* (Anouilh), Arts Theatre, London.
Gigi (Colette and Loos), New Theatre, London.
Love's Labour's Lost (Shakespeare), Shakespeare Memorial Theatre, Stratford-upon-Avon.

1957   *The Rope Dancers* (Wishengrad), Cort Theatre, New York.
Camino Real (T. Williams), Phoenix Theatre, London.
The Moon and Sixpence (opera), Sadler's Wells Theatre, London.
Cymbeline (Shakespeare), Shakespeare Memorial Theatre, Stratford-upon-Avon.

1958   *Cat on a Hot Tin Roof* (T. Williams), London.
Twelfth Night (Shakespeare), Shakespeare Memorial Theatre, Stratford-upon-Avon.
Brouhaha (Tabori), Shakespeare Memorial Theatre, Stratford-upon-Avon.
Shadow of Heroes (Ardrey), Shakespeare Memorial Theatre, Stratford-upon-Avon.

1959   *Madame De . . .* (Anouilh), Shakespeare Memorial Theatre, Stratford-upon-Avon.
A Traveller Without Luggage (Anouilh), Shakespeare Memorial Theatre, Stratford-upon-Avon.
A Midsummer Night's Dream (Shakespeare), Shakespeare Memorial Theatre, Stratford-upon-Avon.
Coriolanus (Shakespeare), Shakespeare Memorial Theatre, Stratford-upon-Avon.
The Wrong Side of the Park (Mortimer), Shakespeare Memorial Theatre, Stratford-upon-Avon.

1960   *The Two Gentlemen of Verona* (Shakespeare), Shakespeare Memorial Theatre, Stratford-upon-Avon.
Twelfth Night (Shakespeare), Shakespeare Memorial Theatre, Stratford-upon-Avon.
Troilus and Cressida (Shakespeare), Shakespeare Memorial Theatre, Stratford-upon-Avon.

1961   *Ondine* (Giraudoux), Royal Shakespeare Theatre, Stratford-upon-Avon, and Aldwych Theatre, London.

337

Peter Hall (credit: Gordon Goode, Stratford-upon-Avon).

Becket (Anouilh), Royal Shakespeare Theatre, Stratford-upon-Avon, and Aldwych Theatre, London.

Romeo and Juliet (Shakespeare), Royal Shakespeare Theatre, Stratford-upon-Avon, and Aldwych Theatre, London.

A Midsummer Night's Dream (Shakespeare), Royal Shakespeare Theatre, Stratford-upon-Avon, and Aldwych Theatre, London.

The Collection (Pinter), Royal Shakespeare Theatre, Stratford-upon-Avon, and Aldwych Theatre, London.

Troilus and Cressida (Shakespeare), Royal Shakespeare Theatre, Stratford-upon-Avon, and Aldwych Theatre, London.

1963   *The Wars of the Roses* (Shakespeare cycle), Royal Shakespeare Theatre, Stratford-upon-Avon, and Aldwych Theatre, London; revived, 1964.

A Midsummer Night's Dream (Shakespeare), Royal Shakespeare Theatre, Stratford-upon-Avon, and Aldwych Theatre, London.

1964   *A Cycle of Seven History Plays* (Shakespeare cycle), Royal Shakespeare Theatre, Stratford-upon-Avon, and Aldwych Theatre, London.

Eh? (Livings), Royal Shakespeare Theatre, Stratford-upon-Avon, and Aldwych Theatre, London.

1965   *The Homecoming* (Pinter), Aldwych Theatre, London, and New York.

Moses and Aaron (Schoenberg), Royal Opera House, Covent Garden, London.

Hamlet (Shakespeare), Royal Shakespeare Theatre, Stratford-upon-Avon, and Aldwych Theatre, London.

The Government Inspector (Gogol), Royal Shakespeare Theatre, Stratford-upon-Avon, and Aldwych Theatre, London.

1966   *The Magic Flute* (Mozart), Royal Opera House, Covent Garden, London.

Staircase (Dyer), Royal Shakespeare Theatre, Stratford-upon-Avon, and Aldwych Theatre, London.

1967   *A Midsummer Night's Dream* (Shakespeare), Royal Shakespeare Theatre, Stratford-upon-Avon, and Aldwych Theatre, London.

Macbeth (Shakespeare), Royal Shakespeare Theatre, Stratford-upon-Avon, and Aldwych Theatre, London.

1969   *A Delicate Balance* (Albee), Royal Shakespeare Theatre, Stratford-upon-Avon, and Aldwych Theatre, London.

Dutch Uncle (Gray), Royal Shakespeare Theatre, Stratford-upon-Avon, and Aldwych Theatre, London.

Landscape and *Silence* (Pinter), Royal Shakespeare Theatre, Stratford-upon-Avon, and Aldwych Theatre, London.

1970   *The Knot Garden* (Tippett), Royal Opera House, Covent Garden, London.

La Calista (Cavalli and Faustini), Glyndebourne Opera House.

The Battle of Shrivings (P. Shaffer), Lyric Theatre, London.

1971   *Eugene Onegin* (Tchaikovsky), Royal Opera House, Covent Garden, London.

Old Times (Pinter), London and New York.

Tristan and Isolde (Wagner), Royal Opera House, Covent Garden, London.

1972   *All Over* (Albee), Aldwych Theatre, London.

Il Ritorno d'Ulisse (Monteverdi), Glyndebourne Opera House.

Alte Zeiten, Burgtheatre, Vienna.

Via Galactica (MacDermot), New York.

1973   *The Marriage of Figaro* (Mozart), Glyndebourne Opera House.

The Tempest (Shakespeare), National Theatre, London.

1974   *John Gabriel Borkman* (Ibsen), National Theatre, London.

Happy Days (Beckett), National Theatre, London.

1975   *No Man's Land* (Pinter), National Theatre, London.

Hamlet (Shakespeare), National Theatre, London.

Judgement (Collins), National Theatre, London.

1976   *Tamburlaine the Great* (Marlowe), National Theatre, London.

1977   *Bedroom Farce* (Ayckbourn), National Theatre, London.

Don Giovanni (Mozart), Glyndebourne Opera House.

1978   *Volpone* (Jonson), National Theatre, London.
The Country Wife (Wycherley), National Theatre, London.
The Cherry Orchard (Chekhov), National Theatre, London.
Macbeth (Shakespeare), National Theatre, London.
Betrayal (Pinter), National Theatre, London.
Cosi Fan Tutte (Mozart), Glyndebourne Opera House.

1979   *Fidelio* (Beethoven), Glyndebourne Opera House.
Amadeus (P. Shaffer), National Theatre, London.

1980   *Betrayal* (Pinter), New York.
Othello (Shakespeare), National Theatre, London.
Amadeus (P. Shaffer), New York.

1981   *Family Voices* (Pinter), National Theatre, London.
Oresteia (Aeschylus, adapted by Harrison), National Theatre, London.

1982   *A Midsummer Night's Dream* (Britten), Glyndebourne Opera House.
The Importance of Being Earnest (Wilde), National Theatre, London.
Macbeth (Verdi), Glyndebourne Opera House and Metropolitan Opera House, New York.
Other Places (Pinter), National Theatre, London.
Orfeo et Euridice (Gluck), Glyndebourne Opera House.

1983   *Der Ring Des Nibelungen* (Wagner), Bayreuth.
Jean Seberg (Hamlisch, Adler, and Barry), National Theatre, London.
The Marriage of Figaro (Mozart), Geneva.

1984   *Animal Farm* (adapted from Orwell), National Theatre, London.
Coriolanus (Shakespeare), National Theatre, London.
Don Giovanni (Mozart), Glyndebourne Opera House.
Cosi Fan Tutte (Mozart), Glyndebourne Opera House.
L'Incoronazione di Poppea, Glyndebourne Opera House; revived there, 1986.

1985   *Yonadab* (P. Shaffer), National Theatre, London.
Carmen (Bizet), Glyndebourne Opera House; Metropolitan Opera House, New York, 1986.
Albert Herring (Britten), Glyndebourne Opera House; revived there, 1986.
Martine (Bernard, translated by Fowles), National Theatre, London.

1986   *The Petition* (Clark), National Theatre, London.
Salome (Strauss), Geneva.
Simon Boccanegra (Verdi), Glyndebourne Opera House.

1987   *Coming in to Land* (Poliakoff), National Theatre, London.

Antony and Cleopatra (Shakespeare), National Theatre, London.
Entertaining Strangers (Edgar), National Theatre, London.
The Marriage of Figaro (Mozart), Chicago.
La Traviata (Verdi), Glyndebourne Opera House; revived there, 1988.

1988   *Cymbeline* (Shakespeare), National Theatre, London.
The Winter's Tale (Shakespeare), National Theatre, London.
The Tempest (Shakespeare), National Theatre, London.
Orpheus Descending (T. Williams), London and New York.
Cosi Fan Tutte (Mozart), Geneva.
Salome (Strauss), Royal Opera House, Covent Garden, London, and Chicago.
Falstaff (Verdi), Glyndebourne Opera House.

1989   *The Merchant of Venice* (Shakespeare), Phoenix Theatre, London.
New World (Dvořák), Houston, Texas.
Albert Herring (Britten), Royal Opera House, Covent Garden, London.
The Marriage of Figaro (Mozart), Glyndebourne Opera House.
A Midsummer Night's Dream (Britten), Glyndebourne Opera House.

1990   *The Wild Duck* (Ibsen), British tour and Phoenix Theatre, London.
Born Again (adapted from Ionesco's *Rhinoceros*), Chichester Festival Theatre.

1991   *The Homecoming* (Pinter), Comedy Theatre, London.
Twelfth Night (Shakespeare), Playhouse, London.
The Rose Tattoo (T. Williams), Playhouse, London.
Tartuffe (Molière), Playhouse, London.

1992   *Four Baboons Adoring the Sun* (Guare), New York.
Sienna Red (Poliakoff), London.
The Magic Flute (Mozart), Geneva.
All's Well That Ends Well (Shakespeare), Swan Theatre, Stratford-upon-Avon; London, 1994.
An Ideal Husband (Wilde), Globe Theatre, London.

1993   *Separate Tables* (Rattigan), Albery Theatre, London.
Lysistrata (Aristophanes, translated by Ranjit Bolt), Old Vic Theatre, London, and Wyndham's Theatre, London.
The Gift of the Gorgon (P. Shaffer), Barbican Pit, London, and Wyndham's Theatre, London.
She Stoops to Conquer (Sheridan), Queen's Theatre, London.
Piaf (Gems), Piccadilly Theatre, London.
An Absolute Turkey (Hall and Frei, translated from Feydeau's *Le Dindon*), Globe Theatre, London.

1994   *Hamlet* (Shakespeare), Gielgud Theatre, London.

Films

Work is a Four-Letter Word, 1968; *A Midsummer Night's Dream*, 1969; *Three into Two Won't Go*, 1969; *Perfect Friday*, 1971; *The Homecoming*, 1973; *Landscape*, 1973; *Akenfield*, 1974; *She's Been Away*, 1989; *Orpheus Descending*, 1991.

Television

The Wars of the Roses, 1964; *Aquarius* (as presenter), 1975–77; *Carmen*, 1985; *The Oresteia*, 1986; *L'Incoronazione di Poppea*, 1986; *Albert Herring*, 1986; *La Traviata*, 1987; *The Marriage of Figaro*, 1989; *The Camomile Lawn* (series), 1992.

Radio

Family Voices, 1981.

Publications

The Wars of the Roses, with John Barton, 1970; *John Gabriel Borkman* (translation), 1975; *Peter Hall's Diaries*, 1983; *Animal Farm* (adaptation), 1986; *The Wild Duck* (adaptation), 1990; *Making an Exhibition of Myself*, 1993.

*

Bibliography

Books:
David Addenbrooke, *The Royal Shakespeare Company: The Peter Hall Years*, London, 1974.
Tirzah Lowen, *Peter Hall Directs "Antony and Cleopatra"*, London, 1990.

* * *

Photographs of Peter Hall in rehearsal sometimes show him with his head down and pen in hand, attending to the script and obviously alert to what he is hearing. This director has spent many hours like this because he insists on speech that is clear in meaning and respectful to the periods of prose and metrical niceties of verse. His production of three of Shakespeare's last plays, *Cymbeline*, *The Winter's Tale*, and *The Tempest*, in 1988 were preceded by days in the National Theatre's Studio, sitting in a circle with his actors and talking about iambic pentameters, caesuras, stress, and phrasing, and about energy, intelligence, and long-nourished skills.

With plays by Shakespeare or Harold Pinter, Hall tells his actors to find their performances while learning to speak the dialogue, allowing the words and their sounds and rhythms to guide both thoughts and feelings, to command and sustain their energy, and to draw them towards action; when the text has been mastered, the characters are free to grow and the actors to find themselves within their roles.

Other rehearsal photographs show Peter Hall standing or crouching behind a star actor, as if pointing the way ahead, up a mountain or through some complex obstacle. These camera shots represent another feature of his work: a respect for performers who are thoroughly in charge of themselves. Many of his productions have had their origin in key-casting: Dustin Hoffman as Shylock, Vanessa Redgrave in *Orpheus Descending*, Ian McKellen as Coriolanus, Judi Dench as Lady Bracknell and Cleopatra, Paul Scofield as Volpone and Othello, Peggy Ashcroft as Winnie in *Happy Days*, Albert Finney as Hamlet and Macbeth.

In Hall's best work, star casting and immaculate speech carry the drama. For Harold Pinter's *No Man's Land* (1975), Ralph Richardson and John Gielgud were rehearsed like two "old lions"; they were held in the cage of the script and fed daily by their keeper, until strength of presence matched finesse of speech. In Marlowe's *Tamburlaine* (1976), Albert Finney was supported and challenged by a large cast used to playing leading roles in Shakespeare and other classical dramas. Delays in the completion of the new building for the National Theatre (of which Hall was now in charge) gave this production a greatly extended rehearsal period, so that actors learned to sustain the long periods and biting ironies of the unfamiliar text.

Opening on the new and spacious stage of the Olivier Theatre, *Tamburlaine* exemplified Peter Hall's ability to take a large number of actors on a journey into new territory. Yet it would be a mistake to think that he had drilled his cast for success with militant authority or led them along a clearly foreseen path. Each member of the company had reached a high pitch of performance by individual powers of discovery and survival. An anxious actor might well have complained of too little leadership, too uncertain or too incomplete instructions. It was so again with the *Oresteia* (1981), which occupied Hall for still longer, in a series of workshop explorations as well as many months of rehearsals.

Shakespeare's history plays at Stratford-upon-Avon in the early 1960's were the most astonishing work of this exploratory kind. After two years of preparation, seven plays were presented in historical sequence, disciplined in speech, controlled in spectacle, and rich with individuality. A long and repetitive drama had been illuminated by a common view of how the text should be spoken and of what it was portraying — the violence, hypocrisy, and heartlessness of political ambition, together with the opposing virtues, briefly seen, of peace and gentleness. In successive roles, the actors took each opportunity to survive and shine, to show both intelligence and committal, and to share with their audience a sense of discovery. As Peter Hall wrote in *Crucial Years*, a pamphlet issued in 1963 by the Royal Shakespeare Company: "Let our motto be: 'Keep open, keep critical' ... We are searching, and whatever we find today, a new search will be necessary tomorrow. The theatre is a quest, not an acceptance".

Both *The Wars of the Roses* and *Tamburlaine* were also eye-catching spectacles, examples of Hall's ability to work with a designer through every step of preparation and rehearsal, and so achieve grand and overwhelming effects. With Lila de Nobili as designer, *A Midsummer Night's Dream* (1959) blended the oak of an old manor house with the living oaks of a wood: both were lit successively with the ravishing glow of early summer sun, mysterious moonlight, or flickering candles. Later productions were never so seductive, but still more impressive: the metallic and wooden setting for the history plays moved and changed to accentuate oppositions, and gave to the more ordered moments an embattled strength; here the obvious scenic glories of heraldry and chivalry gave way to sombre menace and images of cruelty and hardship.

All these qualities were seen together in the *Hamlet* of 1965. The prince was the comparatively inexperienced David Warner, but this young actor had been with the Stratford company all his professional life and gave a new look and sound to the very familiar role. His performance had high definition and an unexpected truth to contemporary sensibility. Elsinore was represented in a dark and sumptuous setting, a place for business and affairs, for established power and desperate innovation. The whole cast was mentally alert and many scenes were staged with more than customary elaboration.

While Shakespeare has been the most constant element in Peter Hall's career, other classic texts have responded to his ability to listen to clues hidden in language, to send actors along difficult terrain and, with the help of a few trusted designers, to turn careful investigation into magnificent shows.

With contemporary texts, the same skills are at work, but the productions have proved more variable. Peter Shaffer's *Amadeus* (1979) had a period setting and required impressiveness and authority, and so responded well; it also drew on Hall's intimate knowledge of Mozart (having staged a series of operas for Glyndebourne during his directorship there). But for Tennessee Williams, Albee, Beckett, Mortimer, Whiting, Anouilh, Poliakoff, and Edgar, a lack of nervous freedom and intimacy has encouraged an unwelcome weight, where the plays might have been served better by more dash and danger. Among contemporary writers Hall has seemed most at home with Pinter — to whose plays he has returned frequently — and with Beckett, although this author's own productions have shown greater lightness and, with that, have awoken more laughter and more tears.

—John Russell Brown

HANDS, Terry. British director. Born Terence David Hands in Aldershot, Hampshire, 9 January 1941. Educated at University of Birmingham; trained for the stage at the Royal Academy of Dramatic Art, London, 1962–64. Married 1) Josephine Barstow in 1964 (divorced); 2) Ludmila Mikael (divorced 1980); one daughter. Co-founder and artistic director, Everyman Theatre, Liverpool, 1964–66; artistic director, Royal Shakespeare Company Theatregoround company, 1966; associate director, Royal Shakespeare Company, 1967–77; consultant director, Comédie-Française, Paris, 1975–77; joint artistic director, with Trevor Nunn, Royal Shakespeare Company, 1978–86; sole artistic director and chief executive, Royal Shakespeare Company, 1986–91. Recipient: French Critics Meilleur Spectacle de l'Année, 1972, 1976; *Plays and Players* Award, 1977; Society of West End Theatre Award, 1978, 1983; New York Drama League Award, 1985. Chevalier, Ordres des Arts et des Lettres, 1975.

Productions

1964–66   *The Importance of Being Earnest* (Wilde), Everyman Theatre, Liverpool.

Look Back in Anger (Osborne), Everyman Theatre, Liverpool.

Richard III (Shakespeare), Everyman Theatre, Liverpool.

Fando and Lis (Arrabal), Everyman Theatre, Liverpool.

1966   *The Proposal* (Chekhov), Theatregoround tour.

The Second Shepherd's Play (trad.), Theatregoround tour.

1967   *The Criminals* (Triana), Aldwych Theatre, London.

The Dumb Waiter (Pinter), Theatregoround tour.

Pleasure and Repentance (Hands), Theatregoround tour.

Under Milk Wood (Thomas), Theatregoround tour.

1968   *The Merry Wives of Windsor* (Shakespeare), Royal Shakespeare Theatre, Stratford-upon-Avon, and Aldwych Theatre, London; Royal Shakespeare Theatre, Stratford-upon-Avon, 1969; Japanese tour, 1970.

The Latent Heterosexual (Chayevsky), Aldwych Theatre, London.

1969   *Pericles* (Shakespeare), Royal Shakespeare Theatre, Stratford-upon-Avon.

Woman Beware Women (Middleton), Royal Shakespeare Theatre, Stratford-upon-Avon.

Bartholomew Fair (Jonson), Aldwych Theatre, London.

1970   *Richard III* (Shakespeare), Royal Shakespeare Theatre, Stratford-upon-Avon.

1971   *The Merchant of Venice* (Shakespeare), Royal Shakespeare Theatre, Stratford-upon-Avon; Aldwych Theatre, London, and British tour, 1972.

The Balcony (Genet), Aldwych Theatre, London.

The Man of Mode (Etherege), Aldwych Theatre, London.

1972   *Murder in the Cathedral* (Eliot), Aldwych Theatre, London.

Richard III (Shakespeare), Comédie-Française, Paris, and Avignon Festival; Aldwych Theatre, London, 1973.

1973   *Romeo and Juliet* (Shakespeare), Royal Shakespeare Theatre, Stratford-upon-Avon.

Cries from Casement (Rudkin), Other Place Theatre, Stratford-upon-Avon.

1974   *Pericles* (Shakespeare), Comédie-Française, Paris.

The Bewitched (Barnes), Aldwych Theatre, London.

The Actor, Australian tour.

1975   *Henry IV, parts 1 and 2* (Shakespeare), Royal Shakespeare Theatre, Stratford-upon-Avon, and Aldwych Theatre, London.

Henry V (Shakespeare), Aldwych Theatre, London, and Brooklyn Academy of Music, New York; British and European tour, 1976.

The Merry Wives of Windsor (Shakespeare), Royal Shakespeare Theatre, Stratford-upon-Avon, and Aldwych Theatre, London.

1976   *Old World* (Arbuzov), Aldwych Theatre, London.
        Twelfth Night (Shakespeare), Comédie-Française, Paris.
        Otello (Verdi), Paris.

1977   *Henry VI, parts 1, 2 and 3* (Shakespeare), Royal Shakespeare Theatre, Stratford-upon-Avon, and Newcastle-upon-Tyne; Aldwych Theatre, London, 1978.
        Coriolanus (Shakespeare), Royal Shakespeare Theatre, Stratford-upon-Avon, and Newcastle-upon-Tyne; Aldwych Theatre, London, 1978; European tour, 1979.
        Henry V (Shakespeare), Royal Shakespeare Theatre, Stratford-upon-Avon; Aldwych Theatre, London, 1978.
        Le Cid (P. Corneille), Comédie-Française, Paris.

1978   *Murder in the Cathedral* (Eliot), Comédie-Française, Paris.
        Troilus and Cressida (Shakespeare), Burgtheater, Vienna.
        The Changeling (Middleton), Aldwych Theatre, London.

1979   *The Children of the Sun* (Gorky), Aldwych Theatre, London.
        As You Like It (Shakespeare), Burgtheater, Vienna.
        Parsifal (Wagner), Covent Garden, London.
        Twelfth Night (Shakespeare), Royal Shakespeare Theatre, Stratford-upon-Avon; Aldwych Theatre, London, 1980.

1980   *As You Like It* (Shakespeare), Royal Shakespeare Theatre, Stratford-upon-Avon; Aldwych Theatre, London, 1981.
        Richard II (Shakespeare), Royal Shakespeare Theatre, Stratford-upon-Avon; Aldwych Theatre, London, 1981.
        Richard III (Shakespeare), Royal Shakespeare Theatre, Stratford-upon-Avon; Aldwych Theatre, London, 1981.

1982   *Much Ado About Nothing* (Shakespeare), Royal Shakespeare Theatre, Stratford-upon-Avon; Barbican Theatre, London, 1983; European and US tour, 1984; Gershwin Theatre, New York, 1985.
        Arden of Faversham (anon.), Other Place Theatre, Stratford-upon-Avon; Barbican Theatre, London, 1983.
        Poppy (Nichols), Barbican Theatre, London; Adelphi Theatre, London, 1983.

1983   *Cyrano de Bergerac* (Rostand), Barbican Theatre, London; US tour, 1984; Gershwin Theatre, New York, 1985.

1985   *Red Noses* (Barnes), Barbican Theatre, London.
        Othello (Shakespeare), Royal Shakespeare Theatre, Stratford-upon-Avon, and Barbican Theatre, London.

1986   *The Winter's Tale* (Shakespeare), Royal Shakespeare Theatre, Stratford-upon-Avon.
        Scenes from a Marriage (Feydeau), Barbican Theatre, London.

1987   *The Balcony* (Genet), Barbican Theatre, London.

1988   *Carrie* (adapted from King), Royal Shakespeare Theatre, Stratford-upon-Avon, London, and New York.

1989   *Romeo and Juliet* (Shakespeare), Swan Theatre, Stratford-upon-Avon.

1991   *Love's Labour's Lost* (Shakespeare), Barbican Theatre, London.
        The Seagull (Chekhov), Royal Shakespeare Theatre, Stratford-upon-Avon.

1992   *Tamburlaine the Great* (Marlowe), Swan Theatre, Stratford-upon-Avon; Barbican Theatre, London, 1993.

1995   *The Importance of Being Earnest* (Wilde), Repertory Theatre, Birmingham.

Publications

The Balcony (translation), with Barbara Wright, 1971; *Pleasure and Repentance* (translation), with Barbara Wright, 1976.

* * *

Terry Hands, one of the foremost directors to emerge in the wake of Sir Peter Hall's stewardship at Stratford, has spent most of his career in senior posts with the Royal Shakespeare Company, beginning with the Theatregoround offshoot in 1966 and culminating in his appointment as sole artistic director and chief executive in 1986. He first came to attention for his participation in 1964 in the founding of Liverpool's Everyman Theatre, which quickly established itself as one of the liveliest provincial theatres under his direction. Subsequent success with the RSC proved that Hands was a director with the "common" touch, able to respond to the challenge of the great Shakespearean classics in a way that would appeal to mass audiences. His very first production for the main theatre in Stratford-upon-Avon, *The Merry Wives of Windsor*, prospered on its transfer to the Aldwych and such was the praise lavished on the show that it was brought back to Stratford the following season.

Though few critics have found much to get excited about in terms of his interpretation of Shakespeare texts, Hands's taste for flamboyant, large-scale spectacle and ambitious projects brought a new sense of exhilaration to the company. In particular, he garnered praise for this collaborations with the actor Alan Howard, who played such parts as Henry IV, Henry V, Coriolanus, Richard II and Richard III under his direction. The cycles of history plays staged by Hands in the 1970's were landmarks in the company's development, and by 1980 he had produced all of Shakespeare's histories; his *Richard III* at the Comédie-Française in 1972 brought similar praise from Continental critics and audiences. Equally distinguished in the annals of the company was his production of *Much Ado About Nothing* with Derek Jacobi in 1982. Among the more notable non-Shakespearean plays were Genet's *The Balcony* (1971), T. S. Eliot's *Murder in the Cathedral* (1972) and Arbuzov's *Old World* (1976). Not all his productions met with unqualified admiration, though: in 1983 his production of *Poppy* by Peter Nichols, which was intended to evoke an uproarious rough-and-ready Victorian pantomime, rather missed the point by rendering the show as a lavishly overproduced West End musical.

Hands was justly rewarded with the joint artistic directorship of the RSC, with Trevor Nunn, in 1978, and eventually with the sole leadership of the company between 1986 and 1991. Unfortunately, Hands experienced mixed fortunes in this period, faced with severe financial pressures that entailed a reduction in the number of productions presented and ultimately the temporary closure of the RSC's Barbican base.

Convinced of the need to push for a more widely-based popular audience, he pursued a somewhat controversial policy of mixing the staple diet of Shakespeare and other classics with large-scale productions that would have strong commercial appeal. Thus, the ill-fated and much-lamented decision to present *Carrie*, an ambitious musical derived from a blockbuster thriller by Stephen King, in the style of the commercial West End. Critics and devotees of the RSC united in decrying the attempts of a major subsidized national company to prove itself as a commercially viable organisation and audiences responded to this bid for "lowbrow" credibility by staying away. The closure of the show, which had been intended for long runs on the London and Broadway stages, after just five performances, was a significant blow to the company and ultimately fatal for Hands's reputation as its head. At any rate, it meant the end of such forays into the commercial sector for the foreseeable future. In Hands's defence, it must be said that the company faced severe financial problems at the time, and perhaps the attempt had to be made if only in order to demonstrate the undesirability of a major national theatre company being obliged to abandon its artistic principles because of serious underfunding.

—David Pickering

————

HAWTREY, (Sir) Charles (Henry). British actor-manager. Born in Eton, Berkshire, 21 September 1858. Educated at St Michael's School, Aldin House, Slough, 1869–72; Eton public school, 1872–73; Rugby public school, 1873–75; under private tutors, 1876–79; Oxford University, 1881. Married 1) Madeline Sheriffe in 1886 (divorced 1893); 2) Katherine Elsie Petre in 1919. Stage debut, Prince of Wales's Theatre, London, 1881; first ventured into management at Her Majesty's Theatre, London, 1885; subsequently managed 16 London venues, including the Globe, Princess, Comedy, and Avenue Theatres; New York debut, 1901; further US visits, 1903 and 1904. Knighted, 1922. Died in London, 30 July 1923.

Roles

1881	Edward Langton in *The Colonel* (Burnand), Prince of Wales's Theatre, London; British tour, 1882; Imperial Theatre, London, 1883.
1882	Jack Merryweather in *The Marble Arch* (Rose), Prince of Wales's Theatre, London.
1883	Charles Livingstone in *That Rascal Pat* (Grover), Gaiety Theatre, London.
	Mr Bultitude's Body in *Vice-Versa* (Rose), Gaiety Theatre, London.

	Herbert in *Equals* (Rose), British tour.
	Maurice Lawley in *Stage Land* (Douglas), British tour.
	Douglas Cattermole in *The Private Secretary* (Hawtrey, adapted from Moser's *Der Bibliothekar*), British tour; Prince's Theatre, London, and Globe Theatre, London, 1884–86; Avenue Theatre, London, 1895.
1884	Geoffrey Wynyard in *Dan'l Druce* (Gilbert), Court Theatre, London.
1886	Osmond Hewitt in *The Pickpocket* (G. P. Hawtrey, adapted from Moser), Globe Theatre, London.
	Basil Brooke in *Harvest* (Fitch), Princess's Theatre, London.
1887	Reginald Sparker in *Lodgers* (Thomas), Globe Theatre, London.
	Felix Featherstone in *The Snowball* (Grundy), Globe Theatre, London.
	Arthur Hummingtop in *The Arabian Nights* (Grundy, adapted from Moser), Globe Theatre, London, and Comedy Theatre, London.
1889	Jasper Quayle in *Tenterhooks* (Paull), Comedy Theatre, London.
	Charles Greythorne in *Pink Dominos* (Albery), Comedy Theatre, London.
1890	Captain Armytage in *Nerves* (Carr), Comedy Theatre, London.
	Captain L'Estrange in *May and December* (Grundy), Comedy Theatre, London.
	Charles Shackleton in *Jane* (Nicholls and Lestocq), Comedy Theatre, London.
1891	Reginald in *Godpapa* (Philips and Brookfield), Comedy Theatre, London.
1892	John Maxwell in *The Grey Mare* (Sims and Raleigh), Comedy Theatre, London.
	Charlie Graham in *Time is Money* (Bell and Cecil), Comedy Theatre, London; Criterion Theatre, London, 1905.
	The Poet in *The Poet and the Puppets* (Brookfield and Glover), Comedy Theatre, London.
	Charles Prothero in *To-Day* (Brookfield), Comedy Theatre, London.
1893	Harry Briscoe in *The Sportsman* (Lestocq), Comedy Theatre, London.
	Tom Stanhope in *Tom, Dick and Harry* (Pacheo), Trafalgar Square Theatre, London.
1894	Major Kildare in *Mrs Dexter* (Darnley), Strand Theatre, London.
	Viscount Oldacre in *The Candidate* (McCarthy), Criterion Theatre, London.
	Chauncey Pottleton in *Hot Water* (Farnie), Criterion Theatre, London.
	Horace Dudley in *A Gay Widow* (Burnand), Court Theatre, London.
	Dr William Brown in *Dr Bill* (Aidé), Court Theatre, London.
1895	Lord Goring in *An Ideal Husband* (Wilde), Haymarket Theatre, London.
	Matthew Ponderbury in *Mrs Ponderbury's Past* (Burnand), Avenue Theatre, London; Vaudeville Theatre, London, 1907.
1896	Martin Heathcote in *Mr Martin* (Hawtrey), Comedy Theatre, London.

Charles Hawtrey

Hon. Stacey Gillam in *A White Elephant* (Carton), Comedy Theatre, London.

1897   Herbert Jocelyn in *Saucy Sally* (Burnand), Comedy Theatre, London.

Major Dick Rudyard in *One Summer's Day* (Esmond), Comedy Theatre, London.

1898   Lord Algernon Chetland in *Lord and Lady Algy* (Carton), Comedy Theatre, London, and Avenue Theatre, London.

1899   Hugh Farrant in *The Cuckoo* (Brookfield), Avenue Theatre, London; Vaudeville Theatre, London, 1907.

Horace Parker in *A Message from Mars* (Ganthony), Avenue Theatre, London; Prince of Wales's Theatre, London, and Garrick Theatre, New York, 1901; Avenue Theatre, London, 1905; Prince of Wales's Theatre, London, 1911; Apollo Theatre, London, 1914.

1901   Lord Strathpeffer in *The Man from Blankley's* (Anstey), Prince of Wales's Theatre, London; Haymarket Theatre, London, and Windsor Castle, 1906; His Majesty's Theatre, London, 1917.

1902   Brooke Trench in *The President* (Stayton), Prince of Wales's Theatre, London.

William Waring in *There and Back* (Arliss), Prince of Wales's Theatre, London.

1905   Frederick Ware in *Lucky Miss Dean* (Bowkett), Coronet Theatre, London, British tour, and Haymarket Theatre, London.

Arthur Kingsbury in *The Indecision of Mr Kingsbury* (Lennox), Haymarket Theatre, London.

1907   Captain Dorvaston in *Lady Huntworth's Experiment* (Carton), Haymarket Theatre, London.

John March in *Mr George* (Parker), Vaudeville Theatre, London.

1908   Charles Ingleton in *Dear Old Charlie* (Brookfield), Vaudeville Theatre, London; Prince of Wales's Theatre, London, and Maxine Elliott Theatre, New York, 1912.

Jack Straw in *Jack Straw* (Maugham), Vaudeville Theatre, London.

1909   Duke of Hermanos in *The Noble Spaniard* (Maugham), Royalty Theatre, London.

Sir Charles Worgan in *What the Public Wants* (Bennett), Royalty Theatre, London.

Recklaw Poole in *The Little Damozel* (Hoffe), Wyndham's Theatre, London, and Windsor Castle.

1910   Bernard Darrell in *The Naked Truth* (Paxton and Maxwell), Wyndham's Theatre, London.

Georges Bullin in *Inconstant George* (Unger), Prince of Wales's Theatre, London.

1911   Edouard Maubrun in *Better Not Enquire* (Unger), Prince of Wales's Theatre, London.

Mr Flat in *Money* (Bulwer-Lytton), Theatre Royal, Drury Lane, London.

Sneer in *The Critic* (Sheridan), His Majesty's Theatre, London.

John Harcourt in *The Great Name* (Feld and Leon, adapted by Hawtrey), Prince of Wales's Theatre, London.

Jacques Calvel in *The Uninvited Guest* (Raphael, adapted from Bernard), Prince of Wales's Theatre, London.

1913   Dr Lucius O'Grady in *General John Regan* (Birmingham), Apollo Theatre, London.

Vincent Cray in *The Perfect Cure* (Houghton), Apollo Theatre, London.

Cool in *London Assurance* (Boucicault), St James's Theatre, London.

Dionysius Woodbury in *Never Say Die* (Post), Apollo Theatre, London.

1914   Richard Gilder in *Things We'd Like to Know* (Titheradge), Apollo Theatre, London.

The Tipsy Passenger in *The Silver King* (H. A. Jones and Herman), Apollo Theatre, London.

Hon. Wylie Walton in *The Compleat Angler*, Coliseum Theatre, London; British tour, 1915.

William Hallowell Magee in *Seven Keys to Baldpate* (Cohan), Apollo Theatre, London.

1915   Lord Charles Temperleigh in *A Busy Day* (Carton), Apollo Theatre, London.

Moses in *The School for Scandal* (Sheridan), Covent Garden, London.

Lord Marston in *Striking*, Apollo Theatre, London.

Sam in *The Haunted Husband*, Coliseum Theatre, London.

Jack Annerley in *Q* (Leacock and Hastings), Coliseum Theatre, London.

1916   Richard Trotter in *Please Help Emily* (Harwood), Playhouse Theatre, London.

Jimmy in *Waiting at the Church*, Coliseum Theatre, London.

1917   Anthony Silvertree in *Anthony in Wonderland* (Hoffe), Prince of Wales's Theatre, London.

Peter in *His Wedding Night*, Coliseum Theatre, London.

Blinn Corbett in *The Saving Grace* (Chambers), Garrick Theatre, London.

1918   Hilary Farrington in *The Naughty Wife* (Jackson), Playhouse Theatre, London.

1919   William in *Home and Beauty* (Maugham), Playhouse Theatre, London.

1920   James Smith in *His Lady Friends* (Nyitray and Mandel), St James's Theatre, London.

1921   Garry Ainsworth in *Up in Mabel's Room* (Collison and Harbach), Playhouse Theatre, London.

Ambrose Applejohn in *Ambrose Applejohn's Adventure* (Hackett), Criterion Theatre, London.

*

Publications

The Truth at Last, 1924.

Bibliography

Books:

Florence Molesworth Hawtrey, *The History of the Hawtrey Family*, London, 1903.

* * *

Charles Hawtrey was knighted in 1922, but he died in 1923 without the chance to build his knighthood into his name and reputation. Hawtrey is significant in the stage history of his time, though, as a rare non-Shakespearean and non-heroic British actor to be honoured with a title. His range came in society drama and he specialized in upper-crust rogues and cads. His skill in slight pieces was unsurpassed and the success he gained as an actor and manager suggests the escapist tastes of many late Victorian, Edwardian, and World War I audiences in both Britain and the USA.

Hawtrey's leading qualities as an actor lay in his ease and apparent effortlessness on the stage. Something of these came as the natural extensions of a boy active in cricket and a man comfortable in the gentlemanly circles of English horse-racing. Even into his portly sixties, Hawtrey maintained his characteristic grace, lightness, and buoyancy on the stage. He stands as one of the pioneers of a style of underplaying which, in fact, diverges from the more general orotundity of the Shakespearean tradition. Together with actors like Gerald du Maurier and A. E. Matthews, Hawtrey refined a style that combined elegant costuming with speaking and movement of such fluidity that it did not look like acting at all.

Hawtrey's charming rascals also signalled a change in definitions of leading men and in the issues considered central to British drama. On one hand, Hawtrey's charac-

ters savoured of traditional farce in that they tended to be immutable, learning little or nothing from their humiliations and failures. On the other hand, they stood at the centre of plays rather than, as in the past, at the periphery. The vogue for "society drama" found its support in audiences of the sort who flocked to see Hawtrey work his wonders within small compass. This vogue was maintained into the years following World War I by the charm of the style that Hawtrey perfected and it was perpetuated even beyond World War II by Hawtrey's heirs in drawing-room style, who included Rex Harrison and Noël Coward (who acted with Hawtrey as a boy).

Hawtrey was also a manager of note, mounting successful and stylish productions on both sides of the Atlantic. He could have gained in this great freedom as an actor, but he chose instead to constrict the range of roles he took — even more than he might have been obliged to do had he hired himself out to other producers. His tastes lay very near to his skill and he seems to have been reluctant to venture very far from what he knew were his strengths. He seems to have worked changes in many of his characters on subtleties of behaviour, of dramatic formula, and as time went on around his audience's anticipation based upon their familiarity with his previous repertoire.

He supported his easy image onstage with a self-deprecating attitude towards his skill. Typically, he chose in his autobiography to dwell on his mistakes on the stage rather than on his many successes. He had no formal training and was instructed during his first engagement by an obliging stage manager, who taught the young actor the rudiments of making entrances, walking, and gesturing. Hawtrey must have been a thorough learner as well as a quick one, for in later years many would remark on his patience in instructing the range of actors in his companies, from the rankest beginners to the most practiced of players.

Hawtrey was the first important British actor to enter US vaudeville, which he essayed in 1904. With characteristic commercial canniness he parlayed his earnings from a half year of vaudeville into a tour of legitimate US theatres for *A Message from Mars*. He seems also to have played one side against the other in the contest between the producers' Syndicate in the USA and the Shuberts, who rivalled it. Hawtrey worked for both during the first decade of the 20th century and then returned to England with both career and finances shored up. The sort of light fare in which he specialized lent itself to long and lucrative runs and his career is based around a rather small number of roles in comparison to most actors of note who came before him.

Hawtrey's ease as an actor was based on the illusion of effortlessness — which he used to advance both his style and his productions. In fact, he was to die at 64, the victim of overwork. He recapitulated in this the pattern of Henry Irving, the first English actor to be knighted, who had also worked until he dropped. Without Shakespearean roles to invite comparisons between himself and such illustrious predecessors as Irving, though, Hawtrey's reputation has lagged behind those of other contemporaries. His legacy, then, lies in the new sort of career he pioneered for leading actors and in a style calculated narrowly for a particular kind of play, and a particular kind of audience.

—Leigh Woods

HAYES, Helen.   US actress. Born Helen Brown in Washington, D.C., 10 October 1900. Educated at the Sacred Heart Convent, Washington. Married playwright Charles MacArthur (died 1956). Stage debut, National Theatre, Washington, 1905; New York debut, Herald Square Theatre, 1909; film debut, 1917; acted with Theatre Guild, New York, from 1925; London debut, Haymarket Theatre, 1948; first appearance at Helen Hayes Theatre, New York, 1958; founder, Helen Hayes Repertory Company, 1964; toured Far East, 1965–66; joined APA Phoenix company, 1966; retired from the stage in 1971 but continued to appear in films and on television. Member: American National Theatre Academy (president, 1951–53). Recipient: Oscar, 1931, 1971; Drama League of New York medal, 1936; Medal of the City of New York; Medal of Arts (Finland); Woman of the Year, United Service Organisation, 1974. DFA: Princeton University, Princeton, New Jersey, 1956; other honorary degrees: Hamilton College, Clinton, New York; Smith College, Northampton, Massachusetts; University of Columbia, New York; Brown University, Providence, Rhode Island; Denver University, Colorado; Brandeis University, Waltham, Massachusetts; University of New York; and Carnegie Institute, Pittsburgh. Died 17 March 1993.

Roles

1905	Prince Charles in *The Royal Family* (Marshall), National Theatre, Washington.
1905–08	Little Lord Fauntleroy in *Little Lord Fauntleroy* (Seeboh, adapted from Burnett), National Theatre, Washington.
1908	Boy Babe in *Babes in the Wood*, National Theatre, Washington.
1909	Gibson Girl and Nell Brinkley Girl in *Jack the Giant Killer* (pantomime), Belasco Theatre, Washington.
	Little Mimi in *Old Dutch* (Herbert), Herald Square Theatre, New York.
1910	Psyche Finnigan in *The Summer Widowers* (Sloane), Broadway Theatre, New York.
1911	Fannie Hicks in *The Never Homes* (Hubbell), Broadway Theatre, New York.
1914	Little Simone in *The Prodigal Husband*, Empire Theatre, New York.
1917–18	Pollyanna Whittier in *Pollyanna* (Cushing), US tour.
1918	Margaret Schofield in *Penrod* (Rose), Globe Theatre, New York.
	Margaret in *Dear Brutus* (Barrie), Empire Theatre, New York.
1919	Dorothy Fessenden in *On the Hiring Line* (O'Higgins and Ford), Washington.
	Cora Wheeler in *Clarence* (Tarkington), Hudson Theatre, New York.
1920	Bab in *Bab* (Carpenter), Park Theatre, New York.
1921	Seeby Olds in *The Wren* (Tarkington), Gaiety Theatre, New York.
	Mary Anne in *Golden Days* (Toler and Short), Gaiety Theatre, New York.
1922	Elsie Beebe in *To the Ladies* (Kaufman and Connelly), Liberty Theatre, New York.

1924	Mary Sundale in *We Moderns* (Zangwill), Gaiety Theatre, New York.
	Constance Neville in *She Stoops to Conquer* (Goldsmith), Empire Theatre, New York.
	Catherine Westcourt in *Dancing Mothers* (Selwyn and Goulding), Booth Theatre, New York.
	Dinah Partlett in *Quarantine* (Jesse), Henry Miller Theatre, New York.
1925	Cleopatra in *Caesar and Cleopatra* (Shaw), Guild Theatre, New York; County Theatre, Suffern, New York, 1935.
	Georgia Bissell in *Young Blood*, Ritz Theatre, New York.
1926	Maggie Wylie in *What Every Woman Knows* (Barrie), Bijou Theatre, New York; County Theatre, Suffern, New York, 1938; City Centre Theatre, New York, 1954.
1927	Norma Besant in *Coquette* (Regnard), Maxine Elliott Theatre, New York; US tour, 1928–29.
1930	Nellie Fitzpatrick in *Mr Gilhooley*, Broadhurst Theatre, New York.
	Peggy Chalfont in *Petticoat Influence* (Grant), Empire Theatre, New York.
1931	Lu in *The Good Fairy* (Molnár), Henry Miller Theatre, New York.
1933	Mary, Queen of Scots in *Mary of Scotland* (Anderson), Alvin Theatre, New York, and US tour.
1935	Queen Victoria in *Victoria Regina* (Housman), Broadhurst Theatre, New York; US tour, 1937–38; Martin Beck Theatre, New York, 1938.
1938	Portia in *The Merchant of Venice* (Shakespeare), Chicago.
1939	Miss Scott in *Ladies and Gentlemen* (Hecht), Martin Beck Theatre, New York.
1940	Viola in *Twelfth Night* (Shakespeare), St James Theatre, New York.
1941	Madeleine Guest in *Candle in the Wind* (M. Anderson), Shubert Theatre, New York.
1943	Harriet Beecher Stowe in *Harriet* (Ryerson and Clements), Henry Miller Theatre, New York; US tour, 1943–45.
1946	Mrs Grey in *Alice Sit-by-the-Fire* (Barrie), Bucks County Playhouse and US tour.
	Addie in *Happy Birthday* (Loos), Broadhurst Theatre, New York.
1948	Amanda Wingfield in *The Glass Menagerie* (T. Williams), Haymarket Theatre, London; City Centre Theatre, New York, 1956; National Theatre, Washington, D.C., and European tour, 1961.
1949	Mrs Burnett in *Good Housekeeping* (McCleery), US tour.
1950	Lucy Andree Ransdell in *The Wisteria Trees* (Logan), Martin Beck Theatre, New York; City Centre Theatre, New York, 1955.
1951	Mary Rose in *Mary Rose* (Barrie), ANTA Playhouse, New York.
1952	Mrs Howard V Larue II in *Mrs McThing* (Chase), ANTA Playhouse, New York.

Helen Hayes (1952).

1955   Mrs Antrobus in *The Skin of Our Teeth* (Wilder), Théâtre Sarah Bernhardt, Paris, and ANTA Playhouse, New York; National Theatre, Washington, D.C., and European tour, 1961.

1956   Mistress of Ceremonies in *Lovers, Villains, and Fools*, Théâtre-de-Lys, New York.

1957   The Duchess in *Time Remembered* (Anouilh), Morosco Theatre, New York.

1958   Nora Melody in *A Touch of the Poet* (O'Neill), Helen Hayes Theatre, New York.

1959   Lulu Spencer in *An Adventure* (Davis), Tappan Zee Theatre, Nyack, New York.

1962   Several roles in *Shakespeare Revisited: A Programme for Two Players* (Shakespeare compilation), American Shakespeare Festival Theatre, Stratford, Connecticut; US tour, 1962–63.

1964   Abigail Adams, Dolly Madison, Mrs Lincoln, Mrs Cleveland, and Mrs Wilson in *The White House* (Murphy), Henry Miller Theatre, New York.

1966   Mrs Candour in *The School for Scandal* (Sheridan), Lyceum Theatre, New York.

          Signora Frola in *Right You Are (If You Think You Are)* (Pirandello), Lyceum Theatre, New York.

1967   Mrs Fisher in *The Show-Off* (Kelly), Lyceum Theatre, New York; revived there and at the Shubert Theatre, Boston, and for US tour, 1968.

1969   Mrs Grant in *The Front Page* (Hecht and MacArthur), Ethel Barrymore Theatre, New York.

1970   Veta Louise Simmons in *Harvey* (Chase), ANTA Theatre, New York.

1971   Mary Tyrone in *Long Day's Journey into Night* (O'Neill), Catholic University, Washington, D.C.

Other roles included: *The Prince Chap* (Peple), National Theatre, Washington, 1905–08; *The Prince and the Pauper*, National Theatre, Washington, 1905–08; *A Poor Relation* (Kidder), National Theatre, Washington, 1909; *The Barrier* (Sutro), National Theatre, Washington, 1911; *The Seven Sisters* (Herczeg), National Theatre, Washington, 1912; *The June Bride*, US tour, 1912; *Lonely Lee*, New York, 1923; *We Comrades Three*, Lyceum Theatre, New York, 1966.

Films

The Weavers of Life, 1917; *Babs*, 1920; *The Sin of Madeline Claudet*, 1931; *Arrowsmith*, 1931; *A Farewell to Arms*, 1932; *The Son Daughter*, 1933; *The White Sister*, 1933; *Another Language*, 1933; *Night Flight*, 1933; *What Every Woman Knows*, 1934; *Crime Without Passion*, 1934; *Vanessa*, 1935; *Stage Door Canteen*, 1943; *My Son John*, 1951; *Main Street to Broadway*, 1953; *Anastasia*, 1956; *Third Man on the Mountain*, 1959; *Airport*, 1971; *Herbie Rides Again*, 1973; *Helen Hayes: Portrait of an American Actress*, 1974; *One of Our Dinosaurs is Missing*, 1975; *Candleshoe*, 1977.

Television

The Glass Menagerie, 1966; *Do Not Fold, Spindle, or Mutilate*, 1971; *The Snoop Sisters* (series), 1973; *Victory at Entebbe*, 1976; *A Family Upside Down*, 1978; *Murder is Easy*, 1982; *A Caribbean Mystery*, 1983. Other productions included: *The Twelve Pound Look*; *Mary of Scotland*; *The Skin of Our Teeth*.

Radio

The Helen Hayes Theatre, 1940–41.

Publications

A Gift of Joy (autobiography), 1965; *On Reflection* (autobiography), 1968; *Twice Over Lightly* (autobiography), with Anita Loos, 1972; *My Life in Three Acts* (autobiography), 1991.

* * *

Helen Hayes made her debut as a performer in 1905, at the age of five; in 1971 she appeared in the film *Airport*. Such a long career, involving the most varied activity, resists neat classification, but it is possible to identify the more striking aspects of her work: her gallery of comic parts, her series of remarkable heroines (including Queen Victoria), and her appearances in the classical repertoire.

Hayes showed versatility as a comic actress. An early success was the Connelly-Kaufman collaboration *To the Ladies* (1922), which gave her the chance to shine as the clever wife in a bright contemporary satire. In 1926 she played Maggie Wylie in Barrie's *What Every Woman Knows* — a challenging test that was bound to attract comparisons with Maude Adams, who had created the role in the USA. But Hayes survived the comparisons with credit; her affinity with Barrie's heroines has been marked. She continued to display her gifts in comedy after World War II. The 1947 Broadway season was enlived by Anita Loos's *Happy Birthday*, which Glenn Hughes described as: "a rollicking holiday for Miss Hayes in the role of a meek little librarian who inadvertently gets drunk and discovers life". Hayes enjoyed playing all varieties of comedy, from the lightest contemporary domestic piece to the lyricism and melancholy of *Twelfth Night*.

The 1930's and 1940's gave Hayes the opportunity of attempting a series of biographical roles. In 1933 there was her Mary Stuart in *Mary of Scotland*, which was followed by her famous impersonation of Queen Victoria in Laurence Housman's *Victoria Regina* two years later. It is not hard to see why Hayes received the medal for most distinguished performance of the year from the New York Drama League: the individual plays that make up *Victoria Regina* require an actress of range and discipline who can convincingly portray Victoria as a girl, a young wife, a middle-aged widow, and finally as the Queen-Empress of her last years. Production photographs preserve something of the completeness of Hayes's assumption — the self-effacing quality that allowed her to subordinate everything to the role. Another biographical portrayal was her Harriet Beecher Stowe in the Ryerson-Clements dramatisation *Harriet* (1942). The play was regarded as "sympathetic but uninspired", its best feature being the central performance. Hayes demonstrated her customary ability to immerse herself in the identity of a dramatic character — to represent, in fact, the antithesis of the "personality" school of acting, in which the role was subordinated to the temperament of the performer.

A capacity to serve the role made Hayes a natural recruit to the Theatre Guild of New York. The organisation had been founded in 1918 to present non-commercial plays of quality. For the opening production at the Guild's own theatre in 1925, Hayes played Cleopatra in Shaw's *Caesar and Cleopatra*. By common consent this was not one of the Guild's best efforts; nor was Hayes's Cleopatra one of her best roles. But the connection with the Guild was to be a fruitful one. Their 1940 *Twelfth Night*, for example, fielded Hayes as Viola and Maurice Evans as Malvolio. The production, by Margaret Webster, did not altogether assist in communicating the spirit of the play, for it intruded the apparatus of Restoration comedy into the world of Illyria, as Robert Speaight recorded: "The sum effect was of merry and picturesque invention, and much individual accomplishment; but the lyrical pulse of the play beat rather faintly, and its underlying melancholy was smothered by the sophistication to which Broadway lends a ready ear". Phyllis Hartnoll, however, noted that Hayes was much admired; Evans showed his usual skill and resource. It was

at any rate satisfying to find Hayes giving her talents to the service of Shakespearean comedy.

Hayes did not, like Evans, work extensively in the Shakespeare-Shaw repertoire. But if complete roles have been few (there was a Chicago Portia in 1938), she compensated for this by recitals and readings. Her Repertory Company (formed in 1964) did valuable work in promoting Shakespearean readings in universities. A similar venture was the Evans-Hayes recital *Shakespeare Revisited*, which toured the USA in 1962–63.

It is a little difficult to speak of a "classical" strain in US 20th-century acting. The best-equipped Shakespearean actor on Broadway in the 1930's and 1940's was the Englishman Maurice Evans. Among actresses, Judith Anderson (Australian-born) occupied a special position; as Medea and Lady Macbeth she rose to the most exacting demands. After Anderson, Helen Hayes and Katharine Cornell have the best claim, in Garff Wilson's phrase, to "kinship with the classic school". He continues: "Although no actress of the period demonstrated the range or the power of Charlotte Cushman or Helena Modjeska, Anderson, Hayes, and Cornell nevertheless gave to their acting an integrity, a devotion, and a quality which resemble the ideals of the classic school". This seems an eminently fair assessment. The last word should come from Hayes herself, who in characteristically unassuming fashion declared: "I'm no high priestess. I'm not in the theatre merely to make a living, or just to have long runs. I'm also in it for fun".

—Charles Calder

HERBERT, Jocelyn. British designer. Born in London, 22 February 1917. Educated at St Paul's Girls' School, London, and in Paris and Vienna; studied art in France and at the Slade School of Art, London; trained for the stage under Michel Saint-Denis and George Devine, London Theatre Studio, 1936–37. Married Anthony B. Lousada in 1937 (divorced 1960), one son and three daughters. Debut as theatre designer, under George Devine at the Royal Court Theatre, London, 1957; freelance designer, from 1958. Fellow, Royal Academy, 1991. Associate, Royal College of Art, 1964; Royal Designer for Industry, 1971.

Productions

1957   *The Chairs* (Ionesco), Royal Court Theatre, London.
        Purgatory (Yeats), Royal Court Theatre, London.
1958   *The Sport of My Mad Mother* (Jellicoe), Royal Court Theatre, London.
        The Lesson (Ionesco), Royal Court Theatre, London.
        Endgame (Beckett), Royal Court Theatre, London.
1959   *Roots* (Wesker), Royal Court Theatre, London.
        Sergeant Musgrave's Dance (Arden), Royal Court Theatre, London.
1960   *Chicken Soup with Barley* (Wesker), Royal Court Theatre, London.

I'm Talking about Jerusalem (Wesker), Royal Court Theatre, London.

Trials by Logue (Logue), Royal Court Theatre, London.

Antigone (Logue), Royal Court Theatre, London.

1961   *The Changeling* (Middleton and Rowley), Royal Court Theatre, London.

The Kitchen (Wesker), Royal Court Theatre, London.

Luther (Osborne), Royal Court Theatre, London.

Richard III (Shakespeare), Royal Shakespeare Theatre, Stratford-upon-Avon.

1962   *A Midsummer Night's Dream* (Shakespeare), Royal Court Theatre, London.

Chips with Everything (Wesker), Royal Court Theatre, London.

Happy Days (Beckett), Royal Court Theatre, London.

1963   *Baal* (Brecht), Royal Court Theatre, London.

Skyvers (Reckford), Royal Court Theatre, London.

Exit the King (Ionesco), Royal Court Theatre, London.

1964   *The Seagull* (Chekhov), Royal Court Theatre, London.

Othello (Shakespeare), National Theatre, London.

Saint Joan of the Stockyards (Brecht), Royal Court Theatre, London.

Inadmissible Evidence (Osborne), Royal Court Theatre, London; Belasco Theatre, New York, 1965.

Julius Caesar (Shakespeare), Royal Court Theatre, London.

1965   *A Patriot for Me* (Osborne), Royal Court Theatre, London.

Mother Courage (Brecht), National Theatre, London.

Ghosts (Ibsen), Aldwych Theatre, London.

1966   *The Lion and the Jewel* (Soyinka), Royal Court Theatre, London.

Orpheus and Euridice (Gluck), Sadler's Wells Theatre, London.

1969   *Life Price* (O'Neill and Seabrook), Royal Court Theatre, London.

Hamlet (Shakespeare), Roundhouse Theatre, London, and Lunt-Fontanne Theatre, New York.

1970   *Three Months Gone* (Howarth), Royal Court Theatre, London.

Home (Storey), Royal Court Theatre, London, and Morosco Theatre, New York.

Beckett 3 (Beckett), Theatre Upstairs, London.

1971   *The Changing Room* (Storey), Royal Court Theatre, London.

A Woman Killed with Kindness (Heywood), National Theatre, London.

Tyger (Mitchell), National Theatre, London.

1973   *Not I* (Beckett), Royal Court Theatre, London.

Krapp's Last Tape (Beckett), Royal Court Theatre, London.

Savages (Hampton), Royal Court Theatre, London.

Cromwell (Storey), Royal Court Theatre, London.

1974   *Life Class* (Storey), Royal Court Theatre, London.

Pygmalion (G. B. Shaw), Albery Theatre, London.

1975   *What the Butler Saw* (Orton), Royal Court Theatre, London.

Teeth 'n' Smiles (Hare), Royal Court Theatre, London.

The Force of Destiny (Verdi), Paris Opera, Paris.

1976   *Footfalls* (Beckett), Royal Court Theatre, London.

That Time (Beckett), Royal Court Theatre, London.

1977   *The Merchant* (Wesker), Plymouth Theatre, New York.

Lulu (Berg), Metropolitan Opera House, New York.

1978   *Saratoga* (Howard), Aldwych Theatre, London.

1979   *Happy Days* (Beckett), Royal Court Theatre, London.

The Abduction from the Seraglio (Mozart), Metropolitan Opera House, New York.

The Rise and Fall of the City of Mahoganny (Brecht and Weill), Metropolitan Opera House, New York.

1980   *Early Days* (Storey), National Theatre, London.

Galileo (Brecht), National Theatre, London.

1981   *The Oresteia* (Aeschylus), National Theatre, London.

1982   *Portage to San Cristobal of Adolph Hitler* (Hampton), Mermaid Theatre, London.

1984   *The Devil and the Good Lord* (Sartre), Lyric Theatre, Hammersmith, London.

1985   *Gigi* (Lerner and Loewe), Lyric Theatre, London.

1986   *The Mask of Orpheus* (Birtwhistle), Coliseum Theatre, London.

1987   *J. J. Farr* (Harwood), Phoenix Theatre, London.

1987–92 *Rum and Coca Cola* (Matura), Royal Court Theatre, London.

Timon of Athens (Shakespeare), Haymarket Theatre, Leicester.

Julius Caesar (Shakespeare), Haymarket Theatre, Leicester.

Creon (Sophocles), Haymarket Theatre, Leicester.

1989   *The March on Russia* (Hare), Royal National Theatre, London.

1990   *The Trackers of Oxyrhynchus* (Harrison), Royal National Theatre, London.

1992   *Square Rounds* (Harrison), Royal National Theatre, London.

Stages (Storey), Royal National Theatre, London.

Heartbreak House (G. B. Shaw), Haymarket Theatre, London.

Films

Tom Jones, 1963; *Isadora*, 1968; *If . . .* , 1969; *Hamlet*, 1970; *Ned Kelly*, 1970; *O, Lucky Man*, 1973; *The Hotel New Hampshire*, 1984; *The Whales of August*, 1987.

* * *

Jocelyn Herbert is the designer most closely associated with the new wave of English drama of the late 1950's and the 1960's and the designer who most consistently exemplified the shift away from decorativeness in British stage design during those years. In this she set a pattern that significantly influenced the work of others (for example, Griffin, Gunter, Dudley, and Napier). It was her work as chief designer with the English Stage Society at the Royal Court Theatre that established a model for settings that most satisfactorily responded to the lean, socially focussed, critically penetrating works of such writers as Osborne, Wesker, Arden, Jellicoe, and, later, Storey, Hampton, and Orton. The directors with whom Herbert worked (John Dexter, Tony Richardson, Lindsay Anderson, John Gaskill, and Peter Gill among others), as well as the basic philosophy of the ESS as shaped by its founder, George Devine, placed primary emphasis on the text and the actors. Settings became unobtrusive, rather austere, and leaned toward the abstract in capturing the essential quality of each work.

This tendency toward an expressive minimalism also proved very suitable for other work at the Royal Court, especially productions of Beckett, Ionesco, and, especially, Brecht. Indeed, it was the Brechtian Epic approach with its non-illusionistic yet theatrically charged spareness and social orientation that in itself affected the Royal Court philosophy and practice of theatre. The other chief inspiration for Herbert and the Royal Court was the theatre tradition of Jacques Copeau, as transmitted by his nephew Michel Saint-Denis, with whom both Herbert and Devine studied in the 1930's in London. Copeau's vision of an austere theatre centring on the work of the actor and totally committed to its art blended effectively with Brecht's anti-romanticism, emphasis on a socially critical text, and functional theatricalism.

Necessity reinforced ideals. The Royal Court always operated on a limited budget in limited quarters. This led Herbert and her collaborators toward the creative use of a relatively bare stage with a neutral cyclorama but more often a stage that was bare to the walls. Herbert's basic premise was clear: "When you have a bare stage it's very beautiful, like a bare canvas. You put one thing on it and it changes the entire dimensions. One chair and you have all sorts of possibilities. And that's how you begin". Within this empty space, Herbert would arrange a few very carefully chosen props and scenic elements (often of authentic materials or else recently developed synthetics) with great care for the placement of the actors in a spatial composition accented by equally precise lighting. The actors became part of the design, not simply performers thrust in front of elaborate sets. The Brechtian practice of exposing lighting units led Herbert and her colleagues to design different lighting grids for each production, to follow the contours of the stage space determined for that production and thus more nearly define the performance space by lighting. Peter Brook referred to her work as a

restoration of "new simplicity and purity to the English theatre". Herbert herself used the term "poetic realism".

Arden's *Sergeant Musgrave's Dance* (1959) centred on a platform with a few stark, symbolic properties within a neutral set of drapes. Gothic arches in the background and a huge crucifix were the key elements for Osborne's *Luther* (1961). Brecht's *Baal* (1963) made use of a white cyclorama, projections on it of house roofs, a red sun, or a forest, and lowered-in walls or red willow branches. Brecht's *Saint Joan of the Stockyards* (1964) was a bit more elaborate: in front of a painted collage of Chicago stockyards that always remained visible in the background, two large periaktoi units were placed midstage at right and left. The various panel surfaces of the rotating periaktoi, plus a few pieces of furniture, created the various scenes of the play.

The fundamental principles of Herbert's work carried over into productions with bigger budgets in larger theatres, as was evident in her scenography for two productions on the Olivier stage of the National Theatre. Although designed to be treated as an amphitheatre in the Greek manner, the Olivier was most often disguised as either a proscenium or thrust stage. For both *Galileo* (1980) and *The Oresteia* (1981), Herbert eliminated all masking and opened up the entire stage to the bare walls. Then, in relation to the rectilinear nature of the theatre interior, she introduced a large raised circle downstage for the main acting area of each production, thus revitalizing the visual effect of an amphitheatre space. In *Galileo* the circle served as a base for a square platform that rode in on rails that ran one hundred feet back into the scene shop. To create an enclosed effect for certain scenes, and to serve as a surface for projections, a large screen was lowered and raised directly behind the circle. The square screen, as well as thin, squared metal frames that backed the circle like a tryptich, offset the circle visually in a striking way. Typical of Herbert's economy and grace was a large armillary sphere occasionally suspended behind the rear of the stage; symbolic of a small one used by Galileo, it was nevertheless an obviously modern artefact, a sculpture of brass, copper, and steel interwoven circles that also supplemented the play of circle and square.

The Oresteia echoed the central use of a circle, here recalling the crucial circular orchestra of Greek theatres. Two diagonal entry paths led offstage right and left, and a low platform with three central steps backed the circle. Recreating the effect of a Greek proscenium facade on this platform was a modernistic metal wall that reflected the three great metal panels permanently at the rear of the stage itself. It was another indication of Herbert's sensitivity to the space of a given theatre in relation to the designer's treatment of the stage within it.

Herbert has also worked in opera, perhaps most notably on *The Force of Destiny* (1975) and *The Abduction from the Seraglio* (1979) at the Met. For the latter, the key design motif was the curved and pointed form of a Turkish arch of domed roof, which was echoed in the selectively chosen architectural structures on stage as well as in the silhouette of the ornamentally perforated teaser outlining the top of the proscenium arch.

Whether working within spatial and budgetary constraints or with ample resources, Herbert's mode of understatement, fine proportion, and evocative essentials characterizes one significant branch of contemporary British stage design.

—Jarka M. Burian

———————

HILLER, (Dame) Wendy. British actress. Born in Bramhall, England, 15 August 1912. Educated at Winceby House, Bexhill; trained for the stage at the Manchester Repertory Theatre, Manchester, England. Married playwright Ronald Gow in 1937 (died 1993), one son and one daughter. Stage debut, Manchester Repertory Theatre, 1930; assistant stage manager, Manchester Repertory Theatre, 1931; London debut, 1935; Broadway debut, Shubert Theatre, 1936; film debut, 1937; actress, Bristol Old Vic Theatre, Bristol, 1946, Old Vic Theatre, London, 1955–56, National Theatre, London, from 1975. Recipient: Oscar, 1959. LL.D: University of Manchester, 1984. OBE (Order of the British Empire), 1971; DBE (Dame Commander of the British Empire), 1975.

Roles

1930	The Maid in *The Ware Case* (Pleydell), Manchester Repertory Theatre, Manchester.
1934	Sally Hardcastle in *Love on the Dole* (Greenwood, adapted by Gow), British tour; Garrick Theatre, London, 1935.
1936	Saint Joan in *Saint Joan* (G. B. Shaw), Malvern Festival, Malvern.
	Eliza Doolittle in *Pygmalion* (G. B. Shaw), Malvern Festival, Malvern.
1943	Viola in *Twelfth Night* (Shakespeare), British tour.
1944	Sister Joanna in *The Cradle Song* (Underhill), Apollo Theatre, London.
1945	Princess Charlotte in *The First Gentleman* (Ginsbury), New Theatre, London.
1946	Portia in *The Merchant of Venice* (Shakespeare), Bristol Old Vic Theatre, Bristol.
	Pegeen Mike in *The Playboy of the Western World* (Synge), Bristol Old Vic Theatre, Bristol.
	Tess Durbyfield in *Tess of the D'Urbervilles* (Gow, adapted from Hardy), Bristol Old Vic Theatre, Bristol; Piccadilly Theatre, London, 1947.
1947	Catherine Sloper in *The Heiress* (Goetz, adapted from H. James's *Washington Square*), Biltmore Theatre, New York; Haymarket Theatre, London, 1950.
1949	Ann Veronica in *Ann Veronica* (Gow), Piccadilly Theatre, London.
1951–53	Evelyn Daly in *Waters of the Moon* (Hunter), Haymarket Theatre, London.
1955	Margaret Tollemache in *Night of the Ball* (Burn), New Theatre, London.
	Portia in *Julius Caesar* (Shakespeare), Old Vic Theatre, London.
	Mistress Page in *The Merry Wives of Windsor* (Shakespeare), Old Vic Theatre, London.

	Hermione in *The Winter's Tale* (Shakespeare), Old Vic Theatre, London.
	Emilia in *Othello* (Shakespeare), Old Vic Theatre, London.
	Helen in *Troilus and Cressida* (Shakespeare), Old Vic Theatre, London.
1957	Josie Hogan in *A Moon for the Misbegotten* (O'Neill), Bijou Theatre, New York.
1958	Isobel Cherry in *Flowering Cherry* (Bolt), Haymarket Theatre, London; Lyceum Theatre, New York, 1959.
1959	Marie Marescaud in *All in the Family* (Hatlen), Gaiety Theatre, Dublin.
1960	Carrie Berniers in *Toys in the Attic* (Hellman), Piccadilly Theatre, London.
1961	Mary Kingsley in *Mr Rhodes*, Royal Windsor Theatre, London.
1962	Miss Tina in *The Aspern Papers* (James, adapted by M. Redgrave), Playhouse Theatre, New York; Haymarket Theatre, London, 1984.
1963	Susan Shepherd in *The Wings of the Dove* (Taylor, adapted from James), Lyric Theatre, London.
1965	Elizabeth in *A Measure of Cruelty* (Passeur), Birmingham Repertory Theatre, Birmingham.
1966	Martha in *A Present for the Past*, Edinburgh Festival, Edinburgh.
1967	Nurse Wayland in *The Sacred Flame* (Maugham), Duke of York's Theatre, London.
1968	Irene in *When We Dead Awaken* (Ibsen), Edinburgh Festival, Edinburgh.
1970	Enid in *The Battle of Shrivings* (Shaffer), Lyric Theatre, London.
1972	Mrs Alving in *Ghosts* (Ibsen), Arts Theatre, Cambridge.
1972	Queen Mary in *Crown Matrimonial* (Ryton), Haymarket Theatre, London.
1975	Edith Grove in *Lies!* (Baxter), Albery Theatre, London.
1975	Gunhild Borkman in *John Gabriel Borkman* (Ibsen), Old Vic Theatre, London; National Theatre, London, 1976.
1977	Mrs Whyte in *Waters of the Moon* (Hunter), Chichester Festival, Chichester; Haymarket Theatre, London, 1978.
1981	Lady Bracknell in *The Importance of Being Earnest* (Wilde), Watford; Royalty Theatre, London, 1987.
1988	Miss Daisy in *Driving Miss Daisy* (Uhry), Apollo Theatre, London.

Other roles included: *Evensong* (Knoblock and Nichols), British tour, 1932; *The Aspen Papers* (adapted from James), Haymarket Theatre, London, 1984.

Films

Lancashire Luck, 1937; *Pygmalion*, 1938; *Major Barbara*, 1940; *I Know Where I'm Going*, 1947; *An Outcast of the Islands*, 1951; *Single Handed/Sailor of the King*, 1953; *Something of Value*, 1957; *How to Murder a Rich Uncle*,

1957; *Separate Tables*, 1958; *Sons and Lovers*, 1960; *Toys in the Attic*, 1963; *A Man for All Seasons*, 1966; *Murder on the Orient Express*, 1974; *Voyage of the Damned*, 1976; *The Cat and the Canary*, 1979; *The Elephant Man*, 1980; *Country*, 1981; *Making Love*, 1982; *The Lonely Passion of Judith Hearne*, 1987.

Television

When We Dead Awaken, 1968; *David Copperfield*, 1969; *Peer Gynt*, 1972; *Clochemerle*, 1973; *Last Wishes*, 1978; *Richard II*, 1979; *The Curse of Tut's Tomb*, 1980; *Miss Morrison's Ghosts*, 1981; *Attracta*, 1982; *Witness for the Prosecution*, 1982; *The Kingfisher*, 1982; *The Comedy of Errors*, 1983; *The Importance of Being Earnest*, 1985; *Darley's Folly*, 1986; *All Passion Spent*, 1986; "Lord Mountbatten: The Last Viceroy", *Masterpiece Theatre*, 1986; *The Death of the Heart*, 1986; *Anne of Avonlea: The Continuing Story of Anne of Green Gables*, 1987; *Ending Up*, 1989; *The Best of Friends*, 1991; *The Countess Alice*, 1992.

* * *

Wendy Hiller is the most surprising of the theatrical Dames in that she has not been constantly before the public as a star actress. Her career has been marked by triumphant phases largely unconnected with each other and divided between stage and screen. In between she has given many performances — nearly all of high quality — in leading roles and small parts in the theatre, on film, and on television, sometimes in otherwise undistinguished or unsuccessful vehicles. It does not look like a career that was carefully planned and nurtured, more like one that has simply happened.

Hiller shot to prominence as the strong-minded Sally in the stage version of Walter Greenwood's classic novel of the Depression, *Love on the Dole*, which she played in the USA as well as in Britain. As an actress from a northern repertory company, she showed how well she had used her quite brief stage experience in learning the technical business of acting, though it was undoubtedly her personality that determined the degree of her success. The young Wendy Hiller was no fashionable sultry beauty; she looked robust and healthy, an outdoor girl, active and vigorous, with spirits capable of rising above adversity. The contours of her face and the way she used her voice suggested the bright directness of a child, the carefulness of a good child, or the mischievousness of a merry one. She was well-equipped to play Shaw's boldly innocent, provincial Saint Joan with Barry Jackson's Birmingham Repertory Company (as guest actress) at the Malvern Festival of 1936. Aided by the dramatist's advice to preserve the down-to-earth quality of Joan and her natural independence of spirit in the trial scene, Wendy Hiller erased the memory of Sybil Thorndike's original performance of Joan as definitive, the first actress to do so. She played Eliza Doolittle in *Pygmalion* during the same Malvern season, but records of that have been obscured by all the publicity attending on the transfer of the play to the screen.

Not only was Gabriel Pascal's production of *Pygmalion* the first film of a Shaw play that faithfully and intelligently represented the qualities of the original to a mass audience

Wendy Hiller (1959).

(except in its treatment of the ending), it was generally regarded as a new kind of triumph for British cinema as a whole, much as Olivier's *Henry V* was later seen. The leading actress's careful enunciation (perhaps a legacy of the time when aspiring young players were required to erase any vestiges of regional speech) was perfect for Eliza, as was her natural vivacity and the quiet dignity into which it was composed. Her facial mobility, expressive of every turn of thought and feeling, particularly delighted Shaw. Plans were made for her to go on and make a film of *Saint Joan*, but they were forestalled by the outbreak of war. Eventually Pascal went ahead with *Major Barbara*, Shaw co-operating fully. The making of this film was a much less happy experience than *Pygmalion* had provided; certainly the direction was less skilled and there were more crises. Her disappointment at the final result has led Hiller to undervalue the whole film and her own achievement in it. Closely argued and involving immensely long speeches, it was altogether a tougher assignment than *Pygmalion*, but this Barbara succeeds in blending the warmth, humour, bossiness, and competence of the heroine with a direct, pure, and passionate spirituality in a highly attractive portrait. Shaw, who had warned her at Malvern that he had not written a play with a "cataleptic Joan, who in her highest moments, goes up out of the world into a trance", gave the actress a chance to do just that in the later part of the film. In a much more modest but intelligent and charming film made at the end of the war, Powell and Pressburger's Hebridean romance *I Know Where I'm Going*, Hiller again demonstrated her ability to play a strong, independent, woman without stridency, making her sexually attractive in her freedom from any Hollywood-style erotic glamour.

Her work in Shakespeare has been limited: touring as Viola in *Twelfth Night* during the war, playing Portia in *The Merchant of Venice* at the Bristol Old Vic in 1946, and appearing as Hermione in Michael Benthall's 1955 Old Vic production are the nearest she has come to taking the great roles. The last of these was an undistinguished production that achieved emotional poignancy only in the scene where Hermione's statue comes to life. Playing alongside Richard Burton and John Neville in *Othello*, she drew from Emilia the effect of truthful feeling that was to be observed almost invariably in her later acting career. However, the triumph of that Old Vic season was Tyrone Guthrie's Edwardian version of *Troilus and Cressida*, during which the scene in Helen's boudoir created the most surprisingly brilliant effect: Wendy Hiller as a blonde incarnation of self-indulgent mischief, sporting a long cigarette-holder, a cocktail glass, and an excessive feather in her hairband.

It seems worth noting how many of Hiller's performances have had a literary basis, in adaptations of novels, where the character may be researched in the book and is not simply inherent in the stage dialogue. She had, of course, married the adaptor of *Love on the Dole*, but too many of the adaptations in which she later appeared were much less lively and skilful than Gow's. One of the best was *The Heiress* (based on Henry James's *Washington Square*), in which Hiller took over from Peggy Ashcroft and gave a quite distinctive but equally touching and powerful performance. Adaptations from Hardy and Wells denied her more opportunities than they gave, and *The Wings of the Dove* proved to be leaden. The bitter force she brought to the ending of *The Heiress* pointed the way to a number of later character parts marked by negative and repressed feelings, or twisted eccentricity, as in films of Rattigan's *Separate Tables* and Lawrence's *Sons and Lovers*, and especially as Gunhild Borkman, with Ralph Richardson and Peggy Ashcroft, in the best production of Ibsen's *John Gabriel Borkman* of its generation; even her Mrs Micawber in a television film of *David Copperfield* can be included here. Two outstanding examples of casting against type paid rich dividends: her Josie Hogan (played against physical type and her noted Englishness) in O'Neill's *Moon for the Misbegotten* in New York, and the eponymous lead in the London stage version of *Driving Miss Daisy* in 1988 ("a Jewish grandmother she ain't", as Milton Shulman commented, recognising that the actress had simply set aside this aspect of her character). For both roles she had dug inside herself to find a general emotional truth, intense, but quite free of sentimentality. A similar approach, combined with the authority she has long been able to command and great skill and sensitivity in impersonation, marked her Queen Mary in *Crown Matrimonial*. Criticisms that she always played Wendy Hiller scarcely take into account the full range of her work. In comparison with post-1956 neo-realism, her acting (like Peggy Ashcroft's) has sometimes been described as mannered, though it is probably the pure vowels and clear voice production of an earlier generation that have seemed most strange.

—Margery Morgan

HIRSCH, John (Stephen). Canadian director, playwright and teacher. Born in Siofolk, Hungary, 1 May 1930. Emigrated to Canada as a war orphan, 1947; educated at the University of Manitoba, until 1952. Established puppet theatre and directed for the Winnipeg Little Theatre, 1949–53; stage manager, Little Theatre, Winnipeg, Manitoba, 1953–57; television producer, Canadian Broadcasting Corporation, 1954; attended Central School of Speech and Drama, London, 1956; founded and directed Theatre 77 company (renamed the Manitoba Theatre Centre, 1958), Winnipeg, 1957–64; also helped found the Rainbow Stage summer theatre, 1957; collaborated with Jean Gascon at the Stratford (Ontario) Festival, 1965–68; associate artistic director, Stratford (Ontario) Festival, 1967–69; Broadway debut, 1968; also worked in New York and in Israel; head of television drama, Canadian Broadcasting Corporation, Toronto, Ontario, 1974–78; directed productions at Stratford, the Shaw Festival, National Arts Centre, Ottawa, and the Mark Taper Forum, Los Angeles, 1975–80; consulting artistic director, Seattle Repertory Theatre, Seattle, Washington, from 1979; artistic director, Stratford Festival, 1980–85; visiting lecturer, Yale Drama School, 1985–89; directed in Dallas, Toronto, New Haven and San Diego, 1985–89; also held posts as lecturer at the Southern Methodist University, 1987, Carleton University, Columbia University, Yale University, National Theatre School of Canada, and New York University. Member: Design Council, National Museums of Canada Discovery Train, 1978; Ontario Arts Council, 1978; History of the American Film Exhibition, National Arts Centre, Ottawa, (director), 1979; Canadian Centre for the Performing Arts; National Endowment of the Arts; National Arts Centre; and board of directors for the Royal Winnipeg Ballet, the Communications Group, the National Ballet of Canada, and Visions — New American Theatre Project. Recipient: Leonard Memorial Scholar, 1952; Poetry Society Award, 1952; National Council of Jewish Women Award, 1958; Outer Circle Critics Award, 1966–67; Canada Service Medal, 1967; Obie Award, 1970–71; Canadian Authors Association Award, 1973; Molson Prize, 1976; Order of Canada, 1976. D.Litt: University of Manitoba, 1966; LL.D: University of Toronto, 1967. Died (complications arising from Aids) in Toronto, 1 August 1989.

Productions

1951   *The Time of Your Life* (Saroyan), Little Theatre, Winnipeg, Manitoba.

1958–64   *A Streetcar Named Desire* (T. Williams), Manitoba Theatre Centre, Winnipeg, Manitoba.
          Mister Roberts (Heggen and Logan), Manitoba Theatre Centre, Winnipeg, Manitoba.
          Visit to a Small Planet (Vidal), Manitoba Theatre Centre, Winnipeg, Manitoba.
          Look Ahead (Peterson), Manitoba Theatre Centre, Winnipeg, Manitoba.
          Names and Nicknames (Reaney), Manitoba Theatre Centre, Winnipeg, Manitoba.

1964   *Who's Afraid of Virginia Woolf?* (Albee), Manitoba Theatre Centre, Winnipeg, Manitoba.
          Mère Courage (Brecht), Manitoba Theatre Centre, Winnipeg, Manitoba, and Théâtre du Nouveau Monde, Montreal, Quebec.

Cat on a Hot Tin Roof (T. Williams), Crest Theatre, Toronto, Ontario.

1965   *The Cherry Orchard* (Chekhov), Shakespeare Festival, Stratford, Ontario.

Andorra (Frisch), Manitoba Theatre Centre, Winnipeg, Manitoba.

1966   *Yerma* (Garcia Lorca), Repertory Theatre of the Lincoln Centre, Vivian Beaumont Theatre, New York.

Henry VI (Shakespeare), Shakespeare Festival, Stratford, Ontario.

1967   *Richard III* (Shakespeare), Shakespeare Festival, Stratford, Ontario.

Colours in the Dark (Reaney), Shakespeare Festival, Stratford, Ontario.

Galileo (Brecht), Repertory Theatre of the Lincoln Centre, Vivian Beaumont Theatre, New York.

1968   *A Midsummer Night's Dream* (Shakespeare), Shakespeare Festival, Stratford, Ontario.

The Three Musketeers (Dumas), Shakespeare Festival, Stratford, Ontario.

We Bombed in New Haven (Heller), Ambassador Theatre, New York.

Saint Joan (G. B. Shaw), Repertory Theatre of the Lincoln Centre, Vivian Beaumont Theatre, New York.

1969   *The Time of Your Life* (Saroyan), Repertory Theatre of the Lincoln Centre, Vivian Beaumont Theatre, New York.

Hamlet (Shakespeare), Shakespeare Festival, Stratford, Ontario, and University of Michigan, Ann Arbor, Michigan.

Satyricon (adapted from Petronius), Shakespeare Festival, Stratford, Ontario.

Tyger! Tyger! and Other Burning Things, National Theatre of the Deaf, Longacre Theatre, New York.

1970   *A Man's a Man* (Brecht), Manitoba Theatre Centre, Winnipeg, Manitoba, and Tyrone Guthrie Theatre, Minneapolis, Minnesota.

The Seagull (Chekhov), Habimah Theatre, Tel Aviv, Israel.

AC/DC (H. Williams), Chelsea Theatre Centre, Brooklyn Academy of Music, Brooklyn, New York.

Beggar on Horseback (Connelly), Repertory Theatre of the Lincoln Centre, Vivian Beaumont Theatre, New York.

1971   *The Playboy of the Western World* (Synge), Repertory Theatre of the Lincoln Centre, Vivian Beaumont Theatre, New York.

Antigone (Sophocles), Repertory Theatre of the Lincoln Centre, Vivian Beaumont Theatre, New York.

What the Butler Saw (Orton), Manitoba Theatre Centre, Winnipeg, Manitoba.

1972   *A Midsummer Night's Dream* (Shakespeare), Tyrone Guthrie Theatre, Minneapolis, Minnesota.

1973   *Guys and Dolls* (Loesser), Manitoba Theatre Centre, Winnipeg, Manitoba.

Lulu Street (Henry), Lennoxville Festival.

John Hirsch

The Dybbuk (Ansky, adapted by Hirsch), Manitoba Theatre Centre, Winnipeg, Manitoba, and St Lawrence Arts Centre, Toronto, Ontario; Centre Theatre Group, Mark Taper Forum, Los Angeles, California, 1975.

1975   *Between Two Worlds* (adapted by Hirsch), Centre Theatre Group, Mark Taper Forum, Los Angeles, California; also choreographed.

1976   *The Three Sisters* (Chekhov), Shakespeare Festival, Stratford, Ontario.

1979   *The Tempest* (Shakespeare), Mark Taper Forum, Los Angeles, California.

Number Our Days, Mark Taper Forum, Los Angeles, California.

Saint Joan (G. B. Shaw), Seattle Repertory Company, Seattle, Washington.

1981   *The Tempest* (Shakespeare), Shakespeare Festival, Stratford, Ontario.

1981–85 *As You Like It* (Shakespeare), Shakespeare Festival, Stratford, Ontario.

Tartuffe (Molière), Shakespeare Festival, Stratford, Ontario.

A Midsummer Night's Dream (Shakespeare), Shakespeare Festival, Stratford, Ontario.

King Lear (Shakespeare), Shakespeare Festival, Stratford, Ontario.

Mary Stuart (Schiller), Avon Theatre, Stratford, Ontario.

The Glass Menagerie (T. Williams), Avon Theatre, Stratford, Ontario.

1987   *Three Men on a Horse* (Abbott), Royal Alexandra Theatre, Toronto, Ontario.

American Dreams: Lost and Found, Alliance Theatre, Atlanta, Georgia.

1988   *Coriolanus* (Shakespeare), San Diego, California.

Odd Jobs, Toronto, Ontario.

Other productions included: *The Boyfriend* (Wilson); *Pal Joey* (Rodgers and Hart); *Peter Pan* (Barrie); *Teach Me How to Cry*; *A Funny Thing Happened on the Way to the Forum* (Sondheim), 1978; *The Alchemist* (Jonson), 1987.

Films

In the Shadow of the City, 1955.

Television

Fifteen Miles of Broken Glass, 1966; *The King of Kensington* (series), 1974–77; *The Three Musketeers*.

* * *

In 1945 John Hirsch watched his grandfather die of starvation in the Budapest ghetto, then learned that his parents and brother had perished at Auschwitz. The pain and horror of these events would haunt him for the rest of his life, in his own words, "influencing everything I am, everything I think about". From his earliest days in Canada Hirsch advocated total commitment to art. The sound of his intense, high-pitched voice demanding deeper involvement and greater passion offended the genteel sensibilities of the artistic establishment; in place of British manners he invoked a Slavic world of intrigue, melancholy and frenzied excitement. His vision brought together pain and frivolity, rage and gaiety and from these elements he concocted a uniquely flavoured theatrical brew.

Actors tell of his treacherous behaviour; he was changeable, demanding, merciless. He began his career with puppets and he sometimes treated actors as though they could be manipulated like dolls dancing on strings. But most of those who worked with him concede that in driving them to dig deeper into themselves he forced them to acheive fuller theatrical expression. He himself was unapologetic about his methods: "If you're striving after electrifying performances you have to unleash temperament and passion. You have to use your soul. In Canada you get along best when you are nice and try to please everybody".

Hirsch could on occasion be charming but he was rarely nice. His longtime collaborator Tom Hendry has said: "It was hard not to love John but sometimes it wasn't easy to like him". Hirsch's best work was full of emotional resonance, notably his Chekhov productions at Stratford, *The Cherry Orchard* in 1965 and *The Three Sisters* in 1978, both of which were finely detailed, meticulously orchestrated and deeply moving. Each character was allowed space to develop, yet was intimately interconnected with all the other characters. An overall shape emerged that was psychologically complex and charged with deep feeling.

These productions embodied a distinctly Canadian sensibility; there was no self-conscious attempt to emulate Russian or British models. Hirsch also acheived a distinctive flavour in his direction of original Canadian plays: Tom Hendry's CBC television drama *Fifteen Miles of Broken Glass* in 1966 and James Reaney's *Colours in the Dark* in 1967. Neither writer ever acheived such satisfying realisations of their work with any other director. Hirsch — the outsider — seemed to have an intuitive grasp of what was unique in the Canadian personality.

For all his intense concern with states of feeling, Hirsch had a strong impulse towards comedy. *Tartuffe*, *A Funny Thing Happened on the Way to the Forum*, *Three Men on a Horse* and *The Alchemist* were among his most successful productions and they illustrate the range of his comic taste and invention. He had a strong affinity for popular entertainment that enabled him to foster the development of such popular television comedies as *The King of Kensington*. He loved the outrageous and this was nowhere given freer rain than in his production of *Satyricon* at Stratford in 1969. A musical based on Petronius's novella, the show featured black performers, nudity and some explicit sexual material. Although it played to full houses, it offended the Stratford governors who complained it was "entertainment, not Art" and that "the people this show attracts are not the kind of people we want in our theatre". Their reaction led Hirsch to resign his position at Stratford and to concentrate his efforts in the USA.

Hirsch rightly believed this would not only open up greater opportunities for theatrical expression but would enhance his prestige at home. Hirsch was the first Canadian director to demonstrate not only the possibility but the positive values of a career that combines US and Canadian influences. His productions of *The Tempest* in Los Angeles in 1978 and at Stratford in 1981 and his *Coriolanus* in San Diego in 1988 displayed a political consciousness that derived at least in part from his experience of straddling the border of both countries.

Hirsch's vision of theatre was a compound of many elements: comedy, pathos, melodrama, argument, gags, tricks. He was not an artistic snob, but a celebrant of theatrical diversity. It is perhaps no accident that the first show he directed was Saroyan's highly theatrical grab-bag, *The Time of Your Life*, a play to which he returned more than once. He became adept at staging melodramas like *The Three Musketeers*, *Yerma* and *The Dybbuk*, musicals like *The Boyfriend* and *Pal Joey*, argumentative plays like *Saint Joan* and *Coriolanus*. He took chances with new scripts from *Teach Me How to Cry* in his first season in Winnipeg to his last production in Toronto, *Odd Jobs*. To all these varied forms he brought insight, invention and a free-ranging intelligence.

As the guiding spirit of large organisations, however, he was a problematic figure. His probing, restless, suspicious personality sometimes bordered on the paranoic. He often made unreasonable demands, drove people beyond their endurance, refused to accept financial realities and sowed discontent among his fellow workers and employees. Consequently his tenure at the Canadian Broadcasting Corporation and at the Stratford Festival was marred by an atmosphere that suggested the court not so much of an enlightened despot as of a power-mad Borgia pope. Hirsch was always a highly theatrical figure, a gadfly who combatted complacency, a stirrer-up of discontents and a seer who expanded the vision of the Canadian theatre community. His best productions displayed a unique sensitivity and some of the most vivid and affecting performances ever seen on the North American stage.

—Martin Hunter

———

HOUSEMAN, John. US director, producer, writer, and actor. Born Jacques Haussman in Bucharest, Romania, 22 September 1902. Educated at Clifton College Junior School, 1913–16, and Clifton College, both in Bristol, England, 1916–18; won scholarship to Trinity College, Cambridge, but did not take place there. Married 1) actress Zita Johan in 1929 (divorced 1931); 2) Joan Courtney in 1950, two sons. Worked in US grain business from 1919 but went bankrupt in stock market crash of 1929; entered theatre as adapter and translator, 1931; made debut as director, New York, 1934; worked for Group Theatre, New York, and Theatre Guild, New York, before appointment as head of the Negro Theatre Project, part of the Federal Theatre Project, 1935; debut as a producer, in collaboration with Orson Welles, 1935; co-founder, with Welles, Project 891, the classical theatre unit of the Federal Theatre Project, 1936; dismissed from Federal Theatre Project as producer of Blitzstein's controversial *The Cradle Will Rock*, directed by Welles, 1937; appointed head of theatre department, Vassar College, Poughkeepsie, New York, 1937; co-founder, with Welles, Mercury Theatre, 1937; worked as Welles's producer, 1936–39; editor, Mercury Theatre on the Air, 1938–39; producer, Office of War Information, 1941; took US nationality and began 20-year stint as a Hollywood producer, 1943; founder, Pelican Productions, based at the Coronet Theatre, Los Angeles, 1947; artistic director: American Shakespeare Festival Theatre and Academy, Stratford, Connecticut, 1956–59, Professional Theatre Group, University of California, Los Angeles, 1959–64, Drama Division, Juilliard School of the Performing Arts, 1966–76, and APA Phoenix, New York, 1967–70; acting debut, 1964; Cockefair Professor, University of Missouri, Kansas City, 1971–72; founder and artistic director, City Centre Acting Company, 1972; Visiting Professor of Performing Arts, University of Southern California, 1977–79. Member: National Theatre Conference, 1970 (president). Recipient: Oscar for Best Supporting Actor, 1973; National Arts Club Gold Drama Award, 1973; Southern Methodist University Alger Meadows Award; Alley Award. Died in Malibu, California, 31 October, 1988.

Productions

As director:
1934   *Four Saints in Three Acts* (Thomson and Stein), Wadsworth Athenaeum, Hartford, Connecticut, and 44th Street Theatre, New York.
1935   *The Lady from the Sea* (Ibsen), Little Theatre, Pennsylvania.
         Valley Forge (Anderson), Guild Theatre, Pittsburgh.
         Panic (McLeish), Imperial Theatre, New York.
1936   *Hamlet* (Shakespeare), Imperial Theatre, New York.

1940   *The Devil and Daniel Webster* (Herrmann), American Lyric Theatre, New York.
1941   *Liberty Jones* (Barry), Lobero Theatre, Santa Barbara, California, and Shubert Theatre, New York.
         Anna Christie (O'Neill), Lobero Theatre, Santa Barbara, California.
         Hello, Out There (Saroyan), Lobero Theatre, Santa Barbara, California.
         The Devil's Disciple (G. B. Shaw), Lobero Theatre, Santa Barbara, California.
1946   *Lute Song* (Scott), Plymouth Theatre, New York.
         Beggar's Holiday (Ellington), New York.
1950   *King Lear* (Shakespeare), National Theatre, New York.
1954   *Coriolanus* (Shakespeare), Phoenix Theatre, New York.
1956   *King John* (Shakespeare), American Shakespeare Festival, Stratford, Connecticut.
         Measure for Measure (Shakespeare), American Shakespeare Festival, Stratford, Connecticut.
1957   *Othello* (Shakespeare), American Shakespeare Festival, Stratford, Connecticut.
         Much Ado About Nothing (Shakespeare), American Shakespeare Festival, Stratford, Connecticut.
1958   *Hamlet* (Shakespeare), American Shakespeare Festival, Stratford, Connecticut.
         The Winter's Tale (Shakespeare), American Shakespeare Festival, Stratford, Connecticut.
1959   *The Merry Wives of Windsor* (Shakespeare), American Shakespeare Festival, Stratford, Connecticut.
         All's Well That Ends Well (Shakespeare), American Shakespeare Festival, Stratford, Connecticut.
         The Devil and Daniel Webster (Herrmann), City Centre, New York.
1960   *Murder in the Cathedral* (Eliot), Los Angeles Professional Theatre Group, University of California.
         The Three Sisters (Chekhov), Los Angeles Professional Theatre Group, University of California.
1961   *Six Characters in Search of an Author* (Pirandello), Los Angeles Professional Theatre Group, University of California.
         The Iceman Cometh (O'Neill), Los Angeles Professional Theatre Group, University of California.
1963   *Measure for Measure* (Shakespeare), Los Angeles Professional Theatre Group, University of California.
         King Lear (Shakespeare), Los Angeles Professional Theatre Group, University of California.
1966   *Murder in the Cathedral* (Eliot), American Shakespeare Festival, Stratford, Connecticut.
1967   *Macbeth* (Shakespeare), American Shakespeare Festival, Stratford, Connecticut.
1967–68 *The Chronicles of Hell* (Ghelderode), APA Phoenix, New York.

John Houseman (1977).

	Pantagleize (Ghelderode), APA Phoenix, New York.
1968	*The Mines of Sulphur* (opera), Civic Opera, Dallas, Texas.
1971	*The Losers* (opera), Juilliard Opera Theatre, New York.
1972	*The Country Girl* (Garrick), Eisenhower Theatre, Washington, D.C.
	Don Juan in Hell (G. B. Shaw), Good Shepherd Faith Church, New York.
1973	*Measure for Measure* (Shakespeare), City Centre and Billy Rose Theatre, New York.
	Clarence Darrow (Rintels), Helen Hayes Theatre, New York.
1975	*The Great American Fourth of July Parade*, Carnegie Music Hall, Pittsburgh, Pennsylvania.
1980	*King Lear* (Shakespeare), Acting Company, New York.
1983	*The Cradle Will Rock* (Blitzstein), Acting Company, New York.

Films

As director:
Voyage to America, 1964.

As actor:
Seven Days in May, 1964; *The Paper Chase*, 1973; *Rollerball*, 1965; *Three Days of the Condor*, 1975; *St Ives*, 1976; *The Cheap Detective*, 1978; *Old Boyfriends*, 1979; *The Fog*, 1980; *My Bodyguard*, 1980; *Wholly Moses*, 1980; *The Bells*, 1982; *Another Woman*, 1988; *Bright Lights, Big City*, 1988; *Scrooged*, 1988.

Television

As actor:
Fear on Trial, 1975; *The Six Million Dollar Man*, 1976; *The Bionic Woman*, 1976; *Captains and the Kings*, 1976; *Hazard's People*, 1976; *Truman at Potsdam*, 1976; *Washington: Behind Closed Doors*, 1977; *Our Town*, 1977; *Six Characters in Search of an Author*, 1978; *The Paper Chase* (series), 1978; *The French Atlantic Affair*, 1979; *The Last Convertible*, 1979; *A Christmas Without Snow*, 1980; *The Babysitter*, 1980; *Gideon's Trumpet*, 1980; *The Associates*, 1980; *Marco Polo*, 1982; *Mork and Mindy*, 1982; *Silver Spoons*, 1982–85; *The Winds of War*, 1983; *Paper Chase*, 1983; *A.D.*, 1985.

Radio

As director:
Theatre USA, 1948–50.

Publications

The American Shakespeare Festival: The Birth of a Theatre, with Jack Landau, 1959; *Run Through — A Memoir*, 1972; *Front and Center*, 1979; *Final Dress*, 1983; *Entertainers and the Entertained: Essays on Theatre, Film, and Television*, 1986; *Unfinished Business, Memoirs: 1902–1989*, 1989.

*

Bibliography

Books:
Roberta Cooper Krensky, *The American Shakespeare Theatre: Stratford, 1955–1985*, Washington, 1986.

Articles:
Chris Chase, "Suddenly They're All Sending for Houseman", *Chicago Tribune*, 21 April 1974.
Arnold Hano, "When Houseman Talks, People Listen", *TV Guide*, 18 November 1978.
Margaret Carroll, "Fear Has a Big Part in Houseman's Life Story", *Chicago Tribune*, 20 December 1979.

* * *

John Houseman embarked on an acting career almost 40 years after he began working in the theatre. Although he started his career as a translator of foreign language plays, he is best known for his portrayal of distinguished curmudgeons. Throughout his half century in the entertainment profession, Houseman alternately (and often simultaneously) worked as a director, producer, writer, educator, and, finally, as an actor. Few people outside the profession realise the significance of Houseman's numerous contributions to the development of institutional theatre and actor training in the USA.

Houseman entered the theatre with virtually no training during the height of the Depression, a time when experienced actors, directors, and playwrights found it increasingly difficult to make a living. Houseman achieved recognition with his first directing job, the all-Black production of *Four Saints in Three Acts*, the very oddity of this commercially dangerous play making it a huge success with audiences. Houseman's association with *Four Saints* created the perception that he was a maverick, a mover against the mainstream of theatre. Houseman embraced this categorization, admitting that a kind of independent recklessness and insanity characterised his professional endeavours.

Houseman's work in the Negro Theatre Project and his subsequent partnership with Orson Welles in Project 891 and the Mercury Theatre centred on his growing belief that Broadway, the theatrical "establishment", was failing to provide any meaningful experience for actors, playwrights, and audiences. As director of the Negro Theatre Project, Houseman witnessed the inability of Black theatre artists to find a viable outlet to perform their craft; professional theatre unions remained closed to Blacks at this time and commercial theatre tended to place Black actors in stereotypical servant and burlesque roles. As producer of Welles's "voodoo" *Macbeth* in 1936, Houseman was indicating his commitment to upgrading the quality of the theatre through non-traditional means. Shakespeare as performed by Black actors seemed an impossibility; changing the context of *Macbeth* to 19th-century Haiti and replacing the weird sisters with authentic witch doctors bordered on the fantastic. Yet the production gained critical and popular accolades, paving the way for a new generation of classical Black actors, such as Alfred Drake.

Houseman's involvement in Project 891 and the Mercury Theatre followed the same pattern. In each instance Houseman attempted to promote creative stagings of accepted classics. He specifically felt that the US fear of the classics stemmed from boring, conventional productions that tried to mirror British theatrical traditions. Houseman and Welles promoted a vital, energetic, almost foolhardy staging of new and traditional works. In 1937, their modern dress *Julius Caesar*, shorn of its battle scenes and placed in the modern context of fascism, played to enthusiastic audiences of divergent socio-economic backgrounds.

Houseman established his reputation as an interpreter of Shakespeare when he directed *King Lear* in 1950. New York audiences had not seen a production of *King Lear* for more than 30 years. Brookes Atkinson, dean of New York critics, believed that Houseman's production shed new light on the most difficult of Shakespeare's works; prior to this 1950 production, Atkinson had held the opinion that *King Lear* simply could not be acted, due to its complex plot, its equivocal protagonist, and its incredible length. Houseman streamlined the text (he had no qualms about the necessity of cutting and adapting) and focused on the storm motif — man caught in a turbulent universe. He also demanded that the cast speak the verse in a very clear, straight-forward manner, rather than the usual clipped stage diction.

The success of this venture led to Houseman's appointment as the artistic director of the fledgling American Shakespeare Festival Theatre and Academy. Houseman saw the ASFTA as a means of creating a national repertory company, an objective he had tried to achieve in the Mercury Theatre. He believed that US actors lacked adequate vocal and physical training; when playing the classics US actors attempted to emulate British accents to compensate for a supposed inferiority when it came to interpreting the texts. Houseman, together with his associate Jack Landau, established an academy in order to train US actors to perform Shakespeare. Noted performers and theorists like John Gielgud and Michel Saint-Denis lectured on classical technique to the ASFTA apprentices as part of the curriculum.

As artistic director of the ASFTA, Houseman made several important contributions. Under his guidance, the ASFTA developed a permanent acting company and gained critical and popular approval. Houseman attempted to make Shakespeare as "seductive" as possible to an audience largely unfamiliar with his works. By developing a system of special previews for elementary, high school, and college students, as well as instigating a series of ASFTA tours, Houseman succeeded in making classical theatre accessible and entertaining to a diverse group of spectators. This period of a single artistic focus marks a golden age in the ASFTA's history.

After his departure from the ASFTA, Houseman continued to search for a permanent repertory company. His goals remained unchanged from his Mercury Theatre days — new works, new stagings of classics, permanent acting company, low prices. As a Hollywood film producer, he certainly recognized the financial risks involved in such an endeavour, yet he always maintained the hope that the theatre could rise above the hurly-burly of commercial realities.

Houseman finally found a medium for his goals in educational theatre. He accepted the offer to head the new drama department at Juilliard with the intention of retiring into respectable academic obscurity. Houseman perceived that the US theatre demanded versatile and flexible actors who could play a wide range of styles and forms. He formulated with Michel Saint-Denis a uniquely American actor-training programme. The curriculum stressed extensive vocal and speech training, as well as dance and movement, circus acrobatics, improvisation, and theatre history. Houseman stated that the Juilliard Acting programme focused on teaching the actor to communicate the author's intent. Despite his penchant of cutting, Houseman always viewed the text as the source of information and inspiration; as a director, he advised his actors to "go back to the text" to find the answers.

Houseman's most satisfying affiliation with a permanent acting company came in 1972, when he founded the City Centre Acting Company. Houseman created this organization to provide employment for the Juilliard graduates; he found it grossly unfair to split up the talented and versatile ensemble of Group 1, Juilliard's first graduating class, and leave them at the mercy of the commercial theatre. Initially based at the Good Shepherd Faith Church in New York, the Acting Company tours regional and university theatres, as well as performing for New York theatre audiences during their regular season. Versatility, range, stage presence, and clarity of diction characterize the Acting Company style; former members include Patti Lupone, Kevin Kline, and William Hurt.

Houseman once remarked "I have always had a passion for starting theatres". During his career Houseman formed these companies as alternatives to the established commercial theatre of Broadway. Although he never affiliated himself with the regional theatre movement, he seems to have pursued the same objectives. While radiating an aura of aloof sophistication, he rejected the notion of theatre as an elite institution. Instead, he pursued the establishment of a theatre that made accessible to the largest possible audience exciting, high quality productions. Houseman viewed his role as a director as that of a mirror or sounding board to actors' explorations; with inexperienced actors he imposed a greater degree of authority. No one particular style defined his productions, although at the ASFTA he focused on elaborate stagings in the Elizabethan style. Much of the commentary pertaining to Houseman focuses on his Hollywood career. A detailed examination of Houseman's personal directing style as well as his contributions to the development of institutional theatre in the USA offers numerous possibilities for scholarship.

—Michelle F. Mazza

HOWARD, Alan (Mackenzie). British actor. Born in London, 5 August 1937; nephew of actor Leslie Howard. Educated at Ardingly College. Married 1) Stephanie Hinchcliffe Davies in 1965 (divorced 1976); 2) Sally Beauman in 1976, one son. Served in Royal Air Force, 1956–60. Stage debut, Belgrade Theatre, Coventry, 1958; assistant stage manager, Belgrade Theatre, 1958; actor, Royal Court Theatre, London, from 1959; film debut, 1961; associate artist, Royal Shakespeare Company, from 1967; Broadway debut, 1971; has since won equal acclaim in Shakespeare history plays and in modern works. Recipient: *Plays and Players* London Theatre Critics Most Promising Actor Award, 1969; *Plays and Players* Best Actor Award, 1977; Society of West End Theatre Managers Award, 1976, 1978; *Evening Standard* Drama Award, 1978, 1981; Variety Club Award, 1980; British Theatre Association Award, 1981.

Roles

1958   Footman in *Half in Earnest* (Ellis, adapted from Wilde), Belgrade Theatre, Coventry.
Lomax in *Major Barbara* (G. B. Shaw), Belgrade Theatre, Coventry.
1959   Frankie Bryant in *Roots* (Wesker), Belgrade Theatre, Coventry, Royal Court Theatre, London, and Duke of York's Theatre, London.
1960   Dave Simmonds in *I'm Talking About Jerusalem* (Wesker), Belgrade Theatre, Coventry.
First removal man in *I'm Talking About Jerusalem* (Wesker), Royal Court Theatre, London.
Monty Blatt in *Chicken Soup with Barley* (Wesker), Royal Court Theatre, London.
1961   Kenny Baird in *A Loss of Roses* (Inge), Pembroke Theatre, Croydon.
De Piraquo in *The Changeling* (Middleton), Royal Court Theatre, London.

1962   Duke of Ferrara in *The Chances* (Fletcher), Chichester Festival Theatre.
Nearchus in *The Broken Heart* (Ford), Chichester Festival Theatre.
1963   Loveless in *Virtue in Danger* (adapted from Vanbrugh), Mermaid Theatre, London, and Strand Theatre, London.
Fotheringham in *Afternoon Men* (Powell), Arts Theatre, London.
1964   Bassanio in *The Merchant of Venice* (Shakespeare), South American and European tour.
Lysander in *A Midsummer Night's Dream* (Shakespeare), South American and European tour.
1965   Simon in *A Heritage and Its History* (Compton-Burnett, adapted by Mitchell), Phoenix Theatre, London.
Angelo in *Measure for Measure* (Shakespeare), Playhouse, Nottingham.
Bolingbroke in *Richard II* (Shakespeare), Playhouse, Nottingham.
1966   Orsino in *Twelfth Night* (Shakespeare), Royal Shakespeare Theatre, Stratford-upon-Avon.
Burgundy in *Henry V* (Shakespeare), Royal Shakespeare Theatre, Stratford-upon-Avon.
Lussurioso in *The Revenger's Tragedy* (Tourneur), Royal Shakespeare Theatre, Stratford-upon-Avon; revived there and at Aldwych Theatre, London, 1969.
1967   Young Fashion in *The Relapse* (Vanbrugh), Aldwych Theatre, London.
Jaques in *As You Like It* (Shakespeare), Royal Shakespeare Theatre, Stratford-upon-Avon; Los Angeles, 1968.
1968   Edgar in *King Lear* (Shakespeare), Royal Shakespeare Theatre, Stratford-upon-Avon, and Aldwych Theatre, London.
Achilles in *Troilus and Cressida* (Shakespeare), Royal Shakespeare Theatre, Stratford-upon-Avon, and Aldwych Theatre, London.
Benedick in *Much Ado About Nothing* (Shakespeare), Royal Shakespeare Theatre, Stratford-upon-Avon, and Aldwych Theatre, London; Los Angeles and San Francisco, 1969.
1969   Bartholomew Cokes in *Bartholomew Fair* (Jonson), Other Place, Stratford-upon-Avon, and Aldwych Theatre, London.
1970   Hamlet in *Hamlet* (Shakespeare), Royal Shakespeare Theatre, Stratford-upon-Avon.
Ceres in *The Tempest* (Shakespeare), Royal Shakespeare Theatre, Stratford-upon-Avon.
Mephistophilis in *Doctor Faustus* (Marlowe), Other Place, Stratford-upon-Avon.
1971   Theseus and Oberon in *A Midsummer Night's Dream* (Shakespeare), Royal Shakespeare Theatre, Stratford-upon-Avon, and Aldwych Theatre, London; world tour, 1972–73.
Nikolai in *Enemies* (Gorky), Aldwych Theatre, London.
Dorimant in *The Man of Mode* (Etherege), Aldwych Theatre, London.
The Envoy in *The Balcony* (Genet), Aldwych Theatre, London.

1972   Cyril Jackson in *The Black and White Minstrels* (Taylor), Traverse Theatre, Edinburgh; Hampstead Theatre Club, London, 1974.

1973   Erich von Stroheim in *The Ride across Lake Constance* (Handke), Hampstead Theatre Club, London, and Mayfair Theatre, London.

1974   Carlos II in *The Bewitched* (Barnes), Aldwych Theatre, London.

1975   Prince Hal in *Henry IV, parts 1 and 2* (Shakespeare), Royal Shakespeare Theatre, Stratford-upon-Avon; Aldwych Theatre, London, 1976.

          Henry V in *Henry V* (Shakespeare), Royal Shakespeare Theatre, Stratford-upon-Avon; Aldwych Theatre, London, Brooklyn Academy of Music, Brooklyn, New York, and world tour, 1976; Royal Shakespeare Theatre, Stratford-upon-Avon, 1977; Aldwych Theatre, London, 1978.

1976   Jack Rover in *Wild Oats* (O'Keeffe), Aldwych Theatre, London, and Piccadilly Theatre, London.

1977   Henry VI in *Henry VI, parts 1, 2, and 3* (Shakespeare), Royal Shakespeare Theatre, Stratford-upon-Avon; Aldwych Theatre, London, 1978.

          Coriolanus in *Coriolanus* (Shakespeare), Royal Shakespeare Theatre, Stratford-upon-Avon; Aldwych Theatre, London, 1978; European tour, 1979.

1978   Mark Antony in *Antony and Cleopatra* (Shakespeare), Royal Shakespeare Theatre, Stratford-upon-Avon; Aldwych Theatre, London, 1979.

1979   Chepurnoy in *Children of the Sun* (Gorky), Aldwych Theatre, London.

1980   Richard II in *Richard II* (Shakespeare), Royal Shakespeare Theatre, Stratford-upon-Avon; Aldwych Theatre, London, 1981.

          Richard III in *Richard III* (Shakespeare), Royal Shakespeare Theatre, Stratford-upon-Avon; Aldwych Theatre, London, 1981.

1981   Neschastlivtsev in *The Forest* (Ostrovsky), Other Place, Stratford-upon-Avon, and Warehouse Theatre, London.

          John Halder in *Good* (Taylor), Warehouse Theatre, London; Booth Theatre, New York, 1982.

1982   Roles in *The Hollow Crown* (Shakespeare compilation), Fortune Theatre, London.

          Roles in *Pleasure and Repentance* (Hands), Fortune Theatre, London.

1985   Nikolai Pesiakoff in *Breaking the Silence* (Poliakoff), Mermaid Theatre, London.

1992   Henry Higgins in *Pygmalion* (G. B. Shaw), Royal National Theatre, London.

1993   Macbeth in *Macbeth* (Shakespeare), Royal National Theatre, London.

Other roles included: *Reluctant Heroes* (Morris), Belgrade Theatre, Coventry, 1959; *Comus* (Milton), Tyneside Theatre, Newcastle-upon-Tyne, 1976; *George and the Dragon* (anon.), Other Place, Stratford-upon-Avon, 1980; *The Swan Down Gloves*, Other Place, Stratford-upon-Avon,

1980; *The Silver King* (H. A. Jones), Chichester Festival Theatre, 1990; *Scenes from a Marriage* (adapted from Feydeau), Chichester Festival Theatre and Wyndham's Theatre, London, 1990; *Kings* (Logue), Royal National Theatre, London, 1991; *Les Parents Terribles* (Cocteau, translated by Sams), Royal National Theatre, London, 1994.

Films

Victim, 1961; *The VIPs*, 1963; *The Americanization of Emily*, 1964; *Heroes of Telemark*, 1965; *Work is a Four Letter Word*, 1968; *Little Big Man*, 1970; *Oxford Blues*, 1984; *The Return of the Musketeers*, 1989; *The Cook, The Thief, His Wife and Her Lover*, 1989; *Strapless*, 1990; *Dakota Road*, 1990.

Television

Notorious Woman (series), 1975; *Cover* (series), 1981; *Coriolanus*, 1983; *Hang Ups*, 1983; *The Strong are Lonely*, 1984; *Poppyland*, 1984; *Too Young to Fight Too Old to Forget*, 1985; *Evensong*, 1986; *The Return of Sherlock Holmes*, 1987; *The Double Helix*, 1987; *The Perfect Spy*, 1987; *Kimberley Carlisle*, 1987; *The Dog it was that Died*, 1988; *Hercule Poirot's Casebook*, 1988; *Frederick Forsythe Presents* ... , 1989. *The Holy Experiment*; *The Way of the World*; *Churchill's People*; *Royal Flash*; *Philoctetes*; *Comets among the Stars*.

Radio

Forsyte Chronicles, 1990–91.

*   *   *

Alan Howard seems the stuff that heroes are made of; on the stage of the Royal Shakespeare Company at least. Since joining the RSC in 1966, he has played a succession of heroic figures for them, including Hamlet, Prince Hal, Henry V, Richard II, Richard III, Henry VI, Benedick, Coriolanus, Theseus, Oberon, Dorimant, Jack Rover, Erich von Stroheim, Achilles, and Mark Antony, and he remains an associate artist. It is an astonishing range of parts, classical in the main. But in no sense have these hero-figures ever been one-dimensional, simplistically gung-ho supermen; Howard heroes are ambivalent figures, reflecting — agonising — over their particular role and function; often more or less morally compromised, riven with a myriad uncertainties; sometimes cool, collected, and somewhat detached, sometimes passionately engaged. And they are never the same, for Howard is never predictable, always fresh and original; yet connections between widely differing figures are perceivable. On occasions, such as his Achilles in *Troilus and Cressida* or his Henry V, his reading has been revelatory. At other times it has seemed a quietly definitive summary, as in his Theseus/Oberon for Peter Brook.

Such a list of leading roles attests to the extraordinary level of dominance held by Howard at the RSC in the late 1960's and 1970's, in fruitful partnership with director Terry Hands, among others. His ascendancy may, in part, be due to a chiming with the times' own interrogation and reinterpretation of the concept of the hero-figure; for Howard embodies brilliantly the dichotomy between heroic and anti-heroic qualities. Physically striking, blond-haired, strong-featured, onstage he exudes poise and a considerable sexual presence, though without particular grace in movement. It is unsurprising that many of his roles have entailed a projection of "manliness", be it in terms of swashbuckling martial stage action, the rakehell masculinity of the assured sexual predator, or the measured self-assertion of the confidently superior male. But counter-balancing these portraits have been parallel explorations of the feminine. His Achilles, mythic warrior of renown, flirted with a daringly camp effeminacy, a forthright homosexuality that was ground-breaking and inconoclastic. His Halder, the mild-mannered intellectual disastrously seduced by Nazism in C. P. Taylor's *Good* offered a portrait of a delicate, well-meaning, insecurity and supreme malleability: an award-winning interpretation. His Theseus, in Brook's *Dream*, and his Oberon, offered alternations of gentleness, mischief, and humane recognition of the Mechanicals' effort. Such explorations of dual concepts of masculinity and femininity have allowed Howard to throw into relief clichéd assertions, demanding reappraisal.

Sometimes, this has happened by virtue of unusual casting. He was, for example, on paper a less than obvious choice for the unassertive, almost saintly Henry VI, and perhaps also for Richard II. He does not immediately suggest "victim", being much more obviously suited to Hamlet or to Mark Antony, to the ebullience of Jack Rover, spilling literary allusions everywhere, or to Etherege's Dorimant in *The Man of Mode*. But his casting as Henry and Richard invited a rethinking of their victim status, allowing him to find within them a deep reservoir of moral strength and dignity, which made them attractive rather than simply pitiable. Conversely, such casting enabled him to suggest a level of human imperfection in the golden Henry V, highlighting both his very human fears and the supreme effort of will and duty Hal must exert in order to become, and remain, Henry.

Howard's ability to suggest such complex characterisations resides primarily in the voice and in his approach to language. Howard's voice is an extraordinary and distinctive tool, alternately deep and warmly resonant or thin and piercingly sharp, commanding or hesitant, always crystal-line in clarity. It bespeaks the presence of strong intellect in a character, but an intellect beset by gusts of powerful emotion. It is a magisterial instrument, teasing out fresh meaning from the language, quizzing its structures and pulses, suggesting a mind always actively engaged in interrogation of itself and its verbal manifestations. Therein lies the key element in a Howard performance: an ironic detachment, redolent of an almost Cartesian split into thinking and reflecting being. He would seem ideally suited to play Brechtian roles, such as Galileo Galilei, though he has never been cast in these; there seems in his work the possibility of successful Epic performance. Such detachment is not merely familiar British aloofness, emotionally held back; Howard is well able to give passionately emotional full measure. Rather, it is more an instinctive capacity for dialectic, enabling him to embody and project, without awkwardness, a character's innate contradictions, the heart of a human being's "mystery". It is this attention to the idea of inconsistency that renders his roles recognisably real.

Television, interestingly, has often read this capacity in terms of the spy-thriller genre, frequently casting him as a member of the Intelligence services, positive or negative. He is most often a 'control' figure in these organisations; sometimes, sinister and oblique, as in Thames TV's *Cover*; sometimes more akin to the lone good deed shining in the naughtiest of worlds. On film, he was rarely given much of interest or magnitude to do until Peter Greenaway cast him as The Lover in *The Cook, The Thief, His Wife, and Her Lover*. In this, he presents a positive antithesis to Michael Gambon's bestially savage and coarse Thief; erudite, cultured, civilised, and capable of genuine affection for the bruised — literally and figuratively — Wife. It is a profoundly violent, often repellent film conceived in terms of a series of visual conundrums of voluptuous richness, in which Howard's passionate illicit liaison with Helen Mirren's Wife stands at the image's centre, in a series of escalatingly erotic sexual encounters. His appearance in this film marked a welcome return to prominence after a period of relative invisibility in the 1980's, punctuated only by a brief portrayal in Stephen Poliakoff's *Breaking the Silence*.

—Val Taylor

IFFLAND, August Wilhelm. German actor-manager, director and playwright. Born in Hanover, Germany, 19 April 1759. Stage debut under Konrad Ekhof at the Gotha Court Theatre, 1777; actor, National Theater, Mannheim, 1779; wrote his first plays for production by the Mannheim company and, while still an actor with the company, embarked on series of guest performances throughout Germany, consolidating reputation as leading actor of his generation, 1784; left Mannheim company, moved to Vienna and was subsequently appointed manager of the Königliches Schauspielhaus, Berlin, 1796; director-general of the royal theatre in Prussia, from 1811. Died in Berlin, 22 September 1814.

Productions

1777   *Diamant* (Engel), Gotha Court Theatre; acted Israel.
1781   *Albert von Thurneisen* (Iffland), National Theater, Mannheim.
        Wilhelm von Schenk (Iffland), National Theater, Mannheim.
        Wie man's treibt, so geht's (Iffland), National Theater, Mannheim.
1782   *Die Räber* (Schiller), National Theater, Mannheim; acted Franz Moor.
1784   *Verbrechen aus Ehrsucht* (Iffland), National Theater, Mannheim.
        Die Mündel (Iffland), National Theater, Mannheim.
1785   *Die Jäger* (Iffland), National Theater, Mannheim; acted Forester Warberger.
        Liebe um Liebe (Iffland), National Theater, Mannheim.
1786   *Das Bewusstsein* (Iffland), National Theater, Mannheim.
1787   *Der Magnetismus* (Iffland), National Theater, Mannheim.
        Don Carlos (Schiller), National Theatre, Hamburg; acted Philip II.
1788   *Mittelweg ist Tugendprobe* (Iffland), National Theater, Mannheim.
1790   *Frauenstand* (Iffland), Burgtheatre, Vienna.
        Herbsttag (Iffland), National Theater, Mannheim.
1791   *Elise von Valberg* (Iffland), National Theater, Mannheim.
        Die Hagestolzen (Iffland), National Theater, Mannheim; acted Councillor Reinhold.

1792   *Der Scheinverdienst* (Iffland), Burgtheatre, Vienna.
        Alte und neue Welt (Iffland), Burgtheatre, Vienna.
1793   *Die Verbrüderung* (Iffland), National Theater, Mannheim.
        Allzu scharf macht schartig (Iffland), Burgtheatre, Vienna.
        Der Genius (Iffland), National Theater, Mannheim.
        Der Vormund (Iffland), National Theater, Mannheim.
1794   Die Reise nach der Stadt (Iffland), Burgtheatre, Vienna.
        Die Aussteuer (Iffland), Burgtheatre, Vienna.
        Dienstpflicht (Iffland), Burgtheatre, Vienna.
1795   *Die Geflüchteten* (Iffland), National Theater, Mannheim.
        Die Advokaten (Iffland), Burgtheatre, Vienna.
        Alte und neue Zeit (Iffland), Königliches Schauspielhaus, Berlin.
        Das Vermächtnis (Iffland), Burgtheatre, Vienna.
        Der Spieler (Iffland), Burgtheatre, Vienna.
1796   *Achmet und Zenide* (Iffland), Burgtheatre, Vienna.
        Der Hausfrieden (Iffland), Königliches Schauspielhaus, Berlin.
1797   *Das gerettete Venedig* (Iffland, adapted from Otway), Königliches Schauspielhaus, Berlin.
        Das Gewissen (Iffland), Königliches Schauspielhaus, Berlin.
        Erinnerung (Iffland), Königliches Schauspielhaus, Berlin.
1798   *Leichter Sinn* (Iffland), National Theater, Mannheim.
        Der Komet (Iffland), Burgtheatre, Vienna.
        Der Veteran (Iffland), Königliches Schauspielhaus, Berlin.
        Der Mann von Wort (Iffland), Königliches Schauspielhaus, Berlin.
        Selbstbeherrschung (Iffland), Königliches Schauspielhaus, Berlin.
        Der Fremde (Iffland), Königliches Schauspielhaus, Berlin.
1799   *Albert von Thurneisen* (Iffland), National Theater, Mannheim.
        Die Künstler (Iffland), Königliches Schauspielhaus, Berlin.

August Wilhelm Iffland as Wallenstein.

Die Piccolomini (Schiller), Königliches Schauspielhaus, Berlin; acted Wallenstein.
Wallensteins Tod (Schiller), Königliches Schauspielhaus, Berlin; acted Wallenstein.
1800　*Das Vaterhaus* (Iffland), Königliches Schauspielhaus, Berlin.
Die Höhen (Iffland), Königliches Schauspielhaus, Berlin.
1801　*Die Familie Lonau* (Iffland), Burgtheatre, Vienna.
Maria Stuart (Schiller), Königliches Schauspielhaus, Berlin.
Die Jungfrau von Orleans (Schiller), Königliches Schauspielhaus, Berlin.
1802　*Das Erbteil des Vaters* (Iffland), Burgtheatre, Vienna.
Hussiten vor Naumburg (Kotzebue), Königliches Schauspielhaus, Berlin.
Weihe der Kraft (Werner), Königliches Schauspielhaus, Berlin.
Götz von Berlichingen (Goethe), Königliches Schauspielhaus, Berlin.
Egmont (Schiller), Königliches Schauspielhaus, Berlin.
1804　*Wilhelm Tell* (Schiller), Königliches Schauspielhaus, Berlin; acted Wilhelm Tell.
1805　*Das Hausfreunde* (Iffland), Burgtheatre, Vienna.
Die Seelenwanderung (Iffland), Königliches Schauspielhaus, Berlin.

1806　*Der Oheim* (Iffland), Burgtheatre, Vienna.
Die Heimkehr (Iffland), Burgtheatre, Vienna.
1807　*Iphigenie* (Goethe), Königliches Schauspielhaus, Berlin.
Die natürliche Tochter (Goethe), Königliches Schauspielhaus, Berlin.
1808　*Heinrichs V: Jugendjahre* (Duval), Königliches Schauspielhaus, Berlin.
Die Brautwahl (Iffland), Burgtheatre, Vienna.
1813　*Die Ringe* (Iffland), Königliches Schauspielhaus, Berlin.
1814　*Liebe und Wille* (Iffland), Königliches Schauspielhaus, Berlin.

Other productions included: *Figaro in Deutschland*, 1790; *Wohin?*, 1806; *Die Marionetten*, 1807; *Der Taufschein* (Picard), 1807; *Picards Duhautcours oder Der Vergleichscontract*, 1808; *Der Flatterhafte oder Die schwierige Heirat*, 1809; *Frau von Sévigné*, 1809; *Die Einung*, 1811; *Der Müssiggänger*, 1812; *Der Haustyrann*, 1812; *Der gutherzige Polterer*, 1812; also played Bittermann in *Menschenhass und Reue* (Kotzebue); Harpagon in *Der Geizige* (Molière); Lear in *Koenig Lear* (Shakespeare).

Publications

Plays:
Albert von Thurneisen oder Liebe und Pflicht im Streit (produced Mannheim, 1781); *Wilhelm von Schenk* (produced Mannheim, 1781); *Wie man's treibt, so geht's* (produced Mannheim, 1781); *Verbrechen aus Ehrsucht* (produced Berlin, Dresden, Hamburg, Leipzig, Mannheim, Munich, Vienna, 1784), 1786; *Die Müdel* (produced Mannheim, 1784), 1786; *Die Jäger* (produced Berlin, Dresden, Leipzig, Mannheim, 1785), 1786; *Das Bewusstsein* (produced Dresden, Frankfurt, Leipzig, Mannheim, 1787), 1788; *Der Magnetismus* (produced Mannheim, 1787), 1799; *Hoffnung der Ruhe* (produced Hamburg, 1788); *Mittelweg ist Tugendprobe* (produced Mannheim, 1788); *Reue versöhnt* (produced Berlin, Bresden, Munich, 1789), 1798; *Frauenstand* (produced Hamburg, Vienna, 1790), 1799; *Der Herbsttag* (produced Hamburg, Mannheim, 1790), 1799; *Friedrich von Österreich* (produced Hamburg, 1790), 1799; *Die Hagelstolzen* (produced Dresden, Hamburg, Mannheim, 1791), 1799; *Elise von Walberg* (produced Frankfurt, Hamburg, Mannheim, Weimar, 1791), 1799; *Allzu scharf macht schartig* (produced Hamburg, 1792), 1800; *Alte und neue Zeit* (produced Frankfurt, Hamburg, Vienna, 1792), 1799; *Die Kokarden* (produced Munich, 1792), 1800; *Der Scheinverdienst* (produced Hamburg, 1792), 1802; *Der Vorsatz* (produced Frankfurt, 1792); *Vorurteile* (produced Dresden, Frankfurt, Leipzig, 1792); *Die Reise nach der Stadt* (produced Dresden, 1793), 1800; *Der Vormund* (produced Berlin, Mannheim, Vienna, 1793), 1800; *Die Aussteuer* (produced Berlin, Dresden, Vienna, 1794), 1799; *Dienstpflicht* (produced Dresden, Vienna, 1794), 1800; *Die Advokaten* (produced Berlin, Dresden, Mannheim, Vienna, 1795), 1800; *Die Geflüchteten* (produced Mannheim, 1795), 1799; *Der Spieler* (produced Dresden, Vienna, 1795), 1800; *Das Vermächtnis* (produced Berlin, Dresden, Frankfurt, Vienna, Weimar, 1795), 1799; *Achmet und Zenide* (produced Vienna, 1796), 1798; *Der*

Hausfrieden (produced berlin, Hamburg, 1796), 1799; *Das Gewissen* (produced Berlin, Dresden, Mannheim, Weimar, 1797), 1799; *Erinnerung* (produced Berlin, Dresden, Hamburg, Vienna, Weimar, 1797), 1799; *Leichter Sinn* (produced Berlin, Dresden, Hamburg, Weimar, 1797), 1799; *Das Fremde* (produced Berlin, Dresden, 1798), 1800; *Der Komet* (produced Vienna, Weimar, 1798), 1799; *Der Mann von Wort* (produced Berlin, Dresden, Vienna, 1798), 1800; *Selbstbeherrschung* (produced Berlin, Vienna, 1798), 1800; *Der Veteran* (produced Berlin, 1798), 1798; *Die Künstler* (produced Berlin, 1799), 1801; *Der Eichenkranz*, 1800; *Die Höhen* (produced Berlin, Vienna, 1800), 1801; *Das Vaterhaus* (produced Berlin, Frankfurt, Mannheim, Vienna, Weimar, 1800), 1802; *Die Vaterfreude*, 1800; *Die Familie Lonau* (produced Vienna, 1801), 1802; *Das Erbteil des Vaters* (produced Berlin, 1800), 1802; *Die Hausfreunde* (produced Berlin, Dresden, Leipzig, Mannheim, Vienna, 1805), 1808; *Die Seelenwanderung* (produced Berlin, 1805); *Die Heimkehr* (produced Berlin, Frankfurt, Mannheim, Vienna, 1806); *Der Oheim* (produced Mannheim, Vienna, 1808) 1808; *Die Brautwahl* (produced Vienna, 1808); *Die Ringe* (produced Berlin, 1813); *Liebe und Wille* (produced Berlin, 1814); *Das Liebe auf dem Lande* (produced Hamburg, 1847).

Other:
Iffland in seine Schriften als Künstler, Lehrer, und Direktor der Berliner Bühne, edited by Carl Duncker, 1859; *Über meine theatralische Laufbahn*, 1798; *Über Schauspieler und Schauspielkunst: Ausgewählte Abhandlungen von August Wilhelm Iffland und Johann Gottfried Seume*, edited by Kurt Böwe, 1954.

*

Bibliography

Books:
Karl Böttiger, *Entwickelung des Ifflandischen Spiels in vierzehn Darstellungen auf dem Weimarischen Hoftheater im Aprillmonath 1796*, Leipzig, 1796.
Wilhelm Koffka, *Iffland und Dalberg*, Leipzig, 1865.
Heinrich Härle, *Ifflands Schauspielkunst*, Berlin, 1926.
Erwin Kliewer, *A. W. Iffland: Ein Wegbereiter in der deutschen Schauspielkunst*, Berlin, 1937.
Heinz Kindermann, *Theatergeschichte der Goethezeit*, Vienna, 1948.
Wilhelm Hermann, *Thaliens liebster Sohn: Iffland und Mannheim*, Mannheim, 1960.
Simon Williams, *German Actors of the 18th and 19th Centuries: Idealism, Romanticism and Realism*, Westport, Connecticut, 1985.

* * *

Perhaps no theatrical personage of the golden age of German theatre in the early 19th century was so celebrated or widely known as August Wilhelm Iffland. As a playwright he contributed over 50 plays to the popular German repertoire at a time when few native works were available. Most of these plays were known as "Rührstücke", sentimental pieces with domestic settings. As all of them were well within the technical and mimetic capacities of all acting companies and as their moralizing tone appealed to the values of the middle classes, they were quickly seen throughout Germany and in other countries, including England. Ultimately, however, they proved to be ephemeral and have now totally disappeared from the repertoire.

Iffland's most lasting contribution to the theatre was as an actor. Trained by Ekhof at the Gotha Court Theatre, his acting represented an extension of the ideals of the Enlightenment theatre into the early 19th century. Essays that he wrote during his early years in Mannheim, at the request of the intendant Baron Heribert von Dalberg, indicate that as an actor he strove to create a harmonious whole within which each detail was carefully placed. Balance, decorum and control were, to his mind, the essence of good acting. Furthermore, the actor should never disturb the audience by too raw a display of passion or violent feeling. He contended that an actor should try to be as noble, educated and refined as the characters he represented, sentiments that prefigure several German actors' meditations on their calling during the 19th century. While the actor should always appear graceful on stage, he should also display the sterling "German" values of honesty and inner nobility.

As an actor, Iffland acquired a formidable reputation. Although he remained at Mannheim as a permanent company member from 1779 to 1796, much of his time was spent giving guest performances in all the major theatres of Germany, including Weimar, where he aroused the intense admiration of Goethe, who used his acting as one of the models for his own widely copied Weimar style of acting. Goethe wrote of Iffland that he "has the advantage of being able to give meaning and variety through the slightest nuances, and everything that appears arises from this deep source. His body is most adroit, and he is master of all his vocal organs, the deficiency of which he knows how to hide, even to exploit. The great capacity of his mind to fasten upon human peculiarities and to represent them with their individual features arouses as much astonishment as does the range of his performance and the speed of his representation. But first and last, what most arouses my admiration is his great understanding, through which he grasps single elements of character and gathers them together so that they make a whole different from all others".

But not everyone was as enthusiastic as Goethe. Some writers, among whom were Schiller, Schröder and Tieck, felt that he lacked imagination and humour and had little understanding of complexity of character. His more negative critics felt that he displayed his formidable technique at the expense of the ensemble in which he played and to the disregard of the play in which he was performing. Iffland, in other words, was considered to be a virtuoso, not a player of character in depth.

Maybe the reason for this striking difference of opinion about Iffland's acting arises from the historic changes that were occurring in the German theatre during his career. Iffland was a contemporary of Friedrich Ludwig Schröder, who was noted for his harsh, realistic style of acting, which has been seen as a theatrical manifestation of Sturm und Drang. Through several guest appearances and the strength of his company in Hamburg, Schröder had become a major presence in the German theatre; in particular, his acting seemed a suitable reflection of the harsher political and social climate created by the French Revolution and the revolutionary wars. In contrast, the wholeness and harmony that Iffland had learnt from Ekhof and Dalberg would have appeared to be somewhat dated and lacking in impact. However, early 19th-century German audiences were no less conservative than audiences of other countries and other times and it is certain that they found the clarity of Iffland's acting and his comfortingly rounded performances more to their taste than the harshly contrasting interpretations of Schröder and actors of the Hamburg school.

By the time he died Iffland had also become an icon for the improved social status of the German actor. When as an 18-year-old he left his family in Hanover to take up the theatre, he would seem to have determined to join a profession in the lowest ranks of society, far below that of the middle classes he had abandoned. However, he maintained the values of his class and ensured that they were displayed both in his playwriting and acting. Crucially, he achieved financial success and social respect for his work. As director of the Berlin National Theatre, where he was responsible for exceptionally lavish productions of plays by Goethe, Schiller and Shakespeare, he won a greatly respected position in the city's social life. He was the first actor to be on intimate terms with members of the aristocratic and court circles. As some of his less fortunate colleagues were still forced to tour under conditions as primitive as anything encountered by actors in the 18th century, this unwonted eminence attracted considerable attention to the profession. Because of Iffland's example several younger people were encouraged to choose the theatre not as a job of last resort, but as a profession that might offer greater fulfilment and, exceptionally, greater rewards than others.

—Simon Williams

IRVING, (Sir) Henry. British actor-manager. Born John Henry Brodribb in Keinton Mandeville, near Glastonbury, Somerset, England, 6 February 1838. Educated at the City Commercial School, London, 1848–51. Married Florence O'Callaghan in 1869 (estranged 1871); two sons. Worked in London counting house before making professional stage debut at the Lyceum Theatre, Sunderland, 1856; acted some 350 roles at Theatre Royal, Queen's Theatre, and Operetta House, all in Edinburgh, 1856–59; London debut, Princess's Theatre, 1859; acted at the Queen's Theatre, Dublin, Theatre Royal, Glasgow (and Greenock), and leading provincial theatres throughout England, as well as at the Théâtre des Italiens, Paris, 1859–1866; joined company at the St James's Theatre, London, 1866; acted at the Queen's Theatre opposite Ellen Terry, 1867–68; acted at the Haymarket Theatre, Standard Theatre, Theatre Royal, Croydon, Surrey Theatre, and Gaiety Theatre, 1868–69; invited to the Lyceum Theatre, London, by Hezekiah Bateman, 1871; first appearance in *The Bells*, 1871; debut as Hamlet, 1874; lessee of Lyceum Theatre, 1878–98; recruited Ellen Terry, 1878; toured with own company to USA and Canada eight times, 1883–1904; suffered failing health in last years but made series of provincial farewell tours, 1904–05; last performance, in *Becket*, at the Midland Hotel, Bradford, 1905. Member: Actors' Benevolent Fund (president); Actors' Association (president); Managers' Association of Great Britain (president). D.Litt: University of Dublin, 1892; University of Cambridge, 1898; LL.D: University of Glasgow, 1899.

First actor to be knighted, 1895. Died in Bradford, 13 October 1905 (buried in Westminster Abbey).

Roles

1856–57	Duc d'Orleans and Louis XIII in *Richelieu* (Bulwer-Lytton), Lyceum Theatre, Sunderland.
	Frederick Storke and Francis in *The Buckle of Brilliants; or, The Crown Prince* (Wilks), Lyceum Theatre, Sunderland.
	A Cook in *The Enchanted Lake* (Baird), Lyceum Theatre, Sunderland.
	Frank Hawthorn in *Extremes* (Falconer), Lyceum Theatre, Sunderland.
	Henry Bertram, Dirk Hatterick, and Colonel Mannering in *Guy Mannering* (adapted from Scott), Lyceum Theatre, Sunderland; Theatre Royal, Manchester (as Colonel Mannering), 1860–65.
	George Heriot and Counsel for the prosecution in *Janet Pride* (Boucicault), Lyceum Theatre, Sunderland.
	Athos in *The King's Musketeers* (anon.), Lyceum Theatre, Sunderland.
	Second Officer, Gervais, Beauseant, and Claude Melnotte in *The Lady of Lyons* (Bulwer-Lytton), Lyceum Theatre, Sunderland; Theatre Royal, Glasgow (as Beauseant), 1860; Theatre Royal, Manchester (as Melnotte), 1860–65; Theatre Royal, Oxford (as Melnotte), 1864; Lyceum Theatre, London (as Melnotte), 1879.
	Count Rodolpho in *La! Somnambula!* (H. J. Byron), Lyceum Theatre, Sunderland.
	Count de Cerny in *Memorandums in the Red Book*, Lyceum Theatre, Sunderland; Theatre Royal, Glasgow, 1860.
	Jonas Downeywag in *Not To Be Done* (Craven), Lyceum Theatre, Sunderland.
	Colonel Campbell in *The Orphan of Glencoe* (Parselle), Lyceum Theatre, Sunderland.
	Jack Wind in *Robinson Crusoe* (adapted from Defoe), Lyceum Theatre, Sunderland.
	Careless in *The School for Scandal* (Sheridan), Lyceum Theatre, Sunderland.
	Count D'Orbani in *The Son of the Night* (anon.), Lyceum Theatre, Sunderland.
1857–59	Herbert in *The Advocate's Daughter* (Ebsworth), Edinburgh.
	Sir Arthur Lassel, Stephen Plum, and Jasper Plum in *All That Glitters Is Not Gold* (Morton and Morton), Edinburgh; Theatre Royal, Manchester (as Lassel), 1860–65; St James's Hall, Liverpool (as Plum), 1865.
	Richard Hargrave in *The Anchor of Hope* (Stirling), Edinburgh.
	Peregrine Pyefinch in *An Hour in Seville* (Selby), Edinburgh.
	Lord Welford in *The Artist's Wife* (anon.), Edinburgh; Theatre Royal, Manchester, 1860–65.

Ferdinand and Count Medora in *Asmodeus* (Scribe), Edinburgh.

Sylvius and Orlando in *As You Like It* (Shakespeare), Edinburgh; Theatre Royal, Manchester (as Orlando), 1860–65; Theatre Royal, Oxford (as Orlando), 1864.

General Duclos in *The Avalanche* (Harris), Edinburgh.

Mr Torrington in *The Balance of Comfort* (Bernard), Edinburgh.

Augustus in *Barney the Baron* (Lover), Edinburgh.

Pester in *The Bashful Irishman* (Lemon), Edinburgh.

John Beauchamp in *Bathing* (Bruton), Edinburgh.

M'Kay and M'Intosh in *The Battle of the Inch* (Milner), Edinburgh.

Tom Tunnell in *The Bay of Biscay* (Rogers/ Somerset), Edinburgh.

Mr Crummy in *Betsy Baker* (Burnand), Edinburgh; Theatre Royal, Manchester, 1860–65; Theatre Royal, Oxford, 1864.

Beauchamp in *The Beulah Spa* (Dance), Edinburgh.

Edmund Earlybird in *The Birthplace of Podgers* (Hollingshead), Edinburgh.

Seaweed, Lieutenant Pyke, and Captain Crosstree in *Black-Eyed Susan* (Jerrold), Edinburgh; Theatre Royal, Glasgow (as Crosstree), 1860; Theatre Royal, Manchester (as Crosstree), 1860–65; Standard Theatre, London (as Crosstree), 1869.

Ned Spanker in *A Blighted Being* (Taylor), Edinburgh.

Prince Rodolph in *The Blind Boy* (Dunlap), Edinburgh.

Lieutenant Varley and Captain Harcourt in *The Boarding School* (Bernard), Edinburgh.

Paul Didier in *The Bohemians of Paris* (Barnett), Edinburgh; Theatre Royal, Glasgow, 1860.

Edmond de Mailly in *Book the Third, Chapter the First* (Webster), Edinburgh.

Wildoates Heartycheer in *The Bonnie Fish Wife* (Selby), Edinburgh; St James's Hall, Liverpool, 1865.

Henry Higgins and Frank Friskly in *Boots at the Swan* (Selby), Edinburgh; Queen's Theatre, Dublin (as Friskly), 1860; Vaudeville Theatre, London (as Friskly), 1871.

Count Manfredi in *Born to Good Luck* (Power), Edinburgh.

Albert in *The Bottle Imp* (Hale and Talfourd), Edinburgh.

Captain Craigengelt in *The Bride of Lammermoor* (adapted from Scott), Edinburgh.

Philip in *A Bright To-Morrow* (anon.), Edinburgh.

Colonel Davenport in *The British Legion; or, The Volunteers* (Bayly), Edinburgh; Queen's Theatre, Dublin, 1860.

Vincent in *The Cabin Boy* (Stirling), Edinburgh.

Henry Irving

Antoine in *The Cagot; or, Heart to Heart* (Falconer), Edinburgh.

De Saubigné in *The Carpenter of Rouen* (Jones), Edinburgh.

Earl Percy in *The Castle Spectre* (Lewis), Edinburgh; Queen's Theatre, Dublin, 1860.

Captain Killingly and Captain Poodle in *Catching an Heiress* (Selby), Edinburgh.

Hortensio and Biondello in *Katherine and Petruchio* (Garrick), Edinburgh.

King Charles in *Charles XII* (Planché), Edinburgh.

Nat Nowlan in *The Charming Polly* (Haines), Edinburgh; Theatre Royal, Manchester, 1860–65.

Duke Vivaldi in *Clari, The Maid of Milan* (Planché), Edinburgh.

Yussuf in *Conrad and Medora* (Brough), Edinburgh.

Alfred Meynard and Baron de Montgiron in *The Corsican Brothers* (Boucicault), Edinburgh; Theatre Royal, Manchester (as Montgiron), 1860–65.

Tam Maxwell, James Birkie, and King James in *Cramond Brig* (Murray), Edinburgh; Theatre Royal, Glasgow (as King James), 1860; Theatre Royal, Manchester (as King James), 1860–65.

Alphonse de Nyon in *The Creole* (Brooks), Edinburgh.

Dangle in *The Critic* (Sheridan), Edinburgh; Queen's Theatre, Dublin.

Frederick Storke and Francis in *The Crown Prince* (anon.), Edinburgh.

Frank in *The Custom of the Country* (Fletcher and Massinger), Edinburgh.

Pisanio in *Cymbeline* (Shakespeare), Edinburgh.

Adolphus Jobling in *Daddy Hardacre* (Simpson), Edinburgh.

Alfred Fitzfrolic and Lord Mincington in *The Dancing Barber* (Selby), Edinburgh.

David Copperfield in *David Copperfield* (Dickens), Edinburgh; Theatre Royal, Manchester, 1860–65.

Colonel Freelove and Lord Rivers in *The Day After the Wedding* (M. T. Kemble), Edinburgh.

Captain Templeton in *Deaf as a Post* (Poole), Edinburgh; Theatre Royal, Manchester, 1860–65.

Captain Seymour in *Diamond Cut Diamond* (Drayton), Edinburgh; Theatre Royal, Manchester, 1860–65.

Mr Dombey in *Dombey and Son* (Dickens), Edinburgh; Theatre Royal, Manchester, 1860–65.

Count D'Anville in *Dominique the Deserter* (Murray), Edinburgh.

Don José in *Don Caesar de Bazan* (Boucicault), Edinburgh.

Octavio in *Don Giovanni* (T. Dibdin), Edinburgh.

Frank Topham in *Don't Judge by Appearances* (Morton), Edinburgh.

Gruff Tackleton in *Dot; or, The Cricket on the Hearth* (Boucicault), Edinburgh; Standard Theatre, London, 1869.

John Timpkins in *Double Dummy* (Yates and Harrington), Edinburgh.

Lord Randolph in *Douglas* (Home), Edinburgh.

Mr Ogler in *The Drapery Question* (Selby), Edinburgh.

Richard Penderell in *The Dream at Sea* (Buckstone), Edinburgh.

Clayton in *Dred* (adapted from H. B. Stowe), Edinburgh.

Rudolphus in *The Drunkard's Doom* (Pitt), Edinburgh.

Count Corvenio, Antonio, and Strapado in *The Dumb Maid of Genoa* (Farrell), Edinburgh.

Mr Palmerston in *The Dumb Man of Manchester* (Rayner), Edinburgh.

Colonel Mountfort in *Ella Rosenberg* (Kenney), Edinburgh.

Claude Frollo in *Esmeralda* (Byron), Edinburgh.

Captain Popham in *The Eton Boy* (Morton), Edinburgh.

Charles Digit in *Every Cloud Has a Silver Lining* (anon.), Edinburgh; Theatre Royal, Glasgow, 1860.

Walmesley in *The Evil Genius* (Bernard), Edinburgh.

Philip Blake in *The Fairy Circle* (Grattan), Edinburgh; Prince of Wales's Theatre, Liverpool, 1865–66.

Kenmure in *The Falls of Clyde* (anon.), Edinburgh.

Captain Thompson in *A Fascinating Individual* (Danvers), Edinburgh.

Philario in *Fazio* (Milman), Edinburgh.

Piers Talbot in *The Fire Raiser* (Almar), Edinburgh.

Linton, Leybourne, Captain Laverock, Alfred, and Ishmael in *The Flowers of the Forest* (Buckstone), Edinburgh; Theatre Royal, Manchester (as Alfred), 1860–65; Theatre Royal, Oxford (as Ishmael), 1864 and 1865.

Lieutenant Mowbray and Toby Varnish in *The Flying Dutchman* (Jerrold), Edinburgh.

Lord Dalgarno in *The Fortunes of Nigel* (adapted from Scott), Edinburgh.

Altamont in *Forty and Fifty* (Bayly), Edinburgh.

Baron Longueville in *The Foundling of the Forest* (Dimond), Edinburgh.

Prince of Piombino in *Frankenstein* (Brough and Brough), Edinburgh.

Count de Valmore and Alfred Seabourne in *Fraud and Its Victims* (Coyne), Edinburgh.

Captain Niddermannersteinchwanchoingen in *Frederick of Prussia* (Selby), Edinburgh.

Didier in *The French Spy* (Haines), Edinburgh.

The Organist in *The Gaberlunzie Man* (Ballantyne), Edinburgh.

Bates in *The Gamester* (Centlivre), Edinburgh.

Sir William Worthey in *The Gentle Shepherd* (Ramsay), Edinburgh.

Carbine, Sergeant Musqueton, and Gilderoy in *Gilderoy* (Murray), Edinburgh; Theatre Royal, Glasgow (as Gilderoy), 1860.

Luke Hatfield in *The Gipsy Farmer* (Johnstone), Edinburgh.

Don Manuel in *Giralda* cribe, adapted by Boucicault), Edinburgh.

Charley, Young Mr Simpson, and Harry Collier in *Good for Nothing* (Yates and Harrington), Edinburgh.

Governor of Surinam in *The Governor's Wife* (Mildenhall), Edinburgh.

Langley in *Grandfather Whitehead* (Lemon), Edinburgh.

Ned Keogh and George O'Kennedy in *The Green Bushes* (Buckstone), Edinburgh.

Marston in *The Green Hills of the Far West* (Wilkins), Edinburgh.

Evan Pritchard in *Gwynneth Vaughan* (Lemon), Edinburgh.

Cyril Baliol in *Hamilton of Bothwellhaugh* (Slous), Edinburgh.

Guildenstern, Horatio, Claudius, The Priest, The Ghost, Osric, and Laertes in *Hamlet* (Shakespeare), Edinburgh; Princess's Theatre, London (as Osric), 1859; Queen's Theatre, Dublin (as Laertes), 1860; Theatre Royal, Manchester (as Laertes and Hamlet), 1860–65; Theatre Royal, Oxford (as Hamlet), 1864; Athenaeum, Bury (as Hamlet), 1865; Prince of Wales's Theatre, Birmingham (as Laertes), 1865; Prince's Theatre, Manchester (as The Ghost), 1866; Lyceum Theatre, London (as Hamlet), 1874 and 1878.

Mr Furlong in *Handy Andy* (Floyd), Edinburgh.

Charles in *The Happiest Day of My Life* (Buckstone), Edinburgh.

Fergus Graham in *A Hard Struggle* (Marston), Edinburgh; Theatre Royal, Manchester, 1860–65.

Black Frank, Duke of Argyll, and Reuben Butler in *The Heart of Midlothian* (adapted from Scott), Edinburgh; Theatre Royal, Manchester (as the Duke of Argyll), 1860–65.

Lord Quaverley in *Helping Hands* (Taylor), Edinburgh.

Earl of Surrey in *Henry VIII* (Shakespeare), Edinburgh.

Philip in *High Life Below Stairs* (Townley), Edinburgh.

Charles in *His Last Legs* (Bernard), Edinburgh; Theatre Royal, Manchester, 1860–65.

Captain Lejoyeux in *Honesty is the Best Policy* (Lemon), Edinburgh.

Lampedo and Lopez in *The Honeymoon* (Tobin), Edinburgh.

Lord Tinsel and Sir Thomas Clifford in *The Hunchback* (Daly), Edinburgh; Theatre Royal, Manchester (as Clifford), 1860–65; Theatre Royal, Oxford (as Clifford), 1864.

Marco in *The Hunter of the Alps* (Dimond), Edinburgh.

Smatter in *Hunting a Turtle* (Selby), Edinburgh.

Victor Dubois in *Ici on Parle Français* (Williams), Edinburgh; Standard Theatre, London, 1869.

Kelly in *Ida May* (Young), Edinburgh.

Earl of Sussex in *The Idiot Witness* (Haines), Edinburgh.

Lykon and Myron in *Ingomar* (Charlton), Edinburgh.

Captain Florville in *The Invincibles* (Morton), Edinburgh.

Connor and M. Voyage in *Ireland As It Was* (anon., adapted from Amherst), Edinburgh.

Malden in *Irish-A-Honey* (anon.), Edinburgh.

Captain Herbert in *Irish Assurance* (Williams), Edinburgh.

Henry Travers in *The Irish Emigrant* (Harrigan), Edinburgh; Theatre Royal, Manchester, 1860–65.

Mackenzie and Captain Dixon in *The Irish Lion* (Buckstone), Edinburgh; Theatre Royal, Manchester (as Dixon), 1860–65.

George Lane in *The Irish Post* (Planché), Edinburgh.

Sir Charles Lavender in *The Irish Tiger* (Morton), Edinburgh.

Charles in *The Irish Tutor* (Butler), Edinburgh.

Armstrong and Orson in *The Iron Chest* (Colman the Younger), Edinburgh.

Coquin in *Isabelle* (Buckstone), Edinburgh.

Sir Reginald Frondebouef in *Ivanhoe* (Byron), Edinburgh.

José Rimiero in *Jack Robinson and His Monkey* (Barrymore), Edinburgh.

Sir Richard Wroughton in *The Jacobite* (Planché), Edinburgh; Theatre Royal, Glasgow, 1860.

Belmont in *Jane Shore* (Rowe), Edinburgh.

Dumouchard in *The Jersey Girl* (Pitt), Edinburgh.

Sigismund Fanshawe in *Jessy Vere* (Hazlewood), Edinburgh.

Florine in *Joan of Arc* (Taylor), Edinburgh.

Baron Fitzjeffrey and Mayfly in *John Overy* (Jerrold), Edinburgh.

Wayland Smith in *Kenilworth* (Planché), Edinburgh.

Philip Faulconbridge and King of France in *King John* (Shakespeare), Edinburgh; Theatre Royal, Manchester (as King of France), 1860–65.

Curan in *King Lear* (Shakespeare), Edinburgh.

Franquille in *The King of the Peacocks* (Planché), Edinburgh.

Sir Almeric in *King René's Daughter* (Martin), Edinburgh.

Colonel Vane in *The King's Wager* (Wilks), Edinburgh.

Duc de Charbonnes in *The Knight of Arva* (Boucicault), Edinburgh; Theatre Royal, Manchester, 1860–65.

Gustave de Grignon in *The Ladies' Battle* (Scribe, adapted by Reade), Edinburgh.

Sir Charles Lavender and Mr Bookly in *The Ladies' Club* (Lemon), Edinburgh; Theatre Royal, Manchester (as Lavender), 1860–65.

Malcolm Graeme in *The Lady of the Lake* (T. Dibdin, adapted from Scott), Edinburgh.

Philip Arnold in *The Lamplighter* (Davis), Edinburgh.

Henry Wentworth in *The Last Man* (anon.), Edinburgh.

Simon Hornblower in *The Laughing Hyena* (anon.), Edinburgh.

Louis in *Like and Unlike* (Langford and Sorrell), Edinburgh.

Scruncher (The Wolf) in *Little Bo-Peep* (anon.), Edinburgh.

Sparkler in *Little Dorrit* (Dickens), Edinburgh.

Sir Charles Howard and Captain Walter Maydenblush in *The Little Treasure* (Harris and Williams), Edinburgh; Theatre Royal, Glasgow (as Howard), 1860; Theatre Royal, Manchester (as Maydenblush), 1860–65.

Captain Amersfort in *The Loan of a Lover* (Planché), Edinburgh.

Charles Courtly and Dazzle in *London Assurance* (Boucicault), Edinburgh; Theatre Royal, Oxford (as Dazzle), 1865.

Wyndham Bowyer in *The Lonely Man of the Ocean* (Blake), Edinburgh.

Lord Darnley, Earl Lumley, and Will Eliott in *Lord Darnley* (Wilks), Edinburgh.

Lorain in *The Lost Husband* (Reade), Edinburgh.

Ned Martin in *The Lost Ship* (anon.), Edinburgh.

Charles in *The Lottery Ticket* (Beazley), Edinburgh.

Tristan and Coitier in *Louis XI* (Boucicault), Edinburgh.

Ulrick in *Love* (Knowles), Edinburgh.

Neville and Master Waller in *The Love Chase* (Knowles), Edinburgh.

André in *Lucille* (anon.), Edinburgh.

Squire Chase and Charles Maydew in *Luke the Labourer* (Buckstone), Edinburgh.

Seyton, Rosse, Banquo, and Macduff in *Macbeth* (Shakespeare), Edinburgh; Theatre Royal, Manchester (as Malcolm and Banquo), 1860–65; Theatre Royal, Oxford (as Macduff), 1864 and 1865.

Fernando and Villabella in *The Maid and the Magpie* (Byron), Edinburgh; Theatre Royal, Liverpool (as Villabella), 1860.

Algernon in *The Maid With the Milking Pail* (Buckstone), Edinburgh.

Egerton in *The Man of the World* (Macklin), Edinburgh.

Wrangle in *The Man With the Carpet Bag* (Á Becket), Edinburgh.

D'Aubigné in *The Man With the Iron Mask* (adapted from Dumas), Edinburgh; Theatre Royal, Glasgow, 1860.

Frederick de Courcy in *The Marble Heart* (Selby), Edinburgh; Theatre Royal, Glasgow, 1860.

Gaston de Montclar in *Marianne the Vivandière* (Phillips), Edinburgh.

Count de Provence in *Marie Antoinette* (anon.), Edinburgh.

Markland in *Marie Ducange* (Bernard), Edinburgh.

Herbert Manifest in *Marriage A Lottery* (Dance), Edinburgh.

Frederick Younghusband and Lionel Lynx in *Married Life* (Buckstone), Edinburgh; Theatre Royal, Glasgow (as Younghusband), 1860.

Lord Lyndsay and Jasper Drysdale in *Mary, Queen of Scots* (St John), Edinburgh.

Selva in *Masaniello* (Kenney), Edinburgh.

Snarl and Soaper in *Masks and Faces* (Reade and Taylor), Edinburgh.

Brozzo, Gianetto, and Sampiero in *Matteo Falcone* (Oxberry), Edinburgh.

Secretary Sampson in *The May Queen* (Buckstone), Edinburgh.

Jason in *Medea* (Glover), Edinburgh; Theatre Royal, Manchester, 1860–65; Prince of Wales's Theatre, Birmingham, 1865.

De Ferney in *Memoirs of the Devil* (Barber), Edinburgh.

Marquis de Brancador in *Mephistopheles* (Brough and Edwards), Edinburgh.

Salarino and Bassanio in *The Merchant of Venice* (Shakespeare), Edinburgh; Theatre Royal, Manchester (as Bassanio), 1860–65.

Phillip D'Arville in *Michael Erle* (Wilks), Edinburgh.

Jupiter in *Midas* (anon.), Edinburgh.

Briefless in *The Middle Temple* (Peake), Edinburgh.

Mr Tonnish in *The Middy Ashore* (Bernard), Edinburgh.

Antoine Deval in *The Midnight Watch* (Morton), Edinburgh.

Fabian Leslie in *The Miller of Whetstone* (Wilks), Edinburgh.

George in *The Miller's Maid* (Faucit), Edinburgh.

Lieutenant Bowling in *The Milliner's Holiday* (Morton), Edinburgh.

Mowbray in *Mind Your Own Business* (Lemon), Edinburgh.

Henri Desgrais in *Mischief Making* (Buckstone), Edinburgh.

James Greenfield in *The Momentous Question* (Fitzball), Edinburgh.

Captain Dudley Smooth in *Money* (Bulwer-Lytton), Edinburgh; Theatre Royal, Manchester, 1860–65.

Maxwell in *Mother and Child are Doing Well* (Morton), Edinburgh.

John Brush in *Mr and Mrs Pringle* (De Trueba), Edinburgh.

Don Pedro in *The Muleteer of Toledo* (Robertson), Edinburgh.

Adrien de Beauval in *Music Hath Charms* (Fisher), Edinburgh; Theatre Royal, Manchester, 1860–65.

Captain Touchwood in *My Aunt's Husband* (Selby), Edinburgh.

Oakheart in *My Poll and My Partner Joe* (Haines), Edinburgh.

Langford in *My Precious Betsy* (Morton), Edinburgh.

Captain Gasconade in *The Mysterious Stranger* (Selby), Edinburgh.

Edward Waverley in *My Wife's Mother* (Harrigan), Edinburgh.

Captain Burnish in *The Nervous Man* (Bernard), Edinburgh.

Nicholas and Mantellini in *Nicholas Nickleby* (Dickens), Edinburgh; Queen's Theatre, Dublin (as Nicholas), 1860; Theatre Royal, Manchester (as Nicholas), 1860–65.

Ned O'Grady in *Norah Creina* (anon.), Edinburgh.

Marquis de Treval in *Not A Bad Judge* (Planché), Edinburgh; Theatre Royal, Manchester, 1860–65.

Duke of Vendome in *Nothing Venture, Nothing Win* (Coyne), Edinburgh.

Flipper in *Number One Round the Corner* (Brough), Edinburgh; Theatre Royal, Manchester, 1860–65.

Sydenham Simmerton in *An Object of Interest* (Stocqueler), Edinburgh.

Hal Harsfield in *The Ocean of Life* (Buckstone), Edinburgh.

Charles Benedict in *The Old Gentleman* (Webster), Edinburgh.

Frederick in *Old Joe and Young Joe* (Courtney), Edinburgh.

Monks and Leeford in *Oliver Twist* (adapted from Dickens), Edinburgh.

Messenger, Montano, and Cassio in *Othello* (Shakespeare), Edinburgh; Queen's Theatre, Dublin (as Cassio), 1860; Theatre Royal, Manchester (as Cassio), 1860–65.

Henry Seymour in *Our Gal* (G. Johnson), Edinburgh.

Colonel Albert in *Our Mary Anne* (Buckstone), Edinburgh.

Marquis de Ligny in *Our Wife* (Morton), Edinburgh.

Henry Coates in *Paddy Miles's Boy* (Pilgrim), Edinburgh; Theatre Royal, Manchester, 1860–65.

Leander in *The Padlock* (Bickerstaff), Edinburgh.

Lister in *The Patrician's Daughter* (Marston), Edinburgh.

Harry Stanley in *Paul Pry* (Jerrold), Edinburgh; Theatre Royal, Glasgow, 1860; Theatre Royal, Manchester, 1860–65; Standard Theatre, London, 1869.

Camillo in *Perdita; or, The Royal Milkmaid* (Brough), Edinburgh.

Charles Paragon in *Perfection* (Bayly), Edinburgh; Theatre Royal, Manchester, 1860–65.

Felix Raymond in *Perourou, The Bellows Mender* (Moncrieff), Edinburgh.

Dubois in *Peter Bell, The Waggoner* (Buckstone), Edinburgh.

Lieutenant Griffiths, Captain Manson, and The Pilot in *The Pilot* (Buckstone), Edinburgh; Theatre Royal, Glasgow, 1860.

Sir George in *A Pleasant Neighbour* (Planché), Edinburgh.

Berthier and M. de Cevennes in *Plot and Passion* (Taylor), Edinburgh.

Minos in *Pluto and Proserpine* (Talfourd), Edinburgh.

Walter Warren in *A Poor Girl's Temptation* (Travers), Edinburgh.

Augustus Burr in *The Porter's Knot* (Oxenford), Edinburgh; Theatre Royal, Glasgow, 1860.

Lieutenant Fusile and Mr Somerhill in *P.P.; or, The Man and the Tiger* (Parry), Edinburgh.

Prince Charles in *Prince Charles Edward Stuart* (Crawford), Edinburgh.

Colonel Pazzi in *A Prince for an Hour* (Morton), Edinburgh.

An Ogre and a Demon in *Puss in Boots* (pantomime), Edinburgh.

Bolding in *Quake, Shake and Simon* (anon.), Edinburgh.

Lieutenant Wentworth in *Queen Mary's Bower* (Planché), Edinburgh.

Frank Floss in *Ruby Rattler* (anon.), Edinburgh.

Count St Fruilan and Baron Hoffman in *The Ragpicker of Paris* (Stirling), Edinburgh.

Raymond and Jacques in *Raymond and Agnes* (Fitzball), Edinburgh.

Captain Bolding in *The Rendezvous* (anon.), Edinburgh; Theatre Royal, Manchester, 1860–65.

Toby Heywood in *The Rent Day* (Jerrold), Edinburgh.

Carlos in *The Revenge* (Young), Edinburgh.

Captain Beaugard in *The Review* (Colman the Younger), Edinburgh.

Catesby, Henry VI, and Richmond in *Richard III* (Shakespeare), Edinburgh; Theatre Royal, Manchester (as Buckingham and Richmond), 1860–65.

Captain Nugent in *The Rifle Brigade* (Selby), Edinburgh.

Marquis de Preville in *The Rival Pages* (Selby), Edinburgh; Theatre Royal, Manchester, 1860–65.

Fag, Faulkland, and Captain Absolute in *The Rivals* (Sheridan), Edinburgh; Theatre Royal, Manchester (as Absolute), 1860–65; British tour (as Absolute), 1867; Queen's Theatre, London (as Faulkland), 1868.

Charles Dumont in *Robert Macaire* (Byron), Edinburgh.

Comyn in *Robert the Bruce* (anon.), Edinburgh.

Francis Osbaldiston, Rashleigh Osbaldiston, and Rob Roy in *Rob Roy* (adapted from Scott), Edinburgh; Theatre Royal, Glasgow (as Rashleigh), 1860; Theatre Royal, Manchester (as Rashleigh), 1860–65.

The Gamekeeper and Alfred Highflyer in *A Roland for an Oliver* (Morton), Edinburgh; Theatre Royal, Manchester (as Highflyer), 1860–65.

Paris and Tybalt in *Romeo and Juliet* (Shakespeare), Edinburgh.

De Lacy in *Rory O'More* (Lover), Edinburgh.

Alonzo and The Duke in *Rule a Wife and Have a Wife* (Fletcher), Edinburgh.

Singleton Unit in *Rural Felicity* (Buckstone), Edinburgh; Theatre Royal, Manchester, 1860–65.

Roskelyn in *Saint Clair of the Isles* (Polack), Edinburgh.

Robert Vaughan in *St Mary's Eve* (Bernard), Edinburgh.

Francis and Baron Trenck in *St Patrick's Eve* (Power), Edinburgh.

Samuel in *Samuel in Search of Himself* (Coyne and Coape), Edinburgh.

Harry Frampton in *Sandy McDonald* (anon.), Edinburgh.

Frederick in *The Scholar* (Buckstone), Edinburgh; Theatre Royal, Manchester, 1860–65.

Dupuis in *The Secret* (Beerbohm), Edinburgh; Theatre Royal, Manchester, 1860–65.

Luke Brandon in *Self Accusation* (Lemon), Edinburgh.

Prince in *The Sentinel* (Boucicault), Edinburgh.

Frank Vincent in *The Serious Family* (Barnett), Edinburgh.

Jeremy in *She Stoops to Conquer* (Goldsmith), Edinburgh.

Captain Spoff in *Shocking Events* (Buckstone), Edinburgh.

Captain Vivid in *The Siamese Twins* (Á Becket), Edinburgh.

Mr Bromley in *Simpson and Co.* (Poole), Edinburgh; Theatre Royal, Manchester, 1860–65.

Charles Chester and Narcissus Boss in *Single Life* (Buckstone), Edinburgh; Theatre Royal, Manchester (as Narcissus Boss), 1860–65.

Horace Mordaunt in *Sixteen String Jack* (Rede/Wilks), Edinburgh.

Somerdyke in *The Slave* (Morton), Edinburgh.

Venoma in *The Sleeping Beauty* (pantomime), Edinburgh.

Young Malfort and Frank Heartall in *The Soldier's Daughter* (Cherry), Edinburgh; Theatre Royal, Manchester (as Heartall), 1860–65.

Hans Moritz in *Somebody Else* (Planché), Edinburgh.

M. de Rosembert in *The Somnambulist* (Scribe), Edinburgh.

Captain Vauntington and Mr Nicodemus in *The Spectre Bridegroom* (Moncrieff), Edinburgh; Theatre Royal, Manchester (as Nicodemus), 1860–65.

Darville in *The Spitalfields Weaver* (Bayly), Edinburgh.

Captain Shortcut in *The Spitfire* (Morton), Edinburgh.

Tagg in *The Spoiled Child* (Bickerstaff), Edinburgh.

Lord Lovel in *Spring Gardens* (Planché), Edinburgh.

Calverton Hall in *State Secrets* (Wilks), Edinburgh.

Dunbilk in *Still Waters Run Deep* (Taylor), Edinburgh.

Count Wintersen and Francis in *The Stranger* (Kotzebue, adapted by Dunlap), Edinburgh; Theatre Royal, Manchester, 1860–65.

Andrew Hopley in *Susan Hopley* (Pitt), Edinburgh.

Sandford and Charles Franklin in *Sweethearts and Wives* (Kenney), Edinburgh; Theatre Royal, Manchester (as Franklin), 1860–65.

Hortensio, Biondello, and Petruchio in *The Taming of the Shrew* (Shakespeare), Edinburgh.

Henry in *Teddy the Tiler* (Rodwell), Edinburgh.

Fontaine in *Thérèse; or, The Orphan of Geneva* (Boucicault), Edinburgh.

Athos in *The Three Musketeers* (Dumas *père*), Edinburgh.

Charles Clinton and Matthew Bates in *Time Tries All* (Courtney), Edinburgh; Theatre Royal, Glasgow (as Bates), 1860.

Alfred and Mat Ironhand in *Tom Cringle* (Fitzball), Edinburgh.

George Acorn and Fenton in *The Toodles* (Raymond), Edinburgh.

Phillipot in *The Trumpeter's Daughter* (Coyne), Edinburgh; Theatre Royal, Manchester, 1860–65.

Delorme in *'Twas I* (Payne), Edinburgh.

John Bull in *The Two Gregories* (T. Dibdin), Edinburgh.

Maillard in *The Vagrant and His Wife* (anon.), Edinburgh; Theatre Royal, Glasgow, 1860.

Herbert Fitzherbert in *Victims* (Taylor), Edinburgh.

Macaire in *Victorine* (Falconer), Edinburgh.

Charles in *The Virginia Mummy* (Rice), Edinburgh.

Appius Claudius and Soldier in *Virginius* (Knowles), Edinburgh.

Monteith in *Wallace: The Hero of Scotland* (Barrymore), Edinburgh.

Gregoire, Comte de Croissy, and Roland in *The Wandering Boys* (Pixérécourt), Edinburgh; Theatre Royal, Manchester (as de Croissy), 1860–65.

Tom Tipton in *Wanted 1,000 Spirited Young Milliners* (Coyne), Edinburgh; Theatre Royal, Manchester, 1860–65.

Clanronald in *Warlock of the Glen* (Walker), Edinburgh; Theatre Royal, Glasgow, 1860.

Charles Chester in *The Water Witches* (Coyne), Edinburgh.

Don Lopez and Don Scipio in *Where There's a Will* (Morton), Edinburgh; Theatre Royal, Manchester, 1860–65.

Mr Twitter in *The Widow's Victim* (Selby), Edinburgh.

Count Florio and Leonardo Gonzago in *The Wife: A Tale of Mantua* (Knowles), Edinburgh; Theatre Royal, Manchester, 1860–65.

Micahel and Gessler in *William Tell* (Taylor), Edinburgh; Theatre Royal, Glasgow (as Gessler), 1860.

Cleomenes, The Third Gentleman, and Florizel in *The Winter's Tale* (Shakespeare), Edinburgh; Queen's Theatre, Dublin (as Florizel), 1860.

Frederick in *The Woman Hater* (Beaumont and Fletcher), Edinburgh.

Frederick in *The Wonder* (Centlivre), Edinburgh.

Charles Alison in *The Wraith of the Lake* (Haines), Edinburgh.

Walter Barnard in *The Wreck Ashore* (Buckstone), Edinburgh.

Sir Philip Eaton and Richard Oliver in *The Writing on the Wall* (Morton and Morton), Edinburgh.

Frank Melrose in *The Young Mother* (Selby), Edinburgh.

Arthur in *The Young Scamp* (Stirling), Edinburgh.

Krakwitz in *Your Life's in Danger* (Morton), Edinburgh.

1859   Johnson in *Ivy Hall* (Oxenford), Princess's Theatre, London.

Jack Bumpus in *The Two Polts* (Courtney), Princess's Theatre, London.

Rudolphe in *A Wonderful Woman* (Dance), Princess's Theatre, London.

1860   Didier in *The Courier of Lyons* (Reade), Queen's Theatre, Dublin.

Titus Quintus Fulvius in *Gisipus; or, The Forgotten Friend* (Griffin), Queen's Theatre, Dublin.

Lucien de Nerval in *Pauline; or, A Night of Terror* (Dumas *père*), Queen's Theatre, Dublin.

Captain Walton in *The Anchor of Hope* (Stirling), Theatre Royal, Glasgow.

Nicola in *The Bottle Imp* (Hale and Talfourd), Theatre Royal, Glasgow.

Sir Harry Lester in *Cool as a Cucumber* (Jerrold), Theatre Royal, Glasgow.

Baron Giordino in *The Corsican Brothers* (Boucicault), Theatre Royal, Glasgow.

Courriol in *The Courier of Lyons* (Reade), Theatre Royal, Glasgow; Theatre Royal, Manchester, 1860–65.

Francis in *The Cross of Gold; or, The Maid of Croissy* (Gore), Theatre Royal, Glasgow.

Mr Aubrey in *A Curious Case* (Reynoldson), Theatre Royal, Glasgow.

Sir Frederick Chasemore in *The Dowager* (Mathews), Theatre Royal, Glasgow; Theatre Royal, Manchester, 1860–65.

El Hyder in *El Hyder* (anon.), Theatre Royal, Glasgow.

Mr Icebrook in *Everybody's Friend* (Coyne), Theatre Royal, Glasgow; Theatre Royal, Glasgow, 1860–65.

Captain M'Intosh in *The Fair Maid of Perth* (Webb), Theatre Royal, Glasgow.

Adelbert in *Frederick of Prussia* (Selby), Theatre Royal, Glasgow.

Strato in *Gis, The Armourer of Tyre* (Selby), Theatre Royal, Glasgow.

Henry Fitzherbert in *A Handsome Husband* (Mrs J. R. Planché), Theatre Royal, Glasgow; Theatre Royal, Manchester, 1860–65.

Captain Darling in *Hercules, King of Clubs* (Cooper), Theatre Royal, Glasgow.

Achmet and Prince Jung Bahadour in *The Indian Revolt* (Glover), Theatre Royal, Glasgow.

Philip Darville in *The Maniac Lover* (anon.), Theatre Royal, Glasgow.

Ned Martin in *The Man o' Warsman* (anon.), Theatre Royal, Glasgow.

Henry Pelham in *The Merchant and the Mendicant* (Rice), Theatre Royal, Glasgow.

Demetrius in *A Midsummer Night's Dream* (Shakespeare), Theatre Royal, Glasgow.

Lieutenant Harry Kingston in *Naval Engagements* (Dance), Theatre Royal, Glasgow; Prince of Wales's Theatre, Liverpool, 1865–66.

Roland Forrester in *Nick of the Woods* (Davis), Theatre Royal, Glasgow.

Sir Lucien de Larrante in *Philip of France* (Marston), Theatre Royal, Glasgow.

Felix Merryweather in *A Pretty Piece of Business* (Morton), Theatre Royal, Glasgow.

Henri Berville in *The Ragpicker of Paris* (Stirling), Theatre Royal, Glasgow.

Captain Blenheim in *A Rough Diamond* (Buckstone), Theatre Royal, Glasgow.

Charles Lovel in *The Ways of the World*, Theatre Royal, Glasgow.

Captain Seymour in *The Witch of Windermere* (Selby), Theatre Royal, Glasgow.

Adolphe in *The Spy* (Besant and Pollock), Theatre Royal, Manchester.

Faust in *Faust and Marguerite* (Boucicault), Theatre Royal, Liverpool; Theatre Royal, Manchester, 1860–65.

1860–65   Arthur Clinton in *The Adventures of a Love Letter* (Mathews), Theatre Royal, Manchester.

Edward Evelyn in *Agnes de Vere* (Buckstone), Theatre Royal, Manchester.

Talbot Bulstrode in *Aurora Floyd* (Webster), Theatre Royal, Manchester.

Adolphus Thornton in *A Bachelor of Arts* (Hardwicke), Theatre Royal, Manchester.

D'Arpinal in *Belphegor* (Boucicault), Theatre Royal, Manchester.

Prince Gonzagues in *Blanche of Nevers* (Hyde), Theatre Royal, Manchester.

Albert in *The Brigand* (Douglass), Theatre Royal, Manchester.

Maurice Warner in *Camilla's Husband* (Phillips), Theatre Royal, Manchester.

Clorinda in *Cinderella* (pantomime), Theatre Royal, Manchester.

Hardress Cregan in *The Colleen Bawn* (Boucicault), Theatre Royal, Manchester.

Antipholus of Syracuse in *The Comedy of Errors* (Shakespeare), Theatre Royal, Manchester.

Mr Wapshott in *The Contested Election* (Taylor), Theatre Royal, Manchester.

Frederick Barkins in *Cool As A Cucumber* (Jerrold), Theatre Royal, Manchester.

Earl of Leicester in *The Critic* (Sheridan), Theatre Royal, Manchester.

Charles in *A Curious Case* (Reynoldson), Theatre Royal, Manchester.

Philip Austin in *The Dark Cloud* (Sketchley), Theatre Royal, Manchester; Prince of Wales Operetta House, Edinburgh, St James's Hall, Liverpool, and Prince of Wales's Theatre, Liverpool, 1865.

Cornelius Nepos in *The Dead Letter* (Pinget), Theatre Royal, Manchester.

Joseph in *Deborah* (adapted from Mosenthal), Theatre Royal, Manchester.

Mr Everton in *Doing the Hansom* (Harris), Theatre Royal, Manchester.

Young Norval in *Douglas* (Home), Theatre Royal, Manchester.

Frederick Crawford in *The Family Secret* (Falconer), Theatre Royal, Manchester.

Paul Weldon in *Flies in the Web* (Brougham), Theatre Royal, Manchester.

Serafino Dell'Aquila and Galeotto Manfredi in *The Fool's Revenge* (Taylor), Theatre Royal, Manchester; Theatre Royal, Oxford (as Manfredi), 1865.

Rattle in *Fortune's Frolic* (Allingham), Theatre Royal, Manchester.

Sir Harry Lester in *A Game of Speculation* (Lewes), Theatre Royal, Manchester; Prince of Wales's Theatre, Liverpool, 1865–66.

George Barnwell in *George Barnwell* (Lillo), Theatre Royal, Manchester; Prince of Wales Operetta House, Edinburgh, 1865.

Walter Tresham in *Guy Faux* (Macfarren), Theatre Royal, Manchester.

Mr Furlong in *Handy Andy* (Montgomery), Theatre Royal, Manchester.

Felix Pottinger in *The Hansom Driver* (anon.), Theatre Royal, Manchester.

Prince of Wales in *Henry IV, part 1* (Shakespeare), Theatre Royal, Manchester.

Pierre Marceau in *A Husband to Order* (Morton), Theatre Royal, Manchester.

Mr Clifton in *Irish Assurance* (Williams), Theatre Royal, Manchester.

Wilford in *The Iron Chest* (Colman the Younger), Theatre Royal, Manchester.

Charles Darrell in *The Island Home* (Calvert), Theatre Royal, Manchester.

John Slipton Stasher in *Jacob's Truck* (anon.), Theatre Royal, Manchester.

Edmund in *King Lear* (Shakespeare), Theatre Royal, Manchester; Prince's Theatre, Manchester, 1865.

Frank Fathom in *A Kiss in the Dark* (Buckstone), Theatre Royal, Manchester.

Joe Smith in *The Knotting'em Brothers* (Coyne), Theatre Royal, Manchester.

Captain Littlepop in *Little Toddlekins* (C. Mathews), Theatre Royal, Manchester.

Henri la Carge in *Lord Flannigan* (anon.), Theatre Royal, Manchester.

Horace Chereyhale in *Love and Lucre* (anon.), Theatre Royal, Manchester.

Eugene de Lorme in *Love's Sacrifice* (Lewes), Theatre Royal, Manchester; Theatre Royal, Oxford, 1864.

Mr Easy in *Manchester Wives* (anon.), Theatre Royal, Manchester.

Digby Spooner in *Married Daughters and Young Husbands* (Besemeres), Theatre Royal, Manchester; St James's Hall, Liverpool, 1865.

Ernest Vane in *Masks and Faces* (Reade and Taylor), Theatre Royal, Manchester.

Mr Page in *The Merry Wives of Windsor* (Shakespeare), Theatre Royal, Manchester.

Marquis de Merville in *The Midnight Watch*(Morton), Theatre Royal, Manchester.

Lothair in *The Miller and His Men* (Byron), Theatre Royal, Manchester.

Bernard Reynolds in *Miriam's Crime* (Craven), Theatre Royal, Manchester; Theatre Royal, Oxford, 1864.

Frank Brown in *Mr and Mrs White* (anon.), Theatre Royal, Manchester.

Claudio in *Much Ado About Nothing* (Shakespeare), Theatre Royal, Manchester; Prince's Theatre, Manchester, 1865; Prince's Theatre, Manchester, 1866.

Charles Arundel in *My Aunt's Advice* (anon.), Theatre Royal, Manchester; Prince of Wales's Theatre, Birmingham, 1865; St James's Theatre, London, 1867.

Wellborn in *A New Way To Pay Old Debts* (Massinger), Theatre Royal, Manchester.

Ryder in *A Nice Firm* (Taylor), Theatre Royal, Manchester.

Rodomont Rolingstone in *Nine Points of the Law* (Taylor), Theatre Royal, Manchester; Prince of Wales's Theatre, Liverpool, 1865–66; Prince of Wales's Theatre, Liverpool, 1867.

Captain Prettyman in *Out of Sight, Out of Mind* (anon.), Theatre Royal, Manchester.

Captain Clavering in *The Overland Route* (Taylor), Theatre Royal, Manchester.

Marquis de St Cast in *Payable on Demand* (Taylor), Theatre Royal, Manchester.

Captain Howard in *Peep O'Day* (Falconer), Theatre Royal, Manchester.

Herbert Waverley in *Playing With Fire* (Brougham), Theatre Royal, Manchester.

Edmund Stubbs in *A Poor Gentleman* (Colman the Younger), Theatre Royal, Manchester.

Oliver Random in *The Poor of Manchester* (Boucicault), Theatre Royal, Manchester.

Stephen Scatter in *The Porter's Knot* (Oxenford), Theatre Royal, Manchester.

Jeremy Diddler in *Raising the Wind* (Kenny), Theatre Royal, Manchester; Free Trade Hall, Manchester and Prince of Wales Operetta House, Edinburgh, 1865; Prince of Wales's Theatre, Liverpool, 1865–66; Prince's Theatre, Manchester, 1866; Lyceum Theatre, London, 1872 and 1879.

Mr Whitewash in *Retained for the Defence*, Theatre Royal, Manchester.

Arthur Aubrey in *Returned to Life* (Hayes), Theatre Royal, Manchester.

De Mauprat in *Richelieu* (Bulwer-Lytton), Theatre Royal, Manchester.

Frank Meredith in *Romance and Reality* (Brougham), Theatre Royal, Manchester.

Benvolio and Mercutio in *Romeo and Juliet* (Shakespeare), Theatre Royal, Manchester.

Count de Brissac in *The Rose of Amiens* (Morton), Theatre Royal, Manchester.

Sir Benjamin Backbite in *The School for Scandal* (Sheridan), Theatre Royal, Manchester.

Charles Torrens in *The Serious Family* (Barnett), Theatre Royal, Manchester; St. James's Theatre, London, 1867.

Young Marlow in *She Stoops to Conquer* (Goldsmith), Theatre Royal, Manchester; British tour, 1867; Queen's Theatre, London, 1869.

Count Theodore in *A Signal Engagement* (anon.), Theatre Royal, Manchester.

Clarence Greyleaf in *Slowtop's Engagements* (Cheltnam), Theatre Royal, Manchester.

Frank Goodenough in *The Soft Sex* (Mathews), Theatre Royal, Manchester.

Mr Brown in *The Spitalfields Weaver* (Bayly), Theatre Royal, Manchester; Drury Lane Theatre, 1869.

Captain Hawksley in *Still Waters Run Deep* (Taylor), Theatre Royal, Manchester.

Henry Travers in *Temptation* (anon.), Theatre Royal, Manchester.

Bob Brierly and Jem Dalton in *The Ticket of Leave Man* (Taylor), Theatre Royal, Manchester; Theatre Royal, Oxford (as Brierly), 1864; Prince of Wales Operetta House, Edinburgh, Theatre Royal, Oxford, and Prince of Wales's Theatre, Birmingham (as Brierly), 1865; Prince's Theatre, Manchester (as Brierly), 1866.

Don Carlos in *Tit for Tat* (Colman the Elder), Theatre Royal, Manchester.

Frank Poppleton in *Too Late for Dinner* (anon.), Theatre Royal, Manchester.

Henry Arncliffe in *An Unequal Match* (Taylor), Theatre Royal, Manchester.

Ironbrace in *Used Up* (Boucicault), Theatre Royal, Manchester; Prince of Wales's Theatre, Birmingham, 1865; Prince of Wales's Theatre, Liverpool, 1865–66.

Captain Charles in *Who Speaks First?* (Dance), Theatre Royal, Manchester; Free Trade Hall, Manchester and St James's Hall, Liverpool, 1865.

Marquis de Frontignac in *A Wonderful Woman* (Dance), Theatre Royal, Manchester; Theatre Royal, Oxford, 1864; Victoria Hall, Douglas, Isle of Man, 1865.

Sir Hubert Denzil in *A Word in Your Ear* (anon.), Theatre Royal, Manchester.

Paul Falconer in *Ye Merchant's Storye* (adapted from the French), Theatre Royal, Manchester.

Mandeville in *The Young Widow* (Rodwell), Theatre Royal, Manchester.

1864 Connor O'Kennedy in *The Green Bushes* (Buckstone), Theatre Royal, Oxford.

Julian St Pierre in *The Wife* (Knowles), Theatre Royal, Oxford.

1865 Doctor Ferguson in *The Exposure of the Davenport Brothers* (anon.), Manchester Athenaeum and Free Trade Hall, Manchester.

Duc de Nemours in *Louis XI* (Boucicault), Prince's Theatre, Manchester.

Robert Macaire in *Robert Macaire* (Byron), Prince of Wales Operetta House, Edinburgh and Theatre Royal, Oxford; Prince of Wales's Theatre, Liverpool, 1865–66; St James's Theatre, London, 1867; Lyceum Theatre, London, 1883.

Dick Hazard in *My Wife's Dentist* (Wilks), Prince's Theatre, Manchester and Athenaeum, Bury.

Major Mortar in *The Ladies' Club* (Lemon), Victoria Hall, Douglas, Isle of Man.

Iago in *Othello* (Shakespeare), Theatre Royal, Oxford; Lyceum Theatre, London, 1881.

Charles Surface in *The School for Scandal* (Sheridan), Theatre Royal, Oxford; Queen's Theatre, London, 1868.

Woodcock in *Woodcock's Little Game* (Morton), Theatre Royal, Oxford and St. James's Hall, Liverpool.

Nettle Croker in *Dearest Mamma* (Gordon), Prince of Wales's Theatre, Birmingham.

Archibald Carlyle in *East Lynne* (Oxenford), Prince of Wales's Theatre, Birmingham; Prince of Wales's Theatre, Liverpool, 1865–66.

Anatole in *The Scrap of Paper* (Sardou), Prince of Wales's Theatre, Birmingham.

John Blunt in *War to the Knife* (Byron), Prince of Wales's Theatre, Birmingham.

Captain Ormond in *Tom Noddy's Secret* (Bayly), St James's Hall, Liverpool.

1865–66 John Brownjohn in *Done on Both Sides* (Morton), Prince of Wales's Theatre, Liverpool.

Scampa in *Ernani* (Brough), Prince of Wales's Theatre, Liverpool.

Fox Bromley in *The Favourite of Fortune* (Marston), Prince of Wales's Theatre, Liverpool.

Captain Freeman in *A Lesson in Love* (Cheltnam), Prince of Wales's Theatre, Liverpool.

Captain Feargus Daly in *The Needful* (Craven), Prince of Wales's Theatre, Liverpool.

Harry Thorncote in *Only A Clod* (Simpson), Prince of Wales's Theatre, Liverpool; St. James's Theatre, London, 1867.

Oenone in *Paris; or, Vive Lempriere* (Burnand), Prince of Wales's Theatre, Liverpool.

Arthur Merivale in *The Silver Lining* (Buckingham), Prince of Wales's Theatre, Liverpool.

1866 Rawdon Scudamore in *Hunted Down (Two Lives of Mary Leigh)* (Boucicault), Prince's Theatre, Manchester and St James's Theatre, London.

Joseph Fouché in *Plot and Passion* (Taylor), Prince's Theatre, Manchester.

Colonel Percy Kirke in *A Sheep in Wolf's Clothing* (Taylor), Prince's Theatre, Manchester; Vaudeville Theatre, London, 1871.

Doricourt in *The Belle's Stratagem* (Daly), St James's Theatre, London; Lyceum Theatre, London, 1876 and 1881.

1867 Harry Dornton in *The Road to Ruin* (Holcroft), St James's Theatre, London.

O'Hooligan in *A Rapid Thaw* (Robertson), St James's Theatre, London.

Joseph Surface in *The School for Scandal* (Sheridan), St James's Theatre, London.

Count Falcon in *Idalia* (Roberts), St James's Theatre, London.

Robert Audley in *Lady Audley's Secret* (Hazlewood), St James's Theatre, London.

Abel Murcott in *Our American Cousin* (Taylor), Théâtre Des Italiens, Paris.

Young Wilding in *The Liar* (Mathews), British tour.

Sir Ashley Merton in *Meg's Diversion* (Craven), Prince of Wales's Theatre, Liverpool.

Felix Featherly in *The Widow Hunt* (Coyne), St James's Theatre, London.

Charles Mowbray in *A Story of Procida* (anon.), St James's Theatre, London.

Ferment in *The School of Reform* (Morton), St James's Theatre, London.

Petruchio in *Katherine and Petruchio* (Garrick), Queen's Theatre, London.

1868   Bob Gassitt in *Dearer Than Life* (Byron), Queen's Theatre, London.

Bill Sykes in *Oliver Twist* (adapted from Dickens), Queen's Theatre, London.

Cool in *London Assurance* (Boucicault), Haymarket Theatre, London.

Robert Redburn in *The Lancashire Lass* (Byron), Queen's Theatre, London.

1869   Robert Arnold in *Not Guilty* (Phillips), Queen's Theatre, London.

De Neuville in *Plot and Passion* (Taylor), Queen's Theatre, London.

Harry in *Doing for the Best* (Lacy), Standard Theatre, London.

Doctor Clipper in *The Steeplechase* (Morton), Theatre Royal, Croydon.

John Perrybingle in *Dot; or, The Cricket on the Hearth* (Boucicault), Surrey Theatre, London.

Captain Robert Fitzherbert in *All For Money* (Thierre), Haymarket Theatre, London.

Compton Kerr in *Formosa* (Boucicault), Drury Lane Theatre, London.

Reginald Chevenix in *Uncle Dick's Darling* (Byron), Gaiety Theatre, London.

1870   Alfred Skimmington in *For Love Or Money* (Halliday), Vaudeville Theatre, London.

Digby Grant in *The Two Roses* (Albery), Vaudeville Theatre, London; Lyceum Theatre, London, 1879 and 1881.

1871   Landry Barbeau in *Fanchette* (Bateman), Lyceum Theatre, London.

Alfred Jingle in *Pickwick* (Albery), Lyceum Theatre, London.

Mathias in *The Bells* (Lewis), Lyceum Theatre, London; revived there, 1879; Lyceum Theatre, Sheffield and Theatre Royal, Bradford, 1905.

1872   Charles I in *Charles I* (Wills), Lyceum Theatre, London; revived there, 1879.

1873   Eugene Aram in *Eugene Aram* (Wills), Lyceum Theatre, London; revived there, 1879.

Cardinal Richelieu in *Richelieu* (Bulwer-Lytton), Lyceum Theatre, London; revived there, 1879.

1874   Philip of Miraflore in *Philip* (Aidé), Lyceum Theatre, London.

1875   Macbeth in *Macbeth* (Shakespeare), Lyceum Theatre, London; revived there, 1888.

1876   Othello in *Othello* (Shakespeare), Lyceum Theatre, London; revived there, 1881.

King Philip in *Queen Mary* (Tennyson), Lyceum Theatre, London.

Count Tristan in *King René's Daughter* (Martin), Lyceum Theatre, London.

1877   Duke of Gloucester in *Richard III* (Shakespeare), Lyceum Theatre, London; revived there, 1879 and 1896.

Dubosc and Lesurques in *The Lyons Mail* (Reade), Lyceum Theatre, London; revived there, 1879.

1878   Louis XI in *Louis XI* (Boucicault), Lyceum Theatre, London; revived there, 1879; Theatre Royal, Drury Lane, London, Lyceum Theatre, Sheffield, and Theatre Royal, Bradford, 1905.

Vanderdecken in *Vanderdecken* (Wills and Fitzgerald), Lyceum Theatre, London.

Alfred Jingle in *Jingle* (Albery), Lyceum Theatre, London.

Sir Edward Mortimer in *The Iron Chest* (Colman the Younger), Lyceum Theatre, London.

Shylock in *The Merchant of Venice* (Shakespeare), Lyceum Theatre, London; revived there, 1902; British tour, 1904–05; Theatre Royal, Drury Lane, London, Lyceum Theatre, Sheffield, and Theatre Royal, Bradford, 1905.

1880   Count Tristan in *Iolanthe* (Wills), Lyceum Theatre, London.

Fabien and Louis dei Franchi in *The Corsican Brothers* (Boucicault), Lyceum Theatre, London.

1881   Synorix in *The Cup* (Tennyson), Lyceum Theatre, London.

Modus in *The Hunchback* (Knowles), Lyceum Theatre, London.

1882   Romeo in *Romeo and Juliet* (Shakespeare), Lyceum Theatre, London.

Benedick in *Much Ado About Nothing* (Shakespeare), Lyceum Theatre, London.

1884   Malvolio in *Twelfth Night* (Shakespeare), Lyceum Theatre, London.

1885   Dr Primrose in *Olivia* (Wills), Lyceum Theatre, London.

Mephistopheles in *Faust* (Wills), Lyceum Theatre, London.

1887   Werner in *Werner* (Lord Byron), Lyceum Theatre, London.

1889   Robert Landry in *The Dead Heart* (Phillips), Lyceum Theatre, London.

1890   Edgar of Ravenswood in *Ravenswood* (Merivale), Lyceum Theatre, London.

1892   Cardinal Wolsey in *Henry VIII* (Shakespeare), Lyceum Theatre, London.

Lear in *King Lear* (Shakespeare), Lyceum Theatre, London.

1893   Thomas Becket in *Becket* (Tennyson), Lyceum Theatre, London; Theatre Royal, Drury Lane, London, Lyceum Theatre, Sheffield, and Theatre Royal, Bradford, 1905.

1894   Corporal Gregory Brewster in *A Story of Waterloo* (Doyle), Prince's Theatre, Bristol and Garrick Theatre, London; Lyceum Theatre, London, 1895; Theatre Royal, Drury Lane, London and His Majesty's Theatre, London, 1905.

1895   Arthur in *King Arthur* (Comyns-Carr), Lyceum Theatre, London.
Don Quixote in *Don Quixote* (Wills), Lyceum Theatre, London.

1896   Iachimo in *Cymbeline* (Shakespeare), Lyceum Theatre, London.

1897   Napoleon in *Madame Sans-Gêne* (Sardou), Lyceum Theatre, London.

1898   Peter the Great in *Peter the Great* (L. Irving), Lyceum Theatre, London.
Dr Tregenna in *The Medicine Man* (Hitchen and Traill), Lyceum Theatre, London.

1899   Robespierre in *Robespierre* (Sardou), Lyceum Theatre, London.

1901   Coriolanus in *Coriolanus* (Shakespeare), Lyceum Theatre, London.

1903   Dante in *Dante* (Sardou), Theatre Royal, Drury Lane, London.

Publications

The Drama: Address by Henry Irving, 1893.

*

Bibliography

Books:
Edward R. Russell, *Irving as Hamlet*, London, 1875.
William Archer and R. W. Lowe, *The Fashionable Tragedian*, Edinburgh, 1877.
William Archer, *Henry Irving: Actor and Manager*, London, 1883.
Frank A. Marshall, *Henry Irving: Actor and Manager*, London, 1883.
Joseph Hatton, *Henry Irving's Impressions of America*, New York, 1884.
Frederic Daly, *Henry Irving in England and America*, London, 1884.
Edwin Drew, *Henry Irving, On and Off the Stage*, London, 1889.
Walter Calvert, *Souvenir of Sir Henry Irving*, London, 1895.
Clement Scott, *From "The Bells" to "King Arthur"*, London, 1896.
Charles Hiatt, *Henry Irving*, London, 1899.
Haldane Macfall, *Sir Henry Irving*, London, 1905.
Percy Fitzgerald, *Sir Henry Irving*, Philadelphia, 1906.
Bram Stoker, *Personal Reminiscences of Henry Irving*, 2 vols., London, 1906.
Austin Brereton, *The Life of Henry Irving*, 2 vols., London, 1908.

W. H. Pollock, *Impressions of Henry Irving*, London, 1908.
Edward Gordon Craig, *Henry Irving*, London, 1930.
Henry Arthur Jones, *The Shadow of Henry Irving*, London, 1931.
H. A. Saintsbury and Cecil Palmer (eds.), *We Saw Him Act: A Symposium on the Art of Sir Henry Irving*, London, 1939.
Laurence Irving, *Henry Irving*, London, 1951.
Madeleine Bingham, *Henry Irving and the Victorian Theatre*, London, 1978.
George Taylor, *Henry Irving at the Lyceum*, London, 1980.
Alan Hughes, *Henry Irving, Shakespearean*, Cambridge, 1981.

* * *

The first actor to be knighted, Henry Irving dominated the English stage for more than a quarter of a century. His rise to fame was, however, hard won and once achieved was always attended by controversy. He served a lengthy and gruelling apprenticeship in stock companies (Sunderland, Edinburgh, and Manchester), but in Shaw's view, expressed in *Our Theatre in the Nineties*, this "so-called training ... failed to give him even those generalities of stage deportment which are common to all styles". Irving's professional progress lay not in the acquisition of conventional accomplishments but in the development of his own distinctive style and personality to the point that he demanded and commanded recognition.

Irving's physique did not equip him for youthful success. His face was composed of a high narrow forehead, dark penetrating eyes, overhanging eyebrows, a thin straight nose, hollow cheeks, a sensitive almost lipless mouth, and a marvellously mobile jaw. These features were particularly suited to the sinister, the melancholy, and the obsessive range of characters to which he brought a compelling intensity. Irving's movements were erratic and rarely graceful. William Archer considered that Irving's locomotion was "not a result of volition, but of an involuntary spasm", but to Ellen Terry's son Edward Gordon Craig the actor's walk was "a whole language". Craig took issue with Archer on Irving's vocal delivery, which Archer had described as "the murder of our mother-tongue". Certainly Irving's voice was not naturally sonorous but creaked and wheezed and he was notorious for indulging in wayward pronunciation. "Good" became "god", "sight" became "seyt", "hand" became "hond" or "hend" and whole lines took on an apparently new vocabulary: "Tack the rup from mey nek" for "Take the rope from my neck" (as Mathias in *The Bells*). It is apparent that Irving succeeded not merely in spite of these mannerisms but because of them. This reflects his approach to acting and the creation of character: "There are only two ways of portraying a character on the stage, either you can try to turn yourself into that person — which is impossible — or, and this is the way to act, you can take that person and turn him into yourself. That is how I do it!"

Inevitably, then, Irving's successes were in a range of characters peculiarly suited to his own personality. Of these roles the most renowned was Mathias in *The Bells*, which marked his assumption of star status in November 1871. After a 15-minute build-up, Irving, accompanied by "hurry music", burst through the door, exclaiming "It is I!" (words which in later years were drowned by the applause). As the action unfolded, Irving presented a mesmerising portrait of a soul eaten up with guilt for his (undetected) murder of a Polish Jew. The motif for Irving's Mathias was not the criminal merely fearing detection, but a whole psyche being destroyed by remorse.

Several of Irving's successes were in a similar vein, including W. G. Wills's *Eugene Aram*, depicting three scenes in the after-life of an undetected murderer, George Colman the Younger's *The Iron Chest*, exploring the disturbed conscience of Sir Edward Mortimer, Boucicault's *The Corsican Brothers*, with Irving in the dual roles of the Franchi twins with their telepathic mutual understanding, and Wills's *Faust*, in which he actually embodied the demonic as Mephistopheles.

From his platform as drama critic of *The Saturday Review*, George Bernard Shaw berated Irving for his failure to espouse the "New Drama", but clearly these social plays had no attraction for him. Inevitably several of Irving's Shakespearean creations pre-dated Shaw's tenure of the critic's chair — his melancholy Hamlet, a bitter but sympathetic Shylock, an original Iago, and a predictably conscience-stricken Macbeth. Of Irving's Iachimo in *Cymbeline* Shaw wrote: "this Iachimo was quite fresh and novel to me. I witnessed it with unqualified delight: it was no vulgar bagful of 'points', but a true impersonation". The opportunity to give credibility to another Shakespearean villain came with *Richard III*. Shaw found elements of Punch in this "craftily mischievous, sardonically impudent ... virtuoso in mischief", but regretted Irving's change in tone to prepare for "a pathetically sublime ending". Shaw was resigned to the fact that Irving's play selection was restricted to vehicles for some fantastic creation of his own. He found Irving's own style often at odds with that of the members of his company, the quality of whose performances was at best variable.

As an actor-manager (which he became when he took over the Lyceum from the Batemans in 1878) Irving undeniably employed some talented actors (George Alexander, Frank Benson, Johnson Forbes-Robertson, and John Martin-Harvey, all of whom were knighted), but there was never any question that their primary function was to support the 'Chief'. Ellen Terry was of course the exception, partnering Irving in some of his greatest successes, as Ophelia, Portia, Lady Macbeth, and so on. However, even with Ellen Terry there was no doubt whose performance was to be pre-eminent and on several occasions (Portia, Lady Macbeth) the leading lady had to modify her original interpretation in deference to Irving's.

Similarly, stage designs, lighting, music, and costumes were created to highlight Irving's performances. The taste for historical accuracy still dominated the stage, but even when he engaged such a stickler for antiquarian detail as Sir Lawrence Alma-Tadema Irving's preference was for what was theatrically effective and expressive of character.

The prestige that Irving's Lyceum management enjoyed made it a national theatre in all but name. Personally he was fêted by the luminaries of society from the Prince of Wales downwards. He declined a knighthood in 1883 because he did not wish to be "put over" the rest of his profession; by 1895 the offer was irresistible. Unhappily, Irving's professional fortunes declined. In 1898 he ceded control to the Lyceum Theatre Company, which had to call in the Receiver in 1902. His professional partnership with Ellen Terry ended in that year. Irving's last years were spent touring, not in the USA as he had done so successfully in his prime, but in the English provinces. Thus it was that in Bradford on 13 October 1905 he uttered what were to be his last words on stage, as Tennyson's Becket: "Into thy Hands, O Lord, into they Hands".

Irving died penniless, but his achievements were not to be judged by such a mercenary measure. After some resistance the Dean of Westminster agreed to his burial in Poet's Corner. Ellen Terry recalled that when during the funeral service "a splendid, tawny sun burst across the solemn misty grey of the Abbey at the moment when the coffin under its superb pall of laurel leaves was carried up the choir, I felt it was an effect which he would have loved".

—Richard Foulkes

J

JACKSON, (Sir) Barry (Vincent). British director, manager, and playwright. Born in Birmingham, 6 September 1879. Educated privately. Founder, Pilgrim Players amateur company, 1907; founder and director of Birmingham Repertory Theatre, 1913; served in Royal Navy, 1914–18; took over the (Royal) Court Theatre, London, 1924, and the Kingsway Theatre, London, 1925; founder and director, Malvern Festival, 1929–37; handed over control of the Birmingham Repertory Theatre to the Barry Jackson Trust, 1935, but resumed active direction of the theatre, 1942; director, Shakespeare Memorial Theatre, Stratford-upon-Avon, 1945–48; director, Royal Opera House, Covent Garden, London, 1949–55. Governing director, Birmingham Repertory Theatre, 1935–61; governing trustee, Birmingham Repertory Trust Company, 1935–61. Recipient: Gold Medal, Birmingham Civic Society, 1922; Freedom of the City of Birmingham, 1955. MA: University of Birmingham, 1923; LL.D: University of St Andrew's, Scotland, 1937; D.Litt: University of Birmingham, 1950; University of Manchester, 1955. Knighted, 1925. Died in Birmingham, 3 April 1961.

Productions

1913	*Twelfth Night* (Shakespeare), Repertory Theatre, Birmingham.
	King John (Shakespeare), Repertory Theatre, Birmingham.
	The Merry Wives of Windsor (Shakespeare), Repertory Theatre, Birmingham.
	The Merchant of Venice (Shakespeare), Repertory Theatre, Birmingham.
	Candida (G. B. Shaw), Repertory Theatre, Birmingham.
	Press Cuttings (G. B. Shaw), Repertory Theatre, Birmingham.
	The Pigeon (Galsworthy), Repertory Theatre, Birmingham.
	The Silver Box (Galsworthy), Repertory Theatre, Birmingham.
	The Importance of Being Earnest (Wilde), Repertory Theatre, Birmingham.
	Tragedy of Nan (Masefield), Repertory Theatre, Birmingham.
	The Cassilis Engagement (Hankin), Repertory Theatre, Birmingham.
	The Constant Lover (Hankin), Repertory Theatre, Birmingham.

	An Enemy of the People (Ibsen), Repertory Theatre, Birmingham.
	The White Cockade (Gregory), Repertory Theatre, Birmingham.
	Countess Cathleen (Yeats), Repertory Theatre, Birmingham.
	The Fantasticks (Rostand), Repertory Theatre, Birmingham.
1919	*Abraham Lincoln* (Drinkwater), Repertory Theatre, Birmingham; Lyric Theatre, Hammersmith, London, 1920.
1922	*The Immortal Hour* (MacLeod and Boughton), Regent Theatre, London.
	Romeo and Juliet (Shakespeare), Regent Theatre, London.
1923	*Cymbeline* (Shakespeare), Repertory Theatre, Birmingham.
1924	*Back to Methuselah* (G. B. Shaw), Court Theatre, London; revived there, 1928.
1924–27	*The Farmer's Wife* (Phillpotts), Court Theatre, London; revived there, 1928.
	Caesar and Cleopatra (G. B. Shaw), Kingsway Theatre, London.
	The New Morality (Chapin), Kingsway Theatre, London.
	Hamlet (Shakespeare), Kingsway Theatre, London.
	The Immortal Hour (MacLeod and Boughton), Kingsway Theatre, London.
	The Marvellous History of St Bernard (Jackson), Kingsway Theatre, London.
	Rosmersholm (Ibsen), Kingsway Theatre, London.
	Yellow Sands (Phillpotts), Haymarket Theatre, London.
1928	*Macbeth* (Shakespeare), Court Theatre, London.
	Harold (Tennyson), Court Theatre, London.
	The Taming of the Shrew (Shakespeare), Court Theatre, London.
	Bird in Hand (Drinkwater), Royalty Theatre, London.
	Six Characters in Search of an Author (Pirandello), Globe Theatre, London.
1929	*The Apple Cart* (G. B. Shaw), Queen's Theatre, London.
1930	*The Barretts of Wimpole Street* (Besier), Queen's Theatre, London.
1931	*A Trip to Scarborough* (Sheridan), St James's Theatre, London.

Caravan (Zuckmayer, adapted by Hamilton), Queen's Theatre, London.

Evensong (Knoblock and Nichols), Queen's Theatre, London.

Too True to be Good (G. B. Shaw), New Theatre, London.

For Services Rendered (Maugham), Globe Theatre, London.

1934   Marriage is No Joke (Bridie), Globe Theatre, London.

A Man's House (Drinkwater), New Theatre, London.

1935   1066 and All That (Arkell), Strand Theatre, London.

1953   Henry VI, parts 1–3 (Shakespeare), Repertory Theatre, Birmingham.

1956   Caesar and Cleopatra (G. B. Shaw), Repertory Theatre, Birmingham.

Publications

Fifinella (play), with Basil Dean, 1911; Ser Taldo's Bride (play), with John Drinkwater, 1911; The Christmas Party (play), 1913; The Theatre and Civic Life, 1922; The Marvellous History of St Bernard (translation), 1925; The Marriage of Figaro (adaptation), 1926; He Who Gets Slapped (play), adapted from the Russian with Gertrude Schurhoff, 1926; Demos, King and Slave (adaptation), 1931; The Swiss Family Robinson (play), with R. H. Baptist, 1938; Backward and Forward (play), with John Ellison, 1939; Doctor's Delight (adapted from Molière), 1944; Too Clever by Half (adapted from Griboyedev), 1944; Jonathan Wild (adapted from Fielding), 1948; The Bears of Bay-Rum (adapted from Scribe), 1948; Love in a Labyrinth (translation from Bertin's Les Prétendants), 1949; The Gay Invalid (adaptation), with Robert Brenon, 1950; Emmy (translation from Edmée), 1952.

*

Bibliography

Books:
George W. Bishop, Barry Jackson and the London Theatre, London, 1933.
J. C. Trewin, The Birmingham Repertory Theatre, 1913–63, London, 1963.

* * *

Sir Barry Jackson was one of the pre-eminent directors and managers of the British theatre during the first half of this century. He received a knighthood for services to the theatre in 1925. His considerable personal wealth enabled him to support the theatre at a time when there was no tradition of subsidy for the arts. George Bernard Shaw joked that he spent so much of his own money (about £100,000) on the Birmingham Repertory Theatre, his own creation, that he would be buried in a pauper's grave. Like his mentors, Harley Granville-Barker and William Poel, Jackson belonged to a tradition of academic theatre practitioners who despised the commercial principles that dominated the theatre business. In many ways he took over where Granville-Barker left off, not only as a director of the

plays of Shakespeare but also as a pioneer of the repertory system. Granville-Barker had promoted the work of writers like Shaw, Ibsen, Galsworthy, and Yeats when he ran the Court Theatre, London, along repertory lines, between 1904 and 1907; Jackson founded the amateur Pilgrim Players in 1907, a company that continued to give support to these writers as well as presenting an annual performance of a play by Shakespeare.

But it was with the creation of the Birmingham Repertory Theatre in 1913 that Jackson was able to develop seriously his plans to present the work of new writers alongside neglected and important classics. He based the designs for his theatre along lines developed by Granville-Barker and Poel, who had convincingly argued and demonstrated the case for performing Shakespeare's plays in a space roughly akin to that of the Elizabethan playhouses. In the early years, especially, Shakespeare and Shaw formed the mainstay of the company's work and between 1914 and 1923 17 of Shakespeare's plays were performed. The Birmingham Repertory Theatre soon established itself as the leading centre for Shakespeare performance outside London's Old Vic, attracting actors like John Gielgud and Ralph Richardson. Amongst his accredited innovations were modern dress productions of Cymbeline in 1923 and Hamlet in 1925, which are considered to be significant landmarks in the history of Shakespeare production (although both plays were actually directed by Henry Ayliff). His tastes were essentially catholic and often remarkably adventurous, as is illustrated by his willingness to risk performances of modern plays by foreign writers like Georg Kaiser, whose expressionistic plays Gas and From Morn to Midnight proved to be too extreme for conservative English tastes of the 1920's. Local indifference constantly threatened to terminate his experiments but his commitment and dedication to a philanthropic ideal of theatre overcame temporary disillusionment and slowly influenced establishment attitudes to the arts, both at a local and a national level.

The history of the Birmingham Repertory Theatre has been described as the story of Jackson versus Birmingham. In a sense Jackson won the battle by finally convincing the civic authorities of the need to support their pioneering local theatre and, in 1935, he handed it over to a public trust. He had always aimed for a national and international reputation for the work of his Birmingham theatre by transferring productions to London and the theatre festival at Malvern, which he established in 1927 and managed for ten years. The Malvern Theatre Festival did much to promote the plays of Shaw, though it was by no means devoted exclusively to his plays. This was another ambitious project that Jackson had to finance out of his own pocket.

At the age of 66, he was chosen as the man to relaunch Stratford's Shakespeare Memorial Theatre after World War II, where the new chairman Fordham Flower had ambitious plans. Jackson's period in office was shortlived, lasting only until 1948 when he was replaced by Anthony Quayle. While in charge at Stratford he tended to avoid stars and demonstrated his skill as a talent spotter by introducing young actors who were then relatively unknown. Under his leadership Peter Brook made his name with productions of Love's Labour's Lost and Romeo and Juliet. (Brook had already been noticed by Jackson, who gave him the opportunity to direct Shaw's Man and Superman at Birmingham, aged only 20). Paul Scofield also emerged from his ranks. But Jackson's slightly aloof manner and academic approach clashed with the aspirations of the new manager, Fordham Flower, as well as the commercially-minded townsfolk; he was not entirely popular with actors either. Fordham Flower was looking for an entrepreneurial figure who would make sweeping changes that, in practice, meant getting rid of some of the old staff and bringing stars to Stratford. Jackson stood out against these commercial pressures but during the two main seasons that he ran the company it made losses. With some bitterness he resigned in 1948 and returned to Birmingham where he continued his work until his death.

—Andy Piasecki

JACKSON, Glenda. British actress. Born in Birkenhead, Cheshire, 9 May 1936. Educated at West Kirby County Grammar School for Girls; trained for the stage at the Royal Academy of Dramatic Art, London. Married Roy Hodges in 1958 (divorced 1976), one son. Stage debut, Worthing, 1957; London debut, 1957; actress, various provincial companies, 1957–63; television debut, 1958; film debut, 1963; joined Royal Shakespeare Company, 1963; New York debut, 1965; director, United British Artists, from 1983; largely retired from stage to concentrate on political career, 1990: Labour Party Member of Parliament for Hampstead and Highgate, since 1992. President, Play Matters, from 1976. Recipient: *Variety* Most Promising Actress Award, 1966; New York Drama Critics Circle Award, 1966; Best Actress Award, Variety Club of Great Britain, 1970, 1971, 1978, 1979; New York Film Critics Award, 1970, 1971, 1981; Oscar for Best Actress, 1971, 1974; National Society of Film Critics' Award, 1971; Society of Film and Television Arts Award, 1972; Étoile de Cristal, French Film Academy, 1972; London *Evening News* Award, 1974; National Board of Review Award, 1981; Montreal Film Festival Award, 1981; Cannes Film Festival Award, 1983. D.Litt: University of Liverpool, 1978. CBE (Commander of the British Empire), 1978.

Roles

1957   Nurse in *Doctor in the House* (Willis, adapted from Gordon), Connaught Theatre, Worthing, Sussex.

Jean Stratton and Jean Tanner in *Separate Tables* (Rattigan), Queen's Theatre, Hornchurch, Essex.

The Maid in *The White Sheep of the Family* (Peach and Hay), Queen's Theatre, Hornchurch, Essex.

Ruby in *All Kinds of Men* (Samuels), Arts Theatre, London.

1962   Alexandra in *The Idiot* (Ruben, adapted from Dostoevsky), Lyric Theatre, Hammersmith, London.

1963   Siddie in *Alfie* (Naughton), Mermaid Theatre, London, and Duchess Theatre, London.

1964   Christine Keeler and Jacqueline Kennedy in "Theatre of Cruelty" season (compilation of Shakespeare, Arden, and others), London Academy of Music and Dramatic Art, London.

Charlotte Corday in *The Marat/Sade* (Weiss), Aldwych Theatre, London; revived there and at the Martin Beck Theatre, New York, 1965.

Bellamira in *The Jew of Malta* (Marlowe), Aldwych Theatre, London.

Princess of France in *Love's Labour's Lost* (Shakespeare), Royal Shakespeare Theatre, Stratford-upon-Avon.

1965   Eva in *Puntila* (Brecht), Aldwych Theatre, London.

Ophelia in *Hamlet* (Shakespeare), Royal Shakespeare Theatre, Stratford-upon-Avon.

Reader in *The Investigation* (Weiss), Aldwych Theatre, London.

1967   Masha in *The Three Sisters* (Chekhov), Royal Court Theatre, London.

Tamara Fanghorn in *Fanghorn* (Pinner), Fortune Theatre, London.

1973   Katherine Winter in *Collaborators* (Mortimer), Duchess Theatre, London.

1974   Solange in *The Maids* (Genet), Greenwich Theatre, London.

1975   Hedda in *Hedda Gabler* (Ibsen), Richmond Theatre, Richmond, Surrey, Australian and US tour, and Aldwych Theatre, London.

1976   Vittoria Corombona in *The White Devil* (Webster), Old Vic Theatre, London.

1977   Stevie Smith in *Stevie* (Whitemore), Vaudeville Theatre, London.

1978   Cleopatra in *Antony and Cleopatra* (Shakespeare), Royal Shakespeare Theatre, Stratford-upon-Avon; Aldwych Theatre, London, 1979.

1980   Rose in *Rose* (Davies), Duke of York's Theatre, London; Cort Theatre, New York, 1981.

1982   Eva Braun in *Summit Conference* (MacDonald), Lyric Theatre, London.

1984   Nina Leeds in *Strange Interlude* (O'Neill), Duke of York's Theatre, London; Nederlander Theatre, New York, 1985.

Phedra in *Phedra* (Racine, translated by MacDonald), Old Vic Theatre, London.

1986   Bernarda Alba in *The House of Bernarda Alba* (Lorca), Lyric Theatre, Hammersmith, London, and Globe Theatre, London.

1988   Lady Macbeth in *Macbeth* (Shakespeare), New York.

1987–90   Martha in *Who's Afraid of Virginia Woolf?* (Albee), Los Angeles.

Galactia in *Scenes from an Execution* (Barker), Almeida Theatre, London.

1990   Mother Courage in *Mother Courage* (Brecht), Citizens' Theatre, Glasgow, and Mermaid Theatre, London.

Other roles included: *Come Back with Diamonds* (Lehmann), Lyric Theatre, Hammersmith, London, 1962; *US* (Cannan, adapted by Kustow and Stott), Aldwych Theatre, London, 1966; *Great and Small* (Strauss), British tour,

Glenda Jackson (1973).

1982, and Vaudeville Theatre, London, 1983; *Across from the Garden of Allah* (Wood), Comedy Theatre, London, 1985.

Films

This Sporting Life, 1963; *The Marat/Sade*, 1967; *Tell Me Lies*, 1968; *Negatives*, 1968; *Women in Love*, 1969; *The Music Lovers*, 1970; *The Boy Friend*, 1971; *Sunday, Bloody Sunday*, 1971; *Mary, Queen of Scots*, 1971; *The Triple Echo*, 1972; *A Touch of Class*, 1972; *Bequest to the Nation/The Nelson Affair*, 1973; *The Tempter*, 1974; *The Maids*, 1974; *The Romantic Englishwoman*, 1975; *Hedda*, 1975; *The Incredible Sarah*, 1976; *Nasty Habits*, 1976; *House Calls*, 1978; *Stevie*, 1978; *The Class of Mrs MacMichael*, 1978; *Lost and Found*, 1979; *Health*, 1979; *Hopscotch*, 1980; *Summit Conference*, 1982; *Return of the Soldier*, 1983; *Great and Small*, 1983; *Sakharov*, 1984; *And Nothing But the Truth*, 1984; *Turtle Diary*, 1985; *Beyond Therapy*, 1987; *Business as Usual*, 1987; *Salome's Last Dance*, 1988; *The Rainbow*, 1989; *The Secret Life of Arnold Bax*, 1992.

Television

A Voice in Vision, 1958; *Dr Everyman's Hour*, 1962; *Let's Murder Vivaldi*, 1968; *Elizabeth R* (series), 1971; *The Patricia Neal Story*, 1981; *Giro City*, 1982.

*

Bibliography

Books:
David Nathan, *Glenda Jackson*, Tunbridge Wells, 1984.
Ian Woodward, *Glenda Jackson: A Study in Fire and Ice*, Dunton Green, 1985.

* * *

Glenda Jackson, one of the most accomplished actresses of the late 20th century, has achieved international recognition in theatre, films, and on television. This is despite being advised when she left the Royal Academy of Dramatic Art not to expect to work much before she was 40 because she was essentially a character actress — the drama school's way of telling her that she did not possess the good looks usually assumed to be necessary for a career as a star performer. She was also rejected early in her career by the Royal Shakespeare Company. The then director, Peter Hall, wrote in his notes: "Interesting but a bit rich for our blood". This was a prophetic observation. When, some years later, she played Ophelia in a production directed by Hall, one reviewer wrote that she was "the first Ophelia I have seen who should play Hamlet ... she has all the qualities of a great prince". When speaking of that production, Jackson herself said: "I don't regard Peter Hall highly as a director ... I wasn't looking for inspiration or guidance from him".

With her strong and interesting, if unconventional, looks and with seemingly little guidance, Glenda Jackson quickly developed a highly successful career. Her work has covered an enormous range, from her Oscar-winning "sexy" role in *A Touch of Class* and her highly acclaimed witty Cleopatra to her more recent powerful portrayal of Mother Courage. In many of her roles she has displayed great skill in the handling of the text, a strength she attributes to a childhood spent listening to the radio: "I grew up with radio as a strong influence. During its heyday, radio brought us an amazing cross-section of plays ... it's the most perfect medium, the purest ... because the imagination is liberated".

Jackson resists the notion that there is anything mysterious about performing. For her it is practical, no-nonsense, concentrated hard work in rehearsal that allows the acting to look "easy" in performance. She is very scathing about actors who show the audience how hard they are working in order to earn their sympathy and applause. She also criticises those who speak lightly of the art of acting and of "the prevailing attitude in this country that it doesn't really matter ... when you're doing it there's nothing else". She has earned a reputation in the profession for toughness and a number of colleagues have called her a "workaholic". Michael Billington intends praise in describing her as being "completely free from that cursed English vice of genteel and ladylike restraint".

Except when absolutely required, such as when she played Queen Elizabeth I from the age of 16 to 69, Jackson makes little effort to change herself physically for a role. Instead she tends to draw the character towards her, knowing clearly what of herself she should deploy to portray the part. Her hallmarks are her catlike eyes, high cheekbones, a deep, throaty voice that can rasp and purr by turns (aided perhaps by her heavy cigarette consumption) and a focussed energy and magnetism. As the director Philip Prowse says: "She is completely watchable, she is 100 per cent there. It's a marvellous face that catches light beautifully. She has this terrific charisma".

In many ways Jackson could be described as quite a technical performer. She claims "acting isn't being" and yet when beginning to work on a part she looks at the character for "a fact which releases the imagination", seeking the "simplicity, immediacy, and totality of a child". In true Stanislavskian style, Jackson searches for the subtext of a role and talks of her need for that "fourth wall" that separates her from the audience. Equally, she stresses her enjoyment of working closely with other actors, of the ensemble: "I have never been interested in 'great' parts ... the one diamond in the garbage". But that is perhaps easy to say when you have already played Elizabeth I, Hedda Gabler, Sarah Bernhardt, and Phedra.

Jackson moved to a different kind of stage in 1992 when she was elected to parliament. She had been a member of the Labour Party since she was 16 and made her political interests clear in the 1960's when she was a key figure in the British anti-Vietnam protests. This culminated in her involvement in *US*, a piece about Vietnam that was directed by Peter Brook. As early as 1980 she foresaw an end to her acting career because, she claimed, there are so few good parts for actresses and she began then to consider a political career instead.

Her political interests did not, however, mean that Jackson only sought to appear in politically committed plays. For her, politics in the theatre has always involved broader issues than polemics. Nonetheless, her appearance as Mother Courage in 1990 seemed the perfect vehicle for her, bringing together her skills as a performer and her political engagement. Jackson herself, though, claimed that for her the play's ideology was less important than its greatness as drama. It was political for her in that it was a "team play ... the total being greater than the sum of the parts is very much for me a political idea". All reviewers of the production agreed this was a role she was born to play. Inevitably, she approached it with complete seriousness. The spark for her imaginative way into the character was Ethel Merman — her "up-front bravado, energy, brooking no argument, you can take it or leave it". Thereafter, it was careful, detailed concentrated work to create a performance that so clearly portrayed "the truculent individualism of an insubordinate spirit ... a feisty, cynical philosopher".

Experience of playing such insubordinate spirits will doubtless be useful to Jackson in her new-found role in the political arena.

—Margaret Eddershaw

JACOBI, (Sir) Derek (George). British actor. Born in London, 22 October 1938. Educated at Leyton County High School; St John's College, Cambridge University. Amateur actor, National Youth Theatre and at Cambridge; professional stage debut, Birmingham, 1961; London debut, National Theatre Company at the Old Vic Theatre, 1963; film debut, 1965; toured with Prospect Theatre company, 1972–78; artistic associate, Old Vic Company, 1976–81; Broadway debut, 1980; actor, Royal Shakespeare Company, from 1982; director, Renaissance Theatre Company, 1988. Fellow, St John's College, Cambridge, 1987. Member: National Youth Theatre, London (vice-president, from 1982). Recipient: Variety Club Award, 1976; Television Personality of the Year Award, 1976; Royal Television Society Award, 1976; Press Guild Award, 1976; British Academy of Film and Television Arts Award, 1977; Society of West End Theatre Award, 1983; *Plays and Players* Award, 1983; *Evening Standard* Award, 1983, 1987; Tony Award, 1985. CBE (Commander of the British Empire), 1985. Knighted, 1994.

Productions

As actor:

1955	Hamlet in *Hamlet* (Shakespeare), Edinburgh Festival; Old Vic Theatre, London, 1977 and 1979.
1959	Edward II in *Edward II* (Marlowe), Marlowe Society, Cambridge.
1960	Role in *Henry VIII* (Shakespeare), Repertory Theatre, Birmingham.
1961	Stanley Honeybone in *One Way Pendulum* (Simpson), Repertory Theatre, Birmingham.
1963	Brother Martin in *Saint Joan* (G. B. Shaw), Chichester Festival Theatre.
	PC Liversedge in *The Workhouse Donkey* (Arden), Chichester Festival Theatre.
	Laertes in *Hamlet* (Shakespeare), Old Vic Theatre, London.
1964	Fellipillo in *The Royal Hunt of the Sun* (P. Shaffer), Old Vic Theatre, London.
	Cassio in *Othello* (Shakespeare), Old Vic Theatre, London.
	Simon Bliss in *Hay Fever* (Coward), Old Vic Theatre, London.
1965	Don John in *Much Ado About Nothing* (Shakespeare), Chichester Festival Theatre.
1966	Brindsley Miller in *Black Comedy* (P. Shaffer), Chichester Festival Theatre, Old Vic Theatre, London, and Queen's Theatre, London.
1967	Tusenbach in *The Three Sisters* (Chekhov), Old Vic Theatre, London.
	Touchstone in *As You Like It* (Shakespeare), Old Vic Theatre, London.
1968	King of Navarre in *Love's Labour's Lost* (Shakespeare), Old Vic Theatre, London.
1969	Edward Hotel in *Macrune's Guevara* (Spurling), Old Vic Theatre, London.
	Adam in *Back to Methuselah* (G. B. Shaw), Old Vic Theatre, London.
1970	Myshkin in *The Idiot* (Dostoevsky), Old Vic Theatre, London.
	Lodovico in *The White Devil* (Webster), Old Vic Theatre, London.
1971	Sir Charles Mountford in *A Woman Killed with Kindness* (Heywood), Old Vic Theatre, London.

Orestes in *Electra* (Sophocles), Greenwich Theatre, London.

1972   Oedipus in *Oedipus Rex* (Sophocles), Repertory Theatre, Birmingham.

Mr Puff in *The Critic* (Sheridan), Repertory Theatre, Birmingham.

Duke of Buckingham in *Richard III* (Shakespeare), Repertory Theatre, Birmingham.

Ivanov in *Ivanov* (Chekhov), Prospect Theatre, London; Old Vic Theatre, 1978.

1973   Sir Andrew Aguecheek in *Twelfth Night* (Shakespeare), Round House Theatre, London, and European and Middle Eastern tour.

Pericles in *Pericles* (Shakespeare), Round House Theatre, London, and European and Middle Eastern tour; Her Majesty's Theatre, London, 1974.

1974   Ratikin in *A Month in the Country* (Turgenev), Chichester Festival Theatre; Albery Theatre, London, 1975.

1975   Will Mossop in *Hobson's Choice* (Brighouse), Yvonne Arnaud Theatre, Guildford.

Cecil Vyse in *A Room with a View* (adapted from Forster), Albery Theatre, London.

Roles in *The Hollow Crown* (Shakespeare compilation), tour.

Roles in *Pleasure and Repentance* (Hands), tour.

1977   Octavius Caesar in *Antony and Cleopatra* (Shakespeare), Old Vic Theatre, London.

1978   Thomas Mendip in *The Lady's Not for Burning* (Fry), Old Vic Theatre, London.

1980   Semyon Semyonovich Podsekalnikov in *The Suicide* (Erdman), American National Theatre, New York, and Academy Theatre, New York.

1982   Benedick in *Much Ado About Nothing* (Shakespeare), Aldwych Theatre, London; Gershwin Theatre, New York, 1984.

Peer Gynt in *Peer Gynt* (Ibsen), Aldwych Theatre, London.

1983   Prospero in *The Tempest* (Shakespeare), Aldwych Theatre, London.

Cyrano in *Cyrano de Bergerac* (Rostand), Aldwych Theatre, London; Gershwin Theatre, New York, 1984.

1986   Alan Turing in *Breaking the Code* (Whitemore), Haymarket Theatre, London, and Eisenhower Theatre, Kennedy Centre for the Performing Arts, Washington, D.C.; Neil Simon Theatre, New York, 1987.

1988   Richard II in *Richard II* (Shakespeare), Phoenix Theatre, London.

1989   Richard III in *Richard III* (Shakespeare), Phoenix Theatre, London.

1990   Edmund Kean in *Kean; or, Disorder and Genius* (Sartre), Old Vic Theatre, London.

1991   Becket in *Becket* (Anouilh), Haymarket Theatre, London.

1992   Byron in *Mad, Bad and Dangerous to Know* (McCulloch), Ambassadors Theatre, London.

1993   Macbeth in *Macbeth* (Shakespeare), Barbican Theatre, London; Royal Shakespeare Theatre, Stratford-upon-Avon, 1994.

Derek Jacobi (1979).

1995   Hadrian in *Hadrian VII* (Luke), Festival Theatre, Chichester.

Other roles included: *The Grand Tour* (Rice), Goldsmith's Hall, London, 1973, and world tour; Old Vic Theatre, London, 1978; *The Lunatic, The Lover, and the Poet*, Old Vic Theatre, London, 1978.

As director:
1988   *Hamlet* (Shakespeare), Phoenix Theatre, London.

Films

Othello, 1965; *Interlude*, 1968; *Blue Blood*, 1973; *The Day of the Jackal*, 1973; *The Odessa File*, 1974; *The Three Sisters*, 1974; *The Medusa Touch*, 1978; *The Human Factor*, 1979; *Mannen som gick upp i rok*, 1980; *Charlotte*, 1980; *The Secret of NIMH*, 1982; *Enigma*, 1983; *Little Dorrit*, 1987; *Henry V*, 1989; *The Fool*, 1990; *Dead Again*, 1991.

Television

Man of Straw, 1971–72; *Budgie*, 1972; *Markheim*, 1973; *Affairs of the Heart*, 1973; *The Strauss Family* (series), 1973; *I, Claudius* (series), 1976; *The Pallisers* (series), 1977; *Paths of the Future*, 1978; *Skin*, 1979; *Richard II*, 1979; *Philby, Burgess, and MacLean*, 1979; *Hamlet*,

1980; *A Stranger in Town*, 1982; *Inside the Third Reich* (series), 1982; *The Hunchback of Notre Dame*, 1982; *Statue of Liberty*, 1985; *Cathedral*, 1986; *Mr Pye*, 1986; *The Secret Garden*, 1987; *Graham Greene's The Tenth Man*, 1988; *Pyramid*, 1988; *The Congress*, 1989.

* * *

In one of his most frequently quoted articles, the critic Kenneth Tynan argued that, in Britain, great actors tend to come in pairs, one either side of a division that can be defined poet/peasant, feminine/masculine, or Hamlet/Macbeth. So, for instance, John Philip Kemble and Edmund Kean, John Gielgud and Laurence Olivier, and, until the latter went to Hollywood, Paul Scofield and Richard Burton. Since the immense growth in the subsidised theatre in the 1960's and 1970's, it has become harder to name individual actors as "the greatest", but the basic division remains sound. Apart from Ian McKellen (whose strongest attribute is neither nobility nor strength but rather an intense, amoral intelligence) most British actors can be placed in one or the other category. On the "peasant" side are performers like Michael Gambon and Brian Cox, while the major "poet" actors have been Alan Howard and, more recently, Derek Jacobi.

Jacobi worked for eight years as a member of the National Theatre Company at the Old Vic, a time which he refers to as "like being at the most wonderful drama school" because of the amount he learnt from other actors. The most important single influence was Olivier ("he was very generous of himself, of his time and his talent"), with whom Jacobi shares a mercurial quality, the ability to switch emotional register with astonishing speed. He also cites as important influences Peter O'Toole, Maggie Smith (from whom he learnt about playing comedy and the art of thinking quickly onstage) and Michael Redgrave, whom he, at the age of 24, understudied in *Uncle Vanya*: "What one learnt from that was what looked so utterly spontaneous was utterly calculated, and to watch that technique in action, so that the handkerchief popped into the top pocket, on the same *breath* almost, and it looked as if he'd just that moment thought of putting it back in, as if he'd never done it before; that's great acting, for me".

After leaving the National, Jacobi joined the Prospect Touring Company, run by Toby Robertson, and stayed with them, on and off, for five years, culminating in his triumphant Hamlet. By this time, his strengths and weaknesses as a performer seemed very clear: his angelic good looks and beautiful voice suited him to parts requiring charm, while his air of innocence made him a natural player of victims, from his first leading role (Brindsley in Peter Shaffer's *Black Comedy*) through to Hamlet, by way of the part that made him a household name, the title role in the BBC's *I, Claudius*.

Some kind of turning-point came in 1982–83, when he took up Terry Hands' invitation to play a season with the Royal Shakespeare Company. Two of his four performances were clearly from within his existing range; his Benedick in Hands' *Much Ado About Nothing* was charismatic and lively, while in the title role of Ron Daniels' chamber production of *Peer Gynt* he showed his skill at visibly conveying thought processes. The first surprise came in Daniels' *The Tempest*, where his Prospero, younger and more vengeful that the part is usually played,

showed a degree of strength that had not been seen in Jacobi before — "deeper tones in his voice, more iron in his soul", as Robert Cushman noted in *The Observer*.

The real triumph came in *Cyrano de Bergerac*, one of the most successful RSC productions of the 1980's. As Cyrano, Jacobi gave his finest performances so far, an apparently effortless reconciliation of contrary impulses — humour, pathos, heroism, irony, dedication, impetuousness — with a vocal and emotional range that exceeded all expectations, including Jacobi's own: "Something like a Cyrano was unknown territory to me, because I didn't think I could acquire the anger that Cyrano needed, that wasn't one of the weapons in my armoury. Terry Hands, who directed it, was wonderful; he said yes ... It opened up a whole new area for me. *Kean*, for instance; if I hadn't played Cyrano, I couldn't have attempted Kean".

Since *Cyrano*, Jacobi has worked as a freelance actor, outside a company structure. He gave a skilful low-key performance as the homosexual mathematical genius Alan Turing in Hugh Whitemore's *Breaking the Code*, one of the very few times he has worked with a living author. *Richard II* and *Richard III*, both directed by Clifford Williams, were self-consciously old-fashioned star vehicles (other members of the cast could be observed taking a step backwards when Jacobi was speaking), with little to recommend them other than his own performances, cold and aristocratic in the first play and, according to Michael Billington, "halfway between Olivier and Frankie Howerd" in the second. During this period he also made a number of memorable appearances on film, playing central roles in Christine Edzard's *Little Dorrit* and *The Fool* and a superb cameo as the Chorus in Kenneth Branagh's *Henry V*.

Jacobi has described himself as essentially a company actor ("I'm not very good at knowing what to do. I need other people to suggest. I'm not a leader, I'm a follower"). Even in a commercial ad hoc company, like that for *Kean*, he is impressive; given skilled direction and a long-term ensemble, he is one of the half-dozen best classical actors in Britain.

—David Cottis

JEFFERSON III, Joseph. US actor-manager. Born in Philadelphia, 20 February 1829. Educated at local schools in New York, until 1838. Married 1) Margaret Clements Lockyer in 1850 (died 1861), four children; 2) Sarah Isabel Warren in 1867, several children. Carried on stage as a baby; toured with family as a child, acting with Junius Brutus Booth and others; New York debut, Franklin Theatre, 1837; visited Mexico, 1846; appeared at Chanfrau's New National Theatre, New York, 1849; actor, Mitchell's Olympic Theatre, New York, 1850; first experience as a theatre manager, Baltimore Museum, 1853; visited Europe, 1856; actor, Laura Keene's company, New York, 1856–59, and Winter Garden Theatre, New York, from 1859; San Francisco debut, 1861; toured Australia, 1861–65; enjoyed greatest success as Rip Van Winkle, 1865; visited England, 1865, 1873, and 1875–77; operated on for glaucoma, 1872; lecturer on acting, from 1892; last appearance, as Caleb Plummer, 7 May 1904. Member: Players' Club (president from 1893). LL.D: Yale University, 1892. Died in Palm Beach, Florida, 23 April 1905.

Roles

1842	Sampson in *The Iron Chest* (Colman the Younger), Mobile, Alabama.
	Glavis in *The Lady of Lyons* (Bulwer-Lytton), US tour.
1846	Chorus in *Antigone* (Sophocles), Arch Street Theatre, Philadelphia.
1849	Hans in *Somebody Else* (Planché), New National Theatre, New York.
1850	Marrall in *A New Way to Pay Old Debts* (Massinger), Chatham Theatre, New York.
1850–53	Dr Pangloss in *The Heir-at-Law* (Colman the Younger), Chestnut Street Theatre, Philadelphia; revived notably, Laura Keene's Theatre, New York, 1857.
1853	Moses and Crabtree in *The School for Scandal* (Sheridan), Baltimore Museum, Baltimore.
1858	Asa Trenchard in *Our American Cousin* (Taylor), Laura Keene's Theatre, New York, and US tour.
	Bottom in *A Midsummer Night's Dream* (Shakespeare), Laura Keene's Theatre, New York.
1859	Caleb Plummer in *Dot; or, The Cricket on the Hearth* (Boucicault), Winter Garden Theatre, New York.
	Salem Scudder in *The Octoroon; or, Life in Louisiana* (Boucicault), Winter Garden Theatre, New York.
	Newman Noggs in *Nicholas Nickleby* (adapted from Dickens), Winter Garden Theatre, New York.
	Rip Van Winkle in *Rip Van Winkle* (adapted from Irving), Carusi's Hall, Washington D.C.; revived notably, in Boucicault version, Adelphi Theatre, London, 1865, US tour, 1866, at Booth's Theatre, New York, 1870–71 and 1873, and at the Princess's Theatre, London, 1875–76.
1861	Bob Brierly in *The Ticket-of-Leave Man* (Taylor), Australian tour.
1880	Bob Acres in *The Rivals* (Sheridan, adapted by Jefferson), Arch Street Theatre, Philadelphia.
1888	First Gravedigger in *Hamlet* (Shakespeare), Metropolitan Opera House, New York.
1904	Mr Golightly in *Lend Me Five Shillings* (Morton), Paterson, New Jersey.

Other roles included: King Arthur in *Tom Thumb* (Fielding); Baptisto in *The Hunter of the Alps* (Dimond); Sir Robert Bramble and Dr Ollapod in *The Poor Gentleman* (Colman the Younger); John Bull in *John Bull* (Colman the Younger); Mr Coddle in *Married Life* (Buckstone); Dogberry in *Much Ado About Nothing* (Shakespeare); Admiral Franklin in *Sweethearts and Wives* (Kenney); Gratiano in *The Merchant of Venice* (Shakespeare); Memno in *Abaellino* (Dunlap); Naudin in *Tom Noddy's Secret* (Bayly); Duke of Norfolk in *Richard III* (Shakespeare, adapted by Cibber); Polonius in *Hamlet* (Shakespeare); Raff in *The Conquering Game* (Bernard); Reef in *Ambrose Gwinett* (Jerrold); Sentinel in *Pizarro* (Sheridan); Sentinel in *The Wandering Boys* (Noah); Spinosa in *Venice Preserved* (Otway); Stanon in *The Blind Boy* (Dunlap); Tapwell in *A New Way to Pay Old*

Joseph Jefferson

Debts (Massinger); Baron Vanderbushel in *The Sentinel* (Boucicault); Monsieur de Villecour in *Promotion; or, The General's Hat* (Planché); First Witch in *Macbeth* (Shakespeare); and roles in *The Parish Clerk* (Boucicault); *Rolla* (Kotzebue); and *The Spectre Bridegroom* (Moncrieff).

Publications

The Autobiography of Joseph Jefferson, New York and London, 1890.

*

Bibliography

Books:
William Winter, *The Jeffersons*, Boston, 1881; revised as *Life and Art of Joseph Jefferson together with some Account of his Ancestry and of the Jefferson Family of Actors*, American Actor Series, New York and London, 1894.
Francis Wilson, *Joseph Jefferson*, London, 1906.
Eugénie Paul Jefferson, *Intimate Recollections of Joseph Jefferson*, New York, 1909.
Gladys Malvern, *Good Troupers All: The Story of Joseph Jefferson*, Philadelphia, 1945.

Articles:
L. Clarke Davis, "Jefferson and Rip Van Winkle", *Lippincott's*, 24, July 1879.

Laurence Hutton, "Recollections of Joseph Jefferson", *Harper's Weekly*, 49, May 1905.

Henri Lauriston, "America's Greatest Actor", *New England Magazine*, 32, June 1905.

Morris Bacheller, "The Dean of the American Stage", *Muncey's*, 12, 1895.

James Huneker, "Joseph Jefferson", *World's Work*, June 1905.

Ernest Bradlee Watson, "Joseph Jefferson", *Theatre Arts*, 13, June 1929.

Rosamond Gilder, "Joseph Jefferson", *Theatre Arts*, 27, June 1943.

* * *

As one of the most endearing personalities of the US stage in the 19th century, Joseph Jefferson III redefined the nature of the theatrical star and built a worldwide reputation on his quaint and comical characterizations of American life. Along with Edwin Forrest, Edwin Booth, and Lawrence Barrett, Jefferson ranked as one of the most popular and successful actors of the US stage. Although he displayed a versatility consistent with the best tragedians, his fame was founded on the sentimentally comic portrayal of Rip Van Winkle, a part he performed throughout his professional life.

Jefferson was descended from a long line of theatrical professionals. His grandfather, Joseph Jefferson I, a minor performer on the London stage, emigrated to the USA in 1795 and became a leading actor at the John Street Theatre in New York and the Chestnut Street Theatre in Philadelphia. Jefferson's father, Joseph Jefferson II, was an actor, theatrical manager, and scene painter. With such a pedigree, Jefferson was inherently well prepared to enter the family trade. He made his theatrical debut at the age of four in a song and dance routine alongside the famed "Jim Crow" performer T. D. Rice. Jefferson spent the next 20 years touring with his family and developing into a top-rate performer. After his father's premature death in 1842, Jefferson continued to tour with his mother, Cornelia Thomas Jefferson, gaining a popular following as a supporting actor to leading stars, including Frank Chanfrau and Edwin Forrest. Beginning in the early 1850's, Jefferson expanded his talents into theatrical management. His first effort was a largely unsuccessful venture, in partnership with John Ellsler, to establish a southern circuit between North Carolina and Georgia. Undaunted by this initial experience, Jefferson secured a position as stage manager at Henry C. Jarrett's Baltimore Museum. It was there in 1853 that he first performed with his mentor, the great comic actor James E. Murdoch, in a production of *The School for Scandal*. Within a year, Jefferson was managing for John T. Ford in Richmond, Virginia, and performing with Agnes Robertson and her husband, Dion Boucicault.

By 1856, Jefferson's professional reputation was well established, though he still sought a clear identity as a starring performer. After a brief trip to England and France, he returned to New York as the leading comic actor in Laura Keens's company. His principle parts included Dr Pangloss in Colman's *The Heir at Law* and Asa Trenchard in *Our American Cousin*. Three years later, he was hired by William Stuart to become part of the new company at the Winter Garden under the management of Dion Boucicault. Here Jefferson first developed the combination of comedy, sentimentality, and pathos that would distinguish his work in such roles as Caleb Plummer, Salem Scudder, and Newman Noggs. He also began work on his initial characterization of Rip Van Winkle, first performed in 1859 at Carusi's Hall in Washington, D.C. The production did not live up to Jefferson's expectations, though he remained convinced that this was his ideal part. The play was in need of substantial rewriting, but revisions were delayed by the death of Jefferson's first wife in March 1861 and his subsequent departure for a shortlived booking in San Francisco and a four-year tour of Australia. Upon Jefferson's arrival in London in 1865, he persuaded Boucicault to undertake the rewriting. The new version, premiered at the Adelphi, was an instant success. By 1866, Jefferson was back in the USA performing Rip in New York City, Chicago, and Detroit. Within a year, he was on a nationwide tour, capitalizing on the success of his new-found play and character.

Jefferson became identified with a role as no other performer had before him and his public never tired of the show. He played Rip continuously for the next 14 years, rarely performing anything else until his adaptation of *The Rivals* in 1880 added Bob Acres to his collection of sympathetic rural wits. As a testament to the unparalleled stature Jefferson had achieved in the theatre, the Players' Club in 1893 awarded them their most singular honour: election as their president in succession to Edwin Booth.

Near the end of his career, Jefferson spent much of his time lecturing and writing. In 1890, he produced his widely-acclaimed autobiography. His last performance was on 7 May 1904, as Caleb Plummer.

Jefferson's greatest contribution to the US stage was his popular portrayal of uniquely American characters. He made the rude country bumpkin into a lovable, sympathetic, and heroic figure. He also helped to pioneer the early combination companies through his many successful tours across the country and became one of the first stars to be identified with a single character, establishing a mode of performance and star appeal still evident today. Above all, Jefferson embodied the spirit of the US theatre in the 19th century and presaged the image of the Broadway and Hollywood stars of the 20th century.

—Peter A. Davis

————————

JODELET. French actor. Born Julien Bedeau, c.1590; brother of comedy actor L'Espy. Began career with touring company in the French provinces, c.1603; acted in Paris in 1625 and 1629; actor, under Montdory at the Théâtre du Marais, Paris, 1634; at the order of Louis XIII, accompanied other members of the troupe to the Théâtre de l'Hôtel de Bourgogne, Paris, 1634; returned to the Marais, 1641–59; immensely popular in comedy, often appearing in parts specially written for him and under his own stagename; shortly before his death, joined Molière's company at the Théâtre du Petit-Bourbon, Paris, 1659. Died in Paris, 26 March 1660.

Principal roles

1643	Cliton in *Le Menteur* (P. Corneille), Théâtre du Marais, Paris.
1644	Cliton in *La Suite du Menteur* (P. Corneille), Théâtre du Marais, Paris.
1645	Jodelet in *Jodelet, ou le Maître-valet* (Scarron), Théâtre du Marais, Paris.
1645–59	Jodelet in *Jodelet souffleté* (Scarron), Théâtre du Marais, Paris.
	Jodelet in *Jodelet astrologue* (D'Ouville), Théâtre du Marais, Paris.
	Jodelet in *Le Déniaisé* (Tessonerie), Théâtre du Marais, Paris.
1647	Dom Japhet in *Dom Japhet d'Arménie* (Scarron), Théâtre du Marais, Paris.
1655	Jodelet in *Comédie sans comédie* (Quinault), Théâtre du Marais, Paris.
	Jodelet in *Jodelet prince* (T. Corneille), Théâtre du Marais, Paris.
1656	Arcas in *Timocrate* (T. Corneille), Théâtre du Marais, Paris.
1659	Jodelet in *La Feinte Mort de Jodelet* (Brécourt), Théâtre du Marais, Paris.
	Vicomte de Jodelet in *Les Précieuses ridicules* (Molière), Théâtre du Petit-Bourbon, Paris.

Other roles included: *Dom Bertrand de Cigarral* (T. Corneille), Théâtre de l'Hôtel de Bourgogne, Paris, 1651; *L'Amour à la mode* (T. Corneille), Théâtre du Marais, Paris, 1651; *Le Geôlier de soi-même* (T. Corneille), Théâtre du Marais, Paris, 1655; *Campagnard* (Tessonerie), Théâtre du Marais, Paris, 1655.

*

Bibliography

Books:

Georges Mongrédien, *Les Grands Comédiens du XVIIe siècle*, Paris, 1927.

Georges Mongrédien, *La Vie quotidienne des comédiens au temps de Molière*, Paris, 1966.

Geoffrey Brereton, *French Comic Drama from the Sixteenth to the Eighteenth Century*, London, 1977.

* * *

Jodelet springs instantly to mind in his role in Molière's farce, *Les Précieuses ridicules*, where, as Viscomte Jodelet, he is the second and coarser of the false noblemen who deceive and make fools of two silly young women. Surprisingly, perhaps, he was already 60 by this time, and had only months to live. Jodelet's career had begun in the provinces, 15 or 20 years before he came to Paris in the 1630's. As an actor of farce, drawing comparison with respected older practitioners such as Turlupin and Gros-Guillaume, he built a formidable reputation for humorous acting that ranged from the visual and crude to the linguistic and subtle, and gradually his name became a guarantee that the public could expect an uproarious experience.

From about 1645, he appeared in numerous plays written as vehicles for his talent which, the better to attract an audience, also featured his name in the title. These included *Jodelet ou le Maître-valet*, *Jodelet prince*, *Jodelet astrologue*, *La Feinte Mort de Jodelet*, *Jodelet souffleté*, later revised as *Jodelet duelliste*, of which perhaps only the first two, by Scarron and Thomas Corneille respectively, are recalled today, let alone performed. Jodelet does not necessarily have the largest part in these plays. They were all written during his second period at the Théâtre du Marais, an 18-year spree beginning in 1641 which followed seven years at the rival Hôtel de Bourgogne. So keenly did the public still regret his departure from the more fashionable Hôtel, indeed, that years afterwards the waspish commentator Tallemant des Réaux could say, without much exaggeration, that farce was dead there, and that it survived only at the Marais and only because of Jodelet.

Jodelet was one of the last of the farinés, so-called because they acted with their faces whitened with flour: Molière makes a joke about it, of course. In Jodelet's case, the flour may also have served to cover the traces of smallpox, but it was as much of a trademark as his black beard and long moustache and his broad mouth, made up to extend like a scar from ear to ear. His face was sometimes called his *visage de dogue* (literally, "mastiff's face"), and his voice had a nasal quality, which he seems deliberately to have exaggerated. He was tall and athletic. Contemporary writers called him "the nasal-voiced Jodelet", "badger-nose", and "the flour-faced fool", and praised the quickness of his acerbic wit. He often affected the character of a greedy, bragging bully, who becomes a coward when put to the test. Such vulgarity, inviting dismay and dislike, contrasted with and heightened the absurdity of his most common stock role as a trickster who deceives a faithless or naive young girl. In other roles, he lusts after female servants, who are wise if they mistrust him.

It is difficult to disentangle the actor Jodelet (whose real name, Julien Bedeau, has been virtually forgotten) from the parts he created under his own stage name. He appeared as Jodelet in many plays which did not name him in the title, including *Les Précieuses ridicules* and Quinault's *Comédie sans comédie*. Nevertheless, Jodelet as actor played other comic roles with great success, such as Cliton in Pierre Corneille's *Le Menteur*. When the company performed tragedies, he took small functional parts such as the confidant Arcas in Thomas Corneille's immensely popular *Timocrate*.

Why did this much loved performer move from the Marais in 1659 to join Molière's fledgling company only months after its arrival in the capital? It is tempting to speculate that the older actor recognized the talent and promise of the younger, but of course we do not know. More likely, Molière went out of his way to secure his services, for Jodelet had only to appear, and the audience would erupt with anticipatory delight, a reaction he is said to have been adept at prolonging by appearing mystified or disconcerted or disgruntled by it, as the fancy took him. Moreover, his stock-in-trade of broad humour and ad libs could enliven matters if ever the audience's high spirits were to flag. Audiences knew what to expect, and yet did not know the extremes to which he might go with his ribaldry. Thus did he seek in *Les Précieuses ridicules*, with his inappropriate nasal tones and hideous appearance, to convince his disbelieving audience and the two silly women of his credentials as a sophisticated nobleman. We presume that much of his humour was extemporized, and that Molière did not write it down, though he left clues in the text. Jodelet, gauging the reaction of his audience, played accordingly, varying his exhibition from performance to performance and, incidentally, setting fellow-actors the problem of playing back to his unscripted gestures and banter. Only those who were consummate actors in their own right, such as Molière himself, could hope to hold the stage in his presence. He must also have been an excellent foil for Mascarille: Molière's marquis takes himself seriously and is stylish and articulate, almost mastering the language and behaviour of his betters, whereas Jodelet, out of his depth and striving to keep up, apes and comically exaggerates his companion's behaviour, threatening to wreck both impostors' chances of being believed and, of course, emphasizing the gullibility of the victims who accept them.

In ending his career as the venerable old stager in a company led by the new comic genius, he also passed on something of his unique character. Molière's Mascarille, a comic type who had emerged some years before, owed nothing to Jodelet, but the older actor's grotesque farce, stripped of its grosser aspects, became fused with the empty self-assurance of Mascarille in Molière's next and finest comic valet, the ugly, self-important, cowardly, self-tormenting rogue Sganarelle, who burst on to the Paris stage only weeks after Julien Bedeau's death.

—William Brooks

JONES, Inigo. English architect and theatrical designer. Born in London, 15 July 1573, son of a clothworker. Studied architecture and theatre design in Italy under patronage of William Herbert, third Earl of Pembroke, 1598–1601; possibly also worked as apprentice to a joiner in Islington. Invited to Denmark by Christian IV, 1604; designed sets, costumes, and machinery for court masques in Oxford and London, 1605–40, often in collaboration with Ben Jonson: introduced use of painted scenery within proscenium arch to English theatre and devised scene changes using revolving flats; designed numerous major public buildings, including the Banqueting House, Whitehall, and travelled widely in royal service; appointed Surveyor to Henry, Prince of Wales, 1611–12; revisited Italy, 1613–15; appointed Surveyor to the King's Works, 1615; studied history of Stonehenge; designed hearses for funerals of Queen Anne, 1619, and of James I, 1625; oversaw first stages in renovation of St Paul's Cathedral, London, from 1630; designed Covent Garden piazza, 1631; partnership with Jonson ended in acrimony, 1631; taken prisoner by Cromwell at siege of Basing House, 1645; fined and property sequestrated by Parliament, later restored. Justice of the Peace for Westminster, 1630. Died in London, 21 June 1652.

Productions

1605	*The Masque of Blackness* (Jonson), Whitehall Palace, London.
	Alba (anon.), Christ Church hall, Oxford.
	Ajax Flagellifer (anon.), Christ Church hall, Oxford.
	Vertumnus (anon.), Christ Church hall, Oxford.
	Arcadia Reformed (anon.), Christ Church hall, Oxford.
1606	*Hymenaei* (Jonson), Whitehall Palace, London.
1607	*The Lord Hay's Masque* (anon.).
	The Penates (anon.), Theobalds Palace, Hertfordshire.
1608	*The Hue and Cry after Cupid* (Jonson), Whitehall Palace, London.
1609	*The Masque of Queens* (Jonson), Whitehall Palace, London.
1610	*The Speeches at Prince Henry's Barriers* (Jonson), Whitehall Palace, London.
	Accession Day Tilt: Elephant Pageant (anon.).
	Tethys' Festival; or, The Queen's Wake (Daniel) Whitehall Palace, London.
	Creation Tilt (anon.).
1611	*Oberon, The Faery Prince* (Jonson), Whitehall Palace, London.
	Love Freed from Ignorance and Folly (Jonson), Whitehall Palace, London.
1613	*The Lords' Masque* (Campion), Whitehall Palace, London.
	The Memorable Masque of the Middle Temple and Lincoln's Inn (Chapman), Whitehall Palace, London.
1615	*The Golden Age Restored* (Jonson), at Court.
1616	*Mercury Vindicated from the Alchemists* (Jonson), Whitehall Palace, London.
	Christmas, His Masque (Jonson), Whitehall Palace, London.
1617	*The Vision of Delight* (Jonson), Whitehall Palace, London.
1618	*Pleasure Reconciled to Virtue* (Jonson), Whitehall Palace, London; revised as *For the Honour of Wales*.
1619	Lost masque for Prince Charles (anon.).
1620	*News from the New World Discovered in the Moon* (Jonson), Whitehall Palace, London.
1621	Lost masque for Prince Charles (anon.).
1622	*The Masque of Augurs* (Jonson), Whitehall Palace, London.
1623	*Time Vindicated to Himself and to His Honours* (Jonson), Whitehall Palace, London.
1624	*Neptune's Triumph for the Return of Albion* (Jonson); revised as *The Fortunate Isles and Their Union*, at Court, 1626.
1625	*Pan's Anniversary; or, The Shepherd's Holiday* (Jonson), Whitehall Palace, London.
1626	*Artenice* (anon.), Denmark House, London.
1627	Lost masque for the Queen (anon.).
1628	Lost masque for the King (anon.).
1631	*French Pastoral* (anon.), Somerset House, London.
	Love's Triumph through Callipolis (Jonson), Whitehall Palace, London.
	Chloridia (Jonson), Whitehall Palace, London.
1632	*Albion's Triumph* (Townshend), Whitehall Palace, London.
	Tempe Restored (Townshend), Whitehall Palace, London.
1633	*The Shepherd's Paradise* (Montagu), Somerset House, London.
1634	*The Faithful Shepherdess* (Fletcher), Denmark House, London.

Inigo Jones

The Triumph of Peace (Shirley), Whitehall Palace, London.

Coelum Britannicum (Carew), Whitehall Palace, London.

Love's Mistress; or, The Queen's Masque (Heywood), Denmark House and Cockpit/Phoenix Theatre, London.

1635   *The Temple of Love* (Davenant), Whitehall Palace, London.

Florimène (anon.), Whitehall Palace, London.

1636   *The Triumphs of the Prince D'Amour* (anon.).

The Floating Island (Strode), Christ Church, Oxford.

The Royal Slave (Cartwright), Christ Church Hall, Oxford and Hampton Court, London.

1638   *Britannia Triumphans* (Jones and Davenant), Whitehall Palace, London.

Luminalia; or, The Festival of Light (Davenant), Whitehall Palace, London.

Aglaura (Suckling).

The Passionate Lovers (Carlell), Somerset House, London.

1640   *Salmacida Spolia* (Davenant), Whitehall Palace, London.

The Queen of Aragon (Habington), Cockpit-in-court, London.

*

Bibliography

Books:

W. Kent, *Designs of Inigo Jones*, London, 1727.

J. Loftie, *Inigo Jones and Wren, or Rise and Decline of Modern Architecture in England*, London, 1893.

H. Inigo Triggs and H. Tanner, *Some Architectural Works of Inigo Jones*, London, 1901.

J. Quincy Adams (ed.), *The Dramatic Records of Sir Henry Herbert*, New Haven, Connecticut, 1917.

T. Ramsey, *Inigo Jones*, London, 1924.

P. Simpson and C. F. Bell, *Designs by Inigo Jones for Masques and Plays*, Oxford, 1924.

E. Welsford, *The Court Masque*, Cambridge, 1927.

G. A. Gotch, *Inigo Jones*, London, 1928.

Sir R. Blomfield, *Six Architects*, London, 1935.

A. Nicoll, *Stuart Masques and The Renaissance Stage*, London, 1937.

H. Tintelnot, *Barocktheater und Barocke Kunst*, Berlin, 1939.

G. E. Bentley, *The Jacobean and Caroline Stage*, Oxford, 1941.

J. Laver, *Drama: Its Costume and Décor*, London, 1951.

R. Southern, *Changeable Scenery*, London, 1952.

J. Lees-Milne, *The Age of Inigo Jones*, 1953.

J. N. Summerson, *Inigo Jones*, Harmondsworth, 1965.

John Harris, Stephen Orgel, Roy Strong, *The King's Arcadia: Inigo Jones and the Stuart Court*, London, 1973.

David Lindley (ed.), *The Court Masque*, Manchester, 1984.

John Orrell, *The Theatres of Inigo Jones and John Webb*, Cambridge, 1985.

John Harris and Gordon Higgott, *Inigo Jones: complete architectural drawings*, New York and London, 1989.

* * *

Although the career of Inigo Jones may be dismissed as being that of an importer of Italian designer products, it was unique for an English artist in that it had a length and consistency of patronage that allowed him to explore the possibilities of his imports and, by the close of his career, to have re-organised, extended, and rendered English his contributions to architecture and to theatre practice. He was the first artist to formulate a theory of architecture, which he exemplified in practice, and this legacy was, through his assistant John Webb, to form the bedrock of English "classical" or Palladian architecture. In his other sphere of influence, the scenic technology that he had developed by *Salmacida Spolia* (1640), the last Stuart court masque, was introduced into professional theatre practice (again by Webb) during the early years of the Restoration. With little essential modification, the technology and the philosophy of representation that it enshrined were to be the cornerstones of scenic practice until the closing decades of the last century.

Architecturally, Jones was consciously innovatory, but theatrically, there is no evidence that he viewed existing professional practice as archaic and needing reform. Although it is customary to speak of Jones as England's first stage designer, his activities in this area were confined to serving the complex philosophical, political, and aesthetic priorities of the court masque. He had no regular relationships with professional play-producing bodies and his closest connection with the theatre industry was as the likely architect of the Cockpit in Drury Lane (c.1618). Further, the architectural drawings of permanent theatre spaces such as this and his later Cockpit-in-court (c.1631) have only tangential relationships with hsi designs for masques.

As the resident artist at the court of a Renaissance prince, it was Jones's duty to be a tireless source of beautiful, significant, and startling iconography that could exemplify the platonic ideal of kingship and courtly living. At the beginning of his career (c.1605), the masque had a long history growing out of the revelry, mummings, and designed tournaments of the middle ages. It served as a celebration of the great public occasion - heightening the significance and giving a spiritual "meaning" to royal birthdays, state rituals, and miportant calendar events. Spectacle reinforced the magnificence of those who watched, and, in so doing, offered a philosophical logic and political rationale for the authority of the monarchy. The masque always concluded by requiring the audience to participate by dancing with the courtly performers, thereby providing a visible acceptance of that authority.

Between 1605 and 1631, Jones and the poet and playwright Ben Jonson established a structure for the masque. This took the form of a riddle or situation that could be solved only by the presence of the monarch sitting in the audience at the very point from which lines of perspective (and authority) radiated and visually controlled the pictures presented. The masque is not drama — there is plot and story, but there is no action — no *praxis*. Evil cannot do battle with good but simply vanish in its presence. The masque presents *absolutes* — beauty, manliness, wit, evil, harmony, and discord — that become essentially *visual* qualities and are defined by costume, scenery, and properties. What is important is the moment of *change* from good to evil, ugliness to beauty.

The scene-change became a central feature of the masque and exemplified its process and political power. For Jones, this meant filling the vision with an image and then, most importantly, transforming that entire image before the very eyes of the spectators. This, of course, required a coherent and repeatable technology of scene-changing, which Jones provided. Jones was not original is attempting this, but he was original in the amalgamation of the many varied Italian techniques that he had no doubt observed in action during his visits to the ducal courts of northern Italy in 1601 and in 1613–15. There were also available to him through such treatises as Sebastiano Serlio's *De archittetura* (1545) and Nicola Sabatini's *Praticar per fabricar il scene* (1634). Within their Italian context, however, they remained as suggestions and individual solutions applicable to specific staging problems. By the late 1630s, Jones had experimented with and selected from this "Italian experience" and produced an elegant and effective scene-changing technique. The simplicity of the groove and shutter (*scaena ductilis*) system meant that it remained fundamentally unchanged whether operating in the extravagantly

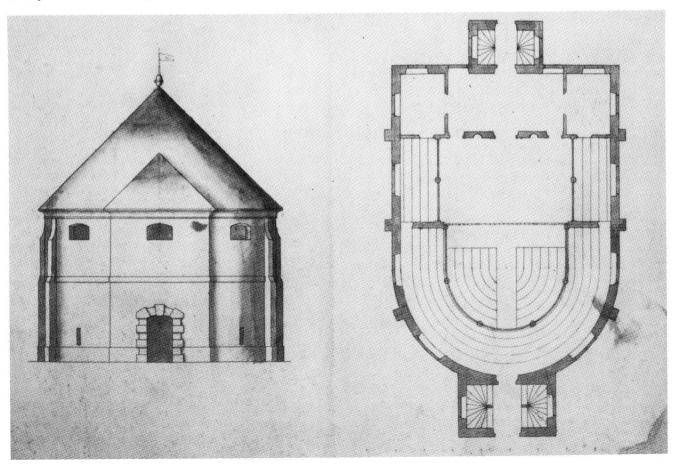

Plans for a conversion to a theatre, designed by **Inigo Jones** and drawn by John Webb (c. 1629).

Inigo Jones's designs for converting the Cockpit in Drury Lane (c. 1616-1618).

patronised world of court art or later within the severe financial constraints of the professional theatre.

Essentially, the complexity of the three dimensional image was broken into a series of flat surfaces ranged one behind the other on either side ("wing") of the stage. They were placed along the lines of the central perspective and hence were closer together towards the back of the stage than at the front. The picture was "closed" in at the rear by larger "flats" that met in the centre. All the surfaces were supported by wooden grooves upon the stage surface, while corresponding grooves were suspended from the ceiling to hold the top edge of the flats. Wings and back scenes could therefore (with the lubrication of black-lead and wax) be slid back and forth upon the stage. The surviving plays for *Salmacida Spolia* indicate that by collecting wing flats into closely spaced groups of five or six, and entire show's worth of scenery could be pre-set in the on-stage position. Disciplined scene-shifting could visually transform the stage by the sliding away of the front wing in each group to reveal the image behind. The suspended upper grooves were hidden by canvas painted borders (cloudings) or by suspended upper shutters whereby blue summer skies could slowly be covered by storm clouds sliding in from the sides. A painted *frontispiece*, the prototype proscenium arch, unified the vision and served to hide the off-stage machinery.

There is no indication that this system was used in a regular way in the professional theatre during Jones's lifetime. It is significant that none of his theatre designs could really accomodate such scenes. Indeed, it was not within his generation's perception of theatre that scenery, such as he designed for the court, should have any place in the presentation of plays. It is probable that very late in the Caroline period one or other of the professional theatres (Blackfriars, Salisbury Court, or the Cockpit) might have occasionally witnessed the use of painted perspective scenery for commissioned, probably private, performances. Less tangible, but no less significant a development for the theatre, was the birth of the philosophy that Jones's work offers of theatre as a place of fantasy and visions, of images into another — usually better — more structured and politically more comforting world.

—Christopher Baugh

JONES, Margo. US director and producer. Born in Livingston, Texas, 12 December 1911. Educated at The Girls Industrial College of Texas, MA. Director, Ojai Community Theatre of California, 1934; assistant director, Houston Federal Theatre, 1935; Texas Centennial delegate to the Moscow Art Theatre Festival, 1936; founder and director, Houston Community Players, 1936–42; taught at University of Texas, Austin, 1942–44; managing director,

Theatre '45–'55, 1945–55. Died (from carbon tetrachloride poisoning) in Dallas, Texas, 25 July 1955.

Productions

1942   *Eve of St Mark* (Anderson), University of Texas, Austin.

1943   *Sporting Pink* (Apstein), University of Texas, Austin.

A Choice of Weapons (Apstein), University of Texas, Austin.

You Touched Me (T. Williams), Pasadena Playhouse, California.

1945   *The Glass Menagerie* (T. Williams), Playhouse, New York.

1946   *On Whitman Avenue* (Wood), Broadway, New York.

Joan of Lorraine (Anderson), Alvin Theatre, New York.

1947   *Farther Off From Heaven/Dark at the Top of the Stairs* (Inge), Theatre '47, Dallas, Texas.

Hedda Gabler (Ibsen), Theatre '47, Dallas, Texas.

How Now Hecate (Coleman), Theatre '47, Dallas, Texas.

Summer and Smoke (Williams), Theatre '47, Dallas, Texas; Music Box Theatre, New York, 1948.

Third Cousin (Matthews), Theatre '47, Dallas, Texas.

1948   *The Master Builder* (Ibsen), Theatre '48, Dallas, Texas.

The Taming of the Shrew (Shakespeare), Theatre '48, Dallas, Texas.

The Importance of Being Earnest (Wilde), Theatre '48, Dallas, Texas.

Summer and Smoke (T. Williams), Broadway, New York.

Last of My Solid Gold Watches, *This Property Condemned*, and *Portrait of a Madonna* (T. Williams), Theatre '48, Dallas, Texas.

Throng o' Scarlet (Connell), Theatre '48, Dallas, Texas.

Lemple's Old Man (Gurian), Theatre '48, Dallas, Texas.

Leaf and Bough (Hayes), Theatre '48, Dallas, Texas.

Black John (MacLane), Theatre '48, Dallas, Texas.

1949   *The Learned Ladies* (Molière), Theatre '49, Dallas, Texas.

Twelfth Night (Shakespeare), Theatre '49, Dallas, Texas.

The Sea Gull (Chekhov), Theatre '49, Dallas, Texas.

She Stoops to Conquer (Goldsmith), Theatre '49, Dallas, Texas.

Here's to Us (Quin), Theatre '49, Dallas, Texas.

Sting in the Tail (Purefoy), Theatre '49, Dallas, Texas.

The Coast of Illyria (Parker and Evans), Theatre '49, Dallas, Texas.

1950   *Heartbreak House* (G. B. Shaw), Theatre '50, Dallas, Texas.

Ghosts (Ibsen), Theatre '50, Dallas, Texas.

An Old Beat-Up Woman (Scott), Theatre '50, Dallas, Texas.

My Granny Van (Disney and Perry), Theatre '50, Dallas, Texas.

Cock-A-Doodle Dandy (O'Casey), Theatre '50, Dallas, Texas.

The Golden Porcupine (Bolton), Theatre '50, Dallas, Texas.

Southern Exposure (Crump), Theatre '50, Dallas, Texas, and Broadway, New York.

A Play for Mary (McLeery), Theatre '50, Dallas, Texas.

An Innocent Time (Caulfield), Theatre '50, Dallas, Texas.

1951   *Lady Windermere's Fan* (Wilde), Theatre '51, Dallas, Texas.

The Merchant of Venice (Shakespeare), Theatre '51, Dallas, Texas.

Candida (G. B. Shaw), Theatre '51, Dallas, Texas.

A Willow Tree (Shiffrin), Theatre '51, Dallas, Texas.

One Bright Day (Miller), Theatre '51, Dallas, Texas.

Walls Rise Up (Duane), Theatre '51, Dallas, Texas.

One Foot in Heaven (Phillips), Theatre '51, Dallas, Texas.

A Gift for Cathy (Alexander), Theatre '51, Dallas, Texas.

1952   *A Midsummer Night's Dream* (Shakespeare), Theatre '52, Dallas, Texas.

Sainted Sisters (Nash), Theatre '52, Dallas, Texas.

The Blind Spot (Caulfield), Theatre '52, Dallas, Texas.

So in Love (Mathews), Theatre '52, Dallas, Texas.

I Am Laughing (Mayer), Theatre '52, Dallas, Texas.

1953   *Hamlet* (Shakespeare), Theatre '53, Dallas, Texas.

The Rivals (Sheridan), Theatre '53, Dallas, Texas.

Goodbye, Your Majesty (Connell), Theatre '53, Dallas, Texas.

The Rising Heifer (Maugham), Theatre '53, Dallas, Texas.

The Last Island (Raskin), Theatre '53, Dallas, Texas.

Late Love (Casey), Theatre '53, Dallas, Texas.

Uncle Marston (Harding), Theatre '53, Dallas, Texas.

The Day's Mischief (Storm), Theatre '53, Dallas, Texas.

1954   *Volpone* (Jonson), Theatre '54, Dallas, Texas.

The Footpath Way (Drake), Theatre '54, Dallas, Texas.

The Guilty (Granick), Theatre '54, Dallas, Texas.

Happy We'll Be (Raphaelson), Theatre '54, Dallas, Texas.

Oracle Junction (Raphaelson), Theatre '54, Dallas, Texas.

The Heel (Raphaelson), Theatre '54, Dallas, Texas.

A Rainbow at Home (Robertson), Theatre 54, Dallas, Texas.

Horatio (Wallach, Baker, and Harnick), Theatre '54, Dallas, Texas.

The Purification (T. Williams), Theatre '54, Dallas, Texas.

The Apollo of Bellac (Giraudoux), Theatre '54, Dallas, Texas.

The Brothers (Rodell), Theatre '54, Dallas, Texas.

A Dash of Bitters (Denham and Sutton-Smith), Theatre '54, Dallas, Texas.

Sea-Change (Case), Theatre '54, Dallas, Texas.

The Inevitable Circle (Alexander), Theatre '54, Dallas, Texas.

Marry Go Round (Dickason), Theatre '54, Dallas, Texas.

The Hemlock Cup (Hunt), Theatre '54, Dallas, Texas.

1955   *As You Like It* (Shakespeare), Theatre '55, Dallas, Texas.

Inherit the Wind (Lawrence and Lee), Theatre '55, Dallas, Texas, and National Theatre, New York.

Whisper to Me (Johnson and Goyen), Theatre '55, Dallas, Texas.

La Belle Lulu (Offenbach and Previn), Theatre '55, Dallas, Texas.

The Girl from Boston (Hayes), Theatre '55, Dallas, Texas.

Publications

Theatre-in-the-Round, 1951.

*

Bibliography

Books:
Helen Sheehy, *Margo: The Life and Theatre of Margo Jones*, Dallas, Texas, 1989.

* * *

Tennessee Williams dubbed Margo Jones "the Texas Tornado", a combination of "Joan of Arc and Gene Autry — and nitroglycerine". Like a tornado she appeared out of nowhere and disappeared just as suddenly, having forged a path for others to follow. Inspired by such examples as the Old Vic, the Abbey Theatre, the Moscow Art Theatre, and the Washington Square Players, Jones created a theatre with an artistic rather than commercial focus. Like Hallie Flanagan, director of the shortlived Federal Theatre Project, Jones dreamed of a national theatre consisting of a network of non-profit, professional, resident theatres providing an outlet for theatre artists of every level of production, an environment for playwrights to experiment

Margo Jones

and mature, and an opportunity for every American to see great plays well done. Although her vision did not come true in her lifetime, her theatre in Dallas, the first non-profit resident professional theatre in the USA, set an example for contemporary regional theatres.

As a director, Jones was self-taught. She developed a collaborative, improvisational style, open to trial and error. To Jones experimentation was necessary in order to avoid the obvious. She trusted her intuition and her need to work instinctively. In rehearsal she sought first to create an environment conducive to creative work, where actors felt free to make contributions and develop their characters. She remained flexible and open to the discoveries that accompany putting a play on its feet.

Jones once described herself as "51 per cent creator and 49 per cent promoter". Except for her involvement with *The Glass Menagerie* and *Inherit the Wind*, her Broadway experience proved financially unsuccessful. It was in spearheading two Texas theatres that she excelled. In 1936 she formed the Houston Community Players out of nine auditioners and six dollars. By 1942, 60 plays later (all directed by Jones), the membership numbered 600, the subscription audience had grown to 3700 and the Players owned equipment valued at $15,000. In Dallas, Jones proved professional theatre could survive as a non-profit corporation guided by a board of civic and social leaders. By converting a building at Dallas's Fair Park into a 198 seat arena playhouse, Jones opened the first professional non-profit resident theatre-in-the-round in the USA, Theatre '47–'55 (the number changed to coincide with the year).

Theatre '45–'55 presented a repertory of classics and new plays. Of the classics, Shakespeare's active, imaginative, and poetic plots were Jones's favourite. She also enjoyed producing Ibsen, Molière, Shaw, Goldsmith, and Sheridan for her audience. But first and foremost her theatre provided a home for dramatists to develop. 75 per cent of the plays produced during her reign as managing director were premieres. Jones declared "the playwright is the star". She approached each new script with "wonderment", not as a critic but as a lover. This love was well-focused. In 1955, four of the playwrights Jones nurtured had productions on Broadway: Williams's *Cat on a Hot Tin Roof*, Inge's *Bus Stop*, Joseph Hayes's *The Desperate Hour*, and Lawrence and Lee's *Inherit the Wind*.

Although ideally Jones wanted a flexible theatre, lack of funds and scarcity of building permits forced her to alter a found space. This resignation to arena staging became a happy circumstance — Jones immediately appreciated the inherent fluidity of movement, the necessity for innovative and experimental design, as well as the intimate relationship with an audience. She also discovered that theatre-in-the-round supported any script.

After five seasons, Jones wrote *Theatre-in-the-Round*, a history of her theatre and a record of her experience with arena staging. According to Jones, a play presented in-the-round becomes a three-dimensional sculpture of which the director must take a bird's-eye view. She followed two basic principles: let the audience's imagination work to fill in the scenic picture, and strive for a simple and honest style of acting from the ensemble.

Jones discovered setting the scene in her theatre-in-the-round depended largely on costumes, props, lights, and sound. These elements plus the language plus the audience's imagination created the spectacle at Theatre '45–55. Lighting provided the curtain, enahanced the mood, and emphasized focus. Sound worked closely with the lighting to provide fluid transitions. Furniture, costumes, and props were totally authentic in every detail as nothing false escaped the scrutiny of the audience in the intimate theatre.

More than anything else, *Theatre-in-the-Round* represented a call to action. With her book in hand on the Columbia lecture circuit, Jones hoped to influence the initiation of at least 20 other theatres like her own: non-profit theatres allowing an artistic rather than a monetary focus, resident theatres offering permanence and stability to actors and technical workers, professional theatres providing a stage and actors for the presentation of original works, and theatres with a subscription audience offering community support.

Although her premature death prevented her witnessing the realisation of her dream, her spirit has been a guiding one for many. In her lifetime she counselled and encouraged Nina Vance of Houston's Alley Theatre, Zelda Fichandler of Washington, D.C.'s Arena Stage, and Mary Johns of the Milwaukee Repertory Theatre. These theatres became models for others and the network grew. How much credit Jones deserves for the present state of regional theatre in the USA is impossible to ascertain. However, her vision of decentralisation has come true in many ways. Currently, regional theatres employ three times as many actors as Broadway and provide steady work for techni-

cians, designers, directors, and administrators. Also, the majority of new plays on Broadway begin their growth in a regional theatre.

Without a doubt, Jones deserves credit for championing playwrights, validating arena staging, and exploring the status of theatre as a non-profit corporation. Her ability to keep a theatre in Dallas in the black for all of the ten seasons she directed and produced, with a repertory of classics and new plays, is a feat few can match.

—Lesley Rathkamp

JONES, Robert Edmond.   US designer and director. Born in Milton, New Hampshire, 12 December 1887. Educated at Nute High School, until 1905; Harvard University, 1906–10. Married Margaret Huston Carrington in 1933 (died 1941). Graduate assistant and instructor in the Department of Fine Arts, Harvard University, 1910–12; first work as a theatrical designer in New York, 1912; studied design in Florence and Berlin, under Max Reinhardt, 1913–14; designed and directed plays, masques, operas, ballets, films, and musical comedies among other productions for the Provincetown Players, Experimental Theatre Inc., and the Theatre Guild among other New York companies; Art Director, Radio City Music Hall, 1932–33; lectured widely on the theatre from 1940. Recipient: Howland Memorial Medal, Yale University, 1925; Fine Arts Medal, American Institute of Architects, 1935. Died in Milton, New Hampshire, 26 November 1954.

Productions

As designer:
1914   *The Glittering Gate* (Dunsany), Washington Square Bookshop, New York.
1915   *The Man Who Married a Dumb Wife* (France), Wallack's Theatre, New York.
    Interior (Maeterlinck), Bandbox Theatre, New York.
    Supressed Desires (Crook), private house, Provincetown, Massachusetts.
    Constancy (Boyce), private house, Provincetown, Massachusetts.
    The Devil's Garden (Ellis), Harris Theatre, New York.
1916   *Caliban by the Yellow Sands* (Mackaye), Lewissohn Stadium, City College, New York; Harvard Stadium, 1917.
    The Happy Ending (Macpherson), Shubert Theatre, New York.
    The Merry Death (Evreinov), Comedy Theatre, New York.
    Til Eulenspiegel (Nijinski ballet), Manhattan Opera House, New York.
    Good Gracious Annabelle (Kummer), Republic Theatre, New York.
1917   *A Successful Calamity* (Kummer), Booth Theatre, New York.
    The Rider of Dreams, *Granny Maumee*, and *Simon the Cyrenian* (Torrence), Garden Theatre, New York; also directed.

The Deluge (Berger), Hudson Theatre, New York; Plymouth Theatre, New York, 1922.

The Rescuing Angel (Kummer), Hudson Theatre, New York.

1918   The Wild Duck (Ibsen), Plymouth Theatre, New York.

Hedda Gabler (Ibsen), Plymouth Theatre, New York.

The Magical City (Akins), Pabst Theatre, Milwaukee.

Fanny's First Play (G. B. Shaw), Pabst Theatre, Milwaukee.

Trilby (Du Maurier), Pabst Theatre, Milwaukee.

The Garden of Paradise (Sheldon), Pabst Theatre, Milwaukee.

The Little Mermaid (adapted from Andersen), Pabst Theatre, Milwaukee.

The Little Shepherd (adapted from Debussy), Pabst Theatre, Milwaukee.

An Ideal Husband (Wilde), Pabst Theatre, Milwaukee.

Hempfield (Thompson), Pabst Theatre, Milwaukee.

Redemption (Tolstoy), Plymouth Theatre, New York.

Be Calm, Camilla (Kummer), Booth Theatre, New York.

The Gentile Wife (Wellman), Venderbilt Theatre, New York.

1919   Guibour (anon., adapted by MacDonald), Neighborhood Playhouse, New York; 39th Street Theatre, New York, 1922.

The Jest (Sheldon), Plymouth Theatre, New York; revived there, 1926.

The Will of Song (Mackaye), The Armory, Orange, New Jersey.

1920   The Birthday of the Infanta (Wilde), Chicago Opera and Lexington Theatre, New York.

The Man Who Made Us (Mackaye), Lyric Theatre, New York.

Richard III (Shakespeare), Plymouth Theatre, New York.

Samson and Delilah (Lange), Greenwich Village Theatre, New York.

1921   Macbeth (Shakespeare), Apollo Theatre, New York.

Daddy's Gone A-Hunting (Akins), Plymouth Theatre, New York.

Swords (Howard), National Theatre, New York.

The Claw (Bernstein), Broadhurst Theatre, New York.

Anna Christie (O'Neill), Vanderbilt Theatre, New York.

The Mountain Man (Kummer), Maxine Elliott's Theatre, New York.

The Idle Inn (Hirschbein), Plymouth Theatre, New York.

1922   The S. S. Tenacity (Vildrac), Belmont Theatre, New York.

The Hairy Ape (O'Neill), Provincetown Playhouse, New York.

Voltaire (Taylor and Purcell), Plymouth Theatre, New York.

Rose Bernd (Hauptmann, adapted by Lewissohn), Longacre Theatre, New York.

Hamlet (Shakespeare), Sam H. Harris Theatre, New York.

Romeo and Juliet (Shakespeare), Longacre Theatre, New York.

1923   The Laughing Lady (Sutro), Longacre Theatre, New York.

Launzi (Molnar, adapted by Millay), Plymouth Theatre, New York.

A Royal Fandango (Akins), Plymouth Theatre, New York.

1924   The Spook Sonata (Strindberg, translated by Björkman), Provincetown Playhouse, New York; also directed.

The Living Mask (Pirandello, translated by Livingston), 44th Street Theatre, New York.

Fashion; or, Life in New York (Mowatt), Provincetown Playhouse, New York; also directed.

Welded (O'Neill), 39th Street Theatre, New York.

George Dandin; or, The Husband Confounded (Molière), Provincetown Playhouse, New York.

The Ancient Mariner (Coleridge, adapted by O'Neill), Provincetown Playhouse, New York; also directed.

At the Gateway (Pirandello), Imperial Theatre, New York.

The Emperor Jones (O'Neill), Provincetown Playhouse, New York.

Hedda Gabler (Ibsen), 48th Street Theatre, New York; also directed.

All God's Chillum Got Wings (O'Neill), Provincetown Playhouse, New York.

The Crime in the Whistler Room (Wilson), Provincetown Playhouse, New York.

The Saint (Young), Greenwich Village Theatre, New York; also directed.

S. S. Glencairn (O'Neill), Provincetown Playhouse, New York.

Desire Under the Elms (O'Neill), Greenwich Village Theatre, New York; also directed.

Patience; or, Bunthorne's Bride (Gilbert and Sullivan), Provincetown Playhouse, New York; also directed.

1925   Beyond (Hasenclever, translated by Matthias), Provincetown Playhouse, New York.

The Triumph of the Egg (Anderson and O'Neil), Provincetown Playhouse, New York.

Diff'rent (O'Neill), Provincetown Playhouse, New York.

Michel Auclair (Vildrac), Provincetown Playhouse, New York; also directed.

Love for Love (Congreve), Greenwich Village Theatre, New York; also directed.

Ruint (Hughes), Provincetown Playhouse, New York.

Trelawny of 'The Wells' (Pinero), Knickerbocker Theatre, New York.

Outside Looking In (Anderson), Greenwich Village Theatre, New York.

The Buccaneer (Anderson and Stallings), Plymouth Theatre, New York.

The Last Night of Don Juan (Rostand, translated by Howard), Greenwich Village Theatre, New York.

In a Garden (Barry), Plymouth Theatre, New York.

The Fountain (O'Neill), Greenwich Village Theatre, New York.

The Great God Brown (O'Neill), Greenwich Village Theatre, New York; also directed.

1926   *Little Eyolf* (Ibsen), Guild Theatre, New York.

Skyscrapers (Carpenter), Metropolitan Opera House, New York; also directed.

Bride of the Lamb (Hurlbut), Greenwich Village Theatre, New York.

Martine (Bernard), American Laboratory Theatre, New York.

The House of Women (Bromfield), Maxine Elliott's Theatre, New York.

Paris Bound (Barry), Music Box Theatre, New York.

1928   *Faust* (Goethe, adapted by Simon), Gallo Theatre, New York.

Salvation (Howard and MacArthur), Empire Theatre, New York.

Machinal (Treadwell), Plymouth Theatre, New York.

Mr Moneypenny (Pollock), Liberty Theatre, New York.

These Days (Clugston), Cort Theatre, New York.

Holiday (Barry), Plymouth Theatre, New York.

1929   *Serena Blandish; or, The Difficulty of Getting Married* (Behrman), Morosco Theatre, New York.

Becky Sharp (Mitchell, adapted from Thackeray), Knickerbocker Theatre, New York.

See Naples and Die (Rice), Vanderbilt Theatre, New York.

Ladies Leave (Treadwell), Charles Hopkins Theatre, New York.

Yolanda of Cyprus (Loomis), Majestic Theatre, Chicago.

The Channel Road (Woollcott and Kaufman), Plymouth Theatre, New York.

Week-End (Parker), John Golden Theatre, New York.

Cross Roads (Flavin), Morosco Theatre, New York.

1930   *Children of Darkness* (Mayer), Biltmore Theatre, New York.

Rebound (Stewart), Plymouth Theatre, New York.

The Green Pastures (Connelly), Mansfield Theatre, New York; Broadway Theatre, New York, 1954.

Die Glückliche Hand (Schönberg), Metropolitan Opera House, New York.

Roadside (Riggs), Longacre Theatre, New York.

Le Preziose Ridicole (Rossato, adapted from Molière's *Les Précieses Ridicules*), Metropolitan Opera House, New York.

1931   *Wozzeck* (Berg), Metropolitan Opera House, Philadelphia.

Oedipus Rex (Stravinsky), Metropolitan Opera House, Philadelphia.

Mourning Becomes Electra (O'Neill), Guild Theatre, New York.

The Lady With a Lamp (Berkeley), Maxine Elliott's Theatre, New York.

The Passing Present (Damrosch), Ethel Barrymore Theatre, New York.

1932   *Night Over Taos* (Anderson), 48th Street Theatre, New York.

Camille (Dumas *fils*), Central City Opera House, Central City, Colorado, and Morosco Theatre, New York; also directed.

Lucrece (Wilder, adapted from Obey), Belasco Theatre, New York.

1933   *Pierrot Lunaire* (Giraud, translated by Hartleben), Town Hall, New York.

Nine Pine Street (Colton and Miles), Longacre Theatre, New York.

The Merry Widow (Lehar), Central City Opera House, Central City, Colorado; also directed.

Ah, Wilderness! (O'Neill), Guild Theatre, New York.

The Green Bay Tree (Shairp), Cort Theatre, New York.

Mary of Scotland (Anderson), Alvin Theatre, New York.

1934   *The Joyous Season* (Barry), Belasco Theatre, New York.

Othello (Shakespeare), Central City Opera House, Central City, Colorado; New Amsterdam Theatre, New York, 1937; also directed.

Dark Victory (Brewer and Bloch), Plymouth Theatre, New York.

1935   *Central City Nights* (review), Central City Opera House, Central City, Colorado; also directed.

1938   *The Seagull* (Chekhov, translated by Young), Shubert Theatre, New York.

Ruy Blas (Hugo, adapted by Hooker), Central City Opera House, Central City, Colorado; also directed.

Everywhere I Roam (Sundgaard and Connelly), National Theatre, New York.

1939   *The Philadelphia Story* (Barry), Shubert Theatre, New York.

The Devil and Daniel Webster (Benét and Moore), Martin Beck Theatre, New York.

Susanna, Don't You Cry (Newmeyer and Loomis), Martin Beck Theatre, New York.

Summer Night (Baum and Glazer), St James Theatre, New York.

Kindred (Carroll), Maxine Elliott's Theatre, New York; also directed.

1940   *Juno and the Paycock* (O'Casey), Mansfield Theatre, New York.

Love for Love (Congreve), Hudson Theatre, New York; also directed.

To-Night at 8:30 (Coward), El Capitan Theatre, Hollywood.

1941   *Orpheus* (Gluck), Central City Opera House, Central City, Colorado.

The Barber of Seville (Rossini), Central City Opera House, Central City, Colorado.

1942   *Without Love* (Barry), St James Theatre, New York.

1943   *The Crucifixion of Christ* (Stokowski), Metropolitan Opera House, New York.

Othello (Shakespeare), Shubert Theatre, New York.

1944   *Jackpot* (Bolton, Sheldon, and Roberts), Alvin Theatre, New York.

Helen Goes to Troy (Reinhardt and Meehan), Alvin Theatre, New York.

The Children's Christmas Story (Stokowski), New York City Centre, New York.

1946   *Lute Song* (Howard and Irwin), Plymouth Theatre, New York.

The Iceman Cometh (O'Neill), Martin Beck Theatre, New York.

1947   *A Moon for the Misbegotten* (O'Neill), US tour.

1949   *Out of Dust* (Riggs), Westport Country Playhouse, Westport, Connecticut.

1950   *The Enchanted* (Giraudoux, adapted by Valency), Lyceum Theatre, New York.

1950   *The Flying Dutchman* (Wagner), Metropolitan Opera House, New York.

Films

As designer:
La Cucaracha, 1934; *Becky Sharp*, 1935; *The Dancing Pirate*, 1936.

Publications

Continental Stagecraft (with Kenneth Macgowan), 1922; *Drawings for the Theatre*, 1925; *The Dramatic Imagination*, 1941.

*

Bibliography

Books:
Ralph Pendleton (ed.), *The Theatre of Robert Edmond Jones*, Middletown, Connecticut, 1958.

* * *

The influence of Robert Edmond Jones on the US theatre is profound. It is acknowledged, although perhaps not that well-known today, that with his 1915 production of *The Man Who Married a Dumb Wife*, Jones brought the 'New Stagecraft' of Europe to the USA. This began the process of a revolution in US stage design, and Jones, along with Norman Bel Geddes and Lee Simonson, established the profession of stage designer in the USA. But it is in his designs and writings, contained in *Drawings for the Theatre*, *The Dramatic Imagination*, and the posthumous *The Theatre of Robert Edmond Jones*, that Jones's influence is most evident. In these books Jones established the first complete aesthetic of stage design in the USA. In addition, through his many assistants, notably Jo Mielziner and Donald Oenslager, Jones shaped the thinking and the attitudes of all the generations of theatrical designers to follow down to the present day.

The effect of Jones's thinking concerning the aesthetics of the profession of stage design is, however, paradoxical. On the one hand, some of the more romantic/mystical concepts found in *The Dramatic Imagination* are so widely accepted today that they have entered into the realm of unexamined assumptions. These ideas have been around so long and have become so much a part of the profession of scene design in the USA that they seem to be like natural phenomena. Foremost among these is the idea that the text of the drama holds within it a universal and eternal truth that it is the duty of the production and the designer to uncover. The work of the designer, then, can always be judged as successful in so far as it approaches and illuminates this eternal truth. Unfortunately, nowhere in Jones's thoughts is there recorded a simple way in which we may recognize this universal truth when we discover it. The designer then is left in a curious situation. He is told by Jones that his profession is in the service of noble and high goals, but what the goals are is never made clear. The designer is encouraged to make himself a conduit through which the message of true theatre may pass, but is not told what the message is or who is sending it.

The result of this is a philosophy of design, very popular in the USA, that stresses the self-abnegation or anonymity of the designer. The designer is taught that personal expression is not encouraged in design. The design must call attention to itself. Instead, all aspects of the production are to be subordinated to the higher eternal truth that is being transmitted through the performance. Unfortunately such intellectual concepts are rarely realised in practical terms in the theatre of today. In fact, these ideas had only a marginal application in Jones's own Symbolist/Impressionist theatre and the idea that theatre design is not self-expression is now dismissed as not accurate. Design is a personal expression and design is a confrontation with the self. Design is a process of discovering what there is to say and thus inevitably a personal expression. It manifests itself in what is identified as style, or attitude — a way of seeing and saying. Style is the expression of self and the work of Jones is, in itself, a refutation of the idea of the anonymity of the designer. No one could ever mistake the work of Jones for that of another designer, transfigured as it is by his own personal style.

The second group of Jones's idead, which are vital for our contemporary theatre, paradoxically, do not enjoy wide circulation in the US theatre. These ideas concern his vision of a 'New Theatre'. As early as 1929 Jones set out his thoughts on this new theatre, which was to be a fusion of film and live action. Jones saw a new theatre that used all the technology of his day. He saw a theatre in which the presence of the live actor existed equally with the motion picture and with still images. Jones saw this as a new theatrical form that would give expression to a new awareness of the duality of life that was being explored in the literature and arts of his era. As Jones foresaw it, ordinary objective reality would be presented on a stage much like our conventional stages by the live actor. Subjective reality, however, would be presented on a projection screen that would surround and enclose this conventional stage. On this screen would be seen the psychological condition of the objective action below and in front of it.

Jones was unable to realise fully his vision of this new theatre, but his restless quest for new ways to present theatrical reality led him to make many experiments along these lines. In 1924 he designed a setting with projected effects for the Provincetown Playhouse production of Eugene O'Neill's version of the Coleridge poem *The Ancient Mariner*. The sketch of this setting shows a large stage with a small ship backed up by a projection cloth on which is projected a menacing skeletal form. In 1931 he designed a production of the Jean Cocteau/Igor Stravinsky *Oedipus Rex* that featured 'Über-Marionettes' towering over a chorus of singers seated at the front of the stage. Even though these giant forms were three-dimensional, mobile, constructions not projected effects, the design is based on the idea of the simultaneous presentation of objective and subjective reality that is the basis of Jones's vision of his 'New Theatre'. In 1941 he completed the design for a project production of *Richard III*. This design featured, essentially, an open stage backed again with a large projection cloth. Jones described this project as a unit setting with projected effects and his renderings show the projection of large heraldic forms for the vision of the crown and an arresting, misty projection of the ghost of Lady Ann.

Unfortunately, Jones's ideas for his new theatre have not enjoyed wide acceptance in the USA except in 'performance art' and at the most experimental and avant-garde theatre venues. Interestingly enough, his ideas about this new theatre have, however, been implemented and brought to fruition in the Laterna Magika of Prague under the directorship of Josef Svoboda.

—Delbert Unruh

JOUVET, Louis. French actor-manager and director. Born Jules-Eugène-Louis Jouvet in Crozon, Finistère, France, 24 December 1887. Educated at the Collège de Lyon, 1898–1902; Collège de Rethel, 1902. Stage debut, Château du Peuple, Bois de Boulogne, 1908, after giving up career as a pharmacist; three times refused admittance to the Paris Conservatoire; actor, Théâtre des Arts, Paris, 1910; joined Jacques Copeau's company at the Théâtre du Vieux-Colombier, Paris, 1913; served in French Army, 1914–17; appeared in New York, 1918–19; director, Comédie des Champs-Élysées, Paris, 1924–34; became one of the Cartel des Quatre, 1927; director, Théâtre de l'Athénée, Paris, from 1934; became a professor at the Paris Conservatoire, 1934; toured South America, 1941–45; also directed for the Comédie-Française and acted at the Edinburgh Festival, 1947. Commander, Légion d'Honneur, 1950. Died in Paris, 16 August 1951.

Productions

1908   Extract from *Les Triumvirs* (Ponsard), Château du Peuple, Bois de Boulogne, Paris; acted Danton.

Les Mauvais Bergers (Mirbeau), Université Populaire du Faubourg Saint-Antoine, Paris; acted Hargand.

Le Moulin des chimères (Marcotte), Université Populaire du Faubourg Saint-Antoine, Paris; acted Don Quichote.

Don Juan (Molière), Université Populaire du Faubourg Saint-Antoine, Paris; acted Don Luis.

Oedipe-roi (Sophocles, translated by Lacroix), Théâtre Municipal, Saint Dizier; acted Le Coryphée.

Les Maîtres de la vie (Mai), Château du Peuple, Bois de Boulogne, Paris; acted Maximilien-Serror.

Le Misanthrope (Molière), Château du Peuple, Bois de Boulogne, Paris; acted Alceste.

Extracts from *Le Moulin des chimères* (Marcotte), Angoulême, Salle des Concerts, Place de le Gendarmerie; acted Don Quichotte.

Extracts from *Un Magistrat comparaît devant un homme libre* (Ryner), L'Hexagramme, Paris; acted Le Prêteur.

Les Revenants (Ibsen), Université Populaire du Faubourg Saint Antoine, Paris; acted Oswald.

Britannicus (Racine), Théâtre de la Ruche des Arts, Paris; acted Burrhus.

Les Triumvirs (Ponsard), Théâtre de la Ruche des Arts, Paris; acted Danton.

Le Principal Témoin (Courteline), Université Populaire du Faubourg Saint Antoine, Paris; acted Grenouillot.

Le Droit au bonheur (Lemonnier and Soulaine), Université Populaire du Faubourg Saint Antoine, Paris; acted Joris Sangue.

Hortense, couche-toi (Courteline), Université Populaire du Faubourg Saint Antoine, Paris; acted M. Saumtre.

La Recommandation (Maury), Théâtre de la Ruche des Arts, Paris; acted Le Directeur.

1909   *La Coeur a ses raisons* (Flers and Caillavet), Théâtre de la Ruche des Arts, Paris; acted Jacques.

Le Combat de cerfs (Bergerat), Université Populaire du Faubourg Saint Antoine, Paris; acted Jacques Séguin.

Le Chien flamberge (Nigond and Jouvet), Théâtre de la Ruche des Arts, Paris.

Jusqu'a l'ame (Ryner), L'Hexagramme, Paris; acted Lucien.

A propos 1909 (Mai), Théâtre d'Action d'Art, Paris; acted Jouvet.

Andromaque (Racine), Théâtre de la Ruche des Arts, Paris; acted Pylade.

L'École des femmes (Molière), Université Populaire du Faubourg Saint Antoine, Paris; acted Arnolphe.

Le Faiseur (Balzac), Trocadéro, Paris; acted August Mercadet.

1910   *Le Colonel Chabert* (Forest, adapted from Balzac), Théâtre de l'Athénée Saint-Germain, Paris; acted Colonel Chabert.

L'Asile de nuit (Maurey), Théâtre de la Ruche des Arts, Paris; acted Ma Soupe.

Poil de carotte (Renard), Université Populaire du Faubourg Saint Antoine, Paris; acted M. Lepic.

Féministe (Pissargewski and Combes), Théâtres d'Idées, Paris; acted Le Rédacteur.

L'Annonce faite à Marie (Claudel), Théâtre d'Idées, Paris; acted The Man.

1911   *Les Frères Karamazov* (Copeau and Croué, adapted from Dostoevsky), Théâtre des Arts, Paris; acted Père Zossima.

Le Pain (Ghéon), Théâtre des Arts, Paris; acted Méteil.

Le Chagrin dans le Palais de Han (Laloy), Théâtre des Arts, Paris; acted Le Ministre.

1912   *Les Dominos* (Couperin and Laloy), Théâtre des Arts, Paris; acted Joueur de vielle.

Fantasio (Musset), Théâtre des Arts, Paris; acted Le Roi.

Mil neuf cent douze (Muller and Gignoux), Théâtre des Arts, Paris; acted Le Maigre, le lion, and le bourgeois.

1913   *Une Femme tuée par le douceur* (Heywood, adapted by Copeau), Théâtre du Vieux-Colombier, Paris; acted Master Cranwell.

L'Amour médecin (Molière), Théâtre du Vieux-Colombier, Paris; acted Macroton.

Les Fils Louverné (Schlumberger), Théâtre du Vieux-Colombier, Paris; acted Grimbosq.

Barberine (Musset), Théâtre du Vieux-Colombier, Paris; acted Uladislas.

L'Avare (Molière), Théâtre du Vieux-Colombier, Paris; acted Maître Simon.

La Farce du savetier enragé (anon.), Théâtre du Vieux-Colombier, Paris; acted Le Savetier.

1914   *La Jalousie du Barbouillé* (Molière), Théâtre du Vieux-Colombier, Paris; acted Le Docteur.

Les Frères Karamazov (Copeau and Croué, adapted from Dostoevsky), Théâtre du Vieux-Colombier, Paris; acted Féodor Pavlovitch Karamazov.

La Nuit des rois (Shakespeare, translated by Lascaris), Théâtre du Vieux-Colombier, Paris; acted Sir Andrew Aguecheek.

1917   *Impromptu du Vieux-Colombier* (Copeau), US tour; acted Jouvet.

Les Fourberies de Scapin (Molière), US tour; acted Géronte.

Le Carosse du Saint-Sacrement (Mérimée), US tour; acted L'Evêque de Lima.

1918   *Les Mauvais Bergers* (Mirbeau), US tour; acted Louis Thieux.

La Petite Marquise (Meilhac and Halévy), US tour; acted Marquis de Keergazon.

Le Paix chez soi (Courteline), US tour; acted Trielle.

Le Mariage de Figaro (Beaumarchais), US tour; acted Brid'Oison.

Blanchette (Brieux), US tour; acted Le Cantonnier.

Crainquebille (France), US tour; acted Crainquebille.

Le Médecin malgré lui (Molière), US tour; acted Sganarelle.

Rosmersholm (Ibsen), US tour; acted Ulric Brendel.

Le Gendre de M. Poirier (Augier and Sandeau), US tour; acted Le Marquis.

Les Caprices de Marianne (Musset), US tour; acted Claudio.

Le Fardeau de la liberté (Bernard), US tour; acted Chambolin.

Les Romanesques (Rostand), US tour; acted Straford.

1919   *La Coupe enchantée* (La Fontaine and Champmeslé), US tour; acted Josselin.

Le Misanthrope (Molière), US tour; acted Philinte.

1920   *A Winter's Tale* (Shakespeare, translated by Bing and Copeau), Théâtre du Vieux-Colombier, Paris; acted Autolycus.

L'Oeuvre des athlètes (Duhamel), Théâtre du Vieux-Colombier, Paris; acted Filliatre Demelin.

Cromedeyre-le-Vieil (Romains), Théâtre du Vieux-Colombier, Paris; acted Anselme.

La Folle Journée (Mazaud), Théâtre du Vieux-Colombier, Paris; acted Truchard.

1921   *La Mort de Sparte* (Schlumberger), Théâtre du Vieux-Colombier, Paris; acted Antigone.

1922   *L'Amour livre d'or* (Tolstoy), Théâtre du Vieux-Colombier, Paris; acted Le Prince.

Saul (Gide), Théâtre du Vieux-Colombier, Paris; acted Grand Prêtre.

1923   *M. Le Trouhadec saisi par la debauche* (Romains), Comédie des Champs-Élysées, Paris; tour, 1941; acted M. Le Trouhadec.

Le Journée des aveux (Duhamel), Comédie des Champs-Élysées, Paris; acted Général Foulon-Dubelair.

Knock; ou, Le Triomphe de la médecine (Romains), tour; acted Dr Knock.

Amédée et les messieurs en rang (Romains), Comédie des Champs-Élysées, Paris.

1924   *La Scintillante* (Romains), Comédie des Champs-Élysées, Paris; acted Le Vicomte.

La Folle Journée (Mazaud), tour; acted Truchard.

Le Pain de ménage (Romains), Comédie des Champs-Élysées, Paris.

Le Testament du Père Leleu (Du Gard), Comédie des Champs-Élysées, Paris.

Malbrough s'en va-t-en guerre (Achard), Comédie des Champs-Élysées, Paris; acted Malbrough.

1925   *Le Mariage de M. Le Trouhadec* (Romains), Comédie des Champs-Élysées, Paris; acted M. Le Trouhadec.

L'Amour qui passe (Quintero, translated by Dubois and Du Gard), Comédie des Champs-Élysées, Paris.

La Jalousie du Barbouillé (Molière), Comédie des Champs-Élysées, Paris; acted Le Docteur.

Tripes d'or (Crommelynck), Comédie des Champs-Élysées, Paris; acted Muscar.

Démétrios (Romains), Comédie des Champs-Élysées, Paris; acted Démétrios.

Louis Jouvet

Madame Béliard (Vildrac), Comédie des Champs-Élysées, Paris.

1926 *Bava L'Africain* (Zimmer), Comédie des Champs-Élysées, Paris; acted Bava.

Deux Paires d'amis (Bost), Comédie des Champs-Élysées, Paris.

Le Carrosse du Saint-Sacrement (Mérimée), Comédie des Champs-Élysées, Paris; acted L'Évêque de Lima.

Le Dictateur (Romains), Comédie des Champs-Élysées, Paris.

Outward Bound (Vane, translated by Verola), Comédie des Champs-Élysées, Paris; acted Tom Prior.

1927 *The Inspector General* (Gogol, translated by Choumanski and Delacre), Comédie des Champs-Élysées, Paris; acted Klestakoff.

Léopold le Bien-aimé (Sarment), tour; acted Léopold.

1928 *Le Coup du deux Décembre* (Zimmer), Comédie des Champs-Élysées, Paris; acted M. Lèbre.

Siegfried (Giraudoux), tour; acted Général de Fontgeloy, Zelten.

1929 *Suzanne* (Passeur), Comédie des Champs-Élysées, Paris; acted Cretai.

Jean de la Lune (Achard), Comédie des Champs-Élysées, Paris; acted Jef.

Amphitryon 38 (Giraudoux), tour; acted Mercure.

1930 *Le Prof d'Anglais* (Gignoux), tour; acted Valfine.

Donogoo-Tonka (Romains), Théâtre Pigalle, Paris.

1931 *Le Médecin malgré lui* (Molière), tour; acted Sganarelle.

L'Eau fraîche (La Rochelle), Comédie des Champs-Élysées, Paris; acted Thomas.

Un Taciturne (Du Gard), Comédie des Champs-Élysées, Paris; acted Armand.

Judith (Giraudoux), tour; acted Le Garde.

Le Roi masqué (Romains), Théâtre Pigalle, Paris.

1932 *Domino* (Achard), Comédie des Champs-Élysées, Paris; acted Domino.

La Pâtissière du village (Savoir), Théâtre Pigalle, Paris.

La Margrave (Savoir), Comédie des Champs-Élysées, Paris; acted Le Margrave.

1933 *Intermezzo* (Giraudoux), Comédie des Champs-Élysées, Paris; acted Le Contrôleur.

Pétrus (Achard), Comédie des Champs-Élysées, Paris; acted Pétrus.

1934 *La Machine infernale* (Cocteau), Comédie des Champs-Élysées, Paris; acted Le Berger de Laïus.

Tessa (Kennedy and Dean, adapted by Giraudoux), Athénée Théâtre Louis Jouvet, Paris; acted Lewis Dodd.

1935 *La Guerre de troie n'aura pas lieu* (Giraudoux), Athénée Théâtre Louis Jouvet, Paris; acted Hector.

Supplément au voyage de Cook (Giraudoux), Athénée Théâtre Louis Jouvet, Paris; acted Outourou.

1936 *L'École des femmes* (Molière), Athénée Théâtre Louis Jouvet, Paris; acted Arnolphe.

1937 *Le Château de Cartes* (Passeur), Athénée Théâtre Louis Jouvet, Paris.

L'Illusion (P. Corneille), Comédie-Française, Paris.

Electre (Giraudoux), Athénée Théâtre Louis Jouvet, Paris; acted Le Mendiant.

L'Impromptu de Paris (Giraudoux), Athénée Théâtre Louis Jouvet, Paris; acted Jouvet.

1938 *Le Corsaire* (Achard), Athénée Théâtre Louis Jouvet, Paris; acted Frank O'Hara and Kid Jackson.

Cantique des cantiques (Giraudoux), Comédie-Française, Paris.

Tricolore (Lestringuez), Comédie-Française, Paris.

1939 *Ondine* (Giraudoux), Athénée Théâtre Louis Jouvet, Paris; acted Chevalier Hans.

1941 *La Coupe enchantée* (La Fontaine and Champmeslé), Rio de Janeiro; acted Josselin.

Je Vivrai un grand amour (Passeur), Buenos Aires; acted Modeste.

1942 *On ne Badine pas avec l'amour* (Musset), Rio de Janeiro; acted Blazius.

L'Apollon de Marsac (Giraudoux), Rio de Janeiro; acted M. de Marsac.

L'Annonce faite à Marie (Claudel), Rio de Janeiro; acted Anne Vercors.

Le Médecin malgré lui (Molière), Rio de Janeiro; acted Sganarelle.

L'Occasion (Mérimée), Rio de Janeiro; acted Fray Eugénio.

La Belle au bois (Supervielle), Rio de Janeiro; acted Barbe Bleue.

Le Misanthrope (Molière), Buenos Aires; acted Philinte and Jouvet.

1945   *La Folle de Chaillot* (Giraudoux), Athénée Théâtre Louis Jouvet, Paris; acted Le Chiffonier.

1946   *L'Annonce faite à Marie* (Claudel), Athénée Théâtre Louis Jouvet, Paris; acted Anne Vercors.

1947   *L'Apollon de Marsac* (Giraudoux), Athénée Théâtre Louis Jouvet, Paris; acted M. de Marsac.

Les Bonnes (Genet), Athénée Théâtre Louis Jouvet, Paris.

Don Juan ou Le Festin de Pierre (Molière), Athénée Théâtre Louis Jouvet, Paris; acted Don Juan.

1949   *Les Fourberies de Scapin* (Molière), Théâtre Marigny, Paris; acted Géronte.

1950   *Le Tartuffe* (Molière), Athénée Théâtre Louis Jouvet, Paris; acted Tartuffe.

1951   *Le Diable et la bon Dieu* (Sartre), Théâtre Antoine, Paris.

Homage to Jean Giraudoux (compilation), Théâtre Bellac, Paris; acted Le Controleur, M. de Marsac, and Hans.

Films

Topaz, 1933; *Knock*, 1933; *Le Kermesse héroïque*, 1935; *Mister Flow*, 1936; *Les Bas-fonds*, 1936; *Mademoiselle docteur*, 1937; *Un Carnet de bal*, 1937; *Drôle de drame*, 1937; *Alibi*, 1937; *La Marseillaise*, 1937–38; *Ramuntcho*, 1937–38; *La Maison du Maltais*, 1938; *Entrée des artistes*, 1938; *Education de Prince*, 1938; *Le Drame à Shanghai*, 1938; *Hôtel du Nord*, 1938; *La Fin du jour*, 1939; *La Charrette fantôme*, 1939; *Volpone*, 1939–40; *Un Tel Père et fils*, 1940; *Sérénade*, 1940; *Un Revenant*, 1946; *Copie conforme*, 1940; *Quai des Orfèvres*, 1947; *Les Amoureux sont seuls au monde*, 1948; *Entre onze heures et minuit*, 1948–49; *Retour à la vie*, 1949; *Miquette et sa mère*, 1949; *Lady Paname*, 1949; *Knock*, 1950; *Une Histoire d'amour*, 1951.

Publications

Réflexions du Comédien, 1938; *Prestige et perspectives du théâtre français*, 1945; *Témoignages sur le théâtre*, 1952; *Le Comédien désincarné*, 1954.

*

Bibliography

Books:
Claude Cézan, *Louis Jouvet et le théâtre d'aujourd'hui*, Paris, 1948.
Valentin Marquetty, *Mon Ami Jouvet*, Paris, 1952.
Bettina Liebowitz Knapp, *Louis Jouvet, Man of the Theatre*, New York, 1957.
Wanda Kérien, *Louis Jouvet, notre patron*, Paris, 1963.
Léo Lapara, *Dix Ans avec Jouvet*, Paris, 1975.
Jean-Marc Loubier, *Louis Jouvet: Biographie*, Paris, 1986.
Paul-Louis Mignon, *Louis Jouvet: qui etes-vous?*, Lyon, 1988.

* * *

Louis Jouvet's career began in earnest in 1913 with the creation of the Vieux-Colombier by Jacques Copeau. He became Copeau's right-hand man, as actor, designer (of sets, costumes, and lights), stage manager, technician (he invented a multi-coloured spot, the "jouvet"), and architect (he designed the stages for the Garrick Theatre, New York, in 1917, for the Vieux-Colombier, 1919, and for his own theatre at the Studio des Champs-Élysées, 1923). After 1924 he devoted most of his time to acting and directing. He also starred in some 24 films, mainly in order to keep his company afloat, although he acquired star status with such films as *Quai des Orfèvres* and *Entrée des artistes*.

At first Jouvet staged fashionable contemporary playwrights, in particular Jules Romains, whose *Knock* became an instant success that Jouvet milked at the rate of 50 performances a year, in Paris and on tour, throughout his life. But, in 1928, his encounter with Jean Giraudoux changed the course of his artistic career. The seminal production of *Siegfried* in 1928 marked the beginning of an exceptional collaboration between the playwright and the director. They shared a passion for "the beauty of the word"; they agreed that a profound and "affective communication" between actors and spectators is necessarily mediated by the playwright's unique style. As Giraudoux's texts were not immediately "stageable" and tended to be over-written and too precious, Jouvet had to inject a strong theatrical quality into the playwright's creations. Giraudoux welcomed the director's collaboration and used to say that he had two muses: Thalia, who inspired him before the writing, and Jouvet, who gave life to his characters. Jouvet directed all 13 plays by Giraudoux, five of which (*Amphitryon 38*, *La Guerre de troie n'aura pas lieu*, *Intermezzo*, *Electre*, and *Ondine*) are arguably the greatest achievements of French theatre during the inter-war years.

Jouvet's other favourite dramatist was Molière, whom he rescued from the doldrums of stultifying tradition. In 1936, having moved to the Théâtre de l'Athénée, he directed a playful and youthful *École des femmes*, with the complicity of his designer Christian Bérard. His *Don Juan* in 1947, with an initial run of 200 performances, rehabilitated a masterpiece that had been neglected for 300 years and offered a new approach to Molière's "grand comedies", away from slapstick towards serious drama with tragic overtones. For Jouvet, Don Juan was no featherbrained womanizer, but a blasphemous Spanish grandee who, like Faustus, challenges divine order. Bérard's lavish baroque sets and costumes and Jouvet's profound reading and authoritative interpretation appealed to audiences. But a similar reappraisal of *Tartuffe* in 1951, with its devilishly seductive hypocrite, failed to please. These productions opened the way for ever more radical directors in the following decades, among them Vilar, Planchon, Sobel, Chéreau, and Bondy. After the war Jouvet directed, without conviction, Genet's *Les Bonnes* and Sartre's *Le Diable et le bon Dieu*.

In 1934 Jouvet began teaching at the celebrated Conservatoire, the acting school of the Comédie-Française, where he had auditioned unsuccessfully three times in his youth. He proved to be a passionate and inspirational teacher, both with his actors and his students, and his example shaped the actors of the future generation. Although preaching absolute fidelity to the text — for actors and directors — he warned against too much intellectualization. He always maintained that he had no opinion on a text or a role, no guiding principle or concept for a mise en scène: actors and directors must never indulge in idle speculations because working in the theatre is a purely practical activity. Understanding his role, for an actor, is not a question of intelligence but of feeling.

Jouvet was also at the heart of the debate on cultural policy. In 1919, when Copeau reopened the Vieux-Colombier, only four stages were state-subsidized in France (the Comédie-Française, the Odéon, the Opéra, and the Opéra-Comique — all in Paris). Art theatres, as well as commercial houses, depended on box office (and the occasional private donation). During the early 1920's, after Copeau had retired to Burgundy, four Parisian directors (Gaston Baty of the Studio Champs-Élysées, Charles Dullin of the Atelier, Jouvet of the Comédie des Champs-Élysées, and Georges Pitoëff of the Mathurins), who were pursuing similar artistic goals — namely the promotion of the best classical and contemporary playwrights, both French and foreign, in well-rehearsed productions — signed an agreement of solidarity on 6 July 1927. Known as the "Cartel des Quatre", the association aimed at harmonizing programmes, publicity, tours, and on occasion casting. The associates also resolved to help and defend each other "whenever professional or moral interests are at stake". They shared Antoine's and Copeau's belief that directing, based on the highest dramatic writing, is the real foundation of the art of theatre. The Cartel achieved official recognition when, in 1936, Jouvet, Dullin, Baty — and their mentor Copeau (but not Pitoëff because he was not French) — were invited to direct at the Comédie-Française.

After the war, on his return from Latin America, Jouvet turned down the artistic directorship of the Comédie-Française, but he joined Dullin in his efforts to promote the idea of "decentralization". Two days before his death, he was appointed to the Ministry of Culture as special adviser on theatre and decentralization.

Jouvet, as actor, teacher, and director, was a living illustration of Diderot's paradox: he used to say that the actor needs "a cool head and a warm heart" and must always accept that "he will never *be* Alceste. He plays the role of Alceste, he is not Alceste." And to play Alceste, or any other part of Molière (or any dramatist), as the playwright wrote it, the actor must learn the words and speak them, over and over again, until he achieves "absolute authenticity". Jouvet's legacy is perhaps best captured in his advice, oft repeated to his actors: "Don't act; say the words".

—Claude Schumacher

K

KACHALOV, Vasili (Ivanovich). Soviet actor. Born Vasili Ivanovich Shverubovich in Vilnius, Lithuania, 30 January 1875. Educated at the University of St Petersburg, 1893–95. Stage debut, A. S. Suvorin Theatre, St Petersburg, 1896; worked with the M. M. Borodai company in Kazan and Saratov, 1897–1900; joined Moscow Art Theatre, 1900, and remained with the company for the rest of his career; led group of Art Theatre actors in Eastern Europe during Russian Civil War, 1919–22; toured Europe with Moscow Art Theatre, 1922–24; made one film appearance, 1928. Recipient: State Prize of the Soviet Union, 1943; two Orders of Lenin; Order of the Red Banner of Labour. People's Artist of USSR, 1936. Died in Moscow, 30 September 1948.

Roles

1897   Boris Godunov in *Smert Ioanna grotznogo* [The Death of Ivan the Terrible] (A. Tolstoy), Suvorin's Theatre, St Petersburg.

Mitya in *Bednost ne porok* [Poverty is No Crime] (Ostrovsky), Suvorin's Theatre, St Petersburg.

Dudukin in *Bezvinny vinovatye* [More Sinned Against Than Sinning] (Ostrovsky), Suvorin's Theatre, St Petersburg.

1898   Tsar Fyodor Ioannovich in *Tsar Fyodor Ioannovich* (A. Tolstoy), Suvorin's Theatre, St Petersburg.

1900   Cassius in *Iulii Tsezar* [Julius Caesar] (Shakespeare), provinces.

Horatio in *Hamlet* (Shakespeare), provinces.

Berendei in *Snegurochka* [The Snow Maiden] (Ostrovsky), Art Theatre, Moscow.

1902   Tuzenbakh in *Tri sestery* [The Three Sisters] (Chekhov), Art Theatre, Moscow.

The Baron in *Na dne* [The Lower Depths] (Gorky), Art Theatre, Moscow.

1903   Johannes Vockerat in *Einsame Menschen* (Hauptmann), Art Theatre, Moscow.

Julius Caesar in *Iulii Tsezar* [Julius Caesar] (Shakespeare), Art Theatre, Moscow.

1904   Petia Trofimov in *Vishnevy sad* [The Cherry Orchard] (Chekhov), Art Theatre, Moscow.

Ivanov in *Ivanov* (Chekhov), Art Theatre, Moscow.

1905   Protasov in *Deti solntsa* [Children of the Sun] (Gorky), Art Theatre, Moscow.

1906   Brand in *Brand* (Ibsen), Art Theatre, Moscow.

Chatsky in *Gore ot Uma* [Woe from Wit] (Griboyedov), Art Theatre, Moscow; revived there, 1914, 1938.

1908   Ivar Kareno in *Ved Rigets Port* [At the Gates of the Kingdom] (Hamsun), Art Theatre, Moscow.

1910   Glumov in *Na vsyakogo dovolno prostoty* [Even a Wise Man Stumbles] (Ostrovsky), Art Theatre, Moscow.

Ivan Karamazov in *Bratja Karamazovy* [The Brothers Karamazov] (Dostoevsky, adapted by Nemirovich-Danchenko), Art Theatre, Moscow.

1911   Karenin in *Zhivoy trup* [The Living Corpse] (L. Tolstoy), Art Theatre, Moscow.

Hamlet in *Hamlet* (Shakespeare), Art Theatre, Moscow.

1912   Gorsky in *Gde tonko, tam i rvetsya* [Where it's Thin, There it Tears] (Turgenev), Art Theatre, Moscow.

1913   Stavrogin in *Nikolai Stavrogin* (Dostoevsky, adapted by Nemirovich-Danchenko), Art Theatre, Moscow.

1915   Don Juan in *Kammeny gost* [The Stone Guest] (Pushkin), Art Theatre, Moscow.

1922–24   Gaev in *Vishnevy sad* [The Cherry Orchard] (Chekhov), European and US tour.

Stockman in *En folkefiende* [An Enemy of the People] (Ibsen), European and US tour.

1926   Nicholas I in *Nicholas I and the Decembrists* (Kugel), Art Theatre, Moscow.

1927   Nikita Vershinin in *Bronepoezd 14–69* [Armoured Train 14–69] (Ivanov), Art Theatre, Moscow.

1928   Artiom Aladyn in *Blokus* [Blockade] (Ivanov), Art Theatre, Moscow.

1930   The Author in *Voskreseniye* [Resurrection] (L. Tolstoy, adapted by Nemirovich-Danchenko), Art Theatre, Moscow.

1930–35   Narokov in *Talanty i poklonniki* [Artists and Admirers] (Ostrovsky), Art Theatre, Moscow.

1935   Zakhar Bardin in *Vragi* [Enemies] (Gorky), Art Theatre, Moscow.

Films

Belyj orël [The White Eagle], 1928.

* * *

405

Vasili Kachalov

Vasili Kachalov began his career in radical student groups in St Petersburg and learned his craft on the provincial stage. When he auditioned at Nemirovich-Danchenko's invitation for the Moscow Art Theatre in March 1900 in the roles of Boris Godunov and Ivan the Terrible in *The Death of Ivan the Terrible* he made an unfavourable impression, not because of lack of talent but because of his personality. Stanislavsky found him actorish and conceited and suggested tactfully that he might not be able to adapt to the Art Theatre's methods and that he might be difficult to cast. Nemirovich, characteristically, was more blunt and told Kachalov he was not wanted. Knipper also confirmed the bad impression Kachalov had made. Nonetheless, Kachalov elected to stay and spent the next two months watching rehearsals and absorbing the company's methods. It was a wise decision. Stanislavsky was having great difficulty in casting the role of King Berendei in Ostrovsky's *The Snow Maiden*. In desperation, he turned to Kachalov, who successfully convinced him that he had learned to put his talent at the service of the ensemble. The production was a failure, but Stanislavsky begged the actor not to be discouraged and they established a close relationship that lasted until Stanislavsky's death in 1938.

Just how valuable an addition Kachalov was to the theatre is evident from the roles he played. Apart from Stanislavsky, who essentially saw him as a character actor, the company did not possess a leading man in the classic sense of the term. Kachalov fitted the bill perfectly. He was tall, handsome, with a good physique and expressive hands. He conveyed, as Knipper described him, a sense of intelligence, sensitivity of feeling and subtlety of mind. During his first ten years he created major roles in plays by Chekhov, Gorky and Turgenev and also appeared in dramas by Shakespeare, Ibsen and Dostoevsky.

Kacholov is best remembered internationally for his performance as Hamlet in the Craig/Stanislavsky production of 1911. Craig originally wanted Stanislavsky to take the role, but he rightly judged that the part had to be played off personality and that Kachalov was ideal. Kachalov was extremely resistant to Craig's approach to the play. He was not comfortable with any form of stylization, but was happier when Stanislavsky took complete charge of the production during Craig's absence. The stenographic records of the rehearsals demonstrate how crucial a role Stanislavsky took in shaping the part and saving Kachalov from the standard clichés of 'classical' acting.

Kachalov's relationship with the Art Theatre was not always unclouded. He would become restless and impatient with the absence of new roles. Rehearsal periods at the Art Theatre were becoming longer and, with unavoidable delays, *Hamlet* was three years in preparation. Yet his loyalty to Stanislavsky kept him in the company. He avoided any responsibilities outside those of an actor and kept apart from the bitter internal battle that set Stanislavsky against Nemirovich but remained true to the former, staging an angry walk-out at one shareholders' meeting in 1911 when he suspected there were moves to squeeze Stanislavsky out of the theatre. Management responsibilities were, however, thrust upon him in 1919 during the Civil War. Part of the company, including Knipper, were cut off from Moscow by the hostilities and spent the next three years touring Eastern Europe. They came to be known as the 'Kachalov Group'. Understandably, perhaps, they were reluctant to return to Russia, where living conditions were harsh and the Art Theatre was under constant attack, but relented so as to allow the Art Theatre's tour of western Europe and the USA to go ahead as planned.

Kachalov proved that he could adapt to the new Soviet society with his appearance in 1927 in Ivanov's *Armoured Train 14–67*, in which for the first time he played a proletarian role, Vershinin, a politically indifferent peasant who becomes a heroic partisan in the Civil War. He was, in his own estimate, less successful in the role of Artiom Aladyn in another revolutionary play, *Blackade*, the following year.

During the 1930's he played fewer new roles. In 1938 he won further plaudits when he recreated the role of Chatsky in *Woe from Wit*, despite the fact that at 63 he was much too old to play a rebellious young man. As Stanislavsky wrote to him in 1935, he had such charm he could get away with anything.

Kachalov never lost the pleasure in being an actor. In 1923 Lee Strasberg had the opportunity to see both Stanislavsky and Kochalov play Vershinin in *The Three Sisters*. While, according to Strasberg, Stanislavsky *was* Vershinin, he could sense the actor behind Kachalov's superlative performance. Kachalov, one suspects, enjoyed acting in a way Stanislavsky was never able to. Questioned about his acting, he made a clear distinction between himself as an individual and the roles he played. He did not become the character until he entered the theatre and stopped being it the moment he left. He never mistook the world of the stage for the real world and never lost himself in the character he was playing. At the same time he fully subscribed to the notion that a role must be 'experienced' each time rather than 'presented'. He was, however, careful to distinguish between emotion experienced in life, in response to actual situations, and emotion on stage, which was created through imagination and recall — a distinction inherent in the Stanislavsky system but often forgotten. He stressed the creative pleasure an actor can take, in performance, in the emotions as they arise. He also took account of the audience's reaction. He fully accepted the notion of the actor's divided consciousness.

—Jean Benedetti

KAINZ, Josef. Austrian actor. Born in Wieselburg, Austria, 2 January 1858. Stage debut, Marburg, 1875; subsequently acted in Leipzig, 1876, and joined the Meiningen Company, 1877–80; actor, Munich Court Theatre, 1880–83; invited by Adolf L'Arronge to become a founding member of the Deutsches Theater, Berlin, 1883; also appeared at the Berliner Theater, 1888, and subsequently made successful tour of the USA; finally resigned as leading actor of the Deutsches Theater, 1899, and joined the Burgtheater, Vienna, where he remained for the rest of his career. Died in Vienna, 20 September 1910.

Principal roles

1878–80	Ferdinand in *Kabale und Liebe* (Schiller), Meiningen Court Theatre.
	Kosinsky in *Die Räuber* (Schiller), Meiningen Court Theatre.
	Prince von Homburg in *Prinz von Homburg* (Kleist), Meiningen Court Theatre.
1883–90	Don Carlos in *Don Carlos* (Schiller), Deutsches Theater, Berlin.
	Romeo in *Romeo und Juliet* (Shakespeare), Deutsches Theater, Berlin.
	Hamlet in *Hamlet* (Shakespeare), Deutsches Theater, Berlin.
	Alfons in *Die Jüdin von Toledo* (Grillparzer), Deutsches Theater, Berlin.
	Franz Moor in *Die Räuber* (Schiller), Deutsches Theater, Berlin.
	Mephistopheles in *Faust* (Goethe), Deutsches Theater, Berlin.
	Mortimer in *Maria Stuart* (Schiller), Deutsches Theater, Berlin.
	Leon in *Weh dem, der lügt* (Grillparzer), Deutsches Theater, Berlin.
	Oswald in *Gespenster* (Ibsen), Lessing-Theater, Berlin.
1890	Wilhelm in *Das Friedenfest* (Hauptmann), Freie Bühne, Ostendtheater, Berlin.
1894	Wurm in *Kabale und Liebe* (Schiller), Deutsches Theater, Berlin.
1896	Heinrich in *Die versunken Glocke* (Hauptmann), Deutsches Theater, Berlin.
	Fritzchen in *Fritzchen* (Sudermann), Burgtheater, Vienna.
1899–1910	Richard II in *Richard II* (Shakespeare), Burgtheater, Vienna.
	Tasso in *Torquato Tasso* (Goethe), Burgtheater, Vienna.

Other roles included: Cyrano in *Cyrano de Bergerac* (Rostand); Ernest in *Galeotto* (Echegaray); Mark Antony in *Julius Caesar* (Shakespeare); Tartuffe in *Tartuffe* (Molière); and roles in *The Winter's Tale* (Shakespeare), 1878; *Morituri* (Sudermann), 1896; *Sardanapal* (Lord Byron), 1897; *Barbier von Sevilla* (Beaumarchais), 1907.

Publications

Briefe von Josef Kainz, 1922.

*

Bibliography

Books:
F. Gregory, *Josef Kainz*, Berlin and Leipzig, 1904.
Julius Bab, *Was ist uns Kainz?*, Berlin and Leipzig, 1905.
Hermann Bahr, *Josef Kainz*, Vienna, 1905.
P. Wilhelm, *Josef Kainz und das Burgtheater*, 1910.
Eugen Isolani, *Josef Kainz, ein Lebensbild*, Berlin, 1910.
Hermann Bang, *Josef Kainz*, Berlin, 1910.
Otto Brahm, *Josef Kainz: Geschehenes und Erlebtes*, Berlin, 1910.
B. Deutsch, *Josef Kainz — Gedenkbuch*, Vienna, 1924.
Helene Richter, *Kainz*, Vienna and Leipzig, 1930.
Paul Wiegler, *Josef Kainz: Ein Genius in seinen Verwandlungen*, Berlin, 1941.
Erich Kober, *Josef Kainz: Mensch unter Masken*, Vienna, 1948.
Marie Mautner-Kalbeck, *Kainz*, Bremen, 1953.

* * *

Josef Kainz, whose career as an actor spanned the period from the detailed concrete realism practised by the Meiningen Court Theatre to the symbolic and poetic drama of the early 20th century, was an almost exact contemporary of the major contributors to naturalist theatre in Germany, the dramatist Gerhart Hauptmann and the theatre director Otto Brahm. Although he worked for and with both of them, he was unlike them in that his talents were not readily accommodated to the dominant style of the 1890's. At times, he has been seen as the last offshoot of the 19th-century style of great individualist acting; at others he has been regarded as the theatrical representative par excellence of fin de siècle aestheticism for, although he secured considerable fame before the turn of the century, it was only after he achieved his personal ambition in the form of an engagement at Vienna's Burgtheater in 1899 that he finally established his reputation and was fêted for his modernity by writers such as Hermann Bahr, Hermann Bang and Hugo von Hofmannsthal.

Kainz joined the Meiningen company as a raw but ambitious young actor in 1877. In this well-drilled and strongly directed company that was lacking in individual talents he clearly stood out as an exceptionally promising actor and was recognised as such by Duke Georg and, especially, his wife Ellen Franz. From the outset he was

Josef Kainz as Hamlet.

entrusted with important parts and figured prominently in the 1878 tour to Berlin in *The Winter's Tale*, Schiller's *The Robbers* and Kleist's *The Prince of Homburg*. Thanks largely to Kainz's interpretation, in which he dared to show a Prussian prince and officer in a state of abject fear of death, this latter production was an object of much contentious debate. It did not win Kainz admiration, but it made him known.

After an engagement of three years in Munich, during which time he enjoyed a short period as a favourite of King Ludwig II of Bavaria, Kainz moved to the newly opened Deutsches Theater in Berlin. Here he rapidly developed the promise he had first shown in the Meiningen production of *The Prince of Homburg* in such roles as Romeo, Ferdinand in Schiller's *Kabale und Liebe*, Mortimer in *Maria Stuart* and, above all, Carlos in Schiller's *Don Carlos*. Kainz became totally absorbed by these parts, all of which bring a young man into passionate conflict with order and authority, with a particular intensity, exploring the extremes of the emotional range with a nervous energy and instability that was new to the German theatre. It was this aspect of his playing that was recognised as particularly 'modern' by his admirers, as exaggerated and mannered by his detractors.

Among his admirers the most important at this time was Otto Brahm, who early on identified him as a potential Oswald in an ideally cast *Ghosts*, and then, after he had taken the role of Wilhelm in the Freie Bühne production of Hauptmann's *Das Friedenfest* (*The Celebration of Peace*), steered Kainz further towards contemporary drama by recruiting him for his company when he took control of the

Deutsches Theater in 1894. Brahm's plans to produce modern interpretations of classic dramas received a setback with the failure of his opening production of *Kabale und Liebe* (1894), in which Kainz played not the emotional Ferdinand but the calculating Wurm. In the short term this meant a setback for Kainz's career, for his particular gift was perceived as his ability to use characters from the dramas of the past as vessels for the anxieties of modern man. With Brahm he did achieve a number of successes in modern works, notably as Heinrich in Hauptmann's poetic drama *Die versunken Glocke* (*The Sunken Bell*), but Brahm was distrustful of Kainz's technical virtuosity, preferring the more restrained, untheatrical style of Emanuel Reicher and Rudolf Rittner; while Kainz himself became increasingly resistant to the restrictions imposed by the demands of mimetic naturalism. Kainz, along with Agnes Sorma, was left to perform in the classic side of the repertoire of the Deutsches Theater, which Brahm left to his assistants to direct.

In Vienna, after 1899, Kainz the mature actor finally came into his own, developing the youthful roles with which he had become identified and extending his range and reputation with memorable interpretations of Hamlet, Richard II, Goethe's Tasso and Grillparzer's Alfons. In the more congenial atmosphere of the Austrian capital, with its openly theatrical culture, Kainz came to be regarded as more than a performing artist; he began during these last years to be seen as a creative artist, and was invested with the creative artist's transformative powers in a poem written on his death by one of his greatest admirers, the poet and dramatist Hugo von Hofmannsthal.

—John Osborne

KANTOR, Tadeusz. Polish director, designer, actor and painter. Born in Wielopole, near Cracow, Poland, 6 April 1915. Educated at the Academy of Fine Arts, Cracow, 1934–39. Married Maria Stangret-Kantor in 1960. Founded underground Independent Theatre during the Nazi Occupation, 1942; worked as designer and director at the Teatr Stary, Cracow, 1945–55; professor, Academy of Fine Arts, Cracow, 1948–49, 1968–69; founder, Teatr Cricot 2, Cracow, 1956; staged series of 'happenings', from 1966; regularly visited France and other countries with the Cricot 2 company, from 1971; also visited Edinburgh, Rome and Shiraz. Member: Association of Polish Plastic Artists. Recipient: Prize for Painting, Sao Paolo, 1967; Premio Marzotto, Rome, 1968; Edinburgh Festival First Prize, 1976; Rembrandt Prize, 1978; Grand Prix, Théâtre des Nations, Caracas, 1978; Obie Award, 1979, 1982; Minister of Culture and Art First Prize, 1981; Diploma of Minister of Foreign Affairs, 1982. Commander's Cross, Order of Polonia Resituta, 1982. Died in Cracow, 8 December 1990.

Productions

As director:
1942   *Balladyna* (Słowacki), Independent Theatre, Cracow.
1944   *Powrót Odysa* [The Return of Odysseus] (Wyspiański), Independent Theatre, Cracow.

1955	*Matwa; czyli, Hyrkaniczny światopogląd* [The Cuttlefish] (Witkiewicz), Teatr Cricot 2, Cracow.
1956	*La zapatera prodigiosa* (Garcia Lorca), Teatr Cricot 2, Cracow.
1957	*Circus* (Mikulski), Teatr Cricot 2, Cracow.
1961	*W ma łym dworku* [In a Small Country House] (Witkiewicz), Teatr Cricot 2, Cracow.
1963	*Wariat i zakonnica* [The Madman and the Nun] (Witkiewicz), Teatr Cricot 2, Cracow. *Chandelier* (Musset), Teatr Stary, Cracow.
1966	*W ma łym dworku* [In a Small Country House] (Witkiewicz), Baden-Baden.
1968	*Kurka wodna* [The Water Hen] (Witkiewicz), Teatr Cricot 2, Cracow; Rome, Modena and Bologna, 1969; World Theatre Festival, Nancy, 1971; Paris and Edinburgh Festival, 1972.
1972	*Szewcy* [The Shoemakers] (Witkiewicz), Théâtre de Malakoff, Paris.
1973	*Nabodnisie i koczkodany* [*Dainty Shapes and Hairy Apes/Lovelies and Dowdies*] (Witkiewicz), Teatr Cricot 2, Cracow, and Edinburgh Festival; Rome, Théâtre National de Chaillot, Paris, Nancy, Shiraz and Essen, 1974.
1975	*The Dead Class* (Kantor), Teatr Cricot 2, Cracow; Edinburgh Festival, National Theatre, Cardiff and Riverside Studio, London, 1976; world tour, 1977–79.
1980	*Wielopole, Wielopole* (Kantor), Florence, Edinburgh Festival, Riverside Studio, London, Théâtre des Bouffes du Nord, Paris, Cracow and Gdansk; world tour, 1981.
1982	*Where are the Snows of Yesteryear?* (Kantor), Teatr Cricot 2, Cracow.
1985	*Let the Artists Die* (Kantor), Nuremberg.
1988	*Je Ne Reviendrai Jamais* (Kantor), Centre Pompidou, Paris.
1990	*Oh Gentle Night* (Kantor), Paris. *Aujourd'hui, c'est mon anniversaire* (Kantor), Teatr Cricot 2, Cracow.

As designer:

1945	*Le Cid* (P. Corneille), Theatr Stary, Cracow.
1946	*The Scales have Fallen from Our Eyes* (Karczewska), Theatr Stary, Cracow.
1954	*Saint Joan* (G. B. Shaw), Theatr Stary, Cracow.
1955	*Measure for Measure* (Shakespeare), Theatr Ludowy, Cracow.
1957	*Antigone* (Anouilh), Theatr Stary, Cracow.
1961	*Rhinoceros* (Ionesco), Theatr Stary, Cracow.
1962	*Don Quixote* (Cervantes), Theatr Stary, Cracow.

Publications

Teatr Śmierci [The Theatre of Death], 1976.

*

Bibliography

Books:
Jan Kott, *The Theatre of Essence*, Evanston, 1984.

* * *

Theatre, for Tadeusz Kantor, was "an activity that occurs when life is pushed to its final limits where all categories and concepts lose their meaning and right to exist, where madness, fever, hysteria and hallucinations are life's last barricades before the approaching troupes of death and its grand theatre". This definition (1980) of theatre as a praxis that takes place in the space of convergence between life and death, can be viewed as the Polish director's response to the modern theatre, which, for him, was grounded in a temporal, ideological discourse. Already in the early 1960's, Kantor rejected the idea of theatre as a public forum and substituted it for theatre as a work of art that constantly acquires new thought dimensions in the process of suppressing illusionistic effects and establishing the priority of the most simple and primitive objects ('objects of low rank').

In its relationship with life, art/theatre functions thus as an analogous or simultaneous rather than reflective structure. Kantor achieved this parallel relationship by destroying the demarcation line between those spaces reserved for stage action and those for spectators. In *The Return of Odysseus*, for example, Kantor placed the audience in a room of a house partially destroyed by the war. This method of breaking theatrical illusion fully emerged in his 'Theatre of Nullification', or 'Zero Theatre' (1963), wherein Kantor evoked negative emotions such as apathy, melancholy and depression by emphasizing 'non-acting', 'surreptitious acting', 'erasing', 'automation' and 'acting under duress'. These 'negative' emotions were employed onstage in order to destroy a traditional dramaturgy grounded in the passions, heroism, conflict, violent reactions and cause-and-effect patterns of traditional plot development.

The 1967 'Theory of a Theatre of Real Space/Theatre Happening' (*The Water Hen*), the 1972 'Impossible Theatre' (*Dainty Shapes and Hairy Apes*), the 1980 'Theatre of Death' (*The Dead Class*), the 1980 'Inn of Memory' (*Wielopole, Wielopole*), the 1985 'Theory of Negatives' (*Let the Artists Die*) and the 1986 'Theory of Hyperspace' (*I Shall Never Return*), mark subsequent stages in Kantor's journey within the boundaries of what Jan Kott calls the 'Theatre of Essence'.

All these theories emphasized the rupture between the traditional and Kantor's theatre, and, as the subsequent productions indicated, were the extension, the elaboration or even the rejection of previously accepted tenets concerning theatrical illusions of space, text, character and time.

The 'Theatre of Real Space' postulates that, during a performance, the actors ought to perform activities and characters in a way that is imposed upon them by the reality of the space and its characteristics. In the 'Theatre of Death', which revealed metaphysical aspects of his theatre, Kantor suggested that a performance was a moment of approaching the border line between life and death. Thus, the present time of the performance is only a self-consistent point of convergence of the past (life) and the future (death). In the *The Dead Class*, old men and woman return to school from the realm of death. They carry with them wax figures of children in school uniforms, a symbol of artistic creation, debased reality and an embodiment of past events or life after death. The 'Inn of Memory' forces the audience to abandon logical analysis and rational thinking for the immaterial memory. Memory is the door to one's imagination, which exists in a different dimension. In the room behind that door, the 'dead', the members of Kantor's family, come to life and populate the 'real'/stage world. In *Wielopole, Wielopole*, the characters who appear on stage, "these dead facades come to life, become real and important through the stubborn repetition of action". They build three-dimensional pictures out of frequently repeated gestures of everyday reality (washing of feet, card playing, lovemaking, praying, travelling, dying, etc.), which create the fabric of the production. The 'Theory of Negatives' can be viewed as an extension of the 'Inn of Memory'. Here, events onstage bring forth and join 'memories', that is, characters, from different past events. These 'memories' cannot be presented in a linear or chronological order because such a representation would not correspond to the process taking place in the mind. Rather, the memories onstage are interimposed as if they were the frames of a film-negative stacked one atop another. Since the negatives are transparent, the audience sees only one frame, but this one frame contains all the elements of all the other frames. The image onstage is thus the image of characters undergoing constant transformation in a space that is alternately expanding or shrinking. In *Let the Artists Die*, one of the recognisable characters on stage is Veit Stoss, a 15th-century sculptor, who was the author of a famous altarpiece in one of Cracow's churches. As various historical records indicate, a nail was driven through Stoss's cheeks as a punishment for his debts. Kantor uses this story as a metaphor for the artist in society. In the 'Room of Memory', that is, *Let the Artists Die*, Kantor created for Veit Stoss, a guest from the other side, an asylum for beggars, Bohemian artists and cutthroats, where Stoss builds the altar that resembles his masterpiece in Cracow. But in a world governed by the 'Theory of Negatives', the altar is transformed into a prison cell and the characters in the asylum become the convicts of the apocalyptic theatre of death. The 'Theory of Hyperspace' focused on the space where all these transformations are taking place.

Space, for Kantor, was not a passive receptacle in which objects and forms are created. Rather, space is energy, which shrinks and expands, which moulds forms and objects posited in it. Thus, it is space that conditions the network of relations and tensions between the objects. Tension is the principal actor of space — a hyperspace. In *I Shall Never Return*, unlike in other productions, Kantor (who was always present on stage during every performance to correct the actors' work) was a true participant in the transformations of the theatrical space. In *I Shall Never Return*, the characters from the past productions keep interrupting Kantor's monologue by asking questions about his life. They do not understand him, since they can only live their lives from his little room of imagination. Scenes from *The Water Hen*, *The Dead Class*, *Wielopole, Wielopole* and *Let the Artists Die* ensue and are interimposed upon each other. At the same time, Kantor's personal history unfolds in front of the audience. The space of the productions is created by the overlapping of all of these

visual sequences. Since logical analysis and rational thinking are abandoned, this space is governed by the laws of unpredictability, probability and uncertainty characterising all unstable systems.

All these theories define Kantor's concept of the autonomous theatre, that is, a theatre that is not a reproductive mechanism intended to present an interpretation of a piece of literature on stage, but a mechanism that has its own independent existence. This independent existence is viewed as the process and the manifestation of a human spiritual activity, rather than as an object/commodity that is presented onstage as a reflection of the external order of things. In this sense, Kantor's theatre was a heterotopia, as the philosopher-historian Michel Foucault defines it, a space which is a counter site to real space, wherein all the rules of real space are recognised, contested and inverted.

Such an attitude toward both the meaning of theatre and theatre itself made Kantor perceive the actor and artist in a new light. As Kantor observed in his *Theatre of Death*: "theatre began with acting, that is, when a man looking like 'them' stood opposite those who stayed on the other side ... Though he looked alike, he was eternally different, shockingly alien, as if dead, cut off by an invisible barrier — no less horrible and inconceivable, whose real meaning and threat appears to us only in dreams". Thus, acting and theatre, according to Kantor, did not originate in a ritual, but in activities that were, as he calls them, 'illegal' and in contradiction to ritual. These 'illegal actions', or 'actions of alterity', are directed against religion, politics, social order and the establishment and its institutions of coercion. Since traditional theatre is for Kantor an institution supporting 'legal actions' only, his theatre, as well as his actors, could not find themselves within those boundaries. His art was *against* rather than *for* the establishment and his artists belonged to the circle of 'artistes maudits' rather than those who enjoyed official recognition.

—Michal Kobialka

KAZAN, Elia. US director, actor and writer. Born Elia Kazanjoglous in Constantinople (now Istanbul), Turkey, 7 September 1909. Educated at New Rochelle High School, New York, 1922–26; Williams College, Williamstown, Massachussetts, 1926–30; Yale University, 1930–32. Married 1) Molly Day Thacher in 1932 (died 1963), two sons and two daughters; 2) Barbara Loden in 1967 (died 1980), one son; 3) Frances Rudge in 1982. Joined Group Theatre, New York, as apprentice and stage manager, 1932; actor, with Group Theatre, 1934–41; film debut, 1940; co-founder, with Cheryl Crawford and Robert Lewis, Actors' Studio, New York, 1947; co-director, Actors' Studio, 1947–62; co-director, Repertory Theatre, Lincoln Centre, New York, 1960–64; subsequently concentrated on film career and writing; formed new playwright/directors unit with Arthur Penn and Joseph Mankiewicz following Lee Strasberg's death, 1982. Recipient: New York Drama Critics Circle Award, 1942, 1947 (twice), 1949, 1955; Donaldson Award, 1946, 1947, 1948, 1953, 1954, 1957; Oscar for Best Director, 1947, 1954; New York Film Critics Best Director Award, 1947, 1951, 1954; Tony Award, 1947 (twice), 1949, 1958; D. W. Griffiths Award, Directors Guild of America, 1987. D.Litt: Wesleyan University, 1955; Carnegie Insti-

Elia Kazan (c. 1949).

tute of Technology, 1962; Williams College, 1964; MFA: Yale University, 1959; Doctor Honoris Causa: Katholieke Universiteit, Leuven, Belgium, 1978.

Productions

As actor:
1932   Louis in *Chrysalis* (Porter), Martin Beck Theatre, New York.
1933   The Orderly in *Men in White* (Kingsley), Broadhurst Theatre, New York.
1934   Polyzoides in *Good Eagle Guy* (Levy), Morosco Theatre, New York.
1935   Agate Keller in *Waiting for Lefty* (Odets), Longacre Theatre, New York.
        Baum in *Till the Day I Die* (Odets), Longacre Theatre, New York.
        Kewpie in *Paradise Lost* (Odets), 44th Street Theatre, New York.
1936   Private Kearns in *Johnny Johnson* (Green), 44th Street Theatre, New York.
1937   Eddie Fuselli in *Golden Boy* (Odets), Belasco Theatre, New York; St James's Theatre, London, 1938.
1938–39 Joe Bonaparte in *Golden Boy* (Odets), tour.
1939   Eli Lieber in *The Gentle People* (I. Shaw), Belasco Theatre, New York.
1940   Steve Takis in *Night Music* (Odets), Broadhurst Theatre, New York.

Ficzur in *Liliom* (Molnár), 44th Street Theatre, New York.
1941   Adam Boguris in *Five Alarm Waltz* (Prumbs), Playhouse Theatre, New York.

As director:
1934   *Dimitroff* (Ivens and Wangenheim), New York.
1935   *The Young Go First* (Martin, Scudder and Friedman), New York.
1936   *The Crime* (Shipman and Hymer), New York.
1938   *Casey Jones* (Ardrey), Fulton Theatre, New York.
1939   *Quiet City* (I. Shaw), New York.
        Thunder Rock (Ardrey), Mansfield Theatre, New York.
1941   *Five Alarm Waltz* (Prumbs), Playhouse Theatre, New York.
1942   *Café Crown* (Kraft), Cort Theatre, New York.
        The Skin of Our Teeth (Wilder), Plymouth Theatre, New York.
1943   *Harriet* (Clements and Ryerson), New York.
        One Touch of Venus (Perelman and Nash), Imperial Theatre, New York.
1944   *Jacobowsky and the Colonel* (Behrman), Martin Beck Theatre, New York.
        Sing Out Sweet Land (Kerr), New York.
1945   *Deep Are the Roots* (D'Usseau and Gow), New York.
        Dunnigan's Daughter (Behrman), John Golden Theatre, New York.
        Strange Bedfellows (Conners), New York.
1947   *All My Sons* (Miller), Coronet Theatre, New York.
        A Streetcar Named Desire (T. Williams), Ethel Barrymore Theatre, New York.
1948   *Sundown Beach* (Breuer), New York.
        Love Life (Lerner and Weill), 46th Street Theatre, New York.
1949   *Death of a Salesman* (Miller), Morosco Theatre, New York.
1952   *Flight into Egypt* (Tabori), New York.
1953   *Camino Real* (T. Williams), Martin Beck Theatre, New York.
        Tea and Sympathy (R. Anderson), Ethel Barrymore Theatre, New York.
1955   *Cat on a Hot Tin Roof* (T. Williams), Morosco Theatre, New York.
1957   *The Dark at the Top of the Stairs* (Inge), Music Box Theatre, New York.
1958   *JB* (MacLeish), New York.
1959   *Sweet Bird of Youth* (T. Williams), New York.
1964   *After the Fall* (Miller), ANTA, Washington Square Theatre, New York.
        But For Whom Charlie (Behrman), ANTA, Washington Square Theatre, New York.
        The Changeling (Middleton and Rowley), ANTA, Washington Square Theatre, New York.

Films

As actor:
Cafe Universal, 1934; *Pie in the Sky*, 1934; *City for Conquest*, 1940; *Blues in the Night*, 1941.

As director:
The People of the Cumberlands, 1937; *It's Up to You*, 1941; *A Tree Grows in Brooklyn*, 1945; *The Sea of Grass*, 1947; *Boomerang*, 1947; *Gentleman's Agreement*, 1947; *Pinky*, 1949; *Panic in the Streets*, 1950; *A Streetcar Named Desire*, 1951; *Viva Zapata!*, 1952; *Man on a Tightrope*, 1953; *On the Waterfront*, 1954; *East of Eden*, 1955; *Baby Doll*, 1956; *A Face in the Crowd*, 1957; *Wild River*, 1960; *Splendour in the Grass*, 1961; *America America*, 1963; *The Arrangement*, 1969; *The Visitors*, 1972; *The Last Tycoon*, 1976; *Acts of Love*, 1978; *The Anatolian*, 1982; *Beyond the Aegean*, 1989.

Publications

America America (novel), 1962; *The Arrangement* (novel), 1967; *The Assassins* (novel), 1972; *The Understudy* (novel), 1975; *A Kazan Reader*, 1977; *Acts of Love* (novel), 1978; *The Anatolian* (novel), 1982; *Elia Kazan: A Life*, 1988.

*

Bibliography

Books:
David Richard Jones, *Great Directors at Work*, Berkeley, California, 1986.
Brenda Murphy, *Tennessee Williams and Elia Kazan*, Cambridge, 1992.

* * *

The greater permanence of film and the director's preference for that medium after the 1950's mean that Elia Kazan will be remembered most vividly as a cinema director. But his theatre work in New York not only established the careers of Arthur Miller and Tennessee Williams, and aided the development of other new dramatists, but contributed massively to the resurgence of drama on Broadway after World War II. His association with Robert Lewis and Lee Strasberg in founding and running the Actors' Studio affected the development of a whole generation of US actors, helped to adapt the teachings of Constantin Stanislavsky for American use and continues to provide a training facility for actors, playwrights and directors.

Kazan's career in theatre and film began with the Group Theatre in New York in the 1930's: he was actor (playing the lead in Clifford Odets's *Golden Boy*), stage-manager, playwright, director, scene-painter and much else, as occasion and his own curiosity and ambition suggested. Here he gained a feeling and respect for popular appeal that never deserted him; Group Theatre productions were searching for new audiences and for ways to ensure the survival of theatre in difficult financial times. He also learnt how to hold people with many diverse talents and aims together. But he did not believe that collaboration and democratic

procedures were appropriate; he came to look for collaborators who would collaborate *with him*, under his thumb. He was the master — the maniac, he would say — who was in charge.

When Orson Welles dropped out from directing Thornton Wilder's *The Skin of Our Teeth* (1942), Kazan had his first Broadway success, and others followed quickly. His choice of scripts seems at first to have been dictated only by opportunity, but he was always guided by an instinct for widening the popularity of theatre. Later he was drawn to Arthur Miller's plays because the two men shared the same backgrounds, their fathers being salesmen and their upbringing lower middle-class and in New York. with Jo Mielziner's design, Kazan placed Miller's hero, Willy Loman, in a sensitively suggested reality, true to the lived experience from which the writing had sprung. Recognising the moral force of Miller's argument, he held back the play's early dramatic appeal to emphasize the strength of its final oppositions.

Tennessee Williams was the writer associated with Kazan for the production of four successive plays. The two men had few qualities in common, except the capacity, and perhaps need, for blazing and sustained emotional confrontations, and for compassion. Kazan visited the South to find the precise lived reality that Williams knew at first hand, almost as if he were researching a piece of social realism for the politically conscious Group Theatre.

Kazan's best productions were dominated by amazing and revelatory performances; they had what was called a 'block-busting' power. He sought for emotional truth and would take great pains to help his actors discover it in their own terms. "The only way to understand any character is through yourself", he would tell his actors: "Even as frantic and fantastic a creature as Blanche is created by things you have felt and known, if you'll dig for them and be honest about what you see". 'Digging' in the selves of the actors was a basic process for rehearsal, and Kazan was always looking for the unexpected: "when an actor tells me he knows just how to do a scene, I have cause for concern". He also wanted emotional power, and would sometimes force the pace and impact by using undue violence: "it's easy to ... make somebody shout, or grab somebody by the neck or throw somebody out, or slam a door, or open a window", he was to admit some years later, adding that the violence that did not spring from emotional truth was all "bullshit".

A further influence upon this director was the ancient tragedy and myths of his family's homeland, Greece. His production notes described Blanche as someone caught by Fate and as an alien in the society in which she found herself: "This is like a classic tragedy. Blanche is Medea or someone pursued by the Harpies, the Harpies being *her own Nature*. Her inner sickness pursues her like *doom* and makes it impossible for her to attain the one thing she needs, the only thing she needs: a safe harbour".

Kazan's grasp of a play's action in his finest productions was bold, and founded on his own deepest feelings and understanding. His signature was unmistakable.

—John Russell Brown

KEAN, Charles (John). British actor-manager. Born in Waterford, Ireland, 18 January 1811, son of the actor Edmund Kean. Educated at Eton public school, until 1827. Married actress Ellen Tree in 1842, one adoptive daughter (actress Agnes Robertson). Stage debut, Theatre Royal, Drury Lane, 1827; subsequently established reputation as actor in the provinces; US tours, 1830, 1839, 1845–47; visited Hamburg, 1832; acted alongside his father on his final appearance (as Othello), 1833; acted in Edinburgh, 1837; first major London success, as Hamlet, 1838; appointed director of Queen Victoria's private theatricals at Windsor, 1848; co-manager, with his wife, of the Princess's Theatre, London, 1850–59; acclaimed for historical plays presented with authentic costumes and scenery; also made innovations in lighting; retired, a wealthy man, 1859; toured Australia, the USA, and Jamaica with his wife, 1863–64; last stage appearance, Liverpool, 1867. Fellow, Society of Antiquaries, 1857. Died in London, 22 January 1868.

Principal productions

1827	*Douglas* (Home), Theatre Royal, Drury Lane, London; acted Young Norval.
1829	*Romeo and Juliet* (Shakespeare), Haymarket Theatre, London; acted Romeo.
	The Iron Chest (Colman the Elder), Haymarket Theatre, London; acted Mortimer.
1830	*Richard III* (Shakespeare), New York; Theatre Royal, Drury Lane, London, 1838; acted Richard.
1833	*Othello* (Shakespeare), Covent Garden, London; acted Iago.
1838	*Hamlet* (Shakespeare), Theatre Royal, Drury Lane, London; acted Hamlet.
	A New Way to Pay Old Debts (Massinger), Theatre Royal, Drury Lane, London; acted Sir Giles Overreach.
1842	*The Gamester* (Moore), Haymarket Theatre, London; Theatre Royal, Drury Lane, London, 1861; acted Beverley.
	As You Like It (Shakespeare), Haymarket Theatre, London; acted Jaques.
1848	*The Wife's Secret* (Lovell), Haymarket Theatre, London; acted Sir Walter Amyott.
1851	*The Merry Wives of Windsor* (Shakespeare), Princess's Theatre, London; acted Ford.
	Pauline (Oxenford), Princess's Theatre, London.
	Love in a Maze (Boucicault), Princess's Theatre, London.
1852	*King John* (Shakespeare), Princess's Theatre, London; acted John.
	Macbeth (Shakespeare), Princess's Theatre, London; acted Macbeth.
	Sardanapalus (Byron), Princess's Theatre, London.
	The Corsican Brothers (Boucicault), Princess's Theatre, London; acted the brothers.
	The Phantom (Boucicault), Princess's Theatre, London.
	The Prima Donna (Boucicault), Princess's Theatre, London.
1854	*The Courier of Lyons* (Reade), Princess's Theatre, London.
	Faust and Marguerite (Boucicault), Princess's Theatre, London.
1855	*Henry VIII* (Shakespeare), Princess's Theatre, London; acted Wolsey.
	Louis XI (Boucicault), Princess's Theatre, London; acted Louis.
	The Critic (Sheridan), Princess's Theatre, London.
1856	*A Midsummer Night's Dream* (Shakespeare), Princess's Theatre, London.
	The Winter's Tale (Shakespeare), Princess's Theatre, London; acted Leontes.
1857	*Richard II* (Shakespeare), Princess's Theatre, London; acted Richard.
1858	*The Merchant of Venice* (Shakespeare), Princess's Theatre, London; acted Shylock.
1859	*Henry V* (Shakespeare), Princess's Theatre, London; acted Henry.

Publications

Emigrant in Motley, edited by J. M. D. Hardwick, 1954.

*

Bibliography

Books:
John William Cole, *The Life and Theatrical Times of Charles Kean*, London, 1860.

* * *

Charles Kean claimed that "If it had not been for my father's fame, I should have made my way with the public twice as easily". Opinion was (and remains) divided on this issue, but indisputably, for all the aura of his family name, Charles Kean was a very different actor (and man) from his mercurial father Edmund. They were both of small stature, but Charles was plump with a rather expressionless face in contrast to his father's energetic figure and electrifying eyes. Charles Kean's voice was nasal, heavy, prone to monotony, often giving the impression that he spoke with a finger pressed against one nostril.

Like his father, Charles Kean was an excellent swordsman, having learnt the art in fencing classes at Eton, whither his father had sent him to secure not only a sound education, but also the social respectability usually denied to the sons of actors. It had not been expected that Charles would pursue a theatrical career, but a downturn in Edmund's fortunes obliged his son to leave Eton at the age of 16 and he concluded that the stage offered the best prospect for him to earn a living and support his mother. Charles's early efforts were not successful, but he prevailed through courageous devotion and a determination to master the skills of his craft. In this endeavour he was greatly assisted by his wife, the former Ellen Tree (1806–80). The couple had known each other since 1828 and both had been on stage for the fateful performance of *Othello* in March 1833, when Edmund collapsed and was unable to complete the play.

Ellen Kean was a more accomplished performer than her husband. Prior to her marriage she had already established a reputation in the USA as well as in England. She possessed a commanding figure (becoming stout in later life), an expressive oval face, and a refined and emotional voice. Her range was considerable, encompassing contemporary, though often historical, drama and progressing through the Shakespearean repertoire from Juliet and Rosalind to Lady Macbeth and Constance. Her forte was the sympathetic expression of turbulent emotions. As Constance, a mother's fondness and indignation gave way to vehement wrath and finally agonised grief. Westland Marston, acknowledging "her fine intensity of feeling", wrote that "She loved to seize those traits which bring a character within the range of actual life" and William Archer recalled an incident, after a performance of *The Gamester*, when Ellen Tree was unable to separate Charles's stage death from reality: "Oh, my Charles! — my poor darling — you are not dead; say you are not dead!" Such emotional identification was not, though, at the expense of vocal clarity. Ellen Terry, a child actress with the Keans, recalled Ellen's coaching and years later commented: "I can hear her now lecturing the ladies of the company on their vowels".

Undoubtedly the improvement in Charles Kean's acting was partly thanks to the example, if not the overt instruction, of his wife. G. H. Lewes observed to Marston:

"Charles Kean is changing his style into a natural one. He will convert me yet". During his management of the Princess's Theatre Kean appeared in a number of 'domestic melodramas', several of them commissioned by him. Boucicault's *The Corsican Brothers* and *Louis XI* afforded Kean many sympathetic opportunities in which he combined the minutest detailed naturalism with intensity of passion. When he applied this approach to Shakespeare, however, his reception was mixed. Not a naturally gifted verse speaker, he concentrated on creating the inmost reality of the character rising to moments of powerfully expressed emotion. Thus, drawing strength from Ellen's performance as his Queen in *Richard II*, Kean made the couple's brief departure scene "heartrending . . . one of the most effective of the whole performance."

Nevertheless, it was the scenery rather than the acting that dominated Kean's Shakespearean revivals. In the decade of the Pre-Raphaelite Brotherhood and the popularisation of photography (Kean's Oxford Street neighbour, the photographer Laroche, created a fine pictorial record of his achievements), Charles concentrated his scholarly disposition on the creation of painstakingly accurate historical settings based on thorough research. Kean's printed playtexts abound with references to scholarly sources; they also reveal how ruthlessly the plays were cut and rearranged to accomodate this scenic extravagance. There was, of course, a link between the realism of the stage scenery and the

Illustration that appeared in the *Illustrated Times* of a scene from a production of *The Winter's Tale,* staged by **Charles Kean.**

From a caricature of **Charles Kean,** manager, seated beneath a portrait of himself as Hamlet.

Keans's acting, the former providing an environment conducive to the latter.

Kean's antiquarianism was recognised by his election as a Fellow of the Society of Antiquaries in 1857. This was the most significant expression of public recognition accorded to an actor up to that time. Throughout his career Kean had been zealous in his pursuit of social respectability for his profession. In this aspiration his Eton education was an undoubted asset, not least in his appointment as director of the Windsor Castle Theatricals in 1848. At that time Kean scarcely commanded the esteem of his profession (Macready, with his republican leanings, was doubly resentful), but Kean set about his task with characteristic conscientiousness and no small sense of his own importance. Through the 1850's Kean enjoyed royal patronage both at Windsor and his own Princess's Theatre. Mrs Kean certainly had hopes of a knighthood for her husband, but no such reward was forthcoming.

The couple travelled far and wide to accumulate the wealth necessary for a comfortable retirement. In 1863–64 they ventured as far as Australia (their letters home form the core of *Emigrant in Motley*), but the experience exhausted Charles. After his death, Ellen acted out her final role, as inconsolable and as protective of her husband's reputation as that other widow (of Windsor) who had denied Charles Kean the accolade that would have provided the greatest consolation.

—Richard Foulkes

KEAN, Edmund. British actor. Born in London, 4 November 1787 (some sources, 17 March 1789). Educated at school in Orange Court, Leicester Square, Mr King's school, Chapel Street, Soho, and Green Street School, Leicester Square, all in London; early theatrical training under ventriloquist uncle and Miss Tidswell, actress at Theatre Royal, Drury Lane, London, from 1795. Married actress Mary Chambers in 1808; two sons (one died in infancy, the other actor Charles (John) Kean). Illegitimate son of strolling players; stage debut as small child, probably as Cupid at either Her Majesty's Theatre, London, in the ballet *Noverre* or at Drury Lane, c.1790; reappeared at Drury Lane playing demons and pageboys, 1791; ran away to sea, 1795; returned to London from Madeira, feigning illness, 1795; acted at Drury Lane, 1801; repeatedly ran away to work in country fairs; broke both legs in Saunder's Circus tumbling act, Bartholomew Fair, c.1801; toured as strolling player as Harlequin and in other roles after parting with mother, 1804; appeared in several small roles at the Haymarket Theatre, 1806; brought to London from Theatre Royal, Exeter, by Robert Elliston to appear at the Olympic Theatre, but instead made sensational debut as Shylock at Drury Lane, 1814; fame consolidated by further Shakespearean roles, 1814–15; first appearance as Sir Giles Overreach, 1816; toured USA, 1820; revisited Paris and Switzerland, 1824; scandal and trial over adulterous affair with alderman's wife Charlotte Cox, 1825; second US tour, 1825; moved to Covent Garden, 1827; appeared in Paris once more, 1828; remaining career disrupted by decline in health and increasing alcohol problem; returned to Drury Lane, 1829; last triumph as Othello with William Charles Macready as Iago, 1832; collapsed while giving last performance of *Othello*, with his son as Iago, March 1833; lived another six weeks. Founder of notorious Wolf Club for actors, 1815. Elected a chief of the Huron Indians, USA, 1825. Died in Richmond, Surrey, 15 May 1833.

Roles

1801	Prince Arthur in *King John* (Shakespeare), Theatre Royal, Drury Lane, London.
1802	Hamlet in *Hamlet* (Shakespeare), York, England.
1803	Norval in *Douglas* (Home), Sheerness, England.
1806	Ganem in *The Mountaineers* (Colman the Younger), Haymarket Theatre, London.
	Peter in *The Iron Chest* (Colman the Younger), Haymarket Theatre, London.
	Simon in *John Bull* (Colman the Younger), Haymarket Theatre, London.
	Rosencrantz, Polonius, and First Gravedigger in *Hamlet* (Shakespeare), Haymarket Theatre, London.
	Osmyn in *The Mourning Bride* (Congreve), Edinburgh.
	Jaffier in *Venice Preserved* (Otway), Edinburgh.
1813	Octavian in *The Mountaineers* (Colman the Younger), Dorchester, England.
1814	Shylock in *The Merchant of Venice* (Shakespeare), Theatre Royal, Drury Lane, London.
	Richard III in *Richard III* (Shakespeare), Theatre Royal, Drury Lane, London.

Othello in *Othello* (Shakespeare), Theatre Royal, Drury Lane, London.

Iago in *Othello* (Shakespeare), Theatre Royal, Drury Lane, London.

Luke Frugal in *The City Madam* (Massinger), Theatre Royal, Drury Lane, London.

1814–15   Macbeth in *Macbeth* (Shakespeare), Theatre Royal, Drury Lane, London.

Romeo in *Romeo and Juliet* (Shakespeare), Theatre Royal, Drury Lane, London.

Glenroy in *Town and Country* (Morton), Theatre Royal, Drury Lane, London.

Richard II in *Richard II* (Shakespeare), Theatre Royal, Drury Lane, London.

Penruddock in *The Wheel of Fortune* (Cumberland), Theatre Royal, Drury Lane, London.

Zanga in *The Revenge* (Young), Theatre Royal, Drury Lane, London.

Abel Drugger in *The Alchemist* (Jonson), Theatre Royal, Drury Lane, London.

1815   Egbert in *Ina* (Wilmot), Theatre Royal, Drury Lane, London.

1815–16   Bajazet in *Tamerlane* (Rowe), Theatre Royal, Drury Lane, London.

Duke Aranza in *The Honey Moon* (Tobin), Theatre Royal, Drury Lane, London.

Goswin or Florez in *The Merchant of Bruges* (Kinnaird, adapted from Beaumont and Fletcher's *The Beggar's Bush*), Theatre Royal, Drury Lane, London.

1816   Sir Giles Overreach in *A New Way to Pay Old Debts* (Massinger), Theatre Royal, Drury Lane, London.

The Duke in *The Maid of Milan* (Massinger), Theatre Royal, Drury Lane, London.

Kitely in *Every Man in his Humour* (Jonson), Theatre Royal, Drury Lane, London.

Bertram in *Bertram* (Maturin), Theatre Royal, Drury Lane, London.

1816–17   Timon in *Timon of Athens* (Shakespeare), Theatre Royal, Drury Lane, London.

Mortimer in *The Iron Chest* (Colman the Younger), Theatre Royal, Drury Lane, London.

Oroonoko in *Oroonoko* (Southerne), Theatre Royal, Drury Lane, London.

Eustace St Pierre in *The Surrender of Calais* (Colman the Younger), Theatre Royal, Drury Lane, London.

Achmet in *Barbarossa* (Brown), Theatre Royal, Drury Lane, London.

Manuel in *Manuel* (Maturin), Theatre Royal, Drury Lane, London.

1817   Paul in *Paul and Virginia* (anon.), Theatre Royal, Drury Lane, London.

Richard in *Richard, Duke of York* (Merivale, adapted from Shakespeare's *Henry VI, parts 1–3*), Theatre Royal, Drury Lane, London.

1818   Selim in *The Bride of Abydos* (Dimond), Theatre Royal, Drury Lane, London.

Barabas in *The Jew of Malta* (Penley, adapted from Marlowe), Theatre Royal, Drury Lane, London.

Edmund Kean (drawing by John Boaden).

Young Norval in *Douglas* (Home), Theatre Royal, Drury Lane, London.

King John in *King John* (Shakespeare), Theatre Royal, Drury Lane, London.

Alexander in *Alexander the Great* (D'Egville), Theatre Royal, Drury Lane, London.

Sylvester Daggerwood in *Sylvester Daggerwood* (Colman the Younger), Theatre Royal, Drury Lane, London.

Orestes in *The Distresst Mother* (Racine), Theatre Royal, Drury Lane, London.

Lucius Junius Brutus in *Brutus* (Payne), Theatre Royal, Drury Lane, London.

Eugene in *Switzerland* (Porter), Theatre Royal, Drury Lane, London.

1818–19   Leon in *Rule a Wife and Have a Wife* (Beaumont and Fletcher), Theatre Royal, Drury Lane, London.

Hotspur in *Henry IV* (Shakespeare), Theatre Royal, Drury Lane, London.

1819   Malvesi in *The Dwarf of Naples* (Soane), Theatre Royal, Drury Lane, London.

Omreah in *The Carib Chief* (Twiss), Theatre Royal, Drury Lane, London.

Rolla in *Pizarro* (Sheridan), Theatre Royal, Drury Lane, London.

1820   Coriolanus in *Coriolanus* (Shakespeare), Theatre Royal, Drury Lane, London.

Lear in *King Lear* (Shakespeare), Theatre Royal, Drury Lane, London.

*

Bibliography

Books:
Francis Phippen, *Authentic Memoirs of Edmund Kean*, London, 1814.
B. Cornwall, *Edmund Kean*, 2 vols., London, 1835.
B. W. Proctor, *The Life of Edmund Kean*, London, 1835; reprinted, 1969.
F. W. Hawkins, *Life of Edmund Kean*, 2 vols., London, 1869.
J. Fitzgerald Molloy, *The Life and Adventures of Edmund Kean, Tragedian*, London, 1881.
N. H. Hillebrand, *Edmund Kean*, New York, 1933.
Giles Playfair, *Kean*, London, 1939.
Julius Berstl, *The Sun's Bright Child*, London, 1946.
Maurice Willson Disher, *Mad Genius*, London, 1950.
W. MacQueen-Pope, *Edmund Kean*, London, 1960.
Joseph Donohue, *Theatre in the Age of Kean*, Oxford, 1975.

Raymond Fitzsimmons, *Edmund Kean — Fire from Heaven*, London, 1976.

* * *

Edmund Kean had a unique impact upon the stage on both sides of the Atlantic over the course of two decades, firstly with the brilliance and later with the notoriety of his acting. Samuel Taylor Coleridge, who saw Kean early on, memorably compared his acting to reading Shakespeare "by flashes of lightning". Much of this brilliance — and inconsistency, it must be added — had its roots in Kean's own erratic temperament and profligate behaviour. Rakish, philandering, alcoholic, and arrogant, Kean cut a swath through London society that put his name in bad odour even as it maintained him as an attraction at the box office well after he had reached his zenith as an actor. His reputation has survived him as the prototype of the Romantic actor, whose very self-destructiveness endows his acting with sexuality, danger, and allure.

If Kean's acting is difficult now to separate from his personality, such confusion can be blamed partly on the actor's own efforts. Kean appears to have believed that any publicity served his interests better than none, a lesson he probably learned in the course of a long and largely unrewarding apprenticeship, and he had no qualms about how he won this attention. A small, dark, man distinguished in appearance only by his burning eyes and feline grace, Kean toiled for years at minor theatres in London and the provinces before mounting a frontal assault on the theatrical establishment with his convulsive performance as Shylock in 1814. This characterization embodied such pain and outrage on the part of a character — like Kean, illegitimate and ill-educated — on the margins of society that it seared its way into the consciousness and writings of such respected critics as William Hazlitt. Hazlitt immediately took up the advocacy of the striking 'new' actor and this early bond between Kean and the journalistic establishment was to have a strong influence upon his subsequent career: he depended on the critics for his fame and they on him for sensation and novelty.

From the earliest days of his renown, Kean set out almost systematically to distort and obfuscate the details of his early life as a London street urchin and to engender an image of himself as scornful of polite society and its strictures. As the novelty of his acting wore off, he (and his chroniclers) came to depend increasingly on the overlaps between his volcanic style as it could be witnessed in the theatre and his notorious personal exploits, enhanced by gossip and hearsay. Kean appears to have served his reputation by his collusion in this process, but also to have increased the pressure on himself to be sensational in life, since he could not always be so on stage. He thus became the first modern actor to be known as much for his private self — or at least the self he believed himself to be — as for his acting.

Not surprisingly, he did best in characters to whom he could relate his own alienation and disaffection. Along these lines, he followed his first great success as Shylock with Richard III and then with Hamlet and Othello — all of whom he played in his inimitably manic and slashing style. One of his few non-Shakespearean successes came as Sir Giles Overreach in Massinger's *A New Way to Pay Old Debts*, in which he achieved apoplectic heights as a character who, like Shylock, loses control over a daughter he has come to regard as tractable and submissive. Kean's record in contemporary plays was, however, less distinguished as, oddly enough, his acrobatic and passionate style did not meld well with the demands of contemporary tragedy. Later in his career, he would endure spectacular failures in several new and highly touted works, his acting progressively undercut by the ravages of his dissipation and by his inability to retain newly-learned lines under the pressure of opening nights.

Nor did Kean age well as an actor. His initial success came as the fruit of faddishness, fed by the long tenure of the stately and stolid John Philip Kemble at the head of tragic actors and by the partisanship of critics like Hazlitt, who polarized themselves around Kean and his sudden ascendancy. Kean rather quickly mined the traditional roles that served the qualities of his style, was subsequently greeted less enthusiastically in such roles as Romeo to which he was less well-suited, and finally languished in his inability to make a success in the often mediocre new plays that came his way.

These misfortunes were exacerbated by Kean's stubborn refusal to undertake comedy. This recalcitrance was odd, because Kean had flourished as Harlequin during his years in the provinces, his athleticism meeting the requisites of the role almost ideally. But Kean apparently associated Harlequin with the long seasons of struggle and frustration at the start of his career and shrank from re-creating the part and, indeed, from any exercise of what must have been considerable skill as a comic actor. A kind of comedy, though, seems to have infiltrated his tragic style in the form of the typically mordant sarcasm he conveyed as Shylock, Richard III, and Hamlet in particular.

Kean's instinct for self-promotion failed him somewhat during the time of his notorious trial for adultery in the mid-1820's. Scorned by polite society and abandoned by his wife, Kean was compelled to continue performing and to undertake exhausting provincial and US tours in order to support his extravagant lifestyle. He seems to have grown to hate acting and discouraged his son, Charles, from pursuing it. In this wish, too, he was to be subverted, as Charles went on to a long and notable career as an actor and producer.

The elder Kean's legacy to the stage lay in the astonishing passion and pain of his performances. At its best between 1814 and 1821, his acting cried out to audiences in the howl of a man whose psyche had been shaped by the backstreets of London, by over-population, and by industrialization.

—Leigh Woods

KEMBLE, Charles. British actor-manager. Born in Brecon, South Wales, 25 November 1775. Educated at English College, Douai, France, 1788–91. Married actress Maria Theresa De Camp in 1806; one daughter (actress Fanny Kemble, *q.v.*). Gave up position in the Post Office to make stage debut in Sheffield, 1792–93; further appearances at Newcastle and Edinburgh before London debut at Theatre Royal, Drury Lane, alongside his brother John Philip Kemble (*q.v.*) and his sister Sarah Siddons (*q.v.*), 1794; engaged for summer season at the Haymarket Theatre,

1794; consolidated reputation at Drury Lane, 1794–1803; toured Germany and Russia, 1803; joined company at Covent Garden, 1803–13; toured England, Scotland, and Ireland and on the Continent, 1813–15; returned to Covent Garden, 1815; wrote several successful plays and adaptations and established reputation as player of romantic leads; acquired control of Covent Garden theatre, 1822–32; introduced historically accurate costumes and after near ruin prospered on strength of his daughter's success, from 1829; toured USA with her after resigning Covent Garden management, 1832–33; farewell appearances, 1836; Examiner of Plays, 1836–40; staged comeback on request of Queen Victoria, 1840; afflicted increasingly by deafness; final appearance, Covent Garden, 1842. Died in London, 12 November 1854.

Principal roles

1792–93	Orlando in *As You Like It* (Shakespeare), Sheffield, England.
1794	Malcolm in *Macbeth* (Shakespeare), Theatre Royal, Drury Lane, London.
	Jaques de Boys in *As You Like It* (Shakespeare), Theatre Royal, Drury Lane, London.
	Cromwell in *Henry VIII* (Shakespeare), Theatre Royal, Drury Lane, London.
	Belville in *The Country Girl* (Garrick), Theatre Royal, Drury Lane, London.
	Count Appiani in *Emilia Galotti* (Lessing), Theatre Royal, Drury Lane, London.
	Jamie in *Auld Robin Gray* (Arnold), Haymarket Theatre, London.
1795	Henry Woodville in *The Wheel of Fortune* (Cumberland), Theatre Royal, Drury Lane, London.
1795–96	Carlos in *Isabella* (Southerne), Theatre Royal, Drury Lane, London.
	Lawson in *The Gamester* (Shirley), Theatre Royal, Drury Lane, London.
	Octavio in *She Would and She Would Not* (Cibber), Theatre Royal, Drury Lane, London.
	Paris in *Romeo and Juliet* (Shakespeare), Theatre Royal, Drury Lane, London.
	Laertes in *Hamlet* (Shakespeare), Theatre Royal, Drury Lane, London.
	Celadon in *Celadon and Florimel* (J. P. Kemble), Theatre Royal, Drury Lane, London.
	Saville in *The Belle's Stratagem* (Cowley), Theatre Royal, Drury Lane, London.
	Pascentius in *Vortigern* (Ireland), Theatre Royal, Drury Lane, London.
	Lovel in *High Life below Stairs* (Townley), Theatre Royal, Drury Lane, London.
	Ferdinand in *The Tempest* (Shakespeare), Theatre Royal, Drury Lane, London.
	Guiderius in *Cymbeline* (Shakespeare), Theatre Royal, Drury Lane, London.
	Philotas in *The Grecian Daughter* (Murphy), Theatre Royal, Drury Lane, London.
	Hotspur in *Henry IV* (Shakespeare), Haymarket Theatre, London.

Wilford in *The Iron Chest* (Colman the Younger), Haymarket Theatre, London.

Vivaldi in *The Italian Monk* (Boaden), Haymarket Theatre, London.

Bassanio in *The Merchant of Venice* (Shakespeare), Haymarket Theatre, London.

Cassio in *Othello* (Shakespeare), Haymarket Theatre, London.

1798   Richmond in *Richard III* (Shakespeare), Theatre Royal, Drury Lane, London.

Claudio in *Measure for Measure* (Shakespeare), Theatre Royal, Drury Lane, London.

Norval in *Douglas* (Home), Theatre Royal, Drury Lane, London.

1799   Alonzo in *Pizarro* (Sheridan), Theatre Royal, Drury Lane, London.

1800   Three-Fingered Jack in *Obi* (Fawcett), Haymarket Theatre, London.

Durimel in *Point of Honour* (C. Kemble, adapted from Mercier's *Le Déserteur*), Haymarket Theatre, London.

Charles Surface in *The School for Scandal* (Sheridan), Haymarket Theatre, London.

Faulconbridge in *King John* (Shakespeare), Haymarket Theatre, London.

Edmund in *King Lear* (Shakespeare), Haymarket Theatre, London.

Young Mirabel in *The Inconstant* (Farquhar), Haymarket Theatre, London.

1801   Adelmorn in *Adelmorn the Outlaw* (Lewis), Theatre Royal, Drury Lane, London.

Lothario in *The Fair Penitent* (Rowe), Theatre Royal, Drury Lane, London.

Florizel in *The Winter's Tale* (Shakespeare), Theatre Royal, Drury Lane, London.

Sir Brilliant Fashion in *The Way to Keep Him* (Murphy), Theatre Royal, Drury Lane, London.

Frederic in *Lovers' Vows* (Inchbald, adapted from Kotzebue), Haymarket Theatre, London.

Dick Dowlas in *The Heir at Law* (Colman the Younger), Haymarket Theatre, London.

1803   Hamlet in *Hamlet* (Shakespeare), Theatre Royal, Drury Lane, London.

Henry in *Speed the Plough* (Morton), Covent Garden, London.

Romeo in *Romeo and Juliet* (Shakespeare), Covent Garden, London.

Pyrrhus in *The Distresst Mother* (Racine, translated by Philips), Covent Garden, London.

1807   Plastic in *Town and Country* (Morton), Covent Garden, London.

Peter the Great in *Peter the Great* (Cherry), Covent Garden, London.

1808   Sigismund in *The Wanderer* (Kotzebue, adapted by C. Kemble), Covent Garden, London.

Fernando in *Plot and Counterplot* (C. Kemble, adapted from Dieulafoi's *Le Portrait de Michel Cervantes*), Haymarket Theatre, London.

1810   Mortimer in *The Iron Chest* (Colman the Younger), Haymarket Theatre, London.

1811   Knight of Snowdoun in *The Lady of the Lake* (Morton), Covent Garden, London.

Antony in *Julius Caesar* (Shakespeare), Covent Garden, London.

Stepanoff in *Kamschatka; or, The Slave's Tribute* (Kotzebue, adapted by C. Kemble), Covent Garden, London.

1813   Frederick in *The Hungarian's Cottage; or, The Brazen Bust* (C. Kemble), Covent Garden, London.

1815   Macbeth in *Macbeth* (Shakespeare), Covent Garden, London.

1817   Doricourt in *The Belle's Stratagem* (Cowley), Covent Garden, London.

Benedick in *Much Ado About Nothing* (Shakespeare), Covent Garden, London.

Young Marlow in *She Stoops to Conquer* (Goldsmith), Covent Garden, London.

1818   Giraldi Fazio in *Fazio* (Milman), Covent Garden, London.

Manfredi in *Bellamira* (Sheil), Covent Garden, London.

1819   Vicentio in *Evadne* (Sheil), Covent Garden, London.

Lord Towneley in *The Provoked Husband* (Farquhar), Covent Garden, London.

Tamerlane in *Tamerlane* (Rowe), Covent Garden, London.

Archer in *The Beaux' Stratagem* (Farquhar), Covent Garden, London.

Sir Edward Mortimer in *Mary Stuart* (adapted from Schiller), Covent Garden, London.

Hastings in *Jane Shore* (Rowe), Covent Garden, London.

Ivanhoe in *Ivanhoe* (adapted from Scott), Covent Garden, London.

Icilius in *Virginius* (Knowles), Covent Garden, London.

Oakley in *The Jealous Wife* (Colman the Elder), Haymarket Theatre, London.

Guido in *Mirandola* (Cornwall), Haymarket Theatre, London.

Don John in *Don John* (Reynolds, adapted from Fletcher's *The Chances*), Haymarket Theatre, London.

1824   Stephen Foster in *A Woman Never Vext* (Rowley, adapted by Planché), Covent Garden, London.

1825   Orestes in *Orestes in Argos* (Bailey), Covent Garden, London.

1825–26   Othello in *Othello* (Shakespeare), Covent Garden, London.

Feignwell in *A Bold Stroke for a Wife* (Centlivre), Covent Garden, London.

1826   Louis Kerneguy in *Woodstock* (Pocock), Covent Garden, London.

Francesco Foscari in *Foscari* (Mitford), Covent Garden, London.

1829   Mercutio in *Romeo and Juliet* (Shakespeare), Covent Garden, London.

Shakespeare in *Shakespeare's Early Days* (anon.), Covent Garden, London.

1832   Sir Thomas Clifford in *The Hunchback* (Knowles), Covent Garden, London.

Other roles included: Don Felix in *The Wonder* (Centlivre); George Barnwell in *The London Merchant* (Lillo); Percy in *The Castle Spectre* (Lewis); Edgar in *King Lear* (Shakespeare); Shylock in *The Merchant of Venice* (Shakespeare); The Stranger in *The Stranger* (Kotzebue); Charles II in *Charles II* (Payne); Macduff in *Macbeth* (Shakespeare).

Publications

Point of Honour (adaptation of Mercier's *Le Déserteur*), 1800; *The Wanderer* (adaptation of Kotzebue), 1808; *Plot and Counterplot* (adaptation of Dieulafoi's *Le Portrait de Michel Cervantes*), 1808; *Kamschatka; or, The Slave's Tribute* (adaptation of Kotzebue), 1811; and *The Hungarian's Cottage; or, The Brazen Bust* (play), 1813.

*

Bibliography

Books:
Percy H. Fitzgerald, *The Kembles*, 2 vols., London, 1871.
Jane Williamson, *Charles Kemble: Man of the Theatre*, Lincoln, Nebraska, 1964.

Articles:
Rosamund Gilder, "Kemble Religion; A Family Portrait", *Theatre Arts Monthly*, 17, 1933.

* * *

Macready called Charles Kemble "a first rate actor in second rate parts". More kindly, W. B. Donne wrote of him that "whenever he played a second part, he made it a first one". His Leartes provided Hamlet, for once, with an adversary worthy of him, while his Cassio in *Othello* was a gentleman trying to conceal his drunkenness rather than the usual drunken sot played for cheap laughs, and his Mercutio was a witty gentleman, not the fop of contemporary stage tradition. His Faulconbridge overshadowed even the title role in *King John*. Leigh Hunt called Kemble "the prince of the genteel comedy" and many remarked on the wit, buoyancy, grace, elegance, and gallantry to be observed in his performances. According to Hunt he was outstanding in three classes of character: the lover, the "spirited gentleman of tragedy", and as a mixture of "the occasional debauchee and the gentleman of feeling". He was also effective in such leading roles as Romeo, Benedick, and Hamlet, but he lacked the voice and passion for the great tragic parts.

There were several reasons for this. His roles were prepared down to the last detail of look, gesture, and intonation, which were then executed very precisely on stage. This gave his acting a finished quality, but it lacked impulsiveness. His attention to minutiae and his use of long pauses, consequently, could make his performances seem laborious. Moreover, actors like Edmund Kean had made the Kemble manner, characterized by a noble bearing, idiosyncratic pronunciation and restraint, seem rather old-fashioned. Westland Marston writes: "His style in passion was uniformly lofty. There was variety, indeed ... but it was a variety confined within what may be called heroic delivery, seldom or never a marked transition from it to colloquial realism." In effect, says Marston, Kemble gave his spectators the typical rather than the individual man.

Nevertheless, despite his failure to scale the peaks of tragedy, Kemble overcame the natural drawbacks of weak voice, awkward legs, and poor posture to excel in witty, gentlemanly roles and as youthful lovers, combining vitality with restraint and demonstrating an intellectual capacity to explore such roles for every possible nuance and subtlety.

As manager of Covent Garden, Kemble was much beset by financial pressures and it was only through the interest of London audiences in the acting of his daughter, Fanny Kemble, that he prolonged his reign there into the 1830's. Most important of the innovations introduced during his regime was the use of historically authentic costumes, first seen in his celebrated production of *King John* in 1823. Using costumes designed by J. R. Planché, this was just the first in a long line of historically accurate presentations of Shakespeare that did much to excite new interest in how established classics might be staged.

—Jim Davis

KEMBLE, Fanny. British actress and writer. Born Frances Anne Kemble in London, 27 November 1809. Educated at Madame Faudier's boarding school in Boulogne, France, 1819–21; Mrs Rowden's school in Paris, 1821–25. Married Pierce Butler in 1834 (divorced 1848), two daughters. Stage debut, Covent Garden, London, 1829; enjoyed immediate acclaim at Covent Garden and during provincial tours, often in roles associated with her aunt, Sarah Siddons (*q.v.*); toured USA with her father, actor-manager Charles Kemble (*q.v.*), 1832–33; retired from stage on marriage, 1834; noted for support for the abolitionist movement; returned to UK, via Rome, 1847; revived acting career in Manchester, Liverpool, and London, 1847; appeared alongside William Charles Macready, 1848; concentrated on highly successful tours of dramatic readings from Shakespeare on both sides of the Atlantic, from 1848; retired to Lennox, Massachusetts, 1848; resumed readings, 1868; returned to UK, 1878; published several bestselling volumes of autobiography. Died in London, 15 January 1893.

Roles

1829	Juliet in *Romeo and Juliet* (Shakespeare), Covent Garden, London.
	Belvidera in *Venice Preserved* (Otway), Covent Garden, London.
1830	Euphrasia in *The Grecian Daughter* (Murphy), Covent Garden, London.
	Mrs Beverly in *The Gamester* (Moore), Covent Garden, London.
	Isabella in *Isabella* (Southerne), Covent Garden, London.
	Lady Townley in *The Provoked Husband* (Farquhar), Covent Garden, London.
1830–31	Mrs Haller in *The Stranger* (Kotzebue), Covent Garden, London.

Calista in *The Fair Penitent* (Rowe), Covent Garden, London.

Juliana in *The Honey Moon* (Tobin), Covent Garden, London.

Lady Macbeth in *Macbeth* (Shakespeare), Covent Garden, London.

Portia in *The Merchant of Venice* (Shakespeare), Covent Garden, London.

Beatrice in *Much Ado About Nothing* (Shakespeare), Covent Garden, London.

Constance in *King John* (Shakespeare), Covent Garden, London.

1832–33   Louise de Savoie in *Francis I* (F. Kemble), Covent Garden, London.

Duchesse de Guise in *Henri III* (Dumas), Covent Garden, London.

Julia in *The Hunchback* (Knowles), Covent Garden, London.

Bianca in *Fazio* (Milman), Park Theatre, New York.

1847   Lady Teazle in *The School for Scandal* (Sheridan), British tour.

Mariana in *Measure for Measure* (Shakespeare), British tour.

Queen Katherine in *Henry V* (Shakespeare), British tour.

1848   Desdemona in *Othello* (Shakespeare), Princess's Theatre, London.

Publications

Francis I (play), 1832; *Journal of Frances Anne Kemble*, 1835 (ed. Monica Young, 1990); *Record of a Girlhood*, 1835; *The Star of Seville* (play), 1837; *Poems*, 1844; *A Year of Consolation* (travel writings), 1847; *Christmas Tree and Other Tales* (translated from German), 1856; *Plays*, 1863; *Journal of a Residence on a Georgian Plantation*, 1863; *Records of Later Life*, 1878; *Notes on Some of Shakespeare's Plays*, 1882; *Far Away and Long Ago*, 1889; *Further Records*, 1891.

*

Bibliography

Books:
Percy H. Fitzgerald, *The Kembles*, 2 vols., London, 1871.
Dorothy de Bear Bobbé, *Fanny Kemble, Actress*, London, 1932.
L. S. Driver, *Fanny Kemble*, Chapel Hill, North Carolina, 1933.
Margaret Armstrong, *Fanny Kemble: A Biography*, London, 1938.
Henry Gibbs, *Affectionately Yours, Fanny*, London, 1947.
Robert Rushmore, *Fanny Kemble*, New York, 1970.
Constance Wright, *Fanny Kemble and the Lovely Land*, New York, 1972.
Dorothy Marshall, *Fanny Kemble*, London, 1977.
J. C. Furnas, *Fanny Kemble — Leading Lady of the Nineteenth Century Stage*, New York, 1982.
Elizabeth Mavor (ed.), *Fanny Kemble: The American Journals*, London, 1990.

Articles:
Rosamund Gilder, "Kemble Religion; A Family Portrait", *Theatre Arts Monthly*, 17, 1933.

* * *

The life of Fanny Kemble, actress, dramatist, poetess, and Shakespearean reader has fascinated many biographers drawn to the multifaceted, often paradoxical nature of her character and experiences. Remembered also as an abolitionist, diarist, and prolific autobiographer, Kemble was accepted within social and intellectual circles in both England and the USA. Her original, though often scathing, wit and spirit of self-determination gained for her respect, if not always approval and affection, from her contemporaries. The transitions in her career, veering from overnight stardom in her youth to the notoriety of her divorce in middle age and culminating in her establishment as an independent admired member of society, project Kemble as a professional and courageous woman, whose stamina overcame the disadvantages of the then ambivalent role of the actress and a highly publicized private life. Her journals, especially *Records of a Girlhood* and *Records of Later Life*, proved immensely popular, ensuring her a comfortable retirement, but more importantly they left to the theatre historian valuable information regarding not only Kemble's direct experiences but also a close view of the contemporary theatrical scene. Eloquent, occasionally elusive, and often self-depreciatory, her writing offers a unique insight into the perceptions and role of a Regency-Victorian actress.

Trained for only three weeks under her mother's tuition, Kemble enjoyed immediate success on her debut in *Romeo and Juliet* on 5 October 1829. Fanny memorabilia, engraved plates, etchings, and nicknacks were purchased throughout fashionable London, a craze that was repeated in the USA upon her first visit there in 1832. She was invited to participate in aristocratic amateur theatricals and attended balls and parties, comingling with circles far superior to her own, as she emphasizes in her diaries. Kemble was very aware of her anachronistic position in such gatherings, being lauded as a novelty rather than as a social equal; indeed, one can argue that this greatly influenced her in her later determination to be accepted unconditionally into middle class society neither as a performer nor as a wife. Kemble's position within the theatre paralleled this situation in that, whilst being trained and supported by her father Charles Kemble on stage, she was chaperoned closely within the theatre, having little contact with fellow performers and being barred from the Green Room. In this context, then, Kemble cannot be said to have been typical of her profession, having the advantages of theatrical renown and a highly protective family unit. The Charles Kembles were actually criticized for the arrangement whereby father and daughter played concomitant roles, Fanny being accused of being unable to play opposite any less capable leading man (a criticism that she heartily ridiculed). However, such criticisms were rare, and plays in which she and Charles Kemble were cast as father and daughter, notably *The Grecian Daughter*, proved highly popular (a gimmick of which Fanny herself wholly disapproved).

In her first season, Kemble was required to master several new parts (she prided herself on her ability to

Fanny Kemble

memorise complete parts in a matter of a few hours), many of which were favourites from the Siddons repertoire. Again, Kemble objected to this manipulation of her own talents for quick financial gain, as she felt she was unsuited to the heavy tragedienne roles that she was required to embody. The physical and emotional demands of such parts as Euphrasia in *The Grecian Daughter*, Bianca in Milman's *Fazio*, Belvidera in Otway's *Venice Preserved*, and Mrs Beverly in Moore's *The Gamester* are immense. Kemble resented the comparisons of herself and her aunt, which were thus forced upon her through managerial policy in reviving what she believed were ponderous and archaic plays suited to Mrs Siddons's particular style. She was also aware that to become stereotyped in parts that were alien to her natural tastes could damage her career prospects were she to continue in them for any length of time. She much preferred Shakespeare's comedy heroines, Portia being her female ideal, and the role of Julia in *The Hunchback* by Sheridan Knowles, the only original leading part that she ever created. Given the opportunity to play Lady Teazle in *The School for Scandal* and Lady Townly in Farquhar's *The Provoked Husband*, Kemble was dissatisfied with her performances, unable to sympathise with the characters and uncomfortable within the superficial and implicitly immoral Restoration setting. Only in her later Shakespearean readings and journal writing was she given scope to develop her natural taste towards comedy; the vitality and humour conveyed in her published works make one regret that such innate qualities were not more encouraged on the stage.

Impressions of Kemble during her early career are mixed (not least because of the various, highly dissimilar portraits that were painted of her). Though famed for her large brown eyes and luxuriant hair, mellow voice, and fluid movements, Kemble was not a beauty. Due to a severe bout of smallpox her complexion was left "muddy" and many admirers were struck by her plain looks upon first personal acquaintance, although commenting upon the animation of her features into a type of beauty when she was enjoying herself. She describes herself as being short, with a tendency towards plumpness, a disadvantage when performing in the enormous Covent Garden auditorium (Kemble much preferred the more intimate houses of Edinburgh and, later, New England). She was painfully aware of her lack of stature when called upon to embody Siddons types such as Euphrasia and Queen Constance and it is remarkable that she could convey the necessary power to an audience with this lack of physical presence. Her elocution and posture were, however, excellent. Kemble argued that she underachieved on the stage due to her lack of enthusiasm and training and affirmed that any success was a result of inherited talents over which she had no control. She relied on nervous energy rather than specific intellectual interpretations of character or mannerisms of the 'Kemble school'. Naturally, this resulted in uneven performances, an indication, Kemble felt, of her inadequacies, and she remained very reliant upon audience approval and response. One can argue, though, that it was exactly her lack of training, the relative absence of marked gestures and 'points' in her acting, that characterised her style and made her an attractive performer. Escaping the rigours of a strict theatrical apprenticeship, Fanny Kemble was adored for her apparent spontaneity and girlishness. The demanding nature of provincial touring certainly tired her but did not detract from this freshness, as her nationwide popularity attests.

Kemble's return to the English stage in 1847 after a 13-year gap and separation from her husband was fraught with difficulties. Now portly and without the direct guidance of her parents, she was required to adapt as best she could to altered modes of acting and new competition. Managing her own business affairs for the first time and desperate to earn a competent livelihood, she toured in the provinces and was engaged to play opposite William Macready at the Princess's Theatre in London in 1848. Typically, her co-star demanded that she play ingenue parts, despite her more mature appearance, choosing plays that highlighted his own talents and made a mockery of hers. Roles foisted upon her included Desdemona, in which she made her debut at the advanced age of 38. Macready's unfavourable comments upon Kemble's acting have cast a shadow over her reputation as an actress, but, simultaneously, it must be remembered that she was highly praised by many well-informed performers and critics, including her exacting parents, Madame Rachel, Ellen Kean, and Brander Matthews. Kemble's re-establishment in the USA and the initiation of her series of Shakespearean readings marked a positive turning point in her career. No longer required to participate in the demeaning business of the theatre, she proceeded to develop her talents with new vigour and satisfaction. 'Playing' all the roles (Ellen Kean disapproved of her acclaimed Falstaff on moral grounds), she won new praise for her ability to invest both minor and major parts with equal pertinence. Although regretting the necessity, she did make use of her father's adaptations of the original texts, as she sought to attract a family audience, gearing her later career towards non-theatregoing members of the public. Without theatrical props, she was said to conjure up scenes with remarkable effect and emotional depth, thus ultimately achieving what she believed to be the ideal means of conveying the beauties of Shakespearean drama.

—S. Johnson

KEMBLE, John Philip. British actor-manager. Born in Prescott, Lancashire, 1 February 1757. Educated at Sedgley Park Roman Catholic school, Staffordshire, from 1767; trained for the priesthood at the English College, Douai, France, 1771–75. Married actress Priscilla Hopkins in 1787. Early stage experience as a child in the touring company of his parents, Roger Kemble and Sarah Ward; adult debut, Chamberlain's company, Wolverhampton, 1776; established reputation in the provinces playing alongside his sister Sarah Siddons (q.v.) and his brother Charles Kemble (q.v.); wrote several unsuccessful plays; actor, Smock Alley Theatre, Dublin, 1781–83; first appearance, Theatre Royal, Drury Lane, London, as Hamlet, 1783; succeeded R. B. Sheridan as Drury Lane manager, 1788–1796, 1800–01; opened rebuilt Drury Lane, 1794; subsequent appearances restricted by asthma and gout; acquired share in Covent Garden and became leading tragedian at the theatre, 1796; visited France and Spain, 1802; co-manager, Covent Garden, 1802–17; hit financially by destruction of Covent Garden by fire, 1808; introduction of new ticket prices at rebuilt Covent Garden under his management sparked notorious O. P. (Old Price) Riots, 1809; made final appearance and retired to Lausanne, 1817. Died in Lausanne, Switzerland, 26 February 1823.

Principal roles

1776	Theodosius in *Theodosius* (N. Lee), Wolverhampton, England.
	Bajazet in *Tamerlane* (Rowe), provincial tour.
	Tancred in *Tancred and Sigismunda* (Thomson), provincial tour.
c.1777	Captain Plume in *The Recruiting Officer* (Farquhar), Wakefield, England.
1778	Macbeth in *Macbeth* (Shakespeare), Hull, England.
	Archer in *The Beaux' Stratagem* (Farquhar), provincial tour.
1779	Orestes in *The Distresst Mother* (Racine, translated by Philips), York, England.
	Ranger in *A Fond Husband* (D'Urfey), York, England.
	Edward in *Edward the Black Prince* (Shirley), York, England.
1780	Hamlet in *Hamlet* (Shakespeare), York, England.
1781	The Master in *The Toy Shop* (Dodsley), Edinburgh.
	Contrast in *The Lord of the Manor*, Edinburgh.
	Puff in *The Critic* (Sheridan), Edinburgh.

	Sir Giles Overreach in *A New Way to Pay Old Debts* (Massinger), Edinburgh.
	Sir George Touchwood in *The Belle's Stratagem* (Cowley), Smock Alley Theatre, Dublin.
	Alexander in *Alexander the Great* (N. Lee), Smock Alley Theatre, Dublin.
	Raymond in *The Count of Narbonne* (Jephson, adapted from Walpole's *The Castle of Otranto*), Smock Alley Theatre, Dublin.
1783	Richard in *Richard III* (Shakespeare), Theatre Royal, Drury Lane, London.
	Beverley in *The Gamester* (Moore), Theatre Royal, Drury Lane, London.
	King John in *King John* (Shakespeare), Theatre Royal, Drury Lane, London.
	Shylock in *The Merchant of Venice* (Shakespeare), Theatre Royal, Drury Lane, London.
	Alwin in *The Countess of Salisbury* (Hartson), Theatre Royal, Drury Lane, London.
	Cato in *Cato* (Addison), Theatre Royal, Drury Lane, London.
	Carlos in *Love Makes a Man* (Cibber), Theatre Royal, Drury Lane, London.
	Jupiter in *Amphitryon* (Dryden), Theatre Royal, Drury Lane, London.
1784	Montgomerie in *The Carmelite* (Cumberland), Theatre Royal, Drury Lane, London.
1785	Adorni in *The Maid of Honour* (Massinger, adapted by J. P. Kemble), Theatre Royal, Drury Lane, London.
	Othello in *Othello* (Shakespeare), Theatre Royal, Drury Lane, London.
	Posthumus in *Cymbeline* (Shakespeare), Theatre Royal, Drury Lane, London.
1786	Orlando in *As You Like It* (Shakespeare), Theatre Royal, Drury Lane, London.
	Richard in *Richard Coeur de Lion* (Burgoyne), Theatre Royal, Drury Lane, London.
1787	Castalio in *The Orphan* (Otway), Theatre Royal, Drury Lane, London.
	Pedro in *The Pilgrim* (Fletcher, adapted by J. P. Kemble), Theatre Royal, Drury Lane, London.
1788	Lear in *King Lear* (Shakespeare), Theatre Royal, Drury Lane, London.
	Cleombrotus in *The Fate of Sparta* (Cowley), Theatre Royal, Drury Lane, London.
	Manuel in *The Regent* (Greatheed), Theatre Royal, Drury Lane, London.
	Benedick in *Much Ado About Nothing* (Shakespeare), Theatre Royal, Drury Lane, London.
	Antony in *Love for Love* (Congreve), Theatre Royal, Drury Lane, London.
	Lord Towneley in *The Provoked Husband* (Cibber), Theatre Royal, Drury Lane, London.
	Biron in *Isabella* (Southerne), Theatre Royal, Drury Lane, London.
	Leon in *Rule a Wife and Have a Wife* (Fletcher), Theatre Royal, Drury Lane, London.
	Sciolto in *The Fair Penitent* (Rowe), Theatre Royal, Drury Lane, London.
	Mirabel in *The Way of the World* (Congreve), Theatre Royal, Drury Lane, London.

Cromwell and Griffith in *Henry VIII* (Shakespeare), Theatre Royal, Drury Lane, London.

1788–89 Norval in *Douglas* (Home), Theatre Royal, Drury Lane, London.

Osmyn in *The Mourning Bride* (Congreve), Theatre Royal, Drury Lane, London.

Zanga in *The Revenge* (Young), Theatre Royal, Drury Lane, London.

Coriolanus in *Coriolanus* (Shakespeare), Theatre Royal, Drury Lane, London.

Paladore in *The Law of Lombardy* (Jephson), Theatre Royal, Drury Lane, London.

Sir Clement Flint in *The Heiress* (Burgoyne), Theatre Royal, Drury Lane, London.

Petruchio in *The Taming of the Shrew* (Shakespeare), Theatre Royal, Drury Lane, London.

Romeo in *Romeo and Juliet* (Shakespeare), Theatre Royal, Drury Lane, London.

Wolsey in *Henry VIII* (Shakespeare), Theatre Royal, Drury Lane, London.

Malvolio in *Twelfth Night* (Shakespeare), Theatre Royal, Drury Lane, London.

Norfolk in *Mary Queen of Scots* (St John), Theatre Royal, Drury Lane, London.

Marquis in *False Appearances* (Conway), Theatre Royal, Drury Lane, London.

1789 Henry in *Henry V* (Shakespeare, adapted by J. P. Kemble), Theatre Royal, Drury Lane, London.

Don Pedro in *The False Friend* (Vanbrugh, adapted by J. P. Kemble), Theatre Royal, Drury Lane, London.

Hernandez in *Marcella* (Hayley), Theatre Royal, Drury Lane, London.

1790 Willmore in *Love in Many Masks* (J. P. Kemble, adapted from Behn's *The Rover*), Theatre Royal, Drury Lane, London.

Raleigh in *Sir Walter Raleigh* (Sewell), Theatre Royal, Drury Lane, London.

Sir Charles Easy in *The Careless Husband* (Cibber), Theatre Royal, Drury Lane, London.

Doricourt in *The Belle's Stratagem* (Cowley), Theatre Royal, Drury Lane, London.

Faulkland in *The Rivals* (Sheridan), Theatre Royal, Drury Lane, London.

Young Marlow in *She Stoops to Conquer* (Goldsmith), Theatre Royal, Drury Lane, London.

1790–91 Charles Surface in *The School for Scandal* (Sheridan), Theatre Royal, Drury Lane, London.

Saville in *Better Late than Never* (Reynolds and Andrews), Theatre Royal, Drury Lane, London.

1791–92 Hotspur in *Henry IV, part 1* (Shakespeare), Haymarket Opera House, London.

Oakley in *The Jealous Wife* (Colman the Elder), Haymarket Opera House, London.

Huniades in *Huniades* (Brand), Haymarket Opera House, London.

1792–93 Pirithous in *The Rival Sisters* (Murphy), Haymarket Opera House, London.

Horatio in *The Fair Penitent* (Rowe), Haymarket Opera House, London.

1793 Octavian in *The Mountaineers* (Colman the Younger), Haymarket Theatre, London.

1794 Prince of Guastalla in *Emilia Galotti* (Lessing), Theatre Royal, Drury Lane, London.

Heraclius in *The Roman Father* (Whitehead), Theatre Royal, Drury Lane, London.

Bertram in *All's Well That Ends Well* (Shakespeare, adapted by J. P. Kemble), Theatre Royal, Drury Lane, London.

The Duke in *Measure for Measure* (Shakespeare), Theatre Royal, Drury Lane, London.

1795 Penruddock in *The Wheel of Fortune* (Cumberland), Theatre Royal, Drury Lane, London.

Edwy in *Edwy and Elgiva* (D'Arblay), Theatre Royal, Drury Lane, London.

Zaphna in *Mahomet* (Voltaire), Theatre Royal, Drury Lane, London.

1796 Sir Edward Mortimer in *The Iron Chest* (Colman the Younger), Theatre Royal, Drury Lane, London.

Vortigern in *Vortigern* (Ireland), Theatre Royal, Drury Lane, London.

Alonzo in *Almeyda* (S. Lee), Theatre Royal, Drury Lane, London.

1796–97 Sextus in *Conspiracy* (Jephson), Theatre Royal, Drury Lane, London.

1797–98 Percy in *The Castle Spectre* (Lewis), Theatre Royal, Drury Lane, London.

The Stranger in *The Stranger* (Kotzebue, adapted by Thompson), Theatre Royal, Drury Lane, London.

1798 Aurelio in *Aurelio and Miranda* (adapted from Lewis's *Ambrosio; or, The Monk*), Theatre Royal, Drury Lane, London.

1799 Rivers in *The East Indian* (Lewis), Theatre Royal, Drury Lane, London.

The Old Count in *The Castle of Montval* (Whalley), Theatre Royal, Drury Lane, London.

Rolla in *Pizarro* (Sheridan), Theatre Royal, Drury Lane, London.

1800 Prince Richard in *Adelaide* (Pye), Theatre Royal, Drury Lane, London.

De Montfort in *De Montfort* (Baillie), Theatre Royal, Drury Lane, London.

Antonio in *Antonio* (Godwin), Theatre Royal, Drury Lane, London.

1801 De L'Epée in *Deaf and Dumb* (Holcroft), Theatre Royal, Drury Lane, London.

1802 Leontes in *The Winter's Tale* (Shakespeare), Theatre Royal, Drury Lane, London.

1803–04 Richmond in *Richard III* (Shakespeare), Covent Garden, London.

Antonio in *The Merchant of Venice* (Shakespeare), Covent Garden, London.

Old Norval in *Douglas* (Home), Covent Garden, London.

Henry in *Henry IV, part 2* (Shakespeare), Covent Garden, London.

Ford in *The Merry Wives of Windsor* (Shakespeare), Covent Garden, London.

1804 Villars in *The Blind Bargain* (Reynolds), Covent Garden, London.

1805   Sir Oswin Mortland in *To Marry or Not to Marry* (Inchbald), Covent Garden, London.
        Barford in *Who Wants a Guinea?* (Colman the Younger), Covent Garden, London.
        Eustace St Pierre in *The Surrender of Calais* (Colman the Younger), Covent Garden, London.
1805–06 Gloster in *Jane Shore* (Rowe), Covent Garden, London.
        Pierre in *Venice Preserved* (Otway), Covent Garden, London.
        The Delinquent in *The Delinquent* (Reynolds), Covent Garden, London.
1806   Prospero in *The Tempest* (Shakespeare, adapted by J. P. Kemble), Covent Garden, London.
1807   Reuben Glenroy in *Town and Country* (Morton), Covent Garden, London.
        Iago in *Othello* (Shakespeare), Covent Garden, London.
        Valentine in *The Two Gentlemen of Verona* (Shakespeare), Covent Garden, London.
1812   Brutus in *Julius Caesar* (Shakespeare), Covent Garden, London.

Other roles included: *Zenobia* (Murphy), York, England, 1778; *Warren Hastings* (Feuchtwanger), Cork, Ireland 1781; *Julia* (Jephson), Theatre Royal, Drury Lane, London, 1787; *The Plain Dealer* (Bickerstaff), Theatre Royal, Drury Lane, London, 1796; *The Roman Actor* (J. P. Kemble, adapted from Massinger), Theatre Royal, Drury Lane, London, 1796.

Publications

Belisarius (play), 1776; *The Female Officer* (play), 1779; *Fugitive Pieces* (verse), 1780; *Oh! It's Impossible* (adaptation of *The Comedy of Errors*), 1780; *The Maid of Honour* (adaptation from Massinger), 1784; *Macbeth Reconsidered*, 1786; *The Pilgrim* (adaptation from Fletcher), 1787; *Coriolanus* (adaptation from Shakespeare), 1789; *The Farm House* (adaptation from Johnson's *Country Lasses; or, The Custom of the Manor*), 1789; *Henry V* (adaptation from Shakespeare), 1789; *The Tempest* (adaptation from Shakespeare), 1789; *The False Friend* (adaptation from Vanbrugh), 1789; *The Pannel* (play), 1789; *Love in Many Masks* (adaptation from Behn's *The Rover*), 1790; *Lodoiska* (adaptation from French original), 1794; *All's Well That Ends Well* (adaptation from Shakespeare), 1794; *The Roman Actor* (adaptation from Massinger), 1794; *The Merchant of Venice* (adaptation from Shakespeare), 1795; *Alexander the Great* (adaptation from N. Lee), 1795; *Celadon and Florimel* (adaptation from Cibber's *The Comical Lovers)*, 1796; *The Plain Dealer*, 1796; *The Merry Wives of Windsor* (adaptation from Shakespeare), 1797; *Much Ado About Nothing* (adaptation from Shakespeare), 1799; *The Way of the World* (adaptation from Congreve), 1800; *Hamlet* (adaptation from Shakespeare), 1800; *King John* (adaptation from Shakespeare), 1800; *King Lear* (adaptation from Shakespeare), 1800; *Henry IV, part 1* (adaptation from Shakespeare), 1803; *Macbeth* (adaptation from Shakespeare), 1803; *Measure for Measure* (adaptation from Shakespeare), 1803; *Othello* (adaptation from Shakespeare), 1804; *Henry IV, part 2* (adaptation from Shakespeare), 1804; *Henry VIII* (adaptation from Shakespeare), 1804; *Two Gentlemen of Verona* (adaptation from Shakespeare), 1805; *Life of John Philip Kemble*, 1809; *Richard III* (adaptation from Shakespeare), 1810; *As You Like It* (adaptation from Shakespeare), 1810; *British Theatre* (collected adaptations of earlier plays), 1815; *Macbeth and King Richard III*, 1817; *An Authentic Narrative of Mr Kemble's Retirement from the Stage*, 1817; *The Double Dealer* (adaptation from Congreve), undated.

*

Bibliography

Books:
John Ambrose Williams, *Memoirs of John Philip Kemble*, 1817.
James Boaden, *Memoirs of the Life of John Philip Kemble, Esq.*, 2 vols., Philadelphia, 1825.
Percy H. Fitzgerald, *The Kembles*, 2 vols., London, 1871.
Herschel C. Baker, *John Philip Kemble: The Actor in His Theatre*, Cambridge, Massachusetts, 1942.

Articles:
H. Martin, "Remarks on the Character of Richard III; as Played by Cooke and Kemble" (pamphlet), London, 1801.
Theodore Martin, "An Eye-witness of John Kemble", *The Nineteenth Century*, 7, 1880.
Rosamund Gilder, "Kemble Religion; A Family Portrait", *Theatre Arts Monthly*, 17, 1933.

* * *

During the 1780's and 1790's, John Philip Kemble and his sister Sarah Siddons, as leading tragedians at Drury Lane, established a style of acting significantly different from that of the mid-18th century actors David Garrick and Charles Macklin. Whilst their predecessors had concentrated on interpreting their roles in terms of sharply contrasted passions and emotions — Garrick, in particular, conveying emotion by an almost feverish animation of physical gesture and facial expression, which prompted George III to describe him as "a great fidget" — Kemble and Siddons formed their interpretations around the singular *ruling passion* of a role, in which, according to Hazlitt, "all the passions move round a central point and are governed by one master-key". Kemble, although capable of great physical agility when required, as in the melodramatic roles of Percy in 'Monk' Lewis's *The Castle Spectre* and the Peruvian warrior Rolla in Sheridan's *Pizarro*, was remarkable for his stillness and dignity upon stage, the grandure of which is evoked in Lawrence's huge portrait of him as Coriolanus, wrapped in the single sweep of a dark cloak.

Theatre historians have categorised Kemble's style as "classical" as opposed to the more emotionally indulgent "romanticism" of Garrick, who preceded him, and Edmund Kean, who, according to Hazlitt writing in 1816, "destroyed the Kemble religion ... in which we were brought up". Whereas both Garrick and Kean were praised for their recreation of "natural" impulses, Kemble was recognised as self-consciously creating a work of art. But his classicism was not emotionless, nor mere rhetorical technique; he too analysed characters in terms of their feelings and strove to move his audience's sympathy, but, by revealing the particular ruling passion that motivated the different characters he played, he gave each interpretation a sense of unity and uniqueness of effect. Kemble's strong sense of the form of a dramatic performance not only led to a differentiation between characters but, by the pacing of his own performance, structured the production as a whole towards a climactic moment of emotional intensity. Macready described how his interpretation of Macbeth was, in the first four acts, "correct, tame, and effective: but in the fifth, when the news was brought 'The queen, my lord, is dead', he seemed struck to the heart ... Then, as if with the inspiration of despair, he hurried out distinctly and pathetically the lines 'Tomorrow and tomorrow and tomorrow ... ' rising to a climax of desperation that brought down the enthusiastic cheers of the closely packed theatre". This emphasis on Macbeth's guilty despair revealed a more perceptive understanding of the psychology of the character and of the meaning of the play than the emphasis Garrick gave to the more obviously exciting moments when Macbeth starts in horror at his visions of the bloody knife and of Banquo's ghost. In a similar comment on Kemble's famous portrayal of Addison's Cato, Macready recorded that "like an eruptive volcano from some level expanse, there was one burst that electrified the house". Walter Scott too was impressed by the tension between "natural" emotion and "intellectual" restraint in Kemble's toga-performances — Cato, Coriolanus, and Brutus — "those lofty Romans, feeling and partly exhibiting, yet on the whole conquering, the passions of nature by the mental discipline to which they have trained themselves".

Kemble's style served him well when playing stoical Romans, but Hazlitt thought that his Hamlet lacked flexibility and the "sensibility which yields to every motive, and is borne away with every breath of fancy ... he played it like a man in armour, with a determined inveteracy of purpose, in one undeviating straight line".

Kemble became manager both at Drury Lane, under the irresponsible proprietorship of Sheridan, and at Covent Garden, in partnership with Thomas Harris. He was responsible for restoring more accuracy to the playing texts of Shakespeare and encouraging the trend towards historically correct costumes and settings, thus earning for himself a reputation for scholarship, which is confirmed by his extensive collection of early play texts and theoretical works, which, having been purchased from him by the Duke of Devonshire, is now to be found in the Huntingdon Library, California. Rather reluctantly, he presided over the enlargement of Drury Lane by Henry Holland in 1794, which Siddons described as making it into a "wilderness of a place", and of Covent Garden in 1808. The attempt to raise prices to help pay for the new building led to the infamous O.P. (Old Price) riots. For 67 nights Kemble confronted the organized mob, his patrician bearing doing little to placate the rowdy champions of "British liberty". During his career as actor and manager he saw a change in the general repertoire, with a decline in the comedies of manners, that had been so well performed by Garrick's ensemble company, and a rise in spectacular melodramas and sentimental domestic tragedies, such as those based on the romantic plays of Kotzebue.

Intelligent, dignified, and responsible — though occasionally indulging in bouts of drunkenness — John Kemble maintained the social respectability that had been won by Garrick and which was to be sacrificed by Edmund Kean. As theatrical taste became more fickle, impressed by spectacle and novelty, Kemble had to suffer the indignity of sharing the stage with Master Betty, the 13-year-old tragedian, and Carlo the Performing Dog, and, in his later years, the majestic delivery of his artistically constructed interpretations seemed increasingly stilted and outdated. Nevertheless, certain elements of the Kemble style were to influence some of the more serious Victorian actors, among them Macready, Helen Faucit, and Samuel Phelps.

—George Taylor

KEMP, Will. English actor. Born William Kemp (or Kempe), possibly in Ipswich, c.1560. Stage debut probably with Leicester's Men, Ipswich, c.1580; travelled with the Earl of Leicester's company to France and the Netherlands, possibly as replacement for clown Richard Tarlton, 1585; acted in Denmark and Saxony, 1586; actor, Strange's Men, 1588–94; inherited roles and fame of Tarlton on the latter's death, 1588; sharer, Lord Chamberlain's Men, 1594–99; celebrated particularly for jigs danced at the close of plays; summoned to act at Court with Shakespeare and Richard Burbage, 1594; famous nine-day jig from London to Norwich, 1600; toured Italy and Germany, 1601; actor, Worcester's Men, from 1601. Freedom of the Merchant Adventurers' Company, 1600. Died (probably in London of plague) c.1603 (possibly 2 November).

Conjectured roles (venues uncertain)

1592	Role in *A Knack to Know a Knave* (anon.).
	Itys in *Seven Deadly Sins* (Tarlton).
	Clown in *Titus Andronicus* (Shakespeare).
1594–99	Launce in *The Two Gentlemen of Verona* (Shakespeare).
	Bottom in *A Midsummer Night's Dream* (Shakespeare).
	Dogberry in *Much Ado About Nothing* (Shakespeare).
	Launcelot Gobbo in *The Merchant of Venice* (Shakespeare).
	Clown/Costard in *Love's Labour's Lost* (Shakespeare).
	Peter in *Romeo and Juliet* (Shakespeare).
	Cob in *Every Man out of his Humour* (Jonson).
	Falstaff in *Henry IV* (Shakespeare).
1601–03	Role in *How a Man May Choose a Good Wife from a Bad* (Heywood).
	Role in *The Royal King and the Loyal Subject* (Smith and Heywood).
	Role in *Sir Thomas Wyatt* (adapted from *Lady Jane* by Dekker, Heywood, Webster, Chettle, and Smith).
	Role in *Sir Thomas More* (Shakespeare, Munday, and others).
	Role in *A Woman Killed with Kindness* (Heywood).

Himself in *Return from Parnassus* (anon.).

Other conjectured roles include: Justice Shallow in *Henry IV, part 2/The Merry Wives of Windsor* (Shakespeare).

Publications

Three Jigs, 1595; *Kemp's Nine Daies Wonder: Performed in a Daunce from London to Norwich* (pamphlet), 1600.

*

Bibliography

Books:
David Wiles, *Shakespeare's Clown. Actor and Text in the Elizabethan Playhouse*, Cambridge, 1987.

* * *

"He calls himself Kemp". Thus was William Kemp introduced onto the stage in *The Travels of The English Brothers*, written by Day, Rowley, and Wilkins in 1607. Writing four years after Kemp's death, Day, who was a firsthand acquaintance, indicates the blunt, straightforward quality of the man. Kemp, the last of the great Elizabethan clowns, was very much a man who had walked if not quite with kings, certainly with earls, but had not lost the common touch. Unlike many of his contemporaries, upward social mobility and financial gain did not interest him. His comedy was anchored in the language and life of the common man.

Though he was to reach the position of leading comic player with The Lord Chamberlain's Men, Kemp began his career as a solo clown and essentially that is what he remained. His first recorded association is with the Earl of Leicester in the Netherlands. As a solo performer or in a small itinerant company, he travelled widely, performing in Denmark (in Elsinore!), France, and Italy. The fact that his comedy crossed linguistic boundaries provides an obvious indication of its nature: it relied more on the physical and visual than on the verbal, though he was evidently able to make jokes in German.

Kemp seems to have looked comical. He had "an ill face". In this he was not alone: Tarlton had a squint, while Armin was deformed. Kemp was clearly also an athlete with huge resources of energy and stamina. He could leap both high and long, jumping ditches and churchyard walls. His *Nine Daies Wonder* records his remarkable feat of morris-dancing from London to Norwich along Elizabethan roads in February.

Such is the power of Shakespeare that any leading player with 'his' company is now accorded some degree of fame by association, but for his contemporaries Kemp's popularity as a clown rested firmly on his jigs rather than in his appearances in scripted plays. These jigs, ultimately derived from folk drama, games, and rituals, were performances given after scripted plays. Jigs provided the stage clown with his chance to present a repertoire of improvisation, direct address, rhyming, singing, and dancing. Dancing was central to the jig, which combined the leaping of the morris with the whirling of courtly galliards. Kemp was clearly an expert dancer. Marston, no fan, mocked this

Title page of *Kemps Nine Daies Wonder,* picturing **William Kemp** in costume for his famous dance.

expertise in the phrase "the orbs celestial will daunce Kempe's jig".

Being largely free of the constraints of a script that could be censored, jigs verged towards the anarchistic. They were of an overtly sexual nature. The verbal wit tended to be obscene, the dancing to be lascivious. David Wiles sums up the evidence: "It is reasonable, therefore, though always insufficient as a final analysis, to regard the jig as a form of soft commercial pornography". Whilst their connection to the scripted play that had preceded them might have been tenuous, the jigs were an integral part of the Elizabethan play-going experience.

Within the scripted repertoire of the Lord Chamberlain's Men, Kemp played such roles as Bottom, Launcelot Gobbo, Peter, Dogberry, and (probably) Falstaff. His roles were plebian, his speech colloquial prose. Even within a script, Kemp was essentially a solo performer. His roles stand independent of the plot and he was frequently provided with monologues. The charge of improvising within a play is often laid against him, as though this was some sort of sacrilege. Was Burbage as Hamlet making a direct reference to Kemp in his famous advice to the players "And let those that play your clowns speak no more than is set down for them"? Richard Brome, in *The Antipodes* in 1636, clearly associates Kemp with altering and diminishing "what the writer with care and skill compos'd". Possibly Kemp did do this. Possibly, as an equal partner in a collaborative venture, he might have believed that clown and playwright had an equal status. If so, he was proved to be wrong for the balance of theatrical power was inexorably shifting towards the playwright.

Around 1599, when the Lord Chamberlain's Men were seeking to please a more socially select and monied audience, Kemp's style of clowning was felt to be out of place. Whether Kemp left the company of his own volition or not, his clowning could no longer be part of the theatrical experience the company was offering at the newly opened Globe. Kemp recorded that "I have daunst my selfe out of the world" (a pun on the Globe), but he might just as easily have been pushed. It is difficult not to see Hamlet's criticism of a clown "that keeps one suit of jests" in the 'bad' First Quarto of 1603, as not being directed at the back of the departing clown. With the rise in importance of the playwright, jigs in particular and improvisation in general was no longer regarded as fare fit for an educated audience. With the replacement of Kemp by Robert Armin, the Lord Chamberlain's Men abandoned jigs and improvisation.

Kemp did not, however. Whatever the circumstances of his departure, he continued unabashed, eventually becoming a member of Worcester's Men and still appealing to those that Hamlet called "barren spectators" but Kemp called "honest fellows". Day wrote of him:

> We neither look for scholarship nor art
> But harmless mirth, for that's thy usual part.

One cannot help feeling that Kemp would have taken that as a huge compliment.

—Christopher Sutcliffe

KOLTAI, Ralph. British designer. Born in Berlin, Germany, 31 July 1924. Educated at schools in Berlin; trained for the stage at the Central School of Arts and Crafts, London, 1948–51. Served in Royal Army Service Corps, 1944–48; attached to Intelligence Corps, Nuremberg War Crimes Trial and War Crimes Interrogation Unit, after World War II. Married Mary Annena Stubbs in 1956 (divorced 1976). Designer, Royal Shakespeare Company, from 1962; associate artist, Royal Shakespeare Theatre, 1963–66 and from 1976; head of theatre design, Central School of Art and Design, London, 1965–72; has also designed, on a freelance basis, plays, operas, and ballets around the world. Recipient: London Drama Critics' Award, 1967, 1981; Individual Gold Medal (co-winner), Prague Quadriennal International Exhibition of Scenography, 1975; Society of West End Theatre Award, 1978, 1984; Golden Troika National Award (co-winner), Prague, 1979; Royal Society of Arts Designer for Industry, 1984; Individual Silver Medal, Prague, 1987. CBE (Commander of the British Empire), 1983.

Productions

1950   *Angelique* (opera), Fortune Theatre, London.
Le Pauvre Matelot, Opera Club, London.

1951   *Werther* (Massenet), Dartington Hall, London.
The Wandering Scholar, English Opera Group, London.

The Sleeping Children, English Opera Group, London.

1952   *Samson and Delilah* (Saint-Saëns), Sadler's Wells Theatre, London.

1954   *The Boatswain's Mate* (Smyth), Dartington Hall, London.
Junior Clerk, Ballet Comique tour.
The Governess, St Pancras Town Hall, London.

1955   *Cosi Fan Tutte* (Mozart), Dartington Hall, London.
Tannhauser (Wagner), Royal Opera House, Covent Garden, London.

1956   *The Medium* (Menotti), Opera School, London.
The Marriage of Figaro (Mozart), Opera School, London.

1957   *Sister Angelica* (Puccini), Opera School, London.

1958   *The Judgement of Paris* (Laing and Weill), Opera School, London.
The Two Brothers, Ballet Rambert.

1959   *Il Campanello*, Opera School, London.
Iphigenia in Aulis (Gluck), Opera School, London.
Hazana, Ballet Rambert.
Il Prigoniero (Dallapiccola), Sadler's Wells Theatre, London.
The Impresario (Mozart), Opera School, London.
The Riders to the Sea (Vaughan Williams), Opera School, London.
Comedy on a Bridge (Martinu), Opera School, London.

1960   *Il Mondo della Luna* (Haydn), Group 8.
Erwartung (Schoenberg), Sadler's Wells Theatre, London.
Dido and Aeneas (Purcell), Opera School, London.
Hercules, Handel Opera Society.

1961   *Volpone*, Sadler's Wells Theatre, London.
A Place in the Desert, Ballet Rambert.
Carmen (Bizet), Sadler's Wells Theatre, London.

1962   *Tales of Hoffmann* (Offenbach), Opera School, London.
Il Tabarro (Puccini), Sadler's Wells Theatre, London.
The Caucasian Chalk Circle (Brecht), Aldwych Theatre, London.
Murder in the Cathedral (Pizzetti), Sadler's Wells Theatre, London.
The Raising of Lazarus, Sadler's Wells Theatre, London.
Boulevard Solitude (Henze and Weil), Sadler's Wells Theatre, London.
Conflicts, Ballet Rambert.
A Midsummer Night's Dream (Shakespeare), Teatro Colon, Buenos Aires.

1963   *The Rise and Fall of the City of Mahagonny* (Brecht and Weill), Sadler's Wells Theatre, London.
Fra Diavolo (Auber), Opera School, London.
Otello (Verdi), Scottish Opera.
Volo de Notte, Scottish Opera.
The Travellers, Ballet Rambert.

The Representative (Hochhuth), Aldwych Theatre, London.

Sgt Dower Must Die, Vaudeville Theatre, London.

Attila, Sadler's Wells Theatre, London.

1964   *Don Giovanni* (Mozart), Scottish Opera.

The Birthday Party (Pinter), Aldwych Theatre, London.

Endgame (Beckett), Aldwych Theatre, London.

Cul de Sac, Ballet Rambert.

Happy End (Brecht), Edinburgh Festival.

The Jew of Malta (Marlowe), Aldwych Theatre, London.

The Man Who Let It Rain, Theatre Royal, Stratford East, London.

1965   *The Tribute*, Royal Ballet.

The Merchant of Venice (Shakespeare), Royal Shakespeare Theatre, Stratford-upon-Avon.

Don Giovanni (Mozart), Los Angeles.

Boris Godunov (Mussorgsky), Scottish Opera.

Timon of Athens (Shakespeare), Royal Shakespeare Theatre, Stratford-upon-Avon.

From the House of the Dead (Janáček), Sadler's Wells Theatre, London.

Raymonda (Glazunov), Australian Ballet.

1966   *Diversities*, Ballet Rambert.

Gaiety of Nations and *Allergy* (Taylor), London Traverse Company.

The Bellow Plays (Bellow), London Traverse Company.

The King's Mare (Canolle, adapted by Loos), Garrick Theatre, London.

Bread and Butter (O'Neill), London Traverse Company.

The General's Tea Party (Vian), London Traverse Company.

1967   *The Rake's Progress* (Stravinsky), Scottish Opera.

Little Murders (Feiffer), Aldwych Theatre, London; Theatre Toronto, 1968.

As You Like It (Shakespeare), Old Vic Theatre, London.

1968   *Raymonda* (Glazunov), Norske Opera.

The Drummer's Boy, Theatre Toronto.

Soldiers (Hochhuth), Theatre Toronto, New York, and Albery Theatre, London.

The Tempest (Shakespeare), Chichester Festival Theatre.

Othello (Shakespeare), Sofia.

1969   *Back to Methuselah* (G. B. Shaw), Old Vic Theatre, London.

1970   *The Bacchae* (Euripides), Schauspielhaus, Dusseldorf.

The Valkyrie (Wagner), Coliseum Theatre, London.

Elegy for Young Lovers (Henze), Scottish Opera.

Major Barbara (G. B. Shaw), Aldwych Theatre, London.

1971   *Gotterdammerung* (Wagner), Coliseum Theatre, London.

Lulu (Berg), Welsh National Opera.

The Rake's Progress (Stravinsky), Scottish Opera.

1972   *Rhinegold* (Wagner), Coliseum Theatre, London.

Duke Bluebeard's Castle (Bartók), Coliseum Theatre, London.

Taverner (Davies), Royal Opera House, Covent Garden, London.

Hullaballoo, Criterion Theatre, London.

Macbeth (Verdi), Burgtheatre, Vienna.

1973   *Siegfried* (Wagner), Coliseum Theatre, London.

Tristan and Isolde, Scottish Opera.

Lulu (Berg), Kassel.

Tannhauser (Wagner), Sydney Opera House.

Wozzeck (Berg), Nederlandsche Opera.

1974   *The Ring Cycle* (Wagner), tour.

Billy (adapted from Hall and Waterhouse's *Billy Liar*), Theatre Royal, Drury Lane, London.

Oedipus Tyrannus (Sophocles), Chichester Festival Theatre.

Fidelio (Beethoven), Bavarian State Opera.

The Highwaymen (Schiller), Round House Theatre, London.

1975   *Otello* (Verdi), Scottish Opera.

Don Giovanni (Mozart), Snape and tour.

The Mouthorgan (devised), The Other Place, Stratford-upon-Avon; co-directed.

Too True to Be Good (G. B. Shaw), Aldwych Theatre, London.

1976   *Billy* (adapted from Hall and Waterhouse's *Billy Liar*), Theatre an der Wien, Vienna.

Macbeth (Verdi), Scottish Opera.

Midsummer Marriage (Tippett), Welsh National Opera.

Old World (Arbuzov), Aldwych Theatre, London, and Royal Shakespeare Theatre, Stratford-upon-Avon.

Wild Oats (O'Keeffe), Aldwych Theatre, London, and Piccadilly Theatre, London.

1977   *King Lear* (Shakespeare), Reyjavik.

State of Revolution (Bolt), National Theatre, London.

Every Good Boy Deserves Favour (Stoppard), Royal Festival Hall, London.

Cruel Garden (Kemp), Ballet Rambert.

The Icebreak (Tippett), Royal Opera House, Covent Garden, London.

Rosmersholm (Ibsen), Haymarket Theatre, London.

Sons of Light (Rudkin), The Other Place, Stratford-upon-Avon.

She Stoops to Conquer (Goldsmith), Hong Kong Festival.

1978   *The Guardsman* (Molnár), National Theatre, London.

Brand (Ibsen), National Theatre, London.

The Tempest (Shakespeare), Royal Shakespeare Company.

Happy Days, Hong Kong Festival.

Love's Labour's Lost (Shakespeare), Royal Shakespeare Company.

The Seven Deadly Sins (Weill and Brecht), Coliseum Theatre, London.

Hippolytus (Rudkin), The Other Place, Stratford-upon-Avon.

1979   *The Threepenny Opera* (Brecht), Aalborg, Denmark.

Don Quixote (adapted from Cervantes), Round House, London.

Baal (Brecht), The Other Place, Stratford-upon-Avon.

The Wild Duck (Ibsen), National Theatre, London.

1980   *The Love Girl and the Innocent*, Aalborg, Denmark; Royal Shakespeare Company, 1981.

Romeo and Juliet (Shakespeare), Royal Shakespeare Company; revived, 1981.

1981   *Man and Superman* (G. B. Shaw), National Theatre, London.

Terra Nova (Tally), Aalborg, Denmark.

Hamlet (Shakespeare), Royal Shakespeare Company.

Anna Karenina (Shchedrin), Coliseum Theatre, London; revived there, 1985.

The Carmelites (Poulenc), Aalborg, Denmark.

1982   *Much Ado About Nothing* (Shakespeare), Aldwych Theatre, London; US tour, 1984.

The Soldier's Tale (Stravinsky) and *Facade* (Walton and Sitwell), Barbican Theatre, London.

Don Giovanni (Mozart), Welsh National Opera.

Molière (Goldoni), Royal Shakespeare Company.

1983   *Die Soldaten*, Lyons Opera.

Bugsy Malone (Williams, adapted by Dolenz), Her Majesty's Theatre, London.

Cyrano de Bergerac (Rostand), Aldwych Theatre, London; US tour, 1984.

Dear Anyone (Whitemore), Cambridge Theatre, London.

Pack of Lies, Lyric Theatre, London; Boston, New York, and Hamburg, 1985.

Custom of the Country (Fletcher and Massinger), Royal Shakespeare Company.

1984   *The Rise and Fall of the City of Mahagonny* (Brecht and Weill), Aalborg, Denmark.

Italian Girl in Algiers (Rossini), Grand Theatre de Geneve.

1985   *Measure for Measure* (Shakespeare), Norrkoping, Sweden.

Troilus and Cressida (Shakespeare), Royal Shakespeare Company.

Othello (Shakespeare), Royal Shakespeare Company.

Tribute to Michael Redgrave, Old Vic Theatre, London.

1986   *Across from the Garden of Allah* (Wood), Comedy Theatre, London.

Tannhauser (Wagner), Geneva.

1987   *The Flying Dutchman* (Wagner), Hong Kong Arts Festival; also directed.

They Shoot Horses, Don't They? (McCoy), Mermaid Theatre, London.

Pacific Overtures, English National Opera.

1988   *Carrie* (adapted from King), Royal Shakespeare Theatre, Stratford-upon-Avon, and Virginia Theatre, New York.

The Seagull (Chekhov), Los Angeles Theatre Centre, Los Angeles.

1989   *Metropolis* (adapted from Lang), Piccadilly Theatre, London.

1990   *La Traviata* (Verdi), Hong Kong Arts Festival and Stockholm; also directed.

E.A.R.W.I.G. (Milne), Barbican Theatre, London.

The Planets (Holst), Royal Opera House, Covent Garden, London.

1991   *The Makropulos Affair* (Janáček), Oslo.

1992   *Cruel Garden* (Kemp), Royal Ballet.

1993   *Tales of Hoffmann* (Offenbach), Houston, Omaha, Minneapolis.

My Fair Lady (Lerner, Loewe, and Hart), New York.

Television

Cruel Garden, 1981; *Cyrano de Bergerac*, 1984; *Man and Superman*, 1986.

*

Bibliography

Articles by: Glenn Loney in *Theatre Crafts*, January/February 1977; David Fingleton in *Arts Review*, March 1979; Beryl McAlhone in *Design and Art*, 12, March 1983; Jarka M. Burian in *Theatre Design and Technology*, vol. 19, 1983; Jarka M. Burian in *Theatre Journal*, 35, May 1983; Debbie Wolfe in *Drama*, vol. 2, 1986.

•   * * *

One of Britain's most important stage designers for well over 30 years, and very significant as a teacher of stage designers during his time at the Central School in London, Ralph Koltai is one who prefers to accentuate the element of sheer design artistry in his works rather than attempt to mirror external reality. Stage design, he emphasizes, is an art, and it should not try to hide that fact; indeed, according to him, theatre today needs more panache in stage design because audiences have been conditioned to expect greater visual stimulation. Essentially intuitive in his approach to production challenges, he nevertheless pays strict attention to the functional requirements of each production as well as to the specific spatial characteristics of each theatre in which he is to design. Central to his creative process is finding the concept that will make a given production work, and he prefers an active role in determining that concept. A logical development of this tendency to want to do more than simply design scenery occurred in 1987, when he himself served as director as well as designer for a production of *The Flying Dutchman* in Hong Kong.

During the first 12 years of his career as stage designer, Koltai worked almost exclusively in opera and ballet, but the balance between those forms and drama was redressed in his subsequent work. Although he has frequently worked independently in commercial theatre, Koltai has also been associated with many opera, ballet, and theatre companies, his most consistent affiliation being with the Royal Shakespeare Company.

Koltai has at times worked very successfully within tight limitations of space and budget, but he comes most fully into his own when working on projects of larger scale. He has concentrated on operas and classics, works that demand creative fantasy and a metaphoric treatment rather than realistic detail, although his work has also encompassed some extremely realistic, functional productions such as *The Love Girl and the Innocent* (1981).

Koltai's career has embodied an impressive range of scenographic methods and ingenious techniques involving contemporary materials and technology. He can move from simple sets with bare wooden floors and sharply controlled lighting to extremely complex structures that have often been admired even when the other elements of the productions drew little praise; above all, this was true in two relatively recent large-scale musicals, *Carrie* (1988) and *Metropolis* (1989), both of which were triumphs of stage engineering as well as design.

Much of Koltai's work has consistently displayed a sculptor's sensibility. *The Jew of Malta* (1964) and *The Merchant of Venice* (1965) used scenery composed of large, moveable blocks of highly textured, deeply carved, and painted styrofoam. In later years Koltai's sculptural sets became more abstract and graceful, and also focussed on the stage floor as well as the elements on it. His *Tempest* (1968) had a saucer-shaped stage floor, a revolving disc, and a sphere, all in white, like marble. Free-form curves distinguished *Terra Nova* (1981): stainless steel laid on plywood formed a curving floor surface, with a metal grillwork sheet extending the floor's curve into a canopy through which light could stream. Even more striking was *Brand* (1978), in which the floor consisted of sections that could move independently in the form of heaving slabs of snow or glacier ice. Another kind of bold sculpture was evident in the opera *Die Soldaten* (1983), the staging of which was dominated by three separate acting platforms in the form of huge, erotically charged parts of female anatomy — sensual lips, a pair of bare breasts, and garter-belted loins.

Koltai has also made effective use of mirrors and projections. In *Man and Superman* (1981), a nearly 50-foot-wide mirrored surface formed an arc over the rear of the upstage area and thereby distorted reflected whatever happened to be lying on the floor upstage of the primary acting area. Projections, although not one of Koltai's favourite devices, have occasionally created impressive stage images for his sets, most notably in the opera *Anna Karenina* (1981). Koltai had two upstage projection surfaces, a front one of scrim for frontal projections, and a translucent one in the rear for rear projections. The variously blended images provided rich atmospheric backgrounds and helped the flow of the action.

To extend his range of sculpture-like expression, Koltai has often drawn on a variety of plastic materials. For an all-male *As You Like It* (1967) and Wagner's *Ring* (1970–73), he used variations of extruded plastic and fibreglass panelling and tubing, which were partially textured and also sprayed with colour to create worlds of artifice, mystery, and magic more true to a dream or fairytale than to worldly reality. In the *Ring* production, he also used certain mirror and projection effects. *Much Ado About Nothing* (1982) was a later refinement on the use of mirrored and transparent plastic panels with appliquéd paint to enclose the stage area and create a fantasy world of airy trees, sun, and moon. "People want to be amazed, not intellectualized at", Koltai explained. Still later, in 1985, for an RSC production of *Othello*, he adopted a more minimal approach with plastics and special lighting: enclosed in black, the entire setting consisted of a few plastic floor panels with white paint-sprayed borders and two moveable vertical plastic panels with their edges outlined by fibreglass optics.

The lasting impression of Koltai's work is that of great inventiveness, variety, and imagination in embodying the essential metaphoric concept underlying each production. Usually preferring the simplest solution, he practises great selectivity in providing directors with the most expressive and yet functional space within which to work. Especially in his use of contemporary materials, instruments, and techniques, he keeps scenography a living art responsive to the times, while his artist's sensitivity to pure form provides a necessary sense of classic coherence and order.

—Jarka M. Burian

KOMMISARJEVSKAYA, Vera (Fedorovna).   Russian actress and manager. Born in St Petersburg, 27 October 1864; half-sister of director Theodore Kommisarjevsky (*q.v.*). Trained for the theatre under V. N. Davydov. Married in 1883 (divorced). Began career as amateur actress in St Petersburg, 1888–89; worked with Stanislavsky's Artistic and Literary Society in Moscow, 1890–91; debut as professional actress, with N. N. Sinelnikov's company, Novocherkassk, 1893; appeared under K. N. Nezlobin in Vilnius, Lithuania, 1894–96; joined company at the Alexandrinksy Theatre, St Petersburg, 1896; appeared in first production of Chekhov's *The Seagull*, 1898; resigned from Alexandrinsky Theatre, 1902, and conducted provincial tour; founder, Kommisarjevskaya 'In the Passage' Theatre, St Petersburg, 1904; with V. E. Meyerhold, opened new theatre in Officer Street, St Petersburg, 1906; dismissed Meyerhold in favour of Nikolai Evreinov and Fyodor Kommisarjevsky, 1907; closed theatre and toured USA, 1908; toured Russia, 1908–10, and announced impending retirement from the stage, 1909. Died (smallpox) in Tashkent, 10 February 1910.

Roles

1891	Betsy in *Plody prosvescheniya* [The Fruits of Enlightenment] (L. Tolstoy), Society of Arts and Literature, Moscow.
1893	Rosina in *Le Barbier de Seville* (Beaumarchais), Novocherkassk.
1894–96	Luise in *Kabale und Liebe* (Schiller), Vilnius, Lithuania.
	Negina in *Talanty i poklonniki* [Artists and Admirers] (Ostrovsky), Vilnius, Lithuania.
	Sofia in *Gore ot uma* [Woe from Wit] (Griboyedov), Vilnius, Lithuania.
1896	Rosa in *Schmetterlingsschlacht* (Sudermann), Alexandrinsky Theatre, St Petersburg.
1898	Larisa in *Bespridannitsa* [The Girl Without a Dowry] (Ostrovsky), Alexandrinsky Theatre, St Petersburg.

Nina in *Chayka* [The Seagull] (Chekhov), Alexandrinsky Theatre, St Petersburg.

1904–06   Sasha in *Ivanov* (Chekhov), Kommisarjevskaya 'In the Passage' Theatre, St Petersburg.

Desdemona in *Othello* (Shakespeare), Kommisarjevskaya 'In the Passage' Theatre, St Petersburg.

Aglaja in *The Idiot* (Dostoevsky), Kommisarjevskaya 'In the Passage' Theatre, St Petersburg.

Maria Vassilievna in *Kholostyak* [The Bachelor] (Turgenev), Kommisarjevskaya 'In the Passage' Theatre, St Petersburg.

Christine in *Liebelei* (Schnitzler), Kommisarjevskaya 'In the Passage' Theatre, St Petersburg.

Ophelia in *Hamlet* (Shakespeare), Kommisarjevskaya 'In the Passage' Theatre, St Petersburg.

Margarete in *Faust I* (Goethe), Kommisarjevskaya 'In the Passage' Theatre, St Petersburg.

Monna Vanna in *Monna Vanna* (Maeterlinck), Kommisarjevskaya 'In the Passage' Theatre, St Petersburg.

Varvara in *Dachniki* [Summerfolk] (Gorky), Kommisarjevskaya 'In the Passage' Theatre, St Petersburg.

Liza in *Deti solntsa* [Children of the Sun] (Gorky), Kommisarjevskaya 'In the Passage' Theatre, St Petersburg.

Nora in *Et dukkehjem* [A Doll's House] (Ibsen), Kommisarjevskaya 'In the Passage' Theatre, St Petersburg.

Hilda in *Bygmester Solness* [The Master Builder] (Ibsen), Kommisarjevskaya 'In the Passage' Theatre, St Petersburg.

Sonja in *Dyadya Vanya* [Uncle Vanya] (Chekhov), Kommisarjevskaya 'In the Passage' Theatre, St Petersburg.

1906   Hedda in *Hedda Gabler* (Ibsen), Kommisarjevsky Theatre, Officer Street, St Petersburg.

Sister Béatrice in *Soeur Béatrice* (Maeterlinck), Kommisarjevsky Theatre, Officer Street, St Petersburg.

1907   Mélisande in *Pelléas et Mélisande* (Maeterlinck, translated by Briusov), Kommisarjevsky Theatre, Officer Street, St Petersburg.

Judith in *Judith* (Hebbel), Officer Street Theatre, St Petersburg.

*

Bibliography

Articles:
Laurence Senelick, "Vera Kommisarjevskaya: The Actress as Symbolist Eidolon", *Theatre Journal*, December 1980.

* * *

Born in St Petersburg, the daughter of the operatic tenor Fyodor Petrovich Kommisarjevsky and a soprano, Vera Kommisarjevskaya grew up in an atmosphere rich in artistic associations, but her parents' divorce caused a trauma that unsettled an already hypersensitive character.

She decided to dedicate herself to the theatre in 1891, after the break-up of her own marriage to a painter she had wed at the age of 19. She took part in amateur productions, some of them at the Moscow Artistic and Literary Society directed by Stanislavsky, imbibing his principle that acting was a mission rather than a trade. Her professional debut took place on 30 August 1893, in N. N. Sinelnikov's company in Novocherkassk, and her vivaciousness and humour rapidly made her a public favourite, especially as comic ingenue in vaudevilles and operettas (for instance, Rosina in *The Barber of Seville*). Between 1894 and 1896 she worked in Vilnius, gaining experience in classical roles.

Sincerity, delicacy and subtlety, the hallmarks of her work, were already apparent. She joined the leading state theatre, the Alexandrinsky in St Petersburg, making her debut on 4 April 1896 as Rosa in Sudermann's *Battle of Butterflies*, and soon enthralled the public with her Larisa in Ostrovsky's *Girl Without a Dowry*, a rendition that expressed the torment of a defenceless creature struggling against a callous society. That same year she also created Nina in the disastrous premiere of *The Seagull*, the only performance in the cast that Chekhov admired. But her idealism regularly clashed with the routine, intrigues and bureaucracy of the imperial stage; she resigned on 1 August 1902, and, after a provincial tour, founded in September 1904 her own Dramatic Theatre 'in the Passage'. Her audience was drawn from the liberal intelligentsia of St Petersburg, and she responded to its demands with a 'progressive' repertory of Ibsen, Gorky and Chekhov. Her intepretations of Nora in *A Doll's House* and Hilda in *The Master Builder*, shaped by the critic Akim Volynsky, contained other-worldly touches that were taken as calls to a new life.

Kommisarjevskaya grew increasingly close to the Russian symbolists and mystical anarchists, and in 1906 the whole complexion of her theatre altered when she opened a new playhouse in Officer Street, with Vsevolod Meyerhold in charge. Under his direction the repertoire shifted to a more avant-garde bill of Maeterlinck, Sologub and Andreyev, with Kommisarjevskaya playing a vampiric Hedda Gabler, a somnambulist Sister Béatrice and a doll-like Mélisande. Propounding a stylized theatre, Meyerhold insisted that the actors move rhythmically and hynogogically, to form static bas-reliefs against the abstract background. The critics opposed this style, maintaining that it was stifling the actress's talent. Gradually Kommisarjevskaya became convinced that her actors were being reduced to marionettes and in October 1907 she sacked Meyerhold. Stipulating her reasons in a famous letter, she clung to the notion of a Symbolist stage but insisted that the bond between actor and audience must be all-important. After continuing a while under the direction of Nikolai Evreinov and her half-brother Fyodor Kommisarjevsky, she closed her theatre and went on a disastrous tour to the USA in 1908. On her return, she consulted with the poet Andrei Bely about a school to train new men of the theatre in transcendental principles, and then embarked on a tour of provincial Russia with her own company. At Kharkov, on 15 November 1909, she announced she would retire from the stage when the tour was over, explaining "I am leaving because the theatre in its present form no longer seems necessary, and the path I followed in the search for new forms no longer seems the right one". Shortly thereafter she succumbed in remote Tashkent to smallpox.

A fragile figure with big blue, melancholy eyes and a chesty, melodious voice that critics compared to a Stradivarius, she was taken as a symbol of that period of retrenchment, doubt and disbelief that runs from Chekhov to Aleksandr Blok. An actress of morbid sensibility, inclined to 'suffer' in her roles, she avidly adopted the personae projected onto her by poets and lived a febrile and neurotic existence, insatiably eager to act and experiment despite a growing sense of impending disaster. The Symbolists saw her as the incarnation of their aesthetic and Blok dedicated one of his best poems to her (1910).

—Laurence Senelick

KOMMISARJEVSKY, Theodore. Russian director and designer. Born Fedor Fedorovich Kommisarjevsky in Venice, Italy, 23 May 1882; half-brother of actress Vera Kommisarjevskaya (q.v.). Educated at the Imperial Institute of Architecture; University of Petrograd; also in Germany. Married 1) Elfriede de Jarosy (divorced); 2) actress Peggy Ashcroft (q.v.) in 1934 (divorced 1936); 3) Ernestine Stodelle. Worked in Vera Kommisarkevskaya's theatre in St Petersburg, from 1906; debut as director there, alongside Nikolai Evreinov, 1907; subsequently directed for K. N. Nezlobin, from 1910, and at the Maly Theatre, Moscow, from 1913; established studio in Moscow, 1910–18; directed for the V. F. Kommisarjevskaya Theatre, 1914–18; worked as director at the Novyi Theatre, Moscow, 1918; also directed opera at S. I. Zimin's theatre and at the Bolshoi Theatre; emigrated to UK, 1919; acclaimed for productions at the Barnes Theatre, London, 1925–26, and at the Shakespeare Memorial Theatre, Stratford-upon-Avon, 1932–39; took British citizenship, 1932; as teacher at the Royal Academy of Dramatic Art in London, promoted the theories of Stanislavsky in British theatre; subsequently lived in France and, from 1939, the USA. Died in Darien, Connecticut, 16 April 1954.

Productions

1908   *Cernye maski* [Black Masks] (Andreyev), Kommisarjevskaya Theatre, Officer Street, St Petersburg.
Bygmester Solness [The Master Builder] (Ibsen), Kommisarjevskaya Theatre, Officer Street, St Petersburg.
Die Maienkonigin (Gluck), Kommisarjevskaya Theatre, Officer Street, St Petersburg.

1910   *Ne bylo ni grosa, da vdrug altyn* [Not a Kopek and Suddenly a Rouble] (Ostrovsky), Nezlobin's Theatre, Moscow.
Le Bourgeois Gentilhomme (Molière), Nezlobin's Theatre, Moscow.
Turandot (Gozzi), Nezlobin's Theatre, Moscow.

1912   *Faust I* (Goethe), Nezlobin's Theatre, Moscow.

1913   *The Idiot* (Dostoevsky), Maly Theatre, Moscow.

1914   *Dmitrii Donskoi* [Dmitri of the Don] (Ozerov), V. F. Kommisarjevskaya Theatre, Moscow.

1914–18   *Gimn Rozdestvu* [A Christmas Carol] (Dickens), V. F. Kommisarjevskaya Theatre, Moscow.
Pan (Van Lerberghe), V. F. Kommisarjevskaya Theatre, Moscow.
Lysistrata (Aristophanes), V. F. Kommisarjevskaya Theatre, Moscow.

1917   *The Golden Cockerel* (Rimsky-Korsakov), Bolshoi Theatre, Moscow.

1918   *Lohengrin* (Wagner), Bolshoi Theatre, Moscow.
Boris Godunov (Mussorgsky), Bolshoi Theatre, Moscow.

1918–19   *The Seraglio* (Mozart), Moscow.
Le Mariage de Figaro (Beaumarchais), Moscow.
The Merry Wives of Windsor (Nicolai), Moscow.
Le Mariage forcé (Molièe), Moscow.
The Tempest (Shakespeare), Novyi Theatre, Moscow.
Les Contes d'Hoffmann (Offenbach), Novyi Theatre, Moscow.

1919   *Prince Igor* (Borodin), Covent Garden, London.

1920   *The Government Inspector* (Gogol), Duke of York's Theatre, London.

1921   *Six Characters in Search of an Author* (Pirandello), Kingsway Theatre, London.
The Love Thief, Comedy Theatre, London.
The Race With a Shadow, Court Theatre, London.
Uncle Vanya (Chekhov), Court Theatre, London.

1922   *At the Gates of the Kingdom* (Hamsun), Court Theatre, London.

1922–23   *The Lucky One*, New York.
The Tidings Brought to Mary (Claudel), New York.
Peer Gynt (Ibsen), New York.
The Dover Road (Milne), Paris.
The Duenna (Sheridan), Paris.
Siegfried (Wagner), Paris.
Walküre (Wagner), Paris.
La Maîtresse du Roy, Paris.

1925   *The Bright Island*, London.
Ivanoff (Chekhov), Barnes Theatre, London.

1926   *Uncle Vanya* (Chekhov), Barnes Theatre, London.
The Three Sisters (Chekhov), Barnes Theatre, London.
Hearts and Diamonds (Jerrold), London.
The Snow Man (Sturgess), London.
Katerina (Andreyev), London.
The Cherry Orchard (Chekhov), London.
Liliom (Molnár), London.

1927   *Naked* (Pirandello), London.
Paul I (Alford and Dale), Court Theatre, London.
Mr Prohack, London.
King Lear (Shakespeare), London.
The 14th of July, London.

1928   *A Man with Red Hair*, London.
The Brass Paperweight (Kommisarjevsky), London.

1929	*Red Sunday*, London.
	The Fair of Sorotchin, Paris.
1930	*The Man with the Portfolio*, London.
1931	*The Queen of Spades* (Scribe), London.
	Take Two from One (Granville-Barker), London.
	Musical Chairs (Mackenzie), Arts Theatre, London.
	Robin Hood (Hamilton and Devereux), Q Theatre, London.
1932	*The Heart Line*, London.
	Le Cocu magnifique (Crommelynck), London.
	Fraulein Elsa (Schnitzler, adapted by Kommisarjevsky), Kingsway Theatre, London.
	The Merchant of Venice (Shakespeare), Shakespeare Memorial Theatre, Stratford-upon-Avon.
	Hatter's Castle (Cronin), Masque Theatre, Edinburgh.
1933	*Escape Me Never* (Kennedy), Apollo Theatre, London.
	Macbeth (Shakespeare), Shakespeare Memorial Theatre, Stratford-upon-Avon.
1934	*Magnolia Street* (Golding and Rawlinson), Adelphi Theatre, London.
	The Maitlands (Mackenzie), Wyndham's Theatre, London.
1935	*Mesmer* (Nichols), British tour.
	Further Outlook, London.
	The Merry Wives of Windsor (Shakespeare), Shakespeare Memorial Theatre, Stratford-upon-Avon.
1936	*The Seagull* (Chekhov), New Theatre, London; also designed costumes.
	Antony and Cleopatra (Shakespeare), London; also designed costumes.
	King Lear (Shakespeare), Shakespeare Memorial Theatre, Stratford-upon-Avon.
	The Comedy of Errors (Shakespeare), Shakespeare Memorial Theatre, Stratford-upon-Avon.
	The Boy David (Barrie), His Majesty's Theatre, London.
1939	*The Taming of the Shrew* (Shakespeare), Shakespeare Memorial Theatre, Stratford-upon-Avon.
1940	*Russian Bank* (Kommisarjevsky), St James Theatre, New York.
1947	*Crime and Punishment* (Dostoevsky), National Theatre, New York.
1950	*Cymbeline* (Shakespeare), Open Air Theatre, Montreal.

Other productions included: *Cosi fan Tutte* (Mozart), Italy; *Mefistofele* (Boito), Riga; *The Wild Duck* (Ibsen), Riga; *Eugene Onegin* (Tchaikovsky).

Films

As director:
The Yellow Stockings, 1928.

Publications

Theatral nye preljudii, 1914; *The Actor and the Theory of Stanislavsky*, 1916; *Myself and the Theatre*, 1929; *The Costume of the Theatre*, 1932; *The Theatre and a Changing Civilization*, 1935.

* * *

Theodore Kommisarjevsky was born in Venice in 1882, but was brought up in Russia, where his elder half-sister, Vera, was a highly acclaimed actress. She became a sort of mentor or patron to him and, having trained as a designer, he went to work at her radical and progressive theatre in the early years of the 20th century.

Kommisarjevskaya's theatre was dedicated to providing a platform for the most advanced artistic drama of the time, and she employed the outstanding but controversial Vsevolod Meyerhold to direct the plays. Watching him at work, and seeing his rebellion against the constrictions of Stanislavsky-based naturalism inspired Kommisarjevsky, so that when his sister sacked Meyerhold, the young man was brought in to work as co-director with the more experienced Nikolai Evreinov.

Kommisarjevsky staged *Black Masks* by Leonid Andreyev and Ibsen's *The Master Builder* at his sister's theatre in 1908, before it was closed with bad debts outstanding. Kommisarjevsky and Evreinov, however, contrived to retain the lease of the building, in which they set up the 'Merry Theatre for Grown-up Children' and presented a series of light entertainments.

In 1910, Kommisarjevsky moved to Moscow, where he worked in many different theatres, including the Maly and Bolshoi, as well as in his own studio, and presented a very large number of plays and operas. Exotic productions of Molière and Dostoevsky were contrasted with a newly sympathetic treatment of the plays of Ostrovsky, in whose work Kommisarjevsky uncovered unexpected philosophical depths and a new sympathy for the Russian way of life.

His approach to any play tended to seek out the philosophical substructure, which he then made into the dominant note in the production. This was, however, likely to be coloured by his own rather romantic outlook on life, and though it was capable of revealing new depths (as in the case of Ostrovsky), it sometimes left a slightly sickly aftertaste in its audiences. His view that art and life were fundamentally different, even if they were not unrelated to one another, led him to a wide variety of styles, but no clear artistic position.

Not that this was necessarily a weakness. As one of the earliest interpreters of Stanislavsky, whose worth he affirmed while refusing to follow in any slavish sense, and as one who trained to be a designer, it is little wonder that in the pre-revolutionary years his work was constantly striking and always interesting, whether it was contemporary drama (he presented work by Andreyev, Kuzmin, Sologub and others) or classical (Goethe and Molière, for instance, as well as many opera productions, especially at the Bolshoi Theatre). His work was thus marked by a desire to express his author's viewpoint, by strong acting and by visual flair.

In 1919, with his reputation as a brilliant theatrical practitioner and innovator at its height, he left Russia for western Europe. Initially, he directed *Prince Igor* at Covent Garden, but found further work hard to come by, and it was not until he started to work in the 'little theatre' in Barnes, west London, that his talents were properly seen.

The Barnes Theatre was a converted cinema with minimal space or facilities and here in 1925 and 1926 Kommisarjevsky created a company that presented a remarkable series of Chekhov productions, as well as plays by Andreyev and Gogol. His actors included the young John Gielgud, Charles Laughton, Claude Rains, Martita Hunt and Jean Forbes-Robertson, and the productions were particularly notable as they really set the style for 'British Chekhov', which is still, some 70 years later, pervasive in the British theatre. Its hallmark is an overriding sense of romantic melancholy, and this is achieved both through the acting and the settings. The acting depends on delicate variations of tone, as one character responds to another, and subtle shifts in tempo. Gielgud himself said that Kommisarjevsky taught him to "work from within to present a character" but noted also that an actor was expected to "absorb the atmosphere and general background" of the play. This was the central feature of Kommisarjevsky's designs — they eschewed detail in favour of 'atmosphere' and mood.

Kommisarjevsky's reputation was enhanced by further 'non-commercial' productions, especially at Stratford-upon-Avon, where his work included *Macbeth* in 1933, with the characters in modern military uniforms and startling aluminium scenery; a Viennese *Merry Wives of Windsor* in 1935, which included at its climax a vision of folk fairies with lighted candles on their heads; and a particularly impressive *King Lear* in 1936 that was very widely acclaimed. Nevertheless, as one critic noted, "his considerable talents were sometimes hampered by his unpredictable temperament", and it is perhaps significant that it was the startling design concepts, worked out in private, which made these shows memorable. As a director, his work was less impressive, and the 'synthesis' he had worked for earlier seemed in danger of being overborne by his artist's imagination. More ordinary plays, which did not yield such possibilities, were less successful, and after *The Boy David* failed in 1936, he moved to the USA, where he continued to write on theatre and where he set up an acting school of some distinction, which he ran until his death.

—Robert Leach

————

LAUBE, Heinrich. German manager and playwright. Born in Sprottau, Silesia, 18 September 1806. Educated at the Schweidnitzer Gymnasium, 1825, and at Halle University, 1826. Married Iduna Hänal (née Buddeus) in 1836 (died 1879), one son. Began career as a journalist and tutor, 1827, and became associated with the Junges Deutschland movement, editing its literary organ, *Die elegante Welt*; imprisoned for radical political writings for nine months, 1834, and again for 18 months, 1837–38; travelled widely after 1839 and writing became less radical; worked as drama critic in Leipzig, 1841, and began to write plays; subsequently worked as drama critic in Vienna, 1845; elected member of Frankfurt Parliament, 1848; director, Burgtheater, Vienna, 1849–67; director, Leipzig Stadttheater, 1869–71; founder, Vienna Stadttheater, 1871; retired as director, 1880. Died in Vienna, 1 August 1884.

Publications

Plays:

Monaldeschi, oder Die Abenteurer (produced Berlin and Dresden, 1842), 1845; *Rokoko, oder die alten Herren* (produced Dresden, 1842), 1846; *Die Bernsteinhexe* (produced Berlin and Hamburg, 1844), 1846; *Struensee* (produced Munich, 1844), 1847; *Gottsched and Gellert* (produced Dresden and Munich, 1845), 1847; *Die Karlsschüler* (produced Dresden, Mannheim and Munich, 1846), 1847; *Prinz Friedrich* (produced Frankfurt, 1848), 1854; *Graf Essex* (produced Berlin, Darmstadt, Frankfurt, Mannheim, Vienna, Weimar, 1856), 1856; *Montrose, der schwarze Markgraf* (produced Vienna, 1859), 1859; *Der Stadtthalter von Bengalen* (produced Hamburg, Leipzig, Mannheim, Munich, Vienna and Weimar, 1867), 1868; *Böse Zungen* (produced Hamburg, Leipzig, Mannheim, Munich and Weimar, 1868), 1868; *Demetrius* (produced Darmstadt, Frankfurt, Leipzig and Munich, 1869), 1872; *Schauspieler* (produced Vienna, 1883).

Other:

Das junge Europa (novel), 1833–37; *Das Burgtheater*, 1868; *Das Norddeutsche Theater*, 1872; *Die Wiener Stadttheater*, 1875; *Gesammelte Schriften*, 16 vols., 1875–82; *Franz Grillparzers Lebensgeschichte*, 1884; *Theaterkritiken und dramaturgische Aufsätze*, 2 vols., edited by Alexander von Weilen, 1906; *Gesammelte Werke*, 50 vols., edited by H. H. Houben, 1908–09; *Schriften über das Theater*, edited by Eva Stahl-Wisten, 1955.

*

Bibliography

Books:

Georg Altman, *Heinrich Laubes Prinzip der Theaterleitung*, Dortmund, 1908.
Maria Moormann, *Die Bühnentechnik Heinrich Laubes*, Leipzig, 1917.

Articles:

Alexander von Weilen, "Heinrich Laube und das Burgtheater", *Bühne und Welt*, 6, 2, 1905.
Marvin Carlson, "Montigny, Laube, Robinson: The Early Realists", *Educational Theatre Journal*, 24, 1972.

* * *

Heinrich Laube was among the most vigorous and prolific writers of his time. A relative latecomer to theatre, as a young man he earned his living as a journalist, a career that reached its zenith in 1833 when he was appointed editor of the influential, radical Leipzig journal *Zeitung für die elegante Welt*. Several of his political essays and the copious accounts of his travels through Germany and Italy have survived as important documents of the social life of the time. During these years Laube also made his mark as a novelist; his three-volume novel *Das junge Europa* was widely read and influenced several of Laube's contemporaries, including the young Richard Wagner, whom Laube befriended and encouraged for a time.

Laube was associated with the Junges Deutschland (Young Germany) movement, a group of writers who rejected the lyricism of the Romantics in order to write a literature that more accurately reflected the social conditions of the time and protested against the repressive political order that emerged after the Congress of Vienna. Because of his radical writings, Laube was sentenced to nine months in prison in Berlin, a sentence which he served. On his release he married, but was soon after sentenced to seven years' further detention that was to take the form of house arrest on the estate of Prince Pückler-Muskau. In the event, Laube had only to serve 18 months and in relative comfort at that, especially as his wife was allowed to stay with him. Both the experience of detention and, probably, the comfort provided by his wife's fortune seem to have matured him. Soon after his final release, he turned to writing dramatic criticism and, subsequently, plays.

As a playwright, Laube helped to acclimatise the French well-made play to German conditions. He did this not so much by translation, though later in life he was responsible for some important translations of Scribe, but by creating

437

his own plays, which, while they owed much to the structure of the French well-made play, drew for their material upon German and Northern European history. Although Laube's plays have disappeared almost entirely from the repertoire today, they could perhaps do with the odd revival as a thorough reading of them suggests they still possess some dramatic life.

Laube's principle contribution to the history of the theatre began in 1849, when he was appointed director of the Vienna Burgtheater. On the face of it, this may seem to have been a puzzling and inappropriate appointment, for the Burgtheater, a royalist theatre par excellence, could hardly be run by an ex-radical. However, one of the reasons why the theatre has maintained its pre-eminence in the German-language world is that the authorities responsible for such appointments have consistently followed the notably enlightened policy of selecting people who do not automatically reflect the ideological beliefs of either the government or the audience.

Laube's appointment came as a result of the riots of 1848, in which Habsburg power was nearly overthrown. No doubt, his leadership of the Burgtheater, which has always been politically a prominent institution, was part of a larger scheme of events that led to the incorporation of the middle classes into influential positions in the socio-political life of Vienna. For several years, it appeared that the strategy was remarkably successful. Laube was both a traditionalist and a radical. As a traditionalist, he maintained and augmented the approach to repertoire that had been initiated by Friedrich Schreyvogel; during his tenure at the Burgtheater, the theatre developed a 'world repertoire' that has since served as a model for national theatres within the German-speaking world and outside it. However, Laube also modernized the repertoire, often over the objections of the censor and court-appointed administrators of the theatre. He ensured that Shakespeare's plays, often suspected in royal circles for their subversive potential, were central to the company's repertoire — 19 of the plays were produced during the 18 years of Laube's directorship. He also introduced, much to the enthusiasm of Viennese audiences, the French well-made play, that turned out to be an ideal vehicle for the style of ensemble developed by the company and a form well-suited to embody actions that drew from the social life of the city. Even Shakespeare, a playwright whose work is as far removed as possible from the rigorously constructed Scribean formula, did not escape adaptation, and several of Laube's versions of his plays were aimed to please audiences who relish the building of suspense, powerful curtain lines and a clearly delineated action.

Laube also capitalized on the changes brought about by Schreyvogel some 20 years before. Several of the older members of Laube's company, especially Heinrich Anschütz, had been recruited by Schreyvogel. Laube built upon this core to form a larger ensemble of remarkable virtuosity. Few of the actors he recruited were able to represent strong passions, destructive emotions or powerful feelings, but they were noted for the finesse of their playing and for their skill in rendering the sophisticated social life of Vienna. The accomplishments of Laube's actors were not confined to the stage. At a time when the aristocracy was declining in power and social influence, the Burgtheater actor became the new setter of trends in fashion and behaviour and accordingly achieved a social eminence no

actors in the German-speaking world so far had been able to acquire. The most distinguished of the many actors and actresses Laube hired for the company was Adolf von Sonnenthal (1834–1909), whose elegant demeanour and soft but sonorous delivery became a byword among the Viennese, a standard by which the quality of all other acting was measured. Sonnenthal continued as an active member of the company until well into the 20th century, which is an indication of the durability of Laube's legacy. Like Schreyvogel before him, Laube eschewed spectacular production and elaborate stage effects. For him the essence of theatre lay in the ensemble of actors.

After his resignation from the Burgtheater for internal political reasons in 1867, Laube resumed his writing career. The three books of theatrical history and memoirs that he produced are among the most valuable documents of his time. He continued his career as a theatre director in Leipzig and then again in Vienna, his most significant achievement during this period being the introduction of Ibsen to the German stage through his production in 1878 of *Pillars of Society*. Unfortunately, he never evolved a methodology by which he trained actors and formed a theatre company. If he had done, we might now consider Laube to be one of the most important innovators in the early years of the modern theatre.

—Simon Williams

LAUGHTON, Charles. British actor and director. Born in Scarborough, Yorkshire, England, 1 July 1899. Educated at local Catholic preparatory school; French convent school at Filey; Stonyhurst College, 1912–15; studied for the stage at the Royal Academy of Dramatic Art, Gold Medal, 1925. Married actress Else Lanchester in 1929. Joined amateur company after army service during World War I; professional stage debut, Barnes Theatre, London, 1926; film debut, 1928; New York debut, 1931; arrived in Hollywood, where he established reputation as a major film star, 1932; actor, under Tyrone Guthrie at the Old Vic Theatre, London, 1933; first British actor to star at the Comédie-Française, Paris, 1937; co-founded Mayflower Picture Corporation, 1937; took US citizenship, 1940; returned to stage, 1947; also toured extensively, giving lectures and readings. Recipient: Oscar, 1933. Died in Los Angeles, 15 December 1962.

Productions

As actor:

1926   Osip in *The Government Inspector* (Gogol), Barnes Theatre, London, and Gaiety Theatre, London.

Rummel in *The Pillars of Society* (Ibsen), Everyman Theatre, London.

Ephikhdof in *The Cherry Orchard* (Chekhov), Barnes Theatre, London.

Vassily Solyony in *The Three Sisters* (Chekhov), Barnes Theatre, London.

Ficsur in *Liliom* (Molnar), Duke of York's Theatre, London.

General Markeloff in *The Greater Love* (Fagan), Prince's Theatre, London.

1927   Sir James Hartley in *Angela* (Bell), Prince's Theatre, London.

Cantavalle in *Naked* (Pirandello), Royalty Theatre, London.

Creon in *Medea* (Euripides, translated by Murray), Prince's Theatre, London.

Frank K. Pratt in *The Happy Husband* (Owen), Criterion Theatre, London.

Count Pahlen in *Paul I* (Merejkovsky, adapted by Alford and Dale), Court Theatre, London.

Mr Prohack in *Mr Prohack* (Bennett), Court Theatre, London.

1928   Mr Crispin in *A Man with Red Hair* (Levy), Little Theatre, London.

Ben Jonson in *The Making of an Immortal* (Moore), Arts Theatre, London.

Hercule Poirot in *Alibi* (Christie), Prince of Wales's Theatre, London; Booth Theatre, New York, 1932.

Pickwick in *Mr Pickwick* (adapted from Dickens), Haymarket Theatre, London.

1929   Jacques Blaise in *Beauty* (Morton, adapted from Deval), Strand Theatre, London.

Harry Heegan and the First Soldier in *The Silver Tassie* (O'Casey), Apollo Theatre, London.

1930   Brigadier-General Archibald Root in *French Leave* (Berkeley), Vaudeville Theatre, London.

Tony Perelli in *On the Spot* (Wallace), Wyndham's Theatre, London.

1931   William Marble in *Payment Deferred* (Forester), St James's Theatre, London, and Lyceum Theatre, New York.

1933   Lopakhin in *The Cherry Orchard* (Chekhov), Old Vic Theatre, London.

Henry in *Henry VIII* (Shakespeare), Old Vic Theatre, London.

Angelo in *Measure for Measure* (Shakespeare), Old Vic Theatre, London.

1934   Prospero in *The Tempest* (Shakespeare), Sadler's Wells Theatre, London, and Old Vic Theatre, London.

Canon Chasuble in *The Importance of Being Earnest* (Wilde), Old Vic Theatre, London.

Tattle in *Love for Love* (Congreve), Sadler's Wells Theatre, London.

Macbeth in *Macbeth* (Shakespeare), Old Vic Theatre, London.

1936   Sganarelle in *Le Médecin malgré lui* (Molière), Comédie-Française, Paris.

Captain Hook in *Peter Pan* (Barrie), London Palladium, London.

1947   Galileo in *Galileo* (Brecht, adapted by Laughton), Coronet Theatre, New York, and Maxine Elliott Theatre, New York.

1951   The Devil in *Don Juan in Hell* (G. B. Shaw), Carnegie Hall, New York; also directed.

1956   Andrew Undershaft in *Major Barbara* (G. B. Shaw), Martin Beck Theatre, New York; also directed.

Charles Laughton (1957).

1958   Richard Brough in *The Party* (Jane Arden), New Theatre, London; also directed.

1959   Bottom in *A Midsummer Night's Dream* (Shakespeare), Shakespeare Memorial Theatre, Stratford-upon-Avon, England.

Lear in *King Lear* (Shakespeare), Shakespeare Memorial Theatre, Stratford-upon-Avon, England.

As director:

1953   *John Brown's Body* (Benét, adapted by Laughton), New Century Theatre, New York.

1954   *The Caine Mutiny Court Martial* (Wouk), Plymouth Theatre, New York.

Films

As actor:

Burglar in *Blue Bottles*, 1928; Eastern potentate in *Day Dreams*, 1928; diner in *Piccadilly*, 1929; The Hero in *Wolves*, 1930; The Skipper in *Down River*, 1931; Porterhouse in *The Old Dark House*, 1932; Commander Charles Sturm in *The Devil and the Deep*, 1932; William Marble in *Payment Deferred*, 1932; Nero in *The Sign of the Cross*, 1932; Phineas V. Lambert in *If I Had a Million*, 1932; Dr Moreau in *Island of Lost Souls*, 1933; Henry VIII in *The Private Life of Henry VIII*, 1933; Horace Prin in *White Woman*, 1933; Barrett in *The Barretts of Wimpole Street*, 1934; Ruggles in *Ruggles of Red Gap*,

1935; Javert in *Les Misérables*, 1935; Captain Bligh in *Mutiny on the Bounty*, 1935; Rembrandt in *Rembrandt*, 1936; Tiberius Claudius in *I, Claudius*, unfinished; Ginger Ted in *Vessel of Wrath*, 1938; Charles in *St Martin's Lane*, 1938; Sir Humphrey Pengallan in *Jamaica Inn*, 1939; Quasimodo in *The Hunchback of Notre Dame*, 1940; Tony Patucci in *They Knew What They Wanted*, 1940; Jonathan Reynolds in *It Started with Eve*, 1941; Jonas in *The Tuttles of Tahiti*, 1942; Charles Smith in *Tales of Manhattan*, 1942; Rear-Admiral Stephen Thomas in *Stand-by for Action*, 1942; Butler in *Forever and a Day*, 1943; Albert Mory in *This Land Is Mine*, 1943; Jacko Wilson in *The Man from Down Under*, 1943; Sir Simon de Canterville in *The Canterville Ghost*, 1944; Philip in *The Suspect*, 1944; Captain William Kidd in *Captain Kidd*, 1945; actor in *Because of Him*, 1946; Lord Horfield in *The Paradine Case*, 1948; Haake in *Arch of Triumph*, 1948; Earl Janoth in *The Big Clock*, 1948; The Bishop in *The Girl from Manhattan*, 1948; J. J. Bealer in *The Bribe*, 1949; Maigret in *The Man on the Eiffel Tower*, 1949; Fred Begley in *The Blue Veil*, 1951; The Squire in *The Strange Door*, 1951; Soapy in *O. Henry's Full House*, 1952; Captain Kidd in *Abbott and Costello Meet Captain Kidd*, 1952; Herod in *Salome*, 1953; Henry VIII in *Young Bess*, 1953; Henry Hobson in *Hobson's Choice*, 1954; Sir Wilfrid Robarts in *Witness for the Prosecution*, 1957; Admiral Russell in *Under Ten Flags*, 1960; Gracchus in *Spartacus*, 1960; Senator Seabright Cooley in *Advise and Consent*, 1962.

As director:
The Night of the Hunter, 1955.

*

Bibliography

Books:

Elsa Lanchester, *Charles Laughton and I*, London, 1938.
Simon Callow, *Charles Laughton: A Difficult Actor*, London, 1987.

* * *

To the cinema-goer Charles Laughton will always be, in this order, Captain Bligh in the 1935 version of *Mutiny on the Bounty* (against Errol Flynn as Fletcher Christian), Henry VIII, picking up a whole roasted chicken and demolishing it with violent greed in *The Private Life of Henry VIII* in 1932, Quasimodo in the 1939 adaptation of *The Hunchback of Notre Dame*, ringing the bells in a frenzy of excited madness in despair at losing Claudette Colbert as Esmeralda, and, in an unfinished attempt to put Robert Graves's *I, Claudius* on to the screen, the most splendidly decadent of Roman emperors, a role which he had previously played in 1932 in *Nero*. On the stage, he will be remembered for one part above all others: Galileo in Brecht's own production of the his play on Broadway in 1954. Laughton was as superb as Galileo as Olivier was to be as Archie Rice in *The Entertainer* a few years later. Just as Olivier's normally suppressed vulgarity came out in his indulgently loving incarnation of a failed music hall star, so Laughton's conflict between a fine intellect and a coarse, overblown physique gave life to Brecht's drama about the man who could have given science an ethical dignity from the very beginning but who could control neither his fear nor his appetite. Laughton devoured the goose that symbolised Galileo's sensuality and consequent vulnerability to torture with the same uninhibited enthusiasm that had endeared him to millions of cinema-goers and he was undoubtedly the actor best suited to bring life to Brecht's best-known male character.

On stage, Laughton's tendency to overact was held in check by his intense professionalism and his perfect English accent was only occasionally allowed to degenerate into ham. This did happen, however, when he made his much-vaunted return to the London stage after an absence of 22 years, directing and appearing as Richard Brough in Jane Arden's *The Party* in 1958. The result was disappointing and reflected Laughton's innate unsuitability for realistic 20th-century drama about people from the suburbs. He was much happier as a magnificently over-sized Bottom in *A Midsummer Night's Dream* at Stratford-upon-Avon in 1959, showing a surprising lightness of movement for such a large man and lending his own natural aptitude for histrionics to the portrayal of the man who wanted to play every part as well. He also did a remarkable Lear at Stratford that year, but he never achieved on the postwar English stage the success he had in the USA. Highlights on the US side of the Atlantic included his direction of Henry Fonda in the stage version of Herman Wouk's novel *The Caine Mutiny* in 1954 and his considerable personal triumph as the self-possessed, affectionately cynical Andrew Undershaft in Shaw's *Major Barbara*. On that occasion, perhaps because he also had to deal with Cornelia Otis Skinner as Lady Britomart and more particularly because he had serious opposition both on the stage and in the play itself from Glynis Johns as Barbara herself, he kept both the play and himself under control and produced an excellent reading of Shaw's most intellectually challenging play.

In the cinema, Laughton rarely found a director prepared to impose the necessary discipline on one of the great 'monstres sacrés' of the screen. He nonetheless made a splendidly bullying lawyer with his heart in the right place in *Witness for the Prosecution* and was given one of the best roles in his career as the worldly wise Southern senator in the political drama *Advise and Consent*. He was three times nominated for an Oscar: for his Bligh, as Barrett in the screen adaptation of Rudolf Besier's play *The Barretts of Wimpole Street*, and for *Witness for the Prosecution*. His failure to win more than the one Academy Award he got as Henry VIII reflected not his own achievements but the difficulty Hollywood has always had in coming to terms with character actors.

Laughton was ugly at a time when the predominant style was the rugged good looks of Clark Gable, the dashing charm of Errol Flynn, or the sophisticated presence of Cary Grant or George Sanders. He had, as he observed, a face like the behind of an elephant. His triumph was to bring the stage character actor on to the screen, providing audiences with somebody to hate or to admire rather than a dream figure with whom they could identify. Unlike the actors of a later period, Laughton could not flaunt his homosexuality, still a taboo subject on the screen. Like the later Orson Welles, whom he resembled in bulk, Laughton was always bigger than the screen, overflowing it in a way that betokened his immense power and authority as a stage actor.

—Philip Thody

LECOUVREUR, Adrienne.   French actress. Born in Damery, Marne, France, 5 April 1692. Two daughters, one by an official of the Duke of Lorena and the other by François de Klinglin. After experience as an amateur actress in Paris and with provincial companies, and with coaching by M. A. Legrand and Michel Baron, she made her professional debut to immediate acclaim with the Comédie-Française, Paris, 1717; made a sociétaire of the company, 1717, and given leading roles in tragedies by Pierre Corneille, Racine, and Voltaire, displacing Mlle Duclos; her life subsequently the basis for a successful play by Scribe and Legouvé, 1849. Died in Paris, 20 March 1730.

Roles

1717	Electre in *Électre* (Crébillon), Comédie-Française, Paris.
	Role in *George Dandin* (Molière), Comédie-Française, Paris.
	Monime in *Mithridate* (Racine), Comédie-Française, Paris.
1720	Artémire in *Artémire* (Voltaire), Comédie-Française, Paris.
1721	Antigone in *Macchabées* (La Motte), Comédie-Française, Paris.
	Zarès in *Esther* (Racine), Comédie-Française, Paris.
1723	Costance in *Inès de Castro* (La Motte), Comédie-Française, Paris.
1724	Mariamne in *Hérode et Mariamne* (Voltaire), Comédie-Française, Paris.
1726	Éricie in *Pyrrhus* (Crébillon), Comédie-Française, Paris.
1727	The Marquise in *La Seconde Surprise de l'Amour* (Marivaux), Comédie-Française, Paris.
1728	Angélique in *Les Fils ingrats* (Piron), Comédie-Française, Paris.

Other roles included: Alcmène in *Amphitryon* (Molière); Atalide in *Bajazet* (Racine); Athalie in *Athalie* (Racine); Bérénice in *Bérénice* (Racine); Célimène in *Le Misanthrope* (Molière); Cornélie in *La Mort de Pompée* (P. Corneille); Élisabeth in *Le Comte d'Essex* (T. Corneille); Elmire in *Tartuffe* (Molière); Ériphile in *Ériphile* (Voltaire); Hermione in *Andromaque* (Racine); Iphigénie in *Iphigénie* (Racine); Pauline in *Polyeucte* (P. Corneille); Phèdre in *Phèdre* (Racine); Roxane in *Bajazet* (Racine).

Publications

Lettres de Adrienne Lecouvreur, edited by Georges Monval, 1892; *Adrienne Lecouvreur et Maurice de Saxe: leurs lettres d'amour*, edited by R. L. Voyer de Paulmy, 1926.

*

Bibliography

Books:
Georges Rivollet, *Adrienne Lecouvreur*, Paris, 1925.
Cécile Sorel, *La Vie amoureuse d'Adrienne Lecouvreur*, Paris, 1925.
Gilberte Lecuyer-Corthis, *Adrienne Lecouvreur*, Paris, 1960.
Barbara Levy, *Adrienne*, New York, 1960.
Jack Richtman, *Adrienne Lecouvreur — The Actress and the Age*, Englewood Cliffs, New Jersey, 1971.

* * *

The life of Adrienne Lecouvreur had all the ingredients required by Hollywood for a showbiz biopic: humble origins, a dizzy rise to stardom, a tumultuous love-life, and a tragically early death at the height of her powers. The mysterious circumstances and suddenness of her death — an internal haemorrhage rumoured to be the result of poison — are also the stuff of legend and help to explain why she was seized on as a suitably romantic subject for drama on several occasions in the nineteenth century, most notably by Scribe and Legouvé in their play of 1849, which provided an affecting role for Rachel and was later adapted as an opera, with music by Francesco Cilea.

The real nature of her achievement as an actress was less sensational but far more substantial. After some experience as an amateur and in the provinces, she is said to have been given formal tuition by the playwright M. A. Legrand and by Molière's famous protégé Michel Baron, though it was also remarked at the time that she was "one of those extraordinary people who create themselves". That her innovations must have been allied to a solid histrionic technique is evident from the rapidity of her advancement in that bastion of traditionalism and orthodoxy, the Comédie-Française. Within weeks of her debut there in the title role of Crébillon's *Electre* in May 1717, she was admitted as a sociétaire of the company and over the next few years she established herself as its leading tragedienne, displacing the majestic but ageing Mlle Duclos in public favour. As such she went on to play most of the heroines in the classic repertoire of Pierre Corneille and Racine, including Pauline in *Polyeucte*, Bérénice, both Roxane and Atalide in *Bajazet*, Monime in *Mithridate*, Iphigénie and Ériphyle, Phèdre, Athalie, and, most triumphantly of all, Cornélie in *La Mort de Pompée* and Hermione in *Andromaque*. At the same time she created tragic roles in contemporary works by Houdar de La Motte, Crébillon, and Voltaire, who became one of her most devoted admirers. She had no pronounced talent for comedy but appeared successfully in a number of plays by Regnard, Piron, and Molière (as Célimène in *Le Misanthrope*, Elmire in *Tartuffe*, Alcmène in *Amphitryon*) and was the original Marquise in Marivaux's *La Seconde Surprise de l'Amour*.

To all these parts she brought a quality of freshness and simplicity that distinguished her playing from the mannered and more emphatic style of her immediate predecessors, who had paid so much attention to the inherent musical qualities of the verse as to assimilate their tragic diction to a form of chant or, in the less complimentary terms of the Italian actor-manager Luigi Riccoboni, a dreadful howling ("urli spaventosi"). In fact, another contemporary, Charles Collé, saw Mlle Lecouvreur's great-

Adrienne Lecouvreur

fluency of inflection that avoided the obvious striving after effect and vocal posturing of many of her fellows. According to her obituary notice in the *Mercure de France*, she was responsible for introducing a "simple, noble, and natural declamation", which must have made for greater delicacy of emotional expressiveness and more finesse in the delineation of character. In fact, there was even a quality of understatement in her playing: as one critic put it, "her voice seemed to be speaking less than her heart". She also took the unusual step of showing some concern for the appropriateness of costume to character, preferring at times to model her own dress on the real world than on theatrical convention.

After her death, not having renounced her profession, she was refused a Christian burial by the Church, and despite the public adulation she had enjoyed her body was simply thrown onto a Paris rubbish dump. Voltaire, who had addressed occasional verse to her during her lifetime, wrote an embittered elegy on the subject, attacking the hypocrisy of his fellow countrymen and contrasting their treatment of Adrienne Lecouvreur with the interment of Anne Oldfield at Westminster Abbey in the same year.

—Donald Roy

LEE, Eugene. US designer. Born in Beloit, Wisconsin, 9 March 1939. Educated at Carnegie Mellon University, Pennsylvania; Yale University, Connecticut. Married designer Franne Newman. Resident designer, Trinity Square Repertory Company, Providence, Rhode Island, 1967; set designer, television's *Saturday Night Live*, 1974–80; has also worked at the Dallas Theatre Centre, 1984–89, with Peter Brook in Shiraz and Paris, with Harold Prince, and as a designer for rock concerts. Recipient: Drama Desk Award, 1970–71, 1973–74; Tony Award, 1974, 1979; Maharam Foundation Award, 1973–74.

Productions

As set designer:
1965   *Endgame* (Beckett), Theatre of the Living Arts, Philadelphia, Pennsylvania.
1966   *Poor Bitos* (Anouilh), Theatre of the Living Arts, Philadelphia, Pennsylvania.
       Fitz and Biscuit, Circle in the Square, New York.
       A Dream of Love, Theatre of the Living Arts, Philadelphia, Pennsylvania.
       Endgame (Beckett), Yale Repertory Theatre, New Haven, Connecticut.
1967   *The Threepenny Opera* (Brecht and Weill), Studio Arena Theatre, Buffalo, New York, and Trinity Square Repertory Company, Providence, Rhode Island.
       The Imaginary Invalid (Molière), Studio Arena Theatre, Buffalo, New York.
       HMS Pinafore (Gilbert and Sullivan), Studio Arena Theatre, Buffalo, New York.
       The Importance of Being Earnest (Wilde), Trinity Square Repertory Company, Providence, Rhode Island.

est gift as precisely her ability to make one forget the actress and to be aware only of the character she was playing. This would seem to be confirmed by Voltaire himself, who described her as having "almost invented the art of speaking to the heart" and replaced mere declamation by sincerity and feeling in a quite inimitable fashion. It imparted to her performances an emotional conviction that audiences found deeply moving: so totally overcome did she seem by grief, tenderness, or anger that they responded as if to something real and, in the words of another commentator, "cried before seeing her tears flow". Significantly, this was just as true when she herself was not speaking, as she had a rare ability to listen and to react expressively to an interlocutor, which had the effect of making the whole situation more convincing.

The secret of Lecouvreur's success appears to have been an intelligent nurturing and deployment of personal resources that were relatively circumscribed. Her health was delicate and she was not physically strong. She did not have conventional good looks, nor many of the charms and anatomical endowments that have been known to enhance an actress's appeal. On the other hand, she possessed a naturally dignified bearing that provided the basis for a striking "presence" on stage and although her vocal powers were of themselves severely limited, this potential weakness was turned into a major source of her strength as a performer. She took particular pains to cultivate her voice and fashioned it into an instrument of considerable sensitivity and subtlety. By all accounts she had complete command of tone and pitch, together with an ease and

1968   *Enrico IV* (Pirandello), Studio Arena Theatre, Buffalo, New York.

    A Delicate Balance (Albee), Studio Arena Theatre, Buffalo, New York.

    Years of the Locust, Trinity Square Repertory Company, Providence, Rhode Island.

    An Enemy of the People (Ibsen), Trinity Square Repertory Company, Providence, Rhode Island.

    Phaedra (Racine), Trinity Square Repertory Company, Providence, Rhode Island.

    Brother to Dragons, Trinity Square Repertory Company, Providence, Rhode Island; also designed lighting.

1969   *Macbeth* (Shakespeare), Trinity Square Repertory Company, Providence, Rhode Island.

    The Homecoming (Pinter), Trinity Square Repertory Company, Providence, Rhode Island.

    Billy Budd (Britten), Trinity Square Repertory Company, Providence, Rhode Island.

    World War 2 1/2, Martinique Theatre, New York.

    Exiles, Trinity Square Repertory Company, Providence, Rhode Island.

    The Old Glory (Lowell), Trinity Square Repertory Company, Providence, Rhode Island; also designed lighting.

    The Recruiting Officer (Farquhar), Theatre of the Living Arts, Philadelphia, Pennsylvania.

    House of Breath and *Black/White*, Trinity Square Repertory Company, Providence, Rhode Island.

    Slave Ship (Baraka), Brooklyn Academy of Music, New York.

    Harry, Noon and Night, Theatre of the Living Arts, Philadelphia, Pennsylvania.

    Gargoyle Cartoons, Theatre of the Living Arts, Philadelphia, Pennsylvania.

    Wilson in the Promise Land, Trinity Square Repertory Company, Providence, Rhode Island.

1970   *Wilson in the Promise Land*, School of Design Theatre, Rhode Island, and ANTA Theatre, New York.

    Slave Ship (Baraka), Theatre-in-the-Church, New York.

    The Skin of Our Teeth (Wilder), Trinity Square Repertory Company, Providence, Rhode Island.

    Lovecraft's Follies, Trinity Square Repertory Company, Providence, Rhode Island.

    The Universal Nigger, Brooklyn Academy of Music, New York.

    Alice in Wonderland, Manhatten Project, Extension Theatre, New York.

    You Can't Take It with You (Kaufman), Trinity Square Repertory Company, Providence, Rhode Island.

    Saved (Bond), Chelsea Theatre Centre, New York.

    Son of Man and the Family, Trinity Square Repertory Company, Providence, Rhode Island.

    Mother Courage and Her Children (Brecht), Arena Stage, Washington, D.C.

    The Taming of the Shrew (Shakespeare), Trinity Square Repertory Company, Providence, Rhode Island.

1971   *The Good and Bad Times of Cady Francis McCullum and Friends*, Trinity Square Repertory Company, Providence, Rhode Island.

    The Threepenny Opera (Brecht and Weill), Trinity Square Repertory Company, Providence, Rhode Island.

    Orghast (Hughes), Shiraz Festival, Iran.

    Troilus and Cressida (Shakespeare), Trinity Square Repertory Company, Providence, Rhode Island.

    Down by the River Where Waterlilies Are Disfigured Every Day, Trinity Square Repertory Company, Providence, Rhode Island.

1972   *Alice in Wonderland*, Manhattan Project, Performing Garage, New York.

    Old Times (Pinter), Trinity Square Repertory Company, Providence, Rhode Island.

    Endgame (Beckett), Manhattan Project, New York.

    Dude, Broadway Theatre, New York.

1973   *The Royal Hunt of the Sun* (Shaffer), Trinity Square Repertory Company, Providence, Rhode Island.

    Feasting with Panthers, Trinity Square Repertory Company, Providence, Rhode Island.

    Ghost Dance, Trinity Square Repertory Company, Providence, Rhode Island.

    Aimee, Trinity Square Repertory Company, Providence, Rhode Island.

    Brother to Dragons, Trinity Square Repertory Company, Providence, Rhode Island.

    Candide (Hellmann), Chelsea Theatre Centre, New York.

1974   *A Man for All Seasons* (Bolt), Trinity Square Repertory Company, Providence, Rhode Island.

    Candide (Hellmann), Broadway Theatre, New York.

    Well Hung, Trinity Square Repertory Company, Providence, Rhode Island; also designed lighting.

    Gabrielle (Augier), Studio Arena Theatre, Buffalo, New York.

1975   *Peer Gynt* (Ibsen), Trinity Square Repertory Company, Providence, Rhode Island; also designed lighting.

    Tom Jones, Trinity Square Repertory Company, Providence, Rhode Island; also designed lighting.

    Seven Keys to Baldpate, Trinity Square Repertory Company, Providence, Rhode Island; also designed lighting.

    The Skin of Our Teeth (Wilder), Mark Hellinger Theatre, New York.

    Cathedral of Ice, Trinity Square Repertory Company, Providence, Rhode Island.

    Two Gentlemen of Verona (Shakespeare), Trinity Square Repertory Company, Providence, Rhode Island.

1976   *Dream on Monkey Mountain* (Walcott), Centre Stage, Baltimore, Maryland.
Bastard Son, Trinity Square Repertory Company, Providence, Rhode Island.
Eustace Chisholm and the Works, Trinity Square Repertory Company, Providence, Rhode Island.
Of Mice and Men (Steinbeck), Trinity Square Repertory Company, Providence, Rhode Island; also designed lighting.

1977   *King Lear* (Shakespeare), Trinity Square Repertory Company, Providence, Rhode Island; also designed lighting.
Some of My Best Friends (Leonard), Longacre Theatre, New York.
Ethan Frome, Trinity Square Repertory Company, Providence, Rhode Island; also designed lighting.
Rosmersholm (Ibsen), Trinity Square Repertory Company, Providence, Rhode Island.
Seduced (Shepard), Trinity Square Repertory Company, Providence, Rhode Island; also designed lighting.

1978   *La Fanciulla del West* (Puccini), Lyric Opera, Chicago, Illinois.

1979   *Sweeney Todd, the Demon Barber of Fleet Street* (Sondheim), Uris Theatre, New York, and London.
Gilda Radner, Live from New York, Winter Garden Theatre, New York.

1980   *Kaspar* (Handke), International Centre for Theatre Research, Paris.

1980–81   *El Grande de Coca-Cola*, Trinity Square Repertory Company, Providence, Rhode Island.
An Almost Perfect Person, Trinity Square Repertory Company, Providence, Rhode Island.
Deathtrap (Levin), Trinity Square Repertory Company, Providence, Rhode Island.
Arsenic and Old Lace (Kesselring), Trinity Square Repertory Company, Providence, Rhode Island.
Betrayal (Pinter), Trinity Square Repertory Company, Providence, Rhode Island.
On Golden Pond (Thompson), Trinity Square Repertory Company, Providence, Rhode Island.
A Christmas Carol (Dickens), Trinity Square Repertory Company, Providence, Rhode Island.
The Iceman Cometh (O'Neill), Trinity Square Repertory Company, Providence, Rhode Island.

1981   *It's Me, Sylvia*, Playhouse Theatre, New York.
Willie Stark, Kennedy Centre Opera House, Washington, D.C.
Inherit the Wind (Lawrence and Lee), Trinity Square Repertory Company, Providence, Rhode Island.
How I Got that Story, Trinity Square Repertory Company, Providence, Rhode Island.
Whose Life Is It, Anyway? (Clark), Trinity Square Repertory Company, Providence, Rhode Island.

The Whales of August (Berry), Trinity Square Repertory Company, Providence, Rhode Island.
Simon and Garfunkel Concert, Central Park, New York.
Faust (Gounod), Opera Company of Boston, Massachusetts.
Of Mice and Men (Steinbeck), tour; also designed lighting.
Buried Child (Shepard), tour.
Merrily We Roll Along (Kaufman), Alvin Theatre, New York.

1982   *Tintypes*, Trinity Square Repertory Company, Providence, Rhode Island; also designed lighting.
The Crucifer of Blood, Trinity Square Repertory Company, Providence, Rhode Island.
13 Rue de L'Amour (Feydeau), Trinity Square Repertory Company, Providence, Rhode Island.
The Dresser (Harwood), Trinity Square Repertory Company, Providence, Rhode Island.
Translations (Friel), Trinity Square Repertory Company, Providence, Rhode Island.
A Christmas Carol (Dickens), Trinity Square Repertory Company, Providence, Rhode Island.
The Front Page (Hecht), Trinity Square Repertory Company, Providence, Rhode Island.
The Tempest (Shakespeare), Trinity Square Repertory Company, Providence, Rhode Island.
Pygmalion (G. B. Shaw), Trinity Square Repertory Company, Providence, Rhode Island.
The Little Prince and the Aviator, Alvin Theatre, New York.
The Hothouse (Pinter), Trinity Square Repertory Company, Providence, Rhode Island, and Playhouse Theatre, New York; also designed lighting.
Agnes of God (Peielmeier), Music Box Theatre, New York.
Some Men Need Help, 47th Street Theatre, New York.
Simon and Garfunkel Concert, Tokyo.
The Web (O'Neill), Trinity Square Repertory Company, Providence, Rhode Island.
Bone Songs, Cubiculo Theatre, New York.

1983   *The Tempest* (Shakespeare), Trinity Square Repertory Company, Providence, Rhode Island; also designed lighting.
Letters from Prison: In the Belly of the Beast, Trinity Square Repertory Company, Providence, Rhode Island; also designed lighting.
Newsweek 50th Anniversary, State Theatre, New York.
Galileo (Brecht), Trinity Square Repertory Company, Providence, Rhode Island; also designed lighting.
The Wild Duck (Ibsen), Trinity Square Repertory Company, Providence, Rhode Island.
The Ballad of Soapy Smith, Seattle Repertory Company, Washington.

Billy Bishop Goes to War (Peterson and Gray), Bradford Theatre, Boston, Massachusetts.

1984 *Beyond Therapy* (Durang), Trinity Square Repertory Company, Providence, Rhode Island.

What the Butler Saw (Orton), Trinity Square Repertory Company, Providence, Rhode Island.

Terra Nova (Tally), Trinity Square Repertory Company, Providence, Rhode Island.

Passion Play (Nichols), Trinity Square Repertory Company, Providence, Rhode Island.

Tartuffe (Molière), Trinity Square Repertory Company, Providence, Rhode Island.

A Christmas Carol (Dickens), Trinity Square Repertory Company, Providence, Rhode Island.

And a Nightingale Sang (Taylor), Trinity Square Repertory Company, Providence, Rhode Island.

The Country Wife (Wycherley), Trinity Square Repertory Company, Providence, Rhode Island.

Master Harold ... and the Boys (Fugard), Trinity Square Repertory Company, Providence, Rhode Island.

Present Laughter (Coward), Trinity Square Repertory Company, Providence, Rhode Island.

The Wild Duck (Ibsen), Arts District Theatre, Dallas, Texas.

Jonestown Express, Trinity Square Repertory Company, Providence, Rhode Island.

Tom Jones, Arts District Theatre, Dallas, Texas.

Seven Keys to Baldpate, Arts District Theatre, Dallas, Texas.

Galileo (Brecht), Kalita Humphreys Theatre, Dallas, Texas.

Fool for Love (Shepard), Kalita Humphreys Theatre, Dallas, Texas.

Misalliance (G. B. Shaw), Kalita Humphreys Theatre, Dallas, Texas.

The Ballad of Soapy Smith, Public Theatre, New York.

1985 *The Normal Heart* (Kramer), Public Theatre, New York.

Amadeus (Shaffer), Theatre Centre, Dallas, Texas.

A Christmas Carol (Dickens), Theatre Centre, Dallas, Texas.

Passion Play (Nichols), Theatre Centre, Dallas, Texas.

The Three Sisters (Chekhov), Theatre Centre, Dallas, Texas.

You Can't Take It with You (Kaufman), Theatre Centre, Dallas, Texas.

Good (Taylor), Theatre Centre, Dallas, Texas.

1985–86 *The Skin of Our Teeth* (Wilder), Theatre Centre, Dallas, Texas.

The Marriage of Bette and Boo (Durang), Theatre Centre, Dallas, Texas.

The Glass Menagerie (T. Williams), Theatre Centre, Dallas, Texas.

The Tavern, Theatre Centre, Dallas, Texas.

The Ups and Downs of Theophilus Maitland, Theatre Centre, Dallas, Texas.

A Folk Tale, Theatre Centre, Dallas, Texas.

Kith and Kin, Theatre Centre, Dallas, Texas.

Cat on a Hot Tin Roof (T. Williams), Trinity Square Repertory Company, Providence, Rhode Island.

The Beauty Part (Behrman), Trinity Square Repertory Company, Providence, Rhode Island.

The Crucible (Miller), Trinity Square Repertory Company, Providence, Rhode Island.

Life and Limb, Trinity Square Repertory Company, Providence, Rhode Island.

Pasta, Trinity Square Repertory Company, Providence, Rhode Island.

The Country Girl (Odets), Trinity Square Repertory Company, Providence, Rhode Island.

Not by Bed Alone (Feydeau), Trinity Square Repertory Company, Providence, Rhode Island.

As costume designer only:
1966 *Belch*, Theatre of the Living Arts, Philadelphia, Pennsylvania.

As lighting designer only:
1970 *Love for Love* (Congreve), School of Design Theatre, Providence, Rhode Island.

1978 *Uncle Tom's Cabin: A History*, Trinity Square Repertory Company, Providence, Rhode Island.

Films

Mr Mike's Mondo Video, 1979; *One Trick Pony*, 1980; *Easy Money*, 1982; *Hammett*, 1982.

Television

Saturday Night Live, 1974–80; *Feasting with Panthers*, 1974; *Brother to Dragons*, 1975; *Life Among the Lowly*, 1976; *The Scarlet Letter*, 1979; *Steve Martin Special*, 1981; *House of Mirth*, 1981; *Randy Newman Live at the Odeon*, 1983; *The New Show*, 1984.

* * *

Eugene Lee is one of the few truly original voices in U.S. scenography. Generally associated with environmental design, he has developed a unique style and refuses to conform to accepted theatrical approaches or practices. Lee has never designed a straightforward box set; nor is the standard post-1950's scenographic vocabulary of scaffolding, collage, wood-plank stage floors, erosion cloth, textured surfaces, emblematic scenic pieces and the like to be found in his settings, at least not in any orthodox manner. The usual precepts of symmetry, order, scale and taste are never starting points or limitations for a Eugene Lee design. As a result, he has worked well with only a few directors, but those collaborations have been longstanding and highly productive, often breaking new theatrical ground. He was also a logical choice for the iconoclastic and even tacky world of television's *Saturday Night Live* in its first seasons, as well as for several rock concert tours.

Whereas most designers evolve their designs from the script or perhaps from the limitations of the stage space, Lee begins with the idea that the theatrical experience resides in the relationship between the performer and spectator. Consequently, he views the stage and auditorium as a whole: a unified space to be totally designed. Each new production is approached as a unique problem to be solved with no preconceived notions or theories about how to design or how to serve the text. His most successful designs, certainly some of his most famous ones, such as *Slave Ship* and *Candide*, have broken through the proscenium to surround, provoke or involve the audience. Although he began his career in the mid-1960's, when the destruction of the fourth wall was becoming commonplace and even chic, he was not interested in the theatre of participation so popular at the time in which the audience was dragged, often unwillingly, into a production; rather, he was interested in involving the audience on a psychological and emotional level by breaking complacent habits of perception. The new spatial arrangements with which he worked were not guided by theory or trendiness but by a desire to revitalize the theatre and to startle the audience into a new awareness. The goal was almost Brechtian, although the means were not. While his environmental designs were not influenced by Richard Schechner, who coined the term and who was producing fairly similar work with the Performance Group at about the same time, Lee's approach was influenced by seeing the work of Jerzy Grotowski at the Edinburgh Festival, and by working with André Gregory in Philadelphia. Gregory encouraged Lee to find new solutions and to explore new ideas. Lee's style thus evolved through trial and error and from an approach to design unhampered by conventional points of view.

But the real exploration of space began with his collaboration with director Adrian Hall at the Trinity Square Repertory Company in Providence, Rhode Island. Beginning in 1967, this became one of the longest director-designer relationships in US theatre history. In dozens upon dozens of productions together they broke through the proscenium, made the audience move from space to space during a production, surrounded audiences with scenery, moved scenic elements at or through the spectators, or built scenery and placed performers literally above the audience. Ideas tried at Providence eventually found their way to other productions. For *Billy Budd* at Providence, the audience was made to feel as it it were on an 18th-century ship; for Amiri Baraka's *Slave Ship* at the Brooklyn Academy of Music the audience felt as if it shared the cramped quarters of the slaves bound for the New World.

Part of Lee's approach derives from an aversion to what he perceives as the phoniness of illusion so prevalent in the commercial theatre. His sets are constructed of, or filled with, real objects and natural textures. Rarely does an illusionistic prop or set piece appear in one of his designs; dirt, wood, functional machinery and rusted tin — all undisguised — are among the many elements to be found in a Lee setting. This was certainly the case with the dirt-floor, tin-roof theatre Lee created for the Dallas Theatre Centre and it could be seen in numerous productions at the Trinity Square Repertory Company, but the most famous example was in the design for the Broadway production of *Sweeney Todd*. Faced with the large and sterile Uris Theatre, Lee filled the stage with factory-like environment created in part from scrap metal and mechanical devices from old Rhode Island factories; but he was unhappy being confined to the proscenium stage. For the same reasons, Lee is also averse, generally, to the typical use of colour and mood in lighting, preferring instead a flat whiteness produced by large lighting instruments. Given the constraints of commercial theatre, however, he has had fewer opportunities to practice lighting design. Needless to say, Lee's style and approach requires a close collaboration with a director who shares his vision, because it is, in fact, a collaborative process. Lee's most successful associations have been with André Gregory in the 1960's, Harold Prince on award-winning productions of *Slave Ship*, *Sweeney Todd* and *Candide* (for which a Broadway theatre was transformed into an environmental space of multiple stages, ramps and platforms), Peter Brook on *Orghast* in Iran and *Kaspar* in Paris, and, of course, with Adrian Hall at Trinity Square and, from 1984 to 1989, the Dallas Theatre Centre.

For a period in the late 1960's and 1970's it appeared as if the traditional theatre was about to undergo a radical transformation. Robin Wagner's design for *Hair*, the productions of many off- and off-off-Broadway companies, and the work of Eugene Lee seemed to presage the demise of the proscenium stage. But economic restraints and changing tastes prevented that from happening. Lee's theatrical output since the mid-1980's has been more limited and less iconoclastic, though in general it remains outside mainstream aesthetics.

—Arnold Aronson

LEE, Ming Cho. US designer. Born in Shanghai, China, 3 October 1930. Emigrated to USA, 1949; educated at Occidental College, Los Angeles, until 1953; School of Applied Arts, University of California, Los Angeles, 1953–54. Married Elizabeth Rapport in 1958, three sons. Assistant designer to Jo Mielziner and Boris Aronson, 1954–59; took US citizenship, 1961; art director and resident designer, San Francisco Opera, 1961; principal designer, Shakespeare Festival, New York, 1962–73; principal designer, Juilliard Opera/American Opera Centre, 1964–70; contributed first of many designs for the Arena Stage, Washington, D.C., 1967; has also designed for the New York City Opera and for various ballet companies; taught scene design at University of New York, 1968–70; head of design, Yale School of Drama, from 1979; set designer, Yale Repertory Theatre, 1981–82. Member: American Theatre Planning Board; Theatre Projects Commission; Advisory Council, International Theatre Institute; US-China Arts Exchange; Board of Directors, Technical Assistance Group Foundation; California Water Colour Society; National Design Archive (trustee). Recipient: Maharam Award, 1965, 1983; Tony Award, 1983; Outer Critics Circle Award, 1983; Drama Desk Award, 1983; Mayor's Award of Honour for Arts and Culture, 1984; China Institute First Qinyan Award, 1984; Los Angeles Drama Critics Award, 1985; Guggenheim Fellowship, 1988. LHD: Occidental College, Los Angeles, California, 1975; DFA: Parsons School of Design, 1986.

Productions

As set designer:

1951   *The Silver Whistle* (McEnroe), Occidental College, Los Angeles.

1955   *Guys and Dolls* (Loesser), Grist Mill Playhouse, Andover, New Jersey.

1958   *The Infernal Machine* (Cocteau), Phoenix Theatre, New York.

Missa Brevis, Juilliard Opera Theatre, New York.

The Crucible (Miller), Martinique Theatre, New York.

Triad (Butler), Theatre Marquee, New York.

1959   *Three Short Dances*, Connecticut College, New London, Connecticut.

The Turk in Italy, Peabody Arts Theatre, Baltimore, Maryland; also designed lighting.

1960   *The Old Maid and the Thief* (Menotti), Peabody Arts Theatre, Baltimore, Maryland; also designed lighting.

The Fall of the City (Cohn), Peabody Arts Theatre, Baltimore, Maryland; also designed lighting.

La Bohème (Puccini), Peabody Arts Theatre, Baltimore, Maryland; also designed lighting.

Kata Kabanova (Janáček), Empire State Music Festival, Bear Mountain, New York.

Peter Ibbetson, Empire State Music Festival, Bear Mountain, New York.

1961   *Amahl and the Night Visitors* (Menotti), Peabody Arts Theatre, Baltimore, Maryland; also designed lighting.

Three by Offenbach, Peabody Arts Theatre, Baltimore, Maryland; also designed lighting.

Don Giovanni (Mozart), Peabody Arts Theatre, Baltimore, Maryland; also designed lighting.

The Pearl Fishers (Bizet), Empire State Music Festival, Bear Mountain, New York.

1962   *Tristan and Isolde* (Wagner), Civic Opera, Baltimore, Maryland; also designed lighting.

Werther (Massenet), Peabody Arts Theatre, Baltimore, Maryland; also designed lighting.

The Merchant of Venice (Shakespeare), Shakespeare Festival, Delacorte Theatre, New York.

The Tempest (Shakespeare), Shakespeare Festival, Delacorte Theatre, New York.

King Lear (Shakespeare), Shakespeare Festival, Delacorte Theatre, New York.

Macbeth (Shakespeare), Shakespeare Festival, Delacorte Theatre, New York.

A Look at Lighting, Martha Graham Dance Company, New York.

The Moon Besieged (Schochen), Lyceum Theatre, New York; also designed lighting.

Hamlet (Shakespeare), Peabody Arts Theatre, Baltimore, Maryland; also designed lighting.

Madama Butterfly (Puccini), Opera Company of Boston, tour; also designed lighting.

1963   *Antony and Cleopatra* (Shakespeare), Shakespeare Festival, Delacorte Theatre, New York.

As You Like It (Shakespeare), Shakespeare Festival, Delacorte Theatre, New York.

The Winter's Tale (Shakespeare), Shakespeare Festival, Delacorte Theatre, New York.

Twelfth Night (Shakespeare), Shakespeare Festival, Delacorte Theatre, New York.

Mother Courage and Her Children (Brecht), Martin Beck Theatre, New York.

Conversation in the Dark (Hanley), Walnut Street Theatre, Philadelphia, Pennsylvania; also designed lighting.

Walk in Darkness (Hairston), Greenwich Mews Theatre, New York; also designed lighting.

Sea Shadow, Joffrey Ballet, New York.

1964   *Hamlet* (Shakespeare), Shakespeare Festival, Delacorte Theatre, New York.

Othello (Shakespeare), Shakespeare Festival, Delacorte Theatre, New York.

Electra (Sophocles), Shakespeare Festival, Delacorte Theatre, New York.

A Midsummer Night's Dream (Shakespeare), Shakespeare Festival, Delacorte Theatre, New York.

Il Tabarro (Puccini), Juilliard Opera Theatre, New York.

Gianni Schicchi (Puccini), Juilliard Opera Theatre, New York.

Kata Kabanova (Janáček), Juilliard Opera Theatre, New York.

1965   *Love's Labour's Lost* (Shakespeare), Shakespeare Festival, Delacorte Theatre, New York.

Coriolanus (Shakespeare), Shakespeare Festival, Delacorte Theatre, New York.

Troilus and Cressida (Shakespeare), Shakespeare Festival, Delacorte Theatre, New York.

The Taming of the Shrew (Shakespeare), Shakespeare Festival, Delacorte Theatre, New York.

Henry V (Shakespeare), Shakespeare Festival, Delacorte Theatre, New York.

Ariadne, Alvin Ailey Dance Company, New York.

The Witch of Endor, Martha Graham Dance Company.

Madama Butterfly (Puccini), Metropolitan Opera, New York.

Fidelio (Beethoven), Juilliard Opera Theatre, New York.

The Magic Flute (Mozart), Juilliard Opera Theatre, New York.

1966   *All's Well That Ends Well* (Shakespeare), Shakespeare Festival, Delacorte Theatre, New York.

Measure for Measure (Shakespeare), Shakespeare Festival, Delacorte Theatre, New York.

Richard III (Shakespeare), Shakespeare Festival, Delacorte Theatre, New York.

Slapstick Tragedy, Longacre Theatre, New York.

A Time for Singing, Broadway Theatre, New York.

Olympics, Joffrey Ballet.

Night Wings, Joffrey Ballet.

Don Rodrigo (Ginastera), City Opera, New York.

Julius Caesar (Handel), City Opera, New York.

The Marriage of Figaro (Mozart), Metropolitan Opera, New York.

The Trial of Lucullus (Sessions), Juilliard Opera Theatre, New York.

1967   *The Comedy of Errors* (Shakespeare), Shakespeare Festival, Delacorte Theatre, New York.

Titus Andronicus (Shakespeare), Shakespeare Festival, Delacorte Theatre, New York.

Hair (Shakespeare), Shakespeare Festival, Public Theatre, New York.

Little Murders (Feiffer), Broadhurst Theatre, New York.

The Crucible (Miller), Arena Stage, Washington D.C.

Elegy, Joffrey Ballet.

The Rape of Lucretia (Britten), Juilliard Opera Theatre, New York.

Bomarzo (Ginastera), Opera Society, Washington D.C.

Le Coq d'or (Rimsky-Korsakov), City Opera, New York.

Boris Godunov (Mussorgsky), Associated Opera Companies of America.

1968   *Henry IV, parts 1 and 2* (Shakespeare), Shakespeare Festival, Delacorte Theatre, New York.

Romeo and Juliet (Shakespeare), Shakespeare Festival, Delacorte Theatre, New York.

Ergo, Shakespeare Festival, Public Theatre, New York.

Here's Where I Belong, Billy Rose Theatre, New York.

The Tenth Man (Chayevsky), Arena Stage, Washington D.C.

Room Service (Murray and Boretz), Arena Stage, Washington D.C.

The Iceman Cometh (O'Neill), Arena Stage, Washington D.C.

King Lear (Shakespeare), Vivian Beaumont Theatre, New York.

A Light Fantastic, Joffrey Ballet.

The Lady of the House of Sleep, Martha Graham Dance Company.

Secret Places, Joffrey Ballet.

Bomarzo (Ginastera), City Opera, New York.

L'Ormindo (Cavalli), Juilliard Opera Theatre, New York.

Faust (Gounod), City Opera, New York.

1969   *Peer Gynt* (Ibsen), Shakespeare Festival, Delacorte Theatre, New York.

Cities in Bezique (Kennedy), Shakespeare Festival, Public Theatre, New York.

Invitation to a Beheading, Shakespeare Festival, Public Theatre, New York.

Electra (Sophocles), Shakespeare Festival, Mobile Unit, New York.

Billy (Barry), Billy Rose Theatre, New York.

Sambo (Tumburella), Shakespeare Festival, Public Theatre, New York.

La Strada, Lunt-Fontanne Theatre, New York.

Animus, Joffrey Ballet.

The Poppet, Joffrey Ballet.

Julius Caesar (Handel), Hamburg State Opera, Hamburg, Germany.

The Barber of Seville (Rossini), American Opera Centre, New York.

Help! Help! The Globolinks, City Centre, New York.

1970   *The Wars of the Roses* (Shakespeare compilation), Shakespeare Festival, Delacorte Theatre, New York.

Jack MacGowran in the Works of Samuel Beckett, Shakespeare Festival, Public Theatre, New York.

Gandhi, Playhouse Theatre, New York.

The Night Thoreau Spent in Jail, Arena Stage, Washington D.C.

Robert Devereux (Donizetti), City Opera, New York.

The Rake's Progress (Stanislavsky), Juilliard Opera Theatre, New York.

Il Giuramento, American Opera Centre, New York.

1971   *Timon of Athens* (Shakespeare), Shakespeare Festival, Delacorte Theatre, New York.

Two Gentlemen of Verona (Shakespeare), Shakespeare Festival, Delacorte Theatre, New York, and St James Theatre, New York.

Lolita, My Love, Shubert Theatre, Philadelphia, Pennsylvania.

Remote Asylum, Ahmanson Theatre, Los Angeles.

Ariodante, Kennedy Centre, Washington D.C.

Susannah, City Opera, New York.

1972   *Hamlet* (Shakespeare), Shakespeare Festival, Delacorte Theatre, New York.

Much Ado About Nothing (Shakespeare), Shakespeare Festival, Delacorte Theatre, New York, and Winter Garden Theatre, New York.

Older People, Shakespeare Festival, Public Theatre, New York.

Wedding Band (Childress), Shakespeare Festival, Public Theatre, New York.

Volpone (Jonson), Mark Taper Forum, Los Angeles.

Henry IV, part 1 (Shakespeare), Mark Taper Forum, Los Angeles.

Our Town (Wilder), Arena Stage, Washington D.C.

Maria Stuarda, City Opera, New York.

Tales of Hoffman (Offenbach), City Opera, New York.

La Bohème (Puccini), American Opera Centre, New York.

Lucia de Lammermoor (Donizetti), Teatro Colon, Buenos Aires.

Bomarzo (Ginastera), Teatro Colon, Buenos Aires.

1973   *Inherit the Wind* (Lawrence and Lee), Arena Stage, Washington D.C.

King Lear (Shakespeare), Yale Repertory Theatre, New Haven, Connecticut.

Don Juan, San Francisco Ballet.

Myth of a Voyage, Martha Graham Dance Company.

Four Saints in Three Acts (Thomson), Forum Theatre, New York.

Syllabaire pour Phèdre, Forum Theatre, New York.

Dido and Aeneas (Purcell), Forum Theatre, New York.

Anna Bolena (Donizetti), City Opera, New York.

St Matthew's Passion (Bach), San Francisco Opera.

La Favorita (Donizetti), San Francisco Opera.

Le Coq d'or (Rimsky-Korsakov), Civic Centre, Dallas, Texas.

1974   *The Seagull* (Chekhov), Shakespeare Festival, Public Theatre, New York.

Whispers of Darkness, National Ballet of Canada.

Boris Godunov (Mussorgsky), Metropolitan Opera, New York.

Idomeneo (Mozart), Kennedy Centre, Washington D.C.

1975   *All God's Chillun Got Wings* (O'Neill), Circle in the Square, New York.

The Glass Menagerie (T. Williams), Circle in the Square, New York.

Julius Caesar (Shakespeare), Arena Stage, Washington D.C.

The Ascent of Mt Fuji (Ajtmatov), Kreeger Theatre, Washington D.C.

In the Quest of the Sun, Royal Winnipeg Ballet, Canada.

The Leaves Are Fading, American Ballet Theatre, New York.

Idomeneo (Mozart), City Opera, New York.

1976   *For Coloured Girls Who Have Considered Suicide* (Shange), Shakespeare Festival, Public Theatre, New York.

Waiting for Godot (Beckett), Arena Stage, Washington D.C.

I Puritani (Bellini), Metropolitan Opera, New York.

Lohengrin (Wagner), Metropolitan Opera, New York.

Bilby's Doll, Grand Opera, Houston, Texas.

1977   *Caesar and Cleopatra* (G. B. Shaw), Palace Theatre, New York.

Romeo and Juliet (Shakespeare), Circle in the Square, New York.

The Shadow Box, Long Wharf Theatre, New Haven, Connecticut, and Morosco Theatre, New York.

Mother Courage and Her Children (Brecht), American Place Theatre, New York.

For Coloured Girls Who Have Considered Suicide (Shange), Mark Taper Forum, Los Angeles.

1978   *Angel*, Minskoff Theatre, New York.

The Grand Tour (Rice), Palace Theatre, New York.

King Lear (Shakespeare), American Place Theatre, New York.

Hamlet (Shakespeare), Arena Stage, Washington D.C.

Twelfth Night (Shakespeare), Shakespeare Festival, Stratford, Connecticut.

The Tiller in the Fields, American Ballet Theatre.

Madama Butterfly (Puccini), Lyric Opera, Chicago.

1979   *Don Juan* (Molière), Arena Stage, Washington D.C.

The Tempest (Shakespeare), Mark Taper Forum, Los Angeles, and Shakespeare Festival, Stratford, Connecticut.

The Glass Menagerie (T. Williams), Guthrie Theatre, Minneapolis, Minnesota.

Saint Joan (G. B. Shaw), Seattle Repertory Theatre, Washington.

1980   *Plenty* (Hare), Arena Stage, Washington D.C.

Boris Godunov (Mussorgsky), Lyric Opera, Chicago.

Attila, Lyric Opera, Chicago.

1981   *Oedipus*, Brooklyn Academy of Music, New York.

Attila, City Opera, New York.

La Donna del Lago (Puccini), Grand Opera, Houston, Texas.

Madama Butterfly, Chilean Opera Society.

1982   *K2*, Kreeger Theatre, Washington D.C.

Mary Stuart (Schiller), Shakespeare Festival, Stratford, Ontario.

Alceste (Gluck), City Opera, New York.

Montezuma, American Opera Centre, New York.

1983   *K2*, Brooks Atkinson Theatre, New York.

Death of a Salesman (Miller), Shakespeare Festival, Stratford, Ontario.

Desire Under the Elms (O'Neill), Indiana Repertory Theatre, Indianapolis.

I Capuleti e I Montecchi (Bellini), American Opera Centre, New York.

The Glass Menagerie (T. Williams), Eugene O'Neill Theatre, New York.

Turandot (Puccini), Opera Company of Boston.

1984   *The Cuban Swimmer* and *Dog Lady*, Intar Theatre, New York.

Other productions have included: *Dream of the Red Chamber*, 1983; *The Entertainer* (Osborne), 1984; *Khovanschina* (Mussorgsky), 1985; *Execution of Justice*, 1985; *Les Noces*, 1985; *Tangled Night*, 1986; *Faust* (Gounod), 1989.

As costume designer only:
1958   *Madama Butterfly* (Puccini), Metropolitan Opera, New York.

* * *

Now in his fifth decade of designing and regarded by many as the dean of US stage designers, Ming Cho Lee has left an indelible impression on the evolution of US stage design as a result not only of his own stage creations but also of his quarter century of teaching at Yale University's School of Drama. His more than 200 stage designs for theatres across the country and abroad reveal an eclectic talent with a number of consistent traits: spareness, a strong sense of structure and spatial proportion and a preference for selective emblems over realistic details.

By his own testimony, Lee is primarily attracted to projects that stress theatricality, which is more likely to be found in dance and opera rather than drama: "The most enjoyable designing ... demands a purely theatrical expression; the least literal is the most satisfying", and to be more precise, "designing for the dance is the most exciting type of design". Of opera, which he finds only somewhat less theatrical than dance, he has said: "Of all forms of theatre, opera is the one I love and live most completely". His key to designing opera is to respond to the 'weight' of the music as the prime influence on the set design rather than the literal story of the opera. Despite Lee's attraction to dance and opera, slightly more than half of his work has been in nonmusical theatre, to which he has brought the same instinct for theatrically expressive settings that he applies to opera and dance. Such settings are most appropriate for works that were written for a nonliteral stage, above all the works of Shakespeare, the Greeks and others of high imagination for which, like opera and dance, "literalness is less important than total statement".

Lee established his reputation most forcefully in his work on Shakespeare and other classics during the 1960's and 1970's for the New York Shakespeare Festival's outdoor Delacorte Theatre in Central Park. Working with minimal budgets, he succeeded in achieving maximal effects that combined theatrical force and functionality with artistic integrity. His signature became the use of steel scaffolding that supported a rectilinear, constructivist-like system of platforms, towers, stairs, bridges and ramps that lent itself to Shakespeare's uninterrupted flow of action (for example, in *Two Gentlemen of Verona* in 1971) or, when modified, to more static scenes in other dramas. At times, the total space had a neutral, universal ambience, but more often the use of carefully selected, symbolically charged emblems (banners, shields, architectural details) attached to the scaffolding created a dominant visual image expressive of the production concept for that play. Variations of this system included the use of turntables (*Peer Gynt* in 1969), actual houses (*The Comedy of Errors* in 1967) and collages of graphic images to create special environments (turn of the century America as the setting for *Much Ado About Nothing* in 1972). In what was Lee's single most celebrated early design, for Sophocles's *Electra* in 1964, a cluster of multi-levelled platforms jutted toward the audience, backed by three deeply eroded slabs of stone mounted above ground level on a number of vertical pipes. The massive fragments captured perfectly the sense of antiquity, power and decay inherent in the text.

A feeling for sculpturesque effects, inherent in many of Lee's designs, is another significant element of his work. Together with his use of highly structured, skeletal elements, the sculptured look may be seen as a symptom of his reaction against the pictorial, poetic tradition of set design associated with Lee's principal mentor, Joel Mielziner, with whom he worked for five years in the 1950's. It also relates to his sensitivity, which owes much to his briefer apprentice work with Boris Aronson. In fact, Lee frequently did his own lighting in opera in the early years, until

technical complexities of production made such dual labour impractical. His special feel for sculpturesque scenery and lighting is also echoed in his attraction to designing for dance, with its emphasis on the human body moving through space. The richest example of the evolution of Lee's skeletal, sculptured work with elements of collage is probably found in his first Metropolitan Opera production, *Boris Godunov*, in 1974.

Lee's tendency toward economy of expression, theatricality and overt use of functional materials also related him to the Brechtian tradition, which, like Lee himself, draws in part on the elegant austerity of Chinese landscape painting. But Lee was not to be confined to only one type of scenography. He eventually wanted to move beyond minimalism and collage toward a more pictorial design that also provided fuller integrity with the text rather than project a primarily visual, mostly abstract statement. He reached a turning point in his production of Ajtmatov's *Ascent of Mt Fuji* in 1975, for which he created what was for Lee an almost realistically detailed mountain meadow. This tendency toward increased pictorial realism was still present, but in more concentrated essence, in *Desire Under the Elms* in 1983 and, more powerfully, in the mammoth facade of mountain ice that he created for *K2* in 1982.

An artist who is never satisfied with his work and who is his own most severe critic, Lee briefly became more interested in pure form and colour in the early and mid-1980's (*Dream of the Red Chamber*, 1983), but also reverted toward his earlier, neo-Brechtian spareness. He was struck by what he called the hard-edged, photographic look of Patrice Chereau's Bayreuth *Ring* cycle and some of Robert Wilson's work. Evidence of Lee's assimilation of this style may be found in his *Turandot* (1983), *The Entertainer* (1984) and *Khovanschina* (1985), all of which seem to express a synthesis of his economy and sense of structure with his greater concern for certain elements of realism.

Although he has had some 20 Broadway productions, Lee has found work with regional resident theatre more satisfying mainly because of its greater emphasis on teamwork and its lessened element of crisis with millions at stake. His extended association with Washington D.C.'s Arena Stage has been particularly fruitful and has led to some interesting experiments with the arena staging form, such as his removal of the stage floor (*Hamlet*, 1978, and Molière's *Don Juan*, 1979) in order to establish the effect of an island with a sunken lower level to create a sense of the life beneath the main action of the play as part of the total set. Lee is especially sensitive to the demands of the various theatre spaces, from arena to proscenium to thrust, not preferring any single spatial arrangement but organically evolving his design from the parameters of each.

In recent years Lee has cut back on the quantity of his own design work because of his increasing involvement with supervising production work at the Yale School of Drama and at the Yale Rep. This work of integrating the creative efforts of directors and designers has led him to think more directorially, to respond to the total world of the play rather than to the play as simply a design challenge. Questions of realism or spatial articulation become secondary to the capturing of the full social and human dimensions inherent in the text. He has cited his recent work on Gounod's *Faust* (1989) as an example of this evolution in his approach.

—Jarka M. Burian

LE GALLIENNE, Eva. US actress, director and producer. Born in London, 11 January 1899. Educated at the Collège de Sevigny, Paris; trained for the stage at the Royal Academy of Dramatic Art, London. Stage debut, as actress at the Queen's Theatre, London, 1914; New York debut, Comedy Theatre, 1915; spent five years on Broadway, 1920–26; founder, Civic Repertory Company, 1926; disbanded Civic Repertory Company after 1581 performances, 1935; co-founder, with Cheryl Crawford and Margaret Webster, of the American Repertory Theatre, at the International Theatre, New York, 1946; film debut, 1955; actress with the National Repertory Theatre, New York, 1961–66. Recipient: Pictorial Review Award, 1926; Town Hall Club Award, 1934; Society of Arts and Sciences Gold Medal, 1934; American Academy of Arts and Letters Gold Medal, 1934; Women's National Press Club Outstanding Woman of the Year, 1947; ANTA Award, 1964; Special Tony Award, 1964; Brandeis University Award, 1966; Handel Medallion, 1976; Drama League Award, 1976; Episcopal Actors' League Award, 1977; Theatre World Award, 1977; Emmy, 1978; National Conference of Christians and Jews Woman of Achievement Award, 1978; Connecticut Commission on the Arts Achievement in Arts Award, 1980. MA: Tufts University, Medford, Massachusetts, 1927; DHL: Smith University, Northampton, Massachusetts, 1930; Ohio Wesleyan University, 1953; University of North Carolina, 1964; Bard University, 1965; Fairfield University, Fairfield, Connecticut, 1966; Litt.D: Russell Sage College, 1930; Brown University, Providence, 1933; Mount Holyoke College, 1937; Goucher College, 1961. Grand Cross of the Royal Order of St Olaf (Norway), 1961. Died in Weston, Massachusetts, 3 June 1991.

Productions

As actress:

1914	Page in *Monna Vanna* (Maeterlinck), Queen's Theatre, London.
1915	Elizabeth in *The Laughter of Fools* (Maltby), Prince of Wales Theatre, London.
	Victorine in *Peter Ibbetson*, His Majesty's Theatre, London.
	Rose in *Mrs Boltay's Daughter*, Comedy Theatre, New York.
1916	Jennie in *Bunny*, Hudson Theatre, New York.
	Mary Powers in *The Melody of Youth* (Tynan), Fulton Theatre, New York.
	Patricia Molloy in *Mr Lazarus* (O'Higgins and Ford), Shubert Theatre, New York.
1916–17	Role in *Rio Grande*, tour.
1917	Dot Carrington in *Saturday to Monday* (Fenn and Pryce), Bijou Theatre, New York.
	Ottiline Mallinson in *Lord and Lady Algy* (Carton), Broadhurst Theatre, New York.
1918	Duchess of Burchester in *The Off-Chance*, Empire Theatre, New York.

	Delia in *Belinda* (Milne), Empire Theatre, New York.
1919	Eithne in *Lusmore*, Henry Miller Theatre, New York.
	Role in *Elsie Janis and Her Gang*, George M. Cohan Theatre, New York.
1920	Elsie Dover in *Not So Long Ago* (Richman), Booth Theatre, New York.
1921	Julie in *Liliom* (Molnár), Garrick Theatre, New York; Civic Repertory Theatre, New York, 1932.
1923	Simonetta in *Sandro Botticelli*, Provincetown, New York.
	Julia in *The Rivals* (Sheridan), 48th Street Theatre, New York.
	Princess Alexandra in *The Swan* (Molnár), Cort Theatre, New York.
1924	The Child in *Hannele* (Hauptmann), Cort Theatre, New York.
	Diane de Charence in *La Vièrge Folle*, Gaiety Theatre, New York.
1925	Marie in *The Call of Life* (Schnitzler), Comedy Theatre, New York.
	Jehanne in *Jehanne d'Arc* (Acosta), Théâtre de la Porte-Saint-Martin, Paris.
	Hilda Wangel in *The Master Builder* (Ibsen), Maxine Elliott's Theatre, New York; Civic Repertory Theatre, New York, 1926; tour, 1933.
1926	Ella Rentheim in *John Gabriel Borkman* (Ibsen), Booth Theatre, New York; Civic Repertory Theatre, New York, 1926; International Theatre, New York, 1946–57, also directed.
	Imperia in *Saturday Night* (Benavente), Civic Repertory Theatre, New York; also directed.
	Masha in *The Three Sisters* (Chekhov), Civic Repertory Theatre, New York; also directed.
	Mirandolina in *La Locandiera* (Goldoni), Civic Repertory Theatre, New York; also directed.
	Viola in *Twelfth Night* (Shakespeare), Civic Repertory Theatre, New York; also directed.
1927	Sister Joanna in *The Cradle Song* (Sierra), Civic Repertory Theatre, New York; Broadhurst Theatre, New York, 1934; also directed.
	Aunt Isobel in *Inheritors* (Glaspell), Civic Repertory Theatre, New York; also directed.
	Jo in *The Good Hope* (Heijermans), Civic Repertory Theatre, New York; also directed.
1928	Sara Peri in *The First Stone* (Ferris), Civic Repertory Theatre, New York; also directed.
	Princess Orloff in *Improvisations in June* (Mohr), Civic Repertory Theatre, New York; also directed.
	Hedda in *Hedda Gabler* (Ibsen), Civic Repertory Theatre, New York; tour, 1933; Broadhurst Theatre, New York, 1934; also directed.
	Marie Louise in *L'Invitation au Voyage* (Bernard), Civic Repertory Theatre, New York; also directed.
	Varya in *The Cherry Orchard* (Chekhov), Civic Repertory Theatre, New York; also directed.
	Peter in *Peter Pan* (Barrie), Civic Repertory Theatre, New York; also directed.

1929   Masha in *The Seagull* (Chekhov), Civic Repertory Theatre, New York; also directed.

Anna Karenina in *The Living Corpse* (Tolstoy), Civic Repertory Theatre, New York; also directed.

1930   Juanita in *The Women Have Their Way* (Quintero), Civic Repertory Theatre, New York; also directed.

Lady Torminster in *The Open Door* (Sutro), Civic Repertory Theatre, New York; also directed.

Juliet in *Romeo and Juliet* (Shakespeare), Civic Repertory Theatre, New York, also directed; tour, 1933.

Genevieve in *Siegfried* (Giraudoux), Civic Repertory Theatre, New York; also directed.

Elsa in *Alison's House* (Glaspell), Civic Repertory Theatre, New York; also directed.

1931   Marguerite in *Camille* (Dumas fils), Civic Repertory Theatre, New York; also directed.

1932   Cassandra Austen in *Dear Jane* (Hinckley), Civic Repertory Theatre, New York; also directed.

The White Queen in *Alice in Wonderland* (Carroll, adapted by Le Gallienne and Friebus), Civic Repertory Theatre, New York, and tour, also directed; International Theatre, New York, 1946–57, also directed; Virginia Theatre, New York, 1982–83.

1934   Duke of Reichstadt in *L'Aiglon* (Rostand), Broadhurst Theatre, New York; also directed.

1935   Rebecca West in *Rosmersholm* (Ibsen), Shubert Theatre, New York.

Donna Laura in *A Sunny Morning*, Broadway Theatre, New York.

Mathilda Wesendonk in *Prelude to Exile*, Guild Theatre, New York.

1936   Angelica in *Love for Love* (Congreve), Westport Country Playhouse, Westport, Connecticut.

1937   Mirandolina in *The Mistress of the Inn*, Mount Kisco, New York.

Hamlet in *Hamlet* (Shakespeare), Cape Playhouse, Dennis, Massachusetts.

1938   Marie Antoinette in *Madame Capet*, Cort Theatre, New York.

1939   Juliet in *Frank Fay's Music Hall*, 44th Street Theatre, New York.

Amanda in *Private Lives* (Coward), tour.

1942   Mrs Malaprop in *The Rivals* (Sheridan), Guild Theatre, New York; also directed.

Lettie in *Uncle Harry* (Job), Broadhurst Theatre, New York.

1944   Andreyevna in *The Cherry Orchard* (Chekhov), National Theatre, New York; also directed.

1945   Thérèse in *Thérèse Raquin* (Zola), Biltmore Theatre, New York.

1946–57   Katherine in *Henry VIII* (Shakespeare), International Theatre, New York.

Comtesse de La Bière in *What Every Woman Knows* (Barrie), International Theatre, New York.

1948   Mrs Alving in *Ghosts* (Ibsen), Cort Theatre, New York.

1949–50   Miss Moffat in *The Corn Is Green* (E, Williams), tour.

1950   Signora Amaranta in *Fortunato* (Granville-Barker), Woodstock Theatre, New York.

1954   Lady Starcross in *The Starcross Story*, Royale Theatre, New York.

1955   Marcia Elder in *The Southwest Corner*, Holiday Theatre, New York.

1957   Narrator in *An Afternoon with Oscar Wilde*, Theatre de Lys, New York.

Queen Elizabeth in *Mary Stuart* (Schiller), Phoenix Theatre, New York; National Repertory Theatre, New York, 1959–60.

1958   Lavinia in *Listen to the Mockingbird*, tour.

1959–60   Queen Elizabeth in *Elizabeth the Queen* (Anderson), National Repertory Theatre, New York.

1963–64   Madame Arkadina in *The Seagull* (Chekhov), National Repertory Theatre, New York.

Madame Desmermortes in *Ring Round the Moon* (Fry), National Repertory Theatre, New York.

1968   Queen Marguerite in *Exit the King* (Ionesco), Lyceum Theatre, New York.

1970   The Countess in *All's Well That Ends Well* (Shakespeare), American Shakespeare Festival, Stratford, Connecticut.

1975   Mrs Woodfin in *The Dream Watcher*, White Barn, Westport, Connecticut; Repertory Theatre, Seattle, 1977.

1975–76   Fanny Cavendish in *The Royal Family* (Marshall), Helen Hayes Theatre, New York; tour, 1977.

1980   Grandmother in *To Grandmother's House We Go*, Alley Theatre, Houston, Texas; Biltmore Theatre, New York, 1980–81.

Also acted role in: *The Trojan Women* (Euripides).

As director only:

1941   *Ah, Wilderness!* (O'Neill), Guild Theatre, New York.

1964–65   *Liliom* (Molnár), tour.

Hedda Gabler (Ibsen), tour.

1968   *The Cherry Orchard* (Chekhov, translated by Le Gallienne), Lyceum Theatre, New York.

1975   *A Doll's House* (Ibsen), Repertory Theatre, Seattle, Washington D.C.

Films

Prince of Players, 1955; *The Devil's Disciple*, 1959; *Resurrection*, 1979.

Television

The Royal Family, 1978.

Publications

Alice in Wonderland (play), with Florida Friebus, 1932; *At 33* (memoir), 1934; *Flossie and Bossie Harper*, 1949; *The*

Strong Are Lonely (play), 1953; *The Master Builder* (translation), 1955; *With a Quiet Heart* (memoir), 1957; *Six Plays of Henrik Ibsen* (translations), 1957; *Seven Tales of Hans Christian Andersen* (translations), 1959; *The Nightingale* (translation), 1959; *The Wild Duck and Other Plays* (translations), 1961; *The Mystic in the Theatre: Eleonora Duse*, 1966; *The Little Mermaid* (translation), 1971; *The Spider and Other Stories* (translations), 1980.

*

Bibliography

Articles:
Ruth Pennybacker, "Eva Le Gallienne, Rebel Actress", *Woman Citizen*, 10, March 1926.
Robert Benchley, "Eva Le Gallienne's Civic Repertory Theatre", *Life*, 11 January 1929.
David Carb, "Eva Le Gallienne", *Theatre Guild Magazine*, 8, February 1931.
May Sarton, "The Genius of Eva Le Gallienne. Acting as a Criticism of Life", *Forum*, 11, Summer 1973–Winter 1974.

* * *

In an acting and producing career spanning almost three-quarters of a century, Eva Le Gallienne established herself as an actress of subtlety and intelligence, and as a dedicated adherent of the repertory system. Part of a generation of remarkable actresses who appeared on the US stage after World War I, Le Gallienne learned her craft in stock companies and as a supporting player on tour with Ethel Barrymore. Her touching performance in the Theatre Guild's production of Ferenc Molnár's play *Liliom* established her as a Broadway star in 1921, and two years later she repeated her success in Molnár's *The Swan*. Her future as a major star of the Broadway stage seemed certain, but Le Gallienne, the daughter of an English poet/novelist, was impatient with the long runs and commercialism of Broadway and after a tour with two Ibsen plays during the 1925–26 season she founded the Civic Repertory Theatre in a decrepit opera house on Manhattan's 14th Street. The company was to give modern and classic plays in a true repertory system where several plays are performed in rotation. Subsidized by wealthy backers, the Civic Repertory Theatre mounted almost 40 productions over eight years at reduced ticket prices that attracted many spectators who had never before attended the live theatre. Le Gallienne directed and acted in almost all the Civic Repertory plays, which included works by Shakespeare, Ibsen, Chekhov and Molière, as well as a memorable adaptation of *Alice in Wonderland* (one of the company's biggest successes). As Le Gallienne's backers suffered financial reversals in the Depression years of the 1930's, her support dried up and the company went out of business in 1935.

After several years of acting and lecturing across the country, in 1946 Le Gallienne formed another repertory company, the American Repertory Theatre, with director Margaret Webster and producer Cheryl Crawford (Le Gallienne was to be the company's leading actress as well as one of the founders). The first season began with a repertory of *John Gabriel Borkman*, *Henry VIII* and *What Every Woman Knows* by James Barrie. Critical reaction

was mixed, and the venture suffered financial losses, which forced the directors to abandon repertory for long runs, and to give up completely at the end of the season. In 1961 the American National Theatre and Academy (ANTA) initiated a National Repertory Theatre, with Le Gallienne as honorary president and leading lady. Despite a successful national tour with Schiller's *Mary Stuart* and Maxwell Anderson's *Elizabeth the Queen* the company could not overcome financial difficulties and gave up the repertory idea. Le Gallienne continued to act, most notably for the APA-Phoenix company in New York, for whom she directed *The Cherry Orchard* and appeared in Ionesco's *Exit the King*; at several major regional theatres, including the American Shakespeare Festival Theatre and the Seattle Repertory Theatre; and on Broadway in *The Royal Family* (1975) and *To Grandmother's House We Go* (1981). In addition to her work as actress, director and producer, Le Gallienne published highly regarded translations of Ibsen's plays, as well as two volumes of autobiography in which she articulated her belief in the value of repertory.

As an actress, Le Gallienne possessed a distinctive style, described by various critics as intellectual, cerebral, cool. While she was quite capable of evincing great passion when a role required it, as in her performances of Julie in *Liliom*, Marguerite Gautier in *Camille* and Elizabeth I in *Mary Stuart*, her greatest success was in parts that benefited from a more repressed, thoughtful performance, and, indeed, these were the roles she most often chose for herself when producing plays. Critics praised the "sobriety, coolness, and logic" of her Rebecca West in *Rosmersholm*, and the "beautiful assurance" of her Madame Ranevskaya in *The Cherry Orchard*. In creating a role, Le Gallienne concentrated on discovering the thought processes of her character, and included numerous pauses in her performance so that the audience could see the act of thinking taking place. Most critics praised her for this ability to draw spectators into the inner life of her characters, but a few, such as George Jean Nathan, assailed what they believed to be her emotionless, excessively cerebral approach to acting. Le Gallienne believed that the best training for actors was an early start on a professional career; she was critical of acting schools and university theatre departments, and felt that 'Method' actors were merely doing what actors had done for centuries — entering into the inner life of their characters.

In the latter part of her career, Le Gallienne's lifetime of theatrical experience and mastery of traditional acting technique resulted in two impressive performances: as Fanny Cavendish, head a Barrymore-like acting clan in *The Royal Family* Le Gallienne had one unforgettable scene in which she passionately described the joys of theatrical life (after which she gave a touching, understated death scene), while as Grandie in *To Grandmother's House We Go* she impressed critics with her stage presence, energy and ironic handling of the play's modern humour.

Eva Le Gallienne stood virtually alone in the 20th-century US theatre in her unrelenting commitment to the ideal of true repertory. Her Civic Repertory Theatre demonstrated that a repertory company performing several plays in rotation could draw large audiences, including many first-time theatregoers, if ticket prices could be kept low. The Depression ended that noble experiment, and her subsequent ventures in repertory were less successful. Nevertheless, her passionate defence of repertory reminded many in the theatre that there were alternatives to the long-run 'hit' philosophy of the commercial producers, and may have helped to prepare the ground for the explosion of regional, modified-repertory companies that began in the late 1940's.

—Margaret M. Knapp

LEKAIN, Henri-Louis. French actor. Born Henri-Louis Cain in Paris, 31 March 1729. Educated at Mazarin College, Paris, 1737–43. Married actress Christine Sirot in 1750, three sons. Stage debut, as an amateur in Paris, 1748; encouraged by Voltaire, who provided him with training and a theatre and arranged his debut with the Comédie-Française, Paris, in 1750; despite hostility of Mlle Clairon, he was acclaimed the finest tragedian of his generation by the late 1750's; important reforms in stage practice included banning audience seating on the stage, 1759; acted primarily at the Comédie-Française, but also toured regularly in the provinces to save himself from bankruptcy; acted before the Prussian court of Frederick II in Berlin, 1775. Died in Paris, 8 February 1778.

Roles

1750   Titus in *Brutus* (Voltaire), Comédie-Française, Paris.
1751–52 Agnelet in *L'Avocat Pathelin* (De Brueys and Palaprat), Comédie-Française, Paris.
         Antiochus in *Rodogune* (P. Corneille), Comédie-Française, Paris.
         Antipater in *Antipater*, Comédie-Française, Paris.
         Catalina in *Rome sauvée* (Voltaire), Comédie-Française, Paris.
         Damon in *Le Préjugé à la mode* (La Chaussée), Comédie-Française, Paris, and Versailles.
         Egisthe in *Mérope* (Voltaire), Comédie-Française, Paris.
         Gustave in *Gustave* (Piron), Comédie-Française, Paris.
         Joad in *Athalie* (Racine), Comédie-Française, Paris.
         Jupiter in *Amphitryon* (Molière), Comédie-Française, Paris.
         Oedipe in *Oedipe* (Voltaire), Comédie-Française, Paris.
         Oreste in *Andromaque* (Racine), Comédie-Française, Paris, and Versailles.
         Orosmane in *Zaïre* (Voltaire), Comédie-Française, Paris, and Fontainebleau.
         Don Pèdre in *Inès de Castro* (La Motte), Comédie-Française, Paris.
         Role in *Atrée et Thyeste* (Crébillon), Comédie-Française, Paris.
         Rhadamisthe in *Rhadamisthe et Zénobie* (Crébillon), Comédie-Française, Paris.
         Rodrigue in *Le Cid* (P. Corneille), Comédie-Française, Paris, and Versailles.
         Séide in *Mahomet* (Voltaire), Comédie-Française, Paris.

         Servilius in *Manlius* (Desjardins), Comédie-Française, Paris, and Fontainebleau.
         Role in *Varron*, Comédie-Française, Paris, and Versailles.
         Télémaque in *Pénélope* (Genest), Comédie-Française, Paris.
         Role in *Le Médecin malgré lui* (Molière), Comédie-Française, Paris.
         Zamore in *Alzire* (Voltaire), Comédie-Française, Paris.
1752–53 Abdéris in *Egyptus* (Marmontel), Comédie-Française, Paris.
         Absalon in *Absalon* (Duché de Vancy), Comédie-Française, Paris, and Versailles.
         Adam in *Le Joueur* (Regnard), Comédie-Française, Paris.
         Agénor in *Démocrite* (Regnard), Comédie-Française, Paris.
         Brama in *Le Prologue de La Métempsycose*, Comédie-Française, Paris.
         Don Carlos in *Le Festin de Pierre* (T. Corneille), Comédie-Française, Paris.
         Clitandre in *Le Misanthrope* (Molière), Comédie-Française, Paris.
         Clitandre in *Le Retour imprévu* (Regnard), Comédie-Française, Paris.
         Drusus in *La Mort de Néron* (Péchantrés), Comédie-Française, Paris.
         Enée in *Didon* (Scudéry), Comédie-Française, Paris.
         Euphémon *fils* in *L'Enfant prodigue* (Voltaire), Comédie-Française, Paris.
         Duc de Foix in *Le Duc de Foix* (Voltaire), Comédie-Française, Paris, Fontainebleau, and Dijon.
         Henrique in *L'Ecole des Femmes* (Molière), Comédie-Française, Paris.
         Don Henrique in *Inès de Castro* (La Motte), Comédie-Française, Paris.
         Hippolyte in *Phèdre* (Racine), Comédie-Française, Paris.
         Jason in *Médée* (Corneille), Comédie-Française, Paris.
         Comte Lisimon in *Les Trois Frères rivaux* (Lafont), Comédie-Française, Paris.
         Mahomet in *Mahomet* (Voltaire), Dijon.
         Mondor in *Le Grondeur* (De Brueys and Palaprat), Comédie-Française, Paris.
         Oreste in *Electre* (Crébillon), Comédie-Française, Paris, Versailles, and Dijon.
         Osmin in *Bajazet* (Racine), Versailles.
         Perithoüs in *Ariane* (T. Corneille), Comédie-Française, Paris, and Versailles.
         Baron Polinville in *Le Français à Londres* (Boissy), Comédie-Française, Paris, and Versailles.
         Le Provincial in *La Nouveauté* (Legrand), Comédie-Française, Paris.
         Role in *Les Héraclides* (Marmontel), Comédie-Française, Paris.
         Xipharès in *Mithridate* (Racine), Comédie-Française, Paris.
1753–54 Bajazet in *Bajazet* (Racine), Comédie-Française, Paris, and Versailles.

Henri-Louis Lekain

Cléon in *Le Triple Mariage* (Destouches), Comédie-Française, Paris, and Versailles.

Le Conseiller in *La Nouveauté* (Legrand), Comédie-Française, Paris.

Eraste in *L'Homme à bonnes fortunes* (Baron), Comédie-Française, Paris.

Essex in *Le Comte d'Essex* (T. Corneille), Gray and Rouen.

Fastidas in *L'Ami de tout le monde*, Versailles.

Giflot in *Les Trois Cousines* (Dancourt), Comédie-Française, Paris.

Horace in *Horace* (P. Corneille), Comédie-Française, Paris, and Versailles.

Don Manrique in *Don Sanche d'Aragon* (P. Corneille), Comédie-Française, Paris, and Versailles.

Orosmane in *Paros*, Comédie-Française, Paris.

Polyeucte in *Polyeucte* (P. Corneille), Comédie-Française, Paris, and Rouen.

Testor in *Les Troyennes* (Chateaubrun), Comédie-Française, Paris, and Versailles.

1754–55   Amalfred in *Amalasonte* (Quinault), Comédie-Française, Paris, and Fontainebleau.

Clitandre in *Le Jaloux désabusé* (Campistron), Versailles.

Crésus in *Esope à la Cour* (Boursault and La Fontaine), Comédie-Française, Paris, and Versailles.

Eraste in *Le Complaisant*, Comédie-Française, Paris, and Fontainebleau.

Ladislas in *Venceslas* (Rotrou), Comédie-Française, Paris, and Versailles.

Lycaste in *L'Usurier gentilhomme* (Legrand), Comédie-Française, Paris.

Mélicerte in *Ino et Mélicerte* (La Grange-Chancel), Versailles.

Octave in *Le Triumvirat* (Voltaire), Comédie-Française, Paris, and Versailles.

Pirrhus in *Philoctète* (Chateaubrun), Comédie-Française, Paris, and Dijon.

Valère in *L'Avocat Pathelin* (De Brueys and Palaprat), Comédie-Française, Paris.

1755–56   Role in *Iphigénie en Aulide* (Algarotti), Comédie-Française, Paris.

Caton in *Le Galant jardinier* (Dancourt), Comédie-Française, Paris.

Damis in *Tartuffe* (Molière), Comédie-Française, Paris.

Dorante in *Le Moulin de Javelle* (Dancourt), Comédie-Française, Paris.

Du Croisy in *Les Précieuses ridicules* (Molière), Comédie-Française, Paris, and Versailles.

Ghengis Khan in *L'Orphelin de la Chine* (Voltaire), Comédie-Française, Paris, Versailles, and Fontainebleau.

Léandre in *L'Aveugle clairvoyant* (Legrand), Comédie-Française, Paris, and Versailles.

Le Marquis in *La Nouveauté* (Legrand), Comédie-Française, Paris, and Fontainebleau.

Le Notaire in *L'Esprit de Contradiction* (Dufresny), Comédie-Française, Paris.

Marius fils in *Marius* (Hénault), Comédie-Française, Paris.

Télégone in *Astianax*, Comédie-Française, Paris.

Timante in *Le Florentin* (La Fontaine), Comédie-Française, Paris, and Versailles.

Valère in *Le Babillard* (Boissy), Comédie-Française, Paris.

1756–57   Hercule in *Hercule* (La Thuillerie), Comédie-Française, Paris.

Jeannot in *La Comtesse d'Escarbagnas* (Molière), Comédie-Française, Paris.

Léandre in *Le Médecin malgré lui* (Molière), Comédie-Française, Paris.

Le Chevalier in *Le Galant coureur* (Legrand), Comédie-Française, Paris.

Le Comte in *La Surprise de l'amour* (Marivaux), Comédie-Française, Paris.

Le Garçon tailleur in *Le Bourgeois Gentilhomme* (Molière), Comédie-Française, Paris.

Lycaste in *Le Mariage forcé* (Molière), Comédie-Française, Paris.

Lisidor in *Le Mariage forcé* (Molière), Comédie-Française, Paris.

Ninias in *Sémiramis* (Voltaire), Comédie-Française, Paris, and Nancy.

Octave in *Les Fourberies de Scapin* (Molière), Comédie-Française, Paris.

Rigaud in *Le Grondeur* (De Brueys and Palaprat), Comédie-Française, Paris.

Théocle in *La Princesse d'Elide* (Molière), Comédie-Française, Paris.

Titus in *Bérénice* (Racine), Comédie-Française, Paris.

1757–58   Abner in *Athalie* (Racine), Comédie-Française, Paris, and Versailles.

Andrès in *L'Etourdi* (Molière), Comédie-Française, Paris, and Fontainebleau.

Bacazar in *Astarbé* (Colardeau), Comédie-Française, Paris.

Mélédin in *Adèle de Ponthieu* (La Place), Comédie-Française, Paris, and Fontainebleau.

Néron in *Britannicus* (Racine), Comédie-Française, Paris, and Versailles.

Oreste in *Iphigénie en Tauride* (La Touche), Comédie-Française, Paris, Versailles, and Fontainebleau.

1758–59   Astrate in *Astrate* (Quinault), Comédie-Française, Paris.

Bobinet in *La Comtesse d'Escarbagnas* (Molière), Versailles.

César in *La Mort de Pompée* (P. Corneille), Comédie-Française, Paris, and Versailles.

Le Coureur in *L'Ecole des mères* (Marivaux), Versailles.

Gelas in *Andronic* (Saint-Réal), Comédie-Française, Paris.

Maître d'hôtel in *L'Ecole des mères* (Marivaux), Versailles.

Lyncée in *Hypermnestre* (Lemierre), Comédie-Française, Paris, Versailles, and Lille.

Pompée in *Sertorius* (P. Corneille), Comédie-Française, Paris, and Versailles.

Sextus in *Titus* (Belloy), Comédie-Française, Paris.

1759–60   Achille in *Iphigénie en Aulide* (Algarotti), Comédie-Française, Paris.

Achille in *Briséis* (Poinsinet de Sivry), Comédie-Française, Paris.

L'Amoureux in *Le Mariage forcé* (Molière), Comédie-Française, Paris.

Andrès in *L'Etourdi* (Molière), Comédie-Française, Paris, and Versailles.

Argatiphontidas in *Amphitryon* (Molière), Comédie-Française, Paris.

L'Exempt in *Le Florentin* (La Fontaine), Comédie-Française, Paris.

Hérode in *Mariamne* (Voltaire), Comédie-Française, Paris.

Namir in *Namir*, Comédie-Française, Paris.

Le Roy in *L'Ambitieux*, Comédie-Française, Paris, and Versailles.

Spartachus in *Spartachus* (Saurin), Comédie-Française, Paris, and Versailles.

Un Suisse in *Monsieur de Pourceaugnac* (Molière), Comédie-Française, Paris.

Zulika in *Zulika* (Dorat), Comédie-Française, Paris.

1760–61   Interlocuteur in *L'Ecossaise* (Voltaire), Comédie-Française, Paris, and Versailles.

Lothario in *Caliste* (Colardeau), Comédie-Française, Paris.

Sésostris in *Amasis* (La Grange-Chancel), Comédie-Française, Paris.

Tancrède in *Tancrède* (Voltaire), Comédie-Française, Paris, and Versailles.

1761–62   Agathyse in *Térée* (Lemierre da Oviedo), Comédie-Française, Paris.

Cicéron in *Rome sauvée* (Voltaire), Comédie-Française, Paris, and Versailles.

Héraclius in *Héraclius* (P. Corneille), Comédie-Française, Paris, and Versailles.

Mathan in *Athalie* (Racine), Comédie-Française, Paris.

Ramire in *Zulime* (Voltaire), Comédie-Française, Paris, and Versailles.

Siamek in *Zarucma*, Comédie-Française, Paris, and Versailles.

Théramène in *Phèdre* (Racine), Comédie-Française, Paris, and Versailles.

1762–63   Ajax in *Ajax* (Poinsinet de Sivry), Comédie-Française, Paris.

Antenor in *Zelmire* (Belloy), Comédie-Française, Paris, and Fontainebleau.

Cinna in *Cinna* (P. Corneille), Comédie-Française, Paris, and Fontainebleau.

Commène in *Irène* (Voltaire), Comédie-Française, Paris, and Choisy.

Mucien in *Eponine* (Chabanon), Comédie-Française, Paris.

Thyamis in *Théagène* (Dorat), Comédie-Française, Paris.

1763–64   Brutus in *La Mort de César* (Voltaire), Comédie-Française, Paris, and Versailles.

Cassandre in *Olympie* (Voltaire), Comédie-Française, Paris.

Criton in *La Mort de Socrate*, Comédie-Française, Paris.

Guiscard in *Blanche et Guiscard* (Saurin), Comédie-Française, Paris, and Versailles.

Huascar in *Manco-Capac* (Guillet), Comédie-Française, Paris, and Choisy.

Idamante in *Idoménée* (Crébillon), Comédie-Française, Paris, and Versailles.

Warwick in *Comte de Warwick* (La Harpe), Comédie-Française, Paris, Versailles, and Rouen.

1764–65   Châtillon in *Zaïre* (Voltaire), Comédie-Française, Paris.

Edouard in *Le Siège de Calais* (Belloy), Comédie-Française, Paris, and Versailles.

Montrose in *Cromwell*, Comédie-Française, Paris.

Timophane in *Timoléon* (La Harpe), Comédie-Française, Paris, and Versailles.

1765–66   Esparville *fils* in *Le Philosophe sans le savoir* (Sedaine), Comédie-Française, Paris.

Valamir in *Pharamond* (La Harpe), Comédie-Française, Paris.

Vendôme in *Adélaïde du Guesclin* (Voltaire), Comédie-Française, Paris, and Fontainebleau.

1766–67   Arbace in *Artaxerce* (Lemierre and Metastasio), Comédie-Française, Paris.

Athamare in *Les Scythes* (Voltaire), Comédie-Française, Paris.

Iarbe in *Didon* (Scudéry), Comédie-Française, Paris.

Tell in *Guillaume Tell* (Lemierre), Comédie-Française, Paris.

1767–68 Cosroès in *Cosroès* (Rotrou), Comédie-Française, Paris.

Hyascar in *Hirza*, Comédie-Française, Paris.

1768–69 Pharnace in *Mithridate* (Racine), Comédie-Française, Paris.

1771–72 Bayard in *Gaston et Bayard* (Belloy), Comédie-Française, Paris, Versailles, and Bordeaux.

Nicomède in *Nicomède* (P. Corneille), Comédie-Française, Paris, and Bordeaux.

Sévère in *Polyeucte* (P. Corneille), Comédie-Française, Paris, and Versailles.

1772–73 Eduoard in *Pierre le Cruel* (Belloy), Comédie-Française, Paris.

Le Général in *La Centenaire de Molière* (Artaud), Comédie-Française, Paris, and Versailles.

Manlius in *Manlius* (Desjardins), Comédie-Française, Paris, and Fontainebleau.

Scévole in *Scévole* (Du Ryer), Lyon.

1773–74 Massinissa in *Sophonsibe* (Voltaire), Comédie-Française, Paris, and Fontainebleau.

Térée in *Térée* (Lemierre da Oviedo), Comédie-Française, Paris.

1775–76 Bourbon in *Le Connétable* (Guibert), Versailles.

Lorédan in *Lorédan*, Comédie-Française, Paris.

Menzikow in *Menzikoff* (La Harpe), Fontainebleau.

1776–77 Léonce in *Andronic* (Saint-Réal), Versailles.

Mustapha in *Mustapha et Zéangir* (Chamfort), Fontainebleau.

1777–78 Arons in *Brutus* (Voltaire), Comédie-Française, Paris, and Versailles.

Publications

Mémoires, edited by Bernardin Lekain, 1801.

*

Bibliography

Books:

F. Talma, *Mémoires de Lekain*, Paris, 1825.

J. J. Olivier, *Henri-Louis Lekain de la Comédie-Française*, Paris, 1907.

* * *

Henri-Louis Lekain affords an object lesson in rising to the top of one's chosen profession by virtue of sheer dedication and skill, in spite of formidable natural disadvantages. By all accounts he was short in stature, rather squat in fact, with an unprepossessing, not to say ugly, face, an over-large mouth, a tendency to bandiness, and, perhaps most damning of all, a weak voice that, initially at least, became hoarse when put under pressure. Nonetheless, he matured into the dominant tragic actor of his age, often compared to his English contemporary, David Garrick, and unarguably the finest exponent of the work of Voltaire.

It was, in fact, Voltaire who launched Lekain on his career: having seen him in an amateur performance, he gave the 22-year-old novice special tuition at his own private theatre and was instrumental in securing him a hearing at the Comédie-Française, where he made his debut in August 1750 as Titus in his benefactor's tragedy *Brutus*. Owing no doubt to his lack of conventional physical graces, and perhaps to the reported hostility of Mlle Clairon, his progress in the company was slow: he was not accepted as a member for almost two years, and then only at the express instance of the King, who had been moved to tears by his playing. In the course of the 1750's, however, a whole succession of personal triumphs — in the title role of Voltaire's *Oedipe*, as the sultan Orosmane in his *Zaire*, as the slave Séide in his *Mahomet*, as Hérode in his *Mariamne*, and as Néron in Racine's *Britannicus* — set the seal on his reputation.

Even so, while his professional debut had created an enormous stir, it had divided the theatregoing public and there continued to be a section of the audience who were repelled, or at least unimpressed, by his appearance or by his acting style. Collé was not alone in expressing surprise that Lekain could take himself seriously as a performer and confided to his journal in 1759 that "the worst, the unpleasantest, the ugliest, and the most ungracious of players ... is our leading tragic actor". Others would reproach him for being too instinctive a performer, drawing inspiration more from his own personality than from the character he portrayed, or were irritated by his abuse of certain mannerisms, such as an over-reliance on grimace and facial working, an over-indulgence in pauses, and a tendency to give undue weight to individual lines or even individual words. The playwright Mercier made a musical notation of a couplet as delivered by Lekain that reveals the degree of emphatic artifice involved.

On the other hand, that perceptive observer Baron Grimm ascribed this to a tendency to "over-think" his interpretation of a role, to ensure that every constituent verse of it was fully felt, and, whatever the effect produced, there can be no doubt about the resourceful intelligence he brought to his reading of every part he played. Several from the classic repertoire were indeed virtually re-invented by Lekain, notably that of Oreste in Racine's *Andromaque*, which he invested with some semblance of ancient Greek dress and a delirious rage that petrified the audience in the fifth act, and later Néron in *Britannicus*, whose ostensibly petulant jealousy he transformed into the mark of an incipient, calculating tyrant. Both these roles, which had hitherto been considered of secondary importance, were thus given a new dramatic prominence (which they were to retain in Talma's hands 40 years later, and thereafter) and Lekain went on to stamp his distinctive imprint on some of Corneille's heroes, particularly Nicomède, though he was not temperamentally equipped for the dignified formalities of Cornelian tragedy.

His power over an audience was of a totally different order: the vast majority of spectators were simply overwhelmed by the sheer energy and excitement of his playing, which more than compensated for any shortcomings of physique. Burning eyes, a surging voice, a gift for mute action that, according to his fellow actor Molé, could be as "eloquent and compelling as spoken action", all generated a passion which could be tender or vehement by turns and was ideally suited to Voltairian tragedy. And for the declamatory diction still regarded as the norm at the Comédie he substituted a way of speaking that Voltaire described as "simple, noble, terrifying, and passionate" and made his Genghis-Khan in *L'Orphelin de la Chine* "a savage tiger". In the same spirit he adopted a signally ethnic costume for this role, consisting of a long tunic with crimson and gold stripes, a lionskin, and a quiverful of arrows over his shoulders, an outsize bow grasped in his hand and on his head a helmet embossed with the head of a lion and a scarlet aigrette. Both by example and by argument he sought to induce his peers to abandon the periwig, white gloves, and knee-breeches of convention in favour of a more rational, historically appropriate style of stage costume.

Lekain's contribution to the affairs of the national theatre was not, however, confined to acting per se. In 1759, with the support of Voltaire, he succeeded in putting an end to the long-established custom of seating spectators on the stage, thus creating a more clear-cut distinction between stage and auditorium and liberating the entire playing area for movement and more elaborate changeable scenery. He himself took full advantage, moving freely about the stage and discarding the conventional practice of delivering important speeches from a downstage centre position. He also canvassed the idea of an acting school under the aegis of the Comédie, for which royal patronage was finally secured in 1774, and made enemies by pressing for reforms in the way in which the theatre was governed by four gentlemen of the royal bedchamber.

Perennially short of money, he endeavoured to augment his income by frequent touring in France and abroad, including several visits to Voltaire's theatre at Ferney. This may have undermined his health and contributed to his untimely death at the age of 48, on the eve of the philosopher-playwright's triumphal return to Paris. Behind him he left a record of professional integrity and innovation that had a significant influence on the development of French theatre.

—Donald Roy

LEMAÎTRE, Frédérick. French actor. Born Antoine-Louis-Prosper Lemaître in Le Havre, 28 July 1800. Educated at Saint-Barbe Collège, Paris; trained for the theatre at the Paris Conservatoire, 1818. Served briefly in French Army, 1815. Stage debut, in pantomime at the Théâtre des Variétés-Amusantes, Boulevard du Temple, Paris, 1815; acted in harlequinades at the Théâtre des Funambules, Paris, 1816; appeared in mimodrames at the Cirque Olympique, Paris, 1817–20; admitted as performer of minor roles to the Théâtre de l'Odéon, 1820; dismissed, 1823; established reputation in the role of Robert Macaire, at the Ambigu-Comique, 1824; subsequently, billed simply as Frédérick, hailed as leading Romantic actor of his era; after fire destroyed the Ambigu-Comique, moved to the Théâtre de la Porte-Saint-Martin, 1827, and acted opposite Marie Dorval, but returned to the Ambigu as actor-director; appeared at the Odéon, 1830, then moved to the Porte-Saint-Martin, 1831–33; subsequently toured then acquired the Folies Dramatiques theatre in Paris, 1834; continued to tour and to appear with success at various Parisian venues into the 1860's; reimposition of censorship restricted roles, 1852; reduced to poverty after a change in tastes in his final years. Died in Paris, 26 January 1876.

Principal roles

1818	Mallorno in *Othello* (adapted from Shakespeare), Cirque Olympique, Paris.
1823	Vivaldi in *L'Homme à Trois Visages* (Pixérécourt), Ambigu-Comique, Paris.
1824	Robert Macaire in *L'Auberge des Adrets*, Ambigu-Comique, Paris.
1827	Georges de Germany in *Trente ans; ou, La Vie d'un joueur* (Ducange), Théâtre de la Porte-Saint-Martin, Paris.
1830	Napoléon in *Napoléon Bonaparte* (Dumas *père*), Théâtre de l'Odéon, Paris.
	Ambrosio in *The Monk* (Lewis), Théâtre de l'Odéon, Paris.
1831	Concini in *La Maréchal d'Ancre* (Vigny), Théâtre de l'Odéon, Paris.
	Richard Darlington in *Richard Darlington* (Dumas *père*, adapted from Scott), Théâtre de la Porte-Saint-Martin, Paris.
1834	Gennaro in *Lucrèce Borgia* (Hugo), Théâtre de la Porte-Saint-Martin, Paris.
	Robert Macaire in *Robert Macaire* (Lemaître), Folies Dramatiques, Paris.
1836	Kean in *Kean; ou, Désordre et génie* (Dumas *père*), Théâtre des Variétés, Paris.
1838	Ruy Blas in *Ruy Blas* (Hugo), Théâtre de la Renaissance, Paris.
1842	Paris in *Paris le Bohémian* (Bouchardy), Paris.
1844	Jacques Ferrand in *Mysteries of Paris* (adapted from Sue), Paris.
	Don César de Bazan in *Don César de Bazan* (Dumanoir and Dennery), Paris.

Also acted roles in: *Le Chiffonier de Paris* (Pyat); *Hamlet* (Shakespeare); *Paillasse*; *Toussaint l'Ouverture*; *Vautrin* (Balzac).

*

Bibliography

Books:
Eugène de Mirecourt, *Frédérick Lemaître*, Havard, 1855.
François de Donville, *Frédérick Lemaître*, Baur, 1876.
Georges Duval, *Frédérick Lemaître et son temps*, Clichy, 1876.
Frédérick Lemaître *fils*, *Souvenirs de Frédérick Lemaître, publiés par son fils*, Ollendorff, 1880.
Eugène Silvain, *Frédérick Lemaître*, Paris, 1930.
Robert Baldick, *The Life and Times of Frédérick Lemaître*, London, 1959.

* * *

Frédérick Lemaître showed a taste for dressing up and for tragic declamation at an early age. He moved to Paris with his mother on his father's death and, after brief army service (he deserted before Waterloo), made his debut as a lion in a pantomime version of *Pyramus and Thisbe*. Calling himself "M. Frédérick" after his maternal grandfather, he began his career on the Boulevard du Temple and also attended classes at the Conservatoire before applying unsuccessfully to the second Théâtre-Français (the Odéon), failing to get in despite a favourable vote from the

Frédérick Lemaître

discerning Talma. He was finally admitted in 1820 but never progressed beyond small parts and in 1823 returned to the "Boulevard du Crime" to join Franconi's company at the Ambigu-Comique.

Almost immediately he imposed himself on admiring audiences as the outstanding melodrama performer of his day. He did this, however, by openly flouting the conventions of the genre, converting the mediocre, cliché-ridden script of *L'Auberge des Adrets* from a vehicle for sentimental moralising into a burlesque travesty of morality and sentiment. This play, which had been transformed out of all recognition by Frédérick's provocatively swaggering interpretation, was banned by the authorities after 85 performances, each of which had been liable to see the addition of ever more outrageous extempore touches; but it was revived in 1832, and followed in 1834 by an even more successful sequel, *Robert Macaire*, of which the actor was himself the principal author, and which consecrated the almost mythical status of the eponymous hero as a universal cult figure in spite of his amoral criminality.

Meanwhile, Frédérick had been diversifying his acting style: if the coarse-grained theatricality of Robert Macaire marks one extreme of his range, the other extreme can be seen in his contributions to the success of the new genre of Romantic drama, more self-consciously "literary" in its manner and aiming at a more permanent kind of success. Thus, he was to play the title role in *Ruy Blas*, of all Victor Hugo's verse plays the one that was to enjoy the most assured and lasting success, both in Paris and on tour in the provinces; though he seems to have been more at home in

prose historical dramas like Alexandre Dumas's *Napoléon Bonaparte*, Alfred de Vigny's *Le Maréchal d'Ancre*, or Hugo's *Lucrèce Borgia*. However, of all the plays by the major dramatists of the 1830's in which he performed, there can be no doubt that it was Dumas's *Kean* that provided him with the most appropriate vehicle for his distinctive talent. The great English actor, who had been seen in Paris in 1827, had become a legend not only on account of his dynamic manner of acting but also because of his life-style: Kean's capacity for wine and his sexual exploits were the subject of extravagant anecdote, and Frédérick was already creating for himself a similar larger-than-life reputation, based as much on his expansive way of life as on his flamboyant acting. In spite of a distinct contrast in physique — Kean had been short and stocky, whereas Frédérick was an imposing figure — a remarkable resemblance was perceived between the two men, and Théophile Gautier paid the French actor a handsome tribute when he wrote that "Kean himself could not have played his own part any better". Dumas's play was subtitled *Désordre et génie*; to the reader at any rate, disorderliness may seem more in evidence that genius, but this is a dramatically convincing illustration of a Romantic stereotype: the great artist, forced to prostitute his talents to a society that patronises and exploits him — a type to which the real Frédérick, just as much as the real Kean, did largely conform.

The late 1830's brought the peak of Frédérick's popularity and success. From the early 1840's onwards, the vogue for Romantic drama was over in the official Paris theatres, which saw a revival of interest in the more formal idiom of Classical tragedy. A proposal that he might enter the Comédie-Française company in 1850 was welcomed by Frédérick himself, but vetoed by the sociétaires; and although a season in Belgium in the following year was successful, a return visit to London was an utter failure. Queen Victoria, shocked by *Ruy Blas* with its portrayal of mutual love between a lackey and the Queen of Spain, found that the hero's part was "very badly acted by Lemaître, who besides being very old … is devoid of all dignity". At home, his faithful public had dwindled away, as changes in theatrical fashion passed him by. The little theatres of the Boulevard du Temple were no more, and employment became hard to find. Long before he was really old, he was affected by ill health and poverty, and his final years are a sorry tale of misery and failure. When he died in 1875, it was nearly 40 years since the period of his greatest triumphs in *Robert Macaire*, *Kean*, and *Ruy Blas*.

In spite of these triumphs, Hugo was later to write that Frédérick had never achieved "the great, undisputed success he deserved"; and Hugo went on to compare the creator of Ruy Blas with his eminent predecessor Talma: "Talma was perfect, Frédérick was uneven. Talma always pleased, Frédérick sometimes shocked. But Frédérick had movements, words, cries, which shook audiences to their very depths, and astonishing flashes of brilliance which completely transfigured him and revealed him in all the dazzling splendour of absolute greatness. In a word, Talma had the more talent and Frédérick had the more genius".

Dumas's *Kean* is no doubt better known today in the form of Sartre's adaptation of 1954, written for Pierre Brasseur just as the original had been written for Frédérick Lemaître. Pierre Brasseur was an actor with a similar kind of panache and gave a memorable performance as the flamboyant Frédérick in that evocative tribute to the "Boulevard du Crime", Marcel Carné's film *Les Enfants du Paradis*.

—William D. Howarth

LINDBERG, Per. Swedish director and actor. Born in Stockholm, Sweden, 5 March 1890, son of the actor and director August Lindberg. Educated at the University of Stockholm, until 1917; studied theatre at Max Reinhardt's studio in Berlin, 1917–18. Stage debut, as an actor, during his father's tour of the USA, 1912; began directorial career in collaboration with designer Knut Ström at the Lorensbergteater, Gothenburg, 1918–23; in Stockholm from 1923, argued for foundation of a People's Theatre to present socially relevant drama; film debut, 1923; directed at the Konserthusteatern [Concert House Theatre], Stockholm, 1926–27 and 1931–32, and at the Klubbteatern [Club Theatre] at the Dramaten [Royal Dramatic Theatre], Stockholm, 1927–29; also worked for the Swedish radio service, 1929–31, with the Riksteatern travelling company, from 1933, and formed partnership with the actor Gösta Ekman at the Vasa Theatre, 1935; director, Bergen, 1934, and Oslo, 1935. Died in Stockholm, Sweden, 7 February 1944.

Productions

1918–23	*Hamlet* (Shakespeare), Lorensbergteater, Gothenburg; later revived in several different productions.
	King Lear (Shakespeare), Lorensbergteater, Gothenburg.
	Othello (Shakespeare), Lorensbergteater, Gothenburg.
	Romeo and Juliet (Shakespeare), Lorensbergteater, Gothenburg.
	Twelfth Night (Shakespeare), Lorensbergteater, Gothenburg.
	Mäster Olof [Master Olof] (Strindberg), Lorensbergteater, Gothenburg.
1920	*Peer Gynt* (Ibsen), Lorensbergteater, Gothenburg; later revived in several different productions.
	Brand (Strindberg), Lorensbergteater, Gothenburg.
	Folkungasagen [The Saga of the Folkungs] (Strindberg), Lorensbergteater, Gothenburg.
	As You Like It (Shakespeare), Lorensbergteater, Gothenburg.
1922	*Till Damaskus III* [To Damaskus III] (Strindberg), Lorensbergteater, Gothenburg.
1923	*Tobie Comedia* (Petri), Nordiska Muséet, Stockholm.
1924	*Till Damaskus II* [To Damaskus II] (Strindberg), Lorensbergteater, Gothenburg.
1925	*Tisbe* (Asteropherus), Nordiska Muséet, Stockholm.
1926–27	*Antony and Cleopatra* (Shakespeare), Konserthusteatern, Stockholm.
	Edipo re (Sophocles), Konserthusteatern, Stockholm.
	The Wolves (Rolland), Konserthusteatern, Stockholm.
	Los Intereses creados (Benavente), Konserthusteatern, Stockholm.
1928	*Strange Interlude* (O'Neill), Klubbteatern, Dramaten, Stockholm.
	Han som fick leva om sitt liv [He Who Got to Live His Life Over] (Lagerkvist), Dramaten, Stockholm.
1929	*Agamemnon* (adapted from Aeschylus's *Oresteia*), Konserthusteatern, Stockholm.
	Hoppla, wir leben (Toller), Klubbteatern, Dramaten, Stockholm.
1931–35	*The Faithful* (Masefield), Konserthusteatern, Stockholm.
1934	*Bödeln* [The Hangman] (Lagerkvist), Vasa Theatre, Stockholm.
1938	*Mannen utan själ* [The Man without a Soul] (Lagerkvist), Dramaten, Stockholm.

Other productions included: *The Merchant of Venice* (Shakespeare), 1929; *The Living Corpse* (L. Tolstoy), 1929; *Hans nads testamente* [His Grace's Last Will] (Bergman), 1931; *Peer Gynt* (Ibsen), 1935–38.

Films

Anna-Clara och hennes bröder [Anna-Clara and Her Brothers], 1923; *Norrtullsligan* [Nortull's Band], 1923; *Gubben kommer* [The Old Man Returns], 1939; *Juninatten* [June Nights], 1938; *Gläd dig i din ungdom* [Joys of the Young], 1939; *Stal* [Steel], 1940; *Hans nads testamente* [His Grace's Last Will], 1940; *Det sägs pa stan* [The Language of the City], 1941; *I paradis* [In Paradise], 1941.

Publications

Regiproblem [Problems of Direction], 1927; *Kring ridan* [Behind the Curtain], 1932; *Gösta Ekman; Skadespelaren och människan* [Gösta Ekman; The Actor and the Man], 1942; *Baletten under fyra sekler* [Four Centuries of Ballet], 1943; *August Lindberg*, 1943; *Anders de Wahl*, 1944; *En bok om Per Lindberg*, 1944; *Bakom masker* [Behind the Mask], 1949.

* * *

Per Lindberg was one of the most visionary and stimulating directors Sweden has ever known. Combining a keen intellect, appreciation of literature and devotion to theatrical art, Lindberg worked tirelessly in pursuit of his ideals. Both Per Lindberg and his father, the great actor and director August Lindberg, often found themselves in controversial situations and without a theatrical home, but with resourcefulness and vigour they continued their significant work.

Growing up with two parents who were professional actors, Per Lindberg understood at an early age the analysis, discipline and creativity that are elements of a successful production. His talents seemed to point to a career as a literary scholar, but in 1912 he appeared as an actor during his father's tour of the United States, the first step that led Per Lindberg to the profession for which he was brilliantly suited. Studying with Max Reinhardt in Berlin increased his understanding of scenic and lighting design and of modern directing. Lindberg admired Reinhardt, but was critical when Reinhardt's productions over-emphasized spectacle. Lindberg stated his allegiance to the principle he learned from his father, of stressing the rhythm and meaning of the text. Although Lindberg himself was accused of over-emphasizing visual scenic elements, he always insisted that the actors should dominate the space. Lindberg was thoroughly acquainted with theatre history and all the contemporary work being done in Germany, France and Russia. He selected the best of what he studied and observed, working with the essence of the styles of historical periods, with technical innovations and psychological insights.

Lindberg's attention was not focussed solely on the aesthetics of dramatic art. He was also concerned about audiences, embracing the concept of a folk theatre that would present theatre to new and larger segments of society. His productions in the monumental concert hall at the Concert House Theatre (the Konserthusteatern) in Stockholm in 1926–27 were contributions to the folk theatre movement. During its brief existence, the Club Theatre (the Klubbteatern) he established at the Royal Dramatic Theatre (the Dramaten) in 1927 attracted 5000 members to see modern experimental drama. Lindberg continued to try to find ways to organise financing, production and distribution of theatre to reach new audiences. His conception of a theatre guild, a network that would span the country, enabling local groups to mount productions and offering tickets at reasonable prices, did not materialize. Instead Lindberg worked with the Riksteatern, the national travelling theatre that was founded in 1933. His philosophy of folk theatre contains principles that still offer guidance for cultural planning.

Per Lindberg's career included producing radio theatre, serving as theatre critic and writing essays and biographies, but his work as a director for the stage overshadows his other accomplishments. Lindberg deserves credit not just as an individual artist, but as a person who established effective partnerships. With designers like Knut Ström and Isaac Grünewald he shared a readiness to bring Continental innovations to Swedish theatre. He worked effectively with such leading composers as Vilhelm Stenhammer and Hilding Rosenberg to make music an integral part of productions. His direction enriched the stage imagery of playwright Pär Lagerkvist's mythical and thought-provoking plays. He guided the actor Gösta Ekman's genius and individuality with patience and friendship. Wherever he worked, Per Lindberg found some members of the ensemble who resisted the challenges and high standards he set, but those with open minds found the director exciting and generous. Lindberg productions did not always please the public or the critics, but they offered a distinctive style and a clear interpretation.

Per Lindberg was affiliated with many different theatres, mostly in Stockholm, but also throughout Sweden and in Norway. Sometimes he worked with outstanding actors, as when he directed Harriet Bosse in *Antony and Cleopatra*, Lars Hanson in *King Lear*, Tora Teje in *Strange Interlude* and Hans Jacob Nilsen in *Hamlet*. He also worked with amateurs or with professionals at the start of their careers,

and taught them to love theatre and the dedication it demands. Sometimes he commanded satisfactory technical resources and appropriate space; at other times he showed great ingenuity in adapting a nontheatrical space or in using the simple decor that a limited budget permitted. Lindberg challenged himself as well as his colleagues — making the chorus an organic part of *Agamemnon*, dealing with the difficult monologues of *Strange Interlude* for its European premiere or staging plays on the open, formal platform of the Concert House and in the large hall of the Nordic Museum (the Nordiska Museet).

The titles of Per Lindberg's productions indicate his good taste and the range of his interests. Because he believed in seeking what was unique in each script and playing it in the appropriate style, it is unfair to present a simplified picture by describing a 'typical' Lindberg production. Nevertheless, one can discover that his mise en scène often exhibited these characteristics: selective, sculptural lighting; effective use of an original music score; scenery with three-dimensional features such as columns, steps and platforms, a striking colour scheme and a style inspired by period art or architecture; excellent composition in placement of a large number of actors; a spirit of experimentation; and thoroughly motivated acting. Most often the plays had intellectual appeal, but they could have emotional power as well. Although Lindberg was never noted for directing comedies, some productions were entertaining and charming.

When surveying Lindberg's career it is difficult to select a few outstanding productions, but the several interpretations of *Hamlet* and *Peer Gynt* and stagings of six plays by Pär Lagerkvist must be named as significant. Lindberg appreciated Lagerkvist's originality, skilful dramatic structure, concern for social problems and compassionate view of humanity. In Lindberg's interpretation the theatrical potential of the plays was made evident: the colloquial dialogue, simple milieu and naive point of view of *Han som fick leva om sitt liv* [He Who Got to Live His Life Over], the skilful structure, universal tragedy and biting satire of *Bödeln* [The Hangman]; the transparent dialogue, classical simplicity and urgent relevance of *Mannen utan själ* [The Man without a Soul].

Why does Lindberg command respect? Not only for the significant productions, but for building his work on a foundation of knowledge and theory, for venturing with other leading practitioners of his era into expressiveness and styles beyond convention and traditional realism, and above all for establishing the director as the artist controlling all elements of a unified total work of theatrical art.

—Carla Waal

LISTON, John. British actor. Born in Soho, London, c.1776. Educated at Soho School, London. Married actress Sarah Tyrer in 1807; one son. Initially teacher, then became strolling player; London debut, 1799; appeared in Dublin, 1799, and then returned to the English provinces; failed in tragic roles but won immediate acclaim at the Newcastle Theatre under Stephen Kemble after switching to character parts in comedy, 1801–05; enjoyed acclaim on London debut at the Haymarket Theatre under Colman the Younger, 1805; actor, Covent Garden, 1805–22; actor, under Elliston, Theatre Royal, Drury Lane, 1823–31;

renewed success with Madame Vestris at the Olympic Theatre, 1831–37; first comedian to earn more than a tragedian; played over 600 roles; final appearance before retirement, Lyceum Theatre, 1837. Died in London, 22 March 1846.

Principal roles

1805   Sheepface in *The Village Lawyer* (Macready), Haymarket Theatre, London.
Zekiel Homespun in *The Heir at Law* (Colman the Younger), Haymarket Theatre, London.
John Lump in *The Review* (Colman the Younger), Haymarket Theatre, London.
Dan in *John Bull* (Colman the Younger), Haymarket Theatre, London.
Motley in *The Castle Spectre* (Lewis), Haymarket Theatre, London.
Frank in *Three and a Deuce* (Hoare), Haymarket Theatre, London.
Stephen in *The Poor Gentleman* (Colman the Younger), Haymarket Theatre, London.
Robin Roughhead in *Fortune's Frolic* (Allingham), Haymarket Theatre, London.
John Grouse in *The School for Prejudice* (T. Dibdin), Haymarket Theatre, London.
Farmer Ashfield in *Speed the Plough* (Morton), Haymarket Theatre, London.
Abel in *Honest Thieves* (Knight), Haymarket Theatre, London.
The Tailor in *Katharine and Petruchio* (Garrick), Haymarket Theatre, London.
Zachariades in *The Tailors* (Colman the Elder), Haymarket Theatre, London.
Fustian in *Sylvester Daggerwood* (Colman the Younger), Haymarket Theatre, London.
Frank Oatland in *A Cure for the Heartache* (Morton), Haymarket Theatre, London.
Antony in *The Village; or, The World's Epitome* (Cherry), Haymarket Theatre, London.
First Gravedigger in *Hamlet* (Shakespeare), Haymarket Theatre, London.
Jacob Gawkey in *The Chapter of Accidents* (S. Lee), Haymarket Theatre, London, and Covent Garden, London.
Solomon in *The Quaker* (Jackman), Covent Garden, London.
Memmo in *Rugantino; or, The Bravo of Venice*(Lewis), Covent Garden, London.
Sim in *Wild Oats* (O'Keeffe), Covent Garden, London.
Nicholas in *The Delinquent* (Reynolds), Covent Garden, London.
Diggory in *All the World's a Stage* (Jackmann), Covent Garden, London.
Master Stephen in *Every Man in His Humour* (Jonson), Covent Garden, London.

1806   Gaby Grim in *We Fly by Night; or, Long Stories* (Colman the Younger), Covent Garden, London.
Slender in *The Merry Wives of Windsor* (Shakespeare), Covent Garden, London.

Governor Tempest in *The Wheel of Fortune* (Cumberland), Covent Garden, London.
Arthur in *The White Plume* (Morton), Covent Garden, London.
Shenkin in *Folly as It Flies* (Morton), Covent Garden, London.
Lord Grizzle in *Tom Thumb* (O'Hara, adapted from Fielding), Covent Garden, London, and Haymarket Theatre, London.
Jeffrio de Pedrillos in *Catch Him Who Can* (Hook), Haymarket Theatre, London.
Flourish in *Five Miles Off* (T. Dibdin), Haymarket Theatre, London.
Jeffrey in *Animal Magnetism* (Inchbald), Haymarket Theatre, London.
Michael in *Adrian and Orilla* (Dimond), Covent Garden, London.
Don Utopio in *The Deserts of Arabia* (Reynolds), Covent Garden, London.
Chequer in *Arbitration* (Reynolds), Covent Garden, London.

1807   Polonius in *Hamlet* (Shakespeare), Covent Garden, London.
Phillip in *The Fortress* (Hook), Haymarket Theatre, London.
Don Whiskerandos in *The Critic* (Sheridan), Haymarket Theatre, London.
Matthew Method in *Music Mad* (Hook), Haymarket Theatre, London.
Hector in *Two Faces under a Hood* (T. Dibdin), Covent Garden, London.
Molino in *The Blind Boy* (Kenney), Covent Garden.

1808   Caper in *Who Wins?; or, The Widow's Choice* (Allingham), Covent Garden, London.
Thurio in *The Two Gentlemen of Verona* (Shakespeare), Covent Garden, London, and Haymarket Theatre, London.
Pedrillo in *Plot and Counterplot* (C. Kemble), Covent Garden, London.
Henry Augustus Mug in *The Africans* (Colman the Younger), Haymarket Theatre, London.
Obadiah Broadbrim in *Yes or No* (Pocock), Haymarket Theatre, London.
Baron Altradoff in *The Exile* (Reynolds), Covent Garden, London.

1809   Octavian in *The Mountaineers* (Colman the Younger), Covent Garden, London.
Scrub in *The Beaux' Stratagem* (Farquhar), Haymarket Theatre, London.
Apollo Belvi in *Killing No Murder* (Hook), Haymarket Theatre, London.
Timothy Quaint in *The Soldier's Daughter* (Cherry), Haymarket Theatre, London.
L'Eclair in *The Foundling of the Forest* (Dimond), Haymarket Theatre, London.
Duke's Servant in *High Life Below Stairs* (Townley), Haymarket Theatre, London.
Launcelot Gobbo in *The Merchant of Venice* (Shakespeare), Haymarket Theatre, London.
Bob Acres in *The Rivals* (Sheridan), Haymarket Theatre, London.
Clod in *The Young Quaker* (O'Keeffe), Haymarket Theatre, London.

1810   Bombastes Furioso in *Bombastes Furioso* (Rhodes), Haymarket Theatre, London.

Neddy Bray in *XYZ* (Colman the Younger), Covent Garden, London.

1811   Malvolio in *Twelfth Night* (Shakespeare), Covent Garden, London.

Macloon in *The Knight of Snowdoun* (Morton), Covent Garden, London.

Rogero in *The Quadrupeds of Quedlinbergh* (Colman the Younger), Haymarket Theatre, London.

Tony Lumpkin in *She Stoops to Conquer* (Goldsmith), Haymarket Theatre, London; revived notably, Theatre Royal, Drury Lane, 1823.

Sir Benjamin Backbite in *The School for Scandal* (Sheridan), Haymarket Theatre, London.

Squire Richard in *The Provoked Husband* (Cibber and Vanbrugh), Haymarket Theatre, London.

Shelty in *The Highland Reel* (O'Keeffe), Covent Garden, London.

1812   Diego in *The Virgin of the Sun* (Reynolds), Covent Garden, London.

Dimdim in *The Secret Mine* (T. Dibdin), Covent Garden, London.

Romeo in *Romeo and Juliet* (Shakespeare), Covent Garden, London.

Midas in *Midas* (O'Hara), Covent Garden, London.

Benmousaff in *The Aethiop* (Dimond), Covent Garden, London.

Moll Flaggon in *The Lord of the Manor* (Burgoyne), Covent Garden, London.

Lubin Log in *Love, Law and Physic* (Kenney), Covent Garden, London.

Jacquez in *The Renegade* (Reynolds, adapted from Dryden's Don Sebastian), Covent Garden, London.

1813   Captain Dash in *At Home* (Dudley), Covent Garden, London.

Suckling in *Education* (Morton), Covent Garden, London.

Ophelia in *Hamlet Travestie* (Poole), Covent Garden, London.

Monsieur de Paris in *The Waltz* (Arnold, adapted from Wycherley's *The Gentleman Dancing Master*), Covent Garden, London.

Karl in *The Miller and His Men* (Pocock), Covent Garden, London.

1814   Peter in *The Farmer's Wife* (C. Dibdin), Covent Garden, London.

Gosling in *Debtor and Creditor* (Kenney), Covent Garden, London.

Solomon Grundy in *Who Wants a Guinea* (Colman the Younger), Covent Garden, London.

Mr Liston/Harlequin in *Harlequin Hoax* (T. Dibdin), Lyceum Theatre, London.

Blaise in *The Forest of Bundi* (Kenney), Covent Garden, London.

Pedrigo Potts in *John of Paris* (Pocock), Covent Garden, London.

1815   Buffardo in *Zembucca* (Pocock), Covent Garden, London.

Martin in *The Magpie; or, The Maid* (Pocock), Covent Garden, London.

Mimiski in *John du Bart* (Pocock), Covent Garden, London.

Justice Dorus in *Cymon* (Garrick), Covent Garden, London.

1816   Bottom in *A Midsummer Night's Dream* (Shakespeare, adapted by Reynolds), Covent Garden, London.

Pompey Bum in *Measure for Measure* (Shakespeare), Covent Garden, London.

Dominie Sampson in *Guy Mannering* (Terry, adapted from Scott), Covent Garden, London.

Fogrun in *The Slave* (Morton), Covent Garden, London.

1817   Humorous Lieutenant in *The Humorous Lieutenant* (Beaumont and Fletcher, adapted by Reynolds), Covent Garden, London.

Leporello in *The Libertine* (Pocock), Covent Garden, London.

Cloten in *Cymbeline* (Shakespeare), Covent Garden, London.

1818   Pequillo in *Zuma* (T. Dibdin), Covent Garden, London.

Baillie Nicol Jarvie in *Rob Roy* (Pocock, adapted from Scott), Covent Garden, London.

Josselin in *Marquis de Carabas* (anon.), Covent Garden, London.

Fitzcloddy in *Who's My Father* (Morton), Covent Garden, London.

Werther in *The Sorrows of Werther* (Lunn), Covent Garden, London.

Old Rapid in *A Cure for the Heartache* (Morton), Covent Garden, London.

Lingo in *The Agreeable Surprise* (O'Keeffe), Haymarket Theatre, London.

Fuddle in *Nine Points of the Law* (Jameson), Haymarket Theatre, London.

Figaro in *The Barber of Seville* (Terry), Covent Garden, London.

1819   Figaro in *The Marriage of Figaro* (Bishop), Covent Garden, London.

Dumbiedikes in *The Heart of Mid-Lothian* (Terry, adapted from Scott), Covent Garden, London.

Sir Onesiphorus Puddefoot in *Wet Weather* (Hook), Haymarket Theatre, London.

Lord Duberley in *The Heir at Law* (Colman the Younger), Haymarket Theatre, London.

Sir Peter Pigwiggin in *Pigeons and Crows* (Moncrieff), Haymarket Theatre, London.

Dromio of Syracuse in *The Comedy of Errors* (Shakespeare), Covent Garden, London.

1820   Jonathan Oldbuck in *The Antiquary* (Terry, adapted from Pocock), Covent Garden, London.

Wamba in *Ivanhoe* (Beazley, adapted from Scott), Covent Garden, London.

Nicholas Twill in *Too Late for Dinner* (Jones), Covent Garden, London.

Jocrisse in *Henri Quatre* (Morton), Covent Garden, London.

Sam Swipes in *Exchange No Robbery* (Hook), Haymarket Theatre, London.

Barnaby Buz in *Dog Days in Bond Street* (Dimond), Haymarket Theatre, London.

Sir Andrew Aguecheek in *Twelfth Night* (Shakespeare, adapted by Reynolds), Covent Garden, London.

1821   Fratioso in *Don John; or, The Two Violettas* (Reynolds, adapted from Beamont and Fletcher's *The Chances*), Covent Garden, London.

Launce in *The Two Gentlemen of Verona* (Shakespeare, adapted by Reynolds), Covent Garden, London.

1822   Captain Dalgetty in *The Legend of Montrose* (Pocock, adapted from Scott), Covent Garden, London.

Pengoose in *The Law of Java* (Colman the Younger), Covent Garden, London.

Sir Bashful Constant in *The Way to Keep Him* (Murphy), Covent Garden, London.

Peter Finn in *Peter Finn* (Jones), Haymarket Theatre, London.

Peeping Tom in *Peeping Tom of Coventry* (O'Keeffe), Haymarket Theatre, London.

Delph in *Family Jars* (Lunn), Haymarket Theatre, London.

Lord Scribbleton in *Morning, Noon and Night* (T. Dibdin), Haymarket Theatre, London.

1823   Tristram Sappy in *Deaf as a Post* (Poole), Theatre Royal, Drury Lane, London.

Mr Smith in *Mrs Smith* (Payne), Haymarket Theatre, London.

Billy Lackaday in *Sweethearts and Wives* (Kenney), Haymarket Theatre, London.

Sam Savory in *Fish out of Water* (Lunn), Haymarket Theatre, London.

Mawworm in *The Hypocrite* (Bickerstaff), Theatre Royal, Drury Lane, London.

1824   Philander in *Philandering* (Beazley), Theatre Royal, Drury Lane, London.

Lucio in *Measure for Measure* (Shakespeare), Theatre Royal, Drury Lane, London.

Pedrosa in *Alcaid* (Kenney), Haymarket Theatre, London.

Van Dunder in *'Twould Puzzle a Conjuror* (Poole), Haymarket Theatre, London.

1825   Grojan in *Quite Correct* (Boaden), Haymarket Theatre, London.

Sir Hilary Heartease in *Roses and Thorns* (Lunn), Haymarket Theatre, London.

Paul Pry in *Paul Pry* (Poole), Haymarket Theatre, London.

1826   Simon Pengander in *'Twixt the Cup and the Lip* (Poole), Haymarket Theatre, London.

Knipper Clipper in *Thirteen to the Dozen* (Kenney), Haymarket Theatre, London.

Oliver Frumpton in *Poor Relations* (anon.), Haymarket Theatre, London.

Pong Wong in *Pong Wong* (C. Mathews the Younger), Haymarket Theatre, London.

Broom Girl in duet with Madame Vestris, Haymarket Theatre, London.

1827   Antonio in *The Trial of Love* (Soane), Theatre Royal, Drury Lane, London.

Sir Hippington Miff in *Comfortable Lodgings* (Peake), Theatre Royal, Drury Lane, London.

Bowbell in *The Illustrious Stranger* (Kenney), Theatre Royal, Drury Lane, London.

1828   Tom Tadpole in *The Haunted Inn* (Peake), Theatre Royal, Drury Lane, London.

Corporal Foss in *The Poor Gentleman* (Colman the Younger), Theatre Royal, Drury Lane, London.

Ben in *Love for Love* (Congreve), Theatre Royal, Drury Lane, London.

Felix Mudberry in *Ups and Downs* (Poole), Theatre Royal, Drury Lane, London.

Adam Brock in *Charles XII* (Planché), Theatre Royal, Drury Lane, London.

1829   Paul Shack in *Master's Rival* (Peake), Theatre Royal, Drury Lane, London.

Jasper Addlewitz in *Peter the Great* (Kenney), Theatre Royal, Drury Lane, London.

Monsieur Papelard in *Partizans* (Planché), Theatre Royal, Drury Lane, London.

Mr Gillman in *The Happiest Day of My Life* (Buckstone), Haymarket Theatre, London.

Mr Cool in *All's Right* (Planché), Haymarket Theatre, London.

Baron Wildenheim in *Lovers' Vows* (Inchbald), Haymarket Theatre, London.

Mr Janus in *Snakes in the Grass* (Buckstone), Theatre Royal, Drury Lane, London.

1830   Achille Bonbon in *The National Guard* (Planché), Theatre Royal, Drury Lane, London.

Jack Humphries in *Turning the Tables* (Poole), Theatre Royal, Drury Lane, London.

1831   Narcissus Stubble in *Highways and Byways* (Webster), Theatre Royal, Drury Lane, London.

Peter Galliard in *Legion of Honour* (Planché), Theatre Royal, Drury Lane, London.

Dominique in *Talk of the Devil* (Beazley), Olympic Theatre, London.

Placid in *I'll be Your Second* (Rodwell), Olympic Theatre, London.

Gervase Skinner in *Gervase Skinner* (anon.), Olympic Theatre, London.

Augustus Galopade in *The Widow* (Allingham), Olympic Theatre, London.

1832   Price Prettyman in *He's Not A-miss* (Dance), Olympic Theatre, London.

Long Singleton in *My Eleventh Day* (Bayly), Olympic Theatre, London.

Von Noodle in *The Young Hopefuls* (Poole), Olympic Theatre, London.

Fluid in *The Water Party* (Dance), Olympic Theatre, London.

Mr Brown in *Kill or Cure* (Dance), Olympic Theatre, London.

1833   Tim Tartlet in *The Cook and the Secretary* (Lunn), Olympic Theatre, London.

Septimus Lovebond in *Look at Home* (Dance), Olympic Theatre, London.

Mortimer Mims in *Paired Off* (Parry), Olympic Theatre, London.

Jasper Touchwood in *Hush Money* (Dance), Olympic Theatre, London.

Mr Flinch in *Fighting by Proxy* (Kenney), Olympic Theatre, London.

1834   Baron Dunderhof in *Dancing for Life* (Kenney), Olympic Theatre, London.

Oliver Sanguine in *Pleasant Dreams* (Dance), Covent Garden, London.

Pequillo in *My Friend the Governor* (Planché), Olympic Theatre, London.

Icarus Hawk in *The Retort Courteous* (anon.), Olympic Theatre, London.

Lucius Lot in *Name the Winner* (Millingen), Olympic Theatre, London.

Edward Dulcimer in *How To Get Off* (Dance), Olympic Theatre, London.

1835   Peter Buzzard in *A Scene of Confusion* (anon.), Olympic Theatre, London.

Tricolore in *Not a Word* (Kenney), Olympic Theatre, London.

Mr Paradise in *Hearts and Diamonds* (Jerrold), Olympic Theatre, London.

Major Limkey in *An Affair of Honour* (Rede), Olympic Theatre, London.

Mr Sedley in *A Gentleman in Difficulties* (Bayly), Olympic Theatre, London.

Magnus Lobb in *The Two Queens* (Buckstone), Olympic Theatre, London.

Becafico in *The Man's an Ass* (Jerrold), Olympic Theatre, London.

Mr Dibbs in *The Beau Ideal* (Lover), Olympic Theatre, London.

Tim Topple in *The Old and Young Stager* (Rede), Olympic Theatre, London.

Maximum Hogflesh in *Barbers at Court* (Mayhew and Smith), Olympic Theatre, London.

1836   Mr Lillywhite in *Forty and Fifty* (Bayly), Olympic Theatre, London.

Christopher Strap in *A Pleasant Neighbour* (Planché), Olympic Theatre, London.

Figaro in *The Two Figaros* (Planché), Olympic Theatre, London.

1837   Monsieur Champignon in *A Peculiar Position* (Planché), Olympic Theatre, London.

*

Bibliography

Books:
Jim Davis, *John Liston, Comedian*, London, 1985.

* * *

John Liston's emergence as the foremost comic actor of his generation was gradual. His debut on the London stage in Charles Kemble's benefit at the Haymarket Theatre on 15 August 1799 failed to make much impression and he was next engaged in Dublin, playing small parts, and subsequently at Taunton, Weymouth, and Exeter. Apart from a brief engagement in York in 1803, where he first met Charles Mathews, he then worked at Newcastle until 1805, rising to a leading position in the company, acclaimed particularly in low comedy roles. Recognition from London audiences followed with appearances at the Haymarket and Covent Garden, where he made his debut on 15 October 1805 and was to remain for the next 17 years. He was initially more successful during his summer seasons at the Haymarket where, teamed with Charles Mathews, he was especially well served by the plays of Theodore Hook. Apollo Belvi in Hook's *Killing No Murder* was typical of the affected coxcomb roles in which he was particularly popular, although his assumption of the role of Lord Grizzle in *Tom Thumb* was arguably the first role in which his originality was noted. In such parts as Henry Augustus Mug in Colman's *The Africans* and Lubin Log in Kenney's *Love, Law and Physic*, he also developed the cockney persona that was to be one of the mainstays of his career. At Covent Garden he played original roles in farce and in time emerged as an unsurpassed performer of Shakespearean clowns such as Bottom, Sir Andrew Aguecheek, and Pompey.

Liston's recruitment to the Drury Lane company under Elliston in 1823 saw his transition from salaried performer to fully-fledged star, whose income reputedly exceeded that of any of the traditionally higher-paid tragedians of the day. Among his most successful new roles at Drury Lane were Mawworm in a revival of *The Hypocrite* (a performance much admired by George IV) and Tristram Sappy in Poole's *Deaf as a Post*. Poole also provided a number of roles for Liston at the Haymarket (where he still played in the summer), including Van Dunder in *'Twould Puzzle a Conjuror* and the phenomenally successful *Paul Pry*. So popular was Liston's personation of Paul Pry, an interfering country busybody always turning up when he's not wanted, and so distinctive his dress (umbrella, lorgnettes, top hat, tail coat, and striped pantaloons) that likenesses began to appear everywhere — in prints, ceramics, snuffboxes, even sweet shops. *Paul Pry* was the zenith of Liston's career, but he was still to add new laurels to it. In 1828, at Drury Lane, he showed that, as the genial Adam Brock in Planché's *Charles XII*, he could perform with a restraint not always possible in his more outré characters, while his sojourn with the Vestris company at the Olympic in the 1830's saw a final golden phase in his career. During his six years at the Olympic he continued to play leading low comedy roles, especially old bachelors and jealous suitors, and added continually to his repertoire rather than relying on old favourites. He contributed significantly to the success of the Olympic venture, not least in introducing Charles Mathews the younger, who became Vestris's husband.

By the time of his retirement in 1837, Liston was unchallenged as the most popular and highly paid low comedian of the early 19th century. Much admired by Leigh Hunt, Crabb Robinson, and particularly Hazlitt, he had demonstrated on countless occasions his extraordinary capacity for suggesting astonishment, stupidity, vulgarity, and self-satisfaction. His performances were detailed and the result of careful study, but to observers he appeared entirely effortless and relaxed. He was doubtless helped by his face, with its snub nose, bulging cheeks, goggle eyes, and sagging chin: his appearance was often sufficient in itself to set the audiences laughing. His posture also helped: a characteristic pose of Liston's was to bend his knees and thrust out his large bottom.

Liston was an original actor, impossible to imitate, and was able to make something unique of any role, whatever its quality. He was accused of 'Listonising' his parts, but he created distinct characters, however much they depended for their impact on his personality and appearance. He was technically adept — able to establish a good relationship with his audiences, but remained utterly unconscious that there was anything humorous about him. The deadpan technique and his restraint rendered him separate from most other low comedians of the period, who relied on grimace, buffoonery, and broad effects. Not surprisingly, Liston was happiest in small theatres such as the Haymarket and the Olympic, in which exaggeration was unnecessary and the subtlest effects could be observed. The word 'natural' was often used to describe his acting and it was this naturalness that made the absurd, grotesque characters he impersonated credible to his audiences.

Liston had reputedly wanted to be a tragedian. His face rendered this impossible, but some felt that his characterisations contained a glimmer of pathos, if only on account of the fact that their ignorance provoked pity as well as laughter. In the later years of his career he was certainly capable of showing a restraint appropriate to the new modes of performance that Vestris was attempting to introduce at the Olympic. Overall, he set the standards by which low comedians were to be judged for the rest of the century and in Paul Pry he created the Hamlet of the 19th-century low comedian.

—Jim Davis

———

LITTLEWOOD, (Maudie) Joan. British director, actress, and writer. Born in Stockwell, London, 1914. Educated at schools in London; trained at the Royal Academy of Dramatic Art, London. Married folksinger and playwright Ewan MacColl in 1935 (divorced). Co-founder and director, with MacColl, Theatre of Action experimental theatre group, Manchester, 1934–37, reformed as the Theatre Union, Manchester, 1937–39; co-founder, with Gerry Raffles, and artistic director of the Theatre Workshop, Kendal, 1945; toured with Theatre Workshop, 1945–53; installed Theatre Workshop at the Theatre Royal, Stratford, East London, 1953; director, Theatre of Nations, Paris, from 1955; Broadway debut, 1960; worked in Africa, 1961–63; returned to Theatre Workshop, 1963, but disbanded company, 1964; worked at the Centre Culturel, Hammamet, Tunisia, 1965–67, and at Image India, Calcutta, India, 1968, before reforming the Theatre Workshop briefly in the early 1970's; final disbandment of Theatre Workshop, 1975; has lived in France since 1975. Member: French Academy of Writers. Recipient: Gold Medal, Berlin, 1958; Olympic Award for Theatre, 1959; Theatre of Nations Best Production of the Year Award, Paris (three times); Society of West End Theatre Special Award, 1983. Honorary doctorate, Open University, Milton Keynes, 1977.

Productions

1947   *Operation Olive Branch* (adapted from Aristophanes' *Lysistrata*), Rudolf Steiner Hall, London.

1952   *Uranium 235* (MacColl), Embassy Theatre, London, and Comedy Theatre, London; acted The Witch.

1953   *Twelfth Night* (Shakespeare), Theatre Royal, Stratford, London.

1954   *The Dutch Courtesan* (Marston), Theatre Royal, Stratford, London.
        The Fire Eaters, Theatre Royal, Stratford, London.
        The Flying Doctor (Molière), Theatre Royal, Stratford, London; acted Marinette.
        Johnny Noble (MacColl), Theatre Royal, Stratford, London.
        The Cruel Daughters (adapted by Littlewood), Theatre Royal, Stratford, London.
        The Chimes (adapted by Littlewood), Theatre Royal, Stratford, London.
        The Prince and the Pauper (adapted by Littlewood), Theatre Royal, Stratford, London.
        The Good Soldier Schweik (McColl), Theatre Royal, Stratford, London, and Embassy Theatre, London.

1955   *Richard II* (Shakespeare), Theatre Royal, Stratford, London; acted the Duchess of Gloucester.
        The Other Animals (MacColl), Theatre Royal, Stratford, London.
        Arden of Feversham (Lillo and Hoadley), Theatre Royal, Stratford, London, and Edinbugh Festival.
        Volpone (Jonson), Theatre Royal, Stratford, London, and Edinbugh Festival.
        The Midwife, Theatre Royal, Stratford, London; acted Mrs Kepes.
        The Legend of Pepito, Theatre Royal, Stratford, London.
        The Sheep Well (Vega), Theatre Royal, Stratford, London.
        The Italian Straw Hat (Labiche), Theatre Royal, Stratford, London.
        Mother Courage (Brecht), Devon Festival, Barnstaple; played Anna Fierling.

1956   *The Good Soldier Schweik* (McColl), Theatre Royal, Stratford, London, and Comedy Theatre, London.
        Edward II (Marlowe), Theatre Royal, Stratford, London.
        The Quare Fellow (Behan), Theatre Royal, Stratford, London, and Comedy Theatre, London.

1957   *You Won't Always Be on Top* (Chapman), Theatre Royal, Stratford, London.
        And the Wind Blew, Theatre Royal, Stratford, London.
        Macbeth (Shakespeare), Theatre Royal, Stratford, London.

1958   *Celestina* (Casona), Theatre Royal, Stratford, London.

Unto Such Glory (Green), Theatre Royal, Stratford, London.

The Respectable Prostitute (Sartre), Theatre Royal, Stratford, London.

A Taste of Honey (Delaney), Theatre Royal, Stratford, London, and Wyndham's Theatre, London.

The Hostage (Behan), Theatre Royal, Stratford, London, and West End, London; Cort Theatre, New York, 1960.

A Christmas Carol (Dickens, adapted by Littlewood), Theatre Royal, Stratford, London.

1959   *Fings Ain't Wot They Used T'Be* (Norman and Bart), Theatre Royal, Stratford, London, and West End, London.

Make Me An Offer (Mankowitz, Norman, and Heneker), Theatre Royal, Stratford, London, and West End, London.

1960   *Ned Kelly*, Theatre Royal, Stratford, London.

Every Man in His Humour (Jonson), Theatre Royal, Stratford, London.

Sparrers Can't Sing (Lewis), Theatre Royal, Stratford, London.

Unternehmen olzweig, Maxim Gorky Theatre, Berlin.

1961   *We're Just Not Practical*, Theatre Royal, Stratford, London.

They Might Be Giants, Theatre Royal, Stratford, London.

1963   *Oh! What a Lovely War* (Theatre Workshop and Chilton), Theatre Royal, Stratford, London, and Wyndham's Theatre, London; Broadhurst Theatre, New York, 1964.

1964   *A Kayf Up West*, Theatre Royal, Stratford, London.

Henry IV (Shakespeare), Edinburgh Festival.

1967   *Macbird!* (Garson), Theatre Royal, Stratford, London.

Intrigues and Amours (adapted from Schiller), Theatre Royal, Stratford, London.

Mrs Wilson's Diary (Wells and Ingrams and Theatre Workshop), Theatre Royal, Stratford, London.

The Marie Lloyd Story, Theatre Royal, Stratford, London.

1970   *Forward, Up Your End*, Theatre Royal, Stratford, London.

The Projector, Theatre Royal, Stratford, London.

1972   *The Londoners*, Theatre Royal, Stratford, London.

The Hostage (Behan), Theatre Royal, Stratford, London.

Costa Packet, Theatre Royal, Stratford, London.

1973   *So You Want to Be in Pictures?*, Theatre Royal, Stratford, London.

Films

As director:
Sparrers Can't Sing, 1962.

Publications

The Cruel Daughters (adaptation), 1954; *The Chimes* (adaptation), 1954; *The Prince and the Pauper* (adaptation), 1954; *A Christmas Carol* (adaptation), 1958.

* * *

The illegitimate daughter of a south London teenager, Joan Littlewood achieved the unlikely feat from such a background of gaining a scholarship to the Royal Academy of Dramatic Arts. Moreover, though she conscientiously rejected almost everything the prestigious drama school stood for, she still won virtually every prize for which she was eligible. On graduation, however, she left the starry lights of London and became assistant stage manager at Rusholme Repertory Theatre, Manchester. At the same time (about 1934) she met Ewan MacColl, an enormously dynamic performer and writer in the Manchester Workers Theatre Movement, whose revolutionary socialism disciplined her innate anarchism and whose commitment fired her energies.

Together, MacColl and Littlewood set up, first, the Theatre of Action, and then, when that closed, the Theatre Union, both dedicated to finding ways of using theatre as a vehicle for the expression of left-wing political ideas and concerns. They shared an absolute conviction that only the finest forms and methods of theatrical practice would suffice for their purpose and from the outset they were as interested in educating and training themselves and their members as they were in presenting plays. Nevertheless, particularly with the Theatre Union, Littlewood created a series of memorable productions out of what might have seemed thoroughly unpromising material — a company consisting largely of untrained working-class enthusiasts.

The last production of the Theatre Union was *Last Edition*, a furious protest against the squalid misery of the 1930's and their degeneration into imperialist war. After five performances the show was closed and Littlewood and MacColl were arrested and fined. The Theatre Union was at an end. Nevertheless, it had in some ways defined the Joan Littlewood style, which embraced the most effective techniques of agitprop theatre — declamation, song, telling tableaux, the unexpected use of personal testimony and apparently dispassionate statistics — as well as utilizing more usual elements, which included a Stanislavskian insistence on truth in acting and a willingness to resort to dance and movement for the expression of abstract or complex ideas. No other theatre in Britain was experimenting so fundamentally.

During World War II, Joan Littlewood worked largely for the BBC and then, in 1945, founded the Theatre Workshop. Dedicated to furthering progressive and socialist understanding, the Theatre Workshop consciously sought to create theatre for the working class and to inaugurate a new golden age through its association with modern-day 'groundlings'. The first period of the company's life entailed exhaustive touring both in Britain and abroad and lasted for seven years, until 1952. The plays, most of which were written by MacColl, were exactly what Littlewood needed, containing fluid rhythms, little or no settings, zany humour, extensive use of dance and song, and hard-fisted political commitment. In some ways, *Johnny Noble, Uranium 235, The Other Animals*, and other works remained unrivalled as vehicles for Littlewood's skills, as the virtuosity and dynamism of her production style and her use of light, music, and movement were precisely what they demanded.

The company, however, lurched from artistic triumph to financial crisis and back with alarming speed. Finally, in 1952, Littlewood and her companion and business manager, Gerry Raffles, took a lease on the old Theatre Royal, Stratford East. Though Littlewood did produce two more Ewan MacColl plays, he disapproved of the move and gave up active participation and the tendency of the repertoire shifted towards the classics. The reception of the work by the London critics and theatregoers was one of amazed delight: perhaps they never realised that 14 or 15 actors could double and treble all the parts in a play like *Richard II* and present it with such attack, vitality, and excitement. But the theatre establishment was shocked when the Theatre Workshop was invited to represent Britain at the Paris International Theatre Festival in 1955, and again the following year. On both occasions Joan Littlewood's productions aroused the highest admiration: "They have brought off the biggest, the most unexpected, the most extraordinary success that a British company has known in France", wrote one critic, while another said: "The acting is miraculous, near perfection".

In the later 1950's, the Theatre Workshop turned again to new authors, such as Brendan Behan and Shelagh Delaney — authors whose drama afforded Littlewood the opportunity to adapt her improvisational methods to help shape their scripts. But when *The Quare Fellow* and *The Hostage* by Behan and Delaney's *A Taste of Honey*, among other shows (notably musicals by Lionel Bart), proved so successful that they were transferred to West End theatres, the company that she had nurtured for so long and kept despite shoestring budgets and derisory wages, began to break up. In 1961, she temporarily gave up the struggle and took a much-needed break.

When Littlewood returned in 1963, it was to use her unique methods of scholarly research coupled with theatrical improvisation to create her greatest single success — *Oh! What a Lovely War*. This brilliant production — "a medley of disparate styles which the genius of Littlewood welded into one" — created an effect "at once epic and intimate, elegantly stylized and grimly realistic, comic and tragi-comic". Popular traditions (the pierrot show and the music hall) fused with a deeply held anti-war conviction to become unforgettable theatre. Though tailored to its creators, it was printed and has continued to be performed by amateur and professional groups, as well as schools, ever since.

This indicates something of Joan Littlewood's enduring influence. She soldiered on for nearly a decade more, but to increasingly little effect, while people who had hardly heard of her used, and misused, her ideas and methods, and her actors and associates spread throughout the British theatre. Even after she gave up work and moved to France, hers was still a name to be conjured with and the sudden flowering of political and agitprop theatre in Britain in the 1970's and 1980's probably owed more to her than to any other single individual.

—Robert Leach

LOUTHERBOURGH, Philip James de. Alsatian-born British artist and stage designer of Polish descent. Born Philippe Jacques de Loutherbourg in Fulda, Germany, 31 October 1740. Educated at theological college of Strasbourg; studied painting of battle scenes and romantic landscapes under his father, a miniaturist, and in Paris. Married Barbe Burlât in 1764; six children. Settled in London, 1771; scene director, Theatre Royal, Drury Lane, 1771–81; collaborated with David Garrick and R. B. Sheridan on scenic and lighting innovations and devised new means of creating sound effects; painted numerous acclaimed naturalistic backcloths, mostly for pantomimes and a variety of other entertainments; also explored possibilities of perspective and introduced reforms in theatrical costume; after retirement from the stage developed the *Eidophusikon* theatre to demonstrate lighting effects; revisited Switzerland, 1783; visited Netherlands as artist with Duke of York's military expedition, 1793; retired to Hammersmith, London, and took up faith-healing. Member: Académie Royale, 1767; Royal Academy, 1781. Died in London, 11 March 1812.

Productions

1773	*Alfred* (Arne), Theatre Royal, Drury Lane, London.
	A Christmas Tale (Garrick), Theatre Royal, Drury Lane, London.
1774	*The Maid of Oaks* (Burgoyne), Theatre Royal, Drury Lane, London.
1776	*Selima and Azor* (Sheridan), Theatre Royal, Drury Lane, London.
1778	*The Camp* (Sheridan), Theatre Royal, Drury Lane, London.
1779	*The Critic* (Sheridan), Theatre Royal, Drury Lane, London.
	The Wonders of Derbyshire; or, Harlequin in the Peak (Sheridan), Theatre Royal, Drury Lane, London.
1780	*Harlequin Fortunatus* (Woodward), Theatre Royal, Drury Lane, London.
1781	*Robinson Crusoe* (Sheridan), Theatre Royal, Drury Lane, London.
1782	*Harlequin Teague; or, The Giant's Causeway* (Colman the Elder and O'Keeffe), Haymarket Theatre, London.
1785	*Omai; or, A Trip round the World* (O'Keeffe), Covent Garden, London.

*

Bibliography

Books:
John O'Keeffe, *Recollections of the Life of John O'Keeffe*, London, 1826.
Christopher Baugh, *Garrick and Loutherbourg*, Cambridge, 1990.

Articles:
John O'Keeffe, *The London Magazine*, November 1774.

* * *

During the 18th century, English theatre did not enjoy the scenic patronage offered by the circuit of court and aristocratic private theatres that formed the focus for theatre activity in continental Europe. Hence, we have few surviving designs from the period and the scant documentary evidence seems to suggest that a rather dour suspicion of scenic spectacle permeated the theatre for most of the period. Pantomimes and subscription seasons of opera at the King's Theatre were alone in offering London audiences imported glimpses of Italian and French scenic attractions in the work of Cipriani and Servandoni. However, towards the close of David Garrick's long management of Drury Lane (1747–76), he and his audience began to develop a new relationship with visual experience. Art and architecture of the past, the relationship between human action and its location, topography, tourism, and the picturesque, all began to find expression within the performance conventions of the theatre.

Besides the interest and significance of the few remaining models and scenic designs of the German-born Philip James de Loutherbourgh, perhaps his primary importance is that he was probably the first artist to be employed in the theatre in the executive and supervisory role that we recognise today. In two letters written to Garrick during 1772–73 (the only scenically relevant writings of Loutherbourgh to survive) the artist makes his role in the theatre quite clear. He will be responsible for all scenery and stage machinery and oversee the lighting of the stage. He will make scenic models, which will serve to instruct the painters and technicians, and he will also supervise the costuming of the entire production. Such overall visual control of production is close to the job description of the modern stage designer and should be contrasted with the prevailing 18th-century system whereby the artist would be hired by the theatre management to supply individual painted scenes, occasionally for an entire production but frequently to satisfy a deficiency within the theatre's stock. These would then be treated as part of the capital assets of the theatre and be re-used, modified, and repainted until age required their replacement. The prevailing system (and therefore the implicit extent of Loutherbourgh's significance) is clearly laid out in *The Case of the Stage in Ireland* (1758): "The stage should be furnished with a competent number of painted scenes sufficient to answer the purpose of all the plays in the stock, in which there is no great variety ... these should be done by a master, if such can be procured; otherwise they should be as simple and unaffected as possible, to avoid offending a judicious eye. If, for some particular purpose, any other scene is necessary, it can be got up occasionally."

It is, of course, highly unlikely that Garrick's original motive in employing Loutherbourgh in 1773 was simply that he shoul 'get up' some scenes, leave the scene-store well stocked for future exploitation, and provide some useful competition for the traditionally more spectacular offerings at Covent Garden. But the financially astute Garrick quickly realised the 'resident' value of such an executive position in the theatre and employed Loutherbourgh regularly until his own retirement in 1776. It is important to note, however, that Loutherbourgh only worked on pantomimes, semi-operas, and the popular 'entertainments' that increasingly occupied Garrick's final years. His most widely praised contributions were for *Alfred*, *A Christmas Tale*, and *The Maid of Oaks*. Sheridan took over the artist's contract when he became manager of Drury Lane in 1776 and the painter contributed to several more productions, perhaps most famously to *The Wonders of Derbyshire*, a travelogue that took the audience on a scenic tour of the Peak district.

A growing reputation as an easel painter and squabbles over payment from Sheridan finally caused Loutherbourgh to end his association with the theatre. For a short period he devoted himself to creating a small actor-less theatre of scenic illusions called the Eidophusikon, which he presented at his home in Lisle Street. In this he could implement the totality of visual experience as the theatre of the day either would or could not. He presented panoramic, atmospheric vistas of London from Greenwich Hill and sublime horror and spectacle in his 'inferno' scenes from *Paradise Lost*. He did return, briefly, to the legitimate theatre to co-devise with John O'Keeffe and to design a travelogue pantomime based upon Captain Cook's voyages and John Webber's drawings as *Omai; or, A Trip round the World* for Covent Garden. It is an enticing, but unproven possibility that he may have been persuaded out of retirement by Sheridan to contribute to his great romantic spectacle *Pizarro* in 1799.

The majority of practical scenic innovations associated with Loutherbourgh had been attempted sporadically on the London stage earlier in the century and, indeed, the basic 'groove and shutter' method of changing scenes, developed by Inigo Jones for the masques, had been used since the early 1660's. Garrick himself, following his Grand Tour of 1764–65, imported the newly designed oil lamps that seem to have formed the basis of the wing lighting that was so important to the success of Loutherbourgh's stage pictures. Loutherbourgh's principal achievement, however, was to develop and integrate a stage technology into what might be termed a pictorial theatre language. Similar to the child's pop-up picture book, he broke up the images of the real world into a series of irregularly shaped two-dimensional pieces, thus breaking up the formal wings and backscenes of the groove and shutter system. Notable also was his use of of low two-dimensional scenery (ground-rows) to give location and character to the stage floor. By placing these elements one behind the other and, most importantly, lighting them carefully with batten-mounted oil lamps behind each surface, the illusion of three-dimensionality could be created for the audience.

Of course, such illusions really require the presence of the harmoniously 'designed' performer to complete the effect. Loutherbourgh's development of this visual possibility for the theatre was ultimately to mean the end of the road for the neutral, scenically undefined forestage of the Renaissance, Restoration and 18th-century theatre. The performer would become inextricably placed within the scenic location and further, location, environment, and of course, spectacle, were themselves to become central to the drama and theatre of the next century.

—Christopher Baugh

LUGNÉ-POË, Aurélien (-François). French actor-manager. Born Aurélien-François-Marie Lugné in Paris, 27 December 1869. Educated at school in Condorcet; trained for the stage under M. Worms at the Paris Conservatoire,

1889–91. Married actress Suzanne Després. Founded amateur theatre group, the Cercle des Escholiers, while still at school; became stage manager of the Théâtre Libre and then joined Paul Fort's Théâtre d'Art, Paris, 1890; co-founded Théâtre de l'Oeuvre, 1893; introduced to French audiences the plays of Maeterlinck and Ibsen, among others; won government subsidy for the Théâtre de l'Oeuvre, 1903; also made numerous world tours and managed tours by Eleonora Duse, Isadora Duncan, and others; wrote theatre criticism for *L'Éclair*; gave up management of Théâtre de l'Oeuvre, 1929. Officier, Lègion d'Honneur. Died in Villeneuve-lès-Avignon, 19 June 1940.

Productions

1893   *Pelléas et Melisande* (Maeterlinck), Théâtre des Bouffes-Parisien, Paris.
    Rosmersholm (Ibsen, translated by Prozor), Théâtre des Bouffes du Nord, Paris.
    Un Ennemi du peuple (Ibsen, translated by Chennevière and Johansen), Théâtre des Bouffes du Nord, Paris.
    Ames solitaires (Hauptmann, translated by Cohen), Théâtre des Bouffes du Nord, Paris.

1894   *L'Araignée de cristal* (Rachilde), Théâtre des Bouffes du Nord, Paris.
    Au-dessus des forces humaines (Björnstjerne-Björnson, translated by Prozor), Théâtre des Bouffes du Nord, Paris.
    Une Nuit d'avril à Céos (Trarieux), Théâtre des Bouffes du Nord, Paris.
    L'Image (Beaubourg), Théâtre des Bouffes du Nord, Paris.
    Solness le construsteur (Ibsen, translated by Prozor), Théâtre des Bouffes du Nord, Paris.
    La Belle au bois dormant (Bataille and d'Humières), Nouveau-Théâtre, Paris.
    Frères (Bang, translated by Colleville and Zepelin), Comédie-Parisienne, Paris.
    La Gardienne (Régnier), Comédie-Parisienne, Paris.
    Les Créanciers (Strindberg, translated by Loiseau), Comédie-Parisienne, Paris.
    Annabella (Ford, translated by Maeterlinck), Nouveau-Théâtre, Paris.
    La Vie muette (Beaubourg), Nouveau-Théâtre, Paris.
    Père (Strindberg, translated by Loiseau), Nouveau-Théâtre, Paris.
    Un Ennemi du peuple (Ibsen, translated by Chennevière and Johansen), Nouveau-Théâtre, Paris.

1895   *Le Chariot de terre cuite* (Barrucand), Nouveau-Théâtre, Paris.
    La Scène (Lebey), Nouveau-Théâtre, Paris.
    La Vrité dans le vin ou les Désagréments de la galanterie (Collé), Nouveau-Théâtre, Paris.
    Intérieur (Maeterlinck), Nouveau-Théâtre, Paris.
    Les Pieds nickelés (Bernard), Nouveau-Théâtre, Paris.
    L'École de l'idéal (Vérola), Théâtre du Ménus-Plaisirs, Paris.

    Le Petit Eyolf (Ibsen, translated by Prozor), Théâtre du Ménus-Plaisirs, Paris.
    Le Volant (Claudel), Théâtre du Ménus-Plaisirs, Paris.
    Carmosine (Musset), Ministère du Commerce, Paris.
    Brand (Ibsen, translated by Prozor), Nouveau-Théâtre, Paris.
    Venise sauvée (Otway, translated by Pène), Comédie-Parisienne, Paris.
    L'Anneau de Çakuntala (Kalidasa, adapted by Hérold), Comédie-Parisienne, Paris.

1896   *Une Mère* (Ameen, translated by Prozor), Comédie-Parisienne, Paris.
    Brocéliande (Lorrain), Comédie-Parisienne, Paris.
    Les Flaireurs (Lerberghe), Comédie-Parisienne, Paris.
    Des mots! des mots! (Quinel and Dubreuil), Comédie-Parisienne, Paris.
    Raphaël (Coolus), Comédie-Parisienne, Paris.
    Salome (Wilde), Comédie-Parisienne, Paris.
    Hérakléa (Villeroy), Nouveau-Théâtre, Paris.
    La Fleur palan enlevée (Arène), Nouveau-Théâtre, Paris.
    L'Errante (Quillard), Nouveau-Théâtre, Paris.
    La Dernière croisade (Gray), Nouveau-Théâtre, Paris.
    La Lépreuse (Bataille), Comédie-Parisienne, Paris.
    Le Grand Galeoto (Echegaray), home of Ruth Rattazzi, Paris.
    Le Tandem (Trézenick and Soulaine), Nouveau-Théâtre, Paris.
    La Brebis (Sée), Nouveau-Théâtre, Paris.
    Les Soutiens de la société (Ibsen, translated by Bertrand and Nevers), Nouveau-Théâtre, Paris.
    Peer Gynt (Ibsen), Nouveau-Théâtre, Paris.
    Ubu roi ou les Polonais (Jarry), Nouveau-Théâtre, Paris.

1897   *La Motte de terre* (Dumur), Nouveau-Théâtre, Paris.
    Au delà des forces humaines (Björnstjerne-Björnson, translated by Monnier and Littmanson), Nouveau-Théâtre, Paris.
    La Cloche engloutie (Hauptmann, translated by Hérold), Nouveau-Théâtre, Paris.
    Ton Sang (Bataille), Nouveau-Théâtre, Paris.
    Le Fils de l'abbesse (Herdey), Nouveau-Théâtre, Paris.
    Le Fardeau de la liberté (Bernard), Nouveau-Théâtre, Paris.
    La Comédie de l'amour (Ibsen, translated by Colleville and Zepelin), Nouveau-Théâtre, Paris.
    Jean-Gabriel Borkman (Ibsen, translated by Prozor), Nouveau-Théâtre, Paris.

1898   *Le Revizor* (Gogol), Nouveau-Théâtre, Paris.
    Rosmersholm (Ibsen, translated by Prozor), Nouveau-Théâtre, Paris.
    Le Gage (Jourdain), Nouveau-Théâtre, Paris.
    L'Échelle (Zype), Nouveau-Théâtre, Paris.

Le Balcon (Heiberg, translated by Prozor), Nouveau-Théâtre, Paris.

Aërt (Rolland), Nouveau-Théâtre, Paris.

Morituri ou les Loups (Rolland), Nouveau-Théâtre, Paris.

La Victoire (Bouhélier), Théâtre des Bouffes-Parisiens, Paris.

Solness le constructeur (Ibsen, translated by Prozor), Théâtre des Bouffes-Parisiens, Paris.

Mesure pour mesure (Shakespeare), Cirque d'Été, Paris.

1899   *Noblesse de la terre* (Faramond), Théâtre de la Renaissance, Paris.

Un Ennemi du peuple (Ibsen, translated by Chennevière and Johansen), Théâtre de la Renaissance, Paris.

Fausta (Sonniès), Nouveau-Théâtre, Paris.

Le Joug (Mayrargue), Nouveau-Théâtre, Paris.

Entretien d'un philosophie avec la maréchale de XXX (Diderot), Théâtre des Bouffes-Parisiens, Paris.

Le Triomphe de la raison (Rolland), Théâtre des Bouffes-Parisiens, Paris.

1900   *Monsieur Bonnet* (Faramond), Théâtre du Gymnase, Paris.

La Cloître (Verhaeren), Nouveau-Théâtre, Paris.

1901   *Le Roi candaule* (Gide), Nouveau-Théâtre, Paris.

1902   *Monna Vanna* (Maeterlinck), Nouveau-Théâtre, Paris.

Manfred (Lord Byron, adapted by Forthuny), Nouveau-Théâtre, Paris.

1903   *La Roussalka* (Schuré), Nouveau-Théâtre, Paris.

Le Maître de Palmyre (Wilbrandt, translated by Renon, Bénon, and Zifferer), Nouveau-Théâtre, Paris.

L'Oasis (Jullien), Nouveau-Théâtre, Paris.

1904   *Philippe II* (Verhaeren), Nouveau-Théâtre, Paris.

Polyphème (Samain), Nouveau-Théâtre, Paris.

Oedipe à Colone (Sophocles, adapted by Gastambide), Nouveau-Théâtre, Paris.

L'Ouvrier de la dernière heure (Guiraud), Nouveau-Théâtre, Paris.

Les Droits du coeur (Jullien), Nouveau-Théâtre, Paris.

Le Jaloux (Bibesco), Nouveau-Théâtre, Paris.

La Prophétie (Toussaint), Théâtre Marigny, Paris.

1905   *La Gioconda* (D'Annunzio, translated by Hérelle), Nouveau-Théâtre, Paris.

La Fille de Jorio (D'Annunzio, translated by Hérelle), Nouveau-Théâtre, Paris.

Dionysos (Gasquet), Nouveau-Théâtre, Paris.

Dans les bas-fonds (Gorky, translated by Halperine-Kaminsky), Nouveau-Théâtre, Paris.

1906   *Madame la marquise* (Sutro), Salle de Trianon, Paris.

Le Troisième Couvert (Savoir), Salle de Trianon, Paris.

Leurs Soucis (Bahr), Salle de Trianon, Paris.

Le Réformateur (Rod), Nouveau-Théâtre, Paris.

Le Cloaque (Labry), Nouveau-Théâtre, Paris.

Pan (Lerberghe), Théâtre Marigny, Paris.

L'Héritier naturel (Keim), Théâtre Marigny, Paris.

1907   *L'Amie des sages* (Allou), Théâtre Marigny, Paris.

Petit Jean (Buysieulx and Max), Théâtre Marigny, Paris.

La Tragédie florentine (Wilde), Théâtre Fémina, Paris.

Philista (Battanchon), Théâtre Fémina, Paris.

Le Droit au bonheur (Lemonnier and Soulaine), Théâtre Fémina, Paris.

Un Rien (Valloton), Théâtre Fémina, Paris.

Une Aventure de Frédérick Lemaître (Basset), Théâtre Grévin, Paris.

Placide (Séverin-Malfayde and Dolley), Théâtre Grévin, Paris.

Zénaïde ou les caprices du destin (Delorme and Gally), Théâtre Grévin, Paris.

Le Baptême (Savoir and Nozière), Théâtre Fémina, Paris.

Mendès est dans la salle (Marchès and Vautel), Théâtre Fémina, Paris.

1908   *Hypatie* (Barlatier), Théâtre Marigny, Paris.

Acquitté (Antona-Traversi, translated by Lécuyer), Théâtre Marigny, Paris.

La Loi (Jourda), Théâtre Fémina, Paris.

Vae Victis (Duterme), Théâtre Fémina, Paris.

Les Amours d'Ovide (Mouézy-Eon, Auzanet, and Faral), Théâtre Fémina, Paris.

Au Temps des fées (Blanchard), Théâtre Fémina, Paris.

Elektra (Hofmannsthal, adapted by Strozzi and Epstein), Théâtre Fémina, Paris.

Le Jeu de la morale et du hasard (Bernard), Théâtre Fémina, Paris.

Les Vieux (Rameil and Saisset), Théâtre Marigny, Paris.

La Madone (Spaak), Théâtre Marigny, Paris.

La Dame qui n'est plus aux camélias (Faramond), Théâtre Fémina, Paris.

1909   *Perce-Neige et les sept gnomes* (Dortzal, adapted from Grimm), Théâtre Fémina, Paris.

La Chaîne (Level and Monnier), Théâtre Fémina, Paris.

Le Roi bombance (Marinetti), Théâtre Marigny, Paris.

Nonotte et Patouillet (du Bois), Théâtre Marigny, Paris.

1910   *La Sonate à Kreutzer* (Savoir and Nozière, adapted from Tolstoy), Théâtre Fémina, Paris.

Le Mauvais Grain (Faramond), Théâtre Fémina, Paris.

L'Amour de Kesa (Humières), Théâtre Fémina, Paris.

Le Poupard (Bouvelet), Théâtre Fémina, Paris.

1911   *Malazarte* (Aranha), Théâtre Fémina, Paris.

Sur le seuil (Battanchon), Théâtre Antoine, Paris.

Un Médecin de campagne (Bordeaux and De-
narié), Théâtre Antoine, Paris.

Les Oiseaux (Nozière), Théâtre Antoine, Paris.

Le Philanthrope ou la Maison des amours
(Bouvelet), Théâtre Réjane, Paris.

1912   *Anne ma soeur* (Auzanet), Théâtre Antoine,
Paris.

La Charité s.v.p. (Speth), Théâtre Antoine,
Paris.

Futile (Bernouard), Théâtre Antoine, Paris.

Le Visionnaire (Renaud), Théâtre Antoine,
Paris.

Ce Bougre d'original (Soulages), Théâtre Antoine, Paris.

Le Candidat Machefer (Hellem and D'Estoc),
Théâtre Antoine, Paris.

Ariane blessée (Allou), Théâtre Antoine, Paris.

Les Derniers Masques (Schnitzler, translated by
Rémon and Valentin), Théâtre Antoine,
Paris.

La Dernière Heure (Frappa), Palais Royal,
Paris.

Grégoire (Falk), Palais Royal, Paris.

Morituri (Prozor), Palais Royal, Paris.

L'Annonce faite á Marie (Claudel), Salle Malakoff, Paris.

1913   *Le Baladin du monde occidental* (Synge, translated by Bourgeois), Salle Berlioz, Paris.

La Brebis égarée (Jammes), Salle Malakoff,
Paris.

1914   *La Danse des fous* (Birinski, adapted by
Rémon), Théâtre Antoine, Paris.

L'Otage (Claudel), Salle Malakoff, Paris.

1920   *La Couronne de carton* (Sarment), Maison de
l'Oeuvre, Cité Monthiers.

Le Cocu magnifique (Crommelynck), Maison
de l'Oeuvre, Cité Monthiers.

1921   *Les Scrupules de Sganarelle* (Régnier), Maison
de l'Oeuvre, Cité Monthiers.

Sophie Arnoux (Nigoud), Maison de l'Oeuvre,
Cité Monthiers.

Le Pêcheur d'ombres (Sarment), Maison de
l'Oeuvre, Cité Monthiers.

La Danse de mort (Strindberg, translated by
Rémon), Maison de l'Oeuvre, Cité Monthiers.

Comité secret (Lourié), Maison de l'Oeuvre,
Cité Monthiers.

Madonna Fiamma (Ségur), Maison de
l'Oeuvre, Cité Monthiers.

1922   *L'Age heureux* (Natanson), Maison de
l'Oeuvre, Cité Monthiers.

Dardamelle (Mazaud), Maison de l'Oeuvre,
Cité Monthiers.

Le Dilemme du docteur (G. B. Shaw), Maison
de l'Oeuvre, Cité Monthiers.

La Dette de Schmil (Orna), Maison de
l'Oeuvre, Cité Monthiers.

Le Visage sans voile (Allou), Maison de
l'Oeuvre, Cité Monthiers.

Le Retour d'Ivering (Holt), Maison de l'Oeuvre,
Cité Monthiers.

Le Lasso (Batty-Weber), Maison de l'Oeuvre,
Cité Monthiers.

L'Enfant truqué (Natanson), Maison de
l'Oeuvre, Cité Monthiers.

1923   *La Dame allègre* (Puig and Ferreter, translated
by Pierat), Maison de l'Oeuvre, Cité Monthiers.

La Messe est dite (Achard), Maison de
l'Oeuvre, Cité Monthiers.

Le Cadi et le cocu (Mille and Loria), Maison de
l'Oeuvre, Cité Monthiers.

Est-ce possible? (Birabeau), Maison de
l'Oeuvre, Cité Monthiers.

Passions de fantoches (San Secondo, translated
by Mortier), Maison de l'Oeuvre, Cité Monthiers.

On finit souvent par où on devrait commencer
(Turpin), Maison de l'Oeuvre, Cité Monthiers.

La Maison avant tout (Hamp), Maison de
l'Oeuvre, Cité Monthiers.

Berniquel (Maeterlinck), Maison de l'Oeuvre,
Cité Monthiers.

L'Autre Messie (Soumagne), Maison de
l'Oeuvre, Cité Monthiers.

1924   *Le Feu à l'Opéra* (Kaiser, translated by Goll),
Maison de l'Oeuvre, Cité Monthiers.

Irène exigeante (Beaunier), Maison de
l'Oeuvre, Cité Monthiers.

Le Mort à cheval (Ghéon), Maison de l'Oeuvre,
Cité Monthiers.

La Farce des encore (Thuysbaert and Ghéon),
Maison de l'Oeuvre, Cité Monthiers.

L'Amour est un Étrange maître (Worms-Barret-
ta), Maison de l'Oeuvre, Cité Monthiers.

Philippe le zélé (Trintzius and Valentin), Maison de l'Oeuvre, Cité Monthiers.

L'Égoïste (Orna), Maison de l'Oeuvre, Cité
Monthiers.

La Profession de Madame Warren (G. B.
Shaw), Maison de l'Oeuvre, Cité Monthiers.

La Maison ouverte (Passeur), Maison de
l'Oeuvre, Cité Monthiers.

1925   *Le Génie camouglé* (Fabri), Maison de
l'Oeuvre, Cité Monthiers.

La Femme de feu (Schoenherr, translated by
Lindauer), Maison de l'Oeuvre, Cité Monthiers.

La Traversée de Paris à la nage (Passeur),
Maison de l'Oeuvre, Cité Monthiers.

Une Demande en mariage (Chekhov), Maison
de l'Oeuvre, Cité Monthiers.

Je Rectifie les visages (Trintzius and Valentin),
Maison de l'Oeuvre, Cité Monthiers.

La Fleur sous les yeux (Martini, translated by
Ponzone), Maison de l'Oeuvre, Cité Monthiers.

Tour à terre (Salacrou), Maison de l'Oeuvre,
Cité Monthiers.

1926   *Les Danseurs de gigue* (Soumagne), Maison de
l'Oeuvre, Cité Monthiers.

Ariel (Marx), Maison de l'Oeuvre, Cité Monthiers.

Poisson d'avril ou les griffes du destin (adapted
from Colpartage, translated by Lindauer),
Maison de l'Oeuvre, Cité Monthiers.

La Jeune Fille de la popote (Passeur), Maison de l'Oeuvre, Cité Monthiers.

L'Ancre noire (Brasseur), Maison de l'Oeuvre, Cité Monthiers.

Ville moderne (Modave), Maison de l'Oeuvre, Cité Monthiers.

1927   *L'Avons-nous tuée?* (Datz), Maison de l'Oeuvre, Cité Monthiers.

Le Déraillement du T.P. 33 (Hamp), Maison de l'Oeuvre, Cité Monthiers.

Le Bourgeois romanesque (Blanchon), Maison de l'Oeuvre, Cité Monthiers.

Un Homme en or (Ferdinand), Maison de l'Oeuvre, Cité Monthiers.

Les Deux Amis (Savoir), Maison de l'Oeuvre, Cité Monthiers.

Le Conditionnel passé (Bruyez), Maison de l'Oeuvre, Cité Monthiers.

Un Homme seul (Sauvage), Maison de l'Oeuvre, Cité Monthiers.

Une Bourgeoise (Francen), Maison de l'Oeuvre, Cité Monthiers.

Télescopage (Demont), Maison de l'Oeuvre, Cité Monthiers.

L'Ile lointaine (Ginisty), Maison de l'Oeuvre, Cité Monthiers.

1928   *Madame Marie* (Soumagne), Maison de l'Oeuvre, Cité Monthiers.

La Halte sur la grand route (Jabès), Maison de l'Oeuvre, Cité Monthiers.

La Foire aux sentiments (Ferdinand), Maison de l'Oeuvre, Cité Monthiers.

Hommes du monde (Brasseur), Maison de l'Oeuvre, Cité Monthiers.

Tu Pourrais ne pas m'aimer (Brasseur), Maison de l'Oeuvre, Cité Monthiers.

Les Trois Langages (Charmel), Maison de l'Oeuvre, Cité Monthiers.

Celui qui voulait jouer avec la vie (François), Maison de l'Oeuvre, Cité Monthiers.

Le Cercle (Maugham, adapted by Carbuccia), Maison de l'Oeuvre, Cité Monthiers.

1929   *Jules, Juliette et Julien* (Bernard), Maison de l'Oeuvre, Cité Monthiers.

Publications

La Parade, 1–3, 1930–33; *Dernière pirouette*, 1946; *Rolland et Lugné-Poë: correspondance, 1894–1901*, edited by Jacques Robichez, 1957.

*

Bibliography

Books:
R. Dupierreux, *Lugné-Poë homme de théâtre*, Paris, 1945.
Gertrude R. Jasper, *Adventure in the Theatre — Lugné-Poë and the Théâtre de l'Oeuvre to 1899*, New Brunswick, 1947.
Jacques Robichez, *Lugné-Poë*, Paris, 1955.

Jacques Robichez, *Le Symbolisme au théâtre: Lugné-Poë et les débuts de l'Oeuvre*, Paris, 1957.

* * *

As director, actor, and theatre manager, Aurélien Lugné-Poë was a key figure in the renovation of nineteenth-century French theatre. His long career stretched from the early heroic days of the avant-garde in the 1880's to the 1930's, when the scenic reforms launched by Copeau were a consolidated fact. For most of this time he worked independently of any school or system, seeking to provide a stage for new playwrights and to introduce interesting foreign dramatists to the French stage. Although he was receptive to innovations in mise en scène, he had a modest conception of the director's role. Believing that the theatre exists to serve playwrights and to foster good dramatic writing, he saw his principal role as being that of a prospector, seeking out new plays of whatever aesthetic tendency.

These ideas made him one of the most eclectic of French directors. He rarely staged the classics, but his early authors included Maeterlinck, Jarry, Bataille, Beaubourg, Gogol, Hauptmann, Rachilde, Rolland, and the Sanskrit writers Soudaka and Kalidasa. Later, he produced Achard, Passeur, Salacrou, and Sarment, and he was the first director to stage Claudel, with *L'Annonce faite à Marie* in 1913 and *L'Otage* in 1914. One of his most lasting contributions was to have introduced French audiences to Scandinavian playwrights: Björnson, Strindberg, and above all Ibsen, with whom he had a particular affinity and to whom he returned time and again. Every season at the Théâtre de l'Oeuvre between 1893 and 1899 included at least one new play by Ibsen.

Unlike many of his theatrically inclined contemporaries, Lugné-Poë was a practical man of the theatre, and his first commitment was to theatre in all its forms, rather than to an aesthetic school. If he turned initially to Symbolist writers, it was not out of a doctrinaire commitment but because he shared their taste for the poetic and the allusive, and because they seemed to represent the most original tendencies of the day. His artistic policy was one of independence, especially independence from the commercial pressures that dictated trends in the regular theatre of the time.

Early productions at the Théâtre de l'Oeuvre were greatly influenced by Symbolist aesthetics. Mixing poetry, painting, and drama, they gave an impression of shadowy forms dimly lit against soft pastel and grey backgrounds. Following Antoine's example, footlights were abolished. Instead of a box set or trompe d'oeil decor an abstract painted backcloth was used, and a transparent gauze curtain was sometimes introduced between the stage and the audience. Such impressionist techniques were seen to best advantage in his first production in 1893, Maeterlinck's *Pelléas et Mélisande*. In reaction to the mimetic acting at the Théâtre Libre, Lugné-Poë emphasised the need for self-effacement by the actors. He introduced an intoning delivery interspersed with long silences, producing a somnambulist effect that in its early extreme phase attracted derision. Lugné-Poë himself acted in many of his productions. He was an excellent and versatile actor, who had been awarded the first prize at the Conservatoire, though his own preference at this time was for the somnambulist style.

Although these were the prevailing characteristics of his production style, they were not always applied systematically. It was noted, for example, that a single production might contain an incongruous mixture of conflicting acting styles. This was partly a result of the director's exploratory method and partly because the troupe depended on a combination of regular company members playing alongside other professionals, such as Firmin Gémier from the Odéon, brought in for specific roles. Some productions abandoned the prevailing house style altogether. There was nothing amorphous or allusive about the celebrated premiere of *Ubu roi*. This production, largely masterminded by Jarry himself, was remarkable as a theatricalist counterblast to the hyper-refined delicacy of perception being offered by Symbolist poets.

Lugné-Poë's growing impatience with the Symbolists' failure to produce genuinely theatrical work resulted in his breaking with them publicly in 1897. By then, his work with Ibsen had led him to develop a more balanced approach to the stage. Without adopting a wholly realistic approach, his later productions of Ibsen's plays paid more attention to the characters and sought to bring out their symbolism through a less abstract, more natural style of acting. He also became conscious of the need to draw theatre closer to social reality, in reaction to the decadent excesses of the 1880's and 1890's. Rolland's historical dramas, raising political themes relevant to contemporary events such as the Dreyfus affair, enabled him to explore this hitherto neglected vein of interest among the theatre public.

Although he relaunched his theatre in 1912 and ran it very successfully until 1929, the main focus of innovation had by now passed to Copeau and the Cartel directors. His most influential work was in the 1890's, when the Théâtre de l'Oeuvre was a beacon for the avant-garde. Ironically, posterity has judged the production, which he undertook reluctantly and regarded as a disaster, to be his most significant contribution.

—David Whitton

LUNT, Alfred and FONTANNE, Lynn. Anglo-American actors. Alfred Lunt born in Milwaukee, Wisconsin, 19 August 1892. Educated at Carroll College, Waukesha, Wisconsin; trained as architect. Married Lynn Fontanne in 1922. Stage debut, Castle Square Theatre, Boston, 1912; remained with the Castle Square stock company until 1914, then toured with Margaret Anglin's company, 1914–15, and appeared in vaudeville; emerged as star in *Clarence*, 1919; film debut, 1923; joined Theatre Guild, New York, and made first appearance with Fontanne, 1924; London debut, 1929; acclaimed alongside his wife in plays by Noël Coward in the 1930's; director, Theatre Guild, 1935; with his wife opened the Lunt-Fontanne Theatre, New York, 1958. Member: Drama Advisory Panel, International Exchange Programme of the American National Theatre and Academy, 1954. Recipient: Peace Medal, 1964; Emmy Award. Honorary degrees: New York University; Carroll College, Waukesha, Wisconsin; Dartmouth College, Hanover, New Hampshire; Beloit College, Wisconsin; Emerson College; Yale University, New Haven, Connecticut; University of Wisconsin. Died 3 August 1977. Lynn Fontanne born Lillie Louise Fontanne in Woodford, Essex, 6 December 1887. Educated at schools in London; studied for the stage under Ellen Terry. Married Alfred Lunt in 1922. London debut, in pantomime at the Theatre Royal, Drury Lane, 1905; New York debut, 1910; returned to USA, joining Laurette Taylor's company, 1916; joined Theatre Guild, New York, and formed stage partnership with Lunt, 1924. Recipient: American Academy of Arts and Letters medal for diction, 1935. Honorary degrees: Russell Sage College, Troy, New York, 1950; New York University; Carroll College, Waukesha, Wisconsin; Yale University, New Haven, Connecticut; Dartmouth College, Hanover, New Hampshire; Beloit College, Wisconsin; Emerson College; University of Wisconsin. Died in Genesee Depot, Wisconsin, 30 July 1983.

Roles

Alfred Lunt:
1912	The Sherriff in *The Aviator* (Montgomery), Castle Square Theatre, Boston, Massachusetts.
1913	William in *Believe Me, Xantippe* (Ballard), Castle Square Theatre, Boston, Massachusetts.
1914–15	Alfred Courtland Redlaw in *Beverly's Balance* (Kester), tour.
	Colonel J. N. Smith in *Green Stockings* (Mason), tour.
	Orlando in *As You Like It* (Shakespeare), tour.
1915	John Belden in *Her Husband's Wife* (Thomas), tour.
	Role in *Iphigenia in Tauris* (Euripides), Greek Theatre, Berkeley, California.
	Role in *Electra* (Sophocles), Greek Theatre, Berkeley, California.
	Role in *Medea* (Sophocles), Greek Theatre, Berkeley, California.
1916	Jaques in *As You Like It* (Shakespeare), Municipal Open Air Theatre, St Louis, Missouri.
	Fred Fowler in *Ashes* (Fendall), Orpheum Theatre, San Francisco, California.
	Eric Huntsdowne in *The Eleventh Hour* (Wolfe), tour.
1917	Trillo in *The Pirate* (Fulda, translated by Parker), Pabst Theatre, Milwaukee, Wisconsin.
	Claude Estabrook in *Romance and Arabella* (Hurlbut), Harris Theatre, New York.
1918	George Tewksbury Reynolds III in *The Country Cousin* (Tarkington and Street), tour.
1919	Clarence in *Clarence* (Tarkington), Hudson Theatre, New York; tour, 1920–21.
1921	Ames in *The Intimate Strangers* (Tarkington), Henry Miller Theatre, New York.
1922	Count Alexandre de Lussac in *Banco* (Savoir, adapted by Kummer), Ritz Theatre, New York.
1923	Charles II in *Sweet Nell of Old Drury* (Kester), 48th Street Theatre, New York.
	David Peel in *Robert E. Lee* (Drinkwater), Ritz Theatre, New York.

1924   Tom Prior in *Outward Bound* (Vane), Ritz Theatre, New York.

The Actor in *The Guardsman* (Molnár), Garrick Theatre, New York; tour, 1927.

1925   Bluntschli in *Arms and the Man* (G. B. Shaw), Guild Theatre, New York.

1926   Juvan in *Goat Song* (Werfel), Guild Theatre, New York.

Mr Dermott in *At Mrs Beam's* (Munro), Guild Theatre, New York.

Maximilian in *Juarez and Maximilian* (Werfel), Guild Theatre, New York.

Babe Callahan in *Ned McCobb's Daughter* (Howard), John Golden Theatre, New York.

1927   Dmitri in *The Brothers Karamazov* (Dostoevsky, adapted by Copeau and Coué), Guild Theatre, New York.

Clark Storey in *The Second Man* (Behrman), Guild Theatre, New York, and tour.

Henry Higgins in *Pygmalion* (G. B. Shaw), Studebaker Theatre, Chicago, Illinois.

Louis Dubedat in *The Doctor's Dilemma* (G. B. Shaw), Studebaker Theatre, Chicago, Illinois, and Guild Theatre, New York.

1928   Marco Polo in *Marco Millions* (O'Neill), Guild Theatre, New York.

Mosca in *Volpone* (Zweig, adapted from Jonson), Guild Theatre, New York.

Albert von Eckhardt in *Caprice* (Sil-Vara), Guild Theatre, New York; St James's Theatre, London, 1929.

1929   Raphael Lord in *Meteor* (Behrman), Guild Theatre, New York.

1930   Essex in *Elizabeth, the Queen* (M. Anderson), Martin Beck Theatre, New York.

1931   Rudolph Maximillian von Hapsburg in *Reunion in Vienna* (Sherwood), Martin Beck Theatre, New York; tour, 1932; Lyric Theatre, London, 1934, also directed.

1933   Otto in *Design for Living* (Coward), Hanna Theatre, Cleveland, and Ethel Barrymore Theatre, New York.

1934   Stefan in *Point Valaine* (Coward), Colonial Theatre, Boston, Massachusetts; Ethel Barrymore Theatre, New York, 1935.

1935   Petruchio in *The Taming of the Shrew* (Shakespeare), tour; Alvin Theatre, New York, 1940.

Harry Van in *Idiot's Delight* (Sherwood), Nixon Theatre, Pittsburgh, Pennsylvania, tour, and Shubert Theatre, New York; tour, 1938–39.

1937   Jupiter in *Amphitryon 38* (Giraudoux, adapted by Behrman), Ford's Theatre, Baltimore, tour, and Shubert Theatre, New York; Lyric Theatre, London, 1938; tour, 1938–39.

1938   Trigorin in *The Seagull* (Chekhov, adapted by Young), Shubert Theatre, New York; tour, 1938–39.

1940   Kaarlo Valkonen in *There Shall Be No Night* (Sherwood), Alvin Theatre, New York, and tour; also directed.

1942   Serafin in *The Pirate* (Behrman, adapted from Fulda), Martin Beck Theatre, New York; also co-directed.

1943   Karilo Valchos in *There Shall Be No Night* (Sherwood, revised version), Court Theatre, Liverpool, and Aldwych Theatre, London; also directed.

1944   Sir John Fletcher in *Love in Idleness/O Mistress Mine* (Rattigan), Lyric Theatre, London; European tour, 1945; Town House Theatre, Toledo, Ohio, 1945–46; Empire Theatre, New York, 1946; tour, 1947–49; also directed.

1949   Thomas Chanler in *I Know My Love* (Behrman, adapted from Achard's *Auprès de ma Blonde*), Shubert Theatre, New York; tour, 1950–51; also directed.

1951   Walk-on role in *Cosi fan Tutte* (Mozart), Metropolitan Opera House, New York; also directed.

1952   Axel Diensen in *Quadrille* (Coward), Opera House, Manchester, and Phoenix Theatre, London; Colonial Theatre, Boston, Massachusetts, and Coronet Theatre, New York, 1954.

1955   Rudi Sebastian in *The Great Sebastians* (Lindsay and Crouse), Playhouse Theatre, Wilmington, Delaware; ANTA Theatre, New York, 1956; tour, 1956–57.

1957   Anton Schill in *Time and Again/The Visit* (Dürrenmatt), British tour; Lunt-Fontanne Theatre, New York, 1958; US tour, 1959–60; Royalty Theatre, London, 1960.

Also directed:

1941   *Candle in the Wind* (M. Anderson), Shubert Theatre, New York.

1954   *Ondine* (Giraudoux, adapted by Valancey), 46th Street Theatre, New York.

1961   *First Love*, Morosco Theatre, New York.

1966   *La Traviata* (Verdi), Lincoln Centre, New York.

Lynn Fontanne:

1905   Chorus girl in *Cinderella* (Burnand, Wood and Collins), Theatre Royal, Drury Lane, London.

1906   Walk-on role in *The Bond of Ninon* (Sutro), Savoy Theatre, London.

1907   Walk-on role in *Monsieur Beaucaire* (Tarkington), Lyric Theatre, London.

1909   Rose Carlisle in *Lady Frederick* (Maugham), British tour.

Joyce in *The Peacemaker* (Bryant), British tour.

Role in *Where Children Rule* (Blow and Hoare), Garrick Theatre, London.

1910   Harriet Budgeon in *Mr Preedy and the Countess* (Carton), British, Canadian and US tours.

Lady Mulberry in *Billy's Bargain* (Lascelles), Garrick Theatre, London.

1911   Gwendolyn in *The Young Lady of Seventeen* (Brookfield), Criterion Theatre, London, and Vaudeville Theatre, London.

1911–12   Mrs Gerrard in *A Storm in a Tea-Shop* (Hilliard), Vaudeville Theatre, London.

1913   Gertrude Rhead in *Milestones* (Bennett and Knoblock), British tour; Royalty Theatre, London, 1914.

1914   Liza and Mrs Collisson in *My Lady's Dress* (Knoblock), Royalty Theatre, London.

1915   Nurse in *Searchlights* (Vachell), Savoy Theatre, London.

The Governor's sister in *The Terrorist* (Irving), Playhouse Theatre, London.

The Maid in *A War Committee* (Knoblock), Haymarket Theatre, London.

Ada Pilbeam in *How to Get On* (Knoblock), Victoria Palace Theatre, London.

A Pleiade in *The Starlight Express* (Blackwood and Pearn), Kingsway Theatre, London.

1916   Winifred in *The Wooing of Eve* (Manners), Lyceum Theatre, Rochester, New York; Liberty Theatre, New York, 1917.

Olive Hood in *The Harp of Life* (Manners), Globe Theatre, New York.

1917   'Princess' Lizzie in *Out There* (Manners), Globe Theatre, New York.

Miss Perkins in *Happiness* (Manners), Criterion Theatre, New York.

1918   Bianca in *The Taming of the Shrew* (Shakespeare), Lyric Theatre, New York.

Nerissa in *The Merchant of Venice* (Shakespeare), Lyric Theatre, New York.

Mrs Rockingham in *A Pair of Petticoats* (Harcourt), 44th Street Theatre, New York.

Mrs Glendinning in *Someone in the House* (Evans, Percival and Kaufman), Knickerbocker Theatre, New York.

1919   Mary Darling Furlong in *A Young Man's Fancy* (MacIntyre), National Theatre, Washington D.C.

1920   Anna Christophersen in *Chris* (O'Neill), Broad Street Theatre, Philadelphia, Pennsylvania.

Zephyr in *One Night in Rome* (Manners), Garrick Theatre, London.

1921   Dulcinea in *Dulcy* (Kaufman and Connelly), Cort Theatre, Chicago, Illinois, and Frazee Theatre, New York.

1923   Lady Castlemaine in *Sweet Nell of Old Drury* (Kester), 48th Street Theatre, New York.

Ann Jordan in *In Love with Love* (Lawrence), Ritz Theatre, New York.

1924   The Actress in *The Guardsman* (Molnár), Garrick Theatre, New York; tour, 1927.

1925   Raina in *Arms and the Man* (G. B. Shaw), Guild Theatre, New York.

1926   Stanja in *Goat Song* (Werfel), Guild Theatre, New York.

Laura in *At Mrs Beam's* (Munro), Guild Theatre, New York.

Eliza Doolittle in *Pygmalion* (G. B. Shaw), Guild Theatre, New York; tour, 1927.

1927   Gruschenka in *The Brothers Karamazov* (Dostoevsky, adapted by Copeau and Coué), Guild Theatre, New York.

Mrs Kendall Frayne in *The Second Man* (Behrman), Guild Theatre, New York, and tour.

Jennifer Dubedat in *The Doctor's Dilemma* (G. B. Shaw), Studebaker Theatre, Chicago, Illinois, and Guild Theatre, New York.

1928   Nina Leeds in *Strange Interlude* (O'Neill), John Golden Theatre, New York.

Ilsa von Ilsen in *Caprice* (Sil-Vara), Guild Theatre, New York; St James's Theatre, London, 1929.

1929   Ann Carr in *Meteor* (Behrman), Guild Theatre, New York.

1930   Elizabeth in *Elizabeth, the Queen* (M. Anderson), Martin Beck Theatre, New York.

1931   Elena in *Reunion in Vienna* (Sherwood), Martin Beck Theatre, New York; US tour, 1932; Lyric Theatre, London, 1934.

1933   Gilda in *Design for Living* (Coward), Hanna Theatre, Cleveland, Ohio, and Ethel Barrymore Theatre, New York.

1934–35 Linda Valaine in *Point Valaine* (Coward), Colonial Theatre, Boston, Massachusetts, and Ethel Barrymore Theatre, New York.

1935   Katherine in *The Taming of the Shrew* (Shakespeare), Nixon Theatre, Pittsburgh, Pennsylvania, and Guild Theatre, New York; US tour, 1936; Alvin Theatre, New York, 1940.

1936   Irene in *Idiot's Delight* (Sherwood), Nixon Theatre, Pittsburgh, Pennsylvania, and Shubert Theatre, New York; US tour, 1938–39.

1937   Alkmena in *Amphitryon 38* (Giraudoux, adapted by Behrman), Ford's Theatre, Baltimore, tour, and Shubert Theatre, New York; Lyric Theatre, London, 1938; US tour, 1938–39.

1938   Irina Arkadina in *The Seagull* (Chekhov, adapted by Young), Shubert Theatre, New York; US tour, 1938–39.

1940   Miranda Valkonen in *There Shall Be No Night* (Sherwood), Alvin Theatre, New York, and US tour.

1942   Manuela in *The Pirate* (Behrman, adapted from Fulda), Martin Beck Theatre, New York.

1943   Miranda Vlachos in *There Shall Be No Night* (Sherwood, revised version), Court Theatre, Liverpool, and Aldwych Theatre, London.

1944   Olivia Brown in *Love in Idleness/O Mistress Mine* (Rattigan), Lyric Theatre, London; European tour, 1945; Town House Theatre, Toledo, Ohio, 1945–46; Empire Theatre, New York, 1946; US tour, 1947–49.

1949   Emily Chanler in *I Know My Love* (Behrman, adapted from Achard's *Auprès de ma Blonde*), Shubert Theatre, New York; US tour, 1950–51.

1952   Serena in *Quadrille* (Coward), Opera House, Manchester, and Phoenix Theatre, London; Colonial Theatre, Boston, Massachusetts, and Coronet Theatre, New York, 1954.

1955   Essie Sebastian in *The Great Sebastians* (Lindsay and Crouse), Playhouse Theatre, Wilmington, Delaware; ANTA Theatre, New York, 1956; US tour, 1956–57.

1957   Claire Zachanassian in *Time and Again/The Visit* (Dürrenmatt), British tour; Lunt-Fontanne Theatre, New York, 1958; US tour, 1959–60; Royalty Theatre, London, 1960.

Films

Alfred Lunt:
The Ragged Edge, 1923; *Backbone*, 1923; *Second Youth*, 1924; *The Guardsman*, 1931; *Stage Door Canteen*, 1943.

Lynn Fontanne:
Second Youth, 1924; *The Guardsman*, 1931; *Stage Door Canteen*, 1943.

Television

Alfred Lunt:
The Great Sebastians, 1957; *The Old Lady Shows Her Medals*, 1963.

Lynn Fontanne:
The Great Sebastians, 1957.

*

Bibliography

Books:
George Freedley, *The Lunts*, London, 1957.
Jared Brown, *The Fabulous Lunts*, New York, 1988.

* * *

Alfred Lunt and Lynn Fontanne, US actor and English actress, hated to be called a team, but were always considered to be two halves of a whole rather than two wholes who co-operated. Although clearly a metaphysical speculation, their careers apart could hardly have been expected to take the kind of meteoric path that their joint efforts produced. Once their joint career was on its way, they were well nigh inseparable and are hardly ever referred to apart.

They were first noticed as individuals: Lunt in Booth Tarkington's *Clarence* in 1919 and Fontanne in George S. Kaufman and Marc Connelly's *Dulcy* in 1921. While they were actors of some means and charisma, they were considered eccentrics, not likely to have enduring stage careers in an age when glamour, rather than idiosyncracy, was paramount. Their joint career started two years after their marriage, in the 1924 production of Ferenc Molnár's *The Guardsman* with the Theatre Guild, formed to present new plays by US writers, in New York. For the next 30 years they appeared almost exclusively together and almost exclusively for the Guild — indeed, their stars rose as did the Guild's. It was perhaps their lustre that made the Theatre Guild a popular success and allowed it to produce many of its more experimental and less popular plays. In one of their rare appearances apart they both played in productions of O'Neill plays, she in *Strange Interlude* and he in *Marco Millions*. The Lunts' specialty, however, was light comedy, a craft they honed to razor perfection.

Fontanne was English, having trained with Ellen Terry, who put her first into pantomime. Lunt, on the other hand, was a midwestern American, having been reared on a farm in Wisconsin. He had knocked about as a small-time repertory player and vaudevillian and their discrete breaks into US show business were considered flukes and unlikely to bear further fruit. As their joint career developed, their corporate creativity grew as well as their individual talents.

Fontanne was, at heart, a technician. She put enormous emphasis on voice and vocal control, and, indeed, conceived her parts as surface performances rather than as inward, psychological excursions. Her English background gave her a sparkling technique upon which she built her dazzling characterizations. She was a master of gesture, and her hands told much about the personality of the character she was portraying. She did not attempt to probe the psychology of her character until she had worked on the part technically, as an actress. For all her emphasis on craft, however, she was rarely faulted for lacking depth. In her maturity, it was only her interpretation of Arkadina in Chekhov's *The Seagull* that belied her working methods. She was almost universally praised for capturing and stylizing the inner life of her characters.

Lunt, on the other hand, saw himself as a servant of the playwright. His characterizations were conceived totally in terms of the play, and the action of the character derived from the text. His upbringing on the stage of the US popular entertainment industry gave him an appreciation for the possibilities of improvisation, a working method he prized. His innate intelligence made him analytical and a bit of a scholar. Thus, his rehearsal method was initially interpretive rather than creative. His method of building his character was assemblage: he observed persons whom he thought exemplified aspects of his character and tried to incorporate their behaviour patterns into a whole. While his method was not the opposite of his wife's, it was very different.

Together, they evolved a sort of synergy, Lunt questioning Fontanne about the motivation behind a theatrical device she wanted to use and Fontanne suggesting ways that a psychological insight Lunt had could be translated into a theatrically viable gesture. Their joint technique was based on a tight, slight overlapping of their lines, so that they seemed to be constantly answering each other before the other was finished talking. This skill solidified their reputation as consummate interpreters of light comedy.

As their careers progressed their skill as performers began to overshadow the vehicles they chose to appear in. It became axiomatic that they were being wasted in whatever play they were currently performing — Coward's *Quadrille*, for example. Their comic style was unmistakable and so seemingly effortless that their audiences began to take their skill for granted.

Late in their careers they gave the US premiere of Freidrich Dürrenmatt's *The Visit*, directed by Peter Brook. Their performances were final testaments to their skills, for they revelled in being really directed and were universally praised for their ensemble work. Fontanne used her reputation as a glittering comedienne to bring irony to her character, and Lunt was proclaimed a master of wordless eloquence. Their careers, thus, ended with a newfound respect for their prowess. They are now remembered as an acting team whose diligent work added considerably to the theatre of their time.

—David Payne-Carter

LYUBIMOV, Yuri (Petrovich). Soviet director and actor. Born in Yaroslavl, Russia, 30 September 1917. Trained for the stage at the Second Moscow Art Theatre Studio, until 1936, and at the Vakhtangov Theatre School, Moscow, until 1940. Married seven times. After army service, 1940-47, joined the Vakhtangov Theatre; taught at the Shchukin Theatre Institute, 1953-63; director, Taganka Theatre, 1964-84; permitted to take Taganka company on foreign tours, 1977; dismissed as director of the Taganka and stripped of Soviet citizenship for criticising Soviet restrictions on the arts while in England, 1983; subsequently worked in Europe and the USA, taking Israeli citizenship in 1984, but returned to the Soviet Union, 1987; Soviet citizenship restored and reappointed director of the Taganka Theatre, 1989; gave up post at the Taganka, 1993. Recipient: State Prizes, 1952. People's Artist of Russia, 1992.

Productions

As actor:
1947-53	Oleg Koshevoy in *Molodaya gvardiya* [The Young Guard] (Fadayev), Vakhtangov Theatre, Moscow.
	Shubin in *Nakanune* [On the Eve] (Turgenev), Vakhtangov Theatre, Moscow.
	Chris in *All My Sons* (Miller), Vakhtangov Theatre, Moscow.
	Benedict in *Much Ado About Nothing* (Shakespeare), Vakhtangov Theatre, Moscow.
1951	Tjatin in *Yegor Bulychov i drugiye* [Yegor Bulychov and others] (Gorky), Vakhtangov Theatre, Moscow.
	Mozart in *Mozart i Salieri* [Mozart and Salieri] (Pushkin), Vakhtangov Theatre, Moscow.

As director:
1963	Der gute Mensch von Sezuan (Brecht), Vakhtangov Theatre, Moscow.
1965	*Ten Days That Shook the World* (Reed), Taganka Theatre, Moscow.
	Antiworlds (Voznesensky), Taganka Theatre, Moscow.
	Under the Skin of the Statue of Liberty (Yevtushenko), Taganka Theatre, Moscow.
	Leben des Galilei (Brecht), Taganka Theatre, Moscow.
	Pugachev (Jessenin), Taganka Theatre, Moscow.
	Mat [The Mother] (Gorky), Taganka Theatre, Moscow.
1967	*Now, Listen!* (Mayakovsky), Taganka Theatre, Moscow.
1969	*Tartuffe* (Molière), Taganka Theatre, Moscow.
	Rush Hour (Stavinsky), Taganka Theatre, Moscow.

1971	*What Is to Be Done?* (Chernyshevsky), Taganka Theatre, Moscow.
1972	*The Dawns Are Silent Here* (Vassiliev), Taganka Theatre, Moscow.
1973	*Comrade, Believe!* (Zelikovskaya and Lyubimov), Taganka Theatre, Moscow.
1974	*The Wooden Horse* (Abramov), Taganka Theatre, Moscow.
	Hamlet (Shakespeare), Taganka Theatre, Moscow.
1975	*Al gran sole carico d'amore* (Nono), La Scala, Milan.
1976	*The Exchange* (Trifonov), Taganka Theatre, Moscow.
1977	*Master i Margarita* [The Master and Margarita] (Bulgakov), Taganka Theatre, Moscow.
1978	*The Inspector's Recounting*, Taganka Theatre, Moscow.
1980	*Death of a Poet (Vladimir Vysotsky)* (compilation from Vysotsky), Taganka Theatre, Moscow.
	The House on the Embankment, Taganka Theatre, Moscow.
1981	*Boris Godunov* (Mussorgsky), La Scala, Milan.
1981-89	*Rigoletto* (Verdi), Florence.
	Eugene Onegin (Tchaikovsky), Bonn.
	Lady Macbeth of Mtsensk (Shostakovitch), Munich and London.
1983	*Prestupleniye i nakazaniye* [Crime and Punishment] (Dostoevsky), Taganka Theatre, Moscow.
1985	*Besy* [The Possessed] (Dostoevsky), Théâtre de l'Europe, Paris, and London.
1987	*Boris Godunov* (Pushkin), Taganka Theatre, Moscow.
1989	*Zhivoy* [The Survivor] (Mozhaev), Taganka Theatre, Moscow.
	Hamlet (Shakespeare), London.
1990	*Self-Murderer*, Taganka Theatre, Moscow.
1992	*Electra* (Sophocles), Taganka Theatre, Moscow, and Athens.

Other productions include: *Jenufa* (Janácek); *Picovaya dama* [The Queen of Spades] (Tchaikovsky); *St Matthew Passion* (Bach), all since 1983.

Films

As actor:
Robinson Crusoe.

Publications

The Sacred Fire (autobiography).

*

Yuri Lyubimov, center, being applauded by the cast following the opening performance of *Under the Skin of the Statue of Liberty,* directed by Lyubimov (1972).

Bibliography

Books:
Birgit Beumers, *Yuri Lyubimov at the Taganka Theatre and in Exile (1964–89),* thesis, Oxford, 1991.

* * *

Yuri Lyubimov is the 'enfant terrible' of postwar Soviet theatre directors, whose relationships with social and critical authority have tended, at best, to be ascerbic. His theatrical life has been spent either offending the Soviet state or, latterly, scandalising the European bourgeoisie. He is also someone like the child in the nursery rhyme, who is usually 'very, very good' but can, on occasion, be 'horrid', especially when over-reliant on repetitive theatrical devices or carried away by formal aspects of a production at the expense of human considerations. This latter tendency has been especially marked in his work outside the Soviet Union, where the formal conception has often served to mask a hollowness, or weakness, in the actors' contribution to the production as a whole.

There is little doubt that Lyubimov is one of the most interesting Soviet directors to have emerged since Meyerhold, with whom he shares a certain biographical resemblance. Like his great predecessor, Lyubimov is something of a director-autocrat, whose approach has brought him into conflict with authority and with his fellow-workers.

The major difference has been that, where Meyerhold's work was made to suffer from society's increasing drift towards Stalinist absolutism, Lyubimov's work has been positively enabled by the emergence of the Soviet state from under the Stalinist cloud. Meyerhold would have gone down in history as a great director even without the enabling fact of the Russian Revolution. Had it not been for the changes in the political and cultural climate under Khruschev in the 1960's, it is doubtful whether Lyubimov would have made any lasting impact on Soviet theatrical history. A crucial difference between Lyubimov and Meyerhold is, therefore, that whereas the latter was a great director in his own right, Lyubimov was made into a great director by his times. His significance lies in his being the means whereby a great theatre came into existence. Without the Taganka Theatre Lyubimov would, in all probability, have been little more than a footnote in theatre history; together with the Taganka Theatre, he has written one of the finest pages in the annals, not just of Soviet theatre, but of world theatre during the second half of the 20th century.

At the end of the 1960's and during the 1970's, on the tiny stage of the former Theatre of Drama and Comedy, Lyubimov and his company accomplished work of truly Wagnerian scope. They gave meaning to the idea of a 'gesamtkunstwerk', staging productions in which every aspect fused in a powerful artistic synthesis that moved and excited both Soviet and international audiences. The success of the productions during what is now viewed, ironically, as a period of political 'stagnation', was very much the result of a collective effort in which the talented and youthful company assembled by Lyubimov combined with designers and composers of outstanding ability. If Lyubimov was the great synthesizer, then crucial components of this synthesis were the acting of Vladimir Vysotsky and Alla Demidova and the lighting of K. Panshin. In this latter respect, the Taganka Theatre may be said to have revolutionised lighting design in the Soviet theatre (where it has never been a strong point), endowing light with a subtlety more usually associated with impressionist painting or a dramatic chiaroscuro redolent of the expressionists. Nowhere was this impressionist/pointillist quality more memorable than in the effect of dappled sunlight achieved in *The Dawns Are Silent Here* or in the effect of expressionist 'grotesquerie' explored to more startling effect in *Ten Days That Shook the World* or in *Crime and Punishment*.

The theatre's reputation is a 'formalist' one in the best sense in so far as a basic tenet of Russian Formalist theory was concerned — the so-called process of 'baring the device' ('obnazhenie priyoma'). Every Lyubimov production appears to take as its starting point a bare stage and the introduction onto that stage of a central 'device', which is the imaginative lynchpin of the production. In *Pugachev* it was a length of heavy convict chain the sound of which being thrown down, violently, in a gesture of revolt reverberated throughout the production. In the production devoted to Mayakovsky, *Now, Listen!*, it was a number of child's alphabet blocks, the basic units of a poet's vocabulary, large enough to stand on and arranged in various vertical and horizontal patterns. In *Tartuffe*, a production performed throughout to musical accompaniment, the central device was a series of full-length screens made of rubber slats on which portraits in period costume were painted and through which the actors could thrust a head, an arm or a leg, or their entire bodies. In *Rush Hour*, the device was a huge pendulum suspended from a pivot above the stage, the base of which formed a clock with Roman numerals that converted into seats on which the actors either sat or swung. In *The Dawns Are Silent Here*, the central device consisted of a series of slatted boards that could be converted into an army lorry, a bathhouse or a forest. In *Hamlet* it was a large woven curtain, filling the proscenium opening and capable of traversing the stage, or swivelling on a central pivot — a symbol of a Fate that, finally, sweeps everyone from the stage whilst reminding the audience of the final curtain call that all have to take. In *The Master and Margarita*, which can be read as Lyubimov's 'confessional' work, a number of these earlier

devices were deliberately reintroduced as a form of postmodern reflection on the devices of the play's own means of production. In *Crime and Punishment*, the central device was the door to the old woman's flat, which appeared to move independently about the stage accompanying the nightmare of Raskolnikov's waking dream. In *Boris Godunov*, the central device was simply a wooden plank and the staff of Tsarist office, the equivalent of a weighty javelin that, when thrown or thrust into the plank or into the stage floor, pierced it with a sickening, authoritarian force.

Of the 40 or so productions staged by Lyubimov at the Taganka between 1964 and 1982, not all were of the standard attained by those mentioned above. Some were removed from the repertoire because Lyubimov himself was not happy with them; others were affected by questions of 'social command', or by the intervention of the censor and, consequently, needed to be modified or adapted. Others were abandoned altogether or called off at the last minute — such was the fate of Erdman's *The Suicide*, Mozhaev's *The Survivor*, Pushkin's *Boris Godunov* and, most crucially, as far as it affected Lyubimov's decision to leave the Soviet Union, the memorial production to Vladimir Vysotsky. This last was permitted two performances a year under Andropov, then banned outright under Chernenko. The years abroad were spent largely staging operatic productions, the most controversial of which were the aborted version of *The Queen of Spades* at the Paris Opera and a *Rigoletto* in Florence that concluded to whistles and catcalls from the audience. Other productions — for example of *Jenufa* and Bach's *St Matthew Passion* — have revealed the surprising fact that Lyubimov, a Party member of some 30 years standing, is a very religious person; a discovery that throws retrospective light on his productions of *The Master and Margarita* as well as *Hamlet*, which he interpreted as a Christian tragedy.

What has been missing of late in Lyubimov's productions is the spirit that animated the Taganka during the first 10 years of its existence. The production of *The Survivor*, premiered in 1989 following Lyubimov's return to the Soviet Union, was, it has to be assumed, merely a pale carbon copy of the banned original. However, nobody who saw this production and can, as a result, compare its impact with the effects produced by the great productions of the earlier period, will ever forget emerging from the tiny theatre off Taganka Square feeling that this is what theatre is all about and that whoever was responsible for creating such a theatre has more than a slight claim to a lasting place in theatre history.

—Nick Worrall

MACKLIN, Charles. Irish actor-manager and playwright. Born Charles MacLaughlin (McLaughlin or Melaghlin) in the parish of Culdaff, County Donegal, Ireland, c.1697. Educated by a Mr Nicholson at Island Bridge, near Dublin, and by his patroness Mrs Pilkington before running away to London. Married 1) actress Ann Grace in 1739 (died 1758), one daughter and one son; 2) Elizabeth Jones in 1759. Strolling player in the provinces, initially at Bristol, c.1717; actor, Lincoln's Inn Fields Theatre, from 1725; actor, Theatre Royal, Drury Lane, from 1733; tried and acquitted of murder of fellow-actor Thomas Hallam in argument over a wig, 1735; acclaimed the finest Shylock of his generation, 1741; clashed with David Garrick over strike against Drury Lane management, after which he was dismissed, 1743; led company at the Haymarket Theatre until re-engagement at Drury Lane, 1744; visited Dublin, 1748–50; actor, Covent Garden, 1750–52; retired from stage to run coffee-house and school of oratory, 1753; forced to return to theatre by bankruptcy, 1759; retired from stage with failing memory at the age of 90, 1789. Died in London, 11 July 1797.

Principal roles

c.1717–25 Richmond in *Richard III* (Shakespeare), provinces.
c.1725 Alcander in *Oedipus* (Dryden and Lee), Lincoln's Inn Fields Theatre, London.
1730 Sir Charles Freeman in *The Beaux' Stratagem* (Farquhar), Harper's Booth, Southwark, London.
  Porer and Brazencourt in *The Coffee-house Politician* (Fielding), Lincoln's Inn Fields Theatre, London.
1733 Captain Brazen in *The Recruiting Officer* (Farquhar), Theatre Royal, Drury Lane, London.
1733–34 Marplot in *The Busy Body* (Centlivre), Theatre Royal, Drury Lane, London.
  Clodio in *Love Makes a Man* (Cibber), Theatre Royal, Drury Lane, London.
  Teague in *The Committee* (Howard), Theatre Royal, Drury Lane, London.
  Brass in *The Confederacy* (Vanbrugh), Theatre Royal, Drury Lane, London.
  Lord Lace in *The Lottery* (Fielding), Theatre Royal, Drury Lane, London.
  The Marquis in *The Country House* (Vanbrugh), Theatre Royal, Drury Lane, London.

  Lord Foppington in *The Careless Husband* (Cibber), Theatre Royal, Drury Lane, London.
  Colonel Bluff in *The Intriguing Chambermaid* (Fielding), Theatre Royal, Drury Lane, London.
1734 Squire Badger in *Don Quixote in England* (Fielding) Haymarket Theatre, London.
  Poins in *Henry IV, parts 1 and 2* (Shakespeare), Theatre Royal, Drury Lane, London.
  Manly in *Cure for a Scold* (Worsdale, adapted from Shakespeare's *The Taming of the Shrew*), Theatre Royal, Drury Lane, London.
1734–48 Snip in *The Merry Cobbler* (Coffey), Theatre Royal, Drury Lane, London.
  Captain Bragg in *The Eunuch; or, The Darby Captain* (Cooke, adapted from Terence), Theatre Royal, Drury Lane, London.
  Zorobabel in *Miss Lucy in Town* (Fielding), Theatre Royal, Drury Lane, London.
  Faddle in *The Foundling* (Moore), Theatre Royal, Drury Lane, London.
  Abel in *The Committee* (Howard), Theatre Royal, Drury Lane, London.
  Sancho in *Love Makes a Man* (Cibber), Theatre Royal, Drury Lane, London.
  Razor in *The Provoked Wife* (Vanbrugh), Theatre Royal, Drury Lane, London.
  Jerry Blackacre in *The Plain Dealer* (Bickerstaff), Theatre Royal, Drury Lane, London.
  Osric in *Hamlet* (Shakespeare), Theatre Royal, Drury Lane, London.
  Jeremy and Ben in *Love for Love* (Congreve), Theatre Royal, Drury Lane, London.
  Sir Hugh Evans in *The Merry Wives of Windsor* (Shakespeare), Theatre Royal, Drury Lane, London.
  Lord Foppington in *The Relapse* (Vanbrugh), Theatre Royal, Drury Lane, London.
  Tattle in *Love for Love* (Congreve), Theatre Royal, Drury Lane, London.
  Old Mirabel in *The Way of the World* (Congreve), Theatre Royal, Drury Lane, London.
  Sir Fopling Flutter in *The Man of Mode* (Etherege), Theatre Royal, Drury Lane, London.
  Sir William Belford in *The Squire of Alsatia* (Shadwell), Theatre Royal, Drury Lane, London.

Trincalo in *The Tempest* (Dryden), Theatre Royal, Drury Lane, London.

Fondlewife in *The Old Bachelor* (Congreve), Theatre Royal, Drury Lane, London.

Sir Novelty Fashion in *Love's Last Shift* (Cibber), Theatre Royal, Drury Lane, London.

Malvolio in *Twelfth Night* (Shakespeare), Theatre Royal, Drury Lane, London.

Touchstone in *As You Like It* (Shakespeare), Theatre Royal, Drury Lane, London.

Corvino in *The Fox* (adapted from Jonson's *Volpone*), Theatre Royal, Drury Lane, London.

Sir Paul Plyant in *The Double-Dealer* (Congreve), Theatre Royal, Drury Lane, London.

Stephano in *The Tempest* (Shakespeare), Theatre Royal, Drury Lane, London.

Lucio in *Measure for Measure* (Shakespeare), Theatre Royal, Drury Lane, London.

Fluellen in *Henry V* (Shakespeare), Theatre Royal, Drury Lane, London.

1736   Peachum in *The Beggar's Opera* (Gay), Theatre Royal, Drury Lane, London.

1741   Shylock in *The Merchant of Venice* (Shakespeare), Theatre Royal, Drury Lane, London.

Drunken Man in *Lethe* (Garrick), Theatre Royal, Drury Lane, London.

1744   Iago in *Othello* (Shakespeare), Haymarket Theatre, London.

Lovelace in *The Relapse* (Vanbrugh), Haymarket Theatre, London.

The Ghost in *Hamlet* (Shakespeare), Haymarket Theatre, London.

1746   Huntley in *King Henry VII; or, The Popish Imposter* (Macklin), Theatre Royal, Drury Lane, London.

1747   Gravedigger in *Hamlet* (Shakespeare), Theatre Royal, Drury Lane, London.

1750–52   Lovegold in *The Miser* (Fielding), Covent Garden, London.

Mercutio in *Romeo and Juliet* (Shakespeare), Covent Garden, London.

Polonius in *Hamlet* (Shakespeare), Covent Garden, London.

Vellum in *The Drummer* (Addison), Covent Garden, London.

Sir Olive Cockwood in *She Would and She Would Not* (Cibber), Covent Garden, London.

Sir Barnaby Brittle in *The Amorous Widow* (Betterton), Covent Garden, London.

Lopez in *The Mistake* (Vanbrugh), Covent Garden, London.

Mad Englishman in *The Pilgrim* (Vanbrugh), Covent Garden, London.

Renault in *Venice Preserved* (Otway), Covent Garden, London.

Buck in *Englishman in Paris* (Foote), Covent Garden, London.

1753   Sir Gilbert Wrangle in *The Refusal* (Cibber), Theatre Royal, Drury Lane, London.

1759   Sir Archy McSarcasm in *Love á la Mode* (Macklin), Theatre Royal, Drury Lane, London.

Charles Macklin

1761   Lord Belville in *Married Libertine* (Macklin), Covent Garden, London.

1763   Murrough O'Dogherty in *True-born Irishman* (Macklin), Smock Alley Theatre, Dublin.

1772   Macbeth in *Macbeth* (Shakespeare), Covent Garden, London.

1775–80   Richard in *Richard III* (Shakespeare), Covent Garden, London.

1781   Sir Pertinax McSycophant in *The Man of the World* (Macklin), Covent Garden, London.

Publications

The Case of Charles Macklin, Comedian (broadside), 1743; *Mr Macklin's Reply to Mr Garrick's Answer*, 1743; *King Henry VII; or, The Popish Imposter* (play), 1746; *A Will and no Will; or, A Bone for the Lawyers* (play), 1746; *The Suspicious Husband Criticised* (play), 1747; *The Fortune Hunters* (play), 1748; *Covent Garden Theatre; or, Pasquin turn'd Drawcansir, Censor of Great Britain* (play), 1752; *M–ckl–n's Answer to Tully*, 1755; *The Married Libertine* (play), 1761; *The True-born Irishman* (play), 1764; *The True-born Scotsman* (play), 1764; *The Whim; or, A Christmas Gambol* (play), 1764; *The Irish Fine Lady* (play), 1767; *The Man of the World* (play), 1785; *Love in a Maze* (play), 1790; *Love á la Mode* (play), 1793.

*

Bibliography

Books:

Francis A. Congreve, *Authentic Memoirs of the Late Mr Charles Macklin, Comedian*, London, 1798.

James T. Kirkman, *Memoirs of the Life of Charles Macklin*, London, 1799.

William Cooke, *Memoirs of Charles Macklin*, London, 1804.

Edmund A. Parry, *Charles Macklin*, London, 1891.

William W. Appleton, *Charles Macklin, an Actor's Life*, Harvard and Oxford, 1960.

Articles:

Esther Raushenbush, "Charles Macklin's Lost Play about Henry Fielding", *Modern Language Notes*, 51, 1936.

Bernard Barrow, "Macklin's Costume and Property Notes for the Character of Lovegold", *Theatre Notebook*, 13, 1958–59.

* * *

With the exception of David Garrick, Charles Macklin was probably the most notable of all 18th-century British actors. Had it not been for Garrick, many of the acting reforms credited to the "English Roscius" might just as easily have been credited to Macklin, the older actor. Maclin seems to have preceded Garrick in the development of the 'natural' style of performance and he may even have coached Garrick for his famous London debut as Richard III in 1741. Certainly Macklin did coach a number of other actors, among whom the actor-manager and playwright Samuel Foote was the most outstanding. Macklin even coached John Hill, the eccentric scientist and actor who published *The Actor* in 1750 and 1755, describing in a precise, scientific way Maclin's methods of actor training, which seem to have been rooted in observation and mimicry. Macklin was primarily a comic actor, but his capacity to reveal his milieu (in fundamental recognizable stereotypes with comic exaggeration) lifted him above the level of most contemporaries.

As a personality, Macklin — renowned for his recklessness as a youth — was often testy, sarcastic, strong-willed, and defensively ill-humoured. He had a passion for argument, displayed in numerous lawsuits arising from both real and imagined slights or injustices in which he was involved. Though Macklin was not always popular with fellow actors or managers during his 70 or so years on the stage, James Boswell, who knew the actor well in his later years, greatly admired Macklin for his straightforwardness, sincerity, and impatience with affectation.

After leaving Ireland for England around 1717, Macklin toured the provinces for a number of years as a strolling player. Though he was engaged at Lincoln's Inn Fields in 1725, his natural style of performance ran so counter to what he himself referred to as "the hoity-toity tone" of playing tragedy that he was released. In 1733, however, he became a member of the company at Drury Lane, performing such roles as Brazen in *The Recruiting Officer* and Teague in *The Committee*. A Green Room altercation with a minor actor named Thomas Hallam over a wig in 1735 brought about Hallam's death and Macklin was put on trial at the Old Bailey. The actor was so skilful in cross-examining witnesses to the event that, within minutes of

retiring, the jury returned to find him guilty only of manslaughter and he was branded on the hand and set free.

Macklin's great success as an actor came on 14 February 1741, when he first performed the role of Shylock in *The Merchant of Venice*. Throughout the Restoration and early 18th century the role had been played in a Jew-baiting, comic manner. Macklin's treatment, on the other hand, was serious — though still far-distant from the sympathetic martyr that Henry Irving would portray some 100 years later. Macklin's Shylock was uncompromisingly evil. George II, upon seeing Macklin's performance, could not sleep that night and suggested to Walpole that the actor be used to frighten the House of Commons. The German Georg Lichtenberg's description of Macklin's performance on seeing it some 30 years later speaks of the actor's "coarse yellow face" and "a nose generously fashioned in all three dimensions". His costume was "a long black gown, long wide trousers, and a red tricorne, after the fashion of Italian Jews". His first words — "Three thousand ducats" — were lisped "as lickerously as if he were savouring the ducats and all they would buy ... "

Despite Macklin's success as Shylock in 1741, that same year also marked the London debut of David Garrick, in whose shadow Macklin thereafter resentfully and jealously stood. At first the two actors were friends, but a bitter dispute with the management at Drury Lane in 1743 (in which Macklin believed Garrick acted without principle) brought about a rift. The dispute also brought about Macklin's exclusion from Drury Lane and seemingly Covent Garden as well. Though the two actors came eventually to tolerate one another (Garrick hired Macklin frequently during his management of Drury Lane between 1747 and 1776), Macklin in private seldom had a good word for Garrick, whose ascendancy as an actor was obvious.

It was at this point, around 1746, that Macklin began to write plays, although his earliest efforts were not particularly notable. He wrote perhaps as many as 40 plays in all, although only a handful are extant either in published form or manuscript: namely, a tragedy, a tragicomedy, two comedies, and six comic afterpieces. He made his breakthrough as a writer for the stage in 1757, with the highly successful afterpiece *Love á la Mode*, developing for himself the role of the avaricious Scotsman, Sir Archy Macsarcasm. Throughout the rest of his career, until his retirement in 1789 at the age of 90, Macklin often gained employment at various theatres both in London and Dublin by offering to perform Shylock and Sir Archy a set number of times in a given season. Because he refused to publish *Love á la Mode* until after his retirement, in order to protect his own acting vehicle, many of his lawsuits were over pirated versions of the play or pirated performances by other actors (modern copyright laws did not come into effect until the 19th century). Macklin's other great success as a playwright was *The Man of the World*, a caustic satire on political corruption, in which the author played the unprincipled Scottish member of Parliament, Sir Pertinax MacSycophant. It was considered by some one of the best plays of the century, originally performed in Dublin in 1764. Because of its political content — the criticism of corrupt Scots in Parliament — the play was denied production in London by the Licencer until 1781.

Despite his great success as an actor over nearly 70 years, Macklin died bankrupt. He was, however, accorded an official mark of respect through burial in St Paul's Cathedral.

—Robert Findlay

———

MACREADY, William Charles. British actor-manager. Born in London, 3 March 1793; son of an actor-manager. Educated at Rugby public school, Rugby, Warwickshire, until 1808. Married 1) actress Catherine Atkins in 1824 (died 1852), four sons and five daughters; 2) Cécile Louise Spencer in 1860, one son. Planned career in law but made reluctant stage debut to assist bankrupt father, Birmingham, 1810; played numerous roles in the provinces before coming to London; actor, Covent Garden, 1816–32; great success as Richard III, 1819; toured USA, 1826; saw François Talma act in Paris, 1828; manager of theatres in Bristol and Bath, 1834, Covent Garden, 1837–39, and Theatre Royal, Drury Lane, 1841–43; introduced numerous reforms at his theatres and promoted dramas of Shakespeare, Bulwer-Lytton, and others; also acted summer seasons at the Haymarket Theatre; conducted provincial tours and visited the USA, 1826, 1843, and 1848; rivalry with US actor Edwin Forrest culminated in infamous Astor Place Opera House riot, 1849; Royal Command Performance, Windsor Castle, 1850; retired, 1851. Died in Cheltenham, Gloucestershire, 27 April 1873.

Roles

1810   Romeo in *Romeo and Juliet* (Shakespeare), New Street Theatre, Birmingham.
        Norval in *Douglas* (Home), New Street Theatre, Birmingham.
        Lothair in *Adelgitha* (Lewis), New Street Theatre, Birmingham.
        Zanga in *The Revenge* (Young), New Street Theatre, Birmingham.
        George Barnwell in *George Barnwell* (Lillo), New Street Theatre, Birmingham.
        Don Felix in *The Wonder* (Centlivre), New Street Theatre, Birmingham.
        Richard in *Richard II* (Shakespeare), Newcastle.
        Mark Antony in *Antony and Cleopatra* (Shakespeare), Newcastle.
1811   Hamlet in *Hamlet* (Shakespeare), Newcastle.
1811–12 Beverley in *The Gamester* (Moore), Newcastle.
1813   Captain Plume in *The Recruiting Officer* (Farquhar), Glasgow.
        Puff in *The Critic* (Sheridan), Glasgow.
        Young Marlow in *She Stoops to Conquer* (Goldsmith), Glasgow.
        Edward IV in *The Earl of Warwick* (Francklin), Glasgow.
1814   Pierre in *Venice Preserved* (Otway), Newcastle.
        Captain Absolute in *The Rivals* (Sheridan), Newcastle.
        Sir Edward Mortimer in *The Iron Chest* (Colman the Younger), Newcastle.
        Othello in *Othello* (Shakespeare), Newcastle.

        The Stranger in *The Stranger* (Kotzebue), Newcastle.
        Mentevole in *Julia; or, The Italian Lover* (Jephson), British provinces.
1816   Orestes in *The Distresst Mother* (Philips), Covent Garden, London.
        Iago in *Othello* (Shakespeare), Covent Garden, London.
        Gambia in *The Slave* (Morton), Covent Garden, London.
        Valentio in *The Conquest of Taranto* (anon.), Covent Garden, London.
1817   Count Pescara in *The Apostate* (Sheil), Covent Garden, London.
1818   Rob Roy in *Rob Roy MacGregor* (Pocock, adapted from Scott), Covent Garden, London.
        Amurath in *Bellamira; or, The Fall of Tunis* (Sheil), Covent Garden, London.
1819   Wallenberg in *Fredolfo* (Maturin), Covent Garden, London.
        Glenalvon in *Douglas* (Home), Covent Garden, London.
        Joseph Surface in *The School for Scandal* (Sheridan), Covent Garden, London.
        Clytus in *Alexander the Great* (Lee), Covent Garden, London.
        Richard in *Richard III* (Shakespeare), Covent Garden, London.
        Coriolanus in *Coriolanus* (Shakespeare), Covent Garden, London.
        Edgar in *King Lear* (Shakespeare), Covent Garden, London.
1820   Virginius in *Virginius* (Knowles), Covent Garden, London.
        Macbeth in *Macbeth* (Shakespeare), Covent Garden, London.
        Iachimo in *Cymbeline* (Shakespeare), Covent Garden, London.
        Prospero in *The Tempest* (Shakespeare), Covent Garden, London.
1821   Henry in *Henry IV, part 2* (Shakespeare), Covent Garden, London.
1822   Cassius in *Julius Caesar* (Shakespeare), Covent Garden, London.
        Hubert in *King John* (Shakespeare), Covent Garden, London.
        Polignac in *The Huguenot* (Sheil), Covent Garden, London.
1823   Cardinal Wolsey in *Henry VIII* (Shakespeare), Covent Garden, London.
        Role in *Julian* (Mitford), Covent Garden, London.
        Shylock in *The Merchant of Venice* (Shakespeare), Covent Garden, London.
        Leontes in *The Winter's Tale* (Shakespeare), Theatre Royal, Drury Lane, London.
        Caius in *Caius Gracchus* (Knowles), Theatre Royal, Drury Lane, London.
1824   The Duke in *Measure for Measure* (Shakespeare), Theatre Royal, Drury Lane, London.
1825   Romont in *The Fatal Dowry* (Massinger, adapted by Sheil), Theatre Royal, Drury Lane, London.

William Charles Macready as Richard III (detail from a print published by Hodgson in 1822).

William Tell in *William Tell* (Knowles), Covent Garden, London.

1826   Hotspur in *Henry IV, part 1* (Shakespeare), Theatre Royal, Drury Lane, London.

1828   Edward the Black Prince in *Edward the Black Prince* (Reynolds), Theatre Royal, Drury Lane, London.

Don Pedro in *Don Pedro* (Porchester), Theatre Royal, Drury Lane, London.

1830   Werner in *Werner* (Lord Byron), Theatre Royal, Bristol.

1831   Don Leo in *The Pledge* (adapted from Hugo's *Hernani*), Theatre Royal, Drury Lane, London.

Mr Oakly in *The Jealous Wife* (Colman the Elder), Theatre Royal, Drury Lane, London.

1832   The Ghost in *Hamlet* (Shakespeare), Covent Garden, London.

1833   Lear in *King Lear* (Shakespeare), Swansea.

Henry V in *Henry V* (Shakespeare), Theatre Royal, Drury Lane, London.

1834   Sardanapalus in *Sardanapalus* (Lord Byron), Theatre Royal, Drury Lane, London.

Melantius in *The Bridal* (Knowles), Dublin.

1835   Ford in *The Merry Wives of Windsor* (Shakespeare), Theatre Royal, Bath.

Jaques in *As You Like It* (Shakespeare), Theatre Royal, Drury Lane, London.

1836   Bertulphe in *The Provost of Bruges* (Lovell), Theatre Royal, Drury Lane, London.

Ion in *Ion* (Talfourd), Covent Garden, London.

Brutus in *Julius Caesar* (Shakespeare), Covent Garden, London.

1837   Bragelone in *The Duchess de la Vallière* (Bulwer-Lytton), Covent Garden, London.

Strafford in *Strafford* (Browning), Covent Garden, London.

Hastings in *Jane Shore* (Rowe), Covent Garden, London.

Luke in *Riches* (adapted from Massinger's *The City Madam*), Covent Garden, London.

1838   Claude Melnotte in *The Lady of Lyons* (Bulwer-Lytton), Covent Garden, London.

Coriolanus in *Coriolanus* (Shakespeare), Covent Garden, London.

Francis Foscari in *The Two Foscari* (Lord Byron), Covent Garden, London.

Friar Lawrence in *Romeo and Juliet* (Shakespeare), Covent Garden, London.

Thoas in *The Athenian Captive* (Talfourd), Haymarket Theatre, London.

Kitely in *Every Man in His Humour* (Jonson), Haymarket Theatre, London.

Walsingham in *The Woman's Wit* (Knowles), Covent Garden, London.

1839   Cardinal Richelieu in *Richelieu* (Bulwer-Lytton), Covent Garden, London.

Norman in *The Sea Captain* (Bulwer-Lytton), Haymarket Theatre, London.

1840   Ruthven in *Mary Stuart* (Haynes), Theatre Royal, Drury Lane, London.

Halbert MacDonald in *The Tragedy of Glencoe* (Talfourd), Theatre Royal, Drury Lane, London.

Sir Oswin Mortland in *To Marry or Not to Marry* (Inchbald), Theatre Royal, Drury Lane, London.

Alfred Evelyn in *Money* (Bulwer-Lytton), Haymarket Theatre, London.

1841   John in *King John* (Shakespeare), Theatre Royal, Drury Lane, London.

Ugonè Spinola in *Nina Sforza* (Troughton), Haymarket Theatre, London.

Harmony in *Every One Has His Fault* (Inchbald), Theatre Royal, Drury Lane, London.

Valentine in *The Two Gentlemen of Verona* (Shakespeare), Theatre Royal, Drury Lane, London.

1842   Gisippus in *Gisippus* (Griffin), Theatre Royal, Drury Lane, London.

Sir Gabriel Grimwood in *Plighted Troth* (Darley), Theatre Royal, Drury Lane, London.

Faliero in *Marino Faliero* (Lord Byron), Theatre Royal, Drury Lane, London.

Mordaunt in *The Patrician's Daughter* (Marston), Theatre Royal, Drury Lane, London.

1843   Benedick in *Much Ado About Nothing* (Shakespeare), Theatre Royal, Drury Lane, London.

Colonel Green in *The Secretary* (Knowles), Theatre Royal, Drury Lane, London.

Athelwold in *Athelwold* (W. Smith), Theatre Royal, Drury Lane, London.

1847   Artevelde in *Philip Van Artevelde* (H. Taylor), Princess's Theatre, London.

Also acted roles in: *Evadne; or, The Statue* (Sheil), Covent Garden, London, 1819; *Hyder Ali; or, The Lions of Mysore* (anon.), Theatre Royal, Drury Lane, London, 1832; *The House of Colberg* (Serle), Theatre Royal, Drury Lane, London, 1832.

Publications

Marmion (play), 1814; *Rokeby* (play), 1814; *Philip van Artevelde* (adaptation from Taylor), 1847; *Macready's Reminiscences and Selections from His Diaries* (edited by Sir Francis Pollock), 1875 (edited by William Toynbee, 1912, and by J. C. Trewin, as *The Journal of William Charles Macready*, 1967).

*

Bibliography

Books:
Lady Pollock, *Macready as I Knew Him*, London, 1884.
William Archer, *William Charles Macready*, London, 1890.
J. C. Trewin, *Mr Macready — A Nineteenth Century Tragedian and His Theatre*, London, 1955.
Alan S. Downer, *The Eminent Tragedian: William Charles Macready*, Oxford, 1966.

Articles:
Alan S. Downer, "The Making of a Great Actor", *Theatre Annual*, 1948–49.

* * *

Born into a theatrical family, William Charles Macready was a reluctant recruit to the acting profession. At Rugby School he took part in recitations and stage plays, but he saw his future in law or one of the other widely esteemed professions. His father's domestic and business difficulties obliged the young Macready to make his stage debut — as Romeo in Birmingham — at the age of 17, but although *Aris's Birmingham Gazette* for 11 June 1810 had "never witnessed a better first appearance" Macready observed that "in other callings the profession confers dignity on the initiated; on the stage the player must contribute respect to the exercise of his art."

As Macready rose inexorably to the leadership of his profession his attitude towards it remained the same. Although his first wife was an actress he made few personal friends (though several enemies including Alfred Bunn and Edwin Forrest) amongst his fellow-actors and ensured that none of his children trod the boards. Politically a republican (unswayed by Queen Victoria's enthusiasm for the theatre), he cultivated the friendships of eminent writers (Browning, Bulwer-Lytton, Dickens, and John Forster), whose interest in the theatre he encouraged as part of his campaign to contribute respect to his art. His periods of personal management accounted for only a small proportion of his career, but at Covent Garden and Drury Lane he made major strides in theatre practice, enforcing full rehearsals, restoring Shakespeare's texts, and introducing high standards of scenery and costume based on thorough historical research.

When, in 1851, Macready retired after a long series of farewell performances he recalled that his ambition had been "to establish a theatre, in regard to decorum and taste, worthy of our country, and to leave in it the plays of our divine Shakespeare fitly illustrated". In this he had been largely successful. Historically, Macready's contribution to reforming the theatre of his day was of far-reaching and lasting significance.

However, in the context of his time, dominated by the actor-manager tradition, Macready's other achievements cannot be separated from his distinction as an actor. Embarking on his acting career as he did, during the ascendancy of Edmund Kean, Macready was inevitably subject to comparison with that mercurial performer. G. H. Lewes, writing of Edmund Kean, established the benchmark with the observation: "The greatest artist is he who is greatest in the highest reaches of his art" and judged Kean as "incomparably the greatest actor I have seen". In contrast to Kean's genius Lewes saw in Macready "only a man of talent, but talent so marked and individual that it approaches very near to genius". Lewes identified as Macready's particular strengths his general flexibility and intellectual sympathy.

Macready's range of roles was remarkable, encompassing in the 1837–38 Covent Garden season alone: Leontes, Hamlet, Melantius in *The Bridal*, Othello, Lord Townly in *The Provoked Husband*, Byron's Werner, Pierre in *Venice Preserved*, Virginius in Knowles's play, Macbeth, Henry V, Luke in *Riches*, Hastings in *Jane Shore*, Lear, Don Felix in *The Wonder*, Claude Melnotte in *The Lady of Lyons*, Brutus, Coriolanus, Francis Foscari in *The Two Foscari*, Friar Lawrence in *Romeo and Juliet*, T. N. Talfourd's Ion, Cardinal Wolsey, and Walsingham in *The Woman's Wit*. Of these Melnotte was the most popular with 33 performances, followed by Walsingham (25), Macbeth (18), and Lear (10).

This is a clear indication of versatility and industry, but varied though the roles were, Macready brought to them certain consistent features, both physically and stylistically. Not even his most fervent admirers could claim natural grace as one of Macready's accomplishments. He was said to resemble portraits of Lorenzo de Medici: his eyebrows swept upwards, his nose was irregular, his mouth depressed at the corners, and his jaw large and square. On stage he favoured a profile position. In his use of make-up and choice of costumes he did nothing to mitigate these characteristics, indeed sometimes he seemed to emphasize them.

Macready's voice was rich and powerful. He avoided the declamation of the Kemble school of acting and though he had a tendency to scream in violent passages (when he lost emotional control) his enunciation was generally precise. His anxiety to avoid any slur between the final consonant of one word and the initial letter of the next, however, resulted in an irritating mannerism in which he inserted *a* or *e*, thus: "Be innocentta of the knowledge, dearestta chuck." Though he was evidently unaware of this mannerism, Macready cultivated another for which he became notorious — making often extremely abrupt transitions from his loudest tones to audible whispers, a practice inherited from Edmund Kean. Early in his career Hazlitt observed of Macready's Coriolanus: "he is also apt to be too sudden and theatrical in his contrasts, from a loud utterance to a low one". These flaws militated against sonorous verse speaking and whilst he was incapable of murdering his metre, the sense of the lines was his overriding priority.

Lewes wrote that Macready's "intelligence always made him follow the winding meetings through the involutions of the verse". His intellectual capacity allowed him penetrating psychological insights into his characters, for whose behaviour he sought to establish convincing reasons. Not

that this was a purely cerebral process. In the case of Shylock he would spend several minutes behind the scenes, lashing himself into an imaginative rage by cursing to himself and violently shaking a ladder fixed to the wall. Thus prepared, he had worked himself up to the proper pitch of excitement to express on stage Shylock's rage over the loss of his daughter and his ducats.

Macready was always his own sternest critic. The pages of his diary are littered with expressions of dissatisfaction, as in the case of his Lear in 1838: "Lay down and tried to think of Lear. Was very nervous in the morning, but prepared for the play much more collected than I had been. I scarcely know how I acted the part. I did not satisfy myself ... was personally pretty good, but I was not what I wished to have been". The consensus of opinion was that Lear was Macready's finest achievement: beginning sovereignly imperious yet imbued with prodigal love for his daughters; striking terror with the curse of Goneril; establishing ties of common humanity in the storm scenes; struggling towards memory in the reconciliation with Cordelia; and in his representation of the father at the end completing, in John Forster's opinion, "the only perfect picture that we have had of Lear since the age of Betterton".

—Richard Foulkes

MAHELOT, Laurent. French designer. No personal details known. Either as principal designer, or as a technical assistant, he contributed designs for the Comédiens du Roi at the Théâtre de l'Hôtel de Bourgogne, Paris; his *Mémoire* gives invaluable information about the scenery used on the Parisian stage in the 1630's.

Conjectured productions

Les Ménechmes (Rotrou, adapted from Plautus), c.1632; *Pyrame et Thisbé* (Théophile), c.1633–34.

Publications

Le Mémoire de Mahelot, Laurent et d'Autres Décorateurs de l'Hôtel de Bourgogne et de la Comédie-Française au XVIIe Siècle, edited by H. C. Lancaster, 1920.

*

Bibliography

Books:
T. E. Lawrenson, *The French Stage in the XVIIth Century: A Study in the Advent of the Italian Order*, Manchester, 1957.

Articles:
T. E. Lawrenson, "The Contemporary Staging of Théophile's *Pyrame et Thisbé*: the Open Stage Imprisoned", *Modern Miscellany Presented to Eugène Vinaver*, Manchester, 1969.
J. D. Golder, "*L'Hypocondriac* de Rotrou: un Essai de Reconstitution d'une des Premières Mises en Scène à

l'Hôtel de Bourgogne", *Revue d'Histoire du Théâtre*, 1979.

* * *

Nothing is known about the author of the document called the *Mémoire de Mahelot* beyond the attribution on the title-page of the manuscript; even the generally held assumption that Laurent Mahelot was employed as the principal "décorateur", or designer, by the Hôtel de Bourgogne theatre in Paris during the 1630's has been challenged by some theatre historians, who have preferred to see him as a "machiniste", or technical assistant to one Georges Buffequin. However, his reputation is identified with the *Mémoire*, or memorandum, of which he was indisputably the original author. Moreover, he is the only one of the three principal known contributors — for the memorandum was to be continued by two successors later in the century — to have provided more than a mere list of the plays composing the company's repertory, and to have supplemented this with the distinctive sketches of theatrical décor that make the *Mémoire* a uniquely valuable record of staging practice during a crucial phase of the evolution of this art. Mahelot's own section of the manuscript lists 71 plays, of which 47 are the subject of illustrative sketches. The completion of his list can be assigned with some confidence to the theatrical season 1633–34: a date at which staging at the Hôtel de Bourgogne (and no doubt at the rival Théâtre du Marais, for which similar visual evidence is lacking) was still following the tradition of the "décor simultané", or multiple set, in its full bloom (as in the *Mystère de la Passion* performed at Valenciennes in 1547, with its 12 very disparate "mansions" existing side by side). The conventions of an indoor secular stage almost 100 years later show considerable modifications. Not only do Mahelot's designs indicate a norm of no more than half this number of compartments, but there is a distinct tendency to "compose" these where possible, producing something like a coherent unity, under the influence of Italian perspective design. In the case of certain plays requiring a more complex setting, Mahelot's comments make it clear that extra locations, additional to the five or six compartments shown, could be created by the drawing of a curtain; however, his sketches chart the progress from the concept of "place whence" (that is, the juxtaposition of independent compartments, each deemed to define the location of the action for the duration of a scene or scenes) to "place where": the portrayal of a unified overall setting, valid for the whole play, including most typically the grouping of the required number of dwelling-houses round a central acting space. The use of perspective — both in the free-standing wing sets and in the backcloth — was an essential part of this development; but although Mahelot's designs frequently reveal an "Italian" symmetry, they stop far short of the stylised complexity of Serlio's Tragic and Comic Scenes.

This evolution can best be illustrated by a comparison between two representative sketches. The design for Théophile de Viau's tragedy *Pyrame et Thisbé* (first performed in 1622, but still in the repertory in the mid-1630's) provides a good example of the genuine multiple set in the final stage of its development; it shows the "town" elements of the décor — the King's palace and the home of Pyramus and Thisbe (with the famous wall apparently

sliding into place when required) — flanked by the out-of-town components: mulberry tree, lion's cave, fountain, and Ninus's tomb. The sketch for Jean Rotrou's adaptation of Plautus's comedy, *Les Ménechmes* (c.1632), on the other hand, shows how the separate but interrelated elements of the déor are now harmoniously linked, by a striking use of perspective, into a homogenous whole. Such a comparison incidentally also suggests a feature that is clearly revealed by several other of the sketches relating to plays produced in the mid-1630's, namely the re-use of stock items from the Hôtel de Bourgogne's store.

With what might appear to be the latest in date of Mahelot's drawings, we are not far from the point at which the symbolic approach to set design — suggesting separate locations for every scene, as required, in however bizarre a conjunction — will give way completely to the representational, embodying the concept of a single unified setting for a whole play. His sketches provide clear visual proof that the replacement of irregular baroque drama by the simplicity of classical tragedy was not merely the work of erudite theoreticians, but that the triumph of the Three Unities on the page was matched by something just as compelling on stage: the move towards a new perception of the possibilities of theatrical illusion.

—William D. Howarth

———

MANSFIELD, Richard.   US actor-manager. Born in Berlin, Germany, 25 May 1854. Educated by private tutors and at schools in London, Jena, Bourbourg, Yverdon, Berlin, and Derby, England; studied painting in London, 1877–80. Married Beatrice Cameron in 1892, one son. Accompanied his mother, soprano Erminia Rudersdorff, to England as an infant and later to USA, 1872; amateur theatre debut, Boston, 1876; engaged by D'Oyly Carte provincial opera touring company in the late 1870's; New York debut, 1882; acclaimed on both sides of Atlantic in a range of classical and modern plays, often at the head of his own company; annual US tours, 1890–1907; reopened Harrigan's Theatre, New York, as the Garrick Theatre, 1895; last stage appearance, as Peer Gynt and Baron Chevrial, 23 March, 1907. Died in New London, Connecticut, 30 August 1907.

Productions

As actor:
1879   Sir Joseph Porter in *H.M.S. Pinafore* (Gilbert and Sullivan), Bristol.
            The Major-General in *The Pirates of Penzance* (Gilbert and Sullivan), Bijou Theatre, Paignton, England.
1880   J. Wellington Wells in *The Sorcerer* (Gilbert and Sullivan), Bijou Theatre, Paignton, England.
1881   Coquebert in *La Boulangère* (Farnie), Globe Theatre, London.
            Monsieur Philippe in *Out of the Hunt* (Reece and Thorpe), Royalty Theatre, London.
            Herbert Colwyn in *Dust* (Grundy), Royalty Theatre, London.

Old Sherman in *The Fisherman's Daughter* (Garvice), Royalty Theatre, London.

1882   Brigard in *Frou Frou* (Webster), Royalty Theatre, London.

Theophilus Woolstone in *Not Registered* (Matthison), Royalty Theatre, London.

The Innkeeper in *The Mascotte* (Farnie and Reece), Comedy Theatre, London.

Dromez in *Les Manteaux Noirs* (Parke and Paulton), Standard Theatre, New York.

Nick Vedder and Jan Vedder in *Rip Van Winkle* (Planquette), Standard Theatre, New York.

Lord High Chancellor in *Iolanthe* (Gilbert and Sullivan), Baltimore.

Tirandel in *A Parisian Romance* (adapted from the French), Union Square Theatre, New York.

1883   Baron Chevrial in *A Parisian Romance* (adapted from the French), Union Square Theatre, New York, and US tour.

1884   Count von Dornfeldt in *Alpine Roses* (Boyesen), Madison Square Theatre, New York.

Baron von Wiener Schnitzel in *La Vie Parisienne* (Burnand), Bijou Theatre, New York.

1885   Baron de Mersac in *Victor Durand* (Carleton), Wallack's Theatre, New York.

Nasoni in *Gasperone* (Millöcker), Standard Theatre, New York.

Louis XI in *Gringoire* (Wills), Princess's Theatre, London.

Herr Kraft in *In Spite of All* (Anderson), Madison Square Theatre, New York.

1886   Ko-Ko in *The Mikado* (Gilbert and Sullivan), Hollis Street Theatre, Boston.

1886–87   Prince Karl in *Prince Karl* (Gunter), Boston Museum, Boston, Madison Square Theatre, New York, and US tour.

1887   Jekyll and Hyde in *Dr Jekyll and Mr Hyde* (Sullivan, adapted from Stevenson), Boston Museum, Boston, Madison Square Theatre, New York, and US tour.

André de Jadot in *Monsieur* (Mansfield), Madison Square Theatre, New York, US tour, and Fifth Avenue Theatre, New York.

1889   Richard in *Richard III* (Shakespeare), Globe Theatre, London, Globe Theatre, Boston, and Palmer's Theatre, New York.

1890   Humphrey Logan in *Master and Man* (Petitt and Sims), Palmer's Theatre, New York.

Beau Brummell in *Beau Brummell* (Fitch), Madison Square Theatre, New York.

1891   Don Juan in *Don Juan* (Mansfield), Garden Theatre, New York.

Nero in *Nero* (Sullivan), Garden Theatre, New York.

1892   Tittlebat Titmouse in *Ten Thousand a Year* (E. Sheridan), Garden Theatre, New York.

Arthur Dimmesdale in *The Scarlet Letter* (Hatton, adapted from Hawthorne), Daly's Theatre, New York.

1893   Shylock in *The Merchant of Venice* (Shakespeare), Hermann's Theatre, New York.

Richard Mansfield

1894   Captain Bluntschli in *Arms and the Man* (G. B. Shaw), Herald Square Theatre, New York.

Napoleon in *Napoleon Bonaparte* (Stoddard), Herald Square Theatre, New York.

1895   Don Pedro XIV in *The King of Peru* (Parker), Garrick Theatre, New York.

Rodion Romanytch in *The Story of Rodion, the Student* (Meltzer), Garrick Theatre, New York.

1896   Sir John Sombras in *Castle Sombras* (Smith), Grand Opera House, Chicago.

1897   Dick Dudgeon in *The Devil's Disciple* (G. B. Shaw), Hermanus Bleeker Hall, Albany, New York.

1898   Eugene Courvoisier in *The First Violin* (Mansfield and Clarke), Hollis Street Theatre, Boston.

Cyrano in *Cyrano de Bergerac* (Rostand, adapted by Kingsbury), Garden Theatre, New York.

1900   Henry in *Henry V* (Shakespeare), Garden Theatre, New York.

1901   Beaucaire in *Monsieur Beaucaire* (Sutherland and Tarkington), Garrick Theatre, Philadelphia.

1902   Brutus in *Julius Caesar* (Shakespeare), Grand Opera House, Chicago, and Herald Square Theatre, New York.

1903   Prince Karl Henry in *Old Heidelberg* (Bleichmann), Lyric Theatre, New York.

1904	Ivan Vassilyevich in *Ivan the Terrible* (Tolstoy), New Amsterdam Theatre, New York.
1905	Alceste in *The Misanthrope* (Molière, translated by Wormeley), New Amsterdam Theatre, New York.
	Don Carlos in *Don Carlos* (Schiller, adapted by Mansfield), Valentine Opera House, Toledo, Ohio.
1906	Peer Gynt in *Peer Gynt* (Ibsen), Grand Opera House, Chicago.

As director:

1888	*A Doll's House* (Ibsen), Globe Theatre, Boston, and Palmer's Theatre, New York.
1895	*Thrilby* (Herbert and Puerner, burlesque of *Trilby*), Garrick Theatre, New York.
	The Man with a Past (Paulton), Garrick Theatre, New York.

Publications

Monsieur (autobiographical play), 1887; *Don Juan* (play), 1891; *Blown Away*, 1897.

*

Bibliography

Books:
Paul Wilstach, *Richard Mansfield: The Man and the Actor*, New York, 1909.
William Winter, *Life and Art of Richard Mansfield*, 2 vols., New York, 1910.

Articles:
Montrose J. Moses, "Richard Mansfield", *Pearson's*, 18, 1905.
James O'Donnell Bennett, "Richard Mansfield", *Munsey's*, 36, 1907.
John Corbin, "The Greatest English Actor", *Appleton's*, 9, 1907.
Lyman B. Glover, "Richard Mansfield", *World To-Day*, 13, 1907.
Paul T. Case, "The Real Richard Mansfield", *Theatre*, 1914.

* * *

Richard Mansfield's efforts to establish himself as a star in the years between 1883 and 1887 were generally unsuccessful, notwithstanding critical acclaim for his performances as Baron Chevrial and Prince Karl. With his sensational dual performance as Dr Jekyll and Mr Hyde, however, Mansfield, as his biographer William Winter noted, "gained an authoritative position ... and at last was able to assert himself in active competition with the potential leaders of the stage." For the next 20 years, Mansfield's career as a starring actor and producer flourished. Each season he would present a repertory consisting of one or two new characters and revivals of previous seasons' successes. Ultimately Mansfield's repertory consisted of 27 roles.

Dr Jekyll and Mr Hyde was well suited to Mansfield's physical capabilities and temperament. Although less than average height, he had an athletic build and an attractive, compelling, appearance. Moreover, his face and body were unusually flexible; his face, in particular, was capable of assuming various expressions or characterizations without resorting to the tricks and devices of stage make-up. His early training as a singer and the tutelage of his mother gave him a voice capable of conveying a wide range of tones or "colours" as he called them: a "blue" voice for prayer, a "yellow" voice for jealousy, a "livid red" voice for rage, and so on. As an individual, furthermore, he was magnetic and energetic, but also contradictory, with more than the normal share of vanity, egotism, and ambition.

Winter described Mansfield's Hyde as "a carnal monster of unqualified evil ... remarkable for loathsome, reptile-like ferocity". But he noted that he also "rose to a nobler height than that ... in the concurrent, associate impersonation of Dr Jekyll." While each character was "distinctively individual", Mansfield was able to blend them into "a single image of human nature" struggling "between inherent forces of good and evil". Mansfield, moreover, transformed himself from the handsome, gracious Jekyll into the hideous Hyde and back again in full sight of the audience without the assistance of make-up.

Throughout his career Mansfield was attracted to forceful, richly histrionic, often historical, characters — both heroes and villains — that offered him the opportunity to display his remarkable versatility, his ability to transform himself, to create realistically detailed, believable personalities. He was most convincing with larger-than-life-sized characters, or with picturesque characters that contained a pronounced element of eccentricity. Certainly among his more effective impersonations was that of Cyrano de Bergerac. Winter thought Mansfield "particularly well fitted" for Cyrano and praised his brilliant portrayal of "the grotesque, ironic, combative, satiric, mental, and practical attributes of the character." Lewis C. Strang thought that Mansfield's Cyrano was "a complete text-book in the art of acting": "It is no exaggeration to say that there was not a turn of phrase, nor a movement of the body that did not bear testimony to the actor's deep delving into details. Cyrano's mind and soul were probed to their innermost recesses, and the actor dragged forth every motive, however hidden, however subtle, that in any way influenced the man in his attitude toward the world."

Mansfield was less successful, however, in capturing the more complex nuances of Shakespearean characters. Of the four Shakespeare roles he played, only Henry V was a qualified critical success, perhaps because Henry, in the words of Charles Shattuck, "plays many roles", changing from scene to scene, variously cunning monarch, resolute soldier, and plain-speaking lover. For "an inveterate character actor like Mansfield he offers a splendid range of opportunities."

Like many contemporaneous 'regisseurs' — Irving, Tree, Sothern, and Marlowe — Mansfield was dedicated to historical accuracy. His major productions were always lavishly and realistically mounted. After Mansfield's visually splendid production of *Henry V*, for example, the New York critic Edward A. Dithmar waxed: "We need not talk now about the Meininger and the management of crowds at Bayreuth."

Though Mansfield was not particularly sympathetic with the then emerging modern drama, he did produce Ibsen's *A Doll's House* in London in 1888 and in New York in 1889, so that his future wife Beatrice Cameron could star as Nora. He also introduced Shaw to the USA with his productions of *Arms and the Man* and *The Devil's Disciple*. His 1907 production of *Peer Gynt* was also the first in the USA.

Mansfield was certainly a forceful presence in the US theatre at the turn of the century, an aspirant to the 'classic' tradition of the 19th century. His repertory, however, was considerably smaller than Booth's or Irving's, nor did it include the major Shakespeare roles in which classical 19th-century tragedians built their reputations. Moreover, as Shattuck writes, Mansfield did not have the depth of experience, nor "the technical proficiency of a Booth or Barrett", nor were his compelling, but essentially melodramatic impersonations, "an intelligent anticipation of the best that would be realised in the 20th century".

Mansfield was, according to writer Garff Wilson, "a product of his times" and perhaps a victim as well. "Pulled in two directions — toward the vanishing traditions of the old century and toward the emerging practices of the new", he both "hastened and represented the transition from one theatrical era to another".

—Daniel J. Watermeier

————

MARLOWE, Julia. US actress. Born Sarah Frances Frost in Upton Caldbeck, Cumberland, England, 17 August 1866. Educated, from 1871, at public schools in Cincinatti, Ohio, and Kansas City, Kansas; trained as an actress under Ada Dow, 1884–87. Married 1) actor Robert Taber in 1894 (divorced 1900); 2) actor Edward Hugh Sothern (*q.v.*) in 1911 (died 1933). Emigrated with her family to the USA, 1871; stage debut at the age of 11 in touring production of *H.M.S. Pinafore*, Vincennes, Indiana, 1877; first starring role, 1887; especially acclaimed in plays by Shakespeare and Sheridan while on tour with Sothern, 1904–07, 1909–14, 1919–24; London debut, 1907; withdrew temporarily from stage, 1916; retired permanently with Sothern, 1924. Member: board of governors, Shakespeare Memorial Association, Stratford-upon-Avon, 1914. Recipient: American Academy of the Arts Gold Medal, 1929. LL.D: George Washington University, Washington DC, 1921; University of Columbia, New York, 1943. Died in New York, 12 November 1950.

Roles

1877	Sir Joseph Porter in *H.M.S. Pinafore* (Gilbert and Sullivan), US tour.
	Suzanne in *The Chimes of Normandy* (Planquette), US tour.
	The Page in *The Little Duke* (Stephenson and Scott), US tour.
1882–83	Heinrich in *Rip Van Winkle* (Farnie), US tour.
1883–84	Balthazar in *Romeo and Juliet* (Shakespeare), US tour.
	Stephen in *The Hunchback* (Knowles), US tour.
	Maria in *Twelfth Night* (Shakespeare), US tour.
	Myrine in *Pygmalion and Galatea* (Gilbert), US tour.

1887	Parthenia in *Ingomar* (Lovell), US tour and Bijou Theatre, New York.
	Pauline in *The Lady of Lyons* (Bulwer-Lytton), US tour.
	Juliet in *Romeo and Juliet* (Shakespeare), Star Theatre, New York.
	Viola in *Twelfth Night* (Shakespeare), Star Theatre, New York; revived notably, London, 1907.
1888	Julia in *The Hunchback* (Knowles), US tour; Fifth Avenue Theatre, New York, 1890.
1889	Rosalind in *As You Like It* (Shakespeare), US tour; Fifth Avenue Theatre, New York, 1890.
1890	Galatea in *Pygmalion and Galatea* (Gilbert), Fifth Avenue Theatre, New York.
1891	Charles Hart in *Rogues and Vagabonds* (revue), Fifth Avenue Theatre, New York.
1892	Constance in *The Love Chase* (Knowles), Fifth Avenue Theatre, New York.
1893	Imogen in *Cymbeline* (Shakespeare), US tour and Fifth Avenue Theatre, New York.
	Letitia Hardy in *The Belle's Stratagem* (Cowley), Fifth Avenue Theatre, New York.
	Thomas Chatterton in *Chatterton* (Jones and Herman), Fifth Avenue Theatre, New York.
1894	Colombe in *Colombe's Birthday* (Browning), Fifth Avenue Theatre, New York.
	Lady Teazle in *The School for Scandal* (Sheridan), Fifth Avenue Theatre, New York.
1895	Prince Hal in *Henry IV, part 1* (Shakespeare), Fifth Avenue Theatre, New York.
1896	Kate Hardcastle in *She Stoops to Conquer* (Goldsmith), Palmer's Theatre, New York.
	Lydia Languish in *The Rivals* (Sheridan), US tour and American Theatre, New York.
	Romola in *Romola* (Barron, adapted from Eliot), US tour.
1897	Mary in *For Bonnie Prince Charlie* (Coppée, translated by Clarke), US tour and Palmer's Theatre, New York.
1898	The Countess in *Countess Valeska* (adapted from the German), Knickerbocker Theatre, New York, and US tour.
1899	Colinette de Bouvray in *Colinette* (Carleton), Knickerbocker Theatre, New York, and US tour.
	Barbara Freitchie in *Barbara Frietchie* (Fitch), Criterion Theatre, New York, and US tour.
1901	Mary Tudor in *When Knighthood Was in Flower* (Kester), US tour.
1902	The Queen in *Queen Fiametta* (Mendès), Boston.
	Charlotte Oliver in *The Cavalier* (Kester, adapted from Cable), Criterion Theatre, New York.
1903	Lady Branchester in *Fools of Nature* (Esmond), Hyperion Theatre, New Haven, Connecticut.
1904	Beatrice in *Much Ado About Nothing* (Shakespeare), Illinois Theatre, Chicago, and Knickerbocker Theatre, New York.
	Ophelia in *Hamlet* (Shakespeare), Illinois Theatre, Chicago, and Knickerbocker Theatre, New York; revived notably, London, 1907

1905	Katherine in *The Taming of the Shrew* (Shakespeare), Cleveland, Ohio, and Knickerbocker Theatre, New York.
	Portia in *The Merchant of Venice* (Shakespeare), Cleveland, Ohio, and Knickerbocker Theatre, New York.
1906	Jeanne D'Arc in *Jeanne D'Arc* (Mackaye), Lyric Theatre, Philadelphia; London, 1907.
	Salome in *John the Baptist* (Sudermann), Lyric Theatre, Philadelphia.
	Rautendelein in *The Sunken Bell* (Hauptmann), Washington.
1907	Role in *Gloria* (Fagan), Philadelphia.
1909	Yvette in *The Goddess of Reason* (Johnston), Majestic Theatre, Boston.
	Cleopatra in *Antony and Cleopatra* (Shakespeare), New Theatre, New York.
1910	Lady Macbeth in *Macbeth* (Shakespeare), New Haven, Connecticut, and Broadway Theatre, New York.

*

Bibliography

Books:
John D. Barry, *Julia Marlowe*, Boston, 1899.
Charles Edward Russell, *Julia Marlowe, Her Life and Art*, New York and London, 1926.
E. H. Sothern (ed. Fairfax Downey), *Julia Marlowe's Story*, New York, 1954.

Articles:
Elizabeth McCracken, "Julia Marlowe", *Century*, 73, 1906.
Wendell Phillips Dodge, "Julia Marlowe", *Strand Magazine*, 45, 1913.
Montrose J. Moses, "Two Interpreters of Shakespeare", *Independent*, 76, 1913.
William Winter, "The Art of Julia Marlowe", *Century*, 90, 1915.
A. Richard Sogluzzio, "Edward H. Sothern and Julia Marlowe on the Art of Acting", *Theatre Survey*, 11, 1970.

* * *

Physically attractive with dark, wavy hair, expressive eyes, and a distinctive mouth and dimpled chin, Julia Marlowe was further blessed with a rich contralto voice that her biographer Charles Russell called an "extraordinary organ" and which was widely regarded as one of the most beautiful voices on the US stage. Building on her natural attributes and her intelligence with diligent study and experience, she became the finest Shakespearean actress of her day. Furthermore, Marlowe and her partner and then husband, E. H. Sothern were universally recognized as the most distinguished acting couple and Shakespearean producers in the USA in the first decade of the 20th century.

Like many performers at the turn of the century, Julia Marlowe rejected the bravura 'point making' style of Romantic acting. Her style tended more towards realism. Critics on both sides of the Atlantic commended her effective 'identification' with her roles, her ability to create "the illusion of really being the character she assumes to be". She created this illusion generally with an economy of means — gesture, movement, and facial expression — and without resort to artificiality or histrionic tricks. In her own writings she conceded that her aim was realism, but that "realism to be effective must be a matter of selection". The true artist "inspired by the genius of selection ... knows what to accept, what to cast aside". Ultimately, it was a "realism enhanced by idealism and uplifted by the spirit of an inner life or purpose" — realism idealized. "Art is beauty" she maintained, and "every exposition of art ... should be subservient to that one great end". There is no doubt that she accomplished this "great end" in her various characterizations. Her Imogen was once described, for example, as "unspeakably beautiful", while her Julet was compared to "a dreamy, mighty impressionistic picture".

While Marlowe had the imagination and technical ability to play a range of characters, she was most effective playing Shakespeare's youthful, romantically tender heroines. The critic William Winter, although not generally an admirer of Marlowe's acting, found her Viola "the most truthful, effective and charming realization of that romantic character which has been placed before the American audience in recent years." Similarly her Rosalind was frequently praised for its "delicious expression" of "arch humour ... brisk wit and above all ... bubbling playfulness". In a different vein, her rendition of Ophelia's mad scene was considered both ingenious in its simplicity and touching in its effect, the only Ophelia in the memory of her biographer who moved an audience to tears.

Marlowe and Sothern staged all of the productions that they toured, but their approach could not be described as "selective realism". Rather, emulating the production style of Henry Irving and Herbert Beerbohm Tree, their productions were models of lavish, historically accurate, generally realistic if somewhat idealized 'mise-en-scène'. To their credit, however, towards the end of their careers they broke with these 19th-century staging practices and adopted the simplified approach to stage decoration being advocated by practitioners of the 'new theatre'. As Charles H. Shattuck noted, Marlowe and Sothern "were a brave and devoted pair of artists who through a troubled and often drab period" struggled and generally succeeded in keeping Shakespeare alive in the USA.

—Daniel J. Watermeier

MAROWITZ, Charles. US director, playwright, and critic. Born in New York, 26 January 1934. Educated at Seward Park High School, New York; trained for the stage at the London Academy of Music and Dramatic Art, 1956–57, Central School of Speech and Drama, 1957–58, University College, London, 1958–59. Served in US Army, 1952–54. Married 1) Julia Costhwait; 2) actress Jane Elizabeth Allsop in 1982. Debut on New York stage, 1948; settled in the UK, 1956; London debut, 1958; director, In-Stage Experimental Theatre, 1958; assistant director, Royal Shakespeare Company, 1963–65; collaborated with Peter Brook, RSC's Theatre of Cruelty season, 1964; associate director, Traverse Theatre Club, London, 1965–67; co-director, with Peter Brook, Royal Shakespeare Company Experimental Group, 1967; founder and director, Open Space Theatre, London, 1968–81; associate director, Los Angeles Theatre Centre, 1982–88; artistic director, Santa

Monica Stage Company, Santa Monica, California, and Malibu Stage Company, from 1990. Drama critic, *Encore Magazine*, 1956–63, *Plays and Players*, 1958–74, *The Village Voice*, from 1955, *The New York Times*, from 1966, *The Los Angeles Herald-Examiner*, 1988–89. Has also taught in Oslo, Stuttgart, Heidelberg, Bergen, Wiesbaden, London, and elsewhere. Member: Dramatists' Guild; Screenwriters' Guild. Recipient: Whitbread Award, 1966; Louis B. Mayer Playwriting Award; Order of the Purple Sash, 1969.

Productions

1948	*Doctor Faustus* (Marlowe), Labour Temple Theatre, New York.
1958	*Marriage* (Gogol), Unity Theatre, London.
	Dominic Behan (Behan), New Arts Theatre, London.
1959	*Crawling Arnold* (Feiffer), New Arts Theatre, London.
1962	*King Lear* (Shakespeare), Royal Shakespeare Theatre, Stratford-upon-Avon, and Aldwych Theatre, London; co-directed with Peter Brook.
1964	*Trigon* (Lynne), New Arts Theatre, London.
	Theatre of Cruelty Season, LAMDA Theatre, London; co-directed with Peter Brook.
	The Screens (Genet), Donmar Rehearsal Rooms, Covent Garden, London; co-directed with Peter Brook.
1965	*The Marowitz Hamlet* (Marowitz, adapted from Shakespeare), Akademie der Kunst, Berlin.
	Woyzeck (Büchner), National Theatre, Bergen, Norway.
1966	*The Bellow Plays* (Bellow), Fortune Theatre, London.
	Loot (Orton), Criterion Theatre, London.
1967	*Fanghorn* (Pinner), Fortune Theatre, London.
	Sclerosis (Barnes), Aldwych Theatre, London.
1968	*Fortune and Men's Eyes* (Herbert), Comedy Theatre, London.
1969	*A Macbeth* (Marowitz, adapted from Shakespeare), May Festival, Staatstheater, Wiesbaden, Germany.
	Blue Comedy, Open Space Theatre, London.
	Muzeeka (Guare), Open Space Theatre, London.
	The Fun War, Open Space Theatre, London.
	Leonardo's Last Supper (Barnes), Open Space Theatre, London.
	Noonday Demons (Barnes), Open Space Theatre, London.
1970	*Chicago Conspiracy*, Open Space Theatre, London.
	Palach, Open Space Theatre, London.
1971	*Sweet Eros* (McNally), Open Space Theatre, London.
	Next, Open Space Theatre, London.
1972	*Four Little Girls* (Picasso), Open Space, Theatre, London.
	Sam Sam (Griffiths), Open Space, Theatre, London.

	The Tooth of Crime (Shepard), Open Space Theatre, London.
	The Old Man's Comforts, Open Space Theatre, London.
	An Othello (Marowitz, adapted from Shakespeare), Open Space Theatre, London.
1973	*Woyzeck* (Büchner), Open Space Theatre, London.
	The Houseboy, Open Space Theatre, London.
	And They Put Handcuffs on the Flowers (Arrabal), Open Space Theatre, London.
	The Shrew (Marowitz, adapted from Shakespeare), Hot Theatre, The Hague, Netherlands.
1974	*Sherlock's Last Case* (Marowitz), Open Space Theatre, London.
1975	*Variations on Measure for Measure* (Marowitz, adapted from Shakespeare), Open Space Theatre, London.
1976	*Artaud at Rodez* (Marowitz), Teatro a Trastavere, Rome, and Open Space Theatre, London; Boston; Amsterdam; Royal Dramatic Theatre, Stockholm; Theatre Centre, Los Angeles, 1981 and 1982.
	Anatol (Schnitzler), Open Space Theatre, London.
	Hanratty in Hell, Open Space Theatre, London.
	The Marowitz Hamlet (Marowitz, adapted from Shakespeare), Great Lakes Shakespeare Festival, Cleveland, Ohio.
1977	*Variations on The Merchant of Venice* (Marowitz, adapted from Shakespeare), Open Space Theatre, London.
	Makbett (Ionesco), Globe Playhouse, London.
1978	*Boo Hoo* (Magdalaney), Open Space Theatre, London.
	Laughter! (Barnes), Royal Court Theatre, London.
	Section Nine (Magdalaney), Aldwych Theatre, London.
	Hedda (Marowitz, adapted from Ibsen), National Theatre, Oslo.
1979	*The Father* (Strindberg), Open Space Theatre, London.
	The Inspector General (Gogol), Bing Theatre, California.
	The Shrew (Marowitz, adapted from Shakespeare), National Theatre, Bergen, Norway.
	Enemy of the People (Ibsen), National Theatre, Oslo.
1980	*Ubu Roi* (Jarry and Milligan), Open Space Theatre, London.
	Hedda (Marowitz, adapted from Ibsen), Round House, London.
1981	*Variations on Measure for Measure* (Marowitz, adapted from Shakespeare), Nye Theatre, Oslo.
	The Father (Strindberg), Trondheim, Norway.
	A Midsummer Night's Dream (Shakespeare), Odense, Denmark.
	Tartuffe (Molière), Molde, Norway.
	Ah, Sweet Mystery of Life (Marowitz), Seattle, Washington.
1982	*Artaud at Rodez* (Marowitz), Los Angeles.

The Marat/Sade (Weiss), Rutgers University, New Brunswick, New Jersey.

The Merry Wives of Windsor (Shakespeare), Shakespeare Festival, Dallas, Texas.

1983   *Enemy of the People* (Ibsen), Theatre Centre, Los Angeles.

1984   *The White Crow* (Freed), Theatre Centre, Los Angeles.

Sherlock's Last Case (Marowitz), Actors' Theatre, Los Angeles.

1985   *The Marowitz Hamlet* (Marowitz, adapted from Shakespeare), Theatre Centre, Los Angeles.

The Petrified Forest (Sherwood), Theatre Centre, Los Angeles.

1986   *The Shrew* (Marowitz, adapted from Shakespeare), Ensemble Studio Theatre, Los Angeles.

1987   *The Fair Penitent* (Rowe), Theatre Centre, Los Angeles.

The Importance of Being Earnest (Wilde), Theatre Centre, Los Angeles.

What the Butler Saw (Orton), Theatre Centre, Los Angeles.

1988   *The Seagull* (Chekhov), Theatre Centre, Los Angeles.

The Marowitz Hamlet (Marowitz, adapted from Shakespeare), Bing Theatre, California.

1989   *Wilde West* (Marowitz), Main Street Theatre, Houston, Texas.

1990   *Variations on Measure for Measure* (Marowitz), Cal State Rep Theatre, Long Beach, California.

1991   *A Macbeth* (Marowitz, adapted from Shakespeare), Los Angeles.

Other productions include: *Cave Dwellers* (Saroyan); *The Tiger* and *The Typists* (Schisgal); *The Snob* (Sternheim); *Investigation* and *Hot Buttered Roll* (Drexler); *Jump!* (Gelbart); *The White Devil* (Webster); *Early Morning* (Bond).

Films

The Method, 1967; *Don Juan: The Legend*, 1967; *Theatre Today*, 1969; *Tonight We Improvise*, 1969; *Hamlet*, 1972; *Macbeth*, 1973; *The Shrew*, 1974; *Omnibus: Open Space Theatre*, 1976; *Crime and Punishment*, 1989.

Radio

Sherlock's Last Case; *The L.A. Scene*; *Movie Makers*; *Bob Hope: Profile*; *The Promising Young Man*; *William Shakespeare: A Sound Portrait*; *Woody Allen: Profile*; *The Austrian Miracle*; *Irresistible Appeal of the Dumb Blonde*; *Shakespeare, The Director*; *Artaud Le Momo*; *Kaleidoscope*; *The BBC Critics*.

Publications

Method as Means: An Acting Survey, 1961; *Theatre at Work: Playwrights and Productions in Modern British Theatre*, with Simon Trussler, 1967; *The Marowitz*

Hamlet, 1967; *A Macbeth* (adaptation), 1970; *Palach* (editor), 1970; *Woyzeck* (adaptation), 1973; *Confessions of a Counterfeit Critic*, 1973; *And They Put Handcuffs on the Flowers* (translation), 1973; *Open Space Plays*, 1974; *Sherlock's Last Case*, 1974; *Artaud at Rodez*, 1975; *The Marowitz Shakespeare: Adaptations and Collage*, 1978; *The Act of Being*, 1978; *The Father* (adaptation), 1979; *New Theatre Voices of the 50s and 60s*, 1981; *Sex Wars: Free Adaptations of Ibsen and Strindberg*, 1982; *Enemy of the People* (adaptation), 1984; *Prospero's Staff: Acting and Directing in the Theatre*, 1986; *Potboilers: Three Black Comedies*, 1986; *Clever Dick*, 1989; *Disciples*, 1989; *Recycling Shakespeare*, 1990; *Burnt Bridges*, 1990; *Directing the Action*, 1992. Other publications include: *Hedda* (adaptation); *An Othello* (adaptation); *Tea with Lady Bracknell*; *Dr Faustus*; *Stanislavsky and the Method*; *The Critic as Artist*; *The Encore Reader* (editor); *New American Drama* (editor); *Alarums and Excursions* (editor).

*   *   *

The theatre of playwright, director, critic, and dramaturg Charles Marowitz is perhaps best characterized by his collaborations with Peter Brook in the Royal Shakespeare Company's Experimental Group, which culminated in the 1964 *Theatre of Cruelty Season*, and by his "radical, freestyled" adaptations of Shakespeare that he began in 1965 with *The Marowitz Hamlet* and continued with five other plays, including *An Othello*, *A Macbeth*, and *The Shrew* (five of which have been collected and published as *The Marowitz Shakespeare*). The Shakespearean collages, in fact, also grew out of the 'Theatre of Cruelty' experiments. As Marowitz notes, "Brook has said it would be fascinating to see *Hamlet* ... reshuffled like a deck of familiar cards". Thus it was that Marowitz spliced up the play "into a collage with lines juxtaposed, sequences rearranged, characters dropped or blended, and the entire thing played out in fragments which appeared like subliminal flashes out of Hamlet's life".

Critics have complained that titles like *The Marowitz Hamlet* demonstrate an unhealthily inflated ego at work, but for Marowitz his adaptations are not Shakespeare's plays. Of *An Othello* he has said, "This really is not Shakespeare's *Othello*, which is just a context into which one has written another play". Certainly, Tom Stoppard's more successful *Rosencrantz and Guildenstern Are Dead* — as well as Edward Bond's violent and political *Lear* — owes something to the Marowitz 'reshuffled' *Hamlet*.

Between 1965 and 1967 Marowitz was associate director of the shortlived London Traverse Theatre at the Jeanetta Cochrane Theatre, an off-shoot of the more successful Traverse Theatre in Edinburgh. From 1968 to 1981 he was founder and artistic director of the Open Space Theatre in London, where he staged the world premiere of Sam Shepard's *Tooth of Crime*, Büchner's *Woyzeck*, and Picasso's *Four Little Girls*, among others. In 1982 he left London to become associate director, playwright, and dramaturg of the Los Angeles Theatre Centre, where he remained until 1989.

As early as 1963 Marowitz began discussing the work of French poet and one-time surrealist Antonin Artaud with Peter Brook, and the following year Marowitz began a notable collaboration with Brook, first as assistant director on the Royal Shakespeare Company's production of *King Lear* at Stratford-upon-Avon and then as co-director of the RSC Experimental Group, which was founded to develop the theatrical theories of Artaud in his influential treatise *The Theatre and Its Double*. "Reading Artaud in my early twenties was like coming across a meteorite from an entirely different solar system", he recalled. The intention behind the Experimental Group was, according to Marowitz, "to explore certain problems of acting and stagecraft in laboratory conditions without the commercial pressures of public performance". But the Group soon moved into public performance, nonetheless, with an evening of short works including "two short nonsense-sketches by Paul Abelman", Artaud's *Jet of Blood*, a dramatization of a short story by Alain Robbe-Grillet, two collages by Brook, *The Public Bath* and *The Guillotine*, three scenes from Genet's *The Screens*, an "anti-Machiavellian mime-sketch" called *The Analysis*, a short play by John Arden and Margaretta D'Arcy, *Ars Longa, Vita Brevis*, and Marowitz's collage-*Hamlet*. The four-week run of short works and improvisations was then followed by a Brook-Marowitz production of Jean Genet's *The Screens* at the Donmar Rehearsal Rooms and culminated in Brook's direction of Peter Weiss's *Marat/Sade*, perhaps the theatrical high point of Artaud's 'Theatre of Cruelty'. The RSC's *Theatre of Cruelty Season* at the LAMDA Theatre was one of the first manifestations of Artaud's profound influence on the contemporary theatre and, in fact, launched the theatrical Age of Artaud. It also launched a new actress on the English stage — Glenda Jackson. Marowitz's interest in Artaud continued after the season ended and, in 1975, having adapted number of classical works, he wrote *Artaud at Rodez*, which premiered at the Teatro a Trastavere in Rome prior to a run at the Open Theatre in London.

As a theorist and teacher of acting, Marowitz is concerned with reconciling or accommodating the Method of Stanislavsky with the acting required for avant-garde, anti-realistic theatre. "Having been brought up on Stanislavsky", he notes, "and the idea of inner truth, it was a major adjustment to discover that there was also *surface truth*". He concludes, finally, that "there is no fundamental disagreement between the Method actor and the Artaudian actor".

Marowitz has also worked extensively with Scandinavian playwrights in Scandinavian theatres, including the Oslo Nye Theatre, the Trondelag Theatre, and the National Theatre of Norway, the Odense Theatre, and the Aarhus Theatre in Denmark and the Folkteatern in Sweden, where he staged the works of Ibsen and Strindberg in addition to his Shakespearean adaptations. His *Free Adaptations of Ibsen and Strindberg* were published as *The Sex Wars* in 1982.

Marowitz has written for various theatre publications as a critic and also for such newspapers as *The Times, The Guardian*, and *The Observer*. His play *Sherlock's Last Case* premiered as part of the Olympic Arts Festival at the Los Angeles Actors' Theatre in 1984 before moving to Broadway. It was published, together with two other Marowitz plays — *Ah, Sweet Mystery of Life* and *Clever Dick* in *Potboilers: Three Black Comedies*.

—S. E. Gontarski

MARS, Mlle. French actress. Born Anne-Françoise-Hippolyte Boutet in Paris, 9 February 1779; illegitimate daughter of the actor Monvel. Never married; had three children by Swiss officer in the French army. Stage debut, under Mlle Montansier, at the age of 12 at the Theatre de Versailles, 1791; admitted to the company of the Théâtre Feydeau, 1795; became a sociétaire, with a part share, of the Comedie-Française, 1799; granted full share in the Comédie-Française, 1807; toured with the company to the Court Theatre in Dresden, 1813; promoted the reintroduction of the comedies of Molière into the repertory and also won acclaim in tragedy; retired from stage, 1841. Died in Paris, 20 March 1847.

Roles

1795	Deaf mute in *L'Abbé de l'Epée* (Bouilly), Théâtre Feydeau, Paris.
1804	Elmire in *Tartuffe* (Molière), Comédie-Française, Paris.
1809	Madame d'Orbeuil in *Le Secret du mariage* (Creuzé de Lesser), Comédie-Française, Paris.
1829	Duchesse de Guise in *Henri III et sa cour* (Dumas père), Comédie-Française, Paris.
	Desdémone in *Le More de Venise* (Vigny, adapted from Shakespeare's *Othello*), Comédie-Française, Paris.
1830	Doña Sol in *Hernani* (Hugo), Comédie-Française, Paris.
1833	Elisabeth in *Les Enfants d'Edouard* (Delavigne), Comédie-Française, Paris.
	Clarisse Harlowe in *Clarisse Harlowe* (Dinaux, adapted from Richardson), Comédie-Française, Paris.
1835	Tisbé in *Angelo, Tyran de Padoue* (Hugo), Comédie-Française, Paris.
1839	Mademoiselle de Belle Isle in *Mademoiselle de Belle-Isle* (Dumas père), Comédie-Française, Paris.

Other roles included: Agnès in *L'École des maris* (Molière); Angélique in *L'Épreuve* (Marivaux); Angélique in *Le Malade imaginaire* (Molière); Caroline in *Caroline*; Célimène in *Le Misanthrope* (Molière); Charlotte in *Deux frères* (Lesage); Éliante in *Le Misanthrope* (Molière); Isabelle in *L'École des maris* (Molière); Rosina in *Le Barbier de Séville* (Beaumarchais); Séraphine in *Minuit*; Silvia in *Jeu de l'amour et du hasard* (Marivaux); Victorine in *Philosophie sans le savoir* (Sedaine); and roles in: *Le Cid d'Andalousie* (Lebrun); *La Femme jalouse* (Desforges); all with the Comédie-Française, Paris, 1795–1839.

Publications

Les Mémoires de Mlle Mars, 2 vols., 1849; *Les Confidences de Mlle Mars*, 3 vols., 1855.

*

Bibliography

Books:
E. Aclocque, *Souvenirs anecdotiques sur Mlle Mars*, Paris, 1847.
E. Briffaut, *Mlle Mars, sa vie, ses succès, sa mort*, Paris, 1847.

* * *

Anne-Françoise-Hippolyte Boutet was born into the theatrical profession as natural daughter of the actor Monvel and of Mlle Salvétat, whose stage name Mars she was to adopt. Making her theatrical debut in 1791 at the age of 12, she profited from the teaching and advice of the actor Walville, her mother's companion, and of the more distinguished actors Dugazon and Louise Contat; and at 16 she was admitted to the company at the Théâtre Feydeau. Despite an initially unpromising physical appearance — she was thin, gauche and shy — she was given a place as sociétaire when the Comédie-Française was reconstituted after the disruption of the Revolutionary years: beginning with a part share (three eighths) in 1799, she progressed rapidly until she was granted a full share in 1807. Unlike most of the legendary performers of French theatrical history, it took Mlle Mars a considerable time to grow into her full stature as an actress: at the age of 20 her prospects were still being assessed in unfavourable terms: "Lovely eyes, a gentle expression, intelligence, sensibility — but her timidity and restraint, which might suit ingénue rules, are fatal to roles which require the lively expression of feeling". Indeed, her first successes were in ingénue roles; but she was still playing Molière's Agnès or Angélique in her mid-twenties; and it was only the retirement of her mentor, Louise Contat, in 1809 that enabled her to seize her chance in roles like Célimène. By 30, her undoubted physical charms were fully developed. "I despaired of ever being beautiful", she is reported to have said at this period; "but Providence must be more favourable in Paris than elsewhere, for I am filling out nicely".

She was instrumental in the revival of Marivaux at the Comédie-Française, where she is said to have been an 'incomparable' Silvia, and also brought many of Molière's plays back into the active repertoire. However, it was in the celebrated roles of Célimène (in *Le Misanthrope*) and Elmire (in *Tartuffe*) that Mars made her reputation — a reputation based on an unparalleled attention to detail, from the perfectly modulated inflections of her voice to the elegance and refinement of her dress, make-up and manner. According to a biographer, "even the smallest ribbon possessed an extraordinary significance for her, and her dress sense and consummate elegance were as important as the qualities of her voice in enabling this charming actress to dominate the stage to the end of her career". Altogether, she showed an instinctive appreciation of what was needed to identify with the great coquette roles of the French comic repertoire, to the extent that for her contemporaries, these roles became so many extensions of her own personality.

Outside the theatre, she soon began to establish herself as an elegant leader of fashion: when the Comédie-Française company visited Dresden in 1813, court and town paid homage to her, and princes, ambassadors and generals were honoured to be given the entrée to her salon; and for the rest of her life she set an example of style and good taste in Paris society.

Although Mlle Mars was a major asset to the Comédie-Française throughout her career in the classical repertory, especially that of Molière and Marivaux, her attitude towards the authors of the new Romantic drama was one of incomprehension and hostility. She did play the Duchesse de Guise in Dumas's *Henri III et sa cour* in 1829, and Desdémone in Vigny's adaptation of *Othello*, *Le More de Venise*, in the same year, without incident, but the production of Hugo's *Hernani* in the following year was quite another matter. *Hernani* was not only to give rise to the celebrated outbreaks of near-rioting in the audience that have become known as the 'battle of *Hernani*', but the rehearsals and the first performances took place in an atmosphere of mistrust and recrimination, with Mlle Mars, who at 51 was to play the young heroine Doña Sol, as the spearhead of the opposition, taking every opportunity to criticise Hugo's innovative handling of the alexandrine metre and his audacious choice of vocabulary, as well as his provocative stagecraft. When the leading lady maintained her refusal to speak such lines as "Vous êtes mon lion superbe et généreux", so that the young author was finally moved to threaten to have her replaced, her active interference was replaced by mute hostility; "She continued to protest by a frosty silence", reported Madame Hugo. In the case of Hugo's *Angelo* (1835), in which Mlle Mars was cast as the courtesan Tisbe, hostility towards the author was compounded by the actress's feud with Marie Dorval, who had been admitted to the Comédie, fresh from her triumphs in the boulevard theatre, in 1834. The campaign against her had begun during rehearsals for Vigny's *Chatterton*, in which Dorval was to score an outstanding success earlier in 1835; and rehearsals and performances of *Angelo* were marked by jealousy and resentment on the part of the older woman, frequently translated into acts of malice.

The opulent lifestyle of Mlle Mars at a series of addresses in Paris, and in the country at Versailles and later at Sceaux, gives some indication of the financial rewards to be had by the leading performers of her day; though in 1832 she judged it expedient to retire as a sociétaire, drawing her retirement pension, and to return the following year as a salaried pensionnaire: an arrangement that enabled her to enjoy a total income of 55,000 francs a year — very handsome indeed for the period. In spite of her wealth and the luxury in which she lived, in her private and domestic affairs she avoided the public eye. She had three children by an army officer, who died young — as did one of her daughters. Mlle Mars retired from the stage in 1841, choosing roles from Molière and Marivaux for her final performances. Her death in 1847 was the occasion for a remarkable public tribute, and over 50,000 mourners are said to have followed her coffin from the Madeleine to Père-Lachaise.

—William D. Howarth

MASSEY, Raymond (Hart). Canadian-born US actor and director. Born in Toronto, Canada, 30 August 1896. Educated at Appleby School, Ontario, 1910–14; Toronto University, and Baliol College, Oxford, 1919–21. Married 1) Margery Fremantle in 1921 (divorced 1929), one son; 2)

Adrianne Allen (divorced 1939), one son (actor Daniel Massey) and one daughter (actress Anna Massey); 3) Dorothy Ludington Whitney in 1939; one step-daughter. Served in Canadian Field Artillery, 1915–19. Stage debut, Everyman Theatre, London, 1922; entered into co-management of Everyman Theatre, 1926; film debut, 1930; New York debut, 1931; served in Canadian Army, 1942–43; took US nationality, 1944; toured with dramatic readings of the poem "John Brown's Body", 1953; final appearance on London stage, 1970. Member: Council, Actors' Equity Association (vice-president); Council, British Actors' Equity Association. Recipient: Delia Austria Medal, 1939. DFA: Ripon College, Ripon, Wisconsin, 1961; Northwestern University, 1959; D.Litt: Lafayette University, 1939; Hobart College, Geneva, New York, 1953; LL.D: Queen's University, Kingston, Canada, 1949; LHD: American International College of Massachusetts, 1960; DHL: College of Wooster, Wooster, Ohio, 1966. Died in Los Angeles, 29 July 1983.

Productions

As actor:

1922	Jack in *In the Zone* (O'Neill), Everyman Theatre, London.
	Roberts in *Glamour* (Bernard), Apollo Theatre, London.
1923	James Bebb in *At Mrs Beam's* (Munro), Everyman Theatre, London, and Royalty Theatre, London.
	Jones in *The Rose and the Ring* (Deans), Wyndham's Theatre, London.
1924	Stanley Pitt in *The Audacious Mr Squire* (Bowkett and Stannard), Criterion Theatre, London.
	Captain La Hire and Canon d'Estivet in *Saint Joan* (G. B. Shaw), New Theatre, London.
1925	Lieutenant Gaythorne in *Tunnel Trench* (Griffith), Prince's Theatre, London; also directed.
	Jonty Drennan in *The Round Table* (Robinson), Wyndham's Theatre, London.
	Captain Rickman in *Prisoners of War* (Ackerley), Court Theatre, London, and Playhouse Theatre, London.
1926	Robert Mayo in *Beyond the Horizon* (O'Neill), Everyman Theatre, London; also directed.
	Rufe Pryor in *Hell-Bent for Heaven* (Hughes), Everyman Theatre, London; also directed.
	Edmund Crowe in *The Rat Trap* (Coward), Everyman Theatre, London.
	Mr Man in *Brer Rabbit* (Dearmer), Everyman Theatre, London.
	Tommy Luttrell in *The White Chateau* (Berkeley), Everyman Theatre, London; also directed.
1927	Khan Aghaba in *The Transit of Venus* (Harwood), Ambassadors' Theatre, London.
	Rev MacMillan in *An American Tragedy*, Apollo Theatre, London; also directed.
	Reuben Manassa in *The Golden Calf* (Jerrold), Globe Theatre, London.
1928	Austin Lowe in *The Second Man* (Behrman), Playhouse Theatre, London.
	Alister Ballantyne in *Four People* (Malleson), St Martin's Theatre, London.
	Joe Cobb in *Spread Eagle* (Brooks and Lister), New Theatre, London; also directed.
	Lewis Dodd in *The Constant Nymph* (Kennedy and Dean), Garrick Theatre, London.
1929	Randolph Calthorpe in *The Black Ace* (Brandon and Farson), Globe Theatre, London.
1930	Smitty in *In the Zone* (O'Neill), Ambassadors' Theatre, London.
	Raymond Dabney in *The Man in Possession* (Harwood), Ambassadors' Theatre, London; also directed.
	Topaze in *Topaze* (Levy), New Theatre, London.
1931	Randall in *Late Night Final* (Weitzenkorn), Phoenix Theatre, London; also directed.
	Hamlet in *Hamlet* (Shakespeare), Broadhurst Theatre, New York.
1932	Smith in *Never Come Back* (Lonsdale), Phoenix Theatre, London.
	Hiram Travers in *Bulldog Drummond* (Munro), Adelphi Theatre, London.
1933	Dr Maclean in *Doctor's Orders* (Verneuil, adapted by Graham), Globe Theatre, London.
	Hugh Sebastian in *The Rats of Norway* (Winter), Playhouse Theatre, London; also directed.
	Kurt von Hagen in *The Ace* (Malleson, adapted from Rossmann), Lyric Theatre, London.
	Cleon in *Acropolis* (Sherwood), Lyric Theatre, London.
1934	David Linden in *The Shining Hour* (Winter), Royal Alexandra Theatre, Toronto, Booth Theatre, New York, and St James's Theatre, London; also directed.
1936	Ethan Frome in *Ethan Frome* (Davis), National Theatre, New York.
1938	Harry Van in *Idiot's Delight* (Sherwood), Apollo Theatre, London; also directed.
1938–40	Abraham Lincoln in *Abe Lincoln in Illinois* (Sherwood), Plymouth Theatre, New York.
1941	Sir Colenso Ridgeon in *The Doctor's Dilemma* (G. B. Shaw), Shubert Theatre, New York.
1942	James Havor Morell in *Candida* (G. B. Shaw), Shubert Theatre, New York.
1943	Rodney Boswell in *Lovers and Friends*, Plymouth Theatre, New York.
1945	Stage Manager in *Our Town* (Wilder), USO European tour.
	Henry Higgins in *Pygmalion* (G. B. Shaw), Ethel Barrymore Theatre, New York.
1947	Professor Lemuel Stevenson in *How in Wonder*, Hudson Theatre, New York.
1949	Role in *The Winslow Boy* (Rattigan), US tour; US tour, 1950; also directed.
	The Captain in *The Father* (Strindberg), Cort Theatre, New York; also directed.
1955	Brutus in *Julius Caesar* (Shakespeare), American Shakespeare Festival Theatre, Stratford, Connecticut.

Raymond Massey (c. 1950)

Prospero in *The Tempest* (Shakespeare), American Shakespeare Festival Theatre, Stratford, Connecticut.

1957   Abraham Lincoln in *The Rivalry* (Corwin), Orpheum Theatre, Seattle; US tour, 1960.

1958   Mr Zuss in *J.B.* (McLeish), ANTA Theatre, New York.

1970   Tom Garrison in *I Never Sang for My Father* (Anderson), Duke of York's Theatre, London.

1975   Nonno in *The Night of the Iguana* (T. Williams), Ahmanson Theatre, Los Angeles.

As director:

1927   *The Wolves* (Rolland), London.
The Crooked Billet (Titheradge), Royalty Theatre, London.
The Squall (Bart), Globe Theatre, London.

1928   *Blackmail* (Bennett), Globe Theatre, London.

1929   *The Sacred Flame* (Maugham), Playhouse Theatre, London.
The Stag (Nichols), Globe Theatre, London.
The Silver Tassie (O'Casey), Apollo Theatre, London.
Symphony in Two Parts (Novello), New Theatre, London.

1930   *Dishonoured Lady* (Barnes and Sheldon), Playhouse Theatre, London.

1931   *Lean Harvest* (Jeans), St Martin's Theatre, London.

Grand Hotel (Baum, adapted by Knoblock), Adelphi Theatre, London.
Full Circle (Pedrolo), London.

1935   *Ringmaster* (Winter), Shaftesbury Theatre, London.
Worse Things Happen at Sea (Winter), St James's Theatre, London.

1936   *Heart's Content* (Strode), Shaftesbury Theatre, London.

1937   *The Orchard Walls* (Hodge), St James's Theatre, London.

Films

The Speckled Band, 1930; *The Face at the Window*, 1931; *The Old Dark House*, 1932; *The Scarlet Pimpernel*, 1934; *Things to Come*, 1936; *Fire Over England*, 1936; *Under the Red Robe*, 1937; *The Prisoner of Zenda*, 1937; *Dreaming Lips*, 1937; *Hurricane*, 1937; *The Drum*, 1938; *Black Limelight*, 1939; *Abe Lincoln in Illinois*, 1940; *Santa Fe Trail*, 1940; *49th Parallel*, 1941; *Dangerously They Live*, 1941; *Desperate Journey*, 1942; *Reap the Wild Wind*, 1942; *Action in the North Atlantic*, 1943; *Arsenic and Old Lace*, 1944; *The Woman in the Window*, 1944; *Hotel in Berlin*, 1945; *God is My Co-Pilot*, 1945; *A Matter of Life and Death*, 1946; *Possessed*, 1947; *Mourning Becomes Electra*, 1947; *The Fountainhead*, 1948; *Roseanna McCoy*, 1949; *Chain Lightning*, 1949; *Barricade*, 1950; *Dallas*, 1950; *Sugarfoot*, 1951; *Come Fill the Cup*, 1951; *David Bathsheba*, 1951; *Carson City*, 1952; *The Desert Song*, 1953; *Prince of Players*, 1955; *Battle Cry*, 1955; *East of Eden*, 1955; *Seven Angry Men*, 1955; *Omar Khayyam*, 1957; *The Naked and the Dead*, 1958; *The Great Imposter*, 1960; *The Fiercest Heart*, 1961; *The Queen's Guard*, 1961; *How the West Was Won*, 1962; *Mackenna's Gold*, 1968.

Television

Our Town, 1948; *I Spy* (series), 1955; *Dr Kildare* (series), 1961–66; *All My Darling Daughters*, 1972; *The President's Plane is Missing*, 1973.

Publications

Hanging Judge (play, produced New Theatre, London, 1952); *When I Was Young* (autobiography), 1976; *A Hundred Different Lives* (autobiography), 1979.

* * *

Raymond Massey was the younger son of a wealthy industrialist in Toronto. His ancestors included Boston preachers as well as Ontario farmers. The family manufactured agricultural machinery and young Raymond spent much of his youth on their private experimental farm, where he indulged his two main passions: horse-riding and amateur theatricals. He was joined in the latter pursuit by his cousins and his older brother Vincent, who later became Governor-General of Canada.

In 1915 Massey joined the Canadian Field Artillery and served as an officer in France and Siberia. His military experience convinced him of the value of both discipline and individual initiative. After the war he attended Balliol College for two years before deciding to become a professional actor. When he informed his family, his strict Methodist father enjoined him to pray before each performance and his austerely discreet brother inquired "What name will you use?"

Massey began his professional career at the Hart House Theatre built by his family but soon went to London, where he concentrated on contemporary plays. He helped to introduce the plays of Eugene O'Neill to British audiences when he appeared as Jack in a production of *In the Zone* at the Everyman Theatre in 1922 and he played Captain La Hire and D'Estivet in the original production of *St Joan* in 1924. Massey began directing the same year and by 1926 was a partner in the management of the Everyman Theatre. Over the next five years he directed and appeared in many new plays, opposite such prominent actresses as Angela Baddeley, Athene Seyler, Isabel Jeans, and Gladys Cooper. He scored a considerable success as Khan Aghaba in *The Transit of Venus* in 1927, a role in which he exploited the romantic potential of his darkly handsome, aquiline features and resonant, metallic voice.

In 1931 Massey went to New York and made his Broadway debut as Hamlet in a production by Norman Bel Geddes that featured a number of innovative touches, including Massey himself speaking the lines of the Ghost to a spectral head. It instantly established him in the USA as an actor of power and presence and also inspired the playwright Robert Sherwood to begin work on a play about Abraham Lincoln, in which Massey would score his greatest stage success. In the meantime he appeared as the repressed New England farmer in *Ethan Frome* opposite Ruth Gordon in New York and as the cynical hoofer Harry Van in *Idiot's Delight* in London. He continued to pursue a transatlantic stage career playing with many of the major actors of the period, including Laurence Olivier, Noël Coward, Sybil Thorndike, and his wife Adrianne Allen.

During the 1930's Massey began to appear in films, initially in costume epics produced by Sir Alexander Korda. Typically he was cast as a saturnine villain: the silky menace of his Chauvelin opposite Leslie Howard's effetely charming Sir Percy Blakeney in *The Scarlet Pimpernel* set a pattern that would be repeated with variations when Massey played Black Michael in *The Prisoner of Zenda* and Oswald Cabal in H. G. Wells's *Things to Come*. His work in these British films led to a Hollywood offer and casting as the sternly oppressive Governor De Laage in John Ford's *Hurricane.*

By 1938 Robert Sherwood had completed his play *Abe Lincoln in Illinois* and Massey opened in it on Broadway before touring throughout the USA in 1939 and 1940. In this role his angular physique, natural reserve, scratchy humour, innate authority, and fierce determination all worked to shape a strongly felt performance that embodied a vision of simple integrity that struck a resonant chord at a time when the USA was heading into another world war.

During the early 1940's Massey continued to tour the USA, playing opposite Katherine Cornell in two Shaw plays, *The Doctor's Dilemma* and *Candida*. His authority and restrained energy provided an excellent foil for her luminous charm. Massey exploited these same qualities in a staged reading of Stephen Vincent Benét's poem 'John Brown's Body', in which he toured with Judith Anderson

and Tyrone Power, and in his portrayals of Prospero and Brutus at the new Shakespearean Festival at Stratford, Connecticut, and his Broadway appearance as the godlike Mr Zuss in Archibald MacLeish's verse drama *J.B.*

Massey continued to appear in films as varied as Michael Powell's historical fantasy *Stairway to Heaven*, the grittily realistic *Action in the North Atlantic*, and the ghoulish comedy *Arsenic and Old Lace*. Perhaps his most memorable film role was the uncompromising father who battles with James Dean in Elia Kazan's *East of Eden*. By now thoroughly identified with the historical and ethical spirit of 19th-century America, Massey became a US citizen in 1944 and settled first in Wilton, Connecticut, and then in California. For five years in the early 1960's he played the genial curmudgeon Dr Gillespie in the long-running television series *Dr Kildare*, opposite Richard Chamberlain.

Massey made two more forays to London: he adapted Bruce Hamilton's novel *The Hanging Judge* for a successful run at the New Theatre, starring Sir Godfrey Tearle, and made a final appearance at the Duke of York's in 1970 in Robert Anderson's *I Never Sang for My Father*, with Catherine Lacey. Severely crippled by arthritis in his last years, he completed two volumes of autobiography: *When I Was Young* is a lively account of life in Edwardian Toronto and his experiences in World War I and *A Hundred Different Lives* is a richly anecdotal reminiscence of his professional career.

—Martin Hunter

MATHEWS, Charles James. British actor and playwright. Born in Liverpool, 26 December 1803; son of the comedian Charles Mathews. Educated at the Merchant Taylors' School, London, and at private school in the Clapham Road, London. Married 1) actress-manager Madame Vestris in 1838 (*q.v.*) (died 1857); 2) actress Lizzie Davenport in 1858. Trained as architect under Augustus Pugin and ran own practice as architect; stage debut as amateur, Lyceum Theatre, London, 1822; further amateur appearances during tour of Italy, 1827; succeeded his father as co-manager, with Frederick Yates, of the Adelphi Theatre, 1835; actor, Vestris's company, Olympic Theatre, from 1835; became popular as urbane gentleman-comedian; toured New York and Philadelphia with Vestris, 1838; co-manager, Covent Garden, 1839–42; produced some 100 plays; declared bankrupt and briefly imprisoned for debt, 1842; actor, Theatre Royal, Drury Lane, and Haymarket Theatre, 1842–47; manager, Lyceum Theatre, 1847–55; imprisoned once more for debt, 1856; second US tour, 1857–58; visited Paris, 1863 and 1865; toured Australia, USA, and Canada, 1870–72, and India, 1875. Died in Manchester, 28 June 1878.

Roles

1822   Dorival in *Le Comédien d'Etampes* (adapted from the French), Lyceum Theatre, London.
    Werther in *The Sorrows of Werther* (Poole), Lyceum Theatre, London.
1835   George Rattleton in *The Humpbacked Lover* (Mathews), Olympic Theatre, London.

The Young Stager in *The Old and Young Stagers* (Rede), Olympic Theatre, London.

Chorus in *Medea* (burlesque), Olympic Theatre, London.

1838   Captain Patter and other roles in *Patter versus Clatter* (Mathews), Olympic Theatre, London.

1839   Slender in *The Merry Wives of Windsor* (Shakespeare), Covent Garden, London.

1840   Dazzle in *London Assurance* (Boucicault), Covent Garden, London.

Puff and Sir Fretful Plagiary in *The Critic* (Sheridan), Covent Garden, London.

1842   Charles Surface in *The School for Scandal* (Sheridan), Haymarket Theatre, London.

1843   Giles in *Who's Your Friend?* (Planché), Haymarket Theatre, London.

Charles Swiftly in *One Hour*, Edinburgh.

1844   Sir Charles Coldstream in *Used Up* (Boucicault), Haymarket Theatre, London.

1845   Chorus in *The Golden Fleece* (Planché), Covent Garden, London.

1848   Daedalus in *Theseus and Ariadne* (Planché), Lyceum Theatre, London.

1851   Lavater in *Cool as a Cucumber* (Jerrold), Lyceum Theatre, London.

Affable Hawk in *A Game of Speculation* (Lewes), Lyceum Theatre, London.

1858   Paul Pry in *Paul Pry* (Poole), Haymarket Theatre, London.

Goldfinch in *The Road to Ruin* (Holcroft), Haymarket Theatre, London.

1860–61   Will Wander in *The Savannah* (Mathews), Theatre Royal, Drury Lane, London.

1861   Himself in *Mr and Mrs Mathews at Home* (Mathews), Theatre Royal, Drury Lane, London.

1872   Sir Simon Simple in *Not Such a Fool as He Looks* (H. J. Byron), Wallack's Theatre, New York.

Also acted roles in: *Woodcock's Little Game* (Morton), St James's Theatre, London, 1864; *Adventures of a Love Letter* (Mathews, adapted from Sardou), St James's Theatre, London, 1864; *A Curious Case*, Gaiety Theatre, London, 1872; *My Awful Dad* (Mathews), Gaiety Theatre, London, 1875; *The Liar* (Foote), Opéra Comique, London, 1877; *The Cosy Couple* (Lewes), Opéra Comique, London.

Publications

Lettre aux Auteurs Dramatiques de la France, 1852; *The Life of Charles James Mathews*, 2 vols., edited by Charles Dickens, 1879. Plays included: *Adventures of a Love Letter*; *Aggravating Sam*; *Bachelor of Arts*; *Black Domino*; *Carlo*; *Chain of Events*; *Cherry and Blue*; *The Court Jesters*; *Cousin German*; *Dead for a Ducat*; *Dowager*; *He Would Be an Actor*; *His Excellency*; *The Humpbacked Lover*; *Impudent Puppy*; *Kill Him Again*; *Little Toddlekins*; *Mandrin*; *Married for Money*; *Match for a King*; *Mathews and Co.*; *Methinks I See My Father*; *Milliner to the King*; *My Awful Dad*; *My Mother's Maid*; *My Usual Luck*; *My Wife's Mother*; *Nothing to Wear*; *Patter versus Clatter*; *Paul Pry Married and Settled*; *Pong-wong*; *Pyramus and Thisbe*; *Ringdoves*; *The Savannah*; *Serve Him Right*; *Soft Sex*; *Striking Likeness*; *Take that Girl Away*; *Too Kind by Half*; *Truth*; *Two in the Morning*; *Who Killed Cock Robin?*; *Why did you Die?*; *The Wolf and the Lamb*; *You Can't Marry Your Grandmother*; *You're Another*.

* * *

In his earliest performances Charles James Mathews relied on the relaxed, elegant manner of a gentlemanly amateur, which indeed he was, as a dilettante architect in the fashionable retinue of Lady Bessborough, travelling through Italy and joining in country house theatricals. However, he was also the son of Charles Mathews, comedian, mimic, and manager of the Adelphi and, in 1835, after his father's retirement, Charles James took employment at the Olympic under Madame Vestris. His socialite background and aimiable personality made him an ideal 'jeune premier' in Planché's extravaganza burlettas, which required poise rather than passion and the turning of a witty phrase rather than vivid characterisation. George Henry Lewes described Mathews at this early stage in his careers as "eminently vivacious; a nimble spirit of mirth sparkled in his eye ... A certain grace tempered his vivacity; an innate sense of elegance rescued him from the exaggerations of animal spirits. 'He wanted weight,' as an old playgoer reproachfully said of him; but he had the qualities of his defects, and the want of weight became a delightful airiness". He was introduced to the Olympic audience in a specially written farce, *The Old and Young Stagers*, in which he played opposite John Liston, and in comparison with that masterly low comedian with his droll manner of button-holing the audience, Mathews's undemonstrative light comedy playing seemed refreshingly modern, even 'naturalistic'. When Mathews performed the Chorus in a burlesque of *Medea*, Lewes pointed out how most actors "would have 'gagged' or made grimaces, would have been extravagant and sought to startle the public into laughter at broad incongruities. Charles Mathews is as quiet, easy, elegant, as free from points and as delightfully humourous as if the part belonged to high comedy ... Probably few who saw Charles Mathews play the Chorus consider there was any art required so to play it; they can understand that to sing patter songs as he sings them may not be easy, but to be quiet and graceful and humorous, to make every line tell, and never show the stress of effort, will not seem wonderful. If they could see another actor in the part it would open their eyes".

This easy relaxed style was perfect for the 'little pieces' — farces, burlettas, and burlesques — presented by Vestris at the Olympic, one of the most successful being Mathews's own farce *Patter versus Clatter* in which, employing a talent for mimicry inherited from his father, he played five different characters, including Captain Patter, whose fast and incessant chattering drove the other actors from the stage. In 1838 Mathews and Vestris were married and although she remained in control of stage production in their partnership, Mathews had to take on responsibility for the financial side of their ventures in theatre management. Their tour of the USA failed to make money and their lease of Covent Garden (1839–42) proved financially disastrous, despite the production of Dion Boucicault's *London Assurance*, in which Mathews played Dazzle with great success. Although he and Vestris were to manage the Lyceum from 1847, Mathews was continually pursued for debt, culminating with a second spell in gaol shortly before Vestris died in 1856. In his account of having to avoid creditors and face bankruptcy, Mathews reveals how his outwardly dilettante manner had to conceal real worries, having to "act, with a merry face, the very part in jest that I was playing behind the scenes in earnest! ... Everyone seemed to believe that I revelled in it, and every allusion I had to make to duns and bailiffs was hailed by the audience as the emanation of a light heart". Thus the fashionable amateur was transformed into the solid professional, whose conscientious reliability as a performer became the hallmark of a career that lasted into his seventies, when he undertook tours of Australia and India with his second wife. Often the couple performed a 'salon entertainment', *Mr and Mrs Mathews at Home*, following the pattern of Charles Mathews Senior's *At Home*. Without costume or scenery they performed sketches and songs, which exploited Mathews's ability to adopt the voice and manner of several characters, though, like many mimics, the impersonations were essentially superficial, as he had no ability to evoke emotions or suggest any great depth of personality. Dutton Cook went so far as to observe: "Even that semblance of feeling by means of which very obtuse players, given a pathetic situation, have been able to move their public, was beyond him".

However, in later life Mathews expanded his repertoire to include some 'straight' comedy and 'genteel' melodrama, although he mainly relied on playing his favourite roles, such as Captain Patter, the socialite Sir Charles Coldstream in *Used Up*, Plumper in *Cool as a Cucumber*, and the doubling of Puff and Sir Fretful Plagiary in Sheridan's prototype burlesque, *The Critic*. In 1851 G. H. Lewes wrote a part specifically to exploit Mathews's 'quiet' manner in a more serious role, and he described the performance of Affable Hawk, a ruthless financier, in *A Game of Speculation* as having such merit that "it almost became an offence against morality, by investing a swindler with irresistable charms, and making the very audacity of deceit a source of pleasurable sympathy ... instead of 'looking the villain', he looked like the man to whom all drawing-rooms would be flung open. Instead of warning away his victims by a countenance and manner significant of villainy, he allured them with the graceful ease of a conscience quite at rest". Westland Marston's account of Affable Hawk gives more detail: "There was not a tone, look, or gesture which might not have been employed by a City man of the time ... A finger inserted in a waistcoat pocket, the deprecatory movement of an arm, or the flourishing of a handkerchief, gave with him as much emphasis in comedy as the heroic gesture or serious actors have given in tragedy". By this kind of unmelodramatic reticence Mathews anticipated the emergence, during the later 19th century, of performers like Squire Bancroft, Edward Willard, George Alexander, Charles Wyndham, and Charles Hawtrey, who, though not trained as actors, became stars of the West End drawing-room comedy by appearing to be entirely at home in high society and by *seeming* to conceal all their emotions behind a facade of suave manners, dry wit, and elegant tailoring.

—George Taylor

McCLINTIC, Guthrie. US director, actor, and producer. Born in Seattle, Washington, 6 August 1893. Educated at local schools in Seattle and at the University of Washington; studied theatre at the American Academy of Dramatic Arts, New York, 1910–12. Married actress Katharine Cornell (*q.v.*) in 1921. Stage debut, as actor, 1912; New York debut, 1914; actor, Grace George's company, Playhouse, New York, 1915–16; actor, Jessie Bonstelle's repertory company, Buffalo, 1918; subsequently assistant director with Winthrop Ames's company, Little Theatre, New York; debut as director, 1921; director, Actors' Theatre, Inc., 1927; directed 28 productions starring his wife. Recipient: Pulitzer Prize, 1935; New York Drama Critics' Award, 1935. Died in Sneden's Landing, New York, 29 October 1961.

Productions

As actor:
1912   Walk-on role in *Oliver Twist* (Dickens), Canadian tour.
1914   Messenger in *The Truth* (Fitch), Little Theatre, New York.
1915–16 Nogam in *The New York Idea* (Mitchell), Playhouse, New York.
        George Nepean in *The Liars* (H. A. Jones), Playhouse, New York.
        Morrison in *Major Barbara* (G. B. Shaw), Playhouse, New York.
        James Bent in *The Earth* (Fagan), Playhouse, New York.
        Marzo in *Captain Brassbound's Conversion* (G. B. Shaw), Playhouse, New York.

As director:
1921   *The Dover Road* (Milne), New York.
1922   *Gringo*, New York.
1923   *A Square Peg* (Beach), New York.
        In the Next Room (Robson and Ford), New York.
1924   *The Way Things Happen* (Dane), Lyceum Theatre, New York.
1925   *Mrs Partridge Presents* (Kennedy and Hawthorne), New York.
        All Dressed Up, New York.
        The Green Hat (Arlen), Broadhurst Theatre, New York.
1926   *Glory Hallelujah*, New York.
        The Shanghai Gesture (Colton), New York.
1927   *Saturday's Children* (M. Anderson), Booth Theatre, New York.
        Mariners (Dane), New York.
        The Letter (Maugham), Morosco Theatre, New York.
        John (Barry), Klaw Theatre, New York.
1928   *Cock Robin* (Barry and Rice), 48th Street Theatre, New York.
        The Age of Innocence, Empire Theatre, New York.
        Jealousy (Walter), New York; also acted Maurice.
1929   *The Skyrocket* (Reed), New York.
        The Cross-Roads (Robinson), New York.

1930	*Dishonoured Lady* (Barnes and Sheldon), Empire Theatre, New York.
1931	*The Barretts of Wimpole Street* (Besier), Empire Theatre, New York.
1932	*Distant Drums* (Totheroh), New York
	The Truth About Blayds (Milne), New York.
	Criminals at Large, New York.
	Lucrece (Obey), Belasco Theatre, New York.
1933	*Alien Corn* (Howard), Belasco Theatre, New York.
	Jezebel (Welsh), New York.
1934	*Yellow Jack* (Howard and De Kruif), Martin Beck Theatre, New York.
	Divided by Three, New York.
	Romeo and Juliet (Shakespeare), US tour.
1935	*The Old Maid* (Akins, adapted from Wharton), New York.
	Winterset (M. Anderson), Martin Beck Theatre, New York.
	Parnell, New York.
1936	*Ethan Frome*, New York.
	Hamlet (Shakespeare), Empire Theatre, New York.
	The Wingless Victory (M. Anderson), Empire Theatre, New York.
	The Ante-Room, London.
1937	*High Tor* (M. Anderson), Martin Beck Theatre, New York.
	Candida (G. B. Shaw), New York.
	The Star-Wagon (M. Anderson), Empire Theatre, New York.
	Barchester Towers, New York.
1938	*How to Get Tough About It*, New York.
	Missouri Legend, New York.
1939	*Mamba's Daughters*, New York.
	No Time for Comedy (Behrman), Ethel Barrymore Theatre, New York.
	Key Largo (M. Anderson), Ethel Barrymore Theatre, New York.
	Christmas Eve (Hecht), New York.
1940	*An International Incident*, New York.
1941	*The Lady Who Came to Stay*, New York.
	The Doctor's Dilemma (G. B. Shaw), Shubert Theatre, New York.
	Spring Again, New York.
1942	*The Morning Star* (E. Williams), New York.
	The Three Sisters (Chekhov), Ethel Barrymore Theatre, New York.
1943	*Lovers and Friends*, Plymouth Theatre, New York.
1945	*You Touched Me!* (T. Williams), New York.
1946	*The Playboy of the Western World* (Synge), New York.
	Antigone (Anouilh), Cort Theatre, New York.
1947	*Antony and Cleopatra* (Shakespeare), Martin Beck Theatre, New York.
1948	*Life with Mother* (Lindsay and Crouse), New York.
1949	*Medea* (Jeffers), New York.
	That Lady (O'Brien), Martin Beck Theatre, New York.
	The Velvet Glove (R. Casey), New York.
1950	*Burning Bright* (Steinbeck), New York.
	Captain Carvallo (Cannan), US tour.

1951	*The Constant Wife* (Maugham), National Theatre, New York.
1952	*Come of Age* (Ashton), New York.
	To Be Continued (Marchant), New York.
	Bernadine (Chase), New York.
1954	*Mrs Patterson*, New York.
1955	*The Dark Is Light Enough* (Fry), ANTA Theatre, New York.
	A Roomful of Roses (Sommer), New York.
1957	*Four Winds* (Atkinson), New York.
1960	*Dear Liar* (Kilty), US tour.

* * *

Guthrie McClintic was one of the most distinguished and prolific US directors of his generation. Although he directed nearly 100 productions over four decades, including the Pulitzer Prize-winning *The Old Maid* and the Critics' Circle Prize-winning *Winterset* and *Hight Tor*, he is most famous for directing his wife, Katharine Cornell, in 28 plays.

McClintic ran away from home in Seattle at an early age to join a repertory company. Stranded, he was rescued by his parents, who thereupon promised to provide him an adequate theatrical education, which he received in New York at the American Academy of Dramatic Art. Although he performed in a number of popular venues, as he later admitted, no-one took him seriously as an actor. His star began to rise, however, when he bluffed his way into the employ of Winthrop Ames, one of the most popular producers and directors on the US stage in the 1920's and 1930's and an impeccable gentleman of considerable taste and efficiency. McClintic's association with Ames proved fruitful not only for the skills and artistic acuity which McClintic developed but also for an offer from Ames of backing in a Broadway venture. Not finding a suitable property, McClintic signed with Jessie Bonstelle's repertory company as the resident director. It was a fortuitous choice, since there he met his wife, who had been engaged as the leading lady (on seeing Cornell years earlier he had written the now famous three words "Interesting, monotonous, watch"). Upon returning to New York in 1921 he found the script he wanted to direct, A. A. Milne's *The Dover Road*, which started him on his distinguished career.

Four years later McClintic first directed Cornell in a drama of intrigue and glamour, *The Green Hat*. A number of similar vehicles followed, in the course of which McClintic developed his skills as a director and, largely on account of his tutelage, Cornell developed a considerable following. It was because of his perceptivity that she was offered her most famous role — by him. She had been given the script of *The Barretts of Wimpole Street* to read and immediately saw that it was the kind of property that her husband could bring to vivid life. He, on the other hand, realised that she was ready to essay the leading role of Elizabeth Barrett. It proved to be their most enduring success.

The production was an artistic as well as commercial success and is emblematic of the contributions McClintic made to the US theatre. His directorial style was gentle and thorough. Rather than lay a concept on an existing vehicle, he contented himself with allowing the plays he directed to fulfil their potential as stage experiences. Typical of his taste and thoroughness was the fact that the incipient incestuous relationship between Miss Barrett and her father, the overbearing and terminally Victorian Edward Moulton-Barrett, was not only perceived but added to the piquancy of the heroine's escape from home into the arms of Robert Browning. In the hands of a lesser artist the turn would either have gone unnoticed or would have been repugnant. It was just the sort of directorial detail that McClintic made popular, finding fascinating and character-ful actions with which to embellish his impeccably cast productions.

But perhaps the heart of McClintic's art lay in his ability to visualize a production. He claimed that as he read a play he could see how each element would contribute to all others and, indeed, it was his scenic designers whom he hired first. He felt that each aspect of a production was essential to the communication of every other aspect. His productions were integrated wholes, despite the fact that his wife was the jewel at the centre of the composition. His 1942 production of Chekhov's *The Three Sisters*, for instance, with Cornell, Judith Anderson, and Ruth Gordon, was praised as surpassing the Moscow Art Theatre in terms of ensemble and insight.

McClintic's contribution was a particular sort of self-respect for the US theatre. Emerging from a tradition of popular entertainment, McClintic took the Broadway stage to new-found heights of artistic achievement that also brought success at the box office, the end all and be all of the US commercial theatre. His faith in Maxwell Anderson, for instance, a playwright who treated complicated and idiomatically American stories in verse, gave that playwright respectable and competent productions. McClintic more than once stretched his audience too far with plays of high artistic goals but little dramatic interest. His productions were often obvious but rarely ineffective. At his best, as *The Barretts of Wimpole Street* or his production of *Romeo and Juliet* with Cornell and Maurice Evans (whom he introduced to the US stage), McClintic was a director who was able to combine artistic integrity, novelty of interpretation, and the show business élan necessary to sell a solid property to Broadway.

—David Payne-Carter

McKELLEN, (Sir) Ian (Murray). British actor and director. Born in Burnley, England, 25 May 1939. Educated at Wigan Grammar School; Bolton school; St Catherine's College, Cambridge University, 1958–61. Stage debut, with Belgrade Theatre Company, Coventry, 1961; London debut, 1964; actor, National Theatre Company at the Old Vic Theatre, London, 1965; television debut, 1965; Broadway debut, 1967; joined Prospect Theatre touring company, 1968; film debut, 1968; founder-member, Actors' Company, 1972–74; actor, Royal Shakespeare Company, 1974–78; organised Royal Shakespeare Company tour of 27 towns and villages, 1978; associate director, National Theatre, London, 1984–86; managed, with Edward Petherbridge, small company within National Theatre organisation, 1985–86; Cameron Mackintosh Professor of Contemporary Theatre, University of Oxford, 1991. Fellow, St Catherine's College, Cambridge, 1982. Member: Marlowe Society (president, 1960–61); Council of Equity, 1971–72. Recipient: Clarence Derwent Award, 1964; *Plays and Players* Award for Most Promising Actor, 1966; Drama Desk Award, 1974, 1981, 1984; *Plays and Players* Best Actor Award, 1976; Society of West End Theatre Award, 1977, 1978, 1979, 1984, 1985; Tony Award, 1981; New York Drama League Award, 1981; Outer Critics Circle Award, 1981; Royal Television Society Performance of the Year Award, 1983; Los Angeles Drama Critics Circle Award, 1984; Laurence Olivier Actor of the Year Award, 1984, 1991; *London Standard* Actor of the Year Award, 1985, 1989; Elliot Norton Award, 1987. D.Litt: University of Nottingham, 1989. CBE (Commander of the British Empire), 1979. Knighted, 1991.

Productions

As actor:

1961–62　Son Roper in *A Man for All Seasons* (Bolt), Belgrade Theatre, Coventry.
Fred Dyson in *When We Are Married* (Priestley), Belgrade Theatre, Coventry.
Philip in *You Never Can Tell* (G. B. Shaw), Belgrade Theatre, Coventry.
Tredwell in *Black Coffee* (Christie), Belgrade Theatre, Coventry.
Stan Dyson in *Celebration* (Hall and Waterhouse), Belgrade Theatre, Coventry.
Mason in *End of Conflict* (England), Belgrade Theatre, Coventry.
Mr Snodgrass in *Mr Pickwick* (Young, adapted from Dickens), Belgrade Theatre, Coventry.
Chief Weasel in *Toad of Toad Hall* (Milne), Belgrade Theatre, Coventry.
Konstantin in *The Seagull* (Chekhov), Belgrade Theatre, Coventry.
Joe Tilney in *The Bride Comes Back* (Millar), Belgrade Theatre, Coventry.
Claudio in *Much Ado About Nothing* (Shakespeare), Belgrade Theatre, Coventry.
Tom in *Semi-Detached* (Turner), Belgrade Theatre, Coventry.
Shem in *Noah* (Wilmurt), Belgrade Theatre, Coventry.

1962–63　Elliott Nash in *The Gazebo* (Coppel), Arts Theatre, Ipswich.
David in *David Copperfield* (Dickens), Arts Theatre, Ipswich.
Chinese Policeman in *Aladdin*, Arts Theatre, Ipswich.
Henry in *Henry V* (Shakespeare), Arts Theatre, Ipswich.
Luther in *Luther* (Osborne), Arts Theatre, Ipswich.
Evans in *The Corn Is Green* (E. Williams), Arts Theatre, Ipswich.
Bridegroom in *All in Good Time* (Naughton), Arts Theatre, Ipswich.

1963　Robin Green in *The Big Contract*, Belgrade Theatre, Coventry.

1963–64　Aufidius in *Coriolanus* (Shakespeare), Playhouse, Nottingham.
John in *The Life in My Hands*, Playhouse, Nottingham.

Winifred Hutchins in *The Bashful Genius* (Green and Dankworth), Playhouse, Nottingham.

The Captain, Don Alvaro in *The Mayor of Zalamea* (Calderón), Playhouse, Nottingham.

Arthur Seaton in *Saturday Night and Sunday Morning* (De Filippo), Playhouse, Nottingham.

More in *Sir Thomas More* (Bolt), Playhouse, Nottingham.

1964   Godfrey in *A Scent of Flowers* (Saunders), Duke of York's Theatre, London.

1965   Claudio in *Much Ado About Nothing* (Shakespeare), Old Vic Theatre, London.

Protestant Evangelist in *Armstrong's Last Goodnight* (Arden), Old Vic Theatre, London, and Chichester Festival Theatre.

Captain de Foenix in *Trelawney of the Wells* (Pinero), Old Vic Theatre, London, and Chichester Festival Theatre.

1965–66   Alvin in *A Lily in Little India* (Howarth), Hampstead Theatre, London, and St Martin's Theatre, London.

1966   Andrew Cobham in *Their Very Own and Golden City* (Wesker), Royal Court Theatre, London.

O'Flaherty in *O'Flaherty, V.C.* (G. B. Shaw), Mermaid Theatre, London.

Napoleon Bonaparte in *The Man of Destiny* (G. B. Shaw), Mermaid Theatre, London.

Leonidik in *The Promise* (Arbuzov), Playhouse, Oxford; Fortune Theatre, London, and Henry Miller Theatre, New York, 1967.

1968   Tom in *White Liars* (P. Shakker), Lyric Theatre, London.

Harold Gorringe in *Black Comedy* (P. Shaffer), Lyric Theatre, London.

Richard in *Richard II* (Shakespeare), British tour; Edinburgh Festival, Mermaid Theatre, London, and Piccadilly Theatre, London, 1969–70.

1969   Pentheus in *The Bacchae* (Euripides), Playhouse, Liverpool.

1969–70   Edward in *Edward II* (Marlowe), Edinburgh Festival, British tour, Mermaid Theatre, London, and Piccadilly Theatre, London.

1970   Darkly in *Billy's Last Stand* (Hines), Theatre Upstairs, London.

Captain Plume in *The Recruiting Officer* (Farquhar), Cambridge Theatre, London, and British tour.

Corporal Hill in *Chips with Everything* (Wesker), Cambridge Theatre, London, and British tour.

1971   Hamlet in *Hamlet* (Shakespeare), British and European tour and Cambridge Theatre, London.

Svetlovidov in *Swan Song* (Hecht and MacArthur), Crucible Theatre, Sheffield.

1972   Page-boy in *Ruling the Roost* (Feydeau), Cambridge Theatre, London, British tour, and Edinburgh Festival.

Ian McKellen (1989).

Giovanni in *'Tis Pity She's a Whore* (Ford), Cambridge Theatre, London, British tour, and Edinburgh Festival; Brooklyn Academy, New York, 1973; Wimbledon Theatre, London, 1974.

Prince Yoremitsu in *The Three Arrows* (Murdoch), Cambridge Theatre, London, British tour, and Edinburgh Festival.

1973   Michael in *The Wood Demon* (Chekhov), Edinburgh Festival and British tour.

Footman in *The Way of the World* (Congreve), Edinburgh Festival, British tour, and Brooklyn Academy, New York; Wimbledon Theatre, London, 1974.

Edgar in *King Lear* (Shakespeare), Brooklyn Academy of Music, New York; Wimbledon Theatre, London, 1974.

Faustus in *Doctor Faustus* (Marlowe), Edinburgh Festival, British tour, and Aldwych Theatre, London.

1974–75   The Marquis in *The Marquis of Keith* (Wedekind), Aldwych Theatre, London.

Philip the Bastard in *King John* (Shakespeare), Aldwych Theatre, London.

Aubrey Bagot in *Too True to Be Good* (G. B. Shaw), Aldwych Theatre, London, and Globe Theatre, London.

1975   Colin in *Ashes* (Rudkin), Young Vic Theatre, London.

1976–77   All roles in *Words, Words, Words* (McKellen), Edinburgh Festival.

Romeo in *Romeo and Juliet* (Shakespeare), Royal Shakespeare Theatre, Stratford-upon-Avon, Newcastle, and Aldwych Theatre, London.

Leontes in *The Winter's Tale* (Shakespeare), Royal Shakespeare Theatre, Stratford-upon-Avon.

Macbeth in *Macbeth* (Shakespeare), The Other Place, Stratford-upon-Avon, Royal Shakespeare Theatre, Stratford-upon-Avon, Warehouse Theatre, London, and Young Vic Theatre, London.

Face in *The Alchemist* (Jonson), The Other Place, Stratford-upon-Avon, and Aldwych Theatre, London.

Karsten Bernick in *Pillars of the Community* (Ibsen), Aldwych Theatre, London.

Langevin in *Days of the Commune* (Brecht), Aldwych Theatre, London.

Alex in *Every Good Boy Deserves Favour* (Stoppard), Royal Shakespeare Theatre, Stratford-upon-Avon, Newcastle, and Aldwych Theatre, London.

All roles in *Ian McKellen Acting Shakespeare* (McKellen), Edinburgh Festival; international and US tours, 1980–83.

1978   Sir Toby Belch in *Twelfth Night* (Shakespeare), British tour; also directed.

Andrei in *The Three Sisters* (Chekhov), British tour; also directed.

1979   Max in *Bent* (Sherman), Royal Court Theatre, London, and Criterion Theatre, London; Royal National Theatre, London, and Garrick Theatre, London, 1989–90.

1980   Salieri in *Amadeus* (P. Shaffer), Broadhurst Theatre, New York, and National Theatre, Washington, D.C.

Narrator in *Eagle in New Mexico* (D. H. Lawrence recital), Sante Fe, New Mexico.

1983   Boy in *Cowardice* (Mathias), Ambassadors' Theatre, London, and British tour.

Terry in *The Short List* (Rudman), Hampstead Theatre, London.

1984–86   Pierre in *Venice Preserved* (Otway), National Theatre, London.

Platonov in *Wild Honey* (Chekhov, adapted by Frayn), National Theatre, London; Ahmanson Theatre, Los Angeles, and Virginia Theatre, New York, 1986–87.

Coriolanus in *Coriolanus* (Shakespeare), National Theatre, London.

Bosola in *The Duchess of Malfi* (Webster), National Theatre, London; Blackstone Theatre, Chicago, 1986.

Inspector Hound in *The Real Inspector Hound* (Stoppard), National Theatre, London; Blackstone Theatre, Chicago, 1986.

Mr Puff in *The Critic* (Sheridan), National Theatre, London; Blackstone Theatre, Chicago, 1986.

Lopakhin in *The Cherry Orchard* (Chekhov), National Theatre, London; Blackstone Theatre, Chicago, 1986.

1987–88   Jerome in *Henceforward...* (Ayckbourn), Vaudeville Theatre, London.

1989   Iago in *Othello* (Shakespeare), The Other Place, Stratford-upon-Avon, and Young Vic Theatre, London.

Richard in *Richard III* (Shakespeare), Royal National Theatre, London, and British tour; US tour, 1992.

1990   Kent in *King Lear* (Shakespeare), Royal National Theatre, London, and world tour.

1991   Gennaro Jovine in *Napoli Milionaria* (De Filippo), Royal National Theatre, London.

1992   Vanya in *Uncle Vanya* (Chekhov, adapted by Gems), Royal National Theatre, London.

Other roles included: *Happy Returns* (revue), Belgrade Theatre, Coventry, 1961–62; *Ten Little Niggers* (Christie), Belgrade Theatre, Coventry, 1961–62; *Irregular Verb to Love* (H. and M. Williams), Belgrade Theatre, Coventry, 1961–62; *Caste* (Robertson), Arts Theatre, Ipswich, 1962–63; *The Big Killing* (Mackie), Arts Theatre, Ipswich, 1962–63; *The Amorous Prawn* (Kimmins), Arts Theatre, Ipswich, 1962–63; *The Keep* (Thomas), Arts Theatre, Ipswich, 1962–63; *How Dare We!*, Arts Theatre, Ipswich, 1962–63; *Arsenic and Old Lace* (Kesselring), Arts Theatre, Ipswich, 1962–63; *Long Day's Journey Into Night* (O'Neill), Arts Theatre, Ipswich, 1962–63; *I, John Brown*, Arts Theatre, Ipswich, 1962–63; *Salad Days* (Reynolds and Slade), Arts Theatre, Ipswich, 1962–63; *Knots*, Shaw Theatre, London, and Brooklyn Academy, New York, 1973, and Wimbledon Theatre, London, 1974.

As director:
1969   *The Prime of Miss Jean Brodie* (Spark), Playhouse, Liverpool.

1972   *The Erpingham Camp* (Orton), Palace Theatre, Watford.

1973   *A Private Matter* (Mavor), Vaudeville Theatre, London.

1975   *The Clandestine Marriage* (Colman the Elder), Savoy Theatre, London.

Films

Alfred the Great, 1968; *Thank You All Very Much*, 1968; *A Touch of Love*, 1969; *The Promise*, 1968; *The Priest of Love*, 1980; *The Keep*, 1982; *Plenty*, 1985; *Zina*, 1985; *Scandal*, 1989; *Last Action Hero*, 1993. Other films included: *I'll Do Anything*; *The Ballad of Little Jo*; *Six Degrees of Separation*.

Television

Sunday out of Season, 1965; *David Copperfield* (serial), 1966; *Ross*, 1970; *Richard II*, 1970; *Edward II*, 1970; *Hamlet*, 1971; *Hedda Gabler*, 1974; *Macbeth*, 1978; *Dying Day*, 1978; *Ian McKellen Acting Shakespeare*, 1981; *Walter*, 1982; *The Scarlet Pimpernel*, 1982; *Walter and June*, 1983; *Countdown to War*, 1989; *Othello*, 1989; *Cold Comfort Farm*, 1994.

*

Bibliography

Books:
Joy Leslie Gibson, *Ian McKellen*, London, 1986.

* * *

Ian McKellen has been widely acknowledged as one of the best British stage actors of his generation. He has played a variety of classical and modern roles for the National Theatre, the Royal Shakespeare Company, and the Royal Court as well as in the West End and on Broadway. He has also twice headed a theatre company: the Actors' Company in the 1970's and his own group under the umbrella of the National Theatre in the 1980's.

McKellen had a conventional start to his career in the 1960's, emerging from the Marlowe Society at Cambridge to gain apprentice experience in the provinces — Coventry, Nottingham, and Ipswich. Through the mid- and later 1960's, he appeared briefly in more prominent venues such as the National and Royal Court Theatres and in the West End, but it was not until he performed the title roles in *Richard II* and *Edward II* for the Prospect Theatre Company in 1969 that he attracted notice as a young classical actor. Edward II in particular provided McKellen with a showcase for his own virtuostic talents. His Edward II was a narcissistic extrovert very willing to make gestures — such as kissing his lover Gaveston in front of his wife — simply to shock. Flailing about the stage like a rebellious teenager, McKellen delivered Marlowe's (patchy) verse with a vocal inventiveness for which he has become well-known (but for which he has also sometimes gained criticism).

In 1974, McKellen joined the Royal Shakespeare Company, playing a variety of roles that included Leontes, Romeo, the Bastard in *King John*, and the Marquis of Keith in Wedekind's play. But it was his two roles, Face in Jonson's *The Alchemist* and Macbeth, that solidified his reputation as an important classical actor. His performance in *Macbeth* perhaps represents McKellen's acting at its best. This role revealed his talent for suggesting extreme passions kept tightly in check through a military demeanour — something he was to draw upon later playing Richard III and Iago. His restrained cinematic performance fitted perfectly into Trevor Nunn's production, which used the intimacy of The Other Place to create an intense, emotionally charged atmosphere. Although his taut acting in *Macbeth* might seem the mirror opposite of his Edward II, both performances exemplified McKellen's bravura style, which makes him a theatrical star and not a company man.

McKellen joined the National in 1984, and enjoyed his most successful sustained relationship with a theatre company there, continuing to work under both the Hall and Eyre regimes. McKellen's first major accomplishment at the National came with his casting at Platonov in *Wild Honey*, Michael Frayn's adaptation from Chekhov. The play's farcical elements allowed McKellen to exercise his extravagant comic talents while still staying true to Chekhov's subtle characterization. His next success at the National followed with the title role in Peter Hall's 1984

production of *Coriolanus*. The production initially received mixed reviews, but over the course of time its reputation has grown so that McKellen's performance is now considered one of his greatest achievements, the equal of the interpretations of Laurence Olivier and Alan Howard in the same role. For his next major classical role, McKellen joined a spate of Richard III's bustling around London in 1989. In Richard Eyre's production, a fantasia on a fascist Britain, McKellen mingled aspects of Edward VIII and Hitler, speaking with a clipped aristocratic accent while imitating Hitler's idiosyncratic hand gestures. From the opening soliloquy, delivered standing at rigid attention, McKellen's Richard, like his Macbeth and Iago, was a professional soldier. Keeping control over his body as well as his situation, this Richard over compensated for his deformities (one side was paralyzed as if from a stroke) by lighting cigarettes, opening wine-bottles, undressing, and wielding weapons one-handed with flourish. In this, as in his Edward II, McKellen melded the magnetic qualities of charismatic actor and character. Perhaps as a result of this, McKellen's acting has sometimes been compared to Olivier's — the highly physical style and the visibility of technique, of virtuosity (although detractors would call this mechanical or mannered). Also like Olivier, McKellen's acting can move stylistically between broad strokes and grand gesture and pointillist detail and restrained naturalism.

Throughout his career, McKellen has remained resolutely a theatre actor, never landing that significant film role or television series that might make him a household name. However, he has gained considerable media attention for his public "role" of gay rights activist. Indeed, this has even impacted his acting career: he revived his portrayal of Max in *Bent* (in which he had originally appeared at the Royal Court in 1979) and has taken cameo roles in television movies. While his political activism opened up new areas in his career, McKellen continued to participate in the National Theatre repertory, touring in *Richard III* and garnering rave reviews for his performance in *Uncle Vanya*. The knighthood he received in 1991, meanwhile, consolidated his public reputation as a theatrical "celebrity".

—Melissa Gibson

———

McMAHON, Gregan. Australian actor and director. Born 2 March 1874. Educated at St Ignatius College, Riverview, Sydney, New South Wales, and at the University of Sydney. Married Mary Hungerford in 1900, one son and one daughter. Stage debut, with the company of Robert Brough; also gained early experience acting with visiting touring companies; co-founder, Melbourne Repertory Company, 1911; presented, with the Gregan McMahon Players at the Melbourne Repertory Theatre, Australian premieres of numerous plays by George Bernard Shaw and other contemporary writers; founded first repertory theatre in Sydney, 1918; staged over 300 productions in all. CBE (Commander of the British Empire), 1938. Died 30 August 1941.

Selected productions

1911–17   *John Gabriel Borkman* (Ibsen), Repertory Theatre, Melbourne.
 The Voysey Inheritance (Granville-Barker), Repertory Theatre, Melbourne; acted George Booth.
 The Madras House (Granville-Barker), Repertory Theatre, Melbourne.
 The Seagull (Chekhov, translated by Calderon), Repertory Theatre, Melbourne.
 The Revolt (Adams), Repertory Theatre, Melbourne.
 Interior (Maeterlinck), Repertory Theatre, Melbourne.
 The Trojan Women (Euripides), Repertory Theatre, Melbourne.
 The Time Is Not Yet Ripe (Esson), Repertory Theatre, Melbourne.
 Candida (G. B. Shaw), Repertory Theatre, Melbourne; acted Burgess.
 Rosmersholm (Ibsen), Repertory Theatre, Melbourne; acted Brendel.
 The Pigeon (Galsworthy), Repertory Theatre, Melbourne; acted Ferrand.
 Man and Superman (G. B. Shaw), Repertory Theatre, Melbourne; acted Tanner.
 What the Public Wants (Bennett), Repertory Theatre, Melbourne; acted Sir Charles Wogan.
1936   *The Millionairess* (G. B. Shaw), King's Theatre, Melbourne.

* * *

After a little over 10 years as a professional actor, Gregan McMahon set out on a 30-year career as Australia's outstanding director. This was incidental to maintaining an indigenous theatre for high quality modern plays. His concerns were not commercial, but artistic, and his inspiration came from the British repertory movement that emerged out of the independent theatre societies of the 1890's (for instance, the Independent Theatre and the Stage Society), through the Vedrenne-Barker seasons at London's Court Theatre (1904–07) and its successors, including Miss Horniman's management at the Gaiety Theatre, Manchester. In the early years of the century, the colonial attitude to culture — as a product of the mother country that might occasionally be imported in small quantities — prevailed in Australia, which was a regular and lucrative destination for overseas touring companies. With no grant or subsidy at any time, McMahon achieved his impressive continuity of work by staying partly outside strictly professional theatre and through a series of ingenious negotiations with leading commercial managements and local amateurs, supplying performers and audiences in Melbourne and, for a shorter time, in Sydney. Late in life, he explained the fact that he had never visited Europe or the USA by saying that his kind of theatre would die out in Australia if he was away for six months.

Having acted at school and while he was at university, he eventually abandoned reading for the Bar in order to turn professional player, joining a series of visiting companies that recruited members from local talent. Both Robert Brough and William Hawtrey offered training to young actors. Gregan seems to have emerged as a skilful comedy actor, excelling in character parts. His features were mobile, his voice flexible, and he had the ability to change shape and appearance using make-up with a light hand. Some clue to his own style may be gathered from principles he adopted in selecting actors for the first Melbourne Repertory Company: "Perfect naturalness with no stage tricks was the end we had in view".

The interests of several groups had combined to give him the opportunity to direct his own company. Supporters of the suffragette cause wanted the plays of Ibsen and Shaw to be publicly presented; a nationalist literary group wanted a stage for new Australian drama; and intellectuals and socialites wanted to see what were then avant-garde successes from Europe. The core of an audience had been built up through a programme of Sunday-night play readings in Melbourne, through the 1890's, which had encompassed all Ibsen's available plays, and, more immediately, by the regular play-readings directed by visiting actress Madge McIntosh (Vivie in the first, Stage Society, production of Shaw's *Mrs Warren's Profession*, and soon to be directing for the Repertory Theatre in Glasgow and, later, director of the Liverpool Repertory Company). The core of McMahon's first acting company graduated from these 1907–09 play-readings. For their first year he personally guaranteed the financial backing. The support of a Repertory Theatre Club enabled him to carry on into 1917 with a regular three seasons a year. He also took pupils in the 'Repertory Theatre School of Dramatic Art', promising them practical experience. Keeping his company together, he built up its reputation as an ensemble of truly professional standard. This was probably the least troubled, most undeniably successful, phase of his work.

Productions presented by the company included nine plays by Shaw, several by Ibsen, works by Galsworthy, Granville-Barker, Chekhov, Villiers de l'Isle Adams, Maeterlinck and Euripides, as well as 13 Australian plays. McMahon's own performances consistently won praise. He preferred to take important minor roles, such as Burgess in *Candida*, Brendel in *Rosmersholm*, or George Booth in *The Voysey Inheritance*. His Ferrand, in Galsworthy's *The Pigeon*, was a "bundle of wistful negatives". Outstanding among the lead roles he took was his Tanner in *Man and Superman*, to which no-one else was equal. A favourite with audiences was Arnold Bennett's *What the Public Wants*, with McMahon playing Sir Charles Wogan in "a very quiet, natural and easy style ... keenly aware of the point of the dialogue. He carried the play along by his bright, quick delivery and his promptness".

The dominant professional managers, J. C. Williamson and Tait, noted his success and encouraged him to extend his activities to Sydney in 1918, with their backing. This was the start of problems — in reconciling commercial management's conditions with the wishes of audiences, amateur actors and champions of Australian plays — only temporarily solved, in various ways, and sometimes by resorting to other managements, up to the day of his death. The Sydney Repertory Theatre Society never fully trusted him and ultimately fell prey to internal dissensions. When his contract obliged him to include professionals employed by the management in his casts, they were sometimes taken away from him at the last moment; less biddable than amateurs, they sometimes gave inferior performances.

McMahon's own services as a director were sometimes required by Williamson's for their own commercial productions. They had no-one else of equal skill and reputation and, given the equipment, he was noted for spectacular stage effects. Eventually, he retreated into once more running a company in Melbourne only, having fought his way through the worst years of threat from the cinema.

Sydney had not liked Ibsen, but otherwise McMahon had continued to expand the range of modern classics he brought to both state capitals: Pirandello became a regular contributor to his repertoire, source of some his chief personal successes, alongside Galsworthy and Shaw. With the latter dramatist he built up a relationship that brought him advice and 'rehearsal copies' for each new play in turn, culminating in permission to mount the world premiere of *The Millionairess*. All along, McMahon's intelligence had shown in his play selection, as well as interpretation, and he belonged to the school of believers in faithful and thorough study of the text. His control over actors was sometimes described as 'Svengali-like', yet numbers of them went on to success in the regular professional theatre and films and continued to voice their indebtedness to him. His chief gift to the English stage was Coral Browne. The stage designer, Loudon Sainthill, also came to England after first being employed by McMahon. Criticised for not giving more Australian plays, he could honestly plead that he went as far as he could in the face of prevailing audience indifference or hostility, and consequent financial disaster, and that he never finally gave up the attempt: even his last season included an Australian item.

—Margery Morgan

MEI LANFANG. Chinese actor, singer, and dancer. Born in Beijing, 1894. Stage debut, aged 14, 1908; acclaimed in female roles in Peking Opera performances throughout China and on tours to the West, 1919–35; visited USA, 1930, and Russia, 1935; widely acknowledged as finest performer in Chinese theatrical history and created many new dance plays, often in collaboration with theatre scholar Qi Rushan, until 1931; remained in Shanghai during Japanese Occupation of China but refused to act; returned to stage, 1949. Died 8 August 1961.

Roles

Deng Xiagu in *Deng Xiagu*; Han Yuniang in *Hongni Guan* [The Rainbow Pass]; Hong Niang in *Xixiang Ji* [The West Wingroom Story]; Jiang Qiulian in *Chun Qui Pei* [The Good Match]; Liang Hongyu in *Kang jinbing* [To Fight Against the Army of the Jing Empire]; Lie Jie in *Tongnu zhan she* [The Maid Who Beheaded a Snake]; Lin Niufen in *Yi lou ma* [A Bundle of Hemp]; Li Shanke in *Laoyu yuanyang* [The Lovebirds in Gaol]; Magu in *Magu Xian Shou* [A Birthday Benediction from Magu]; Mu Guiying in *Mu Guiying gua shuai* [General Mu Guiying]; Sum Furen in *Hui Jingzhou* [Return to Jongzhou]; Tiannu in *Tiannu san hua* [The Nymphs Scattering Flowers]; Xishi in *Xishi*; Yang Yuhuan in *Guifei zuijiu* [The Inebriated Queen]; Yu Ji in *Bawang beiji* [Farewell

Mei Lanfang

My Concubine]; Zhang Jinfeng in *Nengren si* [Nengren Monastery].

*

Bibliography

Books:
George Kin Leung, *Mei Lan-Fang — Foremost Actor of China*, Shanghai, 1929.

* * *

Mei Lanfang (or Lan-Fang) was the most famous and possibly the greatest actor China has ever produced. He was both a transmitter and an innovator and contributed enormously to most of the skills that combine to make up the Peking Opera, including gesture, mime, walking, music, and especially singing, stylized dialogue, make-up, and costume.

His greatest achievements were in the 'qingyi' roles, that is, the respectable, demure, virtuous, and serious female characters. However, he also excelled in the aristocratic and elegant 'Kunqu' drama, and in a variety of female roles other than 'qingyi', such as the military women ('wudan') and the coquettish, lively, 'flower female roles' ('huadan'). Although the ability to perform in more than one role-category was not new to Mei Lanfang, he did help to broaden variety among Chinese performers and to make specialization in only one role-type less fashionable.

Mei Lanfang's contribution to the music of the Peking Opera was extensive. He rearranged the traditional melodies or melodic phrases, giving them his own characteristic style, and also created new ones. Not only his voice, but his own singing style was completely unmistakeable, characterized by unusually clear diction, bright but mellow timbre, in the relevant passages a quite extraordinary mellifluousness, and an effortlessness worthy of note considering he was always singing falsetto. He also instituted changes in the instrumentation that accompanied the sung passages of Peking Opera. For instance, it was largely his innovation to include the low-registered gentle-sounding two-stringed bowed spike fiddle called 'erhu' as auxiliary to the somewhat higher sounding and more piercing but otherwise similar fiddle 'jinghu' in passages for female ('dan') characters.

Many of the items Mei performed early in his career were written or arranged specifically for him by Qi Rushan (1877–1962). But in Peking Opera, performance outstrips libretto and plot in significance. Mei contributed acting and singing skills and innovations important enough to make the plays joint creations.

Among Mei Lanfang's most acclaimed roles from the early part of his career were Yang Guifei in *Guifei zuijiu*, which concerns the favourite concubine of Emperor Minghuang of Tang (who gets drunk when her imperial lover fails to appear for a banquet to which he has invited her), and the heroine of *Yuzhou feng*, a beautiful woman who pretends to be mad in a successful attempt to avoid marrying an emperor. Another notable role, which he performed in the later part of his life, after 1945, was Mu Guiying, one of the most often dramatized female warrior heroes of Chinese history, and a splendid part through which Mei Lanfang could display the important military side of the Peking Opera art.

Mei Lanfang's influence over the Peking Opera remains substantial. He is still regarded as a byword for excellence among Chinese theatre-lovers and he has become something of a cult figure in the People's Republic in recent years. Mei's influence has also been felt in other countries. Among those impressed by him in the West were Stanislavsky and Brecht. His visit to the USA in 1930 also did much to spread knowledge of the Chinese theatre in the West.

By personality, Mei Lanfang was reputed to be modest, despite the fact that he was treated as the star he undoubtedly was, and always anxious to learn from others. He enjoyed unusually good relations with his audiences, seeking and accepting opinions from them on how he might improve his art. He was generous in his admiration of other artists, and was a close friend of Qi Bashi (1863–1957), modern China's greatest painter. His admiration for Charlie Chaplin, whom he met several times in the USA, was such that he promoted some comic actors in the Peking Opera able to perform in a similar style of deadpan humour. Outside the theatre, he was a lover and cultivator of flowers, and kept pigeons. He was also very patriotic and during the Japanese Occupation refused to act as a sign of protest, even growing a moustache to prevent his acting the female roles in which he excelled.

The art of the male impersonator of females is nowadays more or less dead in China, as the roles they once acted are now performed by women. It is a tribute to Mei Lanfang's greatness that the style of acting that he pioneered is still not only carried on but remains popular and a touchstone of excellence. More than any other person, he created lasting artistic images of Chinese femininity, whether of the disappointed drunken lover of *Guifei zuijiu* or of the heroic warrior Mu Guiying. In creating the inner psychology of the women whose roles he performed he surpassed all other Chinese actors. His versatility was also without parallel on the Chinese stage, and his repertoire was of unusual breadth. A great lover and admirer of tradition, he excelled as a transmitter, but was also daring in breaking away from those stereotypes that he perceived as preventing further artistic development. No performer contributed more to the history of Peking Opera than he.

—Colin Mackerras

MERRY, Anne. British actress and manager. Born Anne Brunton in Westminster, London, 30 May 1769. Educated by her mother; trained for the stage by her father, provincial actor-manager John Brunton. Married 1) playwright Robert Merry in 1791 (died 1798); 2) actor Thomas Wignell in 1803 (died seven weeks later); 3) actor-manager William Warren in 1806. Stage debut, Bristol, 1785; actress, Covent Garden, 1785–92; retired after first marriage, 1792; lived in Paris, 1792–93; returned to London, 1793–95; emigrated to USA on Wignell's invitation, appearing at Chestnut Street Theatre, Philadelphia, 1796; first appearance in New York, 1797; consolidated reputation as leading actress in tragic roles; co-manager of Chestnut Street from 1803. Died (following childbirth) in Alexandria, Virginia, 28 June 1808.

Roles

1785 Euphrasia in *The Grecian Daughter* (Murphy), Theatre Royal, Bath.

   Horatia in *The Roman Father* (Corneille, adapted by Whitehead), Theatre Royal, Bath, and Covent Garden, London.

   Palmira in *Mahomet* (Voltaire, adapted by Miller), Theatre Royal, Bath.

   Juliet in *Romeo and Juliet* (Shakespeare), Covent Garden, London.

   Monimia in *The Orphan* (Otway), Covent Garden, London.

1786 Hermione in *The Distresst Mother* (Racine, translated by Philips), Covent Garden, London.

   Athanais in *Theodosius* (N. Lee), 1786, Covent Garden, London.

   Cordelia in *King Lear* (Shakespeare), Covent Garden, London.

   Charlotte in *Werter* (Goethe, adapted by Reynolds), Covent Garden, London.

   Fidelia in *The Foundling* (Moore), Covent Garden, London.

   Zara in *The Mourning Bride* (Congreve), Covent Garden, London.

   Alicia in *Jane Shore* (Rowe), Covent Garden, London.

   Calista in *The Fair Penitent* (Rowe), Covent Garden, London.

Eloisa in *Eloisa* (Reynolds), Covent Garden, London.

1787   Beatrice in *Much Ado About Nothing* (Shakespeare), Covent Garden, London.

Harriet in *The Guardian* (Garrick), Covent Garden, London.

Cecelia in *Chapter of Accidents* (S. Lee), Covent Garden, London.

Perdita in *The Winter's Tale* (Shakespeare), Covent Garden, London.

Statira in *Alexander the Great* (N. Lee), Covent Garden, London.

Louisa in *All on a Summer's Day* (Inchbald), Covent Garden, London.

1788   Panthea in *King and No King* (Beaumont and Fletcher), Covent Garden, London.

Indiana in *The Conscious Lovers* (Steele), Covent Garden, London.

Almeria in *The Mourning Bride* (Congreve), Covent Garden, London.

Julia in *The Rivals* (Sheridan), Covent Garden, London.

Lady Clairville in *Ton; or, The Follies of Fashion* (Wallace), Covent Garden, London.

Harriet in *The Jealous Wife* (Colman), Covent Garden, London.

Leonora in *The Revenge* (Young), Covent Garden, London.

Amanthis in *The Child of Nature* (Inchbald), Covent Garden, London.

1789   Lady Jane in *The Toy; or, Hampton Court Frolics* (O'Keeffe), Covent Garden, London.

Miss Richland in *The Good-Natured Man* (Goldsmith), Covent Garden, London.

Lady Charlot in *The Funeral* (Steele), Covent Garden, London.

Louisa Courtney in *The Dramatist* (Reynolds), Covent Garden, London.

Arabella in *More Ways Than One* (Cowley), Covent Garden, London.

Lady Anne in *Richard III* (Shakespeare), Covent Garden, London.

Fanny in *The Clandestine Marriage* (Garrick and Colman the Elder), Covent Garden, London.

Mrs Strictland in *The Suspicious Husband* (Hoadley), Covent Garden, London.

1790   Penelope in *The Gamester* (Shirley, adapted by Garrick), Covent Garden, London.

Adelaide in *The Count of Narbonne* (Jephson), Covent Garden, London.

Indamora in *The Widow of Malabar* (Starke), Covent Garden, London.

Cleopatra in *All for Love* (Dryden), Covent Garden, London.

Angelina in *Love Makes a Man* (Cibber), Covent Garden, London.

Louisa in *The Picture of Paris* (Robert Merry), Covent Garden, London.

1791   Lydia in *School for Arrogance* (Holcroft), Covent Garden, London.

Zoriana in *Lorenzo* (Robert Merry), Covent Garden, London.

Countess of Rutland in *Earl of Essex* (Jones), Covent Garden, London.

Sylvia in *The Double Gallant* (Cibber), Covent Garden, London.

Lady Amaranth in *Wild Oats* (O'Keeffe), Covent Garden, London.

Sigismunda in *Tancred and Sigismunda* (Thompson), Covent Garden, London.

1792   Sophia in *The Road to Ruin* (Holcroft), Covent Garden, London.

1796   Emily Tempest in *The Wheel of Fortune* (Cumberland), Chestnut Street Theatre, Philadelphia.

1797   Marchioness Merida in *The Child of Nature* (Inchbald), Chestnut Street Theatre, Philadelphia.

Donna Violante in *The Wonder: A Woman Keeps a Secret* (Centlivre), Chestnut Street Theatre, Philadelphia.

Lady Eleanor Irwin in *Every One Has His Fault* (Inchbald), Chestnut Street Theatre, Philadelphia.

Belvidera in *Venice Preserved* (Otway), Chestnut Street Theatre, Philadelphia.

Cora in *Columbus* (Morton), Chestnut Street Theatre, Philadelphia.

Julia Faulkner in *The Way to Get Married* (Morton), Chestnut Street Theatre, Philadelphia.

Julia in *The Abbey of St Augustine* (Robert Merry), Chestnut Street Theatre, Philadelphia.

Portia in *The Merchant of Venice* (Shakespeare), Chestnut Street Theatre, Philadelphia.

Zeraphine in *The Ransomed Slave* (Robert Merry), Chestnut Street Theatre, Philadelphia.

Gertrude in *Hamlet* (Shakespeare), Chestnut Street Theatre, Philadelphia.

Paulina in *Love's Frailties* (Holcroft), Chestnut Street Theatre, Philadelphia.

Helen in *The Iron Chest* (Colman the Younger), Chestnut Street Theatre, Philadelphia.

Charlotte in *Heigh Ho! for a Husband* (Waldron), Chestnut Street Theatre, Philadelphia.

Clarinthia in *An Ancient Day* (Relf), Chestnut Street Theatre, Philadelphia.

Desdemona in *Othello* (Shakespeare), Rickett's Circus, New York.

Miss Dorillon in *Wives as They Were and Maids as They Are* (Inchbald), Rickett's Circus, New York.

Roxana in *Alexander the Great* (N. Lee), Rickett's Circus, New York.

1798   Isabella in *Isabella* (Southerne), Chestnut Street Theatre, Philadelphia.

Eloisa in *Fenelon* (Robert Merry), Chestnut Street Theatre, Philadelphia.

Mrs Beverly in *The Gamester* (Moore), Chestnut Street Theatre, Philadelphia.

Lady Teazle in *The School for Scandal* (Sheridan), Chestnut Street Theatre, Philadelphia.

Cowslip in *The Agreeable Surprise* (O'Keeffe), Chestnut Street Theatre, Philadelphia.

Charlotte in *He Would Be a Soldier* (Pilon), Chestnut Street Theatre, Philadelphia.

Louisa in *The Prodigal* (Waldron), Chestnut Street Theatre, Philadelphia.

Ellena in *The Italian Monk* (Boaden), Chestnut Street Theatre, Philadelphia.

Lady Ann in *The Deserted Daughter* (Holcroft), Chestnut Street Theatre, Philadelphia.

Agnes in *The Fatal Curiosity* (Lillo), Chestnut Street Theatre, Philadelphia.

Elvina in *The Spectre; or, The Castle of the Forest* (Eyre), Chestnut Street Theatre, Philadelphia.

Charlotte in *The Fatal Curiosity* (Lillo), Baltimore.

Mrs Greville in *Secrets Worth Knowing* (Morton), Baltimore.

1799   Cicely Homespun in *The Heir at Law* (Colman the Younger), Chestnut Street Theatre, Philadelphia.

Elinor Bromly in *Cheap Living* (Reynolds), Chestnut Street Theatre, Philadelphia.

Clara Forrester in *Duplicity* (Holcroft), Chestnut Street Theatre, Philadelphia.

Maria in *A Wedding in Wales* (Stock), Chestnut Street Theatre, Philadelphia.

Mrs Haller in *The Stranger* (Kotzebue, adapted by Dunlap), Chestnut Street Theatre, Philadelphia.

Lady Jane in *He's Much to Blame* (Holcroft), Chestnut Street Theatre, Philadelphia.

Countess Rosela in *The Mysterious Marriage* (H. Lee), Chestnut Street Theatre, Philadelphia.

Juliana in *False and True* (Rev. Moultru), Chestnut Street Theatre, Philadelphia.

Julia in *The Mysteries of the Castle* (Andrews), Chestnut Street Theatre, Philadelphia.

Lady Terrendal in *Life's Vagaries; or, Innocence Protected* (O'Keeffe), Chestnut Street Theatre, Philadelphia.

Eleonora in *Edward and Eleanora* (Thomson), Chestnut Street Theatre, Philadelphia.

Amelia in *The Robbers* (adapted from Schiller), Chestnut Street Theatre, Philadelphia.

Emily Fitzallan in *False Impressions* (Cumberland), Chestnut Street Theatre, Philadelphia.

Agatha in *Lovers' Vows* (Inchbald), Chestnut Street Theatre, Philadelphia.

Lady Paragon in *The Natural Son* (Cumberland), Baltimore.

Rosa in *The Secret* (Morris), Chestnut Street Theatre, Philadelphia.

1800   Emma in *The Reconciliation; or, The Birth-Day* (Kotzebue, adapted by Thomas Dibdin), Chestnut Street Theatre, Philadelphia.

Elizabeth von Hailwyl in *The Count of Burgundy* (Kotzebue, adapted by Plumptre), Chestnut Street Theatre, Philadelphia.

Orellana in *Peru Aveng'd* (Murphy), Chestnut Street Theatre, Philadelphia.

Jane Shore in *Jane Shore* (Rowe), Chestnut Street Theatre, Philadelphia.

Angela in *The Castle Spectre* (Lewis), Chestnut Street Theatre, Philadelphia.

Amelia in *False Shame* (Kotzebue, adapted by Dunlap), Chestnut Street Theatre, Philadelphia.

Yarico in *Inkle and Yarico* (Colman the Younger), Chestnut Street Theatre, Philadelphia.

Josephine in *Sighs; or, The Daughter* (Kotzebue, adapted by Hoare), Chestnut Street Theatre, Philadelphia.

Mrs Mortimer in *Laugh When You Can* (Reynolds), Chestnut Street Theatre, Philadelphia.

Lady Percy in *Henry IV* (Shakespeare), Chestnut Street Theatre, Philadelphia.

Constance in *King John* (Shakespeare), Chestnut Street Theatre, Philadelphia.

Ophelia in *Hamlet* (Shakespeare), Chestnut Street Theatre, Philadelphia.

Clarinda in *The Suspicious Husband* (Hoadly), Chestnut Street Theatre, Philadelphia.

Elvira in *Pizarro* (Kotzebue, adapted by Sheridan), Chestnut Street Theatre, Philadelphia.

Juliana in *Management* (Reynolds), Chestnut Street Theatre, Philadelphia.

Sophia in *The Law of Lombardy* (Jephson), Chestnut Street Theatre, Philadelphia.

Zorayda in *The East Indian* (Lewis), Chestnut Street Theatre, Philadelphia.

1801   Elgiva in *Edwy and Elgiva* (Ingersoll), Chestnut Street Theatre, Philadelphia.

1802   Cora in *Virgin of the Sun* (Kotzebue, adapted by Thompson), Chestnut Street Theatre, Philadelphia.

Eloisa in *Joanna of Montfaucon* (Kotzebue, translated by Cumberland), Chestnut Street Theatre, Philadelphia.

Bertha in *Point of Honour* (adapted by Charles Kemble), Chestnut Street Theatre, Philadelphia.

Lady Melmoth in *Folly as It Flies* (Reynolds), Chestnut Street Theatre, Philadelphia.

Cara Bonito in *The Blind Girl* (Morton), Chestnut Street Theatre, Philadelphia.

Innogen in *Adelmorn* (Lewis), Chestnut Street Theatre, Philadelphia.

1803   Rosamunda in *Abaellino, The Great Bandit* (Zschokke, translated by Dunlap), Baltimore.

Amelrosa in *Alfonso, King of Castile* (Lewis), Baltimore.

Lilla in *The Voice of Nature* (Dunlap, adapted from Caigniez's *Le Jugement de Salomon*), Baltimore.

1804   Mrs Ford in *The Merry Wives of Windsor* (Shakespeare), Chestnut Street Theatre, Philadelphia.

Stella in *Maid of Bristol* (Boaden), Chestnut Street Theatre, Philadelphia.

Eliza in *Hear Both Sides* (Holcroft), Chestnut Street Theatre, Philadelphia.

Christina in *Gustavus Vasa* (Brooke), Chestnut Street Theatre, Philadelphia.

Sophia Dove in *The Brothers; or, The Fortunate Shipwreck* (Cumberland), Chestnut Street Theatre, Philadelphia.

Louisa in *The Sailor's Daughter* (Cumberland), Baltimore.

Countess Belfior in *The Wife of Two Husbands* (Pixérecourt, adapted by Cobb), Baltimore.

Suzette in *Guilty or Not Guilty* (Thomas Dibdin), Baltimore.

Umba in *La Perouse; or, The Deserted Island* (Kotzebue, translated by Dunlap), Chestnut Street Theatre, Philadelphia.

1805   Lady Macbeth in *Macbeth* (Shakespeare), Chestnut Street Theatre, Philadelphia.

Cleone in *Cleone* (Dodsley), Chestnut Street Theatre, Philadelphia.

Scander's Daughter in *Selima and Azor* (Sheridan), Chestnut Street Theatre, Philadelphia.

Roxalana in *The Sultan* (Bickerstaff), Chestnut Street Theatre, Philadelphia.

Young Lady in *I'll Tell You What* (Inchbald), Chestnut Street Theatre, Philadelphia.

Mary in *Mary, Queen of Scots* (St. John), Baltimore.

1806   Juliana in *The Honey Moon* (Tobin), Chestnut Street Theatre, Philadelphia.

Mrs Villars in *The Blind Bargain* (Reynolds), Chestnut Street Theatre, Philadelphia.

Seraphina in *Lewis of Monte Blanco* (Dunlap), Chestnut Street Theatre, Philadelphia.

Estifania in *Rule a Wife and Have a Wife* (Beaumont and Fletcher), Chestnut Street Theatre, Philadelphia.

Clarissa in *Lionel and Clarissa* (Bickerstaff), Chestnut Street Theatre, Philadelphia.

Lady Transit in *A Hint to Husbands* (Cumberland), Baltimore.

Mrs Hamilton in *School for Friends* (Chambers), Baltimore.

1807   Lady Townly in *The Provoked Husband* (Cibber), Chestnut Street Theatre, Philadelphia.

Marchioness Merida in *The Travellers* (Cherry), Baltimore.

1808   Madame Clermont in *Adrian and Orilla* (Dimond), Chestnut Street Theatre, Philadelphia.

Olivia Wyndham in *Time's a Tell-Tale* (Siddons), Chestnut Street Theatre, Philadelphia.

Laetitia Hardy in *The Belle's Stratagem* (Cowley), Chestnut Street Theatre, Philadelphia.

*

Bibliography

Books:

Gresdna Ann Doty, *The Career of Mrs Anne Brunton Merry in the American Theatre*, Louisiana State University Press, Baton Rouge, 1971.

Articles:

Thomas Condie, "Biographical Anecdotes of Mrs Merry of the Theatre, Philadelphia", *Philadelphia Monthly Magazine*, 1, 1798.

M. Ray Adams, "Robert Merry and the American Theatre", *Theatre Survey*, 6, 1965.

* * *

The first half of Anne Brunton Merry's career was not unfairly summed up in a contemporary appreciation of her that is quoted in John Genest's *Some Account of the English Stage*: "Mrs Merry left the stage at the end of the season — during her first season she was much followed — after that her attraction ceased — her features were neither delicate nor expressive, but her voice was sonorous, flexible, and sweetly melodious — her deportment was graceful, and her action nicely and judiciously adapted to the situation — her enunciation was animated — she caught the fire of her author, and guided by a feeling heart."

Anne Merry was the eldest daughter of John Brunton, a Norwich man born in 1741 who played Hamlet at Covent Garden before working as an actor-manager in Norwich and Bath. Anne made her own debut on 17 February 1785, while the family was at Bath, playing Euphrasia in a benefit performance of *The Grecian Daughter* for her father. There is a pretty story to the effect that John Brunton was quite unaware that his daughter had any gift for acting until one day he chanced to hear her reciting the part of Calista in Nicholas Rowe's *The Fair Penitent* and was surprised to discover that she had also learned several other roles by heart. How much truth there is in this is hard to say, but it is clear enough that theatrical managers like John Palmer in Bristol and Thomas Harris at Covent Garden were only too ready to give the opportunity to a young actress to rival the success of Sarah Siddons, who had just turned 30 and was sensible opting for more mature roles, such as Lady Macbeth. The story that Anne Brunton was, at least to a degree, self-taught also tallies with the greater naturalness of her interpretations, which made a marked impression on contemporary audiences. On the other hand, the fact that she was able to take on no fewer than 10 roles in her first season might suggest that her catapulting into stardom had been carefully prepared.

At Covent Garden and during arduous tours across England and even across the Irish Sea to Belfast and Cork, Anne Brunton was regularly well received, but it was with provincial audiences that she had her greatest successes. She certainly spoke well in a voice that was clear and sweet and was not hampered by her diminutive stature, which prompted a later admirer (the US critic John Ireland) to comment that "her person was rather undersize" and that she did not possess "great beauty of countenance", even if she made up for this defect with "highly expressive features". For London audiences she had been an interesting beginner, but it was plainly felt that her career had not developed as excitingly as it might have. She did experiment in her choice of roles, even venturing into comedy, but the consensus was that she was no second Sarah Siddons.

At this point, on 27 August 1791, she contracted what must have seemed a highly advantageous marriage. She did not, however, do so well as her sister Louisa, also an actress with some precocious successes to her credit, who in 1807 became the wife of the first Earl of Craven and retiring from the stage opted for the life of the most strait-laced respectability. Robert Merry, though well-connected and educated at Harrow and Christ's College, Cambridge, was a rake and a dilettante, a man with more taste for spending money than skill in making it. Plays were among his many literary efforts and when his *Lorenzo* was put on at Covent Garden the 22-year-old Anne Brunton had a part in it. The wedding took place some five months later. Whether it was for social reasons or on account of her husband's liberal views about the French Revolution that she retired from the stage in 1792 is uncertain. The retirement proved temporary, however, under the financial strain imposed by the costs of a stay in Paris and periods of residence in London, which had finally depleted Merry's fortunes.

Thomas Wignell, who had gone to the USA in 1774 and had had the Chestnut Street Theatre, Philadelphia, built for his company, came back to Europe to recruit talent. Anne Merry, perhaps at her husband's urging and certainly with his consent, accepted a contract and on 5 December 1796 she made her debut in the New World, playing Juliet opposite John Pollard Moreton. She scored an immediate success, in a role, which, it may be noted, was essentially a young one, and the US public clamoured for her not only at the Chestnut Street Theatre but also in New York, at the Greenwich Street Theatre and the Park Theatre, in Baltimore, Annapolis, and Washington. Among her most loyal admirers was William Dunlap and, while not denying that she could have had a more striking physical presence, he never missed an opportunity of lauding "the most perfect actress America has seen". Perhaps her somewhat understated manner was felt to be especially tasteful in theatres where some actors and actresses were tempted into rather gross effects and others, including some who came over from England, were felt to be stiff and affected. Even in the USA, however, Mrs Merry shied away from the heavier tragic roles, either because, as was said, she did not wish to compete with Sarah Siddons or else because she knew her limitations.

Mrs Merry's very considerable success as the first genuine star of the US stage was, sadly, not reflected in her personal life. Robert Merry was carried off by an apoplectic stroke in December 1798 and four years later Thomas Wignell, her second husband, died within two months of their wedding. The final tragedy followed in 1808 with Anne's own death in childbirth. Despite the misfortunes that haunted her in the USA, the second part of the career of Anne Brunton Merry was, in many ways, more notable than the first. She set new standards in acting on the US stage and, by her life and manner, raised the status of the acting profession in the Americas.

—Christopher Smith

MESSEL, Oliver (Hilary Sambourne). British designer. Born in London, 13 January 1905. Educated at Eton public school; Slade School of Art, London, 1922–24. Apprenticed to artist John Wells, 1925; first designed costumes and masks for Diaghilev, 1925; first designed for the revues of C. B. Cochran, 1926; debut as film designer, 1932; engaged by Tyrone Guthrie at the Old Vic Theatre, London, 1932; served in Royal Engineers, 1940–44; first designs for Glyndebourne opera, 1946; went into virtual retirement in Barbados, 1966. Fellow, University College, London, 1956; associate, Regional College of Art, Manchester, 1960.

Recipient: Tony Award, 1955 and 1959. CBE (Commander of the British Empire), 1958. Died in Barbados, 13 July 1978.

Productions

1925   *Zéphyre et Flore* (Diaghilev ballet), Coliseum Theatre, London; designed masks.
1926   'The Masks' in *Cochran's Revue of 1926* (Cochran), Pavilion, London; designed costumes and masks.
1927   *The Great God Brown* (O'Neill), Strand Theatre, London; designed masks.
1928   'Lorelei' in *This Year of Grace* (Cochran), Pavilion, London, and Selwyn Theatre, New York; designed costumes and set.
        'Dance Little Lady' (Coward) in *This Year of Grace* (Cochran), Pavilion, London, and Selwyn Theatre, New York; designed costumes and masks.
        'Nigger Heaven' in *Riverside Nights* (Herbert), Arts Theatre Club, London; designed costumes and masks.
1929   'The Wrong Room in the Wrong House', 'Wake Up and Dream', 'The Dream', and 'A Girl in a Shawl' in *Wake Up and Dream* (Turner and Porter), Pavilion, London; designed costumes and set.
        'What Is This Thing Called Love' in *Wake Up and Dream* (Turner and Porter), Pavilion, London; designed set.
1930   'Piccadilly 1830' and 'Heaven' in *Cochran's Revue of 1930* (Nichols), Pavilion, London; designed costumes and set.
1931   'Stealing Through' and 'Scaramouche' in *Cochran's Revue of 1931* (Coward), Pavilion, London; designed costumes and set.
1932   *Helen* (Herbert), Adelphi Theatre, London; designed costumes and set.
        The Miracle (Volmöller), Lyceum Theatre, London; designed costumes.
1933   *Mother of Pearl* (Herbert), Gaiety Theatre, London; designed set.
1935   *Glamorous Night* (Novello), Theatre Royal, Drury Lane, London; designed set.
1936   *The Country Wife* (Wycherly), Old Vic Theatre, London, and Henry Miller Theatre, New York; designed costumes and set.
1937   *Francesca da Rimini* (Tchaikovsky), Royal Opera House, Covent Garden, London, and Metropolitan Opera House, New York; designed costumes and set.
        A Midsummer Night's Dream (Shakespeare), Old Vic Theatre, London; designed costumes and set.
1940   *The Tempest* (Shakespeare), Old Vic Theatre, London; designed costumes and set.
        The Infernal Machine (Cocteau), Arts Theatre Club, London; designed costumes, masks, and set.
1942   *Comus* (Milton), New Theatre, London; designed costumes and set.

Oliver Messel

       The Big Top (Cochran), His Majesty's Theatre, London; designed costumes.

1945   *The Rivals* (Sheridan), Criterion Theatre, London; designed costumes and set.

1946   *The Sleeping Beauty* (Tchaikovsky), Royal Opera House, Covent Garden, London, and Metropolitan Opera House, New York; Metropolitan Opera House, New York, 1950; Royal Opera House, Covent Garden, London, 1952, 1956, 1958, 1960, and 1976; designed costumes and set.

1947   *The Magic Flute* (Mozart), Royal Opera House, Covent Garden, London; designed costumes and set.

1949   *The Lady's Not for Burning* (Fry), Globe Theatre, London, and Royale Theatre, New York; designed costumes and set.

       Tough at the Top (Herbert), Adelphi Theatre, London; designed costumes and set.

1950   *Ring Round the Moon* (Anouilh), Globe Theatre, London; Martin Beck Theatre, New York, and Folkes Theatre, Copenhagen, 1951; designed costumes and set.

       Ariadne auf Naxos (Hofmannsthal), King's Theatre, Edinburgh.

       The Little Hut (Mitford), Lyric Theatre, London; Coronet Theatre, New York; designed set.

       The Queen of Spades (Tchaikovsky), Royal Opera House, Covent Garden, London; designed costumes and set.

1951   *Romeo and Juliet* (Shakespeare), Broadhurst Theatre, New York; designed costumes and set.

       Idomeneo (Mozart), Glyndebourne; revived, 1952, Edinburgh Festival, 1953, 1956, 1959, and 1964; designed costumes and set.

1952   *Under the Sycamore Tree* (Spewack), Streatham Hill Theatre, London, and Aldwych Theatre, London; designed costumes and set.

       La Cenerentola, Glyndebourne; Edinburgh Festival, 1953; Berlin, 1954; Liverpool, 1956; 1959 and 1960; designed costumes and set.

       Letter from Paris (D. Smith, adapted from H. James), Aldwych Theatre, London; designed costumes and set.

1953   *Homage to the Queen* (Arnold), Royal Opera House, Covent Garden, London, and Metropolitan Opera House, New York, Detroit, and San Francisco; Brussels, 1958; designed costumes and set.

       Ariadne auf Naxos (Hofmannsthal), Glyndebourne; revived there, 1954, 1957, 1958, and 1962.

1954   *The Dark Is Light Enough* (Fry), Aldwych Theatre, London; ANTA Theatre, New York, 1955; designed costumes and set.

       Il Barbiere di Siviglia (Rossini), Glyndebourne; revived there, 1955 and 1961; designed costumes and set.

       Le Comte Ory (Rossini), King's Theatre, Edinburgh; revived 1955, 1957, and 1958; designed costumes and set.

       House of Flowers, Alvin Theatre, New York; designed costumes, masks, and set.

1955   *Zémire et Azor* (opera), Theatre Royal, Bath; designed costumes and set.

       Le Nozze di Figaro (Mozart), Glyndebourne; revived there 1956, 1958, 1962, 1963, and 1965; designed set.

1956   *Die Entführung aus dem Serail* (Mozart), Glyndebourne; revived there, 1957 and 1961; designed costumes and set.

       Die Zauberflöte (Mozart), Glyndebourne; revived there, 1957 and 1960; designed costumes and set.

1958   *Breath of Spring* (Coke), Cambridge Theatre, London, and Duke of York's Theatre, London; designed costumes and set.

       The School for Scandal (Sheridan), Det Ny Theatre, Copenhagen; designed costumes.

       Samson (Handel), Royal Opera House, Covent Garden, London; designed costumes and set.

1959   *Rashomon* (Kanin), Music Box Theatre, New York; designed costumes and set.

       Der Rosenkavalier (Hofmannsthal and Strauss), Glyndebourne; revived there, 1960 and 1965; designed costumes and set.

       The Marriage of Figaro (Mozart), Metropolitan Opera House, New York; designed set.

1960	*The Sleeping Beauty* (Tchaikovsky), Royal Opera House, Covent Garden, London; designed costumes and set.
1962	*Ariadne auf Naxos* (Hofmannsthal), Glyndebourne.
1964	*Traveller Without Luggage* (Anouilh), ANTA Theatre, New York; designed costumes and set.
1965	*Twang!!* (Bart), Shaftesbury Theatre, London; designed costumes and set.
1973	*Gigi* (Colette and Loos), San Francisco, St Louis, Detroit, Toronto, and Uris Theatre, New York.
1976	*The Sleeping Beauty* (Tchaikovsky), Metropolitan Opera House, New York.

Films

The Private Life of Don Juan, 1934; *The Scarlet Pimpernel*, 1935; *Romeo and Juliet*, 1936; *The Thief of Baghdad*, 1940; *Carnival*, 1946; *Caesar and Cleopatra*, 1946; *The Winslow Boy*, 1948; *The Queen of Spades*, 1949; *Arms and the Man*, 1955; *Suddenly Last Summer*, 1960; *Cleopatra*, 1963.

Publications

Stage Designs and Costumes, 1934; *Designs for Romeo and Juliet*, 1936; *Designs for A Midsummer Night's Dream*, 1957; *Designs for Delightful Food*, 1958.

*

Bibliography

Books:
Charles Castle, *Oliver Messel*, New York, 1986.

* * *

"I attempted to use every device to make as much magic as possible", said Oliver Messel of his approach to design and, indeed, the work he did between the mid-1920's and the early 1960's epitomises the best in British Romanticism. Delicate but not cloying, Messel's lambent schemes delighted audiences with their wit and imaginative combinations of styles and colours: flowing lines offset by clean verticals and diagonals, soothing pastel hues judiciously sharpened by tonal discords — for example, orange-vermillion with cyclamen pink. "Designed by Oliver Messel" signalled a distinctive component within a production, for Messel's method was to complement the text or score. Of his *Marriage of Figaro* designs Andrew Porter wrote: "although intensely personal, they reflect and decorate Mozart, whereas less sensitive designers try to interpret him". Messel responded more to mood than meaning.

He conceived three-dimensionally, experimenting with models. Only when satisfied that these, with furniture and characters to scale, were practical, aesthetically appropriate, and excitingly original would he produce groundplans and working drawings. Costume sketches followed — wispy indications of silhouette, colour, and feeling that relied heavily on the sensitivity of the makers to translate

them into garments, headdresses, and jewellery. He therefore campaigned to work with particular craftspeople: Matilda Etches, Margaret Furse, Karinska and Rosemary Vercoe for costumes and Hugh Skillen for masks and headdresses. He (with Carl Toms, his assistant from 1952 to 1958) was closely involved in all the manufacture, for Messel was an adept maker and throughout his career experimented with unorthodox materials and techniques to achieve the surprising effects he visualized.

Messel's first work for the theatre was designing and producing masks. In 1925 Diaghilev commissioned mask-like headdresses and "a few large grotesques" for the ballet *Zéphyre and Flore*, which was designed by Georges Braque. For an item, *The Masks*, in C. B. Cochran's *Revue of 1926*, Messel's costumes and masks for an "extraordinary wealth and range" of ethnic types were praised by the *Daily Telegraph*, as were his hauntingly vacuous masks for Noël Coward's 'Dance Little Lady' number in Cochran's *This Year of Grace* (1928). Over the next three years Messel designed highly distinctive sets and costumes for an increasing number of items in Cochran's productions and in 1932 was entirely responsible for Cochran's lavish *Helen*. This musical, an A. P. Herbert skit on Offenbach's *La Belle Hélène* (1864), itself a skit on classical mythology, challenged Messel to design double-level pastiche. He responded by stylistically marrying the popular conception of Ancient Greece — chaste lines and cool colours — to the refulgent draperies and rich tones of Second Empire rococo in sets and costumes that James Agate hailed as "a triumph of wit, fantasy, and ravishment". They also chimed with the taste of the time and, particularly via the scherzo of slender columns, looped drapery, and wickedly coy statues that was Helen's bedroom, shaped fashions in interior design. *Helen* epitomised the Messel talent for combining meticulous research with his own sense of style to produce schemes that defined period within the context of contemporary taste and were opulent but not oppressive.

Messel could range confidently across time and cultures. For the pseudo-medieval dance-drama *The Miracle* he created some 800 costumes, notable for their elegant line and "fine sense of the heraldic world", in the words of Ivor Brown. Ivor Novello's *Glamorous Night* demonstrated Messel's practical versatility, with its "bewildering succession of rich splendour" that included a sinking ocean liner, a Ruritanian opera-house, and a Balkan gypsy encampment. In researching what *Theatre World* called this "wonderful decor and costumes" Messel travelled widely. For other productions he absorbed archival sources. Painters often inspired schemes: Botticelli for the delicate *Romeo and Juliet* (film), El Greco for an austere *The Tempest*, Inigo Jones for the masque-like *Comus*, Goya for *The Barber of Seville*, and Manet and Renoir for *Letter from Paris*. The conventions of Restoration staging prompted his obviously painted scenery and highly decorated costumes for the Old Vic/Tyrone Guthrie production of Wycherly's *The Country Wife*; these, when seen in New York, were praised for being "at once stylized and fanciful, artificial and amusing". *A Midsummer Night's Dream*, another Old Vic/Guthrie collaboration, placed Shakespeare's comedy in the early Victorian period. In this scheme Messel invoked Pollock's toy theatres. The Athenians' costumes were mock-heroic and Theseus's palace sturdy painted columns and draperies against a sketched-in backcloth. The enchanted wood, with a full moon dominating a glade of cut-cloth trees, exuded fairyland, but Messel wittily disturbed the scale with a foreground of oversized leaves and flowers, so that those playing the sprites could indeed have "crept into acorn cups". Titania and her fairies wafted in white muslin decorated with giant blooms; Oberon and his masked sprites suggested strange insects and animals. The *Observer* critic commended Messel's "double delight in pictorial bravura and practical ingenuity".

A Dream's disruption of scale was repeated for *Under the Sycamore Tree*, a parable about human society set in an ant colony that allowed Messel to make witty visual analogies, and for two Peter Brook productions, *The Little Hut* and the musical *House of Flowers*, which both featured exotically oversized vegetation. Another Brook production, *Ring Round the Moon*, owed much of its success to Messel's capturing of the bitter-sweet tone in his setting of an arched conservatory of slender ribs and delicate trellis against which his flower-like Edwardian gowns glowed. For the film *Suddenly Last Summer* prurient creepiness was evoked by menacing larger-than-life plants (made by Messel and Skillen) surrounding an oppressively ornate mansion in which a staring mask from 'Dance Little Lady' lay on a table.

Messel's many successes included a run of operas for Glyndebourne, fabric designs for Sekers, suites at the Dorchester Hotel, and the design of houses in the West Indies, but he will be remembered most for Tchaikovsky's *The Sleeping Beauty*. His version of this for the Royal Ballet at Covent Garden stayed in the repertoire from 1946 to 1968; it was then recreated for the American Ballet Theatre in 1976. Messel's triumph, in 1946, was to create a scheme that, within the constraints of available materials, lavishly expressed the optimism befitting a nation newly emerged from war. His sets amalgamated the soaring stage architecture of the Bibiena family with the dreamy vistas of Watteau, his costumes suggested the opulence of the late 17th century but incorporated Tudor features, and everywhere typically Messel touches abounded. The evil Carabosse, in black gown and mantilla of bats' wings and cobwebs, arrived in a chariot surmounted by ravens bobbing on wires to confront a court, glittering in silver, blues, and pinks; the Prince travelled to the enchanted castle in a butterfly-drawn car through gauzes that dissolved to reveal vistas of overgrown masonry between giant spiders' legs, and his marriage to Aurora was celebrated in a palace of dizzyingly improbable architecture. This production toured the world and always commanded applause for the designer, who had determined to make "as much magic as possible".

—Raymond Ingram

MEYERHOLD, Vsevolod (Emilievich). Russian director and actor. Born Karl Theodor Kasimir Meyerhold in Penza, Russia, 9 February 1874. Educated at the Penza Gymnasium, from 1884; University of Moscow, 1895–96; trained for the theatre at the Music and Drama School, Moscow Philharmonic Society, 1896–98. Married 1) Olga Munt in 1896 (divorced 1921); 2) Zinaida Raikh in 1922 (murdered 1939). Stage debut, as an amateur, 1892; founder, Penza People's Theatre, 1896; founder-member, Moscow Art Theatre, 1898; quarrelled with Stanislavsky and left Moscow Art Theatre to found own Company of Russian Dramatic Artists, 1902; founded Comrades of the New Drama, 1903; joined Stanislavsky's Moscow Art Studio Theatre, 1905; subsequently worked with Comrades of the New Drama and then as director at Vera Kommisarjevskaya's Theatre, St Petersburg, 1906–07; led company in the provinces and was then appointed to staff of the Imperial Theatres, 1908–18; presented summer season at Terioki, Finland, 1912; directed at the Studio on Borodinskaya Street, St Petersburg, from 1914; published theatrical journal *Love for Three Oranges*, 1914–16; staged much new Soviet drama after Revolution of 1917; head of Petrograd Theatre Section of the People's Commissariat for Education, 1918; escaped arrest and death sentence by White Army and joined Red Army, 1919; head of Theatre Section, People's Commissariat for Education, 1920–21; director, Theatre of the Revolution, Moscow, 1922–23; coined term 'biomechanics', 1922; director, Moscow Theatre of the Revolution, 1922–24; director, Meyerhold Theatre, Moscow, 1923–38; toured Berlin and Paris with Meyerhold State Theatre, 1930; moved company to the Passage Theatre, Moscow, 1932; after 1938, worked as director for Stanislavsky's Opera Theatre; arrested for resisting policy of Socialist Realism, 1942. Member: CPSU, 1918. People's Artist of the RSFSR, 1923. Died (shot in prison on Stalin's orders) in Moscow, 2 February 1942.

Productions

1905   *La Mort de Tintagiles* (Maeterlinck), Art Studio Theatre, Moscow.
        Schluck und Jau (Hauptmann), Art Studio Theatre, Moscow.
        Snow (Przybyszewski), Art Studio Theatre, Moscow.
        Kjaerlighedens komedie [Love's Comedy] (Ibsen), Art Studio Theatre, Moscow.
1906   *Hedda Gabler* (Ibsen), Vera Kommisarjevskaya's Theatre, St Petersburg.
        In the City (Iushkevich), Vera Kommisarjevskaya's Theatre, St Petersburg.
        Soeur Béatrice (Maeterlinck), Vera Kommisarjevskaya's Theatre, St Petersburg.
        The Eternal Fairy Tale (Przybyszewski), Vera Kommisarjevskaya's Theatre, St Petersburg.
        Et dukkehjem [A Doll's House] (Ibsen), Vera Kommisarjevskaya's Theatre, St Petersburg.
        Balaganchik [The Fairground Booth] (Blok), Vera Kommisarjevskaya's Theatre, St Petersburg.
        Le Miracle de Saint-Antoine (Maeterlinck), Vera Kommisarjevskaya's Theatre, St Petersburg.
1907   *The Tragedy of Love* (Heiberg), Vera Kommisarjevskaya's Theatre, St Petersburg.
        Kjaerlighedens komedie [Love's Comedy] (Ibsen), Vera Kommisarjevskaya's Theatre, St Petersburg.
        Die Hochzeit der Sobeide (Hofmannsthal), Vera Kommisarjevskaya's Theatre, St Petersburg.

Vsevolod Meyerhold

Zhizn cheloveka [The Life of Man] (Andreyev), Vera Kommisarjevskaya's Theatre, St Petersburg.
Frühlings Erwachen (Wedekind), Vera Kommisarjevskaya's Theatre, St Petersburg.
Pelléas et Mélisande (Maeterlinck, translated by Briusov), Vera Kommisarjevskaya's Theatre, St Petersburg.
Pobeda smerti [The Victory of Death] (Sologub), Vera Kommisarjevskaya's Theatre, St Petersburg.

1908 *Ved Rigets Port* [At the Gates of the Kingdom] (Hamsun), Alexandrinsky Theatre, St Petersburg.
Salomé (Wilde), Mikhailovsky Theatre, St Petersburg.
Petrushka (Potemkin), Lukomore cabaret, St Petersburg.
Fall of the House of Usher (Poe), Lukomore cabaret, St Petersburg.
Honour and Revenge (Sollogub), Lukomore cabaret, St Petersburg.

1909 *Tyazhba* [The Trial] (Gogol), Alexandrinsky Theatre, St Petersburg.
The Lady from the Box, Foundry Theatre, Moscow.
Tristan und Isolde (Wagner), Marinsky Theatre, St Petersburg.

1910 *Paul I* (Merezhkovsky), private theatre, St Petersburg.

The Fool Tantris (Hardt), Alexandrinsky Theatre, St Petersburg.
La devoción de la cruz (Calderón, translated by Balmont), Tower Theatre, St Petersburg.
Der Schleier der Pierette (Schnitzler), House of Interludes, St Petersburg.
Don Juan (Molière), Alexandrinsky Theatre, St Petersburg.
The Transformed Prince (Znosko-Borovsky), House of Interludes, St Petersburg.

1911 *Boris Godunov*, Marinsky Theatre, St Petersburg.
The Red Tavern (Beliaev), Alexandrinsky Theatre, St Petersburg.
Zhivoy trup [The Living Corpse] (L. Tolstoy), Alexandrinsky Theatre, St Petersburg.
Harlequin, the Marriage Broker (Soloviev), Assembly Rooms, St Petersburg.
Orpheo (Gluck), Marinsky Theatre, St Petersburg.

1912 *Lovers I* (Meyerhold, as Dapertutto), Karabchevsky's Theatre, St Petersburg.
Lovers II (Meyerhold, as Dapertutto), Artists' co-operative, Terioki, Finland.
Harlequin, the Marriage Broker (Soloviev), Artists' co-operative, Terioki, Finland.
La devoción de la cruz (Calderón, translated by Balmont), Artists' co-operative, Terioki, Finland.
Brott och brott [Crimes and Crimes] (Strindberg), Artists' co-operative, Terioki, Finland.
You Never Can Tell (G. B. Shaw), Artists' co-operative, Terioki, Finland.
Zalozhniki zhizni [Hostages of Life] (Sologub), Alexandrinsky Theatre, St Petersburg.

1913 *Elektra* (Strauss and Hofmannsthal, translated by Kuzmin), Marinsky Theatre, St Petersburg.
Pisanella (D'Annunzio), Théâtre du Châtelet, Paris.

1914 *Mid-Channel* (Pinero), Alexandrinsky Theatre, Petrograd.
Balaganchik [The Fairground Booth] (Blok), Tenishevsky Academy, Petrograd.
Neznakomka [The Unknown Woman] (Blok), Tenishevsky Academy, Petrograd.
Mlle Fifi (Maupassant), Suvorin's Theatre, Moscow.
Secret of Suzanna (Wolf-Ferrari), Marinsky Theatre, Petrograd.

1915 *Dve Braty* [The Two Brothers] (Lermontov), Alexandrinsky Theatre, Petrograd.
An Evening at the Studio of Vs Meyerhold (Meyerhold and Solovev), Meyerhold Studio.
The Green Ring (Gippius), Alexandrinsky Theatre, Petrograd.
El principe constante (Calderó), Alexandrinsky Theatre, Petrograd.
Pygmalion (G. B. Shaw), Alexandrinsky Theatre, Petrograd.

1916 *Groza* [The Storm] (Ostrovsky), Alexandrinsky Theatre, Petrograd.

Jota Aragonesa (Glinka), Marinsky Theatre, Petrograd.

Der Schleier der Pierette (Schnitzler), Prival Komediantov, Petrograd.

Romantics (Merezhovsky), Alexandrinsky Theatre, Petrograd.

1917   *Svadba Krechinskogo* [Krechinsky's Wedding] (Sukhovo-Kobylin), Alexandrinsky Theatre, Petrograd.

Kammeny gost [The Stone Guest] (Dargominsky), Marinsky Theatre, Petrograd.

Maskarad [Masquerade] (Lermontov), Alexandrinsky Theatre, Petrograd.

An Ideal Husband (Wilde), Mikhailovsky Theatre, Petrograd.

Delo [The Affair] (Sukhovo-Kobylin), Alexandrinsky Theatre, Petrograd.

Smert Tarelkina [The Death of Tarelkin] (Sukhovo-Kobylin), Alexandrinsky Theatre, Petrograd.

Snegurochka [The Snow Maiden] (Rimsky-Korsakov), Marinsky Theatre, Petrograd.

Fruen fra havet [The Lady from the Sea] (Ibsen), Alexandrinsky Theatre, Petrograd.

1918   *Peter the Baker* (L. Tolstoy), Alexandrinsky Theatre, Petrograd.

The Nightingale (Stravinsky), Marinsky Theatre, Petrograd.

Et dukkehjem [A Doll's House] (Ibsen), Workers' Club, Petrograd.

La Muette de Portici (Auber), Marinsky Theatre, Petrograd.

Misteriya-Buff [Mystery-Bouffe] (Mayakovsky), Conservatoire, Petrograd.

1920   *The Dawns* (Verhaeren), First Theatre of the RSFSR, Moscow.

1921   *Mysteriya-Buff II* [Mystery-Bouffe II] (Mayakovsky), First Theatre of the RSFSR, Moscow.

De unges forbund [The League of Youth] (Ibsen), First Theatre of the RSFSR, Moscow.

1922   *Et dukkehjem* [A Doll's House] (Ibsen), Actors' Theatre, Moscow.

Le Cocu magnifique (Crommelynck), Actors' Theatre, Moscow.

Smert Tarelkina [The Death of Tarelkin] (Sukhovo-Kobylin), GITIS Theatre, Moscow.

1923   *Zemlya dybom* [Earth Rampant] (Tretyakov, adapted from Martinet), Meyerhold Theatre, Moscow.

Dokhodnoye mesto [A Profitable Position] (Ostrovsky), Theatre of the Revolution, Moscow.

Lake Liul (Faiko), Theatre of the Revolution, Moscow.

1924   *Les* [The Forest] (Ostrovsky), Meyerhold Theatre, Moscow.

D.E. (Podgayetsky), Meyerhold Theatre, Moscow.

1925   *Bubus the Teacher* (Faiko), Meyerhold Theatre, Moscow.

The Mandate (Erdman), Meyerhold Theatre, Moscow.

1926   *Revizor* [The Inspector General] (Gogol), Meyerhold State Theatre, Moscow.

Rychi Kitai! [Roar, China!] (Tretyakov), Meyerhold Theatre, Moscow.

1927   *Through a Village Window* (Meyerhold and others), Meyerhold Theatre, Moscow.

1928   *Gore ot uma* [Woe from Wit] (Griboyedov), Meyerhold State Theatre, Moscow.

1929   *Klop* [The Bedbug] (Mayakovsky), Meyerhold State Theatre, Moscow.

Commander of the Second Army (Selvinsky), Meyerhold State Theatre, Moscow.

The Shot (Bezymensky), Meyerhold Theatre, Moscow.

1930   *Banya* [The Bathhouse] (Mayakovsky), Meyerhold Theatre, Moscow.

1931   *Posledny resistelny* [The Last Decisive Battle] (Vishnevsky), Meyerhold Theatre, Moscow.

A List of Assets (Olesha), Meyerhold Theatre, Moscow.

1932   *Don Juan* (Molière), Pushkin Theatre, Leningrad.

1933   *Prelude* (German), Meyerhold Theatre, Moscow.

Svadba Krechinskogo [Krechinsky's Wedding] (Sukovo-Kobylin), Meyerhold Theatre, Moscow.

Maskarad [Masquerade] (Lermontov), Pushkin Theatre, Leningrad.

1934   *Camille* (Dumas fils), Meyerhold State Theatre, Moscow.

1935   *The Queen of Spades* (Tchaikovsky), Maly Opera Theatre, Leningrad.

33 Fainting Fits (Chekhov's *The Jubilee, The Bear* and *The Proposal*), Meyerhold Theatre, Moscow.

Gore ot uma II [Woe from Wit II] (Griboyedov), Meyerhold Theatre, Moscow.

1938   *Maskarad* [Masquerade] (Lermontov), Pushkin Theatre, Leningrad.

1939   *Rigoletto* (Verdi), Stanislavsky Opera Theatre, Moscow.

Films

As director:
The Portrait of Dorian Gray, 1915; *The Strong Man*, 1916; *Witchcraft*, 1917.

Radio

Kammeny gost, 1935; *Russalka*, 1937.

Publications

On Theatre, 1912; *Ampluya Aktera*, with Bebutov and Aksenov, 1922; *Stati. Pisma. Rechi. Besedy*, 1958.

*

Bibliography

Books:
Nina Gourfinkel, *Vsevolod Meyerhold — Le théâtre théâtral*, Paris, 1963.
Edward Braun (ed.), *Meyerhold on Theatre*, London, 1969.
James H. Symons, *Meyerhold's Theatre of the Grotesque*, Cambridge, 1973.
Béatrice Picon-Vallin, *Vsevolod Meyerhold — Écrits sur le Théâtre*, 3 vols., Lausanne, 1973–80.
Marjorie L. Hoover, *Meyerhold: The Art of Conscious Theatre*, Amherst, Massachusetts, 1974.
Edward Braun, *The Theatre of Meyerhold*, London, 1979.
Konstantin Rudnitsky, *Meyerhold the Director*, Ann Arbor, Michigan, 1981.
Paul Schmidt (ed.), *Meyerhold at Work*, Austin, Texas, 1980.
Marjorie L. Hoover, *Meyerhold and His Set Designers*, New York, Bern, Franfurt am Main, and Paris, 1988.
Robert Leach, *Vsevolod Meyerhold*, Cambridge, 1989.

* * *

Vsevolod Meyerhold was a genuine theatrical rebel. In joining the Moscow Art Theatre in 1898 he was in revolt against the clichés and stereotypes of 19th-century Russian theatre. In abandoning the Art Theatre in 1902 he was rebelling against what he saw as the constricting limitations of stage naturalism. In founding a Symbolist theatre of conventionalised gesture and image, he was opposing the 'intimate' theatre of psychological realism that Stanislavsky's 'System' was about to inaugurate. Subsequently, his theory of biomechanics, based on a grammar of physical action reminiscent of gymnastics, advocated a style of acting that was inimical to the school of individualist feeling and emotional identification. In common with other theatrical rebels, such as Edward Gordon Craig, Georg Fuchs and Nikolai Evreinov, Meyerhold began to look for inspiration to forms of pre-Renaissance theatre and towards perennially popular genres such as the pantomime, the harlequinade, commedia dell'arte and the circus, as well as to the Russian 'balagan', or clown-show associated with markets and fairs.

In addition to being a rebel, Meyerhold was also a great innovator and experimenter. Strongly influenced by such art movements of the early 20th century as Cubism, Futurism and Constructivism, he frequently collaborated with many of the leading figures of the Russian and European avant-garde, including the poet, painter and dramatist Vladimir Mayakovsky, who, together with Meyerhold, was among a handful of leading artists who lent their support to the Bolshevik cause after the 1917 Revolution. In many respects, Meyerhold epitomised the exhilarating artistic spirit of those immediate post-revolutionary years, whilst deploying some of the period's less attractive 'command' strategies. Appointed by Lunacharsky to the post of commissar for the theatre arts, Meyerhold sought the militant politicisation of Soviet theatre, leading the way with his own stridently polemical and radically innovative productions of works by both foreign and native dramatists, which he either re-wrote or otherwise restructured in uncompromisingly avant-garde style as programmatic examples of left-wing theatrical practice. In the process he probably offended more people than he pleased, including some on his own side of the political divide.

To the extent that Meyerhold, during these early post-revolutionary years, dressed himself in the uniform of the Red Army and paraded his revolutionary convictions (his production of *Earth Rampant* was dedicated to Trotsky and the Red Army) his subsequent work tended to be viewed as suspect, as 'Trotskyist' or as 'ultra-leftist'. It was almost inevitable, after the 'Sturm und Drang' of the period known as 'October in the Theatre' over which Meyerhold presided, that there should have been a reversion to something like an earlier style and mood. This could be seen in such productions as *Bubus the Teacher* and *The Government Inspector*, which differed in spirit and conception from his earlier 'biomechanical' and 'agit-prop' productions (whilst still bearing traces of their influence). This sense of a reversion to pre-revolutionary 'type' was then compounded (at least in the eyes of Meyerhold's political enemies) by the formal methods employed in his late 1920's productions of *Woe from Wit*, *The Bedbug* and *The Bathhouse*, and by their political implications (the last even being labelled 'anti-Soviet'). There were also abortive attempts, frustrated by state censorship, to stage controversial plays such as Erdman's *The Suicide* and Tretyakov's *I Want a Baby*. It was around this time, in the wake of Trotsky's expulsion and Michael Chekhov's defection, that unfounded rumours were beginning to circulate about Meyerhold's imminent emigration and a number of voices were raised suggesting that the earlier socialist rhetoric had been so much sound and fury signifying opportunism. The tightening of the stranglehold on the arts from 1929 onwards, intensified after 1934, inevitably meant that even Meyerhold's attempts to demonstrate his loyalty, in such productions as *The Last Decisive Battle*, which warned of a future fascist invasion of the Soviet Union, were likely to be construed in hostile terms. It is ironic that his last, banned, production before the closing of his theatre in January 1938 was an adaptation of a classic Soviet text, Nikolai Ostrovsky's *How the Steel Was Tempered*.

Meyerhold's personality was an extremely complex and contradictory one. Rather like Brecht's Galileo, heralding the dawn of a new age, he too found himself caught in the meshes of the past. Comparisons are frequently made between Meyerhold and Brecht. They were both socialist theatre practitioners united in their hostility to the legacy of 19th-century naturalism, both advocates of 'modernism' in the arts and both utilising forms of 'epic' staging, influenced by the Russian Formalists, as part of a search for the redefinition of existing dramatic structures and the alteration of the actor's relationship to both the role and to the audience. However, compared with Brecht, Meyerhold's own Marxism appears to have been instinctive and untutored, none of his theatrical theories having the elaborate theoretical underpinning that characterises those of Brecht. In fact, little that Meyerhold wrote after the Revolution carries the force of his major pre-Revolutionary essays, such as *The Fairground Booth* and *Towards a History of the Theatre and Its Techniques*.

As he was divided in himself, so Meyerhold tended to divide others. A successful production in his terms was one that split an audience down the middle into pro and contra. If the disputes that surrounded his productions are any guide then every one of them must have been a resounding success as far as Meyerhold was concerned. However, if one were to seek out the production that best characterises him and in which he spoke with his most authentic voice, then that would probably have to be of Alexander Ostrovsky's *The Forest* (1924), which he staged as an Eisensteinian 'montage of attractions'. Typically, criticism ranged from the wildly enthusiastic to the hostile and vituperative. One critic, impressed by the "colossal richness" of the production, described its performance as a "miracle" — like watching a six-inch nail being driven in with a ceramic vase. Another commentator delighted in the sequence of "the funny, the touching, the ironic, the angry, the sarcastic, the banal, the amusing, the bourgeois, the heroic, the passionate, the calculated, the primitive, the elegant, the concise, the tender, the seductive, the repulsive". Others thought that Meyerhold had "passed through Ostrovsky like a blind man through a ghost" and that the production "spat in the face of Russian culture". In the final analysis, the negative voices proved dominant — a fact that, even at this stage, can been seen to have anticipated some of the circumstances that lay behind Meyerhold's tragic downfall in the purges 16 years later.

—Nick Worrall

MIELZINER, Jo. US designer and actor. Born in Paris, 19 March 1901. Educated at Pennsylvania Academy; studied design at the National Academy of Design and Art Students and Academy of Fine Arts, Philadelphia. Married Jean Macintyre (divorced). Stage debut as actor, New York, 1923; studied stage design under Joseph Urban, Robert Edmond Jones, and Lee Simonson; debut as designer, Theatre Guild, New York, 1924; subsequently designed over 300 productions, including plays by Shakespeare and Tennessee Williams; designer or consultant on Vivian Beaumont and Forum Theatres at the Lincoln Centre, on the Mark Taper Forum, and the ANTA Washington Square Theatre; consultant, CBS-TV; served as camouflage specialist, US Air Force, 1942–43; designed lighting for first United Nations meeting, San Francisco, 1945. Benjamin Franklin Fellow, Royal Society of Arts, 1969. Member: Board of Directors, US Institute for Theatre Technology; American Theatre Planning Board (chairman). Recipient: Oscar, 1955; New York Drama Critics' Award, 1955–56; Ford Foundation Award, 1960; Tony Awards for design and lighting, 1970; Maharam Awards, 1969 and 1970; Drama Desk Award, 1970; New England Theatre Conference Award, 1957; Brandeis University Award, 1963. DFA: Fordham University, 1947; honorary degrees: University of Michigan; University of Utah; DH: Otterbein College, Westerville, Ohio, 1967. Died 15 March 1976.

Productions

1924   *The Guardsman* (Molnár), Theatre Guild, New York.

1925   *First Flight* (M. Anderson), Plymouth Theatre, New York.

1926   *Lucky Sam McCarver* (Howard), Playhouse, New York.

1927   *Saturday's Children* (M. Anderson), Booth Theatre, New York.
The Second Man (Behrman), Guild Theatre, New York.

1928   *Cock Robin* (Barry and Rice), 48th Street Theatre, New York.
Strange Interlude (O'Neill), John Golden Theatre, New York.

1929   *Street Scene* (Rice), Playhouse Theatre, New York.
The Little Show (Schwartz and Dietz), Music Box Theatre, New York.

1931   *Of Thee I Sing* (Kaufman), Sam H. Harris Theatre, New York.
Brief Moment (Behrman), Belasco Theatre, New York.

1932   *Biography* (Behrman), Guild Theatre, New York.
Gay Divorce (Taylor and Porter), Ethel Barrymore Theatre, New York.

1933   *Emperor Jones* (Gruenberg), Metropolitan Opera House, New York.
The Dark Tower (Kaufman and Woolcott), Morosco Theatre, New York.

1934   *Dodsworth* (Howard, adapted from Lewis), Shubert Theatre, New York.
Yellow Jack (Howard and de Kruif), Martin Beck Theatre, New York.
Merrily We Roll Along (Kaufman and Hart), Music Box Theatre, New York.
The Pure in Heart (Lawson), Longacre Theatre, New York.
Winterset (Anderson), Martin Beck Theatre, New York.

1935   *Panic* (McLeish), Imperial Theatre, New York.

1936   *On Your Toes* (Rodgers, Hart, and Abbott), Imperial Theatre, New York.
Hamlet (Shakespeare), Empire Theatre, New York.
The Wingless Victory (Anderson), Empire Theatre, New York.

1937   *High Tor* (Anderson), Martin Beck Theatre, New York.
The Star Wagon (Anderson), Empire Theatre, New York.
Susan and God (Crothers), Plymouth Theatre, New York.

1938   *I Married an Angel* (Rodgers and Hart), Shubert Theatre, New York.
The Boys from Syracuse (Rodgers, Abbott, and Hart, adapted from Shakespeare's *The Comedy of Errors*), Alvin Theatre, New York.
Knickerbocker Holiday (Anderson), Ethel Barrymore Theatre, New York.
Abe Lincoln in Illinois (Sherwood), Plymouth Theatre, New York.

1939   *No Time for Comedy* (Behrman), Ethel Barrymore Theatre, New York.
Key Largo (Anderson), Ethel Barrymore Theatre, New York.

1940   *Two on an Island* (Rice), Broadhurst Theatre, New York.
Journey to Jerusalem (Anderson), National Theatre, New York.

Jo Mielziner

Pal Joey (Rodgers, Hart, and O'Hara), Ethel Barrymore Theatre, New York.

Flight to the West (Rice), Guild Theatre, New York.

1941 The Talley Method (Behrman), Henry Miller's Theatre, New York.

Watch on the Rhine (Hellman), Martin Beck Theatre, New York.

Best Foot Forward (Martin, Blane, and Hohn), Ethel Barrymore Theatre, New York.

The Land Is Bright (Kaufman and Ferber), Music Box Theatre, New York.

Candle in the Wind (Anderson), Shubert Theatre, New York.

1942 Solitaire (Van Druten, adapted from Corle), Plymouth Theatre, New York.

By Jupiter (Rodgers and Hart), Shubert Theatre, New York.

1945 Foolish Notion (Barry), Martin Beck Theatre, New York.

Carousel (Rodgers and Hammerstein), Majestic Theatre, New York.

Hollywood Pinafore (Kaufman), Alvin Theatre, New York.

The Rugged Path (Sherwood), Plymouth Theatre, New York.

Dream Girl (Rice), Coronet Theatre, New York.

1946 Annie Get Your Gun (Berlin), Imperial Theatre, New York.

Another Part of the Forest (Hellman), Fulton Theatre, New York.

1947 Street Scene (Rice), Adelphi Theatre, New York.

Finian's Rainbow (Lane, Harburg, and Sady), 46th Street Theatre, New York.

Allegro (Rodgers and Hammerstein), Majestic Theatre, New York.

A Streetcar Named Desire (T. Williams), Ethel Barrymore Theatre, New York.

1948 Anne of the Thousand Days (Anderson), Shubert Theatre, New York.

1949 Death of a Salesman (Miller), Morosco Theatre, New York

South Pacific (Rodgers and Hammerstein), Majestic Theatre, New York.

1950 Guys and Dolls (Loesser and Burrows), 46th Street Theatre, New York.

1951 The King and I (Rodgers and Hammerstein), St James Theatre, New York.

A Tree Grows in Brooklyn (Schwartz, Fields, Abbott, and Smith), Alvin Theatre, New York.

1952 Wish You Were Here (Kober, Logan, and Rome), Imperial Theatre, New York.

1953 Picnic (Inge), Music Box Theatre, New York.

Can-Can (Burrows and Porter), Shubert Theatre, New York.

Me and Juliet (Rodgers and Hammerstein), Majestic Theatre, New York.

Tea and Sympathy (R. Anderson), Ethel Barrymore Theatre, New York.

1954 All Summer Long (R. Anderson, adapted from Wetzel), Arena Theatre, Washington D.C.

Fanny (Behrman, Logan, and Rome, adapted from Pagnol), Majestic Theatre, New York.

1955 Silk Stockings (Kaufman, MacGrath, Burrows, and Porter, adapted from Lengyel), Imperial Theatre, New York.

Cat on a Hot Tin Roof (T. Williams), Morosco Theatre, New York.

The Lark (Hellman, adapted from Anouilh), Longacre Theatre, New York.

1956 Middle of the Night (Chayevsky), ANTA Theatre, New York.

The Most Happy Fella (Loesser), Imperial Theatre, New York.

1958 The Day the Money Stopped (Anderson, adapted from Gill), Belasco Theatre, New York.

1959 Rashomon (Kanin), Music Box Theatre, New York; designed lighting.

Gypsy (Sondheim and Styne), Broadway Theatre, New York.

Silent Night, Lonely Night (R. Anderson), Morosco Theatre, New York.

1964 After the Fall (Miller), Washington Square Theatre, New York.

But for Whom Charlie (Behrman), Washington Square Theatre, New York.

1968 The Seven Descents of Myrtle (T. Williams), Ethel Barrymore Theatre, New York.

1969 Galileo (Brecht), University of Illinois, Illinois, Urbana.

1974   *In Praise of Love* (Rattigan), Morosco Theatre, New York.

Other productions included: *Nerves*, 1924; *That Awful Mrs Eaton*, 1924; *Mrs Partridge Presents*, 1925; *Caught*, 1925; *The Call of Life*, 1925; *The Enemy*, 1925; *The Wild Duck* (Ibsen), 1926; *Little Eyolf* (Ibsen); *Masque of Venice*, 1926; *Unseen*, 1926; *Seed of the Brute*, 1926; *Pygmalion* (G. B. Shaw), 1926; *Right You Are (If You Think You Are)* (Pirandello), 1927; *Mariners*, 1927; *Marquise* (Coward), 1927; *The Doctor's Dilemma* (G. B. Shaw), 1927; *Fallen Angels* (Coward), 1927; *The Grey Fox*, 1928; *The Jealous Moon*, 1928; *The Lady Lies*, 1928; *A Most Immoral Lady*, 1928; *The Amorous Antic*, 1929; *Jenny*, 1929; *Karl and Anna*, 1929; *The Sky Rocket*, 1929; *Judas*, 1929; *Meet the Prince*, 1929; *Young Alexander*, 1929; *The First Little Show* (revue), 1929; *First Mortgage*, 1929; *Dread*, 1929; *Mrs Cook's Tour*, 1929; *Uncle Vanya* (Chekhov), 1930; *Mr Gilhooley*, 1930; *Solid South*, 1930; *Sweet and Low* (revue), 1930; *The Second Little Show* (revue), 1930; *The Barretts of Wimpole Street* (Besier), 1931; *I Love an Actress*, 1931; *Anatol* (Schnitzler), 1931; *The House Beautiful*, 1931; *Billy Rose's Crazy Quilt* (revue), 1931; *The Third Little Show* (revue), 1931; *Distant Drums*, 1932; *Never No More*, 1932; *Bloodstream*, 1932; *Bridal Wise*, 1932; *Champagne Sec* (adapted from Strauss's *Die Fledermaus*), 1933; *A Divine Drudge*, 1933; *I Was Waiting for You*, 1933; *The Lake* (Massingham and Macdonald), 1934; *By Your Leave*, 1934; *Spring Song* (T. Williams), 1934; *Romeo and Juliet* (Shakespeare), 1934; *Accent on Youth* (Raphaelson), 1934; *Merrymount*, 1935; *Bird of Our Fathers*, 1935; *It's You I Want* (Braddell), 1935; *De Luxe*, 1935; *Flowers of the Forest* (Van Druten), 1935; *Jubilee* (Chekhov), 1935; *Pride and Prejudice* (Jerome, adapted from Austen), 1935; *A Room in Red and White*, 1935; *Co-Respondent Unknown*, 1935; *The Postman Always Rings Twice*, 1935; *Saint Joan* (G. B. Shaw), 1935; *Daughter of Atreus*, 1935; *The Women* (Boothe), 1935; *Ethan Frome*, 1936; *St Helena* (Sherriff and Casilis), 1936; *Hell Freezes Over*, 1936; *Too Many Heroes*, 1937; *Father Malacky's Miracle*, 1937; *Antony and Cleopatra* (Shakespeare), 1937; *Barchester Towers*, 1937; *Your Obedient Servant*, 1938; *On Borrowed Time*, 1938; *Save Me the Waltz*, 1938; *Sing Out the News* (Kaufman), 1938; *Mrs O'Brien Entertains*, 1939; *Stars in Your Eyes* (Logan and Schwartz), 1939; *Too Many Girls* (Rodgers and Hart), 1939; *Morning's at Seven* (Osborn), 1939; *Christmas Eve* (Hecht), 1939; *Higher and Higher* (Rodgers and Hart), 1940; *The Little Dog Laughed*, 1940; *Mr and Mrs North*, 1941; *The Cream in the Well*, 1941; *The Wookey*, 1941; *The Seventh Trumpet*, 1941; *Pillar of Fire*, 1942; *The Firebrand of Florence* (I. Gershwin and Weill), 1945; *Carib Song*, 1945; *Beggars are Coming to Town*, 1945; *The Glass Menagerie* (T. Williams), 1945; *Jeb* (Ardrey), 1946; *Windy City* (adapted from Hecht's *The Front Page*), 1946; *Happy Birthday* (Mayerl), 1946; *The Big Two*, 1947; *The Chocolate Soldier* (Straus, Bernauer, and Jacobson, adapted from G. B. Shaw's *Arms and the Man*), 1947; *Barefoot Boy with Cheek*, 1947; *Command Decision*, 1947; *Mister Roberts* (Heggen and Logan), 1948; *Shadow of the Wind*, 1948; *Sleepy Hollow*, 1948; *Summer and Smoke* (T. Williams), 1948; *The Man*, 1950; *The Innocents* (Archibald, adapted from James), 1950; *The Wisteria Trees* (Logan, adapted from Chekhov's *The Cherry Orchard*), 1950; *Burning Bright*, 1950; *Dance Me a Song*, 1950; *The Real McCoy*, 1950; *Top Banana* (Mercer), 1951; *Point of No Return*, 1951; *Flight into Egypt* (Wilder), 1952; *The Gambler* (Betti), 1952; *A Month of Sundays*, 1952; *Kind Sir*, 1953; *By the Beautiful Sea* (Fields and Schwartz), 1954; *Island of Goats* (Betti), 1955; *Pipe Dreams* (Rodgers and Hammerstein), 1955; *Happy Hunting* (Burrows, Crouse, Lindsay, and Karr), 1956; *Maiden Voyage*, 1957; *Miss Lonelyhearts*, 1957; *The Square Root of Wonderful*, 1957; *Look Homeward, Angel*, 1957; *Oh, Captain!* (Livingston and Evans), 1958; *Handful of Fire*, 1958; *The World of Susie Wong* (Osborn, adapted from Mason), 1958; *The Gazebo* (Coppel), 1958; *Whoop-up*, 1958; *Sweet Bird of Youth* (T. Williams), 1959; *The Gang's All Here* (Crouse and Hammerstein), 1959; *There Was a Little Girl*, 1960; *The Best Man*, 1960; *Christine* (Fain), 1960; *Little Moon of Alban*, 1960; *Period of Adjustment*, 1960; *White Alice*, 1960; *The Devil's Advocate*, 1961; *A Short Happy Life*, 1961; *Everybody Loves Opal*, 1961; *All American*, 1962; *Mr President*, 1962; *The Milk Train Doesn't Stop Here Anymore* (T. Williams), 1963; *The Owl and the Pussycat*, 1964; *Danton's Death* (Büchner), 1965; *The Playroom*, 1965; *Venus Is*, 1966; *Don't Drink the Water*, 1966; *My Sweet Charlie*, 1966; *The Paisley Convertible*, 1967; *That Summer ... That Fall*, 1967; *Daphne in Cottage D*, 1967; *Mata Hari*, 1967; *The Prime of Miss Jean Brodie* (Spark), 1968; *I Never Sang for My Father* (R. Anderson), 1968; *Slaughter on Tenth Avenue*, 1968; *Possibilities*, 1968; *1776* (Edwards and Stone), 1969; *The Conjuror*, 1969; *The Girl Upstairs*, 1969; *Child's Play* (Minghella), 1970; *Georgy*, 1970; *Look to the Lilies*, 1970; *Who Cares?*, 1970; *Father's Day*, 1971; *Love Me, Love My Children*, 1971; *Children! Children!*, 1972; *Voices*, 1972; *The Crucible* (Miller), 1972; *Sugar* (Merrill and Styne), 1972; *Out Cry* (T. Williams), 1973; *Miss Moffat*, 1974.

Films

Picnic, 1955.

Publications

Designing for the Theatre, 1965; *The Shapes of Our Theatre*, 1970.

* * *

Jo Mielziner designed over 300 productions for theatre, ballet, and opera. The significance lies not in the number alone, but in the fact that this list includes some of the most important dramas and musicals of the US theatre. Especially in the 1940's and 1950's, Mielziner's production credits read like an anthology of great plays. Beginning in 1945, when he returned from the air force, his credits include *The Glass Menagerie, Carousel, Annie Get Your Gun, Finian's Rainbow, A Streetcar Named Desire, Mister Roberts, Death of a Salesman, South Pacific*, and *Guys and Dolls* and continues with more works of Tenessee Williams, Arthur Miller, William Inge, and still more of the classics of the musical stage. This remarkable output was possible because by the 1940's Mielziner had found a visual style that was the perfect embodiment of the plays and musicals of the time. Because of his close involvement with these works, indeed, he often became an equal partner in their creation.

Mielziner was born in Paris, the son of the respected portrait painter Leo Mielziner. He grew up in his father's atelier, training to become an easel painter himself. He began his career in the theatre out of a need to make money, working first in Detroit and then with the Theatre Guild as an actor, stage manager, and finally as a design apprentice. Along the way he discovered that theatrical design was equally as gratifying as painting, perhaps even more so because, as he himself noted, it contained the fourth dimension of "time-space". He apprenticed with the major designers of the New Stagecraft: Joseph Urban, Robert Edmond Jones, and Lee Simonson. It was the latter who developed in him an appreciation for the power of lighting. From these teachers he also learned the desirability of suggestion over literalism. His first Broadway commission was for Ferenc Molnar's *The Guardsman*, produced by the Theatre Guild in 1924. This was, coincidentally, the production that first brought the performers Alfred Lunt and Lynn Fontaine together. Mielziner worked steadily after that, though on mostly undistinguished plays until Elmer Rice's *Street Scene* in 1929. His recreation of a tenement facade and concrete sidewalk for this last play brought him wide recognition. Although this set is often held up as a great example of naturalism in the theatre, Mielziner claimed that it was really an example of selective realism and poeticism.

Mielziner seemed to have an unerring sense of taste and style in regard to most of the plays he designed. A classic example was Maxwell Anderson's *Winterset* (1935), in which the designer's concept eventually overcame the desires of the playwright. Anderson had described the setting as a collection of dilapidated wharves and buildings, but Mielziner felt that the play projected hope, and that the poetry demanded a more poetic setting. He even dragged director Guthrie McClintic and the author out to the Brooklyn waterfront at two o'clock in the morning to test out the lines in different settings. Mielziner's solution of a majestic view of the Brooklyn Bridge soaring over the East River and disappearing into the haze has become one of the most famous images in US design and has outlasted the play, which is no longer considered the classic it once was. Nonetheless, the set never dominated the production; it provided the spare background against which the drama could unfold.

One of Mielziner's main goals was to create a more fluid style of staging, one that would eliminate long and cumbersome scene shifts. His careful organisation and sense of movement allowed him to transform the way both musicals and dramas were produced. It is for this reason that as musicals evolved from what were essentially elaborate vaudevilles into complex and sophisticated book shows that required rapid and fluid changes Mielziner became the logical choice. Likewise, as dramas became more and more cinematic in their structure, Mielziner's ability to create a seamless flow became essential to their success. He exploited standard means, simply making them more efficient, such as the use of two revolves in *Dodsworth* to transform one hotel room into another in a matter of seconds. But he is most closely associated with the use of scrims (gauzes that become transparent under special lighting), which he began experimenting with in the 1920's and perfected in the 1940's. The use of scrims allowed a cinematic-like dissolve from one room or space into another, but also created a dreamlike quality, which fitted in well with the poetic realism emerging in plays in the late 1930's and especially in the plays of Tennessee Williams from the mid-1940's onwards. Mielziner also further developed the art of lighting and was instrumental in creating a style of design in which transformations of locale or mood were effected through changes in lighting and colour. In this he worked closely with Edward F. Kook.

The use of scrims, cinematic scenic dissolves, evocative lighting, and selective realism overlaid with a dreamlike mood — the quintessence of Mielziner's style — was nowhere more evident nor more successful that in the production of *Death of a Salesman*. It in no way detracts from the talents of playwright Arthur Miller to say that this landmark production was a collaborative effort. From the moment the script was turned over to the producers, Mielziner was a part of the realization of the script in production. To this day, one of the hardest tasks for any production is to find a means of staging and a visual vocabulary that does not simply copy or echo the original setting. Much the same is true of *The Glass Menagerie* and *A Streetcar Named Desire*.

Mielziner was never happy with the proscenium stage as it existed and therefore did extensive research into theatre space. As a theatre consultant he was involved in the design of several theatres in the 1960's and was largely responsible for the repopularization of the thrust stage, though his designs for the Vivian Beaumont Theatre at the Lincoln Centre, and the Power Centre in Ann Arbor, Michigan, and elsewhere were plagued by sightline problems.

By the end of the 1960's, Mielziner's painterly style and soft poetic quality was out of step with the grittier and bolder style and materials that were being championed by Ming Cho Lee and his contemporaries. Mielziner's relatively few productions in the 1970's were generally unsuccessful. Nonetheless, his influence remains enormous and his contribution to US theatre virtually unequalled among designers.

—Arnold Aronson

MILLER, Jonathan (Wolfe). British director, actor, writer and physician. Born in London, 21 July 1934. Educated at St John's College, University of Cambridge, until 1959; University College School of Medicine, University of London. Married Helen Rachel Collet in 1956, two sons and one daughter. Stage debut, as actor with the Cambridge Footlights Club, Phoenix Theatre, 1954; first New York appearance, with *Beyond the Fringe* revue, 1962; debut as director, Royal Court Theatre, London, 1962; associate director, National Theatre, 1973–75; associate director, Greenwich Theatre, London, from 1975; artistic director, Old Vic Theatre, 1988–90; has also worked as associate director for the English National Opera and as a teacher of drama at Yale University. Fellow: University College of Medicine, University of London; St John's College, Cambridge University, 1982; University of Sussex, 1985. Member: Arts Council of Great Britain, 1975–76. Recipient: *London Evening Standard* Award, 1961; New York Drama Critics Circle special citation, 1962; Tony Award, 1963; Society of West End Theatre Award, 1976; Royal Television Society Silver Medal, 1981. D.Litt: University of Leicester.

Productions

As actor:
1954 *Out of the Blue*, Phoenix Theatre, London; Lyceum Theatre, Edinburgh, 1960.
1955 *Between the Lines*, Scala Theatre, London.
1961 *Beyond the Fringe*, Fortune Theatre, London; John Golden Theatre, New York, 1962.

As director:
1962 *Under Plain Cover* (Osborne), Royal Court Theatre, London.
1964 *The Old Glory* (Lowell), American Place Theatre, New York.
1965 *Benito Cereno* (Lowell), Theatre de Lys, New York; Mermaid Theatre, London, 1967.
1966 *Come Live with Me*, Yale Repertory Theatre, New Haven, Connecticut.
1967 *Prometheus Bound* (Aeschylus), Yale Repertory Theatre, New Haven, Connecticut.
1968 *The School for Scandal* (Sheridan), Playhouse Theatre, Nottingham.
1969 *King Lear* (Shakespeare), Playhouse Theatre, Nottingham, and Old Vic Theatre, London.
1970 *The Merchant of Venice* (Shakespeare), Old Vic Theatre, London.
  The Tempest (Shakespeare), Mermaid Theatre, London.
  Hamlet (Shakespeare), Arts Theatre, Cambridge.
1971 *Prometheus Bound* (Aeschylus), Mermaid Theatre, London.
  Richard II (Shakespeare), Ahmanson Theatre, Los Angeles.
1972 *Julius Caesar* (Shakespeare), New Theatre, London.
  The Taming of the Shrew (Shakespeare), Chichester Festival.
  The School for Scandal (Sheridan), National Theatre, London.
1973 *Measure for Measure* (Shakespeare), National Theatre, London.
  The Malcontent (Marston), Playhouse Theatre, Nottingham.
  The Seagull (Chekhov), Festival Theatre, Chichester.
  The Devil Is an Ass (Barnes, adapted from Jonson), Playhouse Theatre, Nottingham.
1974 *The Marriage of Figaro* (Beaumarchais), Old Vic Theatre, London.
  The Freeway (Nichols), Old Vic Theatre, London.
  Ghosts (Ibsen), Greenwich Theatre, London.
  The Seagull (Chekhov), Greenwich Theatre, London.
  Hamlet (Shakespeare), Greenwich Theatre, London.
  Arden Must Die, Sadler's Wells Theatre, London.
  Cosi fan Tutte (Mozart), Congress Theatre, Eastbourne.
1975 *The Importance of Being Earnest* (Wilde), Greenwich Theatre, London.

  All's Well That Ends Well (Shakespeare), Greenwich Theatre, London.
  Measure for Measure (Shakespeare), Greenwich Theatre, London.
  Rigoletto (Verdi), Kent Opera Company.
  The Cunning Little Vixen (Janácek), Glyndebourne Theatre, Sussex; revived there, 1977.
1976 *The Three Sisters* (Chekhov), Yvonne Arnaud Theatre, Guildford.
  Orfeo (Monteverdi), Kent Opera Company.
1977 *Eugene Onegin* (Tchaikovsky), Kent Opera Company.
1978 *The Marriage of Figaro* (Mozart), English National Opera, London.
1979 *She Would if She Could* (Etherege), Greenwich Theatre, London.
  La Traviata (Verdi), Kent Opera Company.
  The Turn of the Screw (Britten), English National Opera, London.
1980 *Arabella* (Strauss), English National Opera, London.
  Falstaff (Verdi), Kent Opera Company; revived, 1981.
1982 *The School for Scandal* (Sheridan), American Repertory Theatre, Cambridge, Massachusetts.
  Hamlet (Shakespeare), Warehouse Theatre, London.
  Cosi fan Tutte (Mozart), Opera Theatre, St Louis, Missouri.
  Fidelio (Beethoven), Kent Opera Company; revived, 1983.
1983 *The Magic Flute* (Mozart), Opera House, Glasgow.
1984 *Rigoletto* (Verdi), New York.
1985 *Don Giovanni* (Mozart), English National Opera, London.
1986 *Long Day's Journey into Night* (O'Neill), Broadhurst Theatre, New York.
  Mikado (Gilbert and Sullivan), English National Opera, London.
1988 *Andromache* (Racine), Old Vic Theatre, London.
  The Tutor (Lenz, adapted by Brecht), Old Vic Theatre, London.
  One Way Pendulum (Simpson), Old Vic Theatre, London.
  Too Clever by Half (Ostrovsky), Old Vic Theatre, London.
  The Taming of the Shrew (Shakespeare), Barbican Theatre, London.
  Bussy d'Ambois (Chapman), Old Vic Theatre, London.
1989 *King Lear* (Shakespeare), Old Vic Theatre, London.
  The Liar (P. Corneille), Old Vic Theatre, London.

Other productions include: *The Flying Dutchman* (Wagner); *Tosca* (Puccini).

Films

As actor:
One Way Pendulum, 1964.

As director:
Take a Girl Like You, 1970.

Television

As actor/presenter:
Beyond the Fringe, 1964; *A Trip to the Moon*, 1964; *Monitor*, 1964–65; *Intimations*, 1965; *Review*, 1974; *Books for Our Times*, 1964; *The Body in Question*, 1978; *States of Mind*, 1983.

As director:
What's Going on Here?, 1963; *Plato's Dialogues*, 1966; *Alice in Wonderland*, 1966; *From Chekhov with Love*, 1972; *Whistle and I'll Come to You; The Body in Question*, 1978.

Radio

As director:
Saturday Night on the Light; Monday Night at Home.

Publications

Beyond the Fringe, 1963; *The Anne Hutchinson Story* (teleplay), 1965; *Alice in Wonderland* (teleplay), 1966; *Harvey and the Circulation of the Blood*, 1968; *McLuhan* (biography), 1971; *Freud: The Man, His World, His Influence*, 1972; *The Body in Question*, 1979; *Darwin for Beginners*, 1982; *States of Mind: Conversations with Psychological Investigators*, 1983; *The Human Body*, 1983; *The Facts of Life*, 1984; *Subsequent Performances*, 1986.

* * *

Jonathan Miller's contribution to dramatic production spans theatre, opera, television and film; primarily as director/producer, but also, at various times, as performer, critic, writer and editor. He is also a qualified physician and a writer, researcher and broadcaster on matters medical, with a particular interest in neuropsychology. His theatrical career began in the Cambridge Footlights revue, and continued alongside Alan Bennett, Peter Cook and Dudley Moore in *Beyond the Fringe* in the 1960's, shows which helped spawn a new strain of satirical revue, often imitated but rarely surpassed.

Whilst performing in *Beyond the Fringe*, Miller directed the London premiere of John Osborne's comedy of sexual ill-manners *Under Plain Cover*, thus beginning the transition from actor to director and making a rare excursion into new writing. He has tended to concentrate on classics: Renaissance, 19th and early 20th century, mainly, with occasional forays into modern writing, as in the Absurdist *One Way Pendulum* of N. F. Simpson and Robert Lowell's *The Old Glory* adaptation.

One of Miller's largely unacknowledged strengths is his ability to identify new talent, or a new direction for an existing one. He has, for example, been instrumental in developing such directors as Richard Jones and Elijah Moshinsky, whom he commissioned, though from an opera background, to direct *A Midsummer Night's Dream* in his capacity as producer of the BBC-Time/Life Shakespeare series (1979–81). An early decision as artistic director at the Old Vic was to commission unknown Richard Hudson to design the entire inaugural season, for which Hudson won a major award. Miller's keen eye also serves him in terms of casting, and in textual analysis. One of the many hallmarks of a Miller production is its ability to illuminate hitherto dark corners of familiar texts; or forgotten masterpieces (for example, *Bussy d'Ambois*); or to deliver a newer reading of a character through judicious casting.

In *King Lear*, for instance — a text he has essayed four times — he casts the Fool as Lear's contemporary, juxtaposing them, and reappraises Goneril, Regan and Cordelia: humanising and somewhat rehabilitating the former in the earlier scenes, thereby rendering their descent into later viciousness doubly awful, and toughening Cordelia's early obstinacy, highlighting her 'angel of death' role within the plot, but also offering an arc of development through the play only to be cruelly and the more tragically destroyed. In *Hamlet*, he has cast Claudius as an able statesman ruined only by love of Gertrude, and interpreted Ophelia as a latent schizophrenic, socially crippled by 17th-century mores.

It is in this area that Miller's twin careers of doctor and director overlap and mutually inform each other. Above all, he is a humanist, less concerned with the ways of God to Man that with the ways of man to man, and woman. His encyclopedic knowledge of social history, and the workings of the human psyche and its correlative patterns of external behaviour — normal, deviant or damaged — informs his approach to character. Characters are given precise social contextualisation, sometimes against the grain of fashionable thinking about a famous text. Two examples spring to mind: his rediscovery of Eugene O'Neill's intense realism in *Long Day's Journey into Night* by the simple expedient of overlapping dialogue, a technique familiar in opera singing, thereby reproducing authentic patterns of everyday speech; and a reappraisal of *The Taming of the Shrew*, highlighting its relationship to contemporary English Puritan thinking.

Such detailed socio-historical contextualisation often encourages Miller to transpose the period and/or location of a text, thereby offering fresh insight into both text, period and location. For example, he transposed *Measure for Measure* to Freud's Vienna; *Tosca* was projected to Mussolini's Fascist Italy; *Rigoletto* was reworked in terms of Mafia-dominated 1940's America; Gilbert and Sullivan's 'japonaiserie' was displaced from Titipu to a Marx Brothers-inspired England — Miller's comedic roots surfacing here. Such transpositions are not arbitrary; they are triggered by an extraordinary breadth of intellectual referencing, and function in counterpoint to the original period or location. Likewise, the leavening effect of Miller's humour heightens, clarifies and rounds character and situation; rendering them more real, and in cases of tragedy, therefore more immediately accessible.

Such referencing is often signalled in Miller's visuals. Frequently stimulated by fine art contemporary with either a play's writing, or with the period of transposition, Miller's sets, costumes and lighting reflect this; on screen, this pictorial influence extends to staging and shot composition. Recently he has generated a greater dialectic between the Expressionist or Surrealist design and the psychological naturalism of his actors in working with designers Stefanos Lazaridis (*Tosca, Shrew*) and Richard Hudson (*Andromache*). His boldly intellectual strategies frequently alienate more hidebound critics, and sometimes audience members, and he is often accused of gimmickry and 'unnecessary' experimentation. But whilst his productions are not infallibly successful, they repeatedly expose what is merely fashion, and frequently specious, in current practice: a tendency also visible in his writings on the theatre, such as *Subsequent Performances*, which deals with complex notions of perception, relationships between audience and performance and the origins of his own theoretical and practical approaches. Miller productions rarely fail, at the very least, to provoke lively audience engagement. His work stimulates, sometimes educates, debates: perforce, on occasion, it positively enrages. As artistic director of the Old Vic, he consistently pursued an eclectic repertoire, making that theatre a third classical house alongside the Royal Shakespeare Company and the Vic's near neighbour on the South Bank, the Royal National Theatre.

—Val Taylor

MNOUCHKINE, Ariane. French director. Born in Boulogne-sur-Seine, 1939; daughter of a film producer of Russian extraction. Studied at the University of Oxford, and at the Sorbonne, Paris, 1959–62. Participated in amateur theatre at Oxford; subsequently founded Association Théâtrale des Etudiants de Paris, 1959; toured Far East, 1962–63; founder and co-director, Théâtre du Soleil, Paris, 1964; studied improvisation under Jacques Lecoq; installed company in the Cartoucheries de Vincennes, Paris, 1970; has also directed film versions of several stage successes. Recipient: Prix des Associations de Spectateurs, 1967; Critics' Prize, 1967.

Productions

1959–67	*Noces de Sang* (Lorca), Paris.
	Gengis Khan (Bauchau), Arènes de Lutèce, Paris.
1964	*Les Petits Bourgeois*, Maison des Jeunes et de la Culture, Montreuil; Théâtre Mouffetard, Paris, 1965.
	Philistines (Gorky, adapted by Adamov), Théâtre du Soleil, Paris.
1965	*Capitaine Fracasse* (Gautier, adapted by Léotard), Maison des Jeunes et de la Culture, Montreuil; Théâtre Récamier, Paris, 1966.
1967	*La Cuisine* (Wesker, adapted by Léotard), Antenne Culturelle, Kremlin-Bicêtre, Paris, and Cirque Médrano, Montmartre, Paris.
1968	*Le Songe d'une Nuit d'Été* (Shakespeare, adapted by Léotard), Cirque Médrano, Montmartre, Paris, and Festival des Nuits de Bourgogne.
	L'Arbre sorcier, Jérôme et la Tortue (Dasté), Cirque Medrano, Montmartre, Paris.
1969	*Les Clowns* (collective creation), Théâtre de la Commune, Aubervilliers, and Festival d'Art Dramatique, Avignon.
1970	*1789* (collective creation), Palais des Sports, Milan, and Cartoucheries de Vincennes, Paris.
1972	*1793* (collective creation), Cartoucheries de Vincennes, Paris.
1975	*L'Age d'Or* (collective creation), Cartoucheries de Vincennes, Paris.
1977	*Don Juan* (Molière), Cartoucheries de Vincennes, Paris.
1979	*Mephisto* (Mann, adapted by Mnouchkine), Cartoucheries de Vincennes, Paris.
1981	*Richard II* (Shakespeare), Cartoucheries de Vincennes, Paris.
1982	*Twelfth Night* (Shakespeare), Cartoucheries de Vincennes, Paris.
1984	*Henry IV, part 1* (Shakespeare), Cartoucheries de Vincennes, Paris.
1985	*L'Histoire Terrible mais inachevée de Norodom Sihanouk, Roi du Cambodge* (Cixous), Cartoucheries de Vincennes, Paris.
1987	*L'Indiade, ou l'Inde de leurs rêves* (Cixous), Cartoucheries de Vincennes, Paris.

Films

1789, 1974; *Molière*, 1976; *Mephisto*, 1980.

*

Bibliography

Books:
Denis Bablet and Marie-Louise Bablet, *Le Théâtre du Soleil*, Paris, 1979.
David Bradby, *Modern French Drama*, Cambridge, 1984.

Articles:
"An Interview with Irving Wardle", *Performance*, 2, 1972.
"Différent: Le Théâtre du Soleil", *Travail Théâtral*, February 1976.

* * *

Ariane Mnouchkine first participated in theatrical activities while a student at Oxford University and was subsequently inspired to found the Association Théâtral des Etudiants of Paris, which presented plays and organised acting courses and lectures. The foundation of the Théâtre du Soleil in 1964, with former fellow students, marked the true beginning of her career and her name is now synonymous with that of her company and the revolution in dramatic style and art that they have brought about together.

The Théâtre du Soleil began on an amateur basis, living as a community and rehearsing only in the evenings after work. Their first success came in 1967 with Wesker's *La Cuisine* (*The Kitchen*). Intensive teamwork, a close study of the rhythms of kitchen workers and Mnouchkine's newly acquired expertise in improvisation learnt with Jacques Lecoq brought out the troupe's own house style: stylised gesture and movement based on the observation of certain 'types'. This led the group to attempt a form of collective writing for *Les Clowns*, directed by Mnouchkine in 1969, which was a collage of improvisations using clown masks and comic routines — a development of style within the company that was to last for the next five years and was to attract international renown. The company eventually settled at the Cartoucheries de Vincennes on the outskirts of Paris and also undertook numerous tours of European countries. *1789* and *1793* were the distillations of months of improvisation and historical study, while *L'Age d'Or* (*The Golden Age*) brought the contemporary reality of an immigrant building worker's experiences to the stage.

Under Mnouchkine, the company challenges the traditional notions of theatre as an institution, as a bourgeois enclave reflecting middle-class values, and has put in its place a popular theatre inspired by collaborative writing and infused with collective energies. In Mnouchkine's non-hierarchical troupe, each member receives the same salary and contributes equally to the total work of the group, be it in stage design, costumes, music or performance. The troupe's early penchant for large open auditoria — they made their home in the Cirque Médrano in Montmartre for three productions in 1967 and 1968 — led directly to the development of their house style still apparent today: a theatre of extravagant gesture and energetic movement. At the same time, the events of 1968 demanded a reappraisal of their political stance within the theatre; they adopted some Brechtian techniques (such as the use of mime and a deliberately provocative and political style) while allowing individual actors to develop their personal talents for idiosyncratic accents or stylised movement. Characteristic of the work of the Théâtre du Soleil is the sheer pace of performance; this, together with the vivid use of colour in costume and props, lends the company its uniqueness. Its productions are dazzling, even breathtaking, while at the same time thought-provoking and iconoclastic. As in Kabuki theatre, the inspiration is historical and the form episodic, yet the effect is also intimate and immediate.

At the Cartoucherie de Vincennes, Ariane Mnouchkine and her company completely rebuilt the vast single-storey building — a hangar-like construction measuring 45 metres by 36 — into an open-plan acting area, a dressing space accessible by the public before and after performances, and a large concourse that serves as restaurant, foyer and sales and exhibition area. The dimensions of the Théâtre du Soleil's premises and its manifest encouragement to audiences to participate in the preparation and understanding of each production recall the heady events promoted by Jean VIlar's Théâtre National Populaire in the 1950's.

Mnouchkine's staging innovations will ensure her a place in theatre history in France, whether one thinks of the series of platforms joined by catwalks for *1789*, for which the audience was obliged to stand in the centre of the action, or the shallow craters of *L'Age d'Or*, over which the spectators had to clamber to follow the scenes. In both of these plays, the whole acting space was lit by thousands of tiny ceiling lights that lent a fairground atmosphere to the performance. More recently, Mnouchkine has attracted over a quarter of a million spectators to her 'oriental' Shakespeare cycle and, like Peter Brook before her, has infused the theatre itself with the excitement of novelty, an internationality of scale and mood, and, above all, a universal and popular appeal.

Mnouchkine's great success has been to bring together in one coherent troupe the individual talents of its members; given the initial absence of text in some of the productions of the Théâtre du Soleil, the rigorous discipline of commedia dell'arte and circus forms that they practise, and the pursuit of democracy within theatre structures that they champion, this has been no mean feat.

—David Jeffery

———

MOCHALOV, Pavel (Stepanovich). Russian actor. Born in Moscow, 3 November 1800; son of the actor Stepan Fedorovich Mochalov. Little formal education; trained for the stage under his father. Married; daughter Ekaterina also became an actress. Stage debut, Moscow, 1817; subsequently invited to join the Moscow Imperial Theatre (the Maly Theatre from 1824); first major success, as Othello, 1823; acclaimed in tragedy and remained a star at the Maly Theatre for the rest of his career, as well as touring Russia; last years increasingly disrupted by alcoholism. Died in Moscow, 16 March 1848.

Roles

1817	Polynices in *Edip v Afinach* [Oedipus at Athens] (Ozerov), Moscow.
	Achilles in *Poliksena* (Ozerov), Moscow.
1818	Horace in *Horace* (P. Corneille), Maly Theatre, Moscow.
	Tancrède in *Tancrède* (Voltaire), Maly Theatre, Moscow.
1822	Fingal in *Fingal* (Ozerov), Maly Theatre, Moscow.
1823	Othello in *Othello* (Shakespeare), Maly Theatre, Moscow; revived notably, 1837.
1826	Meinau in *Menschenhass und Reue* (Kotzebue), Maly Theatre, Moscow.
1827	Kerim-Girei in *Bakhchisarai fontan* [The Fountain of Bakhchisarai] (Pushkin, adapted by Shakhovskoi), Maly Theatre, Moscow.
1828	Karl Moor in *Die Raüber* (Schiller), Maly Theatre, Moscow.
1829	Ferdinand in *Kabale und Liebe* (Schiller), Maly Theatre, Moscow.
	Don Carlos in *Don Carlos* (Schiller), Maly Theatre, Moscow.
1831	Chatsky in *Gore ot uma* [Woe from Wit] (Griboyedov), Maly Theatre, Moscow.
1835	Mortimer in *Maria Stuart* (Schiller), Maly Theatre, Moscow.
	Kean in *Kean* (Dumas père), Maly Theatre, Moscow.
1837	Hamlet in *Hamlet* (Shakespeare, translated by Polevoi), Maly Theatre, Moscow.
1839	Lear in *King Lear* (Shakespeare), Maly Theatre, Moscow.
	Richard III in *Richard III* (Shakespeare), Maly Theatre, Moscow.
1841	Romeo in *Romeo and Juliet* (Shakespeare), Maly Theatre, Moscow.

1842   Miller in *Kabale und Liebe* (Schiller), Maly
        Theatre, Moscow.
1844   Almaviva in *Le Barbier de Seville* (Beaumar-
        chais), Maly Theatre, Moscow.
        Franz Moor in *Die Raüber* (Schiller), Maly
        Theatre, Moscow.

Other roles included: Aleko in *The Gypsies* (Pushkin,
adapted by Shakhovskoi); Biderman in *Death or Honour*
(Polevoi); Coriolanus in *Coriolanus* (Shakespeare); Dimitri
in *Dmitri Donskoi* [Dmitri of the Don] (Ozerov); Germani
in *Trente Ans; ou, La Vie d'un Joueur* (Ducange); Julius von
Sassen in *Julius von Sassen* (Zschocke).

Publications

The Circassian Girl (play, produced 1840); *The Black
Shawl* (adaptation from Pushkin); *Zametkh o Teatre*
(treatise on acting), 1953.

* * *

Pavel Mochalov has frequently been compared with
Edmund Kean, whose temperament and drinking habits he
shared. He became the model of the romantic Russian
actor. Unlike Kean, however, he did not play his performances meticulously, but relied on an 'inspirational' approach. His method of acting was influenced by his father,
who finally came to prominence in Moscow in 1812.
Stepan Mochalov had been a serf actor and had received
almost no formal education. As an actor, he had almost no
technique, but he had emotional power. His favourite trick
was to rush downstage and deliver emotional passages with
great feeling and sincerity. This made him popular with
audiences even though it was not always appropriate to the
play.

Pavel Mochalov, whose general education was almost as
scant as his father's, made his debut at the age of 17 in the
role of Polynices in the pseudo-classical drama *Oedipus at
Athens* by Vladislav Ozerov and was an immediate success.
He was well-built, with a large head and a naturally well-
produced, flexible voice. Unlike many actors of the period,
he did not rely on the prompter but always mastered his
lines. This, however, was the full extent of his discipline.
Like his father, he was the master of the sudden burst of
emotion, the flashes of feeling and temperament. He payed
almost no attention to costume or make-up. He played on
the inspiration of the moment and it was his displays of
sensibility and temperament that audiences came to see
and that frequently drew plaudits from informed critics
like Aksakov, Belinski and Herzen. When the inspiration
worked, he was able to illuminate the text from within and
reveal levels of feeling that lesser talents could not achieve.
This was done without pyrotechnics but with simplicity,
sincerity and ease. Moments of brilliance were often
followed by passages in which the playing was distinctly
rough, but Mochalov seemed to exert a magnetic power
over audiences who were willing to forgive the indifferent
passages if they could experience the moments, sometimes
very short, when his talent blazed out. Contemporary
accounts refer to his capacity to reduce an entire house to
tears in Kotzebue's *Menschenhass und Reue* (*The Stranger*)

Pavel Mochalov

or fascinate them with his seductive, irresistible wooing of
Lady Anne in Shakespeare's *Richard III*.

His interpretation of Hamlet stamped the role for the rest
of the century and beyond. This was an active Hamlet, an
essential man of action and not the quiet reflective
philosopher-prince that had been described in German
criticism. His performance was discussed in detail by
Belinski in his classic essay on the play and it was Belinski's
view of the text that Stanislavsky adopted when he came to
collaborate with Gordon Craig on the legendary *Hamlet*
presented at the Art Theatre in 1911.

Mochalov was much less at home in quieter, more
reflective scenes that needed to be paced and controlled or
in comedy and this led to the one major failure of his
career. The general view was that Mochalov was the ideal
actor at the Maly to play Chatsky in Griboyedov's *Woe
from Wit*. Unfortunately, Mochalov played the role on far
too tragic a note, delivering Chatsky's criticisms in much
too savage a manner. In Griboyedov's play, as the title
indicates, Chatsky's problem is that he is not only too
intelligent but incapable of holding his tongue.

Mochalov's inspirational approach was by no means
universally approved and in St Petersburg in particular he
was unfavourably compared to Karatygin, whose performances were minutely prepared in advance. The debate on
the nature of acting, epitomized in Diderot's *Paradoxe sur
le Comedien*, centred on the relative merits of Mochalov
and Karatygin. Yet even within the Maly, Mochalov's own
theatre, there was serious disagreement. Shchepkin, who
favoured the 'actor of feeling' over the 'actor of reason',

required more consistency and discipline in performance than Mochalov would admit and he opposed all attempts to bring his temperament under control in the interests of creating a coherent ensemble. Yet Mochalov shared Shchepkin's conviction that the actor should identify with the thoughts and inner life of the character but this he could only do by instinct, in hit-or-miss fashion. The Mochalov legend became the emblem for those who opposed any attempt to establish a formal acting method or to create regular theatre schools.

Towards the end of his career Mochalov's drinking bouts, which could last up to a month and were, it was claimed, brought on by his unhappy marriage, began to take their toll, affecting his memory and making him more erratic than ever. He was disliked by the theatre management and state officials, but never lost his hold on popular audiences however outrageous his behaviour. Huge crowds attended his funeral when he died as a result of catching a chill.

—Jean Benedetti

MODENA, Gustavo. Italian actor-manager. Born in Venice, Italy, 13 Feburary 1803. Educated at schools in Verona; studied law at the Universities of Padua, from 1818, and Bologna, 1820–21. Married Giulia Calame in 1835. Abandoned career as lawyer and made stage debut, with the touring company of Salvatore Fabbrichesi, 1824; leading actor, company of A. Raftopulo, 1827; founded his own company, with his father Giacomo and Carlotta Polvaro, 1829; subsequently toured throughout Europe, after being obliged to leave Italy because of his revolutionary activities, from 1832; lived in France, Switzerland, Belgium and England, 1832–39; returned to Italy, 1839; formed Compagnia dei Giovani in Milan, 1843; left troupe and resumed touring, 1846; subsequently acted with several companies, including his own; resident in the Kingdom of Piedmont, from 1849; conducted final tour, 1860. Died in Turin, Italy, 20 February 1861.

Productions

1824	*Saul* (Alfieri), Venice; acted David.
1827–31	*Virginia* (Alfieri), tour; acted Icilio.
	Polinice (Alfieri), tour.
	Oreste (Alfieri), tour.
	Gli Innamorati (Goldoni), tour; acted Fulgenzio.
	Pamela nubile (Goldoni), tour; acted Bonfil.
	Maria Stuarda (Schiller), tour; acted Leicester.
	Francesca da Rimini (Pellico), tour; acted Paolo.
	I Due Sergenti (Roti), tour; acted Guglielmo.
	Zaira (Voltaire), tour; acted Orosmane.
	Il Giocatore (Iffland), tour.
	Il Conte Beniowsky, tour.
1830	*Il Cittadino di Gand* (Romand), tour.
1839	*Divina Commedia* (Dante), Queen's Theatre, London.
1847	*Othello* (Shakespeare), tour.
1847–60	*Saul* (Alfieri), tour; acted Saul.
	Louis XI (Delavigne), tour; acted Louis XI.

La Pretendente, ossia Giacomo I Re d'Inghilterra (Dinaux and Sue), tour.
Clothilde Valéry (Soulié), tour.
Claudia (Sand), tour.
La Calunnia (Scribe), tour.
Una Catena (Scribe), tour.
Maometto (Voltaire), tour.
Filippo (Alfieri), tour.
Kean (Dumas), tour; acted Kean.
Il Fornaretto (Dall'Ongara), tour.
Gli Spazzacamini della Valle d'Aosta (Sabbatini), tour.
Bianca Cappello (Sabbatini), tour.
Sampiero (Revere), tour.

*

Bibliography

Books:
Luigi Bonazzi, *Gustavo Modena e l'arte sua*, Castello, 1884.
A. Manzi, *Gustavo Modena, il governo e la Compagnia Reale Sarda*, Genoa, 1936.
T. Grandi, *Scritti e discorsi di Gustavo Modena*, Rome, 1957.
T. Grandi, *Gustavo Modena atore e patriota*, Pisa, 1968.
Claudio Meldolesi, *Profilo di Gustavo Modena*, Rome, 1972.
Leonardo Bragaglia, *Gustavo Modena in il carabiniere*, 1973.

* * *

Born into the profession, Gustavo Modena acquired his early experience acting with his father, Giacomo, a distinguished company manager who gave some of the first performances of Alfieri's lead roles. As much a political activist as an actor and troupe leader, Modena's early career was much disrupted by periods of exile abroad, and later by the restrictions imposed on where he was allowed to act. While in exile he undertook various kinds of work: he taught Italian language and literature, was a professional proof corrector, started a small grocery business. But his political engagement and enthusiasm for the theatre remained constant, and his importance in the history of the 19th-century Italian stage is considerable, for when he finally returned from exile in 1839 he initiated a process of theatrical reform that in the long run was to have a significant influence on the development of acting in Italy and even abroad.

From the beginning Modena used the theatre for educational and socio-political purposes, identifying artistic activity with a firm assertion of the liberty he passionately thought due to Italy and the Italians. He attempted to promote a new national drama and to introduce Italian audiences to the best of European drama. The working practices of the company he formed in 1843 with a group of young actors, the Compagnia dei Giovani, which lasted until 1845, set an example that many players later attempted to follow. Making of his company something of a school, he emphasized the importance of social and historical authenticity; of careful study, preparation and rehearsal; of minute care in the preparation of scenery, costumes and effects; of a disciplined approach to the business of acting, and of the need to banish theatrical crudeness and histrionic excess in the name of greater control over characterisation and a more persuasively naturalistic approach to playing and staging. In essence, his acting reforms consisted of an attempt to elevate what in Italy remained the still largely despised craft of acting into a dignified and recognised creative art.

Part of Modena's high reputation today almost certainly depends on his profound involvement with the struggle for Italian independence, and is not unconnected too with the current fashion for a socially and politically engaged theatre. He himself became somewhat disillusioned, both with the direction Italian politics were to take and with the apparent failure of his theatrical ideas to obtain any firm foothold in Italy. Although he remained true to his republican ideals, he was disillusioned by the Mazzinians and suspicious of the Liberal moderates and the support they provided the Savoy monarchy. He remained, too, strongly committed to theatre, but in the last years achieved little of artistic note, leading several second-rate companies with no conspicuous success and mounting financial exigencies. An actor of powerful physique and expressive features, Modena was a versatile player, good in comedy, tragedy and romantic melodrama, and ever willing to experiment. Particularly intriguing was his attempt to introduce Italian audiences in 1847 to Shakespeare's *Othello*: the text he performed was, in fact, much modified to accommodate Italian taste, but it failed nonetheless, and plans he had to do *Hamlet* were permanently set aside.

To some extent, as far as theatre was concerned, Modena pursued an impossible ideal, and at no time in the century was Italian theatre to achieve the kind of social and cultural status he thought it merited, nor was he able to turn theatre effectively to the business of serving a clearly defined social purpose; the political and economic conditions of the time quite defeated his efforts, as it did those of his successors, who sought inspiration in his example. Yet his influence was in many respects strongly felt and widely diffused. Salvini, Ernesto Rossi and Luigi Bellotti-Bon, later among the leading capo-comici of the Italian stage, learned much from him, and through them, and others, his insistence on a natural, simple, unemphatic yet forceful style of playing, on psychological plausibility in character interpretation, on disciplined preparation and rehearsal, and on the need for uncluttered scenic decoration, were all in innumerable indirect ways to shape stage presentation in Italy for several decades.

—Kenneth Richards

MODJESKA, Helena. Polish actress. Born Helena Opid in Cracow, Poland, 12 October 1840. Educated at convent school in Cracow. Married 1) Gustav Modrzejewski in 1861 (died); 2) Charles Chlapowski, Count Bozenta, in 1868. Stage debut with strolling company organised for her by her first husband, Bochnia, 1861; spent several years touring small Polish towns before returning to Cracow, 1865, and establishing her reputation; subsequently appeared as a star in Warsaw, 1868; obliged to leave Poland for political reasons and emigrated to USA, 1876; learnt English and made her English-speaking debut on the US stage, San Francisco, 1877; European tours, 1879–82, 1894–95 and 1901; London debut, 1880; retired temporarily from the stage due to ill health, 1895; resumed stage career, 1898; toured with Edwin Booth, 1899. Died in Bay Island, East Newport, California, 8 April 1909.

Roles

1861	Hortensja in *Biała kamelia* (adapted from Dumas's *Lady of the Camelias*), Bochnia.
	Signora Roselli in *Primadonna, czyli Mleczna siostra* (Dartois and Jules), Bochnia.
	Hrabina in *Okno na pierwszym pietrze* (Korzeniowski), Bochnia.
	Klara in *Śluby panieńskie* (Fredro), Nowy Sacz.
	Maria in *Maria, corka pułku* (Donizetti), Rzeszów.
	Aniela in *Majatek albo imie* (Korzeniowski), Rzeszów.
1862	Herminia in *Przyjaciółki* (Korzeniowski), Przemyśl.
	Julia in *Pierwsza lepsza* (Fredro), Przemyśl.
	Dorota in *Szkoda wasów* (Dmuszewski), Brzezany.
	Prakseda in *Karpaccy górale* (Korzeniowski), Brody.
	Ksiezniczka in *Zydzi* (Korzeniowski), Brody.
	Basia in *Majatek albo imie* (Korzeniowski), Brody.
	Maria in *Doktor Robin* (Prémaray), Brody.
	Maria in *Domy polskie w XVII wieku* (Majeranowski), Lvov.
	Maria in *Folwark Primerose* (Cormon and Véteuil), Lvov.
	Jadwiga in *Konkurent i maz* (Korzeniowski), Lvov.
	Felusia in *Szlachta czynszowa* (anon.), Lvov.
	Zygmunt Karliński in *Kasper Karliński* (Syrokomla), Lvov.
	Aplikant in *Joanna, która płacze, i Joanna, która sie śmieje* (Dumanoir and Keraniou), Lvov.
	Baronowa in *Filizanka herbaty* (Nuitter and Derley), Lvov.
	Basia in *Podrózomania* (Korzeniowski), Lvov.
	Skierka in *Balladyna* (Słowacki), Lvov.
1863	Fanchon in *Poczwarka* (Birch-Pfeifferowa), Czerniowce.
	Aniela in *Śluby panieńskie* (Fredro), Czerniowce.
	Zofia in *Pierwej mama* (Korzeniowski), Czerniowce.
	Celina in *Tajemnice modnego świata, czyli Tak sie dzieje* (St Bogusławski), Czerniowce.
	Amelia in *Mazepa* (Słowacki), Czerniowce.
	Basia in *Majster i czeladnik* (Korzeniowski), Czerniowce.
	Dziewczyna mazurska in *Cyrulik ze Zwierzynca* (Debicki), Czerniowce.
	Zośka in *Stach i Zośka* (Szymański), Czerniowce.
	Kunegunda in *Wesele przy latarniach* (Offenbach), Czerniowce.
	Barbara Radziwiłłóna in *Barbara Radziwiłłóna* (Feliński), Czerniowce.

Zofia in *Damy i huzary* (Fredro), Czerniowce.

Bronika in *Wiesław* (Ostrovsky), Czerniowce.

Ludwika in *Intryga i miłość* (Schiller), Czerniowce.

Dosia in *Skalmierzanki* (Kamiński), Czerniowce.

Wanda in *Bojomir i Wanda* (Krasiński), Czerniowce.

Amalia in *Nie ma meza w domu* (Scribe, Cormon and Grangé), Czerniowce.

Maria Stuart in *Maria Stuart* (Schiller), Czerniowce.

Berta in *Rece czarodziejskie* (Scribe and Legouvé), Czerniowce.

Precjoza in *Precjoza* (Wolff), Czerniowce.

1864   Murzynka in *Murzynka* (Ziegler), Czerniowce.

Zofia in *Władysław Łokietek, czyli Wiśliczanki* (Dmuszewski), Czerniowce.

Blank in *Garbaty, wygnaniec i mściciel* (Féval and Bourgeois), Czerniowce.

Liliana in *Marnotrawca* (Raimund), Czerniowce.

Klara in *Staroświecczyzna i postep czasu* (anon.), Czerniowce.

Fernanda in *Sto za sto* (Thiboust and Clairville), Czerniowce.

Marco in *Kobiety z kamienia* (Barrière and Thiboust), Czerniowce.

Donna Sol in *Hernani* (Hugo), Czerniowce.

Barbara Zapolska in *Barbara Zapolska* (Creuzé de Lesseur), Czerniowce.

Indiana in *Indiana i Charlemagne* (Bayard and Dumanoir), Czerniowce.

Emilia in *Dwie mezatki* (adapted from the French), Czerniowce.

Ludwik in *Ulicznik paryski* (Bayard and Vanderburch), Czerniowce.

Thisbe in *Angelo Malipieri, tyran Padwy* (Hugo), Czerniowce.

Jenny Laroche in *Chłopiec okretowy* (Souvestre), Czerniowce.

Maria Stuart in *Maria Stuart* (Schiller), Czerniowce.

Teresa in *Zycie snem* (Gauthier, Varennes and Kock), Czerniowce.

Dalila in *Dalila* (Feuillet), Czerniowce.

1865   Floryna in *Floryna* (Pittaud des Forges and St Yves), Czerniowce.

Matylda in *Młyn diabelski* (Hensler), Czerniowce.

Gabriela in *Panna de Belle-Isle* (Dumas, Walewski and Brunswick), Czerniowce.

Sara in *Salomon*, Cracow.

Stefan in *Paziowie królowej Marysieńki* (Duniecki), Cracow.

Leonia in *Szuka siebie* (Decomberousse and Roche), Cracow.

Cecylia in *Panna-mezatka* (Korzeniowski), Cracow.

Łucka in *Maria mulatka* (Pucher and Laurencin), Cracow.

Królowa Anna in *Szklanka wody* (Scribe), Cracow.

Jadwiga in *Michał Sedziwój* (Szymanowski), Cracow.

Celina in *Porzadni ludzie* (Checiński), Cracow.

Anna Oświecimówna in *Anna Oświecimówna* (Bołoz-Antoniewicz), Cracow.

1866   Małgosia in *Pafnucy i Narcyz* (Brisebarre and Marc-Michel), Cracow.

Zuzanna in *Ćwiartka papieru* (Sardou), Cracow.

Ksiezniczka Eboli in *Don Karlos* (Schiller), Cracow.

Antonina in *Ziec pana Poirier* (Augier and Sandeau), Cracow.

Laura in *Dwie wdowy* (Mallefille), Cracow.

Klotylda in *Rodzina Benoiton* (Sardou), Cracow.

Maria in *Drzemka pana Prospera* (Fredro), Cracow.

Pani de Laujoie in *Człowiek słomiany* (Labiche and Lefranc), Cracow.

Zoe in *Niewiniatka* (Grisar), Cracow.

Aniela in *Z małej chmury wielki deszcz* (Gozlan), Cracow.

Maria in *Przez zazdrość* (Musset), Cracow.

Flora in *Diabełki rózowe* (Grangé and Thiboust), Cracow.

Klara in *Stasio* (Szajnocha), Cracow.

Królowa Jadwiga in *Jadwiga, królowa polska* (Szujski), Cracow.

Hrabina in *Pomyślne polowanie* (Decourcelle and Thiboust), Cracow.

Maria in *Sabaudka, czyli Błogosławieństwo matki* (Dennery and Lemoine), Cracow.

Cecylia in *Nasi najserdeczniejsi* (Sardou), Cracow.

Genowefa in *Pokusa* (Duniecki), Cracow.

Paola in *Trefniś* (Mélesville and Xavier), Cracow.

Helena de la Seiglière in *Helena de la Seiglière* (Sandeau), Cracow.

Łucja in *Za piekny* (Plouvier and Adenis), Cracow.

Justysia in *Maz i zona* (Fredro), Cracow.

Berta in *Fortepian Berty* (Barrière and Lorin), Cracow.

Halszka z Ostroga in *Halszka z Ostroga* (Szujski), Cracow.

Barbara Radziwiłłówna in *Twardowski* (Szujski), Cracow.

Margrabina in *Zaraza* (Augier), Cracow.

Gabriela in *Przyparty do ściany* (Najac), Cracow.

Małgosia in *Łobzowianie* (Anczyc), Cracow.

Amelia in *Przed śniadaniem* (Fredro), Poznań.

Helena in *Pan Jowialski* (Fredro), Poznań.

Zosia in *Krakowiacy i Górale* (Kamiński), Poznań.

Kasia in *Gwałtu, co sie dzieje!* (Fredro), Poznań.

Alina in *Paziowie królowej Marysieńki* (Duniecki), Poznań.

Hrabina de Meyran in *Ciezka próba* (Berton), Cracow.

Staróscina in *Ciepła wdówka* (Kraszewski), Cracow.

Amalia in *Zbójcy* (Schiller), Cracow.

Anna in *Po śliskiej drodze* (Koziebrodzki), Cracow.

Kamilla in *Perła uroniona* (Deryng), Cracow.

Julia in *Przesilenie* (Feuillet), Cracow.

Blanka in *Krol sie bawi* (Hugo), Cracow.

Porcja in *Kupiec wenecki* (Shakespeare), Cracow.

1867   Cecylia in *Ojciec Guerin* (Augier), Cracow.

Hero in *Wiele hałasu o nic* (Shakespeare), Cracow.

Genowefa in *Poczciwi wieśniacy* (Sardou), Cracow.

Eponina in *Nedznicy* (Hugo), Cracow.

Adam Kazanowski in *Dwór królewicza Władysława* (Szujski), Cracow.

Antonina in *Starzy kawalerowie* (Sardou), Cracow.

Berta z Bruneku in *Wilhelm Tell* (Schiller), Cracow.

Henryka, później Honoryna in *Lepiej późno niz nigdy* (Tarnowski), Cracow.

Chrystiana in *Czarna perła* (Sardou), Cracow.

Eugenia in *Niebezpieczna ciotunia* (Albini), Cracow.

Emilia in *Na stacji kolei zelaznej* (Müller), Cracow.

Adrianna Lecouvreur in *Adrianna Lecouvreur* (Scribe and Legouvé), Cracow.

Katarzyna Bradigani in *Angelo Malipieri, tyran Padwy* (Hugo), Lvov.

Hrabina in *Zydzi* (Korzeniowski), Poznań.

Wesołowska in *Skalmierzanki* (Kamiński), Poznań.

Hrabina in *Pamietniki szatana* (Arago and Vermond), Poznań.

Hrabina Eliza in *Równy wojewodzie* (Kraszewski), Cracow.

Abigail in *Szklanka wody* (Scribe), Cracow.

Janina in *Pojecia pani Aubray* (Dumas père), Cracow.

Karolina in *Margrabia de Villemer* (Sand), Cracow.

Pani de Léry in *Kaprys* (Musset), Cracow.

Eleonora in *Fiesco* (Schiller), Cracow.

Ofelia in *Hamlet* (Shakespeare), Cracow.

Joanna in *Klucz Metelli* (Meilhac and Halévy), Cracow.

Klara in *Egmont* (Goethe), Cracow.

Paola in *Kabalarka, czyli Zydówka i chrześcijanka* (Séjour), Cracow.

1868   Wanda Marecka in *Poznaj, nim pokochasz* (Fredro), Cracow.

Karolina in *Miłość i dyplomacja* (Feuillet), Cracow.

Goplana in *Balladyna* (Słowacki), Cracow.

Doris Quinault in *Narcyz Rameau* (Brachvogel), Cracow.

Jadwiga Orzelska in *Nazajutrz po balu* (Przezdziecki), Cracow.

Helena in *Zona zołnierza, czyli Bitwa pod Wimpfen* (adapted from the French), Cracow.

Cecylia in *Przeszłość kobiety* (Lafont and Béchard), Cracow.

Hradianka Rutland in *Hrabia Essex* (Laube), Cracow.

Emma in *Zawierucha* (Koziebrodzki), Cracow.

Laura in *Uczniowie Karola, czyli Młodość Fryderkyka Schillera* (Laube), Cracow.

Margrabina d'Auberive in *Bezczelni* (Augier), Cracow.

Anna in *Ryszard III* (Shakespeare), Cracow.

Gryzelda in *Zborowscy* (Szujski), Cracow.

Ludwika in *Posazna jedynaczka* (Fredro), Cracow.

Łucja Percy in *Uzurpator* (Brachvogel), Cracow.

Livia Quintilla in *Livia Quintilla* (Rzetkowski), Cracow.

Pani de Nohan in *Maz na wsi* (Bayard and Vailly), Cracow.

Małgorzata in *Safanduły* (Sardou), Cracow.

Judyta in *Uriel Akosta* (Gutzkow), Poznań.

Julia in *Romeo i Julia* (Shakespeare), Poznań.

Jenny in *Wariatka* (Desnoyers and Gérau), Poznań.

Helena in *List zelazny* (Małecki), Poznań.

Neali in *Paria* (Delavigne), Teatr Wielki, Warsaw.

Margrabina Pompadour in *Narcyz Rameau* (Brachvogel), Teatr Wielki, Warsaw.

1869   Drahomira in *Drahomira* (Weilen), Cracow.

Kordelia in *Król Lir* (Shakespeare), Cracow.

Marta in *Rodzina Benoiton* (Sardou), Cracow.

Joanna Rey in *Płacz i śmiech* (Dumanoir and Keraniou), Cracow.

Małgorzata in *Faust* (Goethe), Cracow.

Jadwiga in *Sto tysiecy* (Bobrowski), Cracow.

Desdemona in *Otello* (Shakespeare), Cracow.

Katarzyna in *Dwaj Radziwiłłowie* (Bełcikowski), Cracow.

Wanda in *Niepokój domowy* (adapted from the French), Cracow.

Amelia in *Gałazka heliopropu* (Asnyk), Cracow.

Joanna de Simerose in *Przyjaciel kobiet* (Dumas père), Teatr Wielki, Warsaw.

Edmea Mauprat in *Mauprat* (Sand), Teatr Wielki, Warsaw.

Donna Diana in *Donna Diana* (Moreto), Teatr Wielki, Warsaw.

1870   Dalia in *Wanda* (Mellerowa), Teatr Rozmaitości, Warsaw.

Hrabina d'Autreval in *Walka kobiet* (Scribe and Legouvé), Cracow.

Maria Delorme in *Maria Delorme* (Hugo), Cracow.

Ksiezna Korecka in *Takie one wszystkie* (Narrey), Cracow.

1871   Gilberta in *Frou-frou* (Meilhac and Halévy), Teatr Wielki, Warsaw.

Pani de Verlière in *Post-scriptum* (Augier), Teatr Rozmaitości, Warsaw.

Małgorzata in *Powieści królowej Nawarry* (Scribe and Legouvé), Teatr Wielki, Warsaw.

1872   Amelia in *Bezinteresowni* (Sarnecki), Teatr Rozmaitości, Warsaw.

Fedra in *Fedra* (Conrad), Teatr Wielki, Warsaw.

Seweryna in *Ksiezna Jerzowa* (Dumas père), Cracow.

Joanna in *Joanna* (Galati), Lvov.

Beatrix Cenci in *Beatrix Cenci* (Słowacki), Lvov.

Lady Tartuffe in *Lady Tartuffe* (Girardin), Teatr Rozmaitości, Warsaw.

1873   Jolanta in *Córka króla René* (Hertz), Teatr Letni, Warsaw.

1874   Joanna in *Czarne diabły* (Sardou), Teatr Rozmaitości, Warsaw.

Sylwina in *Przechodzień* (Coppée), Teatr Rozmaitości, Warsaw.

Marianna in *Kaprysy Marianny* (Musset), Teatr Rozmaitości, Warsaw.

Julia in *Julia* (Feuillet), Lvov.

Bianka de Chelles in *Sfinks* (Feuillet), Lvov.

Donna Dolores in *Ojczyzna* (Sardou), Lvov.

Safo in *Safo* (Grillparzer), Lvov.

Lais in *Flecista* (Augier), Teatr Rozmaitości, Warsaw.

Joanna de Solis in *Akrobata* (Feuillet), Teatr Rozmaitości, Warsaw.

1875   Beata in *Wit Stwosz* (Rapacki), Teatr Wilki, Warsaw.

Hrabina Strzalińska in *Młoda wdowa* (Korzeniowski), Teatr Letni, Warsaw.

Zofia in *Niewinni* (Świetochowski), Teatr Rozmaitości, Warsaw.

1876   Maria in *Maria i Magdalena* (Lindau), Teatr Rozmaitości, Warsaw.

Berta in *Dwie boleści* (Coppée), Teatr Rozmaitości, Warsaw.

Beatrice in *Wiele hałasu o nic* (Shakespeare), Teatr Wielki, Warsaw.

Julia in *Przesady* (Lubowski), Teatr Rozmaitości, Warsaw.

Karolina Wilkenshaw in *Koniec Stuartów* (Falkowski), Teatr Letni, Warsaw.

1877   Camille in *Camille* (Dumas père), National Guard Hall, Virginia City, Nevada.

1878   Peg Woffington in *Peg Woffington* (Reade and Taylor), Arch Street Theatre, Philadelphia.

1879   Pani Hurska in *Miód kasztelański* (Kraszewski), Cracow.

Mistress Clarkson in *Cudzoziemka* (Dumas père), Lvov.

1880   Kleopatra in *Antoniusz i Kleopatra* (Shakespeare), Teatr Wielki, Warsaw.

Leonia de Renat in *Iskierka* (Pailleron), Teatr Wielki, Warsaw.

Fedra in *Fedra* (Racine), Teatr Wielki, Warsaw.

1881   Juana Esteban in *Juana* (Wills), Court Theatre, London.

1882   Zofia in *Dama treflowa* (Zalewski), Teatr Wielki, Warsaw.

Paola in *Posag* (Szymanowski), Teatr Wielki, Warsaw.

Eliza de Chennevières in *Honor domu* (Battu and Desvignes), Teatr Wielki, Warsaw.

Nora in *Nora* (Ibsen), Teatr Wielki, Warsaw.

Odetta in *Odetta* (Sardou), Haymarket Theatre, London.

Rosalind in *As You Like It* (Shakespeare), Globe Theatre, Boston.

Viola in *Twelfth Night* (Shakespeare), National Theatre, Washington D.C.

1883   Imogen in *Cymbeline* (Shakespeare), New Grand Opera House, Des Moines.

1884   Nadiezda in *Nadiezda* (Barrymore), Academy of Music, Baltimore.

1885   Andrea in *Prince Zillah* (Doremus), Academy of Music, Buffalo, New York.

1886   Julia in *Two Gentlemen of Verona* (Shakespeare), Globe Theatre, Boston.

Maria de Verneuil in *The Chouans* (Berton), Union Square Theatre, New York.

Daniela in *Daniela* (Phillipi), Union Square Theatre, New York.

1887   Isabella in *Measure for Measure* (Shakespeare), Tabor Grand Opera House, Denver, Colorado.

1889   Julia de Mortemar in *Richelieu* (Bulwer-Lytton), Grand Opera House, Pittsburgh, Pennsylvania.

Lady Macbeth in *Macbeth* (Shakespeare), Grand Opera House, Pittsburgh, Pennsylvania.

1891   Louise Gréville in *The Tragic Mask* (Reynolds), Globe Theatre, Boston.

1892   Liana in *The Countess Roudine* (Fiske and Kester), Chestnut Street Opera House, Philadelphia.

Katherine in *Henry VIII* (Shakespeare), Garden Theatre, New York.

1893   Magda in *Magda* (Sudermann), Hooley's Theatre, New York.

1894   Fedora in *Fedora* (Sardou), Lvov.

1895   Cyprianna in *Rozwiedźmy sie* (Sardou and Najac), Lvov.

Debora in *Debora* (Mosenthal), Lvov.

Mistress Betty in *Mistress Betty* (Fitch), Garrick Theatre, New York.

1898   Marie Antoinette in *Marie Antoinette* (Stuart), Baldwin Theatre, San Francisco.

1900   Constance in *King John* (Shakespeare), New Wieting Theatre, Syracuse.

1901   Maria in *Warszawianka* (Wyspiański), Lvov.

1902   Hrabina Idalia in *Nowa Dejanira* (Słowacki), Lvov.

1903   Lora in *Jesiennym wieczorem* (Zapolska), Cracow.

Sylwia Settala in *Gioconda* (D'Annunzio), Cracow.

Antygone in *Antygona* (Sophocles), Cracow.

Laodamia in *Protesilas i Laodamia* (Wyspiański), Cracow.

Also acted roles in: *Spotkanie* (adapted from the French), Bochnia, 1861; *Okrezne* (Korzeniowski), Sambor, 1862; *Murzynka* (Ziegler), Sambor, 1862; *Temperamenta, czyli Złe wychowanie* (Decomberousse and d'Epagny), Czerniowce, 1863; *Maria Joanna, kobieta z gminu* (Dennery and Mallian), Czerniowce, 1863; *Ciotunia* (Fredro), Czerniowce, 1863; *Studnia artezyjska* (Raeder), Czerniowce,

1864; *Cyganie no Litwie* (Korzeniowski), Czerniowce, 1864; *East Lynne* (adapted from Wood), Academy of Music, Buffalo, New York, 1878.

Publications

Memories and Impressions of Helena Modjeska: An Autobiography, 1910.

*

Bibliography

Books:
Mabel Collins, *The Story of Helena Modjeska*, London, 1883.
Antoni Granowicz, *Modjeska: Her Life and Loves*, New York, 1956.
Marion Moore Coleman, *Fair Rosalind: The American Career of Helena Modjeska*, Cheshire, Connecticut, 1969.

* * *

It was as an interpreter of Shakespeare's woman that Helena Modjeska made her reputation in the USA and is best remembered today. She had 16 Shakespearean roles in her repertory, two of them — Rosalind and Viola — being popular favourites that she frequently revived. But she also appeared in controversial contemporary plays by Dumas *fils*, Sudermann and D'Annunzio, imparting a modern European sensibility to the US theatre. She gave the US premiere of *A Doll's House* (after first introducing Ibsen's play in Poland a year earlier). By her independence and intelligence, she did much to raise the status of the American actress.

In addition to exceptional beauty and talent, Modjeska brought to the USA the Polish concept of theatre as guardian of national consciousness and a belief in the sacred calling of the artist. At the height of her success she dreamed of creating an American national theatre that would bring together great artists for the cultural betterment of audiences. To her disappointment she failed to establish such a state-financed institution, which she realised went counter to the traditions of her adopted country.

Modjeska came to the USA to embark on an international career that would rival Sarah Bernhardt's. Intensely ambitious, she had early resolved to achieve world fame by switching to a major language. She studied roles in German and was ready to appear in Vienna, but patriotic considerations finally made her abandon any thought of acting in the language of her country's oppressors. Instead she secretly began to learn English and plan her conquest of the new world. Already a highly paid and acclaimed celebrity in the Warsaw Imperial theatres, Modjeska sought freedom from intrigue and opportunity to appear on a world stage. Changing languages at the age of 36 was a formidable task, but after a Polish career lasting 15 years, Modjeska was a fully formed artist by the time she reached California and had only to perfect her craft in America.

In partitioned Poland, censorship and oppression were particularly severe in the Russian sector where the Warsaw theatres were directly under Tsarist administration. Because the use of Polish was strictly forbidden in all public institutions except the theatre and the church, actors and actresses were revered by society, and all productions were closely watched by the authorities. Agents in the audience noted the names of those who applauded too loudly or frequently, on the assumption that there must be hidden political allusions. Shakespeare's tragedies and histories, showing crime in high places and rebellions and conspiracies, were unacceptable to the Russian occupying forces.

Modjeska helped make it possible for Shakespeare to be presented in new Polish translations. Early in her career when she was unknown, she had an affair with a provincial manager resulting in two illegitimate children (her son Ralph Modjeski became an important US engineer and bridge builder), but in Warsaw, after marrying an aristocrat, she occupied an influential social and artistic position, enabling her to reform the trivial repertoire so that for the first time it could include works like the politically daring *Hamlet* (with its subversive regicide) in which she played Ophelia.

Modjeska was a favourite of poets and writers. When she returned to Poland for frequent guest appearances, she moved in the best artistic and intellectual circles. She was close to the novelist Henryk Sienkiewicz and the painter Stanisław Witkiewicz, serving as godmother to his son, Stanisław Ignacy, the future playwright.

Equipped with a slight but silvery voice, which over the years grew more resonant thanks to hard work, Modjeska had the ability to move audiences deeply, but she avoided playing for effect and soliciting applause. For her, Shakespeare's plays were high art, and she wished to introduce this "most difficult and challenging theatre" to US audiences used to pure entertainment.

The basic types of women Modjeska excelled in portraying were the grand lady, the wronged mistress (she played fallen women as a polemical debate with the audience), and the girl who succeeds due to her looks, intelligence and fantasy. She identified completely with the characters she played, idealizing her roles; even her femmes fatales were romantic and aroused deep sympathy. She interpreted Camille as sensitive and cultured, shifting the blame to the men who depraved her. By careful self-discipline she preserved her youthful appearance and physical ability throughout a long career of almost 50 years. Modjeska played Ophelia well into her forties, and she appeared as Cleopatra for the first time at the age of 59.

Modjeska was known for her thorough preparation of roles. The newer style of acting that she introduced in the USA stressed naturalness and credibility. She was frequently and sometimes favourably compared with Bernhardt, who was more sensual and flamboyant. Modjeska anticipated the inner concentration of Duse. Henry James, who saw Modjeska in London in the early 1880's, pointed to her "quiet felicities" and praised her intelligence, charm and grace.

She was restless in her quest for glory. In order to tour with Edwin Booth in 1899 Modjeska broke a contract at a cost of $12,000. The eight-week tour, featuring four of her 16 Shakespearean roles, turned into a match between two domineering personalities, from which both were able to learn and emerge as greater artists. During the "quality of mercy" speech in their *Merchant of Venice* Modjeska approached Shylock and touched him on the shoulder in a direct emotional appeal. Booth drew back in horror at her innovation, his face distorted. The new staging received a round of applause, forcing Booth to admit that Modjeska was right and leading him to adopt the stage business from then on.

Modjeska's portrayal of Lady Macbeth illustrates her originality of interpretation. Known for playing women who aroused sympathy, she made a spirited defence of the character, stressing every extenuating circumstance. Lady Macbeth's dignity, nobility and charm, not her criminality, became the centre of interest. Great love and ambition for her husband, springing from a warm heart, lessened her responsibility for initiating the murder. Her conscience was deadened for only an instant. Modjeska's Lady Macbeth quickly repented and lost her self-possession, arousing profound compassion, not horror.

Modjeska objected to being relegated to a secondary position in the touring organisation, which was advertised as Booth's company. She was forced to accept only half the salary that Booth received, seeing the venture as progress toward the artists' theatre for which she was ready to make material sacrifices. The success of her ideal theatre, Modjeska felt, should not be measured financially as a business, but by the artistic value of the productions and their educational and cultural influence on the people.

Modjeska became a US superstar and celebrity. Streets, mountain peaks, waterfalls and mineral springs were named in her honour; hats and dresses à la Modjeska became fashionable with her many female admirers. But she disapproved of the star system, which she felt was detrimental to both star and public, since it did not permit leading artists to appear together. She favoured the ideal of a harmonious collective without stars. For Modjeska, the theatre of commerce, pandering to the low taste of the audience, was the antithesis of the theatre of art that strove to elevate public taste.

—Daniel Gerould

MOISEIWITSCH, Tanya. British designer. Born in London, 3 December 1914. Educated at private schools and at the Central School of Arts and Crafts, London; trained as apprentice scene painter at the Old Vic Theatre, London. Married Felix Krish in 1942. Debut as designer, 1934; designer, Abbey Theatre, Dublin, 1935–39, Oxford Playhouse, 1941–44, and Old Vic Theatre, London, 1944–49; first designed for Shakespeare Memorial Theatre, Stratford-upon-Avon, 1949; designed stage for Stratford (Ontario) Shakespeare Festival, 1953, and served as the Festival's principal designer, 1953–61; designed for the National Theatre, London, from 1962; designed stage for Tyrone Guthrie Theatre, Minneapolis, and served as its principal designer, 1963–68; designed stage for Crucible Theatre, Sheffield, and served as consultant designer, 1971–73; associate director, Festival Stage, Ontario, since 1974. Fellow, Ontario College of Art, 1979. Member: Canadian Association of Designers, 1984. Recipient: Diploma of Honour, Royal Canadian Academy of Arts, 1964; New York Drama Desk Award for Best Costumes, 1969; Diploma of Honour, Canadian Conference of the Arts, 1975; *Plays and Players* Design Award, 1976; Thomas de Gaetani Award, US Institute for Theatre Technology, 1987. DLitt: University of Birmingham, 1964; University of Waterloo, Ontario, 1977; LLD: University of Toronto, 1976. CBE (Commander of the British Empire), 1976.

Productions

As set designer:

1934   *The Faithful* (Masefield), Westminster Theatre, London.

1935   *A Deuce o' Jacks* (Higgins), Abbey Theatre, Dublin.

1936   *Coriolanus* (Shakespeare), Abbey Theatre, Dublin.
            Hassan (Flecker), Abbey Theatre, Dublin.

1940   *The Golden Cuckoo* (Johnston), Q Theatre, London.
            High Temperature, Q Theatre, London.

1941–44   *Androcles and the Lion* (G. B. Shaw), Oxford Playhouse.
            The Doctor's Dilemma (G. B. Shaw), Oxford Playhouse.
            George and Margaret (Savory), Oxford Playhouse.
            The Merchant of Venice (Shakespeare), Oxford Playhouse.
            Romeo and Juliet (Shakespeare), Oxford Playhouse.
            Rope (Hamilton), Oxford Playhouse.

1944   *Doctor Faustus* (Marlowe), Liverpool Playhouse.
            John Gabriel Borkman (Ibsen), Liverpool Playhouse.
            The Alchemist (Jonson), Liverpool Playhouse.

1945   *Uncle Vanya* (Chekhov), New Theatre, London.
            The School for Scandal (Sheridan), Liverpool Playhouse.
            Point Valaine (Coward), Liverpool Playhouse.
            The Critic (Sheridan), New Theatre, London.

1946   *The Time of Your Life* (Saroyan), Lyric Theatre, Hammersmith, London.
            The Beaux' Stratagem (Farquhar), Old Vic Theatre, Bristol.
            Twelfth Night (Shakespeare), Old Vic Theatre, Bristol.
            Weep for the Cyclops, Old Vic Theatre, Bristol.
            Cyrano de Bergerac (Rostand, translated by Hooker), Old Vic Theatre, Bristol.

1947   *Bless the Bride* (Herbert and Ellis), Adelphi Theatre, London.
            Peter Grimes (Britten), Royal Opera House, Covent Garden, London.

1948   *The Beggar's Opera* (Britten), Aldeburgh Festival.
            Lady Rohesia, Sadler's Wells Theatre, London.
            The Cherry Orchard (Chekhov), New Theatre, London.
            Aine Satire of the Thrie Estaites (Lindsay), Edinburgh Festival.

1949   *Henry VIII* (Shakespeare), Shakespeare Memorial Theatre, Stratford-upon-Avon.
            Treasure Hunt (Farrell and Perry), Apollo Theatre, London.
            Don Giovanni (Mozart), Sadler's Wells Theatre, London.
            A Month in the Country (Turgenev), New Theatre, London.

1950   *Home at Seven* (Sherriff), Wyndham's Theatre, London.

Henry VIII (Shakespeare), Shakespeare Memorial Theatre, Stratford-upon-Avon.

The Holly and the Ivy (Browne), Duchess Theatre, London.

Captain Carvallo (Cannan), St James's Theatre, London.

Rosmersholm (Ibsen), St Martin's Theatre, London.

1951   *The Passing Day* (Shiels), Lyric Theatre, Hammersmith, London.

Richard II (Shakespeare), Shakespeare Memorial Theatre, Stratford-upon-Avon.

Henry IV, parts 1 and 2 (Shakespeare), Shakespeare Memorial Theatre, Stratford-upon-Avon.

Henry V (Shakespeare), Shakespeare Memorial Theatre, Stratford-upon-Avon.

Figure of Fun (Roussin), Aldwych Theatre, London.

A Midsummer Night's Dream (Shakespeare), Old Vic Theatre, London.

1952   *The Deep Blue Sea* (Rattigan), Duchess Theatre, London.

Timon of Athens (Shakespeare), Old Vic Theatre, London.

1953   *Othello* (Shakespeare), tour of Australia and New Zealand.

Julius Caesar (Shakespeare), Old Vic Theatre, London.

Henry VIII (Shakespeare), Old Vic Theatre, London.

Richard III (Shakespeare), Stratford (Ontario) Shakespeare Festival.

All's Well That Ends Well (Shakespeare), Stratford (Ontario) Shakespeare Festival.

1954   *Measure for Measure* (Shakespeare), Stratford (Ontario) Shakespeare Festival.

The Taming of the Shrew (Shakespeare), Stratford (Ontario) Shakespeare Festival.

King Oedipus (Sophocles), Stratford (Ontario) Shakespeare Festival.

Othello (Shakespeare), Shakespeare Memorial Theatre, Stratford-upon-Avon.

The Matchmaker (Wilder), Haymarket Theatre, London.

1955   *The Merchant of Venice* (Shakespeare), Stratford (Ontario) Shakespeare Festival.

Julius Caesar (Shakespeare), Stratford (Ontario) Shakespeare Festival.

King Oedipus (Sophocles), Stratford (Ontario) Shakespeare Festival.

A Life in the Sun (Wilder), Edinburgh Festival.

The Cherry Orchard (Chekhov), Piccolo Teatro, Milan.

1956   *The Matchmaker* (Wilder), Royale Theatre, New York.

Henry V (Shakespeare), Stratford (Ontario) Festival and Edinburgh Festival.

The Merry Wives of Windsor (Shakespeare), Stratford (Ontario) Shakespeare Festival.

Measure for Measure (Shakespeare), Stratford (Ontario) Shakespeare Festival.

King Oedipus (Sophocles), Stratford (Ontario) Shakespeare Festival.

1957   *The Two Gentlemen of Verona* (Shakespeare), Old Vic Theatre, London.

Twelfth Night (Shakespeare), Stratford (Ontario) Shakespeare Festival.

1958   *The Two Gentlemen of Verona* (Shakespeare), Canadian tour and Phoenix Theatre, New York.

The Broken Jug (Kleist), Canadian tour and Phoenix Theatre, New York.

Henry IV, part 1 (Shakespeare), Stratford (Ontario) Shakespeare Festival.

The Winter's Tale (Shakespeare), Stratford (Ontario) Shakespeare Festival.

Much Ado About Nothing (Shakespeare), Shakespeare Memorial Theatre, Stratford-upon-Avon.

The Bright One (Fulton), Winter Garden Theatre, London.

1959   *The Merchant of Venice* (Shakespeare), Habimah Theatre, Tel-Aviv.

Biederman and the Fire-Raisers (Frisch), Habimah Theatre, Tel-Aviv.

All's Well That Ends Well (Shakespeare), Shakespeare Memorial Theatre, Stratford-upon-Avon.

1960   *The Wrong Side of the Park* (Mortimer), Cambridge Theatre, London.

King John (Shakespeare), Stratford (Ontario) Shakespeare Festival.

Romeo and Juliet (Shakespeare), Stratford (Ontario) Shakespeare Festival.

1961   *Ondine* (Giraudoux), Aldwych Theatre, London.

Coriolanus (Shakespeare), Stratford (Ontario) Shakespeare Festival.

Love's Labour's Lost (Shakespeare), Stratford (Ontario) Shakespeare Festival.

1962   *The Taming of the Shrew* (Shakespeare), Stratford (Ontario) Shakespeare Festival.

Cyrano de Bergerac (Rostand), Stratford (Ontario) Shakespeare Festival.

The Alchemist (Jonson), Old Vic Theatre, London.

1963   *Hamlet* (Shakespeare), Tyrone Guthrie Theatre, Minneapolis.

The Miser (Molière), Tyrone Guthrie Theatre, Minneapolis.

The Three Sisters (Chekhov), Tyrone Guthrie Theatre, Minneapolis.

1964   *Saint Joan* (G. B. Shaw), Tyrone Guthrie Theatre, Minneapolis.

Volpone (Jonson), Tyrone Guthrie Theatre, Minneapolis.

Love's Labour's Lost (Shakespeare), Stratford (Ontario) Shakespeare Festival and Chichester Festival Theatre.

1965   *The Way of the World* (Congreve), Tyrone Guthrie Theatre, Minneapolis.

The Cherry Orchard (Chekhov), Tyrone Guthrie Theatre, Minneapolis.

1966   *As You Like It* (Shakespeare), Tyrone Guthrie Theatre, Minneapolis.

The Skin of Our Teeth (Wilder), Tyrone Guthrie Theatre, Minneapolis.

1967   *The House of Atreus* (Aeschylus), Tyrone Guthrie Theatre, Minneapolis.
Antony and Cleopatra (Shakespeare), Stratford (Ontario) Shakespeare Festival.
Peter Grimes (Britten), Metropolitan Opera, New York.

1968   *The House of Atreus* (Aeschylus), Tyrone Guthrie Theatre, Minneapolis, Mark Taper Forum, Los Angeles, and Billy Rose Theatre, New York.
Volpone (Jonson), Old Vic Theatre, London.

1969   *Macook's Corner*, Opera House, Belfast, and Abbey Theatre, Dublin.
Swift, Abbey Theatre, Dublin.
Uncle Vanya (Chekhov), Tyrone Guthrie Theatre, Minneapolis.
The Caucasian Chalk Circle (Brecht), Sheffield Playhouse.

1970   *Cymbeline* (Shakespeare), Stratford (Ontario) Shakespeare Festival.

1971   *The Barber of Seville* (Rossini), Theatre Royal, Brighton.
The Shoemaker's Holiday (Dekker), Crucible Theatre, Sheffield.

1972   *A Man for All Seasons* (Bolt), Crucible Theatre, Sheffield.
The Persians (Aeschylus), Crucible Theatre, Sheffield.

1973   *The Stirrings in Sheffield on Saturday Night*, Crucible Theatre, Sheffield.
The Misanthrope (Molière), Old Vic Theatre, London.

1974   *The Imaginary Invalid* (Molière), Stratford (Ontario) Shakespeare Festival.

1975   *The Misanthrope* (Molière), St James's Theatre, New York.
Phaedra Brittanica (Harrison, adapted from Racine), Old Vic Theatre, London.

1976   *The Voyage of Edgar Allan Poe*, Morris A. Mechanic Theatre, Maryland.

1977   *Rigoletto* (Verdi), Metropolitan Opera, New York.

1978   *Oedipus the King* and *Oedipus at Colonus* (Sophocles), Festival Playhouse, Adelaide.
The Double Dealer (Congreve), National Theatre, London.

1980   *Red Roses for Me* (O'Casey), Abbey Theatre, Dublin.

1981   *La Traviata* (Verdi), Metropolitan Opera, New York.
Kidnapped in London, Children's Theatre, Minnesota.

1983   *Tartuffe* (Molière), Stratford (Ontario) Shakespeare Festival.

1984   *The Clandestine Marriage* (Colman and Garrick), Albery Theatre, London.

1985   *The Government Inspector* (Gogol), Stratford (Ontario) Shakespeare Festival.

As costume designer:
1973   *The Government Inspector* (Gogol), Tyrone Guthrie Theatre, Minneapolis.

1982   *Mary Stuart*, Stratford (Ontario) Shakespeare Festival.

Films

Oedipus Rex, 1957.

Television

King Lear (costumes), 1983.

Publications

"The Production of King Oedipus" (with Tyrone Guthrie) in *Thrice the Brinded Cat Hath Mew'd*, edited by Robertson Davies, 1955.

*

Bibliography

Books:
Audrey Williamson, *Old Vic Drama*, London, 1948.
Denis Bablet, *The Revolutions of Stage Design in the Twentieth Century*, 1977.
John Pettigrew and Jamie Portman, *Stratford: The First Thirty Years*, Toronto, 1985.

Articles:
Elisabethe Coranthiel, "Tanya Moiseiwitsch", *Theatre World*, February 1963.

* * *

In a distinguished career that has spanned 50 years and some 200 productions, Tanya Moiseiwitsch has consistently promoted a design concept that stresses the shared experience of theatre. For works ranging from Greek tragedy to modern musicals, her design schemes have embodied the paradox that theatrical activity is both make-believe and actuality: plays and operas are art but performances are real, actors impersonate characters yet have their own identities, theatre spaces contain the fictional action and the living audience which should be aware, yet unaware, of its role in the creation of an affective event.

Moiseiwitsch's work has sought to foster intellectual engagement; rather than encouraging audiences to sit back and admire, it has embodied the philosophy expressed by *Henry V*'s Chorus, that the "fair beholders" should allow the production team "on your imaginary forces (to) work". This is not to imply that Moiseiwitsch is a minimalist designer but to emphasize that when she uses overt theatricality, be it of colour, form, texture, or mechanics, it is with calculated discrimination. For her, the flamboyant weapons in a designer's armoury must serve the production by heightening the impact of a moment; they should never endanger it by simply proclaiming the designer's contribution. Moiseiwitsch has not articulated this philosophy but the discretion of her design schemes is reflected in her pronouncements on them: "It is not easy for me to analyse how I work. I think it would be a mistake to try. All I know with certainty is that I must wait for the first idea of how a play is to be treated to come to me from the director". This statement records her conviction that a production must be evolved by the team and though she here stresses the importance of the director, copious testimony from performers and theatre craftsmen exists to her skill in accommodating her ideas to theirs and drawing the best from them. Experience nurtured her appreciation of the value of corporate creativity.

Moiseiwitsch began as "a very humble assistant on the paint-frame" at the Old Vic in the early 1930's. She graduated to the rank of resident designer in repertory, first with director Hugh Hunt at the Abbey, Dublin, then with director Peter Ashmore at the Oxford Playhouse. During these 10 years she learned to work efficiently, economically, and responsively, developing her rapport with directors, notably Hunt, with whom she worked again for the Bristol and London Old Vic companies, and Tyrone Guthrie, for whom she designed over 30 plays and operas in Britain, Europe, and the USA. An early success was *Uncle Vanya*, about which one critic commented: "one felt these rooms had been *lived* in ... and the clothes, like her rooms, had characters and utility in addition to revealing an artist's eye for line and colour". Here was Moiseiwitsch creating the fictive reality of Chekhovian Russia for war-torn London. By contrast, in 1947, she celebrated the theatrical actuality of the C. B. Cochran musical *Bless the Bride* in elegant costumes and graceful sets whose witty artificiality complemented the show's "joi de vivre".

Moiseiwitsch's quest for union of play and audience was significantly advanced in two schemes for the Shakespeare Memorial Theatre: *Henry VIII* in 1949 and the "History Cycle", comprising *Richard II, Henry IV parts 1 and 2*, and *Henry V*, in 1951. Both utilised permanent structures of mellow wood, drawn from but not imitating the features of Elizabethan playhouses. They strove to minimise the constrictions of the Memorial Theatre's proscenium arch by organising space in such a way that the action constantly flowed downstage. The set and costumes for *Henry VIII*, directed by Guthrie, had a Tudor solidity that suddenly flowered in the optimistic final scene of the infant Elizabeth's Christening: pale colours and light textures for costumes, floating banners and ribbon-decked wreaths of fresh greenery lightened the atmosphere. Similar "coups de theatre" characterized the History Cycle's scheme (undertaken with Alix Stone). Richard II and his followers, exquisite in pastel silks, confronted older nobles in heavy wools; for Henry V's coronation the spare set was bedecked with streamers and, at the end of the Cycle, reconciliation of English and French was signalled by the descent of drapery that transformed the set's "imposing array of beams" into an airy pavilion.

Moiseiwitsch achieved full union of action and audience in 1953 with her design of the stage for the Stratford (Ontario) Festival. Planned in collaboration with Guthrie, the Festival's first director, this is a five-sided wooden promontory raised above the auditorium on three broad steps; overall it is 36 feet deep and 30 feet wide. At its rear is a prow-like balcony, supported on columns and connected by angled stairways to the main stage. Access is via doorways under the balcony and in the angled rear-stage facias; these latter face correspondingly angled access passages within the seating. Originally, the auditorium embraced the stage with a single tier of 1477 seats, swung in an arc of 240 degrees. Modifications over the years have included the reduction of the seating arc to 220 degrees and

the raising of the on-stage balcony by eight inches, but from its inception this elegantly practical arrangement of levels and angles has proved itself, to quote designer Leslie Hurry, "one of the world's greatest stages". It has accomodated both the Shakespearean repertoire for which it was conceived and the gamut of world drama. It has also inspired a number of newer theatres, notably the Tyrone Guthrie Theatre in Minnesota, designed also by Moiseiwitsch; the Crucible in Sheffield, for which Moiseiwitsch was consultant; the Chichester Festival Theatre, which was built by enthusiasts in response to their visits to Stratford, Ontario; the Olivier stage within the Royal National Theatre complex, for which Moiseiwitsch served on the Consultative Committee; the American Repertory Theatre in Boston; London's Barbican Theatre; and the Swan Theatre at Stratford-upon-Avon. It confirmed for many the long-held beliefs of Moiseiwitsch and Guthrie that drama thrives in an environment that places actors and audience clearly within the same room, thereby allowing the creation of atmosphere to be unequivocally a joint responsibility. Moiseiwitsch's Festival stage must be deemed of paramount significance in the development of later 20th-century design.

Moiseiwitsch herself designed all the productions for the Festival's first four seasons and in many subsequent ones and thus "gave Stratford a distinct visual style from which it has never quite departed", as one critic wrote in 1984. Essentially, this style gives the actors clothes rather than costumes and employs properties that bespeak authenticity. It does not preclude selective histrionic flourishes, as in the Festival's opening production when the vast crimson velvet coronation role of Alec Guinness's Richard III seemingly drenched the platform in blood. Notable in the Festival's early years was the Guthrie/Moiseiwitsch *King Oedipus*, in which the aura of Sophoclean tragedy was impressively communicated by hieratic movement from masked actors of extra-human proportions. Again Moiseiwitsch used theatricality judiciously: no representation of Oedipus's blinding was attempted; more evocatively his golden robe was replaced by one of deep crimson and his imperious gilded mask was veiled in black. This stylized presentation of Greek drama was refined for *The House of Atreus* with Guthrie and, with Colin George, *The Persians* and also for Sophocles's two Oedipus plays. Contrasting with these weighty schemes were her witty designs for *The Matchmaker*, which harked back to *Bless the Bride* in the use of frankly painted scenery and costumes that became ever more riotously coloured as the play progressed, and *Peter Grimes*, which deployed sand, sky, and fishermen's nets to evoke Britten's East Anglian coastal town. Moiseiwitsch neatly married styles for John Dexter's updated production of Molière's *The Misanthrope*: within a framework of rococo drapery that evoked the 17th century, couturier-costumed characters inhabited an elegant apartment in the Paris of President de Gaulle. The audience was led to recognise the affinity of past to present. Moiseiwitsch also makes use of modern stage technology where appropriate. In *The Double Dealer*, for example, the components of her solid Restoration country house revolved and regrouped themselves in visual analogy to the convolutions of Congreve's plot.

Designer Desmond Heely identified as Moiseiwitsch's special quality her fusion of historical research and theatrical responsiveness in schemes that blend the worlds of reality and poetic imaginativeness. Her influence on many designers has been great; her achievement will endure in the thrust stages now to be found throughout the world.

—Raymond Ingram

MOISSI, Alexander. German actor. Born Aleksander Moissiu in Trieste, Austria (now in Italy), 2 April 1879; of Albanian-Italian descent. Educated at schools in Durazzo (now Durrës), Albania, 1885–89; Aquedetto elementary school, Trieste, 1889–97; trained as opera singer in Vienna, 1897. Married actress Johann Terwin. Stage debut, in walk-on roles at the Burgtheater, Vienna, 1899; engaged as actor by Angelo Neumann in Prague, 1902–04; invited to Berlin by Max Reinhardt, 1904; actor in suburban Berlin theatre and subsequently with Reinhardt's company; first recognized by critics as a leading talent, 1906; remained with Reinhardt's company at the Deutsches Theater, Berlin, for the rest of his career and also toured extensively from 1911; also appeared in 12 films, 1910–35. People's Artist (Albania), 1962. Died in Vienna, 22 March, 1935.

Selected roles

1899	An Old Greek in *Die Meister von Palmyra* (Wilbrandt), Burgtheater, Vienna.
	An Old Roman in *Julius Cäsar* (Shakespeare), Burgtheater, Vienna.
	Laurent in *Tartüff* (Molière), Burgtheater, Vienna.
	Gascon cadet in *Cyrano de Bergerac* (Rostand), Burgtheater, Vienna.
1900	Nusdorf in *Die Räuber* (Schiller), Burgtheater, Vienna.
1901	Prince Eco in *König Arlekin* (Lotar), Deutsches Theater, Prague.
	Raul in *Die Jungfrau von Orleans* (Schiller), Deutsches Theater, Prague.
	Franz Moor in *Die Räuber* (Schiller), Deutsches Theatre, Prague.
	Bari in *Narziss* (Brachfogel), Prague.
	Fasel in *Der böse Geist Lumpazivagabundus* (Nestroy), Deutsches Theater, Prague.
	Inquisitor in *Don Carlos* (Schiller), Deutsches Theater, Prague.
1902	Robert in *Richard III* (Shakespeare), Ostend.
	Fshatari in *Götz von Berlichingen* (Goethe), Ostend.
	Deveru in *Wallenstein* (Schiller), Ostend.
	Pilger in *Des Meeres und der Liebe Wellen* (Grillparzer), Ostend.
	Miku in *Pension Schöller* (Jacobi and Laufs), Ostend.
	Lomelino in *Die Verschwörung des Fiesko* (Schiller), Ostend.
	Peshkopi in *Demetrius* (Schiller), Ostend.
	Joel in *Uriel Acosta* (Gutskow), Ostend.
	Tibaldi in *Romeo und Julia* (Shakespeare), Ostend.
1903	Cyrano in *Cyrano de Bergerac* (Rostand), Berlin.

	Don Cesar in *Die Braut von Messina* (Schiller), Berlin.
	Pirro in *Emila Galotti* (Lessing), Berlin.
	Richard II in *Richard II* (Shakespeare), Berlin.
	Sebastian in *Preziosa* (Wolff), Berlin.
	Lancaster in *Henry IV* (Shakespeare), Berlin.
	Salisbury in *Henry IV* (Shakespeare), Berlin.
	Carlos in *Clavigo* (Goethe), Berlin.
	David in *Kean* (Barnai), Berlin.
	Groberg in *Die Wildente* (Ibsen), Berlin.
	Domingo in *Wilhelm Tell* (Schiller), Berlin.
1904	Golo in *Genoveva* (Hebbel), Ostend.
	The Actor in *Nachtasyl* (Gorky), Ostend.
	Philip in *Der Graf von Charolais* (Beer-Hoffman), Neues Theater, Berlin.
	Mortimer in *Maria Stuart* (Schiller), Berlin.
	Orestes in *Elektra* (Hofmannsthal), Berlin.
	Oberon in *Ein Sommernachtstraum* (Shakespeare), Neues Theater, Berlin.
1905	Graciano in *Der Kaufman von Venedig* (Shakespeare), Deutsches Theater, Berlin.
	Prospero in *Der Sturm* (Shakespeare), Deutsches Theater, Berlin.
	Creon in *Oedipus und die Sphinx* (Hofmannsthal), Deutsches Theater, Berlin.
1906	Guido in *A Florentine Tragedy* (Wilde), Deutsches Theater, Berlin.
	Vurm in *Kabale und Liebe* (Schiller), Deutsches Theater, Berlin.
	Riccaut in *Minna von Barnhelm* (Schiller), Deutsches Theater, Berlin.
	Pluto and Aristeus in *Orpheus in der Unterwelt* (Crémieux, Pserhofer and Offenbach), Deutsches Theater, Berlin.
	Oswald in *Gespenster* (Ibsen), Kammerspiele des Deutsches Theater, Berlin.
	Moritz in *Frühlings Erwachen* (Wedekind), Kammerspiele des Deutsches Theater, Berlin.
	Johanson in *Salomé* (Wilde), Kammerspiele des Deutsches Theater, Berlin.
1907	Fool in *Was ihr wollt* (Shakespeare), Deutsches Theater, Berlin.
	Romeo in *Romeo und Julia* (Shakespeare), Deutsches Theater, Berlin.
1908	Poet in *Niau* (Damov), Kammerspiele des Deutsches Theater, Berlin.
	The Fool in *König Lear* (Shakespeare), Deutsches Theater, Berlin.
	Fiesko in *Die Verschwörung des Fiesko* (Schiller), Deutsches Theater, Berlin.
	Dubedat in *The Doctor's Dilemma* (G. B. Shaw), Kammerspiele des Deutsches Theater, Berlin.
1909	Faust in *Faust* (Goethe), Deutsches Theater, Berlin.
	Hamlet in *Hamlet* (Shakespeare), Deutsches Theater, Berlin.
	Marquis of Posa in *Don Carlos* (Schiller), Deutsches Theater, Berlin.
1910	Florindo in *Christinas Heimreise* (Hofmannsthal), Deutsches Theater, Berlin.
	Don Manuel in *Die Braut von Messina* (Schiller), Deutsches Theater, Berlin.

Nuredin in *Sumurún* (Freska), Kammerspiele des Deutsches Theater, Berlin.

Antipholus in *Die Komödie der Irrungen* (Shakespeare), Kammerspiele des Deutsches Theater, Berlin.

Oedipus in *König Ödipus* (Sophocles), Schumann Circus, Berlin.

1911 Achilles in *Pentesilea* (Kleist), Deutsches Theater, Berlin.

Orestes in *Die Orestie* (Aeschylus), Musikfesthalle, Munich.

Caliph in *Turandot* (Gozzi), Deutsches Theater, Berlin.

Jedermann in *Jedermann* (Hofmannsthal), Schumann Circus, Berlin; Salzburg, 1928 and 1931.

Orpheus in *Orpheus in der Unterwelt* (Kremier), Deutsches Theater, Berlin.

1912 Tirsis in *George Dandin* (Molière), Deutsches Theater, Berlin.

Don Juan in *Don Juan* (Molière), Deutsches Theater, Berlin.

1913 Prince Hal in *Henry IV* (Shakespeare), Deutsches Theater, Berlin.

Fedja in *Der Lebende Leichnam* (Tolstoy), Deutsches Theater, Berlin.

Prince Gustala in *Emila Galotti* (Lessing), Deutsches Theater, Berlin.

Tasso in *Torquato Tasso* (Goethe), Kammerspiele des Deutsches Theater, Berlin.

1914 The Alcoholic in *Scheiterhaufen* (Strindberg), Kammerspieles des Deutsches Theater, Berlin.

1916 Danton in *Dantons Tod* (Büchner), Deutsches Theater, Berlin.

1918 Nikita in *Die Macht der Finsternis* (Tolstoy), Deutsches Theater, Berlin.

Gotvald in *Hanele Himmelfahrt* (Hauptmann), Volkstheater, Berlin.

Sarincevi in *Und das Licht scheint in der Finsternis* (Tolstoy), Deutsches Theater, Berlin.

Clavigo in *Clavigo* (Goethe), Kleines Schauspielhaus, Berlin.

1919 Jaques in *Wie es euch gefällt* (Shakespeare), Deutsches Theater, Berlin.

Shylock in *Der Kaufman von Venedig* (Shakespeare), Deutsches Theater, Berlin.

Ivanov in *Ivanov* (Chekhov), Kammerspieles des Deutsches Theater, Berlin.

Jaácob in *Jaácobs traum* (Beer-Hofmann), Deutsches Theater, Berlin.

1920 Montezuma in *Der weisse Heiland* (Hauptmann), Deutsches Theater, Berlin.

Mark Antony in *Julius Cäsar* (Shakespeare), Grosses Schauspielhaus, Berlin.

Zeus in *Europa* (Kaiser), Kammerspiele des Deutsches Theater, Berlin.

1921 Florindo in *Florindo* (Hofmannsthal), Kammerspiele des Deutsches Theater, Berlin.

Henry in *Henry XII* (Strindberg), Stockholm.

Othello in *Othello* (Shakespeare), Volkstheater, Vienna.

Paracelsus in *Paracelsus* (Schnitzler), Volkstheater, Vienna.

1922 Richard II in *Richard II* (Shakespeare), Deutsches Theater, Berlin.

Battler in *Das Salzburger grosse Welttheater* (Hofmannsthal), Salzburg Cathedral.

Alfonse in *Die Jüden von Toledo* (Grillparzer), Prague.

Casanova in *Casanova* (Averhajmer), Volkstheater, Vienna.

1925 Vilibat in *Die schlimmen Buben in der Schule* (Nestroy), Volkstheater, Vienna.

Henry in *Henry IV* (Pirandello), Volkstheater, Vienna.

1926 Mephistopheles in *Faust* (Goethe).

Ekdal in *Die Wildente* (Ibsen), Volkstheater, Vienna.

Oliver in *Zweimal Oliver* (Kaiser), Volkstheater, Vienna.

1928 Orestes in *Iphigenia auf Tauris* (Goethe), Theater in der Josefstadt, Vienna.

Jacques in *Frikacaku* (Lenormand), Volkstheater, Vienna.

1929 Stanhope in *Journey's End* (Sheriff), Volkstheater, Vienna.

1930 Mushkin in *The Idiot* (Dostoevsky), Berlin.

1931 Antony in *Antony und Cleopatra* (Shakespeare), Berlin.

Publications

The Prisoner (play).

*

Bibliography

Books:
Fritz Kreuzig, *Ein Moissi Brevier*, Vienna, 1919.
Emil Faktor, *Alexander Moissi*, Berlin, 1920.
Ludwig Ullmann, *Moissi*, Vienna and Leipzig, 1922.
Hans Böhm (ed.), *Moissi: Der Mensch und der Künstler in Worten und Bildern*, Berlin, 1927.
Vangjel Moïssi, *Aleksander Moïssi*, Unesco, 1979.

Articles:
Julius Bab and Willi Handl, "Alexander Moissi", *Deutsche Schauspieler: Portraits aus Berlin und Wien*, Berlin, 1908.

* * *

In the early 20th century no stage director was more successful at identifying latent talent in young actors than Max Reinhardt. Of all those actors whose careers Reinhardt initiated and nurtured, none was to be more celebrated that Alexander Moissi, and yet Moissi, of all Reinhardt's discoveries, had the greatest inherent obstacle to overcome. Remarkably, he managed to convert that very obstacle into one of the major reasons for his success.

Reinhardt's invitation to Moissi, a neophyte actor in Prague, to join him in Berlin was an act of faith. It must have seemed even more so when Moissi, who began his Berlin career acting in the suburbs, made an unfavourable impression on critics and audiences alike. Only a few critics, among whom was the influential Julius Bab, saw anything impressive in him. Though Bab, like everyone else, had the greatest difficulty in understanding Moissi's German, spoken as it was through a thick Italian dialect, he sensed an unparalleled clarity and power in his facial and gestural expression. Accordingly, he encouraged Reinhardt to stick by the young actor.

In mastering the German language, Moissi overcame the main objection to his acting, yet he still had to fight hard for recognition by the Berlin public. This was due primarily to the unfamiliar quality of his stage presence. By and large, Berlin audiences were accustomed to actors indulging in either the lofty heroics of the Court Theatre or the detailed naturalism associated with the various companies of Otto Brahm. The one actor who seemed free of both these influences was Joseph Kainz, but from 1899 he was only a visitor to the city and he performed mainly in the classic repertoire. Kainz was undoubtedly the point of reference audiences adopted in attempting to come to terms with Moissi, though the younger actor had none of his predecessor's vehemence nor his formidable stage presence. However, his naturally musical voice — he had trained as an opera singer in Vienna — and his striking appearance, which had a touch of androgyny about it, grew in their appeal to audiences reared on Kainz and, when Reinhardt eventually identified those roles that suited Moissi, he quickly became the most celebrated actor in the city.

Moissi's first major Reinhardt role was Philip in Richard Beer-Hoffman's *Der Graf von Charolais*, one of the most accomplished plays written in the neo-romantic vein that was popular with audiences in the first decade of the century. Moissi was the ideal interpreter for such drama. The silken quality of his voice, which earned him countless panegyrics over the years (Raoul Auernheimer called him "the Mozart of the spoken word") his large, soulful eyes, slight build, elegant carriage and lissome gait were well-suited to represent the nervous, often neurasthenic figures that people the plays of Beer-Hoffman and Hugo von Hofmannsthal. Furthermore, the characters Moissi represented often seemed to long for a more perfect world; in so doing they expressed the essence of neo-romantic art.

Once established in the company, Moissi became one of Reinhardt's most frequently used actors. He was noted for several classic roles, above all Hamlet, whom he played as a confused youth, torn between childhood and adulthood, still dependent on his mother but with an awakening awareness and fear of the corruption within and around her. But even though he developed a sizeable classic repertoire — he was a noted Clavigo, Faust, Mephistopheles, Tasso, Franz Moor, Posa, Prince Hal, Romeo, Othello, Shylock and Orestes — his greatest successes remained within the modern repertoire. Felix Salten referred to his performance as Dubedat in Shaw's *The Doctor's Dilemma* as one of the definitive performances of the modern theatre, fit to rank alongside Mitterwurzer's King Philip and Kainz's Tasso. But almost all critics considered his performance as Fedja in Tolstoy's *The Living Corpse* to represent the height of his achievement. As he matured, Moissi gained in power and intensity. In particular, he fastened on darker traits and on fatalistic impulses within his characters that led to their self-destruction. Fedja was Moissi's most extreme manifestation of this mode of acting. While he never adopted the extreme, unidimensional style of contemporary expressionist acting,

roles such as Fedja clearly identified Moissi with whatever was serious and searching in the contemporary theatre.

In addition to acting in Berlin, Moissi enjoyed an international reputation, performing on stages in several countries on both sides of the Atlantic and appearing in a dozen films during the early years of the industry. In 1962, almost 30 years after his death, he was awarded the title of People's Artist by the government of Albania, his father's native country.

—Simon Williams

———

MOLANDER, Olof. Swedish director and actor. Born in Helsinki, Finland, 18 October 1892. Trained for the stage at the theatre school of the Dramaten [Royal Dramatic Theatre], Stockholm, 1912–14. Stage debut, as an actor, Dramaten, Stockholm, 1914; debut as director, 1919; director of the Dramaten, 1934–38; director, Folkets Parker [People's Park] Theatre, 1938–42; concentrated on film work, 1942–46; returned to Dramaten, 1947; also worked as a radio producer. Honorary degree: University of Lund, 1947. Died 1966.

Productions

1919	*The Merchant of Venice* (Shakespeare), Dramaten, Stockholm.
1920	*Danton* (Rolland), Dramaten, Stockholm.
	Hassan (Flecker), Dramaten, Stockholm.
1921	*Turandot* (Gozzi), Dramaten, Stockholm.
	The Tempest (Shakespeare), Dramaten, Stockholm.
1922	*As You Like It* (Shakespeare), Dramaten, Stockholm.
	George Dandin (Molière), Dramaten, Stockholm.
1923	*She Stoops to Conquer* (Goldsmith), Dramaten, Stockholm.
1924	*Othello* (Shakespeare), Dramaten, Stockholm.
	La Dame aux Camélias (Dumas), Dramaten, Stockholm.
	Den Osynlige [The Invisible] (Lagerkvist), Dramaten, Stockholm.
1926	*Advent* (Strindberg), Dramaten, Stockholm.
1927	*Phèdre* (Racine), Dramaten, Stockholm.
1928	*A Midsummer Night's Dream* (Shakespeare), Dramaten, Stockholm.
	Faust (Goethe), Dramaten, Stockholm.
1929	*Erik XIV* (Strindberg), Dramaten, Stockholm.
	Léopold le bien aimé (Sarment), Dramaten, Stockholm.
	Siegfried (Giraudoux), Dramaten, Stockholm.
	Le Maître de son coeur (Raynal), Dramaten, Stockholm.
1930	*L'Âme en peine* (Bernard), Dramaten, Stockholm.
	Fiesco (Schiller), Dramaten, Stockholm.
1931	*Macbeth* (Shakespeare), Dramaten, Stockholm.
1932	*Cant* (Munk), Dramaten, Stockholm.
	Clavigo (Goethe), Dramaten, Stockholm.

Guds grønne enger [Green Pastures] (Connelly), Dramaten, Stockholm.

1933   *Mourning Becomes Electra* (O'Neill), Dramaten, Stockholm.

Mäster Olof (Strindberg), Dramaten, Stockholm.

1934   *Medea* (Euripides), Dramaten, Stockholm.

Lisistrata (Aristophanes), Dramaten, Stockholm.

Amphitryon 38 (Giraudoux), Dramaten, Stockholm.

1935   *Ett drömspel* [A Dream Play] (Strindberg), Dramaten, Stockholm.

1936   *Brott och brott* [Crimes and Crimes] (Strindberg), Dramaten, Stockholm.

1937   *Folkungasagen* [The Saga of the Folkungs] (Strindberg), Dramaten, Stockholm.

Till Damaskus I [To Damascus I] (Strindberg), Dramaten, Stockholm.

Dödsdansen [The Dance of Death] (Strindberg), Dramaten, Stockholm.

1942   *Spöksonaten* [The Ghost Sonata] (Strindberg), Dramaten, Stockholm.

Stora landsvägen [The Great Highway] (Strindberg), Dramaten, Stockholm.

1943   *The Eve of St Mark* (M. Anderson), Dramaten, Stockholm.

Till Damaskus II (Strindberg), Dramaten, Stockholm.

Kronbruden [The Crown Bride] (Strindberg), Dramaten, Stockholm.

1945   *En idealist* [An Idealist] (Munk), Dramaten, Stockholm.

1946   *Brända tomten* [After the Fire] (Strindberg), Dramaten, Stockholm.

Britannicus (Racine), Dramaten, Stockholm.

1947   *Ett drömspel* [A Dream Play] (Strindberg), Dramaten, Stockholm.

1948   *The Iceman Cometh* (O'Neill), Dramaten, Stockholm.

Joan of Arc (M. Anderson), Dramaten, Stockholm.

1949   *Antigone* (Sophocles), Dramaten, Stockholm.

A Streetcar Names Desire (T. Williams), Dramaten, Stockholm.

Stora landsvägen [The Great Highway] (Strindberg), Dramaten, Stockholm.

1950   *Den Galne frå Chaillot* [The Madwoman of Chaillot] (Giraudoux), Dramaten, Stockholm.

The Cocktail Party (Eliot), Dramaten, Stockholm.

1951   *Edipo Re* (Sophocles), Dramaten, Stockholm.

Anne of the Thousand Days (M. Anderson), Dramaten, Stockholm.

1953   *Barabbas* (Lagerkvist), Dramaten, Stockholm.

The Living Room (Greene), Dramaten, Stockholm.

Oresteia (Aeschylus), Dramaten, Stockholm.

1955   *Ett drömspel* [A Dream Play] (Strindberg), Dramaten, Stockholm.

1957   *Partage de midi* (Claudel), Dramaten, Stockholm.

A Touch of the Poet (O'Neill), Dramaten, Stockholm.

1959   *Die Herberge* (Höchwalder), Dramaten, Stockholm.

1960   *Till Damaskus I* [To Damascus I] (Strindberg), Dramaten, Stockholm.

1962   *Spöksonaten* [The Ghost Sonata] (Strindberg), Paris.

Other productions included: *Julius Caesar* (Shakespeare), 1938; *Han sidder ved Smeltedligen* [He Sits at the Melting Pot] (Munk), 1938; *The Gentle People* (I. Shaw), 1940; *A Moon for the Misbegotten* (O'Neill); *Pelikanen* [The Pelican] (Strindberg).

Films

As actor:
Thomas Graals myndling [Thomas Graal's Pupil], 1922; *Gubben kommer* [The Old Man Returns], 1939; *Stora famnen* [Open Arms], 1940; *Vandringmed månen* [Walking under the Moon], 1945; *Galgmannen* [The Executioner], 1945.

As director and designer:
Damen med kameliorna [The Lady with the Camelias], 1925; *Bara en danserska* [Only a Ballerina], 1926; *Giftas*, 1926; *General von Döbeln*, 1942; *Kvinnor i fångenskap* [Women in Prison], 1943; *Jag dräpte* [I Have Seen], 1943; *Appasionata*, 1943; *Oss tjuvar emellan* [Among Thieves], 1945; *Johansson och Vestman*, 1946.

* * *

Himself the son of a distinguished director, Olof Molander trained at the school attached to Stockholm's Royal Dramatic Theatre (the Dramaten), where he played his early roles and directed many productions over a generation, though he was head of the theatre only from 1934 to 1938. He was influenced by the ideas of Gordon Craig and enormously impressed by the productions of Strindberg plays revived in Stockholm by the German director Max Reinhardt. Reinhardt's interpretations were based with great imaginative freedom on Strindberg's scripts and were crucial to the development of the German Expressionist movement. Having absorbed these, Molander went on to work along distinctly different lines, though governed by the concept of a unity of production imposed by a single mind. This involved keeping all the reins in his own hands and gained him the reputation of being a tyrant in the theatre. His justification rests on the lucid consistency and fluid rhythm of performances in which visual, aural and dramatic elements seemed perfectly blended. He liked to work with a resident designer who would take over his own rough sketches. He also saw and took the opportunity to create a distinctively Swedish theatre for his Swedish audiences, rooted in the their own way of life and familiar locations.

Working for a national theatre, he devoted himself to a classical repertoire, including ancient Greek drama, Shakespeare (*The Merchant of Venice* was his first production), Strindberg and outstanding works by leading contemporary dramatists. His productions of Eugene O'Neill, who acknowledged Strindberg as his supreme master, led to the choice of the Dramaten to present the world premieres of the plays left unperformed at O'Neill's death. The inheritance of naturalism — from Strindberg and from Harald Molander — showed in Olof's productions of the Greeks: he went behind classicist tradition, following the archaeologists' scientific interpretations of the ancient world and reproducing the artefacts they had found as key images in his sets. This replacement of idealisation with the suggestion of a more primitive reality, though still retaining a monumental quality, allowed for the psychological approach that was among the hallmarks of his directorial style. The result had the emotional effect of intense, intimate theatre.

He left aside the famous 'naturalistic' plays of Strindberg to concentrate on the later drama, in which fantastic, mystical or dream elements interact with fragments of a more realistic vision. Max Reinhardt had virtually eliminated realism, whereas to Molander it seemed that Strindberg's constant theme was of the everyday world as a place of spiritual pilgrimage and revelation. However he may have begun, his deep involvement in these plays over many years brought about a close identification of the director with the author in what emerged not just as an essentially religious, but a specifically Christian drama. His study of the texts never ceased, leaving him with the sense of yet further possibilities after seven distinct productions of *Ett drömspel* [A Dream Play], four of *Spöksonaten* [The Ghost Sonata], three of *Pelikanen* [The Pelican] and two of *Till Damaskus I* [To Damascus I]. His epoch-making 1935 production of *A Dream Play* used familiar Stockholm locations, in views contemporary with the play, projected in blurred or out-of-focus state, changeable as the action demanded with phantasmagoric smoothness; keeping most of the stage in darkness, he picked out different areas in light, using cross-spotlighting for simultaneous episodes. Though this may have been suggested by Reinhardt's device of dressing his actors in black and focussing on their white mask-like faces, Molander introduced elements of solid realism by lowering from the flies chairs, tables, a door, a picture, whatever might contribute to the effect of detailed realism in the playing out of snatches of experience in what seemed like a corner of a full realistic setting. Lars Hanson's performance as the Officer made the lively Everyman dominant over the Lawyer and Poet, the other two manifestations of the author's psyche, as they appeared in this interpretation of the play. Later, Molander moved the Lawyer to the centre, accentuating Strindberg's hints of a suffering, atoning, Christlike figure, a development anticipated in 1935, when the director went beyond the author's instructions to end the performance with a large reproduction of the cross on Strindberg's grave, inscribed 'O crux, ave spes unica', backed by a sky of faces. After World War II, in the 1947 production, Molander replaced the faces with a skyline of burnt-out, skeletal buildings, against which was set a tall, plain, wooden cross.

Lars Hanson also played the leads (the Unknown and Old Hummel) when Molander first presented *To Damascus I* and *The Ghost Sonata* at the Dramaten, and Sven Erik Skawonius again executed the designs, as he had done for *A Dream Play*. So a consistent, unified approach to Strindberg's work was assured. The reappearance of the same actor incidentally served Molander's view of the plays as documents of spiritual autobiography, an effect driven home in *The Ghost Sonata* by the representation of the house of life, house of secrets, by the facade of a dignified Stockholm building where Strindberg was well-known to have had an apartment. This was an emphasis from which Molander's successors would need to pull away. The chief of these, Alf Sjöberg and Ingmar Bergman, both acknowledged an enormous debt to him, and the overlapping careers of the three helped establish Sweden, and particularly the Dramaten, among the greatest centres of theatre in the 20th century. The Swedish content of Molander's work was extended to its history when he turned from Shakespeare to mount an exciting and spectacular production of *Folkungasagen* [The Saga of the Folkungs], one of the cycle of plays in which Strindberg translated Shakespeare's history plays into Swedish terms. It is generally recognised that this, with its disciplined handling of crowds and succession of strong visual images, its scenes of plague and of a penitent cross-carrying King, influenced Bergman's *The Seventh Seal*.

Molander made a number of films, including a version of Strindberg's ironically humorous short stories of married life, but he was overshadowed as a film director by his brother Gustaf (who 'discovered' Greta Garbo and Ingrid Bergman). He also produced many plays for Swedish radio. His stage work was virtually unseen outside Scandinavia, but in 1962 his production of *The Ghost Sonata* visited Paris and won an international award for best production of the year.

—Margery Morgan

MONTDORY. French actor-manager. Born Guillaume des Gilberts in Thiers. Training for the theatre by 1610. Stage debut, with the provincial touring company of Valleran le Conte, c.1612; continued to tour northern French provinces and Holland before coming to Paris with a new company, 1629; with the support of Cardinal Richelieu, settled at the Théâtre du Marais, Paris, 1634, and won recognition as the leading actor of his generation; created role of Rodrigue in Pierre Corneille's tragedy *Le Cid*, 1637; retired later the same year after being struck down by paralysis of the tongue while on stage, and subsequently lived on a pension granted by Richelieu. Died in Thiers, 10 November 1653.

Productions

1630   *Mélite; ou, Les Fausses Lettres* (P. Corneille), Berthault Tennis Court, Paris.
1631   *Clitandre; ou, L'Innocence délivrée* (P. Corneille), Bertault Tennis Court, Paris.
        Virginie (Mairet), Mlle de Rambouillet's private theatre, Paris.
1632   *La Veuve; ou, Le Traite trahi* (P. Corneille), Berthault Tennis Court, Paris.
        Le Vassal généreux (Scudéry), Théâtre du Marais, Paris.
1633   *Le Galerie du Palais; ou, L'Amie rivale* (P. Corneille), Berthault Tennis Court, Paris.
        La Suivante (P. Corneille), Fontaine Tennis Court, Paris.

La Place Royale; ou, L'Amoureux extravagant
(P. Corneille), Fontaine Tennis Court, Paris.
Le Trompeur puni (Scudéry), Paris.
Orante (Scudéry), Théâtre du Marais, Paris.
Place Royale (Claveret), Forges-les-Eaux.

1634   *La Comédie des comédiens* (Scudéry), Théâtre
du Marais, Paris.
Le Fils supposé (Scudéry), Théâtre du Marais,
Paris.
Le Prince déguisé (Scudéry), Théâtre du Ma-
rais, Paris.

1635   *Médée* (P. Corneille), Paris; acted Jason.
La Comédie des Tuileries (P. Corneille),
Théâtre du Marais, Paris.
La Mort de César (Scudéry), Théâtre du Ma-
rais, Paris; acted Brutus.

1636   *L'Illusion comique* (P. Corneille), Théâtre du
Marais, Paris; acted Clindor.
Didon (Scudéry), Théâtre du Marais, Paris.

1637   *L'Amant libéral* (Scudéry), Théâtre du Marais,
Paris.
Le Cid (P. Corneille), Théâtre du Marais, Paris;
acted Rodrigue.
La Mariane (Tristan), Théâtre du Marais,
Paris; acted Herod.
Les Visionnaires (Desmaretz de Saint-Sorlin),
Théâtre du Marais, Paris.

*

Bibliography

Books:

E. Cottier, *Le Comédien auvergnat Montdory*, Clermont-
Ferrand, 1937.

* * *

Described by Tallemant as "perhaps the most celebrated
actor since Roscius" and by a modern critic as "the first
great French actor", Montdory distinguished himself not
only by his talents as a performer, but also as a producer
and manager. It was he who first brought the works of
Pierre Corneille before the public, performing the title role
in *Le Cid*, and who established the second major Parisian
playhouse in opposition to the Hôtel de Bourgogne.

Montdory first met Corneille while still a strolling player
in the provinces and it was with the playwright's *Mélite*
that he established a reputation with Parisian audiences.
Further successes with plays by Corneille resulted in the
company led by Montdory and Le Noir being given the
lease of the Théâtre du Marais, which was to rival the Hôtel
de Bourgogne for the next 40 years. Corneille remained
loyal to Montdory as long as he continued performing,
giving all his new works to be produced by the actor and his
company. In addition to Corneille, the company also
performed works by Scudéry, Claveret, Mairet, Du Ryer,
Desmarets de Saint-Sorlin, and Tristan l'Hermite.

Montdory and his troupe also performed privately and at
Court at the command of Louis XIII. Such were their links
with the Court that Montdory declined to perform Claveret's *Les Eaux des Forges* on the grounds that it might
offend certain members of the Court to see themselves
depicted on stage. The company was officially called the
Troupe des Comédiens du Roi to distinguish it from the

King's own company or Troupe Royale performing at the
Hôtel de Bourgogne. By 1634, Montdory has succeeded in
establishing a company that, supported as it was by the
major playwrights of the day, constituted a serious threat to
the Troupe Royale, at that time somewhat depleted in
numbers. To remedy this, and, according to Tallemant, to
strike a blow at Richelieu who favoured Montdory and his
troupe, the King ordered that six of Montdory's actors
should join the Troupe Royale. It is a mark of Montdory's
ability that despite this severe blow his troupe retained the
ascendancy over their rivals.

Montdory was clearly an actor of outstanding skill.
Tallement says of him that although of medium height and
unprepossessing appearance, people of discernment would
come to see him in four consecutive performances of
Tristan's *La Mariane*, and each time discover something
new. He adds that the role of Herod was Montdory's
masterpiece, since he was more fitted to play a hero than a
lover. Contributing to this may have been the fact that,
despite the prevalent fashion, he refused to wear a wig, and
played all his roles with his own short-cropped hair. Rapin
remarks that after seeing Montdory in *Le Mariane*, the
members of the audience were always "musing and
thoughtful" and "reflecting on what they had just seen and
at the same time full of great pleasure". Corneille goes so
far in his *Discourse du poème dramatique* as to attribute the
triumph of *Le Mariane* to Montdory's participation. Tristan himself, in his advertisement to *Panthée*, gives a fuller
description of Montdory at work: "Never did a man appear
with more honour on the stage ... the changes in his face
seem to proceed from the movements of his heart; and the
accurate nuances of his speech, and the seemliness of his
actions, form an admirable harmony which delights all his
spectators".

Triumph though *La Mariane* was, it was to have tragic
consequences for the actor, for, in 1637, while exerting
himself in the role of Herod, Montdory suffered some form
of apoplectic fit, which left his tongue and right arm
paralyzed. As Tallemant put it: "he had a powerful
imagination ... he almost believed himself to be what he
represented", which would almost make him a victim of his
own talent. Others have seen Montdory more as a victim of
the tragic acting style of that period, in which an actor was
esteemed above all for the force of his declamation. Studies
of manuals of oratory, however, suggest that this may not
have been the case; which would seem to be borne out by
the descriptions of Montdory's own performances.

For a long time Montdory hoped to make a full recovery.
In 1638, he appeared before the King and Richelieu in a
revival of *L'Aveugle de Smyrne*, but was forced to withdraw
after the second act. He then left the stage permanently,
receiving a pension from Richelieu and other notables of
the Court, and lived the remaining 15 years of his life in
retirement in Paris and Thiers.

In addition to his undoubted gifts, Montdory enjoyed
great good fortune in that his career spanned exciting
times, in terms of the establishment of permanent theatre
companies in the capital, the increasing social acceptability
of the theatre, the development of French classical drama
(Tallemant gives as a sign of Montdory's refinement that he
had never performed in farce), and the early years of the
career of Pierre Corneille. His loss to the stage at the height
of his powers was bitterly regretted, both by his company
and the playwrights he had served so well, so that Scudéry

can be said to be speaking for them all when he wrote that the stage should remain permanently hung in black if there was no longer hope of Montdory appearing on it.

—Janet Clarke

————

N

NAPIER, John. British designer. Born in London, 1 March 1944. Educated at Hornsey College of Art, London; trained for the theatre under Ralph Koltai at the Central School of Arts and Craft, London. Married 1) Andreane Neofitou in 1964, one son and one daughter; 2) actress Donna King in 1985, one son and one daughter. Head of design, Phoenix Theatre, Leicester, 1967–68; London debut, 1968; Broadway debut, 1974; associate designer, Royal Shakespeare Company, from 1976. Member: British Society of Theatre Designers; Royal Shakespeare Company (associate). Recipient: Drama Desk Award, 1981, 1984, 1985; British Academy of Film and Television Arts Award for Costume Design; Society of West End Theatre Award, 1977, 1978, 1980; Tony Award, 1981, 1982, 1987 (twice); *Plays and Players* Award, 1989.

Productions

1967	*A Penny for a Song* (Whiting), Phoenix Theatre, Leicester.
1968	*Fortune and Men's Eyes* (Herbert), Comedy Theatre, London.
1969	*The Ruling Class* (Barnes), Piccadilly Theatre, London.
	The Fun War, Open Space Theatre, London.
	Muzeeka (Guare), Open Space Theatre, London.
	La Turista (Shepard), London.
	George Frederick (ballet), Ballet Rambert, London; revived, 1974.
1970	*Cancer*, London.
	Isabel's a Jezebel (MacDermot), London.
1971	*Mister* (Eveling), Duchess Theatre, London.
	The Foursome (Ionesco), London.
	The Lovers of Viorne (Duras), London.
	Lear (Bond), Royal Court Theatre, London.
1972	*Jump!* (Gelbart), Queen's Theatre, London.
	Sam, Sam (Griffiths), Open Space Theatre, London.
	Big Wolf (Mueller), Royal Court Theatre, London.
	Julius Caesar (Shakespeare), London.
1973	*Equus* (P. Shaffer), Old Vic Theatre, London; Plymouth Theatre, New York, 1974.
	The Party (Griffiths), Old Vic Theatre, London.
	The Devils, English National Opera, London.
1974	*Knuckle* (Hare), Comedy Theatre, London.

	Richard II (Shakespeare), Royal Shakespeare Theatre, Stratford-upon-Avon, and Aldwych Theatre, London.
	King John (Shakespeare), Royal Shakespeare Theatre, Stratford-upon-Avon, and Aldwych Theatre, London.
	Cymbeline (Shakespeare), Royal Shakespeare Theatre, Stratford-upon-Avon, and Aldwych Theatre, London.
	Macbeth (Shakespeare), Royal Shakespeare Theatre, Stratford-upon-Avon.
	Richard III (Shakespeare), Royal Shakespeare Theatre, Stratford-upon-Avon.
	The Devils of Loudon, Sadler's Wells Theatre, London.
	Lohengrin (Wagner), Royal Opera House, Covent Garden, London; revived there, 1978.
1975	*Hedda Gabler* (Ibsen), Aldwych Theatre, London, and Australian and US tour.
1976	*Much Ado About Nothing* (Shakespeare), Royal Shakespeare Theatre, Stratford-upon-Avon, and Aldwych Theatre, London.
	The Comedy of Errors (Shakespeare), Royal Shakespeare Theatre, Stratford-upon-Avon, and Aldwych Theatre, London.
	King Lear (Shakespeare), Royal Shakespeare Theatre, Stratford-upon-Avon, and Aldwych Theatre, London.
	Macbeth (Shakespeare), Royal Shakespeare Theatre, Stratford-upon-Avon, and Aldwych Theatre, London.
1977	*A Midsummer Night's Dream* (Shakespeare), Royal Shakespeare Theatre, Stratford-upon-Avon, and Aldwych Theatre, London.
	As You Like It (Shakespeare), Aldwych Theatre, London.
	King Lear (opera), Royal Opera House, Covent Garden, London.
1978	*Kings and Clowns* (Bricusse), Phoenix Theatre, London.
	The Travelling Music Show (Bricusse and Newley), Her Majesty's Theatre, London.
1979	*The Merry Wives of Windsor* (Shakespeare), Royal Shakespeare Theatre, Stratford-upon-Avon, and Aldwych Theatre, London.
	Twelfth Night (Shakespeare), Royal Shakespeare Theatre, Stratford-upon-Avon, and Aldwych Theatre, London.
	The Three Sisters (Chekhov), The Other Place, Stratford-upon-Avon.

Once in a Lifetime (Kaufman), Aldwych Theatre, London.

1980   *The Greeks* (Barton), Aldwych Theatre, London.

Nicholas Nickleby (adapted from Dickens), Aldwych Theatre, London; Plymouth Theatre, New York, 1981.

1981   *Cats* (Lloyd Webber, adapted from Eliot), New London Theatre, London; Winter Garden Theatre, New York, 1982; world tour.

1982   *Henry IV, parts 1 and 2* (Shakespeare), Barbican Theatre, London.

Peter Pan (Barrie), Barbican Theatre, London.

1983   *Idomeneo* (Mozart), Glyndebourne Opera House.

Macbeth (Verdi), Royal Opera House, Covent Garden, London.

1984   *Mother Courage* (Brecht), Barbican Theatre, London.

Starlight Express (Lloyd Webber and Stilgoe), Apollo Victoria Theatre, London; Gershwin Theatre, New York, 1987.

1985   *Les Misérables* (Schönberg, Boublil, and Kretzmer, adapted from Hugo), Barbican Theatre, London, and Palace Theatre, London; Broadway Theatre, New York, 1987; world tour.

1986   *Time* (Clark), Dominion Theatre, London.

The Fair Maid of the West (Heywood), Swan Theatre, Stratford-upon-Avon.

1989   *Miss Saigon* (Schönberg, Maltby, and Boublil), Theatre Royal, Drury Lane, London.

The Baker's Wife (Stein and Schwartz), Phoenix Theatre, London.

1990   *The Siegfried and Roy Show*, Las Vegas; also co-directed.

Children of God (Caird and Schwartz), Prince Edward Theatre, London.

1993   *Trelawny of the Wells* (Pinero), Royal National Theatre, London.

Sunset Boulevard (Hampton, Black, and Lloyd Webber), Adelphi Theatre, London, and Los Angeles.

Films

Hedda, 1976; *Hook*, 1991.

Television

The Comedy of Errors; *Macbeth*; *The Three Sisters*; *Nicholas Nickleby*.

Publications

Cats, 1981.

*   *   *

John Napier has come to be identified with the design of large-scale musical theatre spectacles, commercial blockbusters that originate in London and achieve perhaps even greater notoriety in New York partly because their staging

has become even more elaborate in the overseas transfer. Yet although Napier's interest in theatre as spectacle is undeniable and may be traced back to his early work, it is also true that his career has included much more conservative, even minimalist, work and that even his most elaborate scenography reflects his need for involvement with a community of collaborative artists rather than a penchant for bravura effects.

Napier's education and training were symptomatic of his later paths in the theatre. In art school he concentrated on sculpture, finding most satisfaction in shaping tangible materials with his hands rather than in drawing and pictorial art. The late 1950's and early 1960's, when Napier was in art school, were an era when traditional approaches in art were rapidly breaking down. Napier's love of working with unconventional materials and shaping new sculptured environments echoed certain broader tendencies in the art world of the time, particularly environmental art and assemblage. But Napier eventually grew tired of what he considered to be the emptiness of abstract art, left art school before finishing, and sought more direct contact with reality and other human beings. The sheer communality of theatre attracted him and he subsequently studied stage design for three years at the Central School during Ralph Koltai's tenure there as head of theatre design. Napier's training in sculpture was of great help: "I could weld, cast, work with any materials, and knew how to use space".

Napier once again left before completing his study. He went directly to work in regional professional theatres in England for a few years before returning to London and work with fringe groups and the vital young English Stage Company at the Royal Court, where chief designer Jocelyn Herbert's economy of expression struck a responsive chord in Napier. One of his most satisfying productions at the Royal Court was Harold Mueller's *Big Wolf* (1972), for which he was able to use an empty warehouse and collect his own random materials to build a set his own way, working with actual objects and materials, but in stage terms.

Most of Napier's work in the 1970's was with the Royal Shakespeare Company, where many of his productions, including *Macbeth* (1973), *A Midsummer Night's Dream* (1976), and *Twelfth Night* (1978), were quite austere and minimal. His design for *The Comedy of Errors* (1976) was significant in another sense, for Napier remodelled the interior of the Stratford theatre to enable the audience seating to extend on two levels to the sides and even rear of the stage; he then filled the stage itself with colourful paraphenalia to convey the atmosphere of a tourist square in Corfu. Two non-RSC productions of the 1970's were also notable. Napier's chief contributions to *Equus* were marvellously abstractly sculpted masks and hooves for the horses, as well as the inclusion of audience seating on an otherwise bare stage. On the other hand, his scenography for the opera *The Devils* (1973) was technically complex in its use of multiple computer-controlled projections of slides and film on several large screens.

Napier achieved international status in the 1980's with a series of large-scale productions, starting with *The Greeks* (1980), a condensed version of some nine Greek dramas adapted and directed by John Barton for the RSC. Here the minimalist and sculptor in Napier was most evident as he used one basic space with a neutral central platform for all the plays, with different locations indicated by relatively sparse, three-dimensional objects that were sometimes recycled in slightly different form for use in more than one play.

Both *Nicholas Nickleby* (1980) and *Cats* (1981) revealed Napier's more extravagant side. For the latter he arranged a mélange of larger-than-life tangible artefacts to create an environment that blended with the audience (often necessitating modifications in the structure of the host theatre). *Nickleby* was relatively more austere, employing a constructivist setting that would serve to unify and facilitate the varied action of the eight-hour spectacle and also bring it into close spatial relationship with the audience. Napier found great satisfaction in the fact that his settings for both productions — and his costumes as well — developed in the semi-improvisational process of rehearsals and to some extent influenced in turn the final shape of the productions. It is precisely that sort of involvement-in-process that gives Napier the greatest satisfaction. And it is the sheer authenticity of the materials used that is also satisfying, although Napier is quick to point out that he is not interested in mere naturalism, but in the artistic shaping and organisation of real objects, as he was earlier when creating environmental sculpture: "I hope the audience feels it's somewhere where every nook and cranny has been thought about and everything, including itself, is part of the design".

Napier's handling of Shakespeare's *Henry IV* as the initial production in the new Barbican home of the RSC (1982) resulted in a blending of the *Nickleby* and *Cats* methods: the constructivist setting of *Nickleby* was broken up into four mobile timber and metal towers that were bedecked with *Cats*-like detritus of the medieval era. Napier wanted to create "a whole teeming world right on the forestage", but he also wanted to be able to get rid of it. The towers were on wheels and each tower had its own electric motor.

His work in *Les Miserables* (1985) was, according to Napier himself, not particularly spectacular: "I think it's conservative. But it gets the job done". Measured against the work of most other designers, it was spectacular enough, chiefly by virtue of its concentric turntables to change scenes and facilitate the movement of actors, and its tour de force employment of kinetic scenery: two separate stage trucks loaded with the debris of revolutionary barricades met in the middle of the stage, lifted, rotated, and meshed to form one huge wall in the climactic scene of the production. Each truck was powered by six large car batteries and had its own concealed driver.

Any fears that Napier was toning down his penchant for spectacle would have been allayed by *Starlight Express* (1985), a flamboyant musical extravaganza centred on a fictive railroad race represented by roller skaters costumed by Napier as personified locomotives whizzing around the interior of a gutted and restructured theatre on a huge spiral track (inspired by roller-coasters) that takes the racers over the stage and around the audience area. Napier's comment on a subsequent musical, *Time* (1986), indicated that he was not cutting back but continuing his involvement with high-tech staging: "A musical that was as close as you could get to a big rock-and-roll event; and because it was also about space it gave me an unmissable chance to use modern technology to the limit". Subsequent projects have continued in a similar vein: another London musical, *Miss Saigon* (1989), the climax of which involves

the onstage descent of a helicopter to rescue a crowd of soldiers who clamber up its rope ladder, and a lavish paratheatrical spectacle, *Siegfried and Roy*, for a Las Vegas hotel (1990).

—Jarka M. Burian

NEMIROVICH-DANCHENKO, Vladimir (Ivanovich). Russian director and playwright. Born in Ozurgety (now Makharadze), Georgia, 11 December 1858. Educated at Moscow University, 1876–79. As a youth, took part in amateur theatricals; subsequently worked as theatre critic, from 1877, and as a playwright, from 1881; director, Moscow Philharmonic Society's Drama Course, 1891–1901; co-founder and co-director, with Stanislavsky, of the Moscow Popular Art Theatre (later renamed the Moscow Art Theatre), 1898; gave up activities as playwright, 1902; championed plays by Soviet dramatists after the Revolution, 1917; founder, Moscow Musical Studio (renamed the Nemirovich-Danchenko Musical Theatre, 1926), 1919; toured Europe and USA with the Musical Studio, 1925–27; visited Paris with the Moscow Art Theatre, 1937; assumed sole directorship of the Moscow Art Theatre on Stanislavsky's death, 1938. Recipient: Griboyedov Prize, 1896; State Prize of the USSR, 1942, 1943. Order of Lenin; Order of the Red Banner of Labour; People's Artist of the Soviet Union, 1936. Died in Moscow, 25 April 1943.

Productions

1898   *Chayka* [The Seagull] (Chekhov), Alexandrinsky Theatre, St Petersburg, and Art Theatre, Moscow.

1899   *Dyadya Vanya* [Uncle Vanya] (Chekhov), Art Theatre, Moscow.

       Einsame Menschen (Hauptmann), Art Theatre, Moscow.

1900   *Når vi døde vågner* [When We Dead Awaken] (Ibsen), Art Theatre, Moscow.

1901   *Tri sestry* [The Three Sisters] (Chekhov), Art Theatre, Moscow.

1902   *Meschane* [The Smug Citizens] (Gorky), Art Theatre, Moscow.

       Na dne [The Lower Depths] (Gorky), Art Theatre, Moscow.

       In Dreams (Nemirovich-Danchenko), Art Theatre, Moscow.

1903   *Samfundets støtter* [The Pillars of Society] (Ibsen), Art Theatre, Moscow.

       Iulii Tsezar [Julius Caesar] (Shakespeare), Art Theatre, Moscow.

1904   *Vishnevy sad* [The Cherry Orchard] (Chekhov), Art Theatre, Moscow.

       Ivanov (Chekhov), Art Theatre, Moscow.

1905–06 *Einsame Menschen* (Hauptmann), Art Theatre, Moscow.

       Deti solntsa [Children of the Sun] (Gorky), Art Theatre, Moscow.

1906   *Brand* (Ibsen), Art Theatre, Moscow.

Gore ot Uma [Woe from Wit] (Griboyedov), Art Theatre, Moscow.

1908   *Rosmersholm* (Ibsen), Art Theatre, Moscow.
Revizor [The Government Inspector] (Gogol), Art Theatre, Moscow.

1909   *Anatema* [Anathema] (Andreyev), Art Theatre, Moscow.

1910   *Na vsyakogo dovolno prostoty* [Even a Wise Man Stumbles] (Ostrovsky), Art Theatre, Moscow.
Boris Godunov (Pushkin), Art Theatre, Moscow.
Bratja Karamazovy [The Brothers Karamazov] (Dostoevsky, adapted by Nemirovich-Danchenko), Art Theatre, Moscow.

1911   *Zhivoy trup* [The Living Corpse] (L. Tolstoy), Art Theatre, Moscow.

1912   *Gde tonko, tam i rvetsya* [Where It's Thin, There It Breaks] (Turgenev), Art Theatre, Moscow.
Ekaterina Ivanovna (Andreyev), Art Theatre, Moscow.

1913   *Nikolai Stavrogin* (Nemirovich-Danchenko, adapted from Dostoevsky's *The Possessed*), Art Theatre, Moscow.

1914   *Smerti Pazukhin* [The Death of Pazukhin] (Saltykov-Shchedrin), Art Theatre, Moscow.
Mysl [Thought] (Andreyev), Art Theatre, Moscow.

1915   *Kamenny gost* [The Statue Guest] (Pushkin), Art Theatre, Moscow.

1916   *There Will Be Joy* (Merezhkovsky), Art Theatre, Moscow.

1925   *Pugachyov Times* (Trenev), Art Theatre, Moscow.

1929   *Blokus* [Blockade] (Ivanov), Art Theatre, Moscow.

1930   *Voskreseniye* [Resurrection] (Tolstoy, adapted by Nemirovich-Danchenko), Art Theatre, Moscow.

1934   *Yegor Bulychov i drugiye* [Yegor Bulychov and Others] (Gorky), Art Theatre, Moscow.

1935   *Groza* [The Storm] (Ostrovsky), Art Theatre, Moscow.
Vragi [Enemies] (Gorky), Art Theatre, Moscow.

1936   *Liubov Iarovaia* (Trenev), Art Theatre, Moscow.

1937   *Anna Karenina* (Tolstoy, adapted by Nemirovich-Danchenko), Art Theatre, Moscow.

1938   *Gore ot Uma* [Woe from Wit] (Griboyedov), Art Theatre, Moscow.

1939   *The Orchards of Polovchansk* (Leonov), Art Theatre, Moscow.

1940   *Tri sestry* [The Three Sisters] (Chekhov), Art Theatre, Moscow.

1942   *Kremlin Chimes* (Pogodin), Art Theatre, Moscow.

Other productions included: *Carmencita and the Soldier* (adapted from Bizet's *Carmen*); *The Daughter of Madame Angot* (Lecocq); *Katerina Izmailova* (Shostakovich); *Lysistrata* (Aristophanes); *La Périchole* (Offenbach); *The Storm*

Vladimir Nemirovich-Danchenko

(Khrennikov); *La Traviata* (Verdi), all at the Musical Studio, Moscow Art Theatre.

Publications

New Business (play), 1890; *Living on Literature* (novella), 1891; *Gold* (play), 1895; *The Worth of Life* (play), 1896; *The Governor's Inspection* (novella), 1896; *Dreams* (novella), 1898; *Drama Behind the Scenes* (novella), 1896; *In Dreams* (play), 1902; *Iz proshlogo*, 1937 (*My Life in the Russian Theatre*, 1937); *Teatral' noe nasledie* [Theatre Legacy], 2 vols., 1952–54; *Pesy*, 1962; *Rezhisserskii plan postanovki tragedii Shekspira "Iulii Tsezar"; Moskovskii khudozhestvennyi teatr, 1903*, 1964.

* * *

Vladimir Nemirovich-Danchenko came from a military family of modest means. His brother was a war correspondent. He became the highly successful author of 11 plays, which were presented at the Alexandrinsky Theatre in St Petersburg and at the Maly in Moscow. They were mostly light comedies and none has survived. He twice won the Griboyedov Prize for play of the year, the second time in 1896 in competition with Chekhov's *The Seagull*, a judgement that he considered absurd. He was a member of the repertoire committee of the Maly, wrote regular dramatic criticism and had occasion to review and commend performances given by Stanislavsky when he was still an amateur.

In 1891 he was appointed head of the drama section of the Philharmonic School. Among his pupils were Olga Knipper, Meyerhold and Moskvin. By the mid-1890's he felt the time had come to play a more active role in reshaping the future of the Russian theatre. The Maly was in serious decline. All effort to reform its practice, including schemes by Ostrovsky, had been ignored. In 1897 Nemirovich prepared a set of proposals for reorganising the theatre in the hope of being given the post of director. At the same time, he was aware that Stanislavsky was planning to turn his amateur Society of Art and Literature into a professional company. In June he arranged to meet Stanislavsky and, after an 18-hour discussion, they laid down an outline policy for the Moscow Art Theatre. It was to be an 'open' theatre, with prices modest enough to encourage audiences.

Basic to the agreement was the division of artistic responsibility: Nemirovich was to have the last word in all literary matters, Stanislavsky in all matters relating to the staging. In Nemirovich's hierarchy of values, literary considerations took precedence over all others. As a writer he believed in the supremacy of the author's text. Stanislavsky saw the actor and director as much more active agents in the creative process and this fundamental disagreement ultimately led to some bitter disputes. Nemirovich also had definite ideas on what the repertoire should be. Ideally, he would have staged only contemporary plays, but given that there were insufficient works of the right quality was prepared to admit classic plays that had relevance. It was Nemirovich who insisted on including Chekhov's *The Seagull* in the first season. After the catastrophic first night of the play in 1896 in St Petersburg, Chekhov was unwilling to let it be seen in Moscow. Much persuasion was needed on Nemirovich's part, but Chekhov's consent was finally secured.

From Nemirovich's point of view his collaboration with Stanislavsky on the play (and on three subsequent Chekhov classics) was ideal. He spent two days analysing the text for Stanislavsky, who admitted that he did not understand the play. Stanislavsky then wrote a detailed production plan, which Nemirovich then rehearsed. Nemirovich admitted that he was at times a rather pedestrian director, whereas Stanislavsky had immense flair. With this method, Stanislavsky's flair could be channelled in the right literary direction.

Nemirovich abandoned the writing of original plays in 1902 and by 1903 had acquired enough confidence as a director to attempt *Julius Caesar* alone. The production was more notable for its historical and archaeological values than for its insights, and Nemirovich was bitterly angry when he discovered how much Stanislavsky disliked it. He was also worried by the increasing influence of Savva Morozov, one of the backers of the Art Theatre, and his sympathy for Gorky and his circle. Nemirovich's attitude towards Gorky was always ambivalent, and culminated in a total breach in 1905. Stanislavsky's wish to experiment with new methods, including improvisation, caused him further alarm, and matters were not helped when, in 1906, Stanislavsky began work on the System. By 1908 the men were at loggerheads and Stanislavsky resigned from the Board, leaving Nemirovich in sole charge of policy (though

he accepted the System as the official working method of the Art Theatre in 1911).

Nemirovich continued his search for a theatre of literary value. In 1910 he made an adaptation of Dostoevsky's *The Brothers Karamazov*, replacing the traditional four acts with scenes of variable length linked by a narrator, and was convinced he had found a new theatrical form. The period 1914-17, however, was one of stagnation for the Art Theatre. New productions became rarer.

After the Revolution, Nemirovich was encouraged by the government to develop an interest in opera and he responded by founding the Musical Studio (1919). Nonetheless, the post-Revolutionary era proved difficult for the Art Theatre, which came under constant attack from the so-called Left. While Stanislavsky and the company were on tour in 1922-24, Nemirovich attempted to redefine and renegotiate the theatre's future. Subsequently he toyed with the idea of emigrating when on tour with the Musical Studio (1925-27) and again with the Art Theatre in 1937.

During the 1930's, now reconciled with Gorky, he directed successful productions of Gorky, Tolstoy, Ostrovsky, Griboyedov and Pogodin. On his death he left an incomplete set of notes for a production of *Hamlet*, which anticipated some of the ideas that emerged in the 1960's. Among his most significant opera productions was the Moscow premiere of *Katerina Izmailova* (or *Lady Macbeth of Mtsenk*), to which Stalin took violent exception.

If the Stanislavsky System was the official method of actor training, Nemirovich's ideas on production methods also became the norm, in particular his emphasis on what he called the 'second level' — the social, historical and political world in which the characters live, their mental 'luggage'. Many later teachers sought to synthesize Stanislavsky's and Nemirovich's methods.

—Jean Benedetti

NEUBER, Friederike Caroline. German actress and manager. Born Carolina Weissenborn in Reichenbach, Saxony, 9 March 1697. Married actor-manager Johann Neuber in 1718 (died 1759). Began career, with her husband, in travelling companies of Christian Spiegelberg, 1717-22, and Karl Caspar Haack, 1722-25; known as 'die Neuberin', acclaimed initially in breeches parts but later also in comedy; founded own company in collaboration with her husband and the critic Johann Christoph Gottsched, based at Leipzig, 1727; presented largely classical repertory throughout Germany through the 1720's and 1730's; returned to Leipzig, 1737, to discover company had lost its patent to rival troupe; performed in Russia at inviation of Empress Anna, 1740; finally quarrelled with Gottsched over the issue of period authenticity, 1741; founded new company, 1748, to tour with plays by Lessing; presented company at the Deutsches Theater, Vienna, 1753-54, with mixed success; formed smaller company in Dresden, 1755-56; spent final years in poverty. Died in Laubegast, near Dresden, 30 November 1760.

Principal productions

1725   *Regulus* (Pradon), Leipzig.

1725–31	*Brutus* (Voltaire), Leipzig.
	Cid (Corneille), Leipzig.
	Cinna (Corneille), Leipzig.
	Iphigénie (Racine), Leipzig.
	Bérénice (Racine), Leipzig.
1732	*Der Sterbende Cato* (Gottsched), Leipzig.
1738	*Polyeucte* (Sheibe), Opernhaus, Hamburg.
	Mithridates (Scheibe), Opernhaus, Hamburg.
1739	*Alzire* (Voltaire), Opernhaus, Hamburg.
1747	*Der Junge Gelehrte* (Lessing), Leipzig.
1749	*Die Juden* (Lessing), Leipzig.

*

Bibliography

Books:

Friedrich von Reden-Esbeck, *Caroline Neuber und ihre Zeitgenossen*, Leipzig, 1881.

Richard Daunicht, *Die Neuberin/Materialien zur Theatergeschichte des 18 Jahrhunderts*, Berlin, 1956.

Simon Williams, *German Actors of the 18th and 19th Centuries*, Westport, Connecticut, 1985.

George W. Brandt (ed.), *German and Dutch Theatre, 1600–1848*, Cambridge, 1993.

* * *

The life of Friederike Caroline Neuber ('die Neuberin' to her contemporaries) was tinged with tragedy — initially fired by ideals, it ended in frustration and obscurity. A key figure on the German stage of the 1730's, her own artistic standing in theatre history is uncertain. As an actress she was variously described as graceful and dignified on the one hand, artificial and mannered on the other. Widely travelled — touring Leipzig, Dresden, Hanover, Hamburg, Kiel, Bremen, Frankfurt-on-Main and other towns, going as far afield as Warsaw and St Petersburg — she was famous in her heyday, appreciated particularly in breeches parts. But she was to outlive her reputation. When she appeared in Vienna in her mid-fifties she was criticised for faulty voice production and described as looking "like a dolled-up Neapolitan princess".

What was remarkable about her was not so much the fact that, in partnership with her husband Johann Neuber (1697–1759), she ran a company of actors — such female enterprise was not unprecedented in Germany — but rather her desire to raise the theatre's cultural status in the teeth of public apathy or downright hostility. However, the advances in style and repertoire that she worked for led up a blind alley and were soon overtaken by events.

The German theatre in the early 18th century, in contrast to that of England and France, was largely divorced from literature. Stage comedy tended to be improvised and coarsely farcical; the 'serious' drama consisted of 'Haupt-und Staatsaktionen', a melodramatic genre that violated the unities and mixed grandiloquent sensationalism with comic interludes. Reputable authors would not write for what was regarded as a crude entertainment for the masses.

These were the defects that die Neuberin and her husband wished to remedy when, in 1727, after some 10 years of stage experience, they set up their own company of strolling players (permanently domiciled companies did not then exist in Germany). In this high endeavour they sought the guidance of Johann Christoph Gottsched

(1700–66), the Professor of Poetry at the University of Leipzig who dominated German literary taste at the time. Gottsched advocated a 'regular' drama along French lines: a clear division of the genres, adherence to the unities of time, place and action, and an avoidance of anything 'low'. So the repertoire of the Neuber company consisted largely of plays supplied by Gottsched, his wife and their friends: translations from the French as well as some original German plays in the French manner. The verse form adopted was the alexandrine, a metre not particularly well-suited to the German language. The performance style was also modelled on the French example.

Such a campaign to elevate taste naturally appealed more to educated than to popular audiences. Frau Neuber often put forward a plea for the acceptance of drama as providing moral uplift in the allegorical plays she wrote herself. The most spectacular endorsement she gave in 1737 or 1738 to Gottsched's ideas was a curtain-raiser in which she 'banished' (not burnt in effigy as is sometimes asserted) Harlequin as the embodiment of improvised theatre. But in fact she could not altogether do without popular crowd-pullers in her repertoire, and included, for instance, a play on the evergreen subject of Doctor Faust (1738).

The inherently unstable link between actress and doctrinaire academic could not last. Die Neuberin, peeved by the professor's attack on her use of anachronistic costumes, publicly ridiculed his — actually forward-looking — call for period authenticity: on 12 June 1741, she put on in Leipzig one act of Gottsched's tragedy *The Death of Cato*, with actors in Roman dress and bare feet. This was considered utterly laughable. A complete breach between the two came about when on 18 September of the same year she staged an allegorical play entitled *The Most Precious of All Treasures*, in which Gottsched was portrayed as 'The Fault-Finder' dressed in a sable star-strewn gown, with bats' wings and a sun of gold tinsel on his head, carrying a dark-lantern. She scored a palpable hit but her own career — and indeed that of Gottsched as well — took a downward plunge thereafter.

Die Neuberin helped to raise the esteem in which actors were held by insisting that members of her company should be seen to conduct themselves decently. Her unmarried actresses lived under her own roof and unmarried actors ate at her table. Three directors who subsequently distinguished themselves in the critical period when German actors graduated from being mere strolling players to performers in fixed venues — Gottfried Heinrich Koch (1703–75), Johann Friedrich Schönemann (1704–82) and Carl Theophil Döbbelin (1727–93) — all learnt much of their craft from their work with the Neuber company. Unfortunately, both Schönemann and Koch were to become her dangerous rivals once they had set up their own companies. Neuber also deserves credit for having staged Gotthold Ephraim Lessing's first play, *The Young Scholar*, written when the author was only 18 years old, in Leipzig in 1747.

Frau Neuber's frequent intemperate outbursts, largely attributable no doubt to the ill-treatment (including until late adolescence physical chastisement) that she received at her father's hands, often did more damage to herself than to anyone else. Thus, a sharply worded valedictory message in verse delivered to the Hamburg public in January 1740 was considered so insulting that the Senate would not allow her to perform in that Hanseatic city ever again.

Konrad Ekhof (1720–78), the great actor whose style was diametrically opposed to that of die Neuberin, summed up his predecessor as follows: "For about 10 years her career was in the ascendant, for 10 years it was in decline, and the last 10 years she spent in misery".

In 1776, 16 years after her death in utter poverty, a monument was put up in the village where she had spent her final days. This praised her "masculine spirit" and called her "the most famous actress of her time, the originator of good taste on the German stage".

—George Brandt

NEVILLE, John. British actor and director. Born in Willesden, London, 2 May 1925. Educated at Willesden and Chiswick County Schools; trained for the stage at the Royal Academy of Dramatic Arts, London. Served in Royal Navy during World War II. Married actress Caroline Hooper in 1949, three sons and three daughters. Stage debut, New Theatre, London, 1947; actor, Lowestoft Repertory Company, 1948, Birmingham Repertory Company, 1949–50; appeared at Bristol Old Vic, 1950–53; actor, Old Vic Theatre, London, 1953–61; Broadway debut, Winter Garden Theatre, 1956; joined Nottingham Playhouse company, 1961; toured South Africa, 1963; director, Nottingham Playhouse, 1963–68; professor of drama, University of Nottingham, from 1967; artistic director, Citadel Theatre, Edmonton, Alberta, 1973–78; artistic director, Neptune Theatre, Halifax, Nova Scotia, 1978–83; artistic director, Festival Theatre, Stratford, Ontario, 1985–89. Doctor of Dramatic Arts, Lethbridge University, Alberta, 1979; DFA: Nova Scotia College of Art and Design, 1981. OBE (Order of the British Empire), 1965.

Productions

As actor:

1947   Walk-on role in *Richard III* (Shakespeare), New Theatre, London.

1948   Lysander in *A Midsummer Night's Dream* (Shakespeare), Open Air Theatre, London.

      Chatillon in *King John* (Shakespeare), Open Air Theatre, London.

1950–53   Gregers Werle in *The Wild Duck* (Ibsen), Old Vic Theatre, Bristol.

      Marlow in *She Stoops to Conquer* (Goldsmith), Old Vic Theatre, Bristol.

      Richard in *The Lady's Not for Burning* (Fry), Old Vic Theatre, Bristol.

      Dunois in *Saint Joan* (G. B. Shaw), Old Vic Theatre, Bristol.

      Edgar in *Venus Observed* (Fry), Old Vic Theatre, Bristol.

      Valentine in *The Two Gentlemen of Verona* (Shakespeare), Old Vic Theatre, Bristol, and London.

      The Duke in *Measure for Measure* (Shakespeare), Old Vic Theatre, Bristol.

      Henry V in *Henry V* (Shakespeare), Old Vic Theatre, Bristol.

1953–54   Fortinbras in *Hamlet* (Shakespeare), Old Vic Theatre, London.

      Bertram in *All's Well That Ends Well* (Shakespeare), Old Vic Theatre, London.

      Ferdinand in *The Tempest* (Shakespeare), Old Vic Theatre, London.

1954–55   Macduff in *Macbeth* (Shakespeare), Old Vic Theatre, London; revived there and for US tour, 1956.

      Richard in *Richard II* (Shakespeare), Old Vic Theatre, London; revived there, 1955–56; US tour, 1956–57; Playhouse, Nottingham, 1965.

      Berowne in *Love's Labour's Lost* (Shakespeare), Old Vic Theatre, London.

      Orlando in *As You Like It* (Shakespeare), Old Vic Theatre, London.

      Henry Percy in *Henry IV, part 1* (Shakespeare), Old Vic Theatre, London.

1955–56   Marc Antony in *Julius Caesar* (Shakespeare), Old Vic Theatre, London.

      Autolycus in *The Winter's Tale* (Shakespeare), Old Vic Theatre, London.

      Othello in *Othello* (Shakespeare), Old Vic Theatre, London; Neptune Theatre, Halifax, Nova Scotia, 1978.

      Iago in *Othello* (Shakespeare), Old Vic Theatre, London; Playhouse, Nottingham, 1967.

      Troilus in *Troilus and Cressida* (Shakespeare), Old Vic Theatre, London.

      Romeo in *Romeo and Juliet* (Shakespeare), Old Vic Theatre, London; Winter Garden Theatre, New York, and US tour, 1956.

1956   Thersites in *Troilus and Cressida* (Shakespeare), Old Vic Theatre, London, Winter Garden Theatre, New York, and US tour.

1957–58   Hamlet in *Hamlet* (Shakespeare), Old Vic Theatre, London; US tour, 1958–59.

      Sir Andrew Aguecheek in *Twelfth Night* (Shakespeare), Old Vic Theatre, London; US tour, 1958–59.

1959   Victor Fabian in *Once More with Feeling* (Kurnitz), New Theatre, London.

      Nestor in *Irma La Douce* (Monnot, More, Heneker, and Norman), Lyric Theatre, London.

1960   Jacko in *The Naked Island* (Braddon), Arts Theatre, London.

1961   Macbeth in *Macbeth* (Shakespeare), Playhouse, Nottingham, and Malta; West African tour, 1963.

      Sir Thomas More in *A Man for All Seasons* (Bolt), Playhouse, Nottingham, and Malta.

      The Stranger in *The Lady from the Sea* (Ibsen), Queen's Theatre, London.

1962   Petruchio in *The Taming of the Shrew* (Shakespeare), Playhouse, Nottingham.

      Joseph Surface in *The School for Scandal* (Sheridan), Playhouse, Nottingham, and Haymarket Theatre, London.

      D'Artagnan in *The Three Musketeers* (Dumas père), Playhouse, Nottingham.

      Don Frederick in *The Chances* (Fletcher), Chichester Festival Theatre.

John Neville as Macbeth.

Orgilus in *The Broken Heart* (Ford), Chichester Festival Theatre.

1963   Coriolanus in *Coriolanus* (Shakespeare), Playhouse, Nottingham.

John Worthing in *The Importance of Being Earnest* (Wilde), Playhouse, Nottingham.

Alfie in *Alfie* (Naughton), Mermaid Theatre, London, and Duchess Theatre, London.

1964   Bernard Shaw in *Boots with Strawberry Jam* (Green and Dankworth), Playhouse, Nottingham.

Moricet in *The Birdwatcher*, Playhouse, Nottingham.

Oedipus in *Oedipus the King* (Sophocles), Playhouse, Nottingham.

1965   Corvino in *Volpone* (Jonson), Playhouse, Nottingham.

1966   Barry Field in *The Spies Are Singing*, Playhouse, Nottingham.

Faustus in *Doctor Faustus* (Marlowe), Playhouse, Nottingham.

1967   Willy Loman in *Death of a Salesman* (Miller), Playhouse, Nottingham.

Kolpakov and others in *Beware of the Dog* (Arout), Playhouse, Nottingham, and St Martin's Theatre, London.

1968   Henry Gow and Alec Harvey in *Mr and Mrs* (Coward), Palace Theatre, London.

1970   King Magnus in *The Apple Cart* (G. B. Shaw), Mermaid Theatre, London.

Garrick in *Boswell's Life of Johnson* (adapted from Boswell), Edinburgh Festival.

Benedick in *Much Ado About Nothing* (Shakespeare), Edinburgh Festival.

Humbert Humbert in *Lolita* (Nabokov), US tour.

1972   Macheath in *The Beggar's Opera* (Gay), Chichester Festival Theatre.

Sir Colenso Ridgeon in *The Doctor's Dilemma* (G. B. Shaw), Chichester Festival Theatre.

Prospero in *The Tempest* (Shakespeare), National Arts Centre Theatre, Ottawa.

Judge Brack in *Hedda Gabler* (Ibsen), Manitoba Theatre Centre, Winnipeg.

Higgins in *Pygmalion* (G. B. Shaw), Citadel Theatre, Edmonton, Alberta.

1975   Sherlock Holmes in *Sherlock Holmes* (Kelly, adapted from Doyle and Gillette), New York.

1977   Willy in *Happy Days* (Beckett), Citadel Theatre, Edmonton, Alberta, and National Theatre, London.

1982   Pastor Manders in *Ghosts* (Ibsen), New York and Washington, D.C.

1983   Don Armado in *Love's Labour's Lost* (Shakespeare), Festival Theatre, Stratford, Ontario.

1984   Shylock in *The Merchant of Venice* (Shakespeare), Festival Theatre, Stratford, Ontario.

1987   Chekhov in *Intimate Admiration*, Festival Theatre, Stratford, Ontario.

1988   Professor Henry Higgins in *My Fair Lady* (Loewe, Lerner, and Hart), Festival Theatre, Stratford, Ontario.

1990   Sir Peter Teazle in *The School for Scandal* (Sheridan), Royal National Theatre, London.

Other roles included: *Oh, Coward* (Coward), Citadel Theatre, Edmonton, Alberta, 1972; *Bethune* (Langley), Citadel Theatre, Edmonton, Alberta, 1972; *Staircase* (Dyer), Neptune Theatre, Halifax, Nova Scotia, 1978; *Dear Antoine*, Grand Theatre, London, Ontario, 1983; *Arsenic and Old Lace* (Kesselring), Grand Theatre, London, Ontario, 1983.

As director:

1960   *Henry V* (Shakespeare), Old Vic Theatre, London.

1962   *Twelfth Night* (Shakespeare), Playhouse, Nottingham.

A Subject of Scandal and Concern (Osborne), Playhouse, Nottingham.

1963   *The Importance of Being Earnest* (Wilde), Playhouse, Nottingham.

1964   *Memento Mori* (Spark), Playhouse, Nottingham.

The Mayor of Zalamea (Calderón), Playhouse, Nottingham.

Listen to the Knocking Bird, Playhouse, Nottingham.

1965   *Richard II* (Shakespeare), Playhouse, Nottingham.

Collapse of Stout Party, Playhouse, Nottingham.

Measure for Measure (Shakespeare), Playhouse, Nottingham.

1966	*Saint Joan* (G. B. Shaw), Playhouse, Nottingham.
	Moll Flanders (adapted from Defoe), Playhouse, Nottingham.
	Antony and Cleopatra (Shakespeare), Playhouse, Nottingham.
	Jack and the Beanstalk (pantomime), Playhouse, Nottingham.
1967	*Death of a Salesman* (Miller), Playhouse, Nottingham.
1969	*Honour and Offer* (Livings), Fortune Theatre, London.
1972	*The Rivals* (Sheridan), National Arts Centre Theatre, Ottawa.
	Romeo and Juliet (Shakespeare), Citadel Theatre, Edmonton, Alberta.
1978	*Les Canadiens* (Salutin), Neptune Theatre, Halifax, Nova Scotia.
	The Seagull (Chekhov), Neptune Theatre, Halifax, Nova Scotia.
1983	*Hamlet* (Shakespeare), Grand Theatre, London, Ontario.
1987	*The Three Sisters* (Chekhov), Festival Theatre, Stratford, Ontario.

Films

Oscar Wilde, 1960; *Mr Topaz*, 1961; *Billy Budd*, 1962; *The Unearthly Stranger*, 1964; *A Study in Terror*, 1966; *The Adventures of Gerrard*, 1970; *The Adventures of Baron Munchhausen*, 1989.

Television

Henry V, 1957; *Romeo and Juliet*, 1957; *Hamlet*, 1959; *The First Churchills* (series), 1969. Other productions included: *Grand* (series).

*

Bibliography

Books:
J. C. Trewin, *John Neville*, London, 1961.
Robert A. Gaines, *John Neville Takes Command*, Stratford, Ontario, 1987.

* * *

John Neville is a pre-eminent exponent of the ensemble. As an actor his performances are attuned to the needs of the productions; as a director he serves the play and its players; and as an artistic director his perception, integrity, and sound management have brought international recognition to the organisations he has led. Significantly, any statements Neville has made about his work have stressed the corporate nature of theatrical activity. In 1968 he wrote, of the Nottingham Playhouse's success under his directorship: "None of this could have been achieved without the company's talent, selfless dedication, strength, and versatility. We have always been essentially a team and naturally I include in that team the continually un-sung people like technicians, makers, builders, etc". 20 years later, welcoming audiences to the Stratford Festival, Ontario, he was quick "to pay tribute to this great acting ensemble". Neville firmly believes that the theatre's duty is "to serve ... as wide and varied a public as possible", a belief that has informed all aspects of his career.

Neville's professional debut in a speaking part was in Shakespearean roles at London's Open Air Theatre, and he has become a leading exponent of Shakespeare. Valentine, in *The Two Gentlemen of Verona*, a Bristol Old Vic production that transferred to London in 1952, first brought him wide recognition for the "ease and aristocracy", the "charm, good looks, poise, fluency and style", with which he played the chivalric lover. Despite successful forays into character parts while at Bristol, notably Gregers Werle in *The Wild Duck*, when Neville joined the London Old Vic he was mainly confined to playing personable young men. This brought him a devoted, sometimes over-demonstrative, fan club; however, this phenomenon signalled qualities that have distinguished Neville throughout his multi-faceted career: his capacity to inspire loyalty in colleagues and audiences and his rapport with and concern for the young. Many of today's eminent theatre practitioners owe their starts in the profession to Neville's discernment and encouragement.

During Neville's years with the Old Vic, the whole Shakespeare canon was produced; Neville's responsiveness to these plays is marked always by his respect for the verse, subtly uniting meaning with cadence, and his indication of the inner forces that prompt speech. He has returned to several plays more than once since then. A romantic Orsino in *Twelfth Night* was surpassed, later, by an Andrew Aguecheek of "rare simplicity", while in *Love's Labour's Lost* his "mocking then rueful" Berowne of 1954 was matched 30 years later by his grand but vulnerable Don Armado. He has successfully embodied Macduff and Macbeth, Benedict and Don Pedro in *Much Ado About Nothing*, Henry V and the Chorus, Troilus and Thersites, Ferdinand and Prospero in *The Tempest*, and, most strikingly, Othello and Iago. These last roles were alternated with Richard Burton at the Old Vic in 1955; at Nottingham in 1967 his Iago, now opposite Robert Ryan's Othello, matured into a chilling study of outwardly amiable malevolence. Neville will be particularly remembered for Richard II and Hamlet. He first played Richard in 1955, then in 1956–57 on the Old Vic's US and Canadian tour, and again at Nottingham in the mid-1960's, adding to the earlier youthful arrogance a stricken dignity that made affecting the king's declining fortunes. His Hamlet, performed several hundred times in London, Europe, and the USA, was romantic but never sentimental; a "sweet prince" who could fence dexterously with wit and rapier, was deeply disturbed but possessed the moral fibre to haul himself back from the brink of madness to do his duty. In contrast, and as evidence of his range, Neville, in these years, also created a flamboyant Pistol in *Henry IV, part 2*, a seedy Thersites in *Troilus and Cressida*, and, in *The Winter's Tale*, a barrow-boy Autolycus whose singing was infectious.

Neville has always enjoyed music — he played pantomime at Bristol and directed it at Nottingham, starred in London in the musical *Irma La Douce*, was a memorable singing and dancing Bernard Shaw in the Benny Green/John Dankworth *Boots with Strawberry Jam* at Nottingham, again in London played contrasting roles in a musical version of a Noël Coward double-bill, *Mr and Mrs*, was Macheath in *The Beggar's Opera* at the Chichester Festival, and Professor Henry Higgins in *My Fair Lady* at the Stratford Festival. In every organisation of which he has been artistic director, Neville has presented a gamut of late night and Sunday programmes of jazz, classical music, and readings. These attracted a public that had shunned conventional repertoires and encouraged them to return to sample more orthodox shows. By these means, and by promoting work specifically for the young, Neville has consistently built audiences. At Nottingham, for example, he championed the Playhouse having a pitch at the annual Goose Fair, and shuttled between playing Richard II in the theatre and doing comic turns in the fairground tent. Also, he has promoted new work. As an actor he secured the success of Russell Braddon's *Naked Island* and Bill Naughton's *Alfie*. Under his directorships plays by Giles Cooper, Richard Epp, Alan Sillitoe, Muriel Spark, Michel Tremblay, Peter Ustinov, and Charles Wood have received their first performances. He has given young actors and directors opportunities to stretch their talents through his staunch support of experimental productions. Examples of his commitment to enthusing the young include playing King Lear with a school group in Somerset in the early 1970's and leading the Stratford Festival Young Company in the early 1980's.

Proof of Neville's talent as an artistic director comes from statistics. In his five years at the Nottingham Playhouse attendance capacity averaged 85 per cent; his six-year directorship of the Citadel, Edmonton, Alberta saw the replacement of the 200-seat ex-Salvation Army meeting hall by a thriving three-auditorium theatre complex; Halifax, Nova Scotia, saw Neville's five-year leadership of the Neptune swell audience figures from 30 per cent to 90 per cent capacity, and as artistic director of the Stratford Festival he cleared a 4.5 million dollar deficit and handed to his successor a flourishing three-venue organisation and a healthy financial reserve. These achievements testify to Neville's artistic judgement and managerial skills, both inside and outside boardrooms. As a cultural ambassador he has led tours by British and Canadian companies throughout Europe, to the USA, to West Africa, and across Canada. Every community within which Neville has worked has been left artistically richer.

Threaded through all his administrative achievements is a rich vein of notable performances: the grey, defeated Willy Loman in *Death of a Salesman*, the sadly camp hairdresser in *Staircase*, an incisive Sherlock Holmes on Broadway, Pastor Manders opposite Liv Ulman in *Ghosts* in Washington and new York, the enigmatic Willy in *Happy Days* opposite Peggy Ashcroft first at Britain's National Theatre and then at the opening of the new Citadel, a dignified Shylock, a compassionate Chekhov in *Intimate Admiration*, and, in a welcome visit to the Royal National Theatre in 1990, Sir Peter Teazle in *The School for Scandal*. This performance was vintage Neville: precise in its placing within the production, elegant and original, leavening the old man's customary irascibility with a sense of humour that could be turned onto himself to reveal the charm that had won him a young wife. Likewise, his intelligence and style have been enjoyed in a variety of film and television roles, most recently in *The Adventures of Baron Munchhausen* and the series *Grand*. Neville is a true polymath of drama, notable, as he said of the Nottingham

company, for "talent, selfless dedication, strength and versatility".

—Raymond Ingram

NILSEN, Hans Jacob. Norwegian director and actor. Born in Fredrikstad, Norway, 8 November 1897. Trained as mechanical engineer, 1921. Stage debut, as an actor, Trondheim, 1922; actor, National Scene, Bergen, 1923–26, Centraltheater, Oslo, 1927–28, and Nationalteatret, Oslo, 1928–33; debut as director, 1932; director of the Norske Teatret, Oslo, 1933–34 and 1946–50, and of the Nationale Scene, Bergen, 1934–39; worked for the Free Norwegian Stage in Sweden during World War II, 1943–45; director, Folketeatret, Oslo, 1952–55; also acted in several films. Died in Oslo, 6 March 1957.

Productions

As actor:
1922   Nils Stensson in *Fru Inger til Østråt* [Lady Inger of Østraat] (Ibsen), tour.
1928   Falk in *Kjaerlighedens komedie* [Love's Comedy] (Ibsen), Centraltheater, Oslo.
1932   Darnley in *Maria Stuart i Skotland* (Bjørnson), Nationalteatret, Oslo.
         Valée in *Spillet om Kjaerlighten og døden* [The Game of Love and Death] (Rolland), Nationalteatret, Oslo.
1943–45 Hamlet in *Hamlet* (Shakespeare), Swedish tour; Nationalteatret, Oslo, and Kronborg Castle, 1946.
1952–55 Othello in *Othello* (Shakespeare), Folketeatret, Oslo.

Other roles included: Peer Gynt in *Peer Gynt* (Ibsen); Masterbuilder Solness in *Bygmester Solness* [The Master Builder] (Ibsen).

As director:
1932   *Reisen Slutt* [Journey's End] (Sherriff), Nationalteatret, Oslo.
1934   *Jeppe på Bierget* [Jeppe of the Hill] (Holberg), Nationalteatret, Oslo.
1934–39 *Brøl Kina* [Roar, China!] (Tretyakov), National Scene, Bergen.
         Lucretias død [The Death of Lucretia] (Obey), National Scene, Bergen.
         Over Aevne II [Beyond Our Power] (Bjørnson), National Scene, Bergen.
1935   *Vår aere og vår makt* [Our Power and Our Glory] (Grieg), National Scene, Bergen.
1936   *Men imorgen* [But Tomorrow] (Grieg), Nationale Scene, Bergen.
1937   *Nederlaget* [The Defeat] (Grieg), Nationalteatret, Oslo.
1939   *Insektliv* [The Insect Play] (Čapek), National Scene, Bergen.
1946–50 *Guds grønne enger* [Green Pastures] (Connelly), Norske Teatret, Oslo.

1948   *Den Galne frå Chaillot* [The Mad Woman of Chaillot] (Giraudoux), Norske Teatret, Oslo.
1948   *Peer Gynt* (Ibsen), Norske Teatret, Oslo.
1952–55 *Brand* (Ibsen), Folketeatret, Oslo.
        Hennes hemmelige våpen [The Road to Rome] (S. Anderson), Folketeatret, Oslo.
        Othello (Shakespeare), Folketeatret, Oslo.

Films

As actor:
Syndere i sommersol [The Sinner and the Summer Sun], 1933; *To levende og en död* [Two Lives and a Death], 1937.

As actor and director:
De svarte hestane [The Black Horses].

* * *

Hans Jacob Nilsen began as an actor, touring in Ibsen's *Lady Inger of Østraat* under the leadership of Agnes Mowinckel, one of Norway's most distinguished directors. His breakthrough as an actor came with an intelligent and sensitive interpretation of Falk in Ibsen's *Love's Comedy* in 1928. Between 1928 and 1933 he was a member of the Oslo National Theatre, appearing mainly in modern plays; the company also gave him the opportunity to direct R. C. Sherriff's *Journey's End*, which was a great success.

In 1934 Nilsen was made artistic director of the Bergen National Theatre, which he remained in charge of until 1939. In this position he was able to demonstrate his considerable artistry, as a director as well as an actor. His leadership of the Bergen National Theatre left its mark on the company to a degree unparalleled in its history.

Nilsen's time in Bergen coincided with the Nazi era in Germany, marked by the persecution of Jews as well as by Germany's rearmament and military aggression. Well versed in the trends of contemporary theatre, particularly the experimental ideas of German and Soviet theatre, Nilsen had spent a period in Moscow and had also visited several major theatre centres in Europe before he took up the leadership of the Bergen company. This background was bound to influence his work in Bergen. His artistic programme was to reflect the political situation of the moment. Expecting a new great war to break out, he felt that the theatre ought to be a battlefield for the ideas of the time. Part of his chosen repertoire could be described as political theatre, produced in a new style, influenced by what was happening on the stages in central and eastern Europe.

The engagement of the Swedish designer Per Schwab established a link with the Expressionist theatre of Sweden. Nilsen also had the Swedish writer Pär Lagerkvist's *The Hangman* adapted for the stage and premiered in Bergen in a production directed by Per Lindberg. A quotation from a contemporary review is characteristic of Nilsen's ideas: "The theatre must never be dusty and drowsy, like a Turkish garden. It should always take up contemporary problems, ask questions, give something positive".

Nilsen himself directed the world premiere of Nordahl Grieg's *Our Power and Our Glory* in 1935, a production that caused an outcry in Bergen because it openly criticised shipowners for their uninhibited speculation during World War I. The 14 scenes were linked together in a way that secured a maximum of propaganda effect. This was the first realisation in Norway of the epic and documentary type of propaganda theatre, as it was known in the Soviet Union and in the Germany of the Weimar Republic. More than any other single production this event gave Nilsen and Grieg a central position in Norwegian theatre history, its importance probably enhanced by the break with the dominating Norwegian Ibsen tradition.

Only a small part of Nilsen's repertoire may be classified as 'propaganda', or is described as such by conservatives. He presented a series of important Norwegian and international plays, attaching particular significance to the creation of new Norwegian plays. Still, he saw it as a major aim for his theatre to warn people against the dangers of the world situation. In addition, he wanted to draw new social groups to the theatre, trying to remove social barriers in the auditorium.

During the German occupation of Norway, Nilsen was a member of the Free Stage in Sweden. As artistic director of Oslo's Norwegian Theatre from 1946 to 1950, he created a sensation with his 'anti-Romantic' version of *Peer Gynt* (1948), in which he replaced Edvard Grieg's incidental music with new music by Harald Saeverud. In 1952 he took over the leadership of the newly established Folk Theatre in Oslo, where his last notable productions included Ibsen's *Brand*.

—Kirsten Broch

———————

NOBLE, Adrian Keith. British director. Born in Chichester, West Sussex, 19 July 1950. Educated at Chichester High School for Boys and University of Bristol; trained for the stage at the Drama Centre, London. Began career working for two years in community and young people's theatre, Birmingham; Associate director, Bristol Old Vic, 1976–79; guest director, Royal Exchange Theatre, Manchester, 1980–81; resident director, Royal Shakespeare Company, 1980–82; associate director, Royal Shakespeare Company, 1982–87; artistic director, Royal Shakespeare Company season at Stratford-upon-Avon, 1988; artistic director, Royal Shakespeare Company season at the Barbican, London, 1989; worked as a freelance director on both sides of the Atlantic, 1990; artistic director, Royal Shakespeare Company, since 1991. Recipient: *Plays and Players* Award, 1980; *Drama* Award, 1980, 1981.

Productions

1977   *Ubu Rex* (Jarry), Old Vic Theatre, Bristol.
        Man Is Man (Brecht), Old Vic Theatre, Bristol.
1978   *The Changeling* (Middleton), Old Vic Theatre, Bristol.
        A View from the Bridge (Miller), Old Vic Theatre, Bristol.
        Titus Andronicus (Shakespeare), Old Vic Theatre, Bristol.
1979   *Timon of Athens* (Shakespeare), Old Vic Theatre, Bristol.

Love for Love (Congreve), Old Vic Theatre, Bristol.

The Recruiting Officer (Farquhar), Edinburgh.

1980   *The Duchess of Malfi* (Webster), Royal Exchange Theatre, Manchester, and Round House, London.

Dr Faustus (Noble), Royal Exchange Theatre, Manchester.

The Forest (Ostrovsky), Other Place Theatre, Stratford-upon-Avon.

1981   *A Doll's House* (Ibsen), Royal Exchange Theatre, Manchester, and Round House, London.

1982   *King Lear* (Shakespeare), Royal Shakespeare Theatre, Stratford-upon-Avon and Barbican Theatre, London.

1983   *The Comedy of Errors* (Shakespeare), Royal Shakespeare Theatre, Stratford-upon-Avon.

Measure for Measure (Shakespeare), Royal Shakespeare Theatre, Stratford-upon-Avon; Barbican Theatre, London, 1984.

Henry V (Shakespeare), Royal Shakespeare Theatre, Stratford-upon-Avon; Barbican, 1984.

Antony and Cleopatra (Shakespeare), Barbican Pit, London.

1984   *A New Way to Pay Old Debts* (Massinger), Barbican Theatre, London.

The Winter's Tale (Shakespeare), Royal Shakespeare Theatre, Stratford-upon-Avon.

Desert Air (Wright), Other Place, Stratford-upon-Avon, and Barbican Pit, London.

1985   *As You Like It* (Shakespeare), Royal Shakespeare Theatre, Stratford-upon-Avon.

1986   *Macbeth* (Shakespeare), Royal Shakespeare Theatre, Stratford-upon-Avon; Barbican Theatre, London, 1987.

Mephisto (Wertenbaker, adapted from Mnouchkine), Barbican Theatre, London.

1987   *The Art of Success* (Dear), Barbican Pit, London; New York, 1990.

Kiss Me, Kate (Porter and Spewack, adapted from Shakespeare's *The Taming of the Shrew*), British tour.

1988   *The Plantagenets* (Wood, adapted from Shakespeare *Henry VI, parts 1, 2 and 3* and *Richard III*), Royal Shakespeare Theatre, Stratford-upon-Avon; Barbican Theatre, London, 1989.

1989   *Macbeth* (Shakespeare), Barbican Theatre, London.

The Master Builder (Ibsen), Barbican Theatre, London.

The Fairy Queen (Purcell), Aix-en-Provence Festival.

1990   *The Three Sisters* (Chekhov), Gate Theatre, Dublin, and Royal Court Theatre, London.

1991   *Henry IV, Parts 1 and 2* (Shakespeare), Royal Shakespeare Theatre, Stratford-upon-Avon; Barbican Theatre, London, 1992.

The Thebans (Sophocles, translated by Wertenbaker), Swan Theatre, Stratford-upon-Avon; Barbican Theatre, London, 1992.

1992   *Hamlet* (Shakespeare), Barbican Theatre, London; Royal Shakespeare Theatre, Stratford-upon-Avon, 1993.

The Winter's Tale (Shakespeare), Royal Shakespeare Theatre, Stratford-upon-Avon; Barbican Theatre, London, 1993.

1993   *King Lear* (Shakespeare), Royal Shakespeare Theatre, Stratford-upon-Avon.

Travesties (Stoppard), Barbican Theatre, London.

Macbeth (Shakespeare), Barbican Theatre, London; Royal Shakespeare Theatre, Stratford-upon-Avon, 1994.

1994   *A Midsummer Night's Dream* (Shakespeare), Royal Shakespeare Theatre, Stratford-upon-Avon.

* * *

Adrian Noble trained at the London Drama Centre and worked in Birmingham before moving to the Bristol Old Vic as resident director with a Thames Television Director's Bursary in 1976. At Bristol he worked on over a dozen productions ranging from Elizabethan standards like *Timon of Athens* and *The Changeling* to modern classics as disparate as Jarry's *Ubu Rex* and Brecht's *Man Is Man*. His breakthrough came with the award-winning production of Webster's *The Duchess of Malfi* at the Manchester Royal Exchange, with Bob Hoskins and Helen Mirren. He made his debut as a director with the Royal Shakespeare Company with Ostrovsky's *The Forest*, which brought him a second *Drama* Award, for best revival of 1981. He stayed at the RSC as an associate director until 1987, establishing a reputation as one of the leading directors of his generation with a string of productions again mixing respected classics with important modern works.

Noble's interest in the theatre dates from his childhood in Chichester, where his enthusiasm was fired by the Festival there, which at that time under Laurence Olivier was an annual rehearsal for the National Theatre that was to come. The Festival introduced him to an international repertoire presented by distinguished company playing close to the audience on an apron stage. One is tempted to see the mark of Chichester in Noble's own style. For him the actors energize the stage space, they give shape to the words and are shaped by them, and it is the director's job to unlock their creativity. So he casts his plays with great care and then builds on what the actors offer him, always on his feet during rehearsals, like a rowing coach feeding in energy and coaxing further efforts from his performers. His is a pragmatic approach, like his RSC predecessors Peter Hall and Trevor Nunn's, and he is not primarily concerned with concepts or with leaving his signature on the play or the production. The show's the thing and the lasting impression he wants the audience to take away is that the production was effective, not that it was an Adrian Noble production.

Noble now mainly directs Shakespeare, whom he modernizes not by imposing a message or style but by forming an idea of what aspects of the play work best for modern audiences and then working them out on a trial and error basis with his actors. His idea of the play sometimes crystallizes in the design: his 1982 *King Lear* opened with a high-walled courtyard into which the commoners peered from small upper windows, an autocrat's court from which the people are excluded, while Justice Shallow's entrance with a beekeeper's net over his head instantly conjured up a vision of rural England in *Henry IV* (1991). Noble likes simple, striking images and bold colours; in *The Plantagenets* (1988) colourful banners were used as iconic splashes of colour to indicate the historical milieu. His productions are uncluttered and often strikingly beautiful. They seem to start from an image, frequently derived from a hunch, which is translated in close collaboration with congenial designers, particularly Bob Crowley, into a visual framework for the play. The design incorporates the spirit, the moral overview, the 'dream' of the play. He is not a naturalistic director. The towering wall of levels, stairs, open rooms, windows and expanses of red cloth for the Eastcheap scenes in *Henry IV*, which attracted much critical approval, was not an architectural space at all, but a bawdy, sensual theatrical space, the feel of a tavern without the actual tavern. He sees making Shakespeare work for big audiences as the main challenge at the RSC, in contrast to, say, Trevor Nunn, whose favourite *Macbeth* of the three he did at the RSC was at the Other Place, which he used as an intimate laboratory to get to the heart of the play. Adrian Noble averages five major productions a year on the main stages at Stratford and the Barbican. Outstanding in the long list are *Hamlet* (1992), with Kenneth Branagh, Sophocles's *The Thebans* (1992), *King Lear* (1993), with Robert Stephens, and *A Midsummer Night's Dream* (1994).

Peter Hall's idea when he founded the RSC in 1962 was that a leavening of modern plays in the repertoire would fertilize contemporary versions of Shakespeare. 30 years later that balanced repertoire had shifted via the magical dramatization of *Nicholas Nickleby* to co-productions of musicals with Cameron Mackintosh. The company was being forced to compete in the marketplace, not least with the National Theatre, which had been founded in the interim with a brief not unlike Hall's concept. The RSC needed to redefine its image. Adrian Noble has turned the company round and attracted sponsorship by taking advice from admen and capitalizing on the company's main asset, Shakespeare. At the same time, he has put verse speaking back at the centre, for example by restoring John Barton's sonnet classes, has broadened the choice of plays in the Swan Theatre and has revitalized the RSC's national and international touring. He combines pragmatic theatricality with theatrical pragmatism. As well as directing five productions a year, each with six weeks rehearsal, he successfully runs the largest theatrical group in the country, offering 35 performances on five stages most weeks of the year.

—Hugh Rorrison

NUNN, Trevor Robert. British director. Born in Ipswich, Suffolk, 14 January 1940. Educated at Northgate Grammar School for Boys, Ipswich; Downing College, University of Cambridge, 1959–62. Married 1) actress Janet Suzman in 1969; 2) Sharon Lee Hill in 1986; 3) actress Imogen Stubbs in 1994; one son and two daughters. Debut as director, with Marlowe Society, Cambridge, 1959–62; director, Belgrade Theatre, Coventry, 1962–65; associate director, Royal Shakespeare Company, 1966–68; artistic director,

Royal Shakespeare Company, 1968–78; chief executive and joint artistic director, with Terry Hands, Royal Shakespeare Company, 1978–86; chief executive and director emeritus, Royal Shakespeare Company, since 1986. Recipient: London Theatre Critics Award, 1966, 1969; Society of Film and Television Arts, 1976; Sydney Edwards Award, 1977–78; *Evening Standard* Award, 1982, 1991; *Drama* Award, 1982; Tony Award, 1982; New York Drama Critics Circle Award, 1982; Society of West End Theatre Award, 1982. Litt.D: University of Warwick, 1982; M.A., University of Newcastle-upon-Tyne. CBE (Commander of the British Empire), 1978.

Productions

1962–65	*The Caucasian Chalk Circle* (Brecht), Belgrade Theatre, Coventry.
	A View from the Bridge (Miller), Belgrade Theatre, Coventry.
	Peer Gynt (Ibsen), Belgrade Theatre, Coventry.
1965	*Henry V* (Shakespeare), Aldwych Theatre, London.
	The Thwarting of Baron Bolligrew (Bolt), Aldwych Theatre, London.
1966	*Henry IV, parts 1 and 2* (Shakespeare), Royal Shakespeare Theatre, Stratford-upon-Avon.
	The Revenger's Tragedy (Tourneur), Royal Shakespeare Theatre, Stratford-upon-Avon.
	Tango (Stoppard), Aldwych Theatre, London.
1967	*The Taming of the Shrew* (Shakespeare), Royal Shakespeare Theatre, Stratford-upon-Avon.
	The Relapse (Vanbrugh), Aldwych Theatre, London.
1968	*King Lear* (Shakespeare), Royal Shakespeare Theatre, Stratford-upon-Avon.
	Much Ado About Nothing (Shakespeare), Royal Shakespeare Theatre, Stratford-upon-Avon, and Aldwych Theatre, London.
1969	*The Winter's Tale* (Shakespeare), Royal Shakespeare Theatre, Stratford-upon-Avon, and Aldwych Theatre, London.
	Henry VIII (Shakespeare), Royal Shakespeare Theatre, Stratford-upon-Avon.
1970	*Hamlet* (Shakespeare), Royal Shakespeare Theatre, Stratford-upon-Avon.
1972	*The Romans* (Shakespeare cycle), Royal Shakespeare Theatre, Stratford-upon-Avon; Aldwych Theatre, London, 1973.
1974	*Macbeth* (Shakespeare), Royal Shakespeare Theatre, Stratford-upon-Avon, and Aldwych Theatre, London.
	Antony and Cleopatra (Shakespeare), Royal Shakespeare Theatre, Stratford-upon-Avon, and Aldwych Theatre, London.
1975	*Hedda Gabler* (Ibsen), Aldwych Theatre, London.
1976	*Romeo and Juliet* (Shakespeare), Royal Shakespeare Theatre, Stratford-upon-Avon.
	The Winter's Tale (Shakespeare), Royal Shakespeare Theatre, Stratford-upon-Avon.
	The Comedy of Errors (Shakespeare), Royal Shakespeare Theatre, Stratford-upon-Avon, and Aldwych Theatre, London.

King Lear (Shakespeare), Royal Shakespeare Theatre, Stratford-upon-Avon, and Aldwych Theatre, London.
Macbeth (Shakespeare), Other Place Theatre, Stratford-upon-Avon, and Aldwych Theatre, London.

1977 *The Alchemist* (Jonson), Other Place Theatre, Stratford-upon-Avon, and Aldwych Theatre, London.
As You Like It (Shakespeare), Royal Shakespeare Theatre, Stratford-upon-Avon, and Aldwych Theatre, London.
Every Good Boy Deserves Favour (Stoppard), Royal Festival Hall, London.

1978 *The Three Sisters* (Chekhov), Aldwych Theatre, London.

1979 *The Merry Wives of Windsor* (Shakespeare), Royal Shakespeare Theatre, Stratford-upon-Avon, and Aldwych Theatre, London.
Once in a Lifetime (Kaufman and Hart), Aldwych Theatre, London; Piccadilly Theatre, London, 1980.

1980 *The Life and Times of Nicholas Nickleby* (Edgar, adapted from Dickens), Aldwych Theatre, London; Plymouth Theatre, New York, 1981.
Juno and the Paycock (O'Casey), Aldwych Theatre, London.

1981 *All's Well That Ends Well* (Shakespeare), Royal Shakespeare Theatre, Stratford-upon-Avon; Martin Beck Theatre, New York, 1982.
Cats (Lloyd Webber, adapted from Eliot), New London Theatre, London; Winter Garden Theatre, New York, 1982.
Henry IV, parts 1 and 2 (Shakespeare), Royal Shakespeare Theatre, Stratford-upon-Avon; Aldwych Theatre, London, 1982.

1982 *Peter Pan* (Barrie), Barbican Theatre, London.
Idomeneo (Mozart), Festival Opera, Glyndebourne.

1984 *Starlight Express* (Lloyd Webber), Apollo Victoria Theatre, London.

1985 *Les Misérables* (adapted from Hugo), Palace Theatre, London; Washington, D.C., New York, and Sydney, Australia, 1987.
The Life and Times of Nicholas Nickleby (Edgar, adapted from Dickens), Royal Shakespeare Theatre, Stratford-upon-Avon.

1986 *Fair Maid of the West* (Heywood), Swan Theatre, Stratford-upon-Avon.
Chess (Rice), Prince Edward Theatre, London; New York, 1988.
Porgy and Bess (Gershwin), Festival Opera, Glyndebourne; revived there, 1987.

1987 *Starlight Express* (Lloyd Webber), New York.
1989 *Othello* (Shakespeare), Other Place Theatre, Stratford-upon-Avon.
Aspects of Love (Lloyd Webber), Prince of Wales Theatre, London; New York, 1990.
The Baker's Wife (Stein and Schwartz), Phoenix Theatre, London.

1990 *Timon of Athens* (Shakespeare), Young Vic Theatre, London.

1991 *The Blue Angel* (Gems), Other Place Theatre, Stratford-upon-Avon.
Measure for Measure (Shakespeare), Other Place Theatre, Stratford-upon-Avon.
1992 *Heartbreak House* (G. B. Shaw), Haymarket Theatre, London.
1993 *Sunset Boulevard* (Lloyd Webber, Hampton and Black), Adelphi Theatre, London.
Arcadia (Stoppard), National Theatre, London.

Films

Hedda Gabler, 1975; *Lady Jane*, 1985.

Television

Antony and Cleopatra, 1974; *The Comedy of Errors*, 1976; *Every Good Boy Deserves Favour*, 1978; *Macbeth*, 1978; *The Three Sisters*, 1978; *Shakespeare Workshops Word of Mouth*, 1979; *Othello*, 1990; *Great Hamlets*, 1983.

Publications

Hedda Gabler (play adaptation), 1975.

* * *

In 1968, at the age of 29, Trevor Nunn succeeded Peter Hall as artistic director of the Royal Shakespeare Company, becoming the youngest-ever artistic director of a major British theatre company. He and Hall have been the dominant influences on the shape of British theatre since the 1960's, Nunn having run the RSC during the period when it achieved international recognition as "the greatest theatre company in the world" and having himself directed two of its four greatest triumphs, *Macbeth* (1976) and the nine-hour two-part *Nicholas Nickleby* (1980). The success of *Nickleby* launched him on an equally illustrious career as director of large-scale musicals, which include *Cats, Starlight Express, Les Misérables, Aspects of Love* and *Sunset Boulevard*. Under his direction, the RSC consolidated and expanded its activities as a major cultural institution by moving from its London base at the Aldwych Theatre to a specially designed home at the Barbican Centre and by the construction within the existing Shakespeare Memorial Theatre building, of the Swan Theatre, conceived by Nunn as a modern version of an Elizabethan public playhouse to provide an appropriate venue for experiments in staging plays written between 1570 and 1750.

Nunn has no recognisable signature as a director; his approach is governed by a scrupulous respect for any text that he would regard as complex and sophisticated rather than dictated by his own individual aesthetic. His work usually expresses a vaguely left-wing point of view, though he has never been a consciously political director in the style of Brecht or Piscator. Working to produce a dramatic experience that is realised in vividly sensuous terms, he aims to celebrate humane and progressive values rather than to politicise an audience in a radical way. While his work is vividly theatrical, his stylistic approach is extremely eclectic. Unlike his mentors at the RSC, John Barton and Peter Hall, who tend to limit the visual dimension of their productions in order to concentrate attention on the complex language of a classic text, Nunn has, from the time of his first production at the RSC, *The Revenger's Tragedy* (1966), sought to exploit the possibilities of visual staging in order to theatricalise fully the world of a play inherent in its written text.

Although his amazingly successful commercial production of Andrew Lloyd Webber's *Cats*, based on poems by T. S. Eliot, made him an international superstar, a showman who could be relied on to conjure up theatrical spectacle in the form of juggernaut productions that are replicated in every major city of the world, he has at regular intervals returned to the 'serious' theatre to direct small-scale productions of Shakespeare (*Othello* in 1989 and *Timon of Athens* in 1990), operas (*Idomeneo, Porgy and Bess, Cosi Fan Tutte*) and prestige productions of literary plays (Shaw's *Heartbreak House* in 1992 and Stoppard's *Arcadia* in 1993), which have received great critical acclaim. His great commercial successes as a director paved the way for a rapprochement between 'popular' and 'serious' theatre, which, under the Thatcher government of the 1980's, moved a little closer together, popular musicals becoming more serious in their artistic aims and subsidised productions of the classics being more intent on having popular appeal.

A kind of English Max Reinhardt, Nunn uses stylisation adventurously, nevertheless allowing the text of a play itself to dictate his approach to its performance. Without sacrificing much of Shakespeare's text, he turned *The Comedy of Errors* (1976) into a musical set in a modern tourist town on a Greek island, while in the same year he directed a sparsely furnished chamber production of *Macbeth* whose intense theatricality derived from its very avoidance of overt spectacle. Lit in shafts of light and shadow with the actors sitting on wooden boxes surrounding the action, the production focussed on relationships between characters staged in the theatrical equivalent of film close-ups.

His unique ability to give productions of the classics the celebratory quality of the best popular theatre was as much in evidence in his stylish production of Kaufman and Hart's satire on Hollywood's treatment of screen writers, *Once in a Lifetime* (1979), with its triumphant ten-minute finale in which a superb cast of classical actors tap-danced their way through a rousing production number, as in his revival at the Swan of Thomas Heywood's neglected *The Fair Maid of the West* (1986), which used a combination of farce and pantomime techniques to evoke the picaresque qualities of Elizabethan romance. It is Nunn's production of *Nicholas Nickleby* that must rank alongside *The Wars of the Roses* (1963) and Brook's *A Midsummer Night's Dream* (1970) as the RSC's most celebrated and innovatory productions. With playwright David Edgar and his co-director John Caird, Nunn devised a form of epic staging to express the picturesque theatricality of Dickens's narrative imagination. Renowned for the tactful way in which he engenders an atmosphere of collaboration in his productions, Nunn managed on this occasion to create an ensemble piece that made no attempt to pretend that it was a stage play. Large sections of the text were narrated by the cast, perched on an intricate web of wooden galleries, bridges and ramps that evoked an environment reminiscent of both a Victorian warehouse or a makeshift theatre in which Vincent Crummles would be likely to appear, its profusion of ropes, theatrical prop baskets and small sliding platforms enabling the panorama of locations to unfold with a minimum of technology. The conscious 'acting-out' of the story became a celebration of the event of theatre, the crippled Smike (hauntingly portrayed by David Threlfall) becoming a powerful symbol to connect the injustices of Victorian England with the inequalities of Thatcher's Britain.

Les Misérables (1985), adapted from Victor Hugo's novel and mounted as a collaboration between the RSC and the commercial producer Cameron Mackintosh, was an attempt to rework the *Nickleby* formula (sentimental presentation of a picaresque melodrama of social protest) utilising the popular format of the rock opera as developed by Tim Rice and Andrew Lloyd Webber to produce what may well be both the most commercially successful and most sophisticated example of the genre.

—Robert Gordon

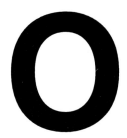

OKHLOPKOV, Nikolai (Pavlovich). Soviet director and actor. Born in Irkutsk, Siberia, 15 May 1900. Educated at the Irkutsk Gymnasium; trained for the stage at the Meyerhold State Theatrical Workshop, Moscow, 1922–23. Married Elena Zotova. Stage debut, as an actor, Irkutsk Municipal Theatre, 1918; acted and studied under Vsevolod Meyerhold at the Meyerhold Theatre, 1923–27; film debut, 1924; artistic director, Realistic Theatre, Moscow, 1930–37; director and actor, Vakhtangov Theatre, Moscow, 1938–43; chief director, Moscow Drama Theatre (renamed the Mayakovsky Moscow Theatre, 1954), 1943–66; toured Poland and Czechoslovakia, 1949; attended International Shakespeare Conference, Stratford-upon-Avon, 1955; also taught as professor at the A. V. Lunacharsky State Institute of Theatrical Arts. Member: CPSU, from 1952. Recipient: State Prize of the USSR, 1941, 1947, 1949 (twice), 1951 (twice); Order of Lenin. People's Artist of the USSR, 1948. Died in Moscow, 8 January 1967.

Principal productions

As director:
1921   *The Struggle Between Labour and Capital* (pageant), Irkutsk.
1923   *Misteriya-Buff* [Mystery-Bouffe] (Mayakovsky), Youth Theatre, Irkutsk.
1932   *A Running Start* (Stavsky), Realistic Theatre, Moscow.
1933   *Mat* [The Mother] (Gorky), Realistic Theatre, Moscow.
        The Iron Flood (adapted from Serafimovich), Realistic Theatre, Moscow.
1934   *Othello* (Shakespeare), Realistic Theatre, Moscow.
1935   *Aristocratici* [The Aristocrats] (Pogodin), Realistic Theatre, Moscow.
        Colas Breugnon (Rolland), Realistic Theatre, Moscow.
1940   *Kutuzov* (Soloviev), Vakhtangov Theatre, Moscow.
1942   *Cyrano de Bergerac* (Rostand), Vakhtangov Theatre, Moscow.
1947   *The Young Guard* (adapted from Fadeyev), Mayakovsky Theatre, Moscow.
1947–54 *Zakon chesti* [The Law of Honour] (Shteyn), Mayakovsky Theatre, Moscow, and Polish and Czech tour.
1949   *Momentous Days* (Virta), Polish and Czech tour.

The Young Guard (Fedeyev), Polish and Czech tour.
The Dog in the Manger (Vega Carpio), Polish and Czech tour.
1950   *Young Guard* (Meitus), Small Opera House, Leningrad.
1952   *Dekabristy* [The Decembrists] (Shaporin), Bolshoi Theatre, Moscow.
1954   *Hamlet* (Shakespeare), Mayakovsky Theatre, Moscow.
1955   *Groza* [The Storm] (Ostrovsky), Mayakovsky Theatre, Moscow.
1956   *Hotel Astoria* (Shteyn), Mayakovsky Theatre, Moscow.
1957   *Mat* [Mother] (Khrennikov), Bolshoi Theatre, Moscow;
1960   *Irkutskaya istoriya* [Irkutsk Story] (Arbuzov), Mayakovsky Theatre, Moscow.
1961   *Medea* (Euripides), Mayakovsky Theatre, Moscow.

Roles as actor included: General Berkovets in *Teacher Bubus* (Faiko); Prince Calaf in *Princess Turandot* (Gozzi); Golub in *Tsar Fyodor Ioannovich* (A. Tolstoy); Kachala in *Smert Tarelkina* [Tarelkin's Death] (Sukhovo-Kobylin); Old Chinese Man in *Rychi Kitai!* [Roar, China!] (Tretyakov).

Films

As actor:
Mitya, 1926; *Alexander Nevsky*, 1938; *Lenin in October*, 1938; *Kutuzov*, 1944; *The Story of a Real Man*, 1949; *Far From Moscow*; *Lenin in 1918*.

Publications

Vsem molodym, 1981.

*

Bibliography

Books:
Nick Worrall, *Modernism to Realism on the Soviet Stage: Tairov — Vakhtangov — Okhlopkov*, Cambridge, 1989.

* * *

563

A scene from a production of *Hamlet,* directed by **Nikolai Okhlopkov** (1954).

Nikolai Okhlopkov's major contribution to Soviet theatre practice dates from the 1930's, rather than the 1920's, but the effect of the revolutionary period on the mental outlook of a young man who was 17 years old in 1917 was permanent and iradicable. Compared with his great counterparts — Stanislavsky, Vakhtangov, Meyerhold, Tairov — all of whom were born in the 19th century, Okhlopkov was quintessentially a 20th-century man, born into a world on the brink of epic events to which his consciousness was uniquely attuned. Okhlopkov was always interested in theatre on an epic scale; his dream was to resurrect a Soviet equivalent of the dramatic festivals of fifth century Athens, to rival open-air performances like those of the medieval mystery plays, or the festivals staged by Leonardo da Vinci with their giant floats, some depicting models of the universe. He wanted a theatre of communal passions that could speak in a universal language to thousands simultaneously. Although Okhlopkov's experiments were restricted to the limits of the small Realistic Theatre, during the 1930's, it was here that foreign visitors such as Bertolt Brecht recorded a sense of authentic theatricality and here that the US director Norris Houghton experienced an excitement unlike any other he had felt in the theatre.

There is little doubt that the greatest claim to be considered the true heir of Meyerhold belongs to Nikolai Okhlopkov. Like his teacher, he was a genuine 'Renaissance man' of the performing arts — an outstanding actor and director who worked successfully in both theatre and film. In no one else did Meyerhold's own universal genius show itself more distinctly than in Okhlopkov. However, it is important to stress that Okhlopkov was no pale imitation of Meyerhold, but someone who made his own unique contribution to the history of Soviet theatre. His uniqueness stems from a deeply rooted Russianness — a quality that speaks through Okhlopkov's productions in ways that cannot be found in the work of other great directors. When Eisenstein was looking to cast the role of Vassily Buslay, the thatch-haired peasant who personifies the epic scale of the Russian spirit, its optimistic boldness in the face of mighty odds (in his film *Alexander Nevsky*), it seemed almost automatic for him to cast Okhlopkov in the role. Okhlopkov *was* larger than life and his vision corresponded to this. He possessed what one critic has described as "telescopic eyes", gigantically intensified vision that enlarged subjects a hundredfold. The singular moments of an Okhlopkov production are those where the grand emotion and the grand gesture are gathered up into an instant of intensity that is both intimate and universal, as if the feeling generated in small scale psychological theatre were raised to the power of 'x' and transferred to a vast amphitheatre, causing thousands to respond with sympathy, even to the point of tears.

Whilst acknowledging a debt to both Meyerhold and Stanislavsky, Okhlopkov did not work according to any particular system. He appeared to master the laws of the stage intuitively and his working methods were uneven, chaotic and tempestuous. He could construct an entire dramatic action in his mind rather than on paper as he seemed uniquely capable of conceiving ideas in images. He loved the art of mise-en-scène like an artist loves colour or a musician loves melody. His theatrical credo can be summarised as 'a passionate love of life', which he learned from his favourite poets — Mayakovsky and Walt Whitman. There is a strongly pantheistic element in his work and a desire, which he shared with Stanislavsky, to restore the word 'nature' to 'human nature', to achieve an organic merging of mind and body, heart and head — a unity of being in the actor, an integral unity in the work of art that was itself a microcosm of the new, communal, post-revolutionary society. It was for this reason that he sought an appropriate form in the mass spectacle. The atmosphere he was seeking could not be found in enclosed buildings, but only on the streets and open platforms. It is ironic, therefore, that only on one occasion did Okhlopkov work under the ideal conditions of which he dreamed all his life when, as a raw youth of 21, he staged a mass spectacle in his home town of Irkutsk.

What appears consistently clear from his work is its ideological commitment. Okhlopkov may be said to have taken up the theme of commitment at a point where that of others was becoming more faint, under pressure from the political and artistic demands being imposed during the 1930's. Okhlopkov chose to celebrate collectivisation, industrialisation and the Bolshevik cause in such productions as *Running Start, Mother, The Iron Flood* and *Aristocrats*, which also sought to redefine the relationship between the play and the audience. Collaborating with Yakov Shtoffer, Okhlopkov reorganised and reformulated notions of theatrical space to accord with the needs of each production. Ironically, the official response to his work was to accuse him of 'formalist' excesses and, finally, to remove him from the artistic leadership of the Realistic Theatre. This might have been understandable had the productions contained any implicit criticism of Party policy — if, for example, the production of *Aristocrats*, a play which deals with the rehabilitation of convicts constructing the White Sea Canal, had contained any suggestion that the action took place in a labour camp that was part of the 'gulag' network. Similarly, it seems clear that the production of *Running Start* was an unambiguously idealised representation of the collectivisation process and contained no suggestion that Okhlopkov might have been aware of the real nature of what was taking place.

Okhlopkov's sense of bitter dismay must, therefore, have been all the more intense when the true facts about the regime he celebrated were promulgated in the mid-1950's. In his production of *The Young Guard*, in 1947, Stalin and the Communist cause had been portrayed as virtually synonymous in the struggle to defeat fascism. However, already by 1954, when Okhlopkov staged *Hamlet*, it was apparent from what he had to say about the work and from the way in which, in Ryndin's cellular setting, Denmark was depicted as a prison, that this was intended as a metaphor for a repressive regime with implications that were nearer home. His meaning became even clearer in what was to be his final major production, of Euripides's *Medea*, which he chose to stage as "a protest against moral monstrosity, lies, arbitrariness and social injustice". In these terms, Okhlopkov saw the production as a manifesto in defence of grand feelings and ideas and the play as a protest against those social relationships that gave rise to crime, evil and even 'demonism' — hyperbole for the destruction of all human connection. Medea expressed, through her actions, how arbitrariness and violence became 'naturalised'. According to Okhlopkov, the meaning of the play was by way of a warning, which is why it should have been staged prior to the rise of fascist dictatorships. By staging the production in the Tchaikovsky Concert Hall, which was to have been Meyerhold's new theatre, Okhlopkov also paid poignant tribute to the memory of his teacher.

—Nick Worrall

OLDFIELD, Anne. English actress. Born probably in London, 1683. Mistress of 1) Arthur Mainwaring (died c.1712), one son, 2) Charles Churchill (to whom she may have been secretly married), one son. Apprentice seamstress and barmaid at the Mitre Tavern, St James's Market, London, before 'discovery' by her admirer, playwright George Farquhar; stage debut under John Rich arranged by Sir John Vanbrugh, Theatre Royal, Drury Lane, London, 1699; acclaimed in major roles in the plays of Colley Cibber and Nicholas Rowe among others; actress, Haymarket Theatre, 1705-08 and 1709; replaced Mrs Bracegirdle as London's leading comedy actress by 1707; returned permanently to Drury Lane, 1708; went on to win wide praise in tragedy. Died in London, 23 October 1730.

Roles

1699-1700 Candiope in *Secret Love; or, The Maiden Queen* (Dryden), Theatre Royal, Drury Lane, London.

1700 Sylvia in *The Grove; or, Love's Paradise* (Oldmixon), Theatre Royal, Drury Lane, London.
Alinda in *The Pilgrim* (Fletcher, adapted by Vanbrugh), Theatre Royal, Drury Lane, London.
Aurelia in *The Perjured Husband; or, The Adventures of Venice* (Centlivre), Theatre Royal, Drury Lane, London.
Lucilia in *Love at a Loss* (Trotter), Theatre Royal, Drury Lane, London.

1701 Ann of Brittanie in *The Unhappy Penitent* (Trotter), Theatre Royal, Drury Lane, London.
Miranda in *The Humour of the Age* (Baker), Theatre Royal, Drury Lane, London.
Helen in *The Virgin Prophetess; or, The Fate of Troy* (Settle), Theatre Royal, Drury Lane, London.
Lady Sharlot in *The Funeral; or, Grief à la Mode* (Steele), Theatre Royal, Drury Lane, London.
Cimene in *The Generous Conqueror; or, Timely Discovery* (Higgons), Theatre Royal, Drury Lane, London.

1702 Camille in *The Modish Husband* (Burnaby), Theatre Royal, Drury Lane, London.
Jacinta in *The False Friend* (Vanbrugh), Theatre Royal, Drury Lane, London.

1703 (Possibly) Hellena in *The Rover* (Behn), Theatre Royal, Drury Lane, London.
Lucia in *The Old Mode and the New* (D'Urfey), Theatre Royal, Drury Lane, London.
Lucia in *The Fair Example* (Estcourt), Theatre Royal, Drury Lane, London.
Belliza in *Love's Contrivance* (Centlivre), Theatre Royal, Drury Lane, London.
Leonora in *Sir Courtly Nice* (Crowne), Bath.
Victoria in *The Lying Lover* (Steele), Theatre Royal, Drury Lane, London.

1703-04 Elvira in *The Spanish Friar* (Dryden), Theatre Royal, Drury Lane, London.
Lady Lurewell in *The Constant Couple* (Farquhar), Theatre Royal, Drury Lane, London.
Narcissa in *Love's Last Shift* (Cibber), Theatre Royal, Drury Lane, London.
Celia in *Volpone* (Jonson), Theatre Royal, Drury Lane, London.
Teresia in *The Squire of Alsatia* (Shadwell), Theatre Royal, Drury Lane, London.
Florella in *Greenwich Park* (Mountfort), Theatre Royal, Drury Lane, London.
Lady Harriet in *The Funeral* (Steele), Theatre Royal, Drury Lane, London.

1704 Lady Betty Modish in *The Careless Husband* (Cibber), Theatre Royal, Drury Lane, London.

1704-05 Second Constantia in *The Chances* (Fletcher, adapted by George Villiers, Duke of Buckingham), Theatre Royal, Drury Lane, London.

1705 Mariana in *Farewell Folly* (Motteux), Theatre Royal, Drury Lane, London.
Biddy Tipkin in *The Tender Husband* (Steele), Theatre Royal, Drury Lane, London.

Arabella in *Hampstead Heath* (Baker), Theatre Royal, Drury Lane, London.

Lady Reveller in *The Basset Table* (Centlivre), Theatre Royal, Drury Lane, London.

Izadora in *Perolla and Izadora* (Cibber), Theatre Royal, Drury Lane, London.

1706   Viletta in *The Fashionable Lover* (anon.), Theatre Royal, Drury Lane, London.

Silvia in *The Recruiting Officer* (Farquhar), Theatre Royal, Drury Lane, London.

Lucina in *Valentinian* (Fletcher, adapted by the Earl of Rochester), Theatre Royal, Drury Lane, London.

Isabella in *The Platonick Lady* (Centlivre), Haymarket Theatre, London.

Mrs Rich in *The Comical Revenge* (Etherege), Haymarket Theatre, London.

1707   Epicoene in *The Silent Woman* (Jonson), Haymarket Theatre, London.

Lady Heartwell in *Wit Without Money* (Fletcher), Haymarket Theatre, London.

Florimel in *Marriage à-la-Mode* (Dryden), Haymarket Theatre, London.

Monimia in *The Orphan* (Otway), Haymarket Theatre, London.

Mrs Sullen in *The Beaux' Stratagem* (Farquhar), Haymarket Theatre, London.

Imoinda in *Oroonoko* (Southerne), Haymarket Theatre, London.

Ismena in *Phaedra and Hippolytus* (Smith), Haymarket Theatre, London.

Maria in *The Fortune Hunters* (Carlisle), Haymarket Theatre, London.

Lady Dainty in *The Double Gallant* (Cibber), Haymarket Theatre, London.

Ethelinda in *The Royal Convert* (Rowe), Haymarket Theatre, London.

Mrs Conquest in *The Lady's Last Stake* (Cibber), Haymarket Theatre, London.

Countess of Nottingham in *The Unhappy Favourite* (Banks), Haymarket Theatre, London.

1708   Estifania in *Rule a Wife and Have a Wife* (Fletcher), Haymarket Theatre, London.

Elvira in *Love Makes a Man* (Cibber), Theatre Royal, Drury Lane, London.

Angelica in *Love for Love* (Congreve), Theatre Royal, Drury Lane, London.

Semandra in *Mithridates* (Lee), Theatre Royal, Drury Lane, London.

Euphronia in *Aesop* (Otway), Theatre Royal, Drury Lane, London.

Lady Rodomont in *The Fine Lady's Airs* (Baker), Theatre Royal, Drury Lane, London.

Carolina in *Epsom Wells* (Shadwell), Theatre Royal, Drury Lane, London.

1709   Lucinda in *The Rival Fools* (Cibber, adapted from Fletcher's *Wit at Several Weapons*), Theatre Royal, Drury Lane, London.

Mrs Loveit in *The Man of Mode* (Etherege), Theatre Royal, Drury Lane, London.

Louisa in *Love Makes a Man* (Cibber), Haymarket Theatre, London.

Countess of Rutland in *The Unhappy Favourite* (Banks), Haymarket Theatre, London.

Mrs Brittle in *The Amorous Widow* (Betterton, adapted from Corneille's *Le Baron d'Albikrac* and Molière's *Georges Dandin*), Haymarket Theatre, London.

Belinda in *The Man's Bewitched* (Centlivre), Haymarket Theatre, London.

1710   Berinthia in *The Relapse* (Vanbrugh), Haymarket Theatre, London.

The Lady in *The Scornful Lady* (Beaumont and Fletcher), Haymarket Theatre, London.

Flora in *Hob; or, The Country Wake* (Cibber), Haymarket Theatre, London.

Laetitia in *The Old Bachelor* (Congreve), Haymarket Theatre, London.

Ruth in *The Committee* (Howard), Haymarket Theatre, London.

1711   Queen Mary in *The Albion Queens* (Banks), Theatre Royal, Drury Lane, London.

Ogle in *Injured Love* (anon.), Theatre Royal, Drury Lane, London.

Arabella in *The Wife's Relief* (C. Johnson, adapted from Shirley's *The Gamester*), Theatre Royal, Drury Lane, London.

Anna Bullen in *Virtue Betrayed* (Banks), Theatre Royal, Drury Lane, London.

1712   Camilla in *The Perplexed Lovers* (Centlivre), Theatre Royal, Drury Lane, London.

Caelia in *The Humorous Lieutenant* (Fletcher), Theatre Royal, Drury Lane, London.

Andromache in *The Distressed Mother* (Philips, adapted from Racine), Theatre Royal, Drury Lane, London.

Ximene in *The Heroick Daughter* (Cibber), Theatre Royal, Drury Lane, London.

1713   Victoria in *The Humours of the Army* (Shadwell), Theatre Royal, Drury Lane, London.

Emilia in *Cinna's Conspiracy* (anon.), Theatre Royal, Drury Lane, London.

Marcia in *Cato* (Addison), Theatre Royal, Drury Lane, London.

1714   Eriphile in *The Victim* (C. Johnson), Theatre Royal, Drury Lane, London.

Jane Shore in *Jane Shore* (Rowe), Theatre Royal, Drury Lane, London.

Donna Violante in *The Wonder! A Woman Keeps a Secret* (Centlivre), Theatre Royal, Drury Lane, London.

1715   Lady Jane Gray in *Lady Jane Gray* (Rowe), Theatre Royal, Drury Lane, London.

1716   Lady Trueman in *The Drummer* (Addison), Theatre Royal, Drury Lane, London.

Arpasia in *Tamerlane* (Rowe), Theatre Royal, Drury Lane, London.

Leonora in *The Cruel Gift* (Centlivre), Theatre Royal, Drury Lane, London.

1717   Mrs Townley in *Three Hours After Marriage* (Gay, Pope, and Arbuthnot), Theatre Royal, Drury Lane, London.

Atalinda in *The Sultaness* (Johnson), Theatre Royal, Drury Lane, London.

Rosalinda in *Lucius* (Manley), Theatre Royal, Drury Lane, London.

Maria in *The Non-Juror* (Cibber), Theatre Royal, Drury Lane, London.

1718   Millimant in *The Way of the World* (Congreve), Theatre Royal, Drury Lane, London.

Cleopatra in *All for Love* (Dryden), Theatre Royal, Drury Lane, London.

1719   Sophronia in *The Masquerade* (Johnson), Theatre Royal, Drury Lane, London.

Florinda in *Chit Chat* (Thomas Killigrew the Younger), Theatre Royal, Drury Lane, London.

Mandane in *Busiris* (Young), Theatre Royal, Drury Lane, London.

Celonia in *The Spartan Dame* (Southerne), Theatre Royal, Drury Lane, London.

1721   Sophronia in *The Refusal* (Cibber), Theatre Royal, Drury Lane, London.

Indamora in *Aureng-Zebe* (Dryden), Theatre Royal, Drury Lane, London.

1722   Amestris in *The Ambitious Stepmother* (Rowe), Theatre Royal, Drury Lane, London.

Mrs Watchit in *The Artifice* (Centlivre), Theatre Royal, Drury Lane, London.

Indiana in *The Conscious Lovers* (Steele), Theatre Royal, Drury Lane, London.

1723   Queen Margaret in *Humphrey, Duke of Gloster* (Philips), Theatre Royal, Drury Lane, London.

Princess Catherine in *Henry V* (Shakespeare, adapted by Hill), Theatre Royal, Drury Lane, London.

1724   Cylene in *The Captives* (Gay), Theatre Royal, Drury Lane, London.

Cleopatra in *Caesar in Egypt* (Cibber), Theatre Royal, Drury Lane, London.

1725   Calista in *The Fair Penitent* (Rowe), Theatre Royal, Drury Lane, London.

Aurelia in *The Twin Rivals* (Farquhar), Theatre Royal, Drury Lane, London.

1726   Lady Brute in *The Provoked Wife* (Vanbrugh), Theatre Royal, Drury Lane, London.

1727   Amoret in *The Rival Modes* (Smythe), Theatre Royal, Drury Lane, London.

1728   Lady Townly in *The Provoked Husband* (Cibber and Vanbrugh), Theatre Royal, Drury Lane, London.

Lady Matchless in *Love in Several Masques* (Fielding), Theatre Royal, Drury Lane, London.

1730   Clarinda in *The Humours of Oxford* (Miller), Theatre Royal, Drury Lane, London.

Sophonisba in *Sophonisba* (Thomson), Theatre Royal, Drury Lane, London.

Also acted role in: (possibly) *Volpone* (Jonson), Theatre Royal, Drury Lane, London, 1700.

Publications

Authentic Memoirs, 1730.

*

Bibliography

Books:

William Egerton, *Faithful Memoirs*, London, 1731.

Colley Cibber, *An Apology for the Life of Mr Colley Cibber*, London, 1740.

Robert W. Lowe (ed.), *A Brief Supplement to Colley Cibber, Esq; His Lives of the Late Famous Actors and Actresses*, London, 1888 (first published, 1747).

William Rufus Chetwood, *A General History of the Stage*, London, 1749.

Edward Robins, *The Palmy Days of Nance Oldfield*, Chicago, 1898.

Robert Gore-Brown, *Gay Was the Pit*, London, 1957.

Joanne Lafler, *The Celebrated Mrs Oldfield*, Carbondale, Illinois, 1989.

* * *

Anne Oldfield is one of the few performers from the Restoration and 18th century whose life and stage career attracted biographers. Some actors, like David Garrick, fully deserved the attention; others, like Nell Gwynn (whose promising stage career was short and only revealed the limits of her acting range) probably did not, at least as theatrical performers. Oldfield had a distinguished 30-year career as an actress and may, indeed, have been one of the two or three best comediennes of the 18th century, and we must accordingly be grateful to the biographers for their attention to her. (One must wish, however, that the equally important careers of, say, Mary Porter or Susannah Verbruggen or Kitty Clive had attracted similar attention.)

The actor and playwright Colley Cibber in his *Apology* in 1740 remembered Anne Oldfield as a slow developer at Drury Lane, where she was first engaged in 1699. Cibber claimed that she was not an important member of the troupe until 1703, though she received a solo benefit on 6 July 1700, which is perhaps a much more reliable indication of a performer's worth to a company than an ageing actor's recollections. On that date she was Alinda, the female lead in Vanbrugh's *The Pilgrim* and the first role, the prompter W. R. Chetwood said, to bring her to prominence. Her early parts were almost exclusively in comedies, in which she exhibited a native intelligence and grace (or is that quality one can see in some of her portraits hauteur?). Cibber wrote Lady Betty Modish in *The Careless Husband* for her and observed of the actress: "Had her Birth plac'd her in a higher Rank of Life she had certainly appear'd in reality what in this Play she only excellently acted, an agreeably gay Woman of Quality a little too conscious of her natural Attractions." Such was the impact she made, indeed, that soon she had become a model for aristocratic ladies in real life.

Though she occasionally acted serious roles (Monimia in *The Orphan*, the title role in *Jane Shore*, and Calista in *The Fair Penitent* are examples), her line was the same as Anne Bracegirdle's before her: the witty, sophisticated, and pretty lady of fashion. It is worth noting that she counted hardly any Shakespearean roles in her repertoire (so far as surviving playbills show) and she readily admitted that tragedy was not her line: "I hate to have a Page dragging my Tail about. Why do they not give Porter these Parts? She can put on a better Tragedy Face than I can". Yet she had a considerable reputation as a tragedienne and Chetwood thought her Calista in Rowe's *The Fair Penitent* "a finish'd Piece of Perfection".

Her voice, according to Cibber, "was sweet, strong, piercing, and melodious; her Pronounciation voluble, distinct, and musical; and her Emphasis always placed where the Spirit of the Sense, in her Periods, only demanded it." "Agreeable" was the word he thought best described her. Chetwood knew Anne in "her meridian lustre, a glow of charms not to be beheld but with a trembling eye!" and he praised her "excellent clear Voice of Passion" and her "piercing Flaming Eye, with Manner and Action suiting". Her charm and hard work brought her money and social contacts and by 1729 she was probably earning more than any other actress in London (Cibber guessed as much as 300 guineas or more in 1725). One of her last benefits, a command performance on 6 March 1729 before the royal family, packed Drury Lane. The *Universal Spectator* two days later ruminated on the takings: "supposing the Tickets which came in at the usual Rates, there was about 240 *l.* in the house: but her Benefit is generally reckoned as 500 *l.* several Persons of Quality, etc., giving five, ten, and twenty Guineas each. There was the greatest Appearance of Ladies of Quality at her Benefit that ever was known, and the House so excessive full, Stage and all, that the Actors had scarce Room to perform."

Mrs Oldfield (for so unmarried women were then styled after they reached maturity) deserved her handsome income, for she was a remarkably hard worker, season after season playing a long list of leading roles and a total of over 110 parts. In her last full season, 1729–30, she appeared in a typical run of characters she had been acting for years: Lady Townly in *The Provoked Husband*, Andromache in *The Distressed Mother*, Berinthia in *The Relapse*, Lady Dainty in *The Double Gallant*, Estifania in *Rule a Wife and Have a Wife*, Laetitia in *The Old Bachelor*, the title role in *Jane Shore*, Lady Brute in *The Provoked Wife*, Biddy Tipkin in *The Tender Husband*, Ruth in *The Committee*, Lady Betty Modish in *The Careless Husband*, Millamant in *The Way of the World*, Mrs Sullen in *The Beaux' Stratagem*, and Indiana in *The Conscious Lovers* — all in the first 60 days of the season. She went to act 13 other old parts and to learn one new one. That was typical and she was a trouper to the last. But she had to end the season a month early, on 28 April 1730 as Lady Brute, for she very sick and in great pain. It is probable that she had cervical cancer ("an inveterate Ulcer *in Matrice*" wrote Lewis Theobald to William Warburton on 3 September). Her death in October that year was followed by burial at Westminster Abbey with great pomp.

Anne Oldfield had an interesting personal life, which largely accounts for the biographical attention she has attracted over the years. But her accomplishments as a skilled and devoted comedienne were sufficient to give her a secure place in acting annals. In 1755 John Hill in *The Actor* wrote that "she was, when she entered the theatre, altogether the actress".

—Edward A. Langhans

OLIVIER, Laurence (Kerr, Baron). British actor-manager and director. Born in Dorking, England, 22 May 1907. Educated at All Saints' School, London, 1916–20, and St Edward's School, Oxford, 1920–23; studied theatre under Elsie Fogerty at the Central School of Speech Training and Dramatic Art, London, 1924. Married 1) actress Jill Esmond in 1930 (divorced 1940), one son; 2) actress Vivien Leigh in 1940 (divorced 1960); 3) actress Joan Plowright in 1961; one son and two daughters. Distinguished himself in school plays and made professional stage debut at the Shakespeare Festival Theatre, Stratford-upon-Avon, 1922; London debut, 1924; joined Lena Ashwell Players, 1925; actor, Birmingham Repertory Theatre, 1926–28; film debut, 1929; New York debut, 1929; admired in Shakespearean roles in London, playing Romeo and Mercutio alternately with John Gielgud, 1935; actor, Old Vic company; joined Royal Naval Volunteer Reserve, as a Lieutenant, 1941; co-director, Old Vic company at the New Theatre, 1944–49; toured Australia and New Zealand with Old Vic company, 1948; acclaimed as the leading actor of his generation; led company at St James's Theatre, London, 1949–53; celebrated season at Stratford-upon-Avon, 1955; director, Chichester Festival Theatre, 1961–63; director, National Theatre, 1962–73; also made many film appearances, sometimes under his own direction. Recipient: Oscar, 1944, 1947, 1948–49; Selznick Golden Laurel Trophy, 1956; British Film Academy Award, 1956; Emmy Award, 1958, 1972, 1973; Olympus Award, Taormina Film Festival, 1962; Special Academy Award, 1979. D.Litt: University of Oxford, 1957, University of Sussex, 1978; LL.D: University of Edinburgh, 1964, University of Manchester, 1968, University of London, 1968. Commander, Order of Dannebrog, 1949; Officier, Légion d'Honneur, 1953; Grand Officer, Ordine al Merito della Republica, 1954; Order of the Yugoslav Flag with Golden Wreath, 1971. Knighted, 1947; ennobled, as Lord Olivier of Brighton, 1970. Died in Steyning, West Sussex, England, 11 July 1989.

Roles

As actor:

1922	Katharina in *The Taming of the Shrew* (Shakespeare), Shakespeare Festival Theatre, Stratford-upon-Avon, England.
1924	Lennox in *Macbeth* (Shakespeare), Letchworth, England.
	Suliot Officer in *Byron* (Law), Century Theatre, London.
1925	Thomas of Clarence and Snare in *Henry IV, part 2* (Shakespeare), Regent Theatre, London.
	Armand St Cyr in *The Unfailing Instinct* (Frank), Century Theatre, London.
	Policeman in *The Ghost Train* (Arnold), Century Theatre, London.
	Flavius in *Julius Caesar* (Shakespeare), Century Theatre, London.
	Second serving-man in *Henry VIII* (Shakespeare), Empire Theatre, London.
1926	Servant in *The Cenci* (Shelley), Empire Theatre, London.
	Minstrel in *The Marvellous History of Saint Bernard* (Ghéon), Kingsway Theatre, London.

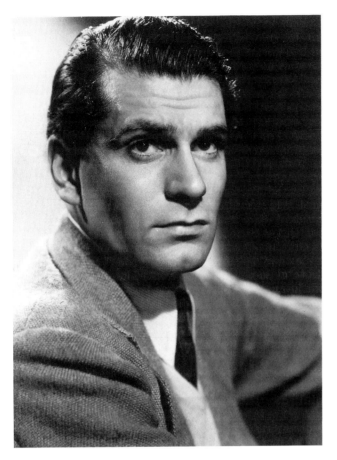

Laurence Olivier

	Role in *The Barber and the Cow* (Davies), British tour.
	Richard Croaker in *The Farmer's Wife* (Phillpotts), British tour.
1927	Guy Sydney in *Something to Talk About* (Phillpotts), Repertory Theatre, Birmingham.
	Mat Simon in *The Well of the Saints* (Synge), Repertory Theatre, Birmingham.
	Tom Hardcastle in *The Third Finger* (Whittaker), Repertory Theatre, Birmingham.
	Peter Mannoch in *The Mannoch Family* (McClymond), Repertory Theatre, Birmingham.
	Role in *The Comedian* (Ghéon), Repertory Theatre, Birmingham.
	Uncle Vanya in *Uncle Vanya* (Chekhov), Repertory Theatre, Birmingham.
	Parolles in *All's Well That Ends Well* (Shakespeare), Repertory Theatre, Birmingham.
	Young Man in *The Pleasure Garden* (Mayor), Repertory Theatre, Birmingham.
	Tony Lumpkin in *She Stoops to Conquer* (Goldsmith), Repertory Theatre, Birmingham.
	Ensign Blades in *Quality Street* (Barrie), Repertory Theatre, Birmingham.
	Gerald Arnwood in *Bird in Hand* (Drinkwater), Repertory Theatre, Birmingham; Royalty Theatre, London, 1928.

	Mervyn Jones in *Advertising April* (Farjeon and Horsnell), Repertory Theatre, Birmingham.
	Jack Barthwick in *The Silver Box* (Galsworthy), Repertory Theatre, Birmingham.
	Young American in *The Adding Machine* (Rice), Repertory Theatre, Birmingham; Royal Court Theatre, London, 1928.
	Ben Hawley in *Aren't Women Wonderful?* (Dean), Repertory Theatre, Birmingham.
	Mr Milford in *The Road to Ruin* (Holcroft), Repertory Theatre, Birmingham.
1928	Malcolm in *Macbeth* (Shakespeare), Royal Court Theatre, London.
	Martellus in *Back to Methuselah* (Shaw), Royal Court Theatre, London.
	Harold in *Harold* (Tennyson), Royal Court Theatre, London.
	The Lord in *The Taming of the Shrew* (Shakespeare), Royal Court Theatre, London.
	Graham Birley in *The Dark Path* (John), Royalty Theatre, London.
	Captain Stanhope in *Journey's End* (Sherriff), Apollo Theatre, London.
1929	Michael Geste in *Beau Geste* (Dean and Mann), His Majesty's Theatre, London.
	Prince Po in *The Circle of Chalk* (Klabund and Laver), New Theatre, London.
	Richard Parish in *Paris Bound* (Barry), Lyric Theatre, London.
	John Hardy in *The Stranger Within* (Wilbur), Garrick Theatre, London.
	Hugh Bromilow in *Murder on the Second Floor* (Vosper), Eltinge Theatre, New York.
	Jerry Warrender in *The Last Enemy* (Harvey), Fortune Theatre, London.
1930	Ralph in *After All* (van Druten), Arts Theatre, London.
	Victor Prynne in *Private Lives* (Coward), Phoenix Theatre, London; Times Square Theatre, New York, 1931.
1933	Steven Beringer in *The Rats of Norway* (Winter), Playhouse Theatre, London.
	Julian Dulcimer in *The Green Bay Tree* (Shairp), Cort Theatre, New York.
1934	Richard Kurt in *Biography* (Behrman), Globe Theatre, London.
	Bothwell in *Queen of Scots* (Daviot), New Theatre, London.
	Anthony Cavendish in *Theatre Royal* (Ferber and Kauffman), Lyric Theatre, London.
1935	Peter Hammond in *Ringmaster* (Winter), Shaftesbury Theatre, London.
	Richard Harben in *Golden Arrow* (Thompson and Cunard), Whitehall Theatre, London.
	Romeo in *Romeo and Juliet* (Shakespeare), New Theatre, London; 51st Street Theatre, New York, 1940.
	Mercutio in *Romeo and Juliet* (Shakespeare), New Theatre, London.
1936	Robert Patch in *Bees on the Boatdeck* (Priestley), Lyric Theatre, London.
1937	Hamlet in *Hamlet* (Shakespeare), Old Vic Theatre, London, and Kronborg Castle, Elsinore, Denmark.

Sir Toby Belch in *Twelfth Night* (Shakespeare), Old Vic Theatre, London.

Henry in *Henry V* (Shakespeare), Old Vic Theatre, London.

Macbeth in *Macbeth* (Shakespeare), Old Vic Theatre, London, and New Theatre, London; Shakespeare Memorial Theatre, Stratford-upon-Avon, England, 1955.

1938   Iago in *Othello* (Shakespeare), Old Vic Theatre, London.

Vivaldi in *The King of Nowhere* (Bridie), Old Vic Theatre, London.

Caius Marcius in *Coriolanus* (Shakespeare), Old Vic Theatre, London.

1939   Gaylord Easterbrook in *No Time for Comedy* (Behrman), Ethel Barrymore Theatre, New York.

1944   Button Moulder in *Peer Gynt* (Ibsen), Old Vic Theatre, London; European tour, 1945.

Sergius Saranoff in *Arms and the Man* (Shaw), Old Vic Theatre, London; European tour, 1945.

Richard in *Richard III* (Shakespeare), Old Vic Theatre, London; European tour, 1945; tour of Australia and New Zealand, 1948; New Theatre, London, 1949.

Astrov in *Uncle Vanya* (Chekhov), Old Vic Theatre, London; Century Theatre, New York, 1946; Chichester Festival Theatre, 1962; Old Vic Theatre, London, and National Theatre, London, 1963.

1945–46   Hotspur in *Henry IV, part 1* (Shakespeare), Old Vic Theatre, London, and Century Theatre, New York.

Justice Shallow in *Henry IV, part 2* (Shakespeare), Old Vic Theatre, London, and Century Theatre, New York.

Oedipus in *Oedipus Rex* (Sophocles, translated by Yeats), Old Vic Theatre, London, Century Theatre, New York.

Mr Puff in *The Critic* (Sheridan), Old Vic Theatre, London, and Century Theatre, New York.

1946   Lear in *King Lear* (Shakespeare), New Theatre, London.

1948   Sir Peter Teazle in *The School for Scandal* (Sheridan), tour of Australia and New Zealand; New Theatre, London, 1949.

Mr Antrobus in *The Skin of Our Teeth* (Wilder), tour of Australia and New Zealand.

1949   Chorus in *Antigone* (Anouilh), New Theatre, London.

1950   Duke of Altair in *Venus Observed* (Fry), St James's Theatre, London.

1951   Caesar in *Caesar and Cleopatra* (Shaw), St James's Theatre, London, and Ziegfeld Theatre, New York.

Antony in *Antony and Cleopatra* (Shakespeare), St James's Theatre, London, and Ziegfeld Theatre, New York.

1953   Grand Duke of Carpathia in *The Sleeping Prince* (Rattigan), Phoenix Theatre, London.

1955   Malvolio in *Twelfth Night* (Shakespeare), Shakespeare Memorial Theatre, Stratford-upon-Avon, England.

Titus in *Titus Andronicus* (Shakespeare), Shakespeare Memorial Theatre, Stratford-upon-Avon, England; European tour, 1957.

1957   Archie Rice in *The Entertainer* (Osborne), Royal Court Theatre, London, and Palace Theatre, London; Royale Theatre, New York, 1958.

1959   Coriolanus in *Coriolanus* (Shakespeare), Shakespeare Memorial Theatre, Stratford-upon-Avon, England.

1960   Berenger in *Rhinoceros* (Ionesco), Royal Court Theatre, London, and Strand Theatre, London.

Becket in *Becket* (Anouilh), St James's Theatre, New York.

1961   Henry II in *Becket* (Anouilh), Hudson Theatre, New York, and US and British tours.

1962   Prologue and Bassanes in *The Broken Heart* (Ford), Chichester Festival Theatre, England.

Fred Midway in *Semi-Detached* (Turner), Saville Theatre, London.

1963   Captain Brazen in *The Recruiting Officer* (Farquhar), National Theatre, London.

1964   Othello in *Othello* (Shakespeare), National Theatre, London, and Chichester Festival Theatre; tour to Moscow and Berlin, 1965.

Halvard Solness in *The Master Builder* (Ibsen), National Theatre, London.

1965   Tattle in *Love for Love* (Congreve), Old Vic Theatre, London; Canadian tour, 1967.

1967   Edgar in *The Dance of Death* (Strindberg), National Theatre, London; Canadian tour, 1967.

Pulcheux in *A Flea in Her Ear* (Feydeau), Canadian tour.

1969   A. B. Raham in *Home and Beauty* (Maugham), National Theatre, London.

Chebutikin in *The Three Sisters* (Chekhov), National Theatre, London, and US tour.

1970   Shylock in *The Merchant of Venice* (Shakespeare), National Theatre, London.

1971   James Tyrone in *Long Day's Journey into Night* (O'Neill), New Theatre, London; Old Vic Theatre, 1972.

1973   Antonio in *Saturday, Sunday, Monday* (Filippo, adapted by Waterhouse and Hall), National Theatre, London.

John Tagg in *The Party* (Griffiths), National Theatre, London.

1986   Akash (hologram) in *Time*, Dominion Theatre, London.

As director:
1935   *Golden Arrow* (Thompson and Cunard), Whitehall Theatre, London.

1936   *Bees on the Boatdeck* (Priestley), Lyric Theatre, London.

1945   *The Skin of Our Teeth* (Wilder), Phoenix Theatre, London; tour of Australia and New Zealand, 1948.

1946	*King Lear* (Shakespeare), New Theatre, London.
1947	*Born Yesterday* (Kanin), Garrick Theatre, London.
1948	*The School for Scandal* (Sheridan), tour of Australia and New Zealand; New Theatre, London, 1949.
1949	*Antigone* (Anoulh), New Theatre, London.
	The Proposal (Chekhov), New Theatre, London.
	A Streetcar Named Desire (T. Williams), Aldwych Theatre, London.
1950	*Venus Observed* (Fry), St James's Theatre, London; New Century Theatre, New York, 1952.
	Captain Carvallo (Cannan), St James's Theatre, London.
1952	*Venus Observed* (Fry), New Century Theatre, New York.
1953	*The Sleeping Prince* (Rattigan), Phoenix Theatre, London.
1960	*The Tumbler* (Levy), Helen Hayes Theatre, New York.
1962	*The Chances* (Villiers), Chichester Festival Theatre, England.
	The Broken Heart (Ford), Chichester Festival Theatre, England.
	Uncle Vanya (Chekhov), Chichester Festival Theatre, England.
1963	*Hamlet* (Shakespeare), National Theatre, London.
1966	*Juno and the Paycock* (O'Casey), National Theatre, London.
1967	*The Three Sisters* (Chekhov), National Theatre, London.
1968	*The Advertisement* (Ginzburg), National Theatre, London.
	Love's Labour's Lost (Shakespeare), National Theatre, London.
1971	*Amphitryon 38* (Giraudoux), New Theatre, London.
1974	*Eden End* (Priestley), National Theatre, London.
1980	*Filumena* (Filippo), St James's Theatre, New York.

Films

As actor:
Peter Bille in *The Temporary Widow*, 1929; The Man in *Too Many Crooks*, 1929; Straker in *Potiphar's Wife*, 1930; Lieutenant Nicholls in *Friends and Lovers*, 1931; Julian Rolphe in *The Yellow Passport*, 1931; Nick Allen in *Westward Passage*, 1932; Nicholas Randall in *Perfect Understanding*, 1932; Clive in *No Funny Business*, 1932; Vincent Lunardi in *Conquest of the Air*, 1935; Ignatoff in *Moscow Nights*, 1935; Orlando in *As You Like It*, 1936; Michael Ingolby in *Fire Over England*, 1936; Logan in *The Divorce of Lady X*, 1938; Larry Durant in *Twenty One Days*, 1938; Tony McVane in *Q Planes*, 1939; Heathcliff in *Wuthering Heights*, 1939; Maxim De Winter in *Rebecca*, 1939; Darcy in *Pride and Prejudice*, 1940; Nelson in *Lady Hamilton*, 1941; Johnnie the Trapper in

49th Parallel, 1941; Ivan Dimitrievitch Kouznetsoff in *The Demi-Paradise*, 1943; George Hurstwood in *Carrie*, 1950; PC 49 in *The Magic Box*, 1951; Macheath in *The Beggar's Opera*, 1952; General Burgoyne in *The Devil's Disciple*, 1958; Marcus Crassus in *Spartacus*, 1959; Archie Rice in *The Entertainer*, 1959; Graham Weir in *Terms of Trial*, 1962; Astrov in *Uncle Vanya*, 1963; Inspector Newhouse in *Bunny Lake is Missing*, 1965; Othello in *Othello*, 1965; The Mahdi in *Khartoum*, 1966; Kamenev in *The Shoes of the Fisherman*, 1968; Sir John French in *Oh! What a Lovely War*, 1968; Edgar in *The Dance of Death*, 1968; Sir Hugh Dowding in *The Battle of Britain*, 1969; Mr Creakle in *David Copperfield*, 1969; Count Witte in *Nicholas and Alexandra*, 1971; Duke of Wellington in *Lady Caroline Lamb*, 1971; Andrew Wyke in *Sleuth*, 1972; James Tyrone in *Long Day's Journey into Night*, 1972; Professor Moriarty in *The Seven Per Cent Solution*, 1976; Dr Christian Szell in *Marathon Man*, 1976; Dr Spaander in *A Bridge Too Far*, 1976; Nicodemus in *Jesus of Nazareth*, 1976; Loren Hardeman Senior in *The Betsy*, 1978; Ezra Lieberman in *The Boys from Brazil*, 1978; Julius in *A Little Romance*, 1979; Professor Van Helsing in *Dracula*, 1979; MacArthur in *Inchon*, 1979; Cantor Rabinovitch in *The Jazz Singer*, 1979; Zeus in *Clash of the Titans*, 1981; Admiral Hood in *The Bounty*, 1984; Sir Gerald Scaith in *The Jigsaw Man*, 1985.

As actor and director:
The Prince in *The Prince and the Showgirl*, 1956; Chebutikin in *The Three Sisters*, 1969.

As actor, producer, and director:
Henry in *Henry V*, 1944; Hamlet in *Hamlet*, 1947; Richard in *Richard III*, 1954.

Television

Borkman in *John Gabriel Borkman*, 1958; Charles Strickland in *The Moon and Sixpence*, 1958; The Priest in *The Power and the Glory*, 1961; Host/Narrator in *Male of the Species*, 1969; Shylock in *The Merchant of Venice*, 1973; Narrator in *The World at War*, 1973; Sir Arthur Granville-Jones in *Love Among the Ruins*, 1973; Harry Kane in *The Collection*, 1976; Big Daddy in *Cat on a Hot Tin Roof*, 1976; Doc Delaney in *Come Back Little Sheba*, 1977; Sir Joseph Pitts in *Daphne Laureola*, 1977; Antonio in *Saturday, Sunday, Monday*, 1977; Lord Marchmain in *Brideshead Revisited*, 1981; Sandor Lukacs in *Wagner*, 1981; Clifford Mortimer in *A Voyage Round My Father*, 1982; Lear in *King Lear*, 1983; Mr Halpern in *Mr Halpern and Mr Johnson*, 1983; Dr Wainwright in *A Talent for Murder*, 1983; Henry Breasley in *The Ebony Tower*, 1984; Gaius in *The Last Days of Pompeii*, 1984; King William III in *Peter the Great*, 1985; Harry Burrard in *Lost Empires*, 1986.

Publications

Confessions of an Actor (autobiography), 1982; *Olivier on Acting*, 1986.

*

Bibliography

Books:

W. A. Darlington, *Laurence Olivier*, London, 1968.
Virginia Fairweather, *Cry God for Larry*, London, 1969.
Logan Gourlay (ed.), *Olivier*, London, 1973.
John Cottrell, *Laurence Olivier*, London, 1975.
Margaret Morley, *The Films and Faces of Laurence Olivier*, Surrey, England, 1978.
Foster Hirsch, *Laurence Olivier*, Boston, 1979.
Daniel Roberts, *Laurence Olivier: Theatre and Cinema*, London, 1980.
Thomas Kiernan, *Sir Larry*, New York, 1981.
Felix Barker, *Laurence Olivier*, Tunbridge Wells, England, 1984.
Melvyn Bragg, *Laurence Olivier*, London, 1984.
Robert Tanitch, *Olivier, The Complete Career*, London, 1985.
Garry O'Connor (ed.), *Olivier: In Celebration*, London, 1987.
Anthony Holden, *Olivier*, London, 1988.

* * *

Posterity is ruthless and Olivier's courage in overcoming a succession of serious illnesses will be of less interest in the future than what he achieved as an actor. Acclaimed as the greatest actor of his time, he is a problem for critical evaluation because of his versatility on stage and the way he adapted to a revolution in visual and electronic media, which by the time of his death threatened to supersede live theatre itself. Striding indefatigably through the decades while those who had seen him in live performance diminished, he eventually became a fragmented image diffused on film in so many character parts that only brief journalistic assessments could be made.

Since Olivier was both an heroic actor and an impersonator, his achievement falls into those two main categories, of which his record in the first would have been superlative if he had done nothing else. The criteria for valuation here are straightforward: a matter of measuring the actor against other interpreters and against accepted masterpieces. Olivier's Henry V, for example, was no better than Godfrey Tearle's of three years before — but it was different, notably in the king's impatience, a leashed-in urge for action obvious when he listened to advisers about the validity of claims on France. This led to a furiously resonant delivery of the patriotic rhetoric, only to be guessed at from the film. In the theatre, an answering excitement was aroused in the audience.

His first Coriolanus, in no way inferior to the complex version of three decades later, was played hard and straight, with equally pounding rhetoric but a contempt for the populace underlined by revulsion, Olivier's facial expression evoking the way they smelt. By this time something deeper than rhetoric, itself compelling enough, was in process of development. His first Macbeth, later to be perfected, was innovative on several counts, with unexpected vocal climaxes on the brief "night thickens" lines and on the farewell to sleep, which emphasized the horrors of insomnia in shattering open vowels rather than the customary low-key delivery, and a subtly oblique briefing of the murderers.

By that time, Olivier's voice had soared free from an apprenticeship in lightweight roles and now testified to initial vocal training by Elsie Fogerty, the only teacher acknowledged in reference books. This training enabled him now to master the long 'operatic' speeches often demanded by Shakespeare. This strength, allied with a magnetic stage presence, athleticism, and unquenchable energy, completed the main armoury of Olivier as a classical actor. Yet at the root of all these qualities was his intelligence, grossly underrated in the 1960's, when admiration for his glamour and virility was at its height and his unforgettable howl as Oedipus was suited to a cult of 'impact'. It was questing intelligence, however, which conditioned his final versions of heroic roles before he was absorbed by the visual media. There was a capricious Lear, too gently psychotic, and a trendily African Othello, in both of which he denied himself grand rhetorical effects (his depiction of Othello's descent into animality was consequently unique). In his final Coriolanus all his gifts, including his sardonic humour, came together, while maintaining total respect for the text.

With Richard III the great impersonator had begun to take over, malevolence often concealed by a fussily pedantic manner. Always aware of the climates outside the theatre, Olivier went on to make the failed music hall comic Archie Rice a symbol of national decline in a performance of unparalleled virtuosity only to be appreciated live. Moreover, he went on to face the challenge of the early modern masters: Ibsen, Chekhov, Strindberg, and O'Neill. Although it cannot be claimed that Olivier excelled Scandinavian, Russian, and US actors in their own field, he rivalled them, at least in translation. A highlight was his Astrov in *Uncle Vanya*, merged in a brilliant ensemble of his own creation, yet allowing him to indulge the impersonator with an accurate portrait of the playwright himself.

Nevertheless, the supreme challenge for an English actor is Shakespeare, not only for human insight but for heightened language, including unsurpassed verse. There the customary predecessor cited in evaluating Olivier was Edmund Kean. In the absence of a Hazlitt to pin down Olivier's achievements in print, we are dependent on responses to what occurred in live performance, the medium after all which Shakespeare had in mind. But for the outside chance of a critic with more than the usual space to do his Coriolanus justice, it is on these reactions that his performances in this (and other roles of which there is no screen version) that his status in the future will depend. Nor can his film roles be adequately classified, in spite of high quality, other than as adaptations of what happened on the stage: the indispensable presence of the actor and his live audience is just not there.

Of Olivier's contemporaries Tearle had more weight and an equal mastery of rhetoric, Gielgud, Scofield, and Redgrave were more suited to Hamlet and a more memorable Lear was Wolfit's. On the dizzy peaks of heroic acting, however, Olivier's Coriolanus, Othello, and definitively Macbeth, stood alone. His reputation was based finally on his mercurial intelligence, allied to his other gifts, in the service of Shakespeare's text, probed to the limit though always with respect. That, though abused by imitators, is his chief claim on posterity.

—Laurence Kitchin

OTTO, Teo. German designer. Born in Remscheid, Germany, 4 February 1904. Educated at the Academy of Fine Arts, Kassel, and at the Bauhaus, Weimar. Began career designing for the Staatstheater, Kassel, 1924–25; subsequently worked as a designer under Otto Klemperer at the Kroll Opera, Berlin, 1927, and at the Staatstheater, Berlin, 1928–33, being appointed chief designer there in 1931; left Germany and settled in Switzerland, working mainly at the Schauspielhaus, Zurich, 1933; produced designs for the premieres of several plays by Bertolt Brecht and subsequently designed for works by Max Frisch and Friedrich Dürrenmatt both in Zurich and elsewhere in Europe; also designed plays and operas for theatres in Basle, Vienna, Salzburg, Munich and back in Berlin as well as in New York. Professor of Stage Design, Academy of Fine Arts, Düsseldorf. Died in Frankfurt-am-Maim, Germany, 9 June 1968.

Principal productions

1924–25	*Vasantasena* (Feuchtwanger), Staatstheater, Kassel.
1941	*Mutter Courage and ihre Kinder* (Brecht), Schauspielhaus, Zurich.
1943	*Der gute Mensch von Sezuan* (Brecht), Schauspielhaus, Zurich.
	Leben des Galilei (Brecht), Schauspielhaus, Zurich.
1945	*Nun Singen sie wieder* (Frisch), Schauspielhaus, Zurich.
1946	*Santa Cruz* (Frisch), Schauspielhaus, Zurich.
	Die chinesische Mauer (Frisch), Schauspielhaus, Zurich.
1949	*Mutter Courage und ihre Kinder* (Brecht), Deutsches Theater, Berlin.
	Wassa Shelesnowa, Deutsches Theater, Berlin.
1951	*Mutter Courage and ihre Kinder* (Brecht), Kammerspiele, Munich.
	Graf Öderland (Frisch), Schauspielhaus, Zurich.
1952–53	*Der gute Mensch von Sezuan* (Brecht), Frankfurt-am-Maim.
1953	*Don Juan* (Frisch), Schauspielhaus, Zurich.
1953–54	*Der gute Mensch von Sezuan* (Brecht), Habimah Theatre, Tel Aviv.
1956	*Der Besuch der alten Dame* (Dürrenmatt), Schauspielhaus, Zurich; Munich and Hamburg, 1956–57.
1956–57	*Der gute Mensch von Sezuan* (Brecht), Royal Court Theatre, London, and Phoenix Theatre, New York.
1957	*Faust* (Goethe), Hamburg and City Centre, New York.
1957–58	*Mutter Courage und ihre Kinder* (Brecht), Frankfurt-am-Maim.
1958	*Biedermann und die Brandstifter* (Frisch), Schauspielhaus, Zurich.
	Der Besuch der alten Dame (Dürrenmatt), New York.
1958–59	*Die Räuber* (Schiller), Schiller-Theater, Berlin.
1959	*Frank V* (Dürrenmatt), Schauspielhaus, Zurich.
	Orestie (Aeschylus), Syracuse.
1960	*Nabucco* (Verdi), Metropolitan Opera, New York.
	Tristan und Isolde (Wagner), Metropolitan Opera, New York.
1961	*Andorra* (Frisch), Schauspielhaus, Zurich.
1962	*Die Physiker* (Dürrenmatt), Schauspielhaus, Zurich.
	Fussgänger der Luft (Ionesco), Schauspielhaus, Zurich.
1963	*Herkules und der Stall des Augias* (Dürrenmatt), Schauspielhaus, Zurich.
1964	*Hunger und Durst* (Ionesco), Schauspielhaus, Zurich.
1966	*Der Meteor* (Dürrenmatt), Schauspielhaus, Zurich.
1967	*Die Wiedertäufer* (Dürrenmatt), Schauspielhaus, Zurich.
1968	*Wallensteins Tod* (Schiller), Düsseldorf.

Publications

Skizen eines Bühnenbildners, with M. Frisch, K. Hirschfeld, O. Waelterlin, H. R. Hilty, 1964; *Meine Szene*, 1965.

*

Bibliography

Books:
J. Mayerhöfer, *Der Bühnenbilder Teo Otto, Inszenierungen in Österreich*, Salzburg, 1977.

Articles:
Kurt Hirschfeld, "Der Bühnenbildner Theo Otto", *Neue Zürcher Zeitung*, 249, 1953.

* * *

Teo Otto began as a student of mechanical engineering before transferring to the study of painting at the academy in Kassel. He worked at the college of architecture in Weimar and then joined the Kroll Opera in Berlin as a set designer. His training, both technical and artistic, gave him a particularly deep and wide-ranging understanding of the potentialities of the materials of stage construction and an excitement in experiment with new materials, as well as in the extending of the application of established methods. He had no fixed style, preferring to adapt his own vision both to the play or opera in hand and the style of the director with whom he was working. This openness to ideas and flexibility of approach allowed him to work with directors whose aims in theatre and requirements of a designer were as disparate as those of Brook and Brecht, Waelterlin and Stroux, and on plays as diverse as those of Brecht and Ionesco.

While in Zurich during the war (he had left Germany in 1933), he designed the world premiere of Brecht's *Mutter Courage und ihre Kinder* (*Mother Courage and her Children*), which he also designed on four subsequent occasions, including Brecht's reworking of the play at the Berliner Ensemble in 1949. His sparse staging, with the cluttered wagon set against an expanse of white cyclorama, established a pattern for many later productions and eloquently expressed the play's central image of the canteen-woman, in the wider context hopelessly drifting through an infinite landscape of war, while the detail of the wagon reinforced the vicious and ultimately futile struggle for survival waged by Courage on behalf of herself and her children. He also designed the premiere production of Brecht's *Der Gute Mensch von Sezuan* (*The Good Person of Setzuan*) in Zurich in 1943, as well as productions of the same play in Tel Aviv in 1953 and in London and New York in 1956–57. In 1943 he designed the German-language premiere of Brecht's *Leben des Galilei* (*The Life of Galileo*), also in Zurich. In 1945, with the premiere of *Nun Singen Sie Wieder* (*Now They're Singing Again*) by Max Frisch, he began a lengthy association with the two Swiss writers Max Frisch and Friedrich Dürrenmatt, during which he designed the Zurich world premieres of each of their major plays until Dürrenmatt's *Die Wiedertäufer* (*The Anabaptists*) the year before his death.

Otto had a complete mastery of technical theatre but frequently wrote of the dangers of designers being seduced by the technical apparatus which he was dismayed to see being installed in increasing complexity in German theatres after the war. He called for a sensitivity to the texture and qualities of materials, as well as an understanding of volume, mass, light and shade in stage design.

In his own career as a designer he fulfilled the demand that: "Designers must remain open to all possibilities, from impressions gained directly from the natural world to ideas deriving from the purest of abstract thought" and set an example of receptivity that has had a considerable impact on the development of stage design in post-war Europe.

—Tony Meech

PAGE, Geraldine (Sue). US actress. Born in Kirksville, Missouri, 22 November 1924. Educated at the Goodman Theatre School, 1942–45; trained for the stage with Sophia Swanstrom Young, Chicago, 1940, with Mira Rostova, New York, 1950, with Uta Hagen, New York, 1949–56, and with Alice Hermes, New York. Married 1) violinist Alexander Scheider (divorced); 2) actor and director Rip Torn; one daughter, two sons. Stage debut, Chicago, 1940; New York debut, 1945; television debut, 1946; film debut, 1947; established reputation in Tennessee Williams's *Summer and Smoke*, 1952; Broadway debut, 1953; London debut, 1956; made many appearances with the Actors' Studio, New York, co-founded the Sanctuary Theatre company, 1976, and worked with the Mirror Repertory Company, New York, from 1983. Recipient: Donaldson Award, 1953; New York Critics Circle Award, 1953, 1959; Drama Desk Award, 1953; Sarah Siddons Award, 1960; Who's Who of American Women Award, 1960; *Cue* Magazine Award, 1961; Cinema Nuova Gold Plaque, Venice, 1961; National Board of Review Award, 1961; Golden Globe Award, 1962, 1964; Donatello Award, 1963; Emmy Award, 1967, 1969; British Academy of Film and Television Arts Award, 1979; Academy Award, 1986. Died in New York, 13 June 1987.

Roles

1945   Sophomore in *Seven Mirrors*, Blackfriars Guild, New York.
1951–52 Pagan Crone in *Yerma* (Lorca), Circle in the Square Theatre, New York.
1952   Alma Winemiller in *Summer and Smoke* (T. Williams), Circle in the Square Theatre, New York.
1953   Lily Barton in *Midsummer* (Delmar), Vanderbilt Theatre, New York.
1954   Marcelline in *The Immoralist* (adapted from Gide), Royale Theatre, New York; Studebaker Theatre, Chicago, 1956.
        Lizzie Curry in *The Rainmaker* (Nash), Cort Theatre, New York; US tour, 1955; St Martin's Theatre, London, 1956.
1956   Amy McGregor in *The Innkeepers* (Apstein), John Golden Theatre, New York.
        Abbie Putnam in *Desire Under the Elms* (O'Neill), Studebaker Theatre, Chicago.
        Natalia Islaev in *A Month in the Country* (Turgenev), Studebaker Theatre, Chicago.

1957   Mrs Shankland and Miss Railton-Bell in *Separate Tables* (Rattigan), Music Box Theatre, New York, and US tour.
1959   Alexandra del Lago in *Sweet Bird of Youth* (Williams), Martin Beck Theatre, New York, and US tour.
1962   Sister Bonaventure in *The Umbrella* (Davis), Locust Theatre, Philadelphia.
1963   Nina Leeds in *Strange Interlude* (O'Neill), Hudson Theatre, New York.
1964   Olga in *Three Sisters* (Chekhov), Morosco Theatre, New York.
        Julie Cunningham in *PS I Love You* (Roman, adapted from Roussin), Henry Miller's Theatre, New York.
1966   Oriane Brice in *The Great Indoors*, Eugene O'Neill Theatre, New York.
1967   Clea in *Black Comedy* (Shaffer), Ethel Barrymore Theatre, New York.
        Baroness Lemberg in *White Lies* (Shaffer), Ethel Barrymore Theatre, New York.
1969   Angela Palmer in *Angela*, Music Box Theatre, New York.
1973   Mary Todd Lincoln in *Look Away*, Playhouse Theatre, New York.
1974   Regina Giddens in *The Little Foxes* (Hellman), Academy Festival Theatre, Lake Forest, Illinois, and Walnut Street Theatre, Philadelphia.
        Marion in *Absurd Person Singular* (Ayckbourn), Music Box Theatre, New York.
1976   Blanche DuBois in *A Streetcar Named Desire* (T. Williams), Academy Festival Theatre, Lake Forest, Illinois.
1977   Tekla in *The Creditors* (Strindberg), Hudson Guild Theatre, New York, and Public/Newman Theatre, New York Shakespeare Festival, New York.
1980   Elberta in *Mixed Couples*, Brooks Atkinson Theatre, New York.
        Zelda Fitzgerald in *Clothes for a Summer Hotel* (T. Williams), Cort Theatre, New York.
1982   Mother Miriam Ruth in *Agnes of God* (Pielmeier), Music Box Theatre, New York; St Peter's Church, New York, 1983–85.
1987   Madame Arcati in *Blithe Spirit* (Coward), Neil Simon Theatre, New York.

Other roles included: Mama in *Papa Is All*; and roles in *Excuse my Dust* (Wood), Englewood Methodist Church,

Geraldine Page (1971).

Chicago, 1940; *The Marriage Proposal* and *The Bear* (Chekhov), Playhouse in the Park, New York, 1971; *Marriage and Money*, US tour, 1971; *Slightly Delayed*, US tour, 1979.

Films

Out of the Night, 1947; *Taxi*, 1953; *Hondo*, 1953; *Summer and Smoke*, 1961; *Sweet Bird of Youth*, 1962; *Toys in the Attic*, 1963; *Dear Heart*, 1964; *The Three Sisters*, 1965; *You're a Big Boy Now*, 1966; *The Happiest Millionaire*, 1967; *Trilogy*, 1969; *Whatever Happened to Aunt Alice?*, 1969; *Beguiled*, 1971; *J. W. Coop*, 1972; *Pete 'n Tillie*, 1972; *The Day of the Locust*, 1974; *The Abbess of Crewe*, 1976; *Nasty Habits*, 1977; *Interiors*, 1978; *Honky Tonk Freeway*, 1980; *Harry's War*, 1980; *I'm Dancing as Fast as I Can*, 1982; *The Pope of Greenwich Village*, 1984; *The Bride*, 1985; *White Nights*, 1985; *The Trip to Bountiful*, 1986; *Native Son*, 1986; *My Little Girl*, 1987.

Television

Easter Story, 1946; *The Turn of the Screw*, 1955; *Barefoot in Athens*, 1966; *A Christmas Memory*, 1966; *A Thanksgiving Visitor*, 1968; *Montserrat*, 1971; *Look Homeward Angel*, 1972; *Live Again, Die Again*, 1974; *Something for Joey*, 1977; *The Parade*, 1984.

Radio

Liliom; The Glass Menagerie; Summer and Smoke.

*

Bibliography

Articles:
Gilbert Millstein, "Portrait of Miss Page, On and Off Stage", *New York Times Magazine*, 29 March 1959.
Rex Reed, "Paging Miss Page: Where Are You?", *Daily News*, 20 March 1977.
Hilary DeVries, "Geraldine Page", *Christian Science Monitor*, 25 March 1986.

* * *

Although she was nominated for eight Academy Awards for her acting in films, Geraldine Page remained dedicated first and foremost to her theatre work. Throughout her 42-year career as an actress, Page consistently sought out the widest range of roles, depsite the natural tendency of producers and directors to typecast her in roles similar to her most recent success. She was particularly identified with the plays of Tennessee Williams. She played Alma, a repressed spinster, in the 1952 Circle in the Square revival of *Summer and Smoke*, a production that many critics point to as the beginning of the rise of Off-Broadway in New York. In 1959, she played Alexandra del Lago, an ageing alcoholic movie star on the skids, in Williams's *Sweet Bird of Youth*. She also created the role of Zelda Fitzgerald in the 1980 production of Williams's last produced play, *Clothes for a Summer Hotel*. In 1962, she recreated her roles in the film versions of *Summer and Smoke* and *Sweet Bird of Youth*, receiving Oscar nominations for Best Actress for both performances.

Throughout her career, she was known as a character actress and frequently played neurotic older women. At five feet seven inches, she was considered too tall to be a leading lady. She was not regarded as a classic beauty, but was able to transform herself to appear quite differently in various roles. Page was quite particular about the roles she played. She preferred to play a small role that excited her rather than a lead in a play or film that she did not believe in. Accordingly, she turned down her share of successes, including the role of Martha in Edward Albee's *Who's Afraid of Virginia Woolf?*, as well as Nurse Ratched in the film version of *One Flew Over the Cuckoo's Nest*.

Her interest in supporting roles was part of her lifetime belief in repertory theatre. After her initial work with the Circle in the Square in the 1950's, she returned to repertory theatre several times in her career. In the mid-1960's, she helped found the Actors' Studio Theatre, along with Paul Newman and her husband Rip Torn. Page starred in the Actors' Studio Theatre's Broadway productions of *Strange Interlude* and *The Three Sisters*. She and Torn quit the Actors' Studio after a feud with Lee Strasberg over artistic direction of the theatre. In 1976, she and Torn went on to found the Sanctuary Theatre in New York as a workshop for actors between jobs. Sanctuary Theatre flourished for several years. Their staging of two one-act plays by Strindberg, *The Creditors* and *The Stronger*, directed by Torn, moved from a workshop production at the Hudson Guild Theatre to a full production at the Public Theatre.

During the 1980's, Page worked as artist-in-residence at the Mirror Repertory Company, founded by John Strasberg (son of Lee Strasberg) and his wife Sabra Jones, for the meagre salary of $15 per performance. As always, it was the love of her acting work that drove her to accept and even seek out these situations. Although she was clearly the most prominent actress connected with the Mirror Repertory Company, she played a wide variety of roles, from the lead in *The Madwoman of Chaillot*, to a small supporting role in *The Circle*, as well as performing in *Paradise Lost, Rain, Inheritors*, and *Ghosts*.

Despite her recognized ability to transform herself dramatically from role to role, certain consistent characteristics made Page's portrayals identifiable. Early in her career, she was praised lavishly for these qualities. The most prominent of these was her voice. Although Page herself noted that her voice was thin, she was able to modulate her voice to great effect. She was known for her eccentric line readings, often shifting pitch and volume drastically within a line or speech. She was also known for her fluttery, almost fidgety, gestures and facial expresssions. Later in her career, though, many reviewers recognized these very same qualities in her performances as mannered. Acknowledging that she was "falling back on her old tricks", Page studiously observed herself in an effort to strip away these habits. In her film work, Page always asked the director to allow her to view the dailies in an effort to control her performances. Most directors allowed her to do so, trusting her ability to observe her own performances without becoming self-conscious.

Her working habits were learned through many years of the study of acting. During the 1970's and 1980's, she shared her wealth of experience with acting students in New York at the Pelican Theatre. According to Page, she taught students "how *not* to act". She believed that if she could rid her students of the burden of trying to act, they would do their best work. Her dedication to sharing her knowledge and experience was further evidence of her passion for theatre and her dedication to the craft of acting.

—Robert Knopf

PALITZSCH, Peter. German director. Born in Deutmannsdorf, Saxony, 11 September 1918. Married Tanja von Oetrzen. Worked as advertising artist for textile company before military service in northern Finland, 1939–45; appointed dramaturg to the Volksbühne, Dresden, after the war; subsequently invited to join the Berliner Ensemble as assistant to Bertolt Brecht and was promoted to chief dramaturg with the company; debut as director with the Berliner Ensemble, 1955; settled in West Germany, 1961; director, Ulm theatre, 1961–62, Theater Bremen, 1962–66; artistic director, Staatstheater, Stuttgart, 1966–72; artistic co-director, Schauspielhaus, Frankfurt-am-Main, 1972–80; has also worked as freelance director with leading theatres in Germany, Austria, Switzerland and Scandinavia since 1957. Member: directorate of the Berliner Ensemble, 1991. Recipient: National Prize (Germany), 1960; Paris Theatre of Nations Prize, 1960; Berlin Theatre Prize, 1991.

Principal productions

1955	*The Day of the Great Scholar Wu* (Palitzsch and Weber, adapted from the Chinese), Berliner Ensemble.
1956	*Der Held der westlichen Welt* (Synge), Berliner Ensemble.
1957	*Furcht und Elend des Dritten Reiches* (Brecht), Berliner Ensemble.
	Leben Eduards des Zweiten von England (Brecht), Staatstheater, Stuttgart.
1958	*Optimische Tragödie* (Vishnevsky), Berliner Ensemble.
	Der aufhaltsame Aufstieg des Arturo Ui (Brecht), Staatstheater, Stuttgart.
	Puntila (Brecht), Wuppertal.
1959	*Der aufhaltsame Aufstieg des Arturo Ui* (Brecht), Berliner Ensemble.
	Mann ist Mann (Brecht), Wuppertal.
	Der kaukasische Kreidekreis (Brecht), Ulm.
1960	*Der gute Mensch von Setzuan* (Brecht), Ulm.
	Der Widerspenstigen Zähmung (Shakespeare), Ulm.
1961	*Frau Flinz* (Baierl), Berliner Ensemble.
	Der Prozess der Jeanne d'Arc zu Rouen 1431 (Brecht and Seghers), Ulm.
1962	*Dantons Tod* (Büchner), Staatstheater, Stuttgart.
1963	*Der kaukasische Kreidekreis* (Brecht), Oslo.
	Der Kaufman von Venedig (Shakespeare), Hanover.
	Der schwarze Schwan (Walser), Staatstheater, Stuttgart.
1964	*Der aufhaltsame Aufstieg des Arturo Ui* (Brecht), Theater Bremen.
	Der kaukasische Kreidekreis (Brecht), Theater Bremen.
	Mutter Courage und ihre Kinder (Brecht), Cologne.
1965	*Die Ermittlung* (Weiss), Staatstheater, Stuttgart.
	Purpurstaub (O'Casey), Cologne.
1966	*Puntila* (Brecht), Cologne.
	The Beggar's Opera (Gay, adapted by Enzensberger and Fortner), Heidelberg.
1967	*The Wars of the Roses* (Shakespeare compilation), Staatstheater, Stuttgart.
	Schweik im zweiten Weltkrieg (Brecht), Ruhrfestspiele, Recklinghausen.
	Marija (Babel), Staatstheater, Stuttgart.
1968	*Toller* (Dorst), Staatstheater, Stuttgart.
1970	*Mutter Courage und ihre Kinder* (Brecht), Staatstheater, Stuttgart.
1971	*Hoelderlin* (Weiss), Staatstheater, Stuttgart.
1972	*Hamlet* (Shakespeare), Staatstheater, Stuttgart.
	Lear (Bond), Schauspielhaus, Frankfurt.
	The Room (Pimyet), Schauspielhaus, Frankfurt.
1973	*Varvary* (Gorky), Schauspielhaus, Frankfurt.
	Frühlings Erwachen (Wedekind), Schauspielhaus, Frankfurt.
1974	*Die Tage des Kommune* (Brecht), Schauspielhaus, Frankfurt.
1975	*Puntila* (Brecht), Schauspielhaus, Frankfurt.

	Zement (Müller), Schauspielhaus, Frankfurt.
1976	*Woyzeck* (Büchner), Schauspielhaus, Frankfurt.
	The Seagull (Chekhov), Schauspielhaus, Frankfurt.
1977	*The Homecoming* (Pinter), Burgtheater, Vienna.
1978	*The Masterbuilder* (Ibsen), Schauspielhaus, Frankfurt.
	Hedda Gabler (Ibsen), Burgtheater, Vienna.
1979	*Don Carlos* (Schiller), Schauspielhaus, Frankfurt.
	Othello (Shakespeare), Schauspielhaus, Frankfurt.
1980	*Kasimir und Karoline* (Horvath).
	Gertrud (Soederberg), Schauspielhaus, Hamburg.
1982	*Othello* (Shakespeare), Staatstheater, Munich.
	Uncle Vanya (Chekhov), Düsseldorf.
	Egmont (Goethe), Bregenz.
1983	*Geherda* (Brecht), Düsseldorf.
	Tales from Hollywood (Hampton), Düsseldorf.
1985	*One for the Road* (Pinter), Bonn.
1986	*Purpurstaub* (O'Casey), Staatstheater, Stuttgart.
1991	*Exiles* (Joyce), Zurich.

Films

Mutter Courage und ihre Kinder, 1961.

Television

Puntila, 1961.

Publications

Theaterarbeit — 6 Auffuehrungen des Berliner Ensembles, editor, 1952; *Puntila* (opera libretto), 1959; *War da Was?*, editor, 1980.

* * *

Of all the directors who determined the aesthetics and politics of the German theatre during the second half of the 20th century, Peter Palitzsch is the one who not only continued Brecht's project in his own work, but — educating a generation of actors and collaborating with a great number of important designers — applied and disseminated the method of his mentor throughout the German-speaking theatre community. While his former co-worker M. Wekwerth tried to uphold at the Berliner Ensemble in East Berlin a tradition that seemed to turn ever more sterile and less creative over the years, Palitzsch never tired in his efforts to adapt Brecht's aesthetic and philosophical heritage to the social currents that were sweeping contemporary society. He never surrendered, however, Brecht's basic principle of a theatre aimed at changing society.

Palitzsch was hired by Brecht as an assistant and dramaturg; together they coined the name 'Berliner Ensemble' for the new company Brecht founded in 1949. Trained as a graphic designer, Palitzsch created the famous logo of the Ensemble and proposed the rotating neon sign mounted on the theatre's roof. As principal dramaturg, he devised the programmes, their format, the artwork and the contents, as well as the company's posters. In such a way, he was greatly responsible for the image the Ensemble presented; this included *Theaterarbeit*, a documentation of the company's first six productions — Palitzsch being the main editor and designer of the volume. Most important, he was Brecht's close collaborator during the preparation of several productions. The thinking and the authorial strategies which went into Brecht's dramaturgical work became Palitzsch's own method.

In 1955, Palitzsch adapted with C. Weber several texts from classic Chinese comedies for a television production. Brecht saw the telecast and proposed the piece as an Ensemble project, which became Palitzsch's first stage production. During the following years, he and Wekwerth formed a team that staged the majority of the Ensemble's productions. When, in 1961, the Berlin Wall was erected, Palitzsch was in Ulm, directing Brecht's *The Trial of Jeanne d'Arc*. He decided to stay in the West, where he had already staged several productions during the late 1950's. Soon he emerged as one of the leading directors in the Federal Republic. With P. Zadek, W. Minks, K. M. Grüber, R. M. Fassbinder and P. Stein he contributed, under the management of K. Hübner in Bremen, to the project that soon became known as the 'Bremen Stil': aesthetic and dramaturgical approaches were developed that broke with prevailing conventions and tried to create a new 'realism', free of the remnants of naturalism as well as of the fashionable West German postwar formalism. The latest discoveries of happening art, photo-realism, and so on were all investigated and adapted to the stage.

When, in 1966, Palitzsch took over the direction of the Schauspiel at Stuttgart's Staatstheater, he assembled a company of committed actors that probably only the Schaubühne, after 1970, was able to surpass. Here he continued his creative evolvement of Brecht's theory and practice, combining it with bold experiments in design, especially in collaboration with Minks. Their outstanding achievement was probably *The Wars of the Roses*, Palitzsch's own adaptation of the Shakespeare histories, firmly sited in the context of contemporary political and social shifts. The Stuttgart years were also devoted to the new generation of German playwrights who had appeared during the 1960's: Weiss, Kipphardt, Walser, Dorst. Palitzsch also began to explore the British tradition aside of Shakespeare, especially the works of O'Casey and Pinter.

In 1972 he was appointed a member of the directorate at the Frankfurt Schauspiel, which implemented an administrative structure that gave all members of the company — be they artists or staff — a democratic voice in the decision-making. The 'Frankfurt model' did not succeed in the long run; nevertheless, it offered a number of younger directors and designers a most nurturing environment that yielded outstanding productions. When the city decided to return the theatre to a traditional administration mode in 1980, Palitzsch left. He continued, as a freelancing director, to employ the stringent dramaturgical approach he had learned from Brecht to his explorations of Ibsen, O'Casey, Joyce, Beckett and Pinter, of Shakespeare and of the German classics.

In Berlin, after Brecht's death, he was once called "the aesthetic conscience of the Ensemble", while the critic P. Iden referred to him in 1991 as "Brecht's heir". The integrity with which Palitzsch pursued and defended Brecht's project — while never turning into a dogmatic purist — is indeed unique. He himself described the theatre as an "instrument of responsibility", an instrument "to change the world, by the millimetre maybe; but still ... ". This Beckettian "But still ... " contains the very definition of Palitzsch's stance as an artist.

—Carl Weber

PAYNE, Ben Iden. British director and actor. Born in Newcastle-upon-Tyne, 5 September 1881. Educated privately and at Manchester Grammar School. Married 1) Mona Limerick (Mary Charlotte Louise Gadney) in 1906 (divorced 1950), one son and two daughters; 2) Barbara Rankin Chiaroni in 1950. Stage debut, under F. R. Benson, Theatre Royal, Worcester, 1899; London debut, 1900; general manager, Abbey Players, Dublin, 1907; director and producer, under Annie Horniman at the Midland and Gaiety Theatres, Manchester, 1907–11; worked in the USA, 1913–34; artistic director, Little Theatre, Philadelphia, 1914; general producer, Charles Frohman (Inc.), 1916–21; head of School of Drama, Carnegie Institute, 1919–34; artistic director, Goodman Theatre, Chicago, 1926; director, Theatre Guild, 1928–29; director, Shakespeare Memorial Theatre, Stratford-upon-Avon, 1934–43; returned to USA, 1943; Professor of Drama, University of Texas, from 1946; founder and director, Summer Shakespeare Festival, Old Globe Theatre, San Diego, 1949–52, 1955, 1957, and 1964; also directed at the Oregon Festival, 1956 and 1961, and at the University of Alberta, 1958–60 and 1962; Visiting Professor of Drama, Banff School of Fine Arts, Alberta, Canada, 1957–64; fund established in his name at University of Texas, to promote productions of Shakespeare, 1962. Member: American Educational Theatre Association, 1965 (Fellow, 1966). Recipient: Southwest Theatre Conference Award of Merit, 1954; American Educational Theatre Association Award of Merit, 1958; Fifth Annual Award, American National Shakespeare Festival and Academy, 1959; University of Texas Students' Association Teaching Excellence Award, 1959; Rodgers and Hammerstein Award, 1962; Consular Law Society Award of Merit, 1968; Theta Alpha Phi Medallion of Honour, 1969; First Annual Award of Austin, Texas Circle of Theatres, 1975. LL.D: University of Alberta, Canada, 1963. OBE (Order of the British Empire), 1976. Died in Austin, Texas, 6 April 1976.

Productions

As actor:
1899   Diggory in *She Stoops to Conquer* (Goldsmith), Theatre Royal, Worcester.
1907   Owen Ford in *The Street*, Manchester.
1908   Mr Ebton-Smith in *The Few and the Many*, Manchester.
    Victor Meux in *The Three Barrows*, Manchester.
    Oscar Eckersley in *Trespassers Will Be Prosecuted*, Manchester.

    Godfrey Rawlings in *When the Devil Was Ill* (McEvoy), Manchester.
    Lickcheese in *Widowers' Houses* (G. B. Shaw), Manchester.
    Eugene Marchbanks in *Candida* (G. B. Shaw), Manchester; Copley Repertory Company, New York, 1923.
1913   Lucio in *Measure for Measure* (Shakespeare), Fine Arts Theatre, Philadelphia; also directed.
1914   Bob Acres in *The Rivals* (Sheridan), Little Theatre, Philadelphia; also directed.
1915   Puff in *The Critic* (Sheridan), Princess Theatre, New York.
1921   James Broxopp in *The Great Broxopp* (Milne), Punch and Judy Theatre, New York; also directed.
1932   Henry Straker in *Man and Superman* (G. B. Shaw), Casino, Newport.

As director:
1907   *The Interior* (Maeterlinck), Abbey Theatre, Dublin.
    Fand (Blunt), Abbey Theatre, Dublin.
1913   *The Master of the House* (Houghton), Fine Arts Theatre, Philadelphia.
    Phipps (Houghton), Fine Arts Theatre, Philadelphia.
    A Florentine Tragedy (Wilde), Fine Arts Theatre, Philadelphia.
    Press Cuttings (G. B. Shaw), Fine Arts Theatre, Philadelphia.
1914   *The Younger Generation* (Houghton), British tour.
    Arms and the Man (G. B. Shaw), British tour.
    The Silver Box (Galsworthy), Little Theatre, Philadelphia.
    Courage, Little Theatre, Philadelphia.
1915   *Hobson's Choice* (Brighouse), Shubert Theatre, New York.
1917   *The Old Lady Shows Her Medals* (Barrie), New Theatre, London.
1920   *At the Villa Rose* (Mason), Strand Theatre, London.
1923   *A Weak Woman* (H. J. Byron), Copley Repertory Company, New York.
    Service for Two, Copley Repertory Company, New York.
1931   *The Way of the World* (Congreve), Guild Theatre, New York.
1935   *Antony and Cleopatra* (Shakespeare), Shakespeare Memorial Theatre, Stratford-upon-Avon.
    The Merry Wives of Windsor (Shakespeare), Shakespeare Memorial Theatre, Stratford-upon-Avon.
    All's Well That Ends Well (Shakespeare), Shakespeare Memorial Theatre, Stratford-upon-Avon.
1936   *King Lear* (Shakespeare), Shakespeare Memorial Theatre, Stratford-upon-Avon.
    Troilus and Cressida (Shakespeare), Shakespeare Memorial Theatre, Stratford-upon-Avon.

1937	*Cymbeline* (Shakespeare), Shakespeare Memorial Theatre, Stratford-upon-Avon.
1938	*The Comedy of Errors* (Shakespeare), Shakespeare Memorial Theatre, Stratford-upon-Avon.
1939	*The Taming of the Shrew* (Shakespeare), Shakespeare Memorial Theatre, Stratford-upon-Avon.
	Coriolanus (Shakespeare), Shakespeare Memorial Theatre, Stratford-upon-Avon.
1940	*King John* (Shakespeare), Shakespeare Memorial Theatre, Stratford-upon-Avon.
1944	*Embezzled Heaven* (Werfel), Theatre Guild, New York.
1945	*The Winter's Tale* (Shakespeare), Theatre Guild, New York.
1946	*Arms and the Man* (G. B. Shaw), University of Texas, Austin.
1947	*The Taming of the Shrew* (Shakespeare), University of Texas, Austin.
1948	*She Stoops to Conquer* (Shakespeare), University of Texas, Austin.
	Romeo and Juliet (Shakespeare), University of Texas, Austin.
	Abraham and Isaac (anon.), University of Texas, Austin.
1949	*The Critic* (Sheridan), University of Texas, Austin.
	Richard II (Shakespeare), University of Texas, Austin.
1950	*Dear Brutus* (Barrie), University of Texas, Austin.
	The Merchant of Venice (Shakespeare), University of Texas, Austin.
1951	*Much Ado About Nothing* (Shakespeare), University of Texas, Austin.
1952	*Henry IV, parts 1 and 2* (Shakespeare), University of Texas, Austin.
1953	*Hobson's Choice* (Brighouse), University of Texas, Austin.
	Cymbeline (Shakespeare), University of Texas, Austin.
1954	*A Midsummer Night's Dream* (Shakespeare), University of Texas, Austin.
1955	*Hamlet* (Shakespeare), University of Texas, Austin.
1956	*Love's Labour's Lost* (Shakespeare), University of Texas, Austin.
1957	*Richard III* (Shakespeare), University of Texas, Austin.
	Love for Love (Congreve), University of Texas, Austin.
1958	*King Lear* (Shakespeare), University of Texas, Austin.
1959	*The Taming of the Shrew* (Shakespeare), University of Texas, Austin.
1960	*The Winter's Tale* (Shakespeare), University of Texas, Austin.
1961	*Macbeth* (Shakespeare), University of Texas, Austin.
1962	*The Merry Wives of Windsor* (Shakespeare), University of Texas, Austin.
1963	*Othello* (Shakespeare), University of Texas, Austin.
1964	*As You Like It* (Shakespeare), University of Texas, Austin.
1965	*Measure for Measure* (Shakespeare), University of Texas, Austin.
	Julius Caesar (Shakespeare), University of Texas, Austin.
1966	*Troilus and Cressida* (Shakespeare), University of Texas, Austin.
1967	*Twelfth Night* (Shakespeare), University of Texas, Austin.
1968	*The Tempest* (Shakespeare), University of Texas, Austin.

Other productions included: *Justice* (Galsworthy), *The Guilty Man* (Willatt), *The Case of Lady Camber* (Vachell), *Pendennis*, *The Lady of the Camellias* (Dumas fils), *The Off-Chance* (Carton), *The Grasshopper* (Hollingshead), *The New World*, *Rambler Rose* (Smith), *Crops and Croppers*, *Dear Brutus* (Barrie), *Blood and Love*, *Déclassée* (Akins), *Caesar's Wife* (Maugham), all 1916–21; *That Day* (Anspacher), 1922; *Dagmar*, 1923; *Hail and Farewell*, 1923; *Children of the Moon*, 1923.

Radio

Variations on a Theatre Theme and *Shakespeare Sidelights* (series), 1956.

Publications

Poe (play, with T. W. Stevens, produced Carnegie Institute, 1920); *Pennie Gay* (play, with T. W. Stevens), 1921; *Dolly Jordan* (play, produced Daly's Theatre, New York, 1922); *Bird in Hand* (play), 1924; *Where Love is, God is also* (play), 1925; *The Ghostly Councillor* (play), 1927; *The Saint's Husband* (play, with Rosemary Casey), 1934; *Shining Armour* (play, with Rosemary Casey), 1935; *Mary Goes to See* (play, with Rosemary Casey, produced Haymarket Theatre, London, 1938); *A Life in a Wooden O: A Memoir of the Theatre*, 1977.

*

Bibliography

Books:
E. Martin Browne, *Two in One*, Cambridge, 1981.

* * *

Ben Iden Payne had a long and honourable career, mostly spent as a university teacher of drama. He was happiest working in an academic setting. Writing on Payne's directorship of the Shakespeare Memorial Theatre, Robert Speaight comments: "a scholarly 'Elizabethan', nurtured on the pure milk of Poel, he was rather too academic for a theatre clamouring for imaginative size both in acting and production". Nevertheless, those nine years were important in the history of Stratford Shakespeare. When Payne took over from William Bridges-Adams, the company included two outstanding male principals — Randle Ayrton and Baliol Holloway. Payne engaged Donald Wolfit for the 1936 and 1937 seasons, while other actors associated with the Payne years were Clement McCallin, Alec Clunes, James Dales, and Joan Sanderson. The presence of such talents, and the directions of Kommisarjevsky suggests that the Memorial Theatre did (at least on occasion) satisfy the demand for "imaginative size ... in acting and production".

Payne's own productions received muted praise. The system then operating did not permit extensive thought and preparation. Payne continued the Bridges-Adams policy of presenting a six-month season containing a repertoire of eight plays. There were eight performances per week; thus in any one week all eight productions could be seen. Rehearsal time was severely limited; just five weeks were allowed for the seven new productions mounted in 1936, for instance. But it is to Payne's credit that he revived a good deal of then unfamiliar Shakespeare, his seasons including *All's Well That Ends Well*, *Troilus and Cressida*, *Cymbeline*, *Coriolanus*, and *King John*. Of *Cymbeline*, J. C. Trewin recorded that it was performed "as a Jacobean court masque in a permanent architectural setting, Inigo Jones fashion; it was visually right, but, a few players aside — Joyce Bland, Wolfit, Baliol Holloway — Payne lacked the cast to fortify his ideas".

The complaint about undercasting is frequently met. The best Stratford principals were very good indeed, the company as a whole less impressive. Unflattering comparisons were often made with the Old Vic company. But it is clear that Stratford could rise to the occasion, as the 1940 *King John* showed. Holloway played the Bastard, George Skillan, King John, Joan Sanderson Constance, while Payne and Andrew Leigh produced. Sidney Charteris felt that the production fielded a better set of performances than had been seen for some time and he particularly commended the fire and vigour of the playing and the "near-greatness" of Sanderson's Constance. The theme of 'commodity' (expediency, self-interest) was strongly established, the Bastard's role as ribald chorus to the doings of a mad world being brought out by the mocking irreverence of Holloway. But there is much more to the Bastard than this, and Holloway conveyed the 'inner iron quality' with rare success. *The Times* noted that Holloway's Faulconbridge "stood truculently and humourously for the English spirit of resistance", gaining in the crisis of 1940 a new momentuousness. *King John* was one of Payne's strongest productions, in which words, music, and spectacle cohered to form a living experience. "The history which makes such hard reading is surprisingly alive on the stage" was the summing-up given by *The Times*.

In general, however, Payne's productions attracted only local praise, London critics showing impatience with the Stratford regime. Charles Morgan complained that "Mr Iden Payne appears to ask little more of his actors save that they should speak their lines clearly and intelligibly". Of his use of modified Elizabethan staging he concluded "he misses both the simplicity of the bare Elizabethan stage, and the persuasiveness of the picture stage".

Clear and intelligible speaking is a laudable aim, indeed, an essential of any performance. The insistence on Elizabethan staging was a more doubtful asset, given the design of the Memorial Theatre. But Payne had been influenced by William Poel and the Elizabethan Stage Society and yearned to return to the swiftness and simplicity of Elizabethan performance. Nugent Monck developed Poel's ideas with the Norwich Players, but Monck's company of amateurs were playing in the Norwich Maddermarket, a theatre seating 300 that was designed to reproduce Elizabethan conditions. Payne's efforts to accommodate a reproduction of the stage of the Swan Theatre within the proscenium arch of the Memorial resulted in "an uneasy and inelegant compromise".

Recalling an Iden Payne production for the Theatre Guild, Robert Speaight noted that "In New York the 'reverential varnish' of traditional Shakespeare production could still gleam agreeably when the brush was in the right hands. It looked a little dull when Iden Payne ... produced *The Winter's Tale* ... His flair was never quite equal to his fidelity, and he returned to the academic theatre in Texas where his profound theatrical scholarship was appreciated at its true worth". Payne was a dedicated teacher, as is shown by his record as a professor of drama at the Carnegie Institute of Technology and later at the University of Texas. If his work in the professional theatre lacked flair, he deserves credit for presenting a wide Shakespearean repertoire and for steering the Memorial Theatre through the first four years of World War II.

—Charles Calder

PEYMANN, Claus. German director. Born 1938. Began career as director at the Theater am Turm, Frankfurt, 1966, where he established his reputation with productions of new dramas by such contemporaries as Peter Handke and Thomas Bernhard; subsequently worked in West Berlin, Hamburg and Salzburg; director, Württemberg Staatstheater, Stuttgart, 1974–79; resigned in wake of scandal, 1979, and moved to Bochum and, from 1986, to the Burgtheater, Vienna.

Productions

1965	*Der schwarze Schwan* (Walser), Theater am Turm, Frankfurt.
1966	*Publikumsbeschimpfung* (Handke), Theater am Turm, Frankfurt.
1968	*Kaspar* (Handke), Theater am Turm, Frankfurt.
1970	*Ein Fest für Boris* (Bernhard), Deutsches Schauspielhaus, Hamburg.
1971	*Der Ritt über den Bodensee* (Handke), Schaubühne am Halleschen Ufer, Berlin.
1972	*Der Ignorant und der Wahnsinnige* (Bernhard), Festspiele, Salzburg.
	Die Hyperchonder (Strauss), Schauspielhaus, Hamburg.
	Pelikan (Strindberg), Schauspielhaus, Hamburg.
1974–79	*Cyanide* (Wolff), Württemberg Staatstheater, Stuttgart.
	Faust (Goethe), Württemberg Staatstheater, Stuttgart.
	Iphigenia (Goethe), Württemberg Staatstheater, Stuttgart.
1974	*Die Jagdgesellschaft* (Bernhard), Burgtheater, Vienna.

Die See (Bond), Theater am Turm, Frankfurt am Maim.

Himmel und Erde (Reinshagen), Württemberg Staatstheater, Stuttgart.

1975   Die Räuber (Schiller), Württemberg Staatstheater, Stuttgart.

Der Präsident (Bernhard), Württemberg Staatstheater, Stuttgart.

Das Käthchen von Heilbronn (Kleist), Württemberg Staatstheater, Stuttgart.

1976   Minetti: Ein Porträt des Künstlers als alter Mann (Bernhard), Württemberg Staatstheater, Stuttgart.

1978   Immanuel Kant (Bernhard), Württemberg Staatstheater, Stuttgart.

1979–86   Bambule (Meinhof), Schauspielhaus, Bochum.

Torquato Tasso (Goethe), Schauspielhaus, Bochum.

Nathan der Weise (Lessing), Schauspielhaus, Bochum.

Prometheus Unbound (Aeschylus, adapted by Handke).

1979   Vor dem Ruhestand (Bernhard), Württemberg Staatstheater, Stuttgart.

Unser Republic, Schauspielhaus, Bochum.

1980   Der Weltverbesserer (Bernhard), Schauspielhaus, Bochum.

1982   Hermannsschlacht (Kleist), Schauspielhaus, Bochum.

1984   Der Schein trügt (Bernhard), Schauspielhaus, Bochum.

1986–94   Wilhelm Tell (Schiller), Burgtheater, Vienna.

Clavigo (Goethe), Burgtheater, Vienna.

Richard III (Shakespeare), Burgtheater, Vienna.

Macbeth (Shakespeare), Burgtheater, Vienna.

Alpine Glow (Turrini), Burgtheater, Vienna.

Raststätte (Jelinek), Burgtheater, Vienna.

Arturo Ui (Brecht), Burgtheater, Vienna.

1988   Heldenplatz (Bernhard), Burgtheater, Vienna.

* * *

Claus Peymann's career began in 1966 when he joined the Frankfurt Theater am Turm, where a young company was trying out democratic self-management as an alternative to the prevalent command structure in which the Intendant or Director was all-powerful and the actors had little say. He came from student theatre and was shaped in many ways by the student protest movement of the 1960's. At the TaT he attracted critical attention when his inventive productions of Peter Handke's unconventional anti-theatre pieces Publikumsbeschimpfung (Offending the Audience) and Kaspar were shown at the Frankfurt 'Experimenta' avant-garde festival. Provocation and inventiveness have remained his stock in trade. In the early 1970's Peymann established a reputation as a specialist in modern plays, directing Bernard's Ein Fest für Boris (A Party for Boris) and Botho Strauss's Der Hyperchonder (Hypochondriacs) in Hamburg, Handke's Der Ritt über den Bodensee (The Ride across Lake Constance) and Bernhard's Der Ignorant und der Wahnsinnige (The Ignorant and the Lunatic) in Salzburg, Bernhard's Die Jagdgesellschaft (The

Shooting Party) at the Vienna Burgtheater and Edward Bond's The Sea in Frankfurt.

In 1974 he was appointed Intendant of the Württemberg State Theatre in Stuttgart, where he built up a team that moved with him to Bochum in 1979 and then to the Vienna Burgtheater in 1986. Among the members were director Alfred Kirchner, dramaturgs Hermann Beil, Uwe Jensen and Vera Sturm, and actors Lore Brunner, Traugott Buhre, Kirsten Dene, Branko Samarovski and Gert Voss. His actors became national stars along the way and the loyalty he gave and received from them applied equally to the string of writers whom he fostered and developed (Gerlind Reinshagen, Thomas Bernhard, Heiner Müller).

Peymann has always been a controversial figure. In Stuttgart he was riding on a wave of artistic success when an appeal came in for dental treatment for Gudrun Ennslin, a left-wing terrorist held in the local high-security prison. Peymann made the first donation, a humanitarian gesture that brought calls for him to be sacked and caused a scandal, in the course of which the prime minister of Württemberg's unknown Nazi past came to light. Both men resigned, Peymann unbowed and with a sense of having been let down all round. Moving on to Bochum, he staged Bambule, a play by the red Army Faction terrorist Ulrike Meinhof. Later, in Vienna, he directed Thomas Bernhard's Heldenplatz (Heroes' Square) as part of the campaign against Kurt Waldheim, the Austrian President who likewise forgot his Nazi past. Peymann has never aligned himself with any party; he belongs to the liberal left.

In Stuttgart, though he continued to premiere new plays (for example, Bernhard's The President and Minetti) and to stage topical revivals, such as Friedrich Wolff's 1928 play Cyanide, on the abortion issue; he also turned his attention to the classics. Thus followed Schiller's Die Räuber (The Robbers), a light, fantastic, circus-like production of Kleist's romantic fairytale Das Käthchen von Heilbronn and Goethe's Faust I and II — the second part as a promenade performance in the theatre's vast foyer, where, in a colourful, jokey, environment and with costumes designed by Achim Freyer, he offered a popular version of the play by introducing a pervasive whimsicality without cheapening the text. He also directed a gripping unclassical production of Goethe's classical dramatic poem Iphigenia.

In Bochum, a medium-sized Ruhr town with a remarkable tradition, especially for Shakespeare, Peymann and his team built up a model municipal repertory company, keeping together a first-class company at a time when productions elsewhere in Germany were being built round peripatetic stars. Almost half the plays produced between 1979 and 1986 were new German or foreign plays, including 24 world premieres. Characteristic of the Bochum Ensemble's critical attitude to the establishment, government and opposition alike, was Our Republic, a political review of West Germany from 1945 to the upcoming 1980 elections. The theatre was at the same time dedicated to entertainment and culture, both high and low — from iambic drama to Arsenic and Old Lace. The programmes included the playtext. The role of Peymann's literary office was to find and encourage new plays and identify classics that were relevant to the time and to Bochum. It nursed new authors like Thomas Brasch, Herbert Achternbusch, Franz-Xaver Kroetz and George Tabori, while Bernhard and Müller virtually became members of the company, the former writing a 'dramolett',

Claus Peymann leaves Bochum and goes to the Burgtheater for Peymann's farewell evening. Bochum also saw a string of classical revivals — Goethe's *Torquato Tasso*, Lessing's *Nathan der Weise*, and, most notable of all, Kleist's *Hermannsschlact* [Hermann's Battle], usually dismissed as an unplayable piece of chauvinism, which Peymann successfully revived as a black comedy, with Gert Voss as Hermann in a Ché Guevara beret.

Peymann took the core members of his Bochum company and part of the repertoire with him when he moved to Vienna, so there were tensions from the start at the Burgtheater, where the large company on lifetime contracts was full of stars who feared being sidelined. Conservative Vienna audiences were not attuned to his style and in any case he was aiming for a younger, less stuffy audience — which he eventually attracted. His run of classical revivals continued with Schiller's *Wilhelm Tell*, Goethe's *Clavigo* and Shakespeare's *Richard III* and *Macbeth*. He staged Bernhard's great anti-Austrian diatribes at the theatrical heart of the nation, then added later Austrian enfants terribles Peter Turrini and Elfriede Jelinek. Alfred Kirchner directed Brecht's *Arturo Ui* with the gangsters/Nazis in loden coats and Tyrolean hats. All this triggered anti-German resentment, and Peymann came under constant fire from a section of the press that felt that a great Austrian institution was degenerating in the hands of a 'Piefke' (Austrian for 'kraut'). Peymann survived the onslaught and continues to attract young talent, though his own productions are now rarely selected for the Berlin Theatertreffen, where he was almost a fixture in the 1970's and 1980's. Stylistically, he lies somewhere between Peter Stein and Peter Zadek. Peymann himself speaks of Stein's *Torquato Tasso* (1970), Zadek's *Othello* (1976) and his own *Hermannsschlacht* (1982) as the stages by which the classics were liberated from the stranglehold of an insidious style that evolved under the Nazis, whom it long outlived. Peymann, Stein and Peter Zadek took over the West German theatre at the end of the 1960's from the generation that had resuscitated it after the war. Peymann is less serious than Stein, less radical than Zadek, but wittier and with far greater organisational stamina than either. In 1994 his contract at the Burgtheater was extended to the end of the millenium.

—Hugh Rorrison

PHELPS, Samuel. British actor-manager. Born in Devonport, Devon, 13 February 1804. Educated at schools in Devonport and at Dr Reed's School, Saltash, Cornwall. Married Sarah Cooper in 1848 (died 1867), three sons and three daughters. Professional stage debut, York, 1826; played in provinces for next 11 years, earning reputation as strong tragedian; first London appearance at the Haymarket Theatre, at the invitation of Ben Webster, 1837; actor, with William Charles Macready's company at Covent Garden, 1837–39, the Haymarket, 1839–41, and the Theatre Royal, Drury Lane, 1841–43, though confined to mainly supporting roles by Macready; co-manager, Sadler's Wells Theatre, London, 1844–62; staged all but four of Shakespeare's plays, raising standards in all respects and restoring original texts; last appearance, Imperial Theatre, London, 1878. Died in Epping, 6 November 1878.

Roles

1837   Shylock in *The Merchant of Venice* (Shakespeare), Haymarket Theatre, London.
        Sir Edward Mortimer in *The Iron Chest* (Colman the Younger), Haymarket Theatre, London.
        Hamlet in *Hamlet* (Shakespeare), Haymarket Theatre, London.
        Othello in *Othello* (Shakespeare), Haymarket Theatre, London.
        Richard in *Richard III* (Shakespeare), Haymarket Theatre, London.
        Jaffier in *Venice Preserved* (Otway), Covent Garden, London.
        Macduff in *Macbeth* (Shakespeare), Covent Garden, London.
        Rob Roy in *Rob Roy* (Ryder, adapted from Scott), Covent Garden, London.

1838   First Lord in *As You Like It* (Shakespeare), Covent Garden, London.
        Cassius in *Julius Caesar* (Shakespeare), Covent Garden, London.
        Dumont in *Jane Shore* (Rowe), Covent Garden, London.
        Adrastus in *Ion* (Talfourd), Covent Garden, London.
        Posthumus in *Cymbeline* (Shakespeare), Covent Garden, London.
        Antonio in *The Tempest* (Shakespeare), Covent Garden, London.
        Tullus Aufidius in *Coriolanus* (Shakespeare), Covent Garden, London.
        Marcus in *Cato* (Addison), Covent Garden, London.

1839   Father Joseph in *Richelieu* (Bulwer-Lytton), Covent Garden, London.
        Kera Khan in *Lodoiska* (J. P. Kemble), Covent Garden, London.
        Constable of France in *Henry V* (Shakespeare), Covent Garden, London.
        Iago in *Othello* (Shakespeare), Haymarket Theatre, London.
        Beauseant in *The Lady of Lyons* (Bulwer-Lytton), Haymarket Theatre, London.
        Jaques in *As You Like It* (Shakespeare), Haymarket Theatre, London.
        Antonio in *The Merchant of Venice* (Shakespeare), Haymarket Theatre, London.
        Louis XV in *King O'Neil* (Gore), Haymarket Theatre, London.
        Walter in *The Hunchback* (Knowles), Haymarket Theatre, London.
        Onslow in *The Sea Captain* (Bulwer-Lytton), Haymarket Theatre, London.
        Faulkland in *The Rivals* (Sheridan), Haymarket Theatre, London.

1840   Peregrine in *John Bull* (Colman the Younger), Haymarket Theatre, London.
        Darnley in *Mary Stuart* (adapted from Schiller), Theatre Royal, Drury Lane, London.
        Rolla in *Pizarro* (Sheridan), Theatre Royal, Drury Lane, London.

The Ghost in *Hamlet* (Shakespeare), Haymarket Theatre, London.

Glenlyon in *Glencoe* (Talfourd), Haymarket Theatre, London.

King Henry in *Richard III* (Shakespeare), Haymarket Theatre, London.

Major Oakley in *The Jealous Wife* (Colman the Elder), Haymarket Theatre, London.

Lavender in *To Marry or not to Marry?* (Inchbald), Haymarket Theatre, London.

Old Dornton in *The Road to Ruin* (Holcroft), Haymarket Theatre, London.

General Distrowe in *Master Clarke* (Serle), Haymarket Theatre, London.

Egerton in *The Man of the World* (Macklin), Haymarket Theatre, London.

Steinfort in *The Stranger* (Kotzebue), Haymarket Theatre, London.

Gabor in *Werner* (Lord Byron), Haymarket Theatre, London.

Joseph Surface in *The School for Scandal* (Sheridan), Haymarket Theatre, London.

Lucius Junius Brutus in *Brutus* (Payne), Surrey Theatre, London.

1841   Count Villiers in *Education* (Morton), Haymarket Theatre, London.

Cardinal Martinuzzi in *Martinuzzi* (Stephens), Lyceum Theatre, London.

Ferrado Gonzaga in *The Wife* (Knowles), Haymarket Theatre, London.

Stukely in *The Gamester* (Moore), Theatre Royal, Drury Lane, London.

Macduff in *Macbeth* (Shakespeare), Theatre Royal, Drury Lane, London.

Norland in *Every One Has His Fault* (Inchbald), Theatre Royal, Drury Lane, London.

Duke of Milan in *The Two Gentlemen of Verona* (Shakespeare), Theatre Royal, Drury Lane, London.

1842   Lewson in *The Gamester* (Moore), Theatre Royal, Drury Lane, London.

St Franc in *A Point of Honour* (C. Kemble), Theatre Royal, Drury Lane, London.

Captain Channel in *The Prisoner of War* (Jerrold), Theatre Royal, Drury Lane, London.

Pierre in *Venice Preserved* (Otway), Theatre Royal, Drury Lane, London.

Andrew Wormall in *Plighted Troth* (Darley), Theatre Royal, Drury Lane, London.

Manly in *The Provoked Husband* (Vanbrugh and Cibber), Theatre Royal, Drury Lane, London.

Israel Bertuccio in *Marino Faliero* (Lord Byron), Theatre Royal, Drury Lane, London.

Almagro in *The Rose of Arragon* (Knowles), Haymarket Theatre, London.

Sir Giles Overreach in *A New Way to Pay Old Debts* (Massinger), Haymarket Theatre, London.

Hubert in *King John* (Shakespeare), Theatre Royal, Drury Lane, London.

Lynterne in *The Patrician's Daughter* (Marston), Theatre Royal, Drury Lane, London.

Samuel Phelps (1826).

Gloster in *Jane Shore* (Rowe), Theatre Royal, Drury Lane, London.

Adam in *As You Like It* (Shakespeare), Theatre Royal, Drury Lane, London.

Duke of Aranza in *The Honeymoon* (Tobin), Haymarket Theatre, London.

Romeo in *Romeo and Juliet* (Shakespeare), British provinces.

Ford in *The Merry Wives of Windsor* (Shakespeare), British provinces.

1843   Damas in *The Lady of Lyons* (Bulwer-Lytton), Theatre Royal, Drury Lane, London.

Belarius in *Cymbeline* (Shakespeare), Theatre Royal, Drury Lane, London.

Thorold Lord Tresham in *A Blot in the 'Scutcheon* (Browning), Theatre Royal, Drury Lane, London.

Leonato in *Much Ado About Nothing* (Shakespeare), Theatre Royal, Drury Lane, London.

Dentatus in *Virginius* (Knowles), Theatre Royal, Drury Lane, London.

Byerdale in *The Secretary* (Knowles), Theatre Royal, Drury Lane, London.

Dunstan in *Athelwold* (Smith), Theatre Royal, Drury Lane, London.

Gascoyne in *Henry IV* (Shakespeare), Theatre Royal, Drury Lane, London.

Antigonus in *The Winter's Tale* (Shakespeare), Theatre Royal, Drury Lane, London.

1844   Macbeth in *Macbeth* (Shakespeare), Sadler's Wells Theatre, London.

Sir Peter Teazle in *The School for Scandal* (Sheridan), Sadler's Wells Theatre, London.

Virginius in *Virginius* (Knowles), Sadler's Wells Theatre, London.

Sir Anthony Absolute in *The Rivals* (Sheridan), Sadler's Wells Theatre, London.

Julian St Pierre in *The Wife* (Knowles), Sadler's Wells Theatre, London.

Melantius in *The Bridal* (Knowles), Sadler's Wells Theatre, London.

King John in *King John* (Shakespeare), Sadler's Wells Theatre, London.

Luke Frugal in *The City Madam* (Massinger), Sadler's Wells Theatre, London.

Claude Melnotte in *The Lady of Lyons* (Bulwer-Lytton), Sadler's Wells Theatre, London.

Don Felix in *The Wonder* (Centlivre), Sadler's Wells Theatre, London.

1845   Role in *The Priest's Daughter* (Serle), Sadler's Wells Theatre, London.

Richard in *Richard III* (Shakespeare), Sadler's Wells Theatre, London.

Rover in *Wild Oats* (Buckstone), Sadler's Wells Theatre, London.

Frank Heartall in *The Soldier's Daughter* (Cherry), Sadler's Wells Theatre, London.

William Tell in *William Tell* (Knowles), Sadler's Wells Theatre, London.

Henry IV, King of France, in *The King's Friend* (Sullivan), Sadler's Wells Theatre, London.

Cardinal Richelieu in *Richelieu* (Bulwer-Lytton), Sadler's Wells Theatre, London.

Beverly in *The Gamester* (Moore), Sadler's Wells Theatre, London.

Romont in *The Fatal Dowry* (Massinger), Sadler's Wells Theatre, London.

Rolla in *Pizarro* (Sheridan), Sadler's Wells Theatre, London.

Lear in *King Lear* (Shakespeare), Sadler's Wells Theatre, London.

Leontes in *The Winter's Tale* (Shakespeare), Sadler's Wells Theatre, London.

1846   Alfred Evelyn in *Money* (Bulwer-Lytton), Sadler's Wells Theatre, London.

Hastings in *Jane Shore* (Rowe), Sadler's Wells Theatre, London.

Falstaff in *Henry IV, part 1* (Shakespeare), Sadler's Wells Theatre, London.

Brutus in *Julius Caesar* (Shakespeare), Sadler's Wells Theatre, London.

Mordaunt in *The Patrician's Daughter* (Marston), Sadler's Wells Theatre, London.

Mercutio in *Romeo and Juliet* (Shakespeare), Sadler's Wells Theatre, London.

The Duke in *Measure for Measure* (Shakespeare), Sadler's Wells Theatre, London.

Damon in *Damon and Pythias* (Banim), Sadler's Wells Theatre, London.

Arbaces in *A King and No King* (Beaumont and Fletcher), Sadler's Wells Theatre, London.

1847   Walter Cochran, Earl of Mar, in *Feudal Times* (White), Sadler's Wells Theatre, London.

Prospero in *The Tempest* (Shakespeare), Sadler's Wells Theatre, London.

Reuben Glenroy in *Town and Country* (Morton), Sadler's Wells Theatre, London.

Bertram in *Bertram* (Maturin), Sadler's Wells Theatre, London.

Bertulphe the Provost in *The Provost of Bruges* (Lovell), Sadler's Wells Theatre, London.

John Savile in *John Savile of Haysted* (White), Sadler's Wells Theatre, London.

Cardinal Wolsey in *Henry VIII* (Shakespeare), Sadler's Wells Theatre, London.

1848   Malvolio in *Twelfth Night* (Shakespeare), Sadler's Wells Theatre, London.

Falstaff in *The Merry Wives of Windsor* (Shakespeare), Sadler's Wells Theatre, London.

Coriolanus in *Coriolanus* (Shakespeare), Sadler's Wells Theatre, London.

Leon in *Rule a Wife and Have a Wife* (Beaumont and Fletcher), Sadler's Wells Theatre, London.

1849   Montagu in *The Honest Man's Fortune* (Beaumont and Fletcher, adapted by Horne), Sadler's Wells Theatre, London.

Calaynos in *Calaynos* (Boker), Sadler's Wells Theatre, London.

Antony in *Antony and Cleopatra* (Shakespeare), Sadler's Wells Theatre, London.

Garcia in *Garcia* (Tomlins), Sadler's Wells Theatre, London.

1850   Blackbourn in *Retribution* (Bennett), Sadler's Wells Theatre, London.

Octavian in *The Mountaineers* (Colman the Younger), Sadler's Wells Theatre, London.

Francesco Agolanti in *The Legend of Florence* (Hunt), Sadler's Wells Theatre, London.

Ferdinand in *The Duchess of Malfi* (Webster), Sadler's Wells Theatre, London.

1851   Jeremiah Bumps in *Turning the Tables*, Sadler's Wells Theatre, London.

Timon in *Timon of Athens* (Shakespeare), Sadler's Wells Theatre, London.

Ingomar in *Ingomar* (Lovell), Sadler's Wells Theatre, London.

Sir Pertinax McSycophant in *The Man of the World* (Macklin), Princess's Theatre, London.

1852   James VI in *James VI* (White), Sadler's Wells Theatre, London.

Parolles in *All's Well That Ends Well* (Shakespeare), Sadler's Wells Theatre, London.

Henry V in *Henry V* (Shakespeare), Sadler's Wells Theatre, London.

1853   The King and Justice Shallow in *Henry IV, part 2* (Shakespeare), Sadler's Wells Theatre, London.

Bottom in *A Midsummer Night's Dream* (Shakespeare), Sadler's Wells Theatre, London.

1854   Pericles in *Pericles* (Shakespeare), Sadler's Wells Theatre, London.

1855   Bailie Nicol Jarvie in *Rob Roy* (Scott), Sadler's Wells Theatre, London.

1856	Christopher Sly in *The Taming of the Shrew* (Shakespeare), Sadler's Wells Theatre, London.
1857	Adriano de Armado in *Love's Labour's Lost* (Shakespeare), Sadler's Wells Theatre, London.
	Lord Ogleby in *The Clandestine Marriage* (Colman and Garrick), Sadler's Wells Theatre, London.
1858	Lord Townley in *The Provoked Husband* (Vanbrugh and Cibber), Sadler's Wells Theatre, London.
	Dr Cantwell in *The Hypocrite* (Bickerstaff), Sadler's Wells Theatre, London.
	Penruddock in *The Wheel of Fortune* (Cumberland), Sadler's Wells Theatre, London.
1859	Job Thornbury in *John Bull* (Colman the Younger), Sadler's Wells Theatre, London.
1860	Bertuccio in *The Fool's Revenge* (Taylor), Sadler's Wells Theatre, London.
1861	Louis in *Louis XI* (Delavigne), Sadler's Wells Theatre, London.
	Falstaff in *Henry IV, part 2* (Shakespeare), Sadler's Wells Theatre, London.
	Dick Stubbs in *Doing for the Best* (Lacy), Sadler's Wells Theatre, London.
1863	Manfred in *Manfred* (Lord Byron), Theatre Royal, Drury Lane, London.
1864	Julian de Vivaldi in *Night and Morn* (Falconer), Theatre Royal, Drury Lane, London.
1866	Mephistopheles in *Faust* (Goethe, adapted by Bernard), Theatre Royal, Drury Lane, London.
1867	The Doge in *The Doge of Venice* (Bernard, adapted from Byron's *Marino Faliero*), Theatre Royal, Drury Lane, London.
1868	James I and Trapbois in *King o'Scots* (Halliday, adapted from Scott's *Fortunes of Nigel*), Theatre Royal, Drury Lane, London.
1870	Mephistopheles in *Faust and Marguerite* (Carrè, adapted by Boucicault), Princess's Theatre, London.
	Isaac of York in *Ivanhoe* (Halliday, adapted from Scott), Theatre Royal, Drury Lane, London.
	Dexter Sanderson in *On the Jury* (Phillips), Princess's Theatre, London.
1876	Henry IV in *Henry V* (Shakespeare), Queen's Theatre, London.

Publications

The Memoirs of Samuel Phelps, edited by John Coleman, 1886.

*

Bibliography

Books:
Westland Marston, *Our Recent Actors*, London, 1890.
W. May Phelps and Johnston Forbes-Robertson, *The Life and Life-work of Samuel Phelps*, London, 1886.

* * *

Born into a well-to-do merchant family in Devonport, Phelps received a good education until he was orphaned at the age of 16. His interest in the theatre already awakened by visits to London, where he saw the Kembles and Edmund Kean, he repaired to the capital working as a journalist and performing as an amateur actor. He took a professional position with a Yorkshire company in 1826 and served a lengthy provincial apprenticeship before making his (professional) London debut as Shylock under Benjamin Webster's management at the Haymarket Theatre on 28 August 1837.

Phelps's performance as Shylock was described as "correct and judicious, but not remarkable or striking". Physically, he was of medium height and slender build (though he filled out in later life) with a high forehead, straight strong nose, broad square chin, and a wide expressive mouth. His voice was powerful with a wide range and musical tone. Capable of intense passion, his particular forte was the pathetic: a worthy man struck down by adverse circumstances. The transcendent heights of tragedy generally eluded him, but his intelligence and judgement ensured that he gave creditable performances in the major Shakespearean roles (in particular Macbeth and Lear). His determination to stay in control is indicated by his reply to the question whether an actor ought to realise the passions of a character as if they were his own: "Good Heaven, if I were to do that, I should never be able to act at all! I should simply lose command of my voice and movements altogether. The very thing I have to fight against is the over-identification of myself with the part."

Phelps spent several formative, if somewhat uneasy, years with Macready at Covent Garden during which, although he had some good opportunities, he chafed under the many minor roles assigned to him by the actor-manager, who was fearful of his younger rival. The repeal — in 1843 — of the Patent Theatres' monopoly meant that legitimate drama was no longer restricted to Covent Garden, Drury Lane, and the Haymarket. Phelps seized upon this opportunity to set up in management, initially with Mr Greenwood and Mrs Warner, at the Sadler's Wells Theatre in the north London suburb of Islington.

Phelps's 18-year tenure of Sadler's Wells remains one of the greatest achievements in the history of the English theatre. Although he was indisputably the star performer, he assembled a loyal and talented company around him, including George Bennett, Henry Marston, Isabella Glyn, and Priscilla Horton. His repertoire was wide-ranging and instead of confining himself to the mainstream of Shakespearean works, he mounted 32 of the plays, including such rarities as *Timon of Athens* and *Pericles*.

His texts, whilst by no means complete, advanced the restorations initiated by Macready. He also produced the plays of Massinger, Beaumont and Fletcher, Webster, and Rowley. His record on new plays was less impressive, but did include works by James White and Tom Taylor (*The Fool's Revenge*). Scenery and costumes were tasteful and appropriate.

As Phelps's reputation grew his audience extended beyond the local populace to include discerning playgoers from further afield. Of these, Professor Henry Morley (Professor of English Literature at London University College), in his capacity as drama critic of the *Examiner*, has left many eloquent testimonials to Phelps's achievements as actor and manager. Perhaps the finest was his 1853 revival of *A Midsummer Night's Dream*. The whole production was conceived as a dream. The scenery made use of two favourite devices: a diorama and gauze, as a result of which "the scenes melt dreamlike one into another". Phelps's Bottom "was completely incorporated with The Midsummer Night's Dream, made an essential part of it, as unsubstantial, as airy and refined as all the rest." Gone was the old "bully Bottom" with his coarse appeals to the audience through exaggerated by-play; in his stead was an uncouth, vain, and bemused mechanical, who accepted what was happening to him quietly, as dreamers do. Thus Phelps created a consummate comic performance anchored in a sense of his character's reality amidst unreal circumstances. Morley considered it doubtful whether the play "has yet, since it was first written, been put upon the stage with so nice an interpretation of its meaning."

Following the termination of his Sadler's Wells management in 1862, Phelps devoted the remainder of his professional life to West End and provincial enagagements as an actor. In Shakespeare's tercentenary year (1864) he took his acknowledged place as head of his profession with a series of commanding performances for Falconer at Drury Lane. Alongside a remarkable success (over 100 performances) as Byron's Manfred (marked by fine elocution and a discriminating display of emotion), he presented a range of old favourites such as Sir Pertinax MacSycophant in Macklin's *The Man of the World*, but the centrepiece was his Falstaff in *Henry IV, part 1*. Morley considered that "If Mr Phelps played nothing than Falstaff, it would be remarkable ... He lays stress not on Falstaff's sensuality, but on the lively intellect that stands for soul as well as mind in his gross body ... The fat knight is not vulgarised in Mr Phelps's reading."

During the next decade Phelps appeared regularly at Charles Calvert's Prince's Theatre in Manchester, usually as a visiting star but on two occasions as a member of the company in revivals of *Henry IV, part 2* (1873) and *Twelfth Night* (1874). As Malvolio his long-standing propensity to present essentially worthy men struck down by circumstances, whilst not negating the character's vanity, made him "less demonstrative, and less directly ridiculous than we sometimes see", according to one review.

In *Henry IV, part 2* he repeated his celebrated diptych as the King and Justice Shallow. As Shallow, he exhibited the vanity (again), the fussiness, the braggadocio, and the senility of the garrulous squire. The high point of his Henry IV came in the Jerusalem Chamber encounter with his errant son Hal. There the limitations that had hedged Phelps's portraits of some of the great, majestic, tragic roles mattered little as he concentrated on the father-son relationship, which he instilled with that domestic pathos that was his true forte. Thus, his broken emphasis on the single word "Harry" in "Come hither, Harry, sit thou by my bed" conveyed "whole volumes of pathos and an affectionate reconciliation which a careful culling of all the words of endearment in an entire language could not equal."

Phelps's Hal on that occasion was the youthful Johnston Forbes-Robertson, whom he had coached in the part. As an author, Forbes-Robertson was Phelps's biographer; as an artist he painted a portrait of the actor as Cardinal Wolsey; as an actor throughout his career he upheld those qualities (fine verse-speaking and controlled emotion based on the truth of the character) that he had learnt from his mentor and thus perpetuated that great tradition of English acting into the 20th century.

—Richard Foulkes

PHILIPE, Gérard. French actor and director. Born Gérard Philip in Cannes, France, 4 December 1922. Educated at the Collegége Stanislas de Cannes, from 1928. Married Nicole Fourcade in 1951, one daughter, one son. Became interested in theatre after appearance at Red Cross charity benefit, 1940; stage debut, Cannes Casino, 1941; film debut, 1943; enrolled as student at the Paris Conservatoire, 1943–45; became hugely popular in young romantic roles on stage and screen; actor, Théâtre National Populaire, from 1951; opposed Korean War and led Comité des Acteurs trade union as president, from 1957. Recipient: Best Actor award, Brussels Film Festival, 1947. Died in Paris (from cancer), 25 November 1959.

Roles

As actor:
1941	Mick in *Une grande fille tout simple* (Roussin), Cannes Casino, Cannes.
1943	Coco in *Une jeune fille savait* (Haguet), French tour.
	The Angel in *Sodome et Gomorrhe* (Giraudoux), Théâtre Hébertot, Paris.
1944	Denis in *Au Petit Bonheur* (Sauvajon), Théâtre Gramont, Paris.
1945	The White Prince in *Fédérigo* (Laporte), Théâtre des Mathurins, Paris.
	Caligula in *Caligula* (Camus), Théâtre Hébertot, Paris.
1947	The Poet in *Epiphanies* (Pichette), Théâtres des Noctambules, Paris.
	Harold in *KMX Labrador* (Deval, adapted from Read's *Petticoat Fever*), Théâtre de la Michodière, Paris.
1949	Albert in *Le Figurant de la Gaîté* (Savoir), Théâtre Montparnasse-Gaston Baty, Paris.
1951	Rodrigo in *Le Cid* (Corneille), Festival d'Avignon.
	Frédéric in *Le Prince de Homburg* (Kleist), Festival d'Avignon; Théâtre des Champs-Eysées, Paris, 1952; Hamburg, 1953.
	Artemona in *La Calandria* (Bibbiena, adapted by Arnaud), Festival d'Avignon.
	Eilif in *Mother Courage* (Brecht), Suresnes Festival.
1952	Tellur in *Nucléa* (Pichette), Palais de Chaillot, Paris; also directed.
	Lorenzo in *Lorenzaccio* (Musset), Festival d'Avignon; Théâtre National Populaire, Paris, 1953; also directed.

Callimaque in *La Nouvelle Mandragore* (Vauthier), Théâtre National Populaire, Paris; also directed.

1954   Richard in *Richard II* (Shakespeare), Théâtre National Populaire, Paris.

Ruy Blas in *Ruy Blas* (Hugo), Théâtre National Populaire, Paris.

1958   Octave in *Les Caprices de Marianne* (Musset), Festival d'Avignon and Palais de Chaillot, Paris.

1959   Perdican in *On ne badine pas avec l'amour* (Musset), Théâtre National Populaire, Paris.

Films

As actor:
Painter's friend in *La Boîte aux rêves*, 1943; Jérôme in *Les Petites fleurs du quai aux Fleurs*, 1944; Simon in *Le Pays sans étoiles*, 1946; Prince Muichkine in *L'Idiot*, 1946; François in *Le Diable au corps*, 1947; Fabrice in *Le Chartreuse de Parme*, 1947; Pierre in *Une si jolie petite plage*, 1949; Gabriel in *Tous les chemins mènent à Rome*, 1949; Henri in *La Beauté du diable*, 1950; The Count in *La Ronde*, 1950; Gérard in *Souvenirs perdus*, 1950; Michel in *Juliette ou la clé des songes*, 1951; Fanfan in *Fanfan-la-tulipe*, 1951; Master of Ceremonies in *Les septs péchés capitaux*, 1951; Claude in *Les Belles-de-nuit*, 1952; Georges in *Les Orgueilleux*, 1953; d'Artagnan in *Si Versailles m'était conté*, 1953; André Ripois in *Knave of Hearts*, 1954; The Lover in *Villa Borghese*, 1954; Julien Sorel in *Le rouge et noir*, 1954; Armand in *Les Grandes manoeuvres*, 1955; Perrin in *La Meilleure part*, 1956; Street singer in *Si Paris nous était conté*, 1956; Octave Mouret in *Pot-Bouille*, 1957; Modigliani in *Montparnasse 19*, 1957; Désiré in *La Vie à Deux*, 1958; Alexei in *Le Joueur*, 1958; Valmont in *Les Liaisons dangereuses*, 1959; Vasquez in *La Fièvre monte à El Pao*, 1960.

As actor and director:
Till in *Les Aventures de Till l'Espiègle*, 1957.

*

Bibliography

Books:
Claude Roy, *Gérard Philipe. Souvenirs et témoignages*, Paris, 1960.
Paul Giannoli, *La Vie inspirée de Gérard Philipe*, Paris, 1960.
Monique Chapelle, *Gérard Philipe, notre Éternelle jeunesse*, Paris, 1965.
Henri Pichette, *Tombeau de Gérard Philipe*, Paris, 1979.
Maurice Périsset, *Gérard Philipe ou la jeunesse sud monde*, Rennes, 1985.
Dominique Nares, *Gérard Philipe — Qui êtes vous?*, Lyon, 1988.

Articles:
Philippe Durant, "Gérard Philipe", *Tétes d'affiche*, 1983.
Pierre Cadars, "Gérard Philipe", *Cinéma*, 1984.

Georges Sadoul, "Gérard Philipe", *Le cinéma en mémoire*, 1984.

*   *   *

Gérard Philipe was probably the handsomest leading man ever to grace both stage and screen. It is said that Albert Camus, who had at one moment considered the possibility of playing the part himself, was not altogether delighted when it was Gérard Philipe in the title role of his *Caligula* who attracted the lion's share of attention when the play was first produced, in 1945; Philipe's portrayal of the maddest of the mad Roman emperors certainly did more for the actor's career than it did for that of the future Nobel prize-winning author.

Most importantly, the prestige Philipe thus obtained allowed him to mount, four years later, the first genuinely theatrical revival of Corneille's *Le Cid* since the early 19th century. Corneille had never been played quite like this before, Philipe making an ideal young and romantic hero in the character of Rodrigo, the young Spanish nobleman who has to make the agonizing decision between love and honour when obliged to challenge the father of his betrothed to a duel. Because Corneille was seen as the father of French Classicism, the tradition had developed, especially under the star system of the Comédie Française, of having Rodrigo played as a slightly elderly Hamlet, arguing the case for love against honour as though it was a French version of "To be, or not to be". Philipe's performance changed all that. His Rodrigo, played in the open air and against the kind of background against which younger members of the audience could imagine the Three Musketeers fighting their duels, knocked the dust off Corneille and made him a playwright for the postwar stage. Similarly, as director and leading actor in the newly established Théâtre National Populaire at the Palais de Chaillot in the 1950's, Philipe showed that even as faulty a play as Victor Hugo's *Ruy Blas* could be made attractive as well as understandable for a modern audience. He performed a comparable miracle for Heinrich von Kleist's *Prince of Homburg* and was predictably outstanding in a new production of Musset's *Lorenzaccio*. The vigour of his acting meant that plays in the French romantic tradition were performed without the self-pity that had characterised their production in the 19th century and Philipe's service to the whole of the French theatrical establishment was thus considerable, more attuned to modern taste than the productions of Louis Jouvet and making use of all the potentialities of the open, curtainless stage of the Palais de Chaillot.

Although Philipe showed himself a very good actor in light comedy on the commercial stage with his 1949 performance in the title role of Savoir's *Le Figurant de la Gaieté* — a revival from 1926 — it is always with the Théâtre National Populaire in Paris and Jean Vilar's Festival d'Avignon that he will be associated. He found the ideal director in Vilar, who taught him to project his voice and especially to take advantage of the much greater space available at Avignon, as at the Palais de Chaillot. Vilar himself described the extraordinarily natural way in which Philipe allowed Hugo's poetry to speak through him in his performance as Ruy Blas, never seeming to look for emotion but allowing it to come through him and reach the audience with a direct spontaneity that other actors nurtured in the more self-consciously dramatic tradition of the French stage could never equal. Almost alone among French actors, Philipe never over-acted, remaining as distant from the mannered preciosity of Jean-Louis Barrault as from the more intelligently self-conscious style of Pierre Brasseur. Even Kenneth Tynan, not an admirer of the French theatrical tradition, wrote enthusiastically of him as "the best jeune premier in the world, a limpid lyrical young animal about whom the only reservation is that animals rarely age well." Cancer made sure of that danger being avoided and prevented audiences from seeing whether an ideal Cid could age into an ideal Lear.

It was a mark of Philipe's genius as a man of the theatre that he did not fall into the trap of allowing himself to be absorbed into the cinema. This could easily have happened, for he was outstanding both as a young, romantic lead, as a comedy player, and as the mature, more cynical Marquis de Valmont in the first 1959 film version of Choderlos de Laclos's *Les Liaisons dangereuses*. This was Philipe's penultimate film and the illness that was shortly to kill him was visible in his face, a kind of outward sign of the inner decay marking the one unsympathetic character that he played. In his other films, he tended to be typecast as the vulnerable teenager in love with an older married woman, as in *Le Diable au corps*, or as the dashing young adventurer, as opposite Gina Lollobrigida in *Fanfan-la-tulipe*. He nevertheless showed a considerable gift for romantic comedy played with a very light touch in *La Ronde* and in *Belles de nuit*. The irony of fate that led to his death in 1959 and Camus's demise in a car crash in January 1960 seems in retrospect to mark the end of an era. The period of the liberation, with its hopes for a fundamental change in French society on the political as well as the cultural front, had come to an end.

—Philip Thody

PISCATOR, Erwin (Friedrich Max). German director. Born in Ulm, Germany, 17 December 1893. Studied for the stage at the König School of Dramatic Art and under Max Reinhardt at the Deutsches Theater, 1918. Joined German Communist party, 1918; founded the Tribunal theatre, Berlin, 1919, and succeeded Karlheinz Martin as director of the Proletarisches Theater, Berlin, 1920, developing concept of epic theatre; director, Volksbühne Theatre, Berlin, until dismissed for left-wing political stance, 1927; founded own Piscator-Bühne theatre in Berlin, 1927–29; worked in Soviet Union, 1933–36; settled in New York, 1938, and became head of the Dramatic Department of the New School for Social Research; returned to Germany, 1951; director, Freie Volksbühne, Berlin, from 1962, winning renewed acclaim for documentary dramas. Died in Starnberg, West Germany, 30 March 1966.

Productions

1920   *Gespenstersonate* (Strindberg), Das Tribunal, Berlin.
     Tod und Teufel (Wedekind), Das Tribunal, Berlin.
     Schloss Wetterstein (Wedekind), Das Tribunal, Berlin.
     Der Centaur (Kaiser), Das Tribunal, Berlin.
     Der Krüppel (Wittvogel), Proletarisches Theater, Berlin.
     Vor dem Tore (Sas), Proletarisches Theater, Berlin.
     Russlands Tag (Barta), Proletarisches Theater, Berlin.
     Die Feinde (Gorky), Proletarisches Theater, Berlin.
     Prinz Hagen (Sinclair), Proletarisches Theater, Berlin.
1921   *Wie Lange noch - du hure Bürgerliche Gerechtigkeit?* (Jung), Proletarisches Theater, Berlin.
     Die Kanaker (Jung), Proletarisches Theater, Berlin.
1922   *Die Kleinbürger* (Gorky), Central-Theater, Berlin.
     Die Zeit wird Kommen (Rolland), Central-Theater, Berlin.
1923   *Die macht der finsternis* (Tolstoy), Central-Theater, Berlin.
1924   *Fahnen* (Paquet), Volksbühne, Berlin.
     Revue Roter Rummel (Gasbarra), Säle, Berlin.
     Unter dem Karibischen Mond (O'Neill), Volksbühne, Berlin.
     Südseespiel (Brust), Volksbühne, Berlin.
1925   *Wer weint um Suckenack?* (Rehfisch), Volksbühne, Berlin.
     Dei Befreiung (Lask), Central-Theater, Berlin.
     Segal am Horizont (Leonhard), Volksbühne, Berlin.
     Hilfe! Ein kind ist vom Himmel Gefallen!, Central-Theater, Berlin
     Trotz Alledem! (Gasbarra), Grosses Schauspielhaus, Berlin.
     Die Fröhliche Stadt (Johst), Kammerspiele, Munich.
1926   *Michael Hundertpfund* (Ortner), Tribüne, Berlin.
     Sturmflut (Paquet), Volksbühne, Berlin.
     Das Trunkene Schiff (Zech), Volksbühne, Berlin.
     Rausch (Strindberg), Kammerspiele, Munich.
     Die Räuber (Schiller), Staatliches Schauspielhaus, Berlin.
     Sturmflut (Paquet), Kammerspiele, Hamburg.
     Nachtasyl (Gorky), Volksbühne, Berlin.
1927   *Das Gastliche Haus* (Mann), Kammerspiele, Munich.
     Die Weber (Hauptmann), Theater Erwerbsloser, Berlin.
     Gewitter über Gottland (Welk), Volksbühne, Berlin.
     Hoppla, Wir Leben! (Toller), Theater am Nollendorfplatz, Berlin.
     Rasputin, die Romanovs, der Krieg und das Volk, das Gegen sie Aufstand (Piscator, Gasbarra, Lania and Brecht, adapted from Tolstoy and Shchegolev), Theater am Nollendorfplatz, Berlin.

1928   *Die Abenteuer des Braven Soldaten Schwejk*
        (Piscator and Brecht, adapted from Hasek),
        Theater am Nollendorfplatz, Berlin.
        Konjunktur (Lania), Lessing-Theater, Berlin.

1929   *Rivalen* (Anderson, adapted by Zuckmayer),
        Königgrätzer Strasse, Berlin.
        Josef (Kalkowska), Volksbühne, Berlin.
        Kaufmann von Berlin (Mehring), Theater am
        Nollendorfplatz, Berlin.
        Die Räuber (Schiller), Theater am Nollendorf-
        platz, Berlin.
        S218 (Frauen in Not) (Credé), Apollotheater,
        Mannheim.

1930   *S218 (Frauen in Not)* (Credé), Wallner-Theater,
        Berlin.
        Des Kaisers Kulis (Plivier), Lessing-Theater,
        Berlin.

1931   *Tai Yang Erwacht* (Wolf), Wallner-Theater,
        Berlin.
        Frau in Front (Glebow), Wallner-Theater, Ber-
        lin.

1940   *Saint Joan* (G. B. Shaw), Belasco Theatre,
        Washington.
        King Lear (Shakespeare), Dramatic Workshop,
        Studio Theatre, New York.

1942   *War and Peace* (Piscator and Neumann), Dra-
        matic Workshop, Studio Theatre, New York.

1943   *Mourning Becomes Electra* (O'Neill), Rooftop
        Theatre, New York.

1944   *Last Stop* (Davis), Ethel Barrymore Theatre,
        New York.

1945   *The Private Life of the Master Race* (Brecht),
        Pauline Edwards Theatre, New York.
        Solomon the King and Shalmai the Cobbler
        (Gronemann), Masters Institute, New York.

1946   *Bar Kochba* (Tschnerichowski), Times Hall,
        New York.

1947   *The Flies* (Sartre), President Theatre, New
        York.
        Twelfth Night (Shakespeare), Placid Manor,
        Lake Placid, New York.

1948   *All the King's Men* (Warren), President The-
        atre, New York.
        Chaff (Bruckner), President Theatre, New
        York.

1949   *Outside the Door* (Borchert), President Theatre,
        New York.
        The Burning Bush (Herald), Rooftop Theatre,
        New York.

1950   *The Scapegoat* (Matthews), President Theatre,
        New York.

1951   *Macbeth* (Shakespeare), DW Technical Insti-
        tute, New York.
        Virginia (Hochwälder), Deutsches Schauspiel-
        haus, Hamburg.

1952   *Nathan der Weise* (Lessing), Schauspielhaus,
        Marburg.
        Die Uebe der Vier Obersten (Ustinov), Schaus-
        spielhaus, Zurich.
        Leonce und Lena (Büchner), Stadttheater,
        Giessen.
        Dantons Tod (Büchner), Schauspielhaus, Mar-
        burg.

Erwin Piscator

1953   *Androklus und der Löwe* (G. B. Shaw),
        Komödie, The Hague.
        Das Heilige Experiment (Hochwälder),
        Komödie, The Hague.
        Macbeth (Shakespeare), Staatstheater, Olden-
        burg.
        Im Räder Werk (Sartre), Städtische Bühnen,
        Frankfurt.

1954   *Caesar und Cleopatra* (G. B. Shaw), Komödie,
        The Hague.
        Hexenjagd (Miller), Nationaltheater, Mann-
        heim; Landestheater, Tübingen, Volksthe-
        ater, Göteborg, and Schauspielhaus, Mar-
        burg, 1955.

1955   *Krieg und Frieden* (Piscator and Neumann),
        Schiller-Theater, Berlin, and Landestheater,
        Darmstadt; Landestheater, Tübingen, and
        Vereinigte Städtische, Mönchen-Gladbach,
        1956.
        Im Räder Werk (Sartre), Landestheater,
        Tübingen.
        Requiem für eine Nonne (Faulkner), Schloss-
        park-Theater, Berlin; Volkstheater, Göteborg,
        1956.
        Die Fall Pinedus (Levi), Nationaltheater,
        Mannheim.

1956   *Dantons Tod* (Büchner), Schiller-Theater, Ber-
        lin.

1957   *Die Räuber* (Schiller), Nationaltheater, Mann-
        heim.

Der Bar (Chekhov), Schlosspark-Theater, Berlin.

Der Heiratsantrag (Chekhov), Schlosspark-Theater, Berlin.

Er ist an allem Schuld (Tolstoy), Schlosspark-Theater, Berlin.

Wie du mich Willst (Pirandello), Landestheater, Tübingen.

Krieg und Frieden (Tolstoy), Upsala.

Totentanz I und II (Strindberg).

1958   *Trauer muss Elektra Tragen* (O'Neill), Bühnen der Stadt, Essen.

Requiem für eine Nonne (Faulkner), Bühnen der Stadt, Essen.

Göttinger Kantate (Weissenborn), Liederhalle, Stuttgart.

Wilhelm Tell (Schiller), Nationaltheater, Mannheim.

Gas I und II (Kaiser), Schauspielhaus, Bochum.

Hexenjagd (Miller), Bühnen der Stadt, Essen.

1959   *Die Räuber* (Schiller), Bühnen der Stadt, Essen.

Nebeneinander (Kaiser), Thalia-Theater, Hamburg.

Biedermann und die Brandstifter (Frisch), Nationaltheater, Mannheim.

Don Carlos (Schiller), Kammerspiele, Munich.

Totentanz I und II (Strindberg), Bühnen der Stadt, Essen.

1960   *Mutter Courage und ihre Kinder* (Brecht), Staatstheater, Kassel.

Die Eingeschlossenen (Sartre), Bühnen der Stadt, Essen, and Schauspielhaus, Marburg; Landestheater, Tübingen.

Rosamunde Floris (Blacher), Städtische Oper, Berlin.

1913 (Sternheim), Kammerspiele, Munich; Städtische Bühnen, Frankfurt, and Bühnen der Stadt, Essen, 1961; Landestheater, Tübingen, 1962.

1961   *Beckett oder Die ehre Gottes* (Anouilh), Bühnen der Stadt, Essen.

Die Staubige Regenbogen (Jahnn), Städtische Bühnen, Frankfurt.

Der Tod des Handlungsreisenden (Miller), Theater am Kurfürstendamm, Berlin.

1962   *Flüchtlingsgespräche* (Brecht), Kammerspiele, Munich.

Der Balkon (Genet), Städtische Bühnen, Frankfurt.

Die Atrieden Tetralogie (Hauptmann), Theater am Kurfürstendamm, Berlin.

Die Grotte (Anouilh), Theater am Kurfürstendamm, Berlin.

1963   *Der Stellvertreter* (Hochhuth), Theater am Kurfürstendamm, Berlin.

Robespierre (Rolland), Freie Volksbühne, Berlin.

Die Räuber (Schiller), Teatro Communale, Florence.

Der Kaufmann von Venedig (Shakespeare), Freie Volksbühne, Berlin.

1964   *Der Teufel und der Liebe Gott* (Sartre), Städtische Bühnen, Frankfurt.

Salome (Wilde), Teatro Communale, Florence.

Mohrenwäsche (Asmodi), Freie Volksbühne, Berlin.

In der Sache J. Robert Oppenheimer (Kipphardt), Freie Volksbühne, Berlin; Théâtre Royal du Parc, Brussels, 1965.

Androklus und der Löwe (G. B. Shaw), Freie Volksbühne, Berlin.

1965   *Fuhrmann Henschel* (Hauptmann), Freie Volksbühne, Berlin.

Nekrassow (Sartre), Freie Volksbühne, Berlin.

Die Ermittlung (Weiss), Freie Volksbühne, Berlin.

1966   *Aufstand der Offiziere* (Kirst), Freie Volksbühne, Berlin.

Films

Aufstand der Fischer von St Barbara, 1934; *Rundfunk Fernsehen*, 1953; *Im Räder Werk*, 1956; *Stellvertreter*, 1963.

Publications

Das Politische Theater, 1929; *Schriften*, edited by Ludwig Hoffmann, 1968.

*

Bibliography

Books:

Maria Ley-Piscator, *The Piscator Experiment*, Carbondale, Illinois, 1970.

Christopher Innes, *Erwin Piscator's Political Theatre*, Cambridge, 1972.

Heinrich Goertz, *Erwin Piscator*, Hamburg, 1974.

John Willett, *The Theatre of Erwin Piscator: Half a Century of Politics in the Theatre*, London, 1978.

Thea Kirfel-Lenk, *Erwin Piscator im Exil in den USA 1939–51*, East Berlin, 1984.

Knut Boeser and Renata Vatková, *Erwin Piscator — Eine Arbeitsbiographie in 2 Bänden*, 2 vols., West Berlin, 1986.

Hugh Rorrison, *Erwin Piscator: Politics on the Stage in the Weimar Republic*, Cambridge, 1987.

* * *

Erwin Piscator was the leading exponent of political theatre in the Weimar Republic. A wartime convert to Communism, he went to Berlin in 1918, where he directed the Proletarian Theatre (1920–21), a seminal German agitprop group that took pro-Soviet pieces like L. Barta's *Russlands Tag* (*Russia's Day*) to pubs and meeting-halls in working-class districts. He later experimented with political revue as direct agitation on a larger scale in *Revue Roter Rummel* (*Red Riot Revue*) and *Trotz Alledem!* (*In Spite of Everything!*), the latter playing to audiences of 3500 at the Grosses Schauspielhaus. It combined scenes and newsreel footage contrapuntally to present the Communist version of German history from the outbreak of war in 1914 to the assassination of Karl Liebknect and Rosa Luxemburg in 1919. All Piscator's main productions were in some degree polemical analyses of these events and what followed from them.

In 1924 he joined the Berlin Volksbühne, a subscription organisation closely linked with the Social-Democratic party. His 11 productions there developed the techniques for "extending the action and clarifying the background of the action and thus continuing the play beyond the dramatic framework" that were to become the basis of his brand of epic theatre (Brecht developed an alternative brand). There being no adequate Communist plays available, he would take plays with a generally socialist drift and use other media to make an explicitly Communist statement. In 1924, Alfons Paquet's *Fahnen* (*Flags*), with its polemical projections and inter-titles between scenes, had the audience on its feet singing the 'Internationale'. By 1926 the management wanted to muzzle Piscator. He was given E. Welk's *Gewitter über Gottland* (*Storm Over Gottland*), ostensibly a pirate play about Klaus Störtebecker, a German seagoing Robin Hood. Piscator made up one of the pirates to look like Lenin and inserted a film prologue with four characters from the play marching towards the viewer, their costumes changing from one revolution to the next (Spartacus, 1789, 1848, 1917) in a series of dissolves, thus identifying the action as a stage in the march of socialism.

In the ensuing furore Piscator resigned. He had found financial backing for a company of his own, the Piscator-Bühne, on whose 1927–28 productions his reputation rests. For Ernst Toller's *Hoppla, Wir Leben!* (*Hurrah, We're Alive!*), which dealt with the failure of the 1918 German revolution, Piscator used a three-tier scaffolding set to present a cross-section of Weimar society and a newsreel summary of events between 1919 and 1927. *Rasputin, die Romanovs, der Krieg und das Volk, das Gegen sie Aufstand* (*Rasputin, the Romanovs, the War, and the People which Rose Against Them*) was an expanded version of the Russian melodrama *Rasputin* by Tolstoy and Shchegolev, which set the mad monk's lurid career in an elaborate framework of military and political data assembled by a script team. The set was a hemisphere of balloon silk stretched over gas piping, which revolved and had flaps that opened to reveal acting areas within. When closed it served, in conjunction with two side-screens and one that came in from the flies, as a projection surface for background (for example, photographs of Flanders fields before and after the battle) and data. The production made international capital responsible for the war, validated the October Revolution and climaxed with Lenin's assumption of power. Piscator's adaptation of Hasek's *Die Abenteuer des Braven Soldaten Schwejk* (*The Adventures of the Good Soldier Shwejk*), with Max Pallenberg as a wonderful pawky Schwejk marching on a conveyor belt, satirised the Austrian army in World War I. Finally, Leo Lania's oil comedy *Konjunktur* (*Boom*) exposed capitalist exploitation of underdeveloped nations' resources. The first three plays were hits, but poor financial control closed the Piscator-Bühne after eight months.

Piscator had demonstrated, not least to Brecht, that theatre could be a political medium. He was among the first to realise the communicative potential of authentic film-clips, now the stock-in-trade of television documentaries. His method was additive — take a fictitious plot and supplement it with factual material to make a political statement. This was the exact opposite of Brecht's reductive 'Lehrstücke'. The technical bravura of play plus documentation combined with film, still projections and constructivist mechanical staging was sensational in its time and remains an occasional source of inspiration.

The Piscator-Bühne's attempted comeback with F. Mehring's *Kaufmann von Berlin* (*The Merchant of Berlin*) in 1929 flopped, partly because polarisation of political stances meant that fashionable audiences (which the box office needed) were no longer open to left-wing theatre. Piscator's company, minus the stars, carried on with low-budget productions like Carl Credé's *S218*, which advocated the liberalisation of the abortion laws, but Brecht commented that in this context Piscator was like a scientist who had had his microscope taken away.

Piscator went to the Soviet Union in 1931 to film Anna Seghers' novella *Aufstand der Fischer von St Barbara* (*The Revolt of the Fishermen of Santa Barbara*). He became involved in a projected German anti-fascist theatre company, but in 1936 went to France, narrowly escaping Stalin's purges. His Communist days were by this time numbered. He moved to the USA and in 1938 founded the Dramatic Workshop at the New School for Social Research in New York. There he propagated his ideas and mounted student productions. Marlon Brando, Tony Curtis and Judith Malina passed, at least briefly, through his hands. In 1951 he returned to the Federal Republic of Germany, where a cool reception awaited him, like other distinguished emigrants. He worked as freelance director, mainly at provincial theatres until, in 1962, he was appointed director of the West Berlin Volksbühne. There he directed Rolf Hochhuth's *Der Stellvertreter* (*The Representative*), H. Kipphardt's *In der Sache J. Robert Oppenheimer* (*In the Matter of J. Robert Oppenheimer*) and P. Weiss's *Die Ermittlung* (*The Investigation*), documentary plays of the kind he needed but did not have in the 1920's.

—Hugh Rorrison

PITOËFF, Georges. French actor-manager, director, and playwright. Born in Tbilisi, Georgia, 4 September 1887. Educated at local schools in Tbilisi. Married actress Ludmilla Pitoëff in 1915, seven children (including actor-manager Sacha Pitoëff). Debut as actor-manager, in Russia, 1908; subsequently worked alongside Vera Kommisarjevskaya, Constantin Stanislavsky and Vsevolod Meyerhold in Moscow and elsewhere, 1913; founded own company, 1915; lived in Geneva, Switzerland, 1915–21; joined Jacques Copeau's company in Paris, 1921; acclaimed for productions presented at the Théâtre des Arts, from 1925, and at the Théâtre des Mathurins, where he installed his company in 1934; founder-member of the Cartel des Quatre, 1927. Died in Geneva, 17 September 1939.

Productions

1915   *Oncle Vania* (Chekhov), Geneva; also acted
            Astrov.
            Hedda Gabler (Ibsen), Comédie de Genève,
            Geneva; also acted Loëvborg.
            Sans Argent (Turgenev), Comédie de Genève,
            Geneva.

Les Tréteaux (Blok), Comédie de Genève, Geneva; also acted Pierrot.

1916 *Le Festin pendant la peste* (Pushkin), Comédie de Genève, Geneva; also acted unidentified role.

Le Demande (Chekhov), Comédie de Genève, Geneva; also acted Stépan Tchouboukov.

Les Revenants (Ibsen), Comédie de Genève, Geneva; also acted Oswald Alving.

Chanson d'amour (Koutschak), Comédie de Genève, Geneva; also acted unidentified role.

Candida (G. B. Shaw), Grand Théâtre de Genève, Geneva; also acted Marchbanks.

Les Violons d'automne (Sourgoutchev), Salle Communale de Plainpalais, Geneva; also acted L'Amant.

1917 *La Neige* (Przybysewsky), Casino de Saint-Pierre, Geneva; also acted Casimir.

Le Revizor (Gogol), Grand Théâtre de Genève, Geneva; also acted Klestakov).

La Puissance des ténèbres (Tolstoy), Salle des Amis de l'Instruction, Geneva; also acted Nikita.

L'Echange (Claudel), Salle des Amis de l'Instruction, Geneva; also acted Louis Laine.

Au-dessus des forces humaines (Björnson), Salle des Amis de l'Instruction, Geneva; also acted Pasteur Sang.

1918 *Soeur Béatrice* (Maeterlinck), Salle Communale de Plainpalais, Geneva; also acted Prince Bellidor.

Les Tréteaux (Blok), Salle Communale de Plainpalais, Geneva; also acted Pierrot.

Celui qui reçoit des gifles (Andreyev), Salle Communale de Plainpalais, Geneva; also acted Celui.

Les Revenants (Ibsen), Salle Communale de Plainpalais, Geneva; also acted Oswald Alving.

La Vénus du lac (Chavannes), Salle Communale de Plainpalais, Geneva; also acted D'Ivrogne.

Halte au village (Chavannes), Salle Communale de Plainpalais, Geneva.

L'Estomac (Brantmay), Salle Communale de Plainpalais, Geneva.

Amour et géographie (Björnson), Salle Communale de Plainpalais, Geneva; also acted Tygesen.

Edifice sur le sable (Schlemmer), Salle Communale de Plainpalais, Geneva; also acted Le Docteur.

Naufrage (Schlemmer), Salle Communale de Plainpalais, Geneva; also acted Daniel.

L'Amour africain (Mérimée), Salle Communale de Plainpalais, Geneva; also acted Zeïn-Ben-Humeida.

Dans l'Ombre des statues (Duhamel), Salle Communale de Plainpalais, Geneva; also acted Robert Bailly.

Le Cadavre vivant (Tolstoy), Salle Communale de Plainpalais, Geneva; also acted Fedia.

La Locandiera (Goldoni), Salle Communale de Plainpalais, Geneva; also acted Chevalier Ripafratta.

Le Soldat de chocolat (G. B. Shaw), Salle Communale de Plainpalais, Geneva; also acted Bluntschli.

La Ville morte (D'Annunzio), Salle Communale de Plainpalais, Geneva; also acted Léonard.

1919 *Le Temps est un songe* (Lenormand), Salle Communale de Plainpalais, Geneva; also acted Nico Van Eyden.

L'Habit vert (Musset and Augier), Salle Communale de Plainpalais, Geneva.

Le Canard sauvage (Ibsen), Salle Communale de Plainpalais, Geneva; also acted Hjalmar Ekdal.

La Puissance des ténèbres (Tolstoy), Salle Communale de Plainpalais, Geneva; also acted Nikita.

L'Orage (Ostrovsky), Salle Communale de Plainpalais, Geneva; also acted Kouliguine.

Mademoiselle Julie (Strindberg), Salle Communale de Plainpalais, Geneva; also acted Jean.

Le Baladin du monde occidental (Synge), Salle Communale de Plainpalais, Geneva; also acted Christy.

Deburau (Guitry), Salle Communale de Plainpalais, Geneva; also acted Deburau.

Sacrifice (Tagore), Théâtre Pitoëff, Geneva; also acted Raghupati.

Le Miracle de Saint Antoine (Maeterlinck), Théâtre Pitoëff, Geneva; also acted Saint Antoine.

Toutes les Ames (Heijermans), Théâtre Pitoëff, Geneva; also acted Curé Nansen.

Deburau (Guitry), Théâtre Pitoëff, Geneva; also acted Deburau.

Le Baladin du monde occidental (Synge), Théâtre Pitoëff, Geneva; also acted Christy.

Mademoiselle Julie (Strindberg), Théâtre Pitoëff, Geneva; also acted Jean.

Le Temps est un songe (Lenormand), Théâtre des Arts, Paris; also acted Nico Van Eyden.

Le Disciple de diable (G. B. Shaw), Théâtre Pitoëff, Geneva; also acted Richard Dudgeon.

Le Temps est un songe (Lenormand), Théâtre Pitoëff, Geneva; also acted Nico Van Eyden.

Vocalises (Morhardt), Théâtre Pitoëff, Geneva.

1920 *Les Ratés* (Lenormand), Théâtre Pitoëff, Geneva; also acted Lui.

Rosmersholm (Ibsen), Théâtre Pitoëff, Geneva; also acted Rosmer.

Ma Femme danseuse (Delluc), Théâtre Pitoëff, Geneva; also acted Jef.

Clarté (Oulmont), Théâtre Pitoëff, Geneva; also acted Lutin.

Les Noces du rétameur (Synge), Théâtre Pitoëff, Geneva.

Toutes les qualités viennent d'Elle (Tolstoy), Théâtre Pitoëff, Geneva; also acted walk-on role.

Père (Strindberg), Théâtre Pitoëff, Geneva; also acted Le Capitaine.

Galatée (Mortier), Théâtre Pitoëff, Geneva.

La Puissance des ténèbres (Tolstoy), Théâtre Pitoëff, Geneva; also acted Nikita.

Mademoiselle Julie (Strindberg), Théâtre Pitoëff, Geneva; also acted Jean.

Les Ratés (Lenormand), Théâtre des Arts, Paris; also acted Lui.

L'Oiseau bleu (Maeterlinck), Théâtre Pitoëff, Geneva.

Lapointe et Ropiteau (Duhamel), Théâtre Pitoëff, Geneva.

Le Chant du cygne (Chekhov), Théâtre Pitoëff, Geneva; also acted Svetlovidov.

La Porte de la prison (Gregory), Théâtre Pitoëff, Geneva.

Mesure pour mesure (Shakespeare), Théâtre Pitoëff, Geneva; also acted Vincentio.

Karma (Prozor and Courtaz), Théâtre Pitoëff, Geneva; also acted Père Saint-Vallier.

Bourg-Saint-Maurice (Chavannes), Théâtre Pitoëff, Geneva; also acted De Farinet.

La Maison du bon Dieu (Fleg), Théâtre Pitoëff, Geneva; also acted Rabbin.

Le Paquebot Tenacity (Vildrac), Théâtre Pitoëff, Geneva.

La Mort de Tintagiles (Maeterlinck), Théâtre Pitoëff, Geneva; also acted D'Agloval.

Hamlet (Shakespeare), Théâtre Pitoëff, Geneva; also acted Hamlet.

La Naissance de la paix (Descartes), Théâtre Pitoëff, Geneva.

Toutes les qualités viennent d'Elle (Tolstoy), Théâtre Pitoëff, Geneva; also acted walk-on role.

Dans les bas-fonds (Gorky), Théâtre Pitoëff, Geneva; also acted Baron.

1921 *Oncle Vania* (Chekhov), Théâtre Pitoëff, Geneva; also acted Astrov.

La Vie d'une femme (Bouhélier), Théâtre Pitoëff, Geneva; also acted Vieux Jude.

Hamlet (Shakespeare), Théâtre Pitoëff, Geneva; also acted Hamlet.

Quand vous voudrez (Duhamel), Théâtre Pitoëff, Geneva, and Théâtre des Arts, Paris; also acted Barnabille.

Lapointe et Ropiteau (Duhamel), Théâtre Pitoëff, Geneva, and Théâtre des Arts, Paris.

Le Temps est un songe (Lenormand), Théâtre Pitoëff, Geneva, and Théâtre des Arts, Paris; also acted Nico Van Eyden.

La Puissance des ténèbres (Tolstoy), Théâtre Moncey, Paris; also acted Nikita.

Oncle Vania (Chekhov), Théâtre du Vieux-Colombier, Paris.

La Mouette (Chekhov), Théâtre Pitoëff, Geneva; also acted Trigorine.

Macbeth (Shakespeare), Théâtre Pitoëff, Geneva; also acted Macbeth.

Celui qui reçoit les gifles (Andreyev), Théâtre des Arts, Paris, and Théâtre Pitoëff, Geneva; also acted Celui.

La Dame aux camélias (Dumas), Théâtre Pitoëff, Geneva.

Salomé (Wilde), Théâtre Pitoëff, Geneva; also acted Hérode Antipas.

La Dame aux camélias (Dumas), Théâtre Pitoëff, Geneva.

Macbeth (Shakespeare), Théâtre Pitoëff, Geneva; also acted Macbeth.

1922 *Androclès et le lion* (G. B. Shaw), Théâtre Pitoëff, Geneva, and Comédie des Champs-Élysées, Paris.

Magie (Chesterton), Théâtre Pitoëff, Geneva, and Comédie des Champs-Élysées, Paris.

Le Mangeur de rêves (Lenormand), Théâtre Pitoëff, Geneva, and Comédie des Champs-Élysées, Paris; also acted Luc de Bronte.

Celui qui reçoit les gifles (Andreyev), Théâtre Pitoëff, Geneva, and Comédie des Champs-Élysées, Paris; also acted Celui.

Hamlet (Shakespeare), Théâtre Pitoëff, Geneva; also acted Hamlet.

Tête à Tête (Traz), Théâtre Pitoëff, Geneva; also acted Lui.

Salomé (Wilde), Comédie des Champs-Élysées, Paris; also acted Hérode Antipas.

Devant les portes d'or (Dunsany), Comédie des Champs-Élysées, Paris.

Mademoiselle Julie (Strindberg), Comédie des Champs-Élysées, Paris; also acted Jean.

Dans le bas-fonds (Gorky), Comédie des Champs-Élysées, Paris; also acted Baron.

Oncle Vania (Chekhov), Comédie des Champs-Élysées, Paris.

La Mouette (Chekhov), Comédie des Champs-Élysées, Paris; also acted Trigorine.

Mesure pour mesure (Shakespeare), Comédie des Champs-Élysées, Paris; also acted Vincentio.

Les Revenants (Ibsen), Comédie des Champs-Élysées, Paris; also acted Oswald Alving.

Les Ratés (Lenormand), Théâtre des Champs-Élysées, Paris; also acted Lui.

Candida (G. B. Shaw), Comédie des Champs-Élysées, Paris; also acted Marchbanks.

Le Portrait de Dorian Gray (Wilde and Nozière), Comédie des Champs-Élysées, Paris.

1923 *Madamoiselle Bourrat* (Anet), Comédie des Champs-Élysées, Paris.

La Puissance des ténèbres (Tolstoy), Comédie des Champs-Élysées, Paris; also acted Nikita.

Six Personages en quête d'auteur (Pirandello), Comédie des Champs-Élysées, Paris; also acted Père.

Androclès et le lion (G. B. Shaw), Comédie des Champs-Élysées, Paris; also acted César.

Liliom (Molnar), Comédie des Champs-Élysées, Paris; also acted Liliom.

La Journée des aveux (Duhamel), Comédie des Champs-Élysées, Paris; also acted Antoine Héglin.

La Petite Baraque (Blok), Comédie des Champs-Élysées, Paris; also acted Pierrot.

L'Indigent (Vildrac), Comédie des Champs-Élysées, Paris.

Toutes les qualités viennent d'Elle (Tolstoy), Comédie des Champs-Élysées, Paris; also acted walk-on role.

Celui qui reçoit les gifles (Andreyev), Comédie des Champs-Élysées, Paris; also acted Celui.

1924   *Au Seuil du royaume* (Hamsun), Comédie des Champs-Élysées, Paris; also acted Ivar Kareno.

Six Personnages en quête d'auteur (Pirandello), Comédie des Champs-Élysées, Paris; also acted Père.

La Puissance des ténèbres (Tolstoy), Théâtre du Vieux-Colombier, Paris; also acted Nikita.

Celui qui reçoit les gifles (Andreyev), Théâtre du Vieux-Colombier, Paris; also acted Celui.

Au Seuil du royaume (Hamsun), Théâtre du Vieux-Colombier, Paris; also acted Ivar Kareno.

L'Histoire du soldat (Ramuz), Théâtre des Champs-Élysées, Paris; also acted Le Lecteur.

1925   *Henri IV* (Pirandello), Théâtre des Arts, Paris; also acted Henri IV.

Sainte Jeanne (G. B. Shaw), Théâtre des Arts, Paris; also acted Le Dauphin.

Le Juif du Pape (Felg), Théâtre des Arts, Paris; also acted Molco.

Le Lâche (Lenormand), Théâtre des Arts, Paris; also acted Jacques.

L'Assoiffée (Derera), Théâtre des Arts, Paris.

Henri IV (Pirandello), Théâtre des Arts, Paris; also acted Henri IV.

La Puissance des ténèbres (Tolstoy), Théâtre des Arts, Paris; also acted Nikita.

1926   *L'Un d'eux* (Mazaud), Théâtre des Arts, Paris.

L'Ame en peine (Bernard), Théâtre des Arts, Paris; also acted Antoine.

Sainte Jeanne (G. B. Shaw), Théâtre des Arts, Paris; also acted Le Dauphin.

Henri IV (Pirandello), Théâtre des Arts, Paris; also acted Henri IV.

Le Juif de Pape (Fleg), Théâtre des Arts, Paris; also acted Molco.

Comme ci (ou comme ça) (Pirandello), Théâtre des Arts, Paris; also acted Diego Cinci.

L'Amour africain (Mérimée), Théâtre des Arts, Paris; also acted Zeïn-Ben-Humeida.

Orphée (Cocteau), Théâtre des Arts, Paris; also acted Orphée.

Séquence (Chaumière), Théâtre des Arts, Paris.

... Et dzim... la... la (Achard), Théâtre des Arts, Paris.

Sardanapale (Saint-Marc), Théâtre des Arts, Paris; also acted Samuel-Samad.

Mademoiselle Bourrat (Anet), Théâtre des Arts, Paris.

Jean Le Maufranc (Romains), Théâtre des Arts, Paris; also acted Jean Le Maufranc.

Hamlet (Shakespeare), Théâtre des Arts, Paris; also acted Hamlet.

1927   *Orphée* (Cocteau), Théâtre des Arts, Paris; also acted Orphée.

L'Indigent (Vildrac), Théâtre des Arts, Paris.

Le Marchand de regrets (Crommelynck), Théâtre des Arts, Paris.

Le Miracle de Saint Antoine (Maeterlinck), Théâtre des Arts, Paris; also acted Saint Antoine.

Mixture (Lenormand), Théâtre des Mathurins, Paris.

La Maison des coeurs brisés (G. B. Shaw), Théâtre des Mathurins, Paris; also acted Capitaine Shotover.

Brand (Ibsen), Théâtre des Mathurins, Paris; also acted Brand.

Les Revenants (Ibsen), Théâtre des Mathurins, Paris; also acted Oswald Alving.

La Célèbre Histoire (Bouhélier), Théâtre des Mathurins, Paris; also acted Jacques Tessler.

Mademoiselle Bourrat (Anet), Théâtre des Mathurins, Paris.

Adam, Eve et Cie (Balgi), Théâtre des Mathurins, Paris; also acted Adam.

La Communion des Saints (Bérubet), Théâtre des Arts, Paris; also acted Simon Tenat.

Le Cadavre vivant (Tolstoy), Théâtre des Arts, Paris; also acted Fedia.

Hamlet (Shakespeare), Théâtre des Arts, Paris; also acted Hamlet.

César et Cléopâtre (G. B. Shaw), Théâtre des Arts, Paris; also acted César.

Sainte Jeanne (G. B. Shaw), Théâtre des Arts, Paris; also acted Le Dauphin.

1929   *Les Trois Soeurs* (Chekhov), Théâtre des Arts, Paris; also acted Tousenbach.

Hamlet (Shakespeare), Théâtre des Arts, Paris; also acted Hamlet.

Vivre (Flurscheim and Le Gouriadec), Théâtre des Arts, Paris.

Sainte Jeanne (G. B. Shaw), Théâtre des Arts, Paris; also acted Le Dauphin.

Le Vray Procès de Jehanne d'Arc (Pitoëff and Arnaud), Théâtre des Arts, Paris; also acted the Narrator.

Le Singe velu (O'Neill), Théâtre des Arts, Paris; also acted Yank.

Magie (Chancerel and Chavannes), Théâtre des Arts, Paris; also acted Jobson.

Mixture (Lenormand), Théâtre des Arts, Paris.

Les Criminels (Bruckner), Théâtre des Arts, Paris; also acted Gustave Tunichgut.

1930   *Sainte Jeanne* (G. B. Shaw), Théâtre des Arts, Paris; also acted Le Dauphin.

Le Cadavre vivant (Tolstoy), Théâtre des Arts, Paris; also acted Fedia.

Maison de Poupée (Ibsen), Théâtre de l'Oeuvre, Paris; also acted Docteur Rank.

1931   *Les Hommes* (Vialar), Théâtre des Arts, Paris; also acted Chose.

La Charrette de pommes (G. B. Shaw), Théâtre des Arts, Paris; also acted Roi Magnus.

Le Vray Procès de Jehanne d'Arc (Pitoëff and Arnaud), Théâtre des Arts, Paris; also acted the Narrator.

La Belle Hôtesse (Goldoni), Théâtre Albert I, Paris.

Maison de Poupée (Ibsen), Théâtre Albert I, Paris; also acted Docteur Rank.

Georges Pitoëff

Sainte Jeanne (G. B. Shaw), Théâtre Albert I, Paris; also acted Le Dauphin.

La Dame aux camélias (Dumas), Grand Théâtre Municipal de Versailles, Paris.

1932   *Oedipe* (Gide), Théâtre de l'Avenue, Paris; also acted Oedipe.

Le Miracle de Saint Antoine (Maeterlinck), Théâtre de l'Avenue, Paris; also acted Saint Antoine.

La Belle au bois (Supervielle), Théâtre de l'Avenue, Paris; also acted Barbe-Bleue.

Les Criminels (Bruckner), Théâtre de l'Avenue, Paris; also acted Gustave Tunichgut.

Maison de Poupée (Ibsen), Théâtre de l'Avenue, Paris; also acted Docteur Rank.

Plus jamais ça (Angermayer), Théâtre de l'Avenue, Paris.

Médée (Seneca), Théâtre de l'Avenue, Paris; also acted Jason.

Joë et Cie (Bergman), Théâtre de l'Avenue, Paris; also acted Joe Meng.

La Louise (Bernard), Théâtre de l'Avenue, Paris; also acted Pierre Garbin.

Fait divers (Gobius), Théâtre de l'Avenue, Paris; also acted Jean.

La Ronde (Schnitzler), Théâtre de l'Avenue, Paris; also acted Le Comte.

1933   *Joë et Cie* (Bergman), Théâtre de l'Avenue, Paris; also acted Joe Meng.

Mademoiselle Julie (Strindberg), Théâtre de l'Avenue, Paris; also acted Jean.

Le Temps est un songe (Lenormand), Théâtre de l'Avenue, Paris; also acted Nico Van Eyden.

Marc-Aurèle (Le Marois), Théâtre de l'Avenue, Paris; also acted Félix.

Les Gants blancs (Bergman), Théâtre de l'Avenue, Paris; also acted Ralf Swedenem.

Les Juifs (Tchirikov), Théâtre du Vieux-Colombier, Paris; also acted Nachman.

Liebeleï (Schnitzler), Théâtre du Vieux-Colombier, Paris.

Les Derniers Masques (Schnitzler), Théâtre du Vieux-Colombier, Paris.

La Polka des chaises (Mackenzie), Théâtre du Vieux-Colombier, Paris; also acted Joseph Schlindler.

1934   *Maison de poupée* (Ibsen), Théâtre du Vieux-Colombier, Paris; also acted Docteur Rank.

Le Canard sauvage (Ibsen), Théâtre du Vieux-Colombier, Paris, and Théâtre des Mathurins, Paris; also acted Hjalmar Ekdal.

Louison (Musset), Château de Coppet, Paris.

Intermèdes (Le Marois), Château de Coppet, Paris.

Les Revenants (Ibsen), Théâtre des Mathurins, Paris; also acted Oswald Alving.

Le Chef (La Rochelle), Théâtre des Mathurins, Paris; also acted Michel.

Sainte Jeanne (G. B. Shaw), Théâtre des Mathurins, Paris; also acted Le Dauphin.

1935   *Ce soir on improvise* (Pirandello), Théâtre des Mathurins, Paris; also acted Hinkfuss.

La Créature (Bruckner), Théâtre des Mathurins, Paris; also acted Alfred Troïk.

Je Vivrai un grand amour (Passeur), Théâtre des Mathurins, Paris; also acted Modeste.

La Complainte de Pranzini et de Thérèse de Lisieux (Ghéon), Théâtre des Mathurins, Paris; also acted Baron Hugues de Craux.

Le Héros et le soldat (G. B. Shaw), Théâtre des Mathurins, Paris; also acted Bluntschli.

1936   *Le Merveilleux alliage* (Kirchon), Théâtre des Mathurins, Paris; also acted Gocha.

La Folle du ciel (Lenormand), Théâtre des Mathurins, Paris; also acted Troll.

Poucette (Vildrac), Théâtre des Mathurins, Paris.

Les Revenants (Ibsen), Théâtre des Mathurins, Paris; also acted Oswald Alving.

Jeanne d'Arc (G. B. Shaw), Salle des Fêtes du Campo Santo, Orléans.

Sainte Jeanne (G. B. Shaw), Salle des Fêtes du Campo Santo, Orléans; also acted Le Dauphin.

Tu ne m'échapperas jamais (Kennedy), Théâtre des Mathurins, Paris; also acted Sébastien Sanger.

Angelica (Ferrero), Théâtre des Mathurins, Paris; also acted Orlando.

Quand vous voudrez (Duhamel), Théâtre des Mathurins, Paris; also acted Barnabille.

Maison de poupée (Ibsen), Théâtre des Mathurins, Paris; also acted Docteur Rank.

1937   *Six Personnages en quête d'auteur* (Pirandello), Théâtre des Mathurins, Paris; also acted Père.

Le Voyageur sans bagage (Anouilh), Théâtre des Mathurins, Paris; also acted Gaston.

Amal et la lettre du roi (Tagore), Théâtre des Mathurins, Paris.

Le Testament de Tante Caroline (Roussel and Nino), Opéra-Comique, Paris.

Lapointe et Ropiteau (Duhamel), Théâtre des Mathurins, Paris.

Roméo et Juliette (Shakespeare), Théâtre des Mathurins, Paris; also acted Roméo.

Eve (Yole), Théâtre des Mathurins, Paris; also acted Jean Fleury.

Kirika (Ciprian), Théâtre des Mathurins, Paris; also acted Kirika.

Des Abailles sur le pont supérieur (Priestley), Théâtre des Mathurins, Paris; also acted Sam Gridley.

Celui qui reçoit les gifles (Andreyev), Théâtre des Mathurins, Paris; also acted Celui.

L'Echange (Claudel), Théâtre des Mathurins, Paris; also acted Louis Laine.

1938   *Le Sauvage* (Anouilh), Théâtre des Mathurins, Paris; also acted Florent.

Mademoiselle Bourrat (Anet), Théâtre des Mathurins, Paris.

Maison de poupée (Ibsen), Théâtre des Mathurins, Paris; also acted Docteur Rank.

L'Argent n'a pas d'odeur (G. B. Shaw), Théâtre des Mathurins, Paris.

La Première famille (Supervielle), Théâtre des Mathurins, Paris.

Là-bas (Titayna), Théâtre des Mathurins, Paris.

La Fenêtre ouverte (Du Gard), Théâtre des Mathurins, Paris; also acted Docteur Marc Galdtz.

1939   *La Mouette* (Chekhov), Théâtre des Mathurins, Paris; also acted Trigorine.

Un Ennemi du peuple (Ibsen), Théâtre des Mathurins, Paris; also acted Dr Stockmann.

La Dame aux camélias (Dumas), Théâtre des Mathurins, Paris.

Publications

Notre Théâtre, edited by O. Lieutier, 1949.

*

Bibliography

Books:
Henri-René Lenormand, *Les Pitoëff: souvenirs*, Paris, 1948.
André Frank, *Georges Pitoëff*, Paris, 1958.
Jean Hort, *La Vie héroïque des Pitoëff* Geneva, 1966.
Jacqueline Jomaron, *Georges Pitoëff, metteur en scène*, Lausanne, 1979.

* * *

Georges Pitoëff was a cosmopolitan artist who brought an important European dimension to the Parisian stage between the wars. He entered the theatre in pre-revolutionary Russia as an actor with Vera Komissarjevsky, then worked as technician and designer under Gaidebourov. He absorbed the theories of Stanislavsky and Meyerhold, but soon took his distance from both, developing a marked antipathy for what he later called the futility of Stanislavsky's search for realistic detail. In Switzerland he followed the Hellerau experiments of Appia and Jaques-Dalcroze, whose ideas on rhythm and simple settings found an echo in his own actor-centred concept of theatre. In France he became the leading producer of plays by Chekhov, Ibsen, and Pirandello, but his vast international repertoire included Gogol, Turgenev, Gorky, Shakespeare, Shaw, Wilde, Strindberg, Hauptmann, and a great many others.

With Pitoëff, the Idealist reaction that generated the French Symbolist theatre at the end of the nineteenth century enjoyed a final fling. He believed that each play had an essence through which it was in touch with the ultimate quasi-divine mysteries at the root of human experience. Like the Idealists he saw the quest for reality in art as a process of peeling off the layers of contingent reality to discover the kernel of truth hidden within. Classical psychology, therefore, did not interest him in the least, nor did historical milieu. In his productions he sought instead to disengage the play and the characters from everyday experience and realistic expression.

He was the most stylistically eclectic, least methodical, of all French directors. His only fixed principle was that in directing there are as many styles as there are plays. The idea was commonplace enough — Antoine, Copeau, Dullin, even Baty all voiced it — but Pitoëff was the only one in practice who approached anything like the adaptability it implied. He really did try to approach each play with a completely open mind, aiming to discover, then communicate, the idea at its core. Similarly, he was the first director to try to give audiences an idea of the distinctive national character of foreign playwrights. His translations of Chekhov were outstandingly successful in making the texts accessible to a French public without sacrificing one bit of their distinctive atmosphere. In producing foreign plays, rather than accommodating them to his own system, as so often happens, he tried to rethink his staging in the spirit of Ibsen, Chekhov, Shakespeare, or whatever.

He was not diffident about asserting the autocratic rights of the director in the theatre, and regarded it as axiomatic that directing constituted an independent art form that only the director, not the playwright, could mastermind. But while proclaiming the director's autonomy in the theatre, he differed from Craig in regarding the director as the servant of the playwright. He saw his first duty as being to enter into communion with the text. His object was to seize the essence of the play, to penetrate the play's form and grasp the ultimate source of its inspiration. For Pitoëff the latter was always of a mystical nature and it came to him not through laborious analysis but as a form of revelation. Like Jouvet, he aimed to interpret the play faithfully, but for Pitoëff this meant something very different from Jouvet's dogged fidelity to textual detail. In practice it meant that each of his productions was a statement by scenic means of what, in his opinion, constituted the irreducible essence of the play. As a result, although he never stamped a consistent personal style on the plays he directed, each of his productions revealed a personal if not idiosyncratic interpretation.

The constant factor in all his productions was the subordination of scenic expression to the actor. He was at pains to avoid exhibitionism, and what he regarded as the excesses of certain theatricalist directors who pinned their faith on scenography, architecture, lighting effects, or any other grand idea. His answer was to focus everything on the actor, whom he regarded as the one indispensable element in theatre. Audiences who went to his theatre were always rewarded with honest un-mannered acting. An important factor in the company's success was his wife and partner Ludmilla, whom Claudel and Shaw considered the greatest actress of the day. Her natural and understated style and her mystical presence ideally complemented Pitoëff's simple productions. Georges himself was also an excellent actor. He was no technical virtuoso, but he had an unsettling presence that made a deep impression on spectators. His forte, like that of Ludmilla, lay in giving expression to the poetic resonances of the characters in a play. His best roles, which included Hamlet, fell within a broad type of troubled psyche that ranged from the madness of Pirandello's Henry IV, through the Freudian depths of Lenormand's plays of the unconscious, to the subtler and sometimes formless anxiety of Chekhov's characters.

Normally he was less guilty of over-accentuation of any one of the scenic components than any other director. His lighting was modest — a few spotlights artfully positioned always sufficed — and his settings were famous for their asceticism. The legendary poverty of his company may have contributed to an impression of slender scenic resources, but its root lay in Pitoëff's conviction that stage designs should be unobtrusive. The stylistic idiom adopted varied greatly according to the play. It might draw on expressionism, symbolism, or decorative arts. Sometimes, as for *The Three Sisters*, it would be nothing more than draped curtains. The aim was always to express the central idea of the play as simply as possible and without competing with the actors for attention.

Pitoëff's inspirational "communion" with the text occasionally went disastrously awry, but at its best it inspired productions that were powerful revelations. His productions of Pirandello's *Six Characters in Search of an Author*, Shaw's *Saint Joan* (both of them French premieres), and Chekhov were among the most significant of the French stage in the 1920's and 1930's.

—David Whitton

PLANCHON, Roger. French director, actor, and playwright. Born in Saint-Chamond, France, 1931. Educated at schools in Lyon. Debut as director, Lyon, 1949; formed own company in Lyon, 1950; opened Théâtre de la Comédie, Lyon, 1953; director, Théâtre Municipal, Villeurbanne, near Lyon, 1957; subsequently made Villeurbanne a centre of French provincial theatre and established himself as the leading director after Jean Vilar; director, Théâtre National Populaire, based at Villeurbanne, 1973–95; also led numerous tours throughout France and Europe; worked chiefly in the cinema in the 1980's.

Productions

1949   *Les Chemins clos* (Lochy), Maison des jeunes, Lyon.

1950   *Bottines et Collets montés* (Courteline, Feydeau and Frédérique), Mâcon and Quai Saint-Antoine, Lyon; La Lorelei, East Germany, 1951.

1951   *La Nuit des Rois* (Shakespeare), Parc de la Tête-d'Or, Lyon, and La Lorelei, East Germany; Hôtel de Ville, Lyon, 1952.
        Les Joyeuses Commèras de Windsor (Shakespeare), French tour.

1952   *Claire* (Char), French tour.
        La Vie est un Songe (Calderón), French tour.

1953   *Rocambole* (Dabril), Théâtre de la Comédie, Lyons.
        La Balade du Grand Macabre (Ghelderode), Théâtre de la Comédie, Lyons.
        Le Sens de la Marche (Adamov), Théâtre de la Comédie, Lyons.
        Le Professeur Taranne (Adamov), Théâtre de la Comédie, Lyons.
        Burlesque-digest (parody of Jean Tardieu), Théâtre de la Comédie, Lyons.
        Liliom (Molnár), Théâtre de la Comédie, Lyons.
        Cartouche (Planchon), Théâtre de la Comédie, Lyons.

1954   *La Cruche cassée* (Kleist), Théâtre de la Comédie, Lyons.
        Edward II (Marlowe, translated by Adamov), Festival de Comédie, Lyons.
        La Bonne Ame de Sé-Tchouan (Brecht), Festival de Lyon.
        Casque d'Or (Cérure), Théâtre de la Comédie, Lyons.

1955   *La Belle Rombière* (Clervers and Hannoteau), Théâtre de la Comédie, Lyons.
        L'Alcade de Zalaméa (Calderón, adapted by Planchon), Musée de Gadagne, Lyon.
        Comment s'en débarrasser (Ionesco), Théâtre de la Comédie, Lyons.
        L'Ombre de la Ravine (Synge), Théâtre de la Comédie, Lyons.
        La Famille Tuyau de Poêle (Prévert), Théâtre de la Comédie, Lyons.
        Victor ou les Enfants au Pouvoir (Vitrac), Théâtre de la Comédie, Lyons.

1956   *Grand-peur et Misères du Troisième Reich* (Brecht), Théâtre de la Comédie, Lyons, and Théâtre d'Aujourd'hui, Paris.
        La Bonne Ame de Sé-Tchouan (Brecht), Théâtre d'Aujourd'hui, Paris.
        Les Soldats (Lenz), Théâtre d'Aujourd'hui, Paris.
        Le Cruche cassée (Kleist), Théâtre d'Aujourd'hui, Paris.
        La Leçon (Ionesco), Théâtre de la Comédie, Lyons.
        Victimes du Devoir (Ionesco), Théâtre de la Comédie, Lyons.
        La Nuit des Rois (Shakespeare), Musée de Gadagne, Lyon.

Aujourd'hui ou les Coréens (Vinaver), Théâtre de la Comédie, Lyons.

1957 *Paolo-Paoli* (Adamov), Théâtre de la Comédie, Lyons, and Théâtre du Vieux Colombier, Paris.

Henri IV, parts 1 and 2 (Shakespeare), Festival des Nuits de Bourgogne and Théâtre de la Cité, Villeurbanne.

1958 *Les Trois Mousquetaires* (Dumas), Théâtre de la Cité, Villeurbanne, and Festival de Liège.

Les Fourberies de Scapin (Molière), Théâtre de la Cité, Villeurbanne.

Henry IV, parts 1 and 2 (Shakespeare), Théâtre de la Cité, Villeurbanne.

1959 *La Seconde Surprise de l'amour* (Marivaux), Théâtre de la Cité, Villeurbanne.

Henry IV, parts 1 and 2 (Shakespeare), Théâtre de la Cité, Villeurbanne and Théâtre de l'Ambigu, Paris.

Les Trois Mousquetaires (Dumas), Théâtre de l'Ambigu, Paris.

1960 *Henry IV, parts 1 and 2* (Shakespeare), Théâtre de la Cité, Villeurbanne, Théâtre de l'Ambigu, Paris, and Orange.

Les Ames mortes (Adamov), Théâtre de la Cité, Villeurbanne, and Théâtre de l'Odéon, Paris.

Les Trois Mousquetaires (Dumas), European tour and Théâtre de la Cité, Villeurbanne.

George Dandin (Molière), French tour and Théâtre de la Cité, Villeurbanne.

Edouard II (Marlowe), Orange and Baalbeck.

Schweik dans la Deuxième Guerre mondiale (Brecht), Théâtre de la Cité, Villeurbanne.

La Seconde Surprise de l'amour (Marivaux), Théâtre de la Cité, Villeurbanne.

1961 *Edouard II* (Marlowe), Théâtre de la Cité, Villeurbanne.

Schweik dans la Deuxième Guerre mondiale (Brecht), Théâtre de la Cité, Villeurbanne.

Les Trois Mousquetaires (Dumas), Théâtre de la Cité, Villeurbanne.

George Dandin (Molière), Théâtre de la Cité, Villeurbanne.

1962 *Schweik dans la Deuxième Guerre mondiale* (Brecht), Théâtre de la Cité, Villeurbanne.

Auguste Geai (Gatti), Théâtre de la Cité, Villeurbanne.

La Remise (Planchon), Théâtre de la Cité, Villeurbanne.

Le Tartuffe (Molière), Théâtre de la Cité, Villeurbanne.

1963 *La Villégiature* (Arnaud, adapted from Goldoni), Théâtre de la Cité, Villeurbanne.

O'Man Chicago, Théâtre de la Cité, Villeurbanne.

George Dandin (Molière), Théâtre de la Cité, Villeurbanne, and East European tour.

Les Trois Mousquetaires (Dumas), East European tour.

Le Tartuffe (Molière), East European tour.

La Remise (Planchon), Théâtre de la Cité, Villeurbanne.

1964 *Troilus et Cressida* (Shakespeare), Théâtre de la Cité, Villeurbanne, and Théâtre de l'Odéon, Paris.

Le Tartuffe (Molière), Théâtre de l'Odéon, Paris.

La Remise (Planchon), Théâtre de l'Odéon, Paris.

Augusta Geai (Gatti), Théâtre de l'Odéon, Paris.

George Dandin (Molière), tour of Middle East.

Schweik dans la Deuxième Guerre mondiale (Brecht), Théâtre de la Cité, Villeurbanne.

1965 *Récital Maupassant*, Théâtre de la Cité, Villeurbanne.

Patte blanche, Théâtre de la Cité, Villeurbanne.

La Fausse Suivante (Marivaux), Théâtre de la Cité, Villeurbanne.

Henry IV, parts 1 and 2 (Shakespeare), Théâtre de la Cité, Villeurbanne.

Falstaff (adapted from Shakespeare), Théâtre de la Cité, Villeurbanne.

1966 *Poussière pourpre* (O'Casey), Théâtre de la Cité, Villeurbanne.

Bérénice (Racine), Théâtre de la Cité, Villeurbanne.

Les Trois Mousquetaires (Dumas), European tour.

Le Tartuffe (Molière), European tour.

Richard III (Shakespeare), Avignon.

George Dandin (Molière), French tour.

1967 *Dernier Adieu d'Armstrong* (Arden), Théâtre de la Cité, Villeurbanne.

Récital Dickens, Théâtre de la Cité, Villeurbanne, and French tour.

Richard III (Shakespeare), Théâtre de la Cité, Villeurbanne.

Bleus, blancs, rouges ou Les Libertins (Planchon), Théâtre de la Cité, Villeurbanne.

Le Tartuffe (Molière), European tour and New York.

1968 *Dans le Vent*, Théâtre de la Cité, Villeurbanne.

Les Trois Mousquetaires (Dumas), Théâtre de la Cité, Villeurbanne, and New York.

George Dandin (Molière), New York.

Le Coup de Trafalgar (Vitrac), Théâtre de la Cité, Villeurbanne.

1969 *La Mise en Pièces*, Théâtre de la Cité, Villeurbanne.

L'Infâme (Planchon), Théâtre de la Cité, Villeurbanne.

Bérénice (Racine), London and Rome.

George Dandin (Molière), London.

1970 *Bérénice* (Racine), Théâtre de la Cité, Villeurbanne, and tour.

L'Infâme (Planchon), tour.

O'Man Chicago, tour.

1971 *Bleus, blancs, rouges ou Les Libertins* (Planchon), Nîmes and European tour.

Le Tartuffe (Molière), European tour.

1972 *The Massacre at Paris* (Marlowe, adapted by Vauthier), Théâtre National Populaire, Villeurbanne.

La Langue au Chat, French tour.

1973   *Toller*, (Dorst), Théâtre National Populaire, Villeurbanne.

Par-dessus bord (Vinaver), Théâtre National Populaire, Villeurbanne.

Le Tartuffe (Molière), South American tour.

La Dispute (Marivaux), Théâtre de la Gaîté-Lyrique, Paris.

Le Cochon noir (Planchon), Caen.

1974   *Le Tartuffe* (Molière), French tour.

La Dispute (Marivaux), French tour.

Toller, (Dorst), Théâtre de l'Odéon, Paris.

Le Cochon noir (Planchon), Théâtre de la Porte Saint-Martin, Paris.

Par-dessus bord (Vinaver), Théâtre de l'Odéon, Paris.

Blues, Whites and Reds (Planchon, translated by Burgess), Repertory Theatre, Birmingham.

1975   *A.A. Théâtres d'Arthur Adamov*, Théâtre National Populaire, Villeurbanne.

Lear (Bond), Théâtre National Populaire, Villeurbanne, and French tour.

Folies bourgeoises, French tour.

Le Tartuffe (Molière), Créteil and Théâtre National Populaire, Villeurbanne.

1976   *Gilles de Rais* (Planchon), Théâtre National Populaire, Villeurbanne.

Folies bourgeoises, Théâtre National Populaire, Villeurbanne and French tour.

Le Tartuffe (Molière), French tour.

La Dispute (Marivaux), French tour.

A.A. Théâtres d'Arthur Adamov, Palais de Chaillot, Paris.

1977   *Gilles de Rais* (Planchon), Palais de Chaillot, Paris.

Loin d'Hagondage (Wenzel), Théâtre de la Porte Saint-Martin, Paris.

Folies bourgeoises, Théâtre de la Porte Saint-Martin, Paris.

1978   *Antony and Cleopatra* (Shakespeare), Théâtre National Populaire, Villeurbanne.

Love's Labour's Lost (Shakespeare), Théâtre National Populaire, Villeurbanne.

Pericles (Shakespeare), Théâtre National Populaire, Villeurbanne.

1979   *No Man's Land* (Pinter), Théâtre National Populaire, Villeurbanne.

Athalie (Racine), Théâtre National Populaire, Villeurbanne.

Dom Juan (Molière), Théâtre National Populaire, Villeurbanne.

1980   *Athalie* (Racine), Théâtre National Populaire, Villeurbanne.

Dom Juan (Molière), Théâtre National Populaire, Villeurbanne.

1983   *Voyages chez les morts* (Ionesco), Théâtre National Populaire, Villeurbanne.

1986   *L'Avare* (Molière), Théâtre National Populaire, Villeurbanne.

Other productions include: *La Bonne Ame de Sé-Tchouan* (Brecht), 1958; *Nicomède* (P. Corneille), 1970; *Homme pour Homme*, 1970.

Publications

Bleus, blancs, rouges (play), 1967; *Le Cochon noir et La Remise* (plays), 1974; *Gilles de Rais et L'Infâme* (plays), 1976.

*

Bibliography

Books:
Emile Copfermann, *Roger Planchon*, Lausanne, 1969.
Jean Duvignaud, *Itinéraire de Roger Planchon*, Paris, 1977.
Yvette Daoust, *Roger Planchon*, Cambridge, 1981.
David Bradby, *The Theatre of Roger Planchon*, Cambridge, 1984.

* * *

After Jean Vilar, Roger Planchon was the most influential French director to emerge in the course of the 1950's and 1960's, and the natural candidate to inherit Vilar's mantle as head of the Théâtre National Populaire, a title he held from 1973 to 1995.

Planchon exhibits all-round creative talents: he is a powerful actor, a prolific inventor of stage images, and a playwright of some originality as well as being a director of both theatre and films. Directing, in his view, involves a mobilisation of all these skills. He has been criticised for setting a trend for all-powerful directors in the French theatre, a charge that has some truth in it since, in 1964, he went so far as to claim that the director's work should be accorded a status equal to that of the playwright. He coined a term — 'scenic writing' — to convey the creative work of the director. By this term he meant the deployment, by the director, of the specific language of theatre: movement, sound, gesture, light, colour, and so on. He was strongly influenced by Brecht, developing his theory of 'scenic writing' out of a meditation on Brecht's work. Since encountering Robert Wilson in the early 1970's, he has placed even greater emphasis on the directing process as the generation of a rich sequence of multi-layered visual and verbal images.

His first company was formed in 1950, before he was 20. Rather than beginning with the classics and modelling himself on Copeau, Planchon sought to discover a form of theatre that would be more immediate, more relevant to popular audiences, with a certain violence (learnt, in part, from Artaud's poetry), in both the comic and the tragic vein. In a disused printing works in the centre of Lyon, with a semi-professional company of young fellow-enthusiasts, his 'Théâtre de la Comédie' developed a rapid-fire burlesque style, drawing on popular comedy, mime and music hall as well as on the American musical comedy films of the 1940's. At the same time he attempted more demanding work, such as Marlowe's *Doctor Faustus* and a version of *Hamlet* attributed to Kydd, approaching these plays with an eye to contemporary relevance, much as Littlewood was doing in England at that time. The contemporary authors he chose were those more or less closely associated with Surrealism: Ghelderode, Ionesco, Adamov, Prévert, Vitrac. From the start, his style was defined by anti-naturalism, acrobatic virtuosity and an interest in dream states.

Then, in 1954 and 1955, came the visits of the Berliner Ensemble to France and Planchon's discovery of the German director's work. In its political directness and its mastery of theatre craft, it seemed to Planchon to come close to perfection. He decided to work an apprenticeship, not literally, but by putting what he understood of the Brechtian methods into practice in his own productions. Though he directed three plays by Brecht, the principal result of this 'apprenticeship' was to be seen in his handling of the classics, especially Shakespeare, Molière and Marivaux, all of whom were revealed in a light that, to contemporaries, appeared shockingly new. This production style gained a special relevance when, in 1957, he and his company moved into the large municipal theatre of Villeurbanne, a working-class suburb some three miles from the centre of Lyon. He renamed it the Théâtre de la Cité and remained there until relieved of his post by the Minister of Culture, Jacques Toubon, in 1995. Here he was best known for his productions of Molière and Shakespeare, in which he recreated the political and ideological realities of the worlds depicted in ways that both respected historical truth and also brought them vividly alive for modern audiences. Notable were *Henry IV*, *Troilus et Cressida* and *Richard III* by Shakespeare and *George Dandin* and *Le Tartuffe* by Molière.

Planchon's Brechtian approach to the classics did not prevent him from working on the modern repertoire as well. In the mid-1950's, he was responsible for two of the most important new productions: of Vinaver's *Les Coréens* (1956) and of Adamov's *Paolo Paoli* (1957). After the move to Villeurbanne, he began writing his own plays, and these became a regular feature of the company's repertoire. They are very varied in their style and subject matter, though all of them display the influence of Brecht, attempting either through historical reconstruction of earlier periods, or through stories taken from contemporary life, to lay bare the ideological structures that govern 20th-century consciousness.

By the end of the 1960's, Planchon was looked up to by a new generation of theatre people as the leader of a revolution in directing, one that combined political commitment with a performance style of great subtlety, complexity and beauty. It was natural that, during the crisis of the summer of 1968, theatre workers from all over France should come to Villeurbanne to discuss the political and cultural crisis sweeping the country. The statement that emerged from these discussions demanded an enhanced level of spending on cultural institutions while at the same time allowing greater artistic freedom to those in charge of them. This priciple was, broadly, accepted by successive governments over the ensuing 25 years.

Planchon's authority was such that he was seen as the only person who could breathe new life into the Théâtre National Populaire, whose fortunes had been declining ever since the resignation of Jean Vilar in 1963. Planchon was pressed to take on the job, but refused to abandon the theatre and the audience he had been nurturing in Villeurbanne. His reward was to have the Théâtre de la Cité designated the Théâtre National Populaire from the start of 1973. He took on a young associate director, Patrice Chéreau, who was responsible for some of the new theatre's most striking successes. Planchon himself failed to find a 'second wind'. He directed a revival of *Le Tartuffe* (1973), which visited London's National Theatre in 1975, and

notable productions of both *Dom Juan* (1975) and *L'Avare* (1986). He also continued to direct his own plays, but these found little critical approval, and with the exception of an extremely original staging of Pinter's *No Man's Land* (1979) and Ionesco's last play, *Voyages chez les morts* (1983), he almost entirely neglected the contemporary repertoire. Most of his energies in the 1980's were taken up with making two films, one based on Molière's *George Dandin*, and the other on the childhood of Louis XIV, but neither of these was successful at the box office. Absorbed by his filming projects, Planchon appears to have neglected the Villeurbanne audience he so carefully built up in previous decades, and the result was the disbanding of the Théâtre National Populaire in 1995.

—David Bradby

PLOWRIGHT, Joan (Anne).   British actress and director. Born in Scunthorpe, Brigg, Lincolnshire, 28 October 1929. Educated at Scunthorpe Grammar School; trained for the stage at the Laban Art of Movement Studio, 1949–50, and under Michel St Denis, Glen Byam Shaw, and George Devine at the Old Vic Theatre School, 1950–52. Married 1) actor Roger Gage in 1954 (divorced 1960); 2) actor and director Laurence Olivier (*q.v.*) in 1961 (died 1989), one son, two daughters. Stage debut, Croydon Repertory Theatre, 1948; joined Bristol Old Vic company, 1952; South African tour with Old Vic Company, 1952; London debut, 1954; actress, Nottingham Playhouse, 1955–56; Broadway debut, 1958; actress, English Stage Company, Royal Court Theatre, London, 1956; first appeared with National Theatre company, 1963. Member: Council, Royal Academy of Dramatic Art. Recipient: Tony Award, 1960; *Evening Standard* Award, 1963; Variety Club Award, 1977; Society of West End Theatres Award, 1978; *Drama Magazine* Award, 1986; Gold Globe Award, 1993 (twice). CBE (Commander of the British Empire), 1970.

Productions

As actress:

1948	Hope in *If Four Walls Told* (Percy), Repertory Theatre, Croydon.
1954	Allison in *The Merry Gentlemen*, Old Vic Theatre, Bristol.
	Donna Clara in *The Duenna* (Sheridan), Westminster Theatre, London.
1955	Pip in *Moby Dick* (Welles, adapted from Melville), Duke of York's Theatre, London.
1956	Mary Warren in *The Crucible* (Miller), Royal Court Theatre, London.
	Baptista in *Don Juan* (Duncan), Royal Court Theatre, London.
	The Receptionist in *The Death of Satan* (Duncan), Royal Court Theatre, London.
	Miss Tray in *Cards of Identity* (Dennis), Royal Court Theatre, London.
	Mrs Shin in *The Good Woman of Setzuan* (Brecht), Royal Court Theatre, London.

Margery Pinchwife in *The Country Wife* (Wycherley), Royal Court Theatre, London; Adelphi Theatre, London, 1957.

1957   Old Woman in *The Chairs* (Ionesco), Royal Court Theatre, London; Phoenix Theatre, New York, 1958.

Elizabeth Compton in *The Making of Moo* (Dennis), Royal Court Theatre, London.

Jean Rice in *The Entertainer* (Osborne), Palace Theatre, London; Royale Theatre, New York, 1958.

1958   Pupil in *The Lesson* (Ionesco), Phoenix Theatre, New York.

Major Barbara in *Major Barbara* (G. B. Shaw), Royal Court Theatre, London.

Arlette in *Hook, Line and Sinker* (Roussin, adapted by Morley), Piccadilly Theatre, London.

1959   Beatie in *Roots* (Wesker), Belgrade Theatre, Coventry, and Royal Court Theatre, London.

1960   Daisy in *Rhinoceros* (Ionesco), Royal Court Theatre, London.

Josephine in *A Taste of Honey* (Delaney), Lyceum Theatre, New York.

1962   Another Constatia in *The Chances* (Fletcher), Chichester Festival Theatre.

Sonya in *Uncle Vanya* (Chekhov), Chichester Festival Theatre and Old Vic Theatre, London.

1963   Joan in *Saint Joan* (G. B. Shaw), Chichester Festival Theatre, Edinburgh Festival, and Old Vic Theatre, London.

1964   Maggie Hobson in *Hobson's Choice* (Brighouse), Old Vic Theatre, London.

Hilda Wangel in *The Master Builder* (Ibsen), Old Vic Theatre, London.

1967   Beatrice in *Much Ado About Nothing* (Shakespeare), Old Vic Theatre, London.

Masha in *The Three Sisters* (Chekhov), Old Vic Theatre, London.

Dorine in *Tartuffe* (Molière), Old Vic Theatre, London.

1968   Teresa in *The Advertisement* (Ginzburg), Old Vic Theatre, London, and Royal Theatre, London.

Rosaline in *Love's Labour's Lost* (Shakespeare), Old Vic Theatre, London.

1969   Voice of Lilith in *Back to Methuselah, part 2* (G. B. Shaw), Old Vic Theatre, London.

1970   Portia in *The Merchant of Venice* (Shakespeare), New Theatre, London.

1971   Mistress Anne Frankford in *A Woman Killed with Kindness* (Heywood), New Theatre, London.

Silla in *The Rules of the Game* (Hare, adapted from Pirandello), New Theatre, London.

1972   Jennifer Dubedat in *The Doctor's Dilemma* (G. B. Shaw), Chichester Festival Theatre.

Katharina in *The Taming of the Shrew* (Shakespeare), Chichester Festival Theatre.

1973   Rebecca West in *Rosmersholm* (Ibsen), Greenwich Theatre, London.

Joan Plowright (1977).

Rosa in *Saturday, Sunday, Monday* (De Filippo), Old Vic Theatre, London; Queen's Theatre, London, 1974.

1974   Stella Kirby in *Eden End* (Priestley), Old Vic Theatre, London.

1975   Irena Arkadina in *The Seagull* (Chekhov), Lyric Theatre, London.

Alma in *The Bed Before Yesterday* (Travers), Lyric Theatre, London.

1977   Filumena Marturano in *Filumena* (De Filippo), Lyric Theatre, London; St James Theatre, New York, 1980.

1980   Mam in *Enjoy* (Bennett), National Theatre, London.

1981   Martha in *Who's Afraid of Virginia Woolf?* (Albee), National Theatre, London.

1983   Madame Ranevskaya in *The Cherry Orchard* (Chekhov), Haymarket Theatre, London.

1984   Lady Wishfort in *The Way of the World* (Congreve), Chichester Festival Theatre and Haymarket Theatre, London.

1985   Mrs Warren in *Mrs Warren's Profession* (G. B. Shaw), National Theatre, London.

1986   Mother in *The House of Bernarda Alba* (Lorca), Globe Theatre, London.

1990   Mrs Conway in *Time and the Conways* (Priestley), Old Vic Theatre, London.

Also acted role in: *Cavell* (Baxter), Chichester Festival Theatre, London, 1982.

As director:

1969   *An Evasion of Women*, Old Vic Theatre, London.

The Travails of Sancho Panza (Sanders), Old Vic Theatre, London.

Rites (Duffy), Old Vic Theatre, London.

1985   *A Prayer for Wings* (Mathias), National Theatre, London.

1988   *Married Love* (Luke), National Theatre, London.

Films

Moby Dick, 1956; *Time Without Pity*, 1957; *The Entertainer*, 1960; *The Three Sisters*, 1969; *Equus*, 1977; *Richard Wagner*, 1987; *Brimstone and Treacle*, 1982; *Britannia Hospital*, 1983; *Wagner*, 1985; *Revolution*, 1985; *Drowning by Numbers*, 1988; *The Dressmaker*, 1988; *I Love You to Death*, 1990; *Avalon*, 1989; *Enchanted April*, 1991; *Stalin*, 1991; *Dennis the Menace*, 1992; *A Place for Annie*, 1992; *A Pin for the Butterfly*, 1993; *Widow's Peak*, 1993; *Last Action Hero*, 1993; *The Summer House*, 1994.

Television

Odd Man In, 1958; *Secret Agent*, 1959; *The School for Scandal*, 1959 and 1964; *Twelfth Night*, 1967; *The Merchant of Venice*, 1973; *Daphne Laureola*, 1977; *Saturday, Sunday, Monday*, 1977; *The Diary of Anne Frank*, 1981; *The Birthday Party*, 1987; *The Importance of Being Earnest*, 1988; *And a Nightingale Sang*, 1989; *The House of Bernarda Alba*, 1991; *Clothes in the Wardrobe*, 1992.

* * *

Joan Plowright (Lady Olivier) is the best-known graduate of the passionately conceived but shortlived Old Vic Theatre School, founded and led by Michel Saint-Denis, Glen Byam-Shaw, and George Devine. Through her connection with Devine she became a member of the English Stage Company at the Royal Court Theatre in its early days and helped to establish the new realism of the 'kitchen sink' drama, which reflected and expressed the changes in postwar Britain, when 'the regions' began to dispute the cultural dominance of London and the upper-middle-class. She belonged to a new generation of actors that found a basis of non-standard accent was an asset in developing a 'real' quality of speech very different from the Chelsea voice prevalent among young actresses of previous years and preserved in British films of the 1940's. Vitality was now rated above glamour.

Plowright did not begin with 'kitchen sink' plays. She had quite a brief apprenticeship at the Old Vic and in the provinces. Her promise and what then seemed boyishness took her into the cast of Orson Welles's stage production of *Moby Dick* in 1955, in the role of Pip. It was not a particularly auspicious start: critics noted her unease, but she was to work with the same director to much happier effect five years later. She appeared in the English Stage Company's second production (Arthur Miller's *The Crucible*) and, through the rest of the year, became familiar to Royal Court audiences as a hard-working and convincing

player. Her first real hit was in another costume drama, the classic Restoration comedy *The Country Wife*, as Margery Pinchwife. Fresh, pert, attractively naive, oddly natural, though staying within the artificial conventions of Wycherley's view of society, she showed a genuine clown's skill in the comic use of facial expression without being clownish. Her gift for combining comedy and character in an artificial style of drama was confirmed when she played the Old Woman in Ionesco's surreal farce *The Chairs* and the 1958 revival of this piece in a single programme with the same playwright's *The Lesson* was evidently designed in part to show the actress's paces: in the interval she transformed herself from a schoolgirl into an old woman. Meanwhile, Laurence Olivier had brought his powerful support to the Company, opening as Archie Rice in Osborne's *The Entertainer*, with Dorothy Tutin playing Archie's daughter Jean, a role Joan Plowright took over from her. So began a strong, though intermittent, stage partnership that continued through their eventual marriage. They appeared together again at the Royal Court in 1960, in Orson Welles's production of another Ionesco absurdist play, *Rhinoceros*, which — not surprisingly — was an outstanding critical and box-office success.

By this time Plowright was known to a wider public, which had never been near Sloane Square, as one of the stars of the new movement in the theatre. This had happened through her performance as Beatie Bryant in Arnold Wesker's *Roots*. Although the Royal Court directorate gave support to Wesker's talents and convictions, they were still nervous about the reception London might give to a play about modern, under-vitalised, working-class rural life. So the play opened at the Belgrade Theatre in Coventry before being brought to the Sloane Square theatre, and Joan Plowright's performance deserved much of the credit for its great success there and on its transfer to the Duke of York's Theatre — and for the consequent widening of the range of theatre in London and England generally. The working atmosphere of the English Stage Company, with its argumentative camaraderie of authors and actors in a play-centred environment, continued into the stage life of *Roots*. Intense sincerity and an achieved ordinariness were hallmarks of Plowright's Beatie, along with a fluctuating but ultimately strong vitality. Although the seemingly artless spontaneity of Beatie dancing to her mother, after her bath, and the final image of defiant self-assertion remain most vividly in the memory, equally touching were the constant, rippling, changes of mood, the warmth and vulnerability of the character. Following this triumph, New York audiences were able to see her as the schoolgirl managing with the help of a gay boy, when she finds herself pregnant with a half-caste baby in Sheila Delaney's *A Taste of Honey*. The play had started its life at Joan Littlewood's east end theatre but needed a star name for US audiences, and this Joan Plowright now had, as well as being obviously suitable for the role.

Plowright's training in the classics undoubtedly helped her avoid a future of type-casting and possible neglect as she grew older. Through a predictably spirited Portia and the lead role in the rarely-seen Elizabethan pathetic tragedy *A Woman Killed with Kindness*, she modulated towards Chekhov. At the first Chichester Festival, *Uncle Vanya* was given with a starry cast that included Michael Redgrave, Laurence Olivier, and, in a tiny part, Sybil Thorndike. It was a memorable ensemble performance, but the greatest surprise was the emergence of Plowright's Sonia as the crowning role, poignant with inner truth, but also blazing with fervour seen by at least one leading critic as revolutionary. When she came to play Arkadina in *The Seagull*, in 1975, and Ranevskaya in *The Cherry Orchard* the rapport with Chekhov was no less evident in the mature roles. Her playing of these mature women combined delicately precise criticism with empathy in a completely authoritative fashion. Although thoroughly competent, she was less happy with Ibsen's drama — possibly her approach was not intellectual enough — and, although her performance as Shaw's Saint Joan was much praised and brought her another of her numerous awards, she allowed too much of the character's down-to-earth common sense to be lost, for strictly Shavian tastes, in a too conventionally mystical playing of some passages. Differently directed, the exact note would surely have been wholly within her range. When she came to play Shaw's Mrs Warren, with a less broad vulgarity and vividness than Coral Browne had displayed, the play was finely served by an evenly matched struggle between mother and daughter as convincing in human terms as in its social thesis; it was one of the rare occasions when their last encounter proved as absorbing as the first and, almost certainly, ended in the mother's victory again.

Joan Plowright's technical assurance in playing farcical or near-farcical actions has not deserted her. It was very evident in the veteran Ben Travers romp *The Bed Before Yesterday* and when she played an Italian housewife in *Saturday, Sunday, Monday* then, later, in *Filomena*. Yet what most strongly distinguished her acting in these parts, as in her Lady Wishfort in *The Way of the World*, was the quality of feeling with which she gave realism to characters that could easily have remained amusing puppets. As a final, most deserved compliment, it can be said that Joan Plowright has never seemed a star on stage, but a most reliable member of a profession at work.

—Margery Morgan

POEL, William. British director and actor. Born William Pole in London, 22 July 1852. Educated privately. Married Ella Constance Locock in 1894. Abandoned office work to launch career as an actor under Charles James Mathews, 1876; co-manager, with Emma Cons, Royal Victoria Hall (later, Old Vic Theatre), 1881–83; stage manager under Frank Benson, 1883–84; general instructor to Shakespeare Reading Society, 1887–97; founder and director, Elizabethan Stage Society, 1894–1905, with whom he attempted to revive the style of the original Elizabethan theatre, directing works by Ford, Marlowe, Fletcher, Jonson, Middleton and Calderón; refused knighthood, 1929. Member: London Shakespeare League (president from 1925). Died in London, 13 December 1934.

Principal productions

As director:
1881   *Hamlet* (Shakespeare), St George's Hall, London; acted Hamlet.
1892   *The Duchess of Malfi* (Webster), Opéra Comique, London.

1893   *Measure for Measure* (Shakespeare), Royalty Theatre, London.
1895   *Twelfth Night* (Shakespeare), St George's Hall, London.
        Measure for Measure (Shakespeare), Shakespeare Festival, Stratford-upon-Avon.
1896   Doctor Faustus (Marlowe), St George's Hall, London.
        Edward III (Shakespeare and others), St George's Hall, London.
1897   *Arden of Feversham* (Lillo), St George's Hall, London.
        Edward II (Marlowe), St George's Hall, London.
1898   *The Broken Heart* (Ford), St George's Hall, London.
        The Spanish Gipsy (Middleton and Rowley), St George's Hall, London.
1899   *The Alchemist* (Jonson), Apothecaries' Hall, London.
        Locrine (Swinburne), St George's Hall, London.
        Sakuntala (Kalidasa), Botanic Gardens, London.
1900   *Samson Agonistes* (Milton), Victoria and Albert Museum, Kensington, London.
1901   *Everyman* (anon.), Charterhouse School, London.
1905   *Romeo and Juliet* (Shakespeare), English Stage Society, London.
1908   *Measure for Measure* (Shakespeare), Gaiety Theatre, Manchester.
1909   *Macbeth* (Shakespeare), Fulham Theatre, London.
        John Bull's Other Island (G. B. Shaw), British tour; revived notably, Kingsway Theatre, London, 1912; acted Father Keegan.
1910   *The Cloister*, Gaiety Theatre, Manchester; acted Dom Balthazar.
1911   *Jacob and Esau* (Udall), Little Theatre, London.
1912   *Troilus and Cressida* (Shakespeare), King's Hall, London; Shakespeare Festival, Stratford-upon-Avon, 1913; acted Pandarus.
1924   *Fratricide Punished* (anon.), Oxford Playhouse, Oxford, and New Oxford Theatre, London.
1925   *Arden of Feversham* (Lillo), Scala Theatre, London.
1926   *Fratricide Punished* (anon.), Apollo Theatre, London.
1927   *When You See Me, You Know Me* (Rowley), Holborn Empire Theatre, London.
1928   *Sejanus His Fall* (Jonson), Holborn Empire, London.
1929   Bonduca (Fletcher), King's Hall, London.
        The Duke of Byron (Chapman), Royalty Theatre, London.
1930   *Caesar and Pompey* (Chapman), Globe Theatre, London.
1932   *David and Bethsabe* (Peele), Mary Ward Settlement.

Other productions included: *The Coxcomb* (anon.), *The Sad Shepherd* (Jonson), *The Good-Natured Man* (Goldsmith), all 1895–1905; *Two Gentlemen of Verona* (Shakespeare), 1910; *Hamlet* (Shakespeare), 1914; *Poetaster* (Jonson), 1916; *The Return from Parnassus*, 1919; *Henry VIII* (Rowley), 1927; *Coriolanus* (Shakespeare), 1931; *Alcestis* (Euripides); *All's Well That Ends Well* (Shakespeare); *Bacchae* (Euripides); *Don Juan* (Molière); *Franciscans*; *Henry VI* (Shakespeare); *Life's a Dream* (Calderón); *Richard II* (Shakespeare); *Wallenstein* (Schiller).

Publications

Priest or Painter (play), 1884; *Mehalah* (play), 1886; *Shakespeare in the Theatre* (essays), 1913; *What is Wrong with the Stage?*, 1920; *Monthly Letters*, 1929; *Absence of Mind* (play); *First Franciscans* (play); *Lilies That Fester* (play); *The Wayside Cottage* (adaptation from Kotzebue); *The Man of Forty* (adaptation from Kotzebue).

*

Bibliography

Books:
Robert Speaight, *William Poel and the Elizabethan Revival*, London, 1954.

* * *

William Poel occupies a crucial place in the development of modern stage practice, specifically in relation to Shakespeare and the classics. Inspired to enter the theatre after witnessing the 'naturalistic' performances of Charles James Mathews as well as productions by touring French companies, he stubbornly dedicated his career to the revival and restaging in the authentic Elizabethan manner of many neglected dramas, returning to the repertoire significant plays by Jonson, Ford, Marlowe, Middleton and of course Shakespeare.

Poel's production of the 'bad' quarto of *Hamlet* at St George's Hall in London in 1888 marked the first step in an obsessive quest to restore an Elizabethan method of presentation to the English stage, in the unshakeable faith that this was appropriate for the plays themselves. He rejected the elaborate staging then fashionable in the main London theatres and championed by the likes of Henry Irving and favoured instead of the conventional proscenium arch setting bare platforms with virtually no scenery. Actors with Poel's controversial but highly influential English Stage Society, founded in 1894, dressed in authentic period costumes and inhabited stage spaces closely modelled on the Elizabethan originals, the acting area protruding into the dress circle and complete with recreations of the Elizabethan 'inner stage'. These efforts extended, in 1893, to the 'reconstruction' of something akin to the stage of the Elizabethan Fortune Theatre actually within the proscenium arch of London's Royalty Theatre, a well-meaning but somewhat awkward compromise of the kind that were to dog Poel's productions over the years. Where possible, rather than staging productions in contemporary theatres, he used the halls of the Inns of Court and other historical locations (his *Twelfth Night* was restaged in the same hall where it was first acted in the reign of Elizabeth I).

With the notable exception of Bernard Shaw, who praised Poel for 'reintellectualizing' the Victorian theatre, the critics were often hostile to his rejection of conventional stage practice. They were less than mollified by his weakness for experimentation with vocal techniques, which led to some very bizarre effects. Poel himself had mixed success as a performer, and his insistence on often eccentric voice production attracted ridicule on more than one occasion. Nonetheless, his ideas, which he promulgated in essays and other writings and through such protegés as Harley Granville-Barker and actress Edith Evans (who made her debut under Poel, as Cressida), were destined to have a lasting impact, as directors of the ensuing generation began to question the limitations of the 'picture-frame' stage of the Victorian and Edwardian eras. His insistence on emphasizing the musicality of the lines, together with continuity of action, fidelity to the text and the establishing of a more intimate relationship between the cast and the audience all had a profound effect.

Official recognition of Poel's work came in 1929 with the offer of a knighthood — which Poel, characteristically, refused on the grounds that no previous recipients of the honour had supported the idea of restoring Elizabethan staging practices.

—David Pickering

———

POPOVA, Lyubov (Sergeevna). Russian designer. Born Lyubov Sergeevna Eding near Moscow, 24 April 1889. Trained as an artist at the private studios of Konstantin Yuon and Stanislav Zhukovsky, 1907–08; studied art and architecture in Italy, 1910; studied modern art at the Tower Studio with Vladimir Tatlin, 1912. Worked as designer in Paris, 1912–13; returned to Russia, 1913, then worked again in France and in Italy, 1914; professor, Free State Art Studios/Higher State Art-Technical Studios, Moscow, 1918; developed concept of constructivism in the theatre, designing first constructivist set for Vsevolod Meyerhold, 1922; also designed textiles and dress designs, 1923–24. Member: Inkhuk (Institute of Artistic Culture), Moscow, 1920. Died (scarlet fever) in Moscow, 25 May 1924.

Productions

1919   *The Tale of the Country Priest and His Dunderhead Servant* (Pushkin), Theatre of Marionettes, Petrouchkas and Shadows, Moscow.

1921   *The Locksmith and the Chancellor* (Lunacharsky), Korsh Theatre, Moscow.

       Romeo and Juliet (Shakespeare), Kamerny Theatre, Moscow.

1922   *Le Cocu magnifique* (Crommelynck), Actors' Theatre, Moscow.

1923   *Zemlya dybom* [Earth Rampant] (Tretyakov, adapted from Martinet), Meyerhold Theatre, Moscow.

*

Bibliography

Articles:
J. Bowlt, "From Surface to Space: The Art of Liubov Popova", *The Structurist*, Saskatoon, Canada, 1976.

* * *

Lyubov Popova was born into a wealthy Moscow family. She studied painting in Moscow, Paris and Italy, and in her early twenties achieved some recognition as a Russian Cubist. By the time of World War I, she had become a Futurist of the school of Kasimir Malevich, and her independent enquiries led her towards the pure abstractionism of Malevich's Suprematism. She supported the Revolution and put her commitment to work by teaching at new institutions such as the Proletkult (Organisation for Proletarian Culture) and VKhTEMAS (Higher State Artistic and Technical Workshop). In the early 1920's she was associated with the Constructivists, and not only executed her stage designs but also designed textiles for mass production.

Popova's first foray into stage design was for a mass spectacle, *The Struggle and Triumph of the Soviets*, to be directed by Meyerhold and performed on the Khodinsky Field in Moscow. It was a fairly schematic but spectacular conception, with on the left a 'Capitalist castle' and on the right a dynamic 'City of the Future', linked by a pair of huge dirigibles, displaying suitably energising slogans, such as "Long Live the Third International" and "Workers of the World, Unite".

The Struggle of the Soviets was never performed, but it led to Popova being invited, first, to teach stage design at Meyerhold's Theatre Workshop, and then to design two of his most striking productions, *Le Cocu magnifique* and *Earth Rampant*. In these she picked up Meyerhold's challenge to the designer implicit in the presentational system he had created. Briefly, this sprang from a new relationship between actor and audience, in which the actor would not shut out the spectator from his consciousness, but would rather use him in the creation of the drama. The actor therefore left the conventional stage setting and centred his performance on the forestage, thus liberating the stage design to contribute in its own way to the meaning of the production, not in any decorative or illustrative manner, but as another dynamic element in the performance.

In accordance with this, the set for *Le Cocu magnifique* was to be primarily a 'machine for acting'. It consisted of open wooden struts assembled to make two large box-like constructions of unequal height, which the actors could enter as if they were largish cubicles or mount to the top of by means of staircases or a slide. Their tops were joined by a gangplank, and behind them were three large wooden wheels, one black with the consonants of the author's name painted on it in white, the other two spoked, not solid, in red and unpainted wood. There was also a propeller-like construction to one side, as though the whole machine might take off at any moment. For the propeller was able to revolve, which it did, like the wheels, at unexpected moments of high drama or emotional intensity. The play was supposedly set in a mill, and the propeller was slightly reminiscent of the windmill sails, as the slide reminded one of the corn chute. It was, however, an allusive, not a

A set from *The Earth Rampant,* designed by **Lyubov Popova.**

representational, creation. The clean lines and skeletal structures were equally like the scaffolding on a construction site, or perhaps the objects found in a children's playground, while also retaining a hint of circus apparatus for the actors to perform their tricks on.

This indeed was the style of performance, and Popova's costumes were designed to encourage it. They were basically loose, blue working garments with characters distinguished usually by small hand props like a riding whip or a monocle, though the central character had red pompoms to suggest, perhaps, a baby or a clown. Set and costumes thus provided 'utilitarian suitability' and were able to 'co-ordinate' the action as well as to contribute to it.

One commentator noted the set was "a kind of machine which takes on a living existence in the course of the production". Meyerhold himself said: "in the creation of the performance, the work of Popova was significant ... much in the tone of the performance was taken from the constructive set".

Popova's final stage design was for Meyerhold's production of *Earth Rampant* by Sergei Tretyakov. This play was less vapid, and more directly concerned with the revolutionary reality of Soviet society, so that where before the machine for acting had been allusive and still therefore partly decorative, now the stage presented a much more utilitarian aspect, which in turn was much more clearly connected to a specific reality. The large gantry crane that dominated the stage was precisely that, and not much action took place on it; rather it provided a convenient place for hanging projection screens and slogans.

The props and costumes were created for their agitational potential, the lighting was provided by military searchlights without colouring, the actors wore no make-up and there were large numbers of simply real things, from typewriters and maps to machine-guns, bicycles and a lorry that brought on the dead hero at the end. The most dynamic element was probably the series of designed slogans to be projected onto the screens (a remarkably early example of this technique), and especially the typically constructivist lettering that Popova created for them. They exemplified the tension between reality and unreality, theatre and the real world, which *Earth Rampant* created for its audience.

Popova's work was important because it addressed a number of problems central to 20th century stage design, such as the contribution the design can make to the dynamic meaning of the drama, the nature of the relationship between real world and theatre world, and the use of theatre as a model for the world. Her first attempts were startlingly original, but it would be impossible to say that she completely solved these problems. Her death at the age of 35 was therefore a real loss.

—Robert Leach

PRITCHARD, Hannah. British actress. Born Hannah Vaughan in London, 1711. Married William Pritchard in 1731, one daughter. May have worked in family staymaking business before making stage debut as strolling player; first appearance at Theatre Royal, Drury Lane, 1733, where she established reputation as comedy actress, 1733–41; first appearance at Covent Garden, 1742; re-engaged by Garrick at Drury Lane, 1748, with husband joining Drury Lane management; widened her range with both comic and tragic roles, notably Lady Macbeth, over next 21 years; later roles restricted by her increasing girth; retired, 1768. Died in Bath, 19 August 1768.

Roles

1733   Phillis in *The Livery Rake Trapped; or, The Disappointed Countrylass* (Phillips), Theatre Royal, Drury Lane, London.

Loveit in *A Cure for Covetousness; or, The Cheats of Scapin* (Otway, adapted from Molière), Bartholomew Fair, London.

Nell in *The Devil to Pay* (Coffey), Haymarket Theatre, London.

Dorcas in *The Mock Doctor* (Fielding), Haymarket Theatre, London.

Ophelia in *Hamlet* (Shakespeare), Haymarket Theatre, London.

Edging in *The Careless Husband* (Cibber), Haymarket Theatre, London.

Sylvia in *The Double Gallant* (Cibber), Haymarket Theatre, London.

Cleora in *The Opera of Operas; or, Tom Thumb the Great* (Fielding), Haymarket Theatre, London.

Lappet in *The Miser* (Fielding, adapted from Molière), Haymarket Theatre, London.

Phaedra in *Amphitryon* (Dryden, adapted from Molière), Haymarket Theatre, London.

Hob's Mother in *Flora* (Hippisley), Haymarket Theatre, London.

1734   Peasant Woman in *The Burgomaster Tricked* (Theobald), Haymarket Theatre, London.

Belina in *The Mother-in-Law* (Miller), Haymarket Theatre, London.

Mrs Fainall in *The Way of the World* (Congreve), Theatre Royal, Drury Lane, London.

Cloe in *The Constant Lovers* (anon.), Bartholomew Fair.

Lady Loverule in *The Devil to Pay* (Coffey), Theatre Royal, Drury Lane, London.

Sylvia in *The Bachelor* (Congreve), Theatre Royal, Drury Lane, London.

Columbine's Maid in *Cupid and Psyche; or, Columbine Courtesan* (anon.), Theatre Royal, Drury Lane, London.

Lady of Pleasure in *Harlot's Progress* (T. Cibber), Theatre Royal, Drury Lane, London.

Isabella in *The Conscious Lovers* (Steele), Theatre Royal, Drury Lane, London.

Mopsophil in *Columbine Courtesan* (anon.), Theatre Royal, Drury Lane, London.

Hortensia in *Junius Brutus* (Duncombe), Theatre Royal, Drury Lane, London.

1735   Patch in *The Busybody* (Centlivre), Theatre Royal, Drury Lane, London.

Cleora in *The Christian Hero* (Lillo), Theatre Royal, Drury Lane, London.

English Lady in *The Plot* (Kelly), Theatre Royal, Drury Lane, London.

Julia in *The Fatal Marriage* (Southerne), Theatre Royal, Drury Lane, London.

Lady Fidget in *The Country Wife* (Wycherley), Theatre Royal, Drury Lane, London.

Flora in *A Cure for a Scold* (Worsdale), Theatre Royal, Drury Lane, London.

Dorothea in *The Man of Taste* (Miller), Theatre Royal, Drury Lane, London.

Florinda in *The Rover* (Behn), Theatre Royal, Drury Lane, London.

Lady Loverule in *The Merry Cobbler* (Coffey), Theatre Royal, Drury Lane, London.

Lady Wou'd be in *Volpone* (Jonson), Theatre Royal, Drury Lane, London.

Eugenia in *Trick for Trick* (Fabian), Theatre Royal, Drury Lane, London.

Margarita in *Rule a Wife and Have a Wife* (Beaumont and Fletcher), Lincoln's Inn Fields Theatre.

Lucy in *The London Merchant* (Lillo), Theatre Royal, Drury Lane, London.

Combrush in *The Honest Yorkshireman* (Carey), Haymarket Theatre, London.

Lady Townly in *The Provoked Husband* (Cibber), Haymarket Theatre, London.

Aurelia in *The Twin Rivals* (Farquhar), Haymarket Theatre, London.

Beatrice in *The Anatomist* (Ravenscroft), Haymarket Theatre, London.

Hannah Pritchard as Lady Macbeth.

1736   Selima in *Zara* (Hill), Theatre Royal, Drury Lane, London.
Ballad Singer in *Harlequin Restored* (anon.), Theatre Royal, Drury Lane, London.
Mrs Freelove in *The Connoisseur* (Connolly), Theatre Royal, Drury Lane, London.
Columbine's Maid in *The Fall of Phaeton* (William Pritchard), Theatre Royal, Drury Lane, London.
Mrs Flareit in *Love's Last Shift* (Cibber), Theatre Royal, Drury Lane, London.
Cephisa in *The Distresst Mother* (Racine, adapted by Philips), Theatre Royal, Drury Lane, London.
Betty in *The Contrivances* (Carey), Theatre Royal, Drury Lane, London.
Fainlove in *The Tender Husband* (Steele), Theatre Royal, Drury Lane, London.
Louisa in *Loves Makes a Man* (Cibber), Theatre Royal, Drury Lane, London.
Mrs Sullen in *The Beaux' Stratagem* (Farquhar), Lincoln's Inn Fields Theatre.
Charlotte in *Oroonoko* (Southerne), Theatre Royal, Drury Lane, London.
Aurelia in *The Wife's Relief* (Johnson), Theatre Royal, Drury Lane, London.
Tippet in *Phebe; or, The Beggar's Wedding* (Coffey), Theatre Royal, Drury Lane, London.

Dol Common in *The Alchemist* (Jonson), Theatre Royal, Drury Lane, London.
Dorinda in *Greenwich Park* (Mountfort), Theatre Royal, Drury Lane, London.
Melissa in *Timon of Athens* (Shakespeare, adapted by Shadwell), Theatre Royal, Drury Lane, London.
Damaris in *The Amorous Widow* (Molière, adapted by Betterton), Theatre Royal, Drury Lane, London.
Lucy in *The Beggar's Opera* (Gay), Theatre Royal, Drury Lane, London.

1737   Peggy in *The King and The Miller of Mansfield* (Dodsley), Theatre Royal, Drury Lane, London.
Delia in *The Universal Passion* (Miller, adapted from Shakespeare's *Much Ado About Nothing*), Theatre Royal, Drury Lane, London.
Ruth in *The Committee* (Howard), Theatre Royal, Drury Lane, London.
Kitty in *The What d'ye Call it* (Gay), Theatre Royal, Drury Lane, London.
Mrs Foresight in *Love for Love* (Congreve), Theatre Royal, Drury Lane, London.
Altea in *Rule a Wife and Have a Wife* (Beaumont and Fletcher), Theatre Royal, Drury Lane, London.
Araminta in *The Old Bachelor* (Congreve), Theatre Royal, Drury Lane, London.
Duchess of York in *Richard III* (Shakespeare), Theatre Royal, Drury Lane, London.
Araminta in *The Confederacy* (Vanbrugh), Theatre Royal, Drury Lane, London.
Mrs Termagant in *The Squire of Alsatia* (Shadwell), Theatre Royal, Drury Lane, London.
Clarinda in *The Double Gallant* (Cibber), Theatre Royal, Drury Lane, London.
Lady Haughty in *The Silent Woman* (Jonson), Theatre Royal, Drury Lane, London.

1738   Pert in *The Man of Mode* (Etherege), Theatre Royal, Drury Lane, London.
Clara in *The Lovers Opera* (Chetwood), Theatre Royal, Drury Lane, London.
Berinthia in *The Relapse* (Vanbrugh), Theatre Royal, Drury Lane, London.
Lady Anne in *Richard III* (Shakespeare), Theatre Royal, Drury Lane, London.
Angelina in *Love Makes a Man* (Cibber), Theatre Royal, Drury Lane, London.
Angelica in *Love for Love* (Congreve), Theatre Royal, Drury Lane, London.
Belina in *The Old Bachelor* (Congreve), Theatre Royal, Drury Lane, London.
Juletta in *The Pilgrims* (Beaumont and Fletcher, adapted by Vanbrugh and Dryden), Theatre Royal, Drury Lane, London.

1739   Mrs Conquest in *The Lady's Last Stake* (Cibber), Theatre Royal, Drury Lane, London.
Dorinda in *The Beaux' Stratagem* (Farquhar), Theatre Royal, Drury Lane, London.
Corinna in *A Match In Newgate* (Bullock), Theatre Royal, Drury Lane, London.

Hypolita in *She Would and She Would Not* (Cibber), Theatre Royal, Drury Lane, London.

Lady Macduff in *Macbeth* (Shakespeare), Theatre Royal, Drury Lane, London.

Anne Bullen in *Henry VIII* (Shakespeare), Theatre Royal, Drury Lane, London.

1740 Leonora in *Don John* (Thadwell), Theatre Royal, Drury Lane, London.

Indiana in *The Conscious Lovers* (Steele), Theatre Royal, Drury Lane, London.

Lady Smart in *Polite Conversation: Morning or Tea Chat; Noon or Table-Talk á-la-mode* (Swift, adapted by Miller), Theatre Royal, Drury Lane, London.

Desdemona in *Othello* (Shakespeare), Theatre Royal, Drury Lane, London.

Bertha in *The Royal Merchant* (Norris), Theatre Royal, Drury Lane, London.

Cordelia in *A Fond Husband* (D'Urfey), Theatre Royal, Drury Lane, London.

Rosalind in *As You Like It* (Shakespeare), Theatre Royal, Drury Lane, London.

1741 Viola in *Twelfth Night* (Shakespeare), Theatre Royal, Drury Lane, London.

Nerissa in *The Merchant of Venice* (Shakespeare), Theatre Royal, Drury Lane, London.

Sylvia in *The Recruiting Officer* (Farquhar), Covent Garden, London.

Elvira in *The Spanish Friar* (Dryden), Covent Garden, London.

Lady Brute in *The Provoked Wife* (Vanbrugh), Covent Garden, London.

Queen Elizabeth in *Richard III* (Shakespeare), Covent Garden, London.

Queen Gertrude in *Hamlet* (Shakespeare), Covent Garden, London.

Lady No in *The London Cuckolds* (Ravenscroft), Covent Garden, London.

The Country Wife in *The Country Wife* (Wycherley), Covent Garden, London.

Lady Lurewell in *The Constant Couple* (Farquhar), Covent Garden, London.

Paulina in *The Winter's Tale* (Shakespeare), Covent Garden, London.

Lady Touchwood in *The Double Dealer* (Congreve), Covent Garden, London.

Mrs Clerimont in *The Tender Husband* (Steele), Covent Garden, London.

Amanda in *Love's Last Shift* (Cibber), Covent Garden, London.

Phillis in *The Conscious Lovers* (Steele), Covent Garden, London.

1742 Lady Sadlife in *The Double Gallant* (Cibber), Covent Garden, London.

Mrs Marwood in *The Way of the World* (Congreve), Covent Garden, London.

Nottingham in *The Unhappy Favourite; or, The Earl of Essex* (Banks), Covent Garden, London.

Mrs Frail in *Love for Love* (Congreve), Covent Garden, London.

Doris in *Aesop* (Vanbrugh), Covent Garden, London.

Monimia in *The Orphan* (Otway), Theatre Royal, Drury Lane, London.

Amanda in *The Relapse* (Vanbrugh), Theatre Royal, Drury Lane, London.

1743 Clarinda in *The Wedding Day* (Fielding), Theatre Royal, Drury Lane, London.

Jane Shore in *Jane Shore* (Rowe), Theatre Royal, Drury Lane, London.

Lady Easy in *The Careless Husband* (Cibber), Theatre Royal, Drury Lane, London.

Constance in *The Twin Rivals* (Farquhar), Theatre Royal, Drury Lane, London.

1744 Isabella in *Measure for Measure* (Shakespeare), Covent Garden, London.

Queen Katharine in *Henry VIII* (Shakespeare), Covent Garden, London.

Eudocia in *The Siege of Damascus* (Hughes), Covent Garden, London.

Calista in *The Fair Penitent* (Rowe), Covent Garden, London.

Hermione in *The Distresst Mother* (Phillips), Covent Garden, London.

Lady in *Comus* (Milton, adapted by Dalton), Covent Garden, London.

Abra Mule in *Abra Mule* (Trapp), Covent Garden, London.

Almeyda in *Don Sebastian* (Dryden), Covent Garden, London.

Lady Macbeth in *Macbeth* (Shakespeare), Covent Garden, London.

Portia in *Julius Caesar* (Shakespeare), Covent Garden, London.

Belvidera in *Venice Preserved* (Otway), Covent Garden, London.

Marcia in *Cato* (Addison), Covent Garden, London.

Mrs Ford in *The Merry Wives of Windsor* (Shakespeare), Covent Garden, London.

Arpasia in *Tamerlane* (Rowe), Covent Garden, London.

Laetitia in *The Bachelor* (Congreve), Covent Garden, London.

Leonora in *The Revenge* (Young), Covent Garden, London.

Queen in *The Spanish Friar* (Dryden), Covent Garden, London.

Evadne in *The Maid's Tragedy* (Beaumont and Fletcher), Covent Garden, London.

Rutland in *The Unhappy Favourite; or, The Earl of Essex* (Banks), Covent Garden, London.

1745 Lady Charlotte in *The Funeral* (Steele), Covent Garden, London.

Lady Constance in *Papal Tyranny in the Reign of King John* (Cibber), Covent Garden, London.

Mariamne in *Mariamne* (Fenton), Covent Garden, London.

Epicoene in *The Silent Woman* (Jonson), Covent Garden, London.

Evandra in *Timon of Athens* (Shakespeare), Covent Garden, London.

Maria in *The Nonjuror* (Cibber), Covent Garden, London.

Antramone in *The Massacre of Paris* (Lee), Covent Garden, London.

Flippanta in *City Wives* (Vanbrugh), Covent Garden, London.

1746   Leonora in *Sir Courtly Nice* (Crowne), Covent Garden, London.

Portia in *The Merchant of Venice* (Shakespeare), Covent Garden, London.

Beatrice in *Much Ado About Nothing* (Shakespeare), Covent Garden, London.

Helena in *All's Well That Ends Well* (Shakespeare), Covent Garden, London.

Imogen in *Cymbeline* (Shakespeare), Covent Garden, London.

Sakia in *Liberty Asserted; or, French Perfidy Displayed* (Dennis), Covent Garden, London.

Anne Lovely in *A Bold Stroke for A Wife* (Centlivre), Covent Garden, London.

1747   Tag in *Miss In Her Teens* (Garrick), Covent Garden, London.

Clarinda in *The Suspicious Husband* (Hoadly), Covent Garden, London.

1748   Emilia in *Othello* (Shakespeare), Theatre Royal, Drury Lane, London.

Oroclea in *Lovers Melancholy* (Ford), Theatre Royal, Drury Lane, London.

Clarissa in *The Confederacy* (Vanbrugh), Theatre Royal, Drury Lane, London.

Lady Allworth in *A New Way to Pay Old Debts* (Massinger), Theatre Royal, Drury Lane, London.

1749   Lady Brumpton in *The Funeral* (Steele), Theatre Royal, Drury Lane, London.

Rosetta in *The Foundling* (Moore), Theatre Royal, Drury Lane, London.

Irene in *Mahomet and Irene* (Johnson), Theatre Royal, Drury Lane, London.

Meropé in *Meropé* (Hill), Theatre Royal, Drury Lane, London.

Millwood in *The London Merchant* (Lillo), Theatre Royal, Drury Lane, London.

1750   Mrs Goodville in *Friendship in Fashion* (Otway), Theatre Royal, Drury Lane, London.

Horatia in *The Roman Father* (Whitehead), Theatre Royal, Drury Lane, London.

Isabella in *The Fatal Marriage* (Southerne), Theatre Royal, Drury Lane, London.

Lady Betty Modish in *The Careless Husband* (Cibber), Theatre Royal, Drury Lane, London.

Cleopatra in *All For Love* (Dryden), Theatre Royal, Drury Lane, London.

Millamant in *The Way of the World* (Congreve), Theatre Royal, Drury Lane, London.

Zara in *The Mourning Bride* (Congreve), Theatre Royal, Drury Lane, London.

1751   Aurora in *Gil Blas* (Moore), Theatre Royal, Drury Lane, London.

Phaedra in *Phaedra and Hippolitus* (Smith), Theatre Royal, Drury Lane, London.

1752   Orphisa in *Eugenia* (Francis), Theatre Royal, Drury Lane, London.

Florimel in *The Comical Lovers* (Dryden, adapted by Cibber), Theatre Royal, Drury Lane, London.

1753   Mrs Beverly in *The Gamester* (Moore), Theatre Royal, Drury Lane, London.

Boadicia in *Boadicia* (Glover), Theatre Royal, Drury Lane, London.

1754   Catherine in *Catherine and Petruchio* (Garrick, adapted from Shakespeare's *The Taming of the Shrew*), Theatre Royal, Drury Lane, London.

Creusa in *Creusa Queen of Athens* (Whitehead), Theatre Royal, Drury Lane, London.

Lady Truman in *The Drummer* (Addison), Theatre Royal, Drury Lane, London.

Volumnia in *Coriolanus* (Shakespeare), Theatre Royal, Drury Lane, London.

1755   Leonora in *The Mistake* (Vanbrugh), Theatre Royal, Drury Lane, London.

Dorcas in *The Schemers* (Mayne), Theatre Royal, Drury Lane, London.

Queen Elizabeth in *The Earl of Essex* (Jones), Theatre Royal, Drury Lane, London.

1756   Hermione in *The Winter's Tale* (Shakespeare, adapted by Garrick), Theatre Royal, Drury Lane, London.

Countess of Rousillon in *All's Well That Ends Well* (Shakespeare), Theatre Royal, Drury Lane, London.

Lady Gentle in *The Lady's Last Stake* (Cibber), Theatre Royal, Drury Lane, London.

Estifania in *Rule a Wife and Have a Wife* (Fletcher), Theatre Royal, Drury Lane, London.

Lady Capulet in *Romeo and Juliet* (Shakespeare), Theatre Royal, Drury Lane, London.

Lady Wealthy in *The Gamester* (Centlivre), Theatre Royal, Drury Lane, London.

1758   Agesistrata in *Agis* (Home), Theatre Royal, Drury Lane, London.

1759   Artemisa in *The Ambitious Step-Mother* (Rowe), Theatre Royal, Drury Lane, London.

Lady Outside in *Woman is a Riddle* (Bullock), Theatre Royal, Drury Lane, London.

1760   Constantia in *The Desert Island* (Murphy), Theatre Royal, Drury Lane, London.

1761   Queen Elizabeth in *The Earl of Essex* (Brooke), Theatre Royal, Drury Lane, London.

Mrs Oakly in *The Jealous Wife* (Colman), Theatre Royal, Drury Lane, London.

Hecuba in *Hecuba* (Delap), Theatre Royal, Drury Lane, London.

1763   Elvira in *Elvira* (Mallett), Theatre Royal, Drury Lane, London.

Lady Medway in *The Discovery* (Frances Sheridan), Theatre Royal, Drury Lane, London.

Mrs Etherdown in *The Dupe* (Frances Sheridan), Theatre Royal, Drury Lane, London.

1764   Roxana in *The Rival Queens* (Lee), Theatre Royal, Drury Lane, London.

1766   Dame Ursula in *Falstaff's Wedding* (Kenrick), Theatre Royal, Drury Lane, London.

1767   Mrs Mildmay in *The Widowed Wife* (Kenrick), Theatre Royal, Drury Lane, London.

*

Bibliography

Books:
Thomas Davies, *Garrick*, London, 1780.
Anthony Vaughan, *Born to Please — Hannah Pritchard, Actress*, London, 1978.

* * *

Hannah Pritchard was the most highly respected actress of her time and was unique among contemporary female performers in her versatility. She excelled in both comedy and tragedy, but she was particularly admired for her comic roles. Rosalind was her first great success and remained one of her most admired characters. In comedy, she was preferred in characters of 'Nature' rather than of 'Affectation', such as Mrs Sullen in Farquhar's *The Beaux' Stratagem* "and in all such parts ... of diversity of humour, wit, and pleasantry", as Benjamin Victor put it.

Pritchard was most celebrated for the characters that she played opposite David Garrick, in which she was considered to be his match. These included Beatrice; Gertrude, which she made a major role; Lady Macbeth, her greatest tragic character; Lady Brute in Vanbrugh and Cibber's *The Provoked Wife*; and the coquette Clarinda in Hoadly's *The Suspicious Husband* and Mrs Oakly, the title character in Colman's *The Jealous Wife*, both of which she originated. Her Clarinda was described by Tate Wilkinson as "so easy, so natural, so spirited and vivacious" that she outdid the much more beautiful Peg Woffington, who played Jacyntha in the first production and subsequently played Clarinda herself. Her performance with Garrick in *The Jealous Wife* was touted as the best comic acting of the time and was praised in Churchill's *Rosciad* as her supreme achievement in the genre. Her impassioned and terrifying Lady Macbeth was the definitive interpretation for the period and Garrick reportedly gave up Macbeth after her retirement because he found her performance indispensable.

In her early years Pritchard was admired for her singing and throughout her career she was distinguished by her clear, harmonious voice, her excellent articulation, and her expressive intonation. As a young woman her movement was "easy, and elegant" and her manner "expressive, yet simple". She was famous for her ability to enter into her characters and particularize their emotions. Like Garrick, she used detailed, pantomimic action to create vivid, concrete performances. One highlight recorded by Thomas Davies in his *Dramatic Miscellanies* (1784) was the banquet scene in Macbeth, in which she: "shewed admirable art in endeavouring to hide Macbeth's frenzy from the observation of the guests, by drawing their attention to conviviality. She smiled on one, whispered to another, and distantly saluted a third; in short, she practised every possible artifice to hide the transaction that passed between her husband and the vision his disturbed imagination had raised. Her reproving and angry looks, which glanced towards Macbeth, at the same time were mixed with marks of inward vexation and uneasiness. When, at last, as if unable to support her feelings any longer, she rose from her seat, and seized his arm, and with a half-whisper of terror, said, 'Are you a man!' she assumed a look of such anger, indignation, and contempt, as cannot be surpassed."

Pritchard's appearance of naturalness on the stage was turned to advantage in Moore's domestic tragedy *The Gamester*, in which she originated the role of Mrs Beverley. Arthur Murphy claimed that her performance was "a specimen of the most natural acting that had ever been seen. She did not appear to be conscious of an audience before her: she seemed to be a gentlewoman in domestic life, walking about in her own parlour, in the deepest distress, and overwhelmed with misery."

She was not without her shortcomings, however. *The Theatrical Review for 1757* found her gesture in tragedy too limited, "being confined to her wrist and fingers", and she was notorious for "a too loud and profuse expression of grief". Although she had been attractive and slender when she was young, from about 1750 onwards she was becoming too corpulent for many of her roles. This problem was considered insuperable only in the starving Jane Shore, however; in her comic roles her "Ease and Viviacity" compensated for her unsuitable figure, while her appearance was considered appropriate for such dignified characters as Lady Macbeth and Gertrude and other wives, mothers, and queens.

Pritchard was one of the very few actresses who were compared to Garrick in terms of versatility and skill. She was also like him in making a conspicuous contribution to the 'respectability' of their profession through her exemplary diligence and morality. She was famous for patiently serving a long apprenticeship in minor roles before achieving prominence and the irreproachable, utterly conventional nature of her private life was well-known and contributed substantially to the praise she received. Davies exemplified the attitude of her contemporaries when he conflated her artistic merit with her probity, writing that "her unblemished conduct in private life justly rendered her the great favourite of the people ... ".

—Nancy Copeland

PROWSE, Philip (John). British designer and director. Born in Warwickshire, 29 December 1937. Educated at King's School, Worcester, Malvern College of Art; Slade School of Fine Art, 1956–59. Freelance designer, at Covent Garden and in Watford and elsewhere, 1960–69; designer/director, in collaboration with Giles Havergal and Robert David MacDonald, Glasgow Citizens' Theatre, from 1970; teacher, Central School of Art, Birmingham College of Art, and Slade School of Art.

Productions

As designer and director:
1961   *Diversions* (Bliss), Royal Opera House, Covent Garden, London.
1972   *The Relapse* (Vanbrugh), Citizens' Theatre, Glasgow.
1973   *Troilus and Cressida* (Shakespeare), Citizens' Theatre, Glasgow.
1974   *Early Morning* (Bond), Citizens' Theatre, Glasgow.
            Comino Real (T. Williams), Citizens' Theatre, Glasgow.

1975   *The Duchess of Malfi* (Webster), Citizens' Theatre, Glasgow, and European tour.

Hamlet (Shakespeare), Citizens' Theatre, Glasgow.

1976   *The Changeling* (Middleton and Rowley), Citizens' Theatre, Glasgow.

1977   *The Country Wife* (Wycherley), Citizens' Theatre, Glasgow.

Chinchilla (MacDonald), Citizens' Theatre, Glasgow, and European tour.

Semi-Monde (Coward), Citizens' Theatre, Glasgow.

1978   *Summit Conference* (MacDonald), Citizens' Theatre, Glasgow, and London.

Painter's Palace of Pleasure (F. Webster), Citizens' Theatre, Glasgow.

The Threepenny Opera (Brecht), Citizens' Theatre, Glasgow.

The Seagull (Chekhov), Citizens' Theatre, Glasgow.

1979   *The Maid's Tragedy* (Beaumont and Fletcher), Citizens' Theatre, Glasgow.

1980   *A Waste of Time* (adapted from Proust's *A la Recherche du Temps Perdu*), Citizens' Theatre, Glasgow, and Amsterdam.

Don Juan (MacDonald), Citizens' Theatre, Glasgow.

1981   *The Massacre at Paris* (Marlowe), Citizens' Theatre, Glasgow, and European tour.

1982   *The Balcony* (Genet), Citizens' Theatre, Glasgow.

The Blacks (Genet), Citizens' Theatre, Glasgow.

The Screens (Genet), Citizens' Theatre, Glasgow.

The Roman Actor (Massinger), Citizens' Theatre, Glasgow.

Philosophy in the Boudoir (De Sade), Citizens' Theatre, Glasgow, and Parma.

Tamerlano (Handel), Welsh National Opera, Opera North, East Berlin, and Halle.

The Threepenny Opera (Brecht and Weill), Opera North.

Aida (Verdi), Opera North.

The Pearl Fishers (Bizet), English National Opera and Opera North.

Daphne (Strauss), Opera North.

1983   *The Merchant of Venice* (Shakespeare), Citizens' Theatre, Glasgow, and Turin.

Sirocco (Coward), Citizens' Theatre, Glasgow.

Webster (MacDonald), Citizens' Theatre, Glasgow.

Der Rosenkavalier (Hoffmanstal), Citizens' Theatre, Glasgow, and Edinburgh.

Oroonoko (Southerne), Citizens' Theatre, Glasgow.

1984   *A Woman of No Importance* (Wilde), Citizens' Theatre, Glasgow.

La Vie Parisienne (Offenbach), Citizens' Theatre, Glasgow.

The White Devil (Webster), Greenwich Theatre, London.

The Seagull (Chekhov), Greenwich Theatre, London.

Phedra (Racine), Old Vic Theatre, London, and Aldwych Theatre, London.

1985   *Mary Stuart* (Schiller), Citizens' Theatre, Glasgow.

The Duchess of Malfi (Webster), National Theatre, London.

1986   *La Celestina* (Rojas), Citizens' Theatre, Glasgow.

The Orphan (Otway), Greenwich Theatre, London.

1987   *Anna Karenina* (Tolstoy), Citizens' Theatre, Glasgow.

1988   *The Vortex* (Coward), Citizens' Theatre, Glasgow, and London.

'Tis Pity She's a Whore (Ford), Citizens' Theatre, Glasgow.

Lady Windermere's Fan (Wilde), Citizens' Theatre, Glasgow.

Phedra (Racine), Citizens' Theatre, Glasgow.

1989   *Tale of Two Cities* (Dickens), Citizens' Theatre, Glasgow.

1990   *Enrico IV* (Pirandello), Citizens' Theatre, Glasgow.

Mother Courage (Brecht), Citizens' Theatre, Glasgow, and Mermaid Theatre, London.

1991   *A Woman of No Importance* (Wilde), Barbican Theatre, London.

Design for Living (Coward), Citizens' Theatre, Glasgow.

1992   *Andromaque* (Racine), Citizens' Theatre, Glasgow.

1993   *The Picture of Dorian Gray* (Wilde, adapted by Prowse), Citizens' Theatre, Glasgow.

The Soldiers (Lenz), Citizens' Theatre, Glasgow.

The Second Mrs Tanqueray (Pinero), Citizens' Theatre, Glasgow.

1994   *Lady Windermere's Fan* (Wilde), Repertory Theatre, Birmingham.

Other productions include: *The Sleeping Beauty*; *Swan Lake*; *La Bayadere*; *The Magic Flute*; *Don Giovanni*.

* * *

Philip Prowse is one of Britain's leading contemporary designers, best known, perhaps, for his work in ballet and opera. Since 1970 he has, however, combined the careers of designer and director, mostly at the Citizens' Theatre in Glasgow, where he has shared the artistic direction of that important regional repertory company with Giles Havergal and Robert David MacDonald. This triumvirate has created an extraordinary repertoire of exciting and provocative work that has gained international recognition, although, as Joyce McMillan observed in *The Guardian* in 1984, "London critics have expressed reservations about its emphasis on visual style at the expense of verbal clarity and its rejection of the Anglo-Saxon tradition of psychological realism". Giles Havergal himself described his colleague as "a creative and original thinker ... who has been the single most important influence on the development of this theatre".

Prowse's theatrical taste lies predominantly in British and foreign classics: Elizabethan and Jacobean drama and plays by such writers as Goldoni, Schiller, and Molière. Although his preference is for drama rather than the 'lyric' forms, there appears to be a cross-fertilization from his work in ballet and opera into his play productions. This is apparent in the way his theatre designs use space and scale, their flamboyance, the importance in his work of rhythm and tempo, and in the way his productions skilfully co-ordinate image, light, and sound. There is a marked theatricality about all Prowse's work.

Paradoxically, he claims that one of the main influences on his design work is the cinema, especially black and white films and those of Visconti and Fellini, because they have "great focus ... they're literate". This accounts for Prowse's extravagant use of space and the frequent employment of black and white in his designs: "I'm not a painter, therefore I'm not a colourist. I can only use colour in a schematic sort of way. I just use tone". Some of his most effective designs have been austere statements in white, grey, or black: his white walled madhouse for *Hamlet* (1981); the black box with star-spangled gauze for *The Massacre at Paris* (1981); the fin-de-siècle drawing-room furnished with grey furniture and framed by a proscenium arch swathed in white chiffon for *The Threepenny Opera* (1978); and the design for Genet's *The Blacks* (1982), in which the stage was dominated by the evocative image of a white, leafless, tree hung with white birdcages containing white dolls.

On the other hand, Prowse can create an exotic, heavy, and suffocating atmosphere, as he did for Oscar Wilde's *A Woman of No Importance* (1984), for which he filled the stage with vases of flowers and flowered furniture and drapes. He can exploit space and dwarf the actors, as he did in his *Don Juan* design (1988) with its wall-to-wall library of books, alcoves, balustrades, and spiral stairs. And he can tease and then dislocate the audience with an effect like his opening of *Mother Courage* (1990), when an idyllic 'Impressionist' cornfield was blasted out of existence and replaced by ruined walls and rubble blackened by the effects of war.

While creating these extraordinarily imaginative, sometimes magical, effects, Prowse remains a very practical man of the theatre, constantly aware of the need to work within budgets. To this end the 50-foot high blackened wall in *Mother Courage* was recycled from his earlier production of *Enrico IV* (1989). As he says of his work at the Citizens' Theatre, "It's not simply a matter of declaring your artistic freedom and getting on with the shows. Our work here would be impossible if we couldn't get on with our Board and balance our books and sustain a good relationship ... with our audience".

The strongest feature of Prowse's work as designer/director is the integration into a unified vision of all aspects of the performance. The actress Glenda Jackson has appeared in three of his productions and particularly admires his approach: "He always starts from the visual. Then that means that the production as a whole IS a whole — the way it looks, the way it moves, the area that it emotionally goes into are interwoven". Prowse is not a dedicated director of actors' acting. To an extent he expects actors to take responsibility for their own part in the creative process, while on the other hand expecting them to tailor their ambitions to fit his directorial concepts: "I'm not very interested if they want to open up their stomachs and show me the contents — then they must go and find a psychiatrist. Where actors interest me is how they respond to the job in hand. When they make a truthful response — what appears truthful to me — I will do my absolute best to incorporate it within the larger truth of what I'm trying to do".

There is no doubt that Philip Prowse's work is controversial. His productions have been criticised for their "exasperating style" and "directorial excesses", for being "wilful" and "too fussy and visually overloaded". But Prowse has also been described as "Britain's most inventive and undervalued director". It is clear that work as bold, risk-taking, and provocative as his is sorely needed to provide contemporary British theatre with a source of excitement and stimulation. His strongly visual approach to the directing of plays is more European than British. His achievements already place him in the ranks of the great designer/directors, alongside Edward Gordon Craig — with the added distinction that, unlike Craig, he has seen almost all his designs come to fruition.

—Margaret Eddershaw

Q

QUAYLE, (Sir John) Anthony. British actor and director. Born in Ainsdale, Lancashire, 7 September 1913. Educated at Rugby public school, Rugby, Warwickshire; trained for the stage at the Royal Academy of Dramatic Art, London. Married 1) Hermione Hannen (divorced); 2) Dorothy Hyson in 1947; one son and two daughters. Stage debut, Q Theatre, London, 1931; played supporting roles at the Old Vic Theatre, London, and elsewhere, 1931–39; Broadway debut, 1936; served in Royal Artillery, British Army, 1939–45; film debut, 1948; actor and company director, Shakespeare Memorial Theatre, Stratford-upon-Avon, 1948–56; guest director and lecturer, University of Tennessee, 1975; joined the Prospect Theatre Company, 1978; founder, Compass Productions touring company, 1984. Recipient: Emmy Award, 1974. D.Litt: University of Hull, 1987; St Andrew's University, St Andrew's, Scotland, 1989. CBE (Commander of the British Empire), 1952. Knighted, 1985. Died in London, 20 October 1989.

Productions

As actor:
1931	Richard Coeur de Lion and Will Scarlet in *Robin Hood* (Hamilton and Devereux), Q Theatre, London.
	Hector in *Troilus and Cressida* (Shakespeare), Festival Theatre, Cambridge.
1932	Ferdinand in *Love's Labour's Lost* (Shakespeare), Westminster Theatre, London.
	Aumerle in *Richard of Bordeaux* (Daviot), New Theatre, London.
1934	Bennie Edelman in *Magnolia Street* (Golding and Rawlinson), Adelphi Theatre, London.
	Matt Burke in *Anna Christie* (O'Neill), Imperial Institute, London, and Embassy Theatre, London.
	Guildenstern in *Hamlet* (Shakespeare), New Theatre, London.
1935	Captain Courtine in *The Soldier's Fortune* (Otway), Ambassadors' Theatre, London.
1936	Mr Harcourt in *The Country Wife* (Wycherley), Henry Miller Theatre, New York.
	St Denis in *St Helena* (Sherriff and Casilis), Old Vic Theatre, London.
	Mr Wickham in *Pride and Prejudice* (Jerome, adapted from Austen), St James's Theatre, London.

1937	Laertes in *Hamlet* (Shakespeare), Elsinore Castle, Denmark; Old Vic Theatre, London, 1938.
	Horatio in *Hamlet* (Shakespeare), Westminster Theatre, London.
	Duke of Surrey in *Richard II* (Shakespeare), Queen's Theatre, London.
	Beppo in *The Silent Knight* (Wolfre, adapted from Heltai), St James's Theatre, London.
1937–38	Demetrius in *A Midsummer Night's Dream* (Shakespeare), Old Vic Theatre, London.
	Cassio in *Othello* (Shakespeare), Old Vic Theatre, London.
1938	Earl of Essex in *Elizabeth, La Femme sans Homme* (Josset, adapted from Pienne), Gate Theatre, London, and Haymarket Theatre, London.
	Ferdinand in *Trelawny of the 'Wells'* (Pinero), Old Vic Theatre, London.
	John Tanner in *Man and Superman* (G. B. Shaw), Old Vic Theatre, London.
	Jack Absolute in *The Rivals* (Sheridan), Old Vic Theatre, London; Criterion Theatre, London, 1945.
1939	Henry in *Henry V* (Shakespeare), European and Egyptian tour.
1946	Enobarbus in *Antony and Cleopatra* (Shakespeare), Piccadilly Theatre, London.
1947	Iago in *Othello* (Shakespeare), Piccadilly Theatre, London; Shakespeare Memorial Theatre, Stratford-upon-Avon, 1948.
1948	Claudius in *Hamlet* (Shakespeare), Shakespeare Memorial Theatre, Stratford-upon-Avon.
	Petruchio in *The Taming of the Shrew* (Shakespeare), Shakespeare Memorial Theatre, Stratford-upon-Avon.
1949–50	Macbeth in *Macbeth* (Shakespeare), tour of Australia and New Zealand.
	Henry in *Henry VIII* (Shakespeare), tour of Australia and New Zealand.
1951	Falstaff in *Henry IV, parts 1 and 2* (Shakespeare), Shakespeare Memorial Theatre, Stratford-upon-Avon.
1954	Othello in *Othello* (Shakespeare), Shakespeare Memorial Theatre, Stratford-upon-Avon.
	Bottom in *A Midsummer Night's Dream* (Shakespeare), Shakespeare Memorial Theatre, Stratford-upon-Avon.

Pandarus in *Troilus and Cressida* (Shakespeare), Shakespeare Memorial Theatre, Stratford-upon-Avon.

1955   Falstaff in *The Merry Wives of Windsor* (Shakespeare), Mermaid Theatre, London.

Aaron in *Titus Andronicus* (Shakespeare), Mermaid Theatre, London; Paris Theatre Festival, Paris, and European tour, 1957.

1956   Tamburlaine in *Tamburlaine the Great* (Marlowe), Winter Garden Theatre, New York.

Eddie in *A View from the Bridge* (Miller), Comedy Theatre, London.

1958   Moses in *The Firstborn* (Fry), Habimah Theatre, Tel Aviv, Israel, and Coronet Theatre, New York.

1959   James in *Long Day's Journey Into Night* (O'Neill), Edinburgh Festival and New Theatre, London.

Marcel Blanchard in *Look After Lulu* (Coward), Edinburgh Festival and New Theatre, London.

1960   Cesareo Grimaldi in *Chin-Chin* (Billetdoux), Wyndham's Theatre, London.

1963   Nachtigall in *Power of Persuasion* (Hofmann), Garrick Theatre, London.

1964   Sir Charles Dilke in *The Right Honourable Gentleman* (Bradley-Dyne), Her Majesty's Theatre, London.

1966   Leduc in *Incident at Vichy* (Miller), Phoenix Theatre, London.

1967   Galileo in *Galileo* (Brecht), Vivian Beaumont Theatre, New York.

General Fitzbuttress in *Halfway up the Tree* (Ustinov), Brooks Atkinson Theatre, New York.

1970   Andrew Wyke in *Sleuth* (A. Shaffer), St Martin's Theatre, London, and Music Box Theatre, New York.

1976   Rodion Nikolayevich in *The Old World/Do You Turn Somersaults?* (Arbuzov), Aldwych Theatre, London; 48th Street Theatre, New York, and US tour, 1978.

1978   Hilary in *The Old Country* (Bennett), Queen's Theatre, London.

Sir Anthony Absolute in *The Rivals* (Sheridan), National Theatre, London.

Lear in *King Lear* (Shakespeare), National Theatre, London.

1984   Lord Ogleby in *The Clandestine Marriage* (Colman the Elder and Garrick), London; also directed.

Also acted roles in: *Heartbreak House* (G. B. Shaw), British tour, 1980; *The Devil's Disciple* (G. B. Shaw), British tour, 1981; *The Skin Game* (Galsworthy), British tour, 1981; *Hobson's Choice* (Brighouse), British tour, 1982; *A Coat of Varnish*, British tour, 1982.

As director:

1946   *Crime and Punishment* (Dostoevsky), New Theatre, London.

1948   *The Relapse* (Vanbrugh), Lyric Theatre, Hammersmith, London.

1949   *Harvey* (Chase), Prince of Wales Theatre, London.

1950   *Who Is Sylvia?* (Rattigan), Criterion Theatre, London.

1951   *Cycle of Histories* (Shakespeare compilation), Shakespeare Memorial Theatre, Stratford-upon-Avon.

1953   *As You Like It* (Shakespeare), tour of Australia and New Zealand.

Othello (Shakespeare), tour of Australia and New Zealand.

Henry IV, part 1 (Shakespeare), tour of Australia and New Zealand.

1954   *Othello* (Shakespeare), Shakespeare Memorial Theatre, Stratford-upon-Avon.

1956   *Measure for Measure* (Shakespeare), Shakespeare Memorial Theatre, Stratford-upon-Avon.

1958   *The Firstborn* (Fry), Habimah Theatre, Tel Aviv, Israel, and Coronet Theatre, New York.

1963   *Power of Persuasion* (Hofmann), Garrick Theatre, London.

1966   *Lady Windermere's Fan* (Wilde), Phoenix Theatre, London.

1970   *The Idiot* (Dostoevsky), National Theatre, London.

1975   *Harvey* (Chase), Prince of Wales Theatre, London.

1978   *The Rivals* (Sheridan), National Theatre, London.

1982   *A Coat of Varnish*, British tour.

Films

Saraband for Dead Lovers, 1948; *Hamlet*, 1948; *Oh, Rosalinda*, 1955; *No Time for Tears*, 1956; *Battle of the River Plate/Pursuit of the Graf Spee*, 1957; *The Wrong Man*, 1957; *Woman in a Dressing Gown*, 1957; *Ice Cold in Alex*, 1957; *Serious Charge*, 1958; *Tarzan's Greatest Adventure*, 1959; *The Challenge*, 1960; *The Man Who Wouldn't Talk*, 1960; *The Guns of Navarone*, 1961; *H.M.S. Defiant*, 1961; *Lawrence of Arabia*, 1962; *The Fall of the Roman Empire*, 1964; *East of Sudan*, 1964; *Operation Crossbow*, 1965; *Fog*, 1965; *A Study in Terror*, 1966; *MacKenna's Gold*, 1969; *Before Winter Comes*, 1969; *Anne of the Thousand Days*, 1970; *Bequest to the Nation*, 1972; *Everything You Always Wanted to Know about Sex*, 1972; *The Tamarind Seed*, 1974; *The Eagle Has Landed*, 1977; *Holocaust 2000*, 1977; *The Chosen*, 1978; *Murder by Decree*, 1979; *After the Ball is Over*, 1985.

Television

As actor:

The Poppy is Also a Flower, 1964; *Strange Report*, 1968; *Destiny of a Spy*, 1969; *Jarrett*, 1973; *QB VII*, 1974; *Great Expectations*, 1974; *Benjamin Franklin*, 1974; *Moses, the Lawgiver*, 1975; *The Story of David*, 1976; *21 Hours at Munich*, 1976; *Ice Age*, 1978; *Last Days of Pompeii*, 1978; *Henry IV, parts 1 and 2*, 1979; *Masada*, 1981; *Dial M for*

Murder, 1981; *The Manions of America*, 1981; *Beethoven*, 1983; *Lace*, 1984; *Testament of John*, 1984; *Quoth the Raven*, 1985; *The Last Bottle in the World*, 1985; *The Key to Rebecca*, 1985; *Oedipus at Colonus*, 1986.

As director:
Caesar and Cleopatra, 1979.

Publications

Eight Hours from England, 1945; *On Such a Night*, 1947; *A Time to Speak* (autobiography), 1990.

* * *

"You've got the wrong face — the wrong mask. You have it in you to be a fine tragic actor — perhaps a great one. But your face will always be in your way. You will always have to play comedy and you're going to find it very frustrating ... Stay in the theatre — but be a director, or go on to the administrative side. But don't break your heart being an actor". It was with these uncompromisingly frank words that Lewis Casson gave his advice to Anthony Quayle when the latter was trying to decide how to relaunch his career after six interesting and at times dangerous years of war service in the course of which he had risen to the not undistinguished rank of major in the Royal Artillery. Quayle himself quotes Casson's words in *A Time to Speak*, a well-written volume of memoirs that recounts much about its author's early years and military experiences but is unfortunately less revealing about his maturity since he had to bring it hurriedly to a conclusion before succumbing to a fatal illness. It is plain that he saw the force of remarks that must, to some extent, have been galling. A man of intelligence and education who had had a good deal of experience in the 1930's and whose qualities were beginning to be appreciated at the Old Vic before the outbreak of the war, he realized that he should accept the verdict of a wise counsellor, and it was as director of the Shakespeare Memorial Theatre (later to be called the Royal Shakespeare Company) at Stratford-upon-Avon from 1948 to 1956 that he made his most significant contribution to British theatrical life in the postwar period.

Another quotation from *A Time to Speak*, in which Quayle compares himself with his mother, gives some idea of his physique: of moderate height like her, he had a build that "could only be called unathletic", his "oval" face "was pleasing, but did not make heads turn", and his eyes, like hers, "could never have been likened to the fishpools in Heshbon". He was a versatile actor, playing serious as well as comic parts in Shakespeare, the 18th-century repertory, and modern plays, and possibly would have made a great impact if he had specialized more. In the postwar phase of his career it was generally to be his lot to play not the dashing romantic leads but rather the important secondary roles and generally rather ageing ones at that, though as Bottom in the 1954 production of *A Midsummer Night's Dream* he could look surprisingly young and decidedly cheeky, with protruding ears. He was only 40 when, looking considerably older, he was well-received as Falstaff at Stratford, but in *Henry IV, part 2* attention was not unnaturally focused on the dynamic Richard Burton. Likewise, though he was outstanding as Aaron the Moore

in Peter Brooks's 1955 production of *Titus Andronicus*, Olivier had the leading role. Among his most impressive modern work was his sympathetic interpretation of the part of Eddie in Miller's *View from the Bridge* in 1956 and that of James Tyrone in O'Neill's *Long Day's Journey into Night* two years later.

Directing the Memorial Theatre at Stratford imposed considerable strains on Quayle. Replacing the revered but reluctant Barry Jackson was not easy at first, and there was much to be done in giving a truly national, not to say international, status to an institution that previously had often seemed to promise more than it could deliver. The premises had to be improved and, in a highly significant change of artistic policy, major stars had to be employed, as directors as well as actors. All this Quayle did with great success, raising the standards of a theatre that had previously tended to be somewhat provincial in tone. He also contributed notably as a performer, but without quite coming to the fore as he might have done if he had been ready to be more selfish and if he had not been shouldering other responsibilities for administration and production at the time. After leaving Stratford Quayle continued to serve the stage as a theatrical administrator, notably for the Prospect and the Compass companies. In his *Diaries*, Peter Hall sums up Quayle's achievement when he writes (on 2 December 1977) that he "was the best theatre runner apart from George Devine I have ever met in my life".

In the cinema, where Quayle might have been expected to be able to challenge such stars as Jack Hawkins as the manly and craggy embodiment of such qualities as British phlegm amidst vicissitudes and an officer-like determination against the odds, he also generally had to be content with significant supporting roles. In 1956 he had an important part as Commodore Harwood in Michael Powell's *Battle of the River Plate* (screened in the USA as *Pursuit of the Graf Spee*), but he could not add much by way of human interest to a film that was largely content to document a naval engagement. After that, in Lean's award-winning *Lawrence of Arabia* (1962), for instance, Quayle gave a very solid and plausible performance as the burly, middle-aged Colonel Brighton, a typical officer-type who is never quite equal to events, but he was patently upstaged, as, of course, the script required, by the charismatic Peter O'Toole in the title-part, and definitely outclassed by Alec Guinness's mesmeric presentation of Faisal. For his Cardinal Wolsey in Charles Jarrott's *Anne of a Hundred Days* seven years later, Quayle won an American Academy nomination, but, once again, it was excellence in a secondary role, with Richard Burton taking the part that really caught the eye.

All in all, then, it seems that Casson's appraisal was accurate. Though far from negligible as an actor, Quayle was destined to do his most significant work in the theatre offstage.

—Christopher Smith

QUIN, James. English actor. Born in London, 24 February 1693. Probably educated at Trinity College, Dublin, until 1710. Stage debut, Smock Alley Theatre, Dublin, 1712; London debut at Theatre Royal, Drury Lane, c.1714, where he established reputation in *Tamerlane*, 1716;

particularly acclaimed in the role of Falstaff, from 1720; became notorious for uncertain temper and twice charged with manslaughter after killing rival actors in duels; engaged at Lincoln's Inn Fields Theatre, 1718–32, Covent Garden, 1732–34, Theatre Royal, Drury Lane, 1734–41; toured Ireland, 1741; closed career at Covent Garden, 1742–51; retired to Bath, 1751; benefit appearances, 1751–54. Died in Bath, 21 January 1766.

Roles

c.1714   Abel in *The Committee* (Howard), Smock Alley Theatre, Dublin.

Cleon in *Timon of Athens* (Shakespeare, adapted by Shadwell), Smock Alley Theatre, Dublin.

The Prince of Tanais in *Tamerlane* (Rowe), Smock Alley Theatre, Dublin.

1715   Vulture in *The Country Lasses* (C. Johnson, adapted from Middleton's *A Mad World, my Masters*), Theatre Royal, Drury Lane, London.

Steward in *The What D'Ye Call It* (Gay), Theatre Royal, Drury Lane, London.

Lieutenant of the Tower in *Lady Jane Gray* (Rowe), Theatre Royal, Drury Lane, London.

Winwife in *Bartholomew Fair* (Jonson), Theatre Royal, Drury Lane, London.

Rovewell in *The Contrivances* (Carey), Theatre Royal, Drury Lane, London.

1716   Lieutenant of the Tower in *Richard III* (Shakespeare, adapted by Cibber), Theatre Royal, Drury Lane, London.

King in *Philaster* (Beaumont and Fletcher), Theatre Royal, Drury Lane, London.

Don Pedro in *The Rover* (Behn), Theatre Royal, Drury Lane, London.

Pedro in *The Pilgrim* (Fletcher, adapted by Vanbrugh), Theatre Royal, Drury Lane, London.

The Cardinal in *The Duke of Guise* (Dryden and Lee), Theatre Royal, Drury Lane, London.

Bajazet in *Tamerlane* (Rowe), Theatre Royal, Drury Lane, London.

Antenor in *The Cruel Gift* (Centlivre), Theatre Royal, Drury Lane, London.

Dervise in *Tamerlane* (Rowe), Theatre Royal, Drury Lane, London.

1717   Gloucester in *King Lear* (Shakespeare, adapted by Tate), Theatre Royal, Drury Lane, London.

Guildenstern in *Hamlet* (Shakespeare), Theatre Royal, Drury Lane, London.

Second Player in *Three Hours After Marriage* (Gay, Pope, and Walsh), Theatre Royal, Drury Lane, London.

Cinna in *Caius Marius* (Otway), Theatre Royal, Drury Lane, London.

Voltore in *Volpone* (Jonson), Theatre Royal, Drury Lane, London.

Flayflint in *The Old Troop* (Lacy), Theatre Royal, Drury Lane, London.

Aaron in *Titus Andronicus* (Shakespeare), Theatre Royal, Drury Lane, London.

Rant in *The Scowrers* (Shadwell), Theatre Royal, Drury Lane, London.

Vincent in *Twice Married and a Maid Still* (anon.), Theatre Royal, Drury Lane, London.

Brumpton in *The Funeral* (Steele), Theatre Royal, Drury Lane, London.

Cato in *Cato* (Addison), Theatre Royal, Drury Lane, London.

Balance in *The Recruiting Officer* (Farquhar), Theatre Royal, Drury Lane, London.

1718   Hotspur in *Henry IV, part 1* (Shakespeare), Lincoln's Inn Fields Theatre, London.

Horatio in *The Fair Penitent* (Rowe), Lincoln's Inn Fields Theatre, London.

Tamerlane in *Tamerlane* (Rowe), Lincoln's Inn Fields Theatre, London.

Morat in *Aureng-Zebe* (Dryden), Lincoln's Inn Fields Theatre, London.

Scipio in *Scipio Africanus* (Beckingham), Lincoln's Inn Fields Theatre, London.

Antony in *Antony and Cleopatra* (Shakespeare), Lincoln's Inn Fields Theatre, London.

Benducar in *Don Sebastian* (Dryden), Lincoln's Inn Fields Theatre, London.

Raymond in *The Spanish Friar* (Dryden), Lincoln's Inn Fields Theatre, London.

Clytus in *The Rival Queens* (Lee), Lincoln's Inn Fields Theatre, London.

Lorenzo in *The Traitor* (Shirley), Lincoln's Inn Fields Theatre, London.

Syphax in *Cato* (Addison), Lincoln's Inn Fields Theatre, London.

Maskwell in *The Double Dealer* (Congreve), Lincoln's Inn Fields Theatre, London.

Brutus in *Julius Caesar* (Shakespeare), Lincoln's Inn Fields Theatre, London.

Macbeth in *Macbeth* (Shakespeare), Lincoln's Inn Fields Theatre, London.

Burleigh in *The Unhappy Favourite* (Banks), Lincoln's Inn Fields Theatre, London.

1719   Sir John Brute in *The Provoked Wife* (Vanbrugh), Lincoln's Inn Fields Theatre, London.

Raleigh in *Sir Walter Raleigh* (Sewell), Lincoln's Inn Fields Theatre, London.

Gerard Clause in *The Royal Merchant* (Beaumont, Fletcher, and Massinger), Lincoln's Inn Fields Theatre, London.

Careful in *'Tis Well If It Takes* (Taverner), Lincoln's Inn Fields Theatre, London.

Dorax in *Don Sebastian* (Dryden), Lincoln's Inn Fields Theatre, London.

Claudius in *Hamlet* (Shakespeare), Lincoln's Inn Fields Theatre, London.

Henry in *Henry IV of France* (Beckingham), Lincoln's Inn Fields Theatre, London.

Sir Edward Belfond in *The Squire of Alsatia* (Shadwell), Lincoln's Inn Fields Theatre, London.

1720   Aboan in *Oroonoko* (Southerne), Lincoln's Inn Fields Theatre, London.

James Quin as Coriolanus.

Genseric in *The Imperial Captives* (Motley), Lincoln's Inn Fields Theatre, London.

Othello in *Othello* (Shakespeare), Lincoln's Inn Fields Theatre, London.

Montezuma in *The Indian Emperor* (Dryden), Lincoln's Inn Fields Theatre, London.

Cymbeline in *Cymbeline* (Shakespeare), Lincoln's Inn Fields Theatre, London.

Falstaff in *The Merry Wives of Windsor* (Shakespeare), Lincoln's Inn Fields Theatre, London.

Hector in *Troilus and Cressida* (Shakespeare), Lincoln's Inn Fields Theatre, London.

The Duke in *Measure for Measure* (Shakespeare, adapted by Gildon), Lincoln's Inn Fields Theatre, London.

1721   Aumerle in *Richard II* (Shakespeare), Lincoln's Inn Fields Theatre, London.

Henry in *Henry IV, part 1* (Shakespeare), Lincoln's Inn Fields Theatre, London.

King in *The Island Princess* (Motteux), Lincoln's Inn Fields Theatre, London.

Mustapha in *The Fair Captive* (Haywood), Lincoln's Inn Fields Theatre, London.

Buckingham in *Richard III* (Shakespeare, adapted by Cibber), Lincoln's Inn Fields Theatre, London.

Solyman in *Abra Mule* (Trapp), Lincoln's Inn Fields Theatre, London.

Roderigo in *The Pilgrim* (Fletcher, adapted by Vanbrugh), Lincoln's Inn Fields Theatre, London.

Seleucus in *Antiochus* (Motley), Lincoln's Inn Fields Theatre, London.

Bellmour in *The Fatal Extravagance* (Mitchell and Hill), Lincoln's Inn Fields Theatre, London.

Winwife in *The Artful Husband* (Taverner), Lincoln's Inn Fields Theatre, London.

Elder Worthy in *Love's Last Shift* (Cibber), Lincoln's Inn Fields Theatre, London.

Chamont in *The Orphan* (Otway), Lincoln's Inn Fields Theatre, London.

Cinthio in *The Emperor of the Moon* (Behn), Lincoln's Inn Fields Theatre, London.

Falstaff in *Henry IV, part 1* (Shakespeare), Lincoln's Inn Fields Theatre, London.

Sullen in *The Beaux' Stratagem* (Farquhar), Lincoln's Inn Fields Theatre, London.

Pierre in *Venice Preserved* (Otway), Lincoln's Inn Fields Theatre, London.

Thrivemore in *Injured Love* (anon.), Lincoln's Inn Fields Theatre, London.

1722   Beaugard in *The Soldier's Fortune* (Otway), Lincoln's Inn Fields Theatre, London.

Heartwell in *The Old Bachelor* (Congreve), Lincoln's Inn Fields Theatre, London.

Lynceus in *Love and Duty* (Sturmy), Lincoln's Inn Fields Theatre, London.

Turgesias in *Hibernia Freed* (Phillips), Lincoln's Inn Fields Theatre, London.

Blunt in *The Committee* (Howard), Lincoln's Inn Fields Theatre, London.

Dominic in *The Spanish Friar* (Dryden), Lincoln's Inn Fields Theatre, London.

Creon in *Oedipus* (Dryden), Lincoln's Inn Fields Theatre, London.

Don Henrique in *The Spanish Curate* (Fletcher and Massinger), Lincoln's Inn Fields Theatre, London.

Aretinus in *Domitian* (anon.), Lincoln's Inn Fields Theatre, London.

1723   Jolly in *Cutter of Coleman Street* (Cowley), Lincoln's Inn Fields Theatre, London.

Lycon in *Phaedra and Hippolytus* (Smith), Lincoln's Inn Fields Theatre, London.

Sohemus in *Mariamne* (Fenton), Lincoln's Inn Fields Theatre, London.

Creon in *Fatal Legacy* (Robe), Lincoln's Inn Fields Theatre, London.

Thersites in *Troilus and Cressida* (Shakespeare), Lincoln's Inn Fields Theatre, London.

Moncado in *Like to Like* (anon.), Lincoln's Inn Fields Theatre, London.

1724   Gomel in *Edwin* (Jeffreys), Lincoln's Inn Fields Theatre, London.

Bessus in *A King and No King* (Beaumont and Fletcher), Lincoln's Inn Fields Theatre, London.

Hermogenes in *Belisarius* (Phillips), Lincoln's Inn Fields Theatre, London.

John in *The False Friend* (Vanbrugh), Lincoln's Inn Fields Theatre, London.

1725   Knowell in *Every Man in His Humour* (Jonson), Lincoln's Inn Fields Theatre, London.

Belville in *The Rover* (Behn), Lincoln's Inn Fields Theatre, London.

Pinchwife in *The Country Wife* (Wycherley), Lincoln's Inn Fields Theatre, London.

Aesop in *Aesop* (Vanbrugh), Lincoln's Inn Fields Theatre, London.

1726   Spring in *The Female Fortune Teller* (Johnson), Lincoln's Inn Fields Theatre, London.

Warcourt in *Money the Mistress* (Southerne), Lincoln's Inn Fields Theatre, London.

Henry in *Henry VIII* (Shakespeare), Lincoln's Inn Fields Theatre, London.

Ranger in *A Fond Husband* (D'Urfey), Lincoln's Inn Fields Theatre, London.

Lord Severne in *The Dissembled Wanton* (Welstead), Lincoln's Inn Fields Theatre, London.

1727   Eurydamas in *The Fall of Saguntum* (Frowde), Lincoln's Inn Fields Theatre, London.

Didas in *Philip of Macedon* (Lewis), Lincoln's Inn Fields Theatre, London.

Volpone in *Volpone* (Jonson), Lincoln's Inn Fields Theatre, London.

1728   Richard in *Richard III* (Shakespeare), Lincoln's Inn Fields Theatre, London.

Axartes in *The Virgin Queen* (Barford), Lincoln's Inn Fields Theatre, London.

1729   Themistocles in *Themistocles* (Madden), Lincoln's Inn Fields Theatre, London.

Count Waldec in *Frederick, Duke of Brunswick Lunenberg* (Haywood), Lincoln's Inn Fields Theatre, London.

Melantius in *The Maid's Tragedy* (Beaumont and Fletcher), Lincoln's Inn Fields Theatre, London.

Alonzo in *The Rape* (Brady), Lincoln's Inn Fields Theatre, London.

1730   Macheath in *The Beggar's Opera* (Gay), Lincoln's Inn Fields Theatre, London.

Young Bevil in *The Conscious Lovers* (Steele), Lincoln's Inn Fields Theatre, London.

1731   Periander in *Periander* (Tracy), Lincoln's Inn Fields Theatre, London.

Clitus in *Philotas* (Frowde), Lincoln's Inn Fields Theatre, London.

Lear in *King Lear* (Shakespeare, adapted by Tate), Lincoln's Inn Fields Theatre, London.

Standard in *The Constant Couple* (Farquhar), Lincoln's Inn Fields Theatre, London.

Glycon in *Merope* (Jeffreys), Lincoln's Inn Fields Theatre, London.

Thoas in *Orestes* (Theobald), Lincoln's Inn Fields Theatre, London.

Dioclesian in *The Prophetess* (Fletcher and Massinger), Lincoln's Inn Fields Theatre, London.

Manly in *The Provoked Husband* (Cibber), Lincoln's Inn Fields Theatre, London.

The Ghost in *Hamlet* (Shakespeare), Lincoln's Inn Fields Theatre, London.

Leon in *Rule a Wife and Have a Wife* (Fletcher), Lincoln's Inn Fields Theatre, London.

1732   Teague in *The Committee* (Howard), Lincoln's Inn Fields Theatre, London.

Old Bellefleur in *The Married Philosopher* (Kelly), Lincoln's Inn Fields Theatre, London.

Fainall in *The Way of the World* (Congreve), Covent Garden, London.

1733	Manly in *The Plain Dealer* (Wycherley), Covent Garden, London.
	Lycomedes in *Achilles* (Gay), Covent Garden, London.
	Caled in *The Siege of Damascus* (Hughes), Covent Garden, London.
	Bosola in *The Fatal Secret* (Theobald, adapted from Webster's *The Duchess of Malfi*), Covent Garden, London.
	Apemantus in *Timon of Athens* (Shakespeare), Covent Garden, London.
1734	Biron in *The Fatal Marriage* (Southerne), Covent Garden, London.
	Gonsalez in *The Mourning Bride* (Congreve), Covent Garden, London.
1735	Amurath in *The Christian Hero* (Lillo), Theatre Royal, Drury Lane, London.
	Mondish in *The Universal Gallant* (Fielding), Theatre Royal, Drury Lane, London.
1736	Lord Constant in *The Connoisseur* (Connolly), Theatre Royal, Drury Lane, London.
	Falstaff in *Henry IV, part 2* (Shakespeare), Theatre Royal, Drury Lane, London.
	Riot in *The Wife's Relief* (Johnson), Theatre Royal, Drury Lane, London.
1737	Protheus in *The Universal Passion* (Miller, adapted from Shakespeare's *Much Ado About Nothing*), Theatre Royal, Drury Lane, London.
1738	Outside in *Art and Nature* (Miller), Theatre Royal, Drury Lane, London.
	Comus in *Comus* (Milton, adapted by Dalton), Theatre Royal, Drury Lane, London.
	Ventidius in *All for Love* (Dryden), Theatre Royal, Drury Lane, London.
	Agamemnon in *Agamemnon* (Thomson), Theatre Royal, Drury Lane, London.
	Pembroke in *Lady Jane Gray* (Rowe), Theatre Royal, Drury Lane, London.
1739	Solyman in *Mustapha* (Mallet), Theatre Royal, Drury Lane, London.
	Gloucester in *Jane Shore* (Rowe), Theatre Royal, Drury Lane, London.
1740	Elmerick in *Elmerick* (Lillo), Theatre Royal, Drury Lane, London.
	Jaques in *As You Like It* (Shakespeare), Theatre Royal, Drury Lane, London.
1741	Antonio in *The Merchant of Venice* (Shakespeare), Theatre Royal, Drury Lane, London.
1742	Pyrrhus in *The Distressed Mother* (Philips), Theatre Royal, Drury Lane, London.
1744	Zanga in *The Revenge* (Young), Covent Garden, London.
1745	King John in *Papal Tyranny* (Cibber), Covent Garden, London.
	Herod in *Mariamne* (Fenton), Covent Garden, London.
1749	Coriolanus in *Coriolanus* (Thomson), Covent Garden, London.
	Gardiner in *Lady Jane Gray* (Rowe), Covent Garden, London.
1750	King Henry in *Virtue Betrayed* (Banks), Covent Garden, London.
1751	John in *King John* (Shakespeare), Covent Garden, London.
	Iago in *Othello* (Shakespeare), Covent Garden, London.

Also acted roles in: *No Fools Like Wits* (adapted from Wright's *The Female Virtuosos*), Lincoln's Inn Fields Theatre, London, 1721; *Much Ado About Nothing* (Shakespeare), Lincoln's Inn Fields Theatre, London, 1721; *The Distressed Wife* (Gay), Covent Garden, London, 1734.

*

Bibliography

Books:
Anon., *The Life of Mr James Quin*, London, 1887.
Joseph Roach, *The Player's Passion*, London, 1985.

* * *

In the first half of the 18th century James Quin was one of England's most popular actors, but he received a decidedly mixed press. He belonged to the 'Baroque' school of Thomas Betterton and Barton Booth, actors whose majestic style had been standard during the Restoration period and was accepted as 'natural' and believable by generations of playgoers. Though audiences loved him, Quin was roundly criticized by experts for his heavy manner. The playwright-critic Aaron Hill called him "All-Weight" and spoke of his "composed air and gravity of ... motion" in *The Prompter* in September 1735, and the author (possibly Fielding) of *An Apology for the Life of Mr T ... C ...* in 1740 said : "Q ... has the Character of a just Speaker, but then it is confin'd to the solemn declamatory Way: He either cannot work himself into the Emotions of a violent Passion, or he will not take the Fatigue of doing it: The partiality of his Friends say he can touch the Passions with great Delicacy *if he will*; but general Opinion affirms he has neither Power of Voice or Sensation to give Love or Pity, Grief or Remorse their proper Tone and Variation of Features." Francis Gentleman in *The Dramatic Censor* in 1770 remembered Quin as a terrible Othello: "his declamation was as heavy as his person, his tones monotonous, his passions bellowing, his emphasis affected, and his under strokes growling ... " Given that kind of criticism, a lesser actor would have been hissed off the stage and advised to find other means of employment.

But Quin's greatest detractors could find qualities in him to praise. Even to the censorious Gentleman Quin's voice was "distinctly sonorous" while his figure was "graceful and important, his countenance open, regular, and authoritative, his eyes expressive ... " Hogarth caught that look in his portrait of Quin, now at the Tate Gallery. Gentleman admired Quin's Falstaff in *Henry IV, Part 1*, especially in his lie about the battle: "There was in this place such a glow of feature and expression, as we shall never see equalled." Thomas Davies in his *Life of David Garrick* (1780) — though he too found many faults in Quin — believed him "the most intelligent and judicious Falstaff since the days of Betterton. In the impudent dignity ... of the character, Quin greatly excelled all competitors." Quin's Pierre in *Venice Preserved* was so good that the critic John Hill in *The Actor* in 1750 thought "the whole compass of the English stage affords nothing greater ... " He said that as

Pierre, Garrick was more the player but Quin "vastly more the man". Garrick, a splendid judge of actors, gave up the role of Pierre in 1744 and left it to Quin, the public's favourite.

Like Betterton before him, Quin is said to have involved himself deeply in the roles he played — or at least he did so in roles he liked. *A Serio-Comic Apology For Part of the Life of Theophilus Cibber* in 1748 claimed that as Falstaff "From the Moment Mr Quin puts on the Dress, he becomes the Man himself; his Mind is never dispossessed of him till the Curtain drops: He looks, he speaks, he thinks the Character. This is evident in his Eye, the Muscles of his Face; and his whole Deportment: — He maintains it throughout with a lively Comic Force, and Flow of Spirit ... His Falstaff seems inimitable yet."

Quin's severest critics were those who had grown theatrically in the age of Garrick. The new style of Garrick (and, to give him his due, Charles Macklin) was smaller, more intense, and athletic, more natural than that of Betterton and Quin. The playwright Richard Cumberland in his *Memoirs* left us the most vivid description of the old style versus the new when he described Quin as Horatio and Garrick as Lothario in Rowe's *The Fair Penitent* at Covent Garden in 1746: "Quin presented himself upon the rising of the curtain in a green velvet coat embroidered down the seams, an enormous full bottomed periwig, rolled stockings, and high-heeled square-toed shoes; with little variation of cadence, and a deep full tone, accompanied by a sawing kind of action, which had more of the senate than of the stage in it, he rolled out his heroics with an air of dignified indifference, that seemed to disdain the plaudits, that were bestowed upon him." This was the style audiences in London (and all over Europe) were accustomed to, and they were not quite ready for Garrick: "When after long and eager expectation I first beheld little Garrick, then young and light and alive in every muscle and every feature, come bounding on the stage and pointing at the ... heavy-paced Horatio — heavens, what a transition! — it seemed as if a whole century had been stept over in the transition of a single scene ... "

Discretion being the better part of valour, one might suppose that Quin would have retired there and then. Remarkably, he did not. He continued performing for 10 years after Garrick's 1741 London debut and frequently acted with Garrick and played roles (like Richard III) in which Garrick excelled — just to remind the public that the old style was not yet dead. But, as Gentleman noted, Quin "found his deficiency, and retired, but rather too late by six or seven years." Quin lived out his retirement in Bath, coming occasionally to London to act at benefits for old friends, but was by the 1750's a relic. He could not have imagined that towards the end of the century the pendulum would swing back with the arrival of John Philip Kemble and his majestic, relatively static, theatrical style.

—Edward A. Langhans

QUINTERO, José (Benjamin). US director. Born in Panama City, Panama, 15 October 1924. Educated at the City College, Los Angeles; University of Southern California, Los Angeles. Debut as director, Woodstock Summer Theatre, New York, 1949; co-founder and artistic director,

Circle in the Square Theatre, New York, 1950–75; London debut, Globe Theatre, 1958; settled in Los Angeles, as artistic director of the Chaplin-O'Neill Theatre, 1980, and has worked with the Scene Study Workshop for Actors in Los Angeles, California, since 1982; lecturer in drama, University of Columbia, 1979–80, California State University, 1983–86, University of Houston, 1989–90, and Florida State University, 1989–90. Member: Theatre Committee for Eugene O'Neill (director). Recipient: Obie Award, 1952, 1953, 1954, 1960; Outer Circle Award, 1955; Drama Desk Award, 1955–56, 1973, 1986; Tony Award, 1956, 1973; Page One Award, 1957; Boston College Centennial Gold Medal Award, 1963; Upward Bound Award, 1973; Eugene O'Neill Gold Medal Award, 1985; Distinguished Performance Award, 1987; Los Angeles Drama Critics Award, 1987; Eugene O'Neill Foundation, Tao House Award, 1990.

Productions

1949	*The Glass Menagerie* (T. Williams), Woodstock Summer Theatre, New York.
1951	*Dark of the Moon* (Richardson and Berney), Circle in the Square Theatre, New York.
	Burning Bright (Steinbeck), Circle in the Square Theatre, New York.
	Bonds of Interest (Benavente y Martínez), Circle in the Square Theatre, New York.
1952	*Yerma* (Lorca), Circle in the Square Theatre, New York.
	Summer and Smoke (T. Williams), Circle in the Square Theatre, New York.
1953	*The Grass Harp* (Capote), Circle in the Square Theatre, New York.
	American Gothic (Wolfson), Circle in the Square Theatre, New York.
	In the Summer House (Bowles), Broadway, New York.
1954	*The Girl on the Via Flaminia* (Hayes), Circle in the Square Theatre, New York.
	Portrait of a Lady (Archibald, adapted from James), ANTA Theatre, New York.
	The Hostage (Behan), Circle in the Square Theatre, New York.
1955	*The Long Christmas Dinner* (Wilder), University of Boston, Massachusetts.
	The King and the Duke, Circle in the Square Theatre, New York.
	La Ronde (Schitzler), Circle in the Square Theatre, New York.
	The Cradle Song (Underhill), Circle in the Square Theatre, New York.
	The Iceman Cometh (O'Neill), Circle in the Square Theatre, New York.
1956	*The Innkeepers* (Apstein), New York.
	Long Day's Journey Into Night (O'Neill), Helen Hayes Theatre, New York.
1957	*Lost in the Stars* (M. Anderson), City Opera, New York.
	The Square Root of Wonderful (McCullers), Princeton University, New Jersey.
1958	*Children of Darkness* (Mayer), Circle in the Square Theatre, New York.

A Moon for the Misbegotten (O'Neill), Festival of Two Worlds, Spoleto, Italy.

Cavalleria Rusticana (Mascagni), Metropolitan Opera, New York.

I Pagliacci (Leoncavallo), Metropolitan Opera, New York.

The Quare Fellow (Behan), Circle in the Square Theatre, New York.

1959   *Our Town* (Wilder), Circle in the Square Theatre, New York.

Macbeth (Shakespeare), Boston, Massachusetts.

1960   *The Balcony* (Genet), Circle in the Square Theatre, New York.

Camino Real (T. Williams), Circle in the Square Theatre, New York.

The Triumph of Saint Joan (Joio), City Opera, New York.

Laurette (Young, adapted from Courtney), New Haven, Connecticut.

1961   *Look, We've Come Through* (Wheeler), New York.

1962   *Plays for Bleecker Street* (Wilder), Circle in the Square Theatre, New York.

Great Day in the Morning (Cannon), New York.

Pullman Car Hiawatha (Wilder), Circle in the Square Theatre, New York.

1963   *Desire Under the Elms* (O'Neill), Circle in the Square Theatre, New York.

Strange Interlude (O'Neill), Broadway, New York.

1964   *Marco Millions* (O'Neill), Lincoln Centre, New York.

Hughie (O'Neill), Royale Theatre, New York.

Susanna, Metropolitan Opera, New York.

La Bohème (Puccini), Metropolitan Opera, New York.

1965   *Diamond Orchid* (Lawrence and Lee), New York.

Matty and the Moron and the Madonna (Leiberman), New York.

A Moon for the Misbegotten (O'Neill), Arena Stage, Buffalo, New York.

1966   *Pousse Cafe*, New York.

1967   *More Stately Mansions* (O'Neill), Ahmanson Theatre, Los Angeles, and New York.

1968   *The Seven Descents of Myrtle* (T. Williams), New York.

1969   *Episode in the Life of an Author* (Anouilh) and *The Orchestra* (Anouilh), Buffalo, New York.

1970   *Gandhi*, Playhouse Theatre, New York.

1971   *Johnny Johnson* (Green), New York.

The Big Coca-Cola Swamp in the Sky, Westport, Connecticut.

1973   *A Moon for the Misbegotten* (O'Neill), Morosco Theatre, New York.

1974   *Gabrielle* (Quintero), Studio Arena, Buffalo, New York, and Washington D.C.

1975   *The Skin of Our Teeth* (Wilder), Washington D.C.

A Moon for the Misbegotten (O'Neill), Oslo, Norway.

1976   *Knock, Knock* (Feiffer), New York.

Hughie (O'Neill), Chicago, Illinois.

José Quintero

1977   *Anna Christie* (O'Neill), New York, Toronto, and Washington D.C.

A Touch of the Poet (O'Neill), New York.

1978   *Same Time, Next Year*, Oslo, Norway.

The Bear (Chekhov) and *The Human Voice* (Cocteau), Melbourne and Sydney, Australia.

1979   *The Human Voice* (Cocteau), Circle in the Square Theatre, New York.

Faith Healer (Friel), Boston, Massachusetts, and Longacre Theatre, New York.

1980   *Clothes for a Summer Hotel* (T. Williams), Washington D.C. and Cort Theatre, New York.

Welded (O'Neill), University of Columbia, New York.

Ah! Wilderness (O'Neill), National Theatre, Mexico City.

1981   *The Time of Your Life* (Saroyan), Brandeis University, Boston, Massachusetts.

Ah! Wilderness (O'Neill), West Palm Beach, Los Angeles.

1983   *Cat on a Hot Tin Roof* (T. Williams), Mark Taper Forum, Los Angeles.

1984   *Rainsnakes*, Long Wharf Theatre, New Haven, Connecticut.

1985   *The Iceman Cometh* (O'Neill), Washington D.C., New York, and Los Angeles.

1988   *Long Day's Journey into Night* (O'Neill), Yale University and New York.

1990   *Private Lives* (Coward), Oslo, Norway.

Films

The Roman Spring of Mrs Stone, 1961.

Television

Our Town, 1959; *The Nurses*, 1963; *Medea*, 1963; *J. F. Kennedy's Profiles in Courage*, 1965; *A Moon for the Misbegotten*, 1973; *The Human Voice*, 1979; *Hughie*, 1981.

Radio

In the Zone, 1988; *The Long Voyage Home*, 1988; *The Moon of the Caribbees*, 1989; *Bound East for Cardiff*, 1989; *The Hairy Ape*, 1989; *The Emperor Jones*, 1990.

Publications

If You Won't Dance, They Beat You (autobiography), 1974; *Gabrielle* (play), 1974.

* * *

José Quintero is known primarily as the pre-eminent director of the plays of Eugene O'Neill. His deeply intuitive and sensitive interpretations of O'Neill would seem surprising for a Panamanian who first came to the USA to study medicine. However, as Quintero himself acknowledges, his own tortured family life and his strict Catholic upbringing engendered in him profound conflicts that were to serve as a rich source of insight into O'Neill's characters.

Tennessee Williams rather than O'Neill first inspired Quintero to pursue a career in theatre when by chance one wintery Chicago night in 1949 he attended a performance of *The Glass Menagerie*. The production touched him on a deeply personal level and revealed to him at once the tragic and poetic possibilities of the theatre. He relates that he felt that the characters knew everything about him — his family, his hopes, his dreams. In 1953, Quintero garnered his first directorial acclaim with a revival of *Summer and Smoke* at the Circle in the Square Theatre that he cofounded with Theodore Mann in 1950. The production, which made a star of Quintero's Goodman classmate Geraldine Page, also sparked a renaissance of the off-Broadway movement.

While Quintero had notable successes at the Circle in the Square from 1950 to 1963 with the plays of Brendan Behan, Thornton Wilder, Tennessee Williams and foreign playwrights like Jean Genet, it was his direction of the mature plays of Eugene O'Neill that secured his place in the theatrical hall of fame and that of the Circle in the Square Theatre in the history of the off-Broadway theatre movement. Quintero's lifelong work with the plays of O'Neill, which he compares to a passionate affair, began in 1956 when he managed to secure the rights for *The Iceman Cometh* from O'Neill's widow, Carlotta Monterey, who had forbidden any productions of her husband's work after his death. Quintero's stunning revival of the play, which ran for almost two years, can be attributed to several factors. First, while O'Neill's plays had been out of fashion with the triumphant post-World War II audiences of the 1940's, the Cold War audiences of the 1950's were ripe for the play's pessimistic message. Secondly, Quintero used the three-quarters arena stage of the Circle in the Square with its proscenium backdrop to special advantage. He created a sense of intimacy by seating the audience around the playing space at tables as an extension of Harry Hope's bar and serving them drinks from the actual bar that remained from the original nightclub at the Circle in the Square. Third, and perhaps most importantly, Quintero's fortunate casting of the then relatively unknown Jason Robards Jr in the pivotal role of Hickey contributed greatly to the production's success. Critics hailed Robards and Quintero as the foremost interpreters of O'Neill and the production as superior to the 1946 Theatre Guild premiere. Subsequently, Carlotte Monterey bestowed upon Quintero and Theodore Mann the most sought-after theatrical property in the USA — the rights to produce the US premiere of *Long Day's Journey into Night*. This 1956 Broadway production cemented Quintero's reputation as a brilliant director and sparked renewed interest in O'Neill both in the USA and abroad. Over the next 30 years Quintero was to direct 11 O'Neill productions in New York alone. The most successful was the 1973 Broadway premiere of *A Moon for the Misbegotten* with Colleen Dewhurst and Jason Robards.

That José Quintero is today considered the foremost interpreter of the plays of Eugene O'Neill is due in large to the fact that he feels a strong emotional connection with O'Neill and his characters. Like O'Neill, Quintero was brought up as a Catholic in a tortured household by a mother who had been raised in a convent and by a famous father who ruled the house with an iron hand. And like many of O'Neill's characters Quintero turned to drink to escape his pain. Such themes as fall and redemption, the conflict between the body and soul — that are central to O'Neill and such playwrights as Tennessee Williams — resonate profoundly within Quintero. In directing O'Neill, Quintero makes himself vulnerable emotionally and psychologically to the play and each person in it. His gifts as a director lie in casting and an ability to convey to his actors the essence of their characters through images wrested from his own experience. Colleen Dewhurst stated that Quintero is an "almost exposed human being. Which makes it incredible to work with because he doesn't have any of the plastic emotions, he feels purely. As a director, he makes you go where in your gut you think you could go but you're a little nervous to go there for fear you'll make an ass of yourself, and José says trust me, and come on, come on, come on, come on, and he makes you break through, and releases something for you".

His directorial style is marked by a preference for slow-paced, hieratical productions interspersed with long silences that owe a great deal to the rigidly stylized and unvarying drama of the Catholic liturgy. From the Catholic ceremonials Quintero gained a special love for gesture rather than broad movement as a means of orchestrating the inner rhythms and feelings of characters. He creates focus by minimizing action in space often using tableaux, pietas and static choral configurations. This technique maximizes the sense of space surrounding the play and charges the character's utterances and gestures with monumental significance. While some critics have been impressed with his slow-paced, evocative style, others have faulted him for static and conventional staging.

When Quintero left the Circle in the Square in 1963 over differences with Theodore Mann on the artistic direction of the theatre, he lost the base that had nurtured his talent. A recovered alcoholic in 1972, he began his own long journey back to the stature he had held during his heyday at the Circle in the Square. However, with the exception of a highly acclaimed and popular Broadway premiere of *A Moon for the Misbegotten*, which established Colleen Dewhurst as one of the greatest interpreters of O'Neill heroines, his post-1963 work has never lived up to the early promise of his productions at the Circle in the Square. Although critics were generally favourable towards his 1985 Broadway premiere of *The Iceman Cometh* and his 1988 revival of *Long Day's Journey into Night*, they closed after only six weeks. *Iceman* lacked the crucial conditions of its 1956 revival at the Circle. Audiences of the late 1980's were resistant to its pessimism, the proscenium staging did not capture the intimacy of the arena staging at the Circle, and overall many critics felt the production lacked the essential spark that a younger Robards had brought to it. Although critics raved about Colleen Dewhurst's tragic and majestic portrayal of Mary Tyrone in *Long Day's Journey into Night*, both productions were faulted for their stark, conventional and static staging. Since these two revivals, Quintero has done very little directing and today devotes his time to teaching and training the next generation of directors at several universities in the South.

—Kathryn Wylie-Marques

R

RACHEL, Élisa. French actress. Born Élisa Félix in Mumpf, Aargau, Switzerland, 1820. Little formal education; trained as an actress at the Conservatoire, Paris, 1836, and, under the actor Joseph Isidore Samson, 1838. Unmarried; her lovers included Véron, the Prince de Joinville, Count Walewski, and Prince Napoleon. Sang in the streets of Lyons and Paris as a child; after leaving the Conservatoire joined the Théâtre du Gymnase, Paris, 1836; debut at the Comédie-Française, 1838; established reputation as a leading tragedienne as Racine's Phèdre, 1843, and consolidated it as Scribe's Adrienne Lecouvreur, 1848; made a pensionnaire of the Comédie-Française, 1849; toured widely and, after resigning from the Comédie-Française, took her own company to the USA, 1855; dissolved company because of ill health, 1856. Died (of tuberculosis) 3 January 1858.

Roles

1837   Geneviève in *La Vendéenne* (Duport), Théâtre du Gymnase, Paris.

     Suzanne in *Le Mariage de raison* (Scribe and Varner), Théâtre du Gymnase, Paris.

1838   Camille in *Horace* (P. Corneille), Comédie-Française, Paris.

     Émilie in *Cinna* (P. Corneille), Comédie-Française, Paris.

     Hermione in *Andromaque* (Racine), Comédie-Française, Paris.

     Aménaïde in *Tancrède* (Voltaire), Comédie-Française, Paris.

     Ériphile in *Iphigénie en Aulide* (Racine), Comédie-Française, Paris.

     Monime in *Mithridate* (Racine), Comédie-Française, Paris.

     Roxane in *Bajazet* (Racine), Comédie-Française, Paris.

1839   Esther in *Esther* (Racine), Comédie-Française, Paris.

     Laodice in *Nicomède* (P. Corneille), Comédie-Française, Paris.

     Dorine in *Tartuffe* (Molière), Comédie-Française, Paris.

1840   Pauline in *Polyeucte, Martyr* (P. Corneille), Comédie-Française, Paris.

     Marie Stuart in *Marie Stuart* (Lebrun), Comédie-Française, Paris.

1842   Chimène in *Le Cid* (P. Corneille), Comédie-Française, Paris.

Ariane in *Ariane* (T. Corneille), Comédie-Française, Paris.

Frédégonde in *Frédégonde et Brunehaut* (Lemercier), Comédie-Française, Paris.

1843   Phèdre in *Phèdre* (Racine), Comédie-Française, Paris.

     Judith in *Judith* (Girardin), Comédie-Française, Paris.

1844   Bérénice in *Bérénice* (Racine), Comédie-Française, Paris.

     Isabelle in *Don Sanche d'Aragon* (P. Corneille), Comédie-Française, Paris.

     Catherine in *Catherine II* (Romand), Comédie-Française, Paris.

     Marinette in *Le Dépit amoureux* (Molière), Comédie-Française, Paris.

1845   Virginie in *Virginie* (Saint-Ybars), Comédie-Française, Paris.

     Électre in *Oreste* (Voltaire), Comédie-Française, Paris.

1846   Jeanne d'Arc in *Jeanne d'Arc* (Soumet), Comédie-Française, Paris.

1847   La Comédie Sérieuse in *L'Ombre de Molière* (Barbier), Comédie-Française, Paris.

     Fatime in *Le Vieux de la Montagne* (Saint-Ybars), Comédie-Française, Paris.

     Athalie in *Athalie* (Racine), Comédie-Française, Paris.

     Cléopâtre in *Cléopâtre* (Girardin), Comédie-Française, Paris.

1848   La Marseillaise in *La Marseillaise* (Lisle), Comédie-Française, Paris.

     La Muse in *Le Roi attend* (Sand), Comédie-Française, Paris.

     Lucrèce in *Lucrèce* (Ponsard), Comédie-Française, Paris.

     Agrippine in *Britannicus* (Racine), Comédie-Française, Paris.

1849   Lesbie in *Le Moineau de Lesbie* (Barthet), Comédie-Française, Paris.

     Adrienne Lecouvreur in *Adrienne Lecouvreur* (Scribe and Legouvé), Comédie-Française, Paris.

1850   Gabrielle de Belle-Isle in *Mlle de Belle-Isle* (Dumas), Comédie-Française, Paris.

     La Tisbé in *Angelo, Tyran de Padoue* (Hugo), Comédie-Française, Paris.

     Lydie in *Horace et Lydie* (Ponsard), Comédie-Française, Paris.

1851   Valeria/Lycisca in *Valeria et Lycisca* (Lacroix and Maquet), Comédie-Française, Paris.

1852   Diane in *Diane* (Augier), Comédie-Française, Paris.

Louise in *Louise de Lignerolles* (Dinaux and Legouvé), Comédie-Française, Paris.

La Muse de l'Histoire in *L'Empire, c'est la paix* (Houssaye), Comédie-Française, Paris.

1853   Virginie de Blossac in *Lady Tartuffe* (Girardin), Comédie-Française, Paris.

1854   Théodore de Banville in *La Muse héroïque* (Banville), Comédie-Française, Paris.

Rosemonde in *Rosemonde* (Saint-Ybars), Comédie-Française, Paris.

1855   Catherine in *La Czarine* (Scribe), Comédie-Française, Paris.

*

Bibliography

Books:

A. Bolot, *Mademoiselle Rachel et l'Avenir du Théâtre-Français*, Paris, 1839.

A. Roussel, *Mlle Rachel et sa Troupe en Province*, Paris, 1849.

Charles Maurice, *La Vérité Rachel*, Paris, 1850.

C. A. de Chambrun, *Quelques Réflexions sur l'Art Dramatique: Mlle Rachel, ses Succès, ses Défauts*, Paris, 1853.

J. Cayla, *Célébrités européennes: Rachel*, Paris, 1854.

R. Trobriand, *Rachel à l'Amerique*, New York, 1855.

Léon Beauvallet, *Rachel et le Nouveau Monde*, Paris, 1856.

Mme de B, *Memoirs of Rachel*, 2 vols., London, 1858.

Jules Janin, *Rachel et la Tragédie*, Paris, 1859.

Eugène de Mirecourt, *Rachel*, Paris, 1869.

G. d'Heylli, *Rachel d'après sa Correspondance*, Paris, 1882.

Mrs Arthur Kennard, *Rachel*, London, 1885.

A. de Faucigny-Lucinge, *Rachel et son Temps*, Paris, 1910.

Hector Fleischmann, *Rachel Intime*, Paris, 1910.

Valentine Thomson, *La Vie Sentimentale de Rachel, d'après des Lettres Inédites*, Paris, 1910.

Francis Gribble, *Rachel: Her Stage Life and Her Real Life*, London, 1911.

J. L. Barthou, *Rachel*, Paris, 1926.

James Agate, *Rachel*, New York, 1928.

Bernard Falk, *Rachel the Immortal*, London, 1935.

J. Lucas-Dubreton, *Rachel*, Paris, 1936.

J. Arnna and P. Briquet, *Rachel et son temps*, Paris, 1939.

M. Cost, *Rachel, an Interpretation*, London, 1947.

Gabriel Laplane, *Rachel: Lettres Inédites*, Paris, 1947.

Martial-Piéchaud, *La Vie Privée de Rachel*, Paris, 1954.

Joanna Richardson, *Rachel*, London, 1956.

Sylvie Chevally, *Rachel en Amérique*, Paris, 1957.

Nicole Toussaint du Wast, *Rachel, Amours et Tragédie*, Paris, 1980.

* * *

The choice of the date 1843 to mark the decline of Romantic drama in France after a brief span of little more than a dozen years is conventionally justified by the coincidence of three significant events: the failure of Hugo's play *Les Burgraves*; the considerable success of Ponsard's *Lucrèce*, a play whose subject and theme were resolutely anti-Romantic; and the consecration of the

young actress Rachel's rise to stardom by her crowning triumph in the title-role of Racine's *Phèdre*.

The story of the beginnings of Rachel's career requires a suspension of disbelief not wholly unlike that which is called into play by the fictional career of Eliza Doolittle. Born in Switzerland of Jewish descent, Élisa Félix was the second eldest of the six children of an itinerant pedlar. She had very little schooling and when the family moved to Paris she and her sister sold oranges in cafés. However, through the good offices of Saint-Aulaire, an actor turned teacher of elocution, she was enabled to enter the Conservatoire; she stayed only three months, but Saint-Aulaire persevered, and she was admitted to the Gymnase company. The first play she appeared in failed, and she made no mark at all; but the turning-point came when she came to the notice of Samson, actor at the Comédie-Française and professor at the Conservatoire, who devoted himself to furthering her career, not only coaching her in the techniques of her craft but transforming her from a young girl hardly literate and with no background of culture — she had a prodigious memory and it is said that she learned her first roles with no knowledge at all of the rest of the play to which they belonged — into an actress whose grace and poise soon took Paris by storm. To quote a contemporary, "Rachel had an unsurpassed grace in her movements and an unrivalled nobility of manner. She wore the tunic and the peplum as if she had been born Roman or Greek, and when she appeared draped in such grace and simplicity, it was like a classical statue in motion". She made her debut at the Comédie-Française in 1838 under Samson's protection, as Camille in Corneille's *Horace*. Her first half-dozen roles made little stir: it was the summer season, with few spectators, and no critics in attendance. But between June and September, there was a remarkable change: the moribund Comédie began to register an almost tenfold increase in its takings, and critics began to produce rave reviews; those of Jules Janin in the *Débats* were to be particularly important. Curiosity about this new phenomenon soon gave way to admiration, and before long the salons of literary and social hostesses were receiving her. Samson was alarmed at the speed of these developments: his protégée's health was not very robust, and there was always the possibility (the comparison with Eliza Doolittle is unavoidable) of social gaffes that would undermine the progress made. But this orange-seller, who in her early teens had sung in cafés, conquered everyone by her innate grace, feminine charm, and modesty.

A much more serious threat was the grasping attitude of the Félix family, and the cupidity with which Rachel herself approached her career. Well aware that she was in a position to exact unheard-of terms from the Comédie-Française, which she had rescued from financial difficulties, she was soon earning 60,000 francs a year. By the early 1840's, she had taken on all the major roles in Racine, and in those plays of Corneille's that were still in the active repertory; by all accounts, her Phèdre in 1843 marked the height of her triumph; though she had already begun to dissipate her energy by arranging demanding tours in the provinces and abroad. Ever more rapacious with regard to fees and conditions of work, she was soon being called "despotic"; by the late 1840's, there were constant quarrels with the Comédie-Française about contracts and money matters. It appeared that her whole professional life was motivated by cupidity, and within the Comédie she refused to attend Marie Dorval's funeral and walked out of the benefit performance for Mlle George. By the time she resigned from the Comédie-Française in 1855 she was no longer the draw that she had been: takings were falling off, and she resented the success of the rising star Ristori. She now sought compensation more and more in overseas tours: Russia in 1853–54, producing profits of 300,000 francs for Rachel herself, and 100,000 for her brother Raphael as her manager; in 1855 to London again, followed by New York (where her financial rewards compared unfavourably with those of Jenny Lind shortly before) and Cuba; and in 1856 to Egypt. Her poor health was aggravated by such a demanding programme and hastened her death from tuberculosis. Her funeral was the occasion of an immense popular demonstration; but though colleagues representing various organisations pronounced funeral orations, the Comédie-Française was not officially represented, and Samson, who wished to deliver an oration, was prevented from doing so by Rachel's father.

Rachel's achievement has been summed up as that of an actress of genius, quick to learn but lacking real originality. She had a marvellous purity of diction, and her unconventional background and training had left her with a relatively natural stage presence, owing more to intuition than to the highly stylised technique produced by the traditional formation. Jules Janin, commenting after her death, looked back with regret to the instinctive and relatively untutored art of her beginnings: "Doubtless at first there were feelings she did not fully comprehend, ideas she misinterpreted, phrases to which she gave a meaning the poet had not intended; but on the other hand everything she said was original, naive, delightful: her misinterpretations could be forgiven in favour of her native inspiration ... ". Beatrice Dussane, in one of the best modern assessments of Rachel's qualities, similarly spoke of "technical faults and imperfections which her regal air, her transparent nobility, her instinctive genius, caused to be overlooked". This genius was endowed with talent by Samson's coaching, but inevitably it became a more cautious genius. According to Gautier in 1842, "Rachel excels above all at the expression of *concentrated* emotions: irony, sarcasm, hatred. The more *expansive* feelings of love, pity and generous affection do not so far come within this young actress's range". And even when she had added, with her Phèdre, what the same observer calls her "marvellous representation of the illusion of tragic grandeur", her talent seems to have remained essentially one-sided, lacking a more universal humane quality. For Dussane, Rachel's career also lacked the "transcendental goal", which might have produced just such a development: instead, she was motivated by the constant pursuit of immediate reward.

It was certainly due to Rachel that the Comédie-Française was able to exploit the declining fortunes of Romanticism in the theatre with a reinvigorated Classical tragedy; and Janin emphasises one particular legacy of Rachel's career at the Comédie when he points out that before her day, "the tragic *actor* reigned supreme in tragedy, and the *actress* invariably had a supporting role. With Rachel, the theatregoing public in France became used to thinking not only of the actor in tragedy, but of actor and actress together".

—William D. Howarth

RADLOV, Sergei (Ernestovich). Soviet actor and director. Born in St Petersburg, 1892. Educated at the University of St Petersburg, until 1916; trained for the theatre at the Meyerhold Studio, St Petersburg, 1913–17. Began career as actor with Vsevolod Meyerhold in Petrograd (formerly St Petersburg) and contributed to the *Love for Three Oranges* theatre journal; debut as director, 1918; subsequently worked with the People's Commissariat for Education's First Communal Troupe and the Petrograd Theatre-Studio, 1918–19; co-founder, with Vladimir Solovyov, of the Theatre of Folk Comedy, Petrograd, 1919–22; subsequently established reputation for productions at the Maly Theatre, Moscow; taught drama, 1922–35; founder, Laboratory for Theatre Research, 1922; director, Pushkin Theatre, Leningrad, 1936–38; also worked for theatres and studios in Petrograd, 1929–42, and in Latvia, 1953–58. Died 1958.

Principal productions

As director:

1918	*Menechmi* (Plautus, translated by Radlov), Theatre-Studio, Petrograd.
1919	*The Corpse's Bride*, Theatre of Folk Comedy, Petrograd.
	The Monkey Who Was an Informer, Theatre of Folk Comedy, Petrograd.
1920	*Towards a World Commune*, Theatre of Folk Comedy, Petrograd.
	The Sultan and the Devil, Theatre of Popular Comedy, Petrograd.
	The Adopted Son, Theatre of Folk Comedy, Petrograd.
1921	*Love and Gold*, Theatre of Folk Comedy, Petrograd.
1923	*Hinkemann* (Toller), Theatre of Folk Comedy, Petrograd.
1925	*Love for Three Oranges* (Prokofiev), Kirov Opera.
1927	*Othello* (Shakespeare), Maly Theatre, Moscow.
1928	*Boris Godunov* (Mussorgsky), Kirov Opera.
1932	*Othello* (Shakespeare), Maly Theatre, Moscow.
1934	*Romeo and Juliet* (Shakespeare), Maly Theatre, Moscow.
1936	*Othello* (Shakespeare), Maly Theatre, Moscow.
	King Lear (Shakespeare), Moscow State Jewish Theatre.
	Salut, Spanien (Afinogenov), Pushkin Theatre, Leningrad.
1937	*An den Ufern der Newa* (Trenev), Pushkin Theatre, Leningrad.
	Mozart i Salieri [Mozart and Salieri] (Pushkin), Pushkin Theatre, Leningrad.
	Pir vo vremya chumy [The Feast During the Plague] (Pushkin), Pushkin Theatre, Leningrad.
	Kammeny gost [The Stone Guest] (Pushkin), Pushkin Theatre, Leningrad.
1938	*Hamlet* (Shakespeare), Pushkin Theatre, Leningrad.

Other productions included: *Lysistrata* (Aristophanes), 1924; *Romeo and Juliet* (Shakespeare), 1939; *Bespridannit-*

sa [The Girl Without a Dowry] (Ostrovsky); *Brave Soldier Shweik* (Hasek); *Der Ferne Klang* (Schreker); *A Servant of Two Masters* (Goldoni); *Zemlia* [Earth] (Markish).

Publications

Ten Years in the Theatre, 1929.

* * *

Even before the Bolshevik Revolution Sergei Radlov was planning radical stage productions for the theatre. After 1917 he was charged with producing three outdoor mass spectacles in Petrograd, with cannon shots and searchlights from destroyers in the river, rockets and parades before an audience estimated at 45,000, three times in successive years, honouring Communist anniversaries. By the mid-1930's, he was nationally famous as a director of classics, including Shakespeare, at Russia's foremost dramatic theatre, the Moscow Maly. He returned to become artistic director of the former Imperial theatres, also directing opera and ballet, in his native St Petersburg, but was in demand to co-direct elsewhere. So famed, he survived the Stalinist terror, dying after World War II at the end of a seemingly contradictory development from far-out radicalism to far-reaching classicism.

Radlov acquired the basis for both extremes simultaneously. While studying for the degree in Greek and Latin that he received from the University of St Petersburg in 1916, he also studied at the innovator Vsevolod Meyerhold's Petersburg studio, and wrote too for the Studio in-house magazine *Love for Three Oranges*. In the magazine's second issue in 1914 he reviewed Professor Faddei Zelinsky's translation of Sophocles's tragedies. To the third issue, which was devoted entirely to the type roles or 'masks' of the commedia dell'arte, Radlov contributed a love poem and article on the many masks added to theatre tradition from the recently rediscovered work of the Roman Menander. The triple number from 1915 then published Radlov's translation of the *Menechmi* by Plautus. The *Menechmi*, in an expressionistically geometric and radically raked Studio staging, was the first production Radlov directed and was designed by his Studio classmate Vladimir Dmitriev.

In the immediate post-revolutionary years Russian intellectuals, among whom were the poet Alexander Blok, Meyerhold and Radlov, responded to cultural commissar's Anatoly Lunacharsky's appeal to work with the Bolsheviks in bringing culture to the people. From their devoted work several theatre groups emerged, including Radlov's Theatre of Folk Comedy, which produced Ernst Toller's *Hinkemann* under the Russian title *Unhappy Eugene*.

In the mid-1920's Radlov directed Prokofiev's *Love for Three Oranges* at the Kirov Opera. Based on material adapted after Carlo Gozzi by Meyerhold and Studio teachers, this production naturally showed some Meyerholdian characteristics, as did Franz Schreker's *Distant Bells*, both operas directed by Radlov and designed by Dmitriev. Yet Radlov rejected Meyerhold's version of Ostrovsky's *The Forest* in 1924, perhaps because he found its use of caricature extreme. Radlov and Dmitriev's collaborative staging of Mussorgsky's *Boris Godunov* at the Kirov in 1928

has been called a turning point away from startling radicalism to a more moderate realism.

In the 1930's Radlov turned to the classics, chosen partly for anniversaries. To honour the centennial of Ostrovsky's birth Radlov directed at the Maly — the theatre marked by Ostrovsky's monument on Theatre Square, Moscow — the dramatist's own favourite, *The Girl Without a Dowry*, concerning the tragedy of a woman auctioned off like a thing to the highest bidder. Radlov marked the 100th anniversary of Pushkin's death with a production of the three 'little tragedies', *Mozart and Salieri*, *The Feast During the Plague* and *The Stone Guest*. But the classic production with which Radlov chose to inaugurate his appointment as artistic director of the former Imperial theatres of St Petersburg, his *Othello* of 1936, became a true national, later international, event.

Radlov's casting of Alexander Ostuzhev as Othello seemed as arbitrary as his insistence on stage curtains, costumes and properties so sumptuous they could hardly be made ready in the few months before the March opening. The gifted actor Ostuzhev had started at the top with membership in the national theatre and playing leading roles, including an unforgettable Romeo, but had fallen into disuse, appearing, if at all, only in non-speaking parts since going deaf in 1910. But he had not lost his intelligence, energy and ability to convey feeling by pose, pantomime and rhythm of body movement. Under Radlov's helpful direction he created an Othello who, as the theatre historian David Zolotnitsky wrote, "killed Desdemona in obedience to the uncompromising purity of his feelings ... neither jealousy nor vengeance nor blinding rage were conceivable to director and actor". Ostuzhev said of Othello, "Everything he does, he does through tears". Radlov continued to direct Shakespeare, *King Lear* and *Romeo and Juliet*, and foreign classics, like Carlo Goldoni's *A Servant of Two Masters* and Jaroslav Hasek's *Brave Soldier Schweik*. He used the smaller Imperial houses to try out recent plays, and he taught young theatre people while also staging opera and ballet.

Radlov also co-directed in Hebrew with Solomon Mikhoels at the theatre Mikhoels founded, the Moscow Jewish Theatre, a contemporary play, *Earth* by Perets Markish, who despite the play's pro-Communist propaganda became a victim of the Stalinist terror.

Radlov's early serious career, the mass spectacles celebrating Communism and his early productions of the Greek and Roman classics resulted from his collaboration with Studio associates like the artist Dmitriev, as well as the wild expressionist challenge of the time and widespread fascination with circus clowns and the commedia dell'arte. While Radlov later continued Meyerhold's effort to bring the theatre back to such forms older than the psychological realism of the Moscow Art Theatre, he also sought his own 'Leningrad way' as director of several performing arts, linguist lover of the classics and sensitive citizen of an all too chaotic period.

—Marjorie L. Hoover

REDGRAVE, (Sir) Michael Scudamore. British actor, author, director, and manager. Born in Bristol, 20 March 1908. Educated at Clifton College, Bristol; Magdalene

College, Cambridge, BA 1931. Married actress Rachel Kempson in 1935, two daughters (actresses Vanessa Redgrave (*q.v.*) and Lynn Redgrave) and one son (actor Corin Redgrave). Employed initially as a school-teacher; made stage debut at the Playhouse, Liverpool, 1934; London debut, Old Vic Theatre, 1936; actor, alongside John Gielgud, Queen's Theatre, London, 1937; film debut, 1939; served in Royal Navy, 1941–42; admired in further Shakespearean roles at Stratford-upon-Avon, 1953–54 and 1958–59; also acted at the Chichester Festival Theatre and at the National Theatre, London; director, opening festival of the Yvonne Arnaud Theatre, Guildford, 1965; repertory theatre in Farnham, Surrey, named after him, 1965; retired on account of ill health, 1975. Member: English Speaking Board, 1953 (president); Questors amateur theatre, Ealing, 1958 (president). Recipient: New York Critics' Award, 1955; *Evening Standard* Award, 1958 and 1963; Variety Club of Great Britain Actor of the Year Award, 1958 and 1963. D.Litt: University of Bristol, 1966. CBE (Commander of the British Empire), 1952; Commander, Order of the Dannebrog (Denmark), 1955. Knighted, 1959. Died in London, 21 March 1985.

Productions

As actor:

1934	Roy Darwin in *Counsellor at Law* (Rice), Playhouse, Liverpool.
	Charles Hubbard in *The Distaff Side* (Van Druten), Playhouse, Liverpool.
	Dr Purley in *A Sleeping Clergyman* (Bridie), Playhouse, Liverpool.
	The Man in *The Perfect Plot* (Ensor), Playhouse, Liverpool.
	Mr Bolton in *Sheppey* (Maugham), Playhouse, Liverpool.
	Ernest Hubbard in *Heaven on Earth* (Johnson), Playhouse, Liverpool.
1935	Melchior Feydak in *Biography* (Behrman), Playhouse, Liverpool.
	Gaston in *Villa for Sale* (Guitry), Playhouse, Liverpool.
	Sir Mark Loddon in *Libel* (Wooll), Playhouse, Liverpool, and Winter Gardens, New Brighton.
	Richard Newton-Clare in *Flowers of the Forest* (Van Druten), Playhouse, Liverpool.
	Horatio in *Hamlet* (Shakespeare), Playhouse, Liverpool.
	Bill Clarke in *Too Young to Marry* (Flavin), Playhouse, Liverpool, and Winter Gardens, New Brighton.
	Oliver Maitland in *The Matriarch* (Stern), Playhouse, Liverpool.
	Charles McFadden in *Counsellor at Law* (Rice), Winter Gardens, New Brighton.
	Randolph Warrender in *Youth at the Helm* (Griffith), Playhouse, Liverpool.
	Richard Barnet in *Barnet's Folly* (Stewer), Playhouse, Liverpool.
	Robert Murrison in *Cornelius* (Priestley), Playhouse, Liverpool.

Michael Redgrave (1956).

	Richard Brinsley Sheridan in *Miss Linley of Bath* (M. Sheridan), Playhouse, Liverpool.
	Max in *The Copy* (Krog), Playhouse, Liverpool.
	Trino in *A Hundred Years Old* (Quintero), Playhouse, Liverpool.
	Gilbert Raymond in *The Wind and the Rain* (Hodge), Playhouse, Liverpool.
	BBC Official in *Circus Boy* (M. Redgrave), Playhouse, Liverpool.
1936	Reverend Ernest Dunwoody in *Boyd's Shop* (Ervine), Playhouse, Liverpool.
	A Radio Announcer in *And So To War* (Corrie), Playhouse, Liverpool.
	Richard II in *Richard of Bordeaux* (Daviot), Playhouse, Liverpool.
	Richard Burdon in *Storm in a Teacup* (Bridie), Playhouse, Liverpool.
	Tom Lambert in *Painted Sparrows* (Paxton and Hoile), Playhouse, Liverpool.
	Malvolio in *Twelfth Night* (Shakespeare), Playhouse, Liverpool.
	Ferdinand in *Love's Labour's Lost* (Shakespeare), Old Vic Theatre, London.
	Mr Horner in *The Country Wife* (Wycherley), Old Vic Theatre, London.
	Orlando in *As You Like It* (Shakespeare), Old Vic Theatre, London; New Theatre, London, 1937; The Barn, Smallhythe, 1938.
	Warbeck in *The Witch of Edmonton* (Dekker), Old Vic Theatre, London.

1937   Laertes in *Hamlet* (Shakespeare), Old Vic Theatre, London.
Anderson in *The Bat* (Rinehart and Hopwood), Embassy Theatre, London.
Iachimo in extract from *Cymbeline* (Shakespeare), Old Vic Theatre, London.
Chorus in *Henry V* (Shakespeare), Old Vic Theatre, London; revived there, 1938; Shakespeare Memorial Theatre, Stratford-upon-Avon, 1951.
Christopher Drew in *A Ship Comes Home* (Fisher), St Martin's Theatre, London.
Larry Starr in *Three Set Out* (Leaver), Embassy Theatre, London.
Bolingbroke in *Richard II* (Shakespeare), Queen's Theatre, London.
Charles Surface in *The School for Scandal* (Sheridan), Queen's Theatre, London.

1938   Baron Tusenbach in *The Three Sisters* (Chekhov), Queen's Theatre, London.
Alexei Turbin in *The White Guard* (Bulgakov), Phoenix Theatre, London.
Sir Andrew Aguecheek in *Twelfth Night* (Shakespeare), Phoenix Theatre, London.

1939   Lord Harry Monchensey in *The Family Reunion* (Eliot), Westminster Theatre, London.
Henry Dewlip in *Springtime for Henry* (Levy), British tour.

1940   Captain Macheath in *The Beggar's Opera* (Gay), Haymarket Theatre, London.
Romeo in extract from *Romeo and Juliet* (Shakespeare), Palace Theatre, London.
Charleston in *Thunder Rock* (Ardrey), Neighbourhood Theatre, London, and Globe Theatre, London.

1942   Gribaud in *The Duke in Darkness* (Hamilton), St James's Theatre, London; also directed.

1943   Rakitin in *A Month in the Country* (Turgenev), St James's Theatre, London; New Theatre, London, 1949; Yvonne Arnaud Theatre, Guildford, and Cambridge Theatre, London, 1965, also directed.
Lafont in *Parisienne* (Becque, adapted by Dukes), St James's Theatre, London; also directed.

1944   Harry in *Uncle Harry* (Job), Garrick Theatre, London; also co-directed.

1945   The Colonel in *Jacobowsky and the Colonel* (Werfel and Behrman), Piccadilly Theatre, London; also directed.

1947   Macbeth in *Macbeth* (Shakespeare), Aldwych Theatre, London; National Theatre, New York, 1948.

1948   The Captain in *The Father* (Strindberg), Embassy Theatre, London; Duchess Theatre, London, 1949.

1949   Etienne in *A Woman in Love* (M. Redgrave and Gould, adapted from Porto-Riche), Embassy Theatre, London; also directed.
Berowne in *Love's Labour's Lost* (Shakespeare), New Theatre, London.
Young Marlow in *She Stoops to Conquer* (Goldsmith), New Theatre, London.

1950   Hamlet in *Hamlet* (Shakespeare), New Theatre, London, and Kronberg Castle, Elsinore, Denmark; Shakespeare Memorial Theatre, Stratford-upon-Avon, and Russian tour, 1958–59.
Filmer Jesson in extract from *His House in Order* (Pinero), Theatre Royal, Drury Lane.

1951   Richard II in *Richard II* (Shakespeare), Shakespeare Memorial Theatre, Stratford-upon-Avon.
Hotspur in *Henry IV, part 1* (Shakespeare), Shakespeare Memorial Theatre, Stratford-upon-Avon.
Prospero in *The Tempest* (Shakespeare), Shakespeare Memorial Theatre, Stratford-upon-Avon.

1952   Frank Elgin in *Winter Journey* (Odets), St James's Theatre, London.

1953   Shylock in *The Merchant of Venice* (Shakespeare), Shakespeare Memorial Theatre, Stratford-upon-Avon; (extract) Waldorf-Astoria, New York, 1955.
Antony in *Antony and Cleopatra* (Shakespeare), Shakespeare Memorial Theatre, Stratford-upon-Avon, and European tour.
Lear in *King Lear* (Shakespeare), Shakespeare Memorial Theatre, Stratford-upon-Avon.

1955   Hector in *Tiger at the Gates* (Giraudoux, translated by Fry), Apollo Theatre, London, and Plymouth Theatre, New York.

1956   The Prince Regent in *The Sleeping Prince* (Rattigan), Coronet Theatre, New York; also directed.

1958   Philip Lester in *A Touch of the Sun* (Hunter), Saville Theatre, London.
Benedick in *Much Ado About Nothing* (Shakespeare), Shakespeare Memorial Theatre, Stratford-upon-Avon.

1959   HJ in *The Aspern Papers* (James, adapted by M. Redgrave), Queen's Theatre, London.

1960   Jack Dean in *The Tiger and the Horse* (Bolt), Queen's Theatre, London.

1961   Victor Rhodes in *The Complaisant Lover* (Greene), Ethel Barrymore Theatre, New York.

1962   Uncle Vanya in *Uncle Vanya* (Chekhov), Chichester Festival Theatre; revived there and at the Old Vic Theatre, London, 1963.
Lancelot Dodd in *Out of Bounds* (Watkyn), Wyndham's Theatre, London.

1963   Claudius in *Hamlet* (Shakespeare), Old Vic Theatre, London.

1964   Henry Hobson in *Hobson's Choice* (Brighouse), Old Vic Theatre, London.
Halvard Solness in *The Master Builder* (Ibsen), Old Vic Theatre, London.

1965   Samson in *Samson Agonistes* (Milton), Yvonne Arnaud Theatre, Guildford.

1971   Mr Jaraby in *The Old Boys* (Trevor), Mermaid Theatre, London.

1972   Father in *A Voyage Round My Father* (Mortimer), Haymarket Theatre, London, and Canadian and Australian tour.

1974–75   Several roles in *The Hollow Crown* (Shakespeare compilation), RSC world tour.

1976–77   Several roles in *Shakespeare's People* (Shakespeare compilation), South American, Canadian, and British tour.

1979   Jasper in *Close of Play* (Gray), National Theatre, London.

As director:

1942   *Lifeline* (Armstrong), Duchess Theatre, London.

1943   *Blow Your Own Trumpet* (Ustinov), Playhouse, London.
        The Wingless Victory (Anderson), Phoenix Theatre, London.

1951   *Henry IV, part 2* (Shakespeare), Shakespeare Memorial Theatre, Stratford-upon-Avon.

1956   *A Month in the Country* (Turgenev), Phoenix Theatre, New York.

1966   *Werther* (Massenet), Glyndebourne Festival Opera.
        La Bohème (Puccini), Glyndebourne Festival Opera.

Films

The Lady Vanishes, 1939; *Stolen Life*, 1939; *Climbing High*, 1939; *The Stars Look Down*, 1940; *A Window in London*, 1940; *Kipps*, 1941; *Atlantic Ferry*, 1941; *Jeannie*, 1941; *The Big Blockade*, 1942; *Thunder Rock*, 1943; *The Way to the Stars*, 1945; *Dead of Night*, 1945; *The Years Between*, 1946; *The Captive Heart*, 1946; *The Man Within*, 1947; *Fame is the Spur*, 1947; *Secret Beyond the Door*, 1948; *The Browning Version*, 1951; *The Magic Box*, 1951; *The Importance of Being Earnest*, 1952; *Mourning Becomes Electra*, 1952; *The Green Scarf*, 1954; *The Sea Shall Not Have Them*, 1955; *Oh, Rosalinda!*, 1955; *The Night My Number Came Up*, 1955; *The Dam Busters*, 1955; *Confidential Report*, 1955; *1984*, 1956; *Time Without Pity*, 1957; *Law and Disorder*, 1958; *Behind the Mask*, 1958; *The Quiet American*, 1958; *Shake Hands with the Devil*, 1959; *The Wreck of the Mary Deare*, 1959; *No, My Darling Daughter*, 1961; *The Innocents*, 1961; *The Loneliness of the Long Distance Runner*, 1963; *Young Cassidy*, 1964; *The Hill*, 1965; *The Heroes of Telemark*, 1965; *The 25th Hour*, 1967; *Assignment K*, 1968; *Oh! What a Lovely War*, 1969; *The Battle of Britain*, 1969; *Goodbye Mr Chips*, 1969; *David Copperfield*, 1970; *Connecting Rooms*, 1970; *Goodbye Gemini*, 1970; *The Go-Between*, 1971; *Nicholas and Alexandra*, 1971.

Publications

The Seventh Man (play, produced Playhouse Liverpool, 1935); *Circus Boy* (play, produced Playhouse, Liverpool, 1935); *A Woman in Love* (adaptation of Porto-Riche's *Amoureuse*, produced Embassy Theatre, London, 1949); *The Aspern Papers* (adaptation from James, produced Queen's Theatre, London, 1959); *The Actor's Ways and Means*, 1955; *Mask or Face — Reflections in an Actor's Mirror*, 1958; *The Mountebank's Tale* (novel), 1959; *In My Mind's Eye* (autobiography), 1983.

*

Bibliography

Books:
Richard Findlater, *Michael Redgrave — Actor*, London, 1956.

* * *

Few this century in the British theatre have matched the multiformity of Michael Redgrave. Educated at Clifton and Cambridge, where besides acquiring some acting experience he gained recognition as a poet, his first ambition was to be a writer and, while his subsequent career as a leading actor overshadowed his other creative gifts, it should not be forgotten that he was the author of an elegant dramatisation of Henry James's *The Aspern Papers* as well as of plays of his own, two volumes of analyses of the craft of acting, and an unsentimental autobiography written towards the end of the long illness that ended his life. He was, moreover, a skilful director, responsible between 1942 and 1945 for the staging of six West End plays, and for others sporadically thereafter, among them a 1951 production of *Henry IV, part 2* at Stratford-upon-Avon. As an actor he played the classics with sensitivity and meticulously persuasive characterisation, sustaining the while a fine career in numerous films. The knighthood conferred in 1959 saluted a protean virtuosity.

Redgrave's manner was full of paradox. Though bookish by inclination and donnish in manner (qualities that took him straight to the heart of a character like Crocker-Harris in the film of Rattigan's *The Browning Version*), he gave release on the stage to emotional extremity. In appearance and manner he was the quintessential Englishman, but his mind was determinedly open to foreign influence, whether from the Compagnie des Quinze or from the teachings of Stanislavsky, on which he wrote and lectured. He was a classical actor who looked at home in contemporary plays and in a succession of modern-dress films. It seemed to some that his status as a leading Shakespearean was at odds with his perennial resort to the more lucrative opportunities of the film studios; his admirers, though, saw in the fractured alternations between stage and screen the ideal pattern of experience for a modern, complete actor. For better or worse, however, his stage work lost continuity. Redgrave — a film star in 1938 on the release of Hitchcock's *The Lady Vanishes*, scarcely three years after he went on the stage — was one of the first actors to be faced with the oppositional pull of theatre and cinema. There was a further paradox too, and a crucial one. He was physically commanding (powerfully built, athletic, and six feet three inches tall) but specialised in the depiction of tenderness, vulnerability, neurosis, and self-doubt. To his biographer, Richard Findlater, his easy charm masked an acting self that showed "a special skill in presenting haunted and divided men on the edge of breakdown and madness". It was the key to the humanity of his Macbeth (1947), Hamlet (1950 and 1958), Vanya (1962), and a host of characters, including — perhaps surprisingly — the hero of *Antony and Cleopatra*: never can an Antony have been so plausibly a triple pillar of the world, never so convincingly a big man inwardly broken.

Redgrave entered the acting profession at 26, following a period teaching at a minor public school, but his advance was uncommonly swift. Within three years he had worked with virtually all the key figures in contemporary British theatre: William Armstrong (who gave him his start at the Liverpool Playhouse), Edith Evans (from whom, over two seasons at the Old Vic, where he was catapulted into major roles, he learnt the precision required for vocal delivery and comic technique), Tyrone Guthrie, Michel Saint-Denis, Laurence Olivier, John Gielgud, and Peggy Ashcroft — the latter two in a celebrated venture of classical repertory instigated and led by Gielgud at the Queen's Theatre, Shaftesbury Avenue. It was Gielgud's company that he deserted for his first film and not until more than a decade later, when in 1949 Hugh Hunt brought him to the Old Vic's temporary home at the New (now the Albery) Theatre, did he return to a classical repertory. There, as Young Marlow in *She Stoops to Conquer*, he made for the first time a consummate mark in a style in which he was otherwise afforded scant opportunity. Then, in 1950, in Hunt's production of *Hamlet*, he portrayed a prince whose depth of feeling and focus of thought were intensified by what T. C. Worsley called an "absolute mastery of the vocal line". Redgrave's authority as a verse-speaker, fastidious but unaffected, was assured.

The work with Hunt marked a turning-point, presaging two mammoth seasons at Stratford — Richard II, Hotspur, Prospero, and Chorus in *Henry V* in 1951 and Shylock, Antony, and Lear in 1953. Redgrave's second Hamlet in 1958 was thought by some to be over the hill, but Michael Billington avers in his recent biography of Peggy Ashcroft that Redgrave at the age of 50 "encompassed more of the character than any actor I have seen before or since". Some of Redgrave's surest acting in *Hamlet* still lay ahead, for his casting as Claudius five years later (to the Hamlet of Peter O'Toole) was the masterstroke of the National Theatre's inaugural production. For two years Redgrave remained a buttress of the National, which he left in 1965 to direct the opening season of the Yvonne Arnaud Theatre, Guildford. By then, however, unbeknown to audiences, he was beginning to suffer from Parkinson's disease, which curtailed his career.

It was said that there were combined in Redgrave the poetry of Gielgud and the fire of Olivier; but his diversity thwarted classification. Repeatedly he obscured his good looks and charm with some morbid sign of instability, like the nervous giggle of his Vanya, or the manic stare in the film *Dead of Night*, in which he played a ventriloquist lethally possessed by the personality of his doll. For a long-legged actor he had curiously short strides, but the trait was well deployed, for instance, in Chekhov and Strindberg, when it seemed the essential expression of a tall man's fear of clumsiness. For years — notwithstanding the emotional intensity of his Hamlet, Lear, and Macbeth — the charge of intellectualism pursued him. No doubt his erudite aestheticism and the persuasive fluency with which he illuminated the processes of his craft led some to suspect in him a non-instinctive approach; but Redgrave's intellectual quest sprang from a deeply instinctive desire to comprehend and articulate.

—Michael Read

REDGRAVE, Vanessa. British actress. Born in London, 30 January 1937; daughter of actor Michael Redgrave (q.v.). Educated at Queensgate School, London; trained for the stage at the Central School of Speech and Drama, London, 1954–57. Married director Tony Richardson (divorced), two daughters. Stage debut, Frinton Summer Theatre, 1957; London debut, 1958; first film and television appearances, 1958; joined Shakespearean Memorial Theatre Company, Stratford-upon-Avon, 1959; concentrated on her film career after stage success in *The Prime of Miss Jean Brodie*, 1966; noted for her commitment to left-wing political ideology and stood unsuccessfully as parliamentary candidate for Workers' Revolutionary Party; returned to stage, 1971. Recipient: Cannes Festival Award, 1966; Golden Globe Award, 1976; Oscar, 1978; *Evening Standard* Award, 1978; Emmy Award, 1981; British Academy of Film and Television Arts Award, 1987; New York Critics' Award, 1987. CBE (Commander of the Order of the British Empire), 1967.

Roles

1957	Clarissa in *The Reluctant Debutante* (Home), Summer Theatre, Frinton.
	Mrs Spottsworth in *Come On, Jeeves* (Wodehouse), Arts Theatre, Cambridge.
1958	Caroline Lester in *A Touch of the Sun* (Hunter), Saville Theatre, London.
	Sarah Undershaft in *Major Barbara* (G. B. Shaw), Royal Court Theatre, London.
	Principal Boy in *Mother Goose*, Leatherhead, Surrey.
1959	Helena in *A Midsummer Night's Dream* (Shakespeare), Shakespeare Memorial Theatre, Stratford-upon-Avon.
	Valeria in *Coriolanus* (Shakespeare), Shakespeare Memorial Theatre, Stratford-upon-Avon.
1960	Rose Sinclair in *Look on Tempests* (Henry), Comedy Theatre, London.
	Stella Dean in *The Tiger and the Horse* (Bolt), Queen's Theatre, London.
1961	Boletta in *The Lady from the Sea* (Ibsen), Queen's Theatre, London.
	Rosalind in *As You Like It* (Shakespeare), Royal Shakespeare Theatre, Stratford-upon-Avon; Aldwych Theatre, London, 1962.
	Katharina in *The Taming of the Shrew* (Shakespeare), Aldwych Theatre, London; Royal Shakespeare Theatre, Stratford-upon-Avon, 1962.
1964	Nina in *The Seagull* (Chekhov), Queen's Theatre, London.
	Imogen in *Cymbeline* (Shakespeare), Royal Shakespeare Theatre, Stratford-upon-Avon.
1966	Jean Brodie in *The Prime of Miss Jean Brodie* (Spark), Wyndham's Theatre, London.
1969	Gwendolen Harleth in *Daniel Deronda*, University Theatre, Manchester.
1971	Susan Thistlewood in *Cato Street*, Young Vic Theatre, London.
1972	Polly Peachum in *The Threepenny Opera* (Brecht), Prince of Wales Theatre, London.
	Viola in *Twelfth Night* (Shakespeare), Shaw Theatre, London.

Vanessa Redgrave (1968).

1973	Cleopatra in *Antony and Cleopatra* (Shakespeare), Bankside Globe Theatre, London; revived, 1986, and Riverside Studios, London, 1995, also directed.
	Gilda in *Design for Living* (Coward), Phoenix Theatre, London.
1975	Lady Macbeth in *Macbeth* (Shakespeare), Los Angeles.
1976	Ellida in *The Lady from the Sea* (Ibsen), Circle in the Square Theatre, New York; Royal Exchange Theatre, Manchester, 1978.
1984	Miss Tina in *The Aspern Papers* (James, adapted by M. Redgrave), London.
1985	Arkadina in *The Seagull* (Chekhov), Queen's Theatre, London.
1986–87	Katherine in *The Taming of the Shrew* (Shakespeare), Haymarket Theatre, London.
	Mrs Alving in *Ghosts* (Ibsen), Young Vic Theatre, London, and Wyndham's Theatre, London.
1988	Nora Melody in *A Touch of the Poet* (O'Neill), Young Vic Theatre, London, and Comedy Theatre, London.
1989	Lady Torrance in *Orpheus Descending* (T. Williams), New York.
1990	Narrator in *Suicide for Love* (Akimoto), National Theatre, London.
1991	Isadora Duncan in *When She Danced* (Sherman), Globe Theatre, London.

1992	Hesione Hushabye in *Heartbreak House* (G. B. Shaw), Haymarket Theatre, London.

Has also acted roles in: *Chekhov's Women* (adapted from Chekhov), Lyric Theatre, London, 1985; *Maybe* (Shatrov, adapted by Reddin), Royal Exchange Theatre, Manchester, 1993.

Films

Behind the Mask, 1958; *Morgan!*, 1965; *Red and Blue*, 1966; *Sailor from Gibralta*, 1966; *A Man for All Seasons*, 1966; *Blow-Up*, 1966; *Camelot*, 1967; *The Charge of the Light Brigade*, 1968; *Isadora*, 1968; *A Quiet Place in the Country*, 1968; *Dropout*, 1969; *Vacation*, 1969; *The Seagull*, 1969; *Oh! What a Lovely War*, 1969; *The Trojan Women*, 1971; *The Devils*, 1971; *Mary, Queen of Scots*, 1972; *Murder on the Orient Express*, 1974; *Out of Season*, 1975; *The Seven Per Cent Solution*, 1976; *Julia*, 1977; *Agatha*, 1979; *Yanks*, 1979; *Bear Island*, 1979; *Snow White and the Seven Dwarfs*, 1983; *The Bostonians*, 1984; *Steaming*, 1985; *Wetherby*, 1985; *Comrades*, 1986; *Prick Up Your Ears*, 1987; *Consuming Passions*, 1988; *The Cook, the Thief, His Wife and Her Lover*, 1989; *Little Odessa*, 1995.

Television

A Farewell to Arms, 1966; *A Midsummer Night's Dream*, 1962; *As You Like It*, 1962; *Maggie*, 1964; *Sally*, 1964; *Playing for Time*, 1980; *My Body, My Child*, 1982; *Occupied Palestine*, 1982; *Wagner*, 1983; *Three Sovereigns for Sarah*, 1985; *Peter the Great*, 1986; *Second Serve*, 1986; *A Man for All Seasons*, 1989.

Publications

Pussies and Tigers (children's anthology), 1963; *Vanessa Redgrave: An Autobiography*, 1991.

* * *

"Ladies and gentlemen, tonight a great actress has been born." Thus was the world informed of the birth of Vanessa Redgrave. The announcement was made by Laurence Olivier during the curtain call of *Hamlet*, in which Olivier and the proud father, Michael Redgrave, were both appearing.

Despite such a high-profile start, family connections can only take an actor so far. Early on, it became apparent that Redgrave's claim to fame was based on far more than her name. By the early 1960's, she was playing leading roles at Stratford and in London. Her interpretations of classical roles were greeted with equal reverence and hysteria. Reviewing these roles — Helena, Valeria, Rosalind, Imogen in Shakespeare; Sarah Undershaft in *Major Barbara*; Nina in *The Seagull* — one is struck by the strange casting. Nearly six feet tall, raw-boned, a voice husky and low, graceful but in a gangly way, vulnerable but powerful: we are now so accustomed to Vanessa Redgrave and the generation of tall, striking-looking leading ladies that followed in her wake, it is easy to forget the unlikeliness of such a figure becoming a convincing ingenue.

Yet all those who have seen Redgrave perform have been struck by her ability to become almost translucent with emotion. It is clearly a gift that she has had for a long time and it accounts for her early success in such parts. Kenneth Tynan wrote in 1961 that watching Redgrave as the daughter in Ibsen's *The Lady from the Sea* "is to relive the painful, illusion-shedding transition that marks the end of youth. If there is better acting than this in London I should like to hear of it".

In a strange way, the greatest compliment an actor can be paid is to be paid no compliment at all. For an audience to assume that an actor is merely being herself is the ideal, if acting is assumed to be an imitation of life. Yet Tynan uses the word "relive", which implies distance. This is appropriate: like any great artist, Vanessa Redgrave does not imitate but illuminate. To pinpoint how Redgrave does this and what makes the actress thrilling and enthralling to watch, it is enlightening to read the words of film critic Pauline Kael (for various reasons, Redgrave worked mainly in films between the mid-1960's and the early 1980's, with mixed artistic and box-office success): "Redgrave often seems to be staring one down, but there's a marvellous romantic excitement about this woman, because one never knows what audacity she will attempt, what heights she'll scale. This may prevent unconscious involvement, because we are always conscious of a *performance* but our conscious involvement in the tension she creates has its own kind of excitement. She seems to act with her whole soul: you don't see a woman trying to play a role — the woman has been consumed by the determination to give the role all she has".

Understandably, this type of acting may seem overwhelming on the screen, although Redgrave has produced some extraordinary screen performances — for instance, in *Blow-Up, Julia* and *Playing for Time*. But in the theatre, the heroic style that Kael identified, and the larger-than-life physiognomy converge (or perhaps the former was borne out of the latter). Redgrave does not reflect human experience, but magnifies it. The impression created is rather like that of watching a trapeze artist perform without a safety net.

Vanessa Redgrave's intensity can lead to the type of bad performance that only the very talented can muster. As Cleopatra in the mid 1980's, her 'kittenish' playing, executed with every fibre of her being, was ghastly to behold. She can be a brittle presence, but not a lightweight one — not surprisingly, she is not noted for her success in comedy. However, it is a measure of her brilliance that, in a theatrical canon notoriously short of leading roles for older women, she has gone from strength to strength. She has found new plays, such as Martin Sherman's *A Madhouse in Goa*, which allow her talent to communicate suffering, ecstacy and endurance. And, in the last decade, she has become the definitive interpreter of Ibsen, O'Neill and Tennessee Williams's older women.

Laurence Olivier's announcement was appropriately flamboyant but also prescient. Vanessa Redgrave is a great actress, not just greater than the rest of the clan, but perhaps the greatest of her generation. It seems unlikely that she would be offered or accept the title of dame. Yet her pre-eminence should be recognised. At her best, she is a performer who sustains one's faith in the magic and power of live theatre.

—Joss Bennathan

REHAN, Ada. US actress. Born Ada Crehan in Limerick, Ireland, 22 April 1860. Emigrated to the USA with her parents, 1865; educated at local schools in Brooklyn, New York, until 1873. Stage debut, Newark, New Jersey, 1873; New York debut, 1873; actress, Mrs John Drew's Arch Street Theatre, Philadelphia company, 1873–74, Barney Macauley's Theatre stock company, Louisville, Kentucky, 1875, Albaugh's Theatre, Albany, New York, 1877, Augustin Daly's company in New York and London, from 1879; London debut, Toole's Theatre, 1884; inherited share in Daly's New York and London theatres on Daly's death, 1899; retired from the stage, 1905. Died in New York, 8 January 1916.

Roles

1873   Clara in *Across the Continent* (O. D. Byron), Newark, New Jersey.
1873–74   Ophelia in *Hamlet* (Shakespeare), Arch Street Theatre, Philadelphia.
    Virginia in *Virginius* (McCullough), Arch Street Theatre, Philadelphia.
1877   Bianca in *The Taming of the Shrew* (Shakespeare), Albany, New York.
1879   Mary Standish in *Pique* (Daly), Grand Opera House, New York.
    Big Clemence in *Big Clemence*, Olympic Theatre, New York.
    Virginie in *L'Assommoir* (Daly, adapted from Zola), Olympic Theatre, New York.
    Nelly Beers in *Love's Young Dream* (Daly), Daly's Theatre, New York.
1880   Cinderella in *Cinderella*, Daly's Theatre, New York.
1885   Sylvia in *The Recruiting Officer* (Farquhar, adapted by Daly), Daly's Theatre, New York.
    Nisbe in *A Night Off* (Schönthan, adapted by Daly), Daly's Theatre, New York.
    Agatha Posket in *The Magistrate* (Pinero), Court Theatre, London.
1886   Mrs Ford in *The Merry Wives of Windsor* (Shakespeare, adapted by Daly), Daly's Theatre, New York.
    Nancy Brasher in *Nancy and Company* (Rosen, adapted by Daly), Daly's Theatre, New York.
1887   Katharine in *The Taming of the Shrew* (Shakespeare, adapted by Daly), Daly's Theatre, New York; Shakespeare Memorial Theatre, Stratford-upon-Avon, 1888; US tour, 1900; Atlantic City, 1903; Lyric Theatre, New York, and Liberty Theatre, New York, 1904.
1888   Helena in *A Midsummer Night's Dream* (Shakespeare, adapted by Daly), Daly's Theatre, New York.
1889   Oriana in *The Inconstant* (Farquhar, adapted by Daly), Daly's Theatre, New York.

Rosalind in *As You Like It* (Shakespeare, adapted by Daly), Daly's Theatre, New York; Lyceum Theatre, London, 1890; British tour, 1897; US tour, 1900.

1891 Lady Teazle in *The School for Scandal* (Sheridan), Daly's Theatre, New York; Daly's Theatre, London, 1893-94; US tour, 1900; Lyric Theatre, New York, and Liberty Theatre, New York, 1904.

1892 Marian Lea in *The Foresters* (Tennyson, adapted by Daly), Daly's Theatre, New York.

Julia in *The Hunchback* (Knowles, adapted by Daly), Daly's Theatre, New York.

1893 Viola in *Twelfth Night* (Shakespeare, adapted by Daly), Daly's Theatre, New York, and Daly's Theatre, London.

Julia in *Two Gentlemen of Verona* (Shakespeare, adapted by Daly), Daly's Theatre, New York.

Juliana in *The Honeymoon* (Tobin), Daly's Theatre, New York.

1896 Beatrice in *Much Ado About Nothing* (Shakespeare, adapted by Daly), Daly's Theatre, New York.

1897 Meg Merrilies in *The Witch of Ellangowan*, Daly's Theatre, New York.

Miranda in *The Tempest* (Shakespeare, adapted by Daly), Daly's Theatre, New York.

1898 Roxane in *Cyrano de Bergerac* (Rostand, adapted by Daly), Daly's Theatre, New York.

1898-99 Portia in *The Merchant of Venice* (Shakespeare, adapted by Daly), Daly's Theatre, New York; Lyric Theatre, New York, 1904.

1899 Catherine in *Madame Sans Gene* (Carr), Daly's Theatre, New York.

Lady Garnet in *The Great Ruby* (Raleigh and Hamilton), Daly's Theatre, New York.

1900 Nell Gwynn in *Sweet Nell of Old Drury* (Kester), Buffalo, New York, and Knickerbocker Theatre, New York.

Also acted roles in: *Thoroughbred* (Lumley), Wood's Museum, New York, 1873; *Wives* (Howard, adapted from Molière), Daly's Theatre, New York, 1879; *An Arabian Night in the 19th Century* (Moser, adapted by Daly), Daly's Theatre, New York, 1879; *Divorce* (Daly, adapted from Trollope), Daly's Theatre, New York, 1879; *Needles and Pins* (Rosen, adapted by Daly), Daly's Theatre, New York, 1880; *The Passing Regiment* (Moser and Schönthan, adapted by Daly), Daly's Theatre, New York, 1880; *Quits* (Daly), Daly's Theatre, New York, 1881; *Royal Youth* (Dumas, adapted by Daly), Daly's Theatre, New York, 1881; *Odette* (Sardou, adapted by Daly), Daly's Theatre, New York, 1882; *The Squire* (Pinero), Daly's Theatre, New York, 1882; *She Would and She Would Not* (Cibber, adapted by Daly), Daly's Theatre, New York, 1883; *7-20-8; or, Casting the Boomerang* (Schönthan, adapted by Daly), Daly's Theatre, New York, 1883; *The Country Girl* (Garrick and Wycherley, adapted by Daly), Daly's Theatre, New York, 1884; *Red Letter Nights* (Jacobson, adapted by Daly), Daly's Theatre, New York, 1884; *Dandy Dick* (Pinero), Daly's Theatre, New York, 1887; *The Countess Gueki* (Schönthan and Koppel-Ellfeld, adapted by Daly), Daly's

Ada Rehan

Theatre, New York, 1893; *Love on Crutches* (Daly), Daly's Theatre, New York, 1893.

*

Bibliography

Books:
William Winter, *Ada Rehan: A Study*, New York, 1891.

Articles:
Fola La Follette, "Ada Rehan: Some Personal Recollections", *Bookman*, 43, July 1916.
Sylvia Golden, "The Romance of Ada Rehan", *Theatre*, 53, January 1931.

* * *

As the premiere female comic performer on the US stage during the last two decades of the 19th century, Ada Rehan was commonly identified with those stars who relied on their charismatic personalities to carry them through their roles. For 20 years, she reigned supreme as one of Augustin Daly's four principal actors, along with Anne Hartley Gilbert, John Drew, and James Lewis. Renowned for her beauty and spirited performances, she was also celebrated for her virtue, wholesomeness, witty charm, and magnetic appeal. In addition to such stars as Gilbert, Maude Adams, Viola Allen, and Julia Marlowe, Rehan is generally credited with instilling a sense of middle-class morality on the stage and providing a model of feminine respectability in a profession popularly perceived as decadent.

Rehan was born in Limerick, Ireland, but came to Brooklyn, New York, with her parents at the age of five. Despite the lack of a theatrical tradition in the family, three of Rehan's siblings eventually entered the profession. Their influence was instrumental in guiding Rehan along a similar course. When Kate, the eldest sister, married the actor and playwright Oliver Doud Byron and joined his company, she was followed in short order by a brother (Arthur) and a sister (Harriet). In 1873, just as the company was suffering the effects of a financial panic, Rehan left school to join her sisters and brother on tour. Although she was not initially employed as an actress, Rehan got her start on stage that year in Newark, New Jersey, when the woman playing the part of Clara in Byron's *Across the Continent* was taken ill.

Later that same year Rehan made her debut on the New York stage in a little-known play, *Thoroughbred*, at Wood's Museum. She did not stay long with Byron's company. With the help of her older sister, Rehan won a place with Louisa Lane Drew's troupe at the Arch Street Theatre in Philadelphia later in the season. It was here that she first gained invaluable experience performing with some of the leading stars of the day. She played Ophelia in Edwin Booth's production of *Hamlet* and was cast as Virginia in John McCullough's *Virginius*. It was also as a member of Drew's company that she became known as Ada C. Rehan, the result of a typographical error in a programme. She remained in Philadelphia through the 1875 season and then spent several years performing for stock companies in Louisville, Kentucky, and Albany, New York.

Ever vigilant for new talent, Augustin Daly had been following Rehan's career for several years when he asked her to join his New York company in 1879. She soon became Daly's leading comedienne and remained with the company until his death in 1899. During that time she performed over 200 major roles and firmly established herself as the most popular comic actress in the country. Despite criticism that she lacked the depth and skill necessary for such roles, she played an enormous variety of parts from both the classical and modern repertory. Daly took every opportunity to advance his new star's career. Aware of her limitations as a tragedienne, he provided her with a wide range of comedies, from Shakespeare to Pinero, and was careful to cast her in roles that would complement her natural beauty, vivacious personality, and melodious voice.

That Daly featured Rehan in his first London production in 1884 is evidence of the confidence he had in his leading star. Yet her London debut was modestly received; London audiences were apparently unaccustomed to her distinctive style. It did not take her long, however, to win over the English audiences. By 1890, she was as popular in London as she was in New York. In 1886, determined to expand her repertoire, she performed Mistress Ford in *The Merry Wives of Windsor* and followed this the next year with one of her best known performances, Katharine in *The Taming of the Shrew*. Rehan also excelled in other Shakespearean parts, including Beatrice, Viola, Helena, and Rosalind, which some critics considered to be her finest role. She won additional praise for her portrayal of Lady Teazle in Sheridan's *The School for Scandal* as well as for her work in

Pinero's US premieres of *The Magistrate* in 1885 and *Dandy Dick* in 1887.

When Daly died in 1899, Rehan retired from the stage. The hiatus was shortlived. Within a year she was back performing the lead in *Sweet Nell of Old Drury*. But she retired again in 1901 after her mother's death. Two years later, Otis Skinner persuaded her to join him on a national tour featuring her classic comedies. In 1905, her health in decline, she quit the stage for the last time.

—Peter A. Davis

REID, (Daphne) Kate. Canadian actress. Born in London, England, 4 November 1930. Emigrated to Canada, 1940; educated at Havergal College; University of Toronto; Royal Conservatory of Music, Toronto; trained for the stage at the Herbert Berghof Studio. Married 1) director Michael Salier; 2) Austin Willis in 1953 (divorced 1962); two sons. Professional stage debut, Gravenhurst, Ontario, 1948; actress, Crest Theatre, Toronto, 1949–56; London debut, 1956; appeared at Stratford, Ontario, 1959–62; subsequently acclaimed in Shakespearean and other roles in UK, USA, and Canada; acted at the Stratford, Ontario, Festival, 1965, 1970, 1980, and also worked with the American Shakespeare Company, 1969 and 1974; has also appeared in many film and television roles. Recipient: Tony Award, 1964, 1966. Ph.D, University of York. Office of the Order of Canada, 1976. Died in Stratford, Ontario, 27 March 1993.

Roles

1949–56	Masha in *The Three Sisters* (Chekhov), Crest Theatre, Toronto.
	Lizzie in *The Rainmaker* (Nash), Crest Theatre, Toronto; St Martin's Theatre, London, and British tour, 1956.
1956	Catherine Ashland in *The Stepmother* (Milne), St Martin's Theatre, London.
1959	Celia in *As You Like It* (Shakespeare), Stratford Shakespeare Festival, Stratford, Ontario.
	Emilia in *Othello* (Shakespeare), Stratford Shakespeare Festival, Stratford, Ontario.
1960	Nurse in *Romeo and Juliet* (Shakespeare), Stratford Shakespeare Festival, Stratford, Ontario; American Shakespeare Festival, Stratford, Connecticut, 1974.
	Helena in *A Midsummer Night's Dream* (Shakespeare), Stratford Shakespeare Festival, Stratford, Ontario.
1961	Katherine of Aragon in *Henry VIII* (Shakespeare), Stratford Shakespeare Festival, Stratford, Ontario.
	Jacquenetta in *Love's Labour's Lost* (Shakespeare), Stratford Shakespeare Festival, Stratford, Ontario.
	Elly Cassidy in *The Canvas Barricade*, Stratford Shakespeare Festival, Stratford, Ontario.
1962	Lady Macbeth in *Macbeth* (Shakespeare), Stratford Shakespeare Festival, Stratford, Ontario.

Katherina in *The Taming of the Shrew* (Shakespeare), Stratford Shakespeare Festival, Stratford, Ontario.

Martha in *Who's Afraid of Virginia Woolf?* (Albee), Billy Rose Theatre, New York; Manitoba Theatre Centre, Winnipeg, Manitoba, 1965.

1963 Cassandra in *Troilus and Cressida* (Shakespeare), Stratford Shakespeare Festival, Stratford, Ontario.

Adriana in *The Comedy of Errors* (Shakespeare), Stratford Shakespeare Festival, Stratford, Ontario.

Lisa, Sister Marthe in *Cyrano de Bergerac* (Rostand), Stratford Shakespeare Festival, Stratford, Ontario.

1964 Caitlin Thomas in *Dylan* (Michael), Plymouth Theatre, New York.

1965 Madame Ranevskaya in *The Cherry Orchard* (Chekhov), Stratford Shakespeare Festival, Stratford, Ontario.

Portia in *Julius Caesar* (Shakespeare), Stratford Shakespeare Festival, Stratford, Ontario.

1966 Moyla and Celeste in *Slapstick Tragedy* (T. Williams), Longacre Theatre, New York.

Medical Officer in *The Adventures of Private Turvey*, Confederation Memorial Centre, Charlottetown, Prince Edward Island.

1967 Writer's Wife in *What Do You Really Know about Your Husband?*, Shubert Theatre, New Haven, Connecticut.

Lady Kitty in *The Circle* (Maugham), Shaw Festival, Court House Theatre, Niagra-on-the-Lake, Ontario.

1968 Esther Franz in *The Price* (Miller), Morosco Theatre, New York; Duke of York's Theatre, London, 1969.

1970 Gertrude in *Hamlet* (Shakespeare), Stratford Shakespeare Festival, Stratford, Ontario.

Masha in *The Three Sisters* (Chekhov), Stratford Shakespeare Festival, Stratford, Ontario.

Esther in *The Friends* (Wesker), Stratford Shakespeare Festival, Stratford, Ontario.

1973 Juno in *Juno and the Paycock* (O'Casey), Walnut Street Theatre, Philadelphia, Pennsylvania.

Mary Mercer in *Leaving Home* (French), Vancouver, British Columbia.

1974 Lily in *The Freedom of the City* (Friel), Eisenhower Theatre, Washington, D.C., and Alvin Theatre, New York.

Big Mama in *Cat on a Hot Tin Roof* (T. Williams), American Shakespeare Festival, Stratford, Connecticut, and American National Theatre Academy Playhouse, New York.

1976 Mrs Warren in *Mrs Warren's Profession* (G. B. Shaw), Shaw Festival.

1978 Rummy Mitchens in *Major Barbara* (G. B. Shaw), Shaw Festival.

Gwyneth Price in *I Sent a Letter to My Love*, Long Wharf Theatre, New Haven, Connecticut.

Kate Reid (1966).

Ella Rentheim in *John Gabriel Borkman* (Ibsen), Shaw Festival.

Henny in *Bosoms and Neglect* (Guare), Longacre Theatre, New York; Stratford Shakespeare Festival, Stratford, Ontario, 1980.

1980 Maria in *Twelfth Night* (Shakespeare), Stratford, Ontario.

Fonsia in *The Gin Game*, Stratford, Ontario.

1982 Ida Bolton in *Morning's at Seven* (Osborn), Lyceum Theatre, New York.

1983 Clytemnestra in *The Oresteia* (Aeschylus), National Arts Centre, New York.

1984 Linda Loman in *Death of a Salesman* (Miller), Broadhurst Theatre, New York.

Has also played roles in: *Years Ago* (Gordon), Gravenhurst, Ontario, 1948; *The Apple Cart* (G. B. Shaw), Shaw Festival, 1976; *The Corn is Green* (E. Williams), Alley Theatre, Houston, Texas, 1977.

Films

One Plus One, 1961; *This Property is Condemned*, 1966; *Pigeons*, 1970; *The Andromeda Strain*, 1971; *A Delicate Balance*, 1973; *The Rainbow Boys*, 1973; *Shoot*, 1976; *Equus*, 1977; *Plague*, 1978; *High Point*, 1979; *Death Ship*, 1980; *Double Negative*, 1980; *Atlantic City*, 1981; *Monkey Grip*, 1983; *Heaven Help Us*, 1984; *No Sad Songs*, 1985; *Fire with Fire*, 1986.

Television

The Invincible Mr Disraeli, 1963; *Abe Lincoln in Illinois*, 1964; *The Holy Terror*, 1965; *An Enemy of the People*, 1966; *Neither Are We Enemies*, 1970; *Friendly Persuasion*, 1972; *Whiteoaks of Jalna*, 1972; *Hawkins on Murder*, 1973; *She Cried Murder*, 1973; *Enemies*, 1974; *Death Among Friends*, 1975; *Loose Change*, 1978; *Happy Birthday to Me*, 1981; *Gavilan*, 1982–83; *Dallas*, 1983–86; *The Blood of Others*, 1984; *Death of a Salesman*, 1985; *Christmas Eve*, 1986. Others include: *Nellie McClung*; *Crossbar*; *Robbers, Rooftops and Witches*.

* * *

Kate Reid spent the first ten years of her life in London, the adored daughter of a retired colonel of the Bengal Lancers and his Canadian wife. After her father's death, her mother returned to Canada and settled in Oakville, a small city with an active upper middle class social life of a highly sporting character. Kate attended several boarding schools where, by her own admission, she was an undistinguished student, though "something of a party girl".

At the age of 15 she enrolled in an acting course at the Royal Conservatory of Music and fell under the influence of Robert Gill, the American-trained director of the Hart House Theatre at the University of Toronto. He was impressed by her emotional openness and cast her in a small role in *Crime and Punishment*, then as Nina in *The Seagull*. This volatile performance attracted the attention of local theatre directors and she was immediately swept up into summer stock companies and appeared at the newly formed Crest Theatre, Toronto's first professional repertory, where she first played Masha in *The Three Sisters* as well as Lizzie in *The Rainmaker*, the role which was to establish her reputation in Britain.

Kate Reid's enthusiasm, freshness and daring were in marked contrast to the mannered posturing of many of her contemporaries. She was invited to join the Stratford company in 1959 and although she tried to opt out during rehearsals of *Othello*, she gave an impassioned rendering of the role of Emilia and soon became a protegé of artistic director Michael Langham, who she claims taught her more about acting than anyone else. She played a number of roles at Stratford in the next four years, culminating in a fiery Katharina in *The Taming of the Shrew* and a dignified, heartsore Katherine of Aragon in *Henry VIII*.

It was this performance especially that attracted the enthusiastic support of Canadian critic Nathan Cohen, who encouraged her to think about trying her luck in England and the USA. Her vigorous portrayal of Lizzie in *The Rainmaker* in the West End brought her to the attention of Alec Guinness, who chose her to play Caitlin opposite his Dylan Thomas. Reid's tempestuous delineation of the poet's wife provided a stunningly effective contrast to Guinness's sensitive, cerebral portrayal of the Welsh bard and contributed significantly to the success of this production on Broadway, where Reid had already made her mark playing matinee performances as Martha in Edward Albee's *Who's Afraid of Virginia Woolf?*. It was in this role that she displayed the combination of brashness and vulnerability that was to become the hallmark of her best work.

Kate Reid soon became a favourite of US playwrights, who chose her to play major roles in their new works: Moyla in Tennessee Williams's *Gnadiges Fraulein*, a one-act play that provided half of the double bill *Slapstick Tragedy*, Julia in the film of Albee's *A Delicate Balance*, Esther Franz in Arthur Miller's *The Price*, Big Mama in the first major revival of Williams's *Cat on a Hot Tin Roof* and Henny in John Guare's *Bosoms and Neglect*, which failed on Broadway but won critical praise when it was revived at Stratford, Ontario, in 1980. This catalogue of American anti-heroines was capped by her intense portrayal of Linda Loman, a woman no less driven and disappoined than her husband in the 1984 revival of *Death of a Salesman* opposite Dustin Hoffman. Arthur Miller singled out this production as the ideal version of his most famous work.

In addition to these American portraits, Kate Reid has played many of the troubled, unsatisfied women in modern European drama, from Casey's embattled Juno to Ibsen's embittered Ella Rentheim, from Maugham's ruefully frivolous Lady Kitty to Shaw's hard-headed Mrs Warren. Reid's depictions of Chekhov's moody, tormented women have been especially memorable, above all her gallantly ineffectual Ranevskaya in John Hirsch's 1965 Stratford production of *The Cherry Orchard*. Reid excels in suggesting the unrealised promise and inexpressible pain of the characters she plays. Her women are frank, impulsive, courageous, given to salty humour but often perplexed by their passions and imprisoned in a web of their own sensibilities. As much as any actress working in the North American theatre today she has explored and expressed the wide range of feminine feelings.

—Martin Hunter

REINHARDT, Max. Austrian director and actor-manager. Born Max Goldmann in Baden, near Vienna, 9 September 1873. Educated at schools in Vienna, from 1877. Married 1) actress Else Heims in 1910 (divorced 1935), two sons; 2) actress Helene Thimig in 1935. Began career as an amateur actor, 1890; undertook two years of formal training at the Sulkowsky Theater, Matzleinsdorf, 1890–92; actor, Volkstheater, Rudolfsheim, Vienna, and Pressburg summer theatre, Bratislava, 1892–93; first full contract as actor, Stadttheater, Salzburg, 1893–94; engaged by Otto Brahm at the Deutsches Theater, Berlin, 1894; summer engagements in Dresden, Prague, Vienna, Budapest and elsewhere, 1895–1901; debut as director, 1900; inaugurated Schall und Rauch cabaret (Kleines Theater from 1902) in the Unten den Linden, Berlin, 1901; left Deutsches Theater and became director of the Kleines Theater and the Neues Theater am Schiffbauerdamm, 1903; first use of revolving stage, 1905; opened school of acting at the Deutsches Theater, 1905; bought Deutsches Theater and opened Kammerspiele next door, 1906; summer tours of Germany and Budapest, 1907–08; summer engagements, Künstler Theater, Munich, 1909–11; promoted revival of ancient Greek drama through European tours, 1910–12; film debut and first visits to New York and Paris, 1912; staged festivals of Shakespearean dramas, 1913–14; visiting director, Stockholm and Christiana, 1915; director, Volksbühne, Berlin, 1915–18; director, Kleines Schauspielhaus, Berlin, 1918; opened Grosses

Schauspielhaus, Berlin, 1919; founder, Salzburg Festival, 1920; gave up control of his theatres in Berlin and moved to Vienna, 1920; opened Redoutensaal at the Imperial Palace, Vienna, 1922; toured USA, opened Komödie in the Kurfürstendamm, Berlin, and once more became director of the Deutsches Theater, 1924; opened Salzburg Festspielhaus, 1925; visits to USA, 1926 and 1927–28; director, Berliner Theater, 1928; Max Reinhardt Seminar founded in Schönbrunn, Vienna, 1928; resumed directorship of his Berlin theatres, 1929; British tour, 1932 and 1933; forced to give up his German theatres by the Nazis, 1933; gave up direction of the Theater in der Josefstadt, 1934; worked as Hollywood film director, 1934–35; last Vienna production, 1937; settled in USA, 1937; opened Max Reinhardt Workshop for Stage, Screen and Radio in Hollywood, 1938; became US citizen, 1940. Member: Shakespeare Association (vice-president). Honorary degrees: Frankfurt-am-Main University and Kiel University, 1930. Died in New York, 31 October 1943.

Productions

As actor:

1890   Paul Hofmeister in *Krieg im Frieden* (Moser and Schönthan), Sulkowsky Theater, Matzleinsdorf.

1891   Burleigh in *Maria Stuart* (Schiller), Sulkowsky Theater, Matzleinsdorf; Stadttheater, Salzburg, 1893.

Zigeunerhauptmann in *Preziosa* (Wolff), Sulkowsky Theater, Matzleinsdorf; Volkstheater, Rudolfsheim, Vienna, 1892.

Rabbi Ben Akiba in *Uriel Acosta* (Gutzkow), Sulkowsky Theater, Matzleinsdorf; Volkstheater, Rudolfsheim, Vienna, 1892.

Dorfschulmeister in *Deborah* (Mosenthal), Sulkowsky Theater, Matzleinsdorf; Volkstheater, Rudolfsheim, Vienna, 1892.

Franz Moor in *Die Räuber* (Schiller), Sulkowsky Theater, Matzleinsdorf; Volkstheater, Rudolfsheim, Vienna, 1892; Sommerarena, Pressburg, 1893; Stadttheater, Salzburg, 1894.

Philipp II in *Don Carlos* (Schiller), Sulkowsky Theater, Matzleinsdorf.

1892   Graf Zdenko von Borotin in *Die Ahnfrau* (Grillparzer), Sulkowsky Theater, Matzleinsdorf.

Azur in *Der Verschwender* (Raimund), Sulkowsky Theater, Matzleinsdorf.

Prinz Eugenius in *Gottfried Prehauser* (Focki), Volkstheater, Rudolfsheim, Vienna.

Herzog d'Amboise in *Narziss* (Brachvogel), Volkstheater, Rudolfsheim, Vienna.

Fabricius in *Die Tochter des Herrn Fabricius* (Wilbrandt), Volkstheater, Rudolfsheim, Vienna.

Role in *Ein glücklicher Kerl* (Netsch), Volkstheater, Rudolfsheim, Vienna.

Zigeunerhauptmann and Peppo in *Der Glöckner von Notre-Dame* (Birch-Pfeiffer), Volkstheater, Rudolfsheim, Vienna.

Blau in *Auf falscher Bahn* (Philippi), Volkstheater, Rudolfsheim, Vienna.

1893   Role in *Der Dreibirkenhof* (Weber), Volkstheater, Rudolfsheim, Vienna.

Kanzler Renard in *Wildfeuer* (Halm), Volkstheater, Rudolfsheim, Vienna.

Spiegelberg in *Die Räuber* (Schiller), Volkstheater, Rudolfsheim, Vienna.

Schlosser Berger in *Fabrik und Werkstatt* (Erwin), Volkstheater, Rudolfsheim, Vienna.

Vinzenz Huber in *Schrankenlos* (Saubermann), Volkstheater, Rudolfsheim, Vienna.

Ein Untreuer Ehemann in *Der Privatdetektiv* (Sachs), Volkstheater, Rudolfsheim, Vienna.

Knorr in *Hasemanns Töchter* (L'Arronge), Volkstheater, Rudolfsheim, Vienna.

Volkmar Quarzhirn in *S'Nullerl* (Morré), Volkstheater, Rudolfsheim, Vienna, and Stadttheater, Salzburg.

Merkur in *Orpheus in der Unterwelt* (Crémieux and Offenbach), Volkstheater, Rudolfsheim, Vienna.

Hettore Gonzaga in *Emilia Galotti* (Lessing), Volkstheater, Rudolfsheim, Vienna.

Baron in *Prinzessin Georges* (Dumas fils), Volkstheater, Rudolfsheim, Vienna.

Role in *Die Bräute von Beach Hall* (Weber), Volkstheater, Rudolfsheim, Vienna.

Schneidermeister Sticherl in *Wo ist der Frack?* (Rotter), Sommerarena, Pressburg.

Henry de Symeux in *Francillon* (Dumas fils), Sommerarena, Pressburg.

Dr Schlicht in *An der schönen blauen Donau* (Berg), Sommerarena, Pressburg.

Michel Grund in *Brave Leut' vom Grund* (Anzengruber), Sommerarena, Pressburg.

Hugo Witte in *Zwei glückliche Tage* (Schönthan and Kadelburg), Sommerarena, Pressburg.

Dr Viktor Ebeling in *Die Sklavin* (Fulda), Sommerarena, Pressburg.

Von Nebenstein in *Der Bettelstudent von Wien* (Braun), Sommerarena, Pressburg.

Role in *Das alte Lied* (Philippi), Sommerarena, Pressburg.

Maler in *Gross-Wien* (Wimmer), Sommerarena, Pressburg.

Emil Nachtigall in *Der Mord in der Schlossbergruine* (Manz), Sommerarena, Pressburg.

Reibstein in *Das ist dem Weana sein Schau!* (Mestrozzi), Sommerarena, Pressburg.

König von Dänemark in *Pamperl's Reiseabenteuer* (Zappert), Sommerarena, Pressburg.

Norbert in *Gengen's baden* (Plowitz and Märtens), Sommerarena, Pressburg.

Balthasar Zwirnspinner in *Die zwölf Himmelszeichen* (Wiesberg), Sommerarena, Pressburg.

Thomas Flanagan in *Dir Reise um die Erde in 80 Tagen* (Verne and D'Ennery), Sommerarena, Pressburg.

Bruno von Weggis in *Ein armes Mädel* (Krenn and Lindau), Sommerarena, Pressburg.

Boulang in *Der Regimentsarzt* (Morré), Sommerarena, Pressburg.

Max Reinhardt

Graf Berkentin in *Der letzte Hanswurst* (Focki), Sommerarena, Pressburg.

Hans Prehauser in *Der letzte Hanswurst* (Focki), Sommerarena, Pressburg.

Elia Combe in *Der Silberkönig* (James and Hermann), Sommerarena, Pressburg.

Charles Schwarz in *Aussi möcht' i!* (Rotter), Sommerarena, Pressburg.

Farkas in *Heisses Blut* (Krenn and Lindau), Sommerarena, Pressburg.

Oberfeldherr Berengar in *Der Talisman* (Fulda), Stadttheater, Salzburg; Deutsches Theater, Berlin, 1895.

Grillhofer in *Der G'wissenswurm* (Anzengruber), Stadttheater, Salzburg.

Vaspik in *Lachende Erben* (Horst and Stein), Stadttheater, Salzburg.

Schöller in *Pension Schöller*, Stadttheater, Salzburg.

Ruperto Corticelli in *Gasparone* (Zell, Genée and Millöcker), Stadttheater, Salzburg.

Dr Crusius in *Grossstadtluft* (Blumenthal and Kadelburg), Stadttheater, Salzburg.

Dr Deik in *Fräulein Frau* (Moser and Misch), Stadttheater, Salzburg.

Octavio Piccolomini in *Wallensteins Tod* (Schiller), Stadttheater, Salzburg.

Bachelin in *Der Hüttenbesitzer* (Ohnet), Stadttheater, Salzburg.

Gerlach in *Das zweite Gesicht* (Blumenthal), Stadttheater, Salzburg.

Wurzelsepp in *Der Pfarrer von Kirchfeld* (Anzengruber), Stadttheater, Salzburg.

Ruschke in *Zwei glückliche Tage* (Schönthan and Kadelburg), Stadttheater, Salzburg.

Hermann Gessler in *Wilhelm Tell* (Schiller), Stadttheater, Salzburg.

Baron Oskar von Hecht in *Einer von der Burgmusik* (Krenn and Chiavacci), Stadttheater, Salzburg.

Dr Hagen in *Aus der Gesellschaft* (Bauernfeld), Stadttheater, Salzburg.

Schmock in *Die Journalisten* (Freytag), Stadttheater, Salzburg; Deutsches Volkstheater, Prague, 1896.

Herr von Frondeville in *Der Attaché* (Meilhac), Stadttheater, Salzburg.

Role in *Ein Blitzmädel* (Costa), Stadttheater, Salzburg.

Schwartze in *Heimat* (Sudermann), Stadttheater, Salzburg.

Mozarts Arzt in *Mozart* (Wartenegg), Stadttheater, Salzburg.

Pimeskern in *Die Gigerln von Wien* (Wimmer), Stadttheater, Salzburg.

Thomas Ritz in *Der Fall Clemenceau* (Dumas fils and D'Artois), Stadttheater, Salzburg.

Sir Walter Raleigh in *Graf Essex* (Laube), Stadttheater, Salzburg.

August in *Ein armes Mädel* (Krenn and Lindau), Stadttheater, Salzburg.

Sigmund von Barkos in *Husarenliebe* (Buchbinder), Stadttheater, Salzburg.

Role in *Ein Tasse Tee* (Neumann), Stadttheater, Salzburg.

Merlin in *Barfüsschen* (Schröder), Stadttheater, Salzburg.

1894   Geheimrat Montius in *Das letzte Wort* (Schönthan), Stadttheater, Salzburg.

Mandelbaum in *Prinz Methusalem* (Delacour), Stadttheater, Salzburg.

Lehrer in *Der Herrgottsschnitzer von Ammergau* (Ganghofer and Neuert), Stadttheater, Salzburg.

Redakteur A. Findeisen in *Eine Palastrevolution* (Skowronnek), Stadttheater, Salzburg.

Herold in *Der Zigeunerbaron* (Schnitzer and Strauss), Stadttheater, Salzburg.

Zanga in *Der Traum ein Leben* (Grillparzer), Stadttheater, Salzburg.

Anastasius Zacherer in *Hans im Glück* (Grube and Koppl-Ellfeld), Stadttheater, Salzburg.

Jago in *Othello* (Shakespeare), Stadttheater, Salzburg.

Ale Schmalenbach in *Die Haubenlerche* (Wildenbruch), Stadttheater, Salzburg.

Obersanitätsrat von Düring in *Rosenkranz und Güldenstern* (Klapp), Stadttheater, Salzburg.

Brasset in *Charleys Tante* (Thomas), Stadttheater, Salzburg.

Professor Spitzmüller in *Der Probepfeil* (Blumenthal), Stadttheater, Salzburg.

Bischof Meinwerk von Paderborn in *Der Graf von Hammerstein* (Wilbrandt), Stadttheater, Salzburg.

Redl in *Vor'm Suppenessen* (Morré), Stadttheater, Salzburg.

Dr Puschel in *Der ungläubige Thomas* (Laufs and Jacobi), Stadttheater, Salzburg.

Stadtrat Kiesel in *Wohltätige Frauen* (L'Arronge), Stadttheater, Salzburg.

Role in *Lumpazivagabundus* (Nestroy), Stadttheater, Salzburg.

Senator Andersen in *Der Herr Senator* (Schönthan and Kadelburg), Stadttheater, Salzburg.

Martin Winter in *Das Lieder des Musikanten* (Kneisel), Stadttheater, Salzburg.

Role in *Der Andere* (Lindau), Stadttheater, Salzburg.

Briefträger Klemm in *Lolo's Vater* (L'Arronge), Stadttheater, Salzburg.

Lord Hamilton Tomkins in *Niobe* (Blumenthal), Stadttheater, Salzburg.

Mundschenk Theres in *Esther* (Grillparzer), Deutsches Theater, Berlin.

Bürger Benedict in *Der Talisman* (Fulda), Deutsches Theater, Berlin.

Ferrante in *Der Talisman* (Fulda), Deutsches Theater, Berlin.

Johann Duncker in *Das vierte Gebot e Der Doppelselbstmord* (Anzengruber), Deutsches Theater, Berlin.

Pastor Kittelhaus in *Die Weber* (Hauptmann), Deutsches Theater, Berlin.

Tubal in *Der Kaufmann von Venedig* (Shakespeare), Deutsches Theater, Berlin.

Erster Schauspieler in *Hamlet* (Shakespeare), Deutsches Theater, Berlin.

Bureaudiener Strack in *Die Katakomben* (Davis), Deutsches Theater, Berlin.

1895   Sigrid in *Weh dem der lügt!* (Grillparzer), Deutsches Theater, Berlin; Deutsches Theater, Berlin, 1898.

Bürgermeister in *Der Mann im Schatten* (Reuling), Deutsches Theater, Berlin.

Poltner in *Der G'wissenswurm* (Anzengruber), Deutsches Theater, Berlin.

Kommerzienrat Dessoir in *Das Lumpengesindel* (Wolzogen), Deutsches Theater, Berlin, and Deutsches Volkstheater, Prague; Raimundtheater, Vienna, and Somossy Theater, Budapest, 1899; Deutsches Theater, Berlin, 1901.

Amandus in *Jugend* (Halbe), Deutsches Volkstheater, Prague; Deutsches Theater, Berlin, 1896; Deutsches Volkstheater, Prague, 1896 and 1897; Somossy Theater, Budapest, 1900.

Tischler Engstrand in *Gespenster* (Ibsen), Deutsches Volkstheater, Prague; revived there, 1896; Neues Deutsches Theater, Prague, 1898; Raimundtheater, Vienna, 1899; Deutsches Theater, Berlin, and Somossy Theater, Budapest, 1900; Vigszinház, Budapest, 1901; Kammerspiele, Berlin, 1906; Künstler-Theater, Munich, 1909.

Don Ramond de Taris in *Don Carlos* (Schiller), Deutsches Theater, Berlin.

Rittmeister von der Goltz in *Prinz Friedrich von Homburg* (Kleist), Deutsches Theater, Berlin.

Vincentio in *Der Widerspenstigen Zähmung* (Shakespeare), Deutsches Theater, Berlin.

Bruder Johannes in *Romeo und Julia* (Shakespeare), Deutsches Theater, Berlin.

Agrippa in *Der Meister von Palmyra* (Wilbrandt), Deutsches Theater, Berlin.

Rechtsanwalt Backhusen in *Robinsons Eiland* (Fulda), Deutsches Theater, Berlin.

Bruder Lorenzo in *Romeo und Julia* (Shakespeare), Deutsches Theater, Berlin.

1896   Rektor Besenmayer in *Florian Geyer* (Hauptmann), Deutsches Theater, Berlin.

Graf Capulet in *Romeo und Julia* (Shakespeare), Deutsches Theater, Berlin.

Gerichtsrat Walter in *Der zerbrochne Krug* (Kleist), Deutsches Theater, Berlin.

Graf von Westmoreland in *König Heinrich IV* (Shakespeare), Deutsches Theater, Berlin.

Sir William Catesby in *König Richard III* (Shakespeare), Deutsches Theater, Berlin.

Selig in *Zu Hause* (Hirschfeld), Deutsches Theater, Berlin.

Tischlergesell in *Lumpazivagabundus* (Nestroy), Deutsches Theater, Berlin.

Zweiter Geselle bei Zwirn in *Lumpazivagabundus* (Nestroy), Deutsches Theater, Berlin.

Prokurist Krapp in *Die Stützen des Gesellschaft* (Ibsen), Deutsches Theater, Berlin.

Fassel in *Lumpazivagabundus* (Nestroy), Deutsches Theater, Berlin.

Herennianos in *Der Meister von Palmyra* (Wilbrandt), Deutsches Theater, Berlin; revived there, 1899.

Ludwig Frey in *Die Mütter* (Hirschfeld), Deutsches Volkstheater, Prague; revived there, 1897; Neues Deutsches Theater, Prague, 1898.

Adolf in *Gläubiger* (Strindberg), Deutsches Volkstheater, Prague.

Fritz Scholz in *Das Friedensfest* (Hauptmann), Deutsches Volkstheater, Prague; Raimundtheater, Vienna, Somossy Theater, Budapest, and Deutsches Theater, Berlin, 1899; Kammerspiele, Berlin, 1906; Vigszinház, Budapest, 1907.

Pfarrer Hoppe in *Jugend* (Halbe), Deutsches Theater, Berlin; Vigszinház, Budapest, and Deutsches Theater, Prague, 1901; Vigszinház, Budapest, 1902.

Cinna in *Julius Cäsar* (Shakespeare), Deutsches Theater, Berlin.

Eurich in *Morituri* (Sudermann), Deutsches Theater, Berlin.

Enderle in *Freiwild* (Schnitzler), Deutsches Theater, Berlin.

Schulmeister in *Die versunkene Glocke* (Hauptmann), Deutsches Theater, Berlin.

1897   Dünnhaariger Herr in *Die Wildente* (Ibsen), Deutsches Theater, Berlin.

Wilhelm Foldal in *John Gabriel Borkmann* (Ibsen), Deutsches Theater, Berlin.

Escalus in *Romeo und Julia* (Shakespeare), Deutsches Theater, Berlin.

Duban in *Der Sohn des Kalifen* (Fulda), Deutsches Theater, Berlin.

Manrique in *Die Jüdin von Toledo* (Grillparzer), Deutsches Theater, Berlin.

Pastor Collin in *Einsame Menschen* (Hauptmann), Deutsches Theater, Berlin.

Wirt in *Das Ewig-Männliche* (Braun and Suppé), Deutsches Theater, Berlin.

Räuber Grimm in *Die Räuber* (Schiller), Deutsches Theater, Berlin.

Ernst Haller in *Gretes Glück* (Mariot), Deutsches Volkstheater, Prague; Neues Deutsches Theater, Prague, 1898.

Vetter in *Die Lore* (Hartleben), Deutsches Volkstheater, Prague.

Der alte Ekdal in *Die Wildente* (Ibsen), Deutsches Volkstheater, Prague; Deutsches Theater, Berlin, 1901; Vigszinház, Budapest, 1902.

Akim in *Die Macht der Finsternis* (Tolstoy), Deutsches Volkstheater, Prague; Raimundtheater, Vienna, and Somossy Theater, Budapest, 1899; Deutsches Theater, Berlin, 1900; Deutsches Theater, Prague, 1901.

Brack in *Hedda Gabler* (Ibsen), Deutsches Volkstheater, Prague.

Girding in *Im Frühfrost* (Rilke), Deutsches Volkstheater, Prague.

Wagner in *Faust* (Goethe), Deutsches Theater, Berlin.

Dr Bodenstein in *Mutter Erde* (Halbe), Deutsches Theater, Berlin.

Herr Sommer in *Agnes Jordan* (Hirschfeld), Deutsches Theater, Berlin.

Graf Otto von der Flühe in *Das Käthchen von Heilbronn* (Kleist), Deutsches Theater, Berlin.

1898   Jünger Amarja in *Johannes* (Sudermann), Deutsches Theater, Berlin.

Schiffer Wulkow in *Der Biberpelz* (Hauptmann), Deutsches Theater, Berlin; Vigszinház, Budapest, and Deutsches Theater, Prague, 1901.

Klosterbruder in *Nathan der Weise* (Lessing), Deutsches Theater, Berlin.

Pietro Caruso in *Pietro Caruso* (Bracco), Neues Deutsches Theater, Prague.

Dr Schimmelpfennig in *Vor Sonnenaufgang* (Hauptmann), Neues Deutsches Theater, Prague.

Lyngstrand in *Die Frau vom Meer* (Ibsen), Neues Deutsches Theater, Prague.

Bernard Voss in *Der Compagnon* (L'Arronge), Neues Deutsches Theater, Prague.

Bellecose in *Cyrano de Bergerac* (Rostand), Deutsches Theater, Berlin.

Arzt in *Das Vermächtnis* (Schnitzler), Deutsches Theater, Berlin.

Hauffe in *Fuhrmann Henschel* (Hauptmann), Deutsches Theater, Berlin; Vigszinház, Budapest, 1901; Vigszinház, Budapest, 1902.

1899   Kanzler in *Die drei Reiherfedern* (Sudermann), Deutsches Theater, Berlin.

Bolle in *Pauline* (Hirschfeld), Deutsches Theater, Berlin.

Schalnassar in *Die Hochzeit der Sobeide* (Hofmannsthal), Deutsches Theater, Berlin.

Franz in *Mutterherz* (Bacano), Deutsches Theater, Berlin.

Grasset in *Der grüne Kakadu* (Schnitzler), Deutsches Theater, Berlin; revived there, 1900 and 1902.

Diomed in *Der Talisman* (Fulda), Deutsches Theater, Berlin.

Vockerat in *Einsame Menschen* (Hauptmann), Deutsches Theater, Berlin.

Oberst Kottwitz in *Prinz Friedrich von Homburg* (Kleist), Deutsches Theater, Berlin.

Maximilian in *Die Räuber* (Schiller), Deutsches Theater, Berlin.

Feist in *College Crampton* (Hauptmann), Deutsches Theater, Berlin.

Peter Mortensgaard in *Rosmersholm* (Ibsen), Deutsches Theater, Berlin.

Müller-Gautsch in *Ein Gastspiel* (Wolzogen and Olden), Deutsches Theater, Berlin.

Oberlehrer Störmer in *Der Probekandidat* (Dreyer), Deutsches Theater, Berlin; Somossy Theater, Budapest, 1900; Vigszinház, Budapest, 1901.

Bürgermeister in *Der Vielgeprüfte* (Meyer-Förster), Deutsches Theater, Berlin.

1900   Huntsman in *Schluck und Jau* (Hauptmann), Deutsches Theater, Berlin.

Korbflechter Grenz in *Das tausendjährige Reich* (Halbe), Deutsches Theater, Berlin.

Der alte Baumert in *Die Weber* (Hauptmann), Somossy Theater, Budapest.

König Arkel in *Pelleas und Melisande* (Maeterlinck), Theater in der Josefstadt, Vienna.

Der Alte in *Interieur* (Maeterlinck), Theater in der Josefstadt, Vienna.

Professor Dühring in *Der Kammersänger* (Wedekind), Theater in der Josefstadt, Vienna.

Dorfrichter Adam in *Der zerbrochne Krug* (Kleist), Theater in der Josefstadt, Vienna.

Carsten Jerven in *An des Reiches Pforten* (Hamsun), Theater in der Josefstadt, Vienna.

Probst in *Brand* (Ibsen), Theater in der Josefstadt, Vienna.

Mephistopheles in *Faust* (Goethe), Deutsches Theater, Berlin.

Kommerzienrat Schmitz in *Rosenmontag* (Hartleben), Deutsches Theater, Berlin.

Michael Kramer in *Michael Kramer* (Hauptmann), Deutsches Theater, Berlin; Deutsches Theater, Prague, 1901.

1901   Stefan Matta in *Der Tag* (Bacano), Deutsches Theater, Berlin.

Leopold Goldner in *Der junge Goldner* (Hirschfeld), Deutsches Theater, Berlin.

Edmund Henckelberg in *Wiederfinden* (Rittner), Deutsches Theater, Berlin.

Pfarrer in *Die versunkene Glocke* (Hauptmann), Vigszinház, Budapest.

Aslaksen in *Ein Volksfeind* (Ibsen), Deutsches Theater, Berlin, and Deutsches Theater, Prague.

Role in *Prolog* (Kayssler), Deutsches Theater, Berlin.

Fremdenführer in *Ein Böhmischer Fremdenführer* (Reinhardt), Deutsches Theater, Berlin, Künstlerhaus, Berlin, and Carltheater, Vienna.

Role in *Kasperltheater* (Vallentin), Künstlerhaus, Berlin.

Role in *Aus der Gemäldegalerie* (Kayssler and Zickel), Carltheater, Vienna.

König in *Don Carlos oder Der Infant von Spanien oder Der unnatürliche Sohn* (Reinhardt, Kayssler and Zickel), Carltheater, Vienna.

Philipp Spanke in *Karle*, Carltheater, Vienna.

Der alte König in *Carleas und Elisande*, Carltheater, Vienna.

Der alte Pierrot in *Carlequin und Carlombine oder l'Ami*, Carltheater, Vienna.

Dichter in *Das Regiekollegium* (Reinhardt), Carltheater, Vienna.

Dramaturg in *Diarrhoesteia des Persiflegeles* (Reinhardt), Carltheater, Vienna.

Ansorge in *Die Weber* (Kayssler), Carltheater, Vienna.

König in *Kasperltheater* (Vallentin), Carltheater, Vienna.

Pharisäer Amaisa in *Johannes* (Sudermann), Deutsches Theater, Berlin.

Günther in *Nora* (Ibsen), Deutsches Theater, Berlin.

Cobus in *Die Hoffnung* (Heijermans), Deutsches Theater, Berlin, and Vigszinház, Budapest.

Schuhmachermeister Fielitz in *Der rote Hahn* (Hauptmann), Deutsches Theater, Berlin.

1902   Anton Hausdorfer in *Lebendige Stunden* (Schnitzler), Deutsches Theater, Berlin, and Vigszinház, Budapest.

Meixner in *Es lebe das Leben* (Sudermann), Deutsches Theater, Berlin.

Petersen in *Ecclesia triumphans* (Dreyer), Deutsches Theater, Berlin.

Hahngikl in *Der Weg zum Licht* (Hirschfeld), Deutsches Theater, Berlin.

Hans Weiring in *Liebelei* (Schnitzler), Deutsches Theater, Berlin.

Karl Rademacher in *Lebendige Stunden* (Schnitzler), Vigszinház, Budapest.

Dr Balduin in *Der Probekandidate* (Dreyer), Vigszinház, Budapest.

Marco Colonna in *Monna Vanna* (Maeterlinck), Deutsches Theater, Berlin.

Vitus Lechner in *D'Mali* (Bernstein), Deutsches Theater, Berlin.

Erster Jude in *Salome* (Wilde), Kleines Theater, Berlin.

Pater Benedikt in *Der arme Heinrich* (Hauptmann), Deutsches Theater, Berlin.

1903   Pilger Luka in *Nachtasyl* (Gorky), Kleines Theater, Berlin, Neues Theater, Berlin, Deutsches Landestheater, Prague, Deutsches Volkstheater, Vienna, and Magyar Szinház, Budapest; Vigszinház, Budapest, 1904; Theater an der Wien, Vienna, and Deutsches Theater, Berlin, 1905.

Alter Brenninger in *Die Kreuzelschreiber* (Anzengruber), Neues Theater, Berlin.

König Arkel in *Pelleas und Melisande* (Maeterlinck), Neues Theater, Berlin, and Deutsches Volkstheater, Vienna.

1904   Just in *Minna von Barnhelm* (Lessing), Neues Theater, Berlin; Vigszinház, Budapest, 1904; Theater an der Wien, Vienna, 1905.

Napoleon in *Der Schlachtenlenker* (G. B. Shaw), Neues Theater, Berlin.

Der alte Vater in *Mutter Landstrasse* (Schmidtbonn), Kleines Theater, Berlin.

Miller in *Kabale und Liebe* (Schiller), Neues Theater, Berlin; Vigszinház, Budapest, 1904; Deutsches Theater, Berlin, 1905.

Bischof Arnesson in *Die Kronprätendenten* (Ibsen), Neues Theater, Berlin.

Abel in *Die Morgenröte* (Ruederer), Neues Theater, Berlin.

Der rote Itzig in *Der Graf von Charolais* (Beer-Hofmann), Neues Theater, Berlin; Theater an der Wien, Vienna, 1905; Deutsches Theater, Berlin, 1906.

1905   Theobald Friedeborn in *Das Käthchen von Heilbronn* (Kleist), Deutsches Theater, Berlin.

1911   Teiresias in *König Ödipus* (Sophocles), Zirkus Busch, Vienna.

1924   Kammerdiener in *Kabale und Liebe* (Schiller), Theater in der Josefstadt, Vienna.

As director:

1903   *Pelleas und Melisande* (Maeterlinck), Neues Theater, Berlin, and Volkstheater, Vienna.

Salome (Wilde), Neues Theater, Berlin; Vigszinház, Budapest, 1908.

Elektra (Hofmannsthal), Kleines Theater, Berlin, and Vigszinház, Budapest; Theater an der Wien, Vienna, 1905.

1904   *Minna von Barnhelm* (Lessing), Neues Theater, Berlin, and Vigszinház, Budapest; Theater an der Wien, Vienna, 1905; Künstler-Theater, Munich, 1910; Kungliga Teatern, Stockholm, National-Theatret, Oslo, Dutch tour, and Vigszinház, Budapest, 1915; Deutsches Theater, Berlin, 1916; Swedish tour, 1917.

Schwester Beatrix (Maeterlinck), Neues Theater, Berlin.

Kabale und Liebe (Schiller), Neues Theater, Berlin, and Vigszinház, Budapest; Austellungstheater, Frankfurt, 1909; Deutsches Theater, Berlin, 1916; Stadttheater, Zurich, 1917; Scandinavian tour, 1920; Stadttheater, Zurich, 1923; Theater in der Josefstadt, Vienna, 1924; Salzburger Festspiele, Salzburg, 1927; Cosmopolitan Theatre, New York, 1928; Residenz-Theater, Munich, 1929; Salzburg Festspiele, Salzburg, 1930; Deutsches Theater, 1931; Schauspielhaus, Zurich, and Rome, 1932.

Einen Jux will er sich machen (Nestroy), Neues Theater, Berlin.

Die Morgenröte (Ruederer), Neues Theater, Berlin.

Der Graf von Charolais (Beer-Hofmann), Neues Theater, Berlin; Theater an der Wien, Vienna, 1905.

1905   *Ein Sommernachtstraum* (Shakespeare), Neues Theater, Berlin, and Theater an der Wien, Vienna; Deutsches Theater, Prague, 1906; Vigszinház, Budapest, 1908; Künstler-Theater, Munich, 1909; Deutsches Theater, Berlin, 1913; Kungliga Teatern, Stockholm, 1915; Stadttheater, Zurich, 1917; Grosses Schauspielhaus, Berlin, 1921; Theater in der Josefstadt, Vienna, 1925; Salzburger Festspiele, Salzburg, and Century Theatre, New York, 1927; Deutsches Theater, Berlin, 1930; Schloss and Park Klessheim, Salzburg, 1932; Boboli Gardens, Florence, and Southpark, Headington, Oxford, 1933; Hollywood Bowl, Los Angeles, and US tour, 1934–35.

Sanna (Bahr), Kleines Theater, Berlin, and Theater an der Wien, Vienna.

Elektra (Hofmannsthal), Theater an der Wien, Vienna.

Das Käthchen von Heilbronn (Kleist), Deutsches Theater, Berlin.

Der Kaufmann von Venedig (Shakespeare), Deutsches Theater, Berlin; Deutsches Theater, Prague, 1906; Vigszinház, Budapest, 1908; Künstler-Theater, Munich, and Austellungstheater, Frankfurt, 1909; Theater an der Wien, Vienna, 1910; Deutsches Theater, Berlin, 1913; Scandinavian tour, 1920; Grosses Schauspielhaus, Berlin, 1921; Theater in der Josefstadt, Vienna, 1924; Campo di San Trovaso, Venice, 1934.

1906 *Ödipus und die Sphinx* (Hofmannsthal), Deutsches Theater, Berlin.

Die Mitschuldigen (Goethe), Deutsches Theater, Berlin; revived there, 1915.

Tartüff (Molière), Deutsches Theater, Berlin.

Orpheus in der Unterwelt (Crémieux and Offenbach), Neues Theater, Berlin; Musikfesthalle, Berlin, 1911; Casino Teatret, Copenhagen, and Grosses Schauspielhaus, Berlin, 1921; Kungliga Teatern, Stockholm, 1922; Kungliga Teatern, Stockholm, 1931.

Das Wintermärchen (Shakespeare), Deutsches Theater, Berlin.

Gespenster (Ibsen), Kammerspiele, Berlin; Künstler-Theater, Munich, and Austellungstheater, Frankfurt, 1909; Vigszinház, Budapest, 1910 and 1914; Dutch tour, 1915; Deutsches Theater, Berlin, 1920.

Frühlings Erwachen (Wedekind), Kammerspiele, Berlin; Vigszinház, Budapest, and Theater an der Wien, Vienna, 1907; Vigszinház, Budapest, 1908 and 1909; Austellungstheater, Frankfurt, 1909; Vigszinház, Budapest, 1913; Kleines Schauspielhaus, Berlin, 1918.

1907 *Das Friedensfest* (Hauptmann), Kammerspiele, Berlin, and Vigszinház, Budapest.

Romeo und Julia (Shakespeare), Deutsches Theater, Berlin; revived there, 1914; Berliner Theater, Berlin, 1928.

Aglavaine und Selysette (Maeterlinck), Kammerspiele, Berlin.

Prinz Friedrich von Homburg (Kleist), Deutsches Theater, Berlin; revived there, 1932.

Was ihr wolt (Shakespeare), Deutsches Theater, Berlin; Vigszinház, Budapest, Künstler-Theater, Munich, and Austellungstheater, Frankfurt, 1909; Theater an der Wien, Vienna, 1910; Deutsches Theater, Berlin, 1914; Kungliga Teatern, Stockholm, 1915; Swiss tour and Volksbühne, Berlin, 1917; Heckentheater im Mirabellgarten, Salzburg, 1930; Gartentheater von Schloss Leopoldskron, and Theater in der Josefstadt, Vienna, 1931.

1908 *Die Räuber* (Schiller), Deutsches Theater, Berlin, and Vigszinház, Budapest; Künstler-Theater, Munich, and Austellungstheater, Frankfurt, 1909; Theater an der Wien, Vienna, 1910; Volksbühne, Berlin, and Kungliga Teatern, Stockholm, 1915; Salzburger Festspiele, Salzburg, 1928.

Lysistrata (Aristophanes), Kammerspiele, Berlin; Vigszinház, Budapest, Künstler-Theater, Munich, and Austellungstheater, Frankfurt, 1909; Theater an der Wien, Vienna, 1910; Grosses Schauspielhaus, Berlin, 1920.

Der Tod und der Tod (Hofmannsthal), Kammerspiele, Berlin.

König Lear (Shakespeare), Deutsches Theater, Berlin; Theater in der Josefstadt, Vienna, 1925.

Clavigo (Goethe), Kammerspiele, Berlin; Kleines Schauspielhaus, Berlin, 1918; Theater im Redoutensaal der Hofburg, Vienna, 1922.

Revolution in Křhwinkel (Nestroy), Deutsches Theater, Berlin; Vigszinház, Budapest, Künstler-Theater, Munich, and Austellungstheater, Frankfurt, 1909.

1909 *Die Lehrerin* (Brody), Deutsches Theater, Berlin, and Vigszinház, Budapest.

Faust (Goethe), Deutsches Theater, Berlin, Vigszinház, Budapest, and Künstler-Theater, Munich, and Austellungstheater, Frankfurt; Deutsches Theater, Berlin, 1911; Kungliga Teatern, Stockholm, 1915; Salzburger Festspiele, Salzburg, and Theater in der Josefstadt, Vienna, 1933; Salzburger Festspiele, Salzburg, 1934, 1935, 1936, 1937; Pilgrimage Outdoor Theatre, Los Angeles, and Civic Auditorium, San Francisco, 1938.

Wolkenkuckucksheim (Ruederer), Kammerspiele, Berlin.

Hamlet (Shakespeare), Vigszinház, Budapest, Künstler-Theater, Munich, and Deutsches Theater, 1909; Theater an der Wien, Vienna, 1910; Deutsches Theater, Berlin, 1913; Grosses Schauspielhaus, Berlin, 1920.

Die Braut von Messina (Schiller), Künstler-Theater, Munich; Deutsches Theater, Berlin, 1910.

Judith (Hebbel), Künstler-Theater, Munich; Deutsches Theater, Berlin, Vigszinház, Budapest, and Theater an der Wien, Vienna, 1910; Deutsches Theater, Berlin, 1915.

Hanneles Himmelfahrt (Hauptmann), Künstler- Theater, Munich; Volksbühne, Berlin, 1918.

Medea (Grillparzer), Austellungstheater, Frankfurt.

Don Carlos (Schiller), Deutsches Theater, Berlin; revived there, 1917.

Der Widerspenstigen Zähmung (Shakespeare), Deutsches Theater, Berlin; Vigszinház, Budapest, 1910.

1910 *Cristinas Heimreise* (Hofmannsthal), Deutsches Theater, Berlin, Vigszinház, Budapest, Theater an der Wien, Vienna, and Künstler-Theater, Munich.

Sumurun (Freksa), Kammerspiele, Berlin, and Künstler-Theater, Munich; Coliseum Theatre, London, Vigszinház, Budapest, and Coliseum Theatre, London, 1911; Casino Theatre, New York, Lyric Theatre, New York, and Théâtre du Vaudeville, Paris, 1912; Lustspieltheater, Vienna, 1913.

Gyges und sein Ring (Hebbel), Künstler-Theater, Munich; Vigszinház, Budapest, 1912.

Komödie der Irrungen (Shakespeare), Künstler-Theater, Munich, and Künstler-Theater, Munich; Vigszinház, Budapest, 1911.

Heirat wider Willen (Molière), Künstler-Theater, Munich; Vigszinház, Budapest, 1911.

König Ödipus (Sophocles), Musikfesthalle, Munich, and Zirkus Schumann, Berlin; European tour, 1911–12; Royal Opera House, Covent Garden, London, 1936.

Der verwundete Vogel (Capus), Kammerspiele, Berlin; Vigszinház, Budapest, 1911.

Othello (Shakespeare), Deutsches Theater, Berlin; Kungliga Teatern, Stockholm, 1917.

Der böse Geist Lumpazivagabundus (Nestroy), Deutsches Theater, Berlin.

1911   *Der Rosenkavalier* (Hofmannsthal and Strauss), Königliches Opernhaus, Dresden.

Bankban (Katona), Vigszinház, Budapest, and Deutsches Theater, Berlin.

Die schöne Helena (Meilhac, Halévy and Offenbach), Künstler-Theater, Berlin, and Theater in der Josefstadt, Vienna; Theater des Westens, 1912; Theater am Kurfürstendamm, Berlin, and Opera House, Manchester, 1931; Volksoper, Vienna, 1932; Alvin Theatre, New York, 1944.

Themidore (Steffan), Künstler-Theater, Berlin.

Die Orestie (Aeschylus), Musikfesthalle, Berlin; Swiss tour, 1917; Grosses Schauspielhaus, Berlin, 1919.

Turandot (Gozzi), Deutsches Theater, Berlin; Vigszinház, Budapest, 1912; Salzburger Festspiele, Salzburg, 1926.

Jedermann (Hofmannsthal), Zirkus Schumann, Berlin; European tour, 1912; Vigszinház, Budapest, 1913; Salzburger Festspiele, Salzburg, and Grosses Schauspielhaus, Berlin, 1920; Salzburger Festspiele, Salzburg, 1921 and 1926; Stadttheater, Basle, 1926; Salzburger Festspiele, Salzburg, and Century Theatre, New York, 1927; Deutsches Theater, Berlin, and Westfalenhalle, Dortmund, 1928; Salzburger Festspiele, Salzburg, and Deutsches Volkstheater, Vienna, 1929; Salzburg Festspiele, Salzburg, 1930, 1931, 1932, 1933, 1934, 1935, 1936, 1937.

Offiziere (Unruh), Deutsches Theater, Berlin.

Das Mirakel (Vollmoeller and Humperdinck), Olympia Hall, London; Theater in der Rotunde, Vienna, 1912; Neues Deutsches Theater, Prague, and German tour, 1913–14; Kungliga Teatern, Stockholm, 1917; Century Theatre, New York, and US tour, 1924; Salzburger Festspiele, Salzburg, 1925; Westfalenhalle, Dortmund, Városi Szinház, Budapest, Divadlo Varieté, Prague, and Zirkus Renz, Vienna, 1927; Lyceum Theatre, London, 1932.

1912   *Viel Lärm um nichts* (Shakespeare), Deutsches Theater, Berlin.

George Dandin (Molière), Deutsches Theater, Berlin.

Totentanz (Strindberg), Deutsches Theater, Berlin; Vigszinház, Budapest, 1913; Kungliga Teatern, Stockholm, National-Theatret, Oslo, Grosses Schauspielhaus, Rotterdam, and Vigszinház, Budapest, 1916; Swiss tour, 1917; Scandinavian tour, 1920.

Heinrich IV (Shakespeare), Deutsches Theater, Berlin.

Ariadne auf Naxos (Hofmannsthal and Strauss), Königliches Hoftheater, Stuttgart.

Eine venetianische Nacht (Vollmoeller), Palace Theatre, London; Kammerspiele, Berlin, 1913.

Der blaue Vogel (Maeterlinck), Deutsches Theater, Berlin; Vigszinház, Budapest, 1913.

1913   *Der lebende Leichnam* (Tolstoy), Deutsches Theater, Berlin, and Vigszinház, Budapest; Stadttheater, Basle, 1926; Cosmopolitan Theatre, New York, Berliner Theater, Berlin, and Theater in der Josefstadt, Vienna, 1928; Residenz-Theater, Munich, 1929.

Bürger Schippel (Sternheim), Kammerspiele, Berlin; Vigszinház, Budapest, 1914.

Festspiel in deutschen Reimen (Hauptmann), Jahrhunderthalle, Breslau.

Torquato Tasso (Goethe), Deutsches Theater, Berlin.

Der verlorene Sohn (Schmidtbonn), Kammerspiele, Berlin; Zirkus Busch, Hamburg, and Vigszinház, Budapest, 1914.

Emilia Galotti (Lessing), Deutsches Theater, Berlin.

Wetterleuchten (Strindberg), Kammerspiele, Berlin; Vigszinház, Budapest, 1914; Scandinavian tour, 1920.

1914   *König Lear* (Shakespeare), Deutsches Theater, Berlin.

Der Snob (Sternheim), Kammerspiele, Berlin, and Vigszinház, Budapest.

Vom Teufel geholt (Hamsun), Kammerspiele, Berlin; Komödie, Berlin, 1929.

Die gelbe Jacke (Cochrane), Kammerspiele, Berlin.

Scheiterhaufen (Strindberg), Deutsches Theater, Berlin, and Vigszinház, Budapest; Scandinavian tour, 1920.

Ein szenischer Prolog (Schmidtbonn), Deutsches Theater, Berlin.

Wallensteins Lager (Schiller), Deutsches Theater, Berlin.

Die Piccolomini (Schiller), Deutsches Theater, Berlin.

Die deutschen Kleinstädter (Kotzebue), Kammerspiele, Berlin; Vigszinház, Budapest, 1916; Swedish and Swiss tours, 1917.

Wallensteins Tod (Schiller), Deutsches Theater, Berlin.

1915   *Rappelkopf* (Raimund), Deutsches Theater, Berlin.

Schluck und Jau (Hauptmann), Deutsches Theater, Berlin.

Die Weibsteufel (Schönherr), Kammerspiele, Berlin.

Das Jahrmarktsfest zu Plundersweilern (Goethe), Deutsches Theater, Berlin.

Der Sturm (Shakespeare), Volksbühne, Berlin.

Maria Stuart (Schiller), Deutsches Theater, Berlin; Theater in der Josefstadt, Vienna, Neues Deutsches Theater, Prague, and Dutch tour, 1934.

Der Stern von Bethlehem (Falckenberg), Deutsches Theater, Berlin.

1916   *Der Biberpelz* (Hauptmann), Deutsches Theater, Berlin, Dutch tour, and Vigszinház, Budapest.

Macbeth (Shakespeare), Deutsches Theater, Berlin, and Grosses Schauspielhaus, Rotterdam.

Der eingebildete Kranke (Molière), Kammerspiele, Berlin; Schloss Leopoldskron, Salzburg, and Salzburger Festspiele, Salzburg, 1923; Komödie, Berlin, 1924.

Das leibende Weib (Klinger), Kammerspiele, Berlin.

Der grüne Flöte (Hofmannsthal, Nilson and Mozart), Deutsches Theater, Berlin; Salzburger Festspiele, Salzburg, 1925.

Die Lästigen (Molière), Deutsches Theater, Berlin.

Hedda Gabler (Ibsen), Kammerspiele, Berlin.

Die Soldaten (Lenz), Deutsches Theater, Berlin.

Gespenstersonate (Strindberg), Kammerspiele, Berlin; Swedish and Swiss tours, 1917; Scandinavian tour, 1920.

Dantons Tod (Büchner), Deutsches Theater, Berlin; Swiss tour, 1917; Grosses Schauspielhaus, Berlin, 1921; Century Theatre, New York, 1927; Arkadenhof des Rathauses, Vienna, and Prinzregententheater, Munich, 1929.

Figaros Hochzeit oder Der tolle Tag (Beaumarchais), Deutsches Theater, Berlin.

1917   *Lillebil's Hochzeitsreise* (Hofmannsthal, Nilson and Bizet), Wintergarten, Berlin.

John Gabriel Borkman (Ibsen), Deutsches Theater, Berlin.

Der Geizige (Molière), Deutsches Theater, Berlin.

Volk in Not (Schönherr), Volksbühne, Berlin.

Prima Ballerina (Hofmannsthal and Offenbach), Lorensbergsteatern, Göteborg.

Winterballade (Hauptmann), Deutsches Theater, Berlin.

Der Bettler (Sorge), Deutsches Theater, Berlin.

1918   *Die Hermannsschlacht* (Kleist), Volksbühne, Berlin.

Die Macht der Finsternis (Tolstoy), Deutsches Theater, Berlin.

Seeschlacht (Goering), Deutsches Theater, Berlin.

Die Bürger als Edelmann (Molière), Deutsches Theater, Berlin.

Und das Licht scheinet in her Finsternis (Tolstoy), Deutsches Theater, Berlin.

1919   *Wie es euch gefällt* (Shakespeare), Deutsches Theater, Berlin.

Jaákobs Traum (Beer-Hofmann), Deutsches Theater, Berlin.

1920   *Judith und Holofernes* (Nestroy), Grosses Schauspielhaus, Berlin.

Danton (Rolland), Grosses Schauspielhaus, Berlin.

Dame Kobold (Calderón), Deutsches Theater, Berlin; Theater im Redoutensaal der Hofburg, Vienna, 1922.

Stella (Goethe), Kammerspiele, Berlin, and Scandinavian tour; Theater im Redoutensaal der Hofburg, Vienna, 1922; Salzburger Festspiele, Salzburg, and Kammerspiele, Munich, 1931.

Julius Cäsar (Shakespeare), Grosses Schauspielhaus, Berlin.

Urfaust (Goethe), Deutsches Theater, Berlin, and Scandinavian tour.

1921   *Woyzeck* (Büchner), Deutsches Theater, Berlin.

Kräfte (Strindberg), Kammerspiele, Berlin.

Ein Traumspiel (Strindberg), Dramatiska Teatern, Stockholm, and Deutsches Theater, Berlin.

1922   *Das Salzburger grosse Welttheater* (Hofmannsthal), Salzburger Festspiele, Salzburg; revived there, 1925; Deutsches Theater, Berlin, 1933.

Schöne Frauen (Rey), Theater im Redoutensaal der Hofburg, Vienna, and Kammerspiele, Berlin.

Die Namenlosen (Lenormand), Deutsches Volkstheater, Vienna.

1924   *Der Diener zweier Herren* (Goldoni), Theater in der Josefstadt, Vienna, and Komödie, Berlin; Landestheater, Meiningen, and Swiss tour, 1926; Cosmopolitan Theatre, New York, 1928; Salzburger Festspiele, Salzburg, 1930; Schauspielhaus, Zurich, Stadttheater, Basle, and Salzburger Festspiele, Salzburg, 1931; Schauspielhaus, Zurich, and Rome, 1932; Dutch tour, 1934.

Der Schwierige (Hofmannsthal), Theater in der Josefstadt, Vienna; Komödie, Berlin, 1930; Salzburger Festspiele, Salzburg, 1931.

Der heilige Johanna (G. B. Shaw), Deutsches Theater, Berlin.

Aimée (Geraldy), Komödie, Berlin.

Sechs Personen suchen einen Autor (Pirandello), Komödie, Berlin; Theater in der Josefstadt, Vienna, Neues Deutsches Theater, Prague, and Dutch and Swiss tours, 1934.

1925   *Gesellschaft* (Galsworthy), Theater in der Josefstadt, Vienna, and Komödie, Berlin.

Juarez und Maximilian (Werfel), Theater in der Josefstadt, Vienna; Deutsches Theater, Berlin, 1926.

Der Kreidekreis (Klabund), Deutsches Theater, Berlin.

Das Apostelspiel (Mell), Kammerspiele, Berlin.

Das Leben hängt an einem Faden (Muffat), Lessing-Theater, Berlin.

Regen (Maugham), Theater am Kurfürstendamm, Berlin.

Riviera (Molnár), Theater in der Josefstaft, Berlin; Renaissance Szinház, Budapest, 1926.

1926   *Viktoria* (Maugham), Komödie, Berlin, and Theater in der Josefstadt, Vienna; Residenz-Theater, Munich, 1929; Komödie, Berlin, and Salzburg Festspiele, Salzburg, 1930; Schauspielhaus, Zurich, Stadttheater, Bern, and Stadttheater, Basle, 1931.

Die Gefangene (Bourdet), Theater in der Josefstadt, Vienna, Magyar Szinház, Budapest, and Komödie, Berlin; Stadttheater, Basle, and Stadttheater, Zurich, 1927

Peripherie (Langer), Deutsches Theater, Berlin; Theater in der Josefstad, Vienna, and Cosmopolitan Theatre, New York, 1928.

Dorothea Angermann (Hauptmann), Theater in der Josefstadt, Vienna; Deutsches Theater, 1927.

1927   *Der gute Kamerad* (Bernard), Theater in der Josefstad, Vienna.

1928   *Er ist an allem schuld* (Tolstoy), Cosmopolitan Theatre, New York.

Artisten (Watters and Hopkins), Deutsches Theater, Berlin; Theater an der Wien, Vienna, 1929.

Die Fledermaus (Meilhac, Halévy and Strauss), Deutsches Theater, Berlin; Kongelige Teatret, Copenhagen, 1930; Latvijas Nacionálá Opera, Riga, 1931; Théâtre Pigalle, Paris, 1933; Italian tour, 1934; 44th Street Theatre, New York, 1942.

Der Kaiser von Amerika (G. B. Shaw), Deutsches Theater, Berlin; Theater in der Josefstadt, Vienna, 1930.

1930   *Die Kreatur* (Bruckner), Komödie, Berlin.

Phaea (Unruh), Deutsches Theater, Berlin.

1931   *Das schwache Geschlecht* (Bourdet), Theater am Kurfürstendamm, Berlin, Oscarsteatern, Stockholm, and Theater in der Josefstadt, Vienna.

Hofmanns Erzählungen (Barbier and Offenbach), Grosses Schauspielhaus, Berlin.

1932   *Vor Sonnenuntergang* (Hauptmann), Deutsches Theater, Berlin.

Mademoiselle (Deval), Theater in der Josefstadt, Vienna.

Harmonie (Molnár), Deutsches Theater, Berlin.

1934   *Die geliebte Stimme* (Cocteau), Theater in der Josefstadt, Vienna.

1937   *The Eternal Road* (Werfel), Manhattan Opera House, New York.

In einer Nacht (Werfel), Theater in der Josefstadt, Vienna.

1938   *The Merchant of Yonkers* (Wilder), Guild Theatre, New York.

1940   *Too Many Husbands* (Maugham), Belasco Theatre, New York.

1943   *Sons and Soldiers* (I. Shaw), Morosco Theatre, New York.

Films

Das Mirakel, 1912; *Die Insel der Seligen*, 1913; *Eine venetianische Nacht*, 1914; *A Midsummer Night's Dream*, 1935.

Publications

Ausgewählte Briefe, Reden, Schriften und Szenen aus Regiebüchern, edited by Franz Hadamowsky, 1963; *Schriften, Briefe, Aufsätze, Interviews, Gespräche, Auszüge aus Regiebüchern*, edited by Hugo Fetting, 1974.

*

Bibliography

Books:
Siegfried Jacobson, *Max Reinhardt*, Berlin, 1910.
Huntly Carter, *The Theatre of Max Reinhardt*, New York, 1914.
Ernst Stern and Heinz Herald (eds.), *Reinhardt und seine Bühne: Bilder von der Arbeit des Deutschen Theaters*, Berlin, 1918.
Oliver M. Sayler, *Max Reinhardt and His Theatre*, New York, 1924.
Hans Rothe (ed.), *Max Reinhardt: 25 Jahre Deutsches Theater*, Munich, 1930.
Hans Horch (ed.), *Die Spielpläne Max Reinhardts 1905–30*, Munich, 1930.
Benno Fleischmann, *Max Reinhardt: Die Wiedererweckung des Barocktheaters*, Vienna, 1948.
Ernst Stern, *Bühnenbildner bei Max Reinhardt*, Berlin, 1955.
Carl Niessen, *Max Reinhardt und seine Bühnenbildner*, Cologne, 1958.
Franz Hadamowsky, *Reinhardt und Salzburg*, Salzburg, 1964.
Heinrich Braulich, *Max Reinhardt: Theater zwischen Traum und Wirklichkeit*, Berlin, 1969.
Fritz Kingenbeck (ed.), *Max Reinhardts Theater in her Josephstadt*, Salzburg, 1972.
Edda Fuhrich-Leisler and Gisela Prossnitz, *Bühnenbild und Raumgestaltung in den Inszenierungen Max Reinhardts*, Salzburg, 1972.
G. E. Wellwarth and A. G. Brooks (eds.), *Max Reinhardt, 1873–1973*, Binghampton, 1973.
Paul Koeppler, *Max Reinhardt auf der Probe: Im Spiegel der zeitgenössischen Autobiographien*, Vienna, 1973.

Leonhard M. Fiedler, *Max Reinhardt in Selbstzeugnissen und Bilddokumenten*, Reinbek, 1975.

Edda Fuhrich-Leisler and Gisela Prossnitz, *Max Reinhardt in Amerika*, Salzburg, 1976.

J. L. Styan, *Max Reinhardt*, Cambridge, 1982.

Heinrich Huesmann, *Welttheater Reinhardt: Bauten, Spielstätten, Inszenierungen*, Munich, 1983.

Knut Boeser and Renata Vatková, *Max Reinhardt in Berlin*, Berlin, 1984.

M. Jacobs and J. Warren (eds.), *Max Reinhardt: The Oxford Symposium*, Oxford, 1986.

Edda Fuhrich and Gisela Prossnitz, *Max Reinhardt: Ein Theater, das den Menschen wieder Freude gibt* ..., Munich, 1987.

* * *

After his training and first acting experiences in Vienna, Max Reinhardt began his career at Otto Brahm's Deutsches Theater in Berlin. Brahm was the first modern director in Germany and had elevated the directing profession from a mere craft to an art form in its own right. Reinhardt developed Brahm's principles further and moved away from the naturalist mode that had been his master's hallmark. When Reinhardt's company took over the Neues Theater in 1902, they found recognition as a separate organisational unit in the Brahm ensemble. In February 1903 they became fully independent and moved into the Neues Theater am Schiffbauerdamm.

In both houses Reinhardt presented a number of productions in an impressionist/symbolist style, in which the acting had a strong gestural content, while novel lighting designs and use of atmospheric music created a sensuous mood and the scenic designs effused a beautiful and captivating quality. Movement, colour, light and music were tightly knit together and used in a non-naturalistic way, not expressing specific meanings but rather interpreting the general ideas behind the plays.

Reinhardt's style won instant recognition. Critics as well as audiences responded very favourably to his productions and in 1905 he took over the Deutsches Theater, replacing his old master Brahm, who had moved to the Lessing Theater. Unlike most theatre managers he actually bought the house he was running, thereby laying the foundation of a theatre empire, which in 1932 included no less than eight leading theatres. Within a few years Reinhardt became Germany's foremost director, residing periodically at the Deutsches Theater (1905–11, 1929–32), the Künstlertheater in Munich (1909–11), the Volksbühne in Berlin (1915–18), the Grosses Schauspielhaus in Berlin (1918–20) and the Theater in der Josefstadt in Vienna (1924–29). In between he produced major works in Salzburg, London, New York, Stockholm and Venice.

His prolific output during these years can be divided into four categories: the intimate theatre, or 'Kammerspiel', where formal divisions between stage and the small auditorium were abolished and the spectator was encouraged to engage fully in the theatrical illusion; the classics and literary comedies, produced in a highly poetic, magical, illusionistic manner combining impressionist, romantic and neo-baroque devices; the scenic experiments with avant-garde plays or classical dramas on the abstract 'reform stage', where the emphasis was on stylized, symbolic actions carried out on a bare stage with a minimum of scenery; and the great spectacles like *Oedipus Rex*, *The Miracle* or *Everyman*.

This extraordinary variety of production styles catered for many different tastes. He explained the fundamental philosophy behind his productions in an essay of 1901: "What I have in mind is a theatre that will again bring joy to people, that leads them out of the grey misery of everyday life, beyond themselves into a gay and pure atmosphere of beauty". For the audiences, going to see a performance directed by Reinhardt always meant a festive experience and a delectation in a world of illusion, where reality was transformed and poetically heightened through the specific means of theatre. Reinhardt's productions appealed to the audience's senses and stimulated their feelings through new and daring theatrical devices. He employed the most up-to-date theatre technology and trained his actors in new performance styles, placing particular emphasis on the mimic and gestural element in acting. But Reinhardt was not a purely visual director. His orchestration of the actors' voices was equally masterful, and in the many classical dramas he produced he always did full justice to their literary and poetic quality. Although the texts were often rewritten and dramaturgically restructured, the director's role in adapting a drama for a stage production served the function of bringing out the author's ideas and intentions on stage. The director never violated the text, but sought to supplement it with his own imagination for the sake of realising its full potential in the performative medium. Reinhardt's productions can be classified as 'director's theatre', but they were also 'actor's theatre'. Reinhardt himself was a consummate performer, who always saw the actor as the first and foremost element in the theatre. He attracted to his theatres the best and most famous actors of the day and took the most talented performers of the younger generation under contract. Although he cast great celebrities in the leading roles, his productions never turned into 'star theatre'. Reinhardt did not accept any undisciplined, egotistical behaviour from his performers. The star was embedded in an ensemble and was obliged to participate in group rehearsals and to fit into the overall concept of the productions like all other members of the company.

The spectrum of Reinhardt's repertoire was extremely wide-ranging: from the classics to the avant-garde, from popular theatre to bourgeois well-made plays. He established many contemporary writers on the German stage and reintroduced others in novel and unconventional productions.

—Günther Berghaus

RÉJANE, Gabrielle-Charlotte. French actress and manager. Born Gabrielle-Charlotte Réju in Paris, 6 June 1856. Trained for the stage at the Paris Conservatoire, 1872–75. Married director Paul Porel in 1893 (divorced 1905). Stage debut, Théâtre de l'Odéon, Paris, 1875; established reputation in boulevard comedy at the Théâtre du Vaudeville, Paris, 1875–82, while also making appearances at the Odéon and elsewhere; London debut, Gaiety Theatre, 1894; New York debut, Abbey's Theatre, 1895; took over the Théâtre Nouveau, renaming it the Théâtre Réjane, 1906; continued to tour internationally as well as throughout Italy to the end of her career; retired, 1915; last stage performance, 1920. Légion d'honneur, 1920. Died in Paris, 14 June 1920.

Productions

1875	*Fanny Lear* (Meilhac and Halévy), Théâtre du Vaudeville, Paris.
	Revue des deux mondes (Clairville and Dreyfus), Théâtre du Vaudeville, Paris.
1882	*L'Aureole* (Normand), Théâtre du Vaudeville, Paris.
	La Nuit de noces (Carré and Labrousse), Théâtres des Variétés, Paris.
1883	*La Glu* (Richepin), Théâtre de l'Ambigu-Comique, Paris.
	Ma Camarade (Meilhac and Gille), Palais-Royal, Paris.
1888	*Décoré* (Meilhac), Théâtres des Variétés, Paris.
	Clara Soleil, Théâtre du Vaudeville, Paris.
	Les Demoiselles Clochard, Théâtres des Variétés, Paris.
	Germinie Lacerteux (adapted from Goncourt), Théâtre de l'Odéon, Paris; acted Germinie Lacerteux.
1889	*La Demi-monde* (Dumas fils), Théâtre du Vaudeville, Paris.
	Marquise! (Sardou), Théâtre du Vaudeville, Paris.
	Shylock (Haracourt, adapted from Shakespeare), Théâtre de l'Odéon, Paris.
1890	*Ma Cousine* (Meilhac), Théâtres des Variétés, Paris.
1891	*Amoureuse* (Porto-Riche), Théâtre de l'Odéon, Paris.
1892	*Fantasio* (Musset), Théâtre de l'Odéon, Paris.
	Lysistrata (Donnay), Théâtre des Variétés, Paris, and Eden-Théâtre, Paris.
1893	*Madame Sans-Gêne* (Sardou and Moreau), Théâtre du Vaudeville, Paris; acted Catherine.
	Viveurs, Théâtre de l'Odéon, Paris.
	La Parisienne (Becque), Théâtre du Vaudeville, Paris.
1894	*Maison de poupée* (Ibsen), Théâtre du Vaudeville, Paris; acted Nora.
1897	*La Douloureuse* (Donnay), Théâtre du Vaudeville, Paris.
1898	*Zaza* (Berton and Simon), Théâtre du Vaudeville, Paris; acted Zaza.
	Delfino in *Pamela, marchande de frivolités* (Sardou), Théâtre du Vaudeville, Paris.
	Le Calice, Théâtre de l'Odéon, Paris.
	Le Lys rouge (France and Caivallet), Théâtre de l'Odéon, Paris.
	Le Partage de midi (Claudel), Théâtre de l'Odéon, Paris.
	Georgette Lemeunier (Donnay), Théâtre de l'Odéon, Paris.
	Divorçons! (Sardou), Théâtre de l'Odéon, Paris.
	Lolotte, Théâtre de l'Odéon, Paris.
	Le Béguin (Courteline and Wolff), Théâtre de l'Odéon, Paris.
	La Robe rouge (Brieux), Théâtre de l'Odéon, Paris.
	Sylvie (Hermant), Théâtre de l'Odéon, Paris.
	Monsieur Betsy (Méténier and Alexis), Théâtre de l'Odéon, Paris.
	Pense douce, Théâtre de l'Odéon, Paris.
1901	*La Course du flambeau* (Hervieu), Théâtre du Vaudeville, Paris.
1902	*Le Masque* (Bataille), Théâtre des Variétés, Paris.
1906	*La Souris* (Pailleron), Théâtre Réjane, Paris.
	Heureuse (Hennequin and Bilhaud), Théâtre Réjane, Paris.
	La Rafale (Bernstein), Théâtre Réjane, Paris.
	La Piste (Sardou), Théâtre des Variétés, Paris.
	La Savelli (Maurey), Théâtre Réjane, Paris.
	Le Joug, Théâtre Réjane, Paris.
	Antoinette Sabrier (Coolus), Théâtre Réjane, Paris.
1907	*Paris—New York* (Croisset), Théâtre Réjane, Paris.
	La Clef (Guitry), Théâtre Réjane, Paris.
	Suzeraine (Niccodemi), Théâtre Réjane, Paris.
	Après le pardon (Decourcelle, adapted from Serao), Théâtre Réjane, Paris.
	Le Monde ou l'on s'ennuie (Pailleron), Théâtre Réjane, Paris.
1908	*Qui perd gagne* (Veber), Théâtre Réjane, Paris.
	Israël (Bernstein), Théâtre Réjane, Paris.
1909	*Trains de luxe* (Hermant), Théâtre Réjane, Paris.
	L'Impératrice (Mendès), Théâtre Réjane, Paris.
	Le Refuge (Niccodemi), Théâtre Réjane, Paris.
	Le Risque (Coolus), Théâtre Réjane, Paris.
	Madame Margot (Moreau and Clairville), Théâtre Réjane, Paris.
	La Risque (Coolus), Théâtre Réjane, Paris.
1910	*La Flamme* (Niccodemi), Théâtre Réjane, Paris.
1911	*La Revue sans-gêne* (Rip and Bousquet), Théâtre Réjane, Paris.
	L'Enfant de l'amour (Bataille), Théâtre de la Porte-Saint-Martin, Paris.
1912	*L'Aigrette* (Niccodemi), Théâtre Réjane, Paris.
1913	*Alsace* (Leroux and Camille), Théâtre Réjane, Paris.
	L'Irrégulière (Sée), Théâtre Réjane, Paris.
1916	*Amazone* (Bataille), Théâtre de la Porte-Saint-Martin, Paris.
1917	*La Treizième chaise* (Veiller), Théâtre Réjane, Paris.
1918	*Notre image* (Bataille), Théâtre Réjane, Paris.
1920	*Le Vierge folle* (Bataille), Théâtre Réjane, Paris.

Other productions included: *La Dame aux camélias* (Dumas); *John Gabriel Borkman* (Ibsen); *Le Passerelle*; *Sapho* (Daudet and Belot).

Films

Madame Sens-Gêne, 1911; *L'Alsace*, 1915; *Miarka, la Fille à l'Ours*, 1920.

*

Bibliography

Books:

Camillo Antona-Traversi, *Réjane*, Paris, 1930.

* * *

Gabrielle-Charlotte Réjane, to use the surname she substituted for the less euphonius Réju at the time of her debut, was one of the most skilled and best loved actresses on the Parisian stage from the time of the Franco-Prussian War until her retirement in 1915. Her background was in the theatre — her father, who died when she was only four years old, had acted in the provinces before returning to Paris to work in the administration of the Théâtre de l'Ambigu where her mother ran the refreshment bar — but it is said that she had had some difficulty in gaining permission to train as an actress. She was, however, fortunate in being able to study at the Conservatoire under the sexagenarian F. J. P. Régnier de la Brière, a notably well-organised actor of comic roles who had made his debut at the Comédie-Française as early as 1831 and had retired to devote himself exclusively to teaching. He is supposed to have been outraged when at the end of her training Gabrielle Réjane was awarded only a second prize. What may well have equally determined the direction her career was to take was the fact that in 1875 she declined the opportunity of undertaking some work suitable for a beginner at the Odéon, the second state-subsidised theatre in Paris, which enjoyed rather more freedom in its choice of plays the the Comédie-Française. Gabrielle Réjane preferred more remunerative employment at the Théâtre des Variétés. This decision by a young Parisian woman who knew what poverty meant is entirely understandable; it did, however, mean that she was not only excluded from the classical repertory but also from certain of the more demanding modern works put on at the Odéon.

Gabrielle Réjane had to make her name in the commercial plays of what is seen in retrospect as a rather inglorious period in French theatrical history.

The list of plays in which she appeared, largely though not exclusively at the Théâtre des Variétés, over a period of more than three decades provides ample proof of her stamina and appetite for work in a time when the Parisian public was ever eager for novelties. But it is hard to work up much enthusiasm these days for the light comedies and drawing-room dramas in which she appeared. Playwrights such as Henri Meilhac and Lavedan spoke enthusiastically of her performances, as did Henri Bataille and Albert Guinon. The name of Goncourt is more famous, but it is more likely to be mentioned by today's critics in connection with novels than with plays. If such triumphs as Dunnoy's *Lysistrata* are now forgotten, Gabrielle Réjane's part in many of the successes of Victorien Sardou — especially her portrayal of a lovable termaganant in *Madame Sans-Gêne* — was, however, a significant factor in Parisian theatrical life in the 1890's. Some degree of sympathy with a more challenging repertory was shown by her readiness to perform in Ibsen's *Doll's House* in 1894, as well as in plays by Becque, Porto-Riche, and Bernstein. She can perhaps hardly be blamed for failing to do much more than make the works of those French dramatists successful at their first performance.

Réjane was not, according to the norms of the age, a regular beauty, and she lacked the fire of her great contemporary Sarah Bernhardt. But she possessed grace and charm — qualities which, it must be said, are hardly photogenic — and she was, by all accounts, equally adept in period costume as in modern dress. From her Montmartre childhood she preserved a volubility of speech and a forthrightness that she could call upon on demand. Knowing her strength in this particular line, audiences could appreciate all the more her restraint and poise when a more genteel manner was required, as was often the case in the drawing-room plays of the age, and her vivacity could evidently enliven what now seem to be the rather prosaic lines she was constantly being asked to speak.

In 1905 she became proprietor of the Nouveau Théâtre in the Rue de Blanche in Paris, and by the time it opened as the Théâtre Réjane in 1906 with the enthusiastic support of many of the authors in whose plays she had appeared, it had been refurbished in the grandest, most luxurious style. A notable event there, in which, however, she did not herself take part, was the French premiere in 1911 of *L'Oiseau bleu*, though it has to be noted that Maeterlinck's poetic drama, which had been given its first performance in Moscow as early as 1908, had even been performed in English in London's Haymarket Theatre two years before Parisian audiences had their chance of seeing it. Sad to relate, it was in any case less of a success in the Théâtre Réjane than Dario Niccodemi's adaptation of E. W. Hornung's *Raffles*. All in all, the financial and artistic experiment of the ageing Réjane's theatre was, like her stage career, vitiated by the relatively low quality of the plays available for performance. At a time when the theatre was brilliant and socially highly rated, French dramatists showed themselves unable to come up to the standard of their contemporaries who were poets, novelists, and visual artists, and what was then often seen as fine drama now seems at best only theatrical, at worst only conventionally stagey. Réjane's parts often appeared tailor-made, but really they had little more to offer than conventional successes.

Something of Réjane's acting is preserved in early films, including scenes from Sardou's *Madame Sans-Gêne* and from *L'Alsace* by Leroux and Camille. Like the studio portraits and posed stills from her stage roles, they give scant impression of an actress whose charm was felt to be very French by audiences both at home and abroad and whose determination carried her right through to the end of a busy, tough career.

—Christopher Smith

RICCOBONI family. Italian actors, comprising Antonio Riccoboni, his son Luigi Riccoboni and his grandson Antoine-François-Valentin Riccoboni, as well as other members of the family. Antonio Riccoboni flourished 1655–98. Married Anastasia Miglioli, five children. Acted the role of Pantalone at the court of Modena and spent in all some 40 years in the part; attained the rank of 'capocomico' at Modena, 1677–89; also appeared as Pantalone in London, 1679. Luigi Andreas Riccoboni was born in Modena, 1676. Married 1) actress Gabriella Gardellini, known as Argentina; 2) actress Elena Balletti in 1706 (1686–1771), known as Flaminia, one son. Acted under the stagename Lélio, initially in comedy at Modena, making his debut at the age of 14; with his second wife, attempted to establish a classical French-influenced theatre in northern Italy in opposition to the commedia dell'arte, 1707; subsequently, with the support of the Duc d'Orléans, reopened the Comédie-Italienne in Paris, 1716, and also appeared in London, 1727–28; retired from the Comédie-Italienne, 1729, and worked briefly as Controller-General of Menus Plaisirs at the court of Parma, 1729–31; returned to Paris, 1733; published several works on contemporary European theatre. Died in Paris, 1753. Antoine-François-Valentin Riccoboni was born in Mantua, 1707, son of Luigi Riccoboni. Educated at Jesuit School in Paris. Married actress Marie-Jeanne de Laboras (born in Paris, 1713; died in Paris, 1792). Acted under the stagename Lélio fils and acted and danced with the Comédie-Italienne, Paris, 1726–50; largely retired from the stage after being insulted by the Duc de Richelieu; also wrote several comedies for the stage among other works. Died in Paris, 1772.

Productions

Luigi Riccoboni:
1710–14   *Sofonisba* (Trissino), Modena.
           L'Ifigenia in Tauride, Modena.
           Rachele (Martello), Modena.
1713   *Merope* (Maffei), Modena; Venice, 1714; Comédie-Italienne, Paris, 1717.
1715   *La Scolastica* (Ariosto), Venice.
1717   *Samson*, Comédie-Italienne, Paris.
           Hercule, Comédie-Italienne, Paris.
           La Vie est un songe (Cicognini), Comédie-Italienne, Paris.
           L'Italian marié à Paris (Cicognini), Comédie-Italienne, Paris.
           Le Libéral malgré lui (Cicognini), Comédie-Italienne, Paris.
1718   *Naufrage au Port-à-l'Anglais* (Autreau), Comédie-Italienne, Paris.
           La Métempsycose d'Arlequin, Comédie-Italienne, Paris.
           Les Deux Arlequins, Comédie-Italienne, Paris.
           Le Père partial, Comédie-Italienne, Paris.
           Le Jugement de Paris, Comédie-Italienne, Paris.
           La Désolation des deux comédies, Comédie-Italienne, Paris.
1719   *La Foire renaissante*, Comédie-Italienne, Paris.
           Colombine mari par complaisance, Comédie-Italienne, Paris.
1721   *Endymion ou L'Amour vengé*, Comédie-Italienne, Paris.
           Le Négligent, Comédie-Italienne, Paris.
           Danaé, Comédie-Italienne, Paris.
1722   *Arlequin camarade du diable*, Comédie-Italienne, Paris.

1729   *L'Italian marié à Paris*, Comédie-Italienne, Paris.

Other conjectured productions include: *L'Amour et la vérité* (Marivaux); *Les Fourberies d'Arlequin*.

Antoine-François-Valentin Riccoboni:
1716   *Surprise de l'amour* (Marivaux), Comédie-Italienne, Paris.
           Serva padrona (Pergolesi), Comédie-Italienne, Paris.
1719   *Oedipe travesti* (adapted from Voltaire's *Oedipe*), Comédie-Italienne, Paris.
1724   *Les Effets de l'éclipse*, Comédie-Italienne, Paris.
1726   *Arcagambis*, Comédie-Italienne, Paris.
           Arlequin toujours Arlequin, Comédie-Italienne, Paris.
           Les Comédiens esclaves, Comédie-Italienne, Paris.
           L'Occasion, Comédie-Italienne, Paris.
           Pyrame et Thisbé (adapted from La Serre), Comédie-Italienne, Paris.
1727   *Médée et Jason* (adapted from Pellegrini), Comédie-Italienne, Paris.
           Zéphire et Flore, Comédie-Italienne, Paris.
           L'Île de la folie, Comédie-Italienne, Paris.
           Le Sincère à contretemps (adapted from L. Riccoboni), Comédie-Italienne, Paris.
1728   *Arlequin Hullo*, Comédie-Italienne, Paris; revived, 1731.
           La Revue des théâtres, Comédie-Italienne, Paris.
           La Suite des Comédiens esclaves, Comédie-Italienne, Paris.
           La Comédie de village, Comédie-Italienne, Paris.
           La Méchante femme (adapted from Longepierre's *Médée*), Comédie-Italienne, Paris.
1732   *Les Catastrophes lyri-tragicomiques* (adapted from Voltaire's *Éryphile* and Pellegrini's *Jephté*), Comédie-Italienne, Paris.
           Les Enfants trouvés (adapted from Voltaire's *Zaïre*), Comédie-Italienne, Paris.
1733   *Le Bouquet*, Comédie-Italienne, Paris.
           Hippolyte et Aricie (adapted from Pellegrini), Comédie-Italienne, Paris.
1734   *Pygmalion*, Comédie-Italienne, Paris.
           L'Heureuse fourberie, Comédie-Italienne, Paris.
1735   *Les Ennuis du carnaval*, Comédie-Italienne, Paris.
           Achille et Déidamia (adapted from Daudet), Comédie-Italienne, Paris.
           Le Conte de fées, Comédie-Italienne, Paris.
           Les Indes galantes (Fuzelier), Comédie-Italienne, Paris.
1736   *Les Sauvages* (adapted from Voltaire's *Alzire*), Comédie-Italienne, Paris.
           Les Compliments, Comédie-Italienne, Paris.
1738   *Castor et Pollux* (adapted from Bernard), Comédie-Italienne, Paris.
           Atys (adapted from Quinault), Comédie-Italienne, Paris.

1739
La Conspiration (adapted from La Chausée's *Maximien*), Comédie-Italienne, Paris.
Les Filets de Vulcan, Comédie-Italienne, Paris.
Orphée, Comédie-Italienne, Paris.
La Dispute du tragique et du comique (adapted from La Noue's *Mahomet II*), Comédie-Italienne, Paris.
Les Muses rivales, Comédie-Italienne, Paris.

1740
Les Rendez-vous nocturnes, Comédie-Italienne, Paris.
Amadis (adapted from Quinault), Comédie-Italienne, Paris.

1741
L'Écho du public, Comédie-Italienne, Paris.

1743
Arlequin Phaéton (adapted from Quinault), Comédie-Italienne, Paris.

1746
Le Prince de Suresnes (adapted from Boissy's *Le Duc de Surrey*), Comédie-Italienne, Paris.

1747
Les Gondoliers vénitiens, Versailles.

1755
La Rancune (adapted from Chateaubrun's *Philoctète*), Comédie-Italienne, Paris.

1760
Le Prétendu, Comédie-Italienne, Paris.

1761
Les Caquets (adapted from Goldoni's *I Pettegolezzi delle danse*), Comédie-Italienne, Paris.
Quand parlera-t-elle? (adapted from Voltaire's *Tancrède*), Comédie-Italienne, Paris.

1762
Armide (adapted from Quinault), Comédie-Italienne, Paris.
Les Trois bossus, Comédie-Italienne, Paris.

1764
Les Amants de village (adapted from Rousseau's *Le Devin du village*), Comédie-Italienne, Paris.

Publications

Luigi Riccoboni:
Dell'arte Rappresentative, 1728; *L'Histoire du Théâtre italien*, 1728, 1731; *Les Réflexions historiques et critiques*, 1738; *Pensées sur la Déclamation*, 1738; *Discorsi della Commedia all'improvviso e scenari inediti*.

Antoine-François-Valentin Riccoboni:
L'Art du Théâtre, 1750.

*

Bibliography

Books:
Xavier De Courville, *Luigi Riccoboni dit Lélio*, 3 vols., Paris, 1943.
Salvatore Cappalletti, *Luigi Riccoboni e la riforma del teatro*, Ravenna, 1986.

* * *

Antonio Riccoboni, who played Pantalone, had a long career of approximately 40 years in the commedia dell'arte troupe sponsored by the court of Modena. According to his son Luigi, he was from a noble family and became an actor "by some strange adventure". This was a common claim, however, by actors seeking social standing in the 17th century; Antonio Riccoboni more probably began his career as he ended it, as a charlatan mountebank. The earliest surviving document that mentions Riccoboni is

from 1674, but an anecdote told by Luigi Riccoboni suggests that his father was already well-known several years earlier. According to the younger Riccoboni, Louis XIV wrote to the Duke of Modena in 1670, asking for his cousin's help in finding a Pantalone for the Paris troupe. The Duke proposed his own Pantalone, but "accompanied this proposal with such affectionate terms for Riccoboni that the actor ... begged the Duke for the favour of remaining in his service". The Duke apparently agreed with the actor's request. From 1677 to 1689, Riccoboni was 'capocomico' of the Modena troupe, a fixture in a company known for its instability. The last document that mentions Antonio Riccoboni is from 1698 and finds him selling medicine on the piazza in Modena, apparently too old to act, but still forced to earn his living.

Luigi Riccoboni, an 'amoroso' known as Lélio, became an actor by paternal fiat after he expressed the desire to join a religious order. Studious by nature and forced to abandon his studies at the age of 14, Luigi Riccoboni was embarrassed by his profession and devoted his life to its reform. A true man of the Enlightenment, Riccoboni set out to reveal the classical nature of the Italian improvisatory theatre, which he believed to have degenerated during the Baroque. He constructed an ideal model of the commedia dell'arte, which influenced historians and critics for many years.

Although he began in the troupe of Modena doing improvised comedy, his heart was in tragedy and tragicomedy. He continued to study the history of drama, under the tutelage of the Marquis Orsi, and made a number of prose translations of great poetic dramas of the past. In 1707, Riccoboni and his second wife, Elena Balletti, formed a troupe that set out to realise the dream of reform. Although their acting style was based on improvisation, lively and natural, their repertory consisted of translations and adaptations of Corneille and Racine, reprises of 16th-century Italian tragedies and modern Italian tragedies by Martelli and Maffei. Riccoboni contributed to the renewal of Italian tragedy, but his efforts to reform Italian comedy were less successful; audiences continued to expect the stratagems and bawdry of the zanni. Riccoboni's attempt to revive Ariosto's *La Scolastica* in Venice in 1715 met with humiliating failure.

The next year, Riccoboni was invited to re-establish the Comédie-Italienne in Paris. He accepted, believing that he could accomplish in France what he had failed to achieve in Italy, the ideal reform of the Italian theatre. He also hoped to make his fortune, leave the stage and get on with his preferred life as a historian and critic. The second goal proved easier than the first. The French audience wanted a reproduction of the theatre that had been dismissed in 1697; like the Italian audience, the French cherished the zanni. For the first two years, the new Comédie-Italienne performed the old farces along with adaptations from Spanish Baroque tragi-comedy. Riccoboni abandoned his project of producing tragedy acted in the natural style. The French, to his disgust, preferred tragedy played in the grand declamatory style of the Comédie-Française. After two years, with revenues falling, the Italians realised that the language barrier was impassable, and began to do new plays in French.

In 1729, Riccoboni retired from the Comédie-Italienne and returned to Italy, hoping to use his new post as Controller-General of Menus Plaisirs at the court of Parma as an agency of reform. But the Prince of Parma died. Riccoboni returned to France; his wife and son rejoined the Comédie-Française, and he continued to write historical and theoretical treatises on the theatre.

Although ashamed of his profession, Luigi Riccoboni was appreciated as one of the great actors of his time. Boindin describes him at the time of his debut in France as having "a sombre face, very apt to paint sad feelings; he does not express joy so well …; he succeeds marvellously in characterizing extremes of feeling". He was not so expressive when it came to more subtle feelings, and was weak in love scenes "where he affects a pitiful tone which is not to the taste of many people". A few months later the *Mercure* reports that "you see a whole troupe in the eyes and on the face of Lélio; his heart and his mind are to be seen there".

Along with his historical studies, Riccoboni published two treatises on acting: *Dell'arte Rappresentativa* (1728) and *Pensées sur la Déclamation* (1738). In these he denounced artificiality, taught that gesture and movement should be based on observation and good sense, and advised actors to live their characters and make the feelings of the characters their own. He was especially interested in the eyes and face and in the agreement of facial and vocal expression. Riccoboni's writings on acting were an important early contribution to the French 18th-century debate on acting that also engaged Voltaire and Diderot.

Luigi Riccoboni's second wife, Elena Balletti (Flaminia), was a 'donna' in the classical tradition. An excellent actress, perhaps one of the greatest of all improvisatory actresses, she was also a scholar and writer and member of several Italian academies. When the Comédie-Italienne opened in Paris in 1716, she made an exceptionally good impression, although she had a sharp and rather disagreeable voice. Nonetheless, she was valued highly for the variety, justness and naturalness of her acting.

The last of the Riccoboni family was Francesco, the only child of Luigi and Elena Balletti, who played as Lélio fils, but without his father's talent or authority. He was considered, like his mother, somewhat cold and pretentious on stage. His life, however, was not conducted according to the precepts of his pious parents. He wrote a number of entertainments for the Comédie-Italienne, some parodies so pointed that the genre was forbidden in 1645. In 1750, Francesco Riccoboni also published a treatise, *Art du Théâtre*, which showed the influence of his father's ideas and foreshadowed those of Diderot's *Paradoxe sur le Comédien*. Francesco Riccoboni married a French woman, Marie de Laboras, who acted at the Comédie-Italienne and was also a very successful writer of romantic novels. The couple had no children, and the Riccoboni family died out when Francesco himself died in 1772.

—Virginia Scott

RICH, John. English actor-manager. Born in London, 19 May 1692 (some sources, 1682). No formal education. Married 1) Henrietta Brerewood in 1716 (died 1725); 2) actress Anne (or Amy) Stevens c.1727 (died 1737); (possibly) 3) Priscilla Wilford; four children. Inherited from his father Christopher Rich three-quarters share in 1660 royal theatrical patent granted to William Davenant as well as control of Lincoln's Inn Fields Theatre, 1714; experienced severe hardship before enjoying commercial success in rivalry with the Theatre Royal, Drury Lane, dropping tragic roles and staging London's first pantomimes, from 1717; highly acclaimed in the (silent) role of Harlequin, using stagename Lun; used profits of John Gay's *The Beggar's Opera* and money from public subscription to build first theatre in Covent Garden, 1732; presented David Garrick at Covent Garden, 1746–47; sold Covent Garden patent, 1759. Founder, Sublime Society of Beefsteaks social and theatrical club, 1735. Died in London, 26 November 1761.

Principal roles

1715	Essex in *The Unhappy Favourite* (Banks), Lincoln's Inn Fields Theatre, London.
1717	Harlequin in *The Cheats; or, The Tavern Bilkers* (Weaver), Lincoln's Inn Fields Theatre, London.
	Underplot (Harlequin) in *The Jealous Doctor* (Rich), Lincoln's Inn Fields Theatre, London.
	Harlequin in *Harlequin Executed* (Rich), Lincoln's Inn Fields Theatre, London.
	Vulcan (Punch) in *The Loves of Mars and Venus* (Weaver), Lincoln's Inn Fields Theatre, London.
	Harlequin in *Colombine* (Weaver), Lincoln's Inn Fields Theatre, London.
1718	Harlequin in *Amadis* (Rich), Lincoln's Inn Fields Theatre, London.
1721	Harlequin in *Harlequin, Scaramouch, and a Countryman* (anon.), Lincoln's Inn Fields Theatre, London.
1722	Harlequin in *Scene Between Harlequin and Countryman* (anon.), Lincoln's Inn Fields Theatre, London.
	Magician in *The Magician; or, Harlequin Director* (Rich), Lincoln's Inn Fields Theatre, London.
1723	Jupiter (Harlequin) in *Jupiter and Europa* (Rich), Lincoln's Inn Fields Theatre, London.
	Harlequin in *The Necromancer; or, Harlequin Doctor Faustus* (Rich), Lincoln's Inn Fields Theatre, London.
1725	Harlequin in *Harlequin a Sorcerer; with the Loves of Pluto and Proserpine* (Theobald), Lincoln's Inn Fields Theatre, London.
1726	Harlequin in *Daphne and Apollo; or, The Burgomaster Tricked* (Theobald), Lincoln's Inn Fields Theatre, London.
1727	Harlequin in *The Rape of Proserpine; with the Birth and Adventures of Harlequin* (Theobald), Lincoln's Inn Fields Theatre, London.
	Harlequin in *The Loves of Damon and Celemen* (anon.), Lincoln's Inn Fields Theatre, London.
1729	Harlequin in *Italian Jealousy* (anon.), Lincoln's Inn Fields Theatre, London.
1730	Harlequin in *Perseus and Andromeda* (Theobald), Lincoln's Inn Fields Theatre, London.
1736	Jupiter (Harlequin) in *The Royal Chace; or, Merlin's Cave* (Phillips), Covent Garden, London.

| 1740 | Harlequin in *Orpheus and Eurydice* (Theobald), Covent Garden, London. |
| 1750 | Harlequin in *The Fair* (Rich), Covent Garden, London. |

Pantomimes (as author/contriver)

Harlequin Executed, 1717; *The Jealous Doctor*, 1717; *Amadis*, 1718; *The Magician; or, Harlequin a Director*, 1721; *Jupiter and Europa*, 1723; *The Necromancer; or, Harlequin Doctor Faustus*, 1723; *The Fair*, 1750; *The Spirit of Contradiction*, 1760; *The Coronation*, 1761.

*

Bibliography

Books:
L. V. Paulin, *John Rich and the Eighteenth Century Stage* (thesis), University of London, 1936.
Paul Sawyer, *John Rich versus Drury Lane* (dissertation), University of Columbia, New York, 1954.
Minnie Lawhon, *'Angel of dulness'. The Career of John Rich* (dissertation), Cornell University, Ithaca, New York, 1969.
Paul Sawyer, *The New Theatre in Lincoln's Inn Fields*, London, 1979.

Articles:
Paul Sawyer, "The Date of John Rich's Birth", *Theatre Notebook*, 1954.
C. F. Burgess, "Some Unpublished Items of John Rich and Something of a Puzzle", *Restoration and 18th Century Theatre Research*, 1968.
Paul Sawyer, "Was John Rich Illiterate?", *Theatre Notebook*, 1972.
Denise Elliott Shane, "John Rich and the Reopening of Lincoln's Inn Fields", *Theatre Notebook*, 1988.

* * *

John Rich as Harlequin.

The second most powerful and influential actor-manager in London in the 18th century (David Garrick being the first), John Rich may have stumbled by accident into his career in theatre management. In 1714 his father left John, then 22, and his brother Christopher a patent and a new playhouse in Lincoln's Inn Fields, and after some touch-and-go seasons at the outset John (apparently with only minimal help from his brother) gradually learned how to run a theatre and a company of performers.

John Rich was a paradox. He was sometimes generous to a fault — in 1745, according to Reed's "Notitia Dramatica", he gave £600 to a charity to which the rival Drury Lane Theatre gave only about £130 — yet at other times he exasperated colleagues and employees with his stinginess. It was said that when an actor died Rich would not promote a performer within the company but hire someone from outside at a lower salary. Rich was also an eccentric. He regularly butchered — perhaps purposely — people's names ('Griskin' for Garrick, 'Williamskin' for Wilkinson) and, as a delightful painting by Smallfield attests, kept a house overrun with cats. Popular tradition has it that he was more or less uneducated, Aaron Hill in *The Prompter* in 1735 explaining that in Rich "Understanding was born

deaf" while the provincial manager Tate Wilkinson spoke in his *Memoirs* of Rich's "natural stupidity" and Alexander Pope in the first *Dunciad* labelled him the "Angel of Dulnes" — yet there is plenty of evidence to suggest that he was quite literate, an enterprising (if sometimes devious) businessman and a shrewd showman.

The Lincoln's Inn Fields Theatre opened on 18 December 1714, with young John (dressed in mourning for his otherwise little-lamented father) delivering a prologue, evidently his first stage appearance. He played the leading role in Banks's *The Unhappy Favourite* a year later, but acting was not apparently his forte, hampered as he was by a natural slowness in delivery. Rich became in time a coach of actors but much of his performing career was spent in his ideal role as Harlequin in pantomimes at both Lincoln's Inn and, from 1732, at the first theatre in Covent Garden. His first such appearance was evidently on 22 April 1717 in *The Cheats* (using the stagename 'Lun'); though nothing is known of his training in dance, it is worth noting that in his company were, among others, the dancers Sandham, Shaw, de la Garde, the Sallées, Hester Santlow, and, most importantly, the young John Thurmond, who became a rival contriver of pantomimes. These light entertainments, usually afterpieces, drew the crowds even if they did not uplift theatre as an art and Rich certainly did well financially.

At the Theatre Royal, Drury Lane in 1759 David Garrick reluctantly paid a compliment to Rich's success when he produced his first pantomime, *Harlequin's Invasion*, for which he wrote a prologue on his rival's ability:

When Lun appeared with matchless art and whim,
He gave the power of speech to every limb;
Tho' mask'd and mute convey'd his quick intent,
And told in frolic gesture what he meant.

A typical Rich pantomime might include Harlequin hatching from an egg, elaborate scene changes, and dazzling machines, Rich imitating a dog, music and dance, a mixed plot of the serious and comic, magic transformations, trick properties, and the like. Frothy stuff, but years later, Horace Walpole for one fondly remembered the high quality of Rich's shows, commenting on what seemed to him a very bad pantomime at Drury Lane in 1782: "How unlike the pantomimes of Rich, which were full of wit, and coherent, and carried on a story!" Rich was, however, also capable of putting on loftier shows. On 22 October 1730 at Kew Gardens he produced a masque for the royal family, while the *Coronation* procession at Covent Garden on 13 November 1761, celebrating the accession of George III, was praised by the *Court Magazine* as being far superior in elegance to a similar show given by Garrick at Drury Lane.

As a manager, Rich had to face the immense popularity (and strong troupe) of Garrick and he understood the necessity of surrounding himself with talent. Over the years he brought to London audiences some fine performances, performers, playwrights, and new and old plays. During his managerial years he was also responsible for presenting Gay's *The Beggar's Opera* (had he produced nothing else of worth during his career, this alone would have secured him a place in British theatre history), importing to Lincoln's Inn Fields the exquisite young French dancer Marie Sallé, building the first theatre in Covent Garden, giving London the Romeo of Spranger Barry (opposite the Juliet of Susanna Maria Cibber and the Mercutio of Charles Macklin), and helping in the production of oratorios at Covent Garden (with Handel usually at the organ, which the composer left to Rich in his will).

Many theatre people have their day and are soon forgotten after they retire (Anne Oldfield, for instance, despite her popularity during her career was rarely mentioned in theatrical records after her death) and John Rich himself was a likely candidate for obscurity, but he left a thriving theatrical enterprise and performing tradition and long after his demise London was still being provided with pantomimes that regularly featured scenes originally developed by his hands.

—Edward A. Langhans

RICHARDSON, (Sir) Ralph (David). British actor. Born in Cheltenham, Gloucestershire, 19 December 1902. Educated at the Xaverian College, Brighton, and privately. Married 1) Muriel Hewitt in 1924 (died 1942); 2) Meriel Forbes-Robertson in 1944, one son. Professional stage debut, with Charles Doran touring company, Marina Theatre, Lowestoft, 1921; toured provinces, 1921–25; joined Birmingham Repertory Company, 1925; London debut, 1926; first appearance at the Old Vic Theatre, London, 1930; film debut, 1933; served in Fleet Air Arm, 1939–44; co-director, Old Vic Company at the New Theatre, London, 1944–47; joined Shakespeare Memorial Theatre Company, 1952; subsequently also appeared at the National Theatre. Member: National Youth Theatre (president, 1959–83). Recipient: New York Film Critics' Award, 1952; British Film Academy Award, 1952; *Evening Standard* Award, 1970; Society of West End Theatre Special Award, 1981. D.Litt: University of Oxford, 1969. Order of St Olaf (Norway), 1950. Knighted, 1947. Died in London, 10 October 1983.

Roles

1921	Lorenzo in *The Merchant of Venice* (Shakespeare), Marina Theatre, Lowestoft.
	Guildenstern and Bernado in *Hamlet* (Shakespeare), British tour.
	Pedant in *The Taming of the Shrew* (Shakespeare), British tour.
	Soothsayer and Strato in *Julius Caesar* (Shakespeare), British tour.
	Oliver in *As You Like It* (Shakespeare), British tour.
	Scroop and Gower in *Henry V* (Shakespeare), British tour.
	Angus and Macduff in *Macbeth* (Shakespeare), British tour.
	Francisco in *The Tempest* (Shakespeare), British tour.
	Lysander in *A Midsummer Night's Dream* (Shakespeare), British tour; British tour, 1922.
	Curio and Valentine in *Twelfth Night* (Shakespeare), British tour.
1922	Banquo in *Macbeth* (Shakespeare), British tour.
	Horatio in *Hamlet* (Shakespeare), British tour.
	Decius Brutus and Octavius Caesar in *Julius Caesar* (Shakespeare), British tour.
	Fabian and Sebastian in *Twelfth Night* (Shakespeare), British tour.
	Vincentio and Lucentio in *The Taming of the Shrew* (Shakespeare), British tour.
1923	Cassio in *Othello* (Shakespeare), British tour.
	Antonio and Gratiano in *The Merchant of Venice* (Shakespeare), British tour.
	Mark Antony in *Julius Caesar* (Shakespeare), British tour.
	Sir Lucius O'Trigger in *The Rivals* (Sheridan), Abbey Theatre, Dublin.
	Bobby in *The Romantic Age* (Milne), Abbey Theatre, Dublin.
1924	Henry in *Outward Bound* (Vane), British tour.
	Fainall in *The Way of the World* (Congreve), British tour.
1925	Richard Coaker in *The Farmer's Wife* (Phillpotts), British tour.
	Dick Whittington in *The Christmas Party* (Merington), Repertory Theatre, Birmingham.
1926	Geoffrey Cassilis in *The Cassilis Engagement* (Hankin), Repertory Theatre, Birmingham.
	Christopher Pegrum in *The Round Table* (Robinson), Repertory Theatre, Birmingham.
	Gentleman in *He Who Gets Slapped* (Andreyev), Repertory Theatre, Birmingham.

Ralph Richardson (1953).

Lane in *The Importance of Being Earnest* (Wilde), Repertory Theatre, Birmingham.

Robert Blanchard in *Devonshire Cream* (Phillpotts), Repertory Theatre, Birmingham, and British tour.

Albert Prosser in *Hobson's Choice* (Brighouse), Repertory Theatre, Birmingham.

Mr Dearth in *Dear Brutus* (Barrie), Repertory Theatre, Birmingham.

Frank Taylor in *The Land of Promise* (Maugham), Repertory Theatre, Birmingham.

Dr Tudor Bevan in *The Barber and the Cow* (Davies), Repertory Theatre, Birmingham.

The Stranger in *Oedipus at Colonus* (Sophocles), Scala Theatre, London.

Albert Titler in *Yellow Sands* (Phillpotts), Haymarket Theatre, London; Garrick Theatre, London, 1927.

1927   Harold Devrill in *Sunday Island*, Strand Theatre, London.

John Bold in *The Warden*, Royalty Theatre, London.

Sophus Meyer in *Samson and Delilah*, Arts Theatre, London.

Frank Liddell in *Chance Acquaintance* (Van Druten), Strand Theatre, London.

1928   Zozim and Pygmalion in *Back to Methuselah* (G. B. Shaw), Court Theatre, London.

Gurth in *Harold* (Tennyson), Court Theatre, London.

Tranio in *The Taming of the Shrew* (Shakespeare), Court Theatre, London.

Hezekiah Brent in *Prejudice*, Arts Theatre, London.

Ben Hawley in *Aren't Women Wonderful?* (Deans), Court Theatre, London.

Alexander Magnus in *The First Performance*, Court Theatre, London.

James Jago in *The Runaways* (Phillpotts), Garrick Theatre, London.

David Llewellyn Davids in *The New Sin* (Hastings), Little Theatre, Epsom.

1929   Duke of Winterset in *Monsieur Beaucaire* (Lonsdale), South African tour.

Joseph Surface in *The School for Scandal* (Sheridan), South African tour.

Squire Chivy in *David Garrick* (Robertson), South African tour.

1930   Gilbert Nash in *Silver Wings* (Titheradge, Furber, Waller, and Tunbridge), Dominion Theatre, London.

Edward in *Cat and Mouse* (Stevenson), Queen's Theatre, London.

Roderigo in *Othello* (Shakespeare), Savoy Theatre, London.

Henry in *Henry IV, part 1* (Shakespeare), Old Vic Theatre, London.

Caliban in *The Tempest* (Shakespeare), Old Vic Theatre, London; revived there, 1931.

Sir Harry Beagle in *The Jealous Wife* (Colman the Elder), Old Vic Theatre, London.

Bolingbroke in *Richard II* (Shakespeare), Old Vic Theatre, London; revived there, 1931.

1931   Sir Toby Belch in *Twelfth Night* (Shakespeare), Old Vic Theatre, London; revived there, 1932.

Bluntschli in *Arms and the Man* (G. B. Shaw), Old Vic Theatre, London; New Theatre, London, 1944.

Don Pedro in *Much Ado About Nothing* (Shakespeare), Old Vic Theatre, London.

Kent in *King Lear* (Shakespeare), Old Vic Theatre, London.

David Regan in *The Mantle*, Arts Theatre, London.

Matthew Merrygreek in *Ralph Roister Doister* (Udall), Malvern Festival; revived there, 1932.

Mr Courtall in *She Would If She Could* (Etherege), Malvern Festival.

Viscount Pascal in *The Switchback* (Bridie), Malvern Festival.

Faulconbridge in *King John* (Shakespeare), Old Vic Theatre, London.

Petruchio in *The Taming of the Shrew* (Shakespeare), Old Vic Theatre, London.

Bottom in *A Midsummer Night's Dream* (Shakespeare), Old Vic Theatre, London; revived there, 1937; tour of South America and Europe, 1964.

Henry in *Henry V* (Shakespeare), Old Vic Theatre, London.

1932   Ralph in *The Knight of the Burning Pestle* (Beaumont and Fletcher), Old Vic Theatre, London.
Brutus in *Julius Caesar* (Shakespeare), Old Vic Theatre, London.
General Grant in *Abraham Lincoln* (Drinkwater), Old Vic Theatre, London.
Iago in *Othello* (Shakespeare), Old Vic Theatre, London.
Ghost and First Grave-digger in *Hamlet* (Shakespeare), Old Vic Theatre, London.
Face in *The Alchemist* (Jonson), Malvern Festival; New Theatre, London, 1947.
Oroonoko in *Oroonoko* (Southerne), Malvern Festival.
Sergeant Fielding in *Too True to Be Good* (G. B. Shaw), Malvern Festival and New Theatre, London.
Collie Stratton in *For Services Rendered* (Maugham), Globe Theatre, London.

1933   Dick Barclay in *Head-on-Crash*, Queen's Theatre, London.
Arthur Bell Nicholls in *Wild Decembers* (Ashton), Apollo Theatre, London.
Sheppey in *Sheppey* (Maugham), Wyndham's Theatre, London.
Captain Hook and Mr Darling in *Peter Pan* (Barrie), Palladium, London.

1934   John MacGregor in *Marriage is no Joke* (Bridie), Globe Theatre, London.
Charles Appleby in *Eden End* (Priestley), Duchess Theatre, London.

1935   Cornelius in *Cornelius* (Priestley), Duchess Theatre, London.
Mercutio and Chorus in *Romeo and Juliet* (Shakespeare), Martin Beck Theatre, New York.

1936   Emile Delbar in *Promise* (Bernstein), Shaftesbury Theatre, London.
Sam Gridley in *Bees on the Boat Deck* (Priestley), Lyric Theatre, London.
Dr Clitterhouse in *The Amazing Dr Clitterhouse* (Lyndon), Haymarket Theatre, London.

1937   Peter Agardi in *The Silent Knight* (Wolfre, adapted from Heltai), St James's Theatre, London.

1938   Othello in *Othello* (Shakespeare), Old Vic Theatre, London.

1939   Johnson in *Johnson Over Jordan* (Priestley), New Theatre, London.

1944   Peer Gynt in *Peer Gynt* (Ibsen), New Theatre, London.
Richmond in *Richard III* (Shakespeare), New Theatre, London.

1945   Vanya in *Uncle Vanya* (Chekhov), New Theatre, London.
Falstaff in *Henry IV, parts 1 and 2* (Shakespeare), New Theatre, London.
Tiresias in *Oedipus* (Sophocles), New Theatre, London.
Lord Burleigh in *The Critic* (Sheridan), New Theatre, London.

1946   Inspector Goole in *An Inspector Calls* (Priestley), New Theatre, London.
Cyrano in *Cyrano de Bergerac* (Rostand), New Theatre, London.

1947   Gaunt in *Richard II* (Shakespeare), New Theatre, London.

1948   Marcus Ivanirex in *Royal Circle* (Cavan), Wyndham's Theatre, London.

1949   Dr Sloper in *The Heiress* (adapted from James), Haymarket Theatre, London.

1950   David Preston in *Home at Seven* (Sherriff), Wyndham's Theatre, London.

1951   Vershinin in *The Three Sisters* (Chekhov), Aldwych Theatre, London.

1952   Prospero in *The Tempest* (Shakespeare), Shakespeare Memorial Theatre, Stratford-upon-Avon.
Macbeth in *Macbeth* (Shakespeare), Shakespeare Memorial Theatre, Stratford-upon-Avon.
Volpone in *Volpone* (Jonson), Shakespeare Memorial Theatre, Stratford-upon-Avon.

1953   John Greenwood in *The White Carnation* (Sherriff), Globe Theatre, London.
Dr Farley in *A Day by the Sea* (Hunter), Haymarket Theatre, London.

1955   Grand Duke in *The Sleeping Prince* (Rattigan), tour of Australia and New Zealand.
Mr Martin and Major Pollock in *Separate Tables* (Rattigan), tour of Australia and New Zealand.

1956   Timon in *Timon of Athens* (Shakespeare), Old Vic Theatre, London.

1957   General St Pé in *The Waltz of the Toreadors* (Anouilh), New York.
Jim Cherry in *Flowering Cherry* (Bolt), Haymarket Theatre, London.

1959   Victor Rhodes in *The Complaisant Lover* (Greene), Globe Theatre, London.

1960   Edward Portal in *The Last Joke* (Bagnold), Phoenix Theatre, London.

1962   Sir Peter Teazle in *The School for Scandal* (Sheridan), Haymarket Theatre, London.

1963   Stepfather in *Six Characters in Search of an Author* (Pirandello), Mayfair Theatre, London.

1964   Shylock in *The Merchant of Venice* (Shakespeare), tour of South America and Europe; Haymarket Theatre, London, 1967.
Father in *Carving a Statue* (Greene), Haymarket Theatre, London.

1966   William in *You Never Can Tell* (G. B. Shaw), Haymarket Theatre, London.
Sir Anthony Absolute in *The Rivals* (Sheridan), Haymarket Theatre, London.

1969   Dr Rance in *What the Butler Saw* (Orton), Queen's Theatre, London.

1970   Jack in *Home* (Storey), Royal Court Theatre, London.

1971   Wyatt Gilman in *West of Suez* (Osborne), Royal Court Theatre, London.

1972   General Sir William Boothroyd in *Lloyd George Knew My Father* (Home), Savoy Theatre, London.

1975	Borkman in *John Gabriel Borkman* (Ibsen), Old Vic Theatre, London.
	Hirst in *No Man's Land* (Pinter), Old Vic Theatre, London.
1977	Cecil in *The Kingfisher* (Home), Lyric Theatre, London.
1978	Firs in *The Cherry Orchard* (Chekhov), National Theatre, London.
	Colonel White in *Alice's Boys*, Savoy Theatre, London.
	Lord Touchwood in *The Double-Dealer* (Congreve), National Theatre, London.
1979	The Master in *The Fruits of Enlightenment* (Frayn), National Theatre, London.
	Old Ekdal in *The Wild Duck* (Ibsen), National Theatre, London.
1980	Kitchen in *Early Days* (Storey), National Theatre, London.
1982	Leonard in *The Understanding* (Huth), Strand Theatre, London.

Films

The Ghoul, 1933; *Friday the Thirteenth*, 1933; *The Return of Bulldog Drummond*, 1934; *Java Head*, 1934; *The King of Paris*, 1934; *Bulldog Jack*, 1935; *Things to Come*, 1936; *The Man Who Could Work Miracles*, 1936; *Thunder in the City*, 1937; *South Riding*, 1938; *The Divorce of Lady X*, 1938; *The Citadel*, 1938; *Smith*, 1938; *Q Planes*, 1939; *The Four Feathers*, 1939; *The Lion Has Wings*, 1939; *On the Night of the Fire*, 1939; *The Day Will Dawn*, 1942; *The Silver Fleet*, 1943; *The Volunteer*, 1943; *School for Secrets*, 1946; *Anna Karenina*, 1948; *The Fallen Idol*, 1948; *The Heiress*, 1949; *An Outcast of the Islands*, 1951; *Home at Seven*, 1952; *The Sound Barrier*, 1952; *The Holly and the Ivy*, 1952; *Richard III*, 1955; *Smiley*, 1956; *The Passionate Stranger*, 1957; *Our Man in Havana*, 1960; *Oscar Wilde*, 1960; *Exodus*, 1960; *The 300 Spartans*, 1962; *Long Day's Journey Into Night*, 1962; *Woman of Straw*, 1964; *Dr Zhivago*, 1965; *Khartoum*, 1966; *The Wrong Box*, 1966; *Oh! What a Lovely War*, 1969; *The Bed-Sitting Room*, 1969; *The Battle of Britain*, 1969; *The Looking Glass War*, 1969; *Midas Run*, 1969; *David Copperfield*, 1969; *Whoever Slew Auntie Roo?*, 1971; *Eagle in a Cage*, 1971; *Tales from the Crypt*, 1972; *Alice's Adventures in Wonderland*, 1972; *Lady Caroline Lamb*, 1972; *A Doll's House*, 1973; *Dr Frankenstein: The True Story*, 1973; *O Lucky Man*, 1973; *Rollerball*, 1975; *Jesus of Nazareth*, 1976; *The Man in the Iron Mask*, 1977; *The Time Bandits*, 1981; *The Dragon Slayer*, 1982; *Wagner*, 1983; *Invitation to the Wedding*, 1983; *Greystoke*, 1984; *Give My Regards to Broad Street*, 1984.

Television

Hedda Gabler, 1962; *Heart to Heart*, 1962; *Voices of Man*, 1963; *Johnson Over Jordan*, 1965; *Blandings Castle*, 1966; *Twelfth Night*, 1968; *Hassan*, 1970; *She Stoops to Conquer*, 1970; *Home*, 1972; *Comets Among the Stars*, 1975; *No Man's Land*, 1978; *Charlie Muffin*, 1979; *Early Days*, 1982.

Radio

The City, 1929; *Twelfth Night*, 1929; *Captain Brassbound's Conversion*, 1929; *The Tempest*, 1931; *Romeo and Juliet*, 1932; *Macbeth*, 1933; *The Tempest*, 1933; *Julius Caesar*, 1933; *A Midsummer Night's Dream*, 1934; *Through the Looking Glass*, 1935; *In Memoriam*, 1936; *The Tempest*, 1936; *Candida*, 1937; *Johnson Over Jordan*, 1940; *Job*, 1941; *The Shoemaker's Holiday*, 1942; *Dr Faustus*, 1942; *Don Quixote*, 1943; *Peer Gynt*, 1944; *Cyrano de Bergerac*, 1945; *Henry IV, parts 1 and 2*, 1945; *Moby Dick*, 1946; *Rubaiyat of Omar Khayyam*, 1947; *Brand*, 1949; *A Midsummer Night's Dream*, 1953; *Noah*, 1958; *Richard II*, 1960; *Hamlet*, 1961; *Arms and the Man*, 1961; *The Ballad of Reading Gaol*, 1963; *The Merchant of Venice*, 1963; *Christmas Carol*, 1964; *Cyrano de Bergerac*, 1966; *Heartbreak House*, 1968; *When We Dead Awaken*, 1969; *Much Ado About Nothing*, 1969; *John Gabriel Borkman*, 1974; *The Phoenix and Turtle*, 1976; *The Passionate Pilgrim*, 1976; *Programme on William Blake*, 1977; *Readings from Andrew Marvell*, 1978; *Little Tich — Giant of the Halls*, 1982.

*

Bibliography

Books:
Gary O'Connor, *Ralph Richardson — An Actor's Life*, London, 1982.
Robert Tanitch, *Ralph Richardson — A Tribute*, London, 1982.
Valerie Clough, *Sir Ralph Richardson: A Life in the Theatre*, Worthing, Sussex, 1989.

* * *

Ralph Richardson was the most eccentric of a triumvirate of great male actors who dominated British theatre from the 1930's to the 1970's: it was his extraordinary ability to transfigure the humanity of the ordinary Englishman that paradoxically distinguished his acting from the athletic romanticism and protean theatricality of Laurence Olivier on the one hand, and the poetic romanticism and high comic sophistication of John Gielgud on the other. Somewhat surprisingly for an actor of his stature, his few performances in Shakespeare's tragedies were not highly regarded.

By the mid-1930's, Richardson's work at the Birmingham Repertory Theatre under Barry Jackson, at the Old Vic, in the West End, and at the Malvern Festival had placed him second only to John Gielgud among the new generation of serious actors. His film contract with Alexander Korda (which ran from 1935 until Korda's death in 1956) ensured his fame and popularity with the general public. His technique of understatement, learned from his heroes Gerald Du Maurier and Charles Hawtrey during the 1930's, transformed a "round, sober cheese face" with its staring eyes and large retroussé nose into a mask of eccentric bluffness, which concealed an intensity of repressed feeling — loneliness, rage, sadness, or romantic passion.

While Gielgud was defining a modern approach to the speaking of Shakespeare in lyrically moving performances at the Old Vic, Richardson complemented him in the 1930 and 1931 seasons with Bolingbroke, Prince Hal, Kent, Caliban, Bottom, Toby Belch, and Henry V. He brought an unaffected sincerity to these roles, an earthy humanity in contrast to Gielgud's more refined intelligence. Gielgud was later to remember his "marvellous performances of shaggy-dog faithfulness ... he was unforgettable as the Bastard and Enobarbus and Kent. And he always gave them a touch of fantasy".

What James Agate described as "his stolid, inexpressive mien, altogether admirable ... in all delineations of the downright" was clearly perceived to limit his range as a classical actor, but Richardson undoubtedly touched a sympathetic chord with West End audiences and critics who were moved by his "impeccable" performance as the hairdresser's assistant Sheppey in Somerset Maugham's play of that name, which ran for three months in 1933. Critics considered this portrayal of a man who wins a sweepstake and decides to give the money away to the poor to be "a kind of masterpiece". His ability to play a "saint with his feet on earth" was recognised by Desmond McCarthy, who claimed that the performance revealed "a rare understanding of human goodness and a rare restraint in expressing it".

In four plays by J. B. Priestley before World War II his memorable performances presented him in different contexts as emblem of a stoical Englishness beset by difficulties; his portrayal of a suburban Everyman in *Johnson Over Jordan* established an indelible impression of his stage persona as "common man glorified by sudden and overwhelming experience". As did Gielgud and Olivier, he moved between the Old Vic and the commercial theatre, his drawing power as a star allowing serious plays to achieve a measure of popularity with the public.

Undoubtedly Ralph Richardson's greatest contribution to the development of the British theatre was his co-directorship with Laurence Olivier and John Burrell of the Old Vic Company from 1944 to 1947. In recognition of what was arguably the summit of his own achievement as an actor he was knighted in 1947, becoming the first of his contemporaries to be thus honoured. By working as a team, Olivier alternately playing supporting roles opposite Richardson's leads and vice-versa, the two actors demonstrated how a company might combine virtuosity with ensemble playing. Among a gallery of superb performances in plays by Shakespeare, Shaw, Chekhov, Ibsen, Ben Jonson, Sophocles, Sheridan, and Edmond Rostand, Richardson's Peer Gynt, Falstaff, and Cyrano de Bergerac were acclaimed as definitive. As Peer Gynt the poetic fancy that had been an undercurrent of his performances was given free rein. This "rare identification of player and part" produced one of the most varied and original performances of the 20th century theatre, the madness of Peer's self-assertion being made wholly understandable through Richardson's "gift of universality". As Falstaff in *Henry IV, parts 1 and 2*, his wonderful comic timing was allied to his great gift for pathos to produce a refined characterisation that though exuberant was never gross. This represented a radical reinterpretation of the role, which was in Tynan's words, "deliciously funny, not riotously so"; there were extraordinary moments of sadness, as if "we had suddenly caught sight of an abyss", according to J. C. Trewin.

Richardson's numerous successful performances on stage and in films in the 1950's and 1960's enhanced his reputation for discovering mystery in the ordinary and for

humanising the strange, villainous, or eccentric. The work that he did at the Royal Court and the National Theatre from 1970 provided him with a wonderful Indian summer in his stage career and enabled him to demonstrate his genius for exposing the secret places of the heart to a new generation of theatregoers in plays by a younger breed of playwrights — *Home* (1970) and *Early Days* (1980) by David Storey, *West of Suez* (1971) by John Osborne, and *No Man's Land* (1975) by Harold Pinter. *Home* and *No Man's Land* provided excellent opportunities for Richardson and Gielgud to highlight each other's complementary personalities as actors, each in his own way miraculously combining a unique gift of pathos with an original comic talent.

As he got older, Richardson's obvious mannerisms became even more obviously the instruments of his art. His odd bearing, described by Tynan as "at once rakish and stately, as of a pirate turned prelate" might appear increasingly clumsy with age, making his strangely guarded vulnerability ever more lovable, yet he was always capable of astonishing acts of physical prowess as a performer. No actor could so devastatingly express emotional or spiritual emptiness, and he quite as effortlessly transformed his "pop-eyed, pole-axed look" to suggest the isolation of Firs, the ancient serf in *The Cherry Orchard* at the National Theatre in 1978, as to signify the ruthlessness of one of his many cool villains in Hollywood films of the 1970's.

—Robert Gordon

RISTORI, Adelaide. Italian actress and manager. Born in Friuli, Austria-Hungary, 29 January 1822. Married Marchese Giuliano Capranica del Grillo in 1847. Stage debut as a baby; first significant success, as Silvio Pellico's Francesca da Rimini, aged 14; joined Campagnia Reale Sarda, Rome, 1837; became the company's leading lady, 1840, and prima donna assoluta, 1841; withdrew temporarily from the theatre on her marriage, 1847; returned to stage, 1853; appeared with Reale Sarda company throughout Italy and also in Paris, 1855 and 1856, London, 1857, and the USA, 1866, 1867, 1875 and 1884, winning high praise in both tragedy and comedy and considered Sarah Bernhardt's equal by many; world tour, 1874; acted Lady Macbeth in English, London, 1882; last stage appearance before retirement, as Maria Stuart, New York, 1885; theatrical collection formed basis of Ristori archive in the Actors' Museum, Genoa. Died in Turin, Italy, 8 October 1906.

Roles

Adrienne Lecouvreur in *Adriana Lecouvreur* (Scribe and Legouvé); Antigone in *Antigone* (Alfieri); Beatrix in *Béatrix* (Legouvé); Elisabeth in *Elisabetta Regina d'Inghilterra* (Giacometti); Francesca da Rimini in *Francesca da Rimini* (Pellico); Lady Macbeth in *Macbeth* (Shakespeare); Maria Stuart in *Maria Stuarda* (Schiller); Marie Antoinette in *Maria Antoinetta* (Giacometti); Mirandolina in *La Locandiera* (Goldoni); Medea in *Medea* (Legouvé); Mirra in *Mirra* (Alfieri); Ottavia in *Ottavia* (Alfieri); Phèdre in *Fedra* (Dall'Ongaro, adapted from Racine); Rosmunda in *Rosmunda* (Alfieri). Also acted roles in: *Il Bicchier d'acqua* (Scribe); *Camma* (Montanelli); *Un Curioso accidente* (Goldoni); *La Gelosie di Lindoro* (Goldoni); *I Gelosi fortunati* (Giraud); *Giulietta e Romeo* (Shakespeare); *Pia de' Tolomei* (Marenco); *La Signora dalle camelie* (Dumas fils); *La Suonatrice d'arpa* (Chiossone).

Publications

Ricordi e studi artistici (autobiography), 1887.

*

Bibliography

Books:
E. Peron Hingston, *Adelaide Ristori: The Siddons of Modern Italy*, London, 1856.
Kate Field, *Ristori, A Biography*, New York, 1867.
Cesare Scoccio, *Adelaide Ristori e Rachel*, Genoa, 1886.
Eduardo Botet, *Adelaide Ristori*, Rome, 1902.
Tommaso Salvini, *Discorsi in commemorazione di Adelaide Ristori*, Rome, 1906.
Leonardo Bragaglia, *Adelaide Ristori*, Friuli, 1972.

* * *

The career of Adelaide Ristori coincided with the development of modern Italy, with the revolutionary fervour of the 1820's and 1830's, and the eventual successful unification in 1870. Ristori's position as prima donna assoluta of the Italian theatre is therefore linked with the birth of the new Italy, and Ristori was indeed a magnificent amabassador. Beautiful, talented, the wife of an aristocrat, and a fervent patriot, Ristori created an image of Italian theatre that revived it from the decline into which it had descended. Her tragic roles took up the theme of revolution, with parts such as Judith, Marie Antoinette, Mary Stuart, or Lady Macbeth.

Ristori's repertoire was relatively limited; she selected plays that served her well and kept them in her repertoire for years. She was an extremely shrewd businesswoman, both in her choice of roles and handling of venues and contract terms. Her success internationally was phenomenal, and contemporary writers spoke of 'Ristori fever', as huge crowds flocked to theatres where she was appearing and her name appeared on products such as 'Ristori eau de Cologne', 'Ristori cosmetics' and 'Ristori sweets'. Her status in Italian society was reflected in her choice of roles, and she played queens and aristocratic women, whilst travelling with an entourage that reinforced the image of her exalted status. Photographs of Ristori show her posed in queenly attitudes, and there are many accounts of her regal bearing and imposing presence both on and off the stage.

It is always difficult to reconstruct performance style, and since Ristori became a myth in her own lifetime that process of reconstruction is particularly hard. In the first stage of her career she was frequently compared to Rachel, her greatest rival, though after Rachel's death in 1858 this (mainly fictitious) rivalry disappeared. The Rachel-Ristori rivalry served much the same purpose as the later Bernhardt-Duse rivalry: it divided audiences into partisan groups and increased public interest in the performers.

Rachel and Ristori came out of completely different traditions and worked in very different ways, so comparison is not especially helpful. Ristori followed the Italian tradition (and there were still a number of handbooks for actors, giving precise instructions on gesture and voice being written in the nineteenth century), but adapted the rules to her own purposes. Contemporary accounts lay a great deal of emphasis on her bearing, on her statuesque appearance, and on her capacity to create powerful often very moving stage pictures. Less kind reviewers might remark that she could do "nothing without pantomime", but others stressed her largeness of gesture, her powers of declamation, and her nobility. Cristina Giorcelli, who has done a detailed survey of contemporary English and Irish reviews, comments that the most frequent terms describing Ristori's work include "impassioned", "rapture", and "fierce" and to these might be added "wildness", "magnificence", and "frenzy", all of which suggest a style of presentation that bordered on the edge of control. Ristori seems to have been able to convey great emotion in terms of grand gestures and a declamatory style of speaking, whilst also creating in her audiences a very definite sense of 'realism' in marked contrast to the work of some of her contemporaries. The paintings of artists such as Delacroix and Courbet reflect a similar concern for the grand scene, where symbolism combines with a particular concept of the realistic.

Ristori also placed great emphasis on careful study of the script, and copies of her own scripts show her detailed notes and careful word-for-word translations. She combined the large gesture with minute changes of facial expression, a technique that audiences throughout the world found fascinating. In a very useful article that examines the relationship between Duse and Ristori, Mirella Schino showed how Ristori helped Duse develop her skill as a performer, even lending her copies of her own annotated scripts. Later, however, Ristori was to provide a detailed critique of Duse's acting style, and from this critique a great deal may be learnt about Ristori's own work. Ristori praises Duse's originality and talent, but states categorically that she is not a realist performer. In contrast to the opinions of most contemporary reviewers, Ristori insists that Duse was anything but a 'natural' player, and gives details of the kind of technical strategies that Duse used to create that impression of naturalness. Ristori objects to Duse's mannered style of acting, and suggests that she is representative of the new woman with her new neuroses; as a representative of the older generation, Ristori saw her own work as more archetypal, not so closely bound up with contemporary society. Her notion of "realism" relates much more to an ideal of universal values, but in her ability to analyze the performance style of another artist she shows the extent of her technical skills and knowledge of theatre.

The photographs of Ristori in old age, playing the scene she made her own, Lady Macbeth's sleepwalking scene, do give a sense of that "realism". The great beauty that is so evident in other roles is completely absent; what we have instead is a haggard woman staring blindly into her own nightmare, and although her hands are prominent, what catches the attention instantly is the expression on her face, the staring eyes, the slightly open mouth, the neck thrust forward. Ristori was an intensely professional woman, a performer who studied her craft and, when she found something that worked for her, stayed with it and refined it to perfection. Her popularity at home and abroad amounted to cult status and Cavour could say with some justification that Adelaide Ristori was the symbol not only of a new phase of development in the Italian theatre but of the new Italy itself.

—Susan Bassnett

ROBARDS, Jason (Nelson). US actor. Born in Chicago, Illinois, 26 July 1922. Educated at Hollywood High School, Los Angeles, until 1940; trained for the stage at the American Academy of Dramatic Arts, 1946–47, and with Uta Hagen in New York. Married 1) Eleanor Pitman in 1947 (divorced 1952), two sons and one daughter; 2) Rachel Taylor in 1959 (divorced); 3) actress Lauren Bacall in 1961 (divorced 1969), one son; 4) Lois O'Connor in 1970, two sons. Served in US Navy, 1939–46. Stage debut, Delyork Theatre, Rehoboth Beach, Delaware, 1947; first Broadway appearance, 1947; subsequently also worked as a stage manager and occasional director; acted in radio serials, 1948–50; emerged as a star in two plays by Eugene O'Neill, 1956; joined Stratford Festival Company, Ontario, 1958; film debut, 1959. Member: Board of Directors, American Academy of Dramatic Arts, since 1957. Recipient: Obie Award, 1956; Theatre World Award, 1957; Tony Award, 1959; ANTA Award, 1959; New York Drama Critics Award, 1960; Cannes Film Festival Award, 1962; Oscar, 1976, 1977; New York Film Critics Award, 1976; presidential citation. DHL, Fairfield University, 1982; DFA, Williams College, 1983.

Roles

1947	Rear end of cow in *Jack and the Beanstalk* (pantomime), Children's World Theatre, New York.
	Buoyant in *Buoyant Billions* (G. B. Shaw), 23rd Street YMCA, New York.
1951	Witherspoon in *Stalag 17* (Bevan and Trzcinski), summer tour.
1953	Ed Moody in *American Gothic* (Wolfson), Circle in the Square, New York.
1956	Hickey in *The Iceman Cometh* (O'Neill), Circle in the Square, New York; Lunt-Fontanne Theatre, New York, 1985; James A Doolittle Theatre, University of California, Los Angeles Centre for the Arts/The Theatre Group, Los Angeles, 1986.
	Jamie in *Long Day's Journey Into Night* (O'Neill), Helen Hayes Theatre, New York.
1958	Hotspur in *Henry IV, part 1* (Shakespeare), Shakespeare Festival, Stratford, Ontario.
	Polixenes in *The Winter's Tale* (Shakespeare), Shakespeare Festival, Stratford, Ontario.
	Manley Halliday in *The Disenchanted* (Schulberg), Coronet Theatre, New York.
1959	Macbeth in *Macbeth* (Shakespeare), Metropolitan Boston Arts Centre, Cambridge, Massachusetts.
1960	Julian Berniers in *Toys in the Attic* (Hellman), Hudson Theatre, New York.
1961	William Baker in *Big Fish, Little Fish* (Wheeler), ANTA Theatre, New York.
1962	Murray Burns in *A Thousand Clowns* (Gardner), Eugene O'Neill Theatre, New York.
1964	Quentin in *After the Fall* (Miller), Washington Square Theatre, New York.
	Seymour Rosenthal in *But for Whom Charlie* (Behrman), Washington Square Theatre, New York.
	Erie Smith in *Hughie* (O'Neill), Royale Theatre, New York; Zellerbach Theatre, Los Angeles, 1975; Lake Forest Theatre, Lake Forest, Illinois, 1976.
1965	Vicar of St Peter's in *The Devils* (Whiting), Broadway Theatre, New York.
1968	Captain Starkey in *We Bombed in New Haven* (Heller), Ambassador Theatre, New York.
1971	Frank Elgin in *The Country Girl* (Odets), Eisenhower Theatre, Washington D.C.; Billy Rose Theatre, New York, 1972.
1973	James Tyrone Jr in *A Moon for the Misbegotten* (O'Neill), Eisenhower Theatre, Washington D.C., and Morosco Theatre, New York; Ahmanson Theatre, Los Angeles, 1974.
1975	James Tyrone Sr in *Long Day's Journey Into Night* (O'Neill), Eisenhower Theatre, Washington D.C.; also directed; Brooklyn Academy of Music, New York, 1976; also directed; Neil Simon Theatre, New York, 1988.
1977	Cornelius Melody in *A Touch of the Poet* (O'Neill), Helen Hayes Theatre, New York.
1983	Martin Vanderhof in *You Can't Take It With You* (Kaufman), Booth Theatre, New York, Plymouth Theatre, New York, and Kennedy Centre, Washington D.C.
1987	Cooper in *A Month of Sundays*, Ritz Theatre, New York.
1988	Nat Miller in *Ah, Wilderness!* (O'Neill), Neil Simon Theatre, New York.

Also acted roles in: *Out of the Frying Pan* (Swann), Delyork Theatre, Rehoboth Beach, Delaware, 1947; *The Mikado* (Gilbert and Sullivan), Century Theatre, New York, 1947; *Iolanthe* (Gilbert and Sullivan), Century Theatre, New York, 1948; *The Yeoman of the Guard* (Gilbert and Sullivan), Century Theatre, New York, 1948; *The Philadelphia Story* (Barry), summer tour, 1951; *Oh, Men! Oh, Women!* (Chodorov), summer tour, 1951; *O'Neill and Carlotta*, Public Theatre, New York, 1979; *Love Letters*, 1989; *Park Your Car in Harvard Yard*, 1991.

Films

The Journey, 1959; *By Love Possessed*, 1961; *Tender Is the Night*, 1961; *Long Day's Journey into Night*, 1962; *Act One*, 1964; *A Thousand Clowns*, 1965; *Any Wednesday*, 1966; *A Big Hand for the Little Lady*, 1966; *Divorce American Style*, 1967; *Hour of the Gun*, 1967; *The St Valentine's Day Massacre*, 1967; *Isadora*, 1968; *The Night They Raided Minsky's*, 1968; *Once Upon a Time in the West*, 1969; *The Ballad of Cable Hogue*, 1970; *Fools,*

Unknown Soldier, 1985; *The Atlanta Child Murders*, 1985; *Johnny Bull*, 1986; *The Last Frontier*, 1986; *Happy Birthday Hollywood*, 1987; *Breaking Home Ties*, 1987; *Laguna Heat*, 1987; *Inherit the Wind*, 1988; *Robert Frost*, 1988; *The Making of Gorillas in the Mist*, 1988; *The Christmas Wife*, 1988; *Chernobyl: The Final Warning*, 1991.

* * *

Jason Robards has built his reputation across a wide territory, encompassing the American repertory, the commercial theatre and Hollywood. He has gained a name for thoughtful and coherent characterization, spellbinding tours de force, fatherly calm and, in films, as a celebrity star specializing in curmudgeons and feisty seniors.

Robards is a part of US dramatic history, having created the role of Jamie Tyrone in Eugene O'Neill's *Long Day's Journey into Night*, of Hickey in *The Iceman Cometh* and the title role in *Hughie*. He has also won two Oscars, for supporting performances in *All the President's Men* and *Julia*; an Obie and various other prestigious awards in the course of his highly successful career.

His first notable part came in *American Gothic*, on which occasion the audience sensed that here was something out of the ordinary in naturalistic acting. His voice was powerful, ruminative and somewhat incantatory, but his performance never seemed to break up into constituent parts of voice, movement and characterization. Robards never seemed very physical, but anyone who saw *American Gothic* would deny that he acted from the neck up. Rather it was — again, partly due to the voice — that he commanded the stage with an authority remarkable in one so young.

Seeing Robards on stage in the plays of Eugene O'Neill is to be in touch with what is certain (even if it is the first performance) to be taken as the definitive word on the character he is just then embodying. O'Neill calls for acting of the US naturalistic actor at its highest reach. Robards's Jamie Tyrone never acted drunk, but he was always a drunkard, whining ever so slightly, baiting those close to him who had heard it before, had heard it for a lifetime. His Hickey, meanwhile, seemed never sober, but never once deviated from his sublime faith in the likelihood that anyone, even someone off the street, would at once take what he said for gospel truth, take him as leader and follow him wherever he said they should go. Robards' realisation of this faith made the confession of that play doubly harrowing: his Hickey knew he could only do this once, and that at first no one would believe him. *Iceman* is a long and rather static, talky play. Robards made it seem like an inevitable formal structure leading to unavoidable truth.

In a way, this power on the stage undercuts some of Robards' film performances. His Howard Hughes of *Melvin and Howard*, perhaps his best performance, is almost too big for the screen, a performance too much projected for the space of a theatre, a portrait to wake up the back rows. The scene with Melvin Dumar (Paul deMat) in the pick-up truck riding back to Las Vegas is a wonderful piece of screen acting and a miraculously blended piece of two entirely different kinds of performing styles. But Robards's performance seems headed for a theatrical denouement we will never get to see. In his stage performances he so surely

Jason Robards (1955).

1970; *Julius Caesar*, 1970; *Tora! Tora!*, 1970; *Johnny Got His Gun*, 1971; *Jud*, 1971; *Murders in the Rue Morgue*, 1971; *The War between Men and Women*, 1972; *Pat Garrett and Billy the Kid*, 1973; *A Boy and His Dog*, 1975; *Mr Sycamore*, 1975; *All the President's Men*, 1976; *Julia*, 1977; *Comes a Horseman*, 1978; *Hurricane*, 1979; *Melvin and Howard*, 1980; *Raise the Titanic*, 1980; *Caboblanco*, 1981; *The Legend of the Lone Ranger*, 1981; *Burden of Dreams*, 1982; *Max Dugan Returns*, 1983; *Something Wicked This Way Comes*, 1983; *America and Lewis Hine*, 1984; *Square Dance*, 1987; *Bright Lights, Big City*, 1988; *The Good Mother*, 1988; *Dream a Little Dream*, 1989; *Black Rainbow*, 1989; *Parenthood*, 1989; *Reunion*, 1990; *Quick Change*, 1990; *Storyville*, 1992.

Television

A Doll's House, 1959; *For Whom the Bell Tolls*, 1959; *People Kill People Sometimes*, 1959; *The Iceman Cometh*, 1960; *One Day in the Life of Ivan Denisovitch*, 1963; *Abe Lincoln in Illinois*, 1964; *Barbra Streisand: The Belle of 14th Street*, 1967; *Ghost Story*, 1970; *The House without a Christmas Tree*, 1972; *The Thanksgiving Treasure*, 1973; *The Country Girl*, 1974; *The Easter Promise*, 1975; *Addie and the King of Hearts*, 1976; *Washington: Behind Closed Doors*, 1977; *A Christmas to Remember*, 1978; *FDR — The Last Year*, 1980; *Haywire*, 1980; *The Magic of David Copperfield*, 1981; *Polar Bear Alert*, 1982; *The Day After*, 1983; *Sakharov*, 1984; *The Long Hot Summer*, 1985; *The* builds such long-fused effects that when he turns to shorter-fused acting we cannot seem to stop expecting them.

Yet he has the kind of acting Americans like to see on the screen: acting they know is acting, either because it is quietly understated or hammily overdone. On stage Robards never overdoes or understates anything. Everything is the product of a careful, studious, slowish actor with ostensibly transparent means. He makes the human kind he embodies seem better than we are, even as we may be thinking of this character as weak. Such powers of characterization have proved eminently suitable for O'Neill's heroes, time and again.

—Joseph Reed

ROBESON, Paul (Leroy). US actor and singer. Born in Princeton, New Jersey, 9 April 1898. Educated at integrated public school in Westfield, New Jersey, 1907–09; Somerville High School, 1911–15; scholar, Rutgers College, New Brunswick, New Jersey, 1915–19; Columbia University Law School, 1920–23. Married Eslanda Cardozo Goode in 1921 (died 1965), one son. Stage debut, New York, 1920, while studying at law school; made first of many British appearances, 1922; singer, Cotton Club, Harlem, New York, 1923; gave up career in law for the stage, 1924; actor, Provincetown Players, New York, 1924; film debut, 1924; established reputation as major recording artist with release of negro spirituals, 1925; European tour, 1929; first of several visits to Soviet Union, 1934; co-founder, with Max Yergan, and chairman, Council on African Affairs, 1937; visited Spain to sing for troops of the International Brigade, 1938; career hampered by hostility to his left-wing politics and support for black civil rights and other causes from the mid-1930's; US concert tour in aid of war effort, 1942; USO-sponsored European tour, 1945; elected vice-president of Civil Rights Congress, 1946; called before various Un-American Activities Committees, 1946, 1948, and 1955; spoke at Paris Peace Conference, 1949; concerts disrupted by violence, 1949; opposed US involvement in Korea, 1950; passport withdrawn, 1950–58; visited UK and Soviet Union, 1958; elected vice-president, British-Soviet Friendship Society, 1959; last concert tour, to Australia and New Zealand, 1960; retired in USA, in ill-health after five years' absence, 1963. Recipient: Abraham Lincoln Medal, 1943; Medal for Good Diction on the Stage, American Academy of Arts and Letters, 1944; Donaldson Award for Outstanding Lead Performance, 1944; NAACP Spingarn Medal, 1945; Artists, Writers, and Printing Workers Congress of Bucharest, Rumania, Award, 1947; Stalin Peace Prize, 1952; Champion of African Freedom, National Church of Nigeria, 1952; Zhitlovsky Award, Zhitlovsky Foundation for Jewish Education, 1970; Black Psychiatrist Association Award, 1972; National Urban League Award, 1972; Emmy Award, 1973; Paul Robeson Award, Actors' Equity Association, 1974. MA: Rutgers University, 1932; degree, Hamilton College, 1940; DHL: Morehouse College, Atlanta, Georgia, 1940; Howard University, Washington D.C., 1945; honorary professor, Moscow State Conservatory of Music, 1958; honorary degree: Humboldt University, German Democratic Republic, 1960; LL.D: Lincoln University, Pennsylvania, 1973. Died in Philadelphia, 27 January 1976.

Roles

1920	Simon in *Simon the Cyrenian* (Torrence), Lafayette Theatre, New York.
1921	Jim in *Taboo/Voodoo* (Wiborg), Sam H. Harris Theatre, New York and British tour.
1924	Jim Harris in *All God's Chillun Got Wings* (O'Neill), Provincetown Playhouse, New York; Embassy Theatre, London, 1933.
	Role in *Rosanne*, Philadelphia.
1925	Brutus Jones in *The Emperor Jones* (O'Neill), Provincetown Playhouse, New York; 52nd Street Theatre, New York; and Ambassadors' Theatre, London; Künstler Theatre, Berlin, 1930; New York, 1939; Philadelphia, 1940.
1926	Black Boy in *Black Boy*, Comedy Theatre, New York.
1927	Crown in *Porgy and Bess* (Heyward and Heyward), Guild Theatre, New York; Republic Theatre, New York, 1928.
	Joe in *Show Boat* (Kern and Hammerstein), Theatre Royal, Drury Lane, London; and Casino Theatre, New York, 1932.
1930	Othello in *Othello* (Shakespeare), Savoy Theatre, London; Brattle Hall, Cambridge, Massachusetts, 1942; Shubert Theatre, New York, 1943; US tour, 1944–45; Shakespeare Memorial Theatre, Stratford-upon-Avon, 1959.
1931	Robert Smith (Yank) in *The Hairy Ape* (O'Neill), Ambassador's Theatre, London.
1935	Workman and Lonnie Thompson in *Stevedore* (Peters and Sklar), Embassy Theatre, London.
	Balu in *Basilik*, Arts Theatre, London.
1936	Toussaint in *Toussaint L'Ouverture* (James), Westminster Theatre, London.
1938	Role in *Plant in the Sun* (Bengal), Unity Theatre, London.
1940	John Henry in *John Henry*, 44th Street Theatre, New York.

Films

Body and Soul, 1924; *Borderline*, 1930; *The Emperor Jones*, 1933; *Sanders of the River*, 1934; *Show Boat*, 1936; *The Song of Freedom*, 1936; *King Solomon's Mines*, 1936; *Big Fella*, 1937; *Jericho*, 1937; *Dark Sands*, 1938; *The Proud Valley*, 1940; *Native Land*, 1942; *Tales of Manhattan*, 1942.

Radio

Ballad for Americans (Corwin, adapted from Latouche's *The Ballad of Uncle Sam*), 1939.

Paul Robeson (1942).

Publications

Here I Stand (autobiography), 1958; *Paul Robeson Speaks: Writings—Speeches—Interviews*, edited by Philip S. Foner, 1978.

*

Bibliography

Books:
Elsanda Goode Robeson, *Paul Robeson, Negro*, New York, 1930.
Earl Schenck Miers, *Big Ben, A Novel*, Philadelphia, 1942.
Shirley Graham, *Paul Robeson, Citizen of the World*, New York, 1946.
Marie Seton, *Paul Robeson*, London, 1958.
Erwin A. Salk, Ernest Kaiser, Paul Robeson, and others, *Paul Robeson: The Great Forerunner*, New York, 1965.
Edwin P. Hoyt, *Paul Robeson: The American Othello*, Cleveland and New York, 1967.
Lloyd L. Brown, *Lift Every Voice for Paul Robeson*, New York, 1971.
Virginia Hamilton, *Paul Robeson: The Life and Times of a Free Black Man*, New York, 1974.
Charles H. Wright, *Robeson: Labor's Forgotten Champion*, Detroit, 1975.
Dorothy Butler Gilliam, *Paul Robeson: All-American*, Washington D.C., 1976.
Ron Ramdin, *Paul Robeson: The Man and his Mission*, London, 1987.
Martin Bauml Duberman, *Paul Robeson*, London, 1989.
Marie Stuart, *Paul Robeson*, Bristol, 1993.

* * *

Paul Robeson was the finest black actor since Ira Aldridge. He had a commanding physical presence and an extraordinary bass-baritone voice, and in a career dogged by racism, he pushed back the boundaries of what was possible for black actors on the stage.

Robeson came to acting almost by accident, being cajoled into playing the title role in *Simon the Cyrenian* for the Amateur Players. This led to his first professional role in *Taboo* (1921). In 1924 he joined the Provincetown Players, to star in *All God's Chillun Got Wings* and *The Emperor Jones*. In playing the role of Jim in *All God's Chillun*, Robeson was, as Martin Bauml Duberman has observed, "already carrying on his head the curses of one race and the hopes of another". When it was reported that a white woman would kiss a black man's hand on the New York stage, both Robeson and playwright Eugene O'Neill became the targets of death threats from the Ku Klux Klan. The *American* carried an article with the headline "Riots Feared from Drama". In the event, however, the performance passed without incident.

At this stage, Robeson, who had no training as an actor, relied less on technique, perhaps, than on the power of his voice. "I was the former college athlete playing on muscle", he recalled; "oratory was the basis of my approach to the theatre". Nevertheless, John Corbin wrote that Robeson had an "admirable directness and dignity ... force too, and even fire" and Ludwig Lewisohn declared: "Mr Paul Robeson is a superb actor, extraordinarily sincere and eloquent".

He repeated the role of Brutus Jones in London and it was here too that he starred in *Show Boat* in 1928. J. A. Rodgers complained that the role of Joe was simply another example of the familiar racial stereotype of the "lazy, good-natured, lolling darkey". Despite this, 'Ol' Man River' was to become Robeson's adopted theme song; in later years he himself changed the lyrics to turn it from a song of despair into one of triumph:

> You show a little grit and land in jail.
> But I keep laughin', instead of cryin',
> I must keep fightin', until I'm dyin'.

It was in London too that he first played the part of Othello (1930). The production was poorly directed and there were mixed reviews for Robeson; some called his performance great, but others argued that he was too subdued, as if "afraid of losing himself". Margaret Webster saw the production and thought him "very bad" in the role. Nevertheless, she fought "hostility and predictions of doom" to bring him to Broadway in 1943. It was the first time in the USA that the role had been played by a black man. The production, Webster said, was "trying to prove something other than itself"; it was "a declaration", an "event": "When Paul Robeson stepped onto the stage for the very first time, when he spoke his very first line, he immediately, by his very presence, brought an incalculable sense of reality to the entire play. Here was a great man, a man of simplicity and strength; here also was a black man. We believed that he could command the armies of Venice; we knew that he would always be alien to its society".

The performance was the pinnacle of Robeson's career, though he still had a tendency to "orate", to concentrate "more on vocal tones than on acting". Webster felt he was at his best in the gentler passages. The scenes of savage jealousy and rage seemed to be beyond him. It was, perhaps, "a triumph of presence, not acting".

"I like to feel", Robeson once remarked, "that my work has a farther reach than its artistic appeal. I consider art as a social weapon". In interviews, he emphasized his view of Othello as a great, and persecuted, "Negro warrior". He described the play as "the problem of my own people. It is a tragedy of racial conflict, a tragedy of honour, rather than of jealousy": "Not simply for art's sake do I try to excel in *Othello*, but more to prove the capacity of the people from whom I've sprung and of all such peoples, of whatever colour, erroneously regarded as backward".

From the early 1930's, Robeson was increasingly committed to the cause of African liberation and anit-imperialism. "I am a Negro with every drop of my blood and with every stir of my soul", he declared. "In my Negro heart lies buried the memories of centuries of oppression". He saw his acting and singing as an extension of this: "In my music, my plays, my films, I want to carry always this central idea: to be African". In the postwar years Robeson was pilloried for his left-wing views and his outspoken affection for the Soviet Union. When he refused to sign an affadavit disclaiming membership of the Communist Party, his passport was withdrawn. The concert halls were closed to him and he became, in his own words, "a prisoner in my native land".

Paul Robeson Jr wrote: "My father survived an unprecedented onslaught. He took all they had to throw at him, came out the other end triumphant, unbowed — his famous comment was, 'I shall not retreat one thousandth part of an inch' ... He never took a word back, and he retired unbowed and undefeated".

"The artist", Robeson declared, "must elect to fight for Freedom or for Slavery. I have made my choice". But the pressure in some ways destroyed his health and his career. He returned to the stage in the role of Othello at Stratford-upon-Avon in 1959, but he was by now, according to Webster, "too old and too fat". It was to be his swan song as illness forced him off the stage more than a decade before his eventual death.

—David and Stanley Allen

ROBSON, (Dame) Flora. British actress. Born in South Shields, County Durham, 28 March 1902. Educated at Palmer's Green High School, London; trained at the Royal Academy of Dramatic Art, 1919–21. Stage debut, Shaftesbury Theatre, London, 1921; actress, Ben Greet's company, 1922, and under J. B. Fagan at the Oxford Playhouse, 1923; appeared at Ambassadors' Theatre, London, 1924, then retired from stage for four years to work as factory welfare officer; actress, Anmer Hall's company at the Festival Theatre, Cambridge, 1929–30; film debut, 1931; joined Old Vic-Sadler's Wells company, 1933; visited New York for first time, 1939; returned to UK, 1944; effectively

retired from the stage, 1969. Fellow: St Anne's College, Oxford; Sunderland Polytechnic, 1975. Member: Actors' Day Society (president, 1950's); Council of the Royal Academy of Dramatic Art (chairman, 1952). Recipient: Bronze Medal, Royal Academy of Dramatic Art, 1921; *Film Weekly* Best Actress Award, 1937; *Evening News* Third Best Actress in International Films, 1938; National Board of Review (US) Best Acting Category, 1939; *News Chronicle* Award for Best Television Actress, 1956 and 1957; *Evening Standard* Best Actress Award, 1960; Cleveland Critics' Circle Award, 1964; Monte Carlo Television Festival Best Actress, 1978. D.Litt: University of London, 1971; University of Wales, 1974; University of Durham, 1974; University of Oxford, 1974. Finnish Order of the White Lion and the White Rose for Services to Humanity, 1949; CBE (Commander of the British Empire), 1952; DBE (Dame Commander of the British Empire), 1960. Died in Brighton, Sussex, 7 July 1984.

Roles

1921	Queen Margaret in *Will Shakespeare* (Dane), Shaftesbury Theatre, London.
1924	Annie in *Fata Morgana* (Vajda, translated by Burrell and Moeller), Ambassadors' Theatre, London.
1931	Tatiana in *Betrayal* (Andreyev, adapted by Troubridge and Hogan), Little Theatre, London.
	Abbie Putnam in *Desire Under the Elms* (O'Neill), Gate Theatre, London.
	Herodias in *Salome* (Wilde), Gate Theatre, London.
	Mary Paterson in *The Anatomist* (Bridie), Westminster Theatre, London.
1932	The Stepdaughter in *Six Characters in Search of an Author* (Pirandello), Westminster Theatre, London.
	Bianca in *Othello* (Shakespeare), St James's Theatre, London.
	Olwen Peel in *Dangerous Corner* (Priestley), Lyric Theatre, London.
	Mercia in *The Storm Fighter*, St Martin's Theatre, London.
	Eva in *For Services Rendered* (Maugham), St Martin's Theatre, London.
1933	Lady Audley in *Lady Audley's Secret* (Roberts), Arts Theatre, London.
	Penelope Otto in *Head-On Crash* (L. Miller), Queen's Theatre, London.
	Ella Downey in *All God's Chillun* (O'Neill), Embassy Theatre, London.
	Narouli Karth in *Vessels Departing*, Embassy Theatre, London.
	Varya in *The Cherry Orchard* (Chekhov), Old Vic Theatre, London.
	Queen Katharine in *Henry VIII* (Shakespeare), Sadler's Wells Theatre, London.
	Isabella in *Measure for Measure* (Shakespeare), Old Vic Theatre, London.
1934	Gwendolen Fairfax in *The Importance of Being Earnest* (Wilde), Old Vic Theatre, London.

Mrs Foresight in *Love for Love* (Congreve), Sadler's Wells Theatre, London.

Ceres in *The Tempest* (Shakespeare), Sadler's Wells Theatre, London.

Lady Macbeth in *Macbeth* (Shakespeare), Old Vic Theatre, London; National Theatre, New York, 1948.

Elizabeth Enticknap in *Touch Wood* (Anthony), Haymarket Theatre, London.

Mary Read in *Mary Read: Dragoon and Pirate* (Bridie), His Majesty's Theatre, London.

1935   Liesa Bergmann in *Close Quarters* (Čapek), Embassy Theatre, London, and Haymarket Theatre, London; British tour, 1963.

Mary Tudor in *Mary Tudor* (Grantham), Playhouse Theatre, London.

1937   Anna Christopherson in *Anna Christie* (O'Neill), Westminster Theatre, London.

Mrs Ellen de Meyer in *Satyr* (Leslie), Shaftesbury Theatre, London.

Lady Catherine Brooke in *Autumn* (Kennedy and Ratoff), St Marin's Theatre, London; Q Theatre, London, 1951.

1938   Anya in *Last Train South* (Hutchinson), St Martin's Theatre, London.

1940   Ellen Creed in *Ladies in Retirement* (Denham and Percy), Henry Miller Theatre, New York.

1941   Duchess of Marlborough in *Anne of England*, St James's Theatre, London.

1942   Elizabeth in *Elizabeth the Queen* (Anderson), US tour.

Rhoda Meldrum in *The Damask Cheek* (Van Druten), Playhouse Theatre, New York.

1943   Several roles in Grand Guignol plays, Belasco Theatre, Los Angeles.

1944   Thérèse Raquin in *Guilty* (Boutall, adapted from Zola), Lyric Theatre, Hammersmith, London.

1945   Ethel Fry in *Ethel Fry*, British tour.

Agnes Isit in *A Man About the House* (Young), British tour; Piccadilly Theatre, London, 1946.

1946   Margaret Hayden in *Message for Margaret* (Parish), Westminster Theatre, London.

1948   Lady Cicely Wayneflete in *Captain Brassbound's Conversion* (G. B. Shaw), Theatre Royal, Windsor, and Lyric Theatre, Hammersmith, London.

1949   Alicia Christie in *Black Chiffon* (Storm), Westminster Theatre, London; 48th Street Theatre, New York, 1950.

1951   Paulina in *The Winter's Tale* (Shakespeare), Phoenix Theatre, London.

1952   Miss Giddens in *The Innocents* (Archibald, adapted from James), Her Majesty's Theatre, London.

1953   Sister Agatha in *The Return*, Duchess Theatre, London.

1954   Rachel Lloyd in *No Escape* (Davies), British tour.

1955   Sarah Ashby in *A Kind of Folly* (Holder), Duchess Theatre, London.

1956   Janet in *The House by the Lake* (Mills), Duke of York's Theatre, London.

Flora Robson

1958   Mrs Alving in *Ghosts* (Ibsen), Old Vic Theatre, London; Prince's Theatre, London, 1959.

1959   Miss Tina in *The Aspern Papers* (Redgrave, adapted from James), Queen's Theatre, London; South African tour, 1960.

1961   Grace Rovarte in *Time and Yellow Roses* (Storm), St Martin's Theatre, London.

Miss Moffat in *The Corn is Green* (E. Williams), Connaught Theatre, Worthing; South African tour and Flora Robson Playhouse, Newcastle-upon-Tyne, 1962.

1963   Gunhild Borkman in *John Gabriel Borkman* (Ibsen), Duchess Theatre, London.

1964   Lady Bracknell in *The Importance of Being Earnest* (Wilde), Duchess Theatre, London.

1966   Hecuba in *The Trojan Women* (Euripides), Edinburgh Festival.

1967   Winifred Brazier in *Brother and Sister* (Bolt), British tour.

1968   Miss Prism in *The Importance of Being Earnest* (Wilde), Haymarket Theatre, London.

The Mother in *Ring Round the Moon* (Anouilh), Haymarket Theatre, London.

1969   Agatha Payne in *The Old Ladies* (Ackland and Walpole), Westminster Theatre, London, and Duchess Theatre, London.

1970   Elizabeth Tudor in *Elizabeth Tudor, Queen of England*, Edinburgh Festival.

1974   Narrator in *Peter and the Wolf* (Prokofiev), Brighton Festival.

Films

A Gentleman of Paris, 1931; *Dance Pretty Lady*, 1932; *One Precious Year*, 1933; *Catherine the Great*, 1933; *Fire Over England*, 1937; *Wuthering Heights*, 1939; *Poison Pen*, 1939; *We Are Not Alone*, 1939; *Invisible Stripes*, 1940; *The Sea Hawk*, 1941; *Bahama Passage*, 1942; *Saratoga Trunk*, 1943; *2000 Women*, 1944; *The Years Between*, 1945; *Great Day*, 1945; *Caesar and Cleopatra*, 1945; *Black Narcissus*, 1947; *Frieda*, 1947; *Holiday Camp*, 1947; *Good Time Girl*, 1948; *Saraband for Dead Lovers*, 1948; *The Tall Headlines*, 1952; *The Malta Story*, 1953; *Romeo and Juliet*, 1954; *High Tide at Noon*, 1957; *No Time for Tears*, 1957; *The Gypsy and the Gentleman*, 1957; *Innocent Sinners*, 1958; *55 Days at Peking*, 1962; *Murder at the Gallop*, 1962; *Guns at Batasi*, 1964; *Young Cassidy*, 1964; *Those Magnificent Men in Their Flying Machines*, 1965; *Seven Women*, 1965; *The Shuttered Room*, 1966; *Cry in the Wind*, 1966; *Eye of the Devil*, 1967; *Fragment of Fear*, 1970; *The Beast in the Cellar*, 1971; *The Beloved*, 1972; *Alice's Adventures in Wonderland*, 1972; *La Grande Scrofa Nera*, 1974; *Dominique*, 1979; *Clash of Titans*, 1981.

Television

Heidi, 1974; *A Legacy*, 1975; *Mr Lollipop*, 1976; *The Shrimp and the Anenome*, 1977; *The Oresteia of Aeschylus*, 1978; *Les Misérables*, 1978; *Eustace and Hilda*, 1979; *A Man Called Intrepid*, 1979; *Gauguin the Savage*, 1980; *A Tale of Two Cities*, 1980.

*

Bibliography

Books:
Janet Dunbar, *Flora Robson*, London, 1960.
Kenneth H. Barrow, *Flora*, London, 1981.

* * *

Flora Robson's career was a paradox. Capable of projecting the outer limits of turpitude or morbid psychology she yet came to be a symbol in the public mind of a certain kind of English woman, dependable and patriotic, not glamorous enough to arouse enthusiasm and envy. She lacked the kind of 'star quality' that leads to journalistic curiosity. Perhaps her most enduring image was associated with Queen Elizabeth I, as embodied in her unforgettable delivery of that monarch's Tilbury oration in the film *Fire Over England*.

She was at her best in the 1930's in O'Neill, Maugham, and Pirandello, always in roles that revealed anarchical power beneath a subdued, almost dowdy exterior. One of these, Eva, a member of Maugham's doomed middle-class family in *For Services Rendered*, not only provided Robson's contrasting images, the prosaic and the outrageous, in sequence but stole the limelight from such distinguished fellow-performers as Cedric Hardwicke and Ralph Richardson. Having introduced Eva in his stage directions as thin, haggard, gentle, subdued, but not seeming at peace with herself, Maugham adds that "behind the placidity is a strange restlessness". If ever there was a cue for the two

aspects of Robson, that was it, and she proceeded to chart the stages of the character's decline to the letter. At 39, her fiancé killed in World War I, Eva has become the family drudge, in and out all the time making tea and ruthlessly exploited by her cynical blind brother. Pathetic rebellion eventually surfaces when she offers her savings to rescue their friend Collie from bankruptcy, suggesting a fake engagement to overcome his reluctance and finally proposing marriage in a series of scenes demanding the most of any actress. The gradations of the slide into humiliation were exactly caught in Robson's performance, which reached new heights at the point where Eva finally becomes mad. When Collie, refused help elsewhere, kills himself, Robson supplied a shriek that was, in obedience to the author's wish, "only just human", then directed a veritable paroxysm of hatred against Eva's father. After that she upended a table and the ornaments on it, shrieked once more, and threw herself down and beat the floor.

But the climax of her performance as Eva was still to come. Supposedly restored to her senses when put under sedation, Robson's Eva ended the play with a distorted rendition of the national anthem. What Maugham wanted from the rest of the family was horror-struck surprise. In Robson's hands, that too was the effect the tune had on the audience.

Robson's gift was different in kind from that of any other English actress of her generation, exploited at routine West End level in, for example, *Black Chiffon*. As Varya in *The Cherry Orchard* it had to be held in abeyance and it was surprisingly absent as a result of the lack of resonance in the verse diction from her Lady Macbeth. For the affectless evil of Zola's Thérèse Raquin it was of course perfect.

But it was in O'Neill's *All God's Chillun Got Wings* that Flora Robson's ability to strike terror into an audience was given full rein. In this play O'Neill exploits his 'compressionist' mode, the cult of enclosure derived from Strindberg, even to the extent of having the set progressively contracted laterally and vertically to increase the tension. It deals with the entrapment of a Black student by his White US wife, unable to cope with the social stresses of a mixed marriage and with her intellectual inferiority to her husband. Hysteria in the closed space becomes inevitable and in this production reached a climax when Robson crept up behind her unsuspecting partner, knife in hand and murder in her eyes. Paul Robeson played the student, his performance finely judged but inevitably less memorable than hers.

That she could stand comparison, given the opportunity, with actors of Paul Robeson's calibre she demonstrated once more in *Close Quarters*, a two character-play by the Čapek brothers. On that occasion her partner was the massively powerful German actor, Oscar Homolka. Gradually, however, the fires were damped in creditable performances in Ibsen and Henry James. In the film of *Wuthering Heights*, meanwhile, she supplied much-needed backbone as the servant Nelly Deans.

—Laurence Kitchin

RONCONI, Luca. Italian director and actor. Born in Susa, Tunisia, 1933. Trained for the theatre at the National Academy of Dramatic Art, Rome. Began career as an actor with several major companies, including those of Vittorio Gassman and the Teatro Stabile in Turin, in the early 1960's; made debut as a director, 1963, and subsequently won acclaim for productions of Renaissance drama; director, Teatro Biennale, Venice, 1973; has also staged numerous operas and directed films since the late 1970's.

Selected productions

As director:
1963	*La Buona Moglie* (Goldoni).
1966	*I Lunatici* (Middleton and Rowley).
1967	*Measure for Measure* (Shakespeare).
	Richard III (Shakespeare).
1968	*Il Candelaoi* (Bruno).
	La Tragedia del vendicatore (Tourneur).
	Orlando Furioso (Ronconi and Sanguinetti, adapted from Ariosto).
1972	*Kätchen von Heillbron* (Kleist).
	Oresteia (Aeschylus).
1975	*Utopia* (compilation from Aristophanes).
	The Birds (Aristophanes).

Other productions have included: *The Barber of Seville* (Rossini); *Faust* (Gounod); *A Game at Chess* (Middleton); *Ghosts* (Ibsen); *Gli straccioni*; *Orpheus and Eurydice* (Gluck); *Siegfried* (Wagner); *The Valkyrie* (Wagner); *XX*.

*

Bibliography

Books:
Cesare Milanese, *Luca Ronconi e la realta del teatro*, Milan, 1973.

* * *

Italian director Luca Ronconi made his greatest impact upon the contemporary theatre through his experiments with non-frontal staging in the late 1960's and 1970's. He exploded onto the scene with the 1968 production of *Orlando Furioso*, an adaptation by Eduardo Sanguinetti of Ludovico Ariosto's epic poem. Ronconi's work often takes on epic proportions; he has a penchant for great theatricality and theatre that occupies vast spaces. His theatre has elements of the frenzy of Eugenio Barba or Jerzy Grotowski, the splendour of Ariane Mnouchkine and the immensity of Robert Wilson. He is a director of great imagination, committed to expanding the standard repertoire.

Ronconi began his career as metteur en scène after working as an actor in Italian companies for a number of years. His first successes as a director were with Italian and Roman comedy, especially Goldoni's *La Buona Moglie* [The Good Wife]. He incites a flamboyant style of performance, highly physical, where the actor utilizes his or her full range of emotions. The tradition of the commedia dell'arte is strongly felt, but modernized for today's audiences. A Latin spirit, à la Fellini, pervades Ronconi's theatre. He applied his individual style to Elizabethan drama in the 1960's, directing Thomas Middleton and William Rowley's *The Changeling* (*I Lunatici*), Cyril Tourneur's *The Revenger's Tragedy* (*La Tragedia del vendicatore*) and Shakespeare's *Measure for Measure* and

Richard III. He also revived the 16th-century playwright Giardano Bruno's only play, *Il Candelaoi* [The Candlemaker], and in 1968 produced one of Carl Sternheim's grotesque comedies. Ronconi's choice of texts tends toward the marginal and the unconventional; his stage pictures speak with a very particular voice.

Orlando Furioso had the atmosphere of a medieval festival, with multiple playing areas and simultaneous scenes; it was magical and extravagant. The spectators moved in and around the performers, and were obliged to avoid the movements of mechanical horses attached to mechanical platforms. There was an intense energy in this production, in which theatre flirted with real danger. As a result, Ronconi jumped into the limelight much as Mnouchkine did after *1789*.

In 1971, Ronconi continued his experiments with alternative uses of space by staging *XX* within a two-storey house placed upon the stage of the Théâtre de l'Odéon in Paris. This environmental production led the spectator from room to room of the house, resulting in different performance experiences for each audience member. The dramas played out in the various rooms created a claustrophobic ambiance, which was altered when the partitions between the rooms were lifted to allow the spectator to view all 20 scenes in one performance space. The following year, Ronconi staged Kleist's *Kätchen von Heillbron* on barges on the lake at Zurich. Also in 1972, he directed the *Oresteia* of Aeschylus in Belgrade on a platform thrust-type stage on two levels. Here the audience was very close to the performance space constructed from blond wood. This production emphasized immobility, in stark contrast to *Orlando Furioso*, for example. Ronconi builds a space for each mise en scène as a significant statement in itself.

At the Edinburgh Festival in 1975, Ronconi staged *Utopia* with spectators on opposite sides of the street. The space thus created the atmosphere of a parade: cars, buses, airplanes and beds on wheels sped past the audience. A large cast of bombarding actors played in this enormous stage area in a style appropriate for the open-air. The text was a collage of Aristophanes' writings arranged to make a social statement against the bourgeoisie. Ronconi continued his work with Greek texts in several new mises en scène of Euripides, Aristophanes and Aeschylus in Vienna.

During the late 1970's and 1980's, Luca Ronconi moved even closer to the Italianate stage. His first opera production, *The Barber of Seville*, was seen at the Odéon in Paris, not in capacity an opera stage. At about the same time that Ronconi's interest moved to opera, he also started staging Ibsen plays in frontal performance spaces, even utilizing a realistic style of acting. Ronconi is a director full of surprises, totally individual and impossible to categorize. His approach to the theatre is unique and inspired.

The greatest testament to Ronconi's abilities as a director is the fact that his theatrical mises en scène were able to play internationally in Italian, without major loss of understanding. His stage action, use of gesture, 'tableaux vivants' and popular spirit made his dynamic productions of the late 1960's and 1970's commercial successes from Spoleto to New York. He was one of the 'star' directors of the era, whose work today has been absorbed into the conventional theatre.

—Ron Popenhagen

ROSENTHAL, Jean. US designer. Born 1912. Began career as collaborator with Orson Welles on the Federal Theatre Project in the 1930's; worked with choreographer Martha Graham, from 1938; acclaimed for innovations in stage lighting design; also worked on lighting designs for auditoria, airports and hotels. Died 1969.

Selected productions

As lighting director:
1947   *The Telephone* (Menotti), New York.
         The Medium (Menotti), New York.
1948   *Joy to the World* (Scott), Plymouth Theatre, New York.
1950   *The Consul* (Menotti), Philadelphia.
1954   *Show Boat* (Hammerstein and Kern), City Opera House, New York.
1956   *King John* (Shakespeare), American Shakespeare Festival, Stratford, Connecticut; Phoenix Theatre, New York, 1957.
         Measure for Measure (Shakespeare), American Shakespeare Festival, Stratford, Connecticut; Phoenix Theatre, New York, 1957.
         The Taming of the Shrew (Shakespeare), American Shakespeare Festival, Stratford, Connecticut; Phoenix Theatre, New York, 1957.
1957   *The Merchant of Venice* (Shakespeare), American Shakespeare Festival, Stratford, Connecticut; Phoenix Theatre, New York, 1957.
         West Side Story (Bernstein, Sondheim and Laurents), Winter Garden Theatre, New York.
         The Dark at the Top of the Stairs (Inge), Music Box Theatre, New York.
1958   *Hamlet* (Shakespeare), American Shakespeare Festival, Stratford, Connecticut; Phoenix Theatre, New York, 1957.
1959   *The Sound of Music* (Rodgers and Hammerstein), Lunt-Fontanne Theatre, New York.
1960   *Caligula* (Camus), 54th Street Theatre, New York.
         West Side Story (Bernstein, Sondheim and Laurents), Winter Garden Theatre, New York.
1961   *The Night of the Iguana* (T. Williams), Royale Theatre, New York.
1962   *A Funny Thing Happened on the Way to the Forum* (Sondheim, Shevelove, and Gelbart), Alvin Theatre, New York.
         Lord Pengo (Behrman), Royale Theatre, New York.
1963   *Barefoot in the Park* (Simon), Biltmore Theatre, New York.
         The Ballad of the Sad Café (Albee), Martin Beck Theatre, New York.
1964   *Hello, Dolly!* (Herman and Stewart), St James Theatre, New York.
         Fiddler on the Roof (Bock and Stein), Imperial Theatre, New York.
         Incident at Vichy (Miller), Washington Square Theatre, New York.
1965   *The Odd Couple* (Simon), Plymouth Theatre, New York.

1966   *Cabaret* (Kander, Ebb and Masteroff), Broadhurst Theatre, New York.
         I do! I do! (Jones and Schmidt), 46th Street Theatre, New York.
         The Star-Spangled Girl (Simon), Plymouth Theatre, New York.
1968   *Plaza Suite* (Simon), Plymouth Theatre, New York.

Other productions included: *The Seventh Trumpet* (Kennedy), 1941; *Richard III* (Shakespeare), 1943; *Sundown Beach* (Breuer), 1948; *Caesar and Cleopatra* (G. B. Shaw), 1949; *The Climate of Eden* (Hart), 1952; *Ondine* (Giraudoux), 1954; *Die Fledermaus* (Strauss), 1954; *Carousel* (Rodgers and Hammerstein), 1954; *Quadrille* (Coward), 1954; *The Saint of Bleecker Street* (Menotti), 1954; *House of Flowers* (Capote), 1954; *The Time of Your Life* (Saroyan), 1955; *Julius Caesar* (Shakespeare), 1955; *The Tempest* (Shakespeare), 1955; *The Great Sebastians* (Lindsay and Crouse), 1956; *The King and I* (Rodgers and Hammerstein), 1956; *Kiss Me, Kate* (Porter and Spewack), 1956; *A Hole in the Head* (Schulman), 1957; *Much Ado About Nothing* (Shakespeare), 1957; *The Beggar's Opera* (Gay), 1957; *The Duchess of Malfi* (Webster), 1957; *Othello* (Shakespeare), 1957; *Jamaica* (Harburg and Saidy), 1957; *Winesburg, Ohio*, 1958; *The Winter's Tale* (Shakespeare), 1958; *The Disenchanted* (Schulberg and Breit), 1958; *Redhead* (Fields, Sheldon and Shaw), 1959; *Destry Rides Again* (Gershe), 1959; *Judy Garland*, 1959; *All's Well That Ends Well* (Shakespeare), 1959; *Take Me Along* (Stein and Russell, adapted from O'Neill), 1959; *Henry IV*, 1960; *Dear Liar* (Kilty), 1960; *A Taste of Honey* (Delaney), 1960; *Becket* (Anouilh), 1960; *The Conquering Hero* (Monkhouse), 1961; *The Gay Life* (Kanin, adapted from Schnitzler), 1961; *Daughter of Silence* (West), 1961; *A Gift of Time*, 1962; *On an Open Roof*, 1963; *The Beast in Me* (Costigan, adapted from Thurber), 1963; *Jennie* (Burton), 1963; *The Chinese Prime Minister* (Bagnold), 1964; *West Side Story* (Bernstein, Sondheim and Laurents), 1964; *Hamlet* (Shakespeare), 1964; *To Broadway With Love*, 1964; *Luv* (Schisgal), 1964; *Poor Bitos* (Anouilh), 1964; *Baker Street*, 1965; *The Country Wife* (Wycherley), 1965; *Happily Never After*, 1966; *Ivanov* (Chekhov), 1966; *A Time for Singing*, 1966; *Show Boat* (Kern and Hammerstein), 1966; *The Diary of Adam and Eve*, 1966; *The Lady or the Tiger?*, 1966; *Passionella*, 1966; *Ilya Darling*, 1967; *Hello, Dolly!* (Herman and Stewart), 1967; *The Happy Time* (Taylor, adapted from Fontaine), 1968; *Weekend*, 1968; *The Exercise*, 1968; *Twelfth Night* (Shakespeare), 1968; *Dear World*, 1969.

Publications

The Magic of Light.

*   *   *

Light has been a key aspect in the development of modern theatre design, figuring centrally in the theories of Adolphe Appia and Edward Gordon Craig. But until Jean Rosenthal there was, essentially, no craft or art of lighting design. Many theatre artists who were known primarily as set designers did their own lighting, but more often the job was done by technicians. One of the first to work as a lighting designer was Abe Feder, but he did not have the effect nor the 'magic' that Rosenthal did. Rosenthal wrote that lighting design emerged out of necessity in the 1930's as the Depression began to limit the lavishness of theatrical design, forcing certain productions to use essentially bare stages in which locales were determined not by scenery but by pools of light. Light, an ephemeral entity, replaced the concrete nature of a tangible set. In this emergent form of design, clearly influenced by Appia, light became the primary design element. Nowhere was this more true than in dance, a field in which Rosenthal had a profound impact. The visual aspect of both modern dance and ballet, virtually throughout the Western world, is largely the result of Rosenthal's contributions.

Rosenthal began as a technical assistant with Project 891 of the Federal Theatre Project, the company headed by John Houseman and Orson Welles. During her experiences there and subsequently with Houseman's production of *Hamlet*, with Welles's Mercury Theatre, with American Ballet Caravan, and with Martha Graham, Rosenthal virtually invented the art of lighting design. By the time of her death in 1969 she had lit some 4000 productions and architectural projects and there were years when as many as one third of the productions on Broadway were designed by her.

Until the 1930's, light had been used primarily for illumination or special effects. The idea of light as a primary element for the shaping of mood or rhythm was not common, though Lee Simonson and Norman Bel Geddes had begun to use it in this way. But Rosenthal saw light as a lyrical element second only to the music in opera, for instance, in terms of its power and flexibility. She talked about it almost as a sculptor talks about clay; it was, said Rosenthal, tactile and possessed shape and dimension. She was also one of the first to note that light on the stage possessed form, colour and movement. While all are important, it is movement that has the greatest effect on the rhythm of a production and contributes greatly to emotional effect. Movement refers to the way in which light changes from scene to scene or even moment to moment. Rosenthal was one of the first to recognise the power of these three components of stage lighting and how they could be manipulated to achieve hitherto unknown effects. Her mastery of the art was such that she was often called a magician and the title of her book is *The Magic of Light*. Audiences and even theatre practitioners are seldom aware of the complexities of light; they know that something is dark or bright. But Rosenthal understood light as a three-dimensional entity. Discussing dance she noted, "Dancers live in light as fish live in water". She understood that the entire volume of the stage was an environment of light through which the performers moved and the success of the dance often hinged on how the light was shaped and how it responded to the movement of the performers.

When Rosenthal began to design for dance the general practice was to light the first ten feet of the stage brightly and to provide minimal illumination for the remaining depth of the stage, resulting in a flat image and poorly defined dancers. Rosenthal lit the whole stage, sculpting the space through the use of light and shadow. She also designed light that 'moved' with the music and the movement of the dancers. The result was a greater sense of three-dimensionality and a greater sense of the performers. In a similar way, when she began to work in opera she

startled many observers by bringing a new sense of life to old sets that were previously perceived as flat and dreary. Rosenthal felt that the key to opera lighting was to give a credibility to a form that is inherently unrealistic in presentation but should carry great emotional weight. Much, if not all, of Rosenthal's approach to design is now common practice.

Rosenthal approached much of her design work in a conceptual way. She looked for the touchstone that would provide the inspiration for the light. It could be a colour, a texture, a word in the script, or a scenic element. Out of this she would work to create a quality that captured the essence of the scene or play. Rosenthal was not concerned that the audience would understand the specific metaphors or concepts — in fact, they should not — but she wanted them to experience the emotional impact of the metaphor through light.

Finally, Rosenthal left a particularly significant legacy beyond her design itself. Set design in the USA is still almost totally a male-dominated field. But because lighting design was begun, in essence, by a woman, it has been wide open to women as a field of endeavour ever since.

—Arnold Aronson

ROSSI, Ernesto (Fortunato Giovanni Maria). Italian actor-manager. Born in Leghorn, Italy, 27 March 1827. Educated at the College di San Sebastiano, Leghorn, until 1845. Stage debut, with the Calloud company after several years with amateur groups, 1845; began in amoroso roles but later concentrated on psychological parts; joined the Modena company, 1846, and the Leigheb company, 1848; became leading man with the Reale Sarda company, 1852, and appeared frequently opposite Adelaide Ristori in Italy and, 1855–56, in Paris; joined Asti company, 1856, and won acclaim acting in and directing Shakespeare; founded own company, 1864; toured widely, visiting the USA, 1865, South America, 1871, and London, 1876 and 1882; last stage appearance, as King Lear, Odessa, 1896. Died in Pescara, Italy, 4 July 1896.

Roles

Il Barone in *Ventaglio* (Goldoni); Bonfil in *Pamela nubile* (Goldoni); Carlo in *Filippo* (Alfieri); Coriolanus in *Coriolanus* (Shakespeare); David in *Saul* (Alfieri); Hamlet in *Hamlet* (Shakespeare); Jacopo Foscari in *Jacopo Foscari* (Vollo); Lear in *Re Lear* (Shakespeare); Macbeth in *Macbeth* (Shakespeare); Mefistofele in *Enrico Faust* (Montazio, adapted from Goethe); Nemours in *Luigi XI* (Delavigne); Oreste in *Oreste* (Alfieri); Othello in *Othello* (Shakespeare); Paolo in *Francesca da Rimini* (Pellico); Rémy in *Claudia* (Sand); Richard in *Richard III* (Shakespeare); Romeo in *Romeo and Juliet* (Shakespeare); Shylock in *The Merchant of Venice* (Shakespeare).

Also acted roles in: *Antonio Foscari* (Niccolini); *Il Bicchier d'acqua* (Scribe); *Il Boccaccio a Napoli* (Bettoli); *Cavelleria rusticana* (Verga); *Cid* (Corneille); *Il Cittadino di Gand* (Romano); *Clavigo* (Goethe); *Colpe e speranze* (Ruta); *La Colunnia* (Scribe); *Il Conte di Essex* (Laube); *Il*

Conte Herman (Dumas père); *La Donna romantica e il medico omeopatico* (Castelvecchio); *I Due Sergenti* (Roti); *Fedeltà alla prova* (Lafontaine); *Filippo* (Alfieri); *Il Fornaretto* (Dall'Ongaro); *Francesca da Rimini* (Pellico); *Le Gelosie di Lindoro* (Goldoni); *Giacomo I* (Sue and Dinaux); *Il Giocatore* (Iffland); *Giorgio Sullivan* (Mélesville); *Giovanni da Procido* (Niccolini); *Giulio Cesar* (Shakespeare); *Gli Innamorati* (Goldoni); *Guglielmo Shakespeare* (Gualtieri); *Kean* (Dumas); *La Mandragola* (Macchiavelli); *Un Milione pagabile a vista* (Montazio); *Montjoie* (Feuillet); *Morte civile* (Giacometti), *Nerone* (Cossa); *Pamela nubile* (Goldoni); *Ruy Blas* (Hugo); *Sardanapalo* (Byron); *Virginia* (Alfieri); *La Vita è sogno* (Calderón).

Publications

Adele (play); *Consorzio parentale* (play); *Il Comico in villeggiatura* (play); *Giulio Cesare* (translation of Shakespeare's *Julius Caesar*); *Studi drammatici e lettere autobiografiche*, 1885; *Quaranta anni di vita artistica*, 3 vols., 1887–89; *Riflessioni sul Teatro Drammatico Italiano*, 1893.

*

Bibliography

Books:
Carlo Guetta, *Ernesto Rossi, Appunti e Ricordi*, Leghorn, 1906.
Aurelio Zanco, *Ernesto Rossi, Interprete e Critico Shakespeariano*, 1939.

* * *

Ernesto Rossi was one of the greatest Italian actors of the nineteenth century, and like Adelaide Ristori and his rival, Tommaso Salvini, he was forced to perform abroad, only making sporadic appearances in Italy. His life spans the period of the struggle for Italian unification, and although many of the actors of the day were actively involved in the fight for independence, the question of subsidy for theatre companies was very low on the list of politicians' priorities. In 1864 Salvini appealed to the new king of Italy, Vittorio Emanuele, for state support of the theatre, but even after unification in 1870 that help was slow in coming. Rossi's career, like that of many of his contemporaries, was shaped in part by the absence of funding and by the subsequent need for actors to tour extensively abroad, both in order to survive financially and in order to extend the range of their work.

In 1865 Rossi was invited by Ristori and Salvini to appear at the Dante festival, where he gave readings from the *Divina Commedia*, and these three actors were generally regarded as Italy's best. The comparisons of Rossi's work with Salvini's are partisan at worst, speculative at best, but what is clear is that Salvini chose to work alongside Ristori for a substantial period of his career, whilst Rossi preferred to work in his own company and chose his leading ladies. This difference in working methods had an impact on the repertoire and on the place of the leading man within the company structure. The 'mattatore' system of star performers with weak companies that became so debased by the

end of the century provided Rossi with an ideal structure in which to work. Moreover, whilst Salvini is generally considered to be a 'classic' actor, Rossi is described most frequently as a 'romantic' actor. Reviewers praised his sense of passion and in particular his spontaneity. He was an outstandingly handsome man with a strong stage presence, although it is generally felt that he had less vocal range than Salvini. When he played Shakespeare in London, he was accused of being unintellectual, bombastic rather than profound, an accusation that greatly offended him.

In his memoirs he discussed the development of his characterisation technique, which seems to have been uniquely his own. He 'felt' his characters, endeavouring to live out their experiences through his own psyche, and in this respect he can be said to have anticipated the kind of detailed character construction work that later came to be associated with naturalism. Rossi was not, however, a naturalistic performer, and time and again reviewers praised his passion and energy whilst noting an absence of a clear acting style or precise technique. When praised for his 'realism', what critics seem to have been trying to say is that Rossi brought strong emotions onto the stage that appeared to be undiluted by obvious technical ploys. That he could carry this off during a career that spanned so many years testifies to his skills as a performer.

Rossi worked with a much larger repertoire than Salvini, and was willing to experiment with new plays, though his Shakespearean roles were an important feature in his international touring programme. In Italy, he had considerable success with plays by Giacometti, Ferrari, and Pietro Cossa, and his appearance in Cossa's *Nerone* (1874) was a triumph. The play failed in France, however, and it is interesting to consider the pattern of successes in Italy and failures abroad in terms of the Italian political scene. Plays that were meaningful for Italian audiences in the revolutionary climate of the mid-nineteenth century were not necessarily the ones that appealed to audiences in London or Paris, where not so much different standards as different expectations prevailed. Ironically, performers like Rossi, Ristori, and Salvini were compelled to tour overseas because of financial constraints, but at home they played a significant part in the revolutionary struggle. Rossi was a 'grand actor', a virtuoso performer able to combine the best of the old improvisation techniques with close character study, and his work spans the period of transition not only from one kind of theatre to another, but from one social order to a new, united Italy.

—Susan Bassnett

RUGGERI, Ruggero. Italian actor-manager. Born in Fano, Italy, 14 November 1871. Educated at local schools; studied singing in Bologna, 1887. Married Germaine D'Arcy in 1926. Stage debut, as juvenile lead with the Benincasa company, Montecassino, 1888; actor, Novelli-Leigheb company, 1891–99; leading actor, Talli-Gramatica-Calabresi company (renamed the Gramatica-Ruggeri company, 1906), 1900–09; with actress Lyda Borelli, led the Ruggeri-Borelli company, visiting Mexico and South America, 1909–12; star of the Compagnia Ruggero Ruggeri, from 1912; appeared with Compagnia Drammatica

Nazionale, 1921–22; joined Luigi Pirandello's Art Theatre project, 1924; toured Europe with Pirandello company, 1925; reformed his own company, 1925–26; acted in New York, 1929; toured South America, 1929 and 1949; continued to appear in theatres throughout Europe until his death. Died in Milan, 20 July 1953.

Roles

1894–98	Iago in *Othello* (Shakespeare), Compagnia Novelli-Leigheb.
	Antonio in *Il mercante di Venezia* (Shakespeare), Compagnia Novelli-Leigheb.
1904	Aligi in *La figlia di Iorio* (D'Annunzio), Teatro Lirico, Milan; Volta Conference, 1934.
1906	Corrado Brando in *Più che l'amore* (D'Annunzio), Teatro Constanzi, Rome.
1909–12	Erode in *Salomé* (Wilde), Compagnia Ruggeri-Borelli; also directed.
1913–14	Don Fiorenzo in *Il piccolo santo* (Bracco), Compagnia Ruggero Ruggeri; Teatro Eliseo, Rome, 1944.
1914–16	Hamlet in *Amleto* (Shakespeare), Compagnia Ruggero Ruggeri; Paris and London, 1925–26; South American tour, 1929.
	Macbeth in *Macbeth* (Shakespeare), Compagnia Ruggero Ruggeri; Compagnia Spettacoli Errepi, 1938–39.
1917–18	Angelo Baldovino in *Il piacere dell'onestà* (Pirandello), Teatro Carignano, Turin; Eiar, 1938; Istituto del Dramma Italiano, Milan, 1947–48.
1918	Leono Gala in *Il giuoco delle parti* (Pirandello), Teatro Quirino, Rome.
1920	Martino Lori in *Tutto per bene* (Pirandello), Compagnia Ruggero Ruggeri; revived, 1949–50; Paris and London, 1953.
	Sly in *Sly* (Forzano), Compagnia Ruggero Ruggeri.
1921–22	Ugo d'Este in *La Parisina* (D'Annunzio), Teatro Manzoni, Milan.
	Enrico IV in *Enrico IV* (Pirandello), Teatro Manzoni, Milan; Paris and London, 1925; German tour, 1942; Rome, 1945; Paris, London and Naples, 1953.
1922	Massimo in *Come le foglie* (Giacosa), Compagnia dei Capocomici.
1938–39	Laudisi in *Così è (si vi pare)* (Pirandello), Compagnia Spettacoli Errepi.
1940	Diacono Martino in *Adelchi* (Manzoni), Boboli Gardens, Florence.
1948–49	Jack in *Rosalinda o Come vi piace* (Shakespeare), Teatro Eliseo, Rome.
	Egisto in *Oreste* (Alfieri), Teatro Quirino, Rome.
1952	Giacomo Gozzi in *Carlo Gozzi* (Simoni), Teatro di Via Manzoni, Milan.

Also acted roles in: *Gli affari sono affari* (Mirbeau); *Agnese* (Cavallotti); *L'albergo dei poveri* (Gorky); *L'altalena* (Varaldo); *Amanti* (Donnay); *Ambizione* (Achille); *L'amico delle donne* (Dumas fils); *Amore senza stima* (Ferrari); *Anitra selvatica* (Ibsen); *Ape regina* (Tieri); *L'arcidiavolo* (Gherardi); *L'arlesiana* (Daudet); *L'artiglio* (Bernstein); *Assassinio nella Cattedrale* (Eliot); *L'attore* (Guitry); *L'avventuriero* (Capus); *Baci perduti* (Birabeau); *Il barone di Gragnano* (Tieri); *Bassano padre geloso* (Bontempelli); *Battaglia di dame* (Scribe); *La bella avventura* (De Flers and Caivallet); *Le bocche inutili* (Vivanti); *Il bosco sacro* (De Flers and Caivallet); *Boubouroche* (Courteline); *Il brutto e le belle* (Lopez); *Il cantico dei cantici* (Cavallotti); *Carita mondana* (Antona-Traversi); *Castelli in aria* (Guitry); *Cera una vilta un prigioniero* (Anouilh); *Chatterton* (De Vigny); *Conflitti* (Carrol); *La crisi* (Praga); *Cyrano de Bergerac* (Rostand); *l tuo al mio* (Verga); *Deburau* (Guitry); *Il delitto di Silvestro Bonnàrd* (France); *Demi-monde* (Dumas fils); *Dialoghi* (Plato); *Divorziamo!* (Sardou); *La dolce follia* (Tieri); *Domino* (Achard); *Il duello* (Ferrari); *Edipo Re* (Sophocles); *La falena* (Bataille); *La famiglia Point-Biquet* (Bisson); *Fedora* (Sardou); *La fiammata* (Kistermakers); *Figaro II* (Tieri); *Fuochi in Arno* (Bandinelli); *Il giorno della cresima* (Rovetta); *Goffredo Mameli* (D'Ambra and Lipparini); *Goldoni e le sue sedici commedie nuove* (Ferrari); *Grengoire* (Banville); *In attesa dell'angelo* (Giannini); *In nome del padre* (Viola); *Ispezione* (Betti); *L'istruttoria* (Henriot); *Jacqueline* (Guitry); *La leggenda di Ognuno* (Hofmansthal); *Luigi XI* (Delavigne); *La luna e tramontata* (Steinbeck); *Il maestro* (Bahr); *Il Marchese di Priola* (Lavedan); *La marcia nuziale* (Bataille); *Marionette* (Wolff); *La maschera e il volto* (Chiarelli); *Maternita* (Bracco); *Mazarino* (D'Ambra and Bonelli); *Il messagero* (Bernstein); *La moglie celebre* (Adami); *La nave* (D'Annunzio); *Noi* (Rocca); *Non fare come me!* (Gherardi); *Non si sa come* (Pirandello); *Non te li puoi portare appresso!* (Kaufman and Hart); *Non tradire!* (Tieri); *La nostra fortuna* (Possenti); *Il nuovo idolo* (De Curel); *Il nuovo testamento* (Guitry); *Occhi azzurri* (Bernstein); *Ombre* (Cantini); *Ondina* (Praga); *Palma e il suo metodo* (De Fonseca); *Pamela nubile* (Goldoni); *Panabò, vita perduta* (Gherardi); *Il pensiero* (Andreyev); *La perla negra* (Sardou); *La piccola fonte* (Bracco); *Pick-up-girl* (Shelley); *Il portafoglio* (Mirbeau); *Poveri davanti a Dio* (Viola); *Il pretore de Minimis* (Giannini); *Qualche cosa di me* (Tieri); *Quella vecchia canaglia* (Nozière); *Questa o quella* (Lopez); *Questi figli* (Tieri); *Questi poveri amanti* (Tieri); *Rabagas* (Sardou); *La raffica* (Bernstein); *Il re* (De Flers and Caivallet); *La resa di Berg-op-zoom* (Guitry); *Il re si diverte* (Terron); *Il rifugio* (Niccodemi); *Robespierre* (Oliva); *Romanticismo* (Rovetta); *I romanzeschi* (Rostand); *Ruy Blas* (Hugo); *Sansone* (Bernstein); *La satira e il Parini* (Ferrari); *Il segreto di Pulcinella* (Wolff); *Sei personaggi in cerca d'autore* (Pirandello); *Servi e padroni* (Tieri); *Sesso debole* (Bourdet); *Siegfried* (Giraudoux); *La signora dalle camelie* (Dumas fils); *Il Signor Beverley* (Verneuilh); *Il signore e la signora Tal dei Tali* (Amiel); *Sogno d'amore* (Kossarotoff); *Sogno (ma forse no)* (Pirandello); *Sole d'ottobre* (Lopez); *Le sorprese del divorzio* (Bisson); *Lo sparviero* (De Croisset); *Sperduti nel buio* (Bracco); *Stelle nel pozzo* (Cavicchiolo); *Sua eccellenza di Falcomarzano* (Martoglio); *Terra inumana* (De Curel); *La modella* (Testoni); *Il titano* (Niccodemi); *Tre tempi, tre maniere* (Lopez and Possenti); *Il tribuno* (Bourget); *Tristi amori* (Giacosa); *L'uomo dal fiore in bocca* (Pirandello); *L'uomo più solo del mondo* (Rocca); *La vergine folle* (Bataille); *Verso l'amore* (Gandillot); *Vita da vendere* (Guitry); *Il voto* (Di Giacomo).

Films

L'istruttoria, 1914; *Il sottomarino 27*, 1915; *Lulù*, 1915;
Amleto, 1917; *Papa*, 1917; *Il principe dell'impossibile*,
1919; *La moglie bella*, 1923; *La casa del peccato*, 1924;
Gli angeli custodi, 1925; *L'uomo più allegro di Vienna*,
1926; *Quella vecchia canaglia*, 1934; *La vedova*, 1938;
Papa Lebonnard, 1939; *Il documento*, 1939; *La gerla di
Papa Martin*, 1940; *Una lampada alla finestra*, 1939; *I
promessi sposi*, 1941; *Gelosia*, 1942; *Si non son matti non
li vogliamo*, 1943; *Sant'Elena piccola isola*, 1943; *Vanità*,
1946; *Quarta pagina*, 1947; *Le due verità*, 1948; (voice
only) *Don Camillo*, 1951; (voice only) *Il ritorno di Don
Camillo*, 1953.

*

Bibliography

Books:
Leonardo Bragaglia, *Ruggero Ruggeri in sessantacinque
anni di storia del teatro rappresentato*, Rome, 1968.
Leonardo Bragaglia, *Carteggio Pirandello-Ruggeri*, Fano,
1987.

* * *

Writing about the production of Pirandello's *Enrico IV*
during the London tour of 1925, the *Times* reviewer
described Ruggero Ruggeri as "a great actor", noting that
his treatment of madness "becomes terrible", as his voice,
hands and gestures "hover on the outer edge of the
uncanny". This comment on Ruggeri's ability to terrify an
audience and freeze the blood of everyone watching him
perform is typical of many such remarks. From his early
portrayals of Hamlet or Iago, through his D'Annunzian
roles (most notably in *La figlia di Iorio* in 1904 and *La nave*
in 1938) and his representations of works by such writers as
Pirandello, Giraudoux, Ugo Betti and T. S. Eliot, Ruggeri
had the presence and the power to dominate the stage.
Contemporary photographs show a darkly brooding figure,
heavily made up according to the conventions of his time,
and in contrast to the other great Pirandellian actor
Lamberto Picasso, there seems to be more weight, less
sense of the playful. Picasso and Ruggeri both performed
Pircandello roles for over 30 years and each had their own
following. The general consensus seems to be that Picasso
embodied Pirandello's characters in terms desired by
Pirandello, that he followed direction well and created roles
conspicuous for their irony, dryness and 'umorismo'.
Ruggeri, on the other hand, used the roles created by
Pirandello as vehicles for his own particular style. That
Pirandello was well aware of this is apparent in the way he
wrote certain parts specifically for Ruggeri. The role of
Henry IV, the mad emperor, was written for Ruggeri, as
was the role of Angelo Baldovino in *Il piacere dell'onestà*,
one of the few Pirandellian plays to have a happy ending.
Pirandello also created the role of Leone Gala for Ruggeri,
the protagonist of *Il giuoco delle parti*, and commented that
"Ruggeri thinks this is the best play I have ever written".
Ruggeri was more than a great interpreter of Pirandellian
roles; he was an inspiration to Pirandello in the crucial
years when he turned increasingly towards the full-length
play. By 1925, when he set up his own company, Pirandello
had begun to write plays built around strong women,
writing expressly for Marta Abba, but the years between
1917 and 1925 saw the creation of many of his best parts
for men, as a result of the collaboration with Ruggeri.
Pirandello seems to have worked well when he was writing
with a specific actor in mind, and the powerful, tormented
images of men locked into desperate relationships or
standing on the edge of madness belong to the period when
he worked mainly with Ruggeri. What Ruggeri excelled at
were roles that demanded the exercise of control over dark,
interior passions.

Ruggeri's elaborate make-up was a deliberate device to
emphasize his use of facial expression. While Lamberto
Picasso used the angularity of his body to create strong
images, jutting out his neck in a stylized movement that
was expressionistic in its distortion of the ordinary gesture,
Ruggeri used the interplay between repressed emotion that
tightened and stiffened the body and mobile facial expression. Contemporary reviewers refer again and again to the
use of his facial muscles, to his changing expressions, to the
way in which he conveyed an inner passion whilst apparently maintaining his physical composure.

Virgilio Marchi, the designer, tells a revealing story about
Ruggeri during the preparations for the revival of *Enrico IV*
in 1925 in the Teatro d'Arte. Marchi had made a new
costume in purple and gold, and Ruggeri at first refused to
wear it. He insisted on his original black costume, since
that was the one in which he had had international success
in the role, and Marchi notes that "it seemed as though
nothing was right for him unless he had already tried it
out". Nevertheless, when the set was finished and fully lit
and the function of the purple costume became clear,
Ruggeri agreed to wear it. What this story reveals is the way
in which Ruggeri was both part of the old tradition and
open to innovation. On the one hand, he was clear about
what he wanted, what he could do and how he should do it,
and at the same time he could be persuaded to try
something new. He belonged to the old 'mattatore' or star
actor tradition, but by agreeing to work with Pirandello,
whose radical ideas of stagecraft involved alternative
company structuring and the abolition of the mattatore
principle, Ruggeri showed that he could hold his own in the
modern world.

Ruggeri's repertoire confirms this view. He has been
accused of having no personal repertoire, of working in too
many different directions and never forming a clear picture
of the kind of plays in which he preferred to perform. But
there is another side to this story; Ruggeri started out at a
particular moment in the late 1880's, when verismo and
the French drama were all the rage, and then gradually
extended his range to include classical tragedy, new plays
by European playwrights and works by the most innovative
of Italian dramatists. When he played the shepherd in *La
figlia Iorio*, he was hugely successful, as he was again later
when he played the mad emperor Henry IV. We have some
notion of the power he could exert, and the sense of the
ironic that went with that power, when we see the Don
Camillo films of the early 1950's, in which the octogenarian
actor's voice is heard on the soundtrack as the voice of
God.

—Susan Bassnett

S

SAINT-DENIS, Michel (Jacques). French director, playwright, and actor. Born in Beauvais, France, 13 September 1897. Educated at the Collège Rollin, Paris; Lycée de Versailles. Married 1) Marie Ostroga in 1923 (divorced), one son and one daughter; 2) Suria Magito. Served in French army, 1914–18. Secretary, and then stage manager and assistant director, to his uncle, Jacques Copeau, at the Théâtre du Vieux-Colombier, Paris; acting debut, Vieux-Colombier, 1922; London debut, 1927; wrote his first plays, in collaboration with Jean Villard, for Copeau's company in Burgundy; founder and director, Compagnie des Quinze, Paris, 1930; toured throughout Europe with the company before disbanding it, 1934; first worked in London with Laurence Olivier and John Gielgud, 1935; founder, London Theatre Studio, 1936–39; served in Infanterie Coloniale, 1939–40; head of French section, BBC, under the pseudonym Jacques Duchesne, 1940–45; worked for Radio-Diffusion Française, 1944–45; director, Old Vic Theatre School, 1946–52; director, Old Vic Theatre, 1950; supervised reconstruction and reopening of Old Vic Theatre, 1950; founder and general director, Centre Nationale Dramatique de l'Est and École Supérieure d'Art Dramatique, Strasbourg, 1952–57; special consultant, Juillard School, Lincoln Centre, New York, 1957; Inspecteur-Général des Spectacles, 1959; general artistic adviser, 1962, and subsequently consultant director, 1966, Royal Shakespeare Company; also founder and artistic adviser, National Theatre School of Canada, Montreal. Honorary Fellow, Royal College of Art, 1963. Recipient: International Award, International Theatre Institute, 1969; International Award, American Educational Theatre, 1969. D.Litt, University of Birmingham, 1962; LHD, Dartmouth College, Hanover, New Hampshire, 1962. Croix de Guerre; Rosette de la Résistance. Officier, Légion d'Honneur; Chevalier, Ordre de Léopold. Honorary CBE (Companion of the British Empire). Died 31 July 1971.

Productions

As actor only:
1922　　Curio in *Twelfth Night* (Shakespeare), Théâtre du Vieux-Colombier, Paris.
1927　　Lucas in *Le Médecin malgré lui* (Molière), St James's Theatre, London.

As director:
1931–34　*Noé* (Obey), Théâtre du Vieux-Colombier, Paris; acted Noah, the Man and the Elephant.

Le Viol de Lucrèce (Obey), Théâtre du Vieux-Colombier, Paris; Arts and Ambassadors Theatre, London, 1931; acted Brutus, the Reciter, and Valère.
Vénus (Obey), Théâtre du Vieux-Colombier, Paris; acted the Gardener.
Loire (Obey), Théâtre du Vieux-Colombier, Paris.
Don Juan (Obey), Théâtre du Vieux-Colombier, Paris; Globe Theatre, London, 1934; acted Catalino.
La Bataille de la Marne (Obey), Théâtre du Vieux-Colombier, Paris; acted the Mayor, the Doctor, and the Taxi-Driver.
La Vie en rose (Salacrou), Théâtre du Vieux-Colombier, Paris; acted the Coachman.
La Mauvaise Conduite, Théâtre du Vieux-Colombier, Paris; acted Legoirfre and Le Commissaire.
Lanceurs de Graines (Giono), Théâtre du Vieux-Colombier, Paris.
Violante (Ghéon), Théâtre du Vieux-Colombier, Paris.
Le Sicilien (Molière), Théâtre du Vieux-Colombier, Paris; acted title role.
La Première Famille (Supervielle), Théâtre du Vieux-Colombier, Paris; acted L'Ours.
Riders to the Sea (Synge), Théâtre du Vieux-Colombier, Paris.
1935　　*Noah* (Obey, translated by Wilmurt), New Theatre, London.
1936　　*The Witch of Edmonton* (Dekker and Ford), Old Vic Theatre, London.
1937　　*Macbeth* (Shakespeare), Old Vic Theatre, London.
1938　　*The Three Sisters* (Chekhov), Queen's Theatre, London.
　　　　The White Guard (Bulgakov), Phoenix Theatre, London.
　　　　Twelfth Night (Shakespeare), Phoenix Theatre, London.
　　　　Electra (Sophocles), London Theatre Studio, London.
1939　　*Alcestis* (Euripides), London Theatre Studio, London.
1945　　*Oedipus Rex* (Sophocles), New Theatre, London and New York.
1949　　*A Month in the Country* (Turgenev), New Theatre, London.
1951　　*Electra* (Sophocles), Old Vic Theatre, London.

1960   *Oedipus Rex* (Stravinsky and Cocteau), Sadler's
        Wells Theatre, London.
1963   *The Hollow Crown* (Shakespeare compilation),
        US tour.
1965   *The Cherry Orchard* (Chekhov), Aldwych The-
        atre, London.
        Squire Puntila and His Servant Matti, Aldwych
        Theatre, London.

Other productions included: *Sowers of the Hills*, 1935;
Marriage of Blood, 1939; *Weep for the Spring*, 1939.

Publications

Theatre: The Rediscovery of Style, 1960.

* * *

Michel Saint-Denis, whose actor training programmes
have had a profound impact upon the theatre in France,
England, Canada, and the USA, was one of the primary
inheritors of Jacques Copeau's theories and "esprit". As
Copeau's nephew, Saint-Denis worked intimately with
Copeau as an actor, director, and teacher. Their collaboration on alternative approaches to text, and their experiments with the improvised theatre of the commedia
dell'arte, masks, mime, and the Noh, became the foundation for a revitalization of classic dramatic literature and a
base for encouraging the work of new playwrights.

Like so many of the prominent French metteurs en scène,
Michel Saint-Denis was an accomplished actor. In the early
1920's, when Copeau was directing both a performance
company and a school, Saint-Denis was his assistant. They
shared the goal of eliminating personal affectations, habits,
and clichés from actors' work, in order to achieve clarity
through simplicity. Saint-Denis was trained with the concept of the actor performing on the "tréteau nu"; he
experienced the phenomenon of amplifying the actor's
presence through a style of performance evolved from the
tradition of the mask. In 1925, for example, Saint-Denis
created the masked personage of Oskar Knie, a comic
companion to Jean Dasté's M. César. This duo performed
as a kind of Sancho Panza/Don Quixote team in a series of
original scenarios. At this time, Michel Saint-Denis was
writing many of the texts, especially in connection with
Jean Villard.

As metteur en scène, Saint-Denis established his reputation with the plays of André Obey, working with the
Compagnie des Quinze. This troupe of actors, trained by
Copeau, continued their training with Saint-Denis, attaining a level of ensemble performance that stunned audiences
in France, Belgium, and England. Saint-Denis's superb
work with diction, voice, and choral singing resulted in a
musicality in the delivery of the text that approached
incantation. In parallel, the actors were skilled with gesture
through mime, gymnastics, and dance training. Sound and
action combined to form a "style" of acting that was
unique. *Noé, Le Viol de Lucrèce, La Bataille de la Marne*,
and Obey's first version of *Don Juan*, produced between
1931 and 1934, were Saint-Denis's most noted mises en
scène with the Compagnie des Quinze.

Prompted by financial difficulties in France, Michel
Saint-Denis settled in England in 1935 and subsequently

formed his first training programme for actors, the London
Theatre Studio. He continued his directing work by presenting *Noah* with John Gielgud in the English version of
Obey's play. A 1938 production of Chekhov's *The Three
Sisters* (with a cast including Peggy Ashcroft, Michael
Redgrave, and Alec Guinness) is remembered as one of the
most successful presentations of Chekhov on the London
stage. Saint-Denis quickly established himself as a director
and teacher of distinction; he stretched his actors to the
maximum of their abilities, instilling an affection for
precision and confidence in the dramatic text.

Following work as the voice to French listeners of BBC
radio during the war, Saint-Denis helped revitalize the Old
Vic, where he started another theatre school. Here Saint-
Denis asserted his belief that a complete school, by
necessity, was accompanied by a professional performing
company that performed both classical and contemporary
texts. "A school is a place to re-invent theatre", he stated.
Unfortunately, the Old Vic Theatre School and the Young
Vic Company lasted only until 1952, when they were
disbanded due to financial problems. Saint-Denis's most
famous mise en scène in the 1940's was his *Oedipus Rex*,
with Laurence Olivier at the Old Vic (1945), which was
taken to New York.

Saint-Denis returned to France in 1952 and immediately
joined the decentralization efforts underway in the French
theatre. His colleague from the Compagnie des Quinze,
Jean Dasté, was now established with a company in St
Etienne. Michel Saint-Denis administered the move of the
Comédie de l'Est from Colmar to Strasbourg and created
alongside the first major training centre for actors outside
Paris. With the assistance of many of the faculty from the
Old Vic Theatre School, the École Supérieure d'Art Dramatique quickly gained notoriety. Saint-Denis departed due to
ill health in 1957, but the school remained a vital force.
Today it continues as a dynamic and innovative training
programme for French actors.

Saint-Denis's final contributions to world theatre were
made in the USA, Canada, and once again, in England. He
advised and co-directed the creation of the Juillard School
at the Lincoln Centre in New York, and also assisted with
the creation of the National Theatre School in Canada.
From 1962 onwards, he also worked as adviser to the Royal
Shakespeare Company, where he had a major influence
upon the acting and directing of Peter Hall. His refreshing
modernization of the French emphasis upon a well-spoken
text and "beaux jestes" provided the English-speaking
theatre with new life. More than any director, Saint-Denis
transferred the best of Jacques Copeau to Britain and the
USA. His balanced training methods — focusing upon the
voice and the body — utilized classical theatre and popular
mask performance to prepare young actors for contemporary playwrights, and the theatre of tomorrow.

—Ron Popenhagen

———

SALVINI, Tommaso. Italian actor-manager. Born in Milan, 1 January 1829. Trained as an actor as apprentice
under Gustavo Modena, 1843–45. Married 1) Carlotta
Sharpe (died in 1878); 2) Jennie Beaman. Stage debut as a
child, Forli, 1842; joined Modena company, 1843; acted
opposite Adelaide Ristori, 1848; fought in Roman uprising,

1849, and imprisoned for political activities; admired particularly as Shakespeare's Othello and Hamlet, 1856; performed in Paris, 1857; founded own company, 1861; joined Compagnia Reale dei Fiorentini, Naples, 1864; toured widely, from 1869, appearing throughout North and South America, Europe, and Russia; British tours, 1875–76 and 1884; played Othello to Edwin Booth's Iago, 1885; came out of retirement to perform in Rome on Ristori's eightieth birthday, 1902. Died in Florence, 31 December 1915.

Roles

1842	Arlecchino in *Donne curiose* (Goldoni), Forli.
1843	Egisto and Polifonte in *Merope* (Alfieri), Compagnia Modena.
	Gionata in *Saul* (Alfieri), Compagnia Modena.
	Perez in *Filippo* (Alfieri), Compagnia Modena.
	Pietro Tasca in *Fornaretto* (Dall'Ongaro), Compagnia Modena.
	Massimiliano Piccolomini in *Wallenstein* (Schiller), Compagnia Modena.
	Macham in *Il Bicchier d'acqua* (Scribe), Compagnia Modena.
1844	David in *Saul* (Alfieri), Compagnia Modena.
	Nemours in *Luigi XI* (Delavigne), Compagnia Modena.
	Carlo in *Filippo* (Alfieri), Compagnia Modena.
1846	Paolo in *Francesca da Rimini* (Pellico), Compagnia Modena.
	Romeo in *Giulietta e Romeo* (Ventignano), Compagnia Modena.
	Rinaldo in *Pia de Tolomei* (Marenco), Compagnia Modena.
	Mortimer in *Maria Stuarda* (Schiller), Compagnia Modena.
	Bonfil in *Pamela nubile* (Goldoni), Compagnia Modena.
1846–53	Domingo in *La Suonatrice d'arpa* (Chiossone), Compagnia Modena.
	Gian Galeazza in *Lodovico il Moro* (Campagna), Compagnia Modena.
	Tartuffe in *Tartufo moderno* (Ferrari), Compagnia Modena.
1848	Oreste in *Oreste* (Alfieri), Teatro Valle, Rome.
1853	Orosmane in *Zaire* (Voltaire), Bologna.
1856	Otello in *Otello* (Shakespeare), Vicenza; revived notably, Boston Conservatoire, 1873, and London, 1875.
	Hamlet in *Hamlet* (Shakespeare), Vicenza.
	Saul in *Saul* (Alfieri), Vicenza.
1860	Ingomaro in *Figlio delle selve* (Halm), Teatro dei Fiorentini, Naples.
1861	Corrado in *La Morte Civile* (Giacometti), Teatro dei Fiorentini, Naples.
1864	Lear in *King Lear* (Shakespeare), Florence.
1865	Lanciotto in *Francesca da Rimini* (Pellico), Florence.
1876	Macbeth in *Macbeth* (Shakespeare).
1885	Coriolanus in *Coriolanus* (Shakespeare), US tour.

Other roles included: *Abimelech* (D'Aste); *Arduino di Ivrea* (Morelli); *La Calunia* (Scribe); *La Colpa vendica la colpa* (Giacometti); *Con gli nomini non si scherza* (Testa); *Fasma e il tesoro* (Dall'Ongaro); *I Gelosi fortunati* (Giraud); *Il Giocatore* (Iffland); *Gio suè il Guardacoste* (Fournier and Meyer); *Il Gladiatore* (Soumet); *Gli Innamorati* (Goldoni); *Il Lapidario* (Dumas fils); *Marco Kralievic* (Dall'Ongaro); *Il Marito e l'amante* (Martini); *I Martiri* (D'Aste); *Milton* (Gattinelli); *La Missione delle donna* (Torelli); *Mosè* (D'Aste); *Il Retorno di Cristoforo Colombo* (Ventignano); *Sansone* (D'Aste); *Scacco matto* (De Angelis); *La Signora delle Camelie* (Dumas fils); *Il Sistema di Giorgio* (Testa); *Sofode* (Giacometti); *Sullivan* (Melesville); *La Verità* (Torelli); *La Vita color di rosa* (Barrière and Kock).

Publications

Sulla Nazionalita dell' arte dramatica, 1883; *In Memoria di Alamanno Morelli*, 1890; *Leaves from the Autobiography of Tommaso Salvini*, 1892; *Riccordi, Aneddoti ed Impressioni*, 1895; *Discorso in Commemorazione de Adelaide Ristori*, 1906.

*

Bibliography

Books:
Edward Tuckerman Mason, *The Othello of Tommaso Salvini*, New York and London, 1890.
Luigi Rasi, *Tommaso Salvini*, Milan, 1904.
Celso Salvini, *Tommaso Salvini nella Storia del Teatro Italiano e nella Vita del suo Tempo*, Rocca San Casciano, 1955.
Marvin Carlson, *The Shakespeare of the Italians*, New York, 1987.

* * *

The greatest Italian actor of the 19th century, Tommaso Salvini acquired an international reputation as one of the great "star" players of the age, and the last two decades of his life are little other than a record of triumphant stage successes in most of the leading cities of the world, from London to Moscow, New York to Buenos Aires. He was also a major innovator in his own country, his performance of Othello at Vicenza in June 1856 and of Hamlet shortly after being among the first stagings of Shakespeare in Italy in a fairly authoritative text. He toured for the first time in 1857 to Paris, hoping to emulate the triumph of his compatriot Adelaide Ristori the year before, but although his Othello was admired, his repertory of mainly Italian plays met with little success, and his international touring career really began only in 1869, by which time he was an acknowledged master in Italy in a wide range of tragic and comic roles, in classic plays by Shakespeare, Alfieri, and Goldoni, and in work by contemporary dramatists like Giacometti and Scribe.

Today he is remembered primarily, perhaps even in Italy itself, for his great Shakespearean interpretations, for Shakespeare provided him with a lingua franca with which to communicate with audiences internationally. The 19th century "star" player was expected to be an histrionic gladiator, competing with rival stars for audience favours.

Such was the case, for example, when Salvini first played in London, after a highly successful visit to the USA. Aware of his triumph in New York, the Drury Lane management invited him on condition he perform Hamlet, in which Henry Irving had triumphed that same season and was still performing at Drury Lane. The rivalry promised good box-office. Salvini's interpretation was admired, the critic G. H. Lewes in *The Athenaeum* remarking that "no actor of our day has brought to the part of Hamlet equal intelligence and mastery of art, equal rigour of judgement and profusion of effort". But in the event Salvini's Hamlet, and rivalry with Irving, were eclipsed by the Italian's performance of Othello, in which he opened on 1 April 1875. This was considered one of the most stunning, if controversial, interpretations of the century: "about the greatest ever witnessed by an English audience", according to the *Illustrated London News*. Since first giving the role in Italy nearly 19 years before, he had progressively refined his performance to draw out, by carefully paced playing, by look, gesture, movement, and "business", and by the modulation of his richly resonant voice, the savage and elemental passions beneath Othello's veneer of civilisation. Desdemona was seized by her hair, dragged to the bed, and strangled "with a ferocity that seems to take delight in its office". Othello slashed his own throat with a scimitar, "hacking and hewing at the flesh, severing all the cords, pipes and ligatures that there meet, and making the hideous noises that escaping air and bubbling blood are likely to produce", as recorded by *The Sunday Times*. The reading was intelligent, imaginative, and persuasive, and was realised by an actor endowed with exceptional resources of which he was in total command: a magnificent physique, a rich and flexible voice, a mobile, expressive face, and grace of movement and gesture.

Not only in this role, but in others too, Salvini was admired by many of the most discriminating theatre practitioners and critics of the mid and late 19th century — George Henry Lewes, Henry James, and Bernard Shaw were but three of the many who thought him the greatest tragic actor they had ever seen. They were particularly enthusiastic about his superbly flexible and musical voice: Lewes, for example, thought his delivery unequalled for "tone, timbre, and rhythm" and the same qualities were admired by James, Shaw, William Poel, and Constantin Stanislavsky. But perhaps what most distinguished his playing was his ability to exercise absolute control over voice and body, and everything in his performance was thought out, related to a consistent, unified reading of a role and expressed with discipline and authority. Stanislavsky, who saw Salvini perform in Moscow in 1891, was but one who keenly admired the manner in which he identified with the roles he played, yet remained always technically in command of movement, gesture, vocal inflection, and the overall pacing and rhythm of his interpretation of a role within the context of the play as a whole.

Characteristic of the high seriousness with which Salvini approached the business of acting was the way in which, as early as 1853, he took a year off in order to prepare new dramatic roles: one of these was Othello, another Hamlet. A third was Alfieri's Saul, later considered to be among his greatest interpretations, as too in his younger days was Alfieri's Oreste. Other major roles included Corrado, in Giacometti's powerful social drama *Morte Civile* and the tragic heroic leads in Soumet's romantically histrionic toga

melodrama *Il Gladiatore* and D'Aste's *Sansone*. He added other Shakespearean parts to his repertory, achieving notable international success with King Lear, which he first acted in the mid-1860's when with the Compagnia Reale dei Fiorentini in Naples, the lead in *Macbeth*, a play he considered "il capolavoro di capolavori", and Coriolanus, prepared for his 1885 tour of the USA. Although he began his career playing in comedy, he rarely acted in lighter drama in maturity, the serious roles being more suited to the powerfully realistic and psychologically subtle playing with which he was identified internationally, and the authority of which is perhaps no better attested than in the admiration expressed by Émile Zola when in Paris in 1878 he saw Salvini perform in *Morte Civile*.

Salvini's influence was such that for decades no later interpretations of Othello, Hamlet, and Macbeth could ignore his readings. But more than that, he helped in mid-century to restore to the stage a dynamic realism that part banished the lachrymosely sentimental tendencies of much late romantic acting; later, when by the 1890's low-key drawing-room naturalism was coming into vogue, his playing was to be cited by innovators as different as Craig, Poel, Shaw, and Stanislavsky, as the conclusive instance of what constituted truly great acting.

—Kenneth Richards

SCHILLER, Leon. Polish director. Born Leon Jerzy Wojciech Schiller de Schildenfeld in Cracow, Poland, 14 March 1887. Educated at the Jagiellonian University, Krakow; University of the Sorbonne, Paris; Akademia Handlowa, Cracow; and in Vienna, all 1906–16; studied theatre under Gordon Craig in Paris, from 1909. Worked as theatre critic, singer in artistic cabaret and as set designer prior to World War I; literary adviser to the Teatr Olski in Warsaw, 1917–20; debut as director, 1917; subsequently directed at the Teatr Reduta, Warsaw; artistic director, Teatr im Bogusławskiego, Warsaw, 1924–26; worked at the Teatr Polski and in Łodź and Lvóv, 1926–30; artistic director, Teatr Miejski, Lvóv, 1930–31; also directed in Wilno, Sofia and Paris; founder and dean, Department of Directing at the Państwowy Instytut Sztuki Teatralnej [National Arts Institute], Warsaw, 1933; co-sponsored reform of Polish theatre by the Związek Artystów Scen Polskich union, 1936; briefly imprisoned by the Nazis in Auschwitz concentration camp, 1941; subsequently worked in the underground organisation of Polish theatre artists in Warsaw and as a member of the Tajna Rada Teatralna [Secret Theatre Council]; entered Roman Catholic Order of St Benedict Fathers as apprentice, 1944; gave concerts for the Home Army soldiers during the Warsaw Uprising, 1944; interned by the Germans at Murnau, Germany, 1944–45; founded company of Polish actors in Germany, 1945; artistic director, Teatr Wojska Polskiego, Łodź, and president of the state theatre school in Łodź, 1945; joined Polska Partia Robotnica [Polish Workers' Party], 1946; delegate to the congress of the Communist Party, 1948; artistic director, Teatr Polski, Warsaw, 1949–50; also appointed president of the state theatre school, Warsaw; dismissed from posts by the communists, 1950; appointed head of the theatre division of the Państwowy Instytut Sztuki [Natonal Arts Institute], 1950.

Member: Stowarzyszenie Polskich Artystów Teatru i Filmu [Association of Polish Artists of Theatre and Film] (president), 1950. Died in Warsaw, 25 March 1954.

Principal productions

As director:

1917   *Królewna Lelijka* [Princess Lelijka] (Tatarkiewiczem), Teatr Polski, Warsaw.
1922   *Pastorałka* [Polish Christmas Carol] (traditional, adapted by Schiller), Teatr Reduta, Warsaw.
1923   *Wielkanoc* [Easter] (traditional), Teatr Reduta, Warsaw.
1924   *Żywoty urojone* (Schwoba), Warsaw.
1925   *Achilleis* [Achilles] (Wyspiański), Teatr im Bogusławskiego, Warsaw.
1926   *Nie-boska komedia* [The Undivine Comedy] (Krasiński), Teatr im Bogusławskiego, Warsaw.
        Róza [The Rose] (Zeromski), Teatr im Bogusławskiego, Warsaw.
1929   *Opery za trzy grosze* [The Threepenny Opera] (Brecht and Weill), Teatr im Bogusławskiego, Warsaw.
1930   *Kordian* [Kordian] (Słowacki), Teatr Wielki, Lvóv.
1932   *Dziady* [Forefather's Eve] (Mickiewicz), Teatr Wielki, Lvóv; Teatr Miejski, Wilno, 1933; Teatr Polski, Warsaw, 1934; National Theatre, Sofia, 1937.
        Krzyczcie Chiny [Roar, China!] (Tretyakov), Teatr Wielki, Lvóv; revived, 1933.
1935   *Kordian* [Kordian] (Słowacki), Teatr Polski, Warsaw.
1938   *Nie-boska komedia* [The Undivine Comedy] (Krasiński), Teatr Polski, Łódź.
1939   *Kordian* [Kordian] (Słowacki), Teatr Miejski, Łódź.
1947   *The Tempest* (Shakespeare), Łódź.
1953   *Halka* [Halka] (Moniuszko), Cracow.
1955   *Krakowiaków i Górali*, Cracow.
1956   *Paryzanka* [La Parisienne] (Becque), Wrocław.

Other productions included: *Dawne czasy w piosence, poezji i zwyczajach* [Old Times in Songs, Poetry and Customs], 1924; *The Winter's Tale* (Shakespeare), 1924; *Kniaź Patiomkin* [Prince Patiomkin] (Miciński), 1925; *As You Like It* (Shakespeare), 1925; *Julius Caesar* (Shakespeare), 1928; *Dzielny wojak Szwjk* [Brave Soldier Shveyk] (Hašek), 1929; *A Midsummer Night's Dream* (Shakespeare), 1934; *King Lear* (Shakespeare), 1935; *Coriolanus* (Shakespeare), 1936; *Kram z piosenkami* [Jumble-shop with Songs] (Schiller), 1945, revived, 1949; *Hrabina* [The Countess] (Moniuszko), 1951.

Publications

Teatr ogromny [Theatre Bigger than Life], edited by Z. Raszewski, 1961; *Na progu nowego teatru* [On the Threshold of a New Theatre], edited by J. Timoszewicz, 1978; *Droga przez teatr* [The Way Through Theatre], edited by J. Timoszewicz, 1983; *Theatrum militans* [A Fighting Theatre], edited by J. Timoszewicz, 1987.

* * *

Considered the best Polish director between the two world wars, Leon Schiller is one of the most important figures in the history of the Polish theatre. He was inspired by the Polish tradition of poetic theatre embodied in the works of the great romantic poets A. Mickiewicz, J. Słowacki, Z. Krasiński and their successor S. Wyspiański, whose productions he saw in Cracow. Second source of Schiller's inspiration was the all-European movement for the reform of the theatre, of which he became one of the leading figures. He was closely associated with Gordon Craig (Schiller published in Craig's *The Mask*), followed in the footsteps of Max Reinhardt and was himself compared to Vsevolod Meyerhold and Erwin Piscator.

Described as a "Renaissance man" by B. Korzeniewski, Schiller expressed himself with great artistic power in three major styles: "monumental theatre", "neo-realistic theatre", and a specific "music theatre"; music was always a fundamental element of all his productions.

Schiller's "monumental theatre" or "theatre bigger than life" (in Polish, "teatr ogromny", a term introduced by Wyspiański), was based on a romantic vision of the universe and history. It used as material poetic dramas (usually Polish verse plays of the 19th and 20th centuries) and expressed these through modern anti-illusionistic means. "Monumental" productions by Schiller were rich and spectacular; they boasted modern cubist stage designs; they featured elaborate lighting plots (based mainly on spotlights); they emphasized rhythm (created mainly by the movement and stage composition of protagonists and crowds); and they relied heavily on music. Thus, Schiller created "monumental", poetic stage visions and built up emotions, intending to transform the audience into participants in a mysterious ceremony.

In his "neo-realistic theatre" Schiller explored contemporary political and social problems and expressed his philosophy and attitude, oscillating from the late 1920's towards Marxism and Communism. He followed the German current of "Zeittheater" ("theatre of momentum"), directing some of the plays of "German Left" writers, as well as other authors (among them several Soviets), concerned with mechanisms of society, revolution and relationships between individuals and institutions. Schiller's "neo-realism" was a combination of real issues and real stage elements and expressive, meticulously selected theatrical means.

"Music theatre" was Schiller's invention, based on his musical education and interest in old Polish songs and in ancient religious theatre. He scripted and directed several productions in which the text was derived from songs, poetry, ancient mysteries and morality plays; the action was created by the director and the music was either found in old songbooks and hymnbooks or composed by Schiller himself. While Schiller's "monumental theatre" related to broad historical and national problems and his "neo-realistic theatre" dealt with soaring contemporary, socio-political issues, his "music theatre" was oriented towards entertainment and enjoyment of the public.

Beside the impact of his directorial work, Schiller influenced Polish theatre greatly as an educator. In his work with students of directing he stressed the necessity of a director's deep humanistic education, of his or her professional preparation in all the major components of theatre (script writing, acting, stage design, music) and of the approach to theatre as an art. He wanted to bring up directors as "theatre artists" and was master and mentor of at least three generations of Polish directors. He contributed vitally to the birth of the specific Polish directorial style.

Not only artistically, but also personally, Schiller was indeed a "Renaissance man", as well as a man of sharp contradictions. An intellectual from the upper class, he became a Communist activist, though by the end of his life he was completely disillusioned with the Communist system. In his youth he was a militant of the avant-garde and later a promoter of poetic theatre, but after World War II he accepted the dogma of Social Realism. During the war he was a strong opponent of the Nazis, but after 1945 he willingly became a member of the Communist Party and joined the elite of the totalitarian regime imposed in Poland by the Soviets, helping the authorities to submit the artistic milieu to the control of the Party. He oscillated between mysticism and materialism. In some periods of his life he was a faithful Roman Catholic, while at other times he declared himself an atheist. According to Z. Raszewski, his nature had two major features: "the call for nobleness and the temperament of an activist". In spite of all the contradictions, he now stands in the history of the Polish theatre as one of its greatest artists.

—Kazimierz Braun

SCHRÖDER, Friedrich Ludwig. German actor-manager. Born in Schwerin, Germany, 2 November 1744; son of actress Sophia Carlotta Schröder. Married actress Anna Christine Hart in 1773. Stage debut, as a child with the company of his stepfather Konrad Ackermann (*q.v.*); subsequently worked as acrobat and ropewalker before establishing himself as an actor, playing chiefly comic roles; rejoined Ackermann's company, 1768; inherited roles of Konrad Ekhof; with his mother, assumed control of the Ackermann company on Ackermann's death, 1771; actor-manager, National Theatre, Hamburg, 1771–78, then toured productions of Shakespeare, Goethe, Lessing and others throughout Germany; joined the Burgtheater, Vienna, 1781–85, then returned to Hamburg, 1785; retired from the stage, 1796. Died in Rellingen, 3 September 1816.

Productions

1772   *Emilia Galotti* (Lessing), National Theatre, Hamburg; acted Marinelli.
1774   *Clavigo* (Goethe), National Theatre, Hamburg; acted Carlos.
        Götz von Berlichingen (Goethe), National Theatre, Hamburg; acted Lerse.
1776   *Stella* (Goethe), National Theatre, Hamburg.
        Die Zwillinge (Klinger), National Theatre, Hamburg.
        Die Reue nach der Tat (Wagner), National Theatre, Hamburg.

Hamlet (Shakespeare), National Theatre, Hamburg; acted The Ghost.
        Othello (Shakespeare), National Theatre, Hamburg; acted Iago.
        Richard II (Shakespeare), National Theatre, Hamburg; acted Richard II.
1777   *Henry IV* (Shakespeare), National Theatre, Hamburg.
1778   *Der Kaufmann von Venedig* (Shakespeare), National Theatre, Hamburg; acted Shylock.
        Die Komedie der Irrungen (Shakespeare), National Theatre, Hamburg.
        Mass für Mass (Shakespeare), National Theatre, Hamburg; acted The Duke.
        Koenig Lear (Shakespeare), National Theatre, Hamburg; acted Lear.
        Der Hofmeister (Lenz), National Theatre, Hamburg.
        Hamlet (Shakespeare), National Theatre, Hamburg; acted Hamlet.
        Richard II (Shakespeare), National Theatre, Hamburg; acted Richard II.
        Henry IV (Shakespeare), National Theatre, Hamburg; acted Falstaff.
1779   *Macbeth* (Shakespeare), National Theatre, Hamburg; acted Macbeth.
1780   *Der Geizige* (Molière), Mannheim; acted Harpagon.
        Emilia Galotti, Mannheim; acted Odoardo.
1781–85 *Portrait der Mutter* (Schröder), Burgtheater, Vienna.
        Victorine (Schröder), Burgtheater, Vienna.
        Orpheus II (Schröder), Burgtheater, Vienna.
        Gustav Vasa (Schröder), Burgtheater, Vienna.
        Adelheid von Salisbury (Schröder), Burgtheater, Vienna.
        Die unglückiche Heirat (Schröder), Burgtheater, Vienna.
        Der Fähndrich (Schröder), Burgtheater, Vienna.
        Der Vetter von Lissabon (Schröder), Burgtheater, Vienna.

Other roles included: Othello in *Othello* (Shakespeare); Philipp II in *Don Carlos* (Schiller); and roles in *The Player* (Moore), 1772; *The London Merchant* (Lillo), 1772.

*

Bibliography

Books:
Joachim Maass, *Stürmischer Morgen*, Bremen, 1937.
P. F. Hoffmann, *Friedrich Ludwig Schröder als Dramaturg und Regisseur*, Berlin, 1939.

* * *

Friedrich Ludwig Schröder was the outstanding character actor of his generation. He was the son of Sophie Schröder, a distinguished tragedienne, and stepson of Konrad Ackermann, a prominent actor-manager. Schröder began as a child actor, graduating first to comic roles as he grew up. He became actor-manager of Ackermann's Hamburg company in 1771, when Sturm und Drang manifestos like

Friedrich Ludwig Schröder as King Lear.

Goethe's *For Shakespeare's Day* and the first prose translations of Shakespeare by C. M. Wieland and J. J. Eschenburg were appearing. Schröder promoted the Sturm und Drang (Storm and Stress) dramatists (Goethe, J. M. R. Lenz, F. M. Klinger) and developed a new style of acting for their plays. The preceding generation of the Enlightenment strove for naturalness and probability and Konrad Ekhof, its most influential actor, had developed a sober, analytical performance style for Lessing's domestic tragedies. Schröder was a nimbler and more mercurial actor, and the watchword of his generation was Nature, glossed by the young Goethe as "colossalistic". Nature was best exemplified by heroic individuals quite above the common run of mankind, and for them Schröder developed a flamboyant style calculated to strike awe into audiences, while at the same time allowing them to empathise with the sublime and grandiose actions on the stage. Schröder invested the tame Shakespeare translations available to him with a passion that on occasion overwhelmed a genteel public brought up on rococo sentimentality. Uncontrolled sobbing, fainting fits and premature labour were audience hazards, and box doors banged as the occupants left or were carried out, all this despite Schröder's efforts to attune the scripts to contemporary taste. He toned down Hamlet's hesitancy and tightened the action of the play so that the duel and Claudius's death followed hard on the play scene that established the king's guilt. Hamlet remained alive to set Denmark to rights, thus defying fate in the approved Sturm und Drang manner. *Othello* was also rewritten after a first night scandal to leave both Othello and Desdemona alive.

Schröder's leading man was J. F. H. Brockmann, a product of the Viennese popular theatre whom he discovered and turned into the leading German heroic actor. Schröder himself played character parts and villains, switching to heroic leads like Hamlet and Macbeth after Brockmann left the company. In four seasons Schröder established a substantial part of the Shakespearean canon on the German stage for the first time. In 1775 he invited writers to send in new plays and guaranteed to produce the best (which turned out to be Klinger's *Twins*) under favourable conditions. During this period Schröder also set up the first pension scheme for German actors.

In 1778 Schröder left the Hamburg theatre and toured his now famous productions triumphantly all over Germany. In Mannheim their impact on Baron Dalberg of the Court Theatre and his leading man A. W. Iffland paved the way for the next development, the Mannheim style for the young Schiller's plays. The history of the German theatre consists of successive phases of predominance in provincial centres: Schröder had taken the torch from Ekhof in Hamburg and now passed it to Iffland.

Schröder did a season at the Vienna Burgtheater, a clannish company that never accepted him. In 1785 he returned to Hamburg, without ever repeating the sensational results of his first management.

Shakespeare had already been identified by Lessing, Herder and Goethe as the appropriate model for German writers, but it was Schröder's dedicated advocacy and his carefully rehearsed productions that first persuaded the public to accept him. When the first performance of *Henry IV* was coolly received he announced as he took his bow: "In the hope that this masterpiece which shows manners much different from ours will be better understood, it will be repeated tomorrow". The practice of including international classics in the German repertoire starts here.

Of his own acting Schröder said: "I feel capable of expressing everything the author has tried to communicate with his words and characters, provided he has been true to Nature. My aim is not to shine on my own account, but to give a full account of the character. I want to give every part its due, no more, no less. Each part must be unique". His tragi-comic Harpagon in Molière's *L'Avare* was a high water-mark in his career. Iffland found his Lear overwhelming: "His look decided all — it blinded all he turned it on — the supporting actors barely dared speak ... Face of fiery red, eyes thunderbolts, every muscle feverishly tensed, lips involuntarily quivering, arms raised as if he meant to tear the fulfilment of his curse out of the heavens, his whole body the expression of the turmoil in his soul". Schröder's technique was incomparable in his day whenever intensity was required.

—Hugh Rorrison

SCOFIELD, (David) Paul. British actor. Born in Hurstpierpoint, Sussex, 21 January 1922. Educated at the Varndean School for Boys, Brighton, Sussex, 1933–39; trained for the stage at the London Mask Theatre and Drama School, in connection with the Westminster Theatre, London, 1940. Married actress Joy Parker in 1943, one son and one daughter. Stage debut, Theatre Royal, Brighton, 1936; London debut, Westminster Theatre, 1940; toured with ENSA, 1940–41; actor, Bideford Repertory Company, 1941, Whitehall Theatre, London, 1943, and Birmingham Repertory Company, 1942–45; first appearance at Stratford-upon-Avon, 1946; film debut, 1954; led company on tour of Soviet Union, 1955; Broadway debut, 1961. Member: Royal Shakespeare Directorate, 1966–68. Recipient: *Evening Standard* Award, 1956, 1962; Tony Award, 1962; Oscar, 1966; New York Film Critics' Award, 1966; London Film Academy Award, 1966; Saint Genesius Gold Medal, Rome, 1966; Bodil Award (Denmark), 1967; Shakespeare Prize (Germany), 1972. LL.D: Glasgow University, 1968; D.Litt: University of Kent, 1973; University of Sussex, 1985. CBE (Commander of the British Empire), 1956.

Roles

1936	Crowd member in *The Only Way* (Wills and Lang), Theatre Royal, Brighton.
1940	Role in *Desire Under the Elms* (O'Neill), Westminster Theatre, London.
	Third clerk and first soldier in *Abraham Lincoln* (Drinkwater), Westminster Theatre, London.
1941	Vincentio and Tranio in *The Taming of the Shrew* (Shakespeare), British tour.
1942	Stephen Undershaft in *Major Barbara* (G. B. Shaw), British tour.
	Horatio in *Hamlet* (Shakespeare), British tour.
1943	Alex Mordon in *The Moon is Down* (Steinbeck), Whitehall Theatre, London.
1944	Reginald in *Getting Married* (G. B. Shaw), Repertory Theatre, Birmingham.
	The Prince in *The Circle of Chalk* (Bagnold), Repertory Theatre, Birmingham.
	The Clown in *The Winter's Tale* (Shakespeare), Repertory Theatre, Birmingham; Shakespeare Memorial Theatre, Stratford-upon-Avon, 1948.
	William D'Albini in *The Empress Maud*, Repertory Theatre, Birmingham.
1945	Valentine in *Doctor's Delight*, Repertory Theatre, Birmingham.
	Young Marlow in *She Stoops to Conquer* (Goldsmith), Repertory Theatre, Birmingham.
	Konstantin in *The Seagull* (Chekhov), Repertory Theatre, Birmingham.
	John Tanner in *Man and Superman* (G. B. Shaw), Repertory Theatre, Birmingham.
	Philip in *King John* (Shakespeare), Repertory Theatre, Birmingham.
1946	Tegeus-Chromis in *A Phoenix Too Frequent* (Fry), Arts Theatre, London.
1946–47	Henry in *Henry V* (Shakespeare), Shakespeare Memorial Theatre, Stratford-upon-Avon.
	Don Armado in *Love's Labour's Lost* (Shakespeare), Shakespeare Memorial Theatre, Stratford-upon-Avon; Stratford Shakespeare Festival, Stratford, Ontario, 1961.
	Malcolm in *Macbeth* (Shakespeare), Shakespeare Memorial Theatre, Stratford-upon-Avon.
	Lucio in *Measure for Measure* (Shakespeare), Shakespeare Memorial Theatre, Stratford-upon-Avon.
	Mercutio in *Romeo and Juliet* (Shakespeare), Shakespeare Memorial Theatre, Stratford-upon-Avon; Her Majesty's Theatre, London, 1947.
	Sir Andrew Aguecheek in *Twelfth Night* (Shakespeare), Shakespeare Memorial Theatre, Stratford-upon-Avon; Her Majesty's Theatre, London, 1947.
	Cloten in *Cymbeline* (Shakespeare), Shakespeare Memorial Theatre, Stratford-upon-Avon.
	Pericles in *Pericles* (Shakespeare), Shakespeare Memorial Theatre, Stratford-upon-Avon; Rudolf Steiner Hall, London, 1950.
	Mephistophilis in *Faust* (Goethe), Shakespeare Memorial Theatre, Stratford-upon-Avon.
1947	Young Fashion in *The Relapse* (Vanbrugh), Lyric Theatre, Hammersmith, London; Phoenix Theatre, London, 1948.
1948	King Philip in *King John* (Shakespeare), Shakespeare Memorial Theatre, Stratford-upon-Avon.

Paul Scofield (1966).

Bassanio in *The Merchant of Venice* (Shakespeare), Shakespeare Memorial Theatre, Stratford-upon-Avon.

Hamlet in *Hamlet* (Shakespeare), Shakespeare Memorial Theatre, Stratford-upon-Avon; Phoenix Theatre, London, and tour of Soviet Union, 1955.

Troilus in *Troilus and Cressida* (Shakespeare), Shakespeare Memorial Theatre, Stratford-upon-Avon.

Roderigo in *Othello* (Shakespeare), Shakespeare Memorial Theatre, Stratford-upon-Avon.

1949 Alexander in *Adventure Story* (Rattigan), St James's Theatre, London.

Treplef in *The Seagull* (Chekhov), Lyric Theatre, Hammersmith, London.

1950 Hugo and Frederic in *Ring Round the Moon* (Anouilh), Globe Theatre, London.

1952 Don Pedro in *Much Ado About Nothing* (Shakespeare), Phoenix Theatre, London.

Philip Sturgess in *The River Line* (Morgan), Edinburgh Festival, Lyric Theatre, Hammersmith, London, and Strand Theatre, London.

Richard in *Richard II* (Shakespeare), Lyric Theatre, Hammersmith, London.

1953 Witwoud in *The Way of the World* (Congreve), Lyric Theatre, Hammersmith, London.

Pierre in *Venice Preserved* (Otway), Lyric Theatre, Hammersmith, London.

Paul Gardiner in *A Question of Fact* (Browne), Piccadilly Theatre, London.

1954 Prince Albert Troubiscoi in *Time Remembered* (Anouilh), Lyric Theatre, Hammersmith, London; New Theatre, London, 1955.

1956 The Priest in *The Power and the Glory* (Greene, adapted by Cannan and Bost), Phoenix Theatre, London.

Harry in *The Family Reunion* (Eliot), Phoenix Theatre, London.

1957 Fred Dyson in *A Dead Secret* (Bramwell), Piccadilly Theatre, London.

1958 Johnnie in *Expresso Bongo* (Mankowitz, More, Heneker, and Norman), Saville Theatre, London.

1959 Clive Root in *The Complaisant Lover* (Greene), Globe Theatre, London.

1960 Thomas More in *A Man for All Seasons* (Bolt), Globe Theatre, London; American National Theatre Academy Theatre, New York, 1961.

Coriolanus in *Coriolanus* (Shakespeare), Stratford Shakespeare Festival, Stratford, Ontario.

1962 Lear in *King Lear* (Shakespeare), Royal Shakespeare Theatre, Stratford-upon-Avon, and Aldwych Theatre, London; Théâtre Sarah Bernhardt, Paris, 1963; State Theatre, New York, and tour of Eastern Europe, 1964.

1965 Timon in *Timon of Athens* (Shakespeare), Royal Shakespeare Theatre, Stratford-upon-Avon.

Ivan Alexandrovitch Khlestakov in *The Government Inspector* (Gogol), Aldwych Theatre, London.

Charlie Dyer in *Staircase* (Dyer), Aldwych Theatre, London.

The Dragon in *The Thwarting of Baron Bolligrew* (Bolt), Aldwych Theatre, London.

1967–68 Macbeth in *Macbeth* (Shakespeare), Aldwych Theatre, London.

1968 Laurie in *The Hotel in Amsterdam* (Osborne), Royal Court Theatre, London, New Theatre, London, and Duke of York's Theatre, London.

1970 Vanya in *Uncle Vanya* (Chekhov), Royal Court Theatre, London.

1971 Wilhelm Voigt in *The Captain of Köpenick* (Mortimer, adapted from Zuckmayer), Old Vic Theatre, London.

Leone in *The Rules of the Game* (Hare, adapted from Pirandello), Old Vic Theatre, London.

1973 Alan West in *Savages* (Hampton), Royal Court Theatre, London, and Comedy Theatre, London.

1974 Prospero in *The Tempest* (Shakespeare), Playhouse, Leeds, and Wyndham's Theatre, London.

1976 Dimetos in *Dimetos* (Fugard), Playhouse, Nottingham, and Comedy Theatre, London.

1977 Volpone in *Volpone* (Jonson), National Theatre, London.

	Constantine Madras in *The Madras House* (Granville-Barker), National Theatre, London.
1978	Freddie Kilner in *A Family* (Harwood), Royal Exchange Theatre, Manchester, and Haymarket Theatre, London.
1979	Salieri in *Amadeus* (P. Shaffer), National Theatre, London.
1980	Othello in *Othello* (Shakespeare), National Theatre, London.
1982	Don Quixote in *Don Quixote* (Dewhurst), National Theatre, London.
	Oberon in *A Midsummer Night's Dream* (Shakespeare), National Theatre, London.
1992	Captain Shotover in *Heartbreak House* (G. B. Shaw), Haymarket Theatre, London.

Other roles included: *I'm Not Rappaport* (Gardner), Apollo Theatre, London, 1986; *Exclusive* (Archer), Strand Theatre, London, 1989.

Films

Carve Her Name with Pride, 1954; *That Lady*, 1955; *The Train*, 1963; *A Man for All Seasons*, 1966; *King Lear*, 1970; *Bartleby*, 1972; *A Delicate Balance*, 1972; *Scorpio*, 1973; *1919*, 1984; *When the Whales Came*, 1989; *Henry V*, 1989; *Hamlet*, 1991; *Utz*, 1992.

Television

The Ambassadors, 1977; *The Curse of King Tut's Tomb*, 1980; *The Potting Shed*, 1981; *If Winter Comes*, 1981; *Song at Twilight*, 1982; *Come into the Garden Maud*, 1982; *A Kind of Alaska*, 1984; *Anna Karenina*, 1985; *The Attic*, 1988; *Martin Chuzzlewit*, 1994.

*

Bibliography

Books:
J. C. Trewin, *Paul Scofield*, London, 1956.

* * *

An elusive but undeniable greatness infuses the acting of Paul Scofield. For nearly half a century critics have tried to define it. His voice, for instance, idiosyncratic and unpredictable, has inspired some of them to vivid evocation. Richard Findlater found it oddly monotonous, but "suddenly cracking and splitting into veins of gold or tin", while to J. C. Trewin it was "a mountain voice, rifted, chasmed, that can glitter on the peak and fall, sombre, in the sudden crevasse". Trewin added that to hear Scofield was to encounter "what a poet long ago called 'the random music of the turning world'".

It is not a comfortable voice to hear, and in certain types of part Scofield is not a comfortable actor to watch. There is a disconcertingly uncompromising truthfulness about what he shows. As Sir Thomas More in Robert Bolt's *A Man for All Seasons* he was a figure of courageous and unsentimental moral goodness, whose adherence to princi-

ple made pygmies of lesser but more powerful men and, by irrefutable force of logic and indomitable strength of character, led the audience to ask of themselves how they might have stood the same test. The directness with which, in Scofield's hands, More strove to justify to his daughter the ineluctibility of his stand — that God made man "to serve Him, wittily, in the tangle of his mind" — bore no trace of affectation or self-regard. Later, when publicly arraigned, one sorrowful look of reproach from his eyes placed his judges on trial before him. Thomas More is the role for which Scofield is best known around the world, having played it on stage in 1960 and in a film performance in 1966 that earned for him an Oscar.

The awe-inspiring stature of such a character seems to touch the actor himself. Effortlessly Scofield embodies moral integrity. The steady gaze of the hooded eyes is framed by a care-worn, grieving face that seems to have witnessed all the follies of humanity. His bearing is languorous but princely. Findlater enumerated some of Scofield's qualities: stillness, weary authority, mesmeric *mana*, eloquent eyes, and a capacity to touch the heart and surprise the mind. They lend him not only something of the aura of a Biblical sage but the form of an archetypal tragic hero: Everyman himself. As the broken whisky priest in a dramatisation of Graham Greene's *The Power and the Glory* (1956) his authentic depiction of an underlying moral goodness lifted the play to the level of classical tragedy and the same trait served him as Hamlet (1948 and 1955) and Lear (1962), which he essayed at Stratford when only 40. As Lear, in Peter Brook's sub-Beckettian interpretation, Scofield was an earthy, close-cropped Titan, muscular in defiance, devastating in the final howl of doom. The Lear was later filmed in snow-blanched desolation. His Timon at Stratford in 1965 reclaimed one of the fiercest dramas in the Shakespearean canon; but his Macbeth, Othello, and Oberon seemed less sure. Some critics found his inflections quirky, but, as W. A. Darlington reminded them, the same had been said of another indelible, self-governing player: "In Scofield today, as in Irving a hundred years ago, there is a force that transcends argument. When he plays Shakespeare, however oddly, Shakespeare is there to meet him".

There are moments in which he electrifies. One such fell in *The Captain of Köpenick* (1971) in the suddenness of the transformation that he wrought from a shambling, whining convict to an erect Prussian officer, gimlet-eyed on parade. It was a *comic* creation, suffused with sardonicism and larded with irony, qualities that he first brought to light at the Birmingham Repertory Theatre in 1945 under Sir Barry Jackson, particularly in plays by Shaw. There he was first directed by Brook: this was a partnership of actor and director that would be oft renewed, variously at Stratford, in the West End, and on film. His eclecticism, though, was apparent when he turned up in a shortlived musical, *Expresso Bongo*, and in 1989 a Jeffrey Archer play.

For all his individuality, Scofield has enjoyed being a company actor. In his fifties he went to Leeds to play Prospero under the direction of John Harrison, a fellow actor from Birmingham 30 years before, and in his sixties, by taking the small part of the French king in *Henry V*, he supported Kenneth Branagh's baptism as a film-maker. In the last 20 years he has sometimes seemed too sparing of himself. Admirers may wonder why he has not tackled Lear again, or Shylock at all, or Marlowe's Jew of Malta, or

Faustus, or Tamburlaine. He is an actor of the highest calibre who rarely in the theatre has been put to his full stretch. He is an Oscar-winning film star seldom seen in films. He is a natural leader, respected by all his fellows, who has apparently never sought to direct a play himself or manage a company of his own.

Paul Scofield has continually resisted conventional expectations. He is indifferent to the trappings of stardom, to the glittering prizes of his profession and the material lure of the cinema. In his youth he was one of the first to be hailed as a second Olivier; to his credit he has remained, in everyone's eyes, palpably the first Scofield.

—Michael Read

<hr>

SCOTT, George C(ampbell). US actor and director. Born in Wise, Virginia, 18 October 1927. Educated at Redford High School and the University of Missouri, 1950. Married 1) actress Patricia Reed (divorced); 2) actress Colleen Dewhurst in 1960 (divorced 1965); remarried Colleen Dewhurst in 1967 (divorced 1972); 3) actress Trish Van Devere in 1972; six children. Served in US Marine Corps, 1945–49. Stage debut, as a student at the University of Missouri, 1950; subsequently acted in some 150 roles with various stock companies; New York debut, New York Shakespeare Festival, 1957; first of many film appearances, 1959; co-founder, Theatre of Michigan company, 1961; London debut, 1965. Recipient: Theatre World Award, 1958; Clarence Derwent Award, 1958; Vernon Rice Award, 1958; Obie Award, 1958, 1963; New York Film Critics Award, 1970; Emmy Award, 1971 (twice); Golden Globe Award, 1971; Oscar, 1971 (refused); Genie Award, Academy of Canadian Cinema and Television, 1980.

Productions

As actor:

1957   Richard in *Richard III* (Shakespeare), Shakespeare Festival, Heckscher Theatre, New York.

1958   Jaques in *As You Like It* (Shakespeare), Shakespeare Festival, Heckscher Theatre, New York.
        Lord Wainwright in *Children of Darkness* (Mayer), Circle in the Square Theatre, New York.
        Tydings Glenn in *Comes a Day* (Lamkin), Ambassador Theatre, New York.

1959   Antony in *Antony and Cleopatra* (Shakespeare), Shakespeare Festival, Heckscher Theatre, New York.
        Lieutenant-Colonel N. P. Chipman in *The Andersonville Trial* (Levitt), Henry Miller Theatre, New York.

1960   Dolek Berson in *The Wall* (Lampell, adapted from Hersey), Billy Rose Theatre, New York.
        Shylock in *The Merchant of Venice* (Shakespeare), Salt Lake City, Utah; Shakespeare Festival., Delacorte Theatre, New York, 1962.

George C. Scott (c. 1966).

1962   General Seeger in *General Seeger* (Levin), Lyceum Theatre, New York.

1963   Ephraim Cabot in *Desire Under the Elms* (O'Neill), Circle in the Square Theatre, New York.

1965   Vershinin in *The Three Sisters* (Chekhov), Aldwych Theatre, London.

1967   Benjamin Hubbard in *The Little Foxes* (Hellman), Vivian Beaumont Theatre, New York.

1968   Sam Nash, Jesse Kiplinger and Roy Hubley in *Plaza Suite* (Simon), Plymouth Theatre, New York.

1973   Michael Astrov in *Uncle Vanya* (Chekhov), Circle in the Square Theatre, New York.

1975   Willy Loman in *Death of a Salesman* (Miller), Circle in the Square Theatre, New York.

1976   Foxwell J. Sly in *Sly Fox* (adapted from Jonson's *Volpone*), Broadhurst Theatre, New York.

1980   Dr August Browning in *Tricks of the Trade*, Brooks Atkinson Theatre, New York.

1982   Garry Essendine in *Present Laughter* (Coward), Circle in the Square Theatre, New York.

1986   Henry Finnegan in *The Boys in Autumn*, Circle in the Square Theatre, New York.

Other roles included: Chester Norton in *Personal Appearance*, Stephens Playhouse, Columbia, Missouri.

As director:

1962   *General Seeger* (Levin), Lyceum Theatre, New York.

1975   *Death of a Salesman* (Miller), Circle in the Square Theatre, New York.

All God's Chillun Got Wings (O'Neill), Circle in the Square Theatre, New York.

1976   *Sly Fox* (adapted from Jonson), Broadhurst Theatre, New York.

1982   *Present Laughter* (Coward), Circle in the Square Theatre, New York.

1984   *Design for Living* (Coward), Circle in the Square Theatre, New York.

1991   *On Borrowed Time*, New York.

Films

As actor:

The Hanging Tree, 1959; *Anatomy of a Murder*, 1959; *The Hustler*, 1961; *The List of Adrian Messenger*, 1963; *Dr Strangelove, or How I Learned to Stop Worrying and Love the Bomb*, 1964; *The Yellow Rolls-Royce*, 1964; *The Bible ... In the Beginning*, 1966; *Not with My Wife, You Don't*, 1966; *The Flim-Flam Man*, 1967; *Petulia*, 1968; *This Savage Land*, 1969; *Patton*, 1970; *The Hospital*, 1971; *Jane Eyre*, 1971; *The Last Run*, 1971; *They Might be Giants*, 1971; *The New Centurions*, 1972; *Rage*, 1972; *The Day of the Dolphin*, 1973; *Oklahoma Crude*, 1973; *Bank Shot*, 1974; *The Savage is Loose*, 1974; *The Hindenberg*, 1975; *Islands in the Stream*, 1977; *Crossed Swords/The Prince and the Pauper*, 1978; *Movie, Movie*, 1978; *Hardcore*, 1979; *Arthur Miller: On Home Ground*, 1979; *The Changeling*, 1980; *The Formula*, 1980; *Taps*, 1981; *The Beastmaster*, 1982; *Firestarter*, 1984; *The Indomitable Teddy Roosevelt*, 1984; *Dick Tracy*, 1989; *The Exorcist III*, 1990.

As director:

Rage, 1972; *The Savage is Loose*, 1975.

Television

As actor:

I Haven't Seen Her Lately, 1958; *The Empty Chair*, 1958; *A Tale of Two Cities*, 1958; *People Kill People Sometimes*, 1959; *Target for Three*, 1959; *Winterset*, 1959; *The Burning Court*, 1960; *Don Juan in Hell*, 1960; *The Power and the Glory*, 1961; *The Picture of Dorian Gray*, 1961; *I Remember a Lemon Tree*, 1961; *East Side/West Side*, 1963–64; *A Time for Killing*, 1965; *The Crucible*, 1967; *Mirror, Mirror, Off the Wall*, 1969; *The Price*, 1971; *Jane Eyre*, 1971; *From Yellowstone to Tomorrow*, 1972; *The Man Who Got a Ticket*, 1972; *Fear on Trial*, 1975; *Beauty and the Beast*, 1976; *Oliver Twist*, 1982; *China Rose*, 1983; *A Christmas Carol*, 1984; *Mussolini: The Untold Story*, 1985; *Choices*, 1986; *The Last Days of Patton*, 1986; *The Murders in the Rue Morgue*, 1986; *Pals*, 1987; *Mr President*, 1987–88; *The Ryan White Story*, 1989; *The Road West*.

As director:
The Andersonville Trial, 1970.

* * *

George C. Scott's contribution to the post-World War II US stage consists of an heroic acting style that reflects traditions that date from the late 18th and early 19th centuries, exemplified by such actors as George Frederick Cooke, surviving images of whom bear a striking resemblance to Scott; Edmund Kean, whose fiery, intense acting strategy demonstrated a continuation of Cooke's powerful stage presence in the heroic style; and Junius Brutus Booth, whose elevated emotionalism won him acclaim as an heroic actor of the same type. Like his historical counterparts, who saw the coming of the end of romanticism and the death of tragedy with the advent of the Industrial Revolution, Scott delivers a brand of realism that mirrors modern man in his ceaseless existential struggle with the depersonalizing forces of late 20th-century society. His performances as Willy Loman in Arthur Miller's *Death of a Salesman* serve as cogent examples.

Additionally, his screen performance as General George S. Patton stands out as perhaps the most effective example of Scott's peculiar ability to play the contemporary epic heroes of the middle class and upper middle class — male partisans who cling to their machismo as a symbol of unity and power. Indeed, his acting in this vein may well reflect the deeper inner struggles Scott himself faced as a soldier-turned-actor following World War II. Oddly, *Patton* was released in 1968 at the height of the protest against US military involvement in the Vietnam War, and it is to Scott's artistic credit that his characterization of the aggressive, arrogant general became a wholesale popular success in the nation's movie houses. To some, *Patton* served to affirm the nobility of a threatened patriotic breed of man. To others, the film exemplified a tragic human condition. Scott's performance succeeded in polarizing both sides of the deeper social issues implied by war consciousness and played a significant role in the ongoing debate of the period.

A third type of role that has become one of the actor's major trademarks takes in characters who rage against social injustice, often as defence attorneys or advocates for various unpopular causes. The most recent example is Scott's 1990 performance in a made-for-television movie as a persuasive attorney who represents a youthful Aids victim's quest for admission to his neighbourhood public school.

The remarkable consistency of character types played by the actor can be traced to the first dramatic role of Scott's career, that of Sir Robert Morton, the barrister who comes to the legal defence of a young schoolboy wrongly accused of theft in *The Winslow Boy*. He played this role while pursuing a degree in journalism at the University of Missouri in 1950, under the auspices of Professor Donovan Rhynsburger. Rhynsburger, one of the first graduates of the Yale School of Drama, began the theatre programme at the University of Missouri in the 1920's. His approach to theatre production embodied a philosophy that saw the stage as a means of exposing societal conditions and situations generally overlooked by the community at large. Scott and Rhynsburger found a unity of purpose in the director's production of *The Winslow Boy*, and the actor earned immediate acclaim from local audiences. Rhynsburger cast Scott in leads of the next six university productions, after which the actor embarked upon his professional career. Now retired, Rhynsburger remembers the young George C. Scott as a quick study, who always worked exhaustingly to perfect his roles. The thespian's self-described approach to acting consisted of four simple words: "To be. To do".

Scott was also given to violent outbursts of anger, a trait that he has carried throughout his career. His obsessive personality, complicated by a lifelong battle with alcoholism and marked by a series of failed marriages, has distinguished him among his peers as an artist of mighty and sometimes fearsome independence. Not only has he snubbed the established theatrical institutions such as the Hollywood Academy of Arts and other dramatic organizations, but he has kept himself apart from the so-called "Method" practitioners who aligned themselves with the Actors' Studio and other "new wave" institutions. Yet, though he denies a conscious association with the Stanislavsky system of actor training advocated by Lee Strasberg, Harold Clurman and others, his transactional approach is clearly close in style to that of many other actors who came out of the 1950's. In practice, he has been professionally associated with most of the Actors' Studio's big names, and despite his claims to the contrary, he has matured over the past decade in much the same fashion as others who shared the discipline of the Stanislavsky tradition. Like his contemporaries Marlon Brando and Lee J. Cobb, Scott brings a strength and power to his acting that has instinctual and emotional roots. Yet the classical approach to which he says he adheres gives his finished performances a polished edge in strange contrast to the raging spirit that appears to seethe beneath the surface. Even in his coolest moments, a fire seems to burn behind his piercing blue eyes. Scott will doubtless be remembered by popular audiences largely for his powerful male machismo, but discerning historians might well keep in mind how his use of this image has been consciously developed to reflect the despair and futility of the innate aggressiveness of human nature. In a sense, it is the anti-hero we find most captivating in Scott's characterizations, a subtext of fear and suffering within the form of bravado and confidence.

—George C. Mielke

SELLARS, Peter. US director. Born 27 September 1957. Educated at Harvard University, until 1981. Attracted attention as a director of promise while at Harvard, 1980–81; ran puppet show for ten years; artistic director, Boston Shakespeare Company, 1983–84; director and manager, American National Theatre Company, Kennedy Centre, Washington, D.C., 1984–86; has since worked as a guest artist with a range of theatres; artistic director, Los Angeles Festival; director, Opera Theatre, Boston, since 1990.

Principal productions

1979	*King Lear* (Shakespeare).
1980–81	*The Inspector General* (Gogol).
1982	*Orlando* (Handel).
1983	*The Visions of Simone Marchard* (Brecht).
	Conversations with Fear and Hope After Death (adapted from Bach).
1984	*Hang On to Me* (compilation from Gorky and Gershwin).
1985	*The Count of Monte Cristo* (Dumas père).
	Julius Caesar in Egypt (Handel).
	The Seagull (Chekhov).
1986	*Ajax* (Sophocles).
	Cosi fan Tutte (Mozart).
1987	*Nixon in China* (Sellars, Adams and Goodman).
	Don Giovanni (Mozart).
1988	*The Marriage of Figaro* (Mozart).
1989	*Don Giovanni* (Mozart).
1990	*The Magic Flute* (Mozart).
	The Death of Klinghoffer (Sellars, Adams and Goodman).
1993	*The Persians* (Aeschylus).

Other productions have included: *The Mikado* (Gilbert and Sullivan); *Zangezi*.

* * *

Peter Sellars is the perennial bad boy of American directing, an intellectual outsider whose anachronistic treatment of classic works — such as *King Lear* (1979) imaged by a disintegrating luxury car, his *Ajax* (1986) staged as a post-Vietnam military trial, or his *The Magic Flute* (1990) set within the fantasy landscape of contemporary Los Angeles — often deflects attention from his deeper originality, his faithfulness to text, and his strong sense of artistic purpose. To his detractors, Sellars is a flashy prankster whose modern restatements are juvenile and reductive. But to his admirers, Sellars is the most conceptually brilliant and innovative US director since Orson Welles, and perhaps the most important figure in the reformulation of opera since Wieland Wagner.

In the best sense of the term, Sellars is an amateur, a self-taught lover of theatre who shuns the conventions of orthodox practice. At Harvard, he avoided what he considered narrow and self-perpetrating theatre studies, devising instead his own curriculum in dramatic theory, Russian literature, psychoacoustics, spatial perception and film. Sellars admires many other directors — especially Elizabeth Le Compte of New York's experimental Wooster Group and film-maker Jean-Luc Godard — but has never served as anyone else's apprentice because he finds directing too inherently idiosyncratic to be learned through imitation. Although deeply American in his love of popular culture and in his ambition to establish a vital national theatre, his true intellectual and artistic roots lie in the theories and practices of the European avant-garde. Brecht, Strehler, Lyubimov, and especially Meyerhold have had a major influence on his socially committed, poetic, openly theatrical style.

The characteristic themes of Sellars's works are political and religious. Like Wagner, he believes that theatre creates social consciousness by providing a prism through which a given culture examines its hidden assumptions and needs. A classical work is especially useful to Sellars's purposes because it distances the emotional immediacy of contemporary issues and reveals the strangeness of the familiar. Thus, in 1985, Sellars used Handel's *Julius Caesar in Egypt* (1724) to examine the issues of terrorism, cultural aggression and President Ronald Reagan's military actions in the Middle East, just as the class conflicts of Mozart's *The Marriage of Figaro* (1786) allowed Sellars to make a statement about social exploitation in the 1988 world of New York billionaire Donald Trump. Beyond any contemporary set of references, Sellars — who was raised a Christian Scientist — tries to locate the eternal or religious coordinates for every production he directs. Even his darkest work, the 1989 revival of *Don Giovanni*, set amid the drugs and pornography of an urban ghetto, ended with an image of heaven and hell inspired by Giotto's *Last Judgement* from the Arena Chapel, Padua.

To witness a Sellars production is an active experience in which deliberate discrepancies between the text and its anachronous performance, serious moments and send-ups, vivid realism and expressionistic choreography challenge audiences to think for themselves. Moreover, abrupt shifts in context reflect an important characteristic of Sellars's theatre in which the realities of contemporary life and poetic invention coexist simultaneously, not in romantic fusion, nor in classical balance, but in zany and often contradictory juxtaposition. For Sellars, simultaneity and contradiction are what the modern world is about. Nevertheless, beneath the contemporary surface, Sellars rigorously adheres to the structure, background and inherent ideas of the original score and text — which he always performs uncut in the original language.

A major unifying factor in his work is the use of symbolic gestures that capture the moral centre of an action and then thread themselves through a production like variations on a theme. Falling is a favourite Sellars motif — he calls it his "Miltonic obsession" — that uses loss of balance as a metaphor for intense spiritual change, such as falling from innocence or falling in love. In expressing the emotional action of *The Marriage of Figaro* (1988), Sellars had the characters repeatedly slip, roll, tumble, teeter, collapse, slide, and fold their lovelorn ways towards the last act, where a final jump from a penthouse ledge was one of joy into each other's arms. This highly developed gestural vocabulary — with its roots in Sellars's love of ballet, sign language and the hand gestures of Pacific island dance — allows Sellars to use his actor-singers abstractly as well as realistically, and thus to have the means of advancing ideas and argument on more levels than the merely psychological. Within the details of a richly conceived design, often developed over a period of months and even years, Sellars places emphasis on the spontaneous reaction of his actor-singers to one another, to the text, and to the audience. Thus, despite Sellars's serious aesthetic and social intentions, the feeling created by his work is playful and immediate.

Sellars's growing international reputation has survived his failure to secure a regular place in the cultural establishment. Since the demise of his short-lived American National Theatre in Washington, D.C., he has worked mainly on the fringe as a guest artist. New York's Metropolitan Opera has twice announced plans for innovative Sellars projects (1987 and 1989), only to cancel them at the last moment. Thus, audiences in New York, London, and Paris must still travel to the suburbs to see a Sellars production. Even his most original work, including his profoundly moving dramatic meditation on Bach cantatas, *Conversations with Fear and Hope After Death* (1983), or his new grand operas on contemporary history devised with composer John Adams and librettist Alice Goodman, *Nixon in China* (1987) and *The Death of Klinghoffer* (1990), will continue to have their debuts in places like Cambridge, Massachusetts; Purchase, New York; Brooklyn; Houston; and Los Angeles.

It is in southern California, where he serves as artistic director of the Los Angeles Festival, that Sellars hopes to establish a new cultural centre in which Pacific, Latin and Euro-American theatre traditions may find a natural meeting ground and help create the international art forms of the 21st century. Simultaneously, as director of the newly-formed Boston Opera Theatre, he intends to continue reformulating the terms of a distinctly American style of contemporary opera.

—Richard Trousdell

SEMIONOVA, Ekaterina (Semionovna).   Russian actress. Born 7 November 1786. Trained for the stage under I. A. Dmitrievich at the St. Petersburg Theatrical School, from 1794. Married Prince I. A. Gagarin in 1826. Stage debut, 1802; joined Imperial Theatre, St. Petersburg, 1803; admitted as member of the St Petersburg company, 1805, and subsequently highly acclaimed with the company in tragic roles by Ozerov, Shakespeare, Racine, Schiller and others; studied drama with poet N. I. Gnedich, from 1807; withdrew temporarily from the stage, 1820–22; officially retired on her marriage, 1826; came briefly out of retirement, 1830. Died in St. Petersburg, 1 March 1849.

Principal roles

1804	Antigone in *Oedipus at Athens* (Ozerov), St. Petersburg.
1805	Moina in *Fingal* (Ozerov), St. Petersburg.
1807	Ksenia in *Dmitri Donskoi* [Dmitri of the Don] (Ozerov), St. Petersburg.
	Cordelia in *King Lear* (Gnedich, adapted from Ducis and Shakespeare), St. Petersburg.
1809	Aménaïde in *Tancrède* (Voltaire), St. Petersburg.
	Polyxena in *Polyxena* (Ozerov), St. Petersburg.
1810	Hermione in *Andromaque* (Racine), St. Petersburg.
	Maria Stuart in *Maria Stuart* (Shpis), St. Petersburg.
	Ophelia in *Hamlet* (Shakespeare), St. Petersburg.
1811	Ariane in *Ariane* (T. Corneille), St. Petersburg.
	Amalia in *Das Kind der Liebe* (Kotzebue), St. Petersburg.
1814	Amelia in *Die Raüber* (Schiller), St. Petersburg.
1824	Phèdre in *Phèdre* (Racine), St. Petersburg.
1830	Sofia in *Gore ot uma* [Woe from Wit] (Griboyedov), St. Petersburg.

Other roles included: Clytemnestra in *Iphigenia in Aulis* (Racine); Medea in *Medea* (Longepierre); Mérope in *Mérope* (Voltaire); Zaïre in *Zaïre* (Voltaire).

* * *

Ekaterina Semionova was a legend in her own time. There was, according to Pushkin, no actress to equal her in tragedy. She entered theatre school at the age of eight, where her teacher was Dmitrievich. Dmitrievich was not only a fine actor but was remarkable for having visited England, at the suggestion of the great French actor Lekain, where he had long conversations on acting with David Garrick. Garrick's approach was radically different from that of his French contemporaries and it was the French "classical" manner that predominated in St. Petersburg at the end of the 18th century. Semionova's rise to prominence occurred at the moment when the classical tradition was beginning to be questioned by the early Romantics. In acting this implied a preference for greater realism and emotional involvement in the character. Semionova is the first notable representative of the new approach and of a specifically Russian school of acting. She was allowed to take part in professional performances while still at school and made her first appearance in 1802, when she was 14. She was fortunate throughout her career in having prominent men of the theatre and of letters as her mentors: first Prince Shakovskoi, who was responsible for repertoire in the imperial theatres, and later the writers Ozerov and Gnedich. All three helped her develop her technique and her sensitivity to literature. Ozerov was considered the leading serious dramatist of his time and a number of his works were specifically written with Semionova in mind. Gnedich was famous as a poet and the translator of the *Iliad*. It was he who made a version of *Lear* for her, translating it from a French adaptation by Ducis. Very much in the classical tradition he coached Semionova in the delivery of verse and in vocal technique.

It was in Ozerov's *Oedipus* that Semionova made her highly successful professional debut in 1804. This was followed by two more plays by the same author. Her repertoire gradually extended to tragedies by Shakespeare, Racine, Voltaire and Schiller, whose plays were beginning to be popular.

Although Semionova was not without her detractors, she was by and large the idol of St. Petersburg society. Those who dared to criticise her openly found themselves virtually hounded down. Semionova herself was no helpless innocent but was ruthless in fighting off potential rivals, making full use of the fact that she enjoyed the "protection" of Prince Gagarin. The teacher of one of her rivals who had dared to voice criticism both of her and of one of her pupils was sent into internal exile on his estates.

The greatest challenge to Semionova's supremacy came from the French actress Mademoiselle George, who took up residence in St Petersburg between 1808 and 1812, having left the Comédie-Française. George was a leading exponent of the method of acting advocated by Diderot in *Le Paradoxe sur le Comédien* and later defined by Stanislavsky as the School of Representation. She possessed a number of vocal tricks that she deployed to great effect, mostly violent contrasts of dynamics and pace. George automatically brought with her the glamour and prestige of La Maison de Molière and Semionova risked being seen as no more than a provincial talent. She attended all of George's performances and with the aid of Gnedich and others mastered all her tricks. In 1809 a theatrical duel was fought. Gnedich made a translation of Voltaire's *Tancrède*, in which Semionova played Aménaïde, one of George's most successful roles. Semionova's triumph, which George was one of the first to acknowledge, saved her from being relegated to the second rank. A similar duel was played out in Moscow the following year.

Some critics maintained that Semionova had damaged her natural gifts by imitating George's mannerisms, but Pushkin took a contrary view. Nothing in his view could obscure Semionova's natural gifts and style. Summing up her career in 1820, he wrote: "Endowed with talent, beauty, truthful, living feelings, she was her own teacher. Semionova never copied any model; the soulless French actress George and the everlastingly enthusiastic Gnedich could only provide her with hints of the secrets of art which she understood thanks to the revelations of her own soul. Her acting was always free, always clear, the nobility of her movement when aroused, her pure, even, pleasing voice, and her frequent bursts of genuine inspiration all these belonged to her and were borrowed from no-one. She adorned the imperfect works of the miserable Ozerov ... Semionova has no rival. Biased gossip, momentary sacrifices, profitable novelties have passed away but she remains the one enduring empress of the tragic stage".

By the mid-1820's, Semionova began to feel that there were fewer major roles for her to play. She had rounded off her demonstration of supremacy in classical drama in 1824 when she played the title role in *Phèdre*. She was less at home with the new style of plays. She could not play romantic young women nor had she the right temperament and technique for light comedy. She tended to swamp them. She retired from the stage in 1826, although she participated in 1830 in a reading of Griboyedov's still incomplete comedy *Woe from Wit*. In 1826 she married her lover of many years, Prince Gagarin, which made it impossible for her, as a member of the aristocracy, to appear on the public stage.

—Jean Benedetti

———

SERBAN, Andrei. Romanian director. Born in Bucharest, Romania, 21 June 1943. Married with two children. Educated at the University of Bucharest; trained for the theatre at the Theatre and Film Institute, Bucharest. Began career as director in Zagreb, Yugoslavia; debut as director on the US stage, 1970; director, La Mama, New York, from 1970; director, Yale Repertory Theatre, New Haven, Connecticut, 1977–78; also worked with Peter Brook in France and Italy; London debut, 1980; has since directed drama and opera at venues throughout the world; general manager, National Theatre of Romania, from 1990. Recipient: Ford scholarship, 1970; Guggenheim scholarship, 1976; Rockefeller scholarship, 1980; Tony Award; prizes at the Avignon, Belgrade, and Shiraz Festivals.

Principal productions

1970	*Arden of Faversham* (anon.), La Mama, New York.
	Ubu Roi (Jarry), La Mama, New York.
1972–74	*Fragments of a Trilogy* (comprising *Medea* and *The Trojan Women* by Euripides and *Electra* by Sophocles), La Mama, New York.
1975	*The Good Woman of Setzuan* (Brecht), La Mama, New York.
1976	*As You Like It* (Shakespeare), La Mama, New York.
1977	*Agamemnon* (Aeschylus), Shakespeare Festival, Delacorte, New York.
	The Cherry Orchard (Chekhov), Vivian Beaumont Theatre, Lincoln Centre, New York.
1977–78	*The Ghost Sonata* (Strindberg), Yale Repertory Theatre, New Haven, Connecticut.
1978	*The Master and Margarita* (adapted by Serban), Shakespeare Festival, Public Theatre, New York.
1979	*The Umbrellas of Cherbourg*, Shakespeare Festival, Public Theatre, New York, and Phoenix Theatre, London.
	Happy Days (Beckett), Shakespeare Festival, Public Theatre, New York.
1980	*The Seagull* (Chekhov), Shakespeare Festival, Public Theatre, New York.
	Eugene Onegin (Tchaikovsky), Welsh National Opera.
1981	*I Puritani* (Bellini), Welsh National Opera.
	La Traviata (Verdi), Juilliard American Opera Centre, New York.
1982	*The Marriage of Figaro* (Mozart), Guthrie Theatre, Minneapolis, Minnesota.
1983	*The Three Sisters* (Chekhov), American Repertory Theatre, Cambridge, Massachusetts.
	Uncle Vanya (Chekhov), La Mama, New York.
	Alcina (Handel), City Opera, New York.
1984	*Turandot* (Puccini), Royal Opera House, London.
1985	*The King Stag* (Gozzi), American Repertory Theatre, Cambridge, Massachussetts.
	Norma (Bellini), Welsh National Opera.
1986	*Fidelio* (Beethoven), Covent Garden, London.
1987	*I Puritani* (Bellini), Opéra, Paris.
1990	*An Ancient Trilogy* (comprising *Medea* and *The Trojan Woman* by Euripides and *Elektra* by Sophocles), National Theatre, Bucharest.

Other productions include: *Ubu Roi* (Jarry), 1966; *Julius Caesar* (Shakespeare), 1968; *Jonah*, 1969; *The Miser* (Molière), 1988; *Twelfth Night* (Shakespeare), 1989; *The Magic Flute* (Mozart).

* * *

Director Andrei Serban is an innovative international artist, whose work synthesizes trends in Europe and the USA. Once the "enfant terrible" of the Bucharest theatre world, Serban was invited to New York by Ellen Stewart at La Mama in 1969. Stewart had seen Serban's work in Zagreb, Yugoslavia, and found him to be a director of great promise. Thrust into the New York experimental scene,

Serban was forced to adapt to a whole new dimension of expectations and performance style. Immediately disturbed by the nature of actor training in the USA, Serban felt that he was starting from point zero in the preparation of a company. The challenge of a new method of work resulted in lively productions of *Arden of Faversham* and Jarry's *Ubu Roi*, two plays that he had already directed in Bucharest. Peter Brook saw these mises en scène in New York and invited Serban to work with him in France and Italy. Brook has had the greatest impact upon Serban's directing. Brook's intimate and profound work with actors and Joseph Chaikin's experiments with ensemble acting have provided an intriguing contrast to Serban's Romanian training at the Theatre and Film Institute.

While preparing *Orghast at Persepolis* with Brook in Iran, Serban led exercises in breathing and physical alignment with the company. Impassioned by the Greek theatre, Serban also helped the company train as a chorus. The experiments with dead languages, sound and Zoroastrian texts were also a major influence upon Serban's subsequent productions. Immediately following the experience with Brook, Serban returned to New York to direct *Medea*, *Electra* and *The Trojan Women* (1972–74). He utilized a kind of gibberish derived from Greek, Latin, American Indian and African languages, which played with the idea of sound as a visual image. Serban saw sound as "energy in movement", a musical and rhythmic element that could paint pictures. Incorporating both subtle and large physical performance styles, Serban created moving drama with intense emotion.

In 1977, Serban directed a controversial production of *The Cherry Orchard* at the Vivian Beaumont Theatre in the Lincoln Centre. Drawing inspiration from one of his favourite directors, Vsevelod Meyerhold, he contested the conventional melancholy, Stanislavsky-inspired approach to Chekhov by interpreting the play as a comedy. He pushed the text to all possible extremes in rehearsal, attempting to discover all possible layers of meaning. And spatially, Serban used the vastness of the Beaumont stage to compose stage pictures of great beauty. The concept of a simple interior and edge of the orchard was expanded to provide an actual orchard upstage, where images of actors wandering provided striking, poetic effects. Serban asserted his belief in the power of non-verbal "text" in this play, putting the drama into action whenever he thought it appropriate. In the 1980's, Lithuanian director Eimuntas Nekrosius took a similar approach in his comic interpretation of *Uncle Vanya*.

Once established in the USA, Serban directed at the American Repertory Theatre, the Guthrie Theatre (where his Romanian colleague Livia Ciulei was artistic director) La Mama, and worldwide for productions of the opera repertoire. Serban's work encompasses a dramatic literature from Beckett to Aeschylus, with special focus upon Chekhov and Gozzi. Serban's love for the commedia dell'arte and improvisation attracted him to the Gozzi plays, and to the operas with libretti based upon a Gozzi "fiabe". Serban's *The King Stag* in 1985 (masks and costumes by Julie Taymor) exhibited a theatricality that paralleled that of Benno Besson's 1982 Gozzi adaptation of *L'Oiseau vert* (*The Green Bird*) in Geneva. The rich visual spectacle of both productions reflects upon the interest in Gozzi that Meyerhold and Vakhtangov had in the 1920's in Russia.

Serban does not confront the dramatic text as a finished entity; he has no fears of cutting the original to suit his needs. This is also reminiscent of Meyerhold. With Serban, productions are in constant transition; changes are possible in the text, the set, or the mise en scène at the very last moment, or even during a show's run. He sees a production as a vital creation, in effect, never finished. For revivals, Serban recreates his mise en scène, because he believes that the tastes of the audience too are in constant transition, subject to the trend of the moment. Serban has an excellent rapport with his actors, and demands great flexibility and adaptability from them. He prefers to prepare and train his actors in a manner suitable to his style of direction. Serban works in all types of performance space — small and large — and occasionally outdoors (as in *As You Like It* in France). He has also experimented with non-frontal staging in his early years of directing. However, in his more recent work with opera, these alternative configurations are not possible. While highly oriented toward the visual image, Serban does not sublimate the actor's position on the stage. He works individually with his performers, adapting the role to the particular personality of the performer. His style requires actors with energy, presence and skills of mime and movement. Serban is an exciting director of original, imaginative and flamboyant theatre.

—Ron Popenhagen

SERLIO, Sebastiano. Italian painter, architect, and designer. Born in Bologna, 1475. Studied as an architect under Baldassare Peruzzi in Rome, from 1514. Introduced innovations in theatrical scenery and lighting and designed first purpose-built theatre at Vicenza in the 1530's; lived in Venice, 1527–40, and then settled in Paris, where he worked on the palace at Fontainebleau, 1541; published his highly influential scenic drawings in the second part, 1545, of *D'Architettura*; fell from favour on death of Françis I, 1547, and was reduced to poverty. Died in Paris, 1554.

Publications

Tutte l'Opere D'Architettura e Prospettiva, six vols., 1537–75; *Libro extraordinaire*, 1551.

* * *

Sebastiano Serlio's immense importance for the development of the theatre of the Italian Renaissance, which in turn determined the nature of theatre practice throughout Europe, rests above all upon his architectural treatise, *D'Architettura*. This was conceived as an elaboration upon the ancient work of Vitruvius, which had been discovered in manuscript in 1414 and, subsequently published in many editions, had had the most profound influence upon the whole of Renaissance architecture.

Serlio's book was not just a commentary and "modern" version of Vitruvius, but was greatly informed too by the extensive practical experience of its author. Serlio had been an assistant to the great painter, architect, and stage designer Baldassare Peruzzi, who had worked widely on theatrical projects within the noble Italian courts, and left

his notes and drawings to Serlio, who in addition to other architectural commissions, constructed a theatre in the 1530's in Vicenza. Beginning in 1537, Serlio's work drawing upon such knowledge was published in six books, the last appearing in 1575.

Book Two, published in 1545, dealt with perspective, and included a section on stagecraft as well as a plan for a typical court theatre and suggested settings. Reflecting the taste of his courtly audiences, Serlio enthusiastically endorsed the wonders of theatrical art, and, in particular, the attractions of illusionistic scenery, asserting that "among all things made by the hand of man, few in my opinion bring greater satisfaction to the spirit than the unveiling to our view of a stage setting. There the art of perspective gives a thousand marvels". As an effective handbook summing up contemporary Italian theatrical stagecraft, and based on and recording his own practical experience, Book Two of *D'Architettura* not only proved extraordinarily effective in disseminating these concepts throughout Europe, but also provides later scholars with an invaluable first-hand account and explanation of historical practice.

In the text and illustrations he describes and demonstrates how to set up perspective flats, angle wings arranged on a raked stage in such a way as to create an illusionistic setting. Because no permanent theatre structures had yet been built (that remained for Palladio and Scamozzi to accomplish), Serlio assumed that a temporary stage would be erected in a rectangular hall. Nevertheless, he imitated ancient practice by placing a semi-circular orchestra and auditorium within such a hall, even though this arrangement was not the best for appreciating the optical illusion of the perspective settings.

In this we can see the confusion that sometimes resulted from Renaissance attempts to reconcile ancient and modern practices that were incompatible. The logic of perspective dictated that the audience itself had to be arranged in relation to sightlines, with the best view being reserved for the most important members of the audience, and everyone else ranked accordingly. With a central vanishing point, the best positions for viewing the setting are those directly opposite that central point: this suggests a horseshoe or bell-shaped auditorium, elongated along the middle axis of the perspective setting. The Roman auditorium, however, was not horseshoe-shaped, but semi-circular, distributing its members in a wide arc opposite the narrow stage upon which were displayed actors, but no perspective scene. Serlio, despite his use of a central vanishing point and perspective angle wings on a deep stage, preserves the Roman semi-circular auditorium and places his most important spectators on the first (bottom) row of it (the place reserved by the Romans for their elite, since it provided a good view of the orchestra and stage) whereas, in fact, the best point for viewing the perspective settings employed by Serlio would be from a row considerable higher up in the auditorium. The desire to emulate Roman practice was thus allowed by Serlio to override pragmatic considerations, which were not incorporated into theatrical architecture until Scamozzi's theatre at Sabbioneta, half a century later.

Taking as his inspiration Vitruvius's highly problematic account of Roman scenic content, Serlio describes and provides drawings of the three types of scenery: comic, tragic, and satyric. He adapts his predecessor's description into equivalent contemporary terms, and elaborates it somewhat in the process; the fundamental concept, however, of three types of conventional "locations" suitable for any play, was retained. In determining how this was to be physically realised, Vitruvius offered little guidance and Serlio drew instead upon practices that had evolved in the Italian courts. The settings were each formed by four sets of wooden angle wings, which were covered with canvas, painted in "trompe d'oeil", and placed before a backdrop. These standard scenes were to be recycled, providing the settings for any work that might be contemplated, and, indeed, they were widely reproduced in later theatrical manuals and endlessly employed with only slight variations in theatres throughout Europe for centuries.

In addition to his treatments of perspective and stage settings, Serlio included descriptions of various lighting and scenic effects, all deliberately intended to enhance the sense of theatrical illusion. Although he evidently did not use a proscenium arch, or envisage a system of changeable settings, his ideas were soon adapted to make use of them, initially with little fundamental change to his symmetrically balanced and harmoniously arranged perspective settings, which drew the eye into them and towards a central vanishing point. Thus, although Serlio did not invent the concept of a theatre of pictorial illusion, his work — more than that of any other individual — ensured that once the theoretical and practical basis for such stagecraft had been formulated in Italy, it was able to spread and dominate European practice virtually to the present day. It was not until Adolphe Appia, Gordon Craig, and other early twentieth-century exponents of "the new art of the theatre" called for a revolutionary stagecraft freed from the tenets of pictorial realism that the Serlian theatre underwent fundamental reform.

—Richard C. Beacham

SERVANDONI, Giovanni (Niccolano Geronimo). French architect, painter and stage designer. Born in Florence, Italy, 2 May 1695. Trained in Rome as an artist, under Giovanni Paolo Pannini, and studied architecture under Guiseppe Iganzio Rossi. Married 1749. Worked chiefly in Paris, from 1724, but also designed several neoclassical theatres and scenery for theatres throughout Europe; principal designer, Académie Royale de Musique et de Danse, Palais Royale, Paris, 1726, and at the Paris Opéra, from 1728; admitted to the Académy de Peinture, 1731; presented designs at the Salle des Machines, Paris, 1738–42 and again in the 1750's; designed scenery for Covent Garden, London, 1749; scene painter to the court at Wurttemberg, 1763; architectural designs included portal of St Sulpice, Paris, 1749. Died in Paris, 19 January 1766.

Productions

As set designer:

1726	*Pyrame et Thisbé* (Rebel and Francoeur), Opéra, Paris.
1727	*Proserpine* (Lulli), Opéra, Paris.
1728	*Orion* (La Coste), Opéra, Paris.
	Pénélope moderne (Gillier), Opéra-Comique, Paris.
	Pénélope française, Opéra-Comique, Paris.
1729	*Tancrède* (Campra), Opéra, Paris.
1730	*Thésée* (Lulli), Opéra, Paris.
	Alcione (Marais), Opéra, Paris.
	Pyrrhus (Royer), Opéra, Paris.
	Phaeton (Lulli), Opéra, Paris.
1733	*L'Empire de l'amour* (Brassac), Opéra, Paris.
1734	*Jephté* (Monteclair), Opéra, Paris.
	Les Éléments (Lalande and Destouches), Opéra, Paris.
	Philomèle (La Coste), Opéra, Paris.
1735	*Les Indes galantes* (Rameau), Opéra, Paris.
	Scanderberg (Rebel and Francoeur), Opéra, Paris.
1739	*Représentation de l'Eglise de Saint-Pierre de Rome* (spectacle), Salle des Machines, Paris.
	Pandore (spectacle), Salle des Machines, Paris.
1740	*La Descent d'Eneé aux enfers* (spectacle), Salle des Machines, Paris.
1741	*Les Diverses Aventures d'Ulysse* (spectacle), Salle des Machines, Paris.
1742	*Hero et Léandre* (spectacle), Salle des Machines, Paris.
	Le Triomphe de l'amour conjugal (spectacle), Salle des Machines, Paris.
1745	*Les Indes galantes* (Rameau), Grand Theatre, Bordeaux.
	Les Fleurs, Grand Theatre, Bordeaux.
	Issé (Destouches), Grand Theatre, Bordeaux.
	Hippolyte et Aricie (Rameau), Grand Theatre, Bordeaux.
1751	*La Tasse* (Bonet), Salle des Machines, Paris.
1754	*La Constance couronnée* (spectacle), Salle des Machines, Paris.
	La Forêt enchantée (spectacle), Salle des Machines, Paris.
1756	*La Conquête du Mogol par Thamas Koull Khan* (spectacle), Salle des Machines, Paris.
1758	*La Chute des angeles rebelles* (spectacle), Salle des Machines, Paris.
1763	*Jason et Medea*, Hoftheater, Stuttgart.
1764	*Demofoonte* (Jommelli), Hoftheater, Stuttgart.

*

Bibliography

Articles:

Jeanne Bouché, "Servandoni à l'Académie Royale de Musique", *Gazette des Beaux-Arts*, 4, August 1910.

R. Mesuret, "Une description imprimée des ouvrages de Servandoni à Bordeaux", *Bulletin de la société des bibliophiles de Guyenne*, 1938.

* * *

Giovanni Servandoni was perhaps the most influential reactionary against the baroque style of stage decoration in France. The characteristically flat and symmetrical scenic style common to 17th-century stage settings shifted in the first quarter of the 18th century, when the perspective vanishing point was placed off centre, at an angle, suggesting a deeper stage space and inviting the audience into a more intimate identification with the performance area. This principle of the "scena per angolo" was popularized by the Bibienas' designs for the Italian aristocracy and many of the European courts as well. However, the Bibienas were never in the service of the Bourbon royalty, possibly due to the presence, ingenuity and artistic skill of Servandoni.

Trained in both the painterly and architectural disciplines, Servandoni was able to combine the qualities of machinist and painter in the service of his designs. After his training, Servandoni lived in Lisbon, where he earned recognition as a stage designer. He travelled to Paris in 1724, and in 1726 succeeded Jean Berain as the "premier peintre décorateur" at the Palais Royale. As an architect, Servandoni brought a technical mastery to the mechanisms of the stage that was in sharp contrast to the more painterly style of Berain. Using angled perspective designs for the Palais Royale, Servandoni overcame the severely limited stage dimensions, giving an unexpected grandeur and spaciousness to the settings. His novel and spectacular designs delighted the French aristocracy and became a powerful impetus for France's acceptance of the Neoclassical style.

Servandoni voluntarily left the Opéra in 1737 in order to design diorama spectacles in the commodious but dilapidated Salle des Machines in the Palais des Tuileries. From 1738 to 1742, he produced and wrote several of these "spectacles muet". Staged without text and music, the first productions were little more than a pretext for displays of spectacular painted scenery, machines and lighting effects. Responsive to criticism, Servandoni added music, silent actors and more machines to add variety to his later spectacles. While working in the Salle des Machines, Servandoni designed and supervised a complete refurbishment of its house decor, machinery and stage. He is also credited at this time with the development and creation of new stage mechanisms.

Servandoni later returned to the conventional stages of the Palais Opéra and Opéra-Comique. Characteristic of his scenographic efforts were scenes depicting ruined castles, gardens, landscapes, architectural colonnades, transparent drops and the combination of light and paint to create highlight and shadow to enhance the sense of three dimensionality. In this manner, Servandoni's theatrical style was reminiscent of the paintings of his master Pannini. Servandoni designed over 60 productions in his life and is known to have worked in Lisbon (1742), Bordeaux (1745), London (1749), Dresden (1755), Brussels (1759), Vienna (1760) and Stuttgart (1762).

Servandoni's services were also in demand for court fêtes including wedding celebrations. His most elaborate fête was on the occasion of the wedding of Madame Élisabeth, niece to Louis XVI (1739), for which he designed a temple dedicated to Hymen, god of weddings, a battle of sea monsters and pyrotechnical displays on the Seine.

While Servandoni made many contributions to French scenography, most seem to stem from his primary contribution of the principles of the "scena per angolo". When Servandoni shifted the symmetrical axis, he appeared to have helped integrate the dramatic action into the scenic area, thereby engaging the figure of the actor with that of the decor. Servandoni is credited with placing architectural obstacles on the stage to prevent actors from moving too close to the forced perspective scenery, which would contradict the illusion of reality. Finally, Servandoni's lavish pantomimic spectacles in the Salle des Machines

mark a high point for illusionistic scenery as an autonomous element in the mise-en-scène. Servandoni also influenced many designers who apprenticed under his mastery, including Antoine Fouré, Jean André, Benoit, Masson, Charles Parrocel and Pierre-Antoine de Machy. Drawings and maquettes attributed to Servandoni are scattered among many private collections and museums. A large collection was acquired by the French government in 1939 from the Château at Versailles and is preserved at the Château de Champs Seine-et-Marne.

—Ronald Naversen

SEYDELMANN, Karl. German actor. Born in Glatz, Upper Silesia, 24 April 1793. Military service in Napoleonic Wars, 1810. Stage debut, Breslau, 1814; subsequently acted with companies in Graz, Prague, Kassel, and Darmstadt, at the Court Theatre, Stuttgart, 1829–38; acclaimed in classic roles; actor, Royal Theatre, Berlin, 1838–43; career much disrupted by ill health. Died in Berlin, 17 March 1843.

Principal roles

Alba in *Egmont* (Goethe); Antonio in *Torquato Tasso* (Goethe); Carlos in *Clavigo* (Goethe); Cromwell in *Cromwell* (Raupach); Franz Moor in *Die Räuber* (Schiller); Frederick the Great in *Order of the Day* (Topfer), Prague; Mephistopheles in *Faust* (Goethe); Othello in *Othello* (Shakespeare); Philip II in *Don Carlos* (Schiller); Richard III in *Richard III* (Shakespeare); Schewa in *Der Jude* (Cumberland); Shylock in *Der Kaufman von Venedig* (Shakespeare); Tartuffe in *Tartuffe* (Molière); President Walter in *Kabale und Liebe* (Schiller).

*

Bibliography

Books:

H. Rötscher, *Seydelmann's Leben und Wirken*, Berlin, 1845.

G. Knispel, *Erinnerungen aus Berlin an Karl Seydelmann*, Darmstadt, 1845.

S. Troizki, *Karl Seydelmann, die Anfänge der realistischen Schauspielkunst*, Berlin, 1950.

* * *

Karl Seydelmann was an innovative and controversial actor during the transition in the early 19th century from idealism — both the idealised formality of Goethe's Weimar style and the inspirational histrionics of romantic actors like Ludwig Devrient — to a realistic style based on nature and observation. After his first engagement in Breslau in 1814 he went via Graz, Prague, Kassel and Darmstadt to the Stuttgart Court Theatre and finally the Royal Playhouse in Berlin. Seydelmann was a conscientious, analytical actor who systematically copied out his own parts, of which eight have been published. On these personal scripts he notes "at 30 a field-marshal, had not only the weaknesses of the mighty — inflexibility, pride, cruelty of soul — but also the vices of the weak — vanity, superstitiousness, envy, cunning and malice". He jots down performance notes on expression, posture, tone of voice and the emotions he wants to convey. In the scene in *The Robbers* between the villain Franz and his twin brother's fiancée Amalia, his Franz starts by "feigning the profound, painful sympathy of the reticent friend who knows all", but when the distraught Amalia puts her arms round his neck he "is in a fever of lust" then "hot, lustful" and finally, when rejected, "cowardly!". The meticulous notes show Seydelmann trying to communicate a carefully analysed sequence of psychological states. There are reminders in his scripts like "Don't declaim, whatever you do!". For Shylock, there is a note: "RB thinks there should not be too much pride in his initial demeanour — and forget tearing out my hair!". Seydelmann's method of synthesizing his parts from details of observed everyday behaviour was exceptional in his time. Preparing for the role of Frederick the Great in Topfer's *Order of the Day*, he spent the preceding night perfecting his make-up with the aid of his wife in the conviction that the first sight had to establish the character and arouse the audience's curiosity.

Seydelmann was active in the years when literature in Germany developed a liberal voice after the Napoleonic wars, and he was regarded as a modern, kindred spirit by "Young Germany", a group of supporters of French democratic ideas with which Georg Büchner was loosely associated.

Seydelmann was a much discussed figure. Heinrich Laube, a leading Young German, later wrote: "About 1829 Seydelmann was new in North Germany, and his amusement at our theoretical infallibility dismayed us. We were struck to the heart by the man's simple, clear, convincing acting, by the power of the word in his mouth. The word! That was the thing, that word was the sword, a protestant sword against the nebulous obfuscation of the romantics". Protestant is to be understood in a political sense here as oppositional and democratic in an as yet unreconstructed aristocratic society. Laube observed that: "it was the power of his intellect that came across the stage ... on his appearance it was as if a fog fell away from all eyes, and with that fog went the twilight of indifference and idle observation which can so easily affect an audience, and everyone felt excited, stimulated to active intellectual participation. It didn't matter that he was just a man of medium build with no great voice and that he was seemingly incapable of sustained passion. He could more than hold his own as the prosaic Antonio against the most glittering and poetic Tasso".

Seydelmann's arrival in Stuttgart coincided with the formation of a new company that revitalised the theatre there, which until then had only been noted for ballet under the guidance of Maria Taglioni. Seydelmann was first cast as jeune premier, but quickly transferred to character parts in which he became outstanding. As well as the great classic roles, he also played leading parts in countless forgotten lesser plays. He has his place in theatrical history as the pioneer of realism on the German stage. He developed his technique by watching people's behaviour, when he then polished and sharpened in a conscious effort to make the commonplace significant, replacing the standard flaccid

Karl Seydelmann as Mephistopheles.

stereotypes with sharply contoured, real figures and declamatory rant with sobriety and clarity of diction.

—Hugh Rorrison

SHCHEPKIN, Mikhail (Semionovich). Russian actor. Born in Krasnoe, near Kursk, Ukraine, 6 November 1788. Educated at Sudzha provincial public school, from 1799. Married Elena Dmitrieva in 1812, three daughters and three sons. Appeared on amateur stage while at school, 1800, and also in private theatre, 1801–03; engaged as prompter at the theatre in Kursk, 1804; made professional debut as actor with the Barsov brothers company in Kursk,

1805; subsequently toured widely with the troupe and also acted with Stein's company at the theatre in Kharkov, 1816; moved to Poltava, 1818; four-year campaign for Shchepkin's emancipation from serfdom resulted in his freedom, 1822; debut at the Maly Theatre, Moscow, 1823; subsequently much admired there in comic roles and for his introduction of a more realistic style of acting; first appearance in St Petersburg, 1825; taught drama at the Maly Theatre School (now the Shchepkin School), Moscow, from 1832; subsequently toured extensively through Russia; visited London and Paris, 1853. Died in Yalta, 11 August 1863.

Roles

1821	Makagonenko in *Natalka Poltavka* [Natalia the Poltavian Lass] (Kotliarevsky), Poltava.
1825	Arnolphe in *L'École des maris* (Molière), Maly Theatre, Moscow.
	Geronte in *Les Fourberies de Scapin* (Molière), Maly Theatre, Moscow.
1826	Aesop.
1827	Hamlet in *Hamlet* (Shakespeare), Maly Theatre, Moscow.
	Gonzales in *Groza* [The Storm] (Ostrovsky), Maly Theatre, Moscow.
1829	Sganarelle in *Sganarelle* (Molière), Maly Theatre, Moscow.
	Dr Bartholo in *Le Barbier de Séville* (Beaumarchais), Maly Theatre, Moscow.
	Antonio in *Le Mariage de Figaro* (Beaumarchais), Maly Theatre, Moscow.
1830	Harpagon in *L'Avare* (Molière, translated by Dmitrevsky), Maly Theatre, Moscow.
1831	Famusov in *Gore ot uma* [Woe from Wit] (Griboyedov), Maly Theatre, Moscow.
1833	Tschub in *Vechera no khutore bliz Dikanka* [Evenings on a Farm Near Didanka] (Gogol), Maly Theatre, Moscow.
1835	Shylock in *The Merchant of Venice* (Shakespeare), Maly Theatre, Moscow.
	The Sailor in *Le Matelot* (adapted from the French), Maly Theatre, Moscow.
1836	The Mayor in *Revizor* [The Government Inspector] (Gogol), Alexandrinsky Theatre, Moscow.
	Don Carlos in *Clavigo* (Goethe), Maly Theatre, Moscow.
1837	Polonius in *Hamlet* (Shakespeare), Maly Theatre, Moscow.
1838	Ford in *The Merry Wives of Windsor* (Shakespeare), Maly Theatre, Moscow.
1839	Grandet in *Eugénie Grandet* (Balzac), Maly Theatre, Moscow.
1841	Capulet in *Romeo and Juliet* (Shakespeare), Maly Theatre, Moscow.
1842	The Postmaster in *Myortvye dushi* [Dead Souls] (Gogol), Maly Theatre, Moscow.
1843	Kochkaryov in *Zhenitba* [The Marriage] (Gogol), Maly Theatre, Moscow.
	Podkolyosin in *Igroki* [The Gamblers] (Gogol), Bolshoi Theatre, Moscow.

	Uteshitelny in *Igroki* [The Gamblers] (Gogol), Maly Theatre, Moscow.
	Burdiukov in *Tyazhbya* [The Lawsuit] (Gogol), Maly Theatre, Moscow.
1845	Wurm in *Kabale und Liebe* (Schiller), Maly Theatre, Moscow.
1846	Drobjeshkin in *Myortvye dushi* [Dead Souls] (Gogol), Maly Theatre, Moscow.
1847	Sancho Panza in *Don Quixote* (Cervantes, translated by Karatagyn), Maly Theatre, Moscow.
1850	Moshkin in *Kholostyak* [The Bachelor] (Turgenev), Alexandrinsky Theatre, Moscow.
1851	Georges Dandin in *Georges Dandin* (Molière), Maly Theatre, Moscow.
	Stupendjev in *Provintsialka* [The Provincial Lady] (Turgenev), Maly Theatre, Moscow.
1853	Taras Bulba in *Taras Bulba* (Gogol), Maly Theatre, Moscow.
	The Baron in *Skupoy rytsar* [The Covetous Knight] (Pushkin), Alexandrinsky Theatre, Moscow.
1854	Salieri in *Mozart i Salieri* [Mozart and Salieri] (Pushkin), Maly Theatre, Moscow.
	Korshunov in *Bednost ne porok* [Poverty's No Crime] (Ostrovsky), Maly Theatre, Moscow.
1855	Menenius Agrippa in *Coriolanus* (Shakespeare), Maly Theatre, Moscow.
	Lyubim Tortsov in *Bednost ne porok* [Poverty's No Crime] (Ostrovsky), provinces.
	Muromsky in *Svadba Krechinskogo* [Krechinsky's Wedding] (Sukhovo-Kobylin), Maly Theatre, Moscow.
1859	The Fool in *King Lear* (Shakespeare), Maly Theatre, Moscow.
1860	Brabantio in *Othello* (Shakespeare), Maly Theatre, Moscow.
1861	Bolchov in *Bankrut/Svoi lyudi-sochtemsya* [The Bankrupt/It's a Family Affair] (Ostrovsky), Maly Theatre, Moscow.
1862	Kuzovkin in *Nakhlebnik* [The Parasite] (Turgenev), Bolshoi Dramatic Theatre, Moscow.

Other roles included: Chuprun in *The Magician Soldier* (Kotliarevsky); Jacquart in *Jacquart's Looms*; Shelmenko in *Shelmenko the Orderly* (Kvitko-Osnovianenko).

Publications

Zapiski, pis'ma — Sovremenniki o Shchepkine, 1952.

*

Bibliography

Books:

Laurence Senelick, *Serf Actor — The Life and Art of Mikhail Shchepkin*, Westport, Connecticut, 1984.

Articles:

Bertha Malnick, "The Actors Shchepkin and Sosnitsky", *Slavonic and East European Review*, 91, June 1960.

Bertha Malnick, "The Actor Shchepkin and His Friends", *Slavonic and East European Review*, 95, June 1962.

Laurence Senelick, "Russian Serf Theatre and the Early Years of Mikhail Shchepkin", *Theatre Quarterly*, 38, 1980.

*   *   *

Mikhail Shchepkin was born a serf on the estate of Count Wolkenstein in the Kursk district of the Ukraine; his parents were trusted family retainers. He made his acting debut in a school theatrical as the tutor Rozmarin in Sumarokov's comedy *The Shrew*. In 1805 he entered the troupe of the Barsov brothers, a mixture of serf-actors and professionals that travelled far and wide in southern Russia; there he learned the provincial actor's trade and quickly revealed a talent that won him attention. From 1816 to 1818 he was a member of Stein's troupe in Kharkov, and when that company split, he moved to Poltava. A subscription taken up by admirers and friends in Poltava ostensibly bought his freedom, though he found himself in debt to one of the subscribers and had to redeem the rest of his large family by his own efforts.

In 1822, the directors of the Imperial Theatre summoned Shchepkin to Moscow. He made his debut at the Maly Theatre with great success, and was accepted into the company in 1823. He rapidly entered the Moscow intellectual circle, in which the theatre played an enormous role at that time, and attracted the sympathies of both leading factions — the conservative Slavophils and the liberal Westernizers. He was befriended by the historian Granovsky, the critic Belinsky, the poet Pushkin and many other notables, and his home became an informal salon. The Russian drama could not satisfy his artistic demands, for the bulk of it was composed of vaudevilles and melodramas adapted from European originals. Moreover, he seemed limited by his short, rotund physique and his pinched voice. But Shchepkin knew how to invest even trivial characters with art and succeeded in making them come to life; his qualities as a comic actor brought acclaim to otherwise mediocre works. To enrich his own repertoire in the 1820's and 1830's, he pleaded with his friends to write and translate plays for him. The results enabled him to shine in Molière (Arnolphe, Harpagon, Sganarelle, Georges Dandin) and Shakespeare (Polonius, Shylock, Ford, the Fool, old Capulet), at the same time he distinguished himself as the lead in a minor French vaudeville, *The Sailor*, which always left the audience in tears.

In original Russian plays, he excelled as the pompous bureaucrat Famusov in Griboyedov's satire *Woe from Wit* (1831) and was the first to play Pushkin's *The Covetous Knight* (1853). Gogol and Turgenev were both close personal friends and enthusiastically developed roles with him in mind. Gogol's Mayor in *The Government Inspector* (1836), Kochkaryov in *The Marriage* and Utelshitelny in *The Gamblers* (both 1843) were all triumphs. The censor forbade Turgenev's *The Charity Case*, written specifically for Shchepkin, but the actor later starred in *The Bachelor* (1850), also tailored for him, and in 1862 was permitted to assume the former role as well. In the latter period of his activity, Shchepkin might have found parts suited to his temperament in Ostrovsky, but he considered the new drama too vulgarly realistic. Although in the provinces he was first-rate as Lyubim Tortsov in *Poverty's No Crime* (1854), in Moscow he felt overshadowed by a new generation of actors, whose naturalism and local colour ran

counter to his own notion of "universally human" emotions. His own penchant led him in these years to gravitate to roles of decent common men caught in pathetic situations, in Dostoevsky's words, "the insulted and injured".

In 1855 the 50th anniversary of Shchepkin's artistic debut was celebrated by the Russian intellectual community. He was extolled as an example of a virtuous self-made man who, despite the humblest beginnings and great adversity, had made major contributions to national culture. His influence was spread not only by his performances in the capitals and on arduous tours of the provinces, but by his masterfully told stories, many of which were adapted by literary men, and by his protests for social change and better conditions for actors. Although he considered himself a loyal subject of the tsar and deplored radicalism, he sympathised with the aims of reformers and jubilated when the serfs were emancipated in 1861.

In acting, Shchepkin stood for a kind of emotional realism based on simplicity and naturalness, and distinct from the verism of the latter half of the 19th century. He insisted on the necessity of delving into the psychology of the part, advised one to "enter, so to speak, the skin of the character, to study his social existence, culture, personal ideas, and also to keep in mind his past life", but "without trying to make the public laugh, because the comic and the serious are derived from a specific way of treating the object"; to "observe all strata of society" and finally "to study the way the stage situation and minute observations of life are wrought". In a trip to Europe in 1853 he managed to become acquainted with the Western stage without being overwhelmed by it, for he found declamation, its basic principle, to be a flaw. He was a major factor in liberating Russian acting from the singsong tradition, and insisted that the theatre was to be respected as a school for society. Without ever being a director, Shchepkin had a sense of ensemble, supported by Gogol, and sought to procure unity of spectacle at the Maly, which was in some sense *his* theatre. Such students of his as Ivan Samarin, Sergei Shumsky and Glikeriya Fedotova illuminated the Russian stage for years. Stanislavsky, who was born in the year Shchepkin died and who studied with Fedotova, declared that "Shchepkin laid the foundations for authentic Russian dramatic art, of which he was the law-maker".

—Laurence Senelick

SIDDONS, Sarah. British actress. Born Sarah Kemble at the Shoulder of Mutton public house, Brecon, 5 July 1755. Educated at Thornloe House, Worcester, 1767, and at day schools in Wolverhampton and other towns. Married actor William Siddons in 1773 (died 1808), two sons, five daughters. Began career in touring company of her parents Roger Kemble and Sarah Ward, becoming child prodigy alongside her brothers John Philip Kemble (*q.v.*) and Charles Kemble (*q.v.*); left company after quarrel with her parents over her intended marriage and worked briefly as a lady's maid in Warwick; returned to Siddons and family, 1773; unsuccessful debut at Theatre Royal, Drury Lane, London, under David Garrick, 1775; returned to provinces, gaining experience in Manchester and on Yorkshire circuit and in Bath, notably as Lady Macbeth; invited back to Drury Lane by R. B. Sheridan, 1782: immediate acclaim as leading tragic actress of her generation (painted as "The Tragic Muse" by Joshua Reynolds, 1784); toured to Dublin and Edinburgh and provinces in summer seasons; played range of Shakespearean and other roles, though never attempted comedy; temporarily left Drury Lane, 1789; visited France and the Netherlands, 1790; co-manager, Covent Garden, with John Philip Kemble, from 1802; no new parts after 1802; retired from stage after last performance as Lady Macbeth, 1812; made several returns for charity performances in ensuing years. "Preceptress in English Reading to the Princesses", from 1782. Died in London, 8 June 1831.

Roles

1767   Rosetta in *Love in a Village* (Bickerstaff), King's Head, Worcester.
Young Princess in *Charles I* (Howard), King's Head, Worcester.
Ariel in *The Tempest; or, The Enchanted Island* (Dryden and Davenant), King's Head, Worcester.

1773   Charlotte Rusport in *The West Indian* (Cumberland), Wolverhampton, England.
Leonora in *The Padlock* (Bickerstaff), Wolverhampton, England.

1774   Belvidera in *Venice Preserved* (Otway), Cheltenham, England.

1775   Portia in *The Merchant of Venice* (Shakespeare), Theatre Royal, Drury Lane, London.

1776   Epicoene in *Epicoene; or, The Silent Woman* (Jonson), Theatre Royal, Drury Lane, London.
Julia in *Blackamoor Washed White* (Bates), Theatre Royal, Drury Lane, London.
Emily in *The Runaway* (Cowley), Theatre Royal, Drury Lane, London.
Maria in *Love's Metamorphoses* (Vaughan), Theatre Royal, Drury Lane, London.
Mrs Strictland in *The Suspicious Husband* (Hoadly), Theatre Royal, Drury Lane, London.
Lady Anne in *Richard III* (Shakespeare), Theatre Royal, Drury Lane, London.

1777   Euphrasia in *The Grecian Daughter* (Murphy), York, England.
Rosalind in *As You Like It* (Shakespeare), York, England.
Matilda in *Matilda* (Francklin), York, England.
Alicia in *Jane Shore* (Rowe), York, England.
Lady Townly in *The Provoked Husband* (Cibber), York, England.
Indiana in *The Conscious Lovers* (Steele), York, England.
Arpasia in *Tamerlane* (Rowe), York, England.
Horatia in *The Roman Father* (Whitehead), York, England.
Semiramis in *Semiramis* (Ayscough), York, England.
Countess of Somerset in *Sir Thomas Overbury* (anon.), Liverpool, England.
Clarinda in *The Suspicious Husband* (Hoadly), Liverpool, England.

Sarah Siddons (portrait by Norm Gainsborough).

Statira in *The Rival Queens; or, Alexander the Great* (N. Lee), Liverpool, England.
Cleopatra in *Antony and Cleopatra* (Shakespeare), Liverpool, England.
Miranda in *The Busy Body* (Centlivre), Liverpool, England.
Miss Richland in *The Good Natured Man* (Goldsmith), Liverpool, England.
Mrs Clerimont in *The Tender Husband* (Steele), Liverpool, England.

1777–78   Mrs Candour in *The School for Scandal* (Sheridan), Theatre Royal, Bath, England.
Mrs Lovemore in *The Way to Keep Him* (Murphy), Theatre Royal, Bath, England.
Elwina in *Percy* (More), Theatre Royal, Bath, England.
Lady Jane in *Know your own Mind* (Murphy), Theatre Royal, Bath, England.
Lady Brumpton in *The Funeral* (Steele), Theatre Royal, Bath, England.
Gertrude in *Hamlet* (Shakespeare), Theatre Royal, Bath, England.
Countess of Salisbury in *The Countess of Salisbury* (Hartson), Theatre Royal, Bath, England.
Millwood in *The London Merchant* (Lillo), Theatre Royal, Bath, England.
Rosamond in *Henry II* (Shakespeare), Theatre Royal, Bath, England.

The Queen in *The Spanish Friar* (Dryden), Theatre Royal, Bath, England.

Juliet in *Romeo and Juliet* (Shakespeare), Theatre Royal, Bath, England.

Imoinda in *Oroonoko* (Southerne), Theatre Royal, Bath, England.

Bellario in *Philaster* (Beaumont and Fletcher), Theatre Royal, Bath, England.

The Princess in *The Law of Lombardy* (Jephson), Theatre Royal, Bath, England.

Imogen in *Cymbeline* (Shakespeare), Theatre Royal, Bath, England.

Miss Aubrey in *The Fashionable Lover* (Cumberland), Theatre Royal, Bath, England.

The Queen in *Richard III* (Shakespeare), Theatre Royal, Bath, England.

Emmeline in *Edgar and Emmeline* (Hawksworth), Theatre Royal, Bath, England.

Sigismunda in *Tancred and Sigismunda* (Thomson), Theatre Royal, Bath, England.

Lady Randolph in *Douglas* (Home), Theatre Royal, Bath, England.

Emmelina in *The Fatal Falsehood* (More), Theatre Royal, Bath, England.

1778–79   Lady Macbeth in *Macbeth* (Shakespeare), Liverpool, England.

1778–81   The Lady in *Comus* (Milton), Theatre Royal, Bath.

Isabella in *Measure for Measure* (Shakespeare), Theatre Royal, Bath.

Beatrice in *Much Ado About Nothing* (Shakespeare), Theatre Royal, Bath.

Queen Katherine in *Henry V* (Shakespeare), Theatre Royal, Bath.

Desdemona in *Othello* (Shakespeare), Theatre Royal, Bath.

Lady Brute in *The Provoked Wife* (Vanbrugh), Theatre Royal, Bath.

Calista in *The Fair Penitent* (Rowe), Theatre Royal, Bath.

Monimia in *The Orphan* (Otway), Theatre Royal, Bath.

Andromache in *The Distresst Mother* (Philips, adapted from Racine), Theatre Royal, Bath.

Elfrida in *Elfrida* (Mason), Theatre Royal, Bath.

Mrs Beverley in *The Gamester* (Moore), Theatre Royal, Bath.

Miss Hardcastle in *She Stoops to Conquer* (Goldsmith), Theatre Royal, Bath.

Zara in *The Mourning Bride* (Congreve), Theatre Royal, Bath.

Zara in *Zara* (Voltaire, adapted by Hill), Theatre Royal, Bath.

Mrs Oakly in *The Jealous Wife* (Colman the Elder), Theatre Royal, Bath.

Nell in *The Devil to Pay* (Coffey), Theatre Royal, Bath.

Countess of Narbonne in *The Countess of Narbonne* (Jephson), Theatre Royal, Bath.

Constance in *King John* (Shakespeare), Theatre Royal, Bath.

1781   Hamlet in *Hamlet* (Shakespeare, adapted by Garrick and Lee), Theatre Royal, Bath.

1782   Isabella in *Isabella; or, The Fatal Marriage* (Southerne, adapted by Garrick), Theatre Royal, Drury Lane, London.

Jane Shore in *Jane Shore* (Rowe), Theatre Royal, Drury Lane, London.

Mrs Montague in *The Fatal Interview* (Hull), Theatre Royal, Drury Lane, London.

1784   Margaret of Anjou in *The Earl of Warwick* (Franklin), Theatre Royal, Drury Lane, London.

Matilda in *The Carmelite* (Cumberland), Theatre Royal, Drury Lane, London.

1785   Camiola in *The Maid of Honour* (Massinger, adapted by J. P. Kemble), Theatre Royal, Drury Lane, London.

1785–86   The Duchess in *Braganza* (Jephson), Theatre Royal, Drury Lane, London.

Hermione in *The Distressed Mother* (Racine, adapted by Phillips), Theatre Royal, Drury Lane, London.

Malvina in *The Captives* (Delap), Theatre Royal, Drury Lane, London.

Ophelia in *Hamlet* (Shakespeare), Theatre Royal, Drury Lane, London.

1786–87   Cleone in *Cleone* (Dodsley), Theatre Royal, Drury Lane, London.

Hortensia in *The Count of Narbonne* (Jephson), Theatre Royal, Drury Lane, London.

Lady Restless in *All in the Wrong* (Murphy), Theatre Royal, Drury Lane, London.

Julia in *Julia; or, The Italian Lover* (Jephson), Theatre Royal, Drury Lane, London.

1787–88   Cordelia in *King Lear* (Shakespeare), Theatre Royal, Drury Lane, London.

Cleopatra in *All for Love* (Dryden), Theatre Royal, Drury Lane, London.

Katharine in *Katharine and Petruchio* (Garrick), Theatre Royal, Drury Lane, London.

1788   Chelonice in *The Fate of Sparta* (Cowley), Theatre Royal, Drury Lane, London.

Dianora in *The Regent* (Greatheed), Theatre Royal, Drury Lane, London.

Queen Katharine in *Henry VIII* (Shakespeare), Theatre Royal, Drury Lane, London.

1788–89   Volumnia in *Coriolanus* (Shakespeare, adapted by Garrick), Theatre Royal, Drury Lane, London.

The Fine Lady in *Lethe* (Garrick), Theatre Royal, Drury Lane, London.

1789   Mary Queen of Scots in *Mary Queen of Scots* (St John), Theatre Royal, Drury Lane, London.

1791–92   The Queen in *Richard II* (Shakespeare), Theatre Royal, Drury Lane, London.

1793   Ariadne in *The Rival Sisters* (Murphy), Theatre Royal, Drury Lane, London.

1794   Countess Orsina in *Emilia Galotti* (translated from Lessing), Theatre Royal, Drury Lane, London.

1795   Elgiva in *Edwy and Elgiva* (D'Arblay), Theatre Royal, Drury Lane, London.

Palmira in *Mahomet the Imposter* (Voltaire, adapted by Miller), Theatre Royal, Drury Lane, London.

Other roles including: *Trials of the Heart* (anon.), Theatre Royal, Drury Lane, London, 1799.

Publications

The Reminiscences of Sarah Siddons (ed. William van Lennep), 1942.

*

Bibliography

Books:
Catherine Galindo, *Mrs. Gallindo's Letters to Mrs Siddons*, London, 1809.
James Boaden, *Memoirs of Mrs. Siddons*, 2 vols., London, 1827.
Thomas Campbell, *Life of Mrs. Siddons*, London, 1834.
Percy Fitzgerald, *The Kembles*, 2 vols., London, 1871.
Nina A. Kennard, *Mrs. Siddons*, London, 1887.
Mrs Clement Parsons, *The Incomparable Mrs. Siddons*, London, 1909.
Henry C. F. Jenkin, *Mrs. Siddons as Lady Macbeth and as Mrs. Siddons*, London, 1915.
Naomi Royde-Smith, *The Private Life of Mrs. Siddons*, London, 1931.
Yvonne Ffrench, *Sarah Siddons — Tragic Actress*, London, 1936.
Kathleen Mackenzie, *The Great Sarah*, London, 1968.
Roger Manvell, *Mrs. Siddons*, London, 1970.
Marian Johnson, *A Troubled Grandeur: The Story of England's Greatest Actress, Mrs. Siddons*, Boston, 1972.

* * *

During her own lifetime Sarah Siddons gained a reputation as the greatest tragic actress Britain had ever produced. This legendary reputation was to persuade many subsequent actresses into emulating her style or reacting against it, but few could combine her noble presence with the emotional vulnerability, even instability, that Siddons achieved in her finest performances. In contradiction to Diderot's famous theoretical paradox, that it is not necessary for the actor to *feel* what has to be portrayed, as well as to the practical technique of her brother, John Philip Kemble, Siddons always sought to experience the emotions of her role — or to bring her own emotion to its playing. She explained to Mrs. Piozzi that "she never acted so well as once when her heart was heavy concerning the loss of a child". Yet emotional involvement did not mean any lack of self-conscious technique and she was never "lost" in her role, even if she wept copiously on its completion. She maintained that she depended on the sympathetic rapport of an audience, whose applause not only inspired her with "the warmth of approbation", but whose prolonged rounds gave her time "to recruit breath and nerve". This ability to inspire applause by the delivery of a single line, gesture, or piece of stage business, smacks more of "point-making" than Stanislavskian naturalism, and yet Siddons has been described as anticipating much of the "Method", not only by her emotional identification but by her *justification* of emotions and motives and by her constructing a *throughline* of development in each performance. This sense of unified effect and structured pacing is a quality she shared with John Kemble, but whereas his style was described as neo-classical in its concern for aesthetic form, her apparent spontaneity suggested a more romantic indulgence in emotion for its own sake. Leigh Hunt felt that, compared to Kemble, she acted with "that natural carelessness which shows it to be the result of genius rather than grave study ... One can hardly imagine there had been any such thing as a rehearsal for power so natural and so spirited." One of the ways in which she maintained her concentration and sense of development was by watching a play throughout from the wings. When playing Constance in *King John* she also wanted the child cast as Prince Arthur to watch with her.

Her ability to combine perceptive character analysis with emotional effect can be illustrated by her greatest creation: Lady Macbeth. She first performed it with William "Gentleman" Smith at Drury Lane in 1785, when the manager, Richard Sheridan, rebuked her for assaying the sleepwalking scene without holding the traditional lighted taper — so that she could better mime the washing of her hands. But her interpretation was not perfected until she acted with her brother. At some stage in her career she recorded her analysis in *Remarks on the Character of Lady Macbeth*, describing her as "fair, feminine, nay, even fragile" — and thus caused many a commentator to express concern, as it seemed to contradict the actual effect of a "turbulent and inhuman strength of spirit". However, Siddons had not always been the grand Tragic Muse of the Reynolds portrait; at her first shortlived appearance at Drury Lane under Garrick in 1775, a critic had described the frightened actress as "very pretty, delicate, and fragile looking". In her subsequent interpretation of Lady Macbeth this fragility was consciously put aside during the evocation of the spirits to "unsex" her. Thus the character underwent its first transformation, the final one being into the madness of the sleepwalking scene. Between these two states she was indeed "inhuman", ruthlessly driving on her husband, whom Kemble interpreted as "a hero, who descends to become an assassin" rather than "a common stabber, who rises to become a royal murderer" and whom Siddons described in her *Remarks* as "aimiable, conscientious, nay pious". To help *justify* the decline into madness she suggested the motivating circumstance that "the last appearance of Banquo's ghost became no less visible to her eyes than it became to those of her husband". This close involvement in the psychological development of the character tended to overshadow Macbeth, even when played by Kemble, and the effect of the hysterical sleepwalking scene was such that, when asked by Edwin Forrest many years later to describe its effect, Sheridan Knowles exclaimed: "I smelt the blood, I swear I smelt the blood". Siddon's greatest achievement was that she made her audiences, as well as herself, identify with the horror of the moment.

Siddons had no talent for comedy, but won an early reputation as the overwrought heroines of Southerne and Otway — in *Isabella*, and as Belvidera in *Venice Preserved*. Later in her career she brought a deep pathos to the suffering wives of such sentimental domestic tragedies as Edward Moore's *The Gamester*, in which Mrs. Beverley lapses into a catatonic trance at the sight of her husband dying in gaol, and *The Stranger*, adapted by Benjamin Thompson from Kotzebue, in which Mrs. Haller is passionately reunited with her estranged husband.

Her own personal life was often unhappy. Married at 18 to William Siddons, a second-rate actor who once admitted "she is too Grand a thing for me", they were continually short of money, particularly as Sheridan tended to pay salaries months in arrears, which forced her into exhausting provincial tours during the summer. Her five children all predeceased her, the longest-living being Maria, who died in 1798 aged 18, Sally, who died in 1805 aged 28, and Henry, who — after a none-too-successful acting career — died in 1815, three years after his mother had retired from the stage. In later life, Siddons became stout and arthritic and when she occasionally returned to perform for the benefits of her brothers, John, Stephen, or Charles, or for poor Henry's widow, she seemed ponderous and affected. Hazlitt sadly reflected: "Players should be immortal ... but they are not." Nevertheless, memories of her finest performances haunted and inspired actresses and critics throughout the century — when Ellen Terry played Lady Macbeth in 1888 she used Siddons's *Remarks* to justify her

own interpretation, which was undoubtedly "fair, feminine, and fragile".

—George Taylor

SIMONSON, Lee. US designer and artist. Born in New York, 26 June 1888. Educated at Ethical Culture School; High School; Harvard University, AB, 1908; studied painting in France, 1908–12. Married 1) Helen Strauss in 1916 (divorced 1926); 2) Caroline Hancock in 1927, one son and one daughter. Scenic designer, Washington Square Players, New York, 1915–17; served in Corps of Interpreters, US Army, 1918; founder and director, Theatre Guild, Garrick Theatre, and Guild Theatre, New York, 1919–40; director, International Exhibition of Theatre Art, 1934; consultant to university theatres of University of Wisconsin, 1939, University of Indiana, 1940, Hunter College, New York, 1940, Rosary College, River Forest, Illinois, 1948; costume instructor, consultant, and Gillender Lecturer, Metropolitan Museum of Art, New York, 1944–45; also created designs for many Broadway shows and operas. Recipient: Ford Foundation fellowship, 1961–62. Died in New York, 23 January 1967.

Productions

1915	*Love of One's Neighbour* (Andreyev), Bandbox Theatre, New York.
1916	*The Seagull* (Chekhov), Bandbox Theatre, New York.
	The Magical City (Akins and Patelin), Bandbox Theatre, New York.
1919	*The Faithful*, Garrick Theatre, New York.
1920	*The Power of Darkness* (Tolstoy), Garrick Theatre, New York.
	Jane Clegg (Ervine), Garrick Theatre, New York.
	The Dance of Death (Strindberg), Garrick Theatre, New York.
	Heartbreak House (G. B. Shaw), Garrick Theatre, New York.
1921	*Mr Pim Passes By* (Milne), Garrick Theatre, New York.
	Liliom (Molnár), Garrick Theatre, New York.
1922	*He Who Gets Slapped* (Andreyev), Garrick Theatre, New York.
	Back to Methuselah (G. B. Shaw), Garrick Theatre, New York.
	From Morn to Midnight (Kaiser), Garrick Theatre, New York.
	R.U.R. (Čapek), Garrick Theatre, New York; Martin Beck Theatre, New York, 1930.
	The Tidings Brought to Mary (Claudel), Garrick Theatre, New York.
1923	*Peer Gynt* (Ibsen), Garrick Theatre, New York.
	The Adding Machine (Rice), Garrick Theatre, New York.
	The Devil's Disciple (G. B. Shaw), Garrick Theatre, New York.
	Les Ratés, Theatre Guild, New York.
	The Failures, Garrick Theatre, New York.

1924	*Fata Morgana* (Vajda, translated by Burrell and Moeller), New York.
	Man and the Masses (Toller), Theatre Guild, New York; also directed.
1926	*The Goat Song*, Theatre Guild, New York.
1927	*The Road to Rome* (Sherwood), Playhouse, New York.
1928	*Marco's Millions* (O'Neill), Guild Theatre, New York.
	Volpone (Jonson), Theatre Guild, New York.
	Faust (Goethe), Guild Theatre, New York.
1929	*Dynamo* (O'Neill), Martin Beck Theatre, New York.
	Damn Your Honour, Cosmopolitan Theatre, New York.
1930	*Roar China!* (Tretyakov), Guild Theatre, New York.
	The Apple Cart (G. B. Shaw), Martin Beck Theatre, New York.
	Hotel Universe (Barry), Martin Beck Theatre, New York.
	Elizabeth the Queen (Anderson), Guild Theatre, New York.
1931	*The Insect Play* (Čapek), New York.
	As You Like It (Shakespeare), New York.
	Lean Harvest (Jeans), Forrest Theatre, New York.
	Pas d'Acier, New York.
1932	*The Good Earth* (Connelly), Guild Theatre, New York.
	Red Planet, New York.
1933	*American Dream*, Guild Theatre, New York.
	The Mask and the Face (Fernald), Guild Theatre, New York.
	The School for Husbands, New York.
1934	*Days Without End* (O'Neill), Henry Miller's Theatre, New York.
	They Shall Not Die, Royale Theatre, New York.
	Jigsaw, Ethel Barrymore Theatre, New York.
	Rain from Heaven (Behrman), John Golden Theatre, New York.
	A Sleeping Clergyman (Bridie), Guild Theatre, New York.
1935	*The Simpleton of the Unexpected Isles* (G. B. Shaw), Guild Theatre, New York.
1936	*Call It a Day* (Anthony), Morosco Theatre, New York.
	End of Summer (Behrman), Guild Theatre, New York.
	Idiot's Delight (Sherwood), Shubert Theatre, New York.
1937	*Virginia* (Schwartz), New York.
1938	*Prelude to Exile*, Guild Theatre, New York.
	The Masque of Kings (Anderson), Shubert Theatre, New York.
	Amphytrion 38 (Giraudoux, adapted by Behrman), Shubert Theatre, New York.
	Madame Bovary (adapted from Flaubert), Broadhurst Theatre, New York.
1938	*Wine of Choice* (Behrman), Guild Theatre, New York.
	Lorelei, Longacre Theatre, New York.
1944	*The Streets Are Guarded*, Henry Miller's Theatre, New York.

Lee Simonson

1945	*Foxhole in the Parlour*, Booth Theatre, New York.
	Portrait in Black (Goff and Roberts), Shubert Theatre, New Haven, Connecticut, and US tour.
1946	*Joan of Lorraine* (Anderson), Alvin Theatre, New York.
1947	*The Ring of the Niebelungen* (Wagner), Metropolitan Opera House, New York.

Publications

Minor Prophecies, 1927; *The Stage is Set*, 1932; *Settings and Costumes of the Modern Stage* (with Theodore Kommissarjevsky), 1933; *Theatre Art*, 1934; *Part of a Lifetime* (autobiography), 1943; *Untended Grove*, 1946; *The Art of Scenic Design*, 1950.

*

Bibliography

Books:
Martin Battersby, *The Decorative Twenties*, London, 1969.

* * *

As a founding director of the Theatre Guild and its primary designer for some 20 years, Lee Simonson played a major role in shaping 20th-century US theatre. During those 20 years, the Theatre Guild was the principle purveyor of serious drama on Broadway — new European drama, new plays by leading US playwrights, and classics — and the Guild's visual style, which is to say Simonson's style, inevitably influenced the direction of US design. If there was, in fact, a US style of theatre and design at this time it could be seen in the works of this organisation. Simonson's influence was further extended through four books and several articles. While he was without question one of the central figures of US design, no one of his creations made the lasting impresssion of many of the works of his contemporaries Robert Edmond Jones, Jo Mielziner, or Boris Aronson; there is no particular play that seems inextricably bound up in his scenography. Nonetheless, it is his style, even more than that of Jones, that shaped the look of the US theatre down to the present day. Because he believed that all theatre involved some degree of illusion he remained wedded to realism, but he evolved a successful style of selective realism in which the inessential elements of the setting were stripped away, leaving primarily iconic or emblematic images within a suggestive space. Although capable of detailed interiors, many of his settings are spare. He was also a pioneer of "island" sets, in which the main scenic piece sits like an island in the midst of the stage, physically unconnected to the wings, and often backed by a cyclorama.

Ironically, Simonson may be remembered best for his passionate denunciations of Edward Gordon Craig and his equally passionate advocacy of the Duke of Saxe-Meiningen and Adolphe Appia. His attacks on Craig seem extreme, especially in the light of Simonson's central role in the development of the New Stagecraft in the USA, to which Craig's theories are fundamental, yet even late in his life Simonson refused to repudiate these views. Some understanding of this might be gleaned from studying his formative influences.

Simonson claims to have discovered his calling as an artist at the age of ten, when he saw the work of Maxfield Parrish. "It was a moment of complete enchantment", he remembered, "as I realised for the first time what the vision of an artist could make of the familiar fragments of the world, the alchemy which could create a realm more perfect than reality, a kind of graphic Utopia". Parrish embodied fantasy and splendour not only through subject and style but through colour. Early in his career Simonson bemoaned what he perceived as a US preoccupation with dark and monochromatic colour schemes. After attending Harvard, where he majored in philosophy and idolized George Santayana, and where he studied playwriting with George Pierce Baker, Simonson went to Europe for three years. In Paris he was a regular attendee at the salon of Gertrude and Leo Stein and was introduced to the wonders of modern art. He was particularly struck by the use of colour by these artists and developed, in his words, a "passion for galaxies of brilliant colour". He was also exposed to a wide range of new theatre that would shape his future aesthetics. He singled out for notice the Ballets Russes, Max Reinhardt's Munich productions of *A Midsummer Night's Dream*, *Lysistrata*, and *Sumurun*, Jacques Rouché's Théâtre des Arts, and a production of *The Life of Man* by the Karlsruhe Theatre. But at the Stein soirées he developed a mistrust of certain artists whom he found pretentious or precious. It was the same response he would have to many theatrical movements and ideas that Simon-

son saw as an attack on the "theatre of illusion". At least some of the work of Jacques Copeau, Max Reinhardt, and Vsevelod Meyerhold were seen as alternatives with "no intrinsic value". He most definitely categorized the work or the style of Craig in this group. Like so many US theatre practitioners of the first part of the century, Simonson was strongly influenced by George Pierce Baker, who instilled in his students an appreciation for the primacy of the playwright and the text. Simonson constantly advocated this view and was therefore suspicious of any person or doctrine that placed the designer at the forefront. In his preface to *The Stage is Set*, he warns against god-like figures and the danger of the design becoming the focal point of a production.

Simonson talked of set design as architecture. He claimed that from the Renaissance to the 18th century the designer was primarily an architect, and in the 20th century the designer was "an architect of stage space". "A setting is a plan of action", he noted; "what will it make an actor do?" He was a pragmatist who admitted that "much of my designing was conceived in technical terms". Rarely does one see a rendering of a Simonson set because he almost never made them; only rarely did he make models. The record of his designs is almost entirely in production photographs. He was a great admirer of German technology and the productions of Leopold Jessner and Jurgen Fehling and frequently bemoaned the lack of facilities and the cramped stage size of most US theatres. As a lighting designer he was virtually the first person to talk of a light plot, pointing out that the word "plot" applied to both the play's story as well as the arrangement of lighting instruments. Referring at times to light as the designer's second brush, and at others comparing it to the score of an opera, Simonson saw this command of light and space as factors making the designer a full collaborator in the creation of a production.

While Simonson may not have the artistic esteem of some of his contemporaries, his work as a scholar and his position as a member of the Board of Directors of the Theatre Guild, together with his prodigious and significant artistic work were major factors in legitimizing the role of design in theatre in the USA and emphasizing its centrality in the production process.

—Arnold Aronson

SJÖBERG, Alf. Swedish director and actor-manager. Born in Stockholm, 21 June 1903. Studied for the stage at the school of the Dramaten [Royal Dramatic Theatre], Stockholm, 1923–25, and in Paris, 1928. Began as an actor at the Dramaten, 1925–29, and made debut as a director there, 1930; subsequently remained with the theatre for some 50 years; debut as film director, 1929. Recipient: Cannes Film Festival Grand Prix, 1951. Died in Stockholm, 17 April 1980.

Productions

As director:
1930   *Baldevins bröllop* [The Marriage of Baldevin] (Krag), Dramaten, Stockholm.

Markurells i Wadköping [The Markurells of Wadköping] (Bergman), Dramaten, Stockholm.

Stor-Klas och Lill-Klas [Big Klas and Little Klas] (Geigerstam, adapted from Andersen), Dramaten, Stockholm.

1931   *Fadershjärtat* [The Breadwinner] (Maugham), Dramaten, Stockholm.

Fru Celias moral [Art and Mrs Bottle] (Levy), Dramaten, Stockholm.

Spekulation [Ces Messieurs de la Santé] (Armont and Marchant), Dramaten, Stockholm.

En Resa i natten [Nocturnal Journey] (Christiansen), Dramaten, Stockholm.

1932   *Revisorn* [The Government Inspector] (Gogol), Dramaten, Stockholm.

Den heliga familjen [The Happy Family] (Värnland), Dramaten, Stockholm.

Den fule Ferrante [Beauty and the Beast] (Lopez), Dramaten, Stockholm.

Kvinnans list [Noughts and Crosses] (Brown), Dramaten, Stockholm.

1933   *Före sol nedgången* [Vor Sonnenuntergang] (Hauptmann), Dramaten, Stockholm.

Oväder [The Storm] (Strindberg), Dramaten, Stockholm.

Blodet ropar under almarna [Desire Under the Elms] (O'Neill), Dramaten, Stockholm.

Cyrano de Bergerac (Rostand), Dramaten, Stockholm.

Spelet om Jesu Krista Glädjerika Födelse [A Play on the Happy Birth of Jesus Christ] (Edelpöck), Dramaten, Stockholm.

1934   *Rivalerna* [The Rivals] (Sheridan), Dramaten, Stockholm.

Ett Brott [A Crime] (Siwertz), Dramaten, Stockholm.

Tiden är en dröm [Life is a Song] (Lenormand), Dramaten, Stockholm.

En hederlig man [An Honest Man] (Siwertz), Dramaten, Stockholm.

1935   *Mordet i Katedralen* [Murder in the Cathedral] (Eliot), Dramaten, Stockholm.

Henry IV (Shakespeare), Dramaten, Stockholm.

Högsta vinsten [Sheppey] (Maugham), Dramaten, Stockholm.

Dagar utan mål [Days Without End] (O'Neill), Dramaten, Stockholm.

Hustrun [The Wife] (Moberg), Dramaten, Stockholm.

1936   *Brott och straff* [Crime and Punishment] (Dostoevsky, adapted by Baty), Dramaten, Stockholm.

Huset vid landsvägen [Nationale Six] (Bernard), Dramaten, Stockholm.

Miljonärskan [The Millionairess] (G. B. Shaw), Dramaten, Stockholm.

1937   *Skönhet* [Beauty] (Siwertz), Dramaten, Stockholm.

Vår ära och vår makt [Our Power and Our Glory] (Grieg), Dramaten, Stockholm.

Hofebar [Hay Fever] (Coward), Dramaten, Stockholm.

Khaki [Le Material humain] (Raynal), Dramaten, Stockholm.

Uppbrott [Departure] (Krog), Dramaten, Stockholm.

Kvinnorna på Niskavuori (Wuolijoki), Dramaten, Stockholm.

1938   *Mannen utan själ* [The Man Without a Soul] (Lagerkvist), Dramaten, Stockholm.

King Lear (Shakespeare), Free Theatre of the USSR.

Spel på havet [The Game by the Sea] (Siwertz), Dramaten, Stockholm.

Mayerlingdramat [The Masque of Kings] (M. Anderson), Dramaten, Stockholm.

1939   *Somni behagar* [As You Like It] (Shakespeare), Free Theatre of the USSR.

Mordet i Katedralen [Murder in the Cathedral] (Eliot), Dramaten, Stockholm.

Ann Sophie Hedvig (Abell), Dramaten, Stockholm.

1940   *Mycket vä sen för ingenting* [Much Abo About Nothing] (Shakespeare), Dramaten, Stockholm.

Seger i mörker [Victory in Darkness] (Lagerqvist), Dramaten, Stockholm.

Möss och människor [Of Mice and Men] (Steinbeck), Dramaten, Stockholm.

Morgondagens män [Key Largo] (M. Anderson), Dramaten, Stockholm.

Karl XII (Strindberg), Dramaten, Stockholm.

1941   *Rovdjuret* (Gierow), Dramaten, Stockholm.

Mästerkatten i stövlar [Puss in Boots] (Werner), Dramaten, Stockholm.

Döbeln (Stolpe), Dramaten, Stockholm.

1942   *Beredskap* [Order of Battle] (Ahlström), Dramaten, Stockholm.

Ut till fåglarna [George Washington Slept Here] (Kaufman), Dramaten, Stockholm.

1943   *Brutus* (Siwertz), Dramaten, Stockholm.

Helgongaga [Legend of a Saint] (Gierow), Dramaten, Stockholm.

Urladdning [Clash by Night] (Odets), Dramaten, Stockholm.

1944   *Köpmannen i Venedig* [The Merchant of Venice] (Shakespeare), Dramaten, Stockholm.

Blodsbröllop [Blood Wedding] (Garcia Lorca), Dramaten, Stockholm.

Attentatet [Attempted Murder] (Stiernstedt), Dramaten, Stockholm.

De vackra människorna [The Beautiful People] (Saroyan), Dramaten, Stockholm.

1945   *Flugorna* [The Flies] (Sartre), Dramaten, Stockholm.

Alla Guds barn ha vingar [All God's Chillun Got Wings] (O'Neill), Dramaten, Stockholm.

Vår ofödde son [Our Unborn Son] (Moberg), Dramaten, Stockholm.

1946   *Somni behagar* [As You Like It] (Shakespeare), Dramaten, Stockholm.

Trettondagsafton [Twelfth Night] (Shakespeare), Dramaten, Stockholm.

Stängda dörrar [Huis clos] (Sartre), Dramaten, Stockholm.

St Antonius visar vägen [This Way to the Tomb] (Duncan), Dramaten, Stockholm.

1947   *Richard III* (Shakespeare), Dramaten, Stockholm.

Den dödsdömde [Sentence of Death] (Dagerman), Dramaten, Stockholm.

Bernardas hus [The House of Bernarda Alba] (Garcia Lorca), Dramaten, Stockholm.

1948   *De vises Sten* [The Philosopher's Stone] (Lagerqvist), Dramaten, Stockholm.

Släkmötet [The Family Reunion] (Eliot), Dramaten, Stockholm.

1949   *En handelsresandes död* [Death of a Salesman] (Miller), Dramaten, Stockholm.

Den Starkare [The Strongest] (Strindberg), Dramaten, Stockholm.

Fröken Julie [Miss Julie] (Strindberg), Dramaten, Stockholm.

Apollo från Bellac [Apollo of Bellac] (Giraudoux), Dramaten, Stockholm.

Tartuffe (Molière), Dramaten, Stockholm.

1950   *Brand* (Ibsen), Dramaten, Stockholm.

Ryttaren [The Cavalier] (Branner), Dramaten, Stockholm.

Erik XIV (Strindberg), Dramaten, Stockholm.

1951   *Amorina* (adapted from Almqvist), Little Stage, Dramaten, Stockholm.

Kvinnan bör inte brännas [The Lady is Not For Burning] (Fry), Dramaten, Stockholm.

Syskon [Brother and Sister] (Branner), Dramaten, Stockholm.

1952   *Pygmalion* (G. B. Shaw), Dramaten, Stockholm.

1953   *Romeo och Julia* [Romeo and Juliet] (Shakespeare), Dramaten, Stockholm.

1954   *Stackars Don Juan* [Platonov] (Chekhov), Dramaten, Stockholm.

Lektionen [The Lesson] (Ionesco), Dramaten, Stockholm.

Escorial (Ghelderode), Dramaten, Stockholm.

Modell Beatrice (Zetterholm), Dramaten, Stockholm.

1955   *Vildanden* [The Wild Duck] (Ibsen), Dramaten, Stockholm.

1956   *En Midsommarnattsdröm* [A Midsummer Night's Dream] (Shakespeare), Dramaten, Stockholm.

Arina (Lidman), Dramaten, Stockholm.

1957   *Drottningensjuvelsmycke* [The Queen's Jewel] (adapted from Almqvist), Little Stage, Dramaten, Stockholm.

Sedig om i vrede [Look Back in Anger] (Osborne), Dramaten, Stockholm.

1958   *Utsikt från en bro* [A View from the Bridge] (Miller), Dramaten, Stockholm.

Don Juan (Molière), Dramaten, Stockholm.

Lika for lika [Measure for Measure] (Shakespeare), Dramaten, Stockholm.

1959   *Rosmersholm* (Ibsen), Dramaten, Stockholm.

Mörkrets makt [The Power of Darkness] (A. Tolstoy), Dramaten, Stockholm.

1960   *Hamlet* (Shakespeare), Dramaten, Stockholm.

1961   *King John* (Shakespeare), Dramaten, Stockholm.

1966   *Ivona, Princess of Burgundy* (Gombrowicz), Dramaten, Stockholm.

1968   *Puntila* (Brecht), Dramaten, Stockholm.

Mother Courage and Her Children (Brecht), Dramaten, Stockholm.

1972   *Mäster Olof* (Strindberg), Dramaten, Stockholm.

Other productions included: *Brända Tomten* [The Burnt Site] (Strindberg).

Roles as actor included: Karl Thomas in *Hoppla! Wir leben* (Toller), Dramaten, Stockholm; Michael in *Riders to the Sea* (Synge), Dramaten, Stockholm; both 1925–29.

Films

As director:

Den Starkaste [The Strongest], 1929; *Med livet soms insats*, 1938; *Den blomstertid* [Blossom Time], 1940; *Hem från Babylon* [Return to Babylon], 1941; *Himlaspelet* [The Road to Heaven], 1942; *Kungajakt* [The Royal Hunt], 1944; *Hets* [Frenzy], 1944; *Resan bort* [The Long Journey], 1945; *Iris och löjtnantshjärta* [Iris Flower of the North], 1946; *Bara en Mor* [Only a Mother], 1949; *Fröken Julie* [Miss Julie], 1951; *Barabbas*, 1953; *Karin Mansdotter*, 1954; *Vildfägler* [Wild Birds], 1955; *Sista paret ut* [Last Pair Out], 1956; *Domaren* [The Judge], 1960; *Ön* [The Island], 1966; *Fadern* [The Father], 1969.

* * *

Alf Sjöberg's brief study of stage design, in Paris in 1928, following his years at the School of Stockholm's Royal Dramatic Theatre (the Dramaten) and a period as an actor in that theatre, set the course of his future work in one important respect: his insistence in precept and practice on the primacy of the visual element in theatre. Moving into direction, on his return to Sweden, he continued working at the Dramaten over five decades, at first designing sets for his own productions or employing the resident designer, Sven Erik Skawonius, and later luring pictorial artists and even sculptors into the theatre in his pursuit of powerfully expressive, distinctively modern stage images. Stellan Mörner, Sven Erixson and Eric Grate were artists who contributed particularly memorably to Sjöberg productions. Spectacle in itself did not interest him. With Max Reinhardt's showmanship in mind, he declared his preference for the simplest means and rejected the marvels of stage machinery — except for modern lighting resources, in which he showed himself a true successor of Appia and Craig. Whatever symbolic values they might have, the visually exciting settings he almost invariably employed were also boldly ingenious, functional treatments of stage space, frequently giving him a multiple stage and a variety of perspectives; though he would happily use bare boards and a bench when this suited his general concept.

Sjöberg was an intellectual of politically radical leanings, and both his stage work and his films challenged the mind even while they delighted the eye. A substantial body of his occasional writings on theatre has been collected and published, providing a theoretical key to his achievement. He accepted that theatre has power to change the world.

This laid upon him the requirement of finding in classic texts, even of remote centuries, an anagogic force whereby the modern world might be revealed, illuminated, to itself. Sjöberg was very much of his generation in his regard for depth-psychology as the mode of interpretation that might explore the unconscious (for example, as embodied in the form of Brechtian drama) to release a new vision into clarity. From Baudelaire he adopted the line: "Au fond de l'Inconnu pour trouver du nouveau" ("Into the depth of the Unknown to discover the new").

Sjöberg's political attitudes found expression in production of such plays as Sartre's *The Flies* and in the film *Frenzy*, scripted by Ingmar Bergman, studies of tyranny in different forms. His treatment of Shakespeare's *Richard III* brought it into the same category, England ravaged by the Wars of the Roses emerging as an analogue of the recent European battleground with a power vacuum to be filled by ambitious opportunists. From *Henry IV* in 1935 to *King John* in 1961, Sjöberg presented Shakespeare's history plays as demonstrations of a long struggle towards democracy. What made such notions, commonplace in their time, the basis for vivid and exciting theatrical experience was Sjöberg's ability to transform ideas into style. While making use of structures that allowed him a freedom and flexibility to match the freedom of Shakespeare's own Elizabethan stage, he turned to the visual arts for a stylistic idiom that might bring out the qualities he perceived in the individual play. Thus, *As You Like It* became a rococo charade haunted by Watteau; the visual world of *The Merchant of Venice* was borrowed from Tiepolo. Although *Twelfth Night* was played in Renaissance costume, the use of a raised platform, screens hinting at period decoration, and gauzes, with changing light dissolving appearances, was a direct yet enchanting translation of the play's theme of illusion; as in an Elizabethan masque, Sjöberg united stage and auditorium in the celebratory ending, when the lighting of candelabra on stage continued with ribbons of light streaming round the edge of the dress circle. With other playwrights of other periods the same basic principles were applied: thus, the lyrical tragedy of Lorca's *Blood Wedding* filtered through a symbolist use of colour; a monumentally simplified, abstract and sculptural set reflected the stark power of Strindberg's *Mäster Olof*, nearly 30 years later, in 1972.

Sjöberg was sometimes criticised for being mainly interested in actors as figures in a stage picture to be posed, grouped, their movements choreographed. If there was any truth in this, it needs to be held in balance with the fact that some very fine actors appeared in his productions, ranging from Lars Hanson as Richard III to Ulf Palme as Hamlet or Max von Sydow in Strindberg's *The Burnt Site*; and, in his films of *Miss Julie* and *Only a Mother*, the performances of Anita Björk and Eva Dahlbeck, respectively, have been assessed as outstanding in cinematic history.

Among the eclectic range of plays he presented at the Dramaten, natural groups emerge: French plays of the 1930's and 1940's (Bernard, Lenormand, Claudel and Giraudoux as well as the existentialists Sartre and Camus), works by Strindberg (history plays, "naturalistic" pieces and late "chamber plays", rather than the pilgrimage plays favoured by the older Dramaten director, Olof Molander), plays of Bertolt Brecht, besides the series of Shakespeare productions at all stages of his career and the otherwise unclassifiable medley of recent foreign plays. In treating Strindberg, he got right away from the narrowness of seeing the plays as documents of biographical or pathological interest, using a recurrent imagery of looking *through* to show the depths of the psyche and the hidden bases of the social world mirroring each other. One of his key ideas was of the transformation of everything into metaphor through putting it on the stage. The intellectual currents of his time carried him on from existentialism to structuralism, and he was fond of citing Lévi-Strauss, or perhaps Foucault, in discussing his own work. In Brecht he found a combination of technical challenge with ideological attraction. Working as he did in the political and social haven of Sweden's premier subsidised theatre, it was hard for him to catch the urgency of crisis, and he was criticised accordingly. His own stage adaptations of mid-19th century novels by C. J. L. Almqvist, which combined realism with presentation of dream states, were among his most popular achievements.

Sjöberg's films have not escaped the label of academicism sometimes attached to his stage work. Easily the best-known of his films outside Scandinavia is the cinematically conceived *Miss Julie*, which won the Cannes Grand Prix (the later film *The Father* was based on his stage production). This is celebrated for its extensive and original adaptation of flashback technique to render the unverifiable monologues of the play in a simultaneity of "memory", dream, fiction, anticipation and present action: triumphantly solving the problem of opening out a theatrical structure for the screen without irrelevance. The elaborate complexity of later films carried them beyond the realm of general comprehension. Yet it is certain that he left a body of creative work in this medium that will continue to be studied, reassessed and better appreciated.

—Margery Morgan

SKINNER, Otis. US actor. Born in Cambridge, Massachusetts, 28 June 1858. Educated at schools in Cambridge, Massachusetts, and at Hartford High School, Connecticut, from 1867. Married actress Maud Durbin in 1895 (died 1936), one daughter (author and actress Cornelia Otis Skinner). Stage debut, Philadelphia Museum, 1877: played numerous minor roles there, 1877–78; actor, Walnut Street Theatre, Philadelphia, 1878–79; New York debut, Niblo's Garden, 1879; actor, companies of Edwin Booth, 1880, Lawrence Barrett, 1881–84, Augustin Daly, 1884–88, and Helen Modjeska, 1889–90 and 1890–94; London debut, 1884; led his own touring company, 1894–1904, then starred under the management of Charles Frohman; toured in revivals of earlier successes into the 1930's; retired, 1940. Member: Players' Club (vice-president); Episcopal Players' Guild (president, 1938). Died in New York, 4 January 1942.

Roles

1877	Old Negro Jim in *Woodleigh* (Stoner), Philadelphia Museum.
1879	Maclow in *The Enchantment* (Law), Niblo's Garden Theatre, New York.

Sir Francis Mobray in *Hearts of Steel* (Falconer), Niblo's Garden Theatre, New York.

1880   Wounded Officer in *Macbeth* (Shakespeare), Booth's Theatre, New York.

François in *Richelieu* (Bulwer-Lytton), Booth's Theatre, New York.

Cassio in *Othello* (Shakespeare), Booth's Theatre, New York.

1882   Pelleas in *Pendragon* (Young), Fifth Avenue Theatre, New York.

1883   Paolo in *Francesca da Rimini* (Boker), Star Theatre, New York.

1884   Paul Hollyhock in *Casting the Boomerang* (Schönthan, adapted by Daly), Toole's Theatre, London.

1884–88   Earl of Caryl in *Lords and Commons* (Pinero), Daly's Theatre, New York.

Guy Roverley in *Love on Crutches* (Daly), Daly's Theatre, New York.

Worthy in *The Recruiting Officer* (Farquhar), Daly's Theatre, New York.

Captain Horace Vale in *The Magistrate* (Pinero), Daly's Theatre, New York.

Master Page in *The Merry Wives of Windsor* (Shakespeare), Daly's Theatre, New York.

Captain Renseller in *Nancy and Co.* (Daly), Daly's Theatre, New York; Strand Theatre, London, 1886.

Charley Hoffman in *Love in Harness* (Valabrègue, adapted by Daly), Daly's Theatre, New York.

Lucentio in *The Taming of the Shrew* (Shakespeare), Daly's Theatre, New York; Strand Theatre, London, 1888.

Benny in *The Railroad of Love* (Daly), Daly's Theatre, New York; Gaiety Theatre, London, 1888.

Lysander in *A Midsummer Night's Dream* (Shakespeare), Daly's Theatre, New York.

1886   Harry Damask in *A Night Off* (Daly), Strand Theatre, London.

1889   Paul Falshawe in *The Love Story* (Leclerq), Tompkins' Fifth Avenue Theatre, New York.

Claudio in *Much Ado About Nothing* (Shakespeare), Broadway Theatre, New York.

Bassanio in *The Merchant of Venice* (Shakespeare), Broadway Theatre, New York.

Laertes in *Hamlet* (Shakespeare), Broadway Theatre, New York.

Macduff in *Macbeth* (Shakespeare), Broadway Theatre, New York.

De Mauprat in *Richelieu* (Bulwer-Lytton), Broadway Theatre, New York.

Serafino Del 'Aquila in *The Fool's Revenge* (Taylor), Broadway Theatre, New York.

1890   Romeo in *Romeo and Juliet* (Shakespeare), Globe Theatre, London.

Percy Gauntlett in *This Woman and That* (Leclerq), Globe Theatre, London.

Thibault and La Hire in *Joan of Arc* (Young), Miner's Fifth Avenue Theatre, New York.

1890–92   Orlando in *As You Like It* (Shakespeare), Broadway Theatre, New York.

Otis Skinner

Henry VIII in *Henry VIII* (Shakespeare), Broadway Theatre, New York.

Sir Edward Mortimer in *Mary Stuart* (Schiller), Broadway Theatre, New York.

Leonatus Posthumous in *Cymbeline* (Shakespeare), Broadway Theatre, New York.

Benedick in *Much Ado About Nothing* (Shakespeare), Broadway Theatre, New York.

Major Schubert in *Magda* (Sudermann), Broadway Theatre, New York.

Captain Jack Absolute in *The Rivals* (Sheridan), Broadway Theatre, New York.

1894   Count of Grammont in *His Grace de Grammont* (Fitch), Grand Opera, Chicago.

1895   François de Villon in *Villon, the Vagabond* (O. and C. Skinner), US tour.

Hamlet in *Hamlet* (Shakespeare), US tour.

1900   Prince Otto in *Prince Otto* (O. Skinner, adapted from Stevenson), Wallack's Theatre, New York.

1901   Lanciotto in *Francesca da Rimini* (Boker), Victorian Theatre, New York.

1904   Charles Surface in *The School for Scandal* (Sheridan), Lyric Theatre, New York.

Shylock in *The Merchant of Venice* (Shakespeare), Lyric Theatre, New York; US tour, 1931–32.

Petruchio in *The Taming of the Shrew* (Shakespeare), Lyric Theatre, New York.

1904	The Harvester in *The Harvester* (C. Skinner, adapted from Richepin's *Le Chemineau*), Lyric Theatre, New York.
1906	Abbé Daniel in *The Duel* (Lavedan), Hudson Theatre, New York, and US tour.
1907	Colonel Philippe Brideau in *The Honour of the Family* (adapted from Balzac's *La Rabouilleuse*), New Rochelle, New York; Hudson Theatre, New York, 1908; Booth Theatre, New York, 1926.
1910	Lafayette Towers in *Your Humble Servant* (Tarkington), Garrick Theatre, New York.
1911	Denis Roulette in *Sire* (Lavedan), Criterion Theatre, New York.
	Hajj the Beggar in *Kismet* (Knobloch), Knickerbocker Theatre, New York; US tour, 1912–14.
1914	Montgomery Starr in *The Silent Voice* (Goodman), Liberty Theatre, New York.
1915	Jean Renaud in *A Celebrated Case* (D'Ennery and Cormon), Empire Theatre, New York.
	Antony Bellchamber in *Cock o' the Walk* (Poole), Cohan Theatre, New York.
1916	Antonio Camaradonio in *Mr Antonio* (Tarkington), Lyceum Theatre, New York; US tour, 1917–18.
1918	Albert Mott in *Humpty-Dumpty* (Bloch), Lyceum Theatre, New York.
1920	Pietro in *Pietro*, Criterion Theatre, New York.
1921	Hanaud in *At the Villa Rose* (Mason), Chicago.
	Juan Gallardo in *Blood and Sand* (Ibanez), Empire Theatre, New York.
1923	Sancho Panza in *Sancho Panza* (Howard), Hudson Theatre, New York.
1926	Falstaff in *Henry IV, part 1* (Shakespeare), Knickerbocker Theatre, New York.
1928	Falstaff in *The Merry Wives of Windsor* (Shakespeare), Knickerbocker Theatre, New York.
1929	Papa Juan in *A Hundred Years Old* (Granville-Barker), Chicago and Lyceum Theatre, New York.
1932	Thersites in *Troilus and Cressida* (Shakespeare), Broadway Theatre, New York.
1933	Uncle Tom in *Uncle Tom's Cabin* (adapted from Stowe), Alvin Theatre, New York.

Other roles included: *Much Ado About Nothing* (Shakespeare), Booth's Theatre, New York, 1880; *Richard III* (Shakespeare), Booth's Theatre, New York, 1880; *The Fool's Revenge* (Taylor), Booth's Theatre, New York, 1880; *Hamlet* (Shakespeare), Booth's Theatre, New York, 1880; *The Merchant of Venice* (Shakespeare), Booth's Theatre, New York, 1880; *The Taming of the Shrew* (Shakespeare), Booth's Theatre, New York, 1880; *Ruy Blas* (Hugo), Booth's Theatre, New York; *Yorick's Love* (Howells), Fifth Avenue Theatre, New York, 1882; *Julius Caesar* (Shakespeare), Fifth Avenue Theatre, New York, 1882; *The Man o' Airlie* (Wills), Fifth Avenue Theatre, New York, 1882; *David Garrick* (Robertson), Fifth Avenue Theatre, New York, 1882; *The Marble Heart* (Selby), Fifth Avenue Theatre, New York, 1882; *A Wooden Spoon* (Schönthan, adapted by Daly), Daly's Theatre, New York, 1884; *The King's Jester* (Leuser), US tour, 1894; *Soldiers of Fortune* (Thomas, adapted from Davies), US tour, 1895; *Prince Rudolph*, US tour, 1895; *The Liars* (H. A. Jones), US tour, 1895; *Rosemary* (Parker and Carson), US tour, 1895; *In a Balcony* (Browning), US tour, 1900; *Lazarre*, US tour, 1901; *The Joy of Peter Barban*, US tour, 1919; *The Nobel Prize* (Bergman), Westport, 1933.

Films

Kismet, 1916 and 1930.

Publications

Footlights and Spotlights: Recollections of My Life on the Stage, 1924; *Mad Folk of the Theatre*, 1928; *One Man in His Home* (edited journal of H. Watkins), 1938; *The Last Tragedian — Booth Tells His Own Story*, 1939.

*

Bibliography

Books:
Cornelia Otis Skinner, *Family Circle*, Boston, 1948.

Articles:
John Mason Brown, "Otis Skinner", *Theatre Arts*, 13, November 1919.

* * *

Otis Skinner's long career spanned a transitional time for the US theatre with significant changes in the dramatic repertory and in the organization of theatrical activity, a movement away from the stable Victorian "old school" and towards a more diverse, eclectic modernity. That Skinner was so successful during this period can be attributed to his considerable physical assets, his training in the time-worn techniques and repertory of the traditional "classical" theatre, and especially his remarkable versatility.

Handsome, with an athletic build and a strong, resonant voice, as a young man Skinner was ideal for juvenile leads. In such roles as Laertes, Cassio, Bassanio, and François in *Richelieu*, he played with many of the leading actors of his era. As he matured, he graduated to leading man parts in support of such stars as Helena Modjeska, Margaret Mather, and Ada Rehan. Eventually he toured with his own company, starring not only as Hamlet and Shylock, but also as romantic, historical heroes and in character roles, often in original plays or dramatic adaptations that he co-authored with his brother Charles. By the early 1900's he was an established and popular star who continued to appear in a varied repertory. Indeed, towards the end of his career, he estimated that he had "played in all, three hundred and twenty-five parts; have appeared in sixteen plays of Shakespeare, acting therein, at various times, thirty-eight parts, and I produced under my own direction thirty-three plays".

Although he was often praised for artistic sincerity and honesty, whatever the role, he was at his most effective in romantic or picturesque parts. In an era when tastes were turning increasingly to the restrained realism of Ibsen and Chekhov, Skinner himself wrote that he liked "plays that require expression rather than repression. I am not anxious for flamboyant roles," he continued, "but I do like to let myself out".

Many of his best qualities were exhibited in his performance as Hajj in *Kismet*. The critic Walter Prichard Eaton described him as amply able to fill the role of Hajj "the more as that slight note of unreality in his acting which sometimes mars his impersonation of serious romantic roles or roles in modern plays, here admirably blends with the glamour of dreamlike fantasy. His impersonation is consistently the beggar, though the part is rather sketched broadly than characterized in detail. Never for an instant is he anything else, be his borrowed robes ever so grand. It is lit with a grim, masculine humour, it is touched with tenderness for his daughter and with fierce passions of revenge. But humour, tenderness, passion, are all held in the key of romantic fable, and so while he counts the bubbles that arise from the drowning Wazir there is no honour in the episode, and when he goes to sleep at last in his beggar's rags there is no sorrow — only a half smile for the round-the-circle logic of it, and the pleasant finish to a good tale told ... "

The critic John Mason Brown praised Skinner's style as "a veteran's method, sure in its devices, conscious of its 'points' and certain in making them ... it is character acting enlarged beyond the ordinary; bold, romantic, mellow but high-tensioned".

It was a method that served Skinner effectively in both the traditional repertory of the Victorian tragedian and in the US commercial theatre in the first third of the 20th century.

—Daniel J. Watermeier

SMITH, (Dame) Maggie. British actress. Born Margaret Natalie Smith in Ilford, Essex, 28 December 1934. Educated at Oxford High School for Girls; trained for the stage at the Oxford Playhouse School. Married 1) actor Robert Stephens in 1967 (divorced 1975), two sons; 2) playwright Beverley Cross in 1975. Acted with the Oxford University Dramatic Society, from 1952; professional stage debut, New York, Ethel Barrymore Theatre, 1956; London debut, Lyric Theatre, Hammersmith, 1957; film debut, 1958; actress, Old Vic company, 1959–60; joined National Theatre Company, 1964; first appeared at Stratford Shakespeare Festival, Stratford, Ontario, 1976; returned to London stage, 1979; director, United British Artists, from 1982. Recipient: London *Evening Standard* Award, 1962, 1970, 1981, 1985; Variety Club Award, 1963, 1968, 1972, 1986; Oscar, 1969, 1979; Society of Film and Television Arts Award, 1969; Golden Globe Award, 1979, 1986; British Academy of Film and Television Arts Award, 1985, 1986, 1988; *Evening Standard* British Film Award, 1988; Royal Television Society Award, 1989; Tony Award, 1990; Shakespeare Prize (Germany), 1991. D.Litt: St Andrew's University, 1971. CBE (Commander of the British Empire), 1970; DBE (Dame Commander of the British Empire), 1990.

Roles

1956	Comedienne in *New Faces of '56 Revue* (Sillman), Ethel Barrymore Theatre, New York.
1957	Comedienne in *Share My Lettuce* (Gascoigne), Lyric Theatre, Hammersmith, London, and Comedy Theatre, London.
1958	Vere Dane in *The Stepmother* (Bennett), St Martin's Theatre, London.
1959–60	Lady Plyant in *The Double-Dealer* (Congreve), Old Vic Theatre, London.
	Celia in *As You Like It* (Shakespeare), Old Vic Theatre, London.
	The Queen in *Richard II* (Shakespeare), Old Vic Theatre, London; Stratford Shakespeare Festival, Stratford, Ontario, 1977–78.
	Mistress Ford in *The Merry Wives of Windsor* (Shakespeare), Old Vic Theatre, London.
	Maggie Wylie in *What Every Woman Knows* (Barrie), Old Vic Theatre, London.
1960	Daisy in *Rhinoceros* (Ionesco), Strand Theatre, London.
1961	Lucile in *The Rehearsal* (Anouilh), Royal Theatre, London, Old Vic Theatre, Bristol, Globe Theatre, London, Queen's Theatre, London, and Apollo Theatre, London.
1962	Doreen in *The Private Ear* and Belinda in *The Public Eye* (P. Shaffer), Globe Theatre, London.
	Narrator in *Pictures in the Hallway* (O'Casey), Mermaid Theatre, London.
1963	Mary in *Mary, Mary* (Kerr), Queen's Theatre, London.
	Silvia in *The Recruiting Officer* (Farquhar), Old Vic Theatre, London.
1964	Desdemona in *Othello* (Shakespeare), Old Vic Theatre, London, and Chichester Festival Theatre.
	Hilda Wangel in *The Master Builder* (Ibsen), Old Vic Theatre, London.
	Myra in *Hay Fever* (Coward), Old Vic Theatre, London.
	Beatrice in *Much Ado About Nothing* (Shakespeare), Old Vic Theatre, London; Stratford Shakespeare Festival, Stratford, Ontario, 1980.
1965	Clea in *Black Comedy* (P. Shaffer), Old Vic Theatre, London.
1965–66	Julie in *Miss Julie* (Strindberg), Old Vic Theatre, London.
1966	Marcela in *A Bond Honoured* (Osborne), Old Vic Theatre, London.
1969	Margery Pinchwife in *The Country Wife* (Wycherley), Old Vic Theatre, London.
1970	Mrs Sullen in *The Beaux' Stratagem* (Farquhar), Old Vic Theatre, London.
	Hedda in *Hedda Gabler* (Ibsen), Old Vic Theatre, London.
	Masha in *The Three Sisters* (Chekhov), Old Vic Theatre, London, and Los Angeles; Stratford Shakespeare Festival, Stratford, Ontario, 1976.

Maggie Smith (1981).

1972	Amanda Prynne in *Private Lives* (Coward), Queen's Theatre, London; Stratford Shakespeare Festival, Stratford, Ontario, 1977–78.
1974	Peter Pan in *Peter Pan* (Barrie), Vaudeville Theatre, London, and 46th Street Theatre, New York.
1976	Cleopatra in *Antony and Cleopatra* (Shakespeare), Stratford Shakespeare Festival, Stratford, Ontario.
	Millamant in *The Way of the World* (Congreve), Stratford Shakespeare Festival, Stratford, Ontario; Chichester Festival Theatre and Haymarket Theatre, London, 1984.
	Lady Macbeth in *Macbeth* (Shakespeare), Stratford Shakespeare Festival, Stratford, Ontario; revived there, 1977–78.
	The Actress in *The Guardsman* (Molnár), Ahmanson Theatre, Los Angeles; Stratford Shakespeare Festival, Stratford, Ontario, 1977–78.
1977–78	Titania and Hippolyta in *A Midsummer Night's Dream* (Shakespeare), Stratford Shakespeare Festival, Stratford, Ontario.
	Judith Bliss in *Hay Fever* (Coward), Stratford Shakespeare Festival, Stratford, Ontario.
	Rosalind in *As You Like It* (Shakespeare), Stratford Shakespeare Festival, Stratford, Ontario.

1979	Ruth Carson in *Night and Day* (Stoppard), Phoenix Theatre, London, and American National Theatre and Academy, New York.
1980	Virginia Woolf in *Virginia* (O'Brien), Stratford Shakespeare Festival, Stratford, Ontario; Haymarket Theatre, London, 1981.
	Masha in *The Seagull* (Chekhov), Stratford Shakespeare Festival, Stratford, Ontario.
1986	Nadia in *Interpreters* (Harwood), Queen's Theatre, London.
	Halina in *Coming in to Land* (Poliakoff), National Theatre, London.
1993	Lady Bracknell in *The Importance of Being Earnest* (Wilde), Aldwych Theatre, London.

Other roles included: *War Plays* (Bond), National Theatre, London, 1985; *Lettice and Lovage* (P. Shaffer), Globe Theatre, London, 1987, and New York, 1990.

Films

Nowhere to Go, 1958; *Go to Blazes*, 1962; *The VIPs*, 1963; *The Pumpkin Eater*, 1964; *Young Cassidy*, 1965; *Othello*, 1965; *The Honey Pot*, 1967; *Oh! What a Lovely War*, 1968; *Hot Millions*, 1968; *The Prime of Miss Jean Brodie*, 1969; *Travels with My Aunt*, 1972; *Love and Pain (and the Whole Damn Thing)*, 1973; *Murder by Death*, 1976; *Death on the Nile*, 1978; *California Suite*, 1978; *Quartet*, 1981; *Clash of the Titans*, 1981; *Evil Under the Sun*, 1982; *The Missionary*, 1982; *Better Late Than Never*, 1983; *Lily in Love*, 1985; *A Private Function*, 1985; *A Room with a View*, 1986; *The Lonely Passion of Judith Hearne*, 1988; *Hook*, 1992; *Sister Act*, 1992.

Television

Miss Silly, 1983; *Talking Heads*, 1989; *Memento Mori*, 1992; *Suddenly Last Summer*, 1993. Other productions include: *Boy Meets Girl*; *A Phoenix Too Frequent*; *For Services Rendered*; *Much Abo About Nothing*; *Man and Superman*; *On Approval*; *Home and Beauty*.

*

Bibliography

Books:
Michael Coveney, *Maggie Smith: A Bright Particular Star*, London, 1992.

* * *

Maggie Smith first made her name in the late 1950's and early 1960's as a comedienne in revue and light comedy. Her London stage debut was *Share My Lettuce*, in which she co-starred with Kenneth Williams. Williams was a master of "high camp", known for his nasal delivery and his range of funny voices. His influence left its mark on her ("I pinch from him all the time", she later confessed). He taught her "clarity and speed" and an "incredible deftness with a line". She may also, however, have picked up some of his faults. The accusation that she too can be mannered and camp has dogged her career.

When, in 1963, Laurence Olivier invited Smith to join the National Theatre to play Desdemona to his Othello, the offer came as a shock — not least to her (she almost refused). It was a turning point, her first real chance to prove that she was more then just a funny voice. Her Desdemona was sensible, serious, a little dull perhaps, but she received respectful reviews.

Comedy remained her strength, however. In *Hay Fever* (1964) she stole the show from, among others, Edith Evans. "Miss Smith possesses an angularity which is temperamental no less than physical", Hugh Leonard wrote; "She seems to belong to the 1920's". When it came to tragic roles, critics questioned if she had sufficient emotional range. As Hedda Gabler (1970), she "lacked the intense, almost oppressive Scandinavian self-absorption". At the climactic moments, the power simply was not there, as Ronald Bryden remarked: "Plunging her fingers into Thea Elvsted's hair, darting towards the flames with Eilert Lovborg's manuscript, she summoned up a swift, angular electricity ... but its effect was of sleight of hand, speed and energy substituting for deep, volcanic force".

In 1972 she played Amanda in *Private Lives*. Sheridan Morley wrote that the performance was pitched "somewhere between Tallulah Bankhead and Kenneth Williams". Smith herself grew increasingly unhappy with her own acting: "What had happened was that, as the run continued, I had gotten so accustomed to laughs that I started playing for them. My performance got broader and broader, and more and more out of touch with Coward".

The danger in Smith's approach has always been that it can turn into a display of technique for technique's sake, a revue-turn. At her best, she blends the comic and the tragic. In the film *Love and Pain and the Whole Damn Thing* (1973), she plays a character who has difficulty with the simpler tasks. Making a telephone call, she is so paralysed with fear that her voice finally breaks into a series of incoherent dysphonic sounds. The character's nervousness and clumsiness are, by turns, comic and deeply affecting.

After *Private Lives* Smith's career seemed to be in limbo. She found a new direction when Robin Phillips asked her to join the Festival Theatre in Stratford, Ontario, where she played Cleopatra, Millamant, Titania, and Lady Macbeth — "the kinds of parts no-one was asking me to do in England". It was perhaps her most productive period as an actress; she was "in her prime".

Working with her on the role of Rosalind, Phillips discouraged her from resorting to comic effects. He asked her to play *against* her natural inclinations — her tendency to pick out the comedy in every role. "Be serious", he told her. "Don't try to make the audience laugh. Try to make them cry".

Stratford saw her most successful performances to date in tragic roles. Her Lady Macbeth (1976) was a chilling study of a woman exercising a terrible control over herself. She had long, it seemed, suppressed her feelings — even sexual feelings had been crushed; she regarded her husband only with a restrained contempt. She lived by will-power — but her will was crushing from within.

London saw Smith in two Stratford roles: as Virginia in the play of the same name and as Millamant. Restoration comedy allows Smith to utilise her dexterity with language (she has an ability to seize on a line, a word, and find comedy where there seems to be none). It allows her to blend artifice and style with inner emotional truth. Milla-

mant is an archetypal Smith role — a character who, like Beatrice in *Much Ado About Nothing*, uses wit and raillery to conceal an inner insecurity. This was a woman hesitating on the verge of matrimony, unwilling to commit herself. In Congreve's famous "proviso" scene, there was a moment when Smith allowed the character's true feelings to show. "When she finally succumbs to her love for Mirabell", Jack Tinker observed, "she sits on a bench utterly shaken, stunned, and drained by the force of her own passions".

Notable performances followed in plays by Poliakoff and Cocteau. In 1987, Smith starred in *Lettice and Lovage*, in a role written for her by Peter Shaffer. It was a return to high camp, to the bad ways she seemed to have left behind her after *Private Lives*. "At least", Michael Radcliffe wrote, "we now know that she is acting like this because she wants to and not because she can no longer do anything else".

—David Allen

SOTHERN, E(dward) H(ugh). US actor. Born in New Orleans, Louisiana, 6 December 1859; son of British comedian Edward Askew Sothern. Educated at Dunchurch, Warwickshire, England, 1863–68; Marylebone Grammar School, London; trained as a painter. Married 1) Virginia Harned in 1896 (divorced 1910); 2) the actress Julia Marlowe (*q.v.*) in 1911. Stage debut, Park Theatre, New York, 1879; subsequently appeared at the Boston Museum and with John McCullough's company, 1879–81; London debut, Royalty Theatre, 1881; toured Britain, 1882–83; returned to McCullough's company in the USA, 1883; actor, under Helen Dauvray and then Daniel Frohman, Lyceum Theatre, New York, 1884–98; acclaimed as Hamlet in his own production of the play, 1900–03; toured with Marlowe, 1904–07, 1909–14, and 1919–24; reappeared on London stage after 24 years' absence, 1907; founded own company, 1907; retired with Marlowe, 1924; presented, with Marlowe, large stock of costumes and scenery to the Shakespeare Memorial Theatre, Stratford-upon-Avon, 1924; last stage appearance, Lyceum Theatre, New York, 1927. Died in New York, 28 October 1933.

Roles

1879   Cabman in *Brother Sam* (Oxenford), Park Theatre, New York.
1881   Mr Sharpe in *False Colours* (Fitzball), Royalty Theatre, London.
        Marshley Bittern in *Out of the Hunt* (Reece and Thorpe), Royalty Theatre, London.
1882   Arthur Spoonbill in *Fourteen Days* (H. J. Byron), Criterion Theatre, London.
1884   Eliphaz Tresham in *The Fatal Letter* (Cazauran), US tour and Union Square Theatre, New York.
        Melchizidec Flighty in *Whose Are They?* (Sothern), Star Theatre, New York.
1885   Alfred Vane in *Favette* (Clayton, adapted from Ouida), Union Square Theatre, New York.
        Knolly Cameron in *Mona* (Hooker), Star Theatre, New York.

John in *In Chancery* (Pinero), Madison Square Theatre, New York.

Jules in *A Moral Crime* (Barron and Bates), Union Square Theatre, New York.

1885   Captain John Gregory in *One of Our Girls* (Howard), Lyceum Theatre, New York.

1886   Prosper Couramont in *A Scrap of Paper* (Simpson), Lyceum Theatre, New York.

1887   Harrington Lee in *Met by Chance* (Howard), Lyceum Theatre, New York.

Ernest Vane in *Masks and Faces* (Reade and Taylor), Lyceum Theatre, New York.

André de Latour in *Walda Lamar* (Wertheimer), Lyceum Theatre, New York.

Wildrake in *The Love Chase* (Knowles), Lyceum Theatre, New York.

Jack Hammerton in *The Highest Bidder* (Morton and Reece), Lyceum Theatre, New York.

Anthony in *The Great Pink Pearl* (Raleigh and Carton), Lyceum Theatre, New York.

Bill Lewis in *Editha's Burglar* (Cleary), Lyceum Theatre, New York; also directed.

1888   Lord Chumley in *Lord Chumley* (De Mille and Belasco), Lyceum Theatre, New York.

1890   Allen Rollit in *The Maister of Woodbarrow* (Jerome), Lyceum Theatre, New York.

1891   Duke of Guisebury in *The Dancing Girl* (H. A. Jones), Lyceum Theatre, New York.

Lettarblair Lytton in *Captain Lettarblair* (Merington), Lyceum Theatre, New York.

All roles in *I Love, thou Lovest, he Loves* (Sothern), Lyceum Theatre, New York.

1892   Reagan in *The Disreputable Mr Reagan*, Lyceum Theatre, New York.

1893   Richard Brinsley Sheridan in *Sheridan; or, The Maid of Bath* (Potter), Lyceum Theatre, New York.

1894   Ralph Seton in *The Victoria Cross* (Potter), Lyceum Theatre, New York.

Harry Halward in *A Way to Win a Woman* (Jerome), Lyceum Theatre, New York.

1895   Rudolf Rassendyl in *The Prisoner of Zenda* (Rose, adapted from Hope), Lyceum Theatre, New York.

1896   Ernanton de Launay in *An Enemy to the King* (Stephens), Lyceum Theatre, New York.

1897   Christopher Heartwright in *Change Alley* (Carson and Parker), Lyceum Theatre, New York.

Claude Melnotte in *The Lady of Lyons* (Bulwer-Lytton), Lyceum Theatre, New York.

1898   George Sylvester in *The Adventure of Lady Ursula* (Hope), Lyceum Theatre, New York.

Godfrey Remsen in *A Colonial Girl* (Furniss and Richardson), Lyceum Theatre, New York.

1890   The Intruder in *An Unwarranted Intrusion* (Morton), Broadway Theatre, New York.

1899   Raoul D'Artagnan in *The King's Musketeers* (adapted from Dumas *père*), Knickerbocker Theatre, New York, and Daly's Theatre, New York.

Captain Egalite in *The Song of the Sword* (Ditrichstein), Daly's Theatre, New York.

E. H. Sothern

1900   Heinrich in *The Sunken Bell* (adapted from Hauptmann), Knickerbocker Theatre, New York; Lyric Theatre, Philadelphia, 1906; Lyric Theatre, New York, 1907; Waldorf Theatre, London, 1907; also directed.

Sir Geoffrey Bloomfield in *Drifting Apart* (Herne), Daly's Theatre, New York.

Hamlet in *Hamlet* (Shakespeare), Garden Theatre, New York; Illinois Theatre, Chicago, and Knickerbocker Theatre, New York, 1904; Lyric Theatre, New York, Waldorf Theatre, London, and Garrick Theatre, Chicago, 1907; also directed.

1901   Richard Lovelace in *Richard Lovelace* (L. Irving), Garden Theatre, New York.

François Villon in *If I Were King* (McCarthy), Garden Theatre, New York; Garrick Theatre, Chicago, 1907; Lyric Theatre, New York, 1908; Shubert Theatre, New York, 1916; also directed.

1903   Markheim in *Markheim* (Courtney), Hollis Street Theatre, Boston.

Robert, King of Sicily in *The Proud Prince* (McCarthy), Herald Square Theatre, New York, and US tour; directed.

1904   Romeo in *Romeo and Juliet* (Shakespeare), Illinois Theatre, Chicago; Lyric Theatre, New York, and Waldorf Theatre, London, 1907; also directed.

Benedick in *Much Ado About Nothing* (Shakespeare), Illinois Theatre, Chicago, and Knickerbocker Theatre, New York.

1905   Petruchio in *The Taming of the Shrew* (Shakespeare), Cleveland, Ohio, and Knickerbocker Theatre, New York.

Shylock in *The Merchant of Venice* (Shakespeare), Cleveland, Ohio, and Knickerbocker Theatre, New York; Lyric Theatre, New York, 1907.

Malvolio in *Twelfth Night* (Shakespeare), Knickerbocker Theatre, New York; Lyric Theatre, New York, and Waldorf Theatre, London, 1907.

1906   Duke D'Alençon in *Jeanne D'Arc* (MacKaye), Lyric Theatre, Philadelphia; Lyric Theatre, New York, and Waldorf Theatre, London, 1907.

John the Baptist in *John the Baptist* (Sudermann), Lyric Theatre, Philadelphia; Lyric Theatre, New York, 1907.

1907   Charles Brandon in *When Knighthood Was in Flower* (Kester), Waldorf Theatre, London.

Rodion Raskelnikoff in *The Fool Hath Said in his Heart* (L. Irving), Garrick Theatre, Chicago; Lyric Theatre, New York, 1908.

Lord Dundreary in *Our American Cousin* (Taylor), Garrick Theatre, Chicago; Lyric Theatre, New York, 1908; Booth Theatre, New York, 1915.

1908   Don Quixote in *Don Quixote* (Wills), Lyric Theatre, New York.

1909   Richelieu in *Richelieu* (Bulwer-Lytton), Daly's Theatre, New York.

Mark Antony in *Antony and Cleopatra* (Shakespeare), New Theatre, New York.

1910   Macbeth in *Macbeth* (Shakespeare), Broadway Theatre, New York.

1914   Charlemagne in *Charlemagne*, Garrick Theatre, Chicago.

1915   Jeffery Panton in *The Two Virtues* (Sutro), Booth Theatre, New York.

1916   Garrick in *David Garrick* (Robertson), Booth Theatre, New York.

1923   Leonatus Posthumous in *Cymbeline* (Shakespeare), Jolson Theatre, New York.

1925   Edmund de Verron in *Accused*, Belasco Theatre, New York.

1926   Tiburtius in *What Never Dies* (P. Wilde), Belasco Theatre, New York.

Other roles included: *Called Back* (Conway and Carr), US tour, 1884; *Lost* (Wyndham), US tour, 1884; *Three Wives to One Husband* (Milliken, adapted from Grenet-Dancourt), US tour, 1884; in *Nita's First* (Warren), Wallack's Theatre, New York, 1884.

Films

The Chattel, 1916; *An Enemy to the King*, 1916; *The Man of Mystery*, 1916.

Publications

Whose Are They?/Domestic Earthquakes (play), 1883; *I Love, Thou Lovest, He Loves* (play), 1891; *Never Trouble Trouble till Trouble Troubles You* (play); *A Luncheon at Nick's* (play); *The Light That Lies in Woman's Eyes* (play); *The Melancholy Tale of 'Me': My Remembrances* (autobiography), 1916; *Matters for a May Morning: Poems Fond and Foolish*, 1929.

*

Bibliography

Books:
Charles H. Shattuck, *Shakespeare on the American Stage: From Booth and Barrettt to Sothern and Marlowe*, Washington, D.C., 1987.

Articles:
Mildred Aldrich, "Edward Hugh Sothern", *Arena*, 6, October, 1892.
Edward Fales Coward, "Edward H. Sothern — An Actor with Ideals", *Theatre*, 3, March 1903.
Matthew White, "Edward H. Sothern", *Munsey's*, 36, October 1906–March 1907.
William Phillips Dodge, "E. H. Sothern", *Strand*, 46, December 1913.
William Winter, "The Art of E. H. Sothern", *Century*, 90, May 1915.
A. Richard Sogluzzio, "Edward H. Sothern and Julia Marlowe on the Art of Acting", *Theatre Survey*, 11, November 1970.

* * *

After a decade of playing light comedic or dashing, romantic roles, which ideally suited his handsome face and trim athletic figure, E. H. Sothern made his mark as a classical actor in his own production of *Hamlet* at New York's Garden Theatre in 1900. Although flawed, Sothern's Hamlet, during a period in the US theatre when Shakespearean acting and production was at a low ebb, "drew full houses, pleased discriminating critics, and proved that the people did want Shakespeare after all". Sothern's success led to a partnership with actress Julia Marlowe. Together they starred in their own touring productions of Shakespeare (and a few modern plays of literary merit) for almost 20 years. In the process, Sothern gained recognition, in the words of Charles H. Shattuck, as the "best all-Shakespeare actor the US stage has produced since Booth".

Apart from Hamlet, Sothern was initially most successful in playing such comic characters as Benedick, Petruchio, and Malvolio. Sothern invested both Petruchio and Benedick with the physical energy and manly charm of the swashbuckling heroes he had played during his years at the Lyceum Theatre. Moreover, he always signalled to the audience with a smile, a wink, or by blowing a kiss that his Petruchio and Benedick were sentimental over their Katherine and Beatrice. One critic called his sense of humour as Petruchio "adroit, suggestive, imaginative, and original and it lifted the part in its finer moments into something very like high comedy". Critics generally agreed that Sothern was at his comic best as Malvolio. The English critic Arthur Symons wrote that Sothern "acts with his eyelids, which move while all the rest of his face is motionless; with his pursed, reticent mouth, with his prim and proper gestures; with that self-consciousness which brings all Malvolio's troubles upon him. It is a fantastic, tragically comic thing, done with rare calculation, and it has its formal, almost cruel share in the immense gaiety of the piece".

Critics were more divided about Sothern's Shylock and Macbeth. William Winter, however, thought Sothern's studied, realistic Shylock came nearer to "tragic stature" than any other role he played. Although not a great actor, Sothern was exceptionally studious and imaginative and he used his physical assets effectively. His Macbeth, for instance, beginning in the prime of middle age and then declining into a haunted, haggard, sometimes hysterical older man, and finally rebounding with a wild surge of energy in his combat with Macduff, was a carefully planned and skilfully executed conception. It failed, however, to win widespread critical praise. One critic called it disparagingly and unfairly "Hamlet in a beard". Generally Sothern was often criticised for being too studious, or lacking in spontaneity or "spiritual depth". During the war years Sothern (joined occasionally by Marlowe) entertained the troops with patriotic recitations and solo scenes from Shakespeare. Sothern had a special flair for scenic design and the highly regarded "mise-en-scène" of Sothern and Marlowe productions owed much to his taste, knowledge, and hard work.

Over 60 years after they retired, Edward Wagenknecht, a distinguished US cultural historian, reminisced that his own standards in Shakespearean production had been set many years ago by E. H. Sothern and Julia Marlowe: "A Sothern and Marlowe production was not, as was said of Edmund Kean, like reading Shakespeare by flashes of lightning. They were both intensely cerebral, even scholarly, actors. Every nuance, every inflection, every gesture had been carefully considered beforehand and gracefully performed on stage: nothing was left to chance. They did not play for 'points'; your satisfaction in one of their performances was that of seeing everything done exactly right".

—Daniel J. Watermeier

SQUARZINA, Luigi. Italian director and playwright. Born in Leghorn, Italy, 18 February 1922. Studied at law school, until 1945, and then trained for the theatre at the Academy of Dramatic Art, Rome. Married actress Zora Piazza in 1948. Assistant director, Teatro Nazionale, Teatro Valle, Rome, 1950–51; studied at the Yale Drama School, USA, 1951–52; subsequently won acclaim for productions of classics, operas and modern plays; artistic director, Teatro Stabile, Genoa, 1962–76; artistic director, Teatro Stabile, Rome, 1976–83; teacher in theatre studies, Dams University of Bologna.

Productions

1947	*Tutti miei figli* (Miller), Teatro Quirino, Rome.
1948	*Un Nemico del popolo* (Ibsen), Teatro Carignano, Turin.

	Pane attrui (Turgenev), Teatro Carignano, Turin.
1949	*Il Costruttore Solness* (Ibsen), Teatro Nuovo, Milan.
1950	*L'Oggetto* (Enrico), Rome.
1951	*Detective Story* (Kingsley), Teatro Valle, Rome.
	La Vedova scaltra (Goldoni), Teatro Nuovo, Milan.
1953	*Amleto* (Shakespeare), Teatro Valle, Rome.
	Tre quarti di luna (Squarzina), Teatro d'Arte, Rome.
	Tieste (Seneca), Teatro Valle, Rome.
	La Fuggitiva (Betti), International Festival, Venice.
	Il Profondo mare azzurro (Rattigan), Teatro Eliseo, Rome.
1954	*Prometeo incatenato* (Eschilo), Teatro Greco, Syracuse.
	È mezzanotte dottor Schweitzer (Cesbron), S. Miniato.
	Corte marziale per l'ammuntinamento del Caine (Wouk), Teatro Valle, Rome.
	Lorenzaccio (Musset), Teatro Valle, Rome.
1955	*La Scala* (San Secondo), International Festival, Venice.
	Il Potere e la gloria (Greene, adapted by Bost and Cannon), S. Miniato and Teatro Valle, Rome.
	Thè e simpatia (R. Anderson), Teatro Valle, Rome.
1956	*Un Cappello pieno di pioggia* (Gazo), Teatro Odeon, Milan.
1957	*Non è una cosa seria* (Pirandello), Rome.
	I Demoni (Fabbri, adapted from Dostoevsky), Teatro Stabile, Genoa.
	Le Donne a parlamento (Aristophanes), Teatro Romano, Renevento.
	La Figlia di Iorio (D'Annunzio), Vittoriale, Gardone.
	Tavole separate (Rattigan), Teatro Politeama, Genoa.
	Misura per misura (Shakespeare), Teatro Stabile, Genoa.
1958	*Serata di gala* (Zardi), Teatro Eliseo, Rome.
	JB (MacLeish), S. Miniato.
1959	*Romagnola* (Squarzina), Teatro d'Arte, Rome.
	Il Benessere (Brusati and Mauri), Teatro Valle, Rome.
	Il Grande statista (Eliot), S. Miniato.
	Il Misantropo (Menander), Teatro Olimpico, Vicenza.
	L'Hurluberlu (Anouilh), Teatro Stabile, Genoa.
1960	*La Congiura* (Prosperi), Piccolo Teatro, Milan.
	La Grande speranza (Rietmann), International Festival, Venice.
	Anna dei miracoli (Gibson), Teatro Odeon, Milan.
1961	*Uomo e superuomo* (G. B. Shaw), Teatro Stabile, Genoa.
	Ciascuno a suo modo (Pirandello), Teatro Carignano, Turin.

Other productions have included: *L'Uomo e il fucile* (Sollima), 1947; *Ifigenia in Tauride*, 1950; *Faust* (Goethe),

1950; *I due gemelli Veneziani* (Goldoni), 1963; *Il Tartufo ovvero vita amori auto-censura e morte in scena del Signor di Molière nostro contemporaneo*, 1970; *Questa sera si recita a soggetto* (Pirandello), 1972; *Cinque giorni al porto*, 1975; *Otto settembre*, 1975; *Rosa Luxemburg*, 1975; *Misura per Misura* (Shakespeare), 1976; *Una delle ultime sere di carnevale* (Goldoni), 1976; *I quattro rusteghi* (Goldoni), 1976; *La Casa nova* (Goldoni), 1976; *Volpone* (Jonson), 1977; *Le Celestina* (Sastre), 1979; *Timon of Athens* (Shakespeare), 1983; *Ciascuno a suo Modo* (Pirandello), 1984; *Romance Romance* (Harman), 1989; *Come prima meglio di prima* (Pirandello), 1990.

Publications

Gli indifferenti (play, adapted from Moravia's novel), 1948; *L'Esposizione universale* (play), 1949; *Tre quarti di luna* (play), 1953; *La sua parte di storia* (play), 1955; *Romagnola* (play), 1957; *Da Dionisio a Brecht*, 1988; *Questa sera Pirandello. Note di regia*, 1990.

*

Bibliography

Books:

T. Reggente, G. Conetti, E. Guagnini, C. Milaic and G. Polacco (eds.), *Il Teatro di Luigi Squarzina*, Trieste, 1962.

Claudio Meldolesi, *Fondamenti del teatro Italiano*, Florence, 1984.

* * *

Luigi Squarzina can rightly be considered one of Italy's leading contemporary directors, having consistently achieved high standards and infused the Italian theatre with renewed vigour. Squarzina's choice of plays reflects his inexorable search for freedom and his faithfulness to the text. He has frequently defined directing as "nothing more than a collection of footnotes, not a philosophical task", though he is also well-known as a commentator on the contemporary Italian stage and the direction he perceives it to be taking.

Squarzina's lasting contribution to the stage is probably in the field of his productions of contemporary and classical Italian plays (though he has also tackled Shakespeare with notable success and his production of *Timon of Athens*, for instance, was only the second such interpretation on the professional stage in Italian theatrical history). He made the first critical revival of D'Annunzio's *La Figlia di Iorio* and achieved imaginative versions of works by other non-contemporaries like Rosso de San Secondo during the postwar period. Critics have hailed his intelligent approach to the texts and in particular the sensitivity he has shown in orchestrating their realisation on stage so as to shed new light on their significance.

In 1961 he defiantly staged Pirandello's *Ciascuno a suo modo*, which had been banned in the Italian theatre for many years. His productions of his own plays, such as *Tre Quarti di luna*, have also been outstanding. During his period as co-director at the Teatro Stabile in Genoa, he presented many new works, including a series of document-plays that made a profound political statement. In that period he also carried out extensive research into Goldoni's theatre, achieving several significant innovative interpretations.

—Margaret Rose

———

STANISLAVSKY, Konstantin (Sergeivich). Russian actor, director, theorist, and teacher. Born Konstantin Sergeivich Alekseev in Moscow, 5 January 1863. Married actress Mariya Petrovna Perevoshchikova (née Lilina) in 1887. Began career as amateur actor, founding the amateur Alekseev Circle, 1877; co-founder, with A. F. Fedotov and Theodore Kommisarjevsky, Society of Art and Literature, Moscow, 1888; debut as director, 1889; co-founder, with Vladimir Nemirovich-Danchenko, of the Moscow Art Theatre, 1898; subsequently introduced hugely influential reforms in acting and opened the Art Theatre's First Studio, 1912, where he developed the Stanislavsky acting "System"; reorganised the Bolshoi Theatre's Opera Studio as the Opera Studio-Theatre (later renamed the Stanislavsky Opera Theatre and then the Moscow Music Theatre), 1918; led Moscow Art Theatre on tour of Europe and the USA, 1922–24; stepped down as the Moscow Art Theatre's leading actor due to ill health, 1928; founded Opera and Drama Studio, Moscow, 1935; ended career as teacher of drama. Recipient: Order of Lenin; Order of the Red Banner of Labour. People's Artist of the USSR, 1936. Died in Moscow, 7 August 1938.

Productions

As actor:

1888   The Baron in *Skupoy rystar* [The Covetous Knight] (Pushkin), Society of Art and Literature, Moscow.

Sotenville in *Georges Dandin* (Molière), Society of Art and Literature, Moscow.

Yakovlev in *A Bitter Fate* (Pisemski), Society of Art and Literature, Moscow.

1889   Don Carlos in *Kamenny gost* [The Stone Guest] (Pushkin), Society of Art and Literature, Moscow.

Don Juan in *Don Juan* (Molière), Society of Art and Literature, Moscow.

Baron Oberheim in *A Cup of Tea* (vaudeville), Society of Art and Literature, Moscow.

Obnovlensky in *The Rouble* (Fedotov), Society of Art and Literature, Moscow.

Krasnokutsky in *Burning Letters* (Pisemski), Society of Art and Literature, Moscow.

Baron von Aldringen in *A Debt of Honour* (Heyse), Society of Art and Literature, Moscow.

Ferdinand in *Kabale und Liebe* (Schiller), Society of Art and Literature, Moscow.

Imshin in *A Law Unto Themselves* (Pisemski), Society of Art and Literature, Moscow; Art Theatre, Moscow, 1898.

1890   Piotr in *Ne tak zhivi, kak khochetsya* [You Can't Just Live as You Please] (Ostrovsky), Society of Art and Literature, Moscow.

Samuel in *King Saul* (Mamontov), Society of Art and Literature, Moscow.

Laviraque in *Honour and Revenge* (Sollogub), Society of Art and Literature, Moscow.

Paratov in *Bespridannitsa* [The Girl Without a Dowry] (Ostrovsky), Society of Art and Literature, Moscow.

1891   Taliski in *Why There was Strife* (Krilov), Society of Art and Literature, Moscow.

Svesdinstsev in *Plody prosvescheniya* [The Fruits of Enlightenment] (L. Tolstoy), Society of Art and Literature, Moscow.

Rostanev in *Foma* (Dostoevsky, adapted by Stanislavsky), Society of Art and Literature, Moscow.

1892   Moréaque in *Anna de Quervilliere* (Legouvé), Society of Art and Literature, Moscow.

Bogusharov in *The Lucky Man* (Nemirovich-Danchenko), Society of Art and Literature, Moscow.

1893   Dulchin in *Poslednyaya zhertva* [The Last Sacrifice] (Ostrovsky), Society of Art and Literature, Moscow.

De Santos in *Uriel Acosta* (Gutzkow), Society of Art and Literature, Moscow.

1894   George Darci in *The Governor* (Dianchenko), Society of Art and Literature, Moscow.

Ashmetiov in *Dikarka* [The Wild Woman] (Ostrovsky and Solovyev), Society of Art and Literature, Moscow.

Agesander in *Aphrodite* (Krotkov and Mamontov), Society of Art and Literature, Moscow.

Rabachev in *Svetit, da ne greyet* [It Lights Up, But Doesn't Heat] (Ostrovsky and Soloviov), Society of Art and Literature, Moscow.

1895   Acosta in *Uriel Acosta* (Gutzkow), Society of Art and Literature, Moscow.

Smirnov in *Medved* [The Bear] (Chekhov), Society of Art and Literature, Moscow.

Police Officer in *Bankrut* [The Bankrupt] (Ostrovsky), Society of Art and Literature, Moscow.

1896   Othello in *Othello* (Shakespeare), Society of Art and Literature, Moscow.

Matthias in *The Polish Jew* (Erckmann-Chatrian), Society of Art and Literature, Moscow.

1897   Benedick in *Much Ado About Nothing* (Shakespeare), Society of Art and Literature, Moscow.

Morozov in *The Appointment*, Society of Art and Literature, Moscow.

Man with a Big Moustache in *Goryachee serdtse* [The Ardent Heart] (Ostrovsky), Society of Art and Literature, Moscow.

Malvolio in *Twelfth Night* (Shakespeare), Society of Art and Literature, Moscow.

1898   Heinrich in *Der versunken Glocke* (Hauptmann), Society of Art and Literature, Moscow, and Art Theatre, Moscow.

Ripafratta in *La Locandiera* (Goldoni), Art Theatre, Moscow; revived there, 1914.

Trigorin in *Chayka* [The Seagull] (Chekhov), Alexandrinsky Theatre, Moscow.

Konstantin Stanislavsky

1899   Lovborg in *Hedda Gabler* (Ibsen), Art Theatre, Moscow.

Tsar Ivan in *Smert Ioanna grotznogo* [The Death of Ivan the Terrible] (A. Tolstoy), Art Theatre, Moscow.

Astrov in *Dyadya Vanya* [Uncle Vanya] (Chekhov), Art Theatre, Moscow.

1900   Dr Stockmann in *En folkefiende* [An Enemy of the People] (Ibsen), Art Theatre, Moscow.

1901   Psaltery Player in *Tsar Fiodor Ioannovich* (A. Tolstoy), Art Theatre, Moscow.

Vershinin in *Tri sestry* [The Three Sisters] (Chekhov), Art Theatre, Moscow.

Kramer in *Michael Kramer* (Hauptmann), Art Theatre, Moscow.

Kostromsky in *In Dreams* (Nemirovich-Danchenko), Art Theatre, Moscow.

1902   Mitrish in *Vlast Tmy; ili, "Kogotok uvyaz, vsey ptishke propast"* [The Power of Darkness] (L. Tolstoy), Art Theatre, Moscow.

Satin in *Na dne* [The Lower Depths] (Gorky), Art Theatre, Moscow.

1903   Consul Bernick in *Samfundets støtten* [The Pillars of Society] (Ibsen), Art Theatre, Moscow.

Brutus in *Iulii Tsezar* [Julius Caesar] (Shakespeare), Art Theatre, Moscow.

1904   Gaev in *Vishnevy sad* [The Cherry Orchard] (Chekhov), Art Theatre, Moscow.

Shabelsky in *Ivanov* (Chekhov), Art Theatre, Moscow.

1906   Famusov in *Gore ot uma* [Woe from Wit] (Griboyedov), Art Theatre, Moscow.

1907   Kareno in *The Drama of Life* (Hamsun), Art Theatre, Moscow.

1909   Ratikin in *Mesyats v derevne* [A Month in the Country] (Turgenev), Art Theatre, Moscow.

1910   Krutitsky in *Na vsyakogo dovolno prostoty* [Even a Wise Man Stumbles] (Ostrovsky), Art Theatre, Moscow.

1912   Liubin in *Provintsialka* [A Provincial Lady] (Turgenev), Art Theatre, Moscow.

1913   Argan in *Le Malade Imaginaire* (Molière), Art Theatre, Moscow.

1915   Salieri in *Mozart i Salieri* [Mozart and Salieri] (Pushkin), Art Theatre, Moscow.

1922   Shuiski in *Tsar Fiodor Ioannovich* (A. Tolstoy), tour to Zagreb.

1924   Metropolitan in *Tsar Fiodor Ioannovich* (A. Tolstoy), US tour.

As director:
1889   *Burning Letters* (Pisemski), Society of Art and Literature, Moscow.

1891   *Plody prosvescheniya* [The Fruits of Enlightenment] (L. Tolstoy), Society of Art and Literature, Moscow.
        Foma (Dostoevsky, adapted by Stanislavsky), Society of Art and Literature, Moscow.

1894   *The Governor* (Diachenko), Society of Art and Literature, Moscow.
        Svetit, da ne greyet [It Lights Up, But Doesn't Heat] (Ostrovsky and Soloviov), Society of Art and Literature, Moscow.

1895   *Uriel Acosta* (Gutzkow), Society of Art and Literature, Moscow.
        A Law Unto Themselves (Pisemski), Society of Art and Literature, Moscow.

1896   *Othello* (Shakespeare), Society of Art and Literature, Moscow.
        The Polish Jew (Erckmann-Chatrian), Society of Art and Literature, Moscow.
        Bespridannitsa [The Girl Without a Dowry] (Ostrovsky), Society of Art and Literature, Moscow.

1897   *Much Ado About Nothing* (Shakespeare), Society of Art and Literature, Moscow.
        Twelfth Night (Shakespeare), Society of Art and Literature, Moscow.

1898   *Der versunken Glocke* (Hauptmann), Society of Art and Literature, Moscow, and Art Theatre, Moscow.
        Tsar Fedor Ioannovich (A. Tolstoy), Art Theatre, Moscow.
        The Merchant of Venice (Shakespeare), Art Theatre, Moscow.
        A Law Unto Themselves (Pisemski), Art Theatre, Moscow.
        La Locandiera (Goldoni), Art Theatre, Moscow.
        Chayka [The Seagull] (Chekhov), Art Theatre, Moscow.

1899   *Hedda Gabler* (Ibsen), Art Theatre, Moscow.

Smert Ioanna grotznogo [The Death of Ivan the Terrible] (A. Tolstoy), Art Theatre, Moscow.

Twelfth Night (Shakespeare), Art Theatre, Moscow.

Drayman Henschel (Hauptmann), Art Theatre, Moscow.

Dyadya Vanya [Uncle Vanya] (Chekhov), Art Theatre, Moscow.

Einsame Menschen (Hauptmann), Art Theatre, Moscow.

1900   *Snegurochka* [The Snow Maiden] (Ostrovsky), Art Theatre, Moscow.
        En folkefiende [An Enemy of the People] (Ibsen), Art Theatre, Moscow.

1901   *Tri sestry* [The Three Sisters] (Chekhov), Art Theatre, Moscow.
        Vildanden [The Wild Duck] (Ibsen), Art Theatre, Moscow.
        Michael Kramer (Hauptmann), Art Theatre, Moscow.
        In Dreams (Nemirovich-Danchenko), Art Theatre, Moscow.

1902   *Meschen* [Smug Citizens] (Gorky), Art Theatre, Moscow.
        Vlast Tmy; ili, "Kogotok uvyaz, vsey ptishke propast" [The Power of Darkness] (L. Tolstoy), Art Theatre, Moscow.
        Na dne [The Lower Depths] (Gorky), Art Theatre, Moscow.

1904   *Vishnevy sad* [The Cherry Orchard] (Chekhov), Art Theatre, Moscow.

1905   *Gengangere* [Ghosts] (Ibsen), Art Theatre, Moscow.
        Deti solntsa [Children of the Sun] (Gorky), Art Theatre, Moscow.

1906   *Gore ot uma* [Woe from Wit] (Griboyedov), Art Theatre, Moscow.

1907   *The Drama of Life* (Hamsun), Art Theatre, Moscow.
        Zhizn cheloveka [The Life of Man] (Andreyev), Art Theatre, Moscow.

1908   *L'Oiseau bleu* (Maeterlinck), Art Theatre, Moscow.
        Revizor [The Inspector General] (Gogol), Art Theatre, Moscow.

1909   *Mesyats v derevne* [A Month in the Country] (Turgenev), Art Theatre, Moscow.

1910   *Na vsyakogo dovolno prostoty* [Even a Wise Man May Stumble] (Ostrovsky), Art Theatre, Moscow.

1911   *Zhivoy trup* [The Living Corpse] (L. Tolstoy), Art Theatre, Moscow.
        Hamlet (Shakespeare), Art Theatre, Moscow.

1912   *Provintsialka* [A Provincial Lady] (Turgenev), Art Theatre, Moscow.

1913   *Le Malade Imaginaire* (Molière), Art Theatre, Moscow.

1914   *La Locandiera* (Goldoni), Art Theatre, Moscow.

1915   *Pir vo vremya chumy* [The Siege During the Plague] (Pushkin), Art Theatre, Moscow.
        Mozart i Salieri [Mozart and Salieri] (Pushkin), Art Theatre, Moscow.

1917	*Twelfth Night* (Shakespeare), Art Theatre, Moscow.
1920	*Cain* (Byron), Art Theatre, Moscow.
1921	*Rimsky-Korsakov Evening*, Art Theatre, Moscow.
	Pushkin Musical Evening, Art Theatre, Moscow.
	Werther (Massenet), Art Theatre, Moscow.
	Revizor [The Inspector General] (Gogol), Art Theatre, Moscow.
1922	*Evgeni Onegin* [Eugene Onegin] (Tchaikovsky), Opera Studio, Moscow.
1925	*Il Matrimonio Segreto* (Cimarosa), Art Theatre, Moscow.
1926	*Goryachee serdtse* [The Ardent Heart] (Ostrovsky), Art Theatre, Moscow.
	Nicholas I and the Decembrists (Kugel), Art Theatre, Moscow.
	Les Marchands de Gloire (Pagnol and Nivoix), Art Theatre, Moscow.
	Dni Turbinykh [The Days of the Turbins] (Bulgakov), Art Theatre, Moscow.
	The Tsar's Bride (Rimsky-Korsakov), Opera Studio, Moscow.
1927	*La Bohème* (Puccini), Opera Studio, Moscow.
	Le Mariage de Figaro (Beaumarchais), Art Theatre, Moscow.
	Les Soeurs Gérard (Ennery and Cormon), Opera Studio, Moscow.
	Bronepoezd 14—69 [Armoured Train 14—69] (Ivanov), Art Theatre, Moscow.
1928	*May Night* (Rimsky-Korsakov), Opera Studio, Moscow.
	Untilovsk (Leonov), Art Theatre, Moscow.
	Boris Godunov (Mussorgsky), Opera Studio, Moscow.
	The Embezzlers (Katayev), Art Theatre, Moscow.
1930	*The Queen of Spades* (Tchaikovsky), Opera Studio, Moscow.
1932	*The Golden Cockerel* (Tchaikovsky), Opera Studio, Moscow.
	Myortvye dushi [Dead Souls] (Gogol), Art Theatre, Moscow.
1933	*Talanty i poklonniki* [Artists and Admirers] (Ostrovsky), Art Theatre, Moscow.
	Il Barbiere di Seviglia (Rossini), Opera Studio, Moscow.
1935	*Carmen* (Bizet), Opera Studio, Moscow.
1936	*Molière* (Bulgakov), Art Theatre, Moscow.
	Don Pasquale (Donizetti), Opera Studio, Moscow.
1939	*Rigoletto* (Verdi), Opera Studio, Moscow.
	Tartuffe (Molière), Art Theatre, Moscow.

Publications

My Life in Art, 1924; *An Actor Prepares*, 1926; *Stanislavsky Rehearses Othello*, 1948; *Building a Character*, 1950; *Sobranie Sochinenii* [Collected Works], 8 vols., 1951–64; *Stanislavsky's Legacy*, edited and translated by Elizabeth Reynolds Hapgood, 1958.

*

Bibliography

Books:
N. Abalkin, *Das Stanislawski-System und das Sowjet Theater*, Berlin, 1953.
Nikolai M. Gorchakov, *Stanislavsky Directs*, New York, 1954.
Nina Gourfinkel, *Constantin Stanislavsky*, Paris, 1955.
Sonia Moore, *The Stanislavsky System*, New York, 1960.
Christine Edwards, *The Stanislavsky Heritage*, New York, 1965.
Jean Benedetti, *Stanislavsky: An Introduction*, London, 1982.
Mel Gordon, *The Stanislavsky Technique: Russia*, New York, 1987.
Jean Benedetti, *Stanislavsky — A Biography*, London, 1988.

* * *

Konstantin Stanislavsky was the second son of a wealthy industrialist and was acquainted with many of the stars of the Maly and Bolshoi theatres in his youth. His acting career began in 1877 at the theatre his father built at his country estate at Liubmovka, near Moscow. Right from the start the young performer kept a working notebook in which he analysed his own performances and artistic problems. Subsequently the Alekseev Circle that he formed and led for 10 years acquired a reputation for the high standards of its productions.

Adopting the stagename Stanislavsky in order to conceal from his parents his work with amateur groups of which they would not have approved, the young actor was substantially self-taught in stagecraft, relying upon his capacity to imitate the professionals. He took singing lessons and at one time considered a career in opera, but was then inspired by his work with the director Aleksandr Fedotov to found the Society of Art and Literature in 1888. Fedotov's methods transformed his acting. He also received lessons from Fedotov's estranged wife Glikeriya, who handed on what she herself had learned form Mikhail Shchepkin. At the Society, Stanislavsky created a series of brilliant and sometimes controversial productions that, despite his amateur status, put him in the forefront of his contemporaries. Many were convinced that he represented the hope for the future of Russian theatre. By 1890 he was convinced that there were laws that governed the art of acting just as there were laws that governed other aspects of life. He defined his problem as the truthful representation of life within the limitations imposed by the nature of the theatre itself.

In 1897 he collaborated with Nemirovich-Danchenko in founding the Moscow Art Theatre. During the first four or five years he and Nemirovich worked together successfully, notably in presenting the plays of Chekhov — both *The Three Sisters* and *The Cherry Orchard* were written for the company. Stanislavsky also directed Gorky's first two plays and Ibsen's *An Enemy of the People*, in which he played one of his favourite roles, Dr Stockman, and *Ghosts*.

By 1904 serious artistic differences were beginning to emerge between Nemirovich and Stanislavsky, who was looking for new methods. His collaboration with Meyerhold, for whom he created a studio at his own expense, merely served to widen the rift. Stanislavsky saw the actor's and the director's contribution to the creation of a performance in much broader, freer terms than Nemirovich, who insisted on the supremacy of the text. Stanislavsky saw no reason not, on occasion, to use an actor's improvised words if they made the dramatic point better than the author's original text.

In 1906 Stanislavsky, now an actor of great technical accomplishment, experienced an artistic crisis. He felt that his playing had become purely mechanical. He needed to find a process by which the personality of the actor became vitally engaged in the problems of the character. The result was a total re-examination of his work and the emergence of what came to be known as the System. Over the next two years he developed his ideas, to the bewilderment of many of his colleagues. As an actor he had previously worked from the outside in. Now he concentrated on psychological processes, on states of feeling and being, which he then found external equivalents for. Important at this period was his discovery of the theory of Affective Memory, developed by the French psychologist Théodule Ribot. According to Ribot, memories of all experiences are stored in the brain and can be evoked by an appropriate stimulus. Stanislavsky believed that by evoking personal experiences analogous to those felt by the character he could create a fusion between the actor's own personality and the fictional character he was portraying that would ensure continued vitality in performance. In 1908 he began rehearsals for Turgenev's *A Month in the Country* using his new method fully for the first time. The vocabulary of the system at that time was a mixture of terms drawn from many sources, including Gogol's writings and Yoga. The production vindicated the new method, which Stanislavsky then went on to apply to such classic plays as *Hamlet* and *Le Malade Imaginaire*. His experiments in this period form the basis for *An Actor Prepares*.

Problems of speech and diction he encountered as an actor in Pushkin's *Mozart and Salieri* and of movement as a director with Byron's *Cain* led him to concentrate more on the actor's physical equipment. This led to the definition of a psycho-technical technique that was later enshrined in *Building a Character*.

With the Revolution Stanislavsky lost his immense wealth and had to face the hostility that was demonstrated towards the Art Theatre as a relic of the bourgeois past. His former pupil and devoted admirer Meyerhold, however, was careful to distinguish Stanislavsky from the dead practices of the Art Theatre, describing him as "the Michelangelo of Theatre".

During 1922–24 Stanislavsky toured with the Art Theatre in Europe and the USA. His impact in the USA led first to the creation of the American Laboratory Theatre, headed by his former pupil Boleslavsky, which in turn led to the development of the Group Theatre and the Actors' Studio.

Stanislavsky's development as a director was governed by two major factors: the quality of the actors he had at his disposal and his own development as a performer. At the Society of Art and Literature he had only amateurs and semi-professionals to work with. In the early days of the Art Theatre most of the company were young artists only just out of theatre school. In order to achieve results, Stanislavsky was obliged to produce meticulous production plans, with detailed indications of moves, gestures, even physical attitudes. The cast were more or less drilled into the set pattern. Many of the effects, particularly the sound effects, were consciously introduced to help actors get into the mood of the scene or the play. Later, the definition of mood and atmosphere and the physical or psychological means of stimulating the actors into greater independence became the major concern during rehearsal. It was in this period that use was made of Emotion Memory. Stanislavsky saw two main phases in the rehearsal process, which was increasingly extended: a first phase in which the actors would explore the characters, followed by a second phase in which they would allow him to shape the raw material into an artistic form, a performance. By the 1930's, however, Stanislavsky had become suspicious of the use of Emotion Memory or what he called an assault on the unconscious. The result was all too often hysteria or severe psychological disturbance, since repressed memories once evoked could not always be controlled.

In the last phase of his work, Stanislavsky developed the Method of Physical Action on the principle that a sequence of actions, carried out with a well-defined purpose in mind, would lead naturally to a series of feelings and emotions. In this method the actor would first define the situation, the "problem" set by the dramatist in a particular scene, in his own person, so that his own interest was engaged. He would then use his own personal reactions as a basis for the character's behaviour. Greater and greater emphasis was laid on the actor's own responsibility for developing his performance and for developing his own methodology.

The Stanislavsky System suffered many distortions. First, it was proclaimed the official method of training under the Stalinist regime and was imposed at all theatre schools. It was codified into an inflexible dogma. Second, outside the USSR, the System has been confused with the "Method", as developed by Lee Strasberg for the Actors' Studio, on the basis of Boleslavsky's teaching. Strasberg was quite clear as to the differences between his own approach and Stanislavsky's Method of Physical Action as explained to him by Stella Adler. Emphasis in the West has always been on the psychological aspects of the System rather than on the fully rounded psycho-physical technique Stanislavsky developed.

—Jean Benedetti

———

STAPLETON, (Lois) Maureen. US actress. Born in Troy, New York, 21 June 1925. Trained for the stage at the Herbert Berghof Studio, New York. Married 1) Max Allentuck in 1949 (divorced 1959), one son and one daughter; 2) playwright David Rayfiel in 1963 (divorced). New York debut, 1946; first film appearance, 1959; particularly acclaimed in plays by Tennessee Williams and Shakespeare among others; has concentrated on film and television career since the mid-1980's. Recipient: Peabody Award, 1951; *Theatre World* Award, 1951; Tony Award, 1951, 1971; Emmy Award, 1967, 1968; National Institute of Arts and Letters Award, 1969; Drama Desk Award, 1971; *Variety* New York Drama Critics Poll Award, 1971; Oscar, 1982.

Roles

1946   Sara Tansey in *The Playboy of the Western World* (Synge), Booth Theatre, New York.

1947   Iras in *Antony and Cleopatra* (Shakespeare), Martin Beck Theatre, New York.

1949   Miss Hatch in *Detective Story* (Kingsley), Hudson Theatre, New York.

1950   Emily Williams in *The Bird Cage* (Laurents), Coronet Theatre, New York.

1951   Serafina in *The Rose Tattoo* (T. Williams), Martin Beck Theatre, New York; City Centre, New York, and Billy Rose Theatre, New York, 1966; Walnut Street Theatre, Philadelphia, 1973.

1953   Elisabeth Proctor in *The Crucible* (Miller), Martin Beck Theatre, New York.

Bella in *The Emperor's Clothes* (Tabori), Ethel Barrymore Theatre, New York.

Anne in *Richard III* (Shakespeare), City Centre, New York.

1954   Masha in *The Seagull* (Chekhov), Phoenix Theatre, New York.

1955   Flora in *27 Wagons Full of Cotton* (T. Williams), Playhouse Theatre, New York.

1957   Lady Torrance in *Orpheus Descending* (T. Williams), Martin Beck Theatre, New York.

1958   Aunt Ida in *The Cold Wind and Warm* (Behrman), Morosco Theatre, New York.

1960   Carrie in *Toys in the Attic* (Hellman), Hudson Theatre, New York.

1965   Amanda Wingfield in *The Glass Menagerie* (T. Williams), Brooks Atkinson Theatre, New York; Circle in the Square, New York, 1975.

1968   Karen Nash, Muriel Tate and Norma Hubley in *Plaza Suite* (Simon), Plymouth Theatre, New York.

1970   Beatrice Chambers in *Norman Is That You?*, Lyceum Theatre, New York.

Evy Meara in *The Gingerbread Lady* (Simon), Plymouth Theatre, New York.

1972   Georgie Elgin in *The Country Girl* (Odets), Billy Rose Theatre, New York.

Mildred Wild in *The Secret Affairs of Mildred Wild*, Ambassador Theatre, New York.

1974   Juno Boyle in *Juno and the Paycock* (O'Casey), Mark Taper Forum, Los Angeles.

1978   Fonsia Dorsey in *The Gin Game*, John Golden Theatre, New York.

1981   Birdie Hubbard in *The Little Foxes* (Hellman), Martin Beck Theatre, New York, and Ahmanson Theatre, Los Angeles.

Films

Lonelyhearts, 1959; *The Fugitive Kind*, 1960; *A View from the Bridge*, 1962; *Bye Bye Birdie*, 1963; *Trilogy*, 1969; *Airport*, 1969; *Plaza Suite*, 1970; *Interiors*, 1978; *The Runner Stumbles*, 1979; *Lost and Found*, 1980; *On the Right Track*, 1981; *Reds*, 1981; *The Fan*, 1981; *Johnny Dangerously*, 1984; *Cocoon*, 1985; *The Money Pit*, 1986; *Made in Heaven*, 1987.

Maureen Stapleton (1958).

Television

All the King's Men, 1958; *For Whom the Bell Tolls*, 1959; *Save Me a Place at Forest Lawn*, 1966; *Among the Paths to Eden*, 1967; *Mirror, Mirror, Off the Wall*, 1969; *Tell Me Where It Hurts*, 1974; *Queen of the Stardust Ballroom*, 1975; *Cat on a Hot Tin Roof*, 1976; *The Gathering*, 1977; *Little Gloria*, 1982; *Happy at Last*, 1982; *The Electric Grandmother*, 1982; *Mother's Day*, 1984; *Sentimental Journey*, 1984; *Private Sessions*, 1985.

* * *

Maureen Stapleton is a versatile stage, film and television character actress of the first magnitude. Overweight much of her career, at five feet four inches Stapleton has often been described as dowdy, dumpy and matronly. Yet her rather unremarkable appearance, which does not call attention to her as a star personality, has allowed her to assume a broad range of dramatic and comedic roles. In a career spanning more than 40 years she has played everything from Jews, Hungarians, Germans, gypsies and dissidents to women of her own Irish Catholic background. What makes this seemingly ordinary woman a remarkable presence in whatever she appears in is her distinctively strong but vulnerable characterizations and the warmth and naturalness of her acting.

Stapleton has some of the straight-talking, tough vulnerability of her favourite actress, Barbara Stanwyck; however, she does not have her emotional elusiveness. While she projects a gritty, down-to-earth no-nonsense quality in her many roles, it is to cover up a deep emotional sensibility. As she puts it, she has what is known as "leaky ducts". When she first began to study at the Actors' Studio, she had to work against a tendency to sink into facile emotionalism towards finding ways to cover up the character's pain. In her personal life Stapleton does constant battle with her own fears and phobias. She is notoriously afraid of flying, loud noises and first night audiences. Disorganised in life, she finds order and structure in the theatre.

Stapleton does little preparatory work in creating a role. She gradually evolves her character during rehearsal by locating the driving force at the centre of its personality and then creating inner subtext to motivate lines and behaviour. Stage business is an important aspect of her style. She is unusually adept at conveying the inner life of her characters through simple gestures and movement. Rarely does she appear on stage or camera with nothing to do. She washes, irons, prunes, tends, picks up, and a myriad of other activities. She even invests basic activities such as walking and sitting with tremendous nuance. Turn off the sound of the movie *Plaza Suite*, and Karen Nash's pain is all present in the orchestration of activity that Stapleton carries out. For example, Stapleton expresses her inner frustration in a struggle to take the plastic boots off her high heels. Then, when she accidentally pulls off a boot with its shoe, she engages in a lopsided walk around the set for the next 10 minutes, conveying the character's lack of inner stability. The activity, gesture and movement that Stapleton creates for her characters serves not only as a barometer of their inner state but as an attempt to mask their pain as well.

Like Karen Nash in *Plaza Suite*, many of Stapleton's characters project a kind of bone weariness and fragility that is counter-balanced by a tough as nails directness and determination. This blend of fragility coupled with a tremendous inner strength and depth has made Stapleton a powerful interpreter of Tennessee Williams's heroines. Williams recognized her unique abilities as a character actress when he cast her as Serafina Delle Rose in *The Rose Tattoo* when she was only 24. Although she was too young to play the middle-aged Italian widow, she achieved overnight stardom for her performance, which was hailed as a tour de force of passion and anguish. She went on to create several other Williams heroines on Broadway: Flora Meighan in *27 Wagons Full of Cotton*, Lady Torrance in *Orpheus Descending* (and its adaptation in the film version, *The Fugitive Kind*) and Amanda Wingfield in *The Glass Menagerie*. In addition, she performed in several television productions of Williams plays — the most notable being *Cat on a Hot Tin Roof*, in which she starred opposite Laurence Olivier. She has been called the American Magnani, because she portrayed roles in Williams plays written for Anna Magnani — Lady Torrance and Serafina. Williams became good friends with Stapleton, whom he called a "genius" and a "total innocent", and subsequently wrote three plays for her, though she never appeared in them.

Part of Stapleton's charm is that she is as refreshingly down to earth both in real life and in her work. In the face of tremendous success as an actress, she has remained steadfastly matter-of-fact about what her craft means to her and how she approaches it. Starry-eyed interviewers have been nonplussed by her statement that acting is "just a job", which she reluctantly does for the money, that she takes roles because "they pay", and that she would prefer not to work at all if she was financially able. To the question of what she would do with all her free time, she has replied without candour, "nothin' . . . just sit around". Stapleton admits to preferring the real life roles of wife, mother and grandmother to that of actress. While she achieved early success as a stage actress, she rapidly moved into film and television work because, she says, she found them less demanding and more lucrative. This no-nonsense attitude is perhaps the key to the secret of what makes Stapleton resonate with her audiences. Austin Pendleton sums it up nicely in his statement: "She has the gift of just being there . . . It's her absolute directness, no embroidery. She has a capacity to make the audience believe everything she says".

—Kathryn Wylie-Marques

STEIN, Peter. German director. Born in Berlin, 1937. Educated at Bad Homburg, near Frankfurt, until 1956; University of Munich, 1956–64. Assistant director and dramaturg, Munich Kammerspiele, from 1964; debut as director, 1967; director, Schaubühne am Halleschen Ufer, Berlin, since 1970, producing both classical and contemporary plays; supervised transfer of Schaubühne to larger theatre in Berlin, 1981.

Productions

1967   *Gerettet* (Bond, adapted by Sperr), Kammerspiele, Munich.
        Kabale und Liebe (Schiller), Theater Bremen.
1968   *Im Dickicht der Städte* (Brecht), Kammerspiele, Munich.
        Viet Nam Diskurs (Weiss), Kammerspiele, Munich.
1969   *Torquato Tasso* (Goethe), Theater Bremen.
        Early Morning (Bond), Schauspielhaus, Zurich.
        Kikeriki (O'Casey), Schauspielhaus, Zurich.
1970   *The Changeling* (Middleton and Rowley), Schauspielhaus, Zurich.
        Die Mutter (Brecht), Schaubühne am Halleschen Ufer, Berlin.
1971   *Das Verhör von Habana* (Hans-Magnus), Schaubühne am Halleschen Ufer, Berlin.
        Die Auseinandersetzung (Kelling), Schaubühne am Halleschen Ufer, Berlin.
        Peer Gynt (Ibsen), Schaubühne am Halleschen Ufer, Berlin.
1972   *Optimistische Tragödie* (Vishnevsky), Schaubühne am Halleschen Ufer, Berlin.
        Prinz Friedrich von Homburg (Kleist), Schaubühne am Halleschen Ufer, Berlin.
        Fegefeuer in Ingolstadt (Fleisser), Schaubühne am Halleschen Ufer, Berlin.
1973   *Das Sparschwein* (Labiche), Schaubühne am Halleschen Ufer, Berlin.
1974   *Antikenprojekt I*, Schaubühne am Halleschen Ufer, Berlin.

1974	*Die Unvernünftigen sterben aus* (Handke), Schaubühne am Halleschen Ufer, Berlin.
	Sommergäste (Gorky), Schaubühne am Halleschen Ufer, Berlin.
1976	*Shakespeare's Memory*, Schaubühne am Halleschen Ufer, Berlin.
	Das Rheingold (Wagner), Opéra, Paris.
1977	*Wie es euch gefällt* (Shakespeare), Schaubühne am Halleschen Ufer, Berlin.
1978	*Trilogie des Wiedersehens* (Strauss), Schaubühne am Halleschen Ufer, Berlin.
	Gross und klein (Strauss), Schaubühne am Halleschen Ufer, Berlin.
1980	*The Oresteia* (Aeschylus), Schaubühne am Halleschen Ufer, Berlin.
1981	*Class Enemy* (N. Williams), Schaubühne am Halleschen Ufer, Berlin.
	Nicht Fisch nicht Fleisch (Kroetz), Schaubühne am Halleschen Ufer, Berlin.
1983	*The Blacks* (Genet), Schaubühne am Halleschen Ufer, Berlin.
1984	*The Three Sisters* (Chekhov), Schaubühne am Halleschen Ufer, Berlin.
	The Park (Strauss), Schaubühne am Halleschen Ufer, Berlin.
1986	*The Hairy Ape* (O'Neill), Schaubühne am Halleschen Ufer, Berlin.
1989	*The Cherry Orchard* (Chekhov), Schaubühne am Halleschen Ufer, Berlin.
	Titus Andronicus (Shakespeare), Rome.

*

Bibliography

Books:

Peter Iden, *Die Schaubühne am Halleschen Ufer, 1970–79*, Munich, 1979.

Michael Patterson, *Peter Stein: Germany's Leading Theatre Director*, Cambridge, 1981.

Articles:

Peter Lackner, "Peter Stein's Path to Shakespeare", *The Drama Review*, 21, 1977.

Jack Zipes, "The Irresistible Rise of the Schaubühne am Halleschen Ufer", *Theater*, 9, 1977.

* * *

Peter Stein achieved a significant following early in his career and is now recognized as one of the most important German directors since Brecht. His work is extremely precise, emotionally controlled and visually compelling, yet he evokes almost fanatical dedication from actors and extraordinary ensemble performances. Though he is a Marxist, he has never been content with Brecht's tendency to convey the world in simple dialectical terms; he is also a product of the capitalist "miracle" of postwar West Germany, and sees that underlying social issues of the dizzying present cannot always be rendered in the theatre as conflicting opposites.

Stein had only brief experience in the theatre when he abandoned his doctoral studies and became an assistant at the Munich Kammerspiele, one of the most consistently adventurous German theatres of the century, where he was strongly influenced by the great actor and director Fritz Kortner. Stein's initial directing opportunities there, in Bremen, and in Zurich set an important pattern: he selected a combination of English plays, of political plays, and of the German classics, presenting them all with clarity and equal political commitment. His first production, an adaptation of Edward Bond's *Saved*, translated into Bavarian dialect and set in a blue-collar district of Munich, was chosen by the influential magazine *Theater Heute* as the best German production of 1967.

This period culminated with a remarkable version of Goethe's *Torquato Tasso* in 1969, in which Stein pointed a way for theatre in the Federal Republic to adapt Brecht's social goals and yet break loose from a mere imitation of the performance style of the Berliner Ensemble. Though the play is a classic in Germany, Stein frankly appropriated it for the present, adapting, rearranging and deconstructing the text so that Goethe's finely structured drama was split open to reveal the social forces operating behind it. Wilfred Minks's setting — a sickly green nylon carpet, plexiglas panels closing off the space on three sides and a plexiglas border at the edge of the apron — made the stage claustrophobic and contemporary. A bust of Goethe, sitting directly on the carpet, was a constant reminder that the performance operated at a distance from Goethe's moral universe, just as Goethe's play operates at a distance from Tasso's. The acting, especially that of Bruno Ganz as Tasso, proceeded from Brecht's notion of the performers "quoting" the characters rather than identifying with them, and suggested a critical attitude not only to the classic status of the text, but also to the "myth of bourgeois individualism" it promotes.

Stein's concern with the structure of society extends into the structure of theatre organisations, and he was given a rare opportunity to establish a new type of company by the government of West Berlin when he was invited to bring his company to the Schaubühne am Halleschen Ufer in 1970; ironically, the extremely high subsidy offered was the result of a policy intended to make Berlin a cultural showplace in the midst of the hostile communist territory of East Germany. In direct opposition to the tradition of dictatorial German theatre management, Stein and his actors created a completely democratic structure. Though subsequent experience has forced modifications to the initial organisation, the Schaubühne has remained a successful participatory collective, like the Théâtre du Soleil. Many of the original members of the ensemble have remained — including the actors Edith Clever, Bruno Ganz, Michael Köning and Jutta Lampe, the dramaturg Dieter Sturm, the designer Karl-Ernst Herrmann, and the costumer designer Moidele Bickel — often doing their best work in collaboration with Stein.

Stein's first production of international note at the new theatre was *Peer Gynt* in 1971, which developed the Marxist approach to the classics indicated in *Tasso*. Performed over two evenings in an environmental set by Herrmann, it further attacked the Romantic ideal of the exceptional man, chiefly by dividing the role of Peer among six actors and stressing how the social and economic environment conditioned the character. A different method was established for a two-year experiment with Shakespeare, though it was also based on historicist principles. The first segment of this work was an unprecedented two-part production in 1976 called *Shakespeare's Money* (the title was given in English) at a film studio in Spandau, which was an amalgamation of dramatic and non-dramatic texts relevant to the Elizabethan period. Performed for a promenade audience, often with two or more events occurring simultaneously, the object was to prepare the ensemble and its audience for a Shakespeare play by recreating some of the material held in the playwright's "memory". The next year *As You Like It* was offered, in the same location and using some of the same physical constructions. The scenes at the court, performed before a standing audience, took place in a narrow hall with brilliant white walls; then the spectators were escorted to a second location, an environmental vision of the Forest of Arden, both beautiful and artificial, where they were often reminded that ideal nature is a dream of the city-dweller, at best a temporary respite from the concerns of society left behind. At the end, the brightly lit court could again be seen through open doors as the characters began their journey home.

Though the excellence of Stein's direction is not dependent on lavish expenditure, it is worth noting that the Schaubühne receives a subsidy that is enormous by British or US standards, and this has permitted work on an adventurous scale. A new period in Stein's career began in 1981, when the Schaubühne transferred operations to Lehniner Platz in the heart of the entertainment district of West Berlin. The new building, a 1927 cinema converted at great expense by the city government, signalled the distinctive success of the theatre as well as its growing participation in mainstream culture. Stein has not abandoned his social orientation, but the fervent revolutionary spirit of the early years has altered as times have changed and he and his original audience have aged. His later work has tended to a more generalized critique of western materialism, as seen in his productions of Chekhov and of Botho Strauss. Recently Stein has given up his administrative position at the theatre to concentrate more completely on artistic matters.

—Dennis Kennedy

STRANITZKY, Josef Anton. Austrian actor and playwright. Born in Graz, Austria, c.1676. Worked from around 1699 as itinerant marionettist and actor in Augsburg, Munich and Nuremberg and probably led company in Monaco before moving to Vienna in 1705; qualified as a dentist from the University of Vienna, 1707; also acted in Vienna with Johann Baptist Hilverding and cofounded the Teutschen Komödianten company with him, 1706; subsequently became famous as creator of the comedy role of Hans Wurst in numerous entertainments and took over the Kärntnertortheater, Vienna, 1711, where he remained for the remainder of his career. Died in Vienna, 1726.

*

Bibliography

Books:

Rudolf Payer von Thurn, *Stranitzky und die Anfänge der Wiener Hanswurst Komödie*, Vienna, 1917.

Nikolaus Britz, *J. A. Stranitzky und Wien*, Vienna and Heidelberg, 1968.

* * *

Josef Anton Stranitsky was the first itinerant actor in the German-speaking world to settle permanently in an urban theatre. Prior to receiving permission to act in Vienna in 1706, he had spent some years travelling in Austria and Bavaria with Johann Baptist Hilverding, with whom he acted and performed marionette plays. Stranitszky and Hilverding found it difficult to establish their company, the "Teutschen Komödianten", in Vienna. Although they had permission to act they were expelled from their first primitive theatres in the Neuer Markt and, later, the Ballhaus in der Teinfaltstrasse due to the complaints of local residents. No doubt, Stranitzky frequently had to depend on his skills as a tooth-drawer to make ends meet. By 1711, however, popular enthusiasm for his acting was so great that the Viennese refused to attend performances given at the newly-opened Kärntnertortheater by the Italian players who performed under Imperial patronage, so that Stranitzky would be granted use of the theatre. The strategy succeeded, and for the next 15 years, until his death in 1726, Stranitzky enjoyed a popular following unprecedented anywhere in central Europe.

It is hard to overestimate Stranitzky's importance to Viennese theatre in particular and German theatre in general. As there were few large cities in Austria and Germany, theatre companies could not find a public big enough to provide audiences throughout the year. Only extremely wealthy aristocrats and royal rulers could afford to maintain regular troupes of players and these were invariably of French or Italian provenance. Stranitzky's victory over the Imperial Italian players was therefore a significant triumph for the nascent German theatre.

Both as actor and playwright, Stranitzky provided the basis for what is possibly the most vigorous local theatrical tradition in the history of modern Europe, a tradition that reached its apogee in the work of Johann Nepomuck Nestroy, well over a century after Stranitzky's death. Stranitzky was most celebrated for creating the generic role of Hans Wurst (literally, "John Sausage"), a comic peasant who spoke in Salzburg dialect and appeared in several of the most popular plays on the Kärntnertortheater stage. Historians have often considered Hans Wurst to be a figure in which were combined the major traits of Harlequin from the commedia dell'arte and comic figures initially associated with the English Comedians, such as Pickelherring. However, Stranitzky may well have relied less on established models, more on his own observation. He did not wear a mask, which would have given the character an unwonted realism. Hans Wurst was noted for the earthy realism of his language, for his wiliness, and for the dogged manner in which he managed to withstand whoever opposed him, however grand their social status. Stranitzky's Hans Wurst stood, therefore, for the common man and, throughout the 18th century, the figure he created would be seen on the popular stages of German-speaking Europe. The tall, conical green hat worn by the character became a widely acknowledged comic symbol.

As an actor, Stranitzky was noted for his powers of improvisation, cultivated during his years as an itinerant player, when improvisation was the norm. In Vienna, however, he needed to create a repertoire that would provide his constant audience with a variety of entertainment, and he developed into a prolific playwright. He adapted several Italian opera libretti, highlighting melodramatic situation and incorporating comedy. His theatre was intensely physical and events that were related in arias in the original operas were afforded vivid, often exaggerated realisation on the stage. He wrote plays on the Amphitryon, Faust and Don Juan themes and several Haupt-und Staatsaktionen, dramas of an epic structure that had their origins in the repertoire of the English Comedians of the early 17th century. These scripts, which allow for generous passages of improvisation, are notable for the way in which the high drama of political life, articulated with pompous rhetoric and rant, is counterpointed with a comic action that is often violent, scabrous and obscene. Indeed, obscenity may have been among the major appeals of Stranitzky's work. It certainly offended that great correspondent Lady Mary Wortley Montagu, who attended a performance at the Kärntnertortheater in 1716. In a letter to Alexander Pope, she claims that she had never laughed so much in her life. Nevertheless, she also found much to which she took exception: "I could not easily pardon the Liberty the Poet has taken of Larding his play with not only indecent expressions, but such grosse Words as I don't think our Mob would suffer from a Mountebank, and the two Sosias very fairly let down their breeches in the direct view of the Boxes, which were full of the first Rank that seem'd very well pleased with their Entertainment, and they assur'd me this was a celebrated Piece".

Lady Mary recommended that Mr Collier should take note of this theatre. Although persons of a like-minded seriousness would later attempt to quench the fire of Viennese popular theatre, for Stranitzky's lifetime the theatre enjoyed an exhilarating freedom.

—Simon Williams

STRASBERG, Lee. US director, actor and teacher. Born Israel Strassberg in Budanov, Galicia, Austria-Hungary, 17 November 1901. Emigrated to USA, 1909; trained for the theatre under Richard Boleslavsky and Maria Ouspenskaya at the American Laboratory Theatre, New York. Married 1) Nora Z. Krecaun in 1926 (died 1929); 2) Paula Miller in 1934 (died 1966); 3) Anna Mizrahi in 1968; three sons and one daughter. Assistant stage manager, Garrick Theatre, from 1924; acting debut in New York, Garrick Theatre, 1925; also worked extensively with the Theatre Guild, New York; co-founder and director, Group Theatre, New York, 1931–37; artistic director, Actors' Studio, New York, from 1951; formulated the Method system from the acting theories of Stanislavsky, 1950's; founded Lee Strasberg Institute of Theatre, New York and Hollywood, California, 1969. Died in New York, 17 February 1982.

Productions

As director:

1931   *The House of Connelly* (Green), Martin Beck Theatre, New York.
1931 (Sifton), Mansfield Theatre, New York.

1932   *Night Over Taos* (Anderson), 48th Street Theatre, New York.
Success Story (Lawson), Maxine Elliot Theatre, New York.

1933   *Hilda Cassidy*, Group Theatre, New York.
Men in White (Kingsley), Broadhurst Theatre, New York.

1934   *Gentlewoman* (Lawson), Cort Theatre, New York.
Gold Eagle Guy (Levy), Morosco Theatre, New York.

1936   *The Case of Clyde Griffith* (Piscator and Goldschmidt, adapted from Dreiser's *An American Tragedy*), Ethel Barrymore Theatre, New York.
Johnny Johnson (Green), 44th Street Theatre, New York.

1937   *Many Mansions* (Godman), Group Theatre, New York.

1938   *Roosty* (Berkeley), Group Theatre, New York.
All the Living (Allbright, adapted from Small), Group Theatre, New York.
Dance Night (Nicholson), Group Theatre, New York.

1939   *Summer Night* (Baum and Glazer), Group Theatre, New York.

1940   *The Fifth Column* (Glazer and Hemingway), Group Theatre, New York.

1941   *Clash by Night* (Odets), Belasco Theatre, New York.

1942   *RUR* (Čapek), New York.

1943   *Apology*, New York.
South Pacific (Rigsby and Heyward), New York.

1948   *Skipper Next to God* (Hartog), New York.

1949   *The Big Knife* (Odets), National Theatre, New York.
The Closing Door (Knox), New York.

1951   *Peer Gynt* (Ibsen, adapted by Green), ANTA Playhouse, New York.

1964   *The Three Sisters* (Chekhov), Actors' Studio, New York; Aldwych Theatre, London, 1965.

1966   *The Country Girl* (Odets), New York.

1972   *Felix*, Actors' Studio, New York.
The Silent Partner (Odets), Actors' Studio, New York.
Siamese Connections, Actors' Studio, New York.
The Masque of St George and the Dragon, Actors' Studio, New York.

1973   *Virility*, Actors' Studio, New York.
Othello (Shakespeare), Actors' Studio, New York.
The Effect of Gamma Rays on Man-in-the-Moon Marigolds (Zindel), Actors' Studio, New York.
A Break in the Skin, Actors' Studio, New York.
Long Day's Journey into Night (O'Neill), Actors' Studio, New York.
The Masque of St George and the Dragon, Actors' Studio, New York.

1974   *People of the Shadows*, Actors' Studio, New York.
American Night Cry, Actors' Studio, New York.

O Glorious Tintinnabulation, Actors' Studio, New York.

Other roles included: *Processional* (Lawson), Garrick Theatre, New York, 1925; *The Garrick Gaieties* (Rodgers and Hart), Garrick Theatre, New York, 1925; *Goat Song* (Werfel), Garrick Theatre, New York, 1926; *The Chief Thing* (Evreinov), Garrick Theatre, New York, 1926; *Four Walls* (Abbott and Burnet), John Golden Theatre, New York, 1927; *Red Dust* (Fleming), Martin Beck Theatre, New York, 1929; *The Garrick Gaieties* (Rodgers and Hart), Garrick Theatre, New York, 1930; *Green Grow the Lilacs* (Riggs), Garrick Theatre, New York, 1931.

Films

As actor:
The Godfather II, 1974; *The Cassandra Crossing*, 1977; *Boardwalk*, 1979; *And Justice for All*, 1979; *Going in Style*, 1979; *And Justice for All*, 1980.

Television

The Last Tenant, 1981; *Skokie*, 1981.

Publications

Famous American Plays of the 1950's, 1963; *A Dream of Passion: The Development of the Method*, 1982.

*

Bibliography

Books:

Harold Clurman, *The Fervent Years: The Group Theatre and the Thirties*, New York, 1945.
Robert H. Hethmon (ed.), *Strasberg at the Actors' Studio*, New York, 1965.
Cindy Adams, *Lee Strasberg: The Imperfect Genius of the Actors' Studio*, New York, 1980.
Wendy Smith, *Real Life Drama: The Group Theatre and America, 1931-40*, New York, 1990.

* * *

Lee Strasberg defined the problem of creation for the actor as "the problem of starting the inspiration". As a teacher of acting and director therefore, Strasberg's task was to "contrive an impulse" from the actor as well as to keep this impulse fresh during the repetitions of the rehearsal process. Strasberg stated that "the central thing that Stanislavsky discovered, and to a certain extent defined and set exercises for, was that the actor can be helped really to think on the stage, instead of thinking only in make-believe fashion. Once the actor begins to think, life starts, and then there cannot be imitation". Thus Strasberg emphasized the importance of the sense of truth for the actor and at the same time suggested, in the manner of Stanislavsky, that the source of this truth is the actor's own self, that is the combination of his or her own personal intellectual and emotional world.

In 1923, Strasberg was greatly impressed by the performances of the Moscow Art Theatre in New York. Yet his first official introduction to Konstantin Stanislavsky's ideas was later, during his studies at the American Laboratory Theatre under Richard Boleslavsky and Maria Ouspenskaya, both students of Stanislavsky's and former members of the Moscow Art Theatre. Also very influential on Strasberg was Vakhtangov's essay "Preparing a Role", in which it is argued that reality in acting means that the actor must live his or her own "temperament on the stage and not the temperament of the character".

With the creation of the Group Theatre out of the Theatre Guild in 1931 — Harold Clurman and Cheryl Crawford together with Strasberg were its co-founders — Strasberg put into practice his own version of Stanislavsky's ideas. He trained the actors of the Group Theatre — among whom were Morris Carnovsky, Stella Adler, Phoebe Brand, Clifford Odets, Stanford Meisner and Elia Kazan — according to his method and directed them in such successful productions as Paul Green's *The House of Connelly*, Maxwell Anderson's *Night over Taos* and Sidney Kingsley's *Men in White*. In his training system, which followed the ensemble approach of Stanislavsky's Moscow Art Theatre, Strasberg stressed in particular the importance of "affective memory" in the actor's creation of "true emotion". Thus the memories and personal experiences of the actor were used as psychoanalytic tools in order for the actor to identify with the character and ultimately to "become" the character on stage instead of simply acting out this character. According to Strasberg, this process entails the employment of "the unconscious or subconscious knowledge that we have, the experiences that we have stored away but which we cannot easily or quickly put our hand on by means of the conscious mind". The goal of getting in touch with one's subconscious was reached in training and rehearsal through exercises and improvisations that Strasberg organized for the actors. These exercises were based on the creation of scenes with situations similar to the emotional background and relationships within the play that the actors rehearsed. In these situations, however, the actors had to recall their personal memories from their past, and thus find analogies between their own original experience and the predicament of the characters they portrayed.

In 1934, Stella Adler, a member of the Group Theatre, visited Stanislavsky in Paris. On her return to New York, she informed other members of the Group that Stanislavsky did not approve of the emphasis that the Group, under Strasberg's direction, put on the emotional memory exercises. At that time, Stanislavsky had set aside his "affective memory" approach in order to experiment with new ideas. In Adler's words, Stanislavsky told her that perhaps the Group Theatre did not use the system properly. Instead of the actor's inner experience and personal memories, imagination and the study of the text should be the major components in the creation of what Stanislavsky called the "magic if".

Strasberg's emphasis on what would personally motivate the actors to express themselves in a situation analogous to the one described in the play should shift, Adler argued, to what the actors imagined they would do if they were the characters within the circumstances of the play. According to Adler, truth and style "must derive from the content of the play — not from mood or feeling ... If you go to your own memories, you create your own play, not the author's". At first, Strasberg's reaction to Adler's report was negative. He stated that "Stanislavsky had gone back on himself" and that the Group Theatre should not be uncritical followers of Stanislavsky but adhere to their own American adaptation of his system. In spite of his initial reaction, however, Strasberg later suggested some modifications to his training system based on Adler's interpretation of Stanislavsky's new approach. But his relationships with the majority of the Group Theatre members had already been stigmatized by the conflicts on the application of Stanislavsky's system and in 1937 he resigned from the company.

In 1947, Elia Kazan founded in New York the Actors' Studio, a workshop for professional actors. At Kazan's suggestion, Strasberg became its artistic director in 1951 and, in the following decade, he directed for the Actors' Studio Theatre a controversial production of Chekhov's *The Three Sisters*. Strasberg's work at the Studio was the high point of his reputation as the most famous acting teacher in the USA. He carried over the legacy of "The Method", as a unique idea of systematic training for the actor and as an alternative to the practices of the commercial theatre, from the Group Theatre to the Actors' Studio. Strasberg's influence on American acting both on stage and on film has been significant. Among the great number of actors who trained with him at the Studio were Marlon Brando, James Dean, Marilyn Monroe, Montgomery Clift, Shelley Winters, Paul Newman, Dustin Hoffman, Robert de Niro, Meryl Streep, Al Pacino and Ellen Burstyn. And when, in 1975, Strasberg applied his Method to himself, he won an Oscar nomination for his acting in Coppola's *Godfather II*.

Lee Strasberg's own version of Stanislavsky's acting system and his approach to discovering an actor's deepest emotion have been both praised and criticised. Perhaps his own words are the best description of his unique contribution to US theatre: "The Method, which seems even more confused than politics, is merely the sum total of the experience of the great actors throughout all ages and countries. The best things in it come from Stanislavsky. The rest come from me".

—Kiki Gounaridou

STREHLER, Giorgio. Italian director and actor. Born in Barcola, Trieste, 14 August 1921. Educated at the University of Milan and at the Geneva Conservatory; trained for the theatre at the Accademia dei Filodrammatici, Milan, until 1940. Married 1) Rosita Lupi; 2) Andrea Jonasson in 1981. Began career as an actor with various companies in Milan, 1940–43; military service, 1943–45; director, Companie des Masques, Geneva, 1943–45; co-founder, with Paolo Grassi, and director, Piccolo Teatro, Milan, 1947–68; debut as opera director, 1947; led politically-motivated Gruppo Teatro e Azione, 1968–71; art director, Salzburg Festival, 1971; director, La Scala, Milan, 1972; returned to Piccolo Teatro as director, 1972; also co-founded and directed Théâtre de l'Europe, Paris, 1982–90; founder, Scuola di Teatro, Milan, 1986, and of the Unione Teatri D'Europa, Paris, 1989; resigned from Piccolo Teatro and announced retirement from the theatre in the wake of

allegations of financial mismanagement of EC funding. Entered European parliament, 1982; senator, Republic of Italy, from 1987. President: Jury of Cannes Film Festival, 1982; Union of Theatres of Europe, 1992. Recipient (selected): Goethe Prize, 1972; Premio Internazionale Pirandello, 1973; Max Reinhardt Award (Salzburg), 1973; French Critics' Prize, 1979; International Theatre Critics' Award, 1985; Piscator Prize (USA), 1987; Goethe Medal (Germany), 1988; Simoni Prize, 1988. Honorary degrees: University of Rome, 1973; University of Salerno, 1983; University of Toronto, 1989. Grand Cross of Merit (Germany), 1974; Cavalier, Grand Cross (Italy), 1982; Commander, Légion d'Honneur (France), 1982; Grand Officer, Ordre des Arts et Lettres (France).

Productions

1943	*L'Uomo dal fiore in bocca, All'uscita* and *Sogno, ma forse no* (Pirandello), Casa Littoria, Novara.
	Un Cielo (Gaudioso), Casa Littoria, Novara.
	Il Cammino (Joppolo), Casa Littoria, Novara.
1943–44	*L'Imbecille, L'Uomo dal fiore in bocca* and *La Patente* (Pirandello), Camp de Murren, Switzerland.
1945	*Meurtre dans la cathédrale* (Eliot), Théâtre de la Comédie, Geneva.
	Caligula (Camus), Théâtre de la Comédie, Geneva.
	Unsere kleine stadt (Wilder), Théâtre de la Comédie, Geneva.
	Il Lutto si addice ad Elettra (O'Neill), Teatro Odeon, Milan.
1946	*Caligola* (Camus), Teatro della Pergola, Florence.
	Giovanna d'Arco al rogo (Honegger), Teatro Lirico, Milan.
	Teresa Raquin (Zola), Teatro Odeon, Milan.
	Desiderio sotto gli olmi (O'Neill), Teatro Odeon, Milan.
	Una Donna libera (Salacrou), Teatro Odeon, Milan.
	Sotto i ponti di New York (M. Anderson), Teatro Odeon, Milan.
	La Guerra spiegata ai poveri (Flaiano), Teatro Excelsior, Milan.
	La Rivolta contro i poveri (Buzzati), Teatro Excelsior, Milan.
	Piccoli Borghese (Gorky), Teatro Excelsior, Milan.
	Pick-Up Girl (Shelley), Teatro Nuovo, Milan.
1947	*La Traviata* (Verdi), Teatro alla Scala, Milan.
	Il Soldato Tanaka (Kaiser), Teatro Olimpia, Milan.
	L'Albergo dei poveri (Gorky), Piccolo Teatro, Milan.
	Le Notti dell'ira (Salacrou), Piccolo Teatro, Milan.
	Il Mago dei prodigi (Calderón), Piccolo Teatro, Milan.
	Il Servitore di due padroni (Goldoni), Piccolo Teatro, Milan.

I Giganti della montagna (Pirandello), Piccolo Teatro, Milan.

L'Uragano (Ostrovsky), Piccolo Teatro, Milan.

L'Amore delle tre melarance (Prokofiev), Teatro alla Scala, Milan.

1948   *Delitto e castigo* (Baty), Piccolo Teatro, Milan.

Riccardo II (Shakespeare), Piccolo Teatro, Milan.

La Tempesta (Shakespeare), Boboli Gardens, Florence.

Romeo e Giulietta (Shakespeare), Teatro Romano, Verona.

Assassinio nella cattedrale (Eliot), Chiesa di San Francesco, San Miniato.

Il Corvo (Gozzi), Teatro La Fenice, Venice.

Il Gabbiano (Chekhov), Piccolo Teatro, Milan.

La Famiglia Antropus (Wilder), Piccolo Teatro, Milan.

1949   *La Bisbetica domata* (Shakespeare), Piccolo Teatro, Milan.

Il Matrimonio segreto (Cimarosa), Teatro alla Scala, Milan.

Pelleas et Melisande (Debussy), Teatro alla Scala, Milan.

Gente nel tempo (Chiesa), Piccolo Teatro, Milan.

Il Cordovano (Petrassi), Teatro alla Scala, Milan.

Lulu (Berg), Teatro La Fenice, Venice.

Die Riesen vom Berge (Pirandello), Schauspielhaus, Zurich.

Questa sera si recita a soggetto (Pirandello), Théâtre de Champs-Élysées, Paris.

Il Piccolo Eyolf (Ibsen), Piccolo Teatro, Milan.

1950   *La Parigina* (Becque), Piccolo Teatro, Milan.

Riccardo III (Shakespeare), Piccolo Teatro, Milan.

Don Juan (Molière), Schauspielhaus, Zurich.

I Giusti (Camus), Piccolo Teatro, Milan.

L'Allegra brigata (Malipiero), Teatro alla Scala, Milan.

Don Pasquale (Donizetti), Teatro alla Scala, Milan.

Arianna a Nasso (Strauss), Teatro alla Scala, Milan.

Alcesti di Samuele (Savinio), Piccolo Teatro, Milan.

Il Nazzareno (Perosi), Teatro alla Scala, Milan.

La Putta onorata (Goldoni), Campo San Trovaso, Venice.

Sofonisba (Trissino), Teatro Olimpico, Vicenza.

Gli Innamorati (Goldoni), Teatro Sciale, Lecco.

Estate e fumo (T. Williams), Piccolo Teatro, Milan.

Il Misantropo (Molière), Teatro Sociale, Lecco.

La Morte di Danton (Büchner), Piccolo Teatro, Milan.

1951   *Casa di Bambola* (Ibsen), Teatro Donizetti, Bergamo.

La Cecchina o La Buona Figliuola (Piccini), Teatro alla Scala, Milan.

L'Elisir d'amore (Donizetti), Teatro alla Scala, Milan.

L'Oro matto (Giovaninetti), Teatro alla Scala, Milan.

Werther (Massenet), Teatro alla Scala, Milan.

Non Giurare su niente (Musset), Piccolo Teatro, Milan.

Frana allo scalo nord (Betti), Piccolo Teatro, Milan.

La Collina (Peragallo), Teatro alla Scala, Milan.

Don Juan (Molière), Freie Volksbühne, Berlin.

Giuditta (Honegger), Teatro alla Scala, Milan.

Re Enrico IV (Shakespeare), Teatro Romano, Verona.

La Dodicesima notte (Shakespeare), Palazzo Grassi, Venice.

Elettra (Sophocles), Teatro Olimpico, Vicenza.

L'Amante militaire (Goldoni), Piccolo Teatro, Milan.

Il Medico volante (Molière), Piccolo Teatro, Milan.

Opla', noi vivamo (Toller), Piccolo Teatro, Milan.

Il Credulo (Cimarosa), Teatro alla Scala, Milan.

1952   *Macbeth* (Shakespeare), Piccolo Teatro, Milan.

Emma (Zardi), Piccolo Teatro, Milan.

Proserpina e lo straniero (Castro), Teatro alla Scala, Milan.

Arlecchino servitore di due padroni (Goldoni), Teatro Quirino, Rome.

Il Cammino sulle acque (Vergani), Teatro La Fenice, Venice.

La Favola del figlio cambiato (Malipiero), Teatro La Fenice, Venice.

Elisabetta d'Inghilterra (Bruckner), Piccolo Teatro, Milan.

Il Revisore (Gogol), Piccolo Teatro, Milan.

1953   *L'Ingranaggio* (Sartre), Piccolo Teatro, Milan.

Sacrilegio massimo (Pirandello), Piccolo Teatro, Milan.

Sei personaggi in cerca d'autore (Pirandello), Théâtre Marigny, Paris.

Lulu (Bertolazzi), Piccolo Teatro, Milan.

Un Caso clinico (Buzzati), Piccolo Teatro, Milan.

La Vedova scaltra (Goldoni), Teatro La Fenice, Venice.

Giulio Cesare (Shakespeare), Piccolo Teatro, Milan.

La Sei giorni (D'Errico), Piccolo Teatro, Milan.

1954   *Il Corvo* (Gozzi), Piccolo Teatro, Milan.

L'Imbecille, La Patente and *La Giara* (Pirandello), Piccolo Teatro, Milan.

La Folle de Chaillot (Giraudoux), Piccolo Teatro, Milan.

La Mascherata (Moravia), Piccolo Teatro, Milan.

La Moglie ideale (Praga), Piccolo Teatro, Milan.

Nostra dea (Bontempelli), Teatro Odeon, Buenos Aires.

La Trilogia della Villegiatura (Goldoni), Piccolo Teatro, Milan.

1955   *Il Giordino dei ciliegi* (Chekhov), Piccolo Teatro, Milan.

La Casa di Bernarda Alba (Lorca), Piccolo Teatro, Milan.

La Linea di condotta (Brecht), Sala Azzurra di Corso Magenta, Milan.

Tre Quarti di luna (Squarzina), Piccolo Teatro, Milan.

L'Angelo di fuoco (Prokofiev), Teatro La Fenice, Venice.

El Nost Milan (Bertolazzi), Piccolo Teatro, Milan.

Il Matrimonio segreto (Cimarosa), Piccola Scala, Milan.

1956   *L'Opera da tre soldi* (Brecht), Piccolo Teatro, Milan.

Dal tuo al mio (Verga), Piccolo Teatro, Milan.

Arlecchino servitore di due padroni (Goldini), Royal Lyceum Theatre, Edinburgh.

Questa sera si recita a soggetto (Pirandello), Royal Lyceum Theatre, Edinburgh.

L'Angelo di fuoco (Prokofiev), Teatro alla Scala, Milan.

1957   *I Giacobini* (Zardi), Piccolo Teatro, Milan.

Luisa (Charpentier), Teatro alla Scala, Milan.

Histoire du soldat (Stravinsky), Piccola Scala, Milan.

Coriolano (Shakespeare), Piccolo Teatro, Milan.

Goldoni e le sue sedici commedie nuove (Ferrari), Piccolo Teatro, Milan.

1958   *L'Anima buona di Sezuan* (Brecht), Piccolo Teatro, Milan.

Die Riesen vom Berge (Pirandello), Schauspielhaus, Düsseldorf.

Un Cappello di paglia di Firenze (Rota), Piccola Scala, Milan.

1959   *Platonov e altri* (Chekhov), Piccolo Teatro, Milan.

Histoire du soldat (Stravinsky), Teatro La Cometa, Rome.

1960   *La Visita del vecchia signora* (Dürrenmatt), Piccolo Teatro, Milan.

L'Egoista (Bertalozzi), Piccolo Teatro, Milan.

1961   *Schweyk nella seconda guerra mondiale* (Brecht), Piccolo Teatro, Milan.

1962   *L'Eccezione e la regola* (Brecht), Piccolo Teatro, Milan.

Ricordo di due lunedi (Miller), Piccolo Teatro, Milan.

1963   *Vita di Galileo* (Brecht), Piccolo Teatro, Milan.

Pierino e il lupo (Prokofiev), Teatro alla Scala, Milan.

Arlecchino servitore di due padroni (Goldoni), Villa Litta ad Affori, Milan.

1964   *Ascesa e caduta della citta' di Mahagonny* (Brecht and Weill), Piccola Scala, Milan.

Le Notti dell'ira (Salacrou), Piccolo Teatro, Milan.

Le Baruffe chiozzotte (Goldoni), Teatro Lirico, Milan.

Sul Caso J. Robert Oppenheimer (Kipphardt), Piccolo Teatro, Milan.

1965   *Bertolt Brecht, poesie e canzoni* (Brecht and Weill), Piccolo Teatro, Milan.

Die Entführung aus dem serail (Mozart), Kleines Festspielhaus, Salzburg.

Il Gioco dei potenti (Strehler, adapted from Shakespeare), Teatro Lirico, Milan.

1966   *Duecentomila e uno* (Cappelli), Piccolo Teatro, Milan.

Cavalleria Rusticana (Mascagni), Teatro alla Scala, Milan.

I Giganti della montagna (Pirandello), Teatro Lirico, Milan.

1967   *Io, Bertolt Brecht* (Brecht, Weill and Eisler), Piccolo Teatro, Milan.

1969   *Il Ratto dal serraglio* (Mozart), Teatro della Pergola, Florence.

Fidelio (Beethoven), Teatro Comunale, Florence.

1970   *Cantata di un mostro lusitano* (Weiss), Teatro Quirino, Rome.

Santa Giovanna dei Macelli (Brecht), Teatro della Pergola, Florence.

Nel Fondo (Gorky), Teatro Metastasio, Prato.

1971   *Referendum per l'assoluzione o la condanna di un criminale di guerra (Walter Reder)* (Pallavicini and Vené), Teatro Manzoni, Pistoia.

Simon Boccanegra (Verdi), Teatro alla Scala, Milan.

1972   *Il Ratto dal serraglio* (Mozart), Teatro alla Scala, Milan.

Re Lear (Shakespeare), Piccolo Teatro, Milan.

1973   *L'Opera da tre soldi* (Brecht and Weill), Teatro Metastasio, Prato.

Le Noces de Figaro (Mozart), Teatrino di Corte, Versailles.

La Condanna di Lucullo (Brecht and Dessau), Teatro Lirico, Milan.

Das Spiel der Mächtigen (Strehler, adapted from Shakespeare), Felsenreitschule, Salzburg.

1974   *Il Giardino del ciliegi* (Chekhov), Piccolo Teatro, Milan.

Die Zauberflöte (Mozart), Grosse Festspielhaus, Salzburg.

L'Amore delle tre melarance (Prokofiev), Teatro alla Scala, Milan.

Die Trilogie der sommerfrische (Goldoni), Burgtheater, Vienna.

1975   *Io, Bertolt Brecht* (Brecht, Weill and Eisler), Piccolo Teatro, Milan.

Il Campiello (Goldoni), Piccolo Teatro, Milan.

Arlecchino servitore di due padroni (Goldoni), Arena Romana, Padua.

Das Spiel der Mächtigen (Strehler, adapted from Shakespeare), Burgtheater, Vienna.

Macbeth (Verdi), Teatro alla Scala, Milan.

1976   *Le Balcon* (Genet), Piccolo Teatro, Milan.

La Storia della bambola abbandonata (Strehler, adapted from Sastre and Brecht), Piccola Scala, Milan.

1977   *Der Gute Mensch von Sezuan* (Brecht), Schauspielhaus, Hamburg.

Arlecchino servitore di due padroni (Goldoni), Théâtre de l'Odéon, Paris.

1978   *La Tempesta* (Shakespeare), Teatro Lirico, Milan.

La Trilogie de la villegiature (Goldoni), Théâtre de l'Odéon, Paris.

1979   *Io, Bertolt Brecht*, Piccolo Teatro, Milan.
El Nost Milan (Bertolazzi), Teatro Lirico, Milan.

1980   *Temporale* (Strindberg), Piccolo Teatro, Milan.
Falstaff (Verdi), Teatro alla Scala, Milan.

1981   *L'Anima buona di Sezuan* (Brecht), Piccolo Teatro, Milan.
Le Nozze di Figaro (Mozart), Teatro alla Scala, Milan.
Lohengrin (Wagner), Teatro alla Scala, Milan.

1982   *Atto senza parole fra Felici Giorni* (Beckett), Piccolo Teatro, Milan.
L'Anima buona di Sezuan (Brecht), Piccolo Teatro, Paris.

1983   *Minna von Barnhelm* (Lessing), Piccolo Teatro, Paris.
La Tempesta (Shakespeare), Théâtre de l'Europe, Paris.

1984   *Minna von Barnhelm* (Lessing), Théâtre de l'Europe, Paris.
L'Illusion (Corneille), Théâtre de l'Europe, Paris.
Arlecchino servitore di due padroni (Goldoni), Olympic Festival of Arts, Los Angeles.

1985   *La Grande Magia* (De Filippo), Piccolo Teatro, Milan.
Temporale (Strindberg), Théâtre de l'Europe, Paris.

1986   *Elvira o la passione teatrale*, Teatro d'Europa, Milan.
L'Opera da tre soldi (Brecht and Weill), Théâtre de l'Europe, Paris.

1988   *Frammenti del Faust parte 1* (Goethe), Teatro d'Europa, Milan.

1990   *Frammenti del Faust parte 2* (Goethe), Teatro d'Europa, Milan.

Other productions included: *Il Giardino dei ciliegi* (Chekhov); *Il Campiello* (Goldoni); *Le Balcon* (Genet); *Come tu mi vuoi* (Pirandello); all since 1980.

Television

Nel Fondo (Gorky), 1971.

Publications

Re Lear, 1973; *Per un teatro umano*, 1974; *Santa Giovanna*, 1974; *Shakespeare, Goldoni, Brecht*, 1984.

*

Bibliography

Books:
Ettore Gaipa, *Giorgio Strehler*, Berlin, 1959.
Eberhard Fechner, *Giorgio Strehler insziniert*, Hanover, 1963.
Fabio Battistini, *Giorgio Strehler*, Rome, 1980.
Odette Aslan, *Strehler*, Paris, 1989.
David L. Hirst, *Giorgio Strehler*, Cambridge, 1993.

*   *   *

Giorgio Strehler, one of the pre-eminent directors of the 20th century, is a celebrated interpreter of Shakespeare, Mozart, Goldoni and especially Brecht. He is also the protean creator of over 200 play and opera productions of notable beauty and intelligence. Founding director from 1947 of Italy's leading art theatre, the Piccolo Teatro of Milan, Strehler established the highly regarded Théâtre de l'Europe of Paris in 1983 as a cultural meeting ground for the most innovative work of theatre companies throughout Europe.

In his landmark productions at the Piccolo, Milan's La Scala, the Paris Opéra, the Théâtre de l'Europe and the Salzburg Festival, Strehler restored an almost lost Italian theatre patrimony to the world scene. He revived the commedia dell'arte as vigorous contemporary technique, most notably through his classic production of Goldoni's *A Servant of Two Masters*, whose five distinct editions (1947, 1952, 1956, 1963 and 1975) have played in every major theatre centre of the world. He led a movement to recover opera as political statement with such highly influential productions as Verdi's *Simon Boccanera* (1971) and Mozart's *The Marriage of Figaro* (1973) that stressed political power and class struggle. And with his designers Luciano Damiani and Ezio Frigerio, Strehler created almost magical stage images that reasserted Italianate scenic illusion as expressive form. Strehler's restoration of Italian theatre to international prominence is comparable to similar achievements by Stanislavsky in Russia and Max Reinhardt in Germany.

Strehler's cosmopolitan background — he was raised in Trieste in a musical family that gave him French, German and Italian as native tongues — has strongly coloured his style. In everything he does there is an Italian flair for earthy improvisation, a French love of reason and language and a vigorous German dedication to theatre as a moral institution. In the best sense, Strehler is an old-fashioned director, an autocratic perfectionist who acknowledges Copeau, Jouvet and Brecht as his great teachers. From Copeau's example, Strehler derives his sense of theatre as a way of life, as well as a reverence for text, which is the cornerstone of his anti-auteur directing style. Jouvet, with whom Strehler studied, reinforced Copeau's lessons through the neoclassical acting techniques that underlie the vivid precision of Strehler's work. From Brecht, who befriended Strehler and called him "the greatest director in Europe", Strehler acquired both a practical model for social commitment and the epic theatre's dialectical process that would animate his productions through an interplay of opposing ideas. In Strehler's theatre, death is made vivid by the struggle for life, light lives in the shadow it casts and powerful feeling is evoked by stillness. From Brecht as well came a distinctive human attitude — at once detached and engaged, serious yet irreverent — with which Strehler's theatre confronts a world it hopes to improve.

Strehler's work is justly famous for its poetic clarity that reveals new and often poignantly beautiful facets of familiar work without distorting the original. In 1956, for example, Brecht was struck by how poetic a production Strehler made of his *The Threepenny Opera*, not by prettifying its sordid milieu, but by shaping grotesque images that suggested contemporary parallels. Similarly, the spare historicity of Strehler's unsentimental approach to Mozart's *The Marriage of Figaro* (1973) or his dreamily minimalist *The Cherry Orchard* (1974) that replaced Chekhov's mysterious sound of a broken string with absolute silence, seemed to spring from deep sources within the text rather than from intrusive directorial invention. The transparency of Strehler's style is also seen in vibrant lighting that evokes the metaphysical through intensity and rhythm, in highly selective alternations between the specificity of colour and the elegant universality of monochrome, and in a sophisticated use of music, including meticulous tuning of actors' voices to the inherent tonal meanings of specific vowels and consonants. Strehler's style evokes the calm lucidity of classicism as a means of bringing to focus the turbulent energies of the modern world.

Theatre itself is the latent subject of every Strehler production, one that lends an elegiac note to even his brightest work. The transitory beauty of theatre, its powers to reveal or transform identity, as well as its ability to deceive, preoccupies Strehler and illuminates his most memorable stagings, including successive versions of Pirandello's *Six Characters in Search of an Author* (1943, 1952) and *The Giants of the Mountain* (1947, 1958 and 1966) that probed the paradoxes of theatre's fragile strength; Shakespeare's *The Tempest* (1977), whose Prospero reflected Strehler's own concerns about the ambiguous uses of his art; Corneille's *The Illusion* (1984) that gorgeously celebrated theatre's ability to transcend bourgeois constraint; De Filippo's *The Great Magic Act* (1986), which cast a rueful look at the power of love's illusions; and finally a metatheatrical staging of Goethe's *Faust*, with Strehler himself in the title role. This vast project, presented as "fragments", was produced over several years and was clearly intended by Strehler to summarize his own spiritual and intellectual history as a scholarly illusionist, and to pay tribute to the similar history of an emerging European cultural identity his theatres have helped to foster.

Strehler's relative lack of celebrity in the English-speaking world results from his qualified interest in touring his work beyond the Continent. "I am naturally European", he often explains. Then too, unlike his more famous contemporaries Peter Brook and Ingmar Bergman, Strehler chooses not to write the books or make the films that would cause his work to be more widely known. By temperament and principle, Strehler chooses to define himself exclusively as a "bete de scène", whose entire art is written in the ephemeral theatre event.

—Richard Trousdell

SUZMAN, Janet. British actress and director. Born in Johannesburg, South Africa, 9 February 1939. Educated at Kingsmead College, Johannesburg; University of the Witwatersrand, South Africa, until 1959; trained for the stage at the London Academy of Music and Dramatic Art, 1959–62. Married director Trevor Nunn (*q.v.*) in 1969 (divorced 1986), one son. Stage debut, Tower Theatre, Ipswich, 1962; London debut, 1962; actress, subsequently associate artist, Royal Shakespeare Company, from 1962;

visiting professor in drama, Westfield College, University of London, 1983–84; debut as director, 1988. Member: Arts Council drama panel, 1975–77; Council of the London Academy of Music and Dramatic Art, from 1978 (vice-chairman, from 1992); trustee, Theatres Trust, London, 1986–87. Recipient: *Evening Standard* Award, 1974, 1976; *Plays and Players* Award, 1976. MA: Open University, 1984; D.Litt: University of Warwick, 1990; University of Leicester, 1992.

Productions

As actress:

| 1962 | Liz in *Billy Liar* (Waterhouse and Hall), Tower Theatre, Ipswich. |

Viola in *Twelfth Night* (Shakespeare), Library Theatre, Manchester.

Luciana in *The Comedy of Errors* (Shakespeare), Aldwych Theatre, London.

1963   Iris in *The Tempest* (Shakespeare), Royal Shakespeare Theatre, Stratford-upon-Avon.

Joan la Pucelle in *The Wars of the Roses* (Shakespeare compilation), Royal Shakespeare Theatre, Stratford-upon-Avon, and Aldwych Theatre, London.

Lady Anne in *Richard III* (Shakespeare), Royal Shakespeare Theatre, Stratford-upon-Avon, and Aldwych Theatre, London.

1964   Lady Percy in *Henry IV, parts 1 and 2* (Shakespeare), Royal Shakespeare Theatre, Stratford-upon-Avon, and Aldwych Theatre, London.

Lulu in *The Birthday Party* (Pinter), Aldwych Theatre, London.

1965   Rosaline in *Love's Labour's Lost* (Shakespeare), Royal Shakespeare Theatre, Stratford-upon-Avon, and Aldwych Theatre, London.

Portia in *The Merchant of Venice* (Shakespeare), Royal Shakespeare Theatre, Stratford-upon-Avon, and Aldwych Theatre, London.

Ophelia in *Hamlet* (Shakespeare), Royal Shakespeare Theatre, Stratford-upon-Avon, and Aldwych Theatre, London.

1966   Kate Hardcastle in *She Stoops to Conquer* (Goldsmith), Playhouse Theatre, Oxford.

Carmen in *The Balcony* (Genet), Playhouse Theatre, Oxford.

1967   Katharina in *The Taming of the Shrew* (Shakespeare), Royal Shakespeare Theatre, Stratford-upon-Avon, and Aldwych Theatre, London; Ahmanson Theatre, Los Angeles, 1968.

Celia in *As You Like It* (Shakespeare), Royal Shakespeare Theatre, Stratford-upon-Avon, and Aldwych Theatre, London.

Berinthia in *The Relapse* (Vanbrugh), Aldwych Theatre, London.

1968–69   Beatrice in *Much Ado About Nothing* (Shakespeare), Royal Shakespeare Theatre, Stratford-upon-Avon, Aldwych Theatre, London, and US tour.

Rosalind in *As You Like It* (Shakespeare), Royal Shakespeare Theatre, Stratford-upon-Avon, and Aldwych Theatre, London.

1970   Roles in *Pleasure and Repentance* (Hands), Edinburgh Festival.

1972–73   Cleopatra in *Antony and Cleopatra* (Shakespeare), Royal Shakespeare Theatre, Stratford-upon-Avon, and Aldwych Theatre, London.

Lavinia in *Titus Andronicus* (Shakespeare), Royal Shakespeare Theatre, Stratford-upon-Avon, and Aldwych Theatre, London.

Hester in *Hello and Goodbye* (Fugard), King's Head Theatre, Islington, London, and The Place, London.

1975   Bessie in *The Death of Bessie Smith* (Albee), Market Theatre, Johannesburg.

1976   Masha in *The Three Sisters* (Chekhov), Cambridge Theatre, London.

1977   Hedda in *Hedda Gabler* (Ibsen), Duke of York's Theatre, London, and Edinburgh Festival.

Shen Te in *The Good Woman of Setzuan* (Brecht), Royal Court Theatre, London.

1978   The Duchess in *The Duchess of Malfi* (Webster), Alexandra Theatre, Birmingham.

Minerva in *Boo Hoo* (Magdalaney), Open Space Theatre, London.

1980   Clytemnestra and Helen of Troy in *The Greeks* (Euripides, adapted by Barton), Aldwych Theatre, London.

1984   Lena in *Boesman and Lena* (Fugard), Hampstead Theatre, London.

1985   Vassa in *Vassa Zheleznova* (Gorky), Greenwich Theatre, London.

1988   Andromache in *Andromache* (Racine), Old Vic Theatre, London.

1989   Belle in *Another Time* (Harwood), Wyndham's Theatre, London.

1991   Phaidra in *Hippolytos* (Euripides), Almeida Theatre, London.

Other roles included: *Irregular Verb to Love* (Williams and Williams), Theatre Royal, Windsor, 1962; *Druids' Circle* (Van Druten), Repertory Theatre, Worthing, 1962; *Cowardice* (Beolco), Ambassadors' Theatre, London, 1983; *The Sisters Rosensweig* (Wasserstein), Greenwich Theatre, London, 1994.

As director:

1987   *Othello* (Shakespeare), Market Theatre, Johannesburg.

1990   *A Dream of People* (Hastings), The Pit, London.

The Provoked Wife (Vanbrugh), London Academy of Music and Dramatic Art, London.

1991   *The Cruel Grasp*, Edinburgh Festival.

1992   *No Flies on Mr Hunter*, Chelsea Centre, London.

1993   *Death of a Salesman* (Miller), Theatr Clwyd, Mold.

Janet Suzman (1974).

Films

Nicholas and Alexandra, 1971; *A Day in the Death of Joe Egg*, 1971; *The Black Windmill*, 1973; *Nijinsky*, 1978; *The House on Garibaldi Street*, 1979; *The Priest of Love*, 1981; *E la Nave Va*, 1983; *The Draughtsman's Contract*, 1983; *A Dry White Season*, 1989; *Nuns on the Run*, 1990; *Leon the Pig Farmer*, 1993.

Television

As actress:
Lord Raingo, 1965; *The Family Reunion*, 1966; *The Battle of Hastings*, 1966; *Saint Joan*, 1968; *The Three Sisters*, 1969; *Macbeth*, 1970; *Hedda Gabler*, 1972; *Twelfth Night*, 1973; *Antony and Cleopatra*, 1974; *Miss Nightingale*, 1975; *Clayhanger* (series), 1975–76; *Solo*, 1977; *Bright Smiler*, 1983; *The Zany Adventures of Robin Hood*, 1983; *Mountbatten, The Last Viceroy*, 1984; *The Singing Detective*, 1986; *The Miser*, 1987; *Revolutionary Witness*, 1989; *Acting Masterclass*, 1990; *Cleopatra*, 1990.

As director:
Othello, 1988; *Cripples*, 1989; *The Amazon*, 1989; *Shakespeare Masterclass*, 1990.

* * *

"Finished" in Switzerland before studying at Witwatersrand University in Johannesburg for a degree in English and French, Janet Suzman clearly hails from a privileged, highly-educated White South African background. That background also contains a powerful strain of oppositional politics, focused principally upon human rights and anti-Apartheid issues; a strain that has clearly shaped both Suzman's own consciousness and her professional approach as actress and director. Leaving South Africa in 1960, after the Sharpeville massacre, Suzman decamped to England, to drama school; nonetheless she kept up strong links with her homeland — a founder-member of the multiracial Market Theatre in Johannesburg, she returned there in 1987 to direct Bantu actor John Kani in *Othello*, a declared "political act" in a society where institutionalized racism was still officially sanctioned. For Suzman, theatre and politics of this kind are inseparable.

Maintaining a personal involvement in human rights issues such as the plight of Soviet Jewry, Suzman has channelled a level of politics into her own theatrical work. Overtly, as in *Othello*, which she videotaped for overseas transmission and dissemination in South African schools, she also filmed and narrated a documentary on the Crossroads squatters' camp (1978), banned in South Africa, and performed in Athol Fugard's plays, notably *Hello and Goodbye*, for which she won the *Evening Standard* Best Actress Award (1974). In 1989 she appeared in Black director Euzhan Palcy's *A Dry White Season* ironically playing the kind of right-winger she has consistently opposed.

But there is a strong sense in which Suzman's impassioned liberalism underpins the rest of her work, in her approach to characterisation. Joining the Royal Shakespeare Company in 1963 after solid repertory experience, her work has embraced a repertoire ranging from Shakespeare, Shaw, and Genet to Chekhov, Restoration Comedy, and the Greeks. On television she was a tigerish Hedda Gabler; a notably myth-debunking Florence Nightingale; a strong and independent Hilda Lessways in the 26-part adaptation of Arnold Bennett's *Clayhanger* novels; and a mysterious, ambivalent wife to Philip Marlow in Dennis Potter's *The Singing Detective*. Less visible on film, she has nonetheless continued to offer complex portrayals of women: as the vulnerable yet enduring mother of a severely handicapped child in *A Day in the Death of Joe Egg*, a role echoed on the grand scale in *Nicholas and Alexandra* as the doomed Tzarina, mother to the haemophiliac Romanov heir, and as the blinkered wife to Donald Sutherland's slowly-awakening radical in *A Dry White Season*.

Throughout her performance work there has been a common thread. Suzman women are always multidimensional: rounded, complicated, women, even where the script itself offers little or ambiguous information, as in the Potter, where her character is seen principally through Marlow's diseased fantasies. Such multidimensionality embraces not only the positive aspects of these women — their courage, passionate vitality, and emotional richness — but also their negative qualities: a capacity for cruelty, physical/mental/emotional potential destructiveness, and a contrasting capacity for emotional repression. Her women may sometimes be poorly educated characters, but are never unintelligent; an especial hallmark is Suzman's ability to convey a character's active intellect — her women think, and are seen to do so. That is not to say they are always wise, or judicious in their actions; they are more often victims, sometimes of a recalcitrant inability to accept prevailing social mores, sometimes of their own natural boldness; often, of their own wild natures, but chiefly, of an unjust and intolerable definition of woman's social role. Her women reek of frustrated potential, combative to a degree.

Notable examples are her portrayals of Cleopatra in *Antony and Cleopatra*, her doubling of Helen and Clytemnestra in John Barton's *The Greeks*, and Masha in Jonathan Miller's production of Chekhov's *The Three Sisters*. Her Cleopatra was a deliberate antithesis to the idealised Roman matron Octavia; alternately subtle and brash, forthright, and deceitful, a glorious forbidden fruit, emotionally unfettered by hidebound convention. Masha, on the other hand, was completely bound by stultifying bourgeois morality, yet was still as volcanically passionate in feeling — a Russian variant on Hedda, without her capacity for ultimate self-destruction. In *The Greeks*, inner violence was turned outward in Clytemnestra, a born leader deprived of power by dint of gender, responding to injury in the martial idiom of her male counterparts; in Helen, sister to Clytemnestra, that violence resurfaced amid arrogant sexuality.

Technically, Suzman achieves her effects through a strong, expressive face, fine-boned and mobile, and a flexible, husky voice of considerable tonal richness, resonance, and clarity. Body language and movement convey a wealth of non-verbal information: perhaps a reason for her less successful Andromache in the augural Old Vic production (1988), where the static Racinian staging offered no such scope. She also brings rigorous intellectual scrutiny to texts, in which she invests ultimate authority — a tendency deriving, she says, from her work with the RSC's John Barton. Such fidelity to the text also underpins her work as a director. Her interpretation of *Othello* married both her political and professional concerns, but final authority for all decisions resided in Shakespeare's text. Casting a Black Othello against a White Iago embodied for her a complete metaphor of South Africa, but was clearly authorized textually. An extra dimension was added by the difficulty imposed on John Kani by the demands of the verse — not by rhyme and metre, but because he is a native speaker of Xhosa, not English.

This production, Suzman's debut, revealed her as a director of promise, but it is to be hoped that her abilities in this field do not lead her to abandon performance.

—Val Taylor

SVOBODA, Josef. Czech designer and architect. Born in Čáslav, Czechoslovakia, 10 May 1920. Trained as architect at the Special School for Interior Architecture, Prague; School of Fine and Applied Arts, Prague, until 1945. Married Libuše Hrubešová in 1948, one daughter. Debut as designer, 1943; designer, National Theatre, Prague, 1947; head designer, National Theatre, Prague, from 1951; collaborated with Alfred Radok on development of multimedia Polyekran and Laterna Magika projects, 1958; won acclaim at the World Theatre Season, London, 1965; has also worked in Belgium, France, Italy, Germany, the Soviet Union, the USA, Canada and elsewhere; artistic director, Laterna Magika company (subsequently merged with the National Theatre), based at the Theatre Behind the Gate,

Prague, from 1973; chief designer, National Theatre, Prague, from 1992. Professor, Academy of Applied Arts, 1968. Member: International Organisation of Scenographers and Theatre Technicians, 1971 (general secretary). Recipient: State Prize, 1954; Order of Labour, 1963; Honoured Artist, 1966; Art Biennale Sao Paulo Best Stage Designer, 1961; London Theatre Critics Award, 1966; National Artist, 1968; Nederlands Sikkenprijs, 1969; Los Angeles Drama Critics Circle Award, 1970; German Photographic Society Kulturpreis, 1971; American Theatre Association International Theatre Award, 1976; Premio Internazionale della Scenorgafia del Costume, Teatro dell'Europa, 1984; Royal Industry Designer, RDIHC (London), 1989. Honorary degrees: Royal College of Art, 1969; Denison University, Ohio, 1977; DFA: University of Ohio, Athens, Ohio, 1978; University of Western Michigan, Kalamazoo, Michigan, 1984. Chevalier, Ordre des Arts et des Lettres, 1976; Légion d'honneur, 1993.

Principal productions

As designer:

1943	*Empedokles* (Hölderlin).
	The Crown Bride (Strindberg).
1946	*La Sposa venduta* (Smetana).
	Tales of Hoffmann (Offenbach).
1947	*Tosca* (Puccini).
1948	*The Government Inspector* (Gogol).
1958	*Hamlet* (Shakespeare).
1961	*The Magic Flute* (Mozart).
1963	*Romeo and Juliet* (Shakespeare).
	Oedipus Rex (Sophocles).
1965	*Intoleranza* (Nono).
1966	*The Storm* (Ostrovsky).
1967	*Three Sisters* (Chekhov).
1970	*The Idiot* (Gray, adapted from Dostoevsky).
	Waiting for Godot (Beckett).
1972	*Carmen* (Bizet).
1974–76	*The Ring* (Wagner).
1975	*Symphonie Fantastique* (Berlioz).
1976	*The Queen of Spades* (Tchaikovsky).
1982	*Idomeneo* (Mozart).
	Hamlet (Shakespeare).
1984	*Partage de Midi* (Claudel).
1986	*The Seagull* (Chekhov).

Other productions have included: *A Sunday in August*, 1959; *The Insect Comedy*, 1965; *The Last Ones*, 1966; *The Wedding*, 1968; *The Magic Circus*, 1977; *Odysseus*, 1987; *Vivisection*, 1987.

As director:

1989	*Minotaur*.

* * *

One of the most highly regarded and certainly most prolific stage designers of the 20th century, Josef Svoboda is a complex theatre artist who has altered the parameters of his craft. Although he has been most celebrated as a high-tech stage designer, such a designation is essentially inadequate and partially misleading. It is true that Svoboda has an extensive background in architecture and, more broadly, science and technology, especially with regard to specialized instruments and materials that can be adapted to theatre production. Indeed, it is this component of his talent and skills that primarily contributes to his preference for the term "scenography" rather than "stage design". A scenographer is a stage designer who does more than simply consider the pictorial aspects of a production in terms usually associated with easel painting. A scenographer has the ability to incorporate the principles and the tangible elements of science and technology (for instance, architecture, physics, mechanics, electronics and contemporary materials beyond those traditionally associated with theatre) into the complex creative process of what is generically called stage design.

Nevertheless, Svoboda is primarily an artist, with an artist's sensitivity to form and style and, most important, metaphoric expression. He is a finely tuned *theatre* artist, which is to say that he does not think in terms of pictorial spectacle but of the organic integration that must occur between his contribution as scenographer and the other production elements during the flow of dramatic action on a stage. The elements of scenography must not only be aesthetically pleasing but also appropriate to the nature of the given stage work and its production concept. Moreover, the scenography should be capable of functioning dynamically with the ongoing flow of the stage action; it should be responsive and capable of being modified or transformed in relation to given moments of the total dramatic action.

Two other characteristics warrant attention. Despite Svoboda's great respect for precision and mastery of craftsmanship, and his dismissal of dilettantism in theatre, he is a notable risk-taker, or, as he sometimes says, a gambler. Rather than rely strictly on tried and true methods or techniques, he often works on intuition and instinct, and he likes to keep certain options open for adjustment or alteration during the rehearsal process. Complementing this characteristic is his tendency to stay with certain scenographic techniques, materials or principles (for instance, kinetic scenic units or special projection effects) during a series of productions, not to make his work easier but to explore the range of expressive possibilities and variations within any given scenographic element, almost like a scientist in a laboratory.

In a career that has extended from the 1940's to the 1990's, his more than 600 productions of drama, opera (including three complete *Ring* cycles) and ballet have been marked by a number of distinctive methods or features, more often than not in combination. Almost always present is his general inclination toward abstract, selective and metaphoric expression rather than literal representation. More than one critic has referred to his basic style as that of "abstract expressionism". Others have noted his echoing of certain principles and techniques of constructivism and the Bauhaus School, two other distinctly non-literal approaches to art and theatre practice. The great secret, according to Svoboda, is stage space: how to shape it, articulate it, modify it and make it expressive.

More specifically, lighting, in all its possibilities, becomes a primary means toward these ends. Whether used by itself from special low voltage, high intensity instruments to create a seeming wall of light, or taking the form of static or cinematic projected images (including laser images) onto a variety of projection surfaces, lighting has been a never-ending source for some of Svoboda's most striking work (*A*

Sunday in August, 1959; *The Queen of Spades*, 1976; *Break of Noon*, 1984). A highly innovative, sophisticated variant of the projection technique is the Laterna Magika (developed by Svoboda with the director Alfred Radok), which combines live action with multiple projected images of the performers themselves. Some original productions were built entirely on this principle (*The Magic Circus*, 1977; *Odysseus*, 1987); others employed the principle in non-traditional stagings of conventionally written plays (*The Last Ones*, 1966; *Vivisection*, 1987).

Svoboda has long had a great interest in the use of mirrors to create special dramatic effects. Sometimes separate panels are suspended or placed at special angles (*The Magic Flute*, 1961); at other times an entire wall is made of semi-transparent mirrors (*The Wedding*, 1968). Sometimes the mirrors reflect one or two actors, sometimes the whole stage (*The Insect Comedy*, 1965), and sometimes the audience (*Waiting for Godot*, 1970). He has even experimented with pneumatic mirrors to create alternating concave and convex surfaces (as in the unperformed *The Fiery Angel*).

Prevalent in much of his work throughout his career is experimentation with kinetic scenery, which is a specific manifestation of his preference for a dynamic scenography, one which is modified or transformed according to the demands of the dramatic action; the scenery itself thus takes on the characteristics of a performer, often by shifts of lighting, or use of projections, but also literally by means of movement (*Romeo and Juliet*, 1963; *The Ring of the Nibelungen*, 1974; *Idomeneo*, 1982).

The sheer range of Svoboda's work also includes extremely simple scenography, when technical elements virtually disappear, and form, line, and spatial composition become paramount (*Symphonie Fantastique*, 1975; *Hamlet*, 1982; *The Seagull*, 1986).

Viewed in retrospect, Svoboda's work represents perhaps the nearest approach to the vision of the great pioneers of modern stage design, Adolphe Appia and Gordon Craig, who first conceived of stage design as an expressive art in its own right, rather than as a mere illustration of locale. Svoboda's special talents and orientation have led him to place emphasis on the idea of scenography as a potentially dramatic *instrument* to be put at the disposal of the stage director. In 1989, Svoboda took what he long felt to be an inevitable step: he himself became the director of a production (*Minotaur*) so as to achieve the fullest orchestration of dramatic action and scenography.

—Jarka M. Burian

SZAJNA, Jósef. Polish director, designer and artist. Born in Rzeszów, Poland, 13 March 1922. Educated at the Gymnasium, Rzeszow, 1933–39; imprisoned in Auschwitz and Buchenwald concentration camps, 1941–45; studied at the Academy of Fine Arts, Cracow, 1947–53. Married Bozena Sieroslawska in 1953, one son. Debut as designer, Opole, Poland, 1953; lecturer, Academy of Fine Arts, Cracow, 1954–65; worked as designer at the Teatr Ludowy, Nowa Huta, 1955–63, and served as managing director of the theatre, 1963–66; also worked with Jerzy Grotowski and what became the Laboratory Theatre in the 1960's; freelance designer and director, Teatr Stary, Cracow, and

elsewhere, 1966–71; managing director, Teatr Studio, Warsaw, 1971–82; professor, Academy of Fine Arts, Warsaw, 1972; director, School for Stage Designers, 1972–78; freelance designer and teacher in Warsaw, since 1982; has also staged numerous art exhibitions. Member: jury of the World Council of Culture, Mexico; International Association of Art. Recipient: Artistic Award of Nowa Huta, 1956; First Prize, All-Poland Short Film Festival, Cracow, 1962; City of Cracow Award, 1971; Gold Medal, Prague Quadriennale, 1971; First Prize and Gold Medal, Fourth Art Festival, Warsaw, 1972; Exempla Silver Medal, Munich, 1974; Special Prize, 8th Kalisz Theatre Encounters, 1977; Chairman's Prize, Council of Ministers, Warsaw, 1979; Golden Centaur Prize, Accademia Italia delle Arti e del lavoro, Salsomaggiore Terme, 1982; Gold Medal, International Parliament for Security and Peace, USA, 1983; Quebec Festival Award, 1986; Meritorious Award for National Culture, 1986; Gold Medal, 40th Anniversary of War Veterans (USSR), 1987; International Honorary Citation from Experimental Theatre, Cairo, 1992. Order of the Banner of Labour (first class); Order of the Builder of Nowa Huta, 1959; Knight's Cross, 1969; Commander's Cross, 1979; Order of Polonia Restituta, Warsaw; Gold Decoraton, City of Cracow, 1965; Gold Decoration of Merited Cultural Activist, Warsaw, 1975; Gold Decoration, Union of Polish Artists, Warsaw, 1975; Medal of the 30th Anniversary of the Polish Republic, Warsaw, 1975; Letter of Honour, Ministry of Foreign Affairs, Warsaw, 1978.

Principal productions

As designer:
1956   *Princess Turandot* (Gozzi), Teatr Ludowy, Nowa Huta.
        Of Mice and Men (Steinbeck), Teatr Ludowy, Nowa Huta.
1957   *Jacobowsky and the Colonel* (Behrman), Teatr Ludowy, Nowa Huta.
1958   *State of Siege* (Camus), Teatr Ludowy, Nowa Huta.
        Pantagleize (Ghelderode), Teatr Stary, Cracow.
1959   *Wariat i zakonnica* [The Madman and the Nun] (Witkiewicz), Teatr Dramatyczny, Warsaw.
        W ma łym dworku [In a Small Country House] (Witkiewicz), Teatr Dramatyczny, Warsaw.
1962   *Dziady* [Forefather's Eve] (Mickiewicz), Teatr Ludowy, Nowa Huta.
        Akropolis (Wyspiański), Theatre of 13 Rows, Opole.
1963–66 *Oresteia* (Aeschylus), Teatr Ludowy, Nowa Huta.
1970   *Macbeth* (Shakespeare), Playhouse, Sheffield.

As director and designer:
1963   *Inspector* [The Government Inspector] (Gogol), Teatr Ludowy, Nowa Huta.
1964   *Smierc na gruszy* [Death on a Pear Tree], Teatr Ludowy, Nowa Huta.
1965   *The Empty Field*, Teatr Ludowy, Nowa Huta, and Pergola Theatre, Florence.

1966   *Mystery-Bouffe* (Mayakovsky), Teatr Ludowy, Nowa Huta.

1966   *The Castle*, Teatr Ludowy, Nowa Huta.

1967   *They, New Liberation*, Teatr Stary, Cracow.

1968   *The Bath-House* (Mayakovsky), Teatr Stary, Cracow, and Bitef.

1971   *Faust* (adapted by Szajna), Teatr Polski, Warsaw.

        Replika I (Szajna), Gothenburg; Teatr Studio, Warsaw, 1973; world tour, 1972–84.

1972   *Witkacy* (Szajna, adapted from Witkiewicz), Teatr Studio, Warsaw; Italy, 1973; West Germany, 1975; Netherlands, 1977.

        Replika II (Szajna), Edinburgh Festival.

1973   *Gulgutiera* (Szajna), Teatr Studio, Warsaw.

        Replika III (Szajna), Nancy Festival.

        Replika IV (Szajna), Poland.

1974   *Dante* (Szajna, adapted from *The Divine Comedy*), Pergola Theatre, Florence, and West Germany; Netherland, 1975; USA, 1976; West Germany and France, 1977; UK, 1979; Dubrovnik, 1982.

1976   *Cervantes* (Szajna, Cervantes compilation), Teatr Studio, Warsaw; Mexico, 1980.

1978   *Mayakovsky* (Szajna), Teatr Studio, Warsaw; Finland, 1979.

        Smierc na gruszy [Death on a Pear Tree], Teatr Studio, Warsaw.

1980   *Replika V* (Szajna), Théâtre des Nations, Paris.

1984   *Replika VI* (Szajna), Istanbul Festival.

1986   *Replika VII* (Szajna), Tel-Aviv.

Other productions have included: *Dante zywy* [Dante Alive] (Szajna), 1981; *Dante III* (Szajna), 1985; *Dante* (Szajna), 1992; *Slady, Slady II* (Szajna), Ankara, 1993; *Workshop, Ziennia* (Szajna), Cairo, 1993; *Vida y muerte del Poeta Cervantes* (Szajna), Alcala.

Publications

Teatr Organiczny [Organic Theatre]; *On the New Function of Scenography*; *The Open Theatre*; *The Matter of Spectacle*; *Visual Narrative*.

*

Bibliography

Articles:

Edward Czerwinski, "Josef Szajna — Polish Messiah in Residence", *New Horizon*, 2, 1976.

* * *

As a very young man during the Nazi occupation of Poland, Józef Szajna was confined to the concentration camps at both Auschwitz and Buchenwald. Sentenced to be executed after an unsuccessful attempt to escape, Szajna nonetheless survived. But the horrific images of the prison camp persisted and found expression on numerous occasions both in his rough-edged and collagic paintings and in his work as a stage designer and director. As critic and historian Roman Szydłowsky says, he is an artist who "can speak only of suffering and the martyrdom of modern man".

After concluding his training at Warsaw's Academy of Fine Arts after World War II, Szajna's first professional work was as a designer in 1953 at the provincial theatre in Opole, Poland. There he met directors Krystyna Skuszanka and Jerzy Krasowski, who shortly thereafter took over the management of the Ludowy Theatre in Nowa Huta, where Szajna became the company's foremost scenic designer. Skuszanka and Krasowsky, together with Szajna, sought to develop a theatre of artistic integrity, with emphasis on experimental approaches. Stressing a surrealist deformity and sometimes draping the stage in rags, Szajna was most resourceful at the Ludowy in designing productions of Steinbeck's *Of Mice and Men*, Mickiewicz's *Forefathers' Eve* and Aeschylus's *Oresteia*. Later, from 1963 to 1966, Szajna became managing and artistic director of the Ludowy.

While in Nowa Huta, Szajna often designed elsewhere, and certainly one of his most notable efforts was in the collaboration in 1962 with director Jerzy Grotowski on the production of Wyspiański's *Akropolis*. Though Wyspiański's original play of 1904 is set in the environs of Wawel castle and cathedral in Cracow, Szajna and Grotowski placed their production in the concentration camp at Auschwitz. Most striking were the costumes Szajna designed: all the actors, prisoners of the camp, wore ragged, coarse, gunny sacking and hightop shoes with thick wooden soles that made a heavy clomping sound in the acting space. Later in a production he titled *Replika*, also concerned with images of the death camp, Szajna used almost precisely the same costumes he had developed for *Akropolis*.

It was at approximately the same time that Szajna collaborated with Grotowski in 1962 that he began also to direct as well as design productions: "In my work as director and designer", he has said, "I think as a painter. I understand stage machinery as integrated elements of light, colour, sound and space". Szajna's great versatility as a theatre artist was most apparent after 1971, when he became managing director of the Studio Theatre in the Palace of Culture in Warsaw. There he began a series of productions that he not only directed and designed but for which he also developed the texts. And it was with several of these works that Szajna gained international recognition during tours throughout Europe and the USA.

The first of these productions at the Studio Theatre was titled *Witkacy*. Here Szajna developed a scenario compiled from many of the proto-absurdist plays of Stanisław Ignacy Witkiewicz, painter and playwright of the interwar years. The production was something of a manifesto for the experimental direction Szajna would take with the Studio Theatre. In *Replika*, Szajna recreated the inhumane world of the concentration camp. Performed in a large room with the audience seated against all four walls, the central playing area was a rubbish pile stacked with newspapers, rags, ropes, shoes, wheels and dirt. Actors spoke few words but voiced groans, wails and inarticulate sounds to the accompaniment of concrete music by Bogusław Schäffer.

The script for *Dante* was developed from *The Divine Comedy* and featured music by Krzysztof Penderecki. Here Szajna seems to have taken his inspiration from Artaud's Theatre of Cruelty. Language served only a secondary function with sounds and surreal images and actions being of primary focus. In *Cervantes*, Szajna chose fragments chiefly from the Spanish writer's lyrical poems, but again the text was secondary to the visual images: a huge puppet with a death's head, books being burned in the fires of the Inquisition, the Knight at one point mounting the Trojan horse and riding it, and eventually the Knight entangled in a spider's web.

Like a number of contemporary experimental directors — namely, Tadeusz Kantor, Robert Wilson and Richard Foreman — Szajna's work grows from the inspiration of the visual arts. His is a theatre less dependent upon the word and linear form than upon striking moments of sight and sound.

—Robert Findlay

T

TAIROV, Alexander (Yakovlevich). Russian director. Born Aleksandr Kornblit in Romny, 24 June 1885. Educated at local secondary schools until 1904. Married actress Alisa Koonen. Stage debut, as an amateur actor, 1904; subsequently appeared with professional companies in Kiev and St Petersburg; joined Vera Kommisarjevskaya's company in St Petersburg, 1906–07; worked with various touring companies, 1907–13, and made debut as director, 1908; founder, Kamerny (Chamber) Theatre, Moscow, 1914; continued as director of the Kamerny Theatre until its closure in 1949. Recipient: Order of Lenin, 1945. People's Artist of the RSFSR, 1935. Died in Moscow, 25 September 1950.

Productions

1907–09	*Hamlet* (Shakespeare), Gaideburov touring company.
	Dyadya Vanya [Uncle Vanya] (Chekhov), Gaideburov touring company.
1913	*The Yellow Jacket* (Hazelton-Benrimo), Svobodny Theatre, Moscow.
	Der Schleier der Pierette (Schnitzler), Svobodny Theatre, Moscow.
1914	*Sakuntala* (Kalidasa, translated by Balmont), Kamerny Theatre, Moscow.
1915	*Il ventaglio* (Goldoni, translated by Boborykine), Kamerny Theatre, Moscow.
	Pentecost Monday in Toledo (Kuzmin), Kamerny Theatre, Moscow.
	Le Mariage de Figaro (Beaumarchais, translated by Platon and Khoudoleyev), Kamerny Theatre, Moscow.
	Cyrano de Bergerac (Rostand, translated by Chtchepkina-Koupernik), Kamerny Theatre, Moscow.
1916	*Der Schleier der Pierette* (Schnitzler), Kamerny Theatre, Moscow.
	Famira-Kifared [Thamira, the Cither Player] (Annensky), Kamerny Theatre, Moscow.
	Un Chapeau de paille d'Italie (Labiche, translated by Fedorov), Kamerny Theatre, Moscow.
1917	*The Blue Carpet* (Stolitsa), Kamerny Theatre, Moscow.
	Salomé (Wilde, translated by Balmont), Kamerny Theatre, Moscow.
	Arlequin-Roi (Lothar, translated by Alexandrov), Kamerny Theatre, Moscow.
	La Boíte à joujoux (Debussy), Kamerny Theatre, Moscow.
1918	*L'Echange* (Claudel, translated by Pann and Vilkina), Kamerny Theatre, Moscow.
1919	*Adrienne Lecouvreur* (Scribe and Legouvé, translated by Ivanov), Kamerny Theatre, Moscow.
1920	*Prinzessin Brambilla* (Hoffmann, adapted by Krasovsky), Kamerny Theatre, Moscow.
	L'Annonce faite à Marie (Claudel, translated by Cherchenevitch), Kamerny Theatre, Moscow.
1921	*Romeo and Juliet* (Shakespeare, translated by Brioussov), Kamerny Theatre, Moscow.
1922	*Phaedra* (Racine, adapted by Vesnin), Kamerny Theatre, Moscow.
	Herr Formica (Hoffmann), Kamerny Theatre, Moscow.
	Giroflé-Girofla (Lecocq, translated by Ardo and Adouev), Kamerny Theatre, Moscow.
1923	*The Man Who Was Thursday* (Chesterton), Kamerny Theatre, Moscow.
1924	*Groza* [The Storm] (Ostrovsky), Kamerny Theatre, Moscow.
	Saint Joan (G. B. Shaw), Kamerny Theatre, Moscow.
1925	*Koukirol* (Antokolsky, Mass, Globa and Zak), Kamerny Theatre, Moscow.
1926	*The Hairy Ape* (O'Neill, translated by Zenkevitch and Krymova), Kamerny Theatre, Moscow.
	Rosita (Globa), Kamerny Theatre, Moscow.
	Desire under the Elms (O'Neill, translated by Zenkevitch and Krymova), Kamerny Theatre, Moscow.
	Le Jour et la Nuit (Lecocq, translated by Mass), Kamerny Theatre, Moscow.
1927	*Antigone* (Hasenclever, translated by Gorodetsky), Kamerny Theatre, Moscow.
	Conspiracy of Equals (Mevidov), Kamerny Theatre, Moscow.
1928	*Sirocco* (Polovinkine, translated by Zak and Dantziguer), Kamerny Theatre, Moscow.
	Bagrovy ostrov [The Crimson Island] (Bulgakov), Kamerny Theatre, Moscow.
1929	*All God's Chillun Got Wings* (O'Neill, translated by Zenkevitch and Krymova), Kamerny Theatre, Moscow.
	Natalia Tarpova (Semyonov), Kamerny Theatre, Moscow.

Alexander Tairov

1930   *Die Dreigroschenoper* (Brecht and Weill), Kamerny Theatre, Moscow.
1931   *The Line of Fire* (Nikitine), Kamerny Theatre, Moscow.
        Sonata pathétique (Koulich), Kamerny Theatre, Moscow.
1932   *The Unknown Soldiers* (Pervomaïsky), Kamerny Theatre, Moscow.
        Who by Whom (Markich), Kamerny Theatre, Moscow.
1933   *The Slavery of the Machine* (Treadwell, translated by Bertenson), Kamerny Theatre, Moscow.
        Optimistecheskaya tragediya [An Optimistic Tragedy] (Vishnevsky), Kamerny Theatre, Moscow.
1935   *Egyptian Nights* (compilation of G. B. Shaw, Pushkin and Shakespeare, translated by Levidov), Kamerny Theatre, Moscow.
        We do not Surrender (Semyonov), Kamerny Theatre, Moscow.
1936   *Les Preux* (Bedny), Kamerny Theatre, Moscow.
1937   *Deti solntsa* [Children of the Sun] (Gorky), Kamerny Theatre, Moscow.
1940   *The Devil's Bridge* (A. Tolstoy), Kamerny Theatre, Moscow.
        Madame Bovary (adapted from Flaubert), Kamerny Theatre, Moscow.
        Klop [The Bedbug] (Mayakovsky), Kamerny Theatre, Moscow.

1941   *Admiral Nakimov* (Loukovsky), Kamerny Theatre, Moscow.
        The Batallion Goes West (Mdivani), Kamerny Theatre, Moscow.
1942   *The Front* (Korneichuk), Kamerny Theatre, Moscow.
1943   *As Long as the Heart Beats* (Paoustovsky), Kamerny Theatre, Moscow.
1944   *Chayka* [The Seagull] (Chekhov), Kamerny Theatre, Moscow.
        Bezvinny vinovatye [More Sinned Against Than Sinning] (Ostrovsky), Kamerny Theatre, Moscow.
1945   *U sten Leningrada* (Vishnevsky), Kamerny Theatre, Moscow.
        He Is Come (Priestley, translated by Koulakovskaya and Hildenbrat), Kamerny Theatre, Moscow.
1946   *Starik* [The Old Man] (Gorky), Kamerny Theatre, Moscow.
1947   *Olga Netchaeva* (Panova), Kamerny Theatre, Moscow.
        The Destiny of Reginald Davis (Kojevnikov and Prout), Kamerny Theatre, Moscow.
1948   *The Lion on the Square* (Ehrenbourg), Kamerny Theatre, Moscow.
        Lady Windermere's Fan (Wilde, translated by Soukhotskaya), Kamerny Theatre, Moscow.
1949   *The Actors* (Vassiliev and Elston), Kamerny Theatre, Moscow.

Publications

Zapiski rezhissera: Stati, besedy, rechi, pisma, 1970; *Le Théâtre libéré*, 1974.

* * *

Alexander Tairov's contribution to Russian theatre needs to be seen alongside the work of such figures as Diaghilev and Meyerhold, with whom he had much in common. Tairov was someone who wished to raise the art of theatre to the level of such sister arts as the ballet, painting and music. With Meyerhold, he shared an antipathy towards post-Renaissance theatre that had culminated in the "cul-de-sac" of late 19th-century naturalism. They both sought to resurrect the archetypal theatre forms of the pantomime and the harlequinade, as well as the improvisatory spirit of the commedia dell'arte. Tairov also imagined a "synthetic" theatre, which united all aspects of the art of the stage, employing actors capable of performing tragedy, farce, opera and pantomime with equal facility. He wished to do away with a specialising tendency that separated the functions of a singer from those of an actor and placed the dancer in a different category from the acrobat. Tairov dreamed of a "universal" artist, a type who had existed in classical antiquity and even during the Middle Ages, but whose art the post-Renaissance theatre had destroyed. The interest in forms of drama that owed their origin to the Roman "mimi", to the commedia dell'arte and to the related forms of music and dance, was something that Tairov shared with many other theatre practitioners before the Revolution. He felt especially drawn towards the art of "pantomime" and would have sympathised with Arthur Symons who, in 1898, wrote of the "gracious, expressive silence, beauty of gesture, a perfectly discreet appeal to the emotions, a transposition of the world into an elegant, accepted convention", characteristic of pantomime. In addition, Tairov sought to derive new theatre forms from ancient Greek and Eastern myth and trained his actors to handle their bodies on stage in such a way that distinctions between a "corps de ballet" and a "corps de drame" were broken down and where the art of the designer, the musician and the actor merged in a unified, aesthetic whole.

Tairov's essentially "modernist" theatre was influenced by symbolist poetry, cubo-futurist painting, constructivism and the avant-garde music of the day. His work at the Kamerny Theatre, which he founded with his wife Alisa Koonen in 1914, became the forum for experiments in "pure theatre" but also a theatre where the formalism never degenerated into "fin-de-siècle" decadence or sterile "art for art's sake". Anti-naturalist theatre practice was supported by a whole range of theories, many of which drew their authority from Renaissance, pre-Renaissance or Greek and Roman theatre practice. It was Tairov who, in his own theoretical work *Notes of a Director*, quoted the Symbolist theorist Fyodor Sologub, when describing the transformation of the ancient theatre of Dionysus into the present "cosy tomb for rabbits". The way out of the present "impasse" was through the rediscovery of mime. In the world of pantomime genuine scenic action was born through eternal figures and eternal passions. Only pantomime could provide the key to the discovery of form saturated with creative emotion, where words die, and scenic synthesis is achieved through emotional gesture and emotional form.

Having insisted on a synthetic unity of the arts, Tairov appreciated how dilettante and amateur was the art of the actor compared with that of the musician or the dancer. Actors needed to be taught how to care for the material of their art — their own natures and their own bodies. The actor needed to learn to be a master of his "instrument" through a mastery of internal and external technique. Real scenic emotion was not gained by an appeal to the spectator's most easily accessible responses. The genuine scenic figure was a synthesis of emotion and form brought alive by the creative fantasy of the actor. The actor's body needed to be to him as the violin is to the player, embodying in clear-cut forms the delicate vibrations of his own creativity. Together with mastery of the body went mastery of the voice. Tairov stressed that there was a particular timbre, key and tonality for every role and that it was the actor's task to find the necessary key and scale for each individual character.

Because the theatre is a collective art, the actor needed to subject himself to voluntary self-restraint and subordination to the director, who creatively strove towards an overall harmonious result. The task of the director was to discover an appropriate form for the production as a whole, then to find literary material and transform it into an effective production structure for which there was need to enlist the help of the poet. The next task involved the use of music, and the final stage of the work involved the scenic atmosphere in which the actor had to function. This could only be worked out in a definite cubic capacity, for which a scale model was required, and the stage floor needed to be broken up into a series of horizontal or vertical surfaces of varying heights. This structure was based on rhythm. The playing area had to be a space where the actor could be incorporated and displayed, as well as somewhere he could play freely — a structural keyboard on which to express his creative will. Colour composition also needed to be in accord with the design of the scenic construction and to harmonise with the costuming. It was necessary to discover for the modern actor the kind of costume that was an integral part of him or her. Style and period entered the basic motif only as an accompaniment.

From 1914 until the closure of the Kamerny Theatre in 1949, Tairov did his best to remain true to these basic principles, staging several remarkable productions of Western and Soviet plays ranging from classical and modern tragedies and revolutionary dramas to propagandist satires, pantomimes, harlequinades and comic operas. In so doing, he collaborated with some of the most outstanding scenic designers of this, or any other, age and, in the course of three foreign tours, established an international reputation for Soviet theatre. However, matters were never easy for a director who, initially, remained singularly unaffected by the Revolution and continued to pursue an independent artistic course in the face of a good deal of hostile criticism, despite the support of the cultural commissar, Lunacharsky. The political turning-point for the Kamerny Theatre came, as it did for so many others, at the end of the 1920's and the beginning of the 1930's, when, in a radically altered artistic climate, experimentation was seen as inimical to the serious political tasks facing the country. Tairov, in common with Meyerhold and others, had to answer criticism levelled at his "formalist" methods and, in response, made strenuous efforts to come to terms with the new mood. In at least one instance (his production of *The Optimistic Tragedy*) he succeeded triumphantly in not only fulfilling what was required of a Soviet artist, but in establishing a model of socialist realist theatre production.

Tairov's career charted a course through one of the most turbulent periods in world history and provides a mirror that reflects these events. Throughout, Tairov remained faithful to certain abiding principles. The first was the principle that he learned from the Greeks — the fact that the harmony of the universe is posited on the co-existence of tragedy and comedy. The second, related, principle consisted in the simultaneous unification and transcendence of these oppositions through the strength of an earthly love that he felt was human and divine.

—Nick Worrall

TALMA, François-Joseph. French actor-manager. Born in Paris, 1763. Educated in London, England; trained as actor at the École de Declamation, Paris, under François-René Molé, 1786–87. Professional debut, Comédie-Française, Paris, 1787; acquired immediate notoriety after appearing in historically appropriate costume, 1789; established reputation after playing the King in Chénier's *Charles IX*, 1789; co-founded breakaway company at the Théâtre de la République, Paris, 1792; acclaimed the leading tragedian of his generation for performances in plays by Pierre Corneille and Shakespeare, often appearing opposite Mlle Duchenois; Talma's company and Comédie-

Française reunited at the Théâtre de la République, 1799; the company's pensions and subsidies restored by Napoleon, 1803; toured Europe with Napoleon, appearing before five crowned heads in Erfurt, Germany, 1803; left Comédie-Française, 1815; continued to tour, acting at Covent Garden, London, 1817; returned to Comédie-Française to play his last role, 1826. Died in Paris, 19 October 1826.

Roles

1787   Walk-on role in *Mahomet* (Voltaire), Comédie-Française, Paris.
1788   Cléandre in *La Jeune Épouse* (Cubières), Comédie-Française, Paris.
        Chevalier Tristan in *Lanval et Vivianne* (Murville), Comédie-Française, Paris.
1789   Comte d'Orsange in *Le Présomptueux* (d'Églantine), Comédie-Française, Paris.
        Garçon Anglais in *Les Deux Pages* (Dezède), Comédie-Française, Paris.
        Chevalier de Sabran in *Raymond V, comte de Toulouse* (Sedaine), Comédie-Française, Paris.
        Charles IX in *Charles IX* (Chénier), Comédie-Française, Paris.
        Juan in *Le Paysan Magistrat* (Herbois), Comédie-Française, Paris.
1790   Titus in *Brutus* (Voltaire), Comédie-Française, Paris.
        D'Harcourt in *Le Réveil d'Épiménide à Paris* (Oliviers), Comédie-Française, Paris.
        Comte d'Amplace in *L'Honnête Criminel* (Falbaire), Comédie-Française, Paris.
        Dorvigny in *Le Comte de Cominges* (Baculard), Comédie-Française, Paris.
        J. J. Rousseau in *Le Journaliste des Ombres* (Aude), Comédie-Française, Paris.
1791   Henri VIII in *Henri VIII* (Chénier), Théâtre de la République, Paris.
        Cléry in *L'Intrigue Épistolaire* (d'Églantine), Théâtre de la République, Paris.
        Jean in *Jean sans Terre* (Ducis), Théâtre de la République, Paris.
        Lasalle in *Jean Calas* (Chénier), Théâtre de la République, Paris.
        Prince Époux de Zuléima in *Abdelazis et Zuléïma* (Murville), Théâtre de la République, Paris.
        Alonzo in *La Vengeance* (adapted by Dumaniant), Théâtre de la République, Paris.
        Monval in *Mélanie* (La Harpe), Théâtre de la République, Paris.
1792   Fulvius Flaccus in *Caius Gracchus* (Chénier), Théâtre de la République, Paris.
        Othello in *Le Maure de Venise* (Ducis), Théâtre de la République, Paris.
1793   Delmance in *Fénélon* (Chénier), Théâtre de la République, Paris.
        Mutius Scévola in *Mutius Scévola* (Lancival), Théâtre de la République, Paris.
1794   Néron in *Épicharis et Néron* (Legouvé), Théâtre de la République, Paris.

1795   Timoléon in *Timoléon* (Chénier), Théâtre de la République, Paris.
        Servilius in *Quintus Cincinnatus* (Arnault), Théâtre de la République, Paris.
        Pharan in *Abufar* (Ducis), Théâtre de la République, Paris.
        Quintus Fabius in *Quintus Fabius* (Legouvé), Théâtre de la République, Paris.
1797   Junius in *Junius* (Monvel), Théâtre de la République, Paris.
        Égisthe in *Agamemnon* (Lemercier), Théâtre de la République, Paris.
        Kaleb in *Falkland* (Laya), Théâtre de la République, Paris.
1798   Moncassin in *Les Vénitiens* (Arnault), Théâtre de la République, Paris.
        Thaulus in *Ophis* (Lemercier), Théâtre de la République, Paris.
1799   Étéocle in *Étéocle et Polynice* (Legouvé), Comédie-Française, Paris.
1800   Pinto in *Pinto* (Lemercier), Comédie-Française, Paris.
        Montmorency in *Montmorency* (Carrion-Nisas), Comédie-Française, Paris.
        Thésée in *Thésée* (Mazoyer), Comédie-Française, Paris.
1801   Phaedor in *Phaedor et Waldamir* (Ducis), Comédie-Française, Paris.
1802   Don Pèdre in *Le Roi et le Laboureur* (Arnault), Comédie-Française, Paris.
        Orovèze in *Ysule et Orovèze* (Lemercier), Comédie-Française, Paris.
1804   Shakespeare in *Shakespeare amoureux* (Duval), Comédie-Française, Paris.
        Ulysse in *Polyxène* (Aignan), Comédie-Française, Paris.
        Harold in *Guillaume le Conquérant* (Duval), Comédie-Française, Paris.
        Pierre le Grand in *Pierre le Grand* (Carrion-Nisas), Comédie-Française, Paris.
        Cyrus in *Cyrus* (Chénier), Comédie-Française, Paris.
1805   Marigny in *Les Templiers* (Raynouard), Comédie-Française, Paris.
1806   Henri IV in *La Mort de Henri IV* (Legouvé), Comédie-Française, Paris.
        Omasis in *Omasis* (Baour-Lormian), Comédie-Française, Paris.
        Manlius in *Manlius Capitolinus* (Lafosse), Comédie-Française, Paris.
1807   Pyrrhus in *Pyrrhus* (Lehoc), Comédie-Française, Paris.
1808   Plaute in *Plaute* (Lemercier), Comédie-Française, Paris.
1809   Hector in *Hector* (Lancival), Comédie-Française, Paris.
1810   Duc de Guise in *Les États de Blois* (Raynouard), Comédie-Française, Paris.
1811   Mahomet in *Mahomet II* (Baour-Lormian), Comédie-Française, Paris.
1813   Tippo-Sahib in *Tippo-Saïb* (Jouy), Comédie-Française, Paris.
        Ninus II in *Ninus II* (Briffaut), Comédie-Française, Paris.

1814	Duguesclin in *La Rançon de Duguesclin* (Arnault), Comédie-Française, Paris.
	Ulysse in *Ulysse* (Lebrun), Comédie-Française, Paris.
1816	Rutland in *Arthur de Bretagne* (Aignan), tour.
1817	Germanicus in *Germanicus* (Arnault), tour.
1820	Leicester in *Marie Stuart* (Lebrun), tour.
	Clovis in *Clovis* (Viennet), tour.
	Jean de Bourgogne in *Jean de Bourgogne* (Formont), tour.
1821	Sylla in *Sylla* (Jouy), tour.
1822	Régulus in *Régulus* (Arnault), tour.
	Oreste in *Clytemnestre* (Soumet), tour.
1823	Ébroïn in *Le Maire du Palais* (Ancelot), tour.
	Danville in *L'Éole des Vieillards* (Lavigne), tour.
1824	Gloucester in *Jane Shore* (Lemercier), tour.
1825	Le Cid in *Le Cid d'Andalousie* (Lebrun), tour.
	Abiatar in *La Clémence de David* (Draparnaud), tour.
	Bélisaire in *Bélisaire* (Jouy), tour.
	Léonidas in *Léonidas* (Pichat), tour.
1826	Charles VI in *Charles VI* (Delaville), Comédie-Française, Paris.

Other roles included: Antiochus in *Rodogune* (P. Corneille); Assuérus in *Esther* (Racine); Auguste and Cinna in *Cinna* (P. Corneille); Hamlet in *Hamlet* (Shakespeare, adapted by Ducis); Macbeth in *Macbeth* (Shakespeare, adapted by Ducis); Néron in *Britannicus* (Racine); Nicomède in *Nicomède* (P. Corneille); Oedipe in *Oedipe* (Voltaire); Oreste in *Andromaque* (Racine); Oreste in *Iphigénie en Tauride* (La Touche).

Publications

Quelques réflexions sur Lekain et sur l'art théâtral, 1826; *Correspondence avec Mme de Staël*, 1928.

*

Bibliography

Books:
Alexandre Dumas, *Mémoires de Talma*, Paris, 1850.
E. D. de Manne, *La Troupe de Talma*, Lyon, 1866.
A. Augustin-Thierry, *Le Tragédien de Napoléon: François-Joseph Talma*, Paris, 1942.
Herbert F. Collins, *Talma*, London, 1964.

* * *

The career of François-Joseph Talma marks a turning-point in the history of French theatre. He can be regarded as a product of his revolutionary times in more ways than one: Republican in his political sympathies and on friendly terms with Napoleon, he also held progressive views on the art of acting and the design of stage costume. Although some of these ideas were shared with his predecessor Lekain, by whom he was strongly influenced, the scale of Talma's enterprise represents the first really radical break with the past and a significant reinterpretation of theatrical values.

His knowledge of the English text of Shakespeare's plays and familiarity with stage practices in London, where he spent most of his youth and had his first experience as an actor, may well have given him a unique perspective on the legacy of neo-classicism that was still deeply ingrained in French dramaturgy and theatrical performance. Certainly the two-year training he underwent at the acting school attached to the Comédie-Française did little to assimilate him to its more prescriptive traditions and he sought additional inspiration from the unorthodox acting style of Lekain through the advice of the latter's erstwhile colleague, Monvel. He made his debut at the Comédie in 1787 while still a pupil of the school, but thereafter found himself playing minor roles until in November 1789, shortly after becoming a full sociétaire, he was cast as the King in Marie-Joseph Chénier's *Charles IX*, a role that no-one else was prepared to undertake in a patently anti-monarchical, anti-clerical play. This not only allowed him to demonstrate his true ability in a leading part but indirectly thrust him into greater prominence by provoking a schism in the company between conservative royalists and a dissident faction of "rouges", including Talma, who 18 months later, with the freeing of the theatres, broke away to join forces with the actors of the recently-built Variétés-Amusantes in the Rue de Richelieu, calling themselves the Théâtre de la République. This new theatre opened in April 1791 with another of Chénier's historical plays, *Henri VIII*, and played in competition with the Comédie until the two companies were amalgamated in 1799 to form a reconstituted Théâtre-Français in the Rue de Richelieu, where it has remained ever since.

It was here that Talma spent most of his residual career, emerging as the undisputed star of the French stage and touring repeatedly in the provinces and abroad. To the statutory classics of the repertoire, as much as to the historical drama of contemporary proto-Romantic playwrights, he brought a distinctive, highly idiosyncratic approach that broke new ground for the actor. The received, strictly formalized manner of speaking Alexandrine verse was finally rejected by him and replaced by a more flexible diction, shorn of declamation, alternately agitated and staccato or relaxed and unaccentuated almost to the point of conversational familiarity at times: apparently it could seem so unregulated and spontaneous as not to be the product of art. Allied to this he made liberal use of gesture, energetic movement, and unconventional posture, devising expressive business to convey mood and state of mind when he was not speaking. Even Stendhal, an ardent admirer of his acting, could complain that he was continually in a state of "movement and exclamation", while others considered that his penchant robbed him of the dignity and solemnity required in a tragic actor. His most persistent critic, Geoffroy, compared him unfavourably with Lekain in this respect, alleging that he "disfigured himself with grimaces" and "seemed convinced that it was necessary simply to *talk* tragedy", a practice that was having a pernicious influence on fellow-players. He was also accused of concentrating on those parts of a play that gave him the opportunity to create "effects" capable of impressing or startling an audience and neglecting the rest, to the detriment of good verse-speaking in both cases.

Audiences were, however, duly impressed and startled, completely won over by a confluence of natural gifts, in terms of voice, face, and figure, with resourceful technique. Mme de Staël avowed that "one was gripped by terror at a distance of two paces from him" and another commentator referred to the "fire from heaven" that at times descended upon him: he could dominate a stage effortlessly. There was also a brooding quality about his playing that temperamentally unsuited him for uncomplicatedly vigorous or heroic roles such as Don Rodrigue in Corneille's *Le Cid*, whom Geoffroy pronounced "too sombre, too heavy" in his hands, but which added a powerful dimension to others. As Antiochus in the same dramatist's *Rodogune*, for instance, he gave a moving portrayal of the character's sufferings, while Oreste's frenzy and despair in Racine's *Andromaque* took on the proportions of genuine madness and his unrequited love for Hermione a shadowy, almost sinister depth, which turned him into a kind of half-brother to Hamlet, a prefiguration of the Romantic hero. Talma was, in fact, particularly drawn to enigmatic or tormented characters or to lovers with the mark of fate on them, as he was quick to acknowledge: "when the love is dark and doom-laden, it accords with me". A similar instinct may have nourished his fondness for certain Shakespearean roles and, despite the rather tame, adulterated versions of the original texts provided by Ducis, he did score notable personal success as Othello, Macbeth, and in particular Hamlet, though he never managed to convert the French public to the unbiddable beauties of Shakespeare.

His other great contribution to the renewal of stagecraft was in the field of costume. It was largely due to his efforts that the French theatre finally turned its back on the conventional dress of the past in favour of a style more in keeping with historical period and geographical location, at least where a play's main personages were concerned; supernumeraries apparently continued to be dressed from stock, an inconsistency tolerated by early nineteenth-century audiences though still falling far short of realism. Talma seems to have envisaged costume as an extension, or even a necessary condition, of character. As early as his first major performance as Charles IX he modelled his appearance on iconographical evidence, complete with gold trimming on a white silk doublet, black velvet cape, ruff, bear and moustaches, and in the following year, for his role in Voltaire's *Brutus*, he ventured to wear a Roman toga and sandals, with his arms bare and his own hair, cropped short. His colleagues were appalled but audience response, after some hesitation, proved enthusiastic and a sartorial revolution was accomplished. He took to frequenting museums and the studio of the painter David, who plied him with suggested designs. As he commented late in life to the young Victor Hugo, who wrote the title role of *Cromwell* for him: "Truth in the plays was unobtainable; I had to be content with putting it in the costumes".

Long before his death Talma had become a legend, fêted in Parisian society, honoured by Napoleon, in demand for performances at the new imperial court or before the crowned heads of Europe, and designated professor of acting at the conservatoire where he had studied. Posterity has recognized him as a pioneer of stage practice, one who hastened the transition from a classical to a Romantic aesthetic and redrew the conventions of performance for a new epoch.

—Donald Roy

TANDY, Jessica. US actress. Born in London, 7 June 1909. Educated at Dame Owen's Girls' School; trained for the stage at the Ben Greet Academy of Acting, 1924–27. Married 1) actor Jack Hawkins in 1932 (divorced 1940), one daughter; 2) actor Hume Cronyn (*q.v.*) in 1942, one son and one daughter. Stage debut, London, 1927; actress, Birmingham Repertory Company, from 1928; New York debut, 1930; film debut, 1932; emigrated to USA, 1940; dramatic adviser, Goddard Neighbourhood Centre, New York, 1948; took US citizenship, 1954; acclaimed in range of classical and modern roles on stage and screen. Recipient: Tony Award, 1948, 1979, 1983; Twelfth Night Club Award, 1948; Comedia Matinee Club Award, 1952; Delia Austria Award, New York Drama League, 1960; two Obie Awards, 1973; Drama Desk Award, 1973, 1979, 1983; Brandeis University Creative Arts Award, 1978; Theatre Arts Medal, 1978; Los Angeles Critics Award, 1979; Sarah Siddons Award, 1979; National Press Club Award, 1979; Outer Circle Critics Award, 1983; Commonwealth Award, 1983; Kennedy Centre Honours, 1986; Alley Theatre Award, 1987; Academy of Science Fiction, Fantasy, and Horror Films Award, 1987; Franklin Haven Sargent Award, American Academy of Dramatic Arts, 1988; Emmy Award, 1988; Oscar, 1990; National Medal of the Arts, 1990. LL.D: University of Western Ontario, London, 1974; LHD: Fordham University, Bronx, New York, 1985. Died in Easton Connecticut, 11 September 1994.

Roles

1927	Sara Manderson in *The Manderson Girls*, Playroom Six, London.
1928	Gladys in *The Comedy of Good and Evil* (Hughes), Repertory Theatre, Birmingham.
	Ginevra in *Alice Sit-by-the-Fire* (Barrie), Repertory Theatre, Birmingham.
	Lydia Blake in *Yellow Sands* (Phillpotts), British tour.
1929	Lena Jackson in *The Rumour* (Munro), Court Theatre, London.
	Typist in *The Theatre of Life*, Arts Theatre, London.
	Maggie in *Water*, Little Theatre, London.
	Aude in *The Unknown Warrior* (Lewis), Haymarket Theatre, London.
1930	Olivia in *Twelfth Night* (Shakespeare), Oxford University Dramatic Society, Oxford.
	Cynthia Perry in *The Last Enemy*, Shubert Theatre, New York.
	Toni Rakonitz in *The Matriarch* (Stern), Longacre Theatre, New York.
1931	Fay in *The Man Who Pays the Piper* (Stern), St Martin's Theatre, London.
	Audrey in *Autumn Crocus* (Smith), Lyric Theatre, London.
	Ruth Blair in *Port Said*, Wyndham's Theatre, London.
	Anna in *Musical Chairs* (Mackenzie), Arts Theatre, London.
1932	Carlotta in *Mutual Benefit*, St Martin's Theatre, London.

Manuela in *Children in Uniform* (Winsloe, adapted by Burnham), Duchess Theatre, London.

1933 Alicia Audley in *Lady Audley's Secret* (Hazlewood), Arts Theatre, London.

Marikke in *Midsummer Fires*, Embassy Theatre, London.

Titania in *A Midsummer Night's Dream* (Shakespeare), Open Air Theatre, London; Stratford Shakespeare Festival, Stratford, Ontario, 1976.

Betty in *Ten Minute Alibi* (Armstrong), Haymarket Theatre, London.

1934 Rosamund in *Birthday*, Cambridge Festival Theatre, Cambridge.

Viola in *Twelfth Night* (Shakespeare), Hippodrome Theatre, Manchester; Old Vic Theatre, London, 1937; Open Air Theatre, London, 1939.

Anne Page in *The Merry Wives of Windsor* (Shakespeare), Hippodrome Theatre, Manchester.

Eva Whiston in *Line Engaged*, Duke of York's Theatre, London.

Ophelia in *Hamlet* (Shakespeare), New Theatre, London.

1935 Ada in *Noah* (Wilmurt), New Theatre, London.

Anna Penn in *Anthony and Anna*, Whitehall Theatre, London.

1936 Marie Rose in *The Ante-Room* (Ervine), Queen's Theatre, London.

Jacqueline in *French Without Tears* (Rattigan), Criterion Theatre, London.

Pamela March in *Honour Thy Father* (Harwood and Tennyson), Arts Theatre, London.

1937 Sebastian in *Twelfth Night* (Shakespeare), Old Vic Theatre, London.

Katherine in *Henry V* (Shakespeare), Old Vic Theatre, London.

Ellen Murray in *Yes, My Darling Daughter*, St James's Theatre, London.

1938 Kay in *Time and the Conways* (Priestley), Ritz Theatre, New York.

1939 Nora Fintry in *The White Steed* (Carroll), Cort Theatre, New York.

1939 Deaconess in *Geneva* (G. B. Shaw), Canadian tour; Henry Miller's Theatre, New York, 1940.

1940 Cordelia in *King Lear* (Shakespeare), Old Vic Theatre, London.

Miranda in *The Tempest* (Shakespeare), Old Vic Theatre, London.

Dr Mary Murray in *Jupiter Laughs* (Cronin), Biltmore Theatre, New York.

1941 Abigail Hill in *Anne of England*, St James's Theatre, New York.

1942 Cattrin in *Yesterday's Magic*, Guild Theatre, New York.

1946 Lucretia Collins in *Portrait of a Madonna* (T. Williams), Las Palmas Theatre, Los Angeles; Playhouse Theatre, New York, 1959.

1947 Blanche Dubois in *A Streetcar Named Desire* (T. Williams), Ethel Barrymore Theatre, New York.

1950 Hilda Crane in *Hilda Crane* (Raphaelson), Coronet Theatre, New York.

1951 Agnes in *The Fourposter* (Hartog), Ethel Barrymore Theatre, New York; City Centre Theatre, New York, 1955.

1953 Mary Doyle in *Madam Will You Walk?* (Howard), Phoenix Theatre, New York.

1955 Mary Honey in *The Honeys*, Longacre Theatre, New York.

Frances Farrar in *A Day By the Sea* (Hunter), American National Theatre, New York, and Academy Theatre, New York.

1957 Martha Walling in *The Man in the Dog Suit* (Beich and Wright), US tour; Coronet Theatre, New York, 1958.

1958 Innocent Bystander in *A Pound on Demand* (O'Casey), US tour; Playhouse Theatre, New York, 1959.

Angela Nightingale in *Bedtime Story* (O'Casey), US tour; Playhouse Theatre, New York, 1959.

1959 Louise Harrington in *Five Finger Exercise* (P. Shaffer), Music Box Theatre, New York; S tour, 1960.

1961 Lady Macbeth in *Macbeth* (Shakespeare), American Shakespeare Festival, Stratford, Connecticut.

Cassandra in *Troilus and Cressida* (Shakespeare), American Shakespeare Festival, Stratford, Connecticut.

1962 Edith Maitland in *Big Fish, Little Fish* (Wheeler), Duke of York's Theatre, London.

1963 Gertrude in *Hamlet* (Shakespeare), Tyrone Guthrie Theatre, Minneapolis.

Olga in *The Three Sisters* (Chekhov), Tyrone Guthrie Theatre, Minneapolis.

Linda Loman in *Death of a Salesman* (Miller), Tyrone Guthrie Theatre, Minneapolis.

1964 Fraulein Doktor Mathilde von Zahnd in *The Physicists* (Dürrenmatt), Martin Beck Theatre, New York.

1965 Lady Wishfort in *The Way of the World* (Congreve), Tyrone Guthrie Theatre, Minneapolis; Stratford Shakespeare Festival, Stratford, Ontario, 1976.

Madame Ranevskaya in *The Cherry Orchard* (Chekhov), Tyrone Guthrie Theatre, Minneapolis.

Mother-in-Law in *The Caucasian Chalk Circle* (Brecht), Tyrone Guthrie Theatre, Minneapolis.

1966 Agnes in *A Delicate Balance* (Albee), Martin Beck Theatre, New York; US tour, 1967.

1968 Froisine in *The Miser* (Molière), Mark Taper Forum, Los Angeles.

Hesione Hushabye in *Heartbreak House* (G. B. Shaw), Shaw Festival, Niagara-on-the-Lake, Ontario.

1969 Pamela Pew-Pickett in *Tchin-Tchin* (Billetdoux), Ivanhoe Theatre, Chicago.

1970 Marguerite Gautier in *Camino Real* (T. Williams), Vivian Beaumont Theatre, New York.

Marjorie in *Home* (Storey), Morosco Theatre, New York.

Jessica Tandy (1989).

1971   Wife in *All Over* (Albee), Martin Beck Theatre, New York.

1972   Winnie in *Happy Days* (Beckett), Forum Theatre, New York.

      The Mouth in *Not I* (Beckett), Forum Theatre, New York; US tour, 1973.

1974   Anna-Mary Conklin in "Come into the Garden, Maud" and Hilde Latymer in "A Song at Twilight" in *Noël Coward in Two Keys* (Coward), Ethel Barrymore Theatre, New York; US tour, 1975.

1976   Hippolyta in *A Midsummer Night's Dream* (Shakespeare), Stratford Shakespeare Festival, Stratford, Ontario.

      Eve in *Eve*, Stratford Shakespeare Festival, Stratford, Ontario.

1977   Mary Tyrone in *Long Day's Journey into Night* (O'Neill), Theatre London, London, Ontario; Stratford Shakespeare Festival, Stratford, Ontario, 1980.

      Fonsia Dorsey in *The Gin Game* (Coburn), Long Wharf Theatre, New Haven, Connecticut, and John Golden Theatre, New York; US and world tour, 1978–79.

1980   Annie Nations in *Foxfire* (Cronyn and Cooper), Stratford Shakespeare Festival, Stratford, Ontario; Tyrone Guthrie Theatre, Minneapolis, 1981; Ethel Barrymore Theatre, New York, 1982; Ahmanson Theatre, Los Angeles, 1985.

1981   Mother in *Rose* (Davies), Cort Theatre, New York.

1984   Amanda Wingfield in *The Glass Menagerie* (T. Williams), Eugene O'Neill Theatre, New York.

1985   Charlotte in *Salonika* (Page), New York Shakespeare Festival, Public Theatre, New York.

1986   Elizabeth Milne in *The Petition* (Clark), John Golden Theatre, New York.

Other roles included: *Below the Surface*, Repertory Players, London, 1932; *Juarez and Maximilian* (Werfel), Phoenix Theatre, London, 1932; *Troilus and Cressida* (Shakespeare), Cambridge Festival Theatre, Cambridge, 1932; *See Naples and Die* (Rice), Cambridge Festival Theatre, Cambridge, 1932; *The Witch* (Masefield), Cambridge Festival Theatre, Cambridge, 1932; *Rose Without a Thorn* (Bax), Cambridge Festival Theatre, Cambridge, 1932; *The Inspector General* (Gogol), Cambridge Festival Theatre, Cambridge, 1932; *The Servant of Two Masters* (Goldoni), Cambridge Festival Theatre, Cambridge, 1932; *The Romantic Young Lady* (Martínez Sierra), Fulham Shilling Theatre, London, 1934; *Charles the King* (Colbourne), Canadian tour, 1939; *Tobias and the Angel* (Bridie), Canadian tour, 1939; *Now I Lay Me Down to Sleep* (Ryan), Stanford University, Palo Alto, California, 1949; *The Little Blue Light* (Wilson), Brattle Theare, Cambridge, Massachusetts, 1950; *Promenade All!* (Robison), US tour, 1972–73; *Many Faces of Love*, US tour, 1974–75.

Films

Indiscretions of Eve, 1932; *Murder in the Family*, 1938; *The Seventh Cross*, 1944; *The Valley of Decision*, 1945; *Dragonwyck*, 1946; *The Green Years*, 1946; *Forever Amber*, 1947; *A Woman's Vengeance*, 1947; *September Affair*, 1950; *Rommel, Desert Fox*, 1951; *The Light in the Desert*, 1958; *Hemingway's Adventures of a Young Man*, 1962; *The Birds*, 1963; *Butley*, 1973; *Honky Tonk Freeway*, 1981; *Best Friends*, 1982; *Still of the Night*, 1982; *The World According to Garp*, 1982; *The Bostonians*, 1984; *Cocoon*, 1985; *The Thrill of Genius*, 1985; *Nobody's Fool*, 1986; **batteries not included*, 1987; *The House on Carroll Street*, 1988; *Cocoon, The Return*, 1988; *Driving Miss Daisy*, 1989; *Fried Green Tomatoes at the Whistle Stop Café*, 1991; *Used People*, 1992; *Camilla*, 1995.

Television

Portrait of a Madonna, 1948; *The Marriage* (series), 1954; *The Fourposter*, 1955; *The Moon and Sixpence*, 1959; *The Fallen Idol*, 1959; *Many Faces of Love*, 1977; *The Gin Game*, 1979; *Foxfire*, 1987.

Radio

The Marriage, 1953–54.

* * *

Jessica Tandy had a long and distinguished career spanning more than six decades as an actress of both stage and screen. She was the recipient of both Broadway and Hollywood's highest awards, with three Tonys, one Emmy, and an Oscar to her credit. It was not so much her versatility as an actress that made her career so remarkable, but rather the fact that she explored many different theatrical strands in her professional life. This was, however, at the expense of wide popular success. When she won her Academy Award in 1990, becoming the oldest actress to date to receive the honour, *Time Magazine* described her as "one of show business's longest overnight success stories".

Recognised as having a natural authority exemplified by her hallmarks of crisp diction and an enduring dignified appearance, Tandy had the ability to engage and move audiences in whichever role she tackled. A product of the Ben Greet Academy, she made her stage debut at the age of 18 and over the next decade was rarely out of work, as she observed in an interview in *Vanity Fair*: "Apart from having my appendix out and having a baby I don't think I stopped for the first ten years, I kept going up the ladder and that's heady stuff". She acted on both sides of the Atlantic in a wide variety of plays, continually displaying and extending her versatility as an actress. Her performances were often described as spellbinding and extremely believable, whatever the role, although her most notable successes were in Shakespeare. She played opposite John Gielgud in three acclaimed productions; firstly, in Gielgud's celebrated *Hamlet*, in which she was Ophelia, secondly, as Cordelia in *King Lear*, and thirdly, as Miranda in *The Tempest*. These three productions marked the pinnacle of her British career.

Tandy moved to the USA in 1940 with her young daughter primarily to avoid the war and to continue working. It was there that she met her second husband, the actor-director Hume Cronyn, with whom she formed a notable and lasting stage partnership.

In 1947 she was the first actress to tackle the role of Blanche DuBois in *A Streetcar Named Desire* by Tennessee Williams. Two years earlier, Cronyn had mounted a production of a short play also by Williams, *Portrait of a Madonna*, at the Actors' Lab in Los Angeles and this became the prototype for the later play when it was directed in New York by Elia Kazan. Cronyn put Tandy in the lead role of *Portrait of a Madonna* and when Kazan saw her he knew she would be ideal for his own production: "She solved our most difficult problem in a flash". Although Williams had initially wanted Lillian Gish for the part of Blanche, Kazan chose Tandy and she went on to win great critical acclaim in the role on Broadway. Brooks Atkinson, of *The New York Times*, concluded that Tandy "was incredibly true".

Tandy's fragility as Blanche is evident from the still photos of the play and her ability to gain the sympathy of the audience for the character as the play progressed was much remarked upon by the critics. She played the role opposite the then unknown Marlon Brando, who appeared as Stanley. Tandy once referred to Brando as "an impossible psychopathic bastard", mainly on the grounds that he often tried to upstage her and rarely did the same thing twice when performing. However, her professionalism was such that her performances in the play established her as one of the leading actresses on the US stage. As Kazan commented on her work with Brando, "She knew that actors give better performances when they work with partners whose talents challenge their own". Tandy also said that until the role of Blanche she had been untested as an actress in the USA. Although Brando, in his autobiography, states that both he and Tandy were miscast in the roles and "threw the play out of balance", the critics disagreed and Tandy received her first Tony Award.

Despite her stage success Tandy did not have the looks that Hollywood correlates with box office profits and the screen role of Blanche was first offered to Olivia de Havilland and then Vivien Leigh, who eventually played the part in the film. The Cronyns, meanwhile, continued to consolidate their stage reputation, often appearing together in such plays as *The Fourposter* and *The Gin Game*, which were ideally suited for married couples. As they aged they specialised increasingly in playing elderly couples full of verve, spirit, and fight. It would have been very easy for their individual talents to have been submerged in such collaborations, but Tandy was more adventurous and occasionally returned to extending stage roles on her own. It was, indeed, on her own that she eventually achieved cinematic acceptance, notably as the southern Jewish matriarch Daisy Werthan in *Driving Miss Daisy*, in which she finally enjoyed popular, albeit somewhat sentimental, success. Tandy played the role with integrity and intelligence. She audaciously stripped away any natural charm the character might have had in order to avoid invoking a maudlin response from the audience and concentrated instead on exploring, with admirable control and definition, the relationship between the cantankerous Werthan and her black chauffeur, thus provoking a more thoughtful and contemplative reading of the film.

Tandy was always pragmatic where acting was concerned. When asked why it had taken her so long to win an Oscar she answered: "I don't think I've ever had a part in a movie that afforded me the opportunity of being nominated for an Oscar". Tandy did not see herself as an actress who was a constructor of a character and did not draw characters derived from her own life experiences. Rather she was a cerebral, interpretive artist, one whose strength and quality lay in her ability to get the very best out of what was written, an imaginative versatility that often put her at odds with the Hollywood star system.

—Sarah-Jane Dickenson

TAYLOR, Laurette. US actress. Born Laurette Cooney in New York, 1 April 1884. Little formal education. Married 1) playwright Charles A. Taylor in 1900 (divorced); 2) playwright John Hartley Manners in 1911 (died in 1928). Stage debut as a child in vaudeville, Gloucester, Massachusetts, and then at the Boston Athenaeum, 1903; New York debut, New Star Theatre, 1903; subsequently toured and appeared in stock repertory in Seattle, Washington, 1903–05; settled in New York after nervous breakdown, 1905; starred in 600-performance run of her second husband's *Peg o' My Heart*, New York, 1912; first appearance on British stage, Eastbourne, 1914; revisited London, 1920; film debut, 1922; retired from the stage on her husband's death, 1928; reappeared sporadically in succeeding years and had last major success in *The Glass Menagerie*, which ran for a year shortly before her death. Died in New York, 8 December 1946.

Roles

1903   Flossie Cooper in *From Rags to Riches* (C. Taylor), New Star Theatre, New York.

1909   May Keating in *The Great John Ganton* (Manners), Lyric Theatre, New York.

Eleanor Hillary in *The Ringmaster* (Porter), Maxine Elliott Theatre, New York.

Ruth Dakon in *Dakon's Daughter*, Hackett Theatre, New York.

1910   Lilian Turner in *The Girl in Waiting* (Manners), Hartford, Connecticut.

Rose Lane in *Alias Jimmy Valentine* (Armstrong), Wallack's Theatre, New York.

1911   Mici in *The Seven Sisters* (Olcott), Lyceum Theatre, New York.

1912   Luana in *The Bird of Paradise* (Tully), Daly's Theatre, New York.

Peg in *Peg o' My Heart* (Manners), Shubert Theatre, Rochester, New York, and Cort Theatre, New York; Devonshire Park Theatre, Eastbourne, and Comedy Theatre, London, 1914; Cort Theatre, New York, 1921.

1914   Doleen Sweetmarsh in *Just as Well*, Cort Theatre, New York.

Jenny in *Happiness* (Manners), Cort Theatre, New York; Theatre Royal, Drury Lane, London, 1915; Criterion Theatre, New York, 1917.

The Dupe in *The Day of Dupes*, Cort Theatre, New York.

Fluff in *The Woman Intervenes*, Empire Theatre, London.

1915   The King's Daughter in *The Monk and the King's Daughter*, St James's Theatre, London.

1916   Sylvia in *The Harp of Life* (Manners), Globe Theatre, New York.

1917   'Aunted Annie in *Out There* (Manners), Globe Theatre, New York.

Miss Alverstone in *The Wooing of Eve* (Manners), Liberty Theatre, New York.

1918   Juliet in extracts from *Romeo and Juliet* (Shakespeare), Criterion Theatre, New York.

Portia in extracts from *The Merchant of Venice* (Shakespeare), Criterion Theatre, New York.

Katherine in extracts from *The Taming of the Shrew* (Shakespeare), Criterion Theatre, New York.

1919   L'Enigme in *One Night in Rome* (Manners), Criterion Theatre, New York; Garrick Theatre, London, 1920.

1922   Marian in *The National Anthem* (Manners), Henry Miller Theatre, New York.

1923   Sarah Kantor in *Humoresque* (Borzage), Vanderbilt Theatre, New York.

Nell Gwynne in *Sweet Nell of Old Drury* (Kester), 48th Street Theatre, New York.

1925   Young Pierrot in *Pierrot the Prodigal*, 48th Street Theatre, New York.

Rose Trelawny in *Trelawny of the Wells* (Pinero), Knickerbocker Theatre, New York.

Lissa Terry in *In a Garden* (Barry), Plymouth Theatre, New York.

Laurette Taylor (c. 1922).

1928   Fifi Sands in *The Furies* (Akins), Shubert Theatre, New York.

1932   Mrs Dowey in *The Old Lady Shows Her Medals* (Barrie), Playhouse Theatre, New York.

Mrs Grey in *Alice-Sit-by-the-Fire* (Barrie), Playhouse Theatre, New York.

1934   Marian Thomas in *At Marian's* (L. Taylor), Ogunquit, Maine.

1938   Miss Midget in *Outward Bound* (Vane), Playhouse Theatre, New York.

1945   Amanda Wingfield in *The Glass Menagerie* (T. Williams), Playhouse Theatre, New York.

Other roles included: *The Comedienne*, Chicago, 1927; *To-Morrow's Sunday*, tour, 1938; *Mary, Mary Quite Contrary* (Ervine), tour, 1938; *Candida* (G. B. Shaw), tour, 1938.

Films

Peg o' My Heart, 1922. *Happiness*, 1924; *One Night in Rome*, 1924.

*

Bibliography

Books:
Marguerite Courtney, *Laurette*, New York and Toronto, 1955.

Articles:
Houghton Norris, "Laurette Taylor", *Theatre Arts*, 29, December 1945.
Day Tuttle, "Recollections of Laurette Taylor", *Theatre Arts*, 34, March 1950.

* * *

Laurette Taylor was called by Helen Hayes, Constantin Stanislavsky, and many others the greatest US actress of her time, and she was extolled by Sarah Bernhardt as a model actress for her generation. Yet, no other actress has ever garnered such fame as a serious artist while performing in so many second-rate plays. Indeed, Laurette Taylor's life story reads like the plot of one of the melodramas she starred in. Raised by an abusive father, Laurette found in the plays to which her stage-struck mother took her a salutory make-believe world. At 13 she became a child performer in the theatres that were the forerunner of vaudeville, and at 16 she began her professional career as a soubrette in the "fifty-cent" road show circuit, starring in the melodramas of Charles A. Taylor, "The King of the Melers", whom she married that year. While Laurette quickly found her husband's plays, with their stilted and lifeless scenes and lurid prose, virtually unplayable, she also learned the secret of acting from them. Her husband warned her that no matter how silly the material seemed, if she believed in it then the audience would believe it too.

Laurette Taylor had a genius for imaginative realism. She once wrote, "It isn't beauty or personality or magnetism that make a really great actress. It is imagination". Laurette was able to embroider a fictional reality around the cardboard and one-dimensional heroines she played and to immerse herself totally in them. In contrast to the many affected ingénues of the time, critics as well as the public found Laurette Taylor to be artless and natural. Playing seven shows in 10 weeks and 50 plays and musical comedies in two years thoroughly grounded Laurette in her craft and taught her the value of hard work. After she had achieved stardom on Broadway, she said of this period: "I looked upon it as a sort of armour to fit me for the fighting I expected and still expect to do ... working hard, never shirking ... its hardships as the test of my ambition". Her work paid off when she achieved stardom while performing in Charles Taylor's *Rags to Riches* in 1903. She continued to perform in her husband's melodramas for the next two years along with the usual stock plays of the period — *Uncle Tom's Cabin*, *Camille*, and *Faust* — until a nervous breakdown prompted her to escape the grind of stock and flee to New York. Here she divorced Charles Taylor and married the most popular Broadway playwright of the time, the dapper Englishman Hartley Manners. His plays, which initially seemed to provide perfect vehicles for Laurette's talent, ultimately proved another mixed blessing for the gifted actress. In 1912 Laurette enjoyed her first Broadway success and international fame in *Peg o' My Heart*, a play written by Manners as a wedding present to her. The character of Peg, with her innocence, impishness, wit, and wisdom, was modelled upon Laurette. While Laurette appeared in more than 10 of Manners's 22 plays over the next 15 years, with only occasional forays into such playwrights as Philip Barrie, Zoe Atkins, and, later, J. M. Barrie, Sutton Vane, and Tennessee Williams, none ever acheived the success of *Peg*. Critic after critic applauded

her acting, while groaning over the waste of her talent in Manners's second-rate plays.

In 1928 the enduring partnership finally came to an end with Manners's death. Devastated, Laurette retired from the stage and took to the bottle. Over the next 16 years she appeared sporadically in revivals of J. M. Barrie and Sutton Vane. In 1944, when fans had thought that Laurette Taylor was finished, phoenix-like she rose up from the despair and alcoholism to play the part of Amanda Wingfield in Williams's *The Glass Menagerie* — "Peg grown old" as Laurette affectionately called her. With this stunning comeback, critics compared her to the great Italian actress Eleonora Duse. The brief and brilliant flare of her final and greatest stage performance lit up the theatre world and secured her lasting recognition in the annals of theatre history.

Laurette Taylor, trained as she was in the "hard knocks" school of melodrama, was a supremely gifted comedienne and mime. She knew how to manipulate her facial expressions and gestures to achieve both the subtle effects of realism as well as to enchant the audience and rivet all eyes on her effortless technique. Critics were unable to pinpoint the reason for Taylor's genius, because she strove to create an illusion so complete that her spectators should be unable to detect how it was done. James O'Donnell Bennett said of her performance in *Dakon's Daughter* on Broadway that "Audiences follow her manoeuvres with intense interest for she exercises in an almost uncanny way the faculty of riveting attention upon herself; and observation is constantly rewarded by the disclosure of fleeting bits of detail, swift changes of mood, little quizzical touches of emphasis and tricks of facial play that are as unexpected as they are right and charming".

In preparing for the soubrette of *Scotty, King of the Desert Mines* she carefully observed the movements of labourers swinging mallets to lay rails so that she could faithfully reproduce them on stage. For the part of Mama Kantor in *Humoresque* she studied the dialects and mannerisms of an old Russian Jewish tailor and his wife and the Jews of the Bronx community where they lived. One critic said, "The character study was authentic, real and living ... Not only did the dialect ring true, but the unwieldy figure, the swaying walk, and the racial gestures were all part of Sarah Kantor and had nothing whatever in common with Laurette Taylor". With *Humoresque*, Laurette proved that she was not only a versatile character actress who could play an old Jewish woman as well as the young impish Peg, but that she also had tremendous abilities as a tragic actress. Constantin Stanislavsky, who saw the motion picture *Peg* in 1922 and *Humoresque* declared her to be the USA's greatest actress.

Ultimately, Laurette Taylor had that indescribable evanescent and luminous quality born of extreme sensitivity that is the hallmark of a great artist. Arthur Hopkins wrote, "Even when that unforgettable face was old and ravaged, it could suddenly be illumined by beauty that is not of this earth. She was a star of celestial illumination". Harold Clurman, who knew her in her old age, wrote that "she expressed a constantly tremulous sensibility that seemed vulnerable to the least breath of vulgarity, coarseness, or cruelty without ever wholly succumbing to the overwhelming persistence of all three ... Her face was always suffused with a look of startled wonder, at once happy, humorous, frightened, and innocent". Finally, Tennessee

Williams wrote perhaps the greatest tribute to her: "There was a radiance about her art which I can compare only to the greatest lines of poetry, and which gave me the same shock of revelation as if the air about us had been momentarily broken through by light from some clear space beyond us".

—Kathryn Wylie-Marques

TERRY, (Dame) Ellen. British actress. Born Ellen Alice Terry in Coventry, 27 February 1847. Married 1) artist George Frederick Watts in 1864 (separated 1865); 2) actor Charles Kelly (Wardell) in 1878 (separated 1881); 3) actor James Carew in 1907 (separated 1909); lived with married architect and designer Edward William Godwin, 1868–75, one son (Edward Gordon Craig, *q.v.*) and one daughter (Edith Craig). Stage debut under Charles Kean, Princess's Theatre, London, 1854; acted with father Benjamin Terry's company and with Kean, 1856–59; toured with sister Kate Terry in father's company, 1859–60; actress, New Royalty Theatre, 1861, Theatre Royal, Bristol, 1862, Haymarket Theatre, London, 1863; left the stage on marriage, 1864, but resumed career, 1866; partnered Henry Irving for first time, Queen's Theatre, 1867; withdrew from the theatre, 1868–74; returned to stage at invitation of Charles Reade and acclaimed as Portia under the Bancrofts, 1875; debut with the Lyceum company as Irving's long-standing leading lady, in the role of Ophelia, 1878; first US tour with Lyceum company, 1883; Royal Command Performances, 1889 and 1893; celebrated correspondence with George Bernard Shaw, 1892–1922; left Lyceum company, 1902; manager, Imperial Theatre, 1903–04; British tour with Imperial company, 1904; celebrated jubilee, Theatre Royal, Drury Lane, 1906; Shakespearean lecture tours of UK, Australia, and USA, 1910–21; Australian tour ended early due to health problems, 1915; virtually blind after operations for cataracts, 1915; film debut, 1916; last stage appearance, Lyric, Hammersmith, 1925. Member: Actors' Orphanage Fund (vice-president). LL.D, University of St Andrew's, 1922. G.B.E. (Dame, Grand Cross of the British Empire), 1925. Died in Tenterden, Kent, 21 July 1928.

Roles

1854   Duke of York in *Richard III* (Shakespeare), Princess's Theatre, London.
1856   Mamillius in *The Winter's Tale* (Shakespeare), Princess's Theatre, London.
    Sun-Worshipper in *Pizarro* (Sheridan), Princess's Theatre, London.
    Puck in *A Midsummer Night's Dream* (Shakespeare), Princess's Theatre, London.
1857   William Waddilove in *To Parents and Guardians* (Taylor), Theatre Royal, Ryde, Isle of Wight.
    Jacob Earwig in *The Boots at the Swan* (Selby), Theatre Royal, Ryde, Isle of Wight.
    Fairy Goldenstar and Dragonetta in *Harlequin and the White Cat*, Princess's Theatre, London.

1858   Karl in *Faust and Margaret* (Boucicault), Princess's Theatre, London.
    A boy in *The Merchant of Venice* (Shakespeare), Princess's Theatre, London.
    Prince Arthur in *King John* (Shakespeare), Princess's Theatre, London.
    Fleance in *Macbeth* (Shakespeare), Princess's Theatre, London.
    Genius of the Jewel in *The King o' the Castle* (Croquill), Princess's Theatre, London.
1859   Katie Mapleton in *Nine Points of the Law* (Taylor), Olympic Theatre, London.
    Fanny Fact in *Time Tries All* (Courtney), Willis's Room, London.
    Tom in *If the Cap Fits* (Harrington and Yates), Princess's Theatre, London.
    An angel in *Henry VIII* (Shakespeare), Princess's Theatre, London.
    Giles, Harry, and James in *Distant Relations* (Courtney), British tour.
    Hector Melrose in *Home for the Holiday* (Moncrieff), British tour.
1860   Mabel Valecrucis in *A Lesson for Life* (Taylor), Lyceum Theatre, London.
1861   Sarah Jane in *Nine Points of the Law* (Taylor), Campden House, London; revived, 1863.
    Puck in *Midsummer's Eve* (Yelland), Lyceum Theatre, London.
    Clementine in *Atar Gull* (Sue), New Royalty Theatre, London.
    Sophia Heinback in *All in the Dark* (Planché), New Royalty Theatre, London.
    Rosetta in *A Thumping Legacy* (Morton), New Royalty Theatre, London.
    Letty Briggs in *The Governor's Wife* (Mildenhall), New Royalty Theatre, London.
    Sophie Western in *Bamboozling* (Wilkes), New Royalty Theatre, London.
    Clara in *Matrimony* (Derby), New Royalty Theatre, London.
    Mrs Laura Brinstone in *A Nice Quiet Day* (Hopkins and Murray), New Royalty Theatre, London.
    Mabel in *Lesson for Husbands* (anon.), New Royalty Theatre, London.
1862   Florence in *Chinese Romance* (Horne), New Royalty Theatre, London.
    Louise Drayton in *Grandfather Whitehead* (Lemon), New Royalty Theatre, London.
    Sally Potts in *The Eton Boy* (Morton), New Royalty Theatre, London.
    Clorinda in *A Family Failing* (Oxenford), St James's Theatre, London.
    Cupid in *Endymion* (Brough), Theatre Royal, Bristol.
    Alice in *Marriage at any Price* (Wooler), Theatre Royal, Bristol.
    Dictys in *Perseus and Andromeda* (Brough), Theatre Royal, Bristol.
    Serena in *Conrad and Medora* (Brough), Theatre Royal, Bristol.
    Gertrude Howard in *The Little Treasure* (Harris and Williams), Theatre Royal, Bristol.

Ellen Terry

1863   Spirit of the Future in *Dramatic Prologue* (Powell), Theatre Royal, Bath.
Titania in *A Midsummer Night's Dream* (Shakespeare), Theatre Royal, Bath.
Hero in *Much Ado About Nothing* (Shakespeare), Haymarket Theatre, London, and Theatre Royal, Bristol.
Britannia in *Mr Buckstone at Home* (Coyne), Haymarket Theatre, London.
Lady Touchwood in *The Belle's Stratagem* (Cowley), Haymarket Theatre, London.
Desdemona in *Othello* (Shakespeare), Princess's Theatre, London; Lyceum Theatre, London, 1881; Grand Theatre, Fulham, London, 1898.
Mary Ford in *A Lesson for Life* (Taylor), St James's Theatre, London.
Isabella in *A Game of Romps* (Morton), Theatre Royal, Bristol.
Flora in *The Duke's Motto* (Feval and Brougham), Theatre Royal, Bristol.
Nerissa in *The Merchant of Venice* (Shakespeare), Theatre Royal, Bristol.
Julia in *The Rivals* (Sheridan), Haymarket Theatre, London.
Mary Meredith in *Our American Cousin* (Taylor), Haymarket Theatre, London.
Sir Tristam in *King Arthur* (Brough), Haymarket Theatre, London.

1866   Helen Heartwell in *The Hunchback* (Knowles), Olympic Theatre, London.

1867   Keziah Mapletop in *A Sheep in Wolf's Clothing* (Taylor), Adelphi Theatre, London.
Madeleine in *The Antipodes* (Taylor), Theatre Royal, Holborn, London.
Kate Dalrymple in *The Little Savage* (Morton), Princess Theatre, Manchester.
Rose de Beaurepaire in *The Double Marriage* (Reade), New Queen's Theatre, London.
Mrs Mildmay in *Still Waters Run Deep* (Taylor), New Queen's Theatre, London.
Katherine in *Katherine and Petruchio* (Garrick), New Queen's Theatre, London.

1868   Kitty in *The Household Fairy* (Talfourd), New Queen's Theatre, London.

1874   Philippa Chester in *The Wandering Heir* (Reade), New Queen's Theatre, London.
Susan Merton in *It's Never Too Late to Mend* (Reade), Astley's Theatre, London.
Helen Rolleston in *Our Seaman* (Reade), Theatre Royal, Birmingham.
Volante in *The Honey Moon* (Tobin), Crystal Palace, London.
Kate Hardcastle in *She Stoops to Conquer* (Goldsmith), Crystal Palace, London.

1875   Portia in *The Merchant of Venice* (Shakespeare), Prince of Wales's Theatre, London; British tour and Lyceum Theatre, London, 1879; British tour, 1880; Lyceum Theatre, London, 1887, 1893, 1894, and 1902; Prince's Theatre, Bristol, 1902; Imperial Theatre, London, 1903; Guild Hall, Winchester, 1909; Shakespeare Memorial Theatre, Stratford-upon-Avon, 1910; Tenterden, Kent, 1915; Old Vic Theatre, London, 1917.
Clara Douglas in *Money* (Bulwer-Lytton), Prince of Wales's Theatre, London.
Mrs Honeyton in *A Happy Pair* (Smith), Prince of Wales's Theatre, London.
Mabel Vance in *Masks and Faces* (Taylor and Reade), Prince of Wales's Theatre, London.

1876   Blanche Haye in *Ours* (Robertson), Prince of Wales's Theatre, London.
Kate Hungerford in *Brothers* (Coghlan), Court Theatre, London.
Lilian Vavasour in *New Men and Old Acres* (Taylor and Dubourg), Court Theatre, London; British tour, 1879 and 1880.

1877   Georgina Vesey in *Money* (Bulwer-Lytton), Theatre Royal, Drury Lane, London.
Lady Teazle in *The School for Scandal* (Sheridan), Gaiety Theatre, London; British tour, 1879 and 1880.
Lady Juliet in *The House of Darnley* (Bulwer-Lytton), Court Theatre, London.

1878   Mrs Merryweather in *Victims* (Taylor), Court Theatre, London.
Olivia in *Olivia* (Wills), Court Theatre, London; Lyceum Theatre, London, 1885, 1891, 1893, and 1897.
Iris in *Cynic's Defeat; or, All Is Vanity* (Thompson), Prince of Wales's Theatre, Liverpool; British tour, 1879.

Ophelia in *Hamlet* (Shakespeare), Lyceum Theatre, London; British tour; revived at the Lyceum, 1879, 1881, and 1885.

1879   Pauline in *The Lady of Lyons* (Bulwer-Lytton), Lyceum Theatre, London.

Lady Anne in *Richard III* (Shakespeare), Gaiety Theatre, London.

Ruth Meadows in *Eugene Aram* (Wills), Lyceum Theatre, London.

Queen Henrietta Maria in *Charles I* (Wills), Lyceum Theatre, London; tour of USA and Canada, 1883; Lyceum Theatre, London, 1891 and 1893.

Peggy in *Raising the Wind* (Kenny), Lyceum Theatre, London; revived there, 1886.

Blanche Beaumont in *Butterfly* (Carr), Gaiety Theatre, Glasgow.

Dora in *Dora* (Reade), Prince of Wales's Theatre, Liverpool.

1880   Iolanthe in *Iolanthe* (Wills), Lyceum Theatre, London.

Beatrice in *Much Ado About Nothing* (Shakespeare), Grand Theatre, Leeds; Lyceum Theatre, London, 1882, 1884, 1891, and 1893; Imperial Theatre, London, 1903; Globe Theatre, Earl's Court, London, 1912; The Middle Temple, London, 1916.

Camma in *The Cup* (Tennyson), Lyceum Theatre, London.

Letitia Hardy in *The Belle's Stratagem* (Cowley), Lyceum Theatre, London.

1882   Juliet in *Romeo and Juliet* (Shakespeare), Lyceum Theatre, London.

1883   Jeanette in *The Lyons Mail* (Reade), Lyceum Theatre, London; revived there, 1893.

Clementine in *Robert Macaire* (Selby), Lyceum Theatre, London.

1884   Viola in *Twelfth Night* (Shakespeare), Lyceum Theatre, London.

1885   Margaret in *Faust* (Wills), Lyceum Theatre, London; revived there, 1888 and 1894.

1887   Josephine in *Werner* (Lord Byron), Lyceum Theatre, London.

Ellaline in *The Amber Heart* (Calmour), Lyceum Theatre, London; revived there, 1888.

Mary Jane in *Wool Gathering* (Longridge), St George's Hall, London.

1888   Mary Jane in *The Secret* (Beerbohm), St George's Hall, London.

Lady Macbeth in *Macbeth* (Shakespeare), British tour.

1889   Catherine Duval in *The Dead Heart* (Phillips), Lyceum Theatre, London.

1890   Lucy Ashton in *Ravenswood* (Merivale), Lyceum Theatre, London.

1891   Nance Oldfield in *Nance Oldfield* (Reade), Lyceum Theatre, London; Coronet Theatre, London, 1901.

1892   Queen Katherine in *Henry VIII* (Shakespeare), Lyceum Theatre, London; revived there, 1893; Shakespeare Memorial Theatre, Stratford-upon-Avon, 1902; Old Vic Theatre, London, 1916.

Cordelia in *King Lear* (Shakespeare), Lyceum Theatre, London.

1893   Rosamund de Clifford in *Becket* (Tennyson), Lyceum Theatre, London; revived there, 1894.

1894   Lady Soupsie in *Journey's End in Lover's Meeting* (Hobbes and Moore), Daly's Theatre, London.

1895   Guinevere in *King Arthur* (Comyns-Carr), Lyceum Theatre, London.

1896   Yolande in *Godefroi and Yolande* (L. Irving), Columbia Theatre, Chicago.

Imogen in *Cymbeline* (Shakespeare), Lyceum Theatre, London; revived there, 1897.

1897   Madame Sans-Gêne in *Madame Sans-Gêne* (Sardou and Moreau), Lyceum Theatre, London.

1898   Catherine in *Peter the Great* (L. Irving), Lyceum Theatre, London.

The Hon. Sylvia Wynford in *The Medicine Man* (Hitchen and Traill), Lyceum Theatre, London.

1899   Clarisse du Malucon in *Robespierre* (Sardou), Lyceum Theatre, London.

Mrs Tresilian in *Variations* (Young), Lyceum Theatre, London; St James's Theatre, London, 1908.

Lady Cicely Wayneflete in *Captain Brassbound's Conversion* (Shaw), Royal Court Theatre, Liverpool; Court Theatre, London, 1906; Grand Theatre, Stockton, 1908.

1901   Volumnia in *Coriolanus* (Shakespeare), Lyceum Theatre, London.

1902   Mistress Page in *The Merry Wives of Windsor* (Shakespeare), His Majesty's Theatre, London; revived there, 1906, 1908, and 1911.

1903   Hiordis in *The Vikings* (Ibsen), Imperial Theatre, London.

Evodia in *The Mistress of the Robes* (Grave), Royal Court Theatre, Liverpool.

1904   Kniertje in *The Good Hope* (Heijermans), Theatre Royal, Nottingham.

Brita in *Eriksson's Wife* (St John), Grand Theatre, Wolverhampton.

1905   Alice in *Alice Sit-By-The-Fire* (Barrie), Duke of York's Theatre, London.

Francesca in *Measure for Measure* (Shakespeare), Adelphi Theatre, London.

Hermione in *The Winter's Tale* (Shakespeare), His Majesty's Theatre, London.

1908   Elizabeth of York in *Henry of Lancaster* (Ungar), Theatre Royal, Nottingham.

Aunt Imogen in *Pinkie and the Fairies* (Robertson), His Majesty's Theatre, London.

1909   Alexia Vane in *At a Junction* (Young), Caxton Hall and Bridgwater House, London.

Nance Oldfield in *Pageant of Famous Women* (Edith Craig and C. Hamilton), Scala Theatre, London.

1910   Drama in *Masque of Shakespeare*, St Dunstan's, London.

1911   Nell Gwynne in *The First Actress* (St John), Kingsway Theatre, London.

1914   The Abbess in *Paphnutis* (Hroswitha), Savoy Theatre, London.

1915   The Queen in *The Princess and the Pea* (Bright), Haymarket Theatre, London.

1916   Darling in *The Admirable Crichton* (Barrie), Coliseum Theatre, London, and London Opera House.

Lady of the Manor in *The Homecoming* (Drinkwater), The Middle Temple, London.

1917   Grand-mère in *Ellen Terry's Bouquet* (Lucas), Lyric, Hammersmith, London.

1919   Prologue in *Nativity Play*, Rye Monastery; Everyman Theatre, Hampstead, London, 1920.

Nurse in *Romeo and Juliet* (Shakespeare), Lyric, Hammersmith, London.

1922   Mrs Long in *Pride and Prejudice* (Squire), Palace Theatre, London.

Ellen Terry in *Thirty Minutes in the Street* (Mayer), Palace Theatre, London.

Old Woman in *The Old Woman Who Lived in a Shoe*, Palace Theatre, London.

1925   The Ghost of Miss Susan Wildersham in *Crossings* (De La Mare), Lyric, Hammersmith, London.

Films

Julia Lovelace in *Her Greatest Performance*, 1917; Mother in *The Invasion of Britain*, 1918; Widow Bernick in *Pillars of Society*, 1918; Lady Merrall in *Potter's Clay*, 1922; Buda in *The Bohemian Girl*, 1922.

Publications

The Story of My Life (autobiography), 1908; *The Russian Ballet*, 1913; *The Heart of Ellen Terry* (autobiography), 1928; *Four Lectures on Shakespeare*, 1932.

*

Bibliography

Books:

Charles Hiatt, *Ellen Terry and Her Impersonations*, London, 1900.

T. Edgar Pemberton, *Ellen Terry and Her Sisters*, London, 1902.

Christopher St John, *Ellen Terry*, 1907.

E. V. Lucas, *Prologue to Ellen Terry's Bouquet*, 1917.

Christopher St John, *Ellen Terry and Bernard Shaw: A Correspondence*, London, 1930.

E. Gordon Craig, *Ellen Terry and Her Secret Self*, London, 1931.

Edith Craig and Christopher St John (eds.), *Ellen Terry's Memoirs*, London, 1933.

Edward Perry, *Remember Ellen Terry and Edith Craig*, London, 1948.

Nina Auerbach, *Ellen Terry – Player in her Time*, London, 1967.

Roger Manvell, *Ellen Terry – A Biography*, London, 1968.

Constance Fechter, *Bright Star: A Portrait of Ellen Terry*, New York, 1970.

Tom Prideaux, *Love or Nothing – The Life and Times of Ellen Terry*, London, 1975.

* * *

Born into a theatrical family, Ellen Terry made her stage debut (aged nine) under the formidable tutelage of Charles and Ellen Kean at the Princess's Theatre. Rehearsals were unrelenting even for so young a performer as Mrs Kean drummed into her the essentials of enunciation: "A, E, I, O, U, my dear, are five distinct vowels, so don't mix them all up together."

Ellen Terry's earliest impersonation was captured by the lens of the photographer Laroche and throughout her life she held a great fascination for artists. Barely 16, she married G. F. Watts, whose portraits ("Choosing", "Ophelia") were the only positive outcome of an ill-matched union. Architect E. W. Godwon, the father of her children Edy and Edward Gordon Craig, drew her and she was subsequently a subject for Graham Robertson, John Collier, John Singer Sargent, and sculptor William Brodie. Graham Robertson described Ellen Terry as "par excellence the Painter's Actress ... (she) appealed to the eye before the ear; her gesture and pose were eloquence itself."

Ellen Terry's most striking physical trait was her hair, variously described as yellow (by Oscar Wilde), golden, flaxen, and blonde. Her eyes were a bewitching grey; her broad nose tilted slightly at the tip; her mouth wide and her chin firm. Such physical beauty was undoubtedly a major asset in Ellen Terry's stage career, especially at a time when pictorialism in both acting and production was reaching its peak. Encased behind the proscenium arch, actors were indeed part of a stage picture, the composition of which often imitated poses from painting.

Ellen Terry's attractions were not merely surface-deep. She was the embodiment of young English womanhood, innately feminine, delicately lady-like, tender, graceful, spontaneous, and essentially innocent. Physically she was restless, fidgety even, but in movement resembled Beatrice "like a lapwing" running "close by the ground". Her vocal training with the Keans stood her in good stead throughout her career. Her articulation was clear and her voice was particularly expressive in scenes of comedy, pathos, and romantic love.

For over 20 years Ellen Terry was the principal jewel in Henry Irving's Lyceum crown. In Shakespeare she was his Ophelia, Juliet, Desdemona, Lady Macbeth, Coredelia, Portia, Imogen, and finally — and improbably — his Voulmnia. The primary imperative in Irving's selection of plays was that there should be a good part for him, hence he never gave Ellen Terry the opportunity to play Rosalind, a role for which she seemed to be singularly well suited. In contemporary plays she had opportunities as Camma in Tennyson's The Cup and as Rosamund de Clifford in the same author's *Becket*. She took the title role in W. G. Wills's *Olivia* (from Goldsmith's *The Vicar of Wakefield*), Queen Henrietta Maria in his *Charles the First*, and Margaret in his *Faust*. But Shaw was not alone in considering that Irving was wasting Ellen Terry's talents.

Not that opinion on those talents was undivided. Ellen Terry's sternest critic was the novelist Henry James, who was adamant that "she is simply not an actress". James was at his most astringent about Terry's Portia, a role in which he found the actress's natural charm inadequate compensation for her lack of artistry. By general consent she began well and won many hearts in the light-hearted banter with Nerissa about her rival suitors. In her encounter with Morocco (Irving's truncated text spared her Arragon) she was cautioned for being over-demonstrative in following his movement from casket to casket. In James's view worse followed in Bassanio's casket scene, where Terry's Portia giggled too much and "too osculatory"; she even entertained the suggestion that Portia was not above giving a hint directing her preferred suitor to the right casket. The expedition to Bellario was little more than a schoolgirl prank and her disguise in a rose-coloured lawyer's gown for the trial scene was rather too becoming. In a late (1911) recording, Terry's delivery of the "quality of mercy" speech emerges as a piece of recitation (her earlier stage performance was described as over-studied by some observers). For her Portia the discovery of the flaw in the bond came only at the last minute and she felt a personal distaste for the "quibble" by which Irving's sympathetic Shylock was ensnared. In her brief scene with Bassanio after the trial she was inappropriately arch, but she blossomed in the romantic dawn of Belmont, except of course when Irving cut the last act. In the final analysis, Ellen Terry's Portia displayed a comic exuberance, female guile and a beauty that evidently charmed all but the most hard-hearted of her critics, who sought in vain for the character's dignity and intellect.

Although Ellen Terry felt that her potential was not fully realised during her Lyceum years, her subsequent career was not marked by great distinction. In part she was the victim of the scarcity of roles available to actresses in later life. Together with her son Edward Gordon Craig, she was briefly involved in an unsuccessful management of the Imperial Theatre, where she produced Ibsen's *The Vikings* alongside *Much Ado About Nothing*. She also appeared in some contemporary plays, most notably Barrie's *Alice-Sit-By-The-Fire* and Shaw's *Captain Brassbound's Conversion*. She was fêted by her profession at a gala to celebrate her 50 years on the stage in 1906, after which her appearances became intermittent. She was among Barrie's nominees for honorary degrees when he was installed as Rector of St Andrew's University in 1922, and (belatedly in the view of many) she became a DBE in 1925.

In death, as in life, Ellen Terry's humanity showed through. Inscribed in her mother's copy of *The Imitation of Christ*, Edy Craig read William Allingham's lines beginning "No funeral gloom, my dears, when I am gone", beneath which 'Our Ellen' had added: "I should wish my children, relatives, and friends to observe this when I die."

—Richard Foulkes

THORNDIKE, (Dame) (Agnes) Sybil. British actress and manager. Born in Gainsborough, Lincolnshire, 24 October 1882. Educated at the High School, Rochester, Kent; Guildhall School of Music, London. Married actor Lewis Casson (*q.v.*) in 1908 (died 1969), two sons and two daughters. Stage debut, with Ben Greet's Pastoral Players, 1904; toured USA with Greet's company, 1904–07; actress, Annie Horniman's company, Manchester, 1908–14; actress, Old Vic Theatre, London, 1914–18; film debut, 1921; manager, with Casson, of the New Theatre, London, from

Sybil Thorndike (1957).

1922; much admired as George Bernard Shaw's St. Joan, 1924; television debut, 1939; toured widely during World War II; retired from stage, 1966; theatre named after her opened in Leatherhead, Surrey, 1969. LL.D: University of Manchester, 1923; D.Litt: University of Oxford, 1966. DBE (Dame of the British Empire), 1931; CH (Companion of Honour), 1970. Died in Chelsea, London, 9 June 1976.

Roles

1904–07   Phyllis in *My Lord from Town* (Paull), Worcester College, Oxford.
           Lucianus in *Hamlet* (Shakespeare), US tour.
           Ceres in *The Tempest* (Shakespeare), US tour.
           Viola in *Twelfth Night* (Shakespeare), US tour; Far East tour, 1954.
           Helena in *All's Well That Ends Well* (Shakespeare), US tour.
           Gertrude in *Hamlet* (Shakespeare), US tour; Lyceum Theatre, London, 1926.
           Rosalind in *As You Like It* (Shakespeare), US tour; Old Vic Theatre, London, 1914–18; Regent Theatre, London, 1924.
           Ophelia in *Hamlet* (Shakespeare), US tour; Old Vic Theatre, London, 1914–18.
           Nerissa in *The Merchant of Venice* (Shakespeare), US tour.
           Everyman in *Everyman* (anon.), US tour.

1907   O Chicka San in *His Japanese Wife* (Griswold),
        Bijou Theatre, London.
1908   Janet Morice in *The Marquis* (Raleigh and
        Dark), Scala Theatre, London.
        Kezia in *The Subjection of Kezia* (Ellis), British
        tour.
        Candida in *Candida* (G. B. Shaw), Gaiety
        Theatre, Manchester; Holborn Empire, London, 1920; British tour, 1940–42.
1908–09 Bessie Carter in *Marriages Are Made in Heaven*
        (Dean), Gaiety Theatre, Manchester.
        Mrs Rawlings in *When the Devil Was Ill*(McEvoy), Gaiety Theatre, Manchester.
        Caroline Blizzard in *Gentlemen of the Road*
        (McEvoy), Gaiety Theatre, Manchester.
        Lady Denison in *The Charity That Began at
        Home* (Hankin), Gaiety Theatre, Manchester;
        revived there, 1912–13.
        Mrs Chartoris in *His Helpmate* (McEvoy),
        Gaiety Theatre, Manchester.
        Mrs Barthwick in *The Silver Box* (Galsworthy),
        Gaiety Theatre, Manchester.
        Artemis in *Hippolytus* (Euripides, adapted by
        Murray), Gaiety Theatre, Manchester; Regent Theatre, London, 1925.
        Nurse Price in *Cupid and the Styx* (Martin),
        Gaiety Theatre, Manchester.
        Thora in *The Feud* (Garnett), Gaiety Theatre,
        Manchester.
        Gertrude Eckersley in *Trespassers Will Be
        Prosecuted* (Arabian), Gaiety Theatre, Manchester.
        Bettina in *The Vale of Content* (Sudermann),
        Gaiety Theatre, Manchester.
1910   Sal Fortescue in *Peg Woffington's Pearls* (Jones
        and Cleugh), Court Theatre, London.
        Columbine in *The Marriage of Columbine*
        (Chapin), Court Theatre, London.
        Winifred in *The Sentimentalists* (Meredith),
        Duke of York's Theatre, London.
        Emma Huxtable in *The Madras House* (Granville Barker), Duke of York's Theatre, London.
        Romp in *Prunella* (Granville Barker and Housman), Duke of York's Theatre, London;
        Gaiety Theatre, Manchester, 1912–13.
        Maggie Massey in *Chains* (Baker), Duke of
        York's Theatre, London.
        Emily Chapman in *Smith* (Maugham), Empire
        Theatre, New York; US tour, 1911.
1912   Beatrice Farrar in *Hindle Wakes* (Houghton),
        Aldwych Theatre, London, and Playhouse,
        London.
        Dolly in *Makeshift* (Robins), Playhouse, London.
1912–13 Jennie Rollins in *The Question* (Wickham),
        Gaiety Theatre, Manchester.
        Renie Dalrymple in *Revolt* (Calderon), Gaiety
        Theatre, Manchester.
        Malkin in *The Whispering Well* (Rose), Gaiety
        Theatre, Manchester.

        Jane Clegg in *Jane Clegg* (Ervine), Gaiety
        Theatre, Manchester; Court Theatre, London, 1913; New Theatre, London, 1922;
        British tour, 1923; South African tour,
        1928–29; Wyndham's Theatre, London,
        1929.
        Privacy in *Prunella* (Granville Barker and
        Housman), Gaiety Theatre, Manchester.
1913   Ann Wellwyn in *The Pigeon* (Galsworthy),
        Court Theatre, London.
        Lady Philox in *Elaine* (Chapin), Court Theatre,
        London.
        Annie Scott in *The Price of Thomas Scott*
        (Baker), Gaiety Theatre, Manchester.
        Miss Stormit in *Nothing Like Leather* (Monkhouse), Gaiety Theatre, Manchester.
        Hester Dunnybrig in *The Shadow* (Phillpotts),
        Gaiety Theatre, Manchester, and Court Theatre, London.
        Portia in *Julius Caesar* (Shakespeare), Gaiety
        Theatre, Manchester.
1914–18 Adriana in *The Comedy of Errors* (Shakespeare), Old Vic Theatre, London.
        Lady Macbeth in *Macbeth* (Shakespeare), Old
        Vic Theatre, London; Théâtre de l'Odéon,
        Paris, 1921; Prince's Theatre, London, 1926;
        South African tour, 1928–29; Australasian
        tour, 1932; British tour, 1940–42; Far East
        tour, 1954.
        Portia in *The Merchant of Venice* (Shakespeare), Old Vic Theatre, London; Lyric
        Theatre, Hammersmith, London, 1927–28.
        Constance in *King John* (Shakespeare), Old Vic
        Theatre, London; New Theatre, London,
        1941.
        Beatrice in *Much Ado About Nothing* (Shakespeare), Old Vic Theatre, London; Lyric
        Theatre, Hammersmith, London, 1927–28;
        South African tour, 1928–29; Far East tour,
        1954.
        Imogen in *Cymbeline* (Shakespeare), Old Vic
        Theatre, London; New Theatre, London,
        1923.
        Chorus and Katharine in *Henry V* (Shakespeare), Old Vic Theatre, London; Lyric
        Theatre, Hammersmith, London, 1927–28;
        South African tour, 1928–29; Far East tour,
        1954.
        Julia in *The Two Gentlemen of Verona* (Shakespeare), Old Vic Theatre, London.
        Queen Margaret in *Richard III* (Shakespeare),
        Old Vic Theatre, London.
        Mrs Ford in *The Merry Wives of Windsor*
        (Shakespeare), Old Vic Theatre, London.
        Prince Hal in *Henry IV, part 1* (Shakespeare),
        Old Vic Theatre, London.
        The Fool in *King Lear* (Shakespeare), Old Vic
        Theatre, London.
        Ferdinand in *The Tempest* (Shakespeare), Old
        Vic Theatre, London.
        Launcelot Gobbo in *The Merchant of Venice*
        (Shakespeare), Old Vic Theatre, London.
        Rugby in *The Merry Wives of Windsor* (Shakespeare), Old Vic Theatre, London.

Puck in *A Midsummer Night's Dream* (Shakespeare), Old Vic Theatre, London.

Lady Teazle in *The School for Scandal* (Sheridan), Old Vic Theatre, London.

Kate Hardcastle in *She Stoops to Conquer* (Goldsmith), Old Vic Theatre, London.

Lydia Languish in *The Rivals* (Sheridan), Old Vic Theatre, London.

Peg Woffington in *Masks and Faces* (Reade and Taylor), Old Vic Theatre, London.

Columbine in *The Sausage String's Romance; or, A New Cut Harlequinade* (R. Thorndike, S. Thorndike, and G. Wilkinson), Old Vic Theatre, London.

Nancy in *Oliver Twist* (Dickens), Portsmouth.

1918   Mrs Lopez in *The Profiteers* (Hackett, adapted from Veber's *Gonzague*), London Pavilion.

Françoise Regnard in *The Kiddies in the Ruins* (Cannot, adapted from Gsell and Poulbot's *Les Gosses dans les Ruines*), New Oxford Theatre, London.

1919   Sygne de Coûfontaine in *The Hostage* (Claudel, translated by Chavannes), Scala Theatre, London.

Naomi Melsham in *The Chinese Puzzle* (Bower and Lion), New Theatre, London.

Dr James Barry in *Dr James Barry* (Racster and Grove), St James's Theatre, London.

Clara Borstwick in *The Great Day* (Parker and Sims), Theatre Royal, Drury Lane, London.

Hecuba in *The Trojan Women* (Murray, adapted from Euripides), Old Vic Theatre, London; Holborn Empire, London, 1920; Palace Theatre, London, and Theatre Royal, Drury Lane, London, 1922; New Theatre, London, 1924; Adelphi Theatre, London, 1937; Far East tour, 1954.

Anne Wickham in *Napoleon* (Trench), Queen's Theatre, London.

Sakuntala in *Sakuntala* (Kalidasa, adapted by Binyon and Das Gupta), Winter Garden Theatre, London.

1920   Medea in *Medea* (Murray, adapted from Euripides), Holborn Empire, London; New Theatre, London, 1922; British tour, 1923; Christ Church, Oxford, 1925; Prince's Theatre, London, and Théâtre des Champs-Elysées, Paris, 1927; Wyndham's Theatre, London, 1929; British tour, 1940–42; New Theatre, London, 1941; Far East tour, 1954.

Mary Hey in *Tom Trouble* (Burley), Holborn Empire, London.

Beryl Napier in *The Showroom* (Bell), Holborn Empire, London.

Mathilde Stangerson in *The Mystery of the Yellow Room* (Leroux, adapted by Bennett), St James's Theatre, London.

Céline in *The Children's Carnival* (Bouhélier, translated by St John), Kingsway Theatre, London.

1920–22   Carmen in *G.H.Q. Love* (Rehm), Little Theatre, London.

Elise Charrier in *The Hand of Death* (Lorde and Binet), Little Theatre, London.

Lea in *Private Room Number Six* (Lorde), Little Theatre, London.

Cinders in *Oh, Hell!!!* (Arkell and R. Thorndike), Little Theatre, London.

Marcelle in *The Medium* (Mille and Vylar, adapted by Levy), Little Theatre, London.

Judy in *The Tragedy of Mr Punch* (R. Thorndike and Arkell), Little Theatre, London.

Daisy in *The Person Unknown* (Maltby), Little Theatre, London.

Liz in *The Love Child* (Fenn and Pryce), Little Theatre, London.

Catherine in *The Kill* (Level, adapted by Harris), Little Theatre, London.

The Girl in *The Chemist* (Maurey, adapted by Harris), Little Theatre, London.

She in *The Vigil* (Lorde), Little Theatre, London.

Louise in *The Old Women* (Lorde, adapted by Holland), Little Theatre, London.

The Wife in *The Unseen* (Renaud, adapted by Casson), Little Theatre, London.

Chou Chou in *Crime* (Level, adapted by Casson), Little Theatre, London.

Millicent Wentworth in *Amends* (Crawshay-Williams), Little Theatre, London.

Mrs Forrest in *Changing Guard* (Nott-Bower), Little Theatre, London.

Katie Cripps in *De Mortuis* (Logan), Little Theatre, London.

Stephanie Meyrick in *Cupboard Love* (Crawshay-Williams), Little Theatre, London.

Amelia Angelfield in *Amelia's Suitors; or, Colonel Chutney's First Defeat* (Maltby), Little Theatre, London.

Rosalie in *The Nutcracker Suite* (Crawshay-Williams), Little Theatre, London.

Mrs Meldon in *Progress* (Ervine), Little Theatre, London.

His Betrothed in *Rounding the Triangle* (Crawshay-Williams), Little Theatre, London.

Madame Jeanne Chabrin in *The Unseen* (Renaud, adapted by Casson), Little Theatre, London.

The Shop Girl in *The Old Story* (Hirsch, adapted by McLellan), Little Theatre, London.

The Girl in *Fear* (Lorde), Little Theatre, London.

1921   Mother Sawyer in *The Witch of Edmonton* (Dekker, Ford, and Rowley), Lyric Theatre, Hammersmith, London.

Evadne in *The Maid's Tragedy* (Beaumont and Fletcher), Lyric Theatre, Hammersmith, London.

Lady Wraithe in *Shall We Join the Ladies?* (Barrie), Palace Theatre, London; Palace Theatre, London, 1929.

1922   An old lady in *Thirty Minutes in the Street* (Meyer), Kingsway Theatre, London, and Palace Theatre, London.

Tosca in extract from *Tosca* (Sardou), Coliseum Theatre, London.

Charlotte Fériol in *Scandal* (Bell, adapted from Bataille), New Theatre, London; British tour, 1923.

Beatrice in *The Cenci* (Shelley), New Theatre, London; Empire Theatre, London, 1926.

1923 April Mawne in *Advertising April* (Farjeon and Horsnell), Criterion Theatre, London, and British tour; Australasian tour, 1932.

Elinor Shale in *The Lie* (H. A. Jones), New Theatre, London; Wyndham's Theatre, London, 1925; South African tour, 1928–29.

1924 Gruach in *Gruach* (Bottomley), St Martin's Theatre, London.

Joan in *St Joan* (Shaw), New Theatre, London; Regent Theatre, London, 1925; Lyceum Theatre, London, 1926; Théâtre des Champs-Elysées, Paris, 1927; South African tour, 1928–29; His Majesty's Theatre, London, 1931; Australasian tour, 1932; Palace Theatre, London, 1941; Far East tour, 1954.

Sonia in *Man and the Masses* (Toller, adapted by Untermeyer), New Theatre, London.

1925 Phaedra in *Hippolytus* (Euripides, adapted by Murray), Regent Theatre, London.

Claire in *The Verge* (Glaspell), Regent Theatre, London.

Daisy Drennan in *The Round Table* (Robinson), Wyndham's Theatre, London.

Queen Katharine in *Henry VIII* (Shakespeare), Empire Theatre, London; Adelphi Theatre, London, 1953; Far East tour, 1954.

1926 Duchess de Croucy in *Israel* (Bernstein, adapted by Isaacs), Strand Theatre, London.

Judith in *Granite* (Dane), Ambassadors Theatre, London; British tour, 1930; Australasian tour, 1932.

Helen Stanley in *The Debit Account* (Crawshay-Williams), New Theatre, London.

1927 Nadejda Ivanovna Pestoff in *The Greater Love* (Fagan), Prince's Theatre, London.

Angela Guiseley in *Angela* (Bell), Prince's Theatre, London.

1927–28 Katharina in *The Taming of the Shrew* (Shakespeare), Lyric Theatre, Hammersmith, London; Far East tour, 1954.

1928 Judith in *Judith of Israel* (Baruch), Strand Theatre, London.

Everyman in *Everyman* (anon.), Rudolf Steiner Hall, London.

Queen Elizabeth in *The Making of an Immortal* (Moore), Arts Theatre, London.

Rosamund Withers in *The Stranger in the House* (Morton and Traill), Wyndham's Theatre, London.

1928–29 Mrs Phelps in *The Silver Cord* (Howard), South African tour.

1929 Barbara Undershaft in *Major Barbara* (G. B. Shaw), Wyndham's Theatre, London.

Lily Cobb in *Mariners* (Dane), Wyndham's Theatre, London.

Lady Lassiter in *The Donkey's Nose* (Crawshay-Williams), Prince of Wales's Theatre, London.

Madame de Beauvais in *Madame Plays Nap* (Girvin and Cozens), New Theatre, London; Australasian tour, 1932.

1930 Dorothy Lister in *The Devil* (Levy), Arts Theatre, London.

Ronnie's Mother in *To Meet the King* (Stevens), Coliseum, London; Hippodrome, London, 1944.

Phèdre in *Phèdre* (Racine), Arts Theatre, London.

Sylvette in *The Fire in the Opera House* (Kaiser), Everyman Theatre, Hampstead, London.

Mrs Alving in *Ghosts* (Ibsen), Everyman Theatre, Hampstead, London, and British tour; Gaiety Theatre, Dublin, 1943.

Emilia in *Othello* (Shakespeare), Savoy Theatre, London; Theatre Royal, Drury Lane, 1935.

Dolores Mendez in *The Squall* (Bart), British tour.

Jess Fortune in *The Matchmaker* (Dukes), British tour.

1931 Marcelle in *The Medium* (Mille and Vylar, adapted by Levy), Palladium, London.

Monica Wilmot in *Dark Hester* (Ferris), New Theatre, London.

Eloise Fontaine in *Marriage by Instalments* (Passeur, adapted by Clive), Embassy Theatre, London.

1932 The Citizen's Wife in *The Knight of the Burning Pestle* (Beaumont and Fletcher), Old Vic Theatre, London.

Julie Renaudin in *The Dark Saint* (Curel, adapted by Ling), Fortune Theatre, London.

Lady Cicely Wayneflete in *Captain Brassbound's Conversion* (G. B. Shaw), Australasian tour; Gaiety Theatre, Dublin, 1943.

Kitty Fane in *The Painted Veil* (Maugham), Australasian tour.

Gertrude Rhead in *Milestones* (Bennett and Knoblock), Australasian tour.

1933 Evie Millward in *The Distaff Side* (Van Druten), Apollo Theatre, London; Booth Theatre, New York, 1934.

Mrs Siddons in *Mrs Siddons* (Smith), Apollo Theatre, London.

1934 Victoria Van Brett in *Double Door* (McFadden), Globe Theatre, London.

Nourmahal in *Aureng-Zebe* (Dryden), Westminster Theatre, London.

Z in *Village Wooing* (G. B. Shaw), Little Theatre, London; British tour, 1936.

1935 Blanche Oldham in *Grief Goes Over* (Hodge), Globe Theatre, London.

Lady Bucktrout in *Short Story* (Morley), Queen's Theatre, London.

Lisha Gerart in *The Farm of Three Echoes* (Langley), Wyndham's Theatre, London.

1936 Mary Herries in *Kind Lady* (Chodorov), Lyric Theatre, London.

Mrs Gascoigne in *My Son, My Son* (Lawrence and Greenwood), British tour.

Lady Maureen Gilpin in *Hands Across the Sea* (Coward), British tour.

Doris Gow in *Fumed Oak* (Coward), British tour.

Aphrodite and the Nurse in *Hippolytus* (Euripides), Streatham Hill, London.

1937   Betsy Loveless in *Six Men of Dorset* (Malleson), British tour.

Ann Murray in *Yes, My Darling Daughter* (Reed), St James's Theatre, London.

1938   Mrs Conway in *Time and the Conways* (Priestley), Ritz Theatre, New York.

Volumnia in *Coriolanus* (Shakespeare), Old Vic Theatre, London.

Miss Moffat in *The Corn is Green* (E. Williams), Duchess Theatre, London.

1941   Rebekah and Chorus in *Jacob* (Housman), Old Vic Theatre, London.

Georgina Jeffreys in *The House of Jeffreys* (R. Thorndike), Playhouse, London.

1943   Mrs Hardcastle in *She Stoops to Conquer* (Goldsmith), Gaiety Theatre, Dublin, and Theatre Royal, Bristol.

Lady Beatrice in *Queen B* (Guthrie), Theatre Royal, Bristol.

Mrs Dundass in *Lottie Dundass* (Bagnold), Vaudeville Theatre, London.

Queen of Hearts and White Queen in *Alice in Wonderland* and *Alice Through the Looking-Glass* (Carroll, adapted by Dane), Scala Theatre, London; Palace Theatre, London, 1944.

1944   Aase in *Peer Gynt* (Ibsen, adapted by Ginsbury), New Theatre, London.

Catherine Petkoff in *Arms and the Man* (G. B. Shaw), New Theatre, London.

Queen Margaret in *Richard III* (Shakespeare), New Theatre, London.

1945   Mistress Quickly in *Henry IV, parts 1 and 2* (Shakespeare), New Theatre, London.

Jocasta in *Oedipus Rex* (Sophocles, translated by Yeats), New Theatre, London.

The Justice's Lady in *The Critic* (Sheridan), New Theatre, London.

1946   Mrs Woodrow Wilson in *In Time to Come* (Koch and Huston), King's Theatre, Hammersmith, London.

Clytemnestra in *Electra* (Euripides, adapted by Murray), King's Theatre, Hammersmith, London.

1947   Mrs Fraser in *Call Home the Heart* (Dane), St James's Theatre, London.

Isobel Linden in *The Linden Tree* (Priestley), Duchess Theatre, London.

1948   Mrs Jackson in *The Return of the Prodigal Son* (Hankin), Globe Theatre, London.

1949   Isabel Brocken in *The Foolish Gentlewoman* (Sharp), Duchess Theatre, London.

Aunt Anna Rose in *Treasure Hunt* (Farrell and Perry), Apollo Theatre, London.

1950   Lady Randolph in *Douglas* (Home), Lyceum Theatre, Edinburgh, and Citizens' Theatre, Glasgow.

1951   Mrs Whyte in *Waters of the Moon* (Hunter), Haymarket Theatre, London.

1953   Laura Anson in *A Day by the Sea* (Hunter), Haymarket Theatre, London.

1954   Queen Elizabeth in extract from *The Lion and the Unicorn* (Dane), Her Majesty's Theatre, London, and Far East tour.

1955   Grand Duchess Charles in *The Sleeping Prince* (Rattigan), Australasian tour.

Mrs Railton-Bell in *Separate Tables* (Rattigan), Australasian tour.

1956   Amy, Lady Monchensey in *The Family Reunion* (Eliot), Phoenix Theatre, London.

1957   Mrs Callifer in *The Potting Shed* (Greene), Bijou Theatre, New York.

1957–58   Mrs St Maugham in *The Chalk Garden* (Bagnold), Australasian tour.

1959   Dame Sophia Carrell in *Eighty in the Shade* (Dane), Globe Theatre, London.

Mrs Kittridge in *The Sea Shell* (Gregg), British tour.

1960   Lotta Bainbridge in *Waiting in the Wings* (Coward), Duke of York's Theatre, London.

1961   Teresa in *Teresa of Avila* (Williamson), Vaudeville Theatre, London.

1962   Marina in *Uncle Vanya* (Chekhov), Chichester Festival Theatre.

Miss Crawley in *Vanity Fair* (Slade), Bristol Old Vic and Queen's Theatre, London.

1963   Dowager Countess of Lister in *The Reluctant Peer* (Douglas-Home), Duchess Theatre, London.

Mrs Storch in *Season of Goodwill* (Marshall), Queen's Theatre, London.

1965   Mrs Doris Tate in *Return Ticket* (Corlett), Duchess Theatre, London.

1966   Abby Brewster in *Arsenic and Old Lace* (Kesselring), Vaudeville Theatre, London.

1967   Claire Ragond in *The Viaduct* (Duras), Yvonne Arnaud Theatre, Guildford, and British tour.

1968   Mrs Basil in *Call Me Jacky* (Bagnold), Yvonne Arnaud Theatre, Guildford.

Mrs Bramson in *Night Must Fall* (E. Williams), British tour.

1969   The Woman in *There Was an Old Woman* (Graham), Thorndike Theatre, Leatherhead.

Other roles included: *The Palace of Truth* (Gilbert), Downing College, Cambridge, 1904; *The Merry Wives of Windsor* (Shakespeare), New Theatre, Cambridge, 1904; *The Rape of the Locks* (Menander), Queen Mary Hall, London, 1943; *No Hurry, Ifor Davies* (E. Williams), Coliseum, London, 1951; *The Winter's Tale* (Shakespeare), Far East tour, 1954.

Films

Mrs Brand in *Moth and Rust*, 1921; Lady Deadlock in *Bleak House*, 1922; Nurse Edith Cavell in *Dawn*, 1928; The Mother in *To What Red Hell*, 1929; Mrs Hawthorn in *Hindle Wakes*, 1931; Madame Duval in *A Gentleman of Paris*, 1932; Ellen in *Tudor Rose*, 1936; The General in *Major Barbara*, 1941; Mrs Squeers in *Nicholas Nickleby*, 1947; Mrs Mouncey in *Britannia Mews*, 1948; Mrs Gill in *Stage Fright*, 1950; Mrs Marston in *Gone to Earth*, 1950;

Miss Bosanquet in *The Lady with the Lamp*, 1951; The Aristocratic Client in *The Magic Box*, 1951; Queen Victoria in *Melba*, 1953; Mabel in *Weak and the Wicked*, 1953; Queen Dowager in *The Prince and the Showgirl*, 1957; Dora in *Alive and Kicking*, 1958; Granny McKinley in *Smiley Gets a Gun*, 1958; Lady Fitzhugh in *Shake Hands with the Devil*, 1959; Lady Caroline in *Hand in Hand*, 1960.

Television

Dame Sophia Carrell in *Eighty in the Shade*, 1959; Mrs Whyte in *Waters of the Moon*, 1959; Maurya in *Riders to the Sea*, 1960; Sara Champline in *A Matter of Age*, 1960; Dowager Countess of Lister in *The Reluctant Peer*, 1964; Mrs Moore in *A Passage to India*, 1965.

Radio

Coriolanus, 1933; *The Winter's Tale*, 1938; *The Persians*, 1939; *Abraham and Isaac*, 1942; *Jane Clegg*, 1944; *Peer Gynt*, 1944; *Henry IV, parts 1 and 2*, 1945; *The Trojan Women*, 1946; *The Cenci*, 1947; *The Blue Bird*, 1947; *The White Devil*, 1948; *Coriolanus*, 1948; *The Corn is Green*, 1948; *Brand*, 1949; *Comedienne*, 1951; *The Women of Troy*, 1952; *Henry VIII*, 1954; *Romeo and Juliet*, 1958; *The Linden Tree*, 1959; *The Sunday Market*, 1961; *A Picture of Autumn*, 1961; *Spooner*, 1962; *For Shakespeare and St George*, 1963; *Waiting in the Wings*, 1963; *God and Kate Murphy*, 1965; *The Sacred Flame*, 1965; *The Loves of Cass McGuire*, 1966; *The Foolish Gentlewoman*, 1966; *Jane Clegg*, 1966; *The Distaff Side*, 1967; *The Potting Shed*, 1967; *Saint Joan*, 1967; *A Passage to India*, 1967; *Captain Brassbound's Conversion*, 1967; *Peace*, 1968; *Night Must Fall*, 1969; *The Son*, 1969; *The Captain's Log*, 1969; *The Viceroy's Wife*, 1971; *Arsenic and Old Lace*, 1971; *The Evening is Calm*, 1975.

Publications

Lilian Baylis, with Russell Thorndike, 1938.

*

Bibliography

Books:
J. C. Trewin, *Sybil Thorndike*, London, 1955.
Elizabeth Sprigge, *Sybil Thorndike Casson*, London, 1971.
John Casson, *Lewis and Sybil*, London, 1972.
Sheridan Morley, *Sybil Thorndike*, London, 1977.

* * *

Sybil Thorndike was one of those children of the clergy who flocked into the theatre after the knighthood of Henry Irving had given a new and honourable image to the stage as a profession. Although her High Anglicanism was hardly ever directly reflected in the plays she graced (T. S. Eliot's *The Family Reunion* was a late exception), a search for spiritual beauty illumined many of her roles, especially in Greek tragedy and the play that made her famous, Shaw's *Saint Joan*. Shaw had written the part for her, catching in it

other qualities in the actress besides the ability to soar into the skies: an enthusiasm for the diversity of life, a rich humanity that seemed to exclude no-one, tremendous energy and humour, and a practical, down-to-earth approach not unknown among those most familiar with God. So she was able to find within herself an extraordinary range of characters: Artemis, Hecuba, Lady Macbeth, Puck, King Lear's Fool (a blank moon face to reflect his master), Mrs Alving, Mistress Quickly, Volumnia, Sakuntala, Launcelot Gobbo, Queen Katherine, madwomen, murderesses, and stern working-class types like Jane Clegg. As her husband, Lewis Casson, liked to recall, she could act a tree superbly. There were limits: as she said herself, "Feminine wiles I can't manage at all — and I don't want to". This, too, Shaw recognised — a kind of emotional androgyny, an unease in erotic situations, which in her younger days closed off the most obvious route to success in the commercial theatre as a conventional leading lady. She could queen it in the West End when advanced years brought her the dowager roles. Before then, she could play Shaw's "virgin mother", Candida, as a perfect woman with straightforward simplicity untouched by any ironic consciousness.

The circumstances that made possible the long working career, eventually recognised in the greatest public honours bestowed on any actress, included the rise of the repertory movement in revolt against West End conditions and poor standards, and the existence of the Old Vic company, specialising in Shakespeare outside the West End system. The first of these had a particular personal aspect in her marriage to Casson, who identified himself with the ideals of the repertory movement and served his wife's genius as director, manager, and general adviser. Motivating Sybil at the start was her mother's ambition for her children, which entailed long hours of practice towards her initial aim of becoming a pianist, before acute and persistent pain in her wrist forced her to relinquish her scholarship to the Guildhall School of Music. When Sybil promptly decided to take up acting, and her brother Russell joined in the decision, their mother's — and father's — support switched immediately to the new aim, and both children found themselves at Ben Greet's Academy of Acting. The early false start had both positive and negative consequences: the love of music remained with Thorndike all her life, as did the daily habit of playing the piano and the ability to keep on working with enjoyment, even through the arthritic pain of her late years. On the other hand, the strain of early overwork and her mother's unremitting perfectionism bequeathed a nervously frenetic quality, liable to surface at intervals, and a related tendency to pull out all the stops, to go straight at a part, giving it all she had, which led to the not-infrequent complaint that she did too much, that she lacked repose. Ben Greet identified the fault early on, told her not to "bounce", and remained alert to this weakness when it recurred in some of her mature performances, for she never finally conquered it and could irritate generally admiring audiences by turning her energy into fussiness.

Greet plunged Thorndike in at the deep end, at almost 22, with a tour of the USA in which she played 112 minor parts and strained her voice so severely that her doctor decreed six weeks of complete vocal silence as the only chance of cure. The remedy worked then, but the trouble recurred until she consulted Elsie Fogerty in 1915–16 and learned from her how to manage her unforgettable musical voice. A daily exercise of reading to her husband, practising the intonational patterns she thought of as his Welsh birthright, stood her in such good stead that at 79, when she played Marina in *Uncle Vanya* at the Chichester Festival, the apparent ease and naturalness of her speech contrasted remarkably with the struggles a younger generation of actors had been having with the theatre's difficult acoustics. She had learnt her naturalism, most artfully contrived, in Miss Horniman's company at the Gaiety Theatre, Manchester, where Casson was the director, acting in plays by "provincial" dramatists, such as Charles McEvoy, Stanley Houghton, and St John Ervine, and in revivals from the Barker-Vedrenne seasons at the Court Theatre. When, in 1910, she played small parts in the shortlived Frohman repertory season at the Duke of York's Theatre, she watched all Granville Barker's rehearsals with close attention, as she had sat next to Bernard Shaw, absorbing his comments and advice, when understudying Candida in 1908. Later directors commented on how quickly she absorbed their suggestions, how ready she was to try anything experimentally, with what precision she responded to any slight modification requested. Given firm handling, she could be powerfully still — as Queen Katharine, or in Ibsen's *Ghosts*, and above all in Greek tragedy.

None of Thorndike's mentors influenced her more than Gilbert Murray, the professor of Greek whose translations of Euripides into English verse enthused audiences of his own day (though they have since fallen from fashion). He taught her to achieve a classic grandeur by expressing idealised emotion, bringing in an impersonal quality that gave universality without losing the capacity to move an audience, and using the visual beauty of movement and gesture as well as musical speech.

Having spent World War I at Lilian Baylis's Old Vic, playing many of the great Shakespearean roles, Thorndike went back in 1938 to match Laurence Olivier's Coriolanus with her Volumnia, and in the later, legendary, phase of the Old Vic in the New Theatre at the end of World War II she played Jocasta to Olivier's Oedipus and Aase to Ralph Richardson's Peer Gynt, in addition to Mistress Quickly. After this, her playing in the classics was largely reserved for overseas tours, with Casson directing.

Throughout her long career Sybil Thorndike enjoyed performing in a large number of non-classic plays and had her share of failures. Early in the 1920's she had kept working continuously, in some 25 roles, in the Grand Guignol plays she and Casson, as joint-managers, presented at the Little Theatre: material that satisfied her instinct to explore extremes of emotion and her taste for horror. Her resounding success as April Mawne in *Advertising April* suggests that she could have had a very different subsequent career if Saint Joan had not come along. Emlyn Williams's *The Corn is Green*, meanwhile, gave her the chance to bring out what was remarkable in an ordinary woman. Apart from her moving silent performance as Edith Cavell in *Dawn*, most of her film appearances were in supporting roles or cameos. She enjoyed filming and appreciated the scaling-down of her style to which film directors held her.

—Margery Morgan

TOOLE, J(ohn) L(aurence). British actor-manager. Born in London, 12 March 1830. Educated at the City of London School; subsequently worked in a wine merchant's. Married Susan Kaslake in 1854 (died 1889), one son and one daughter. Stage debut, at the Queen's Theatre, Dublin, under the stagename John Lavers, 1852; London debut, Haymarket Theatre, 1852; appeared in Edinburgh, 1853–54; actor, Lyceum Theatre, London, 1856, and Adelphi Theatre, London, 1858–67; founded first of a series of summer companies, 1857; first of many appearances as Caleb Plummer in *Dot*, 1862; actor, Gaiety Theatre, London, 1869–77; US tour, 1874–75; manager, Globe Theatre, London, 1874 and 1877, and, 1879–95, Folly Theatre, London (renamed Toole's Theatre 1882); presented first performances of early plays by J. M. Barrie, 1890's; retired temporarily from stage, 1888–89; toured Australia and New Zealand, 1890–91; appearances after 1890 limited by ill health; retired from the stage after last appearance at the Theatre Royal, Rochdale, 1896. Died in Brighton, 30 July 1906.

Roles

1852	Jacob Earwig in *Boots at the Swan* (Selby), Sussex Hall, London.
	Simmons in *The Spitalfields Weaver* (Bayly), Haymarket Theatre, London, and Queen's Theatre, Dublin.
1853	Hector Timid in *A Dead Shot* (Buckstone), Theatre Royal, Edinburgh.
1854	Artful Dodger in *Oliver Twist* (adapted from Dickens), Theatre Royal, Edinburgh.
	Master Willikind in *The Loves of Willikind and His Dinah*, Theatre Royal, Edinburgh.
	Samuel Pepys in *The King's Rival* (Taylor and Reade), St James's Theatre, London.
	Weazle in *My Friend the Major* (Selby), St James's Theatre, London.
1855	Lord Sands in *Henry VIII* (Shakespeare), Theatre Royal, Edinburgh.
	Bottom in *A Midsummer Night's Dream* (Shakespeare), Theatre Royal, Edinburgh.
1856	Felix Rosemary in *Toole's Appeal to the Public*, Theatre Royal, Edinburgh.
	Fanfaronade in *Belphegor the Mountebank* (Webb), Lyceum Theatre, London.
	Autolycus in *Perdita; or, The Royal Milkmaid* (Brough), Lyceum Theatre, London.
1857	Adolphus Spanker in *London Assurance* (Boucicault), Theatre Royal, Edinburgh.
1858	Tom Cranky in *The Birthplace of Podgers* (Hollingshead), Lyceum Theatre, London.
1859	Spriggins in *Ici on parle Français* (T. J. Williams), Adelphi Theatre, London.
	Augustus de Rosherville in *The Willow Copse* (Boucicault), Adelphi Theatre, London.
	Brutus Toupet in *The Dead Heart* (Phillips), Adelphi Theatre, London.
1860	Bob Cratchit in *A Christmas Carol* (Webster, adapted from Dickens), Adelphi Theatre, London.
	Enoch Flicker in *A Story of '45* (Phillips), Adelphi Theatre, London.

1862   Wapshot in *The Life of an Actress* (Boucicault), Adelphi Theatre, London.

Caleb Plummer in *Dot; or, The Cricket on the Hearth* (Boucicault, adapted from Dickens), Adelphi Theatre, London.

Azucena in *Ill-Treated Il Trovatore* (H. J. Byron), Adelphi Theatre, London.

1863   Mr Tetterby in *The Haunted Man* (Robertson), Adelphi Theatre, London.

1864   Policeman in *The Area Belle* (Brough and Halliday), Adelphi Theatre, London.

Stephen Digges in *Stephen Digges* (Oxenford), Adelphi Theatre, London.

1865   Joe Bright in *Through Fire and Water* (Gordon), Adelphi Theatre, London.

1866   Paul Pry in *Paul Pry* (Poole), Adelphi Theatre, London.

1867   Michael Garner in *Dearer Than Life* (H. J. Byron), Alexandra Theatre, Liverpool; Queen's Theatre, London, 1868.

Jack Snipe in *Not Guilty* (Phillips), Queen's Theatre, London.

Dick Dolland in *Uncle Dick's Darling* (H. J. Byron), Gaiety Theatre, London.

Wat Tyler in *Wat Tyler, M.P.* (Sala), Gaiety Theatre, London.

1869–70   Jacques Strop in *Robert Macaire* (Selby), tour; Lyceum Theatre, London, 1883.

1870   Cabriolo in *The Princess of Trebizonde* (Offenbach), Gaiety Theatre, London.

Ko-Kli-Ko in *Aladdin II* (Thompson), Gaiety Theatre, London.

1871   Sergeant Buzfuz in *Bardell v. Pickwick* (Hollingshead), Gaiety Theatre, London.

Thespis in *Thespis; or, The Gods Grown Old* (Gilbert and Sullivan), Gaiety Theatre, London.

1872   Ali Baba in *Ali Baba* (Reece), Gaiety Theatre, London.

1873   Billy Lackaday in *Sweethearts and Wives* (Kenney), Gaiety Theatre, London.

Mawworm in *The Hypocrite* (Bickerstaffe), Gaiety Theatre, London.

Dennis Brulgruddery in *John Bull* (Colman the Younger), Gaiety Theatre, London.

1874   Bob Acres in *The Rivals* (Sheridan), Gaiety Theatre, London.

Hammond Coote in *Wig and Gown* (Albery), Globe Theatre, London.

1875   Himself in *Toole at Sea* (Reece), Gaiety Theatre, London.

Tottles in *Tottles* (H. J. Byron), Gaiety Theatre, London.

Professor Muddle in *A Spelling Bee* (Reece), Gaiety Theatre, London.

1877   Spicer Rumford in *Artful Cards* (Burnand), Gaiety Theatre, London.

Charles Liquorpond in *A Fool and His Money* (H. J. Byron), Globe Theatre, London.

1880   Barnaby Doublechick in *The Upper Crust* (H. J. Byron), Folly Theatre, London.

1882   Benjamin Guffin in *Mr Guffin's Elopement* (Law and Grossmith), Alexandra Theatre, Liverpool, and Toole's Theatre, London.

Solomon Protheroe in *Girls and Boys* (Pinero), Toole's Theatre, London.

1883   Loris Ipanoff in *Stage Dora* (Burnand), Toole's Theatre, London.

1884   Claudian in *Paw Clawdian* (Burnand), Toole's Theatre, London.

1886   Mephistopheles in *Faust and Loose* (Burnand), Toole's Theatre, London.

David Trot in *The Butler* (Merivale), Theatre Royal, Manchester, and Toole's Theatre, London.

1888   Mr Milliken in *The Don* (Merivale), King William Street Theatre.

1891   Ibsen in *Ibsen's Ghost; or, Toole Up-to-Date* (Barrie), Toole's Theatre, London.

1892   Jasper Phipps in *Walker, London* (Barrie), Toole's Theatre, London.

Publications

Reminiscences, 1889.

* * *

J. L. Toole was an actor-manager who specialized in working-class low comedy and farce, played in the style developed in the late 18th and 19th centuries by John Liston and John Baldwin Buckstone. His assets were, for much of the time, his limitations. Short and rascally, he was apt to be free with the text and to "gag" with his audience, whom he could convulse without opening his mouth. When he spoke, it looked to Pinero as if he was trying to bite his ear. By many he was regarded as quaint; but he maintained an unparalleled hold on the affections and the pockets of the theatregoing public, particularly in the provinces, where he was welcomed rapturously for the duration of a career that almost encompassed the second half of the 19th century.

His rise was fast. By 1854, within two years of his professional debut in provincial stock, he was a principal low comedian in the West End. It was, however, in the period between 1858 and 1867 that he became widely admired, earning critical recognition at the Adelphi Theatre not only in farces but melodramas and several plays of domestic sentiment in a quasi-Dickensian vein. In these he generally appeared as a kindhearted father-figure, oppressed by poverty, assaulted by blackmail, or grieving the loss of a dear one. The diminutive Toole struck a sympathetic image, cutting his onlookers to the quick. Dickens himself, not surprisingly, was of their number, recognising "a power of passion very unusual indeed in a comic actor, as such things go, and of a quite remarkable kind". Here was the epitome of Victorian sentiment; and Toole's command of tragical pathos, reminiscent of the serio-comic actor Frederick Robson (1821–64), impelled him in the 1860's to the summit of the acting profession. As the tender old toymaker in *Dot*, a dramatization by Boucicault of Dickens's *The Cricket on the Hearth*, Toole in his scenes with his blind daughter moved the audience to tears. In *Dot* he had found the most durable piece in his non-farce repertoire. Each new role that gained popular favour was added to an ever-increasing personal bevy of old favourites: indeed, in the 1890's he claimed to have played the part of

Spriggins in *Ici on parle Français*, a farce by T. J. Williams, more than 4000 times since 1859. Dickens followed Toole's career with more than passing interest — he had encouraged him initially to adopt the stage and had been instrumental in securing the Adelphi engagement.

At the Gaiety, however, where he was based from 1868 to 1877, Toole's material was almost invariably farce and burlesque-extravaganza, including in 1871 the first collaborative venture from Gilbert and Sullivan, *Thespis*, in which he played the leading character. His position as perhaps the most popular star in the London theatre attracted in 1873 the then phenomenal salary of £100 a week; but it also confirmed his long-held desire to operate a permanent company of his own. Already, in 1867–68, he had run a notable season at the Queen's Theatre, Long Acre, assembling a supporting cast that included his close friend Henry Irving and Charles Wyndham. In 1879, after two spells of management at the Globe, he took the pocket-sized Folly Theatre, near Trafalgar Square, which now became his London base until 1895; and when in 1882 he rechristened it Toole's Theatre he became the first actor to see a West End theatre named after him.

Toole's posthumous reputation has suffered from the fact that he spent his life in a repertoire of subsequently unrevived and forgotten plays; yet he had been a Victorian celebrity, lionized by statesmen and princes, and fairly adored by the masses, who had seen in him the archetypal little man capable of turning any situation to his advantage. To them he personified farce. It was as a celebrity no less than an actor that he toured the USA (1874–75), took his company to Australia and New Zealand (1890–91), and saw his memoirs serialised in the *Sunday Times*.

By 1890, however, his health had broken, and there followed a despairing succession of periods when he was too lame to act. Infirmity precipitated retirement six years later; but in the meantime, indefatigably, he had staged and played the leading roles in the first theatrical writings of J. M. Barrie — *Ibsen's Ghost* and *Walker, London* — much as he had promoted in the previous decade some of Pinero's early work. Among the youthful players he employed during the years of his own decline as an actor were the future Dame Irene Vanbrugh and Sir Seymour Hicks.

Toole's acting style was fully in the tradition of the "mug-cutting" low comedians of previous ages. Like Joseph Munden, he pulled faces to trigger laughter; like Liston, he could be simultaneously amusing and poignant; and, like Buckstone, the croak of his voice from offstage hilariously signalled his entrance. It was Toole the public came to see, not the play he was in. Across the footlights he successfully established with them an apparently confidential relationship; and when at the end of the evening he stepped forward before the curtain, the whimsical speeches he delivered represented the essence of his style. They were a form of solo entertainment, proprietorial and manipulatory, extending the device of direct address upon which his performance in the play had often depended. He excelled in the farcical depiction of bewilderment, of officiousness and social climbing. He was a comic caricaturist and, for innumerable Victorians, the embodiment of humour.

—Michael Read

TORELLI, Giacomo. Italian designer, architect and engineer. Born in Fano, near Rimini, Italy, 1608. Trained as designer under Giambattista Aleotti at the Teatro Farnese. Won acclaim as architect of and designer for the Teatro Novissimo, Venice, 1641–45; arrived in Paris at the request of Cardinal Mazarin and the Queen Regent of France, 1645; executed designs at the Théâtre du Petit-Bourbon, Paris, under Molière, and for several court ballets, 1645–61; invented numerous stage devices, including first set of wings and the carriage-and-pole system of changing scenery; returned to Fano, Italy, 1661, after the demolition of the Théâtre du Petit-Bourbon and the removal of his stage machinery by his rival Gaspare Vigarani. Died in Fano, 17 June 1678.

Productions

1641	*La Finta pazza* (Sacrati), Teatro Novissimo, Venice.
1642	*Bellerofonte* (Sacrati), Teatro Novissimo, Venice.
	Alcate (Manelli), Teatro Novissimo, Venice.
1643	*Venere gelosa* (Sacrati), Teatro Novissimo, Venice; attrib.
1644	*Deidamia* (Cavalli), Teatro Novissimo, Venice.
	Ulisse errante (Sacrati), Teatro di SS Giovanni e Paolo, Venice.
1645	*Ercole in Lidia* (Rovetta), Teatro Novissimo, Venice; attrib.
	La Finta pazza (Sacrati), Théâtre du Petit-Bourbon, Paris.
1647	*Orphée* (Rossi), Théâtre du Palais Royal, Paris.
1650	*Andromède* (P. Corneille), Théâtre du Petit-Bourbon, Paris.
1653	*Ballet de la Nuit* (Benserade), Théâtre du Petit-Bourbon, Paris; attrib.
1654	*Les Noces de Pélé et de Thetis* (Caproli), Théâtre du Petit-Bourbon, Paris.
1656	*Psyché* (Benserade), Louvre, Paris.
1658	*La Rosaure* (Benserade), Théâtre du Petit-Bourbon, Paris.
1661	*Les Fâcheux* (Molière), Vaux-le-Vicomte.
1677	*Il Trionfo della Continenza* (Montevecchio), Teatro della Fortuna, Fano.

Publications

Drawings reproduced in Denis Diderot, *Encyclopédie*, 1772.

*

Bibliography

Books:
Per Bjurström, *Giacomo Torelli and Baroque Stage Design*, Stockholm, 1962.
Raimondo Guarino, *La Tragedie e le machine: Andromède di Corneille e Torelli*, Rome, 1982.

* * *

Giacomo Torelli was important because of his technical innovations and because he brought the techniques of Italian baroque scenery to France in the middle of the 17th century. Unlike such predecessors as Vasari, Buontalenti and Aleotti, who worked principally for the court and academy theatres, Torelli made his reputation in the public theatre in Venice. His first known designs were for the production of *La Finta pazza*, a spectacle play that opened the Theatro Novissimo in January 1641.

Lauded as the "Magician of Fano", Torelli was born into a noble family in that small city on the Adriatic south of Rimini. Nothing is known for certain of him before *La Finta pazza*, but he may have migrated to Venice as a military engineer. He was also responsible for designs for *Bellerofonte* and *Venere gelosa* at the Teatro Novissimo, and probably for several others as well.

Beginning with five settings, two dragons, a ship that sailed into harbour, four descents of the gods and two perspective vistas for *La Finta pazza*, Torelli progressed to eight settings for *Bellerofonte*, which showed Venice rising from the waves, the usual number of glories and an innovative écoveredé scene with wings and borders curving together to create the illusion of a cave. For *Venere gelosa*, Torelli's designs, this time for nine settings, grew in complexity. His design for a city square included a triumphal arch and equestrian statue downstage and a double vista at the rear, the whole made up of 48 pieces of scenery, all rigged for instantaneous, mid-act change.

In 1645 the Queen Regent of France wrote to the Duke of Parma asking for a choreographer and scenic designer to produce something in the mode of Venetian opera at the court of France. The Duke sent Torelli along with the choreographer Balbi. The French court had tasted the delights of Italian baroque scenery in the early 1640's, but the death of Louis XIII interrupted its introduction. By 1645, however, Anne of Austria and her minister, Cardinal Mazarin, had brought both Italian singers and a troupe of commedia dell'arte actors to France, and it was to assist the latter that Torelli was called for. The noble Torelli was appalled at being required to work for a company of common players and sulked for several months, but late in the year he agreed to build a stage and design the settings and machines for a French production of *La Finta pazza*. This production, which was not an exact recreation of the Venetian production, was enormously successful, especially because of the instantaneous scene changes, the lighting effects and the vistas miraculously produced in what Torelli claimed to be a mere five feet of depth. One vista introduced a view of the Pont Neuf with the spire of Sainte-Chapelle and the towers of Notre Dame in the background, although the putative location of the scene was the harbour of Chios.

Between 1647 and 1661, Torelli was responsible for the design of several spectacular entertainments, including Pierre Corneille's machine play *Andromède*, some important ballets, another production by the Italian troupe and the festival at Vaux-le-Vicomte, which included a performance of Molière's *Les Fâcheux*. Because of his passion for self-promotion, Torelli saw to it that engravings were made of a number his Paris designs, including those for *La Finta pazza*, *Andromède* and *Les Noces de Pélée et de Thetis*. Most of the settings are for standard baroque locations: garden, city square and palace. The landscape settings — forests, seascapes, caverns — show more variety. In general, Torelli's work is characterized by the creation of an illusion of great depth. Upstage of the wings is usually an arch with illusion of great depth. Upstage of the wings is usually an arch with a long vista either in place or revealed. Several of the vistas have three vanishing points, enabling audience members seated elsewhere than dead centre to experience some of the effect. The "covered" scene appears several times. Most of the entertainments made substantial use of machines, and it may be justified to suggest that Torelli's reputation was based more on the ingenuity of his machines than on the novelty or magnificence of his settings, which suffered from his lack of contact with new developments in Italy.

Torelli's career also suffered from the conflict between the baroque aesthetic with its taste for "trompe d'oeil", the marvellous, and the magnificent and the classical aesthetique that developed in France in the 1630's. One result of this was a decline in the number of settings used. While Torelli was providing an average five or six settings for each entertainment in Paris, theatres in Venice and Vienna were on a course that would lead to 20 or more settings of great magnificence per production. Torelli's designs also became increasingly abstract, less "necessary" to the action of each particular scene. The tradition of scenery in France was one of symbolic rather than illusionistic staging, while French classical staging relied on scenery that created unspecified milieus. By mid-century, French scenery in the classical mode was restricted to the palais à volonté for tragedy and the scène à quatre portes for comedy. Torelli's work was less influential in the French public theatre than in the tradition that would reach its peak in opera production after 1670, a decade after Torelli's return to Italy.

Torelli's career in France was interrupted for several years by the Fronde and was cut short by the importation in 1659 of Gaspare Vigarani to build a new royal theatre with all the latest in Italian technical marvels. Self-aggrandisement gave way to self-destruction when Torelli provided the settings for Superintendant Fouquet's ill-starred fête at Vaux-le-Vicomte. Shortly after, Fouquet was condemned to life imprisonment and Torelli was asked to leave France. He returned to Fano, where he served on the council and designed a theatre.

Perhaps the most important innovation introduced by Torelli was the machine that permitted instantaneous and simultaneous changes of scenery. Before Torelli's day, scenic wings had been set into grooves and pushed onto the stage by hand. A setting of eight wing positions thus required a crew of 16 to implement each change, and coordination was difficult. Settings were limited and changes took place between the acts. Torelli cut through the stage floor and attached the wings to chariots placed under the stage and connected to a single winch. When the winch was set in motion by a stagehand it released a counterweight and all pairs of wings moved synchronously. The effect was of instantaneous change of scene, a marvel that was then incorporated into the spectacle along with other miraculous transformations characteristic of the baroque stage. Torelli also made significant improvements in the machines used for glories and flight, making it possible for a figure to move up and down stage and side to side, and was a specialist in arranging lighting changes and effects.

—Virginia Scott

TOVSTONOGOV, Georgyi (Alexandrovich). Soviet director. Born in Tbilisi, Georgia, 15 September 1915. Trained for the stage at the State Institute for Theatre Arts (GITIS), 1933–38. Married, with two sons. Began theatrical career as actor and assistant director at the Junior Theatre, Tbilisi, 1931; after training at GITIS, became artistic director of the Tbilisi Griboyedov Russian Theatre, 1938–46; taught at the Rustaveli Georgian Theatrical Institute, 1939–46; director, Moscow Central Children's Theatre, 1946–49; director, Lenin Komsomol Theatre, Leningrad, 1950–56; director, Gorky Bolshoi Drama Theatre, Leningrad, 1956; appointed head of the department of stage directing at the Leningrad Institute of Theatre, Music and Cinematography, 1962. Professor, Leningrad Institute, 1960; deputy to the seventh and eighth convocations of the Supreme Soviet of the USSR, 1966. Recipient: Stalin Prize, 1951; Lenin Prize, 1958; State Prize of the USSR, 1950, 1952, 1968; Order of Lenin (twice); Order of the Red Banner of Labour. Doctorate of Art Studies, 1968. People's Artist of the USSR, 1957. Died 1989.

Productions

1939   *Deti Vanjusina* [Vanjusina's sons], Griboyedov Russian Theatre, Tbilisi.

1940   *Kremlinevskie kuranty* [Kremlin Chimes] (Pogodin), Griboyedov Russian Theatre, Tbilisi.
Polkovec Suvorov [Captain Suvorov] (Bachterov and Razumovsky), Griboyedov Russian Theatre, Tbilisi.

1941   *Paren iznasego goroda* [A Boy of Our City] (Simonov), Griboyedov Russian Theatre, Tbilisi.

1942   *Skola zloslovija* [The School for Scandal] (Sheridan), Griboyedov Russian Theatre, Tbilisi.

1943   *Lenuska* (Leonov), Griboyedov Russian Theatre, Tbilisi.

1944–45   *Lisicki* [Little Foxes] (Hellman), Griboyedov Russian Theatre, Tbilisi.

1946   *Meshchane* [Smug Citizens] (Gorky), Griboyedov Russian Theatre, Tbilisi.

1949   *Gde-to v Sbiri* [Giving Shares in Siberia] (Irosnikova), Central Children's Theatre, Moscow.
Tajna vecnoj noci [The Secret of Our Eternity] (Lukovsky), Central Children's Theatre, Moscow.

1950   *Gde-to v Sbiri* [Giving Shares in Siberia] (Irosnikova), Lenin Komsomol Theatre, Leningrad.
Iz Iskry [By the Spark] (Dadiani), Lenin Komsomol Theatre, Leningrad.
Studenty [The Students] (Lifsin), Lenin Komsomol Theatre, Leningrad.

1951   *Zakon likurga* [The law of Licurgo] (Bazilevsky), Lenin Komsomol Theatre, Leningrad.
Roussalka (Dargomyjsky), Opera of the Palace of Culture, Kirov.
Each Day (Poliakov), Music Hall Theatre.
Groza [The Storm] (Ostrovsky), Lenin Komsomol Theatre, Leningrad.

Dorogoj bes smertija [On the Road to Immortality] (adapted from Fucik's *A Word Before the Execution*), Lenin Komsomol Theatre, Leningrad.

1952   *Scelkovoe sjuzane* [The Silk Dressing-Gown] (Kachchar), Lenin Komsomol Theatre, Leningrad.
Obycnoe delo [An Ordinary Affair] (Tarna), Lenin Komsomol Theatre, Leningrad.
Gibel eskadry [The Destruction of the Squadron] (Korneichuk), Lenin Komsomol Theatre, Leningrad.

1953   *Kto smeetcja poslednij* [He Who Laughs Last] (Krapiva), Lenin Komsomol Theatre, Leningrad.
Stepnaja byl [The History of the Steppes] (Chernyshev), Lenin Komsomol Theatre, Leningrad.
Novye ljudi [The New Men] (adapted from Chernyshevsky's *What Is to Be Done?*), Lenin Komsomol Theatre, Leningrad.

1954   *Na ulice scastlivoj* [Made in the Street] (Princev), Lenin Komsomol Theatre, Leningrad.
Pompadury i pompadursi [The Pompadours, Bureaucrats] (adapted from Saltykov-Schchedrin), Lenin Komsomol Theatre, Leningrad.

1955   *Voskresenie i ponedelnik* [Sunday and Monday] (Slobodsky), Lenin Komsomol Theatre, Leningrad.
Pervaya vesna [The First Spring] (nikolayev and Radzinsky), Lenin Komsomol Theatre, Leningrad.
The Mother of His Children (Afinogenov), Lenin Komsomol Theatre, Leningrad.
Optimisticeskaja tragedija [An Optimistic Tragedy] (Vishnevsky), Pushkin Theatre, Leningrad.

1956   *Umiliatie offesi* [Crime and Punishment] (adapted from Dostoevsky), Lenin Komsomol Theatre, Leningrad.
Bezumnaja zvezda [The Star Without a Name] (Sebastian), Gorky Bolshoi Drama Theatre, Leningrad.
Sestoj etaz [Sixth Stage] (Gehri), Gorky Bolshoi Drama Theatre, Leningrad.
Second Breath (Kron), Pushkin Theatre, Leningrad.

1957   *Lisa i vinograd* [The Fox and the Grapes] (Figueiredo), Gorky Bolshoi Drama Theatre, Leningrad.
Kogda cvetet akacija [When the Acacia Flowers] (Vinnikov), Gorky Bolshoi Drama Theatre, Leningrad.
Idiot [The Idiot] (Dostoevsky), Gorky Bolshoi Drama Theatre, Leningrad.
Optimisticeskaja tragedija [An Optimistic Tragedy] (Vishnevsky), National Theatre, Prague, and Pitoëff Theatre, Budapest.

1958   *Sinor Mario piset Komedija* [Signor Mario Writes a Comedy] (Nicolai), Gorky Bolshoi Drama Theatre, Leningrad.

1959   *Varvary* [The Philistines] (Gorky), Gorky Bolshoi Drama Theatre, Leningrad.

Opening Scene for *Henry IV*, designed by **Georgyi Tovstonogov** (1969).

Pjat vecerov [Five Evenings] (Volodin), Gorky Bolshoi Drama Theatre, Leningrad.

Optimisticeskaja tragedija [An Optimistic Tragedy] (Vishnevsky), Théâtre des Nations, Paris.

Trassa [Traced] (Dvorecky), Gorky Bolshoi Drama Theatre, Leningrad.

1960   *Gibel eskadry* [The Destruction of the Squadron] (Korneichuk), Gorky Bolshoi Drama Theatre, Leningrad.

Irkutskaya istoriya [Irkutz Story] (Arbuzov), Gorky Bolshoi Drama Theatre, Leningrad.

Vospominanie o dvuch ponedelnikach [A Memory of Two Mondays] (Miller), Gorky Bolshoi Drama Theatre, Leningrad.

Semion Kotko (Prokofiev), Opera, Kirov.

Lisa i vinograd [The Fox and the Grapes] (Figueiredo), tour.

1961   *Cetverty* [The Quarter] (Simonov), Gorky Bolshoi Drama Theatre, Leningrad.

Okean [The Ocean] (Shteyn), Gorky Bolshoi Drama Theatre, Leningrad.

Moja starsaja sestra [My Elder Sister] (Volodin), Gorky Bolshoi Drama Theatre, Leningrad.

Nesklonivsie golovy [Of Heads That Do Not Bow] (Douglas and Smith), Gorky Bolshoi Drama Theatre, Leningrad.

Bosest vennaja Komedija [The Divine Comedy] (Stok), Gorky Bolshoi Drama Theatre, Leningrad.

1962   *Pered uzenom* [Before Dinner] (Rozov), Gorky Bolshoi Drama Theatre, Leningrad.

Palata [The Hospital Ward] (Aliochine), Gorky Bolshoi Drama Theatre, Leningrad.

Gore ot uma [Woe from Wit] (Griboyedov), Gorky Bolshoi Drama Theatre, Leningrad.

1963   *Varvary* [The Philistines] (Gorky), tour of Romania and Bulgaria.

Okean [Ocean] (Shteyn), tour of Romania and Bulgaria.

1964   *Esce raz pro lyubov* [Let Us Talk of Love One More Time] (Radzinsky), Gorky Bolshoi Drama Theatre, Leningrad.

Podnjata ja celina [Virgin Soil Upturned] (Sholokhov), Gorky Bolshoi Drama Theatre, Leningrad.

1965   *The Visible Song*, Students Theatre, Leningrad.

Na vsyakogo dovolno prostoty [Even a Wise Man Stumbles] (Ostrovsky), Wspolczesny Theatre, Varsovie.

Tri sestry [The Three Sisters] (Chekhov), Gorky Bolshoi Drama Theatre, Leningrad.

1966   *Of Mice and Men* (Steinbeck), Students Theatre, Leningrad.

Meshchane [Smug Citizens] (Gorky), Gorky Bolshoi Drama Theatre, Leningrad.

Idiot [The Idiot] (Dostoevsky), Gorky Bolshoi Drama Theatre, Leningrad.

1967 *The Reunion* (Rozov), Gorky Bolshoi Drama Theatre, Leningrad.

Lisa i vinograd [The Fox and the Grapes] (Figueiredo), Gorky Bolshoi Drama Theatre, Leningrad.

The Truth and Nothing But the Truth (Al), Students Theatre, Leningrad.

West Side Story (Bernstein), Students Theatre, Leningrad.

La Chanson visible, Festival of University Theatre, Nancy.

1969 *Henry IV* (Shakespeare), Gorky Bolshoi Drama Theatre, Leningrad.

West Side Story (Bernstein), Lenin Komsomol Theatre, Leningrad.

Umiliati e offesi [Crime and Punishment] (adapted from Dostoevsky), Lenin Komsomol Theatre, Leningrad.

The Truth and Nothing But the Truth (Al), Kalinin, Kiev.

1970 *Restless Old Age* (Rakhmanov), Gorky Bolshoi Drama Theatre, Leningrad.

Gibel eskadry [The Destruction of the Squadron] (Korneichuk), Sebastopol.

1971 *Toot* (Erken), Gorky Bolshoi Drama Theatre, Leningrad.

We Drink to Colombia (Joukhovitsky), Gorky Bolshoi Drama Theatre, Leningrad.

Valentin and Valentine (Rochtchine), Gorky Bolshoi Drama Theatre, Leningrad.

Tri sestry [The Three Sisters] (Chekhov), National Theatre, Helsinki.

Henry IV (Shakespeare), Finnish tour.

Restless Old Age (Rakhmanov), Czech tour.

1972 *Revizor* [The Government Inspector] (Gogol), Gorky Bolshoi Drama Theatre, Leningrad.

Hanouma (Tsagareli), Gorky Bolshoi Drama Theatre, Leningrad.

1973 *Balalaikine and Cie* (Saltykov-Schchedrin), Sovremennik Theatre, Moscow.

Public Opinion (Barangui), Gorky Bolshoi Drama Theatre, Leningrad.

1974 Proshlym letom v Chulimske [Last Summer in Chulimsk] (Vampilov), Gorky Bolshoi Drama Theatre, Leningrad.

Energetic People (Choukchine), Gorky Bolshoi Drama Theatre, Leningrad.

Three Sacks of Wheat (Tendryakov), Gorky Bolshoi Drama Theatre, Leningrad.

1975 *Minutes of Meeting* (Gelman), Gorky Bolshoi Drama Theatre, Leningrad.

The Story of a Horse (Rozovsky), Gorky Bolshoi Drama Theatre, Leningrad.

1976 *Dachniki* [Summerfolk] (Gorky), Gorky Bolshoi Drama Theatre, Leningrad.

1977 *The Influence of Gamma Rays on Man-in-the-Moon Marigolds* (Zindel), Gorky Bolshoi Drama Theatre, Leningrad.

Quiet Flows the Don (Sholokov), Gorky Bolshoi Drama Theatre, Leningrad.

Revizor [The Government Inspector] (Gogol), State Theatre, Dresden.

1978 *Zhestokiye igry* [Cruel Games] (Arbuzov), Griboyedov Theatre, Tbilisi.

Na vsyakogo dovolno prostoty [Even a Wise Man Stumbles] (Ostrovsky), National Theatre, Helsinki.

1979 *Idiot* [The Idiot] (Dostoevsky), Hamburg.

We, the Undersigned (Gelman), Gorky Bolshoi Drama Theatre, Leningrad.

Don Carlos (Verdi), International Opera Festival, Finland.

1980 *Volki i ovsty* [Wolves and Sheep] (Ostrovsky), Gorky Bolshoi Drama Theatre, Leningrad.

Card Games (Coburn), Gorky Bolshoi Drama Theatre, Leningrad.

1981 *Optimisticeskaja tragedija* [The Optimistic Tragedy] (Vishnevsky), Gorky Bolshoi Drama Theatre, Leningrad.

Tri sestry [The Three Sisters] (Chekhov), Dramatic Theatre, Belgrade.

1982 *Dyadya Vanya* [Uncle Vanya] (Chekhov), Gorky Bolshoi Drama Theatre, Leningrad.

The Good Mother Samanichvili (Kldiachvili), Gorky Bolshoi Drama Theatre, Leningrad.

1984 *Smert Tarelkina* [Tarelkin's Death] (Sukhovo-Kobylin), Gorky Bolshoi Drama Theatre, Leningrad.

Other productions included: *The Pickwick Club* (Dickens), 1978.

Publications

Sovremennost v sovremennom teatre [Contemporary Direction in the Theatre of Today], 1964; *O professii rejissiora* [On the Stage Director's Profession], 1965; *Kroug myslei* [Circle of Thoughts], 1972; *Klassika i sevremennost* [The Classics and the Modern World], 1975; *Zerkalo stseny* [The Mirror of the Scene], 1980; *Besedy s Kollegami*, 1988.

*

Bibliography

Books:
Odette Aslan and Denis Bablet, *V. Garcia, R. Wilson, G. Tovstonogov, M. Ulosoy*, Paris, 1984.

* * *

Georgyi Tovstonogov became the doyen of modern Soviet theatre directors. He began his career at the age of 16 in his home town of Tbilisi, as an actor and assistant director before going to the State Institute (GITIS) in Moscow from which he graduated just before World War II. He worked in Tbilisi throughout the war but came to real prominence at the Lenin Komsomol Theatre in Leningrad. His 1955 production of Vishnevsky's *Optimistic Tragedy* was awarded a Lenin Prize in 1958. By the time he took over the Gorky Theatre he had already developed a clearly defined approach to both acting and directing. His work tended to be on a large scale. This related both to his desire to find the general behind the particular, to open out domestic situations into a broader context and also to the size of the theatre he worked in.

By the mid-1950's he had become convinced that a new style of acting was necessary to correspond to changes in behaviour in everyday life. He found people more contained, less inclined to express sudden feeling that they had been, a sobriety induced perhaps by wartime experience. Yet, even in contemporary plays, actors were still giving displays of instant emotion, adopting the attitudes of an earlier period. He felt that emotion should grow and develop slowly throughout a scene and that inner depths should emerge in hints and half-tones. In this he followed the essence of the teachings of his acknowledged master, Stanislavsky. Tovstonogov was the first major director of the older generation to attempt to rescue Stanislavsky's teachings from the uniformity imposed on them since they had been made the official doctrine of the Soviet state. In this regard it is significant that he found his new kind of actor in someone who had not been to either GITIS or any of the major metropolitan theatre schools but had trained in Central Siberia, Innokenti Smoktunovsky. His 1957 production of *The Idiot*, taken from Dostoevsky's novel, marked a watershed in his own career and that of his leading actor.

As a director he was concerned on the one hand to escape from the grey uniformity of style that was one of the worst results of the imposition of Socialist Realism and on the other to avoid certain conventions of contemporary staging — the removal of the front curtain, exposure of the mechanics of the production — which represented a new conformity not new thinking. He insisted on the need for an individual approach to each play. Trained in the production methods established by Nemirovich-Danchenko, he followed Nemirovich's dictum that a play in production should be pushed to the limits of its possibilities on condition that its essential meaning was not lost. A production must be logical, justifiable and at the same time surprising. Any reinterpretation should arise from a fresh analysis of the text challenging preconceived notions and expectations. Audiences developed different perceptions from generation to generation and artists needed to be aware of such developments. He was careful to express his ideas in ideologically acceptable terms, claiming that his approach was a contribution to the creation of the communist "new man".

Tovstonogov's aesthetic found its best expression in his productions of classic plays, Chekhov's *The Three Sisters*, Gorky's *Philistines* and Shakespeare's *Henry IV*. In *The Three Sisters* he concentrated attention on the sisters' own responsibility for their failed lives. The original production in 1902 had placed the blame on the state of Russian society of the period, its triviality, its stifling pettiness. In his radical rethink of the play in 1940 Nemirovich-Danchenko had stressed the element of struggle in the characters. Tovstonogov was acutely aware of the selfishness of the characters, their capacity to complain and philosophize without taking any positive action and their failure to feel any genuine sympathy for each other's fate. Each is locked in her own concerns. Thus, while Olga does nothing to prevent the dismissal of a servant, Anfisa, who has been with the family for 30 years, she begs for sympathy for her shattered nerves. Even the fire in Act III fails to produce any positive response.

In staging the play Tovstonogov adopted a "cinematic" approach, setting the play on a revolve that could turn to bring characters into close-up and stress their separation from each other. At the end of Act I the love scene between Andrei and Natasha was brought into focus while the dining-room was faded into the background.

Similarly, Tovstonogov rethought the social and political significance of the characters and their inter-relationships in Gorky's first play *Philistines*. The result was the longest-running production the theatre had staged.

With *Henry IV*, he entered the long-standing controversy over "theatrical" theatre launched by Meyerhold and Vakhtangov. Using a translation by Boris Pasternak, he reduced the two parts to one evening. The evening was presented as a performance given by a troupe of wandering players. The "presentational" aspects of the production were, however, confined to the mechanics of staging. Tovstonogov remarked that he wished to add the realism of the best Russian acting to the methods of Brecht and Peter Brook. He continued to work along these lines with his production in 1972 of Gogol's *Revizor*.

Apart from his rethinking of classic plays, Tovstonogov did his best to encourage the staging of contemporary Russian authors, including Arbuzov and Volodin, as well as foreign plays. Under his management Brecht's *Arturo Ui*, Steinbeck's *Of Mice and Men* and *West Side Story* were also staged.

—Jean Benedetti

TREE, (Sir) Herbert (Draper) Beerbohm. British actor-manager. Born in London, 17 December 1853. Educated at Frant, near Tunbridge Wells, Kent; Dr Stone's school in King's Square, Bristol; Westbourne Collegiate School, Westbourne, London; Schnepfenthal College, Thuringia, Germany. Married Maud Holt in 1882, three daughters. Employed as clerk in father's grain business but became interested in amateur dramatics; professional stage debut, on tour, 1878; actor, various London theatres and in the provinces, 1878–87; manager, Comedy Theatre, London, 1887, and Theatre Royal, Haymarket, London, 1887–96; first US tours, 1895 and 1896; opened Her Majesty's Theatre (later, His Majesty's Theatre), 1897, as manager, 1897–1915; inaugurated annual Shakespeare season, 1905; Royal Command Performances, 1894, 1904, 1909, and 1911; visited Berlin, 1907; visited USA, 1915 and 1916; operated on for knee injury, June 1917. Member, Theatrical Managers' Association (president from 1905); Actors' Benevolent Fund (trustee and vice-president); Actors' Association (president). Founder, (Royal) Academy of Dramatic Art, 1904. Order of the Crown (Germany), 1907; Order of the Crown of Italy, 1909. Knighted, 1909. Died in London, 2 July 1917.

Principal productions

As actor:

1878   Colonel Challice in *Alone* (Simpson and Merivale), Town Hall, Folkestone, and British tour.

Admiral Kingston in *Naval Engagements* (Dance), British tour.

Lord Ingleborough in *Engineering* (Matthison), Old Park Theatre, Camden Town, London.

French Grandfather in *A Congress at Paris* (Rose), Olympic Theatre, London.

Lafleur in *The Two Orphans* (Oxenford), Olympic Theatre, London.

Daniel Gunter in *Jolliboy's Woes* (Fawcett), Olympic Theatre, London.

1879   Algernon Wrigglesworth in *Campaigning* (anon.), Criterion Theatre, London.

Bonneteau in *A Cruise to China* (anon.), Garrick Theatre, London.

Marquis de Pontsablé in *Madame Favart* (Farnie), British tour.

1880   Prince Maleotti in *Forget-Me-Not* (Merivale and Grove), Prince of Wales's Theatre, London.

Mont-Prade in *L'Aventurière* (Augier), Prince of Wales's Theatre, London.

Sir Andrew Aguecheek in *Twelfth Night* (Shakespeare), Imperial Theatre, London.

Scott Ramsay in *Where's the Cat?* (Albery), Criterion Theatre, London.

Earl of Hertford in *A Nine Days' Queen* (Buchanan), Gaiety Theatre, London.

1881   Marquis de Château-Laroche in *Brave Hearts* (Matthison), Criterion Theatre, London.

Sir Benjamin Backbite in *The School for Scandal* (Sheridan), Globe Theatre, London.

Lambert Streyke in *The Colonel* (Burnand), Prince of Wales's Theatre, London, and British tour.

Brigard in *Frou-Frou* (Daly), Globe Theatre, London.

Whittington in *A Thread of Silk* (Matthison), Crystal Palace, London.

1882   Captain Trentham in *The Marble Arch* (Rose and Garroway), Prince of Wales's Theatre, London.

Mont-Gosline in *Led Astray* (Boucicault), Gaiety Theatre, London.

Mr Babblebrook in *A Lesson in Love* (Cheltnam), Gaiety Theatre, London.

Charles Courtly in *London Assurance* (Boucicault), Gaiety Theatre, London.

Scum Goodman in *Clancarty* (Taylor), Gaiety Theatre, London.

Bertolde in *Merely Players* (anon.), Prince of Wales's Theatre, London.

Solon Trippetow in *The Mulberry Bush* (Albery), Theatre Royal, Brighton, and Criterion Theatre, London (as *Little Miss Muffet*).

1883   Harry Spreadbrow in *Sweethearts* (Gilbert), Criterion Theatre, London.

Jabez Greene in *Storm Beaten* (Buchanan), Adelphi Theatre, London.

Lord Boodle in *A Great Catch* (Aidé), Olympic Theatre, London.

Montrichard in *The Ladies' Battle* (Robertson, adapted from Scribe), Gaiety Theatre, London.

Karaloff in *The Decoy* (Eastwood), Gaiety Theatre, London.

Modus in *The Hunchback* (Knowles), Gaiety Theatre, London.

Digby Grant in *Two Roses* (Albery), Theatre Royal, Brighton.

William Roffy in *Knowledge* (Ogilvie), Gaiety Theatre, London.

Sir Fulke Pettigrew in *The Parvenu* (Godfrey), Theatre Royal, Brighton.

Malvolio in *Twelfth Night* (Shakespeare), Gaiety Theatre, London.

John Drummond in *Blow for Blow* (H. J. Byron), Crystal Palace, London.

Prince Borowski in *The Glass of Fashion* (Grundy), Globe Theatre, London.

1884   Chrysal in *The Palace of Truth* (Gilbert), Prince of Wales's Theatre, London.

Philip Dunkley in *Breaking a Butterfly* (Jones), Prince of Wales's Theatre, London.

Herbert in *Six and Eightpence* (H. Tree), Prince of Wales's Theatre, London.

Rev. Robert Spalding in *The Private Secretary* (Hawtrey), Prince of Wales's Theatre, London.

Paolo Macari in *Called Back* (Conway and Comyns Carr), Prince of Wales's Theatre, London.

Michonnet in *Adrienne Lecouvreur* (Scribe), Gaiety Theatre, London.

1885   Joseph Surface in *The School for Scandal* (Sheridan), Prince of Wales's Theatre, London.

Sir Woodbine Grafton in *Peril* (Row and Stephenson), Prince of Wales's Theatre, London.

Mr Poskett in *The Magistrate* (Pinero), Court Theatre, London.

Sir Mervyn Ferrand in *Dark Days* (Carr and Conway), Haymarket Theatre, London.

1886   Prince Zabouroff in *Nadjesda* (Barrymore), Haymarket Theatre, London.

Herr Slowitz in *A Woman of the World* (Stephenson), Haymarket Theatre, London.

Cheviot Hill in *Engaged* (Gilbert), Haymarket Theatre, London.

Baron Hartfeld in *Jim the Penman* (Young), Haymarket Theatre, London.

Paris in *Helena in Troas* (Todhunter), Hengler's Circus, London.

Colonel Abercrombie in *Old Sinners* (Mortimer), Gaiety Theatre, London.

1887   Stephen Cudlip in *Hard Hit* (Jones), Haymarket Theatre, London.

Professor Twiss in *The Professor's Wooing* (Gillette), Royalty Theatre, London.

Silvio in *The Amber Heart* (Calmour), Lyceum Theatre, London.

1888   Falstaff in *The Merry Wives of Windsor* (Shakespeare), Crystal Palace, London.

1889   John in *King John* (Shakespeare), Crystal Palace, London.

1890   Sir Peter Teazle in *The School for Scandal* (Sheridan), Crystal Palace, London.

1891   Hamlet in *Hamlet* (Shakespeare), Theatre Royal, Manchester.

1895   Svengali in *Trilby* (G. Du Maurier, adapted by Potter), Theatre Royal, Manchester.

1896   Hotspur in *Henry IV, part 1* (Shakespeare), Grand Theatre, Islington, London.
       Tinoir Doltaire in *The Seats of the Mighty* (Parker), Knickerbocker Theatre, New York.

1911   Graves in *Money* (Bulwer-Lytton), Theatre Royal, Drury Lane, London.

As actor-manager:

1887   *The Red Lamp* (Tristram), Comedy Theatre, London, and Haymarket Theatre, London; acted Paul Demetrius.
       The Ballad Monger (Pollock, from De Banville's *Gringoire*), Haymarket Theatre, London; acted Gringoire.

1888   *Partners* (Buchanan), Haymarket Theatre, London; acted Heinrich Borgfeldt.
       Incognito (Aidé), Haymarket Theatre, London; acted Vincent.
       Othello (Shakespeare), Haymarket Theatre, London; acted Iago.
       Cupid's Messenger (Calmour), Haymarket Theatre, London.
       Pompadour (Wills and Grundy, from Brachvogel's *Narcisse*), Haymarket Theatre, London; acted Narcisse Rameau.
       A Compromising Case (Smale), Haymarket Theatre, London.
       Captain Swift (Chambers), Haymarket Theatre, London; acted Mr Wilding.
       Masks and Faces (Taylor and Reade), Haymarket Theatre, London; acted Triplet.
       The Duchess of Bayswater and Co. (Heathcote), Haymarket Theatre, London.

1889   *The Merry Wives of Windsor* (Shakespeare), Haymarket Theatre, London; acted Falstaff.
       Wealth (Jones), Haymarket Theatre, London; acted Mathew Ruddock.
       A Man's Shadow (Buchanan), Haymarket Theatre, London; acted Lucien Laroque and Luversan.

1890   *A Village Priest* (Grundy), Haymarket Theatre, London; acted Abbé Dubois.
       Rachel (Graves), Haymarket Theatre, London.
       Comedy and Tragedy (Gilbert), Haymarket Theatre, London.
       Called Back (Conway and Comyns Carr), Haymarket Theatre, London; acted Paolo Macari.
       The Intruder (adapted from Maeterlinck), Haymarket Theatre, London; acted the Grandfather.
       Beau Austin (Henley and Stevenson), Haymarket Theatre, London; acted Beau Austin.
       The Waif (Dick), Haymarket Theatre, London.
       Peril (Row and Stephenson), Haymarket Theatre, London; acted Grafton.

1891   *The Dancing Girl* (Jones), Haymarket Theatre, London; acted the Duke of Guisebury.

1892   *Hamlet* (Shakespeare), Haymarket Theatre, London; acted Hamlet.

1893   *Hypatia* (Ogilvie), Haymarket Theatre, London; acted Issachar.
       A Woman of No Importance (Wilde), Haymarket Theatre, London; acted Lord Illingworth.
       An Enemy of the People (Ibsen), Haymarket Theatre, London; acted Dr Thomas Stockmann.
       The Tempter (Jones), Haymarket Theatre, London; acted the Devil.
       Six Persons (Zangwill), Haymarket Theatre, London.

1894   *The Charlatan* (Buchanan), Haymarket Theatre, London; acted Philip Woodville.
       Once Upon a Time (Parker and Tree, from Ludwig Fulda's *Der Talisman*), Haymarket Theatre, London; acted the King.
       A Bunch of Violets (Grundy, from Feuillet's *Mountjoys*), Haymarket Theatre, London; acted Sir Philip Marchant.
       A Modern Eve (Salaman), Haymarket Theatre, London; acted Kenyon Wargrave.
       John-A-Dreams (Chambers), Haymarket Theatre, London; acted Harold Wynn.

1896   *Fédora* (Sardou, adapted by Merivale), Haymarket Theatre, London; acted Loris Ipanoff.
       Trilby (G. Du Maurier, adapted by Potter), Haymarket Theatre, London; acted Svengali.
       Henry IV, part 1 (Shakespeare), Haymarket Theatre, London; acted Falstaff.

1897   *The Seats of the Mighty* (Parker), Her Majesty's Theatre, London; acted Tinoir Doltaire.
       Chand d'Habits (Mendès), Her Majesty's Theatre, London.
       The Silver Key (Grundy), Her Majesty's Theatre, London; acted Duc de Richelieu.
       Katherine and Petruchio (Garrick), Her Majesty's Theatre, London; acted Petruchio.

1898   *Julius Caesar* (Shakespeare), Her Majesty's Theatre, London; acted Mark Antony.
       Ragged Robin (Parker, from Richepin's *Le Chemineau*), Her Majesty's Theatre, London; acted Robin.
       The Musketeers (Grundy), Her Majesty's Theatre, London; acted D'Artagnan.

1899   *Carnac Sahib* (Jones), Her Majesty's Theatre, London; acted Colonel Stacey Carnac.
       King John (Shakespeare), Her Majesty's Theatre, London; acted John.

1900   *A Midsummer Night's Dream* (Shakespeare), Her Majesty's Theatre, London; acted Bottom.
       Rip Van Winkle, Her Majesty's Theatre, London; acted Rip.
       Herod (Phillips), Her Majesty's Theatre, London; acted Herod.

1901   *Twelfth Night* (Shakespeare), Her Majesty's Theatre, London; acted Malvolio.
       Macaire (Henley and Stevenson), Her Majesty's Theatre, London; acted Robert Macaire.
       The Last of the Dandies (Fitch), Her Majesty's Theatre, London; acted Count D'Orsay.

1902   *Ulysses* (Phillips), His Majesty's Theatre, London; acted Ulysses.

A Midsummer Night's Dream (Shakespeare), His Majesty's Theatre, London; acted Falstaff.

The Eternal City (Caine), His Majesty's Theatre, London; acted Baron Bonelli.

1903   *Resurrection* (Tolstoy, adapted by Bataille and Morton), His Majesty's Theatre, London; acted Prince Dmitri Nehludoff.

The Gordian Knot (Lowther), His Majesty's Theatre, London; acted Roger Martens.

Flodden Field (Austin), His Majesty's Theatre, London.

The Man Who Was (Peile), His Majesty's Theatre, London; acted Austin Limmason.

Richard II (Shakespeare), His Majesty's Theatre, London; acted Richard.

The Darling of the Gods (Belasco and Long), His Majesty's Theatre, London; acted Zakkuri.

1904   *The Tempest* (Shakespeare), His Majesty's Theatre, London; acted Caliban.

1905   *Much Ado About Nothing* (Shakespeare), His Majesty's Theatre, London; acted Benedick.

Business is Business (Grundy, adapted from Mirbeau's *Les Affaires sont les Affaires*), His Majesty's Theatre, London; acted Isidore Izard.

Oliver Twist (Comyns Carr, adapted from Dickens), His Majesty's Theatre, London; acted Fagin.

Agatha, His Majesty's Theatre, London.

1906   *Nero* (Phillips), His Majesty's Theatre, London; acted Nero.

Colonel Newcome (Morton, adapted from Thackeray), His Majesty's Theatre, London; acted Newcome.

The Winter's Tale (Shakespeare), His Majesty's Theatre, London.

Antony and Cleopatra (Shakespeare), His Majesty's Theatre, London; acted Mark Antony.

1907   *The Van Dyke* (Lennox, adapted from Peringue), His Majesty's Theatre, London; acted Arthur Blair-Woldingham.

1908   The Mystery of Edwin Drood (Comyns Carr, adapted from Dickens), His Majesty's Theatre, London; acted John Jasper.

The Beloved Vagabond (Locke), His Majesty's Theatre, London; acted Gaston de Nerac.

Hansel and Gretel (Humperdinck), His Majesty's Theatre, London.

The Merchant of Venice (Shakespeare), His Majesty's Theatre, London; acted Shylock.

Faust (Phillips and Comyns Carr), His Majesty's Theatre, London; acted Mephistopheles.

Pinkie and the Fairies (Robertson), His Majesty's Theatre, London.

1909   *The School for Scandal* (Sheridan), His Majesty's Theatre, London; acted Sir Peter Teazle.

False Gods (Fagan, adapted from Brieux's *La Foi*), His Majesty's Theatre, London; acted the High Priest.

Beethoven (Fauchois, adapted by Parker), His Majesty's Theatre, London; acted Beethoven.

A Russian Tragedy (Glass, adapted by Hamilton), His Majesty's Theatre, London.

The Lethal Hotel (Willner, adapted by Whelen), His Majesty's Theatre, London.

1910   *The O'Flynn* (McCarthy), His Majesty's Theatre, London; acted O'Flynn.

Henry VIII (Shakespeare), His Majesty's Theatre, London; acted Cardinal Wolsey.

1911   *Macbeth* (Shakespeare), His Majesty's Theatre, London; acted Macbeth.

The War God (Zangwill), His Majesty's Theatre, London; acted Count Frithiof.

Orpheus in the Underworld (Norton, Noyes, and Tree, adapted from Offenbach), His Majesty's Theatre, London.

1912   *Othello* (Shakespeare), His Majesty's Theatre, London; acted Othello.

Drake (Parker), His Majesty's Theatre, London; acted Drake.

1913   *The Happy Island* (Lengyel), His Majesty's Theatre, London; acted Derek Arden.

The Perfect Gentleman (Maugham, adapted from Molière's *Le Bourgeois Gentilhomme*), His Majesty's Theatre, London; acted Jourdain.

Romeo and Juliet (Shakespeare), Haymarket Theatre, London; acted Mercutio.

Joseph and His Brethren (Parker), His Majesty's Theatre, London; acted Jacob.

1914   *Pygmalion* (Shaw), His Majesty's Theatre, London; acted Henry Higgins.

The Silver King (Jones), His Majesty's Theatre, London; acted Gaffer Pottle.

David Copperfield (Parker, adapted from Dickens), His Majesty's Theatre, London; acted Wilkins Micawber and Dan'l Peggotty.

1915   *The Right to Kill* (Cannan and Keyzer), His Majesty's Theatre, London; acted Marquis de Sevigné.

Marie Odile (Knoblauch), His Majesty's Theatre, London.

Mavourneen (Parker), His Majesty's Theatre, London.

1916   *Chu Chin Chow* (Asche and Norton), His Majesty's Theatre, London.

Other roles included: Sir Anthony Absolute in *The Rivals* (Sheridan); Captain Mountraffe in *Home* (Robertson, adapted from Augier); and roles in *Bow Bells* (H. J. Byron), *Cymbeline* (Shakespeare), *Henry Dunbar* (Taylor), *Ingomar* (Lovell), *M.D.* (Barri), *Milky White* (Craven), *A Republican Marriage* (Holford), and *The Turn of the Tide* (Burnand).

Films

Macbeth, 1916; *The Old Folks at Home*, 1916.

Publications

An Essay on the Imaginative Faculty, 1893; *Thoughts and Afterthoughts* (essays), 1913; *Nothing Matters* (short stories), 1917.

*

Bibliography

Books:
Max Beerbohm, *Herbert Beerbohm Tree*, London, 1920.
Mrs G. Cran, *Herbert Beerbohm Tree*, London, 1907.
Hesketh Pearson, *Beerbohm Tree: His Life and Laughter*, London, 1956.
Madeleine Bingham, *The Great Lover (The Life and Art of Herbert Beerbohm Tree)*, London, 1978.

* * *

Mrs. Patrick Campbell regarded Herbert Beerbohm Tree as "the best character comedian of his day". Certainly onstage and off he was a commanding figure. His father's family was of Dutch origin and though born and mainly educated in England, Tree always embodied an elegant, rather fantastic, foreign manner. From the age of 17 his ambition was a stage career, but for eight years he deferred to his father by working in the City.

Tree made his professional debut in 1878 and gained early experience in the provinces. In March 1884 he scored a personal success as the Reverend Robert Spalding in Charles Hawtrey's farce *The Private Secretary*. Tree used considerable inventiveness in developing stage business for his character, but he quickly tired of the routine of successive performances and left the cast. Such behaviour was characteristic. Although he had received some coaching from the veteran actor Hermann Vezin essentially Tree remained an amateur in terms of technique. His performances were notoriously uneven. When he was on form — emotionally at one with his character — he could be spellbinding, but the next night he might be dull and remote. Long runs were anathema to him; he began to "gag" the other actors with unseemly jokes and grimaces.

Though not a businessman by nature, Tree assumed the responsibilities of management first at the Comedy Theatre, then the Haymarket, and finally at his own creation, Her Majesty's, which was completed in 1897. In these endeavours he was aided by his wife Maud (Holt), whom he married in 1883. Well-educated and with a forceful personality, Maud Tree shared many of her husband's early successes, including *The Red Lamp* and *The Seats of the Mighty*, with which he opened Her Majesty's.

Tree showed an eclectic flair in his choice of plays. Gilbert Parker, Stephen Phillips, and L. N. Parker furnished him with dramas well suited to the scenic elaboration in which audiences of the day delighted. Oscar Wilde thought (probably rightly) that Tree would have been admirable as Herod in *Salomé*, but instead provided him with *A Woman of No Importance*, in which he played the disreputable Lord Illingworth. Tree's greatest success was as Svengali in an adaptation of George Du Maurier's *Trilby*, by Paul Potter, though Bernard Shaw considered that after a good start Tree declined absurdly into "the stagey, the malignant, the diabolic, the Wandering-Jewish."

Shaw had to wait nearly 20 years for Tree to create Professor Higgins in *Pygmalion*. The temperamental differences between the author and his two stars — Tree and Mrs. Patrick Campbell (as Eliza Doolittle) — made rehearsals highly charged occasions. In contrast, the performances (apart from the excitement over Eliza's use of the world "bloody") were rather ponderous. The pace was funereally slow and Tree's lack of technique was evident in his recurrent dependence upon his own invention rather than the dialogue written for him by Shaw.

Tree was particularly proud of his record in Shakespearean revivals of which he staged 16, four more than Irving with whom he enjoyed a none too friendly rivalry, heightened by Ellen Terry's change of allegiance from the Lyceum to His Majesty's in 1902 to play Mistress Page in *The Merry Wives of Windsor*.

In an essay entitled "The Living Shakespeare" Tree advocated that Shakespeare should be treated "not as a dead author speaking a dead language, but as a living force speaking with the voice of a living humanity". Although Tree counselled that the exponents of stage antiquarianism should not be deferred to uncritically he accepted that 'illusion' was the aim of contemporary stagecraft. The historical painter Alma-Tadema was responsible for the scenery and costumes for *Julius Caesar*, which repaid Tree's lavish investment by running for five months. The scenes in the Senate House and the Forum were fine examples not only of scenic art but also of the management of stage crowds. Shaw acquitted Tree of any belittlement of the parts that competed with his own. As Antony, Tree's memory failed him and technically his performance was haphazard, but he made his character credible. Honours were evenly shared with Louis Calvert (Casca), Lewis Waller (Brutus), and Frank McLeay (Cassius).

Tree's aptitude for eccentric comic characterization found its most complete realisation as Malvolio in *Twelfth Night*. The set for Olivia's garden was copied by Joseph Harker from a picture in *Country Life*. Replete with hedges and statuary, its centre-piece was a flight of steps down which Malvolio descended (and nearly fell) accompanied by four little Malvolios who aped his movements, in particular grimacing at the statues through their monocles.

Tree took his position as a leader of his profession seriously. Despite (or because of) his own lack of training he founded in 1904 what became the Royal Academy of Dramatic Art, lending his theatre for public performances, tendering advice whenever asked, and employing the more promising students. In 1905 he inaugurated his annual Shakespeare Festival at His Majesty's, giving six plays in six days. Over the years he provided a showcase for the work of F. R. Benson, Arthur Bourchier, H. B. Irving, Oscar Asche, Louis Waller, and William Poel's Elizabethan Stage Society.

In his wife's view at least, Tree had earned a knighthood and she asked well-connected friends to use their influence to that end. Following H. H. Asquith's appointment as Prime Minister in 1908 Tree's name appeared in the Birthday Honours of 1909. That evening Tree's delivery of Malvolio's line "Some have greatness thrust upon them", though obviously a contrived coincidence, drew an enthusiastic response from the audience. Maud Tree herself adopted her title with alacrity, but she could not have deluded herself that she was the only woman in her husband's life. His "little lapses" were by then well-known, but like those other lapses — of memory — on stage, they were part and parcel of the larger than life personality of Herbert Beerbohm Tree.

—Richard Foulkes

VAKHTANGOV, Evgeny (Bagrationovich). Russian director and actor. Born in Vladikavkaz (now Ordzhonikidze), Armenia, 1 February 1883. Educated at the Tiflig Gymnasium, 1893–94; Vladikavkaz Gymnasium, 1894–1903; University of Moscow, from 1903; trained for the stage at the School of Drama of A. I. Adashev, Moscow, 1909–11. Married Nadejda Mikhailovna Baitzurova in 1905, one son. Directed and acted in amateur productions, from 1901; joined Moscow Art Theatre, 1911; founder-member, First Studio of the Moscow Art Theatre, 1913; director, Students Drama School (renamed the Moscow Drama Studio, 1917, then the Third Studio of the Moscow Art Theatre, 1921, and finally the Vakhtangov Theatre, 1926), from 1917; co-founder, Habimah Theatre, Moscow, 1918; joined board of Second Studio of the Moscow Art Theatre, 1919; appointed head of the directors' section of the Theatrical Division of the People's Commissariat of Education, 1919. Died in Moscow, 29 May 1922.

Productions

As actor:
1911	The Gypsy in *Zhivoy trup* [The Living Corpse] (L. Tolstoy), Art Theatre, Moscow; tour, 1912.
1912	Second Actor in *Hamlet* (Shakespeare), tour.
1913	The Doctor in *Le Malade Imaginaire* (Molière), tour.
1914	Kraft in *Mysl* [Thought] (Andreyev), Art Theatre, Moscow.
	Guest in *Nikolai Stavrogin* (Dostoevsky), tour.
	Tackleton in *Svercok na peci* [The Cricket on the Hearth] (Dickens), First Studio, Art Theatre, Moscow.
1915	Frazier in *The Deluge* (Berger), First Studio, Art Theatre, Moscow.
1918	Ulric Brendel in *Rosmersholm* (Ibsen), First Studio, Art Theatre, Moscow.
1919	Satin in *Na Dne* [The Lower Depths] (Gorky), tour.
	Feste and other roles in *Twelfth Night* (Shakespeare), First Studio, Art Theatre, Leningrad.

As director:
1913	*Das Friedenfest* (Hauptmann), First Studio, Art Theatre, Moscow.
1914	*Country Estate of Lanins* (Zaitzev), Students' Drama School, Art Theatre, Moscow.
1915	*The Deluge* (Berger), First Studio, Art Theatre, Moscow.

1918	*Rosmersholm* (Ibsen), First Studio, Art Theatre, Moscow.
	Le Miracle de Saint-Antoine (Maeterlinck), Drama Studio, Art Theatre, Moscow.
	The Older Sister (Ash), Habimah Theatre, Moscow.
	The Fire (Peretz), Habimah Theatre, Moscow.
	The Son (Katznelson), Habimah Theatre, Moscow.
	Misfortune (Berkovitch), Habimah Theatre, Moscow.
1920	*Svadba* [A Wedding] (Chekhov), Drama Studio, Moscow.
1921	*Le Miracle de Saint-Antoine* (Maeterlinck), Third Studio, Art Theatre, Moscow.
	Erik XIV (Strindberg), First Studio, Art Theatre, Moscow.
	Svadba [A Wedding] (Chekhov), Third Studio, Art Theatre, Moscow.
1922	*The Dybbuk* (Ansky), Habimah Theatre, Moscow.
	Princess Turandot (Gozzi), Third Studio, Art Theatre, Moscow.

Publications

Zapiski: Pisma, Stati, 1939.

*

Bibliography

Books:
Nikolai Gortchakov, *The Vakhtangov School of Stage Art,* Moscow, not dated.
Reuben Simonov, *Stanislavsky's Protégé: Eugene Vakhtangov,* New York, 1969.
Lyubov Vendrovskaya and Galina Kaptereve, translated by Doris Bradbury, *Evgeny Vakhtangov,* Moscow, 1982.

* * *

Despite the comparative brevity of Evgeny Vakhtangov's theatrical career — a total of about 10 years spent as a professional artist — he has left a permanent mark on the history of world theatre, having established himself, with extraordinary rapidity, as a director of genius. If one seeks for analogies that approximate to Vakhtangov's place in the theatre of his day, one thinks of the leaders of religious sects whose influence on their followers is as much personal

Evgeny Vakhtangov

as it is ideological, a compound of love, fear and intellectual respect. In many ways, Vakhtangov was an artistic fanatic whose standards were maximalist and absolutist. The theatre for Vakhtangov, as it was for Stanislavsky and had been for Nikolai Gogol, was a moral institution and it is not unusual to discover among Vakhtangov's writings connections made between the actor's "calling" and a "sense of mission", references to Stanislavsky as a "god" and a theatrical art that needed to be "served" as part of "service to the people". Acting groups are referred to as 'sects' and the atmosphere of studio work is frequently compared to that of a monastery. The theatre is a place where "the truth" can be sought and "the soul purified" of the imperfections of living and where, eventually, the "meaning of life" can be discovered.

The accounts left by those who knew Vakhtangov both as man and artist bear witness to the fact that he was a remarkable and charismatic individual who left the mark of his personality, permanently, on anyone who came into contact with him. It is also a commonplace of Soviet criticism to say that he represents an important point of intersection between two artistic extremes that had always been at odds with each other, represented by the "realism" of Stanislavsky at one end of the scale and by the "conventionalised theatre" represented by Meyerhold at the other. In actual fact, whilst being critical of both the methods of Stanislavsky and of Meyerhold at various stages in his life, Vakhtangov's development as an artist brought him closer to Meyerhold, of whom he is much quoted as saying: "Meyerhold provided the roots for the theatre of the future. So shall the future honour him". Vakhtangov's artistic career can be described, in one sense, as a journey from Stanislavsky towards Meyerhold. In 1911, the year he entered the Moscow Art Theatre, he spoke of the need to "take the theatre out of the theatre and the actor out of the play", of the need to study the Stanislavsky method intensively so as to produce the kind of performance in which the actors immersed themselves in a role to such an extent that "they ... forget about the audience and create for themselves". By 1921 he had moved away from this position and was talking in terms more reminiscent of Meyerhold: "Theatre is theatre. A play is a performance. The art of performance is acting skill ... the actor — a skilled master possessing internal and external technique ..."

Towards the end of his life he was also developing a theory of "the grotesque", under the influence of Meyerhold's productions. In March 1921 he wrote: "The slice-of-life theatre must die", and that "everyone capable of being a character actor ... must learn to express themselves grotesquely". In August that same year he described the road that he had previously followed (that of Stanislavsky and the Moscow Art Theatre) as the road to a "luxurious cemetery", and a notebook entry for 26 March 1921 stresses that "All theatre in the near future will be built along the main lines that Meyerhold long ago foresaw". In his final conversations with two of his students during April 1922 he spoke for the first time of his theory of "fantastic" or "imaginative" realism, where "form and content harmonise like a musical chord".

The true importance of Vakhtangov's historical position as a "reconciler" of extremes has come into its own since the rehabilitation of Meyerhold, in 1955, and the reopening of the debate surrounding the formal methods that are available and/or tolerable within the parameters of "socialist realism". It has become increasingly common, when comparing the differences between Stanislavsky and Meyerhold, for example, to point to the fact that their principles and methods were merging towards the end of the 1930's, like two people who began digging separate tunnels but discovered that, all the while, they had been tunnelling towards each other and had finally met. According to Brecht, Vakhtangov was this "meeting point" between Stanislavsky and Meyerhold — someone who embraced the other two as contradictory elements but who was, himself, at the same time the most free.

Vakhtangov's symbolic, historical position as a reconciler of formerly irreconcilable opposites is actually more important than his role as a father-figure whose legacy has been taken up and extended by his pupils. The history of Vakhtangov's own theatre, the former Third Studio, would appear to have only a marginal connection with Vakhtangov's own theatrical practice. There were times, indeed, during the troubled 1930's, when Vakhtangov's own contribution to Soviet theatre was being reassessed and his stylised productions downgraded in terms that characterised their "excesses" as "formalistic". Even a life-enhancing and affirmative production such as *Princess Turandot*, which carried the burden of Vakhtangov's acceptance of the Russian Revolution, did not entirely escape formalist strictures during this unhappy period.

The inheritors of the Vakhtangov tradition have, in the most literal sense, been Reuben Simonov and his son Evgeny Simonov, although little that either of them achieved when directors of the Vakhtangov Theatre can stand comparison with the achievements of Vakhtangov himself. The revival of *Princess Turandot* in 1963 was little more than an archival exercise and had little in common with the spirit of the original and was even considered a vulgarisation. Others who have extended Vakhtangov's spiritual legacy have been former pupils and colleagues, such as Boris Zakhava, Yuri Zavadsky and Alexei Popov. Peter Brook, interestingly, has paid tribute to the genuine folk spirit to be found in Vakhtangov's work. In this connection, perhaps the authentic mantle of Vakhtangov's legacy can be seen to have fallen on the shoulders of the outstanding Georgian director Robert Sturua, whose productions of *The Caucasian Chalk Circle*, *Richard III* and *King Lear* amongst others staged at the Rustaveli Theatre during the 1970's and 1980's carry the hallmark of the Vakhtangov style and even manage to extend it in ways of which he would undoubtedly have approved.

—Nick Worrall

VESTRIS, "Madame" Lucia Elizabeth. British actress-manager and singer. Born Lucia Elizabeth Bartolozzi in London, January 1797, of Italian descent. Educated at Manor Hall School, London. Married 1) dancer Armand Vestris in 1812 (separated 1818, died 1825); 2) actor Charles Mathews (*q.v.*) in 1838. Stage debut as opera singer, under Vestris, at the King's Opera House, London, 1815; first appearance as actress in burlesque under William Elliston, Theatre Royal, Drury Lane, 1817; subsequently spent three years in Paris but returned to London after her first husband deserted her, 1820; celebrated in breeches roles for her beautiful legs as much as for her voice at both Drury Lane and Covent Garden, from 1820; manager, Olympic Theatre, 1830–39, staging hugely successful burlesque extravaganzas and introducing numerous reforms in costume and stage decoration in partnership with J. R. Planché; possibly first manager to use a box set, 1832; declared bankruptcy, 1837; US tour with Mathews, 1838; co-manager, with Mathews, Covent Garden, 1839–42, and Lyceum Theatre, 1847–55; brief imprisonment for debt, 1842, followed by gradual decline in health; last stage appearance, 1854. Died in London, 8 August 1856.

Roles

1815	Proserpina in *Il Ratto di Proserpina* (Winter), King's Theatre, London, and Théâtre Italien, Paris, 1816–18.
1816	Zaira in *Zaira* (Winter), King's Theatre, London.
	Dorabella in *Così fan tutte* (Mozart), King's Theatre, London.
	Susanna in *The Marriage of Figaro* (Mozart), King's Theatre, London.
1816–17	Camille in *Horace* (Racine), Comédie-Française, Paris.
1820	Lilla in *The Siege of Belgrade* (Cobb), Theatre Royal, Drury Lane, London.

	Caroline in *Prize* (Hoare), Theatre Royal, Drury Lane, London.
	Artaxerxes in *Artaxerxes* (Arne and Metastasio), Theatre Royal, Drury Lane, London.
	Adela in *The Haunted Tower* (Cobb), Theatre Royal, Drury Lane, London, 1820; Don Giovanni in *Giovanni in London* (Moncrieff), Theatre Royal, Drury Lane, London.
	Dolly Snip and Columbine in *Shakespeare versus Harlequin* (adapted from Garrick's *Harlequin's Invasion*), Theatre Royal, Drury Lane, London.
	Macheath in *The Beggar's Opera* (Gay), Theatre Royal, Drury Lane, London; Covent Garden, London, 1821, 1826, 1828.
	Monsel in *Justice; or, The Caliph and the Cobbler*, Theatre Royal, Drury Lane, London.
	Little Pickle in *The Spoiled Child* (anon.), Theatre Royal, Drury Lane, London.
	Rose Sydney in *Secrets Worth Knowing*, Theatre Royal, Drury Lane, London.
	Edmund in *The Blind Boy*, Theatre Royal, Drury Lane, London.
	Effie Deans in *The Heart of Midlothian* (Scott), Theatre Royal, Drury Lane, London.
	Don Felix in *Alcaid* (Calderón), London.
1821	Don Giovanni in *Giovanni in Ireland* (Moncrieff), Theatre Royal, Drury Lane, London.
	Paul in *Paul and Virginia* (Cobb), Theatre Royal, Drury Lane, London.
	Bell in *The Veteran* (Knight), Theatre Royal, Drury Lane, London.
1822	Betty Blackberry in *The Farmer*, Theatre Royal, Drury Lane, London.
	Nell in *The Devil to Pay* (Coffey), Theatre Royal, Drury Lane, London.
	Lisette in *Love Letters*, Theatre Royal, Drury Lane, London.
	Patrick in *The Poor Soldier* (O'Keeffe), Theatre Royal, Drury Lane, London.
	Ophelia in *Hamlet* (Shakespeare), Theatre Royal, Drury Lane, London.
	Mrs Oakley in *The Jealous Wife* (Colman the Elder), Theatre Royal, Drury Lane, London.
	Herman in *Tale of Other Times* (Dimond), Theatre Royal, Drury Lane, London.
	Florella in *My Grandmother* (Storace), Theatre Royal, Drury Lane, London.
	Maria in *A Roland for an Oliver* (Morton, adapted from Scribe), Theatre Royal, Drury Lane, London.
	Annette in *The Lord of the Manor* (Bishop), Theatre Royal, Drury Lane, London.
	Letitia Hardy in *The Belle's Stratagem* (Cowley), Theatre Royal, Drury Lane, London.
	Pippo in *Gazza ladra* (Rossini), Italian Opera House, London.
	Rosina in *Il Barbiere di Seviglia* (Rossini), Italian Opera House, London.
	Arsace in *Semiramis* (Rossini), Italian Opera House, London.
	Malcolm in *The Lady of the Lake*, Italian Opera House, London.

Zamira in *Richard and Zoraide*, Italian Opera House, London.

Edoardo in *Mathilde of Shabran*, Italian Opera House, London.

Emma in *Zelmira*, Italian Opera House, London.

1824   Pauline in *Philandering* (Beazley), Theatre Royal, Drury Lane, London.

Ariel in *The Tempest* (Shakespeare), Theatre Royal, Drury Lane, London.

Luciana in *The Comedy of Errors* (Shakespeare), Theatre Royal, Drury Lane, London.

Lydia Languish in *The Rivals* (Sheridan), Theatre Royal, Drury Lane, London; Haymarket Theatre, London, 1826.

Rosalind in *As You Like It* (Shakespeare), Theatre Royal, Drury Lane, London.

Lady Teazle in *The School for Scandal* (Sheridan), Theatre Royal, Drury Lane, London; Covent Garden, London, 1825; revived, 1837.

Mrs. Ford and Mrs. Page in *The Merry Wives of Windsor* (Shakespeare), Theatre Royal, Drury Lane, London.

Carlos in *The Duenna* (Linley), Theatre Royal, Drury Lane, London.

Hippolita in *She Would if She Could* (Etherege), Theatre Royal, Drury Lane, London.

Cherubino in *The Marriage of Figaro* (Mozart), Theatre Royal, Drury Lane, London.

1825   Phoebe in *Paul Pry* (Poole), Haymarket Theatre, London.

Georgette Clairville in *'Twas I*, Covent Garden, London.

1826   Fatima in *Oberon* (Planché), Covent Garden, London.

1827   Blonde in *Il Ratto al Serraglio*, Covent Garden, London.

1829   Madame Germance in *Home Sweet Home* (Pocock), Covent Garden, London.

1830   Kate O'Brien in *Perfection* (Bayly), Theatre Royal, Drury Lane, London.

1831   Pandora in *Olympic Revels* (Planché), Olympic Theatre, London.

Orpheus in *The Olympic Devils; or, Orpheus and Eurydice* (Planché), Olympic Theatre, London.

1832   Venus in *The Paphian Bower* (Planché), Olympic Theatre, London.

1833   The Queen of Hearts in *High, Low, Jack, and Game* (Planché), Olympic Theatre, London.

Perseus in *The Deep, Deep Sea*, Olympic Theatre, London.

1834   Calypso in *Telemachus* (Bishop), Olympic Theatre, London.

1836   Princess Emeralda in *Riquet with the Tuft* (Planché), Olympic Theatre, London.

1837   Ralph in *Puss in Boots* (Planché), Olympic Theatre, London.

1838   Praise in *Drama's Levée*, Olympic Theatre, London.

1839   Fleurette in *Blue Beard* (Planché), Olympic Theatre, London.

Catherine in *Love* (Knowles), Covent Garden, London.

Rosaline in *Love's Labour's Lost* (Shakespeare), Covent Garden, London.

Lucy Lockit in *The Beggar's Opera* (Gay), Covent Garden, London.

1840   Oberon in *A Midsummer Night's Dream* (Shakespeare), Covent Garden, London.

Princess Is-a-belle in *The Sleeping Beauty in the Wood* (Planché), Covent Garden, London.

1841   Lady Anne in *Old Maids* (Knowles), Covent Garden, London.

Beauty in *Beauty and the Beast* (Planché), Covent Garden, London.

Grace Harkaway in *London Assurance* (Boucicault), Covent Garden, London.

1842   Prince Paragon in *The White Cat* (Planché), Covent Garden, London.

1845   Medea in *The Golden Fleece* (Planché), Covent Garden, London.

1847   Suivanta in *The Golden Branch* (Planché), Covent Garden, London.

1848   Theseus in *Theseus and Ariadne* (Planché), Lyceum Theatre, London.

Argus in *King of the Peacocks* (Planché), Lyceum Theatre, London.

1850   Charming the First in *King Charming; or, The Blue Bird of Paradise* (Planché), Lyceum Theatre, London.

1852   Dame Goldenhead in *The Good Woman in the Wood*, Lyceum Theatre, London.

1853   Queen Dominantia in *Once Upon a Time There Were Two Kings*, Lyceum Theatre, London.

Other roles included: *Una Cosa rara* (Martín y Soler), King's Theatre, London, 1816; *The Pirate* (Scott), Theatre Royal, Drury Lane, London, 1821; *The Loan of a Lover* (Planché), Olympic Theatre, London, 1834, and US tour, 1838; *Naval Engagements* (Dance), Theatre Royal, Drury Lane, London, 1838; *Comus* (adapted from Milton), Covent Garden, London, 1839; *The Island of Jewels* (Planché), Lyceum Theatre, London, 1847; *Sunshine Through the Clouds* (Girardin, adapted by Lewes, as S. Lawrence), Lyceum Theatre, London, 1849; *Carnival Ball*; *The Rivals* (Sheridan); *You Can't Marry Your Grandmother* (Mathews); *Little Devil* (adapted from Scribe); *Who's Your Friend* (Planché).

Other productions under her management included: *Mary Queen of Scots*, Olympic Theatre, London, 1831; *The Conquering Game* (Bernard), Olympic Theatre, London, 1832; *The Old and Young Stagers* (Rede), Olympic Theatre, London, 1835; *The Humpbacked Lovers* (Mathews), Olympic Theatre, London, 1835; *Court Beauties*, Olympic Theatre, London, 1835; *The Two Queens*, Olympic Theatre, London, 1835; *The Rape of the Lock* (adapted from Pope), Olympic Theatre, London, 1837; *The Idol's Birthday* (Oxenford), Olympic Theatre, London, 1838; *Patter versus Clatter* (Mathews), Olympic Theatre, London, 1838; *Faint Heart Never Won Fair Lady* (Planché), Olympic Theatre, 1839; *Izaak Walton*, 1839; *The Court of Old Fritz,*

1839; *Romeo and Juliet* (Shakespeare), Covent Garden, London, 1840.

*

Bibliography

Books:
Charles E. Pearce, *Madame Vestris and Her Times*, London, 1923.
John Clifford Williams, *Madame Vestris*, London, 1973.

* * *

Lucia Elizabeth Bartolozzi was born into a family of Italian artists who had settled in London. At 15 she married Armand Vestris, 10 years her senior, who was premier danseur at the King's Opera House and also an emigré from Paris, where his father and grandfather had been famous maîtres du ballet. Madame Vestris made her debut in the opera *Il Ratto di Proserpina* for her husband's benefit performance at the King's on 20 July 1815. Her voice was sweet and expressive but untrained in the fashion of ornamenting the vocal line and too low for true soprano roles. She was far more successful with simple ballads such as "Cherry Ripe", with which she was to make a "hit" in *Paul Pry* in 1825, and, after an undistinguished three years singing opera in Paris — where her husband deserted her — she returned to star in musical afterpieces at Drury Lane under William Elliston. Here she developed her speciality of "breeches roles" such as Don Giovanni and Macheath. Her success "en travestie", which allowed her to display her incomparable legs (there was a great scandal in 1831 when "pirated" plaster casts of her leg were offered for sale), combined with a reputation for offstage amours made her a particular favourite with the bucks and blades of Regency society.

However, Vestris was not satisfied with starring in afterpieces and supporting in operas and in 1830 she established her own company at the Olympic Theatre in Wych Street, off Drury Lane. This Minor House was not allowed to present "legitimate" drama, but this was no restriction to Vestris, who wished to make a speciality of the "burlettas" to which the repertoire was restricted. Her original inspiration was the French vaudeville but she wanted to avoid their vulgarity and enhance their visual attraction. In this she was assisted by James Robinson Planché, who was chief dramatist at the Olympic throughout Vestris's management. A Planché extravaganza, like his first *Olympic Revels* in 1830, was not only a theatrical parody with popular songs and punning doggerel but a means of displaying Planché's expert knowledge of period costume and Vestris's meticulously "naturalistic" stage-management. The little Olympic stage was dressed with real furniture and authentic props rather than those painted on the scenery of even the Patent House theatres. It is claimed that Vestris introduced the first "box set" with angled walls and a ceiling replacing the conventional wings and borders.

The whole Olympic programme was planned to attract elegant bourgeois audiences, who had deserted Covent Garden and Drury Lane and who disdained the popular melodrama houses. Bills were shortened to a single performance, prices raised to deter "undesirables", the benefit system replaced by regular and decent salaries, and, in the auditorium, box seats outnumbered the gallery. Thus in several ways the Olympic regime pioneered features that were to become the staple policy of "long run" West End theatres in the second half of the 19th century. As a producer, Vestris not only anticipated the "antiquarian authenticity" of Charles Kean at the Princess's but also his meticulous concern for maintaining a unified production style — when not on stage she "was constantly in her private box, watching the performance, noting the slightest imperfection, and seeking to increase effects instead of allowing them to be gradually destroyed by time and carelessness". In 1840, Vestris and her second husband, Charles James Mathews, took over the management of Covent Garden — much to the horror of Macready: "it is not a fitting spectacle — the national drama in the hands of Mrs Vestris and Mr Charles Mathews!" — though another champion of legitimate drama, James Anderson, recorded years later that: "Madame was an admirable manager, and Charles an aimiable assistant ... Two more capable, competent, and admirable people never before or since managed a theatre". On 4 March 1841 they provided their usual accurate and elegant settings and costumes for Dion Boucicault's first play, *London Assurance*, which, in these production qualities at least, was to inspire the "naturalistic" comedies of Tom Robertson, which were to be presented in the late 1860's by the Bancrofts at the Prince of Wales's. Robertson was briefly a stage manager for Vestris and Mathews in 1854, though it was probably more significant that the Bancrofts's first scene-painter, Charles J. James, had been employed at the Olympic in 1834.

As a performer, however, Vestris was far from naturalistic — if that means creating the illusion that the audience are detached spectators behind an invisible "fourth wall". The Olympic extravaganzas were highly artificial in structure and style and in performing them Vestris employed a style that always acknowledged the absurdity of the theatrical parody in Planché's scripts. According to Westland Marston: "It was her practice of taking the house into her confidence, combined with her coquetry and personal attractions, that rendered Vestris so bewitching to the public. When she sang, she looked with a questioning archness at her audience, as if to ask, 'Do you enjoy that as I do? Did I give it with tolerable effect? And though in the delivery of dialogue she could hardly be called keen or brilliant, she knew what mischief and retort meant. When she had given a sting to the latter, she would glance round, as if to ask for approval, with a smile that seemed to say, 'I was a little severe there. He felt that I suppose?'" This impression that she was sharing a joke with her audience, in condescending to act in these essentially light-weight entertainments, depended on her conveying a sense of effortless ease in performance and cultivating an off-stage sophistication, which had to survive the vicissitudes of financial difficulty, which necessitated long provincial tours and an unsuccessful visit to the USA in 1839.

Comedienne rather than actress, Vestris's appeal declined in middle age as she lost some of her "personal attractions" and after failing to maintain Covent Garden, her last management was at the Lyceum — though Mathews became more than nominally in charge as she succumbed to ill health. Their style of production remained essentially the same and, although they performed some elegant drawing-room comedies, their main success was with Planché's spectacular Christmas and Easter extravaganzas, with transformation scenes designed by William Beverley on a far larger scale than had been possible at the Olympic. However, these productions were no longer unique or pioneering and failed to attract the fashionable audiences to whom Vestris had appealed in her heyday.

—George Taylor

VILAR, Jean. French actor-manager and director. Born in Seté, Hérault, France, 25 March 1912. Educated at the Collège de Sète, until 1930; Universities of Paris and Montpellier, until 1932; studied for the theatre at the theatre school of Charles Dullin in Paris, 1933–36. Married Andrée Schlegel. Stage debut, in minor acting role at the Théâtre de l'Atelier, Paris, 1935; military service, 1937–40; joined La Roulotte touring company, 1941; first appearance in Paris in a leading role, 1942; debut as director, 1942; founded his own Compagnie des Sept, Paris, 1943; subsequently won acclaim for productions of Molière, Strindberg and T. S. Eliot among others; founder, Festival d'Art Dramatique d'Avignon, 1947; director, Théâtre National Populaire, and manager, Palais de Chaillot, 1951–63; first London appearance, Palace Theatre, 1956; New York debut, Broadway Theatre, 1958; also directed opera. Recipient: Prix du Théâtre, 1945; Prix Molière, 1954; Prix Olympo (Italy), 1963; Médaille de l'Université de New York. Died 1971.

Productions

As actor:
1935   Walk-on role in *Le Faiseur* (Balzac), Théâtre de l'Atelier, Paris.
1941–42 Sottenville in *George Dandin* (Molière), French tour.
           Prétendant in *La Farce des filles à marier* (Vilar), French tour.
1942   Thomas Doul in *La Fontaine aux Saints* (Synge), Théâtre Lancry, Paris.
1945   La Capitaine in *La Danse de Mort* (Strindberg), Théâtre des Noctambules, Paris.
           Becket in *Meurtre dans la Cathédral* (Eliot, adapted by Vilar); Théâtre des Noctambules, Paris, and Théâtre du Vieux-Colombier, Paris.
1946   Frédéric in *Roméo et Jeannette* (Anouilh), Théâtre de l'Atelier, Paris.
1947   Richard II in *Richard II* (Shakespeare), Festival d'Art Dramatique, Avignon.
1948   Robespierre in *Mort de Danton* (Büchner), Festival d'Art, Avignon.
1949   Le Roi in *Le Cid* (Corneille), Festival d'Art, Avignon.
           Oedipe in *Oedipe* (Gide), Festival d'Art, Avignon.
1951   Frédéric Guillaume in *Prince de Homburg* (Kleist), Festival d'Art, Avignon.
1952   Gladior in *Nucléa* (Pichette), Palais de Chaillot, Paris.
           Harpagon in *L'Avare* (Molière), Festival d'Art Dramatique, Avignon.

Cardinal Cibo in *Lorenzaccio* (Musset), Palais de Chaillot, Paris.
1953   Thibault in *Le Médecin malgré lui* (Molière), Paris.
           Dom Juan in *Dom Juan* (Molière), Palais de Chaillot, Paris; Palace Theatre, London, 1956; Broadway Theatre, New York, 1958.
           Auguste in *Cinna* (Corneille), Paris.
1954   Macbeth in *Macbeth* (Shakespeare), Festival d'Art Dramatique, Avignon.
1955   Isidore de Besme in *La Ville* (Claudel), Festival d'Art Dramatique, Avignon.
           Hermocrate in *Le Triomphe de l'amour* (Marivaux), Palais de Chaillot, Paris; Palace Theatre, London, 1956; Broadway Theatre, New York, 1958.
1956   Clitandre in *Les Femmes savantes* (Molière), Palais de Chaillot, Paris.
           Platonov in *Ce fou de Platonov* (Chekhov), Festival du Bordeaux.
1957   Mercadet in *Le Faiseur* (Balzac), Palais de Chaillot, Paris.
           Thérামène in *Phèdre* (Racine), Festival de Strasbourg.
           Théramène in *Phèdre* (Racine), Palais de Chaillot, Paris.
           Henri IV in *Henri IV* (Pirandello), Festival d'Art Dramatique, Avignon.
1958   Oedipe in *Oedipe* (Gide), Festival du Bordeaux.
           Don Fernand in *Le Cid* (Corneille), Broadway Theatre, New York.
1959   Obéron in *Le Songe d'une Nuit d'Été* (Shakespeare), Festival d'Art Dramatique, Avignon.
1960   Choryphée in *Antigone* (Sophocles), Festival d'Art Dramatique, Avignon.
           Arturo Ui in *La Résistible Ascension d'Arturo Ui* (Brecht).
1961   Trygée in *La Paix* (Aristophanes, adapted by Vilar), Palais de Chaillot, Paris.
1962   Ulysse in *La Guerre de Troie n'aura pas lieu* (Giraudoux), Festival d'Art Dramatique, Avignon.
1963   Thomas More in *Thomas More* (Bolt), International Theatre Festival, Paris.
1964   Oppenheimer in *Le dossier Oppenheimer* (Vilar), Théâtre de l'Athénée, Paris.

As director:
1942   *La Danse de Mort* (Strindberg), private theatre, Rue Vaneau, Paris.
1943   *Orage* (Strindberg), Théâtre de Poche, Paris.
           Césaire (Schlumberger), Théâtre de Poche, Paris.
1944   *Dom Juan* (Molière), Théâtre la Bruyère, Paris.
           Un voyage dans la nuit (Christiansen), Théâtre la Bruyère, Paris.
1945   *La Danse de Mort* (Strindberg), Théâtre des Noctambules, Paris.
           Meurtre dans la Cathédral (Eliot, adapted by Vilar); Théâtre des Noctambules, Paris, and Théâtre du Vieux-Colombier, Paris.
1946   *Les Voix* (Bernard), Théâtre du Vieux-Colombier, Paris.

1947   *Le Bar du Crépuscule* (Koestler), Théâtre Monceau, Paris.

1947   *Richard II* (Shakespeare), Festival d'Art Dramatique, Avignon.
        La Terrasse de Midi (Clavel), Festival d'Art Dramatique, Avignon.

1948   *La Mort de Danton* (Adamov, adapted by Büchner), Festival d'Art Dramatique, Avignon.
        Sheherazade (Supervielle), Festival d'Art Dramatique, Avignon.

1949   *Le Cid* (Corneille), Festival d'Art Dramatique, Avignon.
        Pasiphae (Montherlant), Festival d'Art Dramatique, Avignon.
        Oedipe (Gide), Festival d'Art Dramatique, Avignon.

1950   *Henry IV, parts 1 and 2* (Shakespeare), Festival d'Art Dramatique, Avignon.
        Le Profanateur (Maulnier), Festival d'Art Dramatique, Avignon.
        L'Invasion (Adamov), Studio de Champs-Élysées, Paris.

1951   *Prince de Homburg* (Kleist), Festival d'Art Dramatique, Avignon.

1952   *L'Avare* (Molière), Festival d'Art Dramatique, Avignon.

1953   *Dom Juan* (Molière), Festival d'Art Dramatique, Avignon.

1954   *Macbeth* (Shakespeare), Festival d'Art Dramatique, Avignon.
        Cinna (Corneille), Festival d'Art Dramatique, Avignon.
        Marie Tudor (Hugo), Palais de Chaillot, Paris.
        Ruy Blas (Hugo), Palais de Chaillot, Paris.

1955   *La Ville* (Claudel), Festival d'Art Dramatique, Avignon.

1956   *Le Mariage de Figaro* (Beaumarchais), Festival d'Art Dramatique, Avignon.

1957   *Meutre dans la Cathédrale* (Eliot), Festival d'Art Dramatique, Avignon.

1958   *Ubu* (Jarry), Palais de Chaillot, Paris.
        Le Carrosse du Saint-Sacrement (Mérimée), Festival du Bordeaux.
        Les Caprices de Marianne (Musset), Festival d'Art Dramatique, Avignon.
        Le Triomphe de l'Amour (Marivaux), Festival d'Art Dramatique, Avignon.
        Marie Tudor (Hugo), Broadway Theatre, New York.

1959   *Le Songe d'une Nuit d'Été* (Shakespeare), Festival d'Art Dramatique, Avignon.
        Mère Courage (Brecht), Festival d'Art Dramatique, Avignon.

1959   *La Crapaud-Buffle* (Gatti), Théâtre Récamier, Paris.

1960   *Lettre Morte* (Pinget), Théâtre Récamier, Paris.
        L'Heureux Stratagème (Marivaux), Palais de Chaillot, Paris.
        Antigone (Sophocles), Festival d'Art Dramatique, Avignon.
        Erik XIV (Strindberg), Festival d'Art Dramatique, Avignon.
        Turcaret (Lesage), Festival du Bordeaux.

1961   *Roses Rouges pour moi* (O'Casey), Palais de Chaillot, Paris.
        Loin de Rueil (Jarre-Pillaudin), Palais de Chaillot, Paris.
        The Mayor of Zalamea (Calderón), Festival d'Art Dramatique, Avignon; Palais de Chaillot, Paris, 1962.
        Les Rustres (Calderón), Festival d'Art Dramatique, Avignon.
        La Paix (Aristophanes, adapted by Vilar), Palais de Chaillot, Paris.

1962   *La Guerre de Troie n'aura pas lieu* (Giraudoux), Festival d'Art Dramatique, Avignon.
        Les Rostres (Goldoni), Palais de Chaillot, Paris.

1963   *Jerusalem* (Verdi), Théâtre de la Fenice, Venice.
        Luces de Bohemia (Valle-Inclán), International Theatre Festival, Paris.
        Thomas More (Bolt), International Theatre Festival, Paris.

1964   *Macbetto* (Verdi), La Scala, Milan.
        Noces de Figaro (Mozart), La Scala, Milan.
        Un banquier sans visage (Weideli), Théâtre de l'Opera, Geneva.
        Le dossier Oppenheimer (Vilar), Théâtre de l'Athénée, Paris.

1965   *Les Hasards du coin du feu* (Crébillon fils), Théâtre de l'Athénée, Paris.

1966   *L'Avare* (Molière), Festival du Marais.
        Le Triomphe de l'amour (Marivaux), Festival du Marais.

Other productions included: *Galileo* (Brecht), 1963.

Films

As actor:
Les Portes de la Nuit, 1946; *Les Frères Bouquinquant; Casabiana; Till l'Espièle.*

Publications

De la tradition théâtrale, 1955; *La Paix* (adaptation), 1961; *Le Dossier Oppenheimer* (play), 1965; *Le Festival a vingt ans*, 1966; *L'Héritage vivant de l'Antiquité grecque*, 1967; *Chronique romanesque*, 1971; *Mot par mot*, 1972; *Du Tableau de Service au Théâtre*, 1975; *Mémento*, edited by D'Armand Delcampe, 1981.

*

Bibliography

Books:
Marie-Thérèse Serrière, *Le T.N.P. et nous*, Paris, 1959.
Claude Roy, *Jean Vilar*, Paris, 1968.
Vera Lee, *Quest for a Public*, Cambridge, Massachussetts, 1970.
Guy Leclerc, *Le Théâtre National Populaire de Jean Vilar*, Paris, 1971.

Philippa Wehle, *Le Théâtre Populaire selon Jean Vilar*, Avignon, 1981.

Alfred Simon, *Jean Vilar: Qui etes-vous?*, Lyons, 1987.

* * *

Jean Vilar's contribution to the renewal of popular interest in the theatre during his 12 years as director of the Théâtre National Populaire (T.N.P.) may be summed up under three headings: technical innovation, freedom of the repertory and support and enthusiasm of the public.

In the technical field, he sounded the death knell for the proscenium arch and released from traditional constraints the arts of lighting, scenery and costumes. As to repertory, he introduced liberty and imagination into the state theatre, which, while incurring the displeasure of some audiences — particularly after 1968 — nevertheless won the support of several ministers and a large proportion of the succeeding generation of theatre directors and practitioners. As an actor, Vilar had striven for simplicity and sobriety in style and this, coupled with his clarity of diction, had led to a nobility in his portrayals of the kings of Corneille and Shakespeare. This royalty of touch and delivery found favour with postwar French audiences and when the dashing young actor Gérard Philipe joined the T.N.P. the duo of sage, mature, king and passionate, handsome, hero set the seal on a great new theatrical venture that attracted thousands of predominantly young people to a theatre hitherto reserved for a wealthy and elite minority. It will be by this success with the general public, and the younger generation in particular, that Vilar will be remembered for, although the T.N.P. had been founded in 1920, it was not until 30 years later that it found its dignity and the realisation of its goals under Jean Vilar.

As a director, Vilar brought a radical approach and a new dimension to the philosophy of popular theatre practised by Copeau before the war. In the Palace of the Popes in Avignon he discovered both the virtues and the constraints of open-air production. The grandeur of the setting and the presence of the elements heightened the drama on stage; Vilar's refusal of subtlety and complication in the acting and the text and his insistence on strong lighting and costume design to compensate inspired powerful and memorable performances from his company.

Vilar's innovative approach to popularising theatre-going comprised both practical measures and theoretical positions. Within the theatre itself, at the Palais de Chaillot in Paris, he eliminated all forms of pomp and ceremonial: he did away with critics' previews and placed full confidence in the general public seeing the first performances of plays, the so-called "avant-premières". The T.N.P. was one of the first theatres to introduce seat booking by telephone; it also began performances for students and schoolchildren on Thursdays and Saturdays; it stopped the customary payment of usherettes by theatregoers and did not charge for cloakroom services; programmes were free; texts of the works played could be purchased in the foyer; a house magazine "Bref" kept people informed of the activities and future productions of the company; seat prices were kept low to attract the young. In a very short space of time, Vilar created a whole house style and company identity: his concept of the theatre as a social milieu and public service had taken shape.

The new mass audiences were easily housed in the enormous auditoria of the Palais de Chaillot and the Palais des Papes and here Vilar made a virtue of necessity: the orchestra pit was abolished, the stage enlarged and the curtain abandoned. The theatre came to the people. The stage set was replaced by props, footlights by a multitude of projectors.

By deritualising theatre, Vilar succeeded in demystifying it. He further promoted the socialising and socialistic influence of the theatre by encouraging workers' groups to come to the T.N.P. and by weekend "packages" when participants would be offered a performance, a meal, a "bal populaire" and a discussion for a modest inclusive sum. In the latter years of his reign at the T.N.P. he brought in more specifically political plays that corresponded to contemporary events. Thus, *Ubu* or *Erik XIV* could have been conceived as attacks on personal power at the time of De Gaulle's struggles during the Algerian wars, while *La Guerre de Troie n'aura pas lieu* and *The Life of Galileo* provoked debates on the morality of war and the use of atomic weapons during the period of testing of these weapons in the early 1960's. Although Vilar was never overtly didactic, he clearly held the view that all works of art contained some element of instruction or exhortation. Moreover, what has been called his "civic sense" predominated in his choice of repertoire.

Vilar's experimental productions in smaller theatres in Paris were not altogether successful, but he did introduce audiences to authors hitherto unknown to the majority — Gatti, Pinget and Obaldia among them. He was also instrumental in bringing Brecht's plays — *The Resistible Rise of Arturo Ui*, *The Good Woman of Setzuan* and *The Life of Galileo* — to Paris audiences in the early 1960's.

Vilar's vision of theatre as a festivity and the peripheral activities of the T.N.P. under his directorship — the lectures, debates and meetings between actors and audience — subsequently influenced the directors of the decentralised theatres over the next two decades.

—David Jeffery

———————

VISCONTI, Luchino (Conte di Modrone).   Italian director and designer. Born in Milan, Italy, 2 November 1906. Worked in Paris as assistant to film director Jean Renoir, 1936; debut as film director, 1943; first stage production as director, 1945; founded Compagnia Italiana di Prosa, 1946; established international reputation as director at the Teatro Eliseo, Rome after World War II; also directed for the Paolo Stoppa-Rina Morelli company and collaborated with Franco Zeffirelli, as well as directing ballet and opera at La Scala, Milan, and elsewhere; largely withdrew from the theatre, 1961. Recipient: Cannes Film Festival Golden Palm, 1963; Venice Golden Lion Award, 1965. Died in Rome, 17 March 1976.

Productions

As director:
1945   *I Parenti terribili* (Cocteau), Teatro Eliseo, Rome.

La Quinta colonna (Hemingway), Teatro Quirino, Rome.
La Machina da scrivere (Cocteau), Teatro Eliseo, Rome.
Antigone (Anouilh), Teatro Eliseo, Rome.
A porte chiusa (Sartre), Teatro Eliseo, Rome.
Adamo (Achard), Teatro Quirino, Rome.
Le Vie del tabacco (Kirkland), Teatro Olimpico, Rome.

1946   *Le Mariage de Figaro* (Beaumarchais), Teatro Quirino, Rome.
Delitto e castigo (Dostoevsky, adapted by Baty), Teatro Eliseo, Rome.
Zoo di vetro (T. Williams), Teatro Eliseo, Rome.

1947   *Euridice* (Anouilh), Pergola, Florence.

1948   *Rosalinda o Come vi piace* (Shakespeare), Teatro Eliseo, Rome.
Vita con padre (Lindsay and Crouse), Teatro Eliseo, Rome.

1949   *Un Tram che si chiamo Desiderio* (T. Williams), Teatro Eliseo, Rome.
Oreste (Alfieri), Teatro Quirino, Rome.
Troilo e Cressida (Shakespeare), Boboli Gardens, Florence.

1951   *Morte di un commesso viaggiatore* (Miller), Teatro Eliseo, Rome; revived, 1955–56.
Il Seduttore (Fabbri), International Festival, Venice.

1952   *La Locandiera* (Goldoni), International Festival, Venice.
Le Tre Sorelle (Chekhov), Teatro Eliseo, Rome.

1953   *Medea* (Euripides), Teatro Manzoni, Milan.
Il Tabacco fa male (Chekhov), Teatro Manzoni, Milan.

1954   *Come le foglie* (Giacosa), Teatro Olimpico, Milan.
La Vestale (Spontini), La Scala, Milan.

1955   *Il Crogiuolo* (Miller), Teatro Quirino, Rome.
Lo Zio Vania (Chekhov), Teatro Eliseo, Rome.
La Sonnambula (Bellini), La Scala, Milan.
La Traviata (Verdi), La Scala, Milan.

1957   *La Contessina Giulia* (Strindberg), Teatro Arti, Rome.
L'Impresario delle Smirne (Goldoni), International Festival, Venice.
Anna Bolena (Donizetti), La Scala, Milan.
Ifigenia in Tauride (Gluck), La Scala, Milan.

1958   *Uno Sguardo dal ponte* (Miller), Teatro Eliseo, Rome.
Immagini e tempi di Eleonora Duse (Guarrieri), Teatro Quirino, Rome.
Veglia la mia casa, angelo (Frings), Teatro Quirino, Rome.
Deux su la balançoire (Gibbons), Théâtre des Ambassadeurs, Paris.
I Ragazzi del signora Gibson (Glickman and Stein), Teatro Eliseo, Rome.
Don Carlos (Verdi), Covent Garden, London.
Macbeth (Verdi), Teatro Nuovo, Spoleto.

1959   *Figli d'arte* (Fabbri), Teatro Eliseo, Rome.
Il Duca d'Alba (Donizetti), Teatro Nuovo, Spoleto.

1960   *L'Arialda* (Testori), Teatro Eliseo, Rome.

1961   *Dommage qu'elle soit une p . . .* (Ford), Théâtre de Paris, Paris.
Salome (Strauss), Teatro Nuovo, Spoleto.

Other productions included: *Il Tredicesimo Albero* (Gide), 1963; *After the Fall* (Miller), 1965; *The Cherry Orchard* (Chekhov), 1965; *La Monaca di Monza* (Testori), 1967; *L'Inserzione* (Ginzberg), 1969; *Old Times* (Pinter), 1973.

Films

As director:
Ossessione/Obsession, 1943; *La Terra Trema/The Earth Trembles*, 1947; *Bellisima*, 1951; *Siamo Donne/We the Women*, 1952; *Senso*, 1954; *Le Notti Bianche/White Nights*, 1957; *Rocco e i sui Fratelli/Rocco and His Brothers*, 1960; *Boccaccio 70*, 1962; *Il Gattopardo/The Leopard*, 1963; *Vaghe stelle dell'orsa*, 1965; *Lo Straniero*, 1967; *La caduta degli dei/The Damned*, 1969; *La Morte a Venzia/Death in Venice*, 1971; *L'Innocente/The Innocent*, 1976; *Conversation Piece*, 1976.

Publications

Visconti: scritti interviste testimonianze documenti, edited by Giuliana Callegari and Nuccio Lodato, 1976; *Luchino Visconti: Il mio teatro*, edited by Caterina d'Amico de Carvalho and Renzo Renzi, 1979.

*

Bibliography

Books:
Laurence Schifano, *I fuochi della passione*, Milan, 1976.
Clarette Tonetti, *Luchino Visconti*, London, 1987.
Paola Fumagalli, *Il gattopardo: dal romanzo al film*, Florence, 1988.
Luciano De Giusti, *I film di Luchino Visconti*, Rome, 1990.

* * *

Like Giorgio Strehler, Luigi Squarzina and Vito Pandolfi, Luchino Visconti was one of a generation of theatre directors who in the immediate postwar period sought to achieve a new interpretation of a text or even to recreate it. In the process they succeeded in renewing the Italian theatre, which had grown stale under Fascism.

Hailing from a privileged background, Visconti inherited a strong artistic sensibility from his mother, a talented musician, and was offered an early introduction to the stage through the passions of his father, who maintained his own private theatre — though by Visconti's own confession he was more interested in art and in horse-breeding as a young man. He made his first foray, as an amateur, into the theatre as a designer at the age of 30 and was subsequently provided with an entrée into the film world as assistant to the celebrated director Jean Renoir.

Over the ensuing decades, Visconti strove to make the Italian stage less provincial by introducing European and American writers whose plays had been banned under the Fascist regime. Among the most significant figures whose writings he brought to the Italian stage were Jean Cocteau,

Luchino Visconti (c. 1975).

Jean-Paul Sartre, Tennessee Williams and Erskine Caldwell.

Visconti's deeply complex personality and left-wing politics often brought his productions to the forefront of public attention: a heated controversy, for example, arose around the incestuous theme of Cocteau's *Les Parents terribles* and around the homosexuality in the Sartre and Achard plays that he chose to direct. Some of the plays he staged reflected his socio-political engagement as a Marxist — the Spanish Civil War in the Hemingway play and the allegory of the German Resistance movement in Anouilh. Time and again the plots he selected depicted the struggles of an antagonist in conflict with the demands of modern society.

Visconti's productions were always impeccable since they incorporated his outstanding professional rigour, a horror of amateurishness and his magnificent aesthetic taste. He also innovated in his working method by calling for longer rehearsals and abolishing the figure of the prompter. Popularly known by admirers of his work in the cinema as the "Father of Neorealism", though he later moved away from the naturalism of his early movies, he sought, and frequently achieved on stage what has been defined as a "realistic lyricism", through an extremely careful textual analysis, followed by his own original interpretation of the play at hand. Giorgio Strehler, in 1976, made the following perspicacious remark concerning Visconti's theatre work:

"A production by Visconti was neither a worldly event nor a game, it meant a reason for living and a way of being".

—Margaret Rose

VITEZ, Antoine. French actor and director. Born in Paris, 20 December 1930. Trained for the theatre under Tania Balachova. Married actress Agnès Vanier in 1952, two daughters. Began career in Marseilles and Caen at the age of 19; joined Communist Party, 1957; engaged as secretary to writer Louis Aragon, 1958; member, Maison de la Culture, Caen, 1964–67; debut as director, 1966; appointed director of studies, Université de la Théâtre des Nations, 1965; also taught at the Jacques Lecoq Mime School, 1966–70; professor, Conservatoire National Supérieur d'Art Dramatique, 1968–81; director, Théâtre des Quartiers d'Ivry, 1971–80; co-artistic director, Théâtre de Chaillot, 1972–74; resigned from French Communist Party in protest at Soviet invasion of Afghanistan, 1980; artistic director, Théâtre National de Chaillot, 1981–88; director, Comédie-Française, Paris, from 1988. Died in Paris, 30 April 1990.

Productions

1966   *Electre* (Sophocles, adapted by Vitez), Maison de la Culture, Caen.

Le Procès d'Emile Henry, Maison de la Culture, Caen.

1967   *Les Bains* (Mayakovsky), Maison de la Culture, Caen.

1968   *Le Dragon* (Shvarts), Comédie de Saint- Etienne.

La Grande enquête de François-Félix Kulpa (Pommeret), Théâtre des Amandiers, Nanterre.

1969   *La Parade* (Anagnostaki), Théâtre de l'Ouest Parisien, Boulogne-sur-Seine.

1970   *Le Précepteur* (Lenz), Théâtre de l'Ouest Parisien, Boulogne-sur-Seine.

La Mouette (Chekhov), Théâtre Municipal, Carcassonne.

1971   *Electre* (Sophocles, adapted by Vitez), Théâtre des Amandiers, Nanterre.

1972   *Faust* (Goethe), Gymnase Joliot-Curie, Ivry.

1973   *Mère Courage* (Brecht), Théâtre des Amandiers, Nanterre.

Vendredi ou la vie sauvage, Château de Vincennes, Théâtre National de Chaillot.

m=M (Pommeret), Festival d'Avignon.

1974   *Les Miracles*, Salle Firmin Gémier, Théâtre National de Chaillot.

La Jalousie du Barbouillé (Molière), Lycée Frédéric Mistral, Fresnes.

Le Pique-nique de Claretta (Kalisky), Studio d'Ivry.

1975   *Phèdre* (Racine), Studio d'Ivry.

Catherine, Festival d'Avignon; Théâtre des Amandiers, Nanterre, 1976.

Partage de midi (Claudel), Théâtre Marigny, Paris.

1976   *La ballade de Mr Punch*, Théâtre Paul Eluard, Choisy-le-Roi.

1977   *Iphigénie Hôtel* (Vinaver), Centre Georges Pompidou, Paris.

Le Tartuffe (Molière), Théâtre de la Satire, Moscow.

Grisélidis, Cloître des Célestins, Festival d'Avignon.

Les Burgraves (Hugo), Gennevilliers.

1978   *L'École des femmes* (Molière), Cloître des Carmes, Festival d'Avignon.

Le Tartuffe (Molière), Cloître des Carmes, Festival d'Avignon.

Dom Juan (Molière), Cloître des Carmes, Festival d'Avignon.

Le Misanthrope (Molière), Cloître des Célestins, Festival d'Avignon.

1979   *Le nozze di Figaro* (Mozart), Florence.

1981   *Faust* (Goethe), Théâtre National de Chaillot.

Britannicus (Racine), Théâtre National de Chaillot.

1983   *Hamlet* (Shakespeare), Théâtre National de Chaillot.

1984   *Macbeth* (Verdi), Opéra, Paris.

1985   *Hernani* (Hugo), Théâtre National de Chaillot.

1987   *Le Soulier de satin* (Claudel), Cour d'Honneur Festival, Avignon.

1988   *Apprentice Sorcerers* (Cleberg), Cour d'Honneur, Avignon; also acted Stanislavsky.

1989   *La Célestine* (Rojas), Festival d'Avignon.

Un Transport amoureux, Théâtre du Petit-Odéon, Paris.

1990   *La Vie de Galilée* (Brecht), Comédie-Française, Paris.

*

Bibliography

Books:

Anne-Françoise Berhamou, *Antoine Vitez: toutes les mises en scène*, Paris, 1981.

Anna Dizier, *Antoine Vitez, Faust, Britannicus, Tombeau pour 50,000 soldats*, Paris, 1982.

* * *

Antoine Vitez, a controversial and highly contemporary director, was head of the Théâtre National de Chaillot for most of the 1980's. He brought surprising new life into this theatre that was the home of Jean Vilar's Théâtre National Populaire. Vitez, a great admirer of Vilar's work at Chaillot, which began in 1951, embarked on his revitalization of this celebrated theatre in 1981. Through continual confrontation between the actor and his or her text, Vitez pushed the boundaries of acting conventions beyond the limitations of realism and the identification of the actor with a role. His work shaped Bertolt Brecht's "Verfremdungsaffekt" into a dynamic style of performance that provided great liberty for the performer. In 1988 Vitez was named administrator of the Comédie-Française; during his tenure at the Comédie-Française, cut short by his sudden death, he invited Dario Fo to direct two plays by Molière.

As an established mentor of the illustrious French metteurs en scène, Vitez distinguished himself from Patrice Chéreau, Roger Planchon, or even Ariane Mnouchkine by his minimizing of the importance of spectacle in favour of progressive work with an ensemble of actors. Most of his performers trained with him at the Conservatoire National Supérieur d'Art Dramatique, where he was a professor from 1968. He utilized his considerable talents as a teacher of acting with classical and contemporary texts. He was not a director who saw actors as one element of a vast stage picture. For Vitez the theatre was the milieu of the actor, and he was the orchestrator of their words and actions. Vitez believed in presenting a great variety of works within a full season of plays. He did not adhere to the current trend of extended rehearsal periods for the production of one chef d'oeuvre per year.

Motivated by his strong political beliefs — he was a Marxist who first directed in the Communist suburbs of Paris — Vitez wanted his theatre to be available to a popular audience. As with Jean Vilar, Jean Dasté, Roger Planchon and Ariane Mnouchkine, he found that this is not always an easy goal to accomplish. The very act of working within an established formal theatre space limits the accessibility of a truly "popular" audience. Vitez was further hampered by the fact that his productions were not readily perceived as approachable for any person at random; rather, they were often most appreciated by the intellectual community. In fact, he conceded that the theatre is often an art form for a chosen few rather than for the masses. He stated that he attempted to create "elitist theatre for everyone".

From 1971 to 1980 Vitez initiated the Théâtre des Quartiers d'Ivry in the Parisian red belt. First working in non-conventional performance spaces like gymnasiums, Vitez produced classical plays like Goethe's *Faust* and Racine's *Phèdre* alongside modern works like Brecht's *Mother Courage* and Michel Vinaver's *Iphigénie-Hôtel*. During the 1978–79 season he directed four Molière plays with a troupe of 13 actors playing before a single scenic drop of painted architecture. This Molière cycle was prepared in only a few short months and then played at the 32nd Festival d'Avignon, the Festival d'Automne and abroad. Vitez sought inspiration from the fairground players of Molière's era, utilizing only the minimum of props and furnishings. All emphasis was upon the "jeu" of the actors within the space of the stage.

In 1980 Vitez directed *Le Revizor* (*The Inspector-General*) by Gogol to show his respect for Vsevelod Meyerhold, who produced a stunning interpretation of this text in 1926. Vitez admired Meyerhold's system of biomechanics as a training for the actor. This distance between the actor and his or her role — which allows the performer to comment upon the action — influenced his pedagogy. Meyerhold's ideas combined with those of Brecht formed the foundation upon which his experiments were built. Also, prior to his teaching at the Conservatoire, Vitez was a professor at Jacques Lecoq's School of Mime and Theatre. This experience with movement and gesture helped formulate his concepts of an internal movement in the drama that can be expressed abstractly by the actor's body. Lecoq's focus upon rhythm and respiration in relation to the text and gesture can also be seen in Vitez's work with actors. He, like Meyerhold, sought performance with a musical design.

To complement his physical approach to acting, Vitez had a refined awareness of the sound of words. He worked comfortably with the Russian, German and Greek languages, and occasionally incorporated foreign language into his productions in French. The sound of the word was integrated into his musical composition, where music itself functioned as an important dramatic element. Sound was not utilized as a decorative or illustrative element, but rather as a living part of the movement of the drama. Text, gesture, sound, chant and the movement of the actors combined to function as a whole. Vitez even found inspiration in such theoretical subjects as semiology and contemporary literary theory. This occasionally resulted in performances that left an audience unmoved, as illustrated by spectators vacating their seats during his presentations.

Among the most notable of his last productions, after opening at the Chaillot Theatre in 1981, were *Faust* (1981), *Britannicus* (1981), *Hamlet* (1983), on which he collaborated with scenographer Yannis Kokkos, *Hernani* (1985), the 12-hour *Soulier de Satin* (1987), *La Célestine* (1989), which starred Jeanne Moreau, and *La Vie de Galilée* (1990). Until the last, he continued to provoke the Paris audience with surprising theatre of social relevance.

—Ron Popenhagen

WEIGEL, Helene. Austrian actress and manager. Born in Vienna, 12 May 1900. Educated at local grammar schools. Married playwright Bertolt Brecht in 1928 (died 1956), one son and one daughter. Stage debut, against the wishes of her family, Neues Theater, Frankfurt, 1919–20; actress, Schauspielhaus, Frankfurt, 1921–23, Staatstheater, Berlin, under Büchner, 1922–24, Deutsches Theater, under Max Reinhardt, 1925–26, Junge Bühne, Berlin, 1926–27; also performed in radio plays and appeared at the Volksbühne, Berlin, 1926–27; subsequently created several leading roles in her husband's plays; accompanied Brecht in exile in Denmark, Sweden, Finland and the USA, making few stage and film appearances, 1933–48; returned to Germany, 1948; founder-member, Berliner Ensemble, 1949; created leading role in *Mutter Courage*, 1949; sole director, Berliner Ensemble, after Brecht's death, 1956. Died in East Berlin, 6 May 1971.

Roles

1918–20	Marie in *Woyzeck* (Büchner), Neues Theater, Frankfurt.
	The Wife in *Weibsteufel* (Schönherr), Neues Theater, Frankfurt.
1920	Griesin in *Gas II* (Kaiser), Neues Theater, Frankfurt.
1921	Piperkarcka in *Die Ratten* (Hauptmann), Neues Theater, Frankfurt.
	Meroe in *Penthesilea* (Kleist), Schauspielhaus, Frankfurt.
1922	Adeline in *Napoleon* (Grabbe), Staatstheater, Berlin.
	Claudine in *George Dandin* (Molière), Staatstheater, Berlin.
	Lucinde in *Arzt wider Willen* (Müller), Staatstheater, Berlin.
	Second Witch in *Macbeth* (Shakespeare), Staatstheater, Berlin.
1923	Lieschen in *Faust I* (Goethe), Staatstheater, Berlin.
	Gänsemagd in *Titus und der Talisman* (Nestroy), Schauspielhaus, Frankfurt.
	Armgard in *Wilhelm Tell* (Schiller), Schauspielhaus, Frankfurt.
1925	Dienstmädchen in *Dardamelle, der Betrogene*, Komödie, Berlin.
	Martha Bernick in *Stützen der Geschellschaft* (Ibsen), Deutsches Theater, Berlin.

	Frau des Landarztes in *Dr Knock* (Romains), Deutsches Theater, Berlin.
	Alte Amme in *Das Leben das ich dir Gab* (Pirandello), Renaissance-Theater, Berlin.
	Klara in *Maria Magdalene* (Hebbel), Renaissance-Theater, Berlin.
1926	Salome in *Herodes und Mariamne* (Hebbel), Staatstheater, Frankfurt.
	Jüngere Schwester in *Fegefuer in Ingolstadt* (Fleisser), Junge Bühne, Berlin.
	Zigarettenverkäferin in *Im Dickicht der Städte* (Brecht), Junge Bühne, Berlin.
1927	Leokadja Begbick in *Mann ist Mann* (Brecht), Rundfunk, Berlin; Staatstheater, Berlin, 1931.
	Grete in *Hinkemann* (Toller), Volksbühne, Berlin.
1929	Magd in *Ödipus* (Sophocles), Staatstheater, Berlin.
	Konstanze in *König Johann* (Shakespeare), Staatstheater, Berlin.
	Fliege in *Happy End* (Lane), Theater am Schiffbauerdamm, Berlin.
1930	Agitator in *Massnahme* (Brecht), Grosses Schauspielhaus, Berlin.
1932	Pelageya Vlassova in *Die Mutter* (Brecht, adapted from Gorky); Komodienhaus am Schiffbauerdamm, Berlin; Berliner Ensemble, 1951; Neue Scala, Vienna, 1953–71.
	Frau Luckerniddle in *Die heilige Johanna der Schlachthöfe* (Brecht), Funkstunde, Berlin; Berliner Ensemble, 1968.
1937	Teresa Carrar in *Die Gewehre der Frau Carrar* (Brecht), Paris; Copenhagen, 1938; Berliner Ensemble, 1952–55.
1938	Judith Keith in *Furcht und Elend des Dritten Reiches* (Brecht), Paris; Berliner Ensemble, 1957–63.
1948	Antigone in *Antigone* (Sophocles, adapted by Brecht), Stadttheater, Chur, Switzerland.
1949	Anna Fierling in *Mutter Courage und ihre Kinder* (Brecht), Berliner Ensemble; Palace Theatre, London, 1956; frequently revived until 1961.
1953	Frau Grossmann in *Katzengraben* (Strittmatter), Berliner Ensemble.
1954	Natella Abaschwili and Mütterchen Grusinien in *Der kaukasische Kreiderkreis* (Brecht), Berliner Ensemble.

1955   Vassilissa in *Ziehtochter* (Ostrovsky, adapted by Brecht), Berliner Ensemble.
1961   Martha Flinz in *Frau Flinz* (Baierl), Berliner Ensemble.
1965   Volumnia in *Coriolan* (Brecht , adapted from Shakespeare), Old Vic Theatre, London.
1968   Marie Soupeau in *Die Gesichte der Simone Machard* (Brecht), Deutsches Fernsehfunk.

Films

The Seventh Cross, 1941; *Mutter Courage und ihre Kinder*, 1961.

*

Bibliography

Books:
Wolfgang Pintzka, *Die Schauspielerin Helene Weigel*, Berlin, 1959.
Werner Hecht and Joachim Tenschert, *Helene Weigel zum 70*, Berlin, 1970.
Vera Tenschert, *Die Weigel*, Berlin, 1981.

* * *

Helene Weigel's strength of character, perhaps encouraged by her attendance at a strongly suffragette school, was evidenced by her determination, against her parents' wishes, to act. She astonished those who heard her first audition at the Vienna Volksbühne, where Artur Rendt described her as "one of the greatest dramatic geniuses ever born". After only three months training with Arthur Holz she began a successful career in the theatre at Frankfurt with a performance of Marie in Büchner's *Woyzeck*. In 1922 she moved to work with Leopold Jessner and Jürgen Fehling in Berlin. She became acquainted with Brecht in 1924, but it was not until 1927 (after two years acting with Max Reinhardt at the Deutsches Theater) that she first appeared in a play by Brecht: *Mann ist Mann* (*Man is Man*).

Weigel developed a formidable reputation as a character actress of considerable emotional power, physical presence and vocal ability. Her performances were frequently described as spellbinding. She was a leading exponent of what Brecht called "culinary theatre". However, during her 30-year association with Brecht she changed her acting style completely to become the outstanding actor of Brecht's "epic theatre". This development began with a number of appearances as Widow Begbick in *Mann ist Mann*, but culminated before the war in her performance as Vlassova in *Die Mutter* (*The Mother*), a role she created in 1932. Her development as an actress was then interrupted for 14 years, during which time in exile she played on only three occasions. However, she returned to Europe in 1947 and consolidated her pre-eminent position as actress as well as embarking on a new career as Intendant (administrative director) of the newly-formed Berliner Ensemble, where she remained the organisational driving force until her death.

The 1949 production by Brecht at the Deutsches Theater in East Berlin of his *Mutter Courage und ihre Kinder* (*Mother Courage and her Children*), in which Weigel played the lead, was a landmark in 20th-century theatre practice.

It provided the immediate impetus for the establishment of the Berliner Ensemble in the Theater am Schiffbauerdamm in Berlin, but Weigel's performance was seen as the clearest embodiment yet of Brecht's ideas on 'gestic' acting and the later form of "epic theatre". Critics appreciated the apparent lack of strain in Weigel's portrayal, the way in which she seemed able to stand apart from the role and show the fate of Courage without losing herself and her own identity as an actress in the role. This critical distance allowed her to comment on the character she was playing, to "alienate" the situation in which Courage found herself and thereby to suggest that it is not the result of inevitable fate. When the production toured to Sweden a Stockholm critic saw her performance as definitive for the role, her dry-eyed hunger-etched face expressing the suffering of a being who had once been a mother. When the production toured to London, the *Times* critic noted in particular salient moments from the performance — the silent scream over the dead body of her son Schweizerkas (Swiss Cheese) and her solitary return to the shafts of the wagon at the end of the play — as being permanently imprinted on the minds of all who saw the production.

The particular strength of Weigel's performances lay in the intensity with which she could invest moments of gestural acting, while at the same time being able to comment on her character. This ability was developed during extended rehearsals in which she would endlessly rework details, more accurately expressing the attitude of her character and her own attitude to the character she was playing. This frequently involved the finding of, and the considered employment of, the right props, each of which had to have the "beauty of use". The tin spoon and patched jacket of Mother Courage grew to become essential items in Weigel's portrayal of the character, and have since become renowned in themselves. But Weigel's use of props was part of a never-ending process of observation and reworking of her roles with the intention of making them truer and more concrete. When playing Vlassova in *Die Mutter* in Moscow 30 years after its first performance, she bought a new prop in a market and was still adding new touches to the role, almost imperceptible to the casual observer.

Her eye for detail helped her not only to be aware of the strengths and weaknesses of each member of the Berliner Ensemble, but also to concern herself with the day to day running of the theatre, even down to the replacement of the ashtrays in the canteen. After Brecht's death she continued to run the company, maintaining the tradition of performance style initiated by Brecht and acting as an example herself on stage to the company. She also expanded the role of the Ensemble as a touring company overseas.

The Berlin critic spoke of the reincarnation of the German language and the German theatre in the work of Brecht the writer and Weigel the actress. Weigel was essential to Brecht for the realisation of his theatre not only for her ability as an actress, but also for the physical, organisational, moral and political support she gave him for the 30 years of their work together.

—Anthony Meech

———

WEKWERTH, Manfred. German director. Born in Köthen, Germany, 3 December 1929. Educated at Humboldt University, Berlin. Married 1) Renate Meiners in 1953; 2) Renate Richter in 1963; one daughter. Worked initially as a teacher, 1949; assistant director to Bertolt Brecht, Berliner Ensemble, 1951–54; appointed chief director, Berliner Ensemble, 1963; subsequently worked as a director in collaboration with Peter Palitzsch, Benno Besson and others; left Berliner Ensemble, 1971; worked with the National Theatre, London, and elsewhere, 1971–77; director, Deutsches Theater, Berlin, 1971; founder, Institut für Schauspielregie, Berlin, 1974; returned to Berliner Ensemble as manager, 1977. Professor, Institut für Schauspielregie, 1975. Member: Akademie der Künste der DDR (president, 1982–90). Recipient: Erich Weinert Medal, 1957; National Prize (Germany), 1959, 1961; Vaterländ ischer Verdienstorden Award, 1969, 1979; Artur Becker Medal, 1973; Heinrich Greif Prize, 1976.

Principal productions

As assistant director:
1953	*Katzgraben* (Strittmatter), Berliner Ensemble.
1954	*Der kaukasische Kreidekreis* (Brecht), Berliner Ensemble.

As director:
1953	*Die Mutter* (Brecht, adapted from Gorky), Neues Theater in der Scala, Vienna.
1954	*Hirse für die Achte* (Brecht, Hauptmann and Wekwerth), Berliner Ensemble.
1955	*Winterschlacht* (Becher), Berliner Ensemble.
1956	*Der Held der westlichen Welt* (Synge), Berliner Ensemble.
	Die Tage der Commune (Brecht), Städtische Theater Karl-Marx-Stadt.
1958	*Optimistische Tragödie* (Vishnevsky), Berliner Ensemble.
1959	*Der aufhaltsame Aufstieg des Arturo Ui* (Brecht), Berliner Ensemble.
1961	*Frau Flinz* (Baierl), Berliner Ensemble.
1962	*Lieder und Gedichte 1914–56* (Brecht and Abend), Berliner Ensemble.
	Die Tage der Commune (Brecht), Berliner Ensemble.
1964	*Coriolan* (Brecht), Berliner Ensemble.
1965	*In der Sache J. Robert Oppenheimer* (Kipphardt), Berliner Ensemble.
1966	*Purpurstaub* (O'Casey), Berliner Ensemble.
	Flüchtlingsgespräche (Brecht), Berliner Ensemble.
1969	*Johanna von Döbeln* (Baierl), Berliner Ensemble.
1968	*Die heilige Johanna der Schlachthöfe* (Brecht), Berliner Ensemble.
1970	*Das Verhör von Habana* (Enzensberger), Deutsches Theater, Berlin.
1971	*Coriolanus* (Shakespeare), National Theatre, London.
1972	*Richard III* (Shakespeare, adapted by Wekwerth), Deutsches Theater, Berlin.
1973	*Jegor Bulytschow und die Anderen* (Gorky, adapted by Wekwerth), Schauspielhaus, Zurich.
1974	*Richard III* (Shakespeare, adapted by Wekwerth), Schauspielhaus, Zurich.
1975	*Der gute Mensch von Setzuan* (Brecht), Schauspielhaus, Zurich.
1985	*Troilus und Cressida* (Shakespeare), Theater am Bertolt Brecht Platz, Berlin.

Films

Katzgraben, 1957; *Die Mutter*, 1958; *Mutter Courage und ihre Kinder*, 1961; *Optimistische Tragödie*, 1971; *Zement*, 1972; *Die unheilige Sophia*, 1975.

Publications

Wir arbeiten an Gerhart Hauptmanns Komödie, 1953; *Auffinden einer ästhetischen Kategorie*, 1957; *Stellungen, Gruppierungen, Gänge auf der Bühne*, 1957; *Über Regiearbeit mit Laienkünstlern*, 1958; *Theater in Veränderung*, 1960; *Notate Über die Arbeit des Berliner Ensembles 1956 bis 1966*, 1967; *Das Theater Brechts*, 1968; *Theater und Wissenschaft*, 1971; *Schriften: Arbeit mit Brecht*, 1973; *Der Vorgang*, 1975; *Brecht?*, 1976; *Erhat Vorschläge gemacht*, 1977; *Brecht-Theater in der Gegenwart*, 1980; *Theater in der Diskussion*, 1982.

* * *

Since 1956, the year of Brecht's death, Manfred Wekwerth has continued and expanded the work of the Berliner Ensemble, first as director, and, since 1977, as Intendant (administrative director), of the Theater am Bertolt Brecht Platz — although he still directs productions on a regular basis.

Wekwerth joined the Ensemble during its first period of existence, while Brecht was trying to wean audiences (many of them former Nazis) away from the elaborate staging of productions mounted during the Nazi era. Wekwerth collaborated on Brecht's production of his *Mutter Courage und ihre Kinder* (*Mother Courage and her Children*), in which an attempt was made, in a simple theatre devoid of decoration and illusion, to present the true horrors of war.

Wekwerth became more active in the Ensemble in what he sees as the next phase of the company's existence, during which they tried to offer a blueprint of a new social order — not Stalinism, but true socialism. This period was marked by struggles with the GDR government censor. Eventually the Ensemble's international success in their 1953 and 1954 visits to France ensured their immunity from governmental attack.

After Brecht's death, Wekwerth maintained the company's commitment to Brecht's work, as well as introducing foreign plays, particularly from Russia and the English-speaking world. Wekwerth selects plays in the production of which he can state his position as citizen and artist in German society, as well as addressing as yet unsolved problems of Brechtian dramaturgy. He has always seen an important role for the Ensemble as ambassadors abroad, both for Brecht's plays and for the company's working methods and performance style. Having defined a socialistic aesthetic with his productions with the Ensemble, he seeks to communicate this via their visits outside the GDR. Following Brecht, Wekwerth places great importance on collective working. He engages in joint productions (in particular with Tenschert), while his many assistants have included now famous names, such as Langhoff and Berghaus.

Wekwerth is noted for his academic approach to research for his productions and his respect for the text — even working as a translator of some foreign plays — although he never allows academic exactitude to take precedence over the theatrical effectiveness of a production. Overall, his work is characterized by the unity he manages to achieve among the wide range of his collaborators and the clarity with which his political and philosophical positions are expressed.

He has always regarded the theatre as a forum for the expression of dissident opinion, and for some three years before the recent collapse of the GDR regime had a policy of staging "problem plays" concerning dissatisfaction with and corruption in German society. Latterly, he organised open-ended political discussions in the Theater am Bertolt Brecht Platz on a weekly basis, on the assumption that a theatre as renowned as his would be (like the Gethsemane Church) immune from attack by the authorities.

After the unification of Germany, Wekwerth aimed to offer, through his theatre work, a third way between the Stalinism of the past and the out-and-out capitalism the GDR seems to have now embraced. He hopes to maintain his critical position on the suffering and repression of humanity and for integrity in politics and society, to replace the false passivity induced in the population by the former regime by reassertion of Brecht's central message: "In praise of doubt" in the face of all forms of authority. In this he sees a new function for the plays of Brecht, which, he feels, will now be able to be played to their full potential. In this respect he quotes his production of Brecht's *Leben des Galilei* (*The Life of Galileo*), premiered in 1978 but revised and still in the Berliner Ensemble repertoire, as a potent warning against the naive belief in the dawning of a new age.

In 1975 Wekwerth founded, and for a while acted as the artistic director of, the Berlin Institut für Schauspielregie, a school for theatre directors, but severed his links with the institution when he felt that it had become too academic and too far removed from the only location where, he believes a theatre director can be trained — the theatre.

—Anthony Meech

———

WELLES, (George) Orson. US actor, director, filmmaker, and writer. Born in Kenosha, Wisconsin, 6 May 1915. Educated at Todd High School, Woodstock, Illinois, 1926–31. Married 1) actress Virginia Nicolson in 1934 (divorced 1940), one daughter; 2) actress Rita Hayworth in 1942 (divorced 1947), one daughter; 3) actress Countess Paula Mori Girlalco in 1955, one daughter. Worked as painter and journalist before making stage debut at the Gate Theatre, Dublin, 1931; actor, Gate Theatre and Abbey Theatre, Dublin, 1931–33; toured USA with Katharine Cornell, 1933–34; organised and managed Woodstock Theatre Festival, Woodstock, Illinois, 1934; New York debut, 1934; director, Negro People's Theatre, New York, 1936; director, Federal Theatre Project, New York, 1937; co-founder, with John Houseman, Mercury Theatre, New

York, 1937; provoked nationwide alarm with radio broadcast of *The War of the Worlds*, 1938; subsequently made numerous film appearances, notably as Harry Lime in *The Third Man*, 1949, and won acclaim for his direction of various Shakespeare films. Recipient: Claire M. Senie Plaque, Drama Study Club, 1938; Oscar (with Herman Mankiewicz), Best Screenplay, 1941; Golden Palm Award, Cannes Film Festival, 1956; Grand Prix, Brussels Film Festival, 1958; Best Actor (shared), Cannes Film Festival, 1959; 20th Anniversary Special Prize, Cannes Film Festival, 1966; Honorary Oscar, 1970; Grammy Award, 1972; Life Achievement Award, American Film Institute, 1974; D. W. Griffith Award, Directors Guild of America, 1984. Officier, Légion d'Honneur, 1982. Died in Hollywood, California, 10 October 1985.

Productions

As actor:

1931	Duke of Württemburg in *Jew Süss* (Dukes), Gate Theatre, Dublin.
1933–34	Mercutio in *Romeo and Juliet* (Shakespeare), US tour.
	Eugene Marchbanks in *Candida* (G. B. Shaw), US tour.
	Octavius Barrett in *The Barretts of Wimpole Street* (Besier), US tour.
	Hamlet in *Hamlet* (Shakespeare), Todd School, Woodstock, Illinois.
	Chorus and Tybalt in *Romeo and Juliet* (Shakespeare), Martin Beck Theatre, New York.
1935	McGafferty in *Panic* (McLeish), Imperial Theatre, New York.
1936	Mugglethorp in *Horse Eats Hat* (Labiche), Maxine Elliott Theatre, New York; also directed.
	André Pequot in *Ten Million Ghosts* (Kingsley), St James's Theatre, New York.
1937	Faustus in *Doctor Faustus* (Marlowe), Maxine Elliott Theatre, New York; also directed.
	Marcus Brutus in *Julius Caesar* (Shakespeare), Mercury Theatre, New York; also directed.
1938	Captain Shotover in *Heartbreak House* (G. B. Shaw), National Theatre, New York; also directed.
	St Just in *Danton's Death* (Buechner, adapted by Welles), Mercury Theatre, New York; also directed.
1939	Bracy and Falstaff in *Five Kings* (Shakespeare compilation by Welles), US tour; also directed.
	Rajah in *The Green Goddess* (Archer), RKO vaudeville circuit, Chicago.
1942	Several roles in *The Mercury Wonder Show* (Welles), US tour; also directed.
1946	Dick Fix in *Around the World* (Porter and Welles), Adelphi Theatre, New York; also directed.
1947	Macbeth in *Macbeth* (Shakespeare), Utah Centennial Festival, Salt Lake City; also directed.
1950–51	Jake in *The Unthinking Lobster* (Welles), Théâtre Edouard VII, Paris.

Dr Faustus in *Time Runs* (Welles, adapted from Marlowe's *Doctor Faustus*), German tour.

1951   Othello in *Othello* (Shakespeare), St James's Theatre, London; also directed.

1955   The Actor-Manager in *Moby Dick* (Welles, adapted from Melville), Duke of York's Theatre, London; also directed.

1956   Lear in *King Lear* (Shakespeare), City Centre, New York; also directed.

1962   Falstaff in *Chimes at Midnight* (Welles, adapted from Shakespeare's *Henry IV* and *Henry V*), Theatre Royal, Belfast, and Gaiety Theatre, Dublin.

Other roles included: *The Dead Ride Fast* (Sears), Gate Theatre, Dublin, 1931; *The Archdupe* (Robinson), Gate Theatre, Dublin, 1931; *Mogu of the Desert* (Colum), Gate Theatre, Dublin, 1931; *Death Takes a Holiday* (Cassella), Gate Theatre, Dublin, 1932; *Hamlet* (Shakespeare), Gate Theatre, Dublin, 1932; *The Chinese Bungalow* (Lang), Gate Theatre, Dublin; also directed, 1932; *Twelfth Night* (Shakespeare), Todd School, Woodstock, Illinois; also co-directed and designed, 1933; *Trilby* (Du Maurier), Todd School, Woodstock, Illinois, 1933–34; *Tsar Paul* (Merezhkovsky), Todd School, Woodstock, Illinois, 1933–34.

As director only:

1932   *The Circle* (Maugham), Gate Theatre, Dublin.

1936   *Macbeth* (Shakespeare), Lafayette Theatre, New York, and Adelphi Theatre, New York.
          Turpentine, Negro People's Theatre, New York.

1937   *The Second Hurricane* (Copland), Playhouse Theatre, New York.
          The Cradle Will Rock (Blitzstein), Venice Theatre, New York.

1938   *The Shoemaker's Holiday* (Dekker, adapted by Welles), Mercury Theatre, New York.
          Too Much Johnson (Gillette, adapted by Welles), Stony Creek Summer Theatre, Stony Creek, Connecticut.

1941   *Native Son* (Green and Wright), St James's Theatre, New York.

1960   *Rhinoceros* (Ionesco), Royal Court Theatre, London; also designed.

As designer:

1953   *The Lady in the Ice* (ballet), Stoll Theatre, London.

Films

As actor:

Swiss Family Robinson, 1940; *Jane Eyre*, 1944; *Follow the Boys*, 1944; *Tomorrow Is Forever*, 1946; *Duel in the Sun*, 1946; *Black Magic*, 1947; *Prince of Roses*, 1949; *The Third Man*, 1949; *The Black Rose*, 1950; *Return to Glennascaul*, 1951; *Trent's Last Case*, 1953; *Royal Affairs of Versailles*, 1953; *Man, Beast, and Virtue*, 1953; *Napoleon*, 1954; *Three Cases of Murder*, 1954; *Trouble in the Glen*, 1955; *Out of Darkness*, 1955; *Moby Dick*, 1956; *Pay the Devil*, 1957; *The Long Hot Summer*, 1957; *The Roots

Orson Welles

of Heaven*, 1958; *Les Seigneurs de la Forêt*, 1958; *The Vikings*, 1958; *Compulsion*, 1959; *David and Goliath*, 1959; *Ferry to Hong Kong*, 1959; *High Journey*, 1959; *South Sea Adventure*, 1959; *Austerlitz*, 1960; *Crack in the Mirror*, 1960; *Lafayette*, 1961; *King of Kings*, 1961; *Désorde*, 1961; *Der Grosse Atlantik*, 1962; *The Tartars*, 1962; *Rogopag*, 1963; *The VIPs*, 1963; *Marco the Magnificent*, 1964; *The Finest Hours*, 1964; *A King's Story*, 1965; *Casino Royale*, 1965; *Is Paris Burning?*, 1966; *A Man for All Seasons*, 1966; *The Sailor from Gibraltar*, 1967; *I'll Never Forget What's 'Is Name*, 1967; *Oedipus the King*, 1968; *House of Cards*, 1968; *The Last Roman*, 1968; *Start the Revolution Without Me*, 1969; *Tepepa*, 1969; *Barbed Water*, 1969; *Michael the Brave*, 1969; *The Southern Star*, 1969; *Twelve Plus One*, 1969; *The Battler of Neretva*, 1969; *The Merchant of Venice*, 1969; *The Kremlin Letter*, 1970; *Catch-22*, 1970; *Waterloo*, 1970; *Directed by John Ford*, 1971; *Sentinels of Silence*, 1971; *A Safe Place*, 1971; *The Canterbury Tales*, 1971; *Ten Days' Wonder*, 1972; *Get to Know Your Rabbit*, 1972; *Necromancy*, 1972; *Treasure Island*, 1972; *Malpertuis*, 1972; *Sutjeska*, 1972; *Bugs Bunny Superstar*, 1975; *Challenge of Greatness*, 1976; *Voyage of the Damned*, 1976; *It Happened One Christmas*, 1977; *The Filming of Othello*, 1978; *The Late Great Planet Earth*, 1979; *The Muppet Movie*, 1979; *The Secret of Nicolai Tesla*, 1979; *Never Trust an Honest Thief*, 1979; *The Muppets Take Manhattan*, 1982; *Butterfly*, 1983; *Where Is Parsifal?*, 1984.

As actor and director:
Citizen Kane, 1941; *The Magnificent Ambersons*, 1942; *Journey into Fear*, 1943; *The Stranger*, 1946; *Macbeth*, 1948; *Othello*, 1952; *Confidential Report/Mr Arkadin*, 1955; *Touch of Evil*, 1957; *The Trial*, 1962; *Chimes at Midnight*, 1966.

As director:
Extracts from *Twelfth Night*, 1933; *Hearts of Age*, 1934; *Too Much Johnson*, 1938; *The Lady from Shanghai*, 1947; *The Immortal Story*, 1968; *F for Fake*, 1973.

Television

As actor:
King Lear, 1953; *I Love Lucy*, 1956; *Four-Star Jubilee: Twentieth Century*, 1956; *The Merchant of Venice*, 1957; *Macbeth*, 1957; *Othello*, 1957; *The Fall of the City*, 1957; *Tempo* (series), 1961; *Around the World* (series), 1961; *Out of Darkness*, 1962; *The Silent Years*, 1971; *Future Shock*, 1971; *The Man Who Came to Dinner*, 1974; *The Big Event*, 1976; *Survival: Magnificent Monsters of the Deep*, 1976; *The Orson Welles Show*, 1979; *Shogun*, 1980; *Scene of the Crime*, 1984; *Moonlighting*, 1985.

As actor and director:
The Orson Welles Sketchbook (series), 1955; *Around the World with Orson Welles* (series), 1955; *Orson Welles's Great Mysteries* (series), 1973.

As director only:
The Fountain of Youth, 1958; *The Method*, 1958.

Radio

As actor:
Panic, 1934; *The March of Time* (series), 1935–36; *The Great McCoy: The Relief of Lucknow*, 1936; *Musical Reveries*, 1936; *Hamlet*, 1936; *The Columbia Workshop*, 1936; *The Shadow* (series), 1937; *Cavalcade of America*, 1937; *Streamlined Shakespeare*, 1937; *America's Hour* (series), 1938; *First Person Singular* (series), 1938; *A Christmas Carol*, 1938; *The Socony Vacuum Hour* (series), 1942–43; *The Texarkana Program*, 1944; *Jane Eyre*, 1944–45; *Exploring the Unknown* (series), 1945–46; *The Adventures of Harry Lime* (series), 1951; *The Black Museum* (series), 1952; *Sherlock Holmes*, 1952; *Song of Myself*, 1953; *Queen of Spades*, 1953; *Sherlock Holmes* (series), 1955.

As actor and director:
Les Misérables, 1937; *The War of the Worlds* (part of *Mercury Theatre of the Air* series), 1938; *The Campbell Playhouse with Orson Welles* (series), 1938–40; *His Honour the Mayor*, 1941; *The Lady Esther Show* (series), 1941; *Ceiling Unlimited* (series), 1942; *The Orson Welles Show* (series), 1942–43; *Suspense* (series), 1942–43; *Orson Welles's Almanack* (series), 1944; *Columbia Presents Corwin*, 1944; *American Eloquence*, 1944; *This Is My Best* (series), 1944–45; *Schlitz Summer Mercury Playhouse* (series), 1946.

Publications

Everybody's Shakespeare, 1933; *Une Grosse Légume*, 1953; *A bon entendeur*, 1953; *Mr Arkadin*, 1954; *Sed de Mal e Il Processo*, 1962; *The Trial*, 1970; *Citizen Kane*, 1971; *This is Orson Welles* (with Peter Bogdanovich and Jonathan Rosenbaum), 1992.

*

Bibliography

Books:
Peter Noble, *The Fabulous Orson Welles*, London, 1956.
Peter Bogdanovich, *The Cinema of Orson Welles*, London, 1961.
Peter Cowie, *The Cinema of Orson Welles*, London, 1965.
Charles Higham, *The Films of Orson Welles*, Berkeley, California, 1970.
Pauline Kael, *The Citizen Kane Book*, London, 1971.
Joseph Mcbride, *Orson Welles: Actor and Director*, London, 1977.
Richard France, *The Theatre of Orson Welles*, London, 1977.
André Bazin, *Orson Welles: A Critical View*, London, 1978.
Barbara Leaming, *Orson Welles: A Biography*, London, 1985.
John Russell Taylor, *Orson Welles: A Celebration*, London, 1986.
Charles Higham, *Orson Welles: The Rise and Fall of an American Genius*, London, 1987.
Frank Brady, *Citizen Welles: A Biography of Orson Welles*, Dunton Green, 1990.
James Howard, *The Complete Films of Orson Welles*, New York, 1991.

*   *   *

Orson Welles lived his life backwards. Aged 26, he turned Hollywood upside down with *Citizen Kane*, his debut film. Two years earlier, he had become a household name after his radio version of H. G. Wells's *The War of the Worlds* caused national panic. His all-Black "voodoo" production of *Macbeth*, which established him as a major theatrical figure, coincided with his 21st birthday. But, having acheived phenomenal success in theatre, radio, and film before most people have started, Welles then spent 40 years of increasing frustration, failure, and living hand-to-mouth.

Everything about Welles was singular — his talent, his precocity, his appearance. Michael MacLiammoir shared his first impression of Welles at the age of 16, when the latter arrived in Dublin and bluffed his way into the renowned Gate Theatre by lying about his age and fabricating theatrical experience: "a very tall young man with a chubby face, full powerful lips and disconcerting Chinese eyes ... His voice, with its brazen transatlantic sonority was already that of a preacher, a leader, a man of power". Back in the USA two years later, John Houseman saw Welles with the Katharine Cornell touring company's production of *Romeo and Juliet*: "a monstrous boy — flat-footed and graceless, yet swift and agile; soft as jelly one moment and uncoiled the next, in a spring of such furious energy that, once released, it could be checked by no human intervention".

The suggestion of an elemental force is appropriate. What Welles conjured up in only five years was only possible for a chronic insomniac, a probably manic depressive, and a man young enough not to understand the concept of impossibility. Welles's phenomenal rise owed much to his charm, his "chutzpah", his ability virtually to hypnotise actors into working long hours for little pay and to entice backers to part with their money. But it is significant that his short and intense career coincided with the equally brief but golden age of subsidized US theatre. As part of President Roosevelt's New Deal, the Federal Theatre Project (FTP) was instituted to provide "bread and circuses": work for unemployed actors, art for the masses. Within months, touring companies, regional theatres, the Living Newspaper revue, and experimental theatre schemes had sprung into being. It was the controversial Negro Theatre Project with which Welles directed his extraordinary "voodoo" *Macbeth*. Although Welles and Houseman's production of *The Cradle Will Rock* was thought too political and the association was severed, the FTP was important not just for financial support but for the aesthetic climate engendered. Welles's political and theatrical ideas were nurtured and consolidated by the European avant-gardism and left-wing principles of many of those who organised and participated in the FTP.

This sustenance should not undermine the fact that Welles was a genius. His magpie sensibility and eclectic education enabled him to borrow and juxtapose ideas in a strikingly original way, always daring and imaginative, if not always wholly realised. His approach to Shakespeare has influenced directors since. Productions such as *The Cradle Will Rock* and *Native Son* turned proletarian fiction and life into popular entertainment. Welles was one of the first to celebrate financial strictures, by making a virtue (pared-down sets) out of a necessity. His choice of material and interpretation was astonishingly diverse. A breakneck version of the Jacobean city comedy, *The Shoemaker's Holiday* (in modern dress) was followed by a respectful, stately production of *Heartbreak House*. Apart from directing this, Welles played a remarkably convincing octogenarian, at the age of 22. A frippery called *Too Much Johnson*, as much like a silent slapstick movie as a play, was followed by the end of his golden period, otherwise known as *Danton's Death*.

Danton's Death featured many of Welles's hallmarks — not least his premature discovery of another artist who was ahead of his time. Platforms rose and fell in front of a cyclorama of skulls lit alternately blood red and steel grey. Music was used to heighten the action, which was updated from the French Revolution to stress the parallels with contemporary Berlin and Moscow. The production flopped, closing after 21 performances having consumed the last of Mercury Theatre's money.

Why did *Danton's Death* fail? Perhaps audiences were exhausted by Welles's productivity, visceral style, and emotional bombardment. Certainly, left-wingers did not wish to hear Welles's grim prophecies about military dictatorship and oppression following revolutionary change and freedom. Or perhaps Welles was already losing interest in theatre and hungered for a new medium to explore and conquer. It is a sobering thought that the bulk of his theatrical work was accomplished before he passed his quarter century.

In retrospect, it seems that in medium after medium, Welles was lauded then reviled, or perhaps given enough rope to hang himself. Like any good tragic hero, he suffered from hubris. Juggling theatre, radio, television, and film as actor, director, and writer (preferably at the same time), Welles's reputation for extravagance and unreliability grew in direct relation to the diminishment of his career. Projects that had occupied him obsessively would be abandoned — interest or financial backing lost (sometimes both). On stage, as with his later films, there were only flashes of brilliance. What was never lost was his talent to polarise. Marlene Dietrich booed his adaptation of *Moby Dick* in 1956 and walked out. Kenneth Tynan called it the most exciting thing to hit London since the Great Fire.

Tynan, hyperbole aside, showed great insight into Welles's central problem: "The trouble is that everything he does is on such a vast scale that it quickly becomes monotonous. He is too big for the boots of any part". Or, indeed, any medium. Orson Welles's life, work, and failure should perhaps be viewed as a cautionary tale, on how the world is unable to deal with visionary mavericks. There has been no one like him, before or since.

—Joss Bennathan

WILLIAMSON, Nicol. British actor and director. Born in Hamilton, Scotland, 14 September 1938. Married Jill Townsend (divorced). Stage debut, Dundee Repertory Theatre, 1960–61; London debut, 1961; actor, Royal Court Theatre, London, 1961–62; first appeared with Royal Shakespeare Company, 1962; New York debut, Belasco Theatre, 1965; rejoined Royal Shakespeare Company, 1973; has returned to the stage only rarely since the early 1980's. Recipient: New York Drama Critics Award, 1966; *Evening Standard* Award, 1965, 1969.

Roles

1961   I-ti in *That's Us* (Chapman), Arts Theatre, Cambridge, and Royal Court Theatre, London.

Black Will in *Arden of Faversham* (Lillo and Hoadley), Royal Court Theatre, London, and tour.

1962   Flute in *A Midsummer Night's Dream* (Shakespeare), Royal Court Theatre, London.

Malvolio in *Twelfth Night* (Shakespeare), Royal Court Theatre, London; Royal Shakespeare Theatre, Stratford-upon-Avon, and Aldwych Theatre, London, 1974–75.

SAC Albert Meakin in *Nil Carborundum* (Livings), New Arts Theatre, London.

Satin in *The Lower Depths* (Gorky), Royal Shakespeare Company.

Leantio in *Women, Beware Women* (Middleton), Royal Shakespeare Company.

Man at the end in *Spring's Awakening* (Wedekind), Royal Court Theatre, London.

1963   Kelly in *Kelly's Eye* (Livings), Royal Court Theatre, London.

Sebastian Dangerfield in *The Ginger Man* (Donleavy), Ashcroft Theatre, Croydon, and Royal Court Theatre, London.

1964   Bill Maitland in *Inadmissible Evidence* (Osborne), Ashcroft Theatre, Croydon; Wyndham's Theatre, London, and Belasco Theatre, New York, 1965; Royal Court Theatre, London, 1978; Roundabout Theatre, New York, 1980.

Peter Wykeham in *A Cuckoo in the Nest* (Travers), Royal Court Theatre, London.

Vladimir in *Waiting for Godot*, (Beckett), Royal Court Theatre, London.

1965   Joe Johnson in *Miniatures* (Cregan), Royal Court Theatre, London.

Sweeney in *Sweeney Agonistes* (Eliot), Globe Theatre, London.

1967   Alexei Ivanovitch Poprichtchine in *Diary of a Madman* (Gogol), Duchess Theatre, London.

1968   Three roles in *Plaza Suite* (Simon), Plymouth Theatre, New York.

1969   Hamlet in *Hamlet* (Shakespeare), Round House Theatre, London, Lunt-Fontanne Theatre, New York, and US tour.

1973   Vanya in *Uncle Vanya* (Chekhov), Circle in the Square Theatre, New York; Other Place, Stratford-upon-Avon, 1974; also directed.

Coriolanus in *Coriolanus* (Shakespeare), Aldwych Theatre, London.

1974   Macbeth in *Macbeth* (Shakespeare), Royal Shakespeare Theatre, Stratford-upon-Avon; Aldwych Theatre, London, 1975; Circle in the Square Theatre, New York, 1982; also directed.

1975   Henry VIII in *Rex*, Lunt-Fontanne Theatre, New York.

1983   Archie Rice in *The Entertainer* (Osborne), Roundabout Theatre, New York.

1985   Henry Boot in *The Real Thing* (Stoppard), Plymouth Theatre, New York.

1994   John Barrymore in *A Night on the Town with John Barrymore* (Williamson and Megahey), Criterion Theatre, London.

Other roles included: *Midwinter Spring*, Queen's Theatre, London, 1969; *The Lark* (Anouilh), Edmonton, Canada; also directed, 1983.

Films

Six Sided Triangle, 1964; *Inadmissible Evidence*, 1967; *The Bofors Gun*, 1968; *Laughter in the Dark*, 1968; *The Reckoning*, 1969; *Hamlet*, 1969; *The Jerusalem File*, 1972; *The Wilby Conspiracy*, 1975; *The Seven Per Cent Solution*, 1976; *Robin and Marian*, 1976; *The Human Factor*, 1979; *Venom*, 1981; *The Goodbye Girl*, 1977; *The Cheap Detective*, 1978; *Excalibur*, 1981; *I'm Dancing as Fast as I Can*, 1982; *Return to Oz*, 1985; *Black Widow*, 1986.

Nicol Williamson (1968).

Television

War and Peace, 1972; *The Word*, 1978; *Macbeth*, 1982; *Christopher Columbus*, 1983; *Mountbatten: The Last Viceroy*, 1985; *Passion Flower*, 1985. Other productions include: *The Lark*; *Arturo Ui*; *I Know What I Meant*.

* * *

Nicol Williamson first played Bill Maitland, the battered hero of John Osborne's *Inadmissible Evidence* in 1964. In retrospect, it may be seen as an archetypal Williamson role: a man on the verge of self-destruction, exploding with nervous energy before he finally burns out.

Maitland was in his forties; Williamson was only 26. It did not matter. The performance was remarkable for its speed, for the actor's ability to switch in an instant from sneering defiance to abject vulnerability. It was remarkable too for its use of physical detail — the nervous movements, the sudden starts and turns, comic at first, but increasingly erratic and unsettling. "He makes Maitland a glass man", Ronald Bryden wrote, "each shift and terror transparent".

In 1969 Williamson was a famous, even infamous, Hamlet. This was not the Hamlet of tradition — the sweet prince, the noble heart. Williamson did not look noble, or sound it. He turned Hamlet from hero to anti-hero; "After all", he observed, "he's quite a frightening man, an unpleasant man in many ways". Ted Kalem called it "a great, mad, doomed, spine-shivering Hamlet" — a Hamlet full of rancour and resentment and a withering contempt, playing with Claudius as if playing with fire, willing his own destruction. What upset purists most was Williamson's voice. It was harsh, nasal, rasping; it lacked "beauty of tone". Williamson himself explained: "I was trying to make an *interesting* noise, not a beautiful one". Kalem wrote: "He cuts through the music of the Shakespearean line to the marrow of its meaning". His approach has often been to find an unusual reading for a line, a scene — and to startle the audience by the unexpected. It is a technique that can be electrifying — but it has also led to charges of idiosyncrasy.

Too many actors want to be liked by audiences. Williamson does not play for easy sympathy. He almost seems to defy the "prejudices and sentimentalities of his audience", as Alan Brien observed. He plays for honesty and truth — however uncomfortable and unpalatable. "I think the only valuable thing you can do as an actor", he argues, "is to make people recognise in themselves what is also there in you. Then they'll hate you because they don't want you to do that to them ... it makes them frightened. But I think you must show these things in order to be true to yourself".

In the late 1960's and early 1970's Williamson played a series of "mad, doomed" characters. Offstage, he was notoriously "difficult". Stories about him multiplied — on one occasion he slugged the Broadway producer David Merrick — and the Williamson legend was born. Indeed, a confusion developed between Williamson the man and the roles he played. John McGrath wrote the role of O'Rourke, the self-destructive sociopath in *The Bofors Gun*, "for and in some minute measure about Nick". The range of his performances, especially in films, has belied any suggestion that his acting is simply an extension of self. Nevertheless, it remains true that he is at his best playing characters who are mad, bad, and dangerous to know. When playing "ordinary" characters (such as Maurice Castle in the film *The Human Factor*) his performance has all too readily been simply "ordinary".

In 1973 he played the title role in *Uncle Vanya* on Broadway, opposite George C. Scott as Astrov. The production offered a fascinating contrast in acting styles, setting Scott's understated performance against Williamson's "free-style agony". "What makes Williamson a great actor", Michael Billington wrote, "is his sheer emotional candour: he has none of the small reticences and checks-and-balances of good taste that inhibit other performers". At the climax of the third act, for example, when Vanya clashes with Serebryakov, Williamson became farcically manic: "he goes brick red with impotent fury, he makes short, nervous stabbing gestures at the Professor and essays aimless kicks like a thwarted infant ... when he reaches the line, 'If I had a normal life, I might have been a Schopenhauer or a Dostoevsky', his body straightens, his eyes bulge, and you feel confronted by temporary insanity".

Williamson has, at times, been deemed a victim of his own excess. His Macbeth (1982) certainly offended the "good taste" of the New York critics. The performance charted Macbeth's precipitate descent, through frenzied madness to the chilling nihilism of the final scenes. But he was criticised for again failing to invest a Shakespearean hero with sufficient "nobility and grandeur" and Frank Rich said the actor was "not in control". The production closed quickly, but Williamson's performance has been recorded as part of the BBC Television Shakespeare series.

In 1983 he played Archie Rice in *The Entertainer*. The role (another of Osborne's world-weary, world-hating, and world-baiting anti-heroes) would seem ideal for him, but he was strangely subdued. Perhaps he feared comparisons with Olivier, or with his own Bill Maitland. "He softens the role", Frank Rich objected, "with his sagging shoulders, mild voice, and vacant, almost cherubic face, he seems defeated before the play begins".

Since then — apart from briefly appearing in (and directing) *The Lark* in Edmonton and a stint in *The Real Thing* on Broadway — Williamson seems to have abandoned the stage and settled for the occasional role in inferior movies. In 1994 the second night of the West End production of his own *A Night on the Town with John Barrymore* ended early with Williamson explaining that he was so dissatisfied with his own performance that the show could not go on. Back in 1978, when playing in the revival of *Inadmissible Evidence*, Williamson observed, "I don't think I can or will act like this very much more". Perhaps the actor who specialised in playing burnt-out cases has, in time, burnt out himself.

—David Allen

———————

WILSON, Robert M. US director, playwright, designer and actor. Born in Waco, Texas, 4 October 1941. Educated at the University of Texas, Austin, 1959–62; studied painting in Paris with George McNeil, 1962; Pratt Institute, Brooklyn, New York, 1965; apprentice to Paolo Soleri, Arcosanti Community, Arizona, 1966. Debut as designer, New York World's Fair, 1965; subsequently collaborated with autistic Christopher Knowles and other handicapped people on several projects over many years; has toured and lectured widely and staged numerous exhibitions of his designs and paintings; artistic director, Byrd Hoffman Foundation, New York. Fellow: Guggenheim Foundation, 1971, 1980; Rockefeller Foundation, 1975, 1981. Member: National Institute of Music Theatre (trustee); American Repertory Theatre (board). Recipient: Syndicat de la Critique Musicale Award, 1970, 1977, 1987; Drama Desk Award, 1971; Obie Award citation, 1974; Maharam Award, 1975; BITEF Grand Prize, 1977; Lumen Award for Design, 1977; German Critics Award, 1979; Der Rosenstrauss citation, 1982; First Prize, San Sebastian Film and Video Festival (Spain), 1984; Berlin Festspiele Theatertreffen, 1984, 1987; Obie Award, 1986; Picasso Award (Spain), 1986; Skowhegan Medal for Drawing, 1987; Bessie Award, 1987; American Theatre Wing Design Award, 1987; Mondello Award (Italy), 1988; Institute Honour, American Institute of Architects, New York, 1988; New York Public Library Lion of the Performing Arts, 1989; Great Prize, Sao Paulo Biennial, 1989; Premio Abbiati, Italian Theatre Critics Award, 1989.

Productions

As director and designer:

1965   *Dance Event*, World's Fair, Queen's, New York.

1966   *Solo Performance* (Wilson), Byrd Hoffman Studio, New York.

1967   *Theatre Activity* (Wilson), Bleecker Street Cinema, New York.

1968   *Theatre Activity* (Wilson), American Theatre Laboratory, New York.

ByrdwoMAN (Wilson), Byrd Hoffman Studio, New York.

Alley Cats (Wilson), University of Continuing Education, New York.

1969   *The King of Spain* (Wilson), Anderson Theatre, New York.

Watermill (Wilson), Spring Palace, New York.

The Life and Times of Sigmund Freud (Wilson), Brooklyn Academy of Music, New York.

1970   *The Life and Times of Sigmund Freud* (Wilson), Brooklyn Academy of Music, New York.

Deafman Glance (Wilson), University of Iowa, Iowa City.

1971   *Program Prologue Now, Overture for a Deafman* (Wilson), Espace Pierre Cardin, Paris.

Deafman Glance (Wilson), Brooklyn Academy of Music, New York, and European tour.

1972   *Overture* (Wilson), Byrd Hoffman Studio, New York, Khaneh-e Zinatolmolk, Shiraz, Iran, and Opéra Comique, Paris.

KA MOUNTAIN AND GUARDenia TERRACE (Wilson), Haft Tan Mountain, Shiraz, Iran.

1973   *The Life and Times of Joseph Stalin* (Wilson), Det Nye Theater, Copenhagen, Denmark, and Brooklyn Academy of Music, New York.

King Lyre and Lady in the Wasteland (Wilson), Byrd Hoffman Studio, New York.

1974   *Prologue to a Letter for Queen Victoria* (Wilson), Teatro 6 O'Clock, Spoleto, Italy.

The Life and Times of Dave Clark (Wilson), Teatro Municipal, Sao Paulo, Brazil.

Dia Log/A Mad Man A Mad Giant A Mad Dog A Mad Urge A Mad Face (Knowles and Wilson), Teatro di Roma, Rome, John F. Kennedy Centre for the Performing Arts, Washington D.C., and Shiraz Festival, Iran.

A Letter for Queen Victoria (Wilson), European tour and ANTA Theatre, New York.

1975   *To Street* (Wilson), Kultur Forum, Bonn Centre, Bonn; also acted.

The $ Value of Man (Wilson), Brooklyn Academy of Music, New York.

Dia Log (Knowles and Wilson), Public Theatre, New York.

1976   *Einstein on the Beach* (Wilson and Glass), European tour and Metropolitan Opera House, New York.

1977   *I Was Sitting on My Patio This Guy Appeared I Thought I Was Hallucinating* (Wilson), US tour.

1978   *Overture to the Fourth Act of Deafman Glance* (Wilson), Manhattanville College, Purchase, New York, and John Drew Theatre, Easthampton, New York.

I Was Sitting on My Patio This Guy Appeared I Thought I Was Hallucinating (Wilson), European tour.

Robert M. Wilson

Dia Log/Network (Knowles and Wilson), US tour.

1979   *Edison* (Wilson), Lion Theatre, New York, Théâtre Nationale Populaire, Lyon, France, Teatro Nazionale, Italy, and Festival d'Automne, Theatre de Paris, France.

Dia Log/Network (Knowles and Wilson), Palais des Beaux Arts, Brussels, Belgium.

Death Destruction and Detroit (Wilson), Schaubühne Theater, Berlin.

1980   *Overture to the Fourth Act of Deafman Glance* (Wilson), Raffinerie Plan K, Brussels, Belgium, and Palais des Congres, Liège, Belgium.

Dia Log/Curious George (Knowles and Wilson), Mitzi E. Newhouse Theatre, New York, and European tour.

1981   *Medea* (Bryars and Wilson), John F. Kennedy Centre for the Performing Arts, Washington D.C.

The Man in the Raincoat (Wilson), Theater der Welt, Cologne.

1982   *Overture to the Fourth Act of Deafman Glance* (Wilson), Japan Performing Arts Centre, Toyama, Japan, and Freiburg University, Germany.

the CIVIL warS/Freiburg Workshop (Wilson and others), Freiburg University, Germany.

Medea (Bryars and Wilson), Aaron Davis Hall, City College, New York.

Great Day in the Morning (Norman and Wilson), Théâtre des Champs-Elysées, Paris.

Golden Windows (Wilson), Kammerspiele, Munich.

1983   *the CIVIL warS/Dutch Section* (Wilson), Schouwburg Theater, Rotterdam, and French tour.

1984   *the CIVIL warS/Japan Section* (Wilson), Workshop, Tokyo.

the CIVIL warS/French Section (Wilson), Office Regionale de la Culture de Provence-Alpes-Côte d'Azur.

the CIVIL warS/Rome Section (Wilson), Teatro dell'Opera, Rome, City Centre, New York, and Pavilion, Los Angeles.

the CIVIL warS/Knee Plays (Wilson), Guthrie Theatre, Minneapolis, Minnesota.

the CIVIL warS/Cologne Section (Wilson), Schauspiel, Cologne, and Berlin Theatre Festival.

Medée (Charpentier), Opéra de Lyon, France.

Medea (Bryars and Wilson), Opéra de Lyon, France, and Festival d'Automne, Théâtre des Champs-Elysées, Paris.

Einstein on the Beach (Wilson and Glass), Brooklyn Academy of Music, New York.

1985   *the CIVIL warS/Cologne Section* (Wilson), American Repertory Theatre, Cambridge, Massachusetts.

King Lear (Shakespeare), University of California, Los Angeles.

the CIVIL warS/Rome Section (Wilson), Saratoga Performing Arts Centre, Saratoga.

Robert Wilson Readings, Dublin Theatre Festival and Museum van Hedendaagse Kunst, Gent, Belgium.

the CIVIL warS/Knee Plays (Wilson), European tour.

The Golden Windows (Wilson), Brooklyn Academy of Music, New York.

1986   *Alcestis* (Euripides, adapted by Wilson and Müller), American Repertory Theatre, Cambridge, Massachusetts, and Festival d'Automne, Théâtre Bobigny, Paris.

the CIVIL warS/Rome Section (Wilson), Netherlands Opera, Amsterdam.

Hamletmachine (Müller), University of New York, Theater in der Kunsthalle, Hamburg, and Brooklyn Academy of Music, New York.

Overture to the Fourth Act of Deafman Glance (Wilson), Theatre Festival, Barcelona, and Theatre Festival, Malaga.

Alceste (Gluck), Staatsoper, Stuttgart.

the CIVIL warS/Knee Plays (Wilson), US tour.

1987   *Salome* (Strauss), Teatro alla Scala, Milan.

Death Destruction and Detroit 2 (Wilson), Schaubühne Theater, Berlin.

Alcestis (Euripides, adapted by Wilson and Müller), Staatstheater, Stuttgart.

Hamletmachine (Müller), Thalia Theater, Hamburg, Almeida Theatre, London, and French/Italian tour.

the CIVIL warS/Knee Plays (Wilson), US tour.

Alceste (Gluck), Staatsoper, Stuttgart.

Quartet (Müller), Staatstheater, Stuttgart.

Overture to the Fourth Act of Deafman Glance (Wilson), International Theatre Conference, Delphi, and Alice Tully Hall, Lincoln Centre, New York.

Parzival (Dorst and Wilson), Thalia Theater, Hamburg.

1988   *Quartet* (Müller), American Repertory Theatre, Cambridge, Massachusetts.

Le Martyre de Saint Sebastian (Debussy and D'Annunzio), Théâtre Bobigny, Paris, Metropolitan Opera, New York, and Barnier Opera House, Paris.

Cosmopolitan Greetings (Wilson and Ginsberg), Theater Kampnagelfabrik, Hamburg.

The Forest (Wilson, Müller and Pinckney), Freien Volksbühne, Berlin, Deutsches Theater, Munich, and Brooklyn Academy of Music, New York.

1989   *Doktor Fausts* (Manzoni and Mann), Teatro alla Scala, Milan.

De Materie (Wilson and Andriessen), Netherlands Opera, Amsterdam; Danstheater aan 't Spui, The Hague, and Schouwburg, Rotterdam.

La Nuit d'avant le jour (musical compilation), Opéra Bastille, Paris.

Orlando (Woolf), adapted by Wilson and Pinckney), Schaubühne Theater, Berlin.

Swan Song (Chekhov), Kammerspiele, Munich.

1990   *The Black Rider: The Casting of the Magic Bullets* (Wilson, Waits and Burroughs), Thalia Theatre, Hamburg.

As designer only:

1963   *America Hurrah* (van Itallie), Pocket Theatre, New York.

1987   *The Man in the Raincoat* (Wilson), Het Muziektheater, Amsterdam.

1988   *The Golden Windows* (Wilson), Centre d'Essai, University of Montreal, Quebec, and Fifth International Festival of University Theatre, Liège, Belgium.

Films

Overture for a Deafman, 1971.

Television/video

The House, 1963; *Slant*, 1967; *Spaceman*, 1976; *Video 50*, 1978; *Deafman Glance*, 1981; *Stations*, 1982; *Spaceman*, 1984; *La Femme à la Cafetiere*, 1989; *The Death of King Lear*, 1989.

Publications

Production Notes on The King of Spain, 1970; *A Letter for Queen Victoria*, 1974; *Einstein on the Beach*, with P. Glass, 1976; *I Was Sitting on My Patio This Guy Appeared I Thought I was Hallucinating*, 1978; *Death Destruction and Detroit*, 1979; *The Golden Windows* (play), 1982; *the CIVIL warS: a tree is best measured when it is down*, with H. Müller, 1983; *Alcestis*, adapted from Euripides, 1987; *Death Destruction and Detroit 2*, with H. Müller, 1987; *Parzival*, with T. Dorst, 1987; *The Forrest*, with H. Müller and D. Pinckney, 1988.

*

Bibliography

Books:
Franco Quadri, *It Teatro di Robert Wilson*, Venice, 1976.
Stefan Brecht, *The Theatre of Visions: Robert Wilson*, Frankfurt, 1979.
Nelson Craig, *Robert Wilson: The Theatre of Images*, Cincinnati, 1980.
Laurence Shyer, *Robert Wilson and His Collaborators*, New York, 1990.

* * *

When critic Bonnie Maranca coined the term "theatre of images" as a label for the avant-garde of the 1970's it was rejected by many as too narrow to encompass the ideas and techniqus of the wide range of theatre creators it meant to describe, but it is a most apt designation for the work of theatre artist Robert Wilson. From the late 1960's, Wilson began creating non-narrative theatre/dance works that were characterized by lush and lavish visual imagery through which performers moved, often at a snail's pace. Unlike much of the avant-garde of Wilson's contemporaries performed in relatively small, makeshift spaces, his work existed on a grand scale, often being performed on opera house stages. A French critic who saw the six-hour *Deafman Glance* in Paris in 1971 referred to it as an "opera", a term that Wilson appropriated for many of his subsequent works. The scope and scale of the works, as well as the derivation of opera from "opus" makes the term most apt. Whereas concurrent works by others were dominated by formalist concepts, structure or ideology, Wilson's works truly foregrounded design and visual motifs. Since the mid-1980's he has done an increasing number of classics or scripts by others, ranging from Gluck's *Alceste* and Richard Strauss's *Salome* to several works by Heiner Müller. Nonetheless, these productions maintain the Wilsonian vocabulary and aesthetics and are unmistakably products of his artistic vision.

The strongest influences on Wilson's work came from choreographers George Balanchine, Merce Cunningham and Jerome Robbins. The first two especially were important for their separation of movement from narrative storyline. This was particularly appealing to Wilson, who from his earliest experiences of theatre found narrative boring and hard to follow, while the visual elements and movement were enormously appealing. This is remarkably like the experience of writer Gertrude Stein, who rejected the narrative theatre in favour of what she dubbed "landscape theatre". Stein's theory of landscape theatre provides a major theoretical basis for Wilson's work. Landscape theatre, like a landscape painting, allows the viewer to perceive the entire image at once or to view it in random order and focus. It is a meditative experience in which time is almost non-existent and the spectator is not pressured or rushed. Once, in response to a question, Wilson described his work as about "nothing", but the sort of nothing that a

child means when asked what he or she is doing and replies "Oh, nothing". The images and actions of his work often comprise a collage; they emerge out of Wilson's mind, images from the world around him, or the creativity and input of his many collaborators and performers and they are put together in ways that make a theatrical, visual, or even personal sense but defy conventional hermeneutics. The desire on the part of spectators and critics to interpret, combined with Wilson's use of socially and culturally charged images and icons, often leads to strained political explications of his work. *The $ Value of Man*, for instance, took as its starting point a newspaper article on the physical value of a human body versus the spiritual value of a human life. But while the performance incorporated images of money and violence, it was not in any way a sociopolitical commentary. Likewise, *Einstein on the Beach*, whose eponymous central figure, like Nero, fiddled at the edge of the stage as an image of an atomic bomb hung behind him, suggested an apocalyptic view of modern technology; yet here, too, structure, rhythm and imagery were more significant than any meaning. Throughout his original creations, Wilson has used Freud, Stalin, Lincoln and Queen Victoria and even radio commercials as unifying elements for his operas, yet he uses them as icons or archetypes stripped of their connotations.

Many of Wilson's techniques come from his work with brain-damaged children. What fascinated him was how these people perceived the world and how they communicated. Some of his early theatre work in New York was done with a deaf mute boy named Raymond Andrews. Later he worked with an autistic child named Christopher Knowles — a collaboration that developed over many years, with Knowles contributing texts and performances to many works. Wilson believed that therapy should not consist of getting the patient to behave in a "normal" way since that was not possible, but should focus on learning how their behaviour is structured. Much of the rehearsal and improvisational work of Wilson's group, the Byrd Hoffman School of Byrds, consisted of imitating the sound and movement of Andrews, Knowles or others. Wilson described how brain-damaged people see the world on an "inner screen", a view that is accessible to most people only in dream states. The almost unbearably slow pace and long duration of his works (*The Life and Times of Joseph Stalin* lasted 12 hours) was intended, at least in part, to induce a trance-like state in the audience in which the objective images on the stage would merge with the dream images of the spectators' "inner screen". Pace and duration in these early pieces also suggested a more Asian than Western spectator response. Full and continuous attention was not necessary and the audience could leave and re-enter the theatre over the course of the performance. *KA MOUNTAIN AND GUARDenia TERRACE* was performed over seven days and a conventional audience/performance relationship was simply not possible. When Louis Aragon, the Surrealist artist, saw *Deafman Glance* in Paris in 1971 he declared that this was the true embodiment of the Surrealist spirit that the movement had been seeking since the 1920's and indeed, the dreamlike juxtaposition of images was perhaps the first successful realisation of Surrealist aesthetics on the stage.

The sheer size of many of Wilson's works, combined with their relative accessibility — they do not require a knowledge of complex theories or rarified aesthetics as do the works of many of his contemporaries; just "listen to the pictures" he once suggested — has made him one of the most popular figures of the avant-garde. As such he has been a major force in gaining acceptance for non-narrative theatre and weaning audiences away from Aristotelian structures and elements. The size of his operas has also made them economically prohibitive, limiting the scope of some of his projects, notably the *CIVIL warS*, which was to have been a multinational epic presented at the 1984 Olympics but never produced and only seen in fragments since then. Some critics and fellow artists have complained that Wilson's more recent work is too slick, lacking the rough edges that gave the early work its power, but it continues to be unlike almost anything else occurring in the contemporary theatre.

—Arnold Aronson

WOFFINGTON, Peg. Irish actress. Born Margaret Woffington in Dublin, c.1714 (some sources, 18 October 1718). Rumoured to have married one Colonel Caesar in secret; her lovers included David Garrick, with whom she lived for a time from 1742. Reputedly worked in tightrope-walking act under Madame Violante as an infant; subsequently sold fruit or vegetables in the street; stage debut with Violante's children's company, c.1724; actress, Aungier Street Theatre, Dublin, and Rainsford Street Theatre, Dublin, 1730's; established reputation at Smock Alley Theatre, Dublin, particularly in breeches parts, 1737–40; acclaimed for her beauty and talent on debut at Covent Garden, London, 1740; joined Garrick at Theatre Royal, Drury Lane, after quarrel with John Rich at Covent Garden, 1741; returned to Covent Garden after quarrel with Garrick, 1749; studied under Mlle Dumesnil in Paris; acted at Smock Alley Theatre, Dublin, 1751–54; closed career at Covent Garden, 1754–57; emnity with rival Mrs Bellamy culminated in Woffington stabbing her rival in the wings, 1756; became invalid after collapsing during performance as Rosalind, 1757. Member: Beefsteak Club, Dublin (president), 1753. Died in London, 28 March 1760.

Principal roles

c.1724	Polly Peachum in *The Beggar's Opera* (Gay), Fawnes' Court, Dublin.
	Nell in *The Devil to Pay* (Coffey), Fawnes' Court, Dublin.
1724–37	Mrs Peachum in *The Beggar's Opera*, Aungier Street Theatre, Dublin.
	Mother Midnight in *The Twin Rivals* (Farquhar), Aungier Street Theatre, Dublin.
1737	Ophelia in *Hamlet* (Shakespeare), Smock Alley Theatre, Dublin.
1737–40	Miss Lucy in *An Old Man Taught Wisdom; or, The Virgin Unmasked* (Fielding), Smock Alley Theatre, Dublin.
	Female Officer and Phillis in *The Conscious Lovers* (Steele), Smock Alley Theatre, Dublin.
1740	Sir Harry Wildair in *The Constant Couple* (Farquhar), Smock Alley Theatre, Dublin, and Covent Garden, London.

	Silvia in *The Recruiting Officer* (Farquhar), Covent Garden, London.
	Lady Sadlife in *The Double Gallant* (Cibber), Covent Garden, London.
	Aura in *The Country Lasses* (C. Johnson), Covent Garden, London.
	Elvira in *The Spanish Friar* (Dryden), Covent Garden, London.
1740–41	Violante in *The Double Falsehood* (Theobald), Covent Garden, London.
	Laetitia in *The Old Bachelor* (Congreve), Covent Garden, London.
	Victoria in *The Fatal Marriage* (Southerne), Covent Garden, London.
	Florella in *Greenwich Park* (Mountfort), Covent Garden, London.
	Angelica in *The Gamester* (Centlivre), Covent Garden, London.
	Cherry in *The Beaux' Stratagem* (Farquhar), Covent Garden, London.
1742	Ruth in *The Committee* (Howard), Theatre Royal, Drury Lane, London.
	Lady Brute in *The Provoked Wife* (Vanbrugh), Theatre Royal, Drury Lane, London.
	Nerissa in *The Merchant of Venice* (Shakespeare), Theatre Royal, Drury Lane, London.
	Rosalind in *As You Like It* (Shakespeare), Theatre Royal, Drury Lane, London.
	Helena in *All's Well That Ends Well* (Shakespeare), Theatre Royal, Drury Lane, London.
	Mrs Sullen in *The Beaux' Stratagem* (Farquhar), Theatre Royal, Drury Lane, London.
	Clarinda in *The Double Gallant* (Cibber), Theatre Royal, Drury Lane, London.
	Berinthia in *The Relapse* (Vanbrugh), Theatre Royal, Drury Lane, London.
	Belinda in *The Man of Mode* (Etherege), Theatre Royal, Drury Lane, London.
	Lady Betty Modish in *The Careless Husband* (Cibber), Theatre Royal, Drury Lane, London.
	Clarissa in *The Confederacy* (Vanbrugh), Theatre Royal, Drury Lane, London.
	Cordelia in *King Lear* (Shakespeare), Theatre Royal, Drury Lane, London.
	Lady Anne in *Richard III* (Shakespeare), Smock Alley Theatre, Dublin.
	Angelina in *Love Makes a Man* (Cibber), Smock Alley Theatre, Dublin.
	Lurewell in *The Constant Couple* (Farquhar), Theatre Royal, Drury Lane, London.
1743	Charlotte in *The Wedding Day* (Fielding), Theatre Royal, Drury Lane, London.
1743–44	Mistress Ford in *The Merry Wives of Windsor* (Shakespeare), Theatre Royal, Drury Lane, London.
	Lady Townley in *The Provoked Husband* (Cibber), Theatre Royal, Drury Lane, London.
	Portia in *The Merchant of Venice* (Shakespeare), Theatre Royal, Drury Lane, London.
	Millamant in *The Way of the World* (Congreve), Theatre Royal, Drury Lane, London.
1744	Laetitia in *The Astrologer* (Ralph), Theatre Royal, Drury Lane, London.

Peg Woffington

1744–45 Mrs Frail in *Love for Love* (Congreve), Theatre Royal, Drury Lane, London.

Oriana in *The Inconstant* (Farquhar), Theatre Royal, Drury Lane, London.

Narcissa in *Love's Last Shift* (Cibber), Theatre Royal, Drury Lane, London.

Belinda in *The Provoked Wife* (Vanbrugh), Theatre Royal, Drury Lane, London.

Maria in *The Non-Juror* (Cibber), Theatre Royal, Drury Lane, London.

Florimel in *The Comical Lovers* (Cibber), Theatre Royal, Drury Lane, London.

Constantia in *The She Gallants* (Lansdowne), Theatre Royal, Drury Lane, London.

The Lady in *The Scornful Lady* (Beaumont), Theatre Royal, Drury Lane, London.

Penelope in *The Lying Lover* (Steele), Theatre Royal, Drury Lane, London.

Mrs Conquest in *The Lady's Last Stake* (Cibber), Theatre Royal, Drury Lane, London.

Isabella in *Measure for Measure* (Shakespeare), Theatre Royal, Drury Lane, London.

Viola in *Twelfth Night* (Shakespeare), Theatre Royal, Drury Lane, London.

Aminta in *The Sea Voyage* (possibly by Fletcher), Theatre Royal, Drury Lane, London.

Belvidera in *The Humours of the Army* (Shadwell) Theatre Royal, Drury Lane, London.

Mariana in *The Miser* (Fielding), Theatre Royal, Drury Lane, London.

1746 Lady Katherine in *Henry VII* (Macklin), Theatre Royal, Drury Lane, London.

1746–47 Charlotte in *The Refusal* (Cibber), Theatre Royal, Drury Lane, London.

Lady Percy in *Henry IV* (Shakespeare), Theatre Royal, Drury Lane, London.

Cleopatra in *All for Love* (Dryden), Theatre Royal, Drury Lane, London.

Belinda in *The Artful Husband* (Tavener), Theatre Royal, Drury Lane, London.

Mrs Loveit in *The Man of Mode* (Etherege), Theatre Royal, Drury Lane, London.

Silvia in *Marry or Do Worse* (Walker), Theatre Royal, Drury Lane, London.

Lady Rhadamont in *A Fine Lady's Airs* (Baker), Theatre Royal, Drury Lane, London.

1748 Rosetta in *The Foundling* (Moore), Theatre Royal, Drury Lane, London.

Sulpitia in *Albumazar* (Tomkis), Theatre Royal, Drury Lane, London.

Jacinthia in *The Suspicious Husband* (Hoadly), Theatre Royal, Drury Lane, London.

Hippolito in *The Tempest* (Shakespeare, adapted by Dryden), Theatre Royal, Drury Lane, London.

Flora in *She Would and She Wouldn't* (Cibber), Theatre Royal, Drury Lane, London.

Jane Shore in *Jane Shore* (Rowe), Theatre Royal, Drury Lane, London.

1749 Veturia in *Coriolanus* (Shakespeare, adapted by Thomson), Covent Garden, London.

Arabella in *The London Cuckolds* (Ravenscroft), Covent Garden, London.

Helena in *The Rover* (Behn), Covent Garden, London.

Portia in *Julius Caesar* (Shakespeare), Covent Garden, London.

The Lady in *Comus* (Milton, adapted by Dalton), Covent Garden, London.

Elvira in *Love Makes a Man* (Cibber), Covent Garden, London.

Bellamente in *The Emperor of the Moon* (Behn), Covent Garden, London.

Andromache in *The Distressed Mother* (Philips), Covent Garden, London.

Calista in *The Fair Penitent* (Rowe), Covent Garden, London.

Lady Touchwood in *The Double Dealer* (Congreve), Covent Garden, London.

Leonora in *Sir Courtly Nice* (Crowne), Covent Garden, London.

Queen Katharine in *Henry VIII* (Shakespeare), Covent Garden, London.

1749–50 Desdemona in *Othello* (Shakespeare), Covent Garden, London.

Lady Macbeth in *Macbeth* (Shakespeare), Covent Garden, London.

Clarinda in *The Suspicious Husband* (Hoadly), Covent Garden, London.

Aspasia in *Tamerlane* (Rowe), Covent Garden, London.

Estifania in *Rule a Wife and Have a Wife* (Fletcher), Covent Garden, London.

Lady Jane Grey in *Lady Jane Grey* (Rowe), Covent Garden, London.

Anne Bullen in *Virtue Betrayed* (Banks), Covent Garden, London.

Queen Mary in *The Albion Queens* (Banks), Covent Garden, London.

1750–51 Gertrude in *Hamlet* (Shakespeare), Covent Garden, London.

Hypolita in *She Would and She Would Not* (Cibber), Covent Garden, London.

Lady Fanciful in *The Provoked Wife* (Vanbrugh), Covent Garden, London.

Hermione in *The Distressed Mother* (Philips), Covent Garden, London.

Constance in *King John* (Shakespeare), Covent Garden, London.

1751–54 Zara in *The Mourning Bride* (Congreve), Smock Alley Theatre, Dublin.

Lothario in *The Fair Penitent* (Rowe), Smock Alley Theatre, Dublin.

Widow Lackit in *The Fair Quaker of Deal* (Shadwell), Smock Alley Theatre, Dublin.

Palmyra in *Mahomet* (Voltaire, translated by Miller), Smock Alley Theatre, Dublin.

Phaedre in *Phaedre and Hippolytus* (Smith), Covent Garden, London.

Lady Pliant in *The Double Dealer* (Congreve), Covent Garden, London.

Aurelia in *The Twin Rivals* (Farquhar), Covent Garden, London.

Jocasta in *Oedipus* (Dryden), Covent Garden, London.

Isabella in *The Fatal Marriage* (Southerne), Covent Garden, London.

1755–56   Angelica in *Love for Love* (Congreve), Covent Garden, London.

Lady Dainty in *The Double Gallant* (Cibber), Covent Garden, London.

Roxana in *Alexander; or, The Rival Queens* (N. Lee), Covent Garden, London.

Penelope in *Ulysses* (Rowe), Covent Garden, London.

Melantha in *The Frenchified Lady* (anon.), Covent Garden, London.

1756–57   Celia in *The Humorous Lieutenant* (Fletcher), Covent Garden, London.

Almeria in *The Mourning Bride* (Congreve), Covent Garden, London.

Queen Margaret in *Richard III* (Shakespeare), Covent Garden, London.

1757   Lady Randolph in *Douglas* (Home), Covent Garden, London.

Other roles included: Adriana in *The Comedy of Errors* (Shakespeare); Alicia in *The Tragedy of Jane Shore* (Rowe); Amanda in *Love's Last Shift* (Cibber); Beatrice in *Much Ado About Nothing* (Shakespeare); Belvidera in *Venice Preserved* (Otway); Calpurnia in *Julius Caesar* (Shakespeare); Mrs Day in *The Committee* (Howard); Queen Elizabeth in *The Earl of Essex* (Brooke); Cicely Grundy in *The Cobbler of Preston* (Bullock); Kate in *Henry V* (Shakespeare); Marcia in *Cato* (Addison); Monimia in *The Orphan* (Otway); Oriana in *The Fair Quaker of Deal* (Shadwell); Phillida in *Damon and Phillida* (Cibber); Sigismunda in *Tancred and Sigismunda* (Thomson); Mrs Trapes in *The Beggar's Opera* (Gay).

*

Bibliography

Books:
J. Hoole, *A Monody: To the Memory of Mrs Margaret Woffington*, London, 1760.
Arthur Maynwaring, *Memoirs of the Celebrated Mrs Woffington*, London, 1760.
J. Fitzgerald Molloy, *The Life and Adventures of Peg Woffington*, 2 vols., London, 1884.
Augustin Daly, *Woffington, A Tribute to the Actress and the Woman*, Philadelphia, 1888.
Janet Camden Lucey, *Lovely Peggy, The Life and Times of Margaret Woffington*, London, 1952.
Janet Dunbar, *Peg Woffington and Her World*, London, 1968.

* * *

Peg Woffington was one of the top three actresses of her time: only Hannah Pritchard and Susanna Cibber were more highly regarded. She was the leading actress in high comedy and in "breeches roles" and in both respects was considered the successor of Anne Oldfield, many of whose parts she played. She was also a noted speaker of prologues and epilogues and a dancer (she occasionally performed dances in character right up to the end of her career).

She was noted especially for her great beauty, her "elegant" figure and bearing, her intelligence, and her wittiness and vivacity as a comic actress. Her unusual dedication to her profession was exemplified for her contemporaries by her willingness to sacrifice her beauty to the demands of characterization by wearing appropriate make-up to play such elderly women as Mrs Day in Howard's *The Committee* and Veturia in Thomson's *Coriolanus*. On the other hand, she was notorious for allowing herself to be distracted from the on-stage action by her admirers in the audience. Her only serious deficiency, however, was her voice, which lacked the harmony that was considered necessary even in comedy, and which became harsh in the declamatory passages of tragedy.

Woffington's personal life had a direct impact on her career: her reputation for off-stage promiscuity not only influenced the reception of her performances but was actively exploited, by herself and others. David Garrick, for example, made use of that reputation in the epilogue he wrote for her to deliver at the opening of Drury Lane in 1747, in which he demonstrated the propriety of forbidding backstage visitors by the ironic means of having her complain that, barred the visits of their "beaux", the actresses' "*occupation's* gone".

Her most famous role, Sir Harry Wildair in Farquhar's *The Constant Couple*, both confirmed her lack of "modesty" and utilized it to create an ambiguous and provocative representation of a fashionable rake; according to Thomas Davies in *Garrick* "she represented with so much ease, elegance, and propriety of deportment, that no male actor equalled her in that part". Her identification with the role is suggested by her appearance in a stage satire as "Peggy Wildair". Wildair was her most successful cross-dressed role, but not her only one: her first London appearance, in 1732, was as Macheath in *The Beggar's Opera* and as a mature actress she also played the villainous rake Lothario in Rowe's *The Fair Penitent* in both London and Dublin.

The masculinity of Woffington's Wildair was reportedly convincing to the degree of having an erotic appeal for the female members of the audience but, inevitably, an awareness of her true gender governed her contemporaries' assessment of her performance. Benjamin Victor, warning other actresses against similar attempts, noted "there is something required so much beyond the Delicacy of your Sex, to arrive at the Point of Perfection, that, if you hit it, you may be condemned as a Woman." John Hill criticized her performance on the grounds that when "she makes love" as Sir Harry "it is insipid, or it is worse; it conveys no ideas at all, or very hateful ones". It should be noted that, according to Victor, she retained control over her acting of this transgressive and lucrative part by having her contract stipulate that she would only perform it "with her own Consent".

Woffington made more conventional use of her erotic appeal and her ability to mime male behaviour in such breeches roles as Rosalind, Portia, and Silvia in Farquhar's *The Recruiting Officer*, which also allowed her to display her skill in representing upper-class ingénues. Her popularity as Silvia was turned to patriotic purposes during the Jacobite Rebellion of 1745, when she spoke on several occasions another characteristic epilogue — "wrote purely for her Manner of Speaking", full of double intendres and delivered in "the Habit of a Volunteer" — entitled *The Female Volunteer; or, An Attempt to Make Our Men Stand*.

Aristocratic coquettes and intriguing wives were equally important to her line and much more numerous. The former group are characterized by vanity, a love of power for its own sake, and affectation, mitigated by an essential goodheartedness. Lady Townly in Cibber's *The Provoked Husband*, whose wilfulness almost leads her into viciousness, was the leading exemplar of this type in Woffington's repertoire, which also included Lady Betty Modish in Cibber's *The Careless Husband*, Maria in his *Non-Juror*, and Millamant in *The Way of the World*. Thomas Davies commented that the "fashionable irregularities and sprightly coquetry" of such characters "were exhibited by Woffington with that happy ease and gaiety, and with such powerful attraction, that the excesses of these characters appeared not only pardonable, but agreeable". The second group of characters featured Mrs Sullen in Farquhar's *The Beaux' Stratagem* and Lady Brute in Vanbrugh's *The Provoked Wife* and included Mistress Ford in *The Merry Wives of Windsor*. Ruth in *The Committee*, another witty ingénue, and Phillis, the maid in Steele's *The Conscious Lovers*, the only low comic character Woffington performed regularly, were also among her most popular roles.

Up until 1748, Woffington appeared in few tragedies, but in the summer of that year she reportedly studied tragic acting in Paris with Dumesnil and thereafter tragic roles formed a more prominent part of her repertoire. Her most important tragic characters both appeared in Philips's *The Distrest Mother*, in which she played at various times both the stoic and rigidly honourable title character, Andromache, and her passionate and unprincipled rival, Hermione. Her other notable tragic roles ran the gamut from Jane Shore to Lady Macbeth and included Cleopatra in Dryden's *All for Love* and Lady Randolph in the London premiere of Home's *Douglas*, but she was not particularly distinguished in any of these. Her comparative lack of success as a tragedienne owed much to her harsh voice, which made her "the screech owl of tragedy" and to her "declamatory tone and laboured gestures" variously attributed to the adverse influence of Dumesnil and Colley Cibber. These limitations prevented her from being the leading actress of her time, but she was unequalled as a "genteel" comedienne and uniquely successful in male roles.

—Nancy Copeland

———

WOLFIT, (Sir) Donald. British actor-manager. Born Donald Woolfitt in New Balderton, near Newark-on-Trent, Nottinghamshire, England, 20 April 1902. Educated at Magnus School, Newark; St George's School, Eastbourne. Married 1) actress Chris Frances Castor in 1928 (divorced), one daughter; 2) Susan Katherine Anthony in 1934 (divorced), one son, one daughter; 3) Rosalind Iden Payne in 1948. Stage debut, Theatre Royal, York, 1920; appeared with various touring and provincial companies, including the Sheffield Repertory Company, 1920–29; London debut, in Matheson Lang's company at the New Theatre, 1924; actor, Old Vic company, 1929–30; first Canadian tour, under Sir Barry Jackson, 1931–32; first appeared under his own management, 1934; film debut, 1934; actor, Shakespeare Memorial Theatre, Stratford-upon-Avon, 1936 and 1937; founded own touring company to present Shakespeare, 1937; led company on annual spring and autumn tours of Britain and the USA and also staged regular London seasons, 1936–60; staged lunchtime Shakespeare performances during the London Blitz, 1940, and toured with ENSA, 1944–45; New York debut, 1947; did not appear in Shakespeare after 1953, but continued to act under his own and other managements; last stage appearance, Lyric Theatre, London, 1967. Member: Royal General Theatrical Fund (president); Carl Rosa Trust (chairman). CBE (Commander of the British Empire), 1950. Knighted, 1957. Died in London, 17 February 1968.

Roles

1920	Biondello in *The Taming of the Shrew* (Shakespeare), Theatre Royal, York.
1920–22	Lancelot Gobbo in *The Merchant of Venice* (Shakespeare), British provinces.
	Trinculo in *The Tempest* (Shakespeare), British provinces.
	Player and Gravedigger in *Hamlet* (Shakespeare), British provinces.
	William, Touchstone, and Sylvius in *As You Like It* (Shakespeare), British provinces.
	Casca, Pindarus, Citizens, Octavius, and Marullus in *Julius Caesar* (Shakespeare), British provinces.
	Witch and Ross in *Macbeth* (Shakespeare), British provinces.
1922	The Policeman in *Pollock's Predicament* (Gimpson), British provinces.
1923	Puck, Snout, and Snug in *A Midsummer Night's Dream* (Shakespeare), British provinces.
	Rosencrantz and Marcellus in *Hamlet* (Shakespeare), British provinces.
	Prince Escalus, Tybalt, and Apothecary in *Romeo and Juliet* (Shakespeare), British provinces.
	Solanio, Tubal, and the Prince of Morocco in *The Merchant of Venice* (Shakespeare), British provinces.
	Amiens, Corin, Oliver, Duke Frederick, and Adam in *As You Like It* (Shakespeare), British provinces.
	Fabian, Sea Captain, and Antonio in *Twelfth Night* (Shakespeare), British provinces.
	Pedant and Vincentio in *The Taming of the Shrew* (Shakespeare), British provinces.
	Doctor Ross Menteith in *Macbeth* (Shakespeare), British provinces.
	Marullus, Octavius, and Metellus in *Julius Caesar* (Shakespeare), British provinces.
	Sebastian and Adrian in *The Tempest* (Shakespeare), British provinces.
	Mr Jones in *David Garrick* (Robertson), British provinces.
	The Mesmerist in *The Bells* (Lewis), British provinces.
1923–24	Armande St Just in *The Scarlet Pimpernel* (Orczy and Barstow), British provinces.
	A Gentleman in *The Borderer*, British provinces.
1924	Japanese Servant in *Bought and Paid For* (Broadhurst), British provinces.
	Andrea in *The Mask and the Face* (Fernald), British provinces.

Phirous in *The Wandering Jew* (Thurston), New Theatre, London.

1925   A Player in *Carnival* (Hardinge and Lang), New Theatre, London.

Swiss Captain in *The Tyrant* (Sabatini), New Theatre, London.

Joseph in *The Sons of Jacob*, Scala Theatre, London.

The King in *The Rose and the Ring* (Clarke and Slaughter), Repertory Theatre, Manchester.

The Mayor in *Hindle Wakes* (Houghton), Repertory Theatre, Manchester.

1927   Trench in *Widower's Houses* (G. B. Shaw), Repertory Theatre, Sheffield.

Anthony in *Anthony and Anna* (Ervine), Repertory Theatre, Sheffield.

Helmer in *The Doll's House* (Ibsen), Repertory Theatre, Sheffield.

Conway Blayds in *The Truth About Blayds* (Milne), Repertory Theatre, Sheffield.

The Magician in *Magic* (Chesterton), Repertory Theatre, Sheffield.

Zack in *Zack* (Brighouse), Repertory Theatre, Sheffield.

Dearth in *Dear Brutus* (Barrie), Repertory Theatre, Sheffield.

Jones in *The Silver Box* (Galsworthy), Repertory Theatre, Sheffield.

Tom Prior in *Outward Bound* (Vane), Repertory Theatre, Sheffield.

Tessman in *Hedda Gabler* (Ibsen), Repertory Theatre, Sheffield.

Mario in *The Mask and the Face* (Fernald), Repertory Theatre, Sheffield.

The Professor in *The Professor's Love Story* (Barrie), Repertory Theatre, Sheffield.

1928   Fritz Winchelman in *The Enemy* (Pollock), Strand Theatre, London.

Stepan in *Such Men Are Dangerous* (Neumann, adapted by Dukes), Duke of York's Theatre, London.

Abdul in *The Chinese Bungalow* (Osmond and Corbet), Duke of York's Theatre, London.

1929   Professor Drysell in *Smoke Persian* (Willoughby), Everyman Theatre, London.

Sir Anthony Absolute in *The Rivals* (Sheridan), Theatre Royal, Huddersfield.

The Man in *Granite* (Dane), Theatre Royal, Huddersfield.

Grandfather in *The Tragedy of Nan* (Masefield), Theatre Royal, Huddersfield.

Mr Horseforse in *The Torchbearers* (Kelly), Theatre Royal, Huddersfield.

Diego Spina in *Lazarro* (Pirandello), Theatre Royal, Huddersfield.

1929–30   Tybalt in *Romeo and Juliet* (Shakespeare), Old Vic Theatre, London.

Lorenzo in *The Merchant of Venice* (Shakespeare), Old Vic Theatre, London.

Mowbray and the Bishop of Carlisle in *Richard II* (Shakespeare), Old Vic Theatre, London.

Cassius in *Julius Caesar* (Shakespeare), Old Vic Theatre, London; Shakespeare Memorial Theatre, Stratford-upon-Avon, 1936.

Touchstone in *As You Like It* (Shakespeare), Old Vic Theatre, London.

Macduff in *Macbeth* (Shakespeare), Old Vic Theatre, London.

Claudius in *Hamlet* (Shakespeare), Old Vic Theatre, London, and Queen's Theatre, London; Sadler's Wells Theatre, London, 1934.

Dr Purgon in *Le Malade Imaginaire* (Molière), Old Vic Theatre, London.

Ferrovius in *Androcles and the Lion* (G. B. Shaw), Old Vic Theatre, London.

1930   Jaroslav Prus in *The Macropulos Secret* (Čapek), Arts Theatre, London.

Cato in *Julius Caesar, the Dictator* (Poel), Globe Theatre, London.

Father Mackintosh in *Count Albany*, Daly's Theatre, London.

A Mortal in *Brain* (Britton), Savoy Theatre, London.

Roger de Berville in *Topaze* (Pagnol), New Theatre, London.

1930–31   Absalom in *The Witch* (Masefield), Embassy Theatre, London.

Blaskovics in *Lady in Waiting*, Embassy Theatre, London.

Dr Carelli in *Black Coffee* (Christie), Embassy Theatre, London.

Beguildy in *Precious Bane* (Lewis), Embassy Theatre, London.

1931   Maurice Mullins in *A Murder Has Been Arranged* (E. Williams), British tour.

Paul Cortot in *Marriage by Purchase* (Passeur), Embassy Theatre, London.

Solness in *The Master Builder* (Ibsen), Repertory Theatre, Croydon; Newark-on-Trent, Westminster Theatre, London, and Embassy Theatre, London, 1934; Westminster Theatre, London, 1943 and 1948; Playhouse, Salisbury, 1955; tour of South Africa and Rhodesia, 1963.

Pierre in *Even She*, Repertory Theatre, Croydon.

1931–32   Robert Browning in *The Barretts of Wimpole Street* (Besier), Canadian tour; Dublin, 1939.

Ive Varwell in *Yellow Sands* (Phillpotts), Canadian tour.

Young Marlow in *She Stoops to Conquer* (Goldsmith), Canadian tour; Q Theatre, London, and Westminster Theatre, London, 1935.

Mr Coade in *Dear Brutus* (Barrie), Canadian tour.

Shakespeare in *The Dark Lady of the Sonnets* (G. B. Shaw), Canadian tour.

1932   The Doctor and the Parson-Burglar in *Too True to Be Good* (G. B. Shaw), New Theatre, London, and British tour.

1933   Thomas Mowbray in *Richard of Bordeaux* (Daviot), New Theatre, London.

Bassanio in *The Lady of Belmont* (Ervine), Cambridge Theatre, London.

The Officer in *A Dream Play* (Strindberg), Grafton Theatre, London.

Hamlet in *Hamlet* (Shakespeare), Arts Theatre, London; Shakespeare Memorial Theatre, Stratford-upon-Avon, 1936 and 1937, British tour, 1937.

1934   Bluntschli in *Arms and the Man* (G. B. Shaw), Newark-on-Trent.

Malvolio in *Twelfth Night* (Shakespeare), Newark-on-Trent; British tour, 1937.

Morat in *Aureng Zebe* (Dryden), Westminster Theatre, London.

The Corporal in *Josephine* (Barrie), His Majesty's Theatre, London.

André Mérin in *The Sulky Fire*, Gate Theatre, London.

1935   Darrell Blake in *The Moon in the Yellow River* (Johnston), Haymarket Theatre, London, Duchess Theatre, London, and Winter Garden Theatre, London.

Leonard Charteris in *The Philanderer* (G. B. Shaw), Q Theatre, London.

Adolphus Cusins in *Major Barbara* (G. B. Shaw), Q Theatre, London.

Kenyon Mallory in *Pirate Mallory*, Arts Theatre, London.

1936   Roland in *Too Famous for Words*, Repertory Theatre, Croydon.

Lucius Cataline in *Cataline* (Ibsen), Repertory Theatre, Croydon, and Royalty Theatre, London.

Tranio and Petruchio in *The Taming of the Shrew* (Shakespeare), Shakespeare Memorial Theatre, Stratford-upon-Avon.

Orsino in *Twelfth Night* (Shakespeare), Shakespeare Memorial Theatre, Stratford-upon-Avon.

Gratiano in *The Merchant of Venice* (Shakespeare), Shakespeare Memorial Theatre, Stratford-upon-Avon.

Ulysses in *Troilus and Cressida* (Shakespeare), Shakespeare Memorial Theatre, Stratford-upon-Avon.

Don Pedro in *Much Ado About Nothing* (Shakespeare), Shakespeare Memorial Theatre, Stratford-upon-Avon.

Kent in *King Lear* (Shakespeare), Shakespeare Memorial Theatre, Stratford-upon-Avon.

Antony in *Antony and Cleopatra* (Shakespeare), New Theatre, London.

1937   Defending Counsel in *Decree Nisi* (Bates), Embassy Theatre, London.

Sir Percy Blakeney in *The Scarlet Pimpernel* (Orczy and Barstow), Q Theatre, London; Dublin, 1939; British tour, 1941.

Iachimo in *Cymbeline* (Shakespeare), Shakespeare Memorial Theatre, Stratford-upon-Avon; British tour, 1944.

Autolycus in *The Winter's Tale* (Shakespeare), Shakespeare Memorial Theatre, Stratford-upon-Avon.

Touchstone in *As You Like It* (Shakespeare), Shakespeare Memorial Theatre, Stratford-upon-Avon.

Chorus in *Henry V* (Shakespeare), Shakespeare Memorial Theatre, Stratford-upon-Avon.

Ford in *The Merry Wives of Windsor* (Shakespeare), Shakespeare Memorial Theatre, Stratford-upon-Avon.

Bobadil in *Every Man in his Humour* (Jonson), Shakespeare Memorial Theatre, Stratford-upon-Avon.

Macbeth in *Macbeth* (Shakespeare), British tour; Caerphilly Castle, 1939.

Shylock in *The Merchant of Venice* (Shakespeare), British tour.

Petruchio in *The Taming of the Shrew* (Shakespeare), British tour.

1938   Volpone in *Volpone* (Jonson), Westminster Theatre, London; Arts Theatre, Cambridge, 1940; St James's Theatre, London, 1942.

The Judge in *Geneva* (G. B. Shaw), Malvern Festival.

The Earl of Warwick in *Saint Joan* (G. B. Shaw), Malvern Festival.

Alexander in *Alexander*, Malvern Festival.

Cyrano in *Cyrano de Bergerac* (Rostand), British tour.

Benedick in *Much Ado About Nothing* (Shakespeare), British tour.

Othello in *Othello* (Shakespeare), British tour; Connaught Theatre, Worthing, 1952.

The Mad Hatter in *Alice in Wonderland* (Dane, adapted from Carroll), British tour; British tour, 1939.

1939   Romeo in *Romeo and Juliet* (Shakespeare), British tour.

Mark Antony in *Julius Caesar* (Shakespeare), British tour.

1940   Giovanni in *'Tis Pity She's a Whore* (Ford), Arts Theatre, Cambridge.

Falstaff in *The Merry Wives of Windsor* (Shakespeare), Strand Theatre, London; British tour, 1941.

1941   Richard in *Richard III* (Shakespeare), British tour.

Bottom in *A Midsummer Night's Dream* (Shakespeare), British tour.

1942   David Garrick in *The Romance of David Garrick*, British tour.

Lear in *King Lear* (Shakespeare), British tour.

1943   Polidor Argan in *The Imaginary Invalid* (Molière), Westminster Theatre, London.

1946   Iago in *Othello* (Shakespeare), Winter Garden Theatre, London.

Fedya in *Redemption*, British tour.

1948   Dean Swift in *The Solitary Lover* (Clewes), Winter Garden Theatre, London; also directed.

1949   Brutus in *Julius Caesar* (Shakespeare), King's Theatre, Hammersmith, London.

Long John Silver in *Treasure Island* (Fagan, adapted from Stevenson), Fortune Theatre, London; Mermaid Theatre, London, 1965.

1950   Sir Giles Overreach in *A New Way to Pay Old Debts* (Massinger), British tour.

1951   The Governor in *His Excellency* (Christie), Piccadilly Theatre, London.

Tamburlaine in *Tamburlaine the Great* (Marlowe), Old Vic Theatre, London.

Lord Ogleby in *The Clandestine Marriage* (Colman and Garrick), Old Vic Theatre, London; King's Theatre, Hammersmith, London, 1953.

1952   Rear-Admiral Sir Benjamin McGuffie in *Lords of Creation* (Percy and Denham), Vaudeville Theatre, London.

1953   Oedipus in *Oedipus the King* (Sophocles), King's Theatre, Hammersmith, London.

Oedipus in *Oedipus in Exile* (Sophocles), King's Theatre, Hammersmith, London.

Mathias in *The Wandering Jew* (Thurston), King's Theatre, Hammersmith, London.

Sir Peter Teazle in *The School for Scandal* (Sheridan), King's Theatre, Hammersmith, London.

Falstaff in *Henry IV, part 1* (Shakespeare), King's Theatre, Hammersmith, London.

Captain Hook in *Peter Pan* (Barrie), Scala Theatre, London.

1954   Marcus McLeod in *Keep in a Cool Place* (Templeton), Saville Theatre, London.

1955   Father Provincial in *The Strong Are Lonely* (Hochwälder), British tour and Piccadilly Theatre, London; Haymarket Theatre, London, and Edinburgh Festival, 1956.

1957   Don Alvaro in *The Master of Santiago* (Montherlant, translated by Griffin), Lyric Theatre, Hammersmith, London; also directed.

Malatesta in *Malatesta* (Montherlant, translated by Griffin), Lyric Theatre, Hammersmith, London; also co-directed.

1958   Adam in *The Broken Jug* (Kleist), British tour; also directed.

The Maestro in *The Court Singer*, British tour.

1959   Pastor Manders in *Ghosts* (Ibsen), Prince's Theatre, London.

Thomas Gainsborough in *Landscape with Figures*, Olympia Theatre, Dublin.

1960   Reverend Richard Jennings in *Stranger in the Tea*, British tour.

1961   Cromwell in *Cromwell at Drogheda*, Theatre Club, Leatherhead.

1962   Archie Pander-Brown in *Fit to Print* (Dunnett), Duke of York's Theatre, London.

1963   John Gabriel Borkman in *John Gabriel Borkman* (Ibsen), Duchess Theatre, London.

1965   Ezra Fitton in *All in Good Time* (Naughton), Royale Theatre, New York.

Screwtape in *Dear Wormwood* (Forsyth), British tour.

1966   Edward Moulton-Barrett in *Robert and Elizabeth*, Lyric Theatre, London.

Films

Inasmuch, 1934; *Death at Broadcasting House*, 1934; *Drake of England*, 1935; *The Ringer*, 1952; *Pickwick Papers*, 1953; *Isn't Life Wonderful?*, 1953; *Svengali*, 1954; *A Prize of Gold*, 1955; *Guilty*, 1956; *I Accuse*, 1957; *The Blood of the Vampire*, 1958; *Trilby*, 1958; *Room at the Top*, 1959; *The House of the Seven Hawks*, 1959; *The Hands of Orlac*, 1960; *The Mark*, 1961; *Lawrence of Arabia*, 1962; *Dr Crippen*, 1963; *Becket*, 1964; *Ninety Degrees in the Shade*, 1965; *Life at the Top*, 1965; *The Sandwich Man*, 1966; *Decline and Fall*, 1968.

Publications

First Interval (autobiography), 1955.

*

Bibliography

Books:
Ronald Harwood, *The Knight Has Been Unruly*, 1971.

* * *

No actor this century, perhaps, has come closer than Donald Wolfit to the personality, manner, and scale of performance most often associated with his Elizabethan theatrical antecedents Edward Alleyn and Richard Burbage. Seeing him play one of the roles that Alleyn or Burbage created, it was not difficult to believe that Wolfit was the kind of actor that Marlowe and Shakespeare had held in their minds when conjuring up their mightiest and most impassioned lines of rhetoric. Though burly of build, particularly in middle age, and lacking in physical grace, he had an astonishing stage presence, compelling unwavering attention and, at his best, enlivening with an almost hypnotic spell, like a weird and strangely possessed magician, the theatrical imaginations of all who watched. Donald Wolfit was an actor for whom the word "bravura" might have been coined.

His voice was exceptionally versatile, rich in timbre and wide in range, capable in its lowest registers of a silky luxuriance, while at greater volume, with his head flung back, it could emit a piercing nasal whine or a barrel-chested roar of venom, defiance, or pain. Lubricated methodically with douches of Guinness, it was the ideal instrument for the expression of emotion in classical tragedy. Never were the limits of its power exposed; always there seemed more in reserve; but only, as he maintained, because he trained himself unsparingly. This was a level of effort that he expected from others.

Of the 47 years spanned by his career on the stage, nearly 30 were spent under his own management. He was in many ways a "self-made man": he altered the spelling of his surname from that of his family, Woolfitt; he produced the dramas of the classical repertoire without concession to contemporary taste or fashion; he grew up in a small town in Nottinghamshire, the son of a brewery clerk, and was raised to an order of knighthood. Ronald Harwood's biography makes essential reading for all who wish to understand the nature of his genius.

After early experience in repertory and in touring companies operated by the actor-managers Charles Doran, Fred Terry, and Matheson Lang, Wolfit shone at the Old Vic in 1929–30 as Claudius, Cassius, Macduff, Tybalt, and Touchstone, and at Stratford in 1936, where his Hamlet was admired as a robust Elizabethan, aware, as John Masefield observed, that danger attended his every turn. In 1937, however, when the Donald Wolfit Shakespeare Company first took the road, he found his métier, not only as a tragedian of high talent but a responsible servant of the public. It was typified by his "Lunch Time Shakespeare", which he instigated and maintained in central London during the Blitz. Here, at the Strand Theatre, was Shakespeare under fire. Alone in the West End, Wolfit provided spoken drama. He acted imperturbably during the raids and his audiences did not desert him as he stood at his post, centre stage, fulfilling the kind of national service that he was best able to give, hurling back against the onslaught of Hitler's bombs the most stirringly defiant, reverberative declamation of the English iambic pentameter. For hundreds of beleaguered Londoners, unable themselves to return the fire of the enemy invading their skies, Wolfit's lunchtime Shakespeare recitals were, no less than Churchill's broadcasts, the metaphor of their resistance.

Having believed in the need for a National Theatre, Wolfit was pained that when it was finally established he was given no chance to participate. Contrary to a reputation for meanness, he had long been concerned for the well-being of the British theatre, its performers and their dependents: when he died at 65, worn out like Irving by overwork, he had served for more than a decade as the president of the Royal General Theatrical Fund. He believed, too, in the objectives of the nascent Theatre Museum, to which he bequeathed a large collection of historic memorabilia, including treasured artefacts that had been worn or carried in performances by some of the most celebrated tragedians of the past. Wolfit had used them in his, and longed most of all to be counted in the pantheon of great actors.

To James Agate, the influential critic, he was great, but there were many, distracted by the lesser quality of the scenery, costumes, and supporting cast, who doubted it. Kenneth Tynan pointed to two flaws in Wolfit the tragedian: a stubby build and a moonlike face, which "shroud it as he may in whiskers and bedizen it with lines, is like Garrick's, essentially a comic face, a comic mask". Yet at the Scala in 1944 he was accounted the greatest Lear of modern times. As Volpone he was furrily vulpine, Jonsonian both in spirit and temper, salivating with physical pleasure at his machinations. All subsequent Volpones have had to be measured against his. Almost every peak of Shakespearean tragedy and comedy was scaled and when, at the Old Vic in 1951, he tackled Marlowe's Tamburlaine he conjured, wrote T. C. Worsley, "the mightiest spectacle of cruelty and lust ever brought to the English stage".

Wolfit's detractors, however, persistently regarded him as a sub-Victorian figure, bedevilled by actor-manager frailties. Agate, on the contrary, was convinced that in Wolfit the English theatre possessed a classical player in a more ancient mould, less Victorian than Elizabethan. For Agate in the 1940's, there had been no actor since Irving comparable to Wolfit in the great roles of drama.

—Michael Read

WORTH, Irene. US actress. Born in Nebraska, 23 June 1916. Educated at the University of California, Los Angeles, until 1937; studied for the stage in London under Elsie Fogarty, 1944–45. Worked initially as a teacher; stage debut, with US touring company, 1942; New York debut, 1943; settled in London, 1944; London debut, 1946; joined Old Vic company, London, 1951; appeared in inaugural season of the Shakespeare Festival Theatre, Stratford, Ontario, 1953; joined Royal Shakespeare Company, 1960. Recipient: *Daily Mail* National Television Award, 1953–54; British Film Academy Award, 1958; Tony Award, 1965, 1975; Whitbread Anglo-American Award, 1967; Jefferson Award, 1975; Obie Award, 1989. Honorary CBE (Commander of the British Empire).

Roles

1942	Fenella in *Escape Me Never* (Kennedy), British tour.
1943	Cecily Harden in *The Two Mrs Carrolls* (Vale), Booth Theatre, New York.
1946	Elsie in *The Time of Your Life* (Saroyan), Lyric Theatre, Hammersmith, London.
	Annabelle Jones in *Love Goes to Press*, Embassy Theatre, London, and Duchess Theatre, London.
	Donna Pascuala in *Drake's Drum*, Embassy Theatre, London.
	Illona Szabo in *The Play's the Thing* (Molnár), British tour; Lyric Theatre, Hammersmith, London, and St James's Theatre, London, 1947.
1947	Olivia Brown in *Love in Idleness* (Parker and Goodman), Q Theatre, London.
	Iris in *Iris* (Pinero), Q Theatre, London.
	Lady Fortrose in *Home is To-Morrow* (Priestley), British tour; Cambridge Theatre, London, 1948.
1948	Mary Dalton in *Native Son* (Green), Bolton's Theatre, London.
	Lucrece in *Lucrece* (Obey), Bolton's Theatre, London.
	Eileen Perry in *Edward My Son* (Morley and Langley), Lyric Theatre, Hammersmith, London.
1949	Olivia Raines in *Champagne for Delilah*, New Theatre, London.
	Delia Coplestone in *The Cocktail Party* (Eliot), Edinburgh Festival; Henry Miller Theatre, New York, 1950.
1951	Desdemona in *Othello* (Shakespeare), Berlin Festival.
1951–52	Helena in *A Midsummer Night's Dream* (Shakespeare), Old Vic Theatre, London; South African tour, 1953.
	Catherine de Vausselles in *The Other Heart*, Old Vic Theatre, London; South African tour, 1953.
1953	Lady Macbeth in *Macbeth* (Shakespeare), Old Vic Theatre, London; Royal Shakespeare Theatre, 1962.
	Portia in *The Merchant of Venice* (Shakespeare), Old Vic Theatre, London.
	Helena in *All's Well That Ends Well* (Shakespeare), Shakespeare Festival Theatre, Stratford, Ontario.
	Queen Margaret in *Richard III* (Shakespeare), Shakespeare Festival Theatre, Stratford, Ontario.

Frances Farrar in *A Day by the Sea* (Hunter), Haymarket Theatre, London.

1955   Argia in *The Queen and the Rebels* (Betti, translated by Reed), Midland Theatre Company, Coventry, and Haymarket Theatre, London.

Alcestis in *A Life in the Sun* (Wilder), Edinburgh Festival.

1956   Marcelle in *Hotel Paradiso* (Feydeau), Winter Garden Theatre, New York.

1957   Mary Stuart in *Mary Stuart* (Schiller), Phoenix Theatre, New York, Assembly Hall, Edinburgh Festival, and Old Vic Theatre, London.

1958   Sara Callifer in *The Potting Shed* (Greene), Globe Theatre, London.

1959   Rosalind in *As You Like It* (Shakespeare), Shakespeare Festival, Stratford, Ontario.

1960   Albertine Prine in *Toys in the Attic* (Hellman), Hudson Theatre, New York.

1962   Marquise de Merteuil in *The Art of Seduction*, Aldwych Theatre, London.

Goneril in *King Lear* (Shakespeare), Royal Shakespeare Theatre, Stratford-upon-Avon; State Theatre, New York, and European, Soviet and Canadian tours, 1964.

Dr Mathilde von Aahnd in *The Physicists* (Dürrenmatt), Aldwych Theatre, London.

Clodia Pulcher in *The Ides of March*, Haymarket Theatre, London.

1964   Tiny Alice in *Tiny Alice* (Albee), Billy Rose Theatre, New York; Aldwych Theatre, London, 1970.

1966   Hilde Latymer in *A Song at Twilight* (Coward), Queen's Theatre, London.

Anne Hilgay and Anna-Mary Conklin in *Suite in Three Keys* (Coward), London.

Several roles in *Men and Women of Shakespeare*, South American and US tours.

1967   Io in *Prometheus Bound* (Aeschylus), Yale University, New Haven, Connecticut.

Hesione Hushabye in *Heartbreak House* (G. B. Shaw), Chichester Festival and Lyric Theatre, London.

1968   Jocasta in *Oedipus* (Seneca), Old Vic Theatre, London.

1970   Hedda Gabler in *Hedda Gabler* (Ibsen), Stratford, Ontario.

1972   Dora Lang in *Notes on a Love Affair* (Marcus), Globe Theatre, London.

1973   Irina Arkadina in *The Seagull* (Chekhov), Chichester Festival; Greenwich, 1974.

1974   Mrs Alving in *Ghosts* (Ibsen), Chichester Festival.

Gertrude in *Hamlet* (Shakespeare), Chichester Festival.

1975   Princess Kosmonopolis in *Sweet Bird of Youth* (T. Williams), Brooklyn Academy, New York, and Harkness Theatre, New York.

1976   Lina in *Misalliance* (G. B. Shaw), Lake Forest, Illinois.

1977   Madame Ranevskaya in *The Cherry Orchard* (Chekhov), Lincoln Centre, New York.

Kate in *Old Times* (Pinter), Lake Forest, Illinois.

Irene Worth (1979).

1979   Winnie in *Happy Days* (Beckett), Public Theatre, New York, and Newman Theatre, New York.

1980   Ella Rentheim in *John Gabriel Borkman* (Ibsen), Circle in the Square, New York.

1982   Miss Madrigal in *The Chalk Garden* (Bagnold), Roundabout Stage One, New York.

1984   Isabel Hastings Hoyt in *The Golden Age*, Jack Lawrence Theatre, New York.

Volumnia in *Coriolanus* (Shakespeare), National Theatre, London.

Other roles included: *This Way to the Tomb* (Duncan), Mercury Theatre, London, 1946; *Return Journey* (Bennett), British tour, 1948; *After the Season*, Lake Forest, Illinois, 1978; *The Bay at Nice* (Hare), National Theatre, London, 1986; *Wrecked Eggs* (Hare), National Theatre, London, 1986.

Films

One Night with You, 1948; *Secret People*, 1951; *Orders to Kill*, 1958; *The Scapegoat*, 1959; *Seven Seas to Calais*, 1963; *King Lear*, 1971; *Nicholas and Alexandra*, 1971; *Rich Kids*, 1979; *Eyewitness*, 1981; *Deathtrap*, 1982.

Television

The Lady from the Lake, 1953; *The Lady from the Sea*, 1953; *Candida*, 1955; *The Duchess of Malfi*, 1955; *Antigone*, 1955; *Prince Orestes*, 1959; *Variations on a Theme*, 1966; *The Way of the World*; *The Displaced Person*; *Forbidden*, 1985.

Radio

The Cocktail Party, 1951; *Major Barbara*, 1954; *All's Well That Ends Well*, 1954; *The Queen and the Rebels*, 1954; *The Merchant of Venice*, 1958; *Scandal at Coventry*, 1959; *Rosmersholm*, 1959; *Duel of Angels*, 1964.

* * *

Irene Worth is as well-known for her talent as organiser and creative director as for her performances as a tragic and character actress of unusual versatility and power. This was especially noticeable in 1949, when shortly after her London debut in Saroyan's *The Time of Your Life* she made an outstanding contribution to modern verse drama in the role of Celia Coplestone in T. S. Eliot's *The Cocktail Party*. In 1953, after two highly successful years with the Old Vic, she collaborated with Tyrone Guthrie and Alec Guinness in founding the Stratford, Ontario, Festival in Canada. This marked the starting point for one of the most interesting experiments in the North American theatre, influencing production techniques everywhere by its abandonment of the proscenium arch and consistent use of an open, uncurtained stage. In 1970, she returned to Canada to perform a Hedda Gabler rich in venom and self-dramatizing power, and she has had some of her greatest successes in portraying human wickedness on stage. This was especially true of her Goneril in Peter Brook's production of *King Lear* for the Royal Shakespeare Company in 1962, and she also played a passionately unhappy Jocasta in Brooks's controversial production of *Oedipus* at the National in 1968. One of her best parts on the stage was as Coriolanus's awesome and dignified mother Volumnia, whom she played with majestic calm at the National in 1984. In the cinema, she played Elizabeth I in *Seven Seas to Calais* in 1963 and repeated her success as Goneril in the 1971 film of *King Lear*.

Although she excels in serious drama rather than light comedy, Worth made an excellent Madame Arkadina in Chekhov's *The Seagull* in 1973. Her Jocasta in Seneca's version of the Orestes legend in the 1968 National Theatre production was exceptionally powerful, as was also her Mrs Alving in the 1974 Greenwich theatre *Ghosts*. She had already perfected her interpretation of this possessive, anguished mother at Stratford, Ontario, and her reading of the part is regarded as one of her greatest triumphs. She exactly conveyed the double guilt felt by Ibsen's heroine at her failure to live her own life satisfactorily and her terror at having transmitted the unmentionable disease of syphilis to her adored son Oswald. Her ability to dominate the stage with a radiant and rather fearsome authority had earlier been evident, in 1953, when she played Queen Margaret in Shakespeare's *Henry VI* at Stratford, Ontario, but she also made a charmingly assertive Rosalind at the same theatre in 1959. Although she worked less in the cinema than many other actresses of her generation, she did win the British Film Academy Award for her performance as Leonie in the 1958 film *Orders to Kill*, a drama set in occupied France in 1944. She has also had a distinguished career as a television actress, and received awards for her performance in *The Lady from the Lake* and *The Lady from the Sea* in 1954. She has played all the great classic roles, and her fame in her native USA was recognised by the Obie Award for Sustained Achievement in the Theatre in 1989.

—Philip Thody

Z

ZACCONI, Ermete. Italian actor–manager. Born in Montecchio, Reggio-Emilia, Italy, 14 September 1857. Married 1) Rosalia Dominici in 1909; 2) Ines Cristina. Stage debut, as a child actor with his father's company; subsequently appeared in the Neapolitan dialect touring troupe of Calia and with various touring companies; actor with the troupe of Giovanni Emanuel, 1884–86, and then with Desare Rossi and Virginia Marini; founded his own company, initially in collaboration with Libero Pilotto, 1894; acted in Vienna, 1897; toured Europe and Russia, 1898; toured Italy with Eleonora Duse, 1899 and 1901; retired from the stage, 1939; continued to direct and to appear in films well into his eighties. Légion d'honneur, 1911. Died in Viareggio, Italy, 14 October 1948.

Productions

As actor:

Boris in *Tsar Boris* (Tolstoy); Corrado in *La morte civile* (Giacometti); Hamlet in *Amleto* (Shakespeare); Henschel in *Il vetturale Henschel* (Hauptmann); Krampton in *Il Collega Krampton* (Hauptmann); Lambertini in *Il Cardinale Lambertini* (Testoni); Lear in *Re Lear* (Shakespeare); Lorenzaccio in *Lorenzaccio* (Musset); Macbeth in *Macbeth* (Shakespeare); Oswald in *Spettri* (Ibsen, adapted by Marini); Othello in *Otello* (Shakespeare); Petruchio in *Il bisbetica delle domata* (Shakespeare); Saul in *Saul* (Alfieri); Wangel in *La donne del mare* (Ibsen).

Other roles included:

L'abate Galliani (Nulli); *Don Abbondio* (Berrini); *Gli affari sono affari* (Mirabeau); *Alla città de Roma* (Rovetta); *Al telefono* (De Lorde); *L'amico delle donne* (Dumas fils); *Anime solitaire* (Hauptmann); *L'apologia di Socrate* (Plato); *L'Aretino* (Nulli); *L'assomoir* (Zola); *Bartel Turasel* (Langmann); *Il bell'Apollo* (Praga); *La bottega del caffè* (Zacconi); *Il brutto e le belle* (Lopez); *Il cantico dei cantici* (Cavallotti); *Il Caporale* (Testoni); *Il capro espiatorio* (Walter and Stein); *La casa dei fanciulli* (Antonelli); *Casa Rosmer* (Ibsen); *Celeste* (Leopoldo); *La città morta* (D'Annunzio); *La colpa vendica la colpa* (Giacometti); *Il corriere di Lione* (D'Aubigny); *Cravatta nera* (Ruggi); *Cristo all festa di Purim* (Bovio); *Il critone* (Plato); *Il cuore e il mondo* (Ruggi); *Il cuore rivelatore* (Poe); *La danza macabre* (Camillo); *Demi-monde* (Dumas fils); *Il diavolo* (Molnár); *Il diritti dell'anima* (Giacosa); *Il diritto di vivere* (Bracco); *I disonesti* (Rovetta); *Don Buonaparte* (Forzano); *La donna romantica* (Castelvecchio); *Don Pietro Caruso* (Bracco); *Il Dottor Muller* (Scalinger); *Il duello* (Ferrari); *Le due orfanelle* (D'Ennery); *I due sargenti* (D'Aubigny, translated by Zacconi); *L'Erede* (Praga); *Fanfulla da Lodi* (Nulli); *Fedone* (Plato); *La figlia unica* (Cicconi); *Il focalare* (Gherardi); *La forza della coscienza* (Gualtieri); *I fourchambault* (Augier); *Francesca da Rimini* (Pellico); *Frate Agostino* (Costamagna); *Il Fratello d'armi* (Giacosa); *Fuorimoda* (Lopez and Possenti); *Garibaldi* (Tumiati); *Le gelosie di Lindoro* (Goldoni); *Giacchino Rossini* (Testoni); *Gian Gabriele Borkmann* (Ibsen); *La Gioconda* (D'Annunzio); *Giorgio Gandi* (Leopoldo); *Giramondo* (Cantini); *Il giudice* (Térésah); *La gloria* (D'Annunzio); *La grande ombra* (Giannino); *Gringoire* (De Bainville); *I guarany* (Barbieri, translated by Zacconi); *La guerra* (Lopez); *Innanzi il levar del sole* (Hauptmann); *L'Interdizione* (Savarese); *L'intrusa* (Maeterlinck); *Jacqueline* (Guitry); *Kean* (Dumas père); *La legge del cuore* (Dominici); *Lontananza* (D'Ambra); *Luce* (Lopez); *Maschere* (Bracco); *Il matrimonio di Figaro* (Beaumarchais); *Messalina* (Cossa); *La meteora* (Tumiati); *Mezzalana* (Ruggi); *Miserabili* (Barbieri); *La moglie di Claudio* (Dumas fils); *Monaldesca* (Somma); *Le montagne* (Romualda); *Morella* (Poe); *Napoleone* (D'Avoine); *Un nemico del popolo* (Ibsen); *Nerone* (Cossa); *Il nuovo idolo* (De Curel); *Occhio di pollo* (Ruggi); *L'onda* (D'Avoine); *Oreste* (Alfieri); *L'ostacolo* (Daudet); *Il padre* (Strindberg); *Il padre prodigo* (Dumas fils); *Il padrone delle ferriere* (Ohnet); *Il pane altrui* (Turgenev); *Paolo* (Bovio); *La parola* (Calandra); *Perla* (Scalinger); *Per l'onore* (Sanfelice); *Pia de' Tolomei* (Carlo); *Il piccolo Eyolf* (Ibsen); *Il piccolo re* (Romualda); *Pietro il grande* (Forzano; *Più che l'amore* (D'Annunzio); *Il poeta* (Rovetta); *La porta chiusa* (Praga); *La posta suprema* (Lopez); *La potenza delle tenebre* (Tolstoy); *Prete pero* (Niccodemi); *La primavera del '99* (Calandra); *Principio di Secolo* (Rovetta); *Un quadro di signorelli* (Phillips); *Realtà* (Rovetta); *Resa a discrezione* (Giacosa); *Romanticismo* (Rovetta); *Romeo e Giulietta* (Shakespeare); *I Rusteghi* (Goldoni); *Lo schiaffo della gloria* (Soldani); *La scuola della maldicenza* (Sheridan); *Il Signor D'Aldrè* (Garzes); *La signorina Giulia* (Strindberg); *Solitudine* (D'Ambra); *Termidore* (Sardou); *Il tessitore* (Tumiati); *Tormento* (Ciaceri); *Il tramonto di un re* (Berrini); *Il trionfo* (Bracco); *Il trionfo d'amore* (Giacosa); *Tristi amori* (Giacosa); *Il tuo sangue* (Bataille); *Tutte si accomoda* (Pirandello); *L'utopia* (Butti); *I vassalli* (Castelveccio); *Il ventaglio* (Goldoni); *La vergine del Lippi* (Augusto); *La villa dei gigli* (Zacconi and Gherardini); *La vista degli altri* (Rampolla); *Le vittime del passato* (Ruggi).

Films

Lo scomparso, 1912; *Il Padre*, 1912; *L'emigrante*, 1915; *Gli spettri*, 1917; *Il Cardinale Lambertini*, 1934; *Cuor di vagabondo*, 1936; *Un colpa divento*, 1936; *Pioggia d'estate*, 1937; *La perle della corona*, 1937; *Processo e morte di Socrate*, 1940; *L'orizzonte di pinto*, 1941; *Don Buonaparte*, 1941; *Il Conte di Monte Cristo*, 1943; *La forza della conscienza*.

Publications

Ricordi e battaglie, 1946.

*

Bibliography

Books:
Polese Santernecchi Enrico, *Ermete Zacconi*, Milan, 1898.
G. V. Cenni, *Arte e vita prodigiosa di Ermete Zacconi*, Milan, 1945.
Leonardo Bragaglia, *Ermete Zacconi e il naturalismo scenico*, Rome, 1973.
Guiseppe Pardieri, *Ermete Zacconi*, Bologna.

* * *

Ermete Zacconi was born to the profession, and two influences were perhaps the most formative: his early touring as a male juvenile lead in companies playing stock romantic drama, and the two years he spent with the great Italian realistic actor Giovanni Emanuel. These helped to foster the romantic naturalism that characterised many of Zacconi's interpretations. He was drawn early to the late 19th-century naturalism of Ibsen and the Italian verists, and after he himself became a capo comico in 1894 included their work in his repertory. Although some of his greatest successes were in commercial stage vehicles calculated to appeal to middle-class audiences, and he was long remembered for his playing in such actor-manager pieces as Alfredo Testoni's *Il Cardinale Lambertini*, he helped to pioneer in Italy a wide range of serious drama, from Tolstoy and Hauptmann to Giacosa and Praga. Although financial exigencies obliged him to include in his repertory many standard romantic pieces, it is scarcely an exaggeration to say that the example of Antoine's Théâtre Libre was strongly felt in the work he was most keen to champion. He was no less pioneering in his Shakespearean interpretations, performing not only the major tragic roles, and excelling as King Lear and Othello, parts already well established on the Italian stage, but also the much less familiar comic parts, like that of Petruchio in *The Taming of the Shrew*. As this last suggests, he was a fairly versatile player, in his early years at least perhaps as good in comedy as in more serious social and domestic drama, achieving some success in Beaumarchais and Goldoni.

Zacconi had a good voice and an imposing presence, which held him in good stead in stock parts, but these qualities were reinforced by what he had acquired from his training under Emanuel: an emphasis in the preparation and interpretation of a role on truth to what was observed as natural in everyday life, on making a part a persuasive reading of an individual temperament, on the accumula-

tion of psychologically plausible detail and on the conceiving of a part as itself a unity, yet an element too in a unified whole. His mode of naturalistic playing in the character of Corrado in Giacometti's *La morte civile* offended the great mid-century player Tommaso Salvini, one of whose stage vehicles it had been. By 1918, Zacconi's acting was perhaps beginning to look somewhat passé, and his playing of Hamlet and Macbeth issued in dispute with the critic Silvio D'Amico. Yet if we bear in mind that Zacconi's stage career spanned some 75 years — years that saw the most radical changes in Italian society and theatre — old-fashioned though his manner came to seem, it is a measure of his innate authority as actor and manager that his work continued to be popular and artistically engaging through to his retirement in 1939, notwithstanding that the size of his repertory by late 19th and early 20th century standards was comparatively small and he added little to it in the 1920's and 1930's. His bias to strong naturalism, together with his presence and voice, enabled him to move from stage to screen, and to survive the shift in film technology from the silent to the sound picture. He recreated on the screen a number of his stage successes, and after he had retired from the theatre continued to act in films in Italy and France.

—Kenneth Richards

———

ZAVADSKY, Yuri (Aleksandrovich). Soviet director, actor and teacher. Born in Moscow, 30 June 1894. Trained for the stage at the theatre studio of Evgeny Vakhtangov, Moscow, from 1915. Married 1) actress Vera Maretskaya; 2) ballerina Galina Ulanova. Began career as actor under Vakhtangov, 1915; subsequently worked with the Moscow Art Theatre under Stanislavsky, 1924–31, and also directed at his own studio, 1924–36; chief director, Central Theatre of the Red Army, Moscow, 1932–35; director, Gorky State Theatre, Rostov, 1936–40; director, Mossoviet Theatre, Moscow, 1940–77; also taught at the National Institute of Theatre Art (GITIS), from 1940; director, GITIS, 1954–58. Professor, State Institute, 1947. Recipient: Stalin Prize, 1946, 1951; Lenin Prize, 1951, 1965; two Orders of Lenin; Order of the Red Banner of Labour. People's Artist of the USSR, 1948. Died in Moscow, 5 April 1977.

Principal productions

As actor:

1921	St Anthony in *Le Miracle de Saint-Antoine* (Maeterlinck), Third Studio, Art Theatre, Moscow.
1922	Calaf in *Princess Turandot* (Gozzi), Third Studio, Art Theatre, Moscow.
1925	Chatsky in *Gore ot uma* [Woe from Wit] (Griboyedov), Art Theatre, Moscow.
	Prince Trubetskoy in *Nicolai I i dekabristy* [Nicholas I and the Decembrists] (Kugel), Art Theatre, Moscow.
1926	Almaviva in *Le Mariage de Figaro* (Beaumarchais), Art Theatre, Moscow.

As director:

1924   *On ne badine pas avec l'amour* (Musset), Zavadsky Studio, Moscow.

     Zhenitba [The Wedding] (Gogol), Central Theatre of the Red Army, Moscow.

1924–36   *Volpone* (Jonson), Zavadsky Studio, Moscow.

     The Devil's Disciple (G. B. Shaw), Zavadsky Studio, Moscow.

1934   *Gibel eskadry* [The Destruction of the Squadron] (Korneichuk), Central Theatre of the Red Army, Moscow.

1936–40   *Lyubov Iarovaia* [Schoolmistress Iarovaia] (Trenev), Gorky Theatre, Rostov.

     The Taming of the Shrew (Shakespeare), Gorky Theatre, Rostov.

1940   *La Locandiera* (Goldoni), Mossoviet Theatre, Moscow.

1941   *Tania* (Arbuzov), Mossoviet Theatre, Moscow.

1942   *Russkie liudi* [Russian People] (Simonov), Alma Ata.

1943   *Nashestvie* [Invasion] (Leonov), Alma Ata.

1950   *Rassvet nad Moskvoy* [Dawn over Moscow] (Surov), Mossoviet Theatre, Moscow.

1952   *Maskarad* [Masquerade] (Lermontov), Mossoviet Theatre, Moscow.

1957   *Othello* (Shakespeare), Mossoviet Theatre, Moscow.

     The Merry Wives of Windsor (Shakespeare), Mossoviet Theatre, Moscow.

     Dali neogladnye [As Far as the Eye Can See] (Virta), Mossoviet Theatre, Moscow.

     Krylia [Wings] (Korneichuk), Mossoviet Theatre, Moscow.

     Personalnoe delo [A Personal Affair] (Shtein), Mossoviet Theatre, Moscow.

     Vechno zhivye [The Cranes are Flying] (Rozov), Mossoviet Theatre, Moscow.

1960   *Vishnevy sad* [The Cherry Orchard] (Chekhov), Theatre Institute, New York.

1964   *Maskarad* [Masquerade] (Lermontov), Mossoviet Theatre, Moscow.

1967   *The Merry Wives of Windsor* (Shakespeare), Mossoviet Theatre, Moscow.

     Maskarad [Masquerade] (Lermontov), Mossoviet Theatre, Moscow.

1969   *Petersburgskie snovideniia* [Petersburg Dreams] (Dostoevsky, adapted from *Crime and Punishment*), Mossoviet Theatre, Moscow.

1973   *Posledniaia zhertva* [The Final Sacrifice] (Ostrovsky), Mossoviet Theatre, Moscow.

Other productions included: *Leotom nebo vysokoye* [In Summer the Sky is High] (Virta); *Meschane* [The Philistines] (Gorky); *Moskovy kharakter* [The Character of Moscow] (Sofronov); *Mstsislav Udaloy* (Prut); *Na beregu Nevy* [On the Banks of the Neva] (Trenev); *Russky vopros* [The Russian Question] (Simonov); *Shtorm* [Storm] (Bill-Belotserkovsky); *Volki i ovtsy* [Wolves and Sheep] (Ostrovsky); *Vragi* [The Enemies] (Gorky); *Vstrecha v temnote* [Meeting in the Dark] (Knorre); *Zakon chesti* [The Law of Honour] (Shteyn).

Publications

O vneshem oformlenii obraza [Creating the Outward Appearance of the Character], 1934; *Ob iskusstve teatra* [On the Art of the Theatre], 1965; *Uchitelia i ucheniki* [Teachers and Pupils], 1975; *Rozhdenie spektaklia* [A Show Is Born], 1975.

* * *

Yuri Zavadsky was the eldest of three children in the family of a well-to-do Moscow cloth merchant. Along with three generations of musically talented relations Yuri too studied music. He took art lessons from the painter Valentin Serov. He graduated from a top Moscow preparatory school, where he stood out in studies and for his artistic talents in amateur theatricals, which his school staged with some professional assistance. Though Yuri went on to study law, he continued studying art too, but then quit both to join the highly unusual theatre studio of Evgeny Vakhtangov. Evidently he failed the audition as an actor, but Vakhtangov nevertheless admitted him for his great height and good looks, promising to employ him only as stage designer. After strict drill, though, Zavadsky found himself acting leads.

Vakhtangov's own genius led him to constant innovative experimentation, sometimes in a second production of the same play in a different manner. So his studio actor Zavadsky went from one extreme to another in the leads he played, St Anthony in Maurice Maeterlinck's *Le Miracle de Saint-Antoine* and the commedia dell'arte figure Calaf in Carlo Gozzi's *Princess Turandot*. Communal living and the commitment to being a good person earned the Vakhtangov Studio the reputation of a monastery. Zavadsky directed the first act of the 1920 *St Anthony* so as to let the fresh air of revolution into the cloistered studio. When he showed it to Vakhtangov, who had had to spend time at a sanatorium, the master agreed with his initiative and completed the production to show the bourgeois relatives of the deceased stripped of realistic detail and streamlined to the point of caricature. Zavadsky as Anthony towered with his great physical height and with psychological intensity, arms extended on high, to challenge the dead aunt to rise from the dead — altogether an expressionist interpretation.

Unlike his St Anthony, Zavadsky and his fellow actors each played against the role in Gozzi's *Turandot*. Not fantastic costumes, but black evening dress would place the actors in reality, while a single property would mark the character each played, like the turban Zavadsky-Calaf wore along with his tuxedo and black tie. The characters' actions and speeches were addressed to the audience, and when each had finished, he sometimes sat down and watched his fellows while eating an orange. That is, the actor did not so much enter into the role as show off the unreality of his merry play.

After Vakhtangov's death the former pupil made his professional debut as director in his deceased teacher's studio with Nikolai Gogol's *Zhenitba* (*The Wedding*), about the escape of a reluctant bridegroom before the marriage. However, Zavadsky overloaded his staging with suggestions of a metaphysical Gogol through ghostly lighting and funereal music, and the production unequivocally failed.

A scene from *Petersburg Dreams,* directed by **Yuri Zavadsky** (1969).

While the neophyte director Zavadsky had sought exaggerated clarity of outline, at the Moscow Art Theatre, of which he became a member for the next half-dozen years, he was coached by Stanislavsky towards inner depth of feeling in successful acting roles: Chatsky in Alexander Griboyedov's *Woe from Wit* and Almaviva in Beaumarchais' *Le Mariage de Figaro* among them.

In a studio of his own, Zavadsky produced some of the international repertory: Alfred de Musset's *On ne badine pas avec l'amour,* Ben Jonson's *Volpone,* George Bernard Shaw's *The Devil's Disciple.* He also took on the chief directorship of a house for mass audiences that had previously had only guest directors, the Central Theatre of the Red Army, and raised it to high standards, as with Alexander Korneichuk's *Destruction of the Squadron.*

Unhappy with the large but poorly equipped building of the Red Army Theatre, Zavadsky accepted the direction of another major house, but in the provinces — the Gorky Theatre of Rostov-on-the-Don. Here again he staged both classics and the contemporary Soviet repertory, thus Konstantin Trenev's *Lyubov Iarovaia* about the Communist victory in the Civil War of the early 1920's and Shakespeare's *The Taming of the Shrew.* In 1940 he was able to return to Moscow, where he received a renovated building and a company, the Mossoviet Theatre, with which he worked imaginatively in an eclectic repertory until his death.

Trained in clarity and outward theatricality by Vakhtangov, the actor Zavadsky learned under Stanislavsky to project inner feeling along with his native external elegance. Zavadsky's direction, like his choice of repertory, was sophisticated and varied. His artist's talent helped in the staging of some memorably colourful, vivid productions, one of which was staged twice (1952 and 1964) very much after the precedent of Meyerhold's 1917 masterpiece, Mikhail Lermontov's *Maskarad.* Zavadsky achieved national acclaim with Soviet awards, as well as international renown with two invitations to direct in the USA, though he failed to make the journey the second time. For over four decades he was a prominent figure in the Soviet theatre in the four functions of designing, acting, directing and teaching.

—Marjorie L. Hoover

ZEFFIRELLI, Franco (Corsi). Italian director and designer. Born in Florence, 12 February 1923. Educated at the Liceo Artistic, Florence; School of Agriculture, Florence. Stage debut, as an actor with the Morelli Stopa company, 1945; began career as a set designer, 1945, and as a costume designer, 1949; worked as assistant to Luchino Visconti and also designed films by Michelangelo Antonioni and Vittorio de Sica; debut as director with the Givi-

Ferzetti-Cimara company, 1951; first of many productions as director and designer at La Scala, Milan, 1953; worked at the Old Vic Theatre, London, and with the National Theatre, London, at Glyndebourne and in New York; also acclaimed as a film director from the late 1960's; entered politics as candidate for Forza Italia, 1994. Recipient: Prix des Nations, 1976.

Productions

As set designer:
1945   *La Patente* (Pirandello), Florence.
        L'Uomo corruppe Hadleyburg (Twain), Florence.
1949   *Un Tram che si chiamo desiderio* (T. Williams), Teatro Eliseo, Roma; also designed costumes.
        Rosalinda o Come vi piace (Shakespeare), Teatro Eliseo, Rome; also designed costumes.
        Troilo e Cressida (Shakespeare), Boboli Gardens, Florence.
1952   *Le Tre Sorelle* (Chekhov), Teatro Eliseo, Rome; also designed costumes.
1953   *L'Italiana in Algeri* (Rossini), La Scala, Milan; also designed costumes.
1957   *Linda di Chamounix* (Donizetti), Teatro Massimo, Palermo; also designed costumes.

Other productions as set designer included: *Livietta e Tracollo* (Pergolesi), 1946; *Serenata a tre* (Vivaldi), 1947; *Il Giocatore* (Orlandini), 1949; *La Zingara* (Capua), 1950; *Le Serve rivali* (Traetta), 1953.

As director and set designer:
1950   *Lulù* (Bertolazzi), Compagnia Gioi-Ferzetti-Cimarci; also designed costumes.
1954   *La Cenerentola* (Rossini), La Scala, Milan; also designed costumes.
1955   *L'Elisir d'amore* (Donizetti), La Scala, Milan; also designed costumes.
        L'Italiana in Algeri (Rossini), Festival of Holland, Amsterdam; also designed costumes.
        Il Turco in Italia (Rossini), La Scala, Milan; also designed costumes.
1956   *Falstaff* (Verdi), Festival of Holland, Amsterdam; also designed costumes.
        Carmen (Bizet), Carlo Felice, Genoa; also designed costumes.
1957   *La Buona figliola* (Piccinni), Piccola Scala, Milan.
        Rigoletto (Verdi), Carlo Felice, Genoa; also designed costumes.
1958   *Don Giovanni* (Mozart), Teatro di Corte, Naples; also designed costumes.
        Il Giuoco del barone (Bucchi), Teatro Caio Melisso, Spoleto; also designed costumes.
        Lo Frate 'nnamurato (Pergolesi), Teatro Caio Melisso, Spoleto; also designed costumes.
        La Traviata (Verdi), Civic Opera, Dallas; also designed costumes.
        L'Italiana in Algeri (Rossini), Civic Opera, Dallas; also designed costumes.
        Norma (Bellini), Teatro Massimo, Palermo; also designed costumes.

1959   *Don Pasquale* (Donizetti), Piccola Scala, Milan; also designed costumes.
        Falstaff (Verdi), Tel-Aviv, Israel; also designed costumes.
        Lucia di Lammermoor (Donizetti), Covent Garden, London; also designed costumes.
        La Forza delle circostanze (Henze), Festival of Two Worlds, Spoleto; also designed costumes.
        Cavelleria Rusticana (Mascagni), Covent Garden, London; also designed costumes.
        I Pagliacci (Leoncavallo), Covent Garden, London, also designed costumes; revived there, 1973.
        La Figlia del reggimento (Donizetti), Teatro Massimo, Palermo.
        Il Barbiere di Siviglio (Rossini), Carlo Felice, Genoa.
        Il Trovatore (Verdi), Carlo Felice, Genoa; also designed costumes.
        L'Elisir d'amore (Donizetti), Glyndebourne, Sussex; also designed costumes.
1960   *Le Astuzie femminili* (Cimarosa), Piccola Scala, Milan.
        Alcina (Handel), La Fenice, Venice.
        Griselda (Scarlatti), Teatro Massimo, Catania; also designed costumes.
        Orfeo (Monteverdi), Teatro della Cometa, Rome.
        Euridice (Peri), Boboli Gardens, Florence.
        Falstaff (Verdi), Teatro Massimo, Palermo, and Covent Garden, London; also designed costumes.
        Romeo and Juliet (Shakespeare), Old Vic Theatre, London.
1961   *I Puritani* (Bellini), Teatro Massimo, Palermo.
        Rigoletto (Verdi), Teatro Massimo, Palermo, and Civic Opera, Dallas; also designed costumes.
        Don Giovanni (Mozart), Covent Garden, London, and Civic Opera, Dallas; also designed costumes.
        Othello (Shakespeare), Royal Shakespeare Theatre, Stratford-upon-Avon.
        Thais (Massenet), Civic Opera, Dallas.
1962   *The Great Gala*, Albert Hall, London; also designed costumes.
        Alcina (Handel), Covent Garden, London.
1964   *Hamlet* (Shakespeare), Old Vic Theatre, London.
        After the Fall (Miller), Rome.
        Falstaff (Verdi), Metropolitan Opera House, New York.
        Who's Afraid of Virginia Woolf? (Albee), Paris; Milan, 1965.
        Tosca (Puccini), Covent Garden, London.
        Rigoletto (Verdi), Covent Garden, London; revived there, 1966 and 1973.
1965   *La Lupa* (Verga), Rome.
        Much Ado About Nothing (Shakespeare), National Theatre, London.
        The Taming of the Shrew (Shakespeare), National Theatre, London.
1967   *Black Comedy* (Shaffer), Rome.

Franco Zeffirelli (1981).

	A Delicate Balance (Albee), Rome.
1971	*Missa Solemnis* (Beethoven), San Pietro, Rome.
1972	*Don Giovanni* (Mozart), Staatsoper, Vienna.
	Otello (Verdi), Metropolitan Opera House, New York.
1973	*Antony and Cleopatra*, Metropolitan Opera House, New York.
	Saturday, Sunday, Monday (De Filippo), National Theatre, London.
1975	*La città morta* (D'Annunzio), Florence.
1976	*Otello* (Verdi), La Scala, Milan.
1977	*Filumena* (De Filippo), Lyric Theatre, London.
1981	*La Bohème* (Puccini), Metropolitan Opera House, New York.
1983	*Turandot* (Puccini), La Scala, Milan.
1985	*Swan Lake* (Tchaikovsky), La Scala, Milan.
	Rigoletto (Verdi), Metropolitan Opera House, New York.
1987	*Turandot* (Puccini), Metropolitan Opera House, New York.
1992	*Don Carlos* (Verdi), Metropolitan Opera House, New York.
	Cerco d'autore (Pirandello), National Theatre, London.

Other productions as director and set designer have included: *La Favola di Orfeo* (Casella), 1959; *Giovedì grasso*, 1959; *Aida* (Verdi), 1963.

Productions as director only have included: *Vivì* (Mannino), 1957; *Mignon* (Thomas), 1958; *Don Pasquale* (Donizetti), 1959; *Boris Godunov* (Mussorgsky), 1959.

Films

The Taming of the Shrew, 1966; *Florence, Days of Destruction*, 1966; *Romeo and Juliet*, 1968; *Fratello Sole, Sorella Luna*, 1973; *The Champ*, 1979; *Endless Love*, 1981; *La Traviata*, 1982; *Cavalleria Rusticana*, 1983; *Otello*, 1986; *The Young Toscanini*, 1988; *Hamlet*, 1990; *Sparrow*, 1994.

Television

Gesù di Nazareth, 1977.

Publications

Zeffirelli by Zeffirelli, 1986.

* * *

Franco Zeffirelli is one of the world's most sought-after designers and directors of plays, opera and film. He is associated with lavish, visually stunning productions. His set and costume designs have won widespread praise; he has produced plays by Verga in Rome, Shakespeare at the Old Vic and Musset at the Comédie-Française. Many of the operas he has mounted stand as landmarks of their kind.

He was working as a set painter when he met Luchino Visconti, who gave him small parts and his first opportunities to design (for *A Streetcar Named Desire* and *Troilus and Cressida*, for example). The first work he directed himself was Bertolazzi's *Lulu*, an Italian play similar to the better known drama by Wedekind. It was a flop — but then came an unexpected break. He was invited to direct Rossini's *The Italian Girl in Algiers* at La Scala. Its success led to further invitations, which included doing Donizetti's *L'Elisir d'amore* and Rossini's *Il Turco in Italia* with Maria Callas, then at the height of her powers. It is impossible to divorce his work for the opera from his work for the theatre.

Zeffirelli's early years in comic opera developed one of the characteristics of his style: an unrelenting, almost exhausting sense of ever-changing fun, bordering on slapstick. The theatrical production that best illustrates this was the *Much Ado About Nothing* that he mounted for the National Theatre in 1965. Instead of concentrating on the sophisticated wit of the central pair, his mock-Sicilian production emphasized visual confusion. Not Shakespeare, the critics cried, but Peter Roberts had to concede Zeffirelli's "ability to persuade English actors to fling their inhibitions into the orchestra pit and to strut, swagger and reel about the stage with their hands gesticulating freely in a way that would have brought a worried frown to the brow of the old generation of RADA teachers". He brought a similar breath of fresh air to *The Taming of the Shrew*, which he filmed immediately afterwards with Richard Burton and Elizabeth Taylor. Whatever he touches, he invigorates and injects with life.

This quality was well defined by Caryl Brahms, who closed her otherwise unfavourable review of the *Romeo and Juliet* that he did for the Old Vic in 1960 by admitting that she enjoyed its visual impact: "He has a way with visuals, a gift for filling the moment of significance with sound, for orchestrating sight, which is rare, and valuable and quite uniquely personal". He was criticized for concentrating too much on successive vignettes and missing the beauty of the poetry. His Romeo and Juliet were young, and terribly in love: that was all — as it was in the later film. It was, however, fresh, even moving: it made excellent theatre because his instinct is first and last that action should speak for itself. The sheer exuberance of his productions invariably carries the audience along. He has little patience with the fashion for discovering ever more relevant social or psychological significance in a work. His love of theatre is a love of "beauty, drama and emotion" for their own sake. The vignettes cumulate, and can be either moving, as in his film of *La Traviata*, or devastatingly funny, as in his 1973 production for the National Theatre of Eduardo de Filippo's *Saturday, Sunday, Monday*, in which Laurence Olivier gave one of his finest cameo roles.

The critics were even more unkind to his next film, *Brother Sun, Sister Moon*, about the life of St Francis of Assisi, which though beautifully filmed makes no pretence of having any interpretative depth. But Zeffirelli's work covers a much broader range than many critics give him credit for. He learned from Visconti how to handle the darker side of social realism. In Paris, he scored a tremendous success with *Who's Afraid of Virginia Woolf?*, where the emotions reached (and even went beyond) boiling point, and his classic Italian production of Verga's *La Lupa* (*The She-Wolf*), with Anna Magnani, was equally rivetting.

The style that came to be associated with him — "lavish in scale and unashamedly theatrical" — was established by his 1963 production of *Aida*. Its 600 singers and dancers, the gigantic idols and the ten horses that appeared were a forecast of things to come. Many decried such opulence, but as one critic wrote of the *La Bohème* that he mounted for the Metropolitan Opera in New York and which took extravagance to its limit: "The gasps of disbelief as the curtain rose were replaced with such sustained applause that half a minute of music was lost". At a time when the combination of soaring production costs and the "zeitgeist" favoured small casts and kitchen-sink drama, Zeffirelli has championed theatre as a magnificent spectacle.

He researched a work carefully, and his aim is to produce (as with his *Aida*, whose designs were a recreation of the sets and costumes of 1871) a work that he feels is akin to the artist's original concept. When invited to direct *Swan Lake*, he did away with the tutus and recreated the powerful symbolist drama that he thought Tchaikovsky wanted. Beneath this conservatism, however, lies a considerable talent for innovation. It may seem obvious to do *Romeo and Juliet* with a cast of very young principals, but it changed people's concepts of the play. His *Swan Lake* horrified a number of balletomanes, but it made better drama than the usual versions. To overcome the static quality of Handel, he mounted *Alcina* as a play within a play. By more than doubling the number of settings in *La Traviata*, and producing it as an extended flashback, he created a dynamic new reading of a classic.

Zeffirelli has been privileged to work with some of the finest talent of his time in the theatre, in film and in opera. Inevitably, he has had some failures. But few directors can boast so many triumphs in such a range of genres. He once wrote: "I have found it an irritating irony that those who espouse populist political views often want art to be 'difficult'; and that the supposedly *avant-garde*, while being politically left-wing, has often proved culturally elitist. Yet I who favour the Right in our democracy, believe passionately in a broad culture made accessible to as many as possible". His *Romeo and Juliet* introduced many young people to Shakespeare, his *Jesus of Nazareth* was watched by an enormous audience throughout the world and his recent opera films of *La Traviata* and *Otello* have shown how this once dusty genre makes spectacular drama.

—Terence Dawson

NOTES ON ADVISERS AND CONTRIBUTORS

AARSETH, Asbjørn. Professor of Scandinavian literature, University of Bergen, Norway. Former editor of *Edda: Scandinavian Journal of Literary Research*, 1986-90. Author of *Peer Gynt*, 1975; *"Peer Gynt" and "Ghosts"* (Text and Performance series), 1989; and of books in Norwegian on the Bergen National Theatre (1901-31), 1969; applied narratology, 1976; realism in Norwegian literary history, 1981; and Romanticism in Scandinavian literary history, 1985. **Essays:** Bjørn Bjørnson; Johannes Finne Brun.

ALLEN, David. Essays: John Barrymore; Paul Robeson; Maggie Smith; Nicol Williamson.

ALLEN, Stanley. Essay: Paul Robeson.

ARONSON, Arnold. Adviser. Chair, Theatre Arts Division, School of the Arts, Columbia University. Formerly professor, Department of Theatre, Hunter College, City University of New York; associate professor of drama, University of Virginia; and professor of drama, University of Michigan, Ann Arbor. Author of *The History and Theory of Environmental Scenography; American Set Design;* and articles on stage design and avant-garde theatre for numerous journals. Contributor to the *Cambridge Guide to World Theatre* and the *Cambridge Guide to American Theatre.* **Essays:** Boris Aronson; Norman Bel Geddes; Lee Breuer; Mordecai Gorelik; Eugene Lee; Jo Mielziner; Jean Rosenthal; Lee Simonson; Robert M. Wilson.

BANFIELD, Chris. Lecturer in theatre arts, University of Birmingham. **Essay:** Albert Finney.

BANHAM, Martin. Adviser. Professor of drama and theatre studies, University of Leeds. Author of *Osborne*, 1969; and *African Theatre Today*, 1976. Editor of *Plays by Tom Taylor*, 1985; and *The Cambridge Guide to World Theatre*, 1988, revised 1992, 2nd edition as *The Cambridge Guide to Theatre*, 1995. Co-editor (with John Hodgson) of three volumes of *Drama in Education*, 1972, 1973, and 1975.

BASSNETT, Susan. Professor of comparative literature and director, Centre for British and Comparative Cultural Studies, University of Warwick. Formerly lecturer in English literature, University of Rome. Author of several books, including *Luigi Pirandello*, 1983; *Magdalena: Experimental Women's Theatre*, 1988; *Shakespeare: The Elizabethan Plays;* and articles on theatre semiotics and women's theatre history. Co-author of *Bernhardt, Terry, Duse: The Actress in Her Time*, 1988. Compiler of *File on Pirandello*, 1989. Translator of plays, poems, and novels. **Essays:** Andreini family; Eleonora Duse; Adelaide Ristori; Ernesto Rossi; Ruggero Ruggeri.

BATTY, Mark. Essay: Constant-Benoît Coquelin.

BAUGH, Christopher. Reader in drama and head of drama department, Goldsmiths' College, University of London. Also a professional designer. Author of *Garrick and Loutherbourg*, 1990. Author of articles and essays on eighteenth-century scenography, Inigo Jones, William Capon, and Edward Gordon Craig. Co-editor (with Simon Trussler) of *The Play of Personality in Restoration Theatre*, 1992. Contributor of "Brecht and Stage Design: The Bühnenbildner and the Bühnenbauer," in *The Cambridge Companion to Brecht*, 1994. **Essays:** William Capon; Gordon Craig; Inigo Jones; Philip James de Loutherbourgh.

BEACHAM, Richard C. Professor in theatre studies, University of Warwick. Author of *Adolphe Appia: Theatre Artist*, 1987; *Adolphe Appia: Essays, Scenarios and Designs*, 1989; *The Roman Theatre and Its Audience*, 1991; *Adolphe Appia: Artist and Visionary of the Modern Theatre*, 1995; *Power into Pageantry: Spectacle Entertainments of Rome*, forthcoming; and articles on theatre history in *Theater, Theatre Research International, Maske and Kothurn, Opera Quarterly*, and *New Theatre Quarterly.* Editor of the video series *Ancient Theatre and Its Legacy.* Translator of Roman comedies. Producer of ancient dramas on replica ancient stages, including Plautus's *Casina* at the J. Paul Getty Museum, 1994. **Essays:** Adolphe Appia; Sebastiano Serlio.

BENEDETTI, Jean. Adviser and consultant, School of Theatre, Manchester Polytechnic, Department of Performing Arts, Middlesex Polytechnic, and Academy of Theatre, Damascus, Syria. Formerly principal, Rose Bruford College, Sidcup, Surrey, 1970-87; also actor and director. Author of *Gilles de Rais, A Biography*, 1972; *Stanislavski: An Introduction*, 1982; *Stanislavski: A Biography*, 1988; *Brecht, Stanislavski and the Art of the Actor in Brechtjahrbuch*, 1995; as well as numerous articles on Stanislavski and plays for radio and television. Editor of *The Moscow Art Letters*, 1992. Translator of Arrabal's *The Architect and the Emperor of Assyria*, 1971; and Brecht's *A Respectable Wedding*, 1980. **Essays:** Oleg Efreimov; Anatoly Efros; Mariya Ermolova; Glikeriya Fedotova; Vasili Kachalov; Pavel Mochalov; Vladimir Nemirovich-Danchenko; Ekaterina Semionova; Konstantin Stanislavsky; Georgyi Tovstonogov.

BENNATHAN, Joss. Freelance writer and drama teacher, actor, and community theatre worker. Contributor to *Contemporary Dramatists.* **Essays:** Vanessa Redgrave; Orson Welles.

BENSON, Eugene. Adviser. Professor of English, University of Guelph, Ontario; editor of the journal *Canadian Drama.* Former chairman of the Writers' Union of Canada, 1983-84. Author of the plays *Joan of Arc's Violin*, 1972; *The Gunners' Rope*, 1973; the novels *The Bulls of Ronda*, 1976; *Power Game*, 1980; and the critical monograph *J.M. Synge*, 1980. Librettist of the operas *Heloise and Abelard*, 1973; *Everyman*, 1974; and *Psycho Red*, 1980. Co-editor (with L.W. Connolly) of *English-Canadian Theatre*, 1980, and the *Oxford Companion to Canadian Theatre*, 1989.

BERGHAUS, Günther. Reader in theatre studies, Drama Department, University of Bristol. Author of books, including *Nestroys Revolutionspossen*, 1978; *A. Gryphius' "Carolus Stuardus,"* 1984; *The Reception of the English Revolution, 1640-1669*, 1989; *Theatre and Film in Exile*, 1989; *The Genesis of Futurism*, 1995; *Theatre and Fascism*, 1996; *Futurism and Politics*, 1996; and many articles on dance history, avant-garde performance, modernist theatre, and Renaissance and Baroque drama. **Essay:** Max Reinhardt.

BILLINGTON, Michael. Adviser. Theatre critic for the *Guardian* since 1971, and London correspondent for the *New York Times* since 1978; author and broadcaster. Formerly theatre, film, and television critic for the *Times*, 1965-71. Author of *The Modern Actor*, 1973; *How Tickled I Am*, 1977; *Alan Ayckbourn,*

1983 (revised 1990); *Tom Stoppard: Playwright,* 1987; *Peggy Ashcroft,* 1988; and *Director's Shakespeare: "Twelfth Night",* 1990. **Essay:** Peggy Ashcroft.

BRADBY, David. Adviser. Professor of drama and theatre studies, Royal Holloway and Bedford New College, University of London. Formerly reader in French theatre studies, University of Kent, Canterbury. Author of *Modern French Drama,* 1984 (revised 1991); *The Theatre of Robert Planchon* (Theatre in Focus series); *The Theatre of Michel Vinaver,* 1993; and various articles on French theatre. Co-author (with John McCormick) of *People's Theatre,* 1978; and (with David Williams) *Director's Theatre,* 1988. Editor of *Landmarks of French Classical Drama,* 1991. Co-editor (with Claude Schumacher) of *New French Plays,* 1989. Compiler of the bibliography *Adamov,* 1975. **Essays:** Jacques Copeau; Roger Planchon.

BRANDON, James. Adviser. Professor of theatre, University of Hawaii, Honolulu. Previously taught at Michigan State University, East Lansing, 1961-68. Author of *Theatre in Southeast Asia,* 1967, and *Brandon's Guide to Theatre in Asia,* 1976. Advisory editor of the *Cambridge Guide to World Theatre,* 1988. Editor of *On Thrones of Gold: Three Javanese Shadow Plays,* 1970; *The Performing Arts in Asia,* 1971; *Traditional Asian Plays,* 1972; and *Chushingura: Studies in Kabuki and the Puppet Theater,* 1982. Co-editor (with Tamako Niwa) of *Kabuki Plays,* 1966, and (with Rachel Baumer) *Sanskrit Drama in Performance,* 1981. Translator of *Kabuki: Five Classic Plays,* 1975.

BRANDT, George. Freelance writer and lecturer. Former professor of radio, film and television studies, Drama Department, University of Bristol. Author of *Memories and Inventions,* 1983. Editor of *British Television Drama,* 1981; *British Television Drama in the 1980s,* 1993; and *German & Dutch Theatre 1600-1848,* 1993. Contributor of articles to *Cassell's Encyclopedia of World Literature,* 1953; and *The Cambridge Guide to World Theatre,* 1995. Translator of Hans Sachs' *The Wandering Scholar in Paradise* and Lope de Rueda's *The Troublesome Olives* (both in *Medieval Interludes,* 1972), and Calderón's *The Great Stage of the World,* 1976. **Essay:** Friederike Caroline Neuber.

BRAUN, Kazimierz. Professor of theater history and directing at State University of New York at Buffalo. Formerly professor at Wrocław University and Wrocław School of Drama, and artistic director and general manager of the Teatr Współczesny (Contemporary Theatre) in Wrocław, Poland. Author of *A History of Polish Theater, 1939-1989, Spheres of Captivity and Freedom,* 1994; twelve other books on history of theatre; and more than 300 articles, as well as dramas and prose works. **Essay:** Leon Schiller.

BROCH, Kirsten. **Essay:** Hans Jacob Nilsen.

BROOKS, William. Senior lecturer in French, University of Bath. Author of *Bibliographie critique du théâtre de Quinault,* 1988; *Bellérophon,* 1990; *The Theatre in France Seen by Elizabeth Charlotte, Duchesse d'Orléans,* 1991; and articles on French theatre, the French *noveau roman,* and British and French detective fiction for *Modern Langauage Review, Seventeenth-Century French Studies,* and other journals. **Essays:** Floridor; Jodelet.

BROWN, John Russell. Adviser. Professor of theatre, University of Michigan, since 1985. Formerly head of drama, University of Birmingham, 1964-71; professor of English, University of Sussex, 1971-82; and literary manager and associate of the National Theatre of Great Britain, 1973-88. Author of *Shakespeare and His Comedies,* 1957; *Shakespeare's "Macbeth",* 1963; *Shakespeare's Plays in Performance,* 1966; *Effective Theatre,* 1969; *Shakespeare's "The Tempest",* 1969; *Shakespeare's Dramatic Style,* 1970; *Theatre Language: A Study of Arden, Osborne, Pinter, Wesker,* 1972; *Free Shakespeare,* 1974; *Shakespeare in Performance,* 1976; *Discovering Shakespeare,* 1981; *Shakespeare and His Theatre,* 1982; *A Short Guide to Modern British Drama,* 1982; and *Shakespeares,* 1991. General editor of Stratford-upon-Avon Studies, 1960-67, and Theatre Production Studies. Editor of Shakespeare's *The Merchant of Venice,* 1955; Webster's *The White Devil,* 1960; *The Duchess of Malfi,* 1965; and Shakespeare's *Henry V,* 1965. **Essays:** Peter Reginald Frederick Hall; Elia Kazan.

BURIAN, Jarka M. Adviser. Professor emeritus of theatre, State University of New York, Albany. Author of *The Scenography of Josef Svoboda,* 1971; *Svoboda: Wagner,* 1983; and many articles on scenography, design, and Czechoslovakian theatre for *Theatre Journal; Theatre Crafts; Drama Review; Modern Drama; American Theater; Theatre Design and Technology; Theatre History Studies;* and other journals. Editor and translator of Svoboda's *The Secret of Theatrical Space.* Contributor to *Contemporary Designers; Contemporary Dramatists;* and *The Cambridge Guide to Theatre.* **Essays:** Emil František Burian; William Dudley; John Forsyth Gunter; Jocelyn Herbert; Ralph Koltai; Ming Cho Lee; John Napier; Josef Svoboda.

CALDER, Charles. Occasional lecturer in English, Aberdeen University, Scotland. Visiting lecturer in drama, Instituto Suor Orsola Benincasa, Naples, 1995-96. Author of articles on Shakespearian and rhetorical topics. **Essays:** Spranger Barry; Maurice Evans; Helen Hayes; Ben Iden Payne.

CARLSON, Marvin. Adviser. Sidney E. Cohn professor of theatre, Graduate School, City University of New York. Formerly taught at Cornell University, Ithaca, New York, 1961-79, and at Indiana University, Bloominton. Author of *The Theatre of the French Revolution,* 1966; *The French Stage in the Nineteenth Century,* 1972; *The German Stage in the Nineteenth Century,* 1972; *Geothe and the Weimar Theatre,* 1978; *The Italian Stage in the Nineteenth Century,* 1980; *Theories of the Theatre: A Historical and Critical Survey from the Greeks to the Present,* 1984; *The Italian Shakespeareans: Performances by Ristori, Salvini and Rossi in England and America,* 1985; *Places of Performance: The Semiotics of Theatre Architecture,* 1989; *Theatre Semiotics,* 1990; and articles on theatre and drama in *Comparative Literature, Modern Drama, Educational Theatre Journal,* and other periodicals. Translator of *André Antoine's Memories of the Théâtre-Libre,* 1964.

CASEY, Roger N. Instructor, Department of English, Florida State University. **Essay:** Harold Clurman.

CLARKE, Janet. Part-time lecturer in French, University of Lancaster. Formerly lecturer, University of Exeter. Author of articles on Evénégaud Theatre for *Seventeenth-Century French*

Studies. Editor of Thomas Corneille's *Circé,* 1989. **Essay:** Montdory.

COPELAND, Nancy. Instructor, Department of Drama, Erindale College, University of Toronto. **Essays:** George Anne Bellamy; Hannah Pritchard; Peg Woffington.

COTTIS, David. Freelance writer, director, and lyricist; artistic director, Instant Classics Theatre Company. Formerly theatre critic for *City Wise* magazine, and part-time lecturer in drama and English literature, University of East Anglia, Norwich. Author of several produced plays. **Essays:** John Dexter; Derek Jacobi.

DACE, Tish. Adviser. Professor of English, University of Massachusetts Dartmouth. Contributor to *Back Stage, Plays International, Plays and Players, Theater Week, Theatre Crafts, Other Stages, Village Voice, New York Times, American Theatre, Playbill,* and other journals. Author of *LeRoi Jones (Imamu Amiri Baraka): A Checklist of Works by and about Him,* 1971; *The Theatre Student: Modern Theatre and Drama,* 1973; and *Langston Hughes: The Contemporary Reviews,* 1996. Executive committee member and foundation vice-president, American Theater Critics Association; and committee chair, American Theater Ring Design Awards.

DAVIS, Peter A. Instructor, Department of Drama, Tufts University, Medford, Massachusetts. **Essays:** Maude Adams; Ira Aldridge; Joseph Jefferson III; Ada Rehan.

DAVIS, Jim. Senior lecturer in theatre studies, University of New South Wales, Sydney. Formerly senior lecturer in drama, Roehampton Institute of Higher Education, London. Author of *John Liston Comedian,* 1985, and articles on 19th-century British theatre for *Theatre Notebook, New Theatre Quarterly,* and other publications. Editor of *Plays* by H.J. Byron, 1984. **Essays:** George Frederick Cooke; Charles Kemble; John Liston.

DAWSON, Terence. Lecturer in English literature, National University of Singapore. Contributor of articles on both English and French literature to numerous journals including *Modern Language Review.* **Essay:** Franco Zeffirelli.

DICKENSON, Sarah-Jane. Lecturer, Drama Department, Hull University; playwright. **Essays:** Alec Guinness; Jessica Tandy.

DIECKMAN, Suzanne Burgoyne. Associate professor of theatre, University of Missouri, Columbia. Formerly chair of department of fine and performing arts, Creighton University, Omaha, Nebraska. Author of articles in *Theatre Topics, Theatre Journal,* and *American Drama.* **Essay:** Roger Blin.

DOLBY, William. Lecturer in Chinese studies, University of Edinburgh. Formerly lecturer in Chinese, University of Malaysia, Kuala Lumpur. Author of *A History of Chinese Drama,* 1976; *Eight Chinese Plays,* 1978; and many other works on Chinese literature and theatre. **Essay:** Cheng Changgeng.

EDDERSHAW, Margaret. Senior lecturer in theatre studies, University of Lancaster. Author of *Grand Fashionable Nights: Kendal Theatre (1575-1985),* 1989, and of articles on Brecht and Stanislavsky for *Brecht in Perspective,* 1982, and on Brecht's

Mother Courage for *New Theatre Quarterly,* 1991. **Essays:** Glenda Jackson; Philip Prowse.

FINDLAY, Robert. Instructor, Department of Theatre and Film, University of Kansas, Lawrence. **Essays:** Jerzy Grotowski; Charles Macklin; Jósef Szajna.

FORSÅS-SCOTT, Helena. Lecturer in Swedish, University College, London. 1978. Author of thesis on modern British drama, 1978. **Essay:** Ingmar Bergman.

FOULKES, Richard. Lecturer, departments of adult education and English, University of Leicester. Author of *The Shakespeare Tercentary of 1864,* 1984; *The Calverts: Actors of Some Importance,* 1992; and *Repertory at the Royal: Sixty-five Years of Theatre in Northampton, 1927-92,* 1992. Editor, *Shakespeare and the Victorian Stage,* 1986; *British Theatre in the 1890's,* 1992; and *Scenes from Provincial Stages,* 1994. Contributor of articles to several journals, including *Shakespeare Survey;* associate editor, *New Dictionary of Biography;* and general editor, *Publications for the Society for Theatre Research.* **Essays:** Frank Benson; Helen Faucit; Johnston Forbes-Robertson; Henry Irving; Charles Kean; William Charles Macready; Samuel Phelps; Ellen Terry; Herbert Beerbohm Tree.

GEROULD, Daniel. Adviser. Lucille Lortel Distinguished Professor of Theatre and Comparative Literature, Graduate School, City University of New York. Author of *Witkacy: Stanisław Ignacy Witkiewicz as an Imaginative Writer,* 1981; and *Guillotine,* 1991. Co-author of *A Life of Solitude: Stanisława Przybyszewska,* 1989. Editor of *America Melodrama,* 1983. Editor and translator of *Twentieth-Century Polish Avant-Garde Drama,* 1977; *Gallant and Libertine: Divertissements & Parades of 18th Century France,* 1983; *Doubles, Demons and Dreamers: An International Collection of Symbolist Drama,* 1985, and *A Witkiewicz Reader,* 1991. **Essay:** Helena Modjeska.

GIBSON, Melissa. Graduate student, Department of Theatre, University of Pittsburgh. **Essay:** Ian McKellen.

GONTARSKI, S.E. Professor of English, Florida State University; editor of *Journal of Beckett Studies.* Formerly visiting distinguished professor of comparative literature, California State University, and visiting associate professor of English, University of California, Riverside. Author of *The Intent of Undoing in Samuel Beckett's Dramatic Texts,* 1985. Editor of *Happy Days,* 1977; *On Beckett: Essays and Criticism,* 1986; and *The Theatrical Notebooks of Samuel Beckett: Endgame,* 1991. Co-editor (with Morris Beja and Pierre Astier) of *Samuel Beckett: Humanistic Perspectives,* 1983, and (with John Calder) *The Surrealist Reader,* 1991. Guest editor of *Modern Fiction Studies,* 1983. **Essay:** Charles Marowitz.

GORDON, Robert. Senior lecturer in drama, Goldsmiths' College, University of London. Professional actor and director in the United Kingdom and South Africa. Author of book on Tom Stoppard for the Macmillan "Text and Performance" series, 1991; of plays, *Red Earth,* about women's experiences with apartheid, 1985, and *Waterloo Road,* 1987, both produced in London; and many articles on post-apartheid South African theatre, modern British drama (Orton, Rattigan, Osborne, Simon Gray, Stoppard, and Pinter), Oscar Wilde, and Strindberg. Currently writing a book on 20th-century acting theories and collaborating with Irish poet and playwright, Anne le Marquand Hartigan, in directing and performing her trilogy *Jersey Lilies.* **Essays:** Judi Dench; Trevor Robert Nunn; Ralph Richardson.

GOTTLEIB, Vera. Adviser. Professor of drama, Goldsmiths' College, University of London; co-director of Magna Carta Productions (theatre company). Author of *Chekhov and the Vaudeville,* 1982; *Chekhov in Performance in Russia and Soviet Russia* (Theatre in Focus series); and articles on contemporary theatre, Chekhov, and farce for *Themes in Drama, New Theatre Quarterly,* and other periodicals. Translator and adapter of *Chekhov Quartet* (produced London, Yalta, and Moscow, 1989). Co-director of *Red Earth* and *Waterloo Road.*

GOUNARIDOU, Kiki. Assistant professor and director of graduate studies, Department of Theatre Studies, University of Pittsburgh. Author of articles and papers on theatre translation theory, ancient Greek theatre, and contemporary theatre. Active as a theatre director in the U.S. and Europe. **Essays:** Morris Carnovsky; Lee Strasberg.

HOLLAND, Peter. Adviser. Judith E. Watson University Lecturer in Drama, Faculty of English, University of Cambridge. Author of *The Ornament of Action: Text and Performance in Restoration Comedy,* and of articles on Shakespeare, Chekhov, and contemporary theatre in *Shakespeare Survey, New Theatre Quarterly, Themes in Drama,* and other journals. Editor of *The Plays of Wycherley,* 1981. Co-editor (with Hanna Scolnicov) of *The Play out of Context,* 1988, and *Reading Plays,* 1991.

HOOVER, Marjorie L. Emeritus professor of German and Russian, Oberlin College, Ohio. Formerly assistant professor of German, Swarthmore College, Pennsylvania, and honored Campbell professor, Wells College, Aurora, New York. Author of *Meyerhold: The Art of Conscious Theater,* 1974; *Alexander Ostrovsky,* 1981; *Meyerhold and His Set Designers,* 1988; and articles and dictionary entries on Brecht, Russian theatre, and other topics. Editor of *Das Tagebuch der Anne Frank, Die Verwandlung* by Kafka, and *Two Plays* by Tankred Dorst. Translator (with George Genereux) of Erdman's *The Mandate* and *The Suicide,* 1975, and of Goncharov's *An Ordinary Story,* 1994. **Essays:** Nikolai Akimov; Gustaf Gründgens; Sergei Radlov; Yuri Zavadsky.

HOWARTH, William D. Adviser. Emeritus professor of French, University of Bristol. Formerly fellow and tutor in modern languages, Jesus College, University of Oxford, 1948-66; professor of classical French literature, Bristol University, 1966-88. Author of *Life and Letters in France: The Seventeenth Century,* 1965; *Sublime and Grotesque: A Study of French Romantic Drama,* 1975; *Molière: A Playwright and His Audience,* 1982; *Anouilh: Antigone,* 1983; *Corneille: Le Cid,* 1988; and many articles on French literature and theatre. Editor of *Comic Drama: The European Heritage,* 1978; and editions of works by Anouilh, Molière, La Chaussée, and Voltaire. Co-editor of *Molière: Stage and Study,* 1973. Member of editorial board for the series *A Documentary History of the European Theatre* (15 vols.), 1989-. **Essays:** Marie Dorval; Frédéric Lemaître; Laurent Mahelot; Mlle Mars; Élisa Rachel.

HUNTER, Martin. **Essays:** Zoë Caldwell; Hume Cronyn; Jean Gascon; John Hirsch; Raymond Massey; Kate Reid.

INGRAM, Raymond. Honorary research fellow, King Alfred's College, Winchester; former head of Drama and Television, King Alfred's College. Author of articles and books on various designers and productions. Exhibitions include *Leslie Hurry* at the Royal Festival Hall, 1990 and *Tanya Moiseiwitsch* at the Theatre Museum, 1996. Productions include Shakespeare in England and the United States of America. **Essays:** John Bury; Oliver Messel; Tanya Moiseiwitsch; John Neville.

INNES, Christopher. Adviser. Professor of English, York Univerity, North York, Ontario; general editor of the "Directors in Perspective" series for Cambridge University Press. Author of *Erwin Piscator's Political Theatre,* 1972; *Modern German Drama,* 1979; *Holy Theatre: Ritual and the Avant Garde,* 1981; *Edward Gordon Craig,* 1983; *Modern British Drama 1980-1990, Avant Garde Theatre,* 1993; and articles on drama and theatre.

JACK, R.D.S. Professor of Scottish and medieval literature, University of Edinburgh. Formerly visiting professor, University of Virginia, Charlottesville. Author of *The Italian Influence on Scottish Literature,* 1972; *Alexander Montgomerie,* 1985; *Scotland's Literary Debt to Italy,* 1986; *Patterns of Divine Comedy in Medieval Drama,* 1989; *Structured Thought: The Road to Never Land,* 1990; and many articles and reviews on Scottish literature for *Studies in Scottish Literature, Comparative Literature, Review of English Studies, Modern Language Review, Scottish Literary Journal,* and other periodicals. Editor of *Scottish Prose (1550-1700),* 1971; *A Choice of Scottish Verse (1550-1660),* 1978; and *The History of Scottish of Scottish Literature: Volume 1, Origins to 1660,* 1988. Co-editor of *Robert Maclellan's "Jamie the Saxt,"* 1971; *The Art of Robert Burns,* 1982; *Sir Thomas Urquhart: "The Jewel,"* 1984; and *Leopardi: A Scottis Quair,* 1987. **Essay:** Fay Compton.

JEFFERY, David. **Essays:** Ariane Mnouchkine; Jean Vilar.

JOHNSON, Samantha. Researcher in 19th-century theatre and culture, Victoria Studies Centre, University of Leeds. **Essays:** Mrs Patrick Campbell; Fanny Kemble.

KENNEDY, Dennis. Samuel Beckett Professor of Drama and Theatre Studies, Trinity College, Dublin. Formerly professor of theatre, University of Pittsburgh, and general editor of *Pittsburgh Studies in Theatre and Culture.* Author of *Granville Barker and the Dream of Theatre,* 1985; *Foreign Shakespeare,* 1994; and *Looking at Shakespeare: A Visual History of 20th Century Performance,* 1993. Editor of *Plays by Harley Granville Barker,* 1987. Author of several plays and dramaturg in the professional theatre. **Essay:** Peter Stein.

KING, Bruce. Adviser. Adjunct professor of English, University of Guelph, Ontario; general editor of the series "Modern Dramatists" and "English Dramatists". Formerly professor and visiting professor at universities in the U.S., Canada, Scotland, France, Israel, Nigeria, and New Zealand. Author of *Dryden's Major Plays,* 1966; *Marvell's Allegorical Poetry,* 1977; *The New English Literatures: Cultural Nationalism in a Changing World,* 1980; *History of Seventeenth Century English Literature,* 1988; *Modern*

Indian Poetry in English, 1987/89; *Coriolanus*, 1991; and *V.S. Naipaul*, 1993. Editor of *Twentieth Century Interpretations of "All for Love"*, 1968; *Dryden's Mind and Art*, 1969; *Introduction to Nigerian Literature*, 1971; *Literatures of the World in English*, 1974; *A Celebration of Black and African Writing*, 1976; *West Indian Literature*, 1979; *Contemporary American Theatre*, 1991; *The Commonwealth Novel Since 1960*, 1991; and *The Later Fiction of Nadine Gordimer*, 1993.

KITCHIN, Laurence. Formerly professor of liberal arts, City University of New York, and visiting professor of drama, Stanford University. Author of *Mid-Century Drama*, 1960; *Drama in the Sixties*, 1966; and numerous articles on drama for *The Times*, 1956-62. **Essays:** John Gielgud; Laurence Olivier; Flora Robson.

KNAPP, Margaret M. Associate professor of theatre, Arizona State University. Co-author of *"The Ancient Famous Cittie": David Rogers and the Chester Mystery Plays;* and author of articles on Minnie Madern Fiske for *Journal of American Drama and Theatre;* on Agnes Morgan, Irene and Alice Lewisohn for *Notable Women in American Theatre: A Biographical Dictionary;* and on musical theatre for the *Cambridge Guide to World Theatre.* **Essays:** Margaret Anglin; Minnie Maddern Fiske; Eva Le Gallienne.

KNOPF, Robert. Theatre instructor and Rackham fellow, University of Michigan, Ann Arbor. **Essay:** Geraldine Page.

KOBIALKA, Michal. Associate professor of theatre, University of Minnesota. Author of *A Journey Through Other Spaces: Essays and Manifestoes, 1944-1990* (on Tadeusz Kantor's theatre), 1993. Contributor of articles and reviews to numerous journals, including *Assaph, Journal of Dramatic Theory and Criticism, Theatre History Studies, Medieval Perspectives, Drama Review, Theatre Journal*, and others. **Essay:** Tadeusz Kantor.

LANGHANS, Edward A. Professor emeritus of drama and theatre, University of Hawaii. Formerly chairman, Department of Drama and Theatre, University of Hawaii. Author of *Restoration Promptbooks*, 1981; *Eighteenth Century British and Irish Promptbooks*, 1987; co-author of *A Biographical Dictionary of Actors, Actresses, Musicians, Dancers, Managers, and Other Stage Personnel in London, 1660-1800*, 1973-93, 16 volumes. Editor of *Five Restoration Theatrical Adaptations*, 1980. Co-author of *An International Dictionary of Theatre Language*, 1985; author of many articles in such journals as *Theatre Notebook, Theatre Survey, On-Stage Studies, Educational Theatre Journal, Essays in Theatre*, and *Studies in Eighteenth-Century Culture.* **Essays:** Thomas Betterton; Bibiena family; Anne Bracegirdle; Anne Oldfield; James Quin; John Rich.

LAVENDER, Andrew. Lecturer in drama, Goldsmiths' College, University of London. Director of theatre productions on the London fringe. Feature writer on the arts for the *Times;* and author of academic writings including "Edge of Darkness" in *British Television Drama in the 1980s*, 1993. **Essay:** Richard Eyre.

LEACH, Robert. Lecturer in drama and theatre arts, University of Birmingham. Formerly director of Cannon Hill Community

Theatre, Birmingham. Author of *Theatre for Youth*, 1970; *The Wellsbourne Tree: A Musical Documentary Play*, 1975; *Theatre Workshop Series*, 1977-83; *The Punch and Judy Show*, 1985; and *Vsevolod Meyerhold*, 1989. **Essays:** Nikolai Evreinov; Theodore Kommisarjevsky; Joan Littlewood; Lyubov Popova.

LINE, Jill. Lecturer, Temenos Academy, London. **Essay:** Ben Greet.

LONDRÉ, Felicia Hardison. Adviser. Curators' professor of theatre, University of Missouri-Kansas City; dramaturg for Missouri Repertory Theatre and Heart of America Shakespeare Festival. Formerly women's chair in humanistic studies, Marquette University, and visiting foreign professor, Hosei University, Tokyo. Author of *Tennessee Williams*, 1979; *Tom Stoppard*, 1981; *Federico García Lorca*, 1984; and *The History of World Theater: From the English Restoration to the Present*, 1991. Associate editor, *Shakespeare Around the Globe*, 1986. Author of articles on European and American theatre history for essay collections and journals, including *Theatre Research International, Theatre History Studies, Theatre Journal, Slavic and East European Arts, Theatre Annual, Elizabethan Review*, and *Comparative Drama.* **Essay:** David Belasco.

MacKERRAS, Colin. Professor and co-director, Key Centre for Asian Languages and Studies, Griffith University, Brisbane. Formerly chairman, School of Modern Asian Studies, Griffith University, 1979-85; and foreign expert, Beijing Institute of Foreign Languages, 1964-66, 1986, 1990, and 1995. Author of *The Rise of the Peking Opera*, 1972; *The Chinese Theatre in Modern Times*, 1975; *The Performing Arts in Contemporary China*, 1981; *Chinese Drama: A Historical Perspective*, 1990; and numerous other books, articles, book chapters, and encyclopedia entries on China and Chinese theatre. Editor of *Chinese Theater From Its Origins to the Present Day*, 1983. **Essay:** Mei Lanfang.

MARKER, Frederick J. Adviser. Professor of English, University College, University of Toronto. Author of articles for *The Revels History of Drama in English, 1750-1800*, 1975; *Ibsen and the Theatre*, 1980; *Ibsen Yearbook; Theatre Survey; Theatre Notebook; Scandinavian Review; Modern Drama;* and other publications. Co-author (with Lise-Lone Marker) of *The Scandinavian Theatre: A Short History*, 1975; *Edward Gordon Craig and "The Pretenders": A Production Revisited*, 1981; and *Ingmar Bergman: Four Decades in the Theatre*, 1982. Editor of *The Heibergs*, 1971, and Hans Christian Andersen's *Den nye Barselstue*, 1975. Co-editor and translator of *Ingmar Bergman: A Project for the Theatre*, 1983.

MAZZA, Michelle F. Essay: John Houseman.

McNAUGHTON, Howard. Reader in English, University of Canterbury, Christchurch, New Zealand. Author of *Bruce Mason*, 1976; *New Zealand Drama*, 1981; and the section on the novel in *The Oxford History of New Zealand Literature*, 1991. Editor of *Contemporary New Zealand Plays*, 1976, and *James K. Baxter: Collected Plays*, 1982. **Essay:** William Gillette.

MEECH, Anthony. Lecturer in drama, University of Hull. Author of articles on German theatre (especially of the former DDR), and a forthcoming history of German theatre for Cambridge University Press. **Essays:** Teo Otto; Helene Weigel; Manfred Wekwerth.

MERWE, Pieter van der. General editor, National Maritime Museum, London, and vice-chairman of the Society for Theatre Research. **Essay:** Grieve family.

MESERVE, Walter J. Adviser. Retired distinguished professor of theatre and English, Graduate School, City University of New York; co-editor of *Journal of American Drama and Theatre.* Formerly professor of theatre and drama and director of the Institute for American Studies, Indiana University, Bloomington. Author of *An Outline History of American Drama,* 1965, revised 1994; *Robert Sherwood: Reluctant Moralist,* 1970; *An Emrging Entertainment: The Drama of the American People to 1828,* 1977; *American Drama* (Volume 8 of the *Revels History*), with others, 1977; *American Drama to 1900: A Guide to Reference Sources,* 1980; and *Heralds of Promise: The Drama of the American People During the Age of Jackson 1829-1849,* 1986. Editor of *The Complete Plays of William Dean Howells,* 1960; *Discussions of Modern American Drama,* 1966; *American Satiric Comedies,* 1969; *Modern Drama from Communist China,* 1970; *The Rise of Silas Lapham by Howells,* 1971; *Studies in Death of a Salesman,* 1972; and *Modern Literature from China,* 1974. Compiler of *Who's Where in the American Theatre,* 1990.

MIELKE, George C. Essay: George C. Scott.

MORGAN, Margery. Emeritus reader in English and theatre studies, University of Lancaster. Formerly lecturer in English, Royal Holloway College, University of London; and reader in English, Monash University, Australia. Author of *A Drama of Political Man: A Study of the Plays of Harley Granville-Barker,* 1961; *The Shavian Playground,* 1972; *York Notes on "Pygmalion",* 1980, and *York Notes on "Major Barbara",* 1982; *Bernard Shaw,* 1982, and *John Galsworthy,* 1982 (Writers and Their Work series); *August Strindberg,* 1985; and *York Handbook on Drama,* 1987. Author of articles on Granville-Barker, Shaw, Wesker, and other topics. Editor of Granville-Barker's *The Madras House,* 1977, and Shaw's *The Doctor's Dilemma,* 1981. Compiler of *File on Shaw,* 1989, and *File on Wilde,* 1990. **Essays:** Claire Bloom; Lewis Casson; Alec Clunes; Edith Evans; Wendy Hiller; Gregan McMahon; Olof Molander; Joan Plowright; Alf Sjöberg; Sybil Thorndike.

MULRYNE, J.R. Professor of English and comparative literary studies, and chairman of the graduate school of Renaissance studies, University of Warwick, Coventry. Formerly reader in English literature, University of Edinburgh, 1962-77. Author of essays of Middleton, Kyd, Shakespeare, Webster, Sir Thomas Browne, and W.B. Yeats. Editor of Middleton's *Women Beware Women,* Webster's *The White Devil,* Kyd's *The Spanish Tragedy,* and *An Honoured Guest: New Essays on W.B. Yeats.* Co-editor of *War Literature and the Arts in Sixteenth Century Europe; English and Italian Theatre of the Renaissance; Italian Renaissance Festival and Its European Influence;* and *Theatre and Government under the Early Stuarts.* Joint editor, compiler, and publisher (with Margaret Shewring) of *This Golden Round: The Royal Shakespeare Company at the Swan.* **Essay:** John Barton.

NAVERSEN, Ronald. Associate professor of theatre, and

department head, design and technical production program, Southern Illinois University at Carbondale. Contributor of articles to *Theater Design and Technology, Theater Crafts,* and *Tech Notes.* Co-chair, American Schools of Scenography exhibit, Prague Quadrennial, 1991; Special Exhibits coordinator, United States Institute for Theater Technology National Conference, 1994. Freelance designer for regional theaters. **Essay:** Giovanni Servandoni.

ODDEY, Alison J.L. Instructor, Eliot College, University of Kent. **Essay:** Augusto Boal.

OLSEN, Tom J.A. Essay: Bengt Ekerot.

OSBORNE, John. Professor of German, University of Warwick, Coventry. Formerly Alexander von Humboldt research fellow, University of Göttingen, 1972-73 and 1975-76; visiting professor, University of Metz, 1985-86. Author of *The Naturalist Drama in Germany,* 1971; *J.M.R. Lenz: The Renunciation of Heroism,* 1975; *Die Meininger: Texte zur Rezeption,* 1980; *The Meiningen Court Theatre (1866-90),* 1988; and articles on German drama and theatre of the 18th and 19th centuries. **Essays:** Otto Brahm; Josef Kainz.

PATTERSON, Michael. Adviser. Professor of theatre and head of Department of Visual and Performing Arts, De Montfort University, Leivester, since 1994. Formerly lecturer in German, Queen's University of Belfast, 1965-70; lecturer in drama, University College of North Wales, Bangor, 1970-74; senior lecturer in drama and theatre arts, University of Leeds, 1974-87; reader in theatre studies, University of Ulster, Coleraine, 1987-74. Author of *German Theatre Today,* 1976; *The Revolution in German Theatre 1900-1933,* 1981; *Peter Stein,* 1981; *The First German Theatre,* 1990. Editor of *Büchner: The Complete Plays,* 1987. Contributed chapters on "Piscator and Brecht" to *Terrorism and Modern Drama,* 1990; "Brecht's Legacy" to *The Cambridge Guide to Brecht,* 1994; "The Eighteenth Century" (with Peter Holland) to *The Oxford Illustrated History of Theatre,* 1995; and articles to *Theatre Quarterly, German Life and Letters, Modern Drama,* and *History of European Ideas.* Currently preparing a comprehensive bibliography of German theatre.

PAYNE-CARTER, David. Essays: Katharine Cornell; John Drew; Alfred Lunt and Lynn Fontanne; Guthrie McClintic.

PIASECKI, Andy. Freelance writer. Formerly lecturer in drama, Royal Holloway and Bedford New College, University of London, 1981-90. Author of articles on Elizabethan theatre for *The Shakespeare Handbook,* 1987, and on modern British drama for *The Bloomsbury Guide to English Literature,* 1989. Compiler of *File on Lorca,* 1991. Contributor to *Plays International.* **Essay:** Barry Jackson.

PICKERING, David. Freelance writer and editor. **Essays:** Eugenio Barba; Ethel Barrymore; Terry Hands; William Poel.

POPENHAGEN, Ron. Assistant professor, Department of Theatre and Film, University of Kansas, Lawrence; professional actor working in the United States, Britain, Canada, France, Lithuania, and Australia. **Essays:** André Acquart; Jean-Louis Barrault; Luigi Bellotti-Bon; Benno Besson; Jean Dasté; Jean-

Baptiste Gaspard Deburau; Luca Ronconi; Michel Saint-Denis; Andrei Serban; Antoine Vitez.

RADFORD, Colin. Emeritus professor of French, Queen's University, Belfast. Former chairman of Arts Council of Northern Ireland. Author of several books, articles, and reviews. **Essay:** William Tyrone Guthrie.

RATHKAMP, Lesley. Essay: Margo Jones.

READ, Michael. Essays: Michael Scudamore Redgrave; Paul Scofield; J.L. Toole; Donald Wolfit.

READ, Leslie du S. Lecturer in drama, University of Exeter, Devon. Contributor to *The Cambridge Guide to World Theatre*, 1988; *The Cambridge Encyclopaedia*, 1990; and to the forthcoming *Literature and Criticism: A New Century Guide*. **Essays:** Edward Alleyn; Elizabeth Barry.

REED, Joseph. Professor of English and American studies, Wesleyan University, Middletown, Connecticut. Author of books on Boswell, Walpole, Faulkner, Charles Ives, John Ford, and American movies. **Essay:** Jason Robards.

RICHARDS, Kenneth. Adviser. Professor of drama and director of University Theatre, University of Manchester; previously taught at universities of Ljubljana (Yugoslavia), Trondheim (Norway), and Uppsala, and has been a fellow of the Folger Shakespeare Library, Washington, D.C.; the Huntington Library, California; and a Jean Monnet fellow, European University Institute, Fiesole (Italy). Author of *Comedy*, 1977; many articles on drama and theatre for *The Oxford Companion to the Theatre*, *The Cambridge Guide to World Theatre*, 1988; *Shakespeare Nas Telas*, 1995; and various journals. Co-author (with Laura Richards) of *The Commedia dell'Arte: A Documentary History*, 1991. Editor of *Nineteenth Century British Theatre*. Co-editor (with Peter Thomson) of *The Eighteenth Century English Stage*, 1973; and (with David Meyer) *Western Popular Theatre*, 1978. **Essays:** Gustavo Modena; Tommaso Salvini; Ermete Zacconi.

RORRISON, Hugh. Senior lecturer in German, University of Leeds. Author of *Erwin Piscator: Politics on the Stage in the Weimar Republic*, 1987; introductions to *Brecht: Plays* (multivolume), regular play reviews for *Plays and Players*, *Drama*, and *Plays International*, and articles on Peter Handke, Wolfgang Bauer, Heiner Müller, Botho Strauss, Ernst Stern, Ibsen, and the Berliner Schaubühne. Editor of plays by Brecht, including *Mother Courage and Her Children*, 1983; *The Caucasian Chalk Circle*, 1984; and *Life of Galileo* 1986. Translator of Piscator's *The Political Theatre*, 1978; Pavel Kohout's *The Maple Tree Game* (produced 1990); and Wedekind's *The Lulu Plays* (produced 1991). **Essays:** Friedrich Ludwig Schröder; Karl Seydelmann; Adrian Keith Noble; Claus Peymann; Erwin Piscator.

ROSE, Margaret. Essays: Luigi Squarzina; Luchino Visconti.

ROSS, Francesca. Freelance lecturer, writer, and translator. Formerly lecturer at universities in Sardinia and Paris, 1986-89. **Essay:** Anton Giulio Bragaglia.

ROTHENBERG, John. Lecturer in French, University of Leeds.

Author of articles on Jean Anouilh, Rochefort, Beckett, and Nathalie Sarraute, for *Modern Languages* and other publications. **Essay:** André Barsacq.

ROY, Donald. Professor emeritus of drama, University of Hull. Formerly lecturer in French at the universities of Glasgow and St. Andrews. Author of *Jacques Copeau and the Cartel des Quatre*, 1993; and of articles on 17th- and 18th-century French theatre and 19th-century British theatre. Editor of *Molière: Five Plays*, 1982, and *Plays by James Robinson Planché*, 1986. **Essays:** Mlle Clairon; Adrienne Lecouvreur; Henri-Louis Lekain; François-Joseph Talma.

SCHUMACHER, Claude. Reader in theatre studies, University of Glasgow; editor of the journal *Theatre Research International*. Author of *Jarry and Apollinaire*, 1984; and articles on Dürrenmatt, Frisch, Appia, Zola, the theatre of the absurd, and other aspects of literature and theatre. Editor of *40 Years of Mise en Scène*, 1986; *Marivaux: Plays*, 1988; *Artaus on Theatre*, 1990; and *Musset: Five Plays*, 1995. Co-editor (with David Bradby) of *New French Plays*, 1989. **Essays:** André Antoine; Antonin Artaud; Charles Dullin; Louis Jouvet.

SCOTT, Virginia. Professor, Department of Theater, University of Massachusetts, Amherst. Formerly editor of *Theatre Journal*. Author of *The Commedia dell'Arte in Paris, 1644-1697*, 1990, and numerous articles on *commedia dell'arte*, pantomime, Molière, and other subjects. **Essays:** Biancolelli family; Tiberio Fiorilli; Riccoboni family; Giacomo Torelli.

SENELICK, Laurence. Adviser. Fletcher Professor of Drama, Tufts University, Medford, Massachusetts; honorary curator of Russian theatre, Harvard Theatre Collection. Author of many books, including *Russian Dramatic Theory from Pushkin to the Symbolists*, 1981; *Gordon Craig's Moscow Hamlet*, 1982; *Anton Chekhov*, 1985; and *National Theatre in Northern and Eastern Europe, 1753-1900*, 1991; a documentary history of Soviet theatre is in progress. **Essays:** Michael Chekhov; Joseph Grimaldi; Vera Kommisarjevskaya; Mikhail Shchepkin.

SHAUGHNESSY, Robert. Senior lecturer in literary studies, University of the West of England. Author of *Three Socialist Plays*, 1992; *Representing Shakespeare: England, History, and the RSC*, 1994; and contributor of articles to *New Theatre Quarterly*, *Studies in Theatre Production*, and *Theatre Notebook*. **Essays:** George Devine; Bill Gaskill; Terence Gray.

SMITH, Christopher. Senior lecturer in French and comparative literature, University of East Anglia. Author of *Jean Anouilh: Life, Work and Criticism; Alabaster, Bikinis and Calvados*, 1985; and numerous articles on drama and translation. Editor of Jean de Taille's *Dramatic Works*, Jacques de la Taille's *Alexandre*, A. Montchrestien's *Two Tragedies*, and of the journal *Seventeenth-Century French Studies*. **Essays:** Junius Brutus Booth; Richard Burbage; Pierre-Luc-Charles Ciceri; Pauline-Virginie Déjazet; Gerald du Maurier; Anne Merry; Anthony Quayle; Gabrielle-Charlotte Réjane.

SUTCLIFFE, Christopher. English instructor, Huntcliff School, Kirton Lindsey, North Lincolnshire. **Essays:** Robert Armin; Will Kemp.

TAYLOR, George. Lecturer in drama, Manchester University; freelance theatre director. Contributor to *The Politics of Theatre and Drama*, and author of articles on Timberlake Wertenbaker's *Our Country's Good* and Britain's National Theatre for *Critical Survey*. **Essays:** Squire and Marie Bancroft; John Philip Kemble; Charles James Mathews; Sarah Siddons; "Madame" Lucia Elizabeth Vestris.

TAYLOR, Val. Lecturer in drama, University of East Anglia; freelance theatre director. Formerly lecturer in drama, Roehampton Institute, London, 1988-92. Author of *Hamlet* (study guide), 1993; essays for *The Politics of Theatre and Drama*, 1992; and *Boxed Sets*, edited by Jeremy Ridgman (forthcoming), and articles on Timberlake Wertenbaker and Britain's National Theatre for *Critical Survey*. **Essays:** Alan Howard; Jonathan Miller; Janet Suzman.

THODY, Philip. Professor of French literature, University of Leeds. Past positions include visiting professorships at the universities of Western Ontario, California (Berkeley), Harvard, Adelaide, Canterbury (New Zealand), Western Australia, and Virginia. Author of *Albert Camus*, 1957; *Jean-Paul Sartre*, 1960; *Albert Camus, 1913-1960*, 1961; *Jean Anouilh*, 1968; *Jean Genet*, 1968; *Jean-Paul Sartre*, 1971; *Aldous Huxley*, 1973; *A True Life Reader for Children and Parents*, 1977; *Dog Days in Babel*, 1979; *Faux Amis and French Caesarism from Napolean to Charles de Gaulle*; and many articles on French language and literature, and a series of teaching tapes on French authors. Editor of Sartre's *Les Séquestrés d'Altona*, 1965; Camus' *Caligula*, 1973; and Christiane Rochefort's *Les Petits Enfants du siècle*, 1982. Translator of works by Camus, Orwell, Lucien Goldmann, and Jacqueline de Romilly. **Essays:** Sarah Bernhardt; Maria Casarès; Charles Laughton; Gérard Philipe; Irene Worth.

THOMSON, Peter. Adviser. Professor of drama, University of Exeter, Devon. Author of *Shakespeare's Theatre*, 1983, revised 1992; *Shakespeare's Professional Career*, 1991; and articles on Shakespeare, 19th-century theatre, and other topics. Co-author (with Jan Needle) of *Brecht*, and (with Gāmini Salgādo) *The Everyman Companion to the Theatre*, 1985. Editor of Shakespeare's *Julius Caeser*, 1970; Malcolm Elwin's *Lord Byron's Family*, 1975; and *Plays by Dion Boucicault*, 1984. Co-editor (with Kenneth Richards) of *Nineteenth Century British Theatre*, 1971, and *The Eighteenth Century English Stage*, 1973.

TROUSDELL, Richard. Instructor, Department of Theatre, University of Massachusetts, Amherst. **Essays:** Peter Sellars; Giorgio Strehler.

UNRUH, Delbert. Professor of theatre, University of Kansas, Lawrence. **Essay:** Robert Edmond Jones.

WAAL, Carla. Professor emeritus of theatre, University of Missouri--Columbia. Formerly, associate professor of theatre, University of Georgia, Athens, and visiting professor, Indiana University at Bloomington. Author of *Johanne Dybwad: Norwegian Actress*, 1967; *Harriet Bosse: Strindberg's Muse and Interpreter*, 1990; and articles on Scandinavian and American theatre, for publications, including *Educational Theatre Journal*, *Theatre History Studies*, and *Theatre Companies of the World*. Translations of some of Bjorg Vik's short stories for *Scandina-*

vian Studies, *Scandinavian Review*, and the anthologies *An Everyday Story*, 1984 and 1995, and *Scandinavian Women Writers*, 1987. **Essays:** Johanne Dybwad; Per Lindberg.

WATERMEIER, Daniel J. Professor of theatre and drama, University of Toledo. Formerly visiting professor of drama, University of Southern California, Los Angeles. Author of articles and reviews on 19th-century actors, American drama, and Shakespearian production for *Theatre History Studies*, *Theatre Research International*, *Shakespeare Quarterly*, and the *Cambridge Guide to World Theatre*. Editor of *Between Actor and Critic: Selected Letters of Edwin Booth to William Winter*, 1971, and *Edwin Booth's Preformances: The Mary Isabella Stone Commentaries*, 1990. Associate editor of *Shakespeare Around the Globe: A Guide to Notable Postwar Revivals*, 1986. **Essays:** Lawrence Barrett; Michael Bogdanov; Edwin Booth; Charlotte Cushman; Edward Loomis Davenport; Mrs John Drew; Edwin Forrest; Richard Mansfield; Julia Marlowe; Otis Skinner; E.H. Sothern.

WEBER, Carl. Professor of drama, Stanford University, California. Author of articles on Brecht, Müller, and other aspects of modern German theatre for *Performing Arts Journal*, *Drama Review*, and other publications. Translator of plays by Müller. **Essay:** Peter Palitzsch.

WEISS, Rudolf. Instructor, Institut fur Anglistik und Ameriknaistik, Der Universitat Vien, Austria. **Essay:** George Alexander.

WELLS, Stanley. Adviser. Professor of Shakespeare studies and director of the Shakespeare Institute, University of Birmingham, since 1988; general editor (with Gary Taylor) of the "Oxford Shakespeare" series; editor of *Shakespeare Survey* since 1981. Formerly reader in English, University of Birmingham, 1962-77; senior research fellow, Balliol College, Oxford, 1980-88. Author of *Literature and Drama, Royal Shakespeare*, 1977; *Shakespeare: An Illustrated Dictionary*, 1978; *Shakespeare: The Writer and His Work*, 1978; and many articles on Shakespeare and Renaissance drama. Editor of *Thomas Nashe: Selected Writings*, 1964; Shakespeare's *A Midsummer Night's Dream*, 1967; *Richard the II*, 1969; *Shakespeare: A Reading Guide*, 1969; *The Comedy of Errors*, 1972; the Select Bibliographical Guides *Shakespeare*, 1973 (revised as *Shakespeare: A Bibliographical Guide*, 1990), and *English Drama Excluding Shakespeare*, 1975; *The Cambridge Companion to Shakespeare Studies*, 1986; and *The Oxford Anthology of Shakespeare*, 1987. General editor, with Gary Taylor, of the *Complete Oxford Shakespeare*, 1986. Co-editor (with R.L. Smallwood) of Dekker's *The Shoemaker's Holiday*, 1979, and (with others) *William Shakespeare: A Textual Companion*, 1987.

WELLWARTH, George E. Adviser. Professor of theatre and comparative literature, State University of New York, Binghampton, since 1970; co-editor, *Modern International Drama*, since 1967. Author of *The Theatre of Protest and Paradox*, 1964, and *Modern Drama and the Death of God*, 1986. Editor of *The New Wave, Spanish Drama*, 1970; *German Drama Between the Wars*, 1972, *New Generation Spanish Drama*, 1974; and *Three Catalan Dramatists*, 1974. Co-editor of *Modern French Theatre*, 1964, and *Modern Spanish Theatre*, 1968. Translator of *Concise Encyclopedia of the Modern Drama*, 1964.

WHITTON, David. Professor of French theatre, University of Lancaster. Author of *Stage Directors in Modern France,* 1987; *Molière: "Le Bourgeois Gentilhomme,"* 1991; *Molière: "Le Misanthrope,"* 1991; *Don Juan in Production,* 1995. Contributor of articles on French playwrights and directors for *Theatre Research International, Forum for Modern Language Studies, Nottingham French Studies,* and other journals. **Essays:** Gaston Baty; Aurélien Lugné-Poë; Georges Pitoëff.

WIINGAARD, Jytte. Instructor, Dte Teatervidenskabelige Institut, Kobenhavn Universitet, Denmark. **Essay:** William Edward Bloch.

WILLIAMS, David. Teacher of performance studies, Victoria University, Melbourne, Australia; also works as a theatre director. Contributor to *International Dictionary of Opera,* St. James Press. **Essay:** Peter Brook.

WILLIAMS, Margaret. Adviser. Senior lecturer in theatre studies, University of New South Wales, Kensington, Australia. Author of *Drama* (Writers and Their Work series); *Australia on the Popular Stage, 1829-1929,* 1983; and many articles on Australian drama for *Contemporary Australian Drama,* 1981, *The Cambridge Guide to World Theatre,* 1988, and various periodicals.

WILLIAMS, Simon. Professor of dramatic art, University of California, Santa Barbara. Previously taught at universities in Sweden, Austria, Libya, Iran, the universities of Regina and Alberta, and Cornell. Author of *German Actors of the Eighteenth and Nineteenth Centuries: Idealism, Romanticism and Realism,* 1985; *Shakespeare on the German Stage, 1587-1914,* 1990; and articles on Irish theatre, 18th- and 19th-century theatre, acting, and opera. **Essays:** Konrad Ackermann; Emil Devrient; Ludwig Devrient; Konrad Ekhof; August Wilhelm Iffland; Heinrich Laube; Alexander Moissi; Josef Anton Stranitzky.

WOODS, Leigh. Head of theatre studies, University of Michigan, Ann Arbor; also a professional actor. Author of books about David Garrick and the traditions of Shakespearean acting. Co-editor of the forthcoming *Actors on Film Acting;* and (with Ágústa Gunnarsdóttir) *Public Selves, Political Stages.* **Essays:** David Garrick; Charles Hawtrey; Edmund Kean.

WOODYARD, George. Adviser. Professor of Spanish, University of Kansas, Lawrence; editor of *Latin American Theatre Review.* Author of articles on Latin American theatre. Editor of *The Modern Stage in Latin America: Six Plays,* 1971. Co-editor (with Leon F. Lyday) of *Dramatists in Revolt: The New Latin American Theatre,* 1976, and *A Bibliography of Latin American Theatre Criticism, 1940-1974,* 1976.

WORRALL, Nick. Principal lecturer in English and drama, Middlesex University (formerly Middlesex Polytechnic). Formerly Soviet correspondent for British centre of the International Theatre Institute; editor of Soviet Union section of *International Theatrelog.* Author of *Nikolai Gogol and Ivan Turgenev,* 1982; *Modernism to Realism on the Soviet Stage,* 1989; and many articles on Russian and Soviet drama. Compiler of *File on Chekhov,* 1986. **Essays:** Yuri Lyubimov; Vsevolod Meyerhold; Nikolai Okhlopkov; Alexander Tairov; Evgeny Vakhtangov.

WORTH, Kathleen. Adviser. Emeritus professor, University of London, and visiting professor at King's College, University of London. Formerly professor of drama and theatre studies, Royal Holloway and Bedford New College, until 1987. Author of *Revolutions in Modern English Drama,* 1973; *The Irish Drama from Yeats to Beckett,* 1978; *Oscar Wilde,* 1983; *Maeterlinck's Plays in Performance,* 1985; *"Waiting for Godot" and "Happy Days"* (Text in Performance Series), 1990; *Sheridan and Goldsmith,* 1992; and many articles on Beckett, Yeats, and Irish and Noh drama for collections and periodicals. Editor, *Where There Is Nothing* (plays by Yeats), 1991. Has co-directed (with David Clark) television versions of Beckett's *Eh Joe, Words and Music, Embers, Cascando,* and made an award-winning adaptation of Beckett's *Company* for the stage in 1987.

WYLIE-MARQUES, Kathryn. Instructor, John Jay College of Criminal Justice, City University, New York. **Essays:** Colleen Dewhurst; José Quintero; Maureen Stapleton; Laurette Taylor.

PICTURE ACKNOWLEDGEMENTS

British Museum: Quin, James.

Alec Clunes: Bellamy, George Anne; Cooke, George Frederick; Kean, Charles; Macready, William Charles; Pritchard, Hannah; Rich, James.

Deutsches Theatermuseum, Munich: Seydelmann, Karl.

Gesellschaft für Theatergeschichte: Devrient, Emil.

Henry E. Huntington Library, San Marino, California: Jones, Inigo (pp. 391, 392).

Metropolitan Museum of Modern Art: Artaud, Antonin; Ashcroft, Peggy; Barrault, Jean-Louis; Barrymore, Ethel; Barrymore, John; Bergman, Ingmar; Bernhardt, Sarah; Bloom, Claire; Brook, Peter; Casarès, Maria; Clurman, Harold; Compton, Fay; Cornell, Katharine; Cronyn, Hume; Dench, Judi; Dewhurst, Colleen; Duse, Eleonora; Evans, Edith; Evans, Maurice; Finney, Albert; Gielgud, John; Guinness, Alec; Hayes, Helen; Hiller, Wendy; Houseman, John; Jackson, Glenda; Jacobi, Derek; Jouvet, Louis; Kazan, Elia; Laughton, Charles; Massey, Raymond; McKellen, Ian; Messel, Oliver; Neville, John; Olivier, Laurence; Page, Geraldine; Plowright, Joan; Redgrave, Michael; Redgrave, Vanessa; Reid, Kate; Reinhardt, Max; Richardson, Ralph; Robards, Jason; Robeson, Paul; Robson, Flora; Scofield, Paul; Scott, George C.; Skinner, Otis; Smith, Maggie; Stapleton, Maureen; Suzman, Janet; Tandy, Jessica; Taylor, Laurette; Terry, Ellen; Thorndike, Sybil; Visconti, Luchino; Welles, Orson; Williamson, Nicol; Worth, Irene; Zeffirelli, Franco.

New York Public Library: Aldridge, Ira; Alexander, George; Antoine, André; Aronson, Boris; Barry, Elizabeth; Belasco, David; Betterton, Thomas; Booth, Edwin; Burbage, Richard; Campbell, Mrs Patrick (credit: Hal Linden, London); Casson, Lewis; Coquelin, Constant-Benoît; Craig, Gordon; Cushman, Charlotte; Daste, Jean (credit: Talbot, New York City); Davenport, Edward Loomis; Déjazet, Pauline-Virginie; Dorval, Marie; Drew, John; Fiske, Minnie Maddern; Forbes-Robertson, Johnston; Forrest, Edwin; Garrick, David; Gaskill, Bill (credit: Hans Wild, London); Gillette, William H.; Guthrie, Tyrone; Hall, Peter (credit: Gordon Goode, Stratford-upon-Avon); Hawtrey, Charles H.; Hirsch, John; Irving, Henry; Jefferson III, Joseph; Jones, Inigo; Jones, Margo; Kachalov, Vasili; Kean, Edmund; Kemble, Fanny; Lemaître, Frederick; Lecouvreur, Adrienne; Lekain, Henri-Louis; Macklin, Charles; Mansfield, Richard; Mei Lanfang; Mielziner, Jo; Phelps, Samuel; Piscator, Erwin; Pitoëff, Georges; Rehan, Ada; Siddons, Sarah; Simonson, Lee; Sothern, E.H.; Woffington, Peg.

Theatermuseum der Universitat zu Köln: Devrient, Ludwig; Kainz, Josef; Ekhof, Konrad; Schröder, Friedrich Ludwig.

Victoria and Albert Museum: Bracegirdle, Anne.